PRESENTED

TO ______________________________

____

BY ______________________________

____

ON ______________________________

____

YOUR WORD IS A LAMP FOR MY FEET,
A LIGHT ON MY PATH.

PSALM 119:105

NEW INTERNATIONAL VERSION

HOLY BIBLE

ZONDERVAN®

NIV Super Giant Print Reference Bible

Published by Zondervan
Grand Rapids, Michigan, USA

www.Zondervan.com

This Bible was set in the Zondervan NIV Typeface, created at the 2K/DENMARK type foundry.

Library of Congress Catalog Card Number 2017932285

Printed in South Korea N030314

25 26 27 28 29 30 31 32 33 /SWK/ 29 28 27 26 25 24 23 22 21 20 19 18 17 16 15 14

A portion of the purchase price of your NIV® Bible is provided to Biblica so together we support the mission of *Transforming lives through God's Word.*

Biblica provides God's Word to people through translation, publishing and Bible engagement in Africa, Asia Pacific, Europe, Latin America, Middle East, and North America. Through its worldwide reach, Biblica engages people with God's Word so that their lives are transformed through a relationship with Jesus Christ.

TABLE OF CONTENTS

OLD TESTAMENT

NEW TESTAMENT

PREFACE

The goal of the New International Version (NIV) is to enable English-speaking people from around the world to read and hear God's eternal Word in their own language. Our work as translators is motivated by our conviction that the Bible is God's Word in written form. We believe that the Bible contains the divine answer to the deepest needs of humanity, sheds unique light on our path in a dark world and sets forth the way to our eternal well-being. Out of these deep convictions, we have sought to recreate as far as possible the experience of the original audience — blending transparency to the original text with accessibility for the millions of English speakers around the world. We have prioritized accuracy, clarity and literary quality with the goal of creating a translation suitable for public and private reading, evangelism, teaching, preaching, memorizing and liturgical use. We have also sought to preserve a measure of continuity with the long tradition of translating the Scriptures into English.

The complete NIV Bible was first published in 1978. It was a completely new translation made by over a hundred scholars working directly from the best available Hebrew, Aramaic and Greek texts. The translators came from the United States, Great Britain, Canada, Australia and New Zealand, giving the translation an international scope. They were from many denominations and churches — including Anglican, Assemblies of God, Baptist, Brethren, Christian Reformed, Church of Christ, Evangelical Covenant, Evangelical Free, Lutheran, Mennonite, Methodist, Nazarene, Presbyterian, Wesleyan and others. This breadth of denominational and theological perspective helped to safeguard the translation from sectarian bias. For these reasons, and by the grace of God, the NIV has gained a wide readership in all parts of the English-speaking world.

The work of translating the Bible is never finished. As good as they are, English translations must be regularly updated so that they will continue to communicate accurately the meaning of God's Word. Updates are needed in order to reflect the latest developments in our understanding of the biblical world and its languages and to keep pace with changes in English usage. Recognizing, then, that the NIV would retain its ability to communicate God's Word accurately only if it were regularly updated, the original translators established the Committee on Bible Translation (CBT). The Committee is a self-perpetuating group of biblical scholars charged with keeping abreast of advances in biblical scholarship and changes in English and issuing periodic updates to the NIV. The CBT is an independent, self-governing body and has sole responsibility for the NIV text. The Committee mirrors the original group of translators in its diverse international and denominational makeup and in its unifying commitment to the Bible as God's inspired Word.

In obedience to its mandate, the Committee has issued periodic updates to the NIV. An initial revision was released in 1984. A more thorough revision process was completed in 2005, resulting in the separately published TNIV. The updated NIV you now have in your hands builds on both the original NIV and the TNIV and represents the latest effort of the Committee to articulate God's unchanging Word in the way the original authors might have said it had they been speaking in English to the global English-speaking audience today.

Translation Philosophy

The Committee's translating work has been governed by three widely accepted principles about the way people use words and about the way we understand them.

First, the meaning of words is determined by the way that users of the language actually use them at any given time. For the biblical languages, therefore, the Committee utilizes the best and most recent scholarship on the way Hebrew, Aramaic and Greek words were being used in biblical times. At the same time, the Committee carefully studies the state of modern English. Good translation is like good communication: one must know the target audience so that the appropriate choices can be made about which English words to use to represent the original words of Scripture. From its inception, the NIV has had as its target the general English-speaking population all over the world, the "International" in its title reflecting this concern. The aim of the Committee is to put the Scriptures into natural English that will communicate effectively with the broadest possible audience of English speakers.

Modern technology has enhanced the Committee's ability to choose the right English words to convey the meaning of the original text. The field of computational linguistics harnesses the power of computers to provide broadly applicable and current data about the state of the language. Translators can now access huge databases of modern English to better understand the current meaning and usage of key words. The Committee utilized this resource in preparing the 2011 edition of the NIV. An area of especially rapid and significant change in English is the way certain nouns and pronouns are used to refer to human beings. The Committee therefore requested experts in computational linguistics at Collins Dictionaries to pose some key questions about this usage to its database of English — the largest in the world, with over 4.4 billion words, gathered from several English-speaking countries and including both spoken and written English. (The Collins Study, called "The Development and Use of Gender Language in Contemporary English," can be accessed at *http://www.thenivbible.com/about-the-niv/about-the-2011-edition/*.) The study revealed that the most popular words to describe the human race in modern U.S. English were "humanity," "man" and "mankind." The Committee then used this data in the updated NIV, choosing from among these three words (and occasionally others also) depending on the context.

A related issue creates a larger problem for modern translations: the move away from using the third-person masculine singular pronouns — "he/him/his" — to refer to men and women equally. This usage does persist in some forms of English, and this revision therefore occasionally uses these pronouns in a generic sense. But the tendency, recognized in day-to-day usage and confirmed by the Collins study, is away from the generic use of "he," "him" and "his." In recognition of this shift in language and in an effort to translate into the natural English that people are actually using, this revision of the NIV generally uses other constructions when the biblical text is plainly addressed to men and women equally. The reader will encounter especially frequently a "they," "their" or "them" to express a generic singular idea. Thus, for instance, Mark 8:36 reads: "What good is it for someone to gain the whole world, yet forfeit their soul?" This generic use of the "distributive" or "singular" "they/them/their" has been used for many centuries by respected writers of English and has now become established as standard English, spoken and written, all over the world.

A second linguistic principle that feeds into the Committee's translation work is that meaning is found not in individual words, as vital as they are, but in larger clusters: phrases, clauses, sentences, discourses. Translation is not, as many people think, a matter of word substitution: English word *x* in place of Hebrew word *y*. Translators must first determine the meaning of the words of the biblical languages in the context of the passage and then select English words that accurately communicate that meaning to modern listeners and readers. This means that accurate translation will not always reflect the exact structure of the original language. To be sure, there is debate over the degree to which translators should try to preserve the "form" of the original text in English. From the beginning, the NIV has taken a mediating position on this issue. The manual produced when the translation that became the NIV was first being planned states: "If the Greek or Hebrew syntax has a good parallel in modern English, it should be used. But if there is no good parallel, the English syntax appropriate to the meaning of the original is to be chosen." It is fine, in other words, to carry over the form of the biblical languages into English — but not at the expense of natural expression. The principle that meaning resides in larger clusters of words means that the Committee has not insisted on a "word-for-word" approach to translation. We certainly believe that every word of Scripture is inspired by God and therefore to be carefully studied to determine what God is saying to us. It is for this reason that the Committee labors over every single word of the original texts, working hard to determine how each of those words contributes to what the text is saying. Ultimately, however, it is how these individual words function in combination with other words that determines meaning.

A third linguistic principle guiding the Committee in its translation work is the recognition that words have a spectrum of meaning. It is popular to define a word by using another word, or "gloss," to substitute for it. This substitute word is then sometimes called the "literal" meaning of a word. In fact, however, words have a range of possible meanings. Those meanings will vary depending on the context, and words in one language will usually not occupy the same semantic range as words in another language. The Committee therefore studies each original word of Scripture in its context to identify its meaning in a particular verse and then chooses an appropriate English word (or phrase) to represent it. It is impossible, then, to translate any given Hebrew, Aramaic or Greek word with the same English word all the time. The Committee does try to translate related occurrences of a word in the original languages with the same English word in order to preserve the connection for the English reader. But the Committee generally privileges clear natural meaning over a concern with consistency in rendering particular words.

Textual Basis

For the Old Testament the standard Hebrew text, the Masoretic Text as published in the latest edition of *Biblia Hebraica*, has been used throughout. The Masoretic Text tradition contains marginal notations that offer variant readings. These have sometimes been followed instead of the text itself. Because such instances involve variants within the Masoretic tradition, they have not been indicated in the textual notes. In a few cases, words in the basic consonantal text have been divided differently than in the Masoretic Text. Such cases are usually indicated in the textual footnotes. The Dead Sea Scrolls contain biblical texts that represent an earlier stage of the transmission of the Hebrew text. They have been consulted, as have been the Samaritan Pentateuch and the ancient scribal traditions concerning deliberate textual changes. The translators also consulted the more important early versions. Readings from these versions, the Dead Sea Scrolls and the scribal traditions were occasionally followed where the Masoretic Text seemed doubtful and where accepted principles of textual criticism showed that one or more of these textual witnesses appeared to provide the correct reading. In rare cases, the translators have emended the Hebrew text where it appears to have become corrupted at an even earlier stage of its transmission. These departures from the Masoretic Text are also indicated in the textual footnotes. Sometimes the vowel indicators (which are later additions to the basic consonantal text) found in the Masoretic Text did not, in the judgment of the translators, represent the correct vowels for the original text. Accordingly, some words have been read with a different set of vowels. These instances are usually not indicated in the footnotes.

The Greek text used in translating the New Testament has been an eclectic one, based on the latest editions of the Nestle-Aland/United Bible Societies' Greek New Testament. The translators have made their choices among the variant readings in accordance with widely accepted principles of New Testament textual criticism. Footnotes call attention to places where uncertainty remains.

The New Testament authors, writing in Greek, often quote the Old Testament from its ancient Greek version, the Septuagint. This is one reason why some of the Old Testament quotations in the NIV New Testament are not identical to the corresponding passages in the NIV Old Testament. Such quotations in the New Testament are indicated with the footnote "(see Septuagint)."

Footnotes and Formatting

Footnotes in this version are of several kinds, most of which need no explanation. Those giving alternative translations begin with "Or" and generally introduce the alternative with the last word preceding it in the text, except when it is a single-word alternative. When poetry is quoted in a footnote a slash mark indicates a line division.

It should be noted that references to diseases, minerals, flora and fauna, architectural details, clothing, jewelry, musical instruments and other articles cannot always be identified with precision. Also, linear measurements and measures of capacity can only be approximated (see the Table of Weights and Measures). Although *Selah*, used mainly in the Psalms, is probably a musical term, its meaning is uncertain. Since it may interrupt reading and distract the reader, this word has not been kept in thc English text, but every occurrence has been signaled by a footnote.

As an aid to the reader, sectional headings have been inserted. They are not to be regarded as part of the biblical text and are not intended for oral reading. It is the Committee's hope that these headings may prove more helpful to the reader than the traditional chapter divisions, which were introduced long after the Bible was written.

Sometimes the chapter and/or verse numbering in English translations of the Old Testament differs from that found in published Hebrew texts. This is particularly the case in the Psalms, where the traditional titles are included in the Hebrew verse numbering. Such differences are indicated in the footnotes at the bottom of the page. In the New Testament, verse numbers that marked off portions of the traditional English text not supported by the best Greek manuscripts now appear in brackets, with a footnote indicating the text that has been omitted (see, for example, Matthew 17:[21]).

Mark 16:9 – 20 and John 7:53 — 8:11, although long accorded virtually equal status with the rest of the Gospels in which they stand, have a questionable standing in the textual history of the New Testament, as noted in the bracketed annotations with which they are set off. A different typeface has been chosen for these passages to indicate their uncertain status.

Basic formatting of the text, such as lining the poetry, paragraphing (both prose and poetry), setting up of (administrative-like) lists, indenting letters and lengthy prayers within narratives and the insertion of sectional headings, has been the work of the Committee. However, the choice between single-column and double-column formats has been left to the publishers. Also the issuing of "red-letter" editions is a publisher's choice — one that the Committee does not endorse.

The Committee has again been reminded that every human effort is flawed — including this revision of the NIV. We trust, however, that many will find in it an improved representation of the Word of God, through which they hear his call to faith in our Lord Jesus Christ and to service in his kingdom. We offer this version of the Bible to him in whose name and for whose glory it has been made.

The Committee on Bible Translation

OLD TESTAMENT

GENESIS

The Beginning

1 In the beginning God created the heavens and the earth.
2Now the earth was formless
and empty, darkness was over
the surface of the deep, and
the Spirit of God was hovering over the waters.
Jn 1:1-2; Isa 45:12,18

3And God said, "Let there be
light," and there was light.
4God saw that the light was
good, and he separated the
light from the darkness. 5God
called the light "day," and the
darkness he called "night."
And there was evening, and
there was morning — the first
day. 2Co 4:6; Ps 33:6,9; 74:16
6And God said, "Let there be a
vault between the waters to
separate water from water."
7So God made the vault and
separated the water under the
vault from the water above
it. And it was so. 8God called
the vault "sky." And there was
evening, and there was morning — the second day.
Ps 148:4; Jer 10:12
9And God said, "Let the water
under the sky be gathered to
one place, and let dry ground
appear." And it was so. 10God
called the dry ground "land,"
and the gathered waters he
called "seas." And God saw
that it was good.
Ps 104:6-9; Jer 5:22; 2Pe 3:5
11Then God said, "Let the
land produce vegetation:
seed-bearing plants and trees
on the land that bear fruit
with seed in it, according to
their various kinds." And it
was so. 12The land produced
vegetation: plants bearing
seed according to their kinds
and trees bearing fruit with
seed in it according to their
kinds. And God saw that it
was good. 13And there was
evening, and there was morning — the third day. Ps 65:9-13
14And God said, "Let there be
lights in the vault of the sky
to separate the day from the
night, and let them serve as
signs to mark sacred times,
and days and years, 15and let
them be lights in the vault of
the sky to give light on the
earth." And it was so. 16God
made two great lights — the
greater light to govern the
day and the lesser light to
govern the night. He also
made the stars. 17God set them
in the vault of the sky to give
light on the earth, 18to govern
the day and the night, and to

separate light from darkness.
And God saw that it was good.
19 And there was evening, and
there was morning — the
fourth day. Ps 74:16; 104:19; 136:9

20 And God said, "Let the water
teem with living creatures,
and let birds fly above the
earth across the vault of the
sky." 21 So God created the
great creatures of the sea and
every living thing with which
the water teems and that
moves about in it, according to their kinds, and every
winged bird according to its
kind. And God saw that it was
good. 22 God blessed them and
said, "Be fruitful and increase
in number and fill the water
in the seas, and let the birds
increase on the earth." 23 And
there was evening, and there
was morning — the fifth day.
Ge 8:17; Ps 104:25-26

24 And God said, "Let the land
produce living creatures according to their kinds: the
livestock, the creatures that
move along the ground, and
the wild animals, each according to its kind." And it was so.
25 God made the wild animals
according to their kinds, the
livestock according to their
kinds, and all the creatures
that move along the ground
according to their kinds. And
God saw that it was good.

26 Then God said, "Let us
make mankind in our image,
in our likeness, so that they
may rule over the fish in the
sea and the birds in the sky,
over the livestock and all the
wild animals,[a] and over all
the creatures that move along
the ground." Ge 29:6; Ps 8:6-8; 100:3

27 So God created mankind in his
own image, 1Co 11:7
in the image of God he
created them;
male and female he created
them. Ge 5:2; Mk 10:6

28 God blessed them and
said to them, "Be fruitful and
increase in number; fill the
earth and subdue it. Rule
over the fish in the sea and
the birds in the sky and over
every living creature that
moves on the ground."
Ge 9:1,7; Lev 26:9

29 Then God said, "I give you
every seed-bearing plant on
the face of the whole earth
and every tree that has fruit
with seed in it. They will be
yours for food. 30 And to all
the beasts of the earth and all
the birds in the sky and all the
creatures that move along the
ground — everything that has
the breath of life in it — I give
every green plant for food."
And it was so. Ps 104:14,27; 145:15

31 God saw all that he had
made, and it was very good.

[a] *26* Probable reading of the original Hebrew text (see Syriac); Masoretic Text *the earth*

And there was evening, and
there was morning — the
sixth day. Ps 104:24

2 Thus the heavens and the
earth were completed in all
their vast array. Isa 44:24

2 By the seventh day God had finished the work he had been
doing; so on the seventh day
he rested from all his work.
3 Then God blessed the seventh day and made it holy,
because on it he rested from
all the work of creating that
he had done. Ex 20:11; Heb 4:4

Adam and Eve

4 This is the account of the heavens and the earth when they were
created, when the LORD God made
the earth and the heavens.

5 Now no shrub had yet appeared on the earth[a] and no plant
had yet sprung up, for the LORD
God had not sent rain on the earth
and there was no one to work
the ground, 6 but streams[b] came
up from the earth and watered
the whole surface of the ground.
7 Then the LORD God formed a
man[c] from the dust of the ground
and breathed into his nostrils the
breath of life, and the man became a living being.
1Co 15:45; Ge 3:19; Ps 103:14

8 Now the LORD God had planted a garden in the east, in Eden;
and there he put the man he had
formed. 9 The LORD God made all
kinds of trees grow out of the
ground — trees that were pleasing to the eye and good for food.
In the middle of the garden were
the tree of life and the tree of the
knowledge of good and evil.
Ge 3:22,24; Rev 2:7; 22:2,14,19

10 A river watering the garden
flowed from Eden; from there it
was separated into four headwa-
ters. 11 The name of the first is the
Pishon; it winds through the entire land of Havilah, where there
is gold. 12 (The gold of that land is
good; aromatic resin[d] and onyx
are also there.) 13 The name of the
second river is the Gihon; it winds
through the entire land of Cush.[e]
14 The name of the third river is the
Tigris; it runs along the east side
of Ashur. And the fourth river is
the Euphrates. Da 10:4

15 The LORD God took the man
and put him in the Garden of
Eden to work it and take care of it.
16 And the LORD God commanded
the man, "You are free to eat from
any tree in the garden; 17 but you
must not eat from the tree of the
knowledge of good and evil, for
when you eat from it you will certainly die." Ro 5:12; 6:23; Dt 30:15,19

18 The LORD God said, "It is not
good for the man to be alone. I
will make a helper suitable for
him." 1Co 11:9

[a] 5 Or *land*; also in verse 6 [b] 6 Or *mist*
[c] 7 The Hebrew for *man (adam)* sounds like and may be related to the Hebrew for *ground (adamah)*; it is also the name *Adam* (see verse 20). [d] 12 Or *good; pearls*
[e] 13 Possibly southeast Mesopotamia

19 Now the LORD God had formed
out of the ground all the wild animals and all the birds in the sky.
He brought them to the man to
see what he would name them;
and whatever the man called each
living creature, that was its name.
20 So the man gave names to all the
livestock, the birds in the sky and
all the wild animals. Ps 8:7

But for Adam[a] no suitable helper was found. 21 So the LORD God
caused the man to fall into a deep
sleep; and while he was sleeping,
he took one of the man's ribs[b]
and then closed up the place with
flesh. 22 Then the LORD God made a
woman from the rib[c] he had tak-
en out of the man, and he brought
her to the man. 1Co 11:8-9,12

23 The man said,

"This is now bone of my bones
and flesh of my flesh;
Eph 5:28-30
she shall be called 'woman,'
for she was taken out of
man."

24 That is why a man leaves his father and mother and is united to
his wife, and they become one
flesh. Mt 19:5; Eph 5:31; Mal 2:15

25 Adam and his wife were both
naked, and they felt no shame.
Ge 3:7,10-11

The Fall

3 Now the serpent was more
crafty than any of the wild animals the LORD God had made. He
said to the woman, "Did God really
say, 'You must not eat from any
tree in the garden'?"
2Co 11:3; Rev 12:9; 20:2

2 The woman said to the serpent,
"We may eat fruit from the trees
in the garden, 3 but God did say,
'You must not eat fruit from the
tree that is in the middle of the
garden, and you must not touch
it, or you will die.'"

4 "You will not certainly die," the
serpent said to the woman. 5 "For
God knows that when you eat
from it your eyes will be opened,
and you will be like God, knowing
good and evil." Jn 8:44; Isa 14:14

6 When the woman saw that the
fruit of the tree was good for food
and pleasing to the eye, and also
desirable for gaining wisdom, she
took some and ate it. She also gave
some to her husband, who was
with her, and he ate it. 7 Then the
eyes of both of them were opened,
and they realized they were naked; so they sewed fig leaves together and made coverings for
themselves. 1Ti 2:14; Jas 1:14-15; 1Jn 2:16

8 Then the man and his wife
heard the sound of the LORD God
as he was walking in the garden in
the cool of the day, and they hid
from the LORD God among the
trees of the garden. 9 But the LORD
God called to the man, "Where are
you?" Job 31:33

10 He answered, "I heard you in
the garden, and I was afraid because I was naked; so I hid." Ge 2:25

[a] 20 Or *the man* [b] 21 Or *took part of the man's side* [c] 22 Or *part*

11 And he said, "Who told you
that you were naked? Have you
eaten from the tree that I commanded you not to eat from?"
Ge 2:17

12 The man said, "The woman
you put here with me — she gave
me some fruit from the tree, and
I ate it."

13 Then the LORD God said to the
woman, "What is this you have
done?"

The woman said, "The serpent
deceived me, and I ate."
2Co 11:3; 1Ti 2:14

14 So the LORD God said to the
serpent, "Because you have done
this,

"Cursed are you above all
livestock Dt 28:15-20
and all wild animals!
You will crawl on your
belly
and you will eat dust Isa 65:25
all the days of your life.
15 And I will put enmity
between you and the
woman,
and between your offspring[a]
and hers; Rev 12:17; 1Jn 3:8
he will crush[b] your head, Ro 16:20
and you will strike his
heel."

16 To the woman he said,

"I will make your pains in
childbearing very
severe;
with painful labor you will
give birth to children.
Your desire will be for your
husband,
and he will rule over you."
1Co 11:3

17 To Adam he said, "Because you
listened to your wife and ate fruit
from the tree about which I commanded you, 'You must not eat
from it,'

"Cursed is the ground because
of you; Ro 8:20-22; Ge 5:29
through painful toil you will
eat food from it
all the days of your life.
Job 5:7; Ecc 2:23
18 It will produce thorns and
thistles for you, Job 31:40
and you will eat the plants of
the field. Ps 104:14
19 By the sweat of your brow
you will eat your food
until you return to the ground,
since from it you were taken;
for dust you are
and to dust you will return."
Ge 2:7; Ps 90:3; Ecc 12:7

20 Adam[c] named his wife Eve,[d]
because she would become the
mother of all the living. 1Ti 2:13

21 The LORD God made garments
of skin for Adam and his wife and
clothed them. 22 And the LORD God
said, "The man has now become
like one of us, knowing good and
evil. He must not be allowed to
reach out his hand and take also
from the tree of life and eat, and

[a] 15 Or *seed* [b] 15 Or *strike* [c] 20 Or *The man* [d] 20 *Eve* probably means *living.*

live forever.” 23So the LORD God
banished him from the Garden
of Eden to work the ground from
which he had been taken. 24After
he drove the man out, he placed
on the east side[a] of the Garden
of Eden cherubim and a flaming
sword flashing back and forth to
guard the way to the tree of life.

Ge 2:9; Rev 22:14; Ex 25:18-22

Cain and Abel

4 Adam[b] made love to his wife
Eve, and she became pregnant
and gave birth to Cain.[c] She said,
“With the help of the LORD I have
brought forth[d] a man.” 2Later she
gave birth to his brother Abel.

Lk 11:51

Now Abel kept flocks, and Cain
worked the soil. 3In the course of
time Cain brought some of the
fruits of the soil as an offering to
the LORD. 4And Abel also brought
an offering — fat portions from
some of the firstborn of his flock.
The LORD looked with favor on
Abel and his offering, 5but on Cain
and his offering he did not look
with favor. So Cain was very angry,
and his face was downcast.

Heb 11:4; Ex 13:2,12; Nu 18:12

6Then the LORD said to Cain,
“Why are you angry? Why is your
face downcast? 7If you do what is
right, will you not be accepted?
But if you do not do what is right,
sin is crouching at your door; it
desires to have you, but you must
rule over it.” Ro 6:16; Nu 32:23

8Now Cain said to his brother
Abel, “Let’s go out to the field.”[e]
While they were in the field, Cain
attacked his brother Abel and
killed him. Mt 23:35; 1Jn 3:12

9Then the LORD said to Cain,
“Where is your brother Abel?”

“I don’t know,” he replied. “Am I
my brother’s keeper?”

10The LORD said, “What have you
done? Listen! Your brother’s blood
cries out to me from the ground.
11Now you are under a curse and
driven from the ground, which
opened its mouth to receive your
brother’s blood from your hand.
12When you work the ground, it
will no longer yield its crops for
you. You will be a restless wanderer on the earth.” Heb 12:24; Rev 6:9-10

13Cain said to the LORD, “My punishment is more than I can bear.
14Today you are driving me from
the land, and I will be hidden from
your presence; I will be a restless
wanderer on the earth, and whoever finds me will kill me.”

Ps 51:11; Nu 35:19,21,27,33

15But the LORD said to him,
“Not so[f]; anyone who kills Cain
will suffer vengeance seven times
over.” Then the LORD put a mark
on Cain so that no one who found
him would kill him. 16So Cain went

[a] 24 Or *placed in front* [b] 1 Or *The man*
[c] 1 *Cain* sounds like the Hebrew for *brought forth* or *acquired.* [d] 1 Or *have acquired*
[e] 8 Samaritan Pentateuch, Septuagint, Vulgate and Syriac; Masoretic Text does not have *“Let’s go out to the field.”*
[f] 15 Septuagint, Vulgate and Syriac; Hebrew *Very well*

out from the LORD's presence and
lived in the land of Nod,[a] east of
Eden. Eze 9:4,6; Ge 2:8
17 Cain made love to his wife,
and she became pregnant and
gave birth to Enoch. Cain was then
building a city, and he named it after his son Enoch. 18 To Enoch was
born Irad, and Irad was the father
of Mehujael, and Mehujael was the
father of Methushael, and Methushael was the father of Lamech.
Ps 49:11
19 Lamech married two women,
one named Adah and the other
Zillah. 20 Adah gave birth to Jabal;
he was the father of those who live
in tents and raise livestock. 21 His
brother's name was Jubal; he was
the father of all who play stringed
instruments and pipes. 22 Zillah
also had a son, Tubal-Cain, who
forged all kinds of tools out of[b]
bronze and iron. Tubal-Cain's sister was Naamah. Ex 35:35
23 Lamech said to his wives,

"Adah and Zillah, listen to me;
wives of Lamech, hear my
words.
I have killed a man for
wounding me, Ex 20:13
a young man for injuring
me.
24 If Cain is avenged seven times,
then Lamech seventy-seven
times." ver 15; Mt 18:22

25 Adam made love to his wife
again, and she gave birth to a son
and named him Seth,[c] saying,
"God has granted me another
child in place of Abel, since Cain
killed him." 26 Seth also had a son,
and he named him Enosh. Ge 5:3
At that time people began to
call on[d] the name of the LORD.
Ge 12:8; Joel 2:32; 1Co 1:2

From Adam to Noah

5 This is the written account of
Adam's family line.

When God created mankind, he
made them in the likeness of God.
2 He created them male and female
and blessed them. And he named
them "Mankind"[e] when they were
created. Ge 1:27; Eph 4:24; Col 3:10
3 When Adam had lived 130
years, he had a son in his own
likeness, in his own image; and he
named him Seth. 4 After Seth was
born, Adam lived 800 years and
had other sons and daughters. 5 Altogether, Adam lived a total of 930
years, and then he died. Ge 3:19
6 When Seth had lived 105 years,
he became the father[f] of Enosh.
7 After he became the father of
Enosh, Seth lived 807 years and
had other sons and daughters. 8 Altogether, Seth lived a total of 912
years, and then he died. Ge 4:26
9 When Enosh had lived 90 years,
he became the father of Kenan.

[a] 16 *Nod* means *wandering* (see verses 12 and 14). [b] 22 Or *who instructed all who work in* [c] 25 *Seth* probably means *granted.* [d] 26 Or *to proclaim* [e] 2 Hebrew *adam* [f] 6 *Father* may mean *ancestor*; also in verses 7-26.

10 After he became the father of Kenan, Enosh lived 815 years and had
other sons and daughters. 11 Altogether, Enosh lived a total of 905
years, and then he died. 1Ch 1:2

12 When Kenan had lived 70
years, he became the father of
Mahalalel. 13 After he became the
father of Mahalalel, Kenan lived
840 years and had other sons and
daughters. 14 Altogether, Kenan
lived a total of 910 years, and then
he died. Lk 3:37

15 When Mahalalel had lived 65
years, he became the father of Jared. 16 After he became the father
of Jared, Mahalalel lived 830 years
and had other sons and daughters.
17 Altogether, Mahalalel lived a total of 895 years, and then he died.
1Ch 1:2

18 When Jared had lived 162 years,
he became the father of Enoch. 19 After he became the father of Enoch,
Jared lived 800 years and had other sons and daughters. 20 Altogether, Jared lived a total of 962 years,
and then he died. Jude 1:14

21 When Enoch had lived 65
years, he became the father of Methuselah. 22 After he became the father of Methuselah, Enoch walked
faithfully with God 300 years and
had other sons and daughters.
23 Altogether, Enoch lived a total of
365 years. 24 Enoch walked faithfully with God; then he was no more,
because God took him away.
Ge 6:9; Mic 6:8; Heb 11:5

25 When Methuselah had lived
187 years, he became the father of
Lamech. 26 After he became the father of Lamech, Methuselah lived
782 years and had other sons and
daughters. 27 Altogether, Methuselah lived a total of 969 years, and
then he died.

28 When Lamech had lived 182
years, he had a son. 29 He named
him Noah[a] and said, "He will comfort us in the labor and painful toil
of our hands caused by the ground
the LORD has cursed." 30 After Noah
was born, Lamech lived 595 years
and had other sons and daughters.
31 Altogether, Lamech lived a total
of 777 years, and then he died.
Ro 8:20

32 After Noah was 500 years old,
he became the father of Shem,
Ham and Japheth. Ge 10:1

Wickedness in the World

6 When human beings began
to increase in number on the
earth and daughters were born to
them, 2 the sons of God saw that
the daughters of humans were
beautiful, and they married any of
them they chose. 3 Then the LORD
said, "My Spirit will not contend
with[b] humans forever, for they are
mortal[c]; their days will be a hundred and twenty years."
Ps 78:39; Isa 57:16

4 The Nephilim were on the
earth in those days — and also
afterward — when the sons of God
went to the daughters of humans

[a] 29 *Noah* sounds like the Hebrew for *comfort.* [b] 3 Or *My spirit will not remain in* [c] 3 Or *corrupt*

and had children by them. They
were the heroes of old, men of renown. Nu 13:33
5The LORD saw how great the
wickedness of the human race
had become on the earth, and that
every inclination of the thoughts
of the human heart was only evil
all the time. 6The LORD regretted
that he had made human beings
on the earth, and his heart was
deeply troubled. 7So the LORD
said, "I will wipe from the face of
the earth the human race I have
created — and with them the animals, the birds and the creatures
that move along the ground — for
I regret that I have made them."
8But Noah found favor in the eyes
of the LORD. Isa 63:10; Ge 8:21; 19:19

Noah and the Flood

9This is the account of Noah and
his family.

Noah was a righteous man,
blameless among the people of
his time, and he walked faithfully
with God. 10Noah had three sons:
Shem, Ham and Japheth.
Ge 5:22; Heb 11:7; 2Pe 2:5
11Now the earth was corrupt in
God's sight and was full of violence. 12God saw how corrupt the
earth had become, for all the people on earth had corrupted their
ways. 13So God said to Noah, "I am
going to put an end to all people,
for the earth is filled with violence
because of them. I am surely
going to destroy both them and
the earth. 14So make yourself an
ark of cypress[a] wood; make rooms
in it and coat it with pitch inside
and out. 15This is how you are to
build it: The ark is to be three hundred cubits long, fifty cubits wide
and thirty cubits high.[b] 16Make a
roof for it, leaving below the roof
an opening one cubit[c] high all
around.[d] Put a door in the side of
the ark and make lower, middle
and upper decks. 17I am going to
bring floodwaters on the earth to
destroy all life under the heavens,
every creature that has the breath
of life in it. Everything on earth
will perish. 18But I will establish
my covenant with you, and you
will enter the ark — you and your
sons and your wife and your sons'
wives with you. 19You are to bring
into the ark two of all living creatures, male and female, to keep
them alive with you. 20Two of every kind of bird, of every kind of
animal and of every kind of creature that moves along the ground
will come to you to be kept alive.
21You are to take every kind of
food that is to be eaten and store
it away as food for you and for
them." Ge 9:9-16; Ps 14:1-3; 2Pe 2:5
22Noah did everything just as
God commanded him. Ge 7:5,9,16

[a] *14* The meaning of the Hebrew for this word is uncertain. [b] *15* That is, about 450 feet long, 75 feet wide and 45 feet high or about 135 meters long, 23 meters wide and 14 meters high [c] *16* That is, about 18 inches or about 45 centimeters [d] *16* The meaning of the Hebrew for this clause is uncertain.

7 The LORD then said to Noah,
"Go into the ark, you and your
whole family, because I have
found you righteous in this generation. 2 Take with you seven pairs
of every kind of clean animal, a
male and its mate, and one pair
of every kind of unclean animal, a
male and its mate, 3 and also seven
pairs of every kind of bird, male
and female, to keep their various
kinds alive throughout the earth.
4 Seven days from now I will send
rain on the earth for forty days
and forty nights, and I will wipe
from the face of the earth every
living creature I have made."

Ge 6:9; Heb 11:7; Lev 10:10

5 And Noah did all that the LORD
commanded him. Ge 6:22

6 Noah was six hundred years old
when the floodwaters came on the
earth. 7 And Noah and his sons and
his wife and his sons' wives entered the ark to escape the waters
of the flood. 8 Pairs of clean and
unclean animals, of birds and of
all creatures that move along the
ground, 9 male and female, came
to Noah and entered the ark, as
God had commanded Noah. 10 And
after the seven days the floodwaters came on the earth. Ge 5:32

11 In the six hundredth year of
Noah's life, on the seventeenth day
of the second month — on that day
all the springs of the great deep
burst forth, and the floodgates of
the heavens were opened. 12 And
rain fell on the earth forty days
and forty nights. Ge 8:2; Eze 26:19

13 On that very day Noah and his
sons, Shem, Ham and Japheth, together with his wife and the wives
of his three sons, entered the
ark. 14 They had with them every
wild animal according to its kind,
all livestock according to their
kinds, every creature that moves
along the ground according to its
kind and every bird according to
its kind, everything with wings.
15 Pairs of all creatures that have
the breath of life in them came to
Noah and entered the ark. 16 The
animals going in were male and
female of every living thing, as
God had commanded Noah. Then
the LORD shut him in. Ge 6:19

17 For forty days the flood kept
coming on the earth, and as the
waters increased they lifted the
ark high above the earth. 18 The
waters rose and increased greatly on the earth, and the ark float-
ed on the surface of the water.
19 They rose greatly on the earth,
and all the high mountains under
the entire heavens were covered.
20 The waters rose and covered the
mountains to a depth of more
than fifteen cubits.[a,b] 21 Every living thing that moved on land perished — birds, livestock, wild animals, all the creatures that swarm
over the earth, and all mankind.
22 Everything on dry land that had
the breath of life in its nostrils

[a] *20* That is, about 23 feet or about 6.8 meters [b] *20* Or *rose more than fifteen cubits, and the mountains were covered*

died. 23 Every living thing on the
face of the earth was wiped out;
people and animals and the creatures that move along the ground
and the birds were wiped from
the earth. Only Noah was left, and
those with him in the ark.
2Pe 2:5; Mt 24:39; Ge 1:30

24 The waters flooded the earth
for a hundred and fifty days. Ge 8:3

8 But God remembered Noah
and all the wild animals and
the livestock that were with him
in the ark, and he sent a wind over
the earth, and the waters receded. 2 Now the springs of the deep
and the floodgates of the heavens
had been closed, and the rain had
stopped falling from the sky. 3 The
water receded steadily from the
earth. At the end of the hundred
and fifty days the water had gone
down, 4 and on the seventeenth
day of the seventh month the ark
came to rest on the mountains
of Ararat. 5 The waters continued
to recede until the tenth month,
and on the first day of the tenth
month the tops of the mountains
became visible. Ge 19:29; 9:15

6 After forty days Noah opened
a window he had made in the
ark 7 and sent out a raven, and it
kept flying back and forth until
the water had dried up from the
earth. 8 Then he sent out a dove
to see if the water had receded
from the surface of the ground.
9 But the dove could find nowhere
to perch because there was water
over all the surface of the earth; so
it returned to Noah in the ark. He
reached out his hand and took the
dove and brought it back to himself in the ark. 10 He waited sev-
en more days and again sent out
the dove from the ark. 11 When the
dove returned to him in the evening, there in its beak was a fresh-
ly plucked olive leaf! Then Noah
knew that the water had receded
from the earth. 12 He waited seven
more days and sent the dove out
again, but this time it did not return to him. Ge 7:12

13 By the first day of the first
month of Noah's six hundred and
first year, the water had dried up
from the earth. Noah then removed
the covering from the ark and saw
that the surface of the ground was
dry. 14 By the twenty-seventh day of
the second month the earth was
completely dry. Ge 7:11

15 Then God said to Noah,
16 "Come out of the ark, you and
your wife and your sons and their
wives. 17 Bring out every kind of
living creature that is with you —
the birds, the animals, and all the
creatures that move along the
ground — so they can multiply on
the earth and be fruitful and increase in number on it." Ge 1:22

18 So Noah came out, together
with his sons and his wife and his
sons' wives. 19 All the animals and
all the creatures that move along
the ground and all the birds — everything that moves on land —
came out of the ark, one kind after
another.

20 Then Noah built an altar to
the LORD and, taking some of all
the clean animals and clean birds,
he sacrificed burnt offerings on it.
21 The LORD smelled the pleasing
aroma and said in his heart: "Never again will I curse the ground
because of humans, even though[a]
every inclination of the human
heart is evil from childhood. And
never again will I destroy all living
creatures, as I have done.
Ge 9:11,15; 12:7-8; 22:2,13

22 "As long as the earth endures,
seedtime and harvest,
cold and heat,
summer and winter,
day and night
will never cease." Jer 33:20,25; Ge 1:14

God's Covenant With Noah

9 Then God blessed Noah and
his sons, saying to them, "Be
fruitful and increase in number
and fill the earth. 2 The fear and
dread of you will fall on all the
beasts of the earth, and on all the
birds in the sky, on every creature
that moves along the ground, and
on all the fish in the sea; they are
given into your hands. 3 Everything that lives and moves about
will be food for you. Just as I gave
you the green plants, I now give
you everything. Ge 1:22,29
4 "But you must not eat meat
that has its lifeblood still in it.
5 And for your lifeblood I will surely demand an accounting. I will
demand an accounting from every
animal. And from each human being, too, I will demand an accounting for the life of another human
being. Ge 4:10; Lev 3:17; 17:10-14

6 "Whoever sheds human blood,
by humans shall their blood
be shed; Ex 21:12,14; Mt 26:52
for in the image of God
has God made mankind. Ge 1:26

7 As for you, be fruitful and increase in number; multiply on the
earth and increase upon it." Ge 1:22
8 Then God said to Noah and to
his sons with him: 9 "I now establish my covenant with you and
with your descendants after you
10 and with every living creature
that was with you — the birds, the
livestock and all the wild animals,
all those that came out of the ark
with you — every living creature
on earth. 11 I establish my covenant
with you: Never again will all life
be destroyed by the waters of a
flood; never again will there be a
flood to destroy the earth."
Ge 6:18; 8:21; Isa 54:9
12 And God said, "This is the sign
of the covenant I am making between me and you and every living creature with you, a covenant
for all generations to come: 13 I
have set my rainbow in the clouds,
and it will be the sign of the covenant between me and the earth.
14 Whenever I bring clouds over the
earth and the rainbow appears in
the clouds, 15 I will remember my

[a] 21 Or *humans, for*

covenant between me and you
and all living creatures of every
kind. Never again will the waters
become a flood to destroy all life.
16Whenever the rainbow appears
in the clouds, I will see it and remember the everlasting covenant
between God and all living creatures of every kind on the earth."
Ge 17:7,13,19; Lev 26:42,45

17So God said to Noah, "This is
the sign of the covenant I have established between me and all life
on the earth." ver 12; Ge 17:11

The Sons of Noah

18The sons of Noah who came
out of the ark were Shem, Ham
and Japheth. (Ham was the father
of Canaan.) 19These were the three
sons of Noah, and from them came
the people who were scattered
over the whole earth. Ge 10:32

20Noah, a man of the soil, proceeded[a] to plant a vineyard.
21When he drank some of its wine,
he became drunk and lay uncovered inside his tent. 22Ham, the
father of Canaan, saw his father
naked and told his two brothers
outside. 23But Shem and Japheth
took a garment and laid it across
their shoulders; then they walked
in backward and covered their
father's naked body. Their faces
were turned the other way so that
they would not see their father
naked. Hab 2:15

24When Noah awoke from his
wine and found out what his
youngest son had done to him,
25he said,

"Cursed be Canaan! ver 18
The lowest of slaves
will he be to his brothers."
Ge 25:23

26He also said,

"Praise be to the LORD, the God
of Shem!
May Canaan be the slave of
Shem. 1Ki 9:21
27May God extend Japheth's[b]
territory; Ge 10:2-5
may Japheth live in the tents
of Shem, Eph 2:13-14
and may Canaan be the slave
of Japheth."

28After the flood Noah lived 350
years. 29Noah lived a total of 950
years, and then he died. Ge 2:17

The Table of Nations

10 This is the account of Shem,
Ham and Japheth, Noah's
sons, who themselves had sons after the flood. Ge 2:4

The Japhethites

2The sons[c] of Japheth:
Gomer, Magog, Madai, Ja-
van, Tubal, Meshek and Tiras. Eze 38:2,6; Rev 20:8
3The sons of Gomer:
Ashkenaz, Riphath and To-
garmah. Eze 38:6; Jer 51:27

[a] 20 Or *soil, was the first* [b] 27 *Japheth* sounds like the Hebrew for *extend.*
[c] 2 *Sons* may mean *descendants* or *successors* or *nations*; also in verses 3, 4, 6, 7, 20-23, 29 and 31.

4 The sons of Javan:
Elishah, Tarshish, the Kittites and the Rodanites.[a]
5 (From these the maritime
peoples spread out into
their territories by their
clans within their nations,
each with its own lan-
guage.) 1Ch 1:5-7; Jnh 1:3

The Hamites

6 The sons of Ham:
Cush, Egypt, Put and Ca-
naan. ver 15; Ge 9:18
7 The sons of Cush:
Seba, Havilah, Sabtah, Raa-
mah and Sabteka.
The sons of Raamah:
Sheba and Dedan.

8 Cush was the father[b] of Nimrod, who became a mighty warrior
on the earth. 9 He was a mighty
hunter before the LORD; that is
why it is said, "Like Nimrod, a
mighty hunter before the LORD."
10 The first centers of his kingdom
were Babylon, Uruk, Akkad and
Kalneh, in[c] Shinar.[d] 11 From that
land he went to Assyria, where he
built Nineveh, Rehoboth Ir,[e] Calah 12 and Resen, which is between
Nineveh and Calah — which is the
great city. Ge 11:9; Mic 5:6; Jnh 1:2

13 Egypt was the father of
the Ludites, Anamites,
Lehabites, Naphtuhites,
14 Pathrusites, Kasluhites
(from whom the Philistines
came) and Caphtorites.
Ge 21:32,34

15 Canaan was the father of
Sidon his firstborn,[f] and
of the Hittites, 16 Jebusites,
Amorites, Girgashites, 17 Hivites, Arkites, Sinites, 18 Ar-
vadites, Zemarites and Hamathites.
Ge 9:18; Eze 28:21; Ge 23:3,20

Later the Canaanite clans scattered 19 and the borders of Canaan
reached from Sidon toward Gerar
as far as Gaza, and then toward
Sodom, Gomorrah, Admah and
Zeboyim, as far as Lasha. Ge 13:12; 17:8
20 These are the sons of Ham by
their clans and languages, in their
territories and nations. 1Ch 1:8-16

The Semites

21 Sons were also born to Shem,
whose older brother was[g] Japheth;
Shem was the ancestor of all the
sons of Eber. Nu 24:24

22 The sons of Shem:
Elam, Ashur, Arphaxad, Lud
and Aram. Jer 49:34; Lk 3:36
23 The sons of Aram:
Uz, Hul, Gether and Me-
shek.[h] Job 1:1

[a] 4 Some manuscripts of the Masoretic Text and Samaritan Pentateuch (see also Septuagint and 1 Chron. 1:7); most manuscripts of the Masoretic Text *Dodanites* [b] 8 *Father* may mean *ancestor* or *predecessor* or *founder*; also in verses 13, 15, 24 and 26. [c] 10 Or *Uruk and Akkad — all of them in* [d] 10 That is, Babylonia [e] 11 Or *Nineveh with its city squares* [f] 15 Or *of the Sidonians, the foremost* [g] 21 Or *Shem, the older brother of* [h] 23 See Septuagint and 1 Chron. 1:17; Hebrew *Mash*.

24 Arphaxad was the father of[a]
Shelah,
and Shelah the father of
Eber. Lk 3:35
25 Two sons were born to Eber:
One was named Peleg,[b] because in his time the earth
was divided; his brother
was named Joktan.
26 Joktan was the father of
Almodad, Sheleph, Hazar-
maveth, Jerah, 27 Hadoram,
Uzal, Diklah, 28 Obal, Abim-
ael, Sheba, 29 Ophir, Havilah
and Jobab. All these were
sons of Joktan.
30 The region where they lived
stretched from Mesha toward Se-
phar, in the eastern hill country.
31 These are the sons of Shem by
their clans and languages, in their
territories and nations.
Ge 11:10-27; 1Ch 1:17-27

32 These are the clans of Noah's
sons, according to their lines of
descent, within their nations.
From these the nations spread out
over the earth after the flood.
Ge 9:19

The Tower of Babel

11 Now the whole world had
one language and a common
speech. 2 As people moved eastward,[c] they found a plain in Shinar[d] and settled there. Ge 10:10
3 They said to each other, "Come,
let's make bricks and bake them
thoroughly." They used brick instead of stone, and tar for mortar.
4 Then they said, "Come, let us build
ourselves a city, with a tower that
reaches to the heavens, so that we
may make a name for ourselves;
otherwise we will be scattered over
the face of the whole earth."
Dt 1:28; Ge 6:4; Dt 4:27
5 But the LORD came down to see
the city and the tower the people
were building. 6 The LORD said, "If
as one people speaking the same
language they have begun to do
this, then nothing they plan to
do will be impossible for them.
7 Come, let us go down and confuse their language so they will
not understand each other."
Ge 18:21; 42:23
8 So the LORD scattered them
from there over all the earth, and
they stopped building the city.
9 That is why it was called Babel[e] —
because there the LORD confused
the language of the whole world.
From there the LORD scattered
them over the face of the whole
earth. Lk 1:51; Ge 10:10

From Shem to Abram

10 This is the account of Shem's
family line.

Two years after the flood, when
Shem was 100 years old, he became the father[f] of Arphaxad.
11 And after he became the father of

[a] 24 Hebrew; Septuagint *father of Cainan, and Cainan was the father of* [b] 25 *Peleg* means *division.* [c] 2 Or *from the east;* or *in the east* [d] 2 That is, Babylonia [e] 9 That is, Babylon; *Babel* sounds like the Hebrew for *confused.* [f] 10 *Father* may mean *ancestor*; also in verses 11-25.

Arphaxad, Shem lived 500 years
and had other sons and daughters.
12 When Arphaxad had lived 35
years, he became the father of
Shelah. 13 And after he became the
father of Shelah, Arphaxad lived
403 years and had other sons and
daughters.[a] Lk 3:35
14 When Shelah had lived 30
years, he became the father of
Eber. 15 And after he became the father of Eber, Shelah lived 403 years
and had other sons and daughters.
Lk 3:35
16 When Eber had lived 34 years,
he became the father of Peleg.
17 And after he became the father
of Peleg, Eber lived 430 years and
had other sons and daughters.
18 When Peleg had lived 30 years,
he became the father of Reu. 19 And
after he became the father of Reu,
Peleg lived 209 years and had other sons and daughters.
20 When Reu had lived 32 years,
he became the father of Serug.
21 And after he became the father
of Serug, Reu lived 207 years and
had other sons and daughters.
22 When Serug had lived 30
years, he became the father of
Nahor. 23 And after he became the
father of Nahor, Serug lived 200
years and had other sons and
daughters.
24 When Nahor had lived 29
years, he became the father of Terah. 25 And after he became the father of Terah, Nahor lived 119 years
and had other sons and daughters.
Lk 3:34
26 After Terah had lived 70 years,
he became the father of Abram,
Nahor and Haran.
Ge 10:21-31; 1Ch 1:17-27; Jos 24:2

Abram's Family

27 This is the account of Terah's
family line.

Terah became the father of
Abram, Nahor and Haran. And
Haran became the father of Lot.
28 While his father Terah was still
alive, Haran died in Ur of the Chaldeans, in the land of his birth.
29 Abram and Nahor both married.
The name of Abram's wife was Sarai, and the name of Nahor's wife
was Milkah; she was the daughter
of Haran, the father of both Milkah and Iskah. 30 Now Sarai was
childless because she was not able
to conceive. Ge 12:4; 16:1; 17:15
31 Terah took his son Abram, his
grandson Lot son of Haran, and
his daughter-in-law Sarai, the wife
of his son Abram, and together
they set out from Ur of the Chaldeans to go to Canaan. But when
they came to Harran, they settled
there. Ge 15:7; Ac 7:4
32 Terah lived 205 years, and he
died in Harran.

[a] 12,13 Hebrew; Septuagint (see also Luke 3:35, 36 and note at Gen. 10:24) *35 years, he became the father of Cainan.* 13 *And after he became the father of Cainan, Arphaxad lived 430 years and had other sons and daughters, and then he died. When Cainan had lived 130 years, he became the father of Shelah. And after he became the father of Shelah, Cainan lived 330 years and had other sons and daughters*

The Call of Abram

12 The LORD had said to Abram,
“Go from your country, your
people and your father’s household to the land I will show you.
Ac 7:3; Heb 11:8

2 “I will make you into a great
nation, Ge 17:2,4; 18:18
and I will bless you; Ge 24:1,35
I will make your name great,
and you will be a blessing.[a]
3 I will bless those who bless you,
and whoever curses you I
will curse; Ge 27:29; Nu 24:9
and all peoples on earth
will be blessed through
you.”[b] Ge 22:18; Ac 3:25; Gal 3:8

4 So Abram went, as the LORD had
told him; and Lot went with him.
Abram was seventy-five years old
when he set out from Harran. 5 He
took his wife Sarai, his nephew
Lot, all the possessions they had
accumulated and the people they
had acquired in Harran, and they
set out for the land of Canaan, and
they arrived there. Ge 11:31; 14:14
6 Abram traveled through the
land as far as the site of the great
tree of Moreh at Shechem. At
that time the Canaanites were
in the land. 7 The LORD appeared
to Abram and said, “To your offspring[c] I will give this land.” So he
built an altar there to the LORD,
who had appeared to him.
Ge 13:15,17; 17:1; Ps 105:9-11
8 From there he went on toward
the hills east of Bethel and pitched
his tent, with Bethel on the west
and Ai on the east. There he built
an altar to the LORD and called on
the name of the LORD.
9 Then Abram set out and continued toward the Negev. Ge 4:26; 13:3

Abram in Egypt

10 Now there was a famine in the
land, and Abram went down to
Egypt to live there for a while because the famine was severe. 11 As
he was about to enter Egypt, he
said to his wife Sarai, “I know what
a beautiful woman you are. 12 When
the Egyptians see you, they will
say, ‘This is his wife.’ Then they will
kill me but will let you live. 13 Say
you are my sister, so that I will be
treated well for your sake and my
life will be spared because of you.”
Ge 20:2
14 When Abram came to Egypt, the
Egyptians saw that Sarai was a very
beautiful woman. 15 And when Pharaoh’s officials saw her, they praised
her to Pharaoh, and she was taken
into his palace. 16 He treated Abram
well for her sake, and Abram acquired sheep and cattle, male and
female donkeys, male and female
servants, and camels. Ge 24:35; Job 1:3
17 But the LORD inflicted serious diseases on Pharaoh and his
household because of Abram’s
wife Sarai. 18 So Pharaoh summoned Abram. “What have you
done to me?” he said. “Why didn’t

[a] 2 Or *be seen as blessed* [b] 3 Or *earth / will use your name in blessings* (see 48:20)
[c] 7 Or *seed*

you tell me she was your wife?
19 Why did you say, 'She is my sister,' so that I took her to be my
wife? Now then, here is your wife.
Take her and go!" 20 Then Pharaoh gave orders about Abram to
his men, and they sent him on his
way, with his wife and everything
he had. Ge 20:1-18; 26:1-11; 1Ch 16:21

Abram and Lot Separate

13 So Abram went up from
Egypt to the Negev, with his
wife and everything he had, and
Lot went with him. 2 Abram had
become very wealthy in livestock
and in silver and gold. Ge 12:5,9

3 From the Negev he went from
place to place until he came to
Bethel, to the place between Bethel and Ai where his tent had been
earlier 4 and where he had first
built an altar. There Abram called
on the name of the LORD. Ge 12:7-8

5 Now Lot, who was moving
about with Abram, also had flocks
and herds and tents. 6 But the land
could not support them while they
stayed together, for their possessions were so great that they were
not able to stay together. 7 And
quarreling arose between Abram's
herders and Lot's. The Canaanites
and Perizzites were also living in
the land at that time.

Ge 26:20-21; 36:7; 12:6

8 So Abram said to Lot, "Let's not
have any quarreling between you
and me, or between your herders
and mine, for we are close relatives. 9 Is not the whole land before
you? Let's part company. If you go
to the left, I'll go to the right; if
you go to the right, I'll go to the
left." Ps 133:1; Pr 15:18

10 Lot looked around and saw
that the whole plain of the Jordan
toward Zoar was well watered, like
the garden of the LORD, like the
land of Egypt. (This was before the
LORD destroyed Sodom and Gomorrah.) 11 So Lot chose for himself
the whole plain of the Jordan and
set out toward the east. The two
men parted company: 12 Abram
lived in the land of Canaan, while
Lot lived among the cities of the
plain and pitched his tents near
Sodom. 13 Now the people of Sodom were wicked and were sinning
greatly against the LORD.

Ge 18:20; 19:17-29; 2Pe 2:8

14 The LORD said to Abram after
Lot had parted from him, "Look
around from where you are, to
the north and south, to the east
and west. 15 All the land that you
see I will give to you and your offspring[a] forever. 16 I will make your
offspring like the dust of the earth,
so that if anyone could count the
dust, then your offspring could be
counted. 17 Go, walk through the
length and breadth of the land, for
I am giving it to you."

Ge 12:7; Nu 13:17-25; Gal 3:16

18 So Abram went to live near the
great trees of Mamre at Hebron,
where he pitched his tents. There
he built an altar to the LORD.

Ge 8:20; 14:13,24

[a] *15* Or *seed*; also in verse 16

Abram Rescues Lot

14 At the time when Amraphel
was king of Shinar,[a] Arioch
king of Ellasar, Kedorlaomer king
of Elam and Tidal king of Goyim,
2these kings went to war against
Bera king of Sodom, Birsha king
of Gomorrah, Shinab king of Admah, Shemeber king of Zeboyim,
and the king of Bela (that is, Zoar).
3All these latter kings joined forces
in the Valley of Siddim (that is, the
Dead Sea Valley). 4For twelve years
they had been subject to Kedorlaomer, but in the thirteenth year
they rebelled. Nu 34:3,12; Jos 3:16

5In the fourteenth year, Kedorlaomer and the kings allied with
him went out and defeated the
Rephaites in Ashteroth Karnaim,
the Zuzites in Ham, the Emites in
Shaveh Kiriathaim 6and the Horites in the hill country of Seir,
as far as El Paran near the desert.
7Then they turned back and went
to En Mishpat (that is, Kadesh),
and they conquered the whole
territory of the Amalekites, as
well as the Amorites who were living in Hazezon Tamar.

Dt 2:12,22; Ge 21:21

8Then the king of Sodom, the
king of Gomorrah, the king of Admah, the king of Zeboyim and the
king of Bela (that is, Zoar) marched
out and drew up their battle lines
in the Valley of Siddim 9against
Kedorlaomer king of Elam, Tidal
king of Goyim, Amraphel king
of Shinar and Arioch king of Ellasar — four kings against five.
10Now the Valley of Siddim was full
of tar pits, and when the kings of
Sodom and Gomorrah fled, some
of the men fell into them and the
rest fled to the hills. 11The four
kings seized all the goods of Sodom and Gomorrah and all their
food; then they went away. 12They
also carried off Abram's nephew
Lot and his possessions, since he
was living in Sodom.

Ge 13:10; 19:17-29; Dt 29:23

13A man who had escaped came
and reported this to Abram the
Hebrew. Now Abram was living
near the great trees of Mamre the
Amorite, a brother[b] of Eshkol and
Aner, all of whom were allied with
Abram. 14When Abram heard that
his relative had been taken captive, he called out the 318 trained
men born in his household and
went in pursuit as far as Dan.
15During the night Abram divided his men to attack them and he
routed them, pursuing them as
far as Hobah, north of Damascus.
16He recovered all the goods and
brought back his relative Lot and
his possessions, together with the
women and the other people.

Ge 13:18; 15:3

17After Abram returned from
defeating Kedorlaomer and the
kings allied with him, the king of
Sodom came out to meet him in
the Valley of Shaveh (that is, the
King's Valley).

[a] *1* That is, Babylonia; also in verse 9
[b] *13* Or *a relative*; or *an ally*

[18]Then Melchizedek king of Salem brought out bread and wine.
He was priest of God Most High,
[19]and he blessed Abram, saying,
Ps 110:4; Heb 7:2,6

"Blessed be Abram by God Most
High,
Creator of heaven and earth.
[20]And praise be to God Most High,
who delivered your enemies
into your hand." Ge 24:27

Then Abram gave him a tenth of
everything. Heb 7:4
[21]The king of Sodom said to
Abram, "Give me the people and
keep the goods for yourself."
[22]But Abram said to the king of
Sodom, "With raised hand I have
sworn an oath to the LORD, God
Most High, Creator of heaven and
earth, [23]that I will accept nothing belonging to you, not even a
thread or the strap of a sandal, so
that you will never be able to say,
'I made Abram rich.' [24]I will accept
nothing but what my men have
eaten and the share that belongs
to the men who went with me — to
Aner, Eshkol and Mamre. Let them
have their share." Ex 6:8; Rev 10:5-6

The LORD's Covenant With Abram

15 After this, the word of the
LORD came to Abram in a vision: Nu 12:6

"Do not be afraid, Abram.
Ge 21:17; 26:24; Isa 41:10,13-14
I am your shield,[a] Dt 33:29
your very great reward.[b]"

[2]But Abram said, "Sovereign
LORD, what can you give me since I
remain childless and the one who
will inherit[c] my estate is Eliezer
of Damascus?" [3]And Abram said,
"You have given me no children;
so a servant in my household will
be my heir." Ac 7:5; Ge 24:2,34
[4]Then the word of the LORD
came to him: "This man will not
be your heir, but a son who is
your own flesh and blood will be
your heir." [5]He took him outside
and said, "Look up at the sky and
count the stars — if indeed you
can count them." Then he said to
him, "So shall your offspring[d] be."
Gal 4:28; Ro 4:18
[6]Abram believed the LORD, and
he credited it to him as righteousness. Ro 4:3,20-24; Gal 3:6; Jas 2:23
[7]He also said to him, "I am the
LORD, who brought you out of Ur
of the Chaldeans to give you this
land to take possession of it."
Ge 13:17
[8]But Abram said, "Sovereign
LORD, how can I know that I will
gain possession of it?" Lk 1:18
[9]So the LORD said to him, "Bring
me a heifer, a goat and a ram, each
three years old, along with a dove
and a young pigeon." Nu 19:2; Dt 21:3
[10]Abram brought all these to
him, cut them in two and arranged
the halves opposite each other;
the birds, however, he did not cut

[a] *1* Or *sovereign* [b] *1* Or *shield; / your reward will be very great* [c] *2* The meaning of the Hebrew for this phrase is uncertain. [d] *5* Or *seed*

in half. 11Then birds of prey came
down on the carcasses, but Abram
drove them away. Lev 1:17; Jer 34:18;
12As the sun was setting, Abram
fell into a deep sleep, and a thick
and dreadful darkness came over
him. 13Then the LORD said to him,
"Know for certain that for four
hundred years your descendants
will be strangers in a country not
their own and that they will be enslaved and mistreated there. 14But
I will punish the nation they serve
as slaves, and afterward they will
come out with great possessions.
15You, however, will go to your
ancestors in peace and be buried
at a good old age. 16In the fourth
generation your descendants will
come back here, for the sin of the
Amorites has not yet reached its
full measure." Ex 12:32-38,40; Ge 25:8
17When the sun had set and darkness had fallen, a smoking firepot
with a blazing torch appeared and
passed between the pieces. 18On
that day the LORD made a covenant with Abram and said, "To
your descendants I give this land,
from the Wadi[a] of Egypt to the
great river, the Euphrates— 19the
land of the Kenites, Kenizzites,
Kadmonites, 20Hittites, Perizzites,
Rephaites, 21Amorites, Canaanites,
Girgashites and Jebusites."
Ge 17:2,4,7

Hagar and Ishmael

16 Now Sarai, Abram's wife, had
borne him no children. But
she had an Egyptian slave named
Hagar; 2so she said to Abram,
"The LORD has kept me from having children. Go, sleep with my
slave; perhaps I can build a family
through her."
Ge 11:30; 30:3-4,9-10; Gal 4:24-25
Abram agreed to what Sarai
said. 3So after Abram had been living in Canaan ten years, Sarai his
wife took her Egyptian slave Hagar and gave her to her husband
to be his wife. 4He slept with Hagar, and she conceived. Ge 12:5
When she knew she was pregnant, she began to despise her
mistress. 5Then Sarai said to
Abram, "You are responsible for
the wrong I am suffering. I put my
slave in your arms, and now that
she knows she is pregnant, she despises me. May the LORD judge between you and me." Ge 31:53
6"Your slave is in your hands,"
Abram said. "Do with her whatever you think best." Then Sarai mistreated Hagar; so she fled from
her. Jos 9:25
7The angel of the LORD found
Hagar near a spring in the desert;
it was the spring that is beside the
road to Shur. 8And he said, "Hagar, slave of Sarai, where have you
come from, and where are you going?" Ge 21:17; 22:11,15
"I'm running away from my
mistress Sarai," she answered.
9Then the angel of the LORD told
her, "Go back to your mistress and
submit to her." 10The angel added,

[a] 18 Or *river*

"I will increase your descendants so much that they will be too numerous to count." Ge 13:16; 17:20

11 The angel of the LORD also said to her:

"You are now pregnant
and you will give birth to a son.
You shall name him Ishmael,[a]
for the LORD has heard of your misery. Ex 2:24; 3:7,9
12 He will be a wild donkey of a man;
his hand will be against everyone
and everyone's hand against him,
and he will live in hostility
toward[b] all his brothers." Ge 25:18

13 She gave this name to the LORD who spoke to her: "You are the God who sees me," for she said, "I have now seen[c] the One who sees me."
14 That is why the well was called Beer Lahai Roi[d]; it is still there, between Kadesh and Bered. Ge 32:30
15 So Hagar bore Abram a son, and Abram gave the name Ishmael to the son she had borne.
16 Abram was eighty-six years old when Hagar bore him Ishmael. Gal 4:22

The Covenant of Circumcision

17 When Abram was ninety-nine years old, the LORD appeared to him and said, "I am God Almighty[e]; walk before me faithfully and be blameless. 2 Then I will make my covenant between me and you and will greatly increase your numbers." Ge 15:18; 28:3; Dt 18:13

3 Abram fell facedown, and God said to him, 4 "As for me, this is my covenant with you: You will be the father of many nations. 5 No longer will you be called Abram[f]; your name will be Abraham,[g] for I have made you a father of many nations. 6 I will make you very fruitful; I will make nations of you, and kings will come from you. 7 I will establish my covenant as an everlasting covenant between me and you and your descendants after you for the generations to come, to be your God and the God of your descendants after you.
8 The whole land of Canaan, where you now reside as a foreigner, I will give as an everlasting possession to you and your descendants after you; and I will be their God." Ge 12:2; 35:11; Ro 4:17

9 Then God said to Abraham, "As for you, you must keep my covenant, you and your descendants after you for the generations to come. 10 This is my covenant with you and your descendants after you, the covenant you are to keep: Every male among you shall be circumcised. 11 You are to undergo

[a] 11 *Ishmael* means *God hears.* [b] 12 Or *live to the east / of* [c] 13 Or *seen the back of* [d] 14 *Beer Lahai Roi* means *well of the Living One who sees me.* [e] 1 Hebrew *El-Shaddai* [f] 5 *Abram* means *exalted father.* [g] 5 *Abraham* probably means *father of many.*

circumcision, and it will be the
sign of the covenant between me
and you. 12 For the generations to
come every male among you who
is eight days old must be circumcised, including those born in your
household or bought with money
from a foreigner — those who are
not your offspring. 13 Whether born
in your household or bought with
your money, they must be circumcised. My covenant in your flesh
is to be an everlasting covenant.
14 Any uncircumcised male, who
has not been circumcised in the
flesh, will be cut off from his people; he has broken my covenant."

Ro 4:11; Lev 12:3; Ge 21:4

15 God also said to Abraham, "As
for Sarai your wife, you are no longer to call her Sarai; her name will
be Sarah. 16 I will bless her and will
surely give you a son by her. I will
bless her so that she will be the
mother of nations; kings of peoples will come from her."

Ge 18:10; Gal 4:31

17 Abraham fell facedown; he
laughed and said to himself, "Will
a son be born to a man a hundred
years old? Will Sarah bear a child
at the age of ninety?" 18 And Abraham said to God, "If only Ishmael
might live under your blessing!"

Ge 21:11; 18:12

19 Then God said, "Yes, but your
wife Sarah will bear you a son, and
you will call him Isaac.[a] I will establish my covenant with him as
an everlasting covenant for his descendants after him. 20 And as for
Ishmael, I have heard you: I will
surely bless him; I will make him
fruitful and will greatly increase
his numbers. He will be the father
of twelve rulers, and I will make
him into a great nation. 21 But my
covenant I will establish with
Isaac, whom Sarah will bear to you
by this time next year." 22 When he
had finished speaking with Abraham, God went up from him.

Ge 16:10; 21:18; 25:12-16

23 On that very day Abraham
took his son Ishmael and all those
born in his household or bought
with his money, every male in
his household, and circumcised
them, as God told him. 24 Abraham
was ninety-nine years old when
he was circumcised, 25 and his son
Ishmael was thirteen; 26 Abraham
and his son Ishmael were both circumcised on that very day. 27 And
every male in Abraham's household, including those born in his
household or bought from a foreigner, was circumcised with him.

Ro 4:11

The Three Visitors

18 The LORD appeared to Abraham near the great trees of
Mamre while he was sitting at the
entrance to his tent in the heat of
the day. 2 Abraham looked up and
saw three men standing nearby.
When he saw them, he hurried
from the entrance of his tent to
meet them and bowed low to the
ground.

Ver 16,22; Heb 13:2

[a] 19 *Isaac* means *he laughs.*

3He said, "If I have found favor in your eyes, my lord,[a] do not pass your servant by. 4Let a little water be brought, and then you may all wash your feet and rest under this tree. 5Let me get you something to eat, so you can be refreshed and then go on your way — now that you have come to your servant."

Ge 43:24; Jdg 13:15

"Very well," they answered, "do as you say."

6So Abraham hurried into the tent to Sarah. "Quick," he said, "get three seahs[b] of the finest flour and knead it and bake some bread."

7Then he ran to the herd and selected a choice, tender calf and gave it to a servant, who hurried to prepare it. 8He then brought some curds and milk and the calf that had been prepared, and set these before them. While they ate, he stood near them under a tree.

Ge 19:3

9"Where is your wife Sarah?" they asked him.

"There, in the tent," he said.

10Then one of them said, "I will surely return to you about this time next year, and Sarah your wife will have a son." Ro 9:9

Now Sarah was listening at the entrance to the tent, which was behind him. 11Abraham and Sarah were already very old, and Sarah was past the age of childbearing. 12So Sarah laughed to herself as she thought, "After I am worn out and my lord is old, will I now have this pleasure?" Ge 17:17; Ro 4:19; 1Pe 3:6

13Then the LORD said to Abraham, "Why did Sarah laugh and say, 'Will I really have a child, now that I am old?' 14Is anything too hard for the LORD? I will return to you at the appointed time next year, and Sarah will have a son."

Jer 32:17,27; Lk 1:37; Ro 4:21

15Sarah was afraid, so she lied and said, "I did not laugh."

But he said, "Yes, you did laugh."

Abraham Pleads for Sodom

16When the men got up to leave, they looked down toward Sodom, and Abraham walked along with them to see them on their way. 17Then the LORD said, "Shall I hide from Abraham what I am about to do? 18Abraham will surely become a great and powerful nation, and all nations on earth will be blessed through him.[c] 19For I have chosen him, so that he will direct his children and his household after him to keep the way of the LORD by doing what is right and just, so that the LORD will bring about for Abraham what he has promised him." Gal 3:8; Dt 4:9-10

20Then the LORD said, "The outcry against Sodom and Gomorrah is so great and their sin so grievous 21that I will go down and see if what they have done is as bad as the outcry that has reached me. If not, I will know." Ge 19:13; Eze 16:46

[a] 3 Or *eyes, Lord* [b] 6 That is, probably about 36 pounds or about 16 kilograms
[c] 18 Or *will use his name in blessings* (see 48:20)

22 The men turned away and
went toward Sodom, but Abraham remained standing before
the LORD.[a] 23 Then Abraham approached him and said: "Will you
sweep away the righteous with
the wicked? 24 What if there are
fifty righteous people in the city?
Will you really sweep it away and
not spare[b] the place for the sake
of the fifty righteous people in it?
25 Far be it from you to do such a
thing — to kill the righteous with
the wicked, treating the righteous
and the wicked alike. Far be it
from you! Will not the Judge of all
the earth do right?" Nu 16:22; Ro 3:6

26 The LORD said, "If I find fifty righteous people in the city
of Sodom, I will spare the whole
place for their sake." Jer 5:1

27 Then Abraham spoke up again:
"Now that I have been so bold
as to speak to the Lord, though I
am nothing but dust and ashes,
28 what if the number of the righteous is five less than fifty? Will
you destroy the whole city for lack
of five people?" Ge 2:7; Job 42:6

"If I find forty-five there," he
said, "I will not destroy it."

29 Once again he spoke to him,
"What if only forty are found
there?"

He said, "For the sake of forty, I
will not do it."

30 Then he said, "May the Lord not
be angry, but let me speak. What if
only thirty can be found there?"

He answered, "I will not do it if
I find thirty there."

31 Abraham said, "Now that I
have been so bold as to speak to
the Lord, what if only twenty can
be found there?"

He said, "For the sake of twenty,
I will not destroy it."

32 Then he said, "May the Lord
not be angry, but let me speak just
once more. What if only ten can be
found there?" Jdg 6:39

He answered, "For the sake of
ten, I will not destroy it."

33 When the LORD had finished
speaking with Abraham, he left,
and Abraham returned home.
Ge 17:22

Sodom and Gomorrah Destroyed

19 The two angels arrived at
Sodom in the evening, and
Lot was sitting in the gateway of
the city. When he saw them, he
got up to meet them and bowed
down with his face to the ground.
2 "My lords," he said, "please turn
aside to your servant's house. You
can wash your feet and spend the
night and then go on your way
early in the morning." Ge 18:22

"No," they answered, "we will
spend the night in the square."
Jdg 19:15,20

3 But he insisted so strongly that
they did go with him and entered
his house. He prepared a meal
for them, baking bread without
yeast, and they ate. 4 Before they

[a] 22 Masoretic Text; an ancient Hebrew scribal tradition *but the LORD remained standing before Abraham* [b] 24 Or *forgive*; also in verse 26

had gone to bed, all the men from
every part of the city of Sodom —
both young and old — surrounded the house. 5They called to Lot,
"Where are the men who came to
you tonight? Bring them out to
us so that we can have sex with
them." Jdg 19:22; Ro 1:24-27

6Lot went outside to meet them
and shut the door behind him 7and
said, "No, my friends. Don't do this
wicked thing. 8Look, I have two
daughters who have never slept
with a man. Let me bring them
out to you, and you can do what
you like with them. But don't do
anything to these men, for they
have come under the protection
of my roof." Jdg 19:24; 2Pe 2:7-8

9"Get out of our way," they replied. "This fellow came here as
a foreigner, and now he wants
to play the judge! We'll treat you
worse than them." They kept
bringing pressure on Lot and
moved forward to break down the
door. Ac 7:27

10But the men inside reached
out and pulled Lot back into the
house and shut the door. 11Then
they struck the men who were at
the door of the house, young and
old, with blindness so that they
could not find the door.
Dt 28:28-29; 2Ki 6:18; Ac 13:11

12The two men said to Lot, "Do
you have anyone else here — sons-
in-law, sons or daughters, or anyone else in the city who belongs
to you? Get them out of here,
13because we are going to destroy
this place. The outcry to the LORD
against its people is so great that
he has sent us to destroy it." 1Ch 21:15

14So Lot went out and spoke to
his sons-in-law, who were pledged
to marry[a] his daughters. He said,
"Hurry and get out of this place,
because the LORD is about to destroy the city!" But his sons-in-law
thought he was joking. Nu 16:21

15With the coming of dawn, the
angels urged Lot, saying, "Hurry! Take your wife and your two
daughters who are here, or you
will be swept away when the city
is punished." Nu 16:26; Rev 18:4

16When he hesitated, the men
grasped his hand and the hands of
his wife and of his two daughters
and led them safely out of the city,
for the LORD was merciful to them.
17As soon as they had brought
them out, one of them said, "Flee
for your lives! Don't look back, and
don't stop anywhere in the plain!
Flee to the mountains or you will
be swept away!" ver 26

18But Lot said to them, "No, my
lords,[b] please! 19Your[c] servant has
found favor in your[c] eyes, and you[c]
have shown great kindness to me
in sparing my life. But I can't flee
to the mountains; this disaster will
overtake me, and I'll die. 20Look,
here is a town near enough to run
to, and it is small. Let me flee to
it — it is very small, isn't it? Then
my life will be spared." Ge 6:8; 24:12

[a] 14 Or *were married to* [b] 18 Or *No, Lord;* or *No, my lord* [c] 19 The Hebrew is singular.

21He said to him, "Very well, I
will grant this request too; I will
not overthrow the town you speak
of. 22But flee there quickly, because I cannot do anything until you reach it." (That is why the
town was called Zoar.[a]) Ge 13:10
23By the time Lot reached Zoar,
the sun had risen over the land.
24Then the LORD rained down
burning sulfur on Sodom and Gomorrah — from the LORD out of
the heavens. 25Thus he overthrew
those cities and the entire plain,
destroying all those living in the
cities — and also the vegetation in
the land. 26But Lot's wife looked
back, and she became a pillar of
salt. ver 17; Lk 17:29,32
27Early the next morning Abraham got up and returned to the
place where he had stood before
the LORD. 28He looked down toward Sodom and Gomorrah, toward all the land of the plain, and
he saw dense smoke rising from
the land, like smoke from a furnace. Ge 18:22; Rev 18:9
29So when God destroyed the
cities of the plain, he remembered
Abraham, and he brought Lot out
of the catastrophe that overthrew
the cities where Lot had lived.
2Pe 2:7

Lot and His Daughters

30Lot and his two daughters left
Zoar and settled in the mountains,
for he was afraid to stay in Zoar.
He and his two daughters lived in
a cave. 31One day the older daughter said to the younger, "Our father is old, and there is no man
around here to give us children —
as is the custom all over the earth.
32Let's get our father to drink wine
and then sleep with him and preserve our family line through our
father." Ge 14:10
33That night they got their father to drink wine, and the older
daughter went in and slept with
him. He was not aware of it when
she lay down or when she got up.
34The next day the older daughter said to the younger, "Last night
I slept with my father. Let's get
him to drink wine again tonight,
and you go in and sleep with
him so we can preserve our family line through our father." 35So
they got their father to drink wine
that night also, and the younger
daughter went in and slept with
him. Again he was not aware of it
when she lay down or when she
got up.
36So both of Lot's daughters became pregnant by their father.
37The older daughter had a son,
and she named him Moab[b]; he is
the father of the Moabites of today. 38The younger daughter also
had a son, and she named him
Ben-Ammi[c]; he is the father of the
Ammonites[d] of today. Dt 2:9,19

[a] 22 *Zoar* means *small.* [b] 37 *Moab* sounds like the Hebrew for *from father.* [c] 38 *Ben-Ammi* means *son of my father's people.* [d] 38 Hebrew *Bene-Ammon*

Abraham and Abimelek

20 Now Abraham moved on
from there into the region
of the Negev and lived between
Kadesh and Shur. For a while he
stayed in Gerar, 2 and there Abraham said of his wife Sarah, "She is
my sister." Then Abimelek king of
Gerar sent for Sarah and took her.
ver 12; Ge 12:13; 26:7

3 But God came to Abimelek in a
dream one night and said to him,
"You are as good as dead because
of the woman you have taken; she
is a married woman." Ge 26:11

4 Now Abimelek had not gone
near her, so he said, "Lord, will you
destroy an innocent nation? 5 Did
he not say to me, 'She is my sister,'
and didn't she also say, 'He is my
brother'? I have done this with a
clear conscience and clean hands."

6 Then God said to him in the
dream, "Yes, I know you did this
with a clear conscience, and so
I have kept you from sinning
against me. That is why I did not
let you touch her. 7 Now return the
man's wife, for he is a prophet, and
he will pray for you and you will
live. But if you do not return her,
you may be sure that you and all
who belong to you will die."
1Sa 7:5; 25:26,34; Job 42:8

8 Early the next morning Abimelek summoned all his officials, and when he told them all
that had happened, they were
very much afraid. 9 Then Abimelek called Abraham in and said,
"What have you done to us? How
have I wronged you that you have
brought such great guilt upon me
and my kingdom? You have done
things to me that should never
be done." 10 And Abimelek asked
Abraham, "What was your reason
for doing this?" Ge 12:18

11 Abraham replied, "I said to
myself, 'There is surely no fear of
God in this place, and they will kill
me because of my wife.' 12 Besides,
she really is my sister, the daughter of my father though not of my
mother; and she became my wife.
13 And when God had me wander
from my father's household, I said
to her, 'This is how you can show
your love to me: Everywhere we
go, say of me, "He is my brother."'" Ps 36:1; Ge 12:12; 26:7

14 Then Abimelek brought sheep
and cattle and male and female
slaves and gave them to Abraham,
and he returned Sarah his wife to
him. 15 And Abimelek said, "My
land is before you; live wherever
you like."

16 To Sarah he said, "I am giving
your brother a thousand shekels[a]
of silver. This is to cover the offense against you before all who
are with you; you are completely
vindicated." Ge 12:16; 13:9

17 Then Abraham prayed to God,
and God healed Abimelek, his
wife and his female slaves so they
could have children again, 18 for
the LORD had kept all the women

[a] 16 That is, about 25 pounds or about 12 kilograms

in Abimelek's household from
conceiving because of Abraham's
wife Sarah. Ge 12:10-20; 26:1-11

The Birth of Isaac

21 Now the LORD was gra-
cious to Sarah as he had
said, and the LORD did for Sarah what he had promised. 2Sarah
became pregnant and bore a son
to Abraham in his old age, at the
very time God had promised him.
3Abraham gave the name Isaac[a]
to the son Sarah bore him. 4When
his son Isaac was eight days old,
Abraham circumcised him, as God
commanded him. 5Abraham was
a hundred years old when his son
Isaac was born to him.
Ge 17:10,12,19; Gal 4:22

6Sarah said, "God has brought
me laughter, and everyone who
hears about this will laugh with
me." 7And she added, "Who would
have said to Abraham that Sarah
would nurse children? Yet I have
borne him a son in his old age."
Ge 17:17; Isa 54:1

Hagar and Ishmael Sent Away

8The child grew and was weaned,
and on the day Isaac was weaned
Abraham held a great feast. 9But
Sarah saw that the son whom Hagar the Egyptian had borne to
Abraham was mocking, 10and she
said to Abraham, "Get rid of that
slave woman and her son, for that
woman's son will never share
in the inheritance with my son
Isaac." Gal 4:30; Ge 16:15

11The matter distressed Abraham greatly because it concerned
his son. 12But God said to him, "Do
not be so distressed about the boy
and your slave woman. Listen to
whatever Sarah tells you, because
it is through Isaac that your offspring[b] will be reckoned. 13I will
make the son of the slave into a
nation also, because he is your offspring." Ro 9:7; Heb 11:18; Ge 17:18

14Early the next morning Abraham took some food and a skin
of water and gave them to Hagar.
He set them on her shoulders and
then sent her off with the boy. She
went on her way and wandered in
the Desert of Beersheba. ver 31,32

15When the water in the skin
was gone, she put the boy under
one of the bushes. 16Then she went
off and sat down about a bowshot
away, for she thought, "I cannot
watch the boy die." And as she sat
there, she[c] began to sob.

17God heard the boy crying, and
the angel of God called to Hagar from heaven and said to her,
"What is the matter, Hagar? Do
not be afraid; God has heard the
boy crying as he lies there. 18Lift
the boy up and take him by the
hand, for I will make him into a
great nation." Ge 17:20; Ex 3:7

19Then God opened her eyes
and she saw a well of water. So she
went and filled the skin with water and gave the boy a drink.
Nu 22:31

[a] 3 *Isaac* means *he laughs.* [b] 12 Or *seed*
[c] 16 Hebrew; Septuagint *the child*

20God was with the boy as he
grew up. He lived in the desert
and became an archer. 21While he
was living in the Desert of Paran,
his mother got a wife for him from
Egypt. Ge 28:15; Lk 1:66; Ge 24:4,38

The Treaty at Beersheba

22At that time Abimelek and
Phicol the commander of his forces said to Abraham, "God is with
you in everything you do. 23Now
swear to me here before God that
you will not deal falsely with me
or my children or my descendants.
Show to me and the country where
you now reside as a foreigner the
same kindness I have shown to
you." Ge 26:28; 39:2,3

24Abraham said, "I swear it."

25Then Abraham complained
to Abimelek about a well of water that Abimelek's servants had
seized. 26But Abimelek said, "I
don't know who has done this. You
did not tell me, and I heard about
it only today." Ge 26:15,18,20-22

27So Abraham brought sheep
and cattle and gave them to Abimelek, and the two men made a
treaty. 28Abraham set apart seven
ewe lambs from the flock, 29and
Abimelek asked Abraham, "What
is the meaning of these seven ewe
lambs you have set apart by themselves?" Ge 26:28,31

30He replied, "Accept these sev-
en lambs from my hand as a witness that I dug this well."
Ge 31:44,47,48,50,52

31So that place was called Beersheba,[a] because the two men
swore an oath there. Ge 26:33

32After the treaty had been
made at Beersheba, Abimelek and
Phicol the commander of his forces returned to the land of the Philistines. 33Abraham planted a tamarisk tree in Beersheba, and there
he called on the name of the LORD,
the Eternal God. 34And Abraham
stayed in the land of the Philistines for a long time. Ge 4:26; Dt 33:27

Abraham Tested

22 Some time later God tested
Abraham. He said to him,
"Abraham!" Dt 8:2,16; Heb 11:17; Jas 1:12-13

"Here I am," he replied.

2Then God said, "Take your son,
your only son, whom you love —
Isaac — and go to the region of
Moriah. Sacrifice him there as a
burnt offering on a mountain I
will show you." Jn 3:16; Heb 11:17; 1Jn 4:9

3Early the next morning Abraham got up and loaded his donkey. He took with him two of his
servants and his son Isaac. When
he had cut enough wood for the
burnt offering, he set out for the
place God had told him about. 4On
the third day Abraham looked up
and saw the place in the distance.
5He said to his servants, "Stay here
with the donkey while I and the
boy go over there. We will worship and then we will come back
to you."

[a] 31 *Beersheba* can mean *well of seven* and *well of the oath.*

[6]Abraham took the wood for the burnt offering and placed it on his son Isaac, and he himself carried the fire and the knife. As the two of them went on together, [7]Isaac spoke up and said to his father Abraham, "Father?" Jn 19:17

"Yes, my son?" Abraham replied.

"The fire and wood are here," Isaac said, "but where is the lamb for the burnt offering?" Lev 1:10

[8]Abraham answered, "God himself will provide the lamb for the burnt offering, my son." And the two of them went on together. Jn 1:29

[9]When they reached the place God had told him about, Abraham built an altar there and arranged the wood on it. He bound his son Isaac and laid him on the altar, on top of the wood. [10]Then he reached out his hand and took the knife to slay his son. [11]But the angel of the LORD called out to him from heaven, "Abraham! Abraham!" Heb 11:17-19; Jas 2:21

"Here I am," he replied.

[12]"Do not lay a hand on the boy," he said. "Do not do anything to him. Now I know that you fear God, because you have not withheld from me your son, your only son." 1Sa 15:22; Jn 3:16; 1Jn 4:9

[13]Abraham looked up and there in a thicket he saw a ram[a] caught by its horns. He went over and took the ram and sacrificed it as a burnt offering instead of his son. [14]So Abraham called that place The LORD Will Provide. And to this day it is said, "On the mountain of the LORD it will be provided." Ro 8:32

[15]The angel of the LORD called to Abraham from heaven a second time [16]and said, "I swear by myself, declares the LORD, that because you have done this and have not withheld your son, your only son, [17]I will surely bless you and make your descendants as numerous as the stars in the sky and as the sand on the seashore. Your descendants will take possession of the cities of their enemies, [18]and through your offspring[b] all nations on earth will be blessed,[c] because you have obeyed me." Ac 3:25; Heb 6:14

[19]Then Abraham returned to his servants, and they set off together for Beersheba. And Abraham stayed in Beersheba.

Nahor's Sons

[20]Some time later Abraham was told, "Milkah is also a mother; she has borne sons to your brother Nahor: [21]Uz the firstborn, Buz his brother, Kemuel (the father of Aram), [22]Kesed, Hazo, Pildash, Jidlaph and Bethuel." [23]Bethuel became the father of Rebekah.

[a] 13 Many manuscripts of the Masoretic Text, Samaritan Pentateuch, Septuagint and Syriac; most manuscripts of the Masoretic Text *a ram behind him* [b] 18 Or *seed* [c] 18 Or *and all nations on earth will use the name of your offspring in blessings* (see 48:20)

Milkah bore these eight sons to
Abraham's brother Nahor. 24His
concubine, whose name was Reu-
mah, also had sons: Tebah, Gaham,
Tahash and Maakah. Ge 24:15

The Death of Sarah

23 Sarah lived to be a hundred
and twenty-seven years
old. 2She died at Kiriath Arba (that
is, Hebron) in the land of Canaan,
and Abraham went to mourn for
Sarah and to weep over her.
Ge 13:18; Jos 14:15

3Then Abraham rose from beside his dead wife and spoke to
the Hittites.[a] He said, 4"I am a foreigner and stranger among you.
Sell me some property for a burial
site here so I can bury my dead."
Ps 105:12; Heb 11:9,13

5The Hittites replied to Abraham, 6"Sir, listen to us. You are a
mighty prince among us. Bury
your dead in the choicest of our
tombs. None of us will refuse you
his tomb for burying your dead."
Ge 14:14-16; 24:35

7Then Abraham rose and bowed
down before the people of the
land, the Hittites. 8He said to
them, "If you are willing to let me
bury my dead, then listen to me
and intercede with Ephron son of
Zohar on my behalf 9so he will sell
me the cave of Machpelah, which
belongs to him and is at the end of
his field. Ask him to sell it to me
for the full price as a burial site
among you." Ge 25:9

10Ephron the Hittite was sitting
among his people and he replied to
Abraham in the hearing of all the
Hittites who had come to the gate
of his city. 11"No, my lord," he said.
"Listen to me; I give[b] you the field,
and I give[b] you the cave that is in
it. I give[b] it to you in the presence
of my people. Bury your dead."
Ru 4:4

12Again Abraham bowed down
before the people of the land 13and
he said to Ephron in their hearing,
"Listen to me, if you will. I will
pay the price of the field. Accept
it from me so I can bury my dead
there."

14Ephron answered Abraham,
15"Listen to me, my lord; the land
is worth four hundred shekels[c] of
silver, but what is that between
you and me? Bury your dead."
Eze 45:12

16Abraham agreed to Ephron's
terms and weighed out for him
the price he had named in the
hearing of the Hittites: four hundred shekels of silver, according
to the weight current among the
merchants. Jer 32:9

17So Ephron's field in Machpelah near Mamre — both the field
and the cave in it, and all the trees
within the borders of the field —
was deeded 18to Abraham as his
property in the presence of all the
Hittites who had come to the gate

[a] 3 Or *the descendants of Heth*; also in verses 5, 7, 10, 16, 18 and 20 [b] 11 Or *sell*
[c] 15 That is, about 10 pounds or about 4.6 kilograms

of the city. [19]Afterward Abraham buried his wife Sarah in the cave in the field of Machpelah near Mamre (which is at Hebron) in the land of Canaan. [20]So the field and the cave in it were deeded to Abraham by the Hittites as a burial site. Ge 25:9; 50:13

Isaac and Rebekah

24 Abraham was now very old, and the LORD had blessed him in every way. [2]He said to the senior servant in his household, the one in charge of all that he had, "Put your hand under my thigh. [3]I want you to swear by the LORD, the God of heaven and the God of earth, that you will not get a wife for my son from the daughters of the Canaanites, among whom I am living, [4]but will go to my country and my own relatives and get a wife for my son Isaac." Ge 12:1; 28:2

[5]The servant asked him, "What if the woman is unwilling to come back with me to this land? Shall I then take your son back to the country you came from?" Heb 11:15

[6]"Make sure that you do not take my son back there," Abraham said. [7]"The LORD, the God of heaven, who brought me out of my father's household and my native land and who spoke to me and promised me on oath, saying, 'To your offspring[a] I will give this land'—he will send his angel before you so that you can get a wife for my son from there. [8]If the woman is unwilling to come back with you, then you will be released from this oath of mine. Only do not take my son back there." [9]So the servant put his hand under the thigh of his master Abraham and swore an oath to him concerning this matter. Ge 12:7; 13:15; Gal 3:16

[10]Then the servant left, taking with him ten of his master's camels loaded with all kinds of good things from his master. He set out for Aram Naharaim[b] and made his way to the town of Nahor. [11]He had the camels kneel down near the well outside the town; it was toward evening, the time the women go out to draw water. 1Sa 9:11

[12]Then he prayed, "LORD, God of my master Abraham, make me successful today, and show kindness to my master Abraham. [13]See, I am standing beside this spring, and the daughters of the townspeople are coming out to draw water. [14]May it be that when I say to a young woman, 'Please let down your jar that I may have a drink,' and she says, 'Drink, and I'll water your camels too'—let her be the one you have chosen for your servant Isaac. By this I will know that you have shown kindness to my master." Ge 26:24; Jdg 6:17,37

[15]Before he had finished praying, Rebekah came out with her jar on her shoulder. She was the daughter of Bethuel son of Milkah, who was the wife of Abraham's

[a] 7 Or *seed* [b] 10 That is, Northwest Mesopotamia

brother Nahor. 16The woman was
very beautiful, a virgin; no man
had ever slept with her. She went
down to the spring, filled her jar
and came up again. Ge 22:23; 26:7
17The servant hurried to meet
her and said, "Please give me a little water from your jar."
18"Drink, my lord," she said,
and quickly lowered the jar to her
hands and gave him a drink.
19After she had given him a
drink, she said, "I'll draw water for
your camels too, until they have
had enough to drink." 20So she
quickly emptied her jar into the
trough, ran back to the well to draw
more water, and drew enough for
all his camels. 21Without saying a
word, the man watched her closely
to learn whether or not the LORD
had made his journey successful.
ver 12,14
22When the camels had finished
drinking, the man took out a gold
nose ring weighing a beka[a] and
two gold bracelets weighing ten
shekels.[b] 23Then he asked, "Whose
daughter are you? Please tell me,
is there room in your father's
house for us to spend the night?"
ver 47
24She answered him, "I am the
daughter of Bethuel, the son that
Milkah bore to Nahor." 25And she
added, "We have plenty of straw
and fodder, as well as room for
you to spend the night."
Ge 11:29; Jdg 19:19
26Then the man bowed down
and worshiped the LORD, 27saying,
"Praise be to the LORD, the God
of my master Abraham, who has
not abandoned his kindness and
faithfulness to my master. As for
me, the LORD has led me on the
journey to the house of my master's relatives." ver 48,52; Ge 32:10
28The young woman ran and
told her mother's household about
these things. 29Now Rebekah had a
brother named Laban, and he hurried out to the man at the spring.
30As soon as he had seen the nose
ring, and the bracelets on his sister's arms, and had heard Rebekah tell what the man said to her,
he went out to the man and found
him standing by the camels near
the spring. 31"Come, you who are
blessed by the LORD," he said.
"Why are you standing out here?
I have prepared the house and a
place for the camels."
Ge 26:29; 29:5,12,13
32So the man went to the house,
and the camels were unloaded.
Straw and fodder were brought for
the camels, and water for him and
his men to wash their feet. 33Then
food was set before him, but he
said, "I will not eat until I have told
you what I have to say." Ge 43:24
"Then tell us," Laban said.
34So he said, "I am Abraham's
servant. 35The LORD has blessed
my master abundantly, and he has
become wealthy. He has given him
sheep and cattle, silver and gold,

[a] 22 That is, about 1/5 ounce or about 5.7 grams [b] 22 That is, about 4 ounces or about 115 grams

male and female servants, and
camels and donkeys. 36My master's wife Sarah has borne him a
son in her old age, and he has giv-
en him everything he owns. 37And
my master made me swear an
oath, and said, 'You must not get
a wife for my son from the daughters of the Canaanites, in whose
land I live, 38but go to my father's
family and to my own clan, and
get a wife for my son.' ver 1; Ge 25:5

39"Then I asked my master,
'What if the woman will not come
back with me?' ver 5

40"He replied, 'The LORD, before
whom I have walked faithfully,
will send his angel with you and
make your journey a success, so
that you can get a wife for my son
from my own clan and from my father's family. 41You will be released
from my oath if, when you go to
my clan, they refuse to give her to
you — then you will be released
from my oath.' ver 7-8

42"When I came to the spring today, I said, 'LORD, God of my master
Abraham, if you will, please grant
success to the journey on which I
have come. 43See, I am standing beside this spring. If a young woman
comes out to draw water and I say
to her, "Please let me drink a little
water from your jar," 44and if she
says to me, "Drink, and I'll draw
water for your camels too," let her
be the one the LORD has chosen for
my master's son.' ver 12-14

45"Before I finished praying in
my heart, Rebekah came out, with
her jar on her shoulder. She went
down to the spring and drew water, and I said to her, 'Please give
me a drink.' 1Sa 1:13

46"She quickly lowered her
jar from her shoulder and said,
'Drink, and I'll water your camels
too.' So I drank, and she watered
the camels also. ver 18-19

47"I asked her, 'Whose daughter
are you?' ver 23

"She said, 'The daughter of Bethuel son of Nahor, whom Milkah
bore to him.' ver 24

"Then I put the ring in her nose
and the bracelets on her arms,
48and I bowed down and worshiped the LORD. I praised the
LORD, the God of my master Abraham, who had led me on the right
road to get the granddaughter of
my master's brother for his son.
49Now if you will show kindness
and faithfulness to my master, tell
me; and if not, tell me, so I may
know which way to turn."

Ge 47:29; Jos 2:14; Eze 16:11-12

50Laban and Bethuel answered,
"This is from the LORD; we can say
nothing to you one way or the other. 51Here is Rebekah; take her and
go, and let her become the wife of
your master's son, as the LORD has
directed." Ps 118:23; Ge 31:7,24,29,42

52When Abraham's servant
heard what they said, he bowed
down to the ground before the
LORD. 53Then the servant brought
out gold and silver jewelry and articles of clothing and gave them to
Rebekah; he also gave costly gifts

to her brother and to her mother.
[54]Then he and the men who were
with him ate and drank and spent
the night there. ver 26

When they got up the next
morning, he said, "Send me on my
way to my master." ver 56,59

[55]But her brother and her mother replied, "Let the young woman remain with us ten days or so;
then you[a] may go." Jdg 19:4

[56]But he said to them, "Do not
detain me, now that the LORD has
granted success to my journey.
Send me on my way so I may go to
my master." ver 12

[57]Then they said, "Let's call the
young woman and ask her about
it." [58]So they called Rebekah and
asked her, "Will you go with this
man?" Jdg 19:3

"I will go," she said. Ru 1:16

[59]So they sent their sister Rebekah on her way, along with her
nurse and Abraham's servant and
his men. [60]And they blessed Rebekah and said to her, Ge 35:8

"Our sister, may you increase
to thousands upon
thousands; Ge 17:16
may your offspring possess
the cities of their enemies."
Ge 22:17

[61]Then Rebekah and her attendants got ready and mounted the
camels and went back with the
man. So the servant took Rebekah
and left.

[62]Now Isaac had come from Beer
Lahai Roi, for he was living in the
Negev. [63]He went out to the field
one evening to meditate,[b] and as
he looked up, he saw camels approaching. [64]Rebekah also looked
up and saw Isaac. She got down
from her camel [65]and asked the
servant, "Who is that man in the
field coming to meet us?"
Ps 1:2; Ge 16:14; 25:11

"He is my master," the servant
answered. So she took her veil and
covered herself.

[66]Then the servant told Isaac all
he had done. [67]Isaac brought her
into the tent of his mother Sarah,
and he married Rebekah. So she
became his wife, and he loved her;
and Isaac was comforted after his
mother's death. Ge 25:20; 29:18,20

The Death of Abraham

25 Abraham had taken another wife, whose name was
Keturah. [2]She bore him Zimran,
Jokshan, Medan, Midian, Ishbak
and Shuah. [3]Jokshan was the father of Sheba and Dedan; the
descendants of Dedan were the
Ashurites, the Letushites and the
Leummites. [4]The sons of Midian
were Ephah, Epher, Hanok, Abida
and Eldaah. All these were descendants of Keturah. 1Ch 1:32-33

[5]Abraham left everything he
owned to Isaac. [6]But while he was
still living, he gave gifts to the
sons of his concubines and sent
them away from his son Isaac to
the land of the east. Ge 24:36; 21:10

[a] 55 Or *she* [b] 63 The meaning of the Hebrew for this word is uncertain.

7 Abraham lived a hundred and
seventy-five years. 8 Then Abraham breathed his last and died
at a good old age, an old man and
full of years; and he was gathered
to his people. 9 His sons Isaac and
Ishmael buried him in the cave
of Machpelah near Mamre, in the
field of Ephron son of Zohar the
Hittite, 10 the field Abraham had
bought from the Hittites.[a] There
Abraham was buried with his wife
Sarah. 11 After Abraham's death,
God blessed his son Isaac, who
then lived near Beer Lahai Roi.
Ge 15:15; 23:16; 49:29,33

Ishmael's Sons

12 This is the account of the family line of Abraham's son Ishmael, whom Sarah's slave, Hagar the
Egyptian, bore to Abraham.
Ge 16:15

13 These are the names of the
sons of Ishmael, listed in the order of their birth: Nebaioth the
firstborn of Ishmael, Kedar, Adbeel, Mibsam, 14 Mishma, Dumah,
Massa, 15 Hadad, Tema, Jetur, Naphish and Kedemah. 16 These were
the sons of Ishmael, and these are
the names of the twelve tribal rulers according to their settlements
and camps. 17 Ishmael lived a hundred and thirty-seven years. He
breathed his last and died, and he
was gathered to his people. 18 His
descendants settled in the area
from Havilah to Shur, near the
eastern border of Egypt, as you go
toward Ashur. And they lived in
hostility toward[b] all the tribes related to them. 1Ch 1:29-31; Ge 16:12; 17:20

Jacob and Esau

19 This is the account of the family line of Abraham's son Isaac.

Abraham became the father of
Isaac, 20 and Isaac was forty years
old when he married Rebekah
daughter of Bethuel the Aramean
from Paddan Aram[c] and sister of
Laban the Aramean. Ge 24:29
21 Isaac prayed to the LORD on
behalf of his wife, because she was
childless. The LORD answered his
prayer, and his wife Rebekah became pregnant. 22 The babies jos-
tled each other within her, and
she said, "Why is this happening
to me?" So she went to inquire of
the LORD. 1Ch 5:20; 1Sa 9:9
23 The LORD said to her,

"Two nations are in your
womb, Ge 17:4
and two peoples from within
you will be separated;
one people will be stronger
than the other,
and the older will serve
the younger."

Ge 27:29,40; Ro 9:11-12; Mal 1:3

24 When the time came for her
to give birth, there were twin boys
in her womb. 25 The first to come
out was red, and his whole body

[a] 10 Or *the descendants of Heth* [b] 18 Or *lived to the east of* [c] 20 That is, Northwest Mesopotamia

was like a hairy garment; so they
named him Esau.[a] 26After this,
his brother came out, with his
hand grasping Esau's heel; so he
was named Jacob.[b] Isaac was sixty years old when Rebekah gave
birth to them. Hos 12:3; Ge 27:11,36

27The boys grew up, and Esau
became a skillful hunter, a man of
the open country, while Jacob was
content to stay at home among
the tents. 28Isaac, who had a taste
for wild game, loved Esau, but Rebekah loved Jacob. Ge 27:3,5

29Once when Jacob was cooking
some stew, Esau came in from the
open country, famished. 30He said
to Jacob, "Quick, let me have some
of that red stew! I'm famished!"
(That is why he was also called
Edom.[c]) Ge 32:3

31Jacob replied, "First sell me
your birthright." Dt 21:16-17

32"Look, I am about to die," Esau
said. "What good is the birthright
to me?"

33But Jacob said, "Swear to me
first." So he swore an oath to him,
selling his birthright to Jacob.
Heb 12:16

34Then Jacob gave Esau some
bread and some lentil stew. He ate
and drank, and then got up and
left.

So Esau despised his birthright.

Isaac and Abimelek

26 Now there was a famine in
the land — besides the previous famine in Abraham's time —
and Isaac went to Abimelek king of
the Philistines in Gerar. 2The LORD
appeared to Isaac and said, "Do not
go down to Egypt; live in the land
where I tell you to live. 3Stay in this
land for a while, and I will be with
you and will bless you. For to you
and your descendants I will give
all these lands and will confirm the
oath I swore to your father Abraham. 4I will make your descendants
as numerous as the stars in the sky
and will give them all these lands,
and through your offspring[d] all nations on earth will be blessed,[e] 5be-
cause Abraham obeyed me and did
everything I required of him, keeping my commands, my decrees and
my instructions." 6So Isaac stayed
in Gerar. Ge 12:1,7,10

7When the men of that place
asked him about his wife, he said,
"She is my sister," because he was
afraid to say, "She is my wife." He
thought, "The men of this place
might kill me on account of Rebekah, because she is beautiful."
Ge 12:13; 20:2,12

8When Isaac had been there a
long time, Abimelek king of the
Philistines looked down from a
window and saw Isaac caressing
his wife Rebekah. 9So Abimelek
summoned Isaac and said, "She is
really your wife! Why did you say,
'She is my sister'?"

Isaac answered him, "Because I

[a] 25 *Esau* may mean *hairy*. [b] 26 *Jacob* means *he grasps the heel*, a Hebrew idiom for *he deceives*. [c] 30 *Edom* means *red*. [d] 4 Or *seed* [e] 4 Or *and all nations on earth will use the name of your offspring in blessings* (see 48:20)

thought I might lose my life on account of her."
10 Then Abimelek said, "What
is this you have done to us? One
of the men might well have slept
with your wife, and you would
have brought guilt upon us." Ge 20:9
11 So Abimelek gave orders to all
the people: "Anyone who harms
this man or his wife shall surely
be put to death." Ge 12:10-20; 20:1-18
12 Isaac planted crops in that land
and the same year reaped a hun-
dredfold, because the LORD blessed
him. 13 The man became rich, and
his wealth continued to grow until
he became very wealthy. 14 He had
so many flocks and herds and servants that the Philistines envied
him. 15 So all the wells that his father's servants had dug in the time
of his father Abraham, the Philistines stopped up, filling them with
earth. ver 3; Ge 21:30
16 Then Abimelek said to Isaac,
"Move away from us; you have become too powerful for us." Ex 1:9
17 So Isaac moved away from
there and encamped in the Valley
of Gerar, where he settled. 18 Isaac
reopened the wells that had been
dug in the time of his father Abraham, which the Philistines had
stopped up after Abraham died,
and he gave them the same names
his father had given them. Ge 21:30
19 Isaac's servants dug in the valley and discovered a well of fresh
water there. 20 But the herders of
Gerar quarreled with those of Isaac
and said, "The water is ours!" So
he named the well Esek,[a] because
they disputed with him. 21 Then
they dug another well, but they
quarreled over that one also; so he
named it Sitnah.[b] 22 He moved on
from there and dug another well,
and no one quarreled over it. He
named it Rehoboth,[c] saying, "Now
the LORD has given us room and
we will flourish in the land." Ge 17:6
23 From there he went up to Beersheba. 24 That night the LORD appeared to him and said, "I am the
God of your father Abraham. Do
not be afraid, for I am with you;
I will bless you and will increase
the number of your descendants
for the sake of my servant Abraham." Ge 17:7; 24:12
25 Isaac built an altar there and
called on the name of the LORD.
There he pitched his tent, and
there his servants dug a well.
Ge 12:7,8; 13:4,18
26 Meanwhile, Abimelek had
come to him from Gerar, with
Ahuzzath his personal adviser and
Phicol the commander of his forces. 27 Isaac asked them, "Why have
you come to me, since you were
hostile to me and sent me away?"
Ge 21:22
28 They answered, "We saw clearly that the LORD was with you;
so we said, 'There ought to be a
sworn agreement between us' —
between us and you. Let us make
a treaty with you 29 that you will

[a] 20 *Esek* means *dispute.* [b] 21 *Sitnah* means *opposition.* [c] 22 *Rehoboth* means *room.*

do us no harm, just as we did not
harm you but always treated you
well and sent you away peacefully. And now you are blessed by the
LORD." Ge 21:22; 24:31
30 Isaac then made a feast for
them, and they ate and drank.
31 Early the next morning the men
swore an oath to each other. Then
Isaac sent them on their way, and
they went away peacefully. Ge 21:31
32 That day Isaac's servants came
and told him about the well they
had dug. They said, "We've found
water!" 33 He called it Shibah,[a] and
to this day the name of the town
has been Beersheba.[b] Ge 21:14

Jacob Takes Esau's Blessing

34 When Esau was forty years
old, he married Judith daughter
of Beeri the Hittite, and also Basemath daughter of Elon the Hittite. 35 They were a source of grief
to Isaac and Rebekah. Ge 27:46; 36:2
27 When Isaac was old and his
eyes were so weak that he
could no longer see, he called for
Esau his older son and said to him,
"My son." Ge 25:25; 48:10
"Here I am," he answered.
2 Isaac said, "I am now an old
man and don't know the day of my
death. 3 Now then, get your equipment — your quiver and bow —
and go out to the open country
to hunt some wild game for me.
4 Prepare me the kind of tasty food
I like and bring it to me to eat, so
that I may give you my blessing
before I die." Ge 49:28; Dt 33:1; Heb 11:20
5 Now Rebekah was listening as
Isaac spoke to his son Esau. When
Esau left for the open country to
hunt game and bring it back, 6 Rebekah said to her son Jacob, "Look,
I overheard your father say to your
brother Esau, 7 'Bring me some
game and prepare me some tasty
food to eat, so that I may give you
my blessing in the presence of the
LORD before I die.' 8 Now, my son,
listen carefully and do what I tell
you: 9 Go out to the flock and bring
me two choice young goats, so I
can prepare some tasty food for
your father, just the way he likes
it. 10 Then take it to your father to
eat, so that he may give you his
blessing before he dies." ver 13,43
11 Jacob said to Rebekah his
mother, "But my brother Esau is
a hairy man while I have smooth
skin. 12 What if my father touches
me? I would appear to be tricking
him and would bring down a curse
on myself rather than a blessing."
ver 22; Ge 25:25
13 His mother said to him, "My
son, let the curse fall on me. Just
do what I say; go and get them
for me." Mt 27:25
14 So he went and got them and
brought them to his mother, and
she prepared some tasty food, just
the way his father liked it. 15 Then
Rebekah took the best clothes of
Esau her older son, which she had
in the house, and put them on her

[a] 33 *Shibah* can mean *oath* or *seven.*
[b] 33 *Beersheba* can mean *well of the oath* and *well of seven.*

younger son Jacob. 16She also covered his hands and the smooth
part of his neck with the goatskins. 17Then she handed to her
son Jacob the tasty food and the
bread she had made. ver 27

18He went to his father and said,
"My father."

"Yes, my son," he answered.
"Who is it?"

19Jacob said to his father, "I am
Esau your firstborn. I have done
as you told me. Please sit up and
eat some of my game, so that you
may give me your blessing."
ver 4; Ge 25:28

20Isaac asked his son, "How did
you find it so quickly, my son?"

"The LORD your God gave me
success," he replied. Ge 24:12

21Then Isaac said to Jacob,
"Come near so I can touch you, my
son, to know whether you really
are my son Esau or not." ver 12

22Jacob went close to his father
Isaac, who touched him and said,
"The voice is the voice of Jacob,
but the hands are the hands of
Esau." 23He did not recognize him,
for his hands were hairy like those
of his brother Esau; so he proceeded to bless him. 24"Are you really
my son Esau?" he asked.
ver 16; Ge 45:4

"I am," he replied.

25Then he said, "My son, bring me
some of your game to eat, so that I
may give you my blessing." ver 4

Jacob brought it to him and he
ate; and he brought some wine
and he drank. 26Then his father
Isaac said to him, "Come here, my
son, and kiss me."

27So he went to him and kissed
him. When Isaac caught the smell
of his clothes, he blessed him and
said, Heb 11:20; SS 4:11

"Ah, the smell of my son
is like the smell of a field
that the LORD has blessed.
28May God give you heaven's dew
Dt 33:13
and earth's richness —
an abundance of grain and
new wine. Dt 33:28
29May nations serve you Isa 49:7,23
and peoples bow down to
you. Ge 9:25; 25:23
Be lord over your brothers,
and may the sons of your
mother bow down to
you.
May those who curse you be
cursed
and those who bless you be
blessed." Ge 12:3

30After Isaac finished blessing
him, and Jacob had scarcely left
his father's presence, his brother
Esau came in from hunting. 31He
too prepared some tasty food and
brought it to his father. Then he
said to him, "My father, please sit
up and eat some of my game, so
that you may give me your blessing." ver 4

32His father Isaac asked him,
"Who are you?"

"I am your son," he answered,
"your firstborn, Esau."

33Isaac trembled violently and

said, "Who was it, then, that hunted game and brought it to me? I
ate it just before you came and I
blessed him — and indeed he will
be blessed!" Ge 28:3,4; Ro 11:29
34 When Esau heard his father's
words, he burst out with a loud
and bitter cry and said to his father, "Bless me — me too, my father!" Heb 12:17
35 But he said, "Your brother
came deceitfully and took your
blessing." Jer 9:4
36 Esau said, "Isn't he rightly
named Jacob[a]? This is the second
time he has taken advantage of
me: He took my birthright, and
now he's taken my blessing!" Then
he asked, "Haven't you reserved
any blessing for me?" Ge 25:26,33
37 Isaac answered Esau, "I have
made him lord over you and have
made all his relatives his servants,
and I have sustained him with
grain and new wine. So what can
I possibly do for you, my son?"
ver 28
38 Esau said to his father, "Do
you have only one blessing, my
father? Bless me too, my father!"
Then Esau wept aloud. Heb 12:17
39 His father Isaac answered him,

"Your dwelling will be
away from the earth's
richness,
away from the dew of heaven
above. ver 28
40 You will live by the sword
and you will serve your
brother. Ge 25:23
But when you grow
restless,
you will throw his yoke
from off your neck." 2Ki 8:20-22

41 Esau held a grudge against
Jacob because of the blessing his
father had given him. He said to
himself, "The days of mourning
for my father are near; then I will
kill my brother Jacob." Ge 32:11
42 When Rebekah was told what
her older son Esau had said, she
sent for her younger son Jacob
and said to him, "Your brother
Esau is planning to avenge himself by killing you. 43 Now then, my
son, do what I say: Flee at once
to my brother Laban in Harran.
44 Stay with him for a while until your brother's fury subsides.
45 When your brother is no longer
angry with you and forgets what
you did to him, I'll send word for
you to come back from there. Why
should I lose both of you in one
day?" ver 8; Ge 11:31
46 Then Rebekah said to Isaac,
"I'm disgusted with living because of these Hittite women. If
Jacob takes a wife from among
the women of this land, from Hittite women like these, my life will
not be worth living." Ge 26:35

28 So Isaac called for Jacob
and blessed him. Then he
commanded him: "Do not marry
a Canaanite woman. 2 Go at once

[a] 36 *Jacob* means *he grasps the heel,* a Hebrew idiom for *he takes advantage of* or *he deceives.*

to Paddan Aram,[a] to the house
of your mother's father Bethuel. Take a wife for yourself there,
from among the daughters of Laban, your mother's brother. 3May
God Almighty[b] bless you and
make you fruitful and increase
your numbers until you become
a community of peoples. 4May he
give you and your descendants
the blessing given to Abraham, so
that you may take possession of
the land where you now reside as
a foreigner, the land God gave to
Abraham." 5Then Isaac sent Jacob
on his way, and he went to Paddan
Aram, to Laban son of Bethuel the
Aramean, the brother of Rebekah,
who was the mother of Jacob and
Esau. Ge 12:2-3; 17:8; 24:3

6Now Esau learned that Isaac
had blessed Jacob and had sent
him to Paddan Aram to take a
wife from there, and that when he
blessed him he commanded him,
"Do not marry a Canaanite woman," 7and that Jacob had obeyed
his father and mother and had
gone to Paddan Aram. 8Esau then
realized how displeasing the Canaanite women were to his father
Isaac; 9so he went to Ishmael and
married Mahalath, the sister of
Nebaioth and daughter of Ishmael son of Abraham, in addition to
the wives he already had.

Ge 26:34-35

Jacob's Dream at Bethel

10Jacob left Beersheba and set
out for Harran. 11When he reached
a certain place, he stopped for the
night because the sun had set.
Taking one of the stones there,
he put it under his head and lay
down to sleep. 12He had a dream
in which he saw a stairway resting
on the earth, with its top reaching
to heaven, and the angels of God
were ascending and descending
on it. 13There above it[c] stood the
LORD, and he said: "I am the LORD,
the God of your father Abraham
and the God of Isaac. I will give you
and your descendants the land on
which you are lying. 14Your descendants will be like the dust of
the earth, and you will spread out
to the west and to the east, to the
north and to the south. All peoples
on earth will be blessed through
you and your offspring.[d] 15I am
with you and will watch over you
wherever you go, and I will bring
you back to this land. I will not
leave you until I have done what I
have promised you."

Jn 1:51; Ge 12:3; Gal 3:8

16When Jacob awoke from his
sleep, he thought, "Surely the
LORD is in this place, and I was not
aware of it." 17He was afraid and
said, "How awesome is this place!
This is none other than the house
of God; this is the gate of heaven."

Ex 3:5; Jos 5:15

18Early the next morning Jacob
took the stone he had placed under

[a] 2 That is, Northwest Mesopotamia; also in verses 5, 6 and 7 [b] 3 Hebrew *El-Shaddai* [c] 13 Or *There beside him* [d] 14 Or *will use your name and the name of your offspring in blessings* (see 48:20)

his head and set it up as a pillar and
poured oil on top of it. 19He called
that place Bethel,[a] though the city
used to be called Luz. Jdg 1:23,26
20Then Jacob made a vow, saying, "If God will be with me and
will watch over me on this journey I am taking and will give me
food to eat and clothes to wear 21so
that I return safely to my father's
household, then the LORD[b] will
be my God 22and[c] this stone that I
have set up as a pillar will be God's
house, and of all that you give me
I will give you a tenth."
Dt 26:17; Ge 14:20; 31:13

Jacob Arrives in Paddan Aram

29 Then Jacob continued on
his journey and came to
the land of the eastern peoples.
2There he saw a well in the open
country, with three flocks of sheep
lying near it because the flocks
were watered from that well. The
stone over the mouth of the well
was large. 3When all the flocks
were gathered there, the shepherds would roll the stone away
from the well's mouth and water
the sheep. Then they would return the stone to its place over the
mouth of the well. Jdg 6:3,33
4Jacob asked the shepherds, "My
brothers, where are you from?"
"We're from Harran," they replied. Ge 28:10
5He said to them, "Do you know
Laban, Nahor's grandson?"
"Yes, we know him," they answered. Ge 11:29
6Then Jacob asked them, "Is he
well?"
"Yes, he is," they said, "and here
comes his daughter Rachel with
the sheep."
7"Look," he said, "the sun is still
high; it is not time for the flocks to
be gathered. Water the sheep and
take them back to pasture." Ex 2:16
8"We can't," they replied, "until
all the flocks are gathered and the
stone has been rolled away from
the mouth of the well. Then we
will water the sheep." Ge 24:13
9While he was still talking with
them, Rachel came with her father's sheep, for she was a shepherd. 10When Jacob saw Rachel
daughter of his uncle Laban, and
Laban's sheep, he went over and
rolled the stone away from the
mouth of the well and watered his
uncle's sheep. 11Then Jacob kissed
Rachel and began to weep aloud.
12He had told Rachel that he was a
relative of her father and a son of
Rebekah. So she ran and told her
father. Ge 24:28
13As soon as Laban heard the
news about Jacob, his sister's son,
he hurried to meet him. He embraced him and kissed him and
brought him to his home, and
there Jacob told him all these
things. 14Then Laban said to him,
"You are my own flesh and blood."
Ge 24:29; Jdg 9:2

[a] 19 *Bethel* means *house of God.*
[b] 20,21 Or *Since God . . . father's household, the LORD*
[c] 21,22 Or *household, and the LORD will be my God, 22then*

Jacob Marries Leah and Rachel

After Jacob had stayed with him for a whole month, 15 Laban said to him, "Just because you are a relative of mine, should you work for me for nothing? Tell me what your wages should be." Ge 31:7,41

16 Now Laban had two daughters; the name of the older was Leah, and the name of the younger was Rachel. 17 Leah had weak[a] eyes, but Rachel had a lovely figure and was beautiful. 18 Jacob was in love with Rachel and said, "I'll work for you seven years in return for your younger daughter Rachel." Hos 12:12

19 Laban said, "It's better that I give her to you than to some other man. Stay here with me." 20 So Jacob served seven years to get Rachel, but they seemed like only a few days to him because of his love for her. Ge 31:15; Hos 12:12

21 Then Jacob said to Laban, "Give me my wife. My time is completed, and I want to make love to her." Jdg 15:1

22 So Laban brought together all the people of the place and gave a feast. 23 But when evening came, he took his daughter Leah and brought her to Jacob, and Jacob made love to her. 24 And Laban gave his servant Zilpah to his daughter as her attendant. Jdg 14:10; Jn 2:1-2

25 When morning came, there was Leah! So Jacob said to Laban, "What is this you have done to me? I served you for Rachel, didn't I? Why have you deceived me?" Ge 12:18; 27:36

26 Laban replied, "It is not our custom here to give the younger daughter in marriage before the older one. 27 Finish this daughter's bridal week; then we will give you the younger one also, in return for another seven years of work." Jdg 14:12

28 And Jacob did so. He finished the week with Leah, and then Laban gave him his daughter Rachel to be his wife. 29 Laban gave his servant Bilhah to his daughter Rachel as her attendant. 30 Jacob made love to Rachel also, and his love for Rachel was greater than his love for Leah. And he worked for Laban another seven years. Ge 31:41

Jacob's Children

31 When the LORD saw that Leah was not loved, he enabled her to conceive, but Rachel remained childless. 32 Leah became pregnant and gave birth to a son. She named him Reuben,[b] for she said, "It is because the LORD has seen my misery. Surely my husband will love me now." Dt 21:15-17; Ps 127:3; Ge 16:11

33 She conceived again, and when she gave birth to a son she said, "Because the LORD heard that I am not loved, he gave me

[a] 17 Or *delicate* [b] 32 *Reuben* sounds like the Hebrew for *he has seen my misery*; the name means *see, a son.*

this one too." So she named him Simeon.[a] Ge 34:25

34 Again she conceived, and when she gave birth to a son she said, "Now at last my husband will become attached to me, because I have borne him three sons." So he was named Levi.[b] Ge 49:5-7

35 She conceived again, and when she gave birth to a son she said, "This time I will praise the LORD." So she named him Judah.[c] Then she stopped having children.

Ge 49:8; Mt 1:2-3

30 When Rachel saw that she was not bearing Jacob any children, she became jealous of her sister. So she said to Jacob, "Give me children, or I'll die!"

Ge 29:31

2 Jacob became angry with her and said, "Am I in the place of God, who has kept you from having children?" Ge 16:2

3 Then she said, "Here is Bilhah, my servant. Sleep with her so that she can bear children for me and I too can build a family through her." Ge 16:2

4 So she gave him her servant Bilhah as a wife. Jacob slept with her, 5 and she became pregnant and bore him a son. 6 Then Rachel said, "God has vindicated me; he has listened to my plea and given me a son." Because of this she named him Dan.[d] Ge 16:3-4; 49:16-17

7 Rachel's servant Bilhah conceived again and bore Jacob a second son. 8 Then Rachel said, "I have had a great struggle with my sister, and I have won." So she named him Naphtali.[e]

Ge 49:21; Hos 12:3-4

9 When Leah saw that she had stopped having children, she took her servant Zilpah and gave her to Jacob as a wife. 10 Leah's servant Zilpah bore Jacob a son. 11 Then Leah said, "What good fortune!"[f] So she named him Gad.[g] ver 4

12 Leah's servant Zilpah bore Jacob a second son. 13 Then Leah said, "How happy I am! The women will call me happy." So she named him Asher.[h] Lk 1:48; Ge 49:20

14 During wheat harvest, Reuben went out into the fields and found some mandrake plants, which he brought to his mother Leah. Rachel said to Leah, "Please give me some of your son's mandrakes."

SS 7:13

15 But she said to her, "Wasn't it enough that you took away my husband? Will you take my son's mandrakes too?" Nu 16:9,13

"Very well," Rachel said, "he can sleep with you tonight in return for your son's mandrakes." Eze 16:33

16 So when Jacob came in from the fields that evening, Leah went out to meet him. "You must sleep with me," she said. "I have hired

[a] 33 *Simeon* probably means *one who hears.* [b] 34 *Levi* sounds like and may be derived from the Hebrew for *attached.*
[c] 35 *Judah* sounds like and may be derived from the Hebrew for *praise.*
[d] 6 *Dan* here means *he has vindicated.*
[e] 8 *Naphtali* means *my struggle.*
[f] 11 Or "A troop is coming!" [g] 11 *Gad* can mean *good fortune* or *a troop.*
[h] 13 *Asher* means *happy.*

you with my son's mandrakes." So he slept with her that night.

17 God listened to Leah, and she became pregnant and bore Jacob a fifth son. 18 Then Leah said, "God has rewarded me for giving my servant to my husband." So she named him Issachar.[a] Ge 46:13; 49:14

19 Leah conceived again and bore Jacob a sixth son. 20 Then Leah said, "God has presented me with a precious gift. This time my husband will treat me with honor, because I have borne him six sons." So she named him Zebulun.[b] 1Pe 3:7

21 Some time later she gave birth to a daughter and named her Dinah. Ge 34:1

22 Then God remembered Rachel; he listened to her and enabled her to conceive. 23 She became pregnant and gave birth to a son and said, "God has taken away my disgrace." 24 She named him Joseph,[c] and said, "May the LORD add to me another son."
Ge 35:17; Isa 4:1; Lk 1:25

Jacob's Flocks Increase

25 After Rachel gave birth to Joseph, Jacob said to Laban, "Send me on my way so I can go back to my own homeland. 26 Give me my wives and children, for whom I have served you, and I will be on my way. You know how much work I've done for you."
Ge 24:54; 29:20,30

27 But Laban said to him, "If I have found favor in your eyes, please stay. I have learned by divination that the LORD has blessed me because of you." 28 He added, "Name your wages, and I will pay them." Ge 26:24; 29:15; 39:3,5

29 Jacob said to him, "You know how I have worked for you and how your livestock has fared under my care. 30 The little you had before I came has increased greatly, and the LORD has blessed you wherever I have been. But now, when may I do something for my own household?" Ge 31:38-40; 1Ti 5:8

31 "What shall I give you?" he asked.

"Don't give me anything," Jacob replied. "But if you will do this one thing for me, I will go on tending your flocks and watching over them: 32 Let me go through all your flocks today and remove from them every speckled or spotted sheep, every dark-colored lamb and every spotted or speckled goat. They will be my wages. 33 And my honesty will testify for me in the future, whenever you check on the wages you have paid me. Any goat in my possession that is not speckled or spotted, or any lamb that is not dark-colored, will be considered stolen." Ge 31:8,12

34 "Agreed," said Laban. "Let it be as you have said." 35 That same day he removed all the male goats that were streaked or spotted, and all the speckled or spotted female goats (all that had white on them)

[a] 18 *Issachar* sounds like the Hebrew for *reward.* [b] 20 *Zebulun* probably means *honor.* [c] 24 *Joseph* means *may he add.*

and all the dark-colored lambs,
and he placed them in the care of
his sons. 36Then he put a three-day
journey between himself and Jacob, while Jacob continued to tend
the rest of Laban's flocks. Ge 31:1
37Jacob, however, took fresh-cut
branches from poplar, almond
and plane trees and made white
stripes on them by peeling the
bark and exposing the white inner
wood of the branches. 38Then he
placed the peeled branches in all
the watering troughs, so that they
would be directly in front of the
flocks when they came to drink.
When the flocks were in heat and
came to drink, 39they mated in
front of the branches. And they
bore young that were streaked
or speckled or spotted. 40Jacob
set apart the young of the flock
by themselves, but made the rest
face the streaked and dark-colored animals that belonged to Laban. Thus he made separate flocks
for himself and did not put them
with Laban's animals. 41Whenever
the stronger females were in heat,
Jacob would place the branches
in the troughs in front of the animals so they would mate near
the branches, 42but if the animals
were weak, he would not place
them there. So the weak animals
went to Laban and the strong ones
to Jacob. 43In this way the man
grew exceedingly prosperous and
came to own large flocks, and female and male servants, and camels and donkeys. Ge 12:16; 13:2; 26:13-14

Jacob Flees From Laban

31 Jacob heard that Laban's sons
were saying, "Jacob has tak-
en everything our father owned
and has gained all this wealth
from what belonged to our father."
2And Jacob noticed that Laban's attitude toward him was not what it
had been. Ge 30:42
3Then the LORD said to Jacob,
"Go back to the land of your fathers and to your relatives, and I
will be with you." Ge 21:22; 26:3; 32:9
4So Jacob sent word to Rachel
and Leah to come out to the fields
where his flocks were. 5He said to
them, "I see that your father's attitude toward me is not what it was
before, but the God of my father
has been with me. 6You know that
I've worked for your father with
all my strength, 7yet your father
has cheated me by changing my
wages ten times. However, God
has not allowed him to harm me.
8If he said, 'The speckled ones will
be your wages,' then all the flocks
gave birth to speckled young; and
if he said, 'The streaked ones will
be your wages,' then all the flocks
bore streaked young. 9So God has
taken away your father's livestock
and has given them to me.
Ge 21:22; 30:32,42
10"In breeding season I once
had a dream in which I looked up
and saw that the male goats mating with the flock were streaked,
speckled or spotted. 11The angel
of God said to me in the dream,

'Jacob.' I answered, 'Here I am.'
12 And he said, 'Look up and see
that all the male goats mating
with the flock are streaked, speckled or spotted, for I have seen all
that Laban has been doing to you.
13 I am the God of Bethel, where
you anointed a pillar and where
you made a vow to me. Now leave
this land at once and go back to
your native land.'" Ge 28:10-22; Ex 3:7

14 Then Rachel and Leah replied,
"Do we still have any share in the
inheritance of our father's estate?
15 Does he not regard us as foreigners? Not only has he sold us, but
he has used up what was paid for
us. 16 Surely all the wealth that God
took away from our father belongs
to us and our children. So do whatever God has told you." Ge 29:20

17 Then Jacob put his children
and his wives on camels, 18 and
he drove all his livestock ahead
of him, along with all the goods
he had accumulated in Paddan
Aram,[a] to go to his father Isaac in
the land of Canaan. Ge 35:27

19 When Laban had gone to shear
his sheep, Rachel stole her father's
household gods. 20 Moreover, Jacob deceived Laban the Aramean
by not telling him he was running
away. 21 So he fled with all he had,
crossed the Euphrates River, and
headed for the hill country of Gilead. Ge 27:36; 35:2; Jdg 17:5

Laban Pursues Jacob

22 On the third day Laban was
told that Jacob had fled. 23 Taking
his relatives with him, he pursued
Jacob for seven days and caught
up with him in the hill country of
Gilead. 24 Then God came to Laban
the Aramean in a dream at night
and said to him, "Be careful not to
say anything to Jacob, either good
or bad." Ge 20:3; 24:50

25 Jacob had pitched his tent in
the hill country of Gilead when
Laban overtook him, and Laban
and his relatives camped there
too. 26 Then Laban said to Jacob,
"What have you done? You've deceived me, and you've carried off
my daughters like captives in war.
27 Why did you run off secretly and
deceive me? Why didn't you tell
me, so I could send you away with
joy and singing to the music of
timbrels and harps? 28 You didn't
even let me kiss my grandchildren and my daughters goodbye.
You have done a foolish thing. 29 I
have the power to harm you; but
last night the God of your father
said to me, 'Be careful not to say
anything to Jacob, either good or
bad.' 30 Now you have gone off because you longed to return to your
father's household. But why did
you steal my gods?" ver 19,55

31 Jacob answered Laban, "I was
afraid, because I thought you
would take your daughters away
from me by force. 32 But if you find
anyone who has your gods, that
person shall not live. In the presence of our relatives, see for yourself whether there is anything of

[a] *18* That is, Northwest Mesopotamia

yours here with me; and if so, take
it." Now Jacob did not know that
Rachel had stolen the gods. Ge 44:9
33 So Laban went into Jacob's
tent and into Leah's tent and into
the tent of the two female servants, but he found nothing. After
he came out of Leah's tent, he entered Rachel's tent. 34 Now Rachel
had taken the household gods and
put them inside her camel's saddle and was sitting on them. Laban searched through everything
in the tent but found nothing.
ver 37; Ge 44:12
35 Rachel said to her father,
"Don't be angry, my lord, that
I cannot stand up in your presence; I'm having my period." So
he searched but could not find the
household gods. Lev 19:3,32
36 Jacob was angry and took Laban to task. "What is my crime?"
he asked Laban. "How have I
wronged you that you hunt
me down? 37 Now that you have
searched through all my goods,
what have you found that belongs
to your household? Put it here in
front of your relatives and mine,
and let them judge between the
two of us. ver 23
38 "I have been with you for
twenty years now. Your sheep
and goats have not miscarried,
nor have I eaten rams from your
flocks. 39 I did not bring you animals torn by wild beasts; I bore
the loss myself. And you demanded payment from me for whatever
was stolen by day or night. 40 This
was my situation: The heat consumed me in the daytime and the
cold at night, and sleep fled from
my eyes. 41 It was like this for the
twenty years I was in your household. I worked for you fourteen
years for your two daughters and
six years for your flocks, and you
changed my wages ten times. 42 If
the God of my father, the God of
Abraham and the Fear of Isaac,
had not been with me, you would
surely have sent me away empty-handed. But God has seen my
hardship and the toil of my hands,
and last night he rebuked you."
Ge 29:30,32; Ex 22:13
43 Laban answered Jacob, "The
women are my daughters, the
children are my children, and the
flocks are my flocks. All you see
is mine. Yet what can I do today
about these daughters of mine,
or about the children they have
borne? 44 Come now, let's make
a covenant, you and I, and let it
serve as a witness between us."
Ge 21:27; Jos 24:27
45 So Jacob took a stone and set
it up as a pillar. 46 He said to his relatives, "Gather some stones." So
they took stones and piled them
in a heap, and they ate there by
the heap. 47 Laban called it Jegar
Sahadutha, and Jacob called it
Galeed.[a] Ge 28:18
48 Laban said, "This heap is a witness between you and me today."
That is why it was called Galeed.

[a] 47 The Aramaic *Jegar Sahadutha* and the Hebrew *Galeed* both mean *witness heap.*

49It was also called Mizpah,[a] because he said, "May the LORD keep
watch between you and me when
we are away from each other. 50If
you mistreat my daughters or if
you take any wives besides my
daughters, even though no one is
with us, remember that God is a
witness between you and me."

Jdg 11:29; 1Sa 7:5-6; Jer 29:23

51Laban also said to Jacob, "Here
is this heap, and here is this pillar I have set up between you and
me. 52This heap is a witness, and
this pillar is a witness, that I will
not go past this heap to your side
to harm you and that you will not
go past this heap and pillar to my
side to harm me. 53May the God of
Abraham and the God of Nahor,
the God of their father, judge between us." Ge 16:5

So Jacob took an oath in the
name of the Fear of his father
Isaac. 54He offered a sacrifice there
in the hill country and invited his
relatives to a meal. After they had
eaten, they spent the night there.

ver 42

55Early the next morning Laban
kissed his grandchildren and his
daughters and blessed them. Then
he left and returned home.[b] Ge 18:33

Jacob Prepares to Meet Esau

32[c] Jacob also went on his way,
and the angels of God met
him. 2When Jacob saw them, he
said, "This is the camp of God!" So
he named that place Mahanaim.[d]

Ps 34:7; 91:11

3Jacob sent messengers ahead
of him to his brother Esau in the
land of Seir, the country of Edom.
4He instructed them: "This is what
you are to say to my lord Esau:
'Your servant Jacob says, I have
been staying with Laban and have
remained there till now. 5I have
cattle and donkeys, sheep and
goats, male and female servants.
Now I am sending this message to
my lord, that I may find favor in
your eyes.'" Ge 12:16; 33:8,10,15

6When the messengers returned
to Jacob, they said, "We went to
your brother Esau, and now he is
coming to meet you, and four hundred men are with him." Ge 33:1

7In great fear and distress Jacob divided the people who were
with him into two groups,[e] and
the flocks and herds and camels as well. 8He thought, "If Esau
comes and attacks one group,[f] the
group[f] that is left may escape."

ver 11

9Then Jacob prayed, "O God of
my father Abraham, God of my father Isaac, LORD, you who said to
me, 'Go back to your country and
your relatives, and I will make
you prosper,' 10I am unworthy of
all the kindness and faithfulness
you have shown your servant. I
had only my staff when I crossed

[a] 49 *Mizpah* means *watchtower.*
[b] 55 In Hebrew texts this verse (31:55) is numbered 32:1. [c] In Hebrew texts 32:1-32 is numbered 32:2-33. [d] 2 *Mahanaim* means *two camps.* [e] 7 Or *camps*
[f] 8 Or *camp*

this Jordan, but now I have become two camps. 11Save me, I pray,
from the hand of my brother Esau,
for I am afraid he will come and
attack me, and also the mothers with their children. 12But you
have said, 'I will surely make you
prosper and will make your descendants like the sand of the sea,
which cannot be counted.'"

Hos 1:10; Ge 24:27; 31:13

13He spent the night there, and
from what he had with him he selected a gift for his brother Esau:
14two hundred female goats and
twenty male goats, two hundred
ewes and twenty rams, 15thirty female camels with their young, forty cows and ten bulls, and twenty female donkeys and ten male
donkeys. 16He put them in the
care of his servants, each herd by
itself, and said to his servants, "Go
ahead of me, and keep some space
between the herds."

Ge 43:11,15,25-26; Pr 18:16

17He instructed the one in the
lead: "When my brother Esau
meets you and asks, 'Who do you
belong to, and where are you going, and who owns all these animals in front of you?' 18then you
are to say, 'They belong to your
servant Jacob. They are a gift sent
to my lord Esau, and he is coming
behind us.'" Ge 18:3

19He also instructed the second,
the third and all the others who
followed the herds: "You are to
say the same thing to Esau when
you meet him. 20And be sure to
say, 'Your servant Jacob is coming behind us.'" For he thought, "I
will pacify him with these gifts I
am sending on ahead; later, when
I see him, perhaps he will receive me." 21So Jacob's gifts went
on ahead of him, but he himself
spent the night in the camp.

Ge 33:10; Pr 21:14

Jacob Wrestles With God

22That night Jacob got up and
took his two wives, his two female
servants and his eleven sons and
crossed the ford of the Jabbok.
23After he had sent them across
the stream, he sent over all his
possessions. 24So Jacob was left
alone, and a man wrestled with
him till daybreak. 25When the
man saw that he could not overpower him, he touched the socket
of Jacob's hip so that his hip was
wrenched as he wrestled with the
man. 26Then the man said, "Let
me go, for it is daybreak."

But Jacob replied, "I will not let
you go unless you bless me."

Hos 12:4

27The man asked him, "What is
your name?"

"Jacob," he answered.

28Then the man said, "Your
name will no longer be Jacob, but
Israel,[a] because you have struggled with God and with humans
and have overcome." Ge 17:5; 35:10

29Jacob said, "Please tell me
your name." Jdg 13:17

[a] 28 *Israel* probably means *he struggles with God.*

But he replied, "Why do you ask
my name?" Then he blessed him
there. Ge 35:9

30So Jacob called the place Peniel,[a] saying, "It is because I saw
God face to face, and yet my life
was spared." Ge 16:13; Ex 24:11; Jdg 6:22

31The sun rose above him as he
passed Peniel,[b] and he was limp-
ing because of his hip. 32Therefore
to this day the Israelites do not eat
the tendon attached to the socket
of the hip, because the socket of
Jacob's hip was touched near the
tendon. ver 25

Jacob Meets Esau

33 Jacob looked up and there
was Esau, coming with his
four hundred men; so he divided the children among Leah, Rachel and the two female servants.
2He put the female servants and
their children in front, Leah and
her children next, and Rachel and
Joseph in the rear. 3He himself
went on ahead and bowed down
to the ground seven times as he
approached his brother. Ge 32:6; 42:6

4But Esau ran to meet Jacob and
embraced him; he threw his arms
around his neck and kissed him.
And they wept. 5Then Esau looked
up and saw the women and children. "Who are these with you?"
he asked. Ge 45:14-15

Jacob answered, "They are the
children God has graciously given
your servant." Ge 48:9; Ps 127:3; Isa 8:18

6Then the female servants and
their children approached and
bowed down. 7Next, Leah and her
children came and bowed down.
Last of all came Joseph and Rachel,
and they too bowed down. Ge 30:24

8Esau asked, "What's the meaning of all these flocks and herds I
met?" Ge 32:14-16

"To find favor in your eyes, my
lord," he said. Ge 24:9

9But Esau said, "I already have
plenty, my brother. Keep what you
have for yourself."

10"No, please!" said Jacob. "If I
have found favor in your eyes, accept this gift from me. For to see
your face is like seeing the face of
God, now that you have received
me favorably. 11Please accept the
present that was brought to you,
for God has been gracious to me
and I have all I need." And because
Jacob insisted, Esau accepted it.
Ge 32:20; 1Sa 25:27

12Then Esau said, "Let us be on
our way; I'll accompany you."

13But Jacob said to him, "My lord
knows that the children are tender
and that I must care for the ewes
and cows that are nursing their
young. If they are driven hard just
one day, all the animals will die.
14So let my lord go on ahead of his
servant, while I move along slow-
ly at the pace of the flocks and
herds before me and the pace of
the children, until I come to my
lord in Seir." Ge 32:3

15Esau said, "Then let me leave
some of my men with you."

[a] *30* *Peniel* means *face of God.*
[b] *31* Hebrew *Penuel*, a variant of *Peniel*

"But why do that?" Jacob asked.
"Just let me find favor in the eyes
of my lord." Ge 34:11

16So that day Esau started on his
way back to Seir. 17Jacob, however,
went to Sukkoth, where he built a
place for himself and made shelters for his livestock. That is why
the place is called Sukkoth.[a]
Jdg 8:4-5,8,14-16

18After Jacob came from Paddan
Aram,[b] he arrived safely at the city
of Shechem in Canaan and camped
within sight of the city. 19For a hundred pieces of silver,[c] he bought
from the sons of Hamor, the father
of Shechem, the plot of ground
where he pitched his tent. 20There
he set up an altar and called it El
Elohe Israel.[d] Jos 24:1,32; Jn 4:5

Dinah and the Shechemites

34 Now Dinah, the daugh-
ter Leah had borne to Ja-
cob, went out to visit the women
of the land. 2When Shechem son
of Hamor the Hivite, the ruler of
that area, saw her, he took her and
raped her. 3His heart was drawn to
Dinah daughter of Jacob; he loved
the young woman and spoke tenderly to her. 4And Shechem said to
his father Hamor, "Get me this girl
as my wife." Ge 30:21

5When Jacob heard that his
daughter Dinah had been defiled,
his sons were in the fields with his
livestock; so he did nothing about
it until they came home.

6Then Shechem's father Hamor went out to talk with Jacob.
7Meanwhile, Jacob's sons had
come in from the fields as soon as
they heard what had happened.
They were shocked and furious,
because Shechem had done an
outrageous thing in[e] Israel by
sleeping with Jacob's daughter —
a thing that should not be done.
Dt 22:21; Jdg 20:6; 2Sa 13:12

8But Hamor said to them, "My
son Shechem has his heart set on
your daughter. Please give her
to him as his wife. 9Intermarry
with us; give us your daughters
and take our daughters for yourselves. 10You can settle among us;
the land is open to you. Live in it,
trade[f] in it, and acquire property
in it." Ge 13:9; 42:34; 47:6,27

11Then Shechem said to Dinah's
father and brothers, "Let me find
favor in your eyes, and I will give
you whatever you ask. 12Make the
price for the bride and the gift I
am to bring as great as you like,
and I'll pay whatever you ask me.
Only give me the young woman as
my wife." Ex 22:16; Dt 22:29; 1Sa 18:25

13Because their sister Dinah had
been defiled, Jacob's sons replied
deceitfully as they spoke to Shechem and his father Hamor. 14They
said to them, "We can't do such a
thing; we can't give our sister to a

[a] 17 *Sukkoth* means *shelters.* [b] 18 That is, Northwest Mesopotamia [c] 19 Hebrew *hundred kesitahs*; a kesitah was a unit of money of unknown weight and value. [d] 20 *El Elohe Israel* can mean *El is the God of Israel* or *mighty is the God of Israel.* [e] 7 Or *against* [f] 10 Or *move about freely*; also in verse 21

man who is not circumcised. That
would be a disgrace to us. 15 We will
enter into an agreement with you
on one condition only: that you
become like us by circumcising
all your males. 16 Then we will give
you our daughters and take your
daughters for ourselves. We'll settle
among you and become one people with you. 17 But if you will not
agree to be circumcised, we'll take
our sister and go." Ge 17:14; Ex 12:48

18 Their proposal seemed good
to Hamor and his son Shechem.
19 The young man, who was the
most honored of all his father's
family, lost no time in doing what
they said, because he was delighted with Jacob's daughter. 20 So Hamor and his son Shechem went
to the gate of their city to speak
to the men of their city. 21 "These
men are friendly toward us," they
said. "Let them live in our land
and trade in it; the land has plenty of room for them. We can marry
their daughters and they can marry ours. 22 But the men will agree
to live with us as one people only
on the condition that our males be
circumcised, as they themselves
are. 23 Won't their livestock, their
property and all their other animals become ours? So let us agree
to their terms, and they will settle
among us." ver 3; Ru 4:1

24 All the men who went out of
the city gate agreed with Hamor
and his son Shechem, and every
male in the city was circumcised.
Ge 23:10

25 Three days later, while all of
them were still in pain, two of Jacob's sons, Simeon and Levi, Dinah's brothers, took their swords
and attacked the unsuspecting
city, killing every male. 26 They
put Hamor and his son Shechem
to the sword and took Dinah from
Shechem's house and left. 27 The
sons of Jacob came upon the
dead bodies and looted the city
where[a] their sister had been defiled. 28 They seized their flocks
and herds and donkeys and everything else of theirs in the city and
out in the fields. 29 They carried off
all their wealth and all their wom-
en and children, taking as plunder
everything in the houses. Ge 49:5,7

30 Then Jacob said to Simeon and
Levi, "You have brought trouble
on me by making me obnoxious
to the Canaanites and Perizzites,
the people living in this land. We
are few in number, and if they join
forces against me and attack me,
I and my household will be destroyed." Ex 5:21; 1Ch 16:19

31 But they replied, "Should he
have treated our sister like a prostitute?"

Jacob Returns to Bethel

35 Then God said to Jacob,
"Go up to Bethel and settle
there, and build an altar there to
God, who appeared to you when
you were fleeing from your brother Esau." Ge 27:43; 28:19

[a] 27 Or *because*

2So Jacob said to his household
and to all who were with him,
"Get rid of the foreign gods you
have with you, and purify yourselves and change your clothes.
3Then come, let us go up to Bethel, where I will build an altar to
God, who answered me in the day
of my distress and who has been
with me wherever I have gone."
4So they gave Jacob all the foreign gods they had and the rings
in their ears, and Jacob buried
them under the oak at Shechem.
5Then they set out, and the terror of God fell on the towns all
around them so that no one pursued them.

Ge 28:15,20-22; 32:7; Ex 19:10,14

6Jacob and all the people with
him came to Luz (that is, Bethel)
in the land of Canaan. 7There he
built an altar, and he called the
place El Bethel,[a] because it was
there that God revealed himself to
him when he was fleeing from his
brother. Ge 28:13,19

8Now Deborah, Rebekah's nurse,
died and was buried under the oak
outside Bethel. So it was named
Allon Bakuth.[b] Ge 24:59

9After Jacob returned from Paddan Aram,[c] God appeared to him
again and blessed him. 10God said
to him, "Your name is Jacob,[d] but
you will no longer be called Jacob;
your name will be Israel.[e]" So he
named him Israel. Ge 17:5; 32:29

11And God said to him, "I am
God Almighty[f]; be fruitful and
increase in number. A nation
and a community of nations will
come from you, and kings will be
among your descendants. 12The
land I gave to Abraham and Isaac
I also give to you, and I will give
this land to your descendants after you." 13Then God went up from
him at the place where he had
talked with him. Ge 13:15; 17:6

14Jacob set up a stone pillar at the
place where God had talked with
him, and he poured out a drink offering on it; he also poured oil on
it. 15Jacob called the place where
God had talked with him Bethel.[g]

Ge 28:18-19

The Deaths of Rachel and Isaac

16Then they moved on from
Bethel. While they were still
some distance from Ephrath, Rachel began to give birth and had
great difficulty. 17And as she was
having great difficulty in childbirth, the midwife said to her,
"Don't despair, for you have another son." 18As she breathed her
last — for she was dying — she
named her son Ben-Oni.[h] But his
father named him Benjamin.[i]

Ge 30:24

19So Rachel died and was buried on the way to Ephrath (that is,

[a] 7 *El Bethel* means *God of Bethel.*
[b] 8 *Allon Bakuth* means *oak of weeping.*
[c] 9 That is, Northwest Mesopotamia; also in verse 26
[d] 10 *Jacob* means *he grasps the heel,* a Hebrew idiom for *he deceives.*
[e] 10 *Israel* probably means *he struggles with God.*
[f] 11 Hebrew *El-Shaddai*
[g] 15 *Bethel* means *house of God.*
[h] 18 *Ben-Oni* means *son of my trouble.*
[i] 18 *Benjamin* means *son of my right hand.*

Bethlehem). 20Over her tomb Jacob set up a pillar, and to this day
that pillar marks Rachel's tomb.

1Sa 10:2

21Israel moved on again and
pitched his tent beyond Migdal
Eder. 22While Israel was living in
that region, Reuben went in and
slept with his father's concubine
Bilhah, and Israel heard of it.

Ge 49:4

Jacob had twelve sons:

23The sons of Leah:

Reuben the firstborn of Jacob, Ge 46:8

Simeon, Levi, Judah, Issachar and Zebulun. Ge 29:35

24The sons of Rachel:

Joseph and Benjamin.

ver 18; Ge 30:24

25The sons of Rachel's servant Bilhah:

Dan and Naphtali.

26The sons of Leah's servant Zilpah:

Gad and Asher. Ge 30:11,13

These were the sons of Jacob,
who were born to him in Paddan
Aram. 1Ch 2:1-2

27Jacob came home to his father
Isaac in Mamre, near Kiriath Arba
(that is, Hebron), where Abraham and Isaac had stayed. 28Isaac
lived a hundred and eighty years.
29Then he breathed his last and
died and was gathered to his people, old and full of years. And his
sons Esau and Jacob buried him.

Ge 15:15; 25:8-9

Esau's Descendants

36 This is the account of the
family line of Esau (that is,
Edom). Ge 25:30

2Esau took his wives from
the women of Canaan: Adah
daughter of Elon the Hittite,
and Oholibamah daughter
of Anah and granddaughter
of Zibeon the Hivite— 3also
Basemath daughter of Ishmael and sister of Nebaioth.

Ge 26:34; 28:8-9

4Adah bore Eliphaz to Esau,
Basemath bore Reuel, 5and
Oholibamah bore Jeush, Jalam and Korah. These were
the sons of Esau, who were
born to him in Canaan. 1Ch 1:35
6Esau took his wives and
sons and daughters and all
the members of his house-
hold, as well as his livestock
and all his other animals
and all the goods he had acquired in Canaan, and moved
to a land some distance from
his brother Jacob. 7Their possessions were too great for
them to remain together; the
land where they were staying
could not support them both
because of their livestock. 8So
Esau (that is, Edom) settled in
the hill country of Seir.

Ge 13:6; 32:3

9This is the account of the fam-
ily line of Esau the father of the
Edomites in the hill country of
Seir.

[10]These are the names of Esau's sons:
Eliphaz, the son of Esau's wife Adah, and Reuel, the son of Esau's wife Basemath.
[11]The sons of Eliphaz:
Teman, Omar, Zepho, Gatam and Kenaz. Am 1:12; Hab 3:3
[12]Esau's son Eliphaz also had a concubine named Timna, who bore him Amalek. These were grandsons of Esau's wife Adah.
Ex 17:8,16; Nu 24:20; 1Sa 15:2
[13]The sons of Reuel:
Nahath, Zerah, Shammah and Mizzah. These were grandsons of Esau's wife Basemath.
[14]The sons of Esau's wife Oholibamah daughter of Anah and granddaughter of Zibeon, whom she bore to Esau:
Jeush, Jalam and Korah.
1Ch 1:35-37

[15]These were the chiefs among
Esau's descendants: Ex 15:15
The sons of Eliphaz the firstborn of Esau:
Chiefs Teman, Omar, Zepho, Kenaz, [16]Korah,[a] Gatam and Amalek. These were the chiefs descended from Eliphaz in Edom; they were grandsons of Adah.
[17]The sons of Esau's son Reuel:
1Ch 1:37
Chiefs Nahath, Zerah, Shammah and Mizzah. These were the chiefs descended from Reuel in Edom; they were grandsons of Esau's wife Basemath.
[18]The sons of Esau's wife Oholibamah:
Chiefs Jeush, Jalam and Korah. These were the chiefs descended from Esau's wife Oholibamah daughter of Anah.
[19]These were the sons of Esau
(that is, Edom), and these were
their chiefs. Ge 25:30

[20]These were the sons of Seir the
Horite, who were living in the re-
gion: Ge 14:6; Dt 2:12,22
Lotan, Shobal, Zibeon, Anah, [21]Dishon, Ezer and Dishan. These sons of Seir in Edom were Horite chiefs.
[22]The sons of Lotan:
Hori and Homam.[b] Timna was Lotan's sister.
[23]The sons of Shobal:
Alvan, Manahath, Ebal, Shepho and Onam.
[24]The sons of Zibeon:
Aiah and Anah. This is the Anah who discovered the hot springs[c] in the desert while he was grazing the donkeys of his father Zibeon.

[a] 16 Masoretic Text; Samaritan Pentateuch (also verse 11 and 1 Chron. 1:36) does not have *Korah*. [b] 22 Hebrew *Hemam*, a variant of *Homam* (see 1 Chron. 1:39)
[c] 24 Vulgate; Syriac *discovered water;* the meaning of the Hebrew for this word is uncertain.

25 The children of Anah:
Dishon and Oholibamah daughter of Anah.
26 The sons of Dishon[a]:
Hemdan, Eshban, Ithran and Keran.
27 The sons of Ezer:
Bilhan, Zaavan and Akan.
28 The sons of Dishan:
Uz and Aran. 1Ch 1:38-42
29 These were the Horite chiefs:
Lotan, Shobal, Zibeon,
Anah, 30 Dishon, Ezer and
Dishan. These were the Horite chiefs, according to their divisions, in the land of Seir.

The Rulers of Edom

31 These were the kings who reigned in Edom before any Israelite king reigned:
32 Bela son of Beor became king of Edom. His city was named Dinhabah. 1Ch 1:43
33 When Bela died, Jobab son of Zerah from Bozrah succeeded him as king. Jer 49:13,22
34 When Jobab died, Husham from the land of the Temanites succeeded him as king. Eze 25:13
35 When Husham died, Hadad son of Bedad, who defeated Midian in the country of Moab, succeeded him as king. His city was named Avith. Ge 19:37; Ru 1:1,6
36 When Hadad died, Samlah from Masrekah succeeded him as king.
37 When Samlah died, Shaul from Rehoboth on the river succeeded him as king.
38 When Shaul died, Baal-Hanan son of Akbor succeeded him as king.
39 When Baal-Hanan son of Akbor died, Hadad[b] succeeded him as king. His city was named Pau, and his wife's name was Mehetabel daughter of Matred, the daughter of Me-Zahab.

40 These were the chiefs descended from Esau, by name, according to their clans and regions:
Timna, Alvah, Jetheth,
41 Oholibamah, Elah, Pinon,
42 Kenaz, Teman, Mibzar,
43 Magdiel and Iram. These were the chiefs of Edom, according to their settlements in the land they occupied.

This is the family line of Esau, the father of the Edomites.
1Ch 1:43-54

Joseph's Dreams

37 Jacob lived in the land where his father had stayed, the land of Canaan. Ge 17:8

2 This is the account of Jacob's family line.

Joseph, a young man of seventeen, was tending the flocks with

[a] 26 Hebrew *Dishan*, a variant of *Dishon*
[b] 39 Many manuscripts of the Masoretic Text, Samaritan Pentateuch and Syriac (see also 1 Chron. 1:50); most manuscripts of the Masoretic Text *Hadar*

his brothers, the sons of Bilhah
and the sons of Zilpah, his father's
wives, and he brought their father
a bad report about them.
1Sa 2:24; Ps 78:71

3 Now Israel loved Joseph more
than any of his other sons, because
he had been born to him in his old
age; and he made an ornate[a] robe
for him. 4 When his brothers saw
that their father loved him more
than any of them, they hated him
and could not speak a kind word
to him. Ge 27:41; 44:20

5 Joseph had a dream, and when
he told it to his brothers, they
hated him all the more. 6 He said
to them, "Listen to this dream I
had: 7 We were binding sheaves of
grain out in the field when suddenly my sheaf rose and stood upright, while your sheaves gathered
around mine and bowed down
to it." Ge 42:6,9; 44:14; 50:18

8 His brothers said to him, "Do
you intend to reign over us? Will
you actually rule us?" And they
hated him all the more because of
his dream and what he had said.
Ge 49:26

9 Then he had another dream,
and he told it to his brothers.
"Listen," he said, "I had another
dream, and this time the sun and
moon and eleven stars were bowing down to me." Ge 28:12

10 When he told his father as well
as his brothers, his father rebuked
him and said, "What is this dream
you had? Will your mother and I
and your brothers actually come
and bow down to the ground before you?" 11 His brothers were jealous of him, but his father kept the
matter in mind.
Ge 27:29; Lk 2:19,51; Ac 7:9

Joseph Sold by His Brothers

12 Now his brothers had gone
to graze their father's flocks near
Shechem, 13 and Israel said to Joseph, "As you know, your brothers
are grazing the flocks near Shechem. Come, I am going to send
you to them."

"Very well," he replied.

14 So he said to him, "Go and see
if all is well with your brothers and
with the flocks, and bring word
back to me." Then he sent him off
from the Valley of Hebron. Ge 13:18

When Joseph arrived at Shechem, 15 a man found him wandering around in the fields and asked
him, "What are you looking for?"

16 He replied, "I'm looking for my
brothers. Can you tell me where
they are grazing their flocks?"

17 "They have moved on from
here," the man answered. "I heard
them say, 'Let's go to Dothan.'"
2Ki 6:13

So Joseph went after his brothers and found them near Dothan.
18 But they saw him in the distance,
and before he reached them, they
plotted to kill him. Mk 14:1

19 "Here comes that dreamer!"
they said to each other. 20 "Come
now, let's kill him and throw him

[a] 3 The meaning of the Hebrew for this word is uncertain; also in verses 23 and 32.

into one of these cisterns and say
that a ferocious animal devoured
him. Then we'll see what comes of
his dreams." Ge 50:20
21 When Reuben heard this, he
tried to rescue him from their
hands. "Let's not take his life,"
he said. 22 "Don't shed any blood.
Throw him into this cistern here
in the wilderness, but don't lay a
hand on him." Reuben said this to
rescue him from them and take
him back to his father. Ge 42:22
23 So when Joseph came to his
brothers, they stripped him of
his robe — the ornate robe he was
wearing — 24 and they took him
and threw him into the cistern.
The cistern was empty; there was
no water in it. Jer 41:7
25 As they sat down to eat their
meal, they looked up and saw a caravan of Ishmaelites coming from
Gilead. Their camels were loaded with spices, balm and myrrh,
and they were on their way to take
them down to Egypt. ver 28
26 Judah said to his brothers,
"What will we gain if we kill our
brother and cover up his blood?
27 Come, let's sell him to the Ishmaelites and not lay our hands
on him; after all, he is our brother, our own flesh and blood." His
brothers agreed. Ge 4:10; 42:21
28 So when the Midianite merchants came by, his brothers pulled
Joseph up out of the cistern and
sold him for twenty shekels[a] of
silver to the Ishmaelites, who took
him to Egypt. Ge 45:4-5; Ps 105:17; Ac 7:9
29 When Reuben returned to the
cistern and saw that Joseph was
not there, he tore his clothes. 30 He
went back to his brothers and said,
"The boy isn't there! Where can I
turn now?" ver 22; Ge 42:13,36; Job 1:20
31 Then they got Joseph's robe,
slaughtered a goat and dipped the
robe in the blood. 32 They took the
ornate robe back to their father
and said, "We found this. Examine
it to see whether it is your son's
robe." ver 3,23
33 He recognized it and said, "It
is my son's robe! Some ferocious
animal has devoured him. Joseph
has surely been torn to pieces."
ver 20; Ge 44:20,28
34 Then Jacob tore his clothes,
put on sackcloth and mourned for
his son many days. 35 All his sons
and daughters came to comfort
him, but he refused to be comforted. "No," he said, "I will continue
to mourn until I join my son in
the grave." So his father wept for
him. Ge 42:38; 44:22,29,31
36 Meanwhile, the Midianites[b]
sold Joseph in Egypt to Potiphar,
one of Pharaoh's officials, the captain of the guard. Ge 39:1

Judah and Tamar

38 At that time, Judah left his
brothers and went down
to stay with a man of Adullam
named Hirah. 2 There Judah met

[a] *28* That is, about 8 ounces or about 230 grams [b] *36* Samaritan Pentateuch, Septuagint, Vulgate and Syriac (see also verse 28); Masoretic Text *Medanites*

the daughter of a Canaanite man
named Shua. He married her and
made love to her; 3she became
pregnant and gave birth to a son,
who was named Er. 4She conceived
again and gave birth to a son and
named him Onan. 5She gave birth
to still another son and named
him Shelah. It was at Kezib that
she gave birth to him. 1Ch 2:3; 4:21

6Judah got a wife for Er, his
firstborn, and her name was Tamar. 7But Er, Judah's firstborn,
was wicked in the LORD's sight; so
the LORD put him to death. 1Ch 2:3

8Then Judah said to Onan,
"Sleep with your brother's wife
and fulfill your duty to her as a
brother-in-law to raise up offspring for your brother." 9But
Onan knew that the child would
not be his; so whenever he slept
with his brother's wife, he spilled
his semen on the ground to keep
from providing offspring for his
brother. 10What he did was wicked in the LORD's sight; so the LORD
put him to death also.
Dt 25:5-6; Mt 22:24-28; Ge 46:12

11Judah then said to his daughter-in-law Tamar, "Live as a widow
in your father's household until
my son Shelah grows up." For he
thought, "He may die too, just like
his brothers." So Tamar went to
live in her father's household.
Ru 1:13

12After a long time Judah's wife,
the daughter of Shua, died. When
Judah had recovered from his
grief, he went up to Timnah, to the
men who were shearing his sheep,
and his friend Hirah the Adullam-
ite went with him. Jos 15:10,57

13When Tamar was told, "Your
father-in-law is on his way to Timnah to shear his sheep," 14she took
off her widow's clothes, covered
herself with a veil to disguise herself, and then sat down at the entrance to Enaim, which is on the
road to Timnah. For she saw that,
though Shelah had now grown up,
she had not been given to him as
his wife. Ge 31:19

15When Judah saw her, he
thought she was a prostitute, for
she had covered her face. 16Not realizing that she was his daughter-
in-law, he went over to her by the
roadside and said, "Come now, let
me sleep with you." Lev 18:15; 20:12

"And what will you give me to
sleep with you?" she asked.

17"I'll send you a young goat
from my flock," he said. Eze 16:33

"Will you give me something
as a pledge until you send it?" she
asked.

18He said, "What pledge should
I give you?"

"Your seal and its cord, and the
staff in your hand," she answered.
So he gave them to her and slept
with her, and she became pregnant by him. 19After she left, she
took off her veil and put on her
widow's clothes again.

20Meanwhile Judah sent the
young goat by his friend the Adul-
lamite in order to get his pledge
back from the woman, but he did

not find her. 21 He asked the men
who lived there, "Where is the
shrine prostitute who was beside
the road at Enaim?" Lev 19:29; Hos 4:14
"There hasn't been any shrine
prostitute here," they said.
22 So he went back to Judah and
said, "I didn't find her. Besides, the
men who lived there said, 'There
hasn't been any shrine prostitute
here.'"
23 Then Judah said, "Let her keep
what she has, or we will become a
laughingstock. After all, I did send
her this young goat, but you didn't
find her."
24 About three months later Judah was told, "Your daughter-in-
law Tamar is guilty of prostitution, and as a result she is now
pregnant."
Judah said, "Bring her out and
have her burned to death!"
Lev 21:9; Dt 22:21,22
25 As she was being brought
out, she sent a message to her father-in-law. "I am pregnant by the
man who owns these," she said.
And she added, "See if you recognize whose seal and cord and staff
these are." ver 18
26 Judah recognized them and
said, "She is more righteous than
I, since I wouldn't give her to my
son Shelah." And he did not sleep
with her again. 1Sa 24:17
27 When the time came for her to
give birth, there were twin boys
in her womb. 28 As she was giving birth, one of them put out his
hand; so the midwife took a scarlet thread and tied it on his wrist
and said, "This one came out first."
29 But when he drew back his hand,
his brother came out, and she said,
"So this is how you have broken
out!" And he was named Perez.[a]
30 Then his brother, who had the
scarlet thread on his wrist, came
out. And he was named Zerah.[b]
Ge 46:12; Nu 26:20-21; Mt 1:3

Joseph and Potiphar's Wife

39 Now Joseph had been tak-
en down to Egypt. Poti-
phar, an Egyptian who was one of
Pharaoh's officials, the captain of
the guard, bought him from the
Ishmaelites who had taken him
there. Ge 37:25,36; Ps 105:17
2 The LORD was with Joseph so
that he prospered, and he lived
in the house of his Egyptian master. 3 When his master saw that the
LORD was with him and that the
LORD gave him success in everything he did, 4 Joseph found favor
in his eyes and became his attendant. Potiphar put him in charge
of his household, and he entrusted
to his care everything he owned.
5 From the time he put him in
charge of his household and of all
that he owned, the LORD blessed
the household of the Egyptian because of Joseph. The blessing of
the LORD was on everything Potiphar had, both in the house and in
the field. 6 So Potiphar left everything he had in Joseph's care; with

[a] 29 *Perez* means *breaking out.*
[b] 30 *Zerah* can mean *scarlet* or *brightness.*

Joseph in charge, he did not concern himself with anything except the food he ate. Ge 21:22; 26:28; Ps 1:3

Now Joseph was well-built and handsome, 7and after a while his master's wife took notice of Joseph and said, "Come to bed with me!" Pr 7:15-18

8But he refused. "With me in charge," he told her, "my master does not concern himself with anything in the house; everything he owns he has entrusted to my care. 9No one is greater in this house than I am. My master has withheld nothing from me except you, because you are his wife. How then could I do such a wicked thing and sin against God?" 10And though she spoke to Joseph day after day, he refused to go to bed with her or even be with her. Ge 20:6; 42:18; Pr 6:23-24

11One day he went into the house to attend to his duties, and none of the household servants was inside. 12She caught him by his cloak and said, "Come to bed with me!" But he left his cloak in her hand and ran out of the house. Pr 7:13

13When she saw that he had left his cloak in her hand and had run out of the house, 14she called her household servants. "Look," she said to them, "this Hebrew has been brought to us to make sport of us! He came in here to sleep with me, but I screamed. 15When he heard me scream for help, he left his cloak beside me and ran out of the house." Dt 22:24,27

16She kept his cloak beside her until his master came home. 17Then she told him this story: "That Hebrew slave you brought us came to me to make sport of me. 18But as soon as I screamed for help, he left his cloak beside me and ran out of the house." Ex 23:1,7; Ps 101:5

19When his master heard the story his wife told him, saying, "This is how your slave treated me," he burned with anger. 20Joseph's master took him and put him in prison, the place where the king's prisoners were confined. Ps 105:18

But while Joseph was there in the prison, 21the LORD was with him; he showed him kindness and granted him favor in the eyes of the prison warden. 22So the warden put Joseph in charge of all those held in the prison, and he was made responsible for all that was done there. 23The warden paid no attention to anything under Joseph's care, because the LORD was with Joseph and gave him success in whatever he did. ver 3; Ex 3:21

The Cupbearer and the Baker

40 Some time later, the cupbearer and the baker of the king of Egypt offended their master, the king of Egypt. 2Pharaoh was angry with his two officials, the chief cupbearer and the chief baker, 3and put them in custody in the house of the captain of the guard, in the same prison where

Joseph was confined. 4The captain
of the guard assigned them to Joseph, and he attended them.
Ge 39:4,20

After they had been in custody for some time, 5each of the
two men — the cupbearer and the
baker of the king of Egypt, who
were being held in prison — had
a dream the same night, and each
dream had a meaning of its own.
Ge 41:11

6When Joseph came to them the
next morning, he saw that they
were dejected. 7So he asked Pharaoh's officials who were in custody with him in his master's house,
"Why do you look so sad today?"
Ne 2:2

8"We both had dreams," they
answered, "but there is no one to
interpret them." Ge 41:8,15

Then Joseph said to them, "Do
not interpretations belong to God?
Tell me your dreams." Ge 41:16

9So the chief cupbearer told Joseph his dream. He said to him,
"In my dream I saw a vine in front
of me, 10and on the vine were
three branches. As soon as it budded, it blossomed, and its clusters
ripened into grapes. 11Pharaoh's
cup was in my hand, and I took
the grapes, squeezed them into
Pharaoh's cup and put the cup in
his hand."

12"This is what it means," Joseph
said to him. "The three branches
are three days. 13Within three days
Pharaoh will lift up your head and
restore you to your position, and
you will put Pharaoh's cup in his
hand, just as you used to do when
you were his cupbearer. 14But
when all goes well with you, remember me and show me kindness; mention me to Pharaoh and
get me out of this prison. 15I was
forcibly carried off from the land
of the Hebrews, and even here I
have done nothing to deserve being put in a dungeon."
Da 2:36; 4:19; Jos 2:12

16When the chief baker saw that
Joseph had given a favorable interpretation, he said to Joseph,
"I too had a dream: On my head
were three baskets of bread.[a] 17In
the top basket were all kinds of
baked goods for Pharaoh, but the
birds were eating them out of the
basket on my head."

18"This is what it means," Joseph
said. "The three baskets are three
days. 19Within three days Pharaoh
will lift off your head and impale
your body on a pole. And the birds
will eat away your flesh." ver 12-13

20Now the third day was Pharaoh's birthday, and he gave a feast
for all his officials. He lifted up the
heads of the chief cupbearer and
the chief baker in the presence
of his officials: 21He restored the
chief cupbearer to his position,
so that he once again put the cup
into Pharaoh's hand — 22but he
impaled the chief baker, just as
Joseph had said to them in his interpretation. ver 13; Ps 105:19

[a] 16 Or *three wicker baskets*

23The chief cupbearer, however,
did not remember Joseph; he forgot him. Job 19:14

Pharaoh's Dreams

41 When two full years had
passed, Pharaoh had a
dream: He was standing by the
Nile, 2when out of the river there
came up seven cows, sleek and fat,
and they grazed among the reeds.
3After them, seven other cows,
ugly and gaunt, came up out of
the Nile and stood beside those on
the riverbank. 4And the cows that
were ugly and gaunt ate up the
seven sleek, fat cows. Then Pharaoh woke up. Ge 20:3; Isa 19:6

5He fell asleep again and had
a second dream: Seven heads of
grain, healthy and good, were
growing on a single stalk. 6After
them, seven other heads of grain
sprouted — thin and scorched by
the east wind. 7The thin heads
of grain swallowed up the seven
healthy, full heads. Then Pharaoh
woke up; it had been a dream.

8In the morning his mind was
troubled, so he sent for all the
magicians and wise men of Egypt.
Pharaoh told them his dreams,
but no one could interpret them
for him. Da 2:1,3; 4:5,19; Ex 7:11,22

9Then the chief cupbearer said
to Pharaoh, "Today I am reminded of my shortcomings. 10Phar-
aoh was once angry with his servants, and he imprisoned me and
the chief baker in the house of the
captain of the guard. 11Each of us
had a dream the same night, and
each dream had a meaning of its
own. 12Now a young Hebrew was
there with us, a servant of the captain of the guard. We told him our
dreams, and he interpreted them
for us, giving each man the interpretation of his dream. 13And
things turned out exactly as he
interpreted them to us: I was restored to my position, and the other man was impaled." Ge 40:2,5,12,22

14So Pharaoh sent for Joseph,
and he was quickly brought from
the dungeon. When he had shaved
and changed his clothes, he came
before Pharaoh. Ps 105:20; Da 2:25

15Pharaoh said to Joseph, "I had
a dream, and no one can interpret
it. But I have heard it said of you
that when you hear a dream you
can interpret it." Da 15:16

16"I cannot do it," Joseph replied
to Pharaoh, "but God will give
Pharaoh the answer he desires."
Ge 40:8; Da 2:30; 2Co 3:5

17Then Pharaoh said to Joseph,
"In my dream I was standing on the
bank of the Nile, 18when out of the
river there came up seven cows, fat
and sleek, and they grazed among
the reeds. 19After them, seven other cows came up — scrawny and
very ugly and lean. I had never
seen such ugly cows in all the land
of Egypt. 20The lean, ugly cows ate
up the seven fat cows that came
up first. 21But even after they ate
them, no one could tell that they
had done so; they looked just as
ugly as before. Then I woke up.

[22]"In my dream I saw seven heads of grain, full and good, growing on a single stalk. [23]After them, seven other heads sprouted — withered and thin and scorched by the east wind. [24]The thin heads of grain swallowed up the seven good heads. I told this to the magicians, but none of them could explain it to me." ver 8

[25]Then Joseph said to Pharaoh, "The dreams of Pharaoh are one and the same. God has revealed to Pharaoh what he is about to do. [26]The seven good cows are seven years, and the seven good heads of grain are seven years; it is one and the same dream. [27]The seven lean, ugly cows that came up afterward are seven years, and so are the seven worthless heads of grain scorched by the east wind: They are seven years of famine.

Da 2:45; 2Ki 8:1

[28]"It is just as I said to Pharaoh: God has shown Pharaoh what he is about to do. [29]Seven years of great abundance are coming throughout the land of Egypt, [30]but seven years of famine will follow them. Then all the abundance in Egypt will be forgotten, and the famine will ravage the land. [31]The abundance in the land will not be remembered, because the famine that follows it will be so severe. [32]The reason the dream was given to Pharaoh in two forms is that the matter has been firmly decided by God, and God will do it soon.

ver 47,54; Ge 47:13

[33]"And now let Pharaoh look for a discerning and wise man and put him in charge of the land of Egypt. [34]Let Pharaoh appoint commissioners over the land to take a fifth of the harvest of Egypt during the seven years of abundance. [35]They should collect all the food of these good years that are coming and store up the grain under the authority of Pharaoh, to be kept in the cities for food. [36]This food should be held in reserve for the country, to be used during the seven years of famine that will come upon Egypt, so that the country may not be ruined by the famine." ver 48,56

[37]The plan seemed good to Pharaoh and to all his officials. [38]So Pharaoh asked them, "Can we find anyone like this man, one in whom is the spirit of God[a]?"

Nu 27:18; Da 4:8-9,18; 5:11,14

[39]Then Pharaoh said to Joseph, "Since God has made all this known to you, there is no one so discerning and wise as you. [40]You shall be in charge of my palace, and all my people are to submit to your orders. Only with respect to the throne will I be greater than you." Ps 105:21-22; Ac 7:10

Joseph in Charge of Egypt

[41]So Pharaoh said to Joseph, "I hereby put you in charge of the whole land of Egypt." [42]Then Pharaoh took his signet ring from his finger and put it on Joseph's finger.

[a] 38 Or *of the gods*

He dressed him in robes of fine lin-
en and put a gold chain around his
neck. 43 He had him ride in a chariot as his second-in-command,[a]
and people shouted before him,
"Make way[b]!" Thus he put him in
charge of the whole land of Egypt.

Ge 42:6; Est 3:10; Da 5:7,16,29

44 Then Pharaoh said to Joseph,
"I am Pharaoh, but without your
word no one will lift hand or foot
in all Egypt." 45 Pharaoh gave Joseph the name Zaphenath-Paneah
and gave him Asenath daughter of
Potiphera, priest of On,[c] to be his
wife. And Joseph went throughout the land of Egypt.

Ps 105:22

46 Joseph was thirty years old
when he entered the service of
Pharaoh king of Egypt. And Joseph went out from Pharaoh's
presence and traveled throughout
Egypt. 47 During the seven years
of abundance the land produced
plentifully. 48 Joseph collected all
the food produced in those seven
years of abundance in Egypt and
stored it in the cities. In each city
he put the food grown in the fields
surrounding it. 49 Joseph stored up
huge quantities of grain, like the
sand of the sea; it was so much
that he stopped keeping records
because it was beyond measure.

Da 1:19

50 Before the years of famine
came, two sons were born to Joseph by Asenath daughter of Potiphera, priest of On. 51 Joseph
named his firstborn Manasseh[d]
and said, "It is because God has
made me forget all my trouble and
all my father's household." 52 The
second son he named Ephraim[e]
and said, "It is because God has
made me fruitful in the land of
my suffering."

Ge 17:6; 49:22

53 The seven years of abundance
in Egypt came to an end, 54 and the
seven years of famine began, just
as Joseph had said. There was famine in all the other lands, but in
the whole land of Egypt there was
food. 55 When all Egypt began to
feel the famine, the people cried
to Pharaoh for food. Then Pharaoh
told all the Egyptians, "Go to Joseph and do what he tells you."

ver 30; Ps 105:11; Ac 7:11

56 When the famine had spread
over the whole country, Joseph
opened all the storehouses and
sold grain to the Egyptians, for
the famine was severe throughout
Egypt. 57 And all the world came to
Egypt to buy grain from Joseph,
because the famine was severe everywhere.

Ge 12:10; 42:5

Joseph's Brothers Go to Egypt

42 When Jacob learned that
there was grain in Egypt, he
said to his sons, "Why do you just
keep looking at each other?" 2 He
continued, "I have heard that there

[a] 43 Or *in the chariot of his second-in-command*; or *in his second chariot*
[b] 43 Or *Bow down*
[c] 45 That is, Heliopolis; also in verse 50
[d] 51 *Manasseh* sounds like and may be derived from the Hebrew for *forget.*
[e] 52 *Ephraim* sounds like the Hebrew for *twice fruitful.*

is grain in Egypt. Go down there
and buy some for us, so that we
may live and not die." Ge 43:8; Ac 7:12
3Then ten of Joseph's broth-
ers went down to buy grain from
Egypt. 4But Jacob did not send
Benjamin, Joseph's brother, with
the others, because he was afraid
that harm might come to him. 5So
Israel's sons were among those
who went to buy grain, for there
was famine in the land of Canaan
also. ver 38; Ac 7:11
6Now Joseph was the governor
of the land, the person who sold
grain to all its people. So when
Joseph's brothers arrived, they
bowed down to him with their
faces to the ground. 7As soon as
Joseph saw his brothers, he recognized them, but he pretended to
be a stranger and spoke harshly to
them. "Where do you come from?"
he asked. Ge 37:7-10; 41:41
"From the land of Canaan," they
replied, "to buy food."
8Although Joseph recognized
his brothers, they did not recognize him. 9Then he remembered
his dreams about them and said
to them, "You are spies! You have
come to see where our land is unprotected." Ge 37:7
10"No, my lord," they answered.
"Your servants have come to buy
food. 11We are all the sons of one
man. Your servants are honest
men, not spies."
12"No!" he said to them. "You
have come to see where our land
is unprotected."
13But they replied, "Your servants were twelve brothers, the
sons of one man, who lives in the
land of Canaan. The youngest is
now with our father, and one is no
more." Ge 37:30,33; 44:20
14Joseph said to them, "It is just
as I told you: You are spies! 15And
this is how you will be tested: As
surely as Pharaoh lives, you will
not leave this place unless your
youngest brother comes here.
16Send one of your number to get
your brother; the rest of you will
be kept in prison, so that your
words may be tested to see if you
are telling the truth. If you are not,
then as surely as Pharaoh lives,
you are spies!" 17And he put them
all in custody for three days.
Ge 40:4; 1Sa 17:55
18On the third day, Joseph said
to them, "Do this and you will live,
for I fear God: 19If you are honest men, let one of your brothers
stay here in prison, while the rest
of you go and take grain back for
your starving households. 20But
you must bring your youngest
brother to me, so that your words
may be verified and that you may
not die." This they proceeded
to do. ver 15,34; Ge 43:5; Lev 25:43
21They said to one another,
"Surely we are being punished because of our brother. We saw how
distressed he was when he pleaded with us for his life, but we
would not listen; that's why this
distress has come on us."
Hos 5:15

22 Reuben replied, “Didn’t I tell
you not to sin against the boy? But
you wouldn’t listen! Now we must
give an accounting for his blood.”
23 They did not realize that Joseph
could understand them, since he
was using an interpreter.
Ge 9:5; 37:21-22

24 He turned away from them
and began to weep, but then came
back and spoke to them again. He
had Simeon taken from them and
bound before their eyes. Ge 45:14-15

25 Joseph gave orders to fill their
bags with grain, to put each man’s
silver back in his sack, and to give
them provisions for their journey. After this was done for them,
26 they loaded their grain on their
donkeys and left. Ro 12:17,20-21

27 At the place where they
stopped for the night one of them
opened his sack to get feed for his
donkey, and he saw his silver in
the mouth of his sack. 28 “My silver
has been returned,” he said to his
brothers. “Here it is in my sack.”
Ge 43:21-22

Their hearts sank and they
turned to each other trembling
and said, “What is this that God
has done to us?” Ge 43:23

29 When they came to their father
Jacob in the land of Canaan, they
told him all that had happened to
them. They said, 30 “The man who
is lord over the land spoke harshly
to us and treated us as though we
were spying on the land. 31 But we
said to him, ‘We are honest men;
we are not spies. 32 We were twelve
brothers, sons of one father. One
is no more, and the youngest is
now with our father in Canaan.’
ver 7

33 “Then the man who is lord
over the land said to us, ‘This is
how I will know whether you are
honest men: Leave one of your
brothers here with me, and take
food for your starving households
and go. 34 But bring your youngest
brother to me so I will know that
you are not spies but honest men.
Then I will give your brother back
to you, and you can trade[a] in the
land.’ ” Ge 34:10

35 As they were emptying their
sacks, there in each man’s sack
was his pouch of silver! When they
and their father saw the money
pouches, they were frightened.
36 Their father Jacob said to them,
“You have deprived me of my children. Joseph is no more and Simeon is no more, and now you want
to take Benjamin. Everything is
against me!” Ge 43:14

37 Then Reuben said to his father,
“You may put both of my sons to
death if I do not bring him back to
you. Entrust him to my care, and I
will bring him back.”

38 But Jacob said, “My son will
not go down there with you; his
brother is dead and he is the only
one left. If harm comes to him on
the journey you are taking, you
will bring my gray head down to
the grave in sorrow.” Ge 37:33,35

[a] 34 Or *move about freely*

The Second Journey to Egypt

43 Now the famine was still severe in the land. 2So when
they had eaten all the grain they
had brought from Egypt, their father said to them, "Go back and
buy us a little more food."

Ge 12:10; 41:56-57

3But Judah said to him, "The
man warned us solemnly, 'You
will not see my face again unless
your brother is with you.' 4If you
will send our brother along with
us, we will go down and buy food
for you. 5But if you will not send
him, we will not go down, because
the man said to us, 'You will not
see my face again unless your
brother is with you.'" Ge 42:15

6Israel asked, "Why did you
bring this trouble on me by telling
the man you had another brother?"

7They replied, "The man questioned us closely about ourselves
and our family. 'Is your father still
living?' he asked us. 'Do you have
another brother?' We simply answered his questions. How were
we to know he would say, 'Bring
your brother down here'?" Ge 42:13

8Then Judah said to Israel his
father, "Send the boy along with
me and we will go at once, so that
we and you and our children may
live and not die. 9I myself will
guarantee his safety; you can hold
me personally responsible for
him. If I do not bring him back to
you and set him here before you,
I will bear the blame before you
all my life. 10As it is, if we had not
delayed, we could have gone and
returned twice."

Ge 42:37; 44:32; Phm 1:18-19

11Then their father Israel said to
them, "If it must be, then do this:
Put some of the best products of
the land in your bags and take
them down to the man as a gift—
a little balm and a little honey,
some spices and myrrh, some pis-
tachio nuts and almonds. 12Take
double the amount of silver with
you, for you must return the silver
that was put back into the mouths
of your sacks. Perhaps it was a
mistake. 13Take your brother also
and go back to the man at once.
14And may God Almighty[a] grant
you mercy before the man so that
he will let your other brother and
Benjamin come back with you. As
for me, if I am bereaved, I am bereaved." Ge 32:20; 37:25; 42:25

15So the men took the gifts and
double the amount of silver, and
Benjamin also. They hurried down
to Egypt and presented themselves to Joseph. 16When Joseph
saw Benjamin with them, he said
to the steward of his house, "Take
these men to my house, slaughter an animal and prepare a meal;
they are to eat with me at noon."

Ge 44:1,4,12

17The man did as Joseph told him
and took the men to Joseph's house.
18Now the men were frightened

[a] 14 Hebrew *El-Shaddai*

when they were taken to his house. They thought, "We were brought here because of the silver that was put back into our sacks the first time. He wants to attack us and overpower us and seize us as slaves and take our donkeys."

19 So they went up to Joseph's steward and spoke to him at the entrance to the house. 20 "We beg your pardon, our lord," they said, "we came down here the first time to buy food. 21 But at the place where we stopped for the night we opened our sacks and each of us found his silver — the exact weight — in the mouth of his sack. So we have brought it back with us. 22 We have also brought additional silver with us to buy food. We don't know who put our silver in our sacks." ver 15; Ge 42:27,35

23 "It's all right," he said. "Don't be afraid. Your God, the God of your father, has given you treasure in your sacks; I received your silver." Then he brought Simeon out to them. Ge 42:28

24 The steward took the men into Joseph's house, gave them water to wash their feet and provided fodder for their donkeys. 25 They prepared their gifts for Joseph's arrival at noon, because they had heard that they were to eat there. ver 16; Ge 18:4; 24:32

26 When Joseph came home, they presented to him the gifts they had brought into the house, and they bowed down before him to the ground. 27 He asked them how they were, and then he said, "How is your aged father you told me about? Is he still living?" Ge 37:7,10; Mt 2:11

28 They replied, "Your servant our father is still alive and well." And they bowed down, prostrating themselves before him. Ge 37:7

29 As he looked about and saw his brother Benjamin, his own mother's son, he asked, "Is this your youngest brother, the one you told me about?" And he said, "God be gracious to you, my son." 30 Deeply moved at the sight of his brother, Joseph hurried out and looked for a place to weep. He went into his private room and wept there. Ge 42:13,24; 45:2,14,15

31 After he had washed his face, he came out and, controlling himself, said, "Serve the food." Ge 45:1

32 They served him by himself, the brothers by themselves, and the Egyptians who ate with him by themselves, because Egyptians could not eat with Hebrews, for that is detestable to Egyptians. 33 The men had been seated before him in the order of their ages, from the firstborn to the youngest; and they looked at each other in astonishment. 34 When portions were served to them from Joseph's table, Benjamin's portion was five times as much as anyone else's. So they feasted and drank freely with him. Ge 37:3; 45:22; 46:34

A Silver Cup in a Sack

44 Now Joseph gave these instructions to the steward
of his house: "Fill the men's sacks
with as much food as they can carry, and put each man's silver in the
mouth of his sack. 2Then put my
cup, the silver one, in the mouth
of the youngest one's sack, along
with the silver for his grain." And
he did as Joseph said. Ge 42:25
3As morning dawned, the men
were sent on their way with their
donkeys. 4They had not gone far
from the city when Joseph said to
his steward, "Go after those men at
once, and when you catch up with
them, say to them, 'Why have you
repaid good with evil? 5Isn't this
the cup my master drinks from
and also uses for divination? This
is a wicked thing you have done.'"
Ge 30:27; Ps 35:12
6When he caught up with them,
he repeated these words to them.
7But they said to him, "Why does
my lord say such things? Far be
it from your servants to do anything like that! 8We even brought
back to you from the land of Canaan the silver we found inside
the mouths of our sacks. So why
would we steal silver or gold from
your master's house? 9If any of
your servants is found to have it,
he will die; and the rest of us will
become my lord's slaves."
Ge 31:32; 42:25; 43:21
10"Very well, then," he said, "let
it be as you say. Whoever is found
to have it will become my slave;
the rest of you will be free from
blame."
11Each of them quickly lowered
his sack to the ground and opened
it. 12Then the steward proceeded
to search, beginning with the oldest and ending with the youngest.
And the cup was found in Benjamin's sack. 13At this, they tore their
clothes. Then they all loaded their
donkeys and returned to the city.
Ge 37:29; Nu 14:6
14Joseph was still in the house
when Judah and his brothers came
in, and they threw themselves to
the ground before him. 15Joseph
said to them, "What is this you
have done? Don't you know that a
man like me can find things out
by divination?" ver 5; Ge 37:7,10
16"What can we say to my lord?"
Judah replied. "What can we say?
How can we prove our innocence?
God has uncovered your servants' guilt. We are now my lord's
slaves — we ourselves and the one
who was found to have the cup."
ver 9; Ge 43:18
17But Joseph said, "Far be it from
me to do such a thing! Only the
man who was found to have the
cup will become my slave. The rest
of you, go back to your father in
peace."
18Then Judah went up to him
and said: "Pardon your servant,
my lord, let me speak a word to
my lord. Do not be angry with your
servant, though you are equal to

Pharaoh himself. 19My lord asked his servants, 'Do you have a father or a brother?' 20And we answered, 'We have an aged father, and there is a young son born to him in his old age. His brother is dead, and he is the only one of his mother's sons left, and his father loves him.'

Ge 37:33; 42:13

21"Then you said to your servants, 'Bring him down to me so I can see him for myself.' 22And we said to my lord, 'The boy cannot leave his father; if he leaves him, his father will die.' 23But you told your servants, 'Unless your youngest brother comes down with you, you will not see my face again.' 24When we went back to your servant my father, we told him what my lord had said.

Ge 42:15; 43:5

25"Then our father said, 'Go back and buy a little more food.' 26But we said, 'We cannot go down. Only if our youngest brother is with us will we go. We cannot see the man's face unless our youngest brother is with us.'

Ge 43:2

27"Your servant my father said to us, 'You know that my wife bore me two sons. 28One of them went away from me, and I said, "He has surely been torn to pieces." And I have not seen him since. 29If you take this one from me too and harm comes to him, you will bring my gray head down to the grave in misery.'

Ge 37:33; 42:38; 46:19

30"So now, if the boy is not with us when I go back to your servant my father, and if my father, whose life is closely bound up with the boy's life, 31sees that the boy isn't there, he will die. Your servants will bring the gray head of our father down to the grave in sorrow. 32Your servant guaranteed the boy's safety to my father. I said, 'If I do not bring him back to you, I will bear the blame before you, my father, all my life!'

Ge 43:9; 1Sa 18:1

33"Now then, please let your servant remain here as my lord's slave in place of the boy, and let the boy return with his brothers. 34How can I go back to my father if the boy is not with me? No! Do not let me see the misery that would come on my father."

Jn 15:13

Joseph Makes Himself Known

45 Then Joseph could no longer control himself before all his attendants, and he cried out, "Have everyone leave my presence!" So there was no one with Joseph when he made himself known to his brothers. 2And he wept so loudly that the Egyptians heard him, and Pharaoh's household heard about it.

Ge 29:11

3Joseph said to his brothers, "I am Joseph! Is my father still living?" But his brothers were not able to answer him, because they were terrified at his presence.

Ac 7:13

4Then Joseph said to his brothers, "Come close to me." When they had done so, he said, "I am

your brother Joseph, the one you
sold into Egypt! 5And now, do not
be distressed and do not be angry with yourselves for selling
me here, because it was to save
lives that God sent me ahead of
you. 6For two years now there has
been famine in the land, and for
the next five years there will be
no plowing and reaping. 7But God
sent me ahead of you to preserve
for you a remnant on earth and to
save your lives by a great deliverance.[a] Ge 37:28; 50:20; Ps 105:17

8"So then, it was not you who
sent me here, but God. He made
me father to Pharaoh, lord of his
entire household and ruler of all
Egypt. 9Now hurry back to my father and say to him, 'This is what
your son Joseph says: God has
made me lord of all Egypt. Come
down to me; don't delay. 10You
shall live in the region of Goshen
and be near me — you, your children and grandchildren, your
flocks and herds, and all you have.
11I will provide for you there, because five years of famine are still
to come. Otherwise you and your
household and all who belong to
you will become destitute.'
Ge 41:41; Jdg 17:10

12"You can see for yourselves,
and so can my brother Benjamin,
that it is really I who am speaking
to you. 13Tell my father about all
the honor accorded me in Egypt
and about everything you have
seen. And bring my father down
here quickly." Ac 7:14

14Then he threw his arms around
his brother Benjamin and wept,
and Benjamin embraced him,
weeping. 15And he kissed all his
brothers and wept over them. Afterward his brothers talked with
him. Lk 15:20

16When the news reached Pharaoh's palace that Joseph's brothers
had come, Pharaoh and all his officials were pleased. 17Pharaoh said
to Joseph, "Tell your brothers, 'Do
this: Load your animals and return to the land of Canaan, 18and
bring your father and your families back to me. I will give you the
best of the land of Egypt and you
can enjoy the fat of the land.'
Ge 27:28; 46:34; 47:6,11,27

19"You are also directed to tell
them, 'Do this: Take some carts
from Egypt for your children and
your wives, and get your father
and come. 20Never mind about
your belongings, because the best
of all Egypt will be yours.'" Ge 46:5

21So the sons of Israel did this.
Joseph gave them carts, as Pharaoh had commanded, and he also
gave them provisions for their
journey. 22To each of them he gave
new clothing, but to Benjamin he
gave three hundred shekels[b] of silver and five sets of clothes. 23And
this is what he sent to his father:
ten donkeys loaded with the best
things of Egypt, and ten female
donkeys loaded with grain and

[a] 7 Or *save you as a great band of survivors*
[b] 22 That is, about 7 1/2 pounds or about 3.5 kilograms

bread and other provisions for his
journey. 24Then he sent his brothers away, and as they were leaving
he said to them, "Don't quarrel on
the way!" Ge 42:21-22
25So they went up out of Egypt
and came to their father Jacob in
the land of Canaan. 26They told
him, "Joseph is still alive! In fact,
he is ruler of all Egypt." Jacob was
stunned; he did not believe them.
27But when they told him everything Joseph had said to them, and
when he saw the carts Joseph had
sent to carry him back, the spirit
of their father Jacob revived. 28And
Israel said, "I'm convinced! My son
Joseph is still alive. I will go and
see him before I die." ver 19; Ge 44:28

Jacob Goes to Egypt

46 So Israel set out with all
that was his, and when
he reached Beersheba, he offered
sacrifices to the God of his father
Isaac. Ge 31:42
2And God spoke to Israel in a vision at night and said, "Jacob! Jacob!" Ge 15:1; Job 33:14-15
"Here I am," he replied. Ge 22:1
3"I am God, the God of your father," he said. "Do not be afraid to
go down to Egypt, for I will make
you into a great nation there. 4I
will go down to Egypt with you,
and I will surely bring you back
again. And Joseph's own hand will
close your eyes." Ge 12:2; 50:1,24
5Then Jacob left Beersheba, and
Israel's sons took their father Jacob
and their children and their wives
in the carts that Pharaoh had sent
to transport him. 6So Jacob and all
his offspring went to Egypt, taking with them their livestock and
the possessions they had acquired
in Canaan. 7Jacob brought with
him to Egypt his sons and grandsons and his daughters and grand-
daughters — all his offspring.
Dt 26:5; Jos 24:4

8These are the names of the
sons of Israel (Jacob and his descendants) who went to Egypt: Ex 1:1

Reuben the firstborn of Jacob.
9The sons of Reuben: 1Ch 5:3
Hanok, Pallu, Hezron and
Karmi.
10The sons of Simeon: Ge 29:33
Jemuel, Jamin, Ohad, Ja-
kin, Zohar and Shaul the
son of a Canaanite woman.
Ex 6:15
11The sons of Levi: Ge 29:34
Gershon, Kohath and Merari.
12The sons of Judah: Ge 29:35
Er, Onan, Shelah, Perez and
Zerah (but Er and Onan had
died in the land of Canaan).
The sons of Perez: 1Ch 2:5
Hezron and Hamul.
13The sons of Issachar: Ge 30:18
Tola, Puah,[a] Jashub[b] and
Shimron.
14The sons of Zebulun: Ge 30:20
Sered, Elon and Jahleel.

[a] 13 Samaritan Pentateuch and Syriac (see also 1 Chron. 7:1); Masoretic Text *Puvah*
[b] 13 Samaritan Pentateuch and some Septuagint manuscripts (see also Num. 26:24 and 1 Chron. 7:1); Masoretic Text *Iob*

15These were the sons Leah bore to Jacob in Paddan Aram,[a] besides his daughter Dinah. These sons and daughters of his were thirty-three in all.

16The sons of Gad: Ge 30:11
Zephon,[b] Haggi, Shuni, Ezbon, Eri, Arodi and Areli. Nu 26:15
17The sons of Asher: Ge 30:13
Imnah, Ishvah, Ishvi and Beriah.
Their sister was Serah.
The sons of Beriah:
Heber and Malkiel.
18These were the children born to Jacob by Zilpah, whom Laban had given to his daughter Leah — sixteen in all.

19The sons of Jacob's wife Rachel:
Joseph and Benjamin.
20In Egypt, Manasseh and Ephraim were born to Joseph by Asenath daughter of Potiphera, priest of On.[c] Ge 41:51-52; 44:27
21The sons of Benjamin: 1Ch 7:6-12
Bela, Beker, Ashbel, Gera, Naaman, Ehi, Rosh, Muppim, Huppim and Ard.
22These were the sons of Rachel who were born to Jacob — fourteen in all.

23The son of Dan:
Hushim.
24The sons of Naphtali:
Jahziel, Guni, Jezer and Shillem.
25These were the sons born to Jacob by Bilhah, whom Laban had given to his daughter Rachel — seven in all. Ge 29:29; 30:8

26All those who went to Egypt with Jacob — those who were his direct descendants, not counting his sons' wives — numbered sixty-six persons.
27With the two sons[d] who had been born to Joseph in Egypt, the members of Jacob's family, which went to Egypt, were seventy[e] in all. Ac 7:14; Ex 1:5; Dt 10:22

28Now Jacob sent Judah ahead of him to Joseph to get directions to Goshen. When they arrived in the region of Goshen,
29Joseph had his chariot made ready and went to Goshen to meet his father Israel. As soon as Joseph appeared before him, he threw his arms around his father[f] and wept for a long time. Ge 45:14-15
30Israel said to Joseph, "Now I am ready to die, since I have seen for myself that you are still alive."
31Then Joseph said to his brothers and to his father's household, "I will go up and speak to Pharaoh and will say to him, 'My brothers and my father's household, who were living in the land of Canaan, have come to me.
32The men are

[a] *15* That is, Northwest Mesopotamia
[b] *16* Samaritan Pentateuch and Septuagint (see also Num. 26:15); Masoretic Text *Ziphion*
[c] *20* That is, Heliopolis
[d] *27* Hebrew; Septuagint *the nine children*
[e] *27* Hebrew (see also Exodus 1:5 and note); Septuagint (see also Acts 7:14) *seventy-five*
[f] *29* Hebrew *around him*

shepherds; they tend livestock,
and they have brought along their
flocks and herds and everything
they own.' 33When Pharaoh calls
you in and asks, 'What is your occupation?' 34you should answer,
'Your servants have tended livestock from our boyhood on, just as
our fathers did.' Then you will be
allowed to settle in the region of
Goshen, for all shepherds are detestable to the Egyptians."
Ge 43:32; Ex 8:26

47 Joseph went and told Pharaoh, "My father and brothers, with their flocks and herds
and everything they own, have
come from the land of Canaan
and are now in Goshen." 2He chose
five of his brothers and presented
them before Pharaoh. Ge 46:31
3Pharaoh asked the brothers,
"What is your occupation?" Ge 46:33
"Your servants are shepherds,"
they replied to Pharaoh, "just as
our fathers were." 4They also said
to him, "We have come to live here
for a while, because the famine is
severe in Canaan and your servants' flocks have no pasture. So
now, please let your servants settle in Goshen." Ge 46:34
5Pharaoh said to Joseph, "Your
father and your brothers have
come to you, 6and the land of
Egypt is before you; settle your father and your brothers in the best
part of the land. Let them live in
Goshen. And if you know of any
among them with special ability, put them in charge of my own
livestock." Ge 45:18; Ex 18:21,25
7Then Joseph brought his father
Jacob in and presented him before Pharaoh. After Jacob blessed[a]
Pharaoh, 8Pharaoh asked him,
"How old are you?"
9And Jacob said to Pharaoh,
"The years of my pilgrimage are
a hundred and thirty. My years
have been few and difficult, and
they do not equal the years of the
pilgrimage of my fathers." 10Then
Jacob blessed[b] Pharaoh and went
out from his presence.
ver 7; Ge 25:7; 35:28
11So Joseph settled his father
and his brothers in Egypt and gave
them property in the best part of
the land, the district of Rameses,
as Pharaoh directed. 12Joseph also
provided his father and his brothers and all his father's household
with food, according to the number of their children. Ex 1:11; 12:37

Joseph and the Famine

13There was no food, however, in
the whole region because the famine was severe; both Egypt and Canaan wasted away because of the
famine. 14Joseph collected all the
money that was to be found in
Egypt and Canaan in payment for
the grain they were buying, and
he brought it to Pharaoh's palace.
15When the money of the people
of Egypt and Canaan was gone, all
Egypt came to Joseph and said,

[a] 7 Or *greeted* [b] 10 Or *said farewell to*

“Give us food. Why should we die
before your eyes? Our money is all
gone.” Ge 41:30,56
16“Then bring your livestock,”
said Joseph. “I will sell you food
in exchange for your livestock,
since your money is gone.” 17So
they brought their livestock to Joseph, and he gave them food in
exchange for their horses, their
sheep and goats, their cattle and
donkeys. And he brought them
through that year with food in exchange for all their livestock. Ex 14:9
18When that year was over, they
came to him the following year
and said, “We cannot hide from
our lord the fact that since our
money is gone and our livestock
belongs to you, there is nothing
left for our lord except our bodies and our land. 19Why should we
perish before your eyes — we and
our land as well? Buy us and our
land in exchange for food, and we
with our land will be in bondage
to Pharaoh. Give us seed so that
we may live and not die, and that
the land may not become desolate.” Ge 42:2
20So Joseph bought all the land
in Egypt for Pharaoh. The Egyptians, one and all, sold their fields,
because the famine was too severe
for them. The land became Pharaoh’s, 21and Joseph reduced the
people to servitude,[a] from one
end of Egypt to the other. 22How-
ever, he did not buy the land of
the priests, because they received
a regular allotment from Pharaoh
and had food enough from the allotment Pharaoh gave them. That
is why they did not sell their land.
Dt 14:28-29; Ezr 7:24
23Joseph said to the people,
“Now that I have bought you and
your land today for Pharaoh, here
is seed for you so you can plant
the ground. 24But when the crop
comes in, give a fifth of it to Pharaoh. The other four-fifths you may
keep as seed for the fields and
as food for yourselves and your
households and your children.”
Ge 41:34
25“You have saved our lives,”
they said. “May we find favor in
the eyes of our lord; we will be in
bondage to Pharaoh.” Ge 32:5
26So Joseph established it as a
law concerning land in Egypt —
still in force today — that a fifth of
the produce belongs to Pharaoh.
It was only the land of the priests
that did not become Pharaoh’s.
ver 22
27Now the Israelites settled in
Egypt in the region of Goshen.
They acquired property there and
were fruitful and increased greatly in number. Ge 17:6
28Jacob lived in Egypt seventeen years, and the years of his
life were a hundred and forty-sev-
en. 29When the time drew near for
Israel to die, he called for his son

[a] *21* Samaritan Pentateuch and Septuagint (see also Vulgate); Masoretic Text *and he moved the people into the cities*

Joseph and said to him, "If I have
found favor in your eyes, put your
hand under my thigh and promise
that you will show me kindness
and faithfulness. Do not bury me
in Egypt, 30but when I rest with
my fathers, carry me out of Egypt
and bury me where they are buried." Ge 49:29-32; 24:2

"I will do as you say," he said.

31"Swear to me," he said. Then
Joseph swore to him, and Israel
worshiped as he leaned on the top
of his staff.[a] Heb 11:21

Manasseh and Ephraim

48 Some time later Joseph
was told, "Your father is
ill." So he took his two sons Manasseh and Ephraim along with
him. 2When Jacob was told, "Your
son Joseph has come to you," Israel rallied his strength and sat up
on the bed. Ge 41:52

3Jacob said to Joseph, "God Almighty[b] appeared to me at Luz in
the land of Canaan, and there he
blessed me 4and said to me, 'I am
going to make you fruitful and increase your numbers. I will make
you a community of peoples, and
I will give this land as an everlasting possession to your descendants after you.' Ge 28:13,19; 35:9-12

5"Now then, your two sons born
to you in Egypt before I came
to you here will be reckoned as
mine; Ephraim and Manasseh will
be mine, just as Reuben and Simeon are mine. 6Any children born
to you after them will be yours; in
the territory they inherit they will
be reckoned under the names of
their brothers. 7As I was returning from Paddan,[c] to my sorrow
Rachel died in the land of Canaan
while we were still on the way, a
little distance from Ephrath. So I
buried her there beside the road
to Ephrath" (that is, Bethlehem).
Ge 35:19; 41:50-52

8When Israel saw the sons of Joseph, he asked, "Who are these?"

9"They are the sons God has
given me here," Joseph said to his
father. Ge 33:5

Then Israel said, "Bring them to
me so I may bless them." Ge 27:4

10Now Israel's eyes were failing
because of old age, and he could
hardly see. So Joseph brought his
sons close to him, and his father
kissed them and embraced them.
Ge 27:1,27

11Israel said to Joseph, "I never
expected to see your face again,
and now God has allowed me to
see your children too."

12Then Joseph removed them
from Israel's knees and bowed
down with his face to the ground.
13And Joseph took both of them,
Ephraim on his right toward Israel's left hand and Manasseh on his
left toward Israel's right hand, and
brought them close to him. 14But
Israel reached out his right hand
and put it on Ephraim's head,

[a] 31 Or *Israel bowed down at the head of his bed* [b] 3 Hebrew *El-Shaddai* [c] 7 That is, Northwest Mesopotamia

though he was the younger, and
crossing his arms, he put his left
hand on Manasseh's head, even
though Manasseh was the firstborn. Ge 41:51
15 Then he blessed Joseph and
said, Ge 17:1

"May the God before whom my
fathers
Abraham and Isaac walked
faithfully,
the God who has been my
shepherd Ge 49:24
all my life to this day,
16 the Angel who has delivered
me from all harm
—may he bless these boys.
Heb 11:21
May they be called by my name
and the names of my fathers
Abraham and Isaac,
Ge 28:13
and may they increase greatly
on the earth."

17 When Joseph saw his father
placing his right hand on Ephraim's head he was displeased; so
he took hold of his father's hand
to move it from Ephraim's head
to Manasseh's head. 18 Joseph said
to him, "No, my father, this one is
the firstborn; put your right hand
on his head." ver 14; Ge 25:23
19 But his father refused and said,
"I know, my son, I know. He too
will become a people, and he too
will become great. Nevertheless,
his younger brother will be greater than he, and his descendants
will become a group of nations."
20 He blessed them that day and
said,

"In your[a] name will Israel
pronounce this
blessing:
'May God make you
like Ephraim and
Manasseh.'" Nu 2:20; Ru 4:11

So he put Ephraim ahead of Manasseh.
21 Then Israel said to Joseph, "I
am about to die, but God will be
with you[b] and take you[b] back to
the land of your[b] fathers. 22 And to
you I give one more ridge of land[c]
than to your brothers, the ridge I
took from the Amorites with my
sword and my bow."
Jn 4:5; Ge 26:3; 28:13

Jacob Blesses His Sons

49 Then Jacob called for his
sons and said: "Gather
around so I can tell you what will
happen to you in days to come.
Nu 24:14

2 "Assemble and listen, sons of
Jacob;
listen to your father Israel.

3 "Reuben, you are my firstborn,
Ge 29:32
my might, the first sign of
my strength, Dt 21:17
excelling in honor, excelling
in power.

[a] 20 The Hebrew is singular. [b] 21 The Hebrew is plural. [c] 22 The Hebrew for *ridge of land* is identical with the place name Shechem.

4 Turbulent as the waters, you
will no longer excel,
for you went up onto your
father's bed,
onto my couch and defiled it.
Ge 35:22; Dt 27:20

5 "Simeon and Levi are
brothers —
their swords[a] are weapons of
violence. Ge 34:25
6 Let me not enter their council,
let me not join their
assembly, Pr 1:15; Eph 5:11
for they have killed men in
their anger Ge 34:26
and hamstrung oxen as they
pleased.
7 Cursed be their anger, so
fierce,
and their fury, so cruel!
I will scatter them in Jacob
and disperse them in Israel.
Jos 19:1,9

8 "Judah,[b] your brothers will
praise you;
your hand will be on the
neck of your enemies;
your father's sons will bow
down to you. 1Ch 5:2
9 You are a lion's cub, Judah;
Nu 24:9
you return from the prey, my
son.
Like a lion he crouches and lies
down,
like a lioness — who dares to
rouse him?
10 The scepter will not
depart from Judah,
Nu 24:17,19; Ps 60:7
nor the ruler's staff from
between his feet,[c]
until he to whom it belongs[d]
shall come
and the obedience of the
nations shall be his.
Ps 2:9; Isa 42:1,4
11 He will tether his donkey to a
vine,
his colt to the choicest branch;
he will wash his garments in
wine,
his robes in the blood of
grapes.
12 His eyes will be darker than
wine,
his teeth whiter than milk.[e]

13 "Zebulun will live by the
seashore Dt 33:18-19
and become a haven for
ships;
his border will extend
toward Sidon.

14 "Issachar is a rawboned[f] donkey
lying down among the sheep
pens.[g]
15 When he sees how good is his
resting place
and how pleasant is his land,
he will bend his shoulder to the
burden
and submit to forced labor.

[a] 5 The meaning of the Hebrew for this word is uncertain. [b] 8 *Judah* sounds like and may be derived from the Hebrew for *praise.* [c] 10 Or *from his descendants* [d] 10 Or *to whom tribute belongs*; the meaning of the Hebrew for this phrase is uncertain. [e] 12 Or *will be dull from wine, / his teeth white from milk* [f] 14 Or *strong* [g] 14 Or *the campfires*; or *the saddlebags*

16 "Dan[a] will provide justice for
his people Dt 33:22
as one of the tribes
of Israel.
17 Dan will be a snake by the
roadside, Jdg 18:27
a viper along the path,
that bites the horse's heels
so that its rider tumbles
backward.

18 "I look for your deliverance,
LORD.

19 "Gad[b] will be attacked by a
band of raiders, Dt 33:20
but he will attack them at
their heels.

20 "Asher's food will be rich; Dt 33:24
he will provide delicacies fit
for a king.

21 "Naphtali is a doe set free Dt 33:23
that bears beautiful fawns.[c]

22 "Joseph is a fruitful vine,
Dt 33:13-17
a fruitful vine near a spring,
whose branches climb over a
wall.[d]
23 With bitterness archers
attacked him;
they shot at him with
hostility.
24 But his bow remained steady,
his strong arms stayed[e]
limber, Ps 18:34
because of the hand of the
Mighty One of Jacob,
Ps 132:2,5; Isa 1:24
because of the Shepherd, the
Rock of Israel, Isa 28:16
25 because of your father's God,
who helps you, Ge 28:13
because of the Almighty,[f]
who blesses you
with blessings of the skies
above,
blessings of the deep springs
below,
blessings of the breast and
womb.
26 Your father's blessings are
greater
than the blessings of the
ancient mountains,
than[g] the bounty of the age-
old hills.
Let all these rest on the head of
Joseph,
on the brow of the prince
among[h] his brothers.
Dt 33:15-16

27 "Benjamin is a ravenous wolf;
in the morning he devours
the prey,
in the evening he divides the
plunder."

28 All these are the twelve tribes
of Israel, and this is what their father said to them when he blessed
them, giving each the blessing appropriate to him. Dt 33:1-29

[a] 16 *Dan* here means *he provides justice.*
[b] 19 *Gad* sounds like the Hebrew for *attack* and also for *band of raiders.*
[c] 21 Or *free; / he utters beautiful words*
[d] 22 Or *Joseph is a wild colt, / a wild colt near a spring, / a wild donkey on a terraced hill*
[e] 23,24 Or *archers will attack . . . will shoot . . . will remain . . . will stay*
[f] 25 Hebrew *Shaddai*
[g] 26 Or *of my progenitors, / as great as*
[h] 26 Or *of the one separated from*

The Death of Jacob

29Then he gave them these instructions: "I am about to be gathered to my people. Bury me with
my fathers in the cave in the field
of Ephron the Hittite, 30the cave
in the field of Machpelah, near
Mamre in Canaan, which Abraham bought along with the field
as a burial place from Ephron
the Hittite. 31There Abraham and
his wife Sarah were buried, there
Isaac and his wife Rebekah were
buried, and there I buried Leah.
32The field and the cave in it were
bought from the Hittites.[a]"

Ge 25:9; 35:29

33When Jacob had finished giving instructions to his sons, he
drew his feet up into the bed,
breathed his last and was gathered to his people. Ge 25:8

50 Joseph threw himself on
his father and wept over
him and kissed him. 2Then Joseph directed the physicians in his
service to embalm his father Israel. So the physicians embalmed
him, 3taking a full forty days, for
that was the time required for
embalming. And the Egyptians
mourned for him seventy days.

Ge 46:4; 2Ch 16:14

4When the days of mourning
had passed, Joseph said to Pharaoh's court, "If I have found favor
in your eyes, speak to Pharaoh for
me. Tell him, 5'My father made
me swear an oath and said, "I am
about to die; bury me in the tomb
I dug for myself in the land of Canaan." Now let me go up and bury
my father; then I will return.'"

Ge 47:31; Isa 22:16

6Pharaoh said, "Go up and bury
your father, as he made you swear
to do."

7So Joseph went up to bury his
father. All Pharaoh's officials accompanied him — the dignitaries
of his court and all the dignitaries
of Egypt — 8besides all the members of Joseph's household and
his brothers and those belonging
to his father's household. Only
their children and their flocks
and herds were left in Goshen.
9Chariots and horsemen[b] also
went up with him. It was a very
large company.

10When they reached the threshing floor of Atad, near the Jordan,
they lamented loudly and bitterly; and there Joseph observed a
seven-day period of mourning for
his father. 11When the Canaanites
who lived there saw the mourning
at the threshing floor of Atad, they
said, "The Egyptians are holding a
solemn ceremony of mourning."
That is why that place near the
Jordan is called Abel Mizraim.[c]

1Sa 31:13; Job 2:13; Ac 8:2

12So Jacob's sons did as he had
commanded them: 13They carried
him to the land of Canaan and
buried him in the cave in the field
of Machpelah, near Mamre, which

[a] 32 Or *the descendants of Heth* [b] 9 Or *charioteers* [c] 11 *Abel Mizraim* means *mourning of the Egyptians.*

Abraham had bought along with
the field as a burial place from
Ephron the Hittite. 14After burying his father, Joseph returned to
Egypt, together with his brothers
and all the others who had gone
with him to bury his father.
Ge 23:20; Ac 7:16

Joseph Reassures His Brothers

15When Joseph's brothers saw
that their father was dead, they
said, "What if Joseph holds a
grudge against us and pays us
back for all the wrongs we did to
him?" 16So they sent word to Joseph, saying, "Your father left
these instructions before he died:
17'This is what you are to say to
Joseph: I ask you to forgive your
brothers the sins and the wrongs
they committed in treating you so
badly.' Now please forgive the sins
of the servants of the God of your
father." When their message came
to him, Joseph wept. Ge 37:28

18His brothers then came and
threw themselves down before
him. "We are your slaves," they
said. Ge 37:7

19But Joseph said to them, "Don't
be afraid. Am I in the place of God?
20You intended to harm me, but
God intended it for good to accomplish what is now being done,
the saving of many lives. 21So then,
don't be afraid. I will provide for
you and your children." And he re-
assured them and spoke kindly to
them. Ro 8:28; 12:19; Ge 45:5

The Death of Joseph

22Joseph stayed in Egypt, along
with all his father's family. He lived
a hundred and ten years 23and saw
the third generation of Ephraim's
children. Also the children of Makir son of Manasseh were placed
at birth on Joseph's knees.[a]
Nu 32:39-40

24Then Joseph said to his brothers, "I am about to die. But God
will surely come to your aid and
take you up out of this land to
the land he promised on oath to
Abraham, Isaac and Jacob." 25And
Joseph made the Israelites swear
an oath and said, "God will surely come to your aid, and then you
must carry my bones up from this
place." Ge 12:7; 26:3

26So Joseph died at the age of a
hundred and ten. And after they
embalmed him, he was placed in
a coffin in Egypt.

[a] *23* That is, were counted as his

EXODUS

The Israelites Oppressed

1 These are the names of the sons of Israel who went to Egypt with Jacob, each with his family: 2Reuben, Simeon, Levi and Judah; 3Issachar, Zebulun and Benjamin; 4Dan and Naphtali; Gad and Asher. 5The descendants of Jacob numbered seventy[a] in all; Joseph was already in Egypt. Ge 46:8,26

6Now Joseph and all his brothers and all that generation died, 7but the Israelites were exceedingly fruitful; they multiplied greatly, increased in numbers and became so numerous that the land was filled with them.

Ge 46:3; Ac 7:17; Ge 50:26

8Then a new king, to whom Joseph meant nothing, came to power in Egypt. 9"Look," he said to his people, "the Israelites have become far too numerous for us. 10Come, we must deal shrewdly with them or they will become even more numerous and, if war breaks out, will join our enemies, fight against us and leave the country." Ps 105:24-25; Ac 7:17-19

11So they put slave masters over them to oppress them with forced labor, and they built Pithom and Rameses as store cities for Pharaoh. 12But the more they were oppressed, the more they multiplied and spread; so the Egyptians came to dread the Israelites 13and worked them ruthlessly. 14They made their lives bitter with harsh labor in brick and mortar and with all kinds of work in the fields; in all their harsh labor the Egyptians worked them ruthlessly.

Ex 3:7; 2:23; Nu 20:15

15The king of Egypt said to the Hebrew midwives, whose names were Shiphrah and Puah, 16"When you are helping the Hebrew women during childbirth on the delivery stool, if you see that the baby is a boy, kill him; but if it is a girl, let her live." 17The midwives, however, feared God and did not do what the king of Egypt had told them to do; they let the boys live. 18Then the king of Egypt summoned the midwives and asked them, "Why have you done this? Why have you let the boys live?" ver 21; Pr 16:6

19The midwives answered Pharaoh, "Hebrew women are not like Egyptian women; they are vigorous and give birth before the midwives arrive." Jos 2:4-6

20So God was kind to the midwives and the people increased and became even more numerous. 21And because the midwives feared God, he gave them families of their own. 1Sa 2:35

[a] *5* Masoretic Text (see also Gen. 46:27); Dead Sea Scrolls and Septuagint (see also Acts 7:14 and note at Gen. 46:27) *seventy-five*

22Then Pharaoh gave this order
to all his people: "Every Hebrew
boy that is born you must throw
into the Nile, but let every girl live."
Ac 7:19

The Birth of Moses

2 Now a man of the tribe of Levi
married a Levite woman, 2and
she became pregnant and gave
birth to a son. When she saw that
he was a fine child, she hid him
for three months. 3But when she
could hide him no longer, she got
a papyrus basket[a] for him and
coated it with tar and pitch. Then
she placed the child in it and put
it among the reeds along the bank
of the Nile. 4His sister stood at a
distance to see what would happen to him. Heb 11:23; Ex 15:20; 6:20
5Then Pharaoh's daughter went
down to the Nile to bathe, and her
attendants were walking along
the riverbank. She saw the basket
among the reeds and sent her female slave to get it. 6She opened it
and saw the baby. He was crying,
and she felt sorry for him. "This
is one of the Hebrew babies," she
said. Ex 7:15
7Then his sister asked Pharaoh's
daughter, "Shall I go and get one
of the Hebrew women to nurse the
baby for you?"
8"Yes, go," she answered. So
the girl went and got the baby's
mother. 9Pharaoh's daughter said
to her, "Take this baby and nurse
him for me, and I will pay you."
So the woman took the baby and
nursed him. 10When the child grew
older, she took him to Pharaoh's
daughter and he became her son.
She named him Moses,[b] saying, "I
drew him out of the water."

Moses Flees to Midian

11One day, after Moses had grown
up, he went out to where his own
people were and watched them at
their hard labor. He saw an Egyptian beating a Hebrew, one of his
own people. 12Looking this way
and that and seeing no one, he
killed the Egyptian and hid him
in the sand. 13The next day he
went out and saw two Hebrews
fighting. He asked the one in the
wrong, "Why are you hitting your
fellow Hebrew?" Ac 7:23; Heb 11:24-26
14The man said, "Who made you
ruler and judge over us? Are you
thinking of killing me as you killed
the Egyptian?" Then Moses was
afraid and thought, "What I did
must have become known." Ac 7:27
15When Pharaoh heard of this,
he tried to kill Moses, but Moses
fled from Pharaoh and went to live
in Midian, where he sat down by a
well. 16Now a priest of Midian had
seven daughters, and they came to
draw water and fill the troughs to
water their father's flock. 17Some
shepherds came along and drove
them away, but Moses got up and
came to their rescue and watered
their flock. Ex 3:1; Ge 29:10

[a] *3* The Hebrew can also mean *ark*, as in Gen. 6:14. [b] *10* *Moses* sounds like the Hebrew for *draw out*.

18When the girls returned to
Reuel their father, he asked them,
"Why have you returned so early
today?" Nu 10:29
19They answered, "An Egyptian
rescued us from the shepherds.
He even drew water for us and watered the flock."
20"And where is he?" Reuel
asked his daughters. "Why did
you leave him? Invite him to have
something to eat." Ge 31:54
21Moses agreed to stay with the
man, who gave his daughter Zipporah to Moses in marriage. 22Zip-
porah gave birth to a son, and Moses named him Gershom,[a] saying,
"I have become a foreigner in a
foreign land." Ex 18:2; Heb 11:13
23During that long period, the
king of Egypt died. The Israelites
groaned in their slavery and cried
out, and their cry for help because
of their slavery went up to God.
24God heard their groaning and he
remembered his covenant with
Abraham, with Isaac and with Jacob. 25So God looked on the Israelites and was concerned about
them. Ex 3:7; Ps 105:10,42

Moses and the Burning Bush

3 Now Moses was tending the
flock of Jethro his father-in-
law, the priest of Midian, and he
led the flock to the far side of the
wilderness and came to Horeb, the
mountain of God. 2There the angel of the LORD appeared to him in
flames of fire from within a bush.
Moses saw that though the bush
was on fire it did not burn up. 3So
Moses thought, "I will go over and
see this strange sight — why the
bush does not burn up."
Dt 33:16; Ac 7:30
4When the LORD saw that he
had gone over to look, God called
to him from within the bush, "Moses! Moses!"
And Moses said, "Here I am."
Ge 31:11
5"Do not come any closer," God
said. "Take off your sandals, for
the place where you are standing is
holy ground." 6Then he said, "I am
the God of your father,[b] the God of
Abraham, the God of Isaac and the
God of Jacob." At this, Moses hid
his face, because he was afraid to
look at God. Ac 7:32-33; Mt 22:32
7The LORD said, "I have indeed
seen the misery of my people in
Egypt. I have heard them crying
out because of their slave drivers,
and I am concerned about their
suffering. 8So I have come down
to rescue them from the hand of
the Egyptians and to bring them
up out of that land into a good
and spacious land, a land flowing
with milk and honey — the home
of the Canaanites, Hittites, Amorites, Perizzites, Hivites and Jebusites. 9And now the cry of the
Israelites has reached me, and I
have seen the way the Egyptians
are oppressing them. 10So now, go.

[a] 22 *Gershom* sounds like the Hebrew for *a foreigner there.* [b] 6 Masoretic Text; Samaritan Pentateuch (see Acts 7:32) *fathers*

I am sending you to Pharaoh to
bring my people the Israelites out
of Egypt." Mic 6:4; Ex 2:25
11But Moses said to God, "Who
am I that I should go to Pharaoh
and bring the Israelites out of
Egypt?" Ex 6:12,30; 1Sa 18:18
12And God said, "I will be with
you. And this will be the sign to
you that it is I who have sent you:
When you have brought the people out of Egypt, you[a] will worship
God on this mountain." Ro 8:31
13Moses said to God, "Suppose
I go to the Israelites and say to
them, 'The God of your fathers
has sent me to you,' and they ask
me, 'What is his name?' Then what
shall I tell them?"
14God said to Moses, "I AM WHO I
AM.[b] This is what you are to say to
the Israelites: 'I AM has sent me to
you.'" Ex 6:2-3; Jn 8:58; Heb 13:8
15God also said to Moses, "Say to
the Israelites, 'The LORD,[c] the God
of your fathers — the God of Abraham, the God of Isaac and the God
of Jacob — has sent me to you.'

"This is my name forever,
the name you shall call me
from generation to
generation. Ps 135:13

16"Go, assemble the elders of Israel and say to them, 'The LORD,
the God of your fathers — the God
of Abraham, Isaac and Jacob —
appeared to me and said: I have
watched over you and have seen
what has been done to you in Egypt.
17And I have promised to bring you
up out of your misery in Egypt into
the land of the Canaanites, Hittites,
Amorites, Perizzites, Hivites and
Jebusites — a land flowing with
milk and honey.' Ge 15:16
18"The elders of Israel will listen
to you. Then you and the elders
are to go to the king of Egypt and
say to him, 'The LORD, the God of
the Hebrews, has met with us. Let
us take a three-day journey into
the wilderness to offer sacrifices
to the LORD our God.' 19But I know
that the king of Egypt will not let
you go unless a mighty hand compels him. 20So I will stretch out my
hand and strike the Egyptians with
all the wonders that I will perform
among them. After that, he will let
you go. Ex 6:1,6; 12:31-33; Dt 6:22
21"And I will make the Egyptians
favorably disposed toward this
people, so that when you leave you
will not go empty-handed. 22Every
woman is to ask her neighbor and
any woman living in her house for
articles of silver and gold and for
clothing, which you will put on
your sons and daughters. And so
you will plunder the Egyptians."
Ps 105:37; Ex 11:2

Signs for Moses

4 Moses answered, "What if they
do not believe me or listen to
me and say, 'The LORD did not appear to you'?" Ex 3:18

[a] 12 The Hebrew is plural. [b] 14 Or *I WILL BE WHAT I WILL BE* [c] 15 The Hebrew for *LORD* sounds like and may be related to the Hebrew for *I AM* in verse 14.

2Then the LORD said to him, "What is that in your hand?"

"A staff," he replied. ver 17,20

3The LORD said, "Throw it on the ground."

Moses threw it on the ground and it became a snake, and he ran from it. 4Then the LORD said to him, "Reach out your hand and take it by the tail." So Moses reached out and took hold of the snake and it turned back into a staff in his hand. 5"This," said the LORD, "is so that they may believe that the LORD, the God of their fathers — the God of Abraham, the God of Isaac and the God of Jacob — has appeared to you." Ex 19:9

6Then the LORD said, "Put your hand inside your cloak." So Moses put his hand into his cloak, and when he took it out, the skin was leprous[a] — it had become as white as snow. Nu 12:10; 2Ki 5:1,27

7"Now put it back into your cloak," he said. So Moses put his hand back into his cloak, and when he took it out, it was restored, like the rest of his flesh. Nu 12:13-15

8Then the LORD said, "If they do not believe you or pay attention to the first sign, they may believe the second. 9But if they do not believe these two signs or listen to you, take some water from the Nile and pour it on the dry ground. The water you take from the river will become blood on the ground." Ex 7:17-21

10Moses said to the LORD, "Pardon your servant, Lord. I have never been eloquent, neither in the past nor since you have spoken to your servant. I am slow of speech and tongue." Ex 6:12; Jer 1:6

11The LORD said to him, "Who gave human beings their mouths? Who makes them deaf or mute? Who gives them sight or makes them blind? Is it not I, the LORD? 12Now go; I will help you speak and will teach you what to say." Isa 50:4; Jer 1:9; Lk 12:12

13But Moses said, "Pardon your servant, Lord. Please send someone else." Jnh 1:1-3

14Then the LORD's anger burned against Moses and he said, "What about your brother, Aaron the Levite? I know he can speak well. He is already on his way to meet you, and he will be glad to see you. 15You shall speak to him and put words in his mouth; I will help both of you speak and will teach you what to do. 16He will speak to the people for you, and it will be as if he were your mouth and as if you were God to him. 17But take this staff in your hand so you can perform the signs with it." Ex 7:1-2,9-21; Nu 23:5,12,16

Moses Returns to Egypt

18Then Moses went back to Jethro his father-in-law and said to him, "Let me return to my own people in Egypt to see if any of them are still alive."

Jethro said, "Go, and I wish you well."

[a] 6 The Hebrew word for *leprous* was used for various diseases affecting the skin.

19Now the LORD had said to Moses in Midian, "Go back to Egypt,
for all those who wanted to kill
you are dead." 20So Moses took
his wife and sons, put them on a
donkey and started back to Egypt.
And he took the staff of God in his
hand. Ex 2:15,23

21The LORD said to Moses,
"When you return to Egypt, see
that you perform before Pharaoh
all the wonders I have given you
the power to do. But I will harden
his heart so that he will not let the
people go. 22Then say to Pharaoh,
'This is what the LORD says: Israel is my firstborn son, 23and I told
you, "Let my son go, so he may
worship me." But you refused to
let him go; so I will kill your firstborn son.'" Ex 12:12,29; Jer 31:9

24At a lodging place on the way,
the LORD met Moses[a] and was
about to kill him. 25But Zipporah
took a flint knife, cut off her son's
foreskin and touched Moses' feet
with it.[b] "Surely you are a bridegroom of blood to me," she said.
26So the LORD let him alone. (At
that time she said "bridegroom of
blood," referring to circumcision.)
Jos 5:2-3

27The LORD said to Aaron, "Go
into the wilderness to meet Moses." So he met Moses at the
mountain of God and kissed him.
28Then Moses told Aaron everything the LORD had sent him to
say, and also about all the signs he
had commanded him to perform.
Ex 3:1

29Moses and Aaron brought together all the elders of the Israelites, 30and Aaron told them everything the LORD had said to Moses.
He also performed the signs before the people, 31and they believed. And when they heard that
the LORD was concerned about
them and had seen their misery,
they bowed down and worshiped.
Ex 3:16,18

Bricks Without Straw

5 Afterward Moses and Aaron went to Pharaoh and said,
"This is what the LORD, the God
of Israel, says: 'Let my people go,
so that they may hold a festival to
me in the wilderness.'" Ex 4:23

2Pharaoh said, "Who is the LORD,
that I should obey him and let Israel go? I do not know the LORD
and I will not let Israel go."
Ex 3:19; Job 21:15

3Then they said, "The God of the
Hebrews has met with us. Now let
us take a three-day journey into
the wilderness to offer sacrifices
to the LORD our God, or he may
strike us with plagues or with the
sword." Ex 3:18-19; Job 21:15

4But the king of Egypt said, "Moses and Aaron, why are you taking
the people away from their labor?
Get back to your work!" 5Then
Pharaoh said, "Look, the people of
the land are now numerous, and
you are stopping them from working." Ex 1:11

[a] 24 Hebrew *him* [b] 25 The meaning of the Hebrew for this clause is uncertain.

6That same day Pharaoh gave
this order to the slave drivers and
overseers in charge of the people: 7"You are no longer to supply
the people with straw for making bricks; let them go and gather their own straw. 8But require
them to make the same number
of bricks as before; don't reduce
the quota. They are lazy; that is
why they are crying out, 'Let us
go and sacrifice to our God.' 9Make
the work harder for the people so
that they keep working and pay
no attention to lies." Ge 15:13

10Then the slave drivers and the
overseers went out and said to the
people, "This is what Pharaoh says:
'I will not give you any more straw.
11Go and get your own straw wherever you can find it, but your work
will not be reduced at all.'" 12So the
people scattered all over Egypt to
gather stubble to use for straw.
13The slave drivers kept pressing
them, saying, "Complete the work
required of you for each day, just as
when you had straw." 14And Pharaoh's slave drivers beat the Israelite overseers they had appointed, demanding, "Why haven't you
met your quota of bricks yesterday
or today, as before?" Isa 10:24

15Then the Israelite overseers
went and appealed to Pharaoh:
"Why have you treated your servants this way? 16Your servants
are given no straw, yet we are told,
'Make bricks!' Your servants are
being beaten, but the fault is with
your own people."

17Pharaoh said, "Lazy, that's
what you are — lazy! That is why
you keep saying, 'Let us go and
sacrifice to the LORD.' 18Now get
to work. You will not be given any
straw, yet you must produce your
full quota of bricks."

19The Israelite overseers realized
they were in trouble when they
were told, "You are not to reduce
the number of bricks required of
you for each day." 20When they left
Pharaoh, they found Moses and
Aaron waiting to meet them, 21and
they said, "May the LORD look on
you and judge you! You have made
us obnoxious to Pharaoh and his
officials and have put a sword in
their hand to kill us." Ge 34:30; Ex 14:11

God Promises Deliverance

22Moses returned to the LORD
and said, "Why, Lord, why have you
brought trouble on this people? Is
this why you sent me? 23Ever since
I went to Pharaoh to speak in your
name, he has brought trouble on
this people, and you have not rescued your people at all." Jer 4:10

6 Then the LORD said to Moses, "Now you will see what I
will do to Pharaoh: Because of my
mighty hand he will let them go;
because of my mighty hand he
will drive them out of his country."
Ex 3:19; 12:31,33,39

2God also said to Moses, "I am
the LORD. 3I appeared to Abraham, to Isaac and to Jacob as God
Almighty,[a] but by my name the

[a] 3 Hebrew *El-Shaddai*

LORD[a] I did not make myself fully
known to them. 4I also established
my covenant with them to give
them the land of Canaan, where
they resided as foreigners. 5More-
over, I have heard the groaning
of the Israelites, whom the Egyptians are enslaving, and I have remembered my covenant.

Ex 2:23; 3:14; Ge 15:18

6"Therefore, say to the Israelites:
'I am the LORD, and I will bring
you out from under the yoke of
the Egyptians. I will free you from
being slaves to them, and I will
redeem you with an outstretched
arm and with mighty acts of judgment. 7I will take you as my own
people, and I will be your God.
Then you will know that I am the
LORD your God, who brought you
out from under the yoke of the
Egyptians. 8And I will bring you
to the land I swore with uplifted
hand to give to Abraham, to Isaac
and to Jacob. I will give it to you as
a possession. I am the LORD.'"

Ge 15:18; Dt 7:8; Ps 136:21-22

9Moses reported this to the Israelites, but they did not listen to
him because of their discourage-
ment and harsh labor.

10Then the LORD said to Moses,
11"Go, tell Pharaoh king of Egypt
to let the Israelites go out of his
country."

12But Moses said to the LORD, "If
the Israelites will not listen to me,
why would Pharaoh listen to me,
since I speak with faltering lips[b]?"

Ex 4:10

Family Record of Moses and Aaron

13Now the LORD spoke to Moses and Aaron about the Israelites
and Pharaoh king of Egypt, and he
commanded them to bring the Israelites out of Egypt.

Ex 3:10

14These were the heads of
their families[c]:

Ge 46:9

The sons of Reuben the
firstborn son of Israel were
Hanok and Pallu, Hezron and
Karmi. These were the clans
of Reuben.

15The sons of Simeon were
Jemuel, Jamin, Ohad, Jakin,
Zohar and Shaul the son of a
Canaanite woman. These were
the clans of Simeon.

1Ch 4:24

16These were the names of
the sons of Levi according to
their records: Gershon, Kohath and Merari. Levi lived
137 years.

Ge 46:11; Nu 3:17

17The sons of Gershon, by
clans, were Libni and Shimei.

1Ch 6:17

18The sons of Kohath were
Amram, Izhar, Hebron and
Uzziel. Kohath lived 133 years.

1Ch 6:2,18

19The sons of Merari were
Mahli and Mushi.

1Ch 6:19

These were the clans of Levi
according to their records.

20Amram married his fa-
ther's sister Jochebed, who

[a] 3 See note at 3:15. [b] 12 Hebrew *I am uncircumcised of lips*; also in verse 30
[c] 14 The Hebrew for *families* here and in verse 25 refers to units larger than clans.

bore him Aaron and Moses.
Amram lived 137 years. Ex 2:1-2
21The sons of Izhar were Korah, Nepheg and Zikri. 1Ch 6:38
22The sons of Uzziel were
Mishael, Elzaphan and Sithri.
Lev 10:4
23Aaron married Elisheba,
daughter of Amminadab and
sister of Nahshon, and she bore
him Nadab and Abihu, Eleazar
and Ithamar. Lev 10:1; Nu 3:2,32
24The sons of Korah were
Assir, Elkanah and Abiasaph.
These were the Korahite clans.
Nu 26:11
25Eleazar son of Aaron married one of the daughters
of Putiel, and she bore him
Phinehas. Nu 25:7,11; Jos 24:33

These were the heads of the
Levite families, clan by clan.

26It was this Aaron and Moses to
whom the LORD said, "Bring the
Israelites out of Egypt by their divisions." 27They were the ones who
spoke to Pharaoh king of Egypt
about bringing the Israelites out
of Egypt — this same Moses and
Aaron. Ex 7:4

Aaron to Speak for Moses

28Now when the LORD spoke to
Moses in Egypt, 29he said to him, "I
am the LORD. Tell Pharaoh king of
Egypt everything I tell you." ver 2,11
30But Moses said to the LORD,
"Since I speak with faltering lips,
why would Pharaoh listen to me?"
ver 12

7 Then the LORD said to Moses,
"See, I have made you like God
to Pharaoh, and your brother Aaron will be your prophet. 2You are
to say everything I command you,
and your brother Aaron is to tell
Pharaoh to let the Israelites go out
of his country. 3But I will hard-
en Pharaoh's heart, and though I
multiply my signs and wonders in
Egypt, 4he will not listen to you.
Then I will lay my hand on Egypt
and with mighty acts of judgment
I will bring out my divisions, my
people the Israelites. 5And the
Egyptians will know that I am the
LORD when I stretch out my hand
against Egypt and bring the Israelites out of it." Ex 3:20; 4:16,21
6Moses and Aaron did just as
the LORD commanded them. 7Mo-
ses was eighty years old and Aaron eighty-three when they spoke
to Pharaoh. Dt 34:7; Ac 7:23,30

Aaron's Staff Becomes a Snake

8The LORD said to Moses and
Aaron, 9"When Pharaoh says to
you, 'Perform a miracle,' then
say to Aaron, 'Take your staff and
throw it down before Pharaoh,'
and it will become a snake."
10So Moses and Aaron went to
Pharaoh and did just as the LORD
commanded. Aaron threw his staff
down in front of Pharaoh and his
officials, and it became a snake.
11Pharaoh then summoned wise
men and sorcerers, and the Egyptian magicians also did the same
things by their secret arts: 12Each

one threw down his staff and it
became a snake. But Aaron's staff
swallowed up their staffs. 13Yet
Pharaoh's heart became hard and
he would not listen to them, just
as the LORD had said.
Ge 41:8; Ex 4:2-5; Isa 7:11

The Plague of Blood

14Then the LORD said to Moses,
"Pharaoh's heart is unyielding; he
refuses to let the people go. 15Go
to Pharaoh in the morning as he
goes out to the river. Confront
him on the bank of the Nile, and
take in your hand the staff that
was changed into a snake. 16Then
say to him, 'The LORD, the God of
the Hebrews, has sent me to say
to you: Let my people go, so that
they may worship me in the wilderness. But until now you have
not listened. 17This is what the
LORD says: By this you will know
that I am the LORD: With the staff
that is in my hand I will strike the
water of the Nile, and it will be
changed into blood. 18The fish in
the Nile will die, and the river will
stink; the Egyptians will not be
able to drink its water.'"
Ex 3:18; 4:9; Rev 16:4

19The LORD said to Moses, "Tell
Aaron, 'Take your staff and stretch
out your hand over the waters of
Egypt — over the streams and canals, over the ponds and all the
reservoirs — and they will turn to
blood.' Blood will be everywhere
in Egypt, even in vessels[a] of wood
and stone."
Ex 14:21

20Moses and Aaron did just as
the LORD had commanded. He
raised his staff in the presence
of Pharaoh and his officials and
struck the water of the Nile, and
all the water was changed into
blood. 21The fish in the Nile died,
and the river smelled so bad that
the Egyptians could not drink its
water. Blood was everywhere in
Egypt.
Ps 78:44; 105:29

22But the Egyptian magicians
did the same things by their secret arts, and Pharaoh's heart became hard; he would not listen to
Moses and Aaron, just as the LORD
had said. 23Instead, he turned and
went into his palace, and did not
take even this to heart. 24And all
the Egyptians dug along the Nile
to get drinking water, because
they could not drink the water of
the river.
ver 11

The Plague of Frogs

25Seven days passed after the
8[b] LORD struck the Nile. 1Then
the LORD said to Moses, "Go
to Pharaoh and say to him, 'This
is what the LORD says: Let my people go, so that they may worship
me. 2If you refuse to let them go, I
will send a plague of frogs on your
whole country. 3The Nile will teem
with frogs. They will come up into
your palace and your bedroom
and onto your bed, into the houses of your officials and on your

[a] 19 Or *even on their idols* [b] In Hebrew texts 8:1-4 is numbered 7:26-29, and 8:5-32 is numbered 8:1-28.

people, and into your ovens and
kneading troughs. 4The frogs will
come up on you and your people
and all your officials.'" Ex 3:12,18; 10:6

5Then the LORD said to Moses,
"Tell Aaron, 'Stretch out your hand
with your staff over the streams
and canals and ponds, and make
frogs come up on the land of
Egypt.'" Ex 7:19

6So Aaron stretched out his
hand over the waters of Egypt, and
the frogs came up and covered the
land. 7But the magicians did the
same things by their secret arts;
they also made frogs come up on
the land of Egypt. Ex 7:11; Ps 78:45

8Pharaoh summoned Moses
and Aaron and said, "Pray to the
LORD to take the frogs away from
me and my people, and I will let
your people go to offer sacrifices
to the LORD." Ex 9:28; 10:17

9Moses said to Pharaoh, "I leave
to you the honor of setting the
time for me to pray for you and
your officials and your people that
you and your houses may be rid of
the frogs, except for those that remain in the Nile."

10"Tomorrow," Pharaoh said.

Moses replied, "It will be as you
say, so that you may know there
is no one like the LORD our God.
11The frogs will leave you and your
houses, your officials and your
people; they will remain only in
the Nile." Ex 9:14; Dt 33:26

12After Moses and Aaron left
Pharaoh, Moses cried out to the
LORD about the frogs he had
brought on Pharaoh. 13And the
LORD did what Moses asked. The
frogs died in the houses, in the
courtyards and in the fields. 14They
were piled into heaps, and the
land reeked of them. 15But when
Pharaoh saw that there was relief,
he hardened his heart and would
not listen to Moses and Aaron, just
as the LORD had said. Ex 7:14

The Plague of Gnats

16Then the LORD said to Moses,
"Tell Aaron, 'Stretch out your staff
and strike the dust of the ground,'
and throughout the land of Egypt
the dust will become gnats."
17They did this, and when Aaron
stretched out his hand with the
staff and struck the dust of the
ground, gnats came on people and
animals. All the dust throughout
the land of Egypt became gnats.
18But when the magicians tried to
produce gnats by their secret arts,
they could not.

Since the gnats were on people and animals everywhere, 19the
magicians said to Pharaoh, "This
is the finger of God." But Pharaoh's
heart was hard and he would not
listen, just as the LORD had said.
Ex 7:5; 9:11; Ps 8:3; 105:31; Lk 11:20

The Plague of Flies

20Then the LORD said to Moses,
"Get up early in the morning and
confront Pharaoh as he goes to the
river and say to him, 'This is what
the LORD says: Let my people go,
so that they may worship me. 21If

you do not let my people go, I will
send swarms of flies on you and
your officials, on your people and
into your houses. The houses of
the Egyptians will be full of flies;
even the ground will be covered
with them. Ex 3:18; 7:15
22"'But on that day I will deal differently with the land of Goshen,
where my people live; no swarms
of flies will be there, so that you
will know that I, the LORD, am in
this land. 23I will make a distinction[a] between my people and your
people. This sign will occur tomorrow.'" Ex 7:5; 9:4,6,26
24And the LORD did this. Dense
swarms of flies poured into Pharaoh's palace and into the houses
of his officials; throughout Egypt
the land was ruined by the flies.
Ps 78:45; 105:31
25Then Pharaoh summoned Moses and Aaron and said, "Go, sacrifice to your God here in the land."
Ex 9:27; 10:16
26But Moses said, "That would
not be right. The sacrifices we offer
the LORD our God would be detestable to the Egyptians. And if we
offer sacrifices that are detestable
in their eyes, will they not stone
us? 27We must take a three-day
journey into the wilderness to offer sacrifices to the LORD our God,
as he commands us." Ge 43:32; Ex 3:18
28Pharaoh said, "I will let you go
to offer sacrifices to the LORD your
God in the wilderness, but you
must not go very far. Now pray
for me." ver 8
29Moses answered, "As soon as I
leave you, I will pray to the LORD,
and tomorrow the flies will leave
Pharaoh and his officials and his
people. Only let Pharaoh be sure
that he does not act deceitfully
again by not letting the people go
to offer sacrifices to the LORD."
30Then Moses left Pharaoh and
prayed to the LORD, 31and the LORD
did what Moses asked. The flies
left Pharaoh and his officials and
his people; not a fly remained.
32But this time also Pharaoh hardened his heart and would not let
the people go. ver 12; Ex 4:21

The Plague on Livestock

9 Then the LORD said to Moses,
"Go to Pharaoh and say to him,
'This is what the LORD, the God of
the Hebrews, says: "Let my people
go, so that they may worship me."
2If you refuse to let them go and
continue to hold them back, 3the
hand of the LORD will bring a terrible plague on your livestock in
the field — on your horses, donkeys and camels and on your cattle, sheep and goats. 4But the LORD
will make a distinction between
the livestock of Israel and that of
Egypt, so that no animal belonging to the Israelites will die.'"
Ex 8:1,22
5The LORD set a time and said,
"Tomorrow the LORD will do this
in the land." 6And the next day
the LORD did it: All the livestock

[a] 23 Septuagint and Vulgate; Hebrew *will put a deliverance*

of the Egyptians died, but not one animal belonging to the Israelites died. 7Pharaoh investigated and found that not even one of the animals of the Israelites had died. Yet his heart was unyielding and he would not let the people go. Ex 7:14; 8:32

The Plague of Boils

8Then the LORD said to Moses and Aaron, "Take handfuls of soot from a furnace and have Moses toss it into the air in the presence of Pharaoh. 9It will become fine dust over the whole land of Egypt, and festering boils will break out on people and animals throughout the land." Rev 16:2

10So they took soot from a furnace and stood before Pharaoh. Moses tossed it into the air, and festering boils broke out on people and animals. 11The magicians could not stand before Moses because of the boils that were on them and on all the Egyptians. 12But the LORD hardened Pharaoh's heart and he would not listen to Moses and Aaron, just as the LORD had said to Moses. Ex 4:21

The Plague of Hail

13Then the LORD said to Moses, "Get up early in the morning, confront Pharaoh and say to him, 'This is what the LORD, the God of the Hebrews, says: Let my people go, so that they may worship me, 14or this time I will send the full force of my plagues against you and against your officials and your people, so you may know that there is no one like me in all the earth. 15For by now I could have stretched out my hand and struck you and your people with a plague that would have wiped you off the earth. 16But I have raised you up[a] for this very purpose, that I might show you my power and that my name might be proclaimed in all the earth. 17You still set yourself against my people and will not let them go. 18Therefore, at this time tomorrow I will send the worst hailstorm that has ever fallen on Egypt, from the day it was founded till now. 19Give an order now to bring your livestock and everything you have in the field to a place of shelter, because the hail will fall on every person and animal that has not been brought in and is still out in the field, and they will die.'" Ro 9:17; Ex 8:10

20Those officials of Pharaoh who feared the word of the LORD hurried to bring their slaves and their livestock inside. 21But those who ignored the word of the LORD left their slaves and livestock in the field. Pr 13:13

22Then the LORD said to Moses, "Stretch out your hand toward the sky so that hail will fall all over Egypt — on people and animals and on everything growing in the fields of Egypt." 23When Moses stretched out his staff toward the sky, the LORD sent thunder and

[a] 16 Or *have spared you*

hail, and lightning flashed down
to the ground. So the LORD rained
hail on the land of Egypt; [24]hail
fell and lightning flashed back
and forth. It was the worst storm
in all the land of Egypt since it
had become a nation. [25]Through-
out Egypt hail struck everything
in the fields — both people and
animals; it beat down everything
growing in the fields and stripped
every tree. [26]The only place it did
not hail was the land of Goshen,
where the Israelites were.
ver 4; Ps 105:32-33; Jos 10:11
[27]Then Pharaoh summoned Moses and Aaron. "This time I have
sinned," he said to them. "The
LORD is in the right, and I and my
people are in the wrong. [28]Pray to
the LORD, for we have had enough
thunder and hail. I will let you go;
you don't have to stay any longer."
Ex 8:8; 10:16; 2Ch 12:6
[29]Moses replied, "When I have
gone out of the city, I will spread
out my hands in prayer to the
LORD. The thunder will stop and
there will be no more hail, so you
may know that the earth is the
LORD's. [30]But I know that you and
your officials still do not fear the
LORD God." 1Ki 8:22,38; Ps 24:1
[31](The flax and barley were destroyed, since the barley had
headed and the flax was in bloom.
[32]The wheat and spelt, however,
were not destroyed, because they
ripen later.) Ru 1:22
[33]Then Moses left Pharaoh and
went out of the city. He spread out
his hands toward the LORD; the
thunder and hail stopped, and the
rain no longer poured down on
the land. [34]When Pharaoh saw that
the rain and hail and thunder had
stopped, he sinned again: He and
his officials hardened their hearts.
[35]So Pharaoh's heart was hard and
he would not let the Israelites go,
just as the LORD had said through
Moses. Ex 4:21

The Plague of Locusts

10 Then the LORD said to Moses, "Go to Pharaoh, for I
have hardened his heart and the
hearts of his officials so that I
may perform these signs of mine
among them [2]that you may tell
your children and grandchildren
how I dealt harshly with the Egyptians and how I performed my
signs among them, and that you
may know that I am the LORD."
Dt 4:9; Ps 44:1
[3]So Moses and Aaron went to
Pharaoh and said to him, "This
is what the LORD, the God of the
Hebrews, says: 'How long will you
refuse to humble yourself before
me? Let my people go, so that
they may worship me. [4]If you refuse to let them go, I will bring locusts into your country tomorrow.
[5]They will cover the face of the
ground so that it cannot be seen.
They will devour what little you
have left after the hail, including
every tree that is growing in your
fields. [6]They will fill your houses
and those of all your officials and

all the Egyptians — something
neither your parents nor your ancestors have ever seen from the
day they settled in this land till
now.' " Then Moses turned and left
Pharaoh. Joel 1:4; Jas 4:10

7 Pharaoh's officials said to him,
"How long will this man be a snare
to us? Let the people go, so that
they may worship the LORD their
God. Do you not yet realize that
Egypt is ruined?" Ex 8:19; 23:33

8 Then Moses and Aaron were
brought back to Pharaoh. "Go,
worship the LORD your God," he
said. "But tell me who will be going." Ex 8:8

9 Moses answered, "We will go
with our young and our old, with
our sons and our daughters, and
with our flocks and herds, because
we are to celebrate a festival to the
LORD."

10 Pharaoh said, "The LORD be
with you — if I let you go, along
with your women and children!
Clearly you are bent on evil.[a] 11 No!
Have only the men go and worship the LORD, since that's what
you have been asking for." Then
Moses and Aaron were driven out
of Pharaoh's presence.

12 And the LORD said to Moses,
"Stretch out your hand over Egypt
so that locusts swarm over the
land and devour everything growing in the fields, everything left by
the hail." Ex 7:19

13 So Moses stretched out his
staff over Egypt, and the LORD
made an east wind blow across
the land all that day and all that
night. By morning the wind had
brought the locusts; 14 they invaded all Egypt and settled down in
every area of the country in great
numbers. Never before had there
been such a plague of locusts, nor
will there ever be again. 15 They
covered all the ground until it was
black. They devoured all that was
left after the hail — everything
growing in the fields and the fruit
on the trees. Nothing green remained on tree or plant in all the
land of Egypt. Joel 2:1-11,25

16 Pharaoh quickly summoned
Moses and Aaron and said, "I have
sinned against the LORD your God
and against you. 17 Now forgive
my sin once more and pray to the
LORD your God to take this deadly
plague away from me." Ex 9:27

18 Moses then left Pharaoh and
prayed to the LORD. 19 And the
LORD changed the wind to a very
strong west wind, which caught
up the locusts and carried them
into the Red Sea.[b] Not a locust was
left anywhere in Egypt. 20 But the
LORD hardened Pharaoh's heart,
and he would not let the Israelites go. Ex 4:21

The Plague of Darkness

21 Then the LORD said to Moses,
"Stretch out your hand toward
the sky so that darkness spreads
over Egypt — darkness that can
be felt." 22 So Moses stretched out

[a] 10 Or *Be careful, trouble is in store for you!*
[b] 19 Or *the Sea of Reeds*

his hand toward the sky, and total darkness covered all Egypt
for three days. 23No one could see
anyone else or move about for
three days. Yet all the Israelites
had light in the places where they
lived. Ps 105:28; Rev 16:10

24Then Pharaoh summoned
Moses and said, "Go, worship the
LORD. Even your women and children may go with you; only leave
your flocks and herds behind."
ver 8-10

25But Moses said, "You must allow us to have sacrifices and burnt
offerings to present to the LORD
our God. 26Our livestock too must
go with us; not a hoof is to be left
behind. We have to use some of
them in worshiping the LORD our
God, and until we get there we will
not know what we are to use to
worship the LORD."

27But the LORD hardened Pharaoh's heart, and he was not willing
to let them go. 28Pharaoh said to
Moses, "Get out of my sight! Make
sure you do not appear before me
again! The day you see my face
you will die."

29"Just as you say," Moses replied. "I will never appear before
you again." Heb 11:27

The Plague on the Firstborn

11 Now the LORD had said to
Moses, "I will bring one more
plague on Pharaoh and on Egypt.
After that, he will let you go from
here, and when he does, he will
drive you out completely. 2Tell the
people that men and women alike
are to ask their neighbors for articles of silver and gold." 3(The LORD
made the Egyptians favorably disposed toward the people, and Moses himself was highly regarded
in Egypt by Pharaoh's officials and
by the people.) Dt 34:11; Ex 3:21-22

4So Moses said, "This is what the
LORD says: 'About midnight I will
go throughout Egypt. 5Every firstborn son in Egypt will die, from
the firstborn son of Pharaoh, who
sits on the throne, to the firstborn
son of the female slave, who is at
her hand mill, and all the firstborn
of the cattle as well. 6There will be
loud wailing throughout Egypt —
worse than there has ever been
or ever will be again. 7But among
the Israelites not a dog will bark
at any person or animal.' Then you
will know that the LORD makes a
distinction between Egypt and Israel. 8All these officials of yours
will come to me, bowing down before me and saying, 'Go, you and
all the people who follow you!' After that I will leave." Then Moses,
hot with anger, left Pharaoh.
Ex 8:22; 12:31-33

9The LORD had said to Moses,
"Pharaoh will refuse to listen to
you — so that my wonders may be
multiplied in Egypt." 10Moses and
Aaron performed all these wonders before Pharaoh, but the LORD
hardened Pharaoh's heart, and he
would not let the Israelites go out
of his country. Ex 4:21; 7:4

The Passover and the Festival of Unleavened Bread

12 The LORD said to Moses and Aaron in Egypt, 2“This month is to be for you the first month, the first month of your year. 3Tell the whole community of Israel that on the tenth day of this month each man is to take a lamb[a] for his family, one for each household. 4If any household is too small for a whole lamb, they must share one with their nearest neighbor, having taken into account the number of people there are. You are to determine the amount of lamb needed in accordance with what each person will eat. 5The animals you choose must be year-old males without defect, and you may take them from the sheep or the goats. 6Take care of them until the fourteenth day of the month, when all the members of the community of Israel must slaughter them at twilight. 7Then they are to take some of the blood and put it on the sides and tops of the doorframes of the houses where they eat the lambs. 8That same night they are to eat the meat roasted over the fire, along with bitter herbs, and bread made without yeast. 9Do not eat the meat raw or boiled in water, but roast it over a fire — with the head, legs and internal organs. 10Do not leave any of it till morning; if some is left till morning, you must burn it. 11This is how you are to eat it: with your cloak tucked into your belt, your sandals on your feet and your staff in your hand. Eat it in haste; it is the LORD's Passover. Dt 16:1,3; Lev 22:18-21

12“On that same night I will pass through Egypt and strike down every firstborn of both people and animals, and I will bring judgment on all the gods of Egypt. I am the LORD. 13The blood will be a sign for you on the houses where you are, and when I see the blood, I will pass over you. No destructive plague will touch you when I strike Egypt. Nu 33:4; Heb 11:28

14“This is a day you are to commemorate; for the generations to come you shall celebrate it as a festival to the LORD — a lasting ordinance. 15For seven days you are to eat bread made without yeast. On the first day remove the yeast from your houses, for whoever eats anything with yeast in it from the first day through the seventh must be cut off from Israel. 16On the first day hold a sacred assembly, and another one on the seventh day. Do no work at all on these days, except to prepare food for everyone to eat; that is all you may do. Ex 13:5,10; 23:15; Lev 23:6

17“Celebrate the Festival of Unleavened Bread, because it was on this very day that I brought your divisions out of Egypt. Celebrate this day as a lasting ordinance for the generations to come. 18In the first month you are to eat bread

[a] 3 The Hebrew word can mean *lamb* or *kid*; also in verse 4.

made without yeast, from the
evening of the fourteenth day until the evening of the twenty-first
day. 19For seven days no yeast is
to be found in your houses. And
anyone, whether foreigner or native-born, who eats anything with
yeast in it must be cut off from the
community of Israel. 20Eat nothing made with yeast. Wherever
you live, you must eat unleavened
bread." Lev 23:4-8; Nu 28:16-25; Dt 16:1-8

21Then Moses summoned all the
elders of Israel and said to them,
"Go at once and select the animals
for your families and slaughter the
Passover lamb. 22Take a bunch of
hyssop, dip it into the blood in the
basin and put some of the blood
on the top and on both sides of
the doorframe. None of you shall
go out of the door of your house
until morning. 23When the LORD
goes through the land to strike
down the Egyptians, he will see
the blood on the top and sides of
the doorframe and will pass over
that doorway, and he will not permit the destroyer to enter your
houses and strike you down.
Mk 14:12-16; 1Co 10:10

24"Obey these instructions as
a lasting ordinance for you and
your descendants. 25When you enter the land that the LORD will give
you as he promised, observe this
ceremony. 26And when your children ask you, 'What does this ceremony mean to you?' 27then tell
them, 'It is the Passover sacrifice
to the LORD, who passed over the
houses of the Israelites in Egypt
and spared our homes when he
struck down the Egyptians.'" Then
the people bowed down and worshiped. 28The Israelites did just
what the LORD commanded Moses
and Aaron. ver 11; Jos 4:6

29At midnight the LORD struck
down all the firstborn in Egypt,
from the firstborn of Pharaoh,
who sat on the throne, to the firstborn of the prisoner, who was in
the dungeon, and the firstborn of
all the livestock as well. 30Phar-
aoh and all his officials and all
the Egyptians got up during the
night, and there was loud wailing
in Egypt, for there was not a house
without someone dead. Ex 4:23; 11:4,6

The Exodus

31During the night Pharaoh
summoned Moses and Aaron and
said, "Up! Leave my people, you
and the Israelites! Go, worship
the LORD as you have requested.
32Take your flocks and herds, as
you have said, and go. And also
bless me." Ex 10:9,26

33The Egyptians urged the people to hurry and leave the country.
"For otherwise," they said, "we will
all die!" 34So the people took their
dough before the yeast was added, and carried it on their shoulders in kneading troughs wrapped
in clothing. 35The Israelites did as
Moses instructed and asked the
Egyptians for articles of silver and
gold and for clothing. 36The LORD
had made the Egyptians favorably

disposed toward the people, and
they gave them what they asked
for; so they plundered the Egyptians. Ex 3:22
37 The Israelites journeyed from
Rameses to Sukkoth. There were
about six hundred thousand men
on foot, besides women and children. 38 Many other people went up
with them, and also large droves
of livestock, both flocks and
herds. 39 With the dough the Israelites had brought from Egypt, they
baked loaves of unleavened bread.
The dough was without yeast because they had been driven out
of Egypt and did not have time to
prepare food for themselves.
Nu 11:13,21; 33:3-5
40 Now the length of time the
Israelite people lived in Egypt[a]
was 430 years. 41 At the end of the
430 years, to the very day, all the
LORD's divisions left Egypt. 42 Because the LORD kept vigil that
night to bring them out of Egypt,
on this night all the Israelites are
to keep vigil to honor the LORD for
the generations to come.
Dt 16:1,6; Ac 7:6

Passover Restrictions

43 The LORD said to Moses and
Aaron, "These are the regulations
for the Passover meal: ver 11
"No foreigner may eat it. 44 Any
slave you have bought may eat it
after you have circumcised him,
45 but a temporary resident or a
hired worker may not eat it.
Ge 17:12-13
46 "It must be eaten inside the
house; take none of the meat outside the house. Do not break any
of the bones. 47 The whole community of Israel must celebrate it.
Nu 9:12; Jn 19:36
48 "A foreigner residing among
you who wants to celebrate the
LORD's Passover must have all the
males in his household circumcised; then he may take part like
one born in the land. No uncircumcised male may eat it. 49 The
same law applies both to the native-born and to the foreigner residing among you." Nu 9:14; 15:15-16,29
50 All the Israelites did just what
the LORD had commanded Moses
and Aaron. 51 And on that very day
the LORD brought the Israelites
out of Egypt by their divisions.
Ex 6:26

Consecration of the Firstborn

13 The LORD said to Moses,
2 "Consecrate to me every
firstborn male. The first offspring
of every womb among the Israelites belongs to me, whether human or animal." Lk 2:23
3 Then Moses said to the people, "Commemorate this day, the
day you came out of Egypt, out of
the land of slavery, because the
LORD brought you out of it with a
mighty hand. Eat nothing containing yeast. 4 Today, in the month of
Aviv, you are leaving. 5 When the

[a] 40 Masoretic Text; Samaritan Pentateuch and Septuagint *Egypt and Canaan*

LORD brings you into the land of
the Canaanites, Hittites, Amorites, Hivites and Jebusites — the
land he swore to your ancestors to
give you, a land flowing with milk
and honey — you are to observe
this ceremony in this month: 6For
seven days eat bread made without yeast and on the seventh day
hold a festival to the LORD. 7Eat
unleavened bread during those
seven days; nothing with yeast
in it is to be seen among you, nor
shall any yeast be seen anywhere
within your borders. 8On that day
tell your son, 'I do this because of
what the LORD did for me when I
came out of Egypt.' 9This observance will be for you like a sign on
your hand and a reminder on your
forehead that this law of the LORD
is to be on your lips. For the LORD
brought you out of Egypt with his
mighty hand. 10You must keep this
ordinance at the appointed time
year after year. Ex 12:15-20; Dt 6:8

11"After the LORD brings you into
the land of the Canaanites and
gives it to you, as he promised on
oath to you and your ancestors,
12you are to give over to the LORD
the first offspring of every womb.
All the firstborn males of your
livestock belong to the LORD. 13Re-
deem with a lamb every firstborn
donkey, but if you do not redeem
it, break its neck. Redeem every
firstborn among your sons.

Nu 18:15; Lk 2:23

14"In days to come, when your
son asks you, 'What does this
mean?' say to him, 'With a mighty
hand the LORD brought us out of
Egypt, out of the land of slavery.
15When Pharaoh stubbornly refused to let us go, the LORD killed
the firstborn of both people and
animals in Egypt. This is why I
sacrifice to the LORD the first male
offspring of every womb and redeem each of my firstborn sons.'
16And it will be like a sign on your
hand and a symbol on your forehead that the LORD brought us out
of Egypt with his mighty hand."

Ex 12:29; Dt 6:20

Crossing the Sea

17When Pharaoh let the people
go, God did not lead them on the
road through the Philistine country, though that was shorter. For
God said, "If they face war, they
might change their minds and return to Egypt." 18So God led the
people around by the desert road
toward the Red Sea.[a] The Israelites went up out of Egypt ready for
battle. Ex 14:11

19Moses took the bones of Joseph with him because Joseph had
made the Israelites swear an oath.
He had said, "God will surely come
to your aid, and then you must
carry my bones up with you from
this place."[b] Ge 50:24-25; Jos 24:32

20After leaving Sukkoth they
camped at Etham on the edge
of the desert. 21By day the LORD
went ahead of them in a pillar of

[a] *18* Or *the Sea of Reeds* [b] *19* See Gen. 50:25.

cloud to guide them on their way
and by night in a pillar of fire to
give them light, so that they could
travel by day or night. 22 Neither
the pillar of cloud by day nor the
pillar of fire by night left its place
in front of the people.
Ex 14:19,24; Ps 78:14; 1Co 10:1

14 Then the LORD said to Moses, 2 "Tell the Israelites to
turn back and encamp near Pi Hahiroth, between Migdol and the
sea. They are to encamp by the
sea, directly opposite Baal Zephon.
3 Pharaoh will think, 'The Israelites
are wandering around the land in
confusion, hemmed in by the desert.' 4 And I will harden Pharaoh's
heart, and he will pursue them.
But I will gain glory for myself
through Pharaoh and all his army,
and the Egyptians will know that I
am the LORD." So the Israelites did
this. Ro 9:17,22-23; Ex 4:21

5 When the king of Egypt was
told that the people had fled, Pharaoh and his officials changed their
minds about them and said, "What
have we done? We have let the Israelites go and have lost their services!" 6 So he had his chariot made
ready and took his army with him.
7 He took six hundred of the best
chariots, along with all the other chariots of Egypt, with officers
over all of them. 8 The LORD hardened the heart of Pharaoh king of
Egypt, so that he pursued the Israelites, who were marching out
boldly. 9 The Egyptians — all Pharaoh's horses and chariots, horsemen[a] and troops — pursued the
Israelites and overtook them as
they camped by the sea near Pi
Hahiroth, opposite Baal Zephon.
Ex 15:9; Nu 33:3

10 As Pharaoh approached, the
Israelites looked up, and there
were the Egyptians, marching after them. They were terrified and
cried out to the LORD. 11 They said
to Moses, "Was it because there
were no graves in Egypt that you
brought us to the desert to die?
What have you done to us by
bringing us out of Egypt? 12 Didn't
we say to you in Egypt, 'Leave us
alone; let us serve the Egyptians'?
It would have been better for us to
serve the Egyptians than to die in
the desert!" Ne 9:9; Ps 34:17

13 Moses answered the people,
"Do not be afraid. Stand firm and
you will see the deliverance the
LORD will bring you today. The
Egyptians you see today you will
never see again. 14 The LORD will
fight for you; you need only to be
still." Ps 46:10; Isa 30:15; Ex 15:3

15 Then the LORD said to Moses, "Why are you crying out to
me? Tell the Israelites to move
on. 16 Raise your staff and stretch
out your hand over the sea to divide the water so that the Israelites can go through the sea on dry
ground. 17 I will harden the hearts
of the Egyptians so that they will
go in after them. And I will gain
glory through Pharaoh and all his

[a] 9 Or *charioteers*; also in verses 17, 18, 23, 26 and 28

army, through his chariots and his
horsemen. 18The Egyptians will
know that I am the LORD when I
gain glory through Pharaoh, his
chariots and his horsemen."
Ex 4:17; Isa 10:26

19Then the angel of God, who
had been traveling in front of Israel's army, withdrew and went behind them. The pillar of cloud also
moved from in front and stood
behind them, 20coming between
the armies of Egypt and Israel.
Throughout the night the cloud
brought darkness to the one side
and light to the other side; so neither went near the other all night
long. Ex 13:21

21Then Moses stretched out his
hand over the sea, and all that
night the LORD drove the sea back
with a strong east wind and turned
it into dry land. The waters were
divided, 22and the Israelites went
through the sea on dry ground,
with a wall of water on their right
and on their left. Heb 11:29; Isa 63:12

23The Egyptians pursued them,
and all Pharaoh's horses and
chariots and horsemen followed
them into the sea. 24During the
last watch of the night the LORD
looked down from the pillar of
fire and cloud at the Egyptian
army and threw it into confusion.
25He jammed[a] the wheels of their
chariots so that they had difficulty driving. And the Egyptians said,
"Let's get away from the Israelites! The LORD is fighting for them
against Egypt." ver 14; Ex 13:21

26Then the LORD said to Moses,
"Stretch out your hand over the
sea so that the waters may flow
back over the Egyptians and their
chariots and horsemen." 27Mo-
ses stretched out his hand over
the sea, and at daybreak the sea
went back to its place. The Egyptians were fleeing toward[b] it, and
the LORD swept them into the sea.
28The water flowed back and covered the chariots and horsemen —
the entire army of Pharaoh that
had followed the Israelites into
the sea. Not one of them survived.
Ex 15:1,21; Ps 106:11

29But the Israelites went
through the sea on dry ground,
with a wall of water on their right
and on their left. 30That day the
LORD saved Israel from the hands
of the Egyptians, and Israel saw
the Egyptians lying dead on the
shore. 31And when the Israelites
saw the mighty hand of the LORD
displayed against the Egyptians,
the people feared the LORD and
put their trust in him and in Moses his servant. Jn 2:11; Ps 106:8,10,21

The Song of Moses and Miriam

15 Then Moses and the Israelites sang this song to the
LORD: Rev 15:3

"I will sing to the LORD, Ps 106:12
  for he is highly exalted.
Both horse and driver
  he has hurled into the sea.

[a] 25 See Samaritan Pentateuch, Septuagint and Syriac; Masoretic Text *removed*
[b] 27 Or *from*

2 "The LORD is my strength and
my defense[a]; Ps 59:17
he has become my salvation.
Ps 18:2,46; Hab 3:18
He is my God, and I will praise
him,
my father's God, and I will
exalt him. Ex 3:6,15-16; Isa 25:1
3 The LORD is a warrior; Rev 19:11
the LORD is his name.
4 Pharaoh's chariots and his
army
he has hurled into the sea.
The best of Pharaoh's officers
are drowned in the Red Sea.[b]
5 The deep waters have covered
them;
they sank to the depths like a
stone. Ne 9:11
6 Your right hand, LORD, Ps 118:15
was majestic in power.
Your right hand, LORD,
shattered the enemy.
7 "In the greatness of your
majesty
you threw down those who
opposed you.
You unleashed your burning
anger;
it consumed them like
stubble.
8 By the blast of your nostrils
the waters piled up. Ps 78:13
The surging waters stood up
like a wall;
the deep waters congealed in
the heart of the sea.
9 The enemy boasted,
'I will pursue, I will overtake
them. Ex 14:5-9
I will divide the spoils;
I will gorge myself on them.
I will draw my sword
and my hand will destroy
them.'
10 But you blew with your
breath,
and the sea covered them.
They sank like lead
in the mighty waters.
11 Who among the gods
is like you, LORD? Ex 8:10
Who is like you —
majestic in holiness, Isa 6:3
awesome in glory, Ps 18:1
working wonders?
12 "You stretch out your right
hand,
and the earth swallows your
enemies.
13 In your unfailing love you will
lead Ne 9:12
the people you have
redeemed.
In your strength you will guide
them
to your holy dwelling. Ps 78:54
14 The nations will hear and
tremble;
anguish will grip the people
of Philistia.
15 The chiefs of Edom will be
terrified,
the leaders of Moab will be
seized with trembling,
Nu 22:3
the people[c] of Canaan will melt
away;

[a] 2 Or *song* in verse 22 [b] 4 Or *the Sea of Reeds*; also [c] 15 Or *rulers*

16 terror and dread will fall on
them.
By the power of your arm
they will be as still as a
stone —
until your people pass by, LORD,
until the people you bought[a]
pass by. Ps 74:2
17 You will bring them in and
plant them Ps 44:2
on the mountain of your
inheritance — Ps 78:54,68
the place, LORD, you made for
your dwelling,
the sanctuary, Lord, your
hands established.

18 "The LORD reigns
for ever and ever."

19 When Pharaoh's horses, chariots and horsemen[b] went into the
sea, the LORD brought the waters
of the sea back over them, but the
Israelites walked through the sea
on dry ground. 20 Then Miriam the
prophet, Aaron's sister, took a timbrel in her hand, and all the wom-
en followed her, with timbrels and
dancing. 21 Miriam sang to them:
Ex 14:28; Nu 26:59; 1Sa 18:6

"Sing to the LORD,
for he is highly exalted.
Both horse and driver
he has hurled into the sea."

The Waters of Marah and Elim

22 Then Moses led Israel from the
Red Sea and they went into the
Desert of Shur. For three days they
traveled in the desert without
finding water. 23 When they came
to Marah, they could not drink its
water because it was bitter. (That
is why the place is called Marah.[c])
24 So the people grumbled against
Moses, saying, "What are we to
drink?" Nu 33:8
25 Then Moses cried out to the
LORD, and the LORD showed him
a piece of wood. He threw it into
the water, and the water became
fit to drink.

There the LORD issued a ruling
and instruction for them and put
them to the test. 26 He said, "If you
listen carefully to the LORD your
God and do what is right in his
eyes, if you pay attention to his
commands and keep all his decrees, I will not bring on you any
of the diseases I brought on the
Egyptians, for I am the LORD, who
heals you." Ex 23:25-26; Dt 28:27,58-60
27 Then they came to Elim, where
there were twelve springs and seventy palm trees, and they camped
there near the water. Nu 33:9

Manna and Quail

16 The whole Israelite community set out from Elim and
came to the Desert of Sin, which
is between Elim and Sinai, on the
fifteenth day of the second month
after they had come out of Egypt.
2 In the desert the whole community grumbled against Moses
and Aaron. 3 The Israelites said to
them, "If only we had died by the

[a] 16 Or *created* [b] 19 Or *charioteers*
[c] 23 *Marah* means *bitter.*

LORD's hand in Egypt! There we sat around pots of meat and ate all the food we wanted, but you have brought us out into this desert to starve this entire assembly to death." Nu 11:4,34; 1Co 10:10

[4]Then the LORD said to Moses, "I will rain down bread from heaven for you. The people are to go out each day and gather enough for that day. In this way I will test them and see whether they will follow my instructions. [5]On the sixth day they are to prepare what they bring in, and that is to be twice as much as they gather on the other days." Dt 8:3; Jn 6:31

[6]So Moses and Aaron said to all the Israelites, "In the evening you will know that it was the LORD who brought you out of Egypt, [7]and in the morning you will see the glory of the LORD, because he has heard your grumbling against him. Who are we, that you should grumble against us?" [8]Moses also said, "You will know that it was the LORD when he gives you meat to eat in the evening and all the bread you want in the morning, because he has heard your grumbling against him. Who are we? You are not grumbling against us, but against the LORD." Nu 16:11; Ro 13:2

[9]Then Moses told Aaron, "Say to the entire Israelite community, 'Come before the LORD, for he has heard your grumbling.'"

[10]While Aaron was speaking to the whole Israelite community, they looked toward the desert, and there was the glory of the LORD appearing in the cloud. Ex 13:21; 1Ki 8:10

[11]The LORD said to Moses, [12]"I have heard the grumbling of the Israelites. Tell them, 'At twilight you will eat meat, and in the morning you will be filled with bread. Then you will know that I am the LORD your God.'"

[13]That evening quail came and covered the camp, and in the morning there was a layer of dew around the camp. [14]When the dew was gone, thin flakes like frost on the ground appeared on the desert floor. [15]When the Israelites saw it, they said to each other, "What is it?" For they did not know what it was. Nu 11:7-9,31; Ps 78:27-28

Moses said to them, "It is the bread the LORD has given you to eat. [16]This is what the LORD has commanded: 'Everyone is to gather as much as they need. Take an omer[a] for each person you have in your tent.'"

[17]The Israelites did as they were told; some gathered much, some little. [18]And when they measured it by the omer, the one who gathered much did not have too much, and the one who gathered little did not have too little. Everyone had gathered just as much as they needed. 2Co 8:15

[a] *16* That is, possibly about 3 pounds or about 1.4 kilograms; also in verses 18, 32, 33 and 36

19 Then Moses said to them, "No
one is to keep any of it until morning." Ex 12:10
20 However, some of them paid
no attention to Moses; they kept
part of it until morning, but it was
full of maggots and began to smell.
So Moses was angry with them.
21 Each morning everyone gathered as much as they needed, and
when the sun grew hot, it melted
away. 22 On the sixth day, they gathered twice as much — two omers[a]
for each person — and the leaders
of the community came and reported this to Moses. 23 He said to
them, "This is what the LORD commanded: 'Tomorrow is to be a day
of sabbath rest, a holy sabbath to
the LORD. So bake what you want
to bake and boil what you want
to boil. Save whatever is left and
keep it until morning.'"
24 So they saved it until morning, as Moses commanded, and it
did not stink or get maggots in it.
25 "Eat it today," Moses said, "because today is a sabbath to the
LORD. You will not find any of it on
the ground today. 26 Six days you
are to gather it, but on the seventh
day, the Sabbath, there will not be
any." Ge 2:3; Ex 20:8
27 Nevertheless, some of the
people went out on the seventh
day to gather it, but they found
none. 28 Then the LORD said to Moses, "How long will you[b] refuse to
keep my commands and my instructions? 29 Bear in mind that
the LORD has given you the Sabbath; that is why on the sixth day
he gives you bread for two days.
Everyone is to stay where they are
on the seventh day; no one is to go
out." 30 So the people rested on the
seventh day. Ps 78:10
31 The people of Israel called the
bread manna.[c] It was white like coriander seed and tasted like wafers
made with honey. 32 Moses said,
"This is what the LORD has commanded: 'Take an omer of manna
and keep it for the generations to
come, so they can see the bread I
gave you to eat in the wilderness
when I brought you out of Egypt.'"
33 So Moses said to Aaron, "Take
a jar and put an omer of manna in
it. Then place it before the LORD
to be kept for the generations to
come." Heb 9:4
34 As the LORD commanded Moses, Aaron put the manna with the
tablets of the covenant law, so that
it might be preserved. 35 The Israelites ate manna forty years, until
they came to a land that was settled; they ate manna until they
reached the border of Canaan.
Ex 25:16,21-22; Jos 5:12
36 (An omer is one-tenth of an
ephah.)

Water From the Rock

17 The whole Israelite community set out from the Desert of Sin, traveling from place to

[a] *22* That is, possibly about 6 pounds or about 2.8 kilograms [b] *28* The Hebrew is plural. [c] *31* *Manna* sounds like the Hebrew for *What is it?* (see verse 15).

place as the LORD commanded. They camped at Rephidim, but there was no water for the people to drink. 2So they quarreled with Moses and said, "Give us water to drink." Nu 20:2

Moses replied, "Why do you quarrel with me? Why do you put the LORD to the test?"

Dt 6:16; Ps 78:18,41; 1Co 10:9

3But the people were thirsty for water there, and they grumbled against Moses. They said, "Why did you bring us up out of Egypt to make us and our children and livestock die of thirst?"

Ex 15:24; 16:2-3

4Then Moses cried out to the LORD, "What am I to do with these people? They are almost ready to stone me." Nu 14:10

5The LORD answered Moses, "Go out in front of the people. Take with you some of the elders of Israel and take in your hand the staff with which you struck the Nile, and go. 6I will stand there before you by the rock at Horeb. Strike the rock, and water will come out of it for the people to drink." So Moses did this in the sight of the elders of Israel. 7And he called the place Massah[a] and Meribah[b] because the Israelites quarreled and because they tested the LORD saying, "Is the LORD among us or not?" Nu 20:11; 1Co 10:4

The Amalekites Defeated

8The Amalekites came and attacked the Israelites at Rephidim. 9Moses said to Joshua, "Choose some of our men and go out to fight the Amalekites. Tomorrow I will stand on top of the hill with the staff of God in my hands."

Dt 25:17-19

10So Joshua fought the Amalekites as Moses had ordered, and Moses, Aaron and Hur went to the top of the hill. 11As long as Moses held up his hands, the Israelites were winning, but whenever he lowered his hands, the Amalekites were winning. 12When Moses' hands grew tired, they took a stone and put it under him and he sat on it. Aaron and Hur held his hands up — one on one side, one on the other — so that his hands remained steady till sunset. 13So Joshua overcame the Amalekite army with the sword. Jas 5:16

14Then the LORD said to Moses, "Write this on a scroll as something to be remembered and make sure that Joshua hears it, because I will completely blot out the name of Amalek from under heaven." Ex 34:27

15Moses built an altar and called it The LORD is my Banner. 16He said, "Because hands were lifted up against[c] the throne of the LORD,[d] the LORD will be at war against the Amalekites from generation to generation."

Ge 22:14; Nu 24:7

[a] 7 *Massah* means *testing.* [b] 7 *Meribah* means *quarreling.* [c] 16 Or *to* [d] 16 The meaning of the Hebrew for this clause is uncertain.

Jethro Visits Moses

18 Now Jethro, the priest of
Midian and father-in-law of
Moses, heard of everything God
had done for Moses and for his
people Israel, and how the LORD
had brought Israel out of Egypt.
Ex 2:16; 3:1

2After Moses had sent away his
wife Zipporah, his father-in-law
Jethro received her 3and her two
sons. One son was named Gershom,[a] for Moses said, "I have
become a foreigner in a foreign
land"; 4and the other was named
Eliezer,[b] for he said, "My father's
God was my helper; he saved me
from the sword of Pharaoh."
Ex 2:22; 4:25; Ac 7:29

5Jethro, Moses' father-in-law,
together with Moses' sons and
wife, came to him in the wilderness, where he was camped near
the mountain of God. 6Jethro had
sent word to him, "I, your father-
in-law Jethro, am coming to you
with your wife and her two sons."
Ex 3:1

7So Moses went out to meet his
father-in-law and bowed down
and kissed him. They greeted
each other and then went into the
tent. 8Moses told his father-in-law
about everything the LORD had
done to Pharaoh and the Egyptians for Israel's sake and about all
the hardships they had met along
the way and how the LORD had
saved them.
Ge 29:13; 43:28

9Jethro was delighted to hear
about all the good things the
LORD had done for Israel in res-
cuing them from the hand of the
Egyptians. 10He said, "Praise be to
the LORD, who rescued you from
the hand of the Egyptians and
of Pharaoh, and who rescued the
people from the hand of the Egyptians. 11Now I know that the LORD
is greater than all other gods, for
he did this to those who had treated Israel arrogantly." 12Then Jethro, Moses' father-in-law, brought a
burnt offering and other sacrifices to God, and Aaron came with all
the elders of Israel to eat a meal
with Moses' father-in-law in the
presence of God.
Lk 1:51; Ps 68:19-20

13The next day Moses took his
seat to serve as judge for the people, and they stood around him
from morning till evening. 14When
his father-in-law saw all that Moses was doing for the people, he
said, "What is this you are doing
for the people? Why do you alone
sit as judge, while all these people
stand around you from morning
till evening?"

15Moses answered him, "Because
the people come to me to seek
God's will. 16Whenever they have a
dispute, it is brought to me, and
I decide between the parties and
inform them of God's decrees and
instructions."
Nu 9:6,8; Dt 17:8-13

17Moses' father-in-law replied,
"What you are doing is not good.
18You and these people who come

[a] 3 *Gershom* sounds like the Hebrew for *a foreigner there.* [b] 4 *Eliezer* means *my God is helper.*

to you will only wear yourselves
out. The work is too heavy for you;
you cannot handle it alone. 19Lis-
ten now to me and I will give you
some advice, and may God be with
you. You must be the people's representative before God and bring
their disputes to him. 20Teach
them his decrees and instructions,
and show them the way they are
to live and how they are to behave.
21But select capable men from all
the people — men who fear God,
trustworthy men who hate dishonest gain — and appoint them
as officials over thousands, hundreds, fifties and tens. 22Have them
serve as judges for the people at all
times, but have them bring every
difficult case to you; the simple
cases they can decide themselves.
That will make your load lighter,
because they will share it with you.
23If you do this and God so commands, you will be able to stand
the strain, and all these people will
go home satisfied." Nu 27:5; Dt 15:1; 16:19

24Moses listened to his father-
in-law and did everything he said.
25He chose capable men from all Israel and made them leaders of the
people, officials over thousands,
hundreds, fifties and tens. 26They
served as judges for the people at
all times. The difficult cases they
brought to Moses, but the simple
ones they decided themselves.
ver 22; Dt 1:13-15

27Then Moses sent his father-in-
law on his way, and Jethro returned
to his own country. Nu 10:29-30

At Mount Sinai

19 On the first day of the third
month after the Israelites
left Egypt — on that very day —
they came to the Desert of Sinai.
2After they set out from Rephidim,
they entered the Desert of Sinai,
and Israel camped there in the
desert in front of the mountain.
Ex 17:1

3Then Moses went up to God,
and the LORD called to him from
the mountain and said, "This is
what you are to say to the descendants of Jacob and what you are
to tell the people of Israel: 4'You
yourselves have seen what I did
to Egypt, and how I carried you on
eagles' wings and brought you to
myself. 5Now if you obey me fully
and keep my covenant, then out
of all nations you will be my treasured possession. Although the
whole earth is mine, 6you[a] will be
for me a kingdom of priests and a
holy nation.' These are the words
you are to speak to the Israelites."
Dt 7:6; 1Pe 2:5

7So Moses went back and summoned the elders of the people
and set before them all the words
the LORD had commanded him to
speak. 8The people all responded together, "We will do everything the LORD has said." So Moses
brought their answer back to the
LORD. Ex 24:3,7; Dt 5:27

9The LORD said to Moses, "I am
going to come to you in a dense

[a] 5,6 Or *possession, for the whole earth is mine.* 6*You*

cloud, so that the people will hear
me speaking with you and will always put their trust in you." Then
Moses told the LORD what the people had said. ver 16; Ex 24:15-16
10And the LORD said to Moses,
"Go to the people and consecrate
them today and tomorrow. Have
them wash their clothes 11and be
ready by the third day, because
on that day the LORD will come
down on Mount Sinai in the sight
of all the people. 12Put limits for
the people around the mountain
and tell them, 'Be careful that
you do not approach the mountain or touch the foot of it. Whoever touches the mountain is to
be put to death. 13They are to be
stoned or shot with arrows; not
a hand is to be laid on them. No
person or animal shall be permitted to live.' Only when the ram's
horn sounds a long blast may
they approach the mountain."

Lev 11:44; Heb 12:20

14After Moses had gone down the
mountain to the people, he consecrated them, and they washed
their clothes. 15Then he said to the
people, "Prepare yourselves for
the third day. Abstain from sexual
relations." Ge 35:2; 1Sa 21:4
16On the morning of the third
day there was thunder and lightning, with a thick cloud over the
mountain, and a very loud trumpet blast. Everyone in the camp
trembled. 17Then Moses led the
people out of the camp to meet
with God, and they stood at the
foot of the mountain. 18Mount
Sinai was covered with smoke, because the LORD descended on it in
fire. The smoke billowed up from
it like smoke from a furnace, and
the whole mountain[a] trembled
violently. 19As the sound of the
trumpet grew louder and louder,
Moses spoke and the voice of God
answered him.[b]

Ps 81:7; 104:32; Heb 12:18-19

20The LORD descended to the
top of Mount Sinai and called Moses to the top of the mountain. So
Moses went up 21and the LORD said
to him, "Go down and warn the
people so they do not force their
way through to see the LORD and
many of them perish. 22Even the
priests, who approach the LORD,
must consecrate themselves, or
the LORD will break out against
them." Lev 10:3; 1Sa 6:19
23Moses said to the LORD, "The
people cannot come up Mount Sinai, because you yourself warned
us, 'Put limits around the mountain and set it apart as holy.' "

ver 12

24The LORD replied, "Go down
and bring Aaron up with you. But
the priests and the people must
not force their way through to
come up to the LORD, or he will
break out against them." Ex 24:1,9
25So Moses went down to the
people and told them.

[a] 18 Most Hebrew manuscripts; a few Hebrew manuscripts and Septuagint *and all the people* [b] 19 Or *and God answered him with thunder*

The Ten Commandments

20 And God spoke all these
words:

[2]"I am the LORD your God,
who brought you out of
Egypt, out of the land of
slavery. Ex 13:3
[3]"You shall have no other gods
before[a] me. Dt 6:14; Jer 35:15
[4]"You shall not make for yourself an image in the form
of anything in heaven
above or on the earth be-
neath or in the waters
below. [5]You shall not bow
down to them or worship
them; for I, the LORD your
God, am a jealous God,
punishing the children
for the sin of the parents
to the third and fourth
generation of those who
hate me, [6]but showing
love to a thousand gener-
ations of those who love
me and keep my com-
mandments.
Dt 4:24; 7:9; Jer 32:18
[7]"You shall not misuse the
name of the LORD your
God, for the LORD will
not hold anyone guiltless
who misuses his name.
Lev 19:12
[8]"Remember the Sabbath day
by keeping it holy. [9]Six
days you shall labor and
do all your work, [10]but the
seventh day is a sabbath
to the LORD your God. On
it you shall not do any
work, neither you, nor
your son or daughter, nor
your male or female ser-
vant, nor your animals,
nor any foreigner residing
in your towns. [11]For in six
days the LORD made the
heavens and the earth,
the sea, and all that is in
them, but he rested on
the seventh day. There-
fore the LORD blessed the
Sabbath day and made it
holy. Ex 31:13-16; Ge 2:2
[12]"Honor your father and your
mother, so that you may
live long in the land the
LORD your God is giving
you. Mt 15:4; Eph 6:2
[13]"You shall not murder. Ro 13:9
[14]"You shall not commit adultery. Mt 19:18
[15]"You shall not steal.
Lev 19:11,13; Mt 19:18
[16]"You shall not give false testimony against your
neighbor. Ex 23:1,7
[17]"You shall not covet your
neighbor's house. You
shall not covet your
neighbor's wife, or his
male or female servant,
his ox or donkey, or any-
thing that belongs to your
neighbor." Dt 5:6-21; Ro 7:7

[18]When the people saw the thunder and lightning and heard the
trumpet and saw the mountain in

[a] 3 Or *besides*

smoke, they trembled with fear.
They stayed at a distance 19and
said to Moses, "Speak to us yourself and we will listen. But do not
have God speak to us or we will
die." Dt 5:5,23-27; Ex 19:16-19

20Moses said to the people, "Do
not be afraid. God has come to test
you, so that the fear of God will be
with you to keep you from sinning." Pr 16:6

21The people remained at a distance, while Moses approached
the thick darkness where God was.
Dt 5:22

Idols and Altars

22Then the LORD said to Moses,
"Tell the Israelites this: 'You have
seen for yourselves that I have
spoken to you from heaven: 23Do
not make any gods to be alongside
me; do not make for yourselves
gods of silver or gods of gold. ver 3

24" 'Make an altar of earth for me
and sacrifice on it your burnt offerings and fellowship offerings,
your sheep and goats and your
cattle. Wherever I cause my name
to be honored, I will come to you
and bless you. 25If you makc an altar of stones for me, do not build
it with dressed stones, for you
will defile it if you use a tool on it.
26And do not go up to my altar on
steps, or your private parts may be
exposed.' Ge 12:2; Dt 27:5-6

21 "These are the laws you are
to set before them: Dt 4:14

Hebrew Servants

2"If you buy a Hebrew servant,
he is to serve you for six years.
But in the seventh year, he shall
go free, without paying anything.
3If he comes alone, he is to go free
alone; but if he has a wife when he
comes, she is to go with him. 4If
his master gives him a wife and
she bears him sons or daughters,
the woman and her children shall
belong to her master, and only the
man shall go free. Jer 34:8,14

5"But if the servant declares, 'I
love my master and my wife and
children and do not want to go
free,' 6then his master must take
him before the judges.[a] He shall
take him to the door or the doorpost and pierce his ear with an
awl. Then he will be his servant
for life. Dt 15:12-18

7"If a man sells his daughter as
a servant, she is not to go free as
male servants do. 8If she does not
please the master who has selected her for himself,[b] he must let
her be redeemed. He has no right
to sell her to foreigners, because
he has broken faith with her. 9If
he selects her for his son, he must
grant her the rights of a daughter.
10If he marries another woman,
he must not deprive the first one
of her food, clothing and marital
rights. 11If he does not provide her
with these three things, she is to
go free, without any payment of
money. Lev 25:39-55; 1Co 7:3-5

[a] 6 Or *before God* [b] 8 Or *master so that he does not choose her*

Personal Injuries

12“Anyone who strikes a person with a fatal blow is to be put to death. 13However, if it is not done intentionally, but God lets it happen, they are to flee to a place I will designate. 14But if anyone schemes and kills someone deliberately, that person is to be taken from my altar and put to death.

Dt 19:11-12; Nu 35:10-34

15“Anyone who attacks[a] their father or mother is to be put to death.

16“Anyone who kidnaps someone is to be put to death, whether the victim has been sold or is still in the kidnapper’s possession.

Dt 24:7

17“Anyone who curses their father or mother is to be put to death.

Mk 7:10

18“If people quarrel and one person hits another with a stone or with their fist[b] and the victim does not die but is confined to bed, 19the one who struck the blow will not be held liable if the other can get up and walk around outside with a staff; however, the guilty party must pay the injured person for any loss of time and see that the victim is completely healed.

20“Anyone who beats their male or female slave with a rod must be punished if the slave dies as a direct result, 21but they are not to be punished if the slave recovers after a day or two, since the slave is their property.

Lev 25:44-46

22“If people are fighting and hit a pregnant woman and she gives birth prematurely[c] but there is no serious injury, the offender must be fined whatever the woman’s husband demands and the court allows. 23But if there is serious injury, you are to take life for life, 24eye for eye, tooth for tooth, hand for hand, foot for foot, 25burn for burn, wound for wound, bruise for bruise.

Mt 5:38

26“An owner who hits a male or female slave in the eye and destroys it must let the slave go free to compensate for the eye. 27And an owner who knocks out the tooth of a male or female slave must let the slave go free to compensate for the tooth.

28“If a bull gores a man or woman to death, the bull is to be stoned to death, and its meat must not be eaten. But the owner of the bull will not be held responsible. 29If, however, the bull has had the habit of goring and the owner has been warned but has not kept it penned up and it kills a man or woman, the bull is to be stoned and its owner also is to be put to death. 30However, if payment is demanded, the owner may redeem his life by the payment of whatever is demanded. 31This law also applies if the bull gores a son or daughter. 32If the bull gores a male or female slave, the owner must pay thirty shekels[d] of silver

[a] 15 Or *kills* [b] 18 Or *with a tool*
[c] 22 Or *she has a miscarriage* [d] 32 That is, about 12 ounces or about 345 grams

to the master of the slave, and the
bull is to be stoned to death.

Zec 11:12-13; Mt 26:15; Ge 9:5

33“If anyone uncovers a pit or
digs one and fails to cover it and
an ox or a donkey falls into it, 34the
one who opened the pit must pay
the owner for the loss and take the
dead animal in exchange.

35“If anyone's bull injures someone else's bull and it dies, the two
parties are to sell the live one and
divide both the money and the
dead animal equally. 36However,
if it was known that the bull had
the habit of goring, yet the owner did not keep it penned up, the
owner must pay, animal for animal, and take the dead animal in
exchange.

Protection of Property

22 [a] “Whoever steals an ox or a
sheep and slaughters it or
sells it must pay back five head of
cattle for the ox and four sheep for
the sheep.

2Sa 12:6

2“If a thief is caught breaking
in at night and is struck a fatal
blow, the defender is not guilty of
bloodshed; 3but if it happens after
sunrise, the defender is guilty of
bloodshed.

Mt 24:43

“Anyone who steals must certainly make restitution, but if
they have nothing, they must be
sold to pay for their theft. 4If the
stolen animal is found alive in
their possession — whether ox or
donkey or sheep — they must pay
back double.

Ge 43:12; Ex 21:2

5“If anyone grazes their livestock in a field or vineyard and
lets them stray and they graze in
someone else's field, the offender
must make restitution from the
best of their own field or vineyard.

ver 1

6“If a fire breaks out and spreads
into thornbushes so that it burns
shocks of grain or standing grain
or the whole field, the one who
started the fire must make restitution.

Jdg 15:5

7“If anyone gives a neighbor silver or goods for safekeeping and
they are stolen from the neighbor's house, the thief, if caught,
must pay back double. 8But if the
thief is not found, the owner of
the house must appear before the
judges, and they must[b] determine
whether the owner of the house
has laid hands on the other person's property. 9In all cases of illegal possession of an ox, a donkey,
a sheep, a garment, or any other
lost property about which somebody says, ‘This is mine,’ both parties are to bring their cases before
the judges.[c] The one whom the
judges declare[d] guilty must pay
back double to the other.

Dt 25:1

10“If anyone gives a donkey, an
ox, a sheep or any other animal
to their neighbor for safekeeping
and it dies or is injured or is tak-
en away while no one is looking,

[a] In Hebrew texts 22:1 is numbered 21:37, and 22:2-31 is numbered 22:1-30. [b] *8* Or *before God, and he will* [c] *9* Or *before God* [d] *9* Or *whom God declares*

11the issue between them will be
settled by the taking of an oath
before the LORD that the neighbor did not lay hands on the other
person's property. The owner is to
accept this, and no restitution is
required. 12But if the animal was
stolen from the neighbor, restitution must be made to the owner.
13If it was torn to pieces by a wild
animal, the neighbor shall bring
in the remains as evidence and
shall not be required to pay for the
torn animal. Ge 31:39; Heb 6:16

14"If anyone borrows an animal
from their neighbor and it is injured or dies while the owner is
not present, they must make restitution. 15But if the owner is with
the animal, the borrower will not
have to pay. If the animal was
hired, the money paid for the hire
covers the loss. Lev 19:13

Social Responsibility

16"If a man seduces a virgin who
is not pledged to be married and
sleeps with her, he must pay the
bride-price, and she shall be his
wife. 17If her father absolutely refuses to give her to him, he must
still pay the bride-price for virgins. Dt 22:28

18"Do not allow a sorceress to
live. Lev 20:27; Dt 18:11

19"Anyone who has sexual relations with an animal is to be put
to death. Lev 18:23

20"Whoever sacrifices to any god
other than the LORD must be destroyed.[a] Dt 17:2-5

21"Do not mistreat or oppress a
foreigner, for you were foreigners
in Egypt. Dt 10:19

22"Do not take advantage of the
widow or the fatherless. 23If you
do and they cry out to me, I will
certainly hear their cry. 24My anger
will be aroused, and I will kill you
with the sword; your wives will
become widows and your children
fatherless. Ps 18:6; 109:9; Lk 18:7

25"If you lend money to one
of my people among you who is
needy, do not treat it like a business deal; charge no interest. 26If
you take your neighbor's cloak as
a pledge, return it by sunset, 27be-
cause that cloak is the only covering your neighbor has. What else
can they sleep in? When they cry
out to me, I will hear, for I am
compassionate. Ex 34:6; Lev 25:35-37

28"Do not blaspheme God[b] or
curse the ruler of your people.
Ac 23:5; Lev 24:11,16

29"Do not hold back offerings
from your granaries or your vats.[c]
Ex 23:15-16,19

"You must give me the firstborn
of your sons. 30Do the same with
your cattle and your sheep. Let
them stay with their mothers for
seven days, but give them to me
on the eighth day.
Ex 13:2; Lev 22:27; Dt 15:19

[a] 20 The Hebrew term refers to the irrevocable giving over of things or persons to the LORD, often by totally destroying them. [b] 28 Or *Do not revile the judges* [c] 29 The meaning of the Hebrew for this phrase is uncertain.

31 “You are to be my holy people.
So do not eat the meat of an animal torn by wild beasts; throw it
to the dogs. Lev 19:2

Laws of Justice and Mercy

23 “Do not spread false reports. Do not help a guilty
person by being a malicious witness. Ex 20:16; Ps 35:11
2 “Do not follow the crowd in doing wrong. When you give testimony in a lawsuit, do not pervert
justice by siding with the crowd,
3 and do not show favoritism to a
poor person in a lawsuit. Dt 16:19
4 “If you come across your enemy’s ox or donkey wandering off,
be sure to return it. 5 If you see the
donkey of someone who hates you
fallen down under its load, do not
leave it there; be sure you help
them with it. Dt 22:4
6 “Do not deny justice to your
poor people in their lawsuits.
7 Have nothing to do with a false
charge and do not put an innocent or honest person to death, for
I will not acquit the guilty. Eph 4:25
8 “Do not accept a bribe, for a
bribe blinds those who see and
twists the words of the innocent.
Dt 10:17
9 “Do not oppress a foreigner;
you yourselves know how it feels
to be foreigners, because you were
foreigners in Egypt. Ex 22:21

Sabbath Laws

10 “For six years you are to sow
your fields and harvest the crops,
11 but during the seventh year let
the land lie unplowed and un-
used. Then the poor among your
people may get food from it, and
the wild animals may eat what is
left. Do the same with your vineyard and your olive grove.
12 “Six days do your work, but on
the seventh day do not work, so
that your ox and your donkey may
rest, and so that the slave born in
your household and the foreigner living among you may be refreshed. Ex 20:9
13 “Be careful to do everything
I have said to you. Do not invoke
the names of other gods; do not let
them be heard on your lips. 1Ti 4:16

The Three Annual Festivals

14 “Three times a year you are to
celebrate a festival to me. Ex 34:23-24
15 “Celebrate the Festival of Unleavened Bread; for seven days
eat bread made without yeast, as
I commanded you. Do this at the
appointed time in the month of
Aviv, for in that month you came
out of Egypt. Ex 12:17
“No one is to appear before me
empty-handed. Ex 34:20
16 “Celebrate the Festival of Harvest with the firstfruits of the
crops you sow in your field. Ex 34:22
“Celebrate the Festival of Ingathering at the end of the year,
when you gather in your crops
from the field. Dt 16:13
17 “Three times a year all the men
are to appear before the Sovereign
LORD. Dt 16:16

18“Do not offer the blood of a
sacrifice to me along with anything containing yeast. Ex 34:25
“The fat of my festival offerings
must not be kept until morning.
Dt 16:4

19“Bring the best of the firstfruits of your soil to the house of
the LORD your God. Dt 26:2,10
“Do not cook a young goat in its
mother’s milk. Dt 14:21

God’s Angel to Prepare the Way

20“See, I am sending an angel
ahead of you to guard you along
the way and to bring you to the
place I have prepared. 21Pay attention to him and listen to what
he says. Do not rebel against him;
he will not forgive your rebellion,
since my Name is in him. 22If you
listen carefully to what he says and
do all that I say, I will be an enemy
to your enemies and will oppose
those who oppose you. 23My angel will go ahead of you and bring
you into the land of the Amorites,
Hittites, Perizzites, Canaanites, Hivites and Jebusites, and I will wipe
them out. 24Do not bow down before their gods or worship them
or follow their practices. You must
demolish them and break their
sacred stones to pieces. 25Worship
the LORD your God, and his blessing will be on your food and water. I will take away sickness from
among you, 26and none will miscarry or be barren in your land. I
will give you a full life span.
Dt 12:30-31; Ps 78:8,40,56; Mt 4:10

27“I will send my terror ahead of
you and throw into confusion every nation you encounter. I will
make all your enemies turn their
backs and run. 28I will send the hornet ahead of you to drive the Hivites, Canaanites and Hittites out
of your way. 29But I will not drive
them out in a single year, because
the land would become desolate
and the wild animals too numerous for you. 30Little by little I will
drive them out before you, until
you have increased enough to take
possession of the land. Dt 7:23; Jos 24:12

31“I will establish your borders
from the Red Sea[a] to the Mediterranean Sea,[b] and from the desert to the Euphrates River. I will
give into your hands the people
who live in the land, and you will
drive them out before you. 32Do
not make a covenant with them or
with their gods. 33Do not let them
live in your land or they will cause
you to sin against me, because the
worship of their gods will certainly be a snare to you.” Dt 7:16; Jos 21:44

The Covenant Confirmed

24 Then the LORD said to Moses, “Come up to the LORD,
you and Aaron, Nadab and Abihu,
and seventy of the elders of Israel.
You are to worship at a distance,
2but Moses alone is to approach
the LORD; the others must not
come near. And the people may
not come up with him.” Nu 11:16

[a] 31 Or *the Sea of Reeds* [b] 31 Hebrew *to the Sea of the Philistines*

[3]When Moses went and told the people all the LORD's words and laws, they responded with one voice, "Everything the LORD has said we will do." [4]Moses then wrote down everything the LORD had said. Ex 19:8; Dt 31:9

He got up early the next morning and built an altar at the foot of the mountain and set up twelve stone pillars representing the twelve tribes of Israel. [5]Then he sent young Israelite men, and they offered burnt offerings and sacrificed young bulls as fellowship offerings to the LORD. [6]Moses took half of the blood and put it in bowls, and the other half he splashed against the altar. [7]Then he took the Book of the Covenant and read it to the people. They responded, "We will do everything the LORD has said; we will obey." Heb 9:19; Ex 19:8

[8]Moses then took the blood, sprinkled it on the people and said, "This is the blood of the covenant that the LORD has made with you in accordance with all these words." Heb 9:20; 1Pe 1:2

[9]Moses and Aaron, Nadab and Abihu, and the seventy elders of Israel went up [10]and saw the God of Israel. Under his feet was something like a pavement made of lapis lazuli, as bright blue as the sky. [11]But God did not raise his hand against these leaders of the Israelites; they saw God, and they ate and drank. Ge 32:30; Eze 1:26; Rev 4:3

[12]The LORD said to Moses, "Come up to me on the mountain and stay here, and I will give you the tablets of stone with the law and commandments I have written for their instruction." Ex 32:15-16

[13]Then Moses set out with Joshua his aide, and Moses went up on the mountain of God. [14]He said to the elders, "Wait here for us until we come back to you. Aaron and Hur are with you, and anyone involved in a dispute can go to them." Ex 3:1; 17:9

[15]When Moses went up on the mountain, the cloud covered it, [16]and the glory of the LORD settled on Mount Sinai. For six days the cloud covered the mountain, and on the seventh day the LORD called to Moses from within the cloud. [17]To the Israelites the glory of the LORD looked like a consuming fire on top of the mountain. [18]Then Moses entered the cloud as he went on up the mountain. And he stayed on the mountain forty days and forty nights. Heb 12:18,29; Ex 19:9

Offerings for the Tabernacle

25 The LORD said to Moses, [2]"Tell the Israelites to bring me an offering. You are to receive the offering for me from everyone whose heart prompts them to give. [3]These are the offerings you are to receive from them: gold, silver and bronze; [4]blue, purple and scarlet yarn and fine linen; goat

hair; 5ram skins dyed red and
another type of durable leather[a]; acacia wood; 6olive oil for the
light; spices for the anointing oil
and for the fragrant incense; 7and
onyx stones and other gems to
be mounted on the ephod and
breastpiece. Ex 35:4-9; 2Co 8:11-12

8"Then have them make a sanctuary for me, and I will dwell
among them. 9Make this tabernacle and all its furnishings exactly
like the pattern I will show you.
Ex 29:45; Rev 21:3

The Ark

10"Have them make an ark[b] of
acacia wood — two and a half cubits long, a cubit and a half wide,
and a cubit and a half high.[c]
11Overlay it with pure gold, both
inside and out, and make a gold
molding around it. 12Cast four gold
rings for it and fasten them to its
four feet, with two rings on one
side and two rings on the other.
13Then make poles of acacia wood
and overlay them with gold. 14In-
sert the poles into the rings on the
sides of the ark to carry it. 15The
poles are to remain in the rings
of this ark; they are not to be removed. 16Then put in the ark the
tablets of the covenant law, which
I will give you. Dt 31:26; Heb 9:4

17"Make an atonement cover of
pure gold — two and a half cubits
long and a cubit and a half wide.
18And make two cherubim out of
hammered gold at the ends of the
cover. 19Make one cherub on one
end and the second cherub on the
other; make the cherubim of one
piece with the cover, at the two
ends. 20The cherubim are to have
their wings spread upward, overshadowing the cover with them.
The cherubim are to face each
other, looking toward the cover.
21Place the cover on top of the ark
and put in the ark the tablets of
the covenant law that I will give
you. 22There, above the cover between the two cherubim that are
over the ark of the covenant law, I
will meet with you and give you all
my commands for the Israelites.
Ex 37:1-9

The Table

23"Make a table of acacia wood —
two cubits long, a cubit wide and
a cubit and a half high.[d] 24Overlay
it with pure gold and make a gold
molding around it. 25Also make
around it a rim a handbreadth[e]
wide and put a gold molding on
the rim. 26Make four gold rings
for the table and fasten them to
the four corners, where the four
legs are. 27The rings are to be close
to the rim to hold the poles used
in carrying the table. 28Make the

[a] *5* Possibly the hides of large aquatic mammals [b] *10* That is, a chest
[c] *10* That is, about 3 3/4 feet long and 2 1/4 feet wide and high or about 1.1 meters long and 68 centimeters wide and high; similarly in verse 17 [d] *23* That is, about 3 feet long, 1 1/2 feet wide and 2 1/4 feet high or about 90 centimeters long, 45 centimeters wide and 68 centimeters high [e] *25* That is, about 3 inches or about 7.5 centimeters

poles of acacia wood, overlay them
with gold and carry the table with
them. 29And make its plates and
dishes of pure gold, as well as its
pitchers and bowls for the pouring
out of offerings. 30Put the bread of
the Presence on this table to be
before me at all times.

Ex 37:10-16; Nu 4:7

The Lampstand

31“Make a lampstand of pure
gold. Hammer out its base and
shaft, and make its flowerlike
cups, buds and blossoms of one
piece with them. 32Six branches are to extend from the sides
of the lampstand — three on
one side and three on the other.
33Three cups shaped like almond
flowers with buds and blossoms
are to be on one branch, three on
the next branch, and the same
for all six branches extending
from the lampstand. 34And on the
lampstand there are to be four
cups shaped like almond flowers
with buds and blossoms. 35One
bud shall be under the first pair
of branches extending from the
lampstand, a second bud under
the second pair, and a third bud
under the third pair — six branches in all. 36The buds and branches
shall all be of one piece with the
lampstand, hammered out of pure
gold.

Zec 4:2; Rev 1:12

37“Then make its seven lamps
and set them up on it so that they
light the space in front of it. 38Its
wick trimmers and trays are to be
of pure gold. 39A talent[a] of pure
gold is to be used for the lampstand and all these accessories.
40See that you make them according to the pattern shown you on
the mountain.

Ex 37:17-24; Ac 7:44; Heb 8:5

The Tabernacle

26 “Make the tabernacle with
ten curtains of finely twisted linen and blue, purple and scarlet yarn, with cherubim woven
into them by a skilled worker. 2All
the curtains are to be the same
size — twenty-eight cubits long
and four cubits wide.[b] 3Join five of
the curtains together, and do the
same with the other five. 4Make
loops of blue material along the
edge of the end curtain in one
set, and do the same with the end
curtain in the other set. 5Make fifty loops on one curtain and fifty
loops on the end curtain of the
other set, with the loops opposite
each other. 6Then make fifty gold
clasps and use them to fasten the
curtains together so that the tabernacle is a unit. Ex 36:8-13

7“Make curtains of goat hair for
the tent over the tabernacle —
eleven altogether. 8All eleven
curtains are to be the same size —
thirty cubits long and four cubits
wide.[c] 9Join five of the curtains

[a] *39* That is, about 75 pounds or about 34 kilograms [b] *2* That is, about 42 feet long and 6 feet wide or about 13 meters long and 1.8 meters wide [c] *8* That is, about 45 feet long and 6 feet wide or about 13.5 meters long and 1.8 meters wide

together into one set and the other six into another set. Fold the
sixth curtain double at the front
of the tent. 10 Make fifty loops
along the edge of the end curtain
in one set and also along the edge
of the end curtain in the other set.
11 Then make fifty bronze clasps
and put them in the loops to fasten the tent together as a unit.
12 As for the additional length of
the tent curtains, the half curtain
that is left over is to hang down
at the rear of the tabernacle. 13 The
tent curtains will be a cubit[a] longer on both sides; what is left will
hang over the sides of the tabernacle so as to cover it. 14 Make for
the tent a covering of ram skins
dyed red, and over that a covering
of the other durable leather.[b]
Ex 36:14-19

15 "Make upright frames of acacia wood for the tabernacle.
16 Each frame is to be ten cubits
long and a cubit and a half wide,[c]
17 with two projections set parallel to each other. Make all the
frames of the tabernacle in this
way. 18 Make twenty frames for the
south side of the tabernacle 19 and
make forty silver bases to go under them — two bases for each
frame, one under each projection.
20 For the other side, the north side
of the tabernacle, make twenty
frames 21 and forty silver bases —
two under each frame. 22 Make six
frames for the far end, that is, the
west end of the tabernacle, 23 and
make two frames for the corners
at the far end. 24 At these two corners they must be double from
the bottom all the way to the top
and fitted into a single ring; both
shall be like that. 25 So there will
be eight frames and sixteen silver
bases — two under each frame.
Ex 36:20-30

26 "Also make crossbars of acacia
wood: five for the frames on one
side of the tabernacle, 27 five for
those on the other side, and five
for the frames on the west, at the
far end of the tabernacle. 28 The
center crossbar is to extend from
end to end at the middle of the
frames. 29 Overlay the frames with
gold and make gold rings to hold
the crossbars. Also overlay the
crossbars with gold. Ex 36:31-34

30 "Set up the tabernacle according to the plan shown you on the
mountain. Ex 25:9,40; Ac 7:44; Heb 8:5

31 "Make a curtain of blue, purple
and scarlet yarn and finely twisted linen, with cherubim woven
into it by a skilled worker. 32 Hang
it with gold hooks on four posts
of acacia wood overlaid with gold
and standing on four silver bases.
33 Hang the curtain from the clasps
and place the ark of the covenant
law behind the curtain. The curtain will separate the Holy Place
from the Most Holy Place. 34 Put
the atonement cover on the ark of

[a] *13* That is, about 18 inches or about 45 centimeters [b] *14* Possibly the hides of large aquatic mammals (see 25:5) [c] *16* That is, about 15 feet long and 2 1/4 feet wide or about 4.5 meters long and 68 centimeters wide

the covenant law in the Most Holy Place. 35Place the table outside the curtain on the north side of the tabernacle and put the lampstand opposite it on the south side. Ex 36:35-36; Heb 9:2-3

36"For the entrance to the tent make a curtain of blue, purple and scarlet yarn and finely twisted linen — the work of an embroiderer. 37Make gold hooks for this curtain and five posts of acacia wood overlaid with gold. And cast five bronze bases for them. Ex 36:37-38

The Altar of Burnt Offering

27 "Build an altar of acacia wood, three cubits[a] high; it is to be square, five cubits long and five cubits wide.[b] 2Make a horn at each of the four corners, so that the horns and the altar are of one piece, and overlay the altar with bronze. 3Make all its utensils of bronze — its pots to remove the ashes, and its shovels, sprinkling bowls, meat forks and firepans. 4Make a grating for it, a bronze network, and make a bronze ring at each of the four corners of the network. 5Put it under the ledge of the altar so that it is halfway up the altar. 6Make poles of acacia wood for the altar and overlay them with bronze. 7The poles are to be inserted into the rings so they will be on two sides of the altar when it is carried. 8Make the altar hollow, out of boards. It is to be made just as you were shown on the mountain. Ex 38:1-7

The Courtyard

9"Make a courtyard for the tabernacle. The south side shall be a hundred cubits[c] long and is to have curtains of finely twisted linen, 10with twenty posts and twenty bronze bases and with silver hooks and bands on the posts. 11The north side shall also be a hundred cubits long and is to have curtains, with twenty posts and twenty bronze bases and with silver hooks and bands on the posts.

12"The west end of the courtyard shall be fifty cubits[d] wide and have curtains, with ten posts and ten bases. 13On the east end, toward the sunrise, the courtyard shall also be fifty cubits wide. 14Curtains fifteen cubits[e] long are to be on one side of the entrance, with three posts and three bases, 15and curtains fifteen cubits long are to be on the other side, with three posts and three bases.

16"For the entrance to the courtyard, provide a curtain twenty cubits[f] long, of blue, purple and scarlet yarn and finely twisted linen — the work of an embroiderer — with four posts and four bases. 17All the posts around the courtyard are to have silver bands

[a] *1* That is, about 4 1/2 feet or about 1.4 meters [b] *1* That is, about 7 1/2 feet or about 2.3 meters long and wide [c] *9* That is, about 150 feet or about 45 meters; also in verse 11 [d] *12* That is, about 75 feet or about 23 meters; also in verse 13 [e] *14* That is, about 23 feet or about 6.8 meters; also in verse 15 [f] *16* That is, about 30 feet or about 9 meters

and hooks, and bronze bases.
18The courtyard shall be a hundred
cubits long and fifty cubits wide,[a]
with curtains of finely twisted
linen five cubits[b] high, and with
bronze bases. 19All the other articles used in the service of the tabernacle, whatever their function,
including all the tent pegs for it
and those for the courtyard, are to
be of bronze. Ex 38:9-20

Oil for the Lampstand

20"Command the Israelites to
bring you clear oil of pressed olives for the light so that the lamps
may be kept burning. 21In the tent
of meeting, outside the curtain
that shields the ark of the covenant law, Aaron and his sons are
to keep the lamps burning before
the LORD from evening till morning. This is to be a lasting ordinance among the Israelites for the
generations to come. Lev 24:1-3

The Priestly Garments

28 "Have Aaron your brother brought to you from
among the Israelites, along with
his sons Nadab and Abihu, Eleazar
and Ithamar, so they may serve
me as priests. 2Make sacred garments for your brother Aaron to
give him dignity and honor. 3Tell
all the skilled workers to whom I
have given wisdom in such matters that they are to make garments for Aaron, for his consecration, so he may serve me as priest.
4These are the garments they are
to make: a breastpiece, an ephod,
a robe, a woven tunic, a turban
and a sash. They are to make these
sacred garments for your brother
Aaron and his sons, so they may
serve me as priests. 5Have them
use gold, and blue, purple and
scarlet yarn, and fine linen. Ex 31:3,6

The Ephod

6"Make the ephod of gold, and of
blue, purple and scarlet yarn, and
of finely twisted linen — the work
of skilled hands. 7It is to have two
shoulder pieces attached to two of
its corners, so it can be fastened.
8Its skillfully woven waistband is
to be like it — of one piece with the
ephod and made with gold, and
with blue, purple and scarlet yarn,
and with finely twisted linen.

9"Take two onyx stones and engrave on them the names of the
sons of Israel 10in the order of their
birth — six names on one stone
and the remaining six on the other. 11Engrave the names of the sons
of Israel on the two stones the way
a gem cutter engraves a seal. Then
mount the stones in gold filigree
settings 12and fasten them on the
shoulder pieces of the ephod as
memorial stones for the sons of
Israel. Aaron is to bear the names
on his shoulders as a memorial before the LORD. 13Make gold filigree
settings 14and two braided chains

[a] *18* That is, about 150 feet long and 75 feet wide or about 45 meters long and 23 meters wide [b] *18* That is, about 7 1/2 feet or about 2.3 meters

of pure gold, like a rope, and attach the chains to the settings.
Ex 39:2-7

The Breastpiece

15“Fashion a breastpiece for
making decisions — the work of
skilled hands. Make it like the
ephod: of gold, and of blue, purple and scarlet yarn, and of finely
twisted linen. 16It is to be square —
a span[a] long and a span wide —
and folded double. 17Then mount
four rows of precious stones on it.
The first row shall be carnelian,
chrysolite and beryl; 18the second
row shall be turquoise, lapis lazuli
and emerald; 19the third row shall
be jacinth, agate and amethyst;
20the fourth row shall be topaz,
onyx and jasper.[b] Mount them in
gold filigree settings. 21There are
to be twelve stones, one for each
of the names of the sons of Israel,
each engraved like a seal with the
name of one of the twelve tribes.
Rev 21:12

22“For the breastpiece make
braided chains of pure gold, like a
rope. 23Make two gold rings for it
and fasten them to two corners of
the breastpiece. 24Fasten the two
gold chains to the rings at the corners of the breastpiece, 25and the
other ends of the chains to the
two settings, attaching them to
the shoulder pieces of the ephod
at the front. 26Make two gold rings
and attach them to the other two
corners of the breastpiece on the
inside edge next to the ephod.
27Make two more gold rings and
attach them to the bottom of the
shoulder pieces on the front of
the ephod, close to the seam just
above the waistband of the ephod.
28The rings of the breastpiece are
to be tied to the rings of the ephod
with blue cord, connecting it to
the waistband, so that the breastpiece will not swing out from the
ephod.
Ex 39:8-21

29“Whenever Aaron enters the
Holy Place, he will bear the names
of the sons of Israel over his heart
on the breastpiece of decision as
a continuing memorial before the
LORD. 30Also put the Urim and the
Thummim in the breastpiece, so
they may be over Aaron's heart
whenever he enters the presence
of the LORD. Thus Aaron will always bear the means of making
decisions for the Israelites over
his heart before the LORD.
Lev 8:8; Nu 27:21

Other Priestly Garments

31“Make the robe of the ephod
entirely of blue cloth, 32with an
opening for the head in its center.
There shall be a woven edge like
a collar[c] around this opening, so
that it will not tear. 33Make pomegranates of blue, purple and scarlet
yarn around the hem of the robe,
with gold bells between them.

[a] *16* That is, about 9 inches or about 23 centimeters [b] *20* The precise identification of some of these precious stones is uncertain. [c] *32* The meaning of the Hebrew for this word is uncertain.

34The gold bells and the pomegranates are to alternate around
the hem of the robe. 35Aaron must
wear it when he ministers. The
sound of the bells will be heard
when he enters the Holy Place before the LORD and when he comes
out, so that he will not die.

36"Make a plate of pure gold and
engrave on it as on a seal: HOLY TO
THE LORD. 37Fasten a blue cord to it
to attach it to the turban; it is to be
on the front of the turban. 38It will
be on Aaron's forehead, and he will
bear the guilt involved in the sacred gifts the Israelites consecrate,
whatever their gifts may be. It will
be on Aaron's forehead continually
so that they will be acceptable to
the LORD. Nu 18:1; Zec 14:20

39"Weave the tunic of fine linen
and make the turban of fine lin-
en. The sash is to be the work of
an embroiderer. 40Make tunics,
sashes and caps for Aaron's sons
to give them dignity and honor.
41After you put these clothes on
your brother Aaron and his sons,
anoint and ordain them. Consecrate them so they may serve me
as priests. Ex 29:7-9; Lev 18:1-36

42"Make linen undergarments
as a covering for the body, reaching from the waist to the thigh.
43Aaron and his sons must wear
them whenever they enter the
tent of meeting or approach the
altar to minister in the Holy Place,
so that they will not incur guilt
and die. Ex 20:26

"This is to be a lasting ordinance
for Aaron and his descendants.
Ex 39:22-31

Consecration of the Priests

29 "This is what you are to do
to consecrate them, so they
may serve me as priests: Take a
young bull and two rams without
defect. 2And from the finest wheat
flour make round loaves without
yeast, thick loaves without yeast
and with olive oil mixed in, and
thin loaves without yeast and
brushed with olive oil. 3Put them
in a basket and present them
along with the bull and the two
rams. 4Then bring Aaron and his
sons to the entrance to the tent of
meeting and wash them with water. 5Take the garments and dress
Aaron with the tunic, the robe of
the ephod, the ephod itself and the
breastpiece. Fasten the ephod on
him by its skillfully woven waistband. 6Put the turban on his head
and attach the sacred emblem to
the turban. 7Take the anointing oil
and anoint him by pouring it on
his head. 8Bring his sons and dress
them in tunics 9and fasten caps
on them. Then tie sashes on Aaron and his sons.[a] The priesthood
is theirs by a lasting ordinance.

"Then you shall ordain Aaron
and his sons.
Nu 18:7; Ex 30:25,30-31; Lev 21:10

10"Bring the bull to the front of
the tent of meeting, and Aaron

[a] 9 Hebrew; Septuagint *on them*

and his sons shall lay their hands
on its head. 11Slaughter it in the
LORD's presence at the entrance to
the tent of meeting. 12Take some
of the bull's blood and put it on
the horns of the altar with your
finger, and pour out the rest of it
at the base of the altar. 13Then take
all the fat on the internal organs,
the long lobe of the liver, and both
kidneys with the fat on them, and
burn them on the altar. 14But burn
the bull's flesh and its hide and its
intestines outside the camp. It is a
sin offering.[a] Lev 1:4; Heb 13:11

15"Take one of the rams, and
Aaron and his sons shall lay their
hands on its head. 16Slaughter it
and take the blood and splash it
against the sides of the altar. 17Cut
the ram into pieces and wash the
internal organs and the legs, putting them with the head and the
other pieces. 18Then burn the entire ram on the altar. It is a burnt
offering to the LORD, a pleasing
aroma, a food offering presented
to the LORD. Ge 8:21

19"Take the other ram, and Aaron and his sons shall lay their
hands on its head. 20Slaughter it,
take some of its blood and put
it on the lobes of the right ears
of Aaron and his sons, on the
thumbs of their right hands, and
on the big toes of their right feet.
Then splash blood against the
sides of the altar. 21And take some
blood from the altar and some of
the anointing oil and sprinkle it
on Aaron and his garments and
on his sons and their garments.
Then he and his sons and their
garments will be consecrated.
Heb 9:22

22"Take from this ram the fat,
the fat tail, the fat on the internal
organs, the long lobe of the liver,
both kidneys with the fat on them,
and the right thigh. (This is the
ram for the ordination.) 23From
the basket of bread made without
yeast, which is before the LORD,
take one round loaf, one thick
loaf with olive oil mixed in, and
one thin loaf. 24Put all these in the
hands of Aaron and his sons and
have them wave them before the
LORD as a wave offering. 25Then
take them from their hands and
burn them on the altar along with
the burnt offering for a pleasing
aroma to the LORD, a food offering presented to the LORD. 26After
you take the breast of the ram for
Aaron's ordination, wave it before
the LORD as a wave offering, and it
will be your share. Lev 7:30

27"Consecrate those parts of
the ordination ram that belong
to Aaron and his sons: the breast
that was waved and the thigh that
was presented. 28This is always to
be the perpetual share from the
Israelites for Aaron and his sons.
It is the contribution the Israelites
are to make to the LORD from their
fellowship offerings. Lev 7:31,34

29"Aaron's sacred garments will
belong to his descendants so that

[a] 14 Or *purification offering*; also in verse 36

they can be anointed and ordained
in them. [30]The son who succeeds
him as priest and comes to the
tent of meeting to minister in the
Holy Place is to wear them seven
days. Nu 20:26,28

[31]"Take the ram for the ordination and cook the meat in a sacred
place. [32]At the entrance to the tent
of meeting, Aaron and his sons are
to eat the meat of the ram and the
bread that is in the basket. [33]They
are to eat these offerings by which
atonement was made for their ordination and consecration. But no
one else may eat them, because
they are sacred. [34]And if any of
the meat of the ordination ram or
any bread is left over till morning,
burn it up. It must not be eaten,
because it is sacred. Lev 22:10,13

[35]"Do for Aaron and his sons everything I have commanded you,
taking seven days to ordain them.
[36]Sacrifice a bull each day as a sin
offering to make atonement. Purify the altar by making atonement
for it, and anoint it to consecrate
it. [37]For seven days make atonement for the altar and consecrate
it. Then the altar will be most holy,
and whatever touches it will be
holy. Lev 8:1-36

[38]"This is what you are to offer
on the altar regularly each day:
two lambs a year old. [39]Offer one
in the morning and the other at
twilight. [40]With the first lamb offer a tenth of an ephah[a] of the finest flour mixed with a quarter of
a hin[b] of oil from pressed olives,
and a quarter of a hin of wine as a
drink offering. [41]Sacrifice the other lamb at twilight with the same
grain offering and its drink offering as in the morning — a pleasing
aroma, a food offering presented
to the LORD. Nu 28:3-8

[42]"For the generations to come
this burnt offering is to be made
regularly at the entrance to the
tent of meeting, before the LORD.
There I will meet you and speak to
you; [43]there also I will meet with
the Israelites, and the place will be
consecrated by my glory.
Ex 25:22; 1Ki 8:11

[44]"So I will consecrate the tent
of meeting and the altar and will
consecrate Aaron and his sons to
serve me as priests. [45]Then I will
dwell among the Israelites and
be their God. [46]They will know
that I am the LORD their God, who
brought them out of Egypt so that
I might dwell among them. I am
the LORD their God.
Ex 25:8; 2Co 6:16; Rev 21:3

The Altar of Incense

30 "Make an altar of acacia
wood for burning incense.
[2]It is to be square, a cubit long
and a cubit wide, and two cubits
high[c] — its horns of one piece with
it. [3]Overlay the top and all the sides
and the horns with pure gold, and

[a] *40* That is, probably about 3 1/2 pounds or about 1.6 kilograms [b] *40* That is, probably about 1 quart or about 1 liter
[c] *2* That is, about 1 1/2 feet long and wide and 3 feet high or about 45 centimeters long and wide and 90 centimeters high

make a gold molding around it.
4Make two gold rings for the altar
below the molding — two on each
of the opposite sides — to hold the
poles used to carry it. 5Make the
poles of acacia wood and overlay
them with gold. 6Put the altar in
front of the curtain that shields
the ark of the covenant law — before the atonement cover that is
over the tablets of the covenant
law — where I will meet with you.
Ex 37:25-28

7"Aaron must burn fragrant incense on the altar every morning when he tends the lamps. 8He
must burn incense again when he
lights the lamps at twilight so incense will burn regularly before
the LORD for the generations to
come. 9Do not offer on this altar
any other incense or any burnt
offering or grain offering, and do
not pour a drink offering on it.
10Once a year Aaron shall make
atonement on its horns. This annual atonement must be made
with the blood of the atoning sin
offering[a] for the generations to
come. It is most holy to the LORD."
Lev 16:18-19,30

Atonement Money

11Then the LORD said to Moses,
12"When you take a census of the
Israelites to count them, each one
must pay the LORD a ransom for
his life at the time he is counted. Then no plague will come on
them when you number them.
13Each one who crosses over to
those already counted is to give
a half shekel,[b] according to the
sanctuary shekel, which weighs
twenty gerahs. This half shekel is
an offering to the LORD. 14All who
cross over, those twenty years old
or more, are to give an offering to
the LORD. 15The rich are not to give
more than a half shekel and the
poor are not to give less when you
make the offering to the LORD to
atone for your lives. 16Receive the
atonement money from the Israelites and use it for the service
of the tent of meeting. It will be a
memorial for the Israelites before
the LORD, making atonement for
your lives."
Nu 1:2,49; 31:50

Basin for Washing

17Then the LORD said to Moses,
18"Make a bronze basin, with its
bronze stand, for washing. Place it
between the tent of meeting and
the altar, and put water in it. 19Aar-
on and his sons are to wash their
hands and feet with water from it.
20Whenever they enter the tent of
meeting, they shall wash with water so that they will not die. Also,
when they approach the altar to
minister by presenting a food offering to the LORD, 21they shall
wash their hands and feet so that
they will not die. This is to be a
lasting ordinance for Aaron and
his descendants for the generations to come."
Ex 27:21; 40:31-32

[a] 10 Or *purification offering* [b] 13 That is, about 1/5 ounce or about 5.8 grams; also in verse 15

Anointing Oil

22Then the LORD said to Moses,
23"Take the following fine spices: 500 shekels[a] of liquid myrrh,
half as much (that is, 250 shekels)
of fragrant cinnamon, 250 shekels[b] of fragrant calamus, 24500
shekels of cassia — all according
to the sanctuary shekel — and a
hin[c] of olive oil. 25Make these into
a sacred anointing oil, a fragrant
blend, the work of a perfumer. It
will be the sacred anointing oil.
26Then use it to anoint the tent of
meeting, the ark of the covenant
law, 27the table and all its articles,
the lampstand and its accessories,
the altar of incense, 28the altar of
burnt offering and all its utensils,
and the basin with its stand. 29You
shall consecrate them so they will
be most holy, and whatever touches them will be holy. Ex 37:29; Lev 8:10

30"Anoint Aaron and his sons
and consecrate them so they may
serve me as priests. 31Say to the Israelites, 'This is to be my sacred
anointing oil for the generations
to come. 32Do not pour it on anyone
else's body and do not make any
other oil using the same formula.
It is sacred, and you are to consider it sacred. 33Whoever makes perfume like it and puts it on anyone
other than a priest must be cut off
from their people.'" Lev 8:2,12,30

Incense

34Then the LORD said to Moses,
"Take fragrant spices — gum resin,
onycha and galbanum — and pure
frankincense, all in equal amounts,
35and make a fragrant blend of incense, the work of a perfumer. It is
to be salted and pure and sacred.
36Grind some of it to powder and
place it in front of the ark of the
covenant law in the tent of meeting, where I will meet with you. It
shall be most holy to you. 37Do not
make any incense with this formula for yourselves; consider it holy
to the LORD. 38Whoever makes incense like it to enjoy its fragrance
must be cut off from their people."
Ex 29:37; Lev 2:3

Bezalel and Oholiab

31 Then the LORD said to Moses,
2"See, I have chosen Bezalel
son of Uri, the son of Hur, of the
tribe of Judah, 3and I have filled
him with the Spirit of God, with
wisdom, with understanding,
with knowledge and with all kinds
of skills — 4to make artistic designs for work in gold, silver and
bronze, 5to cut and set stones, to
work in wood, and to engage in all
kinds of crafts. 6Moreover, I have
appointed Oholiab son of Ahisamak, of the tribe of Dan, to help
him. Also I have given ability to
all the skilled workers to make everything I have commanded you:
7the tent of meeting, the ark of

[a] *23* That is, about 12 1/2 pounds or about 5.8 kilograms; also in verse 24
[b] *23* That is, about 6 1/4 pounds or about 2.9 kilograms [c] *24* That is, probably about 1 gallon or about 3.8 liters

the covenant law with the atonement cover on it, and all the other
furnishings of the tent — 8the table and its articles, the pure gold
lampstand and all its accessories,
the altar of incense, 9the altar of
burnt offering and all its utensils,
the basin with its stand — 10and
also the woven garments, both
the sacred garments for Aaron the
priest and the garments for his
sons when they serve as priests,
11and the anointing oil and fragrant incense for the Holy Place.
They are to make them just as I
commanded you." Ex 35:30-35

The Sabbath

12Then the LORD said to Moses,
13"Say to the Israelites, 'You must
observe my Sabbaths. This will be
a sign between me and you for the
generations to come, so you may
know that I am the LORD, who
makes you holy. Eze 20:12,20
14" 'Observe the Sabbath, because it is holy to you. Anyone
who desecrates it is to be put to
death; those who do any work on
that day must be cut off from their
people. 15For six days work is to be
done, but the seventh day is a day
of sabbath rest, holy to the LORD.
Whoever does any work on the
Sabbath day is to be put to death.
16The Israelites are to observe the
Sabbath, celebrating it for the generations to come as a lasting covenant. 17It will be a sign between
me and the Israelites forever, for
in six days the LORD made the
heavens and the earth, and on the
seventh day he rested and was refreshed.' " Ex 20:8-11
18When the LORD finished speaking to Moses on Mount Sinai, he
gave him the two tablets of the
covenant law, the tablets of stone
inscribed by the finger of God.
Ex 32:15-16

The Golden Calf

32 When the people saw that
Moses was so long in com-
ing down from the mountain,
they gathered around Aaron and
said, "Come, make us gods[a] who
will go before us. As for this fellow Moses who brought us up out
of Egypt, we don't know what has
happened to him." Ac 7:40
2Aaron answered them, "Take
off the gold earrings that your
wives, your sons and your daughters are wearing, and bring them
to me." 3So all the people took off
their earrings and brought them
to Aaron. 4He took what they handed him and made it into an idol
cast in the shape of a calf, fashion-
ing it with a tool. Then they said,
"These are your gods,[b] Israel, who
brought you up out of Egypt."
Dt 9:16
5When Aaron saw this, he built
an altar in front of the calf and
announced, "Tomorrow there
will be a festival to the LORD." 6So
the next day the people rose early
and sacrificed burnt offerings and

[a] 1 Or *a god*; also in verses 23 and 31
[b] 4 Or *This is your god*; also in verse 8

presented fellowship offerings.
Afterward they sat down to eat
and drink and got up to indulge
in revelry. 1Co 10:7
7Then the LORD said to Moses,
"Go down, because your people, whom you brought up out
of Egypt, have become corrupt.
8They have been quick to turn
away from what I commanded
them and have made themselves
an idol cast in the shape of a calf.
They have bowed down to it and
sacrificed to it and have said,
'These are your gods, Israel, who
brought you up out of Egypt.'
Dt 9:12
9"I have seen these people," the
LORD said to Moses, "and they are
a stiff-necked people. 10Now leave
me alone so that my anger may
burn against them and that I may
destroy them. Then I will make
you into a great nation."
Ex 33:3,5; Isa 48:4; Ac 7:51
11But Moses sought the favor of
the LORD his God. "LORD," he said,
"why should your anger burn
against your people, whom you
brought out of Egypt with great
power and a mighty hand? 12Why
should the Egyptians say, 'It was
with evil intent that he brought
them out, to kill them in the
mountains and to wipe them off
the face of the earth'? Turn from
your fierce anger; relent and do
not bring disaster on your people.
13Remember your servants Abraham, Isaac and Israel, to whom
you swore by your own self: 'I will
make your descendants as numerous as the stars in the sky and
I will give your descendants all
this land I promised them, and it
will be their inheritance forever.'"
14Then the LORD relented and did
not bring on his people the disaster he had threatened.
Nu 14:13-16; Dt 9:18
15Moses turned and went down
the mountain with the two tablets
of the covenant law in his hands.
They were inscribed on both sides,
front and back. 16The tablets were
the work of God; the writing was
the writing of God, engraved on
the tablets. Ex 31:18; Dt 9:15
17When Joshua heard the noise
of the people shouting, he said to
Moses, "There is the sound of war
in the camp."
18Moses replied:

"It is not the sound of victory,
it is not the sound of defeat;
it is the sound of singing that
I hear."

19When Moses approached the
camp and saw the calf and the
dancing, his anger burned and he
threw the tablets out of his hands,
breaking them to pieces at the
foot of the mountain. 20And he
took the calf the people had made
and burned it in the fire; then he
ground it to powder, scattered it
on the water and made the Israelites drink it. Dt 9:16,21
21He said to Aaron, "What did
these people do to you, that you
led them into such great sin?"

22“Do not be angry, my lord,” Aaron answered. “You know how prone these people are to evil. 23They said to me, ‘Make us gods who will go before us. As for this fellow Moses who brought us up out of Egypt, we don’t know what has happened to him.’ 24So I told them, ‘Whoever has any gold jewelry, take it off.’ Then they gave me the gold, and I threw it into the fire, and out came this calf!” Dt 9:24

25Moses saw that the people were running wild and that Aaron had let them get out of control and so become a laughingstock to their enemies. 26So he stood at the entrance to the camp and said, “Whoever is for the LORD, come to me.” And all the Levites rallied to him.

27Then he said to them, “This is what the LORD, the God of Israel, says: ‘Each man strap a sword to his side. Go back and forth through the camp from one end to the other, each killing his brother and friend and neighbor.’ ” 28The Levites did as Moses commanded, and that day about three thousand of the people died. 29Then Moses said, “You have been set apart to the LORD today, for you were against your own sons and brothers, and he has blessed you this day.” Nu 25:3,5; Dt 33:9

30The next day Moses said to the people, “You have committed a great sin. But now I will go up to the LORD; perhaps I can make atonement for your sin.”

Lev 1:4; Nu 25:13

31So Moses went back to the LORD and said, “Oh, what a great sin these people have committed! They have made themselves gods of gold. 32But now, please forgive their sin—but if not, then blot me out of the book you have written.”

Ro 9:3; Ps 69:28; Da 12:1

33The LORD replied to Moses, “Whoever has sinned against me I will blot out of my book. 34Now go, lead the people to the place I spoke of, and my angel will go before you. However, when the time comes for me to punish, I will punish them for their sin.”

Dt 29:20; 32:35; Ps 99:8

35And the LORD struck the people with a plague because of what they did with the calf Aaron had made.

33

Then the LORD said to Moses, “Leave this place, you and the people you brought up out of Egypt, and go up to the land I promised on oath to Abraham, Isaac and Jacob, saying, ‘I will give it to your descendants.’ 2I will send an angel before you and drive out the Canaanites, Amorites, Hittites, Perizzites, Hivites and Jebusites. 3Go up to the land flowing with milk and honey. But I will not go with you, because you are a stiff-necked people and I might destroy you on the way.”

Ex 3:8; 32:10

4When the people heard these distressing words, they began to mourn and no one put on any ornaments. 5For the LORD had said

to Moses, "Tell the Israelites, 'You
are a stiff-necked people. If I were
to go with you even for a moment,
I might destroy you. Now take off
your ornaments and I will decide
what to do with you.'" 6So the Israelites stripped off their ornaments
at Mount Horeb. Nu 14:39

The Tent of Meeting

7Now Moses used to take a tent
and pitch it outside the camp
some distance away, calling it the
"tent of meeting." Anyone inquiring of the LORD would go to the
tent of meeting outside the camp.
8And whenever Moses went out to
the tent, all the people rose and
stood at the entrances to their
tents, watching Moses until he
entered the tent. 9As Moses went
into the tent, the pillar of cloud
would come down and stay at the
entrance, while the LORD spoke
with Moses. 10Whenever the people saw the pillar of cloud standing at the entrance to the tent,
they all stood and worshiped, each
at the entrance to their tent. 11The
LORD would speak to Moses face
to face, as one speaks to a friend.
Then Moses would return to the
camp, but his young aide Joshua
son of Nun did not leave the tent.
Nu 12:8; Dt 34:10; Ps 99:7

Moses and the Glory of the LORD

12Moses said to the LORD, "You
have been telling me, 'Lead these
people,' but you have not let me
know whom you will send with
me. You have said, 'I know you by
name and you have found favor
with me.' 13If you are pleased with
me, teach me your ways so I may
know you and continue to find favor with you. Remember that this
nation is your people."
Dt 9:26,29; Ps 25:4

14The LORD replied, "My Presence will go with you, and I will
give you rest." Jos 21:44; Isa 63:9

15Then Moses said to him, "If
your Presence does not go with
us, do not send us up from here.
16How will anyone know that you
are pleased with me and with
your people unless you go with
us? What else will distinguish me
and your people from all the other
people on the face of the earth?"
Ex 34:10; Nu 14:14

17And the LORD said to Moses,
"I will do the very thing you have
asked, because I am pleased with
you and I know you by name."
Jas 5:16

18Then Moses said, "Now show
me your glory." Ex 16:7; Jn 1:14

19And the LORD said, "I will cause
all my goodness to pass in front of
you, and I will proclaim my name,
the LORD, in your presence. I will
have mercy on whom I will have
mercy, and I will have compassion
on whom I will have compassion.
20But," he said, "you cannot see
my face, for no one may see me
and live." Ro 9:15

21Then the LORD said, "There is
a place near me where you may
stand on a rock. 22When my glory

passes by, I will put you in a cleft in the rock and cover you with my hand until I have passed by. 23 Then I will remove my hand and you will see my back; but my face must not be seen." Ps 91:4

The New Stone Tablets

34 The LORD said to Moses, "Chisel out two stone tablets like the first ones, and I will write on them the words that were on the first tablets, which you broke. 2 Be ready in the morning, and then come up on Mount Sinai. Present yourself to me there on top of the mountain. 3 No one is to come with you or be seen anywhere on the mountain; not even the flocks and herds may graze in front of the mountain." Ex 19:11; 32:19

4 So Moses chiseled out two stone tablets like the first ones and went up Mount Sinai early in the morning, as the LORD had commanded him; and he carried the two stone tablets in his hands. 5 Then the LORD came down in the cloud and stood there with him and proclaimed his name, the LORD. 6 And he passed in front of Moses, proclaiming, "The LORD, the LORD, the compassionate and gracious God, slow to anger, abounding in love and faithfulness, 7 maintaining love to thousands, and forgiving wickedness, rebellion and sin. Yet he does not leave the guilty unpunished; he punishes the children and their children for the sin of the parents to the third and fourth generation." Ex 20:6; Ps 103:3

8 Moses bowed to the ground at once and worshiped. 9 "Lord," he said, "if I have found favor in your eyes, then let the Lord go with us. Although this is a stiff-necked people, forgive our wickedness and our sin, and take us as your inheritance." Ps 33:12

10 Then the LORD said: "I am making a covenant with you. Before all your people I will do wonders never before done in any nation in all the world. The people you live among will see how awesome is the work that I, the LORD, will do for you. 11 Obey what I command you today. I will drive out before you the Amorites, Canaanites, Hittites, Perizzites, Hivites and Jebusites. 12 Be careful not to make a treaty with those who live in the land where you are going, or they will be a snare among you. 13 Break down their altars, smash their sacred stones and cut down their Asherah poles.[a] 14 Do not worship any other god, for the LORD, whose name is Jealous, is a jealous God. Ex 33:2; Dt 5:2-3

15 "Be careful not to make a treaty with those who live in the land; for when they prostitute themselves to their gods and sacrifice to them, they will invite you and you will eat their sacrifices. 16 And when you choose some of their daughters as wives for your sons

[a] *13* That is, wooden symbols of the goddess Asherah

and those daughters prostitute
themselves to their gods, they will
lead your sons to do the same.
Nu 25:2; Dt 7:3
17“Do not make any idols. Ex 32:8
18“Celebrate the Festival of Unleavened Bread. For seven days
eat bread made without yeast, as
I commanded you. Do this at the
appointed time in the month of
Aviv, for in that month you came
out of Egypt. Ex 12:2,15,17
19“The first offspring of every
womb belongs to me, including all
the firstborn males of your livestock, whether from herd or flock.
20Redeem the firstborn donkey
with a lamb, but if you do not redeem it, break its neck. Redeem
all your firstborn sons. Ex 13:2
“No one is to appear before me
empty-handed. Dt 16:16
21“Six days you shall labor, but
on the seventh day you shall rest;
even during the plowing season
and harvest you must rest. Ex 20:9
22“Celebrate the Festival of
Weeks with the firstfruits of the
wheat harvest, and the Festival
of Ingathering at the turn of the
year.[a] 23Three times a year all your
men are to appear before the Sovereign LORD, the God of Israel. 24I
will drive out nations before you
and enlarge your territory, and no
one will covet your land when you
go up three times each year to appear before the LORD your God.
Ex 23:14,16
25“Do not offer the blood of a
sacrifice to me along with anything containing yeast, and do
not let any of the sacrifice from
the Passover Festival remain until
morning. Ex 23:18
26“Bring the best of the firstfruits of your soil to the house of
the LORD your God. Ex 22:29
“Do not cook a young goat in its
mother’s milk.” Ex 23:19
27Then the LORD said to Moses, “Write down these words, for
in accordance with these words I
have made a covenant with you
and with Israel.” 28Moses was there
with the LORD forty days and forty nights without eating bread or
drinking water. And he wrote on
the tablets the words of the covenant — the Ten Commandments.
Dt 4:13; 10:4

The Radiant Face of Moses

29When Moses came down from
Mount Sinai with the two tablets
of the covenant law in his hands,
he was not aware that his face was
radiant because he had spoken
with the LORD. 30When Aaron and
all the Israelites saw Moses, his
face was radiant, and they were
afraid to come near him. 31But Moses called to them; so Aaron and
all the leaders of the community
came back to him, and he spoke
to them. 32Afterward all the Israelites came near him, and he gave
them all the commands the LORD
had given him on Mount Sinai.
Mt 17:2; 2Co 3:7,13

[a] 22 That is, in the autumn

33 When Moses finished speaking to them, he put a veil over his
face. 34 But whenever he entered
the LORD's presence to speak with
him, he removed the veil until he
came out. And when he came out
and told the Israelites what he had
been commanded, 35 they saw that
his face was radiant. Then Moses
would put the veil back over his
face until he went in to speak with
the LORD. 2Co 3:13

Sabbath Regulations

35 Moses assembled the whole
Israelite community and
said to them, "These are the
things the LORD has commanded you to do: 2 For six days, work
is to be done, but the seventh day
shall be your holy day, a day of
sabbath rest to the LORD. Whoever
does any work on it is to be put to
death. 3 Do not light a fire in any
of your dwellings on the Sabbath
day." Ex 16:23

Materials for the Tabernacle

4 Moses said to the whole Israelite community, "This is what
the LORD has commanded: 5 From
what you have, take an offering for
the LORD. Everyone who is willing
is to bring to the LORD an offering
of gold, silver and bronze; 6 blue,
purple and scarlet yarn and fine
linen; goat hair; 7 ram skins dyed
red and another type of durable
leather[a]; acacia wood; 8 olive oil for
the light; spices for the anointing
oil and for the fragrant incense;
9 and onyx stones and other gems
to be mounted on the ephod and
breastpiece. Ex 25:1-7

10 "All who are skilled among
you are to come and make everything the LORD has commanded:
11 the tabernacle with its tent and
its covering, clasps, frames, crossbars, posts and bases; 12 the ark
with its poles and the atonement
cover and the curtain that shields
it; 13 the table with its poles and all
its articles and the bread of the
Presence; 14 the lampstand that
is for light with its accessories,
lamps and oil for the light; 15 the
altar of incense with its poles, the
anointing oil and the fragrant incense; the curtain for the doorway
at the entrance to the tabernacle;
16 the altar of burnt offering with
its bronze grating, its poles and
all its utensils; the bronze basin
with its stand; 17 the curtains of the
courtyard with its posts and bases,
and the curtain for the entrance to
the courtyard; 18 the tent pegs for
the tabernacle and for the courtyard, and their ropes; 19 the woven
garments worn for ministering in
the sanctuary — both the sacred
garments for Aaron the priest and
the garments for his sons when
they serve as priests." Ex 39:32-41

20 Then the whole Israelite
community withdrew from Moses' presence, 21 and everyone
who was willing and whose heart
moved them came and brought

[a] 7 Possibly the hides of large aquatic mammals; also in verse 23

an offering to the LORD for the work on the tent of meeting, for all its service, and for the sacred garments. 22All who were willing, men and women alike, came and brought gold jewelry of all kinds: brooches, earrings, rings and ornaments. They all presented their gold as a wave offering to the LORD. 23Everyone who had blue, purple or scarlet yarn or fine linen, or goat hair, ram skins dyed red or the other durable leather brought them. 24Those presenting an offering of silver or bronze brought it as an offering to the LORD, and everyone who had acacia wood for any part of the work brought it. 25Every skilled woman spun with her hands and brought what she had spun — blue, purple or scarlet yarn or fine linen. 26And all the women who were willing and had the skill spun the goat hair. 27The leaders brought onyx stones and other gems to be mounted on the ephod and breastpiece. 28They also brought spices and olive oil for the light and for the anointing oil and for the fragrant incense. 29All the Israelite men and women who were willing brought to the LORD freewill offerings for all the work the LORD through Moses had commanded them to do.

ver 4-9; Ex 25:1-7; 36:3

Bezalel and Oholiab

30Then Moses said to the Israelites, "See, the LORD has chosen Bezalel son of Uri, the son of Hur, of the tribe of Judah, 31and he has filled him with the Spirit of God, with wisdom, with understanding, with knowledge and with all kinds of skills — 32to make artistic designs for work in gold, silver and bronze, 33to cut and set stones, to work in wood and to engage in all kinds of artistic crafts. 34And he has given both him and Oholiab son of Ahisamak, of the tribe of Dan, the ability to teach others. 35He has filled them with skill to do all kinds of work as engravers, designers, embroiderers in blue, purple and scarlet yarn and fine linen, and weavers — all of them

36 skilled workers and designers. 1So Bezalel, Oholiab and every skilled person to whom the LORD has given skill and ability to know how to carry out all the work of constructing the sanctuary are to do the work just as the LORD has commanded." Ex 21:2-6

2Then Moses summoned Bezalel and Oholiab and every skilled person to whom the LORD had given ability and who was willing to come and do the work. 3They received from Moses all the offerings the Israelites had brought to carry out the work of constructing the sanctuary. And the people continued to bring freewill offerings morning after morning. 4So all the skilled workers who were doing all the work on the sanctuary left what they were doing 5and said to Moses, "The people are bringing more than enough for doing the

work the LORD commanded to be
done." 2Ch 24:14; 2Co 8:2-3
6Then Moses gave an order and
they sent this word throughout
the camp: "No man or woman is to
make anything else as an offering
for the sanctuary." And so the people were restrained from bringing
more, 7because what they already
had was more than enough to do
all the work.

The Tabernacle

8All those who were skilled
among the workers made the tabernacle with ten curtains of finely
twisted linen and blue, purple and
scarlet yarn, with cherubim woven
into them by expert hands. 9All
the curtains were the same size —
twenty-eight cubits long and four
cubits wide.[a] 10They joined five of
the curtains together and did the
same with the other five. 11Then
they made loops of blue material
along the edge of the end curtain
in one set, and the same was done
with the end curtain in the other
set. 12They also made fifty loops on
one curtain and fifty loops on the
end curtain of the other set, with
the loops opposite each other.
13Then they made fifty gold clasps
and used them to fasten the two
sets of curtains together so that
the tabernacle was a unit.
14They made curtains of goat
hair for the tent over the tabernacle — eleven altogether. 15All elev-
en curtains were the same size —
thirty cubits long and four cubits
wide.[b] 16They joined five of the
curtains into one set and the other six into another set. 17Then they
made fifty loops along the edge of
the end curtain in one set and also
along the edge of the end curtain
in the other set. 18They made fifty
bronze clasps to fasten the tent together as a unit. 19Then they made
for the tent a covering of ram skins
dyed red, and over that a covering
of the other durable leather.[c]
20They made upright frames
of acacia wood for the tabernacle. 21Each frame was ten cubits
long and a cubit and a half wide,[d]
22with two projections set parallel
to each other. They made all the
frames of the tabernacle in this
way. 23They made twenty frames
for the south side of the tabernacle
24and made forty silver bases to go
under them — two bases for each
frame, one under each projection.
25For the other side, the north side
of the tabernacle, they made twenty frames 26and forty silver bases — two under each frame. 27They
made six frames for the far end,
that is, the west end of the tabernacle, 28and two frames were made
for the corners of the tabernacle at
the far end. 29At these two corners

[a] *9* That is, about 42 feet long and 6 feet wide or about 13 meters long and 1.8 meters wide
[b] *15* That is, about 45 feet long and 6 feet wide or about 14 meters long and 1.8 meters wide
[c] *19* Possibly the hides of large aquatic mammals (see 35:7)
[d] *21* That is, about 15 feet long and 2 1/4 feet wide or about 4.5 meters long and 68 centimeters wide

the frames were double from the
bottom all the way to the top and
fitted into a single ring; both were
made alike. 30 So there were eight
frames and sixteen silver bases—
two under each frame.

31 They also made crossbars of
acacia wood: five for the frames
on one side of the tabernacle,
32 five for those on the other side,
and five for the frames on the
west, at the far end of the tabernacle. 33 They made the center crossbar so that it extended from end
to end at the middle of the frames.
34 They overlaid the frames with
gold and made gold rings to hold
the crossbars. They also overlaid
the crossbars with gold.

35 They made the curtain of blue,
purple and scarlet yarn and finely twisted linen, with cherubim
woven into it by a skilled worker.
36 They made four posts of acacia wood for it and overlaid them
with gold. They made gold hooks
for them and cast their four silver
bases. 37 For the entrance to the
tent they made a curtain of blue,
purple and scarlet yarn and finely twisted linen—the work of an
embroiderer; 38 and they made five
posts with hooks for them. They
overlaid the tops of the posts and
their bands with gold and made
their five bases of bronze. Ex 26:1-37

The Ark

37 Bezalel made the ark of acacia wood—two and a half
cubits long, a cubit and a half wide,
and a cubit and a half high.[a] 2 He
overlaid it with pure gold, both
inside and out, and made a gold
molding around it. 3 He cast four
gold rings for it and fastened them
to its four feet, with two rings on
one side and two rings on the other. 4 Then he made poles of acacia wood and overlaid them with
gold. 5 And he inserted the poles
into the rings on the sides of the
ark to carry it. ver 11,26; Ex 31:2

6 He made the atonement cover of pure gold—two and a half
cubits long and a cubit and a half
wide. 7 Then he made two cherubim out of hammered gold at the
ends of the cover. 8 He made one
cherub on one end and the second cherub on the other; at the
two ends he made them of one
piece with the cover. 9 The cherubim had their wings spread upward, overshadowing the cover
with them. The cherubim faced
each other, looking toward the
cover. Ex 25:10-20

The Table

10 They[b] made the table of acacia wood—two cubits long, a cubit wide and a cubit and a half
high.[c] 11 Then they overlaid it with
pure gold and made a gold mold-

[a] *1* That is, about 3 3/4 feet long and 2 1/4 feet wide and high or about 1.1 meters long and 68 centimeters wide and high; similarly in verse 6 [b] *10* Or *He*; also in verses 11-29 [c] *10* That is, about 3 feet long, 1 1/2 feet wide and 2 1/4 feet high or about 90 centimeters long, 45 centimeters wide and 68 centimeters high

ing around it. 12They also made
around it a rim a handbreadth[a]
wide and put a gold molding on
the rim. 13They cast four gold rings
for the table and fastened them to
the four corners, where the four
legs were. 14The rings were put
close to the rim to hold the poles
used in carrying the table. 15The
poles for carrying the table were
made of acacia wood and were
overlaid with gold. 16And they
made from pure gold the articles
for the table — its plates and dishes and bowls and its pitchers for
the pouring out of drink offerings.
Ex 25:23-29

The Lampstand

17They made the lampstand of
pure gold. They hammered out
its base and shaft, and made its
flowerlike cups, buds and blossoms of one piece with them.
18Six branches extended from the
sides of the lampstand — three on
one side and three on the other.
19Three cups shaped like almond
flowers with buds and blossoms
were on one branch, three on the
next branch and the same for all
six branches extending from the
lampstand. 20And on the lampstand were four cups shaped like
almond flowers with buds and
blossoms. 21One bud was under
the first pair of branches extending from the lampstand, a second
bud under the second pair, and a
third bud under the third pair —
six branches in all. 22The buds and
the branches were all of one piece
with the lampstand, hammered
out of pure gold. Heb 9:2; Rev 1:12
23They made its seven lamps,
as well as its wick trimmers and
trays, of pure gold. 24They made
the lampstand and all its accessories from one talent[b] of pure gold.
Ex 25:31-39

The Altar of Incense

25They made the altar of incense
out of acacia wood. It was square,
a cubit long and a cubit wide and
two cubits high[c] — its horns of
one piece with it. 26They overlaid
the top and all the sides and the
horns with pure gold, and made
a gold molding around it. 27They
made two gold rings below the
molding — two on each of the opposite sides — to hold the poles
used to carry it. 28They made the
poles of acacia wood and overlaid
them with gold. Ex 30:1-5
29They also made the sacred
anointing oil and the pure, fragrant incense — the work of a perfumer. Ex 30:1,25; 31:11

The Altar of Burnt Offering

38 They[d] built the altar of
burnt offering of acacia
wood, three cubits[e] high; it was

[a] *12* That is, about 3 inches or about 7.5 centimeters [b] *24* That is, about 75 pounds or about 34 kilograms [c] *25* That is, about 1 1/2 feet long and wide and 3 feet high or about 45 centimeters long and wide and 90 centimeters high [d] *1* Or *He*; also in verses 2-9 [e] *1* That is, about 4 1/2 feet or about 1.4 meters

square, five cubits long and five
cubits wide.[a] 2They made a horn
at each of the four corners, so that
the horns and the altar were of
one piece, and they overlaid the
altar with bronze. 3They made all
its utensils of bronze — its pots,
shovels, sprinkling bowls, meat
forks and firepans. 4They made a
grating for the altar, a bronze network, to be under its ledge, halfway up the altar. 5They cast bronze
rings to hold the poles for the
four corners of the bronze grating. 6They made the poles of acacia wood and overlaid them with
bronze. 7They inserted the poles
into the rings so they would be
on the sides of the altar for carrying it. They made it hollow, out of
boards. Ex 27:1-8

The Basin for Washing

8They made the bronze basin
and its bronze stand from the mirrors of the women who served at
the entrance to the tent of meeting. Dt 23:17; 1Sa 2:22

The Courtyard

9Next they made the courtyard.
The south side was a hundred cubits[b] long and had curtains of
finely twisted linen, 10with twenty posts and twenty bronze bases,
and with silver hooks and bands
on the posts. 11The north side
was also a hundred cubits long
and had twenty posts and twenty bronze bases, with silver hooks
and bands on the posts.

12The west end was fifty cubits[c]
wide and had curtains, with ten
posts and ten bases, with silver
hooks and bands on the posts.
13The east end, toward the sunrise, was also fifty cubits wide.
14Curtains fifteen cubits[d] long
were on one side of the entrance,
with three posts and three bases, 15and curtains fifteen cubits
long were on the other side of the
entrance to the courtyard, with
three posts and three bases. 16All
the curtains around the courtyard were of finely twisted lin-
en. 17The bases for the posts were
bronze. The hooks and bands on
the posts were silver, and their
tops were overlaid with silver; so
all the posts of the courtyard had
silver bands.

18The curtain for the entrance to
the courtyard was made of blue,
purple and scarlet yarn and finely twisted linen — the work of an
embroiderer. It was twenty cubits[e]
long and, like the curtains of the
courtyard, five cubits[f] high, 19with
four posts and four bronze bases.
Their hooks and bands were silver,
and their tops were overlaid with
silver. 20All the tent pegs of the
tabernacle and of the surrounding
courtyard were bronze. Ex 27:9-19

[a] *1* That is, about 7 1/2 feet or about 2.3 meters long and wide [b] *9* That is, about 150 feet or about 45 meters [c] *12* That is, about 75 feet or about 23 meters [d] *14* That is, about 22 feet or about 6.8 meters [e] *18* That is, about 30 feet or about 9 meters [f] *18* That is, about 7 1/2 feet or about 2.3 meters

The Materials Used

21 These are the amounts of the materials used for the tabernacle, the tabernacle of the covenant law, which were recorded at Moses' command by the Levites under the direction of Ithamar son of Aaron, the priest. 22 (Bezalel son of Uri, the son of Hur, of the tribe of Judah, made everything the LORD commanded Moses; 23 with him was Oholiab son of Ahisamak, of the tribe of Dan — an engraver and designer, and an embroiderer in blue, purple and scarlet yarn and fine linen.) 24 The total amount of the gold from the wave offering used for all the work on the sanctuary was 29 talents and 730 shekels,[a] according to the sanctuary shekel. Nu 1:50,53; 9:15

25 The silver obtained from those of the community who were counted in the census was 100 talents[b] and 1,775 shekels,[c] according to the sanctuary shekel — 26 one beka per person, that is, half a shekel,[d] according to the sanctuary shekel, from everyone who had crossed over to those counted, twenty years old or more, a total of 603,550 men. 27 The 100 talents of silver were used to cast the bases for the sanctuary and for the curtain — 100 bases from the 100 talents, one talent for each base. 28 They used the 1,775 shekels to make the hooks for the posts, to overlay the tops of the posts, and to make their bands. Ex 30:12-14

29 The bronze from the wave offering was 70 talents and 2,400 shekels.[e] 30 They used it to make the bases for the entrance to the tent of meeting, the bronze altar with its bronze grating and all its utensils, 31 the bases for the surrounding courtyard and those for its entrance and all the tent pegs for the tabernacle and those for the surrounding courtyard.

The Priestly Garments

39 From the blue, purple and scarlet yarn they made woven garments for ministering in the sanctuary. They also made sacred garments for Aaron, as the LORD commanded Moses. Ex 35:19,23

The Ephod

2 They[f] made the ephod of gold, and of blue, purple and scarlet yarn, and of finely twisted linen. 3 They hammered out thin sheets of gold and cut strands to be worked into the blue, purple and scarlet yarn and fine linen — the work of skilled hands. 4 They made shoulder pieces for the ephod, which were attached to two of its corners, so it could be fastened. 5 Its skillfully woven waistband

[a] 24 The weight of the gold was a little over a ton or about 1 metric ton. [b] 25 That is, about 3 3/4 tons or about 3.4 metric tons; also in verse 27 [c] 25 That is, about 44 pounds or about 20 kilograms; also in verse 28 [d] 26 That is, about 1/5 ounce or about 5.7 grams [e] 29 The weight of the bronze was about 2 1/2 tons or about 2.4 metric tons. [f] 2 Or *He*; also in verses 7, 8 and 22

was like it — of one piece with the ephod and made with gold, and with blue, purple and scarlet yarn, and with finely twisted linen, as the LORD commanded Moses.

6 They mounted the onyx stones in gold filigree settings and engraved them like a seal with the names of the sons of Israel. 7 Then they fastened them on the shoulder pieces of the ephod as memorial stones for the sons of Israel, as the LORD commanded Moses.

Ex 28:6-14

The Breastpiece

8 They fashioned the breastpiece — the work of a skilled craftsman. They made it like the ephod: of gold, and of blue, purple and scarlet yarn, and of finely twisted linen. 9 It was square — a span[a] long and a span wide — and folded double. 10 Then they mounted four rows of precious stones on it. The first row was carnelian, chrysolite and beryl; 11 the second row was turquoise, lapis lazuli and emerald; 12 the third row was jacinth, agate and amethyst; 13 the fourth row was topaz, onyx and jasper.[b] They were mounted in gold filigree settings. 14 There were twelve stones, one for each of the names of the sons of Israel, each engraved like a seal with the name of one of the twelve tribes.

15 For the breastpiece they made braided chains of pure gold, like a rope. 16 They made two gold filigree settings and two gold rings, and fastened the rings to two of the corners of the breastpiece. 17 They fastened the two gold chains to the rings at the corners of the breastpiece, 18 and the other ends of the chains to the two settings, attaching them to the shoulder pieces of the ephod at the front. 19 They made two gold rings and attached them to the other two corners of the breastpiece on the inside edge next to the ephod. 20 Then they made two more gold rings and attached them to the bottom of the shoulder pieces on the front of the ephod, close to the seam just above the waistband of the ephod. 21 They tied the rings of the breastpiece to the rings of the ephod with blue cord, connecting it to the waistband so that the breastpiece would not swing out from the ephod — as the LORD commanded Moses.

Ex 28:15-28

Other Priestly Garments

22 They made the robe of the ephod entirely of blue cloth — the work of a weaver — 23 with an opening in the center of the robe like the opening of a collar,[c] and a band around this opening, so that it would not tear. 24 They made pomegranates of blue, purple and scarlet yarn and finely twisted linen around the hem of the robe. 25 And they made bells of pure gold

[a] *9* That is, about 9 inches or about 23 centimeters [b] *13* The precise identification of some of these precious stones is uncertain. [c] *23* The meaning of the Hebrew for this word is uncertain.

and attached them around the
hem between the pomegranates.
26The bells and pomegranates alternated around the hem of the
robe to be worn for ministering,
as the LORD commanded Moses.

27For Aaron and his sons, they
made tunics of fine linen — the
work of a weaver — 28and the turban of fine linen, the linen caps
and the undergarments of finely
twisted linen. 29The sash was made
of finely twisted linen and blue,
purple and scarlet yarn — the work
of an embroiderer — as the LORD
commanded Moses. Ex 28:4; Lev 6:10

30They made the plate, the sacred emblem, out of pure gold and
engraved on it, like an inscription on a seal: HOLY TO THE LORD.
31Then they fastened a blue cord to
it to attach it to the turban, as the
LORD commanded Moses. Ex 28:31-43

Moses Inspects the Tabernacle

32So all the work on the tabernacle, the tent of meeting, was completed. The Israelites did everything just as the LORD commanded
Moses. 33Then they brought the tabernacle to Moses: the tent and all
its furnishings, its clasps, frames,
crossbars, posts and bases; 34the
covering of ram skins dyed red and
the covering of another durable
leather[a] and the shielding curtain;
35the ark of the covenant law with
its poles and the atonement cover;
36the table with all its articles and
the bread of the Presence; 37the
pure gold lampstand with its row
of lamps and all its accessories, and
the olive oil for the light; 38the gold
altar, the anointing oil, the fragrant
incense, and the curtain for the
entrance to the tent; 39the bronze
altar with its bronze grating, its
poles and all its utensils; the basin
with its stand; 40the curtains of the
courtyard with its posts and bases,
and the curtain for the entrance to
the courtyard; the ropes and tent
pegs for the courtyard; all the furnishings for the tabernacle, the
tent of meeting; 41and the woven
garments worn for ministering in
the sanctuary, both the sacred garments for Aaron the priest and the
garments for his sons when serving as priests. Ex 35:10-19

42The Israelites had done all the
work just as the LORD had commanded Moses. 43Moses inspected
the work and saw that they had
done it just as the LORD had commanded. So Moses blessed them.
Lev 9:22-23; 2Ch 30:27

Setting Up the Tabernacle

40 Then the LORD said to
Moses: 2"Set up the tab-
ernacle, the tent of meeting, on
the first day of the first month.
3Place the ark of the covenant law
in it and shield the ark with the
curtain. 4Bring in the table and
set out what belongs on it. Then
bring in the lampstand and set up
its lamps. 5Place the gold altar of
incense in front of the ark of the

[a] 34 Possibly the hides of large aquatic mammals

covenant law and put the curtain
at the entrance to the tabernacle.
Ex 26:33; Nu 1:1
6 "Place the altar of burnt offering in front of the entrance to the
tabernacle, the tent of meeting;
7 place the basin between the tent
of meeting and the altar and put
water in it. 8 Set up the courtyard
around it and put the curtain at
the entrance to the courtyard.
Ex 30:18; 2Ki 16:14
9 "Take the anointing oil and
anoint the tabernacle and everything in it; consecrate it and all
its furnishings, and it will be holy.
10 Then anoint the altar of burnt
offering and all its utensils; consecrate the altar, and it will be most
holy. 11 Anoint the basin and its
stand and consecrate them. Ex 30:26
12 "Bring Aaron and his sons to
the entrance to the tent of meeting and wash them with water.
13 Then dress Aaron in the sacred
garments, anoint him and consecrate him so he may serve me as
priest. 14 Bring his sons and dress
them in tunics. 15 Anoint them
just as you anointed their father,
so they may serve me as priests.
Their anointing will be to a priesthood that will continue throughout their generations." 16 Moses did
everything just as the LORD commanded him. Ex 29:9; Nu 25:13
17 So the tabernacle was set up
on the first day of the first month
in the second year. 18 When Moses
set up the tabernacle, he put the
bases in place, erected the frames,
inserted the crossbars and set up
the posts. 19 Then he spread the
tent over the tabernacle and put
the covering over the tent, as the
LORD commanded him. Nu 7:1; 2Ch 1:3
20 He took the tablets of the covenant law and placed them in the
ark, attached the poles to the ark
and put the atonement cover over
it. 21 Then he brought the ark into
the tabernacle and hung the shielding curtain and shielded the ark of
the covenant law, as the LORD commanded him. Ex 16:34; Heb 9:4
22 Moses placed the table in the
tent of meeting on the north side
of the tabernacle outside the curtain 23 and set out the bread on it
before the LORD, as the LORD commanded him. Ex 26:35
24 He placed the lampstand in
the tent of meeting opposite the
table on the south side of the tabernacle 25 and set up the lamps before the LORD, as the LORD commanded him. Ex 26:35
26 Moses placed the gold altar
in the tent of meeting in front of
the curtain 27 and burned fragrant
incense on it, as the LORD commanded him.
28 Then he put up the curtain
at the entrance to the tabernacle.
29 He set the altar of burnt offering near the entrance to the tabernacle, the tent of meeting, and
offered on it burnt offerings and
grain offerings, as the LORD commanded him. ver 6; Ex 29:38-42; 30:6
30 He placed the basin between
the tent of meeting and the altar

and put water in it for washing,
[31]and Moses and Aaron and his
sons used it to wash their hands
and feet. [32]They washed whenever they entered the tent of meeting or approached the altar, as the
LORD commanded Moses. Ex 30:20

[33]Then Moses set up the courtyard around the tabernacle and
altar and put up the curtain at the
entrance to the courtyard. And so
Moses finished the work.
ver 8; Ex 27:9

The Glory of the LORD

[34]Then the cloud covered the
tent of meeting, and the glory
of the LORD filled the tabernacle.
[35]Moses could not enter the tent
of meeting because the cloud had
settled on it, and the glory of the
LORD filled the tabernacle.
Nu 9:15-23

[36]In all the travels of the Israelites, whenever the cloud lifted
from above the tabernacle, they
would set out; [37]but if the cloud
did not lift, they did not set out —
until the day it lifted. [38]So the
cloud of the LORD was over the
tabernacle by day, and fire was in
the cloud by night, in the sight of
all the Israelites during all their
travels. Nu 9:17-23

LEVITICUS

The Burnt Offering

1 The LORD called to Moses and
spoke to him from the tent of
meeting. He said, 2"Speak to the
Israelites and say to them: 'When
anyone among you brings an offering to the LORD, bring as your
offering an animal from either the
herd or the flock. Lev 22:18-19
3" 'If the offering is a burnt offering from the herd, you are to
offer a male without defect. You
must present it at the entrance
to the tent of meeting so that it
will be acceptable to the LORD.
4You are to lay your hand on the
head of the burnt offering, and it
will be accepted on your behalf
to make atonement for you. 5You
are to slaughter the young bull
before the LORD, and then Aaron's
sons the priests shall bring the
blood and splash it against the
sides of the altar at the entrance
to the tent of meeting. 6You are
to skin the burnt offering and cut
it into pieces. 7The sons of Aaron
the priest are to put fire on the altar and arrange wood on the fire.
8Then Aaron's sons the priests
shall arrange the pieces, including the head and the fat, on the
wood that is burning on the altar.
9You are to wash the internal organs and the legs with water, and
the priest is to burn all of it on the
altar. It is a burnt offering, a food
offering, an aroma pleasing to the
LORD. Ge 8:21; Eph 5:2
10" 'If the offering is a burnt offering from the flock, from either
the sheep or the goats, you are to
offer a male without defect. 11You
are to slaughter it at the north
side of the altar before the LORD,
and Aaron's sons the priests shall
splash its blood against the sides
of the altar. 12You are to cut it into
pieces, and the priest shall arrange
them, including the head and the
fat, on the wood that is burning
on the altar. 13You are to wash the
internal organs and the legs with
water, and the priest is to bring
all of them and burn them on the
altar. It is a burnt offering, a food
offering, an aroma pleasing to the
LORD.

14" 'If the offering to the LORD is
a burnt offering of birds, you are
to offer a dove or a young pigeon.
15The priest shall bring it to the altar, wring off the head and burn
it on the altar; its blood shall be
drained out on the side of the altar.
16He is to remove the crop and the
feathers[a] and throw them down
east of the altar where the ashes
are. 17He shall tear it open by the
wings, not dividing it completely,

[a] 16 Or *crop with its contents*; the meaning of the Hebrew for this word is uncertain.

and then the priest shall burn it
on the wood that is burning on
the altar. It is a burnt offering, a
food offering, an aroma pleasing
to the LORD. Lev 5:7; 6:10

The Grain Offering

2 "'When anyone brings a grain
offering to the LORD, their offering is to be of the finest flour.
They are to pour olive oil on it, put
incense on it 2and take it to Aaron's sons the priests. The priest
shall take a handful of the flour
and oil, together with all the incense, and burn this as a memorial[a] portion on the altar, a food
offering, an aroma pleasing to the
LORD. 3The rest of the grain offering belongs to Aaron and his sons;
it is a most holy part of the food
offerings presented to the LORD.
Lev 6:14-18; 10:12-13

4"'If you bring a grain offering
baked in an oven, it is to consist of
the finest flour: either thick loaves
made without yeast and with olive oil mixed in or thin loaves
made without yeast and brushed
with olive oil. 5If your grain offering is prepared on a griddle, it
is to be made of the finest flour
mixed with oil, and without yeast.
6Crumble it and pour oil on it; it is
a grain offering. 7If your grain offering is cooked in a pan, it is to be
made of the finest flour and some
olive oil. 8Bring the grain offering
made of these things to the LORD;
present it to the priest, who shall
take it to the altar. 9He shall take
out the memorial portion from
the grain offering and burn it on
the altar as a food offering, an
aroma pleasing to the LORD. 10The
rest of the grain offering belongs
to Aaron and his sons; it is a most
holy part of the food offerings presented to the LORD. Ex 29:2; Lev 7:9

11"'Every grain offering you
bring to the LORD must be made
without yeast, for you are not to
burn any yeast or honey in a food
offering presented to the LORD.
12You may bring them to the LORD
as an offering of the firstfruits, but
they are not to be offered on the
altar as a pleasing aroma. 13Sea-
son all your grain offerings with
salt. Do not leave the salt of the
covenant of your God out of your
grain offerings; add salt to all your
offerings. Nu 18:19; Eze 43:24

14"'If you bring a grain offering of firstfruits to the LORD, offer
crushed heads of new grain roasted in the fire. 15Put oil and incense
on it; it is a grain offering. 16The
priest shall burn the memorial
portion of the crushed grain and
the oil, together with all the incense, as a food offering presented
to the LORD. Lev 23:10

The Fellowship Offering

3 "'If your offering is a fellowship offering, and you offer an
animal from the herd, whether
male or female, you are to present
before the LORD an animal without defect. 2You are to lay your

[a] 2 Or *representative*; also in verses 9 and 16

hand on the head of your offering
and slaughter it at the entrance to
the tent of meeting. Then Aaron's
sons the priests shall splash the
blood against the sides of the altar. 3From the fellowship offering
you are to bring a food offering
to the LORD: the internal organs
and all the fat that is connected
to them, 4both kidneys with the
fat on them near the loins, and
the long lobe of the liver, which
you will remove with the kidneys.
5Then Aaron's sons are to burn it
on the altar on top of the burnt offering that is lying on the burning
wood; it is a food offering, an aroma pleasing to the LORD.

Lev 7:11-34; 22:21

6"'If you offer an animal from
the flock as a fellowship offering to
the LORD, you are to offer a male
or female without defect. 7If you
offer a lamb, you are to present it
before the LORD, 8lay your hand on
its head and slaughter it in front of
the tent of meeting. Then Aaron's
sons shall splash its blood against
the sides of the altar. 9From the fellowship offering you are to bring a
food offering to the LORD: its fat,
the entire fat tail cut off close to
the backbone, the internal organs
and all the fat that is connected to
them, 10both kidneys with the fat
on them near the loins, and the
long lobe of the liver, which you
will remove with the kidneys. 11The
priest shall burn them on the altar
as a food offering presented to the
LORD.

Lev 21:6,17

12"'If your offering is a goat, you
are to present it before the LORD,
13lay your hand on its head and
slaughter it in front of the tent of
meeting. Then Aaron's sons shall
splash its blood against the sides
of the altar. 14From what you offer you are to present this food
offering to the LORD: the internal
organs and all the fat that is connected to them, 15both kidneys
with the fat on them near the
loins, and the long lobe of the liver, which you will remove with the
kidneys. 16The priest shall burn
them on the altar as a food offering, a pleasing aroma. All the fat is
the LORD's.

Lev 1:9; 1Sa 2:16

17"'This is a lasting ordinance for
the generations to come, wherever you live: You must not eat any
fat or any blood.'"

The Sin Offering

4 The LORD said to Moses, 2"Say
to the Israelites: 'When anyone sins unintentionally and does
what is forbidden in any of the
LORD's commands—

Lev 5:15-18; Heb 9:7

3"'If the anointed priest sins,
bringing guilt on the people, he
must bring to the LORD a young
bull without defect as a sin offering[a] for the sin he has committed.
4He is to present the bull at the entrance to the tent of meeting before the LORD. He is to lay his hand

[a] 3 Or *purification offering*; here and throughout this chapter

on its head and slaughter it there
before the LORD. 5Then the anointed priest shall take some of the
bull's blood and carry it into the
tent of meeting. 6He is to dip his
finger into the blood and sprinkle some of it seven times before
the LORD, in front of the curtain
of the sanctuary. 7The priest shall
then put some of the blood on the
horns of the altar of fragrant incense that is before the LORD in
the tent of meeting. The rest of
the bull's blood he shall pour out
at the base of the altar of burnt offering at the entrance to the tent
of meeting. 8He shall remove all
the fat from the bull of the sin offering — all the fat that is connected to the internal organs, 9both
kidneys with the fat on them near
the loins, and the long lobe of the
liver, which he will remove with
the kidneys — 10just as the fat is
removed from the ox[a] sacrificed
as a fellowship offering. Then the
priest shall burn them on the altar
of burnt offering. 11But the hide of
the bull and all its flesh, as well as
the head and legs, the internal organs and the intestines — 12that
is, all the rest of the bull — he
must take outside the camp to a
place ceremonially clean, where
the ashes are thrown, and burn
it there in a wood fire on the ash
heap. Lev 5:9; Heb 13:11

13" 'If the whole Israelite community sins unintentionally and
does what is forbidden in any
of the LORD's commands, even
though the community is unaware of the matter, when they realize their guilt 14and the sin they
committed becomes known, the
assembly must bring a young bull
as a sin offering and present it before the tent of meeting. 15The elders of the community are to lay
their hands on the bull's head before the LORD, and the bull shall
be slaughtered before the LORD.
16Then the anointed priest is to
take some of the bull's blood into
the tent of meeting. 17He shall
dip his finger into the blood and
sprinkle it before the LORD seven
times in front of the curtain. 18He
is to put some of the blood on
the horns of the altar that is before the LORD in the tent of meeting. The rest of the blood he shall
pour out at the base of the altar of
burnt offering at the entrance to
the tent of meeting. 19He shall remove all the fat from it and burn
it on the altar, 20and do with this
bull just as he did with the bull
for the sin offering. In this way
the priest will make atonement
for the community, and they will
be forgiven. 21Then he shall take
the bull outside the camp and
burn it as he burned the first bull.
This is the sin offering for the
community. ver 3; Nu 15:25

22" 'When a leader sins unintentionally and does what is

[a] *10* The Hebrew word can refer to either male or female.

forbidden in any of the commands
of the LORD his God, when he real-
izes his guilt 23 and the sin he has
committed becomes known, he
must bring as his offering a male
goat without defect. 24 He is to lay
his hand on the goat's head and
slaughter it at the place where the
burnt offering is slaughtered before the LORD. It is a sin offering.
25 Then the priest shall take some
of the blood of the sin offering
with his finger and put it on the
horns of the altar of burnt offering
and pour out the rest of the blood
at the base of the altar. 26 He shall
burn all the fat on the altar as he
burned the fat of the fellowship
offering. In this way the priest will
make atonement for the leader's
sin, and he will be forgiven.

Lev 9:9; Nu 31:13

27 " 'If any member of the community sins unintentionally and
does what is forbidden in any of
the LORD's commands, when they
realize their guilt 28 and the sin
they have committed becomes
known, they must bring as their
offering for the sin they committed a female goat without defect.
29 They are to lay their hand on
the head of the sin offering and
slaughter it at the place of the
burnt offering. 30 Then the priest
is to take some of the blood with
his finger and put it on the horns
of the altar of burnt offering and
pour out the rest of the blood at
the base of the altar. 31 They shall
remove all the fat, just as the fat is
removed from the fellowship offering, and the priest shall burn it
on the altar as an aroma pleasing
to the LORD. In this way the priest
will make atonement for them,
and they will be forgiven.

Ge 8:21; Lev 1:4

32 " 'If someone brings a lamb as
their sin offering, they are to bring
a female without defect. 33 They
are to lay their hand on its head
and slaughter it for a sin offering
at the place where the burnt offering is slaughtered. 34 Then the
priest shall take some of the blood
of the sin offering with his finger
and put it on the horns of the altar of burnt offering and pour out
the rest of the blood at the base of
the altar. 35 They shall remove all
the fat, just as the fat is removed
from the lamb of the fellowship
offering, and the priest shall burn
it on the altar on top of the food
offerings presented to the LORD.
In this way the priest will make
atonement for them for the sin
they have committed, and they
will be forgiven.

Ex 29:38; Lev 1:4; 9:3

5 " 'If anyone sins because they
do not speak up when they
hear a public charge to testify regarding something they have seen
or learned about, they will be held
responsible.

Pr 29:24

2 " 'If anyone becomes aware
that they are guilty — if they un-
wittingly touch anything ceremonially unclean (whether the car-

cass of an unclean animal, wild or
domestic, or of any unclean creature that moves along the ground)
and they are unaware that they
have become unclean, but then
they come to realize their guilt; 3or
if they touch human uncleanness
(anything that would make them
unclean) even though they are unaware of it, but then they learn of
it and realize their guilt; 4or if anyone thoughtlessly takes an oath to
do anything, whether good or evil
(in any matter one might carelessly swear about) even though
they are unaware of it, but then
they learn of it and realize their
guilt — 5when anyone becomes
aware that they are guilty in any
of these matters, they must confess in what way they have sinned.
6As a penalty for the sin they have
committed, they must bring to the
LORD a female lamb or goat from
the flock as a sin offering[a]; and the
priest shall make atonement for
them for their sin. Lev 16:21; 26:40

7"'Anyone who cannot afford a
lamb is to bring two doves or two
young pigeons to the LORD as a
penalty for their sin — one for a
sin offering and the other for a
burnt offering. 8They are to bring
them to the priest, who shall first
offer the one for the sin offering.
He is to wring its head from its
neck, not dividing it completely,
9and is to splash some of the blood
of the sin offering against the side
of the altar; the rest of the blood
must be drained out at the base of
the altar. It is a sin offering. 10The
priest shall then offer the other as
a burnt offering in the prescribed
way and make atonement for
them for the sin they have committed, and they will be forgiven.
Lev 12:8; 14:21

11"'If, however, they cannot afford two doves or two young pigeons, they are to bring as an offering for their sin a tenth of an
ephah[b] of the finest flour for a sin
offering. They must not put olive
oil or incense on it, because it is
a sin offering. 12They are to bring
it to the priest, who shall take a
handful of it as a memorial[c] portion and burn it on the altar on
top of the food offerings presented to the LORD. It is a sin offering.
13In this way the priest will make
atonement for them for any of
these sins they have committed,
and they will be forgiven. The rest
of the offering will belong to the
priest, as in the case of the grain
offering.'" Lev 2:1,3; 4:26

The Guilt Offering

14The LORD said to Moses:
15"When anyone is unfaithful to
the LORD by sinning unintentionally in regard to any of the LORD's
holy things, they are to bring to the
LORD as a penalty a ram from the
flock, one without defect and of the
proper value in silver, according to

[a] 6 Or *purification offering*; here and throughout this chapter [b] 11 That is, probably about 3 1/2 pounds or about 1.6 kilograms [c] 12 Or *representative*

the sanctuary shekel.[a] It is a guilt
offering. 16They must make restitution for what they have failed to do
in regard to the holy things, pay an
additional penalty of a fifth of its
value and give it all to the priest.
The priest will make atonement
for them with the ram as a guilt offering, and they will be forgiven.
Lev 6:4; 22:14; Nu 5:7

17"If anyone sins and does what
is forbidden in any of the LORD's
commands, even though they do
not know it, they are guilty and
will be held responsible. 18They
are to bring to the priest as a guilt
offering a ram from the flock, one
without defect and of the proper
value. In this way the priest will
make atonement for them for the
wrong they have committed unintentionally, and they will be forgiven. 19It is a guilt offering; they
have been guilty of[b] wrongdoing
against the LORD." Lev 6:6; 14:12

6 [c] The LORD said to Moses: 2"If
anyone sins and is unfaithful
to the LORD by deceiving a neighbor about something entrusted to
them or left in their care or about
something stolen, or if they cheat
their neighbor, 3or if they find
lost property and lie about it, or if
they swear falsely about any such
sin that people may commit —
4when they sin in any of these
ways and realize their guilt, they
must return what they have stolen or taken by extortion, or what
was entrusted to them, or the lost
property they found, 5or whatever it was they swore falsely about.
They must make restitution in
full, add a fifth of the value to it
and give it all to the owner on the
day they present their guilt offering. 6And as a penalty they must
bring to the priest, that is, to the
LORD, their guilt offering, a ram
from the flock, one without defect
and of the proper value. 7In this
way the priest will make atonement for them before the LORD,
and they will be forgiven for any
of the things they did that made
them guilty." Lev 5:15; Dt 22:1-3

The Burnt Offering

8The LORD said to Moses: 9"Give
Aaron and his sons this command:
'These are the regulations for the
burnt offering: The burnt offering
is to remain on the altar hearth
throughout the night, till morning, and the fire must be kept
burning on the altar. 10The priest
shall then put on his linen clothes,
with linen undergarments next
to his body, and shall remove the
ashes of the burnt offering that
the fire has consumed on the altar and place them beside the altar. 11Then he is to take off these
clothes and put on others, and carry the ashes outside the camp to a
place that is ceremonially clean.
12The fire on the altar must be

[a] *15* That is, about 2/5 ounce or about 12 grams [b] *19* Or *offering; atonement has been made for their* [c] In Hebrew texts 6:1-7 is numbered 5:20-26, and 6:8-30 is numbered 6:1-23.

kept burning; it must not go out. Every morning the priest is to add firewood and arrange the burnt offering on the fire and burn the fat of the fellowship offerings on it. 13The fire must be kept burning on the altar continuously; it must not go out. Ex 28:39-43; Lev 4:12

The Grain Offering

14" 'These are the regulations for the grain offering: Aaron's sons are to bring it before the LORD, in front of the altar. 15The priest is to take a handful of the finest flour and some olive oil, together with all the incense on the grain offering, and burn the memorial[a] portion on the altar as an aroma pleasing to the LORD. 16Aaron and his sons shall eat the rest of it, but it is to be eaten without yeast in the sanctuary area; they are to eat it in the courtyard of the tent of meeting. 17It must not be baked with yeast; I have given it as their share of the food offerings presented to me. Like the sin offering[b] and the guilt offering, it is most holy. 18Any male descendant of Aaron may eat it. For all generations to come it is his perpetual share of the food offerings presented to the LORD. Whatever touches them will become holy.[c]' "

Lev 2:3; Eze 44:29

19The LORD also said to Moses, 20"This is the offering Aaron and his sons are to bring to the LORD on the day he[d] is anointed: a tenth of an ephah[e] of the finest flour as a regular grain offering, half of it in the morning and half in the evening. 21It must be prepared with oil on a griddle; bring it well-mixed and present the grain offering broken[f] in pieces as an aroma pleasing to the LORD. 22The son who is to succeed him as anointed priest shall prepare it. It is the LORD's perpetual share and is to be burned completely. 23Every grain offering of a priest shall be burned completely; it must not be eaten."

Ex 29:2; Lev 2:5

The Sin Offering

24The LORD said to Moses, 25"Say to Aaron and his sons: 'These are the regulations for the sin offering: The sin offering is to be slaughtered before the LORD in the place the burnt offering is slaughtered; it is most holy. 26The priest who offers it shall eat it; it is to be eaten in the sanctuary area, in the courtyard of the tent of meeting. 27Whatever touches any of the flesh will become holy, and if any of the blood is spattered on a garment, you must wash it in the sanctuary area. 28The clay pot the meat is cooked in must be broken; but if it is cooked in a bronze pot, the pot is to be scoured and rinsed with water. 29Any male in

[a] 15 Or *representative* [b] 17 Or *purification offering*; also in verses 25 and 30 [c] 18 Or *Whoever touches them must be holy*; similarly in verse 27 [d] 20 Or *each* [e] 20 That is, probably about 3 1/2 pounds or about 1.6 kilograms [f] 21 The meaning of the Hebrew for this word is uncertain.

a priest's family may eat it; it is
most holy. 30 But any sin offering
whose blood is brought into the
tent of meeting to make atonement in the Holy Place must not
be eaten; it must be burned up.
Ex 29:37; Lev 1:5,11; 11:33

The Guilt Offering

7 "'These are the regulations
for the guilt offering, which is
most holy: 2 The guilt offering is to
be slaughtered in the place where
the burnt offering is slaughtered,
and its blood is to be splashed
against the sides of the altar. 3 All
its fat shall be offered: the fat tail
and the fat that covers the internal organs, 4 both kidneys with the
fat on them near the loins, and
the long lobe of the liver, which is
to be removed with the kidneys.
5 The priest shall burn them on the
altar as a food offering presented
to the LORD. It is a guilt offering.
6 Any male in a priest's family may
eat it, but it must be eaten in the
sanctuary area; it is most holy.
Ex 29:13; Lev 6:18

7 "'The same law applies to both
the sin offering[a] and the guilt offering: They belong to the priest
who makes atonement with
them. 8 The priest who offers a
burnt offering for anyone may
keep its hide for himself. 9 Every
grain offering baked in an oven
or cooked in a pan or on a griddle
belongs to the priest who offers it,
10 and every grain offering, whether mixed with olive oil or dry, belongs equally to all the sons of
Aaron.
Lev 2:5; 16:17,26

The Fellowship Offering

11 "'These are the regulations for
the fellowship offering anyone
may present to the LORD:

12 "'If they offer it as an expression of thankfulness, then along
with this thank offering they are
to offer thick loaves made without yeast and with olive oil mixed
in, thin loaves made without yeast
and brushed with oil, and thick
loaves of the finest flour well-
kneaded and with oil mixed in.
13 Along with their fellowship offering of thanksgiving they are
to present an offering with thick
loaves of bread made with yeast.
14 They are to bring one of each
kind as an offering, a contribution to the LORD; it belongs to the
priest who splashes the blood of
the fellowship offering against
the altar. 15 The meat of their fellowship offering of thanksgiving
must be eaten on the day it is offered; they must leave none of it
till morning.
Lev 22:30; Am 4:5

16 "'If, however, their offering
is the result of a vow or is a freewill offering, the sacrifice shall be
eaten on the day they offer it, but
anything left over may be eaten
on the next day. 17 Any meat of the
sacrifice left over till the third day
must be burned up. 18 If any meat
of the fellowship offering is eat-
en on the third day, the one who

[a] 7 Or *purification offering*; also in verse 37

offered it will not be accepted. It
will not be reckoned to their credit, for it has become impure; the
person who eats any of it will be
held responsible. Lev 19:5-8; Nu 18:27
19"'Meat that touches anything
ceremonially unclean must not be
eaten; it must be burned up. As for
other meat, anyone ceremonially
clean may eat it. 20But if anyone
who is unclean eats any meat of
the fellowship offering belonging
to the LORD, they must be cut off
from their people. 21Anyone who
touches something unclean —
whether human uncleanness or
an unclean animal or any unclean
creature that moves along the
ground[a] — and then eats any of
the meat of the fellowship offering belonging to the LORD must
be cut off from their people.'"
Lev 22:3-7

Eating Fat and Blood Forbidden

22The LORD said to Moses, 23"Say
to the Israelites: 'Do not eat any
of the fat of cattle, sheep or goats.
24The fat of an animal found dead
or torn by wild animals may be
used for any other purpose, but
you must not eat it. 25Anyone who
eats the fat of an animal from
which a food offering may be[b]
presented to the LORD must be cut
off from their people. 26And wherever you live, you must not eat the
blood of any bird or animal. 27Any-
one who eats blood must be cut
off from their people.'"
Ge 9:4; Lev 17:10-24

The Priests' Share

28The LORD said to Moses, 29"Say
to the Israelites: 'Anyone who
brings a fellowship offering to the
LORD is to bring part of it as their
sacrifice to the LORD. 30With their
own hands they are to present the
food offering to the LORD; they are
to bring the fat, together with the
breast, and wave the breast before
the LORD as a wave offering. 31The
priest shall burn the fat on the altar, but the breast belongs to Aaron and his sons. 32You are to give
the right thigh of your fellowship
offerings to the priest as a contribution. 33The son of Aaron who
offers the blood and the fat of the
fellowship offering shall have the
right thigh as his share. 34From
the fellowship offerings of the Israelites, I have taken the breast
that is waved and the thigh that
is presented and have given them
to Aaron the priest and his sons as
their perpetual share from the Israelites.'" Ex 29:27; Nu 18:18-19
35This is the portion of the food
offerings presented to the LORD
that were allotted to Aaron and his
sons on the day they were presented to serve the LORD as priests.
36On the day they were anointed,
the LORD commanded that the Israelites give this to them as their
perpetual share for the generations to come. Lev 8:12,30

[a] 21 A few Hebrew manuscripts, Samaritan Pentateuch, Syriac and Targum (see 5:2); most Hebrew manuscripts *any unclean, detestable thing* [b] 25 Or *offering is*

37These, then, are the regulations for the burnt offering, the
grain offering, the sin offering,
the guilt offering, the ordination
offering and the fellowship offering, 38which the LORD gave Moses
at Mount Sinai in the Desert of Sinai on the day he commanded the
Israelites to bring their offerings
to the LORD. Lev 1:2; 6:9

The Ordination of Aaron and His Sons

8 The LORD said to Moses,
2"Bring Aaron and his sons,
their garments, the anointing oil,
the bull for the sin offering,[a] the
two rams and the basket containing bread made without yeast,
3and gather the entire assembly at the entrance to the tent of
meeting." 4Moses did as the LORD
commanded him, and the assembly gathered at the entrance to the
tent of meeting. Ex 29:2-3; 30:23-25,30
5Moses said to the assembly,
"This is what the LORD has commanded to be done." 6Then Moses
brought Aaron and his sons forward and washed them with water. 7He put the tunic on Aaron,
tied the sash around him, clothed
him with the robe and put the
ephod on him. He also fastened
the ephod with a decorative waistband, which he tied around him.
8He placed the breastpiece on
him and put the Urim and Thummim in the breastpiece. 9Then he
placed the turban on Aaron's head
and set the gold plate, the sacred
emblem, on the front of it, as the
LORD commanded Moses.
Ex 28:30,36; Ac 22:16
10Then Moses took the anointing oil and anointed the tabernacle and everything in it, and so
consecrated them. 11He sprinkled
some of the oil on the altar sev-
en times, anointing the altar and
all its utensils and the basin with
its stand, to consecrate them. 12He
poured some of the anointing
oil on Aaron's head and anointed him to consecrate him. 13Then
he brought Aaron's sons forward,
put tunics on them, tied sashes
around them and fastened caps
on them, as the LORD commanded Moses. Ex 30:26,30
14He then presented the bull for
the sin offering, and Aaron and his
sons laid their hands on its head.
15Moses slaughtered the bull and
took some of the blood, and with
his finger he put it on all the horns
of the altar to purify the altar. He
poured out the rest of the blood at
the base of the altar. So he consecrated it to make atonement for it.
16Moses also took all the fat around
the internal organs, the long lobe
of the liver, and both kidneys and
their fat, and burned it on the altar.
17But the bull with its hide and its
flesh and its intestines he burned
up outside the camp, as the LORD
commanded Moses. Ps 66:15; Heb 9:22
18He then presented the ram for
the burnt offering, and Aaron and

[a] 2 Or *purification offering*; also in verse 14

his sons laid their hands on its head.
19Then Moses slaughtered the ram
and splashed the blood against the
sides of the altar. 20He cut the ram
into pieces and burned the head,
the pieces and the fat. 21He washed
the internal organs and the legs
with water and burned the whole
ram on the altar. It was a burnt offering, a pleasing aroma, a food
offering presented to the LORD, as
the LORD commanded Moses.

22He then presented the other
ram, the ram for the ordination,
and Aaron and his sons laid their
hands on its head. 23Moses slaughtered the ram and took some of
its blood and put it on the lobe of
Aaron's right ear, on the thumb
of his right hand and on the big
toe of his right foot. 24Moses also
brought Aaron's sons forward and
put some of the blood on the lobes
of their right ears, on the thumbs
of their right hands and on the big
toes of their right feet. Then he
splashed blood against the sides of
the altar. 25After that, he took the
fat, the fat tail, all the fat around
the internal organs, the long lobe
of the liver, both kidneys and their
fat and the right thigh. 26And from
the basket of bread made without
yeast, which was before the LORD,
he took one thick loaf, one thick
loaf with olive oil mixed in, and
one thin loaf, and he put these on
the fat portions and on the right
thigh. 27He put all these in the
hands of Aaron and his sons, and
they waved them before the LORD
as a wave offering. 28Then Moses
took them from their hands and
burned them on the altar on top
of the burnt offering as an ordination offering, a pleasing aroma,
a food offering presented to the
LORD. 29Moses also took the breast,
which was his share of the ordination ram, and waved it before the
LORD as a wave offering, as the
LORD commanded Moses.
Lev 7:31-34; Heb 9:18-22

30Then Moses took some of the
anointing oil and some of the
blood from the altar and sprinkled them on Aaron and his garments and on his sons and their
garments. So he consecrated Aaron and his garments and his sons
and their garments. Nu 3:3

31Moses then said to Aaron and
his sons, "Cook the meat at the entrance to the tent of meeting and
eat it there with the bread from
the basket of ordination offerings, as I was commanded: 'Aaron
and his sons are to eat it.' 32Then
burn up the rest of the meat and
the bread. 33Do not leave the entrance to the tent of meeting for
seven days, until the days of your
ordination are completed, for your
ordination will last seven days.
34What has been done today was
commanded by the LORD to make
atonement for you. 35You must
stay at the entrance to the tent of
meeting day and night for seven
days and do what the LORD requires, so you will not die; for that
is what I have been commanded."

36 So Aaron and his sons did everything the LORD commanded
through Moses. Ex 29:1-37; Dt 11:1

The Priests Begin Their Ministry

9 On the eighth day Moses summoned Aaron and his sons
and the elders of Israel. 2 He said
to Aaron, "Take a bull calf for your
sin offering[a] and a ram for your
burnt offering, both without defect, and present them before the
LORD. 3 Then say to the Israelites:
'Take a male goat for a sin offering, a calf and a lamb — both a
year old and without defect — for
a burnt offering, 4 and an ox[b] and
a ram for a fellowship offering to
sacrifice before the LORD, together
with a grain offering mixed with
olive oil. For today the LORD will
appear to you.'" Ex 29:43; Eze 43:27

5 They took the things Moses
commanded to the front of the
tent of meeting, and the entire assembly came near and stood before the LORD. 6 Then Moses said,
"This is what the LORD has commanded you to do, so that the glory of the LORD may appear to you."
Ex 24:16

7 Moses said to Aaron, "Come to
the altar and sacrifice your sin offering and your burnt offering and
make atonement for yourself and
the people; sacrifice the offering
that is for the people and make
atonement for them, as the LORD
has commanded." Heb 5:1,3; 7:27

8 So Aaron came to the altar and
slaughtered the calf as a sin offering for himself. 9 His sons brought
the blood to him, and he dipped
his finger into the blood and put
it on the horns of the altar; the
rest of the blood he poured out at
the base of the altar. 10 On the altar he burned the fat, the kidneys
and the long lobe of the liver from
the sin offering, as the LORD commanded Moses; 11 the flesh and the
hide he burned up outside the
camp. Lev 4:1-12

12 Then he slaughtered the burnt
offering. His sons handed him the
blood, and he splashed it against
the sides of the altar. 13 They handed him the burnt offering piece
by piece, including the head, and
he burned them on the altar. 14 He
washed the internal organs and the
legs and burned them on top of the
burnt offering on the altar. Lev 1:8

15 Aaron then brought the offering that was for the people. He
took the goat for the people's sin
offering and slaughtered it and offered it for a sin offering as he did
with the first one. Lev 4:27-31

16 He brought the burnt offering
and offered it in the prescribed
way. 17 He also brought the grain
offering, took a handful of it and
burned it on the altar in addition
to the morning's burnt offering.
Lev 1:1-13; 2:1-2

18 He slaughtered the ox and the
ram as the fellowship offering

[a] 2 Or *purification offering*; here and throughout this chapter [b] 4 The Hebrew word can refer to either male or female; also in verses 18 and 19.

for the people. His sons handed
him the blood, and he splashed it
against the sides of the altar. 19But
the fat portions of the ox and the
ram — the fat tail, the layer of fat,
the kidneys and the long lobe of
the liver — 20these they laid on the
breasts, and then Aaron burned
the fat on the altar. 21Aaron waved
the breasts and the right thigh before the LORD as a wave offering,
as Moses commanded.

Lev 3:1-11; 7:30-34

22Then Aaron lifted his hands
toward the people and blessed
them. And having sacrificed the
sin offering, the burnt offering
and the fellowship offering, he
stepped down. Nu 6:23; Lk 24:50

23Moses and Aaron then went
into the tent of meeting. When
they came out, they blessed the
people; and the glory of the LORD
appeared to all the people. 24Fire
came out from the presence of the
LORD and consumed the burnt offering and the fat portions on the
altar. And when all the people saw
it, they shouted for joy and fell
facedown. 1Ki 18:39

The Death of Nadab and Abihu

10 Aaron's sons Nadab and Abihu took their censers, put
fire in them and added incense;
and they offered unauthorized
fire before the LORD, contrary to
his command. 2So fire came out
from the presence of the LORD and
consumed them, and they died
before the LORD. 3Moses then said
to Aaron, "This is what the LORD
spoke of when he said:

Lev 16:12; Nu 3:2-4

"'Among those who
approach me
I will be proved holy;
Ex 30:29; Eze 28:22
in the sight of all the people
I will be honored.'" Isa 49:3

Aaron remained silent.

4Moses summoned Mishael and
Elzaphan, sons of Aaron's uncle
Uzziel, and said to them, "Come
here; carry your cousins outside
the camp, away from the front of
the sanctuary." 5So they came and
carried them, still in their tunics,
outside the camp, as Moses ordered. Ex 6:22

6Then Moses said to Aaron
and his sons Eleazar and Ithamar, "Do not let your hair become
unkempt[a] and do not tear your
clothes, or you will die and the
LORD will be angry with the whole
community. But your relatives,
all the Israelites, may mourn for
those the LORD has destroyed by
fire. 7Do not leave the entrance to
the tent of meeting or you will die,
because the LORD's anointing oil is
on you." So they did as Moses said.

Nu 16:22; Jos 7:1

8Then the LORD said to Aaron,
9"You and your sons are not to
drink wine or other fermented
drink whenever you go into the
tent of meeting, or you will die.
This is a lasting ordinance for the

[a] 6 Or *Do not uncover your heads*

generations to come, 10so that you
can distinguish between the holy
and the common, between the unclean and the clean, 11and so you
can teach the Israelites all the decrees the LORD has given them
through Moses." Lev 20:25; Eze 44:21

12Moses said to Aaron and his
remaining sons, Eleazar and Ithamar, "Take the grain offering
left over from the food offerings
prepared without yeast and presented to the LORD and eat it beside the altar, for it is most holy.
13Eat it in the sanctuary area, because it is your share and your
sons' share of the food offerings
presented to the LORD; for so I
have been commanded. 14But you
and your sons and your daughters
may eat the breast that was waved
and the thigh that was presented.
Eat them in a ceremonially clean
place; they have been given to you
and your children as your share
of the Israelites' fellowship offerings. 15The thigh that was presented and the breast that was waved
must be brought with the fat portions of the food offerings, to be
waved before the LORD as a wave
offering. This will be the perpetual
share for you and your children, as
the LORD has commanded."
Lev 6:14-18; 7:34

16When Moses inquired about
the goat of the sin offering[a] and
found that it had been burned up,
he was angry with Eleazar and Ithamar, Aaron's remaining sons, and
asked, 17"Why didn't you eat the
sin offering in the sanctuary area?
It is most holy; it was given to you
to take away the guilt of the community by making atonement for
them before the LORD. 18Since its
blood was not taken into the Holy
Place, you should have eaten the
goat in the sanctuary area, as I
commanded." Lev 6:26,30; 9:3

19Aaron replied to Moses, "Today they sacrificed their sin offering and their burnt offering before the LORD, but such things as
this have happened to me. Would
the LORD have been pleased if I
had eaten the sin offering today?"
20When Moses heard this, he was
satisfied. Lev 9:12

Clean and Unclean Food

11 The LORD said to Moses and
Aaron, 2"Say to the Israelites:
'Of all the animals that live on
land, these are the ones you may
eat: 3You may eat any animal that
has a divided hoof and that chews
the cud. Ac 10:12-14

4" 'There are some that only
chew the cud or only have a divided hoof, but you must not eat
them. The camel, though it chews
the cud, does not have a divided
hoof; it is ceremonially unclean
for you. 5The hyrax, though it
chews the cud, does not have a divided hoof; it is unclean for you.
6The rabbit, though it chews the
cud, does not have a divided hoof;
it is unclean for you. 7And the pig,

[a] 16 Or *purification offering*; also in verses 17 and 19

though it has a divided hoof, does
not chew the cud; it is unclean for
you. 8You must not eat their meat
or touch their carcasses; they are
unclean for you. Isa 65:4; Heb 9:10

9" 'Of all the creatures living
in the water of the seas and the
streams you may eat any that have
fins and scales. 10But all creatures
in the seas or streams that do not
have fins and scales — whether
among all the swarming things or
among all the other living creatures in the water — you are to regard as unclean. 11And since you
are to regard them as unclean, you
must not eat their meat; you must
regard their carcasses as unclean.
12Anything living in the water that
does not have fins and scales is to
be regarded as unclean by you.
Lev 7:18

13" 'These are the birds you are
to regard as unclean and not eat
because they are unclean: the eagle,[a] the vulture, the black vulture, 14the red kite, any kind of
black kite, 15any kind of raven,
16the horned owl, the screech owl,
the gull, any kind of hawk, 17the
little owl, the cormorant, the great
owl, 18the white owl, the desert
owl, the osprey, 19the stork, any
kind of heron, the hoopoe and the
bat.

20" 'All flying insects that walk
on all fours are to be regarded as
unclean by you. 21There are, however, some flying insects that walk
on all fours that you may eat:
those that have jointed legs for
hopping on the ground. 22Of these
you may eat any kind of locust,
katydid, cricket or grasshopper.
23But all other flying insects that
have four legs you are to regard as
unclean. Dt 14:3-20; Mt 3:4

24" 'You will make yourselves
unclean by these; whoever touches their carcasses will be unclean
till evening. 25Whoever picks up
one of their carcasses must wash
their clothes, and they will be unclean till evening.
Lev 14:8,47; 15:5; Nu 31:24

26" 'Every animal that does not
have a divided hoof or that does
not chew the cud is unclean for
you; whoever touches the carcass
of any of them will be unclean.
27Of all the animals that walk on
all fours, those that walk on their
paws are unclean for you; whoever touches their carcasses will
be unclean till evening. 28Anyone
who picks up their carcasses must
wash their clothes, and they will
be unclean till evening. These animals are unclean for you.

29" 'Of the animals that move
along the ground, these are unclean for you: the weasel, the rat,
any kind of great lizard, 30the
gecko, the monitor lizard, the wall
lizard, the skink and the chame-
leon. 31Of all those that move along
the ground, these are unclean for
you. Whoever touches them when
they are dead will be unclean till

[a] *13* The precise identification of some of the birds, insects and animals in this chapter is uncertain.

evening. 32When one of them dies
and falls on something, that article, whatever its use, will be unclean, whether it is made of wood,
cloth, hide or sackcloth. Put it in
water; it will be unclean till evening, and then it will be clean. 33If
one of them falls into a clay pot,
everything in it will be unclean,
and you must break the pot. 34Any
food you are allowed to eat that
has come into contact with water
from any such pot is unclean, and
any liquid that is drunk from such
a pot is unclean. 35Anything that
one of their carcasses falls on becomes unclean; an oven or cooking pot must be broken up. They
are unclean, and you are to regard
them as unclean. 36A spring, however, or a cistern for collecting water remains clean, but anyone who
touches one of these carcasses is
unclean. 37If a carcass falls on any
seeds that are to be planted, they
remain clean. 38But if water has
been put on the seed and a carcass
falls on it, it is unclean for you.

Lev 15:12

39" 'If an animal that you are
allowed to eat dies, anyone who
touches its carcass will be unclean
till evening. 40Anyone who eats
some of its carcass must wash
their clothes, and they will be unclean till evening. Anyone who
picks up the carcass must wash
their clothes, and they will be unclean till evening. Lev 17:15; 22:8

41" 'Every creature that moves
along the ground is to be regarded as unclean; it is not to be eat-
en. 42You are not to eat any creature that moves along the ground,
whether it moves on its belly or
walks on all fours or on many
feet; it is unclean. 43Do not defile
yourselves by any of these creatures. Do not make yourselves
unclean by means of them or be
made unclean by them. 44I am the
LORD your God; consecrate yourselves and be holy, because I am
holy. Do not make yourselves unclean by any creature that moves
along the ground. 45I am the LORD,
who brought you up out of Egypt
to be your God; therefore be holy,
because I am holy.

Ex 19:6; Lev 19:2; 1Pe 1:16

46" 'These are the regulations
concerning animals, birds, every
living thing that moves about in
the water and every creature that
moves along the ground. 47You
must distinguish between the unclean and the clean, between living creatures that may be eaten
and those that may not be eaten.' "

Lev 10:10

Purification After Childbirth

12 The LORD said to Moses, 2"Say
to the Israelites: 'A woman
who becomes pregnant and gives
birth to a son will be ceremonially unclean for seven days, just as
she is unclean during her monthly period. 3On the eighth day the
boy is to be circumcised. 4Then
the woman must wait thirty-
three days to be purified from her

bleeding. She must not touch anything sacred or go to the sanctuary
until the days of her purification
are over. 5If she gives birth to a
daughter, for two weeks the woman will be unclean, as during her
period. Then she must wait sixty-
six days to be purified from her
bleeding. Ge 17:12; Lk 1:59

6"'When the days of her purification for a son or daughter are
over, she is to bring to the priest at
the entrance to the tent of meeting
a year-old lamb for a burnt offering and a young pigeon or a dove
for a sin offering.[a] 7He shall offer
them before the LORD to make
atonement for her, and then she
will be ceremonially clean from
her flow of blood.

"'These are the regulations for
the woman who gives birth to a
boy or a girl. 8But if she cannot
afford a lamb, she is to bring two
doves or two young pigeons, one
for a burnt offering and the other
for a sin offering. In this way the
priest will make atonement for
her, and she will be clean.'"

Lev 4:26; 5:7; Lk 2:22-24

Regulations About Defiling Skin Diseases

13 The LORD said to Moses and
Aaron, 2"When anyone has a
swelling or a rash or a shiny spot
on their skin that may be a defiling skin disease,[b] they must be
brought to Aaron the priest or to
one of his sons[c] who is a priest.
3The priest is to examine the sore
on the skin, and if the hair in the
sore has turned white and the
sore appears to be more than skin
deep, it is a defiling skin disease.
When the priest examines that
person, he shall pronounce them
ceremonially unclean. 4If the
shiny spot on the skin is white but
does not appear to be more than
skin deep and the hair in it has
not turned white, the priest is to
isolate the affected person for sev-
en days. 5On the seventh day the
priest is to examine them, and if
he sees that the sore is unchanged
and has not spread in the skin, he
is to isolate them for another sev-
en days. 6On the seventh day the
priest is to examine them again,
and if the sore has faded and has
not spread in the skin, the priest
shall pronounce them clean; it is
only a rash. They must wash their
clothes, and they will be clean.
7But if the rash does spread in
their skin after they have shown
themselves to the priest to be pronounced clean, they must appear
before the priest again. 8The priest
is to examine that person, and if
the rash has spread in the skin, he
shall pronounce them unclean; it
is a defiling skin disease.

Lev 11:25; Dt 24:8

9"When anyone has a defiling skin disease, they must be

[a] 6 Or *purification offering*; also in verse 8
[b] 2 The Hebrew word for *defiling skin disease*, traditionally translated "leprosy," was used for various diseases affecting the skin; here and throughout verses 3-46.
[c] 2 Or *descendants*

brought to the priest. [10]The priest
is to examine them, and if there is
a white swelling in the skin that
has turned the hair white and if
there is raw flesh in the swelling,
[11]it is a chronic skin disease and
the priest shall pronounce them
unclean. He is not to isolate them,
because they are already unclean.
Lev 14:8; Nu 12:10

[12]"If the disease breaks out all
over their skin and, so far as the
priest can see, it covers all the skin
of the affected person from head
to foot, [13]the priest is to examine
them, and if the disease has covered their whole body, he shall
pronounce them clean. Since it has
all turned white, they are clean.
[14]But whenever raw flesh appears
on them, they will be unclean.
[15]When the priest sees the raw
flesh, he shall pronounce them
unclean. The raw flesh is unclean;
they have a defiling disease. [16]If
the raw flesh changes and turns
white, they must go to the priest.
[17]The priest is to examine them,
and if the sores have turned white,
the priest shall pronounce the affected person clean; then they will
be clean. ver 2,6

[18]"When someone has a boil on
their skin and it heals, [19]and in the
place where the boil was, a white
swelling or reddish-white spot appears, they must present themselves to the priest. [20]The priest
is to examine it, and if it appears
to be more than skin deep and
the hair in it has turned white,
the priest shall pronounce that
person unclean. It is a defiling
skin disease that has broken out
where the boil was. [21]But if, when
the priest examines it, there is no
white hair in it and it is not more
than skin deep and has faded,
then the priest is to isolate them
for seven days. [22]If it is spreading
in the skin, the priest shall pronounce them unclean; it is a defiling disease. [23]But if the spot is
unchanged and has not spread, it
is only a scar from the boil, and
the priest shall pronounce them
clean. Ex 9:9; Lev 14:37

[24]"When someone has a burn
on their skin and a reddish-white
or white spot appears in the raw
flesh of the burn, [25]the priest is to
examine the spot, and if the hair
in it has turned white, and it appears to be more than skin deep,
it is a defiling disease that has
broken out in the burn. The priest
shall pronounce them unclean; it
is a defiling skin disease. [26]But if
the priest examines it and there
is no white hair in the spot and if
it is not more than skin deep and
has faded, then the priest is to isolate them for seven days. [27]On the
seventh day the priest is to examine that person, and if it is spreading in the skin, the priest shall
pronounce them unclean; it is a
defiling skin disease. [28]If, however, the spot is unchanged and has
not spread in the skin but has faded, it is a swelling from the burn,
and the priest shall pronounce

them clean; it is only a scar from
the burn. ver 4-5
29“If a man or woman has a sore
on their head or chin, 30the priest
is to examine the sore, and if it appears to be more than skin deep
and the hair in it is yellow and
thin, the priest shall pronounce
them unclean; it is a defiling skin
disease on the head or chin. 31But
if, when the priest examines the
sore, it does not seem to be more
than skin deep and there is no
black hair in it, then the priest is
to isolate the affected person for
seven days. 32On the seventh day
the priest is to examine the sore,
and if it has not spread and there
is no yellow hair in it and it does
not appear to be more than skin
deep, 33then the man or woman
must shave themselves, except for
the affected area, and the priest is
to keep them isolated another sev-
en days. 34On the seventh day the
priest is to examine the sore, and
if it has not spread in the skin and
appears to be no more than skin
deep, the priest shall pronounce
them clean. They must wash their
clothes, and they will be clean.
35But if the sore does spread in the
skin after they are pronounced
clean, 36the priest is to examine
them, and if he finds that the sore
has spread in the skin, he does
not need to look for yellow hair;
they are unclean. 37If, however,
the sore is unchanged so far as the
priest can see, and if black hair
has grown in it, the affected person is healed. They are clean, and
the priest shall pronounce them
clean. Lev 11:25
38“When a man or woman has
white spots on the skin, 39the
priest is to examine them, and
if the spots are dull white, it is a
harmless rash that has broken out
on the skin; they are clean.
40“A man who has lost his hair
and is bald is clean. 41If he has
lost his hair from the front of his
scalp and has a bald forehead,
he is clean. 42But if he has a reddish-white sore on his bald head
or forehead, it is a defiling disease
breaking out on his head or forehead. 43The priest is to examine
him, and if the swollen sore on his
head or forehead is reddish-white
like a defiling skin disease, 44the
man is diseased and is unclean.
The priest shall pronounce him
unclean because of the sore on his
head. 2Ki 2:23; Eze 29:18
45“Anyone with such a defiling
disease must wear torn clothes,
let their hair be unkempt,[a] cover the lower part of their face and
cry out, ‘Unclean! Unclean!’ 46As
long as they have the disease they
remain unclean. They must live
alone; they must live outside the
camp. Nu 5:1-4; La 4:15; Lk 17:12

Regulations About Defiling Molds

47“As for any fabric that is spoiled
with a defiling mold — any wool-
en or linen clothing, 48any woven or knitted material of linen

[a] 45 Or *clothes, uncover their head*

or wool, any leather or anything made of leather — 49if the affected area in the fabric, the leather, the woven or knitted material, or any leather article, is greenish or reddish, it is a defiling mold and must be shown to the priest. 50The priest is to examine the affected area and isolate the article for seven days. 51On the seventh day he is to examine it, and if the mold has spread in the fabric, the woven or knitted material, or the leather, whatever its use, it is a persistent defiling mold; the article is unclean. 52He must burn the fabric, the woven or knitted material of wool or linen, or any leather article that has been spoiled; because the defiling mold is persistent, the article must be burned.

Mk 1:44; Lev 14:44

53"But if, when the priest examines it, the mold has not spread in the fabric, the woven or knitted material, or the leather article, 54he shall order that the spoiled article be washed. Then he is to isolate it for another seven days. 55After the article has been washed, the priest is to examine it again, and if the mold has not changed its appearance, even though it has not spread, it is unclean. Burn it, no matter which side of the fabric has been spoiled. 56If, when the priest examines it, the mold has faded after the article has been washed, he is to tear the spoiled part out of the fabric, the leather, or the woven or knitted material. 57But if it reappears in the fabric, in the woven or knitted material, or in the leather article, it is a spreading mold; whatever has the mold must be burned. 58Any fabric, woven or knitted material, or any leather article that has been washed and is rid of the mold, must be washed again. Then it will be clean."

59These are the regulations concerning defiling molds in woolen or linen clothing, woven or knitted material, or any leather article, for pronouncing them clean or unclean.

Cleansing From Defiling Skin Diseases

14 The LORD said to Moses, 2"These are the regulations for any diseased person at the time of their ceremonial cleansing, when they are brought to the priest: 3The priest is to go outside the camp and examine them. If they have been healed of their defiling skin disease,[a] 4the priest shall order that two live clean birds and some cedar wood, scarlet yarn and hyssop be brought for the person to be cleansed. 5Then the priest shall order that one of the birds be killed over fresh water in a clay pot. 6He is then to take the live bird and dip it, together with the cedar wood,

[a] 3 The Hebrew word for *defiling skin disease*, traditionally translated "leprosy," was used for various diseases affecting the skin; also in verses 7, 32, 54 and 57.

the scarlet yarn and the hyssop,
into the blood of the bird that was
killed over the fresh water. 7Sev-
en times he shall sprinkle the one
to be cleansed of the defiling disease, and then pronounce them
clean. After that, he is to release
the live bird in the open fields.
Mt 8:2-4; Nu 19:6; 2Ki 5:10,14

8"The person to be cleansed
must wash their clothes, shave off
all their hair and bathe with water; then they will be ceremonially clean. After this they may come
into the camp, but they must stay
outside their tent for seven days.
9On the seventh day they must
shave off all their hair; they must
shave their head, their beard,
their eyebrows and the rest of
their hair. They must wash their
clothes and bathe themselves
with water, and they will be clean.
Lev 11:25; 13:6

10"On the eighth day they must
bring two male lambs and one
ewe lamb a year old, each without
defect, along with three-tenths
of an ephah[a] of the finest flour
mixed with olive oil for a grain
offering, and one log[b] of oil. 11The
priest who pronounces them
clean shall present both the one
to be cleansed and their offerings
before the LORD at the entrance to
the tent of meeting. Mt 8:4

12"Then the priest is to take one
of the male lambs and offer it as
a guilt offering, along with the
log of oil; he shall wave them before the LORD as a wave offering.
13He is to slaughter the lamb in
the sanctuary area where the sin
offering[c] and the burnt offering
are slaughtered. Like the sin offering, the guilt offering belongs
to the priest; it is most holy. 14The
priest is to take some of the blood
of the guilt offering and put it on
the lobe of the right ear of the
one to be cleansed, on the thumb
of their right hand and on the big
toe of their right foot. 15The priest
shall then take some of the log of
oil, pour it in the palm of his own
left hand, 16dip his right forefinger into the oil in his palm, and
with his finger sprinkle some of
it before the LORD seven times.
17The priest is to put some of the
oil remaining in his palm on the
lobe of the right ear of the one
to be cleansed, on the thumb of
their right hand and on the big
toe of their right foot, on top of
the blood of the guilt offering.
18The rest of the oil in his palm
the priest shall put on the head of
the one to be cleansed and make
atonement for them before the
LORD. Ex 29:11; Lev 5:18

19"Then the priest is to sacrifice
the sin offering and make atonement for the one to be cleansed
from their uncleanness. After
that, the priest shall slaughter the
burnt offering 20and offer it on
the altar, together with the grain

[a] *10* That is, probably about 11 pounds or about 5 kilograms [b] *10* That is, about 1/3 quart or about 0.3 liter; also in verses 12, 15, 21 and 24 [c] *13* Or *purification offering*; also in verses 19, 22 and 31

offering, and make atonement for
them, and they will be clean.
21“If, however, they are poor and
cannot afford these, they must
take one male lamb as a guilt offering to be waved to make atonement for them, together with a
tenth of an ephah[a] of the finest
flour mixed with olive oil for a
grain offering, a log of oil, 22and
two doves or two young pigeons,
such as they can afford, one for
a sin offering and the other for a
burnt offering. Lev 5:7; 12:8
23“On the eighth day they must
bring them for their cleansing to
the priest at the entrance to the
tent of meeting, before the LORD.
24The priest is to take the lamb for
the guilt offering, together with
the log of oil, and wave them before the LORD as a wave offering.
25He shall slaughter the lamb for
the guilt offering and take some
of its blood and put it on the lobe
of the right ear of the one to be
cleansed, on the thumb of their
right hand and on the big toe of
their right foot. 26The priest is
to pour some of the oil into the
palm of his own left hand, 27and
with his right forefinger sprinkle
some of the oil from his palm sev-
en times before the LORD. 28Some
of the oil in his palm he is to put
on the same places he put the
blood of the guilt offering — on
the lobe of the right ear of the
one to be cleansed, on the thumb
of their right hand and on the big
toe of their right foot. 29The rest
of the oil in his palm the priest
shall put on the head of the one
to be cleansed, to make atonement for them before the LORD.
30Then he shall sacrifice the doves
or the young pigeons, such as the
person can afford, 31one as a sin
offering and the other as a burnt
offering, together with the grain
offering. In this way the priest
will make atonement before the
LORD on behalf of the one to be
cleansed.”
32These are the regulations for
anyone who has a defiling skin
disease and who cannot afford
the regular offerings for their
cleansing. Lev 5:7; 13:2; Nu 6:14

Cleansing From Defiling Molds

33The LORD said to Moses and
Aaron, 34“When you enter the
land of Canaan, which I am giving you as your possession, and I
put a spreading mold in a house in
that land, 35the owner of the house
must go and tell the priest, ‘I have
seen something that looks like a
defiling mold in my house.’ 36The
priest is to order the house to be
emptied before he goes in to examine the mold, so that nothing
in the house will be pronounced
unclean. After this the priest is to
go in and inspect the house. 37He
is to examine the mold on the
walls, and if it has greenish or reddish depressions that appear to
be deeper than the surface of the

[a] *21* That is, probably about 3 1/2 pounds or about 1.6 kilograms

wall, 38the priest shall go out the
doorway of the house and close
it up for seven days. 39On the seventh day the priest shall return to
inspect the house. If the mold has
spread on the walls, 40he is to order that the contaminated stones
be torn out and thrown into an
unclean place outside the town.
41He must have all the inside walls
of the house scraped and the material that is scraped off dumped
into an unclean place outside the
town. 42Then they are to take other stones to replace these and take
new clay and plaster the house.

Ge 17:8; Nu 32:22

43"If the defiling mold reappears in the house after the stones
have been torn out and the house
scraped and plastered, 44the priest
is to go and examine it and, if the
mold has spread in the house, it
is a persistent defiling mold; the
house is unclean. 45It must be torn
down — its stones, timbers and all
the plaster — and taken out of the
town to an unclean place. Lev 13:51

46"Anyone who goes into the
house while it is closed up will
be unclean till evening. 47Anyone
who sleeps or eats in the house
must wash their clothes. Lev 11:24-25

48"But if the priest comes to examine it and the mold has not
spread after the house has been
plastered, he shall pronounce the
house clean, because the defiling mold is gone. 49To purify the
house he is to take two birds and
some cedar wood, scarlet yarn and
hyssop. 50He shall kill one of the
birds over fresh water in a clay
pot. 51Then he is to take the cedar wood, the hyssop, the scarlet
yarn and the live bird, dip them
into the blood of the dead bird
and the fresh water, and sprinkle
the house seven times. 52He shall
purify the house with the bird's
blood, the fresh water, the live
bird, the cedar wood, the hyssop
and the scarlet yarn. 53Then he is
to release the live bird in the open
fields outside the town. In this
way he will make atonement for
the house, and it will be clean."

Lev 13:6; Ps 51:7

54These are the regulations for
any defiling skin disease, for a
sore, 55for defiling molds in fabric
or in a house, 56and for a swelling,
a rash or a shiny spot, 57to determine when something is clean or
unclean. Lev 13:2,47-52

These are the regulations for
defiling skin diseases and defiling
molds. Lev 10:10

Discharges Causing Uncleanness

15 The LORD said to Moses and
Aaron, 2"Speak to the Is-
raelites and say to them: 'When
any man has an unusual bodily
discharge, such a discharge is unclean. 3Whether it continues flowing from his body or is blocked,
it will make him unclean. This is
how his discharge will bring about
uncleanness: Lev 22:4; Mt 9:20

4" 'Any bed the man with a discharge lies on will be unclean,

and anything he sits on will be
unclean. 5 Anyone who touches his
bed must wash their clothes and
bathe with water, and they will
be unclean till evening. 6 Whoever
sits on anything that the man with
a discharge sat on must wash their
clothes and bathe with water, and
they will be unclean till evening.
Lev 11:25; 14:8

7 " 'Whoever touches the man
who has a discharge must wash
their clothes and bathe with water, and they will be unclean till
evening. Lev 22:5

8 " 'If the man with the discharge
spits on anyone who is clean, they
must wash their clothes and bathe
with water, and they will be unclean till evening. Nu 12:14

9 " 'Everything the man sits on
when riding will be unclean, 10 and
whoever touches any of the things
that were under him will be unclean till evening; whoever picks
up those things must wash their
clothes and bathe with water, and
they will be unclean till evening.
Nu 19:10

11 " 'Anyone the man with a discharge touches without rinsing
his hands with water must wash
their clothes and bathe with water, and they will be unclean till
evening.

12 " 'A clay pot that the man
touches must be broken, and any
wooden article is to be rinsed with
water. Lev 6:28

13 " 'When a man is cleansed
from his discharge, he is to count
off seven days for his ceremonial cleansing; he must wash his
clothes and bathe himself with
fresh water, and he will be clean.
14 On the eighth day he must take
two doves or two young pigeons
and come before the LORD to the
entrance to the tent of meeting
and give them to the priest. 15 The
priest is to sacrifice them, the one
for a sin offering[a] and the other
for a burnt offering. In this way
he will make atonement before
the LORD for the man because of
his discharge. Lev 8:33; 14:18-19

16 " 'When a man has an emission of semen, he must bathe his
whole body with water, and he
will be unclean till evening. 17 Any
clothing or leather that has semen
on it must be washed with water,
and it will be unclean till evening.
18 When a man has sexual relations
with a woman and there is an
emission of semen, both of them
must bathe with water, and they
will be unclean till evening.
Lev 22:4; Dt 23:10

19 " 'When a woman has her regular flow of blood, the impurity of
her monthly period will last sev-
en days, and anyone who touches
her will be unclean till evening.
Lev 12:2

20 " 'Anything she lies on during her period will be unclean,
and anything she sits on will be
unclean. 21 Anyone who touches her bed will be unclean; they
must wash their clothes and bathe

[a] 15 Or *purification offering;* also in verse 30

with water, and they will be unclean till evening. 22Anyone who
touches anything she sits on will
be unclean; they must wash their
clothes and bathe with water, and
they will be unclean till evening.
23Whether it is the bed or anything
she was sitting on, when anyone
touches it, they will be unclean till
evening.

24"'If a man has sexual relations
with her and her monthly flow
touches him, he will be unclean
for seven days; any bed he lies on
will be unclean. Lev 12:2; 18:19

25"'When a woman has a discharge of blood for many days at a
time other than her monthly period or has a discharge that continues beyond her period, she will be
unclean as long as she has the discharge, just as in the days of her
period. 26Any bed she lies on while
her discharge continues will be
unclean, as is her bed during her
monthly period, and anything she
sits on will be unclean, as during
her period. 27Anyone who touches
them will be unclean; they must
wash their clothes and bathe with
water, and they will be unclean till
evening. Mt 9:20

28"'When she is cleansed from
her discharge, she must count
off seven days, and after that she
will be ceremonially clean. 29On
the eighth day she must take two
doves or two young pigeons and
bring them to the priest at the
entrance to the tent of meeting.
30The priest is to sacrifice one for
a sin offering and the other for a
burnt offering. In this way he will
make atonement for her before
the LORD for the uncleanness of
her discharge. Lev 14:22

31"'You must keep the Israelites
separate from things that make
them unclean, so they will not
die in their uncleanness for defiling my dwelling place,[a] which
is among them.'"

Nu 19:13,20; Eze 5:11; 23:38

32These are the regulations for
a man with a discharge, for anyone made unclean by an emission
of semen, 33for a woman in her
monthly period, for a man or a
woman with a discharge, and for
a man who has sexual relations
with a woman who is ceremonially unclean. ver 2

The Day of Atonement

16 The LORD spoke to Moses after the death of the two sons
of Aaron who died when they approached the LORD. 2The LORD said
to Moses: "Tell your brother Aaron that he is not to come whenever he chooses into the Most Holy
Place behind the curtain in front
of the atonement cover on the ark,
or else he will die. For I will appear
in the cloud over the atonement
cover. Ex 25:22; Lev 10:1

3"This is how Aaron is to enter
the Most Holy Place: He must first
bring a young bull for a sin offering[b] and a ram for a burnt offering.

[a] 31 Or *my tabernacle* [b] 3 Or *purification offering*; here and throughout this chapter

4 He is to put on the sacred linen tunic, with linen undergarments next to his body; he is to tie the linen sash around him and put on the linen turban. These are sacred garments; so he must bathe himself with water before he puts them on. 5 From the Israelite community he is to take two male goats for a sin offering and a ram for a burnt offering. Lev 4:13-21; 2Ch 29:23

6 "Aaron is to offer the bull for his own sin offering to make atonement for himself and his household. 7 Then he is to take the two goats and present them before the LORD at the entrance to the tent of meeting. 8 He is to cast lots for the two goats — one lot for the LORD and the other for the scapegoat.[a] 9 Aaron shall bring the goat whose lot falls to the LORD and sacrifice it for a sin offering. 10 But the goat chosen by lot as the scapegoat shall be presented alive before the LORD to be used for making atonement by sending it into the wilderness as a scapegoat. Lev 9:7; Heb 7:27; 9:7,12

11 "Aaron shall bring the bull for his own sin offering to make atonement for himself and his household, and he is to slaughter the bull for his own sin offering. 12 He is to take a censer full of burning coals from the altar before the LORD and two handfuls of finely ground fragrant incense and take them behind the curtain. 13 He is to put the incense on the fire before the LORD, and the smoke of the incense will conceal the atonement cover above the tablets of the covenant law, so that he will not die. 14 He is to take some of the bull's blood and with his finger sprinkle it on the front of the atonement cover; then he shall sprinkle some of it with his finger seven times before the atonement cover. Lev 10:1; Heb 9:7,13,25

15 "He shall then slaughter the goat for the sin offering for the people and take its blood behind the curtain and do with it as he did with the bull's blood: He shall sprinkle it on the atonement cover and in front of it. 16 In this way he will make atonement for the Most Holy Place because of the uncleanness and rebellion of the Israelites, whatever their sins have been. He is to do the same for the tent of meeting, which is among them in the midst of their uncleanness. 17 No one is to be in the tent of meeting from the time Aaron goes in to make atonement in the Most Holy Place until he comes out, having made atonement for himself, his household and the whole community of Israel. Ex 29:36; Heb 9:7,12

18 "Then he shall come out to the altar that is before the LORD and make atonement for it. He shall take some of the bull's blood and some of the goat's blood and put it on all the horns of the altar. 19 He shall sprinkle some of the

[a] 8 The meaning of the Hebrew for this word is uncertain; also in verses 10 and 26.

blood on it with his finger seven
times to cleanse it and to consecrate it from the uncleanness of
the Israelites. Lev 4:7,25
20“When Aaron has finished
making atonement for the Most
Holy Place, the tent of meeting
and the altar, he shall bring forward the live goat. 21He is to lay
both hands on the head of the live
goat and confess over it all the
wickedness and rebellion of the
Israelites — all their sins — and
put them on the goat’s head. He
shall send the goat away into the
wilderness in the care of someone
appointed for the task. 22The goat
will carry on itself all their sins to
a remote place; and the man shall
release it in the wilderness.
Lev 5:5; Isa 53:12
23“Then Aaron is to go into the
tent of meeting and take off the
linen garments he put on before
he entered the Most Holy Place,
and he is to leave them there. 24He
shall bathe himself with water in
the sanctuary area and put on his
regular garments. Then he shall
come out and sacrifice the burnt
offering for himself and the burnt
offering for the people, to make
atonement for himself and for the
people. 25He shall also burn the fat
of the sin offering on the altar.
Eze 42:14; 44:19
26“The man who releases the
goat as a scapegoat must wash his
clothes and bathe himself with
water; afterward he may come
into the camp. 27The bull and the
goat for the sin offerings, whose
blood was brought into the Most
Holy Place to make atonement,
must be taken outside the camp;
their hides, flesh and intestines
are to be burned up. 28The man
who burns them must wash his
clothes and bathe himself with
water; afterward he may come
into the camp. Lev 11:25; Heb 13:11
29“This is to be a lasting ordinance for you: On the tenth day
of the seventh month you must
deny yourselves[a] and not do any
work — whether native-born or a
foreigner residing among you —
30because on this day atonement
will be made for you, to cleanse
you. Then, before the LORD, you
will be clean from all your sins.
31It is a day of sabbath rest, and
you must deny yourselves; it is
a lasting ordinance. 32The priest
who is anointed and ordained to
succeed his father as high priest
is to make atonement. He is to
put on the sacred linen garments
33and make atonement for the
Most Holy Place, for the tent of
meeting and the altar, and for the
priests and all the members of the
community. Nu 29:7; Eph 5:26
34“This is to be a lasting ordinance for you: Atonement is to be
made once a year for all the sins of
the Israelites.” Heb 9:7,25
And it was done, as the LORD
commanded Moses.
Lev 23:26-32; Nu 29:7-11

[a] *29* Or *must fast*; also in verse 31

Eating Blood Forbidden

17 The LORD said to Moses,
2“Speak to Aaron and his
sons and to all the Israelites and
say to them: ‘This is what the
LORD has commanded: 3Any Israelite who sacrifices an ox,[a] a lamb
or a goat in the camp or outside
of it 4instead of bringing it to the
entrance to the tent of meeting
to present it as an offering to the
LORD in front of the tabernacle of
the LORD — that person shall be
considered guilty of bloodshed;
they have shed blood and must be
cut off from their people. 5This is
so the Israelites will bring to the
LORD the sacrifices they are now
making in the open fields. They
must bring them to the priest,
that is, to the LORD, at the entrance
to the tent of meeting and sacrifice them as fellowship offerings.
6The priest is to splash the blood
against the altar of the LORD at
the entrance to the tent of meeting and burn the fat as an aroma
pleasing to the LORD. 7They must
no longer offer any of their sacrifices to the goat idols[b] to whom
they prostitute themselves. This is
to be a lasting ordinance for them
and for the generations to come.’
Ex 34:15; 1Co 10:20

8“Say to them: ‘Any Israelite
or any foreigner residing among
them who offers a burnt offering
or sacrifice 9and does not bring
it to the entrance to the tent of
meeting to sacrifice it to the LORD
must be cut off from the people of
Israel. Lev 1:3; 3:7

10“ ‘I will set my face against any
Israelite or any foreigner residing
among them who eats blood, and I
will cut them off from the people.
11For the life of a creature is in the
blood, and I have given it to you
to make atonement for yourselves
on the altar; it is the blood that
makes atonement for one’s life.[c]
12Therefore I say to the Israelites,
“None of you may eat blood, nor
may any foreigner residing among
you eat blood.” Ge 9:4; Heb 9:22

13“ ‘Any Israelite or any foreigner residing among you who hunts
any animal or bird that may be eat-
en must drain out the blood and
cover it with earth, 14because the
life of every creature is its blood.
That is why I have said to the Israelites, “You must not eat the blood
of any creature, because the life of
every creature is its blood; anyone
who eats it must be cut off.”
Ge 9:4; Dt 12:16

15“ ‘Anyone, whether native-
born or foreigner, who eats anything found dead or torn by wild
animals must wash their clothes
and bathe with water, and they
will be ceremonially unclean till
evening; then they will be clean.
16But if they do not wash their
clothes and bathe themselves,
they will be held responsible.’ ”
Ex 22:31; Dt 14:21

[a] 3 The Hebrew word can refer to either male or female. [b] 7 Or *the demons*
[c] 11 Or *atonement by the life in the blood*

Unlawful Sexual Relations

18 The LORD said to Moses, 2"Speak to the Israelites and say to them: 'I am the LORD your God. 3You must not do as they do in Egypt, where you used to live, and you must not do as they do in the land of Canaan, where I am bringing you. Do not follow their practices. 4You must obey my laws and be careful to follow my decrees. I am the LORD your God. 5Keep my decrees and laws, for the person who obeys them will live by them. I am the LORD.

Eze 20:11; Ro 10:5; Gal 3:12

6" 'No one is to approach any close relative to have sexual relations. I am the LORD.

7" 'Do not dishonor your father by having sexual relations with your mother. She is your mother; do not have relations with her.

Lev 20:11

8" 'Do not have sexual relations with your father's wife; that would dishonor your father. Lev 20:11; 1Co 5:1

9" 'Do not have sexual relations with your sister, either your father's daughter or your mother's daughter, whether she was born in the same home or elsewhere.

Lev 20:17

10" 'Do not have sexual relations with your son's daughter or your daughter's daughter; that would dishonor you.

11" 'Do not have sexual relations with the daughter of your father's wife, born to your father; she is your sister.

12" 'Do not have sexual relations with your father's sister; she is your father's close relative.

Lev 20:19

13" 'Do not have sexual relations with your mother's sister, because she is your mother's close relative.

14" 'Do not dishonor your father's brother by approaching his wife to have sexual relations; she is your aunt. Lev 20:20

15" 'Do not have sexual relations with your daughter-in-law. She is your son's wife; do not have relations with her. Lev 20:12

16" 'Do not have sexual relations with your brother's wife; that would dishonor your brother.

Lev 20:21

17" 'Do not have sexual relations with both a woman and her daughter. Do not have sexual relations with either her son's daughter or her daughter's daughter; they are her close relatives. That is wickedness. Lev 20:14

18" 'Do not take your wife's sister as a rival wife and have sexual relations with her while your wife is living.

19" 'Do not approach a woman to have sexual relations during the uncleanness of her monthly period. Lev 15:24

20" 'Do not have sexual relations with your neighbor's wife and defile yourself with her.

Ex 20:14; Mt 5:27-28

21" 'Do not give any of your children to be sacrificed to Molek, for

you must not profane the name of
your God. I am the LORD.
Lev 19:12; 20:2-5; Dt 12:31

22“ ‘Do not have sexual relations
with a man as one does with a
woman; that is detestable.
Lev 20;13; Ro 1:27

23“ ‘Do not have sexual relations
with an animal and defile yourself
with it. A woman must not present herself to an animal to have
sexual relations with it; that is a
perversion. Lev 20:15

24“ ‘Do not defile yourselves in
any of these ways, because this is
how the nations that I am going to
drive out before you became defiled. 25Even the land was defiled;
so I punished it for its sin, and the
land vomited out its inhabitants.
26But you must keep my decrees
and my laws. The native-born and
the foreigners residing among you
must not do any of these detestable things, 27for all these things
were done by the people who
lived in the land before you, and
the land became defiled. 28And if
you defile the land, it will vomit
you out as it vomited out the nations that were before you. Dt 18:12

29“ ‘Everyone who does any of
these detestable things — such
persons must be cut off from their
people. 30Keep my requirements
and do not follow any of the detestable customs that were practiced before you came and do not
defile yourselves with them. I am
the LORD your God.’ ” Dt 11:1

Various Laws

19 The LORD said to Moses,
2“Speak to the entire assembly of Israel and say to them: ‘Be
holy because I, the LORD your God,
am holy. Lev 11:44; 1Pe 1:16

3“ ‘Each of you must respect
your mother and father, and you
must observe my Sabbaths. I am
the LORD your God. Ex 20:12

4“ ‘Do not turn to idols or make
metal gods for yourselves. I am
the LORD your God. Ps 96:5

5“ ‘When you sacrifice a fellowship offering to the LORD, sacrifice
it in such a way that it will be accepted on your behalf. 6It shall be
eaten on the day you sacrifice it
or on the next day; anything left
over until the third day must be
burned up. 7If any of it is eaten on
the third day, it is impure and will
not be accepted. 8Whoever eats it
will be held responsible because
they have desecrated what is holy
to the LORD; they must be cut off
from their people. Lev 7:16-17

9“ ‘When you reap the harvest
of your land, do not reap to the
very edges of your field or gather the gleanings of your harvest.
10Do not go over your vineyard a
second time or pick up the grapes
that have fallen. Leave them for
the poor and the foreigner. I am
the LORD your God. Dt 24:19-22

11“ ‘Do not steal. Ex 20:15

“ ‘Do not lie. Eph 4:25

“ ‘Do not deceive one another.
Lev 6:2

[12]"'Do not swear falsely by my name and so profane the name of your God. I am the LORD.
Ex 20:7; Mt 5:33

[13]"'Do not defraud or rob your neighbor. Ex 22:15,25-27

"'Do not hold back the wages of a hired worker overnight.
Dt 24:15; Jas 5:4

[14]"'Do not curse the deaf or put a stumbling block in front of the blind, but fear your God. I am the LORD. Dt 27:18

[15]"'Do not pervert justice; do not show partiality to the poor or favoritism to the great, but judge your neighbor fairly. Ex 23:2,6; Dt 1:17

[16]"'Do not go about spreading slander among your people.
Ps 15:3; Eze 22:9

"'Do not do anything that endangers your neighbor's life. I am the LORD. Ex 23:7

[17]"'Do not hate a fellow Israelite in your heart. Rebuke your neighbor frankly so you will not share in their guilt. Jn 2:9; Mt 18:15

[18]"'Do not seek revenge or bear a grudge against anyone among your people, but love your neighbor as yourself. I am the LORD.
Mt 5:43; Gal 5:14; Ro 12:19

[19]"'Keep my decrees.

"'Do not mate different kinds of animals.

"'Do not plant your field with two kinds of seed.

"'Do not wear clothing woven of two kinds of material. Dt 22:9,11

[20]"'If a man sleeps with a female slave who is promised to another man but who has not been ransomed or given her freedom, there must be due punishment.[a]
Yet they are not to be put to death, because she had not been freed.
[21]The man, however, must bring a ram to the entrance to the tent of meeting for a guilt offering to the LORD. [22]With the ram of the guilt offering the priest is to make atonement for him before the LORD for the sin he has committed, and his sin will be forgiven. Lev 5:15

[23]"'When you enter the land and plant any kind of fruit tree, regard its fruit as forbidden.[b] For three years you are to consider it forbidden[b]; it must not be eaten. [24]In the fourth year all its fruit will be holy, an offering of praise to the LORD.
[25]But in the fifth year you may eat its fruit. In this way your harvest will be increased. I am the LORD your God. Pr 3:9

[26]"'Do not eat any meat with the blood still in it. Lev 17:10

"'Do not practice divination or seek omens. Dt 18:10

[27]"'Do not cut the hair at the sides of your head or clip off the edges of your beard. Lev 21:5

[28]"'Do not cut your bodies for the dead or put tattoo marks on yourselves. I am the LORD.

[29]"'Do not degrade your daughter by making her a prostitute, or the land will turn to prostitution and be filled with wickedness.
Dt 23:18

[a] 20 Or *be an inquiry* [b] 23 Hebrew *uncircumcised*

30“ ‘Observe my Sabbaths and
have reverence for my sanctuary.
I am the LORD. Lev 26:2
31“ ‘Do not turn to mediums or
seek out spiritists, for you will be
defiled by them. I am the LORD
your God. Lev 20:6; Isa 8:19
32“ ‘Stand up in the presence of
the aged, show respect for the elderly and revere your God. I am
the LORD. Job 32:4; 1Ti 5:1
33“ ‘When a foreigner resides
among you in your land, do not
mistreat them. 34The foreigner residing among you must be treated
as your native-born. Love them as
yourself, for you were foreigners
in Egypt. I am the LORD your God.
ver 18; Ex 12:48; Dt 10:19
35“ ‘Do not use dishonest standards when measuring length,
weight or quantity. 36Use honest scales and honest weights,
an honest ephah[a] and an honest
hin.[b] I am the LORD your God, who
brought you out of Egypt. Dt 25:13-15
37“ ‘Keep all my decrees and all
my laws and follow them. I am the
LORD.’ ” 2Ki 17:37

Punishments for Sin

20 The LORD said to Moses,
2“Say to the Israelites: ‘Any
Israelite or any foreigner residing
in Israel who sacrifices any of his
children to Molek is to be put to
death. The members of the community are to stone him. 3I myself
will set my face against him and
will cut him off from his people;
for by sacrificing his children to
Molek, he has defiled my sanctuary and profaned my holy name.
4If the members of the community close their eyes when that man
sacrifices one of his children to
Molek and if they fail to put him
to death, 5I myself will set my face
against him and his family and
will cut them off from their people together with all who follow
him in prostituting themselves to
Molek. Lev 18:21; Dt 17:2-5
6“ ‘I will set my face against anyone who turns to mediums and
spiritists to prostitute themselves
by following them, and I will cut
them off from their people. Lev 19:31
7“ ‘Consecrate yourselves and be
holy, because I am the LORD your
God. 8Keep my decrees and follow
them. I am the LORD, who makes
you holy. Eph 1:4; 1Pe 1:16
9“ ‘Anyone who curses their father or mother is to be put to
death. Because they have cursed
their father or mother, their blood
will be on their own head.
Ex 21:17; Dt 27:16
10“ ‘If a man commits adultery
with another man’s wife — with
the wife of his neighbor — both
the adulterer and the adulteress
are to be put to death. Ex 20:14
11“ ‘If a man has sexual relations
with his father’s wife, he has dishonored his father. Both the man
and the woman are to be put to

[a] 36 An ephah was a dry measure having the capacity of about 3/5 of a bushel or about 22 liters. [b] 36 A hin was a liquid measure having the capacity of about 1 gallon or about 3.8 liters.

death; their blood will be on their own heads. Lev 18:7

12“ ‘If a man has sexual relations with his daughter-in-law, both of them are to be put to death. What they have done is a perversion; their blood will be on their own heads. Lev 18:15

13“ ‘If a man has sexual relations with a man as one does with a woman, both of them have done what is detestable. They are to be put to death; their blood will be on their own heads. Lev 18:22

14“ ‘If a man marries both a woman and her mother, it is wicked. Both he and they must be burned in the fire, so that no wickedness will be among you. Dt 27:23

15“ ‘If a man has sexual relations with an animal, he is to be put to death, and you must kill the animal. Lev 18:23

16“ ‘If a woman approaches an animal to have sexual relations with it, kill both the woman and the animal. They are to be put to death; their blood will be on their own heads.

17“ ‘If a man marries his sister, the daughter of either his father or his mother, and they have sexual relations, it is a disgrace. They are to be publicly removed from their people. He has dishonored his sister and will be held responsible. Lev 18:9

18“ ‘If a man has sexual relations with a woman during her monthly period, he has exposed the source of her flow, and she has also uncovered it. Both of them are to be cut off from their people. Lev 15:24; 18:19

19“ ‘Do not have sexual relations with the sister of either your mother or your father, for that would dishonor a close relative; both of you would be held responsible. Lev 18:12-13

20“ ‘If a man has sexual relations with his aunt, he has dishonored his uncle. They will be held responsible; they will die childless. Lev 18:14

21“ ‘If a man marries his brother's wife, it is an act of impurity; he has dishonored his brother. They will be childless. Lev 18:16

22“ ‘Keep all my decrees and laws and follow them, so that the land where I am bringing you to live may not vomit you out. 23You must not live according to the customs of the nations I am going to drive out before you. Because they did all these things, I abhorred them. 24But I said to you, “You will possess their land; I will give it to you as an inheritance, a land flowing with milk and honey.” I am the Lord your God, who has set you apart from the nations. Ex 33:16; Lev 18:3,25-28

25“ ‘You must therefore make a distinction between clean and unclean animals and between unclean and clean birds. Do not defile yourselves by any animal or bird or anything that moves along the ground — those that I have set apart as unclean for you. 26You

are to be holy to me because I, the
LORD, am holy, and I have set you
apart from the nations to be my
own. Dt 14:3-21
27“ ‘A man or woman who is a
medium or spiritist among you
must be put to death. You are to
stone them; their blood will be on
their own heads.’ ” Lev 19:31

Rules for Priests

21 The LORD said to Moses,
“Speak to the priests, the
sons of Aaron, and say to them:
‘A priest must not make himself
ceremonially unclean for any of
his people who die, 2except for a
close relative, such as his mother
or father, his son or daughter, his
brother, 3or an unmarried sister
who is dependent on him since
she has no husband — for her he
may make himself unclean. 4He
must not make himself unclean
for people related to him by marriage,[a] and so defile himself.
Eze 44:25
5“ ‘Priests must not shave their
heads or shave off the edges of
their beards or cut their bodies.
6They must be holy to their God
and must not profane the name
of their God. Because they present
the food offerings to the LORD, the
food of their God, they are to be
holy. Lev 18:21; 19:28
7“ ‘They must not marry wom-
en defiled by prostitution or divorced from their husbands, because priests are holy to their God.
8Regard them as holy, because
they offer up the food of your God.
Consider them holy, because I the
LORD am holy — I who make you
holy. Eze 44:22
9“ ‘If a priest’s daughter defiles
herself by becoming a prostitute,
she disgraces her father; she must
be burned in the fire.
Ge 38:24; Lev 19:29
10“ ‘The high priest, the one
among his brothers who has had
the anointing oil poured on his
head and who has been ordained
to wear the priestly garments,
must not let his hair become unkempt[b] or tear his clothes. 11He
must not enter a place where
there is a dead body. He must not
make himself unclean, even for
his father or mother, 12nor leave
the sanctuary of his God or desecrate it, because he has been dedicated by the anointing oil of his
God. I am the LORD. Lev 10:6-7
13“ ‘The woman he marries must
be a virgin. 14He must not marry
a widow, a divorced woman, or a
woman defiled by prostitution,
but only a virgin from his own
people, 15so that he will not defile
his offspring among his people.
I am the LORD, who makes him
holy.’ ” Eze 44:22
16The LORD said to Moses, 17“Say
to Aaron: ‘For the generations to
come none of your descendants
who has a defect may come near
to offer the food of his God. 18No
man who has any defect may come

[a] 4 Or *unclean as a leader among his people*
[b] 10 Or *not uncover his head*

near: no man who is blind or lame,
disfigured or deformed; 19 no man
with a crippled foot or hand, 20 or
who is a hunchback or a dwarf, or
who has any eye defect, or who has
festering or running sores or dam-
aged testicles. 21 No descendant of
Aaron the priest who has any defect is to come near to present the
food offerings to the LORD. He has
a defect; he must not come near to
offer the food of his God. 22 He may
eat the most holy food of his God,
as well as the holy food; 23 yet because of his defect, he must not go
near the curtain or approach the
altar, and so desecrate my sanctuary. I am the LORD, who makes
them holy.' " Lev 22:19-25; Dt 23:1

24 So Moses told this to Aaron
and his sons and to all the Israelites.

22 The LORD said to Moses,
2 "Tell Aaron and his sons
to treat with respect the sacred offerings the Israelites consecrate
to me, so they will not profane my
holy name. I am the LORD. Lev 19:8

3 "Say to them: 'For the generations to come, if any of your descendants is ceremonially unclean
and yet comes near the sacred
offerings that the Israelites consecrate to the LORD, that person
must be cut off from my presence.
I am the LORD. Lev 7:20-21

4 " 'If a descendant of Aaron has
a defiling skin disease[a] or a bodily
discharge, he may not eat the sacred offerings until he is cleansed.
He will also be unclean if he touches something defiled by a corpse
or by anyone who has an emission
of semen, 5 or if he touches any
crawling thing that makes him
unclean, or any person who makes
him unclean, whatever the uncleanness may be. 6 The one who
touches any such thing will be unclean till evening. He must not eat
any of the sacred offerings unless
he has bathed himself with water.
7 When the sun goes down, he will
be clean, and after that he may eat
the sacred offerings, for they are
his food. 8 He must not eat anything found dead or torn by wild
animals, and so become unclean
through it. I am the LORD.
Lev 11:24-28,39; Nu 18:11

9 " 'The priests are to perform
my service in such a way that they
do not become guilty and die for
treating it with contempt. I am
the LORD, who makes them holy.
Ex 28:43

10 " 'No one outside a priest's
family may eat the sacred offering, nor may the guest of a priest
or his hired worker eat it. 11 But if
a priest buys a slave with money,
or if slaves are born in his household, they may eat his food. 12 If a
priest's daughter marries anyone
other than a priest, she may not
eat any of the sacred contributions. 13 But if a priest's daughter
becomes a widow or is divorced,

[a] 4 The Hebrew word for *defiling skin disease*, traditionally translated "leprosy," was used for various diseases affecting the skin.

yet has no children, and she returns to live in her father's household as in her youth, she may eat her father's food. No unauthorized person, however, may eat it.

Ge 17:13; Ex 12:44

14 " 'Anyone who eats a sacred offering by mistake must make restitution to the priest for the offering and add a fifth of the value to it. 15 The priests must not desecrate the sacred offerings the Israelites present to the LORD 16 by allowing them to eat the sacred offerings and so bring upon them guilt requiring payment. I am the LORD, who makes them holy.' "

Lev 5:15

Unacceptable Sacrifices

17 The LORD said to Moses, 18 "Speak to Aaron and his sons and to all the Israelites and say to them: 'If any of you — whether an Israelite or a foreigner residing in Israel — presents a gift for a burnt offering to the LORD, either to fulfill a vow or as a freewill offering, 19 you must present a male without defect from the cattle, sheep or goats in order that it may be accepted on your behalf. 20 Do not bring anything with a defect, because it will not be accepted on your behalf. 21 When anyone brings from the herd or flock a fellowship offering to the LORD to fulfill a special vow or as a freewill offering, it must be without defect or blemish to be acceptable. 22 Do not offer to the LORD the blind, the injured or the maimed, or anything with warts or festering or running sores. Do not place any of these on the altar as a food offering presented to the LORD. 23 You may, however, present as a freewill offering an ox[a] or a sheep that is deformed or stunted, but it will not be accepted in fulfillment of a vow. 24 You must not offer to the LORD an animal whose testicles are bruised, crushed, torn or cut. You must not do this in your own land, 25 and you must not accept such animals from the hand of a foreigner and offer them as the food of your God. They will not be accepted on your behalf, because they are deformed and have defects.' "

Lev 3:6; Dt 15:21

26 The LORD said to Moses, 27 "When a calf, a lamb or a goat is born, it is to remain with its mother for seven days. From the eighth day on, it will be acceptable as a food offering presented to the LORD. 28 Do not slaughter a cow or a sheep and its young on the same day.

Ex 22:30; Dt 22:6-7

29 "When you sacrifice a thank offering to the LORD, sacrifice it in such a way that it will be accepted on your behalf. 30 It must be eaten that same day; leave none of it till morning. I am the LORD.

Lev 7:12; Ps 107:22

31 "Keep my commands and follow them. I am the LORD. 32 Do not profane my holy name, for I

[a] 23 The Hebrew word can refer to either male or female.

must be acknowledged as holy by the Israelites. I am the LORD, who made you holy [33]and who brought you out of Egypt to be your God. I am the LORD." Dt 4:2,40; Ps 105:45

The Appointed Festivals

23 The LORD said to Moses, [2]"Speak to the Israelites and say to them: 'These are my appointed festivals, the appointed festivals of the LORD, which you are to proclaim as sacred assemblies. Nu 29:39

The Sabbath

[3]" 'There are six days when you may work, but the seventh day is a day of sabbath rest, a day of sacred assembly. You are not to do any work; wherever you live, it is a sabbath to the LORD. Ex 20:9-10; 31:13-17

The Passover and the Festival of Unleavened Bread

[4]" 'These are the LORD's appointed festivals, the sacred assemblies you are to proclaim at their appointed times: [5]The LORD's Passover begins at twilight on the fourteenth day of the first month. [6]On the fifteenth day of that month the LORD's Festival of Unleavened Bread begins; for seven days you must eat bread made without yeast. [7]On the first day hold a sacred assembly and do no regular work. [8]For seven days present a food offering to the LORD. And on the seventh day hold a sacred assembly and do no regular work.' " Ex 12:14-20; Nu 28:16-25; Dt 16:1-8

Offering the Firstfruits

[9]The LORD said to Moses, [10]"Speak to the Israelites and say to them: 'When you enter the land I am going to give you and you reap its harvest, bring to the priest a sheaf of the first grain you harvest. [11]He is to wave the sheaf before the LORD so it will be accepted on your behalf; the priest is to wave it on the day after the Sabbath. [12]On the day you wave the sheaf, you must sacrifice as a burnt offering to the LORD a lamb a year old without defect, [13]together with its grain offering of two-tenths of an ephah[a] of the finest flour mixed with olive oil — a food offering presented to the LORD, a pleasing aroma — and its drink offering of a quarter of a hin[b] of wine. [14]You must not eat any bread, or roasted or new grain, until the very day you bring this offering to your God. This is to be a lasting ordinance for the generations to come, wherever you live. Ex 23:16,19; Ro 11:16

The Festival of Weeks

[15]" 'From the day after the Sabbath, the day you brought the sheaf of the wave offering, count off seven full weeks. [16]Count off fifty days up to the day after the

[a] *13* That is, probably about 7 pounds or about 3.2 kilograms; also in verse 17
[b] *13* That is, about 1 quart or about 1 liter

seventh Sabbath, and then present an offering of new grain to
the LORD. 17From wherever you
live, bring two loaves made of
two-tenths of an ephah of the finest flour, baked with yeast, as a
wave offering of firstfruits to the
LORD. 18Present with this bread
seven male lambs, each a year old
and without defect, one young
bull and two rams. They will be a
burnt offering to the LORD, together with their grain offerings and
drink offerings — a food offering,
an aroma pleasing to the LORD.
19Then sacrifice one male goat
for a sin offering[a] and two lambs,
each a year old, for a fellowship
offering. 20The priest is to wave
the two lambs before the LORD as
a wave offering, together with the
bread of the firstfruits. They are a
sacred offering to the LORD for the
priest. 21On that same day you are
to proclaim a sacred assembly and
do no regular work. This is to be a
lasting ordinance for the generations to come, wherever you live.

ver 2-3; Ac 2:1

22" 'When you reap the harvest
of your land, do not reap to the
very edges of your field or gather the gleanings of your harvest.
Leave them for the poor and for
the foreigner residing among you.
I am the LORD your God.' "

Nu 28:26-31; Dt 16:9-12

The Festival of Trumpets

23The LORD said to Moses, 24"Say
to the Israelites: 'On the first day
of the seventh month you are to
have a day of sabbath rest, a sacred assembly commemorated
with trumpet blasts. 25Do no regular work, but present a food offering to the LORD.' "

Nu 29:1-6

The Day of Atonement

26The LORD said to Moses,
27"The tenth day of this seventh
month is the Day of Atonement.
Hold a sacred assembly and deny
yourselves,[b] and present a food
offering to the LORD. 28Do not do
any work on that day, because it
is the Day of Atonement, when
atonement is made for you before the LORD your God. 29Those
who do not deny themselves on
that day must be cut off from
their people. 30I will destroy from
among their people anyone who
does any work on that day. 31You
shall do no work at all. This is
to be a lasting ordinance for the
generations to come, wherever
you live. 32It is a day of sabbath
rest for you, and you must deny
yourselves. From the evening of
the ninth day of the month until
the following evening you are to
observe your sabbath."

Lev 16:2-34; Nu 29:7-11

The Festival of Tabernacles

33The LORD said to Moses, 34"Say
to the Israelites: 'On the fifteenth
day of the seventh month the
LORD's Festival of Tabernacles

[a] 19 Or *purification offering* [b] 27 Or *and fast*; similarly in verses 29 and 32

begins, and it lasts for seven days.
35 The first day is a sacred assembly; do no regular work. 36 For sev-
en days present food offerings to
the LORD, and on the eighth day
hold a sacred assembly and present a food offering to the LORD.
It is the closing special assembly;
do no regular work.

Ex 23:16; Dt 16:13; Jn 7:2

37 ("'These are the LORD's appointed festivals, which you are
to proclaim as sacred assemblies
for bringing food offerings to the
LORD — the burnt offerings and
grain offerings, sacrifices and
drink offerings required for each
day. 38 These offerings are in addition to those for the LORD's Sabbaths and[a] in addition to your gifts
and whatever you have vowed and
all the freewill offerings you give
to the LORD.)

ver 2,4; Eze 45:17

39 "'So beginning with the fifteenth day of the seventh month,
after you have gathered the crops
of the land, celebrate the festival
to the LORD for seven days; the
first day is a day of sabbath rest,
and the eighth day also is a day of
sabbath rest. 40 On the first day you
are to take branches from luxuriant trees — from palms, willows
and other leafy trees — and rejoice before the LORD your God
for seven days. 41 Celebrate this
as a festival to the LORD for sev-
en days each year. This is to be a
lasting ordinance for the generations to come; celebrate it in the
seventh month. 42 Live in temporary shelters for seven days: All
native-born Israelites are to live
in such shelters 43 so your descendants will know that I had the Israelites live in temporary shelters
when I brought them out of Egypt.
I am the LORD your God.'"

Nu 29:12-39; Dt 16:13-17

44 So Moses announced to the Israelites the appointed festivals of
the LORD.

Olive Oil and Bread Set Before the LORD

24 The LORD said to Moses,
2 "Command the Israelites
to bring you clear oil of pressed olives for the light so that the lamps
may be kept burning continually.
3 Outside the curtain that shields
the ark of the covenant law in the
tent of meeting, Aaron is to tend
the lamps before the LORD from
evening till morning, continually. This is to be a lasting ordinance
for the generations to come. 4 The
lamps on the pure gold lampstand
before the LORD must be tended
continually.

Ex 27:20-21

5 "Take the finest flour and bake
twelve loaves of bread, using two-
tenths of an ephah[b] for each loaf.
6 Arrange them in two stacks, six
in each stack, on the table of pure
gold before the LORD. 7 By each
stack put some pure incense as a
memorial[c] portion to represent

[a] 38 Or *These festivals are in addition to the LORD's Sabbaths, and these offerings are*
[b] 5 That is, probably about 7 pounds or about 3.2 kilograms
[c] 7 Or *representative*

the bread and to be a food offering presented to the LORD. 8This
bread is to be set out before the
LORD regularly, Sabbath after
Sabbath, on behalf of the Israelites, as a lasting covenant. 9It belongs to Aaron and his sons, who
are to eat it in the sanctuary area,
because it is a most holy part of
their perpetual share of the food
offerings presented to the LORD."
Mt 12:4; Nu 4:7; 2Ch 2:4

A Blasphemer Put to Death

10Now the son of an Israelite
mother and an Egyptian father
went out among the Israelites,
and a fight broke out in the camp
between him and an Israelite.
11The son of the Israelite woman blasphemed the Name with a
curse; so they brought him to Moses. (His mother's name was Shelomith, the daughter of Dibri the
Danite.) 12They put him in custody
until the will of the LORD should
be made clear to them.
Ex 18:16; Nu 15:34

13Then the LORD said to Moses:
14"Take the blasphemer outside
the camp. All those who heard
him are to lay their hands on his
head, and the entire assembly is
to stone him. 15Say to the Israelites: 'Anyone who curses their
God will be held responsible;
16anyone who blasphemes the
name of the LORD is to be put to
death. The entire assembly must
stone them. Whether foreigner
or native-born, when they blaspheme the Name they are to be
put to death. Dt 13:9; 1Ki 21:10,13

17" 'Anyone who takes the life
of a human being is to be put to
death. 18Anyone who takes the life
of someone's animal must make
restitution — life for life. 19Any-
one who injures their neighbor is
to be injured in the same manner:
20fracture for fracture, eye for eye,
tooth for tooth. The one who has
inflicted the injury must suffer
the same injury. 21Whoever kills
an animal must make restitution,
but whoever kills a human being
is to be put to death. 22You are to
have the same law for the foreigner and the native-born. I am the
LORD your God.' " Ex 21:12; Mt 5:38

23Then Moses spoke to the Israelites, and they took the blasphemer outside the camp and
stoned him. The Israelites did as
the LORD commanded Moses.

The Sabbath Year

25 The LORD said to Moses at
Mount Sinai, 2"Speak to the
Israelites and say to them: 'When
you enter the land I am going to
give you, the land itself must observe a sabbath to the LORD. 3For
six years sow your fields, and for
six years prune your vineyards
and gather their crops. 4But in the
seventh year the land is to have a
year of sabbath rest, a sabbath to
the LORD. Do not sow your fields
or prune your vineyards. 5Do not
reap what grows of itself or harvest the grapes of your untended

vines. The land is to have a year
of rest. 6Whatever the land yields
during the sabbath year will be
food for you — for yourself, your
male and female servants, and the
hired worker and temporary resident who live among you, 7as well
as for your livestock and the wild
animals in your land. Whatever
the land produces may be eaten.
Ex 23:10

The Year of Jubilee

8" 'Count off seven sabbath
years — seven times seven years —
so that the seven sabbath years
amount to a period of forty-nine
years. 9Then have the trumpet
sounded everywhere on the tenth
day of the seventh month; on
the Day of Atonement sound the
trumpet throughout your land.
10Consecrate the fiftieth year and
proclaim liberty throughout the
land to all its inhabitants. It shall
be a jubilee for you; each of you is
to return to your family property
and to your own clan. 11The fiftieth year shall be a jubilee for you;
do not sow and do not reap what
grows of itself or harvest the untended vines. 12For it is a jubilee
and is to be holy for you; eat only
what is taken directly from the
fields. Jer 34:8,15,17; Lk 4:19

13" 'In this Year of Jubilee everyone is to return to their own property. ver 10

14" 'If you sell land to any of your
own people or buy land from them,
do not take advantage of each other. 15You are to buy from your own
people on the basis of the number of years since the Jubilee. And
they are to sell to you on the basis of the number of years left for
harvesting crops. 16When the years
are many, you are to increase the
price, and when the years are few,
you are to decrease the price, because what is really being sold to
you is the number of crops. 17Do
not take advantage of each other,
but fear your God. I am the LORD
your God. Lev 19:14,32

18" 'Follow my decrees and be
careful to obey my laws, and you
will live safely in the land. 19Then
the land will yield its fruit, and
you will eat your fill and live there
in safety. 20You may ask, "What
will we eat in the seventh year
if we do not plant or harvest our
crops?" 21I will send you such a
blessing in the sixth year that the
land will yield enough for three
years. 22While you plant during
the eighth year, you will eat from
the old crop and will continue to
eat from it until the harvest of
the ninth year comes in.
Lev 26:10; Hag 2:19

23" 'The land must not be sold
permanently, because the land
is mine and you reside in my
land as foreigners and strangers.
24Throughout the land that you
hold as a possession, you must
provide for the redemption of the
land. Ge 23:4; Ex 19:5; 1Pe 2:11

25" 'If one of your fellow Israelites becomes poor and sells some

of their property, their nearest relative is to come and redeem what
they have sold. 26 If, however, there
is no one to redeem it for them
but later on they prosper and acquire sufficient means to redeem
it themselves, 27 they are to determine the value for the years since
they sold it and refund the balance to the one to whom they sold
it; they can then go back to their
own property. 28 But if they do not
acquire the means to repay, what
was sold will remain in the possession of the buyer until the Year
of Jubilee. It will be returned in
the Jubilee, and they can then go
back to their property.

Lev 27:13,19,31; Ru 2:20

29 " 'Anyone who sells a house in
a walled city retains the right of redemption a full year after its sale.
During that time the seller may
redeem it. 30 If it is not redeemed
before a full year has passed, the
house in the walled city shall belong permanently to the buyer
and the buyer's descendants. It is
not to be returned in the Jubilee.
31 But houses in villages without
walls around them are to be considered as belonging to the open
country. They can be redeemed,
and they are to be returned in the
Jubilee.

32 " 'The Levites always have
the right to redeem their houses in the Levitical towns, which
they possess. 33 So the property of
the Levites is redeemable — that
is, a house sold in any town they
hold — and is to be returned in
the Jubilee, because the houses in
the towns of the Levites are their
property among the Israelites.
34 But the pastureland belonging
to their towns must not be sold; it
is their permanent possession.

Nu 35:1-8

35 " 'If any of your fellow Israelites become poor and are unable
to support themselves among
you, help them as you would a
foreigner and stranger, so they
can continue to live among you.
36 Do not take interest or any profit from them, but fear your God,
so that they may continue to live
among you. 37 You must not lend
them money at interest or sell
them food at a profit. 38 I am the
LORD your God, who brought you
out of Egypt to give you the land
of Canaan and to be your God.

Dt 15:1-11; Ex 22:25

39 " 'If any of your fellow Israelites become poor and sell themselves to you, do not make them
work as slaves. 40 They are to be
treated as hired workers or temporary residents among you; they
are to work for you until the Year
of Jubilee. 41 Then they and their
children are to be released, and
they will go back to their own
clans and to the property of their
ancestors. 42 Because the Israelites
are my servants, whom I brought
out of Egypt, they must not be sold
as slaves. 43 Do not rule over them
ruthlessly, but fear your God.

1Ki 9:22; Eze 34:4; Col 4:1

44“ ‘Your male and female slaves are to come from the nations around you; from them you may buy slaves. 45You may also buy some of the temporary residents living among you and members of their clans born in your country, and they will become your property. 46You can bequeath them to your children as inherited property and can make them slaves for life, but you must not rule over your fellow Israelites ruthlessly.

47“ ‘If a foreigner residing among you becomes rich and any of your fellow Israelites become poor and sell themselves to the foreigner or to a member of the foreigner’s clan, 48they retain the right of redemption after they have sold themselves. One of their relatives may redeem them: 49An uncle or a cousin or any blood relative in their clan may redeem them. Or if they prosper, they may redeem themselves. 50They and their buyer are to count the time from the year they sold themselves up to the Year of Jubilee. The price for their release is to be based on the rate paid to a hired worker for that number of years. 51If many years remain, they must pay for their redemption a larger share of the price paid for them. 52If only a few years remain until the Year of Jubilee, they are to compute that and pay for their redemption accordingly. 53They are to be treated as workers hired from year to year; you must see to it that those to whom they owe service do not rule over them ruthlessly. Ex 21:2-11; Dt 15:12-18

54“ ‘Even if someone is not redeemed in any of these ways, they and their children are to be released in the Year of Jubilee, 55for the Israelites belong to me as servants. They are my servants, whom I brought out of Egypt. I am the LORD your God.

Reward for Obedience

26 “ ‘Do not make idols or set up an image or a sacred stone for yourselves, and do not place a carved stone in your land to bow down before it. I am the LORD your God. Ex 20:4; Dt 5:8

2“ ‘Observe my Sabbaths and have reverence for my sanctuary. I am the LORD. Lev 19:30

3“ ‘If you follow my decrees and are careful to obey my commands, 4I will send you rain in its season, and the ground will yield its crops and the trees their fruit. 5Your threshing will continue until grape harvest and the grape harvest will continue until planting, and you will eat all the food you want and live in safety in your land. Lev 25:18; Dt 28:1,9

6“ ‘I will grant peace in the land, and you will lie down and no one will make you afraid. I will remove wild beasts from the land, and the sword will not pass through your country. 7You will pursue your enemies, and they will fall by the sword before you. 8Five of you will

chase a hundred, and a hundred
of you will chase ten thousand,
and your enemies will fall by the
sword before you. Ps 29:11; 147:14

9"'I will look on you with favor and make you fruitful and increase your numbers, and I will
keep my covenant with you. 10You
will still be eating last year's harvest when you will have to move
it out to make room for the new.
11I will put my dwelling place[a]
among you, and I will not abhor
you. 12I will walk among you and
be your God, and you will be my
people. 13I am the LORD your God,
who brought you out of Egypt so
that you would no longer be slaves
to the Egyptians; I broke the bars
of your yoke and enabled you to
walk with heads held high.

Ge 17:6; 2Co 6:16

Punishment for Disobedience

14"'But if you will not listen to me
and carry out all these commands,
15and if you reject my decrees and
abhor my laws and fail to carry out
all my commands and so violate
my covenant, 16then I will do this
to you: I will bring on you sudden
terror, wasting diseases and fever
that will destroy your sight and sap
your strength. You will plant seed
in vain, because your enemies will
eat it. 17I will set my face against
you so that you will be defeated by
your enemies; those who hate you
will rule over you, and you will flee
even when no one is pursuing you.

Dt 28:15-68; Mal 2:2

18"'If after all this you will not
listen to me, I will punish you for
your sins seven times over. 19I will
break down your stubborn pride
and make the sky above you like
iron and the ground beneath you
like bronze. 20Your strength will
be spent in vain, because your soil
will not yield its crops, nor will the
trees of your land yield their fruit.

Dt 28:23; Ps 127:1; Isa 25:11

21"'If you remain hostile toward
me and refuse to listen to me, I
will multiply your afflictions sev-
en times over, as your sins deserve.
22I will send wild animals against
you, and they will rob you of your
children, destroy your cattle and
make you so few in number that
your roads will be deserted. Dt 32:24

23"'If in spite of these things
you do not accept my correction
but continue to be hostile toward
me, 24I myself will be hostile toward you and will afflict you for
your sins seven times over. 25And
I will bring the sword on you to
avenge the breaking of the covenant. When you withdraw into
your cities, I will send a plague
among you, and you will be given
into enemy hands. 26When I cut
off your supply of bread, ten wom-
en will be able to bake your bread
in one oven, and they will dole out
the bread by weight. You will eat,
but you will not be satisfied.

Ps 105:16; Jer 2:30

27"'If in spite of this you still do
not listen to me but continue to be

[a] 11 Or *my tabernacle*

hostile toward me, 28then in my anger I will be hostile toward you, and I myself will punish you for your sins seven times over. 29You will eat the flesh of your sons and the flesh of your daughters. 30I will destroy your high places, cut down your incense altars and pile your dead bodies[a] on the lifeless forms of your idols, and I will abhor you. 31I will turn your cities into ruins and lay waste your sanctuaries, and I will take no delight in the pleasing aroma of your offerings. 32I myself will lay waste the land, so that your enemies who live there will be appalled. 33I will scatter you among the nations and will draw out my sword and pursue you. Your land will be laid waste, and your cities will lie in ruins. 34Then the land will enjoy its sabbath years all the time that it lies desolate and you are in the country of your enemies; then the land will rest and enjoy its sabbaths. 35All the time that it lies desolate, the land will have the rest it did not have during the sabbaths you lived in it.

Dt 4:27; Ps 74:3-7; Jer 9:11

36" 'As for those of you who are left, I will make their hearts so fearful in the lands of their enemies that the sound of a windblown leaf will put them to flight. They will run as though fleeing from the sword, and they will fall, even though no one is pursuing them. 37They will stumble over one another as though fleeing from the sword, even though no one is pursuing them. So you will not be able to stand before your enemies. 38You will perish among the nations; the land of your enemies will devour you. 39Those of you who are left will waste away in the lands of their enemies because of their sins; also because of their ancestors' sins they will waste away.

Eze 21:7

40" 'But if they will confess their sins and the sins of their ancestors — their unfaithfulness and their hostility toward me, 41which made me hostile toward them so that I sent them into the land of their enemies — then when their uncircumcised hearts are humbled and they pay for their sin, 42I will remember my covenant with Jacob and my covenant with Isaac and my covenant with Abraham, and I will remember the land. 43For the land will be deserted by them and will enjoy its sabbaths while it lies desolate without them. They will pay for their sins because they rejected my laws and abhorred my decrees. 44Yet in spite of this, when they are in the land of their enemies, I will not reject them or abhor them so as to destroy them completely, breaking my covenant with them. I am the LORD their God. 45But for their sake I will remember the covenant with their ancestors whom I brought out of Egypt in the sight

[a] 30 Or *your funeral offerings*

of the nations to be their God. I
am the LORD.'" Dt 4:31; 1Jn 1:9
46These are the decrees, the laws
and the regulations that the LORD
established at Mount Sinai between himself and the Israelites
through Moses. Lev 7:38; 27:34

Redeeming What Is the LORD's

27 The LORD said to Moses,
2"Speak to the Israelites
and say to them: 'If anyone makes
a special vow to dedicate a person
to the LORD by giving the equivalent value, 3set the value of a male
between the ages of twenty and
sixty at fifty shekels[a] of silver, according to the sanctuary shekel[b];
4for a female, set her value at thirty shekels[c]; 5for a person between
the ages of five and twenty, set the
value of a male at twenty shekels[d]
and of a female at ten shekels[e];
6for a person between one month
and five years, set the value of a
male at five shekels[f] of silver and
that of a female at three shekels[g]
of silver; 7for a person sixty years
old or more, set the value of a
male at fifteen shekels[h] and of a
female at ten shekels. 8If anyone
making the vow is too poor to pay
the specified amount, the person
being dedicated is to be presented
to the priest, who will set the value
according to what the one making
the vow can afford. Ex 30;13; Nu 18:16
9" 'If what they vowed is an animal that is acceptable as an offering to the LORD, such an animal
given to the LORD becomes holy.
10They must not exchange it or
substitute a good one for a bad
one, or a bad one for a good one;
if they should substitute one animal for another, both it and the
substitute become holy. 11If what
they vowed is a ceremonially unclean animal—one that is not
acceptable as an offering to the
LORD—the animal must be presented to the priest, 12who will
judge its quality as good or bad.
Whatever value the priest then
sets, that is what it will be. 13If the
owner wishes to redeem the animal, a fifth must be added to its
value. Lev 25:25; Dt 15:19
14" 'If anyone dedicates their
house as something holy to the
LORD, the priest will judge its
quality as good or bad. Whatever
value the priest then sets, so it will
remain. 15If the one who dedicates
their house wishes to redeem it,
they must add a fifth to its value,
and the house will again become
theirs. ver 13,20
16" 'If anyone dedicates to the
LORD part of their family land,
its value is to be set according
to the amount of seed required
for it—fifty shekels of silver to a

[a] 3 That is, about 1 1/4 pounds or about 575 grams; also in verse 16 [b] 3 That is, about 2/5 ounce or about 12 grams; also in verse 25 [c] 4 That is, about 12 ounces or about 345 grams [d] 5 That is, about 8 ounces or about 230 grams [e] 5 That is, about 4 ounces or about 115 grams; also in verse 7 [f] 6 That is, about 2 ounces or about 58 grams [g] 6 That is, about 1 1/4 ounces or about 35 grams [h] 7 That is, about 6 ounces or about 175 grams

homer[a] of barley seed. 17 If they
dedicate a field during the Year of
Jubilee, the value that has been
set remains. 18 But if they dedicate
a field after the Jubilee, the priest
will determine the value according
to the number of years that remain
until the next Year of Jubilee, and
its set value will be reduced. 19 If the
one who dedicates the field wishes to redeem it, they must add a
fifth to its value, and the field will
again become theirs. 20 If, however,
they do not redeem the field, or if
they have sold it to someone else,
it can never be redeemed. 21 When
the field is released in the Jubilee,
it will become holy, like a field devoted to the LORD; it will become
priestly property. Nu 18:14; Eze 44:29

22 " 'If anyone dedicates to the
LORD a field they have bought,
which is not part of their family
land, 23 the priest will determine
its value up to the Year of Jubilee,
and the owner must pay its value
on that day as something holy to
the LORD. 24 In the Year of Jubilee
the field will revert to the person
from whom it was bought, the one
whose land it was. 25 Every value is
to be set according to the sanctuary shekel, twenty gerahs to the
shekel. Ex 30:13; Lev 25:28

26 " 'No one, however, may dedicate the firstborn of an animal,
since the firstborn already belongs to the LORD; whether an ox[b]
or a sheep, it is the LORD's. 27 If it
is one of the unclean animals, it
may be bought back at its set value, adding a fifth of the value to
it. If it is not redeemed, it is to be
sold at its set value. Ex 13:2,12

28 " 'But nothing that a person
owns and devotes[c] to the LORD —
whether a human being or an animal or family land — may be sold
or redeemed; everything so devoted is most holy to the LORD.
Jos 6:17-19

29 " 'No person devoted to destruction[d] may be ransomed; they
are to be put to death.

30 " 'A tithe of everything from
the land, whether grain from the
soil or fruit from the trees, belongs to the LORD; it is holy to the
LORD. 31 Whoever would redeem
any of their tithe must add a fifth
of the value to it. 32 Every tithe of
the herd and flock — every tenth
animal that passes under the
shepherd's rod — will be holy to
the LORD. 33 No one may pick out
the good from the bad or make
any substitution. If anyone does
make a substitution, both the animal and its substitute become
holy and cannot be redeemed.' "
Ge 28:22; Mal 3:8

34 These are the commands the
LORD gave Moses at Mount Sinai
for the Israelites. Lev 26:46

[a] *16* That is, probably about 300 pounds or about 135 kilograms [b] *26* The Hebrew word can refer to either male or female. [c] *28* The Hebrew term refers to the irrevocable giving over of things or persons to the LORD. [d] *29* The Hebrew term refers to the irrevocable giving over of things or persons to the LORD, often by totally destroying them.

NUMBERS

The Census

1 The LORD spoke to Moses in the
tent of meeting in the Desert of
Sinai on the first day of the second
month of the second year after the
Israelites came out of Egypt. He
said: 2“Take a census of the whole
Israelite community by their clans
and families, listing every man by
name, one by one. 3You and Aaron are to count according to their
divisions all the men in Israel who
are twenty years old or more and
able to serve in the army. 4One man
from each tribe, each of them the
head of his family, is to help you.
5These are the names of the men
who are to assist you: Ex 30:11-16; Dt 1:15

from Reuben, Elizur son of
Shedeur; Rev 7:5
6from Simeon, Shelumiel son
of Zurishaddai; Nu 25:14
7from Judah, Nahshon son of
Amminadab; Ge 29:35
8from Issachar, Nethanel son
of Zuar; Ge 30:18
9from Zebulun, Eliab son of
Helon; Nu 10:16
10from the sons of Joseph:
from Ephraim, Elishama
son of Ammihud; Nu 2:18
from Manasseh, Gamaliel
son of Pedahzur; Nu 10:23
11from Benjamin, Abidan son
of Gideoni; Nu 10:24
12from Dan, Ahiezer son of Ammishaddai; Nu 2:25
13from Asher, Pagiel son of Okran; Nu 2:27; 10:26
14from Gad, Eliasaph son of
Deuel; Nu 2:14; 10:20
15from Naphtali, Ahira son of
Enan.” Nu 2:29; 10:27

16These were the men appointed
from the community, the leaders
of their ancestral tribes. They were
the heads of the clans of Israel.
Ex 18:25; Nu 7:2

17Moses and Aaron took these
men whose names had been specified, 18and they called the whole
community together on the first
day of the second month. The
people registered their ancestry
by their clans and families, and
the men twenty years old or more
were listed by name, one by one,
19as the LORD commanded Moses.
And so he counted them in the
Desert of Sinai: Ezr 2:59; Heb 7:3

20From the descendants of Reuben the firstborn son of Israel: Nu 26:5-11; Rev 7:5
All the men twenty years
old or more who were able
to serve in the army were
listed by name, one by one,
according to the records
of their clans and fami-
lies. 21The number from

the tribe of Reuben was 46,500.

22 From the descendants of Simeon: Nu 26:12-14; Rev 7:7
All the men twenty years old or more who were able to serve in the army were counted and listed by name, one by one, according to the records of their clans and families.
23 The number from the tribe of Simeon was 59,300.

24 From the descendants of Gad: Nu 26:15-18; Rev 7:5
All the men twenty years old or more who were able to serve in the army were listed by name, according to the records of their clans and families.
25 The number from the tribe of Gad was 45,650.

26 From the descendants of Judah: Nu 26:19-22; Mt 1:2; Rev 7:5
All the men twenty years old or more who were able to serve in the army were listed by name, according to the records of their clans and families.
27 The number from the tribe of Judah was 74,600.

28 From the descendants of Issachar: Nu 26:23-25; Rev 7:7
All the men twenty years old or more who were able to serve in the army were listed by name, according to the records of their clans and families.
29 The number from the tribe of Issachar was 54,400.

30 From the descendants of Zebulun: Nu 26:26-27; Rev 7:8
All the men twenty years old or more who were able to serve in the army were listed by name, according to the records of their clans and families.
31 The number from the tribe of Zebulun was 57,400.

32 From the sons of Joseph:
From the descendants of Ephraim: Nu 26:35-37
All the men twenty years old or more who were able to serve in the army were listed by name, according to the records of their clans and families.
33 The number from the tribe of Ephraim was 40,500.

34 From the descendants of Manasseh: Nu 26:28-34; Rev 7:6
All the men twenty years old or more who were able to serve in the army were listed by name, according to the records of their clans and families.
35 The number from the tribe of Manasseh was 32,200.

36 From the descendants of Benjamin: Nu 26:38-41; Rev 7:8
All the men twenty years old or more who were able

to serve in the army were
listed by name, according
to the records of their clans
and families. 37The number
from the tribe of Benjamin
was 35,400.

38From the descendants of Dan:
Nu 26:42-43
All the men twenty years
old or more who were able
to serve in the army were
listed by name, according
to the records of their clans
and families. 39The number
from the tribe of Dan was
62,700.

40From the descendants of Asher: Nu 26:44-47; Rev 7:6
All the men twenty years
old or more who were able
to serve in the army were
listed by name, according
to the records of their clans
and families. 41The number
from the tribe of Asher was
41,500.

42From the descendants of
Naphtali: Nu 26:48-50; Rev 7:6
All the men twenty years
old or more who were able
to serve in the army were
listed by name, according
to the records of their clans
and families. 43The number
from the tribe of Naphtali
was 53,400.

44These were the men counted by Moses and Aaron and the
twelve leaders of Israel, each one
representing his family. 45All the
Israelites twenty years old or
more who were able to serve in Israel's army were counted according to their families. 46The total
number was 603,550.
Nu 2:32; 26:64

47The ancestral tribe of the Levites, however, was not counted along with the others. 48The
LORD had said to Moses: 49"You
must not count the tribe of Levi
or include them in the census of
the other Israelites. 50Instead, appoint the Levites to be in charge
of the tabernacle of the covenant
law—over all its furnishings and
everything belonging to it. They
are to carry the tabernacle and all
its furnishings; they are to take
care of it and encamp around it.
51Whenever the tabernacle is to
move, the Levites are to take it
down, and whenever the tabernacle is to be set up, the Levites shall
do it. Anyone else who approaches it is to be put to death. 52The
Israelites are to set up their tents
by divisions, each of them in their
own camp under their standard.
53The Levites, however, are to set
up their tents around the tabernacle of the covenant law so that my
wrath will not fall on the Israelite
community. The Levites are to be
responsible for the care of the tabernacle of the covenant law."
Nu 2:33; 18:2-4

54The Israelites did all this just
as the LORD commanded Moses.

The Arrangement of the Tribal Camps

2
The LORD said to Moses and
Aaron: 2“The Israelites are to
camp around the tent of meeting some distance from it, each
of them under their standard
and holding the banners of their
family.” Nu 1:52; Ps 74:4

3On the east, toward the
sunrise, the divisions of the
camp of Judah are to encamp
under their standard. The
leader of the people of Judah
is Nahshon son of Ammina-
dab. 4His division numbers
74,600. Nu 10:14
5The tribe of Issachar will
camp next to them. The leader of the people of Issachar is
Nethanel son of Zuar. 6His division numbers 54,400.
Nu 1:8; 10:15

7The tribe of Zebulun will
be next. The leader of the
people of Zebulun is Eliab son
of Helon. 8His division numbers 57,400. Nu 1:9
9All the men assigned to
the camp of Judah, according to their divisions, number 186,400. They will set out
first. Nu 10:14

10On the south will be the
divisions of the camp of Reuben under their standard.
The leader of the people of
Reuben is Elizur son of Shedeur. 11His division numbers
46,500. Nu 1:5
12The tribe of Simeon will
camp next to them. The leader of the people of Simeon is
Shelumiel son of Zurishaddai. 13His division numbers
59,300. Nu 1:6
14The tribe of Gad will be
next. The leader of the people
of Gad is Eliasaph son of Deuel.[a] 15His division numbers
45,650. Nu 1:14
16All the men assigned to
the camp of Reuben, according to their divisions, number
151,450. They will set out second. Nu 10:18

17Then the tent of meeting
and the camp of the Levites
will set out in the middle of
the camps. They will set out
in the same order as they encamp, each in their own place
under their standard. Nu 10:21

18On the west will be the divisions of the camp of Ephraim under their standard. The
leader of the people of Ephraim is Elishama son of Ammihud. 19His division numbers
40,500. Ge 48:20; Nu 1:10
20The tribe of Manasseh will
be next to them. The leader of
the people of Manasseh is Gamaliel son of Pedahzur. 21His
division numbers 32,200.
Nu 1:10

[a] 14 Many manuscripts of the Masoretic Text, Samaritan Pentateuch and Vulgate (see also 1:14); most manuscripts of the Masoretic Text *Reuel*

22The tribe of Benjamin
will be next. The leader of the
people of Benjamin is Abidan
son of Gideoni. 23His division
numbers 35,400. Nu 1:11; Ps 68:27
24All the men assigned to
the camp of Ephraim, according to their divisions, number 108,100. They will set out
third. Nu 10:22; Ps 80:2

25On the north will be the
divisions of the camp of Dan
under their standard. The
leader of the people of Dan
is Ahiezer son of Ammishaddai. 26His division numbers
62,700. Nu 1:12
27The tribe of Asher will
camp next to them. The leader of the people of Asher is
Pagiel son of Okran. 28His division numbers 41,500. Nu 1:13
29The tribe of Naphtali will
be next. The leader of the people of Naphtali is Ahira son of
Enan. 30His division numbers
53,400. Nu 1:15
31All the men assigned to
the camp of Dan number
157,600. They will set out last,
under their standards. Nu 10:25

32These are the Israel-
ites, counted according to
their families. All the men
in the camps, by their divisions, number 603,550. 33The
Levites, however, were not
counted along with the other
Israelites, as the LORD commanded Moses.
34So the Israelites did everything the LORD commanded Moses; that is the way they encamped
under their standards, and that is
the way they set out, each of them
with their clan and family.
Ex 38:26; Nu 1:46-47

The Levites

3 This is the account of the family of Aaron and Moses at the
time the LORD spoke to Moses at
Mount Sinai. Ex 6:27
2The names of the sons of Aaron
were Nadab the firstborn and Abihu, Eleazar and Ithamar. 3Those
were the names of Aaron's sons,
the anointed priests, who were
ordained to serve as priests. 4Na-
dab and Abihu, however, died before the LORD when they made an
offering with unauthorized fire
before him in the Desert of Sinai.
They had no sons, so Eleazar and
Ithamar served as priests during
the lifetime of their father Aaron.
Ex 6:23; Lev 10:1-2
5The LORD said to Moses, 6"Bring
the tribe of Levi and present them
to Aaron the priest to assist him.
7They are to perform duties for
him and for the whole community at the tent of meeting by doing
the work of the tabernacle. 8They
are to take care of all the furnishings of the tent of meeting, fulfilling the obligations of the Israelites by doing the work of the
tabernacle. 9Give the Levites to
Aaron and his sons; they are the
Israelites who are to be given

wholly to him.[a] 10 Appoint Aaron
and his sons to serve as priests;
anyone else who approaches the
sanctuary is to be put to death."
Nu 1:51; 8:6-22; 18:1-7

11 The LORD also said to Moses,
12 "I have taken the Levites from
among the Israelites in place of
the first male offspring of every
Israelite woman. The Levites are
mine, 13 for all the firstborn are
mine. When I struck down all the
firstborn in Egypt, I set apart for
myself every firstborn in Israel,
whether human or animal. They
are to be mine. I am the LORD."
Ex 13:12; Nu 8:16,18

14 The LORD said to Moses in the
Desert of Sinai, 15 "Count the Levites by their families and clans.
Count every male a month old or
more." 16 So Moses counted them,
as he was commanded by the word
of the LORD. Nu 26:62

17 These were the names of the
sons of Levi: Ge 46:11
Gershon, Kohath and Me-
rari. Ex 6:16
18 These were the names of the
Gershonite clans:
Libni and Shimei. Ex 6:17
19 The Kohathite clans:
Amram, Izhar, Hebron and
Uzziel. Ex 6:18
20 The Merarite clans:
Mahli and Mushi. Ex 6:19
These were the Levite clans, ac-
cording to their families.

21 To Gershon belonged the clans
of the Libnites and Shimeites;
these were the Gershonite clans.
22 The number of all the males
a month old or more who were
counted was 7,500. 23 The Gershonite clans were to camp on the west,
behind the tabernacle. 24 The leader
of the families of the Gershonites
was Eliasaph son of Lael. 25 At the
tent of meeting the Gershonites
were responsible for the care of
the tabernacle and tent, its coverings, the curtain at the entrance to
the tent of meeting, 26 the curtains
of the courtyard, the curtain at
the entrance to the courtyard surrounding the tabernacle and altar,
and the ropes — and everything related to their use. Ex 6:17; 25:9; Nu 4:25

27 To Kohath belonged the clans
of the Amramites, Izharites, Hebronites and Uzzielites; these were
the Kohathite clans. 28 The number of all the males a month old
or more was 8,600.[b] The Kohathites were responsible for the care
of the sanctuary. 29 The Kohathite
clans were to camp on the south
side of the tabernacle. 30 The leader of the families of the Kohathite
clans was Elizaphan son of Uzziel. 31 They were responsible for the
care of the ark, the table, the lampstand, the altars, the articles of the
sanctuary used in ministering, the
curtain, and everything related to
their use. 32 The chief leader of the

[a] *9* Most manuscripts of the Masoretic Text; some manuscripts of the Masoretic Text, Samaritan Pentateuch and Septuagint (see also 8:16) *to me* [b] *28* Hebrew; some Septuagint manuscripts *8,300*

Levites was Eleazar son of Aaron,
the priest. He was appointed over
those who were responsible for
the care of the sanctuary.
Ex 25:10-22,31; 1Ch 26:23

33 To Merari belonged the clans
of the Mahlites and the Mushites;
these were the Merarite clans.
34 The number of all the males
a month old or more who were
counted was 6,200. 35 The leader of
the families of the Merarite clans
was Zuriel son of Abihail; they
were to camp on the north side
of the tabernacle. 36 The Merarites
were appointed to take care of the
frames of the tabernacle, its crossbars, posts, bases, all its equipment, and everything related to
their use, 37 as well as the posts of
the surrounding courtyard with
their bases, tent pegs and ropes.
Ex 6:19; Nu 4:32

38 Moses and Aaron and his sons
were to camp to the east of the
tabernacle, toward the sunrise, in
front of the tent of meeting. They
were responsible for the care of
the sanctuary on behalf of the
Israelites. Anyone else who approached the sanctuary was to be
put to death. Nu 18:5

39 The total number of Levites
counted at the LORD's command
by Moses and Aaron according to
their clans, including every male
a month old or more, was 22,000.
Nu 26:62

40 The LORD said to Moses,
"Count all the firstborn Israelite males who are a month old
or more and make a list of their
names. 41 Take the Levites for me
in place of all the firstborn of the
Israelites, and the livestock of the
Levites in place of all the firstborn
of the livestock of the Israelites. I
am the LORD." ver 12,15

42 So Moses counted all the firstborn of the Israelites, as the LORD
commanded him. 43 The total number of firstborn males a month
old or more, listed by name, was
22,273.

44 The LORD also said to Moses,
45 "Take the Levites in place of all
the firstborn of Israel, and the
livestock of the Levites in place of
their livestock. The Levites are to
be mine. I am the LORD. 46 To redeem the 273 firstborn Israelites
who exceed the number of the
Levites, 47 collect five shekels[a] for
each one, according to the sanctuary shekel, which weighs twenty
gerahs. 48 Give the money for the
redemption of the additional Israelites to Aaron and his sons."
Ex 13:13; Nu 18:15

49 So Moses collected the redemption money from those who
exceeded the number redeemed
by the Levites. 50 From the firstborn of the Israelites he collected
silver weighing 1,365 shekels,[b] according to the sanctuary shekel.

[a] *47* That is, about 2 ounces or about 58 grams [b] *50* That is, about 35 pounds or about 16 kilograms

51Moses gave the redemption money to Aaron and his sons, as he was
commanded by the word of the
LORD. ver 46-48

The Kohathites

4 The LORD said to Moses and
Aaron: 2"Take a census of the
Kohathite branch of the Levites by
their clans and families. 3Count all
the men from thirty to fifty years
of age who come to serve in the
work at the tent of meeting.
Ex 30:12; Nu 8:25; 1Ch 23:3,24,27

4"This is the work of the Kohathites at the tent of meeting:
the care of the most holy things.
5When the camp is to move, Aaron
and his sons are to go in and take
down the shielding curtain and
put it over the ark of the covenant
law. 6Then they are to cover the
curtain with a durable leather,[a]
spread a cloth of solid blue over
that and put the poles in place.
Ex 25:10,16; 26:31,33

7"Over the table of the Presence
they are to spread a blue cloth and
put on it the plates, dishes and
bowls, and the jars for drink offerings; the bread that is continually there is to remain on it. 8They
are to spread a scarlet cloth over
them, cover that with the durable
leather and put the poles in place.
Ex 25:30; Lev 24:6

9"They are to take a blue cloth
and cover the lampstand that is
for light, together with its lamps,
its wick trimmers and trays, and
all its jars for the olive oil used to
supply it. 10Then they are to wrap
it and all its accessories in a covering of the durable leather and put
it on a carrying frame. Ex 25:31,37-38

11"Over the gold altar they are to
spread a blue cloth and cover that
with the durable leather and put
the poles in place. Ex 30:1

12"They are to take all the articles used for ministering in the
sanctuary, wrap them in a blue
cloth, cover that with the durable
leather and put them on a carrying frame.

13"They are to remove the ashes
from the bronze altar and spread
a purple cloth over it. 14Then they
are to place on it all the utensils
used for ministering at the altar,
including the firepans, meat forks,
shovels and sprinkling bowls.
Over it they are to spread a covering of the durable leather and put
the poles in place. Ex 27:1-8

15"After Aaron and his sons have
finished covering the holy furnishings and all the holy articles,
and when the camp is ready to
move, only then are the Kohathites to come and do the carrying.
But they must not touch the holy
things or they will die. The Kohathites are to carry those things
that are in the tent of meeting.
Nu 1:51; 2Sa 6:6-7

16"Eleazar son of Aaron, the
priest, is to have charge of the oil
for the light, the fragrant incense,

[a] 6 Possibly the hides of large aquatic mammals; also in verses 8, 10, 11, 12, 14 and 25

the regular grain offering and the
anointing oil. He is to be in charge
of the entire tabernacle and everything in it, including its holy
furnishings and articles."

Ex 25:6; 29:41

17The LORD said to Moses and
Aaron, 18"See that the Kohathite tribal clans are not destroyed
from among the Levites. 19So that
they may live and not die when
they come near the most holy
things, do this for them: Aaron
and his sons are to go into the
sanctuary and assign to each man
his work and what he is to carry.
20But the Kohathites must not go
in to look at the holy things, even
for a moment, or they will die."

Ex 19:21; 1Sa 6:19

The Gershonites

21The LORD said to Moses, 22"Take
a census also of the Gershonites by
their families and clans. 23Count
all the men from thirty to fifty
years of age who come to serve in
the work at the tent of meeting.

24"This is the service of the Gershonite clans in their carrying
and their other work: 25They are
to carry the curtains of the tabernacle, that is, the tent of meeting,
its covering and its outer covering
of durable leather, the curtains for
the entrance to the tent of meeting, 26the curtains of the courtyard surrounding the tabernacle
and altar, the curtain for the entrance to the courtyard, the ropes
and all the equipment used in the
service of the tent. The Gershonites are to do all that needs to be
done with these things. 27All their
service, whether carrying or doing other work, is to be done under the direction of Aaron and his
sons. You shall assign to them as
their responsibility all they are to
carry. 28This is the service of the
Gershonite clans at the tent of
meeting. Their duties are to be
under the direction of Ithamar
son of Aaron, the priest.

Ex 27:10-18; Nu 3:25-26

The Merarites

29"Count the Merarites by their
clans and families. 30Count all the
men from thirty to fifty years of
age who come to serve in the work
at the tent of meeting. 31As part of
all their service at the tent, they
are to carry the frames of the tabernacle, its crossbars, posts and
bases, 32as well as the posts of the
surrounding courtyard with their
bases, tent pegs, ropes, all their
equipment and everything related to their use. Assign to each man
the specific things he is to carry.
33This is the service of the Merarite clans as they work at the tent
of meeting under the direction of
Ithamar son of Aaron, the priest."

Ge 46:11; Nu 3:36

The Numbering of the Levite Clans

34Moses, Aaron and the leaders of the community counted
the Kohathites by their clans and
families. 35All the men from thir-

ty to fifty years of age who came
to serve in the work at the tent of
meeting, 36counted by clans, were
2,750. 37This was the total of all
those in the Kohathite clans who
served at the tent of meeting. Moses and Aaron counted them according to the LORD's command
through Moses. Nu 3:27

38The Gershonites were counted by their clans and families.
39All the men from thirty to fifty
years of age who came to serve in
the work at the tent of meeting,
40counted by their clans and families, were 2,630. 41This was the total of those in the Gershonite clans
who served at the tent of meeting.
Moses and Aaron counted them
according to the LORD's command.
Ge 46:11

42The Merarites were counted by
their clans and families. 43All the
men from thirty to fifty years of
age who came to serve in the work
at the tent of meeting, 44counted
by their clans, were 3,200. 45This
was the total of those in the Merarite clans. Moses and Aaron counted them according to the LORD's
command through Moses. ver 29

46So Moses, Aaron and the leaders of Israel counted all the Levites by their clans and families.
47All the men from thirty to fifty
years of age who came to do the
work of serving and carrying the
tent of meeting 48numbered 8,580.
49At the LORD's command through
Moses, each was assigned his work
and told what to carry. Nu 3:39

Thus they were counted, as the
LORD commanded Moses. Nu 1:47

The Purity of the Camp

5 The LORD said to Moses,
2"Command the Israelites to
send away from the camp anyone
who has a defiling skin disease[a] or
a discharge of any kind, or who is
ceremonially unclean because of a
dead body. 3Send away male and
female alike; send them outside
the camp so they will not defile
their camp, where I dwell among
them." 4The Israelites did so; they
sent them outside the camp. They
did just as the LORD had instructed Moses. Lev 26:12; 2Co 6:16

Restitution for Wrongs

5The LORD said to Moses, 6"Say
to the Israelites: 'Any man or
woman who wrongs another in
any way[b] and so is unfaithful to
the LORD is guilty 7and must confess the sin they have committed.
They must make full restitution
for the wrong they have done,
add a fifth of the value to it and
give it all to the person they have
wronged. 8But if that person has
no close relative to whom restitution can be made for the wrong,
the restitution belongs to the
LORD and must be given to the
priest, along with the ram with

[a] 2 The Hebrew word for *defiling skin disease,* traditionally translated "leprosy," was used for various diseases affecting the skin. [b] 6 Or *woman who commits any wrong common to mankind*

which atonement is made for the
wrongdoer. 9All the sacred contributions the Israelites bring to a
priest will belong to him. 10Sacred
things belong to their owners, but
what they give to the priest will
belong to the priest.’ ”

Lev 5:5; 6:2; Lk 19:8

The Test for an Unfaithful Wife

11Then the LORD said to Moses, 12“Speak to the Israelites and
say to them: ‘If a man’s wife goes
astray and is unfaithful to him 13so
that another man has sexual relations with her, and this is hidden
from her husband and her impurity is undetected (since there is no
witness against her and she has
not been caught in the act), 14and
if feelings of jealousy come over
her husband and he suspects his
wife and she is impure — or if he
is jealous and suspects her even
though she is not impure — 15then
he is to take his wife to the priest.
He must also take an offering of a
tenth of an ephah[a] of barley flour
on her behalf. He must not pour
olive oil on it or put incense on it,
because it is a grain offering for
jealousy, a reminder-offering to
draw attention to wrongdoing.

Eze 29:16

16“ ‘The priest shall bring her
and have her stand before the
LORD. 17Then he shall take some
holy water in a clay jar and put
some dust from the tabernacle
floor into the water. 18After the
priest has had the woman stand
before the LORD, he shall loosen
her hair and place in her hands
the reminder-offering, the grain
offering for jealousy, while he
himself holds the bitter water
that brings a curse. 19Then the
priest shall put the woman under oath and say to her, “If no
other man has had sexual relations with you and you have not
gone astray and become impure
while married to your husband,
may this bitter water that brings
a curse not harm you. 20But if you
have gone astray while married
to your husband and you have
made yourself impure by having
sexual relations with a man other
than your husband” — 21here the
priest is to put the woman under
this curse — “may the LORD cause
you to become a curse[b] among
your people when he makes your
womb miscarry and your abdomen swell. 22May this water that
brings a curse enter your body so
that your abdomen swells or your
womb miscarries.” Jos 6:26; Ps 109:18

“ ‘Then the woman is to say,
“Amen. So be it.” Dt 27:15

23“ ‘The priest is to write these
curses on a scroll and then wash
them off into the bitter water. 24He
shall make the woman drink the
bitter water that brings a curse, and
this water that brings a curse and
causes bitter suffering will enter

[a] *15* That is, probably about 3 1/2 pounds or about 1.6 kilograms [b] *21* That is, may he cause your name to be used in cursing (see Jer. 29:22); or, may others see that you are cursed; similarly in verse 27.

her. 25The priest is to take from her
hands the grain offering for jealousy, wave it before the LORD and
bring it to the altar. 26The priest is
then to take a handful of the grain
offering as a memorial[a] offering
and burn it on the altar; after that,
he is to have the woman drink the
water. 27If she has made herself
impure and been unfaithful to her
husband, this will be the result:
When she is made to drink the water that brings a curse and causes
bitter suffering, it will enter her, her
abdomen will swell and her womb
will miscarry, and she will become
a curse. 28If, however, the woman
has not made herself impure, but
is clean, she will be cleared of guilt
and will be able to have children.
Jer 29:18; 42:18

29" 'This, then, is the law of jealousy when a woman goes astray
and makes herself impure while
married to her husband, 30or when
feelings of jealousy come over a
man because he suspects his wife.
The priest is to have her stand before the LORD and is to apply this
entire law to her. 31The husband
will be innocent of any wrongdoing, but the woman will bear the
consequences of her sin.' "
Lev 5:1; 20:17

The Nazirite

6 The LORD said to Moses,
2"Speak to the Israelites and
say to them: 'If a man or woman wants to make a special vow, a
vow of dedication to the LORD as a
Nazirite, 3they must abstain from
wine and other fermented drink
and must not drink vinegar made
from wine or other fermented
drink. They must not drink grape
juice or eat grapes or raisins. 4As
long as they remain under their
Nazirite vow, they must not eat
anything that comes from the
grapevine, not even the seeds or
skins. Jdg 13:5; Am 2:11-12; Ac 21:23

5" 'During the entire period of
their Nazirite vow, no razor may
be used on their head. They must
be holy until the period of their
dedication to the LORD is over;
they must let their hair grow long.

6" 'Throughout the period of
their dedication to the LORD, the
Nazirite must not go near a dead
body. 7Even if their own father or
mother or brother or sister dies,
they must not make themselves
ceremonially unclean on account
of them, because the symbol of
their dedication to God is on their
head. 8Throughout the period of
their dedication, they are consecrated to the LORD. Nu 9:6; 1Sa 1:11

9" 'If someone dies suddenly in
the Nazirite's presence, thus defiling the hair that symbolizes their
dedication, they must shave their
head on the seventh day — the
day of their cleansing. 10Then on
the eighth day they must bring
two doves or two young pigeons
to the priest at the entrance to the
tent of meeting. 11The priest is to

[a] 26 Or *representative*

offer one as a sin offering[a] and the
other as a burnt offering to make
atonement for the Nazirite because they sinned by being in the
presence of the dead body. That
same day they are to consecrate
their head again. 12 They must re-
dedicate themselves to the LORD
for the same period of dedication
and must bring a year-old male
lamb as a guilt offering. The previous days do not count, because
they became defiled during their
period of dedication. Lev 5:7; 14:22

13 " 'Now this is the law of the
Nazirite when the period of their
dedication is over. They are to be
brought to the entrance to the
tent of meeting. 14 There they are
to present their offerings to the
LORD: a year-old male lamb without defect for a burnt offering, a
year-old ewe lamb without defect
for a sin offering, a ram without
defect for a fellowship offering,
15 together with their grain offerings and drink offerings, and a
basket of bread made with the
finest flour and without yeast —
thick loaves with olive oil mixed
in, and thin loaves brushed with
olive oil. Lev 14:10; Ac 21:26

16 " 'The priest is to present all
these before the LORD and make
the sin offering and the burnt offering. 17 He is to present the basket of unleavened bread and is to
sacrifice the ram as a fellowship
offering to the LORD, together
with its grain offering and drink
offering. Lev 1:3; 23:13

18 " 'Then at the entrance to the
tent of meeting, the Nazirite must
shave off the hair that symbolizes
their dedication. They are to take
the hair and put it in the fire that
is under the sacrifice of the fellowship offering. ver 9; Ac 21:24

19 " 'After the Nazirite has shaved
off the hair that symbolizes their
dedication, the priest is to place
in their hands a boiled shoulder
of the ram, and one thick loaf and
one thin loaf from the basket,
both made without yeast. 20 The
priest shall then wave these before the LORD as a wave offering;
they are holy and belong to the
priest, together with the breast
that was waved and the thigh
that was presented. After that,
the Nazirite may drink wine.
Ecc 9:7

21 " 'This is the law of the Nazirite who vows offerings to the
LORD in accordance with their
dedication, in addition to whatever else they can afford. They
must fulfill the vows they have
made, according to the law of the
Nazirite.' " ver 2,13

The Priestly Blessing

22 The LORD said to Moses, 23 "Tell
Aaron and his sons, 'This is how
you are to bless the Israelites. Say
to them: 1Ch 23:13

24 " ' "The LORD bless you Dt 28:3-6
and keep you;

[a] 11 Or *purification offering*; also in verses 14 and 16

25 the LORD make his face shine
on you Ps 80:3; 119:135
and be gracious to you;
Ge 43:29; Ps 25:16
26 the LORD turn his face toward
you Ps 4:6; 44:3
and give you peace."' Ps 29:11

27 "So they will put my name
on the Israelites, and I will bless
them." Dt 28:10; 2Ch 7:14

Offerings at the Dedication of the Tabernacle

7 When Moses finished setting
up the tabernacle, he anointed and consecrated it and all its
furnishings. He also anointed
and consecrated the altar and all
its utensils. 2 Then the leaders of
Israel, the heads of families who
were the tribal leaders in charge
of those who were counted, made
offerings. 3 They brought as their
gifts before the LORD six covered
carts and twelve oxen — an ox
from each leader and a cart from
every two. These they presented
before the tabernacle. Ex 40:9,17
4 The LORD said to Moses, 5 "Accept these from them, that they
may be used in the work at the tent
of meeting. Give them to the Levites as each man's work requires."
6 So Moses took the carts and
oxen and gave them to the Levites.
7 He gave two carts and four oxen
to the Gershonites, as their work
required, 8 and he gave four carts
and eight oxen to the Merarites,
as their work required. They were
all under the direction of Ithamar
son of Aaron, the priest. 9 But Moses did not give any to the Kohathites, because they were to carry on
their shoulders the holy things,
for which they were responsible.
Nu 4:15,31-33
10 When the altar was anointed,
the leaders brought their offerings for its dedication and presented them before the altar. 11 For
the LORD had said to Moses, "Each
day one leader is to bring his offering for the dedication of the
altar." 2Ch 7:9

12 The one who brought his offering on the first day was Nahshon
son of Amminadab of the tribe of
Judah.
13 His offering was one silver
plate weighing a hundred
and thirty shekels[a] and one
silver sprinkling bowl weighing seventy shekels,[b] both
according to the sanctuary
shekel, each filled with the
finest flour mixed with olive
oil as a grain offering; 14 one
gold dish weighing ten shekels,[c] filled with incense; 15 one
young bull, one ram and one
male lamb a year old for a
burnt offering; 16 one male
goat for a sin offering[d]; 17 and

[a] 13 That is, about 3 1/4 pounds or about 1.5 kilograms; also elsewhere in this chapter
[b] 13 That is, about 1 3/4 pounds or about 800 grams; also elsewhere in this chapter
[c] 14 That is, about 4 ounces or about 115 grams; also elsewhere in this chapter
[d] 16 Or *purification offering*; also elsewhere in this chapter

two oxen, five rams, five male
goats and five male lambs a
year old to be sacrificed as a
fellowship offering. This was
the offering of Nahshon son
of Amminadab. Lev 3:1; 4:3,23

18 On the second day Nethanel son
of Zuar, the leader of Issachar,
brought his offering. Nu 1:8

19 The offering he brought was
one silver plate weighing a
hundred and thirty shekels
and one silver sprinkling bowl
weighing seventy shekels,
both according to the sanctuary shekel, each filled with
the finest flour mixed with
olive oil as a grain offering;
20 one gold dish weighing ten
shekels, filled with incense;
21 one young bull, one ram and
one male lamb a year old for
a burnt offering; 22 one male
goat for a sin offering; 23 and
two oxen, five rams, five male
goats and five male lambs a
year old to be sacrificed as a
fellowship offering. This was
the offering of Nethanel son
of Zuar.

24 On the third day, Eliab son of
Helon, the leader of the people of
Zebulun, brought his offering.
Nu 1:9

25 His offering was one silver
plate weighing a hundred and
thirty shekels and one silver
sprinkling bowl weighing
seventy shekels, both according to the sanctuary shekel,
each filled with the finest
flour mixed with olive oil as a
grain offering; 26 one gold dish
weighing ten shekels, filled
with incense; 27 one young
bull, one ram and one male
lamb a year old for a burnt offering; 28 one male goat for a
sin offering; 29 and two oxen,
five rams, five male goats and
five male lambs a year old to
be sacrificed as a fellowship
offering. This was the offering
of Eliab son of Helon.

30 On the fourth day Elizur son of
Shedeur, the leader of the people
of Reuben, brought his offering.
Nu 1:5

31 His offering was one silver
plate weighing a hundred and
thirty shekels and one silver
sprinkling bowl weighing
seventy shekels, both according to the sanctuary shekel, each filled with the finest
flour mixed with olive oil as a
grain offering; 32 one gold dish
weighing ten shekels, filled
with incense; 33 one young
bull, one ram and one male
lamb a year old for a burnt offering; 34 one male goat for a
sin offering; 35 and two oxen,
five rams, five male goats and
five male lambs a year old to
be sacrificed as a fellowship
offering. This was the offering of Elizur son of Shedeur.

36 On the fifth day Shelumiel son
of Zurishaddai, the leader of the

people of Simeon, brought his offering. Nu 1:6
37His offering was one silver
plate weighing a hundred
and thirty shekels and one
silver sprinkling bowl weighing seventy shekels, both
according to the sanctuary
shekel, each filled with the
finest flour mixed with olive
oil as a grain offering; 38one
gold dish weighing ten shekels, filled with incense; 39one
young bull, one ram and one
male lamb a year old for a
burnt offering; 40one male
goat for a sin offering; 41and
two oxen, five rams, five male
goats and five male lambs a
year old to be sacrificed as a
fellowship offering. This was
the offering of Shelumiel son
of Zurishaddai.

42On the sixth day Eliasaph son of
Deuel, the leader of the people of
Gad, brought his offering. Nu 1:14
43His offering was one silver
plate weighing a hundred and
thirty shekels and one silver
sprinkling bowl weighing
seventy shekels, both according to the sanctuary shekel, each filled with the finest
flour mixed with olive oil as a
grain offering; 44one gold dish
weighing ten shekels, filled
with incense; 45one young
bull, one ram and one male
lamb a year old for a burnt offering; 46one male goat for a
sin offering; 47and two oxen,
five rams, five male goats and
five male lambs a year old to
be sacrificed as a fellowship
offering. This was the offering of Eliasaph son of Deuel.

48On the seventh day Elishama
son of Ammihud, the leader of the
people of Ephraim, brought his offering. Nu 1:10
49His offering was one silver
plate weighing a hundred
and thirty shekels and one
silver sprinkling bowl weighing seventy shekels, both
according to the sanctuary
shekel, each filled with the
finest flour mixed with olive
oil as a grain offering; 50one
gold dish weighing ten shekels, filled with incense; 51one
young bull, one ram and one
male lamb a year old for a
burnt offering; 52one male
goat for a sin offering; 53and
two oxen, five rams, five male
goats and five male lambs a
year old to be sacrificed as a
fellowship offering. This was
the offering of Elishama son
of Ammihud.

54On the eighth day Gamaliel son
of Pedahzur, the leader of the people of Manasseh, brought his offering. Nu 1:10; 2:20
55His offering was one silver
plate weighing a hundred
and thirty shekels and one
silver sprinkling bowl weighing seventy shekels, both

according to the sanctuary
shekel, each filled with the
finest flour mixed with olive
oil as a grain offering; 56 one
gold dish weighing ten shekels, filled with incense; 57 one
young bull, one ram and one
male lamb a year old for a
burnt offering; 58 one male
goat for a sin offering; 59 and
two oxen, five rams, five male
goats and five male lambs a
year old to be sacrificed as a
fellowship offering. This was
the offering of Gamaliel son
of Pedahzur.

60 On the ninth day Abidan son of
Gideoni, the leader of the people
of Benjamin, brought his offering.
Nu 1:11

61 His offering was one silver
plate weighing a hundred and
thirty shekels and one silver
sprinkling bowl weighing
seventy shekels, both according to the sanctuary shekel, each filled with the finest
flour mixed with olive oil as a
grain offering; 62 one gold dish
weighing ten shekels, filled
with incense; 63 one young
bull, one ram and one male
lamb a year old for a burnt offering; 64 one male goat for a
sin offering; 65 and two oxen,
five rams, five male goats and
five male lambs a year old to
be sacrificed as a fellowship
offering. This was the offering
of Abidan son of Gideoni.

66 On the tenth day Ahiezer son of
Ammishaddai, the leader of the
people of Dan, brought his offering. Nu 1:12; 2:25

67 His offering was one silver
plate weighing a hundred
and thirty shekels and one
silver sprinkling bowl weighing seventy shekels, both
according to the sanctuary
shekel, each filled with the
finest flour mixed with olive
oil as a grain offering; 68 one
gold dish weighing ten shekels, filled with incense; 69 one
young bull, one ram and one
male lamb a year old for a
burnt offering; 70 one male
goat for a sin offering; 71 and
two oxen, five rams, five male
goats and five male lambs a
year old to be sacrificed as a
fellowship offering. This was
the offering of Ahiezer son of
Ammishaddai.

72 On the eleventh day Pagiel son
of Okran, the leader of the people
of Asher, brought his offering.
Nu 1:13

73 His offering was one silver
plate weighing a hundred and
thirty shekels and one silver
sprinkling bowl weighing
seventy shekels, both according to the sanctuary shekel, each filled with the finest
flour mixed with olive oil as a
grain offering; 74 one gold dish
weighing ten shekels, filled
with incense; 75 one young

bull, one ram and one male
lamb a year old for a burnt offering; 76 one male goat for a
sin offering; 77 and two oxen,
five rams, five male goats and
five male lambs a year old to
be sacrificed as a fellowship
offering. This was the offering of Pagiel son of Okran.

78 On the twelfth day Ahira son of
Enan, the leader of the people of
Naphtali, brought his offering.
Nu 1:15; 2:29

79 His offering was one silver
plate weighing a hundred
and thirty shekels and one
silver sprinkling bowl weighing seventy shekels, both
according to the sanctuary
shekel, each filled with the
finest flour mixed with olive
oil as a grain offering; 80 one
gold dish weighing ten shekels, filled with incense; 81 one
young bull, one ram and one
male lamb a year old for a
burnt offering; 82 one male
goat for a sin offering; 83 and
two oxen, five rams, five male
goats and five male lambs a
year old to be sacrificed as a
fellowship offering. This was
the offering of Ahira son of
Enan.

84 These were the offerings of
the Israelite leaders for the dedication of the altar when it was
anointed: twelve silver plates,
twelve silver sprinkling bowls and
twelve gold dishes. 85 Each silver
plate weighed a hundred and thirty shekels, and each sprinkling
bowl seventy shekels. Altogether, the silver dishes weighed two
thousand four hundred shekels,[a]
according to the sanctuary shekel. 86 The twelve gold dishes filled
with incense weighed ten shekels
each, according to the sanctuary
shekel. Altogether, the gold dishes weighed a hundred and twenty
shekels.[b] 87 The total number of animals for the burnt offering came
to twelve young bulls, twelve rams
and twelve male lambs a year old,
together with their grain offering.
Twelve male goats were used for
the sin offering. 88 The total number of animals for the sacrifice
of the fellowship offering came
to twenty-four oxen, sixty rams,
sixty male goats and sixty male
lambs a year old. These were the
offerings for the dedication of the
altar after it was anointed. ver 1,10

89 When Moses entered the tent
of meeting to speak with the LORD,
he heard the voice speaking to
him from between the two cherubim above the atonement cover
on the ark of the covenant law. In
this way the LORD spoke to him.
Ex 25:21-22; Ps 80:1; 99:1

Setting Up the Lamps

8 The LORD said to Moses,
2 "Speak to Aaron and say to
him, 'When you set up the lamps,

[a] 85 That is, about 60 pounds or about 28 kilograms [b] 86 That is, about 3 pounds or about 1.4 kilograms

see that all seven light up the area
in front of the lampstand.'"
3 Aaron did so; he set up the
lamps so that they faced forward
on the lampstand, just as the
LORD commanded Moses. 4 This is
how the lampstand was made: It
was made of hammered gold—
from its base to its blossoms. The
lampstand was made exactly like
the pattern the LORD had shown
Moses. Ex 25:36-37

The Setting Apart of the Levites

5 The LORD said to Moses: 6 "Take
the Levites from among all the Israelites and make them ceremonially clean. 7 To purify them, do this:
Sprinkle the water of cleansing
on them; then have them shave
their whole bodies and wash their
clothes. And so they will purify
themselves. 8 Have them take a
young bull with its grain offering
of the finest flour mixed with olive oil; then you are to take a second young bull for a sin offering.[a]
9 Bring the Levites to the front of
the tent of meeting and assemble
the whole Israelite community.
10 You are to bring the Levites before the LORD, and the Israelites
are to lay their hands on them.
11 Aaron is to present the Levites
before the LORD as a wave offering
from the Israelites, so that they
may be ready to do the work of the
LORD. Lev 8:3; Isa 52:11; Ac 6:6
12 "Then the Levites are to lay
their hands on the heads of the
bulls, using one for a sin offering to the LORD and the other for
a burnt offering, to make atonement for the Levites. 13 Have the
Levites stand in front of Aaron and
his sons and then present them as
a wave offering to the LORD. 14 In
this way you are to set the Levites
apart from the other Israelites,
and the Levites will be mine. Nu 3:12
15 "After you have purified the
Levites and presented them as a
wave offering, they are to come
to do their work at the tent of
meeting. 16 They are the Israelites who are to be given wholly
to me. I have taken them as my
own in place of the firstborn, the
first male offspring from every
Israelite woman. 17 Every firstborn
male in Israel, whether human
or animal, is mine. When I struck
down all the firstborn in Egypt, I
set them apart for myself. 18 And
I have taken the Levites in place
of all the firstborn sons in Israel.
19 From among all the Israelites, I
have given the Levites as gifts to
Aaron and his sons to do the work
at the tent of meeting on behalf of
the Israelites and to make atonement for them so that no plague
will strike the Israelites when
they go near the sanctuary."
Ex 13:2; Nu 3:12
20 Moses, Aaron and the whole
Israelite community did with
the Levites just as the LORD commanded Moses. 21 The Levites purified themselves and washed their
clothes. Then Aaron presented

[a] 8 Or *purification offering*; also in verse 12

them as a wave offering before
the LORD and made atonement for
them to purify them. 22 After that,
the Levites came to do their work
at the tent of meeting under the
supervision of Aaron and his sons.
They did with the Levites just as
the LORD commanded Moses.

Ge 35:2; Nu 16:47

23 The LORD said to Moses, 24 "This
applies to the Levites: Men twenty-
five years old or more shall come
to take part in the work at the tent
of meeting, 25 but at the age of fifty, they must retire from their regular service and work no longer.
26 They may assist their brothers
in performing their duties at the
tent of meeting, but they themselves must not do the work. This,
then, is how you are to assign the
responsibilities of the Levites."

Nu 4:3; 1Ch 23:3

The Passover

9 The LORD spoke to Moses in
the Desert of Sinai in the first
month of the second year after
they came out of Egypt. He said,
2 "Have the Israelites celebrate the
Passover at the appointed time.
3 Celebrate it at the appointed
time, at twilight on the fourteenth
day of this month, in accordance
with all its rules and regulations."

Ex 12:2-11,43-49; Nu 1:1

4 So Moses told the Israelites to
celebrate the Passover, 5 and they
did so in the Desert of Sinai at
twilight on the fourteenth day of
the first month. The Israelites did
everything just as the LORD commanded Moses.

Ex 12:1-13; Jos 5:10

6 But some of them could not
celebrate the Passover on that day
because they were ceremonially unclean on account of a dead
body. So they came to Moses and
Aaron that same day 7 and said to
Moses, "We have become unclean
because of a dead body, but why
should we be kept from presenting the LORD's offering with the
other Israelites at the appointed
time?"

Ex 18:15; Nu 27:2

8 Moses answered them, "Wait
until I find out what the LORD
commands concerning you."

Nu 27:5,21; Ps 85:8

9 Then the LORD said to Moses,
10 "Tell the Israelites: 'When any of
you or your descendants are unclean because of a dead body or
are away on a journey, they are still
to celebrate the LORD's Passover,
11 but they are to do it on the fourteenth day of the second month at
twilight. They are to eat the lamb,
together with unleavened bread
and bitter herbs. 12 They must not
leave any of it till morning or
break any of its bones. When they
celebrate the Passover, they must
follow all the regulations. 13 But if
anyone who is ceremonially clean
and not on a journey fails to celebrate the Passover, they must be
cut off from their people for not
presenting the LORD's offering at
the appointed time. They will bear
the consequences of their sin.

Ge 17:14; Ex 12:8,15,46

14“ ‘A foreigner residing among
you is also to celebrate the LORD’s
Passover in accordance with its
rules and regulations. You must
have the same regulations for
both the foreigner and the native-
born.’ ” Ex 12:48-49

The Cloud Above the Tabernacle

15On the day the tabernacle, the
tent of the covenant law, was set
up, the cloud covered it. From evening till morning the cloud above
the tabernacle looked like fire.
16That is how it continued to be;
the cloud covered it, and at night
it looked like fire. 17Whenever the
cloud lifted from above the tent,
the Israelites set out; wherever
the cloud settled, the Israelites
encamped. 18At the LORD’s command the Israelites set out, and
at his command they encamped.
As long as the cloud stayed over
the tabernacle, they remained in
camp. 19When the cloud remained
over the tabernacle a long time,
the Israelites obeyed the LORD’s
order and did not set out. 20Some-
times the cloud was over the tabernacle only a few days; at the
LORD’s command they would encamp, and then at his command
they would set out. 21Sometimes
the cloud stayed only from evening till morning, and when it
lifted in the morning, they set
out. Whether by day or by night,
whenever the cloud lifted, they set
out. 22Whether the cloud stayed
over the tabernacle for two days
or a month or a year, the Israelites
would remain in camp and not set
out; but when it lifted, they would
set out. 23At the LORD’s command
they encamped, and at the LORD’s
command they set out. They
obeyed the LORD’s order, in accordance with his command through
Moses. Ex 13:21; 40:36-38; 1Co 10:1

The Silver Trumpets

10 The LORD said to Moses:
2“Make two trumpets of
hammered silver, and use them
for calling the community together and for having the camps set
out. 3When both are sounded, the
whole community is to assemble
before you at the entrance to the
tent of meeting. 4If only one is
sounded, the leaders — the heads
of the clans of Israel — are to assemble before you. 5When a trumpet blast is sounded, the tribes
camping on the east are to set out.
6At the sounding of a second blast,
the camps on the south are to set
out. The blast will be the signal for
setting out. 7To gather the assembly, blow the trumpets, but not
with the signal for setting out.
Ps 47:5; Jer 4:5,19; Joel 2:1,15

8“The sons of Aaron, the priests,
are to blow the trumpets. This is
to be a lasting ordinance for you
and the generations to come.
9When you go into battle in your
own land against an enemy who
is oppressing you, sound a blast
on the trumpets. Then you will
be remembered by the LORD your

God and rescued from your enemies. 10Also at your times of rejoicing — your appointed festivals and New Moon feasts — you
are to sound the trumpets over
your burnt offerings and fellowship offerings, and they will be
a memorial for you before your
God. I am the LORD your God."
Lev 23:24; Ps 106:4

The Israelites Leave Sinai

11On the twentieth day of the
second month of the second year,
the cloud lifted from above the
tabernacle of the covenant law.
12Then the Israelites set out from
the Desert of Sinai and traveled
from place to place until the cloud
came to rest in the Desert of Paran. 13They set out, this first time,
at the LORD's command through
Moses. Nu 9:17; Dt 1:6

14The divisions of the camp of
Judah went first, under their standard. Nahshon son of Amminadab
was in command. 15Nethanel son
of Zuar was over the division of the
tribe of Issachar, 16and Eliab son of
Helon was over the division of the
tribe of Zebulun. 17Then the tabernacle was taken down, and the
Gershonites and Merarites, who
carried it, set out. Nu 2:3-9; 4:21-32

18The divisions of the camp of
Reuben went next, under their
standard. Elizur son of Shedeur
was in command. 19Shelumiel son
of Zurishaddai was over the division of the tribe of Simeon, 20and
Eliasaph son of Deuel was over
the division of the tribe of Gad.
21Then the Kohathites set out, carrying the holy things. The tabernacle was to be set up before they
arrived. Nu 2:10-16; 4:20

22The divisions of the camp of
Ephraim went next, under their
standard. Elishama son of Ammihud was in command. 23Gamaliel
son of Pedahzur was over the division of the tribe of Manasseh,
24and Abidan son of Gideoni was
over the division of the tribe of
Benjamin. Nu 1:10-11; 2:24

25Finally, as the rear guard for
all the units, the divisions of the
camp of Dan set out under their
standard. Ahiezer son of Ammishaddai was in command. 26Pagiel
son of Okran was over the division
of the tribe of Asher, 27and Ahira
son of Enan was over the division
of the tribe of Naphtali. 28This was
the order of march for the Israelite divisions as they set out.
Nu 2:31; Jos 6:9

29Now Moses said to Hobab son
of Reuel the Midianite, Moses' father-in-law, "We are setting out for
the place about which the LORD
said, 'I will give it to you.' Come
with us and we will treat you well,
for the LORD has promised good
things to Israel." Ge 12:7; Ex 2:18

30He answered, "No, I will not
go; I am going back to my own
land and my own people." Mt 21:29

31But Moses said, "Please do
not leave us. You know where we
should camp in the wilderness,
and you can be our eyes. 32If you

come with us, we will share with
you whatever good things the
LORD gives us." Dt 10:18; Ps 22:27-31
33 So they set out from the
mountain of the LORD and traveled for three days. The ark of the
covenant of the LORD went before
them during those three days to
find them a place to rest. 34 The
cloud of the LORD was over them
by day when they set out from the
camp. Nu 9:15-23; Jos 3:3
35 Whenever the ark set out, Moses said,

"Rise up, LORD!
May your enemies be
scattered; Ps 68:1
may your foes flee before
you." Dt 7:10; 32:41

36 Whenever it came to rest, he
said,

"Return, LORD,
to the countless thousands
of Israel." Dt 1:10

Fire From the LORD

11 Now the people complained
about their hardships in the
hearing of the LORD, and when he
heard them his anger was aroused.
Then fire from the LORD burned
among them and consumed some
of the outskirts of the camp.
2 When the people cried out to Moses, he prayed to the LORD and
the fire died down. 3 So that place
was called Taberah,[a] because fire
from the LORD had burned among
them. Lev 10:2; Nu 21:7

Quail From the LORD

4 The rabble with them began to
crave other food, and again the Israelites started wailing and said,
"If only we had meat to eat! 5 We
remember the fish we ate in Egypt
at no cost — also the cucumbers,
melons, leeks, onions and garlic.
6 But now we have lost our appetite; we never see anything but
this manna!" Ex 16:3; Ps 78:18
7 The manna was like coriander
seed and looked like resin. 8 The
people went around gathering it,
and then ground it in a hand mill
or crushed it in a mortar. They
cooked it in a pot or made it into
loaves. And it tasted like something made with olive oil. 9 When
the dew settled on the camp at
night, the manna also came down.
Ex 16:13,31
10 Moses heard the people of every family wailing at the entrance
to their tents. The LORD became
exceedingly angry, and Moses was
troubled. 11 He asked the LORD,
"Why have you brought this trouble on your servant? What have I
done to displease you that you put
the burden of all these people on
me? 12 Did I conceive all these people? Did I give them birth? Why do
you tell me to carry them in my
arms, as a nurse carries an infant,
to the land you promised on oath
to their ancestors? 13 Where can I
get meat for all these people? They
keep wailing to me, 'Give us meat

[a] 3 *Taberah* means *burning.*

to eat!' 14 I cannot carry all these people by myself; the burden is too heavy for me. 15 If this is how you are going to treat me, please go ahead and kill me — if I have found favor in your eyes — and do not let me face my own ruin."

Ex 5:22; 18:18; 1Ki 19:4

16 The LORD said to Moses: "Bring me seventy of Israel's elders who are known to you as leaders and officials among the people. Have them come to the tent of meeting, that they may stand there with you. 17 I will come down and speak with you there, and I will take some of the power of the Spirit that is on you and put it on them. They will share the burden of the people with you so that you will not have to carry it alone.

Ex 18:18; 1Sa 10:6

18 "Tell the people: 'Consecrate yourselves in preparation for tomorrow, when you will eat meat. The LORD heard you when you wailed, "If only we had meat to eat! We were better off in Egypt!" Now the LORD will give you meat, and you will eat it. 19 You will not eat it for just one day, or two days, or five, ten or twenty days, 20 but for a whole month — until it comes out of your nostrils and you loathe it — because you have rejected the LORD, who is among you, and have wailed before him, saying, "Why did we ever leave Egypt?"'"

Ex 19:10; 1Sa 10:19; Ac 7:39

21 But Moses said, "Here I am among six hundred thousand men on foot, and you say, 'I will give them meat to eat for a whole month!' 22 Would they have enough if flocks and herds were slaughtered for them? Would they have enough if all the fish in the sea were caught for them?"

Mt 15:33

23 The LORD answered Moses, "Is the LORD's arm too short? Now you will see whether or not what I say will come true for you."

Isa 50:2; 59:1

24 So Moses went out and told the people what the LORD had said. He brought together seventy of their elders and had them stand around the tent. 25 Then the LORD came down in the cloud and spoke with him, and he took some of the power of the Spirit that was on him and put it on the seventy elders. When the Spirit rested on them, they prophesied — but did not do so again.

Nu 12:5; 1Sa 10:10; Ac 2:17

26 However, two men, whose names were Eldad and Medad, had remained in the camp. They were listed among the elders, but did not go out to the tent. Yet the Spirit also rested on them, and they prophesied in the camp. 27 A young man ran and told Moses, "Eldad and Medad are prophesying in the camp."

28 Joshua son of Nun, who had been Moses' aide since youth, spoke up and said, "Moses, my lord, stop them!"

Mk 9:38-40

29 But Moses replied, "Are you jealous for my sake? I wish that all the LORD's people were prophets

and that the LORD would put his
Spirit on them!" 30Then Moses and
the elders of Israel returned to the
camp. 1Co 14:5
31Now a wind went out from the
LORD and drove quail in from the
sea. It scattered them up to two cubits[a] deep all around the camp, as
far as a day's walk in any direction.
32All that day and night and all
the next day the people went out
and gathered quail. No one gathered less than ten homers.[b] Then
they spread them out all around
the camp. 33But while the meat
was still between their teeth and
before it could be consumed, the
anger of the LORD burned against
the people, and he struck them
with a severe plague. 34Therefore
the place was named Kibroth Hattaavah,[c] because there they buried
the people who had craved other
food. Ex 16:13; Ps 78:30; 106:15
35From Kibroth Hattaavah the
people traveled to Hazeroth and
stayed there. Nu 33:17

Miriam and Aaron Oppose Moses

12 Miriam and Aaron began to
talk against Moses because
of his Cushite wife, for he had
married a Cushite. 2"Has the LORD
spoken only through Moses?" they
asked. "Hasn't he also spoken
through us?" And the LORD heard
this. Ex 2:21; Nu 11:1
3(Now Moses was a very humble
man, more humble than anyone
else on the face of the earth.)
Mt 11:29
4At once the LORD said to Moses,
Aaron and Miriam, "Come out to
the tent of meeting, all three of
you." So the three of them went
out. 5Then the LORD came down
in a pillar of cloud; he stood at
the entrance to the tent and summoned Aaron and Miriam. When
the two of them stepped forward,
6he said, "Listen to my words:
Nu 11:25

"When there is a prophet
among you,
I, the LORD, reveal myself to
them in visions, Ge 15:1; 46:2
I speak to them in dreams.
Ge 31:10; Heb 1:1
7But this is not true of my
servant Moses; Ps 105:26
he is faithful in all my house.
Heb 3:2,5
8With him I speak face to face,
clearly and not in riddles;
Dt 34:10
he sees the form of the LORD.
Ps 17:15
Why then were you not afraid
to speak against my servant
Moses?"

9The anger of the LORD burned
against them, and he left them.
Ge 17:22
10When the cloud lifted from
above the tent, Miriam's skin was
leprous[d] — it became as white as

[a] *31* That is, about 3 feet or about 90 centimeters [b] *32* That is, possibly about 1 3/4 tons or about 1.6 metric tons
[c] *34* *Kibroth Hattaavah* means *graves of craving.* [d] *10* The Hebrew for *leprous* was used for various diseases affecting the skin.

snow. Aaron turned toward her
and saw that she had a defiling
skin disease, 11and he said to Moses, “Please, my lord, I ask you not
to hold against us the sin we have
so foolishly committed. 12Do not
let her be like a stillborn infant
coming from its mother’s womb
with its flesh half eaten away.”
Dt 24:9; 2Sa 19:19; 2Ki 5:1,27

13So Moses cried out to the LORD,
“Please, God, heal her!”
Isa 30:26; Jer 17:14

14The LORD replied to Moses,
“If her father had spit in her face,
would she not have been in disgrace for seven days? Confine her
outside the camp for seven days;
after that she can be brought
back.” 15So Miriam was confined
outside the camp for seven days,
and the people did not move on
till she was brought back.
Lev 13:46; Nu 5:2-3

16After that, the people left Hazeroth and encamped in the Desert of Paran. Nu 11:35

Exploring Canaan

13 The LORD said to Moses,
2“Send some men to ex-
plore the land of Canaan, which I
am giving to the Israelites. From
each ancestral tribe send one of its
leaders.” Dt 1:22

3So at the LORD’s command Moses sent them out from the Desert
of Paran. All of them were leaders
of the Israelites. 4These are their
names: Nu 1:16

from the tribe of Reuben,
Shammua son of Zakkur;
5from the tribe of Simeon,
Shaphat son of Hori;
6from the tribe of Judah, Caleb
son of Jephunneh;
Nu 14:6,24; Jdg 1:12-15
7from the tribe of Issachar, Igal
son of Joseph;
8from the tribe of Ephraim,
Hoshea son of Nun; Nu 11:28
9from the tribe of Benjamin,
Palti son of Raphu;
10from the tribe of Zebulun,
Gaddiel son of Sodi;
11from the tribe of Manasseh (a
tribe of Joseph), Gaddi son
of Susi;
12from the tribe of Dan, Ammiel son of Gemalli;
13from the tribe of Asher, Se-
thur son of Michael;
14from the tribe of Naphtali,
Nahbi son of Vophsi;
15from the tribe of Gad, Geuel
son of Maki.

16These are the names of the men
Moses sent to explore the land.
(Moses gave Hoshea son of Nun
the name Joshua.) Dt 32:44

17When Moses sent them to explore Canaan, he said, “Go up
through the Negev and on into the
hill country. 18See what the land is
like and whether the people who
live there are strong or weak, few
or many. 19What kind of land do
they live in? Is it good or bad?
What kind of towns do they live
in? Are they unwalled or fortified?

20How is the soil? Is it fertile or
poor? Are there trees in it or not?
Do your best to bring back some
of the fruit of the land." (It was the
season for the first ripe grapes.)

Ge 12:9; Dt 1:25

21So they went up and explored
the land from the Desert of Zin
as far as Rehob, toward Lebo Hamath. 22They went up through the
Negev and came to Hebron, where
Ahiman, Sheshai and Talmai, the
descendants of Anak, lived. (Hebron had been built seven years
before Zoan in Egypt.) 23When
they reached the Valley of Eshkol,[a]
they cut off a branch bearing a single cluster of grapes. Two of them
carried it on a pole between them,
along with some pomegranates
and figs. 24That place was called
the Valley of Eshkol because of the
cluster of grapes the Israelites cut
off there. 25At the end of forty days
they returned from exploring the
land.

Jos 15:13-14; Ps 78:12,43

Report on the Exploration

26They came back to Moses and
Aaron and the whole Israelite
community at Kadesh in the Desert of Paran. There they reported
to them and to the whole assembly and showed them the fruit of
the land. 27They gave Moses this
account: "We went into the land
to which you sent us, and it does
flow with milk and honey! Here
is its fruit. 28But the people who
live there are powerful, and the
cities are fortified and very large.
We even saw descendants of Anak
there. 29The Amalekites live in the
Negev; the Hittites, Jebusites and
Amorites live in the hill country;
and the Canaanites live near the
sea and along the Jordan."

Ex 3:8; Dt 1:25,28

30Then Caleb silenced the people before Moses and said, "We
should go up and take possession
of the land, for we can certainly
do it."

31But the men who had gone up
with him said, "We can't attack
those people; they are stronger
than we are." 32And they spread
among the Israelites a bad report
about the land they had explored.
They said, "The land we explored
devours those living in it. All the
people we saw there are of great
size. 33We saw the Nephilim there
(the descendants of Anak come
from the Nephilim). We seemed
like grasshoppers in our own eyes,
and we looked the same to them."

Dt 1:28; 9:1; Jos 14:8

The People Rebel

14 That night all the members
of the community raised
their voices and wept aloud. 2All
the Israelites grumbled against
Moses and Aaron, and the whole
assembly said to them, "If only we
had died in Egypt! Or in this wilderness! 3Why is the LORD bringing us to this land only to let us
fall by the sword? Our wives and
children will be taken as plunder.

[a] 23 *Eshkol* means *cluster*; also in verse 24.

Wouldn't it be better for us to go
back to Egypt?" 4And they said to
each other, "We should choose a
leader and go back to Egypt."
Nu 11:1; Dt 1:39

5Then Moses and Aaron fell
facedown in front of the whole Israelite assembly gathered there.
6Joshua son of Nun and Caleb son
of Jephunneh, who were among
those who had explored the land,
tore their clothes 7and said to the
entire Israelite assembly, "The
land we passed through and explored is exceedingly good. 8If
the LORD is pleased with us, he
will lead us into that land, a land
flowing with milk and honey, and
will give it to us. 9Only do not rebel against the LORD. And do not
be afraid of the people of the land,
because we will devour them.
Their protection is gone, but the
LORD is with us. Do not be afraid
of them." Dt 1:21; 9:7,23,24; 10:15

10But the whole assembly talked
about stoning them. Then the glory of the LORD appeared at the tent
of meeting to all the Israelites.
11The LORD said to Moses, "How
long will these people treat me
with contempt? How long will they
refuse to believe in me, in spite
of all the signs I have performed
among them? 12I will strike them
down with a plague and destroy
them, but I will make you into a
nation greater and stronger than
they." Ex 32:10; Lev 9:23

13Moses said to the LORD, "Then
the Egyptians will hear about it!
By your power you brought these
people up from among them.
14And they will tell the inhabitants of this land about it. They
have already heard that you,
LORD, are with these people and
that you, LORD, have been seen
face to face, that your cloud stays
over them, and that you go before
them in a pillar of cloud by day
and a pillar of fire by night. 15If
you put all these people to death,
leaving none alive, the nations
who have heard this report about
you will say, 16'The LORD was not
able to bring these people into
the land he promised them on
oath, so he slaughtered them in
the wilderness.' Ex 13:21; 15:14; 32:11-14

17"Now may the Lord's strength
be displayed, just as you have declared: 18'The LORD is slow to anger, abounding in love and forgiving sin and rebellion. Yet he does
not leave the guilty unpunished;
he punishes the children for the
sin of the parents to the third
and fourth generation.' 19In accordance with your great love, forgive the sin of these people, just as
you have pardoned them from the
time they left Egypt until now."
Ex 20:5; 34:6,9

20The LORD replied, "I have forgiven them, as you asked. 21Nev-
ertheless, as surely as I live and
as surely as the glory of the LORD
fills the whole earth, 22not one of
those who saw my glory and the
signs I performed in Egypt and in
the wilderness but who disobeyed

me and tested me ten times — 23not one of them will ever see the land I promised on oath to their ancestors. No one who has treated me with contempt will ever see it. 24But because my servant Caleb has a different spirit and follows me wholeheartedly, I will bring him into the land he went to, and his descendants will inherit it. 25Since the Amalekites and the Canaanites are living in the valleys, turn back tomorrow and set out toward the desert along the route to the Red Sea.[a]"

Nu 32:12; Jos 14:8,14; Heb 3:18

26The LORD said to Moses and Aaron: 27"How long will this wicked community grumble against me? I have heard the complaints of these grumbling Israelites. 28So tell them, 'As surely as I live, declares the LORD, I will do to you the very thing I heard you say: 29In this wilderness your bodies will fall — every one of you twenty years old or more who was counted in the census and who has grumbled against me. 30Not one of you will enter the land I swore with uplifted hand to make your home, except Caleb son of Jephunneh and Joshua son of Nun. 31As for your children that you said would be taken as plunder, I will bring them in to enjoy the land you have rejected. 32But as for you, your bodies will fall in this wilderness. 33Your children will be shepherds here for forty years, suffering for your unfaithfulness, until the last of your bodies lies in the wilderness. 34For forty years — one year for each of the forty days you explored the land — you will suffer for your sins and know what it is like to have me against you.' 35I, the LORD, have spoken, and I will surely do these things to this whole wicked community, which has banded together against me. They will meet their end in this wilderness; here they will die."

Nu 13:25; 23:19; 1Co 10:5

36So the men Moses had sent to explore the land, who returned and made the whole community grumble against him by spreading a bad report about it — 37these men who were responsible for spreading the bad report about the land were struck down and died of a plague before the LORD. 38Of the men who went to explore the land, only Joshua son of Nun and Caleb son of Jephunneh survived. Nu 13:32; 1Co 10:10

39When Moses reported this to all the Israelites, they mourned bitterly. 40Early the next morning they set out for the highest point in the hill country, saying, "Now we are ready to go up to the land the LORD promised. Surely we have sinned!" Dt 1:41

41But Moses said, "Why are you disobeying the LORD's command? This will not succeed! 42Do not go up, because the LORD is not with you. You will be defeated by your enemies, 43for the Amalekites

[a] 25 Or *the Sea of Reeds*

and the Canaanites will face you there. Because you have turned away from the LORD, he will not be with you and you will fall by the sword." Dt 1:42; 2Ch 24:20

44 Nevertheless, in their presumption they went up toward the highest point in the hill country, though neither Moses nor the ark of the LORD's covenant moved from the camp. 45 Then the Amalekites and the Canaanites who lived in that hill country came down and attacked them and beat them down all the way to Hormah. Nu 21:3; Dt 1:43-44

Supplementary Offerings

15 The LORD said to Moses, 2 "Speak to the Israelites and say to them: 'After you enter the land I am giving you as a home 3 and you present to the LORD food offerings from the herd or the flock, as an aroma pleasing to the LORD — whether burnt offerings or sacrifices, for special vows or freewill offerings or festival offerings — 4 then the person who brings an offering shall present to the LORD a grain offering of a tenth of an ephah[a] of the finest flour mixed with a quarter of a hin[b] of olive oil. 5 With each lamb for the burnt offering or the sacrifice, prepare a quarter of a hin of wine as a drink offering. Lev 1:2; 6:14; 23:1-44

6 " 'With a ram prepare a grain offering of two-tenths of an ephah[c] of the finest flour mixed with a third of a hin[d] of olive oil, 7 and a third of a hin of wine as a drink offering. Offer it as an aroma pleasing to the LORD. Nu 28:12

8 " 'When you prepare a young bull as a burnt offering or sacrifice, for a special vow or a fellowship offering to the LORD, 9 bring with the bull a grain offering of three-tenths of an ephah[e] of the finest flour mixed with half a hin[f] of olive oil, 10 and also bring half a hin of wine as a drink offering. This will be a food offering, an aroma pleasing to the LORD. 11 Each bull or ram, each lamb or young goat, is to be prepared in this manner. 12 Do this for each one, for as many as you prepare. Lev 1:3; 14:10

13 " 'Everyone who is native-born must do these things in this way when they present a food offering as an aroma pleasing to the LORD. 14 For the generations to come, whenever a foreigner or anyone else living among you presents a food offering as an aroma pleasing to the LORD, they must do exactly as you do. 15 The community is to have the same rules for you and for the foreigner residing among you; this is a lasting ordinance for the generations to come. You and

[a] 4 That is, probably about 3 1/2 pounds or about 1.6 kilograms [b] 4 That is, about 1 quart or about 1 liter; also in verse 5 [c] 6 That is, probably about 7 pounds or about 3.2 kilograms [d] 6 That is, about 1 1/3 quarts or about 1.3 liters; also in verse 7 [e] 9 That is, probably about 11 pounds or about 5 kilograms [f] 9 That is, about 2 quarts or about 1.9 liters; also in verse 10

the foreigner shall be the same
before the LORD: 16 The same laws
and regulations will apply both to
you and to the foreigner residing
among you.' " ver 29; Nu 9:14

17 The LORD said to Moses,
18 "Speak to the Israelites and say
to them: 'When you enter the land
to which I am taking you 19 and you
eat the food of the land, present a
portion as an offering to the LORD.
20 Present a loaf from the first of
your ground meal and present it
as an offering from the threshing
floor. 21 Throughout the generations to come you are to give this
offering to the LORD from the first
of your ground meal.
Jos 5:11-12; Ro 11:16

Offerings for Unintentional Sins

22 " 'Now if you as a community unintentionally fail to keep
any of these commands the LORD
gave Moses — 23 any of the LORD's
commands to you through him,
from the day the LORD gave them
and continuing through the generations to come — 24 and if this
is done unintentionally without
the community being aware of it,
then the whole community is to
offer a young bull for a burnt offering as an aroma pleasing to the
LORD, along with its prescribed
grain offering and drink offering,
and a male goat for a sin offering.[a]
25 The priest is to make atonement
for the whole Israelite community, and they will be forgiven, for
it was not intentional and they
have presented to the LORD for
their wrong a food offering and
a sin offering. 26 The whole Israelite community and the foreigners residing among them will be
forgiven, because all the people
were involved in the unintention-
al wrong. Lev 4:2,14,20

27 " 'But if just one person sins
unintentionally, that person must
bring a year-old female goat for
a sin offering. 28 The priest is to
make atonement before the LORD
for the one who erred by sinning
unintentionally, and when atonement has been made, that person
will be forgiven. 29 One and the
same law applies to everyone who
sins unintentionally, whether a
native-born Israelite or a foreigner residing among you. Lev 4:27,35

30 " 'But anyone who sins defiantly, whether native-born or foreigner, blasphemes the LORD and
must be cut off from the people
of Israel. 31 Because they have despised the LORD's word and broken
his commands, they must surely
be cut off; their guilt remains on
them.' " Lev 5:1; Dt 17:13; 2Sa 12:9

The Sabbath-Breaker Put to Death

32 While the Israelites were in the
wilderness, a man was found gathering wood on the Sabbath day.
33 Those who found him gathering
wood brought him to Moses and
Aaron and the whole assembly,
34 and they kept him in custody,

[a] 24 Or *purification offering*; also in verses 25 and 27

because it was not clear what should be done to him. [35]Then the LORD said to Moses, "The man must die. The whole assembly must stone him outside the camp." [36]So the assembly took him outside the camp and stoned him to death, as the LORD commanded Moses. Ex 31:14-15; Lev 24:14

Tassels on Garments

[37]The LORD said to Moses, [38]"Speak to the Israelites and say to them: 'Throughout the generations to come you are to make tassels on the corners of your garments, with a blue cord on each tassel. [39]You will have these tassels to look at and so you will remember all the commands of the LORD, that you may obey them and not prostitute yourselves by chasing after the lusts of your own hearts and eyes. [40]Then you will remember to obey all my commands and will be consecrated to your God. [41]I am the LORD your God, who brought you out of Egypt to be your God. I am the LORD your God.'" Lev 11:44; Ro 12:1; Col 1:22

Korah, Dathan and Abiram

16 Korah son of Izhar, the son of Kohath, the son of Levi, and certain Reubenites — Dathan and Abiram, sons of Eliab, and On son of Peleth — became insolent[a] [2]and rose up against Moses. With them were 250 Israelite men, well-known community leaders who had been appointed members of the council. [3]They came as a group to oppose Moses and Aaron and said to them, "You have gone too far! The whole community is holy, every one of them, and the LORD is with them. Why then do you set yourselves above the LORD's assembly?" Ex 19:6; Ps 106:16

[4]When Moses heard this, he fell facedown. [5]Then he said to Korah and all his followers: "In the morning the LORD will show who belongs to him and who is holy, and he will have that person come near him. The man he chooses he will cause to come near him. [6]You, Korah, and all your followers are to do this: Take censers [7]and tomorrow put burning coals and incense in them before the LORD. The man the LORD chooses will be the one who is holy. You Levites have gone too far!" Nu 14:5; 17:5

[8]Moses also said to Korah, "Now listen, you Levites! [9]Isn't it enough for you that the God of Israel has separated you from the rest of the Israelite community and brought you near himself to do the work at the LORD's tabernacle and to stand before the community and minister to them? [10]He has brought you and all your fellow Levites near himself, but now you are trying to get the priesthood too. [11]It is against the LORD that you and all your followers have banded together. Who is Aaron that you should grumble against him?" Dt 10:8; 1Co 10:10

[a] 1 Or *Peleth — took men*

[12]Then Moses summoned Dathan and Abiram, the sons of Eliab. But they said, "We will not
come! [13]Isn't it enough that you
have brought us up out of a land
flowing with milk and honey to
kill us in the wilderness? And now
you also want to lord it over us!
[14]Moreover, you haven't brought
us into a land flowing with milk
and honey or given us an inheritance of fields and vineyards. Do
you want to treat these men like
slaves[a]? No, we will not come!"
Lev 20:24; Ac 7:27,35

[15]Then Moses became very angry and said to the LORD, "Do not
accept their offering. I have not
taken so much as a donkey from
them, nor have I wronged any of
them." 1Sa 12:3

[16]Moses said to Korah, "You and
all your followers are to appear
before the LORD tomorrow — you
and they and Aaron. [17]Each man is
to take his censer and put incense
in it — 250 censers in all — and
present it before the LORD. You
and Aaron are to present your
censers also." [18]So each of them
took his censer, put burning coals
and incense in it, and stood with
Moses and Aaron at the entrance
to the tent of meeting. [19]When
Korah had gathered all his followers in opposition to them at the
entrance to the tent of meeting,
the glory of the LORD appeared to
the entire assembly. [20]The LORD
said to Moses and Aaron, [21]"Separate yourselves from this assembly so I can put an end to them at
once." Ex 32:10; Nu 14:10

[22]But Moses and Aaron fell facedown and cried out, "O God, the
God who gives breath to all living
things, will you be angry with the
entire assembly when only one
man sins?" Ge 18:23; Job 21:20

[23]Then the LORD said to Moses,
[24]"Say to the assembly, 'Move away
from the tents of Korah, Dathan
and Abiram.' "

[25]Moses got up and went to
Dathan and Abiram, and the elders of Israel followed him. [26]He
warned the assembly, "Move
back from the tents of these
wicked men! Do not touch anything belonging to them, or you
will be swept away because of all
their sins." [27]So they moved away
from the tents of Korah, Dathan
and Abiram. Dathan and Abiram
had come out and were standing
with their wives, children and little ones at the entrances to their
tents. Ge 19:15; Isa 52:11

[28]Then Moses said, "This is how
you will know that the LORD has
sent me to do all these things and
that it was not my idea: [29]If these
men die a natural death and suffer
the fate of all mankind, then the
LORD has not sent me. [30]But if the
LORD brings about something totally new, and the earth opens its
mouth and swallows them, with
everything that belongs to them,
and they go down alive into the

[a] 14 *Or to deceive these men*; Hebrew *Will you gouge out the eyes of these men*

realm of the dead, then you will
know that these men have treated
the LORD with contempt."

Ex 3:12; Jn 5:36; 6:38

31 As soon as he finished saying all this, the ground under
them split apart 32 and the earth
opened its mouth and swallowed
them and their households, and
all those associated with Korah,
together with their possessions.
33 They went down alive into the
realm of the dead, with everything they owned; the earth closed
over them, and they perished and
were gone from the community.
34 At their cries, all the Israelites
around them fled, shouting, "The
earth is going to swallow us too!"

Nu 26:11; Mic 1:3-4

35 And fire came out from the
LORD and consumed the 250 men
who were offering the incense.

Nu 11:1-3; 26:10

36 The LORD said to Moses, 37 "Tell
Eleazar son of Aaron, the priest,
to remove the censers from the
charred remains and scatter the
coals some distance away, for the
censers are holy — 38 the censers
of the men who sinned at the cost
of their lives. Hammer the censers
into sheets to overlay the altar, for
they were presented before the
LORD and have become holy. Let
them be a sign to the Israelites."

Nu 26:10; Pr 20:2; Eze 14:8

39 So Eleazar the priest collected the bronze censers brought
by those who had been burned
to death, and he had them hammered out to overlay the altar, 40 as
the LORD directed him through
Moses. This was to remind the Israelites that no one except a descendant of Aaron should come to
burn incense before the LORD, or
he would become like Korah and
his followers.

Nu 3:10; 2Ch 26:18; Ex 30:7-10

41 The next day the whole Israelite community grumbled against
Moses and Aaron. "You have killed
the LORD's people," they said.

42 But when the assembly gathered in opposition to Moses and
Aaron and turned toward the tent
of meeting, suddenly the cloud
covered it and the glory of the
LORD appeared. 43 Then Moses and
Aaron went to the front of the tent
of meeting, 44 and the LORD said
to Moses, 45 "Get away from this
assembly so I can put an end to
them at once." And they fell facedown.

ver 19; Nu 20:6

46 Then Moses said to Aaron,
"Take your censer and put incense in it, along with burning
coals from the altar, and hurry
to the assembly to make atonement for them. Wrath has come
out from the LORD; the plague has
started." 47 So Aaron did as Moses
said, and ran into the midst of
the assembly. The plague had already started among the people,
but Aaron offered the incense and
made atonement for them. 48 He
stood between the living and the
dead, and the plague stopped.
49 But 14,700 people died from the

plague, in addition to those who
had died because of Korah. 50Then
Aaron returned to Moses at the
entrance to the tent of meeting,
for the plague had stopped.[a]
Ps 106:30; Nu 8:19; 25:13

The Budding of Aaron's Staff

17[b] The LORD said to Moses,
2"Speak to the Israelites
and get twelve staffs from them,
one from the leader of each of
their ancestral tribes. Write the
name of each man on his staff.
3On the staff of Levi write Aaron's name, for there must be one
staff for the head of each ancestral tribe. 4Place them in the tent
of meeting in front of the ark of
the covenant law, where I meet
with you. 5The staff belonging to
the man I choose will sprout, and
I will rid myself of this constant
grumbling against you by the Israelites." Nu 16:5; Ex 16:7; 25:22
6So Moses spoke to the Israelites, and their leaders gave him
twelve staffs, one for the leader of
each of their ancestral tribes, and
Aaron's staff was among them.
7Moses placed the staffs before the
LORD in the tent of the covenant
law. Ex 38:21; Ac 7:44
8The next day Moses entered
the tent and saw that Aaron's
staff, which represented the tribe
of Levi, had not only sprouted
but had budded, blossomed and
produced almonds. 9Then Moses
brought out all the staffs from
the LORD's presence to all the
Israelites. They looked at them,
and each of the leaders took his
own staff. Eze 17:24; Heb 9:4
10The LORD said to Moses, "Put
back Aaron's staff in front of the
ark of the covenant law, to be kept
as a sign to the rebellious. This
will put an end to their grumbling
against me, so that they will not
die." 11Moses did just as the LORD
commanded him. Dt 9:24
12The Israelites said to Moses,
"We will die! We are lost, we are
all lost! 13Anyone who even comes
near the tabernacle of the LORD
will die. Are we all going to die?"
Nu 1:51

Duties of Priests and Levites

18 The LORD said to Aaron,
"You, your sons and your
family are to bear the responsibility for offenses connected with the
sanctuary, and you and your sons
alone are to bear the responsibility for offenses connected with the
priesthood. 2Bring your fellow Levites from your ancestral tribe to
join you and assist you when you
and your sons minister before the
tent of the covenant law. 3They are
to be responsible to you and are to
perform all the duties of the tent,
but they must not go near the furnishings of the sanctuary or the
altar. Otherwise both they and you
will die. 4They are to join you and
be responsible for the care of the

[a] *50* In Hebrew texts 16:36-50 is numbered 17:1-15. [b] In Hebrew texts 17:1-13 is numbered 17:16-28.

tent of meeting — all the work at
the tent — and no one else may
come near where you are.

Nu 3:10; 4:15

5“You are to be responsible for
the care of the sanctuary and the
altar, so that my wrath will not fall
on the Israelites again. 6I myself
have selected your fellow Levites
from among the Israelites as a gift
to you, dedicated to the LORD to do
the work at the tent of meeting.
7But only you and your sons may
serve as priests in connection with
everything at the altar and inside
the curtain. I am giving you the
service of the priesthood as a gift.
Anyone else who comes near the
sanctuary is to be put to death.”

Ex 29:9; Nu 3:9; Heb 9:3,6

Offerings for Priests and Levites

8Then the LORD said to Aaron,
“I myself have put you in charge
of the offerings presented to me;
all the holy offerings the Israelites give me I give to you and your
sons as your portion, your perpetual share. 9You are to have the part
of the most holy offerings that is
kept from the fire. From all the
gifts they bring me as most holy
offerings, whether grain or sin[a] or
guilt offerings, that part belongs
to you and your sons. 10Eat it as
something most holy; every male
shall eat it. You must regard it as
holy.

Lev 6:16,25

11“This also is yours: whatever is
set aside from the gifts of all the
wave offerings of the Israelites.
I give this to you and your sons
and daughters as your perpetual
share. Everyone in your household who is ceremonially clean
may eat it.

Ex 29:26; Lev 22:1-16

12“I give you all the finest olive
oil and all the finest new wine and
grain they give the LORD as the
firstfruits of their harvest. 13All the
land’s firstfruits that they bring to
the LORD will be yours. Everyone
in your household who is ceremonially clean may eat it.

Ex 23:19; Ne 10:35

14“Everything in Israel that is devoted[b] to the LORD is yours. 15The
first offspring of every womb,
both human and animal, that is
offered to the LORD is yours. But
you must redeem every firstborn
son and every firstborn male of
unclean animals. 16When they are
a month old, you must redeem
them at the redemption price set
at five shekels[c] of silver, according to the sanctuary shekel, which
weighs twenty gerahs.

Ex 13:2; Lev 27:6,28

17“But you must not redeem
the firstborn of a cow, a sheep
or a goat; they are holy. Splash
their blood against the altar and
burn their fat as a food offering,
an aroma pleasing to the LORD.
18Their meat is to be yours, just
as the breast of the wave offering and the right thigh are yours.

[a] 9 Or *purification* [b] 14 The Hebrew term refers to the irrevocable giving over of things or persons to the LORD. [c] 16 That is, about 2 ounces or about 58 grams

19Whatever is set aside from the
holy offerings the Israelites present to the LORD I give to you and
your sons and daughters as your
perpetual share. It is an everlasting covenant of salt before the
LORD for both you and your offspring." 2Ch 13:5; Lev 3:2

20The LORD said to Aaron, "You
will have no inheritance in their
land, nor will you have any share
among them; I am your share and
your inheritance among the Israelites. Dt 10:9; 18:1-2; Jos 13:33

21"I give to the Levites all the
tithes in Israel as their inheritance in return for the work they
do while serving at the tent of
meeting. 22From now on the Israelites must not go near the tent
of meeting, or they will bear the
consequences of their sin and will
die. 23It is the Levites who are to
do the work at the tent of meeting and bear the responsibility for
any offenses they commit against
it. This is a lasting ordinance for
the generations to come. They will
receive no inheritance among the
Israelites. 24Instead, I give to the
Levites as their inheritance the
tithes that the Israelites present
as an offering to the LORD. That is
why I said concerning them: 'They
will have no inheritance among
the Israelites.'" Lev 27:30-33; Nu 1:51

25The LORD said to Moses,
26"Speak to the Levites and say to
them: 'When you receive from the
Israelites the tithe I give you as
your inheritance, you must present a tenth of that tithe as the
LORD's offering. 27Your offering
will be reckoned to you as grain
from the threshing floor or juice
from the winepress. 28In this way
you also will present an offering
to the LORD from all the tithes you
receive from the Israelites. From
these tithes you must give the
LORD's portion to Aaron the priest.
29You must present as the LORD's
portion the best and holiest part
of everything given to you.'
Ne 10:38; Mal 3:8

30"Say to the Levites: 'When you
present the best part, it will be
reckoned to you as the product of
the threshing floor or the winepress. 31You and your households
may eat the rest of it anywhere,
for it is your wages for your work
at the tent of meeting. 32By presenting the best part of it you will
not be guilty in this matter; then
you will not defile the holy offerings of the Israelites, and you will
not die.'" Lev 19:8; 22:15

The Water of Cleansing

19 The LORD said to Moses and
Aaron: 2"This is a requirement of the law that the LORD has
commanded: Tell the Israelites to
bring you a red heifer without defect or blemish and that has never
been under a yoke. 3Give it to Eleazar the priest; it is to be taken
outside the camp and slaughtered
in his presence. 4Then Eleazar the
priest is to take some of its blood
on his finger and sprinkle it seven

times toward the front of the tent
of meeting. 5While he watches, the
heifer is to be burned — its hide,
flesh, blood and intestines. 6The
priest is to take some cedar wood,
hyssop and scarlet wool and throw
them onto the burning heifer. 7Af-
ter that, the priest must wash his
clothes and bathe himself with
water. He may then come into the
camp, but he will be ceremonially unclean till evening. 8The man
who burns it must also wash his
clothes and bathe with water, and
he too will be unclean till evening.
Ex 29:14; Lev 4:12,21; Dt 21:3

9"A man who is clean shall gather up the ashes of the heifer and
put them in a ceremonially clean
place outside the camp. They are
to be kept by the Israelite community for use in the water of cleansing; it is for purification from sin.
10The man who gathers up the
ashes of the heifer must also wash
his clothes, and he too will be unclean till evening. This will be a
lasting ordinance both for the Israelites and for the foreigners residing among them.
ver 13; Nu 8:7; Heb 9:13

11"Whoever touches a human
corpse will be unclean for seven
days. 12They must purify themselves with the water on the third
day and on the seventh day; then
they will be clean. But if they do
not purify themselves on the
third and seventh days, they will
not be clean. 13If they fail to purify themselves after touching a human corpse, they defile the LORD's
tabernacle. They must be cut off
from Israel. Because the water of
cleansing has not been sprinkled
on them, they are unclean; their
uncleanness remains on them.
Lev 7:20; 21:1; Nu 31:19

14"This is the law that applies
when a person dies in a tent: Anyone who enters the tent and anyone who is in it will be unclean for
seven days, 15and every open con-
tainer without a lid fastened on it
will be unclean.

16"Anyone out in the open who
touches someone who has been
killed with a sword or someone
who has died a natural death, or
anyone who touches a human
bone or a grave, will be unclean
for seven days. Nu 31:19; Mt 23:27

17"For the unclean person, put
some ashes from the burned purification offering into a jar and
pour fresh water over them. 18Then
a man who is ceremonially clean is
to take some hyssop, dip it in the
water and sprinkle the tent and
all the furnishings and the people who were there. He must also
sprinkle anyone who has touched
a human bone or a grave or anyone who has been killed or anyone who has died a natural death.
19The man who is clean is to sprinkle those who are unclean on the
third and seventh days, and on the
seventh day he is to purify them.
Those who are being cleansed
must wash their clothes and bathe
with water, and that evening they

will be clean. 20But if those who
are unclean do not purify themselves, they must be cut off from
the community, because they have
defiled the sanctuary of the LORD.
The water of cleansing has not
been sprinkled on them, and they
are unclean. 21This is a lasting ordinance for them. Eze 36:25; Heb 10:22
"The man who sprinkles the water of cleansing must also wash his
clothes, and anyone who touches
the water of cleansing will be unclean till evening. 22Anything that
an unclean person touches becomes unclean, and anyone who
touches it becomes unclean till
evening." Lev 5:2; Hag 2:13-14

Water From the Rock

20 In the first month the
whole Israelite communi-
ty arrived at the Desert of Zin, and
they stayed at Kadesh. There Miriam died and was buried.
Ex 15:20; Nu 33:36
2Now there was no water for the
community, and the people gathered in opposition to Moses and
Aaron. 3They quarreled with Moses and said, "If only we had died
when our brothers fell dead before
the LORD! 4Why did you bring the
LORD's community into this wilderness, that we and our livestock
should die here? 5Why did you
bring us up out of Egypt to this
terrible place? It has no grain or
figs, grapevines or pomegranates.
And there is no water to drink!"
Ex 14:11; 17:1-2
6Moses and Aaron went from
the assembly to the entrance to
the tent of meeting and fell facedown, and the glory of the LORD
appeared to them. 7The LORD said
to Moses, 8"Take the staff, and you
and your brother Aaron gather the
assembly together. Speak to that
rock before their eyes and it will
pour out its water. You will bring
water out of the rock for the community so they and their livestock
can drink." Ex 17:6; Isa 43:20; Nu 14:5
9So Moses took the staff from
the LORD's presence, just as he
commanded him. 10He and Aaron
gathered the assembly together in
front of the rock and Moses said to
them, "Listen, you rebels, must we
bring you water out of this rock?"
11Then Moses raised his arm and
struck the rock twice with his staff.
Water gushed out, and the community and their livestock drank.
Ex 17:6; Nu 17:10; Ps 106:32-33
12But the LORD said to Moses and
Aaron, "Because you did not trust
in me enough to honor me as holy
in the sight of the Israelites, you
will not bring this community into
the land I give them." Nu 27:14; Dt 1:37
13These were the waters of Meribah,[a] where the Israelites quarreled
with the LORD and where he was
proved holy among them. Ex 17:7

Edom Denies Israel Passage

14Moses sent messengers from
Kadesh to the king of Edom, saying: Dt 2:4; Jdg 11:16-17

[a] 13 *Meribah* means *quarreling.*

"This is what your brother
Israel says: You know about
all the hardships that have
come on us. 15Our ancestors
went down into Egypt, and
we lived there many years.
The Egyptians mistreated us
and our ancestors, 16but when
we cried out to the LORD, he
heard our cry and sent an
angel and brought us out of
Egypt. Ex 2:23; 14:19

"Now we are here at Ka-
desh, a town on the edge of
your territory. 17Please let us
pass through your country.
We will not go through any
field or vineyard, or drink water from any well. We will travel along the King's Highway
and not turn to the right or to
the left until we have passed
through your territory."
Nu 21:22

18But Edom answered:

"You may not pass through
here; if you try, we will march
out and attack you with the
sword." Nu 21:23

19The Israelites replied:

"We will go along the main
road, and if we or our livestock drink any of your water, we will pay for it. We
only want to pass through on
foot — nothing else." Dt 2:6,28

20Again they answered:

"You may not pass through."

Then Edom came out against
them with a large and powerful
army. 21Since Edom refused to let
them go through their territory,
Israel turned away from them.
Dt 2:8; Jdg 11:18

The Death of Aaron

22The whole Israelite community set out from Kadesh and came
to Mount Hor. 23At Mount Hor, near
the border of Edom, the LORD said
to Moses and Aaron, 24"Aaron will
be gathered to his people. He will
not enter the land I give the Israelites, because both of you rebelled
against my command at the waters
of Meribah. 25Get Aaron and his son
Eleazar and take them up Mount
Hor. 26Remove Aaron's garments
and put them on his son Eleazar, for
Aaron will be gathered to his people; he will die there." ver 10; Ge 25:8

27Moses did as the LORD commanded: They went up Mount
Hor in the sight of the whole community. 28Moses removed Aaron's
garments and put them on his son
Eleazar. And Aaron died there on
top of the mountain. Then Moses and Eleazar came down from
the mountain, 29and when the
whole community learned that
Aaron had died, all the Israelites
mourned for him thirty days.
Ex 29:29; Nu 33:38; Dt 34:8

Arad Destroyed

21 When the Canaanite king of
Arad, who lived in the Negev,
heard that Israel was coming along

the road to Atharim, he attacked
the Israelites and captured some
of them. 2Then Israel made this
vow to the LORD: "If you will deliver these people into our hands, we
will totally destroy[a] their cities."
3The LORD listened to Israel's plea
and gave the Canaanites over to
them. They completely destroyed
them and their towns; so the place
was named Hormah.[b]

Ex 22:20; Nu 33:40

The Bronze Snake

4They traveled from Mount Hor
along the route to the Red Sea,[c] to
go around Edom. But the people
grew impatient on the way; 5they
spoke against God and against
Moses, and said, "Why have you
brought us up out of Egypt to die
in the wilderness? There is no
bread! There is no water! And we
detest this miserable food!"

Ps 78:19; Nu 20:22

6Then the LORD sent venomous
snakes among them; they bit the
people and many Israelites died.
7The people came to Moses and
said, "We sinned when we spoke
against the LORD and against you.
Pray that the LORD will take the
snakes away from us." So Moses
prayed for the people.

Dt 8:15; Ps 78:34; Ac 8:24

8The LORD said to Moses, "Make
a snake and put it up on a pole;
anyone who is bitten can look
at it and live." 9So Moses made a
bronze snake and put it up on a
pole. Then when anyone was bitten by a snake and looked at the
bronze snake, they lived.

Jn 3:14-15; 2Ki 18:4

The Journey to Moab

10The Israelites moved on and
camped at Oboth. 11Then they set
out from Oboth and camped in Iye
Abarim, in the wilderness that faces Moab toward the sunrise. 12From
there they moved on and camped
in the Zered Valley. 13They set out
from there and camped alongside
the Arnon, which is in the wilderness extending into Amorite territory. The Arnon is the border of
Moab, between Moab and the Amorites. 14That is why the Book of
the Wars of the LORD says:

Nu 33:44; Dt 2:13-14

"... Zahab[d] in Suphah and the
ravines,
the Arnon 15and[e] the slopes
of the ravines
that lead to the settlement of
Ar Dt 2:9,18
and lie along the border of
Moab."

16From there they continued on to
Beer, the well where the LORD said
to Moses, "Gather the people together and I will give them water."

[a] 2 The Hebrew term refers to the irrevocable giving over of things or persons to the LORD, often by totally destroying them; also in verse 3.
[b] 3 *Hormah* means *destruction.*
[c] 4 Or *the Sea of Reeds*
[d] 14 Septuagint; Hebrew *Waheb*
[e] 14,15 Or *"I have been given from Suphah and the ravines / of the Arnon* 15*to*

[17]Then Israel sang this song:
Ex 15:1

"Spring up, O well!
Sing about it,
[18]about the well that the princes dug,
that the nobles of the people sank—
the nobles with scepters and staffs."

Then they went from the wilderness to Mattanah, [19]from Mattanah to Nahaliel, from Nahaliel to
Bamoth, [20]and from Bamoth to
the valley in Moab where the top
of Pisgah overlooks the wasteland.

Defeat of Sihon and Og

[21]Israel sent messengers to say to Sihon king of the Amorites:
Dt 1:4; Jdg 11:19-21

[22]"Let us pass through your country. We will not turn aside into any field or vineyard, or drink water from any well. We will travel along the King's Highway until we have passed through your territory."
Nu 20:17

[23]But Sihon would not let Israel pass through his territory. He
mustered his entire army and
marched out into the wilderness
against Israel. When he reached
Jahaz, he fought with Israel. [24]Is-
rael, however, put him to the
sword and took over his land from
the Arnon to the Jabbok, but only
as far as the Ammonites, because
their border was fortified. [25]Is-
rael captured all the cities of the
Amorites and occupied them, including Heshbon and all its surrounding settlements. [26]Heshbon
was the city of Sihon king of the
Amorites, who had fought against
the former king of Moab and had
taken from him all his land as far
as the Arnon. Dt 2:32; 29:7; Ps 135:10-11
[27]That is why the poets say:

"Come to Heshbon and let it be rebuilt;
let Sihon's city be restored.

[28]"Fire went out from Heshbon,
a blaze from the city of Sihon.
Jer 48:45
It consumed Ar of Moab,
the citizens of Arnon's heights.
Isa 15:2
[29]Woe to you, Moab!
You are destroyed, people of Chemosh!
Jdg 11:24
He has given up his sons as fugitives
and his daughters as captives
to Sihon king of the Amorites.

[30]"But we have overthrown them;
Heshbon's dominion has been destroyed all the way to Dibon.
Nu 32:3; Jer 48:18,22
We have demolished them as far as Nophah,
which extends to Medeba."

[31]So Israel settled in the land of
the Amorites.

32 After Moses had sent spies
to Jazer, the Israelites captured
its surrounding settlements and
drove out the Amorites who were
there. 33 Then they turned and
went up along the road toward Bashan, and Og king of Bashan and
his whole army marched out to
meet them in battle at Edrei.
Nu 32:1,3,35; Dt 13:1,10

34 The LORD said to Moses, "Do
not be afraid of him, for I have delivered him into your hands, along
with his whole army and his land.
Do to him what you did to Sihon
king of the Amorites, who reigned
in Heshbon." Dt 3:2

35 So they struck him down, together with his sons and his whole
army, leaving them no survivors.
And they took possession of his
land.

Balak Summons Balaam

22 Then the Israelites traveled
to the plains of Moab and
camped along the Jordan across
from Jericho. Nu 33:48

2 Now Balak son of Zippor saw
all that Israel had done to the Amorites, 3 and Moab was terrified
because there were so many people. Indeed, Moab was filled with
dread because of the Israelites.
Ex 15:15

4 The Moabites said to the elders
of Midian, "This horde is going to
lick up everything around us, as an
ox licks up the grass of the field."

So Balak son of Zippor, who was
king of Moab at that time, 5 sent
messengers to summon Balaam
son of Beor, who was at Pethor,
near the Euphrates River, in his
native land. Balak said:
Dt 23:4; 2Pe 2:15

"A people has come out of
Egypt; they cover the face
of the land and have settled
next to me. 6 Now come and
put a curse on these people,
because they are too powerful
for me. Perhaps then I will be
able to defeat them and drive
them out of the land. For I
know that whoever you bless
is blessed, and whoever you
curse is cursed." Nu 23:7,11,13

7 The elders of Moab and Midian left, taking with them the fee
for divination. When they came to
Balaam, they told him what Balak
had said. Ge 30:27

8 "Spend the night here," Balaam
said to them, "and I will report
back to you with the answer the
LORD gives me." So the Moabite
officials stayed with him.

9 God came to Balaam and asked,
"Who are these men with you?"
Ge 20:3

10 Balaam said to God, "Balak son
of Zippor, king of Moab, sent me
this message: 11 'A people that has
come out of Egypt covers the face
of the land. Now come and put a
curse on them for me. Perhaps
then I will be able to fight them
and drive them away.'"

12 But God said to Balaam, "Do
not go with them. You must not

put a curse on those people, because they are blessed." Ge 12:2; 22:17
13The next morning Balaam got
up and said to Balak's officials, "Go
back to your own country, for the
LORD has refused to let me go with
you."
14So the Moabite officials returned to Balak and said, "Balaam
refused to come with us."
15Then Balak sent other officials,
more numerous and more distinguished than the first. 16They
came to Balaam and said:

> "This is what Balak son of
> Zippor says: Do not let any-
> thing keep you from com-
> ing to me, 17because I will re-
> ward you handsomely and do
> whatever you say. Come and
> put a curse on these people
> for me."

18But Balaam answered them,
"Even if Balak gave me all the silver and gold in his palace, I could
not do anything great or small to
go beyond the command of the
LORD my God. 19Now spend the
night here so that I can find out
what else the LORD will tell me."
Nu 24:13; 1Ki 22:14; 2Ch 18:13
20That night God came to Balaam and said, "Since these men
have come to summon you, go
with them, but do only what I tell
you." Nu 23:5,12,16,26

Balaam's Donkey

21Balaam got up in the morning, saddled his donkey and went
with the Moabite officials. 22But
God was very angry when he went,
and the angel of the LORD stood in
the road to oppose him. Balaam
was riding on his donkey, and
his two servants were with him.
23When the donkey saw the angel
of the LORD standing in the road
with a drawn sword in his hand,
it turned off the road into a field.
Balaam beat it to get it back on the
road. Ex 23:20
24Then the angel of the LORD
stood in a narrow path through
the vineyards, with walls on both
sides. 25When the donkey saw the
angel of the LORD, it pressed close
to the wall, crushing Balaam's foot
against it. So he beat the donkey
again.
26Then the angel of the LORD
moved on ahead and stood in a
narrow place where there was no
room to turn, either to the right or
to the left. 27When the donkey saw
the angel of the LORD, it lay down
under Balaam, and he was angry
and beat it with his staff. 28Then
the LORD opened the donkey's
mouth, and it said to Balaam,
"What have I done to you to make
you beat me these three times?"
Jas 1:19; 2Pe 2:16
29Balaam answered the donkey,
"You have made a fool of me! If
only I had a sword in my hand, I
would kill you right now."
Pr 12:10; Mt 15:19
30The donkey said to Balaam,
"Am I not your own donkey, which
you have always ridden, to this

day? Have I been in the habit of doing this to you?"

"No," he said.

[31]Then the LORD opened Balaam's eyes, and he saw the angel of the LORD standing in the road with his sword drawn. So he bowed low and fell facedown. Ge 21:19

[32]The angel of the LORD asked him, "Why have you beaten your donkey these three times? I have come here to oppose you because your path is a reckless one before me.[a] [33]The donkey saw me and turned away from me these three times. If it had not turned away, I would certainly have killed you by now, but I would have spared it."

[34]Balaam said to the angel of the LORD, "I have sinned. I did not realize you were standing in the road to oppose me. Now if you are displeased, I will go back." Nu 14:40

[35]The angel of the LORD said to Balaam, "Go with the men, but speak only what I tell you." So Balaam went with Balak's officials.

[36]When Balak heard that Balaam was coming, he went out to meet him at the Moabite town on the Arnon border, at the edge of his territory. [37]Balak said to Balaam, "Did I not send you an urgent summons? Why didn't you come to me? Am I really not able to reward you?" Nu 21:13

[38]"Well, I have come to you now," Balaam replied. "But I can't say whatever I please. I must speak only what God puts in my mouth." Nu 23:5,16,26

[39]Then Balaam went with Balak to Kiriath Huzoth. [40]Balak sacrificed cattle and sheep, and gave some to Balaam and the officials who were with him. [41]The next morning Balak took Balaam up to Bamoth Baal, and from there he could see the outskirts of the Israelite camp. Nu 21:28; 23:13

Balaam's First Message

23 Balaam said, "Build me seven altars here, and prepare seven bulls and seven rams for me." [2]Balak did as Balaam said, and the two of them offered a bull and a ram on each altar. ver 14,30; Nu 22:40

[3]Then Balaam said to Balak, "Stay here beside your offering while I go aside. Perhaps the LORD will come to meet with me. Whatever he reveals to me I will tell you." Then he went off to a barren height. ver 15

[4]God met with him, and Balaam said, "I have prepared seven altars, and on each altar I have offered a bull and a ram."

[5]The LORD put a word in Balaam's mouth and said, "Go back to Balak and give him this word." Dt 18:18; Jer 1:9

[6]So he went back to him and found him standing beside his offering, with all the Moabite officials. [7]Then Balaam spoke his message: ver 18; Nu 24:3,21

[a] *32* The meaning of the Hebrew for this clause is uncertain.

"Balak brought me from Aram,
the king of Moab from the eastern mountains.
'Come,' he said, 'curse Jacob for me;
come, denounce Israel.' Nu 22:6
8 How can I curse
those whom God has not cursed? Nu 22:12
How can I denounce
those whom the LORD has not denounced?
9 From the rocky peaks I see them,
from the heights I view them.
I see a people who live apart
and do not consider themselves one of the nations. Dt 32:8; 33:28
10 Who can count the dust of Jacob
or number even a fourth of Israel?
Let me die the death of the righteous,
and may my final end be like theirs!" Ps 37:37

11 Balak said to Balaam, "What
have you done to me? I brought
you to curse my enemies, but
you have done nothing but bless
them!" Nu 24:10; Ne 13:2
12 He answered, "Must I not
speak what the LORD puts in my
mouth?" Nu 22:20,38

Balaam's Second Message

13 Then Balak said to him, "Come
with me to another place where
you can see them; you will not see
them all but only the outskirts of
their camp. And from there, curse
them for me." 14 So he took him to
the field of Zophim on the top of
Pisgah, and there he built seven
altars and offered a bull and a ram
on each altar.
15 Balaam said to Balak, "Stay
here beside your offering while I
meet with him over there."
16 The LORD met with Balaam
and put a word in his mouth and
said, "Go back to Balak and give
him this word." Nu 22:38
17 So he went to him and found
him standing beside his offering,
with the Moabite officials. Balak
asked him, "What did the LORD
say?"
18 Then he spoke his message:

"Arise, Balak, and listen;
hear me, son of Zippor.
19 God is not human, that he should lie, Isa 55:9; Hos 11:9
not a human being, that he should change his mind. 1Sa 15:29; Mal 3:6; Jas 1:17
Does he speak and then not act?
Does he promise and not fulfill?
20 I have received a command to bless;
he has blessed, and I cannot change it. Ge 22:17; Nu 22:12; Isa 43:13

21 "No misfortune is seen in Jacob, Ps 32:2,5; Ro 4:7-8
no misery observed[a] in Israel.

[a] 21 Or *He has not looked on Jacob's offenses / or on the wrongs found*

The LORD their God is with
them;
the shout of the King is
among them. Ps 89:15-18
22 God brought them out of
Egypt;
they have the strength of a
wild ox. Nu 24:8; Dt 33:17
23 There is no divination against[a]
Jacob,
no evil omens against[a]
Israel. Nu 24:1; Jos 13:22
It will now be said of Jacob
and of Israel, 'See what God
has done!'
24 The people rise like a lioness;
they rouse themselves like a
lion Ge 49:9
that does not rest till it devours
its prey
and drinks the blood of its
victims."

25 Then Balak said to Balaam,
"Neither curse them at all nor
bless them at all!"
26 Balaam answered, "Did I not
tell you I must do whatever the
LORD says?"

Balaam's Third Message

27 Then Balak said to Balaam,
"Come, let me take you to another place. Perhaps it will please God
to let you curse them for me from
there." 28 And Balak took Balaam
to the top of Peor, overlooking the
wasteland. Ps 106:28
29 Balaam said, "Build me sev-
en altars here, and prepare sev-
en bulls and seven rams for me."
30 Balak did as Balaam had said,
and offered a bull and a ram on
each altar.

24 Now when Balaam saw that
it pleased the LORD to bless
Israel, he did not resort to divination as at other times, but turned
his face toward the wilderness.
2 When Balaam looked out and saw
Israel encamped tribe by tribe, the
Spirit of God came on him 3 and he
spoke his message:
Nu 11:25-26; 1Sa 10:10; 19:20

"The prophecy of Balaam son
of Beor,
the prophecy of one whose
eye sees clearly,
4 the prophecy of one who hears
the words of God,
who sees a vision from the
Almighty,[b] Ge 15:1
who falls prostrate, and
whose eyes are opened:

5 "How beautiful are your tents,
Jacob,
your dwelling places, Israel!

6 "Like valleys they spread out,
like gardens beside
a river,
like aloes planted by
the LORD,
like cedars beside the waters.
Ps 1:3; 104:16
7 Water will flow from their
buckets;
their seed will have
abundant water.

[a] 23 Or *in* [b] 4 Hebrew *Shaddai*; also in verse 16

"Their king will be greater than
Agag;
their kingdom will
be exalted.
2Sa 5:12; 1Ch 14:2; Ps 145:11-13

8 "God brought them out of
Egypt;
they have the strength of a
wild ox.
They devour hostile nations
and break their bones in
pieces; Ps 2:9; Jer 50:17
with their arrows they pierce
them. Ps 45:5
9 Like a lion they crouch and lie
down,
like a lioness — who dares to
rouse them?

"May those who bless you be
blessed
and those who curse you be
cursed!" Ge 12:3

10 Then Balak's anger burned
against Balaam. He struck his
hands together and said to him, "I
summoned you to curse my enemies, but you have blessed them
these three times. 11 Now leave at
once and go home! I said I would
reward you handsomely, but the
LORD has kept you from being rewarded." Nu 22:17; 23:11
12 Balaam answered Balak, "Did
I not tell the messengers you sent
me, 13 'Even if Balak gave me all the
silver and gold in his palace, I could
not do anything of my own accord,
good or bad, to go beyond the command of the LORD — and I must say
only what the LORD says'? 14 Now I
am going back to my people, but
come, let me warn you of what this
people will do to your people in
days to come." Nu 22:18,20; Mic 6:5

Balaam's Fourth Message

15 Then he spoke his message:

"The prophecy of Balaam son
of Beor,
the prophecy of one whose
eye sees clearly,
16 the prophecy of one who hears
the words of God,
who has knowledge from the
Most High,
who sees a vision from the
Almighty,
who falls prostrate, and
whose eyes are opened:

17 "I see him, but not now;
I behold him, but not near.
Rev 1:7
A star will come out of Jacob;
Mt 2:2
a scepter will rise out of
Israel. Ge 49:10
He will crush the foreheads of
Moab,
the skulls[a] of[b] all the people
of Sheth.[c]
18 Edom will be conquered;
Seir, his enemy, will be
conquered,
but Israel will grow strong.

[a] 17 Samaritan Pentateuch (see also Jer. 48:45); the meaning of the word in the Masoretic Text is uncertain. [b] 17 Or possibly *Moab, / batter* [c] 17 Or *all the noisy boasters*

19 A ruler will come out of Jacob
and destroy the survivors of
the city." Ge 49:10; Mic 5:2

Balaam's Fifth Message

20 Then Balaam saw Amalek and
spoke his message:

"Amalek was first among the
nations,
but their end will be utter
destruction." Dt 25:19

Balaam's Sixth Message

21 Then he saw the Kenites and
spoke his message:

"Your dwelling place is secure,
your nest is set in a rock;
22 yet you Kenites will be
destroyed
when Ashur takes you
captive." Ge 10:22

Balaam's Seventh Message

23 Then he spoke his message:

"Alas! Who can live when God
does this?[a]
24 Ships will come from the
shores of Cyprus;
they will subdue Ashur and Eber,
but they too will come to
ruin." Ge 10:4,21

25 Then Balaam got up and returned home, and Balak went his
own way. Nu 31:8

Moab Seduces Israel

25 While Israel was staying
in Shittim, the men began
to indulge in sexual immorality
with Moabite women, 2 who invited them to the sacrifices to their
gods. The people ate the sacrificial meal and bowed down before
these gods. 3 So Israel yoked themselves to the Baal of Peor. And
the LORD's anger burned against
them. Ex 20:5; Nu 31:16; Ps 106:28

4 The LORD said to Moses, "Take
all the leaders of these people, kill
them and expose them in broad
daylight before the LORD, so that
the LORD's fierce anger may turn
away from Israel." Dt 4:3; 13:17

5 So Moses said to Israel's judges, "Each of you must put to death
those of your people who have
yoked themselves to the Baal of
Peor."

6 Then an Israelite man brought
into the camp a Midianite woman
right before the eyes of Moses and
the whole assembly of Israel while
they were weeping at the entrance
to the tent of meeting. 7 When Phinehas son of Eleazar, the son of Aaron, the priest, saw this, he left the
assembly, took a spear in his hand
8 and followed the Israelite into the
tent. He drove the spear into both
of them, right through the Israelite
man and into the woman's stomach. Then the plague against the
Israelites was stopped; 9 but those
who died in the plague numbered
24,000. Nu 14:37; 1Co 10:8

10 The LORD said to Moses,
11 "Phinehas son of Eleazar, the son

[a] 23 Masoretic Text; with a different word division of the Hebrew *The people from the islands will gather from the north.*

of Aaron, the priest, has turned
my anger away from the Israelites.
Since he was as zealous for my
honor among them as I am, I did
not put an end to them in my zeal.
12 Therefore tell him I am making
my covenant of peace with him.
13 He and his descendants will have
a covenant of a lasting priesthood,
because he was zealous for the
honor of his God and made atonement for the Israelites."

Isa 54:10; Mal 2:4-5; Ex 20:5

14 The name of the Israelite
who was killed with the Midianite woman was Zimri son of Salu,
the leader of a Simeonite family.
15 And the name of the Midianite woman who was put to death
was Kozbi daughter of Zur, a tribal
chief of a Midianite family.

Nu 31:8; Jos 13:21

16 The LORD said to Moses,
17 "Treat the Midianites as enemies
and kill them. 18 They treated you
as enemies when they deceived
you in the Peor incident involving
their sister Kozbi, the daughter
of a Midianite leader, the woman
who was killed when the plague
came as a result of that incident."

Nu 31:1-3,16

The Second Census

26 After the plague the LORD
said to Moses and Eleazar
son of Aaron, the priest, 2 "Take a
census of the whole Israelite community by families — all those
twenty years old or more who are
able to serve in the army of Israel."
3 So on the plains of Moab by the
Jordan across from Jericho, Moses
and Eleazar the priest spoke with
them and said, 4 "Take a census of
the men twenty years old or more,
as the LORD commanded Moses."

Ex 30:11-16; Nu 22:1

These were the Israelites who
came out of Egypt:

5 The descendants of Reuben, the
firstborn son of Israel, were:
through Hanok, the Hanokite
clan;
through Pallu, the Palluite
clan;
6 through Hezron, the Hezronite clan;
through Karmi, the Karmite
clan.

Nu 1:20; 1Ch 5:3

7 These were the clans of Reuben;
those numbered were 43,730.
8 The son of Pallu was Eliab,
9 and the sons of Eliab were Nemuel, Dathan and Abiram. The
same Dathan and Abiram were
the community officials who rebelled against Moses and Aaron
and were among Korah's followers when they rebelled against
the LORD. 10 The earth opened its
mouth and swallowed them along
with Korah, whose followers died
when the fire devoured the 250
men. And they served as a warning sign. 11 The line of Korah, however, did not die out.

Ex 6:24; Nu 16:2; Dt 24:16

12 The descendants of Simeon by
their clans were:

through Nemuel, the Nemuelite clan;
through Jamin, the Jaminite clan; 1Ch 4:24
through Jakin, the Jakinite clan;
13 through Zerah, the Zerahite clan; Ge 46:10
through Shaul, the Shaulite clan.
14 These were the clans of Simeon; those numbered were 22,200.

15 The descendants of Gad by their clans were:
through Zephon, the Zephonite clan; Ge 46:16
through Haggi, the Haggite clan;
through Shuni, the Shunite clan;
16 through Ozni, the Oznite clan;
through Eri, the Erite clan;
17 through Arodi,[a] the Arodite clan;
through Areli, the Arelite clan.
18 These were the clans of Gad; those numbered were 40,500.
Nu 1:25; Jos 13:24-28

19 Er and Onan were sons of Judah, but they died in Canaan.
Ge 38:2-10; 46:12
20 The descendants of Judah by their clans were:
through Shelah, the Shelanite clan; 1Ch 2:3
through Perez, the Perezite clan;
through Zerah, the Zerahite clan.
21 The descendants of Perez were:
through Hezron, the Hezronite clan;
through Hamul, the Hamulite clan.
22 These were the clans of Judah; those numbered were 76,500.
Nu 1:27

23 The descendants of Issachar by their clans were:
through Tola, the Tolaite clan;
Ge 46:13
through Puah, the Puite[b] clan;
24 through Jashub, the Jashubite clan;
through Shimron, the Shimronite clan.
25 These were the clans of Issachar; those numbered were 64,300.
Nu 1:29

26 The descendants of Zebulun by their clans were:
through Sered, the Seredite clan;
through Elon, the Elonite clan;
through Jahleel, the Jahleelite clan.
27 These were the clans of Zebulun; those numbered were 60,500.
Nu 1:31

28 The descendants of Joseph by their clans through Manasseh and Ephraim were:

[a] *17* Samaritan Pentateuch and Syriac (see also Gen. 46:16); Masoretic Text *Arod*
[b] *23* Samaritan Pentateuch, Septuagint, Vulgate and Syriac (see also 1 Chron. 7:1); Masoretic Text *through Puvah, the Punite*

29The descendants of Manasseh:
through Makir, the Makirite clan (Makir was the father of Gilead); Jos 17:1
through Gilead, the Gileadite clan.
30These were the descendants of Gilead:
through Iezer, the Iezerite clan; Jos 17:2; Jdg 6:11
through Helek, the Helekite clan;
31through Asriel, the Asrielite clan;
through Shechem, the Shechemite clan;
32through Shemida, the Shemidaite clan;
through Hepher, the Hepherite clan.
33(Zelophehad son of Hepher had no sons; he had only daughters, whose names were Mahlah, Noah, Hoglah, Milkah and Tirzah.) Nu 27:1; 36:11
34These were the clans of Manasseh; those numbered were 52,700.

35These were the descendants of Ephraim by their clans:
through Shuthelah, the Shuthelahite clan;
through Beker, the Bekerite clan;
through Tahan, the Tahanite clan.
36These were the descendants of Shuthelah:
through Eran, the Eranite clan.
37These were the clans of Ephraim; those numbered were 32,500. Nu 1:33

These were the descendants of Joseph by their clans.

38The descendants of Benjamin by their clans were: Ge 46:21
through Bela, the Belaite clan;
through Ashbel, the Ashbelite clan;
through Ahiram, the Ahiramite clan;
39through Shupham,[a] the Shuphamite clan;
through Hupham, the Huphamite clan.
40The descendants of Bela through Ard and Naaman were:
through Ard,[b] the Ardite clan;
through Naaman, the Naamite clan.
41These were the clans of Benjamin; those numbered were 45,600. Nu 1:37

42These were the descendants of Dan by their clans:
through Shuham, the Shuhamite clan. Ge 46:23
These were the clans of Dan:
43All of them were Shuhamite clans; and those numbered were 64,400.

[a] 39 A few manuscripts of the Masoretic Text, Samaritan Pentateuch, Vulgate and Syriac (see also Septuagint); most manuscripts of the Masoretic Text *Shephupham* [b] 40 Samaritan Pentateuch and Vulgate (see also Septuagint); Masoretic Text does not have *through Ard.*

[44]The descendants of Asher by their clans were:

through Imnah, the Imnite clan;
through Ishvi, the Ishvite clan;
through Beriah, the Beriite clan;
[45]and through the descendants of Beriah:
through Heber, the Heberite clan;
through Malkiel, the Malkielite clan.
[46](Asher had a daughter named Serah.)

[47]These were the clans of Asher; those numbered were 53,400.

Nu 1:41

[48]The descendants of Naphtali by their clans were:

through Jahzeel, the Jahzeelite clan;
through Guni, the Gunite clan;
[49]through Jezer, the Jezerite clan;
through Shillem, the Shillemite clan.

[50]These were the clans of Naphtali; those numbered were 45,400.

[51]The total number of the men of Israel was 601,730. Ex 12:37; 38:26

[52]The LORD said to Moses, [53]"The
land is to be allotted to them as
an inheritance based on the number of names. [54]To a larger group
give a larger inheritance, and to
a smaller group a smaller one;
each is to receive its inheritance
according to the number of those
listed. [55]Be sure that the land
is distributed by lot. What each
group inherits will be according to the names for its ancestral
tribe. [56]Each inheritance is to be
distributed by lot among the larger and smaller groups."

Nu 33:54; 34:14; Jos 11:23

[57]These were the Levites who were counted by their clans: Ge 46:11

through Gershon, the Gershonite clan;
through Kohath, the Kohathite clan;
through Merari, the Merarite clan.

[58]These also were Levite clans:

the Libnite clan,
the Hebronite clan,
the Mahlite clan,
the Mushite clan,
the Korahite clan.
(Kohath was the forefather of
Amram; [59]the name of Amram's wife was Jochebed, a
descendant of Levi, who was
born to the Levites[a] in Egypt.
To Amram she bore Aaron,
Moses and their sister Miriam. [60]Aaron was the father of
Nadab and Abihu, Eleazar and
Ithamar. [61]But Nadab and Abihu died when they made an
offering before the LORD with
unauthorized fire.)

Ex 6:20; Lev 10:1-2; Nu 3:2

[a] 59 Or *Jochebed, a daughter of Levi, who was born to Levi*

62 All the male Levites a month old
or more numbered 23,000. They
were not counted along with the
other Israelites because they received no inheritance among
them. Nu 1:47; 18:23

63 These are the ones counted by
Moses and Eleazar the priest when
they counted the Israelites on
the plains of Moab by the Jordan
across from Jericho. 64 Not one of
them was among those counted by
Moses and Aaron the priest when
they counted the Israelites in the
Desert of Sinai. 65 For the LORD had
told those Israelites they would
surely die in the wilderness, and
not one of them was left except
Caleb son of Jephunneh and Joshua son of Nun.
Nu 14:28; Dt 2:14-15; Heb 3:17

Zelophehad's Daughters

27 The daughters of Zelophehad son of Hepher, the son
of Gilead, the son of Makir, the
son of Manasseh, belonged to the
clans of Manasseh son of Joseph.
The names of the daughters were
Mahlah, Noah, Hoglah, Milkah
and Tirzah. They came forward
2 and stood before Moses, Eleazar the priest, the leaders and the
whole assembly at the entrance
to the tent of meeting and said,
3 "Our father died in the wilderness. He was not among Korah's
followers, who banded together
against the LORD, but he died for
his own sin and left no sons. 4 Why
should our father's name disappear from his clan because he had
no son? Give us property among
our father's relatives."
Nu 16:2; 26:65; 36:1

5 So Moses brought their case
before the LORD, 6 and the LORD
said to him, 7 "What Zelophehad's
daughters are saying is right. You
must certainly give them property as an inheritance among their
father's relatives and give their father's inheritance to them.
Nu 9:8; Jos 17:4

8 "Say to the Israelites, 'If a man
dies and leaves no son, give his
inheritance to his daughter. 9 If he
has no daughter, give his inheritance to his brothers. 10 If he has no
brothers, give his inheritance to
his father's brothers. 11 If his father
had no brothers, give his inheritance to the nearest relative in his
clan, that he may possess it. This is
to have the force of law for the Israelites, as the LORD commanded
Moses.'" Nu 36:1-12

Joshua to Succeed Moses

12 Then the LORD said to Moses, "Go up this mountain in the
Abarim Range and see the land I
have given the Israelites. 13 After
you have seen it, you too will be
gathered to your people, as your
brother Aaron was, 14 for when the
community rebelled at the waters
in the Desert of Zin, both of you
disobeyed my command to hon-
or me as holy before their eyes."

(These were the waters of Meribah
Kadesh, in the Desert of Zin.)
Nu 20:12; 33:47; Dt 32:48-52
15Moses said to the LORD, 16"May
the LORD, the God who gives
breath to all living things, appoint
someone over this community 17to
go out and come in before them,
one who will lead them out and
bring them in, so the LORD's people will not be like sheep without
a shepherd." Nu 16:22; Dt 31:2; Mt 9:36
18So the LORD said to Moses,
"Take Joshua son of Nun, a man in
whom is the spirit of leadership,[a]
and lay your hand on him. 19Have
him stand before Eleazar the priest
and the entire assembly and commission him in their presence.
20Give him some of your authority so the whole Israelite community will obey him. 21He is to stand
before Eleazar the priest, who will
obtain decisions for him by inquiring of the Urim before the LORD.
At his command he and the entire
community of the Israelites will go
out, and at his command they will
come in." Nu 11:25-29; Dt 34:9; Jos 1:16-17
22Moses did as the LORD com-
manded him. He took Joshua and
had him stand before Eleazar the
priest and the whole assembly.
23Then he laid his hands on him
and commissioned him, as the
LORD instructed through Moses.

Daily Offerings

28 The LORD said to Moses,
2"Give this command to
the Israelites and say to them:
'Make sure that you present to me
at the appointed time my food offerings, as an aroma pleasing to
me.' 3Say to them: 'This is the food
offering you are to present to the
LORD: two lambs a year old without defect, as a regular burnt offering each day. 4Offer one lamb
in the morning and the other at
twilight, 5together with a grain offering of a tenth of an ephah[b] of
the finest flour mixed with a quarter of a hin[c] of oil from pressed
olives. 6This is the regular burnt
offering instituted at Mount Sinai
as a pleasing aroma, a food offering presented to the LORD. 7The
accompanying drink offering is to
be a quarter of a hin of fermented drink with each lamb. Pour out
the drink offering to the LORD at
the sanctuary. 8Offer the second
lamb at twilight, along with the
same kind of grain offering and
drink offering that you offer in the
morning. This is a food offering,
an aroma pleasing to the LORD.
Ex 29:38; Lev 2:1; 3:11

Sabbath Offerings

9" 'On the Sabbath day, make
an offering of two lambs a year
old without defect, together with
its drink offering and a grain offering of two-tenths of an ephah[d]

[a] 18 Or *the Spirit* [b] 5 That is, probably about 3 1/2 pounds or about 1.6 kilograms; also in verses 13, 21 and 29 [c] 5 That is, about 1 quart or about 1 liter; also in verses 7 and 14 [d] 9 That is, probably about 7 pounds or about 3.2 kilograms; also in verses 12, 20 and 28

of the finest flour mixed with olive oil. 10This is the burnt offering
for every Sabbath, in addition to
the regular burnt offering and its
drink offering. Lev 23:13; Mt 12:5

Monthly Offerings

11" 'On the first of every month,
present to the LORD a burnt offering of two young bulls, one ram
and seven male lambs a year old,
all without defect. 12With each bull
there is to be a grain offering of
three-tenths of an ephah[a] of the
finest flour mixed with oil; with
the ram, a grain offering of two-
tenths of an ephah of the finest
flour mixed with oil; 13and with
each lamb, a grain offering of a
tenth of an ephah of the finest
flour mixed with oil. This is for a
burnt offering, a pleasing aroma,
a food offering presented to the
LORD. 14With each bull there is to
be a drink offering of half a hin[b]
of wine; with the ram, a third of a
hin[c]; and with each lamb, a quarter of a hin. This is the monthly
burnt offering to be made at each
new moon during the year. 15Be-
sides the regular burnt offering
with its drink offering, one male
goat is to be presented to the LORD
as a sin offering.[d] Lev 4:3; Nu 10:10

The Passover

16" 'On the fourteenth day of the
first month the LORD's Passover is
to be held. 17On the fifteenth day
of this month there is to be a festival; for seven days eat bread made
without yeast. 18On the first day
hold a sacred assembly and do no
regular work. 19Present to the LORD
a food offering consisting of a
burnt offering of two young bulls,
one ram and seven male lambs a
year old, all without defect. 20With
each bull offer a grain offering of
three-tenths of an ephah of the
finest flour mixed with oil; with
the ram, two-tenths; 21and with
each of the seven lambs, one-
tenth. 22Include one male goat as
a sin offering to make atonement
for you. 23Offer these in addition
to the regular morning burnt offering. 24In this way present the
food offering every day for seven
days as an aroma pleasing to the
LORD; it is to be offered in addition to the regular burnt offering
and its drink offering. 25On the
seventh day hold a sacred assembly and do no regular work.
Ex 12:14-20; Lev 23:4-8; Dt 16:1-8

The Festival of Weeks

26" 'On the day of firstfruits,
when you present to the LORD an
offering of new grain during the
Festival of Weeks, hold a sacred
assembly and do no regular work.
27Present a burnt offering of two
young bulls, one ram and seven
male lambs a year old as an aroma pleasing to the LORD. 28With

[a] *12* That is, probably about 11 pounds or about 5 kilograms; also in verses 20 and 28
[b] *14* That is, about 2 quarts or about 1.9 liters
[c] *14* That is, about 1 1/3 quarts or about 1.3 liters
[d] *15* Or *purification offering*; also in verse 22

each bull there is to be a grain offering of three-tenths of an ephah
of the finest flour mixed with oil;
with the ram, two-tenths; 29and
with each of the seven lambs, one-
tenth. 30Include one male goat to
make atonement for you. 31Offer
these together with their drink offerings, in addition to the regular
burnt offering and its grain offering. Be sure the animals are without defect. Lev 23:15-22; Dt 16:9-12

The Festival of Trumpets

29 "'On the first day of the
seventh month hold a sa-
cred assembly and do no regular work. It is a day for you to
sound the trumpets. 2As an aroma pleasing to the LORD, offer a
burnt offering of one young bull,
one ram and seven male lambs a
year old, all without defect. 3With
the bull offer a grain offering of
three-tenths of an ephah[a] of the
finest flour mixed with olive oil;
with the ram, two-tenths[b]; 4and
with each of the seven lambs, one-
tenth.[c] 5Include one male goat as
a sin offering[d] to make atonement
for you. 6These are in addition to
the monthly and daily burnt offerings with their grain offerings
and drink offerings as specified.
They are food offerings presented
to the LORD, a pleasing aroma.
Lev 23:23-25

The Day of Atonement

7"'On the tenth day of this seventh month hold a sacred assembly. You must deny yourselves[e]
and do no work. 8Present as an
aroma pleasing to the LORD a
burnt offering of one young bull,
one ram and seven male lambs a
year old, all without defect. 9With
the bull offer a grain offering of
three-tenths of an ephah of the
finest flour mixed with oil; with
the ram, two-tenths; 10and with
each of the seven lambs, one-
tenth. 11Include one male goat as
a sin offering, in addition to the
sin offering for atonement and
the regular burnt offering with
its grain offering, and their drink
offerings. Lev 16:2-34; 23:26-32

The Festival of Tabernacles

12"'On the fifteenth day of the
seventh month, hold a sacred assembly and do no regular work.
Celebrate a festival to the LORD for
seven days. 13Present as an aroma
pleasing to the LORD a food offering consisting of a burnt offering of thirteen young bulls, two
rams and fourteen male lambs a
year old, all without defect. 14With
each of the thirteen bulls offer a
grain offering of three-tenths of
an ephah of the finest flour mixed
with oil; with each of the two
rams, two-tenths; 15and with each

[a] 3 That is, probably about 11 pounds or about 5 kilograms; also in verses 9 and 14
[b] 3 That is, probably about 7 pounds or about 3.2 kilograms; also in verses 9 and 14
[c] 4 That is, probably about 3 1/2 pounds or about 1.6 kilograms; also in verses 10 and 15
[d] 5 Or *purification offering*; also elsewhere in this chapter
[e] 7 Or *must fast*

of the fourteen lambs, one-tenth.
16Include one male goat as a sin offering, in addition to the regular
burnt offering with its grain offering and drink offering.

Lev 23:24; 1Ki 8:2

17" 'On the second day offer
twelve young bulls, two rams and
fourteen male lambs a year old, all
without defect. 18With the bulls,
rams and lambs, offer their grain
offerings and drink offerings according to the number specified.
19Include one male goat as a sin offering, in addition to the regular
burnt offering with its grain offering, and their drink offerings.

Nu 28:3,15

20" 'On the third day offer elev-
en bulls, two rams and fourteen
male lambs a year old, all without
defect. 21With the bulls, rams and
lambs, offer their grain offerings
and drink offerings according to
the number specified. 22Include
one male goat as a sin offering, in
addition to the regular burnt offering with its grain offering and
drink offering.

23" 'On the fourth day offer ten
bulls, two rams and fourteen male
lambs a year old, all without defect. 24With the bulls, rams and
lambs, offer their grain offerings
and drink offerings according to
the number specified. 25Include
one male goat as a sin offering, in
addition to the regular burnt offering with its grain offering and
drink offering.

26" 'On the fifth day offer nine
bulls, two rams and fourteen male
lambs a year old, all without defect. 27With the bulls, rams and
lambs, offer their grain offerings
and drink offerings according to
the number specified. 28Include
one male goat as a sin offering, in
addition to the regular burnt offering with its grain offering and
drink offering.

29" 'On the sixth day offer eight
bulls, two rams and fourteen male
lambs a year old, all without defect. 30With the bulls, rams and
lambs, offer their grain offerings
and drink offerings according to
the number specified. 31Include
one male goat as a sin offering, in
addition to the regular burnt offering with its grain offering and
drink offering.

32" 'On the seventh day offer sev-
en bulls, two rams and fourteen
male lambs a year old, all without
defect. 33With the bulls, rams and
lambs, offer their grain offerings
and drink offerings according to
the number specified. 34Include
one male goat as a sin offering, in
addition to the regular burnt offering with its grain offering and
drink offering.

35" 'On the eighth day hold a
closing special assembly and do no
regular work. 36Present as an aroma pleasing to the LORD a food offering consisting of a burnt offering of one bull, one ram and seven
male lambs a year old, all without

defect. 37With the bull, the ram and the lambs, offer their grain offerings and drink offerings according to the number specified. 38Include one male goat as a sin offering, in addition to the regular burnt offering with its grain offering and drink offering. Lev 1:9; 23:36

39" 'In addition to what you vow and your freewill offerings, offer these to the LORD at your appointed festivals: your burnt offerings, grain offerings, drink offerings and fellowship offerings.' "

Lev 23:33-43; Dt 16:13-17

40Moses told the Israelites all that the LORD commanded him.[a]

Vows

30[b] Moses said to the heads of the tribes of Israel: "This is what the LORD commands: 2When a man makes a vow to the LORD or takes an oath to obligate himself by a pledge, he must not break his word but must do everything he said. Dt 23:21-23; Ps 50:14; Pr 20:25

3"When a young woman still living in her father's household makes a vow to the LORD or obligates herself by a pledge 4and her father hears about her vow or pledge but says nothing to her, then all her vows and every pledge by which she obligated herself will stand. 5But if her father forbids her when he hears about it, none of her vows or the pledges by which she obligated herself will stand; the LORD will release her because her father has forbidden her.

6"If she marries after she makes a vow or after her lips utter a rash promise by which she obligates herself 7and her husband hears about it but says nothing to her, then her vows or the pledges by which she obligated herself will stand. 8But if her husband forbids her when he hears about it, he nullifies the vow that obligates her or the rash promise by which she obligates herself, and the LORD will release her.

Ge 3:16; Lev 5:4

9"Any vow or obligation taken by a widow or divorced woman will be binding on her.

10"If a woman living with her husband makes a vow or obligates herself by a pledge under oath 11and her husband hears about it but says nothing to her and does not forbid her, then all her vows or the pledges by which she obligated herself will stand. 12But if her husband nullifies them when he hears about them, then none of the vows or pledges that came from her lips will stand. Her husband has nullified them, and the LORD will release her. 13Her husband may confirm or nullify any vow she makes or any sworn pledge to deny herself.[c] 14But if her husband says nothing to her about it from day to day, then he confirms all her vows or the pledges binding on her. He confirms them

[a] 40 In Hebrew texts this verse (29:40) is numbered 30:1. [b] In Hebrew texts 30:1-16 is numbered 30:2-17. [c] 13 Or *to fast*

by saying nothing to her when he
hears about them. 15If, however,
he nullifies them some time after he hears about them, then he
must bear the consequences of
her wrongdoing." Eph 5:22; Col 3:18
16These are the regulations the
LORD gave Moses concerning relationships between a man and his
wife, and between a father and
his young daughter still living at
home.

Vengeance on the Midianites

31 The LORD said to Moses,
2"Take vengeance on the
Midianites for the Israelites. After
that, you will be gathered to your
people." Nu 20:26; 27:13
3So Moses said to the people,
"Arm some of your men to go to
war against the Midianites so that
they may carry out the LORD's
vengeance on them. 4Send into
battle a thousand men from each
of the tribes of Israel." 5So twelve
thousand men armed for battle,
a thousand from each tribe, were
supplied from the clans of Israel.
6Moses sent them into battle, a
thousand from each tribe, along
with Phinehas son of Eleazar, the
priest, who took with him articles
from the sanctuary and the trumpets for signaling.
Nu 10:9; Jdg 11:36; Ps 94:1
7They fought against Midian, as
the LORD commanded Moses, and
killed every man. 8Among their
victims were Evi, Rekem, Zur, Hur
and Reba — the five kings of Midian. They also killed Balaam son of
Beor with the sword. 9The Israelites captured the Midianite wom-
en and children and took all the
Midianite herds, flocks and goods
as plunder. 10They burned all the
towns where the Midianites had
settled, as well as all their camps.
11They took all the plunder and
spoils, including the people and
animals, 12and brought the captives, spoils and plunder to Moses
and Eleazar the priest and the Israelite assembly at their camp on
the plains of Moab, by the Jordan
across from Jericho.
Dt 20:13; Jdg 21:11; Jos 13:21-22
13Moses, Eleazar the priest and all
the leaders of the community went
to meet them outside the camp.
14Moses was angry with the officers of the army — the commanders of thousands and commanders
of hundreds — who returned from
the battle. Ex 18:21; Dt 1:15
15"Have you allowed all the wom-
en to live?" he asked them. 16"They
were the ones who followed Balaam's advice and enticed the Israelites to be unfaithful to the
LORD in the Peor incident, so that
a plague struck the LORD's people.
17Now kill all the boys. And kill every woman who has slept with a
man, 18but save for yourselves every girl who has never slept with a
man. 2Pe 2:15; Nu 25:1-9; Jdg 21:11
19"Anyone who has killed someone or touched someone who
was killed must stay outside the
camp seven days. On the third

and seventh days you must purify yourselves and your captives.
20 Purify every garment as well as
everything made of leather, goat
hair or wood." Nu 19:12,16

21 Then Eleazar the priest said
to the soldiers who had gone into
battle, "This is what is required by
the law that the LORD gave Moses:
22 Gold, silver, bronze, iron, tin, lead
23 and anything else that can withstand fire must be put through the
fire, and then it will be clean. But
it must also be purified with the
water of cleansing. And whatever
cannot withstand fire must be put
through that water. 24 On the seventh day wash your clothes and
you will be clean. Then you may
come into the camp."
1Co 3:13; Nu 19:9,17; Lev 11:25

Dividing the Spoils

25 The LORD said to Moses, 26 "You
and Eleazar the priest and the
family heads of the community
are to count all the people and animals that were captured. 27 Divide
the spoils equally between the soldiers who took part in the battle
and the rest of the community.
28 From the soldiers who fought
in the battle, set apart as tribute
for the LORD one out of every five
hundred, whether people, cattle, donkeys or sheep. 29 Take this
tribute from their half share and
give it to Eleazar the priest as the
LORD's part. 30 From the Israelites'
half, select one out of every fifty,
whether people, cattle, donkeys,
sheep or other animals. Give them
to the Levites, who are responsible
for the care of the LORD's tabernacle." 31 So Moses and Eleazar the
priest did as the LORD commanded Moses. Nu 3:7; 18:21; Jos 22:8

32 The plunder remaining from
the spoils that the soldiers took
was 675,000 sheep, 33 72,000 cattle, 34 61,000 donkeys 35 and 32,000
women who had never slept with
a man.

36 The half share of those who
fought in the battle was:

337,500 sheep, 37 of which the
tribute for the LORD was
675;
38 36,000 cattle, of which the tribute for the LORD was 72;
39 30,500 donkeys, of which the
tribute for the LORD was
61;
40 16,000 people, of whom the
tribute for the LORD was
32.

41 Moses gave the tribute to Eleazar the priest as the LORD's part,
as the LORD commanded Moses.
Nu 18:8

42 The half belonging to the Israelites, which Moses set apart from
that of the fighting men — 43 the
community's half — was 337,500
sheep, 44 36,000 cattle, 45 30,500
donkeys 46 and 16,000 people.
47 From the Israelites' half, Moses selected one out of every fifty
people and animals, as the LORD
commanded him, and gave them
to the Levites, who were respon-

sible for the care of the LORD's
tabernacle.
48Then the officers who were
over the units of the army — the
commanders of thousands and
commanders of hundreds — went
to Moses 49and said to him, "Your
servants have counted the soldiers
under our command, and not one
is missing. 50So we have brought
as an offering to the LORD the
gold articles each of us acquired —
armlets, bracelets, signet rings,
earrings and necklaces — to make
atonement for ourselves before
the LORD." Ex 30:16; Jer 23:4
51Moses and Eleazar the priest
accepted from them the gold —
all the crafted articles. 52All the
gold from the commanders of
thousands and commanders of
hundreds that Moses and Eleazar presented as a gift to the LORD
weighed 16,750 shekels.[a] 53Each
soldier had taken plunder for
himself. 54Moses and Eleazar the
priest accepted the gold from the
commanders of thousands and
commanders of hundreds and
brought it into the tent of meeting as a memorial for the Israelites before the LORD. Ex 28:12; Dt 20:14

The Transjordan Tribes

32 The Reubenites and Gadites, who had very large
herds and flocks, saw that the
lands of Jazer and Gilead were
suitable for livestock. 2So they
came to Moses and Eleazar the
priest and to the leaders of the
community, and said, 3"Ataroth,
Dibon, Jazer, Nimrah, Heshbon,
Elealeh, Sebam, Nebo and Beon —
4the land the LORD subdued before the people of Israel — are
suitable for livestock, and your
servants have livestock. 5If we
have found favor in your eyes,"
they said, "let this land be given
to your servants as our possession. Do not make us cross the
Jordan." Ex 12:38; Nu 21:32,34
6Moses said to the Gadites and
Reubenites, "Should your fellow
Israelites go to war while you sit
here? 7Why do you discourage the
Israelites from crossing over into
the land the LORD has given them?
8This is what your fathers did when
I sent them from Kadesh Barnea
to look over the land. 9After they
went up to the Valley of Eshkol
and viewed the land, they discouraged the Israelites from entering
the land the LORD had given them.
10The LORD's anger was aroused
that day and he swore this oath:
11'Because they have not followed
me wholeheartedly, not one of
those who were twenty years old
or more when they came up out of
Egypt will see the land I promised
on oath to Abraham, Isaac and Jacob — 12not one except Caleb son
of Jephunneh the Kenizzite and
Joshua son of Nun, for they followed the LORD wholeheartedly.'
13The LORD's anger burned against
Israel and he made them wander

[a] 52 That is, about 420 pounds or about 190 kilograms

in the wilderness forty years, until
the whole generation of those
who had done evil in his sight was
gone. Nu 13:27-14:4; Dt 1:19-25; Ps 63:8
14“And here you are, a brood
of sinners, standing in the place
of your fathers and making the
LORD even more angry with Israel. 15If you turn away from following him, he will again leave all this
people in the wilderness, and you
will be the cause of their destruction.” Dt 30:17-18; 2Ch 7:20
16Then they came up to him and
said, “We would like to build pens
here for our livestock and cities
for our women and children. 17But
we will arm ourselves for battle[a]
and go ahead of the Israelites until we have brought them to their
place. Meanwhile our women and
children will live in fortified cities, for protection from the inhabitants of the land. 18We will not
return to our homes until each of
the Israelites has received their
inheritance. 19We will not receive
any inheritance with them on the
other side of the Jordan, because
our inheritance has come to us on
the east side of the Jordan.”
Jos 4:12-13; 12:1; 22:1-4
20Then Moses said to them, “If
you will do this — if you will arm
yourselves before the LORD for
battle 21and if all of you who are
armed cross over the Jordan before the LORD until he has driv-
en his enemies out before him —
22then when the land is subdued
before the LORD, you may return
and be free from your obligation
to the LORD and to Israel. And this
land will be your possession before the LORD. Dt 3:18-20
23“But if you fail to do this, you
will be sinning against the LORD;
and you may be sure that your sin
will find you out. 24Build cities for
your women and children, and
pens for your flocks, but do what
you have promised.” Ge 4:7
25The Gadites and Reubenites
said to Moses, “We your servants
will do as our lord commands.
26Our children and wives, our
flocks and herds will remain here
in the cities of Gilead. 27But your
servants, every man who is armed
for battle, will cross over to fight
before the LORD, just as our lord
says.” Jos 1:14
28Then Moses gave orders about
them to Eleazar the priest and
Joshua son of Nun and to the family heads of the Israelite tribes.
29He said to them, “If the Gadites and Reubenites, every man
armed for battle, cross over the
Jordan with you before the LORD,
then when the land is subdued before you, you must give them the
land of Gilead as their possession.
30But if they do not cross over with
you armed, they must accept their
possession with you in Canaan.”
Dt 3:18-20; Jos 1:13
31The Gadites and Reubenites
answered, “Your servants will do
what the LORD has said. 32We will

[a] 17 Septuagint; Hebrew *will be quick to arm ourselves*

cross over before the LORD into
Canaan armed, but the property
we inherit will be on this side of
the Jordan."

33 Then Moses gave to the Gadites, the Reubenites and the half-
tribe of Manasseh son of Joseph
the kingdom of Sihon king of the
Amorites and the kingdom of Og
king of Bashan — the whole land
with its cities and the territory
around them. Nu 21:24; Jos 12:6

34 The Gadites built up Dibon, Ataroth, Aroer, 35 Atroth Shophan, Jazer, Jogbehah, 36 Beth Nimrah and
Beth Haran as fortified cities, and
built pens for their flocks. 37 And
the Reubenites rebuilt Heshbon,
Elealeh and Kiriathaim, 38 as well
as Nebo and Baal Meon (these
names were changed) and Sibmah. They gave names to the cities they rebuilt. ver 3; Dt 2:36

39 The descendants of Makir son
of Manasseh went to Gilead, captured it and drove out the Amorites who were there. 40 So Moses
gave Gilead to the Makirites, the
descendants of Manasseh, and
they settled there. 41 Jair, a descendant of Manasseh, captured their
settlements and called them Havvoth Jair.[a] 42 And Nobah captured
Kenath and its surrounding settlements and called it Nobah after
himself. Ge 50:23; Dt 3:14; 2Sa 18:18

Stages in Israel's Journey

33 Here are the stages in the
journey of the Israelites
when they came out of Egypt by
divisions under the leadership of
Moses and Aaron. 2 At the LORD's
command Moses recorded the
stages in their journey. This is their
journey by stages: Ps 77:20; Mic 6:4

3 The Israelites set out from
Rameses on the fifteenth
day of the first month, the
day after the Passover. They
marched out defiantly in full
view of all the Egyptians,
4 who were burying all their
firstborn, whom the LORD had
struck down among them; for
the LORD had brought judgment on their gods. Ex 12:12; 14:8

5 The Israelites left Rameses
and camped at Sukkoth.

6 They left Sukkoth and
camped at Etham, on the
edge of the desert. Ex 13:20

7 They left Etham, turned
back to Pi Hahiroth, to the
east of Baal Zephon, and
camped near Migdol. Ex 14:2

8 They left Pi Hahiroth[b] and
passed through the sea into
the desert, and when they
had traveled for three days
in the Desert of Etham, they
camped at Marah. Ex 14:22

9 They left Marah and went
to Elim, where there were
twelve springs and seventy
palm trees, and they camped
there. Ex 15:27

[a] 41 Or *them the settlements of Jair*
[b] 8 Many manuscripts of the Masoretic Text, Samaritan Pentateuch and Vulgate; most manuscripts of the Masoretic Text *left from before Hahiroth*

10 They left Elim and camped by the Red Sea.[a]

11 They left the Red Sea and camped in the Desert of Sin. Ex 16:1

12 They left the Desert of Sin and camped at Dophkah.

13 They left Dophkah and camped at Alush.

14 They left Alush and camped at Rephidim, where there was no water for the people to drink.

15 They left Rephidim and camped in the Desert of Sinai. Ex 17:1; 19:1

16 They left the Desert of Sinai and camped at Kibroth Hattaavah. Nu 11:34

17 They left Kibroth Hattaavah and camped at Hazeroth. Nu 11:35

18 They left Hazeroth and camped at Rithmah.

19 They left Rithmah and camped at Rimmon Perez.

20 They left Rimmon Perez and camped at Libnah. Jos 10:29

21 They left Libnah and camped at Rissah.

22 They left Rissah and camped at Kehelathah.

23 They left Kehelathah and camped at Mount Shepher.

24 They left Mount Shepher and camped at Haradah.

25 They left Haradah and camped at Makheloth.

26 They left Makheloth and camped at Tahath.

27 They left Tahath and camped at Terah.

28 They left Terah and camped at Mithkah.

29 They left Mithkah and camped at Hashmonah.

30 They left Hashmonah and camped at Moseroth. Dt 10:6

31 They left Moseroth and camped at Bene Jaakan.

32 They left Bene Jaakan and camped at Hor Haggidgad.

33 They left Hor Haggidgad and camped at Jotbathah.

34 They left Jotbathah and camped at Abronah.

35 They left Abronah and camped at Ezion Geber. Dt 2:8

36 They left Ezion Geber and camped at Kadesh, in the Desert of Zin. Nu 20:1

37 They left Kadesh and camped at Mount Hor, on
the border of Edom. 38 At the
LORD's command Aaron the priest went up Mount Hor, where he died on the first day of the fifth month of the fortieth year after the Israelites
came out of Egypt. 39 Aaron
was a hundred and twenty-three years old when he died on Mount Hor. Nu 20:22,25-28; Dt 10:6

40 The Canaanite king of Arad, who lived in the Negev of Canaan, heard that the Israelites were coming. Nu 21:1

41 They left Mount Hor and camped at Zalmonah.

[a] 10 Or *the Sea of Reeds*; also in verse 11

42They left Zalmonah and
camped at Punon.
43They left Punon and
camped at Oboth. Nu 21:10
44They left Oboth and
camped at Iye Abarim, on the
border of Moab.
45They left Iye Abarim and
camped at Dibon Gad.
46They left Dibon Gad and
camped at Almon Diblatha-
im.
47They left Almon Diblathaim and camped in the mountains of Abarim, near Nebo.
48They left the mountains
of Abarim and camped on the
plains of Moab by the Jordan
across from Jericho. 49There
on the plains of Moab they
camped along the Jordan
from Beth Jeshimoth to Abel
Shittim. Nu 22:1; 25:1

50On the plains of Moab by the
Jordan across from Jericho the
LORD said to Moses, 51"Speak to
the Israelites and say to them:
'When you cross the Jordan into
Canaan, 52drive out all the inhabitants of the land before you. Destroy all their carved images and
their cast idols, and demolish all
their high places. 53Take possession of the land and settle in it, for
I have given you the land to possess. 54Distribute the land by lot,
according to your clans. To a larger group give a larger inheritance,
and to a smaller group a smaller
one. Whatever falls to them by lot
will be theirs. Distribute it according to your ancestral tribes.

Ex 23:24; Ps 106:34-36; Nu 26:54

55" 'But if you do not drive out
the inhabitants of the land, those
you allow to remain will become
barbs in your eyes and thorns in
your sides. They will give you trouble in the land where you will live.
56And then I will do to you what I
plan to do to them.' "

Jos 23:13; Jdg 2:3; Ps 106:36

Boundaries of Canaan

34 The LORD said to Moses,
2"Command the Israelites
and say to them: 'When you enter
Canaan, the land that will be allotted to you as an inheritance is to
have these boundaries:

Ge 17:8; Dt 1:7-8; Ps 78:54-55

3" 'Your southern side will include some of the Desert of Zin
along the border of Edom. Your
southern boundary will start in
the east from the southern end of
the Dead Sea, 4cross south of Scorpion Pass, continue on to Zin and
go south of Kadesh Barnea. Then
it will go to Hazar Addar and over
to Azmon, 5where it will turn, join
the Wadi of Egypt and end at the
Mediterranean Sea.

Ge 15:18; Nu 32:8; Jos 15:1-3

6" 'Your western boundary will
be the coast of the Mediterranean
Sea. This will be your boundary on
the west.
7" 'For your northern boundary,
run a line from the Mediterranean

Sea to Mount Hor [8]and from Mount
Hor to Lebo Hamath. Then the
boundary will go to Zedad, [9]con-
tinue to Ziphron and end at Hazar
Enan. This will be your boundary
on the north. Eze 47:15-17; Nu 13:21

[10]" 'For your eastern boundary,
run a line from Hazar Enan to
Shepham. [11]The boundary will go
down from Shepham to Riblah on
the east side of Ain and continue
along the slopes east of the Sea of
Galilee.[a] [12]Then the boundary will
go down along the Jordan and end
at the Dead Sea. Dt 3:17; 2Ki 23:33

" 'This will be your land, with its
boundaries on every side.' "

[13]Moses commanded the Israelites: "Assign this land by lot as an
inheritance. The LORD has ordered
that it be given to the nine and a
half tribes, [14]because the families
of the tribe of Reuben, the tribe of
Gad and the half-tribe of Manasseh
have received their inheritance.
[15]These two and a half tribes have
received their inheritance east of
the Jordan across from Jericho, toward the sunrise." Nu 32:33; Jos 14:1-5

[16]The LORD said to Moses, [17]"These
are the names of the men who are
to assign the land for you as an inheritance: Eleazar the priest and
Joshua son of Nun. [18]And appoint
one leader from each tribe to help
assign the land. [19]These are their
names: Nu 1:4,16; Jos 14:1

Caleb son of Jephunneh,
from the tribe of Judah; Ge 29:35; Nu 26:65

[20]Shemuel son of Ammihud,
from the tribe of Simeon; Ge 49:5

[21]Elidad son of Kislon,
from the tribe of Benjamin; Ge 49:27; Ps 68:27

[22]Bukki son of Jogli,
the leader from the tribe of
Dan;

[23]Hanniel son of Ephod,
the leader from the tribe of
Manasseh son of Joseph;

[24]Kemuel son of Shiphtan,
the leader from the tribe of
Ephraim son of Joseph; Nu 1:32,34

[25]Elizaphan son of Parnak,
the leader from the tribe of
Zebulun;

[26]Paltiel son of Azzan,
the leader from the tribe of
Issachar;

[27]Ahihud son of Shelomi,
the leader from the tribe of
Asher; Nu 1:40

[28]Pedahel son of Ammihud,
the leader from the tribe of
Naphtali."

[29]These are the men the LORD
commanded to assign the inheritance to the Israelites in the land
of Canaan.

Towns for the Levites

35 On the plains of Moab by the
Jordan across from Jericho,
the LORD said to Moses, [2]"Command the Israelites to give the
Levites towns to live in from the

[a] 11 Hebrew *Kinnereth*

inheritance the Israelites will possess. And give them pasturelands
around the towns. 3Then they will
have towns to live in and pasturelands for the cattle they own and
all their other animals.

Lev 25:32-34; Jos 14:3-4

4"The pasturelands around the
towns that you give the Levites
will extend a thousand cubits[a]
from the town wall. 5Outside the
town, measure two thousand cubits[b] on the east side, two thousand on the south side, two thousand on the west and two thousand
on the north, with the town in the
center. They will have this area as
pastureland for the towns.

Cities of Refuge

6"Six of the towns you give the
Levites will be cities of refuge, to
which a person who has killed
someone may flee. In addition,
give them forty-two other towns.
7In all you must give the Levites
forty-eight towns, together with
their pasturelands. 8The towns
you give the Levites from the land
the Israelites possess are to be
given in proportion to the inheritance of each tribe: Take many
towns from a tribe that has many,
but few from one that has few."

Nu 26:54; Jos 20:7-9

9Then the LORD said to Moses:
10"Speak to the Israelites and say
to them: 'When you cross the Jordan into Canaan, 11select some
towns to be your cities of refuge,
to which a person who has killed
someone accidentally may flee.
12They will be places of refuge
from the avenger, so that anyone accused of murder may not
die before they stand trial before
the assembly. 13These six towns
you give will be your cities of refuge. 14Give three on this side of
the Jordan and three in Canaan as
cities of refuge. 15These six towns
will be a place of refuge for Israelites and for foreigners residing
among them, so that anyone who
has killed another accidentally
can flee there.

Ex 21:13; Jos 20:3

16" 'If anyone strikes someone a
fatal blow with an iron object, that
person is a murderer; the murderer is to be put to death. 17Or if anyone is holding a stone and strikes
someone a fatal blow with it, that
person is a murderer; the murderer is to be put to death. 18Or if
anyone is holding a wooden object
and strikes someone a fatal blow
with it, that person is a murderer; the murderer is to be put to
death. 19The avenger of blood shall
put the murderer to death; when
the avenger comes upon the murderer, the avenger shall put the
murderer to death. 20If anyone
with malice aforethought shoves
another or throws something at
them intentionally so that they
die 21or if out of enmity one person hits another with their fist so
that the other dies, that person is

[a] 4 That is, about 1,500 feet or about 450 meters [b] 5 That is, about 3,000 feet or about 900 meters

to be put to death; that person is
a murderer. The avenger of blood
shall put the murderer to death
when they meet. Ex 21:12,14; Lev 24:17

22“ ‘But if without enmity someone suddenly pushes another or
throws something at them unintentionally 23or, without seeing them, drops on them a stone
heavy enough to kill them, and
they die, then since that other
person was not an enemy and no
harm was intended, 24the assembly must judge between the accused and the avenger of blood according to these regulations. 25The
assembly must protect the one accused of murder from the avenger of blood and send the accused
back to the city of refuge to which
they fled. The accused must stay
there until the death of the high
priest, who was anointed with the
holy oil. Ex 21:13; 29:7

26“ ‘But if the accused ever goes
outside the limits of the city of
refuge to which they fled 27and
the avenger of blood finds them
outside the city, the avenger of
blood may kill the accused without being guilty of murder. 28The
accused must stay in the city of
refuge until the death of the high
priest; only after the death of the
high priest may they return to
their own property.

29“ ‘This is to have the force of
law for you throughout the generations to come, wherever you live.

30“ ‘Anyone who kills a person is
to be put to death as a murderer
only on the testimony of witnesses. But no one is to be put to death
on the testimony of only one witness. Dt 17:6; Mt 18:16; 2Co 13:1

31“ ‘Do not accept a ransom for
the life of a murderer, who deserves to die. They are to be put to
death.

32“ ‘Do not accept a ransom for
anyone who has fled to a city of
refuge and so allow them to go
back and live on their own land
before the death of the high
priest.

33“ ‘Do not pollute the land
where you are. Bloodshed pollutes
the land, and atonement cannot
be made for the land on which
blood has been shed, except by the
blood of the one who shed it. 34Do
not defile the land where you live
and where I dwell, for I, the LORD,
dwell among the Israelites.’ ”
Dt 4:41-43; 19:1-14; Jos 20:1-9

Inheritance of Zelophehad's Daughters

36 The family heads of the
clan of Gilead son of Makir,
the son of Manasseh, who were
from the clans of the descendants
of Joseph, came and spoke before
Moses and the leaders, the heads
of the Israelite families. 2They
said, “When the LORD commanded my lord to give the land as an
inheritance to the Israelites by lot,
he ordered you to give the inheritance of our brother Zelophehad
to his daughters. 3Now suppose
they marry men from other Isra-

elite tribes; then their inheritance
will be taken from our ancestral
inheritance and added to that of
the tribe they marry into. And so
part of the inheritance allotted
to us will be taken away. 4When
the Year of Jubilee for the Israelites comes, their inheritance will
be added to that of the tribe into
which they marry, and their property will be taken from the tribal
inheritance of our ancestors."
Lev 25:10; Nu 26:33; 26:29

5Then at the LORD's command
Moses gave this order to the Israelites: "What the tribe of the descendants of Joseph is saying is
right. 6This is what the LORD commands for Zelophehad's daughters: They may marry anyone they
please as long as they marry within their father's tribal clan. 7No inheritance in Israel is to pass from
one tribe to another, for every Israelite shall keep the tribal inheritance of their ancestors. 8Every
daughter who inherits land in any
Israelite tribe must marry someone in her father's tribal clan, so
that every Israelite will possess
the inheritance of their ancestors.
9No inheritance may pass from
one tribe to another, for each Israelite tribe is to keep the land it
inherits." 1Ki 21:3; 1Ch 23:22

10So Zelophehad's daughters did
as the LORD commanded Moses.
11Zelophehad's daughters — Mahlah, Tirzah, Hoglah, Milkah and
Noah — married their cousins on
their father's side. 12They married
within the clans of the descendants of Manasseh son of Joseph,
and their inheritance remained in
their father's tribe and clan.
Nu 27:1-11

13These are the commands
and regulations the LORD gave
through Moses to the Israelites on
the plains of Moab by the Jordan
across from Jericho. Lev 26:46; Nu 22:1

DEUTERONOMY

The Command to Leave Horeb

1 These are the words Moses
spoke to all Israel in the wilderness east of the Jordan — that
is, in the Arabah — opposite Suph,
between Paran and Tophel, Laban,
Hazeroth and Dizahab. 2(It takes
eleven days to go from Horeb to
Kadesh Barnea by the Mount Seir
road.) Dt 19:23

3In the fortieth year, on the first
day of the eleventh month, Moses proclaimed to the Israelites
all that the LORD had commanded
him concerning them. 4This was
after he had defeated Sihon king
of the Amorites, who reigned in
Heshbon, and at Edrei had defeated Og king of Bashan, who reigned
in Ashtaroth. Nu 21:33-35; 33:38; Jos 13:12

5East of the Jordan in the territory of Moab, Moses began to expound this law, saying:

6The LORD our God said to us
at Horeb, "You have stayed long
enough at this mountain. 7Break
camp and advance into the hill
country of the Amorites; go to all
the neighboring peoples in the
Arabah, in the mountains, in the
western foothills, in the Negev
and along the coast, to the land
of the Canaanites and to Lebanon, as far as the great river, the
Euphrates. 8See, I have given you
this land. Go in and take possession of the land the LORD swore
he would give to your fathers — to
Abraham, Isaac and Jacob — and
to their descendants after them."

Ge 12:7; Dt 11:24; Nu 10:13

The Appointment of Leaders

9At that time I said to you, "You
are too heavy a burden for me to
carry alone. 10The LORD your God
has increased your numbers so
that today you are as numerous as
the stars in the sky. 11May the LORD,
the God of your ancestors, increase
you a thousand times and bless
you as he has promised! 12But how
can I bear your problems and your
burdens and your disputes all by
myself? 13Choose some wise, understanding and respected men
from each of your tribes, and I will
set them over you."

Ex 18:18; Ge 15:5; Dt 10:22

14You answered me, "What you
propose to do is good."

15So I took the leading men of
your tribes, wise and respected
men, and appointed them to have
authority over you — as commanders of thousands, of hundreds, of fifties and of tens and
as tribal officials. 16And I charged
your judges at that time, "Hear the
disputes between your people and
judge fairly, whether the case is

between two Israelites or between
an Israelite and a foreigner residing among you. 17 Do not show partiality in judging; hear both small
and great alike. Do not be afraid of
anyone, for judgment belongs to
God. Bring me any case too hard
for you, and I will hear it." 18 And
at that time I told you everything
you were to do. Ex 18:25; Dt 16:18; Jas 2:1

Spies Sent Out

19 Then, as the LORD our God
commanded us, we set out from
Horeb and went toward the hill
country of the Amorites through
all that vast and dreadful wilderness that you have seen, and so we
reached Kadesh Barnea. 20 Then I
said to you, "You have reached
the hill country of the Amorites,
which the LORD our God is giving
us. 21 See, the LORD your God has
given you the land. Go up and take
possession of it as the LORD, the
God of your ancestors, told you. Do
not be afraid; do not be discouraged." Jos 1:6,9,18; Dt 8:15

22 Then all of you came to me
and said, "Let us send men ahead
to spy out the land for us and bring
back a report about the route we
are to take and the towns we will
come to." Nu 13:1-3

23 The idea seemed good to me;
so I selected twelve of you, one
man from each tribe. 24 They left
and went up into the hill country, and came to the Valley of Eshkol and explored it. 25 Taking with
them some of the fruit of the land,
they brought it down to us and reported, "It is a good land that the
LORD our God is giving us."

Nu 13:21-25

Rebellion Against the LORD

26 But you were unwilling to go
up; you rebelled against the command of the LORD your God. 27 You
grumbled in your tents and said,
"The LORD hates us; so he brought
us out of Egypt to deliver us into
the hands of the Amorites to destroy us. 28 Where can we go? Our
brothers have made our hearts
melt in fear. They say, 'The people
are stronger and taller than we
are; the cities are large, with walls
up to the sky. We even saw the Anakites there.'" Nu 14:1-4; Dt 9:28; Nu 13:33

29 Then I said to you, "Do not be
terrified; do not be afraid of them.
30 The LORD your God, who is going
before you, will fight for you, as he
did for you in Egypt, before your
very eyes, 31 and in the wilderness.
There you saw how the LORD your
God carried you, as a father carries
his son, all the way you went until
you reached this place."

Dt 32:10-12; Ac 13:18; Ex 14:14

32 In spite of this, you did not
trust in the LORD your God, 33 who
went ahead of you on your journey, in fire by night and in a cloud
by day, to search out places for you
to camp and to show you the way
you should go. Ps 106:24; Ex 13:21

34 When the LORD heard what
you said, he was angry and solemnly swore: 35 "No one from this

evil generation shall see the good land I swore to give your ancestors, 36except Caleb son of Jephunneh. He will see it, and I will give him and his descendants the land he set his feet on, because he followed the LORD wholeheartedly." Nu 14:23,28-30

37Because of you the LORD became angry with me also and said, "You shall not enter it, either. 38But your assistant, Joshua son of Nun, will enter it. Encourage him, because he will lead Israel to inherit it. 39And the little ones that you said would be taken captive, your children who do not yet know good from bad — they will enter the land. I will give it to them and they will take possession of it. 40But as for you, turn around and set out toward the desert along the route to the Red Sea.[a]" Nu 20:12; 14:3; Dt 3:26

41Then you replied, "We have sinned against the LORD. We will go up and fight, as the LORD our God commanded us." So every one of you put on his weapons, thinking it easy to go up into the hill country.

42But the LORD said to me, "Tell them, 'Do not go up and fight, because I will not be with you. You will be defeated by your enemies.'" Nu 14:41-43

43So I told you, but you would not listen. You rebelled against the LORD's command and in your arrogance you marched up into the hill country. 44The Amorites who lived in those hills came out against you; they chased you like a swarm of bees and beat you down from Seir all the way to Hormah. 45You came back and wept before the LORD, but he paid no attention to your weeping and turned a deaf ear to you. 46And so you stayed in Kadesh many days — all the time you spent there.

Job 27:9; Ps 118:12; Nu 20:1

Wanderings in the Wilderness

2 Then we turned back and set out toward the wilderness along the route to the Red Sea,[a] as the LORD had directed me. For a long time we made our way around the hill country of Seir.

2Then the LORD said to me, 3"You have made your way around this hill country long enough; now turn north. 4Give the people these orders: 'You are about to pass through the territory of your relatives the descendants of Esau, who live in Seir. They will be afraid of you, but be very careful. 5Do not provoke them to war, for I will not give you any of their land, not even enough to put your foot on. I have given Esau the hill country of Seir as his own. 6You are to pay them in silver for the food you eat and the water you drink.'"

Jos 24:4; Nu 20:14-21

7The LORD your God has blessed you in all the work of your hands. He has watched over your journey through this vast wilderness.

[a] 40,1 Or *the Sea of Reeds*

These forty years the LORD your
God has been with you, and you
have not lacked anything. Dt 8:2-4
8So we went on past our relatives the descendants of Esau,
who live in Seir. We turned from
the Arabah road, which comes up
from Elath and Ezion Geber, and
traveled along the desert road of
Moab. 1Ki 9:26; Dt 1:1
9Then the LORD said to me, "Do
not harass the Moabites or provoke them to war, for I will not
give you any part of their land. I
have given Ar to the descendants
of Lot as a possession."
Ge 19:36-38; Nu 21:15
10(The Emites used to live
there — a people strong and numerous, and as tall as the Anakites. 11Like the Anakites, they too
were considered Rephaites, but
the Moabites called them Emites.
12Horites used to live in Seir, but
the descendants of Esau drove
them out. They destroyed the Horites from before them and settled
in their place, just as Israel did in
the land the LORD gave them as
their possession.) ver 22; Ge 14:5
13And the LORD said, "Now get
up and cross the Zered Valley." So
we crossed the valley.
14Thirty-eight years passed from
the time we left Kadesh Barnea
until we crossed the Zered Valley.
By then, that entire generation of
fighting men had perished from
the camp, as the LORD had sworn
to them. 15The LORD's hand was
against them until he had completely eliminated them from the
camp. Nu 14:29-35; Dt 1:34-35; Ps 106:26
16Now when the last of these
fighting men among the people
had died, 17the LORD said to me,
18"Today you are to pass by the
region of Moab at Ar. 19When you
come to the Ammonites, do not
harass them or provoke them to
war, for I will not give you possession of any land belonging to the
Ammonites. I have given it as a
possession to the descendants of
Lot." ver 9; Ge 19:38
20(That too was considered a
land of the Rephaites, who used
to live there; but the Ammonites called them Zamzummites.
21They were a people strong and
numerous, and as tall as the Anakites. The LORD destroyed them
from before the Ammonites, who
drove them out and settled in
their place. 22The LORD had done
the same for the descendants of
Esau, who lived in Seir, when he
destroyed the Horites from before them. They drove them out
and have lived in their place to
this day. 23And as for the Avvites
who lived in villages as far as Gaza,
the Caphtorites coming out from
Caphtor[a] destroyed them and settled in their place.)
Ge 10:14; Jos 13:3; Am 9:7

Defeat of Sihon King of Heshbon

24"Set out now and cross the Arnon Gorge. See, I have given into
your hand Sihon the Amorite,

[a] *23* That is, Crete

king of Heshbon, and his country.
Begin to take possession of it and
engage him in battle. 25 This very
day I will begin to put the terror
and fear of you on all the nations
under heaven. They will hear reports of you and will tremble and
be in anguish because of you."

Ex 15:14-16; Dt 11:25; Jdg 11:13,18

26 From the Desert of Kedemoth
I sent messengers to Sihon king
of Heshbon offering peace and
saying, 27 "Let us pass through
your country. We will stay on the
main road; we will not turn aside
to the right or to the left. 28 Sell us
food to eat and water to drink for
their price in silver. Only let us
pass through on foot — 29 as the
descendants of Esau, who live in
Seir, and the Moabites, who live
in Ar, did for us — until we cross
the Jordan into the land the LORD
our God is giving us." 30 But Sihon
king of Heshbon refused to let us
pass through. For the LORD your
God had made his spirit stubborn
and his heart obstinate in order
to give him into your hands, as he
has now done.

Ex 4:21; Nu 21:21-22

31 The LORD said to me, "See, I
have begun to deliver Sihon and
his country over to you. Now begin to conquer and possess his
land."

Dt 1:8

32 When Sihon and all his army
came out to meet us in battle at
Jahaz, 33 the LORD our God delivered him over to us and we struck
him down, together with his sons
and his whole army. 34 At that time
we took all his towns and completely destroyed[a] them — men,
women and children. We left no
survivors. 35 But the livestock and
the plunder from the towns we
had captured we carried off for
ourselves. 36 From Aroer on the
rim of the Arnon Gorge, and from
the town in the gorge, even as far
as Gilead, not one town was too
strong for us. The LORD our God
gave us all of them. 37 But in accordance with the command of
the LORD our God, you did not
encroach on any of the land of
the Ammonites, neither the land
along the course of the Jabbok
nor that around the towns in the
hills.

Dt 3:6; 7:2; Ge 32:22

Defeat of Og King of Bashan

3 Next we turned and went up
along the road toward Bashan,
and Og king of Bashan with his
whole army marched out to meet
us in battle at Edrei. 2 The LORD
said to me, "Do not be afraid of
him, for I have delivered him into
your hands, along with his whole
army and his land. Do to him what
you did to Sihon king of the Amorites, who reigned in Heshbon."

Nu 21:33

3 So the LORD our God also gave
into our hands Og king of Bashan
and all his army. We struck them
down, leaving no survivors. 4 At

[a] 34 The Hebrew term refers to the irrevocable giving over of things or persons to the LORD, often by totally destroying them.

that time we took all his cities.
There was not one of the sixty
cities that we did not take from
them — the whole region of Argob, Og's kingdom in Bashan. 5All
these cities were fortified with
high walls and with gates and bars,
and there were also a great many
unwalled villages. 6We completely
destroyed[a] them, as we had done
with Sihon king of Heshbon, destroying[a] every city — men, wom-
en and children. 7But all the livestock and the plunder from their
cities we carried off for ourselves.

Dt 2:24,34; 1Ki 4:13

8So at that time we took from
these two kings of the Amorites the territory east of the Jordan, from the Arnon Gorge as far
as Mount Hermon. 9(Hermon is
called Sirion by the Sidonians; the
Amorites call it Senir.) 10We took
all the towns on the plateau, and
all Gilead, and all Bashan as far as
Salekah and Edrei, towns of Og's
kingdom in Bashan. 11(Og king of
Bashan was the last of the Rephaites. His bed was decorated with
iron and was more than nine cubits long and four cubits wide.[b] It is
still in Rabbah of the Ammonites.)

Ge 14:5; 2Sa 12:26; Ps 29:6

Division of the Land

12Of the land that we took over
at that time, I gave the Reubenites and the Gadites the territory north of Aroer by the Arnon
Gorge, including half the hill
country of Gilead, together with
its towns. 13The rest of Gilead and
also all of Bashan, the kingdom of
Og, I gave to the half-tribe of Manasseh. (The whole region of Argob in Bashan used to be known
as a land of the Rephaites. 14Jair, a
descendant of Manasseh, took the
whole region of Argob as far as
the border of the Geshurites and
the Maakathites; it was named after him, so that to this day Bashan
is called Havvoth Jair.[c]) 15And I
gave Gilead to Makir. 16But to the
Reubenites and the Gadites I gave
the territory extending from Gilead down to the Arnon Gorge
(the middle of the gorge being
the border) and out to the Jabbok River, which is the border of
the Ammonites. 17Its western border was the Jordan in the Arabah,
from Kinnereth to the Sea of the
Arabah (that is, the Dead Sea), below the slopes of Pisgah.

Nu 32:32-38; Nu 34:11; Dt 2:36

18I commanded you at that
time: "The LORD your God has giv-
en you this land to take possession of it. But all your able-bodied
men, armed for battle, must cross
over ahead of the other Israelites.
19However, your wives, your children and your livestock (I know
you have much livestock) may
stay in the towns I have given you,

[a] 6 The Hebrew term refers to the irrevocable giving over of things or persons to the LORD, often by totally destroying them. [b] 11 That is, about 14 feet long and 6 feet wide or about 4 meters long and 1.8 meters wide [c] 14 Or *called the settlements of Jair*

20until the LORD gives rest to your
fellow Israelites as he has to you,
and they too have taken over the
land that the LORD your God is giving them across the Jordan. After
that, each of you may go back to
the possession I have given you."
Nu 32:17; Jos 1:14

Moses Forbidden to Cross the Jordan

21At that time I commanded
Joshua: "You have seen with your
own eyes all that the LORD your
God has done to these two kings.
The LORD will do the same to all
the kingdoms over there where
you are going. 22Do not be afraid
of them; the LORD your God him-
self will fight for you." Ex 14:14; Dt 1:29

23At that time I pleaded with the
LORD: 24"Sovereign LORD, you have
begun to show to your servant
your greatness and your strong
hand. For what god is there in
heaven or on earth who can do the
deeds and mighty works you do?
25Let me go over and see the good
land beyond the Jordan — that
fine hill country and Lebanon."
Dt 4:22; Ex 15:11; Dt 11:2

26But because of you the LORD
was angry with me and would not
listen to me. "That is enough," the
LORD said. "Do not speak to me anymore about this matter. 27Go up to
the top of Pisgah and look west and
north and south and east. Look at
the land with your own eyes, since
you are not going to cross this Jordan. 28But commission Joshua, and
encourage and strengthen him, for
he will lead this people across and
will cause them to inherit the land
that you will see." 29So we stayed in
the valley near Beth Peor.
Dt 1:37; Nu 27:12; Dt 34:6

Obedience Commanded

4 Now, Israel, hear the decrees
and laws I am about to teach
you. Follow them so that you may
live and may go in and take possession of the land the LORD, the
God of your ancestors, is giving
you. 2Do not add to what I command you and do not subtract
from it, but keep the commands
of the LORD your God that I give
you. Dt 30:15-20; 12:32; Rev 22:18-19

3You saw with your own eyes
what the LORD did at Baal Peor.
The LORD your God destroyed
from among you everyone who
followed the Baal of Peor, 4but all
of you who held fast to the LORD
your God are still alive today.
Ps 106:28

5See, I have taught you decrees
and laws as the LORD my God commanded me, so that you may follow them in the land you are entering to take possession of it.
6Observe them carefully, for this
will show your wisdom and understanding to the nations, who
will hear about all these decrees
and say, "Surely this great nation
is a wise and understanding people." 7What other nation is so great
as to have their gods near them
the way the LORD our God is near

us whenever we pray to him? [8]And
what other nation is so great as to
have such righteous decrees and
laws as this body of laws I am setting before you today?

2Sa 7:23; Isa 55:6; 2Ti 3:15

[9]Only be careful, and watch
yourselves closely so that you do
not forget the things your eyes
have seen or let them fade from
your heart as long as you live.
Teach them to your children and
to their children after them. [10]Re-
member the day you stood before
the LORD your God at Horeb, when
he said to me, "Assemble the people before me to hear my words
so that they may learn to revere
me as long as they live in the land
and may teach them to their children." [11]You came near and stood
at the foot of the mountain while
it blazed with fire to the very
heavens, with black clouds and
deep darkness. [12]Then the LORD
spoke to you out of the fire. You
heard the sound of words but saw
no form; there was only a voice.
[13]He declared to you his covenant,
the Ten Commandments, which
he commanded you to follow and
then wrote them on two stone tablets. [14]And the LORD directed me at
that time to teach you the decrees
and laws you are to follow in the
land that you are crossing the Jordan to possess. Pr 4:23; Eph 6:4; Ex 34:28

Idolatry Forbidden

[15]You saw no form of any kind
the day the LORD spoke to you at
Horeb out of the fire. Therefore
watch yourselves very carefully, [16]so that you do not become
corrupt and make for yourselves
an idol, an image of any shape,
whether formed like a man or
a woman, [17]or like any animal
on earth or any bird that flies in
the air, [18]or like any creature that
moves along the ground or any
fish in the waters below. [19]And
when you look up to the sky and
see the sun, the moon and the
stars — all the heavenly array —
do not be enticed into bowing
down to them and worshiping
things the LORD your God has apportioned to all the nations under
heaven. [20]But as for you, the LORD
took you and brought you out of
the iron-smelting furnace, out of
Egypt, to be the people of his inheritance, as you now are.

Ex 20:4-5; Dt 5:8; 1Ki 8:51

[21]The LORD was angry with me
because of you, and he solemnly
swore that I would not cross the
Jordan and enter the good land
the LORD your God is giving you
as your inheritance. [22]I will die in
this land; I will not cross the Jordan; but you are about to cross
over and take possession of that
good land. [23]Be careful not to forget the covenant of the LORD your
God that he made with you; do not
make for yourselves an idol in the
form of anything the LORD your
God has forbidden. [24]For the LORD
your God is a consuming fire, a
jealous God. Heb 12:29; Dt 1:37; 3:25

25 After you have had children
and grandchildren and have lived
in the land a long time—if you
then become corrupt and make
any kind of idol, doing evil in
the eyes of the LORD your God
and arousing his anger, 26 I call
the heavens and the earth as witnesses against you this day that
you will quickly perish from the
land that you are crossing the Jordan to possess. You will not live
there long but will certainly be
destroyed. 27 The LORD will scatter
you among the peoples, and only
a few of you will survive among
the nations to which the LORD will
drive you. 28 There you will worship man-made gods of wood and
stone, which cannot see or hear
or eat or smell. 29 But if from there
you seek the LORD your God, you
will find him if you seek him with
all your heart and with all your
soul. 30 When you are in distress
and all these things have happened to you, then in later days
you will return to the LORD your
God and obey him. 31 For the LORD
your God is a merciful God; he
will not abandon or destroy you
or forget the covenant with your
ancestors, which he confirmed to
them by oath.

Dt 30:18-19; 2Ki 17:2,17; 2Ch 15:4

The LORD Is God

32 Ask now about the former
days, long before your time, from
the day God created human beings on the earth; ask from one
end of the heavens to the other.
Has anything so great as this ever
happened, or has anything like it
ever been heard of? 33 Has any other people heard the voice of God[a]
speaking out of fire, as you have,
and lived? 34 Has any god ever tried
to take for himself one nation out
of another nation, by testings, by
signs and wonders, by war, by a
mighty hand and an outstretched
arm, or by great and awesome
deeds, like all the things the LORD
your God did for you in Egypt before your very eyes?

Dt 5:24-26; 7:19; Mt 24:31

35 You were shown these things
so that you might know that the
LORD is God; besides him there is
no other. 36 From heaven he made
you hear his voice to discipline
you. On earth he showed you his
great fire, and you heard his words
from out of the fire. 37 Because he
loved your ancestors and chose
their descendants after them, he
brought you out of Egypt by his
Presence and his great strength,
38 to drive out before you nations
greater and stronger than you and
to bring you into their land to give
it to you for your inheritance, as it
is today. Ex 19:9,19; Dt 10:15; 1Sa 2:2

39 Acknowledge and take to
heart this day that the LORD is God
in heaven above and on the earth
below. There is no other. 40 Keep
his decrees and commands, which
I am giving you today, so that it
may go well with you and your

[a] 33 Or *of a god*

children after you and that you may live long in the land the LORD your God gives you for all time.

Jos 2:11; Lev 22:31; Dt 5:16

Cities of Refuge

41Then Moses set aside three cities east of the Jordan, 42to which anyone who had killed a person could flee if they had unintentionally killed a neighbor without malice aforethought. They could flee into one of these cities and save their life. 43The cities were these: Bezer in the wilderness plateau, for the Reubenites; Ramoth in Gilead, for the Gadites; and Golan in Bashan, for the Manassites.

Nu 35:6-34; Dt 19:1-14; Jos 20:1-9

Introduction to the Law

44This is the law Moses set before the Israelites. 45These are the stipulations, decrees and laws Moses gave them when they came out of Egypt 46and were in the valley near Beth Peor east of the Jordan, in the land of Sihon king of the Amorites, who reigned in Heshbon and was defeated by Moses and the Israelites as they came out of Egypt. 47They took possession of his land and the land of Og king of Bashan, the two Amorite kings east of the Jordan. 48This land extended from Aroer on the rim of the Arnon Gorge to Mount Sirion[a] (that is, Hermon), 49and included all the Arabah east of the Jordan, as far as the Dead Sea,[b] below the slopes of Pisgah.

Nu 21:26

The Ten Commandments

5 Moses summoned all Israel and said:

Hear, Israel, the decrees and laws I declare in your hearing today. Learn them and be sure to follow them. 2The LORD our God made a covenant with us at Horeb. 3It was not with our ancestors[c] that the LORD made this covenant, but with us, with all of us who are alive here today. 4The LORD spoke to you face to face out of the fire on the mountain. 5(At that time I stood between the LORD and you to declare to you the word of the LORD, because you were afraid of the fire and did not go up the mountain.) And he said:

Ex 19:5; 20:18,21; Dt 4:12,33,36

6"I am the LORD your God,
who brought you out of
Egypt, out of the land of
slavery. Lev 26:1

7"You shall have no other gods
before[d] me.
8"You shall not make for yourself an image in the form
of anything in heaven
above or on the earth beneath or in the waters
below. 9You shall not bow
down to them or worship
them; for I, the LORD your
God, am a jealous God,
punishing the children

[a] 48 Syriac (see also 3:9); Hebrew *Siyon*
[b] 49 Hebrew *the Sea of the Arabah*
[c] 3 Or *not only with our parents*
[d] 7 Or *besides*

for the sin of the parents
to the third and fourth
generation of those who
hate me, 10 but showing
love to a thousand gener-
ations of those who love
me and keep my com-
mandments.
Ex 34:7; Jer 32:18

11 "You shall not misuse the
name of the LORD your
God, for the LORD will
not hold anyone guiltless
who misuses his name.
Lev 19:12

12 "Observe the Sabbath day by
keeping it holy, as the
LORD your God has com-
manded you. 13 Six days
you shall labor and do all
your work, 14 but the seventh day is a sabbath to
the LORD your God. On
it you shall not do any
work, neither you, nor
your son or daughter, nor
your male or female ser-
vant, nor your ox, your
donkey or any of your
animals, nor any for-
eigner residing in your
towns, so that your male
and female servants may
rest, as you do. 15 Remember that you were slaves
in Egypt and that the
LORD your God brought
you out of there with a
mighty hand and an out-
stretched arm. Therefore
the LORD your God has
commanded you to ob-
serve the Sabbath day.
Ge 2:2; Heb 4:4; Mk 2:27

16 "Honor your father and your
mother, as the LORD your
God has commanded
you, so that you may live
long and that it may go
well with you in the land
the LORD your God is giv-
ing you. Lev 19:3; Eph 6:2-3

17 "You shall not murder.
Ge 9:6; Mt 5:21-22

18 "You shall not commit adultery. Mt 5:27-30; Jas 2:11

19 "You shall not steal.
Lev 19:11; Mt 19:19

20 "You shall not give false testimony against your
neighbor. Mk 10:19

21 "You shall not covet your
neighbor's wife. You shall
not set your desire on
your neighbor's house or
land, his male or female
servant, his ox or donkey,
or anything that belongs
to your neighbor."
Ex 20:1-17; Ro 7:7

22 These are the command-
ments the LORD proclaimed in a
loud voice to your whole assembly
there on the mountain from out
of the fire, the cloud and the deep
darkness; and he added nothing
more. Then he wrote them on
two stone tablets and gave them
to me. Ex 31:18; Dt 4:13

23 When you heard the voice
out of the darkness, while the

mountain was ablaze with fire,
all the leaders of your tribes and
your elders came to me. 24And
you said, "The LORD our God has
shown us his glory and his majesty, and we have heard his voice
from the fire. Today we have seen
that a person can live even if God
speaks with them. 25But now, why
should we die? This great fire will
consume us, and we will die if we
hear the voice of the LORD our
God any longer. 26For what mortal has ever heard the voice of the
living God speaking out of fire, as
we have, and survived? 27Go near
and listen to all that the LORD our
God says. Then tell us whatever
the LORD our God tells you. We
will listen and obey."

Dt 4:33; 18:16; Ex 19:19

28The LORD heard you when you
spoke to me, and the LORD said to
me, "I have heard what this people
said to you. Everything they said
was good. 29Oh, that their hearts
would be inclined to fear me and
keep all my commands always, so
that it might go well with them
and their children forever!

Ps 81:8,13; Isa 48:18

30"Go, tell them to return to their
tents. 31But you stay here with me
so that I may give you all the commands, decrees and laws you are
to teach them to follow in the land
I am giving them to possess."

Ex 24:12

32So be careful to do what the
LORD your God has commanded
you; do not turn aside to the right
or to the left. 33Walk in obedience
to all that the LORD your God has
commanded you, so that you may
live and prosper and prolong your
days in the land that you will possess.

Dt 17:11,20; Jos 1:7; Jer 7:23

Love the LORD Your God

6 These are the commands, decrees and laws the LORD your
God directed me to teach you to
observe in the land that you are
crossing the Jordan to possess, 2so
that you, your children and their
children after them may fear the
LORD your God as long as you live
by keeping all his decrees and
commands that I give you, and so
that you may enjoy long life. 3Hear,
Israel, and be careful to obey so
that it may go well with you and
that you may increase greatly in a
land flowing with milk and honey,
just as the LORD, the God of your
ancestors, promised you.

Ex 3:8; 20:20; Dt 10:12-13

4Hear, O Israel: The LORD our
God, the LORD is one.[a] 5Love the
LORD your God with all your heart
and with all your soul and with all
your strength. 6These commandments that I give you today are to
be on your hearts. 7Impress them
on your children. Talk about them
when you sit at home and when
you walk along the road, when
you lie down and when you get
up. 8Tie them as symbols on your

[a] 4 Or *The LORD our God is one LORD*; or *The LORD is our God, the LORD is one*; or *The LORD is our God, the LORD alone*

hands and bind them on your foreheads. 9 Write them on the doorframes of your houses and on your gates. Mt 22:37; Dt 11:18; Eph 6:4

10 When the LORD your God brings you into the land he swore to your fathers, to Abraham, Isaac and Jacob, to give you — a land with large, flourishing cities you did not build, 11 houses filled with all kinds of good things you did not provide, wells you did not dig, and vineyards and olive groves you did not plant — then when you eat and are satisfied, 12 be careful that you do not forget the LORD, who brought you out of Egypt, out of the land of slavery.

Dt 8:10; Jos 24:13; Ps 103:2

13 Fear the LORD your God, serve him only and take your oaths in his name. 14 Do not follow other gods, the gods of the peoples around you; 15 for the LORD your God, who is among you, is a jealous God and his anger will burn against you, and he will destroy you from the face of the land. 16 Do not put the LORD your God to the test as you did at Massah. 17 Be sure to keep the commands of the LORD your God and the stipulations and decrees he has given you. 18 Do what is right and good in the LORD's sight, so that it may go well with you and you may go in and take over the good land the LORD promised on oath to your ancestors, 19 thrusting out all your enemies before you, as the LORD said. Mt 4:7; Dt 4:24; Ps 119:4

20 In the future, when your son asks you, "What is the meaning of the stipulations, decrees and laws the LORD our God has commanded you?" 21 tell him: "We were slaves of Pharaoh in Egypt, but the LORD brought us out of Egypt with a mighty hand. 22 Before our eyes the LORD sent signs and wonders — great and terrible — on Egypt and Pharaoh and his whole household. 23 But he brought us out from there to bring us in and give us the land he promised on oath to our ancestors. 24 The LORD commanded us to obey all these decrees and to fear the LORD our God, so that we might always prosper and be kept alive, as is the case today. 25 And if we are careful to obey all this law before the LORD our God, as he has commanded us, that will be our righteousness." Ex 13:14; Jer 32:39; Ro 10:3,5

Driving Out the Nations

7 When the LORD your God brings you into the land you are entering to possess and drives out before you many nations — the Hittites, Girgashites, Amorites, Canaanites, Perizzites, Hivites and Jebusites, seven nations larger and stronger than you — 2 and when the LORD your God has delivered them over to you and you have defeated them, then you must destroy them totally.[a] Make

[a] 2 The Hebrew term refers to the irrevocable giving over of things or persons to the LORD, often by totally destroying them; also in verse 26.

no treaty with them, and show
them no mercy. [3]Do not intermarry with them. Do not give your
daughters to their sons or take
their daughters for your sons, [4]for
they will turn your children away
from following me to serve other gods, and the LORD's anger will
burn against you and will quickly
destroy you. [5]This is what you are
to do to them: Break down their
altars, smash their sacred stones,
cut down their Asherah poles[a] and
burn their idols in the fire. [6]For
you are a people holy to the LORD
your God. The LORD your God has
chosen you out of all the peoples
on the face of the earth to be his
people, his treasured possession.

Ex 23:32; Dt 14:2; 31:3

[7]The LORD did not set his affection on you and choose you because you were more numerous
than other peoples, for you were
the fewest of all peoples. [8]But it
was because the LORD loved you
and kept the oath he swore to your
ancestors that he brought you out
with a mighty hand and redeemed
you from the land of slavery, from
the power of Pharaoh king of
Egypt. [9]Know therefore that the
LORD your God is God; he is the
faithful God, keeping his covenant
of love to a thousand generations
of those who love him and keep
his commandments. [10]But

those who hate him he will
repay to their face by
destruction;
he will not be slow to repay
to their face those who
hate him.

[11]Therefore, take care to follow the
commands, decrees and laws I
give you today.

[12]If you pay attention to these
laws and are careful to follow
them, then the LORD your God will
keep his covenant of love with you,
as he swore to your ancestors. [13]He
will love you and bless you and increase your numbers. He will bless
the fruit of your womb, the crops
of your land — your grain, new
wine and olive oil — the calves of
your herds and the lambs of your
flocks in the land he swore to your
ancestors to give you. [14]You will be
blessed more than any other people; none of your men or women
will be childless, nor will any of
your livestock be without young.
[15]The LORD will keep you free from
every disease. He will not inflict
on you the horrible diseases you
knew in Egypt, but he will inflict
them on all who hate you. [16]You
must destroy all the peoples the
LORD your God gives over to you.
Do not look on them with pity and
do not serve their gods, for that
will be a snare to you.

Dt 28:1-14; Ex 23:26; 15:26

[17]You may say to yourselves,
"These nations are stronger than
we are. How can we drive them
out?" [18]But do not be afraid of

[a] 5 That is, wooden symbols of the goddess Asherah; here and elsewhere in Deuteronomy

them; remember well what the
LORD your God did to Pharaoh and
to all Egypt. 19You saw with your
own eyes the great trials, the signs
and wonders, the mighty hand
and outstretched arm, with which
the LORD your God brought you
out. The LORD your God will do the
same to all the peoples you now
fear. 20Moreover, the LORD your
God will send the hornet among
them until even the survivors who
hide from you have perished. 21Do
not be terrified by them, for the
LORD your God, who is among you,
is a great and awesome God. 22The
LORD your God will drive out those
nations before you, little by little.
You will not be allowed to elimi-
nate them all at once, or the wild
animals will multiply around you.
23But the LORD your God will deliver them over to you, throwing
them into great confusion until
they are destroyed. 24He will give
their kings into your hand, and you
will wipe out their names from under heaven. No one will be able to
stand up against you; you will destroy them. 25The images of their
gods you are to burn in the fire.
Do not covet the silver and gold on
them, and do not take it for yourselves, or you will be ensnared by
it, for it is detestable to the LORD
your God. 26Do not bring a detestable thing into your house or you,
like it, will be set apart for destruction. Regard it as vile and utterly
detest it, for it is set apart for destruction. Dt 4:34; Ex 23:28-30; Ps 105:5

Do Not Forget the LORD

8 Be careful to follow every command I am giving you today,
so that you may live and increase
and may enter and possess the
land the LORD promised on oath to
your ancestors. 2Remember how
the LORD your God led you all the
way in the wilderness these forty
years, to humble and test you in
order to know what was in your
heart, whether or not you would
keep his commands. 3He humbled
you, causing you to hunger and
then feeding you with manna,
which neither you nor your ancestors had known, to teach you that
man does not live on bread alone
but on every word that comes
from the mouth of the LORD. 4Your
clothes did not wear out and your
feet did not swell during these forty years. 5Know then in your heart
that as a man disciplines his son,
so the LORD your God disciplines
you. Dt 4:1; Mt 4:4; Heb 12:5-11

6Observe the commands of the
LORD your God, walking in obedience to him and revering him.
7For the LORD your God is bringing
you into a good land — a land with
brooks, streams, and deep springs
gushing out into the valleys and
hills; 8a land with wheat and barley, vines and fig trees, pomegranates, olive oil and honey; 9a land
where bread will not be scarce
and you will lack nothing; a land
where the rocks are iron and you
can dig copper out of the hills.
Dt 11:9-12; Jer 2:7

10 When you have eaten and are
satisfied, praise the LORD your
God for the good land he has giv-
en you. 11 Be careful that you do
not forget the LORD your God,
failing to observe his commands,
his laws and his decrees that I
am giving you this day. 12 Otherwise, when you eat and are satisfied, when you build fine houses
and settle down, 13 and when your
herds and flocks grow large and
your silver and gold increase and
all you have is multiplied, 14 then
your heart will become proud and
you will forget the LORD your God,
who brought you out of Egypt,
out of the land of slavery. 15 He led
you through the vast and dreadful wilderness, that thirsty and
waterless land, with its venomous
snakes and scorpions. He brought
you water out of hard rock. 16 He
gave you manna to eat in the wilderness, something your ancestors had never known, to humble
and test you so that in the end it
might go well with you. 17 You may
say to yourself, "My power and the
strength of my hands have produced this wealth for me." 18 But
remember the LORD your God, for
it is he who gives you the ability to
produce wealth, and so confirms
his covenant, which he swore to
your ancestors, as it is today.

Dt 6:10-12; Pr 10:22; Hos 2:8

19 If you ever forget the LORD
your God and follow other gods
and worship and bow down to
them, I testify against you today
that you will surely be destroyed.
20 Like the nations the LORD destroyed before you, so you will
be destroyed for not obeying the
LORD your God. Dt 4:26; 30:18

Not Because of Israel's Righteousness

9 Hear, Israel: You are now
about to cross the Jordan to go
in and dispossess nations greater
and stronger than you, with large
cities that have walls up to the sky.
2 The people are strong and tall—
Anakites! You know about them
and have heard it said: "Who can
stand up against the Anakites?"
3 But be assured today that the
LORD your God is the one who goes
across ahead of you like a devouring fire. He will destroy them; he
will subdue them before you. And
you will drive them out and annihilate them quickly, as the LORD
has promised you.

Nu 13:22,28,32-33; Dt 7:23-24; 31:3

4 After the LORD your God has
driven them out before you, do
not say to yourself, "The LORD has
brought me here to take possession of this land because of my
righteousness." No, it is on account
of the wickedness of these nations
that the LORD is going to drive
them out before you. 5 It is not because of your righteousness or
your integrity that you are going
in to take possession of their land;
but on account of the wickedness
of these nations, the LORD your
God will drive them out before

you, to accomplish what he swore
to your fathers, to Abraham, Isaac
and Jacob. 6Understand, then, that
it is not because of your righteousness that the LORD your God is giving you this good land to possess,
for you are a stiff-necked people.
Ge 12:7; Lev 18:21,24-30; Dt 8:17

The Golden Calf

7Remember this and never forget how you aroused the anger
of the LORD your God in the wilderness. From the day you left
Egypt until you arrived here, you
have been rebellious against the
LORD. 8At Horeb you aroused the
LORD's wrath so that he was angry
enough to destroy you. 9When I
went up on the mountain to receive the tablets of stone, the tablets of the covenant that the LORD
had made with you, I stayed on
the mountain forty days and forty
nights; I ate no bread and drank
no water. 10The LORD gave me two
stone tablets inscribed by the finger of God. On them were all the
commandments the LORD proclaimed to you on the mountain
out of the fire, on the day of the
assembly. Ps 106:19; Ex 24:12,15,18

11At the end of the forty days and
forty nights, the LORD gave me the
two stone tablets, the tablets of
the covenant. 12Then the LORD told
me, "Go down from here at once,
because your people whom you
brought out of Egypt have become
corrupt. They have turned away
quickly from what I commanded
them and have made an idol for
themselves." Ex 32:7-8; Jdg 2:17

13And the LORD said to me, "I
have seen this people, and they
are a stiff-necked people indeed!
14Let me alone, so that I may destroy them and blot out their
name from under heaven. And I
will make you into a nation stronger and more numerous than
they." Ex 32:10

15So I turned and went down
from the mountain while it was
ablaze with fire. And the two tablets of the covenant were in my
hands. 16When I looked, I saw that
you had sinned against the LORD
your God; you had made for yourselves an idol cast in the shape of
a calf. You had turned aside quickly from the way that the LORD had
commanded you. 17So I took the
two tablets and threw them out of
my hands, breaking them to pieces before your eyes. Ex 32:15

18Then once again I fell prostrate before the LORD for forty
days and forty nights; I ate no
bread and drank no water, because
of all the sin you had committed,
doing what was evil in the LORD's
sight and so arousing his anger.
19I feared the anger and wrath of
the LORD, for he was angry enough
with you to destroy you. But again
the LORD listened to me. 20And the
LORD was angry enough with Aaron to destroy him, but at that time
I prayed for Aaron too. 21Also I
took that sinful thing of yours, the
calf you had made, and burned it

in the fire. Then I crushed it and
ground it to powder as fine as dust
and threw the dust into a stream
that flowed down the mountain.
Ex 34:28; Heb 12:21; Ex 32:20
[22]You also made the LORD angry
at Taberah, at Massah and at Kibroth Hattaavah. Nu 11:3; Ex 17:7; Nu 11:34
[23]And when the LORD sent you
out from Kadesh Barnea, he said,
"Go up and take possession of the
land I have given you." But you
rebelled against the command of
the LORD your God. You did not
trust him or obey him. [24]You have
been rebellious against the LORD
ever since I have known you.
Dt 31:27; Ps 106:24
[25]I lay prostrate before the
LORD those forty days and forty
nights because the LORD had said
he would destroy you. [26]I prayed
to the LORD and said, "Sovereign
LORD, do not destroy your people,
your own inheritance that you
redeemed by your great power
and brought out of Egypt with a
mighty hand. [27]Remember your
servants Abraham, Isaac and Jacob. Overlook the stubbornness
of this people, their wickedness
and their sin. [28]Otherwise, the
country from which you brought
us will say, 'Because the LORD
was not able to take them into
the land he had promised them,
and because he hated them, he
brought them out to put them
to death in the wilderness.' [29]But
they are your people, your inheritance that you brought out by
your great power and your outstretched arm." Ex 32:11; Dt 4:20; 1Ki 8:51

Tablets Like the First Ones

10 At that time the LORD said
to me, "Chisel out two stone
tablets like the first ones and come
up to me on the mountain. Also
make a wooden ark.[a] [2]I will write
on the tablets the words that were
on the first tablets, which you
broke. Then you are to put them
in the ark." Ex 25:16,21; 34:1-2
[3]So I made the ark out of acacia wood and chiseled out two
stone tablets like the first ones,
and I went up on the mountain
with the two tablets in my hands.
[4]The LORD wrote on these tablets what he had written before,
the Ten Commandments he had
proclaimed to you on the mountain, out of the fire, on the day of
the assembly. And the LORD gave
them to me. [5]Then I came back
down the mountain and put the
tablets in the ark I had made, as
the LORD commanded me, and
they are there now. Ex 20:1; 40:20
[6](The Israelites traveled from
the wells of Bene Jaakan to Mo-
serah. There Aaron died and was
buried, and Eleazar his son succeeded him as priest. [7]From there
they traveled to Gudgodah and on
to Jotbathah, a land with streams
of water. [8]At that time the LORD set
apart the tribe of Levi to carry the
ark of the covenant of the LORD, to

[a] *1* That is, a chest

stand before the LORD to minister
and to pronounce blessings in his
name, as they still do today. 9That
is why the Levites have no share
or inheritance among their fellow
Israelites; the LORD is their inheritance, as the LORD your God told
them.) Nu 33:30-31,38; Dt 18:5; 21:5

10Now I had stayed on the
mountain forty days and forty
nights, as I did the first time, and
the LORD listened to me at this
time also. It was not his will to destroy you. 11"Go," the LORD said to
me, "and lead the people on their
way, so that they may enter and
possess the land I swore to their
ancestors to give them."

Ex 34:28; Dt 9:18-19,25

Fear the LORD

12And now, Israel, what does the
LORD your God ask of you but to
fear the LORD your God, to walk in
obedience to him, to love him, to
serve the LORD your God with all
your heart and with all your soul,
13and to observe the LORD's commands and decrees that I am giving you today for your own good?

Mic 6:8; Dt 6:5

14To the LORD your God belong
the heavens, even the highest
heavens, the earth and everything in it. 15Yet the LORD set his
affection on your ancestors and
loved them, and he chose you,
their descendants, above all the
nations — as it is today. 16Circum-
cise your hearts, therefore, and
do not be stiff-necked any longer.
17For the LORD your God is God of
gods and Lord of lords, the great
God, mighty and awesome, who
shows no partiality and accepts
no bribes. 18He defends the cause
of the fatherless and the widow, and loves the foreigner residing among you, giving them
food and clothing. 19And you are
to love those who are foreigners,
for you yourselves were foreigners in Egypt. 20Fear the LORD your
God and serve him. Hold fast to
him and take your oaths in his
name. 21He is the one you praise;
he is your God, who performed
for you those great and awesome
wonders you saw with your own
eyes. 22Your ancestors who went
down into Egypt were seventy in
all, and now the LORD your God
has made you as numerous as the
stars in the sky.

Lev 19:34; Dt 4:37; 1Ki 8:27

Love and Obey the LORD

11 Love the LORD your God and
keep his requirements, his
decrees, his laws and his commands always. 2Remember today
that your children were not the
ones who saw and experienced
the discipline of the LORD your
God: his majesty, his mighty hand,
his outstretched arm; 3the signs
he performed and the things he
did in the heart of Egypt, both to
Pharaoh king of Egypt and to his
whole country; 4what he did to the
Egyptian army, to its horses and
chariots, how he overwhelmed

them with the waters of the Red Sea[a] as they were pursuing you, and how the LORD brought lasting ruin on them. 5It was not your children who saw what he did for you in the wilderness until you arrived at this place, 6and what he did to Dathan and Abiram, sons of Eliab the Reubenite, when the earth opened its mouth right in the middle of all Israel and swallowed them up with their households, their tents and every living thing that belonged to them. 7But it was your own eyes that saw all these great things the LORD has done. Nu 16:1-35; Dt 5:24; 10:12

8Observe therefore all the commands I am giving you today, so that you may have the strength to go in and take over the land that you are crossing the Jordan to possess, 9and so that you may live long in the land the LORD swore to your ancestors to give to them and their descendants, a land flowing with milk and honey. 10The land you are entering to take over is not like the land of Egypt, from which you have come, where you planted your seed and irrigated it by foot as in a vegetable garden. 11But the land you are crossing the Jordan to take possession of is a land of mountains and valleys that drinks rain from heaven. 12It is a land the LORD your God cares for; the eyes of the LORD your God are continually on it from the beginning of the year to its end.

Jos 1:7; Dt 4:40; 8:7

13So if you faithfully obey the commands I am giving you today—to love the LORD your God and to serve him with all your heart and with all your soul—14then I will send rain on your land in its season, both autumn and spring rains, so that you may gather in your grain, new wine and olive oil. 15I will provide grass in the fields for your cattle, and you will eat and be satisfied.

Dt 4:29; Joel 2:23; Ps 104:14

16Be careful, or you will be enticed to turn away and worship other gods and bow down to them. 17Then the LORD's anger will burn against you, and he will shut up the heavens so that it will not rain and the ground will yield no produce, and you will soon perish from the good land the LORD is giving you. 18Fix these words of mine in your hearts and minds; tie them as symbols on your hands and bind them on your foreheads. 19Teach them to your children, talking about them when you sit at home and when you walk along the road, when you lie down and when you get up. 20Write them on the doorframes of your houses and on your gates, 21so that your days and the days of your children may be many in the land the LORD swore to give your ancestors, as many as the days that the heavens are above the earth.

Dt 4:9-10; 6:6-8; 1Ki 8:35

[a] 4 Or *the Sea of Reeds*

22 If you carefully observe all
these commands I am giving you
to follow — to love the LORD your
God, to walk in obedience to him
and to hold fast to him — 23 then
the LORD will drive out all these
nations before you, and you will
dispossess nations larger and
stronger than you. 24 Every place
where you set your foot will be
yours: Your territory will extend
from the desert to Lebanon, and
from the Euphrates River to the
Mediterranean Sea. 25 No one will
be able to stand against you. The
LORD your God, as he promised
you, will put the terror and fear of
you on the whole land, wherever
you go. Ge 15:18; Dt 7:24; 9:1

26 See, I am setting before you
today a blessing and a curse —
27 the blessing if you obey the
commands of the LORD your God
that I am giving you today; 28 the
curse if you disobey the commands of the LORD your God and
turn from the way that I command you today by following
other gods, which you have not
known. 29 When the LORD your
God has brought you into the land
you are entering to possess, you
are to proclaim on Mount Gerizim
the blessings, and on Mount Ebal
the curses. 30 As you know, these
mountains are across the Jordan,
westward, toward the setting sun,
near the great trees of Moreh, in
the territory of those Canaanites
living in the Arabah in the vicinity of Gilgal. 31 You are about to
cross the Jordan to enter and take
possession of the land the LORD
your God is giving you. When you
have taken it over and are living
there, 32 be sure that you obey all
the decrees and laws I am setting
before you today.
Dt 28:1-14; 30:1,15,19; 27:12-13

The One Place of Worship

12 These are the decrees and
laws you must be careful to
follow in the land that the LORD,
the God of your ancestors, has
given you to possess — as long as
you live in the land. 2 Destroy completely all the places on the high
mountains, on the hills and under every spreading tree, where
the nations you are dispossessing worship their gods. 3 Break
down their altars, smash their sacred stones and burn their Asherah poles in the fire; cut down the
idols of their gods and wipe out
their names from those places.
Dt 4:9-10; Nu 33:52; Ex 23:13

4 You must not worship the LORD
your God in their way. 5 But you are
to seek the place the LORD your
God will choose from among all
your tribes to put his Name there
for his dwelling. To that place you
must go; 6 there bring your burnt
offerings and sacrifices, your
tithes and special gifts, what you
have vowed to give and your freewill offerings, and the firstborn
of your herds and flocks. 7 There,
in the presence of the LORD your
God, you and your families shall

eat and shall rejoice in everything you have put your hand to,
because the LORD your God has
blessed you. Dt 14:26; 2Ch 7:12,16

8 You are not to do as we do here
today, everyone doing as they
see fit, 9 since you have not yet
reached the resting place and the
inheritance the LORD your God is
giving you. 10 But you will cross the
Jordan and settle in the land the
LORD your God is giving you as an
inheritance, and he will give you
rest from all your enemies around
you so that you will live in safety.
11 Then to the place the LORD your
God will choose as a dwelling for
his Name — there you are to bring
everything I command you: your
burnt offerings and sacrifices,
your tithes and special gifts, and
all the choice possessions you
have vowed to the LORD. 12 And
there rejoice before the LORD your
God — you, your sons and daughters, your male and female servants, and the Levites from your
towns who have no allotment
or inheritance of their own. 13 Be
careful not to sacrifice your burnt
offerings anywhere you please.
14 Offer them only at the place the
LORD will choose in one of your
tribes, and there observe everything I command you.

Dt 10:9; 15:20; 3:20

15 Nevertheless, you may slaughter your animals in any of your
towns and eat as much of the meat
as you want, as if it were gazelle
or deer, according to the blessing
the LORD your God gives you. Both
the ceremonially unclean and the
clean may eat it. 16 But you must
not eat the blood; pour it out on
the ground like water. 17 You must
not eat in your own towns the
tithe of your grain and new wine
and olive oil, or the firstborn of
your herds and flocks, or whatever you have vowed to give, or your
freewill offerings or special gifts.
18 Instead, you are to eat them in
the presence of the LORD your
God at the place the LORD your
God will choose — you, your sons
and daughters, your male and female servants, and the Levites
from your towns — and you are to
rejoice before the LORD your God
in everything you put your hand
to. 19 Be careful not to neglect the
Levites as long as you live in your
land. Lev 17:10-12; Dt 14:5,27

20 When the LORD your God
has enlarged your territory as he
promised you, and you crave meat
and say, “I would like some meat,”
then you may eat as much of it as
you want. 21 If the place where the
LORD your God chooses to put his
Name is too far away from you,
you may slaughter animals from
the herds and flocks the LORD has
given you, as I have commanded
you, and in your own towns you
may eat as much of them as you
want. 22 Eat them as you would
gazelle or deer. Both the ceremonially unclean and the clean may
eat. 23 But be sure you do not eat
the blood, because the blood is

the life, and you must not eat the
life with the meat. 24 You must not
eat the blood; pour it out on the
ground like water. 25 Do not eat it,
so that it may go well with you and
your children after you, because
you will be doing what is right in
the eyes of the LORD.

Ge 15:18; Lev 17:11,14; Dt 4:40

26 But take your consecrated
things and whatever you have
vowed to give, and go to the place
the LORD will choose. 27 Present
your burnt offerings on the altar
of the LORD your God, both the
meat and the blood. The blood
of your sacrifices must be poured
beside the altar of the LORD your
God, but you may eat the meat.
28 Be careful to obey all these regulations I am giving you, so that it
may always go well with you and
your children after you, because
you will be doing what is good and
right in the eyes of the LORD your
God. Lev 1:5,9,13

29 The LORD your God will cut
off before you the nations you are
about to invade and dispossess.
But when you have driven them
out and settled in their land, 30 and
after they have been destroyed before you, be careful not to be ensnared by inquiring about their
gods, saying, "How do these nations serve their gods? We will do
the same." 31 You must not worship
the LORD your God in their way,
because in worshiping their gods,
they do all kinds of detestable
things the LORD hates. They even
burn their sons and daughters in
the fire as sacrifices to their gods.

Dt 9:5; 18:10

32 See that you do all I command
you; do not add to it or take away
from it.[a] Dt 4:2

Worshiping Other Gods

13[b] If a prophet, or one who
foretells by dreams, ap-
pears among you and announces to you a sign or wonder, 2 and
if the sign or wonder spoken of
takes place, and the prophet says,
"Let us follow other gods" (gods
you have not known) "and let us
worship them," 3 you must not listen to the words of that prophet
or dreamer. The LORD your God
is testing you to find out whether
you love him with all your heart
and with all your soul. 4 It is the
LORD your God you must follow,
and him you must revere. Keep
his commands and obey him;
serve him and hold fast to him.
5 That prophet or dreamer must be
put to death for inciting rebellion
against the LORD your God, who
brought you out of Egypt and redeemed you from the land of slavery. That prophet or dreamer tried
to turn you from the way the LORD
your God commanded you to follow. You must purge the evil from
among you. Dt 8:2,16; 2Ki 23:3; Mt 24:24

6 If your very own brother, or
your son or daughter, or the wife

[a] 32 In Hebrew texts this verse (12:32) is numbered 13:1. [b] In Hebrew texts 13:1-18 is numbered 13:2-19.

you love, or your closest friend secretly entices you, saying, "Let us
go and worship other gods" (gods
that neither you nor your ancestors have known, 7gods of the peoples around you, whether near or
far, from one end of the land to the
other), 8do not yield to them or listen to them. Show them no pity.
Do not spare them or shield them.
9You must certainly put them to
death. Your hand must be the first
in putting them to death, and then
the hands of all the people. 10Stone
them to death, because they tried
to turn you away from the LORD
your God, who brought you out of
Egypt, out of the land of slavery.
11Then all Israel will hear and be
afraid, and no one among you will
do such an evil thing again.

Dt 17:2-7; 17:13; Pr 1:10

12If you hear it said about one
of the towns the LORD your God
is giving you to live in 13that trou-
blemakers have arisen among
you and have led the people of
their town astray, saying, "Let us
go and worship other gods" (gods
you have not known), 14then you
must inquire, probe and investigate it thoroughly. And if it is true
and it has been proved that this
detestable thing has been done
among you, 15you must certainly put to the sword all who live
in that town. You must destroy it
completely,[a] both its people and
its livestock. 16You are to gather all
the plunder of the town into the
middle of the public square and
completely burn the town and all
its plunder as a whole burnt offering to the LORD your God. That
town is to remain a ruin forever,
never to be rebuilt, 17and none
of the condemned things[a] are
to be found in your hands. Then
the LORD will turn from his fierce
anger, will show you mercy, and
will have compassion on you. He
will increase your numbers, as
he promised on oath to your ancestors — 18because you obey the
LORD your God by keeping all his
commands that I am giving you
today and doing what is right in
his eyes. Jos 8:28; Nu 25:4; Dt 7:25-26

Clean and Unclean Food

14 You are the children of the
LORD your God. Do not cut
yourselves or shave the front of
your heads for the dead, 2for you
are a people holy to the LORD your
God. Out of all the peoples on the
face of the earth, the LORD has
chosen you to be his treasured
possession. Lev 21:5; Ro 8:14; Dt 7:6

3Do not eat any detestable
thing. 4These are the animals you
may eat: the ox, the sheep, the
goat, 5the deer, the gazelle, the
roe deer, the wild goat, the ibex,
the antelope and the mountain
sheep.[b] 6You may eat any animal
that has a divided hoof and that

[a] *15,17* The Hebrew term refers to the irrevocable giving over of things or persons to the LORD, often by totally destroying them. [b] *5* The precise identification of some of the birds and animals in this chapter is uncertain.

chews the cud. 7However, of those
that chew the cud or that have a
divided hoof you may not eat the
camel, the rabbit or the hyrax. Although they chew the cud, they
do not have a divided hoof; they
are ceremonially unclean for you.
8The pig is also unclean; although
it has a divided hoof, it does not
chew the cud. You are not to eat
their meat or touch their carcasses.
Lev 11:2-45; Eze 4:14

9Of all the creatures living in
the water, you may eat any that
has fins and scales. 10But anything
that does not have fins and scales
you may not eat; for you it is unclean.

11You may eat any clean bird.
12But these you may not eat: the
eagle, the vulture, the black vulture, 13the red kite, the black kite,
any kind of falcon, 14any kind of raven, 15the horned owl, the screech
owl, the gull, any kind of hawk,
16the little owl, the great owl, the
white owl, 17the desert owl, the osprey, the cormorant, 18the stork,
any kind of heron, the hoopoe and
the bat.

19All flying insects are unclean
to you; do not eat them. 20But any
winged creature that is clean you
may eat. Lev 11:1-23

21Do not eat anything you find
already dead. You may give it to
the foreigner residing in any of
your towns, and they may eat it,
or you may sell it to any other foreigner. But you are a people holy
to the LORD your God. Lev 17:15

Do not cook a young goat in its
mother's milk. Ex 34:26

Tithes

22Be sure to set aside a tenth of
all that your fields produce each
year. 23Eat the tithe of your grain,
new wine and olive oil, and the
firstborn of your herds and flocks
in the presence of the LORD your
God at the place he will choose as a
dwelling for his Name, so that you
may learn to revere the LORD your
God always. 24But if that place is too
distant and you have been blessed
by the LORD your God and cannot
carry your tithe (because the place
where the LORD will choose to put
his Name is so far away), 25then
exchange your tithe for silver,
and take the silver with you and
go to the place the LORD your God
will choose. 26Use the silver to buy
whatever you like: cattle, sheep,
wine or other fermented drink, or
anything you wish. Then you and
your household shall eat there in
the presence of the LORD your God
and rejoice. 27And do not neglect
the Levites living in your towns,
for they have no allotment or inheritance of their own.
Lev 27:30; Nu 18:20; Dt 12:5

28At the end of every three
years, bring all the tithes of that
year's produce and store it in your
towns, 29so that the Levites (who
have no allotment or inheritance
of their own) and the foreigners,
the fatherless and the widows who
live in your towns may come and

eat and be satisfied, and so that
the LORD your God may bless you
in all the work of your hands.

Dt 15:10; 26:12

The Year for Canceling Debts

15 At the end of every seven
years you must cancel debts.
2This is how it is to be done: Every creditor shall cancel any loan
they have made to a fellow Israelite. They shall not require payment from anyone among their
own people, because the LORD's
time for canceling debts has been
proclaimed. 3You may require
payment from a foreigner, but
you must cancel any debt your
fellow Israelite owes you. 4How-
ever, there need be no poor people among you, for in the land
the LORD your God is giving you
to possess as your inheritance,
he will richly bless you, 5if only
you fully obey the LORD your God
and are careful to follow all these
commands I am giving you today. 6For the LORD your God will
bless you as he has promised, and
you will lend to many nations but
will borrow from none. You will
rule over many nations but none
will rule over you.

Dt 31:10; 23:20; 28:12-13,44

7If anyone is poor among your
fellow Israelites in any of the
towns of the land the LORD your
God is giving you, do not be hard-
hearted or tightfisted toward
them. 8Rather, be openhanded
and freely lend them whatever
they need. 9Be careful not to harbor this wicked thought: "The
seventh year, the year for canceling debts, is near," so that you do
not show ill will toward the needy
among your fellow Israelites and
give them nothing. They may
then appeal to the LORD against
you, and you will be found guilty
of sin. 10Give generously to them
and do so without a grudging
heart; then because of this the
LORD your God will bless you in all
your work and in everything you
put your hand to. 11There will always be poor people in the land.
Therefore I command you to be
openhanded toward your fellow
Israelites who are poor and needy
in your land.

Lev 25:8-38; Mt 26:11; 1Jn 3:17

Freeing Servants

12If any of your people — Hebrew men or women — sell themselves to you and serve you six
years, in the seventh year you
must let them go free. 13And when
you release them, do not send
them away empty-handed. 14Sup-
ply them liberally from your flock,
your threshing floor and your
winepress. Give to them as the
LORD your God has blessed you.
15Remember that you were slaves
in Egypt and the LORD your God
redeemed you. That is why I give
you this command today.

Ex 21:2-6; Lev 25:38-55

16But if your servant says to
you, "I do not want to leave you,"

because he loves you and your
family and is well off with you,
17then take an awl and push it
through his earlobe into the door,
and he will become your servant
for life. Do the same for your female servant.

18Do not consider it a hardship
to set your servant free, because
their service to you these six years
has been worth twice as much as
that of a hired hand. And the LORD
your God will bless you in everything you do.

The Firstborn Animals

19Set apart for the LORD your
God every firstborn male of your
herds and flocks. Do not put the
firstborn of your cows to work,
and do not shear the firstborn of
your sheep. 20Each year you and
your family are to eat them in the
presence of the LORD your God at
the place he will choose. 21If an animal has a defect, is lame or blind,
or has any serious flaw, you must
not sacrifice it to the LORD your
God. 22You are to eat it in your own
towns. Both the ceremonially unclean and the clean may eat it, as
if it were gazelle or deer. 23But you
must not eat the blood; pour it out
on the ground like water.

Ex 13:2; Lev 22:19-25; Dt 12:5-7,17-18

The Passover

16 Observe the month of Aviv
and celebrate the Passover
of the LORD your God, because in
the month of Aviv he brought you
out of Egypt by night. 2Sacrifice as
the Passover to the LORD your God
an animal from your flock or herd
at the place the LORD will choose
as a dwelling for his Name. 3Do
not eat it with bread made with
yeast, but for seven days eat unleavened bread, the bread of affliction, because you left Egypt
in haste — so that all the days
of your life you may remember
the time of your departure from
Egypt. 4Let no yeast be found in
your possession in all your land
for seven days. Do not let any of
the meat you sacrifice on the evening of the first day remain until
morning.

Ex 12:2; 34:25

5You must not sacrifice the
Passover in any town the LORD
your God gives you 6except in the
place he will choose as a dwelling
for his Name. There you must sacrifice the Passover in the evening,
when the sun goes down, on the
anniversary[a] of your departure
from Egypt. 7Roast it and eat it at
the place the LORD your God will
choose. Then in the morning return to your tents. 8For six days eat
unleavened bread and on the seventh day hold an assembly to the
LORD your God and do no work.

Ex 12:14-20; Lev 23:4-8; Nu 28:16-25

The Festival of Weeks

9Count off seven weeks from
the time you begin to put the sickle to the standing grain. 10Then
celebrate the Festival of Weeks

[a] 6 Or *down, at the time of day*

to the LORD your God by giving a freewill offering in proportion to the blessings the LORD your God has given you. 11And rejoice before the LORD your God at the place he will choose as a dwelling for his Name — you, your sons and daughters, your male and female servants, the Levites in your towns, and the foreigners, the fatherless and the widows living among you. 12Remember that you were slaves in Egypt, and follow carefully these decrees.

Lev 23:15-22; Nu 28:26-31; Dt 12:7

The Festival of Tabernacles

13Celebrate the Festival of Tabernacles for seven days after you have gathered the produce of your threshing floor and your winepress. 14Be joyful at your festival — you, your sons and daughters, your male and female servants, and the Levites, the foreigners, the fatherless and the widows who live in your towns. 15For seven days celebrate the festival to the LORD your God at the place the LORD will choose. For the LORD your God will bless you in all your harvest and in all the work of your hands, and your joy will be complete. Lev 23:34

16Three times a year all your men must appear before the LORD your God at the place he will choose: at the Festival of Unleavened Bread, the Festival of Weeks and the Festival of Tabernacles. No one should appear before the LORD empty-handed: 17Each of you must bring a gift in proportion to the way the LORD your God has blessed you.

Lev 23:33-43; Nu 29:12-39; Ex 34:20

Judges

18Appoint judges and officials for each of your tribes in every town the LORD your God is giving you, and they shall judge the people fairly. 19Do not pervert justice or show partiality. Do not accept a bribe, for a bribe blinds the eyes of the wise and twists the words of the innocent. 20Follow justice and justice alone, so that you may live and possess the land the LORD your God is giving you.

Ex 23:2,8; Dt 1:17

Worshiping Other Gods

21Do not set up any wooden Asherah pole beside the altar you build to the LORD your God, 22and do not erect a sacred stone, for these the LORD your God hates.

Lev 26:1

17 Do not sacrifice to the LORD your God an ox or a sheep that has any defect or flaw in it, for that would be detestable to him.

Dt 15:21

2If a man or woman living among you in one of the towns the LORD gives you is found doing evil in the eyes of the LORD your God in violation of his covenant, 3and contrary to my command has worshiped other gods, bowing down to them or to the sun

or the moon or the stars in the
sky, 4and this has been brought
to your attention, then you must
investigate it thoroughly. If it is
true and it has been proved that
this detestable thing has been
done in Israel, 5take the man or
woman who has done this evil
deed to your city gate and stone
that person to death. 6On the testimony of two or three witnesses
a person is to be put to death, but
no one is to be put to death on the
testimony of only one witness.
7The hands of the witnesses must
be the first in putting that person
to death, and then the hands of
all the people. You must purge
the evil from among you.

Nu 35:30; Dt 13:6-11; Mt 18:16

Law Courts

8If cases come before your
courts that are too difficult for
you to judge — whether bloodshed, lawsuits or assaults — take
them to the place the LORD your
God will choose. 9Go to the Levitical priests and to the judge who
is in office at that time. Inquire of
them and they will give you the
verdict. 10You must act according
to the decisions they give you at
the place the LORD will choose.
Be careful to do everything they
instruct you to do. 11Act according to whatever they teach you
and the decisions they give you.
Do not turn aside from what they
tell you, to the right or to the left.
12Anyone who shows contempt
for the judge or for the priest
who stands ministering there to
the LORD your God is to be put to
death. You must purge the evil
from Israel. 13All the people will
hear and be afraid, and will not be
contemptuous again.

Dt 12:5; 19:17; Nu 15:30

The King

14When you enter the land the
LORD your God is giving you and
have taken possession of it and
settled in it, and you say, "Let us
set a king over us like all the nations around us," 15be sure to appoint over you a king the LORD
your God chooses. He must be
from among your fellow Israelites. Do not place a foreigner over
you, one who is not an Israelite.
16The king, moreover, must not
acquire great numbers of horses for himself or make the people return to Egypt to get more of
them, for the LORD has told you,
"You are not to go back that way
again." 17He must not take many
wives, or his heart will be led
astray. He must not accumulate
large amounts of silver and gold.

1Sa 8:5,19-20; 1Ki 10:26; Jer 30:21

18When he takes the throne of
his kingdom, he is to write for
himself on a scroll a copy of this
law, taken from that of the Levitical priests. 19It is to be with him,
and he is to read it all the days of
his life so that he may learn to revere the LORD his God and follow
carefully all the words of this law

and these decrees 20and not consider himself better than his fellow Israelites and turn from the
law to the right or to the left. Then
he and his descendants will reign
a long time over his kingdom in
Israel. Jos 1:8; 1Ki 15:5

Offerings for Priests and Levites

18 The Levitical priests — indeed, the whole tribe of
Levi — are to have no allotment
or inheritance with Israel. They
shall live on the food offerings
presented to the LORD, for that is
their inheritance. 2They shall have
no inheritance among their fellow
Israelites; the LORD is their inheritance, as he promised them.
Dt 10:9; 1Co 9:13

3This is the share due the priests
from the people who sacrifice a
bull or a sheep: the shoulder, the
internal organs and the meat from
the head. 4You are to give them the
firstfruits of your grain, new wine
and olive oil, and the first wool
from the shearing of your sheep,
5for the LORD your God has chosen
them and their descendants out of
all your tribes to stand and minister in the LORD's name always.
Lev 7:28-34; Nu 18:12; Dt 10:8

6If a Levite moves from one of
your towns anywhere in Israel
where he is living, and comes in
all earnestness to the place the
LORD will choose, 7he may minister in the name of the LORD his
God like all his fellow Levites who
serve there in the presence of the
LORD. 8He is to share equally in
their benefits, even though he has
received money from the sale of
family possessions. Ne 12:44,47

Occult Practices

9When you enter the land the
LORD your God is giving you, do
not learn to imitate the detestable
ways of the nations there. 10Let no
one be found among you who sacrifices their son or daughter in the
fire, who practices divination or
sorcery, interprets omens, engages in witchcraft, 11or casts spells,
or who is a medium or spiritist or
who consults the dead. 12Anyone
who does these things is detestable to the LORD; because of these
same detestable practices the
LORD your God will drive out those
nations before you. 13You must be
blameless before the LORD your
God. Dt 12:31; Lev 18:24

The Prophet

14The nations you will dispossess listen to those who practice
sorcery or divination. But as for
you, the LORD your God has not
permitted you to do so. 15The LORD
your God will raise up for you a
prophet like me from among you,
from your fellow Israelites. You
must listen to him. 16For this is
what you asked of the LORD your
God at Horeb on the day of the assembly when you said, "Let us not
hear the voice of the LORD our God
nor see this great fire anymore, or
we will die." Ex 20:19; Jn 1:21; Ac 3:22

17The LORD said to me: “What
they say is good. 18I will raise up
for them a prophet like you from
among their fellow Israelites, and
I will put my words in his mouth.
He will tell them everything I
command him. 19I myself will call
to account anyone who does not
listen to my words that the prophet speaks in my name. 20But a
prophet who presumes to speak
in my name anything I have not
commanded, or a prophet who
speaks in the name of other gods,
is to be put to death.”
Isa 51:16; Jn 4:25-26; Ac 3:23

21You may say to yourselves,
“How can we know when a message has not been spoken by the
LORD?” 22If what a prophet proclaims in the name of the LORD
does not take place or come true,
that is a message the LORD has
not spoken. That prophet has spoken presumptuously, so do not be
alarmed. Jer 28:9

Cities of Refuge

19 When the LORD your God
has destroyed the nations
whose land he is giving you, and
when you have driven them out
and settled in their towns and
houses, 2then set aside for yourselves three cities in the land the
LORD your God is giving you to
possess. 3Determine the distances
involved and divide into three
parts the land the LORD your God
is giving you as an inheritance, so
that a person who kills someone
may flee for refuge to one of these
cities. Dt 12:29

4This is the rule concerning
anyone who kills a person and
flees there for safety — anyone
who kills a neighbor unintentionally, without malice aforethought.
5For instance, a man may go into
the forest with his neighbor to cut
wood, and as he swings his ax to
fell a tree, the head may fly off
and hit his neighbor and kill him.
That man may flee to one of these
cities and save his life. 6Otherwise,
the avenger of blood might pursue him in a rage, overtake him if
the distance is too great, and kill
him even though he is not deserving of death, since he did it to his
neighbor without malice aforethought. 7This is why I command
you to set aside for yourselves
three cities.

8If the LORD your God enlarges
your territory, as he promised on
oath to your ancestors, and gives
you the whole land he promised
them, 9because you carefully follow all these laws I command you
today — to love the LORD your God
and to walk always in obedience
to him — then you are to set aside
three more cities. 10Do this so that
innocent blood will not be shed
in your land, which the LORD your
God is giving you as your inheritance, and so that you will not be
guilty of bloodshed. Dt 21:1-9

11But if out of hate someone lies
in wait, assaults and kills a neighbor, and then flees to one of these

cities, 12the killer shall be sent for
by the town elders, be brought
back from the city, and be handed
over to the avenger of blood to die.
13Show no pity. You must purge
from Israel the guilt of shedding
innocent blood, so that it may go
well with you.
14Do not move your neighbor's
boundary stone set up by your
predecessors in the inheritance
you receive in the land the LORD
your God is giving you to possess.

Nu 35:6-34; Dt 4:41-43; Jos 20:1-9

Witnesses

15One witness is not enough to
convict anyone accused of any
crime or offense they may have
committed. A matter must be established by the testimony of two
or three witnesses.
16If a malicious witness takes
the stand to accuse someone of a
crime, 17the two people involved
in the dispute must stand in the
presence of the LORD before the
priests and the judges who are
in office at the time. 18The judges must make a thorough investigation, and if the witness proves
to be a liar, giving false testimony
against a fellow Israelite, 19then
do to the false witness as that witness intended to do to the other
party. You must purge the evil
from among you. 20The rest of
the people will hear of this and be
afraid, and never again will such
an evil thing be done among you.
21Show no pity: life for life, eye
for eye, tooth for tooth, hand for
hand, foot for foot.

Mt 5:38; Ps 27:12; Pr 19:5,9

Going to War

20 When you go to war against
your enemies and see horses and chariots and an army greater than yours, do not be afraid of
them, because the LORD your God,
who brought you up out of Egypt,
will be with you. 2When you are
about to go into battle, the priest
shall come forward and address
the army. 3He shall say: "Hear,
Israel: Today you are going into
battle against your enemies. Do
not be fainthearted or afraid; do
not panic or be terrified by them.
4For the LORD your God is the one
who goes with you to fight for you
against your enemies to give you
victory." Dt 1:30; 31:6,8; 2Ch 32:7-8
5The officers shall say to the
army: "Has anyone built a new
house and not yet begun to live in
it? Let him go home, or he may die
in battle and someone else may
begin to live in it. 6Has anyone
planted a vineyard and not begun
to enjoy it? Let him go home, or
he may die in battle and someone
else enjoy it. 7Has anyone become
pledged to a woman and not married her? Let him go home, or he
may die in battle and someone
else marry her." 8Then the officers shall add, "Is anyone afraid
or fainthearted? Let him go home
so that his fellow soldiers will not
become disheartened too." 9When

the officers have finished speaking to the army, they shall appoint commanders over it.

Dt 24:5; Jdg 7:3

10 When you march up to attack a city, make its people an offer of peace. 11 If they accept and
open their gates, all the people in
it shall be subject to forced labor
and shall work for you. 12 If they
refuse to make peace and they engage you in battle, lay siege to that
city. 13 When the LORD your God delivers it into your hand, put to the
sword all the men in it. 14 As for the
women, the children, the livestock
and everything else in the city,
you may take these as plunder for
yourselves. And you may use the
plunder the LORD your God gives
you from your enemies. 15 This is
how you are to treat all the cities
that are at a distance from you
and do not belong to the nations
nearby. Nu 31:7; Jos 8:2; 1Ki 9:21

16 However, in the cities of the
nations the LORD your God is giving you as an inheritance, do not
leave alive anything that breathes.
17 Completely destroy[a] them — the
Hittites, Amorites, Canaanites,
Perizzites, Hivites and Jebusites —
as the LORD your God has commanded you. 18 Otherwise, they
will teach you to follow all the
detestable things they do in worshiping their gods, and you will
sin against the LORD your God.

Ex 23:33; Dt 7:2; Jos 11:14

19 When you lay siege to a city for
a long time, fighting against it to
capture it, do not destroy its trees
by putting an ax to them, because
you can eat their fruit. Do not cut
them down. Are the trees people,
that you should besiege them?[b]
20 However, you may cut down
trees that you know are not fruit
trees and use them to build siege
works until the city at war with
you falls.

Atonement for an Unsolved Murder

21 If someone is found slain,
lying in a field in the land
the LORD your God is giving you
to possess, and it is not known
who the killer was, 2 your elders
and judges shall go out and measure the distance from the body
to the neighboring towns. 3 Then
the elders of the town nearest the
body shall take a heifer that has
never been worked and has never
worn a yoke 4 and lead it down to
a valley that has not been plowed
or planted and where there is a
flowing stream. There in the valley they are to break the heifer's
neck. 5 The Levitical priests shall
step forward, for the LORD your
God has chosen them to minister and to pronounce blessings
in the name of the LORD and to
decide all cases of dispute and
assault. 6 Then all the elders of

[a] 17 The Hebrew term refers to the irrevocable giving over of things or persons to the LORD, often by totally destroying them. [b] 19 Or *down to use in the siege, for the fruit trees are for the benefit of people.*

the town nearest the body shall
wash their hands over the heifer
whose neck was broken in the valley, 7and they shall declare: "Our
hands did not shed this blood, nor
did our eyes see it done. 8Accept
this atonement for your people
Israel, whom you have redeemed,
LORD, and do not hold your people guilty of the blood of an innocent person." Then the bloodshed
will be atoned for, 9and you will
have purged from yourselves the
guilt of shedding innocent blood,
since you have done what is right
in the eyes of the LORD.

Dt 17:8-11; 19:13; Mt 27:24

Marrying a Captive Woman

10When you go to war against
your enemies and the LORD your
God delivers them into your
hands and you take captives, 11if
you notice among the captives a
beautiful woman and are attracted to her, you may take her as
your wife. 12Bring her into your
home and have her shave her
head, trim her nails 13and put
aside the clothes she was wearing when captured. After she has
lived in your house and mourned
her father and mother for a full
month, then you may go to her
and be her husband and she shall
be your wife. 14If you are not
pleased with her, let her go wherever she wishes. You must not sell
her or treat her as a slave, since
you have dishonored her.

Lev 14:9; Ps 45:10; Jos 21:44

The Right of the Firstborn

15If a man has two wives, and he
loves one but not the other, and
both bear him sons but the firstborn is the son of the wife he does
not love, 16when he wills his property to his sons, he must not give
the rights of the firstborn to the
son of the wife he loves in pref-
erence to his actual firstborn, the
son of the wife he does not love.
17He must acknowledge the son of
his unloved wife as the firstborn
by giving him a double share of all
he has. That son is the first sign of
his father's strength. The right of
the firstborn belongs to him.

Ge 29:33; 49:3; 1Ch 26:10

A Rebellious Son

18If someone has a stubborn and
rebellious son who does not obey
his father and mother and will not
listen to them when they discipline him, 19his father and mother
shall take hold of him and bring
him to the elders at the gate of his
town. 20They shall say to the elders, "This son of ours is stubborn
and rebellious. He will not obey us.
He is a glutton and a drunkard."
21Then all the men of his town are
to stone him to death. You must
purge the evil from among you.
All Israel will hear of it and be
afraid. Dt 13:11; Eph 6:1-3

Various Laws

22If someone guilty of a capital
offense is put to death and their
body is exposed on a pole, 23you

must not leave the body hanging on the pole overnight. Be sure
to bury it that same day, because
anyone who is hung on a pole is
under God's curse. You must not
desecrate the land the LORD your
God is giving you as an inheritance. Gal 3:13; Jos 8:29; Jn 19:31

22 If you see your fellow Israelite's ox or sheep stray-
ing, do not ignore it but be sure
to take it back to its owner. 2If
they do not live near you or if you
do not know who owns it, take it
home with you and keep it until they come looking for it. Then
give it back. 3Do the same if you
find their donkey or cloak or anything else they have lost. Do not
ignore it. Ex 23:4-5

4If you see your fellow Israelite's
donkey or ox fallen on the road,
do not ignore it. Help the owner
get it to its feet.

5A woman must not wear men's
clothing, nor a man wear women's
clothing, for the LORD your God
detests anyone who does this.

6If you come across a bird's nest
beside the road, either in a tree
or on the ground, and the mother is sitting on the young or on
the eggs, do not take the mother with the young. 7You may take
the young, but be sure to let the
mother go, so that it may go well
with you and you may have a long
life. Lev 22:28; Dt 4:40

8When you build a new house,
make a parapet around your roof
so that you may not bring the
guilt of bloodshed on your house
if someone falls from the roof.

9Do not plant two kinds of seed
in your vineyard; if you do, not
only the crops you plant but also
the fruit of the vineyard will be
defiled.[a] Lev 19:19

10Do not plow with an ox and a
donkey yoked together. 2Co 6:14

11Do not wear clothes of wool
and linen woven together.

12Make tassels on the four corners of the cloak you wear.
Nu 15:37-41; Mt 23:5

Marriage Violations

13If a man takes a wife and, after sleeping with her, dislikes her
14and slanders her and gives her a
bad name, saying, "I married this
woman, but when I approached
her, I did not find proof of her virginity," 15then the young woman's
father and mother shall bring to
the town elders at the gate proof
that she was a virgin. 16Her father
will say to the elders, "I gave my
daughter in marriage to this man,
but he dislikes her. 17Now he has
slandered her and said, 'I did not
find your daughter to be a virgin.' But here is the proof of my
daughter's virginity." Then her
parents shall display the cloth before the elders of the town, 18and
the elders shall take the man and
punish him. 19They shall fine him
a hundred shekels[b] of silver and

[a] 9 Or *be forfeited to the sanctuary*
[b] 19 That is, about 2 1/2 pounds or about 1.2 kilograms

give them to the young woman's
father, because this man has giv-
en an Israelite virgin a bad name.
She shall continue to be his wife;
he must not divorce her as long as
he lives. Ex 18:21; Dt 1:9-18
20If, however, the charge is true
and no proof of the young woman's virginity can be found, 21she
shall be brought to the door of
her father's house and there the
men of her town shall stone her
to death. She has done an outrageous thing in Israel by being promiscuous while still in her father's
house. You must purge the evil
from among you. Ge 34:7; Dt 13:5
22If a man is found sleeping with
another man's wife, both the man
who slept with her and the woman must die. You must purge the
evil from Israel. Lev 20:10; Jn 8:5
23If a man happens to meet in a
town a virgin pledged to be married and he sleeps with her, 24you
shall take both of them to the
gate of that town and stone them
to death — the young woman because she was in a town and did
not scream for help, and the man
because he violated another man's
wife. You must purge the evil from
among you.
25But if out in the country a man
happens to meet a young woman
pledged to be married and rapes
her, only the man who has done
this shall die. 26Do nothing to the
woman; she has committed no sin
deserving death. This case is like
that of someone who attacks and
murders a neighbor, 27for the man
found the young woman out in
the country, and though the betrothed woman screamed, there
was no one to rescue her.
28If a man happens to meet a
virgin who is not pledged to be
married and rapes her and they
are discovered, 29he shall pay her
father fifty shekels[a] of silver. He
must marry the young woman, for
he has violated her. He can never
divorce her as long as he lives.
Ex 22:16
30A man is not to marry his father's wife; he must not dishonor
his father's bed.[b]
Lev 18:8; Dt 27:20; 1Co 5:1

Exclusion From the Assembly

23[c] No one who has been
emasculated by crushing
or cutting may enter the assembly
of the LORD.
2No one born of a forbidden
marriage[d] nor any of their descendants may enter the assembly of
the LORD, not even in the tenth
generation.
3No Ammonite or Moabite or
any of their descendants may
enter the assembly of the LORD,
not even in the tenth generation. 4For they did not come to
meet you with bread and water
on your way when you came out

[a] *29* That is, about 1 1/4 pounds or about 575 grams [b] *30* In Hebrew texts this verse (22:30) is numbered 23:1. [c] In Hebrew texts 23:1-25 is numbered 23:2-26.
[d] *2* Or *one of illegitimate birth*

of Egypt, and they hired Balaam
son of Beor from Pethor in Aram
Naharaim[a] to pronounce a curse
on you. 5However, the LORD your
God would not listen to Balaam
but turned the curse into a blessing for you, because the LORD
your God loves you. 6Do not seek
a treaty of friendship with them
as long as you live.
Nu 22:5-6; Ezr 9:12; Ne 13:2
7Do not despise an Edomite, for
the Edomites are related to you.
Do not despise an Egyptian, because you resided as foreigners in
their country. 8The third generation of children born to them may
enter the assembly of the LORD.
Ge 25:26; Ex 22:21

Uncleanness in the Camp

9When you are encamped
against your enemies, keep away
from everything impure. 10If one
of your men is unclean because of
a nocturnal emission, he is to go
outside the camp and stay there.
11But as evening approaches he is
to wash himself, and at sunset he
may return to the camp. Lev 15:16
12Designate a place outside the
camp where you can go to relieve
yourself. 13As part of your equipment have something to dig with,
and when you relieve yourself,
dig a hole and cover up your excrement. 14For the LORD your God
moves about in your camp to protect you and to deliver your enemies to you. Your camp must be
holy, so that he will not see among
you anything indecent and turn
away from you. Lev 26:12

Miscellaneous Laws

15If a slave has taken refuge
with you, do not hand them over
to their master. 16Let them live
among you wherever they like and
in whatever town they choose. Do
not oppress them. 1Sa 30:15
17No Israelite man or woman
is to become a shrine prostitute.
18You must not bring the earnings
of a female prostitute or of a male
prostitute[b] into the house of the
LORD your God to pay any vow, because the LORD your God detests
them both. Lev 19:29; 20:13
19Do not charge a fellow Israelite interest, whether on money
or food or anything else that may
earn interest. 20You may charge a
foreigner interest, but not a fellow
Israelite, so that the LORD your
God may bless you in everything
you put your hand to in the land
you are entering to possess.
Ex 22:25; Lev 25:35-37
21If you make a vow to the LORD
your God, do not be slow to pay it,
for the LORD your God will certainly demand it of you and you will
be guilty of sin. 22But if you refrain from making a vow, you will
not be guilty. 23Whatever your lips
utter you must be sure to do, because you made your vow freely to
the LORD your God with your own
mouth. Nu 30:1-2; Mt 5:33

[a] *4* That is, Northwest Mesopotamia
[b] *18* Hebrew *of a dog*

[24]If you enter your neighbor's
vineyard, you may eat all the
grapes you want, but do not put
any in your basket. [25]If you enter
your neighbor's grainfield, you
may pick kernels with your hands,
but you must not put a sickle to
their standing grain. Mt 12:1; Mk 2:23

24 If a man marries a woman
who becomes displeasing
to him because he finds something indecent about her, and he
writes her a certificate of divorce,
gives it to her and sends her from
his house, [2]and if after she leaves
his house she becomes the wife of
another man, [3]and her second husband dislikes her and writes her a
certificate of divorce, gives it to
her and sends her from his house,
or if he dies, [4]then her first husband, who divorced her, is not allowed to marry her again after she
has been defiled. That would be
detestable in the eyes of the LORD.
Do not bring sin upon the land the
LORD your God is giving you as an
inheritance. Jer 3:1; Mt 5:31; 19:7-9

[5]If a man has recently married,
he must not be sent to war or have
any other duty laid on him. For
one year he is to be free to stay at
home and bring happiness to the
wife he has married. Dt 20:7

[6]Do not take a pair of millstones — not even the upper
one — as security for a debt, because that would be taking a person's livelihood as security.

[7]If someone is caught kidnap-
ping a fellow Israelite and treating
or selling them as a slave, the kidnapper must die. You must purge
the evil from among you. Ex 21:16

[8]In cases of defiling skin diseases,[a] be very careful to do exactly as
the Levitical priests instruct you.
You must follow carefully what I
have commanded them. [9]Remem-
ber what the LORD your God did to
Miriam along the way after you
came out of Egypt. Lev 13:1-46; Nu 12:10

[10]When you make a loan of any
kind to your neighbor, do not go
into their house to get what is offered to you as a pledge. [11]Stay outside and let the neighbor to whom
you are making the loan bring the
pledge out to you. [12]If the neighbor is poor, do not go to sleep with
their pledge in your possession.
[13]Return their cloak by sunset so
that your neighbor may sleep in
it. Then they will thank you, and
it will be regarded as a righteous
act in the sight of the LORD your
God. Ex 22:26; Dt 6:25; Da 4:27

[14]Do not take advantage of a
hired worker who is poor and
needy, whether that worker is a
fellow Israelite or a foreigner residing in one of your towns. [15]Pay
them their wages each day before
sunset, because they are poor and
are counting on it. Otherwise they
may cry to the LORD against you,
and you will be guilty of sin.
Lev 19:13; Jas 5:4

[a] *8* The Hebrew word for *defiling skin diseases*, traditionally translated "leprosy," was used for various diseases affecting the skin.

16Parents are not to be put to
death for their children, nor children put to death for their parents; each will die for their own
sin. Jer 31:29-30; Eze 18:20
17Do not deprive the foreigner
or the fatherless of justice, or take
the cloak of the widow as a pledge.
18Remember that you were slaves
in Egypt and the LORD your God
redeemed you from there. That is
why I command you to do this.
19When you are harvesting in
your field and you overlook a
sheaf, do not go back to get it. Leave
it for the foreigner, the fatherless
and the widow, so that the LORD
your God may bless you in all the
work of your hands. 20When you
beat the olives from your trees, do
not go over the branches a second
time. Leave what remains for the
foreigner, the fatherless and the
widow. 21When you harvest the
grapes in your vineyard, do not go
over the vines again. Leave what
remains for the foreigner, the fatherless and the widow. 22Remem-
ber that you were slaves in Egypt.
That is why I command you to do
this. Lev 19:9; 23:22

25 When people have a dispute, they are to take it to
court and the judges will decide
the case, acquitting the innocent
and condemning the guilty. 2If the
guilty person deserves to be beat-
en, the judge shall make them lie
down and have them flogged in
his presence with the number of
lashes the crime deserves, 3but
the judge must not impose more
than forty lashes. If the guilty party is flogged more than that, your
fellow Israelite will be degraded in
your eyes. Dt 17:8-13; 19:17; 2Co 11:24
4Do not muzzle an ox while it is
treading out the grain. 1Ti 5:18
5If brothers are living together and one of them dies without
a son, his widow must not marry
outside the family. Her husband's
brother shall take her and marry
her and fulfill the duty of a brother-in-law to her. 6The first son she
bears shall carry on the name of
the dead brother so that his name
will not be blotted out from Israel.
Ru 4:5,10; Mt 22:24; Lk 20:28
7However, if a man does not
want to marry his brother's wife,
she shall go to the elders at the
town gate and say, "My husband's
brother refuses to carry on his
brother's name in Israel. He will
not fulfill the duty of a brother-
in-law to me." 8Then the elders of
his town shall summon him and
talk to him. If he persists in saying, "I do not want to marry her,"
9his brother's widow shall go up to
him in the presence of the elders,
take off one of his sandals, spit
in his face and say, "This is what
is done to the man who will not
build up his brother's family line."
10That man's line shall be known
in Israel as The Family of the Un-
sandaled. Ru 4:1-2,5-6
11If two men are fighting and the
wife of one of them comes to rescue her husband from his assail-

ant, and she reaches out and seizes
him by his private parts, 12you shall
cut off her hand. Show her no pity.
13Do not have two differing
weights in your bag — one heavy,
one light. 14Do not have two differing measures in your house — one
large, one small. 15You must have
accurate and honest weights and
measures, so that you may live
long in the land the LORD your
God is giving you. 16For the LORD
your God detests anyone who does
these things, anyone who deals
dishonestly. Lev 19:35-37; Pr 11:1

17Remember what the Ama-
lekites did to you along the way
when you came out of Egypt.
18When you were weary and worn
out, they met you on your journey and attacked all who were
lagging behind; they had no fear
of God. 19When the LORD your God
gives you rest from all the enemies around you in the land he is
giving you to possess as an inheritance, you shall blot out the name
of Amalek from under heaven. Do
not forget! Ex 17:8; Ps 36:1; 1Sa 15:2-3

Firstfruits and Tithes

26 When you have entered the
land the LORD your God is
giving you as an inheritance and
have taken possession of it and
settled in it, 2take some of the firstfruits of all that you produce from
the soil of the land the LORD your
God is giving you and put them
in a basket. Then go to the place
the LORD your God will choose as
a dwelling for his Name 3and say
to the priest in office at the time,
"I declare today to the LORD your
God that I have come to the land
the LORD swore to our ancestors
to give us." 4The priest shall take
the basket from your hands and
set it down in front of the altar
of the LORD your God. 5Then you
shall declare before the LORD your
God: "My father was a wandering Aramean, and he went down
into Egypt with a few people and
lived there and became a great
nation, powerful and numerous.
6But the Egyptians mistreated us
and made us suffer, subjecting us
to harsh labor. 7Then we cried out
to the LORD, the God of our ancestors, and the LORD heard our voice
and saw our misery, toil and oppression. 8So the LORD brought us
out of Egypt with a mighty hand
and an outstretched arm, with
great terror and with signs and
wonders. 9He brought us to this
place and gave us this land, a land
flowing with milk and honey;
10and now I bring the firstfruits of
the soil that you, LORD, have giv-
en me." Place the basket before
the LORD your God and bow down
before him. 11Then you and the Levites and the foreigners residing
among you shall rejoice in all the
good things the LORD your God
has given to you and your household. Ex 3:8; 23:16,19; Dt 4:34

12When you have finished setting aside a tenth of all your produce in the third year, the year of

the tithe, you shall give it to the
Levite, the foreigner, the fatherless and the widow, so that they
may eat in your towns and be satisfied. 13Then say to the LORD your
God: "I have removed from my
house the sacred portion and have
given it to the Levite, the foreigner, the fatherless and the widow,
according to all you commanded.
I have not turned aside from your
commands nor have I forgotten
any of them. 14I have not eaten any
of the sacred portion while I was
in mourning, nor have I removed
any of it while I was unclean, nor
have I offered any of it to the dead.
I have obeyed the LORD my God;
I have done everything you commanded me. 15Look down from
heaven, your holy dwelling place,
and bless your people Israel and
the land you have given us as you
promised on oath to our ancestors, a land flowing with milk and
honey." Dt 14:28-29; Ps 119:141,153,176

Follow the LORD's Commands

16The LORD your God commands
you this day to follow these decrees and laws; carefully observe
them with all your heart and
with all your soul. 17You have declared this day that the LORD is
your God and that you will walk
in obedience to him, that you will
keep his decrees, commands and
laws — that you will listen to him.
18And the LORD has declared this
day that you are his people, his
treasured possession as he promised, and that you are to keep all
his commands. 19He has declared
that he will set you in praise, fame
and honor high above all the nations he has made and that you
will be a people holy to the LORD
your God, as he promised.

Dt 7:6; 28:1,13,44; 4:7-8

The Altar on Mount Ebal

27 Moses and the elders of Israel commanded the peo-
ple: "Keep all these commands
that I give you today. 2When you
have crossed the Jordan into the
land the LORD your God is giving you, set up some large stones
and coat them with plaster. 3Write
on them all the words of this law
when you have crossed over to enter the land the LORD your God is
giving you, a land flowing with
milk and honey, just as the LORD,
the God of your ancestors, promised you. 4And when you have
crossed the Jordan, set up these
stones on Mount Ebal, as I command you today, and coat them
with plaster. 5Build there an altar
to the LORD your God, an altar of
stones. Do not use any iron tool on
them. 6Build the altar of the LORD
your God with fieldstones and
offer burnt offerings on it to the
LORD your God. 7Sacrifice fellowship offerings there, eating them
and rejoicing in the presence of
the LORD your God. 8And you shall
write very clearly all the words of
this law on these stones you have
set up." Ex 20:25; Dt 26:9; Jos 8:31

Curses From Mount Ebal

9Then Moses and the Levitical
priests said to all Israel, "Be silent, Israel, and listen! You have
now become the people of the
LORD your God. 10Obey the LORD
your God and follow his commands and decrees that I give
you today."

11On the same day Moses commanded the people:

12When you have crossed the
Jordan, these tribes shall stand on
Mount Gerizim to bless the peo-
ple: Simeon, Levi, Judah, Issachar,
Joseph and Benjamin. 13And these
tribes shall stand on Mount Ebal
to pronounce curses: Reuben, Gad,
Asher, Zebulun, Dan and Naphtali.
Jos 8:35

14The Levites shall recite to
all the people of Israel in a loud
voice:

15"Cursed is anyone who
makes an idol — a thing detestable to the LORD, the work
of skilled hands — and sets it
up in secret." Ex 20:4; 34:17

Then all the people
shall say, "Amen!"

16"Cursed is anyone who
dishonors their father or
mother." Ex 21:17

Then all the people
shall say, "Amen!"

17"Cursed is anyone who
moves their neighbor's boundary stone." Pr 22:28

Then all the people
shall say, "Amen!"

18"Cursed is anyone who
leads the blind astray on the
road." Lev 19:14

Then all the people
shall say, "Amen!"

19"Cursed is anyone who
withholds justice from the
foreigner, the fatherless or
the widow." Dt 10:18; 24:19

Then all the people
shall say, "Amen!"

20"Cursed is anyone who
sleeps with his father's wife,
for he dishonors his father's
bed." Lev 18:7; Dt 22:30

Then all the people
shall say, "Amen!"

21"Cursed is anyone who
has sexual relations with any
animal." Lev 18:23

Then all the people
shall say, "Amen!"

22"Cursed is anyone who
sleeps with his sister, the
daughter of his father or the
daughter of his mother."

Then all the people
shall say, "Amen!"

23"Cursed is anyone who
sleeps with his mother-in-
law."

Then all the people
shall say, "Amen!"

24"Cursed is anyone who
kills their neighbor secretly."
Nu 35:31

Then all the people
shall say, "Amen!"

25"Cursed is anyone who accepts a bribe to kill an innocent person." Ex 23:7-8

Then all the people
shall say, "Amen!"
26"Cursed is anyone who
does not uphold the words of
this law by carrying them out."
Gal 3:10
Then all the people
shall say, "Amen!"

Blessings for Obedience

28 If you fully obey the LORD
your God and carefully follow all his commands I give you
today, the LORD your God will set
you high above all the nations
on earth. 2All these blessings will
come on you and accompany you
if you obey the LORD your God:
Dt 26:19; Lev 26:3

3You will be blessed in the
city and blessed in the country. Ge 39:5
4The fruit of your womb
will be blessed, and the crops
of your land and the young of
your livestock — the calves of
your herds and the lambs of
your flocks. Ge 49:25
5Your basket and your
kneading trough will be
blessed.
6You will be blessed when
you come in and blessed
when you go out. Ps 121:8

7The LORD will grant that the
enemies who rise up against you
will be defeated before you. They
will come at you from one direction but flee from you in seven.
Lev 26:8,17

8The LORD will send a blessing
on your barns and on everything
you put your hand to. The LORD
your God will bless you in the land
he is giving you.
9The LORD will establish you as
his holy people, as he promised
you on oath, if you keep the commands of the LORD your God and
walk in obedience to him. 10Then
all the peoples on earth will see
that you are called by the name of
the LORD, and they will fear you.
11The LORD will grant you abundant prosperity — in the fruit of
your womb, the young of your
livestock and the crops of your
ground — in the land he swore to
your ancestors to give you.
Ex 19:6; 2Ch 7:14

12The LORD will open the heavens, the storehouse of his bounty,
to send rain on your land in season and to bless all the work of
your hands. You will lend to many
nations but will borrow from
none. 13The LORD will make you
the head, not the tail. If you pay
attention to the commands of the
LORD your God that I give you this
day and carefully follow them,
you will always be at the top, never at the bottom. 14Do not turn
aside from any of the commands
I give you today, to the right or to
the left, following other gods and
serving them. Lev 26:4; Dt 5:32; 15:3,6

Curses for Disobedience

15However, if you do not obey
the LORD your God and do not

carefully follow all his commands
and decrees I am giving you today,
all these curses will come on you
and overtake you: Lev 26:14; Jos 23:15

16 You will be cursed in the
city and cursed in the country.

17 Your basket and your
kneading trough will be
cursed.

18 The fruit of your womb
will be cursed, and the crops
of your land, and the calves of
your herds and the lambs of
your flocks.

19 You will be cursed when
you come in and cursed when
you go out.

20 The LORD will send on you
curses, confusion and rebuke in
everything you put your hand to,
until you are destroyed and come
to sudden ruin because of the evil
you have done in forsaking him.[a]
21 The LORD will plague you with
diseases until he has destroyed
you from the land you are entering to possess. 22 The LORD will
strike you with wasting disease,
with fever and inflammation,
with scorching heat and drought,
with blight and mildew, which
will plague you until you perish.
23 The sky over your head will be
bronze, the ground beneath you
iron. 24 The LORD will turn the rain
of your country into dust and
powder; it will come down from
the skies until you are destroyed.
Isa 51:20; Am 4:9; Mal 2:2

25 The LORD will cause you to be
defeated before your enemies. You
will come at them from one direction but flee from them in sev-
en, and you will become a thing
of horror to all the kingdoms on
earth. 26 Your carcasses will be food
for all the birds and the wild animals, and there will be no one to
frighten them away. 27 The LORD
will afflict you with the boils of
Egypt and with tumors, festering
sores and the itch, from which you
cannot be cured. 28 The LORD will
afflict you with madness, blindness and confusion of mind. 29 At
midday you will grope about like a
blind person in the dark. You will
be unsuccessful in everything you
do; day after day you will be oppressed and robbed, with no one
to rescue you. Jer 15:4; 7:33; 1Sa 5:6

30 You will be pledged to be married to a woman, but another will
take her and rape her. You will
build a house, but you will not live
in it. You will plant a vineyard, but
you will not even begin to enjoy its
fruit. 31 Your ox will be slaughtered
before your eyes, but you will eat
none of it. Your donkey will be
forcibly taken from you and will
not be returned. Your sheep will
be given to your enemies, and no
one will rescue them. 32 Your sons
and daughters will be given to another nation, and you will wear
out your eyes watching for them
day after day, powerless to lift a

[a] 20 Hebrew *me*

hand. 33 A people that you do not know will eat what your land and labor produce, and you will have nothing but cruel oppression all your days. 34 The sights you see will drive you mad. 35 The LORD will afflict your knees and legs with painful boils that cannot be cured, spreading from the soles of your feet to the top of your head.

Jer 5:15-17; 8:10; Am 5:11

36 The LORD will drive you and the king you set over you to a nation unknown to you or your ancestors. There you will worship other gods, gods of wood and stone. 37 You will become a thing of horror, a byword and an object of ridicule among all the peoples where the LORD will drive you.

Dt 4:28; Jer 16:13; 24:9

38 You will sow much seed in the field but you will harvest little, because locusts will devour it. 39 You will plant vineyards and cultivate them but you will not drink the wine or gather the grapes, because worms will eat them. 40 You will have olive trees throughout your country but you will not use the oil, because the olives will drop off. 41 You will have sons and daughters but you will not keep them, because they will go into captivity. 42 Swarms of locusts will take over all your trees and the crops of your land.

Joel 1:4; Mic 6:15; Hag 1:6,9

43 The foreigners who reside among you will rise above you higher and higher, but you will sink lower and lower. 44 They will lend to you, but you will not lend to them. They will be the head, but you will be the tail.

45 All these curses will come on you. They will pursue you and overtake you until you are destroyed, because you did not obey the LORD your God and observe the commands and decrees he gave you. 46 They will be a sign and a wonder to you and your descendants forever. 47 Because you did not serve the LORD your God joyfully and gladly in the time of prosperity, 48 therefore in hunger and thirst, in nakedness and dire poverty, you will serve the enemies the LORD sends against you. He will put an iron yoke on your neck until he has destroyed you.

Ne 9:35; Isa 8:18; Jer 28:13-14

49 The LORD will bring a nation against you from far away, from the ends of the earth, like an eagle swooping down, a nation whose language you will not understand, 50 a fierce-looking nation without respect for the old or pity for the young. 51 They will devour the young of your livestock and the crops of your land until you are destroyed. They will leave you no grain, new wine or olive oil, nor any calves of your herds or lambs of your flocks until you are ruined. 52 They will lay siege to all the cities throughout your land until the high fortified walls in which you trust fall down. They will besiege all the cities through-

out the land the LORD your God is
giving you. Isa 47:6; Jer 48:40; Zep 1:14-17
53Because of the suffering your
enemy will inflict on you during
the siege, you will eat the fruit of
the womb, the flesh of the sons
and daughters the LORD your God
has given you. 54Even the most
gentle and sensitive man among
you will have no compassion on
his own brother or the wife he
loves or his surviving children,
55and he will not give to one of
them any of the flesh of his children that he is eating. It will be all
he has left because of the suffering your enemy will inflict on you
during the siege of all your cities.
56The most gentle and sensitive
woman among you — so sensitive and gentle that she would
not venture to touch the ground
with the sole of her foot — will be-
grudge the husband she loves and
her own son or daughter 57the af-
terbirth from her womb and the
children she bears. For in her dire
need she intends to eat them secretly because of the suffering
your enemy will inflict on you
during the siege of your cities.
Lev 26:29; Jer 19:9; La 2:20
58If you do not carefully follow
all the words of this law, which
are written in this book, and do
not revere this glorious and awesome name — the LORD your
God — 59the LORD will send fearful plagues on you and your descendants, harsh and prolonged
disasters, and severe and linger-
ing illnesses. 60He will bring on
you all the diseases of Egypt that
you dreaded, and they will cling
to you. 61The LORD will also bring
on you every kind of sickness and
disaster not recorded in this Book
of the Law, until you are destroyed.
62You who were as numerous as
the stars in the sky will be left but
few in number, because you did
not obey the LORD your God. 63Just
as it pleased the LORD to make you
prosper and increase in number,
so it will please him to ruin and
destroy you. You will be uprooted
from the land you are entering to
possess. Dt 10:22; Ne 9:23; Pr 1:26
64Then the LORD will scatter you
among all nations, from one end
of the earth to the other. There
you will worship other gods —
gods of wood and stone, which
neither you nor your ancestors
have known. 65Among those nations you will find no repose, no
resting place for the sole of your
foot. There the LORD will give
you an anxious mind, eyes weary with longing, and a despairing
heart. 66You will live in constant
suspense, filled with dread both
night and day, never sure of your
life. 67In the morning you will
say, "If only it were evening!" and
in the evening, "If only it were
morning!" — because of the terror that will fill your hearts and
the sights that your eyes will see.
68The LORD will send you back in
ships to Egypt on a journey I said
you should never make again.

There you will offer yourselves for
sale to your enemies as male and
female slaves, but no one will buy
you. Dt 4:27; Lev 26:16,36; Job 7:4

Renewal of the Covenant

29[a] These are the terms of the
covenant the LORD com-
manded Moses to make with the
Israelites in Moab, in addition to
the covenant he had made with
them at Horeb. Dt 5:2-3

2Moses summoned all the Israelites and said to them:

Your eyes have seen all that the
LORD did in Egypt to Pharaoh, to
all his officials and to all his land.
3With your own eyes you saw
those great trials, those signs and
great wonders. 4But to this day the
LORD has not given you a mind
that understands or eyes that see
or ears that hear. 5Yet the LORD
says, "During the forty years that
I led you through the wilderness,
your clothes did not wear out, nor
did the sandals on your feet. 6You
ate no bread and drank no wine or
other fermented drink. I did this
so that you might know that I am
the LORD your God."

Dt 8:4; Isa 6:10; Ro 11:8

7When you reached this place,
Sihon king of Heshbon and Og
king of Bashan came out to fight
against us, but we defeated them.
8We took their land and gave it as
an inheritance to the Reubenites,
the Gadites and the half-tribe of
Manasseh. Nu 21:21-24,33-35; 32:33

9Carefully follow the terms of
this covenant, so that you may
prosper in everything you do. 10All
of you are standing today in the
presence of the LORD your God—
your leaders and chief men, your
elders and officials, and all the
other men of Israel, 11together
with your children and your wives,
and the foreigners living in your
camps who chop your wood and
carry your water. 12You are standing here in order to enter into a
covenant with the LORD your God,
a covenant the LORD is making
with you this day and sealing with
an oath, 13to confirm you this day
as his people, that he may be your
God as he promised you and as he
swore to your fathers, Abraham,
Isaac and Jacob. 14I am making
this covenant, with its oath, not
only with you 15who are standing
here with us today in the presence
of the LORD our God but also with
those who are not here today.

Ge 17:7; Jos 1:7; Ac 2:39

16You yourselves know how we
lived in Egypt and how we passed
through the countries on the
way here. 17You saw among them
their detestable images and idols
of wood and stone, of silver and
gold. 18Make sure there is no man
or woman, clan or tribe among
you today whose heart turns away
from the LORD our God to go and
worship the gods of those nations;
make sure there is no root among

[a] In Hebrew texts 29:1 is numbered 28:69, and 29:2-29 is numbered 29:1-28.

you that produces such bitter poison. Dt 28:36; Heb 12:15

19When such a person hears the words of this oath and they invoke a blessing on themselves, thinking, "I will be safe, even though I persist in going my own way," they will bring disaster on the watered land as well as the dry. 20The LORD will never be willing to forgive them; his wrath and zeal will burn against them. All the curses written in this book will fall on them, and the LORD will blot out their names from under heaven. 21The LORD will single them out from all the tribes of Israel for disaster, according to all the curses of the covenant written in this Book of the Law. Dt 9:14; Ps 74:1; 79:5

22Your children who follow you in later generations and foreigners who come from distant lands will see the calamities that have fallen on the land and the diseases with which the LORD has afflicted it. 23The whole land will be a burning waste of salt and sulfur — nothing planted, nothing sprouting, no vegetation growing on it. It will be like the destruction of Sodom and Gomorrah, Admah and Zeboyim, which the LORD overthrew in fierce anger. 24All the nations will ask: "Why has the LORD done this to this land? Why this fierce, burning anger?" Jer 19:8; 22:8-9; Zep 2:9

25And the answer will be: "It is because this people abandoned the covenant of the LORD, the God of their ancestors, the covenant he made with them when he brought them out of Egypt. 26They went off and worshiped other gods and bowed down to them, gods they did not know, gods he had not given them. 27Therefore the LORD's anger burned against this land, so that he brought on it all the curses written in this book. 28In furious anger and in great wrath the LORD uprooted them from their land and thrust them into another land, as it is now." 1Ki 14:15; 2Ki 17:23; Da 9:11,13-14

29The secret things belong to the LORD our God, but the things revealed belong to us and to our children forever, that we may follow all the words of this law. 2Ti 3:16

Prosperity After Turning to the LORD

30 When all these blessings and curses I have set before you come on you and you take them to heart wherever the LORD your God disperses you among the nations, 2and when you and your children return to the LORD your God and obey him with all your heart and with all your soul according to everything I command you today, 3then the LORD your God will restore your fortunes[a] and have compassion on you and gather you again from all the nations where he scattered you. 4Even if you have been banished to the most distant land under the heavens, from there the LORD your God will gather you and bring you

[a] 3 Or *will bring you back from captivity*

back. [5]He will bring you to the
land that belonged to your ancestors, and you will take possession
of it. He will make you more prosperous and numerous than your
ancestors. [6]The LORD your God
will circumcise your hearts and
the hearts of your descendants,
so that you may love him with all
your heart and with all your soul,
and live. [7]The LORD your God will
put all these curses on your enemies who hate and persecute you.
[8]You will again obey the LORD and
follow all his commands I am giving you today. [9]Then the LORD your
God will make you most prosperous in all the work of your hands
and in the fruit of your womb, the
young of your livestock and the
crops of your land. The LORD will
again delight in you and make you
prosperous, just as he delighted in
your ancestors, [10]if you obey the
LORD your God and keep his commands and decrees that are written in this Book of the Law and
turn to the LORD your God with all
your heart and with all your soul.
Dt 11:26; Ps 126:4; Jer 32:39

The Offer of Life or Death

[11]Now what I am commanding
you today is not too difficult for
you or beyond your reach. [12]It is
not up in heaven, so that you have
to ask, "Who will ascend into heav-
en to get it and proclaim it to us
so we may obey it?" [13]Nor is it beyond the sea, so that you have to
ask, "Who will cross the sea to get
it and proclaim it to us so we may
obey it?" [14]No, the word is very
near you; it is in your mouth and
in your heart so you may obey it.
Isa 45:19,23; Ro 10:6

[15]See, I set before you today life
and prosperity, death and destruction. [16]For I command you today
to love the LORD your God, to walk
in obedience to him, and to keep
his commands, decrees and laws;
then you will live and increase,
and the LORD your God will bless
you in the land you are entering
to possess. Dt 4:1; 11:26

[17]But if your heart turns away
and you are not obedient, and if
you are drawn away to bow down
to other gods and worship them,
[18]I declare to you this day that you
will certainly be destroyed. You
will not live long in the land you
are crossing the Jordan to enter
and possess. Dt 8:19

[19]This day I call the heavens and
the earth as witnesses against you
that I have set before you life and
death, blessings and curses. Now
choose life, so that you and your
children may live [20]and that you
may love the LORD your God, listen
to his voice, and hold fast to him.
For the LORD is your life, and he will
give you many years in the land he
swore to give to your fathers, Abraham, Isaac and Jacob. Dt 4:26; Ps 27:1

Joshua to Succeed Moses

31 Then Moses went out and
spoke these words to all Israel: [2]"I am now a hundred and

twenty years old and I am no longer able to lead you. The LORD has
said to me, 'You shall not cross the
Jordan.' 3The LORD your God himself will cross over ahead of you.
He will destroy these nations before you, and you will take possession of their land. Joshua also
will cross over ahead of you, as
the LORD said. 4And the LORD will
do to them what he did to Sihon
and Og, the kings of the Amorites,
whom he destroyed along with
their land. 5The LORD will deliver
them to you, and you must do to
them all that I have commanded
you. 6Be strong and courageous.
Do not be afraid or terrified because of them, for the LORD your
God goes with you; he will never
leave you nor forsake you."

Dt 3:23,26; 7:2; Jos 10:25

7Then Moses summoned Joshua and said to him in the presence of all Israel, "Be strong and
courageous, for you must go with
this people into the land that the
LORD swore to their ancestors to
give them, and you must divide it
among them as their inheritance.
8The LORD himself goes before you
and will be with you; he will never
leave you nor forsake you. Do not
be afraid; do not be discouraged."

Dt 1:38; 3:28; Ex 13:21

Public Reading of the Law

9So Moses wrote down this law
and gave it to the Levitical priests,
who carried the ark of the covenant of the LORD, and to all the
elders of Israel. 10Then Moses
commanded them: "At the end of
every seven years, in the year for
canceling debts, during the Festival of Tabernacles, 11when all Israel comes to appear before the
LORD your God at the place he will
choose, you shall read this law before them in their hearing. 12As-
semble the people — men, women
and children, and the foreigners
residing in your towns — so they
can listen and learn to fear the
LORD your God and follow carefully all the words of this law. 13Their
children, who do not know this
law, must hear it and learn to fear
the LORD your God as long as you
live in the land you are crossing
the Jordan to possess."

Nu 4:15; Dt 15:1; Jos 8:34-35

Israel's Rebellion Predicted

14The LORD said to Moses, "Now
the day of your death is near. Call
Joshua and present yourselves at
the tent of meeting, where I will
commission him." So Moses and
Joshua came and presented themselves at the tent of meeting.

Nu 27:13; Dt 32:49-50

15Then the LORD appeared at
the tent in a pillar of cloud, and
the cloud stood over the entrance
to the tent. 16And the LORD said to
Moses: "You are going to rest with
your ancestors, and these people
will soon prostitute themselves to
the foreign gods of the land they
are entering. They will forsake me
and break the covenant I made

with them. 17And in that day I will become angry with them and forsake them; I will hide my face from them, and they will be destroyed. Many disasters and calamities will come on them, and in that day they will ask, 'Have not these disasters come on us because our God is not with us?' 18And I will certainly hide my face in that day because of all their wickedness in turning to other gods.

Ex 33:9; Nu 14:42; Jdg 10:6,13

19"Now write down this song and teach it to the Israelites and have them sing it, so that it may be a witness for me against them. 20When I have brought them into the land flowing with milk and honey, the land I promised on oath to their ancestors, and when they eat their fill and thrive, they will turn to other gods and worship them, rejecting me and breaking my covenant. 21And when many disasters and calamities come on them, this song will testify against them, because it will not be forgotten by their descendants. I know what they are disposed to do, even before I bring them into the land I promised them on oath." 22So Moses wrote down this song that day and taught it to the Israelites.

Dt 32:15-17; Jn 2:24-25

23The LORD gave this command to Joshua son of Nun: "Be strong and courageous, for you will bring the Israelites into the land I promised them on oath, and I myself will be with you." Jos 1:6

24After Moses finished writing in a book the words of this law from beginning to end, 25he gave this command to the Levites who carried the ark of the covenant of the LORD: 26"Take this Book of the Law and place it beside the ark of the covenant of the LORD your God. There it will remain as a witness against you. 27For I know how rebellious and stiff-necked you are. If you have been rebellious against the LORD while I am still alive and with you, how much more will you rebel after I die! 28Assemble before me all the elders of your tribes and all your officials, so that I can speak these words in their hearing and call the heavens and the earth to testify against them. 29For I know that after my death you are sure to become utterly corrupt and to turn from the way I have commanded you. In days to come, disaster will fall on you because you will do evil in the sight of the LORD and arouse his anger by what your hands have made."

Dt 4:26; 9:6,24; 32:1

The Song of Moses

30And Moses recited the words of this song from beginning to end in the hearing of the whole assembly of Israel:

32 Listen, you heavens, and I
will speak;
hear, you earth, the words of
my mouth. Dt 4:26; Isa 1:2

2 Let my teaching fall like rain
and my words descend like dew,
like showers on new grass,
like abundant rain on tender plants. Isa 55:11

3 I will proclaim the name of the LORD. Ex 33:19
Oh, praise the greatness of our God! Dt 3:24
4 He is the Rock, his works are perfect, 2Sa 22:31
and all his ways are just.
A faithful God who does no wrong,
upright and just is he. Dt 7:9

5 They are corrupt and not his children;
to their shame they are a warped and crooked generation. Dt 31:29; Mt 17:17
6 Is this the way you repay the LORD,
you foolish and unwise people? Ps 74:2; 116:12
Is he not your Father, your Creator,[a]
who made you and formed you? Dt 1:31; Isa 63:16

7 Remember the days of old;
consider the generations long past. Ps 44:1; Job 8:8
Ask your father and he will tell you,
your elders, and they will explain to you. Ex 13:14
8 When the Most High gave the nations their inheritance,
when he divided all mankind,
he set up boundaries for the peoples
according to the number of the sons of Israel.[b] Ge 11:8; Ac 17:26
9 For the LORD's portion is his people,
Jacob his allotted inheritance. Jer 10:16; 1Ki 8:51,53

10 In a desert land he found him,
in a barren and howling waste. Jer 2:6
He shielded him and cared for him;
he guarded him as the apple of his eye, Ps 17:8; Zec 2:8
11 like an eagle that stirs up its nest
and hovers over its young,
that spreads its wings to catch them
and carries them aloft. Ex 19:4
12 The LORD alone led him;
no foreign god was with him. Dt 4:35; Isa 43:12

13 He made him ride on the heights of the land Isa 58:14
and fed him with the fruit of the fields.
He nourished him with honey from the rock,
and with oil from the flinty crag, Dt 8:8; Job 29:6

[a] 6 Or *Father, who bought you*
[b] 8 Masoretic Text; Dead Sea Scrolls (see also Septuagint) *sons of God*

14 with curds and milk from herd
and flock
and with fattened lambs and
goats,
with choice rams of Bashan
and the finest kernels of
wheat.
You drank the foaming
blood of the grape.
Ps 81:16; 147:14; Ge 49:11

15 Jeshurun[a] grew fat and kicked;
filled with food, they became
heavy and sleek. Dt 31:20
They abandoned the God who
made them
and rejected the Rock their
Savior. Isa 1:4,28
16 They made him jealous with
their foreign gods
and angered him with
their detestable idols.
1Co 10:22; Ps 78:58
17 They sacrificed to false gods,
which are not God —
gods they had not known,
gods that recently
appeared,
gods your ancestors did not
fear. Dt 28:64; Jdg 5:8
18 You deserted the Rock, who
fathered you;
you forgot the God who gave
you birth. Ps 106:21; Isa 17:10
19 The LORD saw this and rejected
them Jer 44:21-23
because he was angered by
his sons and daughters.
Ps 106:40
20 "I will hide my face from
them," he said, Dt 31:17,29
"and see what their end will
be;
for they are a perverse
generation,
children who are unfaithful.
21 They made me jealous by what
is no god
and angered me with their
worthless idols. 1Ki 16:13,26
I will make them envious by
those who are not a
people;
I will make them angry by
a nation that has no
understanding. Ro 10:19
22 For a fire will be kindled by my
wrath,
one that burns down to the
realm of the dead
below.
It will devour the earth and its
harvests
and set afire the foundations
of the mountains.
Jer 15:14; La 4:11

23 "I will heap calamities on
them
and spend my arrows against
them. Dt 29:21; Ps 18:14
24 I will send wasting famine
against them,
consuming pestilence and
deadly plague; Dt 28:22
I will send against them the
fangs of wild beasts,
Lev 26:22
the venom of vipers that
glide in the dust. Am 5:18-19

[a] 15 *Jeshurun* means *the upright one*, that is, Israel.

25 In the street the sword
will make them
childless;
in their homes terror will
reign.
The young men and young
women will perish,
the infants and those with
gray hair. 2Ch 36:17; Eze 7:15
26 I said I would scatter them
and erase their name from
human memory, Dt 4:27
27 but I dreaded the taunt of the
enemy,
lest the adversary
misunderstand
and say, 'Our hand has
triumphed;
the LORD has not done all
this.'" Isa 10:13

28 They are a nation without
sense,
there is no discernment in
them. Isa 1:3; 27:11
29 If only they were wise and
would understand this
and discern what their end
will be! Ps 81:13
30 How could one man chase a
thousand,
or two put ten thousand to
flight,
unless their Rock had sold
them,
unless the LORD had given
them up? Lev 26:8; Ps 44:12
31 For their rock is not like our
Rock,
as even our enemies
concede. Ge 49:24
32 Their vine comes from the vine
of Sodom
and from the fields of
Gomorrah.
Their grapes are filled with
poison,
and their clusters with
bitterness. Dt 29:18
33 Their wine is the venom of
serpents,
the deadly poison of cobras.
Ps 58:4

34 "Have I not kept this in reserve
and sealed it in my vaults?
35 It is mine to avenge; I will
repay.
In due time their foot will
slip;
their day of disaster is near
and their doom rushes
upon them."
Ro 12:19; Heb 10:30; Eze 7:8-9

36 The LORD will vindicate his
people
and relent concerning his
servants
when he sees their strength is
gone
and no one is left, slave or
free.[a] Ps 135:14; Joel 2:14
37 He will say: "Now where are
their gods,
the rock they took refuge in,
Jdg 10:14; Jer 2:28
38 the gods who ate the fat of
their sacrifices
and drank the wine of their
drink offerings?

[a] 36 Or *and they are without a ruler or leader*

Let them rise up to
help you!
Let them give you shelter!

39 "See now that I myself am he!
There is no god besides me.
Isa 41:4; 45:5
I put to death and I bring to
life,
I have wounded and I will
heal,
and no one can deliver out of
my hand. Ps 50:22; Hos 6:1
40 I lift my hand to heaven and
solemnly swear:
As surely as I live forever,
41 when I sharpen my flashing
sword
and my hand grasps it in
judgment, Isa 66:16
I will take vengeance on my
adversaries
and repay those who hate
me. Jer 50:29
42 I will make my arrows drunk
with blood,
while my sword devours
flesh:
the blood of the slain and the
captives,
the heads of the enemy
leaders." Jer 12:12; 46:10,14
43 Rejoice, you nations, with his
people,[a,b] Ro 15:10
for he will avenge the blood
of his servants;
he will take vengeance on his
enemies
and make atonement for
his land and people.
Ps 85:1; Rev 19:2

44 Moses came with Joshua[c] son
of Nun and spoke all the words
of this song in the hearing of the
people. 45 When Moses finished re-
citing all these words to all Israel,
46 he said to them, "Take to heart
all the words I have solemnly declared to you this day, so that you
may command your children to
obey carefully all the words of
this law. 47 They are not just idle
words for you — they are your life.
By them you will live long in the
land you are crossing the Jordan
to possess." Eze 40:4; Dt 30:20

Moses to Die on Mount Nebo

48 On that same day the LORD
told Moses, 49 "Go up into the Abarim Range to Mount Nebo in Moab,
across from Jericho, and view Canaan, the land I am giving the Israelites as their own possession.
50 There on the mountain that you
have climbed you will die and be
gathered to your people, just as
your brother Aaron died on Mount
Hor and was gathered to his people.
51 This is because both of you broke
faith with me in the presence of the
Israelites at the waters of Meribah
Kadesh in the Desert of Zin and because you did not uphold my holiness among the Israelites. 52 Therefore, you will see the land only
from a distance; you will not enter

[a] 43 Or *Make his people rejoice, you nations*
[b] 43 Masoretic Text; Dead Sea Scrolls (see also Septuagint) *people, / and let all the angels worship him, /*
[c] 44 Hebrew *Hoshea*, a variant of *Joshua*

the land I am giving to the people of Israel." Ge 25:8; Nu 20:11-13; 27:12

Moses Blesses the Tribes

33 This is the blessing that Moses the man of God pronounced on the Israelites before his death. 2 He said: Jos 14:6

"The LORD came from Sinai
and dawned over them from Seir;
he shone forth from Mount Paran. Ps 50:2; 68:8; Hab 3:3
He came with[a] myriads of holy ones
from the south, from his mountain slopes.[b]
Da 17:10; Rev 5:11
3 Surely it is you who love the people;
all the holy ones are in your hand.
At your feet they all bow down,
and from you receive instruction, Lk 10:39
4 the law that Moses gave us,
the possession of the assembly of Jacob.
Ps 119:111; Jn 1:17
5 He was king over Jeshurun[c]
when the leaders of the people assembled,
along with the tribes of Israel. Nu 23:21

6 "Let Reuben live and not die,
nor[d] his people be few."

7 And this he said about Judah:

"Hear, LORD, the cry of Judah;
bring him to his people.
With his own hands he defends his cause.
Oh, be his help against his foes!" Ge 49:10

8 About Levi he said:

"Your Thummim and Urim belong
to your faithful servant.
Ex 28:30
You tested him at Massah;
you contended with him at the waters of Meribah.
Ex 17:7
9 He said of his father and mother,
'I have no regard for them.'
He did not recognize his brothers
or acknowledge his own children,
but he watched over your word
and guarded your covenant.
Ex 32:26-29; Mal 2:5
10 He teaches your precepts to Jacob
and your law to Israel.
He offers incense before you
and whole burnt offerings on your altar.
Ps 51:19; Lev 10:11; Ne 8:18
11 Bless all his skills, LORD,
and be pleased with the work of his hands.
Strike down those who rise against him,
his foes till they rise no more."

[a] 2 Or *from* [b] 2 The meaning of the Hebrew for this phrase is uncertain. [c] 5 *Jeshurun* means *the upright one,* that is, Israel; also in verse 26. [d] 6 Or *but let*

12 About Benjamin he said:

"Let the beloved of the LORD
rest secure in him,
for he shields him all day
long,
and the one the LORD loves
rests between his
shoulders." Ex 28:12; Dt 12:10

13 About Joseph he said:

"May the LORD bless his land
with the precious dew from
heaven above
and with the deep waters
that lie below;
Ge 27:28; 49:25
14 with the best the sun brings
forth
and the finest the moon can
yield;
15 with the choicest gifts of the
ancient mountains
and the fruitfulness of the
everlasting hills; Hab 3:6
16 with the best gifts of the earth
and its fullness
and the favor of him who
dwelt in the burning
bush.
Let all these rest on the head of
Joseph,
on the brow of the prince
among[a] his brothers.
Ex 3:2
17 In majesty he is like a firstborn
bull;
his horns are the horns of a
wild ox.
With them he will gore the
nations,
even those at the ends
of the earth.
Nu 23:22; 1Ki 22:11; Ps 44:5
Such are the ten thousands of
Ephraim;
such are the thousands of
Manasseh."

18 About Zebulun he said:

"Rejoice, Zebulun, in your
going out,
and you, Issachar, in your
tents. Ge 49:13-15
19 They will summon peoples to
the mountain
and there offer the sacrifices
of the righteous;
Ps 4:5; Isa 2:3
they will feast on the
abundance of the seas,
on the treasures hidden in
the sand." Isa 60:5,11

20 About Gad he said:

"Blessed is he who enlarges
Gad's domain!
Gad lives there like a lion,
tearing at arm or head.
Ge 30:11; 49:19
21 He chose the best land for
himself;
the leader's portion was kept
for him. Nu 32:1-5,31-32
When the heads of the people
assembled,
he carried out the LORD's
righteous will,
and his judgments
concerning Israel." Jos 4:12

[a] 16 Or *of the one separated from*

22 About Dan he said:

"Dan is a lion's cub,
springing out of Bashan."
Ge 49:16

23 About Naphtali he said:

"Naphtali is abounding with
the favor of the LORD
and is full of his blessing;
he will inherit southward to
the lake." Ge 30:8

24 About Asher he said:

"Most blessed of sons is Asher;
let him be favored by his
brothers,
and let him bathe his feet in
oil. Ge 49:21; Job 29:6
25 The bolts of your gates will be
iron and bronze, Ne 3:3
and your strength will equal
your days. Dt 4:40

26 "There is no one like the God of
Jeshurun,
who rides across the heavens
to help you
and on the clouds in his
majesty. Ex 15:11; 2Sa 22:10
27 The eternal God is your refuge,
and underneath are the
everlasting arms. Ps 90:1
He will drive out your enemies
before you,
saying, 'Destroy them!'
Dt 7:2; Jos 24:18
28 So Israel will live in safety;
Jacob will dwell[a] secure
in a land of grain and new wine,
where the heavens drop dew.
Ge 27:28; Jer 23:6
29 Blessed are you, Israel!
Who is like you,
a people saved by the LORD?
2Sa 7:23; Ps 144:15
He is your shield and helper
and your glorious sword.
Your enemies will cower before
you,
and you will tread on their
heights." Ex 18:4; Ps 115:9-11

The Death of Moses

34 Then Moses climbed Mount
Nebo from the plains of
Moab to the top of Pisgah, across
from Jericho. There the LORD
showed him the whole land —
from Gilead to Dan, 2 all of Naphtali, the territory of Ephraim and
Manasseh, all the land of Judah
as far as the Mediterranean Sea,
3 the Negev and the whole region
from the Valley of Jericho, the City
of Palms, as far as Zoar. 4 Then the
LORD said to him, "This is the land
I promised on oath to Abraham,
Isaac and Jacob when I said, 'I will
give it to your descendants.' I have
let you see it with your eyes, but
you will not cross over into it."
Ge 12:7; Dt 32:52; 2Ch 28:15

5 And Moses the servant of the
LORD died there in Moab, as the
LORD had said. 6 He buried him[b]
in Moab, in the valley opposite
Beth Peor, but to this day no one
knows where his grave is. 7 Moses
was a hundred and twenty years
old when he died, yet his eyes

[a] 28 Septuagint; Hebrew *Jacob's spring is*
[b] 6 Or *He was buried*

were not weak nor his strength
gone. 8The Israelites grieved for
Moses in the plains of Moab thirty days, until the time of weeping
and mourning was over. Jos 1:1-2; Jude 1:9; Ge 27:1

9Now Joshua son of Nun was
filled with the spirit[a] of wisdom
because Moses had laid his hands
on him. So the Israelites listened
to him and did what the LORD had
commanded Moses. Nu 27:18,23; Isa 11:2

10Since then, no prophet has ris-
en in Israel like Moses, whom the
LORD knew face to face, 11who did
all those signs and wonders the
LORD sent him to do in Egypt —
to Pharaoh and to all his officials
and to his whole land. 12For no one
has ever shown the mighty power
or performed the awesome deeds
that Moses did in the sight of all
Israel. Dt 18:15,18; Ex 33:11; Nu 12:6,8

[a] 9 Or *Spirit*

JOSHUA

Joshua Installed as Leader

1 After the death of Moses the servant of the LORD, the LORD said to Joshua son of Nun, Moses' aide: 2"Moses my servant is dead. Now then, you and all these people, get ready to cross the Jordan River into the land I am about to give to them — to the Israelites. 3I will give you every place where you set your foot, as I promised Moses. 4Your territory will extend from the desert to Lebanon, and from the great river, the Euphrates — all the Hittite country — to the Mediterranean Sea in the west. 5No one will be able to stand against you all the days of your life. As I was with Moses, so I will be with you; I will never leave you nor forsake you. 6Be strong and courageous, because you will lead these people to inherit the land I swore to their ancestors to give them. Dt 7:24; 11:24; 31:6-8

7"Be strong and very courageous. Be careful to obey all the law my servant Moses gave you; do not turn from it to the right or to the left, that you may be successful wherever you go. 8Keep this Book of the Law always on your lips; meditate on it day and night, so that you may be careful to do everything written in it. Then you will be prosperous and successful. 9Have I not commanded you? Be strong and courageous. Do not be afraid; do not be discouraged, for the LORD your God will be with you wherever you go."

Dt 31:23; Ps 1:1-3; Jer 1:8

10So Joshua ordered the officers of the people: 11"Go through the camp and tell the people, 'Get your provisions ready. Three days from now you will cross the Jordan here to go in and take possession of the land the LORD your God is giving you for your own.'" Jos 3:2; Joel 3:2

12But to the Reubenites, the Gadites and the half-tribe of Manasseh, Joshua said, 13"Remember the command that Moses the servant of the LORD gave you after he said, 'The LORD your God will give you rest by giving you this land.' 14Your wives, your children and your livestock may stay in the land that Moses gave you east of the Jordan, but all your fighting men, ready for battle, must cross over ahead of your fellow Israelites. You are to help them 15until the LORD gives them rest, as he has done for you, and until they too have taken possession of the land the LORD your God is giving them. After that, you may go back and occupy your own land, which Moses the servant of the LORD gave you east of the Jordan toward the sunrise." Nu 32:20-22; Jos 22:1-4; Dt 3:18-20

[16]Then they answered Joshua,
"Whatever you have commanded
us we will do, and wherever you
send us we will go. [17]Just as we fully obeyed Moses, so we will obey
you. Only may the LORD your God
be with you as he was with Moses. [18]Whoever rebels against your
word and does not obey it, whatever you may command them, will
be put to death. Only be strong
and courageous!" ver 5,9; Nu 27:20

Rahab and the Spies

2 Then Joshua son of Nun secretly sent two spies from
Shittim. "Go, look over the land,"
he said, "especially Jericho." So
they went and entered the house
of a prostitute named Rahab and
stayed there. Heb 11:31; Jas 2:25

[2]The king of Jericho was told,
"Look, some of the Israelites have
come here tonight to spy out the
land." [3]So the king of Jericho sent
this message to Rahab: "Bring out
the men who came to you and entered your house, because they
have come to spy out the whole
land."

[4]But the woman had taken the
two men and hidden them. She
said, "Yes, the men came to me,
but I did not know where they
had come from. [5]At dusk, when
it was time to close the city gate,
they left. I don't know which way
they went. Go after them quickly. You may catch up with them."
[6](But she had taken them up to
the roof and hidden them under
the stalks of flax she had laid out
on the roof.) [7]So the men set out
in pursuit of the spies on the road
that leads to the fords of the Jordan, and as soon as the pursuers
had gone out, the gate was shut.
2Sa 17:19-20; Nu 22:1; Jos 6:22

[8]Before the spies lay down for
the night, she went up on the roof
[9]and said to them, "I know that
the LORD has given you this land
and that a great fear of you has
fallen on us, so that all who live
in this country are melting in fear
because of you. [10]We have heard
how the LORD dried up the water of the Red Sea[a] for you when
you came out of Egypt, and what
you did to Sihon and Og, the two
kings of the Amorites east of the
Jordan, whom you completely
destroyed.[b] [11]When we heard of
it, our hearts melted in fear and
everyone's courage failed because
of you, for the LORD your God is
God in heaven above and on the
earth below.
Ex 14:21; 23:27; Nu 21:21,24,34-35

[12]"Now then, please swear to me
by the LORD that you will show
kindness to my family, because I
have shown kindness to you. Give
me a sure sign [13]that you will spare
the lives of my father and mother, my brothers and sisters, and
all who belong to them — and that
you will save us from death."

[a] *10* Or *the Sea of Reeds* [b] *10* The Hebrew term refers to the irrevocable giving over of things or persons to the LORD, often by totally destroying them.

14"Our lives for your lives!" the men assured her. "If you don't tell what we are doing, we will treat you kindly and faithfully when the LORD gives us the land."

Jdg 1:24; Mt 5:7

15So she let them down by a rope through the window, for the house she lived in was part of the city wall. 16She said to them, "Go to the hills so the pursuers will not find you. Hide yourselves there three days until they return, and then go on your way."

Ac 9:25; Jer 38:6,11

17Now the men had said to her, "This oath you made us swear will not be binding on us 18unless, when we enter the land, you have tied this scarlet cord in the window through which you let us down, and unless you have brought your father and mother, your brothers and all your family into your house. 19If any of them go outside your house into the street, their blood will be on their own heads; we will not be responsible. As for those who are in the house with you, their blood will be on our head if a hand is laid on them. 20But if you tell what we are doing, we will be released from the oath you made us swear."

Ge 24:8; Mt 27:25; Eze 33:4

21"Agreed," she replied. "Let it be as you say."

So she sent them away, and they departed. And she tied the scarlet cord in the window.

22When they left, they went into the hills and stayed there three days, until the pursuers had searched all along the road and returned without finding them. 23Then the two men started back. They went down out of the hills, forded the river and came to Joshua son of Nun and told him everything that had happened to them. 24They said to Joshua, "The LORD has surely given the whole land into our hands; all the people are melting in fear because of us."

ver 9

Crossing the Jordan

3 Early in the morning Joshua and all the Israelites set out from Shittim and went to the Jordan, where they camped before crossing over. 2After three days the officers went throughout the camp, 3giving orders to the people: "When you see the ark of the covenant of the LORD your God, and the Levitical priests carrying it, you are to move out from your positions and follow it. 4Then you will know which way to go, since you have never been this way before. But keep a distance of about two thousand cubits[a] between you and the ark; do not go near it."

Dt 31:9; Jos 2:1; 1:11

5Joshua told the people, "Consecrate yourselves, for tomorrow the LORD will do amazing things among you."

Ex 19:10,14; Jos 7:13

6Joshua said to the priests, "Take up the ark of the covenant

[a] 4 That is, about 3,000 feet or about 900 meters

and pass on ahead of the people."
So they took it up and went ahead
of them.

7And the LORD said to Joshua,
"Today I will begin to exalt you
in the eyes of all Israel, so they
may know that I am with you as
I was with Moses. 8Tell the priests
who carry the ark of the covenant:
'When you reach the edge of the
Jordan's waters, go and stand in
the river.'" Jos 1:5; 1Ch 29:25

9Joshua said to the Israelites,
"Come here and listen to the
words of the LORD your God. 10This
is how you will know that the living God is among you and that
he will certainly drive out before
you the Canaanites, Hittites, Hivites, Perizzites, Girgashites, Amorites and Jebusites. 11See, the ark
of the covenant of the Lord of all
the earth will go into the Jordan
ahead of you. 12Now then, choose
twelve men from the tribes of Israel, one from each tribe. 13And as
soon as the priests who carry the
ark of the LORD — the Lord of all
the earth — set foot in the Jordan,
its waters flowing downstream
will be cut off and stand up in a
heap." Dt 5:26; Jos 4:2,4; Zec 6:5

14So when the people broke
camp to cross the Jordan, the
priests carrying the ark of the
covenant went ahead of them.
15Now the Jordan is at flood stage
all during harvest. Yet as soon as
the priests who carried the ark
reached the Jordan and their feet
touched the water's edge, 16the water from upstream stopped flowing. It piled up in a heap a great
distance away, at a town called
Adam in the vicinity of Zarethan,
while the water flowing down to
the Sea of the Arabah (that is, the
Dead Sea) was completely cut off.
So the people crossed over opposite Jericho. 17The priests who carried the ark of the covenant of the
LORD stopped in the middle of the
Jordan and stood on dry ground,
while all Israel passed by until the
whole nation had completed the
crossing on dry ground.

Ex 14:22,29; Jos 4:18; Ac 7:44-45

4 When the whole nation had
finished crossing the Jordan,
the LORD said to Joshua, 2"Choose
twelve men from among the people, one from each tribe, 3and tell
them to take up twelve stones
from the middle of the Jordan,
from right where the priests are
standing, and carry them over
with you and put them down at
the place where you stay tonight."

Dt 27:2; Jos 3:12; ver 20

4So Joshua called together the
twelve men he had appointed
from the Israelites, one from each
tribe, 5and said to them, "Go over
before the ark of the LORD your
God into the middle of the Jordan.
Each of you is to take up a stone
on his shoulder, according to the
number of the tribes of the Israelites, 6to serve as a sign among you.
In the future, when your children
ask you, 'What do these stones
mean?' 7tell them that the flow of

the Jordan was cut off before the
ark of the covenant of the LORD.
When it crossed the Jordan, the
waters of the Jordan were cut off.
These stones are to be a memorial
to the people of Israel forever."

Ex 12:26; 13:14; Jos 3:13

8So the Israelites did as Joshua commanded them. They took
twelve stones from the middle
of the Jordan, according to the
number of the tribes of the Israelites, as the LORD had told Joshua;
and they carried them over with
them to their camp, where they
put them down. 9Joshua set up
the twelve stones that had been[a]
in the middle of the Jordan at the
spot where the priests who carried
the ark of the covenant had stood.
And they are there to this day.

Ex 28:21; 1Sa 7:12

10Now the priests who carried
the ark remained standing in the
middle of the Jordan until everything the LORD had commanded
Joshua was done by the people,
just as Moses had directed Joshua.
The people hurried over, 11and as
soon as all of them had crossed,
the ark of the LORD and the priests
came to the other side while the
people watched. 12The men of
Reuben, Gad and the half-tribe of
Manasseh crossed over, ready for
battle, in front of the Israelites, as
Moses had directed them. 13About
forty thousand armed for battle
crossed over before the LORD to
the plains of Jericho for war.

Ex 13:18; Nu 32:27

14That day the LORD exalted
Joshua in the sight of all Israel;
and they stood in awe of him all
the days of his life, just as they
had stood in awe of Moses. Jos 3:7

15Then the LORD said to Joshua,
16"Command the priests carrying the ark of the covenant law to
come up out of the Jordan."

Ex 25:22

17So Joshua commanded the
priests, "Come up out of the Jordan."

18And the priests came up out
of the river carrying the ark of
the covenant of the LORD. No
sooner had they set their feet on
the dry ground than the waters of
the Jordan returned to their place
and ran at flood stage as before.

Jos 3:15

19On the tenth day of the first
month the people went up from
the Jordan and camped at Gilgal
on the eastern border of Jericho.
20And Joshua set up at Gilgal the
twelve stones they had taken out
of the Jordan. 21He said to the Israelites, "In the future when your
descendants ask their parents,
'What do these stones mean?'
22tell them, 'Israel crossed the Jordan on dry ground.' 23For the LORD
your God dried up the Jordan before you until you had crossed
over. The LORD your God did to the
Jordan what he had done to the
Red Sea[b] when he dried it up before us until we had crossed over.

[a] 9 Or *Joshua also set up twelve stones*
[b] 23 Or *the Sea of Reeds*

24He did this so that all the peoples
of the earth might know that the
hand of the LORD is powerful and
so that you might always fear the
LORD your God."

Ex 15:16; 1Ki 8:42-43; Ps 106:8

5

5 Now when all the Amorite
kings west of the Jordan and
all the Canaanite kings along the
coast heard how the LORD had
dried up the Jordan before the
Israelites until they[a] had crossed
over, their hearts melted in fear
and they no longer had the courage to face the Israelites.

Nu 13:29; Jos 2:9-11

Circumcision and Passover at Gilgal

2At that time the LORD said to
Joshua, "Make flint knives and
circumcise the Israelites again."
3So Joshua made flint knives and
circumcised the Israelites at Gibeath Haaraloth.[b] Ex 4:25
4Now this is why he did so: All
those who came out of Egypt —
all the men of military age — died
in the wilderness on the way after
leaving Egypt. 5All the people that
came out had been circumcised,
but all the people born in the wilderness during the journey from
Egypt had not. 6The Israelites
had moved about in the wilderness forty years until all the men
who were of military age when
they left Egypt had died, since
they had not obeyed the LORD.
For the LORD had sworn to them
that they would not see the land
he had solemnly promised their
ancestors to give us, a land flowing with milk and honey. 7So he
raised up their sons in their place,
and these were the ones Joshua
circumcised. They were still uncircumcised because they had
not been circumcised on the way.
8And after the whole nation had
been circumcised, they remained
where they were in camp until
they were healed.

Dt 2:7,14; Nu 14:23,29-35

9Then the LORD said to Joshua,
"Today I have rolled away the reproach of Egypt from you." So the
place has been called Gilgal[c] to
this day.
10On the evening of the fourteenth day of the month, while
camped at Gilgal on the plains of
Jericho, the Israelites celebrated
the Passover. 11The day after the
Passover, that very day, they ate
some of the produce of the land:
unleavened bread and roasted
grain. 12The manna stopped the
day after[d] they ate this food from
the land; there was no longer any
manna for the Israelites, but that
year they ate the produce of Canaan. Ex 12:6; 16:35; Nu 15:19

The Fall of Jericho

13Now when Joshua was near
Jericho, he looked up and saw a
man standing in front of him with
a drawn sword in his hand. Joshua

[a] 1 Another textual tradition *we*
[b] 3 *Gibeath Haaraloth* means *the hill of foreskins.*
[c] 9 *Gilgal* sounds like the Hebrew for *roll.*
[d] 12 Or *the day*

went up to him and asked, “Are
you for us or for our enemies?”
Ge 18:2; 32:24

14 “Neither,” he replied, “but as
commander of the army of the
LORD I have now come.” Then Joshua fell facedown to the ground in
reverence, and asked him, “What
message does my Lord[a] have for
his servant?” Ge 17:3; 19:1

15 The commander of the LORD’s
army replied, “Take off your sandals, for the place where you are
standing is holy.” And Joshua
did so. Ex 3:5; Ac 7:33

6 Now the gates of Jericho were
securely barred because of the
Israelites. No one went out and no
one came in. Jos 24:11

2 Then the LORD said to Joshua,
“See, I have delivered Jericho into
your hands, along with its king and
its fighting men. 3 March around
the city once with all the armed
men. Do this for six days. 4 Have
seven priests carry trumpets of
rams’ horns in front of the ark. On
the seventh day, march around the
city seven times, with the priests
blowing the trumpets. 5 When you
hear them sound a long blast on
the trumpets, have the whole army
give a loud shout; then the wall of
the city will collapse and the army
will go up, everyone straight in.”
Dt 7:24; Lev 25:9; Isa 42:13

6 So Joshua son of Nun called the
priests and said to them, “Take
up the ark of the covenant of the
LORD and have seven priests carry trumpets in front of it.” 7 And
he ordered the army, “Advance!
March around the city, with an
armed guard going ahead of the
ark of the LORD.” Ex 14:15; 1Sa 4:3

8 When Joshua had spoken to
the people, the seven priests carrying the seven trumpets before
the LORD went forward, blowing
their trumpets, and the ark of the
LORD’s covenant followed them.
9 The armed guard marched ahead
of the priests who blew the trumpets, and the rear guard followed
the ark. All this time the trumpets
were sounding. 10 But Joshua had
commanded the army, “Do not give
a war cry, do not raise your voices,
do not say a word until the day I
tell you to shout. Then shout!” 11 So
he had the ark of the LORD carried
around the city, circling it once.
Then the army returned to camp
and spent the night there. Isa 52:12

12 Joshua got up early the next
morning and the priests took up
the ark of the LORD. 13 The seven
priests carrying the seven trumpets went forward, marching before the ark of the LORD and blowing the trumpets. The armed men
went ahead of them and the rear
guard followed the ark of the
LORD, while the trumpets kept
sounding. 14 So on the second day
they marched around the city
once and returned to the camp.
They did this for six days.

15 On the seventh day, they got up
at daybreak and marched around
the city seven times in the same

[a] 14 Or *lord*

manner, except that on that day
they circled the city seven times.
16 The seventh time around, when
the priests sounded the trumpet blast, Joshua commanded the
army, "Shout! For the LORD has
given you the city! 17 The city and
all that is in it are to be devoted[a]
to the LORD. Only Rahab the prostitute and all who are with her
in her house shall be spared, because she hid the spies we sent.
18 But keep away from the devoted
things, so that you will not bring
about your own destruction by
taking any of them. Otherwise you
will make the camp of Israel liable
to destruction and bring trouble
on it. 19 All the silver and gold and
the articles of bronze and iron are
sacred to the LORD and must go
into his treasury." Lev 27:28; Jos 2:4; 7:1
20 When the trumpets sound-
ed, the army shouted, and at the
sound of the trumpet, when the
men gave a loud shout, the wall
collapsed; so everyone charged
straight in, and they took the city.
21 They devoted the city to the LORD
and destroyed with the sword every living thing in it — men and
women, young and old, cattle,
sheep and donkeys. Dt 20:16; Am 2:2
22 Joshua said to the two men
who had spied out the land, "Go
into the prostitute's house and
bring her out and all who belong
to her, in accordance with your
oath to her." 23 So the young men
who had done the spying went in
and brought out Rahab, her father
and mother, her brothers and sisters and all who belonged to her.
They brought out her entire family and put them in a place outside
the camp of Israel. Jos 2:14; Heb 11:31
24 Then they burned the whole
city and everything in it, but they
put the silver and gold and the articles of bronze and iron into the
treasury of the LORD's house. 25 But
Joshua spared Rahab the prostitute, with her family and all who
belonged to her, because she hid
the men Joshua had sent as spies
to Jericho — and she lives among
the Israelites to this day. Jdg 1:25
26 At that time Joshua pronounced this solemn oath:
"Cursed before the LORD is the one
who undertakes to rebuild this
city, Jericho:

"At the cost of his firstborn son
he will lay its foundations;
at the cost of his youngest
he will set up its gates." 1Ki 16:34

27 So the LORD was with Joshua,
and his fame spread throughout
the land. Jos 1:5; 9:1

Achan's Sin

7 But the Israelites were unfaithful in regard to the devoted
things[b]; Achan son of Karmi, the

[a] *17* The Hebrew term refers to the irrevocable giving over of things or persons to the LORD, often by totally destroying them; also in verses 18 and 21. [b] *1* The Hebrew term refers to the irrevocable giving over of things or persons to the LORD, often by totally destroying them; also in verses 11, 12, 13 and 15.

son of Zimri,[a] the son of Zerah, of
the tribe of Judah, took some of
them. So the LORD's anger burned
against Israel. Jos 6:18

2Now Joshua sent men from
Jericho to Ai, which is near Beth
Aven to the east of Bethel, and
told them, "Go up and spy out the
region." So the men went up and
spied out Ai. Jos 18:12

3When they returned to Joshua,
they said, "Not all the army will
have to go up against Ai. Send two
or three thousand men to take it
and do not weary the whole army,
for only a few people live there."
4So about three thousand went
up; but they were routed by the
men of Ai, 5who killed about thirty-six of them. They chased the
Israelites from the city gate as far
as the stone quarries and struck
them down on the slopes. At this
the hearts of the people melted in
fear and became like water.
Lev 26:17; Dt 28:25

6Then Joshua tore his clothes
and fell facedown to the ground
before the ark of the LORD, remaining there till evening. The
elders of Israel did the same, and
sprinkled dust on their heads.
7And Joshua said, "Alas, Sovereign
LORD, why did you ever bring this
people across the Jordan to deliver us into the hands of the Amorites to destroy us? If only we had
been content to stay on the other
side of the Jordan! 8Pardon your
servant, Lord. What can I say, now
that Israel has been routed by its
enemies? 9The Canaanites and the
other people of the country will
hear about this and they will surround us and wipe out our name
from the earth. What then will you
do for your own great name?"
Ex 32:12; Job 2:12; Rev 18:19

10The LORD said to Joshua,
"Stand up! What are you doing
down on your face? 11Israel has
sinned; they have violated my covenant, which I commanded them
to keep. They have taken some of
the devoted things; they have stolen, they have lied, they have put
them with their own possessions.
12That is why the Israelites cannot stand against their enemies;
they turn their backs and run because they have been made liable
to destruction. I will not be with
you anymore unless you destroy
whatever among you is devoted
to destruction.
Jos 6:17-19; Ac 5:1-2; Dt 29:27

13"Go, consecrate the people. Tell
them, 'Consecrate yourselves in
preparation for tomorrow; for this
is what the LORD, the God of Israel, says: There are devoted things
among you, Israel. You cannot
stand against your enemies until
you remove them. Jos 3:5; 6:18

14" 'In the morning, present
yourselves tribe by tribe. The tribe
the LORD chooses shall come forward clan by clan; the clan the
LORD chooses shall come forward
family by family; and the family

[a] *1* See Septuagint and 1 Chron. 2:6; Hebrew *Zabdi*; also in verses 17 and 18.

the LORD chooses shall come forward man by man. [15]Whoever is caught with the devoted things shall be destroyed by fire, along with all that belongs to him. He has violated the covenant of the LORD and has done an outrageous thing in Israel!'"

Ge 34:7; 1Sa 14:39; Pr 16:33

[16]Early the next morning Joshua
had Israel come forward by tribes,
and Judah was chosen. [17]The clans
of Judah came forward, and the
Zerahites were chosen. He had the
clan of the Zerahites come forward
by families, and Zimri was chosen.
[18]Joshua had his family come forward man by man, and Achan son of Karmi, the son of Zimri, the son of Zerah, of the tribe of Judah, was chosen.

Nu 26:20

[19]Then Joshua said to Achan, "My son, give glory to the LORD, the God of Israel, and honor him. Tell me what you have done; do not hide it from me."

Jer 13:16; Jn 9:24; 1Sa 6:5

[20]Achan replied, "It is true! I
have sinned against the LORD, the
God of Israel. This is what I have
done: [21]When I saw in the plunder a beautiful robe from Babylonia,[a] two hundred shekels[b] of silver and a bar of gold weighing fifty shekels,[c] I coveted them and took them. They are hidden in the ground inside my tent, with the silver underneath."

Eph 5:5; 1Ti 6:10

[22]So Joshua sent messengers, and they ran to the tent, and there it was, hidden in his tent, with the
silver underneath. [23]They took the things from the tent, brought them to Joshua and all the Israelites and spread them out before the LORD.

[24]Then Joshua, together with all Israel, took Achan son of Zerah, the silver, the robe, the gold bar, his sons and daughters, his cattle, donkeys and sheep, his tent and all that he had, to the Valley of Achor.
[25]Joshua said, "Why have you brought this trouble on us? The LORD will bring trouble on you today."

Jos 6:18; 15:7

Then all Israel stoned him, and after they had stoned the rest, they
burned them. [26]Over Achan they heaped up a large pile of rocks, which remains to this day. Then the LORD turned from his fierce anger. Therefore that place has been called the Valley of Achor[d] ever since.

Dt 13:17; 17:5

Ai Destroyed

8 Then the LORD said to Joshua, "Do not be afraid; do not be discouraged. Take the whole army with you, and go up and attack Ai. For I have delivered into your hands the king of Ai, his people,
his city and his land. [2]You shall do to Ai and its king as you did to Jericho and its king, except that you may carry off their plunder and

[a] 21 Hebrew *Shinar* [b] 21 That is, about 5 pounds or about 2.3 kilograms
[c] 21 That is, about 1 1/4 pounds or about 575 grams [d] 26 *Achor* means *trouble.*

livestock for yourselves. Set an
ambush behind the city."
Jos 1:9; 6:2; Dt 1:21
3So Joshua and the whole army
moved out to attack Ai. He chose
thirty thousand of his best fighting men and sent them out at
night 4with these orders: "Listen
carefully. You are to set an ambush behind the city. Don't go very
far from it. All of you be on the
alert. 5I and all those with me will
advance on the city, and when the
men come out against us, as they
did before, we will flee from them.
6They will pursue us until we have
lured them away from the city, for
they will say, 'They are running
away from us as they did before.'
So when we flee from them, 7you
are to rise up from ambush and
take the city. The LORD your God
will give it into your hand. 8When
you have taken the city, set it on
fire. Do what the LORD has commanded. See to it; you have my
orders."
Jdg 7:7; 20:29-38
9Then Joshua sent them off, and
they went to the place of ambush
and lay in wait between Bethel and Ai, to the west of Ai — but
Joshua spent that night with the
people.
2Ch 13:13
10Early the next morning Joshua mustered his army, and he and
the leaders of Israel marched before them to Ai. 11The entire force
that was with him marched up
and approached the city and arrived in front of it. They set up
camp north of Ai, with the valley
between them and the city. 12Josh-
ua had taken about five thousand
men and set them in ambush between Bethel and Ai, to the west of
the city. 13So the soldiers took up
their positions — with the main
camp to the north of the city and
the ambush to the west of it. That
night Joshua went into the valley.
Ge 22:3
14When the king of Ai saw this,
he and all the men of the city hurried out early in the morning to
meet Israel in battle at a certain
place overlooking the Arabah.
But he did not know that an ambush had been set against him
behind the city. 15Joshua and all
Israel let themselves be driven
back before them, and they fled
toward the wilderness. 16All the
men of Ai were called to pursue
them, and they pursued Joshua
and were lured away from the
city. 17Not a man remained in Ai
or Bethel who did not go after Israel. They left the city open and
went in pursuit of Israel.
Jos 15:61; 18:12; Jdg 20:34
18Then the LORD said to Joshua, "Hold out toward Ai the javelin that is in your hand, for into
your hand I will deliver the city."
So Joshua held out toward the city
the javelin that was in his hand.
19As soon as he did this, the men
in the ambush rose quickly from
their position and rushed forward. They entered the city and
captured it and quickly set it on
fire.
Ex 14:16; 17:9-12

[20]The men of Ai looked back and saw the smoke of the city rising up into the sky, but they had no chance to escape in any direction; the Israelites who had been fleeing toward the wilderness had turned back against their pursuers. [21]For when Joshua and all Israel saw that the ambush had taken the city and that smoke was going up from it, they turned around and attacked the men of Ai. [22]Those in the ambush also came out of the city against them, so that they were caught in the middle, with Israelites on both sides. Israel cut them down, leaving them neither survivors nor fugitives. [23]But they took the king of Ai alive and brought him to Joshua. Dt 7:2; 1Sa 15:8

[24]When Israel had finished killing all the men of Ai in the fields and in the wilderness where they had chased them, and when every one of them had been put to the sword, all the Israelites returned to Ai and killed those who were in it. [25]Twelve thousand men and women fell that day — all the people of Ai. [26]For Joshua did not draw back the hand that held out his javelin until he had destroyed[a] all who lived in Ai. [27]But Israel did carry off for themselves the livestock and plunder of this city, as the LORD had instructed Joshua.

Ex 17:12; Dt 20:16-18

[28]So Joshua burned Ai[b] and made it a permanent heap of ruins, a desolate place to this day. [29]He impaled the body of the king of Ai on a pole and left it there until evening. At sunset, Joshua ordered them to take the body from the pole and throw it down at the entrance of the city gate. And they raised a large pile of rocks over it, which remains to this day.

Dt 13:16; 21:23; Jn 19:31

The Covenant Renewed at Mount Ebal

[30]Then Joshua built on Mount Ebal an altar to the LORD, the God of Israel, [31]as Moses the servant of the LORD had commanded the Israelites. He built it according to what is written in the Book of the Law of Moses — an altar of uncut stones, on which no iron tool had been used. On it they offered to the LORD burnt offerings and sacrificed fellowship offerings. [32]There, in the presence of the Israelites, Joshua wrote on stones a copy of the law of Moses. [33]All the Israelites, with their elders, officials and judges, were standing on both sides of the ark of the covenant of the LORD, facing the Levitical priests who carried it. Both the foreigners living among them and the native-born were there. Half of the people stood in front of Mount Gerizim and half of them in front of Mount Ebal, as Moses the servant of the LORD had for-

[a] *26* The Hebrew term refers to the irrevocable giving over of things or persons to the LORD, often by totally destroying them. [b] *28* *Ai* means *the ruin*.

merly commanded when he gave instructions to bless the people of Israel. Ex 20:25; Dt 27:6-7; 11:29

[34]Afterward, Joshua read all the words of the law — the blessings and the curses — just as it is written in the Book of the Law. [35]There was not a word of all that Moses had commanded that Joshua did not read to the whole assembly of Israel, including the women and children, and the foreigners who lived among them.

Dt 31:12; Jos 1:8

The Gibeonite Deception

9 Now when all the kings west of the Jordan heard about these things — the kings in the hill country, in the western foothills, and along the entire coast of the Mediterranean Sea as far as Lebanon (the kings of the Hittites, Amorites, Canaanites, Perizzites, Hivites and Jebusites) — [2]they came together to wage war against Joshua and Israel. Nu 34:6; Ex 3:17

[3]However, when the people of Gibeon heard what Joshua had done to Jericho and Ai, [4]they resorted to a ruse: They went as a delegation whose donkeys were loaded[a] with worn-out sacks and old wineskins, cracked and mended. [5]They put worn and patched sandals on their feet and wore old clothes. All the bread of their food supply was dry and moldy. [6]Then they went to Joshua in the camp at Gilgal and said to him and the Israelites, "We have come from a distant country; make a treaty with us." Jos 5:10; 10:2

[7]The Israelites said to the Hivites, "But perhaps you live near us, so how can we make a treaty with you?" Ex 23:32; Jos 11:19

[8]"We are your servants," they said to Joshua.

But Joshua asked, "Who are you and where do you come from?"

[9]They answered: "Your servants have come from a very distant country because of the fame of the LORD your God. For we have heard reports of him: all that he did in Egypt, [10]and all that he did to the two kings of the Amorites east of the Jordan — Sihon king of Heshbon, and Og king of Bashan, who reigned in Ashtaroth. [11]And our elders and all those living in our country said to us, 'Take provisions for your journey; go and meet them and say to them, "We are your servants; make a treaty with us." ' [12]This bread of ours was warm when we packed it at home on the day we left to come to you. But now see how dry and moldy it is. [13]And these wineskins that we filled were new, but see how cracked they are. And our clothes and sandals are worn out by the very long journey."

Dt 20:15; Jos 2:9; Nu 21:24,35

[14]The Israelites sampled their provisions but did not inquire of

[a] 4 Most Hebrew manuscripts; some Hebrew manuscripts, Vulgate and Syriac (see also Septuagint) *They prepared provisions and loaded their donkeys*

the LORD. 15Then Joshua made a
treaty of peace with them to let
them live, and the leaders of the
assembly ratified it by oath.
Nu 27:21; Ps 106:34

16Three days after they made
the treaty with the Gibeonites, the
Israelites heard that they were
neighbors, living near them. 17So
the Israelites set out and on the
third day came to their cities: Gibeon, Kephirah, Beeroth and Kiriath Jearim. 18But the Israelites did
not attack them, because the leaders of the assembly had sworn an
oath to them by the LORD, the God
of Israel. Jos 18:25; Ps 15:4

The whole assembly grumbled
against the leaders, 19but all the
leaders answered, "We have giv-
en them our oath by the LORD, the
God of Israel, and we cannot touch
them now. 20This is what we will
do to them: We will let them live,
so that God's wrath will not fall on
us for breaking the oath we swore
to them." 21They continued, "Let
them live, but let them be woodcutters and water carriers in the
service of the whole assembly." So
the leaders' promise to them was
kept. Ex 15:24; Dt 29:11

22Then Joshua summoned the
Gibeonites and said, "Why did you
deceive us by saying, 'We live a
long way from you,' while actually you live near us? 23You are now
under a curse: You will never be
released from service as woodcutters and water carriers for the
house of my God." Ge 9:25

24They answered Joshua, "Your
servants were clearly told how the
LORD your God had commanded
his servant Moses to give you the
whole land and to wipe out all its
inhabitants from before you. So
we feared for our lives because of
you, and that is why we did this.
25We are now in your hands. Do to
us whatever seems good and right
to you." Ge 16:6; Jer 26:14

26So Joshua saved them from
the Israelites, and they did not
kill them. 27That day he made the
Gibeonites woodcutters and water
carriers for the assembly, to provide for the needs of the altar of
the LORD at the place the LORD
would choose. And that is what
they are to this day. Dt 12:5

The Sun Stands Still

10 Now Adoni-Zedek king of
Jerusalem heard that Joshua had taken Ai and totally destroyed[a] it, doing to Ai and its
king as he had done to Jericho
and its king, and that the people
of Gibeon had made a treaty of
peace with Israel and had become
their allies. 2He and his people
were very much alarmed at this,
because Gibeon was an important
city, like one of the royal cities; it
was larger than Ai, and all its men
were good fighters. 3So Adoni-Zedek king of Jerusalem appealed

[a] *1* The Hebrew term refers to the irrevocable giving over of things or persons to the LORD, often by totally destroying them; also in verses 28, 35, 37, 39 and 40.

to Hoham king of Hebron, Piram
king of Jarmuth, Japhia king of
Lachish and Debir king of Eglon.
4"Come up and help me attack
Gibeon," he said, "because it has
made peace with Joshua and the
Israelites." Ge 13:18; Jos 8:22; Jdg 1:7

5Then the five kings of the Amorites — the kings of Jerusalem,
Hebron, Jarmuth, Lachish and Eglon — joined forces. They moved
up with all their troops and took
up positions against Gibeon and
attacked it. Nu 13:29

6The Gibeonites then sent word
to Joshua in the camp at Gilgal:
"Do not abandon your servants.
Come up to us quickly and save
us! Help us, because all the Amorite kings from the hill country
have joined forces against us."

7So Joshua marched up from
Gilgal with his entire army, including all the best fighting men. 8The
LORD said to Joshua, "Do not be
afraid of them; I have given them
into your hand. Not one of them
will be able to withstand you."
Jos 1:9; 8:1

9After an all-night march from
Gilgal, Joshua took them by surprise. 10The LORD threw them into
confusion before Israel, so Joshua
and the Israelites defeated them
completely at Gibeon. Israel pursued them along the road going up
to Beth Horon and cut them down
all the way to Azekah and Makkedah. 11As they fled before Israel on
the road down from Beth Horon
to Azekah, the LORD hurled large
hailstones down on them, and
more of them died from the hail
than were killed by the swords of
the Israelites. Dt 7:23; Jdg 5:20; Ps 18:12

12On the day the LORD gave the
Amorites over to Israel, Joshua
said to the LORD in the presence
of Israel:

"Sun, stand still over Gibeon,
and you, moon, over the
Valley of Aijalon." Am 2:9
13So the sun stood still,
and the moon stopped,
till the nation avenged itself
on[a] its enemies,

as it is written in the Book of Jashar. 2Sa 1:18; Hab 3:11

The sun stopped in the middle
of the sky and delayed going down
about a full day. 14There has never
been a day like it before or since,
a day when the LORD listened to
a human being. Surely the LORD
was fighting for Israel!
Ex 14:14; Isa 38:8

15Then Joshua returned with all
Israel to the camp at Gilgal. ver 43

Five Amorite Kings Killed

16Now the five kings had fled
and hidden in the cave at Makkedah. 17When Joshua was told that
the five kings had been found hiding in the cave at Makkedah, 18he
said, "Roll large rocks up to the
mouth of the cave, and post some
men there to guard it. 19But don't
stop; pursue your enemies! Attack
them from the rear and don't let

[a] 13 Or *nation triumphed over*

them reach their cities, for the
LORD your God has given them
into your hand."
20 So Joshua and the Israelites
defeated them completely, but a
few survivors managed to reach
their fortified cities. 21 The whole
army then returned safely to Joshua in the camp at Makkedah, and
no one uttered a word against the
Israelites. Dt 20:16
22 Joshua said, "Open the mouth
of the cave and bring those five
kings out to me." 23 So they brought
the five kings out of the cave — the
kings of Jerusalem, Hebron, Jarmuth, Lachish and Eglon. 24 When
they had brought these kings to
Joshua, he summoned all the men
of Israel and said to the army commanders who had come with him,
"Come here and put your feet on
the necks of these kings." So they
came forward and placed their
feet on their necks. Dt 7:24; Mal 4:3
25 Joshua said to them, "Do not
be afraid; do not be discouraged.
Be strong and courageous. This is
what the LORD will do to all the
enemies you are going to fight."
26 Then Joshua put the kings to
death and exposed their bodies on
five poles, and they were left hanging on the poles until evening.
27 At sunset Joshua gave the order and they took them down
from the poles and threw them
into the cave where they had been
hiding. At the mouth of the cave
they placed large rocks, which are
there to this day. Dt 21:23

Southern Cities Conquered

28 That day Joshua took Makkedah. He put the city and its king
to the sword and totally destroyed
everyone in it. He left no survivors. And he did to the king of
Makkedah as he had done to the
king of Jericho. Dt 20:16; Jos 6:21
29 Then Joshua and all Israel
with him moved on from Makkedah to Libnah and attacked it.
30 The LORD also gave that city and
its king into Israel's hand. The city
and everyone in it Joshua put to
the sword. He left no survivors
there. And he did to its king as he
had done to the king of Jericho.
Nu 33:20
31 Then Joshua and all Israel with
him moved on from Libnah to Lachish; he took up positions against
it and attacked it. 32 The LORD gave
Lachish into Israel's hands, and
Joshua took it on the second day.
The city and everyone in it he put
to the sword, just as he had done
to Libnah. 33 Meanwhile, Horam
king of Gezer had come up to help
Lachish, but Joshua defeated him
and his army — until no survivors
were left.
34 Then Joshua and all Israel
with him moved on from Lachish
to Eglon; they took up positions
against it and attacked it. 35 They
captured it that same day and
put it to the sword and totally destroyed everyone in it, just as they
had done to Lachish.
36 Then Joshua and all Israel
with him went up from Eglon to

Hebron and attacked it. 37They
took the city and put it to the
sword, together with its king, its
villages and everyone in it. They
left no survivors. Just as at Eglon,
they totally destroyed it and everyone in it. Jos 14:13; 15:13; Jdg 1:10

38Then Joshua and all Israel with
him turned around and attacked
Debir. 39They took the city, its king
and its villages, and put them to
the sword. Everyone in it they totally destroyed. They left no survivors. They did to Debir and its
king as they had done to Libnah
and its king and to Hebron.

Jos 15:15; Jdg 1:11

40So Joshua subdued the whole
region, including the hill country,
the Negev, the western foothills
and the mountain slopes, together with all their kings. He left no
survivors. He totally destroyed all
who breathed, just as the LORD,
the God of Israel, had commanded. 41Joshua subdued them from
Kadesh Barnea to Gaza and from
the whole region of Goshen to
Gibeon. 42All these kings and their
lands Joshua conquered in one
campaign, because the LORD, the
God of Israel, fought for Israel.

Dt 7:24; Jos 11:16; ver 14

43Then Joshua returned with all
Israel to the camp at Gilgal.

Northern Kings Defeated

11 When Jabin king of Hazor
heard of this, he sent word to
Jobab king of Madon, to the kings
of Shimron and Akshaph, 2and
to the northern kings who were
in the mountains, in the Arabah
south of Kinnereth, in the western foothills and in Naphoth Dor
on the west; 3to the Canaanites in
the east and west; to the Amorites,
Hittites, Perizzites and Jebusites
in the hill country; and to the Hivites below Hermon in the region
of Mizpah. 4They came out with all
their troops and a large number
of horses and chariots — a huge
army, as numerous as the sand
on the seashore. 5All these kings
joined forces and made camp together at the Waters of Merom to
fight against Israel.

Jdg 7:12; Jos 12:3; Dt 7:1

6The LORD said to Joshua, "Do
not be afraid of them, because by
this time tomorrow I will hand all
of them, slain, over to Israel. You
are to hamstring their horses and
burn their chariots." Jos 10:8; 2Sa 8:4

7So Joshua and his whole army
came against them suddenly at
the Waters of Merom and attacked
them, 8and the LORD gave them
into the hand of Israel. They defeated them and pursued them all
the way to Greater Sidon, to Misrephoth Maim, and to the Valley
of Mizpah on the east, until no
survivors were left. 9Joshua did
to them as the LORD had directed:
He hamstrung their horses and
burned their chariots. Jos 13:6

10At that time Joshua turned
back and captured Hazor and
put its king to the sword. (Hazor
had been the head of all these

kingdoms.) 11 Everyone in it they
put to the sword. They totally destroyed[a] them, not sparing anyone that breathed, and he burned
Hazor itself. Dt 20:16-17

12 Joshua took all these royal cities and their kings and put them
to the sword. He totally destroyed
them, as Moses the servant of the
LORD had commanded. 13 Yet Israel
did not burn any of the cities built
on their mounds — except Hazor,
which Joshua burned. 14 The Israelites carried off for themselves all
the plunder and livestock of these
cities, but all the people they put
to the sword until they completely
destroyed them, not sparing anyone that breathed. 15 As the LORD
commanded his servant Moses,
so Moses commanded Joshua,
and Joshua did it; he left nothing
undone of all that the LORD commanded Moses.

Ex 34:11; Nu 33:50-52; Jos 1:7

16 So Joshua took this entire
land: the hill country, all the Negev, the whole region of Goshen,
the western foothills, the Arabah
and the mountains of Israel with
their foothills, 17 from Mount Halak, which rises toward Seir, to
Baal Gad in the Valley of Lebanon
below Mount Hermon. He captured all their kings and put them
to death. 18 Joshua waged war
against all these kings for a long
time. 19 Except for the Hivites living in Gibeon, not one city made
a treaty of peace with the Israelites, who took them all in battle.
20 For it was the LORD himself who
hardened their hearts to wage war
against Israel, so that he might destroy them totally, exterminating
them without mercy, as the LORD
had commanded Moses.

Ex 14:17; Jos 9:3; 10:41

21 At that time Joshua went and
destroyed the Anakites from the
hill country: from Hebron, Debir
and Anab, from all the hill country of Judah, and from all the hill
country of Israel. Joshua totally
destroyed them and their towns.
22 No Anakites were left in Israelite
territory; only in Gaza, Gath and
Ashdod did any survive.

23 So Joshua took the entire land,
just as the LORD had directed Moses, and he gave it as an inheritance to Israel according to their
tribal divisions. Then the land had
rest from war.

Ex 33:14; Nu 13:22,33; Jos 21:43-45; 1Sa 17:4

List of Defeated Kings

12 These are the kings of the
land whom the Israelites
had defeated and whose territory
they took over east of the Jordan,
from the Arnon Gorge to Mount
Hermon, including all the eastern
side of the Arabah: Dt 3:8

2 Sihon king of the Amorites,
who reigned in Heshbon.
He ruled from Aroer on the
rim of the Arnon Gorge —

[a] 11 The Hebrew term refers to the irrevocable giving over of things or persons to the LORD, often by totally destroying them; also in verses 12, 20 and 21.

from the middle of the
gorge — to the Jabbok River, which is the border of
the Ammonites. This in-
cluded half of Gilead. 3He
also ruled over the eastern
Arabah from the Sea of Galilee[a] to the Sea of the Arabah (that is, the Dead Sea),
to Beth Jeshimoth, and
then southward below the
slopes of Pisgah.

Jos 11:2; 13:20; Jdg 11:19

4And the territory of Og king
of Bashan, one of the last of
the Rephaites, who reigned in
Ashtaroth and Edrei.

5He ruled over Mount Her-
mon, Salekah, all of Bashan
to the border of the people
of Geshur and Maakah, and
half of Gilead to the border
of Sihon king of Heshbon.

Nu 21:21,33; Dt 1:4; 3:10

6Moses, the servant of the LORD,
and the Israelites conquered
them. And Moses the servant of
the LORD gave their land to the
Reubenites, the Gadites and the
half-tribe of Manasseh to be their
possession. Nu 32:29,33

7Here is a list of the kings of the
land that Joshua and the Israelites
conquered on the west side of the
Jordan, from Baal Gad in the Valley of Lebanon to Mount Halak,
which rises toward Seir. Joshua
gave their lands as an inheritance
to the tribes of Israel according to their tribal divisions. 8The
lands included the hill country,
the western foothills, the Arabah,
the mountain slopes, the wilderness and the Negev. These were
the lands of the Hittites, Amorites,
Canaanites, Perizzites, Hivites and
Jebusites. These were the kings:

Jos 11:17; Ezr 9:1

9the king of Jericho one
the king of Ai (near
Bethel) one
10the king of Jerusalem one
the king of Hebron one
11the king of Jarmuth one
the king of Lachish one
12the king of Eglon one
the king of Gezer one
13the king of Debir one
the king of Geder one
14the king of Hormah one
the king of Arad one
15the king of Libnah one
the king of Adullam one
16the king of Makkedah one
the king of Bethel one
17the king of Tappuah one
the king of Hepher one
18the king of Aphek one
the king of Lasharon one
19the king of Madon one
the king of Hazor one
20the king of Shimron
Meron one
the king of Akshaph one
21the king of Taanach one
the king of Megiddo one
22the king of Kedesh one
the king of Jokneam
in Carmel one

[a] 3 Hebrew *Kinnereth*

23 the king of Dor (in
Naphoth Dor) one
the king of Goyim
in Gilgal one
24 the king of Tirzah one
thirty-one kings in all.

Land Still to Be Taken

13 When Joshua had grown old,
the LORD said to him, "You
are now very old, and there are
still very large areas of land to be
taken over. Jos 14:10

2 "This is the land that remains: all the regions of the
Philistines and Geshurites,
3 from the Shihor River on the
east of Egypt to the territory
of Ekron on the north, all of it
counted as Canaanite though
held by the five Philistine rulers in Gaza, Ashdod, Ashkelon,
Gath and Ekron; the territory
of the Avvites 4 on the south;
all the land of the Canaanites,
from Arah of the Sidonians
as far as Aphek and the border of the Amorites; 5 the area
of Byblos; and all Lebanon to
the east, from Baal Gad below
Mount Hermon to Lebo Ha-
math. Dt 2:23; Jdg 3:3; Am 2:10

6 "As for all the inhabitants of
the mountain regions from Lebanon to Misrephoth Maim, that
is, all the Sidonians, I myself will
drive them out before the Israelites. Be sure to allocate this land to
Israel for an inheritance, as I have
instructed you, 7 and divide it as an
inheritance among the nine tribes
and half of the tribe of Manasseh."
Jos 11:8; Nu 33:54

Division of the Land East of the Jordan

8 The other half of Manasseh,[a] the
Reubenites and the Gadites had
received the inheritance that Moses had given them east of the Jordan, as he, the servant of the LORD,
had assigned it to them. Jos 12:6

9 It extended from Aroer on
the rim of the Arnon Gorge,
and from the town in the
middle of the gorge, and included the whole plateau of
Medeba as far as Dibon, 10 and
all the towns of Sihon king of
the Amorites, who ruled in
Heshbon, out to the border
of the Ammonites. 11 It also included Gilead, the territory
of the people of Geshur and
Maakah, all of Mount Her-
mon and all Bashan as far as
Salekah — 12 that is, the whole
kingdom of Og in Bashan,
who had reigned in Ashtaroth
and Edrei. (He was the last of
the Rephaites.) Moses had defeated them and taken over
their land. 13 But the Israelites
did not drive out the people
of Geshur and Maakah, so
they continue to live among
the Israelites to this day.
Dt 2:36; 3:11; Jos 12:4

[a] 8 Hebrew *With it* (that is, with the other half of Manasseh)

14 But to the tribe of Levi he gave
no inheritance, since the food offerings presented to the LORD, the
God of Israel, are their inheritance,
as he promised them. Dt 18:1-2

15 This is what Moses had given to
the tribe of Reuben, according to
its clans:

16 The territory from Aroer on
the rim of the Arnon Gorge,
and from the town in the middle of the gorge, and the whole
plateau past Medeba 17 to
Heshbon and all its towns on
the plateau, including Dibon,
Bamoth Baal, Beth Baal Meon,
18 Jahaz, Kedemoth, Mephaath,
19 Kiriathaim, Sibmah, Zereth
Shahar on the hill in the valley, 20 Beth Peor, the slopes of
Pisgah, and Beth Jeshimoth —
21 all the towns on the plateau
and the entire realm of Sihon
king of the Amorites, who
ruled at Heshbon. Moses had
defeated him and the Midianite chiefs, Evi, Rekem, Zur,
Hur and Reba — princes allied
with Sihon — who lived in that
country. 22 In addition to those
slain in battle, the Israelites
had put to the sword Balaam
son of Beor, who practiced
divination. 23 The boundary of
the Reubenites was the bank
of the Jordan. These towns
and their villages were the inheritance of the Reubenites,
according to their clans.

Nu 21:23; 31:8; 32:37

24 This is what Moses had given to
the tribe of Gad, according to its
clans:

25 The territory of Jazer, all
the towns of Gilead and half
the Ammonite country as
far as Aroer, near Rabbah;
26 and from Heshbon to Ramath Mizpah and Betonim,
and from Mahanaim to the
territory of Debir; 27 and in
the valley, Beth Haram, Beth
Nimrah, Sukkoth and Zaphon
with the rest of the realm of
Sihon king of Heshbon (the
east side of the Jordan, the
territory up to the end of the
Sea of Galilee[a]). 28 These towns
and their villages were the inheritance of the Gadites, according to their clans.

Nu 21:32; 34:11

29 This is what Moses had given to
the half-tribe of Manasseh, that is,
to half the family of the descendants of Manasseh, according to
its clans:

30 The territory extending
from Mahanaim and includ-
ing all of Bashan, the entire
realm of Og king of Bashan —
all the settlements of Jair in
Bashan, sixty towns, 31 half
of Gilead, and Ashtaroth and
Edrei (the royal cities of Og
in Bashan). This was for the
descendants of Makir son of
Manasseh — for half of the

[a] 27 Hebrew *Kinnereth*

sons of Makir, according to
their clans. Nu 32:41; Jos 12:4

32This is the inheritance Moses had given when he was in the
plains of Moab across the Jordan
east of Jericho. 33But to the tribe
of Levi, Moses had given no inheritance; the LORD, the God of Israel,
is their inheritance, as he promised them. Nu 18:20

Division of the Land West of the Jordan

14 Now these are the areas the
Israelites received as an inheritance in the land of Canaan,
which Eleazar the priest, Joshua
son of Nun and the heads of the
tribal clans of Israel allotted to
them. 2Their inheritances were
assigned by lot to the nine and a
half tribes, as the LORD had commanded through Moses. 3Moses
had granted the two and a half
tribes their inheritance east of
the Jordan but had not granted
the Levites an inheritance among
the rest, 4for Joseph's descendants
had become two tribes — Manasseh and Ephraim. The Levites received no share of the land but
only towns to live in, with pasturelands for their flocks and herds.
5So the Israelites divided the land,
just as the LORD had commanded
Moses. Nu 32:33; 34:17-18; Jos 13:14

Allotment for Caleb

6Now the people of Judah approached Joshua at Gilgal, and
Caleb son of Jephunneh the Kenizzite said to him, "You know
what the LORD said to Moses the
man of God at Kadesh Barnea
about you and me. 7I was forty
years old when Moses the servant
of the LORD sent me from Kadesh
Barnea to explore the land. And
I brought him back a report according to my convictions, 8but
my fellow Israelites who went
up with me made the hearts of
the people melt in fear. I, however, followed the LORD my God
wholeheartedly. 9So on that day
Moses swore to me, 'The land on
which your feet have walked will
be your inheritance and that of
your children forever, because
you have followed the LORD my
God wholeheartedly.'[a]

Nu 13:30; 14:6-9,24,30; Dt 1:36

10"Now then, just as the LORD
promised, he has kept me alive
for forty-five years since the time
he said this to Moses, while Israel moved about in the wilderness.
So here I am today, eighty-five
years old! 11I am still as strong today as the day Moses sent me out;
I'm just as vigorous to go out to
battle now as I was then. 12Now
give me this hill country that the
LORD promised me that day. You
yourself heard then that the Anakites were there and their cities were large and fortified, but,
the LORD helping me, I will drive
them out just as he said."

Nu 13:33; Dt 34:7

[a] 9 Deut. 1:36

[13]Then Joshua blessed Caleb son of Jephunneh and gave him Hebron as his inheritance. [14]So Hebron has belonged to Caleb son of Jephunneh the Kenizzite ever since, because he followed the LORD, the God of Israel, wholeheartedly. [15](Hebron used to be called Kiriath Arba after Arba, who was the greatest man among the Anakites.) Jos 22:6-7; Jdg 1:20

Then the land had rest from war. Jos 11:23

Allotment for Judah

15 The allotment for the tribe of Judah, according to its clans, extended down to the territory of Edom, to the Desert of Zin in the extreme south. Nu 34:3

[2]Their southern boundary started from the bay at the southern end of the Dead Sea, [3]crossed south of Scorpion Pass, continued on to Zin and went over to the south of Kadesh Barnea. Then it ran past Hezron up to Addar and curved around to Karka. [4]It then passed along to Azmon and joined the Wadi of Egypt, ending at the Mediterranean Sea. This is their[a] southern boundary.

[5]The eastern boundary is the Dead Sea as far as the mouth of the Jordan. Ge 14:3

The northern boundary started from the bay of the sea at the mouth of the Jordan, [6]went up to Beth Hoglah and continued north of Beth Arabah to the Stone of Bohan son of Reuben. [7]The boundary then went up to Debir from the Valley of Achor and turned north to Gilgal, which faces the Pass of Adummim south of the gorge. It continued along to the waters of En Shemesh and came out at En Rogel. [8]Then it ran up the Valley of Ben Hinnom along the southern slope of the Jebusite city (that is, Jerusalem). From there it climbed to the top of the hill west of the Hinnom Valley at the northern end of the Valley of Rephaim. [9]From the hilltop the boundary headed toward the spring of the waters of Nephtoah, came out at the towns of Mount Ephron and went down toward Baalah (that is, Kiriath Jearim). [10]Then it curved westward from Baalah to Mount Seir, ran along the northern slope of Mount Jearim (that is, Kesalon), continued down to Beth Shemesh and crossed to Timnah. [11]It went to the northern slope of Ekron, turned toward Shikkeron, passed along to Mount Baalah and reached Jabneel. The boundary ended at the sea. Jos 7:24; 18:17; 1Ch 13:6

[12]The western boundary is the coastline of the Mediterranean Sea. Nu 34:6

[a] 4 Septuagint; Hebrew *your*

These are the boundaries around
the people of Judah by their clans.

13In accordance with the LORD's
command to him, Joshua gave to
Caleb son of Jephunneh a portion
in Judah — Kiriath Arba, that is,
Hebron. (Arba was the forefather
of Anak.) 14From Hebron Caleb
drove out the three Anakites —
Sheshai, Ahiman and Talmai, the
sons of Anak. 15From there he
marched against the people living
in Debir (formerly called Kiriath
Sepher). 16And Caleb said, "I will
give my daughter Aksah in marriage to the man who attacks and
captures Kiriath Sepher." 17Othniel
son of Kenaz, Caleb's brother, took
it; so Caleb gave his daughter Aksah to him in marriage.

18One day when she came to
Othniel, she urged him[a] to ask her
father for a field. When she got
off her donkey, Caleb asked her,
"What can I do for you?"

Jos 14:13-15; Jdg 1:12; 3:9,11

19She replied, "Do me a special favor. Since you have given me land
in the Negev, give me also springs
of water." So Caleb gave her the upper and lower springs. Jdg 1:11-15

20This is the inheritance of the
tribe of Judah, according to its
clans:

21The southernmost towns of the
tribe of Judah in the Negev toward the boundary of Edom were:

Kabzeel, Eder, Jagur, 22Ki-
nah, Dimonah, Adadah, 23Ke-
desh, Hazor, Ithnan, 24Ziph,
Telem, Bealoth, 25Hazor Ha-
dattah, Kerioth Hezron (that
is, Hazor), 26Amam, Shema,
Moladah, 27Hazar Gaddah,
Heshmon, Beth Pelet, 28Hazar
Shual, Beersheba, Biziothiah,
29Baalah, Iyim, Ezem, 30Elto-
lad, Kesil, Hormah, 31Ziklag,
Madmannah, Sansannah,
32Lebaoth, Shilhim, Ain and
Rimmon — a total of twenty-
nine towns and their villages.

Ge 21:31; 35:21; 1Sa 27:6

33In the western foothills:

Eshtaol, Zorah, Ashnah,
34Zanoah, En Gannim, Tappuah, Enam, 35Jarmuth, Adullam, Sokoh, Azekah, 36Shaa-
raim, Adithaim and Gederah
(or Gederothaim)[b] — fourteen
towns and their villages.

Jdg 13:25; 16:31; 1Sa 22:1

37Zenan, Hadashah, Migdal
Gad, 38Dilean, Mizpah, Joktheel, 39Lachish, Bozkath, Eglon,
40Kabbon, Lahmas, Kitlish,
41Gederoth, Beth Dagon, Naamah and Makkedah — six-
teen towns and their villages.

Jos 10:3; 2Ki 14:7,19

42Libnah, Ether, Ashan,
43Iphtah, Ashnah, Nezib, 44Ke-
ilah, Akzib and Mareshah —
nine towns and their villages.

1Ch 6:59

[a] 18 Hebrew and some Septuagint manuscripts; other Septuagint manuscripts (see also note at Judges 1:14) *Othniel, he urged her* [b] 36 Or *Gederah and Gederothaim*

45 Ekron, with its surrounding settlements and villages; 46 west of Ekron, all that
were in the vicinity of Ashdod, together with their villages; 47 Ashdod, its surrounding settlements and villages;
and Gaza, its settlements and
villages, as far as the Wadi of
Egypt and the coastline of the
Mediterranean Sea. Nu 34:6

48 In the hill country:
Shamir, Jattir, Sokoh,
49 Dannah, Kiriath Sannah
(that is, Debir), 50 Anab, Eshte-
moh, Anim, 51 Goshen, Holon
and Giloh — eleven towns and
their villages. Jos 10:41; Jdg 10:1
52 Arab, Dumah, Eshan, 53 Ja-
nim, Beth Tappuah, Aphekah,
54 Humtah, Kiriath Arba (that
is, Hebron) and Zior — nine
towns and their villages.
Ge 25:14
55 Maon, Carmel, Ziph, Juttah, 56 Jezreel, Jokdeam, Zanoah, 57 Kain, Gibeah and Timnah — ten towns and their
villages. Jdg 10:12; 1Ch 11:31
58 Halhul, Beth Zur, Gedor,
59 Maarath, Beth Anoth and
Eltekon — six towns and their
villages.[a]
60 Kiriath Baal (that is, Kiriath Jearim) and Rabbah —
two towns and their villages.
Dt 3:11; Jos 18:14

61 In the wilderness:
Beth Arabah, Middin, Se-
kakah, 62 Nibshan, the City of
Salt and En Gedi — six towns
and their villages.
Jos 8:15; Eze 47:10
63 Judah could not dislodge the
Jebusites, who were living in Jerusalem; to this day the Jebusites
live there with the people of Judah. Jdg 1:21; 2Sa 5:6

Allotment for Ephraim and Manasseh

16 The allotment for Jo-
seph began at the Jor-
dan, east of the springs of Jericho, and went up from there
through the desert into the
hill country of Bethel. 2 It went
on from Bethel (that is, Luz),[b]
crossed over to the territory
of the Arkites in Ataroth, 3 descended westward to the territory of the Japhletites as far
as the region of Lower Beth
Horon and on to Gezer, ending at the Mediterranean Sea.
Jos 8:15; 18:13
4 So Manasseh and Ephraim, the
descendants of Joseph, received
their inheritance. Jos 18:5

5 This was the territory of Ephraim, according to its clans:

The boundary of their in-
heritance went from Ataroth
Addar in the east to Upper
Beth Horon 6 and continued
to the Mediterranean Sea.

[a] 59 The Septuagint adds another district of eleven towns, including Tekoa and Ephrathah (Bethlehem). [b] 2 Septuagint; Hebrew *Bethel to Luz*

From Mikmethath on the
north it curved eastward to
Taanath Shiloh, passing by it
to Janoah on the east. 7 Then
it went down from Janoah to
Ataroth and Naarah, touched
Jericho and came out at the
Jordan. 8 From Tappuah the
border went west to the Kanah Ravine and ended at
the Mediterranean Sea. This
was the inheritance of the
tribe of the Ephraimites, according to its clans. 9 It also
included all the towns and
their villages that were set
aside for the Ephraimites
within the inheritance of the
Manassites.

Jos 17:7,9; 2Ki 15:29; 1Ch 7:28

10 They did not dislodge the Canaanites living in Gezer; to this
day the Canaanites live among
the people of Ephraim but are required to do forced labor.

Jos 17:13; Jdg 1:28-29; 1Ki 9:16

17 This was the allotment for
the tribe of Manasseh as Joseph's firstborn, that is, for Makir, Manasseh's firstborn. Makir
was the ancestor of the Gileadites,
who had received Gilead and Bashan because the Makirites were
great soldiers. 2 So this allotment
was for the rest of the people of
Manasseh — the clans of Abiezer,
Helek, Asriel, Shechem, Hepher
and Shemida. These are the other male descendants of Manasseh
son of Joseph by their clans.

Ge 41:51; 50:23; Nu 26:30

3 Now Zelophehad son of Hepher, the son of Gilead, the son
of Makir, the son of Manasseh,
had no sons but only daughters,
whose names were Mahlah, Noah,
Hoglah, Milkah and Tirzah. 4 They
went to Eleazar the priest, Joshua son of Nun, and the leaders
and said, "The LORD commanded
Moses to give us an inheritance
among our relatives." So Joshua
gave them an inheritance along
with the brothers of their father,
according to the LORD's command.
5 Manasseh's share consisted of ten
tracts of land besides Gilead and
Bashan east of the Jordan, 6 because the daughters of the tribe of
Manasseh received an inheritance
among the sons. The land of Gilead belonged to the rest of the descendants of Manasseh.

Nu 27:1,5-7; Jos 13:30-31

7 The territory of Manasseh
extended from Asher to Mikmethath east of Shechem.
The boundary ran southward
from there to include the
people living at En Tappuah.
8 (Manasseh had the land of
Tappuah, but Tappuah itself,
on the boundary of Manas-
seh, belonged to the Ephraimites.) 9 Then the boundary continued south to the
Kanah Ravine. There were
towns belonging to Ephra-
im lying among the towns of
Manasseh, but the boundary
of Manasseh was the northern side of the ravine and

ended at the Mediterranean
Sea. 10On the south the land
belonged to Ephraim, on the
north to Manasseh. The territory of Manasseh reached
the Mediterranean Sea and
bordered Asher on the north
and Issachar on the east.
Jos 16:8; Eze 48:5

11Within Issachar and Asher,
Manasseh also had Beth Shan,
Ibleam and the people of Dor,
Endor, Taanach and Megiddo,
together with their surround-
ing settlements (the third in
the list is Naphoth[a]).
Jos 11:2; 1Sa 31:10; 1Ch 7:29

12Yet the Manassites were not able
to occupy these towns, for the Canaanites were determined to live
in that region. 13However, when
the Israelites grew stronger, they
subjected the Canaanites to forced
labor but did not drive them out
completely. Jos 16:10; Jdg 1:27

14The people of Joseph said to
Joshua, "Why have you given us
only one allotment and one portion for an inheritance? We are a
numerous people, and the LORD
has blessed us abundantly."
Nu 26:28-37

15"If you are so numerous,"
Joshua answered, "and if the hill
country of Ephraim is too small
for you, go up into the forest and
clear land for yourselves there
in the land of the Perizzites and
Rephaites."

16The people of Joseph replied,
"The hill country is not enough
for us, and all the Canaanites who
live in the plain have chariots fitted with iron, both those in Beth
Shan and its settlements and
those in the Valley of Jezreel."
Jdg 1:19; 1Sa 29:1

17But Joshua said to the tribes
of Joseph — to Ephraim and Manasseh — "You are numerous and
very powerful. You will have not
only one allotment 18but the for-
ested hill country as well. Clear
it, and its farthest limits will be
yours; though the Canaanites
have chariots fitted with iron and
though they are strong, you can
drive them out."

Division of the Rest of the Land

18 The whole assembly of the
Israelites gathered at Shiloh and set up the tent of meeting
there. The country was brought
under their control, 2but there
were still seven Israelite tribes
who had not yet received their inheritance. Jos 19:51; Jer 7:12

3So Joshua said to the Israelites:
"How long will you wait before you
begin to take possession of the
land that the LORD, the God of your
ancestors, has given you? 4Appoint
three men from each tribe. I will
send them out to make a survey of
the land and to write a description
of it, according to the inheritance
of each. Then they will return to
me. 5You are to divide the land into
seven parts. Judah is to remain in
its territory on the south and the

[a] *11* That is, Naphoth Dor

tribes of Joseph in their territory
on the north. 6After you have written descriptions of the seven parts
of the land, bring them here to
me and I will cast lots for you in
the presence of the LORD our God.
7The Levites, however, do not get
a portion among you, because the
priestly service of the LORD is their
inheritance. And Gad, Reuben and
the half-tribe of Manasseh have already received their inheritance
on the east side of the Jordan. Moses the servant of the LORD gave it
to them." Jos 13:33; 15:1; 16:1-4

8As the men started on their
way to map out the land, Joshua
instructed them, "Go and make a
survey of the land and write a description of it. Then return to me,
and I will cast lots for you here
at Shiloh in the presence of the
LORD." 9So the men left and went
through the land. They wrote its
description on a scroll, town by
town, in seven parts, and returned
to Joshua in the camp at Shiloh.
10Joshua then cast lots for them in
Shiloh in the presence of the LORD,
and there he distributed the land
to the Israelites according to their
tribal divisions. Jos 19:51; Jer 7:12

Allotment for Benjamin

11The first lot came up for the
tribe of Benjamin according to its
clans. Their allotted territory lay
between the tribes of Judah and
Joseph:

12On the north side their
boundary began at the Jordan,
passed the northern slope of
Jericho and headed west into
the hill country, coming out at
the wilderness of Beth Aven.
13From there it crossed to the
south slope of Luz (that is,
Bethel) and went down to Ataroth Addar on the hill south
of Lower Beth Horon.
Ge 28:19; Jos 16:1; Jdg 1:23

14From the hill facing Beth
Horon on the south the
boundary turned south along
the western side and came
out at Kiriath Baal (that is,
Kiriath Jearim), a town of the
people of Judah. This was the
western side.

15The southern side began at
the outskirts of Kiriath Jearim
on the west, and the boundary came out at the spring of
the waters of Nephtoah. 16The
boundary went down to the
foot of the hill facing the Valley of Ben Hinnom, north of
the Valley of Rephaim. It continued down the Hinnom Valley along the southern slope
of the Jebusite city and so
to En Rogel. 17It then curved
north, went to En Shemesh,
continued to Geliloth, which
faces the Pass of Adummim,
and ran down to the Stone of
Bohan son of Reuben. 18It continued to the northern slope
of Beth Arabah[a] and on down
into the Arabah. 19It then went

[a] 18 Septuagint; Hebrew *slope facing the Arabah*

to the northern slope of Beth
Hoglah and came out at the
northern bay of the Dead Sea,
at the mouth of the Jordan in
the south. This was the southern boundary.

Ge 14:3; Jos 15:9; 2Ki 23:10

20The Jordan formed the
boundary on the eastern side.
These were the boundaries that
marked out the inheritance of the
clans of Benjamin on all sides.

1Sa 9:1

21The tribe of Benjamin, according to its clans, had the following
towns:

Jericho, Beth Hoglah, Emek
Keziz, 22Beth Arabah, Zema-
raim, Bethel, 23Avvim, Parah,
Ophrah, 24Kephar Ammo-
ni, Ophni and Geba — twelve
towns and their villages.

2Ch 13:4; Isa 10:29

25Gibeon, Ramah, Beeroth,
26Mizpah, Kephirah, Mozah,
27Rekem, Irpeel, Taralah, 28Ze-
lah, Haeleph, the Jebusite city
(that is, Jerusalem), Gibeah
and Kiriath — fourteen towns
and their villages.

Jos 15:8; Jdg 4:5; 2Sa 21:14

This was the inheritance of Benjamin for its clans. Eze 48:23

Allotment for Simeon

19 The second lot came out for
the tribe of Simeon according to its clans. Their inheritance
lay within the territory of Judah.
2It included: Ge 49:7

Beersheba (or Sheba),[a] Moladah, 3Hazar Shual, Balah,
Ezem, 4Eltolad, Bethul, Hormah, 5Ziklag, Beth Markaboth,
Hazar Susah, 6Beth Lebaoth
and Sharuhen — thirteen
towns and their villages;

Ge 21:14

7Ain, Rimmon, Ether and
Ashan — four towns and their
villages — 8and all the villages around these towns as far
as Baalath Beer (Ramah in the
Negev). Jos 15:32

This was the inheritance of the
tribe of the Simeonites, according
to its clans. 9The inheritance of the
Simeonites was taken from the
share of Judah, because Judah's
portion was more than they needed. So the Simeonites received
their inheritance within the territory of Judah. Ge 49:7

Allotment for Zebulun

10The third lot came up for Zebulun
according to its clans: 1Ch 4:28-33

The boundary of their in-
heritance went as far as Sarid.
11Going west it ran to Maralah,
touched Dabbesheth, and extended to the ravine near Jokneam. 12It turned east from
Sarid toward the sunrise to
the territory of Kisloth Tabor
and went on to Daberath and
up to Japhia. 13Then it continued eastward to Gath Hepher
and Eth Kazin; it came out at

[a] 2 Or *Beersheba, Sheba*; 1 Chron. 4:28 does not have *Sheba*.

Rimmon and turned toward
Neah. 14There the boundary
went around on the north to
Hannathon and ended at the
Valley of Iphtah El. 15Included
were Kattath, Nahalal, Shimron, Idalah and Bethlehem.
There were twelve towns and
their villages.

Ge 35:19; Jos 12:22; 1Ch 6:72

16These towns and their villages
were the inheritance of Zebulun,
according to its clans. Eze 48:26

Allotment for Issachar

17The fourth lot came out for Issachar according to its clans. 18Their
territory included: Ge 30:18

Jezreel, Kesulloth, Shunem,
19Hapharaim, Shion, Anaha-
rath, 20Rabbith, Kishion, Ebez,
21Remeth, En Gannim, En Had-
dah and Beth Pazzez. 22The
boundary touched Tabor, Sha-
hazumah and Beth Shemesh,
and ended at the Jordan. There
were sixteen towns and their
villages. 1Sa 28:4; 2Ki 4:8; Ps 89:12

23These towns and their villages
were the inheritance of the tribe
of Issachar, according to its clans.

Allotment for Asher

24The fifth lot came out for the
tribe of Asher according to its
clans. 25Their territory included:

Jos 17:7

Helkath, Hali, Beten, Ak-
shaph, 26Allammelek, Amad
and Mishal. On the west the
boundary touched Carmel
and Shihor Libnath. 27It then
turned east toward Beth Dagon, touched Zebulun and the
Valley of Iphtah El, and went
north to Beth Emek and Nei-
el, passing Kabul on the left.
28It went to Abdon,[a] Rehob,
Hammon and Kanah, as far as
Greater Sidon. 29The boundary then turned back toward
Ramah and went to the fortified city of Tyre, turned toward Hosah and came out at
the Mediterranean Sea in the
region of Akzib, 30Ummah,
Aphek and Rehob. There were
twenty-two towns and their
villages. Ge 10:19; Jdg 1:31; 1Ki 9:13

31These towns and their villages
were the inheritance of the tribe
of Asher, according to its clans.

Ge 30:13

Allotment for Naphtali

32The sixth lot came out for Naphtali according to its clans:

33Their boundary went
from Heleph and the large
tree in Zaanannim, passing
Adami Nekeb and Jabne-
el to Lakkum and ending at
the Jordan. 34The boundary
ran west through Aznoth Tabor and came out at Hukkok.
It touched Zebulun on the
south, Asher on the west and
the Jordan[b] on the east. 35The

[a] 28 Some Hebrew manuscripts (see also 21:30); most Hebrew manuscripts *Ebron*
[b] 34 Septuagint; Hebrew *west, and Judah, the Jordan,*

fortified towns were Ziddim,
Zer, Hammath, Rakkath, Kinnereth, 36Adamah, Ramah, Hazor, 37Kedesh, Edrei, En Hazor,
38Iron, Migdal El, Horem, Beth
Anath and Beth Shemesh.
There were nineteen towns
and their villages. Jos 11:1; Jdg 4:11
39These towns and their villages
were the inheritance of the tribe
of Naphtali, according to its clans.
Dt 33:23

Allotment for Dan

40The seventh lot came out for the
tribe of Dan according to its clans.
41The territory of their inheritance
included:

Zorah, Eshtaol, Ir Shemesh,
42Shaalabbin, Aijalon, Ithlah,
43Elon, Timnah, Ekron, 44El-
tekeh, Gibbethon, Baalath,
45Jehud, Bene Berak, Gath
Rimmon, 46Me Jarkon and
Rakkon, with the area facing
Joppa. Jdg 1:35; Jnh 1:3

47(When the territory of the
Danites was lost to them, they
went up and attacked Leshem,
took it, put it to the sword and occupied it. They settled in Leshem
and named it Dan after their ancestor.) Jdg 18:1,27,29
48These towns and their villages
were the inheritance of the tribe
of Dan, according to its clans.

Allotment for Joshua

49When they had finished dividing the land into its allotted portions, the Israelites gave Joshua
son of Nun an inheritance among
them, 50as the LORD had commanded. They gave him the town
he asked for — Timnath Serah[a] in
the hill country of Ephraim. And
he built up the town and settled
there. Jos 24:30

51These are the territories that
Eleazar the priest, Joshua son of
Nun and the heads of the tribal clans of Israel assigned by lot
at Shiloh in the presence of the
LORD at the entrance to the tent
of meeting. And so they finished
dividing the land. Jos 14:1; 18:10

Cities of Refuge

20 Then the LORD said to
Joshua: 2"Tell the Israelites
to designate the cities of refuge, as
I instructed you through Moses,
3so that anyone who kills a person
accidentally and unintentionally
may flee there and find protection
from the avenger of blood. 4When
they flee to one of these cities,
they are to stand in the entrance
of the city gate and state their
case before the elders of that city.
Then the elders are to admit the
fugitive into their city and provide a place to live among them.
5If the avenger of blood comes in
pursuit, the elders must not surrender the fugitive, because the
fugitive killed their neighbor unintentionally and without malice
aforethought. 6They are to stay
in that city until they have stood

[a] 50 Also known as *Timnath Heres* (see Judges 2:9)

trial before the assembly and until
the death of the high priest who
is serving at that time. Then they
may go back to their own home in
the town from which they fled."

Lev 4:2; Nu 35:12; Ru 4:1

7So they set apart Kedesh in Galilee in the hill country of Naphtali, Shechem in the hill country of
Ephraim, and Kiriath Arba (that
is, Hebron) in the hill country of
Judah. 8East of the Jordan (on the
other side from Jericho) they designated Bezer in the wilderness on
the plateau in the tribe of Reuben,
Ramoth in Gilead in the tribe of
Gad, and Golan in Bashan in the
tribe of Manasseh. 9Any of the Israelites or any foreigner residing
among them who killed someone
accidentally could flee to these
designated cities and not be killed
by the avenger of blood prior to
standing trial before the assembly.

Nu 35:9-34; Dt 4:41-43; 19:1-14

Towns for the Levites

21 Now the family heads of the
Levites approached Eleazar
the priest, Joshua son of Nun, and
the heads of the other tribal families of Israel 2at Shiloh in Canaan
and said to them, "The LORD commanded through Moses that you
give us towns to live in, with pasturelands for our livestock." 3So,
as the LORD had commanded, the
Israelites gave the Levites the following towns and pasturelands
out of their own inheritance:

Nu 35:2-3; Jos 14:1; Lev 25:32

4The first lot came out for the Kohathites, according to their clans.
The Levites who were descendants
of Aaron the priest were allotted
thirteen towns from the tribes
of Judah, Simeon and Benjamin.
5The rest of Kohath's descendants
were allotted ten towns from the
clans of the tribes of Ephraim, Dan
and half of Manasseh. Nu 3:17

6The descendants of Gershon
were allotted thirteen towns from
the clans of the tribes of Issachar,
Asher, Naphtali and the half-tribe
of Manasseh in Bashan. Ge 30:18

7The descendants of Merari, according to their clans, received
twelve towns from the tribes of
Reuben, Gad and Zebulun. Ex 6:16

8So the Israelites allotted to the
Levites these towns and their pasturelands, as the LORD had commanded through Moses.

9From the tribes of Judah and
Simeon they allotted the following towns by name 10(these towns
were assigned to the descendants
of Aaron who were from the Kohathite clans of the Levites, because the first lot fell to them):

11They gave them Kiriath
Arba (that is, Hebron), with
its surrounding pastureland,
in the hill country of Judah.
(Arba was the forefather of
Anak.) 12But the fields and villages around the city they had
given to Caleb son of Jephunneh as his possession.

Jos 15:13; 1Ch 6:55; Ge 23:2

[13]So to the descendants of
Aaron the priest they gave
Hebron (a city of refuge for
one accused of murder), Libnah, [14]Jattir, Eshtemoa, [15]Ho-
lon, Debir, [16]Ain, Juttah and
Beth Shemesh, together with
their pasturelands — nine
towns from these two tribes.

Jos 15:42; 1Ch 6:57; Nu 33:20

[17]And from the tribe of Benjamin they gave them Gibeon,
Geba, [18]Anathoth and Almon,
together with their pasturelands — four towns.

Jos 18:24; Ne 11:32; Jer 32:7

[19]The total number of towns for the priests, the descendants of Aaron, came to thirteen, together with their pasturelands.

2Ch 31:15

[20]The rest of the Kohathite clans of the Levites were allotted towns from the tribe of Ephraim:

[21]In the hill country of
Ephraim they were given Shechem (a city of refuge for one
accused of murder) and Gezer, [22]Kibzaim and Beth Horon, together with their pasturelands four towns.

Jos 20:7; 1Sa 1:1

[23]Also from the tribe of Dan
they received Eltekeh, Gibbethon, [24]Aijalon and Gath Rimmon, together with their pasturelands — four towns.

Jos 19:44

[25]From half the tribe of Manasseh they received Taanach and Gath Rimmon, together with their pasturelands — two towns.

[26]All these ten towns and their pasturelands were given to the rest of the Kohathite clans.

[27]The Levite clans of the Gershonites were given:

from the half-tribe of Manasseh,
Golan in Bashan (a city of refuge for one accused of murder) and Be Eshterah, together with their pasturelands — two towns;

Nu 35:6; Jos 12:5

[28]from the tribe of Issachar,
Kishion, Daberath, [29]Jarmuth
and En Gannim, together
with their pasturelands —
four towns;

Ge 30:18

[30]from the tribe of Asher,
Mishal, Abdon, [31]Helkath and
Rehob, together with their
pasturelands — four towns;

Jos 17:7

[32]from the tribe of Naphtali,
Kedesh in Galilee (a city of refuge for one accused of murder), Hammoth Dor and Kartan, together with their pasturelands — three towns.

Jos 20:7; Nu 35:6

[33]The total number of towns of the Gershonite clans came to thirteen, together with their pasturelands.

[34]The Merarite clans (the rest of the Levites) were given:

from the tribe of Zebulun,

Jokneam, Kartah, 35Dimnah
and Nahalal, together with
their pasturelands — four
towns; 1Ch 6:77; Jos 12:22
36from the tribe of Reuben,
Bezer, Jahaz, 37Kedemoth and
Mephaath, together with their
pasturelands — four towns;
Jos 20:8; Nu 21:23
38from the tribe of Gad,
Ramoth in Gilead (a city of
refuge for one accused of
murder), Mahanaim, 39Hesh-
bon and Jazer, together with
their pasturelands — four
towns in all. 1Ch 6:54-80; Dt 4:43
40The total number of towns allotted to the Merarite clans, who
were the rest of the Levites, came
to twelve.

41The towns of the Levites in
the territory held by the Israelites
were forty-eight in all, together
with their pasturelands. 42Each of
these towns had pasturelands surrounding it; this was true for all
these towns. Nu 35:7

43So the LORD gave Israel all the
land he had sworn to give their
ancestors, and they took possession of it and settled there. 44The
LORD gave them rest on every
side, just as he had sworn to their
ancestors. Not one of their enemies withstood them; the LORD
gave all their enemies into their
hands. 45Not one of all the LORD's
good promises to Israel failed; every one was fulfilled.
Dt 11:31; Jos 1:13; 23:14

Eastern Tribes Return Home

22 Then Joshua summoned
the Reubenites, the Gad-
ites and the half-tribe of Manasseh 2and said to them, "You have
done all that Moses the servant of
the LORD commanded, and you
have obeyed me in everything
I commanded. 3For a long time
now — to this very day — you
have not deserted your fellow Israelites but have carried out the
mission the LORD your God gave
you. 4Now that the LORD your God
has given them rest as he promised, return to your homes in the
land that Moses the servant of the
LORD gave you on the other side of
the Jordan. 5But be very careful to
keep the commandment and the
law that Moses the servant of the
LORD gave you: to love the LORD
your God, to walk in obedience
to him, to keep his commands, to
hold fast to him and to serve him
with all your heart and with all
your soul." Dt 3:20; 5:29; Nu 32:18

6Then Joshua blessed them and
sent them away, and they went to
their homes. 7(To the half-tribe of
Manasseh Moses had given land
in Bashan, and to the other half of
the tribe Joshua gave land on the
west side of the Jordan along with
their fellow Israelites.) When Joshua sent them home, he blessed
them, 8saying, "Return to your
homes with your great wealth —
with large herds of livestock, with
silver, gold, bronze and iron, and

a great quantity of clothing — and
divide the plunder from your enemies with your fellow Israelites."
Ex 39:43; Nu 31:27; 1Sa 30:16
9 So the Reubenites, the Gadites
and the half-tribe of Manasseh left
the Israelites at Shiloh in Canaan
to return to Gilead, their own land,
which they had acquired in accordance with the command of the
LORD through Moses. Nu 32:26,29
10 When they came to Geliloth
near the Jordan in the land of Canaan, the Reubenites, the Gadites
and the half-tribe of Manasseh
built an imposing altar there by
the Jordan. 11 And when the Israelites heard that they had built the
altar on the border of Canaan at
Geliloth near the Jordan on the Israelite side, 12 the whole assembly
of Israel gathered at Shiloh to go
to war against them. Jos 18:1
13 So the Israelites sent Phinehas
son of Eleazar, the priest, to the
land of Gilead — to Reuben, Gad
and the half-tribe of Manasseh.
14 With him they sent ten of the
chief men, one from each of the
tribes of Israel, each the head of a
family division among the Israelite clans. Nu 1:4; 25:7
15 When they went to Gilead — to
Reuben, Gad and the half-tribe of
Manasseh — they said to them:
16 "The whole assembly of the
LORD says: 'How could you break
faith with the God of Israel like
this? How could you turn away
from the LORD and build yourselves an altar in rebellion against
him now? 17 Was not the sin of Peor
enough for us? Up to this very
day we have not cleansed ourselves from that sin, even though
a plague fell on the community of
the LORD! 18 And are you now turning away from the LORD?
Nu 25:1-9; Dt 12:13-14
"'If you rebel against the LORD
today, tomorrow he will be angry
with the whole community of Israel. 19 If the land you possess is
defiled, come over to the LORD's
land, where the LORD's tabernacle
stands, and share the land with us.
But do not rebel against the LORD
or against us by building an altar
for yourselves, other than the altar of the LORD our God. 20 When
Achan son of Zerah was unfaithful
in regard to the devoted things,[a]
did not wrath come on the whole
community of Israel? He was not
the only one who died for his sin.'"
Nu 16:22; Jos 7:1
21 Then Reuben, Gad and the
half-tribe of Manasseh replied to
the heads of the clans of Israel:
22 "The Mighty One, God, the LORD!
The Mighty One, God, the LORD! He
knows! And let Israel know! If this
has been in rebellion or disobedience to the LORD, do not spare
us this day. 23 If we have built our
own altar to turn away from the
LORD and to offer burnt offerings
and grain offerings, or to sacrifice

[a] 20 The Hebrew term refers to the irrevocable giving over of things or persons to the LORD, often by totally destroying them.

fellowship offerings on it, may the LORD himself call us to account.

Dt 10:17; 18:19; 1Ki 8:39

24"No! We did it for fear that some day your descendants might say to ours, 'What do you have to do with the LORD, the God of Israel?
25The LORD has made the Jordan a boundary between us and you — you Reubenites and Gadites! You have no share in the LORD.' So your descendants might cause ours to stop fearing the LORD.

26"That is why we said, 'Let us get ready and build an altar — but not for burnt offerings or sacrifices.'
27On the contrary, it is to be a witness between us and you and the generations that follow, that we will worship the LORD at his sanctuary with our burnt offerings, sacrifices and fellowship offerings. Then in the future your descendants will not be able to say to ours, 'You have no share in the LORD.'

Dt 12:6; Jos 24:27

28"And we said, 'If they ever say this to us, or to our descendants, we will answer: Look at the replica of the LORD's altar, which our ancestors built, not for burnt offerings and sacrifices, but as a witness between us and you.'

29"Far be it from us to rebel against the LORD and turn away from him today by building an altar for burnt offerings, grain offerings and sacrifices, other than the altar of the LORD our God that stands before his tabernacle."

Dt 12:13-14; Jos 24:16

30When Phinehas the priest and the leaders of the community — the heads of the clans of the Israelites — heard what Reuben, Gad and Manasseh had to say, they were pleased.
31And Phinehas son of Eleazar, the priest, said to Reuben, Gad and Manasseh, "Today we know that the LORD is with us, because you have not been unfaithful to the LORD in this matter. Now you have rescued the Israelites from the LORD's hand."

Lev 26:11-12; 2Ch 15:2

32Then Phinehas son of Eleazar, the priest, and the leaders returned to Canaan from their meeting with the Reubenites and Gadites in Gilead and reported to the Israelites.
33They were glad to hear the report and praised God. And they talked no more about going to war against them to devastate the country where the Reubenites and the Gadites lived.

1Ch 29:20; Da 2:19

34And the Reubenites and the Gadites gave the altar this name: A Witness Between Us — that the LORD is God. Ge 21:30

Joshua's Farewell to the Leaders

23 After a long time had passed and the LORD had given Israel rest from all their enemies around them, Joshua, by then a very old man,
2summoned all Israel — their elders, leaders, judges and officials — and said to them: "I am very old.
3You yourselves have seen everything the

LORD your God has done to all
these nations for your sake; it was
the LORD your God who fought for
you. [4]Remember how I have allotted as an inheritance for your
tribes all the land of the nations
that remain — the nations I conquered — between the Jordan
and the Mediterranean Sea in the
west. [5]The LORD your God himself
will push them out for your sake.
He will drive them out before you,
and you will take possession of
their land, as the LORD your God
promised you. Jos 13:1; 21:44; Nu 33:53

[6]"Be very strong; be careful
to obey all that is written in the
Book of the Law of Moses, without turning aside to the right or
to the left. [7]Do not associate with
these nations that remain among
you; do not invoke the names of
their gods or swear by them. You
must not serve them or bow down
to them. [8]But you are to hold fast
to the LORD your God, as you have
until now. Ex 23:13; Dt 10:20; Jos 1:7

[9]"The LORD has driven out before you great and powerful nations; to this day no one has been
able to withstand you. [10]One of
you routs a thousand, because the
LORD your God fights for you, just
as he promised. [11]So be very careful to love the LORD your God.

Dt 3:22; 11:23; Lev 26:8

[12]"But if you turn away and
ally yourselves with the survivors of these nations that remain
among you and if you intermarry with them and associate with
them, [13]then you may be sure that
the LORD your God will no longer
drive out these nations before
you. Instead, they will become
snares and traps for you, whips
on your backs and thorns in your
eyes, until you perish from this
good land, which the LORD your
God has given you.

Ex 34:16; Dt 7:3; Ps 106:34-35

[14]"Now I am about to go the way
of all the earth. You know with all
your heart and soul that not one
of all the good promises the LORD
your God gave you has failed. Every promise has been fulfilled;
not one has failed. [15]But just as
all the good things the LORD your
God has promised you have come
to you, so he will bring on you all
the evil things he has threatened,
until the LORD your God has destroyed you from this good land
he has given you. [16]If you violate
the covenant of the LORD your
God, which he commanded you,
and go and serve other gods and
bow down to them, the LORD's anger will burn against you, and you
will quickly perish from the good
land he has given you."

Dt 28:15; Jos 21:45; 1Ki 2:2

The Covenant Renewed at Shechem

24 Then Joshua assembled all
the tribes of Israel at Shechem. He summoned the elders,
leaders, judges and officials of
Israel, and they presented themselves before God. Jos 23:2

2 Joshua said to all the people,
"This is what the LORD, the God of
Israel, says: 'Long ago your ancestors, including Terah the father of
Abraham and Nahor, lived beyond
the Euphrates River and worshiped other gods. 3 But I took your
father Abraham from the land beyond the Euphrates and led him
throughout Canaan and gave him
many descendants. I gave him
Isaac, 4 and to Isaac I gave Jacob
and Esau. I assigned the hill country of Seir to Esau, but Jacob and
his family went down to Egypt.

Ge 11:32; 25:26; 46:5-6

5 " 'Then I sent Moses and Aaron, and I afflicted the Egyptians
by what I did there, and I brought
you out. 6 When I brought your
people out of Egypt, you came
to the sea, and the Egyptians
pursued them with chariots and
horsemen[a] as far as the Red Sea.[b]
7 But they cried to the LORD for
help, and he put darkness between you and the Egyptians; he
brought the sea over them and
covered them. You saw with your
own eyes what I did to the Egyptians. Then you lived in the wilderness for a long time.

Ex 3:10; 14:9; Dt 1:46

8 " 'I brought you to the land of
the Amorites who lived east of the
Jordan. They fought against you,
but I gave them into your hands. I
destroyed them from before you,
and you took possession of their
land. 9 When Balak son of Zippor,
the king of Moab, prepared to
fight against Israel, he sent for Balaam son of Beor to put a curse on
you. 10 But I would not listen to Balaam, so he blessed you again and
again, and I delivered you out of
his hand.

Ex 23:23; Nu 22:2; Dt 23:5

11 " 'Then you crossed the Jordan and came to Jericho. The citizens of Jericho fought against
you, as did also the Amorites,
Perizzites, Canaanites, Hittites,
Girgashites, Hivites and Jebusites, but I gave them into your
hands. 12 I sent the hornet ahead
of you, which drove them out before you — also the two Amorite
kings. You did not do it with your
own sword and bow. 13 So I gave
you a land on which you did not
toil and cities you did not build;
and you live in them and eat
from vineyards and olive groves
that you did not plant.'

Dt 6:10-11; Jos 3:16-17; Ps 44:3,6-7

14 "Now fear the LORD and serve
him with all faithfulness. Throw
away the gods your ancestors worshiped beyond the Euphrates River
and in Egypt, and serve the LORD.
15 But if serving the LORD seems
undesirable to you, then choose
for yourselves this day whom you
will serve, whether the gods your
ancestors served beyond the Euphrates, or the gods of the Amorites, in whose land you are living.
But as for me and my household,
we will serve the LORD."

Dt 10:12; Ru 1:16; 1Sa 12:24

[a] 6 Or *charioteers* [b] 6 Or *the Sea of Reeds*

16 Then the people answered, "Far be it from us to forsake the LORD to serve other gods! 17 It was the LORD our God himself who brought us and our parents up out of Egypt, from that land of slavery, and performed those great signs before our eyes. He protected us on our entire journey and among all the nations through which we traveled. 18 And the LORD drove out before us all the nations, including the Amorites, who lived in the land. We too will serve the LORD, because he is our God."

19 Joshua said to the people, "You are not able to serve the LORD. He is a holy God; he is a jealous God. He will not forgive your rebellion and your sins. 20 If you forsake the LORD and serve foreign gods, he will turn and bring disaster on you and make an end of you, after he has been good to you."

Ex 23:21; Jos 23:15; 1Ch 28:9,20

21 But the people said to Joshua, "No! We will serve the LORD."

22 Then Joshua said, "You are witnesses against yourselves that you have chosen to serve the LORD." Ru 4:10; Ps 119:30,173

"Yes, we are witnesses," they replied. Dt 25:9

23 "Now then," said Joshua, "throw away the foreign gods that are among you and yield your hearts to the LORD, the God of Israel." 1Ki 8:58

24 And the people said to Joshua, "We will serve the LORD our God and obey him." Ex 19:8; 24:3,7

25 On that day Joshua made a covenant for the people, and there at Shechem he reaffirmed for them decrees and laws. 26 And Joshua recorded these things in the Book of the Law of God. Then he took a large stone and set it up there under the oak near the holy place of the LORD. Ex 24:8; Dt 31:24

27 "See!" he said to all the people. "This stone will be a witness against us. It has heard all the words the LORD has said to us. It will be a witness against you if you are untrue to your God."

Jos 22:27; Pr 30:9; Hab 2:11

28 Then Joshua dismissed the people, each to their own inheritance. Jdg 21:23-24

Buried in the Promised Land

29 After these things, Joshua son of Nun, the servant of the LORD, died at the age of a hundred and ten. 30 And they buried him in the land of his inheritance, at Timnath Serah[a] in the hill country of Ephraim, north of Mount Gaash.

Jos 19:50; Jdg 1:1

31 Israel served the LORD throughout the lifetime of Joshua and of the elders who outlived him and who had experienced everything the LORD had done for Israel.

Jdg 2:6-9

32 And Joseph's bones, which the Israelites had brought up from Egypt, were buried at Shechem in the tract of land that Jacob bought

[a] *30* Also known as *Timnath Heres* (see Judges 2:9)

for a hundred pieces of silver[a]
from the sons of Hamor, the father of Shechem. This became the inheritance of Joseph's descendants. Ge 33:19; 50:25; Ex 13:19
33 And Eleazar son of Aaron died
and was buried at Gibeah, which had been allotted to his son Phinehas in the hill country of Ephraim. Jos 22:13; 1Sa 9:4

[a] 32 Hebrew *hundred kesitahs*; a kesitah was a unit of money of unknown weight and value.

JUDGES

Israel Fights the Remaining Canaanites

1 After the death of Joshua, the Israelites asked the LORD, "Who of us is to go up first to fight against the Canaanites?"

Nu 27:21; Jos 24:29; Jdg 3:1-6

[2]The LORD answered, "Judah shall go up; I have given the land into their hands." Ge 49:8

[3]The men of Judah then said to the Simeonites their fellow Israelites, "Come up with us into the territory allotted to us, to fight against the Canaanites. We in turn will go with you into yours." So the Simeonites went with them.

[4]When Judah attacked, the LORD gave the Canaanites and Perizzites into their hands, and they struck down ten thousand men at Bezek. [5]It was there that they found Adoni-Bezek and fought against him, putting to rout the Canaanites and Perizzites. [6]Adoni-Bezek fled, but they chased him and caught him, and cut off his thumbs and big toes. Ge 13:7; Jos 3:10

[7]Then Adoni-Bezek said, "Seventy kings with their thumbs and big toes cut off have picked up scraps under my table. Now God has paid me back for what I did to them." They brought him to Jerusalem, and he died there. Lev 24:19

[8]The men of Judah attacked Jerusalem also and took it. They put the city to the sword and set it on fire. Jos 15:63

[9]After that, Judah went down to fight against the Canaanites living in the hill country, the Negev and the western foothills. [10]They advanced against the Canaanites living in Hebron (formerly called Kiriath Arba) and defeated Sheshai, Ahiman and Talmai. [11]From there they advanced against the people living in Debir (formerly called Kiriath Sepher).

Nu 13:17; Jos 15:14

[12]And Caleb said, "I will give my daughter Aksah in marriage to the man who attacks and captures Kiriath Sepher." [13]Othniel son of Kenaz, Caleb's younger brother, took it; so Caleb gave his daughter Aksah to him in marriage.

[14]One day when she came to Othniel, she urged him[a] to ask her father for a field. When she got off her donkey, Caleb asked her, "What can I do for you?"

[15]She replied, "Do me a special favor. Since you have given me land in the Negev, give me also springs of water." So Caleb gave her the upper and lower springs.

Jos 15:15-19

[a] 14 Hebrew; Septuagint and Vulgate *Othniel, he urged her*

16The descendants of Moses' father-in-law, the Kenite, went up
from the City of Palms[a] with the
people of Judah to live among the
inhabitants of the Desert of Judah
in the Negev near Arad.

Nu 10:29; Dt 34:3; Jdg 4:11

17Then the men of Judah went
with the Simeonites their fellow
Israelites and attacked the Canaanites living in Zephath, and
they totally destroyed[b] the city.
Therefore it was called Hormah.[c]
18Judah also took[d] Gaza, Ashkelon
and Ekron — each city with its territory.

Nu 21:3; Jos 11:22

19The LORD was with the men
of Judah. They took possession of
the hill country, but they were unable to drive the people from the
plains, because they had chariots
fitted with iron. 20As Moses had
promised, Hebron was given to
Caleb, who drove from it the three
sons of Anak. 21The Benjamites,
however, did not drive out the
Jebusites, who were living in Jerusalem; to this day the Jebusites
live there with the Benjamites.

Jos 14:9; 15:63; 17:16

22Now the tribes of Joseph attacked Bethel, and the LORD was
with them. 23When they sent men
to spy out Bethel (formerly called
Luz), 24the spies saw a man coming out of the city and they said
to him, "Show us how to get into
the city and we will see that you
are treated well." 25So he showed
them, and they put the city to the
sword but spared the man and his
whole family. 26He then went to
the land of the Hittites, where he
built a city and called it Luz, which
is its name to this day.

Ge 28:19; Jos 2:12,14; 6:25

27But Manasseh did not drive
out the people of Beth Shan or
Taanach or Dor or Ibleam or Megiddo and their surrounding settlements, for the Canaanites were
determined to live in that land.
28When Israel became strong,
they pressed the Canaanites into
forced labor but never drove them
out completely. 29Nor did Ephraim drive out the Canaanites living
in Gezer, but the Canaanites continued to live there among them.
30Neither did Zebulun drive out
the Canaanites living in Kitron or
Nahalol, so these Canaanites lived
among them, but Zebulun did
subject them to forced labor. 31Nor
did Asher drive out those living
in Akko or Sidon or Ahlab or Akzib or Helbah or Aphek or Rehob.
32The Asherites lived among the
Canaanite inhabitants of the land
because they did not drive them
out. 33Neither did Naphtali drive
out those living in Beth Shemesh
or Beth Anath; but the Naph-
talites too lived among the Canaanite inhabitants of the land,

[a] *16* That is, Jericho [b] *17* The Hebrew term refers to the irrevocable giving over of things or persons to the LORD, often by totally destroying them. [c] *17* *Hormah* means *destruction.* [d] *18* Hebrew; Septuagint *Judah did not take*

and those living in Beth Shemesh
and Beth Anath became forced
laborers for them. [34]The Amorites confined the Danites to the
hill country, not allowing them to
come down into the plain. [35]And
the Amorites were determined
also to hold out in Mount Heres,
Aijalon and Shaalbim, but when
the power of the tribes of Joseph
increased, they too were pressed
into forced labor. [36]The boundary
of the Amorites was from Scorpion Pass to Sela and beyond.

Jos 15:3; 16:10; 17:11

The Angel of the LORD at Bokim

2 The angel of the LORD went
up from Gilgal to Bokim and
said, "I brought you up out of
Egypt and led you into the land
I swore to give to your ancestors.
I said, 'I will never break my covenant with you, [2]and you shall
not make a covenant with the
people of this land, but you shall
break down their altars.' Yet you
have disobeyed me. Why have you
done this? [3]And I have also said,
'I will not drive them out before
you; they will become traps for
you, and their gods will become
snares to you.'"

Ex 20:2; Jos 23:13; Ps 106:36

[4]When the angel of the LORD
had spoken these things to all the
Israelites, the people wept aloud,
[5]and they called that place Bokim.[a] There they offered sacrifices
to the LORD.

Disobedience and Defeat

[6]After Joshua had dismissed
the Israelites, they went to take
possession of the land, each to
their own inheritance. [7]The people served the LORD throughout
the lifetime of Joshua and of the
elders who outlived him and who
had seen all the great things the
LORD had done for Israel.

[8]Joshua son of Nun, the servant
of the LORD, died at the age of a
hundred and ten. [9]And they buried him in the land of his inheritance, at Timnath Heres[b] in the
hill country of Ephraim, north of
Mount Gaash. Jos 24:29-31; 19:50

[10]After that whole generation
had been gathered to their ancestors, another generation grew
up who knew neither the LORD
nor what he had done for Israel.
[11]Then the Israelites did evil in the
eyes of the LORD and served the
Baals. [12]They forsook the LORD, the
God of their ancestors, who had
brought them out of Egypt. They
followed and worshiped various
gods of the peoples around them.
They aroused the LORD's anger
[13]because they forsook him and
served Baal and the Ashtoreths.
[14]In his anger against Israel the
LORD gave them into the hands
of raiders who plundered them.
He sold them into the hands of
their enemies all around, whom

[a] 5 *Bokim* means *weepers.* [b] 9 Also known as *Timnath Serah* (see Joshua 19:50 and 24:30)

they were no longer able to resist. 15Whenever Israel went out to fight, the hand of the LORD was against them to defeat them, just as he had sworn to them. They were in great distress.

Dt 28:25; 31:16; 1Sa 2:12

16Then the LORD raised up judges,[a] who saved them out of the hands of these raiders. 17Yet they would not listen to their judges but prostituted themselves to other gods and worshiped them. They quickly turned from the ways of their ancestors, who had been obedient to the LORD's commands. 18Whenever the LORD raised up a judge for them, he was with the judge and saved them out of the hands of their enemies as long as the judge lived; for the LORD relented because of their groaning under those who oppressed and afflicted them. 19But when the judge died, the people returned to ways even more corrupt than those of their ancestors, following other gods and serving and worshiping them. They refused to give up their evil practices and stubborn ways.

Jos 1:5; Jdg 3:12; Ac 13:20

20Therefore the LORD was very angry with Israel and said, "Because this nation has violated the covenant I ordained for their ancestors and has not listened to me, 21I will no longer drive out before them any of the nations Joshua left when he died. 22I will use them to test Israel and see whether they will keep the way of the LORD and walk in it as their ancestors did." 23The LORD had allowed those nations to remain; he did not drive them out at once by giving them into the hands of Joshua.

Dt 8:2,16; Jos 23:16; Jdg 3:1,14

3 These are the nations the LORD left to test all those Israelites who had not experienced any of the wars in Canaan 2(he did this only to teach warfare to the descendants of the Israelites who had not had previous battle experience): 3the five rulers of the Philistines, all the Canaanites, the Sidonians, and the Hivites living in the Lebanon mountains from Mount Baal Hermon to Lebo Hamath. 4They were left to test the Israelites to see whether they would obey the LORD's commands, which he had given their ancestors through Moses.

Ex 15:25; Jos 13:3; Jdg 2:21-22

5The Israelites lived among the Canaanites, Hittites, Amorites, Perizzites, Hivites and Jebusites. 6They took their daughters in marriage and gave their own daughters to their sons, and served their gods.

Ex 34:16; Dt 7:3-4; Ps 106:35

Othniel

7The Israelites did evil in the eyes of the LORD; they forgot the LORD their God and served the Baals and the Asherahs. 8The anger of the LORD burned against

[a] 16 Or *leaders*; similarly in verses 17-19

Israel so that he sold them into
the hands of Cushan-Rishatha-
im king of Aram Naharaim,[a] to
whom the Israelites were subject
for eight years. 9But when they
cried out to the LORD, he raised up
for them a deliverer, Othniel son
of Kenaz, Caleb's younger brother, who saved them. 10The Spirit of
the LORD came on him, so that he
became Israel's judge[b] and went
to war. The LORD gave Cushan-
Rishathaim king of Aram into the
hands of Othniel, who overpowered him. 11So the land had peace
for forty years, until Othniel son
of Kenaz died.

Nu 11:25,29; Dt 4:9; Jdg 6:34

Ehud

12Again the Israelites did evil in
the eyes of the LORD, and because
they did this evil the LORD gave
Eglon king of Moab power over
Israel. 13Getting the Ammonites
and Amalekites to join him, Eglon came and attacked Israel, and
they took possession of the City
of Palms.[c] 14The Israelites were
subject to Eglon king of Moab for
eighteen years. Jdg 1:16; 2:11,14

15Again the Israelites cried out
to the LORD, and he gave them a
deliverer — Ehud, a left-handed
man, the son of Gera the Benjamite. The Israelites sent him with
tribute to Eglon king of Moab.
16Now Ehud had made a double-
edged sword about a cubit[d] long,
which he strapped to his right
thigh under his clothing. 17He presented the tribute to Eglon king
of Moab, who was a very fat man.
18After Ehud had presented the
tribute, he sent on their way those
who had carried it. 19But on reaching the stone images near Gilgal
he himself went back to Eglon and
said, "Your Majesty, I have a secret
message for you." 1Ch 12:2; Ps 78:34

The king said to his attendants,
"Leave us!" And they all left.

20Ehud then approached him
while he was sitting alone in the
upper room of his palace[e] and
said, "I have a message from God
for you." As the king rose from his
seat, 21Ehud reached with his left
hand, drew the sword from his
right thigh and plunged it into
the king's belly. 22Even the handle sank in after the blade, and
his bowels discharged. Ehud did
not pull the sword out, and the
fat closed in over it. 23Then Ehud
went out to the porch[f]; he shut the
doors of the upper room behind
him and locked them. Am 3:15

24After he had gone, the servants came and found the doors
of the upper room locked. They
said, "He must be relieving himself in the inner room of the palace." 25They waited to the point of

[a] *8* That is, Northwest Mesopotamia
[b] *10* Or *leader* [c] *13* That is, Jericho
[d] *16* That is, about 18 inches or about 45 centimeters [e] *20* The meaning of the Hebrew for this word is uncertain; also in verse 24. [f] *23* The meaning of the Hebrew for this word is uncertain.

embarrassment, but when he did
not open the doors of the room,
they took a key and unlocked
them. There they saw their lord
fallen to the floor, dead.
1Sa 24:3; 2Ki 2:17
[26]While they waited, Ehud got
away. He passed by the stone images and escaped to Seirah. [27]When
he arrived there, he blew a trumpet in the hill country of Ephraim,
and the Israelites went down with
him from the hills, with him leading them. Jdg 6:34
[28]"Follow me," he ordered, "for
the LORD has given Moab, your
enemy, into your hands." So they
followed him down and took possession of the fords of the Jordan
that led to Moab; they allowed no
one to cross over. [29]At that time
they struck down about ten thousand Moabites, all vigorous and
strong; not one escaped. [30]That
day Moab was made subject to Israel, and the land had peace for
eighty years. Jdg 7:9,15,24; 12:5

Shamgar

[31]After Ehud came Shamgar son
of Anath, who struck down six
hundred Philistines with an ox-
goad. He too saved Israel. Jdg 5:6

Deborah

4 Again the Israelites did evil
in the eyes of the LORD, now
that Ehud was dead. [2]So the LORD
sold them into the hands of Jabin
king of Canaan, who reigned in
Hazor. Sisera, the commander of
his army, was based in Harosheth
Haggoyim. [3]Because he had nine
hundred chariots fitted with iron
and had cruelly oppressed the
Israelites for twenty years, they
cried to the LORD for help.
Jdg 1:19; 2:19; Jos 11:1
[4]Now Deborah, a prophet, the
wife of Lappidoth, was leading[a]
Israel at that time. [5]She held court
under the Palm of Deborah between Ramah and Bethel in the
hill country of Ephraim, and the
Israelites went up to her to have
their disputes decided. [6]She sent
for Barak son of Abinoam from
Kedesh in Naphtali and said to
him, "The LORD, the God of Israel, commands you: 'Go, take with
you ten thousand men of Naphtali and Zebulun and lead them up
to Mount Tabor. [7]I will lead Sisera,
the commander of Jabin's army,
with his chariots and his troops to
the Kishon River and give him into
your hands.'" Heb 11:32; Ps 83:9; Ge 35:8
[8]Barak said to her, "If you go
with me, I will go; but if you don't
go with me, I won't go."
[9]"Certainly I will go with you,"
said Deborah. "But because of the
course you are taking, the honor
will not be yours, for the LORD will
deliver Sisera into the hands of a
woman." So Deborah went with
Barak to Kedesh. [10]There Barak
summoned Zebulun and Naphtali, and ten thousand men went up

[a] 4 Traditionally *judging*

under his command. Deborah also
went up with him. Jdg 5:15,18
11 Now Heber the Kenite had left
the other Kenites, the descendants
of Hobab, Moses' brother-in-law,[a]
and pitched his tent by the great
tree in Zaanannim near Kedesh.
Jdg 1:16
12 When they told Sisera that Barak son of Abinoam had gone up to
Mount Tabor, 13 Sisera summoned
from Harosheth Haggoyim to the
Kishon River all his men and his
nine hundred chariots fitted with
iron.
14 Then Deborah said to Barak,
"Go! This is the day the LORD has
given Sisera into your hands. Has
not the LORD gone ahead of you?"
So Barak went down Mount Tabor,
with ten thousand men following
him. 15 At Barak's advance, the LORD
routed Sisera and all his chariots
and army by the sword, and Sisera
got down from his chariot and fled
on foot. Dt 9:3; Jos 10:10; 2Sa 5:24
16 Barak pursued the chariots and
army as far as Harosheth Haggoyim, and all Sisera's troops fell by
the sword; not a man was left. 17 Sisera, meanwhile, fled on foot to the
tent of Jael, the wife of Heber the
Kenite, because there was an alliance between Jabin king of Hazor
and the family of Heber the Kenite.
18 Jael went out to meet Sisera
and said to him, "Come, my lord,
come right in. Don't be afraid." So
he entered her tent, and she covered him with a blanket.
19 "I'm thirsty," he said. "Please
give me some water." She opened
a skin of milk, gave him a drink,
and covered him up. Jdg 5:25
20 "Stand in the doorway of the
tent," he told her. "If someone
comes by and asks you, 'Is anyone
in there?' say 'No.' "
21 But Jael, Heber's wife, picked
up a tent peg and a hammer and
went quietly to him while he lay
fast asleep, exhausted. She drove
the peg through his temple into
the ground, and he died.
22 Just then Barak came by in
pursuit of Sisera, and Jael went
out to meet him. "Come," she said,
"I will show you the man you're
looking for." So he went in with
her, and there lay Sisera with the
tent peg through his temple —
dead.
23 On that day God subdued Jabin king of Canaan before the Israelites. 24 And the hand of the Israelites pressed harder and harder
against Jabin king of Canaan until
they destroyed him. Ne 9:24; Ps 18:47

The Song of Deborah

5 On that day Deborah and Barak son of Abinoam sang this
song: Ex 15:1

2 "When the princes in Israel
take the lead,
when the people willingly
offer themselves —
2Ch 17:16
praise the LORD!

[a] 11 Or *father-in-law*

3 "Hear this, you kings! Listen,
you rulers!
I, even I, will sing to[a] the
LORD;
I will praise the LORD, the
God of Israel, in song.
Ps 27:6

4 "When you, LORD, went out
from Seir,
when you marched
from the land
of Edom, Dt 33:2
the earth shook, the heavens
poured,
the clouds poured down
water. Ps 68:8
5 The mountains quaked before
the LORD, the One of
Sinai,
before the LORD, the God of
Israel. Ex 19:18

6 "In the days of Shamgar
son of Anath, Jdg 3:31
in the days of Jael, the
highways were
abandoned; Jdg 4:17
travelers took to winding
paths.
7 Villagers in Israel would not
fight;
they held back until I,
Deborah, arose,
until I arose, a mother in
Israel.
8 God chose new leaders Dt 32:17
when war came to the city
gates,
but not a shield or spear was
seen
among forty thousand in
Israel.
9 My heart is with Israel's
princes,
with the willing volunteers
among the people.
Praise the LORD!

10 "You who ride on white
donkeys, Jdg 10:4
sitting on your saddle
blankets,
and you who walk along the
road,
consider 11 the voice of the
singers[b] at the watering
places.
They recite the victories of
the LORD, 1Sa 12:7; Mic 6:5
the victories of his villagers
in Israel.
"Then the people of the LORD
went down to the
city gates.
12 'Wake up, wake up,
Deborah! Ps 57:8
Wake up, wake up, break out
in song!
Arise, Barak!
Take captive your captives,
son of Abinoam.'
Ps 68:18; Eph 4:8

13 "The remnant of the nobles
came down;
the people of the LORD
came down to
me against the
mighty.

[a] 3 Or *of* [b] 11 The meaning of the Hebrew for this word is uncertain.

14 Some came from Ephraim,
whose roots were in Amalek;
Benjamin was with the people who followed you.
From Makir captains came down,
from Zebulun those who bear a commander's[a] staff.
15 The princes of Issachar were with Deborah; Jdg 4:10
yes, Issachar was with Barak,
sent under his command into the valley.
In the districts of Reuben
there was much searching of heart.
16 Why did you stay among the sheep pens[b]
to hear the whistling for the flocks? Nu 32:1
In the districts of Reuben
there was much searching of heart.
17 Gilead stayed beyond the Jordan.
And Dan, why did he linger by the ships?
Asher remained on the coast
and stayed in his coves. Jos 19:29
18 The people of Zebulun risked their very lives;
so did Naphtali on the terraced fields. Jdg 4:6,10
19 "Kings came, they fought, Jos 11:5
the kings of Canaan fought.
At Taanach, by the waters of Megiddo, Jdg 1:27
they took no plunder of silver.
20 From the heavens the stars fought,
from their courses
they fought against Sisera. Jos 10:11
21 The river Kishon swept them away,
the age-old river, the river Kishon.
March on, my soul; be strong!
22 Then thundered the horses' hooves—
galloping, galloping go his mighty steeds.
23 'Curse Meroz,' said the angel of the LORD.
'Curse its people bitterly,
because they did not come to help the LORD,
to help the LORD against the mighty.'

24 "Most blessed of women be Jael, Jdg 4:17
the wife of Heber the Kenite,
most blessed of tent-dwelling women.
25 He asked for water, and she gave him milk;
in a bowl fit for nobles she brought him curdled milk.

[a] *14* The meaning of the Hebrew for this word is uncertain. [b] *16* Or *the campfires*; or *the saddlebags*

26 Her hand reached for the tent peg,
her right hand for the workman's hammer.
She struck Sisera, she crushed his head,
she shattered and pierced his temple.
27 At her feet he sank,
he fell; there he lay.
At her feet he sank, he fell;
where he sank, there he fell — dead.

28 "Through the window peered Sisera's mother;
behind the lattice she cried out, Pr 7:6
'Why is his chariot so long in coming?
Why is the clatter of his chariots delayed?'
29 The wisest of her ladies answer her;
indeed, she keeps saying to herself,
30 'Are they not finding and dividing the spoils: Ex 15:9; 1Sa 30:24
a woman or two for each man,
colorful garments as plunder for Sisera,
colorful garments embroidered,
highly embroidered garments for my neck —
all this as plunder?'

31 "So may all your enemies perish, LORD!
But may all who love you be like the sun Ps 19:4; 89:36
when it rises in its strength."

Then the land had peace forty years. Jdg 3:11

Gideon

6 The Israelites did evil in the
eyes of the LORD, and for sev-
en years he gave them into the
hands of the Midianites. 2 Because
the power of Midian was so oppressive, the Israelites prepared
shelters for themselves in mountain clefts, caves and strongholds.
3 Whenever the Israelites planted
their crops, the Midianites, Amalekites and other eastern peoples invaded the country. 4 They
camped on the land and ruined
the crops all the way to Gaza and
did not spare a living thing for
Israel, neither sheep nor cattle
nor donkeys. 5 They came up with
their livestock and their tents like
swarms of locusts. It was impossible to count them or their camels;
they invaded the land to ravage it.
6 Midian so impoverished the Israelites that they cried out to the
LORD for help. Lev 26:16; Jdg 7:12; 1Sa 13:6

7 When the Israelites cried out to
the LORD because of Midian, 8 he
sent them a prophet, who said,
"This is what the LORD, the God of
Israel, says: I brought you up out
of Egypt, out of the land of slavery.
9 I rescued you from the hand of
the Egyptians. And I delivered you
from the hand of all your oppres-

sors; I drove them out before you
and gave you their land. 10 I said to
you, 'I am the LORD your God; do
not worship the gods of the Amorites, in whose land you live.' But
you have not listened to me."
Jdg 2:1; Ps 44:2; Jer 10:2

11 The angel of the LORD came
and sat down under the oak in
Ophrah that belonged to Joash
the Abiezrite, where his son Gideon was threshing wheat in a winepress to keep it from the Midianites. 12 When the angel of the LORD
appeared to Gideon, he said, "The
LORD is with you, mighty warrior."
Jos 1:5; Heb 11:32

13 "Pardon me, my lord," Gideon
replied, "but if the LORD is with us,
why has all this happened to us?
Where are all his wonders that our
ancestors told us about when they
said, 'Did not the LORD bring us up
out of Egypt?' But now the LORD
has abandoned us and given us
into the hand of Midian." Ps 44:1

14 The LORD turned to him and
said, "Go in the strength you have
and save Israel out of Midian's
hand. Am I not sending you?"
Heb 11:34

15 "Pardon me, my lord," Gideon
replied, "but how can I save Israel?
My clan is the weakest in Manasseh, and I am the least in my family." 1Sa 9:21

16 The LORD answered, "I will be
with you, and you will strike down
all the Midianites, leaving none
alive." Ex 3:12

17 Gideon replied, "If now I have
found favor in your eyes, give me
a sign that it is really you talking
to me. 18 Please do not go away until I come back and bring my offering and set it before you."
Ge 24:14

And the LORD said, "I will wait
until you return."

19 Gideon went inside, prepared
a young goat, and from an ephah[a]
of flour he made bread without
yeast. Putting the meat in a basket
and its broth in a pot, he brought
them out and offered them to him
under the oak. Ge 18:7-8

20 The angel of God said to him,
"Take the meat and the unleavened bread, place them on this
rock, and pour out the broth." And
Gideon did so. 21 Then the angel of
the LORD touched the meat and
the unleavened bread with the tip
of the staff that was in his hand.
Fire flared from the rock, consuming the meat and the bread.
And the angel of the LORD disappeared. 22 When Gideon realized
that it was the angel of the LORD,
he exclaimed, "Alas, Sovereign
LORD! I have seen the angel of the
LORD face to face!"
Jdg 13:16,19,21; Lev 9:24; Ge 32:30

23 But the LORD said to him,
"Peace! Do not be afraid. You are
not going to die." Da 10:19

24 So Gideon built an altar to the
LORD there and called it The LORD

[a] 19 That is, probably about 36 pounds or about 16 kilograms

Is Peace. To this day it stands in Ophrah of the Abiezrites. Jdg 8:32

25 That same night the LORD said to him, "Take the second bull from your father's herd, the one seven years old.[a] Tear down your father's altar to Baal and cut down the Asherah pole[b] beside it. 26 Then build a proper kind of[c] altar to the LORD your God on the top of this height. Using the wood of the Asherah pole that you cut down, offer the second[d] bull as a burnt offering." Ex 34:13

27 So Gideon took ten of his servants and did as the LORD told him. But because he was afraid of his family and the townspeople, he did it at night rather than in the daytime.

28 In the morning when the people of the town got up, there was Baal's altar, demolished, with the Asherah pole beside it cut down and the second bull sacrificed on the newly built altar! 1Ki 16:32

29 They asked each other, "Who did this?"

When they carefully investigated, they were told, "Gideon son of Joash did it."

30 The people of the town demanded of Joash, "Bring out your son. He must die, because he has broken down Baal's altar and cut down the Asherah pole beside it."

31 But Joash replied to the hostile crowd around him, "Are you going to plead Baal's cause? Are you trying to save him? Whoever fights for him shall be put to death by morning! If Baal really is a god, he can defend himself when someone breaks down his altar." 32 So because Gideon broke down Baal's altar, they gave him the name Jerub-Baal[e] that day, saying, "Let Baal contend with him." Jdg 7:1; 1Sa 12:11

33 Now all the Midianites, Amalekites and other eastern peoples joined forces and crossed over the Jordan and camped in the Valley of Jezreel. 34 Then the Spirit of the LORD came on Gideon, and he blew a trumpet, summoning the Abiezrites to follow him. 35 He sent messengers throughout Manasseh, calling them to arms, and also into Asher, Zebulun and Naphtali, so that they too went up to meet them. Jos 17:16; Jdg 3:10,27; 4:6

36 Gideon said to God, "If you will save Israel by my hand as you have promised — 37 look, I will place a wool fleece on the threshing floor. If there is dew only on the fleece and all the ground is dry, then I will know that you will save Israel by my hand, as you said." 38 And that is what happened. Gideon rose early the next day; he squeezed the fleece and wrung out the dew — a bowlful of water. Ge 24:14

[a] 25 Or *Take a full-grown, mature bull from your father's herd* [b] 25 That is, a wooden symbol of the goddess Asherah; also in verses 26, 28 and 30 [c] 26 Or *build with layers of stone an* [d] 26 Or *full-grown;* also in verse 28 [e] 32 *Jerub-Baal* probably means *let Baal contend.*

39Then Gideon said to God, "Do not be angry with me. Let me make just one more request. Allow me one more test with the fleece, but this time make the fleece dry and let the ground be covered with dew." 40That night God did so. Only the fleece was dry; all the ground was covered with dew. Ge 18:32

Gideon Defeats the Midianites

7 Early in the morning, Jerub-Baal (that is, Gideon) and all his men camped at the spring of Harod. The camp of Midian was north of them in the valley near the hill of Moreh. 2The LORD said to Gideon, "You have too many men. I cannot deliver Midian into their hands, or Israel would boast against me, 'My own strength has saved me.' 3Now announce to the army, 'Anyone who trembles with fear may turn back and leave Mount Gilead.'" So twenty-two thousand men left, while ten thousand remained. Dt 8:17; 20:8; Jdg 6:32

4But the LORD said to Gideon, "There are still too many men. Take them down to the water, and I will thin them out for you there. If I say, 'This one shall go with you,' he shall go; but if I say, 'This one shall not go with you,' he shall not go." 1Sa 14:6

5So Gideon took the men down to the water. There the LORD told him, "Separate those who lap the water with their tongues as a dog laps from those who kneel down to drink." 6Three hundred of them drank from cupped hands, lapping like dogs. All the rest got down on their knees to drink.

7The LORD said to Gideon, "With the three hundred men that lapped I will save you and give the Midianites into your hands. Let all the others go home." 8So Gideon sent the rest of the Israelites home but kept the three hundred, who took over the provisions and trumpets of the others. Jos 8:7

Now the camp of Midian lay below him in the valley. 9During that night the LORD said to Gideon, "Get up, go down against the camp, because I am going to give it into your hands. 10If you are afraid to attack, go down to the camp with your servant Purah 11and listen to what they are saying. Afterward, you will be encouraged to attack the camp." So he and Purah his servant went down to the outposts of the camp. 12The Midianites, the Amalekites and all the other eastern peoples had settled in the valley, thick as locusts. Their camels could no more be counted than the sand on the seashore. Jos 2:24; 11:4; Jdg 8:10

13Gideon arrived just as a man was telling a friend his dream. "I had a dream," he was saying. "A round loaf of barley bread came tumbling into the Midianite camp. It struck the tent with such force that the tent overturned and collapsed."

14 His friend responded, "This can be nothing other than the sword of Gideon son of Joash, the Israelite. God has given the Midianites and the whole camp into his hands."

15 When Gideon heard the dream and its interpretation, he bowed down and worshiped. He returned to the camp of Israel and called out, "Get up! The LORD has given the Midianite camp into your hands." 16 Dividing the three hundred men into three companies, he placed trumpets and empty jars in the hands of all of them, with torches inside. 1Sa 15:31

17 "Watch me," he told them. "Follow my lead. When I get to the edge of the camp, do exactly as I do. 18 When I and all who are with me blow our trumpets, then from all around the camp blow yours and shout, 'For the LORD and for Gideon.'" Jdg 3:27

19 Gideon and the hundred men with him reached the edge of the camp at the beginning of the middle watch, just after they had changed the guard. They blew their trumpets and broke the jars that were in their hands. 20 The three companies blew the trumpets and smashed the jars. Grasping the torches in their left hands and holding in their right hands the trumpets they were to blow, they shouted, "A sword for the LORD and for Gideon!" 21 While each man held his position around the camp, all the Midianites ran, crying out as they fled. 2Ki 7:7

22 When the three hundred trumpets sounded, the LORD caused the men throughout the camp to turn on each other with their swords. The army fled to Beth Shittah toward Zererah as far as the border of Abel Meholah near Tabbath. 23 Israelites from Naphtali, Asher and all Manasseh were called out, and they pursued the Midianites. 24 Gideon sent messengers throughout the hill country of Ephraim, saying, "Come down against the Midianites and seize the waters of the Jordan ahead of them as far as Beth Barah." Jdg 3:28; 6:35; 1Sa 14:20

So all the men of Ephraim were called out and they seized the waters of the Jordan as far as Beth Barah. 25 They also captured two of the Midianite leaders, Oreb and Zeeb. They killed Oreb at the rock of Oreb, and Zeeb at the winepress of Zeeb. They pursued the Midianites and brought the heads of Oreb and Zeeb to Gideon, who was by the Jordan. Jdg 8:4; Ps 83:11; Isa 10:26

Zebah and Zalmunna

8 Now the Ephraimites asked Gideon, "Why have you treated us like this? Why didn't you call us when you went to fight Midian?" And they challenged him vigorously. Jdg 12:1

2But he answered them, "What
have I accomplished compared
to you? Aren't the gleanings of
Ephraim's grapes better than the
full grape harvest of Abiezer? 3God
gave Oreb and Zeeb, the Midianite
leaders, into your hands. What was
I able to do compared to you?" At
this, their resentment against him
subsided. Jdg 7:25; Pr 15:1

4Gideon and his three hundred
men, exhausted yet keeping up
the pursuit, came to the Jordan
and crossed it. 5He said to the men
of Sukkoth, "Give my troops some
bread; they are worn out, and I am
still pursuing Zebah and Zalmunna, the kings of Midian." Ge 33:17

6But the officials of Sukkoth
said, "Do you already have the
hands of Zebah and Zalmunna in
your possession? Why should we
give bread to your troops?" 1Sa 25:11

7Then Gideon replied, "Just for
that, when the LORD has given Zebah and Zalmunna into my hand,
I will tear your flesh with desert
thorns and briers." Jdg 7:15

8From there he went up to Peniel[a] and made the same request
of them, but they answered as the
men of Sukkoth had. 9So he said
to the men of Peniel, "When I return in triumph, I will tear down
this tower." Ge 32:30; 1Ki 12:25

10Now Zebah and Zalmunna
were in Karkor with a force of
about fifteen thousand men, all
that were left of the armies of the
eastern peoples; a hundred and
twenty thousand swordsmen had
fallen. 11Gideon went up by the
route of the nomads east of Nobah
and Jogbehah and attacked the
unsuspecting army. 12Zebah and
Zalmunna, the two kings of Midian, fled, but he pursued them and
captured them, routing their entire army. Jdg 7:12; Nu 32:42; Isa 9:4

13Gideon son of Joash then returned from the battle by the
Pass of Heres. 14He caught a
young man of Sukkoth and questioned him, and the young man
wrote down for him the names
of the seventy-seven officials of
Sukkoth, the elders of the town.
15Then Gideon came and said
to the men of Sukkoth, "Here
are Zebah and Zalmunna, about
whom you taunted me by saying,
'Do you already have the hands
of Zebah and Zalmunna in your
possession? Why should we give
bread to your exhausted men?' "
16He took the elders of the town
and taught the men of Sukkoth
a lesson by punishing them with
desert thorns and briers. 17He also
pulled down the tower of Peniel
and killed the men of the town.
Jdg 6:11

18Then he asked Zebah and Zalmunna, "What kind of men did
you kill at Tabor?" Jdg 4:6

"Men like you," they answered,
"each one with the bearing of a
prince."

[a] 8 Hebrew *Penuel,* a variant of *Peniel;* also in verses 9 and 17

19Gideon replied, "Those were
my brothers, the sons of my own
mother. As surely as the LORD
lives, if you had spared their lives,
I would not kill you." 20Turning to
Jether, his oldest son, he said, "Kill
them!" But Jether did not draw his
sword, because he was only a boy
and was afraid.

21Zebah and Zalmunna said,
"Come, do it yourself. 'As is the
man, so is his strength.'" So Gideon stepped forward and killed
them, and took the ornaments off
their camels' necks. Ps 83:11

Gideon's Ephod

22The Israelites said to Gideon, "Rule over us — you, your son
and your grandson — because you
have saved us from the hand of
Midian."

23But Gideon told them, "I will
not rule over you, nor will my son
rule over you. The LORD will rule
over you." 24And he said, "I do have
one request, that each of you give
me an earring from your share of
the plunder." (It was the custom of
the Ishmaelites to wear gold earrings.) 1Sa 8:7; 12:12; Ge 25:13

25They answered, "We'll be glad
to give them." So they spread out a
garment, and each of them threw
a ring from his plunder onto it.
26The weight of the gold rings he
asked for came to seventeen hundred shekels,[a] not counting the
ornaments, the pendants and
the purple garments worn by the
kings of Midian or the chains that
were on their camels' necks. 27Gid-
eon made the gold into an ephod,
which he placed in Ophrah, his
town. All Israel prostituted themselves by worshiping it there, and
it became a snare to Gideon and
his family. Jdg 17:5; Dt 7:16; Ps 106:39

Gideon's Death

28Thus Midian was subdued
before the Israelites and did not
raise its head again. During Gideon's lifetime, the land had peace
forty years. Jdg 5:31

29Jerub-Baal son of Joash went
back home to live. 30He had seventy sons of his own, for he had
many wives. 31His concubine, who
lived in Shechem, also bore him
a son, whom he named Abimelek. 32Gideon son of Joash died
at a good old age and was buried
in the tomb of his father Joash in
Ophrah of the Abiezrites.
Jdg 7:1; 9:2,5,18,24

33No sooner had Gideon died
than the Israelites again prostituted themselves to the Baals.
They set up Baal-Berith as their
god 34and did not remember the
LORD their God, who had rescued
them from the hands of all their
enemies on every side. 35They also
failed to show any loyalty to the
family of Jerub-Baal (that is, Gideon) in spite of all the good things
he had done for them.
Jdg 2:11,13,19; 9:16; Dt 4:9

[a] *26* That is, about 43 pounds or about 20 kilograms

Abimelek

9 Abimelek son of Jerub-Baal
went to his mother's brothers
in Shechem and said to them and
to all his mother's clan, 2"Ask all
the citizens of Shechem, 'Which is
better for you: to have all seventy
of Jerub-Baal's sons rule over you,
or just one man?' Remember, I am
your flesh and blood." Ge 29:14; Jdg 8:31
3When the brothers repeated all
this to the citizens of Shechem,
they were inclined to follow Abimelek, for they said, "He is related
to us." 4They gave him seventy
shekels[a] of silver from the temple
of Baal-Berith, and Abimelek used
it to hire reckless scoundrels, who
became his followers. 5He went to
his father's home in Ophrah and
on one stone murdered his seventy brothers, the sons of Jerub-
Baal. But Jotham, the youngest
son of Jerub-Baal, escaped by hiding. 6Then all the citizens of Shechem and Beth Millo gathered beside the great tree at the pillar in
Shechem to crown Abimelek king.
Jdg 8:33; 2Ki 11:2
7When Jotham was told about
this, he climbed up on the top of
Mount Gerizim and shouted to
them, "Listen to me, citizens of
Shechem, so that God may listen
to you. 8One day the trees went
out to anoint a king for themselves. They said to the olive tree,
'Be our king.' Dt 11:29; Jn 4:20
9"But the olive tree answered,
'Should I give up my oil, by which
both gods and humans are honored, to hold sway over the trees?'
10"Next, the trees said to the fig
tree, 'Come and be our king.'
11"But the fig tree replied,
'Should I give up my fruit, so good
and sweet, to hold sway over the
trees?'
12"Then the trees said to the
vine, 'Come and be our king.'
13"But the vine answered,
'Should I give up my wine, which
cheers both gods and humans, to
hold sway over the trees?' Ecc 2:3
14"Finally all the trees said to
the thornbush, 'Come and be our
king.'
15"The thornbush said to the
trees, 'If you really want to anoint
me king over you, come and take
refuge in my shade; but if not, then
let fire come out of the thornbush
and consume the cedars of Lebanon!' Isa 30:2
16"Have you acted honorably
and in good faith by making
Abimelek king? Have you been
fair to Jerub-Baal and his family?
Have you treated him as he deserves? 17Remember that my father fought for you and risked his
life to rescue you from the hand
of Midian. 18But today you have
revolted against my father's family. You have murdered his seventy sons on a single stone and have
made Abimelek, the son of his female slave, king over the citizens

[a] 4 That is, about 1 3/4 pounds or about 800 grams

of Shechem because he is related
to you. 19So have you acted honorably and in good faith toward Jerub-Baal and his family today? If
you have, may Abimelek be your
joy, and may you be his, too! 20But
if you have not, let fire come out
from Abimelek and consume you,
the citizens of Shechem and Beth
Millo, and let fire come out from
you, the citizens of Shechem and
Beth Millo, and consume Abimelek!" Jdg 8:30

21Then Jotham fled, escaping to
Beer, and he lived there because
he was afraid of his brother Abimelek.

22After Abimelek had governed
Israel three years, 23God stirred up
animosity between Abimelek and
the citizens of Shechem so that
they acted treacherously against
Abimelek. 24God did this in order
that the crime against Jerub-Baal's seventy sons, the shedding
of their blood, might be avenged
on their brother Abimelek and on
the citizens of Shechem, who had
helped him murder his brothers.
25In opposition to him these citizens of Shechem set men on the
hilltops to ambush and rob everyone who passed by, and this was
reported to Abimelek.
Nu 35:33; Dt 27:25; 1Sa 16:14,23

26Now Gaal son of Ebed moved
with his clan into Shechem, and
its citizens put their confidence
in him. 27After they had gone out
into the fields and gathered the
grapes and trodden them, they
held a festival in the temple of
their god. While they were eating
and drinking, they cursed Abimelek. 28Then Gaal son of Ebed said,
"Who is Abimelek, and why should
we Shechemites be subject to him?
Isn't he Jerub-Baal's son, and isn't
Zebul his deputy? Serve the family
of Hamor, Shechem's father! Why
should we serve Abimelek? 29If
only this people were under my
command! Then I would get rid of
him. I would say to Abimelek, 'Call
out your whole army!' "[a] 2Sa 15:4

30When Zebul the governor
of the city heard what Gaal son
of Ebed said, he was very angry.
31Under cover he sent messengers
to Abimelek, saying, "Gaal son
of Ebed and his clan have come
to Shechem and are stirring up
the city against you. 32Now then,
during the night you and your
men should come and lie in wait
in the fields. 33In the morning at
sunrise, advance against the city.
When Gaal and his men come out
against you, seize the opportunity
to attack them." 1Sa 10:7

34So Abimelek and all his troops
set out by night and took up concealed positions near Shechem in
four companies. 35Now Gaal son of
Ebed had gone out and was standing at the entrance of the city gate
just as Abimelek and his troops
came out from their hiding place.
Ps 32:7; Jer 49:10

[a] 29 Septuagint; Hebrew *him." Then he said to Abimelek, "Call out your whole army!"*

36When Gaal saw them, he said
to Zebul, "Look, people are coming down from the tops of the
mountains!"

Zebul replied, "You mistake the
shadows of the mountains for
men."

37But Gaal spoke up again:
"Look, people are coming down
from the central hill,[a] and a company is coming from the direction
of the diviners' tree."

38Then Zebul said to him,
"Where is your big talk now, you
who said, 'Who is Abimelek that
we should be subject to him?'
Aren't these the men you ridiculed? Go out and fight them!"

39So Gaal led out[b] the citizens
of Shechem and fought Abimelek. 40Abimelek chased him all the
way to the entrance of the gate,
and many were killed as they fled.
41Then Abimelek stayed in Aru-
mah, and Zebul drove Gaal and his
clan out of Shechem.

42The next day the people of
Shechem went out to the fields,
and this was reported to Abimelek. 43So he took his men, divided them into three companies
and set an ambush in the fields.
When he saw the people coming
out of the city, he rose to attack
them. 44Abimelek and the companies with him rushed forward
to a position at the entrance of
the city gate. Then two companies attacked those in the fields
and struck them down. 45All that
day Abimelek pressed his attack
against the city until he had captured it and killed its people. Then
he destroyed the city and scattered salt over it. Dt 29:23; 2Ki 3:25

46On hearing this, the citizens in
the tower of Shechem went into
the stronghold of the temple of
El-Berith. 47When Abimelek heard
that they had assembled there,
48he and all his men went up
Mount Zalmon. He took an ax and
cut off some branches, which he
lifted to his shoulders. He ordered
the men with him, "Quick! Do
what you have seen me do!" 49So
all the men cut branches and followed Abimelek. They piled them
against the stronghold and set it
on fire with the people still inside.
So all the people in the tower of
Shechem, about a thousand men
and women, also died. Ps 68:14

50Next Abimelek went to Thebez and besieged it and captured
it. 51Inside the city, however, was a
strong tower, to which all the men
and women — all the people of the
city — had fled. They had locked
themselves in and climbed up on
the tower roof. 52Abimelek went
to the tower and attacked it. But
as he approached the entrance to
the tower to set it on fire, 53a woman dropped an upper millstone on
his head and cracked his skull.
2Sa 11:21

54Hurriedly he called to his armor-bearer, "Draw your sword

[a] 37 The Hebrew for this phrase means *the navel of the earth.* [b] 39 Or *Gaal went out in the sight of*

and kill me, so that they can't say, 'A woman killed him.'" So his servant ran him through, and he died. 55When the Israelites saw that Abimelek was dead, they went home. 1Sa 31:4

56Thus God repaid the wickedness that Abimelek had done to his father by murdering his seventy brothers. 57God also made the people of Shechem pay for all their wickedness. The curse of Jotham son of Jerub-Baal came on them.

Tola

10 After the time of Abimelek, a man of Issachar named Tola son of Puah, the son of Dodo, rose to save Israel. He lived in Shamir, in the hill country of Ephraim. 2He led[a] Israel twenty-three years; then he died, and was buried in Shamir. Jdg 2:16; Ge 46:13

Jair

3He was followed by Jair of Gilead, who led Israel twenty-two years. 4He had thirty sons, who rode thirty donkeys. They controlled thirty towns in Gilead, which to this day are called Havvoth Jair.[b] 5When Jair died, he was buried in Kamon. Nu 32:41

Jephthah

6Again the Israelites did evil in the eyes of the LORD. They served the Baals and the Ashtoreths, and the gods of Aram, the gods of Sidon, the gods of Moab, the gods of the Ammonites and the gods of the Philistines. And because the Israelites forsook the LORD and no longer served him, 7he became angry with them. He sold them into the hands of the Philistines and the Ammonites, 8who that year shattered and crushed them. For eighteen years they oppressed all the Israelites on the east side of the Jordan in Gilead, the land of the Amorites. 9The Ammonites also crossed the Jordan to fight against Judah, Benjamin and Ephraim; Israel was in great distress. 10Then the Israelites cried out to the LORD, "We have sinned against you, forsaking our God and serving the Baals."

Jdg 2:13; Dt 31:17; 1Sa 12:10

11The LORD replied, "When the Egyptians, the Amorites, the Ammonites, the Philistines, 12the Sidonians, the Amalekites and the Maonites[c] oppressed you and you cried to me for help, did I not save you from their hands? 13But you have forsaken me and served other gods, so I will no longer save you. 14Go and cry out to the gods you have chosen. Let them save you when you are in trouble!"

Dt 32:37; Jdg 3:13; Ps 106:42

15But the Israelites said to the LORD, "We have sinned. Do with us whatever you think best, but please rescue us now." 16Then they

[a] 2 Traditionally *judged*; also in verse 3
[b] 4 Or *called the settlements of Jair*
[c] 12 Hebrew; some Septuagint manuscripts *Midianites*

got rid of the foreign gods among them and served the LORD. And he could bear Israel's misery no longer. Jos 24:23; 1Sa 3:18; Isa 63:9

17 When the Ammonites were called to arms and camped in Gilead, the Israelites assembled and camped at Mizpah. 18 The leaders of the people of Gilead said to each other, "Whoever will take the lead in attacking the Ammonites will be head over all who live in Gilead." Jdg 11:8,9,29

11 Jephthah the Gileadite was a mighty warrior. His father was Gilead; his mother was a prostitute. 2 Gilead's wife also bore him sons, and when they were grown up, they drove Jephthah away. "You are not going to get any inheritance in our family," they said, "because you are the son of another woman." 3 So Jephthah fled from his brothers and settled in the land of Tob, where a gang of scoundrels gathered around him and followed him. Heb 11:32; 2Sa 10:6,8

4 Some time later, when the Ammonites were fighting against Israel, 5 the elders of Gilead went to get Jephthah from the land of Tob. 6 "Come," they said, "be our commander, so we can fight the Ammonites." Jdg 10:9

7 Jephthah said to them, "Didn't you hate me and drive me from my father's house? Why do you come to me now, when you're in trouble?" Ge 26:27

8 The elders of Gilead said to him, "Nevertheless, we are turning to you now; come with us to fight the Ammonites, and you will be head over all of us who live in Gilead." Jdg 10:18

9 Jephthah answered, "Suppose you take me back to fight the Ammonites and the LORD gives them to me—will I really be your head?"

10 The elders of Gilead replied, "The LORD is our witness; we will certainly do as you say." 11 So Jephthah went with the elders of Gilead, and the people made him head and commander over them. And he repeated all his words before the LORD in Mizpah. Jer 42:5

12 Then Jephthah sent messengers to the Ammonite king with the question: "What do you have against me that you have attacked my country?"

13 The king of the Ammonites answered Jephthah's messengers, "When Israel came up out of Egypt, they took away my land from the Arnon to the Jabbok, all the way to the Jordan. Now give it back peaceably." Nu 21:24

14 Jephthah sent back messengers to the Ammonite king, 15 saying:

"This is what Jephthah says: Israel did not take the land of Moab or the land of the Ammonites. 16 But when they came up out of Egypt, Israel went through the wilderness to the Red Sea[a] and on

[a] 16 Or *the Sea of Reeds*

to Kadesh. 17Then Israel sent
messengers to the king of
Edom, saying, 'Give us permission to go through your
country,' but the king of Edom
would not listen. They sent
also to the king of Moab, and
he refused. So Israel stayed at
Kadesh. Nu 20:14; Dt 1:40; 2:19

18"Next they traveled
through the wilderness,
skirted the lands of Edom
and Moab, passed along the
eastern side of the country
of Moab, and camped on the
other side of the Arnon. They
did not enter the territory of
Moab, for the Arnon was its
border. Nu 21:4; Dt 2:8

19"Then Israel sent mes-
sengers to Sihon king of the
Amorites, who ruled in Heshbon, and said to him, 'Let us
pass through your country to
our own place.' 20Sihon, however, did not trust Israel[a] to
pass through his territory.
He mustered all his troops
and encamped at Jahaz and
fought with Israel.
Nu 21:21-22; Dt 2:32

21"Then the LORD, the God
of Israel, gave Sihon and
his whole army into Isra-
el's hands, and they defeated them. Israel took over all
the land of the Amorites who
lived in that country, 22captur-
ing all of it from the Arnon to
the Jabbok and from the desert to the Jordan. Dt 2:36

23"Now since the LORD, the
God of Israel, has driven the
Amorites out before his people Israel, what right have you
to take it over? 24Will you not
take what your god Chemosh
gives you? Likewise, whatever the LORD our God has giv-
en us, we will possess. 25Are
you any better than Balak son
of Zippor, king of Moab? Did
he ever quarrel with Israel or
fight with them? 26For three
hundred years Israel occupied Heshbon, Aroer, the surrounding settlements and all
the towns along the Arnon.
Why didn't you retake them
during that time? 27I have not
wronged you, but you are doing me wrong by waging war
against me. Let the LORD, the
Judge, decide the dispute this
day between the Israelites
and the Ammonites."
Ge 16:5; 18:25; 1Ki 11:7

28The king of Ammon, however,
paid no attention to the message
Jephthah sent him.

29Then the Spirit of the LORD
came on Jephthah. He crossed Gilead and Manasseh, passed through
Mizpah of Gilead, and from there
he advanced against the Ammonites. 30And Jephthah made a vow
to the LORD: "If you give the Ammonites into my hands, 31what-
ever comes out of the door of my

[a] 20 *Or however, would not make an agreement for Israel*

house to meet me when I return
in triumph from the Ammonites
will be the LORD's, and I will sacrifice it as a burnt offering."

Jdg 3:10; Ge 28:20; Lev 1:3

[32]Then Jephthah went over to
fight the Ammonites, and the
LORD gave them into his hands.
[33]He devastated twenty towns
from Aroer to the vicinity of Minnith, as far as Abel Keramim. Thus
Israel subdued Ammon. Eze 27:17

[34]When Jephthah returned to
his home in Mizpah, who should
come out to meet him but his
daughter, dancing to the sound of
timbrels! She was an only child.
Except for her he had neither
son nor daughter. [35]When he saw
her, he tore his clothes and cried,
"Oh no, my daughter! You have
brought me down and I am devastated. I have made a vow to the
LORD that I cannot break."

Nu 30:2; Ecc 5:2,4-5; Jer 31:4

[36]"My father," she replied, "you
have given your word to the LORD.
Do to me just as you promised,
now that the LORD has avenged
you of your enemies, the Ammonites. [37]But grant me this one
request," she said. "Give me two
months to roam the hills and
weep with my friends, because I
will never marry."

[38]"You may go," he said. And
he let her go for two months. She
and her friends went into the hills
and wept because she would never
marry. [39]After the two months, she
returned to her father, and he did
to her as he had vowed. And she
was a virgin.

From this comes the Israelite tradition [40]that each year the young
women of Israel go out for four
days to commemorate the daughter of Jephthah the Gileadite.

Jephthah and Ephraim

12 The Ephraimite forces were
called out, and they crossed
over to Zaphon. They said to Jephthah, "Why did you go to fight the
Ammonites without calling us to
go with you? We're going to burn
down your house over your head."

Jdg 8:1

[2]Jephthah answered, "I and my
people were engaged in a great
struggle with the Ammonites, and
although I called, you didn't save
me out of their hands. [3]When I
saw that you wouldn't help, I took
my life in my hands and crossed
over to fight the Ammonites, and
the LORD gave me the victory over
them. Now why have you come up
today to fight me?" 1Sa 19:5

[4]Jephthah then called together the men of Gilead and fought
against Ephraim. The Gileadites
struck them down because the
Ephraimites had said, "You Gileadites are renegades from Ephraim and Manasseh." [5]The Gileadites captured the fords of the
Jordan leading to Ephraim, and
whenever a survivor of Ephraim
said, "Let me cross over," the men
of Gilead asked him, "Are you an
Ephraimite?" If he replied, "No,"

6they said, "All right, say 'Shib-
boleth.'" If he said, "Sibboleth,"
because he could not pronounce
the word correctly, they seized
him and killed him at the fords of
the Jordan. Forty-two thousand
Ephraimites were killed at that
time. Jdg 3:28
7Jephthah led[a] Israel six years.
Then Jephthah the Gileadite died
and was buried in a town in Gilead.

Ibzan, Elon and Abdon

8After him, Ibzan of Bethlehem
led Israel. 9He had thirty sons
and thirty daughters. He gave his
daughters away in marriage to
those outside his clan, and for his
sons he brought in thirty young
women as wives from outside his
clan. Ibzan led Israel seven years.
10Then Ibzan died and was buried
in Bethlehem. Ge 35:19
11After him, Elon the Zebulunite
led Israel ten years. 12Then Elon
died and was buried in Aijalon in
the land of Zebulun. Jos 10:12
13After him, Abdon son of Hillel,
from Pirathon, led Israel. 14He had
forty sons and thirty grandsons,
who rode on seventy donkeys.
He led Israel eight years. 15Then
Abdon son of Hillel died and was
buried at Pirathon in Ephraim, in
the hill country of the Amalekites.
Jdg 5:10,14

The Birth of Samson

13 Again the Israelites did evil
in the eyes of the LORD, so
the LORD delivered them into the
hands of the Philistines for forty
years. Jdg 2:11; 14:4
2A certain man of Zorah, named
Manoah, from the clan of the Danites, had a wife who was childless,
unable to give birth. 3The angel
of the LORD appeared to her and
said, "You are barren and childless, but you are going to become
pregnant and give birth to a son.
4Now see to it that you drink no
wine or other fermented drink
and that you do not eat anything
unclean. 5You will become pregnant and have a son whose head
is never to be touched by a razor
because the boy is to be a Nazirite,
dedicated to God from the womb.
He will take the lead in delivering
Israel from the hands of the Philistines." Nu 6:2,13; 1Sa 1:11; Lk 1:13
6Then the woman went to her
husband and told him, "A man of
God came to me. He looked like
an angel of God, very awesome.
I didn't ask him where he came
from, and he didn't tell me his
name. 7But he said to me, 'You
will become pregnant and have
a son. Now then, drink no wine
or other fermented drink and do
not eat anything unclean, because
the boy will be a Nazirite of God
from the womb until the day of
his death.'"
8Then Manoah prayed to the
LORD: "Pardon your servant, Lord.
I beg you to let the man of God
you sent to us come again to teach

[a] 7 Traditionally *judged*; also in verses 8-14

us how to bring up the boy who is
to be born."
9God heard Manoah, and the angel of God came again to the woman
while she was out in the field; but
her husband Manoah was not with
her. 10The woman hurried to tell her
husband, "He's here! The man who
appeared to me the other day!"
11Manoah got up and followed
his wife. When he came to the
man, he said, "Are you the man
who talked to my wife?"
"I am," he said.
12So Manoah asked him, "When
your words are fulfilled, what is to
be the rule that governs the boy's
life and work?"
13The angel of the LORD answered,
"Your wife must do all that I have
told her. 14She must not eat anything that comes from the grapevine, nor drink any wine or other
fermented drink nor eat anything
unclean. She must do everything I
have commanded her." Nu 6:4
15Manoah said to the angel of
the LORD, "We would like you to
stay until we prepare a young goat
for you." Jdg 6:19
16The angel of the LORD replied,
"Even though you detain me, I will
not eat any of your food. But if you
prepare a burnt offering, offer it to
the LORD." (Manoah did not realize
that it was the angel of the LORD.)
17Then Manoah inquired of the
angel of the LORD, "What is your
name, so that we may honor you
when your word comes true?"
Ge 32:29
18He replied, "Why do you ask
my name? It is beyond understanding.[a]" 19Then Manoah took
a young goat, together with the
grain offering, and sacrificed it on
a rock to the LORD. And the LORD
did an amazing thing while Manoah and his wife watched: 20As
the flame blazed up from the altar toward heaven, the angel of
the LORD ascended in the flame.
Seeing this, Manoah and his wife
fell with their faces to the ground.
21When the angel of the LORD did
not show himself again to Manoah
and his wife, Manoah realized that
it was the angel of the LORD.
Lev 9:24; 1Ch 21:16
22"We are doomed to die!" he
said to his wife. "We have seen
God!" Dt 5:26
23But his wife answered, "If
the LORD had meant to kill us, he
would not have accepted a burnt
offering and grain offering from
our hands, nor shown us all these
things or now told us this." Ps 25:14
24The woman gave birth to a boy
and named him Samson. He grew
and the LORD blessed him, 25and
the Spirit of the LORD began to
stir him while he was in Mahaneh
Dan, between Zorah and Eshtaol.
1Sa 3:19; Heb 11:32; Jdg 18:12

Samson's Marriage

14 Samson went down to Timnah and saw there a young
Philistine woman. 2When he

[a] 18 Or *is wonderful*

returned, he said to his father and
mother, "I have seen a Philistine
woman in Timnah; now get her
for me as my wife." Ge 21:21; 34:4

3His father and mother replied,
"Isn't there an acceptable woman
among your relatives or among
all our people? Must you go to the
uncircumcised Philistines to get a
wife?" Ge 24:4; Ex 34:16

But Samson said to his father,
"Get her for me. She's the right
one for me." 4(His parents did not
know that this was from the LORD,
who was seeking an occasion to
confront the Philistines; for at that
time they were ruling over Israel.)
Jos 11:20

5Samson went down to Tim-
nah together with his father and
mother. As they approached the
vineyards of Timnah, suddenly a
young lion came roaring toward
him. 6The Spirit of the LORD came
powerfully upon him so that he
tore the lion apart with his bare
hands as he might have torn a
young goat. But he told neither
his father nor his mother what he
had done. 7Then he went down
and talked with the woman, and
he liked her. Jdg 3:10; 13:1

8Some time later, when he went
back to marry her, he turned aside
to look at the lion's carcass, and
in it he saw a swarm of bees and
some honey. 9He scooped out the
honey with his hands and ate as
he went along. When he rejoined
his parents, he gave them some,
and they too ate it. But he did not
tell them that he had taken the
honey from the lion's carcass.

10Now his father went down to
see the woman. And there Samson held a feast, as was customary
for young men. 11When the people
saw him, they chose thirty men to
be his companions.

12"Let me tell you a riddle," Samson said to them. "If you can give
me the answer within the seven
days of the feast, I will give you
thirty linen garments and thirty
sets of clothes. 13If you can't tell
me the answer, you must give me
thirty linen garments and thirty
sets of clothes." Eze 17:2; Ge 29:27; 2Ki 5:5

"Tell us your riddle," they said.
"Let's hear it."

14He replied,

"Out of the eater, something
to eat;
out of the strong, something
sweet."

For three days they could not give
the answer.

15On the fourth[a] day, they said
to Samson's wife, "Coax your husband into explaining the riddle
for us, or we will burn you and
your father's household to death.
Did you invite us here to steal our
property?" Jdg 15:6; 16:5; Ecc 7:26

16Then Samson's wife threw herself on him, sobbing, "You hate me!
You don't really love me. You've
given my people a riddle, but you
haven't told me the answer." Jdg 16:15

[a] *15* Some Septuagint manuscripts and Syriac; Hebrew *seventh*

"I haven't even explained it to
my father or mother," he replied,
"so why should I explain it to
you?" 17She cried the whole seven
days of the feast. So on the seventh day he finally told her, because she continued to press him.
She in turn explained the riddle to
her people.

18Before sunset on the seventh
day the men of the town said to
him,

"What is sweeter than
honey?
What is stronger than a
lion?"

Samson said to them,

"If you had not plowed with
my heifer,
you would not have solved
my riddle."

19Then the Spirit of the LORD
came powerfully upon him. He
went down to Ashkelon, struck
down thirty of their men, stripped
them of everything and gave
their clothes to those who had
explained the riddle. Burning
with anger, he returned to his father's home. 20And Samson's wife
was given to one of his companions who had attended him at the
feast. Jdg 6:34; 1Sa 11:6; Isa 11:2

Samson's Vengeance on the Philistines

15 Later on, at the time of
wheat harvest, Samson took
a young goat and went to visit his
wife. He said, "I'm going to my
wife's room." But her father would
not let him go in. Ge 38:17

2"I was so sure you hated her,"
he said, "that I gave her to your
companion. Isn't her younger sister more attractive? Take her instead." Jdg 14:20

3Samson said to them, "This
time I have a right to get even
with the Philistines; I will really
harm them." 4So he went out and
caught three hundred foxes and
tied them tail to tail in pairs. He
then fastened a torch to every pair
of tails, 5lit the torches and let the
foxes loose in the standing grain
of the Philistines. He burned up
the shocks and standing grain, together with the vineyards and olive groves.

6When the Philistines asked,
"Who did this?" they were told,
"Samson, the Timnite's son-in-law,
because his wife was given to his
companion."

So the Philistines went up
and burned her and her father
to death. 7Samson said to them,
"Since you've acted like this, I
swear that I won't stop until I get
my revenge on you." 8He attacked
them viciously and slaughtered
many of them. Then he went
down and stayed in a cave in the
rock of Etam. Jdg 14:15; Ge 38:24

9The Philistines went up and
camped in Judah, spreading out
near Lehi. 10The people of Judah
asked, "Why have you come to
fight us?"

"We have come to take Samson
prisoner," they answered, "to do to
him as he did to us."
11 Then three thousand men
from Judah went down to the
cave in the rock of Etam and said
to Samson, "Don't you realize that
the Philistines are rulers over us?
What have you done to us?"

Jdg 13:1; 14:4

He answered, "I merely did to
them what they did to me."
12 They said to him, "We've come
to tie you up and hand you over to
the Philistines."

Samson said, "Swear to me that
you won't kill me yourselves."

Ge 47:31

13 "Agreed," they answered. "We
will only tie you up and hand you
over to them. We will not kill you."
So they bound him with two new
ropes and led him up from the rock.
14 As he approached Lehi, the Philistines came toward him shouting.
The Spirit of the LORD came powerfully upon him. The ropes on
his arms became like charred flax,
and the bindings dropped from his
hands. 15 Finding a fresh jawbone of
a donkey, he grabbed it and struck
down a thousand men.

Lev 26:8; Jos 23:10; Jdg 14:19

16 Then Samson said,

"With a donkey's jawbone
 I have made donkeys of
  them.[a]
With a donkey's jawbone
 I have killed a thousand
  men."

17 When he finished speaking, he
threw away the jawbone; and the
place was called Ramath Lehi.[b]
18 Because he was very thirsty, he
cried out to the LORD, "You have
given your servant this great victory. Must I now die of thirst and
fall into the hands of the uncircumcised?" 19 Then God opened up
the hollow place in Lehi, and water came out of it. When Samson
drank, his strength returned and
he revived. So the spring was called
En Hakkore,[c] and it is still there in
Lehi.

Ge 45:27; Jdg 16:28; Isa 40:29

20 Samson led[d] Israel for twenty years in the days of the Philistines.

Jdg 13:1; 16:31

Samson and Delilah

16 One day Samson went to
Gaza, where he saw a prostitute. He went in to spend the night
with her. 2 The people of Gaza were
told, "Samson is here!" So they
surrounded the place and lay in
wait for him all night at the city
gate. They made no move during
the night, saying, "At dawn we'll
kill him."

1Sa 19:11; Ps 118:10-12

3 But Samson lay there only until
the middle of the night. Then he
got up and took hold of the doors
of the city gate, together with the
two posts, and tore them loose,
bar and all. He lifted them to his

[a] 16 Or *made a heap or two*; the Hebrew for *donkey* sounds like the Hebrew for *heap*.
[b] 17 *Ramath Lehi* means *jawbone hill*.
[c] 19 *En Hakkore* means *caller's spring*.
[d] 20 Traditionally *judged*

shoulders and carried them to the
top of the hill that faces Hebron.

4Some time later, he fell in love
with a woman in the Valley of So-
rek whose name was Delilah. 5The
rulers of the Philistines went to
her and said, "See if you can lure
him into showing you the secret
of his great strength and how we
can overpower him so we may tie
him up and subdue him. Each one
of us will give you eleven hundred
shekels[a] of silver."

Ge 24:67; Jos 13:3; Jdg 14:15

6So Delilah said to Samson,
"Tell me the secret of your great
strength and how you can be tied
up and subdued."

7Samson answered her, "If anyone ties me with seven fresh bowstrings that have not been dried,
I'll become as weak as any other
man."

8Then the rulers of the Philistines brought her seven fresh
bowstrings that had not been
dried, and she tied him with
them. 9With men hidden in the
room, she called to him, "Samson,
the Philistines are upon you!" But
he snapped the bowstrings as easily as a piece of string snaps when
it comes close to a flame. So the
secret of his strength was not discovered.

10Then Delilah said to Samson,
"You have made a fool of me; you
lied to me. Come now, tell me how
you can be tied."

11He said, "If anyone ties me securely with new ropes that have
never been used, I'll become as
weak as any other man." Jdg 15:13

12So Delilah took new ropes
and tied him with them. Then,
with men hidden in the room,
she called to him, "Samson, the
Philistines are upon you!" But he
snapped the ropes off his arms as
if they were threads.

13Delilah then said to Samson,
"All this time you have been mak-
ing a fool of me and lying to me.
Tell me how you can be tied."

He replied, "If you weave the
seven braids of my head into the
fabric on the loom and tighten it
with the pin, I'll become as weak
as any other man." So while he
was sleeping, Delilah took the sev-
en braids of his head, wove them
into the fabric 14and[b] tightened it
with the pin.

Again she called to him, "Samson, the Philistines are upon you!"
He awoke from his sleep and
pulled up the pin and the loom,
with the fabric.

15Then she said to him, "How
can you say, 'I love you,' when you
won't confide in me? This is the
third time you have made a fool
of me and haven't told me the secret of your great strength." 16With
such nagging she prodded him
day after day until he was sick to
death of it. Jdg 14:16

[a] 5 That is, about 28 pounds or about 13 kilograms [b] 13,14 Some Septuagint manuscripts; Hebrew *replied, "I can if you weave the seven braids of my head into the fabric on the loom."* 14*So she*

17 So he told her everything. "No
razor has ever been used on my
head," he said, "because I have
been a Nazirite dedicated to God
from my mother's womb. If my
head were shaved, my strength
would leave me, and I would become as weak as any other man."
Nu 6:2,5; Mic 7:5

18 When Delilah saw that he had
told her everything, she sent word
to the rulers of the Philistines,
"Come back once more; he has
told me everything." So the rulers
of the Philistines returned with
the silver in their hands. 19 After
putting him to sleep on her lap,
she called for someone to shave
off the seven braids of his hair,
and so began to subdue him.[a] And
his strength left him. Pr 7:26-27

20 Then she called, "Samson, the
Philistines are upon you!"

He awoke from his sleep and
thought, "I'll go out as before and
shake myself free." But he did not
know that the LORD had left him.
Nu 14:42; Jos 7:12; 1Sa 16:14

21 Then the Philistines seized
him, gouged out his eyes and
took him down to Gaza. Binding
him with bronze shackles, they
set him to grinding grain in the
prison. 22 But the hair on his head
began to grow again after it had
been shaved. Jer 47:1

The Death of Samson

23 Now the rulers of the Philistines assembled to offer a great
sacrifice to Dagon their god and to
celebrate, saying, "Our god has delivered Samson, our enemy, into
our hands." 1Sa 5:2

24 When the people saw him,
they praised their god, saying,
Da 5:4

"Our god has delivered our
enemy
into our hands, 1Sa 31:9; 1Ch 10:9
the one who laid waste
our land
and multiplied our
slain."

25 While they were in high spirits, they shouted, "Bring out
Samson to entertain us." So they
called Samson out of the prison,
and he performed for them.
Jdg 9:27; Ru 3:7

When they stood him among
the pillars, 26 Samson said to the
servant who held his hand, "Put
me where I can feel the pillars
that support the temple, so that
I may lean against them." 27 Now
the temple was crowded with
men and women; all the rulers of
the Philistines were there, and on
the roof were about three thousand men and women watching
Samson perform. 28 Then Samson
prayed to the LORD, "Sovereign
LORD, remember me. Please, God,
strengthen me just once more,
and let me with one blow get revenge on the Philistines for my
two eyes." 29 Then Samson reached
toward the two central pillars on

[a] *19* Hebrew; some Septuagint manuscripts *and he began to weaken*

which the temple stood. Bracing
himself against them, his right
hand on the one and his left hand
on the other, [30]Samson said, "Let
me die with the Philistines!" Then
he pushed with all his might, and
down came the temple on the rulers and all the people in it. Thus
he killed many more when he
died than while he lived.
Jdg 15:18; Jer 15:15

[31]Then his brothers and his father's whole family went down to
get him. They brought him back
and buried him between Zorah
and Eshtaol in the tomb of Manoah his father. He had led[a] Israel
twenty years. Jdg 13:2; Ru 1:1

Micah's Idols

17 Now a man named Micah
from the hill country of
Ephraim [2]said to his mother, "The
eleven hundred shekels[b] of silver that were taken from you and
about which I heard you utter a
curse — I have that silver with me;
I took it."

Then his mother said, "The
LORD bless you, my son!" Ru 2:20

[3]When he returned the eleven
hundred shekels of silver to his
mother, she said, "I solemnly consecrate my silver to the LORD for
my son to make an image overlaid with silver. I will give it back
to you." Ex 20:4,23

[4]So after he returned the silver
to his mother, she took two hundred shekels[c] of silver and gave
them to a silversmith, who used
them to make the idol. And it was
put in Micah's house. Ex 32:4; Isa 17:8

[5]Now this man Micah had a
shrine, and he made an ephod
and some household gods and
installed one of his sons as his
priest. [6]In those days Israel had
no king; everyone did as they saw
fit. Dt 12:8; Jdg 8:27; 19:1

[7]A young Levite from Bethlehem in Judah, who had been living within the clan of Judah, [8]left
that town in search of some other
place to stay. On his way[d] he came
to Micah's house in the hill country of Ephraim. Jdg 19:1; Mic 5:2; Mt 2:1

[9]Micah asked him, "Where are
you from?"

"I'm a Levite from Bethlehem in
Judah," he said, "and I'm looking
for a place to stay."

[10]Then Micah said to him, "Live
with me and be my father and
priest, and I'll give you ten shekels[e] of silver a year, your clothes
and your food." [11]So the Levite
agreed to live with him, and the
young man became like one of
his sons to him. [12]Then Micah installed the Levite, and the young
man became his priest and lived
in his house. [13]And Micah said,
"Now I know that the LORD will
be good to me, since this Levite
has become my priest."
Nu 18:7; Jdg 18:19

[a] 31 Traditionally *judged* [b] 2 That is, about 28 pounds or about 13 kilograms [c] 4 That is, about 5 pounds or about 2.3 kilograms [d] 8 Or *To carry on his profession* [e] 10 That is, about 4 ounces or about 115 grams

The Danites Settle in Laish

18 In those days Israel had no
king. Jdg 17:6
And in those days the tribe of
the Danites was seeking a place
of their own where they might
settle, because they had not yet
come into an inheritance among
the tribes of Israel. 2So the Danites sent five of their leading men
from Zorah and Eshtaol to spy out
the land and explore it. These men
represented all the Danites. They
told them, "Go, explore the land."
Jos 2:1; 19:47; Jdg 13:25
So they entered the hill country
of Ephraim and came to the house
of Micah, where they spent the
night. 3When they were near Micah's house, they recognized the
voice of the young Levite; so they
turned in there and asked him,
"Who brought you here? What are
you doing in this place? Why are
you here?" Jdg 17:1
4He told them what Micah had
done for him, and said, "He has
hired me and I am his priest."
5Then they said to him, "Please
inquire of God to learn whether
our journey will be successful."
Ge 25:22; 2Sa 5:19; 1Ki 22:5
6The priest answered them, "Go
in peace. Your journey has the
LORD's approval."
7So the five men left and came
to Laish, where they saw that the
people were living in safety, like
the Sidonians, at peace and secure.
And since their land lacked nothing, they were prosperous.[a] Also,
they lived a long way from the Sidonians and had no relationship
with anyone else.[b] Ge 34:25; Jos 19:47
8When they returned to Zorah
and Eshtaol, their fellow Danites
asked them, "How did you find
things?"
9They answered, "Come on, let's
attack them! We have seen the
land, and it is very good. Aren't
you going to do something? Don't
hesitate to go there and take it
over. 10When you get there, you
will find an unsuspecting people
and a spacious land that God has
put into your hands, a land that
lacks nothing whatever."
Nu 13:30; Dt 8:9; 1Ki 22:3
11Then six hundred men of the
Danites, armed for battle, set out
from Zorah and Eshtaol. 12On
their way they set up camp near
Kiriath Jearim in Judah. This is
why the place west of Kiriath Jearim is called Mahaneh Dan[c] to
this day. 13From there they went
on to the hill country of Ephraim
and came to Micah's house.
Jdg 13:25
14Then the five men who had
spied out the land of Laish said
to their fellow Danites, "Do you
know that one of these houses
has an ephod, some household
gods and an image overlaid with
silver? Now you know what to

[a] 7 The meaning of the Hebrew for this clause is uncertain. [b] 7 Hebrew; some Septuagint manuscripts *with the Arameans* [c] 12 *Mahaneh Dan* means *Dan's camp.*

do." 15 So they turned in there and
went to the house of the young
Levite at Micah's place and greeted him. 16 The six hundred Danites, armed for battle, stood at the
entrance of the gate. 17 The five
men who had spied out the land
went inside and took the idol, the
ephod and the household gods
while the priest and the six hundred armed men stood at the entrance of the gate.

Ge 31:19; Jdg 17:5; Mic 5:13

18 When the five men went into
Micah's house and took the idol,
the ephod and the household
gods, the priest said to them,
"What are you doing?"

19 They answered him, "Be quiet! Don't say a word. Come with us,
and be our father and priest. Isn't
it better that you serve a tribe and
clan in Israel as priest rather than
just one man's household?" 20 The
priest was very pleased. He took
the ephod, the household gods
and the idol and went along with
the people. 21 Putting their little
children, their livestock and their
possessions in front of them, they
turned away and left.

Jdg 17:10; Job 21:5; 29:9

22 When they had gone some
distance from Micah's house, the
men who lived near Micah were
called together and overtook the
Danites. 23 As they shouted after
them, the Danites turned and said
to Micah, "What's the matter with
you that you called out your men
to fight?"

24 He replied, "You took the gods
I made, and my priest, and went
away. What else do I have? How
can you ask, 'What's the matter
with you?' "

25 The Danites answered, "Don't
argue with us, or some of the men
may get angry and attack you, and
you and your family will lose your
lives." 26 So the Danites went their
way, and Micah, seeing that they
were too strong for him, turned
around and went back home.

Ps 18:17

27 Then they took what Micah
had made, and his priest, and
went on to Laish, against a people at peace and secure. They attacked them with the sword and
burned down their city. 28 There
was no one to rescue them because they lived a long way from
Sidon and had no relationship
with anyone else. The city was in
a valley near Beth Rehob.

Jos 19:47; 2Sa 10:6

The Danites rebuilt the city and
settled there. 29 They named it Dan
after their ancestor Dan, who was
born to Israel — though the city
used to be called Laish. 30 There
the Danites set up for themselves
the idol, and Jonathan son of Gershom, the son of Moses,[a] and his
sons were priests for the tribe of
Dan until the time of the captivity of the land. 31 They continued to
use the idol Micah had made, all

[a] 30 Many Hebrew manuscripts, some Septuagint manuscripts and Vulgate; many other Hebrew manuscripts and some other Septuagint manuscripts *Manasseh*

the time the house of God was in Shiloh. Ex 2:22; Jos 19:47; 18:1

A Levite and His Concubine

19 In those days Israel had no king.

Now a Levite who lived in a remote area in the hill country of Ephraim took a concubine from Bethlehem in Judah. 2But she was unfaithful to him. She left him and went back to her parents' home in Bethlehem, Judah. After she had been there four months, 3her husband went to her to persuade her to return. He had with him his servant and two donkeys. She took him into her parents' home, and when her father saw him, he gladly welcomed him. 4His father-in-law, the woman's father, prevailed on him to stay; so he remained with him three days, eating and drinking, and sleeping there. Ex 32:6

5On the fourth day they got up early and he prepared to leave, but the woman's father said to his son-in-law, "Refresh yourself with something to eat; then you can go." 6So the two of them sat down to eat and drink together. Afterward the woman's father said, "Please stay tonight and enjoy yourself." 7And when the man got up to go, his father-in-law persuaded him, so he stayed there that night. 8On the morning of the fifth day, when he rose to go, the woman's father said, "Refresh yourself. Wait till afternoon!" So the two of them ate together.

9Then when the man, with his concubine and his servant, got up to leave, his father-in-law, the woman's father, said, "Now look, it's almost evening. Spend the night here; the day is nearly over. Stay and enjoy yourself. Early tomorrow morning you can get up and be on your way home." 10But, unwilling to stay another night, the man left and went toward Jebus (that is, Jerusalem), with his two saddled donkeys and his concubine. 1Ch 11:4-5

11When they were near Jebus and the day was almost gone, the servant said to his master, "Come, let's stop at this city of the Jebusites and spend the night."

12His master replied, "No. We won't go into any city whose people are not Israelites. We will go on to Gibeah." 13He added, "Come, let's try to reach Gibeah or Ramah and spend the night in one of those places." 14So they went on, and the sun set as they neared Gibeah in Benjamin. 15There they stopped to spend the night. They went and sat in the city square, but no one took them in for the night. Ge 19:2; 1Sa 10:26

16That evening an old man from the hill country of Ephraim, who was living in Gibeah (the inhabitants of the place were Benjamites), came in from his work in the fields. 17When he looked and saw the traveler in the city square, the old man asked, "Where are you going? Where did you come from?" Ps 104:23

18 He answered, "We are on our
way from Bethlehem in Judah to
a remote area in the hill country
of Ephraim where I live. I have
been to Bethlehem in Judah and
now I am going to the house of
the LORD.[a] No one has taken me
in for the night. 19 We have both
straw and fodder for our donkeys
and bread and wine for ourselves
your servants — me, the woman
and the young man with us. We
don't need anything." Jdg 18:31
20 "You are welcome at my house,"
the old man said. "Let me supply
whatever you need. Only don't
spend the night in the square." 21 So
he took him into his house and fed
his donkeys. After they had washed
their feet, they had something to
eat and drink. Ge 24:32-33; Lk 7:44
22 While they were enjoying
themselves, some of the wicked men of the city surrounded
the house. Pounding on the door,
they shouted to the old man who
owned the house, "Bring out the
man who came to your house so
we can have sex with him."
Ge 19:4-5; Dt 13:13; Ro 1:26-27
23 The owner of the house went
outside and said to them, "No, my
friends, don't be so vile. Since this
man is my guest, don't do this outrageous thing. 24 Look, here is my
virgin daughter, and his concubine. I will bring them out to you
now, and you can use them and do
to them whatever you wish. But as
for this man, don't do such an outrageous thing." Ge 34:7; Dt 22:21; 2Sa 13:12
25 But the men would not lis-
ten to him. So the man took his
concubine and sent her outside
to them, and they raped her and
abused her throughout the night,
and at dawn they let her go. 26 At
daybreak the woman went back to
the house where her master was
staying, fell down at the door and
lay there until daylight.
Jdg 20:5; 1Sa 31:4
27 When her master got up in the
morning and opened the door of
the house and stepped out to continue on his way, there lay his concubine, fallen in the doorway of
the house, with her hands on the
threshold. 28 He said to her, "Get
up; let's go." But there was no answer. Then the man put her on his
donkey and set out for home.
29 When he reached home, he
took a knife and cut up his concubine, limb by limb, into twelve
parts and sent them into all the
areas of Israel. 30 Everyone who
saw it was saying to one another,
"Such a thing has never been seen
or done, not since the day the Israelites came up out of Egypt. Just
imagine! We must do something!
So speak up!" Jdg 20:7; 1Sa 11:7

The Israelites Punish the Benjamites

20 Then all Israel from Dan
to Beersheba and from
the land of Gilead came together as one and assembled before

[a] 18 Hebrew, Vulgate, Syriac and Targum; Septuagint *going home*

the LORD in Mizpah. 2The leaders
of all the people of the tribes of
Israel took their places in the assembly of God's people, four hundred thousand men armed with
swords. 3(The Benjamites heard
that the Israelites had gone up to
Mizpah.) Then the Israelites said,
"Tell us how this awful thing happened." Jdg 8:10; 21:5; 1Sa 7:5

4So the Levite, the husband of
the murdered woman, said, "I and
my concubine came to Gibeah in
Benjamin to spend the night.
5During the night the men of Gibeah came after me and surrounded the house, intending to kill me.
They raped my concubine, and she
died. 6I took my concubine, cut her
into pieces and sent one piece to
each region of Israel's inheritance,
because they committed this lewd
and outrageous act in Israel. 7Now,
all you Israelites, speak up and tell
me what you have decided to do."
Jos 7:15; Jdg 19:25-26

8All the men rose up together
as one, saying, "None of us will go
home. No, not one of us will return to his house. 9But now this is
what we'll do to Gibeah: We'll go
up against it in the order decided
by casting lots. 10We'll take ten
men out of every hundred from all
the tribes of Israel, and a hundred
from a thousand, and a thousand
from ten thousand, to get provisions for the army. Then, when the
army arrives at Gibeah[a] in Benjamin, it can give them what they
deserve for this outrageous act
done in Israel." 11So all the Israelites got together and united as
one against the city.

12The tribes of Israel sent messengers throughout the tribe of
Benjamin, saying, "What about
this awful crime that was committed among you? 13Now turn those
wicked men of Gibeah over to us
so that we may put them to death
and purge the evil from Israel."
Dt 13:13

But the Benjamites would not
listen to their fellow Israelites.
14From their towns they came together at Gibeah to fight against
the Israelites. 15At once the Benjamites mobilized twenty-six
thousand swordsmen from their
towns, in addition to seven hundred able young men from those
living in Gibeah. 16Among all these
soldiers there were seven hundred
select troops who were left-handed, each of whom could sling a
stone at a hair and not miss.
Jdg 3:15; 1Ch 12:2

17Israel, apart from Benjamin,
mustered four hundred thousand
swordsmen, all of them fit for
battle.

18The Israelites went up to Bethel[b] and inquired of God. They said,
"Who of us is to go up first to fight
against the Benjamites?"
Jos 12:9; Jdg 18:5

The LORD replied, "Judah shall
go first."

[a] *10* One Hebrew manuscript; most Hebrew manuscripts *Geba*, a variant of *Gibeah*
[b] *18* Or *to the house of God*; also in verse 26

[19]The next morning the Israelites got up and pitched camp near Gibeah. [20]The Israelites went out to fight the Benjamites and took up battle positions against them at Gibeah. [21]The Benjamites came out of Gibeah and cut down twenty-two thousand Israelites on the battlefield that day. [22]But the Israelites encouraged one another and again took up their positions where they had stationed themselves the first day. [23]The Israelites went up and wept before the LORD until evening, and they inquired of the LORD. They said, "Shall we go up again to fight against the Benjamites, our fellow Israelites?"

Nu 14:1; Jos 7:6

The LORD answered, "Go up against them."

[24]Then the Israelites drew near to Benjamin the second day. [25]This time, when the Benjamites came out from Gibeah to oppose them, they cut down another eighteen thousand Israelites, all of them armed with swords.

[26]Then all the Israelites, the whole army, went up to Bethel, and there they sat weeping before the LORD. They fasted that day until evening and presented burnt offerings and fellowship offerings to the LORD. [27]And the Israelites inquired of the LORD. (In those days the ark of the covenant of God was there, [28]with Phinehas son of Eleazar, the son of Aaron, ministering before it.) They asked, "Shall we go up again to fight against the Benjamites, our fellow Israelites, or not?"

Dt 18:5; Jdg 21:4

The LORD responded, "Go, for tomorrow I will give them into your hands."

Jdg 7:9

[29]Then Israel set an ambush around Gibeah. [30]They went up against the Benjamites on the third day and took up positions against Gibeah as they had done before. [31]The Benjamites came out to meet them and were drawn away from the city. They began to inflict casualties on the Israelites as before, so that about thirty men fell in the open field and on the roads — the one leading to Bethel and the other to Gibeah. [32]While the Benjamites were saying, "We are defeating them as before," the Israelites were saying, "Let's retreat and draw them away from the city to the roads."

Jos 8:2,4

[33]All the men of Israel moved from their places and took up positions at Baal Tamar, and the Israelite ambush charged out of its place on the west[a] of Gibeah.[b] [34]Then ten thousand of Israel's able young men made a frontal attack on Gibeah. The fighting was so heavy that the Benjamites did not realize how near disaster was. [35]The LORD defeated Benjamin before Israel, and on that day the Israelites struck down 25,100 Benjamites, all armed with swords.

[a] 33 Some Septuagint manuscripts and Vulgate; the meaning of the Hebrew for this word is uncertain. [b] 33 Hebrew *Geba*, a variant of *Gibeah*

36Then the Benjamites saw that
they were beaten. Jos 8:19; 1Sa 9:21

Now the men of Israel had giv-
en way before Benjamin, because
they relied on the ambush they
had set near Gibeah. 37Those who
had been in ambush made a sudden dash into Gibeah, spread
out and put the whole city to the
sword. 38The Israelites had arranged with the ambush that they
should send up a great cloud of
smoke from the city, 39and then
the Israelites would counterat-
tack. Jos 8:15

The Benjamites had begun to
inflict casualties on the Israelites
(about thirty), and they said, "We
are defeating them as in the first
battle." 40But when the column of
smoke began to rise from the city,
the Benjamites turned and saw
the whole city going up in smoke.
41Then the Israelites counterat-
tacked, and the Benjamites were
terrified, because they realized
that disaster had come on them.
42So they fled before the Israelites in the direction of the wilderness, but they could not escape
the battle. And the Israelites who
came out of the towns cut them
down there. 43They surrounded
the Benjamites, chased them and
easily[a] overran them in the vicinity of Gibeah on the east. 44Eigh-
teen thousand Benjamites fell, all
of them valiant fighters. 45As they
turned and fled toward the wilderness to the rock of Rimmon,
the Israelites cut down five thousand men along the roads. They
kept pressing after the Benjamites
as far as Gidom and struck down
two thousand more. Jos 15:32; Jdg 21:13

46On that day twenty-five thousand Benjamite swordsmen fell,
all of them valiant fighters. 47But
six hundred of them turned and
fled into the wilderness to the
rock of Rimmon, where they
stayed four months. 48The men of
Israel went back to Benjamin and
put all the towns to the sword,
including the animals and everything else they found. All the
towns they came across they set
on fire. 1Sa 9:21

Wives for the Benjamites

21 The men of Israel had tak-
en an oath at Mizpah: "Not
one of us will give his daughter in
marriage to a Benjamite."
Jos 9:18; Jdg 20:1

2The people went to Bethel,[b]
where they sat before God until
evening, raising their voices and
weeping bitterly. 3"LORD, God of
Israel," they cried, "why has this
happened to Israel? Why should
one tribe be missing from Israel
today?"

4Early the next day the people
built an altar and presented burnt
offerings and fellowship offerings.
Jdg 20:26; 2Sa 24:25

5Then the Israelites asked,
"Who from all the tribes of Israel

[a] 43 The meaning of the Hebrew for this word is uncertain. [b] 2 Or *to the house of God*

has failed to assemble before the
LORD?" For they had taken a sol-
emn oath that anyone who failed
to assemble before the LORD at
Mizpah was to be put to death.
Jdg 5:23

6Now the Israelites grieved for
the tribe of Benjamin, their fellow Israelites. "Today one tribe
is cut off from Israel," they said.
7"How can we provide wives for
those who are left, since we have
taken an oath by the LORD not to
give them any of our daughters
in marriage?" 8Then they asked,
"Which one of the tribes of Israel
failed to assemble before the LORD
at Mizpah?" They discovered that
no one from Jabesh Gilead had
come to the camp for the assembly. 9For when they counted the
people, they found that none of
the people of Jabesh Gilead were
there. 1Sa 11:1

10So the assembly sent twelve
thousand fighting men with instructions to go to Jabesh Gilead
and put to the sword those living
there, including the women and
children. 11"This is what you are
to do," they said. "Kill every male
and every woman who is not a virgin." 12They found among the people living in Jabesh Gilead four
hundred young women who had
never slept with a man, and they
took them to the camp at Shiloh
in Canaan. Nu 31:17-18; Jos 18:1

13Then the whole assembly sent
an offer of peace to the Benjamites
at the rock of Rimmon. 14So the
Benjamites returned at that time
and were given the women of Jabesh Gilead who had been spared.
But there were not enough for all
of them. Jdg 20:47

15The people grieved for Benjamin, because the LORD had made a
gap in the tribes of Israel. 16And the
elders of the assembly said, "With
the women of Benjamin destroyed,
how shall we provide wives for
the men who are left? 17The Benjamite survivors must have heirs,"
they said, "so that a tribe of Israel will not be wiped out. 18We can't
give them our daughters as wives,
since we Israelites have taken this
oath: 'Cursed be anyone who gives
a wife to a Benjamite.' 19But look,
there is the annual festival of the
LORD in Shiloh, which lies north
of Bethel, east of the road that
goes from Bethel to Shechem, and
south of Lebonah." Jos 16:1; 1Sa 1:3

20So they instructed the Benjamites, saying, "Go and hide in
the vineyards 21and watch. When
the young women of Shiloh come
out to join in the dancing, rush
from the vineyards and each of
you seize one of them to be your
wife. Then return to the land of
Benjamin. 22When their fathers or
brothers complain to us, we will
say to them, 'Do us the favor of
helping them, because we did not
get wives for them during the war.
You will not be guilty of breaking
your oath because you did not
give your daughters to them.' "
Ex 15:20; Jdg 11:34

23So that is what the Benjamites
did. While the young women were
dancing, each man caught one
and carried her off to be his wife.
Then they returned to their inheritance and rebuilt the towns and
settled in them. Jdg 20:48

24At that time the Israelites left
that place and went home to their
tribes and clans, each to his own
inheritance.
25In those days Israel had no
king; everyone did as they saw fit.
Jdg 17:6; 18:1; 19:1

RUTH

Naomi Loses Her Husband and Sons

1 In the days when the judges ruled,[a] there was a famine in the land. So a man from Bethlehem in Judah, together with his wife and two sons, went to live for a while in the country of Moab.
2The man's name was Elimelek,
his wife's name was Naomi, and the names of his two sons were Mahlon and Kilion. They were Ephrathites from Bethlehem, Judah. And they went to Moab and lived there. Ge 35:19; Jdg 2:16-18; 3:30
3Now Elimelek, Naomi's hus-
band, died, and she was left with
her two sons. 4They married Mo-
abite women, one named Orpah and the other Ruth. After they had
lived there about ten years, 5both
Mahlon and Kilion also died, and Naomi was left without her two sons and her husband. Mt 1:5

Naomi and Ruth Return to Bethlehem

6When Naomi heard in Moab
that the LORD had come to the aid of his people by providing food for them, she and her daughters-in-law prepared to return home from there. 7With her
two daughters-in-law she left the place where she had been living and set out on the road that would take them back to the land of Judah. Ex 4:31; Mt 6:11
8Then Naomi said to her two
daughters-in-law, "Go back, each of you, to your mother's home. May the LORD show you kindness, as you have shown kindness to your dead husbands and to me.
9May the LORD grant that each of
you will find rest in the home of another husband." Ru 2:20; 3:1; 2Ti 1:16

Then she kissed them goodbye
and they wept aloud 10and said to
her, "We will go back with you to your people."
11But Naomi said, "Return home,
my daughters. Why would you come with me? Am I going to have any more sons, who could become
your husbands? 12Return home,
my daughters; I am too old to have another husband. Even if I thought there was still hope for me — even if I had a husband tonight and
then gave birth to sons — 13would
you wait until they grew up? Would you remain unmarried for them? No, my daughters. It is more bitter for me than for you, because the LORD's hand has turned against me!" Ge 38:11; Jdg 2:15; Job 19:21
14At this they wept aloud again.
Then Orpah kissed her mother-in-law goodbye, but Ruth clung to her. Pr 17:17; 18:24

[a] *1* Traditionally *judged*

15 "Look," said Naomi, "your sister-in-law is going back to her people and her gods. Go back with her." Jos 24:14; Jdg 11:24

16 But Ruth replied, "Don't urge me to leave you or to turn back from you. Where you go I will go, and where you stay I will stay. Your people will be my people and your God my God. 17 Where you die I will die, and there I will be buried. May the LORD deal with me, be it ever so severely, if even death separates you and me." 18 When Naomi realized that Ruth was determined to go with her, she stopped urging her. 1Sa 3:17; 2Ki 2:2; Ac 21:14

19 So the two women went on until they came to Bethlehem. When they arrived in Bethlehem, the whole town was stirred because of them, and the women exclaimed, "Can this be Naomi?" Mt 21:10

20 "Don't call me Naomi,[a]" she told them. "Call me Mara,[b] because the Almighty[c] has made my life very bitter. 21 I went away full, but the LORD has brought me back empty. Why call me Naomi? The LORD has afflicted[d] me; the Almighty has brought misfortune upon me." Job 1:21

22 So Naomi returned from Moab accompanied by Ruth the Moabite, her daughter-in-law, arriving in Bethlehem as the barley harvest was beginning. Ex 9:31

Ruth Meets Boaz in the Grain Field

2 Now Naomi had a relative on her husband's side, a man of standing from the clan of Elimelek, whose name was Boaz. Ru 1:2; 3:2,12

2 And Ruth the Moabite said to Naomi, "Let me go to the fields and pick up the leftover grain behind anyone in whose eyes I find favor." Lev 19:9; Dt 24:19

Naomi said to her, "Go ahead, my daughter." 3 So she went out, entered a field and began to glean behind the harvesters. As it turned out, she was working in a field belonging to Boaz, who was from the clan of Elimelek.

4 Just then Boaz arrived from Bethlehem and greeted the harvesters, "The LORD be with you!" Lk 1:28; 2Th 3:16

"The LORD bless you!" they answered. Ps 129:7-8

5 Boaz asked the overseer of his harvesters, "Who does that young woman belong to?"

6 The overseer replied, "She is the Moabite who came back from Moab with Naomi. 7 She said, 'Please let me glean and gather among the sheaves behind the harvesters.' She came into the field and has remained here from morning till now, except for a short rest in the shelter." Ru 1:22

8 So Boaz said to Ruth, "My daughter, listen to me. Don't go and glean in another field and don't go away from here. Stay here with the women who work for me.

[a] 20 *Naomi* means *pleasant.* [b] 20 *Mara* means *bitter.* [c] 20 Hebrew *Shaddai*; also in verse 21 [d] 21 Or *has testified against*

9 Watch the field where the men
are harvesting, and follow along
after the women. I have told the
men not to lay a hand on you. And
whenever you are thirsty, go and
get a drink from the water jars the
men have filled."
10 At this, she bowed down with
her face to the ground. She asked
him, "Why have I found such favor
in your eyes that you notice me —
a foreigner?" 1Sa 25:23
11 Boaz replied, "I've been told all
about what you have done for your
mother-in-law since the death of
your husband — how you left your
father and mother and your homeland and came to live with a people
you did not know before. 12 May the
LORD repay you for what you have
done. May you be richly rewarded
by the LORD, the God of Israel, under whose wings you have come to
take refuge." Ru 1:14; 1Sa 24:19; Ps 17:8
13 "May I continue to find favor in
your eyes, my lord," she said. "You
have put me at ease by speaking
kindly to your servant — though I
do not have the standing of one of
your servants." Ge 18:3
14 At mealtime Boaz said to her,
"Come over here. Have some bread
and dip it in the wine vinegar."
When she sat down with the
harvesters, he offered her some
roasted grain. She ate all she wanted and had some left over. 15 As she
got up to glean, Boaz gave orders
to his men, "Let her gather among
the sheaves and don't reprimand
her. 16 Even pull out some stalks
for her from the bundles and leave
them for her to pick up, and don't
rebuke her."
17 So Ruth gleaned in the field
until evening. Then she threshed
the barley she had gathered, and
it amounted to about an ephah.[a]
18 She carried it back to town,
and her mother-in-law saw how
much she had gathered. Ruth also
brought out and gave her what
she had left over after she had eat-
en enough.
19 Her mother-in-law asked her,
"Where did you glean today?
Where did you work? Blessed be
the man who took notice of you!"
Ps 41:1
Then Ruth told her mother-in-
law about the one at whose place
she had been working. "The name
of the man I worked with today is
Boaz," she said.
20 "The LORD bless him!" Naomi
said to her daughter-in-law. "He
has not stopped showing his kindness to the living and the dead."
She added, "That man is our close
relative; he is one of our guardian-
redeemers.[b]" Ru 3:10
21 Then Ruth the Moabite said,
"He even said to me, 'Stay with my
workers until they finish harvesting all my grain.'"
22 Naomi said to Ruth her daughter-in-law, "It will be good for you,

[a] *17* That is, probably about 30 pounds or about 13 kilograms [b] *20* The Hebrew word for *guardian-redeemer* is a legal term for one who has the obligation to redeem a relative in serious difficulty (see Lev. 25:25-55).

my daughter, to go with the wom-
en who work for him, because in
someone else's field you might be
harmed."
23So Ruth stayed close to the
women of Boaz to glean until the
barley and wheat harvests were
finished. And she lived with her
mother-in-law. Dt 16:9

Ruth and Boaz at the Threshing Floor

3 One day Ruth's mother-in-law
Naomi said to her, "My daughter, I must find a home[a] for you,
where you will be well provided
for. 2Now Boaz, with whose wom-
en you have worked, is a relative
of ours. Tonight he will be winnowing barley on the threshing
floor. 3Wash, put on perfume, and
get dressed in your best clothes.
Then go down to the threshing
floor, but don't let him know you
are there until he has finished eating and drinking. 4When he lies
down, note the place where he is
lying. Then go and uncover his
feet and lie down. He will tell you
what to do." Ru 2:1; 2Sa 14:2
5"I will do whatever you say,"
Ruth answered. 6So she went
down to the threshing floor and
did everything her mother-in-law
told her to do. Eph 6:1; Col 3:20
7When Boaz had finished eating and drinking and was in good
spirits, he went over to lie down at
the far end of the grain pile. Ruth
approached quietly, uncovered his
feet and lay down. 8In the middle
of the night something startled
the man; he turned—and there
was a woman lying at his feet!
Jdg 19:6,9,22; 2Sa 13:28; 1Ki 21:7
9"Who are you?" he asked.
"I am your servant Ruth," she
said. "Spread the corner of your
garment over me, since you are
a guardian-redeemer[b] of our
family." Ru 2:20
10"The LORD bless you, my
daughter," he replied. "This kindness is greater than that which you
showed earlier: You have not run
after the younger men, whether
rich or poor. 11And now, my daughter, don't be afraid. I will do for you
all you ask. All the people of my
town know that you are a woman
of noble character. 12Although it is
true that I am a guardian-redeemer of our family, there is another
who is more closely related than
I. 13Stay here for the night, and in
the morning if he wants to do his
duty as your guardian-redeemer,
good; let him redeem you. But if
he is not willing, as surely as the
LORD lives I will do it. Lie here until morning." Dt 25:5; Pr 12:4; Mt 22:24
14So she lay at his feet until
morning, but got up before anyone could be recognized; and he
said, "No one must know that a
woman came to the threshing
floor." Ro 14:16; 2Co 8:21

[a] *1* Hebrew *find rest* (see 1:9) [b] *9* The Hebrew word for *guardian-redeemer* is a legal term for one who has the obligation to redeem a relative in serious difficulty (see Lev. 25:25-55); also in verses 12 and 13.

15 He also said, "Bring me the
shawl you are wearing and hold it
out." When she did so, he poured
into it six measures of barley and
placed the bundle on her. Then
he[a] went back to town.
16 When Ruth came to her mother-in-law, Naomi asked, "How did
it go, my daughter?"
Then she told her everything
Boaz had done for her 17 and added, "He gave me these six measures of barley, saying, 'Don't go
back to your mother-in-law empty-handed.'"
18 Then Naomi said, "Wait, my
daughter, until you find out what
happens. For the man will not rest
until the matter is settled today."

Ps 37:3-5

Boaz Marries Ruth

4 Meanwhile Boaz went up to
the town gate and sat down
there just as the guardian-redeemer[b] he had mentioned came
along. Boaz said, "Come over here,
my friend, and sit down." So he
went over and sat down. Ru 3:12
2 Boaz took ten of the elders
of the town and said, "Sit here,"
and they did so. 3 Then he said to
the guardian-redeemer, "Naomi,
who has come back from Moab, is
selling the piece of land that belonged to our relative Elimelek. 4 I
thought I should bring the matter
to your attention and suggest that
you buy it in the presence of these
seated here and in the presence of
the elders of my people. If you will
redeem it, do so. But if you[c] will
not, tell me, so I will know. For no
one has the right to do it except
you, and I am next in line."

Lev 25:25; Jer 32:7-8; 1Ki 21:8

"I will redeem it," he said.
5 Then Boaz said, "On the day
you buy the land from Naomi,
you also acquire Ruth the Moabite, the[d] dead man's widow, in order to maintain the name of the
dead with his property."

Ge 38:8; Dt 25:5-6; Mt 22:24

6 At this, the guardian-redeemer said, "Then I cannot redeem it
because I might endanger my own
estate. You redeem it yourself. I
cannot do it." Ru 3:13
7 (Now in earlier times in Israel,
for the redemption and transfer of
property to become final, one party took off his sandal and gave it
to the other. This was the method
of legalizing transactions in Israel.) Dt 25:7-9
8 So the guardian-redeemer said
to Boaz, "Buy it yourself." And he
removed his sandal.
9 Then Boaz announced to the
elders and all the people, "Today you are witnesses that I have

[a] *15* Most Hebrew manuscripts; many Hebrew manuscripts, Vulgate and Syriac *she* [b] *1* The Hebrew word for *guardian-redeemer* is a legal term for one who has the obligation to redeem a relative in serious difficulty (see Lev. 25:25-55); also in verses 3, 6, 8 and 14. [c] *4* Many Hebrew manuscripts, Septuagint, Vulgate and Syriac; most Hebrew manuscripts *he* [d] *5* Vulgate and Syriac; Hebrew (see also Septuagint) *Naomi and from Ruth the Moabite, you acquire the*

bought from Naomi all the property of Elimelek, Kilion and Mahlon. 10I have also acquired Ruth
the Moabite, Mahlon's widow, as
my wife, in order to maintain the
name of the dead with his property, so that his name will not disappear from among his family or
from his hometown. Today you
are witnesses!"
11Then the elders and all the
people at the gate said, "We are
witnesses. May the LORD make the
woman who is coming into your
home like Rachel and Leah, who
together built up the family of
Israel. May you have standing in
Ephrathah and be famous in Bethlehem. 12Through the offspring
the LORD gives you by this young
woman, may your family be like
that of Perez, whom Tamar bore
to Judah." Ps 127:3; 128:3; Ge 38:29

Naomi Gains a Son

13So Boaz took Ruth and she
became his wife. When he made
love to her, the LORD enabled her
to conceive, and she gave birth to
a son. 14The women said to Naomi: "Praise be to the LORD, who
this day has not left you without
a guardian-redeemer. May he become famous throughout Israel!
15He will renew your life and sustain you in your old age. For your
daughter-in-law, who loves you
and who is better to you than sev-
en sons, has given him birth."
Ge 29:31; Ru 1:16-17; 1Sa 1:8
16Then Naomi took the child in
her arms and cared for him. 17The
women living there said, "Naomi
has a son!" And they named him
Obed. He was the father of Jesse,
the father of David. 1Sa 16:1,18

The Genealogy of David

18This, then, is the family line of
Perez: Mt 1:3-6

Perez was the father of Hezron,
19Hezron the father of Ram,
Ram the father of Amminadab,
20Amminadab the father of Nahshon,
Nahshon the father of Salmon,[a]
21Salmon the father of Boaz,
Boaz the father of Obed,
22Obed the father of Jesse,
and Jesse the father of David.
1Ch 2:5-15; Mt 1:3-6; Lk 3:31-33

[a] *20* A few Hebrew manuscripts, some Septuagint manuscripts and Vulgate (see also verse 21 and Septuagint of 1 Chron. 2:11); most Hebrew manuscripts *Salma*

1 SAMUEL

The Birth of Samuel

1 There was a certain man from
Ramathaim, a Zuphite[a] from
the hill country of Ephraim, whose
name was Elkanah son of Jeroham, the son of Elihu, the son of
Tohu, the son of Zuph, an Ephraimite. 2He had two wives; one was
called Hannah and the other Peninnah. Peninnah had children,
but Hannah had none.
1Ch 6:27,34; Dt 21:15-17

3Year after year this man went
up from his town to worship and
sacrifice to the LORD Almighty at
Shiloh, where Hophni and Phinehas, the two sons of Eli, were
priests of the LORD. 4Whenever
the day came for Elkanah to sacrifice, he would give portions of the
meat to his wife Peninnah and to
all her sons and daughters. 5But
to Hannah he gave a double portion because he loved her, and the
LORD had closed her womb. 6Be-
cause the LORD had closed Hannah's womb, her rival kept provoking her in order to irritate
her. 7This went on year after year.
Whenever Hannah went up to the
house of the LORD, her rival provoked her till she wept and would
not eat. 8Her husband Elkanah
would say to her, "Hannah, why
are you weeping? Why don't you
eat? Why are you downhearted?
Don't I mean more to you than ten
sons?" Ge 16:1; Ru 4:15; Job 24:21

9Once when they had finished
eating and drinking in Shiloh,
Hannah stood up. Now Eli the
priest was sitting on his chair by
the doorpost of the LORD's house.
10In her deep anguish Hannah
prayed to the LORD, weeping bitterly. 11And she made a vow, saying, "LORD Almighty, if you will
only look on your servant's misery and remember me, and not
forget your servant but give her
a son, then I will give him to the
LORD for all the days of his life,
and no razor will ever be used on
his head." Nu 6:1-21; Jdg 13:5; 1Sa 3:3

12As she kept on praying to the
LORD, Eli observed her mouth.
13Hannah was praying in her heart,
and her lips were moving but her
voice was not heard. Eli thought
she was drunk 14and said to her,
"How long are you going to stay
drunk? Put away your wine."

15"Not so, my lord," Hannah replied, "I am a woman who is deeply troubled. I have not been drinking wine or beer; I was pouring out
my soul to the LORD. 16Do not take
your servant for a wicked woman;
I have been praying here out of my
great anguish and grief." Ps 42:4; 62:8

[a] 1 See Septuagint and 1 Chron. 6:26-27, 33-35; or *from Ramathaim Zuphim.*

17 Eli answered, "Go in peace, and
may the God of Israel grant you
what you have asked of him."

Jdg 18:6; Ps 20:3-5; Mk 5:34

18 She said, "May your servant
find favor in your eyes." Then she
went her way and ate something,
and her face was no longer downcast. Ru 2:13; Ro 15:13
19 Early the next morning they
arose and worshiped before the
LORD and then went back to their
home at Ramah. Elkanah made
love to his wife Hannah, and the
LORD remembered her. 20 So in the
course of time Hannah became
pregnant and gave birth to a son.
She named him Samuel,[a] saying,
"Because I asked the LORD for
him." Ge 30:22; Ex 2:10,22

Hannah Dedicates Samuel

21 When her husband Elkanah
went up with all his family to offer
the annual sacrifice to the LORD
and to fulfill his vow, 22 Hannah
did not go. She said to her husband, "After the boy is weaned,
I will take him and present him
before the LORD, and he will live
there always."[b] Dt 12:11; Lk 2:22
23 "Do what seems best to you,"
her husband Elkanah told her.
"Stay here until you have weaned
him; only may the LORD make
good his[c] word." So the woman
stayed at home and nursed her son
until she had weaned him. Nu 30:7
24 After he was weaned, she took
the boy with her, young as he was,
along with a three-year-old bull,[d] an
ephah[e] of flour and a skin of wine,
and brought him to the house of
the LORD at Shiloh. 25 When the bull
had been sacrificed, they brought
the boy to Eli, 26 and she said to
him, "Pardon me, my lord. As surely as you live, I am the woman who
stood here beside you praying to
the LORD. 27 I prayed for this child,
and the LORD has granted me what
I asked of him. 28 So now I give him
to the LORD. For his whole life he
will be given over to the LORD."
And he worshiped the LORD there.

Nu 15:8-10; Dt 12:5; Ge 24:26,52

Hannah's Prayer

2 Then Hannah prayed and said:

Lk 1:46-55

"My heart rejoices in the LORD;
in the LORD my horn[f] is lifted
high. Isa 12:2-3
My mouth boasts over my
enemies,
for I delight in your
deliverance.

2 "There is no one holy like the
LORD; Ex 15:11
there is no one besides you;
there is no Rock like our God.

Dt 32:30-31

[a] 20 *Samuel* sounds like the Hebrew for *heard by God.* [b] 22 Masoretic Text; Dead Sea Scrolls *always. I have dedicated him as a Nazirite — all the days of his life."* [c] 23 Masoretic Text; Dead Sea Scrolls, Septuagint and Syriac *your* [d] 24 Dead Sea Scrolls, Septuagint and Syriac; Masoretic Text *with three bulls* [e] 24 That is, probably about 36 pounds or about 16 kilograms [f] 1 *Horn* here symbolizes strength; also in verse 10.

3 "Do not keep talking so proudly
or let your mouth speak such
arrogance, Pr 8:13
for the LORD is a God who
knows,
and by him deeds
are weighed.
1Sa 16:7; 1Ki 8:39; Pr 16:2

4 "The bows of the warriors are
broken, Ps 37:15
but those who stumbled are
armed with strength.
5 Those who were full hire
themselves out for food,
but those who were hungry
are hungry no more.
She who was barren has borne
seven children,
but she who has had many
sons pines away.
Ps 113:9; Jer 15:9
6 "The LORD brings death and
makes alive; Dt 32:39
he brings down to the grave
and raises up.
7 The LORD sends poverty and
wealth;
he humbles and he exalts.
Ps 75:7
8 He raises the poor from the dust
and lifts the needy from the
ash heap;
he seats them with princes
and has them inherit a
throne of honor. Job 36:7

"For the foundations of the
earth are the LORD's;
on them he has set the
world. Job 38:4
9 He will guard the feet of his
faithful servants, Ps 91:12
but the wicked will be
silenced in the place of
darkness. Mt 8:12

"It is not by strength that one
prevails;
10 those who oppose the LORD
will be broken. Ex 15:6; Ps 2:9
The Most High will thunder
from heaven;
2Sa 22:14; Ps 18:13
the LORD will judge the
ends of the earth.
Ps 96:13; Mt 25:31-32

"He will give strength to his
king
and exalt the horn of his
anointed." Ps 89:24

11 Then Elkanah went home to
Ramah, but the boy ministered
before the LORD under Eli the
priest. 1Sa 3:1

Eli's Wicked Sons

12 Eli's sons were scoundrels;
they had no regard for the LORD.
13 Now it was the practice of the
priests that, whenever any of the
people offered a sacrifice, the
priest's servant would come with
a three-pronged fork in his hand
while the meat was being boiled
14 and would plunge the fork into
the pan or kettle or caldron or pot.
Whatever the fork brought up the
priest would take for himself. This
is how they treated all the Israelites who came to Shiloh. 15 But even

before the fat was burned, the
priest's servant would come and
say to the person who was sacrificing, "Give the priest some meat to
roast; he won't accept boiled meat
from you, but only raw."

Lev 7:29-34; Jer 2:8

16 If the person said to him, "Let
the fat be burned first, and then
take whatever you want," the servant would answer, "No, hand it
over now; if you don't, I'll take it
by force."

17 This sin of the young men was
very great in the LORD's sight, for
they[a] were treating the LORD's offering with contempt. Mal 2:7-9

18 But Samuel was ministering
before the LORD — a boy wearing a linen ephod. 19 Each year his
mother made him a little robe and
took it to him when she went up
with her husband to offer the annual sacrifice. 20 Eli would bless Elkanah and his wife, saying, "May
the LORD give you children by
this woman to take the place of
the one she prayed for and gave
to[b] the LORD." Then they would
go home. 21 And the LORD was gracious to Hannah; she gave birth
to three sons and two daughters.
Meanwhile, the boy Samuel grew
up in the presence of the LORD.

Ge 21:1; Jdg 13:24; 1Sa 1:3

22 Now Eli, who was very old,
heard about everything his sons
were doing to all Israel and how
they slept with the women who
served at the entrance to the tent
of meeting. 23 So he said to them,
"Why do you do such things? I
hear from all the people about
these wicked deeds of yours. 24 No,
my sons; the report I hear spreading among the LORD's people is
not good. 25 If one person sins
against another, God[c] may mediate for the offender; but if anyone
sins against the LORD, who will intercede for them?" His sons, however, did not listen to their father's
rebuke, for it was the LORD's will
to put them to death.

Ex 38:8; Nu 15:30; Jos 11:20

26 And the boy Samuel continued to grow in stature and in favor
with the LORD and with people.

Lk 2:52

Prophecy Against the House of Eli

27 Now a man of God came to
Eli and said to him, "This is what
the LORD says: 'Did I not clearly
reveal myself to your ancestor's
family when they were in Egypt
under Pharaoh? 28 I chose your ancestor out of all the tribes of Israel to be my priest, to go up to
my altar, to burn incense, and to
wear an ephod in my presence. I
also gave your ancestor's family
all the food offerings presented
by the Israelites. 29 Why do you[d]
scorn my sacrifice and offering
that I prescribed for my dwelling?
Why do you honor your sons more

[a] *17* Dead Sea Scrolls and Septuagint; Masoretic Text *people* [b] *20* Dead Sea Scrolls; Masoretic Text *and asked from* [c] *25* Or *the judges* [d] *29* The Hebrew is plural.

than me by fattening yourselves
on the choice parts of every offering made by my people Israel?’

Ex 4:14-16; 28:1; Dt 12:5

30“Therefore the LORD, the
God of Israel, declares: ‘I promised that members of your family would minister before me forever.’ But now the LORD declares:
‘Far be it from me! Those who
honor me I will honor, but those
who despise me will be disdained.
31The time is coming when I will
cut short your strength and the
strength of your priestly house,
so that no one in it will reach old
age, 32and you will see distress in
my dwelling. Although good will
be done to Israel, no one in your
family line will ever reach old age.
33Every one of you that I do not
cut off from serving at my altar
I will spare only to destroy your
sight and sap your strength, and
all your descendants will die in
the prime of life.

Ex 29:9; 1Sa 4:11-18; Zec 8:4

34“ ‘And what happens to your
two sons, Hophni and Phinehas, will be a sign to you — they
will both die on the same day. 35I
will raise up for myself a faithful priest, who will do according
to what is in my heart and mind.
I will firmly establish his priestly house, and they will minister
before my anointed one always.
36Then everyone left in your family line will come and bow down
before him for a piece of silver and
a loaf of bread and plead, “Appoint
me to some priestly office so I can
have food to eat.” ’ ”

1Sa 4:11; 2Sa 7:11,27; 1Ki 11:38

The LORD Calls Samuel

3 The boy Samuel ministered
before the LORD under Eli. In
those days the word of the LORD
was rare; there were not many visions. Ps 74:9; Am 8:11; 1Sa 2:11

2One night Eli, whose eyes were
becoming so weak that he could
barely see, was lying down in his
usual place. 3The lamp of God had
not yet gone out, and Samuel was
lying down in the house of the
LORD, where the ark of God was.
4Then the LORD called Samuel.

Lev 24:1-4; 1Sa 4:15

Samuel answered, “Here I am.”
5And he ran to Eli and said, “Here
I am; you called me.” Isa 6:8

But Eli said, “I did not call; go
back and lie down.” So he went
and lay down.

6Again the LORD called, “Samuel!” And Samuel got up and went
to Eli and said, “Here I am; you
called me.”

“My son,” Eli said, “I did not call;
go back and lie down.”

7Now Samuel did not yet know
the LORD: The word of the LORD
had not yet been revealed to him.

Ac 19:12

8A third time the LORD called,
“Samuel!” And Samuel got up and
went to Eli and said, “Here I am;
you called me.”

Then Eli realized that the LORD
was calling the boy. 9So Eli told

Samuel, "Go and lie down, and if
he calls you, say, 'Speak, LORD, for
your servant is listening.'" So Samuel went and lay down in his place.
10The LORD came and stood
there, calling as at the other times,
"Samuel! Samuel!"
Then Samuel said, "Speak, for
your servant is listening."
11And the LORD said to Samuel:
"See, I am about to do something
in Israel that will make the ears
of everyone who hears about it
tingle. 12At that time I will carry
out against Eli everything I spoke
against his family — from beginning to end. 13For I told him that
I would judge his family forever
because of the sin he knew about;
his sons blasphemed God,[a] and he
failed to restrain them. 14There-
fore I swore to the house of Eli,
'The guilt of Eli's house will never
be atoned for by sacrifice or offering.'" 1Sa 2:27-36; 2Ki 21:12; Isa 22:14
15Samuel lay down until morn-
ing and then opened the doors
of the house of the LORD. He was
afraid to tell Eli the vision, 16but
Eli called him and said, "Samuel,
my son."
Samuel answered, "Here I am."
17"What was it he said to you?"
Eli asked. "Do not hide it from me.
May God deal with you, be it ever
so severely, if you hide from me
anything he told you." 18So Samuel
told him everything, hiding nothing from him. Then Eli said, "He is
the LORD; let him do what is good
in his eyes." 2Sa 3:35; Isa 39:8
19The LORD was with Samuel
as he grew up, and he let none of
Samuel's words fall to the ground.
20And all Israel from Dan to Beersheba recognized that Samuel was
attested as a prophet of the LORD.
21The LORD continued to appear at
Shiloh, and there he revealed himself to Samuel through his word.
Ge 39:2; 1Sa 9:6; 2:21

4

And Samuel's word came to
all Israel.

The Philistines Capture the Ark

Now the Israelites went out to
fight against the Philistines. The
Israelites camped at Ebenezer,
and the Philistines at Aphek. 2The
Philistines deployed their forces
to meet Israel, and as the battle
spread, Israel was defeated by the
Philistines, who killed about four
thousand of them on the battlefield. 3When the soldiers returned
to camp, the elders of Israel asked,
"Why did the LORD bring defeat
on us today before the Philistines?
Let us bring the ark of the LORD's
covenant from Shiloh, so that he
may go with us and save us from
the hand of our enemies."
Nu 10:35; Jos 7:7; 1Sa 7:12
4So the people sent men to Shiloh, and they brought back the
ark of the covenant of the LORD
Almighty, who is enthroned between the cherubim. And Eli's two
sons, Hophni and Phinehas, were

[a] 13 An ancient Hebrew scribal tradition (see also Septuagint); Masoretic Text *sons made themselves contemptible*

there with the ark of the covenant of God. 2Sa 6:2

5When the ark of the LORD's covenant came into the camp, all Israel raised such a great shout that the ground shook. 6Hearing the uproar, the Philistines asked, "What's all this shouting in the Hebrew camp?" Jos 6:5,10

When they learned that the ark of the LORD had come into the camp, 7the Philistines were afraid. "A god has[a] come into the camp," they said. "Oh no! Nothing like this has happened before. 8We're doomed! Who will deliver us from the hand of these mighty gods? They are the gods who struck the Egyptians with all kinds of plagues in the wilderness. 9Be strong, Philistines! Be men, or you will be subject to the Hebrews, as they have been to you. Be men, and fight!" Ex 15:14; Jdg 13:1; 1Co 16:13

10So the Philistines fought, and the Israelites were defeated and every man fled to his tent. The slaughter was very great; Israel lost thirty thousand foot soldiers. 11The ark of God was captured, and Eli's two sons, Hophni and Phinehas, died. Dt 28:25; 1Sa 2:34; Ps 78:61,64

Death of Eli

12That same day a Benjamite ran from the battle line and went to Shiloh with his clothes torn and dust on his head. 13When he arrived, there was Eli sitting on his chair by the side of the road, watching, because his heart feared for the ark of God. When the man entered the town and told what had happened, the whole town sent up a cry. Jos 7:6; 2Sa 1:2; Ne 9:1

14Eli heard the outcry and asked, "What is the meaning of this uproar?"

The man hurried over to Eli, 15who was ninety-eight years old and whose eyes had failed so that he could not see. 16He told Eli, "I have just come from the battle line; I fled from it this very day." 1Sa 3:2

Eli asked, "What happened, my son?"

17The man who brought the news replied, "Israel fled before the Philistines, and the army has suffered heavy losses. Also your two sons, Hophni and Phinehas, are dead, and the ark of God has been captured."

18When he mentioned the ark of God, Eli fell backward off his chair by the side of the gate. His neck was broken and he died, for he was an old man, and he was heavy. He had led[b] Israel forty years. Jdg 2:16

19His daughter-in-law, the wife of Phinehas, was pregnant and near the time of delivery. When she heard the news that the ark of God had been captured and that her father-in-law and her husband were dead, she went into labor and gave birth, but was overcome by her labor pains. 20As she

[a] 7 Or "*Gods have* (see Septuagint)
[b] 18 Traditionally *judged*

was dying, the women attending
her said, "Don't despair; you have
given birth to a son." But she did
not respond or pay any attention.
21 She named the boy Ichabod,[a]
saying, "The Glory has departed from Israel" — because of the
capture of the ark of God and the
deaths of her father-in-law and
her husband. 22 She said, "The Glory has departed from Israel, for
the ark of God has been captured."
Ps 106:20

The Ark in Ashdod and Ekron

5 After the Philistines had captured the ark of God, they
took it from Ebenezer to Ashdod.
2 Then they carried the ark into
Dagon's temple and set it beside
Dagon. 3 When the people of Ashdod rose early the next day, there
was Dagon, fallen on his face on
the ground before the ark of the
LORD! They took Dagon and put
him back in his place. 4 But the following morning when they rose,
there was Dagon, fallen on his face
on the ground before the ark of
the LORD! His head and hands had
been broken off and were lying
on the threshold; only his body
remained. 5 That is why to this day
neither the priests of Dagon nor
any others who enter Dagon's temple at Ashdod step on the threshold. Jdg 16:23; Isa 46:7; Eze 6:6
6 The LORD's hand was heavy on
the people of Ashdod and its vicinity; he brought devastation on
them and afflicted them with tumors.[b] 7 When the people of Ashdod saw what was happening,
they said, "The ark of the god of
Israel must not stay here with us,
because his hand is heavy on us
and on Dagon our god." 8 So they
called together all the rulers of the
Philistines and asked them, "What
shall we do with the ark of the god
of Israel?" Ex 9:3; Ps 78:66; 1Sa 6:5
They answered, "Have the ark of
the god of Israel moved to Gath."
So they moved the ark of the God
of Israel.
9 But after they had moved it,
the LORD's hand was against that
city, throwing it into a great panic.
He afflicted the people of the city,
both young and old, with an outbreak of tumors.[c] 10 So they sent
the ark of God to Ekron. 1Sa 7:13
As the ark of God was entering
Ekron, the people of Ekron cried
out, "They have brought the ark
of the god of Israel around to us
to kill us and our people." 11 So they
called together all the rulers of the
Philistines and said, "Send the ark
of the god of Israel away; let it go
back to its own place, or it[d] will kill
us and our people." For death had
filled the city with panic; God's
hand was very heavy on it. 12 Those
who did not die were afflicted with
tumors, and the outcry of the city
went up to heaven. 1Sa 4:8

[a] 21 *Ichabod* means *no glory.* [b] 6 Hebrew; Septuagint and Vulgate *tumors. And rats appeared in their land, and there was death and destruction throughout the city*
[c] 9 Or *with tumors in the groin* (see Septuagint) [d] 11 Or *he*

The Ark Returned to Israel

6 When the ark of the LORD had been in Philistine territory seven months, 2the Philistines called for the priests and the diviners and said, "What shall we do with the ark of the LORD? Tell us how we should send it back to its place."

Ge 41:8; Ex 7:11

3They answered, "If you return the ark of the god of Israel, do not send it back to him without a gift; by all means send a guilt offering to him. Then you will be healed, and you will know why his hand has not been lifted from you."

Ex 23:15; Lev 5:15; Dt 16:16

4The Philistines asked, "What guilt offering should we send to him?"

They replied, "Five gold tumors and five gold rats, according to the number of the Philistine rulers, because the same plague has struck both you and your rulers. 5Make models of the tumors and of the rats that are destroying the country, and give glory to Israel's god. Perhaps he will lift his hand from you and your gods and your land. 6Why do you harden your hearts as the Egyptians and Pharaoh did? When Israel's god dealt harshly with them, did they not send the Israelites out so they could go on their way?

Ex 12:31,33; Jos 7:19; 13:3

7"Now then, get a new cart ready, with two cows that have calved and have never been yoked. Hitch the cows to the cart, but take their calves away and pen them up. 8Take the ark of the LORD and put it on the cart, and in a chest beside it put the gold objects you are sending back to him as a guilt offering. Send it on its way, 9but keep watching it. If it goes up to its own territory, toward Beth Shemesh, then the LORD has brought this great disaster on us. But if it does not, then we will know that it was not his hand that struck us but that it happened to us by chance."

2Sa 6:3; Nu 19:2; Jos 15:10

10So they did this. They took two such cows and hitched them to the cart and penned up their calves. 11They placed the ark of the LORD on the cart and along with it the chest containing the gold rats and the models of the tumors. 12Then the cows went straight up toward Beth Shemesh, keeping on the road and lowing all the way; they did not turn to the right or to the left. The rulers of the Philistines followed them as far as the border of Beth Shemesh.

13Now the people of Beth Shemesh were harvesting their wheat in the valley, and when they looked up and saw the ark, they rejoiced at the sight. 14The cart came to the field of Joshua of Beth Shemesh, and there it stopped beside a large rock. The people chopped up the wood of the cart and sacrificed the cows as a burnt offering to the LORD. 15The Levites took down the ark of the LORD, together with the chest containing

the gold objects, and placed them
on the large rock. On that day the
people of Beth Shemesh offered
burnt offerings and made sacrifices to the LORD. 16The five rulers
of the Philistines saw all this and
then returned that same day to
Ekron. 2Sa 24:22; 1Ki 19:21

17These are the gold tumors the
Philistines sent as a guilt offering
to the LORD — one each for Ashdod, Gaza, Ashkelon, Gath and Ekron. 18And the number of the gold
rats was according to the number of Philistine towns belonging
to the five rulers — the fortified
towns with their country villages.
The large rock on which the Levites set the ark of the LORD is a
witness to this day in the field of
Joshua of Beth Shemesh.

19But God struck down some of
the inhabitants of Beth Shemesh,
putting seventy[a] of them to death
because they looked into the ark
of the LORD. The people mourned
because of the heavy blow the
LORD had dealt them. 20And the
people of Beth Shemesh asked,
"Who can stand in the presence of
the LORD, this holy God? To whom
will the ark go up from here?"
Ex 19:21; Lev 11:45; Mal 3:2

21Then they sent messengers
to the people of Kiriath Jearim,
saying, "The Philistines have returned the ark of the LORD. Come
down and take it up to your town."

7 1So the men of Kiriath Jearim
came and took up the ark of
the LORD. They brought it to Abinadab's house on the hill and consecrated Eleazar his son to guard
the ark of the LORD. 2The ark remained at Kiriath Jearim a long
time — twenty years in all. 2Sa 6:3

Samuel Subdues the Philistines at Mizpah

Then all the people of Israel
turned back to the LORD. 3So Samuel said to all the Israelites, "If you
are returning to the LORD with all
your hearts, then rid yourselves
of the foreign gods and the Ashtoreths and commit yourselves to
the LORD and serve him only, and
he will deliver you out of the hand
of the Philistines." 4So the Israelites put away their Baals and Ashtoreths, and served the LORD only.
Jos 24:14; Joel 2:12; Lk 4:8

5Then Samuel said, "Assemble
all Israel at Mizpah, and I will intercede with the LORD for you."
6When they had assembled at Mizpah, they drew water and poured
it out before the LORD. On that day
they fasted and there they confessed, "We have sinned against
the LORD." Now Samuel was serving as leader[b] of Israel at Mizpah.
Jdg 10:10; Ne 9:1; La 2:19

7When the Philistines heard
that Israel had assembled at Mizpah, the rulers of the Philistines
came up to attack them. When the
Israelites heard of it, they were
afraid because of the Philistines.

[a] 19 A few Hebrew manuscripts; most Hebrew manuscripts and Septuagint *50,070*
[b] 6 Traditionally *judge*; also in verse 15

8They said to Samuel, "Do not stop
crying out to the LORD our God for
us, that he may rescue us from
the hand of the Philistines." 9Then
Samuel took a suckling lamb and
sacrificed it as a whole burnt offering to the LORD. He cried out
to the LORD on Israel's behalf, and
the LORD answered him.
1Sa 17:11; Isa 37:4; Ps 99:6

10While Samuel was sacrificing
the burnt offering, the Philistines
drew near to engage Israel in battle. But that day the LORD thundered with loud thunder against
the Philistines and threw them
into such a panic that they were
routed before the Israelites. 11The
men of Israel rushed out of Mizpah and pursued the Philistines,
slaughtering them along the way
to a point below Beth Kar.
Jos 10:10; 1Sa 2:10; 2Sa 22:14-15

12Then Samuel took a stone
and set it up between Mizpah and
Shen. He named it Ebenezer,[a] saying, "Thus far the LORD has helped
us." Jos 4:9; Jdg 13:1,5; 1Sa 13:5

13So the Philistines were subdued and they stopped invading Israel's territory. Throughout
Samuel's lifetime, the hand of the
LORD was against the Philistines.
14The towns from Ekron to Gath
that the Philistines had captured
from Israel were restored to Israel, and Israel delivered the neighboring territory from the hands
of the Philistines. And there was
peace between Israel and the Amorites. Jdg 13:1,5; 1Sa 13:5

15Samuel continued as Isra-
el's leader all the days of his life.
16From year to year he went on a
circuit from Bethel to Gilgal to
Mizpah, judging Israel in all those
places. 17But he always went back
to Ramah, where his home was,
and there he also held court for Israel. And he built an altar there to
the LORD. 1Sa 12:11; Jdg 21:4

Israel Asks for a King

8 When Samuel grew old, he
appointed his sons as Israel's
leaders.[b] 2The name of his firstborn was Joel and the name of
his second was Abijah, and they
served at Beersheba. 3But his
sons did not follow his ways. They
turned aside after dishonest gain
and accepted bribes and perverted
justice. Dt 16:18-19; Ps 15:5

4So all the elders of Israel gathered together and came to Samuel
at Ramah. 5They said to him, "You
are old, and your sons do not follow your ways; now appoint a king
to lead[c] us, such as all the other
nations have." Dt 17:14-20; 1Sa 7:17

6But when they said, "Give us
a king to lead us," this displeased
Samuel; so he prayed to the LORD.
7And the LORD told him: "Listen
to all that the people are saying
to you; it is not you they have rejected, but they have rejected me
as their king. 8As they have done
from the day I brought them up

[a] 12 *Ebenezer* means *stone of help.*
[b] 1 Traditionally *judges* [c] 5 Traditionally *judge*; also in verses 6 and 20

out of Egypt until this day, forsaking me and serving other gods, so
they are doing to you. 9Now listen
to them; but warn them solemnly and let them know what the
king who will reign over them will
claim as his rights."
Ex 16:8; 1Sa 10:19; 15:11

10Samuel told all the words of
the LORD to the people who were
asking him for a king. 11He said,
"This is what the king who will
reign over you will claim as his
rights: He will take your sons and
make them serve with his chariots and horses, and they will run
in front of his chariots. 12Some he
will assign to be commanders of
thousands and commanders of fifties, and others to plow his ground
and reap his harvest, and still others to make weapons of war and
equipment for his chariots. 13He
will take your daughters to be per-
fumers and cooks and bakers. 14He
will take the best of your fields
and vineyards and olive groves
and give them to his attendants.
15He will take a tenth of your grain
and of your vintage and give it to
his officials and attendants. 16Your
male and female servants and the
best of your cattle[a] and donkeys
he will take for his own use. 17He
will take a tenth of your flocks,
and you yourselves will become
his slaves. 18When that day comes,
you will cry out for relief from
the king you have chosen, but the
LORD will not answer you in that
day." 1Sa 14:52; 1Ki 21:7,15; Mic 3:4

19But the people refused to listen to Samuel. "No!" they said.
"We want a king over us. 20Then
we will be like all the other nations, with a king to lead us and
to go out before us and fight our
battles." Isa 66:4; Jer 44:16

21When Samuel heard all that
the people said, he repeated it
before the LORD. 22The LORD answered, "Listen to them and give
them a king." Jdg 11:11

Then Samuel said to the Israelites, "Everyone go back to your
own town."

Samuel Anoints Saul

9 There was a Benjamite, a man
of standing, whose name was
Kish son of Abiel, the son of Ze-
ror, the son of Bekorath, the son
of Aphiah of Benjamin. 2Kish had
a son named Saul, as handsome a
young man as could be found anywhere in Israel, and he was a head
taller than anyone else.
1Sa 10:23; 14:51; 1Ch 9:39

3Now the donkeys belonging to
Saul's father Kish were lost, and
Kish said to his son Saul, "Take one
of the servants with you and go and
look for the donkeys." 4So he passed
through the hill country of Ephraim
and through the area around Sha-
lisha, but they did not find them.
They went on into the district of
Shaalim, but the donkeys were not
there. Then he passed through the
territory of Benjamin, but they did
not find them. Jos 24:33; 2Ki 4:42

[a] 16 Septuagint; Hebrew *young men*

5When they reached the district
of Zuph, Saul said to the servant
who was with him, "Come, let's go
back, or my father will stop thinking about the donkeys and start
worrying about us." 1Sa 10:2
6But the servant replied, "Look,
in this town there is a man of God;
he is highly respected, and everything he says comes true. Let's go
there now. Perhaps he will tell us
what way to take." Dt 33:1; 1Sa 3:19
7Saul said to his servant, "If we
go, what can we give the man? The
food in our sacks is gone. We have
no gift to take to the man of God.
What do we have?" 1Ki 14:3; 2Ki 8:8
8The servant answered him
again. "Look," he said, "I have a
quarter of a shekel[a] of silver. I will
give it to the man of God so that
he will tell us what way to take."
9(Formerly in Israel, if someone
went to inquire of God, they would
say, "Come, let us go to the seer,"
because the prophet of today used
to be called a seer.)
2Sa 24:11; 1Ch 26:28; Isa 30:10
10"Good," Saul said to his servant. "Come, let's go." So they set
out for the town where the man of
God was.
11As they were going up the hill
to the town, they met some young
women coming out to draw water,
and they asked them, "Is the seer
here?"
12"He is," they answered. "He's
ahead of you. Hurry now; he has
just come to our town today, for
the people have a sacrifice at the
high place. 13As soon as you enter
the town, you will find him before he goes up to the high place
to eat. The people will not begin
eating until he comes, because
he must bless the sacrifice; afterward, those who are invited will
eat. Go up now; you should find
him about this time."
Ge 31:54; Nu 28:11-15; Mt 14:19
14They went up to the town, and
as they were entering it, there was
Samuel, coming toward them on
his way up to the high place.
15Now the day before Saul came,
the LORD had revealed this to
Samuel: 16"About this time tomorrow I will send you a man from
the land of Benjamin. Anoint him
ruler over my people Israel; he
will deliver them from the hand
of the Philistines. I have looked
on my people, for their cry has
reached me." Ex 3:7-9; 1Sa 10:1
17When Samuel caught sight of
Saul, the LORD said to him, "This is
the man I spoke to you about; he
will govern my people." 1Sa 16:12
18Saul approached Samuel in
the gateway and asked, "Would
you please tell me where the seer's
house is?"
19"I am the seer," Samuel replied. "Go up ahead of me to the
high place, for today you are to
eat with me, and in the morning I will send you on your way
and will tell you all that is in your
heart. 20As for the donkeys you

[a] 8 That is, about 1/10 ounce or about 3 grams

lost three days ago, do not worry about them; they have been
found. And to whom is all the desire of Israel turned, if not to you
and your whole family line?"
1Sa 8:5; 12:13; Ezr 6:8

21 Saul answered, "But am I not a
Benjamite, from the smallest tribe
of Israel, and is not my clan the
least of all the clans of the tribe of
Benjamin? Why do you say such a
thing to me?" Jdg 20:35,46; 1Sa 15:17
22 Then Samuel brought Saul
and his servant into the hall and
seated them at the head of those
who were invited — about thirty
in number. 23 Samuel said to the
cook, "Bring the piece of meat I
gave you, the one I told you to lay
aside."
24 So the cook took up the thigh
with what was on it and set it in
front of Saul. Samuel said, "Here
is what has been kept for you. Eat,
because it was set aside for you for
this occasion from the time I said,
'I have invited guests.'" And Saul
dined with Samuel that day.
25 After they came down from
the high place to the town, Samuel talked with Saul on the roof of
his house. 26 They rose about daybreak, and Samuel called to Saul
on the roof, "Get ready, and I will
send you on your way." When Saul
got ready, he and Samuel went outside together. 27 As they were going down to the edge of the town,
Samuel said to Saul, "Tell the servant to go on ahead of us" — and
the servant did so — "but you stay
here for a while, so that I may give
you a message from God."
Dt 22:8; Ac 10:9

10 Then Samuel took a flask of
olive oil and poured it on
Saul's head and kissed him, saying,
"Has not the LORD anointed you
ruler over his inheritance?[a] 2 When
you leave me today, you will meet
two men near Rachel's tomb, at
Zelzah on the border of Benjamin.
They will say to you, 'The donkeys
you set out to look for have been
found. And now your father has
stopped thinking about them and
is worried about you. He is asking,
"What shall I do about my son?"'
2Ki 9:1,3,6; Dt 32:9; Ge 35:20

3 "Then you will go on from there
until you reach the great tree of Tabor. Three men going up to worship
God at Bethel will meet you there.
One will be carrying three young
goats, another three loaves of
bread, and another a skin of wine.
4 They will greet you and offer you
two loaves of bread, which you will
accept from them. Ge 35:7-8; Pr 18:16
5 "After that you will go to Gibeah of God, where there is a Philistine outpost. As you approach the
town, you will meet a procession
of prophets coming down from
the high place with lyres, timbrels,
pipes and harps being played before them, and they will be proph-

[a] 1 Hebrew; Septuagint and Vulgate *over his people Israel? You will reign over the LORD's people and save them from the power of their enemies round about. And this will be a sign to you that the LORD has anointed you ruler over his inheritance:*

esying. 6The Spirit of the LORD will
come powerfully upon you, and
you will prophesy with them; and
you will be changed into a different person. 7Once these signs are
fulfilled, do whatever your hand
finds to do, for God is with you.
Nu 11:25; 1Sa 19:23-24; Jdg 6:12

8"Go down ahead of me to Gilgal. I will surely come down to
you to sacrifice burnt offerings
and fellowship offerings, but you
must wait seven days until I come
to you and tell you what you are
to do." 1Sa 11:14-15; 13:8

Saul Made King

9As Saul turned to leave Samuel,
God changed Saul's heart, and all
these signs were fulfilled that day.
10When he and his servant arrived
at Gibeah, a procession of prophets met him; the Spirit of God
came powerfully upon him, and
he joined in their prophesying.
11When all those who had formerly known him saw him prophesying with the prophets, they asked
each other, "What is this that has
happened to the son of Kish? Is
Saul also among the prophets?"
1Sa 19:20,24; Mt 13:54

12A man who lived there answered, "And who is their father?"
So it became a saying: "Is Saul also
among the prophets?" 13After Saul
stopped prophesying, he went to
the high place.

14Now Saul's uncle asked him
and his servant, "Where have you
been?" 1Sa 14:50

"Looking for the donkeys," he
said. "But when we saw they were
not to be found, we went to Samuel."

15Saul's uncle said, "Tell me what
Samuel said to you."

16Saul replied, "He assured us
that the donkeys had been found."
But he did not tell his uncle what
Samuel had said about the kingship. 1Sa 9:20

17Samuel summoned the people of Israel to the LORD at Mizpah 18and said to them, "This is
what the LORD, the God of Israel,
says: 'I brought Israel up out of
Egypt, and I delivered you from
the power of Egypt and all the
kingdoms that oppressed you.'
19But you have now rejected your
God, who saves you out of all
your disasters and calamities.
And you have said, 'No, appoint
a king over us.' So now present
yourselves before the LORD by
your tribes and clans."
Jdg 6:8-9; 1Sa 7:5; 8:5-7

20When Samuel had all Israel
come forward by tribes, the tribe
of Benjamin was taken by lot.
21Then he brought forward the
tribe of Benjamin, clan by clan,
and Matri's clan was taken. Finally Saul son of Kish was taken. But
when they looked for him, he was
not to be found. 22So they inquired
further of the LORD, "Has the man
come here yet?" 1Sa 23:2,4,9-11

And the LORD said, "Yes, he has
hidden himself among the supplies."

23They ran and brought him out, and as he stood among the people he was a head taller than any of the others. 24Samuel said to all the people, "Do you see the man the LORD has chosen? There is no one like him among all the people."

Dt 17:15; 2Sa 21:6

Then the people shouted, "Long live the king!" 1Ki 1:25,34,39

25Samuel explained to the people the rights and duties of kingship. He wrote them down on a scroll and deposited it before the LORD. Then Samuel dismissed the people to go to their own homes.

Dt 17:14-20; 1Sa 8:11-18

26Saul also went to his home in Gibeah, accompanied by valiant men whose hearts God had touched. 27But some scoundrels said, "How can this fellow save us?" They despised him and brought him no gifts. But Saul kept silent.

1Sa 11:4; 1Ki 10:25; 2Ch 17:5

Saul Rescues the City of Jabesh

11 Nahash[a] the Ammonite went up and besieged Jabesh Gilead. And all the men of Jabesh said to him, "Make a treaty with us, and we will be subject to you."

Jdg 21:8; 1Sa 12:12

2But Nahash the Ammonite replied, "I will make a treaty with you only on the condition that I gouge out the right eye of every one of you and so bring disgrace on all Israel." Nu 16:14; 1Sa 17:26

3The elders of Jabesh said to him, "Give us seven days so we can send messengers throughout Israel; if no one comes to rescue us, we will surrender to you."

1Sa 8:4

4When the messengers came to Gibeah of Saul and reported these terms to the people, they all wept aloud. 5Just then Saul was returning from the fields, behind his oxen, and he asked, "What is wrong with everyone? Why are they weeping?" Then they repeated to him what the men of Jabesh had said.

1Sa 10:5,26; Jdg 2:4; 1Sa 30:4

6When Saul heard their words, the Spirit of God came powerfully upon him, and he burned with anger. 7He took a pair of oxen, cut them into pieces, and sent the pieces by messengers throughout Israel, proclaiming, "This is what will be done to the oxen of anyone who does not follow Saul and Samuel." Then the terror of the LORD fell on the people, and they came out together as one. 8When Saul mustered them at Bezek, the men of Israel numbered three hundred thousand and those of Judah thirty thousand.

Jdg 3:10; 19:29; 21:5

[a] 1 Masoretic Text; Dead Sea Scrolls *gifts. Now Nahash king of the Ammonites oppressed the Gadites and Reubenites severely. He gouged out all their right eyes and struck terror and dread in Israel. Not a man remained among the Israelites beyond the Jordan whose right eye was not gouged out by Nahash king of the Ammonites, except that seven thousand men fled from the Ammonites and entered Jabesh Gilead. About a month later,* 1*Nahash*

9They told the messengers who
had come, "Say to the men of Jabesh Gilead, 'By the time the sun
is hot tomorrow, you will be rescued.'" When the messengers
went and reported this to the men
of Jabesh, they were elated. 10They
said to the Ammonites, "Tomorrow we will surrender to you, and
you can do to us whatever you
like."
11The next day Saul separated his men into three divisions;
during the last watch of the night
they broke into the camp of the
Ammonites and slaughtered them
until the heat of the day. Those
who survived were scattered, so
that no two of them were left together. Jdg 7:16

Saul Confirmed as King

12The people then said to Samuel, "Who was it that asked, 'Shall
Saul reign over us?' Turn these
men over to us so that we may put
them to death." 1Sa 10:27; Lk 19:27
13But Saul said, "No one will be
put to death today, for this day the
LORD has rescued Israel."
1Sa 19:5; 2Sa 19:22
14Then Samuel said to the people, "Come, let us go to Gilgal and
there renew the kingship." 15So
all the people went to Gilgal and
made Saul king in the presence
of the LORD. There they sacrificed
fellowship offerings before the
LORD, and Saul and all the Israelites held a great celebration.
1Sa 10:8,17,25

Samuel's Farewell Speech

12 Samuel said to all Israel, "I
have listened to everything
you said to me and have set a king
over you. 2Now you have a king as
your leader. As for me, I am old
and gray, and my sons are here
with you. I have been your leader from my youth until this day.
3Here I stand. Testify against me
in the presence of the LORD and
his anointed. Whose ox have I
taken? Whose donkey have I tak-
en? Whom have I cheated? Whom
have I oppressed? From whose
hand have I accepted a bribe to
make me shut my eyes? If I have
done any of these things, I will
make it right." 1Sa 8:7; 24:6; 2Sa 1:14
4"You have not cheated or oppressed us," they replied. "You
have not taken anything from
anyone's hand." Ex 22:4; Ac 23:9
5Samuel said to them, "The
LORD is witness against you, and
also his anointed is witness this
day, that you have not found anything in my hand."
"He is witness," they said.
6Then Samuel said to the people, "It is the LORD who appointed Moses and Aaron and brought
your ancestors up out of Egypt.
7Now then, stand here, because I
am going to confront you with evidence before the LORD as to all
the righteous acts performed by
the LORD for you and your ancestors. Ex 6:26; Eze 20:35; Mic 6:1-5
8"After Jacob entered Egypt,
they cried to the LORD for help,

and the LORD sent Moses and Aaron, who brought your ancestors
out of Egypt and settled them in
this place. Ex 2:23; 3:10; 4:16

9“But they forgot the LORD their
God; so he sold them into the hand
of Sisera, the commander of the
army of Hazor, and into the hands
of the Philistines and the king of
Moab, who fought against them.
10They cried out to the LORD and
said, ‘We have sinned; we have
forsaken the LORD and served the
Baals and the Ashtoreths. But now
deliver us from the hands of our
enemies, and we will serve you.’
11Then the LORD sent Jerub-Baal,[a]
Barak,[b] Jephthah and Samuel,[c]
and he delivered you from the
hands of your enemies all around
you, so that you lived in safety.
Jdg 3:7; 4:2; 6:14,32

12“But when you saw that Nahash king of the Ammonites was
moving against you, you said to
me, ‘No, we want a king to rule
over us’—even though the LORD
your God was your king. 13Now
here is the king you have chosen,
the one you asked for; see, the
LORD has set a king over you. 14If
you fear the LORD and serve and
obey him and do not rebel against
his commands, and if both you
and the king who reigns over you
follow the LORD your God—good!
15But if you do not obey the LORD,
and if you rebel against his commands, his hand will be against
you, as it was against your ancestors. Jdg 8:23; Jos 24:14; Hos 13:11

16“Now then, stand still and see
this great thing the LORD is about
to do before your eyes! 17Is it not
wheat harvest now? I will call on
the LORD to send thunder and
rain. And you will realize what
an evil thing you did in the eyes
of the LORD when you asked for a
king.” Ex 14:13; 1Sa 8:6-7; Pr 26:1

18Then Samuel called on the
LORD, and that same day the LORD
sent thunder and rain. So all the
people stood in awe of the LORD
and of Samuel. Ex 14:31

19The people all said to Samuel,
“Pray to the LORD your God for
your servants so that we will not
die, for we have added to all our
other sins the evil of asking for a
king.” Ex 9:28

20“Do not be afraid,” Samuel replied. “You have done all this evil;
yet do not turn away from the
LORD, but serve the LORD with all
your heart. 21Do not turn away after useless idols. They can do you
no good, nor can they rescue you,
because they are useless. 22For the
sake of his great name the LORD
will not reject his people, because
the LORD was pleased to make you
his own. 23As for me, far be it from
me that I should sin against the
LORD by failing to pray for you.
And I will teach you the way that
is good and right. 24But be sure to
fear the LORD and serve him faith-

[a] 11 Also called *Gideon* [b] 11 Some Septuagint manuscripts and Syriac; Hebrew *Bedan* [c] 11 Hebrew; some Septuagint manuscripts and Syriac *Samson*

fully with all your heart; consider
what great things he has done for
you. 25Yet if you persist in doing
evil, both you and your king will
perish."
Dt 31:6; Hab 2:18; Col 1:9

Samuel Rebukes Saul

13 Saul was thirty[a] years old
when he became king, and
he reigned over Israel forty-[b] two
years.
2Saul chose three thousand men
from Israel; two thousand were
with him at Mikmash and in the
hill country of Bethel, and a thousand were with Jonathan at Gibeah in Benjamin. The rest of the
men he sent back to their homes.
3Jonathan attacked the Philistine outpost at Geba, and the Philistines heard about it. Then Saul
had the trumpet blown throughout the land and said, "Let the Hebrews hear!" 4So all Israel heard
the news: "Saul has attacked the
Philistine outpost, and now Israel has become obnoxious to the
Philistines." And the people were
summoned to join Saul at Gilgal.
1Sa 10:5; Jdg 3:27
5The Philistines assembled to
fight Israel, with three thousand[c]
chariots, six thousand charioteers,
and soldiers as numerous as the
sand on the seashore. They went
up and camped at Mikmash, east
of Beth Aven. 6When the Israelites
saw that their situation was criti-
cal and that their army was hard
pressed, they hid in caves and
thickets, among the rocks, and in
pits and cisterns. 7Some Hebrews
even crossed the Jordan to the
land of Gad and Gilead.
Jos 11:4; Jdg 6:2; Nu 32:33
Saul remained at Gilgal, and all
the troops with him were quaking
with fear. 8He waited seven days,
the time set by Samuel; but Samuel did not come to Gilgal, and
Saul's men began to scatter. 9So he
said, "Bring me the burnt offering
and the fellowship offerings." And
Saul offered up the burnt offering.
10Just as he finished making the
offering, Samuel arrived, and Saul
went out to greet him.
1Sa 10:8; 15:13; 2Sa 24:25
11"What have you done?" asked
Samuel.
Saul replied, "When I saw that
the men were scattering, and that
you did not come at the set time,
and that the Philistines were as-
sembling at Mikmash, 12I thought,
'Now the Philistines will come
down against me at Gilgal, and I
have not sought the LORD's favor.'
So I felt compelled to offer the
burnt offering."
13"You have done a foolish
thing," Samuel said. "You have not
kept the command the LORD your
God gave you; if you had, he would
have established your kingdom
over Israel for all time. 14But now

[a] *1* A few late manuscripts of the Septuagint; Hebrew does not have *thirty*.
[b] *1* Probable reading of the original Hebrew text (see Acts 13:21); Masoretic Text does not have *forty-*.
[c] *5* Some Septuagint manuscripts and Syriac; Hebrew *thirty thousand*

your kingdom will not endure;
the LORD has sought out a man after his own heart and appointed
him ruler of his people, because
you have not kept the LORD's command." 2Ch 16:9; Ac 7:46; 13:22
15Then Samuel left Gilgal[a] and
went up to Gibeah in Benjamin,
and Saul counted the men who
were with him. They numbered
about six hundred. 1Sa 14:2

Israel Without Weapons

16Saul and his son Jonathan and
the men with them were staying
in Gibeah[b] in Benjamin, while the
Philistines camped at Mikmash.
17Raiding parties went out from
the Philistine camp in three de-
tachments. One turned toward
Ophrah in the vicinity of Shual,
18another toward Beth Horon, and
the third toward the borderland
overlooking the Valley of Zeboyim
facing the wilderness.
Jos 18:23; Ne 11:34
19Not a blacksmith could be
found in the whole land of Israel,
because the Philistines had said,
"Otherwise the Hebrews will make
swords or spears!" 20So all Israel
went down to the Philistines to
have their plow points, mattocks,
axes and sickles[c] sharpened. 21The
price was two-thirds of a shekel[d]
for sharpening plow points and
mattocks, and a third of a shekel[e]
for sharpening forks and axes and
for repointing goads. 2Ki 24:14
22So on the day of the battle not
a soldier with Saul and Jonathan
had a sword or spear in his hand;
only Saul and his son Jonathan
had them. Jdg 5:8

Jonathan Attacks the Philistines

23Now a detachment of Philistines had gone out to the pass at
14 Mikmash. 1One day Jonathan son of Saul said to his
young armor-bearer, "Come, let's
go over to the Philistine outpost
on the other side." But he did not
tell his father.
2Saul was staying on the outskirts of Gibeah under a pomegranate tree in Migron. With him
were about six hundred men,
3among whom was Ahijah, who
was wearing an ephod. He was a
son of Ichabod's brother Ahitub
son of Phinehas, the son of Eli,
the LORD's priest in Shiloh. No one
was aware that Jonathan had left.
1Sa 4:21; 13:15; 22:11,20
4On each side of the pass that
Jonathan intended to cross to
reach the Philistine outpost was a
cliff; one was called Bozez and the
other Seneh. 5One cliff stood to the
north toward Mikmash, the other
to the south toward Geba. 1Sa 13:23
6Jonathan said to his young armor-bearer, "Come, let's go over

[a] 15 Hebrew; Septuagint *Gilgal and went his way; the rest of the people went after Saul to meet the army, and they went out of Gilgal* [b] 16 Two Hebrew manuscripts; most Hebrew manuscripts *Geba,* a variant of *Gibeah* [c] 20 Septuagint; Hebrew *plow points* [d] 21 That is, about 1/4 ounce or about 8 grams [e] 21 That is, about 1/8 ounce or about 4 grams

to the outpost of those uncircumcised men. Perhaps the LORD will
act in our behalf. Nothing can hinder the LORD from saving, whether by many or by few.”
Jdg 7:4; 1Sa 17:46-47; Jer 9:26
7“Do all that you have in mind,”
his armor-bearer said. “Go ahead; I
am with you heart and soul.”
8Jonathan said, “Come on, then;
we will cross over toward them
and let them see us. 9If they say
to us, ‘Wait there until we come
to you,’ we will stay where we are
and not go up to them. 10But if
they say, ‘Come up to us,’ we will
climb up, because that will be our
sign that the LORD has given them
into our hands.” Ge 24:14; Jdg 6:36-37
11So both of them showed themselves to the Philistine outpost.
“Look!” said the Philistines. “The
Hebrews are crawling out of the
holes they were hiding in.” 12The
men of the outpost shouted to
Jonathan and his armor-bearer,
“Come up to us and we’ll teach
you a lesson.” 1Sa 13:6; 17:43-44
So Jonathan said to his armor-
bearer, “Climb up after me; the
LORD has given them into the
hand of Israel.” 2Sa 5:24
13Jonathan climbed up, using
his hands and feet, with his armor-
bearer right behind him. The Philistines fell before Jonathan, and
his armor-bearer followed and
killed behind him. 14In that first
attack Jonathan and his armor-
bearer killed some twenty men in
an area of about half an acre.

Israel Routs the Philistines

15Then panic struck the whole
army — those in the camp and
field, and those in the outposts
and raiding parties — and the
ground shook. It was a panic sent
by God.[a] Ge 35:5; 2Ki 7:5-7; 1Sa 13:17
16Saul’s lookouts at Gibeah in
Benjamin saw the army melting
away in all directions. 17Then Saul
said to the men who were with
him, “Muster the forces and see
who has left us.” When they did, it
was Jonathan and his armor-bearer who were not there.
18Saul said to Ahijah, “Bring the
ark of God.” (At that time it was
with the Israelites.)[b] 19While Saul
was talking to the priest, the tumult in the Philistine camp increased more and more. So Saul
said to the priest, “Withdraw your
hand.” Nu 27:21; 1Sa 30:7
20Then Saul and all his men assembled and went to the battle.
They found the Philistines in total confusion, striking each other with their swords. 21Those Hebrews who had previously been
with the Philistines and had gone
up with them to their camp went
over to the Israelites who were
with Saul and Jonathan. 22When
all the Israelites who had hidden
in the hill country of Ephraim
heard that the Philistines were on
the run, they joined the battle in
hot pursuit. 23So on that day the

[a] 15 *Or a terrible panic* [b] 18 Hebrew; Septuagint *“Bring the ephod.” (At that time he wore the ephod before the Israelites.)*

LORD saved Israel, and the battle
moved on beyond Beth Aven.

Ex 14:30; Jdg 7:22; 1Sa 13:6

Jonathan Eats Honey

24Now the Israelites were in distress that day, because Saul had
bound the people under an oath,
saying, “Cursed be anyone who
eats food before evening comes,
before I have avenged myself
on my enemies!” So none of the
troops tasted food. Jos 6:26

25The entire army entered the
woods, and there was honey on
the ground. 26When they went
into the woods, they saw the honey oozing out; yet no one put his
hand to his mouth, because they
feared the oath. 27But Jonathan
had not heard that his father had
bound the people with the oath,
so he reached out the end of the
staff that was in his hand and
dipped it into the honeycomb. He
raised his hand to his mouth, and
his eyes brightened.[a] 28Then one
of the soldiers told him, “Your father bound the army under a strict
oath, saying, ‘Cursed be anyone
who eats food today!’ That is why
the men are faint.”

1Sa 30:12; Ps 19:10; Pr 16:24

29Jonathan said, “My father has
made trouble for the country. See
how my eyes brightened when I
tasted a little of this honey. 30How
much better it would have been if
the men had eaten today some of
the plunder they took from their
enemies. Would not the slaughter
of the Philistines have been even
greater?” 1Ki 18:18

31That day, after the Israelites
had struck down the Philistines
from Mikmash to Aijalon, they
were exhausted. 32They pounced
on the plunder and, taking sheep,
cattle and calves, they butchered
them on the ground and ate them,
together with the blood. 33Then
someone said to Saul, “Look, the
men are sinning against the LORD
by eating meat that has blood
in it.” Ge 9:4; Lev 17:10-14; 1Sa 15:19

“You have broken faith,” he
said. “Roll a large stone over here
at once.” 34Then he said, “Go out
among the men and tell them,
‘Each of you bring me your cattle and sheep, and slaughter them
here and eat them. Do not sin
against the LORD by eating meat
with blood still in it.’ ”

So everyone brought his ox that
night and slaughtered it there.
35Then Saul built an altar to the
LORD; it was the first time he had
done this. 1Sa 7:17

36Saul said, “Let us go down and
pursue the Philistines by night
and plunder them till dawn, and
let us not leave one of them alive.”

“Do whatever seems best to
you,” they replied.

But the priest said, “Let us inquire of God here.”

37So Saul asked God, “Shall I go
down and pursue the Philistines?
Will you give them into Israel’s

[a] 27 Or *his strength was renewed*; similarly in verse 29

hand?" But God did not answer
him that day. 1Sa 10:22; 28:6,15
38 Saul therefore said, "Come
here, all you who are leaders of the
army, and let us find out what sin
has been committed today. 39 As
surely as the LORD who rescues
Israel lives, even if the guilt lies
with my son Jonathan, he must
die." But not one of them said a
word. 2Sa 12:5
40 Saul then said to all the Israelites, "You stand over there; I and
Jonathan my son will stand over
here."

"Do what seems best to you,"
they replied.
41 Then Saul prayed to the LORD,
the God of Israel, "Why have you
not answered your servant today?
If the fault is in me or my son Jonathan, respond with Urim, but if
the men of Israel are at fault,[a] respond with Thummim." Jonathan
and Saul were taken by lot, and
the men were cleared. 42 Saul said,
"Cast the lot between me and Jonathan my son." And Jonathan was
taken. Ac 1:24; Pr 16:33
43 Then Saul said to Jonathan,
"Tell me what you have done."
Jos 7:19

So Jonathan told him, "I tasted
a little honey with the end of my
staff. And now I must die!"
44 Saul said, "May God deal with
me, be it ever so severely, if you do
not die, Jonathan." Ru 1:17
45 But the men said to Saul,
"Should Jonathan die — he who
has brought about this great deliverance in Israel? Never! As surely as the LORD lives, not a hair of
his head will fall to the ground, for
he did this today with God's help."
So the men rescued Jonathan, and
he was not put to death.
2Sa 14:11; 1Ki 1:52
46 Then Saul stopped pursuing
the Philistines, and they withdrew
to their own land.
47 After Saul had assumed rule
over Israel, he fought against their
enemies on every side: Moab, the
Ammonites, Edom, the kings[b] of
Zobah, and the Philistines. Wherever he turned, he inflicted punishment on them.[c] 48 He fought
valiantly and defeated the Amalekites, delivering Israel from the
hands of those who had plundered
them. 1Sa 11:1-13; 15:2,7

Saul's Family

49 Saul's sons were Jonathan, Ishvi and Malki-Shua. The name of
his older daughter was Merab, and
that of the younger was Michal.
50 His wife's name was Ahinoam
daughter of Ahimaaz. The name
of the commander of Saul's army
was Abner son of Ner, and Ner was
Saul's uncle. 51 Saul's father Kish
and Abner's father Ner were sons
of Abiel. 1Sa 9:1; 18:17-20; 31:2
52 All the days of Saul there was
bitter war with the Philistines, and
whenever Saul saw a mighty or

[a] 41 Septuagint; Hebrew does not have *"Why . . . at fault.* [b] 47 Masoretic Text; Dead Sea Scrolls and Septuagint *king* [c] 47 Hebrew; Septuagint *he was victorious*

brave man, he took him into his
service. 1Sa 8:11

The LORD Rejects Saul as King

15 Samuel said to Saul, "I am
the one the LORD sent to
anoint you king over his people Israel; so listen now to the message
from the LORD. 2This is what the
LORD Almighty says: 'I will punish
the Amalekites for what they did
to Israel when they waylaid them
as they came up from Egypt. 3Now
go, attack the Amalekites and totally destroy[a] all that belongs to
them. Do not spare them; put to
death men and women, children
and infants, cattle and sheep, camels and donkeys.'"

Ex 17:8-14; Nu 24:20; 1Sa 9:16

4So Saul summoned the men
and mustered them at Telaim—
two hundred thousand foot soldiers and ten thousand from
Judah. 5Saul went to the city of
Amalek and set an ambush in the
ravine. 6Then he said to the Kenites, "Go away, leave the Amalekites so that I do not destroy you
along with them; for you showed
kindness to all the Israelites when
they came up out of Egypt." So
the Kenites moved away from the
Amalekites.

Ex 18:10,19; Nu 10:29-32; Jdg 1:16

7Then Saul attacked the Amalekites all the way from Havilah
to Shur, near the eastern border
of Egypt. 8He took Agag king of
the Amalekites alive, and all his
people he totally destroyed with
the sword. 9But Saul and the army
spared Agag and the best of the
sheep and cattle, the fat calves[b]
and lambs—everything that was
good. These they were unwilling
to destroy completely, but everything that was despised and weak
they totally destroyed.

Ge 16:7; 25:17-18; 1Sa 14:48

10Then the word of the LORD
came to Samuel: 11"I regret that I
have made Saul king, because he
has turned away from me and has
not carried out my instructions."
Samuel was angry, and he cried
out to the LORD all that night.

Ge 6:6; Jos 22:16; 1Ki 9:6-7

12Early in the morning Samuel
got up and went to meet Saul, but
he was told, "Saul has gone to Carmel. There he has set up a monument in his own honor and has
turned and gone on down to Gilgal." Jos 15:55

13When Samuel reached him,
Saul said, "The LORD bless you! I
have carried out the LORD's instructions."

14But Samuel said, "What then is
this bleating of sheep in my ears?
What is this lowing of cattle that I
hear?"

15Saul answered, "The soldiers
brought them from the Amalekites; they spared the best of the
sheep and cattle to sacrifice to the

[a] *3* The Hebrew term refers to the irrevocable giving over of things or persons to the LORD, often by totally destroying them; also in verses 8, 9, 15, 18, 20 and 21.
[b] *9* Or *the grown bulls*; the meaning of the Hebrew for this phrase is uncertain.

LORD your God, but we totally destroyed the rest."
16"Enough!" Samuel said to Saul.
"Let me tell you what the LORD
said to me last night."
"Tell me," Saul replied.
17Samuel said, "Although you
were once small in your own eyes,
did you not become the head of the
tribes of Israel? The LORD anointed you king over Israel. 18And he
sent you on a mission, saying,
'Go and completely destroy those
wicked people, the Amalekites;
wage war against them until you
have wiped them out.' 19Why did
you not obey the LORD? Why did
you pounce on the plunder and do
evil in the eyes of the LORD?"

1Sa 9:21; 14:32

20"But I did obey the LORD," Saul
said. "I went on the mission the
LORD assigned me. I completely destroyed the Amalekites and
brought back Agag their king.
21The soldiers took sheep and cattle from the plunder, the best of
what was devoted to God, in order
to sacrifice them to the LORD your
God at Gilgal."
22But Samuel replied:

"Does the LORD delight in
burnt offerings and
sacrifices
as much as in obeying the
LORD?
To obey is better than sacrifice,
and to heed is better
than the fat of rams.

Isa 1:11-15; Hos 6:6; Mic 6:6-8

23For rebellion is like the sin of
divination,
and arrogance like the evil of
idolatry.
Because you have rejected the
word of the LORD,
he has rejected you as king."

1Sa 13:13

24Then Saul said to Samuel, "I
have sinned. I violated the LORD's
command and your instructions.
I was afraid of the men and so I
gave in to them. 25Now I beg you,
forgive my sin and come back
with me, so that I may worship
the LORD." Ex 10:17; 2Sa 12:13; Isa 51:12-13
26But Samuel said to him, "I will
not go back with you. You have rejected the word of the LORD, and
the LORD has rejected you as king
over Israel!" 1Sa 13:14
27As Samuel turned to leave,
Saul caught hold of the hem of his
robe, and it tore. 28Samuel said to
him, "The LORD has torn the kingdom of Israel from you today and
has given it to one of your neighbors — to one better than you. 29He
who is the Glory of Israel does not
lie or change his mind; for he is
not a human being, that he should
change his mind."

Eze 24:14; 1Sa 28:17; 1Ki 11:11,31

30Saul replied, "I have sinned.
But please honor me before the elders of my people and before Israel;
come back with me, so that I may
worship the LORD your God." 31So
Samuel went back with Saul, and
Saul worshiped the LORD. Jn 12:43

[32]Then Samuel said, "Bring me
Agag king of the Amalekites."
Agag came to him in chains.[a]
And he thought, "Surely the bit-
terness of death is past."
[33]But Samuel said,

"As your sword has made
women childless,
so will your mother be
childless among
women." Ge 9:6; Jdg 1:7

And Samuel put Agag to death before the LORD at Gilgal.
[34]Then Samuel left for Ramah,
but Saul went up to his home in
Gibeah of Saul. [35]Until the day
Samuel died, he did not go to
see Saul again, though Samuel
mourned for him. And the LORD
regretted that he had made Saul
king over Israel. 1Sa 11:4; 16:1; 19:24

Samuel Anoints David

16 The LORD said to Samuel,
"How long will you mourn
for Saul, since I have rejected him
as king over Israel? Fill your horn
with oil and be on your way; I am
sending you to Jesse of Bethlehem. I have chosen one of his sons
to be king." Ac 13:22; Ru 4:17; 1Sa 15:23
[2]But Samuel said, "How can I
go? If Saul hears about it, he will
kill me."
The LORD said, "Take a heifer with
you and say, 'I have come to sacrifice to the LORD.' [3]Invite Jesse to the
sacrifice, and I will show you what
to do. You are to anoint for me the
one I indicate." Ex 4:15; Dt 17:15; 1Sa 9:16
[4]Samuel did what the LORD said.
When he arrived at Bethlehem, the
elders of the town trembled when
they met him. They asked, "Do you
come in peace?" 1Ki 2:13; 2Ki 9:17
[5]Samuel replied, "Yes, in peace;
I have come to sacrifice to the
LORD. Consecrate yourselves and
come to the sacrifice with me."
Then he consecrated Jesse and his
sons and invited them to the sacrifice. Ex 19:10,22
[6]When they arrived, Samuel
saw Eliab and thought, "Surely
the LORD's anointed stands here
before the LORD." 1Sa 17:13
[7]But the LORD said to Samuel,
"Do not consider his appearance
or his height, for I have rejected
him. The LORD does not look at
the things people look at. People
look at the outward appearance,
but the LORD looks at the heart."
1Ki 8:39; 1Ch 28:9
[8]Then Jesse called Abinadab
and had him pass in front of Samuel. But Samuel said, "The LORD
has not chosen this one either."
[9]Jesse then had Shammah pass
by, but Samuel said, "Nor has the
LORD chosen this one." [10]Jesse had
seven of his sons pass before Samuel, but Samuel said to him, "The
LORD has not chosen these." [11]So
he asked Jesse, "Are these all the
sons you have?" 1Sa 17:12
"There is still the youngest,"
Jesse answered. "He is tending the
sheep."

[a] 32 The meaning of the Hebrew for this phrase is uncertain.

Samuel said, "Send for him; we will not sit down until he arrives."

12So he sent for him and had him brought in. He was glowing with health and had a fine appearance and handsome features. Ge 39:6; 1Sa 9:17

Then the LORD said, "Rise and anoint him; this is the one."

13So Samuel took the horn of oil and anointed him in the presence of his brothers, and from that day on the Spirit of the LORD came powerfully upon David. Samuel then went to Ramah. 1Sa 10:1,6,9-10

David in Saul's Service

14Now the Spirit of the LORD had departed from Saul, and an evil[a] spirit from the LORD tormented him. Jdg 16:20; 9:23

15Saul's attendants said to him, "See, an evil spirit from God is tormenting you.
16Let our lord command his servants here to search for someone who can play the lyre. He will play when the evil spirit from God comes on you, and you will feel better." 1Sa 18:10; 2Ki 3:15

17So Saul said to his attendants, "Find someone who plays well and bring him to me."

18One of the servants answered, "I have seen a son of Jesse of Bethlehem who knows how to play the lyre. He is a brave man and a warrior. He speaks well and is a fine-looking man. And the LORD is with him." 1Sa 3:19; 17:32-37

19Then Saul sent messengers to Jesse and said, "Send me your son David, who is with the sheep."
20So Jesse took a donkey loaded with bread, a skin of wine and a young goat and sent them with his son David to Saul. 1Sa 10:27; Pr 18:16

21David came to Saul and entered his service. Saul liked him very much, and David became one of his armor-bearers.
22Then Saul sent word to Jesse, saying, "Allow David to remain in my service, for I am pleased with him." Ge 41:46; Pr 22:29

23Whenever the spirit from God came on Saul, David would take up his lyre and play. Then relief would come to Saul; he would feel better, and the evil spirit would leave him. Jdg 9:23

David and Goliath

17 Now the Philistines gathered their forces for war and assembled at Sokoh in Judah. They pitched camp at Ephes Dammim, between Sokoh and Azekah.
2Saul and the Israelites assembled and camped in the Valley of Elah and drew up their battle line to meet the Philistines.
3The Philistines occupied one hill and the Israelites another, with the valley between them. 1Sa 13:5; Jos 15:35

4A champion named Goliath, who was from Gath, came out of the Philistine camp. His height was six cubits and a span.[b]
5He had a bronze helmet on his head

[a] 14 Or *and a harmful*; similarly in verses 15, 16 and 23 [b] 4 That is, about 9 feet 9 inches or about 3 meters

and wore a coat of scale armor of
bronze weighing five thousand
shekels[a]; 6on his legs he wore
bronze greaves, and a bronze javelin was slung on his back. 7His
spear shaft was like a weaver's
rod, and its iron point weighed six
hundred shekels.[b] His shield bearer went ahead of him.

Jos 11:21-22; 2Sa 21:19

8Goliath stood and shouted to
the ranks of Israel, "Why do you
come out and line up for battle?
Am I not a Philistine, and are you
not the servants of Saul? Choose a
man and have him come down to
me. 9If he is able to fight and kill
me, we will become your subjects;
but if I overcome him and kill him,
you will become our subjects and
serve us." 10Then the Philistine
said, "This day I defy the armies
of Israel! Give me a man and let us
fight each other." 11On hearing the
Philistine's words, Saul and all the
Israelites were dismayed and terrified.

1Sa 8:17

12Now David was the son of an
Ephrathite named Jesse, who was
from Bethlehem in Judah. Jesse
had eight sons, and in Saul's time
he was very old. 13Jesse's three oldest sons had followed Saul to the
war: The firstborn was Eliab; the
second, Abinadab; and the third,
Shammah. 14David was the youngest. The three oldest followed
Saul, 15but David went back and
forth from Saul to tend his father's
sheep at Bethlehem.

1Ch 2:13-15; Ge 35:19; 1Sa 16:6

16For forty days the Philistine
came forward every morning and
evening and took his stand.

17Now Jesse said to his son David, "Take this ephah[c] of roasted grain and these ten loaves of
bread for your brothers and hurry
to their camp. 18Take along these
ten cheeses to the commander of
their unit. See how your brothers
are and bring back some assurance[d] from them. 19They are with
Saul and all the men of Israel in
the Valley of Elah, fighting against
the Philistines."

Ge 37:14; 1Sa 25:18

20Early in the morning David left
the flock in the care of a shepherd,
loaded up and set out, as Jesse had
directed. He reached the camp as
the army was going out to its battle positions, shouting the war cry.
21Israel and the Philistines were
drawing up their lines facing each
other. 22David left his things with
the keeper of supplies, ran to the
battle lines and asked his brothers
how they were. 23As he was talking
with them, Goliath, the Philistine
champion from Gath, stepped out
from his lines and shouted his
usual defiance, and David heard
it. 24Whenever the Israelites saw
the man, they all fled from him in
great fear.

25Now the Israelites had been
saying, "Do you see how this man

[a] *5* That is, about 125 pounds or about 58 kilograms [b] *7* That is, about 15 pounds or about 6.9 kilograms [c] *17* That is, probably about 36 pounds or about 16 kilograms [d] *18* Or *some token*; or *some pledge of spoils*

keeps coming out? He comes out
to defy Israel. The king will give
great wealth to the man who kills
him. He will also give him his
daughter in marriage and will exempt his family from taxes in Israel." Jos 15:16; 1Sa 18:17

26David asked the men standing
near him, "What will be done for
the man who kills this Philistine
and removes this disgrace from
Israel? Who is this uncircumcised
Philistine that he should defy the
armies of the living God?"
1Sa 11:2; 14:6; Dt 5:26

27They repeated to him what
they had been saying and told
him, "This is what will be done for
the man who kills him."

28When Eliab, David's oldest
brother, heard him speaking with
the men, he burned with anger
at him and asked, "Why have you
come down here? And with whom
did you leave those few sheep in
the wilderness? I know how conceited you are and how wicked
your heart is; you came down only
to watch the battle." Ge 37:4,8,11; Pr 18:19

29"Now what have I done?" said
David. "Can't I even speak?" 30He
then turned away to someone else
and brought up the same matter,
and the men answered him as before. 31What David said was overheard and reported to Saul, and
Saul sent for him.

32David said to Saul, "Let no one
lose heart on account of this Philistine; your servant will go and
fight him." Dt 20:3; 1Sa 16:18

33Saul replied, "You are not
able to go out against this Philistine and fight him; you are only
a young man, and he has been a
warrior from his youth." Nu 13:31

34But David said to Saul, "Your
servant has been keeping his father's sheep. When a lion or a bear
came and carried off a sheep from
the flock, 35I went after it, struck
it and rescued the sheep from its
mouth. When it turned on me, I
seized it by its hair, struck it and
killed it. 36Your servant has killed
both the lion and the bear; this uncircumcised Philistine will be like
one of them, because he has defied the armies of the living God.
37The LORD who rescued me from
the paw of the lion and the paw of
the bear will rescue me from the
hand of this Philistine."
Jer 49:19; 2Co 1:10; 2Ti 4:17

Saul said to David, "Go, and the
LORD be with you." 1Sa 20:13; 1Ch 22:11,16

38Then Saul dressed David in
his own tunic. He put a coat of armor on him and a bronze helmet
on his head. 39David fastened on
his sword over the tunic and tried
walking around, because he was
not used to them. Ge 41:42

"I cannot go in these," he said
to Saul, "because I am not used to
them." So he took them off. 40Then
he took his staff in his hand, chose
five smooth stones from the
stream, put them in the pouch of
his shepherd's bag and, with his
sling in his hand, approached the
Philistine.

41 Meanwhile, the Philistine,
with his shield bearer in front of
him, kept coming closer to David.
42 He looked David over and saw
that he was little more than a boy,
glowing with health and handsome, and he despised him. 43 He
said to David, "Am I a dog, that
you come at me with sticks?" And
the Philistine cursed David by his
gods. 44 "Come here," he said, "and
I'll give your flesh to the birds and
the wild animals!"
1Sa 24:14; 1Ki 20:10-11; Pr 16:18

45 David said to the Philistine,
"You come against me with sword
and spear and javelin, but I come
against you in the name of the
LORD Almighty, the God of the armies of Israel, whom you have defied. 46 This day the LORD will deliver you into my hands, and I'll
strike you down and cut off your
head. This very day I will give the
carcasses of the Philistine army
to the birds and the wild animals,
and the whole world will know
that there is a God in Israel. 47 All
those gathered here will know
that it is not by sword or spear
that the LORD saves; for the battle
is the LORD's, and he will give all of
you into our hands."
1Ki 18:36; 2Ch 14:11; 32:8

48 As the Philistine moved closer to attack him, David ran quickly toward the battle line to meet
him. 49 Reaching into his bag and
taking out a stone, he slung it and
struck the Philistine on the forehead. The stone sank into his forehead, and he fell facedown on the
ground.

50 So David triumphed over the
Philistine with a sling and a stone;
without a sword in his hand he
struck down the Philistine and
killed him.

51 David ran and stood over him.
He took hold of the Philistine's
sword and drew it from the sheath.
After he killed him, he cut off his
head with the sword. Heb 11:34

When the Philistines saw that
their hero was dead, they turned
and ran. 52 Then the men of Israel
and Judah surged forward with a
shout and pursued the Philistines
to the entrance of Gath[a] and to the
gates of Ekron. Their dead were
strewn along the Shaaraim road
to Gath and Ekron. 53 When the Israelites returned from chasing the
Philistines, they plundered their
camp. Jos 15:36

54 David took the Philistine's
head and brought it to Jerusalem;
he put the Philistine's weapons in
his own tent.

55 As Saul watched David going
out to meet the Philistine, he said
to Abner, commander of the army,
"Abner, whose son is that young
man?" 1Sa 16:21

Abner replied, "As surely as you
live, Your Majesty, I don't know."

56 The king said, "Find out whose
son this young man is."

57 As soon as David returned
from killing the Philistine, Abner

[a] 52 Some Septuagint manuscripts; Hebrew *of a valley*

took him and brought him before
Saul, with David still holding the
Philistine's head.
58 "Whose son are you, young
man?" Saul asked him.
David said, "I am the son of your
servant Jesse of Bethlehem." Ru 4:17

Saul's Growing Fear of David

18 After David had finished
talking with Saul, Jonathan
became one in spirit with David, and he loved him as himself.
2 From that day Saul kept David
with him and did not let him return home to his family. 3 And Jonathan made a covenant with David
because he loved him as himself.
4 Jonathan took off the robe he
was wearing and gave it to David,
along with his tunic, and even his
sword, his bow and his belt.
Ge 41:42; 44:30; 2Sa 1:26
5 Whatever mission Saul sent
him on, David was so successful
that Saul gave him a high rank
in the army. This pleased all the
troops, and Saul's officers as well.
6 When the men were returning home after David had killed
the Philistine, the women came
out from all the towns of Israel to
meet King Saul with singing and
dancing, with joyful songs and
with timbrels and lyres. 7 As they
danced, they sang:
Ex 15:20; Jdg 11:34; Ps 68:25

"Saul has slain his thousands,
and David his tens of
thousands." 1Sa 21:11

8 Saul was very angry; this refrain displeased him greatly. "They
have credited David with tens of
thousands," he thought, "but me
with only thousands. What more
can he get but the kingdom?"
9 And from that time on Saul kept
a close eye on David. 1Sa 15:8
10 The next day an evil[a] spirit
from God came forcefully on Saul.
He was prophesying in his house,
while David was playing the lyre,
as he usually did. Saul had a spear
in his hand 11 and he hurled it, saying to himself, "I'll pin David to
the wall." But David eluded him
twice. 1Sa 16:14; 19:7; 20:7,33
12 Saul was afraid of David, because the LORD was with David
but had departed from Saul. 13 So
he sent David away from him
and gave him command over a
thousand men, and David led the
troops in their campaigns. 14 In everything he did he had great success, because the LORD was with
him. 15 When Saul saw how successful he was, he was afraid of
him. 16 But all Israel and Judah
loved David, because he led them
in their campaigns.
Ge 39:3; Nu 27:17; Jos 6:27
17 Saul said to David, "Here is my
older daughter Merab. I will give
her to you in marriage; only serve
me bravely and fight the battles of
the LORD." For Saul said to himself,
"I will not raise a hand against
him. Let the Philistines do that!"
1Sa 17:25; 25:28

[a] *10* Or *a harmful*

18But David said to Saul, "Who
am I, and what is my family or my
clan in Israel, that I should become
the king's son-in-law?" 19So[a] when
the time came for Merab, Saul's
daughter, to be given to David, she
was given in marriage to Adriel of
Meholah. 2Sa 7:18; 21:8; Jdg 7:22

20Now Saul's daughter Michal
was in love with David, and when
they told Saul about it, he was
pleased. 21"I will give her to him,"
he thought, "so that she may be a
snare to him and so that the hand
of the Philistines may be against
him." So Saul said to David, "Now
you have a second opportunity to
become my son-in-law."

22Then Saul ordered his attendants: "Speak to David privately
and say, 'Look, the king likes you,
and his attendants all love you;
now become his son-in-law.' "

23They repeated these words
to David. But David said, "Do you
think it is a small matter to become the king's son-in-law? I'm
only a poor man and little known."

24When Saul's servants told
him what David had said, 25Saul
replied, "Say to David, 'The king
wants no other price for the bride
than a hundred Philistine foreskins, to take revenge on his enemies.' " Saul's plan was to have
David fall by the hands of the Philistines. Ex 22:17; Jer 20:10

26When the attendants told David these things, he was pleased to
become the king's son-in-law. So
before the allotted time elapsed,
27David took his men with him
and went out and killed two hundred Philistines and brought back
their foreskins. They counted out
the full number to the king so that
David might become the king's
son-in-law. Then Saul gave him his
daughter Michal in marriage.
2Sa 3:14

28When Saul realized that the
LORD was with David and that
his daughter Michal loved David,
29Saul became still more afraid of
him, and he remained his enemy
the rest of his days.

30The Philistine commanders
continued to go out to battle, and
as often as they did, David met
with more success than the rest of
Saul's officers, and his name became well known.

Saul Tries to Kill David

19 Saul told his son Jonathan
and all the attendants to kill
David. But Jonathan had taken a
great liking to David 2and warned
him, "My father Saul is looking for
a chance to kill you. Be on your
guard tomorrow morning; go into
hiding and stay there. 3I will go
out and stand with my father in
the field where you are. I'll speak
to him about you and will tell you
what I find out." 1Sa 18:9; 20:12

4Jonathan spoke well of David to Saul his father and said to
him, "Let not the king do wrong
to his servant David; he has not
wronged you, and what he has

[a] 19 Or *However,*

done has benefited you greatly.
5He took his life in his hands when
he killed the Philistine. The LORD
won a great victory for all Israel,
and you saw it and were glad. Why
then would you do wrong to an innocent man like David by killing
him for no reason?"
Ge 42:22; 1Sa 11:13; Mt 27:4

6Saul listened to Jonathan and
took this oath: "As surely as the
LORD lives, David will not be put
to death."

7So Jonathan called David and
told him the whole conversation.
He brought him to Saul, and David
was with Saul as before. 1Sa 16:21

8Once more war broke out, and
David went out and fought the
Philistines. He struck them with
such force that they fled before
him.

9But an evil[a] spirit from the
LORD came on Saul as he was sitting in his house with his spear in
his hand. While David was playing
the lyre, 10Saul tried to pin him
to the wall with his spear, but David eluded him as Saul drove the
spear into the wall. That night David made good his escape.
1Sa 16:14; 18:10-11

11Saul sent men to David's house
to watch it and to kill him in the
morning. But Michal, David's wife,
warned him, "If you don't run for
your life tonight, tomorrow you'll
be killed." 12So Michal let David
down through a window, and he
fled and escaped. 13Then Michal
took an idol and laid it on the bed,
covering it with a garment and
putting some goats' hair at the
head. Jos 2:15; Ac 9:25

14When Saul sent the men to
capture David, Michal said, "He is
ill." Jos 2:4

15Then Saul sent the men back
to see David and told them, "Bring
him up to me in his bed so that I
may kill him." 16But when the men
entered, there was the idol in the
bed, and at the head was some
goats' hair.

17Saul said to Michal, "Why did
you deceive me like this and send
my enemy away so that he escaped?"

Michal told him, "He said to me,
'Let me get away. Why should I kill
you?' "

18When David had fled and
made his escape, he went to Samuel at Ramah and told him all that
Saul had done to him. Then he and
Samuel went to Naioth and stayed
there. 19Word came to Saul: "David is in Naioth at Ramah"; 20so
he sent men to capture him. But
when they saw a group of prophets prophesying, with Samuel
standing there as their leader, the
Spirit of God came on Saul's men,
and they also prophesied. 21Saul
was told about it, and he sent
more men, and they prophesied
too. Saul sent men a third time,
and they also prophesied. 22Final-
ly, he himself left for Ramah and
went to the great cistern at Seku.

[a] 9 Or *But a harmful*

And he asked, "Where are Samuel
and David?" Nu 11:25; 1Sa 10:5
"Over in Naioth at Ramah," they
said.
23So Saul went to Naioth at Ramah. But the Spirit of God came
even on him, and he walked along
prophesying until he came to
Naioth. 24He stripped off his garments, and he too prophesied in
Samuel's presence. He lay naked
all that day and all that night. This
is why people say, "Is Saul also
among the prophets?"
1Sa 15:35; Isa 20:2; Mic 1:8

David and Jonathan

20 Then David fled from Naioth at Ramah and went to
Jonathan and asked, "What have
I done? What is my crime? How
have I wronged your father, that
he is trying to kill me?" 1Sa 24:9
2"Never!" Jonathan replied.
"You are not going to die! Look,
my father doesn't do anything,
great or small, without letting
me know. Why would he hide this
from me? It isn't so!"
3But David took an oath and
said, "Your father knows very well
that I have found favor in your
eyes, and he has said to himself,
'Jonathan must not know this or
he will be grieved.' Yet as surely
as the LORD lives and as you live,
there is only a step between me
and death." Dt 6:13
4Jonathan said to David, "Whatever you want me to do, I'll do for
you."
5So David said, "Look, tomorrow
is the New Moon feast, and I am
supposed to dine with the king;
but let me go and hide in the field
until the evening of the day after
tomorrow. 6If your father misses
me at all, tell him, 'David earnestly asked my permission to hurry
to Bethlehem, his hometown, because an annual sacrifice is being
made there for his whole clan.'
7If he says, 'Very well,' then your
servant is safe. But if he loses his
temper, you can be sure that he is
determined to harm me. 8As for
you, show kindness to your servant, for you have brought him
into a covenant with you before
the LORD. If I am guilty, then kill
me yourself! Why hand me over to
your father?" 1Sa 18:3; 2Sa 14:32; Nu 10:10
9"Never!" Jonathan said. "If I
had the least inkling that my father was determined to harm you,
wouldn't I tell you?"
10David asked, "Who will tell
me if your father answers you
harshly?"
11"Come," Jonathan said, "let's
go out into the field." So they went
there together.
12Then Jonathan said to David,
"I swear by the LORD, the God of
Israel, that I will surely sound out
my father by this time the day after tomorrow! If he is favorably
disposed toward you, will I not
send you word and let you know?
13But if my father intends to harm
you, may the LORD deal with Jonathan, be it ever so severely, if I

do not let you know and send you
away in peace. May the LORD be
with you as he has been with my
father. [14]But show me unfailing
kindness like the LORD's kindness
as long as I live, so that I may not
be killed, [15]and do not ever cut off
your kindness from my family —
not even when the LORD has cut
off every one of David's enemies
from the face of the earth."
Ru 1:17; 1Sa 3:17; 2Sa 9:7

[16]So Jonathan made a covenant
with the house of David, saying,
"May the LORD call David's enemies to account." [17]And Jonathan
had David reaffirm his oath out
of love for him, because he loved
him as he loved himself. 1Sa 25:22

[18]Then Jonathan said to David, "Tomorrow is the New Moon
feast. You will be missed, because
your seat will be empty. [19]The
day after tomorrow, toward evening, go to the place where you
hid when this trouble began, and
wait by the stone Ezel. [20]I will
shoot three arrows to the side of
it, as though I were shooting at
a target. [21]Then I will send a boy
and say, 'Go, find the arrows.' If I
say to him, 'Look, the arrows are
on this side of you; bring them
here,' then come, because, as
surely as the LORD lives, you are
safe; there is no danger. [22]But if I
say to the boy, 'Look, the arrows
are beyond you,' then you must
go, because the LORD has sent
you away. [23]And about the matter
you and I discussed — remember,
the LORD is witness between you
and me forever." Ge 31:50; 1Sa 19:2

[24]So David hid in the field, and
when the New Moon feast came,
the king sat down to eat. [25]He sat
in his customary place by the wall,
opposite Jonathan,[a] and Abner
sat next to Saul, but David's place
was empty. [26]Saul said nothing
that day, for he thought, "Something must have happened to
David to make him ceremonially
unclean — surely he is unclean."
[27]But the next day, the second day
of the month, David's place was
empty again. Then Saul said to his
son Jonathan, "Why hasn't the son
of Jesse come to the meal, either
yesterday or today?"
Lev 7:20-21; 15:5; 1Sa 16:5

[28]Jonathan answered, "David
earnestly asked me for permission to go to Bethlehem. [29]He said,
'Let me go, because our family is
observing a sacrifice in the town
and my brother has ordered me to
be there. If I have found favor in
your eyes, let me get away to see
my brothers.' That is why he has
not come to the king's table."

[30]Saul's anger flared up at Jonathan and he said to him, "You son
of a perverse and rebellious woman! Don't I know that you have
sided with the son of Jesse to your
own shame and to the shame of
the mother who bore you? [31]As
long as the son of Jesse lives on
this earth, neither you nor your

[a] *25* Septuagint; Hebrew *wall. Jonathan arose*

kingdom will be established. Now send someone to bring him to me, for he must die!"

32 "Why should he be put to death? What has he done?" Jonathan asked his father. 33 But Saul hurled his spear at him to kill him. Then Jonathan knew that his father intended to kill David.

Ge 31:36; 1Sa 18:11,17; 19:4

34 Jonathan got up from the table in fierce anger; on that second day of the feast he did not eat, because he was grieved at his father's shameful treatment of David.

35 In the morning Jonathan went out to the field for his meeting with David. He had a small boy with him, 36 and he said to the boy, "Run and find the arrows I shoot." As the boy ran, he shot an arrow beyond him. 37 When the boy came to the place where Jonathan's arrow had fallen, Jonathan called out after him, "Isn't the arrow beyond you?" 38 Then he shouted, "Hurry! Go quickly! Don't stop!" The boy picked up the arrow and returned to his master. 39 (The boy knew nothing about all this; only Jonathan and David knew.) 40 Then Jonathan gave his weapons to the boy and said, "Go, carry them back to town."

41 After the boy had gone, David got up from the south side of the stone and bowed down before Jonathan three times, with his face to the ground. Then they kissed each other and wept together — but David wept the most.

42 Jonathan said to David, "Go in peace, for we have sworn friendship with each other in the name of the LORD, saying, 'The LORD is witness between you and me, and between your descendants and my descendants forever.'" Then David left, and Jonathan went back to the town.[a]

1Sa 1:17; 2Sa 1:26; Pr 18:24

David at Nob

21 [b] David went to Nob, to Ahimelek the priest. Ahimelek trembled when he met him, and asked, "Why are you alone? Why is no one with you?"

1Sa 14:3; 16:4

2 David answered Ahimelek the priest, "The king sent me on a mission and said to me, 'No one is to know anything about the mission I am sending you on.' As for my men, I have told them to meet me at a certain place. 3 Now then, what do you have on hand? Give me five loaves of bread, or whatever you can find."

4 But the priest answered David, "I don't have any ordinary bread on hand; however, there is some consecrated bread here — provided the men have kept themselves from women." Mt 12:4; Lev 24:8-9; Ex 19:15

5 David replied, "Indeed women have been kept from us, as usual whenever[c] I set out. The men's

[a] 42 In Hebrew texts this sentence (20:42b) is numbered 21:1. [b] In Hebrew texts 21:1-15 is numbered 21:2-16. [c] 5 Or *from us in the past few days since*

bodies are holy even on missions
that are not holy. How much more
so today!" 6So the priest gave him
the consecrated bread, since there
was no bread there except the
bread of the Presence that had
been removed from before the
LORD and replaced by hot bread
on the day it was taken away.

Ex 25:30; 1Th 4:4

7Now one of Saul's servants was
there that day, detained before the
LORD; he was Doeg the Edomite,
Saul's chief shepherd. 1Sa 22:9,22
8David asked Ahimelek, "Don't
you have a spear or a sword here?
I haven't brought my sword or any
other weapon, because the king's
mission was urgent."
9The priest replied, "The sword
of Goliath the Philistine, whom
you killed in the Valley of Elah, is
here; it is wrapped in a cloth behind the ephod. If you want it,
take it; there is no sword here but
that one." 1Sa 17:51

David said, "There is none like
it; give it to me."

David at Gath

10That day David fled from Saul
and went to Achish king of Gath.
11But the servants of Achish said
to him, "Isn't this David, the king
of the land? Isn't he the one they
sing about in their dances:

"'Saul has slain his
thousands,
and David his tens of
thousands'?" 1Sa 18:7; 29:5

12David took these words to
heart and was very much afraid of
Achish king of Gath. 13So he pretended to be insane in their presence; and while he was in their
hands he acted like a madman,
making marks on the doors of the
gate and letting saliva run down
his beard.
14Achish said to his servants,
"Look at the man! He is insane!
Why bring him to me? 15Am I so
short of madmen that you have to
bring this fellow here to carry on
like this in front of me? Must this
man come into my house?"

David at Adullam and Mizpah

22 David left Gath and escaped to the cave of Adullam. When his brothers and his
father's household heard about
it, they went down to him there.
2All those who were in distress or
in debt or discontented gathered
around him, and he became their
commander. About four hundred
men were with him.

1Sa 25:13; 2Sa 23:13; Ps 57 Title

3From there David went to Mizpah in Moab and said to the king
of Moab, "Would you let my father
and mother come and stay with
you until I learn what God will
do for me?" 4So he left them with
the king of Moab, and they stayed
with him as long as David was in
the stronghold.
5But the prophet Gad said to
David, "Do not stay in the stronghold. Go into the land of Judah."

So David left and went to the forest of Hereth.

2Sa 24:11; 1Ch 21:9; 2Ch 29:25

Saul Kills the Priests of Nob

6 Now Saul heard that David and his men had been discovered. And Saul was seated, spear in hand, under the tamarisk tree on the hill at Gibeah, with all his officials standing at his side. 7 He said to them, "Listen, men of Benjamin! Will the son of Jesse give all of you fields and vineyards? Will he make all of you commanders of thousands and commanders of hundreds? 8 Is that why you have all conspired against me? No one tells me when my son makes a covenant with the son of Jesse. None of you is concerned about me or tells me that my son has incited my servant to lie in wait for me, as he does today."

1Sa 8:14; 18:3; Jdg 4:5

9 But Doeg the Edomite, who was standing with Saul's officials, said, "I saw the son of Jesse come to Ahimelek son of Ahitub at Nob. 10 Ahimelek inquired of the LORD for him; he also gave him provisions and the sword of Goliath the Philistine."

1Sa 17:51; 21:7; Nu 27:21

11 Then the king sent for the priest Ahimelek son of Ahitub and all the men of his family, who were the priests at Nob, and they all came to the king. 12 Saul said, "Listen now, son of Ahitub."

"Yes, my lord," he answered.

13 Saul said to him, "Why have you conspired against me, you and the son of Jesse, giving him bread and a sword and inquiring of God for him, so that he has rebelled against me and lies in wait for me, as he does today?"

14 Ahimelek answered the king, "Who of all your servants is as loyal as David, the king's son-in-law, captain of your bodyguard and highly respected in your household? 15 Was that day the first time I inquired of God for him? Of course not! Let not the king accuse your servant or any of his father's family, for your servant knows nothing at all about this whole affair."

16 But the king said, "You will surely die, Ahimelek, you and your whole family."

17 Then the king ordered the guards at his side: "Turn and kill the priests of the LORD, because they too have sided with David. They knew he was fleeing, yet they did not tell me."

But the king's officials were unwilling to raise a hand to strike the priests of the LORD.

Ex 1:17

18 The king then ordered Doeg, "You turn and strike down the priests." So Doeg the Edomite turned and struck them down. That day he killed eighty-five men who wore the linen ephod. 19 He also put to the sword Nob, the town of the priests, with its men and women, its children and infants, and its cattle, donkeys and sheep.

1Sa 2:18,31; 15:3

20 But one son of Ahimelek son of Ahitub, named Abiathar, escaped

and fled to join David. 21He told
David that Saul had killed the
priests of the LORD. 22Then David
said to Abiathar, "That day, when
Doeg the Edomite was there, I
knew he would be sure to tell Saul.
I am responsible for the death of
your whole family. 23Stay with
me; don't be afraid. The man who
wants to kill you is trying to kill
me too. You will be safe with me."

1Sa 2:32; 23:6,9; 1Ki 2:26

David Saves Keilah

23 When David was told, "Look,
the Philistines are fighting
against Keilah and are looting the
threshing floors," 2he inquired of
the LORD, saying, "Shall I go and
attack these Philistines?"

Jos 15:44; 1Sa 30:8

The LORD answered him, "Go,
attack the Philistines and save Keilah."

3But David's men said to him,
"Here in Judah we are afraid. How
much more, then, if we go to Keilah against the Philistine forces!"

4Once again David inquired of
the LORD, and the LORD answered
him, "Go down to Keilah, for I am
going to give the Philistines into
your hand." 5So David and his men
went to Keilah, fought the Philistines and carried off their livestock. He inflicted heavy losses on
the Philistines and saved the people of Keilah. 6(Now Abiathar son of
Ahimelek had brought the ephod
down with him when he fled to David at Keilah.) Jos 8:7; Jdg 7:7; 1Sa 22:20

Saul Pursues David

7Saul was told that David had
gone to Keilah, and he said, "God
has delivered him into my hands,
for David has imprisoned himself
by entering a town with gates and
bars." 8And Saul called up all his
forces for battle, to go down to Keilah to besiege David and his men.

9When David learned that Saul
was plotting against him, he said
to Abiathar the priest, "Bring the
ephod." 10David said, "LORD, God
of Israel, your servant has heard
definitely that Saul plans to come
to Keilah and destroy the town on
account of me. 11Will the citizens
of Keilah surrender me to him?
Will Saul come down, as your servant has heard? LORD, God of Israel, tell your servant."

And the LORD said, "He will."

12Again David asked, "Will the
citizens of Keilah surrender me
and my men to Saul?"

And the LORD said, "They will."

13So David and his men, about
six hundred in number, left Keilah and kept moving from place
to place. When Saul was told that
David had escaped from Keilah, he
did not go there. 1Sa 22:2; 25:13

14David stayed in the wilderness
strongholds and in the hills of the
Desert of Ziph. Day after day Saul
searched for him, but God did not
give David into his hands.

Ps 32:7; 54:3-4

15While David was at Horesh
in the Desert of Ziph, he learned

that[a] Saul had come out to take his life. 16And Saul's son Jonathan went to David at Horesh and helped him find strength in God. 17"Don't be afraid," he said. "My father Saul will not lay a hand on you. You will be king over Israel, and I will be second to you. Even my father Saul knows this." 18The two of them made a covenant before the LORD. Then Jonathan went home, but David remained at Horesh. 1Sa 20:16,42; 24:20; 2Sa 21:7

19The Ziphites went up to Saul at Gibeah and said, "Is not David hiding among us in the strongholds at Horesh, on the hill of Hakilah, south of Jeshimon? 20Now, Your Majesty, come down whenever it pleases you to do so, and we will be responsible for giving him into your hands." 1Sa 26:1

21Saul replied, "The LORD bless you for your concern for me. 22Go and get more information. Find out where David usually goes and who has seen him there. They tell me he is very crafty. 23Find out about all the hiding places he uses and come back to me with definite information. Then I will go with you; if he is in the area, I will track him down among all the clans of Judah." 1Sa 22:8

24So they set out and went to Ziph ahead of Saul. Now David and his men were in the Desert of Maon, in the Arabah south of Jeshimon. 25Saul and his men began the search, and when David was told about it, he went down to the rock and stayed in the Desert of Maon. When Saul heard this, he went into the Desert of Maon in pursuit of David. Jos 15:55; 1Sa 25:2

26Saul was going along one side of the mountain, and David and his men were on the other side, hurrying to get away from Saul. As Saul and his forces were closing in on David and his men to capture them, 27a messenger came to Saul, saying, "Come quickly! The Philistines are raiding the land." 28Then Saul broke off his pursuit of David and went to meet the Philistines. That is why they call this place Sela Hammahlekoth.[b] 29And David went up from there and lived in the strongholds of En Gedi.[c]

1Sa 24:22; Ps 17:9; 2Ch 20:2

David Spares Saul's Life

24 [d] After Saul returned from pursuing the Philistines, he was told, "David is in the Desert of En Gedi." 2So Saul took three thousand able young men from all Israel and set out to look for David and his men near the Crags of the Wild Goats. 1Sa 23:28-29; 26:2

3He came to the sheep pens along the way; a cave was there, and Saul went in to relieve himself. David and his men were far back in the cave. 4The men said,

[a] 15 Or *he was afraid because* [b] 28 *Sela Hammahlekoth* means *rock of parting.* [c] 29 In Hebrew texts this verse (23:29) is numbered 24:1. [d] In Hebrew texts 24:1-22 is numbered 24:2-23.

"This is the day the LORD spoke of
when he said[a] to you, 'I will give
your enemy into your hands for
you to deal with as you wish.' "
Then David crept up unnoticed
and cut off a corner of Saul's robe.
1Sa 25:28-30; Jdg 3:24

5 Afterward, David was conscience-stricken for having cut off
a corner of his robe. 6 He said to
his men, "The LORD forbid that I
should do such a thing to my master, the LORD's anointed, or lay my
hand on him; for he is the anointed of the LORD." 7 With these words
David sharply rebuked his men
and did not allow them to attack
Saul. And Saul left the cave and
went his way. 1Sa 26:11; 2Sa 24:10

8 Then David went out of the
cave and called out to Saul, "My
lord the king!" When Saul looked
behind him, David bowed down
and prostrated himself with his
face to the ground. 9 He said to
Saul, "Why do you listen when
men say, 'David is bent on harming you'? 10 This day you have seen
with your own eyes how the LORD
delivered you into my hands in
the cave. Some urged me to kill
you, but I spared you; I said, 'I will
not lay my hand on my lord, because he is the LORD's anointed.'
11 See, my father, look at this piece
of your robe in my hand! I cut off
the corner of your robe but did
not kill you. See that there is nothing in my hand to indicate that I
am guilty of wrongdoing or rebellion. I have not wronged you, but
you are hunting me down to take
my life. 12 May the LORD judge between you and me. And may the
LORD avenge the wrongs you have
done to me, but my hand will not
touch you. 13 As the old saying goes,
'From evildoers come evil deeds,'
so my hand will not touch you.
Ge 16:5; Jdg 11:27; Mt 7:20

14 "Against whom has the king of
Israel come out? Who are you pursuing? A dead dog? A flea? 15 May
the LORD be our judge and decide
between us. May he consider my
cause and uphold it; may he vindicate me by delivering me from
your hand." 1Sa 17:43; Ps 35:1,23; Mic 7:9

16 When David finished saying this, Saul asked, "Is that your
voice, David my son?" And he
wept aloud. 17 "You are more righteous than I," he said. "You have
treated me well, but I have treated you badly. 18 You have just now
told me about the good you did to
me; the LORD delivered me into
your hands, but you did not kill
me. 19 When a man finds his enemy, does he let him get away unharmed? May the LORD reward you
well for the way you treated me today. 20 I know that you will surely
be king and that the kingdom of
Israel will be established in your
hands. 21 Now swear to me by the
LORD that you will not kill off my
descendants or wipe out my name
from my father's family."
Ge 38:26; 2Sa 21:1-9; Mt 5:44

[a] 4 Or *"Today the LORD is saying*

22 So David gave his oath to Saul.
Then Saul returned home, but David and his men went up to the
stronghold. 1Sa 23:29

David, Nabal and Abigail

25 Now Samuel died, and
all Israel assembled and
mourned for him; and they buried
him at his home in Ramah. Then
David moved down into the Des-
ert of Paran.[a] Dt 34:8; 1Sa 28:3; Ge 21:21
2 A certain man in Maon, who
had property there at Carmel, was
very wealthy. He had a thousand
goats and three thousand sheep,
which he was shearing in Carmel. 3 His name was Nabal and his
wife's name was Abigail. She was
an intelligent and beautiful woman, but her husband was surly and
mean in his dealings — he was a
Calebite. Jos 15:55; Pr 31:10; Ge 31:19
4 While David was in the wilderness, he heard that Nabal was
shearing sheep. 5 So he sent ten
young men and said to them, "Go
up to Nabal at Carmel and greet
him in my name. 6 Say to him:
'Long life to you! Good health to
you and your household! And
good health to all that is yours!
1Ch 12:18; Ps 122:7; Lk 10:5
7 " 'Now I hear that it is
sheep-shearing time. When your
shepherds were with us, we did
not mistreat them, and the whole
time they were at Carmel nothing
of theirs was missing. 8 Ask your
own servants and they will tell
you. Therefore be favorable toward my men, since we come at a
festive time. Please give your servants and your son David whatever you can find for them.' "
9 When David's men arrived,
they gave Nabal this message in
David's name. Then they waited.
10 Nabal answered David's servants, "Who is this David? Who is
this son of Jesse? Many servants
are breaking away from their
masters these days. 11 Why should
I take my bread and water, and the
meat I have slaughtered for my
shearers, and give it to men coming from who knows where?"
Jdg 8:6; 9:28
12 David's men turned around
and went back. When they arrived,
they reported every word. 13 David said to his men, "Each of you
strap on your sword!" So they did,
and David strapped his on as well.
About four hundred men went up
with David, while two hundred
stayed with the supplies.
1Sa 23:13; 30:24
14 One of the servants told Abigail, Nabal's wife, "David sent
messengers from the wilderness
to give our master his greetings,
but he hurled insults at them.
15 Yet these men were very good
to us. They did not mistreat us,
and the whole time we were out
in the fields near them nothing
was missing. 16 Night and day they
were a wall around us the whole

[a] *1* Hebrew and some Septuagint manuscripts; other Septuagint manuscripts *Maon*

time we were herding our sheep
near them. 17 Now think it over
and see what you can do, because
disaster is hanging over our master and his whole household. He
is such a wicked man that no one
can talk to him."

Ex 14:22; 1Sa 20:7; Job 1:10

18 Abigail acted quickly. She took
two hundred loaves of bread, two
skins of wine, five dressed sheep,
five seahs[a] of roasted grain, a
hundred cakes of raisins and two
hundred cakes of pressed figs,
and loaded them on donkeys.
19 Then she told her servants, "Go
on ahead; I'll follow you." But she
did not tell her husband Nabal.

Ge 32:20; 2Sa 16:1; 1Ch 12:40

20 As she came riding her donkey into a mountain ravine, there
were David and his men descending toward her, and she met them.
21 David had just said, "It's been
useless — all my watching over
this fellow's property in the wilderness so that nothing of his was
missing. He has paid me back evil
for good. 22 May God deal with David,[b] be it ever so severely, if by
morning I leave alive one male of
all who belong to him!"

1Sa 3:17; 1Ki 14:10; Ps 109:5

23 When Abigail saw David, she
quickly got off her donkey and
bowed down before David with
her face to the ground. 24 She
fell at his feet and said: "Pardon
your servant, my lord, and let me
speak to you; hear what your servant has to say. 25 Please pay no
attention, my lord, to that wicked man Nabal. He is just like his
name — his name means Fool,
and folly goes with him. And as
for me, your servant, I did not
see the men my lord sent. 26 And
now, my lord, as surely as the
LORD your God lives and as you
live, since the LORD has kept
you from bloodshed and from
avenging yourself with your own
hands, may your enemies and
all who are intent on harming
my lord be like Nabal. 27 And let
this gift, which your servant has
brought to my lord, be given to
the men who follow you.

1Sa 20:41; Pr 14:16; 17:12

28 "Please forgive your servant's
presumption. The LORD your God
will certainly make a lasting dynasty for my lord, because you
fight the LORD's battles, and no
wrongdoing will be found in you
as long as you live. 29 Even though
someone is pursuing you to take
your life, the life of my lord will be
bound securely in the bundle of
the living by the LORD your God,
but the lives of your enemies he
will hurl away as from the pock-
et of a sling. 30 When the LORD has
fulfilled for my lord every good
thing he promised concerning
him and has appointed him ruler
over Israel, 31 my lord will not have
on his conscience the staggering

[a] *18* That is, probably about 60 pounds or about 27 kilograms [b] *22* Some Septuagint manuscripts; Hebrew *with David's enemies*

burden of needless bloodshed
or of having avenged himself.
And when the LORD your God has
brought my lord success, remember your servant."

2Sa 7:11,26; 18:32; Jer 10:18

32 David said to Abigail, "Praise
be to the LORD, the God of Israel,
who has sent you today to meet
me. 33 May you be blessed for your
good judgment and for keeping
me from bloodshed this day and
from avenging myself with my
own hands. 34 Otherwise, as surely as the LORD, the God of Israel, lives, who has kept me from
harming you, if you had not come
quickly to meet me, not one male
belonging to Nabal would have
been left alive by daybreak."

Ge 24:27; Ex 18:10; Lk 1:68

35 Then David accepted from her
hand what she had brought him
and said, "Go home in peace. I
have heard your words and granted your request."

Ge 19:21; 1Sa 20:42; 2Ki 5:19

36 When Abigail went to Nabal,
he was in the house holding a banquet like that of a king. He was in
high spirits and very drunk. So
she told him nothing at all until
daybreak. 37 Then in the morning,
when Nabal was sober, his wife
told him all these things, and his
heart failed him and he became
like a stone. 38 About ten days later, the LORD struck Nabal and he
died.

Pr 20:1; Ecc 10:17; 1Sa 26:10

39 When David heard that Nabal was dead, he said, "Praise be
to the LORD, who has upheld my
cause against Nabal for treating
me with contempt. He has kept
his servant from doing wrong and
has brought Nabal's wrongdoing
down on his own head."

Then David sent word to Abigail,
asking her to become his wife.
40 His servants went to Carmel and
said to Abigail, "David has sent us
to you to take you to become his
wife."

41 She bowed down with her face
to the ground and said, "I am your
servant and am ready to serve you
and wash the feet of my lord's servants." 42 Abigail quickly got on a
donkey and, attended by her five
female servants, went with David's messengers and became his
wife. 43 David had also married
Ahinoam of Jezreel, and they both
were his wives. 44 But Saul had giv-
en his daughter Michal, David's
wife, to Paltiel[a] son of Laish, who
was from Gallim.

Ge 24:61-67; Jos 15:56; 2Sa 3:15

David Again Spares Saul's Life

26 The Ziphites went to Saul
at Gibeah and said, "Is not
David hiding on the hill of Hakilah, which faces Jeshimon?"

1Sa 23:19; Ps 54 Title

2 So Saul went down to the Desert of Ziph, with his three thousand select Israelite troops, to
search there for David. 3 Saul made
his camp beside the road on the

[a] 44 Hebrew *Palti*, a variant of *Paltiel*

hill of Hakilah facing Jeshimon,
but David stayed in the wilderness. When he saw that Saul had
followed him there, 4he sent out
scouts and learned that Saul had
definitely arrived. 1Sa 24:2
5Then David set out and went to
the place where Saul had camped.
He saw where Saul and Abner son
of Ner, the commander of the
army, had lain down. Saul was
lying inside the camp, with the
army encamped around him.
1Sa 17:55
6David then asked Ahimelek the
Hittite and Abishai son of Zeruiah,
Joab's brother, "Who will go down
into the camp with me to Saul?"
2Sa 10:10; Jdg 7:10-11; 1Ch 2:16
"I'll go with you," said Abishai.
7So David and Abishai went to
the army by night, and there was
Saul, lying asleep inside the camp
with his spear stuck in the ground
near his head. Abner and the soldiers were lying around him.
8Abishai said to David, "Today
God has delivered your enemy
into your hands. Now let me pin
him to the ground with one thrust
of the spear; I won't strike him
twice."
9But David said to Abishai,
"Don't destroy him! Who can lay
a hand on the LORD's anointed and be guiltless? 10As surely
as the LORD lives," he said, "the
LORD himself will strike him, or
his time will come and he will
die, or he will go into battle and
perish. 11But the LORD forbid that
I should lay a hand on the LORD's
anointed. Now get the spear and
water jug that are near his head,
and let's go." 1Sa 31:6; 2Sa 1:14; Dt 31:14
12So David took the spear and
water jug near Saul's head, and
they left. No one saw or knew
about it, nor did anyone wake up.
They were all sleeping, because
the LORD had put them into a deep
sleep. Ge 2:21; 15:12
13Then David crossed over to the
other side and stood on top of the
hill some distance away; there was
a wide space between them. 14He
called out to the army and to Abner son of Ner, "Aren't you going
to answer me, Abner?"
Abner replied, "Who are you
who calls to the king?"
15David said, "You're a man,
aren't you? And who is like you in
Israel? Why didn't you guard your
lord the king? Someone came to
destroy your lord the king. 16What
you have done is not good. As
surely as the LORD lives, you and
your men must die, because you
did not guard your master, the
LORD's anointed. Look around
you. Where are the king's spear
and water jug that were near his
head?"
17Saul recognized David's voice
and said, "Is that your voice, David my son?" 1Sa 24:16
David replied, "Yes it is, my
lord the king." 18And he added,
"Why is my lord pursuing his
servant? What have I done, and
what wrong am I guilty of? 19Now

let my lord the king listen to his
servant's words. If the LORD has
incited you against me, then may
he accept an offering. If, however, people have done it, may they
be cursed before the LORD! They
have driven me today from my
share in the LORD's inheritance
and have said, 'Go, serve other
gods.' 20 Now do not let my blood
fall to the ground far from the
presence of the LORD. The king of
Israel has come out to look for a
flea — as one hunts a partridge in
the mountains."

1Sa 24:9,11-14; 2Sa 14:16; 16:11

21 Then Saul said, "I have sinned.
Come back, David my son. Because you considered my life precious today, I will not try to harm
you again. Surely I have acted
like a fool and have been terribly
wrong." Ex 9:27; 1Sa 15:24; 24:17

22 "Here is the king's spear," David answered. "Let one of your
young men come over and get it.
23 The LORD rewards everyone for
their righteousness and faithfulness. The LORD delivered you into
my hands today, but I would not
lay a hand on the LORD's anointed.
24 As surely as I valued your life today, so may the LORD value my life
and deliver me from all trouble."

Ps 7:8; 54:7; 62:12

25 Then Saul said to David, "May
you be blessed, David my son; you
will do great things and surely triumph."

So David went on his way, and
Saul returned home.

David Among the Philistines

27 But David thought to himself, "One of these days I will
be destroyed by the hand of Saul.
The best thing I can do is to escape
to the land of the Philistines. Then
Saul will give up searching for me
anywhere in Israel, and I will slip
out of his hand."

2 So David and the six hundred
men with him left and went over
to Achish son of Maok king of
Gath. 3 David and his men settled
in Gath with Achish. Each man
had his family with him, and David had his two wives: Ahinoam
of Jezreel and Abigail of Carmel,
the widow of Nabal. 4 When Saul
was told that David had fled to
Gath, he no longer searched for
him. 1Sa 25:13; 21:10; 1Ki 2:39

5 Then David said to Achish, "If
I have found favor in your eyes,
let a place be assigned to me in
one of the country towns, that I
may live there. Why should your
servant live in the royal city with
you?"

6 So on that day Achish gave
him Ziklag, and it has belonged
to the kings of Judah ever since.
7 David lived in Philistine territory a year and four months.

Jos 15:31; 19:5; 1Sa 29:3

8 Now David and his men went
up and raided the Geshurites,
the Girzites and the Amalekites.
(From ancient times these peoples had lived in the land extending to Shur and Egypt.) 9 Whenever David attacked an area, he did

not leave a man or woman alive, but took sheep and cattle, donkeys and camels, and clothes. Then he returned to Achish.

Jos 13:2,13; Ex 17:8; 1Sa 15:3

10 When Achish asked, "Where did you go raiding today?" David would say, "Against the Negev of Judah" or "Against the Negev of Jerahmeel" or "Against the Negev of the Kenites." 11 He did not leave a man or woman alive to be brought to Gath, for he thought, "They might inform on us and say, 'This is what David did.'" And such was his practice as long as he lived in Philistine territory. 12 Achish trusted David and said to himself, "He has become so obnoxious to his people, the Israelites, that he will be my servant for life."

Jdg 1:16; 1Ch 2:9,25

28 In those days the Philistines gathered their forces to fight against Israel. Achish said to David, "You must understand that you and your men will accompany me in the army." 1Sa 29:1

2 David said, "Then you will see for yourself what your servant can do."

Achish replied, "Very well, I will make you my bodyguard for life."

Saul and the Medium at Endor

3 Now Samuel was dead, and all Israel had mourned for him and buried him in his own town of Ramah. Saul had expelled the mediums and spiritists from the land.

Lev 19:31; Dt 18:10-11

4 The Philistines assembled and came and set up camp at Shunem, while Saul gathered all Israel and set up camp at Gilboa. 5 When Saul saw the Philistine army, he was afraid; terror filled his heart. 6 He inquired of the LORD, but the LORD did not answer him by dreams or Urim or prophets. 7 Saul then said to his attendants, "Find me a woman who is a medium, so I may go and inquire of her."

Ex 28:30; 1Ch 10:13-14; 2Ki 4:8

"There is one in Endor," they said. Jos 17:11

8 So Saul disguised himself, putting on other clothes, and at night he and two men went to the woman. "Consult a spirit for me," he said, "and bring up for me the one I name." Dt 18:10-11; 2Ch 18:29; Isa 8:19

9 But the woman said to him, "Surely you know what Saul has done. He has cut off the mediums and spiritists from the land. Why have you set a trap for my life to bring about my death?"

10 Saul swore to her by the LORD, "As surely as the LORD lives, you will not be punished for this."

11 Then the woman asked, "Whom shall I bring up for you?"

"Bring up Samuel," he said.

12 When the woman saw Samuel, she cried out at the top of her voice and said to Saul, "Why have you deceived me? You are Saul!"

13 The king said to her, "Don't be afraid. What do you see?"

The woman said, "I see a ghost-
ly figure[a] coming up out of the
earth."
14"What does he look like?" he
asked.
"An old man wearing a robe is
coming up," she said. 1Sa 15:27
Then Saul knew it was Samuel,
and he bowed down and prostrated himself with his face to the
ground.
15Samuel said to Saul, "Why
have you disturbed me by bringing me up?"
"I am in great distress," Saul
said. "The Philistines are fighting against me, and God has departed from me. He no longer answers me, either by prophets or by
dreams. So I have called on you to
tell me what to do." 1Sa 18:12
16Samuel said, "Why do you
consult me, now that the LORD
has departed from you and become your enemy? 17The LORD
has done what he predicted
through me. The LORD has torn
the kingdom out of your hands
and given it to one of your neighbors — to David. 18Because you
did not obey the LORD or carry
out his fierce wrath against the
Amalekites, the LORD has done
this to you today. 19The LORD will
deliver both Israel and you into
the hands of the Philistines, and
tomorrow you and your sons will
be with me. The LORD will also
give the army of Israel into the
hands of the Philistines."
1Sa 15:28; 31:2; 1Ki 20:42

20Immediately Saul fell full
length on the ground, filled with
fear because of Samuel's words.
His strength was gone, for he had
eaten nothing all that day and all
that night.
21When the woman came to Saul
and saw that he was greatly shak-
en, she said, "Look, your servant
has obeyed you. I took my life in
my hands and did what you told
me to do. 22Now please listen to
your servant and let me give you
some food so you may eat and
have the strength to go on your
way." Jdg 12:3; 1Sa 19:5
23He refused and said, "I will not
eat."
But his men joined the woman
in urging him, and he listened to
them. He got up from the ground
and sat on the couch. 2Ki 5:13
24The woman had a fattened
calf at the house, which she butchered at once. She took some flour,
kneaded it and baked bread without yeast. 25Then she set it before
Saul and his men, and they ate.
That same night they got up and
left.

Achish Sends David Back to Ziklag

29 The Philistines gathered
all their forces at Aphek,
and Israel camped by the spring
in Jezreel. 2As the Philistine rulers
marched with their units of hundreds and thousands, David and
his men were marching at the rear

[a] 13 Or *see spirits*; or *see gods*

with Achish. [3]The commanders of the Philistines asked, "What about these Hebrews?" 1Sa 4:1; 28:1; 2Ki 9:30

Achish replied, "Is this not David, who was an officer of Saul king of Israel? He has already been with me for over a year, and from the day he left Saul until now, I have found no fault in him." 1Sa 27:7; Da 6:5

[4]But the Philistine commanders were angry with Achish and said, "Send the man back, that he may return to the place you assigned him. He must not go with us into battle, or he will turn against us during the fighting. How better could he regain his master's favor than by taking the heads of our own men? [5]Isn't this the David they sang about in their dances: 1Sa 14:21; 1Ch 12:19

"'Saul has slain his
thousands,
and David his tens of
thousands'?" 1Sa 18:7; 21:11

[6]So Achish called David and said to him, "As surely as the LORD lives, you have been reliable, and I would be pleased to have you serve with me in the army. From the day you came to me until today, I have found no fault in you, but the rulers don't approve of you. [7]Now turn back and go in peace; do nothing to displease the Philistine rulers." 1Sa 27:8-12

[8]"But what have I done?" asked David. "What have you found against your servant from the day I came to you until now? Why can't I go and fight against the enemies of my lord the king?"

[9]Achish answered, "I know that you have been as pleasing in my eyes as an angel of God; nevertheless, the Philistine commanders have said, 'He must not go up with us into battle.' [10]Now get up early, along with your master's servants who have come with you, and leave in the morning as soon as it is light." 2Sa 14:17,20; 19:27; 1Ch 12:19

[11]So David and his men got up early in the morning to go back to the land of the Philistines, and the Philistines went up to Jezreel.

David Destroys the Amalekites

30 David and his men reached Ziklag on the third day. Now the Amalekites had raided the Negev and Ziklag. They had attacked Ziklag and burned it, [2]and had taken captive the women and everyone else in it, both young and old. They killed none of them, but carried them off as they went on their way. 1Sa 15:7; 27:8

[3]When David and his men reached Ziklag, they found it destroyed by fire and their wives and sons and daughters taken captive. [4]So David and his men wept aloud until they had no strength left to weep. [5]David's two wives had been captured — Ahinoam of Jezreel and Abigail, the widow of Nabal of Carmel. [6]David was greatly distressed because the men were talking of stoning him; each one

was bitter in spirit because of his
sons and daughters. But David
found strength in the LORD his
God. Ex 17:4; Ps 56:3-4,11
7Then David said to Abiathar the
priest, the son of Ahimelek, "Bring
me the ephod." Abiathar brought
it to him, 8and David inquired of
the LORD, "Shall I pursue this raiding party? Will I overtake them?"
1Sa 22:20; 23:2
"Pursue them," he answered.
"You will certainly overtake them
and succeed in the rescue."
9David and the six hundred
men with him came to the Besor
Valley, where some stayed behind.
10Two hundred of them were too
exhausted to cross the valley, but
David and the other four hundred
continued the pursuit. 1Sa 27:2
11They found an Egyptian in a
field and brought him to David.
They gave him water to drink and
food to eat — 12part of a cake of
pressed figs and two cakes of raisins. He ate and was revived, for he
had not eaten any food or drunk
any water for three days and three
nights. Jdg 15:19
13David asked him, "Who do you
belong to? Where do you come
from?"
He said, "I am an Egyptian, the
slave of an Amalekite. My master
abandoned me when I became ill
three days ago. 14We raided the Negev of the Kerethites, some territory belonging to Judah and the
Negev of Caleb. And we burned
Ziklag." Jos 14:13; 2Sa 8:18; Eze 25:16
15David asked him, "Can you
lead me down to this raiding party?"
He answered, "Swear to me before God that you will not kill me
or hand me over to my master,
and I will take you down to them."
16He led David down, and
there they were, scattered over
the countryside, eating, drinking and reveling because of the
great amount of plunder they
had taken from the land of the
Philistines and from Judah. 17Da-
vid fought them from dusk until
the evening of the next day, and
none of them got away, except
four hundred young men who
rode off on camels and fled. 18Da-
vid recovered everything the Amalekites had taken, including his
two wives. 19Nothing was missing:
young or old, boy or girl, plunder
or anything else they had taken.
David brought everything back.
20He took all the flocks and herds,
and his men drove them ahead of
the other livestock, saying, "This
is David's plunder."
Ge 14:16; 1Sa 15:3; Lk 12:19
21Then David came to the two
hundred men who had been too
exhausted to follow him and who
were left behind at the Besor Valley. They came out to meet David
and the men with him. As David and his men approached, he
asked them how they were. 22But
all the evil men and troublemak-
ers among David's followers said,
"Because they did not go out with

us, we will not share with them
the plunder we recovered. However, each man may take his wife
and children and go."

23David replied, "No, my brothers, you must not do that with
what the LORD has given us. He
has protected us and delivered
into our hands the raiding party
that came against us. 24Who will
listen to what you say? The share
of the man who stayed with the
supplies is to be the same as that
of him who went down to the battle. All will share alike." 25David
made this a statute and ordinance
for Israel from that day to this.

Nu 31:27; Jos 22:8

26When David reached Zik-
lag, he sent some of the plunder
to the elders of Judah, who were
his friends, saying, "Here is a gift
for you from the plunder of the
LORD's enemies." Ge 33:11

27David sent it to those who were
in Bethel, Ramoth Negev and Jattir; 28to those in Aroer, Siphmoth,
Eshtemoa 29and Rakal; to those
in the towns of the Jerahmeelites
and the Kenites; 30to those in Hormah, Bor Ashan, Athak 31and Hebron; and to those in all the other
places where he and his men had
roamed. Jos 13:16; 14:13; Jdg 1:17

Saul Takes His Life

31 Now the Philistines fought
against Israel; the Israelites
fled before them, and many fell
dead on Mount Gilboa. 2The Philistines were in hot pursuit of Saul
and his sons, and they killed his
sons Jonathan, Abinadab and Malki-Shua. 3The fighting grew fierce
around Saul, and when the archers
overtook him, they wounded him
critically. 1Sa 28:4; 2Sa 1:6; 1Ch 10:1-12

4Saul said to his armor-bearer, "Draw your sword and run me
through, or these uncircumcised
fellows will come and run me
through and abuse me."

Jdg 9:54; 1Sa 14:6

But his armor-bearer was terrified and would not do it; so Saul
took his own sword and fell on it.
5When the armor-bearer saw that
Saul was dead, he too fell on his
sword and died with him. 6So Saul
and his three sons and his armor-
bearer and all his men died together that same day.

7When the Israelites along the
valley and those across the Jordan
saw that the Israelite army had
fled and that Saul and his sons had
died, they abandoned their towns
and fled. And the Philistines came
and occupied them.

8The next day, when the Philistines came to strip the dead, they
found Saul and his three sons fall-
en on Mount Gilboa. 9They cut off
his head and stripped off his armor,
and they sent messengers throughout the land of the Philistines to
proclaim the news in the temple of
their idols and among their people.
10They put his armor in the temple
of the Ashtoreths and fastened his
body to the wall of Beth Shan.

Jos 17:11; Jdg 2:12-13; 2Sa 1:20

11 When the people of Jabesh
Gilead heard what the Philistines
had done to Saul, 12 all their valiant
men marched through the night
to Beth Shan. They took down the
bodies of Saul and his sons from
the wall of Beth Shan and went to
Jabesh, where they burned them.
13 Then they took their bones and
buried them under a tamarisk tree
at Jabesh, and they fasted seven
days. 1Ch 10:1-12; 2Sa 1:4-12; 21:12-14

2 SAMUEL

David Hears of Saul's Death

1 After the death of Saul, David
returned from striking down
the Amalekites and stayed in Ziklag two days. 2On the third day
a man arrived from Saul's camp
with his clothes torn and dust on
his head. When he came to David,
he fell to the ground to pay him
honor. 1Sa 4:12; 30:17; 31:6

3"Where have you come from?"
David asked him.

He answered, "I have escaped
from the Israelite camp."

4"What happened?" David
asked. "Tell me."

"The men fled from the battle,"
he replied. "Many of them fell and
died. And Saul and his son Jonathan are dead."

5Then David said to the young
man who brought him the report,
"How do you know that Saul and
his son Jonathan are dead?"

6"I happened to be on Mount
Gilboa," the young man said, "and
there was Saul, leaning on his
spear, with the chariots and their
drivers in hot pursuit. 7When he
turned around and saw me, he
called out to me, and I said, 'What
can I do?' 1Sa 31:2-4

8"He asked me, 'Who are you?'

"'An Amalekite,' I answered.
1Sa 15:2

9"Then he said to me, 'Stand
here by me and kill me! I'm in the
throes of death, but I'm still alive.'

10"So I stood beside him and
killed him, because I knew that
after he had fallen he could not
survive. And I took the crown that
was on his head and the band on
his arm and have brought them
here to my lord." Jdg 9:54; 2Ki 11:12

11Then David and all the men
with him took hold of their clothes
and tore them. 12They mourned
and wept and fasted till evening
for Saul and his son Jonathan, and
for the army of the LORD and for
the nation of Israel, because they
had fallen by the sword.
1Sa 31:1-13; 1Ch 10:1-12; Ge 37:29

13David said to the young man
who brought him the report,
"Where are you from?"

"I am the son of a foreigner, an
Amalekite," he answered.

14David asked him, "Why weren't
you afraid to lift your hand to destroy the LORD's anointed?" 1Sa 24:6

15Then David called one of his
men and said, "Go, strike him
down!" So he struck him down,
and he died. 16For David had said
to him, "Your blood be on your
own head. Your own mouth testified against you when you said, 'I
killed the LORD's anointed.'"
2Sa 4:10; Lev 20:9; Mt 27:24-25

David's Lament for Saul and Jonathan

17 David took up this lament concerning Saul and his son Jonathan,
18 and he ordered that the people of Judah be taught this lament of the bow (it is written in the Book of Jashar): Jos 10:13; 2Ch 35:25

19 "A gazelle[a] lies slain on your
heights, Israel.
How the mighty have fallen! 2Sa 3:38

20 "Tell it not in Gath, Mic 1:10
proclaim it not in the streets
of Ashkelon,
lest the daughters of the
Philistines be glad,
lest the daughters of the
uncircumcised rejoice. Ex 15:20; 1Sa 18:6; 31:8

21 "Mountains of Gilboa, 1Sa 31:1
may you have neither dew
nor rain,
may no showers fall on your
terraced fields.[b] Eze 31:15
For there the shield of the
mighty was despised,
the shield of Saul — no
longer rubbed with oil. Isa 21:5

22 "From the blood of the slain,
from the flesh of the mighty, Isa 34:3,7
the bow of Jonathan did not
turn back,
the sword of Saul did
not return unsatisfied. 1Sa 18:4

23 Saul and Jonathan —
in life they were loved and
admired,
and in death they were not
parted.
They were swifter than eagles, Jer 4:13
they were stronger than
lions. Jdg 14:18

24 "Daughters of Israel,
weep for Saul,
who clothed you in scarlet and
finery,
who adorned your
garments with
ornaments of gold.

25 "How the mighty have fallen in
battle!
Jonathan lies slain on your
heights.
26 I grieve for you, Jonathan my
brother; 1Sa 20:42
you were very dear to me.
Your love for me was
wonderful,
more wonderful than that of
women. 1Sa 18:1

27 "How the mighty have fallen!
The weapons of war have
perished!"

David Anointed King Over Judah

2 In the course of time, David inquired of the LORD. "Shall I go up to one of the towns of Judah?" he asked. 1Sa 23:2,11-12

[a] 19 *Gazelle* here symbolizes a human dignitary. [b] 21 Or / *nor fields that yield grain for offerings*

The LORD said, "Go up."
David asked, "Where shall I go?"
"To Hebron," the LORD an-
swered. Ge 13:18; 1Sa 30:31
2 So David went up there with
his two wives, Ahinoam of Jezreel
and Abigail, the widow of Nabal of
Carmel. 3 David also took the men
who were with him, each with his
family, and they settled in Hebron
and its towns. 4 Then the men of
Judah came to Hebron, and there
they anointed David king over the
tribe of Judah. 1Sa 25:42; 27:2; 2Sa 5:3-5
When David was told that it was
the men from Jabesh Gilead who
had buried Saul, 5 he sent messengers to them to say to them, "The
LORD bless you for showing this
kindness to Saul your master by
burying him. 6 May the LORD now
show you kindness and faithfulness, and I too will show you
the same favor because you have
done this. 7 Now then, be strong
and brave, for Saul your master is dead, and the people of Judah have anointed me king over
them." Ex 34:6; 1Sa 23:21; 1Ti 1:16

War Between the Houses of David and Saul

8 Meanwhile, Abner son of Ner,
the commander of Saul's army,
had taken Ish-Bosheth son of Saul
and brought him over to Mahanaim. 9 He made him king over Gilead, Ashuri and Jezreel, and also
over Ephraim, Benjamin and all
Israel. Jdg 1:32; 1Sa 14:50; 1Ch 12:29
10 Ish-Bosheth son of Saul was
forty years old when he became
king over Israel, and he reigned
two years. The tribe of Judah,
however, remained loyal to David. 11 The length of time David
was king in Hebron over Judah
was seven years and six months.
2Sa 5:5
12 Abner son of Ner, together
with the men of Ish-Bosheth son
of Saul, left Mahanaim and went
to Gibeon. 13 Joab son of Zeruiah
and David's men went out and
met them at the pool of Gibeon.
One group sat down on one side
of the pool and one group on the
other side. Jos 18:25; 2Sa 8:16; 1Ch 2:16
14 Then Abner said to Joab, "Let's
have some of the young men get
up and fight hand to hand in front
of us."
"All right, let them do it," Joab
said.
15 So they stood up and were
counted off — twelve men for
Benjamin and Ish-Bosheth son of
Saul, and twelve for David. 16 Then
each man grabbed his opponent
by the head and thrust his dagger
into his opponent's side, and they
fell down together. So that place
in Gibeon was called Helkath Hazzurim.[a]
17 The battle that day was very
fierce, and Abner and the Israelites were defeated by David's men.
2Sa 3:1

[a] 16 *Helkath Hazzurim* means *field of daggers* or *field of hostilities.*

18The three sons of Zeruiah were
there: Joab, Abishai and Asahel.
Now Asahel was as fleet-footed as
a wild gazelle. 19He chased Abner,
turning neither to the right nor to
the left as he pursued him. 20Ab-
ner looked behind him and asked,
"Is that you, Asahel?" 1Ch 2:16; 12:8
"It is," he answered.
21Then Abner said to him, "Turn
aside to the right or to the left;
take on one of the young men and
strip him of his weapons." But Asahel would not stop chasing him.
22Again Abner warned Asahel,
"Stop chasing me! Why should I
strike you down? How could I look
your brother Joab in the face?"
2Sa 3:27
23But Asahel refused to give up
the pursuit; so Abner thrust the
butt of his spear into Asahel's
stomach, and the spear came out
through his back. He fell there
and died on the spot. And every
man stopped when he came to the
place where Asahel had fallen and
died. 2Sa 3:27; 20:12
24But Joab and Abishai pursued
Abner, and as the sun was setting,
they came to the hill of Ammah,
near Giah on the way to the wasteland of Gibeon. 25Then the men of
Benjamin rallied behind Abner.
They formed themselves into a
group and took their stand on top
of a hill.
26Abner called out to Joab,
"Must the sword devour forever?
Don't you realize that this will end
in bitterness? How long before
you order your men to stop pursuing their fellow Israelites?"
Dt 32:42
27Joab answered, "As surely as
God lives, if you had not spoken,
the men would have continued
pursuing them until morning."
28So Joab blew the trumpet,
and all the troops came to a halt;
they no longer pursued Israel,
nor did they fight anymore.
2Sa 18:16; Jdg 3:27
29All that night Abner and his
men marched through the Arabah. They crossed the Jordan,
continued through the morning
hours[a] and came to Mahanaim.
30Then Joab stopped pursuing
Abner and assembled the whole
army. Besides Asahel, nineteen of
David's men were found missing.
31But David's men had killed three
hundred and sixty Benjamites
who were with Abner. 32They took
Asahel and buried him in his father's tomb at Bethlehem. Then
Joab and his men marched all
night and arrived at Hebron by
daybreak. Ge 49:29

3 The war between the house
of Saul and the house of David lasted a long time. David grew
stronger and stronger, while the
house of Saul grew weaker and
weaker. 2Sa 2:17; 5:10; 1Ki 14:30
2Sons were born to David in
Hebron:

[a] 29 See Septuagint; the meaning of the Hebrew for this phrase is uncertain.

His firstborn was Amnon
the son of Ahinoam of Jezreel; 1Sa 25:43; 1Ch 3:1-3
3his second, Kileab the son
of Abigail the widow of Nabal of Carmel; 1Sa 25:42
the third, Absalom the son
of Maakah daughter of Talmai king of Geshur;
1Sa 27:8; 2Sa 13:37
4the fourth, Adonijah the
son of Haggith; 1Ki 1:5,11
the fifth, Shephatiah the
son of Abital;
5and the sixth, Ithream the
son of David's wife Eglah.
These were born to David
in Hebron.

Abner Goes Over to David

6During the war between the
house of Saul and the house of David, Abner had been strengthening his own position in the house
of Saul. 7Now Saul had had a concubine named Rizpah daughter of Aiah. And Ish-Bosheth said to Abner, "Why did you sleep with my father's concubine?"
2Sa 16:21-22; 21:8-11
8Abner was very angry because
of what Ish-Bosheth said. So he answered, "Am I a dog's head — on Judah's side? This very day I am loyal to the house of your father Saul and to his family and friends. I haven't handed you over to David. Yet now you accuse me of an offense involving this woman! 9May God deal with Abner, be
it ever so severely, if I do not do for David what the LORD promised him on oath 10and transfer
the kingdom from the house of Saul and establish David's throne over Israel and Judah from Dan to Beersheba." 11Ish-Bosheth did not
dare to say another word to Abner, because he was afraid of him.
2Sa 9:8; 1Ki 19:2; Jdg 20:1
12Then Abner sent messengers on his behalf to say to David, "Whose land is it? Make an agreement with me, and I will help you bring all Israel over to you."
13"Good," said David. "I will
make an agreement with you. But I demand one thing of you: Do not come into my presence unless you bring Michal daughter of Saul when you come to see me." 14Then
David sent messengers to Ish-Bosheth son of Saul, demanding, "Give me my wife Michal, whom I betrothed to myself for the price of a hundred Philistine foreskins."
Ge 43:5; 1Sa 18:27
15So Ish-Bosheth gave orders
and had her taken away from her husband Paltiel son of Laish. 16Her
husband, however, went with her, weeping behind her all the way to Bahurim. Then Abner said to him, "Go back home!" So he went back.
Dt 24:1-4; 1Sa 25:44; 2Sa 16:5
17Abner conferred with the el-
ders of Israel and said, "For some time you have wanted to make David your king. 18Now do it! For
the LORD promised David, 'By my

servant David I will rescue my people Israel from the hand of the Philistines and from the hand of all their enemies.' "

Jdg 11:11; 1Sa 9:16; 15:28

19 Abner also spoke to the Benjamites in person. Then he went to Hebron to tell David everything that Israel and the whole tribe of Benjamin wanted to do. 20 When Abner, who had twenty men with him, came to David at Hebron, David prepared a feast for him and his men. 21 Then Abner said to David, "Let me go at once and assemble all Israel for my lord the king, so that they may make a covenant with you, and that you may rule over all that your heart desires." So David sent Abner away, and he went in peace.

1Sa 10:20-21; 1Ki 11:37; 1Ch 12:2,16,29

Joab Murders Abner

22 Just then David's men and Joab returned from a raid and brought with them a great deal of plunder. But Abner was no longer with David in Hebron, because David had sent him away, and he had gone in peace. 23 When Joab and all the soldiers with him arrived, he was told that Abner son of Ner had come to the king and that the king had sent him away and that he had gone in peace.

24 So Joab went to the king and said, "What have you done? Look, Abner came to you. Why did you let him go? Now he is gone! 25 You know Abner son of Ner; he came to deceive you and observe your movements and find out everything you are doing."

26 Joab then left David and sent messengers after Abner, and they brought him back from the cistern at Sirah. But David did not know it. 27 Now when Abner returned to Hebron, Joab took him aside into an inner chamber, as if to speak with him privately. And there, to avenge the blood of his brother Asahel, Joab stabbed him in the stomach, and he died.

2Sa 2:22; 20:9-10; 1Ki 2:5

28 Later, when David heard about this, he said, "I and my kingdom are forever innocent before the LORD concerning the blood of Abner son of Ner. 29 May his blood fall on the head of Joab and on his whole family! May Joab's family never be without someone who has a running sore or leprosy[a] or who leans on a crutch or who falls by the sword or who lacks food."

Dt 21:9; Lev 15:2; 1Ki 2:31-33

30 (Joab and his brother Abishai murdered Abner because he had killed their brother Asahel in the battle at Gibeon.)

31 Then David said to Joab and all the people with him, "Tear your clothes and put on sackcloth and walk in mourning in front of Abner." King David himself

[a] 29 The Hebrew for *leprosy* was used for various diseases affecting the skin.

walked behind the bier. 32They
buried Abner in Hebron, and the
king wept aloud at Abner's tomb.
All the people wept also.
Ge 37:34; Pr 24:17; Isa 20:2

33The king sang this lament for
Abner: 2Sa 1:17

"Should Abner have died as the
lawless die?
34 Your hands were not bound,
your feet were not fettered.
You fell as one falls before the
wicked."

And all the people wept over
him again.

35Then they all came and urged
David to eat something while it
was still day; but David took an
oath, saying, "May God deal with
me, be it ever so severely, if I taste
bread or anything else before the
sun sets!" Ru 1:17; 2Sa 1:12; 12:17

36All the people took note and
were pleased; indeed, everything
the king did pleased them. 37So on
that day all the people there and
all Israel knew that the king had
no part in the murder of Abner
son of Ner.

38Then the king said to his men,
"Do you not realize that a commander and a great man has fall-
en in Israel this day? 39And today,
though I am the anointed king, I
am weak, and these sons of Zeruiah are too strong for me. May the
LORD repay the evildoer according
to his evil deeds!"
2Sa 19:5-7; 1Ki 2:5-6,33-34; Ps 41:10

Ish-Bosheth Murdered

4 When Ish-Bosheth son of Saul
heard that Abner had died
in Hebron, he lost courage, and
all Israel became alarmed. 2Now
Saul's son had two men who were
leaders of raiding bands. One was
named Baanah and the other Rekab; they were sons of Rimmon
the Beerothite from the tribe of
Benjamin — Beeroth is considered part of Benjamin, 3because
the people of Beeroth fled to Gittaim and have resided there as
foreigners to this day.
2Sa 3:27; Jos 9:17; Ne 11:33

4(Jonathan son of Saul had a son
who was lame in both feet. He was
five years old when the news about
Saul and Jonathan came from Jezreel. His nurse picked him up and
fled, but as she hurried to leave,
he fell and became disabled. His
name was Mephibosheth.)
1Sa 18:1; 2Sa 9:3,6; 1Ch 8:34

5Now Rekab and Baanah, the
sons of Rimmon the Beerothite,
set out for the house of Ish-Bosheth, and they arrived there in
the heat of the day while he was
taking his noonday rest. 6They
went into the inner part of the
house as if to get some wheat, and
they stabbed him in the stomach.
Then Rekab and his brother Baanah slipped away. 2Sa 2:23

7They had gone into the house
while he was lying on the bed in
his bedroom. After they stabbed
and killed him, they cut off his

head. Taking it with them, they
traveled all night by way of the
Arabah. 8They brought the head
of Ish-Bosheth to David at Hebron
and said to the king, "Here is the
head of Ish-Bosheth son of Saul,
your enemy, who tried to kill you.
This day the LORD has avenged my
lord the king against Saul and his
offspring." 1Sa 24:4; 25:29

9David answered Rekab and his
brother Baanah, the sons of Rimmon the Beerothite, "As surely
as the LORD lives, who has delivered me out of every trouble,
10when someone told me, 'Saul is
dead,' and thought he was bringing good news, I seized him and
put him to death in Ziklag. That
was the reward I gave him for his
news! 11How much more — when
wicked men have killed an innocent man in his own house and
on his own bed — should I not
now demand his blood from your
hand and rid the earth of you!"
1Ki 1:29; 2Sa 1:2-16; Ge 9:5

12So David gave an order to his
men, and they killed them. They
cut off their hands and feet and
hung the bodies by the pool in
Hebron. But they took the head of
Ish-Bosheth and buried it in Abner's tomb at Hebron. 2Sa 1:15

David Becomes King Over Israel

5 All the tribes of Israel came to
David at Hebron and said, "We
are your own flesh and blood. 2In
the past, while Saul was king over
us, you were the one who led Israel on their military campaigns.
And the LORD said to you, 'You
will shepherd my people Israel,
and you will become their ruler.'"
1Sa 16:1; 18:5,13,16

3When all the elders of Israel
had come to King David at Hebron, the king made a covenant
with them at Hebron before the
LORD, and they anointed David
king over Israel. 1Ch 11:1-3; 2Sa 2:4; 3:21

4David was thirty years old
when he became king, and he
reigned forty years. 5In Hebron he
reigned over Judah seven years
and six months, and in Jerusalem
he reigned over all Israel and Judah thirty-three years.
Lk 3:23; 1Ch 3:4; 26:31

David Conquers Jerusalem

6The king and his men marched
to Jerusalem to attack the Jebusites, who lived there. The Jebusites said to David, "You will not
get in here; even the blind and
the lame can ward you off." They
thought, "David cannot get in
here." 7Nevertheless, David captured the fortress of Zion — which
is the City of David.
Jos 15:8; Jdg 1:8; 1Ki 2:10

8On that day David had said,
"Anyone who conquers the Jebusites will have to use the water shaft to reach those 'lame
and blind' who are David's enemies.[a]" That is why they say, "The

[a] 8 Or *are hated by David*

'blind and lame' will not enter the
palace."

9 David then took up residence
in the fortress and called it the
City of David. He built up the area
around it, from the terraces[a] inward. 10 And he became more and
more powerful, because the LORD
God Almighty was with him.

1Ch 11:4-9; 2Sa 3:1; 1Ki 9:15,24

11 Now Hiram king of Tyre sent
envoys to David, along with cedar
logs and carpenters and stonema-
sons, and they built a palace for
David. 12 Then David knew that the
LORD had established him as king
over Israel and had exalted his
kingdom for the sake of his people Israel.

1Ki 5:1,18; 1Ch 14:1

13 After he left Hebron, David
took more concubines and wives
in Jerusalem, and more sons
and daughters were born to him.
14 These are the names of the children born to him there: Shammua, Shobab, Nathan, Solomon,
15 Ibhar, Elishua, Nepheg, Japhia,
16 Elishama, Eliada and Eliphelet.

1Ch 3:5-9; 14:1-7; Dt 17:17

David Defeats the Philistines

17 When the Philistines heard
that David had been anointed
king over Israel, they went up in
full force to search for him, but David heard about it and went down
to the stronghold. 18 Now the Philistines had come and spread out
in the Valley of Rephaim; 19 so David inquired of the LORD, "Shall I
go and attack the Philistines? Will
you deliver them into my hands?"

1Sa 23:2; 2Sa 23:14; Jos 15:8

The LORD answered him, "Go,
for I will surely deliver the Philistines into your hands."

20 So David went to Baal Perazim, and there he defeated them.
He said, "As waters break out, the
LORD has broken out against my
enemies before me." So that place
was called Baal Perazim.[b] 21 The
Philistines abandoned their idols
there, and David and his men carried them off.

1Ch 14:12; Isa 28:21; 46:2

22 Once more the Philistines
came up and spread out in the
Valley of Rephaim; 23 so David inquired of the LORD, and he answered, "Do not go straight up, but
circle around behind them and attack them in front of the poplar
trees. 24 As soon as you hear the
sound of marching in the tops of
the poplar trees, move quickly, because that will mean the LORD has
gone out in front of you to strike
the Philistine army." 25 So David
did as the LORD commanded him,
and he struck down the Philistines
all the way from Gibeon[c] to Gezer.

1Ch 14:8-17; Jdg 4:14; 2Ki 7:6

The Ark Brought to Jerusalem

6 David again brought together
all the able young men of Israel — thirty thousand. 2 He and all

[a] 9 Or *the Millo* [b] 20 *Baal Perazim* means *the lord who breaks out.*
[c] 25 Septuagint (see also 1 Chron. 14:16); Hebrew *Geba*

his men went to Baalah[a] in Judah
to bring up from there the ark of
God, which is called by the Name,[b]
the name of the LORD Almighty,
who is enthroned between the
cherubim on the ark. 3 They set
the ark of God on a new cart and
brought it from the house of Abinadab, which was on the hill. Uzzah
and Ahio, sons of Abinadab, were
guiding the new cart 4 with the ark
of God on it,[c] and Ahio was walking in front of it. 5 David and all Israel were celebrating with all their
might before the LORD, with cas-
tanets,[d] harps, lyres, timbrels, sis-
trums and cymbals.

Lev 24:16; 1Sa 4:4; 6:7

6 When they came to the threshing floor of Nakon, Uzzah reached
out and took hold of the ark of God,
because the oxen stumbled. 7 The
LORD's anger burned against Uzzah because of his irreverent act;
therefore God struck him down,
and he died there beside the ark
of God. Ex 19:22; Nu 4:15,19-20; 1Ch 15:13-15

8 Then David was angry because
the LORD's wrath had broken out
against Uzzah, and to this day that
place is called Perez Uzzah.[e] Ps 7:11

9 David was afraid of the LORD
that day and said, "How can the
ark of the LORD ever come to me?"
10 He was not willing to take the
ark of the LORD to be with him in
the City of David. Instead, he took
it to the house of Obed-Edom the
Gittite. 11 The ark of the LORD remained in the house of Obed-
Edom the Gittite for three months,
and the LORD blessed him and his
entire household.

1Ch 13:1-14; Ge 39:5; 1Ch 26:4-5

12 Now King David was told, "The
LORD has blessed the household
of Obed-Edom and everything he
has, because of the ark of God." So
David went to bring up the ark of
God from the house of Obed-Edom
to the City of David with rejoicing. 13 When those who were carrying the ark of the LORD had taken
six steps, he sacrificed a bull and
a fattened calf. 14 Wearing a linen
ephod, David was dancing before
the LORD with all his might, 15 while
he and all Israel were bringing up
the ark of the LORD with shouts
and the sound of trumpets.

Ex 15:20; 1Ki 8:1,5,62; 1Ch 15:25

16 As the ark of the LORD was entering the City of David, Michal
daughter of Saul watched from a
window. And when she saw King
David leaping and dancing before
the LORD, she despised him in her
heart.

17 They brought the ark of the
LORD and set it in its place inside
the tent that David had pitched for

[a] 2 That is, Kiriath Jearim (see 1 Chron. 13:6)
[b] 2 Hebrew; Septuagint and Vulgate do not have *the Name.*
[c] 3,4 Dead Sea Scrolls and some Septuagint manuscripts; Masoretic Text *cart* [4]*and they brought it with the ark of God from the house of Abinadab, which was on the hill*
[d] 5 Masoretic Text; Dead Sea Scrolls and Septuagint (see also 1 Chron. 13:8) *songs*
[e] 8 *Perez Uzzah* means *outbreak against Uzzah.*

it, and David sacrificed burnt offerings and fellowship offerings
before the LORD. 18After he had finished sacrificing the burnt offerings and fellowship offerings, he
blessed the people in the name of
the LORD Almighty. 19Then he gave
a loaf of bread, a cake of dates and
a cake of raisins to each person in
the whole crowd of Israelites, both
men and women. And all the people went to their homes.

1Ch 15:25-16:3; 2Ch 1:4; Hos 3:1

20When David returned home to
bless his household, Michal daughter of Saul came out to meet him
and said, "How the king of Israel
has distinguished himself today,
going around half-naked in full
view of the slave girls of his servants as any vulgar fellow would!"

21David said to Michal, "It was
before the LORD, who chose me
rather than your father or anyone
from his house when he appointed me ruler over the LORD's people
Israel — I will celebrate before the
LORD. 22I will become even more
undignified than this, and I will
be humiliated in my own eyes.
But by these slave girls you spoke
of, I will be held in honor." 1Sa 13:14

23And Michal daughter of Saul
had no children to the day of her
death.

God's Promise to David

7 After the king was settled in
his palace and the LORD had
given him rest from all his enemies around him, 2he said to Nathan the prophet, "Here I am, living in a house of cedar, while the
ark of God remains in a tent."

Ex 26:1; 2Sa 5:11; 1Ch 17:1

3Nathan replied to the king,
"Whatever you have in mind, go
ahead and do it, for the LORD is
with you."

4But that night the word of the
LORD came to Nathan, saying:

5"Go and tell my servant
David, 'This is what the LORD
says: Are you the one to build
me a house to dwell in? 6I
have not dwelt in a house
from the day I brought the
Israelites up out of Egypt to
this day. I have been moving from place to place with a
tent as my dwelling. 7Wherev-
er I have moved with all the
Israelites, did I ever say to any
of their rulers whom I commanded to shepherd my people Israel, "Why have you not
built me a house of cedar?"'

Ex 40:18,34; Lev 26:11-12; 1Ki 5:3-5

8"Now then, tell my servant
David, 'This is what the LORD
Almighty says: I took you
from the pasture, from tending the flock, and appointed
you ruler over my people Israel. 9I have been with you
wherever you have gone, and
I have cut off all your enemies from before you. Now I
will make your name great,
like the names of the greatest

men on earth. 10And I will
provide a place for my people
Israel and will plant them so
that they can have a home of
their own and no longer be
disturbed. Wicked people will
not oppress them anymore,
as they did at the beginning
11and have done ever since
the time I appointed leaders[a] over my people Israel. I
will also give you rest from all
your enemies.

1Sa 16:11; Ps 18:37-42; Isa 5:1-7

"'The LORD declares to you
that the LORD himself will
establish a house for you:
12When your days are over and
you rest with your ancestors, I
will raise up your offspring to
succeed you, your own flesh
and blood, and I will establish
his kingdom. 13He is the one
who will build a house for my
Name, and I will establish the
throne of his kingdom forever. 14I will be his father, and he
will be my son. When he does
wrong, I will punish him with
a rod wielded by men, with
floggings inflicted by human
hands. 15But my love will never be taken away from him,
as I took it away from Saul,
whom I removed from before
you. 16Your house and your
kingdom will endure forever
before me[b]; your throne will
be established forever.'"

1Ch 17:1-15; 1Sa 15:23,28; 25:28

17Nathan reported to David all
the words of this entire revelation.

David's Prayer

18Then King David went in and
sat before the LORD, and he said:

"Who am I, Sovereign LORD,
and what is my family, that
you have brought me this
far? 19And as if this were not
enough in your sight, Sovereign LORD, you have also spoken about the future of the
house of your servant — and
this decree, Sovereign LORD,
is for a mere human![c]

1Sa 18:18; Isa 55:8-9

20"What more can David
say to you? For you know your
servant, Sovereign LORD. 21For
the sake of your word and according to your will, you have
done this great thing and
made it known to your servant.

1Sa 16:7; Jn 21:17

22"How great you are, Sovereign LORD! There is no one
like you, and there is no God
but you, as we have heard
with our own ears. 23And who
is like your people Israel — the
one nation on earth that God
went out to redeem as a people for himself, and to make
a name for himself, and to

[a] 11 Traditionally *judges* [b] 16 Some Hebrew manuscripts and Septuagint; most Hebrew manuscripts *you* [c] 19 Or *for the human race*

perform great and awesome
wonders by driving out nations and their gods from before your people, whom you
redeemed from Egypt?[a] 24You
have established your people
Israel as your very own forever, and you, LORD, have become their God.

Dt 3:24; 4:32-38; 26:18

25"And now, LORD God, keep
forever the promise you have
made concerning your ser-
vant and his house. Do as
you promised, 26so that your
name will be great forever.
Then people will say, 'The
LORD Almighty is God over Israel!' And the house of your
servant David will be established in your sight.

27"LORD Almighty, God of
Israel, you have revealed this
to your servant, saying, 'I will
build a house for you.' So your
servant has found courage to
pray this prayer to you. 28Sov-
ereign LORD, you are God!
Your covenant is trustworthy,
and you have promised these
good things to your servant.
29Now be pleased to bless the
house of your servant, that
it may continue forever in
your sight; for you, Sovereign
LORD, have spoken, and with
your blessing the house of
your servant will be blessed
forever."

1Ch 17:16-27; Nu 6:23-27; Jn 17:17

David's Victories

8 In the course of time, David
defeated the Philistines and
subdued them, and he took Me-
theg Ammah from the control of
the Philistines.

2David also defeated the Moabites. He made them lie down on
the ground and measured them
off with a length of cord. Every two
lengths of them were put to death,
and the third length was allowed
to live. So the Moabites became
subject to David and brought him
tribute. Nu 24:17

3Moreover, David defeated
Hadadezer son of Rehob, king of
Zobah, when he went to restore
his monument at[b] the Euphrates
River. 4David captured a thousand of his chariots, seven thousand charioteers[c] and twenty
thousand foot soldiers. He hamstrung all but a hundred of the
chariot horses.

Jos 11:9; 1Sa 14:47; 2Sa 10:16,19

5When the Arameans of Da-
mascus came to help Hadadezer
king of Zobah, David struck down
twenty-two thousand of them.
6He put garrisons in the Aramean kingdom of Damascus, and the
Arameans became subject to him
and brought tribute. The LORD

[a] 23 See Septuagint and 1 Chron. 17:21; Hebrew *wonders for your land and before your people, whom you redeemed from Egypt, from the nations and their gods.*
[b] 3 Or *his control along* [c] 4 Septuagint (see also Dead Sea Scrolls and 1 Chron. 18:4); Masoretic Text *captured seventeen hundred of his charioteers*

gave David victory wherever he
went. 2Sa 3:18; 1Ki 11:24
7David took the gold shields that
belonged to the officers of Hadadezer and brought them to Jerusalem. 8From Tebah[a] and Berothai,
towns that belonged to Hadadezer, King David took a great quantity of bronze. 1Ki 10:16; Eze 47:16
9When Tou[b] king of Hamath
heard that David had defeated the
entire army of Hadadezer, 10he
sent his son Joram[c] to King David
to greet him and congratulate him
on his victory in battle over Hadadezer, who had been at war with
Tou. Joram brought with him articles of silver, of gold and of bronze.
11King David dedicated these articles to the LORD, as he had done
with the silver and gold from
all the nations he had subdued:
12Edom[d] and Moab, the Ammonites and the Philistines, and Amalek. He also dedicated the plunder
taken from Hadadezer son of Rehob, king of Zobah. 1Ki 7:51
13And David became famous
after he returned from striking
down eighteen thousand Edom-
ites[e] in the Valley of Salt. 2Ki 14:7
14He put garrisons throughout
Edom, and all the Edomites became subject to David. The LORD
gave David victory wherever he
went. 1Ch 18:1-13; Ge 27:29,37-40; Nu 24:17-18

David's Officials

15David reigned over all Israel,
doing what was just and right for
all his people. 16Joab son of Zeruiah was over the army; Jehoshaphat son of Ahilud was recorder;
17Zadok son of Ahitub and Ahimelek son of Abiathar were priests;
Seraiah was secretary; 18Benaiah
son of Jehoiada was over the Kerethites and Pelethites; and David's
sons were priests.[f]
Ge 18:19; 1Sa 30:14; 1Ch 24:3

David and Mephibosheth

9 David asked, "Is there anyone
still left of the house of Saul
to whom I can show kindness for
Jonathan's sake?" 1Sa 20:14-17,42
2Now there was a servant of
Saul's household named Ziba.
They summoned him to appear
before David, and the king said to
him, "Are you Ziba?"
2Sa 16:1-4; 19:17,26,29
"At your service," he replied.
3The king asked, "Is there no
one still alive from the house of
Saul to whom I can show God's
kindness?"
Ziba answered the king, "There
is still a son of Jonathan; he is
lame in both feet." 2Sa 4:4
4"Where is he?" the king asked.

[a] *8* See some Septuagint manuscripts (see also 1 Chron. 18:8); Hebrew *Betah.*
[b] *9* Hebrew *Toi,* a variant of *Tou;* also in verse 10 [c] *10* A variant of *Hadoram*
[d] *12* Some Hebrew manuscripts, Septuagint and Syriac (see also 1 Chron. 18:11); most Hebrew manuscripts *Aram* [e] *13* A few Hebrew manuscripts, Septuagint and Syriac (see also 1 Chron. 18:12); most Hebrew manuscripts *Aram* (that is, Arameans)
[f] *18* Or *were chief officials* (see Septuagint and Targum; see also 1 Chron. 18:17)

Ziba answered, "He is at the house of Makir son of Ammiel in Lo Debar." 2Sa 17:27-29

5 So King David had him brought from Lo Debar, from the house of Makir son of Ammiel.

6 When Mephibosheth son of Jonathan, the son of Saul, came to David, he bowed down to pay him honor.

David said, "Mephibosheth!"

"At your service," he replied.

7 "Don't be afraid," David said to him, "for I will surely show you kindness for the sake of your father Jonathan. I will restore to you all the land that belonged to your grandfather Saul, and you will always eat at my table." 1Ki 2:7; 2Ki 25:29

8 Mephibosheth bowed down and said, "What is your servant, that you should notice a dead dog like me?" 2Sa 16:9

9 Then the king summoned Ziba, Saul's steward, and said to him, "I have given your master's grandson everything that belonged to Saul and his family. 10 You and your sons and your servants are to farm the land for him and bring in the crops, so that your master's grandson may be provided for. And Mephibosheth, grandson of your master, will always eat at my table." (Now Ziba had fifteen sons and twenty servants.)

11 Then Ziba said to the king, "Your servant will do whatever my lord the king commands his servant to do." So Mephibosheth ate at David's[a] table like one of the king's sons.

12 Mephibosheth had a young son named Mika, and all the members of Ziba's household were servants of Mephibosheth. 13 And Mephibosheth lived in Jerusalem, because he always ate at the king's table; he was lame in both feet. 1Ch 8:34

David Defeats the Ammonites

10 In the course of time, the king of the Ammonites died, and his son Hanun succeeded him as king. 2 David thought, "I will show kindness to Hanun son of Nahash, just as his father showed kindness to me." So David sent a delegation to express his sympathy to Hanun concerning his father. 1Sa 11:1

When David's men came to the land of the Ammonites, 3 the Ammonite commanders said to Hanun their lord, "Do you think David is honoring your father by sending envoys to you to express sympathy? Hasn't David sent them to you only to explore the city and spy it out and overthrow it?" 4 So Hanun seized David's envoys, shaved off half of each man's beard, cut off their garments at the buttocks, and sent them away. Isa 15:2; 20:4

5 When David was told about this, he sent messengers to meet the men, for they were greatly humiliated. The king said, "Stay at Jericho till your beards have grown, and then come back."

[a] 11 Septuagint; Hebrew *my*

6When the Ammonites realized
that they had become obnoxious
to David, they hired twenty thousand Aramean foot soldiers from
Beth Rehob and Zobah, as well as
the king of Maakah with a thousand men, and also twelve thousand men from Tob.

Ge 34:30; 2Sa 8:5; Jdg 18:28

7On hearing this, David sent
Joab out with the entire army of
fighting men. 8The Ammonites
came out and drew up in battle
formation at the entrance of their
city gate, while the Arameans of
Zobah and Rehob and the men of
Tob and Maakah were by themselves in the open country.

9Joab saw that there were battle
lines in front of him and behind
him; so he selected some of the
best troops in Israel and deployed
them against the Arameans. 10He
put the rest of the men under the
command of Abishai his brother
and deployed them against the
Ammonites. 11Joab said, "If the
Arameans are too strong for me,
then you are to come to my rescue; but if the Ammonites are too
strong for you, then I will come to
rescue you. 12Be strong, and let us
fight bravely for our people and
the cities of our God. The LORD
will do what is good in his sight."

Dt 31:6; 1Sa 3:18; 1Co 16:13

13Then Joab and the troops with
him advanced to fight the Arameans, and they fled before him.
14When the Ammonites realized
that the Arameans were fleeing,
they fled before Abishai and went
inside the city. So Joab returned
from fighting the Ammonites and
came to Jerusalem.

15After the Arameans saw that
they had been routed by Israel,
they regrouped. 16Hadadezer had
Arameans brought from beyond
the Euphrates River; they went
to Helam, with Shobak the commander of Hadadezer's army leading them.

17When David was told of this,
he gathered all Israel, crossed the
Jordan and went to Helam. The
Arameans formed their battle
lines to meet David and fought
against him. 18But they fled before Israel, and David killed seven
hundred of their charioteers and
forty thousand of their foot soldiers.[a] He also struck down Shobak the commander of their army,
and he died there. 19When all the
kings who were vassals of Hadadezer saw that they had been routed by Israel, they made peace with
the Israelites and became subject
to them. 2Sa 8:6

So the Arameans were afraid to
help the Ammonites anymore.

1Ch 19:1-19; 1Ki 11:25

David and Bathsheba

11 In the spring, at the time
when kings go off to war, David sent Joab out with the king's

[a] *18* Some Septuagint manuscripts (see also 1 Chron. 19:18); Hebrew *horsemen*

men and the whole Israelite army. They destroyed the Ammonites and besieged Rabbah. But David remained in Jerusalem.

1Ki 20:22,26; 1Ch 20:1

[2]One evening David got up from his bed and walked around on the roof of the palace. From the roof he saw a woman bathing. The woman was very beautiful, [3]and David sent someone to find out about her. The man said, "She is Bathsheba, the daughter of Eliam and the wife of Uriah the Hittite."
[4]Then David sent messengers to get her. She came to him, and he slept with her. (Now she was purifying herself from her monthly uncleanness.) Then she went back home. [5]The woman conceived and sent word to David, saying, "I am pregnant."

Ps 51 Title; Mt 5:28; Jas 1:14-15

[6]So David sent this word to Joab: "Send me Uriah the Hittite." And Joab sent him to David.
[7]When Uriah came to him, David asked him how Joab was, how the soldiers were and how the war was going. [8]Then David said to Uriah, "Go down to your house and wash your feet." So Uriah left the palace, and a gift from the king was sent after him. [9]But Uriah slept at the entrance to the palace with all his master's servants and did not go down to his house.

1Ch 11:41

[10]David was told, "Uriah did not go home." So he asked Uriah, "Haven't you just come from a military campaign? Why didn't you go home?"

[11]Uriah said to David, "The ark and Israel and Judah are staying in tents,[a] and my commander Joab and my lord's men are camped in the open country. How could I go to my house to eat and drink and make love to my wife? As surely as you live, I will not do such a thing!"

2Sa 7:2

[12]Then David said to him, "Stay here one more day, and tomorrow I will send you back." So Uriah remained in Jerusalem that day and the next. [13]At David's invitation, he ate and drank with him, and David made him drunk. But in the evening Uriah went out to sleep on his mat among his master's servants; he did not go home.

[14]In the morning David wrote a letter to Joab and sent it with Uriah. [15]In it he wrote, "Put Uriah out in front where the fighting is fiercest. Then withdraw from him so he will be struck down and die."

1Ki 21:8; 2Sa 12:12

[16]So while Joab had the city under siege, he put Uriah at a place where he knew the strongest defenders were. [17]When the men of the city came out and fought against Joab, some of the men in David's army fell; moreover, Uriah the Hittite died.

[18]Joab sent David a full account of the battle. [19]He instructed the messenger: "When you have finished

[a] 11 Or *staying at Sukkoth*

giving the king this account of the
battle, 20the king's anger may flare
up, and he may ask you, 'Why did
you get so close to the city to fight?
Didn't you know they would shoot
arrows from the wall? 21Who killed
Abimelek son of Jerub-Besheth[a]?
Didn't a woman drop an upper
millstone on him from the wall,
so that he died in Thebez? Why
did you get so close to the wall?' If
he asks you this, then say to him,
'Moreover, your servant Uriah the
Hittite is dead.'" Jdg 9:50-54
22The messenger set out, and
when he arrived he told David everything Joab had sent him to say.
23The messenger said to David, "The
men overpowered us and came
out against us in the open, but we
drove them back to the entrance
of the city gate. 24Then the archers
shot arrows at your servants from
the wall, and some of the king's
men died. Moreover, your servant
Uriah the Hittite is dead."
25David told the messenger,
"Say this to Joab: 'Don't let this
upset you; the sword devours one
as well as another. Press the attack
against the city and destroy it.' Say
this to encourage Joab."
26When Uriah's wife heard
that her husband was dead, she
mourned for him. 27After the time
of mourning was over, David had
her brought to his house, and she
became his wife and bore him a
son. But the thing David had done
displeased the LORD. 2Sa 12:9; Ps 51:4-5

Nathan Rebukes David

12 The LORD sent Nathan to David. When he came to him,
he said, "There were two men in a
certain town, one rich and the other poor. 2The rich man had a very
large number of sheep and cattle,
3but the poor man had nothing
except one little ewe lamb he had
bought. He raised it, and it grew
up with him and his children. It
shared his food, drank from his
cup and even slept in his arms. It
was like a daughter to him.
2Sa 14:4; 1Ki 20:35-41
4"Now a traveler came to the rich
man, but the rich man refrained
from taking one of his own sheep
or cattle to prepare a meal for the
traveler who had come to him. Instead, he took the ewe lamb that
belonged to the poor man and
prepared it for the one who had
come to him."
5David burned with anger
against the man and said to Nathan, "As surely as the LORD lives,
the man who did this must die! 6He
must pay for that lamb four times
over, because he did such a thing
and had no pity." Ex 22:1; Lk 19:8
7Then Nathan said to David,
"You are the man! This is what
the LORD, the God of Israel, says: 'I
anointed you king over Israel, and
I delivered you from the hand of
Saul. 8I gave your master's house
to you, and your master's wives

[a] 21 Also known as *Jerub-Baal* (that is, Gideon)

into your arms. I gave you all Israel and Judah. And if all this had
been too little, I would have giv-
en you even more. 9Why did you
despise the word of the LORD by
doing what is evil in his eyes? You
struck down Uriah the Hittite with
the sword and took his wife to be
your own. You killed him with the
sword of the Ammonites. 10Now,
therefore, the sword will never depart from your house, because you
despised me and took the wife of
Uriah the Hittite to be your own.'

2Sa 11:15; 13:28; 1Ki 20:42

11"This is what the LORD says:
'Out of your own household I am
going to bring calamity on you.
Before your very eyes I will take
your wives and give them to one
who is close to you, and he will
sleep with your wives in broad
daylight. 12You did it in secret, but
I will do this thing in broad daylight before all Israel.' "

Dt 28:30; 2Sa 11:4-15; 16:21-22

13Then David said to Nathan, "I
have sinned against the LORD."

1Sa 15:24; 2Sa 24:10

Nathan replied, "The LORD has
taken away your sin. You are not
going to die. 14But because by doing this you have shown utter contempt for[a] the LORD, the son born
to you will die."

Pr 28:13; Isa 52:5; Mic 7:18-19

15After Nathan had gone home,
the LORD struck the child that Uriah's wife had borne to David, and
he became ill. 16David pleaded
with God for the child. He fasted
and spent the nights lying in sackcloth[b] on the ground. 17The elders
of his household stood beside him
to get him up from the ground,
but he refused, and he would not
eat any food with them.

1Sa 25:38; 2Sa 13:31; Ps 5:7

18On the seventh day the child
died. David's attendants were
afraid to tell him that the child was
dead, for they thought, "While the
child was still living, he wouldn't
listen to us when we spoke to him.
How can we now tell him the child
is dead? He may do something
desperate."

19David noticed that his attendants were whispering among
themselves, and he realized the
child was dead. "Is the child dead?"
he asked.

"Yes," they replied, "he is dead."

20Then David got up from the
ground. After he had washed,
put on lotions and changed his
clothes, he went into the house of
the LORD and worshiped. Then he
went to his own house, and at his
request they served him food, and
he ate. Job 1:20

21His attendants asked him,
"Why are you acting this way?
While the child was alive, you
fasted and wept, but now that the
child is dead, you get up and eat!"

Jdg 20:26

[a] 14 An ancient Hebrew scribal tradition; Masoretic Text *for the enemies of*

[b] 16 Dead Sea Scrolls and Septuagint; Masoretic Text does not have *in sackcloth*.

22 He answered, "While the child
was still alive, I fasted and wept.
I thought, 'Who knows? The LORD
may be gracious to me and let the
child live.' 23 But now that he is
dead, why should I go on fasting?
Can I bring him back again? I will
go to him, but he will not return
to me." Jnh 3:9; Ge 37:35; Isa 38:1-5
24 Then David comforted his wife
Bathsheba, and he went to her and
made love to her. She gave birth
to a son, and they named him Solomon. The LORD loved him; 25 and
because the LORD loved him, he
sent word through Nathan the
prophet to name him Jedidiah.[a]
1Ki 1:11; 1Ch 22:9; Mt 1:6
26 Meanwhile Joab fought
against Rabbah of the Ammonites and captured the royal citadel. 27 Joab then sent messengers
to David, saying, "I have fought
against Rabbah and taken its water supply. 28 Now muster the rest
of the troops and besiege the city
and capture it. Otherwise I will
take the city, and it will be named
after me." Dt 3:11
29 So David mustered the entire
army and went to Rabbah, and
attacked and captured it. 30 David
took the crown from their king's[b]
head, and it was placed on his
own head. It weighed a talent[c] of
gold, and it was set with precious
stones. David took a great quantity of plunder from the city 31 and
brought out the people who were
there, consigning them to labor
with saws and with iron picks and
axes, and he made them work at
brickmaking.[d] David did this to
all the Ammonite towns. Then he
and his entire army returned to
Jerusalem. 1Ch 20:1-3; 1Sa 14:47

Amnon and Tamar

13 In the course of time, Amnon son of David fell in love
with Tamar, the beautiful sister of
Absalom son of David. 2Sa 3:2; 1Ch 3:9
2 Amnon became so obsessed
with his sister Tamar that he made
himself ill. She was a virgin, and it
seemed impossible for him to do
anything to her.
3 Now Amnon had an adviser
named Jonadab son of Shimeah,
David's brother. Jonadab was a
very shrewd man. 4 He asked Amnon, "Why do you, the king's son,
look so haggard morning after
morning? Won't you tell me?"
1Sa 16:9

Amnon said to him, "I'm in love
with Tamar, my brother Absalom's
sister."
5 "Go to bed and pretend to be
ill," Jonadab said. "When your father comes to see you, say to him,
'I would like my sister Tamar to
come and give me something to
eat. Let her prepare the food in my
sight so I may watch her and then
eat it from her hand.' "

[a] *25 Jedidiah* means *loved by the LORD.*
[b] *30* Or *from Milkom's* (that is, Molek's)
[c] *30* That is, about 75 pounds or about 34 kilograms
[d] *31* The meaning of the Hebrew for this clause is uncertain.

6So Amnon lay down and pretended to be ill. When the king came to see him, Amnon said to him, “I would like my sister Tamar to come and make some special bread in my sight, so I may eat from her hand.”

7David sent word to Tamar at the palace: “Go to the house of your brother Amnon and prepare some food for him.” 8So Tamar went to the house of her brother Amnon, who was lying down. She took some dough, kneaded it, made the bread in his sight and baked it. 9Then she took the pan and served him the bread, but he refused to eat.

“Send everyone out of here,” Amnon said. So everyone left him. 10Then Amnon said to Tamar, “Bring the food here into my bedroom so I may eat from your hand.” And Tamar took the bread she had prepared and brought it to her brother Amnon in his bedroom. 11But when she took it to him to eat, he grabbed her and said, “Come to bed with me, my sister.” Ge 39:12; 45:1

12“No, my brother!” she said to him. “Don’t force me! Such a thing should not be done in Israel! Don’t do this wicked thing. 13What about me? Where could I get rid of my disgrace? And what about you? You would be like one of the wicked fools in Israel. Please speak to the king; he will not keep me from being married to you.” 14But he refused to listen to her, and since he was stronger than she, he raped her. Lev 18:9; Dt 22:25; Jdg 19:23

15Then Amnon hated her with intense hatred. In fact, he hated her more than he had loved her. Amnon said to her, “Get up and get out!”

16“No!” she said to him. “Sending me away would be a greater wrong than what you have already done to me.”

But he refused to listen to her. 17He called his personal servant and said, “Get this woman out of my sight and bolt the door after her.” 18So his servant put her out and bolted the door after her. She was wearing an ornate[a] robe, for this was the kind of garment the virgin daughters of the king wore. 19Tamar put ashes on her head and tore the ornate robe she was wearing. She put her hands on her head and went away, weeping aloud as she went.

Ge 37:23; Jos 7:6; Est 4:1

20Her brother Absalom said to her, “Has that Amnon, your brother, been with you? Be quiet for now, my sister; he is your brother. Don’t take this thing to heart.” And Tamar lived in her brother Absalom’s house, a desolate woman.

21When King David heard all this, he was furious. 22And Absalom never said a word to Amnon,

[a] *18* The meaning of the Hebrew for this word is uncertain; also in verse 19.

either good or bad; he hated Amnon because he had disgraced his sister Tamar.

Ge 31:24; Lev 19:17-18; 1Jn 2:9-11

Absalom Kills Amnon

23 Two years later, when Absalom's sheepshearers were at Baal Hazor near the border of Ephraim, he invited all the king's sons to come there.
24 Absalom went to the king and said, "Your servant has had shearers come. Will the king and his attendants please join me?" 1Sa 25:7

25 "No, my son," the king replied. "All of us should not go; we would only be a burden to you." Although Absalom urged him, he still refused to go but gave him his blessing.

26 Then Absalom said, "If not, please let my brother Amnon come with us."

The king asked him, "Why should he go with you?"
27 But Absalom urged him, so he sent with him Amnon and the rest of the king's sons.

28 Absalom ordered his men, "Listen! When Amnon is in high spirits from drinking wine and I say to you, 'Strike Amnon down,' then kill him. Don't be afraid. Haven't I given you this order? Be strong and brave."
29 So Absalom's men did to Amnon what Absalom had ordered. Then all the king's sons got up, mounted their mules and fled. Jdg 19:6,9,22; 1Sa 25:36

30 While they were on their way, the report came to David: "Absalom has struck down all the king's sons; not one of them is left."
31 The king stood up, tore his clothes and lay down on the ground; and all his attendants stood by with their clothes torn. Nu 14:6; 2Sa 1:11

32 But Jonadab son of Shimeah, David's brother, said, "My lord should not think that they killed all the princes; only Amnon is dead. This has been Absalom's express intention ever since the day Amnon raped his sister Tamar.
33 My lord the king should not be concerned about the report that all the king's sons are dead. Only Amnon is dead."

34 Meanwhile, Absalom had fled.

Now the man standing watch looked up and saw many people on the road west of him, coming down the side of the hill. The watchman went and told the king, "I see men in the direction of Horonaim, on the side of the hill."[a]

35 Jonadab said to the king, "See, the king's sons have come; it has happened just as your servant said."

36 As he finished speaking, the king's sons came in, wailing loudly. The king, too, and all his attendants wept very bitterly.

37 Absalom fled and went to Talmai son of Ammihud, the king of

[a] 34 Septuagint; Hebrew does not have this sentence.

Geshur. But King David mourned
many days for his son. 2Sa 3:3; 14:23,32
38After Absalom fled and went
to Geshur, he stayed there three
years. 39And King David longed
to go to Absalom, for he was consoled concerning Amnon's death.
2Sa 12:19-23

Absalom Returns to Jerusalem

14 Joab son of Zeruiah knew
that the king's heart longed
for Absalom. 2So Joab sent someone to Tekoa and had a wise woman brought from there. He said to
her, "Pretend you are in mourning. Dress in mourning clothes,
and don't use any cosmetic lotions. Act like a woman who has
spent many days grieving for the
dead. 3Then go to the king and
speak these words to him." And
Joab put the words in her mouth.
2Sa 12:20; 20:16; 2Ch 11:6
4When the woman from Tekoa
went[a] to the king, she fell with
her face to the ground to pay him
honor, and she said, "Help me,
Your Majesty!"
5The king asked her, "What is
troubling you?"
She said, "I am a widow; my
husband is dead. 6I your servant
had two sons. They got into a
fight with each other in the field,
and no one was there to separate
them. One struck the other and
killed him. 7Now the whole clan
has risen up against your servant;
they say, 'Hand over the one who
struck his brother down, so that
we may put him to death for the
life of his brother whom he killed;
then we will get rid of the heir as
well.' They would put out the only
burning coal I have left, leaving
my husband neither name nor descendant on the face of the earth."
Dt 19:10-13; Nu 35:19; Mt 21:38
8The king said to the woman,
"Go home, and I will issue an order in your behalf." 1Sa 25:35
9But the woman from Tekoa
said to him, "Let my lord the king
pardon me and my family, and let
the king and his throne be without guilt." 1Sa 25:24; 1Ki 2:33; Mt 27:25
10The king replied, "If anyone
says anything to you, bring them
to me, and they will not bother
you again."
11She said, "Then let the king invoke the LORD his God to prevent
the avenger of blood from adding
to the destruction, so that my son
will not be destroyed." Nu 35:12,21
"As surely as the LORD lives," he
said, "not one hair of your son's
head will fall to the ground."
1Sa 14:45
12Then the woman said, "Let
your servant speak a word to my
lord the king."
"Speak," he replied.
13The woman said, "Why then
have you devised a thing like this
against the people of God? When
the king says this, does he not

[a] 4 Many Hebrew manuscripts, Septuagint, Vulgate and Syriac; most Hebrew manuscripts *spoke*

convict himself, for the king has
not brought back his banished son?
14Like water spilled on the ground,
which cannot be recovered, so we must die. But that is not what God desires; rather, he devises ways so that a banished person does not remain banished from him.

2Sa 12:7; Nu 35:15,25-28; Heb 9:27

15"And now I have come to say this to my lord the king because the people have made me afraid. Your servant thought, 'I will speak to the king; perhaps he will grant
his servant's request. 16Perhaps
the king will agree to deliver his servant from the hand of the man who is trying to cut off both me and my son from God's inheritance.'

17"And now your servant says, 'May the word of my lord the king secure my inheritance, for my lord the king is like an angel of God in discerning good and evil. May the LORD your God be with you.'"

2Sa 19:27; 1Ki 3:9

18Then the king said to the woman, "Don't keep from me the answer to what I am going to ask you."

"Let my lord the king speak," the woman said.

19The king asked, "Isn't the hand of Joab with you in all this?"

The woman answered, "As surely as you live, my lord the king, no one can turn to the right or to the left from anything my lord the king says. Yes, it was your servant Joab who instructed me to do this and who put all these words into
the mouth of your servant. 20Your
servant Joab did this to change the present situation. My lord has wisdom like that of an angel of God — he knows everything that happens in the land."

2Sa 18:13; Isa 28:6

21The king said to Joab, "Very well, I will do it. Go, bring back the young man Absalom."

22Joab fell with his face to the ground to pay him honor, and he blessed the king. Joab said, "Today your servant knows that he has found favor in your eyes, my lord the king, because the king has granted his servant's request."

Ge 47:7

23Then Joab went to Geshur and brought Absalom back to Jerusalem. 24But the king said, "He must
go to his own house; he must not see my face." So Absalom went to his own house and did not see the face of the king.

25In all Israel there was not a man so highly praised for his handsome appearance as Absalom. From the top of his head to the sole of his foot there was no
blemish in him. 26Whenever he
cut the hair of his head — he used to cut his hair once a year because it became too heavy for him — he would weigh it, and its weight was two hundred shekels[a] by the royal standard.

Eze 44:20

[a] 26 That is, about 5 pounds or about 2.3 kilograms

27Three sons and a daughter were
born to Absalom. His daughter's
name was Tamar, and she became
a beautiful woman. 2Sa 13:1; 18:18
28Absalom lived two years in Jerusalem without seeing the king's
face. 29Then Absalom sent for Joab
in order to send him to the king,
but Joab refused to come to him.
So he sent a second time, but he refused to come. 30Then he said to his
servants, "Look, Joab's field is next
to mine, and he has barley there.
Go and set it on fire." So Absalom's
servants set the field on fire.
31Then Joab did go to Absalom's
house, and he said to him, "Why
have your servants set my field on
fire?" Jdg 15:5
32Absalom said to Joab, "Look, I
sent word to you and said, 'Come
here so I can send you to the king
to ask, "Why have I come from Geshur? It would be better for me if
I were still there!"' Now then, I
want to see the king's face, and if I
am guilty of anything, let him put
me to death." 1Sa 20:8; 2Sa 3:3
33So Joab went to the king and
told him this. Then the king summoned Absalom, and he came in
and bowed down with his face to
the ground before the king. And
the king kissed Absalom.
Ge 33:4; Lk 15:20

Absalom's Conspiracy

15 In the course of time, Absalom provided himself with
a chariot and horses and with fifty men to run ahead of him. 2He
would get up early and stand by the
side of the road leading to the city
gate. Whenever anyone came with
a complaint to be placed before the
king for a decision, Absalom would
call out to him, "What town are you
from?" He would answer, "Your servant is from one of the tribes of Israel." 3Then Absalom would say to
him, "Look, your claims are valid
and proper, but there is no representative of the king to hear you."
4And Absalom would add, "If only
I were appointed judge in the land!
Then everyone who has a complaint or case could come to me
and I would see that they receive
justice." Jdg 9:29; 2Sa 19:8; Pr 12:2
5Also, whenever anyone approached him to bow down before
him, Absalom would reach out his
hand, take hold of him and kiss
him. 6Absalom behaved in this
way toward all the Israelites who
came to the king asking for justice, and so he stole the hearts of
the people of Israel. Ro 16:18
7At the end of four[a] years, Absalom said to the king, "Let me go to
Hebron and fulfill a vow I made to
the LORD. 8While your servant was
living at Geshur in Aram, I made
this vow: 'If the LORD takes me
back to Jerusalem, I will worship
the LORD in Hebron.[b]'"
Ge 28:20; 2Sa 13:37-38

[a] 7 Some Septuagint manuscripts, Syriac and Josephus; Hebrew *forty* [b] 8 Some Septuagint manuscripts; Hebrew does not have *in Hebron.*

9 The king said to him, "Go in
peace." So he went to Hebron.
10 Then Absalom sent secret
messengers throughout the tribes
of Israel to say, "As soon as you
hear the sound of the trumpets,
then say, 'Absalom is king in Hebron.'" 11 Two hundred men from
Jerusalem had accompanied Absalom. They had been invited as
guests and went quite innocently,
knowing nothing about the matter. 12 While Absalom was offering
sacrifices, he also sent for Ahithophel the Gilonite, David's counselor, to come from Giloh, his
hometown. And so the conspiracy gained strength, and Absalom's
following kept on increasing.
2Sa 16:15,23; 1Ki 1:34,39; Ps 3:1

David Flees

13 A messenger came and told
David, "The hearts of the people
of Israel are with Absalom."
14 Then David said to all his officials who were with him in Jerusalem, "Come! We must flee, or none
of us will escape from Absalom.
We must leave immediately, or he
will move quickly to overtake us
and bring ruin on us and put the
city to the sword." 2Sa 19:9; 1Ki 2:26
15 The king's officials answered
him, "Your servants are ready to
do whatever our lord the king
chooses."
16 The king set out, with his entire household following him; but
he left ten concubines to take care
of the palace. 17 So the king set out,
with all the people following him,
and they halted at the edge of the
city. 18 All his men marched past
him, along with all the Kerethites and Pelethites; and all the six
hundred Gittites who had accompanied him from Gath marched
before the king. 2Sa 8:18; 16:21-22
19 The king said to Ittai the Gittite, "Why should you come along
with us? Go back and stay with
King Absalom. You are a foreigner, an exile from your homeland.
20 You came only yesterday. And
today shall I make you wander
about with us, when I do not know
where I am going? Go back, and
take your people with you. May
the LORD show you kindness and
faithfulness."[a] 1Sa 23:13; 2Sa 2:6; 18:2
21 But Ittai replied to the king,
"As surely as the LORD lives, and as
my lord the king lives, wherever
my lord the king may be, whether it means life or death, there will
your servant be." Ru 1:16-17; Pr 17:17
22 David said to Ittai, "Go ahead,
march on." So Ittai the Gittite
marched on with all his men and
the families that were with him.
23 The whole countryside wept
aloud as all the people passed by.
The king also crossed the Kidron
Valley, and all the people moved
on toward the wilderness. 1Sa 11:4
24 Zadok was there, too, and all
the Levites who were with him

[a] 20 Septuagint; Hebrew *May kindness and faithfulness be with you*

were carrying the ark of the covenant of God. They set down the ark of God, and Abiathar offered sacrifices until all the people had finished leaving the city.

Nu 4:15; 1Sa 22:20; 2Sa 8:17

[25]Then the king said to Zadok, "Take the ark of God back into the city. If I find favor in the LORD's eyes, he will bring me back and let me see it and his dwelling place again. [26]But if he says, 'I am not pleased with you,' then I am ready; let him do to me whatever seems good to him."

Ex 15:13; 1Sa 3:18; Ps 43:3

[27]The king also said to Zadok the priest, "Do you understand? Go back to the city with my blessing. Take your son Ahimaaz with you, and also Abiathar's son Jonathan. You and Abiathar return with your two sons. [28]I will wait at the fords in the wilderness until word comes from you to inform me." [29]So Zadok and Abiathar took the ark of God back to Jerusalem and stayed there. 1Sa 9:9; 2Sa 17:17

[30]But David continued up the Mount of Olives, weeping as he went; his head was covered and he was barefoot. All the people with him covered their heads too and were weeping as they went up. [31]Now David had been told, "Ahithophel is among the conspirators with Absalom." So David prayed, "LORD, turn Ahithophel's counsel into foolishness."

2Sa 16:23; Est 6:12; Isa 20:2-4

[32]When David arrived at the summit, where people used to worship God, Hushai the Arkite was there to meet him, his robe torn and dust on his head. [33]David said to him, "If you go with me, you will be a burden to me. [34]But if you return to the city and say to Absalom, 'Your Majesty, I will be your servant; I was your father's servant in the past, but now I will be your servant,' then you can help me by frustrating Ahithophel's advice. [35]Won't the priests Zadok and Abiathar be there with you? Tell them anything you hear in the king's palace. [36]Their two sons, Ahimaaz son of Zadok and Jonathan son of Abiathar, are there with them. Send them to me with anything you hear." 2Sa 17:15-16; 19:35

[37]So Hushai, David's confidant, arrived at Jerusalem as Absalom was entering the city. 1Ch 27:33

David and Ziba

16 When David had gone a short distance beyond the summit, there was Ziba, the steward of Mephibosheth, waiting to meet him. He had a string of donkeys saddled and loaded with two hundred loaves of bread, a hundred cakes of raisins, a hundred cakes of figs and a skin of wine.

2Sa 9:1-13; 1Sa 25:18

[2]The king asked Ziba, "Why have you brought these?"

Ziba answered, "The donkeys are for the king's household to

ride on, the bread and fruit are
for the men to eat, and the wine is
to refresh those who become exhausted in the wilderness."
2Sa 17:27-29
3The king then asked, "Where is
your master's grandson?" 2Sa 19:26-27
Ziba said to him, "He is staying
in Jerusalem, because he thinks,
'Today the Israelites will restore to
me my grandfather's kingdom.'"
4Then the king said to Ziba, "All
that belonged to Mephibosheth is
now yours."
"I humbly bow," Ziba said. "May
I find favor in your eyes, my lord
the king."

Shimei Curses David

5As King David approached Bahurim, a man from the same clan
as Saul's family came out from
there. His name was Shimei son
of Gera, and he cursed as he came
out. 6He pelted David and all the
king's officials with stones, though
all the troops and the special
guard were on David's right and
left. 7As he cursed, Shimei said,
"Get out, get out, you murderer,
you scoundrel! 8The LORD has repaid you for all the blood you shed
in the household of Saul, in whose
place you have reigned. The LORD
has given the kingdom into the
hands of your son Absalom. You
have come to ruin because you are
a murderer!" 2Sa 19:16-23; 1Ki 2:8-9,36,44
9Then Abishai son of Zeruiah
said to the king, "Why should this
dead dog curse my lord the king?
Let me go over and cut off his
head." Ex 22:28; 2Sa 9:8
10But the king said, "What does
this have to do with you, you sons
of Zeruiah? If he is cursing because the LORD said to him, 'Curse
David,' who can ask, 'Why do you
do this?'" 2Sa 19:22; Ro 9:20
11David then said to Abishai and
all his officials, "My son, my own
flesh and blood, is trying to kill
me. How much more, then, this
Benjamite! Leave him alone; let
him curse, for the LORD has told
him to. 12It may be that the LORD
will look upon my misery and restore to me his covenant blessing
instead of his curse today."
Dt 23:5; 2Sa 12:11; Ro 8:28
13So David and his men continued along the road while Shimei
was going along the hillside opposite him, cursing as he went
and throwing stones at him and
showering him with dirt. 14The
king and all the people with him
arrived at their destination exhausted. And there he refreshed
himself. 2Sa 17:2

The Advice of Ahithophel and Hushai

15Meanwhile, Absalom and all
the men of Israel came to Jerusalem, and Ahithophel was with
him. 16Then Hushai the Arkite, David's confidant, went to Absalom
and said to him, "Long live the
king! Long live the king!" 2Sa 15:37

17 Absalom said to Hushai, "So
this is the love you show your
friend? If he's your friend, why
didn't you go with him?" 2Sa 19:25
18 Hushai said to Absalom, "No,
the one chosen by the LORD, by
these people, and by all the men
of Israel — his I will be, and I will
remain with him. 19 Furthermore,
whom should I serve? Should I
not serve the son? Just as I served
your father, so I will serve you."
2Sa 15:34
20 Absalom said to Ahithophel,
"Give us your advice. What should
we do?"
21 Ahithophel answered, "Sleep
with your father's concubines
whom he left to take care of the
palace. Then all Israel will hear
that you have made yourself obnoxious to your father, and the
hands of everyone with you will be
more resolute." 22 So they pitched a
tent for Absalom on the roof, and
he slept with his father's concubines in the sight of all Israel.
2Sa 12:11-12
23 Now in those days the advice
Ahithophel gave was like that of
one who inquires of God. That was
how both David and Absalom regarded all of Ahithophel's advice.
2Sa 15:12; 17:14,23

17 Ahithophel said to Absalom,
"I would[a] choose twelve
thousand men and set out tonight
in pursuit of David. 2 I would attack
him while he is weary and weak. I
would strike him with terror, and
then all the people with him will
flee. I would strike down only the
king 3 and bring all the people back
to you. The death of the man you
seek will mean the return of all;
all the people will be unharmed."
4 This plan seemed good to Absalom and to all the elders of Israel.
2Sa 16:14; 1Ki 22:31
5 But Absalom said, "Summon
also Hushai the Arkite, so we can
hear what he has to say as well."
6 When Hushai came to him, Absalom said, "Ahithophel has given
this advice. Should we do what he
says? If not, give us your opinion."
2Sa 15:32
7 Hushai replied to Absalom,
"The advice Ahithophel has given
is not good this time. 8 You know
your father and his men; they are
fighters, and as fierce as a wild
bear robbed of her cubs. Besides,
your father is an experienced
fighter; he will not spend the
night with the troops. 9 Even now,
he is hidden in a cave or some
other place. If he should attack
your troops first,[b] whoever hears
about it will say, 'There has been
a slaughter among the troops who
follow Absalom.' 10 Then even the
bravest soldier, whose heart is like
the heart of a lion, will melt with
fear, for all Israel knows that your
father is a fighter and that those
with him are brave.
Jos 2:9,11; 1Sa 16:18; Hos 13:8

[a] 1 Or *Let me* [b] 9 Or *When some of the men fall at the first attack*

[11]"So I advise you: Let all Israel,
from Dan to Beersheba — as numerous as the sand on the seashore — be gathered to you, with
you yourself leading them into
battle. [12]Then we will attack him
wherever he may be found, and
we will fall on him as dew settles
on the ground. Neither he nor any
of his men will be left alive. [13]If he
withdraws into a city, then all Israel will bring ropes to that city, and
we will drag it down to the valley
until not so much as a pebble is
left." Ge 12:2; 22:17; Mic 1:6

[14]Absalom and all the men of
Israel said, "The advice of Hushai the Arkite is better than that
of Ahithophel." For the LORD had
determined to frustrate the good
advice of Ahithophel in order to
bring disaster on Absalom.

2Sa 15:34; Ne 4:15; Ps 9:16

[15]Hushai told Zadok and Abiathar, the priests, "Ahithophel has
advised Absalom and the elders
of Israel to do such and such, but
I have advised them to do so and
so. [16]Now send a message at once
and tell David, 'Do not spend the
night at the fords in the wilderness; cross over without fail, or
the king and all the people with
him will be swallowed up.'"

[17]Jonathan and Ahimaaz were
staying at En Rogel. A female servant was to go and inform them,
and they were to go and tell King
David, for they could not risk being seen entering the city. [18]But
a young man saw them and told
Absalom. So the two of them left
at once and went to the house
of a man in Bahurim. He had a
well in his courtyard, and they
climbed down into it. [19]His wife
took a covering and spread it out
over the opening of the well and
scattered grain over it. No one
knew anything about it.

Jos 2:6; 15:7; 2Sa 3:16

[20]When Absalom's men came
to the woman at the house, they
asked, "Where are Ahimaaz and
Jonathan?"

The woman answered them,
"They crossed over the brook."[a]
The men searched but found no
one, so they returned to Jerusalem.

Ex 1:19; Jos 2:3-5; 1Sa 19:12-17

[21]After they had gone, the two
climbed out of the well and went
to inform King David. They said to
him, "Set out and cross the river
at once; Ahithophel has advised
such and such against you." [22]So
David and all the people with him
set out and crossed the Jordan. By
daybreak, no one was left who had
not crossed the Jordan.

[23]When Ahithophel saw that his
advice had not been followed, he
saddled his donkey and set out
for his house in his hometown. He
put his house in order and then
hanged himself. So he died and
was buried in his father's tomb.

2Sa 15:12; Mt 27:5; 2Ki 20:1

[a] 20 Or *"They passed by the sheep pen toward the water."*

Absalom's Death

[24]David went to Mahanaim, and Absalom crossed the Jordan with all the men of Israel. [25]Absalom had appointed Amasa over the army in place of Joab. Amasa was the son of Jether,[a] an Ishmaelite[b] who had married Abigail,[c] the daughter of Nahash and sister of Zeruiah the mother of Joab. [26]The Israelites and Absalom camped in the land of Gilead.

Ge 32:2; 2Sa 19:13; 1Ch 2:13-17

[27]When David came to Mahanaim, Shobi son of Nahash from Rabbah of the Ammonites, and Makir son of Ammiel from Lo Debar, and Barzillai the Gileadite from Rogelim [28]brought bedding and bowls and articles of pottery. They also brought wheat and barley, flour and roasted grain, beans and lentils,[d] [29]honey and curds, sheep, and cheese from cows' milk for David and his people to eat. For they said, "The people have become exhausted and hungry and thirsty in the wilderness." 2Sa 10:1-2; 16:2; 19:31-39

18 David mustered the men who were with him and appointed over them commanders of thousands and commanders of hundreds. [2]David sent out his troops, a third under the command of Joab, a third under Joab's brother Abishai son of Zeruiah, and a third under Ittai the Gittite. The king told the troops, "I myself will surely march out with you."

1Sa 11:11; 26:6; 2Sa 15:19

[3]But the men said, "You must not go out; if we are forced to flee, they won't care about us. Even if half of us die, they won't care; but you are worth ten thousand of us.[e] It would be better now for you to give us support from the city."

1Sa 18:7; 2Sa 21:17

[4]The king answered, "I will do whatever seems best to you."

So the king stood beside the gate while all his men marched out in units of hundreds and of thousands. [5]The king commanded Joab, Abishai and Ittai, "Be gentle with the young man Absalom for my sake." And all the troops heard the king giving orders concerning Absalom to each of the commanders.

[6]David's army marched out of the city to fight Israel, and the battle took place in the forest of Ephraim. [7]There Israel's troops were routed by David's men, and the casualties that day were great — twenty thousand men. [8]The battle spread out over the whole countryside, and the forest swallowed up more men that day than the sword. Jos 17:18

[a] *25* Hebrew *Ithra*, a variant of *Jether*
[b] *25* Some Septuagint manuscripts (see also 1 Chron. 2:17); Hebrew and other Septuagint manuscripts *Israelite*
[c] *25* Hebrew *Abigal*, a variant of *Abigail*
[d] *28* Most Septuagint manuscripts and Syriac; Hebrew *lentils, and roasted grain*
[e] *3* Two Hebrew manuscripts, some Septuagint manuscripts and Vulgate; most Hebrew manuscripts *care; for now there are ten thousand like us*

9Now Absalom happened to
meet David's men. He was riding
his mule, and as the mule went
under the thick branches of a large
oak, Absalom's hair got caught in
the tree. He was left hanging in
midair, while the mule he was riding kept on going. 2Sa 14:26
10When one of the men saw
what had happened, he told Joab,
"I just saw Absalom hanging in an
oak tree."
11Joab said to the man who had
told him this, "What! You saw him?
Why didn't you strike him to the
ground right there? Then I would
have had to give you ten shekels[a]
of silver and a warrior's belt."
12But the man replied, "Even if
a thousand shekels[b] were weighed
out into my hands, I would not lay
a hand on the king's son. In our
hearing the king commanded you
and Abishai and Ittai, 'Protect the
young man Absalom for my sake.[c]'
13And if I had put my life in jeopardy[d] — and nothing is hidden from
the king — you would have kept
your distance from me." 2Sa 14:19-20
14Joab said, "I'm not going to
wait like this for you." So he took
three javelins in his hand and
plunged them into Absalom's
heart while Absalom was still alive
in the oak tree. 15And ten of Joab's
armor-bearers surrounded Absalom, struck him and killed him.
2Sa 14:30; 12:10
16Then Joab sounded the trumpet, and the troops stopped pursuing Israel, for Joab halted them.
17They took Absalom, threw him
into a big pit in the forest and
piled up a large heap of rocks over
him. Meanwhile, all the Israelites
fled to their homes.
2Sa 2:28; 20:22; Jos 7:26
18During his lifetime Absalom
had taken a pillar and erected it in
the King's Valley as a monument
to himself, for he thought, "I have
no son to carry on the memory of
my name." He named the pillar after himself, and it is called Absalom's Monument to this day.
Ge 14:17; 1Sa 15:12; 2Sa 14:27

David Mourns

19Now Ahimaaz son of Zadok
said, "Let me run and take the
news to the king that the LORD has
vindicated him by delivering him
from the hand of his enemies."
Jdg 11:36; 2Sa 15:36
20"You are not the one to take
the news today," Joab told him.
"You may take the news another time, but you must not do so
today, because the king's son is
dead."
21Then Joab said to a Cushite,
"Go, tell the king what you have
seen." The Cushite bowed down
before Joab and ran off.

[a] *11* That is, about 4 ounces or about 115 grams [b] *12* That is, about 25 pounds or about 12 kilograms [c] *12* A few Hebrew manuscripts, Septuagint, Vulgate and Syriac; most Hebrew manuscripts may be translated *Absalom, whoever you may be.* [d] *13* Or *Otherwise, if I had acted treacherously toward him*

22Ahimaaz son of Zadok again
said to Joab, "Come what may,
please let me run behind the
Cushite."

But Joab replied, "My son, why
do you want to go? You don't have
any news that will bring you a reward."

23He said, "Come what may, I
want to run."

So Joab said, "Run!" Then Ahimaaz ran by way of the plain[a] and
outran the Cushite.

24While David was sitting between the inner and outer gates,
the watchman went up to the roof
of the gateway by the wall. As he
looked out, he saw a man running
alone. 25The watchman called out
to the king and reported it.
2Sa 19:8; 2Ki 9:17

The king said, "If he is alone, he
must have good news." And the
runner came closer and closer.

26Then the watchman saw another runner, and he called down
to the gatekeeper, "Look, another
man running alone!"

The king said, "He must be
bringing good news, too." 1Ki 1:42

27The watchman said, "It seems
to me that the first one runs like
Ahimaaz son of Zadok."

"He's a good man," the king
said. "He comes with good news."

28Then Ahimaaz called out to the
king, "All is well!" He bowed down
before the king with his face to the
ground and said, "Praise be to the
LORD your God! He has delivered
up those who lifted their hands
against my lord the king."

29The king asked, "Is the young
man Absalom safe?"

Ahimaaz answered, "I saw great
confusion just as Joab was about
to send the king's servant and me,
your servant, but I don't know
what it was."

30The king said, "Stand aside
and wait here." So he stepped
aside and stood there.

31Then the Cushite arrived and
said, "My lord the king, hear the
good news! The LORD has vindicated you today by delivering you
from the hand of all who rose up
against you."

32The king asked the Cushite, "Is
the young man Absalom safe?"

The Cushite replied, "May the
enemies of my lord the king and
all who rise up to harm you be like
that young man." Jdg 5:31; 1Sa 25:26

33The king was shaken. He went
up to the room over the gateway
and wept. As he went, he said:
"O my son Absalom! My son, my
son Absalom! If only I had died
instead of you — O Absalom, my
son, my son!"[b] Ex 32:32; Ro 9:3

19[c] Joab was told, "The king
is weeping and mourning
for Absalom." 2And for the whole
army the victory that day was
turned into mourning, because
on that day the troops heard it

[a] *23* That is, the plain of the Jordan
[b] *33* In Hebrew texts this verse (18:33) is numbered 19:1. [c] In Hebrew texts 19:1-43 is numbered 19:2-44.

said, "The king is grieving for his
son." 3The men stole into the city
that day as men steal in who are
ashamed when they flee from battle. 4The king covered his face and
cried aloud, "O my son Absalom!
O Absalom, my son, my son!"
5Then Joab went into the house
to the king and said, "Today you
have humiliated all your men,
who have just saved your life and
the lives of your sons and daughters and the lives of your wives
and concubines. 6You love those
who hate you and hate those who
love you. You have made it clear
today that the commanders and
their men mean nothing to you.
I see that you would be pleased if
Absalom were alive today and all
of us were dead. 7Now go out and
encourage your men. I swear by
the LORD that if you don't go out,
not a man will be left with you
by nightfall. This will be worse
for you than all the calamities
that have come on you from your
youth till now." Pr 14:28
8So the king got up and took
his seat in the gateway. When the
men were told, "The king is sitting
in the gateway," they all came before him. 2Sa 15:2

Meanwhile, the Israelites had
fled to their homes.

David Returns to Jerusalem

9Throughout the tribes of Israel, all the people were arguing
among themselves, saying, "The
king delivered us from the hand
of our enemies; he is the one who
rescued us from the hand of the
Philistines. But now he has fled
the country to escape from Absalom; 10and Absalom, whom we
anointed to rule over us, has died
in battle. So why do you say nothing about bringing the king back?"
2Sa 8:1-14

11King David sent this message
to Zadok and Abiathar, the priests:
"Ask the elders of Judah, 'Why
should you be the last to bring
the king back to his palace, since
what is being said throughout Israel has reached the king at his
quarters? 12You are my relatives,
my own flesh and blood. So why
should you be the last to bring
back the king?' 13And say to Amasa, 'Are you not my own flesh and
blood? May God deal with me, be
it ever so severely, if you are not
the commander of my army for
life in place of Joab.'"
Ge 29:14; 2Sa 2:13; 17:25

14He won over the hearts of the
men of Judah so that they were
all of one mind. They sent word to
the king, "Return, you and all your
men." 15Then the king returned
and went as far as the Jordan.

Now the men of Judah had
come to Gilgal to go out and meet
the king and bring him across the
Jordan. 16Shimei son of Gera, the
Benjamite from Bahurim, hurried
down with the men of Judah to
meet King David. 17With him were

a thousand Benjamites, along
with Ziba, the steward of Saul's
household, and his fifteen sons
and twenty servants. They rushed
to the Jordan, where the king was.
18They crossed at the ford to take
the king's household over and to
do whatever he wished.

Jos 5:9; 2Sa 16:1-2; 1Ki 2:8

When Shimei son of Gera crossed
the Jordan, he fell prostrate before
the king 19and said to him, "May
my lord not hold me guilty. Do
not remember how your servant
did wrong on the day my lord the
king left Jerusalem. May the king
put it out of his mind. 20For I your
servant know that I have sinned,
but today I have come here as the
first from the tribes of Joseph to
come down and meet my lord the
king."

1Sa 22:15; 2Sa 16:6-8

21Then Abishai son of Zeruiah
said, "Shouldn't Shimei be put
to death for this? He cursed the
LORD's anointed."

Ex 22:28

22David replied, "What does this
have to do with you, you sons of
Zeruiah? What right do you have
to interfere? Should anyone be
put to death in Israel today? Don't
I know that today I am king over
Israel?" 23So the king said to Shimei, "You shall not die." And the
king promised him on oath.

1Sa 11:13; 2Sa 16:10; 1Ki 2:8,42

24Mephibosheth, Saul's grandson, also went down to meet the
king. He had not taken care of his
feet or trimmed his mustache or
washed his clothes from the day
the king left until the day he returned safely. 25When he came
from Jerusalem to meet the king,
the king asked him, "Why didn't
you go with me, Mephibosheth?"

2Sa 4:4; 9:6-10

26He said, "My lord the king,
since I your servant am lame, I
said, 'I will have my donkey saddled and will ride on it, so I can
go with the king.' But Ziba my servant betrayed me. 27And he has
slandered your servant to my lord
the king. My lord the king is like
an angel of God; so do whatever
you wish. 28All my grandfather's
descendants deserved nothing
but death from my lord the king,
but you gave your servant a place
among those who eat at your table. So what right do I have to
make any more appeals to the
king?"

2Sa 14:17,20; 2Sa 21:6-9

29The king said to him, "Why
say more? I order you and Ziba to
divide the land."

30Mephibosheth said to the
king, "Let him take everything,
now that my lord the king has returned home safely."

31Barzillai the Gileadite also
came down from Rogelim to cross
the Jordan with the king and to
send him on his way from there.
32Now Barzillai was very old,
eighty years of age. He had provided for the king during his stay
in Mahanaim, for he was a very
wealthy man. 33The king said to

Barzillai, "Cross over with me and
stay with me in Jerusalem, and I
will provide for you." 2Sa 17:27; 1Ki 2:7
34But Barzillai answered the
king, "How many more years will
I live, that I should go up to Jerusalem with the king? 35I am now
eighty years old. Can I tell the difference between what is enjoyable
and what is not? Can your servant
taste what he eats and drinks? Can
I still hear the voices of male and
female singers? Why should your
servant be an added burden to
my lord the king? 36Your servant
will cross over the Jordan with the
king for a short distance, but why
should the king reward me in this
way? 37Let your servant return,
that I may die in my own town
near the tomb of my father and
mother. But here is your servant
Kimham. Let him cross over with
my lord the king. Do for him whatever you wish." 1Ki 2:7; Ps 90:10; Jer 41:17
38The king said, "Kimham shall
cross over with me, and I will do
for him whatever you wish. And
anything you desire from me I
will do for you."
39So all the people crossed the
Jordan, and then the king crossed
over. The king kissed Barzillai and
bid him farewell, and Barzillai returned to his home. Ge 31:55
40When the king crossed over to
Gilgal, Kimham crossed with him.
All the troops of Judah and half
the troops of Israel had taken the
king over.
41Soon all the men of Israel were
coming to the king and saying to
him, "Why did our brothers, the
men of Judah, steal the king away
and bring him and his household
across the Jordan, together with
all his men?" Jdg 8:1; 12:1
42All the men of Judah answered
the men of Israel, "We did this because the king is closely related
to us. Why are you angry about it?
Have we eaten any of the king's
provisions? Have we taken anything for ourselves?"
43Then the men of Israel answered the men of Judah, "We
have ten shares in the king; so
we have a greater claim on David
than you have. Why then do you
treat us with contempt? Weren't
we the first to speak of bringing
back our king?"

But the men of Judah pressed
their claims even more forcefully
than the men of Israel.

Sheba Rebels Against David

20 Now a troublemaker named
Sheba son of Bikri, a Benjamite, happened to be there. He
sounded the trumpet and shouted,

"We have no share in David,
no part in Jesse's son!
1Ki 12:16; 2Ch 10:16
Every man to his tent,
Israel!"

2So all the men of Israel deserted David to follow Sheba son of
Bikri. But the men of Judah stayed

by their king all the way from the
Jordan to Jerusalem.
3 When David returned to his palace in Jerusalem, he took the ten
concubines he had left to take care
of the palace and put them in a
house under guard. He provided for
them but had no sexual relations
with them. They were kept in con-
finement till the day of their death,
living as widows. 2Sa 15:16; 16:21-22
4 Then the king said to Ama-
sa, "Summon the men of Judah
to come to me within three days,
and be here yourself." 5 But when
Amasa went to summon Judah, he
took longer than the time the king
had set for him. 2Sa 19:13
6 David said to Abishai, "Now
Sheba son of Bikri will do us more
harm than Absalom did. Take your
master's men and pursue him, or
he will find fortified cities and
escape from us."[a] 7 So Joab's men
and the Kerethites and Pelethites
and all the mighty warriors went
out under the command of Abishai. They marched out from Jerusalem to pursue Sheba son of Bikri.
2Sa 8:18; 1Ki 1:38
8 While they were at the great
rock in Gibeon, Amasa came to
meet them. Joab was wearing his
military tunic, and strapped over
it at his waist was a belt with a dagger in its sheath. As he stepped forward, it dropped out of its sheath.
Jos 9:3; 2Sa 2:18
9 Joab said to Amasa, "How are
you, my brother?" Then Joab took
Amasa by the beard with his right
hand to kiss him. 10 Amasa was not
on his guard against the dagger in
Joab's hand, and Joab plunged it
into his belly, and his intestines
spilled out on the ground. Without being stabbed again, Amasa
died. Then Joab and his brother Abishai pursued Sheba son of
Bikri. 2Sa 2:23
11 One of Joab's men stood beside
Amasa and said, "Whoever favors
Joab, and whoever is for David, let
him follow Joab!" 12 Amasa lay wallowing in his blood in the middle
of the road, and the man saw that
all the troops came to a halt there.
When he realized that everyone
who came up to Amasa stopped,
he dragged him from the road
into a field and threw a garment
over him. 13 After Amasa had been
removed from the road, everyone
went on with Joab to pursue Sheba son of Bikri. 2Sa 2:23
14 Sheba passed through all the
tribes of Israel to Abel Beth Maakah
and through the entire region of
the Bikrites,[b] who gathered together and followed him. 15 All the troops
with Joab came and besieged Sheba in Abel Beth Maakah. They built
a siege ramp up to the city, and it
stood against the outer fortifica-
tions. While they were battering
the wall to bring it down, 16 a wise
woman called from the city, "Listen! Listen! Tell Joab to come here

[a] 6 Or *and do us serious injury* [b] 14 See Septuagint and Vulgate; Hebrew *Berites.*

so I can speak to him." 17He went toward her, and she asked, "Are you Joab?"
2Sa 14:2; 2Ki 19:32; 1Ki 15:20

"I am," he answered.

She said, "Listen to what your servant has to say."

"I'm listening," he said.

18She continued, "Long ago they used to say, 'Get your answer at Abel,' and that settled it. 19We are the peaceful and faithful in Israel. You are trying to destroy a city that is a mother in Israel. Why do you want to swallow up the LORD's inheritance?"
Dt 2:26; 1Sa 26:19; 2Sa 21:3

20"Far be it from me!" Joab replied, "Far be it from me to swallow up or destroy! 21That is not the case. A man named Sheba son of Bikri, from the hill country of Ephraim, has lifted up his hand against the king, against David. Hand over this one man, and I'll withdraw from the city."

The woman said to Joab, "His head will be thrown to you from the wall."
2Sa 4:8

22Then the woman went to all the people with her wise advice, and they cut off the head of Sheba son of Bikri and threw it to Joab. So he sounded the trumpet, and his men dispersed from the city, each returning to his home. And Joab went back to the king in Jerusalem.
Ecc 9:13

David's Officials

23Joab was over Israel's entire army; Benaiah son of Jehoiada was over the Kerethites and Pelethites; 24Adoniram[a] was in charge of forced labor; Jehoshaphat son of Ahilud was recorder; 25Sheva was secretary; Zadok and Abiathar were priests; 26and Ira the Jairite[b] was David's priest.
2Sa 8:16-18; 1Ki 4:3,6

The Gibeonites Avenged

21 During the reign of David, there was a famine for three successive years; so David sought the face of the LORD. The LORD said, "It is on account of Saul and his blood-stained house; it is because he put the Gibeonites to death."
Ge 12:10; Ex 32:11

2The king summoned the Gibeonites and spoke to them. (Now the Gibeonites were not a part of Israel but were survivors of the Amorites; the Israelites had sworn to spare them, but Saul in his zeal for Israel and Judah had tried to annihilate them.) 3David asked the Gibeonites, "What shall I do for you? How shall I make atonement so that you will bless the LORD's inheritance?"
Jos 9:15; 1Sa 26:19; 2Sa 20:19

4The Gibeonites answered him, "We have no right to demand silver or gold from Saul or his family, nor do we have the right to put anyone in Israel to death."
Nu 35:33-34

[a] 24 Some Septuagint manuscripts (see also 1 Kings 4:6 and 5:14); Hebrew *Adoram*

[b] 26 Hebrew; some Septuagint manuscripts and Syriac (see also 23:38) *Ithrite*

"What do you want me to do for
you?" David asked.
5They answered the king, "As
for the man who destroyed us and
plotted against us so that we have
been decimated and have no place
anywhere in Israel, 6let seven of
his male descendants be given to
us to be killed and their bodies exposed before the LORD at Gibeah
of Saul — the LORD's chosen one."

Nu 25:4; 1Sa 10:24

So the king said, "I will give
them to you."
7The king spared Mephibosheth
son of Jonathan, the son of Saul,
because of the oath before the
LORD between David and Jonathan
son of Saul. 8But the king took Ar-
moni and Mephibosheth, the two
sons of Aiah's daughter Rizpah,
whom she had borne to Saul, together with the five sons of Saul's
daughter Merab,[a] whom she had
borne to Adriel son of Barzillai the
Meholathite. 9He handed them
over to the Gibeonites, who killed
them and exposed their bodies on
a hill before the LORD. All seven of
them fell together; they were put
to death during the first days of
the harvest, just as the barley harvest was beginning.

1Sa 20:8,15; 2Sa 3:7; 4:4

10Rizpah daughter of Aiah took
sackcloth and spread it out for herself on a rock. From the beginning
of the harvest till the rain poured
down from the heavens on the
bodies, she did not let the birds
touch them by day or the wild animals by night. 11When David was
told what Aiah's daughter Rizpah,
Saul's concubine, had done, 12he
went and took the bones of Saul
and his son Jonathan from the
citizens of Jabesh Gilead. (They
had stolen their bodies from the
public square at Beth Shan, where
the Philistines had hung them after they struck Saul down on Gilboa.) 13David brought the bones of
Saul and his son Jonathan from
there, and the bones of those who
had been killed and exposed were
gathered up. Dt 21:23; 1Sa 31:11-13
14They buried the bones of Saul
and his son Jonathan in the tomb
of Saul's father Kish, at Zela in
Benjamin, and did everything the
king commanded. After that, God
answered prayer in behalf of the
land. Jos 7:26; 18:28; 2Sa 24:25

Wars Against the Philistines

15Once again there was a battle
between the Philistines and Israel.
David went down with his men to
fight against the Philistines, and
he became exhausted. 16And Ishbi-
Benob, one of the descendants of
Rapha, whose bronze spearhead
weighed three hundred shekels[b]
and who was armed with a new
sword, said he would kill David.

[a] *8* Two Hebrew manuscripts, some Septuagint manuscripts and Syriac (see also 1 Samuel 18:19); most Hebrew and Septuagint manuscripts *Michal*
[b] *16* That is, about 7 1/2 pounds or about 3.5 kilograms

17 But Abishai son of Zeruiah came
to David's rescue; he struck the
Philistine down and killed him.
Then David's men swore to him,
saying, "Never again will you go
out with us to battle, so that the
lamp of Israel will not be extinguished." 2Sa 18:3; 20:6; 1Ki 11:36
18 In the course of time, there
was another battle with the Philistines, at Gob. At that time Sibbekai
the Hushathite killed Saph, one of
the descendants of Rapha.
1Ch 11:29; 20:4
19 In another battle with the Philistines at Gob, Elhanan son of
Jair[a] the Bethlehemite killed the
brother of[b] Goliath the Gittite,
who had a spear with a shaft like
a weaver's rod. 1Sa 17:7
20 In still another battle, which
took place at Gath, there was a
huge man with six fingers on each
hand and six toes on each foot —
twenty-four in all. He also was descended from Rapha.
21 When he
taunted Israel, Jonathan son of
Shimeah, David's brother, killed
him. 1Ch 20:4-8; 1Sa 16:9
22 These four were descendants
of Rapha in Gath, and they fell at
the hands of David and his men.

David's Song of Praise

22 David sang to the LORD the
words of this song when
the LORD delivered him from the
hand of all his enemies and from
the hand of Saul.
2 He said:
Ex 15:1; Jdg 5:1

"The LORD is my rock,
my fortress and
my deliverer;
Dt 32:4; Ps 31:3; 144:2
3 my God is my rock, in
whom I take refuge,
Dt 32:37; Jer 16:19
my shield[c] and the horn[d] of
my salvation. Ge 15:1; Lk 1:69
He is my stronghold,
my refuge and my
savior — Ps 9:9
from violent people you
save me.

4 "I called to the LORD, who
is worthy of praise,
Ps 48:1; 96:4
and have been saved from
my enemies.
5 The waves of death
swirled about me;
Ps 69:14-15; 93:4; Jnh 2:3
the torrents of destruction
overwhelmed me.
6 The cords of the grave coiled
around me; Ps 116:3
the snares of death
confronted me.
7 "In my distress I called to the
LORD;
I called out to my God.
Ps 116:4; 120:1
From his temple he heard my
voice;
my cry came to his ears.

[a] 19 See 1 Chron. 20:5; Hebrew *Jaare-Oregim.* [b] 19 See 1 Chron. 20:5; Hebrew does not have *the brother of.* [c] 3 Or *sovereign* [d] 3 *Horn* here symbolizes strength.

8 The earth trembled and
quaked, Jdg 5:4; Ps 77:18
the foundations of the
heavens[a] shook; Job 26:11
they trembled because he
was angry.
9 Smoke rose from his nostrils;
consuming fire came from
his mouth, Ps 97:3; Heb 12:29
burning coals blazed out
of it.
10 He parted the heavens and
came down;
dark clouds were under his
feet. 1Ki 8:12; Na 1:3
11 He mounted the cherubim and
flew;
he soared[b] on the wings of
the wind. Ps 104:3
12 He made darkness his canopy
around him —
the dark[c] rain clouds of the
sky.
13 Out of the brightness of his
presence
bolts of lightning blazed
forth. ver 9
14 The LORD thundered from
heaven; 1Sa 2:10
the voice of the Most High
resounded.
15 He shot his arrows and
scattered the enemy,
Dt 32:23
with great bolts of lightning
he routed them.
16 The valleys of the sea were
exposed
and the foundations of the
earth laid bare
at the rebuke of the LORD, Na 1:4
at the blast of breath from
his nostrils.

17 "He reached down from on
high and took hold
of me; Ps 144:7
he drew me out of deep
waters. Ex 2:10
18 He rescued me from my
powerful enemy,
from my foes, who were too
strong for me.
19 They confronted me in the day
of my disaster,
but the LORD was my
support. Ps 23:4
20 He brought me out into a
spacious place; Ps 31:8
he rescued me because
he delighted in me.
2Sa 15:26; Ps 22:8; 118:5

21 "The LORD has dealt with
me according to my
righteousness; 1Sa 26:23
according to the cleanness
of my hands he has
rewarded me. Ps 24:4
22 For I have kept the ways of the
LORD; Ge 18:19; Ps 128:1; Pr 8:32
I am not guilty of turning
from my God.
23 All his laws are before me;
Dt 6:4-9; Ps 119:30-32
I have not turned away from
his decrees. Ps 119:102

[a] *8* Hebrew; Vulgate and Syriac (see also Psalm 18:7) *mountains* [b] *11* Many Hebrew manuscripts (see also Psalm 18:10); most Hebrew manuscripts *appeared* [c] *12* Septuagint (see also Psalm 18:11); Hebrew *massed*

24 I have been blameless before
him Ge 6:9; Eph 1:4
and have kept myself from
sin.
25 The LORD has rewarded
me according to my
righteousness, ver 21
according to my cleanness[a]
in his sight.

26 "To the faithful you show
yourself faithful,
to the blameless you show
yourself blameless,
27 to the pure you show yourself
pure, Mt 5:8
but to the devious you
show yourself shrewd.
Lev 26:23-24
28 You save the humble, Ps 72:12-13
but your eyes are on the
haughty to bring them
low. Isa 2:12,17; 5:15
29 You, LORD, are my lamp; Ps 27:1
the LORD turns my darkness
into light.
30 With your help I can advance
against a troop[b];
with my God I can scale a
wall.
31 "As for God, his way is perfect:
Dt 32:4; Mt 5:48
The LORD's word is flawless;
Ps 12:6; 119:140; Pr 30:5-6
he shields all who take
refuge in him. Ge 15:1
32 For who is God besides the
LORD?
And who is the Rock except
our God? 1Sa 2:2
33 It is God who arms me with
strength[c]
and keeps my way secure.
34 He makes my feet like the feet
of a deer; Hab 3:19
he causes me to stand on the
heights. Dt 32:13
35 He trains my hands for battle;
Ps 144:1
my arms can bend a bow of
bronze.
36 You make your saving help my
shield; Eph 6:16
your help has made[d] me
great.
37 You provide a broad path for
my feet, Pr 4:11
so that my ankles do not give
way.

38 "I pursued my enemies and
crushed them;
I did not turn back
till they were
destroyed.
39 I crushed them completely,
and they could not rise;
Mal 4:3
they fell beneath my feet.
40 You armed me with strength
for battle;
you humbled my adversaries
before me. Ps 44:5

[a] *25* Hebrew; Septuagint and Vulgate (see also Psalm 18:24) *to the cleanness of my hands* [b] *30* Or *can run through a barricade* [c] *33* Dead Sea Scrolls, some Septuagint manuscripts, Vulgate and Syriac (see also Psalm 18:32); Masoretic Text *who is my strong refuge* [d] *36* Dead Sea Scrolls; Masoretic Text *shield; / you stoop down to make*

41 You made my enemies turn
their backs in flight, Ex 23:27
and I destroyed my foes.
42 They cried for help, but there
was no one to save
them — Ps 50:22; Isa 1:15
to the LORD, but he did not
answer.
43 I beat them as fine as the dust
of the earth;
I pounded and trampled
them like mud in the
streets. Isa 10:6; Mic 7:10

44 "You have delivered me from
the attacks of the
peoples; 2Sa 3:1
you have preserved me as
the head of nations.
Dt 28:13
People I did not know now
serve me, Isa 55:3-5
45 foreigners cower before me;
Ps 66:3; 81:15
as soon as they hear of me,
they obey me.
46 They all lose heart;
they come trembling[a] from
their strongholds. Mic 7:17
47 "The LORD lives! Praise be to
my Rock!
Exalted be my God,
the Rock, my Savior!
Ps 89:26
48 He is the God who avenges me,
who puts the nations under
me, Ps 144:2
49 who sets me free from my
enemies. Ps 140:1,4
You exalted me above
my foes;
from a violent man you
rescued me.
50 Therefore I will praise you,
LORD, among the
nations;
I will sing the praises of your
name. Ro 15:9

51 "He gives his king great
victories; Ps 144:9-10
he shows unfailing kindness
to his anointed, Ps 89:20
to David and his
descendants forever."
Ps 18:1-50; 89:24,29; 2Sa 7:13

David's Last Words

23 These are the last words of
David:

"The inspired utterance of
David son of Jesse,
the utterance of the man
exalted by the Most
High, Ps 78:70-71; 89:27
the man anointed by the God
of Jacob, 1Sa 16:12-13; Ps 89:20
the hero of Israel's songs:

2 "The Spirit of the LORD spoke
through me; Mt 22:43; 2Pe 1:21
his word was on my tongue.
3 The God of Israel spoke,
the Rock of Israel said to me:
Dt 32:4; 2Sa 22:2,32
'When one rules over people in
righteousness, Ps 72:2

[a] 46 Some Septuagint manuscripts and Vulgate (see also Psalm 18:45); Masoretic Text *they arm themselves*

when he rules in the fear of
God, 2Ch 19:7,9; Isa 11:1-5
4 he is like the light of morning
at sunrise Jdg 5:31; Ps 89:36
on a cloudless morning,
like the brightness after rain
that brings grass from the
earth.'

5 "If my house were not right
with God,
surely he would not have
made with me an
everlasting covenant,
Ps 89:29; Isa 55:3
arranged and secured in
every part;
surely he would not bring to
fruition my salvation
and grant me my every desire.
6 But evil men are all to be
cast aside like thorns,
Mt 13:40-41
which are not gathered with
the hand.
7 Whoever touches thorns
uses a tool of iron or the
shaft of a spear;
they are burned up where
they lie."

David's Mighty Warriors

8 These are the names of David's
mighty warriors: 2Sa 17:10
Josheb-Basshebeth,[a] a Tahke-
monite,[b] was chief of the Three;
he raised his spear against eight
hundred men, whom he killed[c] in
one encounter. 1Ch 27:2
9 Next to him was Eleazar son
of Dodai the Ahohite. As one of
the three mighty warriors, he was
with David when they taunted the
Philistines gathered at Pas Dammim[d] for battle. Then the Israelites retreated, 10 but Eleazar stood
his ground and struck down the
Philistines till his hand grew tired
and froze to the sword. The LORD
brought about a great victory that
day. The troops returned to Eleazar, but only to strip the dead.
1Ch 8:4; 27:4
11 Next to him was Shammah son
of Agee the Hararite. When the
Philistines banded together at a
place where there was a field full
of lentils, Israel's troops fled from
them. 12 But Shammah took his
stand in the middle of the field. He
defended it and struck the Philistines down, and the LORD brought
about a great victory.
13 During harvest time, three
of the thirty chief warriors came
down to David at the cave of Adullam, while a band of Philistines
was encamped in the Valley of
Rephaim. 14 At that time David was
in the stronghold, and the Philistine garrison was at Bethlehem.
15 David longed for water and said,
"Oh, that someone would get me

[a] 8 Hebrew; some Septuagint manuscripts suggest *Ish-Bosheth*, that is, *Esh-Baal* (see also 1 Chron. 11:11 *Jashobeam*).
[b] 8 Probably a variant of *Hakmonite* (see 1 Chron. 11:11)
[c] 8 Some Septuagint manuscripts (see also 1 Chron. 11:11); Hebrew and other Septuagint manuscripts *Three; it was Adino the Eznite who killed eight hundred men*
[d] 9 See 1 Chron. 11:13; Hebrew *gathered there*.

a drink of water from the well
near the gate of Bethlehem!" 16So
the three mighty warriors broke
through the Philistine lines, drew
water from the well near the gate
of Bethlehem and carried it back
to David. But he refused to drink
it; instead, he poured it out before
the LORD. 17"Far be it from me,
LORD, to do this!" he said. "Is it
not the blood of men who went at
the risk of their lives?" And David
would not drink it.

1Sa 22:4-5; 2Sa 5:18; Ge 35:14

Such were the exploits of the
three mighty warriors.

18Abishai the brother of Joab son
of Zeruiah was chief of the Three.[a]
He raised his spear against three
hundred men, whom he killed,
and so he became as famous as the
Three. 19Was he not held in greater
honor than the Three? He became
their commander, even though he
was not included among them.

2Sa 10:10,14; 1Ch 11:20

20Benaiah son of Jehoiada, a
valiant fighter from Kabzeel, performed great exploits. He struck
down Moab's two mightiest warriors. He also went down into a
pit on a snowy day and killed a
lion. 21And he struck down a huge
Egyptian. Although the Egyptian
had a spear in his hand, Benaiah
went against him with a club. He
snatched the spear from the Egyptian's hand and killed him with
his own spear. 22Such were the exploits of Benaiah son of Jehoiada;
he too was as famous as the three
mighty warriors. 23He was held
in greater honor than any of the
Thirty, but he was not included
among the Three. And David put
him in charge of his bodyguard.

2Sa 8:18; Jos 15:21

24Among the Thirty were:
Asahel the brother of Joab, 2Sa 2:18
Elhanan son of Dodo from Bethlehem,
25Shammah the Harodite, Jdg 7:1; 1Ch 11:27
Elika the Harodite,
26Helez the Paltite, 1Ch 27:10
Ira son of Ikkesh from Tekoa,
27Abiezer from Anathoth, Jos 21:18
Sibbekai[b] the Hushathite,
28Zalmon the Ahohite,
Maharai the Netophathite, 2Ki 25:23; Ne 7:26
29Heled[c] son of Baanah the Netophathite,
Ithai son of Ribai from Gibeah in Benjamin, Jos 15:57
30Benaiah the Pirathonite, Jdg 12:13
Hiddai[d] from the ravines of Gaash, Jos 24:30

[a] 18 Most Hebrew manuscripts (see also 1 Chron. 11:20); two Hebrew manuscripts and Syriac *Thirty* [b] 27 Some Septuagint manuscripts (see also 21:18; 1 Chron. 11:29); Hebrew *Mebunnai* [c] 29 Some Hebrew manuscripts and Vulgate (see also 1 Chron. 11:30); most Hebrew manuscripts *Heleb* [d] 30 Hebrew; some Septuagint manuscripts (see also 1 Chron. 11:32) *Hurai*

31 Abi-Albon the Arbathite,
Azmaveth the Barhumite, 2Sa 3:16
32 Eliahba the Shaalbonite,
the sons of Jashen,
Jonathan 33 son of[a] Shammah the Hararite,
Ahiam son of Sharar[b] the Hararite,
34 Eliphelet son of Ahasbai the Maakathite, Dt 3:14
Eliam son of Ahithophel the Gilonite, 2Sa 11:3; 15:12
35 Hezro the Carmelite,
Paarai the Arbite,
36 Igal son of Nathan from Zobah, 1Sa 14:47
the son of Hagri,[c]
37 Zelek the Ammonite,
Naharai the Beerothite, the armor-bearer of Joab son of Zeruiah,
38 Ira the Ithrite, 1Ch 2:53
Gareb the Ithrite
39 and Uriah the Hittite. 2Sa 11:3
There were thirty-seven in all.

David Enrolls the Fighting Men

24 Again the anger of the LORD burned against Israel, and he incited David against them, saying, "Go and take a census of Israel and Judah." Jos 9:15; 1Ch 27:23

2 So the king said to Joab and the army commanders[d] with him, "Go throughout the tribes of Israel from Dan to Beersheba and enroll the fighting men, so that I may know how many there are." Jdg 20:1; 2Sa 3:10; 2Ch 2:17

3 But Joab replied to the king, "May the LORD your God multiply the troops a hundred times over, and may the eyes of my lord the king see it. But why does my lord the king want to do such a thing?" Dt 1:11

4 The king's word, however, overruled Joab and the army commanders; so they left the presence of the king to enroll the fighting men of Israel.

5 After crossing the Jordan, they camped near Aroer, south of the town in the gorge, and then went through Gad and on to Jazer.
6 They went to Gilead and the region of Tahtim Hodshi, and on to Dan Jaan and around toward Sidon.
7 Then they went toward the fortress of Tyre and all the towns of the Hivites and Canaanites. Finally, they went on to Beersheba in the Negev of Judah. Jos 13:9; 19:29; Nu 21:32

8 After they had gone through the entire land, they came back to Jerusalem at the end of nine months and twenty days.

9 Joab reported the number of the fighting men to the king: In Israel there were eight hundred thousand able-bodied men who

[a] 33 Some Septuagint manuscripts (see also 1 Chron. 11:34); Hebrew does not have *son of.* [b] 33 Hebrew; some Septuagint manuscripts (see also 1 Chron. 11:35) *Sakar* [c] 36 Some Septuagint manuscripts (see also 1 Chron. 11:38); Hebrew *Haggadi* [d] 2 Septuagint (see also verse 4 and 1 Chron. 21:2); Hebrew *Joab the army commander*

could handle a sword, and in Judah five hundred thousand.

Nu 1:44-46; 1Ch 21:5

10 David was conscience-stricken after he had counted the fighting men, and he said to the LORD, "I have sinned greatly in what I have done. Now, LORD, I beg you, take away the guilt of your servant. I have done a very foolish thing."

1Sa 13:13; 24:5; 2Sa 12:13

11 Before David got up the next morning, the word of the LORD had come to Gad the prophet, David's seer:
12 "Go and tell David, 'This is what the LORD says: I am giving you three options. Choose one of them for me to carry out against you.'"

1Sa 9:9; 22:5; 1Ch 29:29

13 So Gad went to David and said to him, "Shall there come on you three[a] years of famine in your land? Or three months of fleeing from your enemies while they pursue you? Or three days of plague in your land? Now then, think it over and decide how I should answer the one who sent me."

Eze 14:21; Lev 26:25

14 David said to Gad, "I am in deep distress. Let us fall into the hands of the LORD, for his mercy is great; but do not let me fall into human hands."

Ps 51:1; 103:8,13

15 So the LORD sent a plague on Israel from that morning until the end of the time designated, and seventy thousand of the people from Dan to Beersheba died.
16 When the angel stretched out his hand to destroy Jerusalem, the LORD relented concerning the disaster and said to the angel who was afflicting the people, "Enough! Withdraw your hand." The angel of the LORD was then at the threshing floor of Araunah the Jebusite.

Ge 6:6; Ex 12:23; 1Ch 27:24

17 When David saw the angel who was striking down the people, he said to the LORD, "I have sinned; I, the shepherd,[b] have done wrong. These are but sheep. What have they done? Let your hand fall on me and my family."

1Ch 21:1-17; Ps 74:1; Jer 49:20

David Builds an Altar

18 On that day Gad went to David and said to him, "Go up and build an altar to the LORD on the threshing floor of Araunah the
Jebusite." 19 So David went up, as the LORD had commanded
through Gad. 20 When Araunah looked and saw the king and his officials coming toward him, he went out and bowed down before the king with his face to the ground.

21 Araunah said, "Why has my lord the king come to his servant?"

"To buy your threshing floor," David answered, "so I can build an altar to the LORD, that the plague on the people may be stopped."

Nu 16:44-50

[a] 13 Septuagint (see also 1 Chron. 21:12); Hebrew *seven* [b] 17 Dead Sea Scrolls and Septuagint; Masoretic Text does not have *the shepherd*.

22 Araunah said to David, "Let
my lord the king take whatever
he wishes and offer it up. Here
are oxen for the burnt offering,
and here are threshing sledges
and ox yokes for the wood. 23 Your
Majesty, Araunah[a] gives all this
to the king." Araunah also said
to him, "May the LORD your God
accept you."

1Ki 19:21; Eze 20:40-41; 1Sa 6:14

24 But the king replied to Araunah, "No, I insist on paying you for
it. I will not sacrifice to the LORD
my God burnt offerings that cost
me nothing." Mal 1:13-14

So David bought the threshing
floor and the oxen and paid fifty
shekels[b] of silver for them. 25 David
built an altar to the LORD there and
sacrificed burnt offerings and fellowship offerings. Then the LORD
answered his prayer in behalf of
the land, and the plague on Israel
was stopped. 1Ch 21:18-26; 2Sa 21:14; 1Sa 7:17

[a] 23 Some Hebrew manuscripts and Septuagint; most Hebrew manuscripts *King Araunah* [b] 24 That is, about 1 1/4 pounds or about 575 grams

1 KINGS

Adonijah Sets Himself Up as King

1 When King David was very old,
he could not keep warm even
when they put covers over him.
2So his attendants said to him, "Let
us look for a young virgin to serve
the king and take care of him. She
can lie beside him so that our lord
the king may keep warm."

3Then they searched throughout Israel for a beautiful young
woman and found Abishag, a Shunammite, and brought her to the
king. 4The woman was very beautiful; she took care of the king and
waited on him, but the king had
no sexual relations with her.

5Now Adonijah, whose mother
was Haggith, put himself forward
and said, "I will be king." So he got
chariots and horses[a] ready, with
fifty men to run ahead of him.
6(His father had never rebuked
him by asking, "Why do you behave as you do?" He was also very
handsome and was born next after Absalom.) 2Sa 3:4; 15:1

7Adonijah conferred with Joab
son of Zeruiah and with Abiathar
the priest, and they gave him their
support. 8But Zadok the priest, Benaiah son of Jehoiada, Nathan the
prophet, Shimei and Rei and David's special guard did not join Adonijah. 2Sa 20:25; 23:8; 1Ki 2:22,28

9Adonijah then sacrificed sheep,
cattle and fattened calves at the
Stone of Zoheleth near En Rogel.
He invited all his brothers, the
king's sons, and all the royal officials of Judah, 10but he did not
invite Nathan the prophet or Benaiah or the special guard or his
brother Solomon. 2Sa 12:24

11Then Nathan asked Bathsheba, Solomon's mother, "Have you
not heard that Adonijah, the son
of Haggith, has become king, and
our lord David knows nothing
about it? 12Now then, let me advise
you how you can save your own
life and the life of your son Solomon. 13Go in to King David and
say to him, 'My lord the king, did
you not swear to me your servant:
"Surely Solomon your son shall be
king after me, and he will sit on
my throne"? Why then has Adonijah become king?' 14While you
are still there talking to the king,
I will come in and add my word to
what you have said."

2Sa 3:4; 1Ch 22:9-13; Pr 15:22

15So Bathsheba went to see the
aged king in his room, where Abishag the Shunammite was attending him. 16Bathsheba bowed
down, prostrating herself before
the king. ver 1

[a] 5 Or *charioteers*

"What is it you want?" the king
asked.

17She said to him, "My lord, you
yourself swore to me your servant
by the LORD your God: 'Solomon
your son shall be king after me,
and he will sit on my throne.' 18But
now Adonijah has become king,
and you, my lord the king, do not
know about it. 19He has sacrificed
great numbers of cattle, fattened
calves, and sheep, and has invited all the king's sons, Abiathar the
priest and Joab the commander
of the army, but he has not invited Solomon your servant. 20My
lord the king, the eyes of all Israel
are on you, to learn from you who
will sit on the throne of my lord
the king after him. 21Otherwise, as
soon as my lord the king is laid to
rest with his ancestors, I and my
son Solomon will be treated as
criminals." ver 13,30; Dt 31:16; 1Ki 2:10

22While she was still speaking
with the king, Nathan the prophet arrived. 23And the king was
told, "Nathan the prophet is here."
So he went before the king and
bowed with his face to the ground.

24Nathan said, "Have you, my
lord the king, declared that Adonijah shall be king after you, and that
he will sit on your throne? 25Today
he has gone down and sacrificed
great numbers of cattle, fattened
calves, and sheep. He has invited
all the king's sons, the commanders of the army and Abiathar the
priest. Right now they are eating
and drinking with him and saying, 'Long live King Adonijah!'
26But me your servant, and Zadok
the priest, and Benaiah son of Jehoiada, and your servant Solomon
he did not invite. 27Is this something my lord the king has done
without letting his servants know
who should sit on the throne of
my lord the king after him?"

David Makes Solomon King

28Then King David said, "Call in
Bathsheba." So she came into the
king's presence and stood before
him.

29The king then took an oath:
"As surely as the LORD lives, who
has delivered me out of every
trouble, 30I will surely carry out
this very day what I swore to you
by the LORD, the God of Israel: Solomon your son shall be king after
me, and he will sit on my throne
in my place." ver 13,17; 2Sa 4:9

31Then Bathsheba bowed down
with her face to the ground, prostrating herself before the king,
and said, "May my lord King David
live forever!"

32King David said, "Call in Zadok
the priest, Nathan the prophet and
Benaiah son of Jehoiada." When
they came before the king, 33he
said to them: "Take your lord's servants with you and have Solomon
my son mount my own mule and
take him down to Gihon. 34There
have Zadok the priest and Nathan
the prophet anoint him king over

Israel. Blow the trumpet and shout,
'Long live King Solomon!' [35]Then
you are to go up with him, and he
is to come and sit on my throne
and reign in my place. I have appointed him ruler over Israel and
Judah." 1Sa 10:1; 2Sa 15:10; 20:6-7

[36]Benaiah son of Jehoiada answered the king, "Amen! May
the LORD, the God of my lord the
king, so declare it. [37]As the LORD
was with my lord the king, so
may he be with Solomon to make
his throne even greater than the
throne of my lord King David!"
ver 47; Jos 1:5,17; 1Sa 20:13

[38]So Zadok the priest, Nathan
the prophet, Benaiah son of Jehoiada, the Kerethites and the Pelethites went down and had Solomon mount King David's mule,
and they escorted him to Gihon.
[39]Zadok the priest took the horn
of oil from the sacred tent and
anointed Solomon. Then they
sounded the trumpet and all the
people shouted, "Long live King
Solomon!" [40]And all the people
went up after him, playing pipes
and rejoicing greatly, so that the
ground shook with the sound.
1Sa 10:24; 2Sa 8:18; Ps 89:20

[41]Adonijah and all the guests
who were with him heard it as
they were finishing their feast. On
hearing the sound of the trumpet,
Joab asked, "What's the meaning
of all the noise in the city?"

[42]Even as he was speaking, Jonathan son of Abiathar the priest
arrived. Adonijah said, "Come in.
A worthy man like you must be
bringing good news." 2Sa 18:26

[43]"Not at all!" Jonathan answered. "Our lord King David
has made Solomon king. [44]The
king has sent with him Zadok the
priest, Nathan the prophet, Benaiah son of Jehoiada, the Kerethites
and the Pelethites, and they have
put him on the king's mule, [45]and
Zadok the priest and Nathan the
prophet have anointed him king
at Gihon. From there they have
gone up cheering, and the city resounds with it. That's the noise
you hear. [46]Moreover, Solomon
has taken his seat on the royal
throne. [47]Also, the royal officials
have come to congratulate our
lord King David, saying, 'May your
God make Solomon's name more
famous than yours and his throne
greater than yours!' And the king
bowed in worship on his bed [48]and
said, 'Praise be to the LORD, the
God of Israel, who has allowed
my eyes to see a successor on my
throne today.'" ver 37; 1Ki 3:6

[49]At this, all Adonijah's guests
rose in alarm and dispersed. [50]But
Adonijah, in fear of Solomon, went
and took hold of the horns of the
altar. [51]Then Solomon was told,
"Adonijah is afraid of King Solomon and is clinging to the horns
of the altar. He says, 'Let King Solomon swear to me today that he
will not put his servant to death
with the sword.'" 1Ki 2:28

52 Solomon replied, “If he shows himself to be worthy, not a hair of his head will fall to the ground; but if evil is found in him, he will die.” 53 Then King Solomon sent men, and they brought him down from the altar. And Adonijah came and bowed down to King Solomon, and Solomon said, “Go to your home.” 1Ch 29:21-25; 1Sa 14:45

David’s Charge to Solomon

2 When the time drew near for David to die, he gave a charge to Solomon his son.

2 “I am about to go the way of all the earth,” he said. “So be strong, act like a man, 3 and observe what the LORD your God requires: Walk in obedience to him, and keep his decrees and commands, his laws and regulations, as written in the Law of Moses. Do this so that you may prosper in all you do and wherever you go 4 and that the LORD may keep his promise to me: ‘If your descendants watch how they live, and if they walk faithfully before me with all their heart and soul, you will never fail to have a successor on the throne of Israel.’ 2Sa 7:13,25; 2Ki 20:3; 1Ch 22:13

5 “Now you yourself know what Joab son of Zeruiah did to me — what he did to the two commanders of Israel’s armies, Abner son of Ner and Amasa son of Jether. He killed them, shedding their blood in peacetime as if in battle, and with that blood he stained the belt around his waist and the sandals on his feet. 6 Deal with him according to your wisdom, but do not let his gray head go down to the grave in peace. 2Sa 2:18; 20:10

7 “But show kindness to the sons of Barzillai of Gilead and let them be among those who eat at your table. They stood by me when I fled from your brother Absalom. 2Sa 9:7; 17:27; 19:31-39

8 “And remember, you have with you Shimei son of Gera, the Benjamite from Bahurim, who called down bitter curses on me the day I went to Mahanaim. When he came down to meet me at the Jordan, I swore to him by the LORD: ‘I will not put you to death by the sword.’ 9 But now, do not consider him innocent. You are a man of wisdom; you will know what to do to him. Bring his gray head down to the grave in blood.” 2Sa 16:5-13; 19:18-23

10 Then David rested with his ancestors and was buried in the City of David. 11 He had reigned forty years over Israel — seven years in Hebron and thirty-three in Jerusalem. 12 So Solomon sat on the throne of his father David, and his rule was firmly established. 1Ch 29:26-28; 2Ch 1:1; 2Sa 5:7

Solomon’s Throne Established

13 Now Adonijah, the son of Haggith, went to Bathsheba, Solomon’s mother. Bathsheba asked him, “Do you come peacefully?” 1Sa 16:4

He answered, "Yes, peacefully."
14 Then he added, "I have something
to say to you."

"You may say it," she replied.

15 "As you know," he said, "the
kingdom was mine. All Israel
looked to me as their king. But
things changed, and the kingdom
has gone to my brother; for it has
come to him from the LORD. 16 Now
I have one request to make of you.
Do not refuse me."

"You may make it," she said.

17 So he continued, "Please ask
King Solomon — he will not re-
fuse you — to give me Abishag the
Shunammite as my wife." 1Ki 1:3

18 "Very well," Bathsheba replied,
"I will speak to the king for you."

19 When Bathsheba went to King
Solomon to speak to him for Adonijah, the king stood up to meet
her, bowed down to her and sat
down on his throne. He had a
throne brought for the king's
mother, and she sat down at his
right hand. Ps 45:9; 1Ki 15:13

20 "I have one small request to
make of you," she said. "Do not refuse me."

The king replied, "Make it, my
mother; I will not refuse you."

21 So she said, "Let Abishag the
Shunammite be given in marriage
to your brother Adonijah." 1Ki 1:3

22 King Solomon answered his
mother, "Why do you request Abishag the Shunammite for Adonijah? You might as well request the
kingdom for him — after all, he is
my older brother — yes, for him
and for Abiathar the priest and
Joab son of Zeruiah!"

2Sa 12:8; 1Ki 1:3; 1Ch 3:2

23 Then King Solomon swore by
the LORD: "May God deal with me,
be it ever so severely, if Adonijah does not pay with his life for
this request! 24 And now, as surely as the LORD lives — he who has
established me securely on the
throne of my father David and
has founded a dynasty for me as
he promised — Adonijah shall be
put to death today!" 25 So King Solomon gave orders to Benaiah son
of Jehoiada, and he struck down
Adonijah and he died.

2Sa 7:11; 8:18; Ru 1:17

26 To Abiathar the priest the king
said, "Go back to your fields in Anathoth. You deserve to die, but I
will not put you to death now, because you carried the ark of the
Sovereign LORD before my father
David and shared all my father's
hardships." 27 So Solomon removed
Abiathar from the priesthood of
the LORD, fulfilling the word the
LORD had spoken at Shiloh about
the house of Eli.

1Sa 2:27-36; 22:20; 2Sa 15:24

28 When the news reached Joab,
who had conspired with Adonijah though not with Absalom, he
fled to the tent of the LORD and
took hold of the horns of the altar.
29 King Solomon was told that Joab
had fled to the tent of the LORD
and was beside the altar. Then

Solomon ordered Benaiah son of
Jehoiada, "Go, strike him down!"
ver 25; 1Ki 1:7,50

30 So Benaiah entered the tent
of the LORD and said to Joab, "The
king says, 'Come out!'" Ex 21:14

But he answered, "No, I will die
here."

Benaiah reported to the king,
"This is how Joab answered me."

31 Then the king commanded Benaiah, "Do as he says. Strike him
down and bury him, and so clear
me and my whole family of the
guilt of the innocent blood that
Joab shed. 32 The LORD will repay
him for the blood he shed, because without my father David
knowing it he attacked two men
and killed them with the sword.
Both of them — Abner son of Ner,
commander of Israel's army, and
Amasa son of Jether, commander of Judah's army — were better
men and more upright than he.
33 May the guilt of their blood rest
on the head of Joab and his descendants forever. But on David
and his descendants, his house
and his throne, may there be the
LORD's peace forever."
Dt 19:13; Jdg 9:24; 2Ch 21:13

34 So Benaiah son of Jehoiada
went up and struck down Joab
and killed him, and he was buried
at his home out in the country.
35 The king put Benaiah son of Jehoiada over the army in Joab's position and replaced Abiathar with
Zadok the priest. 1Ki 4:4; 1Ch 29:22

36 Then the king sent for Shimei
and said to him, "Build yourself a
house in Jerusalem and live there,
but do not go anywhere else. 37 The
day you leave and cross the Kidron Valley, you can be sure you
will die; your blood will be on your
own head." 2Sa 1:16; 15:23

38 Shimei answered the king,
"What you say is good. Your servant will do as my lord the king
has said." And Shimei stayed in
Jerusalem for a long time.

39 But three years later, two of
Shimei's slaves ran off to Achish
son of Maakah, king of Gath, and
Shimei was told, "Your slaves are
in Gath." 40 At this, he saddled his
donkey and went to Achish at Gath
in search of his slaves. So Shimei
went away and brought the slaves
back from Gath. 1Sa 27:2

41 When Solomon was told that
Shimei had gone from Jerusalem
to Gath and had returned, 42 the
king summoned Shimei and said
to him, "Did I not make you swear
by the LORD and warn you, 'On the
day you leave to go anywhere else,
you can be sure you will die'? At
that time you said to me, 'What
you say is good. I will obey.' 43 Why
then did you not keep your oath to
the LORD and obey the command I
gave you?"

44 The king also said to Shimei,
"You know in your heart all the
wrong you did to my father David. Now the LORD will repay you
for your wrongdoing. 45 But King

Solomon will be blessed, and David's throne will remain secure before the LORD forever."

2Sa 7:13; 16:5-13; Pr 25:5

46Then the king gave the order to Benaiah son of Jehoiada, and he went out and struck Shimei down and he died.

The kingdom was now established in Solomon's hands.

ver 12; 2Ch 1:1

Solomon Asks for Wisdom

3 Solomon made an alliance with Pharaoh king of Egypt and married his daughter. He brought her to the City of David until he finished building his palace and the temple of the LORD, and the wall around Jerusalem.
2The people, however, were still sacrificing at the high places, because a temple had not yet been built for the Name of the LORD.
3Solomon showed his love for the LORD by walking according to the instructions given him by his father David, except that he offered sacrifices and burned incense on the high places.

Dt 6:5; 12:2,4-5; 1Ki 2:3

4The king went to Gibeon to offer sacrifices, for that was the most important high place, and Solomon offered a thousand burnt offerings on that altar.
5At Gibeon the LORD appeared to Solomon during the night in a dream, and God said, "Ask for whatever you want me to give you."

Nu 12:6; 1Ki 9:2; 1Ch 16:39

6Solomon answered, "You have shown great kindness to your servant, my father David, because he was faithful to you and righteous and upright in heart. You have continued this great kindness to him and have given him a son to sit on his throne this very day.

1Ki 1:48; 2:4; 9:4

7"Now, LORD my God, you have made your servant king in place of my father David. But I am only a little child and do not know how to carry out my duties.
8Your servant is here among the people you have chosen, a great people, too numerous to count or number.
9So give your servant a discerning heart to govern your people and to distinguish between right and wrong. For who is able to govern this great people of yours?"

Nu 27:17; Pr 2:3-9; Jas 1:5

10The Lord was pleased that Solomon had asked for this.
11So God said to him, "Since you have asked for this and not for long life or wealth for yourself, nor have asked for the death of your enemies but for discernment in administering justice,
12I will do what you have asked. I will give you a wise and discerning heart, so that there will never have been anyone like you, nor will there ever be.
13Moreover, I will give you what you have not asked for — both wealth and honor — so that in your lifetime you will have no equal among kings.
14And if you walk in obedience to

me and keep my decrees and commands as David your father did, I will give you a long life." 15 Then Solomon awoke — and he realized it had been a dream.

1Ki 4:20-34; Pr 3:1-2,16; Jas 4:3

He returned to Jerusalem, stood before the ark of the Lord's covenant and sacrificed burnt offerings and fellowship offerings. Then he gave a feast for all his court. 2Ch 1:2-13; 1Ki 8:65

A Wise Ruling

16 Now two prostitutes came to the king and stood before him. 17 One of them said, "Pardon me, my lord. This woman and I live in the same house, and I had a baby while she was there with me. 18 The third day after my child was born, this woman also had a baby. We were alone; there was no one in the house but the two of us.

19 "During the night this woman's son died because she lay on him. 20 So she got up in the middle of the night and took my son from my side while I your servant was asleep. She put him by her breast and put her dead son by my breast. 21 The next morning, I got up to nurse my son — and he was dead! But when I looked at him closely in the morning light, I saw that it wasn't the son I had borne."

22 The other woman said, "No! The living one is my son; the dead one is yours."

But the first one insisted, "No! The dead one is yours; the living one is mine." And so they argued before the king.

23 The king said, "This one says, 'My son is alive and your son is dead,' while that one says, 'No! Your son is dead and mine is alive.'"

24 Then the king said, "Bring me a sword." So they brought a sword for the king. 25 He then gave an order: "Cut the living child in two and give half to one and half to the other."

26 The woman whose son was alive was deeply moved out of love for her son and said to the king, "Please, my lord, give her the living baby! Don't kill him!"

Ge 43:30; Isa 49:15; Jer 31:20

But the other said, "Neither I nor you shall have him. Cut him in two!"

27 Then the king gave his ruling: "Give the living baby to the first woman. Do not kill him; she is his mother."

28 When all Israel heard the verdict the king had given, they held the king in awe, because they saw that he had wisdom from God to administer justice. ver 9,11-12; Col 2:3

Solomon's Officials and Governors

4 So King Solomon ruled over all Israel. 2 And these were his chief officials:

Azariah son of Zadok — the priest; 1Ch 6:10

3 Elihoreph and Ahijah, sons of Shisha — secretaries;
Jehoshaphat son of Ahilud — recorder; 2Sa 8:16
4 Benaiah son of Jehoiada — commander in chief; 1Ki 2:35
Zadok and Abiathar — priests; 1Ki 2:27
5 Azariah son of Nathan — in charge of the district governors;
Zabud son of Nathan — a priest and adviser to the king;
6 Ahishar — palace administrator;
Adoniram son of Abda — in charge of forced labor.

7 Solomon had twelve district
governors over all Israel, who
supplied provisions for the king
and the royal household. Each
one had to provide supplies for
one month in the year. 8 These are
their names:

Ben-Hur — in the hill country of Ephraim; Jos 24:33
9 Ben-Deker — in Makaz, Shaalbim, Beth Shemesh and Elon Bethhanan; Jdg 1:35; Jos 21:16
10 Ben-Hesed — in Arubboth (Sokoh and all the land of Hepher were his); Jos 12:17; 15:35
11 Ben-Abinadab — in Naphoth Dor (he was married to Taphath daughter of Solomon); Jos 11:2
12 Baana son of Ahilud — in Taanach and Megiddo, and in all of Beth Shan next to Zarethan below Jezreel, from Beth Shan to Abel Meholah across to Jokmeam; Jos 17:11; 1Ki 19:16; 1Ch 6:68
13 Ben-Geber — in Ramoth Gilead (the settlements of Jair son of Manasseh in Gilead were his, as well as the region of Argob in Bashan and its sixty large walled cities with bronze gate bars); Nu 32:41; Dt 3:4
14 Ahinadab son of Iddo — in Mahanaim; Jos 13:26
15 Ahimaaz — in Naphtali (he had married Basemath daughter of Solomon); 2Sa 15:27
16 Baana son of Hushai — in Asher and in Aloth; 2Sa 15:32
17 Jehoshaphat son of Paruah — in Issachar;
18 Shimei son of Ela — in Benjamin; 1Ki 1:8
19 Geber son of Uri — in Gilead (the country of Sihon king of the Amorites and the country of Og king of Bashan). He was the only governor over the district. Dt 3:8-10

Solomon's Daily Provisions

20 The people of Judah and Israel
were as numerous as the sand on
the seashore; they ate, they drank
and they were happy. 21 And Solomon ruled over all the kingdoms
from the Euphrates River to the

land of the Philistines, as far as the border of Egypt. These countries brought tribute and were Solomon's subjects all his life.

2Ch 9:26; Ps 72:8; Ge 15:18

22Solomon's daily provisions were thirty cors[a] of the finest flour and sixty cors[b] of meal, 23ten head of stall-fed cattle, twenty of pasture-fed cattle and a hundred sheep and goats, as well as deer, gazelles, roebucks and choice fowl. 24For he ruled over all the kingdoms west of the Euphrates River, from Tiphsah to Gaza, and had peace on all sides. 25During Solomon's lifetime Judah and Israel, from Dan to Beersheba, lived in safety, everyone under their own vine and under their own fig tree.

Jer 23:6; Mic 4:4; Zec 3:10

26Solomon had four[c] thousand stalls for chariot horses, and twelve thousand horses.[d]

1Ki 10:26; 2Ch 1:14

27The district governors, each in his month, supplied provisions for King Solomon and all who came to the king's table. They saw to it that nothing was lacking. 28They also brought to the proper place their quotas of barley and straw for the chariot horses and the other horses.

Solomon's Wisdom

29God gave Solomon wisdom and very great insight, and a breadth of understanding as measureless as the sand on the seashore. 30Solomon's wisdom was greater than the wisdom of all the people of the East, and greater than all the wisdom of Egypt. 31He was wiser than anyone else, including Ethan the Ezrahite—wiser than Heman, Kalkol and Darda, the sons of Mahol. And his fame spread to all the surrounding nations. 32He spoke three thousand proverbs and his songs numbered a thousand and five. 33He spoke about plant life, from the cedar of Lebanon to the hyssop that grows out of walls. He also spoke about animals and birds, reptiles and fish. 34From all nations people came to listen to Solomon's wisdom, sent by all the kings of the world, who had heard of his wisdom.[e]

1Ki 3:12; Pr 1:1; 2Ch 9:23

Preparations for Building the Temple

5[f] When Hiram king of Tyre heard that Solomon had been anointed king to succeed his father David, he sent his envoys to Solomon, because he had always been on friendly terms with David. 2Solomon sent back this message to Hiram:

2Sa 5:11

3"You know that because of the wars waged against my

[a] 22 That is, probably about 5 1/2 tons or about 5 metric tons [b] 22 That is, probably about 11 tons or about 10 metric tons [c] 26 Some Septuagint manuscripts (see also 2 Chron. 9:25); Hebrew *forty* [d] 26 Or *charioteers* [e] 34 In Hebrew texts 4:21-34 is numbered 5:1-14. [f] In Hebrew texts 5:1-18 is numbered 5:15-32.

father David from all sides,
he could not build a temple
for the Name of the LORD his
God until the LORD put his
enemies under his feet. 4But
now the LORD my God has
given me rest on every side,
and there is no adversary
or disaster. 5I intend, therefore, to build a temple for the
Name of the LORD my God, as
the LORD told my father David, when he said, 'Your son
whom I will put on the throne
in your place will build the
temple for my Name.'

2Sa 7:13; 1Ch 17:12; 22:9

6"So give orders that cedars
of Lebanon be cut for me. My
men will work with yours,
and I will pay you for your
men whatever wages you set.
You know that we have no
one so skilled in felling timber as the Sidonians."

7When Hiram heard Solomon's
message, he was greatly pleased
and said, "Praise be to the LORD today, for he has given David a wise
son to rule over this great nation."
8So Hiram sent word to Solomon:

"I have received the mes-
sage you sent me and will do
all you want in providing the
cedar and juniper logs. 9My
men will haul them down
from Lebanon to the Medi-
terranean Sea, and I will float
them as rafts by sea to the
place you specify. There I will
separate them and you can
take them away. And you are
to grant my wish by providing food for my royal household." Ezr 3:7; Eze 27:17; Ac 12:20

10In this way Hiram kept Solomon supplied with all the cedar
and juniper logs he wanted, 11and
Solomon gave Hiram twenty thousand cors[a] of wheat as food for his
household, in addition to twenty
thousand baths[b,c] of pressed olive
oil. Solomon continued to do this
for Hiram year after year. 12The
LORD gave Solomon wisdom, just
as he had promised him. There
were peaceful relations between
Hiram and Solomon, and the two
of them made a treaty. 1Ki 3:12; Am 1:9

13King Solomon conscripted laborers from all Israel — thirty
thousand men. 14He sent them off
to Lebanon in shifts of ten thousand a month, so that they spent
one month in Lebanon and two
months at home. Adoniram was
in charge of the forced labor. 15Sol-
omon had seventy thousand carriers and eighty thousand stonecutters in the hills, 16as well as
thirty-three hundred[d] foremen
who supervised the project and

[a] *11* That is, probably about 3,600 tons or about 3,250 metric tons [b] *11* Septuagint (see also 2 Chron. 2:10); Hebrew *twenty cors* [c] *11* That is, about 120,000 gallons or about 440,000 liters [d] *16* Hebrew; some Septuagint manuscripts (see also 2 Chron. 2:2,18) *thirty-six hundred*

directed the workers. 17At the
king's command they removed
from the quarry large blocks of
high-grade stone to provide a
foundation of dressed stone for
the temple. 18The craftsmen of
Solomon and Hiram and workers
from Byblos cut and prepared the
timber and stone for the building
of the temple. 1Ki 4:6; 1Ch 22:2

Solomon Builds the Temple

6 In the four hundred and eight-
ieth[a] year after the Israelites
came out of Egypt, in the fourth
year of Solomon's reign over Israel, in the month of Ziv, the second
month, he began to build the temple of the LORD. Ac 7:47

2The temple that King Solomon
built for the LORD was sixty cubits long, twenty wide and thirty
high.[b] 3The portico at the front of
the main hall of the temple extended the width of the temple,
that is twenty cubits,[c] and project-
ed ten cubits[d] from the front of
the temple. 4He made narrow windows high up in the temple walls.
5Against the walls of the main hall
and inner sanctuary he built a
structure around the building, in
which there were side rooms. 6The
lowest floor was five cubits[e] wide,
the middle floor six cubits[f] and the
third floor seven.[g] He made offset
ledges around the outside of the
temple so that nothing would be
inserted into the temple walls.
Eze 40:16; 41:5-6

7In building the temple, only
blocks dressed at the quarry were
used, and no hammer, chisel or
any other iron tool was heard at
the temple site while it was being
built. Ex 20:25; Dt 27:5

8The entrance to the lowest[h]
floor was on the south side of the
temple; a stairway led up to the
middle level and from there to
the third. 9So he built the temple
and completed it, roofing it with
beams and cedar planks. 10And
he built the side rooms all along
the temple. The height of each
was five cubits, and they were attached to the temple by beams of
cedar. ver 14,38

11The word of the LORD came to
Solomon: 12"As for this temple you
are building, if you follow my decrees, observe my laws and keep
all my commands and obey them,
I will fulfill through you the promise I gave to David your father.
13And I will live among the Israelites and will not abandon my people Israel." Dt 31:6; 2Sa 7:12-16; 1Ki 9:5

14So Solomon built the temple
and completed it. 15He lined its

[a] *1* Hebrew; Septuagint *four hundred and fortieth* [b] *2* That is, about 90 feet long, 30 feet wide and 45 feet high or about 27 meters long, 9 meters wide and 14 meters high [c] *3* That is, about 30 feet or about 9 meters; also in verses 16 and 20 [d] *3* That is, about 15 feet or about 4.5 meters; also in verses 23-26 [e] *6* That is, about 7 1/2 feet or about 2.3 meters; also in verses 10 and 24 [f] *6* That is, about 9 feet or about 2.7 meters [g] *6* That is, about 11 feet or about 3.2 meters [h] *8* Septuagint; Hebrew *middle*

interior walls with cedar boards, paneling them from the floor of the temple to the ceiling, and covered the floor of the temple with planks of juniper. 16He partitioned off twenty cubits at the rear of the temple with cedar boards from floor to ceiling to form within the temple an inner sanctuary, the Most Holy Place. 17The main hall in front of this room was forty cubits[a] long. 18The inside of the temple was cedar, carved with gourds and open flowers. Everything was cedar; no stone was to be seen. Ex 26:33; Ps 74:6

19He prepared the inner sanctuary within the temple to set the ark of the covenant of the LORD there. 20The inner sanctuary was twenty cubits long, twenty wide and twenty high. He overlaid the inside with pure gold, and he also overlaid the altar of cedar. 21Solomon covered the inside of the temple with pure gold, and he extended gold chains across the front of the inner sanctuary, which was overlaid with gold. 22So he overlaid the whole interior with gold. He also overlaid with gold the altar that belonged to the inner sanctuary. 1Sa 3:3; Eze 41:3-4

23For the inner sanctuary he made a pair of cherubim out of olive wood, each ten cubits high. 24One wing of the first cherub was five cubits long, and the other wing five cubits—ten cubits from wing tip to wing tip. 25The second cherub also measured ten cubits, for the two cherubim were identical in size and shape. 26The height of each cherub was ten cubits. 27He placed the cherubim inside the innermost room of the temple, with their wings spread out. The wing of one cherub touched one wall, while the wing of the other touched the other wall, and their wings touched each other in the middle of the room. 28He overlaid the cherubim with gold. Ex 25:20; 37:1-9

29On the walls all around the temple, in both the inner and outer rooms, he carved cherubim, palm trees and open flowers. 30He also covered the floors of both the inner and outer rooms of the temple with gold. 2Ch 3:1-14

31For the entrance to the inner sanctuary he made doors out of olive wood that were one fifth of the width of the sanctuary. 32And on the two olive-wood doors he carved cherubim, palm trees and open flowers, and overlaid the cherubim and palm trees with hammered gold. 33In the same way, for the entrance to the main hall he made doorframes out of olive wood that were one fourth of the width of the hall. 34He also made two doors out of juniper wood, each having two leaves that turned in sockets. 35He carved cherubim, palm trees and open flowers on them and overlaid

[a] 17 That is, about 60 feet or about 18 meters

them with gold hammered evenly
over the carvings.
36 And he built the inner courtyard of three courses of dressed
stone and one course of trimmed
cedar beams. 1Ki 7:12; Ezr 6:4
37 The foundation of the temple
of the LORD was laid in the fourth
year, in the month of Ziv. 38 In the
eleventh year in the month of Bul,
the eighth month, the temple was
finished in all its details according
to its specifications. He had spent
seven years building it. Heb 8:5

Solomon Builds His Palace

7 It took Solomon thirteen years,
however, to complete the construction of his palace. 2 He built
the Palace of the Forest of Lebanon a hundred cubits long, fifty
wide and thirty high,[a] with four
rows of cedar columns supporting trimmed cedar beams. 3 It was
roofed with cedar above the beams
that rested on the columns — forty-five beams, fifteen to a row. 4 Its
windows were placed high in sets
of three, facing each other. 5 All the
doorways had rectangular frames;
they were in the front part in sets
of three, facing each other.[b]
1Ki 9:10; 10:17; 2Ch 8:1
6 He made a colonnade fifty cubits long and thirty wide.[c] In front
of it was a portico, and in front of
that were pillars and an overhanging roof.
7 He built the throne hall, the
Hall of Justice, where he was to
judge, and he covered it with cedar from floor to ceiling.[d] 8 And
the palace in which he was to live,
set farther back, was similar in design. Solomon also made a palace
like this hall for Pharaoh's daughter, whom he had married.
1Ki 3:1; 6:15; 2Ch 8:11
9 All these structures, from the
outside to the great courtyard
and from foundation to eaves,
were made of blocks of high-grade
stone cut to size and smoothed on
their inner and outer faces. 10 The
foundations were laid with large
stones of good quality, some measuring ten cubits[e] and some eight.[f]
11 Above were high-grade stones,
cut to size, and cedar beams. 12 The
great courtyard was surrounded by a wall of three courses of
dressed stone and one course of
trimmed cedar beams, as was the
inner courtyard of the temple of
the LORD with its portico. 1Ki 6:36

The Temple's Furnishings

13 King Solomon sent to Tyre and
brought Huram,[g] 14 whose mother was a widow from the tribe of

[a] *2* That is, about 150 feet long, 75 feet wide and 45 feet high or about 45 meters long, 23 meters wide and 14 meters high
[b] *5* The meaning of the Hebrew for this verse is uncertain.
[c] *6* That is, about 75 feet long and 45 feet wide or about 23 meters long and 14 meters wide
[d] *7* Vulgate and Syriac; Hebrew *floor*
[e] *10* That is, about 15 feet or about 4.5 meters; also in verse 23
[f] *10* That is, about 12 feet or about 3.6 meters
[g] *13* Hebrew *Hiram*, a variant of *Huram*; also in verses 40 and 45

Naphtali and whose father was
from Tyre and a skilled craftsman
in bronze. Huram was filled with
wisdom, with understanding and
with knowledge to do all kinds
of bronze work. He came to King
Solomon and did all the work assigned to him. Ex 31:2-5; 2Ch 2:14; 4:11-16
15 He cast two bronze pillars, each
eighteen cubits high and twelve
cubits in circumference.[a] 16 He also
made two capitals of cast bronze
to set on the tops of the pillars;
each capital was five cubits[b] high.
17 A network of interwoven chains
adorned the capitals on top of the
pillars, seven for each capital. 18 He
made pomegranates in two rows[c]
encircling each network to decorate
the capitals on top of the pillars.[d]
He did the same for each capital.
19 The capitals on top of the pillars
in the portico were in the shape of
lilies, four cubits[e] high. 20 On the
capitals of both pillars, above the
bowl-shaped part next to the network, were the two hundred pomegranates in rows all around. 21 He
erected the pillars at the portico of
the temple. The pillar to the south
he named Jakin[f] and the one to the
north Boaz.[g] 22 The capitals on top
were in the shape of lilies. And so
the work on the pillars was completed. 2Ki 25:17; 2Ch 3:16-17; 4:13
23 He made the Sea of cast metal, circular in shape, measuring
ten cubits from rim to rim and
five cubits high. It took a line of
thirty cubits[h] to measure around
it. 24 Below the rim, gourds encircled it — ten to a cubit. The gourds
were cast in two rows in one piece
with the Sea. 2Ki 25:13; 1Ch 18:8; Jer 52:17
25 The Sea stood on twelve bulls,
three facing north, three facing
west, three facing south and three
facing east. The Sea rested on top
of them, and their hindquarters
were toward the center. 26 It was a
handbreadth[i] in thickness, and its
rim was like the rim of a cup, like
a lily blossom. It held two thousand baths.[j] 2Ch 4:2-5; Jer 52:20
27 He also made ten movable
stands of bronze; each was four
cubits long, four wide and three
high.[k] 28 This is how the stands
were made: They had side panels attached to uprights. 29 On the
panels between the uprights were
lions, bulls and cherubim — and

[a] *15* That is, about 27 feet high and 18 feet in circumference or about 8.1 meters high and 5.4 meters in circumference
[b] *16* That is, about 7 1/2 feet or about 2.3 meters; also in verse 23
[c] *18* Two Hebrew manuscripts and Septuagint; most Hebrew manuscripts *made the pillars, and there were two rows*
[d] *18* Many Hebrew manuscripts and Syriac; most Hebrew manuscripts *pomegranates*
[e] *19* That is, about 6 feet or about 1.8 meters; also in verse 38
[f] *21* *Jakin* probably means *he establishes.*
[g] *21* *Boaz* probably means *in him is strength.*
[h] *23* That is, about 45 feet or about 14 meters
[i] *26* That is, about 3 inches or about 7.5 centimeters
[j] *26* That is, about 12,000 gallons or about 44,000 liters; the Septuagint does not have this sentence.
[k] *27* That is, about 6 feet long and wide and about 4 1/2 feet high or about 1.8 meters long and wide and 1.4 meters high

on the uprights as well. Above
and below the lions and bulls
were wreaths of hammered work.
30 Each stand had four bronze
wheels with bronze axles, and
each had a basin resting on four
supports, cast with wreaths on
each side. 31 On the inside of the
stand there was an opening that
had a circular frame one cubit[a]
deep. This opening was round, and
with its basework it measured a
cubit and a half.[b] Around its opening there was engraving. The panels of the stands were square, not
round. 32 The four wheels were under the panels, and the axles of the
wheels were attached to the stand.
The diameter of each wheel was a
cubit and a half. 33 The wheels were
made like chariot wheels; the axles, rims, spokes and hubs were all
of cast metal. 2Ki 16:17; 2Ch 4:14

34 Each stand had four handles,
one on each corner, projecting
from the stand. 35 At the top of the
stand there was a circular band
half a cubit[c] deep. The supports
and panels were attached to the
top of the stand. 36 He engraved
cherubim, lions and palm trees on
the surfaces of the supports and
on the panels, in every available
space, with wreaths all around.
37 This is the way he made the ten
stands. They were all cast in the
same molds and were identical in
size and shape.

38 He then made ten bronze basins, each holding forty baths[d]
and measuring four cubits across,
one basin to go on each of the
ten stands. 39 He placed five of the
stands on the south side of the
temple and five on the north. He
placed the Sea on the south side, at
the southeast corner of the temple.
40 He also made the pots[e] and shovels and sprinkling bowls. 2Ch 4:6

So Huram finished all the work he had undertaken for King Solomon in the temple of the LORD:

41 the two pillars;
the two bowl-shaped capitals on top of the pillars;
the two sets of network decorating the two bowl-shaped capitals on top of the pillars;
42 the four hundred pomegranates for the two sets of network (two rows of pomegranates for each network decorating the bowl-shaped capitals on top of the pillars); ver 20
43 the ten stands with their ten basins;
44 the Sea and the twelve bulls under it;
45 the pots, shovels and sprinkling bowls. Ex 27:3

[a] *31* That is, about 18 inches or about 45 centimeters [b] *31* That is, about 2 1/4 feet or about 68 centimeters; also in verse 32 [c] *35* That is, about 9 inches or about 23 centimeters [d] *38* That is, about 240 gallons or about 880 liters [e] *40* Many Hebrew manuscripts, Septuagint, Syriac and Vulgate (see also verse 45 and 2 Chron. 4:11); many other Hebrew manuscripts *basins*

All these objects that Huram
made for King Solomon for the
temple of the LORD were of burnished bronze. 46The king had
them cast in clay molds in the
plain of the Jordan between Sukkoth and Zarethan. 47Solomon
left all these things unweighed,
because there were so many; the
weight of the bronze was not determined. 1Ch 22:3

48Solomon also made all the furnishings that were in the LORD's
temple:

the golden altar;
the golden table on which was the bread of the Presence; Ex 25:30; 37:10
49the lampstands of pure gold (five on the right and five on the left, in front of the inner sanctuary); Ex 25:31-38
the gold floral work and lamps and tongs;
50the pure gold basins, wick trimmers, sprinkling bowls, dishes and censers; 2Ki 25:13
and the gold sockets for the doors of the innermost room, the Most Holy Place, and also for the doors of the main hall of the temple.

51When all the work King Solomon had done for the temple of
the LORD was finished, he brought
in the things his father David had
dedicated — the silver and gold
and the furnishings — and he
placed them in the treasuries of
the LORD's temple.
2Ch 4:6,10-5:1; 2Sa 8:11

The Ark Brought to the Temple

8 Then King Solomon sum-
moned into his presence at Jerusalem the elders of Israel, all the
heads of the tribes and the chiefs
of the Israelite families, to bring
up the ark of the LORD's covenant
from Zion, the City of David. 2All
the Israelites came together to
King Solomon at the time of the
festival in the month of Ethanim,
the seventh month.
Lev 23:34; 2Sa 5:7; 6:17

3When all the elders of Israel had arrived, the priests took
up the ark, 4and they brought up
the ark of the LORD and the tent
of meeting and all the sacred furnishings in it. The priests and Levites carried them up, 5and King
Solomon and the entire assembly
of Israel that had gathered about
him were before the ark, sacrificing so many sheep and cattle
that they could not be recorded or
counted. 2Sa 6:13; 2Ch 1:3

6The priests then brought the ark
of the LORD's covenant to its place
in the inner sanctuary of the temple, the Most Holy Place, and put
it beneath the wings of the cherubim. 7The cherubim spread their
wings over the place of the ark and
overshadowed the ark and its carrying poles. 8These poles were so
long that their ends could be seen

from the Holy Place in front of the
inner sanctuary, but not from outside the Holy Place; and they are
still there today. 9There was nothing in the ark except the two stone
tablets that Moses had placed in it
at Horeb, where the LORD made a
covenant with the Israelites after
they came out of Egypt.
Ex 25:13-15,21; Dt 10:2-5; 1Ki 6:19,27

10When the priests withdrew
from the Holy Place, the cloud
filled the temple of the LORD.
11And the priests could not perform their service because of the
cloud, for the glory of the LORD
filled his temple. Ex 40:34-35

12Then Solomon said, "The LORD
has said that he would dwell in a
dark cloud; 13I have indeed built
a magnificent temple for you, a
place for you to dwell forever."
Ps 132:13

14While the whole assembly of
Israel was standing there, the king
turned around and blessed them.
15Then he said: 2Sa 6:18

"Praise be to the LORD, the
God of Israel, who with his
own hand has fulfilled what
he promised with his own
mouth to my father David.
For he said, 16'Since the day I
brought my people Israel out
of Egypt, I have not chosen a
city in any tribe of Israel to
have a temple built so that my
Name might be there, but I
have chosen David to rule my
people Israel.' 1Sa 16:1; Lk 1:68

17"My father David had it in
his heart to build a temple for
the Name of the LORD, the God
of Israel. 18But the LORD said
to my father David, 'You did
well to have it in your heart to
build a temple for my Name.
19Nevertheless, you are not
the one to build the temple,
but your son, your own flesh
and blood — he is the one
who will build the temple for
my Name.' 2Sa 7:2,5,13; 1Ki 5:3,5

20"The LORD has kept the
promise he made: I have succeeded David my father and
now I sit on the throne of Israel, just as the LORD promised,
and I have built the temple
for the Name of the LORD, the
God of Israel. 21I have provided a place there for the ark, in
which is the covenant of the
LORD that he made with our
ancestors when he brought
them out of Egypt." 1Ch 28:6

Solomon's Prayer of Dedication

22Then Solomon stood before
the altar of the LORD in front of
the whole assembly of Israel,
spread out his hands toward heav-
en 23and said: Ezr 9:5

"LORD, the God of Isra-
el, there is no God like you
in heaven above or on earth
below — you who keep your
covenant of love with your
servants who continue
wholeheartedly in your way.

24 You have kept your promise to your servant David my father; with your mouth you have promised and with your hand you have fulfilled it — as it is today. Dt 7:9,12; Ne 1:5; 9:32

25 "Now LORD, the God of Israel, keep for your servant David my father the promises you made to him when you said, 'You shall never fail to have a successor to sit before me on the throne of Israel, if only your descendants are careful in all they do to walk before me faithfully as you have done.' 26 And now, God of Israel, let your word that you promised your servant David my father come true.

2Sa 7:25; 1Ki 2:4

27 "But will God really dwell on earth? The heavens, even the highest heaven, cannot contain you. How much less this temple I have built! 28 Yet give attention to your servant's prayer and his plea for mercy, LORD my God. Hear the cry and the prayer that your servant is praying in your presence this day. 29 May your eyes be open toward this temple night and day, this place of which you said, 'My Name shall be there,' so that you will hear the prayer your servant prays toward this place. 30 Hear the supplication of your servant and of your people Israel when they pray toward this place. Hear from heaven, your dwelling place, and when you hear, forgive.

Dt 12:11; 2Ch 2:6; Isa 66:1

31 "When anyone wrongs their neighbor and is required to take an oath and they come and swear the oath before your altar in this temple, 32 then hear from heaven and act. Judge between your servants, condemning the guilty by bringing down on their heads what they have done, and vindicating the innocent by treating them in accordance with their innocence. Ex 22:11; Dt 25:1

33 "When your people Israel have been defeated by an enemy because they have sinned against you, and when they turn back to you and give praise to your name, praying and making supplication to you in this temple, 34 then hear from heaven and forgive the sin of your people Israel and bring them back to the land you gave to their ancestors. Lev 26:17; Dt 28:25

35 "When the heavens are shut up and there is no rain because your people have sinned against you, and when they pray toward this place and give praise to your name and turn from their sin because you have afflicted them, 36 then hear from heaven and forgive the sin of your

servants, your people Israel. Teach them the right way
to live, and send rain on the
land you gave your people for
an inheritance.
Lev 26:19; 1Sa 12:23; Ps 27:11
37“When famine or plague
comes to the land, or blight
or mildew, locusts or grasshoppers, or when an ene-
my besieges them in any
of their cities, whatever disaster or disease may come,
38and when a prayer or plea is
made by anyone among your
people Israel — being aware
of the afflictions of their
own hearts, and spreading
out their hands toward this
temple — 39then hear from
heaven, your dwelling place.
Forgive and act; deal with everyone according to all they
do, since you know their
hearts (for you alone know
every human heart), 40so that
they will fear you all the time
they live in the land you gave
our ancestors.
1Sa 16:7; 1Ch 28:9; Ps 11:4
41“As for the foreigner who
does not belong to your people Israel but has come from
a distant land because of
your name — 42for they will
hear of your great name and
your mighty hand and your
outstretched arm — when
they come and pray toward
this temple, 43then hear from
heaven, your dwelling place.
Do whatever the foreigner
asks of you, so that all the peoples of the earth may know
your name and fear you, as do
your own people Israel, and
may know that this house I
have built bears your Name.
Dt 3:24; 1Sa 17:46; Ps 102:15
44“When your people go to
war against their enemies,
wherever you send them,
and when they pray to the
LORD toward the city you
have chosen and the temple
I have built for your Name,
45then hear from heaven their
prayer and their plea, and uphold their cause. Ps 9:4; 140:12
46“When they sin against
you — for there is no one who
does not sin — and you become angry with them and
give them over to their enemies, who take them captive
to their own lands, far away
or near; 47and if they have a
change of heart in the land
where they are held captive,
and repent and plead with
you in the land of their captors and say, ‘We have sinned,
we have done wrong, we have
acted wickedly’; 48and if they
turn back to you with all their
heart and soul in the land of
their enemies who took them
captive, and pray to you toward the land you gave their
ancestors, toward the city you
have chosen and the temple
I have built for your Name;

49then from heaven, your
dwelling place, hear their
prayer and their plea, and uphold their cause. 50And forgive
your people, who have sinned
against you; forgive all the offenses they have committed
against you, and cause their
captors to show them mercy;
51for they are your people and
your inheritance, whom you
brought out of Egypt, out of
that iron-smelting furnace.

Dt 9:29; Ps 106:6; Da 6:10

52"May your eyes be open to
your servant's plea and to the
plea of your people Israel, and
may you listen to them whenever they cry out to you. 53For
you singled them out from
all the nations of the world to
be your own inheritance, just
as you declared through your
servant Moses when you, Sovereign LORD, brought our ancestors out of Egypt."

2Ch 6:12-40; Ex 19:5

54When Solomon had finished
all these prayers and supplications to the LORD, he rose from before the altar of the LORD, where
he had been kneeling with his
hands spread out toward heaven.
55He stood and blessed the whole
assembly of Israel in a loud voice,
saying: ver 14; 2Sa 6:18

56"Praise be to the LORD,
who has given rest to his
people Israel just as he promised. Not one word has failed
of all the good promises he
gave through his servant Moses. 57May the LORD our God
be with us as he was with
our ancestors; may he never
leave us nor forsake us. 58May
he turn our hearts to him, to
walk in obedience to him and
keep the commands, decrees
and laws he gave our ancestors. 59And may these words
of mine, which I have prayed
before the LORD, be near to
the LORD our God day and
night, that he may uphold
the cause of his servant and
the cause of his people Israel
according to each day's need,
60so that all the peoples of
the earth may know that the
LORD is God and that there
is no other. 61And may your
hearts be fully committed to
the LORD our God, to live by
his decrees and obey his commands, as at this time."

1Ki 11:4; Ps 119:36; Heb 13:5

The Dedication of the Temple

62Then the king and all Israel
with him offered sacrifices before
the LORD. 63Solomon offered a sacrifice of fellowship offerings to the
LORD: twenty-two thousand cattle
and a hundred and twenty thousand sheep and goats. So the king
and all the Israelites dedicated the
temple of the LORD.

64On that same day the king
consecrated the middle part of the
courtyard in front of the temple

of the LORD, and there he offered
burnt offerings, grain offerings
and the fat of the fellowship offerings, because the bronze altar
that stood before the LORD was too
small to hold the burnt offerings,
the grain offerings and the fat of
the fellowship offerings. 2Ch 4:1

65So Solomon observed the festival at that time, and all Israel
with him — a vast assembly, people from Lebo Hamath to the Wadi
of Egypt. They celebrated it before the LORD our God for seven
days and seven days more, fourteen days in all. 66On the following
day he sent the people away. They
blessed the king and then went
home, joyful and glad in heart for
all the good things the LORD had
done for his servant David and his
people Israel. 2Ch 7:1-10; Ge 15:18; Nu 34:8

The LORD Appears to Solomon

9 When Solomon had finished
building the temple of the
LORD and the royal palace, and
had achieved all he had desired to
do, 2the LORD appeared to him a
second time, as he had appeared
to him at Gibeon. 3The LORD said
to him: 1Ki 3:5

"I have heard the prayer
and plea you have made before me; I have consecrated
this temple, which you have
built, by putting my Name
there forever. My eyes and my
heart will always be there.
Dt 11:12; 1Ki 8:29; 2Ki 20:5

4"As for you, if you walk before me faithfully with integrity of heart and uprightness,
as David your father did, and
do all I command and ob-
serve my decrees and laws,
5I will establish your royal
throne over Israel forever, as
I promised David your father
when I said, 'You shall never
fail to have a successor on the
throne of Israel.'
1Ki 2:4; 15:5; 1Ch 22:10

6"But if you[a] or your descendants turn away from me and
do not observe the commands
and decrees I have given you[a]
and go off to serve other gods
and worship them, 7then I will
cut off Israel from the land I
have given them and will reject this temple I have consecrated for my Name. Israel will
then become a byword and
an object of ridicule among
all peoples. 8This temple will
become a heap of rubble. All[b]
who pass by will be appalled
and will scoff and say, 'Why
has the LORD done such a
thing to this land and to this
temple?' 9People will answer,
'Because they have forsak-
en the LORD their God, who
brought their ancestors out
of Egypt, and have embraced
other gods, worshiping and

[a] 6 The Hebrew is plural. [b] 8 See some Septuagint manuscripts, Old Latin, Syriac, Arabic and Targum; Hebrew *And though this temple is now imposing, all*

serving them — that is why
the LORD brought all this disaster on them.' "
2Ch 7:11-22; 2Ki 17:23; Jer 7:14

Solomon's Other Activities

10 At the end of twenty years,
during which Solomon built these
two buildings — the temple of
the LORD and the royal palace —
11 King Solomon gave twenty towns
in Galilee to Hiram king of Tyre,
because Hiram had supplied him
with all the cedar and juniper and
gold he wanted. 12 But when Hiram
went from Tyre to see the towns
that Solomon had given him,
he was not pleased with them.
13 "What kind of towns are these
you have given me, my brother?"
he asked. And he called them the
Land of Kabul,[a] a name they have
to this day. 14 Now Hiram had sent
to the king 120 talents[b] of gold.
Jos 19:27; 2Ch 8:2

15 Here is the account of the
forced labor King Solomon conscripted to build the LORD's temple, his own palace, the terraces,[c]
the wall of Jerusalem, and Hazor, Megiddo and Gezer. 16 (Pharaoh king of Egypt had attacked
and captured Gezer. He had set
it on fire. He killed its Canaanite
inhabitants and then gave it as a
wedding gift to his daughter, Solomon's wife. 17 And Solomon rebuilt
Gezer.) He built up Lower Beth
Horon, 18 Baalath, and Tadmor[d]
in the desert, within his land, 19 as
well as all his store cities and the
towns for his chariots and for his
horses[e] — whatever he desired to
build in Jerusalem, in Lebanon
and throughout all the territory
he ruled.
2Sa 5:9; 1Ki 4:26; 5:13

20 There were still people left
from the Amorites, Hittites, Perizzites, Hivites and Jebusites (these
peoples were not Israelites). 21 Solomon conscripted the descendants
of all these peoples remaining in
the land — whom the Israelites
could not exterminate[f] — to serve
as slave labor, as it is to this day.
22 But Solomon did not make slaves
of any of the Israelites; they were
his fighting men, his government
officials, his officers, his captains,
and the commanders of his chariots and charioteers. 23 They were
also the chief officials in charge of
Solomon's projects — 550 officials
supervising those who did the
work.
Lev 25:39; Jos 15:63; Ezr 2:55,58

24 After Pharaoh's daughter had
come up from the City of David to
the palace Solomon had built for
her, he constructed the terraces.
1Ki 3:1; 11:27; 2Ch 32:5

25 Three times a year Solomon
sacrificed burnt offerings and fellowship offerings on the altar he

[a] *13* *Kabul* sounds like the Hebrew for *good-for-nothing.* [b] *14* That is, about 4 1/2 tons or about 4 metric tons [c] *15* Or *the Millo*; also in verse 24 [d] *18* The Hebrew may also be read *Tamar.* [e] *19* Or *charioteers* [f] *21* The Hebrew term refers to the irrevocable giving over of things or persons to the LORD, often by totally destroying them.

had built for the LORD, burning incense before the LORD along with
them, and so fulfilled the temple
obligations. Ex 23:14; 2Ch 8:12-13,16

26 King Solomon also built ships
at Ezion Geber, which is near Elath
in Edom, on the shore of the Red
Sea.[a] 27 And Hiram sent his men —
sailors who knew the sea — to
serve in the fleet with Solomon's
men. 28 They sailed to Ophir and
brought back 420 talents[b] of gold,
which they delivered to King Solomon. Nu 33:35; 1Ki 10:11; 22:48

The Queen of Sheba Visits Solomon

10 When the queen of Sheba
heard about the fame of
Solomon and his relationship to
the LORD, she came to test Solomon with hard questions. 2 Arriving at Jerusalem with a very great
caravan — with camels carrying
spices, large quantities of gold,
and precious stones — she came
to Solomon and talked with him
about all that she had on her mind.
3 Solomon answered all her questions; nothing was too hard for
the king to explain to her. 4 When
the queen of Sheba saw all the wisdom of Solomon and the palace he
had built, 5 the food on his table,
the seating of his officials, the attending servants in their robes,
his cupbearers, and the burnt offerings he made at[c] the temple of
the LORD, she was overwhelmed.
Mt 12:42; Jdg 14:12; 1Ch 26:16

6 She said to the king, "The report I heard in my own country
about your achievements and
your wisdom is true. 7 But I did not
believe these things until I came
and saw with my own eyes. Indeed, not even half was told me;
in wisdom and wealth you have
far exceeded the report I heard.
8 How happy your people must
be! How happy your officials, who
continually stand before you and
hear your wisdom! 9 Praise be to
the LORD your God, who has delighted in you and placed you on
the throne of Israel. Because of
the LORD's eternal love for Israel,
he has made you king to maintain
justice and righteousness."
2Sa 8:15; Ps 72:2; Pr 8:34

10 And she gave the king 120 talents[d] of gold, large quantities of
spices, and precious stones. Never again were so many spices
brought in as those the queen of
Sheba gave to King Solomon.
1Ki 9:28; Isa 60:6

11 (Hiram's ships brought gold
from Ophir; and from there they
brought great cargoes of almugwood[e] and precious stones. 12 The
king used the almugwood to
make supports[f] for the temple of
the LORD and for the royal palace,

[a] 26 Or *the Sea of Reeds* [b] 28 That is, about 16 tons or about 14 metric tons
[c] 5 Or *the ascent by which he went up to*
[d] 10 That is, about 4 1/2 tons or about 4 metric tons [e] 11 Probably a variant of *algumwood*; also in verse 12 [f] 12 The meaning of the Hebrew for this word is uncertain.

and to make harps and lyres for the musicians. So much almugwood has never been imported or seen since that day.) 1Ki 9:27-28

13King Solomon gave the queen of Sheba all she desired and asked for, besides what he had given her out of his royal bounty. Then she left and returned with her retinue to her own country. 2Ch 9:1-12

Solomon's Splendor

14The weight of the gold that Solomon received yearly was 666 talents,[a] 15not including the revenues from merchants and traders and from all the Arabian kings and the governors of the territories. 1Ki 9:28

16King Solomon made two hundred large shields of hammered gold; six hundred shekels[b] of gold went into each shield. 17He also made three hundred small shields of hammered gold, with three minas[c] of gold in each shield. The king put them in the Palace of the Forest of Lebanon. 1Ki 7:2; 14:26-28

18Then the king made a great throne covered with ivory and overlaid with fine gold. 19The throne had six steps, and its back had a rounded top. On both sides of the seat were armrests, with a lion standing beside each of them. 20Twelve lions stood on the six steps, one at either end of each step. Nothing like it had ever been made for any other kingdom. 21All King Solomon's goblets were gold, and all the household articles in the Palace of the Forest of Lebanon were pure gold. Nothing was made of silver, because silver was considered of little value in Solomon's days. 22The king had a fleet of trading ships[d] at sea along with the ships of Hiram. Once every three years it returned, carrying gold, silver and ivory, and apes and baboons. 1Ki 9:26; Isa 60:17

23King Solomon was greater in riches and wisdom than all the other kings of the earth. 24The whole world sought audience with Solomon to hear the wisdom God had put in his heart. 25Year after year, everyone who came brought a gift — articles of silver and gold, robes, weapons and spices, and horses and mules. 1Ki 3:13; 4:30

26Solomon accumulated chariots and horses; he had fourteen hundred chariots and twelve thousand horses,[e] which he kept in the chariot cities and also with him in Jerusalem. 27The king made silver as common in Jerusalem as stones, and cedar as plentiful as sycamore-fig trees in the foothills. 28Solomon's horses were imported from Egypt and from Kue[f] — the royal merchants

[a] *14* That is, about 25 tons or about 23 metric tons [b] *16* That is, about 15 pounds or about 6.9 kilograms; also in verse 29 [c] *17* That is, about 3 3/4 pounds or about 1.7 kilograms; or perhaps reference is to double minas, that is, about 7 1/2 pounds or about 3.5 kilograms. [d] *22* Hebrew *of ships of Tarshish* [e] *26* Or *charioteers* [f] *28* Probably *Cilicia*

purchased them from Kue at the current price. [29]They imported a chariot from Egypt for six hundred shekels of silver, and a horse for a hundred and fifty.[a] They also exported them to all the kings of the Hittites and of the Arameans.

2Ch 1:14-17; 9:13-28; 1Ki 4:26

Solomon's Wives

11 King Solomon, however, loved many foreign women besides Pharaoh's daughter — Moabites, Ammonites, Edomites, Sidonians and Hittites. [2]They were from nations about which the LORD had told the Israelites, "You must not intermarry with them, because they will surely turn your hearts after their gods." Nevertheless, Solomon held fast to them in love. [3]He had seven hundred wives of royal birth and three hundred concubines, and his wives led him astray. [4]As Solomon grew old, his wives turned his heart after other gods, and his heart was not fully devoted to the LORD his God, as the heart of David his father had been. [5]He followed Ashtoreth the goddess of the Sidonians, and Molek the detestable god of the Ammonites. [6]So Solomon did evil in the eyes of the LORD; he did not follow the LORD completely, as David his father had done.

Ne 13:26; Dt 7:3-4; Jdg 2:13

[7]On a hill east of Jerusalem, Solomon built a high place for Chemosh the detestable god of Moab, and for Molek the detestable god of the Ammonites. [8]He did the same for all his foreign wives, who burned incense and offered sacrifices to their gods.

Nu 21:29; Jdg 11:24; 2Ki 23:13

[9]The LORD became angry with Solomon because his heart had turned away from the LORD, the God of Israel, who had appeared to him twice. [10]Although he had forbidden Solomon to follow other gods, Solomon did not keep the LORD's command. [11]So the LORD said to Solomon, "Since this is your attitude and you have not kept my covenant and my decrees, which I commanded you, I will most certainly tear the kingdom away from you and give it to one of your subordinates. [12]Nevertheless, for the sake of David your father, I will not do it during your lifetime. I will tear it out of the hand of your son. [13]Yet I will not tear the whole kingdom from him, but will give him one tribe for the sake of David my servant and for the sake of Jerusalem, which I have chosen."

2Sa 7:15; 1Ki 12:15-16

Solomon's Adversaries

[14]Then the LORD raised up against Solomon an adversary, Hadad the Edomite, from the royal line of Edom. [15]Earlier when David was fighting with Edom, Joab

[a] 29 That is, about 3 3/4 pounds or about 1.7 kilograms

the commander of the army, who
had gone up to bury the dead,
had struck down all the men in
Edom. 16Joab and all the Israelites
stayed there for six months, until
they had destroyed all the men in
Edom. 17But Hadad, still only a boy,
fled to Egypt with some Edomite officials who had served his
father. 18They set out from Midian and went to Paran. Then taking people from Paran with them,
they went to Egypt, to Pharaoh
king of Egypt, who gave Hadad a
house and land and provided him
with food. 2Sa 8:14; 1Ch 18:12

19Pharaoh was so pleased with
Hadad that he gave him a sister
of his own wife, Queen Tahpenes,
in marriage. 20The sister of Tahpenes bore him a son named Genubath, whom Tahpenes brought
up in the royal palace. There Genubath lived with Pharaoh's own
children.

21While he was in Egypt, Hadad
heard that David rested with his
ancestors and that Joab the commander of the army was also dead.
Then Hadad said to Pharaoh, "Let
me go, that I may return to my
own country."

22"What have you lacked here
that you want to go back to your
own country?" Pharaoh asked.

"Nothing," Hadad replied, "but
do let me go!"

23And God raised up against Solomon another adversary, Rezon
son of Eliada, who had fled from
his master, Hadadezer king of Zobah. 24When David destroyed Zobah's army, Rezon gathered a band
of men around him and became
their leader; they went to Damascus, where they settled and took
control. 25Rezon was Israel's adversary as long as Solomon lived,
adding to the trouble caused by
Hadad. So Rezon ruled in Aram
and was hostile toward Israel.

2Sa 8:3; 10:8,18-19

Jeroboam Rebels Against Solomon

26Also, Jeroboam son of Nebat rebelled against the king. He
was one of Solomon's officials, an
Ephraimite from Zeredah, and his
mother was a widow named Zeruah. 2Sa 20:21; 1Ki 12:2; 2Ch 13:6

27Here is the account of how he
rebelled against the king: Solomon had built the terraces[a] and
had filled in the gap in the wall of
the city of David his father. 28Now
Jeroboam was a man of standing,
and when Solomon saw how well
the young man did his work, he
put him in charge of the whole labor force of the tribes of Joseph.

Ru 2:1; 1Ki 9:24; Pr 22:29

29About that time Jeroboam was
going out of Jerusalem, and Ahijah the prophet of Shiloh met him
on the way, wearing a new cloak.
The two of them were alone out
in the country, 30and Ahijah took
hold of the new cloak he was wearing and tore it into twelve pieces.

[a] 27 Or *the Millo*

31Then he said to Jeroboam, "Take
ten pieces for yourself, for this is
what the LORD, the God of Israel,
says: 'See, I am going to tear the
kingdom out of Solomon's hand
and give you ten tribes. 32But for
the sake of my servant David and
the city of Jerusalem, which I have
chosen out of all the tribes of Israel, he will have one tribe. 33I will
do this because they have[a] forsak-
en me and worshiped Ashtoreth
the goddess of the Sidonians, Chemosh the god of the Moabites, and
Molek the god of the Ammonites,
and have not walked in obedience
to me, nor done what is right in
my eyes, nor kept my decrees and
laws as David, Solomon's father,
did. 1Sa 15:27; 1Ki 3:3; 14:2

34" 'But I will not take the whole
kingdom out of Solomon's hand; I
have made him ruler all the days
of his life for the sake of David my
servant, whom I chose and who
obeyed my commands and decrees. 35I will take the kingdom
from his son's hands and give you
ten tribes. 36I will give one tribe to
his son so that David my servant
may always have a lamp before
me in Jerusalem, the city where I
chose to put my Name. 37However,
as for you, I will take you, and you
will rule over all that your heart
desires; you will be king over Israel. 38If you do whatever I command you and walk in obedience
to me and do what is right in my
eyes by obeying my decrees and
commands, as David my servant
did, I will be with you. I will build
you a dynasty as enduring as the
one I built for David and will give
Israel to you. 39I will humble David's descendants because of this,
but not forever.' "

Jos 1:5; 2Sa 7:11,27; 1Ki 15:4

40Solomon tried to kill Jeroboam, but Jeroboam fled to Egypt, to
Shishak the king, and stayed there
until Solomon's death. 2Ch 12:2

Solomon's Death

41As for the other events of Solomon's reign — all he did and the
wisdom he displayed — are they
not written in the book of the
annals of Solomon? 42Solomon
reigned in Jerusalem over all Israel forty years. 43Then he rested
with his ancestors and was buried
in the city of David his father. And
Rehoboam his son succeeded him
as king. 2Ch 9:29-31; Mt 1:7

Israel Rebels Against Rehoboam

12 Rehoboam went to Shechem, for all Israel had gone
there to make him king. 2When
Jeroboam son of Nebat heard this
(he was still in Egypt, where he
had fled from King Solomon), he
returned from[b] Egypt. 3So they
sent for Jeroboam, and he and the
whole assembly of Israel went to
Rehoboam and said to him: 4"Your
father put a heavy yoke on us, but
now lighten the harsh labor and

[a] 33 Hebrew; Septuagint, Vulgate and Syriac *because he has* [b] 2 Or *he remained in*

the heavy yoke he put on us, and
we will serve you."
1Sa 8:11-18; 1Ki 4:20-28; 11:40
[5]Rehoboam answered, "Go away
for three days and then come back
to me." So the people went away.
[6]Then King Rehoboam consulted the elders who had served his
father Solomon during his lifetime. "How would you advise me
to answer these people?" he asked.
1Ki 4:2
[7]They replied, "If today you will
be a servant to these people and
serve them and give them a favorable answer, they will always be
your servants." Pr 15:1
[8]But Rehoboam rejected the advice the elders gave him and consulted the young men who had
grown up with him and were serving him. [9]He asked them, "What is
your advice? How should we answer these people who say to me,
'Lighten the yoke your father put
on us'?"
[10]The young men who had
grown up with him replied, "These
people have said to you, 'Your father put a heavy yoke on us, but
make our yoke lighter.' Now tell
them, 'My little finger is thicker
than my father's waist. [11]My father
laid on you a heavy yoke; I will
make it even heavier. My father
scourged you with whips; I will
scourge you with scorpions.'"
[12]Three days later Jeroboam and
all the people returned to Rehoboam, as the king had said, "Come
back to me in three days." [13]The
king answered the people harshly. Rejecting the advice given him
by the elders, [14]he followed the
advice of the young men and said,
"My father made your yoke heavy;
I will make it even heavier. My father scourged you with whips; I
will scourge you with scorpions."
[15]So the king did not listen to the
people, for this turn of events was
from the LORD, to fulfill the word
the LORD had spoken to Jeroboam
son of Nebat through Ahijah the
Shilonite. Dt 2:30; 1Ki 11:29; 2Ch 25:20
[16]When all Israel saw that the
king refused to listen to them,
they answered the king:

"What share do we have in
David,
what part in Jesse's son?
To your tents, Israel! 2Sa 20:1
Look after your own house,
David!"

So the Israelites went home. [17]But
as for the Israelites who were living in the towns of Judah, Rehoboam still ruled over them.
1Ki 11:13,36
[18]King Rehoboam sent out Adoniram,[a] who was in charge of
forced labor, but all Israel stoned
him to death. King Rehoboam,
however, managed to get into his
chariot and escape to Jerusalem.
[19]So Israel has been in rebellion
against the house of David to this
day. 1Ki 4:6; 5:14; 2Ki 17:21

[a] *18* Some Septuagint manuscripts and Syriac (see also 4:6 and 5:14); Hebrew *Adoram*

20 When all the Israelites heard that Jeroboam had returned, they sent and called him to the assembly and made him king over all Israel. Only the tribe of Judah remained loyal to the house of David. 1Ki 11:13,32

21 When Rehoboam arrived in Jerusalem, he mustered all Judah and the tribe of Benjamin — a hundred and eighty thousand able young men — to go to war against Israel and to regain the kingdom for Rehoboam son of Solomon. 2Ch 11:1

22 But this word of God came to Shemaiah the man of God: 23 "Say to Rehoboam son of Solomon king of Judah, to all Judah and Benjamin, and to the rest of the people, 24 'This is what the LORD says: Do not go up to fight against your brothers, the Israelites. Go home, every one of you, for this is my doing.' " So they obeyed the word of the LORD and went home again, as the LORD had ordered. 2Ch 10:1-11:4

Golden Calves at Bethel and Dan

25 Then Jeroboam fortified Shechem in the hill country of Ephraim and lived there. From there he went out and built up Peniel.[a] Jdg 8:8,17; 9:45

26 Jeroboam thought to himself, "The kingdom will now likely revert to the house of David. 27 If these people go up to offer sacrifices at the temple of the LORD in Jerusalem, they will again give their allegiance to their lord, Rehoboam king of Judah. They will kill me and return to King Rehoboam." Dt 12:5-6

28 After seeking advice, the king made two golden calves. He said to the people, "It is too much for you to go up to Jerusalem. Here are your gods, Israel, who brought you up out of Egypt." 29 One he set up in Bethel, and the other in Dan. 30 And this thing became a sin; the people came to worship the one at Bethel and went as far as Dan to worship the other.[b] 1Ki 13:34; 2Ki 17:21

31 Jeroboam built shrines on high places and appointed priests from all sorts of people, even though they were not Levites. 32 He instituted a festival on the fifteenth day of the eighth month, like the festival held in Judah, and offered sacrifices on the altar. This he did in Bethel, sacrificing to the calves he had made. And at Bethel he also installed priests at the high places he had made. 33 On the fifteenth day of the eighth month, a month of his own choosing, he offered sacrifices on the altar he had built at Bethel. So he instituted the festival for the Israelites and went up to the altar to make offerings. Nu 29:12; 1Ki 13:32; 2Ki 17:32

The Man of God From Judah

13 By the word of the LORD a man of God came from Judah to Bethel, as Jeroboam was

[a] *25* Hebrew *Penuel,* a variant of *Peniel*
[b] *30* Probable reading of the original Hebrew text; Masoretic Text *people went to the one as far as Dan*

standing by the altar to make an
offering. 2By the word of the LORD
he cried out against the altar: "Altar, altar! This is what the LORD
says: 'A son named Josiah will be
born to the house of David. On
you he will sacrifice the priests of
the high places who make offerings here, and human bones will
be burned on you.'" 3That same
day the man of God gave a sign:
"This is the sign the LORD has declared: The altar will be split apart
and the ashes on it will be poured
out." 2Ki 23:15-16,20; Jn 2:11

4When King Jeroboam heard
what the man of God cried out
against the altar at Bethel, he
stretched out his hand from the
altar and said, "Seize him!" But
the hand he stretched out toward
the man shriveled up, so that he
could not pull it back. 5Also, the
altar was split apart and its ashes
poured out according to the sign
given by the man of God by the
word of the LORD.

6Then the king said to the man
of God, "Intercede with the LORD
your God and pray for me that my
hand may be restored." So the man
of God interceded with the LORD,
and the king's hand was restored
and became as it was before.
Ex 8:8; Ac 8:24

7The king said to the man of
God, "Come home with me for a
meal, and I will give you a gift."
1Sa 9:7; 2Ki 5:15

8But the man of God answered
the king, "Even if you were to give
me half your possessions, I would
not go with you, nor would I eat
bread or drink water here. 9For I
was commanded by the word of
the LORD: 'You must not eat bread
or drink water or return by the
way you came.'" 10So he took another road and did not return by
the way he had come to Bethel.
Nu 22:18; 24:13

11Now there was a certain old
prophet living in Bethel, whose
sons came and told him all that
the man of God had done there
that day. They also told their father what he had said to the king.
12Their father asked them, "Which
way did he go?" And his sons
showed him which road the man
of God from Judah had taken. 13So
he said to his sons, "Saddle the
donkey for me." And when they
had saddled the donkey for him,
he mounted it 14and rode after the
man of God. He found him sitting
under an oak tree and asked, "Are
you the man of God who came
from Judah?"

"I am," he replied.

15So the prophet said to him,
"Come home with me and eat."

16The man of God said, "I cannot
turn back and go with you, nor can
I eat bread or drink water with you
in this place. 17I have been told by
the word of the LORD: 'You must
not eat bread or drink water there
or return by the way you came.'"
ver 8

18The old prophet answered, "I
too am a prophet, as you are. And

an angel said to me by the word
of the LORD: 'Bring him back with
you to your house so that he may
eat bread and drink water.'" (But
he was lying to him.) 19So the man
of God returned with him and ate
and drank in his house. Dt 13:3
20While they were sitting at
the table, the word of the LORD
came to the old prophet who had
brought him back. 21He cried out
to the man of God who had come
from Judah, "This is what the
LORD says: 'You have defied the
word of the LORD and have not
kept the command the LORD your
God gave you. 22You came back
and ate bread and drank water in
the place where he told you not to
eat or drink. Therefore your body
will not be buried in the tomb of
your ancestors.'" ver 26; 1Ki 20:35
23When the man of God had finished eating and drinking, the
prophet who had brought him
back saddled his donkey for him.
24As he went on his way, a lion
met him on the road and killed
him, and his body was left lying
on the road, with both the donkey and the lion standing beside
it. 25Some people who passed by
saw the body lying there, with the
lion standing beside the body, and
they went and reported it in the
city where the old prophet lived.
1Ki 20:36
26When the prophet who had
brought him back from his journey heard of it, he said, "It is the
man of God who defied the word
of the LORD. The LORD has given
him over to the lion, which has
mauled him and killed him, as
the word of the LORD had warned
him."
27The prophet said to his sons,
"Saddle the donkey for me," and
they did so. 28Then he went out
and found the body lying on
the road, with the donkey and
the lion standing beside it. The
lion had neither eaten the body
nor mauled the donkey. 29So the
prophet picked up the body of the
man of God, laid it on the donkey,
and brought it back to his own city
to mourn for him and bury him.
30Then he laid the body in his own
tomb, and they mourned over him
and said, "Alas, my brother!"
Jer 22:18
31After burying him, he said to
his sons, "When I die, bury me in
the grave where the man of God
is buried; lay my bones beside his
bones. 32For the message he declared by the word of the LORD
against the altar in Bethel and
against all the shrines on the high
places in the towns of Samaria will
certainly come true."
Lev 26:30; 1Ki 16:24,28; 2Ki 23:16,18
33Even after this, Jeroboam did
not change his evil ways, but once
more appointed priests for the
high places from all sorts of people. Anyone who wanted to become a priest he consecrated for
the high places. 34This was the sin

of the house of Jeroboam that led to its downfall and to its destruction from the face of the earth.

1Ki 12:30-31; 14:10

Ahijah's Prophecy Against Jeroboam

14 At that time Abijah son of Jeroboam became ill, [2]and Jeroboam said to his wife, "Go, disguise yourself, so you won't be recognized as the wife of Jeroboam. Then go to Shiloh. Ahijah the prophet is there — the one who told me I would be king over this people. [3]Take ten loaves of bread with you, some cakes and a jar of honey, and go to him. He will tell you what will happen to the boy."
[4]So Jeroboam's wife did what he said and went to Ahijah's house in Shiloh.

1Sa 9:7; 1Ki 11:29

Now Ahijah could not see; his sight was gone because of his age. [5]But the LORD had told Ahijah, "Jeroboam's wife is coming to ask you about her son, for he is ill, and you are to give her such and such an answer. When she arrives, she will pretend to be someone else."

[6]So when Ahijah heard the sound of her footsteps at the door, he said, "Come in, wife of Jeroboam. Why this pretense? I have been sent to you with bad news.
[7]Go, tell Jeroboam that this is what the LORD, the God of Israel, says: 'I raised you up from among the people and appointed you ruler over my people Israel. [8]I tore the kingdom away from the house of David and gave it to you, but you have not been like my servant David, who kept my commands and followed me with all his heart, doing only what was right in my eyes.
[9]You have done more evil than all who lived before you. You have made for yourself other gods, idols made of metal; you have aroused my anger and turned your back on me.

1Ki 11:31,33,38; 2Ch 11:15; Ps 50:17

[10]" 'Because of this, I am going to bring disaster on the house of Jeroboam. I will cut off from Jeroboam every last male in Israel — slave or free.[a] I will burn up the house of Jeroboam as one burns dung, until it is all gone. [11]Dogs will eat those belonging to Jeroboam who die in the city, and the birds will feed on those who die in the country. The LORD has spoken!'

1Ki 15:29; 16:4; 21:24

[12]"As for you, go back home. When you set foot in your city, the boy will die. [13]All Israel will mourn for him and bury him. He is the only one belonging to Jeroboam who will be buried, because he is the only one in the house of Jeroboam in whom the LORD, the God of Israel, has found anything good.

2Ch 12:12; 19:3

[14]"The LORD will raise up for himself a king over Israel who will cut off the family of Jeroboam. Even now this is beginning

[a] 10 Or *Israel — every ruler or leader*

to happen.[a] 15 And the LORD will
strike Israel, so that it will be like a
reed swaying in the water. He will
uproot Israel from this good land
that he gave to their ancestors and
scatter them beyond the Euphrates River, because they aroused
the LORD's anger by making Asherah poles.[b] 16 And he will give Israel up because of the sins Jeroboam has committed and has caused
Israel to commit."

Dt 12:3; Jos 23:15-16; 1Ki 12:30

17 Then Jeroboam's wife got
up and left and went to Tirzah.
As soon as she stepped over the
threshold of the house, the boy
died. 18 They buried him, and all Israel mourned for him, as the LORD
had said through his servant the
prophet Ahijah. 1Ki 16:6-9

19 The other events of Jeroboam's reign, his wars and how he
ruled, are written in the book of
the annals of the kings of Israel.
20 He reigned for twenty-two years
and then rested with his ancestors. And Nadab his son succeeded
him as king.

Rehoboam King of Judah

21 Rehoboam son of Solomon was
king in Judah. He was forty-one
years old when he became king,
and he reigned seventeen years in
Jerusalem, the city the LORD had
chosen out of all the tribes of Israel in which to put his Name. His
mother's name was Naamah; she
was an Ammonite. 1Ki 11:1; 2Ch 12:13

22 Judah did evil in the eyes of
the LORD. By the sins they committed they stirred up his jealous
anger more than those who were
before them had done. 23 They also
set up for themselves high places,
sacred stones and Asherah poles
on every high hill and under every spreading tree. 24 There were
even male shrine prostitutes in
the land; the people engaged in
all the detestable practices of the
nations the LORD had driven out
before the Israelites.

Dt 23:17; 32:21; 2Ch 12:1

25 In the fifth year of King Rehoboam, Shishak king of Egypt
attacked Jerusalem. 26 He carried
off the treasures of the temple of
the LORD and the treasures of the
royal palace. He took everything,
including all the gold shields Solomon had made. 27 So King Rehoboam made bronze shields to replace them and assigned these to
the commanders of the guard on
duty at the entrance to the royal
palace. 28 Whenever the king went
to the LORD's temple, the guards
bore the shields, and afterward
they returned them to the guardroom. 1Ki 10:17; 2Ch 12:2

29 As for the other events of Rehoboam's reign, and all he did, are
they not written in the book of
the annals of the kings of Judah?
30 There was continual warfare

[a] *14* The meaning of the Hebrew for this sentence is uncertain. [b] *15* That is, wooden symbols of the goddess Asherah; here and elsewhere in 1 Kings

between Rehoboam and Jeroboam. 31And Rehoboam rested with
his ancestors and was buried with
them in the City of David. His
mother's name was Naamah; she
was an Ammonite. And Abijah[a]
his son succeeded him as king.

2Ch 12:9-16; 1Ki 12:21

Abijah King of Judah

15 In the eighteenth year of the
reign of Jeroboam son of Nebat, Abijah[b] became king of Judah, 2and he reigned in Jerusalem
three years. His mother's name
was Maakah daughter of Abishalom.[c] 2Ch 11:20; 13:2
3He committed all the sins his
father had done before him; his
heart was not fully devoted to the
LORD his God, as the heart of David his forefather had been. 4Nev-
ertheless, for David's sake the
LORD his God gave him a lamp in
Jerusalem by raising up a son to
succeed him and by making Jerusalem strong. 5For David had done
what was right in the eyes of the
LORD and had not failed to keep
any of the LORD's commands all
the days of his life — except in the
case of Uriah the Hittite.

2Sa 11:2-27; 12:9; 1Ki 11:4; 2Ch 21:7

6There was war between Abijah[d] and Jeroboam throughout
Abijah's lifetime. 7As for the other events of Abijah's reign, and all
he did, are they not written in the
book of the annals of the kings of
Judah? There was war between
Abijah and Jeroboam. 8And Abijah rested with his ancestors and
was buried in the City of David.
And Asa his son succeeded him as
king. 2Ch 13:1-2,22-14:1

Asa King of Judah

9In the twentieth year of Jeroboam king of Israel, Asa became
king of Judah, 10and he reigned
in Jerusalem forty-one years. His
grandmother's name was Maakah
daughter of Abishalom. ver 2
11Asa did what was right in the
eyes of the LORD, as his father David had done. 12He expelled the
male shrine prostitutes from the
land and got rid of all the idols
his ancestors had made. 13He even
deposed his grandmother Maakah from her position as queen
mother, because she had made a
repulsive image for the worship
of Asherah. Asa cut it down and
burned it in the Kidron Valley.
14Although he did not remove the
high places, Asa's heart was fully
committed to the LORD all his life.
15He brought into the temple of
the LORD the silver and gold and
the articles that he and his father
had dedicated. 1Ki 7:51; 14:24; 22:43

[a] *31* Some Hebrew manuscripts and Septuagint (see also 2 Chron. 12:16); most Hebrew manuscripts *Abijam* [b] *1* Some Hebrew manuscripts and Septuagint (see also 2 Chron. 12:16); most Hebrew manuscripts *Abijam*; also in verses 7 and 8 [c] *2* A variant of *Absalom*; also in verse 10 [d] *6* Some Hebrew manuscripts and Syriac *Abijam* (that is, Abijah); most Hebrew manuscripts *Rehoboam*

16 There was war between Asa
and Baasha king of Israel throughout their reigns. 17 Baasha king of
Israel went up against Judah and
fortified Ramah to prevent anyone from leaving or entering the
territory of Asa king of Judah.

Jos 18:25; 1Ki 12:27

18 Asa then took all the silver
and gold that was left in the treasuries of the LORD's temple and of
his own palace. He entrusted it to
his officials and sent them to Ben-
Hadad son of Tabrimmon, the son
of Hezion, the king of Aram, who
was ruling in Damascus. 19 "Let
there be a treaty between me and
you," he said, "as there was between my father and your father.
See, I am sending you a gift of
silver and gold. Now break your
treaty with Baasha king of Israel
so he will withdraw from me."

1Ki 11:23-24; 14:26

20 Ben-Hadad agreed with King
Asa and sent the commanders of
his forces against the towns of Israel. He conquered Ijon, Dan, Abel
Beth Maakah and all Kinnereth in
addition to Naphtali. 21 When Baasha heard this, he stopped building Ramah and withdrew to Tirzah. 22 Then King Asa issued an
order to all Judah — no one was
exempt — and they carried away
from Ramah the stones and timber Baasha had been using there.
With them King Asa built up Geba
in Benjamin, and also Mizpah.

2Ch 14:2-3; 15:16-16:6

23 As for all the other events of
Asa's reign, all his achievements,
all he did and the cities he built,
are they not written in the book
of the annals of the kings of Judah? In his old age, however, his
feet became diseased. 24 Then Asa
rested with his ancestors and was
buried with them in the city of his
father David. And Jehoshaphat his
son succeeded him as king. Mt 1:8

Nadab King of Israel

25 Nadab son of Jeroboam became king of Israel in the second
year of Asa king of Judah, and he
reigned over Israel two years. 26 He
did evil in the eyes of the LORD,
following the ways of his father
and committing the same sin his
father had caused Israel to commit. 1Ki 12:30

27 Baasha son of Ahijah from the
tribe of Issachar plotted against
him, and he struck him down
at Gibbethon, a Philistine town,
while Nadab and all Israel were
besieging it. 28 Baasha killed Nadab in the third year of Asa king of
Judah and succeeded him as king.

Jos 19:44; 1Ki 14:14

29 As soon as he began to reign,
he killed Jeroboam's whole family. He did not leave Jeroboam anyone that breathed, but destroyed
them all, according to the word of
the LORD given through his servant Ahijah the Shilonite. 30 This
happened because of the sins Jeroboam had committed and had

caused Israel to commit, and because he aroused the anger of the
LORD, the God of Israel.
1Ki 14:9-10,14,16

31 As for the other events of Nadab's reign, and all he did, are they
not written in the book of the annals of the kings of Israel? 32 There
was war between Asa and Baasha
king of Israel throughout their
reigns. ver 16

Baasha King of Israel

33 In the third year of Asa king of
Judah, Baasha son of Ahijah became king of all Israel in Tirzah,
and he reigned twenty-four years.
34 He did evil in the eyes of the
LORD, following the ways of Jeroboam and committing the same
sin Jeroboam had caused Israel to
commit.

16 Then the word of the LORD
came to Jehu son of Hanani
concerning Baasha: 2 "I lifted you
up from the dust and appointed
you ruler over my people Israel,
but you followed the ways of Jeroboam and caused my people Israel
to sin and to arouse my anger by
their sins. 3 So I am about to wipe
out Baasha and his house, and I
will make your house like that of
Jeroboam son of Nebat. 4 Dogs will
eat those belonging to Baasha who
die in the city, and birds will feed
on those who die in the country."
1Ki 14:7-11

5 As for the other events of Baasha's reign, what he did and his
achievements, are they not written in the book of the annals of
the kings of Israel? 6 Baasha rested
with his ancestors and was buried
in Tirzah. And Elah his son succeeded him as king. 1Ki 15:31,33

7 Moreover, the word of the LORD
came through the prophet Jehu
son of Hanani to Baasha and his
house, because of all the evil he
had done in the eyes of the LORD,
arousing his anger by the things
he did, becoming like the house
of Jeroboam — and also because
he destroyed it. 1Ki 15:27,29

Elah King of Israel

8 In the twenty-sixth year of Asa
king of Judah, Elah son of Baasha became king of Israel, and he
reigned in Tirzah two years.

9 Zimri, one of his officials, who
had command of half his chariots,
plotted against him. Elah was in
Tirzah at the time, getting drunk
in the home of Arza, the palace
administrator at Tirzah. 10 Zimri came in, struck him down and
killed him in the twenty-seventh
year of Asa king of Judah. Then he
succeeded him as king.
1Ki 18:3; 2Ki 9:30-33

11 As soon as he began to reign
and was seated on the throne, he
killed off Baasha's whole family.
He did not spare a single male,
whether relative or friend. 12 So
Zimri destroyed the whole family
of Baasha, in accordance with the
word of the LORD spoken against

Baasha through the prophet
Jehu — [13]because of all the sins
Baasha and his son Elah had committed and had caused Israel to
commit, so that they aroused the
anger of the LORD, the God of Israel, by their worthless idols.

Dt 32:21; 1Sa 12:21; Isa 41:29

[14]As for the other events of Elah's
reign, and all he did, are they not
written in the book of the annals
of the kings of Israel?

Zimri King of Israel

[15]In the twenty-seventh year of
Asa king of Judah, Zimri reigned
in Tirzah seven days. The army was
encamped near Gibbethon, a Philistine town. [16]When the Israelites
in the camp heard that Zimri had
plotted against the king and murdered him, they proclaimed Omri,
the commander of the army, king
over Israel that very day there
in the camp. [17]Then Omri and all
the Israelites with him withdrew
from Gibbethon and laid siege to
Tirzah. [18]When Zimri saw that the
city was taken, he went into the
citadel of the royal palace and set
the palace on fire around him. So
he died, [19]because of the sins he
had committed, doing evil in the
eyes of the LORD and following
the ways of Jeroboam and committing the same sin Jeroboam
had caused Israel to commit.

Jos 19:44; 1Ki 15:27

[20]As for the other events of Zimri's reign, and the rebellion he carried out, are they not written in
the book of the annals of the kings
of Israel?

Omri King of Israel

[21]Then the people of Israel were
split into two factions; half supported Tibni son of Ginath for
king, and the other half supported Omri. [22]But Omri's followers
proved stronger than those of Tibni son of Ginath. So Tibni died and
Omri became king.

[23]In the thirty-first year of Asa
king of Judah, Omri became king
of Israel, and he reigned twelve
years, six of them in Tirzah. [24]He
bought the hill of Samaria from
Shemer for two talents[a] of silver
and built a city on the hill, calling it Samaria, after Shemer, the
name of the former owner of the
hill.

1Ki 13:32; 15:21; Jn 4:4

[25]But Omri did evil in the eyes
of the LORD and sinned more than
all those before him. [26]He followed
completely the ways of Jeroboam
son of Nebat, committing the same
sin Jeroboam had caused Israel to
commit, so that they aroused the
anger of the LORD, the God of Israel, by their worthless idols.

Dt 4:25; 32:21; Mic 6:16

[27]As for the other events of
Omri's reign, what he did and the
things he achieved, are they not
written in the book of the annals
of the kings of Israel? [28]Omri rest-

[a] 24 That is, about 150 pounds or about 68 kilograms

ed with his ancestors and was buried in Samaria. And Ahab his son succeeded him as king.

Ahab Becomes King of Israel

29 In the thirty-eighth year of Asa king of Judah, Ahab son of Omri became king of Israel, and he reigned in Samaria over Israel twenty-two years. 30 Ahab son of Omri did more evil in the eyes of the LORD than any of those before him. 31 He not only considered it trivial to commit the sins of Jeroboam son of Nebat, but he also married Jezebel daughter of Ethbaal king of the Sidonians, and began to serve Baal and worship him. 32 He set up an altar for Baal in the temple of Baal that he built in Samaria. 33 Ahab also made an Asherah pole and did more to arouse the anger of the LORD, the God of Israel, than did all the kings of Israel before him.

1Ki 14:9; 21:25; 2Ki 10:18,21,27

34 In Ahab's time, Hiel of Bethel rebuilt Jericho. He laid its foundations at the cost of his firstborn son Abiram, and he set up its gates at the cost of his youngest son Segub, in accordance with the word of the LORD spoken by Joshua son of Nun.

Jos 6:26

Elijah Announces a Great Drought

17 Now Elijah the Tishbite, from Tishbe[a] in Gilead, said to Ahab, "As the LORD, the God of Israel, lives, whom I serve, there will be neither dew nor rain in the next few years except at my word."

2Ki 3:14; Lk 4:25; Jas 5:17

Elijah Fed by Ravens

2 Then the word of the LORD came to Elijah: 3 "Leave here, turn eastward and hide in the Kerith Ravine, east of the Jordan. 4 You will drink from the brook, and I have directed the ravens to supply you with food there."

Ge 8:7

5 So he did what the LORD had told him. He went to the Kerith Ravine, east of the Jordan, and stayed there. 6 The ravens brought him bread and meat in the morning and bread and meat in the evening, and he drank from the brook.

Ex 16:8

Elijah and the Widow at Zarephath

7 Some time later the brook dried up because there had been no rain in the land. 8 Then the word of the LORD came to him: 9 "Go at once to Zarephath in the region of Sidon and stay there. I have directed a widow there to supply you with food." 10 So he went to Zarephath. When he came to the town gate, a widow was there gathering sticks. He called to her and asked, "Would you bring me a little water in a jar so I may have a drink?" 11 As she was going to get it, he called, "And bring me, please, a piece of bread."

Ge 24:17; Ob 1:20; Lk 4:26

[a] 1 Or *Tishbite, of the settlers*

12 "As surely as the LORD your
God lives," she replied, "I don't
have any bread — only a handful
of flour in a jar and a little olive
oil in a jug. I am gathering a few
sticks to take home and make a
meal for myself and my son, that
we may eat it — and die." 2Ki 4:2

13 Elijah said to her, "Don't be
afraid. Go home and do as you
have said. But first make a small
loaf of bread for me from what
you have and bring it to me, and
then make something for yourself
and your son. 14 For this is what the
LORD, the God of Israel, says: 'The
jar of flour will not be used up and
the jug of oil will not run dry until
the day the LORD sends rain on the
land.' "

15 She went away and did as Elijah had told her. So there was food
every day for Elijah and for the
woman and her family. 16 For the
jar of flour was not used up and
the jug of oil did not run dry, in
keeping with the word of the LORD
spoken by Elijah.

17 Some time later the son of the
woman who owned the house became ill. He grew worse and worse,
and finally stopped breathing.
18 She said to Elijah, "What do you
have against me, man of God? Did
you come to remind me of my sin
and kill my son?" 2Ki 3:13; Lk 5:8

19 "Give me your son," Elijah replied. He took him from her arms,
carried him to the upper room
where he was staying, and laid
him on his bed. 20 Then he cried
out to the LORD, "LORD my God,
have you brought tragedy even on
this widow I am staying with, by
causing her son to die?" 21 Then he
stretched himself out on the boy
three times and cried out to the
LORD, "LORD my God, let this boy's
life return to him!" 2Ki 4:34; Ac 20:10

22 The LORD heard Elijah's cry,
and the boy's life returned to him,
and he lived. 23 Elijah picked up the
child and carried him down from
the room into the house. He gave
him to his mother and said, "Look,
your son is alive!"

24 Then the woman said to Elijah,
"Now I know that you are a man of
God and that the word of the LORD
from your mouth is the truth."
Jn 3:2; 16:30; Ps 119:43

Elijah and Obadiah

18 After a long time, in the
third year, the word of the
LORD came to Elijah: "Go and present yourself to Ahab, and I will
send rain on the land." 2 So Elijah
went to present himself to Ahab.
Dt 28:12; Lk 4:25; Jas 5:17

Now the famine was severe in Samaria, 3 and Ahab had summoned
Obadiah, his palace administrator.
(Obadiah was a devout believer in
the LORD. 4 While Jezebel was killing off the LORD's prophets, Obadiah had taken a hundred prophets
and hidden them in two caves, fifty in each, and had supplied them
with food and water.) 5 Ahab had

said to Obadiah, “Go through the
land to all the springs and valleys.
Maybe we can find some grass to
keep the horses and mules alive
so we will not have to kill any of
our animals.” 6So they divided the
land they were to cover, Ahab going in one direction and Obadiah
in another. 2Ki 9:7; Ne 7:2; Isa 16:3

7As Obadiah was walking along,
Elijah met him. Obadiah recognized him, bowed down to the
ground, and said, “Is it really you,
my lord Elijah?” 2Ki 1:8

8“Yes,” he replied. “Go tell your
master, ‘Elijah is here.’ ”

9“What have I done wrong,”
asked Obadiah, “that you are
handing your servant over to Ahab
to be put to death? 10As surely as
the LORD your God lives, there is
not a nation or kingdom where
my master has not sent someone
to look for you. And whenever a
nation or kingdom claimed you
were not there, he made them
swear they could not find you.
11But now you tell me to go to my
master and say, ‘Elijah is here.’ 12I
don’t know where the Spirit of the
LORD may carry you when I leave
you. If I go and tell Ahab and he
doesn’t find you, he will kill me.
Yet I your servant have worshiped the LORD since my youth.
13Haven’t you heard, my lord, what
I did while Jezebel was killing the
prophets of the LORD? I hid a hundred of the LORD’s prophets in two
caves, fifty in each, and supplied
them with food and water. 14And
now you tell me to go to my master and say, ‘Elijah is here.’ He will
kill me!” 2Ki 2:16; Eze 3:14; Ac 8:39

15Elijah said, “As the LORD Almighty lives, whom I serve, I will
surely present myself to Ahab today.” 1Ki 17:1

Elijah on Mount Carmel

16So Obadiah went to meet Ahab
and told him, and Ahab went to
meet Elijah. 17When he saw Elijah,
he said to him, “Is that you, you
troubler of Israel?” Jos 7:25; 1Ki 21:20

18“I have not made trouble for
Israel,” Elijah replied. “But you
and your father’s family have. You
have abandoned the LORD’s commands and have followed the Baals. 19Now summon the people
from all over Israel to meet me on
Mount Carmel. And bring the four
hundred and fifty prophets of Baal
and the four hundred prophets of
Asherah, who eat at Jezebel’s table.” Jos 19:26; 1Ki 16:31,33

20So Ahab sent word throughout all Israel and assembled the
prophets on Mount Carmel. 21Eli-
jah went before the people and
said, “How long will you waver between two opinions? If the LORD is
God, follow him; but if Baal is God,
follow him.” Jos 24:15; 2Ki 17:41; Mt 6:24

But the people said nothing.

22Then Elijah said to them, “I am
the only one of the LORD’s prophets left, but Baal has four hundred
and fifty prophets. 23Get two bulls

for us. Let Baal's prophets choose
one for themselves, and let them
cut it into pieces and put it on the
wood but not set fire to it. I will
prepare the other bull and put it
on the wood but not set fire to
it. 24 Then you call on the name
of your god, and I will call on the
name of the LORD. The god who
answers by fire — he is God."
1Ki 19:10; 1Ch 21:26

Then all the people said, "What
you say is good."

25 Elijah said to the prophets of
Baal, "Choose one of the bulls and
prepare it first, since there are so
many of you. Call on the name of
your god, but do not light the fire."
26 So they took the bull given them
and prepared it.

Then they called on the name
of Baal from morning till noon.
"Baal, answer us!" they shouted.
But there was no response; no
one answered. And they danced
around the altar they had made.
Ps 115:4-5; Jer 10:5; 1Co 8:4

27 At noon Elijah began to taunt
them. "Shout louder!" he said.
"Surely he is a god! Perhaps he is
deep in thought, or busy, or traveling. Maybe he is sleeping and
must be awakened." 28 So they
shouted louder and slashed themselves with swords and spears, as
was their custom, until their blood
flowed. 29 Midday passed, and they
continued their frantic prophesying until the time for the evening
sacrifice. But there was no response, no one answered, no one
paid attention. Lev 19:28; Hab 2:19

30 Then Elijah said to all the people, "Come here to me." They came
to him, and he repaired the altar
of the LORD, which had been torn
down. 31 Elijah took twelve stones,
one for each of the tribes descended from Jacob, to whom the word
of the LORD had come, saying,
"Your name shall be Israel." 32 With
the stones he built an altar in the
name of the LORD, and he dug a
trench around it large enough to
hold two seahs[a] of seed. 33 He arranged the wood, cut the bull into
pieces and laid it on the wood.
Then he said to them, "Fill four
large jars with water and pour it
on the offering and on the wood."
1Ki 19:10; 2Ki 17:34; Col 3:17

34 "Do it again," he said, and they
did it again.

"Do it a third time," he ordered,
and they did it the third time.
35 The water ran down around the
altar and even filled the trench.

36 At the time of sacrifice, the
prophet Elijah stepped forward
and prayed: "LORD, the God of
Abraham, Isaac and Israel, let it be
known today that you are God in
Israel and that I am your servant
and have done all these things
at your command. 37 Answer me,
LORD, answer me, so these people
will know that you, LORD, are God,
and that you are turning their
hearts back again." Nu 16:28; Jos 4:24

[a] 32 That is, probably about 24 pounds or about 11 kilograms

[38]Then the fire of the LORD fell
and burned up the sacrifice, the
wood, the stones and the soil, and
also licked up the water in the
trench. Lev 9:24; 1Ch 21:26; 2Ch 7:1
[39]When all the people saw this,
they fell prostrate and cried, "The
LORD — he is God! The LORD — he
is God!" ver 24; Ps 46:10
[40]Then Elijah commanded
them, "Seize the prophets of Baal.
Don't let anyone get away!" They
seized them, and Elijah had them
brought down to the Kishon Valley and slaughtered there.
Dt 13:5; 18:20; 2Ki 10:24-25
[41]And Elijah said to Ahab, "Go,
eat and drink, for there is the
sound of a heavy rain." [42]So Ahab
went off to eat and drink, but Elijah climbed to the top of Carmel,
bent down to the ground and put
his face between his knees. Jas 5:18
[43]"Go and look toward the sea,"
he told his servant. And he went
up and looked.

"There is nothing there," he
said.

Seven times Elijah said, "Go
back."
[44]The seventh time the servant
reported, "A cloud as small as a
man's hand is rising from the sea."
Lk 12:54

So Elijah said, "Go and tell Ahab,
'Hitch up your chariot and go
down before the rain stops you.' "
[45]Meanwhile, the sky grew black
with clouds, the wind rose, a heavy
rain started falling and Ahab rode
off to Jezreel. [46]The power of the
LORD came on Elijah and, tucking his cloak into his belt, he ran
ahead of Ahab all the way to Jezreel. 2Ki 3:15; 4:29

Elijah Flees to Horeb

19 Now Ahab told Jezebel everything Elijah had done
and how he had killed all the
prophets with the sword. [2]So Jezebel sent a messenger to Elijah to
say, "May the gods deal with me,
be it ever so severely, if by this
time tomorrow I do not make
your life like that of one of them."
1Ki 18:40; 20:10; 2Ki 6:31
[3]Elijah was afraid[a] and ran for
his life. When he came to Beersheba in Judah, he left his servant
there, [4]while he himself went a
day's journey into the wilderness. He came to a broom bush,
sat down under it and prayed that
he might die. "I have had enough,
LORD," he said. "Take my life; I
am no better than my ancestors."
[5]Then he lay down under the bush
and fell asleep. Nu 11:15; Jnh 4:8; Ge 31:21

All at once an angel touched
him and said, "Get up and eat."
[6]He looked around, and there by
his head was some bread baked
over hot coals, and a jar of water.
He ate and drank and then lay
down again. Ge 16:7
[7]The angel of the LORD came
back a second time and touched
him and said, "Get up and eat,

[a] 3 Or *Elijah saw*

for the journey is too much for
you." 8So he got up and ate and
drank. Strengthened by that food,
he traveled forty days and forty
nights until he reached Horeb, the
mountain of God. 9There he went
into a cave and spent the night.
Ex 3:1; 34:28; Mt 4:2

The LORD Appears to Elijah

And the word of the LORD came
to him: "What are you doing here,
Elijah?"
10He replied, "I have been very
zealous for the LORD God Almighty. The Israelites have rejected your covenant, torn down
your altars, and put your prophets to death with the sword. I am
the only one left, and now they are
trying to kill me too."
1Ki 18:4,22; Ro 11:3*
11The LORD said, "Go out and
stand on the mountain in the
presence of the LORD, for the LORD
is about to pass by." Ex 24:12
Then a great and powerful
wind tore the mountains apart
and shattered the rocks before
the LORD, but the LORD was not in
the wind. After the wind there was
an earthquake, but the LORD was
not in the earthquake. 12After the
earthquake came a fire, but the
LORD was not in the fire. And after the fire came a gentle whisper.
13When Elijah heard it, he pulled
his cloak over his face and went
out and stood at the mouth of the
cave. Zec 4:6; Ex 3:6; Eze 1:4
Then a voice said to him, "What
are you doing here, Elijah?"
14He replied, "I have been very
zealous for the LORD God Almighty. The Israelites have rejected your covenant, torn down
your altars, and put your prophets to death with the sword. I am
the only one left, and now they are
trying to kill me too." Ro 11:3*
15The LORD said to him, "Go
back the way you came, and go
to the Desert of Damascus. When
you get there, anoint Hazael king
over Aram. 16Also, anoint Jehu son
of Nimshi king over Israel, and
anoint Elisha son of Shaphat from
Abel Meholah to succeed you as
prophet. 17Jehu will put to death
any who escape the sword of Hazael, and Elisha will put to death
any who escape the sword of Jehu.
18Yet I reserve seven thousand in
Israel — all whose knees have not
bowed down to Baal and whose
mouths have not kissed him."
Ro 11:4*; 2Ki 8:7-15; 9:14

The Call of Elisha

19So Elijah went from there and
found Elisha son of Shaphat. He
was plowing with twelve yoke of
oxen, and he himself was driving
the twelfth pair. Elijah went up to
him and threw his cloak around
him. 20Elisha then left his oxen
and ran after Elijah. "Let me kiss
my father and mother goodbye,"
he said, "and then I will come with
you." 2Ki 2:8,14; Mt 8:21-22; Lk 9:61

"Go back," Elijah replied. "What have I done to you?"

21So Elisha left him and went back. He took his yoke of oxen and slaughtered them. He burned the plowing equipment to cook the meat and gave it to the people, and they ate. Then he set out to follow Elijah and became his servant. 2Sa 24:22

Ben-Hadad Attacks Samaria

20 Now Ben-Hadad king of Aram mustered his entire army. Accompanied by thirty-two kings with their horses and chariots, he went up and besieged Samaria and attacked it. 2He sent messengers into the city to Ahab king of Israel, saying, "This is what Ben-Hadad says: 3'Your silver and gold are mine, and the best of your wives and children are mine.'" 1Ki 15:18; 22:31; 2Ki 6:24

4The king of Israel answered, "Just as you say, my lord the king. I and all I have are yours."

5The messengers came again and said, "This is what Ben-Hadad says: 'I sent to demand your silver and gold, your wives and your children. 6But about this time tomorrow I am going to send my officials to search your palace and the houses of your officials. They will seize everything you value and carry it away.'"

7The king of Israel summoned all the elders of the land and said to them, "See how this man is looking for trouble! When he sent for my wives and my children, my silver and my gold, I did not refuse him." 2Ki 5:7

8The elders and the people all answered, "Don't listen to him or agree to his demands."

9So he replied to Ben-Hadad's messengers, "Tell my lord the king, 'Your servant will do all you demanded the first time, but this demand I cannot meet.'" They left and took the answer back to Ben-Hadad.

10Then Ben-Hadad sent another message to Ahab: "May the gods deal with me, be it ever so severely, if enough dust remains in Samaria to give each of my men a handful." 1Ki 19:2

11The king of Israel answered, "Tell him: 'One who puts on his armor should not boast like one who takes it off.'" Pr 27:1

12Ben-Hadad heard this message while he and the kings were drinking in their tents,[a] and he ordered his men: "Prepare to attack." So they prepared to attack the city. 1Ki 16:9

Ahab Defeats Ben-Hadad

13Meanwhile a prophet came to Ahab king of Israel and announced, "This is what the LORD says: 'Do you see this vast army? I will give it into your hand today, and then you will know that I am the LORD.'" ver 28; Ex 6:7

[a] 12 Or *in Sukkoth*; also in verse 16

14“But who will do this?” asked
Ahab.
The prophet replied, “This is
what the LORD says: ‘The junior
officers under the provincial commanders will do it.’ ”
“And who will start the battle?”
he asked. Jdg 1:1
The prophet answered, “You
will.”
15So Ahab summoned the 232
junior officers under the provincial commanders. Then he assembled the rest of the Israelites, 7,000 in all. 16They set out at
noon while Ben-Hadad and the 32
kings allied with him were in their
tents getting drunk. 17The junior
officers under the provincial commanders went out first. ver 12; 1Ki 16:9
Now Ben-Hadad had dispatched
scouts, who reported, “Men are advancing from Samaria.”
18He said, “If they have come
out for peace, take them alive; if
they have come out for war, take
them alive.”
19The junior officers under the
provincial commanders marched
out of the city with the army behind them 20and each one struck
down his opponent. At that, the
Arameans fled, with the Israelites
in pursuit. But Ben-Hadad king of
Aram escaped on horseback with
some of his horsemen. 21The king
of Israel advanced and overpowered the horses and chariots and
inflicted heavy losses on the Arameans.

22Afterward, the prophet came
to the king of Israel and said,
“Strengthen your position and see
what must be done, because next
spring the king of Aram will attack you again.” 2Sa 11:1
23Meanwhile, the officials of the
king of Aram advised him, “Their
gods are gods of the hills. That is
why they were too strong for us.
But if we fight them on the plains,
surely we will be stronger than
they. 24Do this: Remove all the
kings from their commands and
replace them with other officers.
25You must also raise an army
like the one you lost — horse for
horse and chariot for chariot — so
we can fight Israel on the plains.
Then surely we will be stronger
than they.” He agreed with them
and acted accordingly.
1Ki 14:23; Ro 1:21-23
26The next spring Ben-Hadad
mustered the Arameans and went
up to Aphek to fight against Israel. 27When the Israelites were
also mustered and given provisions, they marched out to meet
them. The Israelites camped opposite them like two small flocks
of goats, while the Arameans covered the countryside.
Jdg 6:6; 1Sa 13:6; 2Ki 13:17
28The man of God came up and
told the king of Israel, “This is
what the LORD says: ‘Because the
Arameans think the LORD is a
god of the hills and not a god of
the valleys, I will deliver this vast

army into your hands, and you
will know that I am the LORD.'"
ver 13

29For seven days they camped
opposite each other, and on the
seventh day the battle was joined.
The Israelites inflicted a hundred
thousand casualties on the Aramean foot soldiers in one day.
30The rest of them escaped to the
city of Aphek, where the wall collapsed on twenty-seven thousand
of them. And Ben-Hadad fled to
the city and hid in an inner room.
1Ki 22:25; 2Ch 18:24

31His officials said to him, "Look,
we have heard that the kings of
Israel are merciful. Let us go to
the king of Israel with sackcloth
around our waists and ropes
around our heads. Perhaps he will
spare your life." Ge 37:34

32Wearing sackcloth around
their waists and ropes around
their heads, they went to the king
of Israel and said, "Your servant
Ben-Hadad says: 'Please let me
live.'"

The king answered, "Is he still
alive? He is my brother."

33The men took this as a good
sign and were quick to pick up his
word. "Yes, your brother Ben-Hadad!" they said.

"Go and get him," the king said.
When Ben-Hadad came out, Ahab
had him come up into his chariot.

34"I will return the cities my father took from your father," Ben-
Hadad offered. "You may set up
your own market areas in Damascus, as my father did in Samaria."
1Ki 15:20; Jer 49:23-27

Ahab said, "On the basis of a
treaty I will set you free." So he
made a treaty with him, and let
him go. Ex 23:32

A Prophet Condemns Ahab

35By the word of the LORD one of
the company of the prophets said
to his companion, "Strike me with
your weapon," but he refused.
1Ki 13:20; 2Ki 2:3-7

36So the prophet said, "Because
you have not obeyed the LORD, as
soon as you leave me a lion will
kill you." And after the man went
away, a lion found him and killed
him. 1Ki 13:24

37The prophet found another man and said, "Strike me,
please." So the man struck him
and wounded him. 38Then the
prophet went and stood by the
road waiting for the king. He disguised himself with his headband
down over his eyes. 39As the king
passed by, the prophet called out
to him, "Your servant went into
the thick of the battle, and someone came to me with a captive
and said, 'Guard this man. If he is
missing, it will be your life for his
life, or you must pay a talent[a] of
silver.' 40While your servant was
busy here and there, the man disappeared." 2Ki 10:24

[a] 39 That is, about 75 pounds or about 34 kilograms

"That is your sentence," the
king of Israel said. "You have pronounced it yourself."
41 Then the prophet quickly removed the headband from his
eyes, and the king of Israel recognized him as one of the prophets.
42 He said to the king, "This is what
the LORD says: 'You have set free
a man I had determined should
die.[a] Therefore it is your life for
his life, your people for his people.' " 43 Sullen and angry, the king
of Israel went to his palace in Samaria. 1Ki 21:4; 22:31-37

Naboth's Vineyard

21 Some time later there was
an incident involving a
vineyard belonging to Naboth
the Jezreelite. The vineyard was
in Jezreel, close to the palace of
Ahab king of Samaria. 2 Ahab said
to Naboth, "Let me have your
vineyard to use for a vegetable
garden, since it is close to my palace. In exchange I will give you a
better vineyard or, if you prefer, I
will pay you whatever it is worth."
1Ki 18:45-46; 2Ki 9:21
3 But Naboth replied, "The LORD
forbid that I should give you the
inheritance of my ancestors."
Lev 25:23; Nu 36:7; Eze 46:18
4 So Ahab went home, sullen and
angry because Naboth the Jezreelite had said, "I will not give you
the inheritance of my ancestors."
He lay on his bed sulking and refused to eat. 1Ki 20:43
5 His wife Jezebel came in and
asked him, "Why are you so sullen? Why won't you eat?"
6 He answered her, "Because I
said to Naboth the Jezreelite, 'Sell
me your vineyard; or if you prefer,
I will give you another vineyard
in its place.' But he said, 'I will not
give you my vineyard.' "
7 Jezebel his wife said, "Is this
how you act as king over Israel?
Get up and eat! Cheer up. I'll get
you the vineyard of Naboth the
Jezreelite." 1Sa 8:14
8 So she wrote letters in Ahab's
name, placed his seal on them,
and sent them to the elders and
nobles who lived in Naboth's city
with him. 9 In those letters she
wrote: Ge 38:18; Est 3:12; 8:8,10

> "Proclaim a day of fasting
> and seat Naboth in a prom-
> inent place among the peo-
> ple. 10 But seat two scoundrels
> opposite him and have them
> bring charges that he has
> cursed both God and the king.
> Then take him out and stone
> him to death."

Ac 6:11; Ex 22:28; Lev 24:15-16

11 So the elders and nobles who
lived in Naboth's city did as Jezebel directed in the letters she
had written to them. 12 They proclaimed a fast and seated Naboth
in a prominent place among the

[a] 42 The Hebrew term refers to the irrevocable giving over of things or persons to the LORD, often by totally destroying them.

people. 13 Then two scoundrels came and sat opposite him and brought charges against Naboth before the people, saying, "Naboth has cursed both God and the king." So they took him outside the city and stoned him to death. 14 Then they sent word to Jezebel: "Naboth has been stoned to death."

2Ki 9:26; Isa 58:4

15 As soon as Jezebel heard that Naboth had been stoned to death, she said to Ahab, "Get up and take possession of the vineyard of Naboth the Jezreelite that he refused to sell you. He is no longer alive, but dead." 16 When Ahab heard that Naboth was dead, he got up and went down to take possession of Naboth's vineyard. 1Sa 8:14

17 Then the word of the LORD came to Elijah the Tishbite: 18 "Go down to meet Ahab king of Israel, who rules in Samaria. He is now in Naboth's vineyard, where he has gone to take possession of it. 19 Say to him, 'This is what the LORD says: Have you not murdered a man and seized his property?' Then say to him, 'This is what the LORD says: In the place where dogs licked up Naboth's blood, dogs will lick up your blood—yes, yours!'"

1Ki 22:38; 2Ki 9:26; Ps 9:12

20 Ahab said to Elijah, "So you have found me, my enemy!" 1Ki 18:17

"I have found you," he answered, "because you have sold yourself to do evil in the eyes of the LORD. 21 He says, 'I am going to bring disaster on you. I will wipe out your descendants and cut off from Ahab every last male in Israel—slave or free.[a] 22 I will make your house like that of Jeroboam son of Nebat and that of Baasha son of Ahijah, because you have aroused my anger and have caused Israel to sin.'

1Ki 12:30; 14:10; 15:29

23 "And also concerning Jezebel the LORD says: 'Dogs will devour Jezebel by the wall of[b] Jezreel.'

2Ki 9:10,34-36

24 "Dogs will eat those belonging to Ahab who die in the city, and the birds will feed on those who die in the country." 1Ki 14:11; 16:4

25 (There was never anyone like Ahab, who sold himself to do evil in the eyes of the LORD, urged on by Jezebel his wife. 26 He behaved in the vilest manner by going after idols, like the Amorites the LORD drove out before Israel.)

Ge 15:16; 1Ki 16:33

27 When Ahab heard these words, he tore his clothes, put on sackcloth and fasted. He lay in sackcloth and went around meekly.

Ge 37:34; 2Sa 3:31; 2Ki 6:30

28 Then the word of the LORD came to Elijah the Tishbite: 29 "Have you noticed how Ahab has humbled himself before me? Because he has humbled himself, I will not bring this disaster in his

[a] 21 Or *Israel—every ruler or leader*
[b] 23 Most Hebrew manuscripts; a few Hebrew manuscripts, Vulgate and Syriac (see also 2 Kings 9:26) *the plot of ground at*

day, but I will bring it on his house
in the days of his son." 2Ki 9:26

Micaiah Prophesies Against Ahab

22 For three years there was no
war between Aram and Is-
rael. 2But in the third year Jehoshaphat king of Judah went down
to see the king of Israel. 3The king
of Israel had said to his officials,
"Don't you know that Ramoth Gilead belongs to us and yet we are
doing nothing to retake it from
the king of Aram?" Dt 4:43; Jos 21:38
4So he asked Jehoshaphat, "Will
you go with me to fight against
Ramoth Gilead?" 2Ki 3:7
Jehoshaphat replied to the king
of Israel, "I am as you are, my
people as your people, my horses as your horses." 5But Jehoshaphat also said to the king of Israel, "First seek the counsel of the
LORD." Ex 33:7; 2Ki 3:11
6So the king of Israel brought
together the prophets — about
four hundred men — and asked
them, "Shall I go to war against
Ramoth Gilead, or shall I refrain?"
"Go," they answered, "for the
Lord will give it into the king's
hand." 1Ki 18:19
7But Jehoshaphat asked, "Is
there no longer a prophet of
the LORD here whom we can inquire of?" 2Ki 3:11
8The king of Israel answered
Jehoshaphat, "There is still one
prophet through whom we can inquire of the LORD, but I hate him
because he never prophesies anything good about me, but always
bad. He is Micaiah son of Imlah."
Isa 5:20; Am 5:10
"The king should not say such a
thing," Jehoshaphat replied.
9So the king of Israel called one
of his officials and said, "Bring Micaiah son of Imlah at once."
10Dressed in their royal robes,
the king of Israel and Jehoshaphat king of Judah were sitting
on their thrones at the threshing
floor by the entrance of the gate
of Samaria, with all the prophets
prophesying before them. 11Now
Zedekiah son of Kenaanah had
made iron horns and he declared,
"This is what the LORD says: 'With
these you will gore the Arameans
until they are destroyed.'"
Dt 33:17; Zec 1:18-21
12All the other prophets were
prophesying the same thing. "Attack Ramoth Gilead and be victorious," they said, "for the LORD will
give it into the king's hand."
13The messenger who had gone
to summon Micaiah said to him,
"Look, the other prophets without
exception are predicting success
for the king. Let your word agree
with theirs, and speak favorably."
14But Micaiah said, "As surely as
the LORD lives, I can tell him only
what the LORD tells me."
Nu 22:18; 24:13; 1Ki 18:10,15
15When he arrived, the king asked
him, "Micaiah, shall we go to war
against Ramoth Gilead, or not?"

"Attack and be victorious," he
answered, "for the LORD will give
it into the king's hand."
16The king said to him, "How
many times must I make you
swear to tell me nothing but the
truth in the name of the LORD?"
17Then Micaiah answered, "I saw
all Israel scattered on the hills like
sheep without a shepherd, and the
LORD said, 'These people have no
master. Let each one go home in
peace.'" Nu 27:17; Mt 9:36
18The king of Israel said to Jehoshaphat, "Didn't I tell you that
he never prophesies anything
good about me, but only bad?"
19Micaiah continued, "Therefore hear the word of the LORD: I
saw the LORD sitting on his throne
with all the multitudes of heaven
standing around him on his right
and on his left. 20And the LORD
said, 'Who will entice Ahab into
attacking Ramoth Gilead and going to his death there?'
Job 1:6; Isa 6:1; Da 7:9
"One suggested this, and another that. 21Finally, a spirit came forward, stood before the LORD and
said, 'I will entice him.'
22"'By what means?' the LORD
asked.
"'I will go out and be a deceiving spirit in the mouths of all his
prophets,' he said. Jdg 9:23; 2Th 2:11
"'You will succeed in enticing
him,' said the LORD. 'Go and do it.'
23"So now the LORD has put a deceiving spirit in the mouths of all
these prophets of yours. The LORD
has decreed disaster for you."
Eze 14:9
24Then Zedekiah son of Kenaanah went up and slapped Micaiah
in the face. "Which way did the
spirit from[a] the LORD go when he
went from me to speak to you?"
he asked. ver 11; Ac 23:2
25Micaiah replied, "You will find
out on the day you go to hide in an
inner room." 1Ki 20:30
26The king of Israel then ordered, "Take Micaiah and send him
back to Amon the ruler of the city
and to Joash the king's son 27and
say, 'This is what the king says: Put
this fellow in prison and give him
nothing but bread and water until
I return safely.'" 2Ch 16:10
28Micaiah declared, "If you ever
return safely, the LORD has not
spoken through me." Then he
added, "Mark my words, all you
people!" 2Ch 18:1-27; Dt 18:22

Ahab Killed at Ramoth Gilead

29So the king of Israel and Jehoshaphat king of Judah went up
to Ramoth Gilead. 30The king of
Israel said to Jehoshaphat, "I will
enter the battle in disguise, but
you wear your royal robes." So the
king of Israel disguised himself
and went into battle. 2Ch 35:32
31Now the king of Aram had ordered his thirty-two chariot commanders, "Do not fight with anyone, small or great, except the king

[a] 24 Or *Spirit of*

of Israel." 32 When the chariot commanders saw Jehoshaphat, they
thought, "Surely this is the king
of Israel." So they turned to attack
him, but when Jehoshaphat cried
out, 33 the chariot commanders saw
that he was not the king of Israel
and stopped pursuing him. 2Sa 17:2
34 But someone drew his bow at
random and hit the king of Israel
between the sections of his armor.
The king told his chariot driver,
"Wheel around and get me out of
the fighting. I've been wounded."
35 All day long the battle raged, and
the king was propped up in his chariot facing the Arameans. The blood
from his wound ran onto the floor
of the chariot, and that evening he
died. 36 As the sun was setting, a cry
spread through the army: "Every
man to his town. Every man to his
land!" 2Ki 14:12; 2Ch 35:23
37 So the king died and was
brought to Samaria, and they buried him there. 38 They washed the
chariot at a pool in Samaria (where
the prostitutes bathed),[a] and the
dogs licked up his blood, as the
word of the LORD had declared.
1Ki 21:19
39 As for the other events of
Ahab's reign, including all he did,
the palace he built and adorned
with ivory, and the cities he fortified, are they not written in the
book of the annals of the kings of
Israel? 40 Ahab rested with his ancestors. And Ahaziah his son succeeded him as king. 2Ch 9:17; Am 3:15

Jehoshaphat King of Judah

41 Jehoshaphat son of Asa became king of Judah in the fourth
year of Ahab king of Israel. 42 Jehoshaphat was thirty-five years
old when he became king, and he
reigned in Jerusalem twenty-five
years. His mother's name was Azubah daughter of Shilhi. 43 In everything he followed the ways of his
father Asa and did not stray from
them; he did what was right in the
eyes of the LORD. The high places,
however, were not removed, and
the people continued to offer sacrifices and burn incense there.[b]
44 Jehoshaphat was also at peace
with the king of Israel.
1Ki 15:14; 2Ki 12:3; 2Ch 17:3
45 As for the other events of Jehoshaphat's reign, the things he
achieved and his military exploits,
are they not written in the book of
the annals of the kings of Judah?
46 He rid the land of the rest of the
male shrine prostitutes who remained there even after the reign
of his father Asa. 47 There was then
no king in Edom; a provincial governor ruled. 2Sa 8:14; 1Ki 15:12; 2Ki 3:9
48 Now Jehoshaphat built a fleet
of trading ships[c] to go to Ophir
for gold, but they never set sail—
they were wrecked at Ezion Geber.
49 At that time Ahaziah son of Ahab
said to Jehoshaphat, "Let my men

[a] 38 Or *Samaria and cleaned the weapons*
[b] 43 In Hebrew texts this sentence (22:43b) is numbered 22:44, and 22:44-53 is numbered 22:45-54.
[c] 48 Hebrew *of ships of Tarshish*

sail with yours," but Jehoshaphat
refused. 1Ki 9:26

50 Then Jehoshaphat rested with
his ancestors and was buried with
them in the city of David his father. And Jehoram his son succeeded him as king. 2Ch 20:31-21:1

Ahaziah King of Israel

51 Ahaziah son of Ahab became
king of Israel in Samaria in the
seventeenth year of Jehoshaphat
king of Judah, and he reigned
over Israel two years. 52 He did evil
in the eyes of the LORD, because
he followed the ways of his father and mother and of Jeroboam
son of Nebat, who caused Israel
to sin. 53 He served and worshiped
Baal and aroused the anger of the
LORD, the God of Israel, just as his
father had done. 1Ki 15:26; 16:30-32

2 KINGS

The LORD's Judgment on Ahaziah

1 After Ahab's death, Moab rebelled against Israel. 2Now Ahaziah had fallen through the lattice of his upper room in Samaria and injured himself. So he sent messengers, saying to them, "Go and consult Baal-Zebub, the god of Ekron, to see if I will recover from this injury." 2Sa 8:2; 2Ki 3:5; Mk 3:22

3But the angel of the LORD said to Elijah the Tishbite, "Go up and meet the messengers of the king of Samaria and ask them, 'Is it because there is no God in Israel that you are going off to consult Baal-Zebub, the god of Ekron?'
4Therefore this is what the LORD says: 'You will not leave the bed you are lying on. You will certainly die!'" So Elijah went.

Ge 16:7; 1Ki 17:1

5When the messengers returned to the king, he asked them, "Why have you come back?"

6"A man came to meet us," they replied. "And he said to us, 'Go back to the king who sent you and tell him, "This is what the LORD says: Is it because there is no God in Israel that you are sending messengers to consult Baal-Zebub, the god of Ekron? Therefore you will not leave the bed you are lying on. You will certainly die!"'"

7The king asked them, "What kind of man was it who came to meet you and told you this?"

8They replied, "He had a garment of hair[a] and had a leather belt around his waist." Zec 13:4; Mt 3:4; Mk 1:6

The king said, "That was Elijah the Tishbite."

9Then he sent to Elijah a captain with his company of fifty men. The captain went up to Elijah, who was sitting on the top of a hill, and said to him, "Man of God, the king says, 'Come down!'"

Ex 18:25; 2Ki 6:14; Isa 3:3

10Elijah answered the captain, "If I am a man of God, may fire come down from heaven and consume you and your fifty men!" Then fire fell from heaven and consumed the captain and his men. 1Ki 18:38; Lk 9:54

11At this the king sent to Elijah another captain with his fifty men. The captain said to him, "Man of God, this is what the king says, 'Come down at once!'"

12"If I am a man of God," Elijah replied, "may fire come down from heaven and consume you and your fifty men!" Then the fire of God fell from heaven and consumed him and his fifty men.

13So the king sent a third captain with his fifty men. This third

[a] 8 Or *He was a hairy man*

captain went up and fell on his
knees before Elijah. "Man of God,"
he begged, "please have respect
for my life and the lives of these
fifty men, your servants! 14 See, fire
has fallen from heaven and consumed the first two captains and
all their men. But now have respect for my life!" 1Sa 26:21; Ps 72:14
15 The angel of the LORD said to
Elijah, "Go down with him; do not
be afraid of him." So Elijah got up
and went down with him to the
king. Isa 51:12; Jer 1:17; Eze 2:6
16 He told the king, "This is what
the LORD says: Is it because there
is no God in Israel for you to consult that you have sent messengers to consult Baal-Zebub, the
god of Ekron? Because you have
done this, you will never leave
the bed you are lying on. You will
certainly die!" 17 So he died, according to the word of the LORD
that Elijah had spoken.
2Ki 8:15; Jer 20:6; 28:17
Because Ahaziah had no son,
Joram[a] succeeded him as king in
the second year of Jehoram son of
Jehoshaphat king of Judah. 18 As
for all the other events of Ahaziah's reign, and what he did, are
they not written in the book of
the annals of the kings of Israel?
2Ki 3:1; 8:16

Elijah Taken Up to Heaven

2 When the LORD was about to
take Elijah up to heaven in a
whirlwind, Elijah and Elisha were
on their way from Gilgal. 2 Elijah
said to Elisha, "Stay here; the LORD
has sent me to Bethel."
Ge 5:24; 1Ki 19:16,21; Heb 11:5
But Elisha said, "As surely as the
LORD lives and as you live, I will
not leave you." So they went down
to Bethel. Ru 1:16; 1Sa 1:26
3 The company of the prophets
at Bethel came out to Elisha and
asked, "Do you know that the
LORD is going to take your master from you today?"
1Sa 10:5; 2Ki 4:1,38
"Yes, I know," Elisha replied, "so
be quiet."
4 Then Elijah said to him, "Stay
here, Elisha; the LORD has sent me
to Jericho." Jos 3:16; 6:26
And he replied, "As surely as the
LORD lives and as you live, I will
not leave you." So they went to
Jericho.
5 The company of the prophets
at Jericho went up to Elisha and
asked him, "Do you know that the
LORD is going to take your master
from you today?"
"Yes, I know," he replied, "so be
quiet."
6 Then Elijah said to him, "Stay
here; the LORD has sent me to the
Jordan." Jos 3:15
And he replied, "As surely as the
LORD lives and as you live, I will
not leave you." So the two of them
walked on. Ru 1:16
7 Fifty men from the company
of the prophets went and stood at
a distance, facing the place where
Elijah and Elisha had stopped at

[a] 17 Hebrew *Jehoram*, a variant of *Joram*

the Jordan. 8Elijah took his cloak, rolled it up and struck the water with it. The water divided to the right and to the left, and the two of them crossed over on dry ground. Ex 14:21-22,29; 1Ki 19:19

9When they had crossed, Elijah said to Elisha, "Tell me, what can I do for you before I am taken from you?"

"Let me inherit a double portion of your spirit," Elisha replied. Nu 11:17; Dt 21:17

10"You have asked a difficult thing," Elijah said, "yet if you see me when I am taken from you, it will be yours — otherwise, it will not."

11As they were walking along and talking together, suddenly a chariot of fire and horses of fire appeared and separated the two of them, and Elijah went up to heaven in a whirlwind. 12Elisha saw this and cried out, "My father! My father! The chariots and horsemen of Israel!" And Elisha saw him no more. Then he took hold of his garment and tore it in two. Ge 5:24; 2Ki 13:14; Ps 104:3-4

13Elisha then picked up Elijah's cloak that had fallen from him and went back and stood on the bank of the Jordan. 14He took the cloak that had fallen from Elijah and struck the water with it. "Where now is the LORD, the God of Elijah?" he asked. When he struck the water, it divided to the right and to the left, and he crossed over. 1Ki 19:19

15The company of the prophets from Jericho, who were watching, said, "The spirit of Elijah is resting on Elisha." And they went to meet him and bowed to the ground before him. 16"Look," they said, "we your servants have fifty able men. Let them go and look for your master. Perhaps the Spirit of the LORD has picked him up and set him down on some mountain or in some valley." 1Ki 18:12; Ac 8:39; 1Sa 10:5

"No," Elisha replied, "do not send them."

17But they persisted until he was too embarrassed to refuse. So he said, "Send them." And they sent fifty men, who searched for three days but did not find him. 18When they returned to Elisha, who was staying in Jericho, he said to them, "Didn't I tell you not to go?" 2Ki 8:11

Healing of the Water

19The people of the city said to Elisha, "Look, our lord, this town is well situated, as you can see, but the water is bad and the land is unproductive."

20"Bring me a new bowl," he said, "and put salt in it." So they brought it to him.

21Then he went out to the spring and threw the salt into it, saying, "This is what the LORD says: 'I have healed this water. Never again will it cause death or make the land unproductive.' " 22And the water has remained pure to this day, according to the word Elisha had spoken. Ex 15:25; 2Ki 4:41; 6:6

Elisha Is Jeered

23 From there Elisha went up to Bethel. As he was walking along the road, some boys came out of the town and jeered at him. "Get out of here, baldy!" they said. "Get out of here, baldy!" 24 He turned around, looked at them and called down a curse on them in the name of the LORD. Then two bears came out of the woods and mauled forty-two of the boys. 25 And he went on to Mount Carmel and from there returned to Samaria.

1Ki 18:20; Ge 4:11; Ne 13:25-27

Moab Revolts

3 Joram[a] son of Ahab became king of Israel in Samaria in the eighteenth year of Jehoshaphat king of Judah, and he reigned twelve years. 2 He did evil in the eyes of the LORD, but not as his father and mother had done. He got rid of the sacred stone of Baal that his father had made. 3 Nevertheless he clung to the sins of Jeroboam son of Nebat, which he had caused Israel to commit; he did not turn away from them.

1Ki 12:28-32; 14:9,16; 16:30-32

4 Now Mesha king of Moab raised sheep, and he had to pay the king of Israel a tribute of a hundred thousand lambs and the wool of a hundred thousand rams. 5 But after Ahab died, the king of Moab rebelled against the king of Israel. 6 So at that time King Joram set out from Samaria and mobilized all Israel. 7 He also sent this message to Jehoshaphat king of Judah: "The king of Moab has rebelled against me. Will you go with me to fight against Moab?"

1Ki 22:4; 2Ki 1:1; Isa 16:1

"I will go with you," he replied. "I am as you are, my people as your people, my horses as your horses."

8 "By what route shall we attack?" he asked.

"Through the Desert of Edom," he answered.

9 So the king of Israel set out with the king of Judah and the king of Edom. After a roundabout march of seven days, the army had no more water for themselves or for the animals with them.

1Ki 22:47

10 "What!" exclaimed the king of Israel. "Has the LORD called us three kings together only to deliver us into the hands of Moab?"

11 But Jehoshaphat asked, "Is there no prophet of the LORD here, through whom we may inquire of the LORD?" 1Ki 22:7

An officer of the king of Israel answered, "Elisha son of Shaphat is here. He used to pour water on the hands of Elijah.[b]" Ge 20:7; 1Ki 19:16

12 Jehoshaphat said, "The word of the LORD is with him." So the king of Israel and Jehoshaphat and the king of Edom went down to him. Nu 11:17

[a] *1* Hebrew *Jehoram,* a variant of *Joram;* also in verse 6 [b] *11* That is, he was Elijah's personal servant.

13 Elisha said to the king of Israel,
"Why do you want to involve me?
Go to the prophets of your father
and the prophets of your mother."

"No," the king of Israel answered, "because it was the LORD
who called us three kings together to deliver us into the hands of
Moab."

14 Elisha said, "As surely as the
LORD Almighty lives, whom I
serve, if I did not have respect for
the presence of Jehoshaphat king
of Judah, I would not pay any attention to you. 15 But now bring me
a harpist." 1Sa 16:23

While the harpist was playing,
the hand of the LORD came on Elisha 16 and he said, "This is what
the LORD says: I will fill this valley with pools of water. 17 For this
is what the LORD says: You will
see neither wind nor rain, yet this
valley will be filled with water,
and you, your cattle and your other animals will drink. 18 This is an
easy thing in the eyes of the LORD;
he will also deliver Moab into your
hands. 19 You will overthrow every fortified city and every ma-
jor town. You will cut down every
good tree, stop up all the springs,
and ruin every good field with
stones." Ge 18:14; Jer 32:17,27

20 The next morning, about the
time for offering the sacrifice,
there it was — water flowing from
the direction of Edom! And the
land was filled with water.

Ex 29:39-40

21 Now all the Moabites had heard
that the kings had come to fight
against them; so every man, young
and old, who could bear arms was
called up and stationed on the
border. 22 When they got up early
in the morning, the sun was shining on the water. To the Moabites
across the way, the water looked
red — like blood. 23 "That's blood!"
they said. "Those kings must have
fought and slaughtered each other. Now to the plunder, Moab!"

24 But when the Moabites came
to the camp of Israel, the Israelites rose up and fought them until they fled. And the Israelites invaded the land and slaughtered
the Moabites. 25 They destroyed
the towns, and each man threw a
stone on every good field until it
was covered. They stopped up all
the springs and cut down every
good tree. Only Kir Hareseth was
left with its stones in place, but
men armed with slings surrounded it and attacked it.

Isa 16:7; Jer 48:31,36; Eze 1:3

26 When the king of Moab saw
that the battle had gone against
him, he took with him seven hundred swordsmen to break through
to the king of Edom, but they
failed. 27 Then he took his firstborn
son, who was to succeed him as
king, and offered him as a sacrifice
on the city wall. The fury against
Israel was great; they withdrew
and returned to their own land.

Am 2:1; Mic 6:7

The Widow's Olive Oil

4 The wife of a man from the company of the prophets cried out to Elisha, "Your servant my husband is dead, and you know that he revered the LORD. But now his creditor is coming to take my two boys as his slaves."

Lev 25:39-43; Ne 5:3-5; Job 22:6

2 Elisha replied to her, "How can I help you? Tell me, what do you have in your house?"

"Your servant has nothing there at all," she said, "except a small jar of olive oil." 1Ki 17:12

3 Elisha said, "Go around and ask all your neighbors for empty jars. Don't ask for just a few. 4 Then go inside and shut the door behind you and your sons. Pour oil into all the jars, and as each is filled, put it to one side."

5 She left him and shut the door behind her and her sons. They brought the jars to her and she kept pouring. 6 When all the jars were full, she said to her son, "Bring me another one."

But he replied, "There is not a jar left." Then the oil stopped flowing.

7 She went and told the man of God, and he said, "Go, sell the oil and pay your debts. You and your sons can live on what is left." 1Ki 12:22

The Shunammite's Son Restored to Life

8 One day Elisha went to Shunem. And a well-to-do woman was there, who urged him to stay for a meal. So whenever he came by, he stopped there to eat. 9 She said to her husband, "I know that this man who often comes our way is a holy man of God. 10 Let's make a small room on the roof and put in it a bed and a table, a chair and a lamp for him. Then he can stay there whenever he comes to us."

Jos 19:18; Mt 10:41; Ro 12:13

11 One day when Elisha came, he went up to his room and lay down there. 12 He said to his servant Gehazi, "Call the Shunammite." So he called her, and she stood before him. 13 Elisha said to him, "Tell her, 'You have gone to all this trouble for us. Now what can be done for you? Can we speak on your behalf to the king or the commander of the army?'" 2Ki 8:1

She replied, "I have a home among my own people."

14 "What can be done for her?" Elisha asked.

Gehazi said, "She has no son, and her husband is old."

15 Then Elisha said, "Call her." So he called her, and she stood in the doorway. 16 "About this time next year," Elisha said, "you will hold a son in your arms." Ge 18:10

"No, my lord!" she objected. "Please, man of God, don't mislead your servant!"

17 But the woman became pregnant, and the next year about that same time she gave birth to a son, just as Elisha had told her.

18 The child grew, and one day he went out to his father, who was

with the reapers. 19He said to his
father, "My head! My head!" Ru 2:3
His father told a servant, "Carry him to his mother." 20After the
servant had lifted him up and carried him to his mother, the boy sat
on her lap until noon, and then he
died. 21She went up and laid him
on the bed of the man of God, then
shut the door and went out. ver 32

22She called her husband and
said, "Please send me one of the
servants and a donkey so I can go to
the man of God quickly and return."

23"Why go to him today?" he
asked. "It's not the New Moon or
the Sabbath." Nu 10:10; 1Ch 23:31; Ps 81:3

"That's all right," she said.

24She saddled the donkey and
said to her servant, "Lead on; don't
slow down for me unless I tell
you." 25So she set out and came to
the man of God at Mount Carmel.
1Ki 18:20; 2Ki 2:25

When he saw her in the distance, the man of God said to his
servant Gehazi, "Look! There's the
Shunammite! 26Run to meet her
and ask her, 'Are you all right? Is
your husband all right? Is your
child all right?' "

"Everything is all right," she
said.

27When she reached the man
of God at the mountain, she took
hold of his feet. Gehazi came over
to push her away, but the man of
God said, "Leave her alone! She
is in bitter distress, but the LORD
has hidden it from me and has not
told me why." 1Sa 1:15

28"Did I ask you for a son, my
lord?" she said. "Didn't I tell you,
'Don't raise my hopes'?"

29Elisha said to Gehazi, "Tuck
your cloak into your belt, take my
staff in your hand and run. Don't
greet anyone you meet, and if
anyone greets you, do not answer.
Lay my staff on the boy's face."
Ex 7:19; 1Ki 18:46

30But the child's mother said,
"As surely as the LORD lives and as
you live, I will not leave you." So
he got up and followed her.

31Gehazi went on ahead and laid
the staff on the boy's face, but
there was no sound or response.
So Gehazi went back to meet Elisha and told him, "The boy has
not awakened."

32When Elisha reached the
house, there was the boy lying
dead on his couch. 33He went in,
shut the door on the two of them
and prayed to the LORD. 34Then he
got on the bed and lay on the boy,
mouth to mouth, eyes to eyes,
hands to hands. As he stretched
himself out on him, the boy's body
grew warm. 35Elisha turned away
and walked back and forth in the
room and then got on the bed and
stretched out on him once more.
The boy sneezed seven times and
opened his eyes.
1Ki 17:20-21; 2Ki 8:5; Ac 20:10

36Elisha summoned Gehazi and
said, "Call the Shunammite." And
he did. When she came, he said,
"Take your son." 37She came in,
fell at his feet and bowed to the

ground. Then she took her son and went out. Heb 11:35

Death in the Pot

38 Elisha returned to Gilgal and there was a famine in that region. While the company of the prophets was meeting with him, he said to his servant, "Put on the large pot and cook some stew for these prophets." 2Ki 2:1; 8:1

39 One of them went out into the fields to gather herbs and found a wild vine and picked as many of its gourds as his garment could hold. When he returned, he cut them up into the pot of stew, though no one knew what they were. 40 The stew was poured out for the men, but as they began to eat it, they cried out, "Man of God, there is death in the pot!" And they could not eat it.

41 Elisha said, "Get some flour." He put it into the pot and said, "Serve it to the people to eat." And there was nothing harmful in the pot. Ex 15:25; 2Ki 2:21

Feeding of a Hundred

42 A man came from Baal Shalishah, bringing the man of God twenty loaves of barley bread baked from the first ripe grain, along with some heads of new grain. "Give it to the people to eat," Elisha said. 1Sa 9:4,7; Mt 14:17; 15:36

43 "How can I set this before a hundred men?" his servant asked.

But Elisha answered, "Give it to the people to eat. For this is what the LORD says: 'They will eat and have some left over.' " 44 Then he set it before them, and they ate and had some left over, according to the word of the LORD. Lk 9:13; Jn 6:12

Naaman Healed of Leprosy

5 Now Naaman was commander of the army of the king of Aram. He was a great man in the sight of his master and highly regarded, because through him the LORD had given victory to Aram. He was a valiant soldier, but he had leprosy.[a] Lk 4:27; 2Sa 10:19

2 Now bands of raiders from Aram had gone out and had taken captive a young girl from Israel, and she served Naaman's wife. 3 She said to her mistress, "If only my master would see the prophet who is in Samaria! He would cure him of his leprosy." Ge 20:7; 2Ki 6:23; 13:20

4 Naaman went to his master and told him what the girl from Israel had said. 5 "By all means, go," the king of Aram replied. "I will send a letter to the king of Israel." So Naaman left, taking with him ten talents[b] of silver, six thousand shekels[c] of gold and ten sets of clothing. 6 The letter that he took to the king of Israel read: "With this letter I am sending my servant Naaman to you so that you may cure him of his leprosy." 1Sa 9:7

[a] 1 The Hebrew for *leprosy* was used for various diseases affecting the skin; also in verses 3, 6, 7, 11 and 27. [b] 5 That is, about 750 pounds or about 340 kilograms [c] 5 That is, about 150 pounds or about 69 kilograms

7 As soon as the king of Israel
read the letter, he tore his robes
and said, "Am I God? Can I kill and
bring back to life? Why does this
fellow send someone to me to be
cured of his leprosy? See how he is
trying to pick a quarrel with me!"
Ge 30:2; 1Sa 2:6; 1Ki 20:7

8 When Elisha the man of God
heard that the king of Israel had
torn his robes, he sent him this
message: "Why have you torn
your robes? Have the man come
to me and he will know that there
is a prophet in Israel." 9 So Naaman
went with his horses and chariots
and stopped at the door of Elisha's
house. 10 Elisha sent a messenger
to say to him, "Go, wash yourself
seven times in the Jordan, and
your flesh will be restored and
you will be cleansed."
Jn 9:7; Lev 14:7; 1Ki 22:7

11 But Naaman went away angry
and said, "I thought that he would
surely come out to me and stand
and call on the name of the LORD
his God, wave his hand over the
spot and cure me of my leprosy.
12 Are not Abana and Pharpar, the
rivers of Damascus, better than
all the waters of Israel? Couldn't I
wash in them and be cleansed?" So
he turned and went off in a rage.
Pr 14:17,29; 19:11; 29:11

13 Naaman's servants went to
him and said, "My father, if the
prophet had told you to do some
great thing, would you not have
done it? How much more, then,
when he tells you, 'Wash and be
cleansed'!" 14 So he went down
and dipped himself in the Jordan
seven times, as the man of God
had told him, and his flesh was
restored and became clean like
that of a young boy.
Jos 6:15; Job 33:25; Lk 4:27

15 Then Naaman and all his attendants went back to the man
of God. He stood before him and
said, "Now I know that there is no
God in all the world except in Israel. So please accept a gift from
your servant." Jos 4:24; 1Sa 17:46

16 The prophet answered, "As
surely as the LORD lives, whom I
serve, I will not accept a thing."
And even though Naaman urged
him, he refused. ver 20,26; Ge 14:23

17 "If you will not," said Naaman,
"please let me, your servant, be
given as much earth as a pair of
mules can carry, for your servant
will never again make burnt offerings and sacrifices to any other god
but the LORD. 18 But may the LORD
forgive your servant for this one
thing: When my master enters the
temple of Rimmon to bow down
and he is leaning on my arm and
I have to bow there also — when I
bow down in the temple of Rimmon, may the LORD forgive your
servant for this." Ex 20:24; 2Ki 7:2

19 "Go in peace," Elisha said.
1Sa 1:17; Ac 15:33

After Naaman had traveled
some distance, 20 Gehazi, the servant of Elisha the man of God, said
to himself, "My master was too
easy on Naaman, this Aramean,

by not accepting from him what
he brought. As surely as the LORD
lives, I will run after him and get
something from him." Ex 20:7
21So Gehazi hurried after Naaman. When Naaman saw him running toward him, he got down
from the chariot to meet him. "Is
everything all right?" he asked.
22"Everything is all right," Gehazi answered. "My master sent me
to say, 'Two young men from the
company of the prophets have just
come to me from the hill country of Ephraim. Please give them
a talent[a] of silver and two sets of
clothing.'" ver 5; Ge 45:22
23"By all means, take two talents," said Naaman. He urged Gehazi to accept them, and then tied
up the two talents of silver in two
bags, with two sets of clothing. He
gave them to two of his servants,
and they carried them ahead of
Gehazi. 24When Gehazi came to the
hill, he took the things from the
servants and put them away in the
house. He sent the men away and
they left.
25When he went in and stood before his master, Elisha asked him,
"Where have you been, Gehazi?"
"Your servant didn't go anywhere," Gehazi answered.
26But Elisha said to him, "Was
not my spirit with you when the
man got down from his chariot
to meet you? Is this the time to
take money or to accept clothes —
or olive groves and vineyards, or
flocks and herds, or male and female slaves? 27Naaman's leprosy
will cling to you and to your descendants forever." Then Gehazi
went from Elisha's presence and
his skin was leprous — it had become as white as snow.
ver 16; Ex 4:6; Nu 12:10

An Axhead Floats

6 The company of the prophets said to Elisha, "Look, the
place where we meet with you is
too small for us. 2Let us go to the
Jordan, where each of us can get a
pole; and let us build a place there
for us to meet." 1Sa 10:5; 2Ki 4:38
And he said, "Go."
3Then one of them said, "Won't
you please come with your servants?"
"I will," Elisha replied. 4And he
went with them.
They went to the Jordan and
began to cut down trees. 5As one
of them was cutting down a tree,
the iron axhead fell into the water.
"Oh no, my lord!" he cried out. "It
was borrowed!"
6The man of God asked, "Where
did it fall?" When he showed him
the place, Elisha cut a stick and
threw it there, and made the iron
float. 7"Lift it out," he said. Then
the man reached out his hand and
took it. Ex 15:25; 2Ki 2:21

Elisha Traps Blinded Arameans

8Now the king of Aram was at
war with Israel. After conferring

[a] 22 That is, about 75 pounds or about 34 kilograms

with his officers, he said, "I will
set up my camp in such and such
a place."
9The man of God sent word to
the king of Israel: "Beware of passing that place, because the Arameans are going down there." 10So
the king of Israel checked on the
place indicated by the man of God.
Time and again Elisha warned the
king, so that he was on his guard
in such places. ver 12; Jer 11:18
11This enraged the king of Aram.
He summoned his officers and demanded of them, "Tell me! Which
of us is on the side of the king of
Israel?"
12"None of us, my lord the king,"
said one of his officers, "but Elisha,
the prophet who is in Israel, tells
the king of Israel the very words
you speak in your bedroom."
13"Go, find out where he is," the
king ordered, "so I can send men
and capture him." The report came
back: "He is in Dothan." 14Then he
sent horses and chariots and a
strong force there. They went by
night and surrounded the city.
Ge 37:17; 2Ki 1:9
15When the servant of the man
of God got up and went out early the next morning, an army
with horses and chariots had surrounded the city. "Oh no, my lord!
What shall we do?" the servant
asked.
16"Don't be afraid," the prophet
answered. "Those who are with us
are more than those who are with
them." 2Ch 32:7; Ps 55:18; 1Jn 4:4
17And Elisha prayed, "Open his
eyes, LORD, so that he may see."
Then the LORD opened the servant's eyes, and he looked and saw
the hills full of horses and chariots
of fire all around Elisha.
2Ki 2:11-12; Ps 68:17; Zec 6:1-7
18As the enemy came down toward him, Elisha prayed to the
LORD, "Strike this army with
blindness." So he struck them with
blindness, as Elisha had asked.
Ge 19:11; Ac 13:11
19Elisha told them, "This is not
the road and this is not the city.
Follow me, and I will lead you to
the man you are looking for." And
he led them to Samaria.
20After they entered the city, Elisha said, "LORD, open the eyes of
these men so they can see." Then
the LORD opened their eyes and
they looked, and there they were,
inside Samaria.
21When the king of Israel saw
them, he asked Elisha, "Shall I
kill them, my father? Shall I kill
them?" 2Ki 5:13
22"Do not kill them," he answered. "Would you kill those
you have captured with your own
sword or bow? Set food and water
before them so that they may eat
and drink and then go back to their
master." 23So he prepared a great
feast for them, and after they had
finished eating and drinking, he
sent them away, and they returned
to their master. So the bands from
Aram stopped raiding Israel's territory. Dt 20:11; 2Ki 5:2; Ro 12:20

Famine in Besieged Samaria

24Some time later, Ben-Hadad
king of Aram mobilized his entire
army and marched up and laid
siege to Samaria. 25There was a
great famine in the city; the siege
lasted so long that a donkey's
head sold for eighty shekels[a] of
silver, and a quarter of a cab[b] of
seed pods[c] for five shekels.[d]

Lev 26:26; 1Ki 15:18; Isa 36:12

26As the king of Israel was passing by on the wall, a woman cried
to him, "Help me, my lord the
king!"

27The king replied, "If the LORD
does not help you, where can I get
help for you? From the threshing floor? From the winepress?"
28Then he asked her, "What's the
matter?"

She answered, "This woman
said to me, 'Give up your son so we
may eat him today, and tomorrow
we'll eat my son.' 29So we cooked
my son and ate him. The next day
I said to her, 'Give up your son so
we may eat him,' but she had hidden him."

Lev 26:29; Dt 28:53-55

30When the king heard the
woman's words, he tore his robes.
As he went along the wall, the people looked, and they saw that, under his robes, he had sackcloth on
his body. 31He said, "May God deal
with me, be it ever so severely, if
the head of Elisha son of Shaphat
remains on his shoulders today!"

Ge 37:34; 1Ki 21:27

32Now Elisha was sitting in his
house, and the elders were sitting with him. The king sent a
messenger ahead, but before he
arrived, Elisha said to the elders,
"Don't you see how this murderer
is sending someone to cut off my
head? Look, when the messenger
comes, shut the door and hold it
shut against him. Is not the sound
of his master's footsteps behind
him?" 33While he was still talking to them, the messenger came
down to him.

1Ki 18:4; Eze 8:1

The king said, "This disaster is
from the LORD. Why should I wait
for the LORD any longer?"

Job 2:9; 14:14; Isa 40:31

7 Elisha replied, "Hear the word
of the LORD. This is what the
LORD says: About this time tomorrow, a seah[e] of the finest flour will
sell for a shekel[f] and two seahs[g] of
barley for a shekel at the gate of
Samaria."

ver 16

2The officer on whose arm the
king was leaning said to the man
of God, "Look, even if the LORD
should open the floodgates of the
heavens, could this happen?"

2Ki 5:18; Mal 3:10

"You will see it with your own
eyes," answered Elisha, "but you
will not eat any of it!"

ver 17

[a] *25* That is, about 2 pounds or about 920 grams [b] *25* That is, probably about 1/4 pound or about 100 grams [c] *25* Or *of doves' dung* [d] *25* That is, about 2 ounces or about 58 grams [e] *1* That is, probably about 12 pounds or about 5.5 kilograms of flour; also in verses 16 and 18 [f] *1* That is, about 2/5 ounce or about 12 grams; also in verses 16 and 18 [g] *1* That is, probably about 20 pounds or about 9 kilograms of barley; also in verses 16 and 18

The Siege Lifted

[3]Now there were four men with
leprosy[a] at the entrance of the city
gate. They said to each other, "Why
stay here until we die? [4]If we say,
'We'll go into the city' — the famine is there, and we will die. And
if we stay here, we will die. So let's
go over to the camp of the Arameans and surrender. If they spare
us, we live; if they kill us, then we
die." Lev 13:45-46; Nu 5:1-4

[5]At dusk they got up and went
to the camp of the Arameans.
When they reached the edge of
the camp, no one was there, [6]for
the Lord had caused the Arameans to hear the sound of chariots and horses and a great army,
so that they said to one another,
"Look, the king of Israel has hired
the Hittite and Egyptian kings to
attack us!" [7]So they got up and fled
in the dusk and abandoned their
tents and their horses and donkeys. They left the camp as it was
and ran for their lives.

2Sa 5:24; Ps 48:4-6; Pr 28:1

[8]The men who had leprosy
reached the edge of the camp, entered one of the tents and ate and
drank. Then they took silver, gold
and clothes, and went off and hid
them. They returned and entered
another tent and took some things
from it and hid them also.

Isa 33:23; 35:6

[9]Then they said to each other,
"What we're doing is not right.
This is a day of good news and we
are keeping it to ourselves. If we
wait until daylight, punishment
will overtake us. Let's go at once
and report this to the royal palace."

[10]So they went and called out
to the city gatekeepers and told
them, "We went into the Aramean
camp and no one was there — not
a sound of anyone — only teth-
ered horses and donkeys, and the
tents left just as they were." [11]The
gatekeepers shouted the news,
and it was reported within the
palace.

[12]The king got up in the night
and said to his officers, "I will tell
you what the Arameans have done
to us. They know we are starving;
so they have left the camp to hide
in the countryside, thinking, 'They
will surely come out, and then we
will take them alive and get into
the city.'" Jos 8:4; 2Ki 6:25-29

[13]One of his officers answered,
"Have some men take five of the
horses that are left in the city.
Their plight will be like that of
all the Israelites left here — yes,
they will only be like all these Israelites who are doomed. So let us
send them to find out what happened."

[14]So they selected two chariots
with their horses, and the king
sent them after the Aramean
army. He commanded the drivers,
"Go and find out what has happened." [15]They followed them as

[a] 3 The Hebrew for *leprosy* was used for various diseases affecting the skin; also in verse 8.

far as the Jordan, and they found
the whole road strewn with the
clothing and equipment the Arameans had thrown away in their
headlong flight. So the messengers returned and reported to the
king. 16Then the people went out
and plundered the camp of the
Arameans. So a seah of the finest
flour sold for a shekel, and two seahs of barley sold for a shekel, as
the LORD had said. ver 1; Isa 33:4,23

17Now the king had put the officer on whose arm he leaned in
charge of the gate, and the people
trampled him in the gateway, and
he died, just as the man of God
had foretold when the king came
down to his house. 18It happened
as the man of God had said to the
king: "About this time tomorrow,
a seah of the finest flour will sell
for a shekel and two seahs of barley for a shekel at the gate of Samaria." ver 2; 2Ki 6:32

19The officer had said to the man
of God, "Look, even if the LORD
should open the floodgates of the
heavens, could this happen?" The
man of God had replied, "You will
see it with your own eyes, but you
will not eat any of it!" 20And that
is exactly what happened to him,
for the people trampled him in
the gateway, and he died. ver 2

The Shunammite's Land Restored

8 Now Elisha had said to the
woman whose son he had restored to life, "Go away with your
family and stay for a while wherever you can, because the LORD has
decreed a famine in the land that
will last seven years." 2The woman proceeded to do as the man of
God said. She and her family went
away and stayed in the land of the
Philistines seven years.
2Ki 4:8-37; Ps 105:16; Hag 1:11

3At the end of the seven years
she came back from the land of
the Philistines and went to appeal
to the king for her house and land.
4The king was talking to Gehazi, the servant of the man of God,
and had said, "Tell me about all
the great things Elisha has done."
5Just as Gehazi was telling the king
how Elisha had restored the dead
to life, the woman whose son Elisha had brought back to life came
to appeal to the king for her house
and land. 2Ki 4:35

Gehazi said, "This is the woman,
my lord the king, and this is her
son whom Elisha restored to life."
6The king asked the woman about
it, and she told him.

Then he assigned an official to
her case and said to him, "Give
back everything that belonged to
her, including all the income from
her land from the day she left the
country until now."

Hazael Murders Ben-Hadad

7Elisha went to Damascus, and
Ben-Hadad king of Aram was ill.
When the king was told, "The man
of God has come all the way up
here," 8he said to Hazael, "Take a
gift with you and go to meet the

man of God. Consult the LORD
through him; ask him, 'Will I recover from this illness?'"
1Sa 9:7; 1Ki 19:15; 2Ki 1:2

9Hazael went to meet Elisha,
taking with him as a gift forty
camel-loads of all the finest wares
of Damascus. He went in and stood
before him, and said, "Your son
Ben-Hadad king of Aram has sent
me to ask, 'Will I recover from this
illness?'"

10Elisha answered, "Go and say
to him, 'You will certainly recover.' Nevertheless,[a] the LORD has
revealed to me that he will in
fact die." 11He stared at him with a
fixed gaze until Hazael was embarrassed. Then the man of God began
to weep. Jdg 3:25; Isa 38:1; Lk 19:41

12"Why is my lord weeping?"
asked Hazael.

"Because I know the harm you
will do to the Israelites," he answered. "You will set fire to their
fortified places, kill their young
men with the sword, dash their little children to the ground, and rip
open their pregnant women."
2Ki 10:32; 12:17; 13:3,7

13Hazael said, "How could your
servant, a mere dog, accomplish
such a feat?" 1Sa 17:43; 2Sa 3:8

"The LORD has shown me that
you will become king of Aram,"
answered Elisha. 1Ki 19:15

14Then Hazael left Elisha and returned to his master. When Ben-
Hadad asked, "What did Elisha say
to you?" Hazael replied, "He told
me that you would certainly recover." 15But the next day he took
a thick cloth, soaked it in water
and spread it over the king's face,
so that he died. Then Hazael succeeded him as king. 2Ki 1:17

Jehoram King of Judah

16In the fifth year of Joram son
of Ahab king of Israel, when Jehoshaphat was king of Judah, Jehoram son of Jehoshaphat began
his reign as king of Judah. 17He
was thirty-two years old when he
became king, and he reigned in
Jerusalem eight years. 18He followed the ways of the kings of
Israel, as the house of Ahab had
done, for he married a daughter of
Ahab. He did evil in the eyes of the
LORD. 19Nevertheless, for the sake
of his servant David, the LORD was
not willing to destroy Judah. He
had promised to maintain a lamp
for David and his descendants
forever. 2Sa 7:13; 2Ki 1:17; 2Ch 21:1-4

20In the time of Jehoram, Edom
rebelled against Judah and set up
its own king. 21So Jehoram[b] went
to Zair with all his chariots. The
Edomites surrounded him and his
chariot commanders, but he rose
up and broke through by night; his
army, however, fled back home.
22To this day Edom has been in rebellion against Judah. Libnah revolted at the same time.
Ge 27:40; Jos 21:13; 1Ki 22:47

[a] 10 The Hebrew may also be read *Go and say, 'You will certainly not recover,' for.*
[b] 21 Hebrew *Joram*, a variant of *Jehoram*; also in verses 23 and 24

23 As for the other events of Jehoram's reign, and all he did, are
they not written in the book of
the annals of the kings of Judah?
24 Jehoram rested with his ancestors and was buried with them in
the City of David. And Ahaziah his
son succeeded him as king.

2Ch 21:5-10,20

Ahaziah King of Judah

25 In the twelfth year of Joram
son of Ahab king of Israel, Ahaziah son of Jehoram king of Judah began to reign. 26 Ahaziah
was twenty-two years old when
he became king, and he reigned
in Jerusalem one year. His mother's name was Athaliah, a granddaughter of Omri king of Israel. 27 He followed the ways of the
house of Ahab and did evil in the
eyes of the LORD, as the house of
Ahab had done, for he was related
by marriage to Ahab's family.

1Ki 15:26; 16:23,30

28 Ahaziah went with Joram son
of Ahab to war against Hazael
king of Aram at Ramoth Gilead.
The Arameans wounded Joram;
29 so King Joram returned to Jezreel to recover from the wounds
the Arameans had inflicted on
him at Ramoth[a] in his battle with
Hazael king of Aram.

1Ki 19:15,17; 22:3,29; 2Ki 9:15

Then Ahaziah son of Jehoram
king of Judah went down to Jezreel to see Joram son of Ahab, because he had been wounded.

2Ch 22:1-6

Jehu Anointed King of Israel

9 The prophet Elisha sum-
moned a man from the com-
pany of the prophets and said to
him, "Tuck your cloak into your
belt, take this flask of olive oil
with you and go to Ramoth Gilead.
2 When you get there, look for Jehu
son of Jehoshaphat, the son of
Nimshi. Go to him, get him away
from his companions and take
him into an inner room. 3 Then
take the flask and pour the oil on
his head and declare, 'This is what
the LORD says: I anoint you king
over Israel.' Then open the door
and run; don't delay!"

1Ki 19:16; 2Ki 4:29; 8:28

4 So the young prophet went to
Ramoth Gilead. 5 When he arrived,
he found the army officers sitting
together. "I have a message for
you, commander," he said.

"For which of us?" asked Jehu.

"For you, commander," he replied.

6 Jehu got up and went into the
house. Then the prophet poured
the oil on Jehu's head and declared, "This is what the LORD, the
God of Israel, says: 'I anoint you
king over the LORD's people Israel. 7 You are to destroy the house
of Ahab your master, and I will
avenge the blood of my servants
the prophets and the blood of all
the LORD's servants shed by Jezebel. 8 The whole house of Ahab will
perish. I will cut off from Ahab

[a] 29 Hebrew *Ramah*, a variant of *Ramoth*

every last male in Israel — slave or free.[a] 9I will make the house of Ahab like the house of Jeroboam son of Nebat and like the house of Baasha son of Ahijah. 10As for Jezebel, dogs will devour her on the plot of ground at Jezreel, and no one will bury her.' " Then he opened the door and ran.

1Ki 14:10; 15:29; 21:23

11When Jehu went out to his fellow officers, one of them asked him, "Is everything all right? Why did this maniac come to you?"

Jer 29:26; Jn 10:20; Ac 26:24

"You know the man and the sort of things he says," Jehu replied.

12"That's not true!" they said. "Tell us."

Jehu said, "Here is what he told me: 'This is what the LORD says: I anoint you king over Israel.' "

13They quickly took their cloaks and spread them under him on the bare steps. Then they blew the trumpet and shouted, "Jehu is king!" Mt 21:8; 2Sa 15:10

Jehu Kills Joram and Ahaziah

14So Jehu son of Jehoshaphat, the son of Nimshi, conspired against Joram. (Now Joram and all Israel had been defending Ramoth Gilead against Hazael king of Aram, 15but King Joram[b] had returned to Jezreel to recover from the wounds the Arameans had inflicted on him in the battle with Hazael king of Aram.) Jehu said, "If you desire to make me king, don't let anyone slip out of the city to go and tell the news in Jezreel." 16Then he got into his chariot and rode to Jezreel, because Joram was resting there and Ahaziah king of Judah had gone down to see him.

2Ki 8:28-29; 2Ch 22:7

17When the lookout standing on the tower in Jezreel saw Jehu's troops approaching, he called out, "I see some troops coming." Isa 21:6

"Get a horseman," Joram ordered. "Send him to meet them and ask, 'Do you come in peace?' "

1Sa 16:4

18The horseman rode off to meet Jehu and said, "This is what the king says: 'Do you come in peace?' "

"What do you have to do with peace?" Jehu replied. "Fall in behind me."

The lookout reported, "The messenger has reached them, but he isn't coming back."

19So the king sent out a second horseman. When he came to them he said, "This is what the king says: 'Do you come in peace?' "

Jehu replied, "What do you have to do with peace? Fall in behind me."

20The lookout reported, "He has reached them, but he isn't coming back either. The driving is like that of Jehu son of Nimshi — he drives like a maniac." 2Sa 18:27

21"Hitch up my chariot," Joram ordered. And when it was hitched

[a] 8 Or *Israel — every ruler or leader*
[b] 15 Hebrew *Jehoram*, a variant of *Joram*; also in verses 17 and 21-24

up, Joram king of Israel and Ahaziah king of Judah rode out,
each in his own chariot, to meet
Jehu. They met him at the plot of
ground that had belonged to Naboth the Jezreelite. [22]When Joram
saw Jehu he asked, "Have you
come in peace, Jehu?" 1Ki 21:1-7,15-19

"How can there be peace," Jehu
replied, "as long as all the idolatry and witchcraft of your mother
Jezebel abound?"

1Ki 18:19; 2Ch 21:13; Rev 2:20

[23]Joram turned about and fled,
calling out to Ahaziah, "Treachery,
Ahaziah!" 2Ki 11:14

[24]Then Jehu drew his bow and
shot Joram between the shoulders. The arrow pierced his heart
and he slumped down in his chariot. [25]Jehu said to Bidkar, his chariot officer, "Pick him up and throw
him on the field that belonged to
Naboth the Jezreelite. Remember how you and I were riding together in chariots behind Ahab his
father when the LORD spoke this
prophecy against him: [26]'Yesterday I saw the blood of Naboth and
the blood of his sons, declares the
LORD, and I will surely make you
pay for it on this plot of ground,
declares the LORD.'[a] Now then,
pick him up and throw him on
that plot, in accordance with the
word of the LORD."

1Ki 21:19-22,24-29; 22:34

[27]When Ahaziah king of Judah
saw what had happened, he fled
up the road to Beth Haggan.[b] Jehu
chased him, shouting, "Kill him
too!" They wounded him in his
chariot on the way up to Gur near
Ibleam, but he escaped to Megiddo and died there. [28]His servants
took him by chariot to Jerusalem
and buried him with his ancestors
in his tomb in the City of David.
[29](In the eleventh year of Joram
son of Ahab, Ahaziah had become
king of Judah.)

2Ch 22:7-9; 2Ki 23:30; 8:25

Jezebel Killed

[30]Then Jehu went to Jezreel.
When Jezebel heard about it, she
put on eye makeup, arranged her
hair and looked out of a window.
[31]As Jehu entered the gate, she
asked, "Have you come in peace,
you Zimri, you murderer of your
master?"[c] 1Ki 16:9-10; Jer 4:30; Eze 23:40

[32]He looked up at the window
and called out, "Who is on my
side? Who?" Two or three eunuchs
looked down at him. [33]"Throw her
down!" Jehu said. So they threw
her down, and some of her blood
spattered the wall and the horses
as they trampled her underfoot.

Ps 7:5

[34]Jehu went in and ate and drank.
"Take care of that cursed woman,"
he said, "and bury her, for she was
a king's daughter." [35]But when they
went out to bury her, they found
nothing except her skull, her feet
and her hands. [36]They went back

[a] 26 See 1 Kings 21:19. [b] 27 *Or fled by way of the garden house* [c] 31 *Or "Was there peace for Zimri, who murdered his master?"*

and told Jehu, who said, "This is
the word of the LORD that he spoke
through his servant Elijah the
Tishbite: On the plot of ground at
Jezreel dogs will devour Jezebel's
flesh.[a] 37 Jezebel's body will be like
dung on the ground in the plot at
Jezreel, so that no one will be able
to say, 'This is Jezebel.'"

1Ki 21:23; Ps 83:10; Jer 8:2

Ahab's Family Killed

10 Now there were in Samaria
seventy sons of the house
of Ahab. So Jehu wrote letters and
sent them to Samaria: to the officials of Jezreel,[b] to the elders and
to the guardians of Ahab's children.
He said, 2 "You have your master's
sons with you and you have chariots and horses, a fortified city and
weapons. Now as soon as this letter reaches you, 3 choose the best
and most worthy of your master's
sons and set him on his father's
throne. Then fight for your master's house."

1Ki 13:32; 21:1

4 But they were terrified and
said, "If two kings could not resist
him, how can we?"

5 So the palace administrator,
the city governor, the elders and
the guardians sent this message
to Jehu: "We are your servants and
we will do anything you say. We
will not appoint anyone as king;
you do whatever you think best."

Jos 9:8; 1Ki 20:4,32

6 Then Jehu wrote them a second letter, saying, "If you are on
my side and will obey me, take the
heads of your master's sons and
come to me in Jezreel by this time
tomorrow."

Now the royal princes, seventy of them, were with the leading
men of the city, who were rearing
them. 7 When the letter arrived,
these men took the princes and
slaughtered all seventy of them.
They put their heads in baskets
and sent them to Jehu in Jezreel.
8 When the messenger arrived, he
told Jehu, "They have brought the
heads of the princes."

2Sa 4:8; 1Ki 21:21

Then Jehu ordered, "Put them
in two piles at the entrance of the
city gate until morning."

9 The next morning Jehu went
out. He stood before all the people and said, "You are innocent. It
was I who conspired against my
master and killed him, but who
killed all these? 10 Know, then, that
not a word the LORD has spoken
against the house of Ahab will
fail. The LORD has done what he
announced through his servant
Elijah." 11 So Jehu killed everyone
in Jezreel who remained of the
house of Ahab, as well as all his
chief men, his close friends and
his priests, leaving him no survivor.

1Ki 21:29; 2Ki 9:7-10

12 Jehu then set out and went toward Samaria. At Beth Eked of the
Shepherds, 13 he met some relatives of Ahaziah king of Judah and
asked, "Who are you?"

[a] *36* See 1 Kings 21:23. [b] *1* Hebrew; some Septuagint manuscripts and Vulgate *of the city*

They said, “We are relatives of
Ahaziah, and we have come down
to greet the families of the king
and of the queen mother.”
2Ki 8:24,29; 2Ch 22:8

14“Take them alive!” he ordered. So they took them alive
and slaughtered them by the well
of Beth Eked — forty-two of them.
He left no survivor.

15After he left there, he came
upon Jehonadab son of Rekab,
who was on his way to meet him.
Jehu greeted him and said, “Are
you in accord with me, as I am
with you?” 1Ch 2:55; Jer 35:6,14-19

“I am,” Jehonadab answered.

“If so,” said Jehu, “give me your
hand.” So he did, and Jehu helped
him up into the chariot. 16Jehu
said, “Come with me and see my
zeal for the LORD.” Then he had
him ride along in his chariot.
1Ki 19:10; Ezr 10:19; Eze 17:18

17When Jehu came to Samaria,
he killed all who were left there of
Ahab’s family; he destroyed them,
according to the word of the LORD
spoken to Elijah. 2Ki 9:8

Servants of Baal Killed

18Then Jehu brought all the
people together and said to them,
“Ahab served Baal a little; Jehu
will serve him much. 19Now summon all the prophets of Baal, all
his servants and all his priests. See
that no one is missing, because I
am going to hold a great sacrifice
for Baal. Anyone who fails to come
will no longer live.” But Jehu was
acting deceptively in order to destroy the servants of Baal.
1Ki 16:31-32; 18:19

20Jehu said, “Call an assembly in
honor of Baal.” So they proclaimed
it. 21Then he sent word throughout
Israel, and all the servants of Baal
came; not one stayed away. They
crowded into the temple of Baal
until it was full from one end to
the other. 22And Jehu said to the
keeper of the wardrobe, “Bring
robes for all the servants of Baal.”
So he brought out robes for them.
Ex 32:5; Joel 1:14

23Then Jehu and Jehonadab son
of Rekab went into the temple of
Baal. Jehu said to the servants of
Baal, “Look around and see that no
one who serves the LORD is here
with you — only servants of Baal.”
24So they went in to make sacrifices and burnt offerings. Now Jehu
had posted eighty men outside
with this warning: “If one of you
lets any of the men I am placing in
your hands escape, it will be your
life for his life.” 1Ki 20:39

25As soon as Jehu had finished
making the burnt offering, he ordered the guards and officers: “Go
in and kill them; let no one escape.” So they cut them down with
the sword. The guards and officers
threw the bodies out and then entered the inner shrine of the temple of Baal. 26They brought the
sacred stone out of the temple of
Baal and burned it. 27They demolished the sacred stone of Baal and
tore down the temple of Baal, and

people have used it for a latrine to
this day. 1Ki 14:23; 18:40; 2Ki 11:18
28So Jehu destroyed Baal worship in Israel. 29However, he did
not turn away from the sins of
Jeroboam son of Nebat, which he
had caused Israel to commit — the
worship of the golden calves at
Bethel and Dan. 1Ki 12:28-29; 19:17
30The LORD said to Jehu, "Because you have done well in accomplishing what is right in my
eyes and have done to the house
of Ahab all I had in mind to do,
your descendants will sit on the
throne of Israel to the fourth generation." 31Yet Jehu was not careful to keep the law of the LORD,
the God of Israel, with all his
heart. He did not turn away from
the sins of Jeroboam, which he
had caused Israel to commit.
2Ki 15:12; Pr 4:23
32In those days the LORD began
to reduce the size of Israel. Hazael overpowered the Israelites
throughout their territory 33east
of the Jordan in all the land of Gilead (the region of Gad, Reuben
and Manasseh), from Aroer by the
Arnon Gorge through Gilead to
Bashan. 2Ki 8:12; 13:25
34As for the other events of Jehu's reign, all he did, and all his
achievements, are they not written in the book of the annals of
the kings of Israel? 1Ki 15:31
35Jehu rested with his ancestors and was buried in Samaria.
And Jehoahaz his son succeeded
him as king. 36The time that Jehu
reigned over Israel in Samaria was
twenty-eight years.

Athaliah and Joash

11 When Athaliah the mother of
Ahaziah saw that her son was
dead, she proceeded to destroy the
whole royal family. 2But Jehosheba, the daughter of King Jehoram[a]
and sister of Ahaziah, took Joash
son of Ahaziah and stole him away
from among the royal princes,
who were about to be murdered.
She put him and his nurse in a
bedroom to hide him from Athaliah; so he was not killed. 3He remained hidden with his nurse
at the temple of the LORD for six
years while Athaliah ruled the
land. 2Ki 12:1; Jdg 9:5
4In the seventh year Jehoiada
sent for the commanders of units
of a hundred, the Carites and the
guards and had them brought to
him at the temple of the LORD. He
made a covenant with them and
put them under oath at the temple of the LORD. Then he showed
them the king's son. 5He commanded them, saying, "This is
what you are to do: You who are
in the three companies that are
going on duty on the Sabbath —
a third of you guarding the royal palace, 6a third at the Sur Gate,
and a third at the gate behind the
guard, who take turns guarding
the temple — 7and you who are
in the other two companies that
normally go off Sabbath duty are

[a] 2 Hebrew *Joram,* a variant of *Jehoram*

all to guard the temple for the
king. 8Station yourselves around
the king, each of you with weapon
in hand. Anyone who approaches
your ranks[a] is to be put to death.
Stay close to the king wherever he
goes." 1Ch 9:25

9The commanders of units of
a hundred did just as Jehoiada
the priest ordered. Each one took
his men — those who were going on duty on the Sabbath and
those who were going off duty —
and came to Jehoiada the priest.
10Then he gave the commanders
the spears and shields that had
belonged to King David and that
were in the temple of the LORD.
11The guards, each with weapon
in hand, stationed themselves
around the king — near the altar
and the temple, from the south
side to the north side of the temple. 2Sa 8:7; 1Ch 18:7

12Jehoiada brought out the
king's son and put the crown on
him; he presented him with a copy
of the covenant and proclaimed
him king. They anointed him, and
the people clapped their hands
and shouted, "Long live the king!"
Ex 25:16; 1Sa 10:24; 1Ki 1:39

13When Athaliah heard the noise
made by the guards and the people, she went to the people at the
temple of the LORD. 14She looked
and there was the king, standing
by the pillar, as the custom was.
The officers and the trumpeters
were beside the king, and all the
people of the land were rejoicing
and blowing trumpets. Then Athaliah tore her robes and called out,
"Treason! Treason!"
Ge 37:29; 1Ki 1:39; 2Ki 9:23

15Jehoiada the priest ordered
the commanders of units of a hundred, who were in charge of the
troops: "Bring her out between
the ranks[b] and put to the sword
anyone who follows her." For the
priest had said, "She must not be
put to death in the temple of the
LORD." 16So they seized her as she
reached the place where the horses enter the palace grounds, and
there she was put to death.
Ge 4:14; 1Ki 2:30

17Jehoiada then made a covenant between the LORD and the
king and people that they would
be the LORD's people. He also made
a covenant between the king and
the people. 18All the people of the
land went to the temple of Baal
and tore it down. They smashed
the altars and idols to pieces and
killed Mattan the priest of Baal in
front of the altars.
1Ki 18:40; 2Ki 10:25; 23:3

Then Jehoiada the priest posted
guards at the temple of the LORD.
19He took with him the commanders of hundreds, the Carites, the
guards and all the people of the
land, and together they brought
the king down from the temple
of the LORD and went into the palace, entering by way of the gate of
the guards. The king then took his

[a] 8 Or *approaches the precincts* [b] 15 Or *out from the precincts*

place on the royal throne. 20All the people of the land rejoiced, and the city was calm, because Athaliah had been slain with the sword at the palace. Pr 11:10; 28:12; 29:2

21Joash[a] was seven years old when he began to reign.[b] 2Ch 22:10-23:21

Joash Repairs the Temple

12[c] In the seventh year of Jehu, Joash[d] became king, and he reigned in Jerusalem forty years. His mother's name was Zibiah; she was from Beersheba. 2Joash did what was right in the eyes of the LORD all the years Jehoiada the priest instructed him. 3The high places, however, were not removed; the people continued to offer sacrifices and burn incense there. 2Ki 14:4; 15:35; 18:4

4Joash said to the priests, "Collect all the money that is brought as sacred offerings to the temple of the LORD — the money collected in the census, the money received from personal vows and the money brought voluntarily to the temple. 5Let every priest receive the money from one of the treasurers, then use it to repair whatever damage is found in the temple." Ex 35:5; 2Ki 22:4; 1Ch 29:3-9

6But by the twenty-third year of King Joash the priests still had not repaired the temple. 7Therefore King Joash summoned Jehoiada the priest and the other priests and asked them, "Why aren't you repairing the damage done to the temple? Take no more money from your treasurers, but hand it over for repairing the temple." 8The priests agreed that they would not collect any more money from the people and that they would not repair the temple themselves.

9Jehoiada the priest took a chest and bored a hole in its lid. He placed it beside the altar, on the right side as one enters the temple of the LORD. The priests who guarded the entrance put into the chest all the money that was brought to the temple of the LORD. 10Whenever they saw that there was a large amount of money in the chest, the royal secretary and the high priest came, counted the money that had been brought into the temple of the LORD and put it into bags. 11When the amount had been determined, they gave the money to the men appointed to supervise the work on the temple. With it they paid those who worked on the temple of the LORD — the carpenters and builders, 12the masons and stonecutters. They purchased timber and blocks of dressed stone for the repair of the temple of the LORD, and met all the other expenses of restoring the temple. Mk 12:41; Lk 21:1

[a] *21* Hebrew *Jehoash*, a variant of *Joash*
[b] *21* In Hebrew texts this verse (11:21) is numbered 12:1. [c] In Hebrew texts 12:1-21 is numbered 12:2-22. [d] *1* Hebrew *Jehoash*, a variant of *Joash*; also in verses 2, 4, 6, 7 and 18

13 The money brought into the
temple was not spent for making silver basins, wick trimmers,
sprinkling bowls, trumpets or any
other articles of gold or silver for
the temple of the LORD; 14 it was
paid to the workers, who used it to
repair the temple. 15 They did not
require an accounting from those
to whom they gave the money to
pay the workers, because they acted with complete honesty. 16 The
money from the guilt offerings
and sin offerings[a] was not brought
into the temple of the LORD; it belonged to the priests.

Lev 7:7; 2Ki 22:7; 2Ch 24:14

17 About this time Hazael king of
Aram went up and attacked Gath
and captured it. Then he turned
to attack Jerusalem. 18 But Joash
king of Judah took all the sacred
objects dedicated by his predecessors — Jehoshaphat, Jehoram and
Ahaziah, the kings of Judah — and
the gifts he himself had dedicated
and all the gold found in the treasuries of the temple of the LORD
and of the royal palace, and he
sent them to Hazael king of Aram,
who then withdrew from Jerusalem.

1Ki 15:18; 2Ki 8:12

19 As for the other events of the
reign of Joash, and all he did, are
they not written in the book of
the annals of the kings of Judah?
20 His officials conspired against
him and assassinated him at
Beth Millo, on the road down to
Silla. 21 The officials who murdered him were Jozabad son of
Shimeath and Jehozabad son of
Shomer. He died and was buried
with his ancestors in the City of
David. And Amaziah his son succeeded him as king.

2Ch 24:1-14; 24:23-27

Jehoahaz King of Israel

13 In the twenty-third year of
Joash son of Ahaziah king
of Judah, Jehoahaz son of Jehu
became king of Israel in Samaria,
and he reigned seventeen years.
2 He did evil in the eyes of the
LORD by following the sins of Jeroboam son of Nebat, which he had
caused Israel to commit, and he
did not turn away from them. 3 So
the LORD's anger burned against
Israel, and for a long time he kept
them under the power of Hazael
king of Aram and Ben-Hadad his
son.

Jdg 2:14; 1Ki 12:26-33

4 Then Jehoahaz sought the
LORD's favor, and the LORD listened
to him, for he saw how severely
the king of Aram was oppressing
Israel. 5 The LORD provided a deliverer for Israel, and they escaped
from the power of Aram. So the Israelites lived in their own homes
as they had before. 6 But they did
not turn away from the sins of the
house of Jeroboam, which he had
caused Israel to commit; they continued in them. Also, the Asherah
pole[b] remained standing in Samaria.

1Ki 16:33; 2Ki 14:26

[a] 16 Or *purification offerings* [b] 6 That is, a wooden symbol of the goddess Asherah; here and elsewhere in 2 Kings

7 Nothing had been left of the
army of Jehoahaz except fifty
horsemen, ten chariots and ten
thousand foot soldiers, for the
king of Aram had destroyed the
rest and made them like the dust
at threshing time. 2Ki 10:32-33

8 As for the other events of the
reign of Jehoahaz, all he did and
his achievements, are they not
written in the book of the annals
of the kings of Israel? 9 Jehoahaz
rested with his ancestors and was
buried in Samaria. And Jehoash[a]
his son succeeded him as king.

Jehoash King of Israel

10 In the thirty-seventh year of
Joash king of Judah, Jehoash son
of Jehoahaz became king of Israel in Samaria, and he reigned sixteen years. 11 He did evil in the eyes
of the LORD and did not turn away
from any of the sins of Jeroboam
son of Nebat, which he had caused
Israel to commit; he continued in
them.

12 As for the other events of the
reign of Jehoash, all he did and his
achievements, including his war
against Amaziah king of Judah,
are they not written in the book
of the annals of the kings of Israel? 13 Jehoash rested with his ancestors, and Jeroboam succeeded
him on the throne. Jehoash was
buried in Samaria with the kings
of Israel. 2Ki 14:15,23; 14:23; Hos 1:1

14 Now Elisha had been suffering
from the illness from which he
died. Jehoash king of Israel went
down to see him and wept over
him. "My father! My father!" he
cried. "The chariots and horsemen
of Israel!" 2Ki 2:12

15 Elisha said, "Get a bow and
some arrows," and he did so.
16 "Take the bow in your hands," he
said to the king of Israel. When he
had taken it, Elisha put his hands
on the king's hands. 1Sa 20:20

17 "Open the east window," he
said, and he opened it. "Shoot!"
Elisha said, and he shot. "The
LORD's arrow of victory, the arrow
of victory over Aram!" Elisha declared. "You will completely destroy the Arameans at Aphek."
1Ki 20:26

18 Then he said, "Take the arrows," and the king took them.
Elisha told him, "Strike the
ground." He struck it three times
and stopped. 19 The man of God
was angry with him and said, "You
should have struck the ground five
or six times; then you would have
defeated Aram and completely destroyed it. But now you will defeat
it only three times." ver 25

20 Elisha died and was buried.

Now Moabite raiders used to enter the country every spring. 21 Once
while some Israelites were burying
a man, suddenly they saw a band
of raiders; so they threw the man's
body into Elisha's tomb. When the
body touched Elisha's bones, the
man came to life and stood up on
his feet. Mt 27:52; 2Ki 3:7; 24:2

[a] 9 Hebrew *Joash*, a variant of *Jehoash*; also in verses 12-14 and 25

22 Hazael king of Aram oppressed Israel throughout the
reign of Jehoahaz. 23 But the LORD
was gracious to them and had
compassion and showed concern
for them because of his covenant
with Abraham, Isaac and Jacob. To
this day he has been unwilling to
destroy them or banish them from
his presence. Ex 2:24; 1Ki 19:17; 2Ki 8:12
24 Hazael king of Aram died, and
Ben-Hadad his son succeeded him
as king. 25 Then Jehoash son of Jehoahaz recaptured from Ben-Hadad son of Hazael the towns he
had taken in battle from his father Jehoahaz. Three times Jehoash defeated him, and so he recovered the Israelite towns.

ver 18-19; 2Ki 10:32

Amaziah King of Judah

14 In the second year of Jehoash[a] son of Jehoahaz king of
Israel, Amaziah son of Joash king
of Judah began to reign. 2 He was
twenty-five years old when he became king, and he reigned in Jerusalem twenty-nine years. His
mother's name was Jehoaddan;
she was from Jerusalem. 3 He did
what was right in the eyes of the
LORD, but not as his father David
had done. In everything he followed the example of his father
Joash. 4 The high places, however, were not removed; the people
continued to offer sacrifices and
burn incense there.
5 After the kingdom was firmly
in his grasp, he executed the officials who had murdered his father
the king. 6 Yet he did not put the
children of the assassins to death,
in accordance with what is written in the Book of the Law of Moses where the LORD commanded:
"Parents are not to be put to death
for their children, nor children put
to death for their parents; each
will die for their own sin."[b]

Jer 31:30; Eze 18:4,20

7 He was the one who defeated ten thousand Edomites in the
Valley of Salt and captured Sela
in battle, calling it Joktheel, the
name it has to this day.

2Ch 25:1-4,11-12

8 Then Amaziah sent messengers to Jehoash son of Jehoahaz,
the son of Jehu, king of Israel,
with the challenge: "Come, let us
face each other in battle."
9 But Jehoash king of Israel replied to Amaziah king of Judah:
"A thistle in Lebanon sent a message to a cedar in Lebanon, 'Give
your daughter to my son in marriage.' Then a wild beast in Lebanon came along and trampled
the thistle underfoot. 10 You have
indeed defeated Edom and now
you are arrogant. Glory in your
victory, but stay at home! Why ask
for trouble and cause your own
downfall and that of Judah also?"

Dt 8:14; Jdg 9:8-15; 2Ch 26:16

11 Amaziah, however, would not
listen, so Jehoash king of Israel
attacked. He and Amaziah king

[a] *1* Hebrew *Joash*, a variant of *Jehoash*; also in verses 13, 23 and 27 [b] *6* Deut. 24:16

of Judah faced each other at Beth
Shemesh in Judah. 12 Judah was
routed by Israel, and every man
fled to his home. 13 Jehoash king
of Israel captured Amaziah king of
Judah, the son of Joash, the son of
Ahaziah, at Beth Shemesh. Then
Jehoash went to Jerusalem and
broke down the wall of Jerusalem
from the Ephraim Gate to the Corner Gate — a section about four
hundred cubits long.[a] 14 He took
all the gold and silver and all the
articles found in the temple of the
LORD and in the treasuries of the
royal palace. He also took hostages
and returned to Samaria.

Jos 15:10; Jer 31:38; Zec 14:10

15 As for the other events of the
reign of Jehoash, what he did and
his achievements, including his
war against Amaziah king of Judah, are they not written in the
book of the annals of the kings of
Israel? 16 Jehoash rested with his
ancestors and was buried in Samaria with the kings of Israel. And
Jeroboam his son succeeded him
as king. 2Ki 13:12

17 Amaziah son of Joash king of
Judah lived for fifteen years after
the death of Jehoash son of Jehoahaz king of Israel. 18 As for the other events of Amaziah's reign, are
they not written in the book of the
annals of the kings of Judah?

19 They conspired against him in
Jerusalem, and he fled to Lachish,
but they sent men after him to Lachish and killed him there. 20 He
was brought back by horse and
was buried in Jerusalem with his
ancestors, in the City of David.

2Ki 9:28; 18:14,17

21 Then all the people of Judah
took Azariah,[b] who was sixteen
years old, and made him king in
place of his father Amaziah. 22 He
was the one who rebuilt Elath and
restored it to Judah after Amaziah
rested with his ancestors.

2Ch 25:17-26:2

Jeroboam II King of Israel

23 In the fifteenth year of Amaziah son of Joash king of Judah,
Jeroboam son of Jehoash king of
Israel became king in Samaria,
and he reigned forty-one years.
24 He did evil in the eyes of the
LORD and did not turn away from
any of the sins of Jeroboam son
of Nebat, which he had caused Israel to commit. 25 He was the one
who restored the boundaries of
Israel from Lebo Hamath to the
Dead Sea,[c] in accordance with the
word of the LORD, the God of Israel, spoken through his servant
Jonah son of Amittai, the prophet
from Gath Hepher.

Jnh 1:1; Mt 12:39; Dt 3:17

26 The LORD had seen how bitterly everyone in Israel, whether
slave or free, was suffering;[d] there
was no one to help them. 27 And
since the LORD had not said he
would blot out the name of Israel

[a] 13 That is, about 600 feet or about 180 meters [b] 21 Also called *Uzziah*
[c] 25 Hebrew *the Sea of the Arabah*
[d] 26 Or *Israel was suffering. They were without a ruler or leader, and*

from under heaven, he saved them by the hand of Jeroboam son of Jehoash. 2Ki 13:4; Ps 18:41; Dt 32:36

28 As for the other events of Jeroboam's reign, all he did, and his military achievements, including how he recovered for Israel both Damascus and Hamath, which had belonged to Judah, are they not written in the book of the annals of the kings of Israel? 29 Jeroboam rested with his ancestors, the kings of Israel. And Zechariah his son succeeded him as king.

2Sa 8:5; 1Ki 11:24; 2Ch 8:3

Azariah King of Judah

15 In the twenty-seventh year of Jeroboam king of Israel, Azariah[a] son of Amaziah king of Judah began to reign. 2 He was sixteen years old when he became king, and he reigned in Jerusalem fifty-two years. His mother's name was Jekoliah; she was from Jerusalem. 3 He did what was right in the eyes of the LORD, just as his father Amaziah had done. 4 The high places, however, were not removed; the people continued to offer sacrifices and burn incense there. 2Ki 14:21

5 The LORD afflicted the king with leprosy[b] until the day he died, and he lived in a separate house.[c] Jotham the king's son had charge of the palace and governed the people of the land.

Lev 13:46; 2Ch 27:1

6 As for the other events of Azariah's reign, and all he did, are they not written in the book of the annals of the kings of Judah? 7 Azariah rested with his ancestors and was buried near them in the City of David. And Jotham his son succeeded him as king.

2Ch 26:3-4,21-23

Zechariah King of Israel

8 In the thirty-eighth year of Azariah king of Judah, Zechariah son of Jeroboam became king of Israel in Samaria, and he reigned six months. 9 He did evil in the eyes of the LORD, as his predecessors had done. He did not turn away from the sins of Jeroboam son of Nebat, which he had caused Israel to commit. 1Ki 15:26

10 Shallum son of Jabesh conspired against Zechariah. He attacked him in front of the people,[d] assassinated him and succeeded him as king. 11 The other events of Zechariah's reign are written in the book of the annals of the kings of Israel. 12 So the word of the LORD spoken to Jehu was fulfilled: "Your descendants will sit on the throne of Israel to the fourth generation."[e] 1Ki 15:31; 2Ki 10:30

Shallum King of Israel

13 Shallum son of Jabesh became king in the thirty-ninth year

[a] *1* Also called *Uzziah*; also in verses 6, 7, 8, 17, 23 and 27 [b] *5* The Hebrew for *leprosy* was used for various diseases affecting the skin. [c] *5* Or *in a house where he was relieved of responsibilities* [d] *10* Hebrew; some Septuagint manuscripts *in Ibleam* [e] *12* 2 Kings 10:30

of Uzziah king of Judah, and he
reigned in Samaria one month.
14 Then Menahem son of Gadi went
from Tirzah up to Samaria. He attacked Shallum son of Jabesh in
Samaria, assassinated him and
succeeded him as king.
1Ki 14:17; 2Ki 12:20

15 The other events of Shallum's
reign, and the conspiracy he led,
are written in the book of the annals of the kings of Israel. 1Ki 15:31
16 At that time Menahem, starting out from Tirzah, attacked
Tiphsah and everyone in the city
and its vicinity, because they refused to open their gates. He
sacked Tiphsah and ripped open
all the pregnant women.
1Ki 4:24; 2Ki 8:12; Hos 13:16

Menahem King of Israel

17 In the thirty-ninth year of Azariah king of Judah, Menahem
son of Gadi became king of Israel, and he reigned in Samaria ten
years. 18 He did evil in the eyes of
the LORD. During his entire reign
he did not turn away from the sins
of Jeroboam son of Nebat, which
he had caused Israel to commit.

19 Then Pul[a] king of Assyria invaded the land, and Menahem
gave him a thousand talents[b]
of silver to gain his support and
strengthen his own hold on the
kingdom. 20 Menahem exacted
this money from Israel. Every
wealthy person had to contribute
fifty shekels[c] of silver to be given
to the king of Assyria. So the king
of Assyria withdrew and stayed in
the land no longer. 2Ki 12:18; 1Ch 5:6,26
21 As for the other events of Menahem's reign, and all he did, are
they not written in the book of
the annals of the kings of Israel?
22 Menahem rested with his ancestors. And Pekahiah his son succeeded him as king.

Pekahiah King of Israel

23 In the fiftieth year of Azariah king of Judah, Pekahiah son of
Menahem became king of Israel in
Samaria, and he reigned two years.
24 Pekahiah did evil in the eyes of
the LORD. He did not turn away
from the sins of Jeroboam son of
Nebat, which he had caused Israel to commit. 25 One of his chief
officers, Pekah son of Remaliah,
conspired against him. Taking fifty men of Gilead with him, he assassinated Pekahiah, along with
Argob and Arieh, in the citadel of
the royal palace at Samaria. So Pekah killed Pekahiah and succeeded
him as king. 2Ki 12:20; 2Ch 28:6; Isa 7:1,4
26 The other events of Pekahiah's
reign, and all he did, are written in
the book of the annals of the kings
of Israel.

Pekah King of Israel

27 In the fifty-second year of Azariah king of Judah, Pekah son of
Remaliah became king of Israel

[a] *19* Also called *Tiglath-Pileser* [b] *19* That is, about 38 tons or about 34 metric tons
[c] *20* That is, about 1 1/4 pounds or about 575 grams

in Samaria, and he reigned twenty years. 28He did evil in the eyes
of the LORD. He did not turn away
from the sins of Jeroboam son of
Nebat, which he had caused Israel
to commit. 2Ch 28:6; Isa 7:1,4
29In the time of Pekah king of
Israel, Tiglath-Pileser king of Assyria came and took Ijon, Abel
Beth Maakah, Janoah, Kedesh and
Hazor. He took Gilead and Galilee,
including all the land of Naphtali,
and deported the people to Assyria. 30Then Hoshea son of Elah conspired against Pekah son of Remaliah. He attacked and assassinated
him, and then succeeded him as
king in the twentieth year of Jotham son of Uzziah. 2Ki 16:9; 17:1,6
31As for the other events of Pekah's reign, and all he did, are they
not written in the book of the annals of the kings of Israel?

Jotham King of Judah

32In the second year of Pekah
son of Remaliah king of Israel,
Jotham son of Uzziah king of Judah began to reign. 33He was twenty-five years old when he became
king, and he reigned in Jerusalem
sixteen years. His mother's name
was Jerusha daughter of Zadok.
34He did what was right in the eyes
of the LORD, just as his father Uzziah had done. 35The high places,
however, were not removed; the
people continued to offer sacrifices and burn incense there. Jotham
rebuilt the Upper Gate of the temple of the LORD. ver 3; 2Ch 26:4-5
36As for the other events of Jotham's reign, and what he did, are
they not written in the book of the
annals of the kings of Judah? 37(In
those days the LORD began to send
Rezin king of Aram and Pekah son
of Remaliah against Judah.) 38Jo-
tham rested with his ancestors
and was buried with them in the
City of David, the city of his father.
And Ahaz his son succeeded him
as king. 2Ch 27:1-4,7-9

Ahaz King of Judah

16 In the seventeenth year
of Pekah son of Remaliah,
Ahaz son of Jotham king of Judah began to reign. 2Ahaz was
twenty years old when he became
king, and he reigned in Jerusalem sixteen years. Unlike David
his father, he did not do what was
right in the eyes of the LORD his
God. 3He followed the ways of the
kings of Israel and even sacrificed
his son in the fire, engaging in the
detestable practices of the nations
the LORD had driven out before
the Israelites. 4He offered sacrifices and burned incense at the high
places, on the hilltops and under
every spreading tree.
Lev 18:21; Dt 12:2,31
5Then Rezin king of Aram and
Pekah son of Remaliah king of Israel marched up to fight against
Jerusalem and besieged Ahaz, but
they could not overpower him. 6At
that time, Rezin king of Aram recovered Elath for Aram by driving
out the people of Judah. Edomites

then moved into Elath and have
lived there to this day.
2Ki 14:22; Isa 7:1,4

7Ahaz sent messengers to say to
Tiglath-Pileser king of Assyria, "I
am your servant and vassal. Come
up and save me out of the hand of
the king of Aram and of the king
of Israel, who are attacking me."
8And Ahaz took the silver and gold
found in the temple of the LORD
and in the treasuries of the royal
palace and sent it as a gift to the
king of Assyria. 9The king of Assyria complied by attacking Damascus and capturing it. He deported its inhabitants to Kir and
put Rezin to death.
2Ki 12:18; 15:29; Am 1:5

10Then King Ahaz went to Damascus to meet Tiglath-Pileser
king of Assyria. He saw an altar in
Damascus and sent to Uriah the
priest a sketch of the altar, with
detailed plans for its construction.
11So Uriah the priest built an altar
in accordance with all the plans
that King Ahaz had sent from
Damascus and finished it before
King Ahaz returned. 12When the
king came back from Damascus
and saw the altar, he approached
it and presented offerings[a] on it.
13He offered up his burnt offering
and grain offering, poured out
his drink offering, and splashed
the blood of his fellowship offerings against the altar. 14As for the
bronze altar that stood before the
LORD, he brought it from the front
of the temple — from between the
new altar and the temple of the
LORD — and put it on the north
side of the new altar.
2Ch 4:1; 26:16; Isa 8:2

15King Ahaz then gave these orders to Uriah the priest: "On the
large new altar, offer the morning
burnt offering and the evening
grain offering, the king's burnt
offering and his grain offering,
and the burnt offering of all the
people of the land, and their grain
offering and their drink offering.
Splash against this altar the blood
of all the burnt offerings and sacrifices. But I will use the bronze
altar for seeking guidance." 16And
Uriah the priest did just as King
Ahaz had ordered. Ex 29:38-41; 1Sa 9:9

17King Ahaz cut off the side panels and removed the basins from
the movable stands. He removed
the Sea from the bronze bulls that
supported it and set it on a stone
base. 18He took away the Sabbath
canopy[b] that had been built at the
temple and removed the royal entryway outside the temple of the
LORD, in deference to the king of
Assyria. 1Ki 7:27; Eze 16:28

19As for the other events of the
reign of Ahaz, and what he did,
are they not written in the book of
the annals of the kings of Judah?
20Ahaz rested with his ancestors
and was buried with them in the
City of David. And Hezekiah his
son succeeded him as king.
2Ch 28:1-27

[a] 12 Or *and went up* [b] 18 Or *the dais of his throne* (see Septuagint)

Hoshea Last King of Israel

17 In the twelfth year of Ahaz
king of Judah, Hoshea son
of Elah became king of Israel in
Samaria, and he reigned nine
years. 2He did evil in the eyes of
the LORD, but not like the kings of
Israel who preceded him.
3Shalmaneser king of Assyria
came up to attack Hoshea, who
had been Shalmaneser's vassal
and had paid him tribute. 4But the
king of Assyria discovered that
Hoshea was a traitor, for he had
sent envoys to So[a] king of Egypt,
and he no longer paid tribute
to the king of Assyria, as he had
done year by year. Therefore Shalmaneser seized him and put him
in prison. 5The king of Assyria invaded the entire land, marched
against Samaria and laid siege to
it for three years. 6In the ninth
year of Hoshea, the king of Assyria captured Samaria and deported
the Israelites to Assyria. He settled them in Halah, in Gozan on
the Habor River and in the towns
of the Medes. 2Ki 18:9-12; Hos 10:14

Israel Exiled Because of Sin

7All this took place because the
Israelites had sinned against the
LORD their God, who had brought
them up out of Egypt from under the power of Pharaoh king of
Egypt. They worshiped other gods
8and followed the practices of the
nations the LORD had driven out
before them, as well as the practices that the kings of Israel had introduced. 9The Israelites secretly
did things against the LORD their
God that were not right. From
watchtower to fortified city they
built themselves high places in
all their towns. 10They set up sacred stones and Asherah poles
on every high hill and under every spreading tree. 11At every
high place they burned incense,
as the nations whom the LORD
had driven out before them had
done. They did wicked things that
aroused the LORD's anger. 12They
worshiped idols, though the LORD
had said, "You shall not do this."[b]
13The LORD warned Israel and Judah through all his prophets and
seers: "Turn from your evil ways.
Observe my commands and decrees, in accordance with the entire Law that I commanded your
ancestors to obey and that I delivered to you through my servants
the prophets." 1Sa 9:9; Jer 18:11
14But they would not listen and
were as stiff-necked as their ancestors, who did not trust in the
LORD their God. 15They rejected his
decrees and the covenant he had
made with their ancestors and
the statutes he had warned them
to keep. They followed worthless idols and themselves became
worthless. They imitated the nations around them although the
LORD had ordered them, "Do not
do as they do." Dt 12:30-31; 29:25; 32:21

[a] 4 *So* is probably an abbreviation for *Osorkon.* [b] 12 Exodus 20:4,5

16They forsook all the commands of the LORD their God and
made for themselves two idols
cast in the shape of calves, and an
Asherah pole. They bowed down
to all the starry hosts, and they
worshiped Baal. 17They sacrificed
their sons and daughters in the
fire. They practiced divination
and sought omens and sold themselves to do evil in the eyes of the
LORD, arousing his anger.

1Ki 21:20; Ro 7:14

18So the LORD was very angry
with Israel and removed them
from his presence. Only the tribe
of Judah was left, 19and even Judah did not keep the commands
of the LORD their God. They followed the practices Israel had introduced. 20Therefore the LORD rejected all the people of Israel; he
afflicted them and gave them into
the hands of plunderers, until he
thrust them from his presence.

2Ki 15:29; 16:3

21When he tore Israel away from
the house of David, they made Jeroboam son of Nebat their king. Jeroboam enticed Israel away from
following the LORD and caused
them to commit a great sin. 22The
Israelites persisted in all the sins
of Jeroboam and did not turn
away from them 23until the LORD
removed them from his presence,
as he had warned through all his
servants the prophets. So the people of Israel were taken from their
homeland into exile in Assyria,
and they are still there. 1Ki 11:11; 12:20

Samaria Resettled

24The king of Assyria brought
people from Babylon, Kuthah,
Avva, Hamath and Sepharvaim
and settled them in the towns of
Samaria to replace the Israelites.
They took over Samaria and lived
in its towns. 25When they first
lived there, they did not worship
the LORD; so he sent lions among
them and they killed some of the
people. 26It was reported to the
king of Assyria: "The people you
deported and resettled in the
towns of Samaria do not know
what the god of that country requires. He has sent lions among
them, which are killing them off,
because the people do not know
what he requires."

Ge 37:20; 2Ki 18:34; Ezr 4:2,10

27Then the king of Assyria
gave this order: "Have one of the
priests you took captive from Samaria go back to live there and
teach the people what the god of
the land requires." 28So one of the
priests who had been exiled from
Samaria came to live in Bethel and
taught them how to worship the
LORD.

29Nevertheless, each national
group made its own gods in the
several towns where they settled,
and set them up in the shrines
the people of Samaria had made
at the high places. 30The people
from Babylon made Sukkoth Be-
noth, those from Kuthah made
Nergal, and those from Hamath

made Ashima; [31]the Avvites made
Nibhaz and Tartak, and the Se-
pharvites burned their children
in the fire as sacrifices to Adrammelek and Anammelek, the gods
of Sepharvaim. [32]They worshiped
the LORD, but they also appointed all sorts of their own people to
officiate for them as priests in the
shrines at the high places. [33]They
worshiped the LORD, but they also
served their own gods in accordance with the customs of the nations from which they had been
brought. ver 24; 1Ki 12:31
[34]To this day they persist in
their former practices. They neither worship the LORD nor ad-
here to the decrees and regulations, the laws and commands
that the LORD gave the descendants of Jacob, whom he named
Israel. [35]When the LORD made a
covenant with the Israelites, he
commanded them: "Do not worship any other gods or bow down
to them, serve them or sacrifice
to them. [36]But the LORD, who
brought you up out of Egypt with
mighty power and outstretched
arm, is the one you must worship.
To him you shall bow down and
to him offer sacrifices. [37]You must
always be careful to keep the decrees and regulations, the laws
and commands he wrote for you.
Do not worship other gods. [38]Do
not forget the covenant I have
made with you, and do not worship other gods. [39]Rather, worship
the LORD your God; it is he who
will deliver you from the hand of
all your enemies." Dt 44:23; 5:32
[40]They would not listen, however, but persisted in their former practices. [41]Even while these
people were worshiping the LORD,
they were serving their idols. To
this day their children and grandchildren continue to do as their
ancestors did. 1Ki 18:21; Mt 6:24

Hezekiah King of Judah

18 In the third year of Hoshea
son of Elah king of Israel,
Hezekiah son of Ahaz king of Judah began to reign. [2]He was twenty-five years old when he became
king, and he reigned in Jerusalem
twenty-nine years. His mother's
name was Abijah[a] daughter of
Zechariah. [3]He did what was right
in the eyes of the LORD, just as his
father David had done. [4]He removed the high places, smashed
the sacred stones and cut down
the Asherah poles. He broke into
pieces the bronze snake Moses had
made, for up to that time the Israelites had been burning incense to
it. (It was called Nehushtan.[b])
2Ch 29:1-2; 31:1
[5]Hezekiah trusted in the LORD,
the God of Israel. There was no
one like him among all the kings
of Judah, either before him or after him. [6]He held fast to the LORD
and did not stop following him;
he kept the commands the LORD

[a] 2 Hebrew *Abi*, a variant of *Abijah*
[b] 4 *Nehushtan* sounds like the Hebrew for both *bronze* and *snake*.

had given Moses. 7And the LORD
was with him; he was successful
in whatever he undertook. He rebelled against the king of Assyria and did not serve him. 8From
watchtower to fortified city, he
defeated the Philistines, as far as
Gaza and its territory. 2Ch 31:20-21

9In King Hezekiah's fourth
year, which was the seventh year
of Hoshea son of Elah king of Israel, Shalmaneser king of Assyria marched against Samaria and
laid siege to it. 10At the end of
three years the Assyrians took it.
So Samaria was captured in Hezekiah's sixth year, which was the
ninth year of Hoshea king of Israel. 11The king of Assyria deported
Israel to Assyria and settled them
in Halah, in Gozan on the Habor
River and in towns of the Medes.
12This happened because they had
not obeyed the LORD their God,
but had violated his covenant—
all that Moses the servant of the
LORD commanded. They neither
listened to the commands nor
carried them out.

2Ki 17:3-7; Da 9:6,10; 1Ki 9:6

13In the fourteenth year of King
Hezekiah's reign, Sennacherib
king of Assyria attacked all the
fortified cities of Judah and captured them. 14So Hezekiah king
of Judah sent this message to the
king of Assyria at Lachish: "I have
done wrong. Withdraw from me,
and I will pay whatever you demand of me." The king of Assyria exacted from Hezekiah king of
Judah three hundred talents[a] of
silver and thirty talents[b] of gold.
15So Hezekiah gave him all the silver that was found in the temple
of the LORD and in the treasuries
of the royal palace. 1Ki 15:18; 2Ki 16:8

16At this time Hezekiah king of
Judah stripped off the gold with
which he had covered the doors
and doorposts of the temple of
the LORD, and gave it to the king
of Assyria.

Sennacherib Threatens Jerusalem

17The king of Assyria sent his supreme commander, his chief officer and his field commander with
a large army, from Lachish to King
Hezekiah at Jerusalem. They came
up to Jerusalem and stopped at
the aqueduct of the Upper Pool, on
the road to the Washerman's Field.
18They called for the king; and Eliakim son of Hilkiah the palace administrator, Shebna the secretary,
and Joah son of Asaph the recorder went out to them.

2Ki 19:2; Isa 20:1; 22:15

19The field commander said to
them, "Tell Hezekiah:

"'This is what the great
king, the king of Assyria,
says: On what are you basing this confidence of yours?
20You say you have the counsel and the might for war—
but you speak only empty
words. On whom are you

[a] *14* That is, about 11 tons or about 10 metric tons [b] *14* That is, about 1 ton or about 1 metric ton

depending, that you rebel
against me? 21Look, I know
you are depending on Egypt,
that splintered reed of a staff,
which pierces the hand of
anyone who leans on it! Such
is Pharaoh king of Egypt
to all who depend on him.
22But if you say to me, "We
are depending on the LORD
our God" — isn't he the one
whose high places and altars
Hezekiah removed, saying to
Judah and Jerusalem, "You
must worship before this altar in Jerusalem"?

Isa 30:5,7; Eze 29:6

23" 'Come now, make a bar-
gain with my master, the king
of Assyria: I will give you two
thousand horses — if you can
put riders on them! 24How can
you repulse one officer of the
least of my master's officials,
even though you are depending on Egypt for chariots and
horsemen[a]? 25Furthermore,
have I come to attack and destroy this place without word
from the LORD? The LORD
himself told me to march
against this country and destroy it.' " 2Ki 19:6,22

26Then Eliakim son of Hilkiah,
and Shebna and Joah said to the
field commander, "Please speak to
your servants in Aramaic, since we
understand it. Don't speak to us in
Hebrew in the hearing of the people on the wall." Ezr 4:7

27But the commander replied,
"Was it only to your master and
you that my master sent me to
say these things, and not to the
people sitting on the wall — who,
like you, will have to eat their own
excrement and drink their own
urine?"

28Then the commander stood
and called out in Hebrew, "Hear
the word of the great king, the
king of Assyria! 29This is what the
king says: Do not let Hezekiah deceive you. He cannot deliver you
from my hand. 30Do not let Hezekiah persuade you to trust in the
LORD when he says, 'The LORD will
surely deliver us; this city will not
be given into the hand of the king
of Assyria.'

31"Do not listen to Hezekiah. This
is what the king of Assyria says:
Make peace with me and come
out to me. Then each of you will
eat fruit from your own vine and
fig tree and drink water from your
own cistern, 32until I come and take
you to a land like your own — a
land of grain and new wine, a land
of bread and vineyards, a land of
olive trees and honey. Choose life
and not death!

"Do not listen to Hezekiah,
for he is misleading you when
he says, 'The LORD will deliver us.' 33Has the god of any nation ever delivered his land from
the hand of the king of Assyria?
34Where are the gods of Hamath
and Arpad? Where are the gods of

[a] 24 Or *charioteers*

Sepharvaim, Hena and Ivvah? Have they rescued Samaria from my hand? 35 Who of all the gods of these countries has been able to save his land from me? How then can the LORD deliver Jerusalem from my hand?" 2Ch 32:9-19

36 But the people remained silent and said nothing in reply, because the king had commanded, "Do not answer him."

37 Then Eliakim son of Hilkiah the palace administrator, Shebna the secretary, and Joah son of Asaph the recorder went to Hezekiah, with their clothes torn, and told him what the field commander had said. Isa 36:1-22

Jerusalem's Deliverance Foretold

19 When King Hezekiah heard this, he tore his clothes and put on sackcloth and went into the temple of the LORD. 2 He sent Eliakim the palace administrator, Shebna the secretary and the leading priests, all wearing sackcloth, to the prophet Isaiah son of Amoz. 3 They told him, "This is what Hezekiah says: This day is a day of distress and rebuke and disgrace, as when children come to the moment of birth and there is no strength to deliver them. 4 It may be that the LORD your God will hear all the words of the field commander, whom his master, the king of Assyria, has sent to ridicule the living God, and that he will rebuke him for the words the LORD your God has heard. Therefore pray for the remnant that still survives." 2Sa 16:12; 2Ki 18:35

5 When King Hezekiah's officials came to Isaiah, 6 Isaiah said to them, "Tell your master, 'This is what the LORD says: Do not be afraid of what you have heard — those words with which the underlings of the king of Assyria have blasphemed me. 7 Listen! When he hears a certain report, I will make him want to return to his own country, and there I will have him cut down with the sword.' " ver 37; 2Ki 18:25

8 When the field commander heard that the king of Assyria had left Lachish, he withdrew and found the king fighting against Libnah. 2Ki 18:14

9 Now Sennacherib received a report that Tirhakah, the king of Cush,[a] was marching out to fight against him. So he again sent messengers to Hezekiah with this word: 10 "Say to Hezekiah king of Judah: Do not let the god you depend on deceive you when he says, 'Jerusalem will not be given into the hands of the king of Assyria.' 11 Surely you have heard what the kings of Assyria have done to all the countries, destroying them completely. And will you be delivered? 12 Did the gods of the nations that were destroyed by my predecessors deliver them — the gods of Gozan, Harran, Rezeph and the people of Eden who were in Tel Assar? 13 Where is the king

[a] 9 That is, the upper Nile region

of Hamath or the king of Arpad?
Where are the kings of Lair, Sepharvaim, Hena and Ivvah?" Isa 37:1-13

Hezekiah's Prayer

14 Hezekiah received the letter
from the messengers and read it.
Then he went up to the temple of
the LORD and spread it out before
the LORD. 15 And Hezekiah prayed
to the LORD: "LORD, the God of Israel, enthroned between the cherubim, you alone are God over all
the kingdoms of the earth. You
have made heaven and earth.
16 Give ear, LORD, and hear; open
your eyes, LORD, and see; listen to
the words Sennacherib has sent to
ridicule the living God.
17 "It is true, LORD, that the Assyrian kings have laid waste these
nations and their lands. 18 They
have thrown their gods into the
fire and destroyed them, for they
were not gods but only wood and
stone, fashioned by human hands.
19 Now, LORD our God, deliver us
from his hand, so that all the kingdoms of the earth may know that
you alone, LORD, are God."
Isa 37:14-20; Ps 83:18

Isaiah Prophesies Sennacherib's Fall

20 Then Isaiah son of Amoz sent
a message to Hezekiah: "This is
what the LORD, the God of Israel, says: I have heard your prayer
concerning Sennacherib king of
Assyria. 21 This is the word that the
LORD has spoken against him:
2Ki 20:5; Isa 10:5

"'Virgin Daughter Zion La 2:13
despises you and mocks you.
Ps 22:7-8
Daughter Jerusalem
tosses her head as you flee.
Ps 109:25
22 Who is it you have ridiculed
and blasphemed?
Against whom have you
raised your voice
and lifted your eyes in pride?
Against the Holy One of
Israel! Ps 71:22; Isa 5:24
23 By your messengers
you have ridiculed the Lord.
And you have said, Isa 10:18
"With my many chariots
Ps 20:7
I have ascended the heights of
the mountains,
the utmost heights of
Lebanon.
I have cut down its tallest
cedars, Isa 10:34
the choicest of its junipers.
I have reached its remotest
parts,
the finest of its forests.
24 I have dug wells in foreign
lands
and drunk the water there.
With the soles of my feet
I have dried up all the
streams of Egypt."

25 "'Have you not heard? Isa 40:21,28
Long ago I ordained it.
In days of old I planned it;
Isa 10:5; 45:7
now I have brought it to
pass,

that you have turned fortified
cities
into piles of stone. Mic 1:6
26 Their people, drained of power,
are dismayed and put to
shame. Ps 6:10
They are like plants in the field,
like tender green shoots, Isa 4:2
like grass sprouting on the
roof,
scorched before it grows up.
Ps 129:6

27 " 'But I know where you are
Ps 139:1-4
and when you come and go
and how you rage against
me.
28 Because you rage against me
and because your insolence
has reached my ears,
I will put my hook in your nose
Eze 29:4
and my bit in your mouth,
and I will make you return
by the way you came.' ver 33

29 "This will be the sign for you, Hezekiah: Lk 2:12

"This year you will eat what
grows by itself, Lev 25:5
and the second year what
springs from that.
But in the third year sow and
reap,
plant vineyards and eat their
fruit. Ps 107:37
30 Once more a remnant of the
kingdom of Judah
will take root below and bear
fruit above. 2Ch 32:22-23
31 For out of Jerusalem will come
a remnant, Ge 45:7
and out of Mount Zion
a band of survivors.
Isa 66:19

"The zeal of the LORD Almighty will accomplish this. Isa 9:7

32 "Therefore this is what the
LORD says concerning the king of
Assyria:

" 'He will not enter this city
or shoot an arrow here.
He will not come before it with
shield
or build a siege ramp
against it.
33 By the way that he came he will
return; ver 28
he will not enter this city,
declares the LORD.
34 I will defend this city and
save it, 2Ki 20:6
for my sake and for the sake
of David my servant.' "
1Ki 11:12-13

35 That night the angel of the
LORD went out and put to death a
hundred and eighty-five thousand
in the Assyrian camp. When the
people got up the next morning —
there were all the dead bodies! 36 So
Sennacherib king of Assyria broke
camp and withdrew. He returned
to Nineveh and stayed there.
Ex 12:23; Job 24:24; Jnh 1:2

37 One day, while he was worshiping in the temple of his god
Nisrok, his sons Adrammelek
and Sharezer killed him with the

sword, and they escaped to the land of Ararat. And Esarhaddon his son succeeded him as king.

2Ch 32:20-21; Isa 37:21-38

Hezekiah's Illness

20 In those days Hezekiah became ill and was at the point of death. The prophet Isaiah son of Amoz went to him and said, "This is what the LORD says: Put your house in order, because you are going to die; you will not recover."

[2]Hezekiah turned his face to the wall and prayed to the LORD, [3]"Remember, LORD, how I have walked before you faithfully and with wholehearted devotion and have done what is good in your eyes." And Hezekiah wept bitterly.

2Ki 18:3-6; Ne 13:22

[4]Before Isaiah had left the middle court, the word of the LORD came to him: [5]"Go back and tell Hezekiah, the ruler of my people, 'This is what the LORD, the God of your father David, says: I have heard your prayer and seen your tears; I will heal you. On the third day from now you will go up to the temple of the LORD. [6]I will add fifteen years to your life. And I will deliver you and this city from the hand of the king of Assyria. I will defend this city for my sake and for the sake of my servant David.'"

2Ki 19:20,34; Ps 39:12

[7]Then Isaiah said, "Prepare a poultice of figs." They did so and applied it to the boil, and he recovered.

Isa 38:21

[8]Hezekiah had asked Isaiah, "What will be the sign that the LORD will heal me and that I will go up to the temple of the LORD on the third day from now?"

[9]Isaiah answered, "This is the LORD's sign to you that the LORD will do what he has promised: Shall the shadow go forward ten steps, or shall it go back ten steps?"

Dt 13:2; Jer 44:29

[10]"It is a simple matter for the shadow to go forward ten steps," said Hezekiah. "Rather, have it go back ten steps."

[11]Then the prophet Isaiah called on the LORD, and the LORD made the shadow go back the ten steps it had gone down on the stairway of Ahaz.

2Ch 32:24-26; Isa 38:1-8

Envoys From Babylon

[12]At that time Marduk-Baladan son of Baladan king of Babylon sent Hezekiah letters and a gift, because he had heard of Hezekiah's illness. [13]Hezekiah received the envoys and showed them all that was in his storehouses — the silver, the gold, the spices and the fine olive oil — his armory and everything found among his treasures. There was nothing in his palace or in all his kingdom that Hezekiah did not show them.

[14]Then Isaiah the prophet went to King Hezekiah and asked, "What did those men say, and where did they come from?"

"From a distant land," Hezekiah replied. "They came from Babylon."

15The prophet asked, "What did
they see in your palace?"
"They saw everything in my
palace," Hezekiah said. "There is
nothing among my treasures that
I did not show them."

16Then Isaiah said to Hezekiah,
"Hear the word of the LORD: 17The
time will surely come when everything in your palace, and all that
your predecessors have stored up
until this day, will be carried off
to Babylon. Nothing will be left,
says the LORD. 18And some of your
descendants, your own flesh and
blood who will be born to you, will
be taken away, and they will become eunuchs in the palace of the
king of Babylon." 2Ki 24:15; 2Ch 33:11

19"The word of the LORD you
have spoken is good," Hezekiah replied. For he thought, "Will
there not be peace and security in
my lifetime?" Isa 39:1-8

20As for the other events of Hezekiah's reign, all his achievements
and how he made the pool and the
tunnel by which he brought water
into the city, are they not written
in the book of the annals of the
kings of Judah? 21Hezekiah rested
with his ancestors. And Manasseh
his son succeeded him as king.
Ne 3:16

Manasseh King of Judah

21 Manasseh was twelve years
old when he became king,
and he reigned in Jerusalem fif-
ty-five years. His mother's name
was Hephzibah. 2He did evil in the
eyes of the LORD, following the detestable practices of the nations
the LORD had driven out before
the Israelites. 3He rebuilt the high
places his father Hezekiah had destroyed; he also erected altars to
Baal and made an Asherah pole, as
Ahab king of Israel had done. He
bowed down to all the starry hosts
and worshiped them. 4He built altars in the temple of the LORD, of
which the LORD had said, "In Jerusalem I will put my Name." 5In
the two courts of the temple of the
LORD, he built altars to all the starry hosts. 6He sacrificed his own
son in the fire, practiced divination, sought omens, and consulted mediums and spiritists. He did
much evil in the eyes of the LORD,
arousing his anger.
Jer 15:4; Lev 18:21; 19:31

7He took the carved Asherah
pole he had made and put it in the
temple, of which the LORD had said
to David and to his son Solomon,
"In this temple and in Jerusalem,
which I have chosen out of all the
tribes of Israel, I will put my Name
forever. 8I will not again make the
feet of the Israelites wander from
the land I gave their ancestors, if
only they will be careful to do everything I commanded them and
will keep the whole Law that my
servant Moses gave them." 9But
the people did not listen. Manasseh led them astray, so that they
did more evil than the nations the
LORD had destroyed before the Israelites. 2Ch 33:1-10

10The LORD said through his
servants the prophets: 11"Manasseh king of Judah has committed
these detestable sins. He has done
more evil than the Amorites who
preceded him and has led Judah
into sin with his idols. 12Therefore
this is what the LORD, the God of
Israel, says: I am going to bring
such disaster on Jerusalem and
Judah that the ears of everyone
who hears of it will tingle. 13I will
stretch out over Jerusalem the
measuring line used against Samaria and the plumb line used
against the house of Ahab. I will
wipe out Jerusalem as one wipes
a dish, wiping it and turning it
upside down. 14I will forsake the
remnant of my inheritance and
give them into the hands of enemies. They will be looted and
plundered by all their enemies;
15they have done evil in my eyes
and have aroused my anger from
the day their ancestors came out
of Egypt until this day."

2Ki 19:4; Ps 78:58-60; Isa 34:11

16Moreover, Manasseh also shed
so much innocent blood that
he filled Jerusalem from end to
end — besides the sin that he had
caused Judah to commit, so that
they did evil in the eyes of the
LORD. 2Ki 24:4

17As for the other events of Manasseh's reign, and all he did, including the sin he committed, are
they not written in the book of
the annals of the kings of Judah?
18Manasseh rested with his ancestors and was buried in his palace
garden, the garden of Uzza. And
Amon his son succeeded him as
king.

Amon King of Judah

19Amon was twenty-two years
old when he became king, and he
reigned in Jerusalem two years.
His mother's name was Meshulle-
meth daughter of Haruz; she was
from Jotbah. 20He did evil in the
eyes of the LORD, as his father Manasseh had done. 21He followed
completely the ways of his father,
worshiping the idols his father
had worshiped, and bowing down
to them. 22He forsook the LORD,
the God of his ancestors, and did
not walk in obedience to him.

ver 2-6; 1Ki 11:33

23Amon's officials conspired
against him and assassinated the
king in his palace. 24Then the people of the land killed all who had
plotted against King Amon, and
they made Josiah his son king in
his place. 2Ch 33:21-25

25As for the other events of
Amon's reign, and what he did,
are they not written in the book of
the annals of the kings of Judah?
26He was buried in his tomb in the
garden of Uzza. And Josiah his son
succeeded him as king.

The Book of the Law Found

22 Josiah was eight years old
when he became king, and
he reigned in Jerusalem thirty-
one years. His mother's name was

Jedidah daughter of Adaiah; she
was from Bozkath. 2He did what
was right in the eyes of the LORD
and followed completely the ways
of his father David, not turning
aside to the right or to the left.

Dt 5:32; 17:19; Jos 15:39

3In the eighteenth year of his
reign, King Josiah sent the secretary, Shaphan son of Azaliah, the
son of Meshullam, to the temple
of the LORD. He said: 4"Go up to
Hilkiah the high priest and have
him get ready the money that has
been brought into the temple of
the LORD, which the doorkeepers have collected from the people. 5Have them entrust it to the
men appointed to supervise the
work on the temple. And have
these men pay the workers who
repair the temple of the LORD—
6the carpenters, the builders and
the masons. Also have them purchase timber and dressed stone to
repair the temple. 7But they need
not account for the money entrusted to them, because they are
honest in their dealings."

2Ki 12:4-5,11-15

8Hilkiah the high priest said
to Shaphan the secretary, "I have
found the Book of the Law in the
temple of the LORD." He gave it to
Shaphan, who read it. 9Then Shaphan the secretary went to the
king and reported to him: "Your
officials have paid out the money
that was in the temple of the LORD
and have entrusted it to the workers and supervisors at the temple." 10Then Shaphan the secretary
informed the king, "Hilkiah the
priest has given me a book." And
Shaphan read from it in the presence of the king. Dt 31:24; Jer 36:21

11When the king heard the words
of the Book of the Law, he tore his
robes. 12He gave these orders to
Hilkiah the priest, Ahikam son of
Shaphan, Akbor son of Micaiah,
Shaphan the secretary and Asaiah the king's attendant: 13"Go and
inquire of the LORD for me and
for the people and for all Judah
about what is written in this book
that has been found. Great is the
LORD's anger that burns against us
because those who have gone before us have not obeyed the words
of this book; they have not acted
in accordance with all that is written there concerning us."

Dt 29:24-28; 2Ki 25:22

14Hilkiah the priest, Ahikam, Akbor, Shaphan and Asaiah went to
speak to the prophet Huldah, who
was the wife of Shallum son of
Tikvah, the son of Harhas, keeper
of the wardrobe. She lived in Jerusalem, in the New Quarter.

15She said to them, "This is what
the LORD, the God of Israel, says:
Tell the man who sent you to me,
16'This is what the LORD says: I am
going to bring disaster on this
place and its people, according to
everything written in the book
the king of Judah has read. 17Be-
cause they have forsaken me and
burned incense to other gods and
aroused my anger by all the idols

their hands have made,[a] my anger will burn against this place
and will not be quenched.' 18Tell
the king of Judah, who sent you to
inquire of the LORD, 'This is what
the LORD, the God of Israel, says
concerning the words you heard:
19Because your heart was responsive and you humbled yourself
before the LORD when you heard
what I have spoken against this
place and its people — that they
would become a curse[b] and be
laid waste — and because you tore
your robes and wept in my presence, I also have heard you, declares the LORD. 20Therefore I will
gather you to your ancestors, and
you will be buried in peace. Your
eyes will not see all the disaster I
am going to bring on this place.'"

2Ch 34:1-2,8-28

So they took her answer back to the king.

Josiah Renews the Covenant

23 Then the king called together all the elders of Judah and Jerusalem. 2He went up
to the temple of the LORD with
the people of Judah, the inhabitants of Jerusalem, the priests
and the prophets — all the people from the least to the greatest. He read in their hearing all
the words of the Book of the Covenant, which had been found in
the temple of the LORD. 3The king
stood by the pillar and renewed
the covenant in the presence of
the LORD — to follow the LORD
and keep his commands, statutes
and decrees with all his heart and
all his soul, thus confirming the
words of the covenant written
in this book. Then all the people
pledged themselves to the covenant.

2Ch 34:29-32; 2Ki 22:8

4The king ordered Hilkiah the
high priest, the priests next in
rank and the doorkeepers to remove from the temple of the
LORD all the articles made for
Baal and Asherah and all the starry hosts. He burned them outside
Jerusalem in the fields of the
Kidron Valley and took the ashes to Bethel. 5He did away with
the idolatrous priests appointed
by the kings of Judah to burn incense on the high places of the
towns of Judah and on those
around Jerusalem — those who
burned incense to Baal, to the
sun and moon, to the constellations and to all the starry hosts.
6He took the Asherah pole from
the temple of the LORD to the
Kidron Valley outside Jerusalem
and burned it there. He ground it
to powder and scattered the dust
over the graves of the common
people. 7He also tore down the
quarters of the male shrine prostitutes that were in the temple
of the LORD, the quarters where
women did weaving for Asherah.

1Ki 14:24; 15:12; Eze 16:16

[a] 17 Or *by everything they have done*
[b] 19 That is, their names would be used in cursing (see Jer. 29:22); or, others would see that they are cursed.

8 Josiah brought all the priests
from the towns of Judah and desecrated the high places, from Geba
to Beersheba, where the priests
had burned incense. He broke
down the gateway at the entrance
of the Gate of Joshua, the city governor, which was on the left of the
city gate. 9 Although the priests of
the high places did not serve at
the altar of the LORD in Jerusalem,
they ate unleavened bread with
their fellow priests.

1Ki 15:22; Eze 44:10-14

10 He desecrated Topheth, which
was in the Valley of Ben Hinnom,
so no one could use it to sacrifice
their son or daughter in the fire to
Molek. 11 He removed from the entrance to the temple of the LORD
the horses that the kings of Judah
had dedicated to the sun. They
were in the court[a] near the room
of an official named Nathan-Me-
lek. Josiah then burned the chariots dedicated to the sun.

Isa 30:33; Jer 7:31-32; 19:6

12 He pulled down the altars the
kings of Judah had erected on the
roof near the upper room of Ahaz,
and the altars Manasseh had built
in the two courts of the temple of
the LORD. He removed them from
there, smashed them to pieces and
threw the rubble into the Kidron
Valley. 13 The king also desecrated the high places that were east
of Jerusalem on the south of the
Hill of Corruption — the ones Solomon king of Israel had built for
Ashtoreth the vile goddess of the
Sidonians, for Chemosh the vile
god of Moab, and for Molek the detestable god of the people of Ammon. 14 Josiah smashed the sacred
stones and cut down the Asherah
poles and covered the sites with
human bones. Dt 7:5,25; 1Ki 11:7

15 Even the altar at Bethel, the
high place made by Jeroboam son
of Nebat, who had caused Israel
to sin — even that altar and high
place he demolished. He burned
the high place and ground it to
powder, and burned the Asherah
pole also. 16 Then Josiah looked
around, and when he saw the
tombs that were there on the hillside, he had the bones removed
from them and burned on the altar to defile it, in accordance with
the word of the LORD proclaimed
by the man of God who foretold
these things. 1Ki 13:2

17 The king asked, "What is that
tombstone I see?"

The people of the city said, "It
marks the tomb of the man of God
who came from Judah and pronounced against the altar of Bethel the very things you have done
to it."

18 "Leave it alone," he said. "Don't
let anyone disturb his bones." So
they spared his bones and those of
the prophet who had come from
Samaria. 1Ki 13:31

19 Just as he had done at Bethel, Josiah removed all the shrines
at the high places that the kings

[a] 11 The meaning of the Hebrew for this word is uncertain.

of Israel had built in the towns of
Samaria and that had aroused the
LORD's anger. 20 Josiah slaughtered
all the priests of those high places
on the altars and burned human
bones on them. Then he went back
to Jerusalem. 2Ch 34:3-7,33
21 The king gave this order to all
the people: "Celebrate the Passover to the LORD your God, as it
is written in this Book of the Covenant." 22 Neither in the days of
the judges who led Israel nor in
the days of the kings of Israel and
the kings of Judah had any such
Passover been observed. 23 But in
the eighteenth year of King Josiah, this Passover was celebrated
to the LORD in Jerusalem.

2Ch 35:1,18-19

24 Furthermore, Josiah got rid of
the mediums and spiritists, the
household gods, the idols and all
the other detestable things seen
in Judah and Jerusalem. This he
did to fulfill the requirements of
the law written in the book that
Hilkiah the priest had discovered
in the temple of the LORD. 25 Neither before nor after Josiah was
there a king like him who turned
to the LORD as he did — with all
his heart and with all his soul and
with all his strength, in accordance with all the Law of Moses.

Dt 18:11; 2Ki 18:5

26 Nevertheless, the LORD did
not turn away from the heat of his
fierce anger, which burned against
Judah because of all that Manasseh had done to arouse his anger.
27 So the LORD said, "I will remove
Judah also from my presence as
I removed Israel, and I will reject
Jerusalem, the city I chose, and
this temple, about which I said,
'My Name shall be there.'[a]"

2Ki 18:11; 21:13

28 As for the other events of Josiah's reign, and all he did, are they
not written in the book of the annals of the kings of Judah?
29 While Josiah was king, Pharaoh Necho king of Egypt went up
to the Euphrates River to help
the king of Assyria. King Josiah marched out to meet him in
battle, but Necho faced him and
killed him at Megiddo. 30 Josiah's
servants brought his body in a
chariot from Megiddo to Jerusalem and buried him in his own
tomb. And the people of the land
took Jehoahaz son of Josiah and
anointed him and made him
king in place of his father.

2Ch 35:20-36:1

Jehoahaz King of Judah

31 Jehoahaz was twenty-three
years old when he became king,
and he reigned in Jerusalem three
months. His mother's name was
Hamutal daughter of Jeremiah;
she was from Libnah. 32 He did evil
in the eyes of the LORD, just as his
predecessors had done. 33 Pharaoh
Necho put him in chains at Riblah in the land of Hamath so that
he might not reign in Jerusalem,
and he imposed on Judah a levy

[a] 27 1 Kings 8:29

of a hundred talents[a] of silver and
a talent[b] of gold. 34Pharaoh Necho
made Eliakim son of Josiah king
in place of his father Josiah and
changed Eliakim's name to Jehoiakim. But he took Jehoahaz
and carried him off to Egypt, and
there he died. 35Jehoiakim paid
Pharaoh Necho the silver and
gold he demanded. In order to do
so, he taxed the land and exacted
the silver and gold from the people of the land according to their
assessments.

2Ch 36:2-4; Jer 22:12; Eze 19:3-4

Jehoiakim King of Judah

36Jehoiakim was twenty-five
years old when he became king,
and he reigned in Jerusalem elev-
en years. His mother's name was
Zebidah daughter of Pedaiah; she
was from Rumah. 37And he did
evil in the eyes of the LORD, just
as his predecessors had done.

Jer 26:1

24 During Jehoiakim's reign,
Nebuchadnezzar king of
Babylon invaded the land, and
Jehoiakim became his vassal for
three years. But then he turned
against Nebuchadnezzar and rebelled. 2The LORD sent Babylonian,[c] Aramean, Moabite and Ammonite raiders against him to
destroy Judah, in accordance with
the word of the LORD proclaimed
by his servants the prophets.
3Surely these things happened
to Judah according to the LORD's
command, in order to remove
them from his presence because
of the sins of Manasseh and all
he had done, 4including the shedding of innocent blood. For he had
filled Jerusalem with innocent
blood, and the LORD was not willing to forgive.

2Ki 21:16; 23:26

5As for the other events of Jehoiakim's reign, and all he did, are
they not written in the book of the
annals of the kings of Judah? 6Je-
hoiakim rested with his ancestors.
And Jehoiachin his son succeeded
him as king.

2Ch 36:5-8; Jer 22:19

7The king of Egypt did not
march out from his own country
again, because the king of Babylon had taken all his territory,
from the Wadi of Egypt to the Euphrates River.

Jer 37:5-7; 46:2

Jehoiachin King of Judah

8Jehoiachin was eighteen years
old when he became king, and
he reigned in Jerusalem three
months. His mother's name was
Nehushta daughter of Elnathan;
she was from Jerusalem. 9He did
evil in the eyes of the LORD, just as
his father had done.

1Ch 3:16

10At that time the officers of
Nebuchadnezzar king of Babylon
advanced on Jerusalem and laid
siege to it, 11and Nebuchadnezzar himself came up to the city
while his officers were besieging
it. 12Jehoiachin king of Judah, his

[a] 33 That is, about 3 3/4 tons or about 3.4 metric tons [b] 33 That is, about 75 pounds or about 34 kilograms
[c] 2 Or *Chaldean*

mother, his attendants, his nobles
and his officials all surrendered to
him. Jer 24:1; 29:2; Da 1:1
In the eighth year of the reign
of the king of Babylon, he took Jehoiachin prisoner. 13As the LORD
had declared, Nebuchadnezzar
removed the treasures from the
temple of the LORD and from the
royal palace, and cut up the gold
articles that Solomon king of Israel had made for the temple of
the LORD. 14He carried all Jerusalem into exile: all the officers and
fighting men, and all the skilled
workers and artisans — a total of
ten thousand. Only the poorest
people of the land were left.
2Ki 25:12; Jer 40:7; 52:16
15Nebuchadnezzar took Jehoiachin captive to Babylon. He also
took from Jerusalem to Babylon
the king's mother, his wives, his
officials and the prominent people of the land. 16The king of Babylon also deported to Babylon the
entire force of seven thousand
fighting men, strong and fit for
war, and a thousand skilled workers and artisans. 17He made Mattaniah, Jehoiachin's uncle, king in
his place and changed his name
to Zedekiah. 2Ch 36:9-10

Zedekiah King of Judah

18Zedekiah was twenty-one years
old when he became king, and he
reigned in Jerusalem eleven years.
His mother's name was Hamutal daughter of Jeremiah; she was
from Libnah. 19He did evil in the
eyes of the LORD, just as Jehoiakim
had done. 20It was because of the
LORD's anger that all this happened
to Jerusalem and Judah, and in the
end he thrust them from his presence. 2Ch 36:11-16; Jer 52:1-3; 2Ki 23:31

The Fall of Jerusalem

Now Zedekiah rebelled against
the king of Babylon.
25 So in the ninth year of Zedekiah's reign, on the tenth
day of the tenth month, Nebuchadnezzar king of Babylon
marched against Jerusalem with
his whole army. He encamped
outside the city and built siege
works all around it. 2The city was
kept under siege until the eleventh year of King Zedekiah.
3By the ninth day of the fourth[a]
month the famine in the city had
become so severe that there was
no food for the people to eat. 4Then
the city wall was broken through,
and the whole army fled at night
through the gate between the
two walls near the king's garden,
though the Babylonians[b] were
surrounding the city. They fled
toward the Arabah,[c] 5but the Babylonian[d] army pursued the king
and overtook him in the plains of
Jericho. All his soldiers were separated from him and scattered,
6and he was captured. Jer 34:21-22

[a] 3 Probable reading of the original Hebrew text (see Jer. 52:6); Masoretic Text does not have *fourth*. [b] 4 Or *Chaldeans*; also in verses 13, 25 and 26 [c] 4 Or *the Jordan Valley* [d] 5 Or *Chaldean*; also in verses 10 and 24

He was taken to the king of Babylon at Riblah, where sentence was pronounced on him. 7They killed the sons of Zedekiah before his eyes. Then they put out his eyes, bound him with bronze shackles and took him to Babylon.

2Ki 23:33; Eze 33:21

8On the seventh day of the fifth month, in the nineteenth year of Nebuchadnezzar king of Babylon, Nebuzaradan commander of the imperial guard, an official of the king of Babylon, came to Jerusalem. 9He set fire to the temple of the LORD, the royal palace and all the houses of Jerusalem. Every important building he burned down. 10The whole Babylonian army under the commander of the imperial guard broke down the walls around Jerusalem. 11Nebuzaradan the commander of the guard carried into exile the people who remained in the city, along with the rest of the populace and those who had deserted to the king of Babylon. 12But the commander left behind some of the poorest people of the land to work the vineyards and fields.

Jer 39:1-10; 2Ki 24:14

13The Babylonians broke up the bronze pillars, the movable stands and the bronze Sea that were at the temple of the LORD and they carried the bronze to Babylon. 14They also took away the pots, shovels, wick trimmers, dishes and all the bronze articles used in the temple service. 15The commander of the imperial guard took away the censers and sprinkling bowls — all that were made of pure gold or silver.

Ex 27:3; 1Ki 7:47-50

16The bronze from the two pillars, the Sea and the movable stands, which Solomon had made for the temple of the LORD, was more than could be weighed. 17Each pillar was eighteen cubits[a] high. The bronze capital on top of one pillar was three cubits[b] high and was decorated with a network and pomegranates of bronze all around. The other pillar, with its network, was similar.

1Ki 7:15-22

18The commander of the guard took as prisoners Seraiah the chief priest, Zephaniah the priest next in rank and the three doorkeepers. 19Of those still in the city, he took the officer in charge of the fighting men, and five royal advisers. He also took the secretary who was chief officer in charge of conscripting the people of the land and sixty of the conscripts who were found in the city. 20Nebuzaradan the commander took them all and brought them to the king of Babylon at Riblah. 21There at Riblah, in the land of Hamath, the king had them executed.

Jer 21:1; 29:25

So Judah went into captivity, away from her land.

2Ch 36:17-20; Jer 52:4-27

22Nebuchadnezzar king of Babylon appointed Gedaliah son of Ahikam, the son of Shaphan, to be

[a] *17* That is, about 27 feet or about 8.1 meters [b] *17* That is, about 4 1/2 feet or about 1.4 meters

over the people he had left behind
in Judah. 23When all the army officers and their men heard that the
king of Babylon had appointed
Gedaliah as governor, they came
to Gedaliah at Mizpah — Ishmael son of Nethaniah, Johanan son
of Kareah, Seraiah son of Tanhumeth the Netophathite, Jaazaniah the son of the Maakathite, and
their men. 24Gedaliah took an oath
to reassure them and their men.
"Do not be afraid of the Babylonian officials," he said. "Settle down
in the land and serve the king of
Babylon, and it will go well with
you." Jer 40:5,7
25In the seventh month, however, Ishmael son of Nethaniah, the
son of Elishama, who was of royal
blood, came with ten men and assassinated Gedaliah and also the
men of Judah and the Babylonians who were with him at Mizpah.
26At this, all the people from the
least to the greatest, together with
the army officers, fled to Egypt for
fear of the Babylonians.
Jer 40:7-9; 41:1-3,16-18

Jehoiachin Released

27In the thirty-seventh year of
the exile of Jehoiachin king of Judah, in the year Awel-Marduk became king of Babylon, he released
Jehoiachin king of Judah from
prison. He did this on the twenty-
seventh day of the twelfth month.
28He spoke kindly to him and gave
him a seat of honor higher than
those of the other kings who were
with him in Babylon. 29So Jehoiachin put aside his prison clothes
and for the rest of his life ate regularly at the king's table. 30Day
by day the king gave Jehoiachin
a regular allowance as long as he
lived. Jer 52:31-34

1 CHRONICLES

Historical Records From Adam to Abraham

To Noah's Sons

1 Adam, Seth, Enosh, [2]Kenan, Mahalalel, Jared, [3]Enoch, Methuselah, Lamech, Noah. Ge 5:1-32; Lk 3:36-38

[4]The sons of Noah:[a]
Shem, Ham and Japheth.
Ge 5:32; 6:10

The Japhethites

[5]The sons[b] of Japheth:
Gomer, Magog, Madai, Javan, Tubal, Meshek and Tiras.
[6]The sons of Gomer:
Ashkenaz, Riphath[c] and Togarmah.
[7]The sons of Javan:
Elishah, Tarshish, the Kittites and the Rodanites.
Ge 10:2-5

The Hamites

[8]The sons of Ham:
Cush, Egypt, Put and Canaan.
[9]The sons of Cush:
Seba, Havilah, Sabta, Raamah and Sabteka.
The sons of Raamah:
Sheba and Dedan.
[10]Cush was the father[d] of
Nimrod, who became a mighty warrior on earth.
[11]Egypt was the father of
the Ludites, Anamites, Lehabites, Naphtuhites,
[12]Pathrusites, Kasluhites (from whom the Philistines came) and Caphtorites.
[13]Canaan was the father of
Sidon his firstborn,[e] and of the Hittites, [14]Jebusites,
Amorites, Girgashites, [15]Hivites, Arkites, Sinites, [16]Arvadites, Zemarites and Hamathites.
Ge 10:6-20

The Semites

[17]The sons of Shem:
Elam, Ashur, Arphaxad, Lud and Aram.
The sons of Aram:[f]
Uz, Hul, Gether and Meshek.
[18]Arphaxad was the father of Shelah,
and Shelah the father of Eber.

[a] 4 Septuagint; Hebrew does not have this line. [b] 5 *Sons* may mean *descendants* or *successors* or *nations*; also in verses 6-9, 17 and 23. [c] 6 Many Hebrew manuscripts and Vulgate (see also Septuagint and Gen. 10:3); most Hebrew manuscripts *Diphath* [d] 10 *Father* may mean *ancestor* or *predecessor* or *founder*; also in verses 11, 13, 18 and 20. [e] 13 Or *of the Sidonians, the foremost* [f] 17 One Hebrew manuscript and some Septuagint manuscripts (see also Gen. 10:23); most Hebrew manuscripts do not have this line.

19 Two sons were born to Eber:
One was named Peleg,[a] because in his time the earth
was divided; his brother
was named Joktan.
20 Joktan was the father of
Almodad, Sheleph, Hazar-
maveth, Jerah, 21 Hadoram,
Uzal, Diklah, 22 Obal,[b] Abim-
ael, Sheba, 23 Ophir, Havilah
and Jobab. All these were
sons of Joktan.
Ge 10:21-31; 11:10-27

24 Shem, Arphaxad,[c] Shelah,
Lk 3:34-36
25 Eber, Peleg, Reu,
26 Serug, Nahor, Terah
27 and Abram (that is, Abraham).

The Family of Abraham

28 The sons of Abraham:
Isaac and Ishmael.

Descendants of Hagar

29 These were their descendants:
Nebaioth the firstborn of
Ishmael, Kedar, Adbeel,
Mibsam, 30 Mishma, Du-
mah, Massa, Hadad, Tema,
31 Jetur, Naphish and Kedemah. These were the sons
of Ishmael. Ge 25:12-16

Descendants of Keturah

32 The sons born to Keturah,
Abraham's concubine:
Ge 22:24
Zimran, Jokshan, Medan,
Midian, Ishbak and Shuah.
The sons of Jokshan:
Sheba and Dedan. Ge 10:7
33 The sons of Midian:
Ephah, Epher, Hanok, Abi-
da and Eldaah.
All these were descendants of
Keturah. Ge 25:1-4

Descendants of Sarah

34 Abraham was the father of
Isaac. Ge 21:2-3; Mt 1:2; Ac 7:8
The sons of Isaac:
Esau and Israel. Ge 17:5; 25:25-26

Esau's Sons

35 The sons of Esau: Ge 36:19
Eliphaz, Reuel, Jeush, Jalam and Korah. Ge 36:4
36 The sons of Eliphaz:
Teman, Omar, Zepho,[d] Gatam and Kenaz;
by Timna: Amalek.[e] Ex 17:14
37 The sons of Reuel: Ge 36:17
Nahath, Zerah, Shammah
and Mizzah. Ge 36:10-14

The People of Seir in Edom

38 The sons of Seir:
Lotan, Shobal, Zibeon,
Anah, Dishon, Ezer and Di-
shan.

[a] 19 *Peleg* means *division.* [b] 22 Some Hebrew manuscripts and Syriac (see also Gen. 10:28); most Hebrew manuscripts *Ebal* [c] 24 Hebrew; some Septuagint manuscripts *Arphaxad, Cainan* (see also note at Gen. 11:10) [d] 36 Many Hebrew manuscripts, some Septuagint manuscripts and Syriac (see also Gen. 36:11); most Hebrew manuscripts *Zephi* [e] 36 Some Septuagint manuscripts (see also Gen. 36:12); Hebrew *Gatam, Kenaz, Timna and Amalek*

39 The sons of Lotan:
Hori and Homam. Timna was Lotan's sister.
40 The sons of Shobal:
Alvan,[a] Manahath, Ebal, Shepho and Onam.
The sons of Zibeon:
Aiah and Anah. Ge 36:2
41 The son of Anah:
Dishon.
The sons of Dishon:
Hemdan,[b] Eshban, Ithran and Keran.
42 The sons of Ezer:
Bilhan, Zaavan and Akan.[c]
The sons of Dishan[d]:
Uz and Aran. Ge 36:20-28

The Rulers of Edom

43 These were the kings who reigned in Edom before any Israelite king reigned:
Bela son of Beor, whose city was named Dinhabah.
44 When Bela died, Jobab son of Zerah from Bozrah succeeded him as king.
45 When Jobab died, Husham from the land of the Temanites succeeded him as king. Ge 36:11
46 When Husham died, Hadad son of Bedad, who defeated Midian in the country of Moab, succeeded him as king. His city was named Avith.
47 When Hadad died, Samlah from Masrekah succeeded him as king.
48 When Samlah died, Shaul from Rehoboth on the river[e] succeeded him as king.
49 When Shaul died, Baal-Hanan son of Akbor succeeded him as king.
50 When Baal-Hanan died, Hadad succeeded him as king. His city was named Pau,[f] and his wife's name was Mehetabel daughter of Matred, the daughter of Me-
Zahab. 51 Hadad also died.

The chiefs of Edom were:
Timna, Alvah, Jetheth,
52 Oholibamah, Elah, Pinon,
53 Kenaz, Teman, Mibzar,
54 Magdiel and Iram. These were the chiefs of Edom.
Ge 36:31-43

Israel's Sons

2 These were the sons of Israel:
Reuben, Simeon, Levi, Judah, Issachar, Zebulun,
2 Dan, Joseph, Benjamin,
Naphtali, Gad and Asher.
Ge 35:23-26

[a] *40* Many Hebrew manuscripts and some Septuagint manuscripts (see also Gen. 36:23); most Hebrew manuscripts *Alian*
[b] *41* Many Hebrew manuscripts and some Septuagint manuscripts (see also Gen. 36:26); most Hebrew manuscripts *Hamran*
[c] *42* Many Hebrew and Septuagint manuscripts (see also Gen. 36:27); most Hebrew manuscripts *Zaavan, Jaakan*
[d] *42* See Gen. 36:28; Hebrew *Dishon,* a variant of *Dishan*
[e] *48* Possibly the Euphrates
[f] *50* Many Hebrew manuscripts, some Septuagint manuscripts, Vulgate and Syriac (see also Gen. 36:39); most Hebrew manuscripts *Pai*

Judah

To Hezron's Sons

[3]The sons of Judah: Ge 38:2-10
Er, Onan and Shelah. These
three were born to him by
a Canaanite woman, the
daughter of Shua. Er, Ju-
dah's firstborn, was wicked
in the LORD's sight; so the
LORD put him to death. [4]Ju-
dah's daughter-in-law Ta-
mar bore Perez and Zerah
to Judah. He had five sons
in all. Ge 38:11-30

[5]The sons of Perez: Ge 46:12
Hezron and Hamul. Nu 26:21
[6]The sons of Zerah:
Zimri, Ethan, Heman, Kal-
kol and Darda[a] — five in all.
[7]The son of Karmi:
Achar,[b] who brought trouble on Israel by violating
the ban on taking devoted
things.[c] Jos 6:18; 7:1
[8]The son of Ethan:
Azariah.
[9]The sons born to Hezron were:
Jerahmeel, Ram and Caleb.[d]
Nu 26:21

From Ram Son of Hezron

[10]Ram was the father of Lk 3:32-33
Amminadab, and Ammina-
dab the father of Nahshon,
the leader of the people of
Judah. [11]Nahshon was the
father of Salmon,[e] Salmon
the father of Boaz, [12]Boaz
the father of Obed and Obed
the father of Jesse. Ru 2:1; 4:17
[13]Jesse was the father of Ru 4:17
Eliab his firstborn; the second son was Abinadab, the
third Shimea, [14]the fourth
Nethanel, the fifth Raddai,
[15]the sixth Ozem and the
seventh David. [16]Their sisters were Zeruiah and Ab-
igail. Zeruiah's three sons
were Abishai, Joab and Asahel. [17]Abigail was the mother of Amasa, whose father
was Jether the Ishmaelite.
Ru 4:18-22; Mt 1:3-6

Caleb Son of Hezron

[18]Caleb son of Hezron had children by his wife Azubah
(and by Jerioth). These
were her sons: Jesher, Shobab and Ardon. [19]When
Azubah died, Caleb mar-
ried Ephrath, who bore him
Hur. [20]Hur was the father
of Uri, and Uri the father of
Bezalel. ver 42,50; Ex 31:2
[21]Later, Hezron, when he was
sixty years old, married the
daughter of Makir the fa-
ther of Gilead. He made love
to her, and she bore him
Segub. [22]Segub was the father of Jair, who controlled

[a] 6 Many Hebrew manuscripts, some Septuagint manuscripts and Syriac (see also 1 Kings 4:31); most Hebrew manuscripts *Dara* [b] 7 *Achar* means *trouble*; *Achar* is called *Achan* in Joshua. [c] 7 The Hebrew term refers to the irrevocable giving over of things or persons to the LORD, often by totally destroying them. [d] 9 Hebrew *Kelubai*, a variant of *Caleb* [e] 11 Septuagint (see also Ruth 4:21); Hebrew *Salma*

twenty-three towns in Gilead. [23]
(But Geshur and Aram captured Havvoth Jair,[a] as well as Kenath with its surrounding settlements — sixty towns.) All these were descendants of Makir the father of Gilead.

Nu 32:41; Dt 3:14; Jos 13:30

[24]After Hezron died in Caleb Ephrathah, Abijah the wife of Hezron bore him Ashhur the father[b] of Tekoa. 1Ch 4:5

Jerahmeel Son of Hezron

[25]The sons of Jerahmeel the firstborn of Hezron:
Ram his firstborn, Bunah, Oren, Ozem and[c] Ahijah.
[26]Jerahmeel had another wife, whose name was Atarah; she was the mother of Onam.

[27]The sons of Ram the firstborn of Jerahmeel:
Maaz, Jamin and Eker.

[28]The sons of Onam:
Shammai and Jada.
The sons of Shammai:
Nadab and Abishur.

[29]Abishur's wife was named Abihail, who bore him Ahban and Molid.

[30]The sons of Nadab:
Seled and Appaim. Seled died without children.

[31]The son of Appaim:
Ishi, who was the father of Sheshan.
Sheshan was the father of Ahlai.

[32]The sons of Jada, Shammai's brother:
Jether and Jonathan. Jether died without children.

[33]The sons of Jonathan:
Peleth and Zaza.
These were the descendants of Jerahmeel.

[34]Sheshan had no sons — only daughters.
He had an Egyptian servant named Jarha.
[35]Sheshan gave his daughter in marriage to his servant Jarha, and she bore him Attai.

[36]Attai was the father of Nathan,
Nathan the father of Zabad, 1Ch 11:41
[37]Zabad the father of Ephlal,
Ephlal the father of Obed,
[38]Obed the father of Jehu,
Jehu the father of Azariah,
[39]Azariah the father of Helez,
Helez the father of Eleasah,
[40]Eleasah the father of Sismai,
Sismai the father of Shallum,
[41]Shallum the father of Jekamiah,
and Jekamiah the father of Elishama.

The Clans of Caleb

[42]The sons of Caleb the brother of Jerahmeel: ver 19

[a] 23 Or *captured the settlements of Jair*
[b] 24 *Father* may mean *civic leader* or *military leader*; also in verses 42, 45, 49-52 and possibly elsewhere.
[c] 25 Or *Oren and Ozem, by*

Mesha his firstborn, who
was the father of Ziph, and
his son Mareshah,[a] who
was the father of Hebron.
43 The sons of Hebron:
Korah, Tappuah, Rekem
and Shema. 44 Shema was
the father of Raham, and
Raham the father of Jorke-
am. Rekem was the father
of Shammai. 45 The son of
Shammai was Maon, and
Maon was the father of
Beth Zur. Jos 15:55,58
46 Caleb's concubine Ephah was
the mother of Haran, Moza
and Gazez. Haran was the
father of Gazez.
47 The sons of Jahdai:
Regem, Jotham, Geshan,
Pelet, Ephah and Shaaph.
48 Caleb's concubine Maakah
was the mother of She-
ber and Tirhanah. 49 She
also gave birth to Shaaph
the father of Madmannah
and to Sheva the father of
Makbenah and Gibea. Ca-
leb's daughter was Aksah.
50 These were the descen-
dants of Caleb. Jos 15:16,31

The sons of Hur the firstborn
of Ephrathah: 1Ch 4:4
Shobal the father of Kiriath
Jearim, 51 Salma the father of
Bethlehem, and Hareph the
father of Beth Gader. ver 19
52 The descendants of Shobal
the father of Kiriath Jearim
were:
Haroeh, half the Manahathites, 53 and the clans of Kiriath Jearim: the Ithrites,
Puthites, Shumathites and
Mishraites. From these descended the Zorathites and
Eshtaolites. 2Sa 23:38
54 The descendants of Salma:
Bethlehem, the Netopha-
thites, Atroth Beth Joab,
half the Manahathites, the
Zorites, 55 and the clans of
scribes[b] who lived at Jabez:
the Tirathites, Shimeath-
ites and Sucathites. These
are the Kenites who came
from Hammath, the father
of the Rekabites.[c]
Jdg 1:16; Jer 35:2-19

The Sons of David

3 These were the sons of David
born to him in Hebron:
1Ch 14:3; 28:5
The firstborn was Amnon
the son of Ahinoam of Jezreel; Jos 15:56
the second, Daniel the son
of Abigail of Carmel; 1Sa 25:42
2 the third, Absalom the son
of Maakah daughter of Talmai king of Geshur;
the fourth, Adonijah the
son of Haggith; 1Ki 2:22
3 the fifth, Shephatiah the
son of Abital;
and the sixth, Ithream, by
his wife Eglah.

[a] *42* The meaning of the Hebrew for this phrase is uncertain. [b] *55* Or *of the Sopherites* [c] *55* Or *father of Beth Rekab*

[4]These six were born to David in Hebron, where he
reigned seven years and six
months. 2Sa 3:2-5
David reigned in Jerusalem thirty-three years, [5]and these were the
children born to him there:
Shammua,[a] Shobab, Na-
than and Solomon. These
four were by Bathshe-
ba[b] daughter of Ammiel.
[6]There were also Ibhar, Elishua,[c] Eliphelet, [7]Nogah,
Nepheg, Japhia, [8]Elisha-
ma, Eliada and Eliphelet —
nine in all. [9]All these were
the sons of David, besides
his sons by his concubines.
And Tamar was their sister.
2Sa 5:14-16; 1Ch 14:4-7

The Kings of Judah

[10]Solomon's son was Rehobo-
am, 1Ki 11:43; 14:21-31
Abijah his son,
Asa his son,
Jehoshaphat his son,
2Ch 17:1-21:3
[11]Jehoram[d] his son,
2Ki 8:16-24; 2Ch 21:1
Ahaziah his son, 2Ch 22:1-10
Joash his son, 2Ki 11:1-12:21
[12]Amaziah his son, 2Ki 14:1-22
Azariah his son,
Jotham his son, Isa 1:1; Hos 1:1
[13]Ahaz his son, Isa 7:1
Hezekiah his son, Jer 26:19
Manasseh his son, 2Ch 33:1
[14]Amon his son, 2Ki 21:19-26
Josiah his son. Jer 1:2; 25:3
[15]The sons of Josiah:
Johanan the firstborn,
Jehoiakim the second son,
2Ki 23:34
Zedekiah the third, Jer 37:1
Shallum the fourth. 2Ki 23:31
[16]The successors of Jehoiakim:
Jehoiachin[e] his son, Mt 1:11
and Zedekiah. 2Ki 24:18

The Royal Line After the Exile

[17]The descendants of Jehoia-
chin the captive:
Shealtiel his son, [18]Malki-
ram, Pedaiah, Shenazzar,
Jekamiah, Hoshama and
Nedabiah. Ezr 1:8; 5:14; Jer 22:30
[19]The sons of Pedaiah:
Zerubbabel and Shimei.
Ezr 5:2; Ne 7:7; Hag 1:1
The sons of Zerubbabel:
Meshullam and Hananiah.
Shelomith was their sister.
[20]There were also five others:
Hashubah, Ohel, Berekiah,
Hasadiah and Jushab-He-
sed.
[21]The descendants of Hanani-
ah:
Pelatiah and Jeshaiah, and
the sons of Rephaiah, of
Arnan, of Obadiah and of
Shekaniah.

[a] 5 Hebrew *Shimea*, a variant of *Shammua*
[b] 5 One Hebrew manuscript and Vulgate (see also Septuagint and 2 Samuel 11:3); most Hebrew manuscripts *Bathshua*
[c] 6 Two Hebrew manuscripts (see also 2 Samuel 5:15 and 1 Chron. 14:5); most Hebrew manuscripts *Elishama*
[d] 11 Hebrew *Joram*, a variant of *Jehoram*
[e] 16 Hebrew *Jeconiah*, a variant of *Jehoiachin*; also in verse 17

22 The descendants of Shekaniah:
Shemaiah and his sons:
Hattush, Igal, Bariah, Neariah and Shaphat — six in
all. Ezr 8:2-3
23 The sons of Neariah:
Elioenai, Hizkiah and Azrikam — three in all.
24 The sons of Elioenai:
Hodaviah, Eliashib, Pelaiah,
Akkub, Johanan, Delaiah
and Anani — seven in all.

Other Clans of Judah

4 The descendants of Judah:
Ge 46:12; 1Ch 2:3
Perez, Hezron, Karmi, Hur
and Shobal. Nu 26:21
2 Reaiah son of Shobal was the
father of Jahath, and Ja-
hath the father of Ahumai
and Lahad. These were the
clans of the Zorathites.
3 These were the sons[a] of Etam:
Jezreel, Ishma and Idbash.
Their sister was named
Hazzelelponi. 4 Penuel was
the father of Gedor, and
Ezer the father of Hushah.
These were the descendants
of Hur, the firstborn of Ephrathah and father[b] of Bethlehem. Ru 1:19; 1Ch 2:50
5 Ashhur the father of Tekoa
had two wives, Helah and
Naarah. 1Ch 2:24
6 Naarah bore him Ahuzzam,
Hepher, Temeni and Haa-
hashtari. These were the
descendants of Naarah.
7 The sons of Helah:
Zereth, Zohar, Ethnan, 8 and
Koz, who was the father of
Anub and Hazzobebah and
of the clans of Aharhel son
of Harum.

9 Jabez was more honorable
than his brothers. His mother
had named him Jabez,[c] saying, "I
gave birth to him in pain." 10 Jabez
cried out to the God of Israel, "Oh,
that you would bless me and enlarge my territory! Let your hand
be with me, and keep me from
harm so that I will be free from
pain." And God granted his request.

11 Kelub, Shuhah's brother, was
the father of Mehir, who
was the father of Eshton.
12 Eshton was the father of
Beth Rapha, Paseah and Te-
hinnah the father of Ir Nahash.[d] These were the men
of Rekah.

13 The sons of Kenaz:
Othniel and Seraiah.
Jos 15:17
The sons of Othniel:
Hathath and Meonothai.[e]
14 Meonothai was the father
of Ophrah.

[a] 3 Some Septuagint manuscripts (see also Vulgate); Hebrew *father* [b] 4 *Father* may mean *civic leader* or *military leader*; also in verses 12, 14, 17, 18 and possibly elsewhere. [c] 9 *Jabez* sounds like the Hebrew for *pain.* [d] 12 Or *of the city of Nahash* [e] 13 Some Septuagint manuscripts and Vulgate; Hebrew does not have *and Meonothai.*

Seraiah was the father of Joab,
the father of Ge Harashim.[a]
It was called this because its
people were skilled workers.
15 The sons of Caleb son of Jephunneh:
Iru, Elah and Naam.
The son of Elah:
Kenaz.
16 The sons of Jehallelel:
Ziph, Ziphah, Tiria and Asarel.
17 The sons of Ezrah:
Jether, Mered, Epher and
Jalon. One of Mered's
wives gave birth to Miriam,
Shammai and Ishbah the
father of Eshtemoa.
18 (His
wife from the tribe of Judah gave birth to Jered the
father of Gedor, Heber the
father of Soko, and Jekuthiel the father of Zanoah.)
These were the children of
Pharaoh's daughter Bithiah,
whom Mered had married.
Ex 15:20; Jos 15:34
19 The sons of Hodiah's wife, the
sister of Naham:
the father of Keilah the
Garmite, and Eshtemoa the
Maakathite. Dt 3:14; Jos 15:44
20 The sons of Shimon:
Amnon, Rinnah, Ben-Hanan and Tilon.
The descendants of Ishi:
Zoheth and Ben-Zoheth.
21 The sons of Shelah son of Judah:
Er the father of Lekah, Laadah the father of Mareshah and the clans of the
linen workers at Beth Ashbea,
22 Jokim, the men of
Kozeba, and Joash and Saraph, who ruled in Moab
and Jashubi Lehem. (These
records are from ancient
times.)
23 They were the potters who lived at Netaim
and Gederah; they stayed
there and worked for the
king. Ge 38:5

Simeon

24 The descendants of Simeon:
Ge 29:33
Nemuel, Jamin, Jarib, Zerah and Shaul; Nu 26:12
25 Shallum was Shaul's son,
Mibsam his son and Mishma his son.
26 The descendants of Mishma:
Hammuel his son, Zakkur
his son and Shimei his son.
27 Shimei had sixteen sons and
six daughters, but his brothers did
not have many children; so their
entire clan did not become as numerous as the people of Judah.
28 They lived in Beersheba, Mola-
dah, Hazar Shual,
29 Bilhah, Ezem,
Tolad,
30 Bethuel, Hormah, Ziklag,
31 Beth Markaboth, Hazar Susim,
Beth Biri and Shaaraim. These
were their towns until the reign of
David.
32 Their surrounding villages were Etam, Ain, Rimmon, Token
and Ashan — five towns —
33 and
all the villages around these towns

[a] 14 *Ge Harashim* means *valley of skilled workers.*

as far as Baalath.[a] These were their
settlements. And they kept a genealogical record. Jos 19:2-10

[34]Meshobab, Jamlech, Joshah
son of Amaziah, [35]Joel, Jehu
son of Joshibiah, the son of
Seraiah, the son of Asiel, [36]also
Elioenai, Jaakobah, Jeshoha-
iah, Asaiah, Adiel, Jesimiel,
Benaiah, [37]and Ziza son of Shi-
phi, the son of Allon, the son
of Jedaiah, the son of Shimri,
the son of Shemaiah.

[38]The men listed above by name
were leaders of their clans. Their
families increased greatly, [39]and
they went to the outskirts of Gedor to the east of the valley in
search of pasture for their flocks.
[40]They found rich, good pasture,
and the land was spacious, peaceful and quiet. Some Hamites had
lived there formerly. Jdg 18:7-10
[41]The men whose names were
listed came in the days of Hezekiah king of Judah. They attacked
the Hamites in their dwellings and
also the Meunites who were there
and completely destroyed[b] them,
as is evident to this day. Then they
settled in their place, because
there was pasture for their flocks.
[42]And five hundred of these Simeonites, led by Pelatiah, Neariah,
Rephaiah and Uzziel, the sons of
Ishi, invaded the hill country of
Seir. [43]They killed the remaining
Amalekites who had escaped, and
they have lived there to this day.
1Sa 15:8; 30:17; 2Sa 8:12

Reuben

5 The sons of Reuben the firstborn of Israel (he was the firstborn, but when he defiled his father's marriage bed, his rights as
firstborn were given to the sons of
Joseph son of Israel; so he could
not be listed in the genealogical record in accordance with his
birthright, [2]and though Judah
was the strongest of his brothers
and a ruler came from him, the
rights of the firstborn belonged
to Joseph) — [3]the sons of Reuben
the firstborn of Israel:
Ps 60:7; Mic 5:2; Mt 2:6

Hanok, Pallu, Hezron and
Karmi. Nu 26:5
[4]The descendants of Joel:
Shemaiah his son, Gog his
son,
Shimei his son, [5]Micah his
son,
Reaiah his son, Baal his son,
[6]and Beerah his son, whom
Tiglath-Pileser[c] king of Assyria took into exile. Beerah was a leader of the
Reubenites.
2Ki 15:19; 16:10; 2Ch 28:20
[7]Their relatives by clans, listed
according to their genealogical records: ver 17
Jeiel the chief, Zechari-
ah, [8]and Bela son of Azaz,

[a] 33 Some Septuagint manuscripts (see also Joshua 19:8); Hebrew *Baal* [b] 41 The Hebrew term refers to the irrevocable giving over of things or persons to the LORD, often by totally destroying them. [c] 6 Hebrew *Tilgath-Pilneser,* a variant of *Tiglath-Pileser*; also in verse 26

the son of Shema, the son
of Joel. They settled in the
area from Aroer to Nebo
and Baal Meon. 9To the
east they occupied the land
up to the edge of the desert that extends to the Euphrates River, because their
livestock had increased in
Gilead. Nu 32:26; Jos 22:9
10During Saul's reign they
waged war against the Hagrites, who were defeated at
their hands; they occupied
the dwellings of the Hagrites
throughout the entire region
east of Gilead. ver 18-21

Gad

11The Gadites lived next to
them in Bashan, as far as
Salekah: Jos 13:11,24-28
12Joel was the chief, Sha-
pham the second, then Ja-
nai and Shaphat, in Bashan.
13Their relatives, by families,
were:
Michael, Meshullam, She-
ba, Jorai, Jakan, Zia and
Eber — seven in all.
14These were the sons of Abihail son of Huri, the son of
Jaroah, the son of Gilead,
the son of Michael, the son
of Jeshishai, the son of Jah-
do, the son of Buz.
15Ahi son of Abdiel, the son
of Guni, was head of their
family.
16The Gadites lived in Gilead,
in Bashan and its outlying
villages, and on all the pasturelands of Sharon as far
as they extended.
17All these were entered in the
genealogical records during the
reigns of Jotham king of Judah
and Jeroboam king of Israel.
2Ki 14:16,28; 15:32

18The Reubenites, the Gadites
and the half-tribe of Manasseh
had 44,760 men ready for military
service — able-bodied men who
could handle shield and sword,
who could use a bow, and who
were trained for battle. 19They
waged war against the Hagrites,
Jetur, Naphish and Nodab. 20They
were helped in fighting them, and
God delivered the Hagrites and all
their allies into their hands, because they cried out to him during the battle. He answered their
prayers, because they trusted in
him. 21They seized the livestock
of the Hagrites — fifty thousand
camels, two hundred fifty thousand sheep and two thousand
donkeys. They also took one hundred thousand people captive,
22and many others fell slain, because the battle was God's. And
they occupied the land until the
exile. 2Ki 15:29; 17:6; Da 6:23

The Half-Tribe of Manasseh

23The people of the half-tribe of
Manasseh were numerous; they
settled in the land from Bashan
to Baal Hermon, that is, to Senir
(Mount Hermon). Dt 3:8-9; SS 4:8

24 These were the heads of their
families: Epher, Ishi, Eliel, Azriel,
Jeremiah, Hodaviah and Jahdiel.
They were brave warriors, famous
men, and heads of their families.
25 But they were unfaithful to the
God of their ancestors and prostituted themselves to the gods of
the peoples of the land, whom God
had destroyed before them. 26 So
the God of Israel stirred up the
spirit of Pul king of Assyria (that
is, Tiglath-Pileser king of Assyria), who took the Reubenites, the
Gadites and the half-tribe of Manasseh into exile. He took them to
Halah, Habor, Hara and the river
of Gozan, where they are to this
day. 2Ki 15:29; 17:6; 18:11

Levi

6 [a] The sons of Levi: Ge 46:11; Ex 6:16; Nu 26:57
Gershon, Kohath and Merari.
2 The sons of Kohath:
Amram, Izhar, Hebron and Uzziel.
3 The children of Amram:
Aaron, Moses and Miriam.
The sons of Aaron:
Nadab, Abihu, Eleazar and Ithamar. Lev 10:1
4 Eleazar was the father of Phinehas,
Phinehas the father of Abishua,
5 Abishua the father of Bukki,
Bukki the father of Uzzi,
6 Uzzi the father of Zerahiah,
Zerahiah the father of Meraioth,
7 Meraioth the father of Amariah,
Amariah the father of Ahitub,
8 Ahitub the father of Zadok, 2Sa 8:17; 15:27; Ezr 7:2
Zadok the father of Ahimaaz,
9 Ahimaaz the father of Azariah,
Azariah the father of Johanan,
10 Johanan the father of Azariah (it was he who served as priest in the temple Solomon built in Jerusalem), 1Ki 6:1; 2Ch 3:1; 26:17-18
11 Azariah the father of Amariah,
Amariah the father of Ahitub,
12 Ahitub the father of Zadok,
Zadok the father of Shallum,
13 Shallum the father of Hilkiah, 2Ki 22:1-20; 2Ch 34:9; 35:8
Hilkiah the father of Azariah,
14 Azariah the father of Seraiah,
and Seraiah the father of Jozadak.[b] Ezr 2:2; Ne 11:11
15 Jozadak was deported when
the LORD sent Judah and Jerusalem into exile by the
hand of Nebuchadnezzar.
2Ki 25:18; Hag 1:1,14; Zec 6:11

[a] In Hebrew texts 6:1-15 is numbered 5:27-41, and 6:16-81 is numbered 6:1-66.
[b] 14 Hebrew *Jehozadak*, a variant of *Jozadak*; also in verse 15

16 The sons of Levi: Ge 29:34; Ex 6:16
Gershon,[a] Kohath and Merari. Nu 26:57
17 These are the names of the sons of Gershon:
Libni and Shimei.
18 The sons of Kohath:
Amram, Izhar, Hebron and Uzziel.
19 The sons of Merari: 1Ch 23:21; 24:26
Mahli and Mushi.
These are the clans of the Levites listed according to their fathers:
20 Of Gershon:
Libni his son, Jahath his son,
Zimmah his son, 21 Joah his son,
Iddo his son, Zerah his son
and Jeatherai his son.
22 The descendants of Kohath:
Amminadab his son, Korah his son, Ex 6:24
Assir his son, 23 Elkanah his son,
Ebiasaph his son, Assir his son,
24 Tahath his son, Uriel his son, 1Ch 15:5
Uzziah his son and Shaul his son.
25 The descendants of Elkanah:
Amasai, Ahimoth,
26 Elkanah his son,[b] Zophai his son,
Nahath his son, 27 Eliab his son,
Jeroham his son, Elkanah his son 1Sa 1:1
and Samuel his son.[c] 1Sa 1:20
28 The sons of Samuel:
Joel[d] the firstborn ver 33; 1Sa 8:2
and Abijah the second son.
29 The descendants of Merari:
Mahli, Libni his son,
Shimei his son, Uzzah his son,
30 Shimea his son, Haggiah his son
and Asaiah his son.

The Temple Musicians

31 These are the men David put in
charge of the music in the house
of the LORD after the ark came to
rest there. 32 They ministered with
music before the tabernacle, the
tent of meeting, until Solomon
built the temple of the LORD in
Jerusalem. They performed their
duties according to the regulations laid down for them.
1Ch 15:19; Ezr 3:10; Ps 68:25

33 Here are the men who served,
together with their sons:
From the Kohathites:
Heman, the musician, 1Ki 4:31; 1Ch 15:17
the son of Joel, the son of Samuel,

[a] *16* Hebrew *Gershom,* a variant of *Gershon;* also in verses 17, 20, 43, 62 and 71
[b] *26* Some Hebrew manuscripts, Septuagint and Syriac; most Hebrew manuscripts *Ahimoth [26]and Elkanah. The sons of Elkanah:*
[c] *27* Some Septuagint manuscripts (see also 1 Samuel 1:19,20 and 1 Chron. 6:33,34); Hebrew does not have *and Samuel his son.*
[d] *28* Some Septuagint manuscripts and Syriac (see also 1 Samuel 8:2 and 1 Chron. 6:33); Hebrew does not have *Joel.*

34 the son of Elkanah, the son
of Jeroham, 1Sa 1:1
the son of Eliel, the son of
Toah,
35 the son of Zuph, the son of
Elkanah,
the son of Mahath, the son
of Amasai,
36 the son of Elkanah, the son
of Joel,
the son of Azariah, the son
of Zephaniah,
37 the son of Tahath, the son
of Assir,
the son of Ebiasaph, the
son of Korah, Ex 6:24
38 the son of Izhar, the son of
Kohath, Ex 6:21
the son of Levi, the son of
Israel;
39 and Heman's associate Asaph,
who served at his right
hand: 1Ch 25:1,9; 2Ch 29:13
Asaph son of Berekiah, the
son of Shimea, 1Ch 15:17
40 the son of Michael, the son
of Baaseiah,[a]
the son of Malkijah, 41 the
son of Ethni,
the son of Zerah, the son of
Adaiah,
42 the son of Ethan, the son of
Zimmah,
the son of Shimei, 43 the son
of Jahath,
the son of Gershon, the son
of Levi;
44 and from their associates, the
Merarites, at his left hand:
Ethan son of Kishi, the son
of Abdi,
the son of Malluk, 45 the son
of Hashabiah,
the son of Amaziah, the son
of Hilkiah,
46 the son of Amzi, the son of
Bani,
the son of Shemer, 47 the son
of Mahli,
the son of Mushi, the son of
Merari,
the son of Levi.

48 Their fellow Levites were assigned to all the other duties of
the tabernacle, the house of God.
49 But Aaron and his descendants
were the ones who presented offerings on the altar of burnt offering and on the altar of incense in
connection with all that was done
in the Most Holy Place, making
atonement for Israel, in accordance with all that Moses the servant of God had commanded.
Ex 27:1-8; 30:1-7,10; 1Ch 23:32

50 These were the descendants
of Aaron:
Eleazar his son, Phinehas
his son,
Abishua his son, 51 Bukki his
son,
Uzzi his son, Zerahiah his
son,
52 Meraioth his son, Amariah
his son,
Ahitub his son, 53 Zadok his
son 2Sa 8:17
and Ahimaaz his son.

[a] *40* Most Hebrew manuscripts; some Hebrew manuscripts, one Septuagint manuscript and Syriac *Maaseiah*

54These were the locations of their settlements allotted as their territory (they were assigned to the descendants of Aaron who were from the Kohathite clan, because the first lot was for them): Nu 31:10

55They were given Hebron
in Judah with its surrounding
pasturelands. 56But the fields
and villages around the city
were given to Caleb son of Jephunneh. Jos 14:13; 15:13
57So the descendants of
Aaron were given Hebron (a
city of refuge), and Libnah,[a]
Jattir, Eshtemoa, 58Hilen, Debir, 59Ashan, Juttah[b] and Beth
Shemesh, together with their
pasturelands. 60And from the
tribe of Benjamin they were
given Gibeon,[c] Geba, Alemeth
and Anathoth, together with
their pasturelands. Jos 10:3; Jer 1:1

The total number of towns distributed among the Kohathite clans came to thirteen.

61The rest of Kohath's descendants were allotted ten towns from the clans of half the tribe of Manasseh.

62The descendants of Gershon, clan by clan, were allotted thirteen towns from the tribes of Issachar, Asher and Naphtali, and from the part of the tribe of Manasseh that is in Bashan.

63The descendants of Merari, clan by clan, were allotted twelve towns from the tribes of Reuben, Gad and Zebulun.

64So the Israelites gave the Levites these towns and their pasturelands. 65From the tribes of Ju-
dah, Simeon and Benjamin they allotted the previously named towns. Nu 35:1-8; Jos 21:3,41-42

66Some of the Kohathite clans were given as their territory towns from the tribe of Ephraim.

67In the hill country of
Ephraim they were given Shechem (a city of refuge), and
Gezer,[d] 68Jokmeam, Beth Ho-
ron, 69Aijalon and Gath Rimmon, together with their pasturelands. Jos 10:10,12; 19:45

70And from half the tribe of Manasseh the Israelites gave Aner and Bileam, together with their pasturelands, to the rest of the Kohathite clans.

71The Gershonites received the following: 1Ch 23:7

From the clan of the half-tribe of Manasseh
they received Golan in Bashan and also Ashtaroth, together with their pasturelands; Jos 20:8

72from the tribe of Issachar
they received Kedesh, Dab-
erath, 73Ramoth and Anem, together with their pasturelands; Jos 19:12

[a] 57 See Joshua 21:13; Hebrew *given the cities of refuge: Hebron, Libnah.*
[b] 59 Syriac (see also Septuagint and Joshua 21:16); Hebrew does not have *Juttah.*
[c] 60 See Joshua 21:17; Hebrew does not have *Gibeon.* [d] 67 See Joshua 21:21; Hebrew *given the cities of refuge: Shechem, Gezer.*

74 from the tribe of Asher
they received Mashal, Abdon, 75 Hukok and Rehob, together with their pasturelands; Nu 13:21; Jos 19:28,34
76 and from the tribe of Naphtali
they received Kedesh in Galilee, Hammon and Kiriathaim, together with their pasturelands.
Nu 32:37; Jos 19:28

77 The Merarites (the rest of the Levites) received the following:
From the tribe of Zebulun they received Jokneam, Kartah,[a] Rimmono and Tabor, together with their pasturelands;
78 from the tribe of Reuben across the Jordan east of Jericho
they received Bezer in the wilderness, Jahzah, 79 Kedemoth and Mephaath, together with their pasturelands; Dt 2:26; Jos 20:8
80 and from the tribe of Gad
they received Ramoth in Gilead, Mahanaim, 81 Heshbon and Jazer, together with their pasturelands.
Jos 21:4-39; 2Ch 11:14

Issachar

7 The sons of Issachar: Nu 26:23
Tola, Puah, Jashub and Shimron — four in all.
Ge 46:13

2 The sons of Tola:
Uzzi, Rephaiah, Jeriel, Jahmai, Ibsam and Samuel — heads of their families. During the reign of David, the descendants of Tola listed as fighting men in their genealogy numbered 22,600.
3 The son of Uzzi:
Izrahiah.
The sons of Izrahiah:
Michael, Obadiah, Joel and Ishiah. All five of them were chiefs.
4 According to their family genealogy, they had 36,000 men ready for battle, for they had many wives and children.
5 The relatives who were fighting men belonging to all the clans of Issachar, as listed in their genealogy, were 87,000 in all.

Benjamin

6 Three sons of Benjamin:
Ge 46:21; Nu 26:38; 1Ch 8:1-40
Bela, Beker and Jediael.
7 The sons of Bela:
Ezbon, Uzzi, Uzziel, Jerimoth and Iri, heads of families — five in all. Their genealogical record listed 22,034 fighting men.
8 The sons of Beker:
Zemirah, Joash, Eliezer, Elioenai, Omri, Jeremoth, Abijah, Anathoth and Alemeth.

[a] 77 See Septuagint and Joshua 21:34; Hebrew does not have *Jokneam, Kartah.*

All these were the sons of
Beker. 9Their genealogical
record listed the heads of
families and 20,200 fighting men.
10The son of Jediael:
Bilhan.
The sons of Bilhan:
Jeush, Benjamin, Ehud, Kenaanah, Zethan, Tarshish
and Ahishahar. 11All these
sons of Jediael were heads
of families. There were
17,200 fighting men ready
to go out to war.
12The Shuppites and Huppites
were the descendants of Ir,
and the Hushites[a] the descendants of Aher.

Naphtali

13The sons of Naphtali:

Ge 30:8; 46:24

Jahziel, Guni, Jezer and
Shillem[b] — the descen-
dants of Bilhah.

Manasseh

14The descendants of Manasseh: Ge 41:51; Jos 17:1; 1Ch 5:23
Asriel was his descendant
through his Aramean concubine. She gave birth to Makir
the father of Gilead. 15Makir
took a wife from among the
Huppites and Shuppites. His
sister's name was Maakah.

Nu 26:30

Another descendant was
named Zelophehad, who had
only daughters. Nu 36:1-12
16Makir's wife Maakah gave
birth to a son and named
him Peresh. His brother was
named Sheresh, and his sons
were Ulam and Rakem.
17The son of Ulam:
Bedan.
These were the sons of Gilead
son of Makir, the son of Manasseh. 18His sister Ham-
moleketh gave birth to Ish-
hod, Abiezer and Mahlah.

1Sa 12:11; Jos 17:2

19The sons of Shemida were:
Ahian, Shechem, Likhi and
Aniam.

Ephraim

20The descendants of Ephraim:

Nu 1:33; 26:35

Shuthelah, Bered his son,
Tahath his son, Eleadah his
son,
Tahath his son, 21Zabad his
son
and Shuthelah his son.
Ezer and Elead were killed
by the native-born men of
Gath, when they went down
to seize their livestock. 22Their
father Ephraim mourned for
them many days, and his relatives came to comfort him.
23Then he made love to his
wife again, and she became
pregnant and gave birth to a

[a] 12 Or *Ir. The sons of Dan: Hushim,* (see Gen. 46:23); Hebrew does not have *The sons of Dan.* [b] 13 Some Hebrew and Septuagint manuscripts (see also Gen. 46:24 and Num. 26:49); most Hebrew manuscripts *Shallum*

son. He named him Beriah,[a]
because there had been misfortune in his family. 24His
daughter was Sheerah, who
built Lower and Upper Beth
Horon as well as Uzzen Sheerah. Jos 16:3,5

25Rephah was his son, Resheph
his son,[b]
Telah his son, Tahan his
son,
26Ladan his son, Ammihud
his son,
Elishama his son, 27Nun his
son
and Joshua his son.

28Their lands and settlements
included Bethel and its surrounding villages, Naaran to the east,
Gezer and its villages to the west,
and Shechem and its villages all
the way to Ayyah and its villages.
29Along the borders of Manasseh
were Beth Shan, Taanach, Megiddo and Dor, together with their
villages. The descendants of Joseph son of Israel lived in these
towns. Jos 16:7; 17:11

Asher

30The sons of Asher: Ge 46:17; Nu 26:44

Imnah, Ishvah, Ishvi and
Beriah. Their sister was Serah.

31The sons of Beriah:
Heber and Malkiel, who
was the father of Birzaith.

32Heber was the father of Japhlet, Shomer and Hotham
and of their sister Shua.

33The sons of Japhlet:
Pasak, Bimhal and Ashvath.
These were Japhlet's sons.

34The sons of Shomer:
Ahi, Rohgah,[c] Hubbah and
Aram.

35The sons of his brother He-
lem:
Zophah, Imna, Shelesh and
Amal.

36The sons of Zophah:
Suah, Harnepher, Shual,
Beri, Imrah, 37Bezer, Hod,
Shamma, Shilshah, Ithran[d]
and Beera.

38The sons of Jether:
Jephunneh, Pispah and
Ara.

39The sons of Ulla:
Arah, Hanniel and Rizia.

40All these were descendants of
Asher — heads of families, choice
men, brave warriors and outstanding leaders. The number of
men ready for battle, as listed in
their genealogy, was 26,000.

The Genealogy of Saul the Benjamite

8 Benjamin was the father of
Bela his firstborn, Ge 46:21; 1Ch 7:6

Ashbel the second son,
Aharah the third,
2Nohah the fourth and Rapha
the fifth.

[a] 23 *Beriah* sounds like the Hebrew for *misfortune.* [b] 25 Some Septuagint manuscripts; Hebrew does not have *his son.* [c] 34 Or *of his brother Shomer: Rohgah* [d] 37 Possibly a variant of *Jether*

3The sons of Bela were:
Addar, Gera, Abihud,[a]
4Abishua, Naaman, Ahoah, 5Gera, Shephuphan and Huram. 2Sa 23:9
6These were the descendants of Ehud, who were heads of families of those living in Geba and were deported to Manahath: 1Ch 2:52
7Naaman, Ahijah, and Gera, who deported them and who was the father of Uzza and Ahihud.
8Sons were born to Shaharaim in Moab after he had divorced his wives Hushim and Baara. 9By his wife Hodesh he had Jobab, Zibia, Mesha, Malkam, 10Jeuz, Sakia and Mirmah. These were his sons, heads of families. 11By Hushim he had Abitub and Elpaal.
12The sons of Elpaal:
Eber, Misham, Shemed (who built Ono and Lod with its surrounding villages), 13and Beriah and Shema, who were heads of families of those living in Aijalon and who drove out the inhabitants of Gath. Ezr 2:33; Ne 6:2
14Ahio, Shashak, Jeremoth, 15Zebadiah, Arad, Eder, 16Michael, Ishpah and Joha were the sons of Beriah.
17Zebadiah, Meshullam, Hizki, Heber, 18Ishmerai, Izliah and Jobab were the sons of Elpaal.
19Jakim, Zikri, Zabdi, 20Elienai, Zillethai, Eliel, 21Adaiah, Beraiah and Shimrath were the sons of Shimei.
22Ishpan, Eber, Eliel, 23Abdon, Zikri, Hanan, 24Hananiah, Elam, Anthothijah, 25Iphdeiah and Penuel were the sons of Shashak.
26Shamsherai, Shehariah, Athaliah, 27Jaareshiah, Elijah and Zikri were the sons of Jeroham.
28All these were heads of families, chiefs as listed in their genealogy, and they lived in Jerusalem.

29Jeiel[b] the father[c] of Gibeon lived in Gibeon. Jos 9:3
His wife's name was Maakah, 30and his firstborn son was Abdon, followed by Zur, Kish, Baal, Ner,[d] Nadab, 31Gedor, Ahio, Zeker 32and Mikloth, who was the father of Shimeah. They too lived near their relatives in Jerusalem.
33Ner was the father of Kish, Kish the father of Saul, and Saul the father of Jonathan, Malki-Shua, Abinadab and Esh-Baal.[e]

1Sa 9:1; 2Sa 2:8

[a] 3 Or *Gera the father of Ehud* [b] 29 Some Septuagint manuscripts (see also 9:35); Hebrew does not have *Jeiel.* [c] 29 *Father* may mean *civic leader* or *military leader.* [d] 30 Some Septuagint manuscripts (see also 9:36); Hebrew does not have *Ner.* [e] 33 Also known as *Ish-Bosheth*

34 The son of Jonathan: 2Sa 9:12
Merib-Baal,[a] who was the father of Micah. 2Sa 4:4
35 The sons of Micah:
Pithon, Melek, Tarea and Ahaz.
36 Ahaz was the father of Jehoaddah, Jehoaddah was the
father of Alemeth, Azmaveth
and Zimri, and Zimri was the
father of Moza. 37 Moza was
the father of Binea; Raphah
was his son, Eleasah his son
and Azel his son.
38 Azel had six sons, and these were their names:
Azrikam, Bokeru, Ishmael, Sheariah, Obadiah and Hanan. All these were the sons of Azel. 1Ch 9:34-44
39 The sons of his brother Eshek:
Ulam his firstborn, Jeush
the second son and Eliphelet the third. 40 The sons of
Ulam were brave warriors
who could handle the bow.
They had many sons and
grandsons — 150 in all.
All these were the descendants of Benjamin. Nu 26:38

9 All Israel was listed in the genealogies recorded in the book of the kings of Israel and Judah. They were taken captive to Babylon because of their unfaithfulness.

The People in Jerusalem

2 Now the first to resettle on their own property in their own towns were some Israelites, priests, Levites and temple servants. 1Ch 5:25; Ezr 2:43,58,70

3 Those from Judah, from Benjamin, and from Ephraim and Manasseh who lived in Jerusalem were:

4 Uthai son of Ammihud, the son of Omri, the son of Imri, the son of Bani, a descendant of Perez son of Judah. Ge 46:12
5 Of the Shelanites[b]:
Asaiah the firstborn and his sons.
6 Of the Zerahites:
Jeuel.
The people from Judah numbered 690.
7 Of the Benjamites:
Sallu son of Meshullam, the son of Hodaviah, the son of Hassenuah;
8 Ibneiah son of Jeroham; Elah son of Uzzi, the son of Mikri; and Meshullam son of Shephatiah, the son of Reuel, the son of Ibnijah.
9 The people from Benjamin, as listed in their genealogy, numbered 956. All these men were heads of their families.
10 Of the priests:
Jedaiah; Jehoiarib; Jakin;
11 Azariah son of Hilkiah, the son of Meshullam, the son of Zadok, the son of Meraioth, the son of Ahitub,

[a] 34 Also known as *Mephibosheth*
[b] 5 See Num. 26:20; Hebrew *Shilonites*.

the official in charge of the
house of God;
12 Adaiah son of Jeroham, the
son of Pashhur, the son of
Malkijah; and Maasai son
of Adiel, the son of Jahze-
rah, the son of Meshullam,
the son of Meshillemith,
the son of Immer.

Ezr 2:38; 10:22; Ne 10:3

13 The priests, who were
heads of families, num-
bered 1,760. They were able
men, responsible for ministering in the house of God.

14 Of the Levites:
Shemaiah son of Hasshub,
the son of Azrikam, the son
of Hashabiah, a Merarite;
15 Bakbakkar, Heresh, Galal
and Mattaniah son of Mika,
the son of Zikri, the son of
Asaph; 16 Obadiah son of
Shemaiah, the son of Galal,
the son of Jeduthun; and
Berekiah son of Asa, the
son of Elkanah, who lived
in the villages of the Netophathites.

2Ch 20:14; Ne 11:22; 12:28

17 The gatekeepers: ver 22; 1Ch 26:1
Shallum, Akkub, Talmon,
Ahiman and their fellow
Levites, Shallum their chief
18 being stationed at the
King's Gate on the east, up
to the present time. These
were the gatekeepers be-
longing to the camp of the
Levites. 19 Shallum son of
Kore, the son of Ebiasaph,
the son of Korah, and his
fellow gatekeepers from
his family (the Korahites)
were responsible for guarding the thresholds of the
tent just as their ancestors
had been responsible for
guarding the entrance to
the dwelling of the LORD.
20 In earlier times Phinehas
son of Eleazar was the official in charge of the gatekeepers, and the LORD was
with him. 21 Zechariah son
of Meshelemiah was the
gatekeeper at the entrance
to the tent of meeting.

Ne 11:3-19; 1Ch 26:2,14; Jer 35:4

22 Altogether, those chosen to
be gatekeepers at the thresholds
numbered 212. They were registered by genealogy in their villages. The gatekeepers had been assigned to their positions of trust
by David and Samuel the seer.
23 They and their descendants
were in charge of guarding the
gates of the house of the LORD —
the house called the tent of meeting. 24 The gatekeepers were on
the four sides: east, west, north
and south. 25 Their fellow Levites
in their villages had to come from
time to time and share their duties for seven-day periods. 26 But
the four principal gatekeepers,
who were Levites, were entrusted with the responsibility for the
rooms and treasuries in the house
of God. 27 They would spend the
night stationed around the house

of God, because they had to guard
it; and they had charge of the key
for opening it each morning.
1Ch 23:8,30-32; 26:22

28 Some of them were in charge
of the articles used in the temple service; they counted them
when they were brought in and
when they were taken out. 29 Others were assigned to take care of
the furnishings and all the other
articles of the sanctuary, as well
as the special flour and wine, and
the olive oil, incense and spices.
30 But some of the priests took care
of mixing the spices. 31 A Levite
named Mattithiah, the firstborn
son of Shallum the Korahite, was
entrusted with the responsibility for baking the offering bread.
32 Some of the Kohathites, their
fellow Levites, were in charge of
preparing for every Sabbath the
bread set out on the table.
Lev 24:5-8; 1Ch 23:29

33 Those who were musicians,
heads of Levite families, stayed in
the rooms of the temple and were
exempt from other duties because
they were responsible for the work
day and night. 1Ch 6:31; Ps 134:1

34 All these were heads of Levite
families, chiefs as listed in their
genealogy, and they lived in Jerusalem.

The Genealogy of Saul

35 Jeiel the father[a] of Gibeon
lived in Gibeon. 1Ch 8:29
His wife's name was Ma-
akah, 36 and his firstborn
son was Abdon, followed
by Zur, Kish, Baal, Ner, Nadab, 37 Gedor, Ahio, Zechariah and Mikloth. 38 Mikloth
was the father of Shimeam.
They too lived near their
relatives in Jerusalem.

39 Ner was the father of Kish,
Kish the father of Saul, and
Saul the father of Jona-
than, Malki-Shua, Abina-
dab and Esh-Baal.[b]
1Sa 9:1; 13:22; 1Ch 8:33

40 The son of Jonathan:
Merib-Baal,[c] who was the
father of Micah. 2Sa 4:4

41 The sons of Micah:
Pithon, Melek, Tahrea and
Ahaz.[d]

42 Ahaz was the father of Jadah, Jadah[e] was the father
of Alemeth, Azmaveth and
Zimri, and Zimri was the
father of Moza. 43 Moza was
the father of Binea; Rephaiah was his son, Eleasah his
son and Azel his son.

44 Azel had six sons, and these
were their names:
Azrikam, Bokeru, Ishmael,
Sheariah, Obadiah and Ha-
nan. These were the sons of
Azel. 1Ch 8:28-38

[a] 35 *Father* may mean *civic leader* or *military leader.* [b] 39 Also known as *Ish-Bosheth* [c] 40 Also known as *Mephibosheth* [d] 41 Vulgate and Syriac (see also Septuagint and 8:35); Hebrew does not have *and Ahaz.* [e] 42 Some Hebrew manuscripts and Septuagint (see also 8:36); most Hebrew manuscripts *Jarah, Jarah*

Saul Takes His Life

10 Now the Philistines fought against Israel; the Israelites fled before them, and many fell dead on Mount Gilboa. [2]The Philistines were in hot pursuit of Saul and his sons, and they killed his sons Jonathan, Abinadab and Malki-Shua. [3]The fighting grew fierce around Saul, and when the archers overtook him, they wounded him.

[4]Saul said to his armor-bearer, "Draw your sword and run me through, or these uncircumcised fellows will come and abuse me."

But his armor-bearer was terrified and would not do it; so Saul took his own sword and fell on it. [5]When the armor-bearer saw that Saul was dead, he too fell on his sword and died. [6]So Saul and his three sons died, and all his house died together.

[7]When all the Israelites in the valley saw that the army had fled and that Saul and his sons had died, they abandoned their towns and fled. And the Philistines came and occupied them.

[8]The next day, when the Philistines came to strip the dead, they found Saul and his sons fallen on Mount Gilboa. [9]They stripped him and took his head and his armor, and sent messengers throughout the land of the Philistines to proclaim the news among their idols and their people. [10]They put his armor in the temple of their gods and hung up his head in the temple of Dagon. Jdg 16:23

[11]When all the inhabitants of Jabesh Gilead heard what the Philistines had done to Saul, [12]all their valiant men went and took the bodies of Saul and his sons and brought them to Jabesh. Then they buried their bones under the great tree in Jabesh, and they fasted seven days. 1Sa 31:1-13; 2Sa 1:4-12; Jdg 21:8

[13]Saul died because he was unfaithful to the LORD; he did not keep the word of the LORD and even consulted a medium for guidance, [14]and did not inquire of the LORD. So the LORD put him to death and turned the kingdom over to David son of Jesse. 1Sa 15:28; 2Sa 1:1; 1Ch 12:23

David Becomes King Over Israel

11 All Israel came together to David at Hebron and said, "We are your own flesh and blood. [2]In the past, even while Saul was king, you were the one who led Israel on their military campaigns. And the LORD your God said to you, 'You will shepherd my people Israel, and you will become their ruler.'" 1Sa 18:5,16; 1Ch 5:2; Mt 2:6

[3]When all the elders of Israel had come to King David at Hebron, he made a covenant with them at Hebron before the LORD, and they anointed David king over Israel, as the LORD had promised through Samuel. 2Sa 5:1-3; 1Sa 16:1-13

David Conquers Jerusalem

[4]David and all the Israelites marched to Jerusalem (that is,

Jebus). The Jebusites who lived there 5said to David, “You will not get in here.” Nevertheless, David captured the fortress of Zion — which is the City of David.

Jdg 1:21; 19:10

6David had said, “Whoever leads the attack on the Jebusites will become commander in chief.” Joab son of Zeruiah went up first, and so he received the command.

2Sa 8:16

7David then took up residence in the fortress, and so it was called the City of David. 8He built up the city around it, from the terraces[a] to the surrounding wall, while Joab restored the rest of the city. 9And David became more and more powerful, because the LORD Almighty was with him.

2Sa 3:1; 4:6-10

David's Mighty Warriors

10These were the chiefs of David's mighty warriors — they, together with all Israel, gave his kingship strong support to extend it over the whole land, as the LORD had promised — 11this is the list of David's mighty warriors:

ver 3; 2Sa 17:10

Jashobeam,[b] a Hakmonite, was chief of the officers[c]; he raised his spear against three hundred men, whom he killed in one encounter.

12Next to him was Eleazar son of Dodai the Ahohite, one of the three mighty warriors. 13He was with David at Pas Dammim when the Philistines gathered there for battle. At a place where there was a field full of barley, the troops fled from the Philistines. 14But they took their stand in the middle of the field. They defended it and struck the Philistines down, and the LORD brought about a great victory.

Ex 14:30; 1Sa 11:13

15Three of the thirty chiefs came down to David to the rock at the cave of Adullam, while a band of Philistines was encamped in the Valley of Rephaim. 16At that time David was in the stronghold, and the Philistine garrison was at Bethlehem. 17David longed for water and said, “Oh, that someone would get me a drink of water from the well near the gate of Bethlehem!” 18So the Three broke through the Philistine lines, drew water from the well near the gate of Bethlehem and carried it back to David. But he refused to drink it; instead, he poured it out to the LORD. 19“God forbid that I should do this!” he said. “Should I drink the blood of these men who went at the risk of their lives?” Because they risked their lives to bring it back, David would not drink it.

2Sa 5:17; 1Ch 14:9; Isa 17:5

Such were the exploits of the three mighty warriors.

20Abishai the brother of Joab was chief of the Three. He raised his spear against three hundred

[a] 8 Or *the Millo* [b] 11 Possibly a variant of *Jashob-Baal* [c] 11 Or *Thirty*; some Septuagint manuscripts *Three* (see also 2 Samuel 23:8)

men, whom he killed, and so he
became as famous as the Three.
21 He was doubly honored above
the Three and became their commander, even though he was not
included among them. 1Sa 26:6

22 Benaiah son of Jehoiada, a
valiant fighter from Kabzeel, performed great exploits. He struck
down Moab's two mightiest warriors. He also went down into a pit
on a snowy day and killed a lion.
23 And he struck down an Egyptian
who was five cubits[a] tall. Although
the Egyptian had a spear like a
weaver's rod in his hand, Benaiah
went against him with a club. He
snatched the spear from the Egyptian's hand and killed him with
his own spear.
24 Such were the exploits of Benaiah son of Jehoiada;
he too was as famous as the three
mighty warriors.
25 He was held
in greater honor than any of the
Thirty, but he was not included
among the Three. And David put
him in charge of his bodyguard.
1Sa 17:7,36; Jos 15:21

26 The mighty warriors were:
Asahel the brother of Joab, 2Sa 2:18
Elhanan son of Dodo from Bethlehem,
27 Shammoth the Harorite, 1Ch 27:8
Helez the Pelonite,
28 Ira son of Ikkesh from Tekoa,
Abiezer from Anathoth, 1Ch 27:12
29 Sibbekai the Hushathite, 2Sa 21:18
Ilai the Ahohite,
30 Maharai the Netophathite,
Heled son of Baanah the Netophathite,
31 Ithai son of Ribai from Gibeah in Benjamin,
Benaiah the Pirathonite, Jdg 12:13; 1Ch 27:14
32 Hurai from the ravines of Gaash,
Abiel the Arbathite,
33 Azmaveth the Baharumite,
Eliahba the Shaalbonite,
34 the sons of Hashem the Gizonite,
Jonathan son of Shagee the Hararite,
35 Ahiam son of Sakar the Hararite,
Eliphal son of Ur,
36 Hepher the Mekerathite,
Ahijah the Pelonite,
37 Hezro the Carmelite,
Naarai son of Ezbai,
38 Joel the brother of Nathan,
Mibhar son of Hagri,
39 Zelek the Ammonite,
Naharai the Berothite, the armor-bearer of Joab son of Zeruiah,
40 Ira the Ithrite,
Gareb the Ithrite,
41 Uriah the Hittite, 2Sa 11:6
Zabad son of Ahlai, 2Sa 23:8-39
42 Adina son of Shiza the Reubenite, who was chief of the

[a] *23* That is, about 7 feet 6 inches or about 2.3 meters

Reubenites, and the thirty
with him,
43 Hanan son of Maakah,
Joshaphat the Mithnite,
44 Uzzia the Ashterathite,
Dt 1:4
Shama and Jeiel the sons of
Hotham the Aroerite,
45 Jediael son of Shimri,
his brother Joha the Tizite,
46 Eliel the Mahavite,
Jeribai and Joshaviah the
sons of Elnaam,
Ithmah the Moabite,
47 Eliel, Obed and Jaasiel the
Mezobaite.

Warriors Join David

12 These were the men who
came to David at Ziklag,
while he was banished from the
presence of Saul son of Kish (they
were among the warriors who
helped him in battle; 2 they were
armed with bows and were able
to shoot arrows or to sling stones
right-handed or left-handed; they
were relatives of Saul from the
tribe of Benjamin):
Jdg 3:15; 20:16; 1Sa 27:2-6

3 Ahiezer their chief and Joash the sons of Shemaah the
Gibeathite; Jeziel and Pelet
the sons of Azmaveth; Berakah, Jehu the Anathothite,
4 and Ishmaiah the Gibeonite,
a mighty warrior among the
Thirty, who was a leader of the
Thirty; Jeremiah, Jahaziel,
Johanan, Jozabad the Gederathite,[a] 5 Eluzai, Jerimoth, Bea-
liah, Shemariah and Shephatiah the Haruphite; 6 Elkanah,
Ishiah, Azarel, Joezer and Jashobeam the Korahites; 7 and
Joelah and Zebadiah the sons
of Jeroham from Gedor.
Jos 15:36,58

8 Some Gadites defected to David at his stronghold in the wilderness. They were brave warriors, ready for battle and able to
handle the shield and spear. Their
faces were the faces of lions, and
they were as swift as gazelles in
the mountains. 2Sa 2:18; 17:10
9 Ezer was the chief,
Obadiah the second in command, Eliab the third,
10 Mishmannah the fourth, Jeremiah the fifth,
11 Attai the sixth, Eliel the seventh,
12 Johanan the eighth, Elzabad
the ninth,
13 Jeremiah the tenth and Mak-
bannai the eleventh.
14 These Gadites were army commanders; the least was a match
for a hundred, and the greatest
for a thousand. 15 It was they who
crossed the Jordan in the first
month when it was overflowing
all its banks, and they put to flight
everyone living in the valleys, to
the east and to the west.
Dt 32:30; Jos 3:15

[a] 4 In Hebrew texts the second half of this verse (*Jeremiah . . . Gederathite*) is numbered 12:5, and 12:5-40 is numbered 12:6-41.

16Other Benjamites and some
men from Judah also came to
David in his stronghold. 17David
went out to meet them and said
to them, "If you have come to me
in peace to help me, I am ready
for you to join me. But if you have
come to betray me to my enemies
when my hands are free from violence, may the God of our ancestors see it and judge you." 2Sa 3:19
18Then the Spirit came on Amasai, chief of the Thirty, and he said:
Jdg 6:34; 2Sa 17:25

"We are yours, David!
We are with you, son of
Jesse!
Success, success to you, 1Sa 25:5-6
and success to those who
help you,
for your God will help you."

So David received them and
made them leaders of his raiding
bands.
19Some of the tribe of Manasseh defected to David when he
went with the Philistines to fight
against Saul. (He and his men did
not help the Philistines because,
after consultation, their rulers
sent him away. They said, "It will
cost us our heads if he deserts to
his master Saul.") 20When David
went to Ziklag, these were the
men of Manasseh who defected
to him: Adnah, Jozabad, Jediael,
Michael, Jozabad, Elihu and Zillethai, leaders of units of a thousand in Manasseh. 21They helped
David against raiding bands, for
all of them were brave warriors,
and they were commanders in his
army. 22Day after day men came
to help David, until he had a great
army, like the army of God.[a]
1Sa 27:6; 29:2-11

Others Join David at Hebron

23These are the numbers of the
men armed for battle who came
to David at Hebron to turn Saul's
kingdom over to him, as the LORD
had said: 1Sa 16:1; 2Sa 2:3-4; 1Ch 10:14

24from Judah, carrying shield and spear — 6,800 armed for battle;
25from Simeon, warriors ready for battle — 7,100;
26from Levi — 4,600, 27including Jehoiada, leader of the family of Aaron, with 3,700 men, 28and Zadok, a brave young warrior, with 22 officers from his family; 2Sa 8:17; 1Ch 6:8
29from Benjamin, Saul's tribe — 3,000, most of whom had remained loyal to Saul's house until then; 2Sa 2:8-9; 3:19
30from Ephraim, brave warriors, famous in their own clans — 20,800;
31from half the tribe of Manasseh, designated by name to come and make David king — 18,000;
32from Issachar, men who understood the times and knew what Israel should

[a] 22 Or *a great and mighty army*

do — 200 chiefs, with all their relatives under their command; Est 1:13

33 from Zebulun, experienced soldiers prepared for battle with every type of weapon, to help David with undivided loyalty — 50,000;

34 from Naphtali — 1,000 officers, together with 37,000 men carrying shields and spears;

35 from Dan, ready for battle — 28,600;

36 from Asher, experienced soldiers prepared for battle — 40,000;

37 and from east of the Jordan, from Reuben, Gad and the half-tribe of Manasseh, armed with every type of weapon — 120,000.

38 All these were fighting men
who volunteered to serve in the
ranks. They came to Hebron fully
determined to make David king
over all Israel. All the rest of the
Israelites were also of one mind
to make David king. 39 The men
spent three days there with David, eating and drinking, for their
families had supplied provisions
for them. 40 Also, their neighbors
from as far away as Issachar, Zebulun and Naphtali came bringing
food on donkeys, camels, mules
and oxen. There were plentiful
supplies of flour, fig cakes, raisin
cakes, wine, olive oil, cattle and
sheep, for there was joy in Israel.
1Sa 25:18; 2Sa 5:1-3

Bringing Back the Ark

13 David conferred with each of his officers, the commanders of thousands and commanders of hundreds.
2 He then said to
the whole assembly of Israel, "If
it seems good to you and if it is
the will of the LORD our God, let
us send word far and wide to the
rest of our people throughout the
territories of Israel, and also to the
priests and Levites who are with
them in their towns and pasturelands, to come and join us.
3 Let us
bring the ark of our God back to
us, for we did not inquire of[a] it[b]
during the reign of Saul."
4 The
whole assembly agreed to do this,
because it seemed right to all the
people. 1Sa 7:1-2; 2Ch 1:5

5 So David assembled all Israel,
from the Shihor River in Egypt
to Lebo Hamath, to bring the ark
of God from Kiriath Jearim.
6 David and all Israel went to Baalah
of Judah (Kiriath Jearim) to bring
up from there the ark of God the
LORD, who is enthroned between
the cherubim — the ark that is
called by the Name.
Jos 15:9; 2Ki 19:15; 1Ch 15:3

7 They moved the ark of God
from Abinadab's house on a new
cart, with Uzzah and Ahio guiding
it.
8 David and all the Israelites were
celebrating with all their might
before God, with songs and with
harps, lyres, timbrels, cymbals and
trumpets. Nu 4:15; 1Sa 7:1; 2Sa 6:5

[a] 3 Or *we neglected* [b] 3 Or *him*

9When they came to the threshing floor of Kidon, Uzzah reached
out his hand to steady the ark, because the oxen stumbled. 10The
LORD's anger burned against Uzzah, and he struck him down because he had put his hand on the
ark. So he died there before God.
Lev 10:2; 1Ch 15:13,15

11Then David was angry because
the LORD's wrath had broken out
against Uzzah, and to this day that
place is called Perez Uzzah.[a]
1Ch 15:13; Ps 7:11

12David was afraid of God that
day and asked, "How can I ever
bring the ark of God to me?" 13He
did not take the ark to be with
him in the City of David. Instead,
he took it to the house of Obed-
Edom the Gittite. 14The ark of
God remained with the family of
Obed-Edom in his house for three
months, and the LORD blessed his
household and everything he had.
2Sa 6:1-11; 1Ch 26:4-5

David's House and Family

14 Now Hiram king of Tyre
sent messengers to David,
along with cedar logs, stonema-
sons and carpenters to build a palace for him. 2And David knew that
the LORD had established him as
king over Israel and that his kingdom had been highly exalted for
the sake of his people Israel.
Nu 24:7; Dt 26:19

3In Jerusalem David took more
wives and became the father of
more sons and daughters. 4These
are the names of the children born
to him there: Shammua, Shobab,
Nathan, Solomon, 5Ibhar, Elishua,
Elpelet, 6Nogah, Nepheg, Japhia,
7Elishama, Beeliada[b] and Eliphelet.
2Sa 5:11-16; 1Ch 3:5-8

David Defeats the Philistines

8When the Philistines heard
that David had been anointed king
over all Israel, they went up in full
force to search for him, but David
heard about it and went out to
meet them. 9Now the Philistines
had come and raided the Valley
of Rephaim; 10so David inquired
of God: "Shall I go and attack the
Philistines? Will you deliver them
into my hands?"
1Ch 11:1,15

The LORD answered him, "Go, I
will deliver them into your hands."

11So David and his men went up
to Baal Perazim, and there he defeated them. He said, "As waters
break out, God has broken out
against my enemies by my hand."
So that place was called Baal Perazim.[c] 12The Philistines had abandoned their gods there, and David
gave orders to burn them in the
fire.
Ex 32:20; Jos 7:15; Isa 28:21

13Once more the Philistines
raided the valley; 14so David inquired of God again, and God answered him, "Do not go directly after them, but circle around
them and attack them in front of

[a] 11 *Perez Uzzah* means *outbreak against Uzzah.*
[b] 7 A variant of *Eliada*
[c] 11 *Baal Perazim* means *the lord who breaks out.*

the poplar trees. 15 As soon as you
hear the sound of marching in the
tops of the poplar trees, move out
to battle, because that will mean
God has gone out in front of you
to strike the Philistine army."
16 So David did as God commanded him, and they struck down the
Philistine army, all the way from
Gibeon to Gezer. ver 9; Jos 9:3; 10:33
17 So David's fame spread
throughout every land, and the
LORD made all the nations fear
him. 2Sa 5:17-25

The Ark Brought to Jerusalem

15 After David had constructed
buildings for himself in the
City of David, he prepared a place
for the ark of God and pitched a
tent for it. 2 Then David said, "No
one but the Levites may carry
the ark of God, because the LORD
chose them to carry the ark of the
LORD and to minister before him
forever." Nu 4:15; Dt 10:8; 1Ch 16:1
3 David assembled all Israel in
Jerusalem to bring up the ark of
the LORD to the place he had prepared for it. 4 He called together
the descendants of Aaron and the
Levites: 1Ki 8:1; 1Ch 13:5

5 From the descendants of Kohath,
Uriel the leader and 120 relatives;
6 from the descendants of Merari,
Asaiah the leader and 220 relatives;
7 from the descendants of Gershon,[a]
Joel the leader and 130 relatives;
8 from the descendants of Elizaphan, Ex 6:22
Shemaiah the leader and 200 relatives;
9 from the descendants of Hebron, Ex 6:18
Eliel the leader and 80 relatives;
10 from the descendants of Uzziel,
Amminadab the leader and 112 relatives.

11 Then David summoned Zadok
and Abiathar the priests, and Uriel,
Asaiah, Joel, Shemaiah, Eliel and
Amminadab the Levites. 12 He said
to them, "You are the heads of the
Levitical families; you and your
fellow Levites are to consecrate
yourselves and bring up the ark of
the LORD, the God of Israel, to the
place I have prepared for it. 13 It was
because you, the Levites, did not
bring it up the first time that the
LORD our God broke out in anger
against us. We did not inquire of
him about how to do it in the prescribed way." 14 So the priests and
Levites consecrated themselves
in order to bring up the ark of the
LORD, the God of Israel. 15 And the
Levites carried the ark of God with
the poles on their shoulders, as
Moses had commanded in accordance with the word of the LORD.
Ex 25:14; 2Sa 6:3; 1Ch 13:7-10

[a] 7 Hebrew *Gershom*, a variant of *Gershon*

16 David told the leaders of the
Levites to appoint their fellow Levites as musicians to make a joyful
sound with musical instruments:
lyres, harps and cymbals.

1Ch 25:1; Ne 12:27,36; Ps 68:25

17 So the Levites appointed Heman son of Joel; from his relatives, Asaph son of Berekiah; and
from their relatives the Merarites,
Ethan son of Kushaiah; 18 and with
them their relatives next in rank:
Zechariah,[a] Jaaziel, Shemiramoth,
Jehiel, Unni, Eliab, Benaiah, Maaseiah, Mattithiah, Eliphelehu,
Mikneiah, Obed-Edom and Jeiel,[b]
the gatekeepers. 1Ch 6:33,39,44; 26:4-5

19 The musicians Heman, Asaph
and Ethan were to sound the
bronze cymbals; 20 Zechariah, Jaaziel,[c] Shemiramoth, Jehiel, Unni,
Eliab, Maaseiah and Benaiah were
to play the lyres according to *alamoth*,[d] 21 and Mattithiah, Eliphelehu, Mikneiah, Obed-Edom, Jeiel
and Azaziah were to play the harps,
directing according to *sheminith*.[d]
22 Kenaniah the head Levite was
in charge of the singing; that was
his responsibility because he was
skillful at it. 1Ch 25:6

23 Berekiah and Elkanah were to
be doorkeepers for the ark. 24 Shebaniah, Joshaphat, Nethanel, Amasai, Zechariah, Benaiah and Eliezer
the priests were to blow trumpets
before the ark of God. Obed-Edom
and Jehiah were also to be doorkeepers for the ark. ver 28; 1Ch 16:6

25 So David and the elders of Israel and the commanders of units
of a thousand went to bring up the
ark of the covenant of the LORD
from the house of Obed-Edom,
with rejoicing. 26 Because God had
helped the Levites who were carrying the ark of the covenant of
the LORD, seven bulls and seven
rams were sacrificed. 27 Now David was clothed in a robe of fine
linen, as were all the Levites who
were carrying the ark, and as were
the musicians, and Kenaniah, who
was in charge of the singing of
the choirs. David also wore a lin-
en ephod. 28 So all Israel brought
up the ark of the covenant of the
LORD with shouts, with the sounding of rams' horns and trumpets,
and of cymbals, and the playing of
lyres and harps. 1Ch 13:8,13; 2Ch 1:4

29 As the ark of the covenant of
the LORD was entering the City
of David, Michal daughter of Saul
watched from a window. And
when she saw King David dancing
and celebrating, she despised him
in her heart.

Ministering Before the Ark

16 They brought the ark of God
and set it inside the tent that
David had pitched for it, and they
presented burnt offerings and fellowship offerings before God. 2 Af-

[a] *18* Three Hebrew manuscripts and most Septuagint manuscripts (see also verse 20 and 16:5); most Hebrew manuscripts *Zechariah son and* or *Zechariah, Ben and*
[b] *18* Hebrew; Septuagint (see also verse 21) *Jeiel and Azaziah*
[c] *20* See verse 18; Hebrew *Aziel*, a variant of *Jaaziel*.
[d] *20,21* Probably a musical term

ter David had finished sacrificing
the burnt offerings and fellowship
offerings, he blessed the people
in the name of the LORD. 3Then
he gave a loaf of bread, a cake of
dates and a cake of raisins to each
Israelite man and woman.

2Sa 6:12-19; 1Ch 15:1

4He appointed some of the Levites to minister before the ark
of the LORD, to extol,[a] thank, and
praise the LORD, the God of Israel:
5Asaph was the chief, and next to
him in rank were Zechariah, then
Jaaziel,[b] Shemiramoth, Jehiel,
Mattithiah, Eliab, Benaiah, Obed-
Edom and Jeiel. They were to play
the lyres and harps, Asaph was to
sound the cymbals, 6and Benaiah and Jahaziel the priests were
to blow the trumpets regularly
before the ark of the covenant of
God. 1Ch 15:2

7That day David first appointed
Asaph and his associates to give
praise to the LORD in this manner:

2Sa 23:1

8Give praise to the LORD,
proclaim his name;

ver 34; Ps 136:1

make known among the
nations what he has
done. 2Ki 19:19
9Sing to him, sing praise to him;
tell of all his wonderful acts.

Ex 15:1

10Glory in his holy name;
let the hearts of those who
seek the LORD rejoice.
11Look to the LORD and his
strength;
seek his face always.

Ps 24:6; 119:2,58

12Remember the wonders he has
done, Ps 77:11
his miracles, and the
judgments he
pronounced, Ps 78:43
13you his servants, the
descendants of Israel,
his chosen ones, the children
of Jacob.
14He is the LORD our God;
his judgments are in all the
earth. Isa 26:9

15He remembers[c] his covenant
forever,
the promise he made, for a
thousand generations,
16the covenant he made with
Abraham, Ge 17:2; 26:3
the oath he swore to Isaac.
17He confirmed it to Jacob as a
decree, Ge 35:9-12
to Israel as an everlasting
covenant:
18"To you I will give the land of
Canaan Ge 13:14-17
as the portion you will
inherit."

19When they were but few in
number, Ge 34:30; Dt 7:7
few indeed, and strangers
in it,

[a] 4 Or *petition*; or *invoke* [b] 5 See 15:18,20; Hebrew *Jeiel*, possibly another name for *Jaaziel*. [c] 15 Some Septuagint manuscripts (see also Psalm 105:8); Hebrew *Remember*

20 they[a] wandered from nation to nation,
from one kingdom to another.
21 He allowed no one to oppress them;
for their sake he rebuked kings: Ge 12:17; 20:3; Ex 7:15-18
22 "Do not touch my anointed ones;
do my prophets no harm."
Ps 105:1-15; Ge 20:7

23 Sing to the LORD, all the earth;
proclaim his salvation day after day.
24 Declare his glory among the nations,
his marvelous deeds among all peoples.
25 For great is the LORD and most worthy of praise; Ps 48:1
he is to be feared above all gods. Ps 89:7
26 For all the gods of the nations are idols,
but the LORD made the heavens. Lev 19:4; Ps 102:25
27 Splendor and majesty are before him;
strength and joy are in his dwelling place.

28 Ascribe to the LORD, all you families of nations,
ascribe to the LORD glory and strength. Ps 29:1-2
29 Ascribe to the LORD the glory due his name;
bring an offering and come before him.
Worship the LORD in the splendor of his[b] holiness.
30 Tremble before him, all the earth! Ps 114:7
The world is firmly established; it cannot be moved.

31 Let the heavens rejoice, let the earth be glad; Isa 49:13
let them say among the nations, "The LORD reigns!" Ps 93:1
32 Let the sea resound, and all that is in it; Ps 98:7
let the fields be jubilant, and everything in them!
33 Let the trees of the forest sing,
let them sing for joy before the LORD,
for he comes to judge the earth. Ps 96:1-13

34 Give thanks to the LORD, for he is good;
his love endures forever.
Ezr 3:11; Ps 136:1-26; Jer 33:11
35 Cry out, "Save us, God our Savior; Mic 7:7
gather us and deliver us from the nations,
that we may give thanks to your holy name,
and glory in your praise."

[a] *18-20* One Hebrew manuscript, Septuagint and Vulgate (see also Psalm 105:12); most Hebrew manuscripts *inherit, / [19]though you are but few in number, / few indeed, and strangers in it." / [20]They*
[b] *29* Or *LORD with the splendor of*

[36]Praise be to the LORD, the God
of Israel,
from everlasting to
everlasting.

Then all the people said "Amen"
and "Praise the LORD." Ps 106:1,47-48

[37]David left Asaph and his associates before the ark of the covenant of the LORD to minister
there regularly, according to each
day's requirements. [38]He also left
Obed-Edom and his sixty-eight
associates to minister with them.
Obed-Edom son of Jeduthun, and
also Hosah, were gatekeepers.
1Ch 13:13; 26:10; 2Ch 8:14

[39]David left Zadok the priest and
his fellow priests before the tabernacle of the LORD at the high place
in Gibeon [40]to present burnt offerings to the LORD on the altar of
burnt offering regularly, morning
and evening, in accordance with
everything written in the Law of
the LORD, which he had given Israel. [41]With them were Heman and
Jeduthun and the rest of those
chosen and designated by name
to give thanks to the LORD, "for his
love endures forever." [42]Heman
and Jeduthun were responsible
for the sounding of the trumpets
and cymbals and for the playing
of the other instruments for sacred song. The sons of Jeduthun
were stationed at the gate.
Ex 29:38; 2Ch 5:13; 7:6

[43]Then all the people left, each
for their own home, and David returned home to bless his family.

God's Promise to David

17 After David was settled in
his palace, he said to Nathan
the prophet, "Here I am, living in
a house of cedar, while the ark of
the covenant of the LORD is under
a tent." 1Ch 15:1

[2]Nathan replied to David,
"Whatever you have in mind, do
it, for God is with you." 2Ch 6:7

[3]But that night the word of God
came to Nathan, saying:

[4]"Go and tell my servant
David, 'This is what the LORD
says: You are not the one to
build me a house to dwell in.
[5]I have not dwelt in a house
from the day I brought Israel
up out of Egypt to this day. I
have moved from one tent site
to another, from one dwelling
place to another. [6]Wherever I
have moved with all the Israelites, did I ever say to any of
their leaders[a] whom I commanded to shepherd my people, "Why have you not built
me a house of cedar?"' 1Ch 28:3

[7]"Now then, tell my servant
David, 'This is what the LORD
Almighty says: I took you
from the pasture, from tending the flock, and appointed
you ruler over my people Israel. [8]I have been with you
wherever you have gone, and
I have cut off all your enemies from before you. Now I
will make your name like the

[a] 6 Traditionally *judges*; also in verse 10

names of the greatest men
on earth. 9And I will provide
a place for my people Israel
and will plant them so that
they can have a home of their
own and no longer be dis-
turbed. Wicked people will
not oppress them anymore,
as they did at the beginning
10and have done ever since
the time I appointed leaders
over my people Israel. I will
also subdue all your enemies.

Jdg 2:16; 2Sa 6:21

"'I declare to you that the
LORD will build a house for
you: 11When your days are over
and you go to be with your ancestors, I will raise up your offspring to succeed you, one of
your own sons, and I will establish his kingdom. 12He is
the one who will build a house
for me, and I will establish
his throne forever. 13I will be
his father, and he will be my
son. I will never take my love
away from him, as I took it
away from your predecessor.
14I will set him over my house
and my kingdom forever; his
throne will be established forever.'"

1Ki 2:12; Jer 33:17; 2Ch 6:18

15Nathan reported to David all
the words of this entire revelation.

2Sa 7:1-17

David's Prayer

16Then King David went in and
sat before the LORD, and he said:

"Who am I, LORD God,
and what is my family, that
you have brought me this
far? 17And as if this were not
enough in your sight, my
God, you have spoken about
the future of the house of
your servant. You, LORD God,
have looked on me as though
I were the most exalted of
men.

18"What more can David say
to you for honoring your servant? For you know your servant, 19LORD. For the sake of
your servant and according to
your will, you have done this
great thing and made known
all these great promises.

20"There is no one like you,
LORD, and there is no God but
you, as we have heard with
our own ears. 21And who is
like your people Israel — the
one nation on earth whose
God went out to redeem a
people for himself, and to
make a name for yourself,
and to perform great and
awesome wonders by driving
out nations from before your
people, whom you redeemed
from Egypt? 22You made your
people Israel your very own
forever, and you, LORD, have
become their God.

Ex 9:14; 19:5-6; Isa 44:6

23"And now, LORD, let the
promise you have made concerning your servant and his
house be established forever.

Do as you promised, 24so that
it will be established and that
your name will be great forever. Then people will say, 'The
LORD Almighty, the God over
Israel, is Israel's God!' And
the house of your servant David will be established before
you. 1Ki 8:25
25"You, my God, have re-
vealed to your servant that
you will build a house for him.
So your servant has found
courage to pray to you. 26You,
LORD, are God! You have promised these good things to your
servant. 27Now you have been
pleased to bless the house of
your servant, that it may continue forever in your sight;
for you, LORD, have blessed it,
and it will be blessed forever."
2Sa 7:18-29; Ps 21:6

David's Victories

18 In the course of time, David
defeated the Philistines and
subdued them, and he took Gath
and its surrounding villages from
the control of the Philistines.
2David also defeated the Moabites, and they became subject to
him and brought him tribute.
Nu 21:29
3Moreover, David defeated Hadadezer king of Zobah, in the vicinity of Hamath, when he went
to set up his monument at[a] the
Euphrates River. 4David captured
a thousand of his chariots, seven
thousand charioteers and twenty
thousand foot soldiers. He hamstrung all but a hundred of the
chariot horses. Ge 2:14; 49:6; 1Ch 19:6
5When the Arameans of Da-
mascus came to help Hadadezer
king of Zobah, David struck down
twenty-two thousand of them.
6He put garrisons in the Aramean kingdom of Damascus, and
the Arameans became subject to
him and brought him tribute. The
LORD gave David victory wherever
he went. 1Ch 19:6
7David took the gold shields carried by the officers of Hadadezer
and brought them to Jerusalem.
8From Tebah[b] and Kun, towns
that belonged to Hadadezer, David
took a great quantity of bronze,
which Solomon used to make the
bronze Sea, the pillars and various
bronze articles. 1Ki 7:23; 2Ch 4:12,15-16
9When Tou king of Hamath
heard that David had defeated the
entire army of Hadadezer king of
Zobah, 10he sent his son Hadoram
to King David to greet him and
congratulate him on his victory in battle over Hadadezer, who
had been at war with Tou. Hadoram brought all kinds of articles
of gold, of silver and of bronze.
11King David dedicated these
articles to the LORD, as he had
done with the silver and gold he
had taken from all these nations:
Edom and Moab, the Ammonites
and the Philistines, and Amalek.
Nu 24:18,20

[a] *3* Or *to restore his control over*
[b] *8* Hebrew *Tibhath*, a variant of *Tebah*

12 Abishai son of Zeruiah struck
down eighteen thousand Edomites in the Valley of Salt. 13 He put
garrisons in Edom, and all the
Edomites became subject to David. The LORD gave David victory
wherever he went. 2Sa 8:1-14; 1Ki 11:15

David's Officials

14 David reigned over all Israel,
doing what was just and right for
all his people. 15 Joab son of Zeruiah was over the army; Jehoshaphat son of Ahilud was recorder;
16 Zadok son of Ahitub and Ahimelek[a] son of Abiathar were priests;
Shavsha was secretary; 17 Benaiah
son of Jehoiada was over the Kerethites and Pelethites; and David's
sons were chief officials at the
king's side. 2Sa 8:15-18; 1Ch 29:26

David Defeats the Ammonites

19 In the course of time, Nahash king of the Ammonites
died, and his son succeeded him as
king. 2 David thought, "I will show
kindness to Hanun son of Nahash,
because his father showed kindness to me." So David sent a delegation to express his sympathy to
Hanun concerning his father.
Ge 19:38; Jdg 10:17-11:33

When David's envoys came to
Hanun in the land of the Ammonites to express sympathy to him,
3 the Ammonite commanders said
to Hanun, "Do you think David is
honoring your father by sending
envoys to you to express sympathy? Haven't his envoys come to
you only to explore and spy out
the country and overthrow it?"
4 So Hanun seized David's envoys,
shaved them, cut off their garments at the buttocks, and sent
them away. Nu 21:32

5 When someone came and told
David about the men, he sent
messengers to meet them, for
they were greatly humiliated.
The king said, "Stay at Jericho till
your beards have grown, and then
come back."

6 When the Ammonites realized
that they had become obnoxious
to David, Hanun and the Ammonites sent a thousand talents[b] of
silver to hire chariots and charioteers from Aram Naharaim,[c] Aram
Maakah and Zobah. 7 They hired
thirty-two thousand chariots and
charioteers, as well as the king of
Maakah with his troops, who came
and camped near Medeba, while
the Ammonites were mustered
from their towns and moved out
for battle. Jos 13:9,16; 1Ch 18:3,5,9

8 On hearing this, David sent
Joab out with the entire army of
fighting men. 9 The Ammonites
came out and drew up in battle
formation at the entrance to their
city, while the kings who had come
were by themselves in the open
country.

10 Joab saw that there were battle lines in front of him and be-

[a] *16* Some Hebrew manuscripts, Vulgate and Syriac (see also 2 Samuel 8:17); most Hebrew manuscripts *Abimelek* [b] *6* That is, about 38 tons or about 34 metric tons [c] *6* That is, Northwest Mesopotamia

hind him; so he selected some of
the best troops in Israel and deployed them against the Arameans. 11He put the rest of the men
under the command of Abishai
his brother, and they were deployed against the Ammonites.
12Joab said, "If the Arameans are
too strong for me, then you are to
rescue me; but if the Ammonites
are too strong for you, then I will
rescue you. 13Be strong, and let us
fight bravely for our people and
the cities of our God. The LORD
will do what is good in his sight."
1Sa 26:6

14Then Joab and the troops with
him advanced to fight the Arameans, and they fled before him.
15When the Ammonites realized
that the Arameans were fleeing,
they too fled before his brother
Abishai and went inside the city.
So Joab went back to Jerusalem.

16After the Arameans saw that
they had been routed by Israel,
they sent messengers and had Arameans brought from beyond the
Euphrates River, with Shophak
the commander of Hadadezer's
army leading them.

17When David was told of this,
he gathered all Israel and crossed
the Jordan; he advanced against
them and formed his battle lines
opposite them. David formed his
lines to meet the Arameans in battle, and they fought against him.
18But they fled before Israel, and
David killed seven thousand of
their charioteers and forty thousand of their foot soldiers. He also
killed Shophak the commander of
their army.

19When the vassals of Hadadezer
saw that they had been routed by
Israel, they made peace with David and became subject to him.

So the Arameans were not willing to help the Ammonites anymore.
2Sa 10:1-19

The Capture of Rabbah

20 In the spring, at the time
when kings go off to war,
Joab led out the armed forces. He
laid waste the land of the Ammonites and went to Rabbah and besieged it, but David remained in
Jerusalem. Joab attacked Rabbah
and left it in ruins. 2David took
the crown from the head of their
king[a] — its weight was found to
be a talent[b] of gold, and it was set
with precious stones — and it was
placed on David's head. He took a
great quantity of plunder from the
city 3and brought out the people
who were there, consigning them
to labor with saws and with iron
picks and axes. David did this to
all the Ammonite towns. Then David and his entire army returned
to Jerusalem.
2Sa 11:1; 12:29-31

War With the Philistines

4In the course of time, war broke
out with the Philistines, at Gezer. At that time Sibbekai the Hushathite killed Sippai, one of the

[a] 2 Or *of Milkom*, that is, Molek [b] 2 That is, about 75 pounds or about 34 kilograms

descendants of the Rephaites, and
the Philistines were subjugated.
5 In another battle with the Philistines, Elhanan son of Jair killed
Lahmi the brother of Goliath the
Gittite, who had a spear with a
shaft like a weaver's rod.
6 In still another battle, which
took place at Gath, there was a huge
man with six fingers on each hand
and six toes on each foot — twenty-four in all. He also was descended from Rapha. 7 When he taunted
Israel, Jonathan son of Shimea,
David's brother, killed him.
8 These were descendants of Rapha in Gath, and they fell at the
hands of David and his men.
2Sa 21:15-22

David Counts the Fighting Men

21 Satan rose up against Israel
and incited David to take a
census of Israel. 2 So David said to
Joab and the commanders of the
troops, "Go and count the Israelites from Beersheba to Dan. Then
report back to me so that I may
know how many there are."
1Ch 27:23-24; 2Ch 18:21
3 But Joab replied, "May the
LORD multiply his troops a hundred times over. My lord the king,
are they not all my lord's subjects?
Why does my lord want to do this?
Why should he bring guilt on Israel?" Dt 1:11
4 The king's word, however, overruled Joab; so Joab left and went
throughout Israel and then came
back to Jerusalem. 5 Joab reported
the number of the fighting men to
David: In all Israel there were one
million one hundred thousand
men who could handle a sword,
including four hundred and seventy thousand in Judah. 1Ch 9:1
6 But Joab did not include Levi
and Benjamin in the numbering,
because the king's command was
repulsive to him. 7 This command
was also evil in the sight of God; so
he punished Israel.
8 Then David said to God, "I have
sinned greatly by doing this. Now,
I beg you, take away the guilt of
your servant. I have done a very
foolish thing."
9 The LORD said to Gad, David's
seer, 10 "Go and tell David, 'This is
what the LORD says: I am giving
you three options. Choose one of
them for me to carry out against
you.'" 1Sa 9:9; 22:5
11 So Gad went to David and said
to him, "This is what the LORD
says: 'Take your choice: 12 three
years of famine, three months of
being swept away[a] before your enemies, with their swords overtak-
ing you, or three days of the sword
of the LORD — days of plague in
the land, with the angel of the
LORD ravaging every part of Israel.' Now then, decide how I should
answer the one who sent me."
Dt 32:24; Eze 30:25
13 David said to Gad, "I am in
deep distress. Let me fall into the
hands of the LORD, for his mercy

[a] *12* Hebrew; Septuagint and Vulgate (see also 2 Samuel 24:13) *of fleeing*

is very great; but do not let me fall into human hands." Ps 130:4,7

14 So the LORD sent a plague on Israel, and seventy thousand men of Israel fell dead. 15 And God sent an angel to destroy Jerusalem. But as the angel was doing so, the LORD saw it and relented concerning the disaster and said to the angel who was destroying the people, "Enough! Withdraw your hand." The angel of the LORD was then standing at the threshing floor of Araunah[a] the Jebusite. Ge 6:6; Ex 32:14; 1Ch 27:24

16 David looked up and saw the angel of the LORD standing between heaven and earth, with a drawn sword in his hand extended over Jerusalem. Then David and the elders, clothed in sackcloth, fell facedown. Nu 14:5; Jos 7:6

17 David said to God, "Was it not I who ordered the fighting men to be counted? I, the shepherd,[b] have sinned and done wrong. These are but sheep. What have they done? LORD my God, let your hand fall on me and my family, but do not let this plague remain on your people." 2Sa 7:8; Ps 74:1

David Builds an Altar

18 Then the angel of the LORD ordered Gad to tell David to go up and build an altar to the LORD on the threshing floor of Araunah the Jebusite. 19 So David went up in obedience to the word that Gad had spoken in the name of the LORD. 2Ch 3:1

20 While Araunah was threshing wheat, he turned and saw the angel; his four sons who were with him hid themselves. 21 Then David approached, and when Araunah looked and saw him, he left the threshing floor and bowed down before David with his face to the ground. Jdg 6:11

22 David said to him, "Let me have the site of your threshing floor so I can build an altar to the LORD, that the plague on the people may be stopped. Sell it to me at the full price."

23 Araunah said to David, "Take it! Let my lord the king do whatever pleases him. Look, I will give the oxen for the burnt offerings, the threshing sledges for the wood, and the wheat for the grain offering. I will give all this."

24 But King David replied to Araunah, "No, I insist on paying the full price. I will not take for the LORD what is yours, or sacrifice a burnt offering that costs me nothing."

25 So David paid Araunah six hundred shekels[c] of gold for the site. 26 David built an altar to the LORD there and sacrificed burnt offerings and fellowship offerings. He called on the LORD, and the LORD answered him with fire from heaven on the altar of burnt offering. 2Sa 24:1-25

[a] *15* Hebrew *Ornan*, a variant of *Araunah*; also in verses 18-28 [b] *17* Probable reading of the original Hebrew text (see 2 Samuel 24:17 and note); Masoretic Text does not have *the shepherd*. [c] *25* That is, about 15 pounds or about 6.9 kilograms

27 Then the LORD spoke to the angel, and he put his sword back into its sheath. 28 At that time, when David saw that the LORD had answered him on the threshing floor of Araunah the Jebusite, he offered sacrifices there. 29 The tabernacle of the LORD, which Moses had made in the wilderness, and the altar of burnt offering were at that time on the high place at Gibeon. 30 But David could not go before it to inquire of God, because he was afraid of the sword of the angel of the LORD. 1Ki 3:4; 1Ch 16:39

22 Then David said, "The house of the LORD God is to be here, and also the altar of burnt offering for Israel." 1Ch 21:18-29; 2Ch 3:1

Preparations for the Temple

2 So David gave orders to assemble the foreigners residing in Israel, and from among them he appointed stonecutters to prepare dressed stone for building the house of God. 3 He provided a large amount of iron to make nails for the doors of the gateways and for the fittings, and more bronze than could be weighed. 4 He also provided more cedar logs than could be counted, for the Sidonians and Tyrians had brought large numbers of them to David. 1Ki 5:6; 9:21

5 David said, "My son Solomon is young and inexperienced, and the house to be built for the LORD should be of great magnificence and fame and splendor in the sight of all the nations. Therefore I will make preparations for it." So David made extensive preparations before his death. 1Ch 29:1

6 Then he called for his son Solomon and charged him to build a house for the LORD, the God of Israel. 7 David said to Solomon: "My son, I had it in my heart to build a house for the Name of the LORD my God. 8 But this word of the LORD came to me: 'You have shed much blood and have fought many wars. You are not to build a house for my Name, because you have shed much blood on the earth in my sight. 9 But you will have a son who will be a man of peace and rest, and I will give him rest from all his enemies on every side. His name will be Solomon,[a] and I will grant Israel peace and quiet during his reign. 10 He is the one who will build a house for my Name. He will be my son, and I will be his father. And I will establish the throne of his kingdom over Israel forever.' 2Sa 7:13; 1Ch 17:12

11 "Now, my son, the LORD be with you, and may you have success and build the house of the LORD your God, as he said you would. 12 May the LORD give you discretion and understanding when he puts you in command over Israel, so that you may keep the law of the LORD your God. 13 Then you will have success if you are careful to observe the decrees and laws that the LORD gave Moses for Israel. Be

[a] 9 *Solomon* sounds like and may be derived from the Hebrew for *peace.*

strong and courageous. Do not be
afraid or discouraged.

Jos 1:6-9; 1Ki 3:9-12; 1Ch 28:7

14"I have taken great pains to
provide for the temple of the LORD
a hundred thousand talents[a] of
gold, a million talents[b] of silver,
quantities of bronze and iron too
great to be weighed, and wood and
stone. And you may add to them.
15You have many workers: stonecutters, masons and carpenters, as
well as those skilled in every kind
of work 16in gold and silver, bronze
and iron — craftsmen beyond
number. Now begin the work, and
the LORD be with you." ver 11; 2Ch 2:7

17Then David ordered all the
leaders of Israel to help his son
Solomon. 18He said to them, "Is
not the LORD your God with you?
And has he not granted you rest
on every side? For he has given the
inhabitants of the land into my
hands, and the land is subject to
the LORD and to his people. 19Now
devote your heart and soul to
seeking the LORD your God. Begin
to build the sanctuary of the LORD
God, so that you may bring the ark
of the covenant of the LORD and
the sacred articles belonging to
God into the temple that will be
built for the Name of the LORD."

2Ch 5:7; 1Ch 23:25; 28:1-6

The Levites

23 When David was old and
full of years, he made his
son Solomon king over Israel.

1Ki 1:33-39; 1Ch 28:5; 29:28

2He also gathered together all
the leaders of Israel, as well as
the priests and Levites. 3The Levites thirty years old or more were
counted, and the total number of
men was thirty-eight thousand.
4David said, "Of these, twenty-four
thousand are to be in charge of the
work of the temple of the LORD
and six thousand are to be officials
and judges. 5Four thousand are to
be gatekeepers and four thousand
are to praise the LORD with the musical instruments I have provided
for that purpose." 1Ch 15:16; 2Ch 19:8

6David separated the Levites
into divisions corresponding to
the sons of Levi: Gershon, Kohath
and Merari. 2Ch 8:14; 29:25

Gershonites

7Belonging to the Gershonites:
Ladan and Shimei.
8The sons of Ladan:
Jehiel the first, Zetham and
Joel — three in all.
9The sons of Shimei:
Shelomoth, Haziel and Ha-
ran — three in all.
These were the heads of the
families of Ladan.
10And the sons of Shimei:
Jahath, Ziza,[c] Jeush and Be-
riah.
These were the sons of
Shimei — four in all.

[a] *14* That is, about 3,750 tons or about 3,400 metric tons [b] *14* That is, about 37,500 tons or about 34,000 metric tons
[c] *10* One Hebrew manuscript, Septuagint and Vulgate (see also verse 11); most Hebrew manuscripts *Zina*

[11]Jahath was the first and Ziza the second, but Jeush and Beriah did not have many sons; so they were counted as one family with one assignment.

Kohathites

[12]The sons of Kohath:
Amram, Izhar, Hebron and Uzziel — four in all. Ex 6:18
[13]The sons of Amram: Ex 6:20; 28:1
Aaron and Moses.
Aaron was set apart, he and his descendants forever, to consecrate the most holy things, to offer sacrifices before the LORD, to minister before him and to pronounce blessings in his name forever. [14]The sons of Moses the man of God were counted as part of the tribe of Levi. Ex 30:7-10; Dt 33:1
[15]The sons of Moses:
Gershom and Eliezer. Ex 18:4
[16]The descendants of Gershom: 1Ch 26:24-28
Shubael was the first.
[17]The descendants of Eliezer:
Rehabiah was the first.
Eliezer had no other sons, but the sons of Rehabiah were very numerous.
[18]The sons of Izhar:
Shelomith was the first.
[19]The sons of Hebron: 1Ch 24:23
Jeriah the first, Amariah the second, Jahaziel the third and Jekameam the fourth.
[20]The sons of Uzziel:
Micah the first and Ishiah the second.

Merarites

[21]The sons of Merari: 1Ch 24:26
Mahli and Mushi.
The sons of Mahli:
Eleazar and Kish.
[22]Eleazar died without having sons: he had only daughters. Their cousins, the sons of Kish, married them.
[23]The sons of Mushi:
Mahli, Eder and Jerimoth — three in all.

[24]These were the descendants of Levi by their families — the heads of families as they were registered under their names and counted individually, that is, the workers twenty years old or more who served in the temple of the LORD. [25]For David had said, "Since the LORD, the God of Israel, has granted rest to his people and has come to dwell in Jerusalem forever, [26]the Levites no longer need to carry the tabernacle or any of the articles used in its service." [27]According to the last instructions of David, the Levites were counted from those twenty years old or more. Nu 4:5,15; Dt 10:8

[28]The duty of the Levites was to help Aaron's descendants in the service of the temple of the LORD: to be in charge of the courtyards, the side rooms, the purification of all sacred things and

the performance of other duties
at the house of God. 29 They were
in charge of the bread set out on
the table, the special flour for the
grain offerings, the thin loaves
made without yeast, the baking
and the mixing, and all measurements of quantity and size.
30 They were also to stand every
morning to thank and praise the
LORD. They were to do the same
in the evening 31 and whenever
burnt offerings were presented
to the LORD on the Sabbaths, at
the New Moon feasts and at the
appointed festivals. They were to
serve before the LORD regularly in
the proper number and in the way
prescribed for them.

Ex 25:30; Lev 19:35-36; 23:4

32 And so the Levites carried out
their responsibilities for the tent
of meeting, for the Holy Place and,
under their relatives the descendants of Aaron, for the service of
the temple of the LORD.

Nu 1:53; 3:6-8,38

The Divisions of Priests

24 These were the divisions of
the descendants of Aaron:

Nu 3:2-4; 1Ch 23:6

The sons of Aaron were Nadab,
Abihu, Eleazar and Ithamar. 2 But
Nadab and Abihu died before their
father did, and they had no sons;
so Eleazar and Ithamar served as
the priests. 3 With the help of Zadok a descendant of Eleazar and
Ahimelek a descendant of Ithamar, David separated them into
divisions for their appointed order of ministering. 4 A larger number of leaders were found among
Eleazar's descendants than among
Ithamar's, and they were divided
accordingly: sixteen heads of families from Eleazar's descendants
and eight heads of families from
Ithamar's descendants. 5 They divided them impartially by casting lots, for there were officials of
the sanctuary and officials of God
among the descendants of both
Eleazar and Ithamar.

Ex 6:23; Lev 10:1-2; Nu 3:4

6 The scribe Shemaiah son of
Nethanel, a Levite, recorded their
names in the presence of the king
and of the officials: Zadok the
priest, Ahimelek son of Abiathar
and the heads of families of the
priests and of the Levites — one
family being taken from Eleazar
and then one from Ithamar.

1Ch 18:16

7 The first lot fell to Jehoiarib,
the second to Jedaiah,

Ezr 2:36; Ne 12:6

8 the third to Harim,

Ezr 2:39; Ne 10:5

the fourth to Seorim,
9 the fifth to Malkijah,
the sixth to Mijamin,
10 the seventh to Hakkoz,
the eighth to Abijah,

Ne 12:4,17; Lk 1:5

11 the ninth to Jeshua,
the tenth to Shekaniah,
12 the eleventh to Eliashib,
the twelfth to Jakim,

13 the thirteenth to Huppah,
the fourteenth to Jeshebeab,
14 the fifteenth to Bilgah,
the sixteenth to Immer, Jer 20:1
15 the seventeenth to Hezir,
the eighteenth to Happizzez,
16 the nineteenth to Pethahiah,
the twentieth to Jehezkel,
17 the twenty-first to Jakin,
the twenty-second to Gamul,
18 the twenty-third to Delaiah
and the twenty-fourth to Maaziah.

19 This was their appointed order
of ministering when they entered
the temple of the LORD, according
to the regulations prescribed
for them by their ancestor Aaron,
as the LORD, the God of Israel, had
commanded him.

The Rest of the Levites

20 As for the rest of the descendants of Levi: 1Ch 23:6
from the sons of Amram: Shubael;
from the sons of Shubael: Jehdeiah.
21 As for Rehabiah, from his sons: 1Ch 23:17
Ishiah was the first.
22 From the Izharites: Shelomoth;
from the sons of Shelomoth: Jahath.
23 The sons of Hebron: Jeriah the first,[a] Amariah the second, Jahaziel the third and Jekameam the fourth. 1Ch 23:19
24 The son of Uzziel: Micah;
from the sons of Micah: Shamir.
25 The brother of Micah: Ishiah;
from the sons of Ishiah: Zechariah.
26 The sons of Merari: Mahli and Mushi. 1Ch 6:19; 23:21
The son of Jaaziah: Beno.
27 The sons of Merari:
from Jaaziah: Beno, Shoham, Zakkur and Ibri.
28 From Mahli: Eleazar, who had no sons.
29 From Kish: the son of Kish: Jerahmeel.
30 And the sons of Mushi: Mahli, Eder and Jerimoth.

These were the Levites, according
to their families. 31 They also
cast lots, just as their relatives the
descendants of Aaron did, in the presence of King David and of Zadok, Ahimelek, and the heads of families of the priests and of the Levites. The families of the oldest brother were treated the same as those of the youngest.

The Musicians

25 David, together with the commanders of the army, set apart some of the sons of Asaph, Heman and Jeduthun for the ministry of prophesying, accompanied by harps, lyres and

[a] 23 Two Hebrew manuscripts and some Septuagint manuscripts (see also 23:19); most Hebrew manuscripts *The sons of Jeriah:*

cymbals. Here is the list of the
men who performed this service:
1Sa 10:5; 1Ch 6:33,39; 15:16

2 From the sons of Asaph:
Zakkur, Joseph, Nethaniah and Asarelah. The sons of Asaph were under the supervision of Asaph, who prophesied under the king's supervision.
3 As for Jeduthun, from his sons:
1Ch 16:41-42
Gedaliah, Zeri, Jeshaiah, Shimei,[a] Hashabiah and Mattithiah, six in all, under the supervision of their father Jeduthun, who prophesied, using the harp in thanking and praising the LORD. Ge 4:21; Ps 33:2
4 As for Heman, from his sons:
Bukkiah, Mattaniah, Uzziel, Shubael and Jerimoth; Hananiah, Hanani, Eliathah, Giddalti and Romamti-Ezer; Joshbekashah, Mallothi, Hothir and Mahazioth.
5 (All these were sons of Heman the king's seer. They were given him through the promises of God to exalt him. God gave Heman fourteen sons and three daughters.)

6 All these men were under the
supervision of their father for the
music of the temple of the LORD,
with cymbals, lyres and harps, for
the ministry at the house of God.
Asaph, Jeduthun and Heman
were under the supervision of the
king.
7 Along with their relatives —
all of them trained and skilled in
music for the LORD — they numbered 288.
8 Young and old alike,
teacher as well as student, cast lots
for their duties. 1Ch 15:16,19; 26:13

9 The first lot, which was for Asaph, fell to Joseph,
1Ch 6:39
his sons and relatives[b] 12[c]
the second to Gedaliah, him and his relatives and sons 12
10 the third to Zakkur, his sons and relatives 12
11 the fourth to Izri,[d] his sons and relatives 12
12 the fifth to Nethaniah, his sons and relatives 12
13 the sixth to Bukkiah, his sons and relatives 12
14 the seventh to Jesarelah,[e] his sons and relatives 12
15 the eighth to Jeshaiah, his sons and relatives 12
16 the ninth to Mattaniah, his sons and relatives 12
17 the tenth to Shimei, his sons and relatives 12
18 the eleventh to Azarel,[f] his sons and relatives 12
19 the twelfth to Hashabiah, his sons and relatives 12

[a] 3 One Hebrew manuscript and some Septuagint manuscripts (see also verse 17); most Hebrew manuscripts do not have *Shimei.* [b] 9 See Septuagint; Hebrew does not have *his sons and relatives.* [c] 9 See the total in verse 7; Hebrew does not have *twelve.* [d] 11 A variant of *Zeri* [e] 14 A variant of *Asarelah* [f] 18 A variant of *Uzziel*

20 the thirteenth to Shubael,
his sons and relatives 12
21 the fourteenth to
Mattithiah,
his sons and relatives 12
22 the fifteenth to Jerimoth,
his sons and relatives 12
23 the sixteenth to Hananiah,
his sons and relatives 12
24 the seventeenth to
Joshbekashah,
his sons and relatives 12
25 the eighteenth to Hanani,
his sons and relatives 12
26 the nineteenth to Mallothi,
his sons and relatives 12
27 the twentieth to Eliathah,
his sons and relatives 12
28 the twenty-first to Hothir,
his sons and relatives 12
29 the twenty-second to
Giddalti,
his sons and relatives 12
30 the twenty-third to
Mahazioth,
his sons and relatives 12
31 the twenty-fourth to
Romamti-Ezer,
his sons and relatives 12.

The Gatekeepers

26 The divisions of the gatekeepers: 1Ch 9:17

From the Korahites: Meshelemiah son of Kore, one of the sons of Asaph.
2 Meshelemiah had sons:
Zechariah the firstborn, 1Ch 9:21
Jediael the second,
Zebadiah the third,
Jathniel the fourth,
3 Elam the fifth,
Jehohanan the sixth
and Eliehoenai the seventh.
4 Obed-Edom also had sons:
Shemaiah the firstborn,
Jehozabad the second,
Joah the third,
Sakar the fourth,
Nethanel the fifth,
5 Ammiel the sixth,
Issachar the seventh
and Peullethai the eighth.
(For God had blessed Obed-Edom.) 2Sa 6:10; 1Ch 13:13

6 Obed-Edom's son Shemaiah
also had sons, who were
leaders in their father's
family because they were
very capable men. 7 The
sons of Shemaiah: Othni,
Rephael, Obed and Elza-
bad; his relatives Elihu and
Semakiah were also able
men. 8 All these were de-
scendants of Obed-Edom;
they and their sons and
their relatives were capable
men with the strength to
do the work — descendants
of Obed-Edom, 62 in all.
9 Meshelemiah had sons and
relatives, who were able
men — 18 in all.
10 Hosah the Merarite had sons:
Shimri the first (although he
was not the firstborn, his father had appointed him the
first), 11 Hilkiah the second,

Tabaliah the third and Zechariah the fourth. The sons
and relatives of Hosah were
13 in all. Dt 21:16; 1Ch 5:1

12 These divisions of the gatekeepers, through their leaders, had
duties for ministering in the temple of the LORD, just as their relatives had. 13 Lots were cast for each
gate, according to their families,
young and old alike. 1Ch 24:5,31; 25:8

14 The lot for the East Gate fell to
Shelemiah.[a] Then lots were cast
for his son Zechariah, a wise counselor, and the lot for the North
Gate fell to him. 15 The lot for the
South Gate fell to Obed-Edom,
and the lot for the storehouse fell
to his sons. 16 The lots for the West
Gate and the Shalleketh Gate on
the upper road fell to Shuppim
and Hosah. 1Ch 9:18,21; 13:13

Guard was alongside of guard:
17 There were six Levites a day on
the east, four a day on the north,
four a day on the south and two at
a time at the storehouse. 18 As for
the court[b] to the west, there were
four at the road and two at the
court[b] itself.

19 These were the divisions of
the gatekeepers who were descendants of Korah and Merari.
2Ch 35:15; Ne 7:1; Eze 44:11

The Treasurers and Other Officials

20 Their fellow Levites were[c] in
charge of the treasuries of the
house of God and the treasuries
for the dedicated things.
1Ch 28:12; 2Ch 24:5

21 The descendants of Ladan,
who were Gershonites through Ladan and who were heads of families belonging to Ladan the Gershonite, were Jehieli, 22 the sons
of Jehieli, Zetham and his brother
Joel. They were in charge of the
treasuries of the temple of the
LORD. 1Ch 23:7; 29:8

23 From the Amramites, the Izharites, the Hebronites and the
Uzzielites: Nu 3:27

24 Shubael, a descendant of Gershom son of Moses, was
the official in charge of the
treasuries. 25 His relatives
through Eliezer: Rehabiah
his son, Jeshaiah his son,
Joram his son, Zikri his
son and Shelomith his son.
26 Shelomith and his relatives were in charge of all
the treasuries for the things
dedicated by King David, by
the heads of families who
were the commanders of
thousands and command-
ers of hundreds, and by the
other army commanders.
27 Some of the plunder taken
in battle they dedicated for
the repair of the temple of
the LORD. 28 And everything
dedicated by Samuel the
seer and by Saul son of
Kish, Abner son of Ner and
Joab son of Zeruiah, and all

[a] 14 A variant of *Meshelemiah* [b] 18 The meaning of the Hebrew for this word is uncertain. [c] 20 Septuagint; Hebrew *As for the Levites, Ahijah was*

the other dedicated things
were in the care of Shelomith and his relatives.
1Sa 9:9; 2Sa 8:11; 1Ch 23:18
29 From the Izharites: Kenaniah
and his sons were assigned
duties away from the tem-
ple, as officials and judges
over Israel. 1Ch 23:4; Ne 11:16
30 From the Hebronites: Hashabiah and his relatives—
seventeen hundred able
men—were responsible in
Israel west of the Jordan
for all the work of the LORD
and for the king's service.
31 As for the Hebronites, Jeriah was their chief according to the genealogical records of their families. In
the fortieth year of David's
reign a search was made
in the records, and capable
men among the Hebronites
were found at Jazer in Gilead. 32 Jeriah had twenty-sev-
en hundred relatives, who
were able men and heads
of families, and King David
put them in charge of the
Reubenites, the Gadites and
the half-tribe of Manasseh
for every matter pertaining
to God and for the affairs of
the king. 1Ch 23:19; 27:17

Army Divisions

27 This is the list of the Israelites—heads of families,
commanders of thousands and
commanders of hundreds, and
their officers, who served the king
in all that concerned the army divisions that were on duty month by
month throughout the year. Each
division consisted of 24,000 men.

2 In charge of the first division,
for the first month, was Jashobeam son of Zabdiel.
There were 24,000 men in his
division. 3 He was a descendant of Perez and chief of all
the army officers for the first
month. 2Sa 23:8; 1Ch 11:11
4 In charge of the division for
the second month was Dodai
the Ahohite; Mikloth was the
leader of his division. There
were 24,000 men in his division. 2Sa 23:9
5 The third army commander, for
the third month, was Benaiah son of Jehoiada the priest.
He was chief and there were
24,000 men in his division.
6 This was the Benaiah who
was a mighty warrior among
the Thirty and was over the
Thirty. His son Ammizabad
was in charge of his division.
7 The fourth, for the fourth
month, was Asahel the brother of Joab; his son Zebadiah
was his successor. There were
24,000 men in his division.
2Sa 2:18; 1Ch 11:26
8 The fifth, for the fifth month,
was the commander Sham-
huth the Izrahite. There were
24,000 men in his division.
1Ch 11:27

9 The sixth, for the sixth month, was Ira the son of Ikkesh the Tekoite. There were 24,000 men in his division.
2Sa 23:26; 1Ch 11:28

10 The seventh, for the seventh month, was Helez the Pelonite, an Ephraimite. There were 24,000 men in his division. 2Sa 23:26; 1Ch 11:27

11 The eighth, for the eighth month, was Sibbekai the Hushathite, a Zerahite. There were 24,000 men in his division. 2Sa 21:18

12 The ninth, for the ninth month, was Abiezer the Anathothite, a Benjamite. There were 24,000 men in his division.
2Sa 23:27; 1Ch 11:28

13 The tenth, for the tenth month, was Maharai the Netophathite, a Zerahite. There were 24,000 men in his division.
2Sa 23:28; 1Ch 11:30

14 The eleventh, for the eleventh month, was Benaiah the Pirathonite, an Ephraimite. There were 24,000 men in his division. 1Ch 11:31

15 The twelfth, for the twelfth month, was Heldai the Netophathite, from the family of Othniel. There were 24,000 men in his division.
Jos 15:17; 2Sa 23:29

Leaders of the Tribes

16 The leaders of the tribes of Israel:
over the Reubenites: Eliezer son of Zikri;
over the Simeonites: Shephatiah son of Maakah;
17 over Levi: Hashabiah son of Kemuel; 1Ch 26:30
over Aaron: Zadok; 1Ch 12:28
18 over Judah: Elihu, a brother of David;
over Issachar: Omri son of Michael;
19 over Zebulun: Ishmaiah son of Obadiah;
over Naphtali: Jerimoth son of Azriel;
20 over the Ephraimites: Hoshea son of Azaziah;
over half the tribe of Manasseh: Joel son of Pedaiah;
21 over the half-tribe of Manasseh in Gilead: Iddo son of Zechariah;
over Benjamin: Jaasiel son of Abner;
22 over Dan: Azarel son of Jeroham.

These were the leaders of the tribes of Israel.

23 David did not take the number of the men twenty years old or less, because the LORD had promised to make Israel as numerous as the stars in the sky.
24 Joab son of Zeruiah began to count the men but did not finish. God's wrath came on Israel on account of this numbering, and the number was not entered in the book[a] of the annals of King David. Ge 15:5; 2Sa 24:15

[a] 24 Septuagint; Hebrew *number*

The King's Overseers

25 Azmaveth son of Adiel was in charge of the royal storehouses.

Jonathan son of Uzziah was in charge of the storehouses in the outlying districts, in the towns, the villages and the watchtowers.

26 Ezri son of Kelub was in charge of the workers who farmed the land.

27 Shimei the Ramathite was in charge of the vineyards.

Zabdi the Shiphmite was in charge of the produce of the vineyards for the wine vats.

28 Baal-Hanan the Gederite was in charge of the olive and sycamore-fig trees in the western foothills. 1Ki 10:27

Joash was in charge of the supplies of olive oil.

29 Shitrai the Sharonite was in charge of the herds grazing in Sharon.

Shaphat son of Adlai was in charge of the herds in the valleys.

30 Obil the Ishmaelite was in charge of the camels.

Jehdeiah the Meronothite was in charge of the donkeys.

31 Jaziz the Hagrite was in charge of the flocks. 1Ch 5:10

All these were the officials in charge of King David's property.

32 Jonathan, David's uncle, was a counselor, a man of insight and a scribe. Jehiel son of Hakmoni took care of the king's sons.

33 Ahithophel was the king's counselor. 2Sa 15:12

Hushai the Arkite was the king's confidant. 34 Ahithophel was succeeded by Jehoiada son of Benaiah and by Abiathar. 2Sa 15:37; 1Ki 1:7

Joab was the commander of the royal army. 1Ch 11:6

David's Plans for the Temple

28 David summoned all the officials of Israel to assemble at Jerusalem: the officers over the tribes, the commanders of the divisions in the service of the king, the commanders of thousands and commanders of hundreds, and the officials in charge of all the property and livestock belonging to the king and his sons, together with the palace officials, the warriors and all the brave fighting men. 1Ch 27:1-31

2 King David rose to his feet and said: "Listen to me, my fellow Israelites, my people. I had it in my heart to build a house as a place of rest for the ark of the covenant of the LORD, for the footstool of our God, and I made plans to build it. 3 But God said to me, 'You are not to build a house for my Name, because you are a warrior and have shed blood.' 1Ch 22:8; Ps 132:7

4 "Yet the LORD, the God of Israel, chose me from my whole family to be king over Israel forever. He chose Judah as leader, and from the tribe of Judah he chose my family, and from my father's sons he was pleased to make me king over all Israel. 5 Of all my sons — and the LORD has given me many — he has chosen my son Solomon to sit on

the throne of the kingdom of the
LORD over Israel. 6He said to me:
'Solomon your son is the one who
will build my house and my courts,
for I have chosen him to be my son,
and I will be his father. 7I will establish his kingdom forever if he
is unswerving in carrying out my
commands and laws, as is being
done at this time.' 2Sa 7:13; 1Ch 22:13

8"So now I charge you in the
sight of all Israel and of the assembly of the LORD, and in the
hearing of our God: Be careful to
follow all the commands of the
LORD your God, that you may possess this good land and pass it on
as an inheritance to your descendants forever. Dt 4:1; 6:1

9"And you, my son Solomon, acknowledge the God of your father,
and serve him with wholehearted
devotion and with a willing mind,
for the LORD searches every heart
and understands every desire and
every thought. If you seek him, he
will be found by you; but if you
forsake him, he will reject you forever. 10Consider now, for the LORD
has chosen you to build a house
as the sanctuary. Be strong and do
the work." 1Sa 16:7; 2Ch 15:2

11Then David gave his son Solomon the plans for the portico of
the temple, its buildings, its storerooms, its upper parts, its inner
rooms and the place of atonement.
12He gave him the plans of all that
the Spirit had put in his mind for
the courts of the temple of the LORD
and all the surrounding rooms, for
the treasuries of the temple of God
and for the treasuries for the dedicated things. 13He gave him instructions for the divisions of the priests
and Levites, and for all the work of
serving in the temple of the LORD,
as well as for all the articles to be
used in its service. 14He designated
the weight of gold for all the gold
articles to be used in various kinds
of service, and the weight of silver
for all the silver articles to be used
in various kinds of service: 15the
weight of gold for the gold lampstands and their lamps, with the
weight for each lampstand and
its lamps; and the weight of silver for each silver lampstand and
its lamps, according to the use of
each lampstand; 16the weight of
gold for each table for consecrated
bread; the weight of silver for the
silver tables; 17the weight of pure
gold for the forks, sprinkling bowls
and pitchers; the weight of gold for
each gold dish; the weight of silver for each silver dish; 18and the
weight of the refined gold for the
altar of incense. He also gave him
the plan for the chariot, that is, the
cherubim of gold that spread their
wings and overshadow the ark of
the covenant of the LORD.
Ex 25:18-22; 30:1-10; 1Ch 24:1

19"All this," David said, "I have
in writing as a result of the LORD's
hand on me, and he enabled me
to understand all the details of the
plan." Ex 25:9; 1Ki 6:38

20David also said to Solomon his
son, "Be strong and courageous,

and do the work. Do not be afraid
or discouraged, for the LORD God,
my God, is with you. He will not
fail you or forsake you until all the
work for the service of the temple
of the LORD is finished. 21The divisions of the priests and Levites are
ready for all the work on the temple of God, and every willing person skilled in any craft will help
you in all the work. The officials
and all the people will obey your
every command." Ex 35:25-36:5; Dt 31:6

Gifts for Building the Temple

29 Then King David said to
the whole assembly: "My
son Solomon, the one whom God
has chosen, is young and inexperienced. The task is great, because
this palatial structure is not for
man but for the LORD God. 2With all
my resources I have provided for
the temple of my God — gold for
the gold work, silver for the silver,
bronze for the bronze, iron for the
iron and wood for the wood, as well
as onyx for the settings, turquoise,[a]
stones of various colors, and all
kinds of fine stone and marble —
all of these in large quantities. 3Be-
sides, in my devotion to the temple
of my God I now give my personal
treasures of gold and silver for the
temple of my God, over and above
everything I have provided for
this holy temple: 4three thousand
talents[b] of gold (gold of Ophir)
and seven thousand talents[c] of refined silver, for the overlaying of
the walls of the buildings, 5for the
gold work and the silver work, and
for all the work to be done by the
craftsmen. Now, who is willing to
consecrate themselves to the LORD
today?" 1Ch 22:14; Isa 54:11
6Then the leaders of families,
the officers of the tribes of Israel,
the commanders of thousands and
commanders of hundreds, and
the officials in charge of the king's
work gave willingly. 7They gave toward the work on the temple of
God five thousand talents[d] and ten
thousand darics[e] of gold, ten thousand talents[f] of silver, eighteen
thousand talents[g] of bronze and a
hundred thousand talents[h] of iron.
8Anyone who had precious stones
gave them to the treasury of the
temple of the LORD in the custody
of Jehiel the Gershonite. 9The people rejoiced at the willing response
of their leaders, for they had given
freely and wholeheartedly to the
LORD. David the king also rejoiced
greatly. 1Ki 8:61; 1Ch 26:21; 2Co 9:7

David's Prayer

10David praised the LORD in the
presence of the whole assembly,
saying,

[a] 2 The meaning of the Hebrew for this word is uncertain. [b] 4 That is, about 110 tons or about 100 metric tons [c] 4 That is, about 260 tons or about 235 metric tons [d] 7 That is, about 190 tons or about 170 metric tons [e] 7 That is, about 185 pounds or about 84 kilograms [f] 7 That is, about 380 tons or about 340 metric tons [g] 7 That is, about 675 tons or about 610 metric tons [h] 7 That is, about 3,800 tons or about 3,400 metric tons

"Praise be to you, LORD,
the God of our father Israel,
from everlasting to
everlasting.
11Yours, LORD, is the greatness
and the power Ps 24:8; 59:17
and the glory and the
majesty and the
splendor,
for everything in heaven and
earth is yours. Ps 89:11
Yours, LORD, is the kingdom;
you are exalted as head over
all. Rev 5:12-13
12Wealth and honor come from
you; 2Ch 1:12
you are the ruler of all
things. 2Ch 20:6; Ro 11:36
In your hands are strength and
power
to exalt and give strength to
all.
13Now, our God, we give you
thanks,
and praise your glorious
name.

14"But who am I, and who are
my people, that we should be able
to give as generously as this? Everything comes from you, and we
have given you only what comes
from your hand. 15We are foreigners and strangers in your sight, as
were all our ancestors. Our days
on earth are like a shadow, without hope. 16LORD our God, all this
abundance that we have provided for building you a temple for
your Holy Name comes from your
hand, and all of it belongs to you.
17I know, my God, that you test the
heart and are pleased with integrity. All these things I have given
willingly and with honest intent.
And now I have seen with joy how
willingly your people who are
here have given to you. 18LORD, the
God of our fathers Abraham, Isaac
and Israel, keep these desires and
thoughts in the hearts of your people forever, and keep their hearts
loyal to you. 19And give my son Solomon the wholehearted devotion
to keep your commands, statutes
and decrees and to do everything
to build the palatial structure for
which I have provided."
1Ch 22:14; 28:9; Ps 72:1

20Then David said to the whole
assembly, "Praise the LORD your
God." So they all praised the LORD,
the God of their fathers; they bowed
down, prostrating themselves before the LORD and the king.

Solomon Acknowledged as King

21The next day they made sacrifices to the LORD and presented
burnt offerings to him: a thousand bulls, a thousand rams and
a thousand male lambs, together with their drink offerings, and
other sacrifices in abundance for
all Israel. 22They ate and drank
with great joy in the presence of
the LORD that day. 1Ki 8:62; 1Ch 23:1

Then they acknowledged Solomon son of David as king a second time, anointing him before
the LORD to be ruler and Zadok to
be priest. 23So Solomon sat on the

throne of the LORD as king in place
of his father David. He prospered
and all Israel obeyed him. 24All the
officers and warriors, as well as all
of King David's sons, pledged their
submission to King Solomon.
1Ki 1:33-39; 2:12

25The LORD highly exalted Solomon in the sight of all Israel and
bestowed on him royal splendor
such as no king over Israel ever
had before. 1Ki 1:28-53; 3:13

The Death of David

26David son of Jesse was king
over all Israel. 27He ruled over Israel forty years — seven in Hebron
and thirty-three in Jerusalem.
28He died at a good old age, having enjoyed long life, wealth and
honor. His son Solomon succeeded him as king.
Ge 15:15; 1Ki 2:10-12; 1Ch 23:1

29As for the events of King David's reign, from beginning to end,
they are written in the records of
Samuel the seer, the records of Nathan the prophet and the records
of Gad the seer, 30together with
the details of his reign and power,
and the circumstances that surrounded him and Israel and the
kingdoms of all the other lands.
1Sa 9:9; 22:5; 2Sa 7:2

2 CHRONICLES

Solomon Asks for Wisdom

1 Solomon son of David established himself firmly over his
kingdom, for the LORD his God
was with him and made him exceedingly great.

Ge 39:2; 1Ki 2:12,26; 1Ch 29:25

2Then Solomon spoke to all
Israel — to the commanders of
thousands and commanders of
hundreds, to the judges and to all
the leaders in Israel, the heads of
families — 3and Solomon and the
whole assembly went to the high
place at Gibeon, for God's tent of
meeting was there, which Moses
the LORD's servant had made in
the wilderness. 4Now David had
brought up the ark of God from
Kiriath Jearim to the place he had
prepared for it, because he had
pitched a tent for it in Jerusalem.
5But the bronze altar that Bezalel son of Uri, the son of Hur, had
made was in Gibeon in front of
the tabernacle of the LORD; so Solomon and the assembly inquired
of him there. 6Solomon went up to
the bronze altar before the LORD
in the tent of meeting and offered
a thousand burnt offerings on it.

Ex 36:8; 38:2; 2Sa 6:17

7That night God appeared to
Solomon and said to him, "Ask
for whatever you want me to give
you."

2Ch 7:12

8Solomon answered God, "You
have shown great kindness to David my father and have made me
king in his place. 9Now, LORD God,
let your promise to my father David be confirmed, for you have
made me king over a people who
are as numerous as the dust of
the earth. 10Give me wisdom and
knowledge, that I may lead this
people, for who is able to govern
this great people of yours?"

Nu 27:17; 1Ch 28:5

11God said to Solomon, "Since
this is your heart's desire and
you have not asked for wealth,
possessions or honor, nor for the
death of your enemies, and since
you have not asked for a long life
but for wisdom and knowledge
to govern my people over whom
I have made you king, 12there-
fore wisdom and knowledge will
be given you. And I will also give
you wealth, possessions and hon-
or, such as no king who was before you ever had and none after
you will have."

1Ch 29:25; 2Ch 9:22; Ne 13:26

13Then Solomon went to Jerusalem from the high place at Gibeon,
from before the tent of meeting.
And he reigned over Israel.

14Solomon accumulated chariots and horses; he had fourteen
hundred chariots and twelve

thousand horses,[a] which he kept
in the chariot cities and also with
him in Jerusalem. 15The king
made silver and gold as common
in Jerusalem as stones, and cedar
as plentiful as sycamore-fig trees
in the foothills. 16Solomon's horses were imported from Egypt and
from Kue[b] — the royal merchants
purchased them from Kue at the
current price. 17They imported a
chariot from Egypt for six hundred shekels[c] of silver, and a horse
for a hundred and fifty.[d] They also
exported them to all the kings of
the Hittites and of the Arameans.

1Ki 3:4-15; 10:26-29; 2Ch 9:25-28

Preparations for Building the Temple

2[e] Solomon gave orders to build
a temple for the Name of the
LORD and a royal palace for himself. 2He conscripted 70,000 men
as carriers and 80,000 as stonecutters in the hills and 3,600 as
foremen over them.

ver 18; 2Ch 10:4; Ecc 2:4

3Solomon sent this message to
Hiram[f] king of Tyre:

"Send me cedar logs as you
did for my father David when
you sent him cedar to build
a palace to live in. 4Now I am
about to build a temple for
the Name of the LORD my God
and to dedicate it to him for
burning fragrant incense before him, for setting out the
consecrated bread regularly,
and for making burnt offerings every morning and evening and on the Sabbaths, at
the New Moons and at the appointed festivals of the LORD
our God. This is a lasting ordinance for Israel.

Ex 25:30; Nu 28:9-10; Dt 12:5

5"The temple I am going to
build will be great, because
our God is greater than all
other gods. 6But who is able to
build a temple for him, since
the heavens, even the highest
heavens, cannot contain him?
Who then am I to build a temple for him, except as a place
to burn sacrifices before him?

1Ki 8:27; 1Ch 16:25

7"Send me, therefore, a
man skilled to work in gold
and silver, bronze and iron,
and in purple, crimson and
blue yarn, and experienced in
the art of engraving, to work
in Judah and Jerusalem with
my skilled workers, whom
my father David provided.

1Ch 22:16

8"Send me also cedar, ju-
niper and algum[g] logs from
Lebanon, for I know that your
servants are skilled in cutting
timber there. My servants will

[a] 14 Or *charioteers* [b] 16 Probably Cilicia [c] 17 That is, about 15 pounds or about 6.9 kilograms [d] 17 That is, about 3 3/4 pounds or about 1.7 kilograms [e] In Hebrew texts 2:1 is numbered 1:18, and 2:2-18 is numbered 2:1-17. [f] 3 Hebrew *Huram*, a variant of *Hiram*; also in verses 11 and 12 [g] 8 Probably a variant of *almug*

work with yours 9to provide
me with plenty of lumber, because the temple I build must
be large and magnificent. 10I
will give your servants, the
woodsmen who cut the tim-
ber, twenty thousand cors[a] of
ground wheat, twenty thousand cors[b] of barley, twenty
thousand baths[c] of wine and
twenty thousand baths of olive oil." Ezr 3:7

11Hiram king of Tyre replied by
letter to Solomon:

"Because the LORD loves his
people, he has made you their
king." 1Ki 10:9; 2Ch 9:8

12And Hiram added:

"Praise be to the LORD, the
God of Israel, who made heav-
en and earth! He has given
King David a wise son, endowed with intelligence and
discernment, who will build a
temple for the LORD and a palace for himself. Ps 33:6; 102:25

13"I am sending you Hu-
ram-Abi, a man of great skill,
14whose mother was from Dan
and whose father was from
Tyre. He is trained to work in
gold and silver, bronze and
iron, stone and wood, and
with purple and blue and
crimson yarn and fine linen.
He is experienced in all kinds
of engraving and can execute
any design given to him. He
will work with your skilled
workers and with those of my
lord, David your father.
Ex 31:6; 1Ki 7:13

15"Now let my lord send his
servants the wheat and barley
and the olive oil and wine he
promised, 16and we will cut all
the logs from Lebanon that
you need and will float them
as rafts by sea down to Joppa.
You can then take them up to
Jerusalem." Jos 19:46; Jnh 1:3

17Solomon took a census of all
the foreigners residing in Israel,
after the census his father David
had taken; and they were found to
be 153,600. 18He assigned 70,000 of
them to be carriers and 80,000 to
be stonecutters in the hills, with
3,600 foremen over them to keep
the people working. 1Ki 5:1-16; 1Ch 22:2

Solomon Builds the Temple

3 Then Solomon began to build
the temple of the LORD in Jerusalem on Mount Moriah, where
the LORD had appeared to his father David. It was on the threshing floor of Araunah[d] the Jebusite,
the place provided by David. 2He
began building on the second day
of the second month in the fourth
year of his reign. 1Ch 21:18; Ac 7:47

[a] *10* That is, probably about 3,600 tons or about 3,200 metric tons of wheat
[b] *10* That is, probably about 3,000 tons or about 2,700 metric tons of barley
[c] *10* That is, about 120,000 gallons or about 440,000 liters
[d] *1* Hebrew *Ornan,* a variant of *Araunah*

3 The foundation Solomon laid
for building the temple of God was
sixty cubits long and twenty cubits wide[a] (using the cubit of the
old standard). 4 The portico at the
front of the temple was twenty cubits[b] long across the width of the
building and twenty[c] cubits high.
Eze 41:2

He overlaid the inside with pure
gold. 5 He paneled the main hall
with juniper and covered it with
fine gold and decorated it with
palm tree and chain designs. 6 He
adorned the temple with precious
stones. And the gold he used was
gold of Parvaim. 7 He overlaid the
ceiling beams, doorframes, walls
and doors of the temple with gold,
and he carved cherubim on the
walls. Ge 3:24; 1Ki 6:29-35; Eze 40:16

8 He built the Most Holy Place, its
length corresponding to the width
of the temple — twenty cubits
long and twenty cubits wide. He
overlaid the inside with six hundred talents[d] of fine gold. 9 The
gold nails weighed fifty shekels.[e]
He also overlaid the upper parts
with gold. Ex 26:32-33

10 For the Most Holy Place he
made a pair of sculptured cherubim and overlaid them with gold.
11 The total wingspan of the cherubim was twenty cubits. One wing
of the first cherub was five cubits[f]
long and touched the temple wall,
while its other wing, also five cubits long, touched the wing of the
other cherub. 12 Similarly one wing
of the second cherub was five cubits long and touched the other
temple wall, and its other wing,
also five cubits long, touched the
wing of the first cherub. 13 The
wings of these cherubim extended twenty cubits. They stood on
their feet, facing the main hall.[g]
Ex 25:18

14 He made the curtain of blue,
purple and crimson yarn and
fine linen, with cherubim worked
into it. 1Ki 6:1-29

15 For the front of the temple he
made two pillars, which together
were thirty-five cubits[h] long, each
with a capital five cubits high. 16 He
made interwoven chains[i] and put
them on top of the pillars. He also
made a hundred pomegranates
and attached them to the chains.
17 He erected the pillars in the front
of the temple, one to the south
and one to the north. The one to
the south he named Jakin[j] and the
one to the north Boaz.[k]
1Ki 7:15,17,20

[a] *3* That is, about 90 feet long and 30 feet wide or about 27 meters long and 9 meters wide [b] *4* That is, about 30 feet or about 9 meters; also in verses 8, 11 and 13 [c] *4* Some Septuagint and Syriac manuscripts; Hebrew *and a hundred and twenty* [d] *8* That is, about 23 tons or about 21 metric tons [e] *9* That is, about 1 1/4 pounds or about 575 grams [f] *11* That is, about 7 1/2 feet or about 2.3 meters; also in verse 15 [g] *13* Or *facing inward* [h] *15* That is, about 53 feet or about 16 meters [i] *16* Or possibly *made chains in the inner sanctuary*; the meaning of the Hebrew for this phrase is uncertain. [j] *17* *Jakin* probably means *he establishes.* [k] *17* *Boaz* probably means *in him is strength.*

The Temple's Furnishings

4 He made a bronze altar twenty cubits long, twenty cubits
wide and ten cubits high.[a] 2 He
made the Sea of cast metal, circular in shape, measuring ten cubits
from rim to rim and five cubits[b]
high. It took a line of thirty cubits[c]
to measure around it. 3 Below the
rim, figures of bulls encircled it—
ten to a cubit.[d] The bulls were cast
in two rows in one piece with the
Sea. Ex 27:1-2; 2Ki 16:14
4 The Sea stood on twelve bulls,
three facing north, three facing
west, three facing south and three
facing east. The Sea rested on top
of them, and their hindquarters
were toward the center. 5 It was a
handbreadth[e] in thickness, and its
rim was like the rim of a cup, like
a lily blossom. It held three thousand baths.[f]
6 He then made ten basins for
washing and placed five on the
south side and five on the north.
In them the things to be used for
the burnt offerings were rinsed,
but the Sea was to be used by the
priests for washing. 1Ki 7:23-26,38-51
7 He made ten gold lampstands
according to the specifications for
them and placed them in the temple, five on the south side and five
on the north. Ex 25:31,40
8 He made ten tables and placed
them in the temple, five on the
south side and five on the north.
He also made a hundred gold
sprinkling bowls. Ex 25:23; Nu 4:14
9 He made the courtyard of the
priests, and the large court and
the doors for the court, and overlaid the doors with bronze. 10 He
placed the Sea on the south side,
at the southeast corner.
1Ki 6:36; 2Ki 21:5
11 And Huram also made the
pots and shovels and sprinkling
bowls.

So Huram finished the work he
had undertaken for King Solomon
in the temple of God: 1Ki 7:14

12 the two pillars;
the two bowl-shaped capitals
on top of the pillars;
the two sets of network decorating the two bowl-shaped
capitals on top of the pillars;
13 the four hundred pome-
granates for the two sets
of network (two rows of
pomegranates for each network, decorating the bowl-
shaped capitals on top of
the pillars);
14 the stands with their basins;
1Ki 7:27-30
15 the Sea and the twelve bulls
under it;
16 the pots, shovels, meat forks
and all related articles.

[a] *1* That is, about 30 feet long and wide and 15 feet high or about 9 meters long and wide and 4.5 meters high [b] *2* That is, about 7 1/2 feet or about 2.3 meters [c] *2* That is, about 45 feet or about 14 meters [d] *3* That is, about 18 inches or about 45 centimeters [e] *5* That is, about 3 inches or about 7.5 centimeters [f] *5* That is, about 18,000 gallons or about 66,000 liters

All the objects that Huram-Abi
made for King Solomon for the
temple of the LORD were of polished bronze. 17The king had them
cast in clay molds in the plain
of the Jordan between Sukkoth
and Zarethan.[a] 18All these things
that Solomon made amounted
to so much that the weight of the
bronze could not be calculated.
1Ki 7:13,23

19Solomon also made all the furnishings that were in God's temple:

the golden altar;
the tables on which was the
bread of the Presence;
Ex 25:23,30
20the lampstands of pure gold
with their lamps, to burn in
front of the inner sanctuary
as prescribed; Ex 25:31
21the gold floral work and
lamps and tongs (they were
solid gold);
22the pure gold wick trimmers,
sprinkling bowls, dishes
and censers; and the gold
doors of the temple: the inner doors to the Most Holy
Place and the doors of the
main hall. Lev 10:1; Nu 7:14

5 When all the work Solomon
had done for the temple of the
LORD was finished, he brought in
the things his father David had
dedicated — the silver and gold
and all the furnishings — and he
placed them in the treasuries of
God's temple. 2Sa 8:11; 1Ki 6:14

The Ark Brought to the Temple

2Then Solomon summoned to
Jerusalem the elders of Israel, all
the heads of the tribes and the
chiefs of the Israelite families, to
bring up the ark of the LORD's covenant from Zion, the City of David. 3And all the Israelites came
together to the king at the time of
the festival in the seventh month.
2Sa 6:12; 1Ch 9:1; 15:25

4When all the elders of Israel
had arrived, the Levites took up
the ark, 5and they brought up the
ark and the tent of meeting and
all the sacred furnishings in it.
The Levitical priests carried them
up; 6and King Solomon and the
entire assembly of Israel that had
gathered about him were before
the ark, sacrificing so many sheep
and cattle that they could not be
recorded or counted. Nu 3:31; 1Ch 15:2

7The priests then brought the
ark of the LORD's covenant to its
place in the inner sanctuary of the
temple, the Most Holy Place, and
put it beneath the wings of the
cherubim. 8The cherubim spread
their wings over the place of the
ark and covered the ark and its
carrying poles. 9These poles were
so long that their ends, extending
from the ark, could be seen from
in front of the inner sanctuary, but
not from outside the Holy Place;
and they are still there today.
10There was nothing in the ark ex-

[a] 17 Hebrew *Zeredatha,* a variant of *Zarethan*

cept the two tablets that Moses
had placed in it at Horeb, where
the LORD made a covenant with
the Israelites after they came out
of Egypt. Dt 10:2; Ge 3:24; Rev 11:19

11 The priests then withdrew
from the Holy Place. All the priests
who were there had consecrated
themselves, regardless of their
divisions. 12 All the Levites who
were musicians — Asaph, Heman,
Jeduthun and their sons and relatives — stood on the east side
of the altar, dressed in fine linen
and playing cymbals, harps and
lyres. They were accompanied by
120 priests sounding trumpets.
13 The trumpeters and musicians
joined in unison to give praise and
thanks to the LORD. Accompanied
by trumpets, cymbals and other
instruments, the singers raised
their voices in praise to the LORD
and sang: 1Ch 15:24; 25:1

"He is good;
his love endures forever."

1Ch 16:34,41; 2Ch 7:3

Then the temple of the LORD
was filled with the cloud, 14 and
the priests could not perform
their service because of the cloud,
for the glory of the LORD filled the
temple of God. Ex 29:43; 2Ch 7:2

6 Then Solomon said, "The LORD
has said that he would dwell in
a dark cloud; 2 I have built a magnificent temple for you, a place for
you to dwell forever."

1Ki 8:12-50; Ps 135:21

3 While the whole assembly of
Israel was standing there, the king
turned around and blessed them.
4 Then he said:

"Praise be to the LORD, the
God of Israel, who with his
hands has fulfilled what he
promised with his mouth to
my father David. For he said,
5 'Since the day I brought my
people out of Egypt, I have
not chosen a city in any tribe
of Israel to have a temple
built so that my Name might
be there, nor have I chosen
anyone to be ruler over my
people Israel. 6 But now I have
chosen Jerusalem for my
Name to be there, and I have
chosen David to rule my people Israel.' 1Ch 28:4; 2Ch 12:13

7 "My father David had it in
his heart to build a temple for
the Name of the LORD, the God
of Israel. 8 But the LORD said
to my father David, 'You did
well to have it in your heart to
build a temple for my Name.
9 Nevertheless, you are not the
one to build the temple, but
your son, your own flesh and
blood — he is the one who
will build the temple for my
Name.' 1Sa 10:7; Ac 7:46

10 "The LORD has kept the
promise he made. I have succeeded David my father and
now I sit on the throne of Israel, just as the LORD promised,
and I have built the temple for

the Name of the LORD, the God
of Israel. 11There I have placed
the ark, in which is the covenant of the LORD that he made
with the people of Israel."

1Ki 8:1-21; 2Ch 5:10

Solomon's Prayer of Dedication

12Then Solomon stood before
the altar of the LORD in front of
the whole assembly of Israel and
spread out his hands. 13Now he
had made a bronze platform, five
cubits long, five cubits wide and
three cubits high,[a] and had placed
it in the center of the outer court.
He stood on the platform and then
knelt down before the whole assembly of Israel and spread out
his hands toward heaven. 14He
said: Ne 8:4; Ps 95:6

"LORD, the God of Isra-
el, there is no God like you
in heaven or on earth — you
who keep your covenant of
love with your servants who
continue wholeheartedly in
your way. 15You have kept
your promise to your servant
David my father; with your
mouth you have promised
and with your hand you have
fulfilled it — as it is today.

Dt 7:9; 1Ch 22:10

16"Now, LORD, the God of
Israel, keep for your servant
David my father the promises you made to him when you
said, 'You shall never fail to
have a successor to sit before
me on the throne of Israel,
if only your descendants are
careful in all they do to walk
before me according to my
law, as you have done.' 17And
now, LORD, the God of Israel,
let your word that you promised your servant David come
true. 2Sa 7:13,15; 1Ki 2:4; 2Ch 7:18

18"But will God really dwell
on earth with humans? The
heavens, even the highest
heavens, cannot contain you.
How much less this temple
I have built! 19Yet, LORD my
God, give attention to your
servant's prayer and his plea
for mercy. Hear the cry and
the prayer that your servant
is praying in your presence.
20May your eyes be open toward this temple day and
night, this place of which
you said you would put your
Name there. May you hear
the prayer your servant prays
toward this place. 21Hear the
supplications of your servant and of your people Israel when they pray toward
this place. Hear from heav-
en, your dwelling place; and
when you hear, forgive.

Isa 43:25; Mic 7:18

22"When anyone wrongs
their neighbor and is required
to take an oath and they
come and swear the oath be-

[a] *13* That is, about 7 1/2 feet long and wide and 4 1/2 feet high or about 2.3 meters long and wide and 1.4 meters high

fore your altar in this temple,
23 then hear from heaven and
act. Judge between your servants, condemning the guilty
and bringing down on their
heads what they have done,
and vindicating the innocent
by treating them in accordance with their innocence.
Ex 22:11; Isa 3:11

24 "When your people Israel
have been defeated by an enemy because they have sinned
against you and when they
turn back and give praise to
your name, praying and making supplication before you in
this temple, 25 then hear from
heaven and forgive the sin of
your people Israel and bring
them back to the land you
gave to them and their ancestors. Lev 26:17

26 "When the heavens are
shut up and there is no rain
because your people have
sinned against you, and
when they pray toward this
place and give praise to your
name and turn from their sin
because you have afflicted
them, 27 then hear from heav-
en and forgive the sin of your
servants, your people Israel. Teach them the right way
to live, and send rain on the
land you gave your people for
an inheritance. 1Ki 17:1

28 "When famine or plague
comes to the land, or blight
or mildew, locusts or grasshoppers, or when enemies
besiege them in any of their
cities, whatever disaster or
disease may come, 29 and
when a prayer or plea is made
by anyone among your peo-
ple Israel — being aware of
their afflictions and pains,
and spreading out their
hands toward this temple —
30 then hear from heaven,
your dwelling place. Forgive,
and deal with everyone according to all they do, since
you know their hearts (for
you alone know the human
heart), 31 so that they will fear
you and walk in obedience to
you all the time they live in
the land you gave our ancestors. 1Sa 16:7; 1Ch 28:9; 2Ch 20:9

32 "As for the foreigner who
does not belong to your people Israel but has come from
a distant land because of your
great name and your mighty
hand and your outstretched
arm — when they come and
pray toward this temple,
33 then hear from heaven,
your dwelling place. Do whatever the foreigner asks of you,
so that all the peoples of the
earth may know your name
and fear you, as do your own
people Israel, and may know
that this house I have built
bears your Name.
2Ch 7:14; Jn 12:20

34 "When your people go to
war against their enemies,

wherever you send them, and
when they pray to you toward
this city you have chosen and
the temple I have built for
your Name, 35then hear from
heaven their prayer and their
plea, and uphold their cause.
Dt 28:7; 1Ch 5:20

36"When they sin against
you — for there is no one who
does not sin — and you become angry with them and
give them over to the enemy,
who takes them captive to a
land far away or near; 37and if
they have a change of heart in
the land where they are held
captive, and repent and plead
with you in the land of their
captivity and say, 'We have
sinned, we have done wrong
and acted wickedly'; 38and if
they turn back to you with
all their heart and soul in the
land of their captivity where
they were taken, and pray
toward the land you gave
their ancestors, toward the
city you have chosen and toward the temple I have built
for your Name; 39then from
heaven, your dwelling place,
hear their prayer and their
pleas, and uphold their cause.
And forgive your people, who
have sinned against you.
Job 15:14; Jas 3:1; 1Jn 1:8-10

40"Now, my God, may your
eyes be open and your ears attentive to the prayers offered
in this place. 1Ki 8:22-53

41"Now arise, LORD God,
and come to your
resting place,
1Ch 28:2; Isa 33:10
you and the ark of your
might.
May your priests, LORD
God, be clothed
with salvation,
Ps 132:16
may your faithful people
rejoice in your
goodness. Ps 116:12
42LORD God, do not reject
your anointed one.
Remember the great
love promised to
David your servant."
Ps 132:8-10

The Dedication of the Temple

7 When Solomon finished praying, fire came down from
heaven and consumed the burnt
offering and the sacrifices, and
the glory of the LORD filled the
temple. 2The priests could not
enter the temple of the LORD because the glory of the LORD filled
it. 3When all the Israelites saw the
fire coming down and the glory of the LORD above the temple,
they knelt on the pavement with
their faces to the ground, and they
worshiped and gave thanks to the
LORD, saying, Ex 29:43; 40:35; 2Ch 5:14

"He is good;
his love endures forever."

4Then the king and all the people offered sacrifices before the

LORD. 5And King Solomon offered
a sacrifice of twenty-two thousand head of cattle and a hundred
and twenty thousand sheep and
goats. So the king and all the people dedicated the temple of God.
6The priests took their positions,
as did the Levites with the LORD's
musical instruments, which King
David had made for praising the
LORD and which were used when
he gave thanks, saying, "His love
endures forever." Opposite the Levites, the priests blew their trumpets, and all the Israelites were
standing. 1Ch 15:16; 2Ch 5:12-13

7Solomon consecrated the middle part of the courtyard in front
of the temple of the LORD, and
there he offered burnt offerings
and the fat of the fellowship offerings, because the bronze altar
he had made could not hold the
burnt offerings, the grain offerings and the fat portions.

8So Solomon observed the festival at that time for seven days,
and all Israel with him — a vast
assembly, people from Lebo Hamath to the Wadi of Egypt. 9On the
eighth day they held an assembly,
for they had celebrated the dedication of the altar for seven days
and the festival for seven days
more. 10On the twenty-third day
of the seventh month he sent the
people to their homes, joyful and
glad in heart for the good things
the LORD had done for David and
Solomon and for his people Israel.
Lev 23:36; 2Ch 30:26

The LORD Appears to Solomon

11When Solomon had finished
the temple of the LORD and the
royal palace, and had succeeded in
carrying out all he had in mind to
do in the temple of the LORD and
in his own palace, 12the LORD appeared to him at night and said:

"I have heard your prayer
and have chosen this place for
myself as a temple for sacrifices. Dt 12:5

13"When I shut up the heavens so that there is no rain, or
command locusts to devour
the land or send a plague
among my people, 14if my
people, who are called by my
name, will humble them-
selves and pray and seek
my face and turn from their
wicked ways, then I will hear
from heaven, and I will forgive their sin and will heal
their land. 15Now my eyes will
be open and my ears attentive to the prayers offered in
this place. 16I have chosen and
consecrated this temple so
that my Name may be there
forever. My eyes and my heart
will always be there.
2Ch 6:27,37,40

17"As for you, if you walk
before me faithfully as David
your father did, and do all I
command, and observe my
decrees and laws, 18I will establish your royal throne, as
I covenanted with David your

father when I said, 'You shall never fail to have a successor to rule over Israel.'

1Ki 9:4; 2Ch 6:16

19 "But if you[a] turn away and forsake the decrees and commands I have given you[a] and go off to serve other gods and worship them, 20 then I will uproot Israel from my land, which I have given them, and will reject this temple I have consecrated for my Name. I will make it a byword and an object of ridicule among all peoples. 21 This temple will become a heap of rubble. All[b] who pass by will be appalled and say, 'Why has the LORD done such a thing to this land and to this temple?' 22 People will answer, 'Because they have forsaken the LORD, the God of their ancestors, who brought them out of Egypt, and have embraced other gods, worshiping and serving them — that is why he brought all this disaster on them.' "

1Ki 9:1-9; Dt 29:24

Solomon's Other Activities

8 At the end of twenty years, during which Solomon built the temple of the LORD and his own palace, 2 Solomon rebuilt the villages that Hiram[c] had given him, and settled Israelites in them. 3 Solomon then went to Hamath Zobah and captured it. 4 He also built up Tadmor in the desert and all the store cities he had built in Hamath. 5 He rebuilt Upper Beth Horon and Lower Beth Horon as fortified cities, with walls and with gates and bars, 6 as well as Baalath and all his store cities, and all the cities for his chariots and for his horses[d] — whatever he desired to build in Jerusalem, in Lebanon and throughout all the territory he ruled.

1Ch 7:24; 2Ch 14:7

7 There were still people left from the Hittites, Amorites, Perizzites, Hivites and Jebusites (these people were not Israelites). 8 Solomon conscripted the descendants of all these people remaining in the land — whom the Israelites had not destroyed — to serve as slave labor, as it is to this day. 9 But Solomon did not make slaves of the Israelites for his work; they were his fighting men, commanders of his captains, and commanders of his chariots and charioteers. 10 They were also King Solomon's chief officials — two hundred and fifty officials supervising the men.

Ge 10:16; 1Ki 4:6; 9:21

11 Solomon brought Pharaoh's daughter up from the City of David to the palace he had built for her, for he said, "My wife must not live in the palace of David king of Israel, because the places

[a] *19* The Hebrew is plural. [b] *21* See some Septuagint manuscripts, Old Latin, Syriac, Arabic and Targum; Hebrew *And though this temple is now so imposing, all* [c] *2* Hebrew *Huram*, a variant of *Hiram*; also in verse 18 [d] *6* Or *charioteers*

the ark of the LORD has entered
are holy." 1Ki 3:1; 7:8
12On the altar of the LORD that
he had built in front of the portico, Solomon sacrificed burnt offerings to the LORD, 13according
to the daily requirement for offerings commanded by Moses for
the Sabbaths, the New Moons and
the three annual festivals — the
Festival of Unleavened Bread, the
Festival of Weeks and the Festival of Tabernacles. 14In keeping
with the ordinance of his father
David, he appointed the divisions
of the priests for their duties, and
the Levites to lead the praise and
to assist the priests according to
each day's requirement. He also
appointed the gatekeepers by divisions for the various gates, because this was what David the
man of God had ordered. 15They
did not deviate from the king's
commands to the priests or to the
Levites in any matter, including
that of the treasuries.
Nu 28:3; 1Ch 25:1; Ne 12:24,36
16All Solomon's work was carried
out, from the day the foundation
of the temple of the LORD was laid
until its completion. So the temple of the LORD was finished.
17Then Solomon went to Ezion Geber and Elath on the coast
of Edom. 18And Hiram sent him
ships commanded by his own
men, sailors who knew the sea.
These, with Solomon's men,
sailed to Ophir and brought back
four hundred and fifty talents[a]
of gold, which they delivered to
King Solomon. 1Ki 9:10-28; 2Ch 9:9

The Queen of Sheba Visits Solomon

9 When the queen of Sheba
heard of Solomon's fame,
she came to Jerusalem to test
him with hard questions. Arriving with a very great caravan —
with camels carrying spices, large
quantities of gold, and precious
stones — she came to Solomon
and talked with him about all she
had on her mind. 2Solomon answered all her questions; nothing
was too hard for him to explain
to her. 3When the queen of Sheba saw the wisdom of Solomon,
as well as the palace he had built,
4the food on his table, the seating
of his officials, the attending servants in their robes, the cupbearers in their robes and the burnt offerings he made at[b] the temple of
the LORD, she was overwhelmed.
1Ki 5:12; Mt 12:42; Lk 11:31
5She said to the king, "The report I heard in my own country
about your achievements and
your wisdom is true. 6But I did
not believe what they said until I
came and saw with my own eyes.
Indeed, not even half the greatness of your wisdom was told me;
you have far exceeded the report
I heard. 7How happy your people
must be! How happy your officials,

[a] 18 That is, about 17 tons or about 15 metric tons [b] 4 Or *and the ascent by which he went up to*

who continually stand before you
and hear your wisdom! [8]Praise be
to the LORD your God, who has delighted in you and placed you on
his throne as king to rule for the
LORD your God. Because of the
love of your God for Israel and his
desire to uphold them forever, he
has made you king over them, to
maintain justice and righteousness." 1Ch 28:5; 29:23; 2Ch 2:11

[9]Then she gave the king 120 talents[a] of gold, large quantities of
spices, and precious stones. There
had never been such spices as
those the queen of Sheba gave to
King Solomon. 2Ch 8:18

[10](The servants of Hiram and the
servants of Solomon brought gold
from Ophir; they also brought algumwood[b] and precious stones.
[11]The king used the algumwood to
make steps for the temple of the
LORD and for the royal palace, and
to make harps and lyres for the
musicians. Nothing like them had
ever been seen in Judah.) 2Ch 8:18

[12]King Solomon gave the queen
of Sheba all she desired and asked
for; he gave her more than she
had brought to him. Then she left
and returned with her retinue to
her own country. 1Ki 10:1-13

Solomon's Splendor

[13]The weight of the gold that
Solomon received yearly was 666
talents,[c] [14]not including the revenues brought in by merchants and
traders. Also all the kings of Arabia and the governors of the territories brought gold and silver to
Solomon. 2Ch 17:11; Isa 21:13; Jer 25:24

[15]King Solomon made two hundred large shields of hammered
gold; six hundred shekels[d] of
hammered gold went into each
shield. [16]He also made three hundred small shields of hammered
gold, with three hundred shekels[e]
of gold in each shield. The king
put them in the Palace of the Forest of Lebanon. 1Ki 7:2; 2Ch 12:9

[17]Then the king made a great
throne covered with ivory and
overlaid with pure gold. [18]The
throne had six steps, and a footstool of gold was attached to it. On
both sides of the seat were armrests, with a lion standing beside
each of them. [19]Twelve lions stood
on the six steps, one at either end
of each step. Nothing like it had
ever been made for any other kingdom. [20]All King Solomon's goblets
were gold, and all the household
articles in the Palace of the Forest
of Lebanon were pure gold. Nothing was made of silver, because silver was considered of little value
in Solomon's day. [21]The king had
a fleet of trading ships[f] manned
by Hiram's[g] servants. Once every
three years it returned, carrying

[a] *9* That is, about 4 1/2 tons or about 4 metric tons [b] *10* Probably a variant of *almugwood* [c] *13* That is, about 25 tons or about 23 metric tons [d] *15* That is, about 15 pounds or about 6.9 kilograms [e] *16* That is, about 7 1/2 pounds or about 3.5 kilograms [f] *21* Hebrew *of ships that could go to Tarshish* [g] *21* Hebrew *Huram*, a variant of *Hiram*

gold, silver and ivory, and apes
and baboons. 1Ki 22:39
22King Solomon was greater in
riches and wisdom than all the
other kings of the earth. 23All the
kings of the earth sought audience
with Solomon to hear the wisdom
God had put in his heart. 24Year
after year, everyone who came
brought a gift—articles of silver
and gold, and robes, weapons and
spices, and horses and mules.
1Ki 3:13; 2Ch 1:12
25Solomon had four thousand
stalls for horses and chariots, and
twelve thousand horses,[a] which he
kept in the chariot cities and also
with him in Jerusalem. 26He ruled
over all the kings from the Euphrates River to the land of the Philistines, as far as the border of Egypt.
27The king made silver as common
in Jerusalem as stones, and cedar
as plentiful as sycamore-fig trees
in the foothills. 28Solomon's horses were imported from Egypt and
from all other countries.
1Ki 10:14-29; 2Ch 1:14-17

Solomon's Death

29As for the other events of Solomon's reign, from beginning to
end, are they not written in the
records of Nathan the prophet, in
the prophecy of Ahijah the Shilonite and in the visions of Iddo the
seer concerning Jeroboam son of
Nebat? 30Solomon reigned in Jerusalem over all Israel forty years.
31Then he rested with his ancestors
and was buried in the city of David
his father. And Rehoboam his son
succeeded him as king.
1Ki 2:10; 11:41-43; 1Ch 29:29

Israel Rebels Against Rehoboam

10 Rehoboam went to She-
chem, for all Israel had gone
there to make him king. 2When
Jeroboam son of Nebat heard this
(he was in Egypt, where he had
fled from King Solomon), he returned from Egypt. 3So they sent
for Jeroboam, and he and all Israel went to Rehoboam and said
to him: 4"Your father put a heavy
yoke on us, but now lighten the
harsh labor and the heavy yoke he
put on us, and we will serve you."
1Ki 11:40; 1Ch 9:1
5Rehoboam answered, "Come
back to me in three days." So the
people went away.
6Then King Rehoboam consulted the elders who had served his
father Solomon during his lifetime. "How would you advise me
to answer these people?" he asked.
Job 8:8-9; 12:12
7They replied, "If you will be
kind to these people and please
them and give them a favorable
answer, they will always be your
servants." Pr 15:1
8But Rehoboam rejected the advice the elders gave him and consulted the young men who had
grown up with him and were serving him. 9He asked them, "What is
your advice? How should we answer these people who say to me,

[a] 25 Or *charioteers*

'Lighten the yoke your father put
on us'?" 2Sa 17:14; Pr 13:20
10 The young men who had
grown up with him replied, "The
people have said to you, 'Your father put a heavy yoke on us, but
make our yoke lighter.' Now tell
them, 'My little finger is thicker
than my father's waist. 11 My father
laid on you a heavy yoke; I will
make it even heavier. My father
scourged you with whips; I will
scourge you with scorpions.'"
12 Three days later Jeroboam
and all the people returned to
Rehoboam, as the king had said,
"Come back to me in three days."
13 The king answered them harshly. Rejecting the advice of the elders, 14 he followed the advice of
the young men and said, "My father made your yoke heavy; I will
make it even heavier. My father
scourged you with whips; I will
scourge you with scorpions." 15 So
the king did not listen to the people, for this turn of events was
from God, to fulfill the word the
LORD had spoken to Jeroboam son
of Nebat through Ahijah the Shilonite. 1Ki 11:29; 2Ch 25:16-20
16 When all Israel saw that the
king refused to listen to them,
they answered the king: 1Ch 9:1

"What share do we have in
David, 2Sa 20:1
what part in Jesse's son?
To your tents, Israel!
Look after your own house,
David!"

So all the Israelites went home.
17 But as for the Israelites who were
living in the towns of Judah, Rehoboam still ruled over them.
18 King Rehoboam sent out Adoniram,[a] who was in charge of
forced labor, but the Israelites
stoned him to death. King Rehoboam, however, managed to get
into his chariot and escape to Jerusalem. 19 So Israel has been in rebellion against the house of David
to this day. 1Ki 5:14

11 When Rehoboam arrived in
Jerusalem, he mustered Judah and Benjamin — a hundred
and eighty thousand able young
men — to go to war against Israel
and to regain the kingdom for Rehoboam. 1Ki 12:21
2 But this word of the LORD came
to Shemaiah the man of God: 3 "Say
to Rehoboam son of Solomon king
of Judah and to all Israel in Judah
and Benjamin, 4 'This is what the
LORD says: Do not go up to fight
against your fellow Israelites. Go
home, every one of you, for this
is my doing.'" So they obeyed the
words of the LORD and turned
back from marching against Jeroboam. 1Ki 12:1-24; 2Ch 12:5-7,15

Rehoboam Fortifies Judah

5 Rehoboam lived in Jerusalem
and built up towns for defense
in Judah: 6 Bethlehem, Etam, Tekoa, 7 Beth Zur, Soko, Adullam,
8 Gath, Mareshah, Ziph, 9 Adoraim,

[a] 18 Hebrew *Hadoram*, a variant of *Adoniram*

Lachish, Azekah, 10Zorah, Aijalon
and Hebron. These were fortified
cities in Judah and Benjamin.
11He strengthened their defenses and put commanders in them,
with supplies of food, olive oil and
wine. 12He put shields and spears
in all the cities, and made them
very strong. So Judah and Benjamin were his.

13The priests and Levites from
all their districts throughout Israel sided with him. 14The Levites
even abandoned their pasturelands and property and came to
Judah and Jerusalem, because
Jeroboam and his sons had rejected them as priests of the LORD
15when he appointed his own
priests for the high places and
for the goat and calf idols he had
made. 16Those from every tribe
of Israel who set their hearts on
seeking the LORD, the God of Israel, followed the Levites to Jerusalem to offer sacrifices to the LORD,
the God of their ancestors. 17They
strengthened the kingdom of Judah and supported Rehoboam son
of Solomon three years, following
the ways of David and Solomon
during this time. 2Ch 12:1; 13:9; 15:9

Rehoboam's Family

18Rehoboam married Maha-
lath, who was the daughter of David's son Jerimoth and of Abihail,
the daughter of Jesse's son Eliab.
19She bore him sons: Jeush, Shemariah and Zaham. 20Then he married Maakah daughter of Absalom, who bore him Abijah, Attai,
Ziza and Shelomith. 21Rehoboam
loved Maakah daughter of Absalom more than any of his other
wives and concubines. In all, he
had eighteen wives and sixty concubines, twenty-eight sons and
sixty daughters. Dt 17:17; 1Ki 15:2

22Rehoboam appointed Abijah
son of Maakah as crown prince
among his brothers, in order to
make him king. 23He acted wisely, dispersing some of his sons
throughout the districts of Judah
and Benjamin, and to all the fortified cities. He gave them abundant provisions and took many
wives for them. Dt 21:15-17

Shishak Attacks Jerusalem

12 After Rehoboam's position
as king was established and
he had become strong, he and all
Israel[a] with him abandoned the
law of the LORD. 2Because they
had been unfaithful to the LORD,
Shishak king of Egypt attacked Jerusalem in the fifth year of King
Rehoboam. 3With twelve hundred
chariots and sixty thousand horsemen and the innumerable troops
of Libyans, Sukkites and Cushites[b]
that came with him from Egypt,
4he captured the fortified cities of
Judah and came as far as Jerusalem. 2Ch 11:10; 16:8

5Then the prophet Shemaiah
came to Rehoboam and to the

[a] *1* That is, Judah, as frequently in 2 Chronicles [b] *3* That is, people from the upper Nile region

leaders of Judah who had assembled in Jerusalem for fear of Shishak, and he said to them, "This
is what the LORD says, 'You have
abandoned me; therefore, I now
abandon you to Shishak.'"

2Ch 11:2; 15:2

6The leaders of Israel and the
king humbled themselves and
said, "The LORD is just."

Ex 9:27; Da 9:14

7When the LORD saw that they
humbled themselves, this word
of the LORD came to Shemaiah:
"Since they have humbled themselves, I will not destroy them but
will soon give them deliverance.
My wrath will not be poured out
on Jerusalem through Shishak.
8They will, however, become subject to him, so that they may learn
the difference between serving
me and serving the kings of other
lands." Dt 28:48; 1Ki 21:29; Ps 78:38

9When Shishak king of Egypt
attacked Jerusalem, he carried
off the treasures of the temple
of the LORD and the treasures of
the royal palace. He took everything, including the gold shields
Solomon had made. 10So King Rehoboam made bronze shields to
replace them and assigned these
to the commanders of the guard
on duty at the entrance to the
royal palace. 11Whenever the king
went to the LORD's temple, the
guards went with him, bearing
the shields, and afterward they
returned them to the guardroom.

2Ch 9:16

12Because Rehoboam humbled
himself, the LORD's anger turned
from him, and he was not totally destroyed. Indeed, there was
some good in Judah. 2Ch 19:3

13King Rehoboam established
himself firmly in Jerusalem and
continued as king. He was forty-
one years old when he became
king, and he reigned seventeen
years in Jerusalem, the city the
LORD had chosen out of all the
tribes of Israel in which to put his
Name. His mother's name was Naamah; she was an Ammonite. 14He
did evil because he had not set his
heart on seeking the LORD.

Dt 12:5; 2Ch 6:6

15As for the events of Rehoboam's reign, from beginning to end,
are they not written in the records
of Shemaiah the prophet and of
Iddo the seer that deal with genealogies? There was continual warfare between Rehoboam and Jeroboam. 16Rehoboam rested with his
ancestors and was buried in the
City of David. And Abijah his son
succeeded him as king.

1Ki 14:21,25-31; 2Ch 9:29

Abijah King of Judah

13 In the eighteenth year of
the reign of Jeroboam, Abijah became king of Judah, 2and he
reigned in Jerusalem three years.
His mother's name was Maakah,[a]
a daughter[b] of Uriel of Gibeah.

[a] 2 Most Septuagint manuscripts and Syriac (see also 11:20 and 1 Kings 15:2); Hebrew *Micaiah* [b] 2 Or *granddaughter*

There was war between Abijah
and Jeroboam. 3Abijah went into
battle with an army of four hundred thousand able fighting men,
and Jeroboam drew up a battle
line against him with eight hundred thousand able troops.
1Ki 15:6; 2Ch 11:20

4Abijah stood on Mount Zema-
raim, in the hill country of Ephraim, and said, "Jeroboam and all
Israel, listen to me! 5Don't you
know that the LORD, the God of Israel, has given the kingship of Israel to David and his descendants
forever by a covenant of salt? 6Yet
Jeroboam son of Nebat, an official
of Solomon son of David, rebelled
against his master. 7Some worthless scoundrels gathered around
him and opposed Rehoboam son
of Solomon when he was young
and indecisive and not strong
enough to resist them.
Nu 18:19; 1Ki 11:26

8"And now you plan to resist
the kingdom of the LORD, which
is in the hands of David's descendants. You are indeed a vast army
and have with you the golden
calves that Jeroboam made to be
your gods. 9But didn't you drive
out the priests of the LORD, the
sons of Aaron, and the Levites,
and make priests of your own as
the peoples of other lands do?
Whoever comes to consecrate
himself with a young bull and
seven rams may become a priest
of what are not gods.
1Ki 12:28; 2Ch 11:15; Jer 2:11

10"As for us, the LORD is our God,
and we have not forsaken him.
The priests who serve the LORD
are sons of Aaron, and the Levites
assist them. 11Every morning and
evening they present burnt offerings and fragrant incense to the
LORD. They set out the bread on
the ceremonially clean table and
light the lamps on the gold lampstand every evening. We are observing the requirements of the
LORD our God. But you have forsaken him. 12God is with us; he is
our leader. His priests with their
trumpets will sound the battle
cry against you. People of Israel,
do not fight against the LORD, the
God of your ancestors, for you will
not succeed." Nu 10:8-9; Ac 5:39

13Now Jeroboam had sent troops
around to the rear, so that while
he was in front of Judah the ambush was behind them. 14Judah
turned and saw that they were
being attacked at both front and
rear. Then they cried out to the
LORD. The priests blew their trumpets 15and the men of Judah raised
the battle cry. At the sound of their
battle cry, God routed Jeroboam
and all Israel before Abijah and
Judah. 16The Israelites fled before
Judah, and God delivered them
into their hands. 17Abijah and his
troops inflicted heavy losses on
them, so that there were five hundred thousand casualties among
Israel's able men. 18The Israelites
were subdued on that occasion,
and the people of Judah were

victorious because they relied on the LORD, the God of their ancestors. 2Ch 14:11; 16:8; Ps 22:5

19 Abijah pursued Jeroboam and took from him the towns of Bethel, Jeshanah and Ephron, with their surrounding villages. 20 Jeroboam did not regain power during the time of Abijah. And the LORD struck him down and he died.

21 But Abijah grew in strength. He married fourteen wives and had twenty-two sons and sixteen daughters.

22 The other events of Abijah's reign, what he did and what he said, are written in the annotations of the prophet Iddo.

14 [a] And Abijah rested with his ancestors and was buried in the City of David. Asa his son succeeded him as king, and in his days the country was at peace for ten years. 1Ki 15:1-2,6-8

Asa King of Judah

2 Asa did what was good and right in the eyes of the LORD his God. 3 He removed the foreign altars and the high places, smashed the sacred stones and cut down the Asherah poles.[b] 4 He commanded Judah to seek the LORD, the God of their ancestors, and to obey his laws and commands. 5 He removed the high places and incense altars in every town in Judah, and the kingdom was at peace under him. 6 He built up the fortified cities of Judah, since the land was at peace. No one was at war with him during those years, for the LORD gave him rest. 1Ki 15:11-12; 2Ch 34:4,7

7 "Let us build up these towns," he said to Judah, "and put walls around them, with towers, gates and bars. The land is still ours, because we have sought the LORD our God; we sought him and he has given us rest on every side." So they built and prospered.

8 Asa had an army of three hundred thousand men from Judah, equipped with large shields and with spears, and two hundred and eighty thousand from Benjamin, armed with small shields and with bows. All these were brave fighting men.

9 Zerah the Cushite marched out against them with an army of thousands upon thousands and three hundred chariots, and came as far as Mareshah. 10 Asa went out to meet him, and they took up battle positions in the Valley of Zephathah near Mareshah. 2Ch 11:8; 16:8

11 Then Asa called to the LORD his God and said, "LORD, there is no one like you to help the powerless against the mighty. Help us, LORD our God, for we rely on you, and in your name we have come against this vast army. LORD, you are our God; do not let mere mortals prevail against you." 1Sa 17:45; 2Ch 13:14

12 The LORD struck down the Cushites before Asa and Judah.

[a] In Hebrew texts 14:1 is numbered 13:23, and 14:2-15 is numbered 14:1-14. [b] 3 That is, wooden symbols of the goddess Asherah; here and elsewhere in 2 Chronicles

The Cushites fled, [13]and Asa and
his army pursued them as far as
Gerar. Such a great number of
Cushites fell that they could not
recover; they were crushed before the LORD and his forces. The
men of Judah carried off a large
amount of plunder. [14]They destroyed all the villages around
Gerar, for the terror of the LORD
had fallen on them. They looted
all these villages, since there was
much plunder there. [15]They also
attacked the camps of the herders
and carried off droves of sheep
and goats and camels. Then they
returned to Jerusalem.

Ge 10:19; 35:5; 2Ch 13:15

Asa's Reform

15 The Spirit of God came on Azariah son of Oded. [2]He went
out to meet Asa and said to him,
"Listen to me, Asa and all Judah
and Benjamin. The LORD is with
you when you are with him. If you
seek him, he will be found by you,
but if you forsake him, he will forsake you. [3]For a long time Israel
was without the true God, without a priest to teach and without
the law. [4]But in their distress they
turned to the LORD, the God of Israel, and sought him, and he was
found by them. [5]In those days it
was not safe to travel about, for all
the inhabitants of the lands were
in great turmoil. [6]One nation was
being crushed by another and one
city by another, because God was
troubling them with every kind of
distress. [7]But as for you, be strong
and do not give up, for your work
will be rewarded." Jos 1:7,9; Jas 4:8

[8]When Asa heard these words
and the prophecy of Azariah son
of[a] Oded the prophet, he took
courage. He removed the detestable idols from the whole land of
Judah and Benjamin and from the
towns he had captured in the hills
of Ephraim. He repaired the altar
of the LORD that was in front of
the portico of the LORD's temple.

2Ch 13:19

[9]Then he assembled all Judah
and Benjamin and the people
from Ephraim, Manasseh and Simeon who had settled among them,
for large numbers had come over
to him from Israel when they saw
that the LORD his God was with
him. 2Ch 11:16-17

[10]They assembled at Jerusalem
in the third month of the fifteenth
year of Asa's reign. [11]At that time
they sacrificed to the LORD seven
hundred head of cattle and seven
thousand sheep and goats from
the plunder they had brought
back. [12]They entered into a covenant to seek the LORD, the God of
their ancestors, with all their heart
and soul. [13]All who would not seek
the LORD, the God of Israel, were to
be put to death, whether small or
great, man or woman. [14]They took
an oath to the LORD with loud ac-
clamation, with shouting and with

[a] *8* Vulgate and Syriac (see also Septuagint and verse 1); Hebrew does not have *Azariah son of.*

trumpets and horns. 15 All Judah
rejoiced about the oath because
they had sworn it wholeheartedly.
They sought God eagerly, and he
was found by them. So the LORD
gave them rest on every side.

Ex 22:20; Dt 13:9-16; 2Ch 14:13

16 King Asa also deposed his
grandmother Maakah from her
position as queen mother, because she had made a repulsive
image for the worship of Asherah. Asa cut it down, broke it up
and burned it in the Kidron Valley. 17 Although he did not remove
the high places from Israel, Asa's
heart was fully committed to the
LORD all his life. 18 He brought into
the temple of God the silver and
gold and the articles that he and
his father had dedicated.

Ex 34:13; 2Ch 14:2-5

19 There was no more war until
the thirty-fifth year of Asa's reign.

1Ki 15:13-16

Asa's Last Years

16 In the thirty-sixth year of
Asa's reign Baasha king of
Israel went up against Judah and
fortified Ramah to prevent anyone from leaving or entering the
territory of Asa king of Judah.

Jer 41:9

2 Asa then took the silver and
gold out of the treasuries of the
LORD's temple and of his own palace and sent it to Ben-Hadad king
of Aram, who was ruling in Damascus. 3 "Let there be a treaty between me and you," he said, "as
there was between my father and
your father. See, I am sending you
silver and gold. Now break your
treaty with Baasha king of Israel
so he will withdraw from me."

2Ch 20:35

4 Ben-Hadad agreed with King
Asa and sent the commanders of
his forces against the towns of Israel. They conquered Ijon, Dan,
Abel Maim[a] and all the store cities
of Naphtali. 5 When Baasha heard
this, he stopped building Ramah
and abandoned his work. 6 Then
King Asa brought all the men of
Judah, and they carried away from
Ramah the stones and timber Baasha had been using. With them he
built up Geba and Mizpah.

1Ki 15:17-22

7 At that time Hanani the seer
came to Asa king of Judah and
said to him: "Because you relied
on the king of Aram and not on
the LORD your God, the army of
the king of Aram has escaped
from your hand. 8 Were not the
Cushites[b] and Libyans a mighty
army with great numbers of chariots and horsemen[c]? Yet when you
relied on the LORD, he delivered
them into your hand. 9 For the eyes
of the LORD range throughout the
earth to strengthen those whose
hearts are fully committed to him.
You have done a foolish thing, and
from now on you will be at war."

1Sa 13:13; Pr 15:3; Zec 4:10

[a] 4 Also known as *Abel Beth Maakah*
[b] 8 That is, people from the upper Nile region [c] 8 Or *charioteers*

[10]Asa was angry with the seer
because of this; he was so enraged
that he put him in prison. At the
same time Asa brutally oppressed
some of the people.

[11]The events of Asa's reign, from
beginning to end, are written in
the book of the kings of Judah
and Israel. [12]In the thirty-ninth
year of his reign Asa was afflicted
with a disease in his feet. Though
his disease was severe, even in his
illness he did not seek help from
the LORD, but only from the physicians. [13]Then in the forty-first
year of his reign Asa died and
rested with his ancestors. [14]They
buried him in the tomb that he
had cut out for himself in the City
of David. They laid him on a bier
covered with spices and various
blended perfumes, and they made
a huge fire in his honor.

Ge 50:2; 2Ch 21:19; Jer 17:5-6

Jehoshaphat King of Judah

17 Jehoshaphat his son succeeded him as king and
strengthened himself against Israel. [2]He stationed troops in all
the fortified cities of Judah and
put garrisons in Judah and in the
towns of Ephraim that his father
Asa had captured. 1Ki 15:23-24; 2Ch 15:8

[3]The LORD was with Jehoshaphat because he followed the ways
of his father David before him.
He did not consult the Baals [4]but
sought the God of his father and
followed his commands rather
than the practices of Israel. [5]The
LORD established the kingdom
under his control; and all Judah
brought gifts to Jehoshaphat, so
that he had great wealth and hon-
or. [6]His heart was devoted to the
ways of the LORD; furthermore, he
removed the high places and the
Asherah poles from Judah.

2Ch 15:17; 19:3; 22:9

[7]In the third year of his reign he
sent his officials Ben-Hail, Obadiah, Zechariah, Nethanel and Micaiah to teach in the towns of Judah.
[8]With them were certain Levites—
Shemaiah, Nethaniah, Zebadiah,
Asahel, Shemiramoth, Jehonathan, Adonijah, Tobijah and Tob-
Adonijah—and the priests Elishama and Jehoram. [9]They taught
throughout Judah, taking with
them the Book of the Law of the
LORD; they went around to all the
towns of Judah and taught the
people. Dt 6:4-9; 2Ch 15:3; 19:8

[10]The fear of the LORD fell on
all the kingdoms of the lands surrounding Judah, so that they did
not go to war against Jehoshaphat. [11]Some Philistines brought
Jehoshaphat gifts and silver as
tribute, and the Arabs brought
him flocks: seven thousand sev-
en hundred rams and seven thousand seven hundred goats.

Ge 35:5; 2Ch 9:14; 26:8

[12]Jehoshaphat became more
and more powerful; he built forts
and store cities in Judah [13]and
had large supplies in the towns
of Judah. He also kept experienced fighting men in Jerusalem.

14 Their enrollment by families was as follows: 2Sa 24:2

From Judah, commanders of units of 1,000:
Adnah the commander, with 300,000 fighting men;
15 next, Jehohanan the commander, with 280,000;
16 next, Amasiah son of Zikri, who volunteered himself for the service of the LORD, with 200,000. Jdg 5:9; 1Ch 29:9

17 From Benjamin: Nu 1:36
Eliada, a valiant soldier, with 200,000 men armed with bows and shields;
18 next, Jehozabad, with 180,000 men armed for battle.

19 These were the men who served the king, besides those he stationed in the fortified cities throughout Judah. 2Ch 11:10; 25:5

Micaiah Prophesies Against Ahab

18 Now Jehoshaphat had great wealth and honor, and he allied himself with Ahab by marriage. 2 Some years later he went down to see Ahab in Samaria. Ahab slaughtered many sheep and cattle for him and the people with him and urged him to attack Ramoth Gilead. 3 Ahab king of Israel asked Jehoshaphat king of Judah, "Will you go with me against Ramoth Gilead?" 2Ch 17:5; 21:6

Jehoshaphat replied, "I am as you are, and my people as your people; we will join you in the war." 4 But Jehoshaphat also said to the king of Israel, "First seek the counsel of the LORD."

5 So the king of Israel brought together the prophets — four hundred men — and asked them, "Shall we go to war against Ramoth Gilead, or shall I not?"

"Go," they answered, "for God will give it into the king's hand."

6 But Jehoshaphat asked, "Is there no longer a prophet of the LORD here whom we can inquire of?"

7 The king of Israel answered Jehoshaphat, "There is still one prophet through whom we can inquire of the LORD, but I hate him because he never prophesies anything good about me, but always bad. He is Micaiah son of Imlah."

"The king should not say such a thing," Jehoshaphat replied.

8 So the king of Israel called one of his officials and said, "Bring Micaiah son of Imlah at once."

9 Dressed in their royal robes, the king of Israel and Jehoshaphat king of Judah were sitting on their thrones at the threshing floor by the entrance of the gate of Samaria, with all the prophets prophesying before them. 10 Now Zedekiah son of Kenaanah had made iron horns, and he declared, "This is what the LORD says: 'With these you will gore the Arameans until they are destroyed.'"

11 All the other prophets were prophesying the same thing. "Attack Ramoth Gilead and be victori-

ous," they said, "for the LORD will
give it into the king's hand." 2Ch 22:5
12The messenger who had gone
to summon Micaiah said to him,
"Look, the other prophets without
exception are predicting success
for the king. Let your word agree
with theirs, and speak favorably."
13But Micaiah said, "As surely as
the LORD lives, I can tell him only
what my God says." Nu 22:18,20,35
14When he arrived, the king
asked him, "Micaiah, shall we go
to war against Ramoth Gilead, or
shall I not?"
"Attack and be victorious," he
answered, "for they will be given
into your hand."
15The king said to him, "How
many times must I make you
swear to tell me nothing but the
truth in the name of the LORD?"
16Then Micaiah answered, "I saw
all Israel scattered on the hills like
sheep without a shepherd, and the
LORD said, 'These people have no
master. Let each one go home in
peace.'" Nu 27:17; Eze 34:5-8
17The king of Israel said to Jehoshaphat, "Didn't I tell you that
he never prophesies anything
good about me, but only bad?"
18Micaiah continued, "Therefore hear the word of the LORD: I
saw the LORD sitting on his throne
with all the multitudes of heaven
standing on his right and on his
left. 19And the LORD said, 'Who will
entice Ahab king of Israel into attacking Ramoth Gilead and going
to his death there?' Da 7:9
"One suggested this, and another that. 20Finally, a spirit came forward, stood before the LORD and
said, 'I will entice him.'
"'By what means?' the LORD
asked.
21"'I will go and be a deceiving spirit in the mouths of all his
prophets,' he said. Job 1:6; Jn 8:44
"'You will succeed in enticing
him,' said the LORD. 'Go and do it.'
22"So now the LORD has put a
deceiving spirit in the mouths of
these prophets of yours. The LORD
has decreed disaster for you."
Job 12:16; Eze 14:9
23Then Zedekiah son of Kenaanah went up and slapped Micaiah
in the face. "Which way did the
spirit from[a] the LORD go when he
went from me to speak to you?"
he asked. Jer 20:2; Mk 14:65; Ac 23:2
24Micaiah replied, "You will find
out on the day you go to hide in an
inner room."
25The king of Israel then ordered, "Take Micaiah and send
him back to Amon the ruler of the
city and to Joash the king's son,
26and say, 'This is what the king
says: Put this fellow in prison and
give him nothing but bread and
water until I return safely.'"
2Ch 16:10; Heb 11:36
27Micaiah declared, "If you ever
return safely, the LORD has not
spoken through me." Then he
added, "Mark my words, all you
people!" 1Ki 22:1-28

[a] 23 Or *Spirit of*

Ahab Killed at Ramoth Gilead

28 So the king of Israel and Jehoshaphat king of Judah went up
to Ramoth Gilead. 29 The king of
Israel said to Jehoshaphat, "I will
enter the battle in disguise, but
you wear your royal robes." So the
king of Israel disguised himself
and went into battle.

30 Now the king of Aram had ordered his chariot commanders,
"Do not fight with anyone, small
or great, except the king of Israel."
31 When the chariot commanders
saw Jehoshaphat, they thought,
"This is the king of Israel." So they
turned to attack him, but Jehoshaphat cried out, and the LORD
helped him. God drew them away
from him, 32 for when the chariot
commanders saw that he was not
the king of Israel, they stopped
pursuing him.

33 But someone drew his bow at
random and hit the king of Israel between the breastplate and
the scale armor. The king told the
chariot driver, "Wheel around and
get me out of the fighting. I've
been wounded." 34 All day long the
battle raged, and the king of Israel propped himself up in his chariot facing the Arameans until evening. Then at sunset he died.

1Ki 22:29-36; 2Ch 13:14

19 When Jehoshaphat king of
Judah returned safely to
his palace in Jerusalem, 2 Jehu the
seer, the son of Hanani, went out
to meet him and said to the king,
"Should you help the wicked and
love[a] those who hate the LORD?
Because of this, the wrath of the
LORD is on you. 3 There is, however, some good in you, for you have
rid the land of the Asherah poles
and have set your heart on seeking God."

2Ch 17:6; 32:25; Ps 139:21-22

Jehoshaphat Appoints Judges

4 Jehoshaphat lived in Jerusalem, and he went out again
among the people from Beersheba to the hill country of Ephraim and turned them back to the
LORD, the God of their ancestors.
5 He appointed judges in the land,
in each of the fortified cities of
Judah. 6 He told them, "Consider carefully what you do, because
you are not judging for mere mortals but for the LORD, who is with
you whenever you give a verdict.
7 Now let the fear of the LORD be on
you. Judge carefully, for with the
LORD our God there is no injustice
or partiality or bribery."

Ge 18:25; Dt 10:17; 16:18-20

8 In Jerusalem also, Jehoshaphat appointed some of the Levites, priests and heads of Israelite families to administer the law
of the LORD and to settle disputes.
And they lived in Jerusalem. 9 He
gave them these orders: "You
must serve faithfully and wholeheartedly in the fear of the LORD.
10 In every case that comes before
you from your people who live in

[a] 2 Or *and make alliances with*

the cities — whether bloodshed or
other concerns of the law, commands, decrees or regulations —
you are to warn them not to sin
against the LORD; otherwise his
wrath will come on you and your
people. Do this, and you will not
sin. Dt 17:8-13; 2Ch 17:8-9
11“Amariah the chief priest will
be over you in any matter concerning the LORD, and Zebadiah
son of Ishmael, the leader of the
tribe of Judah, will be over you in
any matter concerning the king,
and the Levites will serve as officials before you. Act with courage,
and may the LORD be with those
who do well.” 1Ch 28:20

Jehoshaphat Defeats Moab and Ammon

20 After this, the Moabites
and Ammonites with some
of the Meunites[a] came to wage
war against Jehoshaphat. 1Ch 4:41
2Some people came and told Jehoshaphat, “A vast army is coming
against you from Edom,[b] from the
other side of the Dead Sea. It is already in Hazezon Tamar” (that is,
En Gedi). 3Alarmed, Jehoshaphat
resolved to inquire of the LORD,
and he proclaimed a fast for all
Judah. 4The people of Judah came
together to seek help from the
LORD; indeed, they came from every town in Judah to seek him.
Ge 14:7; 1Sa 7:6; 2Ch 19:3
5Then Jehoshaphat stood up in
the assembly of Judah and Jerusalem at the temple of the LORD
in the front of the new courtyard
6and said:

“LORD, the God of our an-
cestors, are you not the God
who is in heaven? You rule
over all the kingdoms of the
nations. Power and might are
in your hand, and no one can
withstand you. 7Our God, did
you not drive out the inhabitants of this land before your
people Israel and give it forever to the descendants of
Abraham your friend? 8They
have lived in it and have built
in it a sanctuary for your
Name, saying, 9‘If calamity
comes upon us, whether the
sword of judgment, or plague
or famine, we will stand in
your presence before this
temple that bears your Name
and will cry out to you in our
distress, and you will hear us
and save us.’
Dt 4:39; 1Ch 29:11-12; Isa 41:8
10“But now here are men
from Ammon, Moab and
Mount Seir, whose territory you would not allow Israel to invade when they came
from Egypt; so they turned
away from them and did not
destroy them. 11See how they
are repaying us by coming to
drive us out of the possession
you gave us as an inheritance.

[a] *1* Some Septuagint manuscripts; Hebrew *Ammonites* [b] *2* One Hebrew manuscript; most Hebrew manuscripts, Septuagint and Vulgate *Aram*

12Our God, will you not judge
them? For we have no power
to face this vast army that is
attacking us. We do not know
what to do, but our eyes are
on you." Ps 25:15; 83:1-12; 121:1-2

13All the men of Judah, with
their wives and children and little
ones, stood there before the LORD.
14Then the Spirit of the LORD
came on Jahaziel son of Zechariah, the son of Benaiah, the son of
Jeiel, the son of Mattaniah, a Levite and descendant of Asaph, as
he stood in the assembly. 2Ch 15:1
15He said: "Listen, King Jehoshaphat and all who live in Judah and Jerusalem! This is what
the LORD says to you: 'Do not be
afraid or discouraged because of
this vast army. For the battle is
not yours, but God's. 16Tomorrow
march down against them. They
will be climbing up by the Pass
of Ziz, and you will find them at
the end of the gorge in the Desert of Jeruel. 17You will not have to
fight this battle. Take up your positions; stand firm and see the deliverance the LORD will give you,
Judah and Jerusalem. Do not be
afraid; do not be discouraged. Go
out to face them tomorrow, and
the LORD will be with you.'"
Ex 14:13; 1Sa 17:47; 2Ch 32:7
18Jehoshaphat bowed down
with his face to the ground, and
all the people of Judah and Jerusalem fell down in worship before
the LORD. 19Then some Levites
from the Kohathites and Korahites
stood up and praised the LORD,
the God of Israel, with a very loud
voice. Ex 4:31
20Early in the morning they left
for the Desert of Tekoa. As they set
out, Jehoshaphat stood and said,
"Listen to me, Judah and people of
Jerusalem! Have faith in the LORD
your God and you will be upheld;
have faith in his prophets and you
will be successful." 21After consulting the people, Jehoshaphat appointed men to sing to the LORD
and to praise him for the splendor
of his[a] holiness as they went out
at the head of the army, saying:
1Ch 16:29; Isa 7:9

"Give thanks to the LORD,
for his love endures forever."
2Ch 5:13; Ps 136:1

22As they began to sing and
praise, the LORD set ambushes
against the men of Ammon and
Moab and Mount Seir who were
invading Judah, and they were
defeated. 23The Ammonites and
Moabites rose up against the men
from Mount Seir to destroy and
annihilate them. After they finished slaughtering the men from
Seir, they helped to destroy one
another. Jdg 7:22; 1Sa 14:20; 2Ch 23:13
24When the men of Judah came
to the place that overlooks the
desert and looked toward the vast
army, they saw only dead bodies
lying on the ground; no one had
escaped. 25So Jehoshaphat and his

[a] 21 Or *him with the splendor of*

men went to carry off their plunder, and they found among them
a great amount of equipment and
clothing[a] and also articles of value — more than they could take
away. There was so much plunder
that it took three days to collect
it. 26On the fourth day they assembled in the Valley of Berakah,
where they praised the LORD. This
is why it is called the Valley of Berakah[b] to this day.

27Then, led by Jehoshaphat, all
the men of Judah and Jerusalem
returned joyfully to Jerusalem, for
the LORD had given them cause to
rejoice over their enemies. 28They
entered Jerusalem and went to
the temple of the LORD with harps
and lyres and trumpets.

29The fear of God came on all the
surrounding kingdoms when they
heard how the LORD had fought
against the enemies of Israel.
30And the kingdom of Jehoshaphat was at peace, for his God had
given him rest on every side.
2Ch 15:15; 17:10

The End of Jehoshaphat's Reign

31So Jehoshaphat reigned over
Judah. He was thirty-five years
old when he became king of Judah, and he reigned in Jerusalem
twenty-five years. His mother's
name was Azubah daughter of
Shilhi. 32He followed the ways of
his father Asa and did not stray
from them; he did what was right
in the eyes of the LORD. 33The
high places, however, were not removed, and the people still had
not set their hearts on the God of
their ancestors. 2Ch 17:6; 19:3

34The other events of Jehoshaphat's reign, from beginning to
end, are written in the annals of
Jehu son of Hanani, which are recorded in the book of the kings of
Israel. 1Ki 16:1

35Later, Jehoshaphat king of Judah made an alliance with Ahaziah king of Israel, whose ways were
wicked. 36He agreed with him to
construct a fleet of trading ships.[c]
After these were built at Ezion Geber, 37Eliezer son of Dodavahu of
Mareshah prophesied against Jehoshaphat, saying, "Because you
have made an alliance with Ahaziah, the LORD will destroy what
you have made." The ships were
wrecked and were not able to set
sail to trade.[d]

21 Then Jehoshaphat rested
with his ancestors and was
buried with them in the City of
David. And Jehoram his son succeeded him as king. 2Jehoram's
brothers, the sons of Jehoshaphat,
were Azariah, Jehiel, Zechariah,
Azariahu, Michael and Shephatiah. All these were sons of Jehoshaphat king of Israel.[e] 3Their father
had given them many gifts of silver and gold and articles of value,
as well as fortified cities in Judah,

[a] 25 Some Hebrew manuscripts and Vulgate; most Hebrew manuscripts *corpses*
[b] 26 *Berakah* means *praise.*
[c] 36 Hebrew *of ships that could go to Tarshish*
[d] 37 Hebrew *sail for Tarshish*
[e] 2 That is, Judah, as frequently in 2 Chronicles

but he had given the kingdom to
Jehoram because he was his firstborn son. 2Ch 9:21; 11:10

Jehoram King of Judah

4When Jehoram established
himself firmly over his father's
kingdom, he put all his brothers to
the sword along with some of the
officials of Israel. 5Jehoram was
thirty-two years old when he became king, and he reigned in Jerusalem eight years. 6He followed
the ways of the kings of Israel, as
the house of Ahab had done, for
he married a daughter of Ahab.
He did evil in the eyes of the LORD.
7Nevertheless, because of the covenant the LORD had made with
David, the LORD was not willing to
destroy the house of David. He had
promised to maintain a lamp for
him and his descendants forever.

8In the time of Jehoram, Edom
rebelled against Judah and set
up its own king. 9So Jehoram
went there with his officers and
all his chariots. The Edomites
surrounded him and his chariot
commanders, but he rose up and
broke through by night. 10To this
day Edom has been in rebellion
against Judah.

Libnah revolted at the same
time, because Jehoram had forsaken the LORD, the God of his ancestors. 11He had also built high
places on the hills of Judah and
had caused the people of Jerusalem to prostitute themselves and
had led Judah astray.

12Jehoram received a letter from
Elijah the prophet, which said:
2Ki 1:16-17

"This is what the LORD, the
God of your father David,
says: 'You have not followed
the ways of your father Jehoshaphat or of Asa king of
Judah. 13But you have followed the ways of the kings
of Israel, and you have led
Judah and the people of Jerusalem to prostitute themselves, just as the house of
Ahab did. You have also murdered your own brothers,
members of your own fami-
ly, men who were better than
you. 14So now the LORD is
about to strike your people,
your sons, your wives and everything that is yours, with
a heavy blow. 15You yourself
will be very ill with a linger-
ing disease of the bowels,
until the disease causes your
bowels to come out.'"

1Ki 16:29-33; 2Ch 17:3-6

16The LORD aroused against Jehoram the hostility of the Philistines and of the Arabs who lived
near the Cushites. 17They attacked
Judah, invaded it and carried off
all the goods found in the king's
palace, together with his sons and
wives. Not a son was left to him
except Ahaziah,[a] the youngest.
2Ch 17:10-11; 22:1; 26:7

[a] 17 Hebrew *Jehoahaz*, a variant of *Ahaziah*

18 After all this, the LORD afflicted Jehoram with an incurable disease of the bowels. 19 In the course
of time, at the end of the second
year, his bowels came out because
of the disease, and he died in great
pain. His people made no funeral
fire in his honor, as they had for
his predecessors. 2Ch 16:14
20 Jehoram was thirty-two years
old when he became king, and he
reigned in Jerusalem eight years.
He passed away, to no one's regret,
and was buried in the City of David, but not in the tombs of the
kings. 2Ki 8:16-24; 2Ch 24:25

Ahaziah King of Judah

22 The people of Jerusalem
made Ahaziah, Jehoram's
youngest son, king in his place,
since the raiders, who came with
the Arabs into the camp, had
killed all the older sons. So Ahaziah son of Jehoram king of Judah
began to reign.
2 Ahaziah was twenty-two[a] years
old when he became king, and he
reigned in Jerusalem one year.
His mother's name was Athaliah,
a granddaughter of Omri.
3 He too followed the ways of the
house of Ahab, for his mother encouraged him to act wickedly. 4 He
did evil in the eyes of the LORD, as
the house of Ahab had done, for after his father's death they became
his advisers, to his undoing. 5 He
also followed their counsel when
he went with Joram[b] son of Ahab
king of Israel to wage war against
Hazael king of Aram at Ramoth
Gilead. The Arameans wounded
Joram; 6 so he returned to Jezreel
to recover from the wounds they
had inflicted on him at Ramoth[c]
in his battle with Hazael king of
Aram. 2Ch 18:1; 21:6
Then Ahaziah[d] son of Jehoram
king of Judah went down to Jezreel
to see Joram son of Ahab because
he had been wounded. 2Ki 8:25-29
7 Through Ahaziah's visit to Joram, God brought about Ahaziah's
downfall. When Ahaziah arrived,
he went out with Joram to meet
Jehu son of Nimshi, whom the
LORD had anointed to destroy the
house of Ahab. 8 While Jehu was
executing judgment on the house
of Ahab, he found the officials of
Judah and the sons of Ahaziah's
relatives, who had been attending Ahaziah, and he killed them.
9 He then went in search of Ahaziah, and his men captured him
while he was hiding in Samaria.
He was brought to Jehu and put to
death. They buried him, for they
said, "He was a son of Jehoshaphat, who sought the LORD with
all his heart." So there was no one
in the house of Ahaziah powerful
enough to retain the kingdom.
2Ki 9:21-29; 2Ch 10:15

[a] *2* Some Septuagint manuscripts and Syriac (see also 2 Kings 8:26); Hebrew *forty-two* [b] *5* Hebrew *Jehoram*, a variant of *Joram*; also in verses 6 and 7 [c] *6* Hebrew *Ramah*, a variant of *Ramoth* [d] *6* Some Hebrew manuscripts, Septuagint, Vulgate and Syriac (see also 2 Kings 8:29); most Hebrew manuscripts *Azariah*

Athaliah and Joash

[10]When Athaliah the mother of
Ahaziah saw that her son was dead,
she proceeded to destroy the whole
royal family of the house of Judah.
[11]But Jehosheba,[a] the daughter of
King Jehoram, took Joash son of
Ahaziah and stole him away from
among the royal princes who were
about to be murdered and put
him and his nurse in a bedroom.
Because Jehosheba,[a] the daughter
of King Jehoram and wife of the
priest Jehoiada, was Ahaziah's sister, she hid the child from Athaliah so she could not kill him. [12]He
remained hidden with them at the
temple of God for six years while
Athaliah ruled the land.

23 In the seventh year Jehoiada showed his strength. He
made a covenant with the commanders of units of a hundred:
Azariah son of Jeroham, Ishmael son of Jehohanan, Azariah son
of Obed, Maaseiah son of Adaiah,
and Elishaphat son of Zikri. [2]They
went throughout Judah and gathered the Levites and the heads
of Israelite families from all the
towns. When they came to Jerusalem, [3]the whole assembly made
a covenant with the king at the
temple of God. Nu 35:2-5; 2Ki 11:17

Jehoiada said to them, "The
king's son shall reign, as the LORD
promised concerning the descendants of David. [4]Now this is what
you are to do: A third of you priests
and Levites who are going on duty
on the Sabbath are to keep watch at
the doors, [5]a third of you at the royal palace and a third at the Foundation Gate, and all the others are
to be in the courtyards of the temple of the LORD. [6]No one is to enter
the temple of the LORD except the
priests and Levites on duty; they
may enter because they are consecrated, but all the others are to observe the LORD's command not to
enter.[b] [7]The Levites are to station
themselves around the king, each
with weapon in hand. Anyone who
enters the temple is to be put to
death. Stay close to the king wherever he goes." 2Sa 7:12; 1Ki 2:4; 2Ch 6:16

[8]The Levites and all the men
of Judah did just as Jehoiada the
priest ordered. Each one took his
men — those who were going on
duty on the Sabbath and those
who were going off duty — for Jehoiada the priest had not released
any of the divisions. [9]Then he gave
the commanders of units of a hundred the spears and the large and
small shields that had belonged
to King David and that were in the
temple of God. [10]He stationed all
the men, each with his weapon in
his hand, around the king — near
the altar and the temple, from the
south side to the north side of the
temple. 2Ki 11:9; 1Ch 24:1

[11]Jehoiada and his sons brought
out the king's son and put the
crown on him; they presented

[a] *11* Hebrew *Jehoshabeath,* a variant of *Jehosheba* [b] *6* Or *are to stand guard where the LORD has assigned them*

him with a copy of the covenant
and proclaimed him king. They
anointed him and shouted, “Long
live the king!” Dt 17:18; 1Sa 10:24

12When Athaliah heard the noise
of the people running and cheering the king, she went to them
at the temple of the LORD. 13She
looked, and there was the king,
standing by his pillar at the entrance. The officers and the trumpeters were beside the king, and
all the people of the land were rejoicing and blowing trumpets, and
musicians with their instruments
were leading the praises. Then
Athaliah tore her robes and shouted, “Treason! Treason!” 1Ki 1:41; 7:15

14Jehoiada the priest sent out
the commanders of units of a
hundred, who were in charge
of the troops, and said to them:
“Bring her out between the ranks[a]
and put to the sword anyone who
follows her.” For the priest had
said, “Do not put her to death at
the temple of the LORD.” 15So they
seized her as she reached the entrance of the Horse Gate on the
palace grounds, and there they
put her to death. Ne 3:28; Jer 31:40

16Jehoiada then made a covenant that he, the people and the
king[b] would be the LORD’s people.
17All the people went to the temple of Baal and tore it down. They
smashed the altars and idols and
killed Mattan the priest of Baal in
front of the altars. Dt 13:6-9; 2Ch 29:10

18Then Jehoiada placed the
oversight of the temple of the
LORD in the hands of the Levitical
priests, to whom David had made
assignments in the temple, to
present the burnt offerings of the
LORD as written in the Law of Moses, with rejoicing and singing, as
David had ordered. 19He also stationed gatekeepers at the gates
of the LORD’s temple so that no
one who was in any way unclean
might enter. 1Ch 9:22; 23:6,28-32

20He took with him the commanders of hundreds, the nobles,
the rulers of the people and all the
people of the land and brought
the king down from the temple
of the LORD. They went into the
palace through the Upper Gate
and seated the king on the royal
throne. 21All the people of the land
rejoiced, and the city was calm,
because Athaliah had been slain
with the sword. 2Ki 11:1-21; 15:35

Joash Repairs the Temple

24 Joash was seven years old
when he became king, and
he reigned in Jerusalem forty
years. His mother’s name was Zibiah; she was from Beersheba. 2Jo-
ash did what was right in the eyes
of the LORD all the years of Jehoiada the priest. 3Jehoiada chose two
wives for him, and he had sons
and daughters. 2Ch 26:5

4Some time later Joash decided
to restore the temple of the LORD.
5He called together the priests and

[a] 14 *Or out from the precincts* [b] 16 *Or covenant between the LORD and the people and the king that they* (see 2 Kings 11:17)

Levites and said to them, "Go to
the towns of Judah and collect the
money due annually from all Israel, to repair the temple of your
God. Do it now." But the Levites
did not act at once.
Ex 30:16; 1Ch 11:1; 26:20

6 Therefore the king summoned
Jehoiada the chief priest and said
to him, "Why haven't you required
the Levites to bring in from Judah
and Jerusalem the tax imposed by
Moses the servant of the LORD and
by the assembly of Israel for the
tent of the covenant law?"
Ex 30:12-16; Nu 1:50

7 Now the sons of that wicked
woman Athaliah had broken into
the temple of God and had used
even its sacred objects for the Baals.

8 At the king's command, a chest
was made and placed outside, at
the gate of the temple of the LORD.
9 A proclamation was then issued
in Judah and Jerusalem that they
should bring to the LORD the tax
that Moses the servant of God had
required of Israel in the wilderness. 10 All the officials and all the
people brought their contributions gladly, dropping them into
the chest until it was full. 11 Whenever the chest was brought in by
the Levites to the king's officials
and they saw that there was a
large amount of money, the royal secretary and the officer of the
chief priest would come and empty the chest and carry it back to its
place. They did this regularly and
collected a great amount of money. 12 The king and Jehoiada gave it
to those who carried out the work
required for the temple of the
LORD. They hired masons and carpenters to restore the LORD's temple, and also workers in iron and
bronze to repair the temple.

13 The men in charge of the
work were diligent, and the repairs progressed under them.
They rebuilt the temple of God
according to its original design
and reinforced it. 14 When they
had finished, they brought the
rest of the money to the king and
Jehoiada, and with it were made
articles for the LORD's temple: articles for the service and for the
burnt offerings, and also dishes and other objects of gold and
silver. As long as Jehoiada lived,
burnt offerings were presented
continually in the temple of the
LORD. 2Ki 12:1-16; 1Ch 29:3,6,9

15 Now Jehoiada was old and full
of years, and he died at the age
of a hundred and thirty. 16 He was
buried with the kings in the City
of David, because of the good he
had done in Israel for God and his
temple.

The Wickedness of Joash

17 After the death of Jehoiada, the
officials of Judah came and paid
homage to the king, and he listened to them. 18 They abandoned
the temple of the LORD, the God
of their ancestors, and worshiped
Asherah poles and idols. Because

of their guilt, God's anger came on
Judah and Jerusalem. 19 Although
the LORD sent prophets to the
people to bring them back to him,
and though they testified against
them, they would not listen.
Ex 34:13; 2Ch 19:2; Jer 7:25

20 Then the Spirit of God came
on Zechariah son of Jehoiada the
priest. He stood before the people
and said, "This is what God says:
'Why do you disobey the LORD's
commands? You will not prosper.
Because you have forsaken the
LORD, he has forsaken you.'"
Nu 14:41; 2Ch 15:2; 20:14

21 But they plotted against him,
and by order of the king they
stoned him to death in the courtyard of the LORD's temple. 22 King
Joash did not remember the kindness Zechariah's father Jehoiada
had shown him but killed his son,
who said as he lay dying, "May the
LORD see this and call you to account." Ge 9:5; Ne 9:26; Ac 7:58-59

23 At the turn of the year,[a] the
army of Aram marched against
Joash; it invaded Judah and Jerusalem and killed all the leaders of the people. They sent all
the plunder to their king in Damascus. 24 Although the Aramean army had come with only a
few men, the LORD delivered into
their hands a much larger army.
Because Judah had forsaken the
LORD, the God of their ancestors,
judgment was executed on Joash.
25 When the Arameans withdrew,
they left Joash severely wounded.
His officials conspired against him
for murdering the son of Jehoiada
the priest, and they killed him in
his bed. So he died and was buried
in the City of David, but not in the
tombs of the kings.
Lev 26:23-25; 2Ki 12:17-18; 2Ch 14:9

26 Those who conspired against
him were Zabad,[b] son of Shimeath
an Ammonite woman, and Jehozabad, son of Shimrith[c] a Moabite
woman. 27 The account of his sons,
the many prophecies about him,
and the record of the restoration
of the temple of God are written
in the annotations on the book of
the kings. And Amaziah his son
succeeded him as king. 2Ki 12:17-21

Amaziah King of Judah

25 Amaziah was twenty-five
years old when he became
king, and he reigned in Jerusalem twenty-nine years. His mother's name was Jehoaddan; she was
from Jerusalem. 2 He did what was
right in the eyes of the LORD, but
not wholeheartedly. 3 After the
kingdom was firmly in his control, he executed the officials who
had murdered his father the king.
4 Yet he did not put their children
to death, but acted in accordance
with what is written in the Law,
in the Book of Moses, where the
LORD commanded: "Parents shall
not be put to death for their children, nor children be put to death

[a] *23* Probably in the spring [b] *26* A variant of *Jozabad* [c] *26* A variant of *Shomer*

for their parents; each will die for
their own sin."[a] 2Ki 14:1-6; Dt 24:16; 28:61
5Amaziah called the people
of Judah together and assigned
them according to their families to commanders of thousands
and commanders of hundreds for
all Judah and Benjamin. He then
mustered those twenty years old
or more and found that there were
three hundred thousand men fit
for military service, able to handle the spear and shield. 6He also
hired a hundred thousand fighting men from Israel for a hundred
talents[b] of silver. Nu 1:3; 1Ch 21:1
7But a man of God came to him
and said, "Your Majesty, these
troops from Israel must not march
with you, for the LORD is not with
Israel — not with any of the people of Ephraim. 8Even if you go
and fight courageously in battle,
God will overthrow you before the
enemy, for God has the power to
help or to overthrow." 2Ch 14:11; 20:6
9Amaziah asked the man of
God, "But what about the hundred
talents I paid for these Israelite
troops?"

The man of God replied, "The
LORD can give you much more
than that." Dt 8:18; Pr 10:22
10So Amaziah dismissed the
troops who had come to him from
Ephraim and sent them home.
They were furious with Judah and
left for home in a great rage.
11Amaziah then marshaled his
strength and led his army to the
Valley of Salt, where he killed ten
thousand men of Seir. 12The army
of Judah also captured ten thousand men alive, took them to the
top of a cliff and threw them down
so that all were dashed to pieces.
2Ki 14:7; Ps 141:6
13Meanwhile the troops that
Amaziah had sent back and had
not allowed to take part in the
war raided towns belonging to Judah from Samaria to Beth Horon.
They killed three thousand people
and carried off great quantities of
plunder.
14When Amaziah returned from
slaughtering the Edomites, he
brought back the gods of the people of Seir. He set them up as his
own gods, bowed down to them
and burned sacrifices to them.
15The anger of the LORD burned
against Amaziah, and he sent a
prophet to him, who said, "Why
do you consult this people's gods,
which could not save their own
people from your hand?"
Ex 20:3; Ps 96:5; Isa 44:15
16While he was still speaking,
the king said to him, "Have we
appointed you an adviser to the
king? Stop! Why be struck down?"

So the prophet stopped but said,
"I know that God has determined
to destroy you, because you have
done this and have not listened to
my counsel."
17After Amaziah king of Judah
consulted his advisers, he sent

[a] 4 Deut. 24:16 [b] 6 That is, about 3 3/4 tons or about 3.4 metric tons; also in verse 9

this challenge to Jehoash[a] son of Jehoahaz, the son of Jehu, king of Israel: "Come, let us face each other in battle."

18 But Jehoash king of Israel replied to Amaziah king of Judah: "A thistle in Lebanon sent a message to a cedar in Lebanon, 'Give your daughter to my son in marriage.' Then a wild beast in Lebanon came along and trampled the thistle underfoot. 19 You say to yourself that you have defeated Edom, and now you are arrogant and proud. But stay at home! Why ask for trouble and cause your own downfall and that of Judah also?" Jdg 9:8-15

20 Amaziah, however, would not listen, for God so worked that he might deliver them into the hands of Jehoash, because they sought the gods of Edom. 21 So Jehoash king of Israel attacked. He and Amaziah king of Judah faced each other at Beth Shemesh in Judah. 22 Judah was routed by Israel, and every man fled to his home. 23 Jehoash king of Israel captured Amaziah king of Judah, the son of Joash, the son of Ahaziah,[b] at Beth Shemesh. Then Jehoash brought him to Jerusalem and broke down the wall of Jerusalem from the Ephraim Gate to the Corner Gate—a section about four hundred cubits[c] long. 24 He took all the gold and silver and all the articles found in the temple of God that had been in the care of Obed-Edom, together with the palace treasures and the hostages, and returned to Samaria. 1Ki 12:15; 2Ch 22:7; Jer 31:38

25 Amaziah son of Joash king of Judah lived for fifteen years after the death of Jehoash son of Jehoahaz king of Israel. 26 As for the other events of Amaziah's reign, from beginning to end, are they not written in the book of the kings of Judah and Israel? 27 From the time that Amaziah turned away from following the LORD, they conspired against him in Jerusalem and he fled to Lachish, but they sent men after him to Lachish and killed him there. 28 He was brought back by horse and was buried with his ancestors in the City of Judah.[d] 2Ki 14:8-20

Uzziah King of Judah

26 Then all the people of Judah took Uzziah,[e] who was sixteen years old, and made him king in place of his father Amaziah. 2 He was the one who rebuilt Elath and restored it to Judah after Amaziah rested with his ancestors.

3 Uzziah was sixteen years old when he became king, and he reigned in Jerusalem fifty-two years. His mother's name was

[a] *17* Hebrew *Joash*, a variant of *Jehoash*; also in verses 18, 21, 23 and 25 [b] *23* Hebrew *Jehoahaz*, a variant of *Ahaziah* [c] *23* That is, about 600 feet or about 180 meters [d] *28* Most Hebrew manuscripts; some Hebrew manuscripts, Septuagint, Vulgate and Syriac (see also 2 Kings 14:20) *David* [e] *1* Also called *Azariah*

Jekoliah; she was from Jerusalem.
4He did what was right in the eyes
of the LORD, just as his father Amaziah had done. 5He sought God
during the days of Zechariah, who
instructed him in the fear[a] of God.
As long as he sought the LORD, God
gave him success. 2Ki 14:21-22; 15:1-3

6He went to war against the Philistines and broke down the walls
of Gath, Jabneh and Ashdod. He
then rebuilt towns near Ashdod
and elsewhere among the Philistines. 7God helped him against
the Philistines and against the
Arabs who lived in Gur Baal and
against the Meunites. 8The Ammonites brought tribute to Uzziah, and his fame spread as far as
the border of Egypt, because he
had become very powerful.

2Ch 17:11; 21:16; Isa 14:29

9Uzziah built towers in Jerusalem at the Corner Gate, at the Valley Gate and at the angle of the
wall, and he fortified them. 10He
also built towers in the wilderness
and dug many cisterns, because
he had much livestock in the foothills and in the plain. He had people working his fields and vineyards in the hills and in the fertile
lands, for he loved the soil.

2Ch 25:23; Ne 3:13

11Uzziah had a well-trained
army, ready to go out by divisions
according to their numbers as
mustered by Jeiel the secretary
and Maaseiah the officer under
the direction of Hananiah, one
of the royal officials. 12The total
number of family leaders over
the fighting men was 2,600. 13Un-
der their command was an army
of 307,500 men trained for war,
a powerful force to support the
king against his enemies. 14Uzziah
provided shields, spears, helmets,
coats of armor, bows and slingstones for the entire army. 15In
Jerusalem he made devices in-
vented for use on the towers and
on the corner defenses so that
soldiers could shoot arrows and
hurl large stones from the walls.
His fame spread far and wide, for
he was greatly helped until he became powerful. Jer 46:4

16But after Uzziah became powerful, his pride led to his downfall. He was unfaithful to the LORD
his God, and entered the temple
of the LORD to burn incense on
the altar of incense. 17Azariah
the priest with eighty other courageous priests of the LORD followed him in. 18They confronted
King Uzziah and said, "It is not
right for you, Uzziah, to burn incense to the LORD. That is for the
priests, the descendants of Aaron, who have been consecrated
to burn incense. Leave the sanctuary, for you have been unfaithful; and you will not be honored
by the LORD God."

Ex 30:7; Dt 32:15; 1Ch 6:10

19Uzziah, who had a censer in
his hand ready to burn incense,

[a] 5 Many Hebrew manuscripts, Septuagint and Syriac; other Hebrew manuscripts *vision*

became angry. While he was raging at the priests in their presence before the incense altar in the LORD's temple, leprosy[a] broke out on his forehead. 20When Azariah the chief priest and all the other priests looked at him, they saw that he had leprosy on his forehead, so they hurried him out. Indeed, he himself was eager to leave, because the LORD had afflicted him. 2Ki 5:25-27

21King Uzziah had leprosy until the day he died. He lived in a separate house[b] — leprous, and banned from the temple of the LORD. Jotham his son had charge of the palace and governed the people of the land.

22The other events of Uzziah's reign, from beginning to end, are recorded by the prophet Isaiah son of Amoz. 23Uzziah rested with his ancestors and was buried near them in a cemetery that belonged to the kings, for people said, "He had leprosy." And Jotham his son succeeded him as king.

2Ki 15:5-7; Isa 6:1

Jotham King of Judah

27 Jotham was twenty-five years old when he became king, and he reigned in Jerusalem sixteen years. His mother's name was Jerusha daughter of Zadok. 2He did what was right in the eyes of the LORD, just as his father Uzziah had done, but unlike him he did not enter the temple of the LORD. The people, however, continued their corrupt practices. 3Jotham rebuilt the Upper Gate of the temple of the LORD and did extensive work on the wall at the hill of Ophel. 4He built towns in the hill country of Judah and forts and towers in the wooded areas.

2Ch 33:14; Ne 3:26; 1Ch 3:12

5Jotham waged war against the king of the Ammonites and conquered them. That year the Ammonites paid him a hundred talents[c] of silver, ten thousand cors[d] of wheat and ten thousand cors[e] of barley. The Ammonites brought him the same amount also in the second and third years. Ge 19:38

6Jotham grew powerful because he walked steadfastly before the LORD his God. 2Ch 26:5

7The other events in Jotham's reign, including all his wars and the other things he did, are written in the book of the kings of Israel and Judah. 8He was twenty-five years old when he became king, and he reigned in Jerusalem sixteen years. 9Jotham rested with his ancestors and was buried in the City of David. And Ahaz his son succeeded him as king.

2Ki 15:33-38

[a] *19* The Hebrew for *leprosy* was used for various diseases affecting the skin; also in verses 20, 21 and 23. [b] *21* Or *in a house where he was relieved of responsibilities* [c] *5* That is, about 3 3/4 tons or about 3.4 metric tons [d] *5* That is, probably about 1,800 tons or about 1,600 metric tons of wheat [e] *5* That is, probably about 1,500 tons or about 1,350 metric tons of barley

Ahaz King of Judah

28 Ahaz was twenty years old when he became king, and he reigned in Jerusalem sixteen years. Unlike David his father, he did not do what was right in the eyes of the LORD. 2He followed the ways of the kings of Israel and also made idols for worshiping the Baals. 3He burned sacrifices in the Valley of Ben Hinnom and sacrificed his children in the fire, engaging in the detestable practices of the nations the LORD had driven out before the Israelites. 4He offered sacrifices and burned incense at the high places, on the hilltops and under every spreading tree. Lev 18:21; 2Ch 33:2,6

5Therefore the LORD his God delivered him into the hands of the king of Aram. The Arameans defeated him and took many of his people as prisoners and brought them to Damascus. Isa 7:1

He was also given into the hands of the king of Israel, who inflicted heavy casualties on him. 6In one day Pekah son of Remaliah killed a hundred and twenty thousand soldiers in Judah — because Judah had forsaken the LORD, the God of their ancestors. 7Zikri, an Ephraimite warrior, killed Maaseiah the king's son, Azrikam the officer in charge of the palace, and Elkanah, second to the king. 8The men of Israel took captive from their fellow Israelites who were from Judah two hundred thousand wives, sons and daughters. They also took a great deal of plunder, which they carried back to Samaria.

2Ki 15:25,27; 2Ch 11:4

9But a prophet of the LORD named Oded was there, and he went out to meet the army when it returned to Samaria. He said to them, "Because the LORD, the God of your ancestors, was angry with Judah, he gave them into your hand. But you have slaughtered them in a rage that reaches to heaven. 10And now you intend to make the men and women of Judah and Jerusalem your slaves. But aren't you also guilty of sins against the LORD your God? 11Now listen to me! Send back your fellow Israelites you have taken as prisoners, for the LORD's fierce anger rests on you."

Lev 25:39-46; Ezr 9:6; Isa 47:6

12Then some of the leaders in Ephraim — Azariah son of Jehohanan, Berekiah son of Meshillemoth, Jehizkiah son of Shallum, and Amasa son of Hadlai — confronted those who were arriving from the war. 13"You must not bring those prisoners here," they said, "or we will be guilty before the LORD. Do you intend to add to our sin and guilt? For our guilt is already great, and his fierce anger rests on Israel."

14So the soldiers gave up the prisoners and plunder in the presence of the officials and all the assembly. 15The men designated by name took the prisoners, and from the plunder they clothed all who were naked. They provided them with clothes and sandals, food and drink, and healing balm. All those who were weak they put on donkeys. So they took them back to their fellow Israelites at Jericho, the City of Palms, and returned to Samaria. Jdg 1:16; 2Ki 6:22

16 At that time King Ahaz sent to the kings[a] of Assyria for help. 17 The Edomites had again come and attacked Judah and carried away prisoners, 18 while the Philistines had raided towns in the foothills and in the Negev of Judah. They captured and occupied Beth Shemesh, Aijalon and Gederoth, as well as Soko, Timnah and Gimzo, with their surrounding villages. 19 The LORD had humbled Judah because of Ahaz king of Israel,[b] for he had promoted wickedness in Judah and had been most unfaithful to the LORD. 20 Tiglath-Pileser[c] king of Assyria came to him, but he gave him trouble instead of help. 21 Ahaz took some of the things from the temple of the LORD and from the royal palace and from the officials and presented them to the king of Assyria, but that did not help him.

2Ki 16:7; 2Ch 21:2; Eze 16:27,57

22 In his time of trouble King Ahaz became even more unfaithful to the LORD. 23 He offered sacrifices to the gods of Damascus, who had defeated him; for he thought, "Since the gods of the kings of Aram have helped them, I will sacrifice to them so they will help me." But they were his downfall and the downfall of all Israel.

2Ch 25:14; Jer 44:17-18

24 Ahaz gathered together the furnishings from the temple of God and cut them in pieces. He shut the doors of the LORD's temple and set up altars at every street corner in Jerusalem. 25 In every town in Judah he built high places to burn sacrifices to other gods and aroused the anger of the LORD, the God of his ancestors.

2Ki 16:18; 2Ch 29:7

26 The other events of his reign and all his ways, from beginning to end, are written in the book of the kings of Judah and Israel. 27 Ahaz rested with his ancestors and was buried in the city of Jerusalem, but he was not placed in the tombs of the kings of Israel. And Hezekiah his son succeeded him as king. 2Ki 16:1-20

Hezekiah Purifies the Temple

29 Hezekiah was twenty-five years old when he became king, and he reigned in Jerusalem twenty-nine years. His mother's name was Abijah daughter of Zechariah. 2 He did what was right in the eyes of the LORD, just as his father David had done.

2Ki 18:1-3; 2Ch 34:2

[a] 16 Most Hebrew manuscripts; one Hebrew manuscript, Septuagint and Vulgate (see also 2 Kings 16:7) *king*
[b] 19 That is, Judah, as frequently in 2 Chronicles [c] 20 Hebrew *Tilgath-Pilneser*, a variant of *Tiglath-Pileser*

3In the first month of the first
year of his reign, he opened the
doors of the temple of the LORD
and repaired them. 4He brought in
the priests and the Levites, assembled them in the square on the
east side 5and said: "Listen to me,
Levites! Consecrate yourselves
now and consecrate the temple
of the LORD, the God of your ancestors. Remove all defilement
from the sanctuary. 6Our parents
were unfaithful; they did evil in
the eyes of the LORD our God and
forsook him. They turned their
faces away from the LORD's dwelling place and turned their backs
on him. 7They also shut the doors
of the portico and put out the
lamps. They did not burn incense
or present any burnt offerings at
the sanctuary to the God of Israel.
8Therefore, the anger of the LORD
has fallen on Judah and Jerusalem; he has made them an object
of dread and horror and scorn, as
you can see with your own eyes.
9This is why our fathers have fall-
en by the sword and why our sons
and daughters and our wives are
in captivity. 10Now I intend to
make a covenant with the LORD,
the God of Israel, so that his fierce
anger will turn away from us. 11My
sons, do not be negligent now, for
the LORD has chosen you to stand
before him and serve him, to minister before him and to burn incense." Nu 3:6; 2Ch 23:16; Jer 25:9,18
12Then these Levites set to
work: Nu 3:17-20

from the Kohathites,
Mahath son of Amasai and
Joel son of Azariah;
from the Merarites,
Kish son of Abdi and Azariah son of Jehallelel;
from the Gershonites,
Joah son of Zimmah and
Eden son of Joah; 2Ch 31:15
13from the descendants of Elizaphan,
Shimri and Jeiel;
from the descendants of
Asaph, 1Ch 6:39
Zechariah and Mattaniah;
14from the descendants of Heman,
Jehiel and Shimei;
from the descendants of Jeduthun,
Shemaiah and Uzziel.

15When they had assembled
their fellow Levites and consecrated themselves, they went in
to purify the temple of the LORD,
as the king had ordered, following the word of the LORD. 16The
priests went into the sanctuary
of the LORD to purify it. They
brought out to the courtyard of
the LORD's temple everything unclean that they found in the temple of the LORD. The Levites took
it and carried it out to the Kidron
Valley. 17They began the consecration on the first day of the first
month, and by the eighth day of
the month they reached the portico of the LORD. For eight more
days they consecrated the temple of the LORD itself, finishing

on the sixteenth day of the first month. 1Ch 23:28; 2Ch 30:12

18 Then they went in to King Hezekiah and reported: "We have purified the entire temple of the LORD, the altar of burnt offering with all its utensils, and the table for setting out the consecrated bread, with all its articles. 19 We have prepared and consecrated all the articles that King Ahaz removed in his unfaithfulness while he was king. They are now in front of the LORD's altar." 2Ch 28:24

20 Early the next morning King Hezekiah gathered the city officials together and went up to the temple of the LORD. 21 They brought seven bulls, seven rams, seven male lambs and seven male goats as a sin offering[a] for the kingdom, for the sanctuary and for Judah. The king commanded the priests, the descendants of Aaron, to offer these on the altar of the LORD. 22 So they slaughtered the bulls, and the priests took the blood and splashed it against the altar; next they slaughtered the rams and splashed their blood against the altar; then they slaughtered the lambs and splashed their blood against the altar. 23 The goats for the sin offering were brought before the king and the assembly, and they laid their hands on them. 24 The priests then slaughtered the goats and presented their blood on the altar for a sin offering to atone for all Israel, because the king had ordered the burnt offering and the sin offering for all Israel. Lev 4:13-15,26

25 He stationed the Levites in the temple of the LORD with cymbals, harps and lyres in the way prescribed by David and Gad the king's seer and Nathan the prophet; this was commanded by the LORD through his prophets. 26 So the Levites stood ready with David's instruments, and the priests with their trumpets. 1Ch 15:24; 23:5; 25:6

27 Hezekiah gave the order to sacrifice the burnt offering on the altar. As the offering began, singing to the LORD began also, accompanied by trumpets and the instruments of David king of Israel. 28 The whole assembly bowed in worship, while the musicians played and the trumpets sounded. All this continued until the sacrifice of the burnt offering was completed. 2Ch 23:18

29 When the offerings were finished, the king and everyone present with him knelt down and worshiped. 30 King Hezekiah and his officials ordered the Levites to praise the LORD with the words of David and of Asaph the seer. So they sang praises with gladness and bowed down and worshiped. 2Ch 20:18

31 Then Hezekiah said, "You have now dedicated yourselves to the LORD. Come and bring sacrifices

[a] 21 Or *purification offering*; also in verses 23 and 24

and thank offerings to the temple of the LORD." So the assembly brought sacrifices and thank offerings, and all whose hearts were willing brought burnt offerings.

Ex 35:22; Heb 13:15-16

32 The number of burnt offerings the assembly brought was seventy bulls, a hundred rams and two hundred male lambs — all of them for burnt offerings to the LORD. 33 The animals consecrated as sacrifices amounted to six hundred bulls and three thousand sheep and goats. 34 The priests, however, were too few to skin all the burnt offerings; so their relatives the Levites helped them until the task was finished and until other priests had been consecrated, for the Levites had been more conscientious in consecrating themselves than the priests had been. 35 There were burnt offerings in abundance, together with the fat of the fellowship offerings and the drink offerings that accompanied the burnt offerings.

Lev 3:16; Nu 15:5-10; 2Ch 30:3,15

So the service of the temple of the LORD was reestablished. 36 Hezekiah and all the people rejoiced at what God had brought about for his people, because it was done so quickly.

Hezekiah Celebrates the Passover

30 Hezekiah sent word to all Israel and Judah and also wrote letters to Ephraim and Manasseh, inviting them to come to the temple of the LORD in Jerusalem and celebrate the Passover to the LORD, the God of Israel. 2 The king and his officials and the whole assembly in Jerusalem decided to celebrate the Passover in the second month. 3 They had not been able to celebrate it at the regular time because not enough priests had consecrated themselves and the people had not assembled in Jerusalem. 4 The plan seemed right both to the king and to the whole assembly. 5 They decided to send a proclamation throughout Israel, from Beersheba to Dan, calling the people to come to Jerusalem and celebrate the Passover to the LORD, the God of Israel. It had not been celebrated in large numbers according to what was written.

Jdg 20:1; Nu 9:10; 2Ch 29:34

6 At the king's command, couriers went throughout Israel and Judah with letters from the king and from his officials, which read:

> "People of Israel, return to the LORD, the God of Abraham, Isaac and Israel, that he may return to you who are left, who have escaped from the hand of the kings of Assyria. 7 Do not be like your parents and your fellow Israelites, who were unfaithful to the LORD, the God of their ancestors, so that he made them an object of horror, as you see. 8 Do not be stiff-necked,

as your ancestors were; submit to the LORD. Come to his
sanctuary, which he has consecrated forever. Serve the
LORD your God, so that his
fierce anger will turn away
from you. 9If you return to
the LORD, then your fellow
Israelites and your children
will be shown compassion by
their captors and will return
to this land, for the LORD your
God is gracious and compassionate. He will not turn his
face from you if you return to
him." Dt 30:2-5; Mic 7:18

10The couriers went from town
to town in Ephraim and Manasseh, as far as Zebulun, but people scorned and ridiculed them.
11Nevertheless, some from Asher,
Manasseh and Zebulun humbled
themselves and went to Jerusalem. 12Also in Judah the hand of
God was on the people to give
them unity of mind to carry out
what the king and his officials had
ordered, following the word of the
LORD. 2Ch 36:16; Jer 32:39

13A very large crowd of people
assembled in Jerusalem to celebrate the Festival of Unleavened
Bread in the second month. 14They
removed the altars in Jerusalem
and cleared away the incense altars and threw them into the Kidron Valley. Nu 28:16; 2Ch 28:24

15They slaughtered the Passover
lamb on the fourteenth day of the
second month. The priests and the
Levites were ashamed and consecrated themselves and brought
burnt offerings to the temple of
the LORD. 16Then they took up their
regular positions as prescribed in
the Law of Moses the man of God.
The priests splashed against the
altar the blood handed to them
by the Levites. 17Since many in the
crowd had not consecrated themselves, the Levites had to kill the
Passover lambs for all those who
were not ceremonially clean and
could not consecrate their lambs[a]
to the LORD. 18Although most of
the many people who came from
Ephraim, Manasseh, Issachar and
Zebulun had not purified themselves, yet they ate the Passover,
contrary to what was written. But
Hezekiah prayed for them, saying, "May the LORD, who is good,
pardon everyone 19who sets their
heart on seeking God — the LORD,
the God of their ancestors — even if
they are not clean according to the
rules of the sanctuary." 20And the
LORD heard Hezekiah and healed
the people. 2Ch 7:14; Mal 4:2; Jas 5:16

21The Israelites who were present in Jerusalem celebrated the
Festival of Unleavened Bread
for seven days with great rejoicing, while the Levites and priests
praised the LORD every day with
resounding instruments dedicated to the LORD.[b]

[a] 17 Or *consecrate themselves* [b] 21 Or *priests sang to the LORD every day, accompanied by the LORD's instruments of praise*

22 Hezekiah spoke encouraging-
ly to all the Levites, who showed
good understanding of the service
of the LORD. For the seven days
they ate their assigned portion
and offered fellowship offerings
and praised[a] the LORD, the God of
their ancestors. Ex 12:15,17; 13:6
23 The whole assembly then
agreed to celebrate the festival
seven more days; so for another
seven days they celebrated joyfully. 24 Hezekiah king of Judah
provided a thousand bulls and
seven thousand sheep and goats
for the assembly, and the officials
provided them with a thousand
bulls and ten thousand sheep and
goats. A great number of priests
consecrated themselves. 25 The entire assembly of Judah rejoiced,
along with the priests and Levites
and all who had assembled from
Israel, including the foreigners
who had come from Israel and
also those who resided in Judah.
26 There was great joy in Jerusalem, for since the days of Solomon
son of David king of Israel there
had been nothing like this in Jerusalem. 27 The priests and the Levites stood to bless the people, and
God heard them, for their prayer
reached heaven, his holy dwelling
place. Nu 6:23; Dt 26:15; 2Ch 23:18

31 When all this had ended, the
Israelites who were there
went out to the towns of Judah,
smashed the sacred stones and
cut down the Asherah poles. They
destroyed the high places and the
altars throughout Judah and Benjamin and in Ephraim and Manasseh. After they had destroyed all
of them, the Israelites returned to
their own towns and to their own
property. 2Ki 18:4; 2Ch 32:12; Isa 36:7

Contributions for Worship

2 Hezekiah assigned the priests
and Levites to divisions — each of
them according to their duties as
priests or Levites — to offer burnt
offerings and fellowship offerings, to minister, to give thanks
and to sing praises at the gates
of the LORD's dwelling. 3 The king
contributed from his own possessions for the morning and evening burnt offerings and for the
burnt offerings on the Sabbaths,
at the New Moons and at the appointed festivals as written in
the Law of the LORD. 4 He ordered
the people living in Jerusalem to
give the portion due the priests
and Levites so they could devote themselves to the Law of the
LORD. 5 As soon as the order went
out, the Israelites generously
gave the firstfruits of their grain,
new wine, olive oil and honey
and all that the fields produced.
They brought a great amount, a
tithe of everything. 6 The people
of Israel and Judah who lived in
the towns of Judah also brought a
tithe of their herds and flocks and
a tithe of the holy things dedicated to the LORD their God, and they
piled them in heaps. 7 They began

[a] 22 Or *and confessed their sins to*

doing this in the third month and
finished in the seventh month.
[8]When Hezekiah and his officials
came and saw the heaps, they
praised the LORD and blessed his
people Israel. Dt 14:28; Ps 144:13-15

[9]Hezekiah asked the priests and
Levites about the heaps; [10]and Azariah the chief priest, from the
family of Zadok, answered, "Since
the people began to bring their
contributions to the temple of the
LORD, we have had enough to eat
and plenty to spare, because the
LORD has blessed his people, and
this great amount is left over."

Mal 3:10-12

[11]Hezekiah gave orders to prepare storerooms in the temple
of the LORD, and this was done.
[12]Then they faithfully brought in
the contributions, tithes and dedicated gifts. Konaniah, a Levite,
was the overseer in charge of these
things, and his brother Shimei was
next in rank. [13]Jehiel, Azaziah, Nahath, Asahel, Jerimoth, Jozabad,
Eliel, Ismakiah, Mahath and Benaiah were assistants of Konaniah
and Shimei his brother. All these
served by appointment of King
Hezekiah and Azariah the official
in charge of the temple of God.

2Ch 35:9

[14]Kore son of Imnah the Levite, keeper of the East Gate, was
in charge of the freewill offerings
given to God, distributing the contributions made to the LORD and
also the consecrated gifts. [15]Eden,
Miniamin, Jeshua, Shemaiah,
Amariah and Shekaniah assisted
him faithfully in the towns of the
priests, distributing to their fellow priests according to their divisions, old and young alike.

Jos 21:9-19; 2Ch 29:12

[16]In addition, they distributed to the males three years old or
more whose names were in the
genealogical records — all who
would enter the temple of the
LORD to perform the daily duties
of their various tasks, according to
their responsibilities and their divisions. [17]And they distributed to
the priests enrolled by their families in the genealogical records
and likewise to the Levites twenty years old or more, according
to their responsibilities and their
divisions. [18]They included all the
little ones, the wives, and the sons
and daughters of the whole community listed in these genealogical records. For they were faithful
in consecrating themselves.

1Ch 23:3; Ezr 3:4

[19]As for the priests, the descendants of Aaron, who lived on the
farmlands around their towns or
in any other towns, men were designated by name to distribute portions to every male among them
and to all who were recorded in
the genealogies of the Levites.

[20]This is what Hezekiah did
throughout Judah, doing what was
good and right and faithful before
the LORD his God. [21]In everything
that he undertook in the service
of God's temple and in obedience

to the law and the commands, he
sought his God and worked wholeheartedly. And so he prospered.
2Ki 18:5-7

Sennacherib Threatens Jerusalem

32 After all that Hezekiah had
so faithfully done, Sen-
nacherib king of Assyria came
and invaded Judah. He laid siege
to the fortified cities, thinking to
conquer them for himself. 2When
Hezekiah saw that Sennacherib
had come and that he intended to
wage war against Jerusalem, 3he
consulted with his officials and
military staff about blocking off
the water from the springs outside the city, and they helped him.
4They gathered a large group of
people who blocked all the springs
and the stream that flowed
through the land. "Why should
the kings[a] of Assyria come and
find plenty of water?" they said.
5Then he worked hard repairing
all the broken sections of the wall
and building towers on it. He built
another wall outside that one and
reinforced the terraces[b] of the City
of David. He also made large numbers of weapons and shields.
1Ki 9:24; 1Ch 11:8; Isa 22:8

6He appointed military officers
over the people and assembled
them before him in the square at
the city gate and encouraged them
with these words: 7"Be strong and
courageous. Do not be afraid or
discouraged because of the king
of Assyria and the vast army with
him, for there is a greater power
with us than with him. 8With him
is only the arm of flesh, but with
us is the LORD our God to help us
and to fight our battles." And the
people gained confidence from
what Hezekiah the king of Judah
said. 2Ki 6:16; 2Ch 20:17; Jer 17:5

9Later, when Sennacherib king
of Assyria and all his forces were
laying siege to Lachish, he sent
his officers to Jerusalem with this
message for Hezekiah king of Judah and for all the people of Judah who were there: Jos 10:3,31

> 10"This is what Sennacherib
> king of Assyria says: On what
> are you basing your confi-
> dence, that you remain in Je-
> rusalem under siege? 11When
> Hezekiah says, 'The LORD our
> God will save us from the
> hand of the king of Assyria,'
> he is misleading you, to let
> you die of hunger and thirst.
> 12Did not Hezekiah himself
> remove this god's high plac-
> es and altars, saying to Judah
> and Jerusalem, 'You must
> worship before one altar and
> burn sacrifices on it'?
> 2Ch 31:1; Isa 37:10; Eze 29:16
>
> 13"Do you not know what
> I and my predecessors have
> done to all the peoples of the
> other lands? Were the gods of
> those nations ever able to de-
> liver their land from my hand?

[a] 4 Hebrew; Septuagint and Syriac *king*
[b] 5 Or *the Millo*

14 Who of all the gods of these
nations that my predecessors
destroyed has been able to
save his people from me? How
then can your god deliver you
from my hand? 15 Now do not
let Hezekiah deceive you and
mislead you like this. Do not
believe him, for no god of any
nation or kingdom has been
able to deliver his people
from my hand or the hand of
my predecessors. How much
less will your god deliver you
from my hand!" Ex 5:2; Da 3:15

16 Sennacherib's officers spoke
further against the LORD God and
against his servant Hezekiah.
17 The king also wrote letters ridi-
culing the LORD, the God of Israel, and saying this against him:
"Just as the gods of the peoples
of the other lands did not rescue
their people from my hand, so the
god of Hezekiah will not rescue
his people from my hand." 18 Then
they called out in Hebrew to the
people of Jerusalem who were
on the wall, to terrify them and
make them afraid in order to capture the city. 19 They spoke about
the God of Jerusalem as they did
about the gods of the other peoples of the world — the work of
human hands. 2Ki 18:17-35; Isa 36:2-20

20 King Hezekiah and the prophet Isaiah son of Amoz cried out in
prayer to heaven about this. 21 And
the LORD sent an angel, who annihilated all the fighting men and
the commanders and officers in
the camp of the Assyrian king. So
he withdrew to his own land in
disgrace. And when he went into
the temple of his god, some of his
sons, his own flesh and blood, cut
him down with the sword.
2Ki 19:35-37; Isa 37:36-38

22 So the LORD saved Hezekiah
and the people of Jerusalem from
the hand of Sennacherib king of
Assyria and from the hand of all
others. He took care of them[a] on
every side. 23 Many brought offerings to Jerusalem for the LORD and
valuable gifts for Hezekiah king of
Judah. From then on he was highly regarded by all the nations.
2Ch 17:5; Isa 45:14

Hezekiah's Pride, Success and Death

24 In those days Hezekiah became ill and was at the point of
death. He prayed to the LORD, who
answered him and gave him a miraculous sign. 25 But Hezekiah's
heart was proud and he did not
respond to the kindness shown
him; therefore the LORD's wrath
was on him and on Judah and Jerusalem. 26 Then Hezekiah repented of the pride of his heart, as did
the people of Jerusalem; therefore
the LORD's wrath did not come on
them during the days of Hezekiah.
2Ch 26:16; Jer 26:18-19

27 Hezekiah had very great
wealth and honor, and he made

[a] 22 Hebrew; Septuagint and Vulgate *He gave them rest*

treasuries for his silver and gold
and for his precious stones, spices,
shields and all kinds of valuables.
28He also made buildings to store
the harvest of grain, new wine and
olive oil; and he made stalls for
various kinds of cattle, and pens
for the flocks. 29He built villages
and acquired great numbers of
flocks and herds, for God had giv-
en him very great riches. 1Ch 29:12

30It was Hezekiah who blocked
the upper outlet of the Gihon
spring and channeled the water
down to the west side of the City
of David. He succeeded in everything he undertook. 31But when
envoys were sent by the rulers of
Babylon to ask him about the miraculous sign that had occurred in
the land, God left him to test him
and to know everything that was
in his heart. Dt 8:16; Isa 39:1

32The other events of Hezekiah's
reign and his acts of devotion are
written in the vision of the prophet Isaiah son of Amoz in the book
of the kings of Judah and Israel.
33Hezekiah rested with his ancestors and was buried on the hill
where the tombs of David's descendants are. All Judah and the
people of Jerusalem honored him
when he died. And Manasseh his
son succeeded him as king.

2Ki 20:1-21; Isa 37:21-38; 38:1-8

Manasseh King of Judah

33 Manasseh was twelve years
old when he became king,
and he reigned in Jerusalem fifty-
five years. 2He did evil in the eyes
of the LORD, following the detestable practices of the nations the
LORD had driven out before the
Israelites. 3He rebuilt the high
places his father Hezekiah had
demolished; he also erected altars
to the Baals and made Asherah
poles. He bowed down to all the
starry hosts and worshiped them.
4He built altars in the temple of
the LORD, of which the LORD had
said, "My Name will remain in Jerusalem forever." 5In both courts
of the temple of the LORD, he
built altars to all the starry hosts.
6He sacrificed his children in the
fire in the Valley of Ben Hinnom,
practiced divination and witchcraft, sought omens, and consulted mediums and spiritists. He did
much evil in the eyes of the LORD,
arousing his anger.

Lev 18:21; 19:31; 1Sa 28:13

7He took the image he had made
and put it in God's temple, of
which God had said to David and
to his son Solomon, "In this temple and in Jerusalem, which I have
chosen out of all the tribes of Israel, I will put my Name forever. 8I
will not again make the feet of the
Israelites leave the land I assigned
to your ancestors, if only they will
be careful to do everything I commanded them concerning all the
laws, decrees and regulations giv-
en through Moses." 9But Manasseh led Judah and the people of
Jerusalem astray, so that they did
more evil than the nations the

LORD had destroyed before the Israelites. 2Ki 21:1-10; Jer 15:4
10The LORD spoke to Manasseh
and his people, but they paid no
attention. 11So the LORD brought
against them the army commanders of the king of Assyria,
who took Manasseh prisoner, put
a hook in his nose, bound him
with bronze shackles and took
him to Babylon. 12In his distress
he sought the favor of the LORD
his God and humbled himself
greatly before the God of his ancestors. 13And when he prayed to
him, the LORD was moved by his
entreaty and listened to his plea;
so he brought him back to Jerusalem and to his kingdom. Then
Manasseh knew that the LORD is
God. 2Ch 32:26; 1Pe 5:6
14Afterward he rebuilt the outer
wall of the City of David, west of
the Gihon spring in the valley, as
far as the entrance of the Fish Gate
and encircling the hill of Ophel; he
also made it much higher. He stationed military commanders in all
the fortified cities in Judah.
1Ki 1:33; 2Ch 27:3
15He got rid of the foreign gods
and removed the image from the
temple of the LORD, as well as all
the altars he had built on the temple hill and in Jerusalem; and he
threw them out of the city. 16Then
he restored the altar of the LORD
and sacrificed fellowship offerings
and thank offerings on it, and told
Judah to serve the LORD, the God
of Israel. 17The people, however,
continued to sacrifice at the high
places, but only to the LORD their
God. ver 3-7; Lev 7:11-18
18The other events of Manasseh's reign, including his prayer
to his God and the words the seers
spoke to him in the name of the
LORD, the God of Israel, are written in the annals of the kings of
Israel.[a] 19His prayer and how God
was moved by his entreaty, as well
as all his sins and unfaithfulness,
and the sites where he built high
places and set up Asherah poles
and idols before he humbled himself — all these are written in the
records of the seers.[b] 20Manasseh
rested with his ancestors and was
buried in his palace. And Amon
his son succeeded him as king.
2Ki 21:17-18

Amon King of Judah

21Amon was twenty-two years
old when he became king, and
he reigned in Jerusalem two
years. 22He did evil in the eyes of
the LORD, as his father Manasseh
had done. Amon worshiped and
offered sacrifices to all the idols
Manasseh had made. 23But unlike
his father Manasseh, he did not
humble himself before the LORD;
Amon increased his guilt.
24Amon's officials conspired
against him and assassinated him
in his palace. 25Then the people of

[a] *18* That is, Judah, as frequently in 2 Chronicles [b] *19* One Hebrew manuscript and Septuagint; most Hebrew manuscripts *of Hozai*

the land killed all who had plotted against King Amon, and they
made Josiah his son king in his
place. 2Ki 21:19-24

Josiah's Reforms

34 Josiah was eight years old
when he became king, and
he reigned in Jerusalem thirty-
one years. 2He did what was right
in the eyes of the LORD and followed the ways of his father David, not turning aside to the right
or to the left. 2Ki 22:1-2; 1Ch 3:14; 2Ch 29:2

3In the eighth year of his reign,
while he was still young, he began to seek the God of his father
David. In his twelfth year he began to purge Judah and Jerusalem of high places, Asherah
poles and idols. 4Under his direction the altars of the Baals were
torn down; he cut to pieces the
incense altars that were above
them, and smashed the Asherah poles and the idols. These he
broke to pieces and scattered over
the graves of those who had sacrificed to them. 5He burned the
bones of the priests on their altars, and so he purged Judah and
Jerusalem. 6In the towns of Manasseh, Ephraim and Simeon, as
far as Naphtali, and in the ruins
around them, 7he tore down the
altars and the Asherah poles and
crushed the idols to powder and
cut to pieces all the incense altars
throughout Israel. Then he went
back to Jerusalem.
Lev 26:30; 1Ki 13:2; 2Ch 31:1

8In the eighteenth year of Josiah's reign, to purify the land and
the temple, he sent Shaphan son
of Azaliah and Maaseiah the ruler of the city, with Joah son of Joahaz, the recorder, to repair the
temple of the LORD his God.

9They went to Hilkiah the high
priest and gave him the money
that had been brought into the
temple of God, which the Levites
who were the gatekeepers had
collected from the people of Manasseh, Ephraim and the entire
remnant of Israel and from all
the people of Judah and Benjamin and the inhabitants of Jerusalem. 10Then they entrusted it to
the men appointed to supervise
the work on the LORD's temple.
These men paid the workers who
repaired and restored the temple.
11They also gave money to the carpenters and builders to purchase
dressed stone, and timber for joists
and beams for the buildings that
the kings of Judah had allowed to
fall into ruin. 2Ch 33:4-7; 35:8

12The workers labored faithfully. Over them to direct them were
Jahath and Obadiah, Levites descended from Merari, and Zechariah and Meshullam, descended
from Kohath. The Levites — all
who were skilled in playing musical instruments — 13had charge
of the laborers and supervised all
the workers from job to job. Some
of the Levites were secretaries,
scribes and gatekeepers.
2Ki 12:15; 1Ch 23:4; 25:1

The Book of the Law Found

14 While they were bringing out the money that had been taken into the temple of the LORD, Hilkiah the priest found the Book of the Law of the LORD that had been given through Moses. 15 Hilkiah said to Shaphan the secretary, "I have found the Book of the Law in the temple of the LORD." He gave it to Shaphan. 2Ki 22:8; Ezr 7:6; Ne 8:1

16 Then Shaphan took the book to the king and reported to him: "Your officials are doing everything that has been committed to them. 17 They have paid out the money that was in the temple of the LORD and have entrusted it to the supervisors and workers." 18 Then Shaphan the secretary informed the king, "Hilkiah the priest has given me a book." And Shaphan read from it in the presence of the king.

19 When the king heard the words of the Law, he tore his robes. 20 He gave these orders to Hilkiah, Ahikam son of Shaphan, Abdon son of Micah,[a] Shaphan the secretary and Asaiah the king's attendant: 21 "Go and inquire of the LORD for me and for the remnant in Israel and Judah about what is written in this book that has been found. Great is the LORD's anger that is poured out on us because those who have gone before us have not kept the word of the LORD; they have not acted in accordance with all that is written in this book." 2Ch 29:8; La 2:4; Eze 36:18

22 Hilkiah and those the king had sent with him[b] went to speak to the prophet Huldah, who was the wife of Shallum son of Tokhath,[c] the son of Hasrah,[d] keeper of the wardrobe. She lived in Jerusalem, in the New Quarter. Ex 15:20; Ne 6:14

23 She said to them, "This is what the LORD, the God of Israel, says: Tell the man who sent you to me, 24 'This is what the LORD says: I am going to bring disaster on this place and its people — all the curses written in the book that has been read in the presence of the king of Judah. 25 Because they have forsaken me and burned incense to other gods and aroused my anger by all that their hands have made,[e] my anger will be poured out on this place and will not be quenched.' 26 Tell the king of Judah, who sent you to inquire of the LORD, 'This is what the LORD, the God of Israel, says concerning the words you heard: 27 Because your heart was responsive and you humbled yourself before God when you heard what he spoke against this place and its people, and because you humbled yourself before me and tore your robes and wept in my presence, I have heard you, declares the LORD. 28 Now I will gather you

[a] 20 Also called *Akbor son of Micaiah*
[b] 22 One Hebrew manuscript, Vulgate and Syriac; most Hebrew manuscripts do not have *had sent with him.*
[c] 22 Also called *Tikvah*
[d] 22 Also called *Harhas*
[e] 25 Or *by everything they have done*

to your ancestors, and you will
be buried in peace. Your eyes will
not see all the disaster I am going to bring on this place and on
those who live here.' "
2Ch 12:7; 32:26; 35:20-25

So they took her answer back to
the king. 2Ki 22:8-20

[29]Then the king called together
all the elders of Judah and Jerusalem. [30]He went up to the temple
of the LORD with the people of Judah, the inhabitants of Jerusalem,
the priests and the Levites — all
the people from the least to the
greatest. He read in their hearing
all the words of the Book of the
Covenant, which had been found
in the temple of the LORD. [31]The
king stood by his pillar and renewed the covenant in the presence of the LORD — to follow the
LORD and keep his commands,
statutes and decrees with all his
heart and all his soul, and to obey
the words of the covenant written
in this book.

[32]Then he had everyone in Jerusalem and Benjamin pledge themselves to it; the people of Jerusalem did this in accordance with
the covenant of God, the God of
their ancestors. 2Ki 23:1-3; 2Ch 23:16

[33]Josiah removed all the detestable idols from all the territory
belonging to the Israelites, and he
had all who were present in Israel
serve the LORD their God. As long
as he lived, they did not fail to follow the LORD, the God of their ancestors. ver 3-7; Dt 18:9

Josiah Celebrates the Passover

35 Josiah celebrated the Passover to the LORD in Jerusalem, and the Passover lamb was
slaughtered on the fourteenth
day of the first month. [2]He appointed the priests to their duties and encouraged them in the
service of the LORD's temple. [3]He
said to the Levites, who instructed all Israel and who had been
consecrated to the LORD: "Put the
sacred ark in the temple that Solomon son of David king of Israel
built. It is not to be carried about
on your shoulders. Now serve the
LORD your God and his people Israel. [4]Prepare yourselves by families in your divisions, according to
the instructions written by David
king of Israel and by his son Solomon. Ex 12:1-30; 2Ch 17:7; Ezr 6:18

[5]"Stand in the holy place with a
group of Levites for each subdivi-
sion of the families of your fellow
Israelites, the lay people. [6]Slaugh-
ter the Passover lambs, consecrate yourselves and prepare the
lambs for your fellow Israelites,
doing what the LORD commanded through Moses."
Lev 11:44; 2Ch 29:5,15

[7]Josiah provided for all the lay
people who were there a total of
thirty thousand lambs and goats
for the Passover offerings, and
also three thousand cattle — all
from the king's own possessions.
2Ch 30:24; 31:3

[8]His officials also contributed
voluntarily to the people and the

priests and Levites. Hilkiah, Zechariah and Jehiel, the officials in
charge of God's temple, gave the
priests twenty-six hundred Passover offerings and three hundred cattle. 9 Also Konaniah along
with Shemaiah and Nethanel,
his brothers, and Hashabiah, Jeiel and Jozabad, the leaders of the
Levites, provided five thousand
Passover offerings and five hundred head of cattle for the Levites.

2Ch 31:12-13

10 The service was arranged and
the priests stood in their places
with the Levites in their divisions
as the king had ordered. 11 The
Passover lambs were slaughtered,
and the priests splashed against
the altar the blood handed to
them, while the Levites skinned
the animals. 12 They set aside the
burnt offerings to give them to the
subdivisions of the families of the
people to offer to the LORD, as it is
written in the Book of Moses. They
did the same with the cattle. 13 They
roasted the Passover animals over
the fire as prescribed, and boiled
the holy offerings in pots, caldrons
and pans and served them quickly to all the people. 14 After this,
they made preparations for themselves and for the priests, because
the priests, the descendants of
Aaron, were sacrificing the burnt
offerings and the fat portions until nightfall. So the Levites made
preparations for themselves and
for the Aaronic priests.

Ex 12:2-11; 29:13; 2Ch 29:22,34

15 The musicians, the descendants of Asaph, were in the places prescribed by David, Asaph,
Heman and Jeduthun the king's
seer. The gatekeepers at each gate
did not need to leave their posts,
because their fellow Levites made
the preparations for them.

1Ch 25:1; 26:12-19; 2Ch 29:30

16 So at that time the entire service of the LORD was carried out
for the celebration of the Passover
and the offering of burnt offerings
on the altar of the LORD, as King
Josiah had ordered. 17 The Israelites who were present celebrated the Passover at that time and
observed the Festival of Unleavened Bread for seven days. 18 The
Passover had not been observed
like this in Israel since the days of
the prophet Samuel; and none of
the kings of Israel had ever celebrated such a Passover as did Josiah, with the priests, the Levites
and all Judah and Israel who were
there with the people of Jerusalem. 19 This Passover was celebrated in the eighteenth year of Josiah's reign.

2Ki 23:21-23

The Death of Josiah

20 After all this, when Josiah
had set the temple in order, Necho king of Egypt went up to fight
at Carchemish on the Euphrates,
and Josiah marched out to meet
him in battle. 21 But Necho sent
messengers to him, saying, "What
quarrel is there, king of Judah,
between you and me? It is not

you I am attacking at this time,
but the house with which I am at
war. God has told me to hurry; so
stop opposing God, who is with
me, or he will destroy you."
1Ki 13:18; Isa 10:9

22 Josiah, however, would not
turn away from him, but disguised himself to engage him in
battle. He would not listen to what
Necho had said at God's command
but went to fight him on the plain
of Megiddo. 1Sa 28:8; 2Ch 18:29

23 Archers shot King Josiah, and
he told his officers, "Take me
away; I am badly wounded." 24 So
they took him out of his chariot,
put him in his other chariot and
brought him to Jerusalem, where
he died. He was buried in the
tombs of his ancestors, and all Judah and Jerusalem mourned for
him. 1Ki 22:34

25 Jeremiah composed laments
for Josiah, and to this day all the
male and female singers commemorate Josiah in the laments.
These became a tradition in Israel
and are written in the Laments.
Jer 22:10,15-16

26 The other events of Josiah's
reign and his acts of devotion in
accordance with what is written
in the Law of the LORD — 27 all the
events, from beginning to end, are
written in the book of the kings of

36 Israel and Judah. 1 And the
people of the land took Jehoahaz son of Josiah and made
him king in Jerusalem in place of
his father. 2Ki 23:28-30

Jehoahaz King of Judah

2 Jehoahaz[a] was twenty-three
years old when he became king,
and he reigned in Jerusalem three
months. 3 The king of Egypt de-
throned him in Jerusalem and
imposed on Judah a levy of a
hundred talents[b] of silver and a
talent[c] of gold. 4 The king of Egypt
made Eliakim, a brother of Jehoahaz, king over Judah and Jerusalem and changed Eliakim's name
to Jehoiakim. But Necho took Eliakim's brother Jehoahaz and carried him off to Egypt. 2Ki 23:31-34

Jehoiakim King of Judah

5 Jehoiakim was twenty-five
years old when he became king,
and he reigned in Jerusalem elev-
en years. He did evil in the eyes
of the LORD his God. 6 Nebuchadnezzar king of Babylon attacked
him and bound him with bronze
shackles to take him to Babylon.
7 Nebuchadnezzar also took to Babylon articles from the temple of
the LORD and put them in his temple[d] there. 2Ki 24:13; Jer 26:1; 35:1

8 The other events of Jehoiakim's
reign, the detestable things he
did and all that was found against
him, are written in the book of the
kings of Israel and Judah. And Jehoiachin his son succeeded him as
king. 2Ki 23:36-24:6

[a] 2 Hebrew *Joahaz*, a variant of *Jehoahaz*; also in verse 4 [b] 3 That is, about 3 3/4 tons or about 3.4 metric tons [c] 3 That is, about 75 pounds or about 34 kilograms [d] 7 Or *palace*

Jehoiachin King of Judah

9 Jehoiachin was eighteen[a] years old when he became king, and he reigned in Jerusalem three months and ten days. He did evil in the eyes of the LORD.
10 In the spring, King Nebuchadnezzar sent for him and brought him to Babylon, together with articles of value from the temple of the LORD, and he made Jehoiachin's uncle,[b] Zedekiah, king over Judah and Jerusalem. Jer 22:25; 37:1; Eze 17:12

Zedekiah King of Judah

11 Zedekiah was twenty-one years old when he became king, and he reigned in Jerusalem eleven years.
12 He did evil in the eyes of the LORD his God and did not humble himself before Jeremiah the prophet, who spoke the word of the LORD.
13 He also rebelled against King Nebuchadnezzar, who had made him take an oath in God's name. He became stiff-necked and hardened his heart and would not turn to the LORD, the God of Israel.
14 Furthermore, all the leaders of the priests and the people became more and more unfaithful, following all the detestable practices of the nations and defiling the temple of the LORD, which he had consecrated in Jerusalem.

2Ki 24:18-20; Jer 52:1-3

The Fall of Jerusalem

15 The LORD, the God of their ancestors, sent word to them through his messengers again and again, because he had pity on his people and on his dwelling place.
16 But they mocked God's messengers, despised his words and scoffed at his prophets until the wrath of the LORD was aroused against his people and there was no remedy.
17 He brought up against them the king of the Babylonians,[c] who killed their young men with the sword in the sanctuary, and did not spare young men or young women, the elderly or the infirm. God gave them all into the hands of Nebuchadnezzar.
18 He carried to Babylon all the articles from the temple of God, both large and small, and the treasures of the LORD's temple and the treasures of the king and his officials.
19 They set fire to God's temple and broke down the wall of Jerusalem; they burned all the palaces and destroyed everything of value there.

1Ki 9:8-9; Ps 79:1-3

20 He carried into exile to Babylon the remnant, who escaped from the sword, and they became servants to him and his successors until the kingdom of Persia came to power.
21 The land enjoyed its sabbath rests; all the time of its desolation it rested, until the seventy years were completed

[a] 9 One Hebrew manuscript, some Septuagint manuscripts and Syriac (see also 2 Kings 24:8); most Hebrew manuscripts *eight* [b] 10 Hebrew *brother,* that is, relative (see 2 Kings 24:17) [c] 17 Or *Chaldeans*

in fulfillment of the word of the
LORD spoken by Jeremiah.

Ezr 1:1-3; Jer 25:11; 29:10

22In the first year of Cyrus king
of Persia, in order to fulfill the
word of the LORD spoken by Jeremiah, the LORD moved the heart
of Cyrus king of Persia to make
a proclamation throughout his
realm and also to put it in writing:

Isa 44:28; Jer 25:12; 29:10

23"This is what Cyrus king of Persia says:

" 'The LORD, the God of heaven, has given me all the kingdoms of the earth and he has appointed me to build a temple for him at Jerusalem in Judah. Any of his people among you may go up, and may the LORD their God be with them.' "

Jdg 4:10

EZRA

Cyrus Helps the Exiles to Return

1 In the first year of Cyrus king
of Persia, in order to fulfill the
word of the LORD spoken by Jeremiah, the LORD moved the heart
of Cyrus king of Persia to make
a proclamation throughout his
realm and also to put it in writing:
Jer 25:11-12; 29:10-14

2 "This is what Cyrus king of
Persia says: 2Ch 36:22-23
" 'The LORD, the God of heav-
en, has given me all the kingdoms of the earth and he has
appointed me to build a temple for him at Jerusalem in Judah. 3 Any of his people among
you may go up to Jerusalem in
Judah and build the temple of
the LORD, the God of Israel, the
God who is in Jerusalem, and
may their God be with them.
4 And in any locality where survivors may now be living, the
people are to provide them
with silver and gold, with
goods and livestock, and with
freewill offerings for the temple of God in Jerusalem.' "
Ezr 4:3; 5:13; 6:3,14

5 Then the family heads of Judah
and Benjamin, and the priests and
Levites — everyone whose heart
God had moved — prepared to go
up and build the house of the LORD
in Jerusalem. 6 All their neighbors
assisted them with articles of silver
and gold, with goods and livestock,
and with valuable gifts, in addition
to all the freewill offerings.

7 Moreover, King Cyrus brought
out the articles belonging to the
temple of the LORD, which Nebuchadnezzar had carried away from
Jerusalem and had placed in the
temple of his god.[a] 8 Cyrus king of
Persia had them brought by Mithredath the treasurer, who counted them out to Sheshbazzar the
prince of Judah. 2Ki 24:13; Ezr 5:14
9 This was the inventory:

gold dishes	30
silver dishes	1,000
silver pans[b]	29
10 gold bowls	30
matching silver bowls	410
other articles	1,000

11 In all, there were 5,400 articles
of gold and of silver. Sheshbazzar
brought all these along with the
exiles when they came up from
Babylon to Jerusalem.

The List of the Exiles Who Returned

2 Now these are the people of
the province who came up
from the captivity of the exiles,

[a] 7 Or *gods* [b] 9 The meaning of the Hebrew for this word is uncertain.

whom Nebuchadnezzar king of
Babylon had taken captive to Babylon (they returned to Jerusalem and Judah, each to their own
town, [2]in company with Zerubbabel, Joshua, Nehemiah, Seraiah,
Reelaiah, Mordecai, Bilshan, Mis-
par, Bigvai, Rehum and Baanah):
2Ch 36:20; Ne 7:6,73

The list of the men of the people of Israel:

[3]the descendants of Parosh 2,172
[4]of Shephatiah 372
[5]of Arah 775
[6]of Pahath-Moab (through the line of Jeshua and Joab) 2,812
[7]of Elam 1,254
[8]of Zattu 945
[9]of Zakkai 760
[10]of Bani 642
[11]of Bebai 623
[12]of Azgad 1,222
[13]of Adonikam 666
[14]of Bigvai 2,056
[15]of Adin 454
[16]of Ater (through Hezekiah) 98
[17]of Bezai 323
[18]of Jorah 112
[19]of Hashum 223
[20]of Gibbar 95

[21]the men of Bethlehem 123
[22]of Netophah 56
[23]of Anathoth 128
[24]of Azmaveth 42
[25]of Kiriath Jearim,[a] Kephirah and Beeroth 743
[26]of Ramah and Geba 621
[27]of Mikmash 122
[28]of Bethel and Ai 223
[29]of Nebo 52
[30]of Magbish 156
[31]of the other Elam 1,254
[32]of Harim 320
[33]of Lod, Hadid and Ono 725
[34]of Jericho 345
[35]of Senaah 3,630

[36]The priests:

the descendants of Jedaiah (through the family of Jeshua) 973
[37]of Immer 1,052
[38]of Pashhur 1,247
[39]of Harim 1,017

[40]The Levites:
Ge 29:34; Nu 3:9; Dt 18:6-7

the descendants of Jeshua and Kadmiel (of the line of Hodaviah) 74

[41]The musicians: 1Ch 15:16

the descendants of Asaph 128

[42]The gatekeepers of the temple: 1Sa 3:15; 1Ch 9:17

the descendants of Shallum, Ater, Talmon, Akkub, Hatita and Shobai 139

[a] 25 See Septuagint (see also Neh. 7:29); Hebrew *Kiriath Arim*.

[43]The temple servants: 1Ch 9:2; Ne 11:21

the descendants of
Ziha, Hasupha,
Tabbaoth,
[44]Keros, Siaha, Padon,
[45]Lebanah, Hagabah,
Akkub,
[46]Hagab, Shalmai, Hanan,
[47]Giddel, Gahar, Reaiah,
[48]Rezin, Nekoda, Gazzam,
[49]Uzza, Paseah, Besai,
[50]Asnah, Meunim,
Nephusim,
[51]Bakbuk, Hakupha,
Harhur,
[52]Bazluth, Mehida, Harsha,
[53]Barkos, Sisera, Temah,
[54]Neziah and Hatipha

[55]The descendants of the servants of Solomon:

the descendants of
Sotai, Hassophereth,
Peruda,
[56]Jaala, Darkon, Giddel,
[57]Shephatiah, Hattil,
Pokereth-Hazzebaim
and Ami

[58]The temple servants
and the descendants
of the servants of
Solomon 392

[59]The following came up
from the towns of Tel Melah,
Tel Harsha, Kerub, Addon and
Immer, but they could not
show that their families were
descended from Israel: Nu 1:18

[60]The descendants of
Delaiah, Tobiah and
Nekoda 652

[61]And from among the priests:

The descendants of
Hobaiah, Hakkoz and
Barzillai (a man who had
married a daughter of
Barzillai the Gileadite
and was called by that
name). 2Sa 17:27

[62]These searched for their
family records, but they could
not find them and so were excluded from the priesthood
as unclean. [63]The governor
ordered them not to eat any
of the most sacred food until
there was a priest ministering with the Urim and Thummim. Ex 28:30; Lev 2:3,10

[64]The whole company numbered 42,360, [65]besides their
7,337 male and female slaves;
and they also had 200 male
and female singers. [66]They
had 736 horses, 245 mules,
[67]435 camels and 6,720 donkeys. Isa 66:20

[68]When they arrived at the
house of the LORD in Jerusalem,
some of the heads of the families
gave freewill offerings toward the
rebuilding of the house of God on
its site. [69]According to their ability
they gave to the treasury for this
work 61,000 darics[a] of gold, 5,000

[a] 69 That is, about 1,100 pounds or about 500 kilograms

minas[a] of silver and 100 priestly
garments. Ex 25:2

70 The priests, the Levites, the
musicians, the gatekeepers and
the temple servants settled in their
own towns, along with some of the
other people, and the rest of the Israelites settled in their towns.
Ne 7:6-73; 11:3-4

Rebuilding the Altar

3 When the seventh month came
and the Israelites had settled
in their towns, the people assembled together as one in Jerusalem.
2 Then Joshua son of Jozadak and
his fellow priests and Zerubbabel son of Shealtiel and his associates began to build the altar of
the God of Israel to sacrifice burnt
offerings on it, in accordance with
what is written in the Law of Moses the man of God. 3 Despite their
fear of the peoples around them,
they built the altar on its foundation and sacrificed burnt offerings
on it to the LORD, both the morning and evening sacrifices. 4 Then
in accordance with what is written, they celebrated the Festival
of Tabernacles with the required
number of burnt offerings prescribed for each day. 5 After that,
they presented the regular burnt
offerings, the New Moon sacrifices and the sacrifices for all the
appointed sacred festivals of the
LORD, as well as those brought as
freewill offerings to the LORD. 6 On
the first day of the seventh month
they began to offer burnt offerings
to the LORD, though the foundation of the LORD's temple had not
yet been laid. Ex 23:16; Nu 29:12-39

Rebuilding the Temple

7 Then they gave money to the
masons and carpenters, and gave
food and drink and olive oil to the
people of Sidon and Tyre, so that
they would bring cedar logs by sea
from Lebanon to Joppa, as autho-
rized by Cyrus king of Persia.
Ezr 1:2-4; 6:3

8 In the second month of the
second year after their arrival at
the house of God in Jerusalem, Zerubbabel son of Shealtiel, Joshua
son of Jozadak and the rest of the
people (the priests and the Levites
and all who had returned from
the captivity to Jerusalem) began
the work. They appointed Levites
twenty years old and older to supervise the building of the house
of the LORD. 9 Joshua and his sons
and brothers and Kadmiel and
his sons (descendants of Hodaviah[b]) and the sons of Henadad and
their sons and brothers — all Levites — joined together in supervising those working on the house
of God. 1Ch 23:24; Ezr 2:40

10 When the builders laid the
foundation of the temple of the
LORD, the priests in their vest-
ments and with trumpets, and
the Levites (the sons of Asaph)
with cymbals, took their places to

[a] 69 That is, about 3 tons or about 2.8 metric tons [b] 9 Hebrew *Yehudah*, a variant of *Hodaviah*

praise the LORD, as prescribed by David king of Israel. 11With praise and thanksgiving they sang to the LORD: 1Ch 6:31; 25:1; Zec 6:12

"He is good;
his love toward Israel
endures forever."
1Ch 16:34,41; 2Ch 7:3; Ps 107:1

And all the people gave a great shout of praise to the LORD, because the foundation of the house of the LORD was laid. 12But many of the older priests and Levites and family heads, who had seen the former temple, wept aloud when they saw the foundation of this temple being laid, while many others shouted for joy. 13No one could distinguish the sound of the shouts of joy from the sound of weeping, because the people made so much noise. And the sound was heard far away.
Ne 12:24; Isa 16:9

Opposition to the Rebuilding

4 When the enemies of Judah and Benjamin heard that the exiles were building a temple for the LORD, the God of Israel, 2they came to Zerubbabel and to the heads of the families and said, "Let us help you build because, like you, we seek your God and have been sacrificing to him since the time of Esarhaddon king of Assyria, who brought us here."
2Ki 17:24,41

3But Zerubbabel, Joshua and the rest of the heads of the families of Israel answered, "You have no part with us in building a temple to our God. We alone will build it for the LORD, the God of Israel, as King Cyrus, the king of Persia, commanded us." Ezr 1:1-4; Ne 2:20

4Then the peoples around them set out to discourage the people of Judah and make them afraid to go on building.[a] 5They bribed officials to work against them and frustrate their plans during the entire reign of Cyrus king of Persia and down to the reign of Darius king of Persia. Ezr 3:3

Later Opposition Under Xerxes and Artaxerxes

6At the beginning of the reign of Xerxes,[b] they lodged an accusation against the people of Judah and Jerusalem. Est 1:1; Da 9:1

7And in the days of Artaxerxes king of Persia, Bishlam, Mithredath, Tabeel and the rest of his associates wrote a letter to Artaxerxes. The letter was written in Aramaic script and in the Aramaic language.[c,d] 2Ki 18:26; Da 2:4

8Rehum the commanding officer and Shimshai the secretary wrote a letter against Jerusalem to Artaxerxes the king as follows:

9Rehum the commanding officer and Shimshai the secretary, together with the rest of their associates — the judges,

[a] 4 Or *and troubled them as they built*
[b] 6 Hebrew *Ahasuerus*
[c] 7 Or *written in Aramaic and translated*
[d] 7 The text of 4:8 – 6:18 is in Aramaic.

officials and administrators
over the people from Persia,
Uruk and Babylon, the Elamites of Susa, [10]and the other
people whom the great and
honorable Ashurbanipal deported and settled in the city
of Samaria and elsewhere in
Trans-Euphrates. Ezr 5:6; Ne 4:2

[11](This is a copy of the letter they sent him.)

To King Artaxerxes,

From your servants in Trans-Euphrates:

[12]The king should know
that the people who came up
to us from you have gone to
Jerusalem and are rebuilding that rebellious and wicked city. They are restoring the
walls and repairing the foundations. Ezr 5:3,9
[13]Furthermore, the king
should know that if this city
is built and its walls are restored, no more taxes, tribute or duty will be paid, and
eventually the royal revenues
will suffer.[a] [14]Now since we
are under obligation to the
palace and it is not proper for
us to see the king dishonored,
we are sending this message
to inform the king, [15]so that
a search may be made in the
archives of your predecessors.
In these records you will find
that this city is a rebellious
city, troublesome to kings
and provinces, a place with
a long history of sedition.
That is why this city was destroyed. [16]We inform the king
that if this city is built and its
walls are restored, you will be
left with nothing in Trans-Euphrates. Ezr 7:24; Ne 5:4; Est 3:8

[17]The king sent this reply:

To Rehum the commanding officer, Shimshai the secretary and the rest of their associates living in Samaria and elsewhere in Trans-Euphrates:

Greetings.

[18]The letter you sent us has
been read and translated in
my presence. [19]I issued an order and a search was made,
and it was found that this city
has a long history of revolt
against kings and has been
a place of rebellion and sedition. [20]Jerusalem has had
powerful kings ruling over
the whole of Trans-Euphrates,
and taxes, tribute and duty
were paid to them. [21]Now issue an order to these men to
stop work, so that this city
will not be rebuilt until I so
order. [22]Be careful not to neglect this matter. Why let this
threat grow, to the detriment
of the royal interests?
1Ki 4:21; 2Ki 18:7; Da 6:2

[a] *13* The meaning of the Aramaic for this clause is uncertain.

23 As soon as the copy of the letter of King Artaxerxes was read
to Rehum and Shimshai the secretary and their associates, they
went immediately to the Jews in
Jerusalem and compelled them by
force to stop.

24 Thus the work on the house of
God in Jerusalem came to a stand-
still until the second year of the
reign of Darius king of Persia.

Ne 2:1-8; Da 9:25; Hag 1:1,15

Tattenai's Letter to Darius

5 Now Haggai the prophet and
Zechariah the prophet, a descendant of Iddo, prophesied to
the Jews in Judah and Jerusalem
in the name of the God of Israel,
who was over them. 2 Then Zerubbabel son of Shealtiel and Joshua
son of Jozadak set to work to rebuild the house of God in Jerusalem. And the prophets of God were
with them, supporting them.

Ezr 3:2; Zec 1:1

3 At that time Tattenai, governor of Trans-Euphrates, and Shethar-Bozenai and their associates
went to them and asked, "Who au-
thorized you to rebuild this temple and to finish it?" 4 They[a] also
asked, "What are the names of
those who are constructing this
building?" 5 But the eye of their
God was watching over the elders
of the Jews, and they were not
stopped until a report could go to
Darius and his written reply be received.

Ezr 1:3; 6:6; Ps 33:18

6 This is a copy of the letter that
Tattenai, governor of Trans-Euphrates, and Shethar-Bozenai and
their associates, the officials of
Trans-Euphrates, sent to King Darius. 7 The report they sent him
read as follows:

To King Darius:

Cordial greetings.

8 The king should know that
we went to the district of Judah, to the temple of the great
God. The people are building
it with large stones and placing the timbers in the walls.
The work is being carried on
with diligence and is making
rapid progress under their direction.

9 We questioned the elders
and asked them, "Who au-
thorized you to rebuild this
temple and to finish it?" 10 We
also asked them their names,
so that we could write down
the names of their leaders for
your information.

Ezr 4:12

11 This is the answer they
gave us:

"We are the servants of the
God of heaven and earth, and
we are rebuilding the temple that was built many years
ago, one that a great king of
Israel built and finished. 12 But
because our ancestors an-
gered the God of heaven, he
gave them into the hands of

[a] 4 See Septuagint; Aramaic *We*.

Nebuchadnezzar the Chaldean, king of Babylon, who destroyed this temple and deported the people to Babylon.
2Ki 24:1; 25:8-9,11; 2Ch 36:16

13 "However, in the first year
of Cyrus king of Babylon,
King Cyrus issued a decree to
rebuild this house of God. 14 He
even removed from the temple[a] of Babylon the gold and
silver articles of the house
of God, which Nebuchadnezzar had taken from the temple in Jerusalem and brought
to the temple[a] in Babylon.
Then King Cyrus gave them
to a man named Sheshbaz-
zar, whom he had appointed
governor, 15 and he told him,
'Take these articles and go
and deposit them in the temple in Jerusalem. And rebuild
the house of God on its site.'
Ezr 1:7; 6:5

16 "So this Sheshbazzar
came and laid the founda-
tions of the house of God in
Jerusalem. From that day to
the present it has been under
construction but is not yet
finished." Ezr 3:10; 6:15

17 Now if it pleases the king,
let a search be made in the royal archives of Babylon to see if
King Cyrus did in fact issue a
decree to rebuild this house
of God in Jerusalem. Then let
the king send us his decision
in this matter. Ezr 4:15; 6:1-2

The Decree of Darius

6 King Darius then issued an order, and they searched in the
archives stored in the treasury at
Babylon. 2 A scroll was found in the
citadel of Ecbatana in the province of Media, and this was written on it: Ezr 5:17

Memorandum:

3 In the first year of King Cyrus, the king issued a decree
concerning the temple of God
in Jerusalem:

Let the temple be rebuilt as
a place to present sacrifices,
and let its foundations be laid.
It is to be sixty cubits[b] high
and sixty cubits wide, 4 with
three courses of large stones
and one of timbers. The costs
are to be paid by the royal
treasury. 5 Also, the gold and
silver articles of the house of
God, which Nebuchadnezzar
took from the temple in Jerusalem and brought to Babylon, are to be returned to
their places in the temple in
Jerusalem; they are to be deposited in the house of God.
Ezr 1:7; 5:14

6 Now then, Tattenai, governor of Trans-Euphrates,
and Shethar-Bozenai and you
other officials of that province, stay away from there.

[a] 14 Or *palace* [b] 3 That is, about 90 feet or about 27 meters

7Do not interfere with the
work on this temple of God.
Let the governor of the Jews
and the Jewish elders rebuild
this house of God on its site.

Ezr 5:3

8Moreover, I hereby decree
what you are to do for these
elders of the Jews in the construction of this house of God:

Their expenses are to be
fully paid out of the royal
treasury, from the revenues
of Trans-Euphrates, so that
the work will not stop. 9What-
ever is needed — young bulls,
rams, male lambs for burnt
offerings to the God of heav-
en, and wheat, salt, wine and
olive oil, as requested by the
priests in Jerusalem — must
be given them daily without
fail, 10so that they may offer
sacrifices pleasing to the God
of heaven and pray for the
well-being of the king and his
sons.

Ezr 7:23; 1Ti 2:1-2

11Furthermore, I decree
that if anyone defies this
edict, a beam is to be pulled
from their house and they
are to be impaled on it. And
for this crime their house is
to be made a pile of rubble.
12May God, who has caused
his Name to dwell there, overthrow any king or people who
lifts a hand to change this decree or to destroy this temple
in Jerusalem.

Dt 12:5; Ezr 7:26; Da 2:5

I Darius have decreed it. Let
it be carried out with diligence.

Completion and Dedication of the Temple

13Then, because of the decree
King Darius had sent, Tattenai,
governor of Trans-Euphrates, and
Shethar-Bozenai and their associates carried it out with diligence.
14So the elders of the Jews continued to build and prosper under the preaching of Haggai the
prophet and Zechariah, a descendant of Iddo. They finished building the temple according to the
command of the God of Israel and
the decrees of Cyrus, Darius and
Artaxerxes, kings of Persia. 15The
temple was completed on the
third day of the month Adar, in
the sixth year of the reign of King
Darius.

Ezr 5:1; 7:1; Zec 1:1

16Then the people of Israel —
the priests, the Levites and the
rest of the exiles — celebrated
the dedication of the house of
God with joy. 17For the dedication
of this house of God they offered
a hundred bulls, two hundred
rams, four hundred male lambs
and, as a sin offering[a] for all Israel, twelve male goats, one for
each of the tribes of Israel. 18And
they installed the priests in their
divisions and the Levites in their
groups for the service of God at
Jerusalem, according to what is
written in the Book of Moses.

1Ki 8:63; 2Ch 7:5; 35:4

[a] 17 Or *purification offering*

The Passover

[19]On the fourteenth day of the
first month, the exiles celebrated the Passover. [20]The priests and
Levites had purified themselves
and were all ceremonially clean.
The Levites slaughtered the Passover lamb for all the exiles, for
their relatives the priests and for
themselves. [21]So the Israelites
who had returned from the exile
ate it, together with all who had
separated themselves from the
unclean practices of their Gentile
neighbors in order to seek the
LORD, the God of Israel. [22]For sev-
en days they celebrated with joy
the Festival of Unleavened Bread,
because the LORD had filled them
with joy by changing the attitude
of the king of Assyria so that he
assisted them in the work on the
house of God, the God of Israel.

Ex 12:11; Ezr 1:1

Ezra Comes to Jerusalem

7 After these things, during the
reign of Artaxerxes king of
Persia, Ezra son of Seraiah, the son
of Azariah, the son of Hilkiah, [2]the
son of Shallum, the son of Zadok,
the son of Ahitub, [3]the son of Amariah, the son of Azariah, the son
of Meraioth, [4]the son of Zerahiah,
the son of Uzzi, the son of Bukki, [5]the son of Abishua, the son of
Phinehas, the son of Eleazar, the
son of Aaron the chief priest—
[6]this Ezra came up from Babylon.
He was a teacher well versed in
the Law of Moses, which the LORD,
the God of Israel, had given. The
king had granted him everything
he asked, for the hand of the LORD
his God was on him. [7]Some of the
Israelites, including priests, Levites, musicians, gatekeepers and
temple servants, also came up to
Jerusalem in the seventh year of
King Artaxerxes.

Ezr 8:1; Ne 12:36; Isa 41:20

[8]Ezra arrived in Jerusalem in
the fifth month of the seventh
year of the king. [9]He had begun
his journey from Babylon on the
first day of the first month, and he
arrived in Jerusalem on the first
day of the fifth month, for the gracious hand of his God was on him.
[10]For Ezra had devoted himself to
the study and observance of the
Law of the LORD, and to teaching
its decrees and laws in Israel.

Dt 33:10; Ne 8:1-8

King Artaxerxes' Letter to Ezra

[11]This is a copy of the letter King
Artaxerxes had given to Ezra the
priest, a teacher of the Law, a man
learned in matters concerning
the commands and decrees of the
LORD for Israel:

[12]Artaxerxes, king of kings,

Eze 26:7; Da 2:37

To Ezra the priest, teacher of
the Law of the God of heaven:
Greetings.

[13]Now I decree that any of
the Israelites in my kingdom,
including priests and Levites,

who volunteer to go to Jerusalem with you, may go. 14You
are sent by the king and his
seven advisers to inquire
about Judah and Jerusalem
with regard to the Law of your
God, which is in your hand.
15Moreover, you are to take
with you the silver and gold
that the king and his advisers
have freely given to the God
of Israel, whose dwelling is in
Jerusalem, 16together with all
the silver and gold you may
obtain from the province of
Babylon, as well as the freewill offerings of the people
and priests for the temple of
their God in Jerusalem. 17With
this money be sure to buy
bulls, rams and male lambs,
together with their grain offerings and drink offerings,
and sacrifice them on the altar of the temple of your God
in Jerusalem.

2Ch 6:2; Zec 6:10; Dt 12:5-11

18You and your fellow Israelites may then do whatever
seems best with the rest of
the silver and gold, in accordance with the will of your
God. 19Deliver to the God of
Jerusalem all the articles entrusted to you for worship in
the temple of your God. 20And
anything else needed for the
temple of your God that you
are responsible to supply, you
may provide from the royal
treasury.

Ezr 6:4; Jer 27:22

21Now I, King Artaxerxes,
decree that all the treasurers of Trans-Euphrates are
to provide with diligence
whatever Ezra the priest, the
teacher of the Law of the God
of heaven, may ask of you —
22up to a hundred talents[a]
of silver, a hundred cors[b] of
wheat, a hundred baths[c] of
wine, a hundred baths[c] of olive oil, and salt without limit.
23Whatever the God of heaven
has prescribed, let it be done
with diligence for the temple
of the God of heaven. Why
should his wrath fall on the
realm of the king and of his
sons? 24You are also to know
that you have no authority to
impose taxes, tribute or duty
on any of the priests, Levites,
musicians, gatekeepers, temple servants or other workers
at this house of God.

Ezr 6:10; 8:36

25And you, Ezra, in accordance with the wisdom of
your God, which you pos-
sess, appoint magistrates and
judges to administer justice
to all the people of Trans-Euphrates — all who know the
laws of your God. And you
are to teach any who do not
know them. 26Whoever does
not obey the law of your God

[a] *22* That is, about 3 3/4 tons or about 3.4 metric tons [b] *22* That is, probably about 18 tons or about 16 metric tons [c] *22* That is, about 600 gallons or about 2,200 liters

and the law of the king must
surely be punished by death,
banishment, confiscation of
property, or imprisonment.[a]
Ex 18:21,26; Dt 16:18; Ezr 6:11

27 Praise be to the LORD, the God
of our ancestors, who has put it
into the king's heart to bring hon-
or to the house of the LORD in Jerusalem in this way 28 and who has
extended his good favor to me before the king and his advisers and
all the king's powerful officials.
Because the hand of the LORD my
God was on me, I took courage and
gathered leaders from Israel to go
up with me. Ezr 5:5; 9:9

List of the Family Heads Returning With Ezra

8 These are the family heads
and those registered with
them who came up with me from
Babylon during the reign of King
Artaxerxes: Ezr 7:7

2 of the descendants of Phinehas, Gershom;
of the descendants of Ithamar, Daniel;
of the descendants of David, Hattush 3 of the descendants of Shekaniah; 1Ch 3:22

of the descendants of Parosh, Zechariah, and with him were registered 150 men; Ezr 2:3

4 of the descendants of Pahath-Moab, Eliehoenai son of Zerahiah, and with him 200 men; Ezr 2:6

5 of the descendants of Zattu,[b] Shekaniah son of Jahaziel, and with him 300 men;

6 of the descendants of Adin, Ebed son of Jonathan, and with him 50 men; Ezr 2:15; Ne 7:20; 10:16

7 of the descendants of Elam, Jeshaiah son of Athaliah, and with him 70 men;

8 of the descendants of Shephatiah, Zebadiah son of Michael, and with him 80 men;

9 of the descendants of Joab, Obadiah son of Jehiel, and with him 218 men;

10 of the descendants of Bani,[c] Shelomith son of Josiphiah, and with him 160 men;

11 of the descendants of Bebai, Zechariah son of Bebai, and with him 28 men;

12 of the descendants of Azgad, Johanan son of Hakkatan, and with him 110 men;

13 of the descendants of Adonikam, the last ones, whose names were Eliphelet, Jeuel and Shemaiah, and with them 60 men; Ezr 2:13

14 of the descendants of Bigvai, Uthai and Zakkur, and with them 70 men.

The Return to Jerusalem

15 I assembled them at the canal
that flows toward Ahava, and we

[a] *26* The text of 7:12-26 is in Aramaic.
[b] *5* Some Septuagint manuscripts (also 1 Esdras 8:32); Hebrew does not have *Zattu*.
[c] *10* Some Septuagint manuscripts (also 1 Esdras 8:36); Hebrew does not have *Bani*.

camped there three days. When I checked among the people and the priests, I found no Levites there. 16So I summoned Eliezer, Ariel, Shemaiah, Elnathan, Jarib, Elnathan, Nathan, Zechariah and Meshullam, who were leaders, and Joiarib and Elnathan, who were men of learning, 17and I ordered them to go to Iddo, the leader in Kasiphia. I told them what to say to Iddo and his fellow Levites, the temple servants in Kasiphia, so that they might bring attendants to us for the house of our God. 18Because the gracious hand of our God was on us, they brought us Sherebiah, a capable man, from the descendants of Mahli son of Levi, the son of Israel, and Sherebiah's sons and brothers, 18 in all; 19and Hashabiah, together with Jeshaiah from the descendants of Merari, and his brothers and nephews, 20 in all. 20They also brought 220 of the temple servants — a body that David and the officials had established to assist the Levites. All were registered by name. Ezr 2:43; 5:5

21There, by the Ahava Canal, I proclaimed a fast, so that we might humble ourselves before our God and ask him for a safe journey for us and our children, with all our possessions. 22I was ashamed to ask the king for soldiers and horsemen to protect us from enemies on the road, because we had told the king, "The gracious hand of our God is on everyone who looks to him, but his great anger is against all who forsake him." 23So we fasted and petitioned our God about this, and he answered our prayer. 2Ch 33:13; Ezr 7:6,9,28

24Then I set apart twelve of the leading priests, namely, Sherebiah, Hashabiah and ten of their brothers, 25and I weighed out to them the offering of silver and gold and the articles that the king, his advisers, his officials and all Israel present there had donated for the house of our God. 26I weighed out to them 650 talents[a] of silver, silver articles weighing 100 talents,[b] 100 talents[b] of gold, 2720 bowls of gold valued at 1,000 darics,[c] and two fine articles of polished bronze, as precious as gold. Ezr 7:15-16

28I said to them, "You as well as these articles are consecrated to the LORD. The silver and gold are a freewill offering to the LORD, the God of your ancestors. 29Guard them carefully until you weigh them out in the chambers of the house of the LORD in Jerusalem before the leading priests and the Levites and the family heads of Israel." 30Then the priests and Levites received the silver and gold and sacred articles that had been weighed out to be taken to the house of our God in Jerusalem. Lev 21:6; 22:2-3

[a] *26* That is, about 24 tons or about 22 metric tons [b] *26* That is, about 3 3/4 tons or about 3.4 metric tons [c] *27* That is, about 19 pounds or about 8.4 kilograms

31On the twelfth day of the first
month we set out from the Ahava Canal to go to Jerusalem. The
hand of our God was on us, and he
protected us from enemies and
bandits along the way. 32So we arrived in Jerusalem, where we rested three days. Ge 40:13; Ne 2:11

33On the fourth day, in the house
of our God, we weighed out the silver and gold and the sacred articles into the hands of Meremoth
son of Uriah, the priest. Eleazar
son of Phinehas was with him,
and so were the Levites Jozabad
son of Jeshua and Noadiah son of
Binnui. 34Everything was account-
ed for by number and weight, and
the entire weight was recorded at
that time. Ne 3:4,21,24

35Then the exiles who had returned from captivity sacrificed
burnt offerings to the God of Israel: twelve bulls for all Israel,
ninety-six rams, seventy-seven
male lambs and, as a sin offering,[a]
twelve male goats. All this was a
burnt offering to the LORD. 36They
also delivered the king's orders to
the royal satraps and to the governors of Trans-Euphrates, who
then gave assistance to the people
and to the house of God.
Ezr 7:21-24; Est 9:3

Ezra's Prayer About Intermarriage

9 After these things had been
done, the leaders came to
me and said, "The people of Israel, including the priests and
the Levites, have not kept themselves separate from the neighboring peoples with their detestable practices, like those of the
Canaanites, Hittites, Perizzites,
Jebusites, Ammonites, Moabites,
Egyptians and Amorites. 2They
have taken some of their daughters as wives for themselves and
their sons, and have mingled
the holy race with the peoples
around them. And the leaders
and officials have led the way in
this unfaithfulness."
Ex 22:31; 34:16; Ezr 10:2

3When I heard this, I tore my tunic and cloak, pulled hair from my
head and beard and sat down appalled. 4Then everyone who trembled at the words of the God of Israel gathered around me because
of this unfaithfulness of the exiles. And I sat there appalled until
the evening sacrifice. Ezr 10:3

5Then, at the evening sacrifice,
I rose from my self-abasement,
with my tunic and cloak torn, and
fell on my knees with my hands
spread out to the LORD my God
6and prayed: Ex 29:41

"I am too ashamed and disgraced, my God, to lift up my
face to you, because our sins
are higher than our heads
and our guilt has reached to
the heavens. 7From the days
of our ancestors until now,
our guilt has been great. Because of our sins, we and our
kings and our priests have

[a] 35 Or *purification offering*

been subjected to the sword and captivity, to pillage and humiliation at the hand of foreign kings, as it is today.

Dt 28:37; 2Ch 28:9; Rev 18:5

[8]"But now, for a brief moment, the LORD our God has been gracious in leaving us a remnant and giving us a firm place[a] in his sanctuary, and so our God gives light to our eyes and a little relief in our bondage.
[9]Though we are slaves, our God has not forsaken us in our bondage. He has shown us kindness in the sight of the kings of Persia: He has granted us new life to rebuild the house of our God and repair its ruins, and he has given us a wall of protection in Judah and Jerusalem.

Ne 9:36; Ps 13:3; Isa 22:23

[10]"But now, our God, what can we say after this? For we have forsaken the commands
[11]you gave through your servants the prophets when you said: 'The land you are entering to possess is a land polluted by the corruption of its peoples. By their detestable practices they have filled it with their impurity from one end to the other.
[12]Therefore, do not give your daughters in marriage to their sons or take their daughters for your sons. Do not seek a treaty of friendship with them at any time, that you may be strong and eat the good things of the land and leave it to your children as an everlasting inheritance.'

Dt 7:3; 23:6

[13]"What has happened to us is a result of our evil deeds and our great guilt, and yet, our God, you have punished us less than our sins deserved and have given us a remnant like this.
[14]Shall we then break your commands again and intermarry with the peoples who commit such detestable practices? Would you not be angry enough with us to destroy us, leaving us no remnant or survivor?
[15]LORD, the God of Israel, you are righteous! We are left this day as a remnant. Here we are before you in our guilt, though because of it not one of us can stand in your presence."

1Ki 8:47; Ps 130:3

The People's Confession of Sin

10 While Ezra was praying and confessing, weeping and throwing himself down before the house of God, a large crowd of Israelites — men, women and children — gathered around him. They too wept bitterly.
[2]Then Shekaniah son of Jehiel, one of the descendants of Elam, said to Ezra, "We have been unfaithful to our God by marrying foreign women from the peoples around us. But in spite of this, there is still

[a] 8 Or *a foothold*

hope for Israel. 3Now let us make
a covenant before our God to send
away all these women and their
children, in accordance with the
counsel of my lord and of those
who fear the commands of our
God. Let it be done according to
the Law. 4Rise up; this matter is in
your hands. We will support you,
so take courage and do it."

Dt 7:2-3; Ezr 9:4

5So Ezra rose up and put the
leading priests and Levites and all
Israel under oath to do what had
been suggested. And they took the
oath. 6Then Ezra withdrew from
before the house of God and went
to the room of Jehohanan son of
Eliashib. While he was there, he
ate no food and drank no water,
because he continued to mourn
over the unfaithfulness of the exiles.

Dt 9:18; Ne 5:12; 13:25

7A proclamation was then issued throughout Judah and Jerusalem for all the exiles to assem-
ble in Jerusalem. 8Anyone who
failed to appear within three days
would forfeit all his property, in
accordance with the decision of
the officials and elders, and would
himself be expelled from the assembly of the exiles.

9Within the three days, all the
men of Judah and Benjamin had
gathered in Jerusalem. And on the
twentieth day of the ninth month,
all the people were sitting in the
square before the house of God,
greatly distressed by the occasion
and because of the rain. 10Then
Ezra the priest stood up and said
to them, "You have been unfaithful; you have married foreign
women, adding to Israel's guilt.
11Now honor[a] the LORD, the God
of your ancestors, and do his will.
Separate yourselves from the peoples around you and from your
foreign wives."

Dt 24:1; Mal 2:10-16

12The whole assembly responded with a loud voice: "You are
right! We must do as you say. 13But
there are many people here and
it is the rainy season; so we cannot stand outside. Besides, this
matter cannot be taken care of
in a day or two, because we have
sinned greatly in this thing. 14Let
our officials act for the whole assembly. Then let everyone in our
towns who has married a foreign woman come at a set time,
along with the elders and judges of each town, until the fierce
anger of our God in this matter is
turned away from us." 15Only Jonathan son of Asahel and Jahzeiah
son of Tikvah, supported by Meshullam and Shabbethai the Levite, opposed this.

2Ch 29:10; 30:8; Ne 11:16

16So the exiles did as was proposed. Ezra the priest selected
men who were family heads, one
from each family division, and all
of them designated by name. On
the first day of the tenth month
they sat down to investigate the
cases, 17and by the first day of the

a 11 Or *Now make confession to*

first month they finished dealing with all the men who had married foreign women.

Those Guilty of Intermarriage

18 Among the descendants of the priests, the following had married foreign women: Jdg 3:6

From the descendants of Joshua son of Jozadak, and his brothers: Maaseiah, Eliezer, Jarib and Gedaliah.
19 (They all gave their hands in pledge to put away their wives, and for their guilt they each presented a ram from the flock as a guilt offering.) Lev 5:15; 2Ki 10:15; Ezr 2:2

20 From the descendants of Immer: 1Ch 24:14
Hanani and Zebadiah.

21 From the descendants of Harim: 1Ch 24:8
Maaseiah, Elijah, Shemaiah, Jehiel and Uzziah.

22 From the descendants of Pashhur: 1Ch 9:12
Elioenai, Maaseiah, Ishmael, Nethanel, Jozabad and Elasah.

23 Among the Levites: Ne 8:7; 9:4

Jozabad, Shimei, Kelaiah (that is, Kelita), Pethahiah, Judah and Eliezer.

24 From the musicians:
Eliashib. Ne 3:1; 12:10; 13:7,28

From the gatekeepers:
Shallum, Telem and Uri.

25 And among the other Israelites:

From the descendants of Parosh: Ezr 2:3
Ramiah, Izziah, Malkijah, Mijamin, Eleazar, Malkijah and Benaiah.

26 From the descendants of Elam:
Mattaniah, Zechariah, Jehiel, Abdi, Jeremoth and Elijah.

27 From the descendants of Zattu:
Elioenai, Eliashib, Mattaniah, Jeremoth, Zabad and Aziza.

28 From the descendants of Bebai:
Jehohanan, Hananiah, Zabbai and Athlai.

29 From the descendants of Bani:
Meshullam, Malluk, Adaiah, Jashub, Sheal and Jeremoth.

30 From the descendants of Pahath-Moab:
Adna, Kelal, Benaiah, Maaseiah, Mattaniah, Bezalel, Binnui and Manasseh.

31 From the descendants of Harim:
Eliezer, Ishijah, Malkijah, Shemaiah, Shimeon,
32 Benjamin, Malluk and Shemariah.

33 From the descendants of Hashum:
Mattenai, Mattattah, Zabad,

Eliphelet, Jeremai, Manasseh and Shimei.
34 From the descendants of Bani:
Maadai, Amram, Uel, 35 Benaiah, Bedeiah, Keluhi,
36 Vaniah, Meremoth, Eliashib,
37 Mattaniah, Mattenai and Jaasu.
38 From the descendants of Binnui:[a]
Shimei, 39 Shelemiah, Nathan, Adaiah,
40 Maknadebai, Shashai, Sharai,
41 Azarel, Shelemiah, Shemariah,
42 Shallum, Amariah and Joseph.
43 From the descendants of Nebo:
Jeiel, Mattithiah, Zabad, Zebina, Jaddai, Joel and Benaiah.

44 All these had married foreign women, and some of them had children by these wives.[b]

[a] *37,38* See Septuagint (also 1 Esdras 9:34); Hebrew *Jaasu* [38]*and Bani and Binnui,*
[b] 44 Or *and they sent them away with their children*

NEHEMIAH

Nehemiah's Prayer

1 The words of Nehemiah son of
Hakaliah:

In the month of Kislev in the
twentieth year, while I was in the
citadel of Susa, 2Hanani, one of my
brothers, came from Judah with
some other men, and I questioned
them about the Jewish remnant
that had survived the exile, and
also about Jerusalem. Ne 10:1; Zec 7:1

3They said to me, "Those who
survived the exile and are back in
the province are in great trouble
and disgrace. The wall of Jerusalem is broken down, and its gates
have been burned with fire."
Ne 2:3,13,17

4When I heard these things, I
sat down and wept. For some days
I mourned and fasted and prayed
before the God of heaven. 5Then I
said: Ezr 9:4; Ps 137:1; Da 9:3

"LORD, the God of heaven,
the great and awesome God,
who keeps his covenant of
love with those who love him
and keep his commandments,
6let your ear be attentive and
your eyes open to hear the
prayer your servant is praying
before you day and night for
your servants, the people of
Israel. I confess the sins we Israelites, including myself and
my father's family, have committed against you. 7We have
acted very wickedly toward
you. We have not obeyed the
commands, decrees and laws
you gave your servant Moses.
Dt 28:14-15; Ne 4:14; Da 9:17

8"Remember the instruc-
tion you gave your servant
Moses, saying, 'If you are
unfaithful, I will scatter you
among the nations, 9but if
you return to me and obey
my commands, then even if
your exiled people are at the
farthest horizon, I will gather them from there and bring
them to the place I have
chosen as a dwelling for my
Name.' Lev 26:33; Dt 30:4

10"They are your servants
and your people, whom you
redeemed by your great
strength and your mighty
hand. 11Lord, let your ear be
attentive to the prayer of this
your servant and to the prayer
of your servants who delight
in revering your name. Give
your servant success today
by granting him favor in the
presence of this man." Dt 9:29

I was cupbearer to the king.
Ge 40:1

Artaxerxes Sends Nehemiah to Jerusalem

2 In the month of Nisan in the
twentieth year of King Artaxerxes, when wine was brought
for him, I took the wine and gave
it to the king. I had not been sad
in his presence before, 2so the
king asked me, "Why does your
face look so sad when you are not
ill? This can be nothing but sad-
ness of heart." Ezr 7:1

I was very much afraid, 3but I
said to the king, "May the king live
forever! Why should my face not
look sad when the city where my
ancestors are buried lies in ruins,
and its gates have been destroyed
by fire?" Ne 1:3; Da 2:4

4The king said to me, "What is it
you want?"

Then I prayed to the God of
heaven, 5and I answered the king,
"If it pleases the king and if your
servant has found favor in his
sight, let him send me to the city
in Judah where my ancestors are
buried so that I can rebuild it."

6Then the king, with the queen
sitting beside him, asked me,
"How long will your journey take,
and when will you get back?" It
pleased the king to send me; so I
set a time. Ne 5:14; 13:6

7I also said to him, "If it pleases the king, may I have letters to
the governors of Trans-Euphrates,
so that they will provide me safe-
conduct until I arrive in Judah?
8And may I have a letter to Asaph,
keeper of the royal park, so he will
give me timber to make beams for
the gates of the citadel by the temple and for the city wall and for
the residence I will occupy?" And
because the gracious hand of my
God was on me, the king granted my requests. 9So I went to the
governors of Trans-Euphrates and
gave them the king's letters. The
king had also sent army officers
and cavalry with me. Ezr 7:6; 8:22,36

10When Sanballat the Horonite
and Tobiah the Ammonite official
heard about this, they were very
much disturbed that someone
had come to promote the welfare
of the Israelites. Ne 4:3; 13:4-7; Est 10:3

Nehemiah Inspects Jerusalem's Walls

11I went to Jerusalem, and after
staying there three days 12I set out
during the night with a few others. I had not told anyone what my
God had put in my heart to do for
Jerusalem. There were no mounts
with me except the one I was riding on. Ge 40:13

13By night I went out through
the Valley Gate toward the Jackal[a] Well and the Dung Gate, examining the walls of Jerusalem,
which had been broken down,
and its gates, which had been destroyed by fire. 14Then I moved
on toward the Fountain Gate and
the King's Pool, but there was
not enough room for my mount
to get through; 15so I went up the
valley by night, examining the

[a] 13 Or *Serpent* or *Fig*

wall. Finally, I turned back and reentered through the Valley Gate. 16 The officials did not know where I had gone or what I was doing, because as yet I had said nothing to the Jews or the priests or nobles or officials or any others who would be doing the work. Ne 1:3; 3:13,15

17 Then I said to them, "You see the trouble we are in: Jerusalem lies in ruins, and its gates have been burned with fire. Come, let us rebuild the wall of Jerusalem, and we will no longer be in disgrace." 18 I also told them about the gracious hand of my God on me and what the king had said to me. 2Sa 2:7; Ne 1:3

They replied, "Let us start rebuilding." So they began this good work.

19 But when Sanballat the Horonite, Tobiah the Ammonite official and Geshem the Arab heard about it, they mocked and ridiculed us. "What is this you are doing?" they asked. "Are you rebelling against the king?" Ps 44:13-16

20 I answered them by saying, "The God of heaven will give us success. We his servants will start rebuilding, but as for you, you have no share in Jerusalem or any claim or historic right to it." Ezr 4:3

Builders of the Wall

3 Eliashib the high priest and his fellow priests went to work and rebuilt the Sheep Gate. They dedicated it and set its doors in place, building as far as the Tower of the Hundred, which they dedicated, and as far as the Tower of Hananel. 2 The men of Jericho built the adjoining section, and Zakkur son of Imri built next to them. Ne 7:36; 12:39; Jer 31:38

3 The Fish Gate was rebuilt by the sons of Hassenaah. They laid its beams and put its doors and bolts and bars in place. 4 Meremoth son of Uriah, the son of Hakkoz, repaired the next section. Next to him Meshullam son of Berekiah, the son of Meshezabel, made repairs, and next to him Zadok son of Baana also made repairs. 5 The next section was repaired by the men of Tekoa, but their nobles would not put their shoulders to the work under their supervisors.[a] 2Sa 14:2; Ne 12:39

6 The Jeshanah[b] Gate was repaired by Joiada son of Paseah and Meshullam son of Besodeiah. They laid its beams and put its doors with their bolts and bars in place. 7 Next to them, repairs were made by men from Gibeon and Mizpah — Melatiah of Gibeon and Jadon of Meronoth — places under the authority of the governor of Trans-Euphrates. 8 Uzziel son of Harhaiah, one of the goldsmiths, repaired the next section; and Hananiah, one of the perfume-makers, made repairs next to that. They restored Jerusalem as far as the Broad Wall. 9 Rephaiah son of

[a] 5 Or *their Lord* or *the governor*
[b] 6 Or *Old*

Hur, ruler of a half-district of Jerusalem, repaired the next section. 10 Adjoining this, Jedaiah son
of Harumaph made repairs opposite his house, and Hattush son of
Hashabneiah made repairs next
to him. 11 Malkijah son of Harim
and Hasshub son of Pahath-Moab
repaired another section and the
Tower of the Ovens. 12 Shallum son
of Hallohesh, ruler of a half-district of Jerusalem, repaired the
next section with the help of his
daughters. Ne 2:7; 12:38-39

13 The Valley Gate was repaired
by Hanun and the residents of Zanoah. They rebuilt it and put its
doors with their bolts and bars in
place. They also repaired a thousand cubits[a] of the wall as far as
the Dung Gate. Ne 2:13; 2Ch 26:9

14 The Dung Gate was repaired by
Malkijah son of Rekab, ruler of the
district of Beth Hakkerem. He rebuilt it and put its doors with their
bolts and bars in place. Jer 6:1

15 The Fountain Gate was repaired by Shallun son of Kol-Hozeh, ruler of the district of Mizpah.
He rebuilt it, roofing it over and
putting its doors and bolts and
bars in place. He also repaired the
wall of the Pool of Siloam,[b] by the
King's Garden, as far as the steps
going down from the City of David. 16 Beyond him, Nehemiah son
of Azbuk, ruler of a half-district
of Beth Zur, made repairs up to a
point opposite the tombs[c] of David, as far as the artificial pool and
the House of the Heroes.
Jos 15:58; Isa 8:6; Ac 2:29

17 Next to him, the repairs were
made by the Levites under Rehum
son of Bani. Beside him, Hashabiah, ruler of half the district of
Keilah, carried out repairs for his
district. 18 Next to him, the repairs
were made by their fellow Levites
under Binnui[d] son of Henadad,
ruler of the other half-district of
Keilah. 19 Next to him, Ezer son of
Jeshua, ruler of Mizpah, repaired
another section, from a point facing the ascent to the armory as far
as the angle of the wall. 20 Next to
him, Baruch son of Zabbai zeal-
ously repaired another section,
from the angle to the entrance
of the house of Eliashib the high
priest. 21 Next to him, Meremoth
son of Uriah, the son of Hakkoz,
repaired another section, from the
entrance of Eliashib's house to the
end of it. Jos 15:44; Ezr 8:33

22 The repairs next to him were
made by the priests from the surrounding region. 23 Beyond them,
Benjamin and Hasshub made repairs in front of their house; and
next to them, Azariah son of Maaseiah, the son of Ananiah, made
repairs beside his house. 24 Next

[a] *13* That is, about 1,500 feet or about 450 meters [b] *15* Hebrew *Shelah*, a variant of *Shiloah*, that is, Siloam [c] *16* Hebrew; Septuagint, some Vulgate manuscripts and Syriac *tomb* [d] *18* Two Hebrew manuscripts and Syriac (see also Septuagint and verse 24); most Hebrew manuscripts *Bavvai*

to him, Binnui son of Henadad repaired another section, from Azariah's house to the angle and the corner, 25and Palal son of Uzai worked opposite the angle and the tower projecting from the upper palace near the court of the guard. Next to him, Pedaiah son of Parosh 26and the temple servants living on the hill of Ophel made repairs up to a point opposite the Water Gate toward the east and the projecting tower. 27Next to them, the men of Tekoa repaired another section, from the great projecting tower to the wall of Ophel.

Ne 8:1,3,16; Jer 32:2

28Above the Horse Gate, the priests made repairs, each in front of his own house. 29Next to them, Zadok son of Immer made repairs opposite his house. Next to him, Shemaiah son of Shekaniah, the guard at the East Gate, made repairs. 30Next to him, Hananiah son of Shelemiah, and Hanun, the sixth son of Zalaph, repaired another section. Next to them, Meshullam son of Berekiah made repairs opposite his living quarters. 31Next to him, Malkijah, one of the goldsmiths, made repairs as far as the house of the temple servants and the merchants, opposite the Inspection Gate, and as far as the room above the corner; 32and between the room above the corner and the Sheep Gate the goldsmiths and merchants made repairs.

2Ch 23:15; Jn 5:2

Opposition to the Rebuilding

4 [a] When Sanballat heard that we were rebuilding the wall, he became angry and was greatly incensed. He ridiculed the Jews, 2and in the presence of his associates and the army of Samaria, he said, "What are those feeble Jews doing? Will they restore their wall? Will they offer sacrifices? Will they finish in a day? Can they bring the stones back to life from those heaps of rubble — burned as they are?"

Ne 2:10; Ps 79:1

3Tobiah the Ammonite, who was at his side, said, "What they are building — even a fox climbing up on it would break down their wall of stones!"

Ne 2:10; Job 13:12

4Hear us, our God, for we are despised. Turn their insults back on their own heads. Give them over as plunder in a land of captivity. 5Do not cover up their guilt or blot out their sins from your sight, for they have thrown insults in the face of[b] the builders.

Ps 69:27-28; Jer 18:23

6So we rebuilt the wall till all of it reached half its height, for the people worked with all their heart.

7But when Sanballat, Tobiah, the Arabs, the Ammonites and the people of Ashdod heard that the repairs to Jerusalem's walls had gone ahead and that the gaps were being closed, they were very

[a] In Hebrew texts 4:1-6 is numbered 3:33-38, and 4:7-23 is numbered 4:1-17. [b] 5 Or *have aroused your anger before*

angry. [8]They all plotted together
to come and fight against Jerusalem and stir up trouble against
it. [9]But we prayed to our God and
posted a guard day and night to
meet this threat. Ps 2:2; 83:1-18
[10]Meanwhile, the people in Judah said, "The strength of the laborers is giving out, and there is
so much rubble that we cannot rebuild the wall." 1Ch 23:4
[11]Also our enemies said, "Before
they know it or see us, we will be
right there among them and will
kill them and put an end to the
work."
[12]Then the Jews who lived near
them came and told us ten times
over, "Wherever you turn, they
will attack us."
[13]Therefore I stationed some
of the people behind the lowest
points of the wall at the exposed
places, posting them by families, with their swords, spears
and bows. [14]After I looked things
over, I stood up and said to the
nobles, the officials and the rest
of the people, "Don't be afraid of
them. Remember the Lord, who is
great and awesome, and fight for
your families, your sons and your
daughters, your wives and your
homes." Nu 14:9; Dt 1:29; 2Sa 10:12
[15]When our enemies heard that
we were aware of their plot and
that God had frustrated it, we all
returned to the wall, each to our
own work. 2Sa 17:14; Job 5:12
[16]From that day on, half of my
men did the work, while the other half were equipped with spears,
shields, bows and armor. The officers posted themselves behind
all the people of Judah [17]who were
building the wall. Those who carried materials did their work with
one hand and held a weapon in
the other, [18]and each of the builders wore his sword at his side as he
worked. But the man who sounded the trumpet stayed with me.
Nu 10:2; Ps 149:6
[19]Then I said to the nobles, the
officials and the rest of the people,
"The work is extensive and spread
out, and we are widely separated
from each other along the wall.
[20]Wherever you hear the sound
of the trumpet, join us there. Our
God will fight for us!"
Ex 14:14; Dt 1:30; 20:4
[21]So we continued the work with
half the men holding spears, from
the first light of dawn till the stars
came out. [22]At that time I also said
to the people, "Have every man
and his helper stay inside Jerusalem at night, so they can serve us
as guards by night and as workers
by day." [23]Neither I nor my brothers nor my men nor the guards
with me took off our clothes; each
had his weapon, even when he
went for water.[a]

Nehemiah Helps the Poor

5 Now the men and their wives
raised a great outcry against
their fellow Jews. [2]Some were say-

[a] *23* The meaning of the Hebrew for this
clause is uncertain.

ing, "We and our sons and daughters are numerous; in order for us to eat and stay alive, we must get grain."

3Others were saying, "We are mortgaging our fields, our vineyards and our homes to get grain during the famine." Ge 47:23; Ps 109:11

4Still others were saying, "We have had to borrow money to pay the king's tax on our fields and vineyards. 5Although we are of the same flesh and blood as our fellow Jews and though our children are as good as theirs, yet we have to subject our sons and daughters to slavery. Some of our daughters have already been enslaved, but we are powerless, because our fields and our vineyards belong to others." Lev 25:39-43,47; Ezr 4:13

6When I heard their outcry and these charges, I was very angry. 7I pondered them in my mind and then accused the nobles and officials. I told them, "You are charging your own people interest!" So I called together a large meeting to deal with them 8and said: "As far as possible, we have bought back our fellow Jews who were sold to the Gentiles. Now you are selling your own people, only for them to be sold back to us!" They kept quiet, because they could find nothing to say.

Ex 22:25-27; Lev 25:35-37,47

9So I continued, "What you are doing is not right. Shouldn't you walk in the fear of our God to avoid the reproach of our Gentile enemies? 10I and my brothers and my men are also lending the people money and grain. But let us stop charging interest! 11Give back to them immediately their fields, vineyards, olive groves and houses, and also the interest you are charging them — one percent of the money, grain, new wine and olive oil." Ex 22:25; Isa 52:5; 58:6

12"We will give it back," they said. "And we will not demand anything more from them. We will do as you say."

Then I summoned the priests and made the nobles and officials take an oath to do what they had promised. 13I also shook out the folds of my robe and said, "In this way may God shake out of their house and possessions anyone who does not keep this promise. So may such a person be shaken out and emptied!"

At this the whole assembly said, "Amen," and praised the LORD. And the people did as they had promised. Ezr 10:5; Mt 10:14; Ac 18:6

14Moreover, from the twentieth year of King Artaxerxes, when I was appointed to be their governor in the land of Judah, until his thirty-second year — twelve years — neither I nor my brothers ate the food allotted to the governor. 15But the earlier governors — those preceding me — placed a heavy burden on the people and took forty shekels[a] of silver from

[a] *15* That is, about 1 pound or about 460 grams

them in addition to food and wine. Their assistants also lorded it over the people. But out of reverence for God I did not act like that. 16 Instead, I devoted myself to the work on this wall. All my men were assembled there for the work; we[a] did not acquire any land. Ne 13:6; Jer 40:7; 2Th 3:7-10

17 Furthermore, a hundred and fifty Jews and officials ate at my table, as well as those who came to us from the surrounding nations. 18 Each day one ox, six choice sheep and some poultry were prepared for me, and every ten days an abundant supply of wine of all kinds. In spite of all this, I never demanded the food allotted to the governor, because the demands were heavy on these people. 1Ki 4:23

19 Remember me with favor, my God, for all I have done for these people. Ge 8:1; Ne 1:8; 13:14,22,31

Further Opposition to the Rebuilding

6 When word came to Sanballat, Tobiah, Geshem the Arab and the rest of our enemies that I had rebuilt the wall and not a gap was left in it — though up to that time I had not set the doors in the gates — 2 Sanballat and Geshem sent me this message: "Come, let us meet together in one of the villages[b] on the plain of Ono." 1Ch 8:12; Ne 2:10,19

But they were scheming to harm me; 3 so I sent messengers to them with this reply: "I am carrying on a great project and cannot go down. Why should the work stop while I leave it and go down to you?" 4 Four times they sent me the same message, and each time I gave them the same answer.

5 Then, the fifth time, Sanballat sent his aide to me with the same message, and in his hand was an unsealed letter 6 in which was written: Ne 2:10

> "It is reported among the nations — and Geshem[c] says it is true — that you and the Jews are plotting to revolt, and therefore you are building the wall. Moreover, according to these reports you are about to become their king 7 and have even appointed prophets to make this proclamation about you in Jerusalem: 'There is a king in Judah!' Now this report will get back to the king; so come, let us meet together." Ne 2:19

8 I sent him this reply: "Nothing like what you are saying is happening; you are just making it up out of your head."

9 They were all trying to frighten us, thinking, "Their hands will get too weak for the work, and it will not be completed."

But I prayed, "Now strengthen my hands."

[a] *16* Most Hebrew manuscripts; some Hebrew manuscripts, Septuagint, Vulgate and Syriac *I* [b] *2* Or *in Kephirim*
[c] *6* Hebrew *Gashmu,* a variant of *Geshem*

10 One day I went to the house of
Shemaiah son of Delaiah, the son
of Mehetabel, who was shut in at
his home. He said, "Let us meet in
the house of God, inside the temple, and let us close the temple
doors, because men are coming to
kill you — by night they are coming to kill you." Nu 18:7

11 But I said, "Should a man like
me run away? Or should someone
like me go into the temple to save
his life? I will not go!" 12 I realized
that God had not sent him, but
that he had prophesied against me
because Tobiah and Sanballat had
hired him. 13 He had been hired to
intimidate me so that I would commit a sin by doing this, and then
they would give me a bad name to
discredit me. Ne 2:10; Eze 13:22-23

14 Remember Tobiah and Sanballat, my God, because of what they
have done; remember also the
prophet Noadiah and how she and
the rest of the prophets have been
trying to intimidate me. 15 So the
wall was completed on the twenty-fifth of Elul, in fifty-two days.
Ne 13:29; Eze 13:17-23

Opposition to the Completed Wall

16 When all our enemies heard
about this, all the surrounding
nations were afraid and lost their
self-confidence, because they realized that this work had been done
with the help of our God.

17 Also, in those days the nobles of
Judah were sending many letters
to Tobiah, and replies from Tobiah
kept coming to them. 18 For many
in Judah were under oath to him,
since he was son-in-law to Shekaniah son of Arah, and his son Jehohanan had married the daughter of Meshullam son of Berekiah.
19 Moreover, they kept reporting to
me his good deeds and then telling him what I said. And Tobiah
sent letters to intimidate me.

7 After the wall had been rebuilt and I had set the doors
in place, the gatekeepers, the musicians and the Levites were appointed. 2 I put in charge of Jerusalem my brother Hanani, along
with Hananiah the commander
of the citadel, because he was a
man of integrity and feared God
more than most people do. 3 I said
to them, "The gates of Jerusalem
are not to be opened until the sun
is hot. While the gatekeepers are
still on duty, have them shut the
doors and bar them. Also appoint
residents of Jerusalem as guards,
some at their posts and some near
their own houses." Ne 1:2; 8:9; Ps 68:25

The List of the Exiles Who Returned

4 Now the city was large and
spacious, but there were few people in it, and the houses had not
yet been rebuilt. 5 So my God put
it into my heart to assemble the
nobles, the officials and the common people for registration by
families. I found the genealogical
record of those who had been the

first to return. This is what I found written there:

[6]These are the people of the province who came up from the captivity of the exiles whom Nebuchadnezzar king of Babylon had taken captive (they returned to Jerusalem and Judah, each to his own
town, [7]in company with Zerubbabel, Joshua, Nehemiah, Azariah, Raamiah, Nahamani, Mordecai, Bilshan, Mispereth, Bigvai, Nehum and Baanah):

Ezr 2:1-70; Ne 1:2

The list of the men of Israel:

[8]the descendants of Parosh 2,172
[9]of Shephatiah 372
[10]of Arah 652
[11]of Pahath-Moab (through the line of Jeshua and Joab) 2,818
[12]of Elam 1,254
[13]of Zattu 845
[14]of Zakkai 760
[15]of Binnui 648
[16]of Bebai 628
[17]of Azgad 2,322
[18]of Adonikam 667
[19]of Bigvai 2,067
[20]of Adin 655
[21]of Ater (through Hezekiah) 98
[22]of Hashum 328
[23]of Bezai 324
[24]of Hariph 112
[25]of Gibeon 95
[26]the men of Bethlehem and Netophah 188
[27]of Anathoth 128
[28]of Beth Azmaveth 42
[29]of Kiriath Jearim, Kephirah and Beeroth 743
[30]of Ramah and Geba 621
[31]of Mikmash 122
[32]of Bethel and Ai 123
[33]of the other Nebo 52
[34]of the other Elam 1,254
[35]of Harim 320
[36]of Jericho 345
[37]of Lod, Hadid and Ono 721
[38]of Senaah 3,930

[39]The priests:

the descendants of Jedaiah (through the family of Jeshua) 973
[40]of Immer 1,052
[41]of Pashhur 1,247
[42]of Harim 1,017

[43]The Levites:

the descendants of Jeshua (through Kadmiel through the line of Hodaviah) 74

[44]The musicians: Ne 11:23

the descendants of Asaph 148

[45]The gatekeepers: 1Ch 9:17

the descendants of Shallum, Ater, Talmon, Akkub, Hatita and Shobai 138

46The temple servants: Ne 3:26

the descendants of
Ziha, Hasupha,
Tabbaoth,
47Keros, Sia, Padon,
48Lebana, Hagaba,
Shalmai,
49Hanan, Giddel, Gahar,
50Reaiah, Rezin, Nekoda,
51Gazzam, Uzza, Paseah,
52Besai, Meunim,
Nephusim,
53Bakbuk, Hakupha,
Harhur,
54Bazluth, Mehida, Harsha,
55Barkos, Sisera, Temah,
56Neziah and Hatipha

57The descendants of the servants of Solomon:

the descendants of
Sotai, Sophereth, Perida,
58Jaala, Darkon, Giddel,
59Shephatiah, Hattil,
Pokereth-Hazzebaim
and Amon

60The temple servants
and the descendants
of the servants of
Solomon 392

61The following came up
from the towns of Tel Melah,
Tel Harsha, Kerub, Addon and
Immer, but they could not
show that their families were
descended from Israel:

62the descendants of
Delaiah, Tobiah and
Nekoda 642

63And from among the priests:

the descendants of
Hobaiah, Hakkoz and
Barzillai (a man who had
married a daughter of
Barzillai the Gileadite and
was called by that name).

64These searched for their
family records, but they could
not find them and so were excluded from the priesthood
as unclean. 65The governor,
therefore, ordered them not
to eat any of the most sacred
food until there should be a
priest ministering with the
Urim and Thummim.

Ex 28:30; Ne 8:9

66The whole company num-
bered 42,360, 67besides their
7,337 male and female slaves;
and they also had 245 male and
female singers. 68There were
736 horses, 245 mules,[a] 69435
camels and 6,720 donkeys.

70Some of the heads of the
families contributed to the
work. The governor gave to
the treasury 1,000 darics[b] of
gold, 50 bowls and 530 garments for priests. 71Some of
the heads of the families gave
to the treasury for the work
20,000 darics[c] of gold and

[a] *68* Some Hebrew manuscripts (see also Ezra 2:66); most Hebrew manuscripts do not have this verse. [b] *70* That is, about 19 pounds or about 8.4 kilograms [c] *71* That is, about 375 pounds or about 170 kilograms; also in verse 72

2,200 minas[a] of silver. 72 The total given by the rest of the people was 20,000 darics of gold, 2,000 minas[b] of silver and 67 garments for priests.

Ex 25:2; 1Ch 29:7

73 The priests, the Levites, the gatekeepers, the musicians and the temple servants, along with certain of the people and the rest of the Israelites, settled in their own towns. Ezr 3:1; Ne 1:10

Ezra Reads the Law

When the seventh month came and the Israelites had settled in

8 their towns, 1 all the people came together as one in the square before the Water Gate. They told Ezra the teacher of the Law to bring out the Book of the Law of Moses, which the LORD had commanded for Israel.

Dt 28:61; Ne 3:26; Ezr 7:6

2 So on the first day of the seventh month Ezra the priest brought the Law before the assembly, which was made up of men and women and all who were able to understand. 3 He read it aloud from daybreak till noon as he faced the square before the Water Gate in the presence of the men, women and others who could understand. And all the people listened attentively to the Book of the Law.

Lev 23:23-25; Dt 31:11; Ne 3:26

4 Ezra the teacher of the Law stood on a high wooden platform built for the occasion. Beside him on his right stood Mattithiah, Shema, Anaiah, Uriah, Hilkiah and Maaseiah; and on his left were Pedaiah, Mishael, Malkijah, Hashum, Hashbaddanah, Zechariah and Meshullam. 2Ch 6:13

5 Ezra opened the book. All the people could see him because he was standing above them; and as he opened it, the people all stood up. 6 Ezra praised the LORD, the great God; and all the people lifted their hands and responded, "Amen! Amen!" Then they bowed down and worshiped the LORD with their faces to the ground.

Ex 4:31; Ezr 9:5; 1Ti 2:8

7 The Levites — Jeshua, Bani, Sherebiah, Jamin, Akkub, Shabbethai, Hodiah, Maaseiah, Kelita, Azariah, Jozabad, Hanan and Pelaiah — instructed the people in the Law while the people were standing there. 8 They read from the Book of the Law of God, making it clear[c] and giving the meaning so that the people understood what was being read. Lev 10:11; 2Ch 17:7

9 Then Nehemiah the governor, Ezra the priest and teacher of the Law, and the Levites who were instructing the people said to them all, "This day is holy to the LORD your God. Do not mourn or weep." For all the people had been weeping as they listened to the words of the Law. Ne 7:1,65,70; Dt 12:7,12; 16:14-15

[a] 71 That is, about 1 1/3 tons or about 1.2 metric tons [b] 72 That is, about 1 1/4 tons or about 1.1 metric tons
[c] 8 Or *God, translating it*

10 Nehemiah said, "Go and enjoy choice food and sweet drinks,
and send some to those who have
nothing prepared. This day is holy
to our Lord. Do not grieve, for the
joy of the LORD is your strength."

Lev 23:40; Dt 12:18; Lk 14:12-14

11 The Levites calmed all the people, saying, "Be still, for this is a
holy day. Do not grieve."

12 Then all the people went away
to eat and drink, to send portions
of food and to celebrate with great
joy, because they now understood
the words that had been made
known to them. Est 9:22

13 On the second day of the
month, the heads of all the families, along with the priests and the
Levites, gathered around Ezra the
teacher to give attention to the
words of the Law. 14 They found
written in the Law, which the
LORD had commanded through
Moses, that the Israelites were to
live in temporary shelters during
the festival of the seventh month
15 and that they should proclaim
this word and spread it throughout their towns and in Jerusalem:
"Go out into the hill country and
bring back branches from olive
and wild olive trees, and from
myrtles, palms and shade trees, to
make temporary shelters" — as it
is written.[a]

16 So the people went out and
brought back branches and built
themselves temporary shelters
on their own roofs, in their courtyards, in the courts of the house of
God and in the square by the Water Gate and the one by the Gate
of Ephraim. 17 The whole company
that had returned from exile built
temporary shelters and lived in
them. From the days of Joshua
son of Nun until that day, the Israelites had not celebrated it like
this. And their joy was very great.

2Ch 30:21; Ne 12:39

18 Day after day, from the first
day to the last, Ezra read from the
Book of the Law of God. They celebrated the festival for seven days,
and on the eighth day, in accordance with the regulation, there
was an assembly. Nu 29:35; Dt 31:11

The Israelites Confess Their Sins

9 On the twenty-fourth day of
the same month, the Israelites gathered together, fasting
and wearing sackcloth and putting dust on their heads. 2 Those
of Israelite descent had separated themselves from all foreigners. They stood in their places and
confessed their sins and the sins of
their ancestors. 3 They stood where
they were and read from the Book
of the Law of the LORD their God
for a quarter of the day, and spent
another quarter in confession and
in worshiping the LORD their God.
4 Standing on the stairs of the Levites were Jeshua, Bani, Kadmiel, Shebaniah, Bunni, Sherebiah,
Bani and Kenani. They cried out
with loud voices to the LORD their
God. 5 And the Levites — Jeshua,

[a] *15* See Lev. 23:37-40.

Kadmiel, Bani, Hashabneiah,
Sherebiah, Hodiah, Shebaniah and
Pethahiah — said: "Stand up and
praise the LORD your God, who is
from everlasting to everlasting.[a]"

1Sa 4:12; Ezr 10:11; Ne 13:3,30

"Blessed be your glorious
name, and may it be exalted
above all blessing and praise.
6 You alone are the LORD. You
made the heavens, even the
highest heavens, and all their
starry host, the earth and all
that is on it, the seas and all
that is in them. You give life
to everything, and the multitudes of heaven worship you.

Ge 1:1; 2Ki 19:15; Ps 95:5

7 "You are the LORD God,
who chose Abram and
brought him out of Ur of the
Chaldeans and named him
Abraham. 8 You found his
heart faithful to you, and you
made a covenant with him to
give to his descendants the
land of the Canaanites, Hittites, Amorites, Perizzites,
Jebusites and Girgashites.
You have kept your promise
because you are righteous.

Ge 15:6,18-21; Ezr 9;15

9 "You saw the suffering of
our ancestors in Egypt; you
heard their cry at the Red
Sea.[b] 10 You sent signs and
wonders against Pharaoh,
against all his officials and
all the people of his land, for
you knew how arrogantly
the Egyptians treated them.
You made a name for your-
self, which remains to this
day. 11 You divided the sea before them, so that they passed
through it on dry ground, but
you hurled their pursuers
into the depths, like a stone
into mighty waters. 12 By day
you led them with a pillar of
cloud, and by night with a pillar of fire to give them light
on the way they were to take.

Ex 13:21; 14:21; 15:4-5,10

13 "You came down on
Mount Sinai; you spoke to
them from heaven. You gave
them regulations and laws
that are just and right, and decrees and commands that are
good. 14 You made known to
them your holy Sabbath and
gave them commands, de-
crees and laws through your
servant Moses. 15 In their hunger you gave them bread from
heaven and in their thirst you
brought them water from the
rock; you told them to go in
and take possession of the
land you had sworn with uplifted hand to give them.

Ex 16:4; 17:6; Dt 1:8,21

16 "But they, our ances-
tors, became arrogant and
stiff-necked, and they did not
obey your commands. 17 They
refused to listen and failed
to remember the miracles

[a] 5 Or *God for ever and ever* [b] 9 Or *the Sea of Reeds*

you performed among them.
They became stiff-necked and
in their rebellion appointed a
leader in order to return to
their slavery. But you are a
forgiving God, gracious and
compassionate, slow to anger and abounding in love.
Therefore you did not desert
them, 18even when they cast
for themselves an image of
a calf and said, 'This is your
god, who brought you up out
of Egypt,' or when they committed awful blasphemies.

Ex 32:4; Nu 14:1-4; Ps 78:11

19"Because of your great
compassion you did not
abandon them in the wil-
derness. By day the pillar of
cloud did not fail to guide
them on their path, nor the
pillar of fire by night to shine
on the way they were to take.
20You gave your good Spirit
to instruct them. You did not
withhold your manna from
their mouths, and you gave
them water for their thirst.
21For forty years you sustained
them in the wilderness; they
lacked nothing, their clothes
did not wear out nor did their
feet become swollen.

Nu 11:17; Dt 2:7; Isa 63:11,14

22"You gave them king-
doms and nations, allotting
to them even the remotest
frontiers. They took over
the country of Sihon[a] king
of Heshbon and the country
of Og king of Bashan. 23You
made their children as numerous as the stars in the sky,
and you brought them into
the land that you told their
parents to enter and possess.
24Their children went in and
took possession of the land.
You subdued before them the
Canaanites, who lived in the
land; you gave the Canaanites into their hands, along
with their kings and the peoples of the land, to deal with
them as they pleased. 25They
captured fortified cities and
fertile land; they took possession of houses filled with
all kinds of good things,
wells already dug, vineyards,
olive groves and fruit trees
in abundance. They ate to
the full and were well-nour-
ished; they reveled in your
great goodness.

Dt 6:10-12; 32:12-15

26"But they were disobe-
dient and rebelled against
you; they turned their backs
on your law. They killed your
prophets, who had warned
them in order to turn them
back to you; they commit-
ted awful blasphemies. 27So
you delivered them into the
hands of their enemies, who
oppressed them. But when
they were oppressed they

[a] *22* One Hebrew manuscript and Septuagint; most Hebrew manuscripts *Sihon, that is, the country of the*

cried out to you. From heaven
you heard them, and in your
great compassion you gave
them deliverers, who rescued
them from the hand of their
enemies. Jdg 2:12-14; 1Ki 14:9

28“But as soon as they were
at rest, they again did what
was evil in your sight. Then
you abandoned them to the
hand of their enemies so that
they ruled over them. And
when they cried out to you
again, you heard from heav-
en, and in your compassion
you delivered them time after
time. Ps 106:43

29“You warned them in
order to turn them back to
your law, but they became arrogant and disobeyed your
commands. They sinned
against your ordinances, of
which you said, ‘The person
who obeys them will live
by them.’ Stubbornly they
turned their backs on you,
became stiff-necked and refused to listen. 30For many
years you were patient with
them. By your Spirit you
warned them through your
prophets. Yet they paid no
attention, so you gave them
into the hands of the neighboring peoples. 31But in your
great mercy you did not put
an end to them or abandon
them, for you are a gracious
and merciful God.
Dt 30:16; 2Ki 17:13-18; Zec 7:11-12

32“Now therefore, our God,
the great God, mighty and
awesome, who keeps his covenant of love, do not let all
this hardship seem trifling in
your eyes — the hardship that
has come on us, on our kings
and leaders, on our priests
and prophets, on our ancestors and all your people, from
the days of the kings of Assyria until today. 33In all that has
happened to us, you have remained righteous; you have
acted faithfully, while we acted wickedly. 34Our kings, our
leaders, our priests and our
ancestors did not follow your
law; they did not pay attention to your commands or the
statutes you warned them to
keep. 35Even while they were
in their kingdom, enjoying
your great goodness to them
in the spacious and fertile
land you gave them, they did
not serve you or turn from
their evil ways.
Ge 18:25; Dt 28:45-48; Da 9:7-8,14

36“But see, we are slaves
today, slaves in the land you
gave our ancestors so they
could eat its fruit and the
other good things it produces. 37Because of our sins, its
abundant harvest goes to the
kings you have placed over
us. They rule over our bodies
and our cattle as they please.
We are in great distress.
Dt 28:33,48; Ezr 9:9

The Agreement of the People

38"In view of all this, we are making a binding agreement, putting it in writing, and our leaders, our Levites and our priests are affixing their seals to it."[a]

2Ch 23:16; Isa 44:5

10 [b] Those who sealed it were:

Nehemiah the governor, the son of Hakaliah.

Zedekiah, 2Seraiah, Azariah, Jeremiah, Ezr 2:2
3Pashhur, Amariah, Malkijah, 1Ch 9:12
4Hattush, Shebaniah, Malluk,
5Harim, Meremoth, Obadiah, 1Ch 24:8
6Daniel, Ginnethon, Baruch,
7Meshullam, Abijah, Mijamin,
8Maaziah, Bilgai and Shemaiah.
These were the priests.

9The Levites: Ne 12:1

Jeshua son of Azaniah, Binnui of the sons of Henadad, Kadmiel,
10and their associates: Shebaniah,
Hodiah, Kelita, Pelaiah, Hanan,
11Mika, Rehob, Hashabiah,
12Zakkur, Sherebiah, Shebaniah,
13Hodiah, Bani and Beninu.

14The leaders of the people:

Parosh, Pahath-Moab, Elam, Zattu, Bani,
15Bunni, Azgad, Bebai,
16Adonijah, Bigvai, Adin, Ezr 8:6
17Ater, Hezekiah, Azzur,
18Hodiah, Hashum, Bezai,
19Hariph, Anathoth, Nebai,
20Magpiash, Meshullam, Hezir, 1Ch 24:15
21Meshezabel, Zadok, Jaddua,
22Pelatiah, Hanan, Anaiah,
23Hoshea, Hananiah, Hasshub,
24Hallohesh, Pilha, Shobek,
25Rehum, Hashabnah, Maaseiah,
26Ahiah, Hanan, Anan,
27Malluk, Harim and Baanah.

28"The rest of the people — priests, Levites, gatekeepers, musicians, temple servants and all who separated themselves from the neighboring peoples for the sake of the Law of God, together with their wives and all their sons and daughters who are able
to understand —
29all these now join their fellow Israelites the nobles, and bind themselves with a curse and an oath to follow the Law of God given through Moses the servant of God and to obey carefully all the commands, regulations and decrees of the LORD our Lord.

Ne 9:2; Ps 119:106; 135:1

30"We promise not to give our daughters in marriage to

[a] 38 In Hebrew texts this verse (9:38) is numbered 10:1. [b] In Hebrew texts 10:1-39 is numbered 10:2-40.

the peoples around us or take
their daughters for our sons.
Ex 34:16; Dt 7:3

31 "When the neighboring
peoples bring merchandise or
grain to sell on the Sabbath,
we will not buy from them
on the Sabbath or on any holy
day. Every seventh year we
will forgo working the land
and will cancel all debts.
Ex 23:11; Dt 15:1; Ne 13:16,18

32 "We assume the respon-
sibility for carrying out the
commands to give a third of a
shekel[a] each year for the service of the house of our God:
33 for the bread set out on the
table; for the regular grain
offerings and burnt offerings; for the offerings on the
Sabbaths, at the New Moon
feasts and at the appointed festivals; for the holy offerings; for sin offerings[b] to
make atonement for Israel;
and for all the duties of the
house of our God.
Lev 24:6; 2Ch 24:5

34 "We — the priests, the Levites and the people — have
cast lots to determine when
each of our families is to
bring to the house of our God
at set times each year a contribution of wood to burn on
the altar of the LORD our God,
as it is written in the Law.
Ne 13:31

35 "We also assume responsibility for bringing to the
house of the LORD each year
the firstfruits of our crops
and of every fruit tree.
Ex 23:19; Nu 18:12

36 "As it is also written in the
Law, we will bring the firstborn of our sons and of our
cattle, of our herds and of
our flocks to the house of our
God, to the priests ministering there.
Ex 13:2; Nu 18:14-16

37 "Moreover, we will bring
to the storerooms of the
house of our God, to the
priests, the first of our ground
meal, of our grain offerings,
of the fruit of all our trees and
of our new wine and olive oil.
And we will bring a tithe of
our crops to the Levites, for it
is the Levites who collect the
tithes in all the towns where
we work. 38 A priest descended
from Aaron is to accompany
the Levites when they receive
the tithes, and the Levites are
to bring a tenth of the tithes
up to the house of our God,
to the storerooms of the treasury. 39 The people of Israel,
including the Levites, are to
bring their contributions of
grain, new wine and olive oil
to the storerooms, where the
articles for the sanctuary and
for the ministering priests,
the gatekeepers and the musicians are also kept.
Lev 23:17; Nu 18:21,26

[a] 32 That is, about 1/8 ounce or about 4 grams [b] 33 Or *purification offerings*

"We will not neglect the house of our God."

Dt 12:6; Ne 13:11-12

The New Residents of Jerusalem

11 Now the leaders of the people settled in Jerusalem. The rest of the people cast lots to bring one out of every ten of them to live in Jerusalem, the holy city, while the remaining nine were to stay in their own towns. 2The people commended all who volunteered to live in Jerusalem.

Ne 7:4,73; Isa 48:2

3These are the provincial leaders who settled in Jerusalem (now some Israelites, priests, Levites, temple servants and descendants of Solomon's servants lived in the towns of Judah, each on their own property in the various towns, 4while other people from both Judah and Benjamin lived in Jerusalem):

1Ch 9:2-3; Ezr 2:1

From the descendants of Judah:

Athaiah son of Uzziah, the son of Zechariah, the son of Amariah, the son of Shephatiah, the son of Mahalalel, a descendant of Perez; 5and Maaseiah son of Baruch, the son of Kol-Hozeh, the son of Hazaiah, the son of Adaiah, the son of Joiarib, the son of Zechariah, a descendant of Shelah. 6The descendants of Perez who lived in Jerusalem totaled 468 men of standing.

7From the descendants of Benjamin:

Sallu son of Meshullam, the son of Joed, the son of Pedaiah, the son of Kolaiah, the son of Maaseiah, the son of Ithiel, the son of Jeshaiah, 8and his followers, Gabbai and Sallai — 928 men. 9Joel son of Zikri was their chief officer, and Judah son of Hassenuah was over the New Quarter of the city.

10From the priests:

Jedaiah; the son of Joiarib; Jakin; 11Seraiah son of Hilkiah, the son of Meshullam, the son of Zadok, the son of Meraioth, the son of Ahitub, the official in charge of the house of God, 12and their associates, who carried on work for the temple — 822 men; Adaiah son of Jeroham, the son of Pelaliah, the son of Amzi, the son of Zechariah, the son of Pashhur, the son of Malkijah, 13and his associates, who were heads of families — 242 men; Amashsai son of Azarel, the son of Ahzai, the son of Meshillemoth, the son of Immer, 14and his[a] associates, who were men of standing — 128. Their chief officer was Zabdiel son of Haggedolim.

2Ki 25:18; Ezr 2:2

[a] 14 Most Septuagint manuscripts; Hebrew *their*

15 From the Levites:

Shemaiah son of Hasshub,
the son of Azrikam, the son of
Hashabiah, the son of Bunni;
16 Shabbethai and Jozabad, two
of the heads of the Levites, who
had charge of the outside work
of the house of God; 17 Mattaniah son of Mika, the son of Zabdi, the son of Asaph, the director who led in thanksgiving
and prayer; Bakbukiah, second among his associates; and
Abda son of Shammua, the son
of Galal, the son of Jeduthun.
18 The Levites in the holy city
totaled 284. 1Ch 9:15; 25:1; Rev 21:2

19 The gatekeepers:

Akkub, Talmon and their associates, who kept watch at
the gates — 172 men. 1Ch 9:1-17

20 The rest of the Israelites, with
the priests and Levites, were in all
the towns of Judah, each on their
ancestral property.
21 The temple servants lived on
the hill of Ophel, and Ziha and
Gishpa were in charge of them.
Ezr 2:43; Ne 3:26
22 The chief officer of the Levites
in Jerusalem was Uzzi son of Bani,
the son of Hashabiah, the son of
Mattaniah, the son of Mika. Uzzi
was one of Asaph's descendants,
who were the musicians responsible for the service of the house of
God. 23 The musicians were under
the king's orders, which regulated
their daily activity. 1Ch 9:15; Ne 7:44
24 Pethahiah son of Meshezabel,
one of the descendants of Zerah
son of Judah, was the king's agent
in all affairs relating to the people.
Ge 38:30
25 As for the villages with their
fields, some of the people of Judah lived in Kiriath Arba and its
surrounding settlements, in Dibon and its settlements, in Jekab-
zeel and its villages, 26 in Jeshua, in
Moladah, in Beth Pelet, 27 in Hazar
Shual, in Beersheba and its settlements, 28 in Ziklag, in Mekonah and
its settlements, 29 in En Rimmon,
in Zorah, in Jarmuth, 30 Zanoah,
Adullam and their villages, in Lachish and its fields, and in Azekah
and its settlements. So they were
living all the way from Beersheba
to the Valley of Hinnom.
Ge 21:14; Jos 10:3; 1Sa 27:6
31 The descendants of the Benjamites from Geba lived in Mikmash, Aija, Bethel and its settlements, 32 in Anathoth, Nob and
Ananiah, 33 in Hazor, Ramah and
Gittaim, 34 in Hadid, Zeboim and
Neballat, 35 in Lod and Ono, and in
Ge Harashim. Jos 11:1; 21:17; 1Sa 13:18
36 Some of the divisions of the
Levites of Judah settled in Benjamin.

Priests and Levites

12 These were the priests and
Levites who returned with
Zerubbabel son of Shealtiel and
with Joshua: 1Ch 3:19; Ezr 2:2

Seraiah, Jeremiah, Ezra, Ezr 2:2
2 Amariah, Malluk, Hattush,

3 Shekaniah, Rehum, Meremoth,
4 Iddo, Ginnethon,[a] Abijah,
Lk 1:5; Zec 1:1
5 Mijamin,[b] Moadiah, Bilgah,
6 Shemaiah, Joiarib, Jedaiah,
1Ch 24:7
7 Sallu, Amok, Hilkiah and Jedaiah.

These were the leaders of the priests and their associates in the days of Joshua.

8 The Levites were Jeshua, Binnui, Kadmiel, Sherebiah, Judah,
and also Mattaniah, who, together
with his associates, was in charge
of the songs of thanksgiving.
9 Bakbukiah and Unni, their associates, stood opposite them in the
services. Ne 11:17
10 Joshua was the father of Joiakim, Joiakim the father of Eliashib,
Eliashib the father of Joiada, 11 Joiada the father of Jonathan, and Jonathan the father of Jaddua. Ezr 10:24
12 In the days of Joiakim, these
were the heads of the priestly
families:

of Seraiah's family, Meraiah;
of Jeremiah's, Hananiah;
13 of Ezra's, Meshullam;
of Amariah's, Jehohanan;
14 of Malluk's, Jonathan;
of Shekaniah's,[c] Joseph;
15 of Harim's, Adna;
of Meremoth's,[d] Helkai;
16 of Iddo's, Zechariah;
of Ginnethon's, Meshullam;
17 of Abijah's, Zikri;
of Miniamin's and of Moadiah's, Piltai;
18 of Bilgah's, Shammua;
of Shemaiah's, Jehonathan;
19 of Joiarib's, Mattenai;
of Jedaiah's, Uzzi;
20 of Sallu's, Kallai;
of Amok's, Eber;
21 of Hilkiah's, Hashabiah;
of Jedaiah's, Nethanel.

22 The family heads of the Levites in the days of Eliashib, Joiada, Johanan and Jaddua, as well as
those of the priests, were recorded
in the reign of Darius the Persian.
23 The family heads among the descendants of Levi up to the time of
Johanan son of Eliashib were recorded in the book of the annals.
24 And the leaders of the Levites
were Hashabiah, Sherebiah, Jeshua son of Kadmiel, and their associates, who stood opposite them
to give praise and thanksgiving,
one section responding to the other, as prescribed by David the man
of God. Ezr 2:40
25 Mattaniah, Bakbukiah, Obadiah, Meshullam, Talmon and Akkub were gatekeepers who guarded the storerooms at the gates.
26 They served in the days of Joiakim son of Joshua, the son of Jozadak, and in the days of Nehemiah the governor and of Ezra the
priest, the teacher of the Law.

[a] 4 Many Hebrew manuscripts and Vulgate (see also verse 16); most Hebrew manuscripts *Ginnethoi* [b] 5 A variant of *Miniamin* [c] 14 Very many Hebrew manuscripts, some Septuagint manuscripts and Syriac (see also verse 3); most Hebrew manuscripts *Shebaniah's* [d] 15 Some Septuagint manuscripts (see also verse 3); Hebrew *Meraioth's*

Dedication of the Wall of Jerusalem

27 At the dedication of the wall
of Jerusalem, the Levites were
sought out from where they lived
and were brought to Jerusalem to
celebrate joyfully the dedication
with songs of thanksgiving and
with the music of cymbals, harps
and lyres. 28 The musicians also
were brought together from the
region around Jerusalem — from
the villages of the Netophathites,
29 from Beth Gilgal, and from the
area of Geba and Azmaveth, for
the musicians had built villages for themselves around Jerusalem. 30 When the priests and
Levites had purified themselves
ceremonially, they purified the
people, the gates and the wall.

1Ch 25:6; Ps 92:3

31 I had the leaders of Judah go
up on top of[a] the wall. I also assigned two large choirs to give
thanks. One was to proceed on
top of[b] the wall to the right, toward the Dung Gate. 32 Hoshaiah
and half the leaders of Judah
followed them, 33 along with Azariah, Ezra, Meshullam, 34 Judah,
Benjamin, Shemaiah, Jeremiah, 35 as well as some priests with
trumpets, and also Zechariah
son of Jonathan, the son of Shemaiah, the son of Mattaniah, the
son of Micaiah, the son of Zakkur,
the son of Asaph, 36 and his associates — Shemaiah, Azarel, Mil-
alai, Gilalai, Maai, Nethanel, Judah and Hanani — with musical
instruments prescribed by David
the man of God. Ezra the teacher
of the Law led the procession. 37 At
the Fountain Gate they continued
directly up the steps of the City
of David on the ascent to the wall
and passed above the site of David's palace to the Water Gate on
the east.

Ne 2:13-14; 3:15,26

38 The second choir proceeded in
the opposite direction. I followed
them on top of[c] the wall, together with half the people — past the
Tower of the Ovens to the Broad
Wall, 39 over the Gate of Ephraim,
the Jeshanah[d] Gate, the Fish Gate,
the Tower of Hananel and the
Tower of the Hundred, as far as
the Sheep Gate. At the Gate of the
Guard they stopped.

Ne 3:1,3,8,11; 8:16

40 The two choirs that gave
thanks then took their places in
the house of God; so did I, together with half the officials, 41 as well
as the priests — Eliakim, Maaseiah, Miniamin, Micaiah, Elioenai,
Zechariah and Hananiah with
their trumpets — 42 and also Maaseiah, Shemaiah, Eleazar, Uzzi,
Jehohanan, Malkijah, Elam and
Ezer. The choirs sang under the direction of Jezrahiah. 43 And on that
day they offered great sacrifices,
rejoicing because God had given
them great joy. The women and
children also rejoiced. The sound
of rejoicing in Jerusalem could be
heard far away.

[a] 31 Or *go alongside* [b] 31 Or *proceed alongside* [c] 38 Or *them alongside* [d] 39 Or *Old*

44At that time men were appointed to be in charge of the storerooms for the contributions, firstfruits and tithes. From the fields around the towns they were to bring into the storerooms the portions required by the Law for the priests and the Levites, for Judah was pleased with the ministering priests and Levites. 45They performed the service of their God and the service of purification, as did also the musicians and gatekeepers, according to the commands of David and his son Solomon. 46For long ago, in the days of David and Asaph, there had been directors for the musicians and for the songs of praise and thanksgiving to God. 47So in the days of Zerubbabel and of Nehemiah, all Israel contributed the daily portions for the musicians and the gatekeepers. They also set aside the portion for thc other Levites, and the Levites set aside the portion for the descendants of Aaron.

Nu 18:21; Dt 18:8; 1Ch 25:1

Nehemiah's Final Reforms

13 On that day the Book of Moses was read aloud in the hearing of the people and there it was found written that no Ammonite or Moabite should ever be admitted into the assembly of God, 2because they had not met the Israelites with food and water but had hired Balaam to call a curse down on them. (Our God, however, turned the curse into a blessing.) 3When the people heard this law, they excluded from Israel all who were of foreign descent.

Dt 23:3; Nu 22:3-11; 23:11

4Before this, Eliashib the priest had been put in charge of the storerooms of the house of our God. He was closely associated with Tobiah, 5and he had provided him with a large room formerly used to store the grain offerings and incense and temple articles, and also the tithes of grain, new wine and olive oil prescribed for the Levites, musicians and gatekeepers, as well as the contributions for the priests.

Nu 18:21; Ne 2:10; 12:44

6But while all this was going on, I was not in Jerusalem, for in the thirty-second year of Artaxerxes king of Babylon I had returned to the king. Some time later I asked his permission 7and came back to Jerusalem. Here I learned about the evil thing Eliashib had done in providing Tobiah a room in the courts of the house of God. 8I was greatly displeased and threw all Tobiah's household goods out of the room. 9I gave orders to purify the rooms, and then I put back into them the equipment of the house of God, with the grain offerings and the incense.

2Ch 29:5; Ne 5:14; Mt 21:12-13

10I also learned that the portions assigned to the Levites had not been given to them, and that all the Levites and musicians responsible for the service had gone

back to their own fields. 11So I rebuked the officials and asked
them, "Why is the house of God
neglected?" Then I called them together and stationed them at their
posts. Ne 10:37-39; Hag 1:1-9

12All Judah brought the tithes of
grain, new wine and olive oil into
the storerooms. 13I put Shelemiah
the priest, Zadok the scribe, and
a Levite named Pedaiah in charge
of the storerooms and made Hanan son of Zakkur, the son of Mattaniah, their assistant, because
they were considered trustworthy. They were made responsible
for distributing the supplies to
their fellow Levites.

Ne 10:37-39; 12:44; Ac 6:1-5

14Remember me for this, my
God, and do not blot out what I
have so faithfully done for the
house of my God and its services.

Ge 8:1

15In those days I saw people in
Judah treading winepresses on
the Sabbath and bringing in grain
and loading it on donkeys, together with wine, grapes, figs and all
other kinds of loads. And they were
bringing all this into Jerusalem on
the Sabbath. Therefore I warned
them against selling food on that
day. 16People from Tyre who lived
in Jerusalem were bringing in fish
and all kinds of merchandise and
selling them in Jerusalem on the
Sabbath to the people of Judah. 17I
rebuked the nobles of Judah and
said to them, "What is this wicked
thing you are doing — desecrating
the Sabbath day? 18Didn't your ancestors do the same things, so that
our God brought all this calamity
on us and on this city? Now you
are stirring up more wrath against
Israel by desecrating the Sabbath."

Ex 20:8-11; Ne 10:31; Jer 17:21-23

19When evening shadows fell on
the gates of Jerusalem before the
Sabbath, I ordered the doors to be
shut and not opened until the Sabbath was over. I stationed some of
my own men at the gates so that
no load could be brought in on the
Sabbath day. 20Once or twice the
merchants and sellers of all kinds
of goods spent the night outside
Jerusalem. 21But I warned them
and said, "Why do you spend the
night by the wall? If you do this
again, I will arrest you." From that
time on they no longer came on
the Sabbath. 22Then I commanded
the Levites to purify themselves
and go and guard the gates in order to keep the Sabbath day holy.

Lev 23:32; Ne 12:30

Remember me for this also, my
God, and show mercy to me according to your great love.

23Moreover, in those days I saw
men of Judah who had married
women from Ashdod, Ammon
and Moab. 24Half of their children
spoke the language of Ashdod or
the language of one of the other
peoples, and did not know how to
speak the language of Judah. 25I
rebuked them and called curses

down on them. I beat some of the
men and pulled out their hair. I
made them take an oath in God's
name and said: "You are not to
give your daughters in marriage
to their sons, nor are you to take
their daughters in marriage for
your sons or for yourselves. [26]Was
it not because of marriages like
these that Solomon king of Israel sinned? Among the many nations there was no king like him.
He was loved by his God, and God
made him king over all Israel, but
even he was led into sin by foreign
women. [27]Must we hear now that
you too are doing all this terrible
wickedness and are being unfaithful to our God by marrying foreign
women?" 1Ki 11:3; 2Ch 1:12; Ezr 10:2

[28]One of the sons of Joiada son
of Eliashib the high priest was son-
in-law to Sanballat the Horonite.
And I drove him away from me.
Ezr 10:24; Ne 2:10

[29]Remember them, my God, because they defiled the priestly office and the covenant of the priesthood and of the Levites. Ne 6:14

[30]So I purified the priests and
the Levites of everything foreign,
and assigned them duties, each
to his own task. [31]I also made provision for contributions of wood
at designated times, and for the
firstfruits. Ne 10:30,34-36

Remember me with favor, my
God. ver 14,22; Ge 8:1

ESTHER

Queen Vashti Deposed

1 This is what happened during
the time of Xerxes,[a] the Xerxes who ruled over 127 provinces
stretching from India to Cush[b]:
2At that time King Xerxes reigned
from his royal throne in the citadel of Susa, 3and in the third year
of his reign he gave a banquet for
all his nobles and officials. The
military leaders of Persia and Media, the princes, and the nobles of
the provinces were present.
Est 8:9; 9:30; Da 9:1

4For a full 180 days he displayed
the vast wealth of his kingdom
and the splendor and glory of his
majesty. 5When these days were
over, the king gave a banquet,
lasting seven days, in the enclosed
garden of the king's palace, for all
the people from the least to the
greatest who were in the citadel
of Susa. 6The garden had hangings
of white and blue linen, fastened
with cords of white linen and
purple material to silver rings on
marble pillars. There were couches of gold and silver on a mosaic
pavement of porphyry, marble,
mother-of-pearl and other costly
stones. 7Wine was served in goblets of gold, each one different
from the other, and the royal wine
was abundant, in keeping with
the king's liberality. 8By the king's
command each guest was allowed
to drink with no restrictions, for
the king instructed all the wine
stewards to serve each man what
he wished. Est 2:18; 7:7-8; Eze 23:41

9Queen Vashti also gave a banquet for the women in the royal
palace of King Xerxes. 1Ki 3:15

10On the seventh day, when King
Xerxes was in high spirits from
wine, he commanded the seven
eunuchs who served him — Me-
human, Biztha, Harbona, Bigtha,
Abagtha, Zethar and Karkas — 11to
bring before him Queen Vashti,
wearing her royal crown, in order
to display her beauty to the people
and nobles, for she was lovely to
look at. 12But when the attendants
delivered the king's command,
Queen Vashti refused to come.
Then the king became furious and
burned with anger. Jdg 16:25; Est 2:21

13Since it was customary for the
king to consult experts in matters
of law and justice, he spoke with
the wise men who understood
the times 14and were closest to the
king — Karshena, Shethar, Adma-
tha, Tarshish, Meres, Marsena and
Memukan, the seven nobles of Persia and Media who had special access to the king and were highest in
the kingdom. 2Ki 25:19; 1Ch 12:32; Jer 10:7

[a] *1* Hebrew *Ahasuerus*; here and throughout Esther [b] *1* That is, the upper Nile region

15 "According to law, what must
be done to Queen Vashti?" he
asked. "She has not obeyed the
command of King Xerxes that the
eunuchs have taken to her."
16 Then Memukan replied in
the presence of the king and the
nobles, "Queen Vashti has done
wrong, not only against the king
but also against all the nobles and
the peoples of all the provinces of
King Xerxes. 17 For the queen's conduct will become known to all the
women, and so they will despise
their husbands and say, 'King Xerxes commanded Queen Vashti to
be brought before him, but she
would not come.' 18 This very day
the Persian and Median women of
the nobility who have heard about
the queen's conduct will respond
to all the king's nobles in the same
way. There will be no end of disrespect and discord. Pr 19:13; 27:15
19 "Therefore, if it pleases the
king, let him issue a royal decree
and let it be written in the laws of
Persia and Media, which cannot be
repealed, that Vashti is never again
to enter the presence of King Xerxes. Also let the king give her royal position to someone else who
is better than she. 20 Then when
the king's edict is proclaimed
throughout all his vast realm, all
the women will respect their husbands, from the least to the greatest." Est 8:8; Da 6:8,12
21 The king and his nobles were
pleased with this advice, so the
king did as Memukan proposed.
22 He sent dispatches to all parts of
the kingdom, to each province in
its own script and to each people
in their own language, proclaiming that every man should be ruler
over his own household, using his
native tongue. Ne 13:24; Eph 5:22-24

Esther Made Queen

2 Later when King Xerxes' fury
had subsided, he remembered
Vashti and what she had done and
what he had decreed about her.
2 Then the king's personal attendants proposed, "Let a search be
made for beautiful young virgins
for the king. 3 Let the king appoint
commissioners in every province of his realm to bring all these
beautiful young women into the
harem at the citadel of Susa. Let
them be placed under the care of
Hegai, the king's eunuch, who is
in charge of the women; and let
beauty treatments be given to
them. 4 Then let the young woman who pleases the king be queen
instead of Vashti." This advice
appealed to the king, and he followed it. Est 1:19-20; 7:10
5 Now there was in the citadel of
Susa a Jew of the tribe of Benjamin, named Mordecai son of Jair,
the son of Shimei, the son of Kish,
6 who had been carried into exile
from Jerusalem by Nebuchadnezzar king of Babylon, among those
taken captive with Jehoiachin[a]
king of Judah. 7 Mordecai had a

[a] 6 Hebrew *Jeconiah*, a variant of *Jehoiachin*

cousin named Hadassah, whom
he had brought up because she
had neither father nor mother.
This young woman, who was also
known as Esther, had a lovely figure and was beautiful. Mordecai
had taken her as his own daughter
when her father and mother died.
2Ki 24:6,15; 2Ch 36:10,20; Est 3:2

8 When the king's order and
edict had been proclaimed, many
young women were brought to
the citadel of Susa and put under
the care of Hegai. Esther also was
taken to the king's palace and entrusted to Hegai, who had charge
of the harem. 9 She pleased him
and won his favor. Immediately
he provided her with her beauty
treatments and special food. He
assigned to her seven female attendants selected from the king's
palace and moved her and her attendants into the best place in the
harem. 2Ki 25:30; Est 1:2

10 Esther had not revealed her nationality and family background,
because Mordecai had forbidden
her to do so. 11 Every day he walked
back and forth near the courtyard
of the harem to find out how Esther was and what was happening
to her. ver 20

12 Before a young woman's turn
came to go in to King Xerxes, she
had to complete twelve months of
beauty treatments prescribed for
the women, six months with oil of
myrrh and six with perfumes and
cosmetics. 13 And this is how she
would go to the king: Anything
she wanted was given her to take
with her from the harem to the
king's palace. 14 In the evening she
would go there and in the morning
return to another part of the harem to the care of Shaashgaz, the
king's eunuch who was in charge
of the concubines. She would not
return to the king unless he was
pleased with her and summoned
her by name. 1Ki 11:3; Est 4:11; Pr 27:9

15 When the turn came for Esther
(the young woman Mordecai had
adopted, the daughter of his uncle Abihail) to go to the king, she
asked for nothing other than what
Hegai, the king's eunuch who was
in charge of the harem, suggested. And Esther won the favor of
everyone who saw her. 16 She was
taken to King Xerxes in the royal
residence in the tenth month, the
month of Tebeth, in the seventh
year of his reign. Est 9:29; Ps 45:14

17 Now the king was attracted
to Esther more than to any of the
other women, and she won his favor and approval more than any of
the other virgins. So he set a royal
crown on her head and made her
queen instead of Vashti. 18 And the
king gave a great banquet, Esther's
banquet, for all his nobles and officials. He proclaimed a holiday
throughout the provinces and distributed gifts with royal liberality.
Est 1:3,7,11

Mordecai Uncovers a Conspiracy

19 When the virgins were assembled a second time, Mordecai was

sitting at the king's gate. 20But Esther had kept secret her family
background and nationality just
as Mordecai had told her to do, for
she continued to follow Mordecai's instructions as she had done
when he was bringing her up.
Est 3:2; 4:2; 5:13

21During the time Mordecai was
sitting at the king's gate, Bigthana[a] and Teresh, two of the king's
officers who guarded the doorway, became angry and conspired
to assassinate King Xerxes. 22But
Mordecai found out about the
plot and told Queen Esther, who in
turn reported it to the king, giving
credit to Mordecai. 23And when the
report was investigated and found
to be true, the two officials were
impaled on poles. All this was recorded in the book of the annals
in the presence of the king.
Est 6:1-2; Ps 7:14-16

Haman's Plot to Destroy the Jews

3 After these events, King Xerxes
honored Haman son of Ham-
medatha, the Agagite, elevating
him and giving him a seat of hon-
or higher than that of all the other nobles. 2All the royal officials
at the king's gate knelt down and
paid honor to Haman, for the king
had commanded this concerning him. But Mordecai would not
kneel down or pay him honor.
Nu 24:7; Dt 25:17-19

3Then the royal officials at the
king's gate asked Mordecai, "Why
do you disobey the king's command?" 4Day after day they spoke
to him but he refused to comply.
Therefore they told Haman about
it to see whether Mordecai's behavior would be tolerated, for he
had told them he was a Jew.
Ge 39:10; Est 5:9

5When Haman saw that Mor-
decai would not kneel down or
pay him honor, he was enraged.
6Yet having learned who Mordecai's people were, he scorned the
idea of killing only Mordecai. Instead Haman looked for a way to
destroy all Mordecai's people, the
Jews, throughout the whole kingdom of Xerxes. Est 5:9; Ps 83:4

7In the twelfth year of King Xerxes, in the first month, the month
of Nisan, the *pur* (that is, the lot)
was cast in the presence of Haman
to select a day and month. And the
lot fell on[b] the twelfth month, the
month of Adar. Est 9:24,26

8Then Haman said to King Xerxes, "There is a certain people dispersed among the peoples in all
the provinces of your kingdom
who keep themselves separate.
Their customs are different from
those of all other people, and they
do not obey the king's laws; it is
not in the king's best interest to
tolerate them. 9If it pleases the
king, let a decree be issued to destroy them, and I will give ten
thousand talents[c] of silver to the

[a] 21 Hebrew *Bigthan*, a variant of *Bigthana*
[b] 7 Septuagint; Hebrew does not have *And the lot fell on.*
[c] 9 That is, about 375 tons or about 340 metric tons

king's administrators for the royal
treasury." Ezr 4:15; Ac 16:20-21
10So the king took his signet
ring from his finger and gave it to
Haman son of Hammedatha, the
Agagite, the enemy of the Jews.
11"Keep the money," the king said
to Haman, "and do with the peo-
ple as you please." Ge 41:42; Est 7:6; 8:2
12Then on the thirteenth day
of the first month the royal secretaries were summoned. They
wrote out in the script of each
province and in the language of
each people all Haman's orders
to the king's satraps, the governors of the various provinces and
the nobles of the various peoples.
These were written in the name
of King Xerxes himself and sealed
with his own ring. 13Dispatches
were sent by couriers to all the
king's provinces with the order
to destroy, kill and annihilate all
the Jews — young and old, wom-
en and children — on a single day,
the thirteenth day of the twelfth
month, the month of Adar, and to
plunder their goods. 14A copy of
the text of the edict was to be issued as law in every province and
made known to the people of every nationality so they would be
ready for that day.
1Ki 21:8; Est 8:10-14; 9:10
15The couriers went out, spurred
on by the king's command, and
the edict was issued in the citadel
of Susa. The king and Haman sat
down to drink, but the city of Susa
was bewildered. Est 1:10; 8:15

Mordecai Persuades Esther to Help

4 When Mordecai learned of all
that had been done, he tore
his clothes, put on sackcloth and
ashes, and went out into the city,
wailing loudly and bitterly. 2But
he went only as far as the king's
gate, because no one clothed in
sackcloth was allowed to enter it.
3In every province to which the
edict and order of the king came,
there was great mourning among
the Jews, with fasting, weeping
and wailing. Many lay in sackcloth
and ashes. Nu 14:6; Est 2:19; Eze 27:30-31
4When Esther's eunuchs and fe-
male attendants came and told
her about Mordecai, she was in
great distress. She sent clothes for
him to put on instead of his sackcloth, but he would not accept
them. 5Then Esther summoned
Hathak, one of the king's eunuchs
assigned to attend her, and ordered him to find out what was
troubling Mordecai and why.
6So Hathak went out to Mordecai in the open square of the city
in front of the king's gate. 7Mor-
decai told him everything that
had happened to him, including
the exact amount of money Haman had promised to pay into the
royal treasury for the destruction
of the Jews. 8He also gave him a
copy of the text of the edict for
their annihilation, which had
been published in Susa, to show
to Esther and explain it to her,
and he told him to instruct her to
go into the king's presence to beg

for mercy and plead with him for
her people. Est 3:9; 7:4
9Hathak went back and reported to Esther what Mordecai had
said. 10Then she instructed him to
say to Mordecai, 11"All the king's
officials and the people of the royal provinces know that for any
man or woman who approaches
the king in the inner court without being summoned the king has
but one law: that they be put to
death unless the king extends the
gold scepter to them and spares
their lives. But thirty days have
passed since I was called to go to
the king." Da 2:9; Est 5:1-2; 8:4
12When Esther's words were
reported to Mordecai, 13he sent
back this answer: "Do not think
that because you are in the king's
house you alone of all the Jews
will escape. 14For if you remain
silent at this time, relief and deliverance for the Jews will arise
from another place, but you and
your father's family will perish.
And who knows but that you have
come to your royal position for
such a time as this?"
Ge 50:20; Dt 28:29; Am 5:13
15Then Esther sent this reply to
Mordecai: 16"Go, gather together
all the Jews who are in Susa, and
fast for me. Do not eat or drink
for three days, night or day. I and
my attendants will fast as you do.
When this is done, I will go to the
king, even though it is against the
law. And if I perish, I perish."
Ge 43:14; 2Ch 20:3; Est 9:31
17So Mordecai went away and
carried out all of Esther's instructions.

Esther's Request to the King

5 On the third day Esther put on
her royal robes and stood in the
inner court of the palace, in front
of the king's hall. The king was
sitting on his royal throne in the
hall, facing the entrance. 2When
he saw Queen Esther standing in
the court, he was pleased with her
and held out to her the gold scepter that was in his hand. So Esther
approached and touched the tip of
the scepter. Est 4:11,16; 8:4
3Then the king asked, "What is
it, Queen Esther? What is your request? Even up to half the kingdom, it will be given you."
Est 7:2; Mk 6:23
4"If it pleases the king," replied
Esther, "let the king, together with
Haman, come today to a banquet I
have prepared for him."
5"Bring Haman at once," the
king said, "so that we may do what
Esther asks."
So the king and Haman went to
the banquet Esther had prepared.
6As they were drinking wine, the
king again asked Esther, "Now
what is your petition? It will be
given you. And what is your request? Even up to half the kingdom, it will be granted." Est 7:2; 9:12
7Esther replied, "My petition
and my request is this: 8If the
king regards me with favor and
if it pleases the king to grant my

petition and fulfill my request, let
the king and Haman come tomorrow to the banquet I will prepare
for them. Then I will answer the
king's question." Est 2:15; 6:14

Haman's Rage Against Mordecai

[9]Haman went out that day happy and in high spirits. But when
he saw Mordecai at the king's gate
and observed that he neither rose
nor showed fear in his presence,
he was filled with rage against
Mordecai. [10]Nevertheless, Haman restrained himself and went
home. Est 2:21; 3:3,5; Pr 14:17

Calling together his friends and
Zeresh, his wife, [11]Haman boasted
to them about his vast wealth, his
many sons, and all the ways the
king had honored him and how
he had elevated him above the
other nobles and officials. [12]"And
that's not all," Haman added. "I'm
the only person Queen Esther invited to accompany the king to
the banquet she gave. And she has
invited me along with the king tomorrow. [13]But all this gives me no
satisfaction as long as I see that
Jew Mordecai sitting at the king's
gate." Est 6:13; 9:7-10,13

[14]His wife Zeresh and all his
friends said to him, "Have a pole
set up, reaching to a height of fifty cubits,[a] and ask the king in the
morning to have Mordecai impaled
on it. Then go with the king to the
banquet and enjoy yourself." This
suggestion delighted Haman, and
he had the pole set up. Est 6:4; 7:9

Mordecai Honored

6 That night the king could not
sleep; so he ordered the book
of the chronicles, the record of his
reign, to be brought in and read to
him. [2]It was found recorded there
that Mordecai had exposed Bigthana and Teresh, two of the king's
officers who guarded the doorway,
who had conspired to assassinate
King Xerxes. Est 2:23; Da 6:18

[3]"What honor and recognition
has Mordecai received for this?"
the king asked.

"Nothing has been done for
him," his attendants answered.

[4]The king said, "Who is in the
court?" Now Haman had just entered the outer court of the palace
to speak to the king about impal-
ing Mordecai on the pole he had
set up for him.

[5]His attendants answered, "Haman is standing in the court."

"Bring him in," the king ordered.

[6]When Haman entered, the king
asked him, "What should be done
for the man the king delights to
honor?"

Now Haman thought to him-
self, "Who is there that the king
would rather honor than me?"
[7]So he answered the king, "For
the man the king delights to hon-
or, [8]have them bring a royal robe
the king has worn and a horse the
king has ridden, one with a royal crest placed on its head. [9]Then

[a] 14 That is, about 75 feet or about 23 meters

let the robe and horse be entrusted to one of the king's most noble princes. Let them robe the man the king delights to honor, and lead him on the horse through the city streets, proclaiming before him, 'This is what is done for the man the king delights to honor!'"

Ge 41:43; 1Ki 1:33

10 "Go at once," the king commanded Haman. "Get the robe and the horse and do just as you have suggested for Mordecai the Jew, who sits at the king's gate. Do not neglect anything you have recommended."

11 So Haman got the robe and the horse. He robed Mordecai, and led him on horseback through the city streets, proclaiming before him, "This is what is done for the man the king delights to honor!"

Ge 41:42

12 Afterward Mordecai returned to the king's gate. But Haman rushed home, with his head covered in grief,
13 and told Zeresh his wife and all his friends everything that had happened to him.

2Sa 15:30; Est 5:10

His advisers and his wife Zeresh said to him, "Since Mordecai, before whom your downfall has started, is of Jewish origin, you cannot stand against him — you will surely come to ruin!"
14 While they were still talking with him, the king's eunuchs arrived and hurried Haman away to the banquet Esther had prepared.

1Ki 3:15; Est 5:8

Haman Impaled

7 So the king and Haman went to Queen Esther's banquet,
2 and as they were drinking wine on the second day, the king again asked, "Queen Esther, what is your petition? It will be given you. What is your request? Even up to half the kingdom, it will be granted."

Est 5:3; 9:12; Mt 22:1-14

3 Then Queen Esther answered, "If I have found favor with you, Your Majesty, and if it pleases you, grant me my life — this is my petition. And spare my people — this is my request.
4 For I and my people have been sold to be destroyed, killed and annihilated. If we had merely been sold as male and female slaves, I would have kept quiet, because no such distress would justify disturbing the king.[a]"

Est 2:15; 3:9

5 King Xerxes asked Queen Esther, "Who is he? Where is he — the man who has dared to do such a thing?"

6 Esther said, "An adversary and enemy! This vile Haman!"

Then Haman was terrified before the king and queen.
7 The king got up in a rage, left his wine and went out into the palace garden. But Haman, realizing that the king had already decided his fate, stayed behind to beg Queen Esther for his life.

2Ki 21:18; Est 1:12; 6:13

[a] 4 *Or quiet, but the compensation our adversary offers cannot be compared with the loss the king would suffer*

8 Just as the king returned from
the palace garden to the banquet
hall, Haman was falling on the
couch where Esther was reclining.
Est 1:6

The king exclaimed, "Will he
even molest the queen while she
is with me in the house?" Ge 34:7

As soon as the word left the
king's mouth, they covered Haman's face. 9 Then Harbona, one of
the eunuchs attending the king,
said, "A pole reaching to a height
of fifty cubits[a] stands by Haman's
house. He had it set up for Mordecai, who spoke up to help the
king." Est 1:10; 5:14

The king said, "Impale him on
it!" 10 So they impaled Haman on
the pole he had set up for Mordecai. Then the king's fury subsided.
Ps 7:14-16; Pr 11:5-6

The King's Edict in Behalf of the Jews

8 That same day King Xerxes
gave Queen Esther the estate
of Haman, the enemy of the Jews.
And Mordecai came into the presence of the king, for Esther had
told how he was related to her.
2 The king took off his signet ring,
which he had reclaimed from Haman, and presented it to Mordecai. And Esther appointed him
over Haman's estate.
Est 2:7; 3:10; Pr 13:22

3 Esther again pleaded with the
king, falling at his feet and weeping. She begged him to put an
end to the evil plan of Haman the
Agagite, which he had devised
against the Jews. 4 Then the king
extended the gold scepter to Esther and she arose and stood before him. Est 4:11; 5:2

5 "If it pleases the king," she
said, "and if he regards me with
favor and thinks it the right thing
to do, and if he is pleased with
me, let an order be written over-
ruling the dispatches that Haman
son of Hammedatha, the Agagite,
devised and wrote to destroy the
Jews in all the king's provinces.
6 For how can I bear to see disaster
fall on my people? How can I bear
to see the destruction of my family?" Est 7:4; 9:1

7 King Xerxes replied to Queen
Esther and to Mordecai the Jew,
"Because Haman attacked the
Jews, I have given his estate to Esther, and they have impaled him
on the pole he set up. 8 Now write
another decree in the king's name
in behalf of the Jews as seems
best to you, and seal it with the
king's signet ring — for no docu-
ment written in the king's name
and sealed with his ring can be revoked." Est 1:19; 3:12-14; Da 6:15

9 At once the royal secretaries
were summoned — on the twenty-
third day of the third month, the
month of Sivan. They wrote out all
Mordecai's orders to the Jews, and
to the satraps, governors and nobles of the 127 provinces stretching from India to Cush.[b] These or-

[a] 9 That is, about 75 feet or about 23 meters
[b] 9 That is, the upper Nile region

ders were written in the script of
each province and the language of
each people and also to the Jews
in their own script and language.
10 Mordecai wrote in the name of
King Xerxes, sealed the dispatches with the king's signet ring, and
sent them by mounted couriers,
who rode fast horses especially
bred for the king. Est 1:1,22

11 The king's edict granted the
Jews in every city the right to assemble and protect themselves;
to destroy, kill and annihilate the
armed men of any nationality or
province who might attack them
and their women and children,[a]
and to plunder the property of
their enemies. 12 The day appointed for the Jews to do this in all
the provinces of King Xerxes was
the thirteenth day of the twelfth
month, the month of Adar. 13 A
copy of the text of the edict was
to be issued as law in every province and made known to the people of every nationality so that the
Jews would be ready on that day
to avenge themselves on their enemies. Est 3:14; 9:10,15,16

14 The couriers, riding the royal
horses, went out, spurred on by
the king's command, and the edict
was issued in the citadel of Susa.

The Triumph of the Jews

15 When Mordecai left the king's
presence, he was wearing royal garments of blue and white, a
large crown of gold and a purple
robe of fine linen. And the city of
Susa held a joyous celebration.
16 For the Jews it was a time of happiness and joy, gladness and hon-
or. 17 In every province and in every
city to which the edict of the king
came, there was joy and gladness
among the Jews, with feasting
and celebrating. And many people of other nationalities became
Jews because fear of the Jews had
seized them. Est 9:3; Ps 97:10-12

9 On the thirteenth day of the
twelfth month, the month of
Adar, the edict commanded by the
king was to be carried out. On this
day the enemies of the Jews had
hoped to overpower them, but
now the tables were turned and
the Jews got the upper hand over
those who hated them. 2 The Jews
assembled in their cities in all the
provinces of King Xerxes to attack
those determined to destroy them.
No one could stand against them,
because the people of all the other
nationalities were afraid of them.
3 And all the nobles of the provinces, the satraps, the governors and
the king's administrators helped
the Jews, because fear of Mordecai had seized them. 4 Mordecai
was prominent in the palace; his
reputation spread throughout the
provinces, and he became more
and more powerful.

2Sa 3:1; Est 3:12-14; Pr 22:22-23

5 The Jews struck down all their
enemies with the sword, killing
and destroying them, and they did

[a] *11* Or *province, together with their women and children, who might attack them;*

what they pleased to those who
hated them. 6 In the citadel of Susa,
the Jews killed and destroyed five
hundred men. 7 They also killed
Parshandatha, Dalphon, Aspatha,
8 Poratha, Adalia, Aridatha, 9 Par-
mashta, Arisai, Aridai and Vaiza-
tha, 10 the ten sons of Haman son
of Hammedatha, the enemy of the
Jews. But they did not lay their
hands on the plunder. Est 5:11; 8:11

11 The number of those killed in
the citadel of Susa was reported to
the king that same day. 12 The king
said to Queen Esther, "The Jews
have killed and destroyed five
hundred men and the ten sons
of Haman in the citadel of Susa.
What have they done in the rest of
the king's provinces? Now what is
your petition? It will be given you.
What is your request? It will also
be granted." Est 5:6; 7:2

13 "If it pleases the king," Esther answered, "give the Jews in
Susa permission to carry out this
day's edict tomorrow also, and let
Haman's ten sons be impaled on
poles." Dt 21:22-23; Est 5:11

14 So the king commanded that
this be done. An edict was issued
in Susa, and they impaled the ten
sons of Haman. 15 The Jews in Susa
came together on the fourteenth
day of the month of Adar, and
they put to death in Susa three
hundred men, but they did not lay
their hands on the plunder.
Ge 14:23; Ezr 6:11; Est 8:11

16 Meanwhile, the remainder of
the Jews who were in the king's
provinces also assembled to protect themselves and get relief
from their enemies. They killed
seventy-five thousand of them
but did not lay their hands on the
plunder. 17 This happened on the
thirteenth day of the month of
Adar, and on the fourteenth they
rested and made it a day of feasting and joy. Dt 25:19; 1Ki 3:15; 1Ch 4:43

18 The Jews in Susa, however,
had assembled on the thirteenth
and fourteenth, and then on the
fifteenth they rested and made it
a day of feasting and joy.

19 That is why rural Jews — those
living in villages — observe the
fourteenth of the month of Adar
as a day of joy and feasting, a day
for giving presents to each other.
ver 22; Dt 16:11,14; Ne 8:10,12

Purim Established

20 Mordecai recorded these
events, and he sent letters to all
the Jews throughout the provinces of King Xerxes, near and far, 21 to
have them celebrate annually the
fourteenth and fifteenth days of
the month of Adar 22 as the time
when the Jews got relief from
their enemies, and as the month
when their sorrow was turned into
joy and their mourning into a day
of celebration. He wrote them to
observe the days as days of feasting and joy and giving presents of
food to one another and gifts to
the poor. Ne 8:12; Ps 30:11-12

23 So the Jews agreed to continue
the celebration they had begun,

doing what Mordecai had written
to them. [24]For Haman son of Hammedatha, the Agagite, the enemy
of all the Jews, had plotted against
the Jews to destroy them and had
cast the *pur* (that is, the lot) for
their ruin and destruction. [25]But
when the plot came to the king's attention,[a] he issued written orders
that the evil scheme Haman had
devised against the Jews should
come back onto his own head, and
that he and his sons should be impaled on poles. [26](Therefore these
days were called Purim, from the
word *pur*.) Because of everything
written in this letter and because
of what they had seen and what
had happened to them, [27]the Jews
took it on themselves to establish
the custom that they and their descendants and all who join them
should without fail observe these
two days every year, in the way
prescribed and at the time appointed. [28]These days should be
remembered and observed in
every generation by every family, and in every province and in
every city. And these days of Purim should never fail to be celebrated by the Jews — nor should
the memory of these days die out
among their descendants.

Est 3:7; 7:10; Ps 7:16

[29]So Queen Esther, daughter
of Abihail, along with Mordecai
the Jew, wrote with full authority to confirm this second letter
concerning Purim. [30]And Mordecai sent letters to all the Jews in
the 127 provinces of Xerxes' kingdom — words of goodwill and assurance — [31]to establish these
days of Purim at their designated
times, as Mordecai the Jew and
Queen Esther had decreed for
them, and as they had established
for themselves and their descendants in regard to their times of
fasting and lamentation. [32]Es-
ther's decree confirmed these regulations about Purim, and it was
written down in the records.

Est 4:1-3,16

The Greatness of Mordecai

10 King Xerxes imposed tribute throughout the empire,
to its distant shores. [2]And all his
acts of power and might, together with a full account of the greatness of Mordecai, whom the king
had promoted, are they not written in the book of the annals of
the kings of Media and Persia?
[3]Mordecai the Jew was second in
rank to King Xerxes, preeminent
among the Jews, and held in high
esteem by his many fellow Jews,
because he worked for the good
of his people and spoke up for the
welfare of all the Jews.

Ne 2:10; Jer 29:4-7; Da 6:3

[a] 25 Or *when Esther came before the king*

JOB

Prologue

1 In the land of Uz there lived
a man whose name was Job.
This man was blameless and upright; he feared God and shunned
evil. 2He had seven sons and three
daughters, 3and he owned seven
thousand sheep, three thousand
camels, five hundred yoke of oxen
and five hundred donkeys, and
had a large number of servants.
He was the greatest man among
all the people of the East.
Ge 6:9; 17:1; Ex 18:21

4His sons used to hold feasts in
their homes on their birthdays,
and they would invite their three
sisters to eat and drink with them.
5When a period of feasting had
run its course, Job would make arrangements for them to be purified. Early in the morning he would
sacrifice a burnt offering for each
of them, thinking, "Perhaps my
children have sinned and cursed
God in their hearts." This was Job's
regular custom. Ge 8:20; 1Ki 21:10,13

6One day the angels[a] came to
present themselves before the
LORD, and Satan[b] also came with
them. 7The LORD said to Satan,
"Where have you come from?"
Job 2:1; 38:7

Satan answered the LORD, "From
roaming throughout the earth,
going back and forth on it." 1Pe 5:8

8Then the LORD said to Satan,
"Have you considered my servant
Job? There is no one on earth like
him; he is blameless and upright,
a man who fears God and shuns
evil." Jos 1:7; Job 42:7-8

9"Does Job fear God for nothing?" Satan replied. 10"Have you
not put a hedge around him and
his household and everything he
has? You have blessed the work of
his hands, so that his flocks and
herds are spread throughout the
land. 11But now stretch out your
hand and strike everything he
has, and he will surely curse you
to your face." Job 2:5; 29:6; Ps 34:7

12The LORD said to Satan, "Very
well, then, everything he has is in
your power, but on the man himself do not lay a finger."

Then Satan went out from the
presence of the LORD.

13One day when Job's sons and
daughters were feasting and
drinking wine at the oldest brother's house, 14a messenger came to
Job and said, "The oxen were plowing and the donkeys were grazing
nearby, 15and the Sabeans attacked
and made off with them. They put
the servants to the sword, and I
am the only one who has escaped
to tell you!" Ge 10:7; Job 6:19

[a] 6 Hebrew *the sons of God* [b] 6 Hebrew *satan* means *adversary.*

16While he was still speaking,
another messenger came and
said, "The fire of God fell from the
heavens and burned up the sheep
and the servants, and I am the
only one who has escaped to tell
you!" Lev 10:2; Nu 11:1-3
17While he was still speaking,
another messenger came and
said, "The Chaldeans formed
three raiding parties and swept
down on your camels and made
off with them. They put the servants to the sword, and I am the
only one who has escaped to tell
you!" Ge 11:28,31
18While he was still speaking, yet
another messenger came and said,
"Your sons and daughters were
feasting and drinking wine at the
oldest brother's house, 19when
suddenly a mighty wind swept
in from the desert and struck the
four corners of the house. It collapsed on them and they are dead,
and I am the only one who has escaped to tell you!" Jer 4:11; 13:24
20At this, Job got up and tore his
robe and shaved his head. Then he
fell to the ground in worship 21and
said: Ge 37:29; 1Pe 5:6

"Naked I came from my
mother's womb,
and naked I will depart.[a]
Ecc 5:15; 1Ti 6:7
The LORD gave and the LORD
has taken away;
may the name of the
LORD be praised."
Job 2:10; Eph 5:20; 1Th 5:18

22In all this, Job did not sin by
charging God with wrongdoing.
Job 2:10

2 On another day the angels[b]
came to present themselves
before the LORD, and Satan also
came with them to present himself before him. 2And the LORD
said to Satan, "Where have you
come from?" Job 1:6
Satan answered the LORD,
"From roaming throughout the
earth, going back and forth on it."
3Then the LORD said to Satan,
"Have you considered my servant
Job? There is no one on earth like
him; he is blameless and upright,
a man who fears God and shuns
evil. And he still maintains his
integrity, though you incited me
against him to ruin him without
any reason." Job 9:17; 27:6
4"Skin for skin!" Satan replied.
"A man will give all he has for his
own life. 5But now stretch out
your hand and strike his flesh and
bones, and he will surely curse
you to your face." Job 1:11; 19:20
6The LORD said to Satan, "Very
well, then, he is in your hands; but
you must spare his life."
7So Satan went out from the
presence of the LORD and afflicted Job with painful sores from the
soles of his feet to the crown of his
head. 8Then Job took a piece of
broken pottery and scraped himself with it as he sat among the
ashes. Job 42:6; Eze 27:30; Mt 11:21

[a] 21 Or *will return there* [b] 1 Hebrew *the sons of God*

9His wife said to him, "Are you
still maintaining your integrity?
Curse God and die!"

10He replied, "You are talking like
a foolish[a] woman. Shall we accept
good from God, and not trouble?"

Job 1:21

In all this, Job did not sin in
what he said. Jas 1:12; 5:11

11When Job's three friends, Eliphaz the Temanite, Bildad the
Shuhite and Zophar the Naamathite, heard about all the troubles
that had come upon him, they set
out from their homes and met together by agreement to go and
sympathize with him and comfort him. 12When they saw him
from a distance, they could hardly recognize him; they began to
weep aloud, and they tore their
robes and sprinkled dust on their
heads. 13Then they sat on the
ground with him for seven days
and seven nights. No one said a
word to him, because they saw
how great his suffering was.

Ge 50:10; Pr 17:28

Job Speaks

3 After this, Job opened his
mouth and cursed the day of
his birth. 2He said:

3"May the day of my birth
perish,
and the night that said,
'A boy is conceived!'

Jer 20:14-18

4That day — may it turn to
darkness;
may God above not care
about it;
may no light shine on it.
5May gloom and utter darkness
claim it once more;

Job 10:21-22; Jer 2:6; 13:16

may a cloud settle over it;
may blackness overwhelm it.
6That night — may thick
darkness seize it; Job 23:17
may it not be included
among the days of the
year
nor be entered in any of the
months.
7May that night be barren;
may no shout of joy be heard
in it.
8May those who curse days[b]
curse that day,
those who are ready to
rouse Leviathan.

Job 41:1,8,10,25

9May its morning stars become
dark;
may it wait for daylight in
vain
and not see the first rays of
dawn, Job 41:18
10for it did not shut the doors of
the womb on me
to hide trouble from my
eyes.

11"Why did I not perish at
birth,
and die as I came from the
womb? Job 10:18

[a] *10* The Hebrew word rendered *foolish* denotes moral deficiency. [b] *8* Or *curse the sea*

12 Why were there knees
to receive me Ge 30:3; Isa 66:12
and breasts that I might be
nursed?
13 For now I would be lying down
in peace; Job 17:13
I would be asleep and at rest
Job 7:8-10,21; 14:10-12
14 with kings and rulers of the
earth, Job 12:17
who built for themselves
places now lying in
ruins, Job 15:28
15 with princes who had gold,
Job 12:21
who filled their houses with
silver. Job 27:17
16 Or why was I not hidden
away in the ground
like a stillborn child,
Ps 58:8; Ecc 6:3
like an infant who never saw
the light of day?
17 There the wicked cease from
turmoil,
and there the weary are at
rest. Job 17:16
18 Captives also enjoy their ease;
they no longer hear the
slave driver's shout.
Job 39:7
19 The small and the great are
there,
and the slaves are freed from
their owners.
20 "Why is light given to those in
misery,
and life to the bitter of soul,
1Sa 1:10; Jer 20:18; Eze 27:30-31
21 to those who long for
death that does
not come, Rev 9:6
who search for it more
than for hidden
treasure, Pr 2:4
22 who are filled with gladness
and rejoice when they reach
the grave?
23 Why is life given to a man
whose way is hidden,
whom God has hedged in?
Job 19:6,8,12; La 3:7
24 For sighing has become my
daily food; Job 6:7
my groans pour out like
water. Ps 42:3-4
25 What I feared has come
upon me;
what I dreaded has
happened to me. Job 30:15
26 I have no peace,
no quietness;
I have no rest, but only
turmoil." Job 7:4,14

Eliphaz

4 Then Eliphaz the Temanite replied:

2 "If someone ventures a word
with you, will you be
impatient?
But who can keep from
speaking? Job 32:20
3 Think how you have instructed
many,
how you have strengthened
feeble hands.
Isa 35:3; Heb 12:12

4 Your words have supported
those who stumbled;
you have strengthened
faltering knees.
Isa 35:3; Heb 12:12
5 But now trouble comes to
you, and you are
discouraged;
it strikes you, and you are
dismayed. Job 6:14; 19:21
6 Should not your piety be your
confidence Pr 3:26
and your blameless ways
your hope? Job 1:1

7 "Consider now: Who, being
innocent, has ever
perished? Job 36:7
Where were the upright ever
destroyed? Job 8:20; Ps 37:25
8 As I have observed, those who
plow evil Job 15:35
and those who sow
trouble reap it.
Pr 22:8; Hos 10:13; Gal 6:7-8
9 At the breath of God they
perish; Isa 30:33; 2Th 2:8
at the blast of his anger they
are no more. Job 40:13
10 The lions may roar and growl,
yet the teeth of the great
lions are broken.
Job 5:15; Ps 58:6
11 The lion perishes for lack of
prey, Ps 34:10
and the cubs of the lioness
are scattered.

12 "A word was secretly brought to
me,
my ears caught a whisper of
it. Job 26:14; 33:14
13 Amid disquieting dreams in
the night,
when deep sleep falls on
people, Job 33:15
14 fear and trembling seized me
and made all my bones
shake. Jer 23:9; Hab 3:16
15 A spirit glided past my face,
and the hair on my body
stood on end.
16 It stopped,
but I could not tell what it
was.
A form stood before my eyes,
and I heard a hushed voice:
17 'Can a mortal be more
righteous than God?
Job 9:2
Can even a strong man be
more pure than his
Maker? Job 35:10
18 If God places no trust in his
servants,
if he charges his angels with
error, Job 15:15
19 how much more those
who live in houses
of clay, Job 10:9
whose foundations are
in the dust, Ge 2:7; Job 22:16
who are crushed more
readily than a moth!
20 Between dawn and dusk
they are broken to
pieces;
unnoticed, they perish
forever. Job 20:7; Ps 90:5-6
21 Are not the cords of their tent
pulled up,
so that they die without
wisdom?' Job 36:12

5 "Call if you will, but who will
answer you?
To which of the holy ones
will you turn? Job 15:15
2 Resentment kills a fool,
and envy slays the simple.
Pr 12:16
3 I myself have seen a fool taking
root, Jer 12:2
but suddenly his house was
cursed. Job 24:18
4 His children are far from safety,
Job 4:11
crushed in court without a
defender. Am 5:12
5 The hungry consume his
harvest, Job 18:8-10
taking it even from among
thorns,
and the thirsty pant after his
wealth.
6 For hardship does not spring
from the soil,
nor does trouble sprout from
the ground.
7 Yet man is born to trouble
Job 14:1
as surely as sparks fly upward.

8 "But if I were you, I would
appeal to God;
I would lay my cause before
him. Ps 35:23; 50:15
9 He performs wonders that
cannot be fathomed,
Job 42:3; Ps 40:5
miracles that cannot be
counted.
10 He provides rain for the earth;
he sends water on the
countryside. Job 36:28
11 The lowly he sets on high,
Ps 113:7-8
and those who mourn are
lifted to safety.
12 He thwarts the plans
of the crafty,
Ne 4:15; Ps 33:10
so that their hands achieve
no success.
13 He catches the wise in their
craftiness, 1Co 3:19
and the schemes of
the wily are swept
away.
14 Darkness comes upon
them in the daytime;
Job 12:25
at noon they grope as in the
night. Dt 28:29
15 He saves the needy from the
sword in their mouth;
Ps 35:10
he saves them from the
clutches of the powerful.
Job 4:10
16 So the poor have hope,
and injustice shuts its
mouth. Ps 107:42

17 "Blessed is the one whom God
corrects; Jas 1:12
so do not despise
the discipline of
the Almighty.[a]
Ps 94:12; Pr 3:11; Heb 12:5-11
18 For he wounds, but he also
binds up; Isa 30:26
he injures, but his hands
also heal. 1Sa 2:6

[a] 17 Hebrew *Shaddai*; here and throughout Job

19 From six calamities he will
rescue you;
in seven no harm will touch
you. Ps 34:19; 91:10
20 In famine he will deliver you
from death, Ps 33:19
and in battle from the stroke
of the sword. Ps 144:10
21 You will be protected from the
lash of the tongue, Ps 31:20
and need not fear when
destruction comes. Ps 91:5
22 You will laugh at destruction
and famine,
and need not fear the wild
animals. Ps 91:13
23 For you will have a covenant
with the stones of the
field, Ps 91:12
and the wild animals will be
at peace with you. Isa 11:6-9
24 You will know that your tent is
secure;
you will take stock of your
property and find
nothing missing. Job 8:6
25 You will know that your
children will be many,
Ps 112:2
and your descendants like
the grass of the earth.
Ps 72:16; Isa 44:3-4
26 You will come to the grave in
full vigor, Ge 15:15
like sheaves gathered in
season.
27 "We have examined this, and it
is true.
So hear it and apply it to
yourself." Job 8:5; 32:10,17

Job

6 Then Job replied:

2 "If only my anguish could be
weighed
and all my misery be placed
on the scales! Job 31:6
3 It would surely outweigh
the sand of the seas —
Pr 27:3
no wonder my words
have been impetuous.
Job 23:2
4 The arrows of the Almighty are
in me, Job 16:12-13; Ps 38:2
my spirit drinks in their
poison; Job 21:20
God's terrors are marshaled
against me. Ps 88:15-18
5 Does a wild donkey bray when
it has grass,
or an ox bellow when it has
fodder?
6 Is tasteless food eaten without
salt,
or is there flavor in the sap of
the mallow[a]?
7 I refuse to touch it;
such food makes me ill.
Job 3:24

8 "Oh, that I might have my
request,
that God would grant what I
hope for, Job 14:13
9 that God would be willing to
crush me,
to let loose his hand and cut
off my life! Nu 11:15; 1Ki 19:4

[a] 6 The meaning of the Hebrew for this phrase is uncertain.

10 Then I would still have this
consolation —
my joy in unrelenting pain —
that I had not denied the
words of the Holy One. Job 23:12

11 "What strength do I have,
that I should still hope?
What prospects, that I should
be patient? Job 21:4
12 Do I have the strength of
stone?
Is my flesh bronze?
13 Do I have any power to help
myself, Job 26:2
now that success has been
driven from me?

14 "Anyone who withholds
kindness from a friend Job 4:5; 15:4
forsakes the fear of the
Almighty.
15 But my brothers are as
undependable as
intermittent streams, Ps 38:11; Jer 15:18
as the streams that overflow
16 when darkened by thawing
ice
and swollen with melting
snow,
17 but that stop flowing in the dry
season,
and in the heat vanish
from their channels. Job 24:19
18 Caravans turn aside from their
routes;
they go off into the
wasteland and perish.
19 The caravans of Tema look for
water, Ge 25:15; Isa 21:14
the traveling merchants of
Sheba look in hope.
20 They are distressed, because
they had been confident;
they arrive there, only to be
disappointed. Jer 14:3
21 Now you too have proved to be
of no help;
you see something dreadful
and are afraid. Ps 38:11
22 Have I ever said, 'Give
something on my
behalf,
pay a ransom for me from
your wealth,
23 deliver me from the hand of
the enemy,
rescue me from the clutches
of the ruthless'?

24 "Teach me, and I will be quiet; Ps 39:1
show me where I have been
wrong.
25 How painful are honest words! Ecc 12:11
But what do your arguments
prove?
26 Do you mean to correct what
I say,
and treat my desperate
words as wind? Job 8:2; 15:3
27 You would even cast lots for the
fatherless Joel 3:3; Na 3:10
and barter away your friend.

28 "But now be so kind as to look
at me.
Would I lie to your face? Job 27:4

29 Relent, do not be unjust;
reconsider, for my integrity
is at stake.[a]
Job 23:7,10; 34:5,36
30 Is there any wickedness on my
lips? Job 27:4
Can my mouth not discern
malice? Job 12:11

7 "Do not mortals have hard
service on earth?
Job 14:14; Isa 40:2
Are not their days like
those of hired laborers?
Job 14:6
2 Like a slave longing for the
evening shadows,
or a hired laborer waiting to
be paid, Lev 19:13
3 so I have been allotted months
of futility,
and nights of misery have
been assigned to me.
Job 16:7; Ps 6:6
4 When I lie down I think, 'How
long before I get up?'
Dt 28:67
The night drags on, and
I toss and turn until
dawn.
5 My body is clothed with worms
and scabs, Job 17:14
my skin is broken and
festering.

6 "My days are swifter than a
weaver's shuttle, Job 9:25
and they come to an end
without hope. Job 13:15
7 Remember, O God, that my
life is but a breath;
Ps 78:39; Jas 4:14
my eyes will never see
happiness again. Job 9:25
8 The eye that now sees me will
see me no longer;
you will look for me, but
I will be no more.
Job 20:7,9,21
9 As a cloud vanishes and is
gone,
so one who goes down to the
grave does not return.
2Sa 12:23; Job 11:8
10 He will never come to his
house again;
his place will know him no
more. Job 8:18; 27:21,23

11 "Therefore I will not keep
silent; Ps 40:9
I will speak out in the
anguish of my spirit,
I will complain in the
bitterness of my soul.
1Sa 1:10
12 Am I the sea, or the monster of
the deep, Eze 32:2-3
that you put me under
guard?
13 When I think my bed will
comfort me
and my couch will ease my
complaint, Job 9:27
14 even then you frighten me
with dreams
and terrify me with visions,
Job 9:34
15 so that I prefer strangling and
death, 1Ki 19:4
rather than this body of
mine.

[a] 29 Or *my righteousness still stands*

16 I despise my life; I would not
live forever. Job 10:1
Let me alone; my days have
no meaning.
17 "What is mankind that you
make so much of them,
that you give them so much
attention, Ps 8:4; 144:3; Heb 2:6
18 that you examine them every
morning
and test them every
moment? Job 14:3
19 Will you never look away from
me,
or let me alone even for an
instant? Job 9:18
20 If I have sinned, what have I
done to you, Job 35:6
you who see everything we
do?
Why have you made me your
target? Job 16:12
Have I become a burden to
you?[a]
21 Why do you not pardon my
offenses
and forgive my sins? Job 10:14
For I will soon lie down in the
dust; Ps 104:29
you will search for me, but I
will be no more."

Bildad

8 Then Bildad the Shuhite replied:

2 "How long will you say such
things?
Your words are a blustering
wind. Job 6:26
3 Does God pervert justice?
Dt 32:4; Ro 3:5
Does the Almighty pervert
what is right? Ge 18:25
4 When your children sinned
against him,
he gave them over to the
penalty of their sin.
Job 1:19
5 But if you will seek God earnestly
and plead with the Almighty,
Job 11:13
6 if you are pure and upright,
even now he will rouse
himself on your behalf
Ps 7:6
and restore you to your
prosperous state. Job 5:24
7 Your beginnings will seem
humble,
so prosperous will your
future be. Job 42:12
8 "Ask the former generation
Dt 32:7; Job 15:18
and find out what their
ancestors learned,
9 for we were born only yesterday
and know nothing, Ge 47:9
and our days on earth
are but a shadow.
1Ch 29:15; Job 7:6
10 Will they not instruct you and
tell you?
Will they not bring forth
words from their
understanding? Pr 4:1

[a] 20 A few manuscripts of the Masoretic Text, an ancient Hebrew scribal tradition and Septuagint; most manuscripts of the Masoretic Text *I have become a burden to myself.*

11 Can papyrus grow tall
where there is no marsh?
Can reeds thrive without water?
12 While still growing and uncut,
they wither more quickly than grass. Ps 129:6; Jer 17:6
13 Such is the destiny of all who forget God; Ps 9:17
so perishes the hope of the godless. Job 11:20; Pr 10:28
14 What they trust in is fragile[a];
what they rely on is a spider's web. Isa 59:5
15 They lean on the web, but it gives way; Job 27:18
they cling to it, but it does not hold. Ps 49:11
16 They are like a well-watered plant in the sunshine,
spreading its shoots over the garden; Ps 37:35; 80:11
17 it entwines its roots around a pile of rocks
and looks for a place among the stones.
18 But when it is torn from its spot,
that place disowns it and says, 'I never saw you.'
Job 7:8; Ps 37:36
19 Surely its life withers away,
Job 20:5
and[b] from the soil other plants grow. Ecc 1:4
20 "Surely God does not reject one who is blameless Job 1:1
or strengthen the hands of evildoers. Job 21:30
21 He will yet fill your mouth with laughter Job 5:22
and your lips with shouts of joy. Ps 126:2
22 Your enemies will be clothed in shame,
Ps 35:26; 109:29
and the tents of the wicked will be no more."
Job 18:6,14,21

Job

9 Then Job replied:

2 "Indeed, I know that this is true.
But how can mere mortals prove their innocence before God? Ro 3:20
3 Though they wished to dispute with him,
they could not answer him one time out of a thousand. Job 10:2
4 His wisdom is profound,
his power is vast.
Job 11:6; 36:5
Who has resisted him and come out unscathed?
2Ch 13:12
5 He moves mountains without their knowing it
and overturns them in his anger. Mic 1:4
6 He shakes the earth from its place Isa 2:21; Heb 12:26
and makes its pillars tremble. Job 26:11

[a] 14 The meaning of the Hebrew for this word is uncertain. [b] 19 Or *Surely all the joy it has / is that*

7 He speaks to the sun and it
does not shine;
he seals off the light of the
stars. Isa 13:10; Eze 32:8
8 He alone stretches out the
heavens Ge 1:6; Ps 104:2-3
and treads on the waves of
the sea. Job 38:16; Ps 77:19
9 He is the Maker of the Bear[a]
and Orion,
the Pleiades and the
constellations of the
south. Ge 1:16; Job 38:31
10 He performs wonders that
cannot be fathomed,
Ps 71:15
miracles that cannot be
counted. Job 5:9
11 When he passes me, I cannot
see him;
when he goes by, I
cannot perceive him.
Job 23:8-9; 35:14
12 If he snatches away, who can
stop him? Job 11:10
Who can say to him, 'What
are you doing?' Isa 45:9
13 God does not restrain his anger;
even the cohorts of Rahab
cowered at his feet.
Job 26:12; Isa 30:7

14 "How then can I dispute with
him?
How can I find words to
argue with him?
15 Though I were innocent, I
could not answer him;
Job 10:15
I could only plead with my
Judge for mercy. Job 8:5
16 Even if I summoned him and
he responded,
I do not believe he would
give me a hearing.
17 He would crush me with a
storm Job 16:12; 30:22
and multiply my wounds for
no reason. Job 2:3; 16:14
18 He would not let me catch my
breath
but would overwhelm me
with misery. Job 7:19
19 If it is a matter of strength, he
is mighty! Ne 9:32
And if it is a matter of justice,
who can challenge him[b]?
20 Even if I were innocent,
my mouth would
condemn me;
if I were blameless, it would
pronounce me guilty.

21 "Although I am blameless, Job 1:1
I have no concern for myself;
I despise my own life. Job 7:16
22 It is all the same; that is why I
say,
'He destroys both the
blameless and the
wicked.' Ecc 9:2-3; Eze 21:3
23 When a scourge brings sudden
death, Heb 11:36
he mocks the despair of the
innocent. Job 24:1,12
24 When a land falls into the
hands of the wicked,
Job 10:3
he blindfolds its judges. Job 12:6
If it is not he, then who is it?

[a] 9 Or *of Leo* [b] 19 See Septuagint; Hebrew *me.*

25 "My days are swifter than a
runner; Job 7:6
they fly away without a
glimpse of joy.
26 They skim past like boats of
papyrus, Isa 18:2
like eagles swooping down
on their prey. Hab 1:8
27 If I say, 'I will forget my
complaint, Job 7:11
I will change my expression,
and smile,'
28 I still dread all my sufferings,
Ps 119:120
for I know you will not hold
me innocent. Job 7:21
29 Since I am already found guilty,
why should I struggle in
vain? Ps 37:33
30 Even if I washed myself with
soap
and my hands with cleansing
powder, Jer 2:22
31 you would plunge me into a
slime pit
so that even my clothes
would detest me.

32 "He is not a mere mortal like
me that I might answer
him, Ro 9:20
that we might confront each
other in court. Ecc 6:10
33 If only there were someone
to mediate between us,
1Sa 2:25
someone to bring us together,
34 someone to remove God's rod
from me, Ps 39:10
so that his terror would
frighten me no more.
35 Then I would speak up without
fear of him,
but as it now stands with me,
I cannot. Job 13:21

10

"I loathe my very life; 1Ki 19:4
therefore I will give free
rein to my complaint
and speak out in the
bitterness of my soul.
Job 7:11
2 I say to God: Do not declare me
guilty,
but tell me what charges
you have against me.
Job 9:29
3 Does it please you to oppress
me, Job 9:22
to spurn the work of your
hands, Job 14:15; Ps 138:8
while you smile on the
plans of the wicked?
Job 21:16; 22:18
4 Do you have eyes of flesh?
Do you see as a mortal sees?
1Sa 16:7
5 Are your days like those of a
mortal
or your years like those
of a strong man,
Ps 90:2,4; 2Pe 3:8
6 that you must search out my
faults
and probe after my sin —
Job 14:16
7 though you know that I am not
guilty
and that no one can rescue
me from your hand?

8 "Your hands shaped me and
made me. Ps 119:73

Will you now turn and
destroy me?
9 Remember that you molded
me like clay. Isa 64:8
Will you now turn me to dust
again? Ge 2:7
10 Did you not pour me out like
milk
and curdle me like cheese,
11 clothe me with skin and flesh
and knit me together with
bones and sinews?
Ps 139:13,15
12 You gave me life and showed
me kindness, Job 33:4
and in your providence
watched over my spirit.

13 "But this is what you concealed
in your heart,
and I know that this was in
your mind: Job 23:13
14 If I sinned, you would be
watching me
and would not let my
offense go unpunished.
Job 7:21
15 If I am guilty — woe to me!
Job 9:13
Even if I am innocent, I
cannot lift my head,
Job 9:15
for I am full of shame
and drowned in[a] my
affliction.
16 If I hold my head high, you
stalk me like a lion
Isa 38:13; La 3:10
and again display your
awesome power against
me.
17 You bring new witnesses
against me Job 16:8
and increase your anger
toward me; Ru 1:21
your forces come against me
wave upon wave.

18 "Why then did you bring me
out of the womb? Job 3:11
I wish I had died before any
eye saw me.
19 If only I had never come into
being,
or had been carried straight
from the womb to the
grave!
20 Are not my few days almost
over? Job 7:19; 14:1
Turn away from me so I can
have a moment's joy
Job 7:16
21 before I go to the place of no
return, Job 3:13; 16:22
to the land of gloom
and utter darkness,
Ps 23:4; 88:12
22 to the land of deepest night,
of utter darkness and
disorder,
where even the light is like
darkness."

Zophar

11 Then Zophar the Naamathite
replied:

2 "Are all these words to go
unanswered? Job 8:2
Is this talker to be
vindicated?

[a] 15 Or *and aware of*

3 Will your idle talk reduce
others to silence?
Will no one rebuke you
when you mock?
Job 17:2; 21:3
4 You say to God, 'My beliefs are
flawless Job 6:10
and I am pure in your sight.'
Job 10:7
5 Oh, how I wish that God would
speak,
that he would open his lips
against you
6 and disclose to you the secrets
of wisdom, Job 9:4
for true wisdom has two
sides.
Know this: God has even
forgotten some of your
sin. Ezr 9:13; Job 15:5

7 "Can you fathom the
mysteries of God?
Ecc 3:11; Ro 11:33
Can you probe the limits of
the Almighty?
8 They are higher than the
heavens above — what
can you do? Job 22:12
They are deeper than the
depths below — what
can you know? Ps 139:8
9 Their measure is longer than
the earth
and wider than the sea.
Isa 40:26

10 "If he comes along and
confines you in prison
and convenes a court,
who can oppose him?
Job 9:12; Rev 3:7
11 Surely he recognizes deceivers;
and when he sees evil,
does he not take note?
Job 34:21-25; Ps 10:14
12 But the witless can no more
become wise
than a wild donkey's colt can
be born human.[a]

13 "Yet if you devote your heart to
him 1Sa 7:3; Ps 78:8
and stretch out your hands
to him, Ps 88:9
14 if you put away the sin that is
in your hand
and allow no evil to dwell
in your tent,
Job 22:23; Ps 101:4
15 then, free of fault, you will lift
up your face; Jn 3:21
you will stand firm and
without fear.
16 You will surely forget your
trouble, Isa 65:16
recalling it only as waters
gone by. Job 22:11
17 Life will be brighter than
noonday, Ps 37:6; Isa 58:8,10
and darkness will become
like morning.
18 You will be secure, because
there is hope;
you will look about you and
take your rest in safety.
Lev 26:6; Ps 3:5; Pr 3:24
19 You will lie down, with no one
to make you afraid,
Lev 26:6
and many will court your
favor. Isa 45:14

[a] 12 Or *wild donkey can be born tame*

20 But the eyes of the wicked will
fail, Dt 28:65; Job 17:5
and escape will elude them;
their hope will become a
dying gasp." Job 8:13

Job 12

12 Then Job replied:

2 "Doubtless you are the only
people who matter,
and wisdom will die with
you! Job 17:10
3 But I have a mind as well as
you;
I am not inferior to you.
Who does not know all these
things? Job 13:2

4 "I have become a
laughingstock to my
friends, Job 21:3
though I called on God and
he answered — Ps 91:15
a mere laughingstock,
though righteous and
blameless! Job 6:29
5 Those who are at ease have
contempt for misfortune
as the fate of those whose
feet are slipping.
6 The tents of marauders are
undisturbed, Job 22:18
and those who provoke
God are secure —
Job 9:24; 21:9
those God has in his hand.[a]

7 "But ask the animals, and they
will teach you,
or the birds in the sky, and
they will tell you; Mt 6:26
8 or speak to the earth, and it
will teach you,
or let the fish in the sea
inform you.
9 Which of all these does not
know
that the hand of the LORD
has done this? Isa 41:20
10 In his hand is the life of every
creature
and the breath of
all mankind.
Job 27:3; 33:4; Ac 17:28
11 Does not the ear test words
as the tongue tastes food?
Job 34:3
12 Is not wisdom found among
the aged? Job 15:10
Does not long life bring
understanding? Job 32:7,9

13 "To God belong wisdom and
power; Job 9:4
counsel and understanding
are his. Job 32:8
14 What he tears down cannot
be rebuilt;
Job 19:10; 37:7; Isa 25:2
those he imprisons cannot
be released.
15 If he holds back the waters,
there is drought;
1Ki 8:35; 17:1
if he lets them loose,
they devastate the land.
Ge 7:11
16 To him belong strength and
insight;
both deceived and deceiver
are his. Job 13:7,9

[a] 6 Or *those whose god is in their own hand*

17 He leads rulers away stripped
Job 19:9
and makes fools of judges.
Job 3:14
18 He takes off the shackles put
on by kings Ps 116:16
and ties a loincloth[a] around
their waist.
19 He leads priests away stripped
and overthrows officials
long established.
Job 24:12,22
20 He silences the lips of trusted
advisers
and takes away the
discernment of elders.
Job 32:9
21 He pours contempt on nobles
and disarms the mighty.
22 He reveals the deep things of
darkness 1Co 4:5
and brings utter darkness
into the light. Job 3:5; Da 2:22
23 He makes nations great, and
destroys them; Jer 25:9
he enlarges nations, and
disperses them.
Ps 107:38; Isa 9:3
24 He deprives the leaders of the
earth of their reason;
he makes them wander in a
trackless waste.
25 They grope in darkness with no
light; Job 5:14
he makes them stagger
like drunkards.
Ps 107:27; Isa 24:20

13 "My eyes have seen all this,
my ears have heard and
understood it.
2 What you know, I also know;
I am not inferior to you.
Job 12:3
3 But I desire to speak to the
Almighty
and to argue my case with
God. Job 23:3-4
4 You, however, smear me with
lies; Ps 119:69; Jer 23:32
you are worthless physicians,
all of you!
5 If only you would be altogether
silent!
For you, that would be
wisdom. Pr 17:28
6 Hear now my argument;
listen to the pleas of my
lips.
7 Will you speak wickedly on
God's behalf?
Will you speak deceitfully for
him? Job 36:4
8 Will you show him partiality?
Lev 19:15
Will you argue the case for
God?
9 Would it turn out well if he
examined you?
Could you deceive him as
you might deceive a
mortal? Job 12:16; Gal 6:7
10 He would surely call you to
account
if you secretly showed
partiality.
11 Would not his splendor terrify
you? Job 31:23
Would not the dread of him
fall on you?

[a] 18 Or *shackles of kings / and ties a belt*

[12]Your maxims are proverbs of ashes;
your defenses are defenses of clay.

[13]"Keep silent and let me speak;
then let come to me what may. Job 9:21
[14]Why do I put myself in jeopardy
and take my life in my hands?
[15]Though he slay me, yet will I hope in him; Job 7:6; Ps 23:4; Pr 14:32
I will surely[a] defend my ways to his face. Job 27:5
[16]Indeed, this will turn out for my deliverance, Isa 12:1
for no godless person would dare come before him!
[17]Listen carefully to what I say; Job 21:2
let my words ring in your ears.
[18]Now that I have prepared my case, Job 23:4
I know I will be vindicated.
[19]Can anyone bring charges against me? Isa 50:8
If so, I will be silent and die. Job 10:8

[20]"Only grant me these two things, God,
and then I will not hide from you:
[21]Withdraw your hand far from me, Ps 39:10
and stop frightening me with your terrors.
[22]Then summon me and I will answer, Job 14:15
or let me speak, and you reply to me. Job 9:16
[23]How many wrongs and sins have I committed? 1Sa 26:18
Show me my offense and my sin.
[24]Why do you hide your face Dt 32:20; Ps 13:1; Isa 8:17
and consider me your enemy? Job 19:11; La 2:5
[25]Will you torment a windblown leaf?
Will you chase after dry chaff? Job 21:18; Isa 42:3
[26]For you write down bitter things against me
and make me reap the sins of my youth. Ps 25:7
[27]You fasten my feet in shackles; Job 33:11
you keep close watch on all my paths
by putting marks on the soles of my feet.

[28]"So man wastes away like something rotten,
like a garment eaten by moths. Isa 50:9; Jas 5:2

14 "Mortals, born of woman,
are of few days and full of trouble. Job 5:7; Ecc 2:23
[2]They spring up like flowers and wither away; Ps 90:5-6; Jas 1:10
like fleeting shadows, they do not endure. Job 8:9

[a] 15 *Or He will surely slay me; I have no hope — / yet I will*

3 Do you fix your eye on them? Ps 144:3
Will you bring them[a]
before you for
judgment? Ps 143:2
4 Who can bring what is pure
from the impure?
Ps 51:10; Eph 2:1-3
No one! Jn 3:6; Ro 5:12
5 A person's days are
determined;
you have decreed the
number of his months
Job 21:21
and have set limits he cannot
exceed.
6 So look away from him and let
him alone, Job 7:19
till he has put in his time like
a hired laborer. Job 7:1-2
7 "At least there is hope for a
tree:
If it is cut down, it will
sprout again,
and its new shoots will not
fail.
8 Its roots may grow old in the
ground
and its stump die in the soil,
Isa 6:13
9 yet at the scent of water it will
bud
and put forth shoots like a
plant. Lev 26:4
10 But a man dies and is laid low;
he breathes his last and is no
more. Job 13:19
11 As the water of a lake dries up
or a riverbed becomes
parched and dry, Isa 19:5
12 so he lies down and does not
rise;
till the heavens are no more,
people will not awake
Rev 20:11; 21:1
or be roused from their
sleep. Ac 3:21
13 "If only you would hide me in
the grave
and conceal me till
your anger has passed!
Isa 26:20
If only you would set me a
time
and then remember me!
14 If someone dies, will they live
again?
All the days of my hard
service
I will wait for my renewal[b] to
come.
15 You will call and I will answer
you; Job 13:22
you will long for the
creature your hands
have made.
16 Surely then you will count my
steps Pr 5:21; Jer 32:19
but not keep track of my sin.
Job 10:6
17 My offenses will be sealed up in
a bag; Dt 32:34
you will cover over my sin.
Hos 13:12

18 "But as a mountain erodes and
crumbles
and as a rock is moved from
its place, Job 18:4

[a] 3 Septuagint, Vulgate and Syriac; Hebrew *me* [b] 14 Or *release*

19 as water wears away stones
and torrents wash away the soil, Job 7:6
so you destroy a person's hope.
20 You overpower them once for all, and they are gone;
you change their countenance and send them away. Job 12:19; Jas 1:10
21 If their children are honored, they do not know it;
if their offspring are brought low, they do not see it. Ecc 9:5; Isa 63:16
22 They feel but the pain of their own bodies
and mourn only for themselves." Job 21:21

Eliphaz

15 Then Eliphaz the Temanite replied:

2 "Would a wise person answer with empty notions
or fill their belly with the hot east wind? Job 6:26
3 Would they argue with useless words,
with speeches that have no value?
4 But you even undermine piety
and hinder devotion to God.
5 Your sin prompts your mouth; Pr 16:23
you adopt the tongue of the crafty. Job 5:13
6 Your own mouth condemns you, not mine;
your own lips testify against you. Lk 19:22

7 "Are you the first man ever born? Job 38:21
Were you brought forth before the hills? Ps 90:2; Pr 8:25
8 Do you listen in on God's council? Ro 11:34; 1Co 2:11
Do you have a monopoly on wisdom?
9 What do you know that we do not know?
What insights do you have that we do not have? Job 13:2
10 The gray-haired and the aged are on our side, Job 32:6-7
men even older than your father.
11 Are God's consolations not enough for you, 2Co 1:3-4
words spoken gently to you? Job 36:16
12 Why has your heart carried you away, Job 11:13
and why do your eyes flash,
13 so that you vent your rage against God Pr 29:11
and pour out such words from your mouth?

14 "What are mortals, that they could be pure,
or those born of woman, that they could be righteous? Job 14:4; Pr 20:9; Ecc 7:20
15 If God places no trust in his holy ones,
if even the heavens are not pure in his eyes, Job 25:5

16 how much less mortals, who are
vile and corrupt, Ps 14:1
who drink up evil like water!
Job 34:7; Pr 19:28

17 "Listen to me and I will explain
to you;
let me tell you what I have
seen,
18 what the wise have declared,
hiding nothing received
from their ancestors
Job 8:8
19 (to whom alone the land was
given
when no foreigners moved
among them):
20 All his days the wicked man
suffers torment,
the ruthless man through all
the years stored up for
him. Job 24:1; 27:13-23
21 Terrifying sounds fill his ears;
Job 18:11; 20:25
when all seems well,
marauders attack him.
1Th 5:3
22 He despairs of escaping the
realm of darkness;
he is marked for the sword.
Job 27:14
23 He wanders about for food like
a vulture; Ps 109:10
he knows the day of
darkness is at hand.
Job 18:12
24 Distress and anguish fill him
with terror;
troubles overwhelm him,
like a king poised to
attack,
25 because he shakes his fist at God
and vaunts himself against
the Almighty, Job 36:9
26 defiantly charging against him
with a thick, strong shield.

27 "Though his face is covered
with fat
and his waist bulges with
flesh, Ps 17:10
28 he will inhabit ruined towns
and houses where no one
lives, Isa 5:9
houses crumbling to rubble.
Job 3:14
29 He will no longer be rich and
his wealth will not
endure, Job 27:16-17
nor will his possessions
spread over the land.
30 He will not escape the
darkness; Job 5:14
a flame will wither his
shoots, Job 22:20
and the breath of God's
mouth will carry him
away. Job 4:9
31 Let him not deceive himself
by trusting what is
worthless, Isa 59:4
for he will get nothing in
return.
32 Before his time he will wither,
Job 22:16; Ps 55:23
and his branches will not
flourish. Job 18:16
33 He will be like a vine stripped
of its unripe grapes,
Hab 3:17
like an olive tree shedding
its blossoms.

34 For the company of the godless
will be barren,
and fire will consume the
tents of those who love
bribes. Job 8:22
35 They conceive trouble and
give birth to evil;
Ps 7:14; Isa 59:4; Hos 10:13
their womb fashions deceit."

Job 16

16 Then Job replied:

2 "I have heard many things like
these;
you are miserable
comforters, all of you!
Job 13:4
3 Will your long-winded
speeches never end?
What ails you that you keep
on arguing? Job 6:26
4 I also could speak like you,
if you were in my place;
I could make fine speeches
against you
and shake my head at you.
Ps 22:7; 109:25; Mt 27:39
5 But my mouth would
encourage you;
comfort from my lips would
bring you relief.

6 "Yet if I speak, my pain is not
relieved;
and if I refrain, it does not go
away.
7 Surely, God, you have worn me
out; Job 7:3
you have devastated my
entire household.
8 You have shriveled me up — and
it has become a witness;
my gauntness rises up and
testifies against me.
Job 10:17; 19:20
9 God assails me and tears me in
his anger Hos 6:1
and gnashes his teeth at me;
Ps 35:16; La 2:16
my opponent fastens on me
his piercing eyes. Job 13:24
10 People open their mouths to
jeer at me; Ps 22:13
they strike my cheek in scorn
La 3:30; Mic 5:1; Ac 23:2
and unite together against
me. Ps 35:15
11 God has turned me over to the
ungodly
and thrown me into the
clutches of the wicked.
Job 1:15,17
12 All was well with me, but he
shattered me;
he seized me by the neck and
crushed me. Job 9:17
He has made me his target; La 3:12
13 his archers surround me.
Without pity, he pierces my
kidneys Job 20:24
and spills my gall on the
ground.
14 Again and again he bursts
upon me; Job 9:17
he rushes at me like a
warrior. Joel 2:7

15 "I have sewed sackcloth over
my skin Ge 37:34
and buried my brow in the
dust.

16 My face is red with weeping,
dark shadows ring my eyes;
17 yet my hands have been free of
violence Isa 59:6; Jnh 3:8
and my prayer is pure.

18 "Earth, do not cover my blood;
Isa 26:21
may my cry never be laid to
rest! Ps 66:18-19
19 Even now my witness is in
heaven; Ro 1:9; 1Th 2:5
my advocate is on high.
20 My intercessor is my friend[a]
as my eyes pour out tears to
God; La 2:19
21 on behalf of a man he pleads
with God Ps 9:4
as one pleads for a friend.

22 "Only a few years will pass
before I take the path of no
return. Ecc 12:5

17 1 My spirit is broken, Ps 143:4
my days are cut short,
the grave awaits me. Ps 88:3-4
2 Surely mockers surround me;
1Sa 1:6-7
my eyes must dwell on their
hostility.

3 "Give me, O God, the pledge
you demand. Ps 119:122
Who else will put up security
for me? Isa 38:14
4 You have closed their minds to
understanding;
therefore you will not let
them triumph.
5 If anyone denounces their
friends for reward,
the eyes of their children will
fail. Job 11:20

6 "God has made me a byword to
everyone, Job 30:9
a man in whose face people
spit.
7 My eyes have grown dim with
grief; Job 16:8
my whole frame is but a
shadow.
8 The upright are appalled at
this;
the innocent are aroused
against the ungodly.
Job 22:19
9 Nevertheless, the righteous
will hold to their ways,
Pr 4:18
and those with clean hands
will grow stronger.
Job 22:30

10 "But come on, all of you, try
again!
I will not find a wise man
among you. Job 12:2
11 My days have passed, my plans
are shattered.
Yet the desires of my heart
Job 7:6
12 turn night into day;
in the face of the darkness
light is near.
13 If the only home I hope for is
the grave, Job 3:13
if I spread out my bed in the
realm of darkness,
14 if I say to corruption, 'You are
my father,' Job 13:28
and to the worm, 'My
mother' or 'My sister,'
Job 21:26

[a] 20 Or *My friends treat me with scorn*

[15]where then is my hope — Job 7:6
who can see any hope for me?
[16]Will it go down to the gates of death? Job 3:17-19; Jnh 2:6
Will we descend together into the dust?"

Bildad

18 Then Bildad the Shuhite replied:

[2]"When will you end these speeches? Job 16:3
Be sensible, and then we can talk.
[3]Why are we regarded as cattle
and considered stupid in your sight? Ps 73:22
[4]You who tear yourself to pieces in your anger, Job 13:14
is the earth to be abandoned for your sake?
Or must the rocks be moved from their place?

[5]"The lamp of a wicked man is snuffed out; Pr 13:9; 20:20; 24:20
the flame of his fire stops burning.
[6]The light in his tent becomes dark;
the lamp beside him goes out. Job 11:17
[7]The vigor of his step is weakened; Pr 4:12
his own schemes throw him down. Job 5:13; 15:6
[8]His feet thrust him into a net; Job 22:10; Ps 9:15; 35:7
he wanders into its mesh.
[9]A trap seizes him by the heel; Pr 5:22
a snare holds him fast.
[10]A noose is hidden for him on the ground;
a trap lies in his path.
[11]Terrors startle him on every side Job 15:21
and dog his every step. Job 20:8
[12]Calamity is hungry for him; Isa 8:21
disaster is ready for him when he falls.
[13]It eats away parts of his skin;
death's firstborn devours his limbs. Zec 14:12
[14]He is torn from the security of his tent Job 8:22
and marched off to the king of terrors.
[15]Fire resides[a] in his tent;
burning sulfur is scattered over his dwelling. Ps 11:6
[16]His roots dry up below Isa 5:24; Am 2:9
and his branches wither above. Mal 4:1
[17]The memory of him perishes from the earth;
he has no name in the land. Ps 34:16; Pr 10:7
[18]He is driven from light into the realm of darkness Job 5:14
and is banished from the world.
[19]He has no offspring or descendants among his people, Isa 14:22; Jer 22:30
no survivor where once he lived.

[a] 15 Or *Nothing he had remains*

20 People of the west are
appalled at his fate; Ps 37:13; Jer 50:27
those of the east are seized
with horror.
21 Surely such is the dwelling of
an evil man;
such is the place of one who
does not know God." 1Th 4:5

Job 19

19 Then Job replied:

2 "How long will you torment me Job 13:25
and crush me with words?
3 Ten times now you have
reproached me;
shamelessly you attack me.
4 If it is true that I have gone
astray,
my error remains my
concern alone. Job 6:24
5 If indeed you would exalt
yourselves above me Ps 35:26; 38:16; 55:12
and use my humiliation
against me,
6 then know that God has
wronged me Job 27:2
and drawn his net around
me. Job 18:8

7 "Though I cry, 'Violence!' I get
no response; Job 30:20
though I call for help,
there is no justice. Job 9:24; Hab 1:2-4
8 He has blocked my way so I
cannot pass; Job 3:23; La 3:7
he has shrouded my paths in
darkness. Job 30:26
9 He has stripped me of my
honor Job 12:17
and removed the crown from
my head. Ps 89:39,44; La 5:16
10 He tears me down on every
side till I am gone; Job 12:14
he uproots my hope like a
tree. Job 7:6; 24:20
11 His anger burns against me; Job 16:9
he counts me among his
enemies. Job 13:24
12 His troops advance in force; Job 16:13
they build a siege ramp
against me Job 30:12
and encamp around my tent.

13 "He has alienated my family
from me; Ps 69:8
my acquaintances are
completely estranged
from me. Job 16:7; Ps 88:8
14 My relatives have gone away;
my closest friends have
forgotten me. Ps 88:18
15 My guests and my female
servants count me a
foreigner;
they look on me as on a
stranger.
16 I summon my servant, but he
does not answer,
though I beg him with my
own mouth.
17 My breath is offensive to my
wife;
I am loathsome to my own
family.

18 Even the little boys scorn me; 2Ki 2:23
when I appear, they ridicule
me.
19 All my intimate friends detest
me; Ps 38:11; 55:12-13
those I love have turned
against me. Jn 13:18
20 I am nothing but skin and
bones; Job 33:21; Ps 102:5
I have escaped only by the
skin of my teeth.[a]

21 "Have pity on me, my friends,
have pity, Job 6:14
for the hand of God has
struck me.
22 Why do you pursue me as God
does? Job 13:25; 16:11
Will you never get enough of
my flesh? Ps 69:26

23 "Oh, that my words were
recorded,
that they were written on a
scroll, Isa 30:8
24 that they were inscribed with
an iron tool on[b] lead,
or engraved in rock forever!
25 I know that my redeemer[c] lives,
Job 16:19; Ps 78:35; Isa 43:14
and that in the end he will
stand on the earth.[d]
26 And after my skin has been
destroyed,
yet[e] in[f] my flesh I will see
God; Mt 5:8; 1Co 13:12; 1Jn 3:2
27 I myself will see him
with my own eyes—I, and
not another.
How my heart yearns within
me! Ps 73:26

28 "If you say, 'How we will hound
him, Job 13:25
since the root of the trouble
lies in him,[g]'
29 you should fear the sword
yourselves;
for wrath will bring
punishment by the
sword, Job 15:22
and then you will know that
there is judgment.[h]"
Job 22:4; Ps 1:5

Zophar

20 Then Zophar the Naamathite replied: Job 2:11

2 "My troubled thoughts prompt
me to answer
because I am greatly
disturbed. Ps 42:5
3 I hear a rebuke that dishonors
me, Job 19:3
and my understanding
inspires me to reply.

4 "Surely you know how it has
been from of old, Dt 4:32
ever since mankind[i] was
placed on the earth,
5 that the mirth of the wicked is
brief,
the joy of the godless lasts but
a moment. Ps 37:35-36; 73:19

[a] 20 Or *only by my gums* [b] 24 Or *and* [c] 25 Or *vindicator* [d] 25 Or *on my grave* [e] 26 Or *And after I awake, / though this body has been destroyed, / then* [f] 26 Or *destroyed, / apart from* [g] 28 Many Hebrew manuscripts, Septuagint and Vulgate; most Hebrew manuscripts *me* [h] 29 Or *sword, / that you may come to know the Almighty* [i] 4 Or *Adam*

6 Though the pride of the
godless person reaches
to the heavens
and his head touches the
clouds, Isa 14:13-14; Ob 1:3-4
7 he will perish forever, like his
own dung; Job 4:20
those who have seen him
will say, 'Where is he?'
8 Like a dream he flies away, no
more to be found, Ps 73:20
banished like a vision of the
night. Ps 90:5
9 The eye that saw him will not
see him again;
his place will look on him no
more. Job 7:8
10 His children must make
amends to the poor;
his own hands must give
back his wealth.
11 The youthful vigor that fills his
bones Job 13:26
will lie with him in the dust.

12 "Though evil is sweet in his
mouth
and he hides it under his
tongue,
13 though he cannot bear to let
it go
and lets it linger in his
mouth, Nu 11:18-20
14 yet his food will turn sour in
his stomach;
it will become the venom of
serpents within him.
15 He will spit out the riches he
swallowed;
God will make his stomach
vomit them up.
16 He will suck the poison of
serpents; Dt 32:32
the fangs of an adder will kill
him.
17 He will not enjoy the streams,
the rivers flowing with
honey and cream.
Job 29:6
18 What he toiled for he must give
back uneaten;
he will not enjoy the profit
from his trading.
19 For he has oppressed the poor
and left them destitute;
Job 24:4,14; 35:9
he has seized houses he did
not build.

20 "Surely he will have no
respite from his craving;
Ecc 5:12-14
he cannot save himself by his
treasure.
21 Nothing is left for him to
devour;
his prosperity will not
endure. Job 15:29
22 In the midst of his plenty,
distress will overtake
him;
the full force of misery will
come upon him.
23 When he has filled his belly,
God will vent his burning
anger against him
and rain down his blows on
him. Ps 78:30-31
24 Though he flees from an iron
weapon, Isa 24:18; Am 5:19
a bronze-tipped arrow
pierces him.

25 He pulls it out of his back,
the gleaming point out of his liver.
Terrors will come over him; Job 16:13; 18:11
26 total darkness lies in wait for his treasures. Job 18:18
A fire unfanned will consume him Ps 21:9
and devour what is left in his tent.
27 The heavens will expose his guilt;
the earth will rise up against him.
28 A flood will carry off his house, Dt 28:31
rushing waters[a] on the day of God's wrath. Job 21:17,20,30
29 Such is the fate God allots the wicked,
the heritage appointed for them by God." Job 27:13

Job 21

1 Then Job replied:

2 "Listen carefully to my words; Job 13:17
let this be the consolation you give me.
3 Bear with me while I speak,
and after I have spoken, mock on. Job 16:10

4 "Is my complaint directed to a human being?
Why should I not be impatient? Job 6:11
5 Look at me and be appalled;
clap your hand over your mouth. Jdg 18:19; Job 40:4
6 When I think about this, I am terrified;
trembling seizes my body.
7 Why do the wicked live on,
growing old and increasing in power? Ps 73:3; Jer 12:1
8 They see their children established around them,
their offspring before their eyes. Ps 17:14
9 Their homes are safe and free from fear; Ps 73:5
the rod of God is not on them.
10 Their bulls never fail to breed;
their cows calve and do not miscarry. Ex 23:26
11 They send forth their children as a flock;
their little ones dance about.
12 They sing to the music of timbrel and lyre; Ps 33:2
they make merry to the sound of the pipe. Ps 81:2
13 They spend their years in prosperity Job 36:11
and go down to the grave in peace.[b]
14 Yet they say to God, 'Leave us alone! Job 22:17
We have no desire to know your ways. Pr 1:29
15 Who is the Almighty, that we should serve him?

[a] 28 Or *The possessions in his house will be carried off, / washed away* [b] 13 Or *in an instant*

What would we gain by
praying to him?' Job 34:9
16 But their prosperity is not in
their own hands,
so I stand aloof from the
plans of the wicked.

17 "Yet how often is the lamp of
the wicked snuffed out?
Job 18:5
How often does calamity
come upon them,
the fate God allots in his
anger?
18 How often are they like straw
before the wind,
like chaff swept away by a
gale? Ps 1:4
19 It is said, 'God stores up
the punishment of
the wicked for their
children.' Ex 20:5
Let him repay the wicked,
so that they themselves
will experience it!
20 Let their own eyes see their
destruction;
let them drink the cup of the
wrath of the Almighty.
Isa 51:17; Jer 25:15; Rev 14:10
21 For what do they care about
the families they leave
behind
when their allotted months
come to an end?

22 "Can anyone teach knowledge
to God, Isa 40:13-14; Ro 11:34
since he judges even the
highest? Ps 82:1
23 One person dies in full vigor,
completely secure and at ease,
24 well nourished in body,[a]
bones rich with marrow.
Pr 3:8
25 Another dies in bitterness of
soul,
never having enjoyed
anything good.
26 Side by side they lie in the
dust,
and worms cover them both.
Job 24:20; Ecc 9:2-3

27 "I know full well what you are
thinking,
the schemes by which you
would wrong me.
28 You say, 'Where now is the
house of the great,
Job 1:3; 12:21
the tents where the wicked
lived?' Job 8:22
29 Have you never questioned
those who travel?
Have you paid no regard to
their accounts —
30 that the wicked are spared
from the day of calamity,
Pr 16:4
that they are delivered
from[b] the day of wrath?
Job 20:22,28; 2Pe 2:9
31 Who denounces their conduct
to their face?
Who repays them for what
they have done?
32 They are carried to the grave,
and watch is kept over their
tombs.

[a] 24 The meaning of the Hebrew for this word is uncertain. [b] 30 Or *wicked are reserved for the day of calamity, / that they are brought forth to*

33 The soil in the valley is sweet
to them; Job 3:22; 17:16; 24:24
everyone follows after them,
and a countless throng goes[a]
before them. Job 3:19

34 "So how can you console me
with your nonsense?
Job 16:2
Nothing is left of your
answers but falsehood!"

Eliphaz

22 Then Eliphaz the Temanite replied:

2 "Can a man be of benefit to
God? Lk 17:10
Can even a wise person
benefit him?
3 What pleasure would it give
the Almighty if you were
righteous? Isa 1:11
What would he gain if your
ways were blameless?

4 "Is it for your piety that he
rebukes you
and brings charges against
you? Job 14:3; 19:29
5 Is not your wickedness great?
Are not your sins endless?
Job 11:6
6 You demanded security from
your relatives for no
reason; Ex 22:26
you stripped people of their
clothing, leaving them
naked.
7 You gave no water to the weary
and you withheld food from
the hungry, Job 31:17,21,31
8 though you were a powerful
man, owning land —
an honored man, living on it.
Isa 3:3
9 And you sent widows
away empty-handed
Job 24:3,21
and broke the strength of the
fatherless.
10 That is why snares are all
around you,
why sudden peril terrifies
you,
11 why it is so dark you cannot
see, Job 5:14
and why a flood of water
covers you. Ps 69:1-2; 124:4-5

12 "Is not God in the heights of
heaven? Job 11:8
And see how lofty are the
highest stars!
13 Yet you say, 'What does God
know? Ps 10:11
Does he judge through such
darkness? Eze 8:12
14 Thick clouds veil him, so he
does not see us Job 26:9
as he goes about in the
vaulted heavens.'
15 Will you keep to the old path
that the wicked have trod?
16 They were carried off before
their time, Job 15:32
their foundations washed
away by a flood. Mt 7:26-27
17 They said to God, 'Leave us
alone!
What can the Almighty do
to us?'

[a] 33 Or *them, / as a countless throng went*

18 Yet it was he who filled their
houses with good things, Job 12:6
so I stand aloof from the
plans of the wicked.
19 The righteous see their ruin
and rejoice; Ps 58:10; 107:42
the innocent mock them,
saying, Ps 52:6
20 'Surely our foes are destroyed,
and fire devours their
wealth.' Job 15:30

21 "Submit to God and be at peace
with him;
in this way prosperity will
come to you. Ps 34:8-10
22 Accept instruction from his
mouth
and lay up his words in your
heart.
23 If you return to the Almighty,
you will be restored:
Isa 19:22; Ac 20:32
If you remove wickedness
far from your tent
Job 11:14
24 and assign your nuggets to the
dust,
your gold of Ophir to the
rocks in the ravines,
Job 31:25
25 then the Almighty will be your
gold,
the choicest silver for you.
Isa 33:6
26 Surely then you will find
delight in the Almighty
Job 27:10; Isa 58:14
and will lift up your face to
God.
27 You will pray to him, and he
will hear you, Isa 58:9
and you will fulfill your
vows.
28 What you decide on will be
done,
and light will shine on your
ways.
29 When people are brought low
and you say, 'Lift them
up!'
then he will save the
downcast. Mt 23:12; 1Pe 5:5
30 He will deliver even one who is
not innocent,
who will be delivered
through the cleanness of
your hands." Job 42:7-8

Job

23 Then Job replied:

2 "Even today my complaint is
bitter; Job 6:3
his hand[a] is heavy in
spite of[b] my groaning.
Ps 6:6
3 If only I knew where to find
him;
if only I could go to his
dwelling!
4 I would state my case before
him Job 13:18
and fill my mouth with
arguments.
5 I would find out what he would
answer me,
and consider what he would
say to me.

[a] 2 Septuagint and Syriac; Hebrew / *the hand on me* [b] 2 Or *heavy on me in*

6 Would he vigorously oppose
me? Job 9:4
No, he would not press
charges against me.
7 There the upright can establish
their innocence before
him, Job 13:3
and there I would be
delivered forever from
my judge.

8 "But if I go to the east, he is not
there;
if I go to the west, I do not
find him.
9 When he is at work in the
north, I do not see him;
when he turns to the south, I
catch no glimpse of him.
Job 9:11
10 But he knows the way that I
take;
when he has tested me, I
will come forth as gold.
Ps 139:1-3; 1Pe 1:7
11 My feet have closely followed
his steps;
I have kept to his way
without turning aside.
Ps 44:18
12 I have not departed from the
commands of his lips;
Job 6:10
I have treasured the words
of his mouth more
than my daily bread.
Jn 4:32,34

13 "But he stands alone, and who
can oppose him?
He does whatever he pleases.
Ps 115:3
14 He carries out his decree
against me,
and many such plans he still
has in store. 1Th 3:3
15 That is why I am terrified
before him;
when I think of all this, I fear
him.
16 God has made my heart faint;
Ps 22:14; Jer 51:46
the Almighty has terrified me.
17 Yet I am not silenced by the
darkness, Job 19:8
by the thick darkness that
covers my face.

24 "Why does the Almighty
not set times for
judgment? Jer 46:10
Why must those who know
him look in vain for
such days? Ac 1:7
2 There are those who move
boundary stones;
Dt 19:14; 27:17
they pasture flocks they have
stolen.
3 They drive away the orphan's
donkey
and take the widow's ox in
pledge. Job 22:6
4 They thrust the needy from the
path
and force all the poor of the
land into hiding. Pr 28:28
5 Like wild donkeys in the
desert,
the poor go about their labor
of foraging food; Ps 104:23
the wasteland provides food
for their children.

6 They gather fodder in the fields
and glean in the vineyards of
the wicked. Ru 2:22
7 Lacking clothes, they spend the
night naked;
they have nothing to cover
themselves in the cold.
Ex 22:27; Job 22:6
8 They are drenched by
mountain rains
and hug the rocks for lack of
shelter. La 4:5
9 The fatherless child is snatched
from the breast; Dt 24:17
the infant of the poor is
seized for a debt.
10 Lacking clothes, they go about
naked;
they carry the sheaves, but
still go hungry. Lev 19:9
11 They crush olives among the
terraces[a];
they tread the winepresses,
yet suffer thirst.
12 The groans of the dying rise
from the city,
and the souls of the
wounded cry out for
help. Eze 26:15
But God charges no one with
wrongdoing. Job 9:23
13 "There are those who rebel
against the light, Jn 3:19-20
who do not know its ways
or stay in its paths. Isa 5:20
14 When daylight is gone, the
murderer rises up,
kills the poor and needy,
and in the night steals forth
like a thief. Ps 10:9
15 The eye of the adulterer
watches for dusk; Pr 7:8-9
he thinks, 'No eye will see
me,' Ps 10:11
and he keeps his face
concealed.
16 In the dark, thieves break into
houses, Ex 22:2
but by day they shut
themselves in;
they want nothing to do with
the light. Jn 3:20
17 For all of them, midnight is
their morning;
they make friends with the
terrors of darkness.

18 "Yet they are foam on the
surface of the water;
Job 9:26; 22:16
their portion of the land is
cursed,
so that no one goes to the
vineyards.
19 As heat and drought snatch
away the melted snow,
Job 6:17
so the grave snatches away
those who have sinned.
20 The womb forgets them,
the worm feasts on them;
the wicked are no longer
remembered Pr 10:7
but are broken like a tree.
Ps 31:12
21 They prey on the barren and
childless woman,
and to the widow they show
no kindness. Job 22:9

[a] *11* The meaning of the Hebrew for this word is uncertain.

22 But God drags away the mighty by his power;
though they become established, they have no assurance of life. Dt 28:66
23 He may let them rest in a feeling of security,
but his eyes are on their ways. Job 12:6
24 For a little while they are exalted, and then they are gone; Ps 37:10
they are brought low and gathered up like all others;
they are cut off like heads of grain. Isa 17:5

25 "If this is not so, who can prove me false
and reduce my words to nothing?" Job 6:28; 27:4

Bildad

25 Then Bildad the Shuhite replied:

2 "Dominion and awe belong to God; Job 9:4; Rev 1:6
he establishes order in the heights of heaven.
3 Can his forces be numbered?
On whom does his light not rise? Jas 1:17
4 How then can a mortal be righteous before God?
How can one born of woman be pure? Job 4:17
5 If even the moon is not bright
and the stars are not pure in his eyes, Job 15:15
6 how much less a mortal, who is but a maggot —
a human being, who is only a worm!" Ps 22:6

Job

26 Then Job replied:

2 "How you have helped the powerless! Job 6:12
How you have saved the arm that is feeble! Ps 71:9
3 What advice you have offered to one without wisdom!
And what great insight you have displayed! Job 34:35
4 Who has helped you utter these words?
And whose spirit spoke from your mouth?

5 "The dead are in deep anguish, Ps 88:10
those beneath the waters and all that live in them.
6 The realm of the dead is naked before God; Ps 139:8
Destruction[a] lies uncovered. Heb 4:13
7 He spreads out the northern skies over empty space; Job 9:8
he suspends the earth over nothing.
8 He wraps up the waters in his clouds, Pr 30:4
yet the clouds do not burst under their weight.

[a] 6 Hebrew *Abaddon*

9 He covers the face of the full
moon,
spreading his clouds over it.
10 He marks out the horizon on
the face of the waters
for a boundary between light
and darkness. Job 38:8-11
11 The pillars of the heavens
quake,
aghast at his rebuke.
12 By his power he churned up
the sea; Isa 51:15; Jer 31:35
by his wisdom he cut Rahab
to pieces.
13 By his breath the skies became
fair;
his hand pierced the gliding
serpent. Isa 27:1
14 And these are but the outer
fringe of his works;
how faint the whisper we
hear of him!
Who then can understand
the thunder of his
power?" Job 36:29

Job's Final Word to His Friends

27 And Job continued his discourse:

2 "As surely as God lives, who has
denied me justice, Job 34:5
the Almighty, who has made
my life bitter, Job 9:18
3 as long as I have life within me,
the breath of God in my
nostrils, Job 32:8; 33:4
4 my lips will not say anything
wicked,
and my tongue will not utter
lies. Job 6:28
5 I will never admit you are in
the right;
till I die, I will not deny my
integrity. Job 2:9; 13:15
6 I will maintain my innocence
and never let go of it;
my conscience will not
reproach me as long
as I live. Job 2:3

7 "May my enemy be like the
wicked,
my adversary like the
unjust!
8 For what hope have the godless
when they are cut off,
Job 8:13
when God takes away their
life? Job 11:20; Lk 12:20
9 Does God listen to their cry
when distress comes
upon them?
Job 35:12; Pr 1:28; Isa 1:15
10 Will they find delight in the
Almighty? Job 22:26
Will they call on God at all
times?

11 "I will teach you about the
power of God;
the ways of the Almighty I
will not conceal. Job 36:23
12 You have all seen this
yourselves.
Why then this meaningless
talk?

13 "Here is the fate God allots to
the wicked,
the heritage a ruthless
man receives from the
Almighty: Job 20:29

14 However many his children,
their fate is the sword; Dt 28:41; Hos 9:13
his offspring will never have
enough to eat. Job 20:10
15 The plague will bury those who
survive him,
and their widows will not
weep for them. Ps 78:64
16 Though he heaps up silver like
dust
and clothes like piles of clay, Zec 9:3
17 what he lays up the righteous
will wear, Pr 28:8; Ecc 2:26
and the innocent will divide
his silver.
18 The house he builds is like a
moth's cocoon, Job 8:14
like a hut made by a
watchman. Isa 1:8
19 He lies down wealthy, but will
do so no more; Job 7:8
when he opens his eyes, all is
gone.
20 Terrors overtake him like a
flood; Job 15:21
a tempest snatches him away
in the night. Job 20:8
21 The east wind carries him off,
and he is gone;
it sweeps him out of his
place. Job 7:10
22 It hurls itself against him
without mercy Jer 13:14; Eze 5:11
as he flees headlong from its
power.
23 It claps its hands in derision
and hisses him out of his
place." Job 18:18

Interlude: Where Wisdom Is Found

28 There is a mine for silver
and a place where gold is
refined. Ps 12:6
2 Iron is taken from the earth,
and copper is smelted from
ore. Dt 8:9
3 Mortals put an end to the
darkness; Ecc 1:13
they search out the farthest
recesses
for ore in the blackest
darkness. Job 26:10
4 Far from human dwellings they
cut a shaft, 2Sa 5:8
in places untouched by
human feet;
far from other people they
dangle and sway.
5 The earth, from which food
comes, Ps 104:14
is transformed below as by
fire;
6 lapis lazuli comes from its
rocks, Isa 54:11
and its dust contains nuggets
of gold. Job 22:24
7 No bird of prey knows that
hidden path,
no falcon's eye has seen it.
8 Proud beasts do not set foot
on it, Job 41:34
and no lion prowls there.
9 People assault the flinty rock
with their hands Dt 8:15
and lay bare the roots of the
mountains. Jnh 2:6
10 They tunnel through the rock;
their eyes see all its
treasures.

11 They search[a] the sources of the
rivers Ge 7:11
and bring hidden things to
light. Isa 48:6
12 But where can wisdom be
found? Pr 1:20; 8:1; Ecc 7:24
Where does understanding
dwell?
13 No mortal comprehends its
worth; Pr 3:15; Mt 13:44-46
it cannot be found in
the land of the living.
Dt 29:29
14 The deep says, "It is not in me";
Ps 42:7
the sea says, "It is not with
me." Dt 30:13
15 It cannot be bought with the
finest gold,
nor can its price be
weighed out in silver.
Pr 3:13-14; 8:10-11; 16:16
16 It cannot be bought
with the gold of Ophir,
Ge 10:29
with precious onyx or lapis
lazuli. Ex 24:10
17 Neither gold nor crystal
can compare with it,
Ps 119:72
nor can it be had for jewels
of gold. Pr 16:16
18 Coral and jasper are not worthy
of mention;
the price of wisdom is
beyond rubies. Pr 3:15
19 The topaz of Cush cannot
compare with it; Ex 28:17
it cannot be bought with
pure gold. Pr 8:19

20 Where then does wisdom come
from?
Where does understanding
dwell? ver 23,28
21 It is hidden from the eyes of
every living thing,
concealed even from the
birds in the sky.
22 Destruction[b] and Death say,
Job 26:6
"Only a rumor of it has
reached our ears."
23 God understands the way
to it
and he alone knows where it
dwells, Pr 8:22-31
24 for he views the ends of the
earth Ps 33:13-14
and sees everything under
the heavens. Pr 15:3
25 When he established the force
of the wind
and measured out the
waters, Job 12:15; Ps 135:7
26 when he made a decree for the
rain
and a path for the
thunderstorm, Job 37:3,8,11
27 then he looked at wisdom and
appraised it;
he confirmed it and tested it.
Pr 3:19; 8:22-31
28 And he said to the human
race,
"The fear of the Lord — that
is wisdom,
and to shun evil is
understanding." Dt 4:6; Pr 1:7

[a] 11 Septuagint, Aquila and Vulgate; Hebrew *They dam up* [b] 22 Hebrew *Abaddon*

Job's Final Defense

29 Job continued his discourse: Job 13:12

2 "How I long for the months
gone by,
for the days when God
watched over me, Jer 31:28
3 when his lamp shone on my
head
and by his light I walked
through darkness! Job 11:17
4 Oh, for the days when I was in
my prime,
when God's intimate
friendship blessed my
house, Ps 25:14
5 when the Almighty was still
with me
and my children were
around me,
6 when my path was drenched
with cream Job 20:17
and the rock poured out for
me streams of olive oil.
Dt 32:13; Ps 81:16

7 "When I went to the gate of the
city Job 31:21
and took my seat in the
public square,
8 the young men saw me and
stepped aside
and the old men rose to their
feet;
9 the chief men refrained from
speaking
and covered their
mouths with their
hands; Job 21:5
10 the voices of the nobles were
hushed,
and their tongues stuck to
the roof of their mouths.
Ps 137:6
11 Whoever heard me spoke well
of me,
and those who saw me
commended me,
12 because I rescued the poor who
cried for help, Job 24:4
and the fatherless who had
none to assist them.
Job 31:17,21; Ps 72:12; Pr 21:13
13 The one who was dying blessed
me;
I made the widow's heart
sing. Job 22:9
14 I put on righteousness
as my clothing;
Isa 59:17; 61:10; Eph 6:14
justice was my robe and my
turban.
15 I was eyes to the blind Nu 10:31
and feet to the lame.
16 I was a father to the needy;
Pr 29:7
I took up the case of the
stranger.
17 I broke the fangs of the wicked
and snatched the victims
from their teeth. Ps 3:7
18 "I thought, 'I will die in my
own house,
my days as numerous as the
grains of sand. Ps 30:6
19 My roots will reach to the
water, Jer 17:8
and the dew will lie all night
on my branches.

20 My glory will not fade;
the bow will be ever new in my hand.' Ge 49:24; Ps 18:34

21 "People listened to me expectantly,
waiting in silence for my counsel.
22 After I had spoken, they spoke no more;
my words fell gently on their ears. Dt 32:2
23 They waited for me as for showers
and drank in my words as the spring rain.
24 When I smiled at them, they scarcely believed it;
the light of my face was precious to them.[a]
25 I chose the way for them and sat as their chief;
I dwelt as a king among his troops; Job 1:3
I was like one who comforts mourners. Job 4:4

30

"But now they mock me, Job 12:4
men younger than I,
whose fathers I would have disdained
to put with my sheep dogs.
2 Of what use was the strength of their hands to me,
since their vigor had gone from them?
3 Haggard from want and hunger,
they roamed[b] the parched land Isa 8:21
in desolate wastelands at night. Job 24:5
4 In the brush they gathered salt herbs, Job 39:6
and their food[c] was the root of the broom bush. 1Ki 19:4
5 They were banished from human society,
shouted at as if they were thieves.
6 They were forced to live in the dry stream beds,
among the rocks and in holes in the ground.
7 They brayed among the bushes Job 39:5-6
and huddled in the undergrowth.
8 A base and nameless brood,
they were driven out of the land. Job 18:18

9 "And now those young men mock me in song; Job 12:4; Ps 69:11; La 3:14,63
I have become a byword among them. Job 17:6
10 They detest me and keep their distance;
they do not hesitate
to spit in my face. Nu 12:14; Dt 25:9; Isa 50:6
11 Now that God has unstrung my bow and afflicted me, Ru 1:21
they throw off restraint in my presence. Ps 32:9
12 On my right the tribe[d] attacks;
they lay snares for my feet, Ps 140:4-5

[a] 24 The meaning of the Hebrew for this clause is uncertain. [b] 3 Or *gnawed* [c] 4 Or *fuel* [d] 12 The meaning of the Hebrew for this word is uncertain.

they build their siege ramps
against me. Job 19:12
13 They break up my road; Isa 3:12
they succeed in destroying
me.
'No one can help him,' they
say.
14 They advance as through a
gaping breach;
amid the ruins they come
rolling in.
15 Terrors overwhelm me; Ps 55:4-5
my dignity is driven away as
by the wind,
my safety vanishes like a
cloud. Job 3:25; Hos 13:3
16 "And now my life ebbs away;
Ps 42:4
days of suffering grip me.
17 Night pierces my bones;
my gnawing pains never rest.
18 In his great power God becomes
like clothing to me[a];
he binds me like the neck of
my garment.
19 He throws me into the mud,
Ps 69:2,14
and I am reduced to dust and
ashes.
20 "I cry out to you, God, but you
do not answer; Job 19:7
I stand up, but you merely
look at me.
21 You turn on me ruthlessly;
Job 19:6,22
with the might of your hand
you attack me.
22 You snatch me up and drive
me before the wind;
Job 27:21
you toss me about in the
storm. Job 9:17
23 I know you will bring me down
to death, Job 9:22; 10:8
to the place appointed for all
the living.

24 "Surely no one lays a hand on a
broken man
when he cries for help in his
distress. Job 19:7
25 Have I not wept for those in
trouble?
Has not my soul grieved
for the poor?
Job 24:4; Ps 35:13-14; Ro 12:15
26 Yet when I hoped for good, evil
came;
when I looked for light, then
came darkness. Jer 8:15
27 The churning inside me never
stops; La 2:11
days of suffering confront
me.
28 I go about blackened, but not
by the sun; Ps 42:9
I stand up in the assembly
and cry for help. Job 19:7
29 I have become a brother of
jackals, Ps 44:19
a companion of owls. Mic 1:8
30 My skin grows black and peels;
La 4:8
my body burns with fever.
Ps 102:3
31 My lyre is tuned to mourning,
Isa 24:8
and my pipe to the sound of
wailing.

[a] 18 Hebrew; Septuagint *power he grasps my clothing*

31 "I made a covenant with my
eyes
not to look lustfully at a
young woman. Mt 5:28
2 For what is our lot from God
above,
our heritage from the
Almighty on high?
Job 20:29
3 Is it not ruin for the wicked,
Job 21:30
disaster for those who do
wrong? Job 34:22
4 Does he not see my ways
2Ch 16:9
and count my every step?
Pr 5:21

5 "If I have walked with
falsehood
or my foot has hurried after
deceit — Mic 2:11
6 let God weigh me in honest
scales Job 6:2
and he will know that I am
blameless —
7 if my steps have turned from
the path, Job 23:11
if my heart has been led by
my eyes,
or if my hands have been
defiled, Job 9:30
8 then may others eat what I
have sown, Lev 26:16
and may my crops be
uprooted. Mic 6:15

9 "If my heart has been
enticed by a woman,
Job 24:15
or if I have lurked at my
neighbor's door,
10 then may my wife grind
another man's grain,
and may other men sleep
with her. Jer 8:10
11 For that would have been
wicked,
a sin to be judged. Ge 38:24
12 It is a fire that burns to
Destruction[a]; Job 15:30
it would have uprooted my
harvest. Job 20:28

13 "If I have denied justice to any
of my servants,
whether male or female,
when they had a grievance
against me, Dt 24:14-15
14 what will I do when God
confronts me?
What will I answer when
called to account?
Ps 10:13,15
15 Did not he who made me
in the womb make
them?
Did not the same one form
us both within our
mothers? Job 10:3

16 "If I have denied the desires of
the poor Job 5:16
or let the eyes of the widow
grow weary, Job 22:9
17 if I have kept my bread to
myself,
not sharing it with the
fatherless — Job 22:7
18 but from my youth I reared
them as a father would,
and from my birth I guided
the widow —

[a] 12 Hebrew *Abaddon*

19 if I have seen anyone perishing
for lack of clothing, Job 22:6
or the needy without
garments, Job 24:4
20 and their hearts did not
bless me
for warming them with the
fleece from my sheep,
21 if I have raised my hand
against the fatherless, Job 22:9
knowing that I had influence
in court,
22 then let my arm fall from the
shoulder,
let it be broken off at the
joint. Job 38:15
23 For I dreaded destruction from
God,
and for fear of his splendor
I could not do such
things. Job 13:11

24 "If I have put my trust in gold Job 22:25
or said to pure gold, 'You
are my security,' Mt 6:24; Mk 10:24
25 if I have rejoiced over my great
wealth, Ps 62:10
the fortune my hands had
gained,
26 if I have regarded the sun in its
radiance Eze 8:16
or the moon moving in
splendor,
27 so that my heart was secretly
enticed
and my hand offered them a
kiss of homage,
28 then these also would be sins
to be judged, Dt 17:2-7
for I would have been
unfaithful to God on
high.

29 "If I have rejoiced at my
enemy's misfortune Ob 1:12
or gloated over the trouble
that came to him —
Pr 17:5; 24:17-18
30 I have not allowed my mouth
to sin
by invoking a curse against
their life —
31 if those of my household have
never said,
'Who has not been filled
with Job's meat?' —
Job 22:7
32 but no stranger had to spend
the night in the street,
for my door was always
open to the traveler —
Ge 19:2-3; Ro 12:13
33 if I have concealed my sin as
people do,[a] Pr 28:13
by hiding my guilt in my
heart Ge 3:8
34 because I so feared the crowd
Ex 23:2
and so dreaded the contempt
of the clans
that I kept silent and would
not go outside —
35 ("Oh, that I had someone to
hear me! Job 19:7; 30:28
I sign now my defense —
let the Almighty
answer me;

[a] 33 *Or as Adam did*

let my accuser put his
indictment in writing. Job 35:14
36 Surely I would wear it on my
shoulder,
I would put it on like a
crown.
37 I would give him an account of
my every step;
I would present it to him as
to a ruler.) — Job 1:3; 29:25
38 "if my land cries out against
me Ge 4:10
and all its furrows are wet
with tears,
39 if I have devoured its yield
without payment 1Ki 21:19
or broken the spirit of its
tenants, Jas 5:4
40 then let briers come up instead
of wheat Ge 3:18
and stinkweed instead of
barley."

The words of Job are ended. Ps 72:20

Elihu

32 So these three men stopped
answering Job, because he
was righteous in his own eyes.
2 But Elihu son of Barakel the Bu-
zite, of the family of Ram, became
very angry with Job for justifying
himself rather than God. 3 He was
also angry with the three friends,
because they had found no way
to refute Job, and yet had condemned him.[a] 4 Now Elihu had
waited before speaking to Job
because they were older than he.
5 But when he saw that the three
men had nothing more to say, his
anger was aroused. Ge 22:21; Job 33:9
6 So Elihu son of Barakel the Bu-
zite said:

"I am young in years,
and you are old; Job 15:10
that is why I was fearful,
not daring to tell you what I
know.
7 I thought, 'Age should speak;
advanced years should teach
wisdom.'
8 But it is the spirit[b] in a
person,
the breath of the Almighty,
that gives them
understanding. Job 27:3; Pr 2:6
9 It is not only the old[c] who are
wise, 1Co 1:26
not only the aged who
understand what is
right. Job 12:12,20; Lk 2:47

10 "Therefore I say: Listen to me;
I too will tell you what I
know. Job 5:27
11 I waited while you spoke,
I listened to your reasoning;
while you were searching for
words,
12 I gave you my full attention.
But not one of you has proved
Job wrong;
none of you has answered
his arguments.

[a] *3* Masoretic Text; an ancient Hebrew scribal tradition *Job, and so had condemned God* [b] *8* Or *Spirit*; also in verse 18
[c] *9* Or *many*; or *great*

13 Do not say, 'We have found wisdom; Jer 9:23
let God, not a man, refute him.'
14 But Job has not marshaled his words against me, Job 23:4
and I will not answer him with your arguments.

15 "They are dismayed and have no more to say;
words have failed them.
16 Must I wait, now that they are silent,
now that they stand there with no reply?
17 I too will have my say;
I too will tell what I know. Job 33:3
18 For I am full of words,
and the spirit within me compels me; Ac 4:20; 1Co 9:16
19 inside I am like bottled-up wine,
like new wineskins ready to burst.
20 I must speak and find relief;
I must open my lips and reply.
21 I will show no partiality, Lev 19:15; Mt 22:16
nor will I flatter anyone;
22 for if I were skilled in flattery,
my Maker would soon take me away. Ps 12:2-4

33 "But now, Job, listen to my words;
pay attention to everything I say. Job 13:6
2 I am about to open my mouth;
my words are on the tip of my tongue.
3 My words come from an upright heart;
my lips sincerely speak what I know. Job 6:28; 27:4; 36:4
4 The Spirit of God has made me; Ge 2:7
the breath of the Almighty gives me life. Job 27:3
5 Answer me then, if you can;
stand up and argue your case before me. Job 13:18
6 I am the same as you in God's sight;
I too am a piece of clay. Job 4:19
7 No fear of me should alarm you,
nor should my hand be heavy on you. Job 9:34; 13:21

8 "But you have said in my hearing —
I heard the very words —
9 'I am pure, I have done no wrong; Job 10:7
I am clean and free from sin.
10 Yet God has found fault with me;
he considers me his enemy. Job 13:24
11 He fastens my feet in shackles; Job 13:27
he keeps close watch on all my paths.' Job 14:16

12 "But I tell you, in this you are not right,
for God is greater than any mortal. Ecc 7:20

13 Why do you complain to him
Isa 45:9
that he responds to no one's
words[a]?
14 For God does speak — now one
way, now another —
Ps 62:11
though no one perceives it.
15 In a dream, in a vision of the
night, Job 4:13
when deep sleep falls on
people
as they slumber in their
beds,
16 he may speak in their ears
Job 36:10,15
and terrify them with
warnings,
17 to turn them from wrongdoing
and keep them from pride,
18 to preserve them from the pit,
their lives from perishing by
the sword.[b] Job 15:22

19 "Or someone may be chastened
on a bed of pain
with constant distress in
their bones,
20 so that their body finds food
repulsive Ps 107:18
and their soul loathes the
choicest meal. Job 3:24
21 Their flesh wastes away to
nothing,
and their bones, once
hidden, now stick out.
Job 16:8
22 They draw near to the pit,
and their life to the
messengers of death.[c]
Ps 88:3
23 Yet if there is an angel at their
side,
a messenger, one out of a
thousand,
sent to tell them how to be
upright, Mic 6:8
24 and he is gracious to that
person and says to God,
'Spare them from going
down to the pit; Isa 38:17
I have found a ransom for
them —
25 let their flesh be renewed like a
child's;
let them be restored as in the
days of their youth' —
2Ki 5:14
26 then that person can pray to
God and find favor with
him, Job 34:28
they will see God's face and
shout for joy; Job 22:26
he will restore them to full
well-being. Ps 50:15; 51:12
27 And they will go to others and
say,
'I have sinned, I have
perverted what is right,
2Sa 12:13; Lk 15:21
but I did not get what I
deserved. Ro 6:21
28 God has delivered me from
going down to the pit,
and I shall live to enjoy the
light of life.' Job 22:28

29 "God does all these things to a
person — Eph 1:11; Php 2:13
twice, even three times —

[a] 13 *Or that he does not answer for any of his actions* [b] 18 *Or from crossing the river* [c] 22 *Or to the place of the dead*

30 to turn them back from the pit,
that the light of life may shine on them. Ps 56:13

31 "Pay attention, Job, and listen to me;
be silent, and I will speak.
32 If you have anything to say, answer me;
speak up, for I want to vindicate you.
33 But if not, then listen to me;
be silent, and I will teach you wisdom." Ps 34:11

34

Then Elihu said:

2 "Hear my words, you wise men;
listen to me, you men of learning.
3 For the ear tests words
as the tongue tastes food. Job 12:11
4 Let us discern for ourselves what is right;
let us learn together what is good. 1Th 5:21

5 "Job says, 'I am innocent, Job 33:9
but God denies me justice. Job 27:2
6 Although I am right,
I am considered a liar;
although I am guiltless,
his arrow inflicts an incurable wound.' Job 6:4
7 Is there anyone like Job,
who drinks scorn like water? Job 15:16
8 He keeps company with evildoers;
he associates with the wicked. Ps 50:18
9 For he says, 'There is no profit
in trying to please God.' Job 21:15

10 "So listen to me, you men of understanding.
Far be it from God to do evil, Ge 18:25
from the Almighty to do wrong. Dt 32:4; Job 8:3
11 He repays everyone for what they have done; Ps 62:12; Mt 16:27
he brings on them what their conduct deserves. Jer 32:19; Eze 33:20
12 It is unthinkable that God would do wrong,
that the Almighty would pervert justice. Job 8:3
13 Who appointed him over the earth?
Who put him in charge of the whole world? Job 38:4,6
14 If it were his intention
and he withdrew his spirit[a]
and breath, Ps 104:29
15 all humanity would perish together
and mankind would return to the dust. Ge 3:19; Job 9:22

16 "If you have understanding, hear this;
listen to what I say.

[a] 14 Or *Spirit*

17 Can someone who hates justice govern? 2Sa 23:3-4
Will you condemn the just and mighty One? Job 40:8
18 Is he not the One who says to kings, 'You are worthless,'
and to nobles, 'You are wicked,' Ex 22:28
19 who shows no partiality to princes Dt 10:17; Ac 10:34
and does not favor the rich over the poor,
for they are all the work of his hands? Job 10:3
20 They die in an instant, in the middle of the night; Ex 12:29
the people are shaken and they pass away; Job 12:19
the mighty are removed without human hand.

21 "His eyes are on the ways of mortals;
he sees their every step. Job 31:4
22 There is no deep shadow, no utter darkness, Ps 139:12; Am 9:2-3
where evildoers can hide.
23 God has no need to examine people further,
that they should come before him for judgment. Job 11:11
24 Without inquiry he shatters the mighty Job 12:19
and sets up others in their place. Da 2:21
25 Because he takes note of their deeds,
he overthrows them in the night and they are crushed. Pr 5:21-23
26 He punishes them for their wickedness
where everyone can see them,
27 because they turned from following him Ps 28:5; Isa 5:12
and had no regard for any of his ways. 1Sa 15:11
28 They caused the cry of the poor to come before him,
so that he heard the cry of the needy. Ex 22:23; Jas 5:4
29 But if he remains silent, who can condemn him?
If he hides his face, who can see him?
Yet he is over individual and nation alike,
30 to keep the godless from ruling,
from laying snares for the people. Pr 29:2-12

31 "Suppose someone says to God,
'I am guilty but will offend no more.
32 Teach me what I cannot see; Job 35:11; Ps 25:4
if I have done wrong, I will not do so again.' Job 33:27
33 Should God then reward you on your terms,
when you refuse to repent? Job 41:11

You must decide, not I;
so tell me what you know.

34 "Men of understanding declare,
wise men who hear me say to me,
35 'Job speaks without knowledge; Job 35:16
his words lack insight.'
36 Oh, that Job might be tested to the utmost
for answering like a wicked man! Job 22:15
37 To his sin he adds rebellion;
scornfully he claps his hands among us Job 27:23
and multiplies his words against God." Job 23:2

35

Then Elihu said:

2 "Do you think this is just?
You say, 'I am in the right, not God.' Job 32:2
3 Yet you ask him, 'What profit is it to me,[a]
and what do I gain by not sinning?' Job 9:29-31; 34:9

4 "I would like to reply to you
and to your friends with you.
5 Look up at the heavens and see; Ge 15:5
gaze at the clouds so high above you. Job 22:12
6 If you sin, how does that affect him?
If your sins are many, what does that do to him? Pr 8:36
7 If you are righteous, what do you give to him, Ro 11:35
or what does he receive from your hand? Job 22:2-3; Pr 9:12; Lk 17:10
8 Your wickedness only affects humans like yourself,
and your righteousness only other people.

9 "People cry out under a load of oppression; Ex 2:23
they plead for relief from the arm of the powerful. Job 12:19
10 But no one says, 'Where is God my Maker,
who gives songs in the night, Ps 42:8; Ac 16:25
11 who teaches us more than he teaches[b] the beasts of the earth Ps 94:12
and makes us wiser than[c] the birds in the sky?'
12 He does not answer when people cry out Pr 1:28
because of the arrogance of the wicked.
13 Indeed, God does not listen to their empty plea;
the Almighty pays no attention to it. Isa 1:15; Jer 11:11
14 How much less, then, will he listen
when you say that you do not see him, Job 9:11
that your case is before him Ps 37:6
and you must wait for him,

[a] 3 Or *you* [b] 10,11 Or *night, /* [11]*who teaches us by* [c] 11 Or *us wise by*

15 and further, that his anger
never punishes
and he does not take
the least notice of
wickedness.[a] Ps 10:11
16 So Job opens his mouth with
empty talk;
without knowledge he
multiplies words." Job 34:35,37

36

Elihu continued:

2 "Bear with me a little
longer and I will
show you
that there is more to be said
in God's behalf.
3 I get my knowledge from
afar;
I will ascribe justice to my
Maker. Job 8:3
4 Be assured that my words are
not false; Job 33:3
one who has perfect
knowledge is with you. Job 37:5,16,23

5 "God is mighty, but despises no
one; Ps 22:24
he is mighty, and firm in his
purpose. Job 12:13
6 He does not keep the wicked
alive Job 8:22
but gives the afflicted their
rights. Job 5:15
7 He does not take his eyes off
the righteous; Ps 33:18
he enthrones them with
kings Ps 113:8
and exalts them forever.
8 But if people are bound in
chains, Ps 107:10,14
held fast by cords of
affliction,
9 he tells them what they have
done —
that they have sinned
arrogantly. Job 15:25
10 He makes them listen to
correction Job 33:16
and commands them to
repent of their evil.
11 If they obey and serve him, Isa 1:19
they will spend the rest
of their days in
prosperity
and their years in
contentment.
12 But if they do not listen,
they will perish by the
sword[b] Job 15:22
and die without knowledge. Job 4:21

13 "The godless in heart harbor
resentment; Ro 2:5
even when he fetters
them, they do not
cry for help.
14 They die in their youth,
among male prostitutes of
the shrines. Dt 23:17
15 But those who suffer he
delivers in their
suffering;
he speaks to them in their
affliction.

[a] *15* Symmachus, Theodotion and Vulgate; the meaning of the Hebrew for this word is uncertain. [b] *12* Or *will cross the river*

16 "He is wooing you from the
jaws of distress Hos 2:14
to a spacious place free from
restriction,
to the comfort of your table
laden with choice food.
Ps 23:5
17 But now you are laden with
the judgment due the
wicked;
judgment and justice have
taken hold of you. Job 22:11
18 Be careful that no one entices
you by riches;
do not let a large bribe turn
you aside. Job 34:33
19 Would your wealth or even all
your mighty efforts
sustain you so you would not
be in distress?
20 Do not long for the night,
Job 34:20,25
to drag people away from
their homes.[a]
21 Beware of turning to evil, Ps 66:18
which you seem to prefer to
affliction. Heb 11:25

22 "God is exalted in his power.
Who is a teacher like him?
Isa 40:13
23 Who has prescribed his ways
for him, Job 34:13
or said to him, 'You have
done wrong'?
24 Remember to extol his work,
Ps 92:5
which people have praised in
song. Rev 15:3
25 All humanity has seen it;
mortals gaze on it from afar.
26 How great is God — beyond our
understanding! 1Co 13:12
The number of his years is
past finding out. Heb 1:12

27 "He draws up the drops of
water,
which distill as rain to the
streams[b]; Job 38:28; Ps 147:8
28 the clouds pour down their
moisture
and abundant showers fall
on mankind. Job 5:10
29 Who can understand how he
spreads out the clouds,
how he thunders from his
pavilion? Job 37:16
30 See how he scatters his
lightning about him,
bathing the depths of the
sea.
31 This is the way he governs[c] the
nations Job 37:13
and provides food in
abundance. Ac 14:17
32 He fills his hands with
lightning
and commands it to strike its
mark. Job 37:12,15
33 His thunder announces the
coming storm;
even the cattle make known
its approach.[d] Job 28:26

37 "At this my heart pounds
Ps 38:10
and leaps from its place.

[a] 20 The meaning of the Hebrew for verses 18-20 is uncertain. [b] 27 Or *distill from the mist as rain* [c] 31 Or *nourishes* [d] 33 Or *announces his coming — / the One zealous against evil*

2 Listen! Listen to the roar of his
voice, Job 32:10
to the rumbling that comes
from his mouth. Ps 29:3-9
3 He unleashes his lightning
beneath the whole
heaven
and sends it to the ends of
the earth. Job 36:32
4 After that comes the sound of
his roar;
he thunders with his
majestic voice. Ex 20:19
When his voice resounds,
he holds nothing back.
5 God's voice thunders in
marvelous ways;
he does great things
beyond our
understanding. Job 5:9
6 He says to the snow, 'Fall on the
earth,' Job 38:22
and to the rain shower, 'Be
a mighty downpour.'
Job 36:27
7 So that everyone he has made
may know his work,
he stops all people from their
labor.[a] Job 12:14
8 The animals take cover;
they remain in their dens.
Ps 104:22
9 The tempest comes out from
its chamber,
the cold from the driving
winds.
10 The breath of God produces
ice,
and the broad waters
become frozen.
Job 38:29-30; Ps 147:17
11 He loads the clouds with
moisture;
he scatters his lightning
through them. Job 36:27,29
12 At his direction they swirl
around
over the face of the whole
earth
to do whatever he
commands them. Ps 148:8
13 He brings the clouds to punish
people, 1Sa 12:17
or to water his earth
and show his love.
Ex 9:18; 1Ki 18:45; Job 38:27

14 "Listen to this, Job; Job 32:10
stop and consider God's
wonders. Job 5:9
15 Do you know how God controls
the clouds
and makes his lightning
flash? Job 36:30,32
16 Do you know how the clouds
hang poised,
those wonders of him
who has perfect
knowledge? Job 36:4
17 You who swelter in your
clothes
when the land lies
hushed under the
south wind,
18 can you join him in spreading
out the skies, Isa 44:24
hard as a mirror of cast
bronze? Dt 28:23

19 "Tell us what we should say to
him; Ro 8:26

[a] 7 *Or work, / he fills all people with fear by his power*

we cannot draw up our case
because of our darkness.
20 Should he be told that I want to
speak?
Would anyone ask to be
swallowed up?
21 Now no one can look at the
sun, Jdg 5:31
bright as it is in the skies
after the wind has swept
them clean.
22 Out of the north he comes in
golden splendor; Ps 19:5
God comes in awesome
majesty.
23 The Almighty is beyond our
reach and exalted in
power; Job 9:4; 1Ti 6:16
in his justice and great
righteousness, he
does not oppress.
Isa 63:9; Eze 18:23,32
24 Therefore, people revere him,
Mt 10:28
for does he not have regard
for all the wise in
heart?[a]" Mt 11:25

The LORD Speaks

38 Then the LORD spoke to Job out of the storm. He said:
Job 40:6

2 "Who is this that obscures my
plans
with words without
knowledge? 1Ti 1:7
3 Brace yourself like a man;
I will question you,
and you shall answer me.
Job 40:7
4 "Where were you when I laid
the earth's foundation?
Ps 104:5; Pr 8:29
Tell me, if you understand.
5 Who marked off its
dimensions? Surely you
know! Pr 8:29; Isa 40:12
Who stretched a measuring
line across it?
6 On what were its footings set,
or who laid its cornerstone —
Job 26:7
7 while the morning stars sang
together
and all the angels[b] shouted
for joy?
8 "Who shut up the sea behind
doors Jer 5:22
when it burst forth from the
womb, Ge 1:9-10
9 when I made the clouds its
garment
and wrapped it in thick
darkness,
10 when I fixed limits for it
Ps 33:7; 104:9
and set its doors and bars in
place, Job 26:10
11 when I said, 'This far you
may come and no
farther;
here is where your proud
waves halt'? Ps 89:9
12 "Have you ever given orders to
the morning,
or shown the dawn its
place,

[a] 24 Or *for he does not have regard for any who think they are wise.* [b] 7 Hebrew *the sons of God*

13 that it might take the earth by
the edges
and shake the wicked out of
it? Ps 104:35
14 The earth takes shape like clay
under a seal;
its features stand out like
those of a garment.
15 The wicked are denied their
light, Job 18:5
and their upraised arm is
broken. Ps 10:15

16 "Have you journeyed to the
springs of the sea
or walked in the recesses of
the deep? Ps 77:19
17 Have the gates of death been
shown to you? Ps 9:13
Have you seen the gates of
the deepest darkness?
18 Have you comprehended the
vast expanses of the
earth? Job 28:24
Tell me, if you know all this.

19 "What is the way to the abode
of light?
And where does darkness
reside?
20 Can you take them to their
places?
Do you know the paths to
their dwellings? Job 26:10
21 Surely you know, for you were
already born! Job 15:7
You have lived so many
years!

22 "Have you entered the
storehouses of the snow
Job 37:6
or seen the storehouses of
the hail,
23 which I reserve for times of
trouble, Isa 30:30; Eze 13:11
for days of war and battle?
Ex 9:18; Jos 10:11; Rev 16:21
24 What is the way to the place
where the lightning is
dispersed,
or the place where the east
winds are scattered over
the earth?
25 Who cuts a channel for the
torrents of rain,
and a path for the
thunderstorm, Job 28:26
26 to water a land where no one
lives, Job 36:27
an uninhabited desert,
27 to satisfy a desolate wasteland
and make it sprout with
grass? Ps 104:14
28 Does the rain have a father?
Ps 147:8; Jer 14:22
Who fathers the drops of
dew?
29 From whose womb comes the
ice?
Who gives birth to the
frost from the heavens
Ps 147:16-17
30 when the waters become hard
as stone,
when the surface of the deep
is frozen? Job 37:10

31 "Can you bind the chains[a] of
the Pleiades?
Can you loosen Orion's belt?
Job 9:9; Am 5:8

[a] 31 Septuagint; Hebrew *beauty*

32 Can you bring forth the constellations in their seasons[a]
or lead out the Bear[b] with its cubs?
33 Do you know the laws of the heavens? Ps 148:6; Jer 31:36
Can you set up God's[c] dominion over the earth?

34 "Can you raise your voice to the clouds
and cover yourself with a flood of water? Job 22:11
35 Do you send the lightning bolts on their way? Job 36:32
Do they report to you, 'Here we are'?
36 Who gives the ibis wisdom[d] Job 9:4
or gives the rooster understanding?[e] Job 32:8; Ps 51:6; Ecc 2:26
37 Who has the wisdom to count the clouds?
Who can tip over the water jars of the heavens Jos 3:16
38 when the dust becomes hard
and the clods of earth stick together? 1Ki 18:45

39 "Do you hunt the prey for the lioness
and satisfy the hunger of the lions Ps 104:21
40 when they crouch in their dens Job 37:8
or lie in wait in a thicket?
41 Who provides food for the raven Lk 12:24
when its young cry out to God
and wander about for lack of food? Ps 147:9; Mt 6:26

39

"Do you know when the mountain goats give birth? Dt 14:5
Do you watch when the doe bears her fawn?
2 Do you count the months till they bear?
Do you know the time they give birth?
3 They crouch down and bring forth their young;
their labor pains are ended.
4 Their young thrive and grow strong in the wilds;
they leave and do not return.

5 "Who let the wild donkey go free? Job 6:5
Who untied its ropes?
6 I gave it the wasteland as its home, Job 24:5; Jer 2:24
the salt flats as its habitat. Hos 8:9
7 It laughs at the commotion in the town;
it does not hear a driver's shout. Job 3:18
8 It ranges the hills for its pasture
and searches for any green thing.

[a] 32 Or *the morning star in its season*
[b] 32 Or *out Leo* [c] 33 Or *their*
[d] 36 That is, wisdom about the flooding of the Nile [e] 36 That is, understanding of when to crow; the meaning of the Hebrew for this verse is uncertain.

9 "Will the wild ox consent
to serve you?
Nu 23:22; Dt 33:17
Will it stay by your manger at
night?
10 Can you hold it to the furrow
with a harness?
Will it till the valleys behind
you?
11 Will you rely on it for its great
strength? Ps 147:10
Will you leave your heavy
work to it?
12 Can you trust it to haul in your
grain
and bring it to your
threshing floor?

13 "The wings of the ostrich flap
joyfully,
though they cannot
compare
with the wings and feathers
of the stork. Zec 5:9
14 She lays her eggs on the
ground
and lets them warm in the
sand,
15 unmindful that a foot may
crush them,
that some wild animal may
trample them.
16 She treats her young harshly,
as if they were not hers;
La 4:3
she cares not that her labor
was in vain,
17 for God did not endow her with
wisdom
or give her a share of good
sense. Job 35:11
18 Yet when she spreads her
feathers to run,
she laughs at horse and
rider.

19 "Do you give the horse its
strength
or clothe its neck with a
flowing mane?
20 Do you make it leap like a
locust, Joel 2:4-5
striking terror with its proud
snorting? Jer 8:16
21 It paws fiercely, rejoicing in its
strength,
and charges into the fray.
Jer 8:6
22 It laughs at fear, afraid of
nothing;
it does not shy away from
the sword.
23 The quiver rattles against its
side,
along with the flashing spear
and lance.
24 In frenzied excitement it eats
up the ground;
it cannot stand still when
the trumpet sounds.
Jer 4:5,19; Eze 7:14
25 At the blast of the trumpet it
snorts, 'Aha!' Jos 6:5
It catches the scent of battle
from afar,
the shout of commanders
and the battle cry.
Am 1:14; 2:2

26 "Does the hawk take flight by
your wisdom
and spread its wings toward
the south?

27 Does the eagle soar at your
command
and build its nest on high?
Ob 1:4
28 It dwells on a cliff and stays
there at night;
a rocky crag is its
stronghold.
29 From there it looks for food;
Job 9:26
its eyes detect it from afar.
30 Its young ones feast on
blood,
and where the slain are,
there it is." Mt 24:28

40

The LORD said to Job:
Job 33:13

2 "Will the one who contends
with the Almighty
correct him? Job 9:15
Let him who accuses God
answer him!" Job 9:3

3 Then Job answered the LORD:

4 "I am unworthy — how can I
reply to you? Job 42:6
I put my hand over my
mouth. Job 29:9
5 I spoke once, but I have no
answer — Job 9:3
twice, but I will say no
more."

6 Then the LORD spoke to Job out
of the storm: Job 38:1

7 "Brace yourself like a man;
I will question you,
and you shall answer me.
Job 42:4
8 "Would you discredit my
justice? Ro 3:3
Would you condemn
me to justify
yourself?
9 Do you have an arm like God's,
2Ch 32:8
and can your voice
thunder like his?
Job 37:5; Ps 29:3-4
10 Then adorn yourself with glory
and splendor,
and clothe yourself in honor
and majesty. Ps 93:1; 104:1
11 Unleash the fury of your wrath,
Isa 42:25; Na 1:6
look at all who are proud
and bring them low,
Isa 2:11-12,17; Da 4:37
12 look at all who are proud and
humble them, 1Sa 2:7
crush the wicked where they
stand. Isa 13:11; 63:2-3,6
13 Bury them all in the dust
together;
shroud their faces in the
grave.
14 Then I myself will admit
to you
that your own right hand can
save you. Ps 20:6

15 "Look at Behemoth,
which I made along with you
Job 9:9
and which feeds on grass like
an ox. Isa 11:7
16 What strength it has in its
loins, Job 39:11
what power in the muscles of
its belly! Job 41:9

17 Its tail sways like a cedar;
the sinews of its thighs are close-knit.
18 Its bones are tubes of bronze,
its limbs like rods of iron.
19 It ranks first among the works of God, Job 41:33
yet its Maker can approach it with his sword.
20 The hills bring it their produce, Ps 104:14
and all the wild animals play nearby. Ps 104:26
21 Under the lotus plants it lies,
hidden among the reeds in the marsh.
22 The lotuses conceal it in their shadow;
the poplars by the stream surround it. Isa 44:4
23 A raging river does not alarm it; Isa 8:7
it is secure, though the Jordan should surge against its mouth. Jos 3:1
24 Can anyone capture it by the eyes,
or trap it and pierce its nose? Job 41:2,7,26

41 [a] "Can you pull in Leviathan with a fishhook Ps 104:26; Isa 27:1
or tie down its tongue with a rope?
2 Can you put a cord through its nose
or pierce its jaw with a hook? Isa 37:29
3 Will it keep begging you for mercy?
Will it speak to you with gentle words?
4 Will it make an agreement with you
for you to take it as your slave for life? Ex 21:6
5 Can you make a pet of it like a bird
or put it on a leash for the young women in your house?
6 Will traders barter for it?
Will they divide it up among the merchants?
7 Can you fill its hide with harpoons
or its head with fishing spears? Job 40:24
8 If you lay a hand on it,
you will remember the struggle and never do it again! Job 3:8
9 Any hope of subduing it is false;
the mere sight of it is overpowering. Job 40:16
10 No one is fierce enough to rouse it. Job 3:8
Who then is able to stand against me? Jer 50:44
11 Who has a claim against me that I must pay? Ro 11:35
Everything under heaven belongs to me. Ex 19:5; Dt 10:14; 1Co 10:26

[a] In Hebrew texts 41:1-8 is numbered 40:25-32, and 41:9-34 is numbered 41:1-26.

12 "I will not fail to speak
of Leviathan's limbs, Job 40:18
its strength and its graceful
form. Job 39:11
13 Who can strip off its outer
coat?
Who can penetrate its
double coat of armor[a]?
Job 30:11
14 Who dares open the doors of its
mouth, Ps 22:13
ringed about with fearsome
teeth?
15 Its back has[b] rows of shields
tightly sealed together;
Job 40:17
16 each is so close to the next
that no air can pass
between.
17 They are joined fast to one
another;
they cling together and
cannot be parted.
18 Its snorting throws out flashes
of light;
its eyes are like the rays of
dawn. Job 3:9
19 Flames stream from its mouth;
Da 10:6
sparks of fire shoot out.
20 Smoke pours from its nostrils
Ps 18:8
as from a boiling pot over
burning reeds.
21 Its breath sets coals ablaze,
Isa 40:7
and flames dart from its
mouth. Ps 18:8
22 Strength resides in its neck;
dismay goes before it.
23 The folds of its flesh are tightly
joined;
they are firm and
immovable.
24 Its chest is hard as rock,
hard as a lower millstone.
25 When it rises up, the mighty
are terrified; Job 39:20
they retreat before its
thrashing. Job 3:8
26 The sword that reaches it has
no effect,
nor does the spear or the
dart or the javelin. Jos 8:18
27 Iron it treats like straw
and bronze like rotten wood.
28 Arrows do not make it flee;
Ps 91:5
slingstones are like chaff to it.
29 A club seems to it but a piece of
straw;
it laughs at the rattling of the
lance. Job 5:22
30 Its undersides are jagged
potsherds,
leaving a trail in the mud
like a threshing sledge.
Isa 41:15
31 It makes the depths churn like
a boiling caldron
and stirs up the sea like a pot
of ointment. Eze 32:2
32 It leaves a glistening wake
behind it;
one would think the deep
had white hair.
33 Nothing on earth is its equal —
Job 40:19
a creature without fear.

[a] 13 Septuagint; Hebrew *double bridle*
[b] 15 Or *Its pride is its*

34It looks down on all that are
haughty;
it is king over all that are
proud." Job 28:8

Job

42 Then Job replied to the
LORD:

2"I know that you can do all
things; Ge 18:14; Mt 19:26
no purpose of yours can be
thwarted. 2Ch 20:6
3You asked, 'Who is this that
obscures my plans
without knowledge?'
Job 38:2
Surely I spoke of things I did
not understand,
things too wonderful for me
to know. Ps 40:5
4"You said, 'Listen now, and I
will speak;
I will question you,
and you shall answer me.'
Job 38:3; 40:7
5My ears had heard of you
Job 26:14; Ro 10:17
but now my eyes have
seen you.
Jdg 13:22; Isa 6:5; Eph 1:17-18
6Therefore I despise myself
and repent in dust and
ashes." Job 40:4; Ro 12:3

Epilogue

7After the LORD had said these
things to Job, he said to Eliphaz
the Temanite, "I am angry with
you and your two friends, because
you have not spoken the truth
about me, as my servant Job has.
8So now take seven bulls and sev-
en rams and go to my servant Job
and sacrifice a burnt offering for
yourselves. My servant Job will
pray for you, and I will accept his
prayer and not deal with you according to your folly. You have not
spoken the truth about me, as my
servant Job has." 9So Eliphaz the
Temanite, Bildad the Shuhite and
Zophar the Naamathite did what
the LORD told them; and the LORD
accepted Job's prayer.
Job 22:30; Jas 5:15-16; 1Jn 5:16

10After Job had prayed for his
friends, the LORD restored his fortunes and gave him twice as much
as he had before. 11All his brothers
and sisters and everyone who had
known him before came and ate
with him in his house. They comforted and consoled him over all
the trouble the LORD had brought
on him, and each one gave him a
piece of silver[a] and a gold ring.
Dt 30:3; Ps 14:7

12The LORD blessed the latter
part of Job's life more than the
former part. He had fourteen
thousand sheep, six thousand
camels, a thousand yoke of oxen
and a thousand donkeys. 13And
he also had seven sons and three
daughters. 14The first daughter he
named Jemimah, the second Kezi-
ah and the third Keren-Happuch.

[a] 11 Hebrew *him a kesitah*; a kesitah was a unit of money of unknown weight and value.

[15]Nowhere in all the land were
there found women as beautiful
as Job's daughters, and their father granted them an inheritance
along with their brothers.

[16]After this, Job lived a hundred
and forty years; he saw his children
and their children to the fourth
generation. [17]And so Job died, an
old man and full of years. Ge 25:8

PSALMS

BOOK I

Psalms 1 – 41

Psalm 1

1 Blessed is the one
who does not walk in step
with the wicked Pr 4:14
or stand in the way that sinners
take
or sit in the company of
mockers, Ps 26:4; Jer 15:17
2 but whose delight is in
the law of the LORD,
Ps 119:16,35
and who meditates on
his law day and night.
Jos 1:8
3 That person is like a tree
planted by streams of
water, Jer 17:8
which yields its fruit in
season
and whose leaf does not
wither —
whatever they do prospers.
Ge 39:3

4 Not so the wicked!
They are like chaff
that the wind blows away.
Job 21:18; Isa 17:13
5 Therefore the wicked will not
stand in the judgment,
nor sinners in the assembly
of the righteous.
6 For the LORD watches over the
way of the righteous,
Ps 37:18; 2Ti 2:19
but the way of the wicked
leads to destruction.

Psalm 2

1 Why do the nations conspire[a]
and the peoples plot in vain?
Ps 21:11
2 The kings of the earth rise up
and the rulers band
together
against the LORD and against
his anointed, saying,
Jn 1:41; Ac 4:25-26*
3 "Let us break their chains
and throw off their shackles."

4 The One enthroned in heaven
laughs;
the Lord scoffs at them. Ps 37:13
5 He rebukes them in his anger
and terrifies them in his
wrath, saying,
6 "I have installed my king
on Zion, my holy mountain."
Ex 15:17

7 I will proclaim the LORD's decree:

He said to me, "You are my
son;
today I have become your
father. Ac 13:33*

[a] *1* Hebrew; Septuagint *rage*

8 Ask me,
and I will make the nations
your inheritance,
the ends of the earth your
possession. Ps 22:27
9 You will break them with a rod
of iron[a];
you will dash them to
pieces like pottery."
Ps 89:23; Rev 2:27*

10 Therefore, you kings, be wise;
be warned, you rulers of the
earth.
11 Serve the LORD with fear
and celebrate his rule with
trembling. Heb 12:28
12 Kiss his son, or he will be
angry
and your way will lead to
your destruction,
for his wrath can flare up in a
moment. Rev 6:16
Blessed are all who
take refuge in him.
Ps 34:8; Ro 9:33

Psalm 3[b]

A psalm of David. When he fled from his son Absalom.

1 LORD, how many are my foes!
How many rise up against
me!
2 Many are saying of me,
"God will not deliver him."[c]
Ps 71:11

3 But you, LORD, are a shield
around me, Ge 15:1; Ps 28:7
my glory, the One who lifts
my head high. Ps 27:6
4 I call out to the LORD,
and he answers me from his
holy mountain.

5 I lie down and sleep; Lev 26:6
I wake again, because the
LORD sustains me.
6 I will not fear though tens of
thousands
assail me on every side. Ps 27:3

7 Arise, LORD!
Deliver me, my God!
Strike all my enemies on the
jaw;
break the teeth of the
wicked. Job 16:10

8 From the LORD comes
deliverance. Isa 43:3,11
May your blessing be on your
people.

Psalm 4[d]

For the director of music. With stringed instruments. A psalm of David.

1 Answer me when I call
to you,
my righteous God.
Give me relief from my
distress;
have mercy on me and hear
my prayer. Ps 17:6

2 How long will you people
turn my glory into
shame?

[a] 9 Or *will rule them with an iron scepter* (see Septuagint and Syriac) [b] In Hebrew texts 3:1-8 is numbered 3:2-9. [c] 2 The Hebrew has *Selah* (a word of uncertain meaning) here and at the end of verses 4 and 8. [d] In Hebrew texts 4:1-8 is numbered 4:2-9.

How long will you love
delusions and seek false
gods[a]?[b]
3 Know that the LORD has set
apart his faithful servant
for himself; Ps 31:23
the LORD hears when I call to
him. Ps 6:8

4 Tremble and[c] do not sin; Eph 4:26*
when you are on your beds, Ps 77:6
search your hearts and be
silent.
5 Offer the sacrifices of the
righteous
and trust in the LORD. Dt 33:19; Ps 37:3
6 Many, LORD, are asking, "Who
will bring us prosperity?"
Let the light of your face
shine on us. Nu 6:25
7 Fill my heart with joy Isa 9:3
when their grain and new
wine abound.
8 In peace I will lie down and
sleep, Ps 3:5
for you alone, LORD,
make me dwell in safety. Lev 25:18

Psalm 5[d]

For the director of music. For pipes. A psalm of David.

1 Listen to my words, LORD,
consider my lament.
2 Hear my cry for help, Ps 3:4
my King and my God, Ps 84:3
for to you I pray.
3 In the morning, LORD, you hear
my voice;
in the morning I lay my
requests before you
and wait expectantly.
4 For you are not a God who
is pleased with
wickedness;
with you, evil people are not
welcome. Ps 11:5; 92:15
5 The arrogant cannot stand
in your presence. Ps 1:5; 73:3
You hate all who do
wrong; Ps 11:5
6 you destroy those who tell
lies. Ps 55:23
The bloodthirsty and deceitful
you, LORD, detest.
7 But I, by your great love,
can come into your house;
in reverence I bow down
toward your holy temple. Ps 138:2
8 Lead me, LORD, in your
righteousness Ps 31:1
because of my enemies —
make your way straight
before me. Ps 27:11
9 Not a word from their mouth
can be trusted;
their heart is filled with
malice.
Their throat is an open grave; Lk 11:44
with their tongues they tell
lies. Ro 3:13*

[a] 2 Or *seek lies* [b] 2 The Hebrew has *Selah* (a word of uncertain meaning) here and at the end of verse 4. [c] 4 Or *In your anger* (see Septuagint) [d] In Hebrew texts 5:1-12 is numbered 5:2-13.

10 Declare them guilty, O God!
Let their intrigues be their downfall.
Banish them for their many sins, Ps 9:16
for they have rebelled against you. Ps 107:11
11 But let all who take refuge in you be glad;
let them ever sing for joy. Ps 2:12
Spread your protection over them,
that those who love your name may rejoice in you. Ps 69:36; Isa 65:13

12 Surely, LORD, you bless the righteous;
you surround them with your favor as with a shield. Ps 32:7

Psalm 6[a]

For the director of music. With stringed instruments. According to *sheminith.*[b] A psalm of David.

1 LORD, do not rebuke me in your anger Ps 38:1
or discipline me in your wrath.
2 Have mercy on me, LORD, for I am faint;
heal me, LORD, for my bones are in agony. Ps 22:14
3 My soul is in deep anguish. Jn 12:27
How long, LORD, how long?

4 Turn, LORD, and deliver me;
save me because of your unfailing love. Ps 17:13
5 Among the dead no one proclaims your name.
Who praises you from the grave? Ps 30:9; Isa 38:18

6 I am worn out from my groaning.

All night long I flood my bed with weeping
and drench my couch with tears. Ps 42:3
7 My eyes grow weak with sorrow; Ps 31:9
they fail because of all my foes.

8 Away from me, all you who do evil, Ps 119:115
for the LORD has heard my weeping.
9 The LORD has heard my cry for mercy; Ps 116:1
the LORD accepts my prayer.
10 All my enemies will be overwhelmed with shame and anguish;
they will turn back and suddenly be put to shame. Ps 71:24; 73:19

Psalm 7[c]

A *shiggaion*[d] of David, which he sang to the LORD concerning Cush, a Benjamite.

1 LORD my God, I take refuge in you;
save and deliver me from all who pursue me, Ps 31:15

[a] In Hebrew texts 6:1-10 is numbered 6:2-11. [b] Title: Probably a musical term [c] In Hebrew texts 7:1-17 is numbered 7:2-18. [d] Title: Probably a literary or musical term

2 or they will tear me apart like a lion
and rip me to pieces with no one to rescue me.

3 LORD my God, if I have done this
and there is guilt on my hands — 1Sa 24:11; Isa 59:3
4 if I have repaid my ally with evil
or without cause have robbed my foe —
5 then let my enemy pursue and overtake me;
let him trample my life to the ground
and make me sleep in the dust.[a]

6 Arise, LORD, in your anger; Ps 94:2
rise up against the rage of my enemies.
Awake, my God; decree justice. Ps 44:23
7 Let the assembled peoples gather around you,
while you sit enthroned over them on high.
8 Let the LORD judge the peoples.
Vindicate me, LORD, according to my righteousness, Ps 18:20
according to my integrity, O Most High.
9 Bring to an end the violence of the wicked
and make the righteous secure —
you, the righteous God Jer 11:20
who probes minds and hearts. Rev 2:23

10 My shield[b] is God Most High,
who saves the upright in heart. Ps 125:4
11 God is a righteous judge,
a God who displays his wrath every day.
12 If he does not relent,
he[c] will sharpen his sword; Dt 32:41
he will bend and string his bow.
13 He has prepared his deadly weapons;
he makes ready his flaming arrows.

14 Whoever is pregnant with evil
conceives trouble and gives birth to disillusionment. Isa 59:4; Jas 1:15
15 Whoever digs a hole and scoops it out
falls into the pit they have made. Job 4:8
16 The trouble they cause recoils on them;
their violence comes down on their own heads.

17 I will give thanks to the LORD because of his righteousness; Ps 71:15-16
I will sing the praises of the name of the LORD Most High.

[a] 5 The Hebrew has *Selah* (a word of uncertain meaning) here. [b] 10 Or *sovereign* [c] 12 Or *If anyone does not repent, / God*

Psalm 8[a]

For the director of music. According to *gittith.*[b] A psalm of David.

1 LORD, our Lord,
how majestic is your name in all the earth! 1Ch 16:10

You have set your glory
in the heavens. Ps 113:4; 148:13
2 Through the praise of children and infants
you have established a stronghold against your enemies, Mt 21:16*
to silence the foe and the avenger. Ps 44:16
3 When I consider your heavens, Ps 89:11
the work of your fingers,
the moon and the stars,
which you have set in place,
4 what is mankind that you are mindful of them,
human beings that you care for them?[c] Job 7:17

5 You have made them[d] a little lower than the angels[e]
and crowned them[d] with glory and honor. Ps 21:5; 103:4
6 You made them rulers over the works of your hands;
you put everything under their[f] feet: Heb 2:6-8*
7 all flocks and herds,
and the animals of the wild,
8 the birds in the sky,
and the fish in the sea,
all that swim the paths of the seas. Ge 1:26

9 LORD, our Lord,
how majestic is your name in all the earth! ver 1

Psalm 9[g,h]

For the director of music. To the tune of "The Death of the Son." A psalm of David.

1 I will give thanks to you, LORD,
with all my heart; Ps 86:12
I will tell of all your wonderful deeds.
2 I will be glad and rejoice in you; Ps 5:11
I will sing the praises of your name, O Most High. Ps 83:18

3 My enemies turn back;
they stumble and perish before you.
4 For you have upheld my right and my cause, Ps 140:12
sitting enthroned as the righteous judge. 1Pe 2:23
5 You have rebuked the nations and destroyed the wicked;
you have blotted out their name for ever and ever. Pr 10:7

[a] In Hebrew texts 8:1-9 is numbered 8:2-10.
[b] Title: Probably a musical term
[c] 4 Or *what is a human being that you are mindful of him, / a son of man that you care for him?*
[d] 5 Or *him*
[e] 5 Or *than God*
[f] 6 Or *made him ruler . . . ; / . . . his*
[g] Psalms 9 and 10 may originally have been a single acrostic poem in which alternating lines began with the successive letters of the Hebrew alphabet. In the Septuagint they constitute one psalm.
[h] In Hebrew texts 9:1-20 is numbered 9:2-21.

6 Endless ruin has overtaken my
enemies,
you have uprooted their
cities;
even the memory of them
has perished. Ps 34:16
7 The LORD reigns forever;
he has established his throne
for judgment.
8 He rules the world in
righteousness Ps 96:13
and judges the peoples with
equity.
9 The LORD is a refuge for the
oppressed,
a stronghold in times of
trouble. Ps 32:7
10 Those who know your name
trust in you, Ps 91:14
for you, LORD, have
never forsaken those
who seek you.

11 Sing the praises of the LORD,
enthroned in Zion;
proclaim among the nations
what he has done. Ps 105:1
12 For he who avenges blood
remembers; Ge 9:5
he does not ignore the cries
of the afflicted.

13 LORD, see how my enemies
persecute me! Ps 38:19
Have mercy and lift me up
from the gates of death,
14 that I may declare your praises
Ps 106:2
in the gates of Daughter Zion,
and there rejoice in your
salvation. Ps 13:5

15 The nations have fallen into
the pit they have dug;
Ps 7:15-16
their feet are caught in
the net they have
hidden.
16 The LORD is known by his acts
of justice;
the wicked are ensnared
by the work of their
hands.[a]
17 The wicked go down to the
realm of the dead,
all the nations that forget
God. Job 8:13
18 But God will never forget the
needy;
the hope of the afflicted will
never perish. Pr 23:18

19 Arise, LORD, do not let mortals
triumph;
let the nations be judged in
your presence. Ps 110:6
20 Strike them with terror,
LORD;
let the nations know they are
only mortal.

Psalm 10[b]

1 Why, LORD, do you stand far
off? Ps 22:1,11
Why do you hide yourself in
times of trouble? Ps 13:1

[a] 16 The Hebrew has *Higgaion* and *Selah* (words of uncertain meaning) here; *Selah* occurs also at the end of verse 20.
[b] Psalms 9 and 10 may originally have been a single acrostic poem in which alternating lines began with the successive letters of the Hebrew alphabet. In the Septuagint they constitute one psalm.

[2]In his arrogance the wicked
man hunts down the
weak,
who are caught in the
schemes he devises.
[3]He boasts about the cravings of
his heart; Ps 94:4
he blesses the greedy and
reviles the LORD.
[4]In his pride the wicked man
does not seek him;
in all his thoughts there is no
room for God. Ps 14:1; 36:1
[5]His ways are always
prosperous;
your laws are rejected by[a]
him;
he sneers at all his enemies.
[6]He says to himself, "Nothing
will ever shake me."
He swears, "No one will ever
do me harm." Rev 18:7

[7]His mouth is full of lies and
threats; Ro 3:14*
trouble and evil are under
his tongue.
[8]He lies in wait near the villages;
from ambush he murders
the innocent. Ps 94:6
His eyes watch in secret for his
victims;
9 like a lion in cover he lies in
wait.
He lies in wait to catch the
helpless; Ps 17:12
he catches the helpless and
drags them off in his net.
[10]His victims are crushed, they
collapse;
they fall under his strength.
[11]He says to himself, "God will
never notice; Job 22:13
he covers his face and never
sees."

[12]Arise, LORD! Lift up your hand,
O God. Mic 5:9
Do not forget the helpless.
Ps 9:12
[13]Why does the wicked man
revile God?
Why does he say to himself,
"He won't call me to
account"?
[14]But you, God, see the
trouble of the afflicted;
Ps 22:11
you consider their grief and
take it in hand.
The victims commit
themselves to you;
you are the helper of the
fatherless. Ps 68:5
[15]Break the arm of the wicked
man; Ps 37:17
call the evildoer to
account for his
wickedness
that would not otherwise be
found out.

[16]The LORD is King for ever and
ever; Ps 29:10
the nations will perish from
his land. Dt 8:20
[17]You, LORD, hear the desire of
the afflicted;
you encourage them, and
you listen to their cry,
Ps 34:15

[a] 5 See Septuagint; Hebrew / *they are haughty, and your laws are far from*

18 defending the fatherless
and the oppressed, Ps 9:9; 82:3
so that mere earthly mortals
will never again strike terror.

Psalm 11

For the director of music. Of David.

1 In the LORD I take refuge. Ps 56:11
How then can you say to me:
"Flee like a bird to your
mountain.
2 For look, the wicked bend their
bows;
they set their arrows against
the strings Ps 7:13
to shoot from the shadows
at the upright in heart. Ps 64:3-4
3 When the foundations are
being destroyed, Ps 82:5
what can the righteous do?"

4 The LORD is in his holy temple; Ps 18:6
the LORD is on his heavenly
throne.
He observes everyone on earth;
his eyes examine them. Ps 34:15-16
5 The LORD examines the
righteous, Ge 22:1
but the wicked, those who
love violence,
he hates with a passion. Ps 5:5
6 On the wicked he will rain
fiery coals and burning
sulfur; Eze 38:22
a scorching wind will be their
lot. Jer 4:11-12

7 For the LORD is righteous,
he loves justice;
the upright will see his face. Ps 17:15

Psalm 12[a]

For the director of music. According to *sheminith*.[b] A psalm of David.

1 Help, LORD, for no one is
faithful anymore; Isa 57:1
those who are loyal have
vanished from the
human race.
2 Everyone lies to their neighbor;
they flatter with their lips
but harbor deception in their
hearts. Ps 10:7; Ro 16:18

3 May the LORD silence all
flattering lips
and every boastful tongue — Da 7:8; Rev 13:5
4 those who say,
"By our tongues we will
prevail;
our own lips will defend
us — who is lord over
us?"

5 "Because the poor are
plundered and the
needy groan,
I will now arise," says the
LORD.
"I will protect them from
those who malign
them." Ps 10:18; 34:6
6 And the words of the
LORD are flawless, 2Sa 22:31; Ps 18:30; Pr 30:5

[a] In Hebrew texts 12:1-8 is numbered 12:2-9.
[b] Title: Probably a musical term

like silver purified in a
crucible,
like gold[a] refined seven
times.

7 You, LORD, will keep the needy
safe
and will protect us forever
from the wicked, Ps 37:28
8 who freely strut about
when what is vile is honored
by the human race.
Ps 55:10-11

Psalm 13[b]

For the director of music. A psalm of David.

1 How long, LORD? Will you
forget me forever?
How long will you hide
your face from me?
Job 13:24
2 How long must I wrestle with
my thoughts Ps 42:4
and day after day have
sorrow in my heart?
How long will my enemy
triumph over me? Ps 42:9

3 Look on me and answer, LORD
my God.
Give light to my eyes, or
I will sleep in death,
Ezr 9:8; Jer 51:39
4 and my enemy will say, "I have
overcome him," Ps 25:2
and my foes will rejoice
when I fall.

5 But I trust in your unfailing
love;
my heart rejoices in your
salvation. Ps 9:14
6 I will sing the LORD's praise,
for he has been good to me.
Ps 116:7

Psalm 14

For the director of music. Of David.

1 The fool[c] says in his heart,
"There is no God." Ps 10:4
They are corrupt, their deeds
are vile;
there is no one who does
good.

2 The LORD looks down from
heaven Ps 33:13
on all mankind
to see if there are any who
understand, Ps 92:6
any who seek God.
3 All have turned away, all have
become corrupt; Ps 58:3
there is no one who does
good,
not even one. Ro 3:10-12*

4 Do all these evildoers know
nothing?

They devour my people as
though eating bread;
they never call on the LORD.
Isa 64:7
5 But there they are,
overwhelmed with
dread,
for God is present in
the company of the
righteous.

[a] *6* Probable reading of the original Hebrew text; Masoretic Text *earth* [b] In Hebrew texts 13:1-6 is numbered 13:2-6. [c] *1* The Hebrew words rendered *fool* in Psalms denote one who is morally deficient.

6 You evildoers frustrate the
plans of the poor,
but the LORD is their refuge. Ps 9:9

7 Oh, that salvation for Israel
would come out of
Zion!
When the LORD restores his
people, Ps 53:6
let Jacob rejoice and Israel be
glad!

Psalm 15

A psalm of David.

1 LORD, who may dwell in your
sacred tent? Ps 27:5-6
Who may live on your holy
mountain? Ps 24:3-5
2 The one whose walk is
blameless,
who does what is righteous,
who speaks the truth from
their heart; Eph 4:25
3 whose tongue utters no
slander, Ex 23:1
who does no wrong to a
neighbor,
and casts no slur on others;
4 who despises a vile person
but honors those who fear
the LORD; Ac 28:10
who keeps an oath even when
it hurts,
and does not change their
mind;
5 who lends money to the poor
without interest; Ex 22:25
who does not accept a bribe
against the innocent.
Whoever does these things
will never be shaken. 2Pe 1:10

Psalm 16

A *miktam*[a] of David.

1 Keep me safe, my God,
for in you I take refuge. Ps 7:1

2 I say to the LORD, "You are my
Lord;
apart from you I have no
good thing." Ps 73:25
3 I say of the holy people who are
in the land,
"They are the noble ones in
whom is all my delight." Ps 101:6
4 Those who run after other gods
will suffer more and
more. Ps 32:10
I will not pour out libations
of blood to such gods
or take up their names on
my lips. Ex 23:13

5 LORD, you alone are my portion
and my cup; Ps 23:5
you make my lot secure.
6 The boundary lines have fallen
for me in pleasant places;
surely I have a delightful
inheritance. Ps 78:55
7 I will praise the LORD, who
counsels me; Ps 73:24
even at night my heart
instructs me.
8 I keep my eyes always on the
LORD.
With him at my right hand, I
will not be shaken. Ps 73:23

[a] Title: Probably a literary or musical term

[9]Therefore my heart is glad
and my tongue rejoices; Ps 4:7
my body also will rest secure,
[10]because you will not abandon
me to the realm of the dead,
nor will you let your faithful[a]
one see decay. Ac 13:35*
[11]You make known to me the
path of life; Mt 7:14
you will fill me with joy in
your presence, Ac 2:25-28*
with eternal pleasures at
your right hand.

Psalm 17

A prayer of David.

[1]Hear me, LORD, my plea is just;
listen to my cry. Ps 61:1
Hear my prayer —
it does not rise from
deceitful lips. Isa 29:13
[2]Let my vindication come from
you;
may your eyes see what is
right.
[3]Though you probe my heart,
though you examine me at
night and test me,
you will find that I have
planned no evil; Job 23:10
my mouth has not
transgressed.
[4]Though people tried to bribe
me,
I have kept myself from the
ways of the violent
through what your lips have
commanded.
[5]My steps have held to your
paths; Ps 44:18
my feet have not stumbled.
[6]I call on you, my God, for you
will answer me; Ps 86:7
turn your ear to me and hear
my prayer. Ps 116:2
[7]Show me the wonders of your
great love, Ps 31:21
you who save by your right
hand
those who take refuge in you
from their foes.
[8]Keep me as the apple of your
eye; Dt 32:10
hide me in the shadow of
your wings
[9]from the wicked who are out to
destroy me,
from my mortal enemies
who surround me. Ps 109:3
[10]They close up their callous
hearts, Ps 73:7
and their mouths speak with
arrogance. 1Sa 2:3
[11]They have tracked me down,
they now surround me,
Ps 88:17
with eyes alert, to throw me
to the ground.
[12]They are like a lion hungry for
prey, Ps 7:2
like a fierce lion crouching in
cover.
[13]Rise up, LORD, confront them,
bring them down; Ps 73:18
with your sword rescue me
from the wicked.

[a] 10 Or *holy*

14 By your hand save me from
such people, LORD,
from those of this world
whose reward is in this
life. Lk 16:8
May what you have stored up
for the wicked fill their
bellies;
may their children gorge
themselves on it,
and may there be leftovers
for their little ones.
Ps 73:3-7

15 As for me, I will be vindicated
and will see your face;
when I awake, I will be
satisfied with seeing your
likeness. Ps 4:6-7; 16:11; 1Jn 3:2

Psalm 18[a]

For the director of music. Of David the servant of the LORD. He sang to the LORD the words of this song when the LORD delivered him from the hand of all his enemies and from the hand of Saul. He said:

1 I love you, LORD, my strength.
Ex 15:2

2 The LORD is my rock, my
fortress and my
deliverer; Ps 19:14
my God is my rock, in whom
I take refuge,
my shield[b] and the horn[c]
of my salvation, my
stronghold. Ps 59:11; 75:10

3 I called to the LORD, who is
worthy of praise, Ps 48:1
and I have been saved from
my enemies.

4 The cords of death entangled
me; Ps 116:3
the torrents of destruction
overwhelmed me. Ps 124:4
5 The cords of the grave coiled
around me;
the snares of death
confronted me. Ps 116:3

6 In my distress I called to the
LORD;
I cried to my God for help.
From his temple he heard my
voice; Ps 34:15
my cry came before him, into
his ears.
7 The earth trembled and
quaked, Jdg 5:4
and the foundations of the
mountains shook;
they trembled because he
was angry. Ps 68:7-8
8 Smoke rose from his nostrils;
consuming fire came from
his mouth, Ps 50:3
burning coals blazed out of it.
9 He parted the heavens and
came down; Ps 144:5
dark clouds were under his
feet.
10 He mounted the cherubim and
flew;
he soared on the wings of the
wind. Ps 104:3
11 He made darkness his
covering, his canopy
around him —
the dark rain clouds of the
sky. Ps 97:2

[a] In Hebrew texts 18:1-50 is numbered 18:2-51.
[b] 2 Or *sovereign* [c] 2 *Horn* here symbolizes strength.

12 Out of the brightness of
his presence clouds
advanced, Ps 104:2
with hailstones and bolts of
lightning.
13 The LORD thundered from
heaven;
the voice of the Most High
resounded.[a] Ps 29:3
14 He shot his arrows and
scattered the enemy,
with great bolts of lightning
he routed them. Ps 144:6
15 The valleys of the sea were
exposed
and the foundations of the
earth laid bare
at your rebuke, LORD, Ps 76:6; 106:9
at the blast of breath from
your nostrils.

16 He reached down from on
high and took hold of
me;
he drew me out of deep
waters. Ps 144:7
17 He rescued me from my
powerful enemy,
from my foes, who were too
strong for me. Ps 35:10
18 They confronted me in the day
of my disaster,
but the LORD was my
support. Ps 59:16
19 He brought me out into a
spacious place; Ps 31:8
he rescued me because he
delighted in me. Ps 118:5

20 The LORD has dealt with
me according to my
righteousness;
according to the cleanness
of my hands he has
rewarded me. Ps 24:4
21 For I have kept the ways of the
LORD; 2Ch 34:33
I am not guilty of turning
from my God.
22 All his laws are before me;
I have not turned away from
his decrees. Ps 119:30
23 I have been blameless before
him
and have kept myself from
sin.
24 The LORD has rewarded
me according to my
righteousness, 1Sa 26:23
according to the cleanness
of my hands in his
sight.

25 To the faithful you show
yourself faithful,
1Ki 8:32; Mt 5:7
to the blameless you show
yourself blameless,
26 to the pure you show yourself
pure, Mt 5:8
but to the devious you
show yourself shrewd.
Pr 3:34
27 You save the humble
but bring low those whose
eyes are haughty. Pr 6:17
28 You, LORD, keep my lamp
burning;
my God turns my darkness
into light. Job 18:6

[a] *13* Some Hebrew manuscripts and Septuagint (see also 2 Samuel 22:14); most Hebrew manuscripts *resounded, / amid hailstones and bolts of lightning*

29 With your help I can advance
against a troop[a]; Heb 11:34
with my God I can scale a
wall.

30 As for God, his way is perfect: Dt 32:4
The LORD's word is flawless; Ps 12:6
he shields all who take
refuge in him.
31 For who is God besides the
LORD? Dt 32:39; Ps 86:8; Isa 45:5-6,14,18,21
And who is the Rock except
our God? Dt 32:31
32 It is God who arms me with
strength
and keeps my way secure.
33 He makes my feet like the feet
of a deer; Hab 3:19
he causes me to stand on the
heights. Dt 32:13
34 He trains my hands for battle; Ps 144:1
my arms can bend a bow of
bronze.
35 You make your saving help my
shield,
and your right hand sustains
me; Ps 119:116
your help has made me
great.
36 You provide a broad path for
my feet,
so that my ankles do not give
way.

37 I pursued my enemies and
overtook them; Ps 37:20
I did not turn back till they
were destroyed.
38 I crushed them so that they
could not rise; Ps 36:12
they fell beneath my feet.
39 You armed me with strength
for battle;
you humbled my adversaries
before me.
40 You made my enemies turn
their backs in flight, Ps 21:12
and I destroyed my foes.
41 They cried for help, but there
was no one to save
them — Ps 50:22
to the LORD, but he did not
answer. Pr 1:28
42 I beat them as fine as
windblown dust;
I trampled them[b] like mud
in the streets.
43 You have delivered me from
the attacks of the people;
you have made me the head
of nations. 2Sa 8:1-14
People I did not know now
serve me, Isa 52:15; 55:5
44 foreigners cower before me;
as soon as they hear of me,
they obey me. Ps 66:3
45 They all lose heart;
they come trembling from
their strongholds. Mic 7:17

46 The LORD lives! Praise be to my
Rock!
Exalted be God my Savior! Ps 51:14

[a] 29 Or *can run through a barricade*
[b] 42 Many Hebrew manuscripts, Septuagint, Syriac and Targum (see also 2 Samuel 22:43); Masoretic Text *I poured them out*

[47]He is the God who avenges
me,
who subdues nations under
me, Ps 47:3
48 who saves me from my
enemies. Ps 59:1
You exalted me above my foes;
from a violent man you
rescued me.
[49]Therefore I will praise you,
LORD, among the
nations;
I will sing the praises of your
name. Ps 108:1; Ro 15:9*

[50]He gives his king great
victories;
he shows unfailing love to
his anointed,
to David and to his
descendants forever.
Ps 144:10

Psalm 19[a]

For the director of music. A psalm of David.

[1]The heavens declare the glory
of God; Isa 40:22; Ro 1:19
the skies proclaim the work
of his hands.
[2]Day after day they pour forth
speech;
night after night they reveal
knowledge. Ps 74:16
[3]They have no speech, they use
no words;
no sound is heard from
them.
[4]Yet their voice[b] goes out into
all the earth,
their words to the ends of
the world. Ro 10:18*
In the heavens God has pitched
a tent for the sun. Ps 104:2
5 It is like a bridegroom
coming out of his
chamber,
like a champion rejoicing to
run his course.
[6]It rises at one end of the
heavens
and makes its circuit to the
other; Ps 113:3
nothing is deprived of its
warmth.

[7]The law of the LORD is perfect,
refreshing the soul. Ps 23:3
The statutes of the LORD are
trustworthy, Ps 93:5; 111:7
making wise the simple.
Ps 119:98-100
[8]The precepts of the LORD are
right, Ps 119:128
giving joy to the heart.
The commands of the LORD are
radiant,
giving light to the eyes.
[9]The fear of the LORD is pure,
enduring forever.
The decrees of the LORD are
firm,
and all of them are
righteous. Ps 119:138,142

[10]They are more precious than
gold, Pr 8:10
than much pure gold;
they are sweeter than honey,
than honey from the
honeycomb.

[a] In Hebrew texts 19:1-14 is numbered 19:2-15.
[b] 4 Septuagint, Jerome and Syriac; Hebrew *measuring line*

[11]By them your servant is
warned;
in keeping them there is
great reward.
[12]But who can discern their own
errors?
Forgive my hidden faults.
Ps 51:2; 90:8
[13]Keep your servant also from
willful sins;
may they not rule over me.
Then I will be blameless,
innocent of great
transgression.
[14]May these words of my mouth
and this meditation of
my heart
be pleasing in your sight,
Ps 104:34
LORD, my Rock and my
Redeemer. Ps 18:2; Isa 47:4

Psalm 20[a]

For the director of music. A psalm of David.

[1]May the LORD answer you when
you are in distress;
may the name of the God of
Jacob protect you. Ps 91:14
[2]May he send you help from the
sanctuary
and grant you support from
Zion.
[3]May he remember all your
sacrifices Ac 10:4
and accept your burnt
offerings.[b] Ps 51:19
[4]May he give you the desire of
your heart Ps 21:2; 145:16,19
and make all your plans
succeed.
[5]May we shout for joy over your
victory
and lift up our banners in
the name of our God.
Ps 59:14; 60:4
May the LORD grant all your
requests. 1Sa 1:17
[6]Now this I know:
The LORD gives victory to his
anointed. Ps 28:8
He answers him from his
heavenly sanctuary
with the victorious power of
his right hand.
[7]Some trust in chariots and
some in horses,
but we trust in the name
of the LORD our God.
2Ch 32:8
[8]They are brought to their knees
and fall,
but we rise up and stand
firm. Ps 37:23
[9]LORD, give victory to the king!
Answer us when we call! Ps 17:6

Psalm 21[c]

For the director of music. A psalm of David.

[1]The king rejoices in your
strength, LORD.
How great is his joy in the
victories you give!
Ps 59:16-17
[2]You have granted him his
heart's desire Ps 37:4

[a] In Hebrew texts 20:1-9 is numbered 20:2-10.
[b] 3 The Hebrew has *Selah* (a word of uncertain meaning) here.
[c] In Hebrew texts 21:1-13 is numbered 21:2-14.

and have not withheld the
request of his lips.[a]
3 You came to greet him with
rich blessings
and placed a crown of pure
gold on his head. 2Sa 12:30
4 He asked you for life, and you
gave it to him —
length of days, for ever and
ever. Ps 133:3
5 Through the victories you gave,
his glory is great; Ps 18:50
you have bestowed on him
splendor and majesty.
6 Surely you have granted him
unending blessings
and made him glad with the
joy of your presence.
1Ch 17:27
7 For the king trusts in the LORD;
through the unfailing love of
the Most High
he will not be shaken. Ps 15:5

8 Your hand will lay hold on all
your enemies;
your right hand will seize
your foes. Isa 10:10
9 When you appear for battle,
you will burn them up as
in a blazing furnace.
Ps 50:3; La 2:2; Mal 4:1
The LORD will swallow them up
in his wrath,
and his fire will consume
them.
10 You will destroy their
descendants from the
earth,
their posterity from
mankind. Dt 28:18
11 Though they plot evil against
you Ps 2:1
and devise wicked schemes,
they cannot succeed.
Ps 10:2
12 You will make them turn their
backs Ps 7:12-13; 18:40
when you aim at them with
drawn bow.

13 Be exalted in your strength,
LORD; Ps 18:46
we will sing and praise your
might.

Psalm 22[b]

For the director of music. To the tune of "The Doe of the Morning." A psalm of David.

1 My God, my God, why have you
forsaken me? Mt 27:46*
Why are you so far from
saving me,
so far from my cries of
anguish?
2 My God, I cry out by day, but
you do not answer,
by night, but I find no rest.[c]
Ps 42:3

3 Yet you are enthroned as the
Holy One; Ps 99:9
you are the one Israel
praises.[d] Dt 10:21
4 In you our ancestors put their
trust;
they trusted and you
delivered them.

[a] 2 The Hebrew has *Selah* (a word of uncertain meaning) here. [b] In Hebrew texts 22:1-31 is numbered 22:2-32. [c] 2 Or *night, and am not silent* [d] 3 Or *Yet you are holy, / enthroned on the praises of Israel*

5 To you they cried out and were
saved;
in you they trusted and were
not put to shame. Isa 49:23

6 But I am a worm and not a
man, Job 25:6
scorned by everyone,
despised by the people.
Ps 31:11

7 All who see me mock me;
they hurl insults, shaking
their heads. Mt 27:39,44
8 "He trusts in the LORD," they
say,
"let the LORD rescue him.
Ps 91:14

Let him deliver him,
since he delights in him."
Mt 27:43

9 Yet you brought me out of the
womb; Ps 71:6
you made me trust in you,
even at my mother's
breast.
10 From birth I was cast on you;
Isa 46:3
from my mother's womb you
have been my God.

11 Do not be far from me,
for trouble is near
and there is no one to help.
Ps 72:12

12 Many bulls surround me; Ps 68:30
strong bulls of Bashan
encircle me.
13 Roaring lions that tear their
prey Ps 17:12
open their mouths wide
against me.

14 I am poured out like water,
and all my bones are out of
joint.
My heart has turned to wax;
it has melted within me. Da 5:6
15 My mouth[a] is dried up like a
potsherd,
and my tongue sticks to the
roof of my mouth;
you lay me in the dust of
death. Ps 104:29

16 Dogs surround me,
a pack of villains encircles
me;
they pierce[b] my hands and
my feet. Isa 53:5; Jn 19:34
17 All my bones are on display;
people stare and gloat over
me. Lk 23:35
18 They divide my clothes among
them
and cast lots for my garment.
Jn 19:24*

19 But you, LORD, do not be far
from me.
You are my strength; come
quickly to help me. Ps 70:5
20 Deliver me from the sword,
my precious life from the
power of the dogs. Ps 35:17
21 Rescue me from the mouth of
the lions;
save me from the horns of
the wild oxen.

[a] 15 Probable reading of the original Hebrew text; Masoretic Text *strength*
[b] 16 Dead Sea Scrolls and some manuscripts of the Masoretic Text, Septuagint and Syriac; most manuscripts of the Masoretic Text *me, / like a lion*

22 I will declare your name to my people;
in the assembly I will praise you. Heb 2:12*
23 You who fear the LORD, praise him! Ps 135:19
All you descendants of Jacob, honor him!
Revere him, all you descendants of Israel! Ps 33:8
24 For he has not despised or scorned
the suffering of the afflicted one;
he has not hidden his face from him Ps 69:17
but has listened to his cry for help. Heb 5:7

25 From you comes the theme of my praise in the great assembly; Ps 35:18
before those who fear you[a] I will fulfill my vows.
26 The poor will eat and be satisfied; Ps 107:9
those who seek the LORD will praise him — Ps 40:16
may your hearts live forever!

27 All the ends of the earth Ps 2:8
will remember and turn to the LORD,
and all the families of the nations
will bow down before him, Ps 86:9
28 for dominion belongs to the LORD
and he rules over the nations. Ps 47:7-8

29 All the rich of the earth will feast and worship; Ps 45:12
all who go down to the dust will kneel before him — Isa 26:19
those who cannot keep themselves alive.
30 Posterity will serve him; Ps 102:28
future generations will be told about the Lord.
31 They will proclaim his righteousness,
declaring to a people yet unborn: Ps 78:6
He has done it!

Psalm 23

A psalm of David.

1 The LORD is my shepherd,
I lack nothing. Isa 40:11; Jn 10:11; Php 4:19
2 He makes me lie down in green pastures,
he leads me beside quiet waters, Eze 34:14; Rev 7:17
3 he refreshes my soul.
He guides me along the right paths Ps 5:8
for his name's sake.
4 Even though I walk
through the darkest valley,[b] Job 10:21-22
I will fear no evil, Ps 3:6; 27:1
for you are with me; Isa 43:2
your rod and your staff,
they comfort me.

[a] 25 Hebrew *him* [b] 4 Or *the valley of the shadow of death*

5 You prepare a table before me
in the presence of my
enemies.
You anoint my head with oil; Ps 92:10
my cup overflows. Ps 16:5
6 Surely your goodness and love
will follow me
all the days of my life,
and I will dwell in the house of
the LORD
forever.

Psalm 24

Of David. A psalm.

1 The earth is the LORD's, and
everything in it, Ps 89:11
the world, and all who live in
it; 1Co 10:26
2 for he founded it on the seas
and established it on the
waters.

3 Who may ascend the mountain
of the LORD?
Who may stand in his holy
place? Ps 15:1
4 The one who has clean hands
and a pure heart,
Job 17:9; Mt 5:8
who does not trust in an idol
or swear by a false god.[a]

5 They will receive blessing from
the LORD
and vindication from God
their Savior. Ps 17:2
6 Such is the generation of those
who seek him,
who seek your face, God of
Jacob.[b,c] Ps 27:8

7 Lift up your heads, you gates;
Isa 26:2
be lifted up, you ancient
doors,
that the King of glory may
come in. Ps 97:6; 1Co 2:8
8 Who is this King of glory?
The LORD strong and mighty,
the LORD mighty in battle.
Ps 76:3-6
9 Lift up your heads, you gates;
lift them up, you ancient
doors,
that the King of glory may
come in.
10 Who is he, this King of glory?
The LORD Almighty— 1Sa 1:11
he is the King of glory.

Psalm 25[d]

Of David.

1 In you, LORD my God,
I put my trust. Ps 86:4

2 I trust in you;
do not let me be put to shame,
nor let my enemies triumph
over me.
3 No one who hopes in you
will ever be put to shame,
Isa 49:23
but shame will come on those
who are treacherous without
cause.

[a] 4 Or *swear falsely* [b] 6 Two Hebrew manuscripts and Syriac (see also Septuagint); most Hebrew manuscripts *face, Jacob* [c] 6 The Hebrew has *Selah* (a word of uncertain meaning) here and at the end of verse 10. [d] This psalm is an acrostic poem, the verses of which begin with the successive letters of the Hebrew alphabet.

[4] Show me your ways, LORD,
teach me your paths. Ex 33:13
[5] Guide me in your truth and teach me,
for you are God my Savior,
and my hope is in you all day long.
[6] Remember, LORD, your great mercy and love, Ps 103:17; Isa 63:7,15
for they are from of old.
[7] Do not remember the sins of my youth Job 13:26; Jer 3:25
and my rebellious ways;
according to your love remember me, Ps 51:1
for you, LORD, are good.
[8] Good and upright is the LORD; Ps 92:15
therefore he instructs sinners in his ways. Ps 32:8
[9] He guides the humble in what is right Ps 23:3
and teaches them his way.
[10] All the ways of the LORD are loving and faithful
toward those who keep the demands of his covenant. Ps 103:18
[11] For the sake of your name, LORD, Ps 31:3; 79:9
forgive my iniquity, though it is great.

[12] Who, then, are those who fear the LORD?
He will instruct them in the ways they should choose.[a] Ps 37:23
[13] They will spend their days in prosperity, Pr 19:23
and their descendants will inherit the land.
[14] The LORD confides in those who fear him; Pr 3:32
he makes his covenant known to them.
[15] My eyes are ever on the LORD, Ps 141:8
for only he will release my feet from the snare.

[16] Turn to me and be gracious to me, Ps 69:16
for I am lonely and afflicted.
[17] Relieve the troubles of my heart
and free me from my anguish. Ps 107:6
[18] Look on my affliction and my distress 2Sa 16:12
and take away all my sins.
[19] See how numerous are my enemies Ps 3:1
and how fiercely they hate me!
[20] Guard my life and rescue me; Ps 86:2
do not let me be put to shame,
for I take refuge in you.
[21] May integrity and uprightness protect me, Ps 41:12
because my hope, LORD,[b] is in you.

[22] Deliver Israel, O God,
from all their troubles! Ps 130:8

[a] 12 Or *ways he chooses* [b] 21 Septuagint; Hebrew does not have *LORD*.

Psalm 26

Of David.

[1]Vindicate me, LORD,
for I have led a blameless
life; Ps 7:8
I have trusted in the LORD
and have not faltered.
2Ki 20:3; Heb 10:23

[2]Test me, LORD, and try me,
examine my heart and my
mind; Ps 7:9
[3]for I have always been
mindful of your
unfailing love
and have lived in reliance on
your faithfulness. 2Ki 20:3

[4]I do not sit with the deceitful,
Ps 1:1
nor do I associate with
hypocrites.
[5]I abhor the assembly of
evildoers Ps 139:21
and refuse to sit with the
wicked.
[6]I wash my hands in innocence,
Ps 73:13
and go about your altar,
LORD,
[7]proclaiming aloud your praise
and telling of all your
wonderful deeds. Ps 9:1

[8]LORD, I love the house where
you live, Ps 27:4
the place where your glory
dwells.
[9]Do not take away my soul
along with sinners,
my life with those who are
bloodthirsty, Ps 28:3
[10]in whose hands are wicked
schemes,
whose right hands are full of
bribes. 1Sa 8:3
[11]I lead a blameless life;
deliver me and be merciful
to me. Ps 69:18

[12]My feet stand on level ground;
Ps 27:11; 40:2
in the great congregation I
will praise the LORD.

Psalm 27

Of David.

[1]The LORD is my light and my
salvation — Ex 15:2; Isa 60:19
whom shall I fear?
The LORD is the stronghold of
my life —
of whom shall I be afraid?
Ps 118:6

[2]When the wicked advance
against me
to devour[a] me,
it is my enemies and my foes
who will stumble and fall.
Ps 14:4
[3]Though an army besiege me,
my heart will not fear; Ps 3:6
though war break out against
me,
even then I will be confident.

[4]One thing I ask from the LORD,
Ps 90:17
this only do I seek:
that I may dwell in the house
of the LORD
all the days of my life, Ps 26:8

[a] 2 Or *slander*

to gaze on the beauty of the
LORD
and to seek him in his
temple.
5 For in the day of trouble
he will keep me safe in his
dwelling;
he will hide me in the shelter
of his sacred tent Ps 17:8
and set me high upon a rock.
Ps 40:2

6 Then my head will be exalted
Ps 3:3
above the enemies who
surround me;
at his sacred tent I will sacrifice
with shouts of joy; Ps 107:22
I will sing and make music to
the LORD.

7 Hear my voice when I call,
LORD;
be merciful to me and
answer me. Ps 13:3
8 My heart says of you, "Seek his
face!"
Your face, LORD, I will seek.
9 Do not hide your face from me,
Ps 69:17
do not turn your servant
away in anger;
you have been my helper.
Do not reject me or forsake me,
God my Savior.
10 Though my father and mother
forsake me,
the LORD will receive me.
11 Teach me your way, LORD;
lead me in a straight path
Ps 25:4
because of my oppressors.
12 Do not turn me over to the
desire of my foes,
for false witnesses rise
up against me,
Mt 26:60; Ac 9:1
spouting malicious
accusations.

13 I remain confident of this:
I will see the goodness of the
LORD Ps 31:19
in the land of the living.
Jer 11:19; Eze 26:20
14 Wait for the LORD;
be strong and take heart
and wait for the LORD. Ps 40:1

Psalm 28

Of David.

1 To you, LORD, I call;
you are my Rock,
do not turn a deaf ear
to me.
For if you remain silent, Ps 83:1
I will be like those who go
down to the pit. Ps 88:4
2 Hear my cry for mercy Ps 138:2
as I call to you for help,
as I lift up my hands
toward your Most Holy Place.
Ps 5:7

3 Do not drag me away with the
wicked,
with those who do evil,
who speak cordially with their
neighbors
but harbor malice in their
hearts. Ps 12:2
4 Repay them for their deeds
and for their evil work;

repay them for what their
hands have done 2Ti 4:14
and bring back on them
what they deserve.
Rev 18:6

5 Because they have no regard
for the deeds of the
LORD
and what his hands have
done, Isa 5:12
he will tear them down
and never build them up
again.

6 Praise be to the LORD,
for he has heard my cry for
mercy.
7 The LORD is my strength and
my shield; Ps 18:1
my heart trusts in him, and
he helps me. Ps 13:5
My heart leaps for joy,
and with my song I praise
him. Ps 40:3; 69:30

8 The LORD is the strength of his
people,
a fortress of salvation for his
anointed one. Ps 20:6
9 Save your people and bless
your inheritance; Dt 9:29
be their shepherd and
carry them forever.
Dt 1:31; Isa 40:11

Psalm 29

A psalm of David.

1 Ascribe to the LORD, you
heavenly beings, 1Ch 16:28
ascribe to the LORD glory and
strength. Ps 96:7-9
2 Ascribe to the LORD the glory
due his name;
worship the LORD in the
splendor of his[a]
holiness. 2Ch 20:21

3 The voice of the LORD is over
the waters; Job 37:5
the God of glory thunders,
the LORD thunders over the
mighty waters.
4 The voice of the LORD is
powerful; Ps 68:33
the voice of the LORD is
majestic.
5 The voice of the LORD breaks
the cedars;
the LORD breaks in pieces the
cedars of Lebanon. Jdg 9:15
6 He makes Lebanon leap like a
calf, Ps 114:4
Sirion[b] like a young wild ox.
Dt 3:9

7 The voice of the LORD strikes
with flashes of lightning.
8 The voice of the LORD shakes
the desert;
the LORD shakes the Desert
of Kadesh. Nu 13:26
9 The voice of the LORD twists
the oaks[c]
and strips the forests bare.
And in his temple all cry,
"Glory!" Ps 26:8

10 The LORD sits enthroned over
the flood;
the LORD is enthroned as
King forever. Ps 10:16

[a] 2 Or *LORD with the splendor of* [b] 6 That is, Mount Hermon [c] 9 Or *LORD makes the deer give birth*

[11]The LORD gives strength to his
people; Ps 28:8
the LORD blesses his people
with peace. Ps 37:11

Psalm 30[a]

A psalm. A song. For the dedication of the temple.[b] Of David.

[1]I will exalt you, LORD,
for you lifted me out of the
depths
and did not let my enemies
gloat over me. Ps 25:2
[2]LORD my God, I called to you
for help,
and you healed me. Ps 6:2
[3]You, LORD, brought me up from
the realm of the dead;
you spared me from going
down to the pit. Ps 86:13

[4]Sing the praises of the LORD,
you his faithful people; Ps 149:1
praise his holy name.
[5]For his anger lasts only a
moment, Ps 103:9
but his favor lasts a lifetime;
weeping may stay for the night,
but rejoicing comes in the
morning. 2Co 4:17

[6]When I felt secure, I said,
"I will never be shaken."
[7]LORD, when you favored me,
you made my royal
mountain[c] stand firm;
but when you hid your face,
I was dismayed. Ps 104:29

[8]To you, LORD, I called;
to the Lord I cried for mercy:
[9]"What is gained if I am
silenced,
if I go down to the pit?
Will the dust praise you?
Will it proclaim your
faithfulness? Ps 6:5
[10]Hear, LORD, and be merciful to
me; Ps 4:1
LORD, be my help."

[11]You turned my wailing into
dancing;
you removed my sackcloth
and clothed me with joy,
Ps 4:7; Jer 31:4,13
[12]that my heart may sing your
praises and not be silent.
LORD my God, I will praise
you forever. Ps 16:9; 44:8

Psalm 31[d]

For the director of music. A psalm of David.

[1]In you, LORD, I have taken
refuge; Ps 7:1
let me never be put to
shame;
deliver me in your
righteousness.
[2]Turn your ear to me,
come quickly to my rescue;
be my rock of refuge,
a strong fortress to save me.
[3]Since you are my rock and my
fortress, Ps 18:2
for the sake of your
name lead and
guide me. Ps 23:3

[a] In Hebrew texts 30:1-12 is numbered 30:2-13. [b] Title: Or *palace* [c] 7 That is, Mount Zion [d] In Hebrew texts 31:1-24 is numbered 31:2-25.

4 Keep me free from the trap
that is set for me,
for you are my refuge. Ps 71:1-3
5 Into your hands I commit my
spirit; Lk 23:46
deliver me, LORD, my faithful
God.

6 I hate those who cling to
worthless idols;
as for me, I trust in the LORD.
Jnh 2:8
7 I will be glad and rejoice in
your love,
for you saw my affliction
and knew the anguish of my
soul. Ps 10:14; Jn 10:27
8 You have not given me into
the hands of the enemy
Dt 32:30
but have set my feet in a
spacious place.

9 Be merciful to me, LORD, for I
am in distress;
my eyes grow weak with
sorrow, Ps 6:7
my soul and body with grief.
10 My life is consumed by anguish
and my years by groaning;
my strength fails because of
my affliction,[a]
and my bones grow weak.
Ps 38:3; 39:11
11 Because of all my enemies,
I am the utter contempt
of my neighbors
Ps 38:11; Isa 53:4
and an object of dread to my
closest friends —
those who see me on the
street flee from me.
12 I am forgotten as though I were
dead; Ps 88:4
I have become like broken
pottery.
13 For I hear many whispering,
"Terror on every side!" Jer 20:3,10
They conspire against me
and plot to take my life. Mt 27:1

14 But I trust in you, LORD; Ps 140:6
I say, "You are my God."
15 My times are in your hands;
deliver me from the hands of
my enemies,
from those who pursue me.
16 Let your face shine on your
servant; Ps 4:6
save me in your unfailing
love.
17 Let me not be put to shame,
LORD, Ps 25:2-3
for I have cried out to you;
but let the wicked be put to
shame
and be silent in the realm of
the dead.
18 Let their lying lips be silenced,
Ps 120:2
for with pride and contempt
they speak arrogantly
against the righteous.
Ps 94:4

19 How abundant are the good
things
that you have stored up for
those who fear you,
that you bestow in the sight of
all, Isa 64:4
on those who take refuge in
you.

[a] 10 Or *guilt*

[20] In the shelter of your presence
you hide them Ps 27:5
from all human intrigues; Job 5:21
you keep them safe in your dwelling
from accusing tongues.

[21] Praise be to the LORD,
for he showed me the wonders of his love Ps 17:7
when I was in a city under siege. 1Sa 23:7
[22] In my alarm I said, Ps 116:11
"I am cut off from your sight!"
Yet you heard my cry for mercy
when I called to you for help. Ps 145:19

[23] Love the LORD, all his faithful people! Ps 34:9
The LORD preserves those who are true to him,
but the proud he pays back in full. Ps 94:2
[24] Be strong and take heart, Ps 27:14
all you who hope in the LORD.

Psalm 32

Of David. A *maskil*.[a]

[1] Blessed is the one
whose transgressions are forgiven,
whose sins are covered. Ps 85:2
[2] Blessed is the one
whose sin the LORD does not count against them 2Co 5:19
and in whose spirit is no deceit. Jn 1:47

[3] When I kept silent,
my bones wasted away Ps 31:10
through my groaning all day long.
[4] For day and night
your hand was heavy on me; Job 33:7
my strength was sapped
as in the heat of summer.[b]

[5] Then I acknowledged my sin to you
and did not cover up my iniquity.
I said, "I will confess Pr 28:13
my transgressions to the LORD."
And you forgave
the guilt of my sin. Lev 26:40

[6] Therefore let all the faithful pray to you
while you may be found; Ps 69:13
surely the rising of the mighty waters
will not reach them.
[7] You are my hiding place;
you will protect me from trouble Ps 9:9
and surround me with songs of deliverance. Ex 15:1

[8] I will instruct you and teach you in the way you should go;
I will counsel you with my loving eye on you. Ps 33:18

[a] Title: Probably a literary or musical term
[b] 4 The Hebrew has *Selah* (a word of uncertain meaning) here and at the end of verses 5 and 7.

9 Do not be like the horse or the mule,
which have no understanding
but must be controlled by bit and bridle
or they will not come to you. Pr 26:3

10 Many are the woes of the wicked, Ro 2:9
but the LORD's unfailing love
surrounds the one who trusts in him. Pr 16:20

11 Rejoice in the LORD and be glad, you righteous; Ps 64:10
sing, all you who are upright in heart!

Psalm 33

1 Sing joyfully to the LORD, you righteous;
it is fitting for the upright to praise him. Ps 32:11; 147:1
2 Praise the LORD with the harp;
make music to him on the ten-stringed lyre.
3 Sing to him a new song; Ps 96:1
play skillfully, and shout for joy.

4 For the word of the LORD is right and true; Ps 19:8
he is faithful in all he does.
5 The LORD loves righteousness and justice; Ps 11:7
the earth is full of his unfailing love. Ps 119:64

6 By the word of the LORD the heavens were made, Heb 11:3
their starry host by the breath of his mouth.
7 He gathers the waters of the sea into jars[a];
he puts the deep into storehouses.
8 Let all the earth fear the LORD;
let all the people of the world revere him. Ps 67:7; 96:9
9 For he spoke, and it came to be;
he commanded, and it stood firm. Ge 1:3

10 The LORD foils the plans of the nations; Isa 8:10
he thwarts the purposes of the peoples.
11 But the plans of the LORD stand firm forever,
the purposes of his heart through all generations. Job 23:13

12 Blessed is the nation whose God is the LORD,
the people he chose for his inheritance. Ex 19:5; Dt 7:6
13 From heaven the LORD looks down
and sees all mankind; Job 28:24; Ps 11:4
14 from his dwelling place he watches
all who live on earth —
15 he who forms the hearts of all,
who considers everything they do. Jer 32:19

[a] 7 Or *sea as into a heap*

[16]No king is saved by the size of
his army;
no warrior escapes by his
great strength.
[17]A horse is a vain hope for
deliverance; Ps 20:7
despite all its great strength
it cannot save.
[18]But the eyes of the LORD are
on those who fear him,
Ps 34:15
on those whose hope is in his
unfailing love, Ps 147:11
[19]to deliver them from death
and keep them alive in
famine. Job 5:20
[20]We wait in hope for the LORD;
Ps 130:6
he is our help and our shield.
[21]In him our hearts rejoice, Jn 16:22
for we trust in his holy name.
[22]May your unfailing love be
with us, LORD,
even as we put our hope in
you. Ps 6:4

Psalm 34[a,b]

Of David. When he pretended to be insane before Abimelek, who drove him away, and he left.

[1]I will extol the LORD at all
times;
his praise will always be on
my lips. Ps 71:6; Eph 5:20
[2]I will glory in the LORD; Jer 9:24
let the afflicted hear and
rejoice.
[3]Glorify the LORD with me;
let us exalt his name
together. Lk 1:46
[4]I sought the LORD, and he
answered me; Mt 7:7
he delivered me from all my
fears.
[5]Those who look to him are
radiant; Ps 36:9
their faces are never covered
with shame.
[6]This poor man called, and the
LORD heard him;
he saved him out of all his
troubles. Ps 25:17
[7]The angel of the LORD
encamps around
those who fear him,
Da 6:22
and he delivers them.
[8]Taste and see that the LORD is
good; 1Pe 2:3
blessed is the one who takes
refuge in him. Ps 2:12
[9]Fear the LORD, you his holy
people,
for those who fear him lack
nothing. Ps 23:1
[10]The lions may grow weak and
hungry,
but those who seek the
LORD lack no good thing.
Ps 84:11
[11]Come, my children, listen to
me;
I will teach you the fear of
the LORD.
[12]Whoever of you loves life 1Pe 3:10
and desires to see many good
days,

[a] This psalm is an acrostic poem, the verses of which begin with the successive letters of the Hebrew alphabet. [b] In Hebrew texts 34:1-22 is numbered 34:2-23.

13 keep your tongue from evil
and your lips from telling lies.
14 Turn from evil and do good; Ps 37:27
seek peace and pursue it. Heb 12:14

15 The eyes of the LORD are on the righteous, Job 36:7
and his ears are attentive to their cry;
16 but the face of the LORD is against those who do evil,
to blot out their name from the earth. Pr 10:7

17 The righteous cry out, and the LORD hears them; Ps 145:19
he delivers them from all their troubles.
18 The LORD is close to the brokenhearted Isa 57:15
and saves those who are crushed in spirit.

19 The righteous person may have many troubles,
but the LORD delivers him from them all; Pr 24:16
20 he protects all his bones,
not one of them will be broken. Jn 19:36

21 Evil will slay the wicked; Ps 94:23
the foes of the righteous will be condemned.
22 The LORD will rescue his servants; 1Ki 1:29
no one who takes refuge in him will be condemned.

Psalm 35

Of David.

1 Contend, LORD, with those who contend with me;
fight against those who fight against me. Ps 43:1
2 Take up shield and armor;
arise and come to my aid. Ps 62:2
3 Brandish spear and javelin[a]
against those who pursue me.
Say to me,
"I am your salvation."

4 May those who seek my life
be disgraced and put to shame; Ps 70:2
may those who plot my ruin
be turned back in dismay.
5 May they be like chaff before the wind, Job 21:18
with the angel of the LORD driving them away;
6 may their path be dark and slippery,
with the angel of the LORD pursuing them.

7 Since they hid their net for me without cause
and without cause dug a pit for me, Ps 7:4
8 may ruin overtake them by surprise — 1Th 5:3
may the net they hid entangle them,
may they fall into the pit, to their ruin.

[a] 3 Or *and block the way*

9 Then my soul will rejoice in the
LORD Lk 1:47
and delight in his salvation.
Isa 61:10
10 My whole being will exclaim,
"Who is like you, LORD? Ex 15:11
You rescue the poor from
those too strong for
them,
the poor and needy from
those who rob them."
Ps 37:14
11 Ruthless witnesses come
forward;
they question me on
things I know nothing
about.
12 They repay me evil for good
Jn 10:32
and leave me like one
bereaved.
13 Yet when they were ill, I put on
sackcloth
and humbled myself with
fasting. Job 30:25
When my prayers returned to
me unanswered,
14 I went about mourning Ps 38:6
as though for my friend or
brother.
I bowed my head in grief
as though weeping for my
mother.
15 But when I stumbled, they
gathered in glee;
assailants gathered against
me without my
knowledge.
They slandered me without
ceasing. Job 30:1,8
16 Like the ungodly they
maliciously mocked;[a]
they gnashed their teeth at
me. La 2:16
17 How long, Lord, will you look
on? Hab 1:13
Rescue me from their
ravages,
my precious life from these
lions. Ps 22:20
18 I will give you thanks in the
great assembly;
among the throngs I will
praise you. Ps 22:22
19 Do not let those gloat over me
who are my enemies without
cause;
do not let those who hate
me without reason
Ps 38:19; 69:4
maliciously wink the eye.
Ps 13:4
20 They do not speak peaceably,
but devise false accusations
against those who live
quietly in the land.
21 They sneer at me and say,
"Aha! Aha! Ps 22:13; 40:15
With our own eyes we have
seen it."
22 LORD, you have seen this; do
not be silent. Ex 3:7
Do not be far from me, Lord.
Ps 10:1
23 Awake, and rise to my defense!
Ps 44:23
Contend for me, my God and
Lord.

[a] 16 Septuagint; Hebrew may mean *Like an ungodly circle of mockers,*

24 Vindicate me in your
righteousness, LORD my
God;
do not let them gloat over
me. Ps 22:17
25 Do not let them think,
"Aha, just what we
wanted!"
or say, "We have swallowed
him up." La 2:16

26 May all who gloat over my
distress
be put to shame and
confusion; Ps 40:14; 109:29
may all who exalt themselves
over me
be clothed with shame and
disgrace.
27 May those who delight in my
vindication Ps 9:4
shout for joy and gladness;
may they always say, "The LORD
be exalted,
who delights in the well-
being of his servant."
Ps 147:11

28 My tongue will proclaim your
righteousness, Ps 51:14
your praises all day long.

Psalm 36[a]

For the director of music. Of David
the servant of the LORD.

1 I have a message from God in
my heart
concerning the sinfulness of
the wicked:[b]
There is no fear of God
before their eyes. Ro 3:18*
2 In their own eyes they flatter
themselves
too much to detect or hate
their sin.
3 The words of their mouths are
wicked and deceitful;
Ps 10:7
they fail to act wisely or do
good. Jer 4:22
4 Even on their beds they plot
evil; Pr 4:16
they commit themselves to a
sinful course Isa 65:2
and do not reject what is
wrong.

5 Your love, LORD, reaches to the
heavens,
your faithfulness to the
skies. Ps 57:10
6 Your righteousness is like
the highest
mountains,
your justice like the great
deep. Ro 11:33
You, LORD, preserve
both people and
animals.
7 How priceless is your unfailing
love, O God!
People take refuge in the
shadow of your wings.
Ru 2:12; Ps 17:8
8 They feast on the abundance of
your house; Ps 65:4
you give them drink from
your river of delights.
Job 20:17; Rev 22:1

[a] In Hebrew texts 36:1-12 is numbered 36:2-13. [b] 1 Or *A message from God: The transgression of the wicked / resides in their hearts.*

[9]For with you is the fountain of
life; Jer 2:13
in your light we see light.
1Pe 2:9

[10]Continue your love to those
who know you,
your righteousness to the
upright in heart. Ps 7:10
[11]May the foot of the proud not
come against me,
nor the hand of the
wicked drive me away.
Ps 71:4
[12]See how the evildoers lie
fallen —
thrown down, not able to
rise! Ps 140:10

Psalm 37[a]

Of David.

[1]Do not fret because of those
who are evil
or be envious of those
who do wrong;
Ps 73:3; Pr 23:17-18
[2]for like the grass they will soon
wither,
like green plants they will
soon die away. Ps 90:6
[3]Trust in the LORD and do
good;
dwell in the land and enjoy
safe pasture.
[4]Take delight in the LORD, Isa 58:14
and he will give you the
desires of your heart.
[5]Commit your way to the LORD;
trust in him and he will do
this: Ps 55:22
[6]He will make your righteous
reward shine like the
dawn, Job 11:17
your vindication like the
noonday sun.
[7]Be still before the LORD
and wait patiently for him;
do not fret when people
succeed in their ways,
when they carry out their
wicked schemes.
Ps 40:1; 62:5
[8]Refrain from anger and
turn from wrath;
Eph 4:31; Col 3:8
do not fret — it leads only to
evil.
[9]For those who are evil will be
destroyed,
but those who hope in the
LORD will inherit the
land. Isa 57:13; 60:21
[10]A little while, and the
wicked will be no more;
Job 7:10
though you look for
them, they will not be
found.
[11]But the meek will inherit the
land Mt 5:5
and enjoy peace and
prosperity.
[12]The wicked plot against the
righteous
and gnash their teeth at
them; Ps 35:16

[a] This psalm is an acrostic poem, the stanzas of which begin with the successive letters of the Hebrew alphabet.

[13]but the Lord laughs at the
wicked,
for he knows their day is
coming. 1Sa 26:10; Ps 2:4

[14]The wicked draw the sword
and bend the bow Ps 11:2
to bring down the poor and
needy, Ps 35:10
to slay those whose ways are
upright.
[15]But their swords will pierce
their own hearts, Ps 9:16
and their bows will be
broken.

[16]Better the little that the
righteous have
than the wealth of many
wicked; Pr 15:16
[17]for the power of the wicked will
be broken, Ps 10:15
but the LORD upholds the
righteous.

[18]The blameless spend their days
under the LORD's care,
Ps 1:6
and their inheritance will
endure forever.
[19]In times of disaster they will
not wither;
in days of famine they will
enjoy plenty.

[20]But the wicked will perish:
Ps 34:21
Though the LORD's enemies
are like the flowers of
the field,
they will be consumed, they
will go up in smoke.
Ps 102:3

[21]The wicked borrow and do not
repay,
but the righteous give
generously; Ps 112:5
[22]those the LORD blesses will
inherit the land,
but those he curses will be
destroyed. Pr 3:33

[23]The LORD makes firm the steps
of the one who delights in
him; 1Sa 2:9
[24]though he may stumble, he
will not fall, Pr 24:16
for the LORD upholds him
with his hand.

[25]I was young and now I am old,
yet I have never seen the
righteous forsaken Heb 13:5
or their children begging
bread.
[26]They are always generous and
lend freely;
their children will be a
blessing.[a] Ps 147:13

[27]Turn from evil and do good;
Ps 34:14
then you will dwell in the
land forever.
[28]For the LORD loves the just
and will not forsake his
faithful ones. Ps 21:10

Wrongdoers will be completely
destroyed[b];
the offspring of the wicked
will perish.

[a] 26 Or *freely; / the names of their children will be used in blessings* (see Gen. 48:20); or *freely; / others will see that their children are blessed* [b] 28 See Septuagint; Hebrew *They will be protected forever*

29 The righteous will inherit the
land
and dwell in it forever.

30 The mouths of the righteous
utter wisdom,
and their tongues speak
what is just.
31 The law of their God is in their
hearts; Dt 6:6; Ps 40:8
their feet do not slip.

32 The wicked lie in wait for the
righteous, Ps 10:8
intent on putting them to
death;
33 but the LORD will not leave
them in the power of the
wicked
or let them be condemned
when brought to trial.
Ps 109:31; 2Pe 2:9

34 Hope in the LORD Ps 27:14
and keep his way.
He will exalt you to inherit the
land;
when the wicked are
destroyed, you will
see it. Ps 52:6

35 I have seen a wicked and
ruthless man
flourishing like a luxuriant
native tree, Job 5:3
36 but he soon passed away and
was no more;
though I looked for him,
he could not be found.
Job 20:5

37 Consider the blameless,
observe the upright;
a future awaits those who
seek peace.[a] Isa 57:1-2
38 But all sinners will be
destroyed;
there will be no future[b] for
the wicked. Ps 1:4

39 The salvation of the righteous
comes from the LORD;
Ps 3:8
he is their stronghold in time
of trouble. Ps 9:9
40 The LORD helps them
and delivers them;
1Ch 5:20; Isa 31:5
he delivers them from the
wicked and saves them,
because they take refuge in
him.

Psalm 38[c]

A psalm of David. A petition.

1 LORD, do not rebuke me in your
anger
or discipline me in your
wrath. Ps 6:1
2 Your arrows have pierced me,
Job 6:4; Ps 32:4
and your hand has come
down on me.
3 Because of your wrath there is
no health in my body;
there is no soundness in my
bones because of my sin.
Ps 6:2; Isa 1:6
4 My guilt has overwhelmed me
like a burden too heavy to
bear. Ezr 9:6

[a] 37 Or *upright; / those who seek peace will have posterity* [b] 38 Or *posterity* [c] In Hebrew texts 38:1-22 is numbered 38:2-23.

5 My wounds fester and are loathsome
because of my sinful folly. Ps 69:5
6 I am bowed down and brought very low;
all day long I go about mourning. Ps 35:14
7 My back is filled with searing pain;
there is no health in my body.
8 I am feeble and utterly crushed;
I groan in anguish of heart. Ps 22:1
9 All my longings lie open before you, Lord;
my sighing is not hidden from you. Job 3:24
10 My heart pounds, my strength fails me;
even the light has gone from my eyes. Ps 6:7
11 My friends and companions avoid me because of my wounds;
my neighbors stay far away. Ps 31:11
12 Those who want to kill me set their traps, Ps 140:5
those who would harm me talk of my ruin;
all day long they scheme and lie. Ps 35:20
13 I am like the deaf, who cannot hear,
like the mute, who cannot speak;
14 I have become like one who does not hear,
whose mouth can offer no reply.
15 LORD, I wait for you; Ps 39:7
you will answer, Lord my God.
16 For I said, "Do not let them gloat Ps 35:26
or exalt themselves over me when my feet slip."
17 For I am about to fall,
and my pain is ever with me.
18 I confess my iniquity; Ps 32:5
I am troubled by my sin.
19 Many have become my enemies without cause[a]; Ps 18:17
those who hate me without reason are numerous. Ps 35:19
20 Those who repay my good with evil Ps 35:12
lodge accusations against me,
though I seek only to do what is good.
21 LORD, do not forsake me;
do not be far from me, my God. Ps 35:22
22 Come quickly to help me,
my Lord and my Savior. Ps 27:1

Psalm 39[b]

For the director of music. For Jeduthun. A psalm of David.

1 I said, "I will watch my ways 1Ki 2:4
and keep my tongue from sin;

[a] 19 One Dead Sea Scrolls manuscript; Masoretic Text *my vigorous enemies* [b] In Hebrew texts 39:1-13 is numbered 39:2-14.

I will put a muzzle on my
mouth
while in the presence of the
wicked."
2 So I remained utterly silent, Ps 38:13
not even saying anything
good.
But my anguish increased;
3 my heart grew hot within me.
While I meditated, the fire
burned; Jer 20:9
then I spoke with my tongue:
4 "Show me, LORD, my life's end
and the number of my days; Ps 90:12
let me know how fleeting my
life is. Ps 103:14
5 You have made my days a mere
handbreadth; Ps 89:45
the span of my years is as
nothing before you.
Everyone is but a breath,
even those who seem
secure.[a] Ps 62:9
6 "Surely everyone goes around
like a mere phantom; 1Pe 1:24
in vain they rush about,
heaping up wealth Ps 127:2
without knowing whose it
will finally be. Lk 12:20
7 "But now, Lord, what do I look
for?
My hope is in you.
8 Save me from all my
transgressions; Ps 44:13
do not make me the scorn of
fools.
9 I was silent; I would not open
my mouth, Job 2:10
for you are the one who has
done this.
10 Remove your scourge
from me;
I am overcome by the
blow of your hand. Job 9:34; Ps 32:4
11 When you rebuke and
discipline anyone for
their sin,
you consume their wealth
like a moth — Job 13:28
surely everyone is but a
breath.
12 "Hear my prayer, LORD,
listen to my cry for help;
do not be deaf to my
weeping.
I dwell with you as a foreigner, 1Pe 2:11
a stranger, as all my
ancestors were. Heb 11:13
13 Look away from me,
that I may enjoy life
again
before I depart and am no
more." Job 10:21

Psalm 40[b]

For the director of music.
Of David. A psalm.

1 I waited patiently for the LORD; Ps 27:14
he turned to me and heard
my cry.

[a] 5 The Hebrew has *Selah* (a word of uncertain meaning) here and at the end of verse 11. [b] In Hebrew texts 40:1-17 is numbered 40:2-18.

2 He lifted me out of the slimy pit,
out of the mud and mire; Ps 69:14
he set my feet on a rock Ps 27:5
and gave me a firm place to stand.
3 He put a new song in my mouth, Ps 33:3
a hymn of praise to our God.
Many will see and fear the LORD
and put their trust in him.

4 Blessed is the one
who trusts in the LORD, Ps 84:12
who does not look to the proud,
to those who turn aside to false gods.[a]
5 Many, LORD my God,
are the wonders you have done, Ps 136:4
the things you planned for us.
None can compare with you; Isa 55:8
were I to speak and tell of your deeds,
they would be too many to declare.

6 Sacrifice and offering you did not desire — 1Sa 15:22
but my ears you have opened[b] —
burnt offerings and sin offerings[c] you did not require. Isa 1:11
7 Then I said, "Here I am, I have come —
it is written about me in the scroll.[d]
8 I desire to do your will, my God; Jn 4:34
your law is within my heart." Ps 37:31

9 I proclaim your saving acts
in the great assembly; Ps 22:25
I do not seal my lips, LORD,
as you know. Ps 119:13
10 I do not hide your righteousness in my heart;
I speak of your faithfulness
and your saving help. Ps 89:1
I do not conceal your love and your faithfulness
from the great assembly. Ac 20:20

11 Do not withhold your mercy from me, LORD;
may your love and faithfulness always protect me. Ps 43:3
12 For troubles without number surround me;
my sins have overtaken me,
and I cannot see. Ps 38:4
They are more than the hairs of my head,
and my heart fails within me. Ps 73:26
13 Be pleased to save me, LORD;
come quickly, LORD, to help me. Ps 70:1

[a] 4 Or *to lies* [b] 6 Hebrew; some Septuagint manuscripts *but a body you have prepared for me* [c] 6 Or *purification offerings* [d] 7 Or *come / with the scroll written for me*

14 May all who want to take my life
be put to shame and confusion;
may all who desire my ruin
be turned back in disgrace. Ps 35:4

15 May those who say to me, "Aha! Aha!"
be appalled at their own shame.

16 But may all who seek you Ps 9:10
rejoice and be glad in you;
may those who long for your saving help always say,
"The LORD is great!" Ps 35:27

17 But as for me, I am poor and needy;
may the Lord think of me. Ps 144:3
You are my help and my deliverer;
you are my God, do not delay. Ps 70:5

Psalm 41[a]

For the director of music.
A psalm of David.

1 Blessed are those who have regard for the weak; Ps 82:3-4; Pr 14:21
the LORD delivers them in times of trouble.

2 The LORD protects and preserves them —
they are counted among the blessed in the land — Ps 37:22
he does not give them over to the desire of their foes. Ps 27:12

3 The LORD sustains them on their sickbed
and restores them from their bed of illness.

4 I said, "Have mercy on me, LORD; Ps 6:2
heal me, for I have sinned against you." Ps 51:4

5 My enemies say of me in malice,
"When will he die and his name perish?" Ps 38:12

6 When one of them comes to see me,
he speaks falsely, while his heart gathers slander; Ps 12:2; Pr 26:24
then he goes out and spreads it around.

7 All my enemies whisper together against me; Ps 56:5
they imagine the worst for me, saying,

8 "A vile disease has afflicted him;
he will never get up from the place where he lies." 2Ki 1:4

9 Even my close friend, someone I trusted, Ps 55:12
one who shared my bread,
has turned[b] against me. Job 19:19; Jn 13:18*

[a] In Hebrew texts 41:1-13 is numbered 41:2-14.
[b] 9 Hebrew *has lifted up his heel*

10 But may you have mercy on
me, LORD;
raise me up, that I may repay
them. Ps 3:3
11 I know that you are pleased
with me, Ps 147:11
for my enemy does not
triumph over me.
12 Because of my integrity you
uphold me Ps 37:17
and set me in your presence
forever. Job 36:7

13 Praise be to the LORD, the God
of Israel,
from everlasting to
everlasting.
Amen and Amen.

BOOK II

Psalms 42 – 72

Psalm 42[a,b]

For the director of music. A *maskil*[c] of the Sons of Korah.

1 As the deer pants for streams
of water,
so my soul pants for you,
my God. Ps 119:131
2 My soul thirsts for God, for the
living God. Ps 63:1
When can I go and meet with
God?
3 My tears have been my food
day and night, Ps 80:5
while people say to me all day
long,
"Where is your God?"
4 These things I remember
as I pour out my soul:
how I used to go to the house
of God Isa 30:29
under the protection of the
Mighty One[d]
with shouts of joy and praise
Ps 100:4
among the festive throng.

5 Why, my soul, are you
downcast? Ps 38:6; 77:3
Why so disturbed within me?
Put your hope in God, La 3:24
for I will yet praise him,
my Savior and my God. Ps 44:3

6 My soul is downcast within me;
therefore I will remember
you
from the land of the Jordan,
the heights of Hermon —
from Mount Mizar.
7 Deep calls to deep
in the roar of your waterfalls;
all your waves and breakers
have swept over me. Ps 88:7

8 By day the LORD directs his
love,
at night his song is with
me — Job 35:10
a prayer to the God of my
life.

9 I say to God my Rock,
"Why have you forgotten me?
Why must I go about
mourning, Ps 38:6
oppressed by the enemy?"

[a] In many Hebrew manuscripts Psalms 42 and 43 constitute one psalm. [b] In Hebrew texts 42:1-11 is numbered 42:2-12. [c] Title: Probably a literary or musical term [d] 4 See Septuagint and Syriac; the meaning of the Hebrew for this line is uncertain.

10 My bones suffer mortal agony Ps 6:2
as my foes taunt me,
saying to me all day long,
"Where is your God?"

11 Why, my soul, are you
downcast?
Why so disturbed within
me?
Put your hope in God,
for I will yet praise him,
my Savior and my God. Ps 43:5

Psalm 43[a]

1 Vindicate me, my God,
and plead my cause
against an unfaithful nation.
Ps 26:1
Rescue me from those
who are
deceitful and wicked.
2 You are God my stronghold.
Why have you rejected me?
Why must I go about
mourning,
oppressed by the enemy?
Ps 42:9
3 Send me your light and your
faithful care, Ps 36:9
let them lead me;
let them bring me to your holy
mountain, Ps 42:4
to the place where you dwell.
Ps 84:1
4 Then I will go to the altar of
God, Ps 26:6
to God, my joy and my
delight.
I will praise you with the lyre,
O God, my God. Ps 33:2

5 Why, my soul, are you
downcast?
Why so disturbed within me?
Put your hope in God,
for I will yet praise him,
my Savior and my God. Ps 42:6

Psalm 44[b]

For the director of music. Of the Sons of Korah. A *maskil*.[c]

1 We have heard it with our ears,
O God;
our ancestors have told us
Ex 12:26; Ps 78:3
what you did in their days,
in days long ago.
2 With your hand you drove out
the nations
and planted our ancestors;
Ex 15:17
you crushed the peoples
and made our ancestors
flourish. Ps 80:9
3 It was not by their sword that
they won the land, Jos 24:12
nor did their arm bring them
victory;
it was your right hand, your
arm,
and the light of your face, for
you loved them. Dt 7:7-8

4 You are my King and my God,
Ps 74:12
who decrees[d] victories for
Jacob.

[a] In many Hebrew manuscripts Psalms 42 and 43 constitute one psalm. [b] In Hebrew texts 44:1-26 is numbered 44:2-27. [c] Title: Probably a literary or musical term [d] 4 Septuagint, Aquila and Syriac; Hebrew *King, O God; / command*

5 Through you we push back our
enemies;
through your name we
trample our foes.
6 I put no trust in my bow, Ps 33:16
my sword does not bring me
victory;
7 but you give us victory over our
enemies, Ps 136:24
you put our adversaries to
shame. Ps 53:5
8 In God we make our boast all
day long, Ps 34:2
and we will praise your name
forever.[a]

9 But now you have rejected and
humbled us; Ps 60:1,10
you no longer go out with
our armies.
10 You made us retreat before the
enemy, Lev 26:17
and our adversaries have
plundered us.
11 You gave us up to be devoured
like sheep Ro 8:36
and have scattered us
among the nations.
Dt 28:64
12 You sold your people for a
pittance, Isa 52:3; Jer 15:13
gaining nothing from their
sale.

13 You have made us a reproach
to our neighbors,
the scorn and derision of
those around us. Dt 28:37
14 You have made us a byword
among the nations;
the peoples shake their
heads at us. Jer 24:9
15 I live in disgrace all day long,
and my face is covered with
shame
16 at the taunts of those who
reproach and revile me,
Ps 74:10
because of the enemy, who is
bent on revenge.

17 All this came upon us,
though we had not forgotten
you; Ps 78:7,57
we had not been false to your
covenant.
18 Our hearts had not turned
back; Job 23:11
our feet had not strayed
from your path.
19 But you crushed us and made
us a haunt for jackals;
Ps 51:8
you covered us over with
deep darkness.

20 If we had forgotten the name
of our God Ps 78:11
or spread out our hands
to a foreign god,
Dt 6:14; Ps 81:9
21 would not God have discovered
it,
since he knows the secrets of
the heart? Ps 139:1-2
22 Yet for your sake we face death
all day long;
we are considered as sheep
to be slaughtered. Ro 8:36*

23 Awake, Lord! Why do you
sleep? Ps 7:6

[a] 8 The Hebrew has *Selah* (a word of uncertain meaning) here.

Rouse yourself! Do not reject
us forever.
24 Why do you hide your face Job 13:24
and forget our misery and
oppression?

25 We are brought down to the
dust; Ps 119:25
our bodies cling to the
ground.
26 Rise up and help us;
rescue us because of your
unfailing love. Ps 25:22

Psalm 45[a]

For the director of music. To the tune of "Lilies." Of the Sons of Korah. A *maskil.*[b] A wedding song.

1 My heart is stirred by a noble
theme
as I recite my verses for the
king;
my tongue is the pen of a
skillful writer.

2 You are the most excellent of
men
and your lips have been
anointed with grace, Lk 4:22
since God has blessed you
forever.
3 Gird your sword on your side,
you mighty one; Isa 9:6
clothe yourself with splendor
and majesty.
4 In your majesty ride forth
victoriously Rev 6:2
in the cause of truth,
humility and justice;
let your right hand achieve
awesome deeds. Dt 4:34; Ps 65:5
5 Let your sharp arrows pierce
the hearts of the king's
enemies;
let the nations fall beneath
your feet.
6 Your throne, O God,[c] will last
for ever and ever; Ps 93:2
a scepter of justice will be
the scepter of your
kingdom.
7 You love righteousness
and hate wickedness; Ps 33:5
therefore God, your God,
has set you above your
companions
by anointing you with the oil
of joy. Heb 1:8-9*
8 All your robes are fragrant with
myrrh and aloes and
cassia; SS 1:3
from palaces adorned with
ivory
the music of the strings
makes you glad.
9 Daughters of kings are among
your honored women;
at your right hand is the
royal bride in gold of
Ophir. 1Ki 2:19

10 Listen, daughter, and pay
careful attention:
Forget your people and your
father's house. Dt 21:13

[a] In Hebrew texts 45:1-17 is numbered 45:2-18.
[b] Title: Probably a literary or musical term
[c] 6 Here the king is addressed as God's representative.

[11]Let the king be enthralled by
your beauty;
honor him, for he is your
lord. Ps 95:6; Isa 54:5
[12]The city of Tyre will come with
a gift,[a]
people of wealth will seek
your favor. Ps 22:29
[13]All glorious is the princess
within her chamber;
Isa 61:10
her gown is interwoven with
gold.
[14]In embroidered garments she
is led to the king; SS 1:4
her virgin companions
follow her —
those brought to be with
her.
[15]Led in with joy and gladness,
they enter the palace of the
king.

[16]Your sons will take the place of
your fathers;
you will make them princes
throughout the land.
Ps 68:27

[17]I will perpetuate your memory
through all generations;
Mal 1:11
therefore the nations will
praise you for ever and
ever. Ps 138:4

Psalm 46[b]

For the director of music. Of the Sons of Korah. According to *alamoth*.[c] A song.

[1]God is our refuge and strength,
an ever-present help in
trouble. Dt 4:7
[2]Therefore we will not fear,
though the earth give
way Ps 23:4; 82:5
and the mountains fall
into the heart of
the sea, Ps 18:7
[3]though its waters roar and
foam Ps 93:3
and the mountains
quake with their
surging.[d]

[4]There is a river whose streams
make glad the city of
God, Ps 48:1,8; Isa 60:14
the holy place where the
Most High dwells.
[5]God is within her, she will not
fall; Isa 12:6
God will help her at break of
day.
[6]Nations are in uproar,
kingdoms fall; Ps 2:1
he lifts his voice, the earth
melts.

[7]The LORD Almighty is with us;
the God of Jacob is our
fortress. Ps 9:9

[8]Come and see what the LORD
has done, Ps 66:5
the desolations he has
brought on the earth.
[9]He makes wars cease
to the ends of the earth.
Isa 2:4

[a] 12 Or *A Tyrian robe is among the gifts*
[b] In Hebrew texts 46:1-11 is numbered 46:2-12.
[c] Title: Probably a musical term
[d] 3 The Hebrew has *Selah* (a word of uncertain meaning) here and at the end of verses 7 and 11.

He breaks the bow and shatters
the spear; Ps 76:3
he burns the shields[a] with
fire. Eze 39:9
10 He says, "Be still, and
know that I am God; Ps 100:3
I will be exalted among the
nations,
I will be exalted in the
earth." Isa 2:11

11 The LORD Almighty is with us;
the God of Jacob is our
fortress. Ps 20:1

Psalm 47[b]

For the director of music. Of the Sons of Korah. A psalm.

1 Clap your hands, all you
nations; Ps 98:8; Isa 55:12
shout to God with cries of
joy.

2 For the LORD Most High is
awesome, Dt 7:21
the great King over all the
earth.
3 He subdued nations under us,
peoples under our feet. Ps 18:39,47
4 He chose our inheritance
for us, 1Pe 1:4
the pride of Jacob, whom he
loved.[c]

5 God has ascended amid shouts
of joy,
the LORD amid the sounding
of trumpets. Ps 68:33; 98:6
6 Sing praises to God, sing
praises;
sing praises to our King,
sing praises. Ps 68:4
7 For God is the King of all the
earth;
sing to him a psalm of praise. Col 3:16

8 God reigns over the nations; 1Ch 16:31
God is seated on his holy
throne.
9 The nobles of the nations
assemble
as the people of the God of
Abraham,
for the kings[d] of the earth
belong to God; Ps 89:18
he is greatly exalted.

Psalm 48[e]

A song. A psalm of the Sons of Korah.

1 Great is the LORD, and
most worthy of praise, Ps 96:4
in the city of our God, his
holy mountain. Mic 4:1

2 Beautiful in its loftiness, Ps 50:2
the joy of the whole earth,
like the heights of Zaphon[f] is
Mount Zion,
the city of the Great King. Mt 5:35

3 God is in her citadels;
he has shown himself to be
her fortress. Ps 46:7

[a] 9 Or *chariots* [b] In Hebrew texts 47:1-9 is numbered 47:2-10. [c] 4 The Hebrew has *Selah* (a word of uncertain meaning) here. [d] 9 Or *shields* [e] In Hebrew texts 48:1-14 is numbered 48:2-15. [f] 2 *Zaphon* was the most sacred mountain of the Canaanites.

4 When the kings joined forces,
when they advanced
together, 2Sa 10:1-19
5 they saw her and were
astounded;
they fled in terror. Ex 15:16
6 Trembling seized them there,
pain like that of a woman in
labor.
7 You destroyed them like ships
of Tarshish
shattered by an east wind.
Jer 18:17

8 As we have heard,
so we have seen
in the city of the LORD
Almighty,
in the city of our God:
God makes her secure
forever.[a] Ps 87:5

9 Within your temple, O God,
we meditate on your
unfailing love. Ps 26:3
10 Like your name, O God, Jos 7:9
your praise reaches to the
ends of the earth;
your right hand is filled with
righteousness.
11 Mount Zion rejoices,
the villages of Judah are glad
because of your judgments.
Ps 97:8

12 Walk about Zion, go around
her,
count her towers,
13 consider well her ramparts,
view her citadels, Ps 122:7
that you may tell of them
to the next generation. Ps 78:6

14 For this God is our God for ever
and ever;
he will be our guide even to
the end. Ps 23:4

Psalm 49[b]

For the director of music. Of the
Sons of Korah. A psalm.

1 Hear this, all you peoples; Ps 78:1
listen, all who live in this
world, Ps 33:8
2 both low and high,
rich and poor alike:
3 My mouth will speak words of
wisdom; Ps 37:30
the meditation of my
heart will give you
understanding.
4 I will turn my ear to a proverb;
Ps 78:2
with the harp I will expound
my riddle:

5 Why should I fear when evil
days come, Ps 23:4
when wicked deceivers
surround me —
6 those who trust in their wealth
Job 31:24
and boast of their great
riches?
7 No one can redeem the life of
another
or give to God a ransom for
them —
8 the ransom for a life is costly,
no payment is ever
enough — Mt 16:26

[a] 8 The Hebrew has *Selah* (a word of uncertain meaning) here. [b] In Hebrew texts 49:1-20 is numbered 49:2-21.

[9]so that they should live on
forever
and not see decay. Ps 89:48
[10]For all can see that the wise die,
Ecc 2:16
that the foolish and the
senseless also perish,
leaving their wealth to
others. Ecc 2:18,21
[11]Their tombs will remain their
houses[a] forever,
their dwellings for endless
generations,
though they had[b] named
lands after themselves.
Ge 4:17; Dt 3:14

[12]People, despite their wealth, do
not endure;
they are like the beasts that
perish.

[13]This is the fate of those who
trust in themselves,
Lk 12:20
and of their followers, who
approve their sayings.[c]
[14]They are like sheep and
are destined to die;
Job 24:19; Ps 9:17
death will be their
shepherd
(but the upright will prevail
over them in the
morning). Da 7:18; Mal 4:3
Their forms will decay in the
grave,
far from their princely
mansions.
[15]But God will redeem me from
the realm of the dead;
Hos 13:14
he will surely take me to
himself.
[16]Do not be overawed when
others grow rich,
when the splendor of their
houses increases;
[17]for they will take nothing
with them when
they die,
their splendor will not
descend with them.
Ps 17:14
[18]Though while they live they
count themselves
blessed — Lk 12:19
and people praise you when
you prosper —
[19]they will join those who have
gone before them,
who will never again see the
light of life. Job 33:30
[20]People who have wealth but
lack understanding
are like the beasts that
perish. Ecc 3:19

Psalm 50

A psalm of Asaph.

[1]The Mighty One, God,
the LORD,
speaks and summons the
earth
from the rising of the sun to
where it sets. Ps 113:3
[2]From Zion, perfect in beauty,
God shines forth. Dt 33:2; Ps 80:1

[a] *11* Septuagint and Syriac; Hebrew *In their thoughts their houses will remain* [b] *11* Or *generations, / for they have* [c] *13* The Hebrew has *Selah* (a word of uncertain meaning) here and at the end of verse 15.

3 Our God comes
and will not be silent;
a fire devours before him,
Ps 97:3; Da 7:10
and around him a tempest
rages.
4 He summons the heavens
above,
and the earth, that he
may judge his people:
Dt 4:26
5 "Gather to me this consecrated
people,
who made a covenant
with me by sacrifice."
Ex 24:7
6 And the heavens proclaim his
righteousness,
for he is a God of justice.[a,b]
Ps 75:7

7 "Listen, my people, and I will
speak;
I will testify against you,
Israel:
I am God, your God. Ex 20:2
8 I bring no charges against
you concerning your
sacrifices
or concerning your burnt
offerings, which are ever
before me. Hos 6:6
9 I have no need of a bull from
your stall
or of goats from your pens,
10 for every animal of the forest is
mine,
and the cattle on a thousand
hills. Ps 104:24
11 I know every bird in the
mountains, Mt 6:26
and the insects in the fields
are mine.
12 If I were hungry I would not
tell you,
for the world is mine, and all
that is in it. Ex 19:5
13 Do I eat the flesh of bulls
or drink the blood of
goats?

14 "Sacrifice thank offerings to
God, Heb 13:15
fulfill your vows to the Most
High, Dt 23:21
15 and call on me in the day of
trouble;
I will deliver you, and you
will honor me." Ps 22:23

16 But to the wicked person, God
says:

"What right have you to recite
my laws
or take my covenant on your
lips? Isa 29:13
17 You hate my instruction
and cast my words behind
you. Ne 9:26; Ro 2:21-22
18 When you see a thief,
you join with him;
Ro 1:32; 1Ti 5:22
you throw in your lot with
adulterers.
19 You use your mouth for evil
and harness your tongue to
deceit. Ps 52:2
20 You sit and testify against your
brother

[a] 6 With a different word division of the Hebrew; Masoretic Text *for God himself is judge* [b] 6 The Hebrew has *Selah* (a word of uncertain meaning) here.

and slander your own
mother's son.
21 When you did these things and
I kept silent, Ecc 8:11
you thought I was exactly[a]
like you.
But I now arraign you
and set my accusations
before you. Ps 90:8

22 "Consider this, you who forget
God, Job 8:13; Ps 9:17
or I will tear you to pieces,
with no one to rescue
you:
23 Those who sacrifice thank
offerings honor me,
and to the blameless[b] I will
show my salvation."
Ps 91:16

Psalm 51[c]

For the director of music. A psalm of David. When the prophet Nathan came to him after David had committed adultery with Bathsheba.

1 Have mercy on me, O God,
according to your unfailing
love;
according to your great
compassion
blot out my transgressions.
Isa 43:25; Ac 3:19
2 Wash away all my iniquity
and cleanse me from my sin.
Heb 9:14

3 For I know my transgressions,
and my sin is always before
me. Isa 59:12
4 Against you, you only, have I
sinned
and done what is evil in your
sight; Ge 20:6; Lk 15:21
so you are right in your verdict
and justified when you
judge. Ro 3:4
5 Surely I was sinful at birth,
Job 14:4
sinful from the time
my mother
conceived me.
6 Yet you desired faithfulness
even in the womb;
you taught me wisdom
in that secret place.
Ps 15:2; Pr 2:6

7 Cleanse me with hyssop,
and I will be clean;
Lev 14:4; Heb 9:19
wash me, and I will be whiter
than snow. Isa 1:18
8 Let me hear joy and gladness;
Isa 35:10
let the bones you have
crushed rejoice.
9 Hide your face from my sins
Jer 16:17
and blot out all my
iniquity.

10 Create in me a pure heart,
O God, Ac 15:9
and renew a steadfast spirit
within me. Eze 18:31
11 Do not cast me from your
presence
or take your Holy Spirit from
me. Eph 4:30

[a] 21 Or *thought the 'I AM' was*
[b] 23 Probable reading of the original Hebrew text; the meaning of the Masoretic Text for this phrase is uncertain. [c] In Hebrew texts 51:1-19 is numbered 51:3-21.

12 Restore to me the joy of your
salvation Ps 13:5
and grant me a willing spirit,
to sustain me.

13 Then I will teach transgressors
your ways, Ac 9:21-22
so that sinners will turn back
to you.
14 Deliver me from the guilt
of bloodshed, O God,
2Sa 12:9
you who are God my
Savior,
and my tongue will sing of
your righteousness.
Ps 35:28
15 Open my lips, Lord, Ps 9:14
and my mouth will declare
your praise.
16 You do not delight in sacrifice,
or I would bring it;
1Sa 15:22; Ps 40:6
you do not take pleasure in
burnt offerings.
17 My sacrifice, O God, is[a] a
broken spirit;
a broken and contrite heart
Ps 34:18
you, God, will not despise.

18 May it please you to prosper
Zion, Ps 102:16; Isa 51:3
to build up the walls of
Jerusalem.
19 Then you will delight in
the sacrifices of the
righteous, Ps 4:5
in burnt offerings offered
whole;
then bulls will be offered on
your altar. Ps 66:15

Psalm 52[b]

For the director of music. A *maskil*[c] of David. When Doeg the Edomite had gone to Saul and told him: "David has gone to the house of Ahimelek."

1 Why do you boast of evil, you
mighty hero?
Why do you boast all day
long, Ps 94:4
you who are a disgrace in the
eyes of God?
2 You who practice deceit,
your tongue plots
destruction;
it is like a sharpened razor.
Ps 57:4
3 You love evil rather than
good,
falsehood rather than
speaking the truth.[d]
Jer 9:5
4 You love every harmful word,
you deceitful tongue! Ps 120:2-3
5 Surely God will bring you
down to everlasting
ruin:
He will snatch you up and
pluck you from your
tent; Isa 22:19
he will uproot you from the
land of the living. Pr 2:22
6 The righteous will see and
fear;
they will laugh at you,
saying, Job 22:19; Ps 37:34

[a] *17* Or *The sacrifices of God are* [b] In Hebrew texts 52:1-9 is numbered 52:3-11. [c] Title: Probably a literary or musical term [d] *3* The Hebrew has *Selah* (a word of uncertain meaning) here and at the end of verse 5.

7 "Here now is the man
who did not make God his stronghold
but trusted in his great wealth Ps 49:6
and grew strong by destroying others!"

8 But I am like an olive tree Jer 11:16
flourishing in the house of God;
I trust in God's unfailing love
for ever and ever.
9 For what you have done
I will always praise you Ps 30:12
in the presence of your faithful people.
And I will hope in your name,
for your name is good. Ps 54:6

Psalm 53[a]

For the director of music. According to *mahalath.*[b] A *maskil*[c] of David.

1 The fool says in his heart, Ro 3:10
"There is no God." Ps 10:4
They are corrupt, and their ways are vile;
there is no one who does good.

2 God looks down from heaven Ps 33:13
on all mankind
to see if there are any who understand,
any who seek God. 2Ch 15:2
3 Everyone has turned away, all have become corrupt;
there is no one who does good,
not even one. Ro 3:10-12*

4 Do all these evildoers know nothing?

They devour my people as though eating bread;
they never call on God.
5 But there they are, overwhelmed with dread,
where there was nothing to dread. Lev 26:17
God scattered the bones of those who attacked you; Eze 6:5
you put them to shame,
for God despised them.

6 Oh, that salvation for Israel would come out of Zion!
When God restores his people,
let Jacob rejoice and Israel be glad!

Psalm 54[d]

For the director of music. With stringed instruments. A *maskil*[c] of David. When the Ziphites had gone to Saul and said, "Is not David hiding among us?"

1 Save me, O God, by your name; Ps 20:1
vindicate me by your might. 2Ch 20:6
2 Hear my prayer, O God;
listen to the words of my mouth. Ps 5:1; 55:1

[a] In Hebrew texts 53:1-6 is numbered 53:2-7. [b] Title: Probably a musical term [c] Title: Probably a literary or musical term [d] In Hebrew texts 54:1-7 is numbered 54:3-9.

3 Arrogant foes are attacking me; Ps 86:14
ruthless people are trying to kill me—
people without regard for God.[a] Ps 36:1

4 Surely God is my help; Ps 118:7
the Lord is the one who sustains me. Ps 41:12

5 Let evil recoil on those who slander me;
in your faithfulness destroy them. Ps 89:49

6 I will sacrifice a freewill offering to you;
I will praise your name, LORD, for it is good. Ps 52:9
7 You have delivered me from all my troubles,
and my eyes have looked in triumph on my foes. Ps 59:10

Psalm 55[b]

For the director of music. With stringed instruments. A *maskil*[c] of David.

1 Listen to my prayer, O God,
do not ignore my plea; Ps 27:9
2 hear me and answer me.
My thoughts trouble me and I am distraught Isa 38:14
3 because of what my enemy is saying,
because of the threats of the wicked;
for they bring down suffering on me 2Sa 16:6-8
and assail me in their anger.

4 My heart is in anguish within me;
the terrors of death have fallen on me. Ps 116:3
5 Fear and trembling have beset me; Job 21:6; Ps 119:120
horror has overwhelmed me.
6 I said, "Oh, that I had the wings of a dove!
I would fly away and be at rest.
7 I would flee far away
and stay in the desert;[d]
8 I would hurry to my place of shelter,
far from the tempest and storm." Isa 4:6

9 Lord, confuse the wicked, confound their words,
for I see violence and strife in the city. Jer 6:7
10 Day and night they prowl about on its walls;
malice and abuse are within it.
11 Destructive forces are at work in the city; Ps 5:9
threats and lies never leave its streets. Ps 10:7

12 If an enemy were insulting me,
I could endure it;

[a] 3 The Hebrew has *Selah* (a word of uncertain meaning) here. [b] In Hebrew texts 55:1-23 is numbered 55:2-24. [c] Title: Probably a literary or musical term [d] 7 The Hebrew has *Selah* (a word of uncertain meaning) here and in the middle of verse 19.

if a foe were rising against me,
I could hide.
[13]But it is you, a man like
myself,
my companion, my close
friend, Ps 41:9
[14]with whom I once enjoyed
sweet fellowship
at the house of God,
as we walked about
among the worshipers. Ps 42:4

[15]Let death take my enemies by
surprise;
let them go down alive to
the realm of the dead, Nu 16:30,33
for evil finds lodging among
them.

[16]As for me, I call to God,
and the LORD saves me.
[17]Evening, morning and noon Ps 5:3; 141:2
I cry out in distress,
and he hears my voice.
[18]He rescues me unharmed
from the battle waged
against me,
even though many
oppose me.
[19]God, who is enthroned from
of old, Dt 33:27
who does not change —
he will hear them and humble
them,
because they have no fear of
God. Ps 36:1

[20]My companion attacks his
friends; Ps 7:4
he violates his covenant.
[21]His talk is smooth as butter,
yet war is in his heart;
his words are more soothing
than oil,
yet they are drawn swords. Ps 28:3

[22]Cast your cares on the LORD
and he will sustain you; Ps 37:5
he will never let
the righteous be shaken. Ps 37:24
[23]But you, God, will bring down
the wicked
into the pit of decay;
the bloodthirsty and deceitful Ps 5:6
will not live out half their
days. Job 15:32; Pr 10:27

But as for me, I trust in you. Ps 25:2

Psalm 56[a]

For the director of music. To the tune of "A Dove on Distant Oaks." Of David. A *miktam*.[b] When the Philistines had seized him in Gath.

[1]Be merciful to me, my God,
for my enemies are in hot
pursuit; Ps 57:1-3
all day long they press their
attack.
[2]My adversaries pursue me all
day long; Ps 57:3
in their pride many are
attacking me.

[3]When I am afraid, I put my
trust in you. Ps 55:4-5

[a] In Hebrew texts 56:1-13 is numbered 56:2-14.
[b] Title: Probably a literary or musical term

4 In God, whose word I
praise —
in God I trust and am not
afraid.
What can mere mortals do
to me? Ps 118:6; Heb 13:6

5 All day long they twist my
words; Ps 41:7
all their schemes are for my
ruin.
6 They conspire, they lurk, Ps 59:3
they watch my steps,
hoping to take my life.
7 Because of their wickedness
do not[a] let them
escape;
in your anger, God, bring
the nations down.
Ps 36:12; 55:23

8 Record my misery;
list my tears on your
scroll[b] —
are they not in your record?
Mal 3:16
9 Then my enemies will turn
back Ps 9:3
when I call for help. Ps 102:2
By this I will know that God
is for me. Ro 8:31

10 In God, whose word I praise,
in the LORD, whose word I
praise —
11 in God I trust and am not
afraid.
What can man do to me?

12 I am under vows to you, my
God; Ps 50:14
I will present my thank
offerings to you.

13 For you have delivered me
from death Ps 116:8
and my feet from stumbling,
that I may walk before God
in the light of life. Job 33:30

Psalm 57[c]

For the director of music. To the tune of "Do Not Destroy." Of David. A *miktam.*[d] When he had fled from Saul into the cave.

1 Have mercy on me, my God,
have mercy on me,
for in you I take refuge. Ps 2:12
I will take refuge in the shadow
of your wings Ps 17:8
until the disaster has passed.
Isa 26:20

2 I cry out to God Most High,
to God, who vindicates me.
Ps 138:8
3 He sends from heaven and
saves me, Ps 18:9,16
rebuking those who hotly
pursue me —[e] Ps 56:1
God sends forth his love and
his faithfulness.

4 I am in the midst of lions; Ps 35:17
I am forced to dwell among
ravenous beasts —
men whose teeth are spears
and arrows,
whose tongues are sharp
swords. Pr 30:14

[a] 7 Probable reading of the original Hebrew text; Masoretic Text does not have *do not.* [b] 8 Or *misery; / put my tears in your wineskin* [c] In Hebrew texts 57:1-11 is numbered 57:2-12. [d] Title: Probably a literary or musical term [e] 3 The Hebrew has *Selah* (a word of uncertain meaning) here and at the end of verse 6.

5 Be exalted, O God, above the
heavens;
let your glory be over all the
earth. Ps 108:5

6 They spread a net for my
feet —
I was bowed down in
distress. Ps 145:14
They dug a pit in my path —
but they have fallen into
it themselves.
Ps 7:15; Pr 28:10

7 My heart, O God, is steadfast,
my heart is steadfast; Ps 108:1
I will sing and make music.
8 Awake, my soul!
Awake, harp and lyre! Ps 16:9
I will awaken the dawn.

9 I will praise you, Lord, among
the nations;
I will sing of you among the
peoples.
10 For great is your love, reaching
to the heavens;
your faithfulness reaches to
the skies. Ps 36:5

11 Be exalted, O God, above the
heavens;
let your glory be over all the
earth. ver 5

Psalm 58[a]

For the director of music. To the tune of "Do Not Destroy." Of David. A *miktam*.[b]

1 Do you rulers indeed speak
justly? Ps 82:2
Do you judge people with
equity?
2 No, in your heart you devise
injustice,
and your hands mete out
violence on the earth.
Ps 94:20

3 Even from birth the wicked go
astray;
from the womb they are
wayward, spreading lies.
4 Their venom is like the venom
of a snake, Ps 140:3; Ecc 10:11
like that of a cobra that has
stopped its ears,
5 that will not heed the tune of
the charmer,
however skillful the
enchanter may be.

6 Break the teeth in their
mouths, O God;
LORD, tear out the fangs of
those lions! Job 4:10
7 Let them vanish like water
that flows away;
Jos 7:5; Ps 112:10
when they draw the bow, let
their arrows fall short.
8 May they be like a slug that
melts away as it moves
along,
like a stillborn child that
never sees the sun. Job 3:16

9 Before your pots can feel the
heat of the thorns —
whether they be green or
dry — the wicked will be
swept away.[c] Pr 10:25

[a] In Hebrew texts 58:1-11 is numbered 58:2-12.
[b] Title: Probably a literary or musical term
[c] 9 The meaning of the Hebrew for this verse is uncertain.

10 The righteous will be glad
when they are avenged,
when they dip their feet in
the blood of the wicked.
Ps 68:23

11 Then people will say,
"Surely the righteous still are
rewarded;
surely there is a God who
judges the earth."
Ps 9:8; 18:20

Psalm 59[a]

For the director of music. To the tune of "Do Not Destroy." Of David. A *miktam*.[b] When Saul had sent men to watch David's house in order to kill him.

1 Deliver me from my enemies,
O God; Ps 143:9
be my fortress against those
who are attacking me.
2 Deliver me from evildoers
and save me from those who
are after my blood. Ps 139:19

3 See how they lie in wait for me!
Fierce men conspire against
me Ps 56:6
for no offense or sin of mine,
LORD.
4 I have done no wrong, yet they
are ready to attack me.
Ps 35:19,23
Arise to help me; look on my
plight!
5 You, LORD God Almighty,
you who are the God of
Israel,
rouse yourself to punish all the
nations;
show no mercy to wicked
traitors.[c] Jer 18:23

6 They return at evening,
snarling like dogs, ver 14
and prowl about the city.
7 See what they spew from their
mouths —
the words from their
lips are sharp as swords,
Ps 57:4
and they think, "Who can
hear us?" Ps 10:11
8 But you laugh at them, LORD;
Ps 37:13
you scoff at all those nations.
Ps 2:4

9 You are my strength, I watch
for you;
you, God, are my fortress,
10 my God on whom
I can rely. Ps 62:2

God will go before me
and will let me gloat over
those who slander me.
11 But do not kill them, Lord our
shield,[d] Ps 84:9
or my people will forget. Dt 4:9
In your might uproot them
and bring them down.
12 For the sins of their mouths,
for the words of their lips,
Pr 12:13
let them be caught in their
pride.
For the curses and lies they utter,
13 consume them in your wrath,
consume them till they are
no more. Ps 104:35

[a] In Hebrew texts 59:1-17 is numbered 59:2-18.
[b] Title: Probably a literary or musical term
[c] 5 The Hebrew has *Selah* (a word of uncertain meaning) here and at the end of verse 13.
[d] 11 Or *sovereign*

Then it will be known to the
ends of the earth
that God rules over Jacob.
Ps 83:18

14 They return at evening,
snarling like dogs,
and prowl about the city.
15 They wander about for food
Job 15:23
and howl if not satisfied.
16 But I will sing of your strength,
in the morning I will sing of
your love; Ps 101:1
for you are my fortress,
my refuge in times of
trouble. Ps 46:1

17 You are my strength, I sing
praise to you;
you, God, are my fortress,
my God on whom I can rely.
ver 10

Psalm 60[a]

For the director of music. To the tune of "The Lily of the Covenant." A *miktam*[b] of David. For teaching. When he fought Aram Naharaim[c] and Aram Zobah,[d] and when Joab returned and struck down twelve thousand Edomites in the Valley of Salt.

1 You have rejected us, God, and
burst upon us; Ps 44:9
you have been angry — now
restore us! Ps 79:5; 80:3
2 You have shaken the land and
torn it open; Ps 18:7
mend its fractures, for it is
quaking. 2Ch 7:14
3 You have shown your people
desperate times; Ps 71:20
you have given us wine that
makes us stagger.

4 But for those who fear you, you
have raised a banner
Isa 11:10,12
to be unfurled against the
bow.[e]

5 Save us and help us with your
right hand, Ps 108:6
that those you love may be
delivered.
6 God has spoken from his
sanctuary:
"In triumph I will parcel out
Shechem Ge 12:6
and measure off the Valley of
Sukkoth.
7 Gilead is mine, and Manasseh
is mine; Jos 13:31
Ephraim is my helmet,
Judah is my scepter.
Ge 49:10; Dt 33:17
8 Moab is my washbasin,
on Edom I toss my sandal;
over Philistia I shout in
triumph." 2Sa 8:1

9 Who will bring me to the
fortified city?
Who will lead me to Edom?
10 Is it not you, God, you who
have now rejected us
and no longer go out with
our armies? Jos 7:12
11 Give us aid against the
enemy,
for human help is worthless.
Ps 146:3

[a] In Hebrew texts 60:1-12 is numbered 60:3-14.
[b] Title: Probably a literary or musical term
[c] Title: That is, Arameans of Northwest Mesopotamia
[d] Title: That is, Arameans of central Syria
[e] 4 The Hebrew has *Selah* (a word of uncertain meaning) here.

12 With God we will gain the
victory,
and he will trample down
our enemies. Nu 24:18

Psalm 61[a]

For the director of music. With stringed instruments. Of David.

1 Hear my cry, O God; Ps 64:1
listen to my prayer.

2 From the ends of the earth I
call to you,
I call as my heart grows
faint; Ps 77:3
lead me to the rock that is
higher than I. Ps 18:2
3 For you have been my refuge,
a strong tower against the
foe. Pr 18:10

4 I long to dwell in your tent
forever
and take refuge in the
shelter of your wings.[b]
Ps 91:4
5 For you, God, have heard my
vows; Ps 56:12
you have given me the
heritage of those who
fear your name. Ps 86:11
6 Increase the days of the king's
life,
his years for many
generations. Ps 21:4
7 May he be enthroned in
God's presence forever;
Ps 41:12
appoint your love and
faithfulness to protect
him.

8 Then I will ever sing in praise
of your name Ps 65:1
and fulfill my vows day after
day.

Psalm 62[c]

For the director of music. For Jeduthun. A psalm of David.

1 Truly my soul finds rest in God;
Dt 23:21
my salvation comes from
him.
2 Truly he is my rock and my
salvation; Ps 89:26
he is my fortress, I will never
be shaken. Ps 59:9

3 How long will you assault me?
Would all of you throw me
down—
this leaning wall, this
tottering fence? Isa 30:13
4 Surely they intend to topple
me
from my lofty place;
they take delight in lies.
With their mouths they bless,
but in their hearts they
curse.[d] Ps 28:3

5 Yes, my soul, find rest in God;
my hope comes from him.
6 Truly he is my rock and my
salvation;
he is my fortress, I will not
be shaken.

[a] In Hebrew texts 61:1-8 is numbered 61:2-9. [b] 4 The Hebrew has *Selah* (a word of uncertain meaning) here. [c] In Hebrew texts 62:1-12 is numbered 62:2-13. [d] 4 The Hebrew has *Selah* (a word of uncertain meaning) here and at the end of verse 8.

7 My salvation and my honor
depend on God[a];
he is my mighty rock, my
refuge. Ps 46:1; 85:9
8 Trust in him at all times, you
people;
pour out your hearts to him,
1Sa 1:15; La 2:19
for God is our refuge.

9 Surely the lowborn are but a
breath, Ps 39:5,11
the highborn are but a lie.
If weighed on a balance, they
are nothing; Isa 40:15
together they are only a
breath.
10 Do not trust in extortion
or put vain hope in stolen
goods;
though your riches increase,
do not set your heart on
them. Job 31:25; 1Ti 6:6-10

11 One thing God has spoken,
two things I have heard:
"Power belongs to you, God,
1Ch 29:11
12 and with you, Lord, is
unfailing love"; Ps 86:5
and, "You reward everyone
according to what they have
done." Mt 16:27

Psalm 63[b]

A psalm of David. When he was in the Desert of Judah.

1 You, God, are my God,
earnestly I seek you;
I thirst for you, Ps 42:2
my whole being longs for
you,
in a dry and parched land
where there is no water.
Ps 143:6

2 I have seen you in the
sanctuary Ps 27:4
and beheld your power and
your glory.
3 Because your love is better
than life, Ps 69:16
my lips will glorify you.
4 I will praise you as long as I
live, Ps 104:33
and in your name I will lift
up my hands.
5 I will be fully satisfied as
with the richest of
foods; Ps 36:8
with singing lips my mouth
will praise you.

6 On my bed I remember you;
I think of you through the
watches of the night.
Ps 42:8
7 Because you are my help, Ps 27:9
I sing in the shadow of your
wings.
8 I cling to you;
your right hand upholds me.
Ps 18:35

9 Those who want to kill me will
be destroyed; Ps 40:14
they will go down to the
depths of the earth. Ps 55:15
10 They will be given over to the
sword
and become food for jackals.

[a] 7 Or / *God Most High is my salvation and my honor* [b] In Hebrew texts 63:1-11 is numbered 63:2-12.

[11]But the king will rejoice in God;
all who swear by God will
glory in him, Dt 6:13; Isa 45:23
while the mouths of liars will
be silenced.

Psalm 64[a]

For the director of music. A psalm of David.

[1]Hear me, my God, as I voice my
complaint; Ps 55:2
protect my life from the
threat of the enemy.
Ps 140:1
[2]Hide me from the conspiracy of
the wicked, Ps 56:6; 59:2
from the plots of evildoers.
[3]They sharpen their tongues
like swords
and aim cruel words like
deadly arrows. Ps 58:7
[4]They shoot from ambush at the
innocent; Ps 11:2
they shoot suddenly, without
fear. Ps 55:19
[5]They encourage each other in
evil plans,
they talk about hiding their
snares;
they say, "Who will see it[b]?"
Ps 10:11
[6]They plot injustice and say,
"We have devised a perfect
plan!"
Surely the human mind and
heart are cunning.
[7]But God will shoot them with
his arrows;
they will suddenly be struck
down.
[8]He will turn their own
tongues against them
Pr 18:7
and bring them to ruin;
all who see them will shake
their heads in scorn.
Ps 22:7
[9]All people will fear;
they will proclaim the works
of God
and ponder what he has
done. Jer 51:10
[10]The righteous will rejoice in
the LORD
and take refuge in him; Ps 25:20
all the upright in heart will
glory in him! Ps 32:11

Psalm 65[c]

For the director of music.
A psalm of David. A song.

[1]Praise awaits[d] you, our God, in
Zion;
to you our vows will be
fulfilled. Ps 116:18
[2]You who answer prayer,
to you all people will come.
Isa 66:23
[3]When we were overwhelmed
by sins, Ps 38:4
you forgave[e] our
transgressions. Heb 9:14
[4]Blessed are those you choose
Ps 33:12
and bring near to live in your
courts!

[a] In Hebrew texts 64:1-10 is numbered 64:2-11.
[b] *5* Or *us* [c] In Hebrew texts 65:1-13 is numbered 65:2-14. [d] *1* Or *befits*; the meaning of the Hebrew for this word is uncertain. [e] *3* Or *made atonement for*

We are filled with the good
things of your house,
Ps 36:8
of your holy temple.

5 You answer us with awesome
and righteous deeds,
God our Savior, Ps 85:4
the hope of all the ends of the
earth
and of the farthest seas,
Ps 107:23
6 who formed the mountains by
your power,
having armed yourself with
strength, Ps 93:1
7 who stilled the roaring of the
seas, Mt 8:26
the roaring of their waves,
and the turmoil of the
nations. Isa 17:12-13
8 The whole earth is filled
with awe at your
wonders;
where morning dawns,
where evening fades,
you call forth songs of joy.

9 You care for the land and water
it; Ps 68:9-10
you enrich it abundantly.
The streams of God are filled
with water
to provide the people with
grain, Ps 46:4; 104:14
for so you have ordained
it.[a]
10 You drench its furrows and
level its ridges;
you soften it with
showers and bless
its crops.
11 You crown the year with your
bounty,
and your carts overflow with
abundance.
12 The grasslands of the
wilderness overflow;
Job 28:26
the hills are clothed with
gladness.
13 The meadows are covered with
flocks Ps 144:13
and the valleys are mantled
with grain; Ps 72:16
they shout for joy and sing.
Ps 98:8; Isa 55:12

Psalm 66

For the director of music. A song. A psalm.

1 Shout for joy to God, all the
earth! Ps 100:1
2 Sing the glory of his name;
make his praise glorious.
3 Say to God, "How awesome are
your deeds! Ps 65:5
So great is your power
that your enemies cringe
before you. Ps 18:44
4 All the earth bows down to
you;
they sing praise to you,
they sing the praises of your
name."[b]

5 Come and see what God has
done,
his awesome deeds for
mankind!

[a] 9 Or *for that is how you prepare the land*
[b] 4 The Hebrew has *Selah* (a word of uncertain meaning) here and at the end of verses 7 and 15.

6 He turned the sea into dry
land, Ex 14:22
they passed through the
waters on foot—
come, let us rejoice in him.
7 He rules forever by his power, Ps 145:13
his eyes watch the nations—
let not the rebellious rise up
against him. Ps 140:8

8 Praise our God, all peoples, Ps 98:4
let the sound of his praise be
heard;
9 he has preserved our lives
and kept our feet from
slipping. Ps 121:3
10 For you, God, tested us;
you refined us like silver. Ps 17:3; 1Pe 1:6-7
11 You brought us into prison
and laid burdens on our
backs. La 1:13
12 You let people ride over our
heads; Isa 51:23
we went through fire and
water,
but you brought us to a place
of abundance. Isa 43:2

13 I will come to your temple with
burnt offerings
and fulfill my vows to you— Ecc 5:4
14 vows my lips promised and my
mouth spoke
when I was in trouble.
15 I will sacrifice fat animals to you
and an offering of rams;
I will offer bulls and goats. Nu 6:14; Ps 51:19

16 Come and hear, all you who
fear God;
let me tell you what he has
done for me. Ps 71:15,24
17 I cried out to him with my
mouth;
his praise was on my
tongue.
18 If I had cherished sin in my
heart,
the Lord would not have
listened; Jas 4:3
19 but God has surely listened
and has heard my prayer. Ps 116:1-2

20 Praise be to God,
who has not rejected my
prayer Ps 22:24; 68:35
or withheld his love from
me!

Psalm 67[a]

For the director of music. With stringed instruments. A psalm. A song.

1 May God be gracious to us and
bless us
and make his face shine on
us—[b] Nu 6:24-26
2 so that your ways may be
known on earth,
your salvation among all
nations. Titus 2:11

3 May the peoples praise you,
God;
may all the peoples praise
you.

[a] In Hebrew texts 67:1-7 is numbered 67:2-8.
[b] 1 The Hebrew has *Selah* (a word of uncertain meaning) here and at the end of verse 4.

[4]May the nations be glad and
sing for joy, Ps 100:1-2
for you rule the peoples with
equity Ps 96:10-13
and guide the nations of the
earth.
[5]May the peoples praise you, God;
may all the peoples praise
you.

[6]The land yields its harvest;
Lev 26:4; Eze 34:27
God, our God, blesses us.
[7]May God bless us still,
so that all the ends of the
earth will fear him. Ps 33:8

Psalm 68[a]

For the director of music.
Of David. A psalm. A song.

[1]May God arise, may his
enemies be scattered;
may his foes flee before him.
Nu 10:35
[2]May you blow them away like
smoke — Hos 13:3
as wax melts before the fire,
Isa 9:18; Mic 1:4
may the wicked perish
before God.
[3]But may the righteous be glad
and rejoice before God; Ps 32:11
may they be happy and
joyful.

[4]Sing to God, sing in praise of
his name, Ps 66:2
extol him who rides on the
clouds[b]; Dt 33:26
rejoice before him — his
name is the LORD.
Ex 6:3; Ps 83:18
[5]A father to the fatherless, a
defender of widows,
Ps 10:14
is God in his holy dwelling.
Dt 26:15
[6]God sets the lonely in families,[c]
Ps 113:9
he leads out the prisoners
with singing; Ac 12:6
but the rebellious live in
a sun-scorched land.
Ps 107:34

[7]When you, God, went out
before your people, Ex 13:21
when you marched through
the wilderness,[d]
[8]the earth shook, the heavens
poured down rain,
before God, the One of Sinai,
before God, the God of Israel.
[9]You gave abundant showers,
O God; Dt 11:11
you refreshed your weary
inheritance.
[10]Your people settled in it,
and from your bounty, God,
you provided for the
poor. Ps 74:19

[11]The Lord announces the word,
and the women who proclaim
it are a mighty throng:
[12]"Kings and armies flee in
haste; Jos 10:16
the women at home divide
the plunder.

[a] In Hebrew texts 68:1-35 is numbered 68:2-36.
[b] 4 Or *name, / prepare the way for him who rides through the deserts*
[c] 6 Or *the desolate in a homeland*
[d] 7 The Hebrew has *Selah* (a word of uncertain meaning) here and at the end of verses 19 and 32.

13 Even while you sleep
among the sheep pens,[a] Ge 49:14
the wings of my dove are
sheathed with silver,
its feathers with shining
gold."
14 When the Almighty[b] scattered
the kings in the land, Jos 10:10
it was like snow fallen on
Mount Zalmon.

15 Mount Bashan, majestic
mountain, ver 22; Nu 21:33
Mount Bashan, rugged
mountain,
16 why gaze in envy, you rugged
mountain,
at the mountain where God
chooses to reign, Dt 12:5
where the LORD himself will
dwell forever?
17 The chariots of God are tens of
thousands
and thousands of thousands; Dt 33:2
the Lord has come from Sinai
into his sanctuary.[c]
18 When you ascended on high,
you took many captives; Jdg 5:12
you received gifts from
people, Eph 4:8
even from[d] the rebellious —
that you,[e] LORD God, might
dwell there.
19 Praise be to the Lord, to God
our Savior, Ps 65:5
who daily bears our burdens. Ps 55:22
20 Our God is a God who saves;
from the Sovereign LORD
comes escape from
death. Ps 56:13
21 Surely God will crush the heads
of his enemies,
the hairy crowns of
those who go on in
their sins.
22 The Lord says, "I will bring
them from Bashan;
I will bring them from
the depths of the sea, Nu 21:33
23 that your feet may wade in
the blood of your foes, Ps 58:10
while the tongues of your
dogs have their share." 1Ki 21:19

24 Your procession, God, has come
into view,
the procession of my God
and King into the
sanctuary. Ps 63:2
25 In front are the singers,
after them the
musicians;
with them are the young
women playing the
timbrels. 1Ch 13:8
26 Praise God in the great
congregation;
praise the LORD in the
assembly of Israel. Isa 48:1

[a] 13 Or *the campfires;* or *the saddlebags*
[b] 14 Hebrew *Shaddai* [c] 17 Probable reading of the original Hebrew text; Masoretic Text *Lord is among them at Sinai in holiness* [d] 18 Or *gifts for people, / even* [e] 18 Or *they*

27 There is the little tribe of
Benjamin, leading them, 1Sa 9:21
there the great throng of
Judah's princes,
and there the princes of
Zebulun and of Naphtali.
Jdg 5:18

28 Summon your power, God[a];
show us your strength, our
God, as you have done
before.
29 Because of your temple at
Jerusalem
kings will bring you gifts.
Ps 72:10
30 Rebuke the beast among the
reeds,
the herd of bulls among the
calves of the nations.
Ps 22:12
Humbled, may the beast bring
bars of silver.
Scatter the nations who
delight in war.
31 Envoys will come from Egypt;
Isa 45:14
Cush[b] will submit herself to
God.

32 Sing to God, you kingdoms of
the earth,
sing praise to the Lord,
33 to him who rides across the
highest heavens, the
ancient heavens, Ps 18:10
who thunders with mighty
voice.
34 Proclaim the power of God,
Ps 29:1
whose majesty is over Israel,
whose power is in the
heavens.
35 You, God, are awesome in your
sanctuary;
the God of Israel gives power
and strength to his
people. Ps 29:11

Praise be to God! Ps 66:20

Psalm 69[c]

For the director of music. To the tune of "Lilies." Of David.

1 Save me, O God,
for the waters have come up
to my neck. Jnh 2:5
2 I sink in the miry depths,
Ps 40:2
where there is no foothold.
I have come into the deep
waters;
the floods engulf me.
3 I am worn out calling for help;
Ps 6:6
my throat is parched.
My eyes fail, Ps 119:82; Isa 38:14
looking for my God.
4 Those who hate me without
reason Jn 15:25*
outnumber the hairs of my
head;
many are my enemies without
cause, Ps 35:19
those who seek to destroy
me.
I am forced to restore
what I did not steal.

[a] *28* Many Hebrew manuscripts, Septuagint and Syriac; most Hebrew manuscripts *Your God has summoned power for you*
[b] *31* That is, the upper Nile region [c] In Hebrew texts 69:1-36 is numbered 69:2-37.

5 You, God, know my folly; Ps 38:5
my guilt is not hidden from you. Ps 44:21

6 Lord, the LORD Almighty,
may those who hope in you
not be disgraced because of me;
God of Israel,
may those who seek you
not be put to shame because of me.
7 For I endure scorn for your sake, Jer 15:15
and shame covers my face. Ps 44:15
8 I am a foreigner to my own family,
a stranger to my own mother's children; Ps 31:11; Isa 53:3
9 for zeal for your house consumes me, Jn 2:17
and the insults of those who insult you fall on me.
10 When I weep and fast, Ps 35:13
I must endure scorn;
11 when I put on sackcloth,
people make sport of me.
12 Those who sit at the gate mock me,
and I am the song of the drunkards. Job 30:9

13 But I pray to you, LORD,
in the time of your favor; Isa 49:8
in your great love, O God,
answer me with your sure salvation.
14 Rescue me from the mire,
do not let me sink;
deliver me from those who hate me,
from the deep waters. Ps 144:7
15 Do not let the floodwaters engulf me
or the depths swallow me up Nu 16:33
or the pit close its mouth over me.

16 Answer me, LORD, out of the goodness of your love; Ps 63:3
in your great mercy turn to me.
17 Do not hide your face from your servant; Ps 27:9
answer me quickly, for I am in trouble.
18 Come near and rescue me;
deliver me because of my foes.

19 You know how I am scorned,
disgraced and shamed; Ps 22:6
all my enemies are before you.
20 Scorn has broken my heart
and has left me helpless;
I looked for sympathy, but there was none,
for comforters, but I found none. Job 16:2; Isa 63:5
21 They put gall in my food
and gave me vinegar for my thirst. Jn 19:28-30

22 May the table set before them become a snare;

may it become retribution
and[a] a trap.
23 May their eyes be darkened so
they cannot see,
and their backs be bent
forever. Ro 11:9-10*
24 Pour out your wrath on
them;
let your fierce anger overtake
them.
25 May their place be deserted;
Mt 23:38
let there be no one to dwell
in their tents.
26 For they persecute those you
wound
and talk about the pain of
those you hurt. Isa 53:4
27 Charge them with crime upon
crime;
do not let them share in your
salvation.
28 May they be blotted out
of the book of life
Ex 32:32-33; Php 4:3
and not be listed with the
righteous.
29 But as for me, afflicted and in
pain —
may your salvation, God,
protect me. Ps 59:1; 70:5
30 I will praise God's name in song
Ps 28:7
and glorify him with
thanksgiving.
31 This will please the LORD more
than an ox,
more than a bull with its
horns and hooves.
Ps 50:9-13
32 The poor will see and be glad —
Ps 34:2
you who seek God, may your
hearts live! Ps 22:26
33 The LORD hears the needy
and does not despise his
captive people.
34 Let heaven and earth praise
him,
the seas and all that move in
them, Ps 96:11; Isa 44:23
35 for God will save Zion
and rebuild the cities of
Judah. Ps 51:18; Isa 44:26
Then people will settle there
and possess it;
36 the children of his servants
will inherit it,
and those who love his name
will dwell there. Ps 102:28

Psalm 70[b]

For the director of music.
Of David. A petition.

1 Hasten, O God, to save me;
come quickly, LORD, to help
me. Ps 40:13
2 May those who want to take my
life Ps 35:4
be put to shame and
confusion;
may all who desire my ruin
be turned back in disgrace.
Ps 35:26
3 May those who say to me, "Aha!
Aha!"
turn back because of their
shame.

[a] 22 Or *snare / and their fellowship become*
[b] In Hebrew texts 70:1-5 is numbered 70:2-6.

4 But may all who seek you Ps 9:10
rejoice and be glad in you;
may those who long for your
saving help always say,
"The LORD is great!" Ps 35:27

5 But as for me, I am poor and
needy; Ps 40:17
come quickly to me, O God.
You are my help and my
deliverer; Ps 18:2
LORD, do not delay.

Psalm 71

1 In you, LORD, I have taken
refuge;
let me never be put to
shame. Ps 25:2-3; 31:1
2 In your righteousness, rescue
me and deliver me;
turn your ear to me and save
me. Ps 17:6
3 Be my rock of refuge,
to which I can always go;
give the command to save me,
for you are my rock and my
fortress. Ps 18:2; 31:2-3
4 Deliver me, my God, from the
hand of the wicked,
Ps 140:4
from the grasp of those who
are evil and cruel.

5 For you have been my hope,
Sovereign LORD,
my confidence since my
youth. Jer 17:7
6 From birth I have relied on
you; Ps 22:10
you brought me forth from
my mother's womb.
Isa 46:3
I will ever praise you. Ps 34:1
7 I have become a sign to many;
Isa 8:18; 1Co 4:9
you are my strong refuge.
Ps 61:3
8 My mouth is filled with your
praise,
declaring your splendor all
day long. Ps 35:28
9 Do not cast me away when I am
old; ver 18
do not forsake me when my
strength is gone.
10 For my enemies speak against
me;
those who wait to kill me
conspire together.
Ps 10:8; 31:13
11 They say, "God has forsaken him;
pursue him and seize him,
for no one will rescue him."
Ps 7:2
12 Do not be far from me, my God;
Ps 35:22
come quickly, God, to
help me. Ps 70:1
13 May my accusers perish in
shame;
may those who want to harm
me
be covered with scorn and
disgrace. ver 24

14 As for me, I will always have
hope; Ps 130:7
I will praise you more and
more.

15 My mouth will tell of your
righteous deeds,
Ps 35:28; 40:5

of your saving acts all day
long —
though I know not how to
relate them all.
16 I will come and proclaim your
mighty acts, Sovereign
LORD; Ps 106:2
I will proclaim your
righteous deeds, yours
alone.
17 Since my youth, God, you have
taught me,
and to this day I declare your
marvelous deeds. Ps 26:7
18 Even when I am old and gray,
do not forsake me, my God,
till I declare your power to the
next generation,
your mighty acts to all who
are to come. Ps 22:30,31; 78:4
19 Your righteousness, God,
reaches to the heavens,
Ps 57:10
you who have done great
things.
Who is like you, God? Ps 35:10
20 Though you have made me see
troubles, Ps 60:3
many and bitter,
you will restore my life
again; Hos 6:2
from the depths of the earth
you will again bring me up.
21 You will increase my honor
Ps 18:35
and comfort me once more.
Ps 23:4
22 I will praise you with the harp
for your faithfulness, my
God;
I will sing praise to you with
the lyre,
Holy One of Israel. 2Ki 19:22
23 My lips will shout for joy
when I sing praise to you —
I whom you have delivered.
Ps 103:4
24 My tongue will tell of your
righteous acts
all day long, Ps 35:28
for those who wanted to harm
me
have been put to shame and
confusion.

Psalm 72

Of Solomon.

1 Endow the king with your
justice, O God,
the royal son with your
righteousness.
2 May he judge your people in
righteousness, Isa 9:7
your afflicted ones with
justice.

3 May the mountains bring
prosperity to the
people,
the hills the fruit of
righteousness.
4 May he defend the afflicted
among the people
and save the children of the
needy; Isa 11:4
may he crush the oppressor.
5 May he endure[a] as long as the
sun,
as long as the moon, through
all generations.

[a] 5 Septuagint; Hebrew *You will be feared*

6 May he be like rain falling on a
mown field, Hos 6:3
like showers watering the
earth.
7 In his days may the righteous
flourish Ps 92:12; Isa 2:4
and prosperity abound
till the moon is no
more.

8 May he rule from sea to sea
and from the River[a] to
the ends of the earth.
Ex 23:31; Zec 9:10
9 May the desert tribes bow
before him
and his enemies lick the
dust.
10 May the kings of Tarshish and
of distant shores
bring tribute to him.
May the kings of Sheba and
Seba Ge 10:7
present him gifts. 2Ch 9:24
11 May all kings bow down to
him
and all nations serve him.

12 For he will deliver the needy
who cry out,
the afflicted who have no
one to help.
13 He will take pity on the weak
and the needy
and save the needy from
death.
14 He will rescue them from
oppression and violence,
Ps 69:18
for precious is their blood in
his sight. Ps 116:15

15 Long may he live!
May gold from Sheba be
given him. Isa 60:6
May people ever pray for
him
and bless him all day long.
16 May grain abound throughout
the land;
on the tops of the hills may it
sway.
May the crops flourish like
Lebanon Ps 104:16
and thrive[b] like the grass of
the field.
17 May his name endure forever;
Ex 3:15
may it continue as long as
the sun. Ps 89:36

Then all nations will be blessed
through him,[c]
and they will call him
blessed. Ge 12:3; Lk 1:48

18 Praise be to the LORD God, the
God of Israel, 1Ch 29:10
who alone does marvelous
deeds.
19 Praise be to his glorious name
forever;
may the whole earth be
filled with his glory.
Nu 14:21; Ne 9:5
Amen and Amen.

20 This concludes the prayers
of David son of Jesse.

[a] *8* That is, the Euphrates [b] *16* Probable reading of the original Hebrew text; Masoretic Text *Lebanon, / from the city* [c] *17* Or *will use his name in blessings* (see Gen. 48:20)

BOOK III
Psalms 73 – 89

Psalm 73

A psalm of Asaph.

1 Surely God is good to Israel,
to those who are pure in heart. Mt 5:8

2 But as for me, my feet had almost slipped;
I had nearly lost my foothold.
3 For I envied the arrogant Ps 37:1
when I saw the prosperity of the wicked. Job 21:7

4 They have no struggles;
their bodies are healthy and strong.[a]
5 They are free from common human burdens; Job 21:9
they are not plagued by human ills.
6 Therefore pride is their necklace;
they clothe themselves with violence. Ps 109:18
7 From their callous hearts comes iniquity[b]; Ps 17:10
their evil imaginations have no limits.
8 They scoff, and speak with malice;
with arrogance they threaten oppression. Jude 16
9 Their mouths lay claim to heaven,
and their tongues take possession of the earth.
10 Therefore their people turn to them
and drink up waters in abundance.[c]
11 They say, "How would God know?
Does the Most High know anything?"

12 This is what the wicked are like —
always free of care, they go on amassing wealth. Ps 49:6

13 Surely in vain I have kept my heart pure Job 34:9
and have washed my hands in innocence. Ps 26:6
14 All day long I have been afflicted,
and every morning brings new punishments.

15 If I had spoken out like that,
I would have betrayed your children.
16 When I tried to understand all this,
it troubled me deeply Ecc 8:17
17 till I entered the sanctuary of God; Ps 77:13
then I understood their final destiny. Ps 37:38

18 Surely you place them on slippery ground; Ps 35:6
you cast them down to ruin.

[a] 4 With a different word division of the Hebrew; Masoretic Text *struggles at their death; / their bodies are healthy*
[b] 7 Syriac (see also Septuagint); Hebrew *Their eyes bulge with fat*
[c] 10 The meaning of the Hebrew for this verse is uncertain.

19 How suddenly are they
destroyed, Isa 47:11
completely swept away by
terrors!
20 They are like a dream when
one awakes; Job 20:8
when you arise, Lord,
you will despise them as
fantasies.

21 When my heart was grieved
and my spirit embittered,
22 I was senseless and ignorant;
Ps 49:10
I was a brute beast before
you. Ecc 3:18

23 Yet I am always with you;
you hold me by my right
hand.
24 You guide me with your
counsel, Ps 32:8; 48:14
and afterward you will take
me into glory.
25 Whom have I in heaven but
you?
And earth has nothing
I desire besides you.
Php 3:8
26 My flesh and my heart may fail,
Ps 84:2
but God is the strength of my
heart
and my portion forever.

27 Those who are far from you
will perish; Ps 119:155
you destroy all who are
unfaithful to you.
28 But as for me, it is good
to be near God.
Heb 10:22; Jas 4:8
I have made the Sovereign
LORD my refuge;
I will tell of all your deeds.
Ps 40:5

Psalm 74

A *maskil*[a] of Asaph.

1 O God, why have you rejected
us forever? Dt 29:20
Why does your anger
smolder against the
sheep of your pasture?
Ps 95:7
2 Remember the nation you
purchased long ago,
Ex 15:16
the people of your
inheritance, whom you
redeemed —
Mount Zion, where you
dwelt. Ps 68:16
3 Turn your steps toward these
everlasting ruins,
all this destruction the
enemy has brought on
the sanctuary.

4 Your foes roared in the place
where you met with us;
La 2:7
they set up their standards as
signs.
5 They behaved like men
wielding axes
to cut through a thicket of
trees. Jer 46:22
6 They smashed all the carved
paneling
with their axes and
hatchets.

[a] Title: Probably a literary or musical term

[7]They burned your sanctuary to
the ground;
they defiled the
dwelling place of
your Name. Ps 75:1
[8]They said in their hearts,
"We will crush them
completely!" Ps 83:4
They burned every place
where God was
worshiped in the land.

[9]We are given no signs from
God;
no prophets are left, 1Sa 3:1
and none of us knows how
long this will be.
[10]How long will the enemy mock
you, God?
Will the foe revile your name
forever? Ps 44:16
[11]Why do you hold back your
hand, your right hand?
La 2:3
Take it from the folds of your
garment and destroy
them!

[12]But God is my King from long
ago; Ps 44:4
he brings salvation on the
earth.

[13]It was you who split open the
sea by your power; Ex 14:21
you broke the heads of the
monster in the waters.
Isa 51:9
[14]It was you who crushed the
heads of Leviathan
and gave it as food to the
creatures of the desert.
[15]It was you who opened up
springs and streams;
Ex 17:6; Nu 20:11
you dried up the ever-
flowing rivers. Jos 43:13
[16]The day is yours, and yours also
the night;
you established the sun and
moon. Ge 1:16; Ps 136:7-9
[17]It was you who set all the
boundaries of the earth;
you made both summer and
winter. Ge 8:22

[18]Remember how the enemy has
mocked you, LORD,
how foolish people have
reviled your name. Ps 39:8
[19]Do not hand over the life
of your dove to wild
beasts;
do not forget the lives of
your afflicted people
forever. Ps 9:18
[20]Have regard for your covenant,
Ge 17:7; Ps 106:45
because haunts of violence
fill the dark places of the
land.
[21]Do not let the oppressed retreat
in disgrace; Ps 103:6
may the poor and needy
praise your name. Ps 35:10
[22]Rise up, O God, and defend
your cause;
remember how fools mock
you all day long. Ps 53:1
[23]Do not ignore the clamor of
your adversaries, Ps 65:7
the uproar of your enemies,
which rises continually.

Psalm 75[a]

For the director of music. To the tune of "Do Not Destroy." A psalm of Asaph. A song.

1We praise you, God,
we praise you, for your Name is near; Ps 145:18
people tell of your wonderful deeds. Ps 44:1; 71:16

2You say, "I choose the appointed time;
it is I who judge with equity. Ps 7:11
3When the earth and all its people quake, Isa 24:19
it is I who hold its pillars firm.[b] 1Sa 2:8
4To the arrogant I say, 'Boast no more,'
and to the wicked, 'Do not lift up your horns.[c] Zec 1:21
5Do not lift your horns against heaven;
do not speak so defiantly.' "

6No one from the east or the west
or from the desert can exalt themselves.
7It is God who judges: Ps 50:6
He brings one down,
he exalts another. 1Sa 2:7; Da 2:21
8In the hand of the LORD is a cup
full of foaming wine mixed with spices; Pr 23:30
he pours it out, and all the wicked of the earth
drink it down to its very dregs. Jer 25:15

9As for me, I will declare this forever; Ps 40:10
I will sing praise to the God of Jacob,
10who says, "I will cut off the horns of all the wicked,
but the horns of the righteous will be lifted up." Ps 89:17; 148:14

Psalm 76[d]

For the director of music. With stringed instruments. A psalm of Asaph. A song.

1God is renowned in Judah;
in Israel his name is great. Ps 99:3
2His tent is in Salem, Ge 14:18
his dwelling place in Zion.
3There he broke the flashing arrows,
the shields and the swords,
the weapons of war.[e] Ps 46:9

4You are radiant with light, Ps 36:9
more majestic than mountains rich with game.
5The valiant lie plundered,
they sleep their last sleep; Ps 13:3
not one of the warriors
can lift his hands.

[a] In Hebrew texts 75:1-10 is numbered 75:2-11.
[b] 3 The Hebrew has *Selah* (a word of uncertain meaning) here.
[c] 4 *Horns* here symbolize strength; also in verses 5 and 10.
[d] In Hebrew texts 76:1-12 is numbered 76:2-13.
[e] 3 The Hebrew has *Selah* (a word of uncertain meaning) here and at the end of verse 9.

[6]At your rebuke, God of Jacob,
both horse and chariot lie still. Ex 15:1

[7]It is you alone who are to be feared.
Who can stand before you when you are angry? Na 1:6

[8]From heaven you pronounced judgment,
and the land feared and was quiet — 2Ch 20:29-30
[9]when you, God, rose up to judge, Ps 9:8
to save all the afflicted of the land.
[10]Surely your wrath against mankind brings you praise, Ex 9:16; Ro 9:17
and the survivors of your wrath are restrained.[a]

[11]Make vows to the LORD your God and fulfill them; Ps 50:14; Ecc 5:4-5
let all the neighboring lands
bring gifts to the One to be feared. Ps 68:29
[12]He breaks the spirit of rulers;
he is feared by the kings of the earth.

Psalm 77[b]

For the director of music. For Jeduthun. Of Asaph. A psalm.

[1]I cried out to God for help; Ps 3:4
I cried out to God to hear me.
[2]When I was in distress,
I sought the Lord; Ps 50:15; Isa 26:9,16
at night I stretched out untiring hands, Job 11:13
and I would not be comforted. Ge 37:35

[3]I remembered you, God, and I groaned;
I meditated, and my spirit grew faint.[c] Ps 143:4
[4]You kept my eyes from closing;
I was too troubled to speak.
[5]I thought about the former days, Dt 32:7; Ps 143:5; Isa 51:9
the years of long ago;
[6]I remembered my songs in the night.
My heart meditated and my spirit asked:

[7]"Will the Lord reject forever?
Will he never show his favor again? Ps 85:1
[8]Has his unfailing love vanished forever?
Has his promise failed for all time? 2Pe 3:9
[9]Has God forgotten to be merciful?
Has he in anger withheld his compassion?" Isa 49:15

[a] 10 Or *Surely the wrath of mankind brings you praise, / and with the remainder of wrath you arm yourself* [b] In Hebrew texts 77:1-20 is numbered 77:2-21.
[c] 3 The Hebrew has *Selah* (a word of uncertain meaning) here and at the end of verses 9 and 15.

[10]Then I thought, "To this I will
appeal:
the years when the
Most High stretched
out his right hand.
Ps 31:22
[11]I will remember the deeds of
the LORD;
yes, I will remember your
miracles of long ago.
Ps 143:5
[12]I will consider all your works
and meditate on all your
mighty deeds."
[13]Your ways, God, are holy.
What god is as great as our
God? Ex 15:11
[14]You are the God who performs
miracles;
you display your power
among the peoples.
[15]With your mighty arm you
redeemed your people,
Ex 6:6; Dt 9:29
the descendants of Jacob and
Joseph.
[16]The waters saw you, God,
Ex 14:21,28
the waters saw you and
writhed; Ps 114:4
the very depths were
convulsed.
[17]The clouds poured down water,
Jdg 5:4
the heavens resounded with
thunder;
your arrows flashed back and
forth.
[18]Your thunder was heard in the
whirlwind,
your lightning lit up the
world;
the earth trembled and
quaked. Jdg 5:4
[19]Your path led through the sea,
Hab 3:15
your way through the
mighty waters,
though your footprints were
not seen.
[20]You led your people like a flock
Ex 13:21; Isa 63:11
by the hand of Moses and
Aaron.

Psalm 78

A *maskil*[a] of Asaph.

[1]My people, hear my teaching;
Isa 51:4
listen to the words of my
mouth.
[2]I will open my mouth with a
parable; Mt 13:35*
I will utter hidden things,
things from of old —
[3]things we have heard and
known,
things our ancestors have
told us. Ps 44:1
[4]We will not hide them
from their descendants;
Dt 11:19
we will tell the next
generation
the praiseworthy deeds of the
LORD, Ps 26:7; 71:17
his power, and the wonders
he has done.

[a] Title: Probably a literary or musical term

[5] He decreed statutes for Jacob Ps 147:19
and established the law in Israel,
which he commanded our ancestors
to teach their children,
[6] so the next generation would know them,
even the children yet to be born, Ps 102:18
and they in turn would tell their children.
[7] Then they would put their trust in God
and would not forget his deeds
but would keep his commands.
[8] They would not be like their ancestors —
a stubborn and rebellious generation, Ex 32:9
whose hearts were not loyal to God,
whose spirits were not faithful to him.

[9] The men of Ephraim,
though armed with bows,
turned back on the day of battle; Jdg 20:39
[10] they did not keep God's covenant 2Ki 17:15
and refused to live by his law.
[11] They forgot what he had done, Ps 106:13
the wonders he had shown them.
[12] He did miracles in the sight of their ancestors
in the land of Egypt, in the region of Zoan. Nu 13:22
[13] He divided the sea and led them through; Ex 14:21
he made the water stand up like a wall. Ex 15:8
[14] He guided them with the cloud by day
and with light from the fire all night. Ex 13:21
[15] He split the rocks in the wilderness Nu 20:11
and gave them water as abundant as the seas;
[16] he brought streams out of a rocky crag
and made water flow down like rivers.

[17] But they continued to sin against him, Heb 3:16
rebelling in the wilderness against the Most High.
[18] They willfully put God to the test 1Co 10:9
by demanding the food they craved. Nu 11:4
[19] They spoke against God; Nu 21:5
they said, "Can God really spread a table in the wilderness?
[20] True, he struck the rock,
and water gushed out, Nu 20:11
streams flowed abundantly,
but can he also give us bread?
Can he supply meat for his people?" Nu 11:18

21 When the LORD heard them, he
was furious;
his fire broke out against
Jacob, Nu 11:1
and his wrath rose against
Israel,
22 for they did not believe in God
or trust in his deliverance.
Heb 3:19
23 Yet he gave a command to the
skies above
and opened the doors of the
heavens; Ge 7:11; Mal 3:10
24 he rained down manna for the
people to eat, Jn 6:31*
he gave them the grain of
heaven.
25 Human beings ate the bread of
angels;
he sent them all the food
they could eat.
26 He let loose the east wind from
the heavens Nu 11:31
and by his power made the
south wind blow.
27 He rained meat down on them
like dust,
birds like sand on the
seashore.
28 He made them come down
inside their camp,
all around their tents.
29 They ate till they were
gorged — Nu 11:20
he had given them what they
craved.
30 But before they turned from
what they craved,
even while the food was
still in their mouths,
Nu 11:33
31 God's anger rose against
them;
he put to death the sturdiest
among them, Isa 10:16
cutting down the young men
of Israel.

32 In spite of all this, they kept on
sinning;
in spite of his wonders,
they did not believe.
ver 11,22
33 So he ended their days in
futility Nu 14:29,35
and their years in terror.
34 Whenever God slew them,
they would seek him;
Hos 5:15
they eagerly turned to him
again.
35 They remembered that God
was their Rock, Dt 32:4
that God Most High was their
Redeemer. Dt 9:26
36 But then they would flatter
him with their mouths,
Eze 33:31
lying to him with their
tongues;
37 their hearts were not loyal to
him,
they were not faithful to his
covenant. Ac 8:21
38 Yet he was merciful; Ex 34:6
he forgave their iniquities
Isa 48:10
and did not destroy them.
Time after time he restrained
his anger
and did not stir up his full
wrath.

39 He remembered that they were
but flesh, Ps 103:14
a passing breeze that does
not return. Job 7:7
40 How often they rebelled against
him in the wilderness
and grieved him in the
wasteland! Ps 95:8
41 Again and again they put God
to the test; Nu 14:22
they vexed the Holy One of
Israel. Ps 89:18
42 They did not remember his
power —
the day he redeemed them
from the oppressor,
43 the day he displayed his signs
in Egypt,
his wonders in the region of
Zoan.
44 He turned their river into
blood; Ex 7:20-21
they could not drink from
their streams.
45 He sent swarms of flies
that devoured them,
Ex 8:24; Ps 105:31
and frogs that devastated
them. Ex 8:2,6
46 He gave their crops to the
grasshopper,
their produce to the locust.
47 He destroyed their vines with
hail Ex 9:23
and their sycamore-figs with
sleet.
48 He gave over their cattle to the
hail,
their livestock to bolts of
lightning.
49 He unleashed against them his
hot anger, Ex 15:7
his wrath, indignation and
hostility —
a band of destroying angels.
50 He prepared a path for his
anger;
he did not spare them from
death
but gave them over to the
plague.
51 He struck down all the
firstborn of Egypt, Ex 12:29
the firstfruits of manhood in
the tents of Ham.
52 But he brought his people out
like a flock; Ps 77:20
he led them like sheep
through the wilderness.
53 He guided them safely, so they
were unafraid;
but the sea engulfed their
enemies. Ex 14:28
54 And so he brought them to
the border of his holy
land,
to the hill country his right
hand had taken. Ps 44:3
55 He drove out nations before
them Ps 44:2
and allotted their lands
to them as an
inheritance;
he settled the tribes of Israel
in their homes.

56 But they put God to the test
and rebelled against the
Most High;
they did not keep his
statutes.

57 Like their ancestors they were
disloyal and faithless,
Eze 20:27
as unreliable as a faulty bow.
58 They angered him with
their high places;
Lev 26:30; Jdg 2:12
they aroused his jealousy
with their idols. Dt 32:21
59 When God heard them, he was
furious;
he rejected Israel completely.
Dt 32:19
60 He abandoned the tabernacle
of Shiloh, Jos 18:1
the tent he had set up among
humans.
61 He sent the ark of his might
into captivity, Ps 132:8
his splendor into the hands
of the enemy.
62 He gave his people over to the
sword;
he was furious with his
inheritance.
63 Fire consumed their young
men, Nu 11:1
and their young women had
no wedding songs; Jer 7:34
64 their priests were put to the
sword, 1Sa 22:18
and their widows could not
weep.

65 Then the Lord awoke as from
sleep,
as a warrior wakes from the
stupor of wine.
66 He beat back his enemies;
he put them to everlasting
shame. 1Sa 5:6
67 Then he rejected the tents of
Joseph,
he did not choose the tribe of
Ephraim;
68 but he chose the tribe of
Judah,
Mount Zion, which he loved.
Ps 87:2
69 He built his sanctuary like the
heights,
like the earth that he
established forever.
70 He chose David his servant
1Sa 16:1
and took him from the sheep
pens;
71 from tending the sheep he
brought him
to be the shepherd of his
people Jacob, 2Sa 5:2
of Israel his inheritance.
72 And David shepherded them
with integrity of heart;
1Ki 9:4
with skillful hands he led
them.

Psalm 79

A psalm of Asaph.

1 O God, the nations have
invaded your
inheritance; Ps 74:2
they have defiled your holy
temple,
they have reduced Jerusalem
to rubble. 2Ki 25:9
2 They have left the dead bodies
of your servants
as food for the birds of the
sky,

the flesh of your own people
for the animals of the
wild. Jer 7:33
3 They have poured out blood
like water
all around Jerusalem,
and there is no one to bury
the dead. Jer 16:4
4 We are objects of contempt to
our neighbors,
of scorn and derision
to those around us.
Ps 44:13; 80:6
5 How long, LORD? Will you
be angry forever?
Ps 74:1,10
How long will your jealousy
burn like fire? Zep 3:8
6 Pour out your wrath on the
nations
that do not acknowledge
you, Jer 10:25; 2Th 1:8
on the kingdoms
that do not call on your
name; Ps 14:4
7 for they have devoured Jacob
and devastated his
homeland.
8 Do not hold against us the sins
of past generations;
Isa 64:9
may your mercy come
quickly to meet us,
for we are in desperate need.
Ps 116:6; 142:6
9 Help us, God our Savior,
for the glory of your name;
deliver us and forgive our
sins
for your name's sake. Jer 14:7
10 Why should the nations say,
"Where is their God?" Ps 42:10
Before our eyes, make
known among the
nations
that you avenge the
outpoured blood of your
servants. Ps 94:1
11 May the groans of the
prisoners come before
you;
with your strong arm
preserve those
condemned to die.
12 Pay back into the laps of our
neighbors seven times
Ge 4:15; Isa 65:6; Jer 32:18
the contempt they have
hurled at you, Lord.
13 Then we your people,
the sheep of your
pasture, Ps 74:1; 95:7
will praise you forever;
from generation to
generation
we will proclaim your
praise.

Psalm 80[a]

For the director of music. To the tune of "The Lilies of the Covenant." Of Asaph. A psalm.

1 Hear us, Shepherd of Israel,
you who lead Joseph like a
flock. Ps 77:20
You who sit enthroned
between the cherubim,
Ex 25:22

[a] In Hebrew texts 80:1-19 is numbered 80:2-20.

shine forth [2]before
Ephraim, Benjamin and
Manasseh. Nu 2:18-24
Awaken your might;
come and save us.

3 Restore us, O God; Nu 6:25; La 5:21
make your face shine on us,
that we may be saved.

4 How long, LORD God Almighty,
will your anger smolder Dt 29:20
against the prayers of your
people?
5 You have fed them with the
bread of tears;
you have made them drink
tears by the bowlful. Ps 42:3
6 You have made us an object
of derision[a] to our
neighbors,
and our enemies mock us. Ps 79:4

7 Restore us, God Almighty;
make your face shine
on us,
that we may be saved.

8 You transplanted a vine from
Egypt; Isa 5:1-2
you drove out the nations
and planted it. Jos 13:6
9 You cleared the ground
for it,
and it took root and filled
the land.
10 The mountains were covered
with its shade,
the mighty cedars with its
branches.
11 Its branches reached as far as
the Sea,[b]
its shoots as far as the River.[c] Ps 72:8

12 Why have you broken down its
walls
so that all who pass by pick
its grapes?
13 Boars from the forest ravage it, Jer 5:6
and insects from the fields
feed on it.
14 Return to us, God Almighty!
Look down from heaven and
see! Isa 63:15
Watch over this vine,
15 the root your right hand has
planted,
the son[d] you have raised up
for yourself.

16 Your vine is cut down, it is
burned with fire;
at your rebuke your people
perish. Ps 39:11; 76:6
17 Let your hand rest on the man
at your right hand,
the son of man you have
raised up for yourself.
18 Then we will not turn away
from you;
revive us, and we will
call on your name. Ps 5:6; Isa 57:15

19 Restore us, LORD God Almighty;
make your face shine on us,
that we may be saved.

[a] 6 Probable reading of the original Hebrew text; Masoretic Text *contention*
[b] 11 Probably the Mediterranean
[c] 11 That is, the Euphrates
[d] 15 Or *branch*

Psalm 81[a]

For the director of music. According to *gittith*.[b] Of Asaph.

1 Sing for joy to God our strength;
shout aloud to the God of Jacob! Ps 66:1
2 Begin the music, strike the timbrel,
play the melodious harp and lyre. Ps 92:3

3 Sound the ram's horn at the New Moon,
and when the moon is full, on the day of our festival;
4 this is a decree for Israel,
an ordinance of the God of Jacob.
5 When God went out against Egypt, Ex 11:4
he established it as a statute for Joseph.

I heard an unknown voice say: Ps 114:1

6 "I removed the burden from their shoulders; Isa 9:4
their hands were set free from the basket.
7 In your distress you called and I rescued you, Ex 2:23; Ps 50:15
I answered you out of a thundercloud; Ex 19:19
I tested you at the waters of Meribah.[c] Ex 17:7
8 Hear me, my people,
and I will warn you — Ps 50:7
if you would only listen to me, Israel!
9 You shall have no foreign god among you; Ex 20:3; Dt 32:12; Isa 43:12
you shall not worship any god other than me.
10 I am the LORD your God,
who brought you up out of Egypt. Ex 20:2
Open wide your mouth and I will fill it. Ps 107:9

11 "But my people would not listen to me;
Israel would not submit to me.
12 So I gave them over to their stubborn hearts Ac 7:42
to follow their own devices.

13 "If my people would only listen to me, Dt 5:29; Isa 48:18
if Israel would only follow my ways,
14 how quickly I would subdue their enemies Ps 47:3
and turn my hand against their foes! Am 1:8
15 Those who hate the LORD would cringe before him,
and their punishment would last forever.
16 But you would be fed with the finest of wheat; Dt 32:14
with honey from the rock I would satisfy you."

[a] In Hebrew texts 81:1-16 is numbered 81:2-17. [b] Title: Probably a musical term [c] 7 The Hebrew has *Selah* (a word of uncertain meaning) here.

Psalm 82

A psalm of Asaph.

[1]God presides in the great
assembly;
he renders judgment
among the "gods": Ps 58:11; Isa 3:13

[2]"How long will you[a] defend the
unjust
and show partiality to the
wicked?[b] Dt 1:17
[3]Defend the weak and the
fatherless; Dt 24:17
uphold the cause of the poor
and the oppressed.
[4]Rescue the weak and the
needy;
deliver them from the hand
of the wicked.

[5]"The 'gods' know nothing, they
understand nothing. Mic 3:1
They walk about in
darkness;
all the foundations of the
earth are shaken. Ps 11:3

[6]"I said, 'You are "gods"; Jn 10:34*
you are all sons of the Most
High.'
[7]But you will die like mere
mortals; Ps 49:12
you will fall like every other
ruler."

[8]Rise up, O God, judge the
earth,
for all the nations are
your inheritance. Ps 2:8; Rev 11:15

Psalm 83[c]

A song. A psalm of Asaph.

[1]O God, do not remain silent; Ps 28:1
do not turn a deaf ear,
do not stand aloof, O God.
[2]See how your enemies growl, Ps 2:1
how your foes rear their
heads. Ps 81:15
[3]With cunning they conspire
against your people; Ps 31:13
they plot against those you
cherish.
[4]"Come," they say, "let us
destroy them as a
nation, Est 3:6
so that Israel's name is
remembered no
more."

[5]With one mind they plot
together; Ps 2:2
they form an alliance against
you —
[6]the tents of Edom and the
Ishmaelites,
of Moab and the Hagrites, 2Ch 20:1
[7]Byblos, Ammon and Amalek, Jos 13:5
Philistia, with the people of
Tyre.
[8]Even Assyria has joined them
to reinforce Lot's
descendants.[b] Dt 2:9

[a] 2 The Hebrew is plural. [b] 2,8 The Hebrew has *Selah* (a word of uncertain meaning) here. [c] In Hebrew texts 83:1-18 is numbered 83:2-19.

[9]Do to them as you did to
Midian, Jdg 7:1-23
as you did to Sisera and Jabin
at the river Kishon,
Jdg 4:23-24
[10]who perished at Endor
and became like dung on the
ground. Zep 1:17
[11]Make their nobles like Oreb
and Zeeb,
all their princes like Zebah
and Zalmunna, Jdg 8:12,21
[12]who said, "Let us take
possession
of the pasturelands of God."
[13]Make them like tumbleweed,
my God,
like chaff before the wind.
Ps 35:5; Isa 17:13
[14]As fire consumes the forest
or a flame sets the
mountains ablaze, Dt 32:22
[15]so pursue them with your
tempest
and terrify them with your
storm.
[16]Cover their faces with shame,
LORD, Ps 109:29; 132:18
so that they will seek your
name.
[17]May they ever be ashamed and
dismayed;
may they perish in disgrace.
Ps 35:4
[18]Let them know that you,
whose name is the
LORD —
that you alone are the Most
High over all the earth.
Ps 59:13

Psalm 84[a]

For the director of music. According to *gittith*.[b] Of the Sons of Korah. A psalm.

[1]How lovely is your dwelling
place, Ps 27:4
LORD Almighty!
[2]My soul yearns, even faints,
Ps 42:1-2
for the courts of the LORD;
my heart and my flesh cry
out
for the living God. Jos 3:10
[3]Even the sparrow has found a
home,
and the swallow a nest for
herself,
where she may have her
young —
a place near your altar, Ps 43:4
LORD Almighty, my King and
my God. Ps 5:2
[4]Blessed are those who dwell in
your house;
they are ever praising you.[c]
[5]Blessed are those whose
strength is in you, Ps 81:1
whose hearts are set on
pilgrimage. Jer 31:6
[6]As they pass through the Valley
of Baka,
they make it a place of
springs;
the autumn rains also cover
it with pools.[d] Joel 2:23

[a] In Hebrew texts 84:1-12 is numbered 84:2-13.
[b] Title: Probably a musical term [c] 4 The Hebrew has *Selah* (a word of uncertain meaning) here and at the end of verse 8.
[d] 6 Or *blessings*

7 They go from strength to
strength, Pr 4:18
till each appears before God
in Zion. Dt 16:16

8 Hear my prayer, LORD God
Almighty;
listen to me, God of Jacob.
9 Look on our shield,[a] O God;
Ps 59:11
look with favor on
your anointed one.
1Sa 16:6; Ps 2:2; 132:17

10 Better is one day in your
courts
than a thousand elsewhere;
I would rather be a doorkeeper
in the house of my God
1Ch 23:5
than dwell in the tents of the
wicked.
11 For the LORD God is a sun and
shield; Isa 60:19
the LORD bestows favor and
honor;
no good thing does he
withhold Ps 34:10
from those whose walk is
blameless.

12 LORD Almighty,
blessed is the one who trusts
in you. Ps 2:12

Psalm 85[b]

For the director of music. Of the Sons of Korah. A psalm.

1 You, LORD, showed favor to
your land;
you restored the fortunes of
Jacob. Jer 30:18; Eze 39:25
2 You forgave the iniquity of your
people Nu 14:19; Ps 78:38
and covered all their sins.[c]
3 You set aside all your wrath
and turned from your fierce
anger. Dt 13:17

4 Restore us again, God our
Savior, Ps 80:3,7
and put away your
displeasure toward us.
5 Will you be angry with us
forever? Ps 79:5
Will you prolong your anger
through all generations?
6 Will you not revive us again,
Ps 80:18; Hab 3:2
that your people may rejoice
in you?
7 Show us your unfailing love,
LORD,
and grant us your salvation.

8 I will listen to what God the
LORD says;
he promises peace to his
people, his faithful
servants — Zec 9:10
but let them not turn to folly.
9 Surely his salvation is near
those who fear him,
Isa 46:13
that his glory may dwell in
our land. Zec 2:5

10 Love and faithfulness meet
together;
righteousness and peace kiss
each other. Ps 72:2-3; Isa 32:17

[a] 9 Or *sovereign* [b] In Hebrew texts 85:1-13 is numbered 85:2-14. [c] 2 The Hebrew has *Selah* (a word of uncertain meaning) here.

[11]Faithfulness springs forth from
the earth,
and righteousness looks
down from heaven.
Isa 45:8
[12]The LORD will indeed give what
is good, Ps 84:11; Jas 1:17
and our land will yield its
harvest. Ps 67:6; Zec 8:12
[13]Righteousness goes before
him
and prepares the way for his
steps.

Psalm 86

A prayer of David.

[1]Hear me, LORD, and answer me,
Ps 17:6
for I am poor and needy.
[2]Guard my life, for I am faithful
to you;
save your servant who trusts
in you.
You are my God; [3]have mercy
on me, Lord, Ps 57:1
for I call to you all day long.
[4]Bring joy to your servant,
Lord,
for I put my trust in you.
Ps 143:8
[5]You, Lord, are forgiving and
good,
abounding in love to all
who call to you.
Ps 145:8; Joel 2:13
[6]Hear my prayer, LORD;
listen to my cry for mercy.
[7]When I am in distress, I call to
you, Ps 50:15
because you answer me.

[8]Among the gods there is
none like you, Lord;
Ex 15:11; Dt 3:24; Ps 89:6
no deeds can compare with
yours.
[9]All the nations you have made
will come and worship
before you, Lord; Rev 15:4
they will bring glory to your
name.
[10]For you are great and do
marvelous deeds; Ps 72:18
you alone are God.
Dt 6:4; Mk 12:29
[11]Teach me your way, LORD, Ps 25:5
that I may rely on your
faithfulness;
give me an undivided heart,
Jer 32:39
that I may fear your name.
[12]I will praise you,
Lord my God,
with all my heart; Ps 9:1
I will glorify your name
forever.
[13]For great is your love toward
me;
you have delivered me from
the depths,
from the realm of the dead.
Ps 16:10
[14]Arrogant foes are attacking me,
O God;
ruthless people are trying to
kill me —
they have no regard for you.
Ps 54:3
[15]But you, Lord, are a
compassionate and
gracious God, Ps 103:8

slow to anger, abounding in
love and faithfulness.
Ex 34:6; Ne 9:17; Joel 2:13
16 Turn to me and have mercy on
me;
show your strength in behalf
of your servant;
save me, because I serve you
just as my mother did. Ps 116:16
17 Give me a sign of your
goodness,
that my enemies may
see it and be put to
shame,
for you, LORD, have helped
me and comforted me.

Psalm 87

Of the Sons of Korah. A psalm. A song.

1 He has founded his city on the
holy mountain. Ps 48:1
2 The LORD loves the gates of
Zion Ps 78:68
more than all the other
dwellings of Jacob.

3 Glorious things are said of you,
city of God:[a] Isa 60:1
4 "I will record Rahab[b] and
Babylon Job 9:13
among those who
acknowledge me —
Philistia too, and Tyre, along
with Cush[c] —
and will say, 'This one was
born in Zion.' "[d] Isa 19:25
5 Indeed, of Zion it will be said,
"This one and that one were
born in her,
and the Most High himself
will establish her."
6 The LORD will write in the
register of the peoples:
Eze 13:9
"This one was born in Zion."

7 As they make music they will
sing,
"All my fountains are in you."
Ps 36:9

Psalm 88[e]

A song. A psalm of the Sons
of Korah. For the director of music.
According to *mahalath leannoth*.[f]
A *maskil*[g] of Heman the Ezrahite.

1 LORD, you are the God who
saves me; Ps 51:14
day and night I cry out to
you. Ps 22:2
2 May my prayer come before
you;
turn your ear to my cry.
3 I am overwhelmed with
troubles
and my life draws near to
death. Ps 107:18,26
4 I am counted among those
who go down to the pit;
Ps 28:1
I am like one without
strength.

[a] *3* The Hebrew has *Selah* (a word of uncertain meaning) here and at the end of verse 6. [b] *4* A poetic name for Egypt [c] *4* That is, the upper Nile region [d] *4* Or *"I will record concerning those who acknowledge me: / 'This one was born in Zion.' / Hear this, Rahab and Babylon, / and you too, Philistia, Tyre and Cush."* [e] In Hebrew texts 88:1-18 is numbered 88:2-19. [f] Title: Possibly a tune, "The Suffering of Affliction" [g] Title: Probably a literary or musical term

5 I am set apart with the dead,
like the slain who lie in the grave,
whom you remember no more,
who are cut off from your care. Isa 53:8

6 You have put me in the lowest pit,
in the darkest depths. Ps 69:15; La 3:55
7 Your wrath lies heavily on me;
you have overwhelmed me with all your waves.[a] Ps 42:7
8 You have taken from me my closest friends Job 19:13
and have made me repulsive to them.
I am confined and cannot escape;
9 my eyes are dim with grief. Ps 38:10

I call to you, LORD, every day; Ps 86:3
I spread out my hands to you. Ps 143:6
10 Do you show your wonders to the dead?
Do their spirits rise up and praise you? Ps 6:5
11 Is your love declared in the grave,
your faithfulness in Destruction[b]? Ps 30:9
12 Are your wonders known in the place of darkness,
or your righteous deeds in the land of oblivion?

13 But I cry to you for help, LORD; Ps 30:2
in the morning my prayer comes before you. Ps 5:3
14 Why, LORD, do you reject me
and hide your face from me? Job 13:24; Ps 13:1

15 From my youth I have suffered and been close to death;
I have borne your terrors and am in despair. Job 6:4
16 Your wrath has swept over me;
your terrors have destroyed me.
17 All day long they surround me like a flood; Ps 22:16
they have completely engulfed me.
18 You have taken from me friend and neighbor — Job 19:13
darkness is my closest friend.

Psalm 89[c]

A *maskil*[d] of Ethan the Ezrahite.

1 I will sing of the LORD's great love forever; Ps 101:1
with my mouth I will make your faithfulness known Ps 36:5
through all generations.
2 I will declare that your love stands firm forever,
that you have established your faithfulness in heaven itself. Ps 36:5

[a] 7 The Hebrew has *Selah* (a word of uncertain meaning) here and at the end of verse 10. [b] *11* Hebrew *Abaddon* [c] In Hebrew texts 89:1-52 is numbered 89:2-53. [d] Title: Probably a literary or musical term

3 You said, "I have made a
covenant with my
chosen one,
I have sworn to David my
servant,
4 'I will establish your line
forever
and make your throne
firm through all
generations.'"[a]
2Sa 7:12-16; Lk 1:33

5 The heavens praise your
wonders, LORD, Ps 19:1
your faithfulness too, in the
assembly of the holy
ones.
6 For who in the skies above
can compare with the
LORD?
Who is like the LORD among
the heavenly beings?
Ps 113:5

7 In the council of the holy
ones God is greatly
feared;
he is more awesome than
all who surround him.
Ps 47:2
8 Who is like you, LORD God
Almighty? Ps 71:19
You, LORD, are mighty,
and your faithfulness
surrounds you.

9 You rule over the surging sea;
when its waves mount up,
you still them. Ps 65:7
10 You crushed Rahab like one of
the slain; Ps 87:4
with your strong arm you
scattered your enemies.

11 The heavens are yours, and
yours also the earth;
1Ch 29:11; Ps 24:1
you founded the world and
all that is in it. Ge 1:1
12 You created the north and the
south;
Tabor and Hermon sing
for joy at your name.
Jos 12:1; 19:22
13 Your arm is endowed with
power;
your hand is strong, your
right hand exalted.

14 Righteousness and justice are
the foundation of your
throne;
love and faithfulness go
before you. Ps 97:2
15 Blessed are those who have
learned to acclaim you,
who walk in the light of
your presence, LORD.
Ps 44:3
16 They rejoice in your name all
day long;
they celebrate your
righteousness.
17 For you are their glory and
strength,
and by your favor you
exalt our horn.[b]
Ps 75:10; 148:14
18 Indeed, our shield[c] belongs to
the LORD,
our king to the Holy One of
Israel. Ps 47:9

[a] 4 The Hebrew has *Selah* (a word of uncertain meaning) here and at the end of verses 37, 45 and 48. [b] 17 *Horn* here symbolizes strong one. [c] 18 Or *sovereign*

19 Once you spoke in a vision,
to your faithful people you said:
"I have bestowed strength on a warrior;
I have raised up a young man from among the people.
20 I have found David my servant; Ac 13:22
with my sacred oil I have anointed him. 1Sa 16:1,12
21 My hand will sustain him;
surely my arm will strengthen him. Ps 18:35
22 The enemy will not get the better of him;
the wicked will not oppress him. 2Sa 7:10
23 I will crush his foes before him
and strike down his adversaries. 2Sa 7:9
24 My faithful love will be with him,
and through my name his horn[a] will be exalted.
25 I will set his hand over the sea,
his right hand over the rivers. Ps 72:8
26 He will call out to me, 'You are my Father,
my God, the Rock my Savior.' 2Sa 22:47
27 And I will appoint him to be my firstborn,
the most exalted of the kings of the earth. Nu 24:7
28 I will maintain my love to him forever,
and my covenant with him will never fail. ver 33-34; Isa 55:3
29 I will establish his line forever,
his throne as long as the heavens endure. Dt 11:21; Jer 33:17

30 "If his sons forsake my law
and do not follow my statutes,
31 if they violate my decrees
and fail to keep my commands,
32 I will punish their sin with the rod,
their iniquity with flogging;
33 but I will not take my love from him, 2Sa 7:15
nor will I ever betray my faithfulness.
34 I will not violate my covenant
or alter what my lips have uttered. Nu 23:19
35 Once for all, I have sworn by my holiness —
and I will not lie to David —
36 that his line will continue forever
and his throne endure before me like the sun;
37 it will be established forever like the moon,
the faithful witness in the sky."

38 But you have rejected, you have spurned, Dt 32:19; 1Ch 28:9
you have been very angry with your anointed one.

[a] 24 *Horn* here symbolizes strength.

39 You have renounced the
covenant with your
servant
and have defiled his crown
in the dust. La 5:16
40 You have broken through all
his walls
and reduced his strongholds
to ruins. La 2:2
41 All who pass by have plundered
him;
he has become the scorn of
his neighbors. Ps 44:13
42 You have exalted the right
hand of his foes;
you have made all his
enemies rejoice.
Ps 13:2; 80:6
43 Indeed, you have turned back
the edge of his sword
and have not supported him
in battle. Ps 44:10
44 You have put an end to his
splendor
and cast his throne to the
ground.
45 You have cut short the days of
his youth;
you have covered him with
a mantle of shame.
Ps 44:15; 109:29

46 How long, LORD? Will you hide
yourself forever?
How long will your wrath
burn like fire? Ps 79:5
47 Remember how fleeting is my
life. Job 7:7
For what futility you
have created all
humanity!
48 Who can live and not see death,
or who can escape the power
of the grave? Ps 49:9
49 Lord, where is your former
great love,
which in your faithfulness
you swore to David?
50 Remember, Lord, how your
servant has[a] been
mocked, Ps 69:19
how I bear in my heart the
taunts of all the nations,
51 the taunts with which your
enemies, LORD, have
mocked,
with which they have
mocked every step
of your anointed one.
Ps 74:10

52 Praise be to the LORD forever!
Amen and Amen.

BOOK IV

Psalms 90 – 106

Psalm 90

A prayer of Moses the man of God.

1 Lord, you have been our
dwelling place Eze 11:16
throughout all generations.
2 Before the mountains were
born Pr 8:25
or you brought forth the
whole world,
from everlasting to
everlasting you are God.
Ps 102:24-27

[a] 50 Or *your servants have*

3 You turn people back to
dust,
saying, "Return to dust, you
mortals." Ge 3:19
4 A thousand years in your sight
are like a day that has just
gone by,
or like a watch in the night.
2Pe 3:8
5 Yet you sweep people away
in the sleep of death —
Isa 40:6
they are like the new grass of
the morning:
6 In the morning it springs up
new,
but by evening it is dry
and withered.
Mt 6:30; Jas 1:10
7 We are consumed by your
anger
and terrified by your
indignation.
8 You have set our iniquities
before you,
our secret sins in the
light of your presence.
Ps 19:12
9 All our days pass away under
your wrath;
we finish our years with a
moan. Ps 78:33
10 Our days may come to seventy
years,
or eighty, if our strength
endures;
yet the best of them are but
trouble and sorrow,
for they quickly pass, and we
fly away. Job 20:8
11 If only we knew the power of
your anger!
Your wrath is as great as the
fear that is your due.
Ps 76:7
12 Teach us to number our days,
Ps 39:4
that we may gain a heart of
wisdom.
13 Relent, LORD! How long will it
be?
Have compassion on your
servants. Dt 32:36
14 Satisfy us in the morning with
your unfailing love,
Ps 103:5
that we may sing for joy and
be glad all our days. Ps 85:6
15 Make us glad for as many days
as you have afflicted us,
for as many years as we have
seen trouble.
16 May your deeds be shown to
your servants,
your splendor to their
children. Hab 3:2
17 May the favor[a] of the Lord our
God rest on us; Isa 26:12
establish the work of our
hands for us —
yes, establish the work of our
hands.

Psalm 91

1 Whoever dwells in the shelter
of the Most High Ps 31:20
will rest in the shadow of the
Almighty.[b] Ps 17:8

[a] 17 Or *beauty* [b] 1 Hebrew *Shaddai*

[2]I will say of the LORD, "He is my
refuge and my fortress,
Ps 142:5
my God, in whom I trust."

[3]Surely he will save you
from the fowler's snare Ps 124:7
and from the deadly
pestilence. 1Ki 8:37
[4]He will cover you with his
feathers,
and under his wings you will
find refuge; Ps 17:8
his faithfulness will be
your shield and rampart.
Ps 35:2
[5]You will not fear the terror of
night, Job 5:21
nor the arrow that flies by
day,
[6]nor the pestilence that stalks in
the darkness,
nor the plague that destroys
at midday.
[7]A thousand may fall at your
side,
ten thousand at your right
hand,
but it will not come near you.
[8]You will only observe with your
eyes
and see the punishment of
the wicked. Mal 1:5

[9]If you say, "The LORD is my
refuge,"
and you make the Most High
your dwelling,
[10]no harm will overtake you,
Pr 12:21
no disaster will come near
your tent.
[11]For he will command his angels
concerning you Heb 1:14
to guard you in all your ways;
Ps 34:7
[12]they will lift you up in their
hands,
so that you will not strike
your foot against a
stone. Mt 4:6*; Lk 4:10-11*
[13]You will tread on the lion and
the cobra;
you will trample the great
lion and the serpent.
Da 6:22; Lk 10:19

[14]"Because he[a] loves me," says
the LORD, "I will rescue
him;
I will protect him, for he
acknowledges my name.
[15]He will call on me, and I will
answer him;
I will be with him in trouble,
I will deliver him and honor
him. 1Sa 2:30; Ps 50:15
[16]With long life I will satisfy him
Dt 6:2; Ps 21:4
and show him my salvation."
Ps 50:23

Psalm 92[b]

A psalm. A song. For the Sabbath day.

[1]It is good to praise the LORD
and make music to your
name, O Most High, Ps 147:1
[2]proclaiming your love in the
morning
and your faithfulness at
night, Ps 89:1

[a] *14* That is, probably the king [b] In Hebrew texts 92:1-15 is numbered 92:2-16.

[3]to the music of the ten-
stringed lyre
and the melody of the harp.
Ps 33:2

[4]For you make me glad by your
deeds, LORD;
I sing for joy at what your
hands have done.
Ps 8:6; 143:5
[5]How great are your works, LORD,
how profound your
thoughts! Ps 40:5; Ro 11:33
[6]Senseless people do not know,
Ps 73:22
fools do not understand,
[7]that though the wicked spring
up like grass
and all evildoers flourish,
they will be destroyed
forever. Ps 37:2

[8]But you, LORD, are forever
exalted.

[9]For surely your enemies, LORD,
surely your enemies will
perish;
all evildoers will be
scattered. Ps 68:1
[10]You have exalted my horn[a] like
that of a wild ox; Ps 89:17
fine oils have been poured
on me. Ps 23:5
[11]My eyes have seen the defeat of
my adversaries;
my ears have heard the rout
of my wicked foes. Ps 54:7

[12]The righteous will flourish like
a palm tree,
they will grow like a cedar of
Lebanon; Ps 52:8; Hos 14:6
[13]planted in the house of the
LORD,
they will flourish in
the courts of our God.
Ps 100:4
[14]They will still bear fruit in old
age, Jn 15:2
they will stay fresh and
green,
[15]proclaiming, "The LORD is
upright;
he is my Rock, and there is
no wickedness in him."
Job 34:10

Psalm 93

[1]The LORD reigns, he is robed in
majesty; Ps 97:1; 104:1
the LORD is robed in majesty
and armed with
strength; Ps 65:6
indeed, the world is
established, firm and
secure. Ps 96:10
[2]Your throne was established
long ago;
you are from all eternity.
Ps 45:6

[3]The seas have lifted up, LORD,
Ps 96:11
the seas have lifted up their
voice;
the seas have lifted up their
pounding waves.
[4]Mightier than the thunder of
the great waters, Ps 65:7
mightier than the breakers
of the sea —
the LORD on high is mighty.

[a] *10* *Horn* here symbolizes strength.

[5]Your statutes, LORD, stand firm;
holiness adorns your house Ps 29:2
for endless days.

Psalm 94

[1]The LORD is a God who avenges. Na 1:2
O God who avenges, shine forth.
[2]Rise up, Judge of the earth; Ge 18:25
pay back to the proud what they deserve. Ps 31:23
[3]How long, LORD, will the wicked,
how long will the wicked be jubilant? Ps 13:2
[4]They pour out arrogant words; Ps 31:18
all the evildoers are full of boasting.
[5]They crush your people, LORD; Isa 3:15
they oppress your inheritance.
[6]They slay the widow and the foreigner;
they murder the fatherless.
[7]They say, "The LORD does not see; Ps 10:11
the God of Jacob takes no notice."

[8]Take notice, you senseless ones among the people; Ps 92:6
you fools, when will you become wise?
[9]Does he who fashioned the ear not hear?
Does he who formed the eye not see? Ex 4:11
[10]Does he who disciplines nations not punish?
Does he who teaches mankind lack knowledge? Job 35:11; Isa 28:26
[11]The LORD knows all human plans;
he knows that they are futile. 1Co 3:20*

[12]Blessed is the one you discipline, LORD, Job 5:17; Heb 12:5
the one you teach from your law;
[13]you grant them relief from days of trouble,
till a pit is dug for the wicked. Ps 55:23
[14]For the LORD will not reject his people; 1Sa 12:22; Ro 11:2
he will never forsake his inheritance.
[15]Judgment will again be founded on righteousness, Ps 97:2
and all the upright in heart will follow it.

[16]Who will rise up for me against the wicked? Nu 10:35; Ps 17:13
Who will take a stand for me against evildoers? Ps 59:2
[17]Unless the LORD had given me help, Ps 124:2
I would soon have dwelt in the silence of death.
[18]When I said, "My foot is slipping," Ps 38:16
your unfailing love, LORD, supported me.

[19]When anxiety was great within
me, Ecc 11:10
your consolation brought me
joy.
[20]Can a corrupt throne be allied
with you —
a throne that brings on
misery by its decrees?
Ps 58:2
[21]The wicked band together
against the righteous
Ps 56:6
and condemn the innocent
to death. Pr 17:15,26
[22]But the LORD has become my
fortress,
and my God the rock in
whom I take refuge.
Ps 59:9
[23]He will repay them for their
sins Ps 7:16
and destroy them for their
wickedness;
the LORD our God will
destroy them.

Psalm 95

[1]Come, let us sing for joy to the
LORD; Ps 5:11
let us shout aloud to the
Rock of our salvation.
2Sa 22:47; Ps 81:1
[2]Let us come before him with
thanksgiving Mic 6:6
and extol him with music
and song. Ps 81:2; Eph 5:19
[3]For the LORD is the great God,
the great King above all
gods. Ps 96:4
[4]In his hand are the depths of
the earth,
and the mountain peaks
belong to him.
[5]The sea is his, for he made it,
and his hands formed the
dry land. Ge 1:9; Ps 146:6

[6]Come, let us bow down in
worship, Php 2:10
let us kneel before the
LORD our Maker;
Ps 100:3; 149:2; Isa 17:7
[7]for he is our God
and we are the people of his
pasture, Ps 79:13
the flock under his care.

Today, if only you would hear
his voice,
[8]"Do not harden your hearts as
you did at Meribah,[a] Ex 17:7
as you did that day at
Massah[b] in the
wilderness,
[9]where your ancestors tested
me; Ps 78:18; 1Co 10:9
they tried me, though they
had seen what I did.
[10]For forty years I was angry with
that generation;
I said, 'They are a people
whose hearts go astray,
Ps 119:67,176
and they have not known my
ways.' Dt 8:6
[11]So I declared on oath in my
anger,
'They shall never enter my
rest.'" Heb 4:3*

[a] 8 *Meribah* means *quarreling*.
[b] 8 *Massah* means *testing*.

Psalm 96

1 Sing to the LORD a new song; 1Ch 16:23
sing to the LORD, all the earth.
2 Sing to the LORD, praise his name;
proclaim his salvation day after day. Ps 71:15
3 Declare his glory among the nations, Ps 8:1
his marvelous deeds among all peoples. Ps 71:17

4 For great is the LORD and most worthy of praise; Ps 18:3; 145:3
he is to be feared above all gods. Ps 95:3
5 For all the gods of the nations are idols,
but the LORD made the heavens. Ps 115:15
6 Splendor and majesty are before him;
strength and glory are in his sanctuary. Ps 29:1

7 Ascribe to the LORD, all you families of nations, Ps 29:1
ascribe to the LORD glory and strength.
8 Ascribe to the LORD the glory due his name;
bring an offering and come into his courts. Ps 45:12; 72:10
9 Worship the LORD in the splendor of his[a] holiness; Ps 29:2
tremble before him, all the earth.

10 Say among the nations, "The LORD reigns." Ps 97:1
The world is firmly established, it cannot be moved; Ps 93:1
he will judge the peoples with equity. Ps 67:4

11 Let the heavens rejoice, let the earth be glad;
let the sea resound, and all that is in it.
12 Let the fields be jubilant, and everything in them;
let all the trees of the forest sing for joy. Ps 65:13
13 Let all creation rejoice before the LORD, for he comes,
he comes to judge the earth. Rev 19:11

He will judge the world in righteousness
and the peoples in his faithfulness. Ps 86:11

Psalm 97

1 The LORD reigns, let the earth be glad; Ps 96:10
let the distant shores rejoice.
2 Clouds and thick darkness surround him; Ps 18:11
righteousness and justice are the foundation of his throne. Ps 89:14
3 Fire goes before him
and consumes his foes on every side. Ps 18:8
4 His lightning lights up the world;
the earth sees and trembles.

[a] 9 Or *LORD with the splendor of*

[5]The mountains melt like
wax before the LORD, Mic 1:4
before the Lord of all the
earth.
[6]The heavens proclaim his
righteousness, Ps 50:6
and all peoples see his glory. Ps 19:1

[7]All who worship images are put
to shame,
those who boast in idols —
worship him, all you gods! Heb 1:6

[8]Zion hears and rejoices
and the villages of Judah are
glad
because of your judgments,
LORD. Ps 48:11
[9]For you, LORD, are the Most
High over all the earth; Ps 83:18; 95:3
you are exalted far above all
gods. Ex 18:11
[10]Let those who love the
LORD hate evil, Ps 34:14; Am 5:15
for he guards the lives of his
faithful ones
and delivers them from the
hand of the wicked. Ps 37:40; Da 3:28
[11]Light shines[a] on the righteous Job 22:28
and joy on the upright in
heart.
[12]Rejoice in the LORD, you who
are righteous,
and praise his holy name. Ps 30:4

Psalm 98

A psalm.

[1]Sing to the LORD a new song, Ps 96:1
for he has done marvelous
things;
his right hand and his holy arm Ex 15:6; Isa 52:10
have worked salvation for
him.
[2]The LORD has made
his salvation known Isa 52:10
and revealed his
righteousness to the
nations.
[3]He has remembered his love Lk 1:54
and his faithfulness to
Israel;
all the ends of the earth have
seen
the salvation of our God. Ps 50:23

[4]Shout for joy to the LORD, all
the earth, Isa 44:23
burst into jubilant song with
music;
[5]make music to the LORD with
the harp, Ps 92:3
with the harp and the sound
of singing,
[6]with trumpets and the blast
of the ram's horn — Nu 10:10
shout for joy before the
LORD, the King. Ps 47:7

[a] *11* One Hebrew manuscript and ancient versions (see also 112:4); most Hebrew manuscripts *Light is sown*

7 Let the sea resound, and everything in it,
the world, and all who live in it. Ps 24:1
8 Let the rivers clap their hands,
let the mountains sing together for joy; Isa 55:12
9 let them sing before the LORD,
for he comes to judge the earth.
He will judge the world in righteousness
and the peoples with equity. Ps 96:10

Psalm 99

1 The LORD reigns, Ps 97:1
let the nations tremble;
he sits enthroned between the cherubim, Ex 25:22
let the earth shake.
2 Great is the LORD in Zion;
he is exalted over all the nations. Ps 97:9
3 Let them praise your great and awesome name — Ps 76:1
he is holy.

4 The King is mighty, he loves justice — Ps 11:7
you have established equity; Ps 98:9
in Jacob you have done what is just and right.
5 Exalt the LORD our God Ps 132:7
and worship at his footstool;
he is holy.

6 Moses and Aaron were among his priests,
Samuel was among those who called on his name; Jer 15:1
they called on the LORD
and he answered them. 1Sa 7:9
7 He spoke to them from the pillar of cloud; Ex 33:9
they kept his statutes and the decrees he gave them.

8 LORD our God,
you answered them;
you were to Israel a forgiving God, Nu 14:20
though you punished their misdeeds.[a]
9 Exalt the LORD our God
and worship at his holy mountain,
for the LORD our God is holy.

Psalm 100

A psalm. For giving grateful praise.

1 Shout for joy to the LORD, all the earth. Ps 98:4
2 Worship the LORD with gladness;
come before him with joyful songs. Ps 95:2
3 Know that the LORD is God. Ps 46:10
It is he who made us, and we are his[b];
we are his people, the sheep of his pasture. Ps 74:1; Eze 34:31

[a] 8 *Or God, / an avenger of the wrongs done to them* [b] 3 *Or and not we ourselves*

4 Enter his gates with
thanksgiving
and his courts with praise;
give thanks to him and
praise his name. Ps 116:17
5 For the LORD is good and his
love endures forever; Ps 25:8
his faithfulness continues
through all generations. Ps 119:90

Psalm 101

Of David. A psalm.

1 I will sing of your love and
justice; Ps 89:1
to you, LORD, I will sing
praise.
2 I will be careful to lead a
blameless life — Ge 17:1
when will you come to me?

I will conduct the affairs of my
house
with a blameless heart.
3 I will not look with approval
on anything that is vile. Dt 15:9
I hate what faithless people do; Ps 40:4
I will have no part in it.
4 The perverse of heart shall be
far from me; Pr 11:20
I will have nothing to do
with what is evil.

5 Whoever slanders their
neighbor in secret, Ps 50:20
I will put to silence;
whoever has haughty eyes and
a proud heart, Pr 6:17
I will not tolerate.

6 My eyes will be on the faithful
in the land,
that they may dwell with
me;
the one whose walk is
blameless Ps 119:1
will minister to me.

7 No one who practices deceit
will dwell in my house;
no one who speaks falsely
will stand in my
presence.

8 Every morning I will put to
silence Jer 21:12
all the wicked in the land; Ps 75:10
I will cut off every evildoer Ps 118:10-12
from the city of the LORD.

Psalm 102[a]

A prayer of an afflicted person who has grown weak and pours out a lament before the LORD.

1 Hear my prayer, LORD;
let my cry for help come to
you. Ex 2:23
2 Do not hide your face from me Ps 69:17
when I am in distress.
Turn your ear to me; 2Ki 19:16
when I call, answer me
quickly.

3 For my days vanish like smoke; Jas 4:14
my bones burn like glowing
embers.

[a] In Hebrew texts 102:1-28 is numbered 102:2-29.

4My heart is blighted and
withered like grass; Ps 37:2
I forget to eat my food.
5In my distress I groan aloud
and am reduced to skin and
bones.
6I am like a desert owl, Isa 34:11
like an owl among the ruins.
7I lie awake; I have become
Ps 77:4
like a bird alone on a roof.
8All day long my enemies
taunt me; Ps 42:10
those who rail against me
use my name as a curse.
9For I eat ashes as my food
and mingle my drink with
tears Ps 42:3
10because of your great wrath,
for you have taken me up
and thrown me aside.
11My days are like the evening
shadow; Job 14:2
I wither away like grass.

12But you, LORD, sit enthroned
forever; Ps 9:7
your renown endures
through all generations.
Ps 135:13
13You will arise and have
compassion on Zion,
Isa 60:10
for it is time to show favor
to her;
the appointed time has
come. Ex 13:10
14For her stones are dear to your
servants;
her very dust moves them to
pity.
15The nations will fear the name
of the LORD, 1Ki 8:43
all the kings of the earth will
revere your glory.
16For the LORD will rebuild Zion
and appear in his glory.
Isa 60:1-2
17He will respond to the prayer of
the destitute;
he will not despise their plea.

18Let this be written for a future
generation, Ro 15:4
that a people not yet created
may praise the LORD:
Ps 22:31
19"The LORD looked down from
his sanctuary on high,
Dt 26:15
from heaven he viewed the
earth,
20to hear the groans of the
prisoners
and release those
condemned to death."
21So the name of the LORD will be
declared in Zion Ps 22:22
and his praise in Jerusalem
22when the peoples and the
kingdoms
assemble to worship the
LORD. Ps 22:27

23In the course of my life[a] he
broke my strength;
he cut short my days. Ps 39:5
24So I said:
"Do not take me away, my God,
in the midst of my days;
your years go on through all
generations. Ps 90:2

[a] 23 Or *By his power*

25 In the beginning you laid
the foundations of the
earth, Heb 1:10-12*
and the heavens are the work
of your hands.
26 They will perish, but you
remain; Isa 34:4
they will all wear out like a
garment.
Like clothing you will change
them
and they will be discarded.
27 But you remain the same, Mal 3:6
and your years will never end.
28 The children of your servants
will live in your
presence; Ps 69:36
their descendants will be
established before you."
Ps 89:4

Psalm 103

Of David.

1 Praise the LORD, my soul; Ps 104:1
all my inmost being, praise
his holy name. Ps 30:4
2 Praise the LORD, my soul, Ps 106:1
and forget not all his
benefits —
3 who forgives all your sins Ps 130:8
and heals all your diseases,
Ex 15:26
4 who redeems your life from
the pit Ps 34:22
and crowns you with love
and compassion, Ps 8:5
5 who satisfies your desires with
good things Ps 90:14
so that your youth is
renewed like the eagle's.
Isa 40:31

6 The LORD works righteousness
and justice for all the
oppressed. Ps 74:21
7 He made known his ways to
Moses, Ex 33:13
his deeds to the people of
Israel: Ps 106:22
8 The LORD is compassionate
and gracious,
Ex 34:6; Ps 86:15; Jas 5:11
slow to anger, abounding in
love.
9 He will not always accuse,
nor will he harbor his anger
forever; Ps 30:5
10 he does not treat us as our sins
deserve Ezr 9:13
or repay us according to our
iniquities.
11 For as high as the heavens are
above the earth,
so great is his love for those
who fear him; Ps 57:10
12 as far as the east is from the
west,
so far has he removed our
transgressions from us.
2Sa 12:13

13 As a father has compassion on
his children, Mal 3:17
so the LORD has compassion
on those who fear him;
14 for he knows how we are
formed, Isa 29:16
he remembers that we are
dust.
15 The life of mortals is like
grass,
they flourish like a flower of
the field; Job 14:2; 1Pe 1:24

16 the wind blows over it and it is gone, Isa 40:7
and its place remembers it no more. Job 7:10
17 But from everlasting to everlasting
the LORD's love is with those who fear him,
and his righteousness with their children's children — Ge 48:11
18 with those who keep his covenant Dt 29:9
and remember to obey his precepts. Dt 7:9

19 The LORD has established his throne in heaven,
and his kingdom rules over all. Ps 47:2

20 Praise the LORD, you his angels, Ps 148:2; Heb 1:14
you mighty ones who do his bidding,
who obey his word.
21 Praise the LORD, all his heavenly hosts, 1Ki 22:19
you his servants who do his will.
22 Praise the LORD, all his works Ps 145:10
everywhere in his dominion.

Praise the LORD, my soul. ver 1; Ps 104:1

Psalm 104

1 Praise the LORD, my soul. Ps 103:22

LORD my God, you are very great;
you are clothed with splendor and majesty.
2 The LORD wraps himself in light as with a garment; Da 7:9
he stretches out the heavens like a tent Isa 40:22
3 and lays the beams of his upper chambers on their waters. Am 9:6
He makes the clouds his chariot Isa 19:1
and rides on the wings of the wind. Ps 18:10
4 He makes winds his messengers,[a] Heb 1:7*
flames of fire his servants.

5 He set the earth on its foundations; Job 26:7; Ps 24:1-2
it can never be moved.
6 You covered it with the watery depths as with a garment; Ge 1:2; 7:19
the waters stood above the mountains.
7 But at your rebuke the waters fled, Ps 18:15
at the sound of your thunder they took to flight; Ex 9:23
8 they flowed over the mountains,
they went down into the valleys,
to the place you assigned for them. Ps 33:7
9 You set a boundary they cannot cross;
never again will they cover the earth.

[a] 4 Or *angels*

10 He makes springs pour water
into the ravines; Ps 107:33; Isa 41:18
it flows between the
mountains.
11 They give water to all
the beasts of the
field;
the wild donkeys quench
their thirst. Ge 16:12
12 The birds of the sky nest by the
waters; Mt 8:20
they sing among the
branches.
13 He waters the mountains from
his upper chambers; Ps 147:8; Jer 10:13
the land is satisfied by the
fruit of his work.
14 He makes grass grow
for the cattle, Job 38:27; Ps 147:8
and plants for people to
cultivate —
bringing forth food from the
earth: Ge 1:30; Job 28:5
15 wine that gladdens human
hearts, Jdg 9:13
oil to make their
faces shine, Ps 23:5; 92:10; Lk 7:46
and bread that sustains their
hearts.
16 The trees of the LORD are well
watered,
the cedars of Lebanon that
he planted. Ps 72:16
17 There the birds make their
nests; ver 12
the stork has its home in the
junipers.
18 The high mountains
belong to the wild
goats;
the crags are a refuge for the
hyrax. Pr 30:26
19 He made the moon to mark the
seasons, Ge 1:14
and the sun knows when to
go down.
20 You bring darkness, it becomes
night, Isa 45:7
and all the beasts of the
forest prowl.
21 The lions roar for their prey
and seek their food from
God. Job 38:39
22 The sun rises, and they steal
away;
they return and lie down in
their dens.
23 Then people go out to their
work, Ge 3:19
to their labor until evening.
24 How many are your works,
LORD!
In wisdom you made them
all; Pr 3:19
the earth is full of your
creatures.
25 There is the sea, vast and
spacious, Ps 69:34
teeming with creatures
beyond number —
living things both large and
small.
26 There the ships go to and
fro,
and Leviathan, which you
formed to frolic there. Job 41:1

27 All creatures look to you
to give them their food at the proper time. Ps 136:25
28 When you give it to them,
they gather it up;
when you open your hand,
they are satisfied with good things. Ps 145:16
29 When you hide your face,
they are terrified; Dt 31:17
when you take away their breath,
they die and return to the dust. Job 34:14; Ecc 12:7
30 When you send your Spirit, Ge 1:2
they are created,
and you renew the face of the ground.

31 May the glory of the LORD endure forever;
may the LORD rejoice in his works — Ge 1:31
32 he who looks at the earth, and it trembles,
who touches the mountains, and they smoke. Ps 144:5

33 I will sing to the LORD all my life; Ps 63:4
I will sing praise to my God as long as I live.
34 May my meditation be pleasing to him, Ps 9:2
as I rejoice in the LORD.
35 But may sinners vanish from the earth Ps 37:38
and the wicked be no more.

Praise the LORD, my soul.

Praise the LORD.[a] Ps 105:45; 106:48

Psalm 105

1 Give praise to the LORD,
proclaim his name; 1Ch 16:34; Ps 99:6
make known among the nations what he has done.
2 Sing to him, sing praise to him; Ps 96:1
tell of all his wonderful acts.
3 Glory in his holy name;
let the hearts of those who seek the LORD rejoice.
4 Look to the LORD and his strength;
seek his face always. Ps 27:8

5 Remember the wonders he has done, Ps 40:5
his miracles, and the judgments he pronounced, Ps 77:11
6 you his servants, the descendants of Abraham,
his chosen ones, the children of Jacob. Ps 106:5
7 He is the LORD our God;
his judgments are in all the earth.

8 He remembers his covenant forever, Lk 1:72
the promise he made, for a thousand generations,
9 the covenant he made with Abraham, Ge 17:2; 22:16-18
the oath he swore to Isaac.

[a] *35* Hebrew *Hallelu Yah*; in the Septuagint this line stands at the beginning of Psalm 105.

10 He confirmed it to Jacob as a
decree, Ge 28:13-15
to Israel as an everlasting
covenant:
11 "To you I will give the land of
Canaan Ge 13:15; 15:18
as the portion you will
inherit." Nu 34:2

12 When they were but few in
number, Ge 34:30; Dt 7:7
few indeed, and strangers in
it, Heb 11:9
13 they wandered from nation to
nation,
from one kingdom to another.
14 He allowed no one to oppress
them; Ge 35:5
for their sake he rebuked
kings: Ge 12:17-20
15 "Do not touch my anointed
ones;
do my prophets no harm."

16 He called down famine on the
land Lev 26:26; Isa 3:1
and destroyed all their
supplies of food;
17 and he sent a man before
them —
Joseph, sold as a slave. Ge 37:28
18 They bruised his feet with
shackles,
his neck was put in irons,
19 till what he foretold came to
pass, Ge 40:20-22
till the word of the LORD
proved him true.
20 The king sent and released
him,
the ruler of peoples set him
free. Ge 41:14
21 He made him master of his
household,
ruler over all he possessed,
22 to instruct his princes as he
pleased Ge 41:43-44
and teach his elders wisdom.

23 Then Israel entered Egypt;
Ge 46:6
Jacob resided as a foreigner
in the land of Ham.
24 The LORD made his people very
fruitful;
he made them too numerous
for their foes, Ex 1:7,9
25 whose hearts he turned to hate
his people,
to conspire against his
servants.
26 He sent Moses his servant, Ex 3:10
and Aaron, whom he had
chosen.
27 They performed his signs
among them, Ex 7:8-12:51
his wonders in the land of
Ham.
28 He sent darkness and made the
land dark — Ex 10:22
for had they not rebelled
against his words?
29 He turned their waters into
blood,
causing their fish to die. Ex 7:21
30 Their land teemed with frogs,
Ex 8:2,6
which went up into the
bedrooms of their rulers.
31 He spoke, and there came
swarms of flies,
and gnats throughout their
country. Ex 8:16-18

[32]He turned their rain into hail, Ex 9:22-25
with lightning throughout their land;
[33]he struck down their vines and fig trees Ps 78:47
and shattered the trees of their country.
[34]He spoke, and the locusts came, Ex 10:4,12-15
grasshoppers without number;
[35]they ate up every green thing in their land,
ate up the produce of their soil.
[36]Then he struck down all the firstborn in their land, Ex 12:29
the firstfruits of all their manhood.
[37]He brought out Israel, laden with silver and gold, Ex 12:35
and from among their tribes no one faltered.
[38]Egypt was glad when they left,
because dread of Israel had fallen on them. Ex 15:16

[39]He spread out a cloud as a covering, Ex 13:21
and a fire to give light at night.
[40]They asked, and he brought them quail; Ex 16:13
he fed them well with the bread of heaven.
[41]He opened the rock, and water gushed out; 1Co 10:4
it flowed like a river in the desert.

[42]For he remembered his holy promise Ge 15:13-16
given to his servant Abraham.
[43]He brought out his people with rejoicing, Ex 15:1-18; Ps 106:12
his chosen ones with shouts of joy;
[44]he gave them the lands of the nations, Jos 13:6-7
and they fell heir to what others had toiled for —
[45]that they might keep his precepts
and observe his laws. Dt 4:40; 6:21-24

Praise the LORD.[a] Ps 104:35

Psalm 106

[1]Praise the LORD.[b] Ps 22:23

Give thanks to the LORD, for he is good; Ps 100:5; 105:1
his love endures forever. Jer 33:11

[2]Who can proclaim the mighty acts of the LORD Ps 145:4,12
or fully declare his praise?
[3]Blessed are those who act justly,
who always do what is right. Ps 15:2

[4]Remember me, LORD, when you show favor to your people, Ps 119:132
come to my aid when you save them,

[a] 45 Hebrew *Hallelu Yah* [b] 1 Hebrew *Hallelu Yah*; also in verse 48

[5]that I may enjoy the
prosperity of your
chosen ones, Ps 1:3
that I may share in the joy of
your nation Ps 118:15
and join your inheritance in
giving praise.

[6]We have sinned, even as our
ancestors did; Da 9:5
we have done wrong and
acted wickedly.
[7]When our ancestors were in
Egypt,
they gave no thought to your
miracles;
they did not remember your
many kindnesses,
Ps 78:11,42
and they rebelled by the sea,
the Red Sea.[a] Ex 14:11-12
[8]Yet he saved them for his
name's sake, Ex 9:16
to make his mighty power
known.
[9]He rebuked the Red Sea,
and it dried up;
Ex 14:21; Ps 18:15
he led them through the
depths as through a
desert. Isa 63:11-14
[10]He saved them from the hand
of the foe; Ex 14:30
from the hand of the enemy
he redeemed them.
[11]The waters covered their
adversaries; Ex 14:28; 15:5
not one of them survived.
[12]Then they believed his
promises
and sang his praise.

[13]But they soon forgot what he
had done Ex 15:24
and did not wait for his plan
to unfold.
[14]In the desert they gave in to
their craving;
in the wilderness they
put God to the test.
1Co 10:9
[15]So he gave them what they
asked for, Nu 11:31
but sent a wasting disease
among them. Isa 10:16

[16]In the camp they grew envious
of Moses Nu 16:1-3
and of Aaron, who was
consecrated to the
LORD.
[17]The earth opened up and
swallowed Dathan; Dt 11:6
it buried the company of
Abiram.
[18]Fire blazed among their
followers;
a flame consumed the
wicked. Nu 16:35
[19]At Horeb they made a calf
Ex 32:4
and worshiped an idol cast
from metal.
[20]They exchanged their glorious
God Jer 2:11; Ro 1:23
for an image of a bull, which
eats grass.
[21]They forgot the God who saved
them, Ps 78:11
who had done great things in
Egypt,

[a] 7 Or *the Sea of Reeds*; also in verses 9 and 22

22 miracles in the land of Ham Ps 105:27
and awesome deeds by the Red Sea.
23 So he said he would destroy them — Ex 32:10
had not Moses, his chosen one,
stood in the breach before him
to keep his wrath from destroying them.

24 Then they despised the pleasant land; Dt 8:7
they did not believe his promise. Heb 3:18-19
25 They grumbled in their tents Nu 14:2
and did not obey the LORD.
26 So he swore to them
with uplifted hand Eze 20:15; Heb 3:11
that he would make them
fall in the wilderness, Nu 14:28-35
27 make their descendants fall
among the nations
and scatter them throughout
the lands. Ps 44:11

28 They yoked themselves to the Baal of Peor Nu 25:2-3
and ate sacrifices offered to lifeless gods;
29 they aroused the LORD's anger
by their wicked deeds,
and a plague broke out among them.
30 But Phinehas stood up and intervened,
and the plague was checked. Nu 25:8
31 This was credited to him as righteousness Nu 25:11-13
for endless generations to come.
32 By the waters of Meribah
they angered the LORD, Nu 20:2-13
and trouble came to Moses
because of them;
33 for they rebelled against the Spirit of God, Ex 23:21
and rash words came from Moses' lips.[a] Nu 20:8-12

34 They did not destroy the peoples Jdg 1:21
as the LORD had commanded them, Dt 7:16
35 but they mingled with the nations Jdg 3:5-6
and adopted their customs.
36 They worshiped their idols, Jdg 2:12
which became a snare to them.
37 They sacrificed their sons
and their daughters to false gods.
38 They shed innocent blood,
the blood of their sons and daughters, Nu 35:33
whom they sacrificed to the idols of Canaan,
and the land was desecrated by their blood.
39 They defiled themselves by what they did; Eze 20:18
by their deeds they prostituted themselves. Lev 17:7; Nu 15:39

[a] 33 Or *against his spirit, / and rash words came from his lips*

[40]Therefore the LORD was angry
with his people
and abhorred his inheritance.
[41]He gave them into the hands of
the nations, Jdg 2:14; Ne 9:27
and their foes ruled over
them.
[42]Their enemies oppressed them
and subjected them to their
power.
[43]Many times he delivered them,
but they were bent on
rebellion Jdg 2:16-19
and they wasted away in
their sin.
[44]Yet he took note of their distress
when he heard their cry;
Jdg 10:10
[45]for their sake he remembered
his covenant Lev 26:42
and out of his great love he
relented. Jdg 2:18
[46]He caused all who held them
captive
to show them mercy.
Ezr 9:9; Jer 42:12

[47]Save us, LORD our God,
and gather us from the
nations, Ps 147:2
that we may give thanks to
your holy name
and glory in your praise.

[48]Praise be to the LORD, the God
of Israel,
from everlasting to
everlasting.

Let all the people say, "Amen!"
Ps 41:13

Praise the LORD.

BOOK V
Psalms 107 – 150

Psalm 107

[1]Give thanks to the LORD, for he
is good; Ps 106:1
his love endures forever.

[2]Let the redeemed of the LORD
tell their story — Ps 106:10
those he redeemed from the
hand of the foe,
[3]those he gathered from the
lands, Ps 106:47
from east and west, from
north and south.[a]

[4]Some wandered in desert
wastelands, Nu 14:33; 32:13
finding no way to a city
where they could
settle.
[5]They were hungry and thirsty,
Ex 15:22
and their lives ebbed away.
[6]Then they cried out to the
LORD in their trouble,
Ps 50:15
and he delivered them from
their distress.
[7]He led them by a straight way
Ezr 8:21
to a city where they could
settle.
[8]Let them give thanks to the
LORD for his unfailing
love Ps 6:4
and his wonderful deeds for
mankind, Ps 75:1

[a] 3 Hebrew *north and the sea*

9 for he satisfies the thirsty Lk 1:53
and fills the hungry with
good things. Ps 34:10

10 Some sat in darkness, in utter
darkness, Lk 1:79
prisoners suffering in iron
chains, Job 36:8
11 because they rebelled
against God's
commands
and despised the plans of the
Most High. 2Ch 36:16
12 So he subjected them to bitter
labor;
they stumbled, and
there was no one to
help. Ps 22:11
13 Then they cried to the LORD in
their trouble,
and he saved them from
their distress.
14 He brought them out of
darkness, the utter
darkness,
and broke away their chains.
Ac 12:7
15 Let them give thanks to the
LORD for his unfailing
love Ps 105:1
and his wonderful deeds for
mankind, Ps 75:1
16 for he breaks down gates of
bronze
and cuts through bars of
iron.

17 Some became fools through
their rebellious ways
and suffered affliction
because of their
iniquities. Isa 65:6-7; La 3:39
18 They loathed all food
and drew near the gates of
death. Ps 9:13
19 Then they cried to the LORD in
their trouble,
and he saved them from
their distress.
20 He sent out his word
and healed them;
Ps 103:3; Mt 8:8
he rescued them from the
grave. Ps 30:3
21 Let them give thanks to the
LORD for his unfailing
love
and his wonderful deeds for
mankind.
22 Let them sacrifice thank
offerings Lev 7:12
and tell of his works
with songs of joy.
Ps 9:11; 73:28; 118:17

23 Some went out on the sea in
ships;
they were merchants on the
mighty waters.
24 They saw the works of the
LORD, Ps 64:9
his wonderful deeds in the
deep.
25 For he spoke and stirred up a
tempest Jnh 1:4
that lifted high the waves.
Ps 93:3
26 They mounted up to
the heavens and
went down to the
depths;
in their peril their courage
melted away. Ps 22:14

27 They reeled and staggered like
drunkards;
they were at their wits'
end.
28 Then they cried out to the
LORD in their trouble,
and he brought them out of
their distress. Jnh 1:6
29 He stilled the storm to a
whisper; Mt 8:26
the waves of the sea[a] were
hushed. Ps 89:9
30 They were glad when it grew
calm,
and he guided them to their
desired haven.
31 Let them give thanks to the
LORD for his unfailing
love Ps 6:4
and his wonderful deeds for
mankind.
32 Let them exalt him in the
assembly of the people
Ps 22:22,25; 35:18
and praise him in the council
of the elders.

33 He turned rivers into a desert,
1Ki 17:1; Ps 74:15
flowing springs into thirsty
ground,
34 and fruitful land into a salt
waste, Ge 13:10
because of the wickedness
of those who lived
there.
35 He turned the desert into
pools of water
Ps 114:8; Isa 41:18
and the parched ground into
flowing springs;
36 there he brought the hungry to
live,
and they founded a city
where they could
settle.
37 They sowed fields and planted
vineyards Isa 65:21
that yielded a fruitful
harvest;
38 he blessed them, and their
numbers greatly
increased, Ge 12:2
and he did not let their herds
diminish.

39 Then their numbers
decreased, and
they were humbled
2Ki 10:32; Eze 5:12
by oppression, calamity and
sorrow;
40 he who pours contempt on
nobles Job 12:21
made them wander in a
trackless waste. Job 12:24
41 But he lifted the needy out
of their affliction
1Sa 2:8; Ps 113:7-9
and increased their families
like flocks.
42 The upright see and rejoice,
Job 22:19
but all the wicked shut their
mouths. Job 5:16; Ro 3:19

43 Let the one who is wise
heed these things
Jer 9:12; Hos 14:9
and ponder the loving deeds
of the LORD. Ps 64:9

[a] 29 Dead Sea Scrolls; Masoretic Text / *their waves*

Psalm 108[a]

A song. A psalm of David.

1 My heart, O God, is steadfast;
I will sing and make
music with all my soul.
Ps 18:49
2 Awake, harp and lyre! Job 21:12
I will awaken the dawn.
3 I will praise you, LORD, among
the nations;
I will sing of you among the
peoples.
4 For great is your love,
higher than the
heavens;
your faithfulness reaches to
the skies. Ps 36:5
5 Be exalted, O God, above the
heavens; Ps 8:1
let your glory be over all the
earth. Ps 57:5

6 Save us and help us with your
right hand, Job 40:14
that those you love may be
delivered.
7 God has spoken from his
sanctuary: Ps 68:35
"In triumph I will parcel out
Shechem Ge 12:6
and measure off the Valley of
Sukkoth. Ge 33:17
8 Gilead is mine, Manasseh is
mine;
Ephraim is my helmet,
Judah is my scepter. Ge 49:10
9 Moab is my washbasin,
on Edom I toss my sandal;
2Sa 8:13-14
over Philistia I shout in
triumph." 2Sa 8:1
10 Who will bring me to the
fortified city?
Who will lead me to Edom?
11 Is it not you, God, you who
have rejected us
and no longer go out with
our armies? Ps 44:9
12 Give us aid against the
enemy,
for human help is worthless.
Ps 118:8
13 With God we will gain the
victory,
and he will trample down
our enemies. Ps 44:5

Psalm 109

For the director of music.
Of David. A psalm.

1 My God, whom I praise,
do not remain silent, Ps 83:1
2 for people who are wicked and
deceitful Ps 43:1
have opened their mouths
against me;
they have spoken against
me with lying tongues.
Ps 120:2
3 With words of hatred they
surround me; Ps 69:4
they attack me without
cause.
4 In return for my friendship
they accuse me,
but I am a man of prayer.
5 They repay me evil for good,
Ps 35:12; 38:20
and hatred for my
friendship.

[a] In Hebrew texts 108:1-13 is numbered 108:2-14.

6 Appoint someone evil to
oppose my enemy;
let an accuser stand at his
right hand. Zec 3:1
7 When he is tried, let him be
found guilty,
and may his prayers
condemn him. Pr 28:9
8 May his days be few;
may another take his place of
leadership. Ac 1:20*
9 May his children be fatherless
and his wife a widow. Ex 22:24
10 May his children be wandering
beggars;
may they be driven[a] from
their ruined homes.
11 May a creditor seize all he has;
may strangers plunder
the fruits of his labor.
Job 5:5
12 May no one extend kindness to
him
or take pity on his fatherless
children.
13 May his descendants be cut off,
Ps 37:28
their names blotted out from
the next generation.
Pr 10:7
14 May the iniquity of his fathers
be remembered
before the LORD;
Ex 20:5; Ne 4:5; Jer 18:23
may the sin of his mother
never be blotted out.
15 May their sins always remain
before the LORD,
that he may blot out their
name from the earth.
Ps 34:16

16 For he never thought of doing
a kindness,
but hounded to death the poor
and the needy and the
brokenhearted.
Ps 34:18; 37:14,32
17 He loved to pronounce a curse —
may it come back on him.
Pr 14:14
He found no pleasure in
blessing —
may it be far from him.
18 He wore cursing as his garment;
it entered into his body like
water, Nu 5:22
into his bones like oil.
19 May it be like a cloak wrapped
about him,
like a belt tied forever
around him.
20 May this be the LORD's
payment to my accusers,
Ps 94:23; 2Ti 4:14
to those who speak evil of
me. Ps 71:10

21 But you, Sovereign LORD,
help me for your name's
sake; Ps 79:9
out of the goodness of your
love, deliver me. Ps 69:16
22 For I am poor and needy,
and my heart is wounded
within me.
23 I fade away like an evening
shadow; Ps 102:11
I am shaken off like a locust.
24 My knees give way from
fasting; Heb 12:12
my body is thin and gaunt.

[a] 10 Septuagint; Hebrew *sought*

25 I am an object of scorn to my
accusers; Ps 22:6
when they see me, they
shake their heads. Mt 27:39

26 Help me, LORD my God;
save me according to your
unfailing love.
27 Let them know that it is your
hand, Job 37:7
that you, LORD, have done it.
28 While they curse, may you
bless; 2Sa 16:12
may those who attack me be
put to shame,
but may your servant rejoice.
Isa 65:14
29 May my accusers be clothed
with disgrace
and wrapped in shame as in
a cloak. Ps 35:26

30 With my mouth I will greatly
extol the LORD;
in the great throng of
worshipers I will praise
him.
31 For he stands at the right hand
of the needy, Ps 16:8
to save their lives from those
who would condemn
them.

Psalm 110

Of David. A psalm.

1 The LORD says to my lord:[a]
Mt 22:44*; Ac 2:34*

"Sit at my right hand
until I make your enemies
a footstool for your feet."
1Co 15:25

2 The LORD will extend your
mighty scepter from
Zion, saying, Ps 45:6
"Rule in the midst of your
enemies!"
3 Your troops will be willing
on your day of battle.
Arrayed in holy splendor,
Jdg 5:2; Ps 96:9
your young men will come to
you
like dew from the morning's
womb.[b] Mic 5:7

4 The LORD has sworn
and will not change his
mind: Nu 23:19
"You are a priest forever,
Heb 5:6*; 7:21*
in the order of Melchizedek."
Heb 7:15-17*

5 The Lord is at your right hand[c];
Ps 16:8
he will crush kings on
the day of his wrath.
Ps 2:5,12; Ro 2:5
6 He will judge the nations,
heaping up the dead
Isa 2:4
and crushing the rulers
of the whole earth.
Ps 68:21
7 He will drink from a brook
along the way,[d]
and so he will lift his head
high. Ps 27:6

[a] *1* Or *Lord* [b] *3* The meaning of the Hebrew for this sentence is uncertain.
[c] *5* Or *My lord is at your right hand, LORD*
[d] *7* The meaning of the Hebrew for this clause is uncertain.

Psalm 111[a]

[1]Praise the LORD.[b]

I will extol the LORD with all
my heart Ps 34:1
in the council of the
upright and in the
assembly.

[2]Great are the works of the
LORD; Ps 92:5
they are pondered by
all who delight in
them.
[3]Glorious and majestic are his
deeds,
and his righteousness
endures forever. Ps 112:3,9
[4]He has caused his wonders to
be remembered;
the LORD is gracious
and compassionate.
Ps 103:8
[5]He provides food for
those who fear him;
Mt 6:26,31-33
he remembers his covenant
forever.

[6]He has shown his people
the power of his
works,
giving them the lands of
other nations. Ps 105:44
[7]The works of his hands are
faithful and just;
all his precepts are
trustworthy. Ps 19:7
[8]They are established for ever
and ever,
enacted in faithfulness and
uprightness.

[9]He provided redemption for
his people; Lk 1:68
he ordained his covenant
forever—
holy and awesome is his
name. Ps 99:3

[10]The fear of the LORD is the
beginning of wisdom;
Pr 9:10
all who follow his
precepts have good
understanding. Ecc 12:13
To him belongs eternal
praise. Ps 145:2

Psalm 112[a]

[1]Praise the LORD.[b] Ps 33:2

Blessed are those who fear the
LORD, Ps 128:1
who find great delight in
his commands.
Ps 119:14,16,47,92

[2]Their children will be mighty
in the land; Ps 25:13
the generation of the
upright will be
blessed.
[3]Wealth and riches are in their
houses, Dt 8:18
and their righteousness
endures forever. Ps 37:6
[4]Even in darkness light dawns
for the upright, Job 11:17
for those who are gracious
and compassionate and
righteous. Ps 97:11

[a] This psalm is an acrostic poem, the lines of which begin with the successive letters of the Hebrew alphabet. [b] *1* Hebrew *Hallelu Yah*

5 Good will come to those who
are generous and lend
freely, Ps 37:21,26
who conduct their affairs
with justice.

6 Surely the righteous will never
be shaken;
they will be remembered
forever. Pr 10:7
7 They will have no fear of bad
news;
their hearts are steadfast,
trusting in the LORD.
Ps 57:7
8 Their hearts are secure, they
will have no fear;
in the end they will
look in triumph on
their foes.
9 They have freely scattered
their gifts to the poor,
2Co 9:9
their righteousness endures
forever;
their horn[a] will be lifted high
in honor. Ps 75:10

10 The wicked will see and be
vexed,
they will gnash their teeth
and waste away; Ps 37:12
the longings of the wicked
will come to nothing.
Pr 11:7

Psalm 113

1 Praise the LORD.[b]

Praise the LORD, you his
servants; Ps 135:1
praise the name of the LORD.
2 Let the name of the LORD be
praised,
both now and forevermore.
Da 2:20
3 From the rising of the sun to
the place where it sets,
Isa 59:19; Mal 1:11
the name of the LORD is to be
praised.
4 The LORD is exalted over all the
nations, Ps 99:2
his glory above the heavens.
Ps 8:1
5 Who is like the LORD our God,
the One who sits enthroned
on high,
6 who stoops down to look
Ps 11:4; 138:6; Isa 57:15
on the heavens and the earth?
7 He raises the poor from the
dust 1Sa 2:8
and lifts the needy from the
ash heap; Ps 107:41
8 he seats them with princes,
with the princes of his
people.
9 He settles the childless woman
in her home 1Sa 2:5
as a happy mother of
children.

Praise the LORD.

Psalm 114

1 When Israel came out of Egypt,
Ex 13:3
Jacob from a people of
foreign tongue,

[a] 9 *Horn* here symbolizes dignity.
[b] 1 Hebrew *Hallelu Yah*; also in verse 9

2 Judah became God's sanctuary, Ex 15:17
Israel his dominion.

3 The sea looked and fled, Ex 14:21
the Jordan turned back;
4 the mountains leaped like rams,
the hills like lambs.

5 Why was it, sea, that you fled? Ex 14:21
Why, Jordan, did you turn back?
6 Why, mountains, did you leap like rams,
you hills, like lambs?

7 Tremble, earth, at the presence of the Lord, Ps 96:9
at the presence of the God of Jacob,
8 who turned the rock into a pool,
the hard rock into springs of water. Ex 17:6; Nu 20:11

Psalm 115

1 Not to us, LORD, not to us
but to your name be the glory, Ps 96:8
because of your love and faithfulness. Ex 34:6

2 Why do the nations say,
"Where is their God?" Ps 42:3
3 Our God is in heaven; Ps 103:19
he does whatever pleases him. Ps 135:6
4 But their idols are silver and gold,
made by human hands. Jer 10:3-5
5 They have mouths, but cannot speak, Jer 10:5
eyes, but cannot see.
6 They have ears, but cannot hear,
noses, but cannot smell.
7 They have hands, but cannot feel,
feet, but cannot walk,
nor can they utter a sound with their throats.
8 Those who make them will be like them,
and so will all who trust in them.

9 All you Israelites, trust in the LORD — Ps 37:3
he is their help and shield.
10 House of Aaron, trust in the LORD — Ps 118:3
he is their help and shield.
11 You who fear him, trust in the LORD — Ps 22:23
he is their help and shield.

12 The LORD remembers us and will bless us:
He will bless his people Israel,
he will bless the house of Aaron,
13 he will bless those who fear the LORD — Ps 128:1,4
small and great alike.

14 May the LORD cause you to flourish,
both you and your children.
15 May you be blessed by the LORD,
the Maker of heaven and earth. Ps 96:5

16 The highest heavens belong to
the LORD, Ps 89:11
but the earth he has given to
mankind.
17 It is not the dead who praise
the LORD, Ps 6:5
those who go down to the
place of silence;
18 it is we who extol the LORD,
both now and forevermore.
Ps 113:2

Praise the LORD.[a] Ps 28:6

Psalm 116

1 I love the LORD, for he heard
my voice; Ps 18:1
he heard my cry for mercy.
Ps 66:19
2 Because he turned his ear to
me, Ps 40:1
I will call on him as long as I
live.

3 The cords of death entangled
me, Ps 18:4-5
the anguish of the grave
came over me;
I was overcome by distress
and sorrow.
4 Then I called on the name of
the LORD: Ps 118:5
"LORD, save me!" Ps 22:20

5 The LORD is gracious and
righteous; Ezr 9:15; Ps 103:8
our God is full of
compassion.
6 The LORD protects the
unwary;
when I was brought low, he
saved me. Ps 19:7; 79:8

7 Return to your rest, my soul,
Mt 11:29
for the LORD has been good
to you. Ps 13:6

8 For you, LORD, have delivered
me from death, Ps 56:13
my eyes from tears,
my feet from stumbling,
9 that I may walk before the
LORD
in the land of the living.
Ps 27:13

10 I trusted in the LORD when I
said, 2Co 4:13*
"I am greatly afflicted";
11 in my alarm I said,
"Everyone is a liar." Ro 3:4

12 What shall I return to the LORD
for all his goodness to me?

13 I will lift up the cup of
salvation
and call on the name of the
LORD.
14 I will fulfill my vows to the
LORD Ps 22:25
in the presence of all his
people.

15 Precious in the sight of the
LORD Ps 72:14
is the death of his faithful
servants.
16 Truly I am your servant, LORD;
Ps 119:125; 143:12
I serve you just as my
mother did; Ps 86:16
you have freed me from my
chains.

[a] 18 Hebrew *Hallelu Yah*

[17]I will sacrifice a thank offering
to you Ps 50:14
and call on the name of the
LORD.
[18]I will fulfill my vows to the
LORD
in the presence of all his
people,
[19]in the courts of the house of
the LORD — Ps 96:8
in your midst, Jerusalem.

Praise the LORD.[a]

Psalm 117

[1]Praise the LORD, all you
nations; Ro 15:11*
extol him, all you peoples.
[2]For great is his love toward us,
and the faithfulness of the
LORD endures forever.
Ps 100:5

Praise the LORD.[a]

Psalm 118

[1]Give thanks to the LORD, for he
is good; 1Ch 16:8
his love endures forever.
Ps 106:1; 136:1
[2]Let Israel say: Ps 115:9
"His love endures forever."
[3]Let the house of Aaron say:
"His love endures forever."
[4]Let those who fear the LORD
say: Ps 115:11
"His love endures forever."

[5]When hard pressed, I cried to
the LORD; Ps 120:1
he brought me into a
spacious place.
[6]The LORD is with me;
I will not be afraid.
Heb 13:6*
What can mere mortals do
to me? Ps 56:4
[7]The LORD is with me; he is my
helper.
I look in triumph on my
enemies. Ps 59:10
[8]It is better to take refuge in the
LORD
than to trust in humans.
Ps 40:4
[9]It is better to take refuge in the
LORD
than to trust in princes.
Ps 146:3
[10]All the nations surrounded me,
but in the name of the
LORD I cut them
down.
[11]They surrounded me on every
side, Ps 3:6; 88:17
but in the name of the LORD
I cut them down.
[12]They swarmed around me like
bees, Dt 1:44
but they were consumed
as quickly as burning
thorns;
in the name of the LORD I cut
them down.
[13]I was pushed back and about to
fall,
but the LORD helped me.
[14]The LORD is my strength and
my defense[b]; Ex 15:2
he has become my salvation.
Isa 12:2

[a] 19,2 Hebrew *Hallelu Yah* [b] 14 Or *song*

15 Shouts of joy and victory
resound in the tents of the righteous:
"The LORD's right hand has done mighty things!
Ps 89:13
16 The LORD's right hand is lifted high;
the LORD's right hand has done mighty things!"
17 I will not die but live, Hab 1:12
and will proclaim what the LORD has done. Ps 73:28
18 The LORD has chastened me severely,
but he has not given me over to death. 2Co 6:9
19 Open for me the gates of the righteous; Isa 26:2
I will enter and give thanks to the LORD.
20 This is the gate of the LORD
through which the righteous may enter. Rev 22:14
21 I will give you thanks, for you answered me; Ps 116:1
you have become my salvation.
22 The stone the builders rejected
has become the cornerstone;
Mt 21:42; Lk 20:17*; Ac 4:11*
23 the LORD has done this,
and it is marvelous in our eyes. Mt 21:42*
24 The LORD has done it this very day;
let us rejoice today and be glad. Ps 70:4

25 LORD, save us!
LORD, grant us success!
26 Blessed is he who comes in the name of the LORD.
Mt 21:9*; Jn 12:13*
From the house of the LORD we bless you.[a]
27 The LORD is God,
and he has made his light shine on us. 1Pe 2:9
With boughs in hand, join in the festal procession
up[b] to the horns of the altar.
Ex 27:2

28 You are my God, and I will praise you;
you are my God, and I will exalt you. Ex 15:2; Isa 25:1
29 Give thanks to the LORD, for he is good;
his love endures forever.

Psalm 119[c]

א Aleph

1 Blessed are those whose ways are blameless,
Ge 17:1; Pr 11:20
who walk according to the law of the LORD. Ps 128:1
2 Blessed are those who keep his statutes
and seek him with all their heart— Dt 6:5
3 they do no wrong Jn 3:9; 5:18
but follow his ways. Ps 128:1

[a] *26* The Hebrew is plural. [b] *27* Or *Bind the festal sacrifice with ropes / and take it*
[c] This psalm is an acrostic poem, the stanzas of which begin with successive letters of the Hebrew alphabet; moreover, the verses of each stanza begin with the same letter of the Hebrew alphabet.

[4]You have laid down precepts Ps 103:18
that are to be fully obeyed. Dt 6:17
[5]Oh, that my ways were steadfast
in obeying your decrees! Lev 19:37
[6]Then I would not be put to shame
when I consider all your commands. ver 117
[7]I will praise you with an upright heart
as I learn your righteous laws. Dt 4:8
[8]I will obey your decrees;
do not utterly forsake me. Ps 38:21

ב Beth

[9]How can a young person stay on the path of purity? Ps 39:1
By living according to your word. 2Ch 6:16
[10]I seek you with all my heart; 2Ch 15:15
do not let me stray from your commands.
[11]I have hidden your word in my heart Ps 37:31; Lk 2:19,51
that I might not sin against you.
[12]Praise be to you, LORD;
teach me your decrees.
[13]With my lips I recount
all the laws that come from your mouth. Ps 40:9
[14]I rejoice in following your statutes
as one rejoices in great riches.
[15]I meditate on your precepts Ps 1:2
and consider your ways.
[16]I delight in your decrees; Ps 1:2
I will not neglect your word.

ג Gimel

[17]Be good to your servant while I live, Ps 13:6; 116:7
that I may obey your word.
[18]Open my eyes that I may see
wonderful things in your law.
[19]I am a stranger on earth; 1Ch 29:15; Ps 39:12; Heb 11:13
do not hide your commands from me.
[20]My soul is consumed with longing Ps 42:2; 84:2
for your laws at all times. Ps 63:1
[21]You rebuke the arrogant, who are accursed, Job 30:1; Ps 5:5
those who stray from your commands. ver 10
[22]Remove from me their scorn and contempt, Ps 39:8
for I keep your statutes.
[23]Though rulers sit together and slander me,
your servant will meditate on your decrees.
[24]Your statutes are my delight;
they are my counselors.

ד Daleth

[25]I am laid low in the dust; Ps 44:25
preserve my life according to your word. Ps 143:11

26 I gave an account of my
ways and you
answered me;
teach me your decrees. Ps 25:4
27 Cause me to understand the
way of your precepts,
that I may meditate on your
wonderful deeds. Ps 145:5
28 My soul is weary with sorrow;
Ps 107:26
strengthen me according to
your word. Ps 20:2; 1Pe 5:10
29 Keep me from deceitful ways;
Ps 26:4
be gracious to me and teach
me your law. Nu 6:25
30 I have chosen the way of
faithfulness; Ps 26:3
I have set my heart on your
laws. Ps 108:1
31 I hold fast to your statutes,
LORD; Dt 10:20; 11:22
do not let me be put to
shame.
32 I run in the path of your
commands,
for you have broadened my
understanding.

ה He

33 Teach me, LORD, the way of
your decrees, ver 12
that I may follow it to the
end.[a]
34 Give me understanding, so
that I may keep your law
Dt 6:25
and obey it with all my heart.
35 Direct me in the path of your
commands,
for there I find delight. Ps 1:2
36 Turn my heart toward your
statutes
and not toward selfish gain.
Lk 12:15; Heb 13:5
37 Turn my eyes away from
worthless things;
preserve my life according
to your word.[b]
Ps 71:20; Isa 33:15
38 Fulfill your promise to your
servant, 2Sa 7:25
so that you may be feared.
39 Take away the disgrace I dread,
Ps 69:9
for your laws are good.
40 How I long for your precepts!
ver 20
In your righteousness
preserve my life.

ו Waw

41 May your unfailing love come
to me, LORD, Ps 6:4
your salvation, according
to your promise;
ver 76,116,154,170
42 then I can answer anyone who
taunts me, Pr 27:11
for I trust in your word.
43 Never take your word of truth
from my mouth,
for I have put my
hope in your laws.
ver 74,81,114,147
44 I will always obey your law,
Dt 6:25
for ever and ever.

[a] 33 Or *follow it for its reward* [b] 37 Two manuscripts of the Masoretic Text and Dead Sea Scrolls; most manuscripts of the Masoretic Text *life in your way*

45 I will walk about in freedom,
for I have sought out your
precepts. ver 94,155
46 I will speak of your statutes
before kings
Mt 10:18; Ac 26:1-2
and will not be put to shame,
47 for I delight in your commands
Ps 112:1
because I love them.
48 I reach out for your commands,
which I love,
that I may meditate on your
decrees. Ge 24:63

ז Zayin

49 Remember your word to your
servant,
for you have given me hope.
ver 43
50 My comfort in my suffering is
this:
Your promise preserves my
life. Ro 15:4
51 The arrogant mock me
unmercifully, Jer 20:7
but I do not turn from your
law. Job 23:11
52 I remember, LORD, your
ancient laws, Ps 103:18
and I find comfort in them.
53 Indignation grips me because
of the wicked, Ezr 9:3
who have forsaken your law.
Ps 89:30
54 Your decrees are the theme of
my song
wherever I lodge.
55 In the night, LORD, I remember
your name, Ps 63:6
that I may keep your law.
56 This has been my practice:
I obey your precepts. Nu 15:40

ח Heth

57 You are my portion, LORD;
Ps 16:5; La 3:24
I have promised to obey your
words.
58 I have sought your face with all
my heart;
be gracious to me according
to your promise. 1Ki 13:6
59 I have considered my ways
Lk 15:17-18
and have turned my steps to
your statutes.
60 I will hasten and not delay
to obey your commands.
61 Though the wicked bind me
with ropes,
I will not forget your law.
Ps 140:5
62 At midnight I rise to give you
thanks Ac 16:25
for your righteous laws.
63 I am a friend to all who fear
you, Ps 101:6-7
to all who follow your
precepts.
64 The earth is filled with your
love, LORD; Ps 33:5
teach me your decrees.

ט Teth

65 Do good to your servant
according to your word,
LORD. Ps 125:4; Mic 2:7
66 Teach me knowledge and good
judgment, Ps 51:6
for I trust your commands.

67 Before I was afflicted I went
astray, Jer 31:18-19; Heb 12:11
but now I obey your word.
68 You are good, and what you
do is good;
Ps 106:1; 107:1; Mt 19:17
teach me your decrees.
69 Though the arrogant have
smeared me with lies,
Job 13:4
I keep your precepts with all
my heart.
70 Their hearts are callous and
unfeeling, Ps 17:10; Ac 28:27
but I delight in your law.
71 It was good for me to be
afflicted ver 67,75
so that I might learn your
decrees.
72 The law from your mouth is
more precious to me
than thousands of pieces
of silver and gold.
Ps 19:10; Pr 8:10-11,19

י Yodh

73 Your hands made me
and formed me;
Job 10:8; Ps 138:8; 139:13-16
give me understanding to
learn your commands.
74 May those who fear you
rejoice when they
see me, Ps 34:2
for I have put my hope in
your word.
75 I know, LORD, that your laws
are righteous,
and that in faithfulness
you have afflicted me.
Heb 12:5-11
76 May your unfailing love be my
comfort,
according to your promise to
your servant. ver 41
77 Let your compassion come
to me that I may live,
ver 41; Ps 90:13
for your law is my delight.
78 May the arrogant be put to
shame for wronging
me without cause;
ver 86,161; Ps 35:19; Jer 50:32
but I will meditate on your
precepts.
79 May those who fear you turn to
me,
those who understand your
statutes. ver 27,125
80 May I wholeheartedly follow
your decrees, Ge 26:5
that I may not be put to
shame.

כ Kaph

81 My soul faints with longing for
your salvation, Ps 84:2
but I have put my hope in
your word.
82 My eyes fail, looking
for your promise;
Ps 69:3; La 2:11
I say, "When will you comfort
me?"
83 Though I am like a wineskin in
the smoke,
I do not forget your
decrees.
84 How long must your servant
wait? Ps 39:4; Rev 6:10
When will you punish my
persecutors?

[85]The arrogant dig pits to trap
me, Ps 35:7; Jer 18:20,22
contrary to your law.
[86]All your commands are
trustworthy; Ps 35:19
help me, for I am being
persecuted without
cause. Ps 109:26
[87]They almost wiped me from
the earth,
but I have not forsaken your
precepts. Isa 58:2
[88]In your unfailing love preserve
my life,
that I may obey the statutes
of your mouth.
ver 2,100,129,134,168

ל Lamedh

[89]Your word, LORD, is eternal;
Mt 24:34-35; 1Pe 1:25
it stands firm in the heavens.
[90]Your faithfulness continues
through all generations;
you established the
earth, and it endures.
Ps 148:6; Ecc 1:4
[91]Your laws endure to this day,
Jer 33:25
for all things serve you.
[92]If your law had not been my
delight, Ps 37:4
I would have perished in my
affliction.
[93]I will never forget your
precepts,
for by them you have
preserved my life. Ps 103:5
[94]Save me, for I am yours;
I have sought out your
precepts.
[95]The wicked are waiting to
destroy me, Ps 69:4
but I will ponder your
statutes.
[96]To all perfection I see a limit,
but your commands are
boundless. Ps 19:7

מ Mem

[97]Oh, how I love your law!
I meditate on it all day long.
Ps 1:2
[98]Your commands are always
with me Dt 4:6
and make me wiser than my
enemies.
[99]I have more insight than all my
teachers,
for I meditate on your
statutes. ver 15
[100]I have more understanding
than the elders,
for I obey your precepts.
Job 32:7-9
[101]I have kept my feet from every
evil path Pr 1:15
so that I might obey your
word.
[102]I have not departed from your
laws,
for you yourself have taught
me.
[103]How sweet are your words to
my taste,
sweeter than honey to
my mouth!
Ps 19:10; Pr 8:11; 24:13-14
[104]I gain understanding from
your precepts;
therefore I hate every wrong
path. ver 128

נ Nun

105 Your word is a lamp for my feet,
a light on my path. Pr 6:23
106 I have taken an oath and confirmed it, Ne 10:29
that I will follow your righteous laws.
107 I have suffered much;
preserve my life, LORD,
according to your word. ver 25
108 Accept, LORD, the willing praise of my mouth, Hos 14:2; Heb 13:15
and teach me your laws.
109 Though I constantly take my life in my hands, Jdg 12:3; Job 13:14
I will not forget your law.
110 The wicked have set a snare for me, Ps 140:5; 141:9
but I have not strayed from your precepts.
111 Your statutes are my heritage forever;
they are the joy of my heart.
112 My heart is set on keeping your decrees Ps 108:1
to the very end.[a]

ס Samekh

113 I hate double-minded people, Jas 1:8
but I love your law.
114 You are my refuge and my shield; Ps 32:7; 91:1
I have put my hope in your word.
115 Away from me, you evildoers, Ps 6:8; Mt 7:23
that I may keep the commands of my God!
116 Sustain me, my God, according to your promise, and I will live; Ps 54:4
do not let my hopes be dashed. Ps 25:2; Ro 5:5
117 Uphold me, and I will be delivered; Isa 41:10
I will always have regard for your decrees.
118 You reject all who stray from your decrees,
for their delusions come to nothing.
119 All the wicked of the earth you discard like dross; Eze 22:18-19
therefore I love your statutes.
120 My flesh trembles in fear of you; Hab 3:16
I stand in awe of your laws.

ע Ayin

121 I have done what is righteous and just; 2Sa 8:15
do not leave me to my oppressors.
122 Ensure your servant's well-being; Job 17:3
do not let the arrogant oppress me.
123 My eyes fail, looking for your salvation,
looking for your righteous promise. ver 82

[a] 112 Or *decrees / for their enduring reward*

124 Deal with your servant
according to your love
and teach me your decrees.
ver 12
125 I am your servant; give me
discernment Ps 116:16
that I may understand your
statutes.
126 It is time for you to act, LORD;
your law is being broken.
127 Because I love your
commands
more than gold, more than
pure gold, Ps 19:10
128 and because I consider all your
precepts right,
I hate every wrong path.
ver 104,163

פ Pe

129 Your statutes are wonderful;
ver 18
therefore I obey them.
130 The unfolding of your words
gives light; Pr 6:23
it gives understanding to the
simple. Ps 19:7
131 I open my mouth and pant,
Ps 42:1
longing for your
commands.
132 Turn to me and have mercy
on me, Ps 25:16; 106:4
as you always do to those
who love your name.
133 Direct my footsteps according
to your word; Ps 17:5
let no sin rule over me.
Ps 19:13; Ro 6:12
134 Redeem me from human
oppression, Ps 142:6; Lk 1:74
that I may obey your
precepts.
135 Make your face shine on your
servant Ps 4:6
and teach me your decrees.
136 Streams of tears flow from my
eyes, Jer 9:1,18
for your law is not obeyed.
Eze 9:4

צ Tsadhe

137 You are righteous, LORD,
Ezr 9:15; Jer 12:1
and your laws are right. Ne 9:13
138 The statutes you have laid
down are righteous;
Ps 19:7
they are fully trustworthy.
139 My zeal wears me out,
Ps 69:9; Jn 2:17
for my enemies ignore your
words.
140 Your promises have been
thoroughly tested, Ps 12:6
and your servant loves
them.
141 Though I am lowly and
despised, Ps 22:6
I do not forget your
precepts.
142 Your righteousness is
everlasting
and your law is true. Ps 19:7
143 Trouble and distress have come
upon me,
but your commands give me
delight.
144 Your statutes are always
righteous;
give me understanding that I
may live. Ps 19:9

ק Qoph

145 I call with all my heart; answer
me, LORD,
and I will obey your decrees.
ver 22,55
146 I call out to you; save me
and I will keep your statutes.
147 I rise before dawn and cry for
help; Ps 5:3; 57:8; 108:2
I have put my hope in your
word.
148 My eyes stay open through the
watches of the night,
Ps 63:6
that I may meditate on your
promises.
149 Hear my voice in accordance
with your love; Ps 27:7
preserve my life, LORD,
according to your laws.
150 Those who devise wicked
schemes are near,
but they are far from your
law.
151 Yet you are near, LORD, Ps 145:18
and all your commands are
true. ver 142
152 Long ago I learned from your
statutes
that you established them to
last forever. Lk 21:33

ר Resh

153 Look on my suffering and
deliver me, La 5:1
for I have not forgotten your
law. Pr 3:1
154 Defend my cause and
redeem me; 1Sa 24:15
preserve my life according to
your promise.
155 Salvation is far from the
wicked,
for they do not seek out your
decrees. Job 5:4
156 Your compassion, LORD, is
great;
preserve my life according to
your laws. 2Sa 24:14
157 Many are the foes who
persecute me, Ps 7:1
but I have not turned from
your statutes.
158 I look on the faithless with
loathing, Ps 139:21
for they do not obey your
word.
159 See how I love your precepts;
preserve my life, LORD, in
accordance with your
love. Ps 41:2
160 All your words are true;
all your righteous laws are
eternal. ver 89; Ps 111:8

ש Sin and Shin

161 Rulers persecute me without
cause, 1Sa 24:11
but my heart trembles at
your word.
162 I rejoice in your promise
like one who finds great
spoil. 1Sa 30:16
163 I hate and detest falsehood
but I love your law. ver 47
164 Seven times a day I praise you
for your righteous laws.
165 Great peace have those
who love your law,
Pr 3:2; Isa 32:17
and nothing can make them
stumble.

166 I wait for your salvation, LORD, Ge 49:18
and I follow your commands.
167 I obey your statutes,
for I love them greatly.
168 I obey your precepts and your statutes,
for all my ways are known to you. Pr 5:21

ת Taw

169 May my cry come before you, LORD; Ps 18:6
give me understanding according to your word.
170 May my supplication come before you; Ps 28:2
deliver me according to your promise. Ps 31:2
171 May my lips overflow with praise, Ps 51:15
for you teach me your decrees.
172 May my tongue sing of your word,
for all your commands are righteous.
173 May your hand be ready to help me, Ps 37:24
for I have chosen your precepts. Jos 24:22
174 I long for your salvation, LORD,
and your law gives me delight.
175 Let me live that I may praise you, Isa 55:3
and may your laws sustain me.
176 I have strayed like a lost sheep. Isa 53:6
Seek your servant,
for I have not forgotten your commands. Ps 44:17

Psalm 120

A song of ascents.

1 I call on the LORD in my distress, Jnh 2:2
and he answers me.
2 Save me, LORD,
from lying lips Pr 12:22
and from deceitful tongues. Ps 52:4

3 What will he do to you,
and what more besides,
you deceitful tongue?
4 He will punish you with a warrior's sharp arrows, Ps 45:5
with burning coals of the broom bush.

5 Woe to me that I dwell in Meshek,
that I live among the tents of Kedar! Ge 25:13; Jer 49:28
6 Too long have I lived
among those who hate peace.
7 I am for peace;
but when I speak, they are for war.

Psalm 121

A song of ascents.

1 I lift up my eyes to the mountains —
where does my help come from?

[2]My help comes from the
LORD,
the Maker of heaven and
earth. Ps 124:8

[3]He will not let your foot
slip —
he who watches over you will
not slumber;
[4]indeed, he who watches over
Israel Ps 127:1
will neither slumber nor
sleep.

[5]The LORD watches over you —
Isa 25:4
the LORD is your shade at
your right hand;
[6]the sun will not harm you by
day, Ps 91:5; Isa 49:10
nor the moon by night.

[7]The LORD will keep you from
all harm — Ps 41:2; 91:10-12
he will watch over your
life;
[8]the LORD will watch over your
coming and going
both now and forevermore.
Dt 28:6

Psalm 122

A song of ascents. Of David.

[1]I rejoiced with those who said
to me,
"Let us go to the house of the
LORD."
[2]Our feet are standing
in your gates, Jerusalem.

[3]Jerusalem is built like a city
that is closely compacted
together.
[4]That is where the tribes
go up —
the tribes of the LORD —
to praise the name of the LORD
according to the statute
given to Israel.
[5]There stand the thrones for
judgment,
the thrones of the house
of David.

[6]Pray for the peace of
Jerusalem:
"May those who love you be
secure. Ps 51:18
[7]May there be peace within your
walls 1Sa 25:6
and security within your
citadels." Ps 48:3
[8]For the sake of my family and
friends,
I will say, "Peace be within
you."
[9]For the sake of the house of the
LORD our God,
I will seek your prosperity.
Ne 2:10

Psalm 123

A song of ascents.

[1]I lift up my eyes to you,
to you who sit enthroned in
heaven. Ps 11:4; 121:1; 141:8
[2]As the eyes of slaves look to the
hand of their master,
as the eyes of a female slave
look to the hand of her
mistress,
so our eyes look to the LORD
our God, Ps 25:15
till he shows us his mercy.

3 Have mercy on us, LORD, have
mercy on us,
for we have endured no end
of contempt.
4 We have endured no end
of ridicule from the
arrogant,
of contempt from the
proud.

Psalm 124

A song of ascents. Of David.

1 If the LORD had not been on
our side —
let Israel say — Ps 129:1
2 if the LORD had not been on
our side
when people attacked us,
3 they would have swallowed us
alive
when their anger flared
against us;
4 the flood would have
engulfed us,
the torrent would have
swept over us,
5 the raging waters
would have swept us away.

6 Praise be to the LORD,
who has not let us be torn by
their teeth.
7 We have escaped like a bird
from the fowler's snare; Ps 91:3; Pr 6:5
the snare has been broken,
and we have escaped.
8 Our help is in the name of the
LORD,
the Maker of heaven and
earth. Ge 1:1; Ps 121:2

Psalm 125

A song of ascents.

1 Those who trust in the LORD
are like Mount Zion, Ps 46:5
which cannot be shaken
but endures
forever.
2 As the mountains surround
Jerusalem,
so the LORD surrounds his
people Ps 121:8; Zec 2:4-5
both now and forevermore.

3 The scepter of the wicked
will not remain Pr 22:8; Isa 14:5
over the land allotted to the
righteous,
for then the righteous might
use
their hands to do evil. 1Sa 24:10
4 LORD, do good to those who are
good, Ps 119:68
to those who are upright in
heart. Ps 7:10; 94:15
5 But those who turn to crooked
ways Pr 2:15; Isa 59:8
the LORD will banish with the
evildoers.

Peace be on Israel. Ps 128:6

Psalm 126

A song of ascents.

1 When the LORD restored the
fortunes of[a] Zion, Ps 85:1
we were like those who
dreamed.[b]

[a] *1* Or *LORD brought back the captives to*
[b] *1* Or *those restored to health*

2 Our mouths were filled with laughter,
our tongues with songs of joy. Ps 51:14
Then it was said among the nations,
"The LORD has done great things for them." Ps 71:19
3 The LORD has done great things for us,
and we are filled with joy. Isa 25:9

4 Restore our fortunes,[a] LORD,
like streams in the Negev. Isa 43:19
5 Those who sow with tears
will reap with songs of joy. Isa 35:10
6 Those who go out weeping,
carrying seed to sow,
will return with songs of joy,
carrying sheaves with them.

Psalm 127

A song of ascents. Of Solomon.

1 Unless the LORD builds the house, Ps 78:69
the builders labor in vain.
Unless the LORD watches over the city, Ps 121:4
the guards stand watch in vain.
2 In vain you rise early
and stay up late,
toiling for food to eat — Ge 3:17
for he grants sleep to[b] those he loves. Job 11:18

3 Children are a heritage from the LORD,
offspring a reward from him. Ge 33:5
4 Like arrows in the hands of a warrior Ps 112:2
are children born in one's youth.
5 Blessed is the man
whose quiver is full of them. Ps 128:2-3

They will not be put to shame
when they contend with their opponents in court. Pr 27:11

Psalm 128

A song of ascents.

1 Blessed are all who fear the LORD, Ps 112:1
who walk in obedience to him. Ps 119:1-3
2 You will eat the fruit of your labor; Isa 3:10
blessings and prosperity will be yours. Ecc 8:12
3 Your wife will be like a fruitful vine
within your house; Eze 19:10
your children will be like olive shoots
around your table. Ps 52:8; 144:12
4 Yes, this will be the blessing
for the man who fears the LORD.

5 May the LORD bless you from Zion; Ps 134:3

[a] 4 Or *Bring back our captives* [b] 2 Or *eat — / for while they sleep he provides for*

may you see the prosperity
of Jerusalem
all the days of your life.
6 May you live to see your
children's children —
Job 42:16
peace be on Israel. Ps 125:5

Psalm 129

A song of ascents.

1 "They have greatly oppressed
me from my youth,"
Ps 88:15
let Israel say; Ps 124:1
2 "they have greatly oppressed
me from my youth,
but they have not gained
the victory over me.
Mt 16:18
3 Plowmen have plowed my
back
and made their furrows
long.
4 But the LORD is righteous;
Ps 119:137
he has cut me free from the
cords of the wicked."
5 May all who hate Zion Mic 4:11
be turned back in shame.
Ps 71:13
6 May they be like grass on the
roof,
which withers before it can
grow; Ps 37:2
7 a reaper cannot fill his hands
with it, Dt 28:38
nor one who gathers fill his
arms.
8 May those who pass by not say
to them,
"The blessing of the LORD be
on you;
we bless you in the name of
the LORD." Ru 2:4; Ps 118:26

Psalm 130

A song of ascents.

1 Out of the depths I cry to you,
LORD; Ps 42:7; 69:2; La 3:55
2 Lord, hear my voice. Ps 28:2
Let your ears be attentive Ps 64:1
to my cry for mercy.

3 If you, LORD, kept a record of
sins,
Lord, who could stand? Ps 143:2
4 But with you there is
forgiveness, Ex 34:7; Jer 33:8
so that we can, with
reverence, serve you.
1Ki 8:40

5 I wait for the LORD, my
whole being waits,
Ps 27:14; 33:20; Isa 8:17
and in his word I put my
hope. Ps 119:81
6 I wait for the Lord
more than watchmen wait
for the morning,
more than watchmen wait
for the morning. Ps 119:147

7 Israel, put your hope in the
LORD, Ps 131:3
for with the LORD is unfailing
love
and with him is full
redemption.
8 He himself will redeem Israel
Lk 1:68
from all their sins.

Psalm 131

A song of ascents. Of David.

[1] My heart is not proud, LORD, Ro 12:16
my eyes are not haughty;
I do not concern myself with great matters Jer 45:5
or things too wonderful for me.
[2] But I have calmed and quieted myself, Ps 116:7
I am like a weaned child with its mother;
like a weaned child I am content. Mt 18:3; 1Co 14:20

[3] Israel, put your hope in the LORD Ps 130:7
both now and forevermore.

Psalm 132

A song of ascents.

[1] LORD, remember David
and all his self-denial. 1Sa 18:11

[2] He swore an oath to the LORD,
he made a vow to the Mighty One of Jacob: Ge 49:24
[3] "I will not enter my house
or go to my bed,
[4] I will allow no sleep to my eyes
or slumber to my eyelids,
[5] till I find a place for the LORD, Ac 7:46
a dwelling for the Mighty One of Jacob."

[6] We heard it in Ephrathah, 1Sa 17:12
we came upon it in the fields of Jaar:[a] 1Sa 7:2
[7] "Let us go to his dwelling place, Ps 5:7
let us worship at his footstool, saying, Ps 99:5
[8] 'Arise, LORD, and come to your resting place, Nu 10:35
you and the ark of your might.
[9] May your priests be clothed with your righteousness; Job 29:14; Isa 61:3,10
may your faithful people sing for joy.' "

[10] For the sake of your servant David,
do not reject your anointed one.

[11] The LORD swore an oath to David, Ps 89:3-4,35
a sure oath he will not revoke:
"One of your own descendants 2Sa 7:12
I will place on your throne.
[12] If your sons keep my covenant
and the statutes I teach them,
then their sons will sit
on your throne for ever and ever."

[13] For the LORD has chosen Zion, Ps 48:1-2
he has desired it for his dwelling, saying,

[a] 6 Or *heard of it in Ephrathah, / we found it in the fields of Jearim.* (See 1 Chron. 13:5,6) (And no quotation marks around verses 7-9)

14 “This is my resting place for
ever and ever; Ps 68:16
here I will sit enthroned, for
I have desired it.
15 I will bless her with abundant
provisions;
her poor I will satisfy with
food. Ps 147:14
16 I will clothe her priests with
salvation,
and her faithful people will
ever sing for joy.

17 “Here I will make a horn[a] grow
for David Eze 29:21; Lk 1:69
and set up a lamp for my
anointed one.
18 I will clothe his enemies with
shame, Ps 35:26; 109:29
but his head will be adorned
with a radiant crown.”

Psalm 133

A song of ascents. Of David.

1 How good and pleasant it is
when God’s people live
together in unity! Ge 13:8

2 It is like precious oil poured on
the head, Ex 30:25
running down on the beard,
running down on Aaron’s
beard,
down on the collar of his
robe.
3 It is as if the dew of Hermon
Dt 4:48
were falling on Mount Zion.
For there the LORD bestows his
blessing, Lev 25:21
even life forevermore. Ps 42:8

Psalm 134

A song of ascents.

1 Praise the LORD, all you
servants of the LORD
Ps 135:1-2
who minister by night in the
house of the LORD. 1Ch 9:33
2 Lift up your hands in the
sanctuary 1Ti 2:8
and praise the LORD.

3 May the LORD bless you from
Zion, Ps 128:5
he who is the Maker of
heaven and earth. Ps 124:8

Psalm 135

1 Praise the LORD.[b]

Praise the name of the LORD;
praise him, you servants of
the LORD, Ps 113:1; 134:1
2 you who minister in the house
of the LORD, Lk 2:37
in the courts of the house of
our God. Ps 116:19

3 Praise the LORD, for the LORD is
good; Ps 119:68
sing praise to his name, for
that is pleasant. Ps 147:1
4 For the LORD has chosen Jacob
to be his own, 1Pe 2:9
Israel to be his treasured
possession. Ex 19:5; Dt 7:6

5 I know that the LORD is great,
Ps 48:1
that our Lord is greater than
all gods.

[a] 17 *Horn* here symbolizes strong one, that is, king. [b] 1 Hebrew *Hallelu Yah*; also in verses 3 and 21

6 The LORD does whatever
pleases him, Ps 115:3
in the heavens and on the
earth,
in the seas and all their
depths.
7 He makes clouds rise from the
ends of the earth;
he sends lightning with the
rain Jer 10:13; Zec 10:1
and brings out the wind
from his storehouses.

8 He struck down the firstborn of
Egypt, Ex 12:12
the firstborn of people and
animals.
9 He sent his signs and wonders
into your midst, Egypt,
against Pharaoh and all his
servants. Ps 136:10-15
10 He struck down many nations
Nu 21:21-25; Ps 136:17-21
and killed mighty kings —
11 Sihon king of the Amorites,
Nu 21:21
Og king of Bashan,
and all the kings of
Canaan — Jos 12:7-24
12 and he gave their land as an
inheritance,
an inheritance to his people
Israel.

13 Your name, LORD, endures
forever, Ex 3:15
your renown, LORD, through
all generations. Ps 102:12
14 For the LORD will vindicate his
people Heb 10:30
and have compassion on his
servants. Dt 32:36

15 The idols of the nations are
silver and gold, Ps 96:5
made by human hands.
16 They have mouths, but cannot
speak, 1Ki 18:26
eyes, but cannot see.
17 They have ears, but cannot
hear,
nor is there breath in their
mouths. Jer 10:14
18 Those who make them will be
like them,
and so will all who trust in
them.

19 All you Israelites, praise the
LORD; Ps 22:23
house of Aaron, praise the
LORD;
20 house of Levi, praise the LORD;
you who fear him, praise the
LORD.
21 Praise be to the LORD from
Zion, Ps 134:3
to him who dwells in
Jerusalem.

Praise the LORD.

Psalm 136

1 Give thanks to the LORD, for he
is good. Ps 106:1
His love endures forever.
2 Give thanks to the God of gods.
Dt 10:17
His love endures forever.
3 Give thanks to the Lord of lords:
His love endures forever.

4 to him who alone does great
wonders, Ps 72:18
His love endures forever.

[5]who by his understanding
made the heavens,
Ge 1:1; Pr 3:19; Jer 51:15
His love endures forever.
[6]who spread out the earth upon
the waters, Jer 10:12
His love endures forever.
[7]who made the great lights —
Ge 1:14,16
His love endures forever.
[8]the sun to govern the day,
His love endures forever.
[9]the moon and stars to govern
the night;
His love endures forever.

[10]to him who struck down the
firstborn of Egypt
Ex 12:29; Ps 135:8
His love endures forever.
[11]and brought Israel out from
among them Ex 6:6; 12:51
His love endures forever.
[12]with a mighty hand and
outstretched arm;
Dt 4:34; Ps 44:3
His love endures forever.

[13]to him who divided the Red
Sea[a] asunder Ex 14:21; Ps 78:13
His love endures forever.
[14]and brought Israel through the
midst of it,
His love endures forever.
[15]but swept Pharaoh and his army
into the Red Sea; Ex 14:27
His love endures forever.

[16]to him who led his people
through the wilderness;
Ex 13:18
His love endures forever.

[17]to him who struck
down great kings,
Ps 135:9-12
His love endures forever.
[18]and killed mighty kings —
Dt 29:7
His love endures forever.
[19]Sihon king of the Amorites
His love endures forever.
[20]and Og king of Bashan —
His love endures forever.
[21]and gave their land as an
inheritance, Jos 12:1
His love endures forever.
[22]an inheritance to his servant
Israel.
His love endures forever.

[23]He remembered us in our low
estate Ps 113:7
His love endures forever.
[24]and freed us from our enemies.
Ps 107:2
His love endures forever.
[25]He gives food to every creature.
Ps 104:27; 145:15
His love endures forever.

[26]Give thanks to the God of
heaven. Ps 115:3
His love endures forever.

Psalm 137

[1]By the rivers of Babylon
we sat and wept
Eze 1:1,3; Ne 1:4
when we remembered
Zion.
[2]There on the poplars
we hung our harps, Job 30:31

[a] 13 Or *the Sea of Reeds*; also in verse 15

3 for there our captors asked us
for songs,
our tormentors demanded
songs of joy; Ps 80:6
they said, "Sing us
one of the songs of
Zion!"

4 How can we sing the songs of
the LORD Ne 12:46
while in a foreign land?
5 If I forget you, Jerusalem,
may my right hand forget its
skill.
6 May my tongue cling to
the roof of my mouth
Eze 3:26
if I do not remember you,
if I do not consider Jerusalem
my highest joy.

7 Remember, LORD, what
the Edomites did
Jer 49:7; La 4:21-22
on the day Jerusalem fell.
Ob 1:11
"Tear it down," they cried,
"tear it down to its
foundations!"
8 Daughter Babylon, doomed
to destruction,
Isa 13:1,19; Jer 25:12,26; Rev 18:6
happy is the one who repays
you
according to what you have
done to us.
9 Happy is the one who seizes
your infants
and dashes them
against the rocks.
2Ki 8:12; Isa 13:16

Psalm 138

Of David.

1 I will praise you, LORD, with all
my heart;
before the "gods" I will sing
your praise. Ps 95:3; 96:4
2 I will bow down toward
your holy temple
1Ki 8:29; Ps 5:7; 28:2
and will praise your name
for your unfailing love and
your faithfulness,
for you have so exalted your
solemn decree
that it surpasses your fame.
Isa 42:21
3 When I called, you answered
me;
you greatly emboldened me.
Ps 28:7

4 May all the kings of the earth
praise you, LORD, Ps 102:15
when they hear what you
have decreed.
5 May they sing of the ways of
the LORD,
for the glory of the LORD is
great.

6 Though the LORD is exalted,
he looks kindly on the
lowly; Ps 113:6; Isa 57:15
though lofty, he sees them
from afar. Pr 3:34; Jas 4:6
7 Though I walk in the midst of
trouble, Ps 23:4
you preserve my life.
You stretch out your hand
against the anger of my
foes; Jer 51:25

with your right hand you
save me. Ps 71:20
8 The LORD will vindicate me; Ps 57:2; Php 1:6
your love, LORD, endures
forever —
do not abandon the
works of your hands. Job 10:3,8

Psalm 139

For the director of music.
Of David. A psalm.

1 You have searched me, LORD, Ps 17:3
and you know me. Jer 12:3
2 You know when I sit and when
I rise; 2Ki 19:27
you perceive my thoughts
from afar. Mt 9:4; Jn 2:24
3 You discern my going out and
my lying down;
you are familiar with all my
ways. Job 31:4
4 Before a word is on my
tongue
you, LORD, know it
completely. Heb 4:13
5 You hem me in behind and
before, Ps 34:7
and you lay your hand upon
me.
6 Such knowledge is too
wonderful for me,
too lofty for me to attain. Job 42:3

7 Where can I go from your
Spirit?
Where can I flee from your
presence? Jer 23:24; Jnh 1:3
8 If I go up to the heavens, you
are there; Am 9:2-3
if I make my bed in the
depths, you are there. Pr 15:11
9 If I rise on the wings of the
dawn,
if I settle on the far side of
the sea,
10 even there your hand will
guide me, Ps 23:3
your right hand will hold me
fast.
11 If I say, "Surely the darkness
will hide me
and the light become night
around me,"
12 even the darkness will not be
dark to you; Job 34:22; Da 2:22
the night will shine like the
day,
for darkness is as light to you.
13 For you created my inmost
being; Ps 119:73
you knit me together in
my mother's womb. Job 10:11; Isa 44:2,24
14 I praise you because I
am fearfully and
wonderfully made;
your works are wonderful, Ps 40:5
I know that full well.
15 My frame was not hidden from
you
when I was made in the
secret place,
when I was woven together
in the depths of the
earth. Job 10:11

16 Your eyes saw my unformed
body;
all the days ordained for me
were written in your
book
before one of them came to
be.
17 How precious to me are your
thoughts,[a] God! Ps 40:5
How vast is the sum of them!
18 Were I to count them,
they would outnumber the
grains of sand —
when I awake, I am still with
you. Ps 3:5
19 If only you, God, would slay the
wicked! Isa 11:4
Away from me, you who are
bloodthirsty! Ps 119:115
20 They speak of you with evil
intent;
your adversaries misuse your
name. Jude 15
21 Do I not hate those who hate
you, LORD, Ps 119:158
and abhor those who
are in rebellion against
you?
22 I have nothing but hatred for
them;
I count them my enemies.
23 Search me, God, and know
my heart;
Job 31:6; Ps 26:2; Jer 11:20
test me and know my
anxious thoughts.
24 See if there is any offensive
way in me,
and lead me in the way
everlasting. Ps 5:8; 143:10

Psalm 140[b]

For the director of music. A psalm of David.

1 Rescue me, LORD, from
evildoers; Ps 17:13
protect me from the violent,
Ps 18:48
2 who devise evil plans in their
hearts Ps 56:6
and stir up war every day.
3 They make their tongues
as sharp as a serpent's;
Ps 57:4
the poison of vipers is on
their lips.[c] Ps 58:4; Jas 3:8

4 Keep me safe, LORD, from the
hands of the wicked;
Ps 71:4
protect me from the violent,
who devise ways to trip my
feet.
5 The arrogant have hidden a
snare for me; Job 34:30
they have spread out
the cords of their net
Job 18:8
and have set traps for me
along my path. Ps 31:4; 35:7

6 I say to the LORD, "You are my
God." Ps 16:2
Hear, LORD, my cry for mercy.
Ps 116:1; 143:1
7 Sovereign LORD, my strong
deliverer, Ps 28:8
you shield my head in the
day of battle.

[a] *17* Or *How amazing are your thoughts concerning me* [b] In Hebrew texts 140:1-13 is numbered 140:2-14. [c] *3* The Hebrew has *Selah* (a word of uncertain meaning) here and at the end of verses 5 and 8.

8 Do not grant the wicked their
desires, LORD; Ps 10:2-3
do not let their plans
succeed.

9 Those who surround me
proudly rear their
heads;
may the mischief of their lips
engulf them. Ps 7:16
10 May burning coals fall on
them;
may they be thrown into the
fire, Ps 11:6; 21:9
into miry pits, never to rise.
11 May slanderers not be
established in the land;
may disaster hunt down the
violent. Ps 34:21

12 I know that the LORD secures
justice for the poor
and upholds the cause of the
needy. Ps 9:4; 35:10
13 Surely the righteous will praise
your name, Ps 97:12
and the upright will live in
your presence. Ps 11:7

Psalm 141

A psalm of David.

1 I call to you, LORD, come
quickly to me; Ps 70:5
hear me when I call to you.
Ps 143:1
2 May my prayer be set before
you like incense;
Rev 5:8; 8:3
may the lifting up of my
hands be like the
evening sacrifice.
Ex 29:39,41; 1Ti 2:8

3 Set a guard over my mouth,
LORD; Ps 34:13
keep watch over the door of
my lips. Ps 12:2
4 Do not let my heart be drawn
to what is evil Jos 24:23
so that I take part in wicked
deeds
along with those who are
evildoers;
do not let me eat their
delicacies. Pr 23:6

5 Let a righteous man strike
me — that is a
kindness;
let him rebuke me — that
is oil on my head.
Ps 23:5; Pr 9:8
My head will not refuse it,
for my prayer will still be
against the deeds of
evildoers.

6 Their rulers will be thrown
down from the cliffs,
2Ch 25:12
and the wicked will learn
that my words were well
spoken.
7 They will say, “As one plows
and breaks up the earth,
Ps 129:3
so our bones have been
scattered at the mouth
of the grave.” Ps 53:5

8 But my eyes are fixed on you,
Sovereign LORD; Ps 25:15
in you I take refuge — do not
give me over to death.
Ps 2:12

[9]Keep me safe from the traps set
by evildoers, Ps 140:4
from the snares they have
laid for me. Ps 38:12
[10]Let the wicked fall into their
own nets, Ps 35:8
while I pass by in safety.

Psalm 142[a]

A *maskil*[b] of David. When he was in the cave. A prayer.

[1]I cry aloud to the LORD;
I lift up my voice to the LORD
for mercy. Ps 30:8
[2]I pour out before him my
complaint; Isa 26:16
before him I tell my trouble.

[3]When my spirit grows faint
within me, Ps 140:5; 143:4,7
it is you who watch over my
way.
In the path where I walk
people have hidden a snare
for me.
[4]Look and see, there is no one at
my right hand;
no one is concerned for me.
I have no refuge;
no one cares for my life. Ps 31:11

[5]I cry to you, LORD;
I say, "You are my refuge,
my portion in the land of the
living." Ps 27:13

[6]Listen to my cry, Ps 17:1
for I am in desperate need;
Ps 116:6
rescue me from those who
pursue me, Ps 25:20
for they are too strong for me.
[7]Set me free from my prison,
Ps 146:7
that I may praise your
name.
Then the righteous will gather
about me
because of your goodness to
me. Ps 13:6

Psalm 143

A psalm of David.

[1]LORD, hear my prayer,
listen to my cry for mercy;
Ps 140:6
in your faithfulness and
righteousness Ps 71:2; 89:1-2
come to my relief.
[2]Do not bring your servant into
judgment,
for no one living is
righteous before you.
Ps 14:3; Ecc 7:20; Ro 3:20
[3]The enemy pursues me,
he crushes me to the
ground;
he makes me dwell in the
darkness Ps 107:10
like those long dead.
[4]So my spirit grows faint within
me;
my heart within me is
dismayed. Ps 142:3
[5]I remember the days of long
ago; Ps 77:6
I meditate on all your
works
and consider what your
hands have done.

[a] In Hebrew texts 142:1-7 is numbered 142:2-8.
[b] Title: Probably a literary or musical term

[6]I spread out my hands to you;
Ps 63:1; 88:9
I thirst for you like a parched land.[a]

[7]Answer me quickly, LORD;
Ps 69:17
my spirit fails.
Do not hide your face from me
Ps 28:1
or I will be like those who go down to the pit.
[8]Let the morning bring me word of your unfailing love,
Ps 46:5
for I have put my trust in you.
Show me the way I should go,
Ps 27:11
for to you I entrust my life.
Ps 25:1-2
[9]Rescue me from my enemies, LORD,
Ps 31:15
for I hide myself in you.
[10]Teach me to do your will,
for you are my God;
may your good Spirit
lead me on level ground.
Ne 9:20; 25:4-5

[11]For your name's sake, LORD, preserve my life;
Ps 119:25
in your righteousness, bring me out of trouble.
Ps 31:1
[12]In your unfailing love, silence my enemies;
destroy all my foes,
Ps 54:5
for I am your servant.
Ps 116:16

Psalm 144

Of David.

[1]Praise be to the LORD my Rock,
Ps 18:2,34
who trains my hands for war,
my fingers for battle.
[2]He is my loving God and my fortress,
Ps 59:9; 91:2
my stronghold and my deliverer,
my shield, in whom I take refuge,
Ps 84:9
who subdues peoples[b] under me.

[3]LORD, what are human beings that you care for them,
Ps 8:4; Heb 2:6
mere mortals that you think of them?
[4]They are like a breath;
their days are like a fleeting shadow.
Ps 102:11

[5]Part your heavens, LORD, and come down;
Ps 18:9; Isa 64:1
touch the mountains, so that they smoke.
Ps 104:32
[6]Send forth lightning and scatter the enemy;
shoot your arrows and rout them.
Ps 18:14
[7]Reach down your hand from on high;
deliver me and rescue me

[a] 6 The Hebrew has *Selah* (a word of uncertain meaning) here. [b] 2 Many manuscripts of the Masoretic Text, Dead Sea Scrolls, Aquila, Jerome and Syriac; most manuscripts of the Masoretic Text *subdues my people*

from the mighty waters,
from the hands of foreigners Ps 18:44
8 whose mouths are full of lies, Ps 12:2; 41:6
whose right hands are deceitful.

9 I will sing a new song to you, my God;
on the ten-stringed lyre I will make music to you, Ps 33:2-3
10 to the One who gives victory to kings,
who delivers his servant David. Ps 18:50

From the deadly sword 11 deliver me;
rescue me from the hands of foreigners
whose mouths are full of lies,
whose right hands are deceitful. Ps 12:2; Isa 44:20

12 Then our sons in their youth
will be like well-nurtured plants, Ps 128:3
and our daughters will be like pillars SS 4:4
carved to adorn a palace.
13 Our barns will be filled Pr 3:10
with every kind of provision.
Our sheep will increase by thousands,
by tens of thousands in our fields;
14 our oxen will draw heavy loads.[a] Pr 14:4
There will be no breaching of walls, 2Ki 25:11
no going into captivity,
no cry of distress in our streets. Isa 24:11
15 Blessed is the people of whom this is true; Ps 33:12
blessed is the people whose God is the LORD.

Psalm 145[b]

A psalm of praise. Of David.

1 I will exalt you, my God the King; Ps 30:1; 34:1
I will praise your name for ever and ever.
2 Every day I will praise you Ps 71:6
and extol your name for ever and ever.

3 Great is the LORD and most worthy of praise;
his greatness no one can fathom. Job 5:9; Ro 11:33
4 One generation commends your works to another; Isa 38:19
they tell of your mighty acts.
5 They speak of the glorious splendor of your majesty —
and I will meditate on your wonderful works.[c] Ps 119:27

[a] 14 Or *our chieftains will be firmly established* [b] This psalm is an acrostic poem, the verses of which (including verse 13b) begin with the successive letters of the Hebrew alphabet. [c] 5 Dead Sea Scrolls and Syriac (see also Septuagint); Masoretic Text *On the glorious splendor of your majesty / and on your wonderful works I will meditate*

[6] They tell of the power of your
awesome works — Ps 66:3
and I will proclaim your
great deeds. Dt 32:3
[7] They celebrate your abundant
goodness Isa 63:7
and joyfully sing of your
righteousness. Ps 51:14

[8] The LORD is gracious and
compassionate, Ps 86:15
slow to anger and rich in
love.

[9] The LORD is good to all; Ps 100:5
he has compassion on all he
has made.
[10] All your works praise you,
LORD; Ps 19:1
your faithful people extol
you. Ps 68:26
[11] They tell of the glory of your
kingdom
and speak of your might,
[12] so that all people may know
of your mighty acts
Ps 105:1
and the glorious splendor of
your kingdom.
[13] Your kingdom is an everlasting
kingdom, 1Ti 1:17; 2Pe 1:11
and your dominion
endures through all
generations.

The LORD is trustworthy in all
he promises Dt 7:9
and faithful in all he does.[a]
[14] The LORD upholds all who fall
Ps 37:24
and lifts up all who are
bowed down. Ps 146:8

[15] The eyes of all look to you,
and you give them their
food at the proper time.
Ps 104:27
[16] You open your hand
and satisfy the desires of
every living thing. Ps 104:28

[17] The LORD is righteous in all his
ways
and faithful in all he does.
[18] The LORD is near to all who call
on him, Dt 4:7; Jn 4:24
to all who call on him in
truth.
[19] He fulfills the desires of those
who fear him; Ps 37:4
he hears their cry and saves
them. Pr 15:29
[20] The LORD watches over
all who love him,
Ps 31:23; 97:10
but all the wicked he will
destroy. Ps 9:5

[21] My mouth will speak in praise
of the LORD. Ps 71:8
Let every creature praise his
holy name
for ever and ever.

Psalm 146

[1] Praise the LORD.[b]

Praise the LORD, my soul. Ps 103:1

[2] I will praise the LORD all my
life; Ps 104:33

[a] *13* One manuscript of the Masoretic Text, Dead Sea Scrolls and Syriac (see also Septuagint); most manuscripts of the Masoretic Text do not have the last two lines of verse 13. [b] *1* Hebrew *Hallelu Yah*; also in verse 10

I will sing praise to my God
as long as I live.
3 Do not put your trust in
princes, Ps 118:9
in human beings, who
cannot save. Isa 2:22
4 When their spirit departs, they
return to the ground; Ecc 12:7
on that very day their
plans come to nothing. Ps 33:10; 1Co 2:6
5 Blessed are those whose help
is the God of Jacob, Ps 144:15; Jer 17:7
whose hope is in the LORD
their God.

6 He is the Maker of heaven and
earth, Rev 14:7
the sea, and everything in
them —
he remains faithful forever. Ps 117:2
7 He upholds the cause of the
oppressed Ps 103:6
and gives food to the hungry. Ps 107:9
The LORD sets prisoners free, Ps 68:6
8 the LORD gives sight to the
blind, Mt 9:30
the LORD lifts up those who are
bowed down,
the LORD loves the
righteous.
9 The LORD watches over the
foreigner
and sustains the fatherless
and the widow, Dt 10:18; Ps 68:5
but he frustrates the ways of
the wicked.

10 The LORD reigns forever, Ex 15:18; Ps 10:16
your God, O Zion, for all
generations.

Praise the LORD.

Psalm 147

1 Praise the LORD.[a]

How good it is to sing praises
to our God,
how pleasant and fitting to
praise him! Ps 33:1; 135:3

2 The LORD builds up Jerusalem; Ps 102:16
he gathers the exiles of
Israel. Dt 30:3
3 He heals the brokenhearted
and binds up their
wounds.
4 He determines the number of
the stars Isa 40:26
and calls them each by
name.
5 Great is our Lord and mighty in
power; Ps 48:1
his understanding has no
limit. Isa 40:28
6 The LORD sustains the humble Ps 146:8-9
but casts the wicked to the
ground.

7 Sing to the LORD with grateful
praise; Ps 33:3
make music to our God on
the harp.

[a] 1 Hebrew *Hallelu Yah*; also in verse 20

8 He covers the sky with clouds;
he supplies the earth with rain Job 38:26
and makes grass grow on the hills. Ps 104:14
9 He provides food for the cattle Ps 104:27-28
and for the young ravens when they call. Job 38:41
10 His pleasure is not in the strength of the horse, 1Sa 16:7; Ps 33:16-17
nor his delight in the legs of the warrior;
11 the LORD delights in those who fear him, Ps 33:18
who put their hope in his unfailing love. Ps 119:43
12 Extol the LORD, Jerusalem; Ps 48:1
praise your God, Zion.
13 He strengthens the bars of your gates Dt 33:25
and blesses your people within you. Lev 25:21
14 He grants peace to your borders Isa 60:17-18
and satisfies you with the finest of wheat. Ps 132:15
15 He sends his command to the earth;
his word runs swiftly.
16 He spreads the snow like wool Job 37:6
and scatters the frost like ashes.
17 He hurls down his hail like pebbles.
Who can withstand his icy blast?
18 He sends his word and melts them; Ps 33:9
he stirs up his breezes, and the waters flow.
19 He has revealed his word to Jacob,
his laws and decrees to Israel. Mal 4:4
20 He has done this for no other nation; Dt 4:7-8,32-34
they do not know his laws.[a]

Praise the LORD.

Psalm 148

1 Praise the LORD.[b] Ps 33:2; 103:1

Praise the LORD from the heavens;
praise him in the heights above.
2 Praise him, all his angels; Ps 103:20
praise him, all his heavenly hosts.
3 Praise him, sun and moon; Ps 19:1
praise him, all you shining stars.
4 Praise him, you highest heavens
and you waters above the skies. Ge 1:7
5 Let them praise the name of the LORD,
for at his command they were created, Ge 1:1,6; Ps 33:6,9

[a] *20* Masoretic Text; Dead Sea Scrolls and Septuagint *nation; / he has not made his laws known to them* [b] *1* Hebrew *Hallelu Yah*; also in verse 14

6 and he established them for
ever and ever —
he issued a decree that
will never pass away. Ps 89:37; Jer 33:25

7 Praise the LORD from the
earth,
you great sea creatures and
all ocean depths, Ps 74:13-14
8 lightning and hail, snow and
clouds,
stormy winds that do his
bidding, Ps 147:15-18
9 you mountains and all hills, Isa 44:23; 49:13; 55:12
fruit trees and all cedars,
10 wild animals and all cattle,
small creatures and flying
birds,
11 kings of the earth and all
nations,
you princes and all rulers on
earth,
12 young men and women,
old men and children.

13 Let them praise the name of
the LORD, Isa 12:4
for his name alone is
exalted;
his splendor is above the
earth and the heavens. Ps 113:4
14 And he has raised up for his
people a horn,[a] Ps 75:10
the praise of all his faithful
servants,
of Israel, the people close to
his heart. Dt 26:19

Praise the LORD.

Psalm 149

1 Praise the LORD.[b] Ps 33:2

Sing to the LORD a new song,
his praise in the assembly
of his faithful people. Ps 35:18

2 Let Israel rejoice in their
Maker; Ps 95:6
let the people of Zion be
glad in their King. Ps 47:6; Zec 9:9
3 Let them praise his name with
dancing
and make music to him
with timbrel and harp. Ps 81:2; 150:4
4 For the LORD takes delight in
his people; Ps 35:27
he crowns the humble with
victory. Ps 132:16
5 Let his faithful people rejoice
in this honor
and sing for joy on their
beds. Job 35:10

6 May the praise of God be in
their mouths
and a double-edged sword
in their hands, Heb 4:12; Rev 1:16
7 to inflict vengeance on the
nations Nu 31:3
and punishment on the
peoples, Ps 81:15
8 to bind their kings with fetters, 2Sa 3:34
their nobles with shackles of
iron, 2Ch 33:11

[a] 14 *Horn* here symbolizes strength.
[b] 1 Hebrew *Hallelu Yah*; also in verse 9

[9]to carry out the sentence
written against them — Dt 7:1; Eze 28:26
this is the glory of all his
faithful people. Ps 148:14

Praise the LORD.

Psalm 150

[1]Praise the LORD.[a]

Praise God in his sanctuary; Ps 102:19
praise him in his mighty
heavens.
[2]Praise him for his acts of
power; Dt 3:24
praise him for his surpassing
greatness. Ps 145:5-6
[3]Praise him with the sounding
of the trumpet,
praise him with the harp and
lyre, Ps 149:3
[4]praise him with timbrel and
dancing, Ex 15:20
praise him with the strings
and pipe, Isa 38:20
[5]praise him with the clash of
cymbals, 1Ch 15:16
praise him with resounding
cymbals.

[6]Let everything that has
breath praise the LORD. Ps 145:21

Praise the LORD.

[a] 1 Hebrew *Hallelu Yah*; also in verse 6

PROVERBS

Purpose and Theme

1 The proverbs of Solomon son of David, king of Israel:
1Ki 4:29-34; Pr 10:1; 25:1

2 for gaining wisdom and instruction;
for understanding words of insight;
3 for receiving instruction in prudent behavior,
doing what is right and just and fair;
4 for giving prudence to those who are simple,[a]
Pr 8:5
knowledge and discretion to the young —
Pr 8:12
5 let the wise listen and add to their learning,
Pr 9:9
and let the discerning get guidance —
6 for understanding proverbs and parables,
Ps 78:2
the sayings and riddles of the wise.[b]

7 The fear of the LORD is the beginning of knowledge,
Job 28:28; Ps 111:10; Ecc 12:13
but fools[c] despise wisdom and instruction.
Pr 8:33-36

Prologue: Exhortations to Embrace Wisdom

Warning Against the Invitation of Sinful Men

8 Listen, my son, to your father's instruction
Pr 4:1
and do not forsake your mother's teaching.
Pr 6:20
9 They are a garland to grace your head
and a chain to adorn your neck.
Pr 4:1-9

10 My son, if sinful men entice you,
Ge 39:7
do not give in to them.
Dt 13:8
11 If they say, "Come along with us;
let's lie in wait for innocent blood,
let's ambush some harmless soul;
12 let's swallow them alive, like the grave,
and whole, like those who go down to the pit;
Ps 28:1

[a] 4 The Hebrew word rendered *simple* in Proverbs denotes a person who is gullible, without moral direction and inclined to evil. [b] 6 Or *understanding a proverb, namely, a parable, / and the sayings of the wise, their riddles* [c] 7 The Hebrew words rendered *fool* in Proverbs, and often elsewhere in the Old Testament, denote a person who is morally deficient.

[13] we will get all sorts of valuable
things
and fill our houses with
plunder;
[14] cast lots with us;
we will all share the loot" —
[15] my son, do not go along with
them,
do not set foot on their
paths; Ps 1:1; 119:101
[16] for their feet rush into evil,
they are swift to shed blood.
Isa 59:7
[17] How useless to spread a net
where every bird can see it!
[18] These men lie in wait for their
own blood; Ps 71:10
they ambush only
themselves!
[19] Such are the paths of all
who go after ill-gotten
gain;
it takes away the life of those
who get it. Pr 15:27

Wisdom's Rebuke

[20] Out in the open wisdom calls
aloud, Pr 8:1
she raises her voice in the
public square;
[21] on top of the wall[a] she cries
out,
at the city gate she makes
her speech:

[22] "How long will you who are
simple love your simple
ways? Pr 8:5
How long will mockers
delight in mockery
and fools hate knowledge?
[23] Repent at my rebuke!
Then I will pour out my
thoughts to you,
I will make known to you my
teachings.
[24] But since you refuse to
listen when I call
Isa 65:12; 66:4; Zec 7:11
and no one pays attention
when I stretch out my
hand, 1Sa 8:19
[25] since you disregard all my
advice
and do not accept my
rebuke,
[26] I in turn will laugh when
disaster strikes you; Ps 2:4
I will mock when calamity
overtakes you — Pr 10:24
[27] when calamity overtakes you
like a storm,
when disaster sweeps over
you like a whirlwind,
when distress and trouble
overwhelm you.

[28] "Then they will call to me
but I will not answer;
Isa 1:15; Mic 3:4
they will look for me but
will not find me,
Eze 8:18; Zec 7:13
[29] since they hated knowledge
and did not choose to fear
the LORD. Job 21:14
[30] Since they would not accept my
advice
and spurned my rebuke,
Ps 81:11

[a] 21 Septuagint; Hebrew / *at noisy street corners*

[31] they will eat the fruit of their
ways
and be filled with the fruit
of their schemes.
Isa 3:11; Jer 6:19
[32] For the waywardness of the
simple will kill them,
and the complacency of fools
will destroy them;
[33] but whoever listens to me will
live in safety Ps 25:12
and be at ease, without fear
of harm." Ps 112:8

Moral Benefits of Wisdom

2 My son, if you accept my
words
and store up my commands
within you,
[2] turning your ear to wisdom
and applying your heart
to understanding —
Pr 22:17
[3] indeed, if you call out for
insight
and cry aloud for
understanding,
[4] and if you look for it as for
silver
and search for it as for
hidden treasure,
Pr 3:14; Mt 13:44
[5] then you will understand the
fear of the LORD
and find the knowledge of
God. Pr 1:7
[6] For the LORD gives wisdom;
1Ki 3:9,12; Jas 1:5
from his mouth come
knowledge and
understanding.
[7] He holds success in store for
the upright,
he is a shield to those whose
walk is blameless,
Ps 84:11; Pr 30:5-6
[8] for he guards the course of the
just
and protects the way of
his faithful ones.
1Sa 2:9; Ps 66:9
[9] Then you will understand what
is right and just Dt 1:16
and fair — every good path.
[10] For wisdom will enter your
heart, Pr 14:33
and knowledge will be
pleasant to your soul.
[11] Discretion will protect you,
and understanding will
guard you. Pr 6:22
[12] Wisdom will save you from the
ways of wicked men,
from men whose words are
perverse,
[13] who have left the straight
paths
to walk in dark ways, Jn 3:19
[14] who delight in doing wrong
and rejoice in the
perverseness of evil,
Jer 11:15
[15] whose paths are crooked Ps 125:5
and who are devious in their
ways. Pr 21:8
[16] Wisdom will save you also from
the adulterous woman,
from the wayward woman
with her seductive
words,

17 who has left the partner of her
youth
and ignored the covenant
she made before God.[a]
Mal 2:14

18 Surely her house leads down to
death
and her paths to the spirits
of the dead. Pr 7:27

19 None who go to her return
or attain the paths of life.
Ecc 7:26

20 Thus you will walk in the ways
of the good
and keep to the paths of the
righteous.

21 For the upright will live in the
land, Ps 37:29
and the blameless will
remain in it;

22 but the wicked will be cut off
from the land, Job 18:17
and the unfaithful will be torn
from it. Dt 28:63; Pr 10:30

Wisdom Bestows Well-Being

3 My son, do not forget my
teaching, Pr 4:5
but keep my commands in
your heart,

2 for they will prolong your life
many years Pr 4:10
and bring you peace and
prosperity.

3 Let love and faithfulness never
leave you;
bind them around your
neck,
write them on the tablet of
your heart. Pr 6:21; 2Co 3:3

4 Then you will win favor and a
good name
in the sight of God and man.
1Sa 2:26; Lk 2:52

5 Trust in the LORD with all your
heart Ps 37:3,5
and lean not on your own
understanding;

6 in all your ways submit to
him,
and he will make your
paths straight.[b]
1Ch 28:9; Pr 16:3; Isa 45:13

7 Do not be wise in your own
eyes; Ro 12:16
fear the LORD and shun evil.
Pr 16:6

8 This will bring health to your
body Pr 4:22
and nourishment to your
bones. Job 21:24

9 Honor the LORD with your
wealth,
with the firstfruits of all
your crops;
Ex 22:29; Dt 26:1-15

10 then your barns will be
filled to overflowing,
Dt 28:8
and your vats will brim
over with new wine.
Joel 2:24

11 My son, do not despise
the LORD's discipline,
Job 5:17
and do not resent his
rebuke,

[a] 17 Or *covenant of her God* [b] 6 Or *will direct your paths*

12 because the LORD disciplines
those he loves,
Pr 13:24; Rev 3:19
as a father the son
he delights in.[a]
Dt 8:5; Heb 12:5-6*

13 Blessed are those who find
wisdom,
those who gain
understanding,
14 for she is more profitable than
silver
and yields better returns
than gold. Job 28:15; Pr 8:19
15 She is more precious than
rubies; Job 28:18
nothing you desire can
compare with her. Pr 8:11
16 Long life is in her right
hand;
in her left hand are riches
and honor. Pr 8:18
17 Her ways are pleasant ways,
and all her paths are peace.
Pr 16:7; Mt 11:28-30
18 She is a tree of life to those
who take hold of her;
Ge 2:9; Pr 11:30
those who hold her fast will
be blessed.

19 By wisdom the LORD laid the
earth's foundations,
Ps 104:24
by understanding he set
the heavens in place;
Pr 8:27-29
20 by his knowledge the watery
depths were divided,
and the clouds let drop the
dew.

21 My son, do not let wisdom and
understanding out of
your sight,
preserve sound judgment
and discretion; Pr 4:20-22
22 they will be life for you,
an ornament to grace your
neck. Pr 1:8-9
23 Then you will go on your way
in safety,
and your foot will not
stumble. Pr 4:12
24 When you lie down, you will
not be afraid; Ps 3:5
when you lie down, your
sleep will be sweet.
Job 11:18
25 Have no fear of sudden
disaster
or of the ruin that overtakes
the wicked,
26 for the LORD will be at your
side
and will keep your foot from
being snared. 1Sa 2:9

27 Do not withhold good from
those to whom it is
due,
when it is in your power to
act.
28 Do not say to your neighbor,
"Come back tomorrow and
I'll give it to you" —
when you already have it
with you. Lev 19:13
29 Do not plot harm against your
neighbor,
who lives trustfully near you.

[a] 12 Hebrew; Septuagint *loves, / and he chastens everyone he accepts as his child*

30Do not accuse anyone for no reason —
when they have done you no harm.

31Do not envy the violent Ps 37:1; Pr 24:1-2
or choose any of their ways.
32For the LORD detests the perverse Pr 11:20
but takes the upright into his confidence. Ps 25:14
33The LORD's curse is on the house of the wicked, Zec 5:4; Mal 2:2
but he blesses the home of the righteous. Ps 1:3
34He mocks proud mockers
but shows favor to the humble and oppressed. Jas 4:6*; 1Pe 5:5*
35The wise inherit honor,
but fools get only shame.

Get Wisdom at Any Cost

4 Listen, my sons, to a father's instruction; Pr 1:8
pay attention and gain understanding.
2I give you sound learning,
so do not forsake my teaching.
3For I too was a son to my father,
still tender, and cherished by my mother.
4Then he taught me, and he said to me,
"Take hold of my words with all your heart;
keep my commands, and you will live. Pr 7:2
5Get wisdom, get understanding; Pr 16:16
do not forget my words or turn away from them.
6Do not forsake wisdom, and she will protect you; 2Th 2:10
love her, and she will watch over you.
7The beginning of wisdom is this: Get[a] wisdom.
Though it cost all you have,[b] get understanding. Pr 23:23; Mt 13:44-46
8Cherish her, and she will exalt you;
embrace her, and she will honor you. 1Sa 2:30; Pr 3:18
9She will give you a garland to grace your head
and present you with a glorious crown." Pr 1:8-9

10Listen, my son, accept what I say,
and the years of your life will be many. Pr 3:2
11I instruct you in the way of wisdom 1Sa 12:23
and lead you along straight paths.
12When you walk, your steps will not be hampered;
when you run, you will not stumble. Job 18:7; Pr 3:23
13Hold on to instruction, do not let it go;
guard it well, for it is your life. Pr 3:22

[a] 7 Or *Wisdom is supreme; therefore get*
[b] 7 Or *wisdom. / Whatever else you get*

14 Do not set foot on the path of
the wicked
or walk in the way of
evildoers. Ps 1:1; Pr 1:15
15 Avoid it, do not travel on it;
turn from it and go on your
way.
16 For they cannot rest until they
do evil; Ps 36:4; Mic 2:1
they are robbed of sleep till
they make someone
stumble.
17 They eat the bread of
wickedness
and drink the wine of
violence. Pr 1:10-19

18 The path of the righteous is
like the morning sun,
Isa 26:7
shining ever brighter till
the full light of day.
2Sa 23:4; Php 2:15
19 But the way of the wicked is
like deep darkness;
Job 18:5; Isa 59:9-10; Jn 12:35
they do not know
what makes them
stumble.

20 My son, pay attention to what I
say;
turn your ear to my words.
Pr 5:1
21 Do not let them out of your
sight, Pr 3:21
keep them within your
heart;
22 for they are life to those who
find them
and health to one's whole
body. Pr 3:8; 12:18
23 Above all else, guard your
heart,
for everything you do
flows from it.
Mt 12:34; Lk 6:45
24 Keep your mouth free of
perversity;
keep corrupt talk far from
your lips.
25 Let your eyes look straight
ahead;
fix your gaze directly before
you.
26 Give careful thought to the[a]
paths for your feet
Heb 12:13*
and be steadfast in all your
ways.
27 Do not turn to the right or the
left; Dt 5:32; 28:14
keep your foot from evil.

Warning Against Adultery

5 My son, pay attention to my
wisdom,
turn your ear to my words of
insight, Pr 4:20
2 that you may maintain
discretion
and your lips may preserve
knowledge.
3 For the lips of the adulterous
woman drip honey,
and her speech is smoother
than oil; Ps 55:21; Pr 2:16
4 but in the end she is bitter as
gall, Ecc 7:26
sharp as a double-edged
sword.

[a] 26 Or *Make level*

5 Her feet go down to death;
her steps lead straight to the grave. Pr 7:26-27
6 She gives no thought to the way of life;
her paths wander aimlessly, but she does not know it. Pr 30:20

7 Now then, my sons, listen to me; Pr 7:24
do not turn aside from what I say.
8 Keep to a path far from her, Pr 7:1-27
do not go near the door of her house,
9 lest you lose your honor to others
and your dignity[a] to one who is cruel,
10 lest strangers feast on your wealth
and your toil enrich the house of another. Pr 29:3
11 At the end of your life you will groan,
when your flesh and body are spent.
12 You will say, "How I hated discipline!
How my heart spurned correction! Pr 1:29; 12:1
13 I would not obey my teachers
or turn my ear to my instructors.
14 And I was soon in serious trouble Pr 1:24-27
in the assembly of God's people."

15 Drink water from your own cistern,
running water from your own well.
16 Should your springs overflow in the streets,
your streams of water in the public squares?
17 Let them be yours alone,
never to be shared with strangers.
18 May your fountain be blessed, SS 4:12-15
and may you rejoice in the wife of your youth. Ecc 9:9; Mal 2:14
19 A loving doe, a graceful deer — SS 2:9; 4:5
may her breasts satisfy you always,
may you ever be intoxicated with her love.
20 Why, my son, be intoxicated with another man's wife?
Why embrace the bosom of a wayward woman?

21 For your ways are in full view of the LORD, Hos 7:2
and he examines all your paths. Job 31:4; 34:21; Pr 15:3
22 The evil deeds of the wicked ensnare them; Ps 9:16
the cords of their sins hold them fast. Nu 32:23; Ps 7:15-16
23 For lack of discipline they will die, Job 4:21; 36:12
led astray by their own great folly.

[a] 9 Or *years*

Warnings Against Folly

6 My son, if you have put
up security for your
neighbor, Pr 17:18
if you have shaken hands in
pledge for a stranger,
Pr 11:15; 22:26-27
2 you have been trapped by what
you said,
ensnared by the words of
your mouth.
3 So do this, my son, to free
yourself,
since you have fallen into
your neighbor's hands:
Go — to the point of
exhaustion — [a]
and give your neighbor no
rest!
4 Allow no sleep to your eyes,
no slumber to your eyelids.
Ps 132:4
5 Free yourself, like a gazelle
from the hand of the
hunter,
like a bird from the snare of
the fowler. Ps 91:3

6 Go to the ant, you sluggard;
Pr 20:4
consider its ways and be wise!
7 It has no commander,
no overseer or ruler,
8 yet it stores its provisions in
summer
and gathers its food at
harvest. Pr 10:4

9 How long will you lie there, you
sluggard? Pr 24:30-34
When will you get up from
your sleep?
10 A little sleep, a little
slumber,
a little folding of the hands
to rest — Pr 24:33
11 and poverty will come on you
like a thief Pr 24:30-34
and scarcity like an armed
man.

12 A troublemaker and a villain,
who goes about with a
corrupt mouth,
13 who winks maliciously with
his eye, Ps 35:19
signals with his feet
and motions with his
fingers,
14 who plots evil with deceit in
his heart — Mic 2:1
he always stirs up conflict.
ver 16-19
15 Therefore disaster will
overtake him in an
instant;
he will suddenly be
destroyed — without
remedy. 2Ch 36:16

16 There are six things the LORD
hates,
seven that are detestable to
him:
17 haughty eyes,
a lying tongue, Ps 120:2; Pr 12:22
hands that shed innocent
blood, Isa 1:15
18 a heart that devises wicked
schemes,
feet that are quick to rush
into evil, Ge 6:5

[a] 3 Or *Go and humble yourself,*

19 a false witness who pours
out lies Ps 27:12
and a person who stirs
up conflict in the
community. ver 12-15

Warning Against Adultery

20 My son, keep your father's
command
and do not forsake your
mother's teaching. Pr 1:8
21 Bind them always on your
heart;
fasten them around your
neck. Pr 3:3; 7:1-3
22 When you walk, they will guide
you;
when you sleep, they will
watch over you;
when you awake, they will
speak to you.
23 For this command is a lamp,
this teaching is a light,
Ps 19:8; 119:105
and correction and instruction
are the way to life,
24 keeping you from your
neighbor's wife,
from the smooth talk of
a wayward woman.
Pr 2:16; 7:5

25 Do not lust in your heart after
her beauty
or let her captivate you with
her eyes.

26 For a prostitute can be had for
a loaf of bread,
but another man's wife
preys on your very life.
Pr 7:22-23; 29:3

27 Can a man scoop fire into his
lap
without his clothes being
burned?
28 Can a man walk on hot coals
without his feet being
scorched?
29 So is he who sleeps with
another man's wife;
Pr 2:16-19
no one who touches her will
go unpunished.

30 People do not despise a thief if
he steals
to satisfy his hunger when
he is starving.
31 Yet if he is caught, he must pay
sevenfold, Ex 22:1-14
though it costs him all
the wealth of his
house.
32 But a man who commits
adultery has no sense;
Pr 7:7
whoever does so destroys
himself.
33 Blows and disgrace are his
lot,
and his shame will never be
wiped away. Pr 5:9-14

34 For jealousy arouses a
husband's fury, Ge 34:7
and he will show no
mercy when he takes
revenge.
35 He will not accept any
compensation;
he will refuse a bribe,
however great it is.
Job 31:9-11

Warning Against the Adulterous Woman

7 My son, keep my words Pr 2:1
and store up my commands
within you.
2 Keep my commands and you
will live; Pr 4:4
guard my teachings as the
apple of your eye.
3 Bind them on your fingers;
write them on the tablet of
your heart. Dt 6:8; Pr 3:3
4 Say to wisdom, "You are my
sister,"
and to insight, "You are my
relative."
5 They will keep you from the
adulterous woman,
from the wayward woman
with her seductive
words. Pr 2:16; 6:24

6 At the window of my house
I looked down through the
lattice.
7 I saw among the simple,
I noticed among the young
men,
a youth who had no sense.
Pr 6:32
8 He was going down the street
near her corner,
walking along in the
direction of her house
9 at twilight, as the day was
fading, Job 24:15
as the dark of night set in.

10 Then out came a woman to
meet him,
dressed like a prostitute and
with crafty intent.
11 (She is unruly and defiant,
Pr 9:13; 1Ti 5:13
her feet never stay at
home;
12 now in the street, now in the
squares,
at every corner she lurks.)
Pr 8:1-36
13 She took hold of him and
kissed him Ge 39:12
and with a brazen face she
said:

14 "Today I fulfilled my vows,
and I have food from my
fellowship offering at
home. Lev 7:11-18
15 So I came out to meet you;
I looked for you and have
found you!
16 I have covered my bed
with colored linens from
Egypt.
17 I have perfumed my bed Est 1:6
with myrrh, aloes and
cinnamon. Ge 37:25
18 Come, let's drink deeply of love
till morning;
let's enjoy ourselves with
love! Ge 39:7
19 My husband is not at home;
he has gone on a long
journey.
20 He took his purse filled with
money
and will not be home till full
moon."
21 With persuasive words she led
him astray;
she seduced him with her
smooth talk. Pr 5:3

22 All at once he followed her
like an ox going to the slaughter,
like a deer[a] stepping into a noose[b] Job 18:10
23 till an arrow pierces his liver, Job 15:22
like a bird darting into a snare,
little knowing it will cost him his life. Ecc 9:12

24 Now then, my sons, listen to me; Pr 1:8-9
pay attention to what I say.
25 Do not let your heart turn to her ways
or stray into her paths. Pr 5:7-8
26 Many are the victims she has brought down;
her slain are a mighty throng.
27 Her house is a highway to the grave,
leading down to the chambers of death.
Pr 2:18; 5:5; 9:18

Wisdom's Call

8 Does not wisdom call out? Pr 1:20; 9:3
Does not understanding raise her voice?
2 At the highest point along the way,
where the paths meet, she takes her stand;
3 beside the gate leading into the city,
at the entrance, she cries aloud: Job 29:7
4 "To you, O people, I call out;
I raise my voice to all mankind.
5 You who are simple, gain prudence; Pr 1:4,22
you who are foolish, set your hearts on it.[c]
6 Listen, for I have trustworthy things to say;
I open my lips to speak what is right.
7 My mouth speaks what is true, Ps 37:30; Jn 8:14
for my lips detest wickedness.
8 All the words of my mouth are just;
none of them is crooked or perverse.
9 To the discerning all of them are right;
they are upright to those who have found knowledge.
10 Choose my instruction instead of silver,
knowledge rather than choice gold, Pr 3:14-15
11 for wisdom is more precious than rubies, Job 28:17-19
and nothing you desire can compare with her.
Pr 3:13-15

12 "I, wisdom, dwell together with prudence;
I possess knowledge and discretion. Pr 1:4

[a] 22 Syriac (see also Septuagint); Hebrew *fool* [b] 22 The meaning of the Hebrew for this line is uncertain. [c] 5 Septuagint; Hebrew *foolish, instruct your minds*

13 To fear the LORD is to hate evil; Pr 16:6
I hate pride and arrogance, Jer 44:4
evil behavior and perverse speech.
14 Counsel and sound judgment are mine;
I have insight, I have power. Ecc 7:19
15 By me kings reign
and rulers issue decrees that are just; Da 2:21; Ro 13:1
16 by me princes govern,
and nobles — all who rule on earth.[a]
17 I love those who love me, 1Sa 2:30; Jn 14:21-24
and those who seek me find me. Pr 1:28; Jas 1:5
18 With me are riches and honor, Pr 3:16
enduring wealth and prosperity. Mt 6:33
19 My fruit is better than fine gold;
what I yield surpasses choice silver. Pr 3:13-14; 10:20
20 I walk in the way of righteousness,
along the paths of justice,
21 bestowing a rich inheritance on those who love me
and making their treasuries full. Pr 15:6; 24:4

22 "The LORD brought me forth as the first of his works,[b,c]
before his deeds of old;
23 I was formed long ages ago,
at the very beginning, when the world came to be.
24 When there were no watery depths, I was given birth,
when there were no springs overflowing with water; Ge 7:11
25 before the mountains were settled in place,
before the hills, I was given birth, Job 15:7
26 before he made the world or its fields
or any of the dust of the earth. Ps 90:2
27 I was there when he set the heavens in place, Pr 3:19
when he marked out the horizon on the face of the deep,
28 when he established the clouds above
and fixed securely the fountains of the deep,
29 when he gave the sea its boundary Ge 1:9; Job 38:10; Ps 16:6
so the waters would not overstep his command, Ps 104:9
and when he marked out the foundations of the earth. Job 38:5
30 Then I was constantly[d] at his side. Jn 1:1-3

[a] 16 Some Hebrew manuscripts and Septuagint; other Hebrew manuscripts *all righteous rulers* [b] 22 Or *way*; or *dominion* [c] 22 Or *The LORD possessed me at the beginning of his work*; or *The LORD brought me forth at the beginning of his work* [d] 30 Or *was the artisan*; or *was a little child*

I was filled with delight day after day,
rejoicing always in his presence,
[31] rejoicing in his whole world
and delighting in mankind. Ps 16:3; 104:1-30

[32] "Now then, my children, listen to me;
blessed are those who keep my ways. Ps 119:1-2; Lk 11:28
[33] Listen to my instruction and be wise;
do not disregard it.
[34] Blessed are those who listen to me, Pr 3:13,18
watching daily at my doors,
waiting at my doorway.
[35] For those who find me find life Pr 3:13-18
and receive favor from the LORD. Pr 12:2
[36] But those who fail to find me harm themselves; Pr 15:32
all who hate me love death."

Invitations of Wisdom and Folly

9 Wisdom has built her house; Eph 2:20-22; 1Pe 2:5
she has set up[a] its seven pillars.
[2] She has prepared her meat and mixed her wine;
she has also set her table. Lk 14:16-23
[3] She has sent out her servants, and she calls Pr 8:1-3
from the highest point of the city,
[4] "Let all who are simple come to my house!"
To those who have no sense she says, Pr 6:32
[5] "Come, eat my food
and drink the wine I have mixed. Isa 55:1
[6] Leave your simple ways and you will live; Pr 8:35
walk in the way of insight."

[7] Whoever corrects a mocker invites insults;
whoever rebukes the wicked incurs abuse. Pr 23:9
[8] Do not rebuke mockers or they will hate you;
rebuke the wise and they will love you. Ps 141:5
[9] Instruct the wise and they will be wiser still;
teach the righteous and they will add to their learning. Pr 1:5,7

[10] The fear of the LORD is the beginning of wisdom, Job 28:28; Pr 1:7
and knowledge of the Holy One is understanding. Dt 4:6
[11] For through wisdom[b] your days will be many,
and years will be added to your life. Pr 3:16
[12] If you are wise, your wisdom will reward you;
if you are a mocker, you alone will suffer.

[a] 1 Septuagint, Syriac and Targum; Hebrew *has hewn out* [b] 11 Septuagint, Syriac and Targum; Hebrew *me*

[13] Folly is an unruly woman; Pr 7:11
she is simple and knows nothing. Pr 5:6
[14] She sits at the door of her house,
on a seat at the highest point of the city, ver 3
[15] calling out to those who pass by,
who go straight on their way,
16 "Let all who are simple come to my house!"
To those who have no sense she says, Pr 1:22
17 "Stolen water is sweet;
food eaten in secret is delicious!" Pr 20:17
[18] But little do they know that the dead are there,
that her guests are deep in the realm of the dead. Pr 2:18; 7:26-27

Proverbs of Solomon

10 The proverbs of Solomon: Pr 1:1

A wise son brings joy to his father, Pr 15:20
but a foolish son brings grief to his mother.

[2] Ill-gotten treasures have no lasting value, Pr 21:6
but righteousness delivers from death.

[3] The LORD does not let the righteous go hungry, Mt 6:25-34
but he thwarts the craving of the wicked.

[4] Lazy hands make for poverty, Pr 19:15
but diligent hands bring wealth. Pr 13:4

[5] He who gathers crops in summer is a prudent son,
but he who sleeps during harvest is a disgraceful son.

[6] Blessings crown the head of the righteous,
but violence overwhelms the mouth of the wicked.[a]

[7] The name of the righteous is used in blessings,[b] Ps 112:6
but the name of the wicked will rot. Ps 109:13

[8] The wise in heart accept commands,
but a chattering fool comes to ruin. Mt 7:24-27

[9] Whoever walks in integrity walks securely, Ps 23:4; Isa 33:15
but whoever takes crooked paths will be found out. Pr 28:18

[10] Whoever winks maliciously causes grief,
and a chattering fool comes to ruin.

[11] The mouth of the righteous is a fountain of life, Ps 37:30
but the mouth of the wicked conceals violence.

[a] 6 Or *righteous, / but the mouth of the wicked conceals violence* [b] 7 See Gen. 48:20.

12 Hatred stirs up conflict,
but love covers over all wrongs. 1Pe 4:8

13 Wisdom is found on the lips of the discerning,
but a rod is for the back of one who has no sense. Pr 26:3

14 The wise store up knowledge,
but the mouth of a fool invites ruin. Pr 18:6-7

15 The wealth of the rich is their fortified city, Pr 18:11
but poverty is the ruin of the poor. Pr 19:7

16 The wages of the righteous is life,
but the earnings of the wicked are sin and death. Pr 11:18-19

17 Whoever heeds discipline shows the way to life, Pr 6:23
but whoever ignores correction leads others astray.

18 Whoever conceals hatred with lying lips Ps 31:18
and spreads slander is a fool.

19 Sin is not ended by multiplying words,
but the prudent hold their tongues. Pr 17:28; Ecc 5:3; Jas 3:2-12

20 The tongue of the righteous is choice silver,
but the heart of the wicked is of little value.

21 The lips of the righteous nourish many,
but fools die for lack of sense. Hos 4:1,6,14

22 The blessing of the LORD brings wealth, Ge 24:35
without painful toil for it.

23 A fool finds pleasure in wicked schemes, Pr 15:21
but a person of understanding delights in wisdom.

24 What the wicked dread will overtake them; Isa 66:4
what the righteous desire will be granted. Ps 145:17-19; Mt 5:6; 1Jn 5:14-15

25 When the storm has swept by, the wicked are gone,
but the righteous stand firm forever. Ps 15:5

26 As vinegar to the teeth and smoke to the eyes,
so are sluggards to those who send them. Pr 26:6

27 The fear of the LORD adds length to life, Pr 9:10-11
but the years of the wicked are cut short. Job 15:32

28 The prospect of the righteous is joy,
but the hopes of the wicked come to nothing. Job 8:13; Pr 11:7

29 The way of the LORD is a refuge for the blameless,
but it is the ruin of those who do evil. Pr 21:15

30 The righteous will never be
uprooted,
but the wicked will not
remain in the land.
Ps 37:9,28-29

31 From the mouth of the
righteous comes the
fruit of wisdom, Ps 37:30
but a perverse tongue will be
silenced.

32 The lips of the righteous know
what finds favor, Ecc 10:12
but the mouth of the wicked
only what is perverse.

11 The LORD detests dishonest
scales, Lev 19:36; Dt 25:13-16
but accurate weights find
favor with him. Pr 16:11

2 When pride comes, then comes
disgrace, Pr 16:18
but with humility comes
wisdom. Pr 18:12

3 The integrity of the upright
guides them,
but the unfaithful are
destroyed by their
duplicity. Pr 13:6

4 Wealth is worthless in the day
of wrath, Eze 7:19; Zep 1:18
but righteousness delivers
from death. Ge 7:1

5 The righteousness of the
blameless makes their
paths straight,
but the wicked are brought
down by their own
wickedness. Pr 5:21-23

6 The righteousness of the
upright delivers them,
but the unfaithful are
trapped by evil desires.
Est 7:9

7 Hopes placed in mortals die
with them;
all the promise of[a] their
power comes to nothing.
Pr 10:28

8 The righteous person is
rescued from trouble,
and it falls on the wicked
instead. Pr 21:18

9 With their mouths the
godless destroy their
neighbors,
but through knowledge the
righteous escape. Jer 45:5

10 When the righteous prosper,
the city rejoices; Pr 28:12
when the wicked perish,
there are shouts of joy.

11 Through the blessing of the
upright a city is exalted,
but by the mouth of the
wicked it is destroyed.
Pr 29:8

12 Whoever derides their
neighbor has no sense,
Pr 14:21
but the one who has
understanding holds
their tongue.

[a] 7 Two Hebrew manuscripts; most Hebrew manuscripts, Vulgate, Syriac and Targum *When the wicked die, their hope perishes; / all they expected from*

[13]A gossip betrays a confidence, Lev 19:16; Pr 20:19
but a trustworthy person keeps a secret.

[14]For lack of guidance a nation falls,
but victory is won through many advisers. Pr 15:22; 24:6

[15]Whoever puts up security for a stranger will surely suffer, Pr 6:1
but whoever refuses to shake hands in pledge is safe.

[16]A kindhearted woman gains honor, Pr 31:31
but ruthless men gain only wealth.

[17]Those who are kind benefit themselves,
but the cruel bring ruin on themselves.

[18]A wicked person earns deceptive wages,
but the one who sows righteousness reaps a sure reward. Hos 10:12-13

[19]Truly the righteous attain life, Dt 30:15
but whoever pursues evil finds death. Pr 1:18-19

[20]The LORD detests those whose hearts are perverse,
but he delights in those whose ways are blameless. Ps 119:1; Pr 12:2,22

[21]Be sure of this: The wicked will not go unpunished,
but those who are righteous will go free. Pr 16:5

[22]Like a gold ring in a pig's snout
is a beautiful woman who shows no discretion.

[23]The desire of the righteous ends only in good,
but the hope of the wicked only in wrath.

[24]One person gives freely, yet gains even more;
another withholds unduly, but comes to poverty.

[25]A generous person will prosper;
whoever refreshes others will be refreshed. Mt 5:7; 2Co 9:6-9

[26]People curse the one who hoards grain,
but they pray God's blessing on the one who is willing to sell.

[27]Whoever seeks good finds favor,
but evil comes to one who searches for it. Est 7:10; Ps 7:15-16

[28]Those who trust in their riches will fall, Mk 10:25; 1Ti 6:17
but the righteous will thrive like a green leaf. Ps 1:3; Jer 17:8

29 Whoever brings ruin on their
family will inherit only
wind,
and the fool will be servant
to the wise. Pr 14:19

30 The fruit of the righteous is a
tree of life, Jas 5:20
and the one who is wise
saves lives.

31 If the righteous receive
their due on earth,
Pr 13:21; 1Pe 4:18
how much more the ungodly
and the sinner!

12 Whoever loves discipline
loves knowledge,
but whoever hates correction
is stupid. Pr 9:7-9

2 Good people obtain favor from
the LORD, Ps 84:11
but he condemns those
who devise wicked
schemes.

3 No one can be established
through wickedness,
but the righteous cannot be
uprooted. Pr 10:25

4 A wife of noble character
is her husband's
crown,
but a disgraceful wife is
like decay in his bones.
Pr 14:30

5 The plans of the righteous are
just,
but the advice of the wicked
is deceitful.

6 The words of the wicked lie in
wait for blood,
but the speech of the
upright rescues them.
Pr 14:3

7 The wicked are overthrown
and are no more, Ps 37:36
but the house of the
righteous stands firm.
Pr 10:25

8 A person is praised according
to their prudence,
and one with a warped mind
is despised.

9 Better to be a nobody and yet
have a servant
than pretend to be
somebody and have no
food.

10 The righteous care for the
needs of their animals,
Nu 22:29
but the kindest acts of the
wicked are cruel.

11 Those who work their land
will have abundant
food,
but those who chase
fantasies have no sense.
Pr 28:19

12 The wicked desire the
stronghold of evildoers,
but the root of the righteous
endures.

13 Evildoers are trapped by their
sinful talk, Pr 18:7
and so the innocent escape
trouble. 2Pe 2:9

[14]From the fruit of their lips
people are filled with
good things, Pr 13:2
and the work of their hands
brings them reward.
Isa 3:10-11

[15]The way of fools seems right to
them, Pr 14:12; 16:2,25
but the wise listen to advice.

[16]Fools show their annoyance at
once,
but the prudent overlook an
insult. Pr 29:11

[17]An honest witness tells the
truth,
but a false witness tells lies.
Pr 14:5,25

[18]The words of the reckless
pierce like swords, Ps 57:4
but the tongue of the wise
brings healing. Pr 15:4

[19]Truthful lips endure forever,
but a lying tongue lasts only
a moment.

[20]Deceit is in the hearts of those
who plot evil,
but those who promote
peace have joy.

[21]No harm overtakes the
righteous, Ps 91:10
but the wicked have their fill
of trouble.

[22]The LORD detests lying lips,
Pr 6:17; Rev 22:15
but he delights in people
who are trustworthy.
Pr 11:20

[23]The prudent keep their
knowledge to
themselves, Pr 13:16
but a fool's heart blurts out
folly.

[24]Diligent hands will rule,
but laziness ends in forced
labor. Pr 10:4

[25]Anxiety weighs down the
heart, Pr 15:13; Isa 50:4
but a kind word cheers
it up.

[26]The righteous choose their
friends carefully,
but the way of the
wicked leads them
astray.

[27]The lazy do not roast[a] any
game,
but the diligent feed on the
riches of the hunt.

[28]In the way of righteousness
there is life; Dt 30:15
along that path is
immortality.

13

A wise son heeds his
father's instruction,
but a mocker does not
respond to rebukes. Pr 10:1

[2]From the fruit of their lips
people enjoy good
things, Pr 12:14
but the unfaithful have
an appetite for
violence.

[a] 27 The meaning of the Hebrew for this word is uncertain.

3 Those who guard their lips
preserve their lives, Pr 21:23; Jas 3:2
but those who speak rashly
will come to ruin. Pr 18:7,20-21

4 A sluggard's appetite is never
filled, Pr 21:25-26
but the desires of the
diligent are fully
satisfied.

5 The righteous hate what is
false, Ps 119:128
but the wicked make
themselves a stench
and bring shame on
themselves.

6 Righteousness guards the
person of integrity,
but wickedness overthrows
the sinner. Pr 11:3,5

7 One person pretends to be rich,
yet has nothing;
another pretends to be poor,
yet has great wealth. 2Co 6:10

8 A person's riches may ransom
their life,
but the poor cannot respond
to threatening rebukes.

9 The light of the righteous
shines brightly,
but the lamp of the wicked is
snuffed out. Job 18:5; Pr 24:20

10 Where there is strife, there is
pride,
but wisdom is found in those
who take advice.

11 Dishonest money dwindles
away, Pr 10:2
but whoever gathers money
little by little makes it
grow.

12 Hope deferred makes the heart
sick,
but a longing fulfilled is a
tree of life.

13 Whoever scorns instruction
will pay for it, Nu 15:31; 2Ch 36:16
but whoever respects a
command is rewarded.

14 The teaching of the wise is a
fountain of life, Pr 10:11
turning a person from the
snares of death. Pr 14:27

15 Good judgment wins favor,
but the way of the
unfaithful leads to their
destruction.[a]

16 All who are prudent act with[b]
knowledge,
but fools expose their folly. Pr 12:23

17 A wicked messenger falls into
trouble,
but a trustworthy envoy
brings healing. Pr 25:13

18 Whoever disregards discipline
comes to poverty and
shame,
but whoever heeds correction
is honored. Pr 15:5,31-32

[a] *15* Septuagint and Syriac; the meaning of the Hebrew for this phrase is uncertain.
[b] *16* Or *prudent protect themselves through*

19 A longing fulfilled is sweet to
the soul,
but fools detest turning from
evil.

20 Walk with the wise and become
wise,
for a companion of fools
suffers harm. Pr 15:31

21 Trouble pursues the sinner,
but the righteous are
rewarded with good
things. Ps 32:10

22 A good person leaves an
inheritance for their
children's children,
but a sinner's wealth is
stored up for the
righteous. Job 27:17; Ecc 2:26

23 An unplowed field produces
food for the poor,
but injustice sweeps it away.

24 Whoever spares the rod hates
their children,
but the one who loves their
children is careful
to discipline them.
Pr 19:18; 22:15; 29:15,17

25 The righteous eat to their
hearts' content,
but the stomach of the
wicked goes hungry.
Ps 34:10; Pr 10:3

14 The wise woman builds her
house, Pr 24:3
but with her own hands the
foolish one tears hers
down.

2 Whoever fears the LORD walks
uprightly,
but those who despise him
are devious in their ways.

3 A fool's mouth lashes out with
pride, Pr 10:14; Ecc 10:12
but the lips of the wise
protect them. Pr 12:6

4 Where there are no oxen, the
manger is empty,
but from the strength of
an ox come abundant
harvests.

5 An honest witness does not
deceive,
but a false witness pours out
lies. Pr 6:19; 12:17

6 The mocker seeks wisdom and
finds none,
but knowledge comes easily
to the discerning. Pr 9:9

7 Stay away from a fool,
for you will not find
knowledge on their lips.

8 The wisdom of the prudent is
to give thought to their
ways, Pr 15:28
but the folly of fools is
deception. ver 24

9 Fools mock at making amends
for sin,
but goodwill is found among
the upright.

10 Each heart knows its own
bitterness,
and no one else can share its
joy.

11 The house of the wicked will be
destroyed,
but the tent of the upright
will flourish. Pr 3:33; 12:7

12 There is a way that appears to
be right, Pr 12:15
but in the end it leads to
death. Pr 16:25

13 Even in laughter the heart may
ache, Ecc 2:2
and rejoicing may end in
grief.

14 The faithless will be fully
repaid for their ways,
Pr 1:31
and the good rewarded for
theirs. Pr 12:14

15 The simple believe anything,
but the prudent give thought
to their steps.

16 The wise fear the LORD and
shun evil, Pr 22:3
but a fool is hotheaded and
yet feels secure. 1Sa 25:25

17 A quick-tempered person
does foolish things,
ver 29; Pr 15:18
and the one who devises evil
schemes is hated.

18 The simple inherit folly,
but the prudent are crowned
with knowledge.

19 Evildoers will bow down in
the presence of the
good,
and the wicked at the gates
of the righteous. Pr 11:29

20 The poor are shunned even by
their neighbors,
but the rich have many
friends. Pr 19:4,7

21 It is a sin to despise one's
neighbor, Pr 11:12
but blessed is the one who
is kind to the needy.
Ps 41:1; Pr 19:17

22 Do not those who plot evil go
astray? Pr 4:16-17
But those who plan what
is good find[a] love and
faithfulness.

23 All hard work brings a profit,
but mere talk leads only to
poverty.

24 The wealth of the wise is their
crown,
but the folly of fools yields
folly. ver 8

25 A truthful witness saves lives,
but a false witness is
deceitful. ver 5

26 Whoever fears the LORD has a
secure fortress, Pr 18:10; 19:23
and for their children it will
be a refuge.

27 The fear of the LORD is a
fountain of life, Pr 10:11
turning a person from the
snares of death. Pr 13:14

28 A large population is a king's
glory,
but without subjects a prince
is ruined. 2Sa 19:7

[a] 22 Or *show*

29 Whoever is patient has great
understanding, Pr 17:27
but one who is quick-
tempered displays folly.
Ecc 7:8-9; Jas 1:19

30 A heart at peace gives life to
the body,
but envy rots the bones. Pr 12:4

31 Whoever oppresses the poor
shows contempt for
their Maker, Pr 17:5
but whoever is kind to
the needy honors God.
Dt 24:14

32 When calamity comes, the
wicked are brought
down, Pr 6:15
but even in death the
righteous seek refuge in
God. Job 13:15; 2Ti 4:18

33 Wisdom reposes in the heart of
the discerning Pr 2:6-10
and even among fools she
lets herself be known.[a]

34 Righteousness exalts a nation,
Pr 11:11
but sin condemns any
people.

35 A king delights in a wise
servant,
but a shameful servant
arouses his fury.
Mt 24:45-51; 25:14-30

15 A gentle answer turns away
wrath, Pr 25:15
but a harsh word stirs up
anger.

2 The tongue of the wise adorns
knowledge, Pr 10:31
but the mouth of the fool
gushes folly. Pr 12:23

3 The eyes of the LORD are
everywhere,
2Ch 16:9; Heb 4:13
keeping watch on the wicked
and the good. Jer 16:17

4 The soothing tongue is a tree
of life, Ps 5:9
but a perverse tongue
crushes the spirit. Pr 12:18

5 A fool spurns a parent's
discipline,
but whoever heeds correction
shows prudence. Pr 13:1

6 The house of the righteous
contains great treasure,
Pr 8:21
but the income of the wicked
brings ruin. Pr 10:16

7 The lips of the wise spread
knowledge, Pr 10:13
but the hearts of fools are
not upright.

8 The LORD detests the sacrifice
of the wicked,
Pr 21:27; Isa 1:11; Jer 6:20
but the prayer of the upright
pleases him. ver 29

9 The LORD detests the way of
the wicked, Pr 6:16
but he loves those who
pursue righteousness.
Pr 21:21; 1Ti 6:11

[a] 33 Hebrew; Septuagint and Syriac *discerning / but in the heart of fools she is not known*

10 Stern discipline awaits
anyone who leaves the path;
the one who hates correction
will die. Pr 1:31-32

11 Death and Destruction[a] lie
open before the LORD — Job 26:6; Ps 139:8
how much more do human
hearts! 2Ch 6:30; Ps 44:21

12 Mockers resent correction, Am 5:10
so they avoid the wise.

13 A happy heart makes the face
cheerful,
but heartache crushes the
spirit. Pr 12:25; 17:22

14 The discerning heart seeks
knowledge, Pr 18:15
but the mouth of a fool feeds
on folly.

15 All the days of the oppressed
are wretched,
but the cheerful heart has a
continual feast. ver 13

16 Better a little with the fear of
the LORD
than great wealth with
turmoil. Ps 37:16-17; 1Ti 6:6

17 Better a small serving of
vegetables with love
than a fattened calf with
hatred. Pr 17:1

18 A hot-tempered person stirs up
conflict, Pr 26:21
but the one who is patient
calms a quarrel. Ge 13:8

19 The way of the sluggard is
blocked with thorns, Pr 22:5
but the path of the upright is
a highway.

20 A wise son brings joy to his
father, Pr 10:1
but a foolish man despises
his mother.

21 Folly brings joy to one who has
no sense, Pr 10:23
but whoever has
understanding keeps a
straight course.

22 Plans fail for lack of counsel,
but with many advisers they
succeed. Pr 11:14

23 A person finds joy in giving an
apt reply — Pr 12:14
and how good is a timely
word! Pr 25:11

24 The path of life leads upward
for the prudent
to keep them from going
down to the realm of the
dead.

25 The LORD tears down
the house of the proud, Pr 12:7
but he sets the widow's
boundary stones in
place. Ps 68:5-6

26 The LORD detests the thoughts
of the wicked, Pr 6:16
but gracious words are pure
in his sight.

[a] 11 Hebrew *Abaddon*

27 The greedy bring ruin to their households,
but the one who hates bribes will live. Ex 23:8; Isa 33:15

28 The heart of the righteous weighs its answers, 1Pe 3:15
but the mouth of the wicked gushes evil.

29 The LORD is far from the wicked,
but he hears the prayer of the righteous. Ps 145:18-19

30 Light in a messenger's eyes brings joy to the heart,
and good news gives health to the bones. Pr 25:25

31 Whoever heeds life-giving correction
will be at home among the wise. ver 5

32 Those who disregard discipline despise themselves, Pr 1:7
but the one who heeds correction gains understanding. Pr 9:7-9

33 Wisdom's instruction is to fear the LORD, Pr 1:7
and humility comes before honor. Pr 18:12

16 To humans belong the plans of the heart,
but from the LORD comes the proper answer of the tongue. Pr 19:21

2 All a person's ways seem pure to them, Pr 12:15
but motives are weighed by the LORD. Pr 21:2

3 Commit to the LORD whatever you do,
and he will establish your plans. Ps 37:5-6; Pr 3:5-6

4 The LORD works out everything to its proper end — Isa 43:7
even the wicked for a day of disaster. Ro 9:22

5 The LORD detests all the proud of heart. Pr 6:16
Be sure of this: They will not go unpunished. Pr 11:20-21

6 Through love and faithfulness sin is atoned for;
through the fear of the LORD evil is avoided. Pr 14:16

7 When the LORD takes pleasure in anyone's way,
he causes their enemies to make peace with them. Ps 105:15

8 Better a little with righteousness
than much gain with injustice. Ps 37:16

9 In their hearts humans plan their course,
but the LORD establishes their steps. Jer 10:23

10 The lips of a king speak as an oracle,
and his mouth does not betray justice. Pr 17:7

11 Honest scales and balances
belong to the LORD;
all the weights in the bag are
of his making. Pr 11:1

12 Kings detest wrongdoing,
for a throne is established
through righteousness.
Pr 25:5

13 Kings take pleasure in honest
lips;
they value the one who
speaks what is right.
Pr 14:35

14 A king's wrath is a messenger
of death, Pr 19:12
but the wise will appease it.
Ecc 10:4

15 When a king's face brightens, it
means life; Job 29:24
his favor is like a rain cloud
in spring. Pr 19:12

16 How much better to get
wisdom than gold,
to get insight rather than
silver! Ps 49:20; Pr 8:10,19

17 The highway of the upright
avoids evil;
those who guard their ways
preserve their lives.
Pr 19:16

18 Pride goes before destruction,
1Sa 17:42
a haughty spirit before a fall.
Pr 11:2; 18:12

19 Better to be lowly in spirit
along with the oppressed
than to share plunder with
the proud.

20 Whoever gives heed to
instruction prospers,[a]
Pr 13:13
and blessed is the one who
trusts in the LORD.
Ps 34:8; Jer 17:7

21 The wise in heart are called
discerning,
and gracious words promote
instruction.[b] ver 23

22 Prudence is a fountain of life to
the prudent, Pr 13:14
but folly brings punishment
to fools.

23 The hearts of the wise make
their mouths prudent,
Job 15:5
and their lips promote
instruction.[c] ver 21

24 Gracious words are a
honeycomb, 1Sa 14:27
sweet to the soul and
healing to the bones.
Pr 24:13-14

25 There is a way that appears to
be right, Pr 12:15
but in the end it leads to
death. Pr 14:12

26 The appetite of laborers works
for them;
their hunger drives them on.

27 A scoundrel plots evil, Ps 140:2
and on their lips it is like a
scorching fire. Jas 3:6

[a] 20 Or *whoever speaks prudently finds what is good* [b] 21 Or *words make a person persuasive* [c] 23 Or *prudent / and make their lips persuasive*

28 A perverse person stirs up
conflict, Pr 15:18
and a gossip separates close
friends. Pr 17:9

29 A violent person entices their
neighbor
and leads them down a path
that is not good.
Pr 1:10; 12:26

30 Whoever winks with their eye
is plotting perversity;
Pr 6:13
whoever purses their lips is
bent on evil.

31 Gray hair is a crown of
splendor; Pr 20:29
it is attained in the way of
righteousness.

32 Better a patient person than a
warrior,
one with self-control than
one who takes a city.

33 The lot is cast into the lap,
1Sa 10:21; Eze 21:21
but its every decision is from
the LORD. Pr 18:18

17 Better a dry crust with peace
and quiet
than a house full of feasting,
with strife. Pr 15:16-17

2 A prudent servant will rule
over a disgraceful son
and will share the inheritance
as one of the family.

3 The crucible for silver and the
furnace for gold, Pr 27:21
but the LORD tests the heart.
Ps 26:2; Jer 17:10

4 A wicked person listens to
deceitful lips;
a liar pays attention to a
destructive tongue.

5 Whoever mocks the poor shows
contempt for their
Maker; Pr 14:31
whoever gloats over disaster
will not go unpunished.
Ob 1:12

6 Children's children are a crown
to the aged, Pr 13:22
and parents are the pride of
their children.

7 Eloquent lips are unsuited to a
godless fool —
how much worse lying lips to
a ruler! Pr 16:10

8 A bribe is seen as a charm by
the one who gives it;
they think success will come
at every turn. Ex 23:8

9 Whoever would foster love
covers over an offense,
Pr 10:12
but whoever repeats the
matter separates close
friends. Pr 16:28

10 A rebuke impresses a
discerning person
more than a hundred lashes
a fool.

11 Evildoers foster rebellion
against God;
the messenger of death
will be sent against
them.

12 Better to meet a bear robbed of her cubs
than a fool bent on folly. 1Sa 25:25

13 Evil will never leave the house
of one who pays back evil for good. Ps 109:4-5; Jer 18:20

14 Starting a quarrel is like breaching a dam;
so drop the matter before a dispute breaks out. Pr 20:3

15 Acquitting the guilty and condemning the innocent — Pr 18:5
the LORD detests them both. Ex 23:6-7; Isa 5:23

16 Why should fools have money in hand to buy wisdom,
when they are not able to understand it? Pr 23:23

17 A friend loves at all times,
and a brother is born for a time of adversity. Pr 27:10

18 One who has no sense shakes hands in pledge
and puts up security for a neighbor. Pr 6:1-5; 11:15

19 Whoever loves a quarrel loves sin;
whoever builds a high gate invites destruction.

20 One whose heart is corrupt does not prosper;
one whose tongue is perverse falls into trouble.

21 To have a fool for a child brings grief;
there is no joy for the parent of a godless fool. Pr 10:1

22 A cheerful heart is good medicine,
but a crushed spirit dries up the bones. Ps 22:15; Pr 15:13

23 The wicked accept bribes in secret Ex 23:8
to pervert the course of justice. Job 34:33

24 A discerning person keeps wisdom in view,
but a fool's eyes wander to the ends of the earth. Ecc 2:14

25 A foolish son brings grief to his father
and bitterness to the mother who bore him. Pr 10:1

26 If imposing a fine on the innocent is not good, Pr 18:5
surely to flog honest officials is not right.

27 The one who has knowledge uses words with restraint, Job 6:24
and whoever has understanding is even-tempered. Pr 14:29; Jas 1:19

28 Even fools are thought wise if they keep silent,
and discerning if they hold their tongues. Job 13:5

18 An unfriendly person
pursues selfish ends
and against all sound
judgment starts
quarrels.

2 Fools find no pleasure in
understanding
but delight in airing their
own opinions. Pr 12:23

3 When wickedness comes, so
does contempt,
and with shame comes
reproach.

4 The words of the mouth are
deep waters, Ps 18:16
but the fountain of wisdom
is a rushing stream.

5 It is not good to be partial to
the wicked Lev 19:15
and so deprive the innocent
of justice. Pr 17:15

6 The lips of fools bring them
strife,
and their mouths invite a
beating.

7 The mouths of fools are their
undoing,
and their lips are a snare
to their very lives.
Ps 140:9; Pr 10:14

8 The words of a gossip are like
choice morsels;
they go down to the inmost
parts. Pr 26:22

9 One who is slack in his work
is brother to one who
destroys. Pr 28:24

10 The name of the LORD is
a fortified tower;
2Sa 22:3; Ps 61:3
the righteous run to it and
are safe. Pr 14:26

11 The wealth of the rich is their
fortified city; Pr 10:15
they imagine it a wall too
high to scale.

12 Before a downfall the heart is
haughty,
but humility comes before
honor. Pr 11:2; 16:18

13 To answer before listening —
that is folly and shame.
Pr 20:25; Jn 7:51

14 The human spirit can endure
in sickness,
but a crushed spirit who can
bear? Pr 15:13; 17:22

15 The heart of the discerning
acquires knowledge,
Pr 15:14
for the ears of the wise seek
it out.

16 A gift opens the way Ge 32:20
and ushers the giver into the
presence of the great.

17 In a lawsuit the first to speak
seems right,
until someone comes
forward and cross-
examines.

18 Casting the lot settles disputes
Pr 16:33
and keeps strong opponents
apart.

19 A brother wronged is more
unyielding than a
fortified city; 1Sa 17:28
disputes are like the barred
gates of a citadel.

20 From the fruit of their mouth
a person's stomach is
filled;
with the harvest of their lips
they are satisfied. Pr 12:14

21 The tongue has the power of
life and death, Ps 12:4
and those who love it will eat
its fruit. Mt 12:37

22 He who finds a wife finds what
is good Pr 12:4
and receives favor from the
LORD. Pr 19:14

23 The poor plead for mercy,
but the rich answer harshly.

24 One who has unreliable friends
soon comes to ruin,
but there is a friend who
sticks closer than a
brother. Pr 17:17; Jn 15:13-15

19 Better the poor whose walk
is blameless
than a fool whose lips are
perverse. Pr 28:6

2 Desire without knowledge is
not good—
how much more will hasty
feet miss the way! Pr 29:20

3 A person's own folly leads to
their ruin, Ps 14:1
yet their heart rages against
the LORD. Jas 1:13-15

4 Wealth attracts many friends,
but even the closest friend of
the poor person deserts
them. Pr 14:20

5 A false witness will not go
unpunished, Ex 23:1
and whoever pours out lies
will not go free. Dt 19:19

6 Many curry favor with a ruler,
Pr 29:26
and everyone is the friend
of one who gives gifts.
Pr 17:8

7 The poor are shunned by all
their relatives—
how much more do
their friends avoid
them! Pr 10:15
Though the poor pursue them
with pleading,
they are nowhere to be
found.[a] Ps 38:11

8 The one who gets wisdom loves
life;
the one who cherishes
understanding will soon
prosper. Pr 16:20

9 A false witness will not go
unpunished,
and whoever pours out lies
will perish. ver 5

10 It is not fitting for a fool to live
in luxury— Pr 26:1
how much worse for a slave
to rule over princes!
Pr 30:21-23

[a] 7 The meaning of the Hebrew for this sentence is uncertain.

11 A person's wisdom yields
patience; Pr 16:32
it is to one's glory to
overlook an offense.

12 A king's rage is like the roar of
a lion, Pr 20:2
but his favor is like dew on
the grass. Pr 16:14-15

13 A foolish child is a father's ruin,
Pr 10:1
and a quarrelsome wife is
like
the constant dripping of a
leaky roof. Pr 21:9

14 Houses and wealth are
inherited from parents,
2Co 12:14
but a prudent wife is from
the LORD. Pr 18:22

15 Laziness brings on deep sleep,
and the shiftless go hungry.
Pr 6:9; 10:4

16 Whoever keeps
commandments keeps
their life,
but whoever shows contempt
for their ways will die.
Lk 10:28

17 Whoever is kind to the poor
lends to the LORD, Dt 24:14
and he will reward them for
what they have done.
Mt 10:42; 2Co 9:6-8

18 Discipline your children, for in
that there is hope;
do not be a willing party to
their death. Pr 13:24

19 A hot-tempered person must
pay the penalty;
rescue them, and you will
have to do it again.

20 Listen to advice and accept
discipline, Pr 4:1
and at the end you will be
counted among the
wise. Pr 12:15

21 Many are the plans in a
person's heart,
but it is the LORD's purpose
that prevails. Ps 33:11; Pr 16:9

22 What a person desires is
unfailing love[a];
better to be poor than a liar.

23 The fear of the LORD leads to
life;
then one rests content,
untouched by trouble.
Pr 12:21; 1Ti 4:8

24 A sluggard buries his hand in
the dish;
he will not even bring
it back to his mouth!
Pr 26:15

25 Flog a mocker, and the simple
will learn prudence;
rebuke the discerning,
and they will gain
knowledge. Pr 9:9

26 Whoever robs their father and
drives out their mother
Pr 28:24
is a child who brings shame
and disgrace.

[a] 22 Or *Greed is a person's shame*

27 Stop listening to instruction,
my son, Pr 1:8
and you will stray from the
words of knowledge.

28 A corrupt witness mocks at
justice,
and the mouth of the
wicked gulps down
evil. Job 15:16

29 Penalties are prepared for
mockers,
and beatings for the backs of
fools. Pr 26:3

20 Wine is a mocker and beer
a brawler; 1Sa 25:36
whoever is led astray
by them is not wise.
Pr 31:4

2 A king's wrath strikes terror
like the roar of a lion;
Pr 19:12
those who anger him forfeit
their lives. Pr 8:36

3 It is to one's honor to avoid
strife,
but every fool is quick to
quarrel. Pr 17:14

4 Sluggards do not plow in
season; Pr 6:6
so at harvest time they
look but find nothing.
Ecc 10:18

5 The purposes of a person's
heart are deep waters,
Ps 18:16
but one who has insight
draws them out.

6 Many claim to have unfailing
love,
but a faithful person who can
find? Ps 12:1

7 The righteous lead blameless
lives; Ps 26:1
blessed are their children
after them. Ps 37:25-26

8 When a king sits on his throne
to judge, 1Ki 7:7
he winnows out all evil with
his eyes. ver 26; Pr 25:4-5

9 Who can say, "I have kept my
heart pure; Job 15:14
I am clean and without sin"?
1Ki 8:46

10 Differing weights and differing
measures —
the LORD detests them both.
ver 23; Pr 11:1

11 Even small children are known
by their actions,
so is their conduct
really pure and
upright? Mt 7:16

12 Ears that hear and eyes that
see —
the LORD has made them
both. Ps 94:9

13 Do not love sleep or you will
grow poor; Pr 6:11; 19:15
stay awake and you will have
food to spare.

14 "It's no good, it's no good!" says
the buyer —
then goes off and boasts
about the purchase.

15 Gold there is, and rubies in abundance,
but lips that speak knowledge are a rare jewel.

16 Take the garment of one who puts up security for a stranger;
hold it in pledge if it is done for an outsider. Ex 22:26; Pr 27:13

17 Food gained by fraud tastes sweet, Pr 9:17
but one ends up with a mouth full of gravel. Job 20:14

18 Plans are established by seeking advice;
so if you wage war, obtain guidance. Pr 24:6

19 A gossip betrays a confidence; Pr 11:13
so avoid anyone who talks too much.

20 If someone curses their father or mother, Pr 30:11
their lamp will be snuffed out in pitch darkness. Job 18:5

21 An inheritance claimed too soon
will not be blessed at the end.

22 Do not say, "I'll pay you back for this wrong!" Pr 24:29
Wait for the LORD, and he will avenge you. Ro 12:19

23 The LORD detests differing weights,
and dishonest scales do not please him. ver 10

24 A person's steps are directed by the LORD. Ps 90:12
How then can anyone understand their own way? Jer 10:23

25 It is a trap to dedicate something rashly
and only later to consider one's vows. Ecc 5:2,4-5

26 A wise king winnows out the wicked;
he drives the threshing wheel over them. ver 8

27 The human spirit is[a] the lamp of the LORD Ps 119:105
that sheds light on one's inmost being. Pr 16:2

28 Love and faithfulness keep a king safe;
through love his throne is made secure. Pr 29:14

29 The glory of young men is their strength,
gray hair the splendor of the old. Pr 16:31

30 Blows and wounds scrub away evil, Pr 22:15
and beatings purge the inmost being. Isa 1:5

[a] 27 Or *A person's words are*

21 In the LORD's hand the
king's heart is a stream
of water
that he channels toward all
who please him. Est 5:1

2 A person may think their own
ways are right,
but the LORD weighs the
heart. Pr 16:2; 24:12; Lk 16:15

3 To do what is right and just
is more acceptable to the
LORD than sacrifice.
1Sa 15:22; Isa 1:11; Mic 6:6-8

4 Haughty eyes and a proud
heart — Pr 6:17
the unplowed field of the
wicked — produce sin.

5 The plans of the diligent lead
to profit Pr 10:4
as surely as haste leads to
poverty.

6 A fortune made by a lying
tongue
is a fleeting vapor and a
deadly snare.[a] 2Pe 2:3

7 The violence of the wicked will
drag them away, Pr 11:5
for they refuse to do what is
right.

8 The way of the guilty is
devious, Pr 2:15
but the conduct of the
innocent is upright.

9 Better to live on a corner of the
roof
than share a house with a
quarrelsome wife. Pr 25:24

10 The wicked crave evil;
their neighbors get no mercy
from them.

11 When a mocker is punished,
the simple gain wisdom;
by paying attention to
the wise they get
knowledge. Pr 19:25

12 The Righteous One[b] takes
note of the house of the
wicked
and brings the wicked to
ruin. Pr 14:11

13 Whoever shuts their ears to the
cry of the poor
will also cry out and not be
answered. Mt 18:30-34; Jas 2:13

14 A gift given in secret soothes
anger,
and a bribe concealed in
the cloak pacifies great
wrath. Pr 18:16; 19:6

15 When justice is done, it brings
joy to the righteous
but terror to evildoers. Pr 10:29

16 Whoever strays from the path
of prudence
comes to rest in the company
of the dead. Ps 49:14

17 Whoever loves pleasure will
become poor;
whoever loves wine and
olive oil will never be
rich. Pr 23:20-21,29-35

[a] 6 Some Hebrew manuscripts, Septuagint and Vulgate; most Hebrew manuscripts *vapor for those who seek death* [b] 12 Or *The righteous person*

18 The wicked become a ransom
for the righteous, Pr 11:8
and the unfaithful for the
upright.

19 Better to live in a desert
than with a quarrelsome and
nagging wife. ver 9

20 The wise store up choice food
and olive oil,
but fools gulp theirs down.

21 Whoever pursues
righteousness and love
finds life, prosperity[a] and
honor. Mt 5:6

22 One who is wise can go up
against the city of the
mighty Ecc 9:15-16
and pull down the
stronghold in which
they trust.

23 Those who guard their
mouths and their
tongues Jas 3:2
keep themselves from
calamity. Pr 12:13

24 The proud and arrogant
person — "Mocker" is his
name — Ps 1:1
behaves with insolent fury.

25 The craving of a sluggard
will be the death of him,
Pr 13:4
because his hands refuse to
work.

26 All day long he craves for more,
but the righteous give
without sparing. Ps 37:26

27 The sacrifice of the wicked
is detestable —
Jer 6:20; Am 5:22
how much more so when
brought with evil intent!
Pr 15:8

28 A false witness will perish, Pr 19:5
but a careful listener
will testify
successfully.

29 The wicked put up a bold
front,
but the upright give thought
to their ways. Pr 14:8

30 There is no wisdom, no insight,
no plan Jer 9:23
that can succeed against the
LORD. Isa 8:10; Ac 5:39

31 The horse is made ready for the
day of battle,
but victory rests with the
LORD. Ps 3:8

22 A good name is more
desirable than great
riches;
to be esteemed is better than
silver or gold. Ecc 7:1

2 Rich and poor have this in
common:
The LORD is the Maker of
them all. Job 31:15

3 The prudent see danger and
take refuge, Pr 14:16
but the simple keep going
and pay the penalty.
Pr 27:12

[a] 21 Or *righteousness*

4 Humility is the fear of the
LORD;
its wages are riches and
honor and life. Pr 10:27; 15:33

5 In the paths of the wicked are
snares and pitfalls, Pr 15:19
but those who would
preserve their life stay
far from them.

6 Start children off on the way
they should go, Eph 6:4
and even when they are
old they will not turn
from it. Dt 6:7

7 The rich rule over the poor,
and the borrower is slave to
the lender.

8 Whoever sows injustice reaps
calamity, Job 4:8
and the rod they wield in fury
will be broken. Ps 125:3

9 The generous will themselves
be blessed, 2Co 9:6
for they share their food with
the poor. Pr 19:17

10 Drive out the mocker, and out
goes strife;
quarrels and insults are
ended. Pr 26:20

11 One who loves a pure heart and
who speaks with grace
will have the king for a
friend. Mt 5:8

12 The eyes of the LORD keep
watch over knowledge,
but he frustrates the words
of the unfaithful.

13 The sluggard says, "There's a
lion outside! Pr 26:13
I'll be killed in the public
square!"

14 The mouth of an adulterous
woman is a deep pit;
Pr 2:16; 5:3-5
a man who is under the
LORD's wrath falls into it.
Ecc 7:26

15 Folly is bound up in the heart
of a child,
but the rod of discipline
will drive it far away.
Pr 13:24; 23:14

16 One who oppresses the poor to
increase his wealth
and one who gives gifts to
the rich — both come to
poverty.

Thirty Sayings of the Wise

Saying 1

17 Pay attention and turn your
ear to the sayings of the
wise; Pr 5:1
apply your heart to what I
teach, Pr 2:2
18 for it is pleasing when you keep
them in your heart
and have all of them ready
on your lips.
19 So that your trust may be in
the LORD,
I teach you today, even you.
20 Have I not written thirty
sayings for you,
sayings of counsel and
knowledge,

21 teaching you to be honest
and to speak the truth, Lk 1:3-4; 1Pe 3:15
so that you bring back
truthful reports
to those you serve?

Saying 2

22 Do not exploit the poor
because they are poor Zec 7:10
and do not crush the needy
in court, Ex 23:6; Mal 3:5
23 for the LORD will take up their
case Ps 12:5
and will exact life for life.
Pr 23:10-11

Saying 3

24 Do not make friends with a
hot-tempered person,
do not associate with one
easily angered,
25 or you may learn their ways
and get yourself ensnared.
1Co 15:33

Saying 4

26 Do not be one who shakes
hands in pledge Pr 11:15
or puts up security for
debts;
27 if you lack the means to pay,
your very bed will be
snatched from under
you. Pr 17:18

Saying 5

28 Do not move an ancient
boundary stone Dt 19:14
set up by your ancestors.

Saying 6

29 Do you see someone skilled in
their work?
They will serve before kings;
Ge 41:46
they will not serve before
officials of low rank.

Saying 7

23 When you sit to dine with a
ruler,
note well what[a] is before you,
2 and put a knife to your throat
if you are given to gluttony.
3 Do not crave his delicacies,
ver 6-8
for that food is deceptive.

Saying 8

4 Do not wear yourself out to get
rich;
do not trust your own
cleverness.
5 Cast but a glance at riches, and
they are gone, Mt 6:19
for they will surely sprout
wings
and fly off to the sky like an
eagle. Pr 27:24

Saying 9

6 Do not eat the food of a
begrudging host,
do not crave his delicacies;
Ps 141:4
7 for he is the kind of person
who is always thinking about
the cost.[b]

[a] 1 Or *who* [b] 7 Or *for as he thinks within himself, / so he is*; or *for as he puts on a feast, / so he is*

"Eat and drink," he says to you,
but his heart is not with you.
8 You will vomit up the little you have eaten
and will have wasted your compliments.

Saying 10

9 Do not speak to fools,
for they will scorn your prudent words.
Pr 9:7; Mt 7:6

Saying 11

10 Do not move an ancient boundary stone
Dt 19:14; Pr 22:28
or encroach on the fields of the fatherless,
11 for their Defender is strong;
Job 19:25
he will take up their case against you. Pr 22:22-23

Saying 12

12 Apply your heart to instruction
Pr 2:2
and your ears to words of knowledge.

Saying 13

13 Do not withhold discipline from a child;
if you punish them with the rod, they will not die.
14 Punish them with the rod
and save them from death.
Pr 13:24

Saying 14

15 My son, if your heart is wise,
then my heart will be glad indeed;
16 my inmost being will rejoice
when your lips speak what is right. ver 24; Pr 27:11

Saying 15

17 Do not let your heart envy sinners, Ps 37:1; Pr 28:14
but always be zealous for the fear of the LORD.
18 There is surely a future hope for you,
and your hope will not be cut off. Pr 24:14,19-20

Saying 16

19 Listen, my son, and be wise, Dt 4:9
and set your heart on the right path:
20 Do not join those who drink too much wine Isa 5:11,22
or gorge themselves on meat,
21 for drunkards and gluttons become poor, Pr 21:17
and drowsiness clothes them in rags.

Saying 17

22 Listen to your father, who gave you life,
and do not despise your mother when she is old.
Pr 1:8; Eph 6:1-2
23 Buy the truth and do not sell it —
wisdom, instruction and insight as well. Pr 4:7

24 The father of a righteous child
has great joy;
a man who fathers a wise
son rejoices in him.
ver 15-16; Pr 10:1
25 May your father and mother
rejoice;
may she who gave you birth
be joyful! Pr 10:1

Saying 18

26 My son, give me your heart
Pr 5:1-6
and let your eyes delight in
my ways, Ps 18:21
27 for an adulterous woman is a
deep pit, Pr 22:14
and a wayward wife is a
narrow well.
28 Like a bandit she lies in wait
Pr 7:11-12; Ecc 7:26
and multiplies the unfaithful
among men.

Saying 19

29 Who has woe? Who has
sorrow?
Who has strife? Who has
complaints?
Who has needless bruises?
Who has bloodshot
eyes?
30 Those who linger over wine,
Ps 75:8; Isa 5:11; Eph 5:18
who go to sample bowls of
mixed wine.
31 Do not gaze at wine when it is
red,
when it sparkles in the cup,
when it goes down
smoothly!
32 In the end it bites like a snake
and poisons like a viper.
33 Your eyes will see strange
sights,
and your mind will imagine
confusing things.
34 You will be like one sleeping on
the high seas,
lying on top of the rigging.
35 "They hit me," you will say,
"but I'm not hurt!
They beat me, but I don't feel
it!
When will I wake up
so I can find another drink?"
Pr 20:1

Saying 20

24 Do not envy the wicked,
Ps 37:1; Pr 3:31-32
do not desire their company;
2 for their hearts plot violence,
Ps 2:1; Isa 32:6
and their lips talk about
making trouble. Ps 10:7

Saying 21

3 By wisdom a house is built, Pr 14:1
and through understanding
it is established;
4 through knowledge its rooms
are filled
with rare and beautiful
treasures. Pr 8:21

Saying 22

5 The wise prevail through great
power,
and those who have
knowledge muster their
strength.

6 Surely you need guidance to
wage war,
and victory is won through
many advisers. Pr 11:14

Saying 23

7 Wisdom is too high for fools;
in the assembly at the gate
they must not open
their mouths.

Saying 24

8 Whoever plots evil
will be known as a schemer.
9 The schemes of folly are sin,
and people detest a mocker.

Saying 25

10 If you falter in a time of trouble,
how small is your strength!
Jer 51:46; Heb 12:3
11 Rescue those being led away to
death;
hold back those staggering
toward slaughter.
Ps 82:4; Isa 58:6-7
12 If you say, "But we knew
nothing about this,"
does not he who weighs the
heart perceive it? Pr 21:2
Does not he who guards your
life know it?
Will he not repay everyone
according to what they
have done? Ro 2:6

Saying 26

13 Eat honey, my son, for it is
good;
honey from the comb is
sweet to your taste.
14 Know also that wisdom is like
honey for you:
If you find it, there is a
future hope for you,
and your hope will not be
cut off. Ps 119:103; Pr 16:24

Saying 27

15 Do not lurk like a thief near
the house of the
righteous,
do not plunder their
dwelling place;
16 for though the righteous fall
seven times, they rise
again,
but the wicked stumble
when calamity strikes.
Mic 7:8

Saying 28

17 Do not gloat when your enemy
falls; Ob 1:12
when they stumble, do not
let your heart rejoice,
Job 31:29
18 or the LORD will see and
disapprove
and turn his wrath away
from them. Job 31:29

Saying 29

19 Do not fret because of evildoers
Ps 37:1
or be envious of the
wicked,
20 for the evildoer has no future
hope,
and the lamp of the wicked
will be snuffed out.
Pr 23:17-18

Saying 30

21 Fear the LORD and the king, my
son, Ro 13:1-5; 1Pe 2:17
and do not join with
rebellious officials,
22 for those two will send sudden
destruction on them, Ps 73:19
and who knows what
calamities they can
bring?

Further Sayings of the Wise

23 These also are sayings of the
wise: Pr 1:6

To show partiality in judging is
not good: Lev 19:15; Pr 28:21
24 Whoever says to the guilty,
"You are innocent," Pr 17:15
will be cursed by peoples
and denounced by
nations.
25 But it will go well with
those who convict the
guilty,
and rich blessing will come
on them.

26 An honest answer
is like a kiss on the lips.

27 Put your outdoor work in
order
and get your fields ready;
after that, build your house.

28 Do not testify against your
neighbor without
cause — Eph 4:25
would you use your lips to
mislead?
29 Do not say, "I'll do to them as
they have done to me;
I'll pay them back for what
they did." Pr 20:22; Mt 5:38-41

30 I went past the field of a
sluggard, Pr 6:6-11
past the vineyard of
someone who has no
sense;
31 thorns had come up
everywhere,
the ground was covered with
weeds,
and the stone wall was in
ruins.
32 I applied my heart to what I
observed
and learned a lesson from
what I saw:
33 A little sleep, a little slumber,
a little folding of the hands
to rest — Pr 6:10
34 and poverty will come on you
like a thief
and scarcity like an armed
man. Pr 10:4; Ecc 10:18

More Proverbs of Solomon

25 These are more proverbs of
Solomon, compiled by the
men of Hezekiah king of Judah:
1Ki 4:32; Pr 1:1

2 It is the glory of God to conceal
a matter;
to search out a matter is the
glory of kings. Pr 16:10-15
3 As the heavens are high and
the earth is deep,
so the hearts of kings are
unsearchable.

4 Remove the dross from the silver,
and a silversmith can produce a vessel;
5 remove wicked officials from the king's presence, Pr 20:8
and his throne will be established through righteousness. Pr 16:12

6 Do not exalt yourself in the king's presence,
and do not claim a place among his great men;
7 it is better for him to say to you, "Come up here," Lk 14:7-10
than for him to humiliate you before his nobles.

What you have seen with your eyes
8 do not bring[a] hastily to court,
for what will you do in the end
if your neighbor puts you to shame? Mt 5:25-26

9 If you take your neighbor to court,
do not betray another's confidence,
10 or the one who hears it may shame you
and the charge against you will stand.

11 Like apples[b] of gold in settings of silver Pr 15:23
is a ruling rightly given.
12 Like an earring of gold or an ornament of fine gold
is the rebuke of a wise judge to a listening ear. Pr 15:31

13 Like a snow-cooled drink at harvest time
is a trustworthy messenger to the one who sends him;
he refreshes the spirit of his master. Pr 13:17
14 Like clouds and wind without rain
is one who boasts of gifts never given.

15 Through patience a ruler can be persuaded, Ecc 10:4
and a gentle tongue can break a bone. Pr 15:1

16 If you find honey, eat just enough —
too much of it, and you will vomit. ver 27
17 Seldom set foot in your neighbor's house —
too much of you, and they will hate you.

18 Like a club or a sword or a sharp arrow
is one who gives false testimony against a neighbor. Pr 12:18
19 Like a broken tooth or a lame foot
is reliance on the unfaithful in a time of trouble.
20 Like one who takes away a garment on a cold day,

[a] 7,8 Or *nobles / on whom you had set your eyes. / [8]Do not go* [b] 11 Or possibly *apricots*

or like vinegar poured on a
wound,
is one who sings songs to a
heavy heart.

21 If your enemy is hungry, give
him food to eat;
if he is thirsty, give him
water to drink.
22 In doing this, you will heap
burning coals on his
head, Ps 18:8
and the LORD will reward
you. 2Sa 16:12; Ro 12:20

23 Like a north wind that brings
unexpected rain
is a sly tongue — which
provokes a horrified
look.

24 Better to live on a corner of the
roof
than share a house with a
quarrelsome wife. Pr 21:9

25 Like cold water to a weary soul
is good news from a distant
land. Pr 15:30
26 Like a muddied spring or a
polluted well
are the righteous who give
way to the wicked.

27 It is not good to eat too much
honey, ver 16
nor is it honorable to search
out matters that are too
deep. Pr 27:2

28 Like a city whose walls are
broken through
is a person who lacks self-
control.

26 Like snow in summer or
rain in harvest, 1Sa 12:17
honor is not fitting for a fool.
Pr 19:10

2 Like a fluttering sparrow or a
darting swallow,
an undeserved curse
does not come to rest.
Dt 23:5
3 A whip for the horse, a bridle
for the donkey, Ps 32:9
and a rod for the backs of
fools! Pr 10:13
4 Do not answer a fool according
to his folly,
or you yourself will be just
like him. ver 5; Isa 36:21
5 Answer a fool according to his
folly,
or he will be wise in his own
eyes. ver 4; Pr 3:7
6 Sending a message
by the hands of a fool
Pr 10:26
is like cutting off one's feet
or drinking poison.
7 Like the useless legs of one
who is lame
is a proverb in the mouth of
a fool. ver 9
8 Like tying a stone in a sling
is the giving of honor to a
fool. ver 1
9 Like a thornbush in a
drunkard's hand
is a proverb in the mouth of
a fool. ver 7
10 Like an archer who wounds at
random
is one who hires a fool or any
passer-by.

11 As a dog returns to its vomit, 2Pe 2:22*
so fools repeat their folly. Ex 8:15
12 Do you see a person wise in their own eyes? Pr 3:7
There is more hope for a fool than for them. Pr 29:20

13 A sluggard says, "There's a lion in the road, Pr 6:6-11
a fierce lion roaming the streets!" Pr 22:13
14 As a door turns on its hinges,
so a sluggard turns on his bed. Pr 6:9
15 A sluggard buries his hand in the dish;
he is too lazy to bring it back to his mouth. Pr 19:24
16 A sluggard is wiser in his own eyes
than seven people who answer discreetly.

17 Like one who grabs a stray dog by the ears
is someone who rushes into a quarrel not their own.

18 Like a maniac shooting
flaming arrows of death
19 is one who deceives their neighbor
and says, "I was only joking!"
20 Without wood a fire goes out;
without a gossip a quarrel dies down. Pr 22:10
21 As charcoal to embers and as wood to fire,
so is a quarrelsome person for kindling strife. Pr 15:18
22 The words of a gossip are like choice morsels;
they go down to the inmost parts. Pr 18:8

23 Like a coating of silver dross on earthenware
are fervent[a] lips with an evil heart.
24 Enemies disguise themselves with their lips, Ps 31:18
but in their hearts they harbor deceit. Ps 41:6
25 Though their speech is charming, do not believe them, Ps 28:3
for seven abominations fill their hearts. Jer 9:4-8
26 Their malice may be concealed by deception,
but their wickedness will be exposed in the assembly.
27 Whoever digs a pit will fall into it; Ps 7:15; Est 6:13
if someone rolls a stone, it will roll back on them. Pr 28:10; 29:6
28 A lying tongue hates those it hurts,
and a flattering mouth works ruin. Pr 29:5

27

Do not boast about tomorrow, 1Ki 20:11
for you do not know what a day may bring. Lk 12:19-20; Jas 4:13-16

[a] 23 Hebrew; Septuagint *smooth*

2 Let someone else praise you,
and not your own mouth;
an outsider, and not your own lips. Pr 25:27
3 Stone is heavy and sand a burden, Job 6:3
but a fool's provocation is heavier than both.
4 Anger is cruel and fury overwhelming,
but who can stand before jealousy? Nu 5:14

5 Better is open rebuke
than hidden love.

6 Wounds from a friend can be trusted,
but an enemy multiplies kisses. Ps 141:5
7 One who is full loathes honey from the comb,
but to the hungry even what is bitter tastes sweet.
8 Like a bird that flees its nest Isa 16:2
is anyone who flees from home.
9 Perfume and incense bring joy to the heart, Est 2:12; Ps 45:8
and the pleasantness of a friend
springs from their heartfelt advice.

10 Do not forsake your friend or a friend of your family,
and do not go to your relative's house when disaster strikes you — Pr 17:17; 18:24
better a neighbor nearby than a relative far away.
11 Be wise, my son, and bring joy to my heart; Pr 10:1; 23:15-16
then I can answer anyone who treats me with contempt. Ge 24:60
12 The prudent see danger and take refuge,
but the simple keep going and pay the penalty. Pr 22:3

13 Take the garment of one who puts up security for a stranger;
hold it in pledge if it is done for an outsider. Pr 20:16

14 If anyone loudly blesses their neighbor early in the morning,
it will be taken as a curse.
15 A quarrelsome wife is like the dripping
of a leaky roof in a rainstorm; Pr 19:13
16 restraining her is like restraining the wind
or grasping oil with the hand.

17 As iron sharpens iron,
so one person sharpens another.

[18]The one who guards a fig tree
will eat its fruit, 1Co 9:7
and whoever protects their
master will be honored.
Lk 19:12-27

[19]As water reflects the face,
so one's life reflects the
heart.[a]

[20]Death and Destruction[b] are
never satisfied, Hab 2:5
and neither are human eyes.
Ecc 1:8

[21]The crucible for silver and the
furnace for gold, Pr 17:3
but people are tested by their
praise.

[22]Though you grind a fool in a
mortar,
grinding them like grain
with a pestle,
you will not remove their
folly from them.

[23]Be sure you know the condition
of your flocks, Pr 12:10
give careful attention to your
herds;
[24]for riches do not endure
forever, Pr 23:5
and a crown is not secure for
all generations.
[25]When the hay is removed and
new growth appears
and the grass from the hills
is gathered in,
[26]the lambs will provide you
with clothing,
and the goats with the price
of a field.
[27]You will have plenty of goats'
milk to feed your family
and to nourish your female
servants.

28 The wicked flee though no
one pursues, Lev 26:17; Ps 53:5
but the righteous are as bold
as a lion. Ps 138:3

[2]When a country is rebellious, it
has many rulers,
but a ruler with discernment
and knowledge
maintains order.

[3]A ruler[c] who oppresses the
poor
is like a driving rain that
leaves no crops.

[4]Those who forsake instruction
praise the wicked,
but those who heed it resist
them.

[5]Evildoers do not understand
what is right,
but those who seek the LORD
understand it fully.

[6]Better the poor whose walk is
blameless
than the rich whose ways are
perverse. Pr 19:1

[7]A discerning son heeds
instruction,
but a companion of gluttons
disgraces his father.
Pr 23:19-21

[a] 19 Or *so others reflect your heart back to you* [b] 20 Hebrew *Abaddon* [c] 3 Or *A poor person*

8 Whoever increases wealth by
taking interest or profit
from the poor Ex 18:21
amasses it for another, who
will be kind to the poor.
Pr 13:22; Lk 14:12-14

9 If anyone turns a deaf ear to
my instruction,
even their prayers
are detestable.
Ps 66:18; 109:7; Pr 15:8

10 Whoever leads the upright
along an evil path
will fall into their own trap,
Pr 26:27
but the blameless will
receive a good
inheritance.

11 The rich are wise in their own
eyes;
one who is poor and
discerning sees how
deluded they are.

12 When the righteous triumph,
there is great elation;
2Ki 11:20
but when the wicked rise to
power, people go into
hiding. Pr 11:10

13 Whoever conceals their sins
does not prosper, Job 31:33
but the one who confesses
and renounces them
finds mercy. Ps 32:1-5; 1Jn 1:9

14 Blessed is the one who always
trembles before God,
but whoever hardens their
heart falls into trouble.

15 Like a roaring lion or a
charging bear
is a wicked ruler over a
helpless people.

16 A tyrannical ruler practices
extortion,
but one who hates ill-gotten
gain will enjoy a long
reign.

17 Anyone tormented by the guilt
of murder
will seek refuge in the grave;
Ge 9:6
let no one hold them back.

18 The one whose walk is
blameless is kept safe,
Jer 39:18
but the one whose ways are
perverse will fall into
the pit.[a] Pr 10:9

19 Those who work their land
will have abundant
food,
but those who chase
fantasies will have their
fill of poverty. Pr 12:11

20 A faithful person will be richly
blessed,
but one eager to get rich
will not go unpunished.
ver 22; 1Ti 6:9

21 To show partiality is not
good — Pr 18:5
yet a person will do wrong
for a piece of bread.
Eze 13:19

[a] 18 Syriac (see Septuagint); Hebrew *into one*

22 The stingy are eager to get rich
and are unaware that poverty
awaits them. Pr 23:6

23 Whoever rebukes a person will
in the end gain favor
rather than one who has a
flattering tongue. Pr 27:5-6

24 Whoever robs their father or
mother Pr 19:26
and says, "It's not wrong,"
is partner to one who
destroys. Pr 18:9

25 The greedy stir up conflict, Pr 14:17
but those who trust in the
LORD will prosper. Pr 29:25

26 Those who trust in themselves
are fools, Ps 4:5
but those who walk in
wisdom are kept safe. 1Co 3:18

27 Those who give to the poor will
lack nothing, Dt 24:19
but those who close their
eyes to them receive
many curses. Ps 109:17

28 When the wicked rise to power,
people go into hiding; ver 12
but when the wicked perish,
the righteous thrive.

29 Whoever remains stiff-
necked after many
rebukes Ex 32:9
will suddenly be
destroyed — without
remedy. 2Ch 36:16; Pr 6:15

2 When the righteous thrive, the
people rejoice; Est 8:15
when the wicked rule, the
people groan. Pr 28:12

3 A man who loves wisdom
brings joy to his father, Pr 10:1
but a companion of
prostitutes
squanders his wealth. Pr 5:8-10; Lk 15:11-32

4 By justice a king gives
a country stability, Pr 8:15-16
but those who are greedy
for[a] bribes tear it down.

5 Those who flatter their
neighbors
are spreading nets for their
feet. Pr 26:28

6 Evildoers are snared by their
own sin, Ecc 9:12
but the righteous shout for
joy and are glad.

7 The righteous care about
justice for the poor, Job 29:16
but the wicked have no such
concern.

8 Mockers stir up a city,
but the wise turn away
anger. Pr 11:11; 16:14

9 If a wise person goes to court
with a fool,
the fool rages and scoffs, and
there is no peace.

[a] 4 Or *who give*

[10] The bloodthirsty hate a person
of integrity
and seek to kill the upright. 1Jn 3:12

[11] Fools give full vent to their
rage, Job 15:13
but the wise bring calm in
the end. Pr 12:16

[12] If a ruler listens to lies, 2Ki 21:9
all his officials become
wicked. Job 34:30

[13] The poor and the oppressor
have this in
common:
The LORD gives sight
to the eyes of both.
Pr 22:2; Mt 5:45

[14] If a king judges the poor with
fairness,
his throne will be
established forever.
Ps 72:1-5; Pr 16:12

[15] A rod and a reprimand impart
wisdom,
but a child left undisciplined
disgraces its mother.
Pr 13:24

[16] When the wicked thrive, so
does sin,
but the righteous will
see their downfall.
Ps 37:35-36; 91:8

[17] Discipline your children, and
they will give you
peace;
they will bring you the
delights you desire. Pr 10:1

[18] Where there is no revelation,
people cast off restraint;
but blessed is the one
who heeds wisdom's
instruction. Ps 1:1-2; 119:1-2

[19] Servants cannot be corrected
by mere words;
though they understand,
they will not respond.

[20] Do you see someone who
speaks in haste?
There is more hope for a fool
than for them. Pr 26:12

[21] A servant pampered from
youth
will turn out to be insolent.

[22] An angry person stirs up
conflict,
and a hot-tempered person
commits many sins.
Pr 14:17

[23] Pride brings a person low,
Est 5:12
but the lowly in spirit gain
honor. Pr 11:2; Isa 66:2; Mt 23:12

[24] The accomplices of thieves are
their own enemies;
they are put under oath and
dare not testify. Lev 5:1

[25] Fear of man will prove to be a
snare, 1Sa 15:24
but whoever trusts in the
LORD is kept safe. Pr 28:25

[26] Many seek an audience with a
ruler, Pr 19:6
but it is from the LORD that
one gets justice. Pr 16:33

27 The righteous detest the
dishonest;
the wicked detest the
upright. ver 10

Sayings of Agur

30 The sayings of Agur son of
Jakeh — an inspired utterance. Pr 22:17

This man's utterance to Ithiel:

"I am weary, God,
but I can prevail.[a]
2 Surely I am only a brute, not a
man;
I do not have human
understanding.
3 I have not learned wisdom,
nor have I attained to the
knowledge of the Holy
One. Pr 9:10
4 Who has gone up to heaven
and come down?
Ps 24:1-2; Jn 3:13
Whose hands have gathered
up the wind? Isa 40:12
Who has wrapped up the
waters in a cloak?
Ge 1:2; Job 26:8
Who has established all the
ends of the earth?
What is his name, and what
is the name of his son?
Rev 19:12
Surely you know!

5 "Every word of God is flawless;
Ps 12:6; 18:30
he is a shield to those who
take refuge in him. Ps 84:11
6 Do not add to his words,
Dt 4:2; Rev 22:18
or he will rebuke you and
prove you a liar.

7 "Two things I ask of you,
LORD;
do not refuse me before I
die:
8 Keep falsehood and lies far
from me;
give me neither poverty nor
riches,
but give me only my daily
bread. Mt 6:11
9 Otherwise, I may have too
much and disown you
Jos 24:27
and say, 'Who is the LORD?'
Dt 8:10-14; Hos 13:6
Or I may become poor and
steal,
and so dishonor the name of
my God. Dt 8:12

10 "Do not slander a servant to
their master,
or they will curse you,
and you will pay
for it.

11 "There are those who curse
their fathers
and do not bless their
mothers; Pr 20:20
12 those who are pure in their
own eyes Lk 18:11
and yet are not cleansed of
their filth; Jer 2:23,35

[a] *1* With a different word division of the Hebrew; Masoretic Text *utterance to Ithiel, / to Ithiel and Ukal:*

13 those whose eyes are ever so
haughty, Pr 6:17
whose glances are so
disdainful;
14 those whose teeth are swords
Job 29:17
and whose jaws are set with
knives Ps 57:4
to devour the poor from the
earth Ps 14:4; Am 8:4
and the needy from among
mankind. Job 19:22

15 "The leech has two daughters.
'Give! Give!' they cry.

"There are three things
that are never satisfied,
Pr 27:20
four that never say,
'Enough!':
16 the grave, the barren womb,
Pr 27:20; Hab 2:5
land, which is never satisfied
with water,
and fire, which never says,
'Enough!'

17 "The eye that mocks a father,
Dt 21:18-21
that scorns an aged mother,
will be pecked out by the
ravens of the valley,
will be eaten by the vultures.
Job 15:23

18 "There are three things
that are too amazing
for me,
four that I do not
understand:
19 the way of an eagle in the sky,
the way of a snake on a rock,
the way of a ship on the high
seas,
and the way of a man with a
young woman.

20 "This is the way of an
adulterous woman:
She eats and wipes her
mouth
and says, 'I've done nothing
wrong.' Pr 5:6

21 "Under three things the earth
trembles,
under four it cannot bear up:
22 a servant who becomes king,
Pr 19:10
a godless fool who gets
plenty to eat,
23 a contemptible woman who
gets married,
and a servant who displaces
her mistress.

24 "Four things on earth are
small,
yet they are extremely wise:
25 Ants are creatures of little
strength,
yet they store up their food
in the summer; Pr 6:6-8
26 hyraxes are creatures of little
power, Ps 104:18
yet they make their home in
the crags;
27 locusts have no king, Ex 10:4
yet they advance together in
ranks;
28 a lizard can be caught with the
hand,
yet it is found in kings'
palaces.

29 "There are three things that
are stately in their
stride,
four that move with stately
bearing:
30 a lion, mighty among beasts,
who retreats before nothing;
31 a strutting rooster, a he-goat,
and a king secure against
revolt.[a]

32 "If you play the fool and exalt
yourself,
or if you plan evil,
clap your hand over your
mouth! Job 21:5
33 For as churning cream
produces butter,
and as twisting the nose
produces blood,
so stirring up anger produces
strife."

Sayings of King Lemuel

31 The sayings of King Lemuel — an inspired utterance
his mother taught him. Pr 22:17

2 Listen, my son! Listen, son of
my womb!
Listen, my son, the answer to
my prayers! Isa 49:15
3 Do not spend your strength[b] on
women,
your vigor on those who
ruin kings.
Dt 17:17; Ne 13:26; Pr 5:1-14

4 It is not for kings, Lemuel —
it is not for kings to drink
wine, Pr 20:1; Ecc 10:16-17
not for rulers to crave beer,
5 lest they drink and forget
what has been decreed,
1Ki 16:9; Pr 16:12
and deprive all the oppressed
of their rights.
6 Let beer be for those who are
perishing,
wine for those who are in
anguish! Ge 14:18
7 Let them drink and forget their
poverty Est 1:10
and remember their misery
no more.
8 Speak up for those who cannot
speak for themselves,
Job 29:12-17
for the rights of all who are
destitute.
9 Speak up and judge fairly;
defend the rights of the
poor and needy.
Lev 19:15; Isa 1:17; Jer 22:16

Epilogue: The Wife of Noble Character

10 [c]A wife of noble character who
can find? Ru 3:11; Pr 19:14
She is worth far more than
rubies.
11 Her husband has full
confidence in her Ge 2:18
and lacks nothing of value.
Pr 12:4
12 She brings him good, not
harm,
all the days of her life.

[a] *31* The meaning of the Hebrew for this phrase is uncertain. [b] *3* Or *wealth*
[c] *10* Verses 10-31 are an acrostic poem, the verses of which begin with the successive letters of the Hebrew alphabet.

[13]She selects wool and flax
and works with eager hands.
1Ti 2:9-10
[14]She is like the merchant ships,
bringing her food from afar.
[15]She gets up while it is still
night;
she provides food for her
family
and portions for her female
servants.
[16]She considers a field and buys
it;
out of her earnings she
plants a vineyard.
[17]She sets about her work
vigorously;
her arms are strong for her
tasks.
[18]She sees that her trading is
profitable,
and her lamp does not go out
at night.
[19]In her hand she holds the
distaff
and grasps the spindle with
her fingers.
[20]She opens her arms to the poor
and extends her hands
to the needy.
Dt 15:11; Eph 4:28; Heb 13:16
[21]When it snows, she has no fear
for her household;
for all of them are clothed in
scarlet.
[22]She makes coverings for her
bed;
she is clothed in fine linen
and purple.
[23]Her husband is respected at the
city gate,
where he takes his seat
among the elders of the
land. Ru 4:1,11; Pr 12:4
[24]She makes linen garments and
sells them,
and supplies the merchants
with sashes.
[25]She is clothed with strength
and dignity;
she can laugh at the days to
come.
[26]She speaks with wisdom,
and faithful instruction is on
her tongue. Pr 10:31
[27]She watches over the affairs of
her household
and does not eat the bread of
idleness.
[28]Her children arise and call her
blessed;
her husband also, and he
praises her:
[29]"Many women do noble things,
but you surpass them all."
[30]Charm is deceptive, and beauty
is fleeting;
but a woman who fears the
LORD is to be praised.
[31]Honor her for all that her
hands have done,
and let her works bring her
praise at the city gate.
Pr 11:16

ECCLESIASTES

Everything Is Meaningless

1 The words of the Teacher,[a] son of David, king in Jerusalem:
Pr 1:1; Ecc 7:27

2 "Meaningless! Meaningless!"
says the Teacher.
"Utterly meaningless!
Everything is meaningless."
Ps 39:5-6; 62:9; Ecc 12:8

3 What do people gain from all their labors
at which they toil under the sun? Ecc 2:11,22
4 Generations come and generations go,
but the earth remains forever. Ps 104:5; 119:90
5 The sun rises and the sun sets,
and hurries back to where it rises. Ps 19:5-6
6 The wind blows to the south
and turns to the north;
round and round it goes,
ever returning on its course.
7 All streams flow into the sea,
yet the sea is never full.
To the place the streams come from,
there they return again.
Job 36:28
8 All things are wearisome,
more than one can say.
The eye never has enough of seeing, Pr 27:20
nor the ear its fill of hearing.
9 What has been will be again,
what has been done will be done again; Ecc 3:15
there is nothing new under the sun.
10 Is there anything of which one can say,
"Look! This is something new"?
It was here already, long ago;
it was here before our time.
11 No one remembers the former generations,
and even those yet to come
will not be remembered
by those who follow them.
Ecc 2:16

Wisdom Is Meaningless

12 I, the Teacher, was king over
Israel in Jerusalem. 13 I applied my
mind to study and to explore by
wisdom all that is done under the
heavens. What a heavy burden
God has laid on mankind! 14 I have
seen all the things that are done
under the sun; all of them are
meaningless, a chasing after the
wind. Ecc 3:10; 4:4

15 What is crooked cannot be straightened; Ecc 7:13
what is lacking cannot be counted.

[a] *1* Or *the leader of the assembly*; also in verses 2 and 12

16 I said to myself, "Look, I have
increased in wisdom more than
anyone who has ruled over Jerusalem before me; I have experienced
much of wisdom and knowledge."
17 Then I applied myself to the understanding of wisdom, and also
of madness and folly, but I learned
that this, too, is a chasing after the
wind. 1Ki 3:12; Ecc 2:3,12

18 For with much wisdom comes
much sorrow;
the more knowledge, the
more grief. Ecc 12:12

Pleasures Are Meaningless

2 I said to myself, "Come now, I
will test you with pleasure to
find out what is good." But that
also proved to be meaningless.
2 "Laughter," I said, "is madness.
And what does pleasure accomplish?" 3 I tried cheering myself
with wine, and embracing folly—
my mind still guiding me with
wisdom. I wanted to see what was
good for people to do under the
heavens during the few days of
their lives. Ecc 1:17; 7:6; Lk 12:19

4 I undertook great projects: I
built houses for myself and planted vineyards. 5 I made gardens
and parks and planted all kinds of
fruit trees in them. 6 I made reservoirs to water groves of flourishing trees. 7 I bought male and female slaves and had other slaves
who were born in my house. I
also owned more herds and flocks
than anyone in Jerusalem before
me. 8 I amassed silver and gold for
myself, and the treasure of kings
and provinces. I acquired male
and female singers, and a harem[a]
as well—the delights of a man's
heart. 9 I became greater by far
than anyone in Jerusalem before
me. In all this my wisdom stayed
with me. 1Ki 9:28; 10:10,14,21

10 I denied myself nothing my
eyes desired;
I refused my heart no
pleasure.
My heart took delight in all my
labor,
and this was the reward for
all my toil.
11 Yet when I surveyed all that
my hands had done
and what I had toiled to
achieve,
everything was meaningless, a
chasing after the wind;
Ecc 1:14
nothing was gained under
the sun. Ecc 1:3

Wisdom and Folly Are Meaningless

12 Then I turned my thoughts to
consider wisdom,
and also madness and folly.
Ecc 1:17
What more can the king's
successor do
than what has already been
done? Ecc 1:9
13 I saw that wisdom is better
than folly, Ecc 7:11-12

[a] 8 The meaning of the Hebrew for this phrase is uncertain.

just as light is better than
darkness.
14 The wise have eyes in their
heads,
while the fool walks in the
darkness;
but I came to realize
that the same fate
overtakes them both.
Ps 49:10; Ecc 9:3,11-12

15 Then I said to myself,

"The fate of the fool will
overtake me also.
What then do I gain by being
wise?" Ecc 6:8
I said to myself,
"This too is meaningless."
16 For the wise, like the fool,
will not be long
remembered;
the days have already come
when both have been
forgotten. Ecc 1:11
Like the fool, the wise too must
die! Ps 49:10

Toil Is Meaningless

17 So I hated life, because the
work that is done under the sun
was grievous to me. All of it is
meaningless, a chasing after the
wind. 18 I hated all the things I had
toiled for under the sun, because
I must leave them to the one who
comes after me. 19 And who knows
whether that person will be wise
or foolish? Yet they will have control over all the fruit of my toil
into which I have poured my effort and skill under the sun. This
too is meaningless. 20 So my heart
began to despair over all my toilsome labor under the sun. 21 For a
person may labor with wisdom,
knowledge and skill, and then
they must leave all they own to
another who has not toiled for
it. This too is meaningless and a
great misfortune. 22 What do people get for all the toil and anxious
striving with which they labor under the sun? 23 All their days their
work is grief and pain; even at
night their minds do not rest. This
too is meaningless. Job 5:7; Ecc 1:3,18
24 A person can do nothing better than to eat and drink and find
satisfaction in their own toil. This
too, I see, is from the hand of God,
25 for without him, who can eat
or find enjoyment? 26 To the person who pleases him, God gives
wisdom, knowledge and happiness, but to the sinner he gives
the task of gathering and storing
up wealth to hand it over to the
one who pleases God. This too is
meaningless, a chasing after the
wind. Job 27:17; Pr 13:22; Ecc 3:12-13

A Time for Everything

3 There is a time for everything,
ver 11,17; Ecc 8:6
and a season for every
activity under the
heavens:

2 a time to be born and a time
to die,
a time to plant and a time to
uproot, Isa 28:24

3 a time to kill and a time to
heal, Dt 5:17
a time to tear down and a
time to build,
4 a time to weep and a time to
laugh,
a time to mourn and a time
to dance,
5 a time to scatter stones and a
time to gather them,
a time to embrace and a
time to refrain from
embracing,
6 a time to search and a time
to give up,
a time to keep and a time to
throw away,
7 a time to tear and a time to
mend,
a time to be silent and a time
to speak, Am 5:13
8 a time to love and a time to
hate,
a time for war and a time for
peace.

9 What do workers gain from
their toil? 10 I have seen the burden God has laid on the human
race. 11 He has made everything
beautiful in its time. He has also
set eternity in the human heart;
yet[a] no one can fathom what God
has done from beginning to end.
12 I know that there is nothing better for people than to be happy
and to do good while they live.
13 That each of them may eat and
drink, and find satisfaction in all
their toil — this is the gift of God.
14 I know that everything God does
will endure forever; nothing can
be added to it and nothing taken
from it. God does it so that people
will fear him. Ro 11:33; Jas 1:17; Ecc 2:24

15 Whatever is has already been,
Ecc 6:10
and what will be has been
before; Ecc 1:9
and God will call the past to
account.[b]

16 And I saw something else under the sun:

In the place of judgment —
wickedness was there,
in the place of justice —
wickedness was there.

17 I said to myself,

"God will bring into judgment
Ro 2:6-8; 2Th 1:6-7
both the righteous and the
wicked,
for there will be a time for
every activity,
a time to judge every deed."
ver 1

18 I also said to myself, "As for humans, God tests them so that they
may see that they are like the animals. 19 Surely the fate of human
beings is like that of the animals;
the same fate awaits them both:
As one dies, so dies the other. All
have the same breath[c]; humans
have no advantage over animals.
Everything is meaningless. 20 All

[a] 11 Or *also placed ignorance in the human heart, so that* [b] 15 Or *God calls back the past* [c] 19 Or *spirit*

go to the same place; all come
from dust, and to dust all return.
21Who knows if the human spirit rises upward and if the spirit
of the animal goes down into the
earth?" Ps 73:22; Ge 3:19; Ecc 12:7
22So I saw that there is nothing
better for a person than to enjoy
their work, because that is their
lot. For who can bring them to see
what will happen after them?
Job 31:2; Ecc 2:24; 5:18

Oppression, Toil, Friendlessness

4 Again I looked and saw all the
oppression that was taking
place under the sun: Ps 12:5; Ecc 3:16

I saw the tears of the
oppressed —
and they have no comforter;
power was on the side of their
oppressors —
and they have no comforter.
La 1:16
2And I declared that the dead,
Jer 20:17-18; 22:10
who had already died,
are happier than the living,
who are still alive. Job 3:17; 10:18
3But better than both
is the one who has never
been born, Job 3:16; Ecc 6:3
who has not seen the evil
that is done under the sun.
Job 3:22

4And I saw that all toil and all
achievement spring from one person's envy of another. This too is
meaningless, a chasing after the
wind. Ecc 1:14

5Fools fold their hands Pr 6:10
and ruin themselves.
6Better one handful with
tranquillity
than two handfuls with toil
Pr 15:16-17; 16:8
and chasing after the wind.

7Again I saw something meaningless under the sun:

8There was a man all alone;
he had neither son nor
brother.
There was no end to his toil,
yet his eyes were not
content with his wealth.
Pr 27:20
"For whom am I toiling," he
asked,
"and why am I depriving
myself of enjoyment?"
This too is meaningless —
a miserable business!

9Two are better than one,
because they have a good
return for their labor:
10If either of them falls down,
one can help the other up.
But pity anyone who falls
and has no one to help them
up.
11Also, if two lie down together,
they will keep warm.
But how can one keep warm
alone?
12Though one may be
overpowered,
two can defend themselves.
A cord of three strands is not
quickly broken.

Advancement Is Meaningless

13Better a poor but wise youth
than an old but foolish king who
no longer knows how to heed a
warning. 14The youth may have
come from prison to the kingship,
or he may have been born in poverty within his kingdom. 15I saw
that all who lived and walked under the sun followed the youth,
the king's successor. 16There was
no end to all the people who were
before them. But those who came
later were not pleased with the
successor. This too is meaningless,
a chasing after the wind.

Fulfill Your Vow to God

5[a] Guard your steps when you
go to the house of God. Go
near to listen rather than to offer
the sacrifice of fools, who do not
know that they do wrong.

2Do not be quick with your
mouth,
do not be hasty in your heart
to utter anything before God.
Jdg 11:35
God is in heaven
and you are on earth,
so let your words be few.
Pr 10:19; 20:25
3A dream comes when there are
many cares, Job 20:8
and many words mark the
speech of a fool. Ecc 10:14

4When you make a vow to God,
do not delay to fulfill it. He has no
pleasure in fools; fulfill your vow.
5It is better not to make a vow than
to make one and not fulfill it. 6Do
not let your mouth lead you into
sin. And do not protest to the temple messenger, "My vow was a mistake." Why should God be angry at
what you say and destroy the work
of your hands? 7Much dreaming
and many words are meaningless.
Therefore fear God. Pr 20:25; Ac 5:4

Riches Are Meaningless

8If you see the poor oppressed
in a district, and justice and rights
denied, do not be surprised at
such things; for one official is eyed
by a higher one, and over them
both are others higher still. 9The
increase from the land is taken by
all; the king himself profits from
the fields. Ps 12:5; Ecc 4:1

10Whoever loves money never
has enough;
whoever loves wealth is
never satisfied with
their income.
This too is meaningless.

11As goods increase,
so do those who consume
them.
And what benefit are they to
the owners
except to feast their eyes on
them?

12The sleep of a laborer is sweet,
whether they eat little or
much,

[a] In Hebrew texts 5:1 is numbered 4:17, and 5:2-20 is numbered 5:1-19.

but as for the rich, their
abundance
permits them no sleep. Job 20:20

13 I have seen a grievous evil under the sun: Ecc 6:1-2

wealth hoarded to the harm of
its owners,
14 or wealth lost through some
misfortune,
so that when they have
children
there is nothing left for them
to inherit.
15 Everyone comes naked
from their mother's
womb,
and as everyone comes, so
they depart. Job 1:21
They take nothing from their
toil Ps 49:17; 1Ti 6:7
that they can carry in their
hands. Ecc 1:3

16 This too is a grievous evil:

As everyone comes, so they
depart,
and what do they gain,
since they toil for the wind?
Pr 11:29; Ecc 1:3
17 All their days they eat in
darkness,
with great frustration,
affliction and anger.

18 This is what I have observed to be good: that it is appropriate for a person to eat, to drink and to find satisfaction in their toilsome labor under the sun during the few days of life God has given them — for this is their lot.
19 Moreover, when God gives someone wealth and possessions, and the ability to enjoy them, to accept their lot and be happy in their toil — this is a gift of God.
20 They seldom reflect on the days of their life, because God keeps them occupied with gladness of heart. Dt 12:7,18; Ecc 2:24; 3:13

6 I have seen another evil under the sun, and it weighs heavily on mankind:
2 God gives some people wealth, possessions and honor, so that they lack nothing their hearts desire, but God does not grant them the ability to enjoy them, and strangers enjoy them instead. This is meaningless, a grievous evil. Ps 17:14; Ecc 5:13,19

3 A man may have a hundred children and live many years; yet no matter how long he lives, if he cannot enjoy his prosperity and does not receive proper burial, I say that a stillborn child is better off than he.
4 It comes without meaning, it departs in darkness, and in darkness its name is shrouded.
5 Though it never saw the sun or knew anything, it has more rest than does that man —
6 even if he lives a thousand years twice over but fails to enjoy his prosperity. Do not all go to the same place? Job 3:16; Ecc 4:3

7 Everyone's toil is for their
mouth,
yet their appetite is never
satisfied. Pr 16:26; 27:20

[8]What advantage have the wise
over fools? Ecc 2:15
What do the poor gain
by knowing how to conduct
themselves before
others?
[9]Better what the eye sees
than the roving of the
appetite.
This too is meaningless,
a chasing after the wind.
Ecc 1:14

[10]Whatever exists has
already been named,
Ecc 3:15
and what humanity is has
been known;
no one can contend
with someone who is
stronger.
[11]The more the words,
the less the meaning,
and how does that profit
anyone?

[12]For who knows what is good
for a person in life, during the few
and meaningless days they pass
through like a shadow? Who can
tell them what will happen under
the sun after they are gone?
Ps 39:6; Jas 4:14

Wisdom

7 A good name is better than
fine perfume, Ps 22:1; SS 1:3
and the day of death better
than the day of birth.
Job 10:18
[2]It is better to go to a house of
mourning
than to go to a house of
feasting,
for death is the destiny of
everyone; Ps 90:12; Pr 11:19
the living should take this to
heart.
[3]Frustration is better than
laughter, Pr 14:13
because a sad face is good for
the heart.
[4]The heart of the wise is in the
house of mourning,
but the heart of fools is in
the house of pleasure.
Ecc 2:1; Jer 16:8
[5]It is better to heed the rebuke
of a wise person
Ps 141:5; Pr 15:31-32
than to listen to the song of
fools.
[6]Like the crackling of
thorns under the pot,
Ps 58:9; 118:12
so is the laughter of fools.
Ecc 2:2

This too is meaningless.

[7]Extortion turns a wise person
into a fool,
and a bribe corrupts the
heart. Ex 23:8; Dt 16:19
[8]The end of a matter is better
than its beginning,
and patience is better
than pride.
Pr 14:29; Gal 5:22; Eph 4:2
[9]Do not be quickly provoked
in your spirit,
Pr 14:17; Jas 1:19
for anger resides in the lap of
fools. Pr 14:29

10 Do not say, "Why were the old
days better than these?"
Ps 77:5
For it is not wise to ask such
questions.

11 Wisdom, like an inheritance,
is a good thing
Pr 8:10-11; Ecc 2:13
and benefits those who see
the sun. Ecc 11:7
12 Wisdom is a shelter
as money is a shelter,
but the advantage of
knowledge is this:
Wisdom preserves those who
have it.

13 Consider what God has done:
Ecc 2:24

Who can straighten
what he has made crooked?
Ecc 1:15
14 When times are good, be
happy;
but when times are bad,
consider this:
God has made the one
as well as the other.
Job 1:21; Ecc 2:24
Therefore, no one can discover
anything about their
future.

15 In this meaningless life of mine
I have seen both of these:

the righteous perishing in their
righteousness,
and the wicked living long
in their wickedness.
Ecc 8:12-14; Jer 12:1
16 Do not be overrighteous,
neither be overwise —
why destroy yourself?
17 Do not be overwicked,
and do not be a fool —
why die before your time?
Job 15:32; Ps 55:23
18 It is good to grasp the one
and not let go of the other.
Whoever fears God will avoid
all extremes.[a] Ecc 3:14

19 Wisdom makes one wise
person more powerful
Ecc 9:13-18
than ten rulers in a city.
20 Indeed, there is no one on
earth who is righteous,
Ps 14:3
no one who does what is
right and never sins.
1Ki 8:46; 2Ch 6:36; Pr 20:9

21 Do not pay attention to every
word people say,
or you may hear your servant
cursing you — Pr 30:10
22 for you know in your heart
that many times you
yourself have cursed
others.

23 All this I tested by wisdom and
I said,

"I am determined to be
wise" — Ecc 1:17; Ro 1:22
but this was beyond me.
24 Whatever exists is far off and
most profound —
who can discover it? Job 28:12

[a] 18 Or *will follow them both*

25 So I turned my mind to
understand,
to investigate and to
search out wisdom and
the scheme of things Job 28:3
and to understand the
stupidity of wickedness
and the madness of folly. Ecc 1:17

26 I find more bitter than death
the woman who is a snare, Ex 10:7; Jdg 14:15
whose heart is a trap
and whose hands are chains.
The man who pleases God will
escape her,
but the sinner she will
ensnare. Pr 5:3-5; 7:23; 22:14

27 "Look," says the Teacher,[a] "this
is what I have discovered: Ecc 1:1

"Adding one thing to another
to discover the scheme
of things —
28 while I was still searching
but not finding —
I found one upright man
among a thousand,
but not one upright
woman among
them all. 1Ki 11:3
29 This only have I found:
God created mankind
upright,
but they have gone in search
of many schemes."

8 Who is like the wise?
Who knows the explanation
of things?
A person's wisdom brightens
their face
and changes its hard
appearance.

Obey the King

2 Obey the king's command, I
say, because you took an oath before God. 3 Do not be in a hurry to
leave the king's presence. Do not
stand up for a bad cause, for he
will do whatever he pleases. 4 Since
a king's word is supreme, who can
say to him, "What are you doing?"
Job 9:12; Est 1:19; Da 4:35

5 Whoever obeys his command
will come to no harm,
and the wise heart will know
the proper time and
procedure.
6 For there is a proper time and
procedure for every
matter, Ecc 3:1
though a person may be
weighed down by
misery.

7 Since no one knows the future,
who can tell someone else
what is to come?
8 As no one has power over the
wind to contain it,
so[b] no one has power over
the time of their death.
As no one is discharged in time
of war,
so wickedness will not
release those who
practice it.

[a] 27 *Or the leader of the assembly* [b] 8 Or *over the human spirit to retain it, / and so*

9All this I saw, as I applied my
mind to everything done under
the sun. There is a time when a
man lords it over others to his
own[a] hurt. 10Then too, I saw the
wicked buried — those who used
to come and go from the holy
place and receive praise[b] in the
city where they did this. This too
is meaningless. Ecc 1:11

11When the sentence for a crime
is not quickly carried out, people's
hearts are filled with schemes
to do wrong. 12Although a wicked person who commits a hundred crimes may live a long time,
I know that it will go better with
those who fear God, who are reverent before him. 13Yet because the
wicked do not fear God, it will not
go well with them, and their days
will not lengthen like a shadow.

Dt 4:40; Isa 3:11

14There is something else meaningless that occurs on earth: the
righteous who get what the wicked deserve, and the wicked who
get what the righteous deserve.
This too, I say, is meaningless. 15So
I commend the enjoyment of life,
because there is nothing better for
a person under the sun than to eat
and drink and be glad. Then joy
will accompany them in their toil
all the days of the life God has giv-
en them under the sun.

Ecc 2:24; 3:12-13; 5:18

16When I applied my mind to
know wisdom and to observe the
labor that is done on earth — people getting no sleep day or night —
17then I saw all that God has done.
No one can comprehend what
goes on under the sun. Despite
all their efforts to search it out,
no one can discover its meaning.
Even if the wise claim they know,
they cannot really comprehend it.

Ecc 3:11; Ro 11:33

A Common Destiny for All

9 So I reflected on all this and
concluded that the righteous
and the wise and what they do are
in God's hands, but no one knows
whether love or hate awaits them.
2All share a common destiny —
the righteous and the wicked, the
good and the bad,[c] the clean and
the unclean, those who offer sacrifices and those who do not.

Dt 33:3; Ecc 10:14

As it is with the good,
so with the sinful;
as it is with those who take
oaths,
so with those who are
afraid to take them.

Job 9:22; Ecc 2:14

3This is the evil in everything
that happens under the sun: The
same destiny overtakes all. The
hearts of people, moreover, are
full of evil and there is madness
in their hearts while they live,
and afterward they join the dead.

[a] 9 Or *to their* [b] 10 Some Hebrew manuscripts and Septuagint (Aquila); most Hebrew manuscripts *and are forgotten* [c] 2 Septuagint (Aquila), Vulgate and Syriac; Hebrew does not have *and the bad.*

4Anyone who is among the living has hope[a] — even a live dog is better off than a dead lion!
Job 21:26; Ecc 2:14

5For the living know that they
will die,
but the dead know nothing;
Job 14:21
they have no further reward,
and even their name
is forgotten.
Ps 9:6; Ecc 1:11; Isa 26:14
6Their love, their hate
and their jealousy
have long since
vanished;
never again will they have a
part
in anything that
happens under the sun.
Job 21:21

7Go, eat your food with gladness, and drink your wine with a
joyful heart, for God has already
approved what you do. 8Always
be clothed in white, and always
anoint your head with oil. 9En-
joy life with your wife, whom you
love, all the days of this meaningless life that God has given you
under the sun — all your meaningless days. For this is your lot
in life and in your toilsome labor
under the sun. 10Whatever your
hand finds to do, do it with all
your might, for in the realm of the
dead, where you are going, there
is neither working nor planning
nor knowledge nor wisdom.
1Sa 10:7; Ecc 2:24; Ro 12:11

11I have seen something else under the sun:

The race is not to the swift
or the battle to the strong,
Am 2:14-15
nor does food come to the wise
Job 32:13; Jer 9:23
or wealth to the brilliant
or favor to the learned;
but time and chance happen to
them all. Dt 8:18; Ecc 2:14

12Moreover, no one knows when their hour will come:

As fish are caught in a cruel
net,
or birds are taken in a snare,
so people are trapped by evil
times Pr 29:6
that fall unexpectedly upon
them. Ps 73:22; Ecc 8:7

Wisdom Better Than Folly

13I also saw under the sun this
example of wisdom that greatly
impressed me: 14There was once a
small city with only a few people
in it. And a powerful king came
against it, surrounded it and built
huge siege works against it. 15Now
there lived in that city a man poor
but wise, and he saved the city by
his wisdom. But nobody remembered that poor man. 16So I said,
"Wisdom is better than strength."
But the poor man's wisdom is despised, and his words are no longer heeded. Pr 21:22; Ecc 7:19

[a] 4 Or *What then is to be chosen? With all who live, there is hope*

17 The quiet words of the wise are
more to be heeded
than the shouts of a ruler of
fools.
18 Wisdom is better than weapons
of war, ver 16; Ecc 2:13
but one sinner destroys
much good.

10 As dead flies give perfume
a bad smell,
so a little folly outweighs
wisdom and honor.
Pr 13:16; 18:2
2 The heart of the wise inclines
to the right,
but the heart of the fool to
the left.
3 Even as fools walk along the
road,
they lack sense
and show everyone
how stupid they are.
Pr 13:16; 18:2

4 If a ruler's anger rises against
you,
do not leave your post; Ecc 8:3
calmness can lay great
offenses to rest. Pr 25:15

5 There is an evil I have seen
under the sun,
the sort of error that arises
from a ruler:
6 Fools are put in many high
positions, Pr 29:2
while the rich occupy the low
ones.
7 I have seen slaves on
horseback,
while princes go on foot like
slaves. Pr 19:10

8 Whoever digs a pit may fall
into it; Ps 7:15; Pr 26:27
whoever breaks through
a wall may be bitten
by a snake.
Est 2:23; Ps 9:16; Am 5:19
9 Whoever quarries stones may
be injured by them;
whoever splits logs may be
endangered by them.
Pr 26:27

10 If the ax is dull
and its edge unsharpened,
more strength is needed,
but skill will bring success.

11 If a snake bites before it is
charmed,
the charmer receives no fee.
Ps 58:5; Isa 3:3

12 Words from the mouth of the
wise are gracious, Pr 10:32
but fools are consumed
by their own lips.
Pr 10:14; 14:3; 18:7
13 At the beginning their words
are folly;
at the end they are wicked
madness —
14 and fools multiply words.
Pr 15:2; Ecc 5:3; 8:7

No one knows what is
coming —
who can tell someone else
what will happen after
them? Ecc 9:1
15 The toil of fools wearies them;
they do not know the way to
town.

16 Woe to the land whose king
was a servant[a] Isa 3:4-5,12
and whose princes feast in
the morning.
17 Blessed is the land whose king
is of noble birth
and whose princes eat at a
proper time —
for strength and not
for drunkenness.
1Sa 25:36; Pr 31:4

18 Through laziness, the rafters
sag;
because of idle hands, the
house leaks. Pr 20:4; 24:30-34

19 A feast is made for laughter,
wine makes life merry,
Ge 14:18; Jdg 9:13
and money is the answer for
everything.

20 Do not revile the king even in
your thoughts, Ex 22:28
or curse the rich in your
bedroom,
because a bird in the sky may
carry your words,
and a bird on the wing may
report what you say.

Invest in Many Ventures

11 Ship your grain across the
sea; ver 6; Isa 32:20
after many days you may
receive a return.
Pr 19:17; Mt 10:42

2 Invest in seven ventures, yes,
in eight;
you do not know what
disaster may come upon
the land.

3 If clouds are full of water,
they pour rain on the
earth.
Whether a tree falls to
the south or to the
north,
in the place where it falls,
there it will lie.
4 Whoever watches the wind will
not plant;
whoever looks at the clouds
will not reap.

5 As you do not know the path of
the wind, Jn 3:8-10
or how the body is formed[b]
in a mother's womb,
Ps 139:14-16
so you cannot understand the
work of God,
the Maker of all things.

6 Sow your seed in the morning,
and at evening let your
hands not be idle, Ecc 9:10
for you do not know which will
succeed,
whether this or that,
or whether both will do
equally well.

Remember Your Creator While Young

7 Light is sweet,
and it pleases the eyes to see
the sun. Ecc 7:11
8 However many years anyone
may live,
let them enjoy them all.

[a] 16 Or *king is a child* [b] 5 Or *know how life* (or *the spirit*) / *enters the body being formed*

But let them remember the
days of darkness, Ecc 12:1
for there will be many.
Everything to come is
meaningless.

9 You who are young, be
happy while you are
young,
and let your heart give you
joy in the days of your
youth.
Follow the ways of your heart
and whatever your eyes see,
but know that for all these
things
God will bring you into
judgment. Ecc 12:14; Ro 14:10
10 So then, banish anxiety from
your heart Ps 94:19
and cast off the troubles of
your body,
for youth and vigor are
meaningless. Ecc 2:24

12 Remember your Creator
Ecc 11:8
in the days of your youth,
before the days of trouble
come 2Sa 19:35
and the years approach when
you will say,
"I find no pleasure in
them" —
2 before the sun and the light
and the moon and the stars
grow dark,
and the clouds return after
the rain;
3 when the keepers of the house
tremble,
and the strong men stoop,
when the grinders cease
because they are
few,
and those looking
through the windows
grow dim;
4 when the doors to the street
are closed
and the sound of grinding
fades;
when people rise up at the
sound of birds,
but all their songs grow
faint; Jer 25:10
5 when people are afraid of
heights
and of dangers in the streets;
when the almond tree
blossoms
and the grasshopper drags
itself along
and desire no longer is
stirred.
Then people go to their eternal
home Job 17:13; 10:21
and mourners go about the
streets. Jer 9:17; Am 5:16

6 Remember him — before the
silver cord is severed,
and the golden bowl is
broken;
before the pitcher is shattered
at the spring,
and the wheel broken at the
well,
7 and the dust returns to the
ground it came from,
Ge 3:19; Job 34:15; Ps 146:4
and the spirit returns to God
who gave it. Ecc 3:21; Zec 12:1

8 “Meaningless! Meaningless!”
says the Teacher.[a]
“Everything is meaningless!”
Ecc 1:2

The Conclusion of the Matter

9 Not only was the Teacher wise,
but he also imparted knowledge to the people. He pondered
and searched out and set in order many proverbs. 10 The Teacher searched to find just the right
words, and what he wrote was upright and true. 1Ki 4:32; Pr 22:20-21
11 The words of the wise are like
goads, their collected sayings like
firmly embedded nails — given
by one shepherd.[b] 12 Be warned,
my son, of anything in addition to
them. Ezr 9:8

Of making many books there is
no end, and much study wearies
the body. Ecc 1:18

13 Now all has been heard;
here is the conclusion of the
matter:
Fear God and keep his
commandments,
Dt 4:2; 10:12
for this is the duty of all
mankind. Mic 6:8
14 For God will bring every
deed into judgment,
Ecc 3:17
including every hidden
thing, Mt 10:26; 1Co 4:5
whether it is good or evil.

[a] 8 Or *the leader of the assembly*; also in verses 9 and 10 [a] 11 Or *Shepherd*

SONG OF SONGS

1 Solomon's Song of Songs. 1Ki 4:32

She[a]

[2]Let him kiss me with the kisses
of his mouth —
for your love is more
delightful than wine. SS 4:10
[3]Pleasing is the fragrance of
your perfumes; SS 4:10
your name is like perfume
poured out. Ecc 7:1
No wonder the young
women love you! Ps 45:14
[4]Take me away with you — let
us hurry!
Let the king bring me into
his chambers. Ps 45:15

Friends

We rejoice and delight in you[b]; SS 2:3
we will praise your love more
than wine. ver 2

She

How right they are to adore
you!

[5]Dark am I, yet lovely, SS 2:14; 4:3
daughters of Jerusalem, SS 2:7; 5:8
dark like the tents of Kedar, Ge 25:13
like the tent curtains of
Solomon.[c]
[6]Do not stare at me because I
am dark,
because I am darkened by
the sun.
My mother's sons were angry
with me
and made me take care of
the vineyards; Ps 69:8
my own vineyard I had to
neglect.
[7]Tell me, you whom I love,
where you graze your flock
and where you rest
your sheep at midday. SS 3:1-4
Why should I be like a veiled
woman Ge 24:65
beside the flocks of your
friends?

Friends

[8]If you do not know, most
beautiful of women, SS 5:9; 6:1
follow the tracks of the
sheep
and graze your young goats
by the tents of the
shepherds.

[a] The main male and female speakers (identified primarily on the basis of the gender of the relevant Hebrew forms) are indicated by the captions *He* and *She* respectively. The words of others are marked *Friends*. In some instances the divisions and their captions are debatable.
[b] *4* The Hebrew is masculine singular.
[c] *5* Or *Salma*

He

9 I liken you, my darling, to a mare
among Pharaoh's chariot
horses. 2Ch 1:17
10 Your cheeks are beautiful with
earrings, SS 5:13
your neck with strings of
jewels. Isa 61:10
11 We will make you earrings of
gold,
studded with silver.

She

12 While the king was at his table,
my perfume spread its
fragrance. SS 4:11-14
13 My beloved is to me a sachet of
myrrh Ge 37:25
resting between my breasts.
14 My beloved is to me a cluster
of henna blossoms
SS 2:3,17; 4:13
from the vineyards of En
Gedi. 1Sa 23:29

He

15 How beautiful you are, my
darling! SS 4:7; 7:6
Oh, how beautiful!
Your eyes are doves. SS 14:1; 5:2,12

She

16 How handsome you are, my
beloved!
Oh, how charming!
And our bed is verdant.

He

17 The beams of our house are
cedars; 1Ki 6:9
our rafters are firs.

She[a]

2 I am a rose[b] of Sharon, Isa 35:1
a lily of the valleys.
SS 5:13; Hos 14:5

He

2 Like a lily among thorns
is my darling among the
young women.

She

3 Like an apple[c] tree among the
trees of the forest
is my beloved among the
young men. SS 1:14
I delight to sit in his shade, SS 1:4
and his fruit is sweet to my
taste. SS 4:16
4 Let him lead me to the banquet
hall, Est 1:11
and let his banner over me
be love. Nu 1:52
5 Strengthen me with raisins,
refresh me with apples, SS 7:8
for I am faint with love. SS 5:8
6 His left arm is under my
head,
and his right arm embraces
me. SS 8:3
7 Daughters of Jerusalem, I
charge you SS 5:8
by the gazelles and by the
does of the field:
Do not arouse or awaken love
until it so desires. SS 3:5; 8:4

8 Listen! My beloved!
Look! Here he comes,

[a] Or *He* [b] *1* Probably a member of the crocus family [c] *3* Or possibly *apricot;* here and elsewhere in Song of Songs

leaping across the mountains,
bounding over the hills. ver 17; SS 8:14
9 My beloved is like a gazelle
or a young stag. ver 17; SS 8:14
Look! There he stands
behind our wall,
gazing through the windows,
peering through the lattice.
10 My beloved spoke and said to me,
"Arise, my darling,
my beautiful one, come with me.
11 See! The winter is past;
the rains are over and gone.
12 Flowers appear on the earth;
the season of singing has come,
the cooing of doves
is heard in our land.
13 The fig tree forms its early fruit; Isa 28:4; Jer 24:2
the blossoming vines
spread their fragrance. SS 7:12
Arise, come, my darling;
my beautiful one, come with me."

He

14 My dove in the clefts of the rock, Ge 8:8; SS 1:15
in the hiding places on the mountainside,
show me your face,
let me hear your voice;
for your voice is sweet,
and your face is lovely. SS 1:5; 8:13
15 Catch for us the foxes, Jdg 15:4
the little foxes
that ruin the vineyards, SS 1:6
our vineyards that are in bloom. SS 7:12

She

16 My beloved is mine and I am his; SS 7:10
he browses among the lilies. SS 6:3
17 Until the day breaks
and the shadows flee, SS 4:6
turn, my beloved, SS 1:14
and be like a gazelle
or like a young stag ver 9
on the rugged hills.[a] ver 8

3

All night long on my bed
I looked for the one
my heart loves; SS 5:6; Isa 26:9
I looked for him but did not find him.
2 I will get up now and go about the city,
through its streets and squares;
I will search for the one my heart loves.
So I looked for him but did not find him.
3 The watchmen found me
as they made their rounds in the city. SS 5:7
"Have you seen the one my heart loves?"
4 Scarcely had I passed them
when I found the one my heart loves.

[a] 17 Or *the hills of Bether*

I held him and would not let
him go
till I had brought him
to my mother's house,
SS 8:2
to the room of the one who
conceived me. SS 6:9
5 Daughters of Jerusalem, I
charge you SS 2:7
by the gazelles and by the
does of the field:
Do not arouse or awaken love
until it so desires. SS 8:4
6 Who is this coming up from the
wilderness SS 8:5
like a column of smoke,
perfumed with myrrh and
incense SS 1:13; 4:6,14
made from all the spices of
the merchant? Ex 30:34
7 Look! It is Solomon's carriage,
escorted by sixty warriors,
1Sa 8:11
the noblest of Israel,
8 all of them wearing the
sword,
all experienced in battle,
each with his sword at his
side,
prepared for the terrors of
the night. Job 15:22; Ps 91:5
9 King Solomon made for
himself the carriage;
he made it of wood from
Lebanon.
10 Its posts he made of silver,
its base of gold.
Its seat was upholstered with
purple,
its interior inlaid with love.
Daughters of Jerusalem, 11 come
out,
and look, you daughters of
Zion. Isa 4:4
Look[a] on King Solomon
wearing a crown,
the crown with which his
mother crowned him
on the day of his wedding,
the day his heart rejoiced.
Isa 62:5

He

4 How beautiful you are, my
darling!
Oh, how beautiful!
Your eyes behind your veil
are doves. SS 1:15; 5:12
Your hair is like a flock of goats
descending from the hills of
Gilead. Mic 7:14
2 Your teeth are like a flock of
sheep just shorn,
coming up from the washing.
Each has its twin;
not one of them is alone.
SS 6:6
3 Your lips are like a scarlet
ribbon;
your mouth is lovely. SS 5:16
Your temples behind your veil
are like the halves of a
pomegranate. SS 6:7
4 Your neck is like the tower of
David, SS 7:4
built with courses of stone[b];

[a] 10,11 Or *interior lovingly inlaid / by the daughters of Jerusalem. / 11Come out, you daughters of Zion, / and look* [b] 4 The meaning of the Hebrew for this phrase is uncertain.

on it hang a thousand shields, Eze 27:10
all of them shields of warriors.
5 Your breasts are like two fawns, SS 7:3
like twin fawns of a gazelle Pr 5:19
that browse among the lilies. SS 2:16
6 Until the day breaks
and the shadows flee, SS 2:17
I will go to the mountain of myrrh
and to the hill of incense.
7 You are altogether beautiful, my darling; SS 1:15
there is no flaw in you.

8 Come with me from Lebanon, my bride, SS 5:1
come with me from Lebanon.
Descend from the crest of Amana,
from the top of Senir, the summit of Hermon, Dt 3:9; 1Ch 5:23
from the lions' dens
and the mountain haunts of leopards.
9 You have stolen my heart, my sister, my bride;
you have stolen my heart
with one glance of your eyes,
with one jewel of your necklace. Ge 41:42
10 How delightful is your love, my sister, my bride! SS 1:2; 7:6
How much more pleasing is your love than wine,
and the fragrance of your perfume Ps 45:8
more than any spice!
11 Your lips drop sweetness as the honeycomb, my bride;
milk and honey are under your tongue. Ps 19:10; SS 5:1
The fragrance of your garments
is like the fragrance of Lebanon. Hos 14:6
12 You are a garden locked up, my sister, my bride;
you are a spring enclosed, a sealed fountain. Pr 5:15-18
13 Your plants are an orchard of pomegranates SS 6:11; 7:12
with choice fruits,
with henna and nard, SS 1:14
14 nard and saffron,
calamus and cinnamon, Ex 30:23
with every kind of incense tree,
with myrrh and aloes SS 3:6
and all the finest spices. SS 1:12
15 You are[a] a garden fountain,
a well of flowing water
streaming down from Lebanon.

She

16 Awake, north wind,
and come, south wind!
Blow on my garden,
that its fragrance may spread everywhere.
Let my beloved come into his garden
and taste its choice fruits. SS 2:3; 5:1

[a] 15 Or *I am* (spoken by *She*)

He

5 I have come into my garden,
my sister, my bride; SS 4:8
I have gathered my myrrh
with my spice.
I have eaten my honeycomb
and my honey;
I have drunk my wine and
my milk. SS 4:11; Isa 55:1

Friends

Eat, friends, and drink;
drink your fill of love.

She

2 I slept but my heart was awake.
Listen! My beloved is
knocking:
"Open to me, my sister, my
darling,
my dove, my flawless one.
SS 4:7; 6:9
My head is drenched with dew,
my hair with the dampness
of the night."
3 I have taken off my robe —
must I put it on again?
I have washed my feet —
must I soil them again?
4 My beloved thrust his hand
through the latch-
opening;
my heart began to pound for
him.
5 I arose to open for my
beloved,
and my hands dripped with
myrrh,
my fingers with flowing
myrrh,
on the handles of the bolt.
6 I opened for my beloved, SS 6:1
but my beloved had left; he
was gone. SS 6:2
My heart sank at his
departure.[a]
I looked for him but did not
find him. SS 3:1
I called him but he did not
answer.
7 The watchmen found me
as they made their rounds in
the city. SS 3:3
They beat me, they bruised me;
they took away my cloak,
those watchmen of the walls!
8 Daughters of Jerusalem, I
charge you — SS 2:7; 3:5
if you find my beloved,
what will you tell him?
Tell him I am faint with love.
SS 2:5

Friends

9 How is your beloved better
than others,
most beautiful of women?
SS 1:8; 6:1
How is your beloved better
than others,
that you so charge us?

She

10 My beloved is radiant and
ruddy,
outstanding among ten
thousand. Ps 45:2
11 His head is purest gold;
his hair is wavy
and black as a raven.

[a] 6 Or *heart had gone out to him when he spoke*

[12]His eyes are like doves SS 1:15; 4:1
by the water streams,
washed in milk, Ge 49:12
mounted like jewels.
[13]His cheeks are like beds of
spice SS 1:10; 6:2
yielding perfume.
His lips are like lilies SS 2:1
dripping with myrrh.
[14]His arms are rods of gold
set with topaz.
His body is like polished
ivory
decorated with lapis lazuli.
Job 28:6
[15]His legs are pillars of marble
set on bases of pure gold.
His appearance is like Lebanon,
1Ki 4:33; SS 7:4
choice as its cedars.
[16]His mouth is sweetness itself;
SS 4:3
he is altogether lovely.
This is my beloved, this is my
friend, SS 7:9
daughters of Jerusalem. SS 1:5

Friends

6

Where has your beloved gone,
SS 5:6
most beautiful of women?
SS 1:8
Which way did your beloved
turn,
that we may look for him
with you?

She

[2]My beloved has gone down to
his garden, SS 4:12; 5:6
to the beds of spices, SS 5:13
to browse in the gardens
and to gather lilies.
[3]I am my beloved's and my
beloved is mine; SS 7:10
he browses among the lilies.
SS 2:16

He

[4]You are as beautiful as Tirzah,
my darling, Jos 12:24
as lovely as Jerusalem,
Ps 48:2; 50:2
as majestic as troops with
banners. ver 10
[5]Turn your eyes from me;
they overwhelm me.
Your hair is like a flock of
goats
descending from Gilead. SS 4:1
[6]Your teeth are like a flock of
sheep
coming up from the
washing.
Each has its twin,
not one of them is missing.
SS 4:2
[7]Your temples behind your veil
Ge 24:65
are like the halves of a
pomegranate. SS 4:3
[8]Sixty queens there may be,
Ps 45:9
and eighty concubines, Ge 22:24
and virgins beyond
number;
[9]but my dove, my perfect one, is
unique, SS 1:15; 5:2
the only daughter of her
mother,
the favorite of the one who
bore her. SS 3:4

The young women saw her and
called her blessed;
the queens and concubines
praised her.

Friends

10 Who is this that appears like
the dawn,
fair as the moon, bright as
the sun,
majestic as the stars in
procession?

He

11 I went down to the grove of nut
trees
to look at the new growth in
the valley,
to see if the vines had budded
or the pomegranates were in
bloom. SS 7:12
12 Before I realized it,
my desire set me among
the royal chariots of my
people.[a]

Friends

13 Come back, come back,
O Shulammite;
come back, come back, that
we may gaze on you!

He

Why would you gaze on the
Shulammite
as on the dance of
Mahanaim?[b] Ex 15:20

7[c] How beautiful your sandaled
feet,
O prince's daughter! Ps 45:13
Your graceful legs are like
jewels,
the work of an artist's hands.
2 Your navel is a rounded goblet
that never lacks blended
wine.
Your waist is a mound of wheat
encircled by lilies.
3 Your breasts are like two fawns,
SS 4:5
like twin fawns of a gazelle.
4 Your neck is like an ivory
tower. Ps 144:12; SS 4:4
Your eyes are the pools of
Heshbon Nu 21:26
by the gate of Bath Rabbim.
Your nose is like the tower of
Lebanon SS 5:15
looking toward Damascus.
5 Your head crowns you like
Mount Carmel. Isa 35:2
Your hair is like royal
tapestry;
the king is held captive by its
tresses.
6 How beautiful you are and how
pleasing, SS 1:15
my love, with your delights!
SS 4:10
7 Your stature is like that of the
palm,
and your breasts like clusters
of fruit. SS 4:5
8 I said, "I will climb the palm
tree;
I will take hold of its fruit."

[a] 12 Or *among the chariots of Amminadab;* or *among the chariots of the people of the prince* [b] 13 In Hebrew texts this verse (6:13) is numbered 7:1. [c] In Hebrew texts 7:1-13 is numbered 7:2-14.

May your breasts be like
clusters of grapes on the vine,
the fragrance of your breath
like apples, SS 2:5
9 and your mouth like the best wine.

She

May the wine go straight to my
beloved, SS 5:16
flowing gently over lips and
teeth.[a]
10 I belong to my beloved,
and his desire is for me.
Ps 45:11; SS 2:16; 6:3
11 Come, my beloved, let us go to
the countryside,
let us spend the night in the
villages.[b]
12 Let us go early to the vineyards
SS 1:6
to see if the vines have
budded, SS 2:15
if their blossoms have opened,
SS 2:13
and if the pomegranates are
in bloom — SS 4:13; 6:11
there I will give you my love.
13 The mandrakes send out their
fragrance, Ge 30:14
and at our door is every
delicacy,
both new and old,
that I have stored up for you,
my beloved. SS 4:16

8 If only you were to me like a
brother,
who was nursed at my
mother's breasts!
Then, if I found you outside,
I would kiss you,
and no one would despise me.
2 I would lead you
and bring you to my
mother's house — SS 3:4
she who has taught me.
I would give you spiced wine to
drink,
the nectar of my
pomegranates.
3 His left arm is under my head
and his right arm embraces
me.
4 Daughters of Jerusalem, I
charge you:
Do not arouse or awaken love
until it so desires. SS 2:7; 3:5

Friends

5 Who is this coming up from the
wilderness SS 3:6
leaning on her beloved?

She

Under the apple tree I roused
you;
there your mother conceived
you, SS 3:4
there she who was in labor
gave you birth.
6 Place me like a seal over your
heart,
like a seal on your arm;
for love is as strong as death,
SS 1:2
its jealousy[c] unyielding as
the grave.

[a] 9 Septuagint, Aquila, Vulgate and Syriac; Hebrew *lips of sleepers* [b] 11 Or *the henna bushes* [c] 6 Or *ardor*

It burns like blazing fire,
like a mighty flame.[a] Nu 5:14
7 Many waters cannot quench
love;
rivers cannot sweep it away.
If one were to give
all the wealth of one's house
for love,
it[b] would be utterly scorned.
Pr 6:35

Friends

8 We have a little sister,
and her breasts are not yet
grown.
What shall we do for our sister
on the day she is spoken for?
9 If she is a wall,
we will build towers of silver
on her.
If she is a door,
we will enclose her with
panels of cedar.

She

10 I am a wall,
and my breasts are like
towers.
Thus I have become in his eyes
like one bringing
contentment.
11 Solomon had a vineyard in
Baal Hamon; Ecc 2:4
he let out his vineyard to
tenants.
Each was to bring for its
fruit
a thousand shekels[c] of silver.
Isa 7:23
12 But my own vineyard is mine
to give; SS 1:6
the thousand shekels are for
you, Solomon,
and two hundred[d] are
for those who tend its
fruit.

He

13 You who dwell in the gardens
with friends in attendance,
let me hear your voice!

She

14 Come away, my beloved,
and be like a gazelle Pr 5:19
or like a young stag SS 2:9
on the spice-laden
mountains. SS 2:8,17

[a] 6 Or *fire, / like the very flame of the* LORD
[b] 7 Or *he*
[c] 11 That is, about 25 pounds or about 12 kilograms; also in verse 12
[d] 12 That is, about 5 pounds or about 2.3 kilograms

ISAIAH

1 The vision concerning Judah
and Jerusalem that Isaiah son
of Amoz saw during the reigns of
Uzziah, Jotham, Ahaz and Hezekiah, kings of Judah. Isa 2:1; 2Ki 16:1

A Rebellious Nation

2 Hear me, you heavens! Listen,
earth!
For the LORD has spoken: Mic 1:2
"I reared children and brought
them up,
but they have rebelled
against me. Isa 30:1,9; 65:2
3 The ox knows its master,
the donkey its owner's
manger,
but Israel does not know, Jer 9:3,6; Hos 2:8
my people do not
understand." Dt 32:28; Isa 42:25
4 Woe to the sinful nation,
a people whose guilt is great, Isa 5:18
a brood of evildoers, Isa 14:20; Jer 23:14
children given to corruption! Ps 14:3
They have forsaken the LORD; Ps 119:87
they have spurned the Holy
One of Israel Isa 5:19,24
and turned their backs on
him. Pr 30:9
5 Why should you be beaten
anymore? Pr 20:30
Why do you persist
in rebellion? Isa 31:6; Heb 3:16
Your whole head is injured,
your whole heart afflicted. Isa 33:6,24
6 From the sole of your
foot to the top of
your head
there is no soundness — Ps 38:3
only wounds and welts
and open sores,
not cleansed or bandaged Isa 30:26; Jer 8:22
or soothed with olive oil. Lk 10:34
7 Your country is desolate, Lev 26:34
your cities burned with fire; Lev 26:31
your fields are being
stripped by foreigners Lev 26:16; Jdg 6:3-6
right before you,
laid waste as when
overthrown by
strangers. Ps 109:11
8 Daughter Zion is left Ps 9:14
like a shelter in a
vineyard,
like a hut in a cucumber field, Job 27:18
like a city under siege.

9 Unless the LORD Almighty
had left us some survivors, Isa 10:20-22; 37:4,31-32
we would have become like Sodom,
we would have been like Gomorrah. Ge 19:24; Ro 9:29*

10 Hear the word of the LORD, Isa 28:14
you rulers of Sodom; Eze 16:49; Rev 11:8
listen to the instruction of our God, Isa 8:20
you people of Gomorrah! Isa 13:19
11 "The multitude of your sacrifices —
what are they to me?" says the LORD.
"I have more than enough of burnt offerings,
of rams and the fat of fattened animals; Ps 50:8
I have no pleasure
in the blood of bulls and lambs and goats. 1Sa 15:22; Jer 6:20; Mal 1:10
12 When you come to appear before me,
who has asked this of you, Ex 23:17; Dt 31:11
this trampling of my courts?
13 Stop bringing meaningless offerings! Isa 66:3
Your incense is detestable to me. Jer 7:9
New Moons, Sabbaths and convocations — 1Ch 23:31
I cannot bear your worthless assemblies.
14 Your New Moon feasts and your appointed festivals Nu 28:11-29:39; Isa 29:1
I hate with all my being. Ps 11:5
They have become a burden to me;
I am weary of bearing them. Isa 43:22,24
15 When you spread out your hands in prayer,
I hide my eyes from you; Isa 8:17; 59:2; Mic 3:4
even when you offer many prayers,
I am not listening. Isa 59:3; Jer 2:34

Your hands are full of blood!

16 Wash and make yourselves clean. Mt 27:24; Jas 4:8
Take your evil deeds out of my sight; Isa 52:11
stop doing wrong. Isa 55:7; Jer 25:5
17 Learn to do right; seek justice. Ps 34:14; Zep 2:3
Defend the oppressed.[a] Dt 14:29
Take up the cause of the fatherless; Ps 82:3; 94:6
plead the case of the widow. Ex 22:22; Jas 1:27

18 "Come now, let us settle the matter," Isa 41:1; 43:9,26
says the LORD.
"Though your sins are like scarlet,
they shall be as white as snow; Ps 51:7; Rev 7:14

[a] 17 Or *justice. / Correct the oppressor*

though they are red as
crimson,
they shall be like wool. Isa 55:7
19 If you are willing and obedient,
Job 36:11; Isa 50:10
you will eat the good
things of the land;
Dt 30:15-16; Isa 55:2
20 but if you resist and rebel,
1Sa 12:15
you will be devoured by the
sword." Isa 3:25; 65:12
For the mouth of the
LORD has spoken.

21 See how the faithful city
has become a prostitute!
Jer 2:20
She once was full of justice;
righteousness used
to dwell in her—
Isa 5:7; 46:13
but now murderers! Pr 6:17
22 Your silver has become dross,
Ps 119:119
your choice wine is diluted
with water.
23 Your rulers are rebels,
partners with thieves;
Dt 19:14; Mic 2:1-2
they all love bribes Ex 23:8; Am 5:12
and chase after gifts.
They do not defend the cause
of the fatherless;
the widow's case does not
come before them.
Jer 5:28; Eze 22:6-7; Zec 7:10

24 Therefore the Lord, the LORD
Almighty,
the Mighty One of Israel,
declares: Ge 49:24
"Ah! I will vent my wrath on
my foes
and avenge myself on my
enemies. Isa 35:4; 59:17; 61:2
25 I will turn my hand against
you;[a] Dt 28:63
I will thoroughly purge away
your dross
and remove all your
impurities. Eze 22:22; Mal 3:3
26 I will restore your leaders as in
days of old, Jer 33:7,11
your rulers as at the
beginning.
Afterward you will be called
the City of Righteousness,
Isa 33:5; Zec 8:3
the Faithful City." Isa 60:14; 62:2
27 Zion will be delivered with
justice,
her penitent ones with
righteousness.
Isa 35:10; 62:12; 63:4
28 But rebels and sinners will
both be broken,
and those who forsake
the LORD will perish.
Ps 9:5; Isa 24:20; 2Th 1:8-9

29 "You will be ashamed
because of the sacred
oaks Isa 57:5
in which you have delighted;
you will be disgraced
because of the gardens
Isa 65:3; 66:17
that you have chosen.
30 You will be like an oak with
fading leaves,
like a garden without water.

[a] *25* That is, against Jerusalem

[31]The mighty man will become tinder
and his work a spark;
both will burn together,
with no one to quench the fire." Isa 5:24; 9:18-19; 26:11

The Mountain of the LORD

2 This is what Isaiah son of Amoz saw concerning Judah and Jerusalem: Isa 1:1

[2]In the last days
the mountain of the LORD's temple will be established Mic 4:7
as the highest of the mountains;
it will be exalted above the hills, Zec 14:10
and all nations will stream to it. Ps 102:15

[3]Many peoples will come and say,

"Come, let us go up to the mountain of the LORD, Ps 137:5; Isa 45:14
to the temple of the God of Jacob.
He will teach us his ways,
so that we may walk in his paths."
The law will go out from Zion, Isa 51:4,7
the word of the LORD from Jerusalem. Lk 24:47
[4]He will judge between the nations Isa 1:27; Joel 3:14
and will settle disputes for many peoples. Ge 49:10
They will beat their swords into plowshares
and their spears into pruning hooks. Joel 3:10
Nation will not take up sword against nation, Isa 32:18; Hos 2:18
nor will they train for war anymore. Mic 4:1-3

[5]Come, descendants of Jacob, Isa 58:1
let us walk in the light of the LORD. Isa 60:1,19-20; 1Jn 1:5,7

The Day of the LORD

[6]You, LORD, have abandoned your people, Dt 31:17
the descendants of Jacob.
They are full of superstitions from the East;
they practice divination like the Philistines 2Ki 1:2; 2Ch 26:6
and embrace pagan customs. 2Ki 16:7; Pr 6:1
[7]Their land is full of silver and gold; Dt 17:17
there is no end to their treasures. Ps 17:14
Their land is full of horses; Dt 17:16
there is no end to their chariots. Isa 31:1; Mic 5:10
[8]Their land is full of idols; Isa 10:9-11
they bow down to the work of their hands, Ps 135:15; Mic 5:13
to what their fingers have made. Isa 17:8

9 So people will be brought low Ps 62:9
and everyone humbled — Isa 5:15
do not forgive them.[a] Ne 4:5

10 Go into the rocks, hide in the ground
from the fearful presence of the LORD
and the splendor of his majesty! 2Th 1:9; Rev 6:15-16
11 The eyes of the arrogant will be humbled Ne 9:29; Hab 2:5
and human pride brought low; Isa 5:15; 37:23
the LORD alone will be exalted in that day. Ps 46:10

12 The LORD Almighty has a day in store Am 5:18; Zep 1:14
for all the proud and lofty, 2Sa 22:28
for all that is exalted Isa 24:4,21; Mal 4:1
(and they will be humbled), Job 40:11
13 for all the cedars of Lebanon, tall and lofty,
and all the oaks of Bashan, Zec 11:2
14 for all the towering mountains
and all the high hills, Isa 30:25; 40:4
15 for every lofty tower Isa 30:25
and every fortified wall, Isa 25:2,12
16 for every trading ship[b] 1Ki 10:22
and every stately vessel.
17 The arrogance of man will be brought low
and human pride humbled; ver 9
the LORD alone will be exalted in that day, ver 11
18 and the idols will totally disappear. Isa 21:9

19 People will flee to caves in the rocks Isa 7:19
and to holes in the ground
from the fearful presence of the LORD Dt 2:25
and the splendor of his majesty, Ps 145:12
when he rises to shake the earth. Heb 12:26
20 In that day people will throw away
to the moles and bats Lev 11:19
their idols of silver and idols of gold, Rev 9:20
which they made to worship. Eze 7:19-20
21 They will flee to caverns in the rocks
and to the overhanging crags
from the fearful presence of the LORD
and the splendor of his majesty, Ps 145:12
when he rises to shake the earth. ver 19; Isa 33:10

22 Stop trusting in mere humans, Ps 146:3
who have but a breath in their nostrils.
Why hold them in esteem? Ps 8:4; Jas 4:14

[a] 9 Or *not raise them up* [b] 16 Hebrew *every ship of Tarshish*

Judgment on Jerusalem and Judah

3 See now, the Lord,
the LORD Almighty,
is about to take from Jerusalem
and Judah
both supply and support:
Ps 18:18
all supplies of food and all
supplies of water,
Lev 26:26; Eze 4:16
2 the hero and the warrior,
Eze 17:13
the judge and the prophet,
the diviner and the elder,
2Ki 24:14; Isa 9:14-15
3 the captain of fifty and the
man of rank,
the counselor, skilled
craftsman and clever
enchanter. 2Ki 24:14; Ecc 10:11

4 "I will make mere youths their
officials;
children will rule over them."
Ecc 10:16 *fn*

5 People will oppress each other—
man against man, neighbor
against neighbor.
Mic 7:2,6; Isa 9:19; Jer 9:8
The young will rise up against
the old,
the nobody against the
honored.

6 A man will seize one of his
brothers
in his father's house, and say,
"You have a cloak, you be our
leader;
take charge of this heap of
ruins!"
7 But in that day he will cry out,
"I have no remedy.
Eze 34:4; Hos 5:13
I have no food or clothing in
my house;
do not make me the leader
of the people." Isa 24:2

8 Jerusalem staggers,
Judah is falling; Isa 1:7
their words and deeds are
against the LORD, Isa 9:15,17
defying his glorious
presence. Ps 73:9,11
9 The look on their faces testifies
against them;
they parade their sin like
Sodom; Ge 13:13
they do not hide it.
Woe to them!
They have brought disaster
upon themselves.
Pr 8:36; Ro 6:23

10 Tell the righteous it will be well
with them, Dt 28:1-14
for they will enjoy the fruit
of their deeds. Ps 128:2
11 Woe to the wicked!
Disaster is upon them!
Dt 28:15-68
They will be paid back
for what their hands have
done. 2Ch 6:23

12 Youths oppress my
people, ver 4
women rule over them.
My people, your guides lead
you astray; Isa 9:16
they turn you from the
path.

13 The LORD takes his place in court;
he rises to judge the people. Mic 6:2
14 The LORD enters into judgment Job 22:4
against the elders and leaders of his people:
"It is you who have ruined my vineyard;
the plunder from the poor is in your houses. Jas 2:6
15 What do you mean by crushing my people Ps 94:5
and grinding the faces of the poor?" Isa 10:6; 11:4
declares the Lord,
the LORD Almighty.

16 The LORD says,
"The women of Zion are haughty, SS 3:11
walking along with outstretched necks,
flirting with their eyes,
strutting along with swaying hips,
with ornaments jingling on their ankles.
17 Therefore the Lord will bring sores on the heads of the women of Zion;
the LORD will make their scalps bald."

18 In that day the Lord will snatch
away their finery: the bangles and
headbands and crescent necklaces, 19 the earrings and bracelets
and veils, 20 the headdresses and
anklets and sashes, the perfume
bottles and charms, 21 the signet
rings and nose rings, 22 the fine
robes and the capes and cloaks,
the purses 23 and mirrors, and the
linen garments and tiaras and
shawls. Isa 2:11; Eze 16:10

24 Instead of fragrance there will be a stench; Est 2:12
instead of a sash, a rope; Pr 31:24
instead of well-dressed hair, baldness; Isa 22:12
instead of fine clothing, sackcloth; La 2:10; Eze 27:30-31
instead of beauty, branding. 1Pe 3:3
25 Your men will fall by the sword, Isa 1:20
your warriors in battle.
26 The gates of Zion will lament and mourn; Jer 14:2
destitute, she will sit on the ground. La 2:10

4 1 In that day seven women will take hold of one man Isa 13:12
and say, "We will eat our own food 2Th 3:12
and provide our own clothes;
only let us be called by your name.
Take away our disgrace!" Ge 30:23

The Branch of the LORD

2 In that day the Branch of the
LORD will be beautiful and glorious, and the fruit of the land
will be the pride and glory of the
survivors in Israel. 3 Those who
are left in Zion, who remain in

Jerusalem, will be called holy, all
who are recorded among the living in Jerusalem. 4The Lord will
wash away the filth of the women
of Zion; he will cleanse the blood-
stains from Jerusalem by a spirit[a]
of judgment and a spirit[a] of fire.
5Then the LORD will create over all
of Mount Zion and over those who
assemble there a cloud of smoke
by day and a glow of flaming fire
by night; over everything the glory[b] will be a canopy. 6It will be a
shelter and shade from the heat of
the day, and a refuge and hiding
place from the storm and rain.
Jer 23:5-6; Isa 25:4

The Song of the Vineyard

5 I will sing for the one I love
a song about his vineyard: Ps 80:8-9
My loved one had a vineyard
on a fertile hillside.
2He dug it up and cleared it of stones
and planted it with the choicest vines. Jer 2:21
He built a watchtower in it
and cut out a winepress as well.
Then he looked for a crop of good grapes,
but it yielded only bad fruit. Lk 13:6

3"Now you dwellers in Jerusalem and people of Judah,
judge between me and my vineyard. Mt 21:40
4What more could have been done for my vineyard
than I have done for it? Mt 23:37
When I looked for good grapes,
why did it yield only bad?
5Now I will tell you
what I am going to do to my vineyard:
I will take away its hedge,
and it will be destroyed;
I will break down its wall, Ps 80:12
and it will be trampled. Lk 21:24
6I will make it a wasteland,
neither pruned nor cultivated,
and briers and thorns will grow there.
Isa 7:23-24; Heb 6:8
I will command the clouds
not to rain on it."

7The vineyard of the LORD Almighty
is the nation of Israel, Ps 80:8
and the people of Judah
are the vines he delighted in.
And he looked for justice, but saw bloodshed; Isa 59:15
for righteousness, but heard cries of distress.

Woes and Judgments

8Woe to you who add house to house Jer 22:13
and join field to field
Mic 2:2; Hab 2:9-12
till no space is left
and you live alone in the land.

[a] 4 *Or the Spirit* [b] 5 *Or over all the glory there*

9 The LORD Almighty has declared in my hearing: Isa 22:14

"Surely the great houses
will become desolate, Isa 6:11-12; Mt 23:38
the fine mansions left
without occupants.
10 A ten-acre vineyard will
produce only a bath[a] of wine;
a homer[b] of seed will yield
only an ephah[c] of grain." Lev 26:26

11 Woe to those who rise early in
the morning
to run after their drinks,
who stay up late at night
till they are inflamed with
wine. Pr 23:29-30
12 They have harps and lyres at
their banquets,
pipes and timbrels and wine,
but they have no regard for
the deeds of the LORD, Job 34:27
no respect for the work of his
hands. Ps 28:5; Am 6:5-6
13 Therefore my people will go
into exile
for lack of understanding; Isa 1:3; Hos 4:6
those of high rank will die of
hunger
and the common people
will be parched with
thirst.
14 Therefore Death expands its
jaws, Pr 30:16
opening wide its mouth; Nu 16:30
into it will descend their nobles
and masses
with all their brawlers and
revelers.
15 So people will be brought low Isa 10:33
and everyone humbled, Isa 2:9
the eyes of the arrogant
humbled. Isa 2:11
16 But the LORD Almighty will be
exalted by his justice, Isa 28:17; 30:18; 33:5
and the holy God will be
proved holy by his
righteous acts. Isa 29:23
17 Then sheep will graze as in
their own pasture; Isa 7:25; Zep 2:6,14
lambs will feed[d] among the
ruins of the rich.

18 Woe to those who draw sin
along with cords of
deceit,
and wickedness as with cart
ropes, Isa 59:4-8; Jer 23:14
19 to those who say, "Let God
hurry;
let him hasten his work
so we may see it.
The plan of the Holy One of
Israel —
let it approach, let it come
into view,
so we may know it." Jer 17:15; Eze 12:22; 2Pe 3:4

[a] *10* That is, about 6 gallons or about 22 liters [b] *10* That is, probably about 360 pounds or about 160 kilograms [c] *10* That is, probably about 36 pounds or about 16 kilograms [d] *17* Septuagint; Hebrew / *strangers will eat*

20 Woe to those who call evil good
and good evil,
who put darkness for light
and light for darkness,
Mt 6:22-23; Lk 11:34-35
who put bitter for sweet
and sweet for bitter. Am 5:7
21 Woe to those who are wise
in their own eyes
Ro 12:16; 1Co 3:18-20
and clever in their own sight.
22 Woe to those who are heroes at
drinking wine Pr 23:20
and champions at mixing
drinks,
23 who acquit the guilty for a
bribe, Ex 23:8
but deny justice to the
innocent. Ps 94:21; Jas 5:6
24 Therefore, as tongues of fire
lick up straw
and as dry grass sinks down
in the flames,
so their roots will decay Job 18:16
and their flowers blow away
like dust;
for they have rejected the law
of the LORD Almighty
and spurned the word of
the Holy One of Israel.
Isa 8:6; 30:9,12
25 Therefore the LORD's anger
burns against his
people; 2Ki 22:13
his hand is raised and he
strikes them down.
The mountains shake,
and the dead bodies are like
refuse in the streets.
2Ki 9:37

Yet for all this, his anger is not
turned away, Jer 4:8; Da 9:16
his hand is still upraised.
Isa 9:12,17,21; 10:4

26 He lifts up a banner for the
distant nations,
he whistles for those at
the ends of the earth.
Isa 7:18; Dt 28:49
Here they come,
swiftly and speedily!
27 Not one of them grows tired or
stumbles,
not one slumbers or sleeps;
not a belt is loosened at the
waist, Job 12:18
not a sandal strap is broken.
Joel 2:7-8
28 Their arrows are sharp, Ps 45:5
all their bows are strung;
Ps 7:12
their horses' hooves seem like
flint,
their chariot wheels like a
whirlwind.
29 Their roar is like that of the
lion, Jer 51:38; Zep 3:3
they roar like young lions;
they growl as they seize their
prey Isa 10:6; 49:24-25
and carry it off with no one
to rescue. Isa 42:22; Mic 5:8
30 In that day they will roar over it
like the roaring of the sea.
Lk 21:25
And if one looks at the land,
there is only darkness and
distress; Isa 8:22; Jer 4:23-28
even the sun will be darkened
by clouds. Joel 2:10

Isaiah's Commission

6 In the year that King Uzziah died, I saw the Lord, high
and exalted, seated on a throne;
and the train of his robe filled the
temple. 2Above him were seraphim, each with six wings: With
two wings they covered their faces, with two they covered their
feet, and with two they were flying. 3And they were calling to one
another: 2Ch 6:22-23; Rev 4:8

"Holy, holy, holy is the LORD
Almighty; Ex 15:11; Ps 89:8
the whole earth is full of his
glory." Ps 72:19; Rev 4:8

4At the sound of their voices the
doorposts and thresholds shook
and the temple was filled with
smoke.

5"Woe to me!" I cried. "I am ruined! For I am a man of unclean
lips, and I live among a people of
unclean lips, and my eyes have
seen the King, the LORD Almighty."
Jer 9:3-8; 51:57

6Then one of the seraphim flew
to me with a live coal in his hand,
which he had taken with tongs
from the altar. 7With it he touched
my mouth and said, "See, this has
touched your lips; your guilt is
taken away and your sin atoned
for." Jer 1:9; 1Jn 1:7

8Then I heard the voice of the
Lord saying, "Whom shall I send?
And who will go for us?" Ac 9:4
And I said, "Here am I. Send me!"
Ge 22:1; Ex 3:4

9He said, "Go and tell this people: Eze 3:11

"'Be ever hearing, but never
understanding;
be ever seeing, but
never perceiving.'
Mt 13:15*; Lk 8:10*
10Make the heart of this people
calloused; Ps 119:70
make their ears dull
and close their eyes.[a]
Otherwise they might see with
their eyes,
hear with their ears, Jer 5:21
understand with their
hearts,
and turn and be healed."
Mk 4:12*; Ac 28:26-27*

11Then I said, "For how long,
Lord?" Ps 79:5
And he answered:

"Until the cities lie ruined
Lev 26:31
and without inhabitant,
until the houses are left
deserted
and the fields ruined and
ravaged, Ps 79:1; 109:11
12until the LORD has sent
everyone far away Dt 28:64
and the land is utterly
forsaken. Jer 4:29; 30:17
13And though a tenth remains in
the land, Isa 1:9
it will again be laid waste.

[a] 9,10 Hebrew; Septuagint *'You will be ever hearing, but never understanding; / you will be ever seeing, but never perceiving.' / 10This people's heart has become calloused; / they hardly hear with their ears, / and they have closed their eyes*

But as the terebinth and oak
leave stumps when they are
cut down,
so the holy seed will be the
stump in the land."
Dt 14:2; Job 14:7

The Sign of Immanuel

7 When Ahaz son of Jotham, the
son of Uzziah, was king of Judah, King Rezin of Aram and Pekah son of Remaliah king of Israel
marched up to fight against Jerusalem, but they could not overpower it. 2Ki 15:25,37; 2Ch 28:5
2 Now the house of David was
told, "Aram has allied itself with[a]
Ephraim"; so the hearts of Ahaz
and his people were shaken, as
the trees of the forest are shaken
by the wind. ver 13; Isa 9:9; 22:22
3 Then the LORD said to Isaiah, "Go out, you and your son
Shear-Jashub,[b] to meet Ahaz at
the end of the aqueduct of the Upper Pool, on the road to the Launderer's Field. 4 Say to him, 'Be careful, keep calm and don't be afraid.
Do not lose heart because of these
two smoldering stubs of firewood — because of the fierce anger of Rezin and Aram and of the
son of Remaliah. 5 Aram, Ephraim
and Remaliah's son have plotted
your ruin, saying, 6 "Let us invade
Judah; let us tear it apart and divide it among ourselves, and
make the son of Tabeel king over
it." 7 Yet this is what the Sovereign
LORD says: Isa 10:24; 30:15

" 'It will not take place,
it will not happen, Isa 8:10; Ac 4:25
8 for the head of Aram is
Damascus, Ge 14:15
and the head of Damascus is
only Rezin.
Within sixty-five years
Ephraim will be too
shattered to be a people.
Isa 17:1-3
9 The head of Ephraim is
Samaria,
and the head of Samaria is
only Remaliah's son.
If you do not stand firm in your
faith, 2Ch 20:20
you will not stand at all.' "
Isa 8:6-8; 30:12-14

10 Again the LORD spoke to Ahaz,
11 "Ask the LORD your God for a sign,
whether in the deepest depths or
in the highest heights." Ex 7:9; Dt 13:2
12 But Ahaz said, "I will not ask; I
will not put the LORD to the test."
Dt 6:16; Mt 4:7
13 Then Isaiah said, "Hear now,
you house of David! Is it not
enough to try the patience of humans? Will you try the patience
of my God also? 14 Therefore the
Lord himself will give you[c] a sign:
The virgin[d] will conceive and give
birth to a son, and[e] will call him
Immanuel.[f] 15 He will be eating
curds and honey when he knows

[a] 2 Or *has set up camp in* [b] 3 *Shear-Jashub* means *a remnant will return.*
[c] 14 The Hebrew is plural. [d] 14 Or *young woman* [e] 14 Masoretic Text; Dead Sea Scrolls *son, and he* or *son, and they*
[f] 14 *Immanuel* means *God with us.*

enough to reject the wrong and
choose the right, 16for before the
boy knows enough to reject the
wrong and choose the right, the
land of the two kings you dread
will be laid waste. 17The LORD will
bring on you and on your people
and on the house of your father
a time unlike any since Ephraim
broke away from Judah — he will
bring the king of Assyria."

Isa 8:8,10; Mt 1:23*

Assyria, the LORD's Instrument

18In that day the LORD will whis-
tle for flies from the Nile delta in
Egypt and for bees from the land
of Assyria. 19They will all come
and settle in the steep ravines
and in the crevices in the rocks,
on all the thornbushes and at all
the water holes. 20In that day the
Lord will use a razor hired from
beyond the Euphrates River — the
king of Assyria — to shave your
head and private parts, and to cut
off your beard also. 21In that day,
a person will keep alive a young
cow and two goats. 22And because
of the abundance of the milk they
give, there will be curds to eat. All
who remain in the land will eat
curds and honey. 23In that day,
in every place where there were
a thousand vines worth a thousand silver shekels,[a] there will be
only briers and thorns. 24Hunters
will go there with bow and arrow,
for the land will be covered with
briers and thorns. 25As for all the
hills once cultivated by the hoe,
you will no longer go there for
fear of the briers and thorns; they
will become places where cattle
are turned loose and where sheep
run. Isa 5:6,17; 10:15

Isaiah and His Children as Signs

8 The LORD said to me, "Take
a large scroll and write on it
with an ordinary pen: Maher-Shalal-Hash-Baz."[b] 2So I called in Uriah the priest and Zechariah son of
Jeberekiah as reliable witnesses
for me. 3Then I made love to the
prophetess, and she conceived
and gave birth to a son. And the
LORD said to me, "Name him Maher-Shalal-Hash-Baz. 4For before
the boy knows how to say 'My father' or 'My mother,' the wealth
of Damascus and the plunder of
Samaria will be carried off by the
king of Assyria." Isa 7:8,16; 30:8; Hab 2:2

5The LORD spoke to me again:

6"Because this people has
rejected Isa 5:24
the gently flowing waters of
Shiloah Jn 9:7
and rejoices over Rezin
and the son of Remaliah, Isa 7:1
7therefore the Lord is about to
bring against them
the mighty floodwaters
of the Euphrates —
Isa 17:12-13
the king of Assyria with all
his pomp. Isa 7:20

[a] *23* That is, about 25 pounds or about 12 kilograms [b] *1* *Maher-Shalal-Hash-Baz* means *quick to the plunder, swift to the spoil*; also in verse 3.

It will overflow all its
channels,
run over all its banks
8 and sweep on into Judah,
swirling over it,
passing through it and
reaching up to the neck.
Its outspread wings will cover
the breadth of your land,
Immanuel[a]!" Isa 7:14

9 Raise the war cry,[b] you nations,
and be shattered!
Isa 17:12-13
Listen, all you distant lands.
Prepare for battle, and be
shattered! Joel 3:9
Prepare for battle, and be
shattered!
10 Devise your strategy, but it will
be thwarted; Job 5:12
propose your plan, but it will
not stand, Isa 7:7
for God is with us.[c] Ro 8:31

11 This is what the LORD says to
me with his strong hand upon me,
warning me not to follow the way
of this people: Eze 2:8; 3:14

12 "Do not call conspiracy Isa 7:2
everything this people calls a
conspiracy;
do not fear what they fear,
Isa 7:4; Mt 10:28
and do not dread it. 1Pe 3:14*
13 The LORD Almighty is the one
you are to regard as
holy, Nu 20:12
he is the one you are to fear,
he is the one you are to
dread. Isa 29:23
14 He will be a holy place;
Isa 4:6; Eze 11:16
for both Israel and Judah he
will be
a stone that causes
people to stumble
Lk 2:34; Ro 9:33*; 1Pe 2:8*
and a rock that makes them
fall. Isa 24:17-18
And for the people of
Jerusalem he will be
a trap and a snare.
15 Many of them will stumble;
Lk 20:18; Ro 9:32
they will fall and be broken,
they will be snared and
captured."

16 Bind up this testimony of
warning
and seal up God's instruction
among my disciples.
Isa 29:11-12
17 I will wait for the LORD, Hab 2:3
who is hiding his face from
the descendants of
Jacob. Dt 31:17; Isa 54:8
I will put my trust in him.
Heb 2:13*

18 Here am I, and the children
the LORD has given me. We are
signs and symbols in Israel from
the LORD Almighty, who dwells on
Mount Zion. Heb 2:13*; Ps 9:11

The Darkness Turns to Light

19 When someone tells you to
consult mediums and spiritists,
who whisper and mutter, should

[a] 8 *Immanuel* means *God with us.* [b] 9 Or *Do your worst* [c] 10 Hebrew *Immanuel*

not a people inquire of their God?
Why consult the dead on behalf
of the living? [20]Consult God's instruction and the testimony of
warning. If anyone does not speak
according to this word, they have
no light of dawn. [21]Distressed and
hungry, they will roam through
the land; when they are famished,
they will become enraged and,
looking upward, will curse their
king and their God. [22]Then they
will look toward the earth and see
only distress and darkness and
fearful gloom, and they will be
thrust into utter darkness.
Mic 3:6; Lk 16:29

9 [a] Nevertheless, there will be
no more gloom for those
who were in distress. In the past
he humbled the land of Zebulun
and the land of Naphtali, but in
the future he will honor Galilee of
the nations, by the Way of the Sea,
beyond the Jordan— 2Ki 15:29

[2]The people walking in
darkness Isa 8:20
have seen a great light; Eph 5:8
on those living in the land of
deep darkness Lk 1:79
a light has dawned. Mt 4:15-16*
[3]You have enlarged the nation
Job 12:23
and increased their joy; Isa 25:9
they rejoice before you
as people rejoice at the
harvest,
as warriors rejoice
when dividing the plunder.
Ps 119:162
[4]For as in the day of Midian's
defeat, Jdg 7:25
you have shattered Job 34:24
the yoke that burdens them,
Isa 14:25
the bar across their
shoulders, Isa 10:27
the rod of their oppressor.
Isa 14:4; 49:26
[5]Every warrior's boot used in
battle
and every garment rolled in
blood
will be destined for burning,
Isa 2:4
will be fuel for the fire.
[6]For to us a child is born, Lk 2:11
to us a son is given, Jn 3:16
and the government will be
on his shoulders. Mt 28:18
And he will be called
Wonderful Counselor, Mighty
God, Isa 10:21; 11:2; 28:29
Everlasting Father, Prince of
Peace. Lk 2:14; Jn 14:9-10
[7]Of the greatness of his
government and peace
there will be no end.
Da 2:44; Lk 1:33
He will reign on David's throne
and over his kingdom,
establishing and upholding it
with justice and
righteousness Isa 11:4; 16:5
from that time on and
forever.
The zeal of the LORD Almighty
will accomplish this.
Isa 37:32; 59:17

[a] In Hebrew texts 9:1 is numbered 8:23, and 9:2-21 is numbered 9:1-20.

The LORD's Anger Against Israel

8 The Lord has sent a message
against Jacob;
it will fall on Israel.
9 All the people will know it —
Ephraim and the inhabitants
of Samaria — Isa 7:9
who say with pride
and arrogance of heart, Isa 46:12
10 "The bricks have fallen down,
but we will rebuild with
dressed stone;
the fig trees have been felled,
Lk 19:4
but we will replace them
with cedars." 1Ki 7:2-3
11 But the LORD has strengthened
Rezin's foes against
them Isa 7:8
and has spurred their
enemies on.
12 Arameans from the east and
Philistines from the west
2Ch 28:18
have devoured Israel with
open mouth. Ps 79:7

Yet for all this, his anger is not
turned away,
his hand is still upraised.
Isa 5:25

13 But the people have not
returned to him who
struck them, Jer 5:3
nor have they sought
the LORD Almighty.
Isa 31:1; Hos 7:7,10
14 So the LORD will cut off from
Israel both head and tail,
both palm branch and reed in
a single day; Isa 19:15; Rev 18:8
15 the elders and dignitaries are
the head, Isa 3:2-3
the prophets who teach lies
are the tail. Eze 13:22; Mt 24:24
16 Those who guide this
people mislead them,
Mt 15:14; 23:16,24
and those who are guided
are led astray. Isa 3:12
17 Therefore the Lord will take no
pleasure in the young
men, Jer 18:21
nor will he pity the fatherless
and widows, Isa 27:11
for everyone is ungodly and
wicked, Isa 1:4; 10:6
every mouth speaks folly.
Mt 12:34

Yet for all this, his anger is not
turned away,
his hand is still upraised.
Isa 5:25

18 Surely wickedness burns like a
fire; Mal 4:1
it consumes briers and thorns,
it sets the forest thickets
ablaze, Ps 83:14
so that it rolls upward in a
column of smoke.
19 By the wrath of the LORD
Almighty Isa 13:9,13
the land will be scorched
and the people will be fuel for
the fire; Isa 1:31
they will not spare one
another. Mic 7:2,6
20 On the right they will devour,
but still be hungry; Lev 26:26
on the left they will eat, Isa 49:26
but not be satisfied.

Each will feed on the flesh of
their own offspring[a]:
21 Manasseh will feed on
Ephraim, and Ephraim
on Manasseh;
together they will turn
against Judah. 2Ch 28:6

Yet for all this, his anger is not
turned away,
his hand is still upraised.
Isa 5:25

10 Woe to those who make
unjust laws,
to those who issue
oppressive decrees, Ps 58:2
2 to deprive the poor of their
rights
and withhold justice from
the oppressed of my
people, Isa 5:23
making widows their prey
and robbing the fatherless.
Dt 10:18; Isa 1:17
3 What will you do on the day of
reckoning, Job 31:14; Hos 9:7
when disaster comes from
afar? Lk 19:44
To whom will you run for help?
Isa 20:6
Where will you leave your
riches?
4 Nothing will remain but to
cringe among the
captives Isa 24:22
or fall among the slain.
Isa 22:2; 66:16

Yet for all this, his anger is not
turned away, Isa 5:25
his hand is still upraised.

God's Judgment on Assyria

5 "Woe to the Assyrian, the
rod of my anger,
Isa 14:25; Zep 2:13
in whose hand is the
club of my wrath!
Isa 30:30; 66:14; Jer 51:20
6 I send him against a godless
nation, Isa 9:17
I dispatch him against a
people who anger me,
Isa 9:19
to seize loot and snatch
plunder, Isa 5:29
and to trample them
down like mud in the
streets.
7 But this is not what he intends,
Ge 50:20; Ac 4:23-28
this is not what he has in
mind;
his purpose is to destroy,
to put an end to many
nations.
8 'Are not my commanders
all kings?' he says.
2Ki 18:24
9 'Has not Kalno fared like
Carchemish? 2Ch 35:20
Is not Hamath like Arpad,
and Samaria like Damascus?
2Ki 16:9; 17:6
10 As my hand seized the
kingdoms of the idols,
2Ki 19:18
kingdoms whose images
excelled those of
Jerusalem and
Samaria —

[a] 20 Or *arm*

[11]shall I not deal with Jerusalem
and her images
as I dealt with Samaria and
her idols?'" 2Ki 19:13; Isa 2:8

[12]When the Lord has finished all his work against Mount Zion and Jerusalem, he will say, "I will punish the king of Assyria for the willful pride of his heart and the haughty look in his eyes. [13]For he says: 2Ki 19:31; Jer 50:18

"'By the strength of my
hand I have done this, Isa 37:24; Da 4:30
and by my wisdom, because I
have understanding.
I removed the boundaries of
nations,
I plundered their treasures; Eze 28:4
like a mighty one I subdued[a]
their kings.
[14]As one reaches into a nest, Jer 49:16; Ob 1:4
so my hand reached for the
wealth of the nations; Job 31:25
as people gather abandoned
eggs,
so I gathered all the
countries;
not one flapped a wing,
or opened its mouth to
chirp.'"

[15]Does the ax raise itself
above the person who
swings it,
or the saw boast against the
one who uses it? Ro 9:20-21
As if a rod were to wield the
person who lifts it up,
or a club brandish the one
who is not wood! ver 5
[16]Therefore, the Lord, the LORD
Almighty,
will send a wasting disease
upon his sturdy
warriors; ver 18; Isa 17:4
under his pomp a fire will be
kindled Isa 8:7
like a blazing flame.
[17]The Light of Israel will become
a fire, Isa 31:9
their Holy One a flame; Isa 37:23
in a single day it will burn and
consume
his thorns and his briers. Nu 11:1-3; Isa 9:18
[18]The splendor of his forests and
fertile fields 2Ki 19:23
it will completely destroy,
as when a sick person wastes
away.
[19]And the remaining trees of his
forests will be so few Isa 21:17
that a child could write them
down.

The Remnant of Israel

[20]In that day the remnant of
Israel, Isa 11:10-11
the survivors of Jacob,
will no longer rely on him 2Ki 16:7
who struck them down 2Ch 28:20
but will truly rely on the LORD, Isa 17:7
the Holy One of Israel.

[a] 13 Or *treasures; / I subdued the mighty,*

21 A remnant will return,[a]
a remnant of Jacob
Isa 6:13
will return to the Mighty
God. Isa 9:6
22 Though your people be like the
sand by the sea, Israel,
Ge 12:2; Isa 48:19
only a remnant will return.
Ro 9:27-28
Destruction has been decreed,
Isa 28:22; Da 9:27
overwhelming and
righteous.
23 The Lord, the LORD Almighty,
will carry out
the destruction decreed
upon the whole land.
Isa 28:22; Ro 9:27-28*

24 Therefore this is what the
Lord, the LORD Almighty, says:

"My people who live in Zion,
Ps 87:5-6
do not be afraid of the
Assyrians,
who beat you with a rod Ex 5:14
and lift up a club against you,
as Egypt did.
25 Very soon my anger against
you will end Isa 17:14
and my wrath will be
directed to their
destruction." Da 11:36
26 The LORD Almighty will lash
them with a whip,
Isa 37:36-38
as when he struck down
Midian at the rock
of Oreb; Isa 9:4
and he will raise his staff over
the waters, Ex 14:16
as he did in Egypt.
27 In that day their burden will
be lifted from your
shoulders,
their yoke from your neck;
Isa 9:4; 14:25
the yoke will be broken
because you have grown so
fat.[b]
28 They enter Aiath;
they pass through Migron;
1Sa 14:2
they store supplies at
Mikmash. 1Sa 13:2
29 They go over the pass, and say,
"We will camp overnight at
Geba."
Ramah trembles; Jos 18:25
Gibeah of Saul flees. Jdg 19:14
30 Cry out, Daughter Gallim!
1Sa 25:44
Listen, Laishah!
Poor Anathoth! Ne 11:32
31 Madmenah is in flight;
the people of Gebim take
cover.
32 This day they will halt at Nob;
1Sa 21:1
they will shake their fist
at the mount of Daughter Zion,
Jer 6:23
at the hill of Jerusalem.

33 See, the Lord, the LORD Almighty,
will lop off the boughs with
great power.

[a] 21 Hebrew *shear-jashub* (see 7:3 and note); also in verse 22 [b] 27 Hebrew; Septuagint *broken / from your shoulders*

The lofty trees will be felled,
the tall ones will be brought low. Am 2:9
[34]He will cut down the forest thickets with an ax;
Lebanon will fall before the Mighty One.
2Ki 19:23; Isa 33:21

The Branch From Jesse

11 A shoot will come up from the stump of Jesse; Rev 5:5
from his roots a Branch will bear fruit. Isa 4:2
[2]The Spirit of the LORD
will rest on him —
Mt 3:16; Jn 1:32-33; Isa 61:1
the Spirit of wisdom and of understanding, Eph 1:17
the Spirit of counsel and of might, 2Ti 1:7
the Spirit of the knowledge and fear of the LORD —
[3]and he will delight in the fear of the LORD.

He will not judge by what he sees with his eyes, Jn 7:24
or decide by what he hears with his ears; Jn 2:25
[4]but with righteousness he will judge the needy, Ps 72:2
with justice he will give decisions for the poor of the earth. Isa 3:14; 9:7
He will strike the earth with the rod of his mouth;
Mal 4:6
with the breath of his lips he will slay the wicked.
Job 4:9; 2Th 2:8
[5]Righteousness will be his belt
and faithfulness the sash around his waist.
Isa 25:1; Eph 6:14

[6]The wolf will live with the lamb, Isa 65:25
the leopard will lie down with the goat,
the calf and the lion and the yearling[a] together;
and a little child will lead them.
[7]The cow will feed with the bear,
their young will lie down together,
and the lion will eat straw like the ox.
[8]The infant will play near the cobra's den, Isa 65:20
and the young child will put its hand into the viper's nest. Isa 14:29
[9]They will neither harm nor destroy Job 5:23
on all my holy mountain,
for the earth will be filled with the knowledge of the LORD
Hab 2:14; Ps 98:2-3
as the waters cover the sea.

[10]In that day the Root of Jesse
will stand as a banner for the peoples; the nations will rally to him,
and his resting place will be glorious. [11]In that day the Lord will
reach out his hand a second time
to reclaim the surviving remnant
of his people from Assyria, from
Lower Egypt, from Upper Egypt,

[a] 6 Hebrew; Septuagint *lion will feed*

from Cush,[a] from Elam, from Babylonia,[b] from Hamath and from the islands of the Mediterranean. Ro 15:12*; Mic 7:12; Zec 10:10

12 He will raise a banner for the nations Ps 20:5
and gather the exiles of Israel; Ps 106:47; Isa 14:1
he will assemble the scattered people of Judah Zep 3:10
from the four quarters of the earth. Ps 48:10; Rev 7:1
13 Ephraim's jealousy will vanish,
and Judah's enemies[c] will be destroyed;
Ephraim will not be jealous of Judah,
nor Judah hostile toward Ephraim. Jer 3:18; Eze 37:16-17,22; Hos 1:11
14 They will swoop down on the slopes of Philistia to the west;
together they will plunder the people to the east.
They will subdue Edom and Moab, Da 11:41; Joel 3:19
and the Ammonites will be subject to them.
15 The LORD will dry up
the gulf of the Egyptian sea;
with a scorching wind he will sweep his hand Isa 19:16
over the Euphrates River. Isa 7:20
He will break it up into seven streams
so that anyone can cross over in sandals.
16 There will be a highway for the remnant of his people Isa 19:23; 62:10
that is left from Assyria,
as there was for Israel
when they came up from Egypt. Ex 14:26-31

Songs of Praise

12 In that day you will say:

"I will praise you, LORD. Isa 25:1
Although you were angry with me,
your anger has turned away Job 13:16
and you have comforted me. Ps 71:21
2 Surely God is my salvation; Isa 17:10
I will trust and not be afraid. Isa 26:3
The LORD, the LORD himself,
is my strength and my defense[d]; Ps 18:1
he has become my salvation." Ex 15:2; Ps 118:14
3 With joy you will draw water Jn 4:10,14
from the wells of salvation. Ex 15:25

4 In that day you will say:

"Give praise to the LORD,
proclaim his name; Ps 105:1; Isa 24:15
make known among the nations what he has done, Isa 54:5; 60:3

[a] 11 That is, the upper Nile region
[b] 11 Hebrew *Shinar*
[c] 13 Or *hostility*
[d] 2 Or *song*

and proclaim that his name
is exalted. Ps 113:2
[5]Sing to the LORD, for he has
done glorious things;
Ex 15:1; Ps 98:1
let this be known to all the
world.
[6]Shout aloud and sing for joy,
people of Zion,
for great is the Holy One
of Israel among you."
Isa 49:26; Zep 3:14-17

A Prophecy Against Babylon

13 A prophecy against Babylon
that Isaiah son of Amoz saw:
Ge 10:10; Isa 14:4; 20:2; Rev 14:8

[2]Raise a banner on a bare
hilltop, Jer 50:2; 51:27
shout to them;
beckon to them
to enter the gates of the
nobles.
[3]I have commanded those I
prepared for battle;
I have summoned my
warriors to carry out my
wrath — Joel 3:11
those who rejoice in my
triumph. Ps 149:2

[4]Listen, a noise on the
mountains,
like that of a great
multitude! Joel 3:14
Listen, an uproar among the
kingdoms, Ps 46:6
like nations massing
together!
The LORD Almighty is mustering
an army for war. Isa 47:4; Jer 50:41
[5]They come from faraway lands,
from the ends of the
heavens — Isa 5:26
the LORD and the weapons of
his wrath — Isa 10:25
to destroy the whole country.
Isa 24:1

[6]Wail, for the day of the LORD is
near; Eze 30:2; Joel 1:15
it will come like destruction
from the Almighty.[a] Ge 17:1
[7]Because of this, all hands will
go limp, 2Ki 19:26
every heart will melt with
fear. Eze 21:7
[8]Terror will seize them, Isa 21:4
pain and anguish will grip
them; Ex 15:14
they will writhe like a
woman in labor. Jn 16:21
They will look aghast at each
other,
their faces aflame. Na 2:10

[9]See, the day of the LORD is
coming Isa 2:12; Jer 51:2
— a cruel day, with wrath
and fierce anger —
Isa 9:19; Joel 3:2
to make the land desolate
and destroy the sinners
within it.
[10]The stars of heaven and their
constellations
will not show their light.
The rising sun will be darkened
Isa 5:30; Rev 8:12
and the moon will
not give its light.
Eze 32:7; Mt 24:29*; Mk 13:24*

[a] 6 Hebrew *Shaddai*

11 I will punish the world for its
evil, Isa 3:11
the wicked for their sins.
I will put an end to the
arrogance of the
haughty Ps 10:5; Pr 16:18
and will humble the pride of
the ruthless. Isa 25:3,5
12 I will make people scarcer than
pure gold, Isa 4:1
more rare than the gold of
Ophir. Ge 10:29
13 Therefore I will make the
heavens tremble;
Isa 34:4; 51:6; Hag 2:6
and the earth will shake
from its place
Isa 14:16; Mt 24:7
at the wrath of the LORD
Almighty, Isa 9:19
in the day of his burning
anger. Job 9:5

14 Like a hunted gazelle,
like sheep without a
shepherd, 1Ki 22:17
they will all return to their own
people,
they will flee to their native
land. Jer 50:16
15 Whoever is captured will be
thrust through;
all who are caught will
fall by the sword.
Isa 14:19; Jer 50:25; 51:4
16 Their infants will be dashed to
pieces before their eyes;
Ps 137:9
their houses will be looted
and their wives violated.
Ge 34:29; Hos 13:16

17 See, I will stir up against them
the Medes, Jer 51:1
who do not care for silver
and have no delight in gold.
Pr 6:34-35
18 Their bows will strike down the
young men; Ps 7:12
they will have no mercy on
infants, Isa 47:6
nor will they look with
compassion on children.
Isa 14:22
19 Babylon, the jewel of
kingdoms,
the pride and glory of the
Babylonians,[a] Da 4:30
will be overthrown by God
Rev 14:8
like Sodom and Gomorrah.
Ge 19:24
20 She will never be inhabited
Isa 14:23; 34:10-15
or lived in through all
generations;
there no nomads will pitch
their tents, 2Ch 17:11
there no shepherds will rest
their flocks.
21 But desert creatures will lie
there, Rev 18:2
jackals will fill her houses;
there the owls will dwell,
Dt 14:15-17
and there the wild goats will
leap about.
22 Hyenas will inhabit her
strongholds, Isa 25:2
jackals her luxurious palaces.
Isa 34:13

[a] *19* Or *Chaldeans*

Her time is at hand, Jer 51:33
and her days will not be
prolonged.

14 The LORD will have
compassion on Jacob;
Ps 102:13; Isa 49:10,13
once again he will choose
Israel Zec 1:17; 2:12
and will settle them in their
own land.
Foreigners will join them
Eph 2:12-19
and unite with the
descendants of Jacob.
2 Nations will take them
and bring them to their own
place. Isa 60:9
And Israel will take
possession of the
nations Isa 49:7,23
and make them male and
female servants in the
LORD's land.
They will make captives of
their captors Isa 45:14
and rule over their
oppressors. Isa 60:14

3 On the day the LORD gives you
relief from your suffering and
turmoil and from the harsh labor
forced on you, 4 you will take up
this taunt against the king of Babylon: Hab 2:6; Isa 11:10

How the oppressor has come to
an end! Isa 9:4
How his fury[a] has ended!
5 The LORD has broken the rod of
the wicked, Ps 125:3
the scepter of the rulers,
6 which in anger struck down
peoples Isa 10:14
with unceasing blows,
and in fury subdued nations
with relentless aggression.
Isa 47:6
7 All the lands are at rest and at
peace; Ps 98:1; 126:1-3
they break into singing.
8 Even the junipers and the
cedars of Lebanon Eze 31:16
gloat over you and say,
"Now that you have been laid
low,
no one comes to cut us
down."
9 The realm of the dead below is
all astir Eze 32:21
to meet you at your coming;
it rouses the spirits of the
departed to greet you —
all those who were leaders in
the world; Zec 10:3
it makes them rise from their
thrones —
all those who were kings
over the nations. Job 3:14
10 They will all respond,
they will say to you,
"You also have become weak,
as we are;
you have become like us."
Eze 32:21
11 All your pomp has been
brought down to the
grave,
along with the noise of your
harps;

[a] 4 Dead Sea Scrolls, Septuagint and Syriac; the meaning of the word in the Masoretic Text is uncertain.

maggots are spread out
beneath you
and worms cover you. Isa 51:8

12 How you have fallen from
heaven, Isa 34:4; Lk 10:18
morning star, son of the
dawn! 2Pe 1:19; Rev 2:28; 8:10
You have been cast down to the
earth,
you who once laid low the
nations!
13 You said in your heart,
"I will ascend to the heavens;
Da 8:10; Mt 11:23
I will raise my throne
Eze 28:2; 2Th 2:4
above the stars of God;
I will sit enthroned on the
mount of assembly,
on the utmost heights of
Mount Zaphon.[a]
14 I will ascend above the tops of
the clouds;
I will make myself like the
Most High." Isa 47:8; 2Th 2:4
15 But you are brought down to
the realm of the dead,
to the depths of the pit.
Mt 11:23; Lk 10:15

16 Those who see you stare at you,
they ponder your fate: Jer 50:23
"Is this the man who shook the
earth
and made kingdoms tremble,
17 the man who made the world a
wilderness, Joel 2:3
who overthrew its cities Ps 52:7
and would not let his
captives go home?"
2Ki 15:29
18 All the kings of the nations lie
in state,
each in his own tomb.
19 But you are cast out of your
tomb Isa 22:16-18
like a rejected branch;
you are covered with the slain,
with those pierced by the
sword,
those who descend to the
stones of the pit. Jer 41:7-9
Like a corpse trampled
underfoot,
20 you will not join them in
burial,
for you have destroyed your land
and killed your people.

Let the offspring of the wicked
Job 18:19; Isa 1:4
never be mentioned again.
Ps 21:10
21 Prepare a place to slaughter his
children
for the sins of their
ancestors; Ex 20:5; Lev 26:39
they are not to rise to inherit
the land
and cover the earth with
their cities.

22 "I will rise up against them,"
declares the LORD Almighty.
"I will wipe out Babylon's name
and survivors,
her offspring and
descendants,"
1Ki 14:10; Job 18:19
declares the LORD.

[a] *13* Or *of the north*; Zaphon was the most sacred mountain of the Canaanites.

23 "I will turn her into a place for
owls Isa 34:11-15; Zep 2:14
and into swampland;
I will sweep her with the
broom of destruction,"
declares the LORD Almighty.

24 The LORD Almighty has sworn,
Isa 45:23

"Surely, as I have planned, so it
will be,
and as I have purposed, so it
will happen. Ac 4:28
25 I will crush the Assyrian in my
land; Isa 10:5,12
on my mountains I will
trample him down.
His yoke will be taken from my
people, Isa 9:4
and his burden removed
from their shoulders."
Isa 10:27

26 This is the plan determined for
the whole world; Isa 23:9
this is the hand stretched out
over all nations. Ex 15:12
27 For the LORD Almighty has
purposed, and who can
thwart him?
His hand is stretched out, and
who can turn it back?
2Ch 20:6; Isa 43:13; Da 4:35

A Prophecy Against the Philistines

28 This prophecy came in the
year King Ahaz died: 2Ki 16:20; Isa 13:1

29 Do not rejoice, all you
Philistines, 2Ch 26:6
that the rod that struck you
is broken;
from the root of that snake will
spring up a viper, Isa 11:8
its fruit will be a darting,
venomous serpent. Dt 8:15
30 The poorest of the poor will
find pasture,
and the needy will lie down
in safety. Isa 3:15; 7:21-22
But your root I will destroy by
famine; Isa 8:21; 9:20
it will slay your survivors.
Jer 25:16

31 Wail, you gate! Howl, you city!
Isa 3:26
Melt away, all you Philistines!
A cloud of smoke comes from
the north, Jer 1:14
and there is not a straggler in
its ranks.
32 What answer shall be given
to the envoys of that nation?
Isa 37:9
"The LORD has established
Zion, Ps 87:2,5; Isa 44:28
and in her his afflicted
people will find refuge."
Isa 4:6; Jas 2:5

A Prophecy Against Moab

15 A prophecy against Moab:
Isa 11:14

Ar in Moab is ruined, Jer 48:24,41
destroyed in a night!
Kir in Moab is ruined, 2Ki 3:25
destroyed in a night!
2 Dibon goes up to its temple,
to its high places to weep;
Jer 48:35
Moab wails over Nebo and
Medeba.

Every head is shaved Lev 21:5
and every beard cut off. 2Sa 10:4
3 In the streets they wear sackcloth;
on the roofs and in the public squares Jer 48:38
they all wail,
prostrate with weeping. Isa 22:4
4 Heshbon and Elealeh cry out, Nu 32:3
their voices are heard all the way to Jahaz.
Therefore the armed men of Moab cry out,
and their hearts are faint.
5 My heart cries out over Moab; Jer 48:31
her fugitives flee as far as Zoar,
as far as Eglath Shelishiyah.
They go up the hill to Luhith,
weeping as they go;
on the road to Horonaim Jer 48:3,34
they lament their destruction. Jer 48:5
6 The waters of Nimrim are dried up Isa 19:5-7; Jer 48:34
and the grass is withered; Joel 1:12
the vegetation is gone
and nothing green is left. Jer 14:5
7 So the wealth they have acquired and stored up Isa 30:6; Jer 48:36
they carry away over the Ravine of the Poplars.
8 Their outcry echoes along the border of Moab;
their wailing reaches as far as Eglaim,
their lamentation as far as Beer Elim. Nu 21:16
9 The waters of Dimon[a] are full of blood,
but I will bring still more upon Dimon[a] —
a lion upon the fugitives of Moab 2Ki 17:25
and upon those who remain in the land.

16 Send lambs as tribute 2Ki 3:4
to the ruler of the land,
from Sela, across the desert, 2Ki 14:7
to the mount of Daughter Zion. Isa 10:32
2 Like fluttering birds
pushed from the nest, Pr 27:8
so are the women of Moab
at the fords of the Arnon. Nu 21:13-14; Jer 48:20
3 "Make up your mind," Moab says.
"Render a decision.
Make your shadow like night —
at high noon.
Hide the fugitives, 1Ki 18:4
do not betray the refugees.
4 Let the Moabite fugitives stay with you;
be their shelter from the destroyer."

[a] 9 *Dimon*, a wordplay on *Dibon* (see verse 2), sounds like the Hebrew for *blood*.

The oppressor will come to an
end, Isa 9:4
and destruction will cease;
Isa 2:2-4
the aggressor will vanish
from the land.
5 In love a throne will be
established; Da 7:14; Mic 4:7
in faithfulness a man will sit
on it —
one from the house[a] of
David — Lk 1:32
one who in judging seeks
justice Isa 9:7
and speeds the cause of
righteousness.
6 We have heard of Moab's
pride — Am 2:1; Ob 1:3; Zep 2:8,10
how great is her arrogance! —
of her conceit, her pride and
her insolence;
but her boasts are empty.
7 Therefore the Moabites wail,
Jer 48:20
they wail together for Moab.
Lament and grieve
for the raisin cakes of Kir
Hareseth. 2Ki 3:25; 1Ch 16:3
8 The fields of Heshbon wither,
Isa 15:6
the vines of Sibmah also.
The rulers of the nations
have trampled down the
choicest vines, Isa 5:2
which once reached Jazer
and spread toward the
desert.
Their shoots spread out Job 8:16
and went as far as the sea.[b]
Ps 80:11
9 So I weep, as Jazer weeps, Isa 15:3
for the vines of Sibmah.
Heshbon and Elealeh,
I drench you with tears! Job 7:3
The shouts of joy over your
ripened fruit
and over your harvests have
been stilled. Jer 40:12
10 Joy and gladness are taken
away from the orchards;
Isa 24:7-8
no one sings or shouts in the
vineyards;
no one treads out wine at the
presses, Jdg 9:27; Job 24:11
for I have put an end to the
shouting.
11 My heart laments for Moab like
a harp, Isa 15:5
my inmost being for
Kir Hareseth.
Isa 63:15; Hos 11:8; Php 2:1
12 When Moab appears at her
high place,
she only wears herself out;
when she goes to her shrine to
pray, Isa 15:2
it is to no avail.
Jer 48:29-36; 1Ki 18:29

13 This is the word the LORD has
already spoken concerning Moab.
14 But now the LORD says: "Within
three years, as a servant bound
by contract would count them,
Moab's splendor and all her many
people will be despised, and her
survivors will be very few and
feeble." Isa 21:17; 25:10; Jer 48:42

[a] 5 Hebrew *tent* [b] 8 Probably the Dead Sea

A Prophecy Against Damascus

17 A prophecy against Damascus: Jer 49:23; Ac 9:2

"See, Damascus will no longer
be a city
but will become a heap of
ruins. Am 1:3; Zec 9:1
2 The cities of Aroer will be
deserted
and left to flocks, which will
lie down, Isa 7:21; Eze 25:5
with no one to make them
afraid. Jer 7:33; Mic 4:4
3 The fortified city will disappear
from Ephraim,
and royal power from
Damascus;
the remnant of Aram will be
like the glory of the Israelites,"
ver 4; Isa 7:8,16; 8:4; Hos 9:11
declares the LORD
Almighty.

4 "In that day the glory of Jacob
will fade;
the fat of his body will waste
away. Isa 10:16
5 It will be as when reapers
harvest the standing
grain,
gathering the grain
in their arms —
Jer 51:33; Joel 3:13; Mt 13:30
as when someone gleans heads
of grain
in the Valley of Rephaim.
1Ch 11:15
6 Yet some gleanings will
remain, Isa 24:13
as when an olive tree is
beaten, Isa 27:12
leaving two or three olives on
the topmost branches,
four or five on the fruitful
boughs,"
declares the LORD,
the God of Israel.

7 In that day people will look to
their Maker Isa 10:20
and turn their eyes to the
Holy One of Israel. Mic 7:7
8 They will not look to the
altars,
the work of their hands,
Isa 2:18,20; 30:22
and they will have no regard
for the Asherah poles[a]
Jdg 3:7; 2Ki 17:10
and the incense altars
their fingers have made.
Isa 2:8

9 In that day their strong cities,
which they left because of the Israelites, will be like places abandoned to thickets and undergrowth. And all will be desolation.
Isa 7:19

10 You have forgotten God your
Savior; Ps 68:19; Isa 12:2
you have not remembered
the Rock, your fortress.
Ps 18:2
Therefore, though you set out
the finest plants
and plant imported vines,
11 though on the day you set
them out, you make
them grow,

[a] *8* That is, wooden symbols of the goddess Asherah

and on the morning when
you plant them, you
bring them to bud, Ps 90:6
yet the harvest will be as
nothing Hos 8:7
in the day of disease and
incurable pain. Job 4:8

12 Woe to the many nations that
rage —
they rage like the raging sea!
Ps 18:4; Jer 6:23; Lk 21:25
Woe to the peoples who roar —
they roar like the roaring of
great waters!
13 Although the peoples roar
like the roar of surging
waters,
when he rebukes them they
flee far away, Ps 9:5; Isa 13:14
driven before the wind like
chaff on the hills,
Isa 41:2,15-16
like tumbleweed before a
gale. Job 21:18
14 In the evening, sudden terror!
Before the morning, they are
gone! 2Ki 19:35
This is the portion of those
who loot us,
the lot of those who
plunder us.

A Prophecy Against Cush

18 Woe to the land of whirring
wings[a]
along the rivers of Cush,[b]
Isa 20:3-5; Eze 30:4-5,9; Zep 2:12
2 which sends envoys by sea
in papyrus boats over the
water. Ex 2:3

Go, swift messengers,
to a people tall and smooth-
skinned,
to a people feared far and
wide,
an aggressive nation of strange
speech, Ge 10:8-9; 2Ch 12:3
whose land is divided by
rivers. ver 7
3 All you people of the world,
you who live on the
earth,
when a banner is raised on the
mountains, Isa 5:26
you will see it,
and when a trumpet sounds,
you will hear it.
4 This is what the LORD says
to me:
"I will remain quiet and
will look on from
my dwelling place,
Isa 26:21; Hos 5:15
like shimmering heat in the
sunshine,
like a cloud of dew in
the heat of harvest."
Isa 26:19; Hos 14:5
5 For, before the harvest,
when the blossom is
gone
and the flower becomes a
ripening grape,
he will cut off the shoots with
pruning knives,
and cut down and take away
the spreading branches.
Isa 17:10-11; Eze 17:6

[a] 1 Or *of locusts* [b] 1 That is, the upper Nile region

6 They will all be left to
the mountain birds
of prey
and to the wild animals;
Isa 56:9; Jer 7:33; Eze 32:4
the birds will feed on them all
summer,
the wild animals all winter.

7 At that time gifts will be brought
to the LORD Almighty 2Ch 9:24

from a people tall and smooth-
skinned, Ge 41:14
from a people feared far and
wide, Hab 1:7
an aggressive nation of strange
speech,
whose land is divided by
rivers —

the gifts will be brought to Mount
Zion, the place of the Name of the
LORD Almighty. Ps 68:31

A Prophecy Against Egypt

19 A prophecy against Egypt:
Ex 12:12; Jer 43:12; Joel 3:19

See, the LORD rides on a
swift cloud
Ps 18:10; 104:3; Rev 1:7
and is coming to Egypt.
The idols of Egypt tremble
before him,
and the hearts of the
Egyptians melt with
fear. Jos 2:11
2 "I will stir up Egyptian against
Egyptian —
brother will fight against
brother, Jdg 7:22; Mt 10:21,36
neighbor against neighbor,
city against city,
kingdom against kingdom.
2Ch 20:23
3 The Egyptians will lose heart,
Ps 18:45
and I will bring their plans to
nothing; 1Ch 10:13
they will consult the idols
and the spirits of the
dead,
the mediums and the
spiritists. Isa 8:19; 47:13
4 I will hand the Egyptians
over
to the power of a cruel
master,
and a fierce king will
rule over them,"
Isa 20:4; Jer 46:26; Eze 29:19
declares the Lord, the LORD
Almighty.

5 The waters of the river will
dry up, Jer 51:36
and the riverbed will be
parched and dry.
6 The canals will stink; Ex 7:18
the streams of Egypt will
dwindle and dry up.
Isa 37:25; Eze 30:12
The reeds and rushes will
wither, Isa 15:6
7 also the plants along the
Nile, Isa 23:3
at the mouth of the river.
Every sown field along the
Nile
will become parched, will
blow away and be no
more.

8 The fishermen will groan and
lament, Eze 47:10
all who cast hooks into the
Nile; Hab 1:15
those who throw nets on the
water
will pine away.
9 Those who work with combed
flax will despair,
the weavers of fine linen will
lose hope. Pr 7:16; Eze 27:7
10 The workers in cloth will be
dejected,
and all the wage earners will
be sick at heart.

11 The officials of Zoan are
nothing but fools; Nu 13:22
the wise counselors of
Pharaoh give senseless
advice. Ge 41:37
How can you say to Pharaoh,
"I am one of the wise men,
1Ki 4:30; Ac 7:22
a disciple of the ancient
kings"?
12 Where are your wise men now?
1Co 1:20
Let them show you and make
known
what the LORD Almighty
has planned against Egypt.
Isa 14:24; Ro 9:17
13 The officials of Zoan have
become fools,
the leaders of Memphis
are deceived;
Jer 2:16; Eze 30:13,16
the cornerstones of her
peoples
have led Egypt astray.
14 The LORD has poured into them
a spirit of dizziness; Mt 17:17
they make Egypt stagger in all
that she does,
as a drunkard staggers
around in his vomit.
15 There is nothing Egypt can do —
head or tail, palm branch or
reed. Isa 9:14

16 In that day the Egyptians will
become weaklings. They will shudder with fear at the uplifted hand
that the LORD Almighty raises
against them. 17 And the land of Judah will bring terror to the Egyptians; everyone to whom Judah
is mentioned will be terrified, because of what the LORD Almighty is
planning against them. Isa 11:15; 14:24
18 In that day five cities in Egypt
will speak the language of Canaan
and swear allegiance to the LORD
Almighty. One of them will be
called the City of the Sun.[a] Zep 3:9
19 In that day there will be an altar
to the LORD in the heart of Egypt,
and a monument to the LORD at its
border. 20 It will be a sign and witness to the LORD Almighty in the
land of Egypt. When they cry out
to the LORD because of their oppressors, he will send them a savior and defender, and he will rescue them. 21 So the LORD will make
himself known to the Egyptians,
and in that day they will acknowledge the LORD. They will worship

[a] *18* Some manuscripts of the Masoretic Text, Dead Sea Scrolls, Symmachus and Vulgate; most manuscripts of the Masoretic Text *City of Destruction*

with sacrifices and grain offerings;
they will make vows to the LORD
and keep them. 22The LORD will
strike Egypt with a plague; he will
strike them and heal them. They
will turn to the LORD, and he will
respond to their pleas and heal
them. Isa 45:14; 49:24-26

23In that day there will be a highway from Egypt to Assyria. The
Assyrians will go to Egypt and the
Egyptians to Assyria. The Egyptians and Assyrians will worship
together. 24In that day Israel will
be the third, along with Egypt and
Assyria, a blessing[a] on the earth.
25The LORD Almighty will bless
them, saying, "Blessed be Egypt
my people, Assyria my handiwork,
and Israel my inheritance."
Hos 2:23; Eph 2:10; Ps 100:3

A Prophecy Against Egypt and Cush

20 In the year that the supreme commander, sent
by Sargon king of Assyria, came
to Ashdod and attacked and captured it— 2at that time the LORD
spoke through Isaiah son of Amoz.
He said to him, "Take off the sackcloth from your body and the sandals from your feet." And he did
so, going around stripped and
barefoot. 1Sa 19:24; Mic 1:8; Zec 13:4

3Then the LORD said, "Just as my
servant Isaiah has gone stripped
and barefoot for three years, as a
sign and portent against Egypt and
Cush,[b] 4so the king of Assyria will
lead away stripped and barefoot
the Egyptian captives and Cushite
exiles, young and old, with buttocks bared—to Egypt's shame.
5Those who trusted in Cush and
boasted in Egypt will be dismayed
and put to shame. 6In that day the
people who live on this coast will
say, 'See what has happened to
those we relied on, those we fled to
for help and deliverance from the
king of Assyria! How then can we
escape?'" 2Ki 18:21; Jer 30:15-17; Mt 23:33

A Prophecy Against Babylon

21 A prophecy against the Desert by the Sea: Isa 13:21; Jer 51:43

Like whirlwinds sweeping
through the southland,
Zec 9:14
an invader comes from the
desert,
from a land of terror.

2A dire vision has been shown
to me: Ps 60:3
The traitor betrays, the
looter takes loot. Isa 33:1
Elam, attack! Media, lay siege!
Jer 49:34
I will bring to an end all the
groaning she caused.

3At this my body is racked with
pain,
pangs seize me, like those
of a woman in labor;
Ps 48:6; Isa 26:17
I am staggered by what I hear,
I am bewildered by what I see.

[a] 24 Or *Assyria, whose names will be used in blessings* (see Gen. 48:20); or *Assyria, who will be seen by others as blessed* [b] 3 That is, the upper Nile region; also in verse 5

4 My heart falters,
fear makes me tremble; Isa 13:8
the twilight I longed for
has become a horror to me. Ps 55:5

5 They set the tables,
they spread the rugs,
they eat, they drink! Jer 51:39,57; Da 5:2
Get up, you officers,
oil the shields! 2Sa 1:21; 1Ki 10:16-17

6 This is what the Lord says to me:

"Go, post a lookout 2Ki 9:17
and have him report what he sees.
7 When he sees chariots ver 9
with teams of horses,
riders on donkeys
or riders on camels,
let him be alert,
fully alert."

8 And the lookout[a] shouted, Hab 2:1

"Day after day, my lord, I stand
on the watchtower;
every night I stay at my post.
9 Look, here comes a man in a chariot
with a team of horses.
And he gives back the answer:
'Babylon has fallen, has fallen! Jer 51:8; Rev 14:8; 18:2
All the images of its gods Isa 46:1; Jer 50:2; 51:44
lie shattered on the ground!'"
10 My people who are crushed
on the threshing floor, Jer 51:33
I tell you what I have heard
from the LORD Almighty,
from the God of Israel.

A Prophecy Against Edom

11 A prophecy against Dumah[b]: Ge 25:14

Someone calls to me from Seir, Ge 32:3
"Watchman, what is left of the night?
Watchman, what is left of the night?"
12 The watchman replies,
"Morning is coming, but also the night.
If you would ask, then ask;
and come back yet again."

A Prophecy Against Arabia

13 A prophecy against Arabia: Isa 13:1

You caravans of Dedanites,
who camp in the thickets of Arabia,
14 bring water for the thirsty;
you who live in Tema, Ge 25:15
bring food for the fugitives.
15 They flee from the sword, Isa 13:14
from the drawn sword,
from the bent bow
and from the heat of battle.

[a] 8 Dead Sea Scrolls and Syriac; Masoretic Text *A lion* [b] 11 *Dumah*, a wordplay on *Edom*, means *silence* or *stillness*.

16This is what the Lord says to
me: "Within one year, as a servant
bound by contract would count
it, all the splendor of Kedar will
come to an end. 17The survivors of
the archers, the warriors of Kedar,
will be few." The LORD, the God of
Israel, has spoken.

Ps 120:5; Isa 16:14; 60:7

A Prophecy About Jerusalem

22 A prophecy against the Valley of Vision:

Isa 13:1; Joel 3:2,12,14

What troubles you now,
that you have all gone up on the roofs,
2you town so full of commotion,
you city of tumult and revelry? Isa 32:13
Your slain were not killed by the sword,
2Ki 25:3; Isa 10:4
nor did they die in battle.
3All your leaders have fled together;
they have been captured without using the bow.
2Ki 25:6
All you who were caught were taken prisoner together,
having fled while the enemy was still far away.
4Therefore I said, "Turn away from me;
let me weep bitterly.
Isa 15:3; Lk 19:41
Do not try to console me
over the destruction of my people." Jer 9:1

5The Lord, the LORD Almighty, has a day Isa 2:12
of tumult and trampling and terror La 1:5; Zep 1:15
in the Valley of Vision,
a day of battering down walls
Jer 39:8; Eze 13:14
and of crying out to the mountains.
6Elam takes up the quiver,
Isa 21:2; Jer 49:35
with her charioteers and horses;
Kir uncovers the shield.
2Ki 16:9
7Your choicest valleys are full of chariots,
and horsemen are posted at the city gates. 2Ch 32:1-2

8The Lord stripped away the defenses of Judah,
and you looked in that day
to the weapons in the Palace of the Forest.
1Ki 7:2; 2Ch 32:5
9You saw that the walls of the City of David
were broken through in many places;
you stored up water
in the Lower Pool. 2Ch 32:4
10You counted the buildings in Jerusalem
and tore down houses to strengthen the wall.
2Ch 32:5

[11]You built a reservoir
between the two walls
2Ki 25:4; Jer 39:4
for the water of the Old Pool,
2Ch 32:4
but you did not look to the One
who made it,
or have regard for the One
who planned it long ago.
2Ki 19:25

[12]The Lord, the LORD Almighty,
called you on that day
to weep and to wail, Joel 2:17
to tear out your hair and put
on sackcloth. Joel 1:13; Mic 1:16
[13]But see, there is joy and revelry,
slaughtering of cattle and
killing of sheep,
eating of meat and drinking
of wine! Isa 56:12; Lk 17:26-29
"Let us eat and drink," you say,
"for tomorrow we die!"
1Co 15:32*

[14]The LORD Almighty has revealed this in my hearing: "Till your dying day this sin will not be atoned for," says the Lord, the LORD Almighty. Isa 5:9; 13:11; 26:21

[15]This is what the Lord, the LORD Almighty, says:

"Go, say to this steward,
to Shebna the palace
administrator:
2Ki 18:18; Isa 36:3
[16]What are you doing here
and who gave you
permission
to cut out a grave for yourself
here, Mt 27:60
hewing your grave on the
height
and chiseling your resting
place in the rock?
[17]"Beware, the LORD is about to
take firm hold of you
and hurl you away, you
mighty man.
[18]He will roll you up tightly like a
ball
and throw you into a large
country. Isa 17:13
There you will die
and there the chariots you
were so proud of
will become a disgrace to
your master's house.
[19]I will depose you from your
office,
and you will be ousted
from your position.
1Sa 2:7; Lk 16:3

[20]"In that day I will summon
my servant, Eliakim son of Hilkiah. [21]I will clothe him with your
robe and fasten your sash around
him and hand your authority over
to him. He will be a father to those
who live in Jerusalem and to the
people of Judah. [22]I will place on
his shoulder the key to the house
of David; what he opens no one
can shut, and what he shuts no
one can open. [23]I will drive him
like a peg into a firm place; he will
become a seat[a] of honor for the
house of his father. [24]All the glory
of his family will hang on him: its

[a] 23 Or *throne*

offspring and offshoots — all its lesser vessels, from the bowls to all the jars. Job 36:7; Ezr 9:8; Rev 3:7

25 "In that day," declares the LORD Almighty, "the peg driven into the firm place will give way; it will be sheared off and will fall, and the load hanging on it will be cut down." The LORD has spoken. ver 23; Isa 46:11; Mic 4:4

A Prophecy Against Tyre

23 A prophecy against Tyre: Jer 47:4; Zec 9:2-4

Wail, you ships of Tarshish! Ge 10:4; 1Ki 10:22; Isa 2:16 *fn*
For Tyre is destroyed
and left without house or harbor.
From the land of Cyprus
word has come to them.

2 Be silent, you people of the island
and you merchants of Sidon, Jdg 1:31; Eze 27:5-24
whom the seafarers have enriched.
3 On the great waters
came the grain of the Shihor;
the harvest of the Nile[a] was the revenue of Tyre, Isa 19:7; Eze 27:3
and she became the marketplace of the nations.

4 Be ashamed, Sidon, and you fortress of the sea, Ge 10:15,19
for the sea has spoken:
"I have neither been in labor
nor given birth;
I have neither reared
sons nor brought up daughters."
5 When word comes to Egypt,
they will be in anguish at the report from Tyre. Eze 26:17-18

6 Cross over to Tarshish;
wail, you people of the island.
7 Is this your city of revelry, Isa 22:2; 32:13
the old, old city,
whose feet have taken her
to settle in far-off lands?
8 Who planned this against Tyre,
the bestower of crowns,
whose merchants are princes,
whose traders are renowned in the earth? Eze 28:5; Rev 18:23
9 The LORD Almighty planned it,
to bring down her pride
in all her splendor Job 40:11
and to humble all who are
renowned on the earth. Isa 5:13; 13:11

10 Till[b] your land as they do along the Nile,
Daughter Tarshish,
for you no longer have a harbor.

[a] 2,3 Masoretic Text; Dead Sea Scrolls *Sidon, / who cross over the sea; / your envoys 3are on the great waters. / The grain of the Shihor, / the harvest of the Nile,*
[b] 10 Dead Sea Scrolls and some Septuagint manuscripts; Masoretic Text *Go through*

[11]The LORD has stretched out
his hand over the sea
Ex 14:21
and made its kingdoms
tremble. Ps 46:6
He has given an order
concerning Phoenicia
that her fortresses be
destroyed. Isa 25:2; Zec 9:3-4
[12]He said, "No more of your
reveling, Rev 18:22
Virgin Daughter Sidon, now
crushed! Isa 47:1

"Up, cross over to Cyprus;
even there you will find no
rest."
[13]Look at the land of the
Babylonians,[a]
this people that is now of no
account!
The Assyrians have made it
Isa 10:5
a place for desert
creatures;
they raised up their siege
towers,
they stripped its fortresses
bare
and turned it into a ruin.
Isa 10:7
[14]Wail, you ships of Tarshish;
Isa 2:16 *fn*
your fortress is destroyed!

[15]At that time Tyre will be forgotten for seventy years, the span of a king's life. But at the end of these seventy years, it will happen to Tyre as in the song of the prostitute: Jer 25:22

[16]"Take up a harp, walk through
the city,
you forgotten prostitute;
play the harp well, sing many a
song,
so that you will be
remembered."

[17]At the end of seventy years, the LORD will deal with Tyre. She will return to her lucrative prostitution and will ply her trade with all the kingdoms on the face of the earth.
[18]Yet her profit and her earnings will be set apart for the LORD; they will not be stored up or hoarded. Her profits will go to those who live before the LORD, for abundant food and fine clothes.
Isa 60:5-9; Eze 16:26; Rev 17:1

The LORD's Devastation of the Earth

24 See, the LORD is going
to lay waste the earth
Isa 2:19-21; 33:9
and devastate it;
he will ruin its face
and scatter its
inhabitants —
[2]it will be the same
for priest as for people, Hos 4:9
for the master as for his
servant,
for the mistress as for her
servant,
for seller as for buyer, Eze 7:12
for borrower as for lender,
for debtor as for creditor.
Lev 25:35-37; Dt 23:19-20

[a] 13 Or *Chaldeans*

3 The earth will be completely
laid waste
and totally plundered. Isa 6:11-12
The LORD has spoken
this word.

4 The earth dries up and
withers,
the world languishes and
withers,
the heavens languish with
the earth. Isa 2:12
5 The earth is defiled by its
people; Ge 3:17; Nu 35:33
they have disobeyed the
laws, Isa 10:6; 59:12
violated the statutes
and broken the everlasting
covenant.
6 Therefore a curse consumes
the earth;
its people must bear their
guilt.
Therefore earth's inhabitants
are burned up, Isa 1:31
and very few are left.
7 The new wine dries up
and the vine withers;
Joel 1:10-12
all the merrymakers groan.
Isa 16:8-10
8 The joyful timbrels are stilled,
Isa 5:12
the noise of the revelers has
stopped, Hos 2:11
the joyful harp is silent.
Eze 26:13; Rev 18:22
9 No longer do they drink wine
with a song; Isa 5:11,22
the beer is bitter to its
drinkers. Isa 5:20
10 The ruined city lies desolate;
Isa 6:11
the entrance to every house
is barred.
11 In the streets they cry out for
wine;
all joy turns to gloom,
Isa 16:10; 32:13; Jer 14:3
all joyful sounds are
banished from the earth.
12 The city is left in ruins, Isa 19:18
its gate is battered to pieces.
Isa 3:26
13 So will it be on the earth
and among the nations,
as when an olive tree is beaten,
Isa 17:6
or as when gleanings are left
after the grape harvest.
14 They raise their voices, they
shout for joy; Isa 12:6
from the west they acclaim
the LORD's majesty.
15 Therefore in the east give glory
to the LORD; Isa 66:19
exalt the name of the LORD,
the God of Israel, Mal 1:11
in the islands of the sea.
16 From the ends of the earth
we hear singing:
Ps 48:10; 65:8
"Glory to the Righteous One."
Isa 28:5

But I said, "I waste away, I
waste away!
Woe to me!
The treacherous betray!
With treachery the
treacherous betray!"
Isa 21:2; Jer 5:11

17 Terror and pit and snare await
you, Jer 48:43
people of the earth. Lk 21:35
18 Whoever flees at the sound of
terror Job 20:24
will fall into a pit;
whoever climbs out of the pit
will be caught in a snare.

The floodgates of the heavens
are opened, Ge 7:11
the foundations of the earth
shake. Ps 18:7
19 The earth is broken up,
the earth is split asunder,
Dt 11:6
the earth is violently
shaken.
20 The earth reels like a drunkard,
Isa 19:14
it sways like a hut in the
wind;
so heavy upon it is the guilt
of its rebellion
Isa 1:2,28; 43:27
that it falls — never to rise
again. Ps 46:2

21 In that day the LORD will
punish Isa 10:12
the powers in the heavens
above
and the kings on the earth
below. Isa 2:12
22 They will be herded together
like prisoners bound
in a dungeon;
Isa 10:4; 42:7,22
they will be shut up in
prison
and be punished[a] after many
days. Eze 38:8
23 The moon will be dismayed,
the sun ashamed; Isa 13:10
for the LORD Almighty will
reign Rev 22:5
on Mount Zion and in
Jerusalem, Heb 12:22
and before its elders — with
great glory. Isa 60:19

Praise to the LORD

25 LORD, you are my God; Isa 7:13
I will exalt you and praise
your name, Ps 145:2
for in perfect faithfulness Isa 11:5
you have done wonderful
things, Ps 98:1
things planned long ago.
Nu 23:19; Eph 1:11
2 You have made the city a heap
of rubble, Isa 17:1
the fortified town a ruin,
Isa 17:3
the foreigners' stronghold a
city no more; Isa 13:22
it will never be rebuilt.
3 Therefore strong peoples
will honor you;
Ex 6:2; Ps 22:23
cities of ruthless nations will
revere you. Isa 13:11
4 You have been a refuge for the
poor, Isa 4:6; 17:10
a refuge for the needy in
their distress, Isa 14:30
a shelter from the storm Ps 55:8
and a shade from the heat.
For the breath of the ruthless
Isa 29:5; 49:25
is like a storm driving
against a wall

[a] 22 Or *released*

5 and like the heat of the
desert.
You silence the uproar of
foreigners; Jer 51:55
as heat is reduced by the
shadow of a cloud,
so the song of the ruthless is
stilled.

6 On this mountain the LORD
Almighty will prepare
Isa 2:2
a feast of rich food for all
peoples, Mt 8:11; 22:4
a banquet of aged wine —
the best of meats and the
finest of wines. Pr 9:2
7 On this mountain he will
destroy
the shroud that enfolds all
peoples, 2Co 3:15-16; Eph 4:18
the sheet that covers all
nations;
8 he will swallow up death
forever. Hos 13:14; 1Co 15:54-55*
The Sovereign LORD will wipe
away the tears Rev 7:17; 21:4
from all faces;
he will remove his people's
disgrace Mt 5:11; 1Pe 4:14
from all the earth.
The LORD has spoken.

9 In that day they will say,

"Surely this is our God; Isa 40:9
we trusted in him, and he
saved us. Ps 20:5; Isa 33:22
This is the LORD, we trusted in
him;
let us rejoice and be glad in
his salvation." Isa 35:2,10

10 The hand of the LORD will rest
on this mountain; Isa 2:2
but Moab will be trampled in
their land Am 2:1-3
as straw is trampled down in
the manure.
11 They will stretch out their
hands in it,
as swimmers stretch out
their hands to swim.
God will bring down their pride
Job 40:12; Isa 5:25
despite the cleverness[a] of
their hands.
12 He will bring down your high
fortified walls
and lay them low; Isa 15:1
he will bring them down to the
ground,
to the very dust.

A Song of Praise

26 In that day this song will be
sung in the land of Judah:

We have a strong city; Isa 14:32
God makes salvation
its walls and ramparts.
Isa 60:18; Zec 2:5
2 Open the gates
that the righteous nation
may enter, Isa 54:14; 58:8
the nation that keeps faith.
3 You will keep in perfect peace
Php 4:7
those whose minds are
steadfast,
because they trust in you.
Ps 22:5; Isa 12:2

[a] *11* The meaning of the Hebrew for this word is uncertain.

[4]Trust in the LORD forever,
Isa 12:2; 50:10
for the LORD, the LORD
himself, is the Rock
eternal. Ge 49:24
[5]He humbles those who dwell
on high,
he lays the lofty city low;
he levels it to the ground Isa 25:12
and casts it down to the dust.
[6]Feet trample it down —
the feet of the oppressed,
the footsteps of the poor.
Isa 3:15

[7]The path of the righteous is
level;
you, the Upright One, make
the way of the righteous
smooth. Isa 42:16
[8]Yes, LORD, walking in the way
of your laws,[a] Isa 56:1
we wait for you; Ps 37:9
your name and renown Isa 12:4
are the desire of our hearts.
[9]My soul yearns for you in the
night;
in the morning my
spirit longs for you.
Ps 63:1; 78:34; Isa 55:6
When your judgments come
upon the earth,
the people of the world learn
righteousness. Mt 6:33
[10]But when grace is shown to the
wicked,
they do not learn
righteousness;
even in a land of uprightness
they go on doing evil
Isa 32:6

and do not regard the
majesty of the LORD.
Isa 22:12-13; Hos 11:7; Jn 5:37-38
[11]LORD, your hand is lifted
high,
but they do not see it. Isa 44:9,18
Let them see your zeal for your
people and be put to
shame;
let the fire reserved for your
enemies consume them.
Heb 10:27

[12]LORD, you establish peace
for us; Ps 119:165; Isa 9:6
all that we have
accomplished you have
done for us. Ps 68:28
[13]LORD our God, other lords
besides you have ruled
over us, Isa 2:8; 10:5,11
but your name alone do we
honor. Isa 63:7
[14]They are now dead, they live
no more; Dt 4:28
their spirits do not rise.
You punished them and
brought them to ruin;
Isa 10:3
you wiped out all memory of
them.
[15]You have enlarged the nation,
LORD;
you have enlarged the
nation. Isa 14:2
You have gained glory for
yourself;
you have extended all the
borders of the land.
Isa 33:17

[a] 8 Or *judgments*

16 LORD, they came to you in their
distress; Hos 5:15
when you disciplined them,
they could barely whisper a
prayer.[a]
17 As a pregnant woman about to
give birth Jn 16:21
writhes and cries out in her
pain,
so were we in your presence,
LORD.
18 We were with child, we writhed
in labor,
but we gave birth to wind.
Isa 33:11; 59:4
We have not brought
salvation to the earth,
Ps 17:14
and the people of the world
have not come to life.
Isa 42:6
19 But your dead will live, LORD;
Isa 25:8; Eph 5:14
their bodies will rise —
let those who dwell in the dust
Ps 22:29
wake up and shout for
joy —
your dew is like the dew of the
morning;
the earth will give birth to
her dead. Eze 37:1-14; Da 12:2

20 Go, my people, enter your
rooms
and shut the doors behind
you; Ex 12:23
hide yourselves for a little
while Ps 91:1,4
until his wrath has passed by.
Ps 30:5; Isa 54:7-8
21 See, the LORD is coming out of
his dwelling Mic 1:3; Jude 1:14
to punish the people of the
earth for their sins.
Isa 13:9,11; 30:12-14
The earth will disclose the
blood shed on it;
Job 16:18; Lk 11:50-51
the earth will conceal its
slain no longer.

Deliverance of Israel

27 In that day,

the LORD will punish with his
sword — Isa 34:6; 66:16
his fierce, great and powerful
sword —
Leviathan the gliding serpent,
Job 3:8
Leviathan the coiling serpent;
he will slay the monster of the
sea. Ps 74:13; Rev 12:9
2 In that day —

"Sing about a fruitful vineyard:
Jer 2:21
3 I, the LORD, watch over it;
I water it continually. Isa 58:11
I guard it day and night Ps 91:4
so that no one may harm it.
Jn 6:39
4 I am not angry.
If only there were briers and
thorns confronting me!
I would march against them
in battle;
I would set them all on fire.
Isa 10:17; Mt 3:12; Heb 6:8

[a] *16* The meaning of the Hebrew for this clause is uncertain.

5 Or else let them come to me for
refuge; Isa 25:4
let them make peace
with me,
Job 22:21; Ro 5:1; 2Co 5:20
yes, let them make peace
with me."
6 In days to come Jacob will take
root, Isa 11:10
Israel will bud and blossom
Hos 14:5-6
and fill all the world with
fruit. Isa 37:31

7 Has the LORD struck her
as he struck down those who
struck her? Isa 37:36-38
Has she been killed
as those were killed who
killed her?
8 By warfare[a] and exile you
contend with her —
Isa 50:1; 54:7
with his fierce blast he drives
her out,
as on a day the east wind
blows.
9 By this, then, will Jacob's guilt
be atoned for, Ps 78:38
and this will be the full fruit
of the removal of his sin:
Ro 11:27*
When he makes all the altar
stones
to be like limestone crushed
to pieces,
no Asherah poles[b] or incense
altars Ex 34:13
will be left standing.
10 The fortified city stands
desolate, Isa 32:14; Jer 26:6
an abandoned settlement,
forsaken like the
wilderness; Isa 5:5
there the calves graze,
there they lie down; Isa 17:2
they strip its branches bare.
11 When its twigs are dry, they are
broken off
and women come and make
fires with them.
For this is a people without
understanding;
Dt 32:28; Isa 1:3; Jer 8:7
so their Maker has no
compassion on them,
and their Creator shows
them no favor.
Dt 32:18; Isa 43:1,7,15

12 In that day the LORD will thresh
from the flowing Euphrates to the
Wadi of Egypt, and you, Israel, will
be gathered up one by one. 13 And
in that day a great trumpet will
sound. Those who were perishing
in Assyria and those who were exiled in Egypt will come and worship the LORD on the holy mountain in Jerusalem.
Isa 2:2; Lev 25:9; Mt 24:31

Woe to the Leaders of Ephraim and Judah

28 Woe to that wreath, the
pride of Ephraim's
drunkards, ver 3; Isa 9:9
to the fading flower, his
glorious beauty,

[a] 8 See Septuagint; the meaning of the Hebrew for this word is uncertain.
[b] 9 That is, wooden symbols of the goddess Asherah

set on the head of a fertile
valley — ver 4
to that city, the pride of
those laid low by wine! Hos 7:5
2 See, the Lord has one who is
powerful and strong. Isa 40:10
Like a hailstorm and a
destructive wind, Isa 29:6; 30:30; Eze 13:11
like a driving rain and
a flooding downpour, Isa 8:7
he will throw it forcefully to
the ground.
3 That wreath, the pride of
Ephraim's drunkards,
will be trampled underfoot. Job 40:12; Isa 5:5
4 That fading flower, his glorious
beauty,
set on the head of a fertile
valley,
will be like figs ripe before
harvest — Hos 9:10; Na 3:12
as soon as people see
them and take them in
hand,
they swallow them.
5 In that day the LORD Almighty
will be a glorious crown, Isa 62:3
a beautiful wreath
for the remnant of his
people. Isa 1:9
6 He will be a spirit of justice Isa 11:2-4
to the one who sits in
judgment, Jn 5:30
a source of strength
to those who turn back the
battle at the gate. 2Ch 32:8
7 And these also stagger from
wine Isa 22:13
and reel from beer: Isa 56:10-12
Priests and prophets stagger
from beer Isa 9:15; 24:2
and are befuddled with wine;
they reel from beer,
they stagger when seeing
visions, Isa 29:11; Hos 4:11
they stumble when
rendering decisions.
8 All the tables are covered with
vomit Jer 48:26
and there is not a spot
without filth.
9 "Who is it he is trying to teach? ver 26; Isa 30:20
To whom is he explaining his
message? Isa 53:1
To children weaned from their
milk, Ps 131:2; Heb 5:12-13
to those just taken from the
breast?
10 For it is:
Do this, do that,
a rule for this, a rule for
that[a];
a little here, a little there."
11 Very well then, with foreign
lips and strange tongues Isa 33:19
God will speak to this people, 1Co 14:21*

[a] 10 Hebrew / *sav lasav sav lasav / kav lakav kav lakav* (probably meaningless sounds mimicking the prophet's words); also in verse 13

12 to whom he said,
"This is the resting
place, let the
weary rest"; Mt 11:28-29; Isa 11:10
and, "This is the place of
repose" —
but they would not
listen.
13 So then, the word of the
LORD to them will
become:
Do this, do that,
a rule for this, a rule for
that;
a little here, a little there —
so that as they go they will fall
backward;
they will be injured and
snared and captured. Mt 21:44; Isa 8:15

14 Therefore hear the word
of the LORD, you scoffers Isa 1:10
who rule this people in
Jerusalem.
15 You boast, "We have entered
into a covenant with
death,
with the realm of the dead
we have made an
agreement.
When an overwhelming
scourge sweeps by, ver 2,18; Isa 8:7-8; Da 11:22
it cannot touch us,
for we have made a lie our
refuge Isa 9:15
and falsehood[a] our hiding
place." Isa 29:15

16 So this is what the Sovereign
LORD says:

"See, I lay a stone in Zion,
a tested stone, Ps 118:22; Ac 4:11; Eph 2:20
a precious cornerstone for
a sure foundation; Jer 51:26; 1Co 3:11
the one who relies on it
will never be stricken
with panic. Ro 9:33*; 10:11*; 1Pe 2:6*
17 I will make justice the
measuring line Isa 5:16
and righteousness the plumb
line; 2Ki 21:13
hail will sweep away your
refuge, the lie,
and water will overflow your
hiding place.
18 Your covenant with death will
be annulled;
your agreement with the
realm of the dead will
not stand. Isa 7:7
When the overwhelming
scourge sweeps by, ver 15
you will be beaten down
by it. Da 8:13
19 As often as it comes it will carry
you away; 2Ki 24:2
morning after morning, by
day and by night,
it will sweep through."

The understanding of this
message
will bring sheer terror. Job 18:11

[a] 15 Or *false gods*

20 The bed is too short to stretch
out on,
the blanket too narrow to
wrap around you. Isa 59:6
21 The LORD will rise up as he did
at Mount Perazim, 1Ch 14:11
he will rouse himself as in
the Valley of Gibeon —
Jos 10:10,12; 1Ch 14:16
to do his work, his strange
work, Isa 10:12; Lk 19:41-44
and perform his task, his
alien task.
22 Now stop your mocking,
or your chains will become
heavier;
the Lord, the LORD Almighty,
has told me
of the destruction decreed
against the whole land.
Isa 10:22-23
23 Listen and hear my voice; Isa 32:9
pay attention and hear what
I say.
24 When a farmer plows for
planting, does he plow
continually? Ecc 3:2
Does he keep on breaking up
and working the soil?
25 When he has leveled the
surface,
does he not sow caraway and
scatter cumin? Mt 23:23
Does he not plant wheat in its
place,[a]
barley in its plot,[a]
and spelt in its field? Ex 9:32
26 His God instructs him
and teaches him the right
way. Ps 94:10
27 Caraway is not threshed with a
sledge, Job 41:30
nor is the wheel of a cart
rolled over cumin;
caraway is beaten out with
a rod, Isa 10:5
and cumin with a stick.
28 Grain must be ground to make
bread;
so one does not go on
threshing it forever.
The wheels of a threshing cart
may be rolled over it,
Isa 21:10
but one does not use horses
to grind grain.
29 All this also comes from the
LORD Almighty,
whose plan is wonderful,
whose wisdom is
magnificent. Isa 9:6; Ro 11:33

Woe to David's City

29 Woe to you, Ariel, Ariel,
2Sa 5:9; Isa 22:12-13
the city where David settled!
2Sa 5:7
Add year to year
and let your cycle of festivals
go on. Isa 1:14
2 Yet I will besiege Ariel;
she will mourn and lament,
Isa 3:26; La 2:5
she will be to me like an altar
hearth.[b]
3 I will encamp against you on
all sides;

[a] 25 The meaning of the Hebrew for this word is uncertain. [b] 2 The Hebrew for *altar hearth* sounds like the Hebrew for *Ariel*.

I will encircle you with
towers Lk 19:43-44
and set up my siege works
against you. 2Ki 25:1
4 Brought low, you will speak
from the ground;
your speech will mumble out
of the dust. Isa 8:19
Your voice will come ghostlike
from the earth;
out of the dust your speech
will whisper. Isa 26:16

5 But your many enemies
will become like fine
dust,
the ruthless hordes like
blown chaff. Isa 17:13
Suddenly, in an instant,
Isa 17:14; 1Th 5:3
6 the LORD Almighty will come
Zec 14:1-5
with thunder and earthquake
and great noise,
Mt 24:7; Rev 11:19
with windstorm and
tempest and flames of a
devouring fire. Ps 83:13-15
7 Then the hordes of all
the nations that
fight against Ariel,
Mic 4:11-12; Zec 12:9
that attack her and her
fortress and besiege her,
will be as it is with a dream,
Job 20:8
with a vision in the night —
8 as when a hungry person
dreams of eating,
but awakens hungry still;
Ps 73:20
as when a thirsty person
dreams of drinking,
but awakens faint and
thirsty still.
So will it be with the
hordes of all the
nations
that fight against Mount
Zion. Isa 17:12-14; 54:17

9 Be stunned and amazed,
Jer 4:9; Hab 1:5
blind yourselves and be
sightless; Isa 6:10
be drunk, but not from wine,
Isa 51:21-22
stagger, but not from beer.
Isa 3:12
10 The LORD has brought over you
a deep sleep:
He has sealed your eyes
(the prophets);
Ps 69:23; Isa 6:9-10; Ro 11:8*
he has covered your heads
(the seers). 1Sa 9:9

11 For you this whole vision is
nothing but words sealed in a
scroll. And if you give the scroll
to someone who can read, and
say, “Read this, please,” they will
answer, “I can’t; it is sealed.” 12 Or
if you give the scroll to someone
who cannot read, and say, “Read
this, please,” they will answer, “I
don’t know how to read.”
Isa 8:16; Mt 13:11; Rev 5:1-2

13 The Lord says:

“These people come near to
me with their mouth
Jer 14:11; Hag 1:2

and honor me with their lips, Ps 50:16
but their hearts are far from me. Eze 33:31
Their worship of me
is based on merely human rules they have been taught.[a] Mt 15:8-9*; Col 2:22
14 Therefore once more I will astound these people
with wonder upon wonder; Hab 1:5
the wisdom of the wise will perish, Jer 49:7
the intelligence of the intelligent will vanish." 1Co 1:19*
15 Woe to those who go to great depths
to hide their plans from the LORD, Isa 28:15
who do their work in darkness and think,
"Who sees us? Who will know?" Job 22:13; Ps 94:7; Isa 57:12
16 You turn things upside down,
as if the potter were thought to be like the clay! Job 10:9
Shall what is formed say to the one who formed it, Ge 2:7
"You did not make me"?
Can the pot say to the potter, Isa 45:9; Ro 9:20-21*
"You know nothing"? Job 9:12
17 In a very short time, will not Lebanon be turned into a fertile field Ps 84:6
and the fertile field seem like a forest? Isa 32:15
18 In that day the deaf will hear the words of the scroll, Mk 7:37
and out of gloom and darkness
the eyes of the blind will see. Isa 35:5; Mt 11:5
19 Once more the humble will rejoice in the LORD; Isa 61:1; Mt 5:5; 11:29
the needy will rejoice in the Holy One of Israel. Jas 2:5; Isa 14:30
20 The ruthless will vanish,
the mockers will disappear, Isa 28:22
and all who have an eye for evil will be cut down — Isa 59:4; Mic 2:1
21 those who with a word make someone out to be guilty,
who ensnare the defender in court Am 5:10,15
and with false testimony deprive the innocent of justice. Isa 32:7

22 Therefore this is what the LORD, who redeemed Abraham, says to the descendants of Jacob: Isa 41:8

"No longer will Jacob be ashamed; Isa 49:23
no longer will their faces grow pale. Jer 30:6,10

[a] 13 Hebrew; Septuagint *They worship me in vain; / their teachings are merely human rules*

23 When they see among
them their children, Isa 49:20-26
the work of my hands, Isa 19:25
they will keep my name holy; Mt 6:9
they will acknowledge the
holiness of the Holy One
of Jacob, Isa 5:19
and will stand in awe of the
God of Israel.
24 Those who are wayward
in spirit will gain
understanding; Isa 28:7; Heb 5:2; Isa 41:20
those who complain will
accept instruction." Isa 30:21

Woe to the Obstinate Nation

30 "Woe to the obstinate
children," Isa 29:15
declares the LORD,
"to those who carry out plans
that are not mine,
forming an alliance, but not
by my Spirit, Isa 8:12
heaping sin upon sin;
2 who go down to Egypt Isa 31:1
without consulting me; Nu 27:21
who look for help to Pharaoh's
protection, Isa 36:9
to Egypt's shade for refuge.
3 But Pharaoh's protection will
be to your shame,
Egypt's shade will bring you
disgrace. Isa 20:4-5; 36:6
4 Though they have officials in
Zoan Isa 19:11
and their envoys have
arrived in Hanes,
5 everyone will be put to
shame
because of a people
useless to them, ver 7; 2Ki 18:21
who bring neither help nor
advantage, Jer 37:3-5
but only shame and
disgrace." 2Ki 18:21

6 A prophecy concerning the animals of the Negev: Isa 13:1

Through a land of hardship
and distress, Ex 5:10,21; Isa 8:22; Jer 11:4
of lions and lionesses,
of adders and darting snakes, Dt 8:15
the envoys carry their riches on
donkeys' backs, 1Sa 25:18
their treasures on the humps
of camels, Isa 15:7
to that unprofitable nation,
7 to Egypt, whose help is
utterly useless. 2Ki 18:21
Therefore I call her
Rahab the Do-Nothing. Job 9:13
8 Go now, write it on a tablet for
them, Dt 27:8
inscribe it on a scroll, Isa 8:1; Hab 2:2
that for the days to come
it may be an everlasting
witness. Jos 24:26-27
9 For these are rebellious people,
deceitful children, Isa 28:15; 59:3-4
children unwilling to
listen to the LORD's
instruction. Isa 1:10

10 They say to the seers,
"See no more visions!" Jer 11:21; Am 7:13
and to the prophets,
"Give us no more visions of what is right!
Tell us pleasant things, 1Ki 22:8
prophesy illusions. Eze 13:7; Ro 16:18
11 Leave this way, ver 21; Pr 3:6
get off this path,
and stop confronting us Job 21:14
with the Holy One of Israel!" Isa 29:19

12 Therefore this is what the Holy One of Israel says: Isa 5:19

"Because you have rejected this message, Isa 5:24
relied on oppression Isa 5:7
and depended on deceit,
13 this sin will become for you
like a high wall, cracked and bulging, Ps 62:3
that collapses suddenly, in an instant. 1Ki 20:30; Isa 29:5
14 It will break in pieces like pottery, Ps 2:9; Jer 19:10-11
shattered so mercilessly
that among its pieces not a fragment will be found
for taking coals from a hearth
or scooping water out of a cistern."

15 This is what the Sovereign LORD, the Holy One of Israel, says:

"In repentance and rest is your salvation, Ex 14:14; Jos 1:13
in quietness and trust is your strength, Isa 32:17; 2Ch 20:12
but you would have none of it. Isa 8:6; 42:24
16 You said, 'No, we will flee on horses.' Isa 31:1,3
Therefore you will flee!
You said, 'We will ride off on swift horses.'
Therefore your pursuers will be swift!
17 A thousand will flee
at the threat of one;
at the threat of five Lev 26:8; Jos 23:10
you will all flee away, Dt 28:25
till you are left Isa 1:8
like a flagstaff on a mountaintop,
like a banner on a hill." Ps 20:5

18 Yet the LORD longs to be gracious to you; Isa 42:14; 2Pe 3:9,15
therefore he will rise up to show you compassion. Ps 78:38; Jnh 3:10
For the LORD is a God of justice. Isa 5:16
Blessed are all who wait for him! Isa 25:9; La 3:25

19 People of Zion, who live in Jerusalem, you will weep no more.
How gracious he will be when you
cry for help! As soon as he hears,
he will answer you. 20 Although
the Lord gives you the bread of
adversity and the water of affliction, your teachers will be hidden
no more; with your own eyes you

will see them. 21 Whether you turn
to the right or to the left, your ears
will hear a voice behind you, saying, "This is the way; walk in it."
22 Then you will desecrate your
idols overlaid with silver and your
images covered with gold; you will
throw them away like a menstrual
cloth and say to them, "Away with
you!" Ps 74:9; Isa 29:24; Am 8:11

23 He will also send you rain for
the seed you sow in the ground,
and the food that comes from the
land will be rich and plentiful. In
that day your cattle will graze in
broad meadows. 24 The oxen and
donkeys that work the soil will eat
fodder and mash, spread out with
fork and shovel. 25 In the day of
great slaughter, when the towers
fall, streams of water will flow on
every high mountain and every
lofty hill. 26 The moon will shine
like the sun, and the sunlight will
be seven times brighter, like the
light of seven full days, when the
LORD binds up the bruises of his
people and heals the wounds he
inflicted. Isa 1:5; 60:19-20; Rev 21:23

27 See, the Name of the LORD
comes from afar, Isa 59:19
with burning anger and
dense clouds of smoke; Isa 66:14
his lips are full of wrath, Isa 10:5
and his tongue is a
consuming fire. Job 41:21
28 His breath is like a rushing
torrent, Isa 11:4
rising up to the neck. Isa 8:8
He shakes the nations in the
sieve of destruction; Am 9:9
he places in the jaws of the
peoples
a bit that leads them astray. 2Ki 19:28; Isa 37:29
29 And you will sing
as on the night you
celebrate a holy festival; Isa 25:6
your hearts will rejoice Isa 12:1
as when people playing pipes
go up
to the mountain of the LORD, Ps 42:4
to the Rock of Israel. Ge 49:24
30 The LORD will cause people to
hear his majestic voice Ps 68:33
and will make them see
his arm coming down Isa 9:12; 40:10
with raging anger and
consuming fire, Isa 10:25
with cloudburst,
thunderstorm and hail. Ex 20:18; Ps 29:3
31 The voice of the LORD will
shatter Assyria; Isa 10:5,12
with his rod he will strike
them down. Isa 11:4
32 Every stroke the LORD lays on
them
with his punishing club
will be to the music of timbrels
and harps,
as he fights them in
battle with the
blows of his arm. Isa 11:15; Eze 32:10

33 Topheth has long been
prepared;
it has been made ready for
the king.
Its fire pit has been made deep
and wide,
with an abundance of fire
and wood;
the breath of the LORD,
like a stream of
burning sulfur,
Ge 19:24; Rev 9:17
sets it ablaze. Isa 1:31

Woe to Those Who Rely on Egypt

31 Woe to those who go
down to Egypt for help,
Isa 30:2,5
who rely on horses,
who trust in the multitude of
their chariots Isa 2:7
and in the great strength of
their horsemen,
but do not look to the Holy One
of Israel,
or seek help from the LORD.
Ps 20:7; Da 9:13
2 Yet he too is wise and can
bring disaster;
Isa 45:7; Ro 16:27
he does not take back his
words. Nu 23:19
He will rise up against that
wicked nation, Isa 32:6
against those who help
evildoers.
3 But the Egyptians are mere
mortals and not God;
Eze 28:9
their horses are flesh and not
spirit. Isa 30:16
When the LORD stretches out
his hand, Isa 9:17,21
those who help will stumble,
those who are helped will
fall; Isa 30:5-7
all will perish together.
Isa 20:6; Jer 17:5

4 This is what the LORD says
to me:

"As a lion growls, Am 3:8
a great lion over its prey —
and though a whole band of
shepherds
is called together against it,
it is not frightened by their
shouts
or disturbed by their
clamor —
so the LORD Almighty will
come down Isa 42:13
to do battle on Mount Zion
and on its heights.
5 Like birds hovering overhead,
the LORD Almighty will
shield Jerusalem; Ps 91:4
he will shield it and deliver it,
Isa 37:35; 38:6
he will 'pass over' it and will
rescue it." Ex 12:23

6 Return, you Israelites, to the
One you have so greatly revolted
against. 7 For in that day every one
of you will reject the idols of silver
and gold your sinful hands have
made. Isa 2:20; 30:22

8 "Assyria will fall by no human
sword; Isa 10:12
a sword, not of mortals, will
devour them. Isa 14:25; 37:7

They will flee before the sword
and their young men will
be put to forced labor. Ge 49:15
9 Their stronghold will
fall because of terror; Dt 32:31,37
at the sight of the battle
standard their
commanders will panic," Isa 18:3; Jer 51:9
declares the LORD,
whose fire is in Zion, Isa 10:17
whose furnace is in
Jerusalem. Mal 4:1

The Kingdom of Righteousness

32 See, a king will reign in
righteousness Eze 37:24
and rulers will rule with
justice. Isa 9:7
2 Each one will be like a shelter
from the wind Isa 4:6
and a refuge from the storm, Ps 55:8
like streams of water in the
desert Ps 23:2; 107:35; Jer 31:9
and the shadow of a great
rock in a thirsty land.
3 Then the eyes of those who see
will no longer be closed, Isa 29:18
and the ears of those who
hear will listen. Dt 29:4
4 The fearful heart will
know and understand, Isa 29:24
and the stammering tongue
will be fluent and clear. Isa 35:6
5 No longer will the fool be called
noble 1Sa 25:25
nor the scoundrel be highly
respected.
6 For fools speak folly, Pr 19:3
their hearts are bent on evil: Pr 24:2; Isa 26:10
They practice ungodliness Isa 9:17
and spread error concerning
the LORD; Isa 9:16
the hungry they leave empty Isa 3:15
and from the thirsty they
withhold water.
7 Scoundrels use wicked
methods, Jer 5:26-28
they make up evil schemes Mic 7:3
to destroy the poor with lies,
even when the plea of the
needy is just. Isa 61:1
8 But the noble make noble
plans,
and by noble deeds they
stand. Pr 11:25

The Women of Jerusalem

9 You women who are so
complacent,
rise up and listen to me; Isa 28:23
you daughters who feel secure, Isa 47:8; Am 6:1; Zep 2:15
hear what I have to say!
10 In little more than a year
you who feel secure will
tremble;
the grape harvest will fail, Isa 5:5-6; 24:7
and the harvest of fruit will
not come.

11 Tremble, you complacent
women;
shudder, you daughters who
feel secure!
Strip off your fine clothes Isa 47:2
and wrap yourselves in rags.
Isa 3:24
12 Beat your breasts for the
pleasant fields, Na 2:7
for the fruitful vines Isa 16:9
13 and for the land of my
people,
a land overgrown with
thorns and briers —
Isa 5:6
yes, mourn for all houses of
merriment
and for this city of revelry.
Isa 22:2
14 The fortress will be abandoned,
Isa 13:22
the noisy city deserted; Isa 6:11
citadel and watchtower will
become a wasteland
forever, Isa 34:13
the delight of donkeys,
a pasture for flocks,
Ps 104:11
15 till the Spirit is poured on us
from on high, Joel 2:28
and the desert becomes
a fertile field,
Ps 107:35; Isa 35:1-2
and the fertile field
seems like a forest.
Isa 29:17
16 The LORD's justice will dwell
in the desert,
Isa 9:7; 35:1,6; 42:11
his righteousness live in the
fertile field. Ps 48:1
17 The fruit of that righteousness
will be peace;
Ps 119:165; Jas 3:18
its effect will be quietness
and confidence forever.
Isa 30:15
18 My people will live in peaceful
dwelling places, Isa 2:4
in secure homes, Isa 26:1; Am 9:14
in undisturbed places of rest.
Hos 2:18-23
19 Though hail flattens the forest
Isa 30:30; Zec 11:2
and the city is leveled
completely, Isa 24:10; 27:10
20 how blessed you will be,
sowing your seed by every
stream, Ecc 11:1
and letting your cattle and
donkeys range free.
Isa 30:24

Distress and Help

33 Woe to you, destroyer,
you who have not been
destroyed!
Woe to you, betrayer,
you who have not been
betrayed!
When you stop destroying,
you will be destroyed;
Hab 2:8; Mt 7:2
when you stop betraying,
you will be betrayed. Isa 21:2

2 LORD, be gracious to us;
we long for you.
Be our strength every morning,
Isa 40:10; 51:9
our salvation in time of
distress. Isa 5:30; 25:9

3 At the uproar of your army, the
peoples flee; Ps 68:1
when you rise up, the
nations scatter. Isa 59:16-18
4 Your plunder, O nations, is
harvested as by young
locusts; Joel 1:4
like a swarm of locusts
people pounce on it.

5 The LORD is exalted, for he
dwells on high; Ps 97:9
he will fill Zion with
his justice and
righteousness. Isa 1:26; 28:6
6 He will be the sure foundation
for your times,
a rich store of salvation and
wisdom and knowledge; Isa 51:6
the fear of the LORD is the
key to this treasure.[a] Isa 11:2-3; Mt 6:33

7 Look, their brave men cry
aloud in the streets;
the envoys of peace weep
bitterly. 2Ki 18:37
8 The highways are deserted,
no travelers are on the roads. Jdg 5:6; Isa 35:8
The treaty is broken,
its witnesses[b] are despised,
no one is respected.
9 The land dries up and wastes
away, Isa 3:26
Lebanon is ashamed and
withers; Isa 2:13; 24:4
Sharon is like the Arabah, 1Ch 27:29
and Bashan and Carmel drop
their leaves. 1Ki 18:19; Na 1:4

10 "Now will I arise," says the
LORD. Ps 12:5; Isa 2:21
"Now will I be exalted; Isa 5:16
now will I be lifted up.
11 You conceive chaff, Ps 7:14; Isa 59:4
you give birth to straw; Isa 26:18
your breath is a fire that
consumes you. Isa 1:31
12 The peoples will be burned to
ashes;
like cut thornbushes they
will be set ablaze." Isa 10:17

13 You who are far away, hear
what I have done; Ps 49:1; Isa 49:1
you who are near,
acknowledge my power!
14 The sinners in Zion are
terrified;
trembling grips the godless: Isa 32:11
"Who of us can dwell with
the consuming fire? Isa 30:30; Heb 12:29
Who of us can dwell with
everlasting burning?"
15 Those who walk righteously Isa 58:8
and speak what is right, Ps 15:2; 24:4
who reject gain from extortion
and keep their hands from
accepting bribes, Pr 15:27
who stop their ears against
plots of murder
and shut their eyes against
contemplating evil — Ps 119:37

[a] 6 Or *is a treasure from him* [b] 8 Dead Sea Scrolls; Masoretic Text / *the cities*

16 they are the ones who will
dwell on the heights,
whose refuge will be the
mountain fortress.
Isa 25:4; 26:1
Their bread will be supplied,
and water will not fail them.
Isa 49:10

17 Your eyes will see the king in
his beauty Isa 6:5
and view a land that
stretches afar. Isa 26:15
18 In your thoughts you will
ponder the former
terror: Isa 17:14
"Where is that chief
officer?
Where is the one who took the
revenue?
Where is the officer in
charge of the towers?"
Isa 2:15
19 You will see those arrogant
people no more,
people whose speech is
obscure,
whose language is
strange and
incomprehensible.
Isa 28:11; Jer 5:15

20 Look on Zion, the city of our
festivals;
your eyes will see
Jerusalem,
a peaceful abode, a tent
that will not be moved;
Ps 46:5; 125:1-2; Isa 32:18
its stakes will never be pulled
up,
nor any of its ropes broken.
21 There the LORD will be our
Mighty One.
It will be like a place of broad
rivers and streams.
Isa 41:18; 48:18
No galley with oars will ride
them,
no mighty ship will sail
them.
22 For the LORD is our judge, Isa 11:4
the LORD is our lawgiver,
Isa 2:3; Jas 4:12
the LORD is our king; Ps 89:18
it is he who will save us. Isa 25:9

23 Your rigging hangs loose:
The mast is not held secure,
the sail is not spread.
Then an abundance of spoils
will be divided
and even the lame will carry
off plunder. 2Ki 7:8,16
24 No one living in Zion will say,
"I am ill"; Isa 30:26
and the sins of those who
dwell there will be
forgiven. Jer 50:20; 1Jn 1:7-9

Judgment Against the Nations

34 Come near, you nations,
and listen;
pay attention, you peoples!
Isa 41:1; 43:9
Let the earth hear, and all that
is in it, Ps 49:1
the world, and all that comes
out of it! Dt 32:1
2 The LORD is angry with all
nations;
his wrath is on all their
armies.

He will totally destroy[a] them,
Isa 13:5
he will give them over to
slaughter. Isa 30:25
3 Their slain will be thrown out,
their dead bodies will stink;
Joel 2:20; Am 4:10
the mountains will be
soaked with their blood.
Eze 14:19; 35:6; 38:22
4 All the stars in the sky will be
dissolved Isa 13:13; 2Pe 3:10
and the heavens rolled up
like a scroll; Eze 32:7-8
all the starry host will fall
Joel 2:31; Mt 24:29*; Rev 6:13
like withered leaves from the
vine, Isa 15:6; Mt 21:19
like shriveled figs from the
fig tree.

5 My sword has drunk its fill in
the heavens; Jer 46:10
see, it descends in judgment
on Edom, Am 1:11-12
the people I have totally
destroyed. Mal 1:4; Isa 24:6
6 The sword of the LORD is
bathed in blood, Dt 32:41
it is covered with fat —
the blood of lambs and goats,
fat from the kidneys of
rams.
For the LORD has a sacrifice in
Bozrah Ge 36:33
and a great slaughter in the
land of Edom. Isa 30:25
7 And the wild oxen will fall with
them,
the bull calves and the great
bulls. Ps 68:30
Their land will be drenched
with blood,
and the dust will be soaked
with fat.

8 For the LORD has a day of
vengeance, Isa 63:4
a year of retribution, to
uphold Zion's cause.
Isa 59:18; Joel 3:4
9 Edom's streams will be turned
into pitch,
her dust into burning sulfur;
Ge 19:24
her land will become blazing
pitch!
10 It will not be quenched night
or day;
its smoke will rise forever.
Rev 14:10-11; 19:3
From generation to
generation it
will lie desolate;
Isa 13:20; Eze 29:12; Mal 1:3
no one will ever pass
through it again.
11 The desert owl[b] and screech
owl[b] will possess it;
Zep 2:14
the great owl[b] and the raven
will nest there.
God will stretch out over Edom
Isa 21:11; Eze 35:15
the measuring line of
chaos
and the plumb line of
desolation. 2Ki 21:13; La 2:8

[a] 2 The Hebrew term refers to the irrevocable giving over of things or persons to the LORD, often by totally destroying them; also in verse 5. [b] 11 The precise identification of these birds is uncertain.

12 Her nobles will have nothing
there to be called a
kingdom,
all her princes will vanish
away. Isa 41:11-12; Jer 27:20
13 Thorns will overrun her
citadels,
nettles and brambles
her strongholds.
Isa 13:22; 32:13
She will become a haunt for
jackals, Ps 44:19; Jer 9:11
a home for owls.
14 Desert creatures will meet with
hyenas, Isa 13:22
and wild goats will bleat to
each other;
there the night creatures will
also lie down Rev 18:2
and find for themselves
places of rest.
15 The owl will nest there and lay
eggs,
she will hatch them, and care
for her young
under the shadow of her
wings;
there also the falcons will
gather, Dt 14:13
each with its mate.

16 Look in the scroll of the LORD
and read: Isa 30:8

None of these will be missing,
Isa 40:26
not one will lack her mate.
For it is his mouth that
has given the order,
Isa 1:20; 58:14
and his Spirit will gather
them together.
17 He allots their portions;
Isa 17:14; Jer 13:25
his hand distributes them by
measure.
They will possess it forever
and dwell there from
generation to
generation. ver 10

Joy of the Redeemed

35 The desert and the parched
land will be glad;
Isa 27:10; 41:18-19
the wilderness will rejoice
and blossom. Isa 51:3
Like the crocus, 2 it will burst
into bloom; SS 2:1
it will rejoice greatly and
shout for joy. Isa 25:9; 55:12
The glory of Lebanon will be
given to it, Isa 32:15
the splendor of Carmel and
Sharon; SS 7:5
they will see the glory of the
LORD, Ex 16:7; Isa 4:5
the splendor of our God.
Isa 25:9

3 Strengthen the feeble hands,
steady the knees that give
way; Job 4:4; Heb 12:12
4 say to those with fearful hearts,
Isa 40:2; Zec 1:13
"Be strong, do not fear;
Isa 7:4; Da 10:19
your God will come, Isa 62:11
he will come with vengeance;
Isa 1:24
with divine retribution
he will come to save you."
Isa 25:9

[5]Then will the eyes of the blind
be opened Mt 11:5; Jn 9:6-7
and the ears of the deaf
unstopped. Isa 29:18
[6]Then will the lame leap like a
deer, Mt 15:30; Jn 5:8-9
and the mute tongue shout
for joy. Mt 9:32-33
Water will gush forth in the
wilderness
and streams in the desert.
Isa 41:18; Jn 7:38
[7]The burning sand will become
a pool,
the thirsty ground bubbling
springs. Isa 49:10
In the haunts where jackals
once lay, Isa 13:22
grass and reeds and papyrus
will grow. Job 8:11
[8]And a highway will be there;
Isa 11:16; Mt 7:13-14
it will be called the Way of
Holiness; Isa 4:3; 1Pe 1:15
it will be for those who walk
on that Way.
The unclean will not journey
on it; Isa 52:1
wicked fools will not go
about on it.
[9]No lion will be there, Isa 30:6
nor any ravenous beast;
Isa 34:14
they will not be found there.
But only the redeemed
will walk there,
Isa 51:11; 62:12; 63:4
10 and those the LORD
has rescued will return.
Isa 1:27
They will enter Zion with
singing;
everlasting joy will crown
their heads. Isa 25:9
Gladness and joy will overtake
them, Ps 51:8; Isa 51:3
and sorrow and sighing
will flee away.
Isa 51:11; Rev 7:17; 21:4

Sennacherib Threatens Jerusalem

36 In the fourteenth year of
King Hezekiah's reign, Sennacherib king of Assyria attacked
all the fortified cities of Judah and
captured them. [2]Then the king of
Assyria sent his field commander with a large army from Lachish
to King Hezekiah at Jerusalem.
When the commander stopped at
the aqueduct of the Upper Pool,
on the road to the Launderer's
Field, [3]Eliakim son of Hilkiah the
palace administrator, Shebna the
secretary, and Joah son of Asaph
the recorder went out to him.
2Ch 32:1; Isa 22:20-21

[4]The field commander said to
them, "Tell Hezekiah:

"'This is what the great
king, the king of Assyria, says:
On what are you basing this
confidence of yours? [5]You say
you have counsel and might
for war — but you speak only
empty words. On whom are
you depending, that you rebel against me? [6]Look, I know
you are depending on Egypt,
that splintered reed of a staff,

which pierces the hand of
anyone who leans on it! Such
is Pharaoh king of Egypt to
all who depend on him. 7But
if you say to me, "We are depending on the LORD our
God" — isn't he the one whose
high places and altars Hezekiah removed, saying to Judah
and Jerusalem, "You must
worship before this altar"?

2Ki 18:4; Isa 30:2,5; Eze 29:6-7

8"'Come now, make a bar-
gain with my master, the king
of Assyria: I will give you two
thousand horses — if you can
put riders on them! 9How then
can you repulse one officer of
the least of my master's officials, even though you are depending on Egypt for chariots
and horsemen[a]? 10Further-
more, have I come to attack
and destroy this land without
the LORD? The LORD himself
told me to march against this
country and destroy it.'"

Isa 30:2-5; 31:3

11Then Eliakim, Shebna and
Joah said to the field commander,
"Please speak to your servants in
Aramaic, since we understand it.
Don't speak to us in Hebrew in the
hearing of the people on the wall."

Ezr 4:7

12But the commander replied,
"Was it only to your master and
you that my master sent me to
say these things, and not to the
people sitting on the wall — who,
like you, will have to eat their own
excrement and drink their own
urine?"

13Then the commander stood
and called out in Hebrew, "Hear
the words of the great king, the
king of Assyria! 14This is what the
king says: Do not let Hezekiah deceive you. He cannot deliver you!
15Do not let Hezekiah persuade
you to trust in the LORD when he
says, 'The LORD will surely deliver
us; this city will not be given into
the hand of the king of Assyria.'

2Ch 32:18; Isa 37:10

16"Do not listen to Hezekiah.
This is what the king of Assyria says: Make peace with me and
come out to me. Then each of you
will eat fruit from your own vine
and fig tree and drink water from
your own cistern, 17until I come
and take you to a land like your
own — a land of grain and new
wine, a land of bread and vineyards. Pr 5:15; Zec 3:10

18"Do not let Hezekiah mislead
you when he says, 'The LORD will
deliver us.' Have the gods of any
nations ever delivered their lands
from the hand of the king of Assyria? 19Where are the gods of Hamath and Arpad? Where are the
gods of Sepharvaim? Have they
rescued Samaria from my hand?
20Who of all the gods of these
countries have been able to save
their lands from me? How then
can the LORD deliver Jerusalem
from my hand?" 1Ki 20:23

[a] 9 Or *charioteers*

21 But the people remained silent
and said nothing in reply, because
the king had commanded, "Do not
answer him." Pr 9:7-8

22 Then Eliakim son of Hilkiah
the palace administrator, Shebna the secretary and Joah son of
Asaph the recorder went to Hezekiah, with their clothes torn, and
told him what the field commander had said. 2Ki 18:17-37; 2Ch 32:9-19

Jerusalem's Deliverance Foretold

37 When King Hezekiah heard
this, he tore his clothes and
put on sackcloth and went into
the temple of the LORD. 2 He sent
Eliakim the palace administrator, Shebna the secretary, and the
leading priests, all wearing sackcloth, to the prophet Isaiah son
of Amoz. 3 They told him, "This is
what Hezekiah says: This day is
a day of distress and rebuke and
disgrace, as when children come
to the moment of birth and there
is no strength to deliver them. 4 It
may be that the LORD your God
will hear the words of the field
commander, whom his master,
the king of Assyria, has sent to ridicule the living God, and that he
will rebuke him for the words the
LORD your God has heard. Therefore pray for the remnant that still
survives." 1Sa 7:8; Isa 36:13,18-20

5 When King Hezekiah's officials came to Isaiah, 6 Isaiah said
to them, "Tell your master, 'This
is what the LORD says: Do not be
afraid of what you have heard —
those words with which the underlings of the king of Assyria have
blasphemed me. 7 Listen! When he
hears a certain report, I will make
him want to return to his own
country, and there I will have him
cut down with the sword.' " Isa 7:4

8 When the field command-
er heard that the king of Assyria
had left Lachish, he withdrew and
found the king fighting against
Libnah. Nu 33:20

9 Now Sennacherib received a
report that Tirhakah, the king of
Cush,[a] was marching out to fight
against him. When he heard it, he
sent messengers to Hezekiah with
this word: 10 "Say to Hezekiah king
of Judah: Do not let the god you
depend on deceive you when he
says, 'Jerusalem will not be giv-
en into the hands of the king of
Assyria.' 11 Surely you have heard
what the kings of Assyria have
done to all the countries, destroying them completely. And will you
be delivered? 12 Did the gods of the
nations that were destroyed by
my predecessors deliver them —
the gods of Gozan, Harran, Rezeph and the people of Eden who
were in Tel Assar? 13 Where is the
king of Hamath or the king of Arpad? Where are the kings of Lair,
Sepharvaim, Hena and Ivvah?"
2Ki 19:1-13

Hezekiah's Prayer

14 Hezekiah received the letter
from the messengers and read it.

[a] 9 That is, the upper Nile region

Then he went up to the temple of
the LORD and spread it out before
the LORD. 15 And Hezekiah prayed
to the LORD: 16 "LORD Almighty, the
God of Israel, enthroned between
the cherubim, you alone are God
over all the kingdoms of the earth.
You have made heaven and earth.
17 Give ear, LORD, and hear; open
your eyes, LORD, and see; listen to
all the words Sennacherib has sent
to ridicule the living God.

Dt 10:17; Ps 86:10; Da 9:18

18 "It is true, LORD, that the Assyrian kings have laid waste all these
peoples and their lands. 19 They
have thrown their gods into the fire
and destroyed them, for they were
not gods but only wood and stone,
fashioned by human hands. 20 Now,
LORD our God, deliver us from his
hand, so that all the kingdoms of
the earth may know that you, LORD,
are the only God.[a]" 2Ki 19:14-19; Ps 46:10

Sennacherib's Fall

21 Then Isaiah son of Amoz sent
a message to Hezekiah: "This is
what the LORD, the God of Israel,
says: Because you have prayed to
me concerning Sennacherib king
of Assyria, 22 this is the word the
LORD has spoken against him:

"Virgin Daughter Zion
despises and mocks you.
Daughter Jerusalem
tosses her head as you flee.
Job 16:4

23 Who is it you have ridiculed
and blasphemed?
Against whom have you
raised your voice
and lifted your eyes in pride?
Isa 2:11
Against the Holy One of
Israel! Isa 1:4; 12:6

24 By your messengers
you have ridiculed the Lord.
And you have said,
'With my many chariots
I have ascended the heights of
the mountains,
the utmost heights of
Lebanon. Isa 14:8
I have cut down its tallest
cedars,
the choicest of its junipers.
1Ki 5:8-10; Isa 41:19
I have reached its remotest
heights,
the finest of its forests.
25 I have dug wells in foreign
lands[b]
and drunk the water there.
With the soles of my feet
I have dried up all the
streams of Egypt.' Dt 11:10

26 "Have you not heard?
Long ago I ordained it.
Ac 2:23; 4:27-28; 1Pe 2:8
In days of old I planned it;
Isa 10:6; 25:1
now I have brought it to pass,
that you have turned fortified
cities
into piles of stone. Isa 25:2

[a] 20 Dead Sea Scrolls (see also 2 Kings 19:19); Masoretic Text *you alone are the LORD* [b] 25 Dead Sea Scrolls (see also 2 Kings 19:24); Masoretic Text does not have *in foreign lands.*

[27]Their people, drained of
power,
are dismayed and put to
shame.
They are like plants in the
field,
like tender green shoots,
like grass sprouting on the
roof, Ps 129:6
scorched[a] before it
grows up.

[28]"But I know where you are
and when you come and go
Ps 139:1-3
and how you rage
against me. Ps 2:1
[29]Because you rage against me
and because your insolence
has reached my ears,
Isa 10:12
I will put my hook in your
nose Isa 30:28; Eze 38:4
and my bit in your mouth,
and I will make you return
by the way you came. ver 34

[30]"This will be the sign for you, Hezekiah: Isa 20:3

"This year you will eat what
grows by itself,
and the second year what
springs from that.
But in the third year sow and
reap, Isa 16:14
plant vineyards and eat their
fruit. Ps 107:37; Isa 30:23
[31]Once more a remnant of the
kingdom of Judah
will take root below and bear
fruit above. Isa 27:6
[32]For out of Jerusalem will come
a remnant,
and out of Mount Zion a
band of survivors.
The zeal of the LORD
Almighty
will accomplish this. Isa 9:7

[33]"Therefore this is what the LORD says concerning the king of Assyria:

"He will not enter this city
or shoot an arrow here.
He will not come before it with
shield
or build a siege ramp
against it.
[34]By the way that he came he will
return; ver 29
he will not enter this city,"
declares the LORD.
[35]"I will defend this city and
save it, Isa 38:6
for my sake and for the sake
of David my servant!"
2Ki 20:6; Isa 43:25

[36]Then the angel of the LORD
went out and put to death a hundred and eighty-five thousand in
the Assyrian camp. When the people got up the next morning—
there were all the dead bodies! [37]So
Sennacherib king of Assyria broke
camp and withdrew. He returned
to Nineveh and stayed there.
Ge 10:11; Isa 10:12

[a] *27* Some manuscripts of the Masoretic Text, Dead Sea Scrolls and some Septuagint manuscripts (see also 2 Kings 19:26); most manuscripts of the Masoretic Text *roof / and terraced fields*

38One day, while he was worshiping in the temple of his god
Nisrok, his sons Adrammelek
and Sharezer killed him with the
sword, and they escaped to the
land of Ararat. And Esarhaddon
his son succeeded him as king.
2Ki 19:20-37; 2Ch 32:20-21

Hezekiah's Illness

38 In those days Hezekiah
became ill and was at the
point of death. The prophet Isaiah son of Amoz went to him and
said, "This is what the LORD says:
Put your house in order, because
you are going to die; you will not
recover." 2Sa 17:23; 2Ki 8:10; Isa 37:2
2Hezekiah turned his face to the
wall and prayed to the LORD, 3"Remember, LORD, how I have walked
before you faithfully and with
wholehearted devotion and have
done what is good in your eyes."
And Hezekiah wept bitterly.
Ne 13:14; Ps 6:8
4Then the word of the LORD
came to Isaiah: 5"Go and tell Hezekiah, 'This is what the LORD, the
God of your father David, says: I
have heard your prayer and seen
your tears; I will add fifteen years
to your life. 6And I will deliver you
and this city from the hand of the
king of Assyria. I will defend this
city. 2Ki 18:2; Isa 37:35
7" 'This is the LORD's sign to you
that the LORD will do what he has
promised: 8I will make the shadow cast by the sun go back the
ten steps it has gone down on the
stairway of Ahaz.' " So the sunlight
went back the ten steps it had
gone down. 2Ki 20:1-11; 2Ch 32:24-26

9A writing of Hezekiah king of
Judah after his illness and recovery:

10I said, "In the prime of my life Ps 102:24
  must I go through the gates
    of death Ps 107:18; 2Co 1:9
  and be robbed of the rest of
    my years?" Job 17:11
11I said, "I will not again see the
    LORD himself
  in the land of the living; Ps 27:13; 116:9
no longer will I look on my
    fellow man,
  or be with those who
    now dwell in this
    world.
12Like a shepherd's tent my
    house 2Co 5:1,4; 2Pe 1:13-14
  has been pulled down and
    taken from me. Job 4:21
Like a weaver I have rolled up
    my life, Heb 1:12
  and he has cut me off from
    the loom; Job 7:6
  day and night you made an
    end of me. Ps 73:14
13I waited patiently till dawn,
  but like a lion he broke
    all my bones; Job 10:16; Ps 51:8; Da 6:24
  day and night you made an
    end of me.
14I cried like a swift or thrush,
  I moaned like a mourning
    dove. Isa 59:11

My eyes grew weak as I looked
to the heavens. Ps 6:7
I am being threatened; Lord,
come to my aid!" Job 17:3
15 But what can I say?
He has spoken to me, and he
himself has done this.
Ps 39:9
I will walk humbly all my years
1Ki 21:27
because of this anguish of
my soul. Job 7:11
16 Lord, by such things people
live;
and my spirit finds life in
them too.
You restored me to health
and let me live. Ps 119:25
17 Surely it was for my benefit
Heb 12:11
that I suffered such anguish.
In your love you kept me
from the pit of destruction;
Ps 30:3
you have put all my sins Jer 31:34
behind your back.
Isa 43:25; Mic 7:19
18 For the grave cannot praise
you, Ecc 9:10
death cannot sing your
praise; Ps 6:5; 88:10-11
those who go down to the pit
Ps 30:9
cannot hope for your
faithfulness.
19 The living, the living — they
praise you, Dt 6:7; Ps 118:17
as I am doing today;
parents tell their children Dt 11:19
about your faithfulness.
20 The LORD will save me,
and we will sing with
stringed instruments
Ps 33:2
all the days of our lives Ps 116:2
in the temple of the LORD.
Ps 116:17-19

21 Isaiah had said, "Prepare a
poultice of figs and apply it to the
boil, and he will recover."
22 Hezekiah had asked, "What
will be the sign that I will go up to
the temple of the LORD?" 2Ch 32:31

Envoys From Babylon

39 At that time Marduk-Baladan son of Baladan king
of Babylon sent Hezekiah letters
and a gift, because he had heard
of his illness and recovery. 2 Hezekiah received the envoys gladly
and showed them what was in his
storehouses — the silver, the gold,
the spices, the fine olive oil — his
entire armory and everything
found among his treasures. There
was nothing in his palace or in all
his kingdom that Hezekiah did
not show them. 2Ki 18:15; 2Ch 32:31
3 Then Isaiah the prophet went
to King Hezekiah and asked, "What
did those men say, and where did
they come from?"
"From a distant land," Hezekiah
replied. "They came to me from
Babylon." Dt 28:49
4 The prophet asked, "What did
they see in your palace?"
"They saw everything in my
palace," Hezekiah said. "There is

nothing among my treasures that
I did not show them."
5Then Isaiah said to Hezekiah, "Hear the word of the LORD
Almighty: 6The time will surely
come when everything in your
palace, and all that your predecessors have stored up until this
day, will be carried off to Babylon.
Nothing will be left, says the LORD.
7And some of your descendants,
your own flesh and blood who will
be born to you, will be taken away,
and they will become eunuchs in
the palace of the king of Babylon."
Jer 20:5; Da 1:1-7

8"The word of the LORD you
have spoken is good," Hezekiah
replied. For he thought, "There
will be peace and security in my
lifetime." 2Ki 20:12-19; 2Ch 32:26

Comfort for God's People

40 Comfort, comfort my
people, Isa 12:1; 49:13
says your God.
2Speak tenderly to Jerusalem, Isa 35:4
and proclaim to her
that her hard service has been
completed, Isa 41:11-13
that her sin has been paid
for,
that she has received from the
LORD's hand
double for all her sins.
Isa 61:7; Jer 16:18

3A voice of one calling:
"In the wilderness prepare
the way for the LORD[a]; Mal 3:1
make straight in the
desert Pr 3:5-6
a highway for our God.[b]
Mt 3:3*; Mk 1:3*; Jn 1:23*
4Every valley shall be raised up,
every mountain and hill
made low;
the rough ground shall become
level, Isa 45:2,13
the rugged places a plain.
5And the glory of the LORD will
be revealed,
and all people will see it
together.
For the mouth of the
LORD has spoken."

6A voice says, "Cry out."
And I said, "What shall I cry?"

"All people are like grass, Job 14:2
and all their faithfulness is
like the flowers of the
field.
7The grass withers and the
flowers fall, Isa 15:6
because the breath of the
LORD blows on them.
Job 41:21; Ps 103:16
Surely the people are grass.
8The grass withers and the
flowers fall,
but the word of our God
endures forever."
Isa 55:11; Mt 5:18; 1Pe 1:24-25*

9You who bring good news to
Zion, Isa 52:7-10; Ro 10:15
go up on a high mountain.

[a] 3 Or *A voice of one calling in the wilderness: / "Prepare the way for the LORD* [b] 3 Hebrew; Septuagint *make straight the paths of our God*

You who bring good news to
Jerusalem,[a]
lift up your voice with a
shout,
lift it up, do not be afraid;
say to the towns of Judah,
"Here is your God!" Isa 25:9
10 See, the Sovereign LORD comes
with power, Rev 22:7
and he rules with a mighty
arm. Isa 9:6-7; 59:16
See, his reward is with him,
Isa 62:11; Rev 22:12
and his recompense
accompanies him.
11 He tends his flock like
a shepherd:
Eze 34:23; Mic 5:4; Jn 10:11
He gathers the lambs in his
arms Nu 11:12
and carries them close to his
heart; Dt 26:19
he gently leads those that
have young. Ge 33:13; Isa 49:10

12 Who has measured the waters
in the hollow of his
hand, Job 38:10; Pr 30:4
or with the breadth of his
hand marked off the
heavens? Heb 1:10-12
Who has held the dust of the
earth in a basket,
or weighed the mountains
on the scales
and the hills in a balance?
Pr 16:11
13 Who can fathom the Spirit[b] of
the LORD,
or instruct the LORD as his
counselor? Ro 11:34*; 1Co 2:16*
14 Whom did the LORD consult to
enlighten him,
and who taught him the
right way?
Who was it that taught him
knowledge, Job 21:22; Col 2:3
or showed him the path of
understanding? Job 12:13

15 Surely the nations are like a
drop in a bucket;
they are regarded as dust on
the scales; Ps 62:9
he weighs the islands as
though they were fine
dust. Dt 9:21
16 Lebanon is not sufficient for
altar fires,
nor its animals enough
for burnt offerings.
Ps 50:9-11; Mic 6:7; Heb 10:5-9
17 Before him all the nations
are as nothing;
Isa 29:7; 30:28
they are regarded by him as
worthless
and less than nothing. Da 4:35

18 With whom, then, will
you compare God?
Ex 8:10; Isa 46:5
To what image will you liken
him? Ac 17:29
19 As for an idol, a metalworker
casts it, Ps 115:4
and a goldsmith overlays it
with gold Isa 2:20; 41:7
and fashions silver chains
for it.

[a] 9 *Or Zion, bringer of good news, / go up on a high mountain. / Jerusalem, bringer of good news* [b] 13 *Or mind*

20 A person too poor to
present such an
offering
selects wood that will not
rot;
they look for a skilled worker
to set up an idol that will
not topple. 1Sa 5:3

21 Do you not know?
Have you not heard?
Has it not been told you
from the beginning?
Ps 19:1; Ac 14:17
Have you not understood
since the earth
was founded?
Ro 1:19; Isa 48:13; 51:13
22 He sits enthroned above the
circle of the earth,
and its people are like
grasshoppers.
Ps 104:2; Isa 42:5; Nu 13:33
He stretches out the heavens
like a canopy, Job 22:14
and spreads them out like a
tent to live in. Job 36:29
23 He brings princes to naught
Isa 34:12
and reduces the rulers of
this world to nothing.
Job 12:21; Ps 107:40
24 No sooner are they planted,
no sooner are they sown,
no sooner do they take root
in the ground,
than he blows on them and
they wither, Isa 41:16
and a whirlwind sweeps
them away like chaff.
Job 24:24; Isa 41:2

25 "To whom will you compare
me? ver 18; 1Ch 16:25
Or who is my equal?" says
the Holy One. Isa 1:4
26 Lift up your eyes and look to
the heavens: Isa 51:6
Who created all these?
Ps 89:11-13; Isa 42:5
He who brings out the
starry host one by one
Ps 147:4
and calls forth each of them
by name.
Because of his great power
and mighty strength,
Isa 45:24; Eph 1:19
not one of them is missing.
Isa 34:16

27 Why do you complain, Jacob?
Why do you say, Israel,
"My way is hidden from the
LORD;
my cause is disregarded
by my God"?
Job 27:2; Lk 18:7-8
28 Do you not know?
Have you not heard?
The LORD is the everlasting
God, Ps 90:2
the Creator of the ends of the
earth. Isa 37:16
He will not grow tired or weary,
Isa 44:12
and his understanding
no one can fathom.
Ps 147:5; Ro 11:33
29 He gives strength to the weary
Isa 50:4; Jer 31:25
and increases the power of
the weak.

30 Even youths grow tired and
weary,
and young men stumble and
fall; Isa 9:17; Jer 6:11; 9:21
31 but those who hope in the
LORD Lk 18:1
will renew their strength.
2Co 4:16
They will soar on wings like
eagles; Ps 103:5
they will run and not grow
weary,
they will walk and not be
faint. 2Co 4:1; Heb 12:1-3

The Helper of Israel

41 "Be silent before me, you
islands! Zec 2:13
Let the nations renew their
strength!
Let them come forward and
speak; Isa 48:16
let us meet together at the
place of judgment.
Isa 34:1; 50:8

2 "Who has stirred up one from
the east, Ezr 1:2; Isa 45:1,13
calling him in righteousness
to his service[a]?
He hands nations over to him
and subdues kings before
him.
He turns them to dust with his
sword, 2Sa 22:43
to windblown chaff with his
bow. Isa 40:24
3 He pursues them and moves on
unscathed,
by a path his feet have not
traveled before.
4 Who has done this and carried
it through,
calling forth the generations
from the beginning?
Isa 46:10
I, the LORD—with the first of
them
and with the last—I am he."
Isa 44:6; Rev 1:8,17; 22:13

5 The islands have seen it and
fear; Eze 26:17-18
the ends of the earth
tremble. Isa 11:12
They approach and come
forward;
6 they help each other
and say to their
companions,
"Be strong!" Jos 1:6
7 The metalworker encourages
the goldsmith, Isa 40:19
and the one who
smooths with the
hammer
spurs on the one who strikes
the anvil.
One says of the welding, "It is
good."
The other nails down the
idol so it will not topple.
1Sa 5:3

8 "But you, Israel, my servant,
Ps 136:22; Isa 27:11
Jacob, whom I have chosen,
Isa 14:1
you descendants of
Abraham my friend,
2Ch 20:7; Jas 2:23

[a] 2 Or *east, / whom victory meets at every step*

9 I took you from the ends of the
earth, Isa 11:12
from its farthest corners I
called you.
I said, 'You are my servant';
I have chosen you and have
not rejected you. Dt 7:6
10 So do not fear, for I am with
you; Isa 43:2,5; Ro 8:31
do not be dismayed, for I am
your God.
I will strengthen you and help
you; ver 13-14; Isa 44:2
I will uphold you with my
righteous right hand.
Ps 18:35; 119:117

11 "All who rage against you Isa 17:12
will surely be ashamed and
disgraced; Isa 45:24
those who oppose you Ex 23:22
will be as nothing and
perish. Isa 29:8
12 Though you search for your
enemies,
you will not find them.
Ps 37:35-36
Those who wage war against
you
will be as nothing at all.
Isa 17:14
13 For I am the LORD your God
who takes hold of your right
hand Isa 42:6; 45:1
and says to you, Do not fear;
I will help you. ver 10
14 Do not be afraid, you worm
Jacob, Ge 15:1; Job 4:19
little Israel, do not fear,
for I myself will help you,"
declares the LORD,
your Redeemer, the Holy One
of Israel. Ex 15:13; Isa 1:4
15 "See, I will make you into a
threshing sledge, Mic 4:13
new and sharp, with many
teeth.
You will thresh the mountains
and crush them,
Ex 19:18; Ps 107:33
and reduce the hills to chaff.
16 You will winnow them, the
wind will pick them up,
Jer 51:2
and a gale will blow them
away. Isa 40:24
But you will rejoice in the LORD
Isa 25:9
and glory in the Holy One of
Israel. Isa 45:25; Mi 1:24

17 "The poor and needy search for
water, Isa 43:20
but there is none;
their tongues are parched
with thirst.
But I the LORD will answer
them; Isa 30:19
I, the God of Israel, will not
forsake them. Dt 31:6; Ps 27:9
18 I will make rivers flow on
barren heights, Isa 30:25
and springs within the
valleys.
I will turn the desert into pools
of water, Isa 43:19
and the parched ground into
springs. Isa 35:7
19 I will put in the desert Isa 35:1
the cedar and the acacia, the
myrtle and the olive.
Ex 25:5,10,13

I will set junipers in the
wasteland,
the fir and the cypress
together, Isa 60:13
20 so that people may see and
know, Ex 6:7
may consider and
understand, Isa 29:24
that the hand of the LORD has
done this, Ezr 7:6; 8:31
that the Holy One of Israel
has created it. Job 12:9

21 "Present your case," says the
LORD.
"Set forth your arguments,"
says Jacob's King.
Isa 43:15; 44:6
22 "Tell us, you idols,
what is going to happen.
Isa 45:21
Tell us what the former things
were,
so that we may consider
them
and know their final outcome.
Or declare to us the things to
come, Isa 46:10; Jn 13:19
23 tell us what the future holds,
so we may know that you are
gods. Isa 42:9; 44:7-8; 45:3
Do something, whether good or
bad, Jer 10:5
so that we will be dismayed
and filled with fear.
24 But you are less than nothing
Isa 44:9; 1Co 8:4
and your works are utterly
worthless;
whoever chooses you is
detestable. Ps 115:8

25 "I have stirred up one from the
north, and he comes —
ver 2; Jer 50:9,41
one from the rising sun who
calls on my name.
He treads on rulers as if they
were mortar, 2Sa 22:43
as if he were a potter
treading the clay.
26 Who told of this from the
beginning, so we could
know,
or beforehand, so we could
say, 'He was right'?
No one told of this,
no one foretold it,
no one heard any words
from you. Hab 2:18-19
27 I was the first to tell Zion,
'Look, here they are!'
Isa 48:3,16
I gave to Jerusalem a
messenger of good
news. Isa 40:9
28 I look but there is no one —
Isa 63:5
no one among the gods to
give counsel, Isa 40:13-14
no one to give answer when I
ask them.
29 See, they are all false!
Their deeds amount to
nothing; ver 24
their images are but wind
and confusion. Jer 5:13

The Servant of the LORD

42 "Here is my servant, whom
I uphold, Isa 20:3; Mt 20:28
my chosen one in whom I
delight; Isa 43:10; 1Pe 2:4,6

I will put my Spirit on him, Mt 3:16-17; Jn 3:34
and he will bring justice
to the nations. Ge 49:10; Isa 9:7
2 He will not shout or cry out,
or raise his voice in the
streets.
3 A bruised reed he will not
break, Isa 36:6
and a smoldering wick he
will not snuff out.
In faithfulness he will bring
forth justice; Ps 72:2; 96:13
4 he will not falter or be
discouraged
till he establishes justice on
earth. Isa 2:4
In his teaching the islands
will put their hope."
Mt 12:18-21*; Ge 49:10

5 This is what God the LORD
says —
the Creator of the heavens,
who stretches them out,
Ge 1:6; Ps 102:25
who spreads out the earth
with all that springs
from it, Ps 24:2
who gives breath to its
people, Ac 17:25
and life to those who walk
on it:
6 "I, the LORD, have called
you in righteousness;
Isa 43:1; Jer 23:6
I will take hold of your
hand.
I will keep you and will make
you Isa 26:3
to be a covenant for the
people Isa 49:8
and a light for the Gentiles,
Lk 2:32; Ac 13:47
7 to open eyes that are blind,
Isa 35:5
to free captives from prison
Isa 61:1; Lk 4:19
and to release from the
dungeon those who sit
in darkness. Ps 107:10,14

8 "I am the LORD; that is my
name! Ex 3:15
I will not yield my glory to
another Isa 48:11
or my praise to idols. Ex 8:10
9 See, the former things have
taken place, Isa 41:22
and new things I declare;
before they spring into
being
I announce them to you."
Isa 40:21

Song of Praise to the LORD

10 Sing to the LORD a new song,
Ps 33:3; 40:3; 98:1
his praise from the ends of
the earth, Isa 49:6
you who go down to the sea,
and all that is in it,
1Ch 16:32; Ps 96:11
you islands, and all who live
in them. Isa 11:11
11 Let the wilderness and its
towns raise their voices;
Isa 32:16
let the settlements
where Kedar lives
rejoice. Isa 60:7

Let the people of Sela sing for
joy;
let them shout from
the mountaintops.
Isa 52:7; Na 1:15
12 Let them give glory to the LORD
Isa 24:15
and proclaim his praise in
the islands. Ps 26:7; 66:2
13 The LORD will march out like a
champion, Isa 9:6
like a warrior he will stir up
his zeal; Isa 26:11
with a shout he will raise the
battle cry Hos 11:10
and will triumph over his
enemies. Isa 66:14

14 "For a long time I have kept
silent, Ps 50:21
I have been quiet and held
myself back. Ge 43:31
But now, like a woman in
childbirth,
I cry out, I gasp and pant.
Jer 4:31
15 I will lay waste the mountains
and hills Eze 38:20
and dry up all their
vegetation;
I will turn rivers into islands
and dry up the pools.
Isa 50:2; Na 1:4-6
16 I will lead the blind by
ways they have
not known,
Lk 1:78-79; Isa 32:3
along unfamiliar paths I will
guide them;
I will turn the darkness into
light before them
and make the rough places
smooth. Lk 3:5
These are the things I will do;
I will not forsake them. Heb 13:5
17 But those who trust in idols,
who say to images, 'You are
our gods,'
will be turned back in utter
shame. Ps 97:7; Isa 1:29; 44:11

Israel Blind and Deaf

18 "Hear, you deaf; Isa 35:5
look, you blind, and see!
19 Who is blind but my servant,
Isa 43:8; Eze 12:2
and deaf like the messenger
I send? Isa 44:26
Who is blind like the one
in covenant with me,
Isa 26:3
blind like the servant of the
LORD?
20 You have seen many things,
but you pay no
attention;
your ears are open, but you
do not listen." Jer 6:10
21 It pleased the LORD
for the sake of his
righteousness
to make his law great and
glorious. ver 4; 2Co 3:7
22 But this is a people plundered
and looted, 2Ki 24:13
all of them trapped in pits
Isa 24:18
or hidden away in prisons.
Isa 24:22
They have become plunder,
with no one to rescue them;
Isa 5:29

they have been made loot,
with no one to say, "Send
them back."
23 Which of you will listen to
this
or pay close attention in time
to come? Isa 48:18
24 Who handed Jacob over to
become loot,
and Israel to the plunderers?
2Ki 17:6
Was it not the LORD,
against whom we have
sinned?
For they would not follow his
ways; Isa 30:15
they did not obey his law.
Ps 119:136
25 So he poured out on them
his burning anger,
2Ki 22:13; Job 40:11
the violence of war.
It enveloped them in flames,
yet they did not
understand; 2Ki 25:9
it consumed them, but they
did not take it to heart.
Isa 29:13; Hos 7:9

Israel's Only Savior

43 But now, this is what the
LORD says —
he who created you, Jacob,
he who formed you, Israel:
Isa 44:21
"Do not fear, for I have
redeemed you; Isa 44:2,6
I have summoned you by
name; you are mine.
Isa 45:3-4
2 When you pass through the
waters, Isa 8:7
I will be with you; Dt 31:6,8
and when you pass through the
rivers,
they will not sweep over
you.
When you walk through the
fire, Isa 29:6; 30:27
you will not be burned;
the flames will not set you
ablaze. Ps 66:12; Da 3:25-27
3 For I am the LORD your God,
Ex 20:2
the Holy One of Israel, your
Savior; Ps 3:8; Isa 41:20
I give Egypt for your ransom,
Ps 68:31
Cush[a] and Seba in your
stead. Pr 21:18; Isa 20:3
4 Since you are precious and
honored in my sight,
Isa 49:5
and because I love you, Isa 63:9
I will give people in exchange
for you,
nations in exchange for your
life.
5 Do not be afraid, for I am with
you; Isa 44:2; Jer 30:10-11
I will bring your children
from the east Isa 41:8
and gather you from the
west. Isa 24:14; Zec 8:7
6 I will say to the north, 'Give
them up!'
and to the south,
'Do not hold them back.'
Ps 107:3

[a] 3 That is, the upper Nile region

Bring my sons from afar
and my daughters from the ends of the earth — 2Co 6:18
[7] everyone who is called by my name, Isa 56:5; Jas 2:7
whom I created for my glory,
whom I formed and made." Ps 100:3; Eph 2:10

[8] Lead out those who have eyes but are blind, Isa 6:9-10
who have ears but are deaf. Isa 42:20; Eze 12:2
[9] All the nations gather together Isa 41:1
and the peoples assemble.
Which of their gods foretold this
and proclaimed to us the former things? Isa 41:26
Let them bring in their witnesses to prove they were right,
so that others may hear and say, "It is true."
[10] "You are my witnesses," declares the LORD,
"and my servant whom I have chosen, Isa 41:8-9
so that you may know and believe me Ex 6:7
and understand that I am he.
Before me no god was formed, Isa 44:6,8
nor will there be one after me. Dt 4:35; Jer 14:22
[11] I, even I, am the LORD,
and apart from me there is no savior. Isa 45:21
[12] I have revealed and saved and proclaimed —
I, and not some foreign god among you. Dt 32:12; Ps 81:9
You are my witnesses," declares the LORD, "that I am God. Isa 44:8
[13] Yes, and from ancient days I am he. Ps 90:2
No one can deliver out of my hand.
When I act, who can reverse it?" Isa 14:27

God's Mercy and Israel's Unfaithfulness

[14] This is what the LORD says —
your Redeemer, the Holy One of Israel: Ex 15:13; Isa 1:4
"For your sake I will send to Babylon
and bring down as fugitives all the Babylonians,[a] Isa 23:13
in the ships in which they took pride.
[15] I am the LORD, your Holy One, Isa 42:8
Israel's Creator, your King." Isa 27:11; 41:21

[16] This is what the LORD says —
he who made a way through the sea,
a path through the mighty waters, Isa 51:10
[17] who drew out the chariots and horses, Ps 118:12; Isa 1:31
the army and reinforcements together, Ex 14:9

[a] 14 Or *Chaldeans*

and they lay there, never to rise
again,
extinguished, snuffed
out like a wick:
Job 13:25; Jer 51:21
18 "Forget the former things;
Isa 41:22
do not dwell on the past.
19 See, I am doing a new thing!
2Co 5:17; Rev 21:5
Now it springs up; do you
not perceive it?
I am making a way in
the wilderness
Ex 17:6; Nu 20:11
and streams in the
wasteland. Ps 126:4
20 The wild animals honor me,
the jackals and the owls,
Isa 13:22
because I provide water in the
wilderness Isa 48:21
and streams in the
wasteland,
to give drink to my people, my
chosen,
21 the people I formed for
myself Mal 3:17
that they may proclaim my
praise. Ps 102:18; 1Pe 2:9

22 "Yet you have not called on me,
Jacob,
you have not wearied
yourselves for[a] me,
Israel. Isa 30:11
23 You have not brought me
sheep for burnt
offerings,
nor honored me with your
sacrifices. Am 5:25; Zec 7:5-6
I have not burdened you with
grain offerings
nor wearied you with
demands for incense.
Ex 30:35; Lev 2:1; Jer 7:22
24 You have not bought any
fragrant calamus for me,
Ex 30:23
or lavished on me the fat of
your sacrifices.
But you have burdened me
with your sins
and wearied me with
your offenses.
Isa 1:14; Mal 2:17

25 "I, even I, am he who blots out
your transgressions,
for my own sake,
Ac 3:19; Eze 36:22
and remembers your sins no
more. Jer 31:34
26 Review the past for me,
let us argue the matter
together; Isa 1:18
state the case for your
innocence. Isa 41:1; 50:8
27 Your first father sinned;
those I sent to teach you
rebelled against me.
Isa 9:15; 28:7; Jer 5:31
28 So I disgraced the dignitaries
of your temple;
I consigned Jacob to
destruction[b]
and Israel to scorn.
Jer 24:9; Eze 5:15

[a] 22 Or *Jacob; / surely you have grown weary of* [b] 28 The Hebrew term refers to the irrevocable giving over of things or persons to the LORD, often by totally destroying them.

Israel the Chosen

44 "But now listen, Jacob, my
servant, Jer 30:10; 46:27-28
Israel, whom I have chosen.
2 This is what the LORD says —
he who made you, who
formed you in the
womb, Ps 139:13; 149:2
and who will help you: Isa 41:10
Do not be afraid, Jacob, my
servant,
Jeshurun,[a] whom I have
chosen. Dt 32:15
3 For I will pour water on the
thirsty land, Joel 3:18
and streams on the dry
ground; Isa 32:2
I will pour out my Spirit
on your offspring,
Joel 2:28; Ac 2:17
and my blessing on your
descendants. Isa 61:9; 65:23
4 They will spring up like grass
in a meadow,
like poplar trees by flowing
streams. Lev 23:40; Job 40:22
5 Some will say, 'I belong to the
LORD'; Ps 116:16
others will call themselves by
the name of Jacob;
still others will write on their
hand, 'The LORD's,'
Ex 13:9; Zec 8:20-22
and will take the name
Israel.

The LORD, Not Idols

6 "This is what the LORD says —
Israel's King and Redeemer,
the LORD Almighty: Isa 43:1
I am the first and I am the last;
Isa 41:4; Rev 1:8,17; 22:13
apart from me there is no
God. Dt 6:4; 1Ch 17:20
7 Who then is like me? Let him
proclaim it.
Let him declare and lay out
before me
what has happened since I
established my ancient
people,
and what is yet to come —
yes, let them foretell what
will come. Isa 41:22,26
8 Do not tremble, do not be afraid.
Did I not proclaim this and
foretell it long ago?
You are my witnesses. Is there
any God besides me?
Isa 43:10
No, there is no other Rock;
I know not one."
Dt 4:35; 1Sa 2:2

9 All who make idols are nothing,
and the things they treasure
are worthless. Isa 41:24
Those who would speak up for
them are blind;
they are ignorant, to their
own shame. Isa 1:29
10 Who shapes a god and casts an
idol,
which can profit nothing?
Isa 41:29; Jer 10:5; Ac 19:26
11 People who do that will be put
to shame; Isa 1:29
such craftsmen are only
human beings.

[a] 2 *Jeshurun* means *the upright one,* that is, Israel.

Let them all come together and
take their stand;
they will be brought down
to terror and shame.
Isa 42:17

12 The blacksmith takes a tool
Isa 40:19; 41:6-7
and works with it in the
coals;
he shapes an idol with
hammers,
he forges it with the might of
his arm. Ac 17:29
He gets hungry and loses his
strength;
he drinks no water and
grows faint. Isa 40:28
13 The carpenter measures with a
line Isa 41:7
and makes an outline with a
marker;
he roughs it out with chisels
and marks it with compasses.
He shapes it in human form,
Ps 115:4-7
human form in all its glory,
that it may dwell in a shrine.
Jdg 17:4-5
14 He cut down cedars,
or perhaps took a cypress or
oak.
He let it grow among the trees
of the forest,
or planted a pine, and the
rain made it grow.
15 It is used as fuel for burning;
some of it he takes and
warms himself,
he kindles a fire and bakes
bread.
But he also fashions a god and
worships it;
he makes an idol and bows
down to it. 2Ch 25:14
16 Half of the wood he burns in
the fire;
over it he prepares his
meal,
he roasts his meat and eats
his fill.
He also warms himself and
says,
"Ah! I am warm; I see the
fire."
17 From the rest he makes a god,
his idol;
he bows down to it and
worships.
He prays to it and says, 1Ki 18:26
"Save me! You are my god!"
Isa 45:20
18 They know nothing,
they understand
nothing; Isa 1:3
their eyes are plastered over
so they cannot see,
Isa 6:9-10
and their minds closed
so they cannot
understand.
19 No one stops to think,
no one has the knowledge
or understanding to say,
Isa 45:20
"Half of it I used for fuel;
I even baked bread over its
coals,
I roasted meat and I ate.
Shall I make a detestable
thing from what is left?
Dt 27:15

Shall I bow down to a block
of wood?"
20 Such a person feeds on
ashes; a deluded
heart misleads him;
Ps 102:9; Job 15:31; Ro 1:21-23,28
he cannot save himself, or
say,
"Is not this thing in my
right hand a lie?"
Isa 59:3-4,13; Ro 1:25

21 "Remember these things,
Jacob, Isa 46:8; Zec 10:9
for you, Israel, are my
servant.
I have made you, you are my
servant; ver 1-2
Israel, I will not forget you.
Isa 49:15
22 I have swept away your
offenses like a cloud,
Ac 3:19
your sins like the morning
mist.
Return to me, Isa 55:7
for I have redeemed you."
1Co 6:20

23 Sing for joy, you heavens, for
the LORD has done this;
Isa 42:10
shout aloud, you earth
beneath. Ps 148:7
Burst into song, you
mountains, Ps 98:8
you forests and all your
trees,
for the LORD has redeemed
Jacob,
he displays his glory in
Israel. Isa 61:3

Jerusalem to Be Inhabited

24 "This is what the LORD says —
your Redeemer, who formed
you in the womb:
Ps 139:13; Isa 43:14

I am the LORD,
the Maker of all things,
who stretches out the
heavens, Isa 42:5
who spreads out the earth by
myself,
25 who foils the signs of false
prophets Ps 33:10
and makes fools of diviners,
Isa 47:13
who overthrows the learning of
the wise 1Co 1:27
and turns it into nonsense,
2Sa 15:31; 1Co 1:19-20
26 who carries out the
words of his servants
Zec 1:6
and fulfills the predictions
of his messengers,
Isa 55:11; Mt 5:18

who says of Jerusalem, 'It shall
be inhabited,'
of the towns of Judah, 'They
shall be rebuilt,'
and of their ruins, 'I will
restore them,' Isa 49:8-21
27 who says to the watery deep,
'Be dry,
and I will dry up your
streams,' Isa 11:15
28 who says of Cyrus, 'He is my
shepherd 2Ch 36:22
and will accomplish all that I
please;

he will say of Jerusalem, "Let it
be rebuilt," Isa 14:32
and of the temple, "Let its
foundations be laid."'
Ezr 1:2-4

45 "This is what the LORD
says to his anointed,
to Cyrus, whose right
hand I take hold of
Ps 73:23; Isa 41:13; 42:6
to subdue nations before him
Jer 50:35
and to strip kings of their
armor,
to open doors before him
so that gates will not be shut:
2 I will go before you Ex 23:20
and will level the
mountains[a]; Isa 40:4
I will break down gates of
bronze
and cut through bars of iron.
Ps 107:16; Jer 51:30
3 I will give you hidden
treasures, Jer 50:37
riches stored in secret places,
Jer 41:8
so that you may know that I
am the LORD, Isa 41:23
the God of Israel, who
summons you by name.
Ex 33:12; Isa 43:1
4 For the sake of Jacob my
servant, Isa 41:8-9
of Israel my chosen,
I summon you by name
and bestow on you a title of
honor,
though you do not
acknowledge me. Ac 17:23
5 I am the LORD, and there is no
other; Isa 44:8
apart from me there is no
God. Ps 18:31
I will strengthen you, Ps 18:39
though you have not
acknowledged me,
6 so that from the rising of the sun
to the place of its setting
Isa 43:5; Mal 1:11
people may know there is none
besides me. Isa 11:9
I am the LORD, and there is
no other.
7 I form the light and create
darkness,
I bring prosperity and create
disaster; Isa 31:2; Am 3:6
I, the LORD, do all these things.

8 "You heavens above, rain
down my righteousness;
Ps 72:6; 85:11
let the clouds shower it down.
Let the earth open wide,
let salvation spring up, Isa 12:3
let righteousness flourish with
it;
I, the LORD, have created it.

9 "Woe to those who quarrel with
their Maker, Job 15:25; 33:13
those who are nothing but
potsherds
among the potsherds on the
ground.
Does the clay say to the potter,
Isa 29:16; Ro 9:20-21*
'What are you making?'

[a] 2 Dead Sea Scrolls and Septuagint; the meaning of the word in the Masoretic Text is uncertain.

Does your work say,
'The potter has no hands'?
10 Woe to the one who says to a father,
'What have you begotten?'
or to a mother,
'What have you brought to birth?'

11 "This is what the LORD says —
the Holy One of Israel, and its Maker: Isa 1:4; 51:13
Concerning things to come,
do you question me about my children,
or give me orders about the work of my hands? Isa 19:25
12 It is I who made the earth
and created mankind on it.
My own hands stretched out the heavens; Ge 2:1; Isa 42:5
I marshaled their starry hosts. Ne 9:6
13 I will raise up Cyrus[a] in my righteousness: Isa 41:2
I will make all his ways straight. Ps 26:12; Isa 40:4
He will rebuild my city
and set my exiles free,
but not for a price or reward, Isa 52:3
says the LORD Almighty."
14 This is what the LORD says:

"The products of Egypt and the merchandise of Cush,[b] 2Sa 8:2
and those tall Sabeans — Isa 2:3
they will come over to you
and will be yours;
they will trudge behind you,
coming over to you in chains. Isa 14:1-2
They will bow down before you
and plead with you, saying, Jer 16:19; Zec 8:20-23
'Surely God is with you,
and there is no other; 1Co 14:25
there is no other god.'" Ps 18:31
15 Truly you are a God who has been hiding himself, Ps 44:24
the God and Savior of Israel.
16 All the makers of idols will be put to shame and disgraced; Isa 44:9,11
they will go off into disgrace together.
17 But Israel will be saved by the LORD Ro 11:26
with an everlasting salvation; Isa 26:4
you will never be put to shame or disgraced, Ge 30:23
to ages everlasting.

18 For this is what the LORD says —
he who created the heavens,
he is God;
he who fashioned and made the earth,
he founded it;
he did not create it to be empty, Ge 1:2
but formed it to be inhabited — Ge 1:26; Isa 42:5

[a] 13 Hebrew *him* [b] 14 That is, the upper Nile region

he says:
"I am the LORD,
and there is no other.
ver 5; Dt 4:35
19 I have not spoken in secret,
Isa 48:16
from somewhere in a land of
darkness;
I have not said to Jacob's
descendants, Isa 41:8
'Seek me in vain.' 2Ch 15:2
I, the LORD, speak the truth;
I declare what is right. Dt 30:11

20 "Gather together and come;
Isa 43:9
assemble, you fugitives from
the nations.
Ignorant are those who carry
about idols of wood,
Isa 44:19; Jer 10:5
who pray to gods that cannot
save. Isa 46:6-7
21 Declare what is to be, present
it —
let them take counsel
together.
Who foretold this long ago,
Isa 41:22
who declared it from the
distant past?
Was it not I, the LORD?
And there is no God apart
from me, ver 5; Ps 46:10
a righteous God and a Savior;
Ps 11:7; Isa 25:9
there is none but me.

22 "Turn to me and be saved,
Nu 21:8-9; Zec 12:10
all you ends of the earth;
Isa 49:6,12
for I am God, and there is no
other. Hos 13:4
23 By myself I have sworn, Ge 22:16
my mouth has uttered in all
integrity Heb 6:13
a word that will not be
revoked: Isa 55:11
Before me every knee will
bow;
by me every tongue will
swear. Ro 14:11*; Php 2:10-11
24 They will say of me, 'In the
LORD alone
are deliverance and
strength.'" Jer 33:16
All who have raged against him
will come to him and be put
to shame. Isa 41:11
25 But all the descendants of
Israel
will find deliverance in the
LORD
and will make their boast in
him. Isa 41:16

Gods of Babylon

46 Bel bows down, Nebo
stoops low; Isa 21:9; Jer 50:2
their idols are borne by
beasts of burden.[a] 1Sa 5:2
The images that are carried
about are burdensome,
Isa 45:20
a burden for the weary.
2 They stoop and bow down
together;
unable to rescue the burden,
they themselves go off into
captivity. Jdg 18:17-18; 2Sa 5:21

[a] 1 Or *are but beasts and cattle*

3 "Listen to me, you
descendants of Jacob, ver 12; Isa 48:12
all the remnant of the people
of Israel, Isa 1:9
you whom I have upheld since
your birth, Ps 139:13
and have carried since you
were born. Ps 22:10
4 Even to your old age and gray
hairs Ps 71:18
I am he, I am he who will
sustain you. Isa 43:13
I have made you and I will
carry you;
I will sustain you and I will
rescue you. Ps 18:35

5 "With whom will you
compare me or count
me equal?
To whom will you liken
me that we may be
compared? Isa 40:18,25
6 Some pour out gold from their
bags
and weigh out silver on the
scales;
they hire a goldsmith to make
it into a god, Isa 40:19
and they bow down and
worship it. Isa 44:17
7 They lift it to their shoulders
and carry it; ver 1
they set it up in its place, and
there it stands.
From that spot it cannot
move.
Even though someone cries out
to it, it cannot answer; 1Ki 18:26
it cannot save them
from their troubles. Isa 44:17; 45:20

8 "Remember this, keep it in
mind, Isa 44:21
take it to heart, you rebels.
9 Remember the former
things, those of
long ago; Dt 32:7
I am God, and there is no
other;
I am God, and there is none
like me. Isa 45:5,21
10 I make known the end from
the beginning,
from ancient times, what is
still to come. Isa 45:21
I say, 'My purpose will stand, Pr 19:21; Ac 5:39
and I will do all that I please.'
11 From the east I summon a bird
of prey;
from a far-off land, a man to
fulfill my purpose.
What I have said, that I will
bring about;
what I have planned, that I
will do. Isa 25:1; Jer 44:28
12 Listen to me, you stubborn-
hearted, ver 3; Isa 9:9
you who are now far from
my righteousness. Jer 2:5
13 I am bringing my
righteousness near, Isa 1:26
it is not far away;
and my salvation will not be
delayed. Ps 85:9
I will grant salvation to Zion, Ps 74:2
my splendor to Israel. Isa 44:23

The Fall of Babylon

47 "Go down, sit in the dust,
Virgin Daughter Babylon; Isa 23:12
sit on the ground without a throne,
queen city of the Babylonians.[a] Jer 51:33; Zec 2:7
No more will you be called
tender or delicate. Dt 28:56
2 Take millstones and grind flour; Ex 11:5; Mt 24:41
take off your veil. Ge 24:65
Lift up your skirts, bare your legs, Isa 32:11
and wade through the streams.
3 Your nakedness will be exposed Eze 16:37; Na 3:5
and your shame uncovered. Isa 20:4
I will take vengeance; Isa 34:8
I will spare no one."

4 Our Redeemer — the LORD Almighty is his name — Jer 50:34; Am 4:13
is the Holy One of Israel. Isa 1:4

5 "Sit in silence, go into darkness, Isa 13:10
queen city of the Babylonians; Isa 21:9
no more will you be called
queen of kingdoms. Isa 13:19; Rev 17:18
6 I was angry with my people 2Ch 28:9
and desecrated my inheritance; Dt 13:15; Isa 42:24
I gave them into your hand, Isa 10:13
and you showed them no mercy. Isa 14:6
Even on the aged
you laid a very heavy yoke.
7 You said, 'I am forever —
the eternal queen!' ver 5; Rev 18:7
But you did not consider these things
or reflect on what might happen. Dt 32:29; Isa 42:23,25

8 "Now then, listen, you lover of pleasure,
lounging in your security Isa 32:9
and saying to yourself,
'I am, and there is none besides me. Isa 45:6; Zep 2:15
I will never be a widow Rev 18:7
or suffer the loss of children.'
9 Both of these will overtake you
in a moment, on a single day: 1Th 5:3; Rev 18:8-10
loss of children and widowhood. Isa 13:18
They will come upon you in full measure,
in spite of your many sorceries Na 3:4
and all your potent spells. Rev 18:23
10 You have trusted in your wickedness Ps 52:7; 62:10
and have said, 'No one sees me.' Isa 29:15

[a] *1* Or *Chaldeans*; also in verse 5

Your wisdom and knowledge
mislead you Isa 5:21; 44:20
when you say to yourself,
'I am, and there is none
besides me.'
11 Disaster will come upon you,
Isa 10:3; 14:15
and you will not know how
to conjure it away.
A calamity will fall upon you
that you cannot ward off
with a ransom;
a catastrophe you cannot
foresee
will suddenly come upon
you. 1Th 5:3

12 "Keep on, then, with your
magic spells
and with your many
sorceries, ver 9; Ex 7:11
which you have labored at
since childhood.
Perhaps you will succeed,
perhaps you will cause
terror.
13 All the counsel you have
received has only
worn you out!
Isa 57:10; Jer 51:58
Let your astrologers come
forward, Isa 44:25
those stargazers who make
predictions month by
month,
let them save you from what
is coming upon you.
Isa 5:29
14 Surely they are like stubble;
Isa 5:24; Na 1:10
the fire will burn them up.
They cannot even save
themselves
from the power of the flame.
Isa 10:17; Jer 51:30,32,58
These are not coals for warmth;
this is not a fire to sit by.
15 That is all they are to you —
these you have dealt with
and labored with since
childhood. Rev 18:11
All of them go on in their error;
there is not one that can save
you. ver 13; Isa 44:17

Stubborn Israel

48 "Listen to this, you
descendants of Jacob,
you who are called by the
name of Israel Ge 17:5
and come from the line of
Judah,
you who take oaths in the
name of the LORD 1Sa 20:42
and invoke the God of
Israel — Isa 58:2
but not in truth or
righteousness — Jer 4:2
2 you who call yourselves
citizens of the holy city
Isa 52:1
and claim to rely on the God
of Israel — Mic 3:11; Ro 2:17
the LORD Almighty is his
name: Isa 47:4
3 I foretold the former things
long ago, Isa 41:22
my mouth announced
them and I made them
known; Isa 45:21
then suddenly I acted, and
they came to pass.

4 For I knew how stubborn you
were; Dt 31:27
your neck muscles were iron, Ex 32:9; Ac 7:51
your forehead was bronze. Eze 3:9
5 Therefore I told you these
things long ago;
before they happened I
announced them to you Isa 40:21
so that you could not say,
'My images brought them
about; Jer 44:15-18
my wooden image and
metal god ordained
them.'
6 You have heard these things;
look at them all.
Will you not admit them?

"From now on I will tell you
of new things, Isa 41:22; Ro 16:25
of hidden things unknown
to you.
7 They are created now, and not
long ago; Isa 45:21
you have not heard of them
before today.
So you cannot say,
'Yes, I knew of them.' Ex 6:7
8 You have neither heard nor
understood; Isa 1:3
from of old your ears have
not been open. Dt 29:4
Well do I know how
treacherous you are;
you were called a
rebel from birth. Dt 9:7,24; Ps 58:3
9 For my own name's sake
I delay my wrath; Ps 78:38; Isa 30:18
for the sake of my praise I
hold it back from you,
so as not to destroy you
completely. Ne 9:31
10 See, I have refined you, though
not as silver;
I have tested you in the
furnace of affliction. 1Ki 8:51
11 For my own sake, for my
own sake, I do this. 1Sa 12:22; Isa 37:35
How can I let myself
be defamed? Dt 32:27; Eze 20:9,14,22,44
I will not yield my glory to
another. Isa 42:8

Israel Freed

12 "Listen to me, Jacob, Isa 46:3
Israel, whom I have called:
I am he; Isa 43:13
I am the first and I am the
last. Isa 41:4; Rev 1:17; 22:13
13 My own hand laid the
foundations of the
earth, Heb 1:10-12
and my right hand spread
out the heavens; Ex 20:11
when I summon them,
they all stand up together. Isa 40:26
14 "Come together, all of you, and
listen: Isa 43:9
Which of the idols has
foretold these things? Isa 41:22

The LORD's chosen ally
will carry out his purpose
against Babylon; Isa 46:10-11
his arm will be against the
Babylonians.[a]
15 I, even I, have spoken;
yes, I have called him. Isa 45:1
I will bring him,
and he will succeed in his
mission.

16 "Come near me and listen to
this: Isa 41:1

"From the first announcement
I have not spoken in
secret; Isa 45:19
at the time it happens, I am
there."

And now the Sovereign LORD
has sent me, Zec 2:9,11
endowed with his Spirit.
Isa 11:2

17 This is what the LORD says —
your Redeemer, the Holy One
of Israel: Isa 43:14; 49:7
"I am the LORD your God,
who teaches you what
is best for you,
Isa 28:9; Jer 7:13
who directs you in the
way you should go.
Ps 32:8; Isa 49:10
18 If only you had paid attention
to my commands, Dt 32:29
your peace would have
been like a river,
Ps 119:165; Isa 66:12
your well-being like the
waves of the sea. Isa 45:8
19 Your descendants would
have been like the sand,
Ge 12:2
your children like its
numberless grains; Ge 22:17
their name would never be
blotted out Isa 56:5; 66:22
nor destroyed from before
me."

20 Leave Babylon,
flee from the Babylonians!
Jer 50:8; 51:6,45
Announce this with shouts of
joy Isa 49:13
and proclaim it.
Send it out to the ends of the
earth;
say, "The LORD has redeemed
his servant Jacob."
Isa 52:9; 63:9
21 They did not thirst when he
led them through the
deserts; Isa 41:17
he made water flow for them
from the rock; Isa 30:25
he split the rock
and water gushed out.
Ex 17:6; Nu 20:11; Ps 105:41

22 "There is no peace," says the
LORD, "for the wicked."
Isa 57:21

The Servant of the LORD

49 Listen to me, you islands;
hear this, you distant
nations:
Before I was born the
LORD called me;
Isa 44:24; 46:3; Mt 1:20

[a] 14 Or *Chaldeans*; also in verse 20

from my mother's womb he
has spoken my name.
Isa 43:1
2He made my mouth like a
sharpened sword,
Isa 11:4; Rev 1:16
in the shadow of his hand he
hid me; Ps 91:1
he made me into a polished
arrow Dt 32:23; Zec 9:13
and concealed me in his
quiver.
3He said to me, "You are my
servant, Zec 3:8
Israel, in whom I will display
my splendor." Isa 44:23
4But I said, "I have labored in
vain;
I have spent my strength for
nothing at all. Isa 65:23
Yet what is due me is in the
LORD's hand,
and my reward is with my
God." Isa 35:4

5And now the LORD says —
he who formed me in the
womb to be his servant
Ps 139:13
to bring Jacob back to him
and gather Israel to himself,
Isa 11:12
for I am[a] honored in the eyes
of the LORD Isa 43:4
and my God has been my
strength — Ps 18:1
6he says:
"It is too small a thing for you
to be my servant
to restore the tribes of
Jacob
and bring back those of
Israel I have kept. Isa 1:9
I will also make you a light
for the Gentiles,
Lk 2:32; Jn 1:9
that my salvation may reach
to the ends of the earth."
Jn 11:52; Ac 13:47*

7This is what the LORD says —
the Redeemer and Holy One
of Israel — Isa 48:17
to him who was despised and
abhorred by the nation,
Ps 22:6; 69:7-9
to the servant of rulers:
"Kings will see you and stand
up, Isa 52:15
princes will see and bow
down,
because of the LORD, who is
faithful, 1Co 1:9
the Holy One of Israel, who
has chosen you." Isa 14:1

Restoration of Israel

8This is what the LORD says:

"In the time of my favor I will
answer you, Ps 69:13
and in the day of salvation I
will help you; 2Co 6:2*
I will keep you and will make
you Isa 26:3
to be a covenant for the
people, Isa 42:6
to restore the land Isa 44:26
and to reassign its
desolate inheritances,
Isa 60:21

[a] 5 Or him, / but Israel would not be gathered; / yet I will be

9 to say to the captives, 'Come
out,' Isa 42:7; Lk 4:19
and to those in darkness, 'Be
free!'

"They will feed beside the roads
and find pasture on every
barren hill. Isa 41:18
10 They will neither hunger nor
thirst, Isa 33:16
nor will the desert heat or
the sun beat down on
them. Ps 121:6; Rev 7:16
He who has compassion on them
will guide them Isa 14:1
and lead them beside springs
of water. Isa 35:7
11 I will turn all my mountains
into roads,
and my highways will be
raised up. Isa 11:16; 40:4
12 See, they will come from afar —
Isa 43:5-6
some from the north, some
from the west,
some from the region of
Aswan.[a]"

13 Shout for joy, you heavens;
Isa 48:20
rejoice, you earth;
burst into song, you
mountains! Isa 44:23
For the LORD comforts his
people Isa 40:1; 2Co 1:4
and will have compassion
on his afflicted ones.
Ps 9:12; Isa 14:1

14 But Zion said, "The LORD has
forsaken me, Ps 9:10; 71:11
the Lord has forgotten me."

15 "Can a mother forget the baby
at her breast
and have no compassion on
the child she has borne?
1Ki 3:26
Though she may forget,
I will not forget you! Isa 44:21
16 See, I have engraved you on the
palms of my hands; SS 8:6
your walls are ever before
me. Ps 48:12-13; Isa 62:6
17 Your children hasten back,
and those who laid you waste
depart from you. Isa 10:6
18 Lift up your eyes and look
around;
all your children gather
and come to you.
Isa 60:4; 43:5; 54:7
As surely as I live," declares the
LORD, Ro 14:11*
"you will wear them all as
ornaments; Isa 52:1
you will put them on, like a
bride.

19 "Though you were ruined and
made desolate Isa 54:1,3
and your land laid waste,
Isa 5:6
now you will be too small for
your people, Zec 10:10
and those who devoured you
will be far away. Isa 1:20
20 The children born during your
bereavement
will yet say in your hearing,
'This place is too small for us;
give us more space to live in.'
Isa 54:1-3

[a] 12 Dead Sea Scrolls; Masoretic Text *Sinim*

21 Then you will say in your heart,
'Who bore me these?
I was bereaved and barren;
I was exiled and rejected. Isa 5:13
Who brought these up?
I was left all alone, Isa 1:8
but these — where have they come from?' "

22 This is what the Sovereign LORD says: Ge 15:2

"See, I will beckon to the nations,
I will lift up my banner to the peoples; Isa 11:10
they will bring your sons in their arms Isa 11:12
and carry your daughters on their hips. Isa 60:4
23 Kings will be your foster fathers, Isa 60:3,10-11
and their queens your nursing mothers. Isa 60:16
They will bow down before you with their faces to the ground;
they will lick the dust at your feet. Ps 72:9
Then you will know that I am the LORD; Mic 7:17
those who hope in me will not be disappointed." Ps 37:9; Isa 41:11

24 Can plunder be taken from warriors, Mt 12:29; Lk 11:21
or captives be rescued from the fierce[a]?

25 But this is what the LORD says:

"Yes, captives will be taken from warriors, Isa 14:2; Jer 50:33-34
and plunder retrieved from the fierce;
I will contend with those who contend with you, Jer 50:34
and your children I will save. Isa 25:9; 35:4
26 I will make your oppressors eat their own flesh; Isa 9:4,20
they will be drunk on their own blood, as with wine. Rev 16:6
Then all mankind will know Eze 39:7
that I, the LORD, am your Savior, Isa 25:9
your Redeemer, the Mighty One of Jacob." Isa 48:17

Israel's Sin and the Servant's Obedience

50 This is what the LORD says:

"Where is your mother's certificate of divorce Dt 24:1; Jer 3:8
with which I sent her away?
Or to which of my creditors did I sell you? Ne 5:5; Mt 18:25
Because of your sins you were sold; Dt 32:30; Isa 52:3
because of your transgressions your mother was sent away.

[a] 24 Dead Sea Scrolls, Vulgate and Syriac (see also Septuagint and verse 25); Masoretic Text *righteous*

2 When I came, why was there no
one?
When I called, why was
there no one to answer? Isa 41:28
Was my arm too short
to deliver you? Nu 11:23; Isa 59:1
Do I lack the strength to
rescue you? Ge 18:14
By a mere rebuke I dry up the
sea, Ex 14:22; Jos 3:16
I turn rivers into a desert; Ps 107:33
their fish rot for lack of water
and die of thirst.
3 I clothe the heavens with
darkness
and make sackcloth its
covering." Rev 6:12

4 The Sovereign LORD has given
me a well-instructed
tongue, Ex 4:12
to know the word that
sustains the weary. Mt 11:28
He wakens me morning by
morning, Ps 5:3; 119:147
wakens my ear to listen like
one being instructed. Isa 28:9
5 The Sovereign LORD has
opened my ears; Isa 35:5
I have not been rebellious, Mt 26:39; Jn 14:31
I have not turned away.
6 I offered my back to those who
beat me, Isa 53:5; Mt 27:30
my cheeks to those who
pulled out my beard; 2Sa 10:4
I did not hide my face
from mocking and spitting. La 3:30; Mt 26:67
7 Because the Sovereign LORD
helps me, Isa 42:1
I will not be disgraced.
Therefore have I set my face
like flint, Eze 3:8-9
and I know I will not be put
to shame. Isa 28:16
8 He who vindicates me is near. Ia 26:2; 49:4
Who then will bring
charges against me? Isa 43:26; Ro 8:32-34
Let us face each other! Isa 41:1
Who is my accuser?
Let him confront me!
9 It is the Sovereign LORD who
helps me. Isa 41:10
Who will condemn me? Ro 8:1,34
They will all wear out like a
garment;
the moths will eat them up. Job 13:28; Isa 51:8

10 Who among you fears the
LORD
and obeys the word of his
servant? Isa 49:3
Let the one who walks in the
dark,
who has no light, Ps 107:14
trust in the name of the LORD Isa 26:4
and rely on their God.
11 But now, all you who light
fires
and provide yourselves with
flaming torches, Pr 26:18

go, walk in the light of your
fires Jas 3:6
and of the torches you have
set ablaze.
This is what you shall receive
from my hand: Pr 26:27
You will lie down in torment.
Isa 65:13-15

Everlasting Salvation for Zion

51 "Listen to me, you who
pursue righteousness
Ps 94:15; Isa 46:3; Ro 9:30-31
and who seek the LORD:
Isa 55:6
Look to the rock from which
you were cut Isa 17:10
and to the quarry from
which you were hewn;
2 look to Abraham, your father,
Heb 11:11; Isa 29:22
and to Sarah, who gave you
birth.
When I called him he was only
one man,
and I blessed him and made
him many. Ge 12:2
3 The LORD will surely comfort
Zion Isa 40:1
and will look with
compassion on all her
ruins; Isa 52:9
he will make her deserts like
Eden, Ge 2:8
her wastelands like
the garden of the LORD.
Isa 5:6
Joy and gladness will be found
in her, Isa 25:9; 66:10
thanksgiving and the sound
of singing. Jer 17:26

4 "Listen to me, my people; Ps 50:7
hear me, my nation:
Instruction will go out from
me; Dt 18:18
my justice will become a
light to the nations.
Isa 2:4; 42:4,6
5 My righteousness draws near
speedily,
my salvation is on the way,
Isa 46:13
and my arm will bring
justice to the nations.
Isa 40:10; 63:1,5
The islands will look to me
Isa 11:11
and wait in hope for my arm.
Ge 49:10; Ps 37:9
6 Lift up your eyes to the
heavens,
look at the earth beneath;
the heavens will vanish like
smoke, Mt 24:35; 2Pe 3:10
the earth will wear out like a
garment Ps 102:25-26
and its inhabitants die like
flies.
But my salvation will last
forever, Ps 119:89
my righteousness will never
fail. Ps 89:33
7 "Hear me, you who know what
is right,
you people who have taken
my instruction to heart:
Ps 37:31
Do not fear the reproach of
mere mortals
or be terrified by their
insults. Mt 5:11; Ac 5:41

8 For the moth will eat them up
like a garment; Isa 50:9
the worm will devour them
like wool. Isa 14:11
But my righteousness will last
forever, ver 6
my salvation through all
generations."

9 Awake, awake, arm of the
LORD,
clothe yourself with
strength! Isa 52:1
Awake, as in days gone by,
as in generations of old. Dt 4:34
Was it not you who cut Rahab
to pieces, Job 9:13
who pierced that monster
through? Ps 74:13
10 Was it not you who dried up
the sea, Ex 14:22
the waters of the great deep,
who made a road in the depths
of the sea Job 36:30
so that the redeemed might
cross over? Ex 15:13
11 Those the LORD has rescued
will return. Isa 35:9
They will enter Zion with
singing; Ps 109:28
everlasting joy will crown
their heads.
Gladness and joy will overtake
them, Jer 33:11
and sorrow and sighing will
flee away. Rev 7:17

12 "I, even I, am he who comforts
you. 2Co 1:4
Who are you that you
fear mere mortals,
Ps 118:6; Isa 2:22
human beings who are but
grass, 1Pe 1:24
13 that you forget the LORD your
Maker, Isa 17:10; 45:11
who stretches out the
heavens Ps 104:2; Isa 48:13
and who lays the
foundations of the
earth,
that you live in constant terror
every day Isa 7:4
because of the wrath of the
oppressor,
who is bent on destruction?
For where is the wrath of the
oppressor? Isa 9:4
14 The cowering prisoners will
soon be set free;
they will not die in their
dungeon,
nor will they lack bread.
Isa 49:10
15 For I am the LORD your God,
who stirs up the sea so that
its waves roar — Jer 31:35
the LORD Almighty is his
name. Isa 13:4
16 I have put my words in your
mouth Dt 18:18; Isa 59:21
and covered you with the
shadow of my hand —
Ex 33:22
I who set the heavens in place,
who laid the foundations of
the earth, Isa 48:13
and who say to Zion, 'You are
my people.'" Jer 7:23

The Cup of the LORD's Wrath

17 Awake, awake! Isa 52:1
Rise up, Jerusalem,

you who have drunk from the
hand of the LORD
the cup of his wrath,
Job 21:20; Rev 14:10
you who have drained to its
dregs Ps 75:8
the goblet that makes people
stagger. Ps 60:3
18 Among all the children she
bore Ps 88:18
there was none to guide her;
Isa 49:21
among all the children she
reared
there was none to take her
by the hand.
19 These double calamities have
come upon you — Isa 47:9
who can comfort you? —
Isa 49:13; Jer 15:5
ruin and destruction, famine
and sword — Isa 14:30
who can[a] console you?
20 Your children have fainted;
they lie at every street
corner, Isa 5:25; Jer 14:16
like antelope caught in a
net.
They are filled with the wrath
of the LORD, Job 40:11
with the rebuke of your God.
Dt 28:20
21 Therefore hear this, you
afflicted one, Isa 14:32
made drunk, but not with
wine. Isa 29:9
22 This is what your Sovereign
LORD says,
your God, who defends his
people: Isa 49:25
"See, I have taken out of your
hand
the cup that made you
stagger; ver 17; Jer 25:15
from that cup, the goblet of my
wrath,
you will never drink again.
23 I will put it into the hands
of your tormentors,
Jer 25:15-17,26,28; 49:12
who said to you,
'Fall prostrate that we
may walk on you.'
Zec 12:2; Jos 10:24
And you made your back like
the ground,
like a street to be walked on."
Ps 66:12

52 Awake, awake, Zion, Isa 51:17
clothe yourself with
strength! Isa 51:9
Put on your garments of
splendor, Ps 110:3
Jerusalem, the holy city.
Ne 11:1; Mt 4:5
The uncircumcised and
defiled
will not enter you again.
Rev 21:27
2 Shake off your dust; Isa 29:4
rise up, sit enthroned,
Jerusalem.
Free yourself from the chains
on your neck, Ps 81:6
Daughter Zion, now a
captive. Ps 9:14

3 For this is what the LORD says:

[a] 19 Dead Sea Scrolls, Septuagint, Vulgate and Syriac; Masoretic Text / *how can I*

"You were sold for nothing, Ps 44:12
and without money you will be redeemed." Isa 45:13

4 For this is what the Sovereign LORD says:

"At first my people went down to Egypt to live; Ge 46:6
lately, Assyria has oppressed them.

5 "And now what do I have here?" declares the LORD.

"For my people have been taken away for nothing,
and those who rule them mock,[a]"
declares the LORD.
"And all day long
my name is constantly blasphemed. Eze 36:20; Ro 2:24*
6 Therefore my people will know my name; Isa 49:23
therefore in that day they will know Isa 10:20
that it is I who foretold it. Isa 41:26
Yes, it is I."

7 How beautiful on the mountains
are the feet of those
who bring good news, Ro 10:15*
who proclaim peace, Eph 6:15
who bring good tidings,
who proclaim salvation,
who say to Zion,
"Your God reigns!" Ps 93:1
8 Listen! Your watchmen lift up their voices; Isa 62:6
together they shout for joy. Isa 12:6
When the LORD returns to Zion, Isa 59:20
they will see it with their own eyes.
9 Burst into songs of joy together, Ps 98:4
you ruins of Jerusalem, Isa 51:3
for the LORD has comforted his people, Lk 2:25
he has redeemed Jerusalem. Isa 48:20
10 The LORD will lay bare his holy arm Ps 44:3
in the sight of all the nations, Isa 66:18
and all the ends of the earth will see Isa 11:9
the salvation of our God. Ps 98:2-3; Lk 3:6

11 Depart, depart, go out from there! Isa 48:20
Touch no unclean thing! 2Co 6:17*
Come out from it and be pure, 2Ti 2:19
you who carry the articles of the LORD's house. 2Ch 36:10
12 But you will not leave in haste Ex 12:11
or go in flight;
for the LORD will go before you, Mic 2:13
the God of Israel will be your rear guard. Ex 14:19

[a] 5 Dead Sea Scrolls and Vulgate; Masoretic Text *wail*

The Suffering and Glory of the Servant

13 See, my servant will act
wisely[a]; Isa 42:1
he will be raised and lifted
up and highly exalted.
Php 2:9
14 Just as there were many who
were appalled at him[b] —
Job 18:20
his appearance was so
disfigured beyond that
of any human being
2Sa 10:4
and his form marred beyond
human likeness — Job 2:12
15 so he will sprinkle many
nations,[c] Lev 14:7; 16:14-15
and kings will shut their
mouths because of him.
Isa 49:7
For what they were not told,
they will see,
and what they have not heard,
they will understand.
Ro 15:21*; Eph 3:4-5

53 Who has believed our
message Ro 10:16*
and to whom has the arm of
the LORD been revealed?
Jn 12:38*
2 He grew up before him like a
tender shoot, 2Ki 19:26
and like a root out of dry
ground. Isa 11:10
He had no beauty or majesty to
attract us to him,
nothing in his appearance
that we should desire
him. Isa 52:14
3 He was despised and rejected
by mankind,
a man of suffering, and
familiar with pain.
Lk 18:31-33
Like one from whom people
hide their faces Dt 31:17
he was despised, and we
held him in low esteem.
Ps 22:6; Jn 1:10-11
4 Surely he took up our pain
and bore our suffering, Mt 8:17*
yet we considered him
punished by God, Jn 19:7
stricken by him, and
afflicted. Ge 12:17; Ru 1:21
5 But he was pierced for
our transgressions,
Ro 4:25; 1Co 15:3
he was crushed for our
iniquities; Ps 34:18
the punishment that brought
us peace was on him,
Isa 9:6; 50:6
and by his wounds we are
healed. 1Pe 2:24-25
6 We all, like sheep, have gone
astray, Ps 95:10; 1Pe 2:24-25
each of us has turned to our
own way; 1Sa 8:3
and the LORD has laid on him
the iniquity of us all.
Ex 28:38; Ro 4:25
7 He was oppressed and afflicted,
Isa 49:26
yet he did not open his
mouth; Mk 14:61

[a] 13 Or *will prosper* [b] 14 Hebrew *you*
[c] 15 Or *so will many nations be amazed at him* (see also Septuagint)

he was led like a lamb to the
slaughter, Ps 44:22
and as a sheep before
its shearers is
silent,
so he did not open his
mouth.
8 By oppression[a] and judgment
he was taken away.
Mk 14:49
Yet who of his generation
protested?
For he was cut off from the
land of the living;
Da 9:26; Ac 8:32-33*
for the transgression of
my people he was
punished.[b] Ps 39:8
9 He was assigned a grave with
the wicked,
and with the rich in his
death, Mt 27:57-60
though he had done no
violence, Isa 42:1-3
nor was any deceit in his
mouth. 1Pe 2:22*
10 Yet it was the LORD's will
to crush him and
cause him to suffer,
Isa 46:10; Ge 12:17
and though the LORD
makes[c] his life an
offering for sin,
Lev 5:15; Jn 3:17
he will see his offspring
and prolong his days,
Ps 22:30
and the will of the LORD will
prosper in his hand.
Isa 49:4
11 After he has suffered, Jn 10:14-18
he will see the light of life[d]
and be satisfied[e]; Job 33:30
by his knowledge[f] my
righteous servant will
justify many, Ro 5:18-19
and he will bear their
iniquities. Ex 28:38
12 Therefore I will give him a
portion among the
great,[g] Php 2:9
and he will divide the spoils
with the strong,[h] Lk 11:22
because he poured out his
life unto death,
Mt 26:28,38-39,42
and was numbered with
the transgressors.
Lk 22:37*; 23:32
For he bore the sin of many,
1Pe 2:24
and made intercession for
the transgressors. Ro 8:34

The Future Glory of Zion

54 "Sing, barren woman, Ge 30:1
you who never bore a
child;
burst into song, shout for joy,
Ge 21:6
you who were never in labor;
Isa 66:7

[a] 8 Or *From arrest* [b] 8 Or *generation considered / that he was cut off from the land of the living, / that he was punished for the transgression of my people?* [c] 10 Hebrew *though you make* [d] 11 Dead Sea Scrolls (see also Septuagint); Masoretic Text does not have *the light of life.* [e] 11 Or (with Masoretic Text) [11] *He will see the fruit of his suffering / and will be satisfied* [f] 11 Or *by knowledge of him* [g] 12 Or *many* [h] 12 Or *numerous*

because more are the children
of the desolate woman Isa 49:20
than of her who has a
husband," Gal 4:27*
says the LORD.
2 "Enlarge the place of your tent, Isa 49:19-20
stretch your tent curtains
wide,
do not hold back;
lengthen your cords,
strengthen your stakes. Ex 35:18; 39:40
3 For you will spread out to the
right and to the left;
your descendants will
dispossess nations Isa 14:2; 60:4-11
and settle in their desolate
cities. Isa 49:19
4 "Do not be afraid; you will
not be put to shame. Isa 28:16; 29:22
Do not fear disgrace;
you will not be
humiliated. Ge 30:23
You will forget the shame of
your youth Jer 2:2
and remember no more
the reproach of your
widowhood. Isa 51:7
5 For your Maker is your
husband — Jer 3:14
the LORD Almighty is his
name —
the Holy One of Israel is your
Redeemer; Isa 48:17
he is called the God of all the
earth. Isa 6:3
6 The LORD will call you back Isa 49:14-21
as if you were a wife deserted
and distressed in
spirit — Isa 62:4,12
a wife who married young, Ex 20:14; Mal 2:15
only to be rejected," says
your God.
7 "For a brief moment I
abandoned you, Isa 26:20
but with deep compassion
I will bring you back. Isa 49:18
8 In a surge of anger Isa 60:10
I hid my face from you for a
moment, Isa 1:15
but with everlasting kindness Ps 25:6; Isa 55:3
I will have compassion on
you," Ps 102:13; Isa 14:1
says the LORD your
Redeemer. Isa 48:17
9 "To me this is like the days of
Noah,
when I swore that the waters
of Noah would never
again cover the earth. Ge 8:21
So now I have sworn not
to be angry with you, Isa 12:1; 57:16
never to rebuke you again. Dt 28:20
10 Though the mountains be
shaken Ps 46:2; Rev 6:14
and the hills be removed,
yet my unfailing love for you
will not be shaken Isa 51:6; Ps 6:4

nor my covenant of peace be
removed," Ps 89:34; Isa 42:6
says the LORD, who has
compassion on you.
ver 8; Isa 14:1

11 "Afflicted city, lashed by storms
and not comforted,
Isa 14:32; 28:2; 51:19
I will rebuild you with
stones of turquoise,[a]
1Ch 29:2; Rev 21:18
your foundations with lapis
lazuli. Isa 28:16; Rev 21:19-20
12 I will make your battlements of
rubies,
your gates of sparkling
jewels,
and all your walls of precious
stones.
13 All your children will be taught
by the LORD, Jn 6:45*; Heb 8:11
and great will be their peace.
Isa 48:18
14 In righteousness you will be
established: Isa 26:2
Tyranny will be far from you;
Isa 9:4
you will have nothing to fear.
Zep 3:15
Terror will be far removed;
Isa 17:14
it will not come near you.
15 If anyone does attack you, it
will not be my doing;
whoever attacks you will
surrender to you. Isa 41:11-16

16 "See, it is I who created the
blacksmith Isa 44:12
who fans the coals into
flame
and forges a weapon fit for
its work. Isa 10:5
And it is I who have created
the destroyer to wreak
havoc; Isa 13:5
17 no weapon forged against
you will prevail, Isa 29:8
and you will refute every
tongue that accuses you.
Isa 45:24-25
This is the heritage of the
servants of the LORD,
Isa 56:6-8
and this is their vindication
from me," Ps 17:2
declares the LORD.

Invitation to the Thirsty

55 "Come, all you who are
thirsty, Jn 4:14; 7:37
come to the waters; Jer 2:13
and you who have no money,
come, buy and eat! Rev 3:18
Come, buy wine and milk SS 5:1
without money and
without cost.
Hos 14:4; Mt 10:8
2 Why spend money on what is
not bread,
and your labor on what
does not satisfy?
Ps 22:26; Hos 8:7
Listen, listen to me, and eat
what is good, Isa 1:19
and you will delight in the
richest of fare. Isa 30:23
3 Give ear and come to me;
listen, that you may live.
Lev 18:5; Ro 10:5

[a] 11 The meaning of the Hebrew for this word is uncertain.

I will make an everlasting
covenant with you, Isa 61:8
my faithful love promised to
David. Ac 13:34*; Isa 54:8
4 See, I have made him a
witness to the peoples,
Jer 30:9; Eze 34:23-24
a ruler and commander of
the peoples.
5 Surely you will summon
nations you know not,
Isa 49:6
and nations you do not know
will come running to
you, Isa 2:3
because of the LORD your
God,
the Holy One of Israel, Isa 12:6
for he has endowed you with
splendor." Isa 60:9

6 Seek the LORD while he may be
found; Ps 32:6; 2Co 6:1-2
call on him while he is near.
Isa 65:24
7 Let the wicked forsake their
ways 2Ch 7:14
and the unrighteous their
thoughts. Isa 32:7; 59:7
Let them turn to the LORD, and
he will have mercy on
them, Isa 44:22; 54:10
and to our God, for he will
freely pardon. Isa 1:18; 40:2
8 "For my thoughts are not your
thoughts, Php 2:5; 4:8
neither are your ways my
ways," Isa 53:6; Mic 4:12
declares the LORD.
9 "As the heavens are higher
than the earth, Ps 103:11
so are my ways higher than
your ways
and my thoughts than your
thoughts. Isa 40:13-14
10 As the rain and the snow
Isa 30:23
come down from heaven,
and do not return to it
without watering the earth
and making it bud and
flourish, Ps 67:6
so that it yields seed for the
sower and bread for the
eater, 2Co 9:10
11 so is my word that goes
out from my mouth:
Dt 32:2; Jn 1:1
It will not return to me
empty, Isa 45:23
but will accomplish what I
desire
and achieve the purpose for
which I sent it. Isa 44:26
12 You will go out in joy Ps 98:4
and be led forth in peace;
Isa 54:10,13
the mountains and hills
will burst into song before
you, Ps 65:12-13
and all the trees of the field
1Ch 16:33
will clap their hands. Ps 98:8
13 Instead of the thornbush will
grow the juniper,
and instead of briers the
myrtle will grow.
Isa 5:6; 41:19
This will be for the LORD's
renown, Isa 63:12
for an everlasting sign,
that will endure forever."

Salvation for Others

56 This is what the LORD says:

"Maintain justice Isa 1:17
and do what is right, Isa 26:8
for my salvation is close at
hand Ps 85:9
and my righteousness will
soon be revealed. Jer 23:6
2 Blessed is the one who does
this — Ps 119:2
the person who holds it
fast,
who keeps the Sabbath
without desecrating it,
Ex 20:8,10; Isa 58:13
and keeps their hands from
doing any evil."
3 Let no foreigner who is
bound to the LORD say,
Ex 12:43
"The LORD will surely
exclude me from his
people." Dt 23:3
And let no eunuch complain,
Ac 8:27
"I am only a dry tree."

4 For this is what the LORD says:

"To the eunuchs who keep my
Sabbaths,
who choose what pleases me
and hold fast to my
covenant — Ex 31:13
5 to them I will give within my
temple and its walls
Isa 26:1; 60:18
a memorial and a name
better than sons and
daughters;
I will give them an everlasting
name
that will endure forever.
Isa 48:19; 55:13
6 And foreigners who bind
themselves to the LORD
to minister to him,
Isa 60:7,10; 61:5
to love the name of the LORD,
Mal 1:11
and to be his servants,
all who keep the Sabbath
without desecrating it
ver 2,4
and who hold fast to my
covenant —
7 these I will bring to my holy
mountain Isa 2:2
and give them joy in my
house of prayer.
Their burnt offerings and
sacrifices Ro 12:1; Heb 13:15
will be accepted on my
altar;
for my house will be called
a house of prayer for all
nations." Mt 21:13*; Mk 11:17*
8 The Sovereign LORD declares —
he who gathers the exiles of
Israel:
"I will gather still others to
them Isa 11:12; Jn 10:16
besides those already
gathered."

God's Accusation Against the Wicked

9 Come, all you beasts of the
field, Jer 12:9
come and devour, all you
beasts of the forest!

10 Israel's watchmen are blind, Eze 3:17
they all lack knowledge; Jer 2:8
they are all mute dogs,
they cannot bark;
they lie around and dream,
they love to sleep. Na 3:18
11 They are dogs with mighty appetites;
they never have enough.
They are shepherds who lack understanding; Isa 1:3; Eze 34:2
they all turn to their own way, Isa 53:6
they seek their own gain. Mic 3:11
12 "Come," each one cries, "let me get wine! Lev 10:9
Let us drink our fill of beer!
And tomorrow will be like today,
or even far better." Lk 12:18-19

57 The righteous perish, Ps 12:1
and no one takes it to heart; Isa 42:25
the devout are taken away,
and no one understands
that the righteous are taken away
to be spared from evil. 2Ki 22:20
2 Those who walk uprightly Isa 26:7
enter into peace;
they find rest as they lie in death. Da 12:13
3 "But you — come here, you children of a sorceress, Ex 22:18
you offspring of adulterers and prostitutes! Isa 1:21; Mt 16:4
4 Who are you mocking?
At whom do you sneer
and stick out your tongue?
Are you not a brood of rebels, Isa 1:2
the offspring of liars?
5 You burn with lust among the oaks
and under every spreading tree; 2Ki 16:4
you sacrifice your children in the ravines Lev 18:21; Ps 106:37-38
and under the overhanging crags.
6 The idols among the smooth stones of the ravines are your portion; Jer 3:9
indeed, they are your lot.
Yes, to them you have poured out drink offerings Jer 7:18
and offered grain offerings.
In view of all this, should I relent? Jer 5:9,29; 9:9
7 You have made your bed on a high and lofty hill; Jer 3:6; Eze 16:16
there you went up to offer your sacrifices. Jer 13:27; Eze 6:13
8 Behind your doors and your doorposts
you have put your pagan symbols.
Forsaking me, you uncovered your bed,
you climbed into it and opened it wide;

you made a pact with those
whose beds you love,
Eze 16:26; 23:7
and you looked with lust
on their naked bodies.
Eze 23:18
9 You went to Molek[a] with olive
oil 1Ki 11:5
and increased your
perfumes.
You sent your ambassadors[b] far
away; Eze 23:16,40
you descended to the very
realm of the dead! Isa 8:19
10 You wearied yourself by such
going about,
but you would not say, 'It is
hopeless.' Jer 2:25; 18:12
You found renewal of your
strength,
and so you did not faint.

11 "Whom have you so dreaded
and feared Pr 29:25
that you have not been true
to me,
and have neither remembered
me Jer 2:32; 3:21
nor taken this to heart?
Isa 42:23
Is it not because I have long
been silent Ps 50:21
that you do not fear me?
12 I will expose your
righteousness and your
works, Isa 29:15; Mic 3:2-4,8
and they will not benefit you.
13 When you cry out for help,
Jer 22:20; 30:15
let your collection of idols
save you!
The wind will carry all of them
off,
a mere breath will blow
them away. Is 40:7,24
But whoever takes refuge
in me Ps 118:8
will inherit the land Ps 37:9
and possess my holy
mountain." Isa 65:9-11

Comfort for the Contrite

14 And it will be said:
"Build up, build up, prepare the
road!
Remove the obstacles out of
the way of my people."
Isa 62:10; Jer 18:15
15 For this is what the high and
exalted One says —
Isa 52:13
he who lives forever, whose
name is holy: Dt 33:27
"I live in a high and holy place,
Job 16:19
but also with the one who
is contrite and lowly in
spirit, Ps 34:18; 51:17; 147:3
to revive the spirit of the
lowly
and to revive the heart of the
contrite. Isa 61:1
16 I will not accuse them
forever,
nor will I always be angry,
Ps 85:5; 103:9; Mic 7:18
for then they would faint away
because of me —
the very people I have
created. Ge 2:7; Zec 12:1

[a] 9 Or *to the king* [b] 9 Or *idols*

17 I was enraged by their sinful
greed; Isa 56:11
I punished them, and
hid my face in anger,
Isa 1:15
yet they kept on in their
willful ways. Isa 1:4
18 I have seen their ways, but I
will heal them; Isa 30:26
I will guide them and restore
comfort to Israel's
mourners, Isa 61:1-3
19 creating praise on their lips.
Heb 13:15
Peace, peace, to those far and
near," Ac 2:39; Eph 2:17
says the LORD. "And I will
heal them."
20 But the wicked are like the
tossing sea, Job 18:5-21
which cannot rest,
whose waves cast up mire
and mud. Ps 69:14
21 "There is no peace," says my
God, "for the wicked."
Isa 48:22; 59:8

True Fasting

58 "Shout it aloud, do not
hold back. Isa 40:6
Raise your voice like a
trumpet. Ex 20:18
Declare to my people their
rebellion Isa 48:8
and to the descendants of
Jacob their sins. Isa 57:12
2 For day after day they seek
me out;
Isa 48:1; Titus 1:16; Jas 4:8
they seem eager to know my
ways,
as if they were a nation that
does what is right
and has not forsaken the
commands of its God.
Ps 119:87
They ask me for just decisions
and seem eager for God to
come near them. Isa 29:13
3 'Why have we fasted,' they say,
Lev 16:29
'and you have not seen it?
Why have we humbled
ourselves, Ex 10:3
and you have not noticed?'
Mal 3:14
"Yet on the day of your fasting,
you do as you please
Isa 22:13; Zec 7:5-6
and exploit all your workers.
4 Your fasting ends in quarreling
and strife, 1Ki 21:9-13; Isa 59:6
and in striking each other
with wicked fists.
You cannot fast as you do
today
and expect your voice to be
heard on high. Isa 59:2
5 Is this the kind of fast I have
chosen, Zec 7:5
only a day for people to
humble themselves?
1Ki 21:27
Is it only for bowing one's head
like a reed
and for lying in sackcloth
and ashes? Job 2:8
Is that what you call a fast,
a day acceptable to the LORD?
6 "Is not this the kind of fasting I
have chosen: Joel 2:12-14

to loose the chains of injustice Ne 5:10-11
and untie the cords of the
yoke,
to set the oppressed free Jer 34:9
and break every yoke? Isa 9:4
7 Is it not to share your food
with the hungry Eze 18:16; Lk 3:11
and to provide the poor
wanderer with shelter — Isa 16:4; Heb 13:2
when you see the naked,
to clothe them, Job 31:19-20; Mt 25:36
and not to turn away from
your own flesh and
blood? Ge 29:14; Lk 10:31-32
8 Then your light will break forth
like the dawn, Job 11:17
and your healing will quickly
appear; Isa 30:26
then your righteousness[a] will
go before you, Isa 26:2
and the glory of the LORD
will be your rear guard. Ex 14:19
9 Then you will call, and the
LORD will answer; Ps 50:15
you will cry for help, and he
will say: Here am I.

"If you do away with the yoke
of oppression,
with the pointing finger
and malicious talk, Ps 12:2; Isa 59:13
10 and if you spend yourselves in
behalf of the hungry
and satisfy the needs of the
oppressed, Dt 15:7-8
then your light will rise in the
darkness, Isa 42:16
and your night will become
like the noonday. Job 11:17
11 The LORD will guide you
always; Ps 48:14
he will satisfy your needs
in a sun-scorched land Ps 107:9
and will strengthen your
frame. Ps 72:16
You will be like a well-watered
garden, SS 4:15
like a spring whose waters
never fail. Jn 4:14
12 Your people will rebuild the
ancient ruins Isa 49:8
and will raise up the
age-old foundations; Isa 44:28
you will be called Repairer of
Broken Walls, Ne 2:17
Restorer of Streets with
Dwellings.

13 "If you keep your feet from
breaking the Sabbath Isa 56:2
and from doing as
you please on
my holy day,
if you call the Sabbath a delight Ps 84:2,10
and the LORD's holy day
honorable,
and if you honor it by not
going your own way
and not doing as you
please or speaking idle
words,

[a] 8 Or *your righteous One*

[14]then you will find your joy in
the LORD, Job 22:26
and I will cause you to
ride in triumph on
the heights of the land
Dt 32:13
and to feast on the
inheritance of your
father Jacob." Ps 105:10-11
For the mouth of the
LORD has spoken.

Sin, Confession and Redemption

59 Surely the arm of the LORD
is not too short to save,
Nu 11:23; Isa 50:2
nor his ear too dull to hear.
Isa 58:9; 65:24
[2]But your iniquities have
separated
you from your God;
your sins have hidden his face
from you,
so that he will not hear.
Isa 1:15; 58:4
[3]For your hands are stained with
blood, Isa 1:15
your fingers with guilt. Ps 7:3
Your lips have spoken falsely,
Isa 3:8
and your tongue mutters
wicked things.
[4]No one calls for justice; Isa 5:23
no one pleads a case with
integrity.
They rely on empty
arguments, they
utter lies; Isa 44:20
they conceive trouble
and give birth to evil.
Job 15:35; Ps 7:14

[5]They hatch the eggs of vipers
Isa 11:8
and spin a spider's web.
Job 8:14
Whoever eats their eggs will
die,
and when one is broken, an
adder is hatched.
[6]Their cobwebs are useless for
clothing;
they cannot cover
themselves with what
they make. Isa 28:20
Their deeds are evil deeds,
and acts of violence are in
their hands. Isa 58:4
[7]Their feet rush into sin;
they are swift to shed
innocent blood. Pr 6:17
They pursue evil schemes;
Mk 7:21-22
acts of violence mark their
ways. Ro 3:15-17*
[8]The way of peace they do not
know; Ro 3:15-17*
there is no justice in their
paths.
They have turned them into
crooked roads;
no one who walks along
them will know peace.
Isa 57:21; Lk 1:79

[9]So justice is far from us,
and righteousness does not
reach us.
We look for light, but all is
darkness; Isa 5:30
for brightness, but we
walk in deep
shadows.

10 Like the blind we grope along
the wall, Dt 28:29
feeling our way like people
without eyes.
At midday we stumble as if it
were twilight; Isa 8:15
among the strong, we are
like the dead. La 3:6
11 We all growl like bears;
we moan mournfully like
doves. Isa 38:14; Eze 7:16
We look for justice, but find
none;
for deliverance, but it is far
away.

12 For our offenses are many in
your sight, Ezr 9:6
and our sins testify against
us. Isa 3:9
Our offenses are ever with us,
and we acknowledge our
iniquities: Ps 51:3
13 rebellion and treachery against
the LORD, Isa 46:8
turning our backs on our
God, Titus 1:16
inciting revolt and oppression,
Isa 5:7
uttering lies our hearts have
conceived. Mk 7:21-22
14 So justice is driven back, Isa 29:21
and righteousness stands at
a distance; Isa 1:21
truth has stumbled in the
streets, Isa 48:1
honesty cannot enter.
15 Truth is nowhere to be found,
Jer 7:28
and whoever shuns evil
becomes a prey.

The LORD looked and was
displeased
that there was no justice.
Isa 5:7
16 He saw that there was no one,
Isa 41:28
he was appalled that there
was no one to intervene;
Isa 53:12
so his own arm achieved
salvation for him,
Ps 98:1; Isa 63:5
and his own righteousness
sustained him. Isa 45:8,13
17 He put on righteousness as his
breastplate, Eph 6:14
and the helmet of salvation
on his head; 1Th 5:8
he put on the garments of
vengeance Isa 63:3
and wrapped himself in zeal
as in a cloak. Isa 9:7
18 According to what they have
done,
so will he repay Mt 16:27
wrath to his enemies
and retribution to his foes;
he will repay the islands
their due.
19 From the west, people will fear
the name of the LORD,
Isa 49:12
and from the rising of the
sun, they will revere his
glory. Ps 113:3
For he will come like a pent-up
flood
that the breath of the LORD
drives along.[a] Isa 11:4

[a] 19 Or *When enemies come in like a flood, / the Spirit of the LORD will put them to flight*

20 "The Redeemer will come to
Zion, Job 19:25; Isa 52:8
to those in Jacob who
repent of their sins,"
Ro 11:26-27*; Ac 2:38-39
declares the LORD.

21 "As for me, this is my covenant
with them," says the LORD. "My
Spirit, who is on you, will not depart from you, and my words that
I have put in your mouth will always be on your lips, on the lips
of your children and on the lips
of their descendants — from this
time on and forever," says the
LORD. Isa 11:2

The Glory of Zion

60 "Arise, shine, for your
light has come,
Eph 5:14; Isa 52:2
and the glory of the
LORD rises upon you.
Isa 4:5; Rev 21:11
2 See, darkness covers the
earth
and thick darkness is over
the peoples, Col 1:13; Jer 13:16
but the LORD rises upon you
and his glory appears over
you.
3 Nations will come to your light,
Isa 45:14; Rev 21:24
and kings to the
brightness of your
dawn. Isa 49:23

4 "Lift up your eyes and look
about you:
All assemble and come to
you; Isa 11:12
your sons come from afar,
Jer 30:10
and your daughters are
carried on the hip.
Isa 43:6; 49:20-22
5 Then you will look and be
radiant, Ex 34:29
your heart will throb and
swell with joy; Isa 35:2
the wealth on the seas will be
brought to you, Dt 33:19
to you the riches of the
nations will come.
6 Herds of camels will cover your
land,
young camels of Midian and
Ephah. Ge 25:2,4
And all from Sheba will come,
Ps 72:10
bearing gold and incense
Isa 43:23; Mt 2:11
and proclaiming the
praise of the LORD.
Isa 42:10
7 All Kedar's flocks will be
gathered to you, Ge 25:13
the rams of Nebaioth will
serve you;
they will be accepted as
offerings on my altar,
and I will adorn my glorious
temple. Hag 2:3,7,9

8 "Who are these that fly along
like clouds, Isa 49:21
like doves to their nests?
9 Surely the islands look to me;
Isa 11:11
in the lead are the ships of
Tarshish,[a] Isa 2:16 *fn*

[a] 9 Or *the trading ships*

bringing your children from
afar, Isa 14:2; 43:6
with their silver and gold,
to the honor of the LORD your
God, Ps 22:23
the Holy One of Israel,
for he has endowed you
with splendor.
Isa 55:5; Jer 30:19

10 "Foreigners will rebuild your
walls, Isa 14:1-2
and their kings will serve
you. Isa 49:23; Rev 21:24
Though in anger I struck you,
in favor I will show you
compassion. Isa 54:8
11 Your gates will always stand
open, Isa 62:10; Rev 21:25
they will never be shut, day
or night,
so that people may bring
you the wealth of the
nations — Rev 21:26
their kings led in triumphal
procession. Ps 149:8
12 For the nation or kingdom
that will not
serve you will perish;
Isa 14:2
it will be utterly ruined.
Ps 110:5; Da 2:34

13 "The glory of Lebanon will
come to you, Isa 35:2
the juniper, the fir and the
cypress together, Isa 41:19
to adorn my sanctuary;
and I will glorify the
place for my feet.
1Ch 28:2; Ps 132:7

14 The children of your
oppressors will come
bowing before you;
Isa 14:2
all who despise you will
bow down at your feet
Isa 49:23; Rev 3:9
and will call you the City of the
LORD, Isa 1:26
Zion of the Holy One of
Israel. Heb 12:22

15 "Although you have been
forsaken and hated,
Isa 1:7-9; 6:12
with no one traveling
through, Isa 33:8
I will make you the everlasting
pride Isa 4:2
and the joy of all
generations. Isa 65:18
16 You will drink the milk of
nations
and be nursed at royal
breasts. Isa 49:23; 66:11-12
Then you will know that I, the
LORD, am your Savior,
Ex 14:30
your Redeemer, the
Mighty One of Jacob.
Isa 59:20
17 Instead of bronze I will bring
you gold,
and silver in place of iron.
Instead of wood I will bring
you bronze,
and iron in place of stones.
I will make peace your
governor Ps 85:8; Isa 66:12
and well-being your ruler.
Isa 9:7

18 No longer will violence be
heard in your land, Isa 9:4
nor ruin or destruction
within your borders,
but you will call your walls
Salvation Isa 26:1
and your gates Praise.
Isa 61:11; Zep 3:20
19 The sun will no more be your
light by day,
nor will the brightness of the
moon shine on you,
for the LORD will be your
everlasting light, Rev 22:5
and your God will be your
glory. Zec 2:5; Rev 21:23
20 Your sun will never set again,
Isa 30:26
and your moon will wane no
more;
the LORD will be your
everlasting light,
and your days of sorrow will
end. Isa 35:10
21 Then all your people will be
righteous Rev 21:27
and they will possess the land
forever. Ps 37:11,22; Isa 57:13; 61:7
They are the shoot I have
planted, Mt 15:13
the work of my hands,
Isa 29:23; Eph 2:10
for the display of my
splendor. Isa 52:1
22 The least of you will become a
thousand,
the smallest a mighty nation.
Ge 12:2
I am the LORD;
in its time I will do this
swiftly." Isa 5:19

The Year of the LORD's Favor

61 The Spirit of the Sovereign
LORD is on me, Isa 11:2
because the LORD has
anointed me Ps 45:7
to proclaim good news to the
poor. Mt 11:5; Lk 7:22
He has sent me to bind up the
brokenhearted, Isa 57:15
to proclaim freedom for the
captives Isa 42:7; 49:9
and release from darkness
for the prisoners,[a]
2 to proclaim the year of the
LORD's favor Lk 4:18-19*
and the day of vengeance of
our God, Isa 34:8
to comfort all who mourn,
Isa 57:18; Mt 5:4
3 and provide for those who
grieve in Zion —
to bestow on them a crown of
beauty Isa 3:23
instead of ashes,
the oil of joy Isa 1:6
instead of mourning,
and a garment of praise
instead of a spirit of despair.
They will be called oaks of
righteousness,
a planting of the LORD
Ps 1:3; 92:12-13
for the display of his
splendor. Isa 60:20-21
4 They will rebuild the
ancient ruins
Isa 49:8; Eze 36:33; Am 9:14
and restore the places long
devastated;

[a] 1 Hebrew; Septuagint *the blind*

they will renew the ruined cities
that have been devastated
for generations.
5 Strangers will shepherd your
flocks; Isa 14:1-2
foreigners will work your
fields and vineyards.
6 And you will be called priests
of the LORD, Ex 19:6; 1Pe 2:5
you will be named ministers
of our God.
You will feed on the wealth of
nations, Isa 60:11
and in their riches you will
boast.

7 Instead of your shame
you will receive a double
portion, Isa 40:2; Zec 9:12
and instead of disgrace
you will rejoice in your
inheritance.
And so you will inherit a
double portion in your
land, Isa 60:21
and everlasting joy will be
yours. Isa 25:9

8 "For I, the LORD, love justice; Ps 11:7; Isa 5:16
I hate robbery and
wrongdoing.
In my faithfulness I will reward
my people
and make an everlasting
covenant with them. Isa 55:3
9 Their descendants will be
known among the
nations Isa 43:5
and their offspring among
the peoples.
All who see them will
acknowledge
that they are a people the
LORD has blessed." Dt 28:3-12

10 I delight greatly in the LORD;
my soul rejoices in my God. Isa 25:9; Hab 3:18
For he has clothed me with
garments of salvation
and arrayed me in a robe
of his righteousness, Ps 132:9; Isa 52:1
as a bridegroom adorns his
head like a priest,
and as a bride adorns
herself with her jewels. Isa 49:18; Rev 21:2
11 For as the soil makes the sprout
come up
and a garden causes seeds to
grow,
so the Sovereign LORD will
make righteousness Ps 85:11
and praise spring up before
all nations.

Zion's New Name

62 For Zion's sake I will not
keep silent, Ps 50:21
for Jerusalem's sake I will
not remain quiet,
till her vindication shines out
like the dawn, Isa 1:26
her salvation like a blazing
torch. Ps 67:2
2 The nations will see your
vindication, Isa 52:10; 60:3
and all kings your glory;

you will be called by a new
name ver 4,12; Isa 1:26
that the mouth of the LORD
will bestow.
3 You will be a crown of splendor
in the LORD's hand,
Zec 9:16; 1Th 2:19
a royal diadem in the hand
of your God.
4 No longer will they call you
Deserted, Isa 54:6
or name your land Desolate.
Isa 49:19
But you will be called
Hephzibah,[a]
and your land Beulah[b];
for the LORD will take delight
in you, Jer 32:41; Zep 3:17
and your land will be
married. Jer 3:14; Hos 2:19
5 As a young man marries a
young woman,
so will your Builder marry
you;
as a bridegroom rejoices over
his bride,
so will your God rejoice over
you. Isa 65:19; Zep 3:17

6 I have posted watchmen on
your walls, Jerusalem;
Isa 52:8; Eze 3:17
they will never be silent day
or night.
You who call on the LORD,
give yourselves no rest,
7 and give him no rest till he
establishes Jerusalem
Mt 15:21-28; Lk 18:1-8
and makes her the praise of
the earth. Dt 26:19

8 The LORD has sworn by his
right hand
and by his mighty arm:
"Never again will I give your
grain
as food for your enemies,
Dt 28:30-33; Isa 1:7; Jer 5:17
and never again will foreigners
drink the new wine
for which you have toiled;
9 but those who harvest it will
eat it Isa 1:19
and praise the LORD,
Dt 12:7; Joel 2:26
and those who gather the
grapes will drink it
in the courts of my
sanctuary." Lev 23:39

10 Pass through, pass through the
gates! Isa 60:11
Prepare the way for the
people.
Build up, build up the highway!
Isa 11:16; 57:14
Remove the stones.
Raise a banner for the nations.
Isa 11:10

11 The LORD has made
proclamation
to the ends of the earth: Dt 30:4
"Say to Daughter Zion,
Zec 9:9; Mt 21:5
'See, your Savior comes!
Rev 22:12
See, his reward is with him,
and his recompense
accompanies him.'"
Isa 40:10

[a] 4 *Hephzibah* means *my delight is in her.*
[b] 4 *Beulah* means *married.*

12 They will be called the Holy
People, ver 4; Ge 32:28; 1Pe 2:9
the Redeemed of the LORD; Isa 35:9
and you will be called Sought
After,
the City No Longer Deserted. Isa 42:16

God's Day of Vengeance and Redemption

63 Who is this coming from
Edom, 2Ch 28:17
from Bozrah, with his
garments stained
crimson? Am 1:12
Who is this, robed in splendor,
striding forward in the
greatness of his
strength? Isa 45:24

"It is I, proclaiming victory,
mighty to save." Isa 46:13; Zep 3:17

2 Why are your garments red,
like those of one treading
the winepress? Ge 49:11

3 "I have trodden the winepress
alone; Rev 14:20; 19:15
from the nations no one was
with me.
I trampled them in my anger
and trod them down in my
wrath; Isa 22:5
their blood spattered my
garments, Rev 19:13
and I stained all my clothing.
4 It was for me the day of
vengeance; Jer 50:15
the year for me to redeem
had come.
5 I looked, but there was no one
to help, Isa 41:28
I was appalled that no one
gave support;
so my own arm achieved
salvation for me, Ps 44:3; 98:1
and my own wrath sustained
me. Isa 59:16
6 I trampled the nations in my
anger; Ps 108:13
in my wrath I made them
drunk Isa 29:9
and poured their blood on
the ground." Isa 34:3

Praise and Prayer

7 I will tell of the kindnesses of
the LORD, Isa 54:8
the deeds for which he is to
be praised,
according to all the LORD has
done for us —
yes, the many good things
he has done for Israel, Ex 18:9
according to his compassion
and many kindnesses. Ps 51:1; Eph 2:4
8 He said, "Surely they are my
people, Isa 51:4
children who will be true to
me";
and so he became their
Savior. Isa 25:9
9 In all their distress he too was
distressed,
and the angel of his presence
saved them.[a] Ex 33:14

[a] 9 Or *Savior* [9]*in their distress. / It was no envoy or angel / but his own presence that saved them*

In his love and mercy he
redeemed them; Dt 7:7-8
he lifted them up and carried
them Dt 1:31
all the days of old.
Dt 32:7; Job 37:23
10 Yet they rebelled Ps 78:40
and grieved his Holy Spirit.
Ps 51:11; Ac 7:51; Eph 4:30
So he turned and became their
enemy Ps 106:40
and he himself fought
against them. Jos 10:14
11 Then his people recalled[a] the
days of old,
the days of Moses and his
people —
where is he who brought them
through the sea, Ex 14:22,30
with the shepherd of his
flock?
Where is he who set
his Holy Spirit among them,
Nu 11:17
12 who sent his glorious arm of
power
to be at Moses' right hand,
who divided the waters before
them, Ex 14:21-22; Isa 11:15
to gain for himself
everlasting renown,
Ps 102:12; Isa 55:13
13 who led them through the
depths? Dt 32:12
Like a horse in open country,
they did not stumble; Jer 31:9
14 like cattle that go down to the
plain,
they were given rest by the
Spirit of the LORD. Dt 12:9
This is how you guided your
people
to make for yourself a
glorious name.
15 Look down from heaven and
see, Dt 26:15; Ps 80:14
from your lofty throne, holy
and glorious. Ps 123:1
Where are your zeal and your
might? Isa 9:7
Your tenderness and
compassion are
withheld from us.
Jer 31:20; Hos 11:8
16 But you are our Father, Ex 4:22
though Abraham does not
know us
or Israel acknowledge us;
Job 14:21
you, LORD, are our Father,
our Redeemer from of
old is your name.
Isa 41:14; 44:6
17 Why, LORD, do you make
us wander from your
ways
and harden our hearts so we
do not revere you? Isa 29:13
Return for the sake of your
servants, Nu 10:36
the tribes that are your
inheritance. Ex 34:9
18 For a little while your people
possessed your holy
place, Dt 4:26; 11:17
but now our enemies
have trampled
down your sanctuary.
Ps 74:3-8

[a] 11 Or *But may he recall*

19 We are yours from of old;
but you have not ruled over them,
they have not been called[a] by your name. Isa 43:7; Jer 14:9

64 [b] Oh, that you would rend the heavens and come down, Ps 144:5; Mic 1:3
that the mountains would tremble before you! Ex 19:18
2 As when fire sets twigs ablaze
and causes water to boil,
come down to make your name known to your enemies
and cause the nations to quake before you! Ps 99:1; Jer 5:22; 33:9
3 For when you did awesome things that we did not expect, Ps 65:5
you came down, and the mountains trembled before you.
4 Since ancient times no one has heard,
no ear has perceived,
no eye has seen any God besides you, Isa 43:10-11
who acts on behalf of those who wait for him. Isa 30:18; 1Co 2:9*
5 You come to the help of those who gladly do right, Isa 26:8
who remember your ways.
But when we continued to sin against them,
you were angry. Isa 10:4
How then can we be saved?
6 All of us have become like one who is unclean, Lev 5:2
and all our righteous acts are like filthy rags; Isa 46:12; 48:1
we all shrivel up like a leaf, Ps 90:5-6
and like the wind our sins sweep us away. Jer 4:12
7 No one calls on your name Isa 59:4
or strives to lay hold of you;
for you have hidden your face from us Dt 31:18; Isa 1:15; 54:8
and have given us over to[c] our sins. Isa 9:18

8 Yet you, LORD, are our Father. Isa 63:16
We are the clay, you are the potter; Isa 29:16
we are all the work of your hand. Isa 19:25
9 Do not be angry beyond measure, LORD; Isa 57:17; 60:10
do not remember our sins forever. Isa 43:25
Oh, look on us, we pray,
for we are all your people. Isa 51:4
10 Your sacred cities have become a wasteland; Isa 1:26
even Zion is a wasteland,
Jerusalem a desolation. Dt 29:23

[a] 19 Or *We are like those you have never ruled, / like those never called* [b] In Hebrew texts 64:1 is numbered 63:19b, and 64:2-12 is numbered 64:1-11.
[c] 7 Septuagint, Syriac and Targum; Hebrew *have made us melt because of*

11 Our holy and glorious temple,
where our ancestors
praised you, Ps 74:3-7
has been burned with fire,
and all that we treasured lies
in ruins. La 1:7,10
12 After all this, LORD, will you
hold yourself back?
Ps 74:10-11; Isa 42:14
Will you keep silent and
punish us beyond
measure? Ps 83:1

Judgment and Salvation

65 "I revealed myself to
those who did not ask
for me;
I was found by those who did
not seek me. Ro 10:20*
To a nation that did not call on
my name, Eph 2:12
I said, 'Here am I, here am I.'
2 All day long I have held out my
hands
to an obstinate people,
Ro 10:21*; Isa 1:2,23
who walk in ways not good,
pursuing their own
imaginations —
Ps 81:11-12; Isa 66:18
3 a people who continually
provoke me
to my very face, Job 1:11
offering sacrifices in gardens
Isa 1:29
and burning incense on
altars of brick;
4 who sit among the graves
Lev 19:31
and spend their nights
keeping secret vigil;
who eat the flesh of pigs, Lev 11:7
and whose pots hold broth of
impure meat;
5 who say, 'Keep away; don't
come near me,
for I am too sacred for you!'
Mt 9:11; Lk 18:9-12
Such people are smoke in my
nostrils,
a fire that keeps burning all
day.

6 "See, it stands written before
me:
I will not keep silent but
will pay back in full;
Ps 50:3; Jer 16:18
I will pay it back into their
laps — Ps 79:12
7 both your sins and the sins
of your ancestors,"
Ex 20:5; Isa 22:14
says the LORD.
"Because they burned sacrifices
on the mountains
and defied me on the hills,
Isa 57:7
I will measure into their laps
the full payment for
their former deeds."
Pr 10:24; Isa 10:12

8 This is what the LORD says:

"As when juice is still found in
a cluster of grapes
and people say, 'Don't
destroy it,
there is still a blessing in it,'
so will I do in behalf of my
servants; Isa 54:17
I will not destroy them all.

9 I will bring forth descendants
from Jacob, Isa 45:19
and from Judah those
who will possess my
mountains; Am 9:11-15
my chosen people will inherit
them, Isa 14:1
and there will my servants
live. Isa 32:18
10 Sharon will become a pasture
for flocks, Isa 35:2
and the Valley of Achor a
resting place for herds,
Jos 7:26
for my people who seek me.
Isa 51:1

11 "But as for you who forsake the
LORD Dt 29:24-25; Isa 1:28
and forget my holy
mountain, Ps 137:5
who spread a table for Fortune
and fill bowls of mixed wine
for Destiny, Isa 5:22
12 I will destine you for the sword,
Isa 27:1
and all of you will fall in the
slaughter;
for I called but you did not
answer, Pr 1:24-25; Isa 41:28
I spoke but you did not
listen. 2Ch 36:15-16; Jer 7:13
You did evil in my sight
and chose what displeases
me." Isa 1:24; 66:4

13 Therefore this is what the Sovereign LORD says:

"My servants will eat, Isa 1:19
but you will go hungry;
Job 18:12
my servants will drink, Isa 33:16
but you will go thirsty; Isa 41:17
my servants will rejoice, Isa 60:5
but you will be put to shame.
Isa 44:9

14 My servants will sing
out of the joy of their
hearts,
but you will cry out
Mt 8:12; Lk 13:28
from anguish of heart
and wail in brokenness of
spirit.
15 You will leave your name
for my chosen ones to use in
their curses; Zec 8:13
the Sovereign LORD will put
you to death,
but to his servants he
will give another name.
Rev 2:17
16 Whoever invokes a blessing in
the land Dt 29:19
will do so by the one true
God; Ps 31:5
whoever takes an oath in the
land
will swear by the one true
God. Isa 19:18
For the past troubles will be
forgotten Job 11:16
and hidden from my eyes.

New Heavens and a New Earth

17 "See, I will create
new heavens and a new
earth. Isa 66:22; 2Pe 3:13
The former things will not
be remembered,
Isa 43:18; Jer 3:16
nor will they come to mind.

18 But be glad and rejoice forever Ps 98:1-9; Isa 25:9
in what I will create,
for I will create Jerusalem to be
a delight
and its people a joy.
19 I will rejoice over Jerusalem Isa 35:10; 62:5
and take delight in my
people;
the sound of weeping and of
crying Isa 25:8; Rev 7:17
will be heard in it no more.

20 "Never again will there be in it
an infant who lives but a few
days,
or an old man who does not
live out his years; Ecc 8:13
the one who dies at a hundred
will be thought a mere child;
the one who fails to reach[a] a
hundred
will be considered accursed.
21 They will build houses and
dwell in them; Isa 32:18
they will plant vineyards
and eat their fruit. Isa 37:30; Am 9:14
22 No longer will they build
houses and others live
in them, Dt 28:30
or plant and others eat.
For as the days of a tree, Ps 92:12-14
so will be the days of my
people; Ps 21:4; 91:16
my chosen ones will long enjoy Isa 14:1
the work of their hands.
23 They will not labor in vain, Isa 49:4
nor will they bear children
doomed to misfortune; Jer 16:3-4
for they will be a people
blessed by the LORD, Dt 28:3-12; Isa 61:9
they and their descendants
with them. Ac 2:39
24 Before they call I will answer; Isa 55:6
while they are still speaking
I will hear. Da 9:20-23; 10:12
25 The wolf and the lamb will feed
together, Isa 11:6
and the lion will eat straw
like the ox,
and dust will be the serpent's
food. Ge 3:14; Mic 7:17
They will neither harm nor
destroy
on all my holy mountain,"
says the LORD.

Judgment and Hope

66 This is what the LORD says:

"Heaven is my throne, Mt 23:22
and the earth is my footstool. 1Ki 8:27; Mt 5:34-35
Where is the house you
will build for me? 2Sa 7:7; Jn 4:20-21; Ac 7:49*
Where will my resting place
be?
2 Has not my hand made all
these things, Ac 7:50*
and so they came into
being?"
declares the LORD.

[a] 20 Or *the sinner who reaches*

"These are the ones I look on
with favor:
those who are humble
and contrite in spirit, Isa 57:15; Mt 5:3-4; Lk 18:13-14
and who tremble at my
word. Ezr 9:4
3 But whoever sacrifices a bull Isa 1:11
is like one who kills a
person,
and whoever offers a lamb
is like one who breaks a dog's
neck;
whoever makes a grain
offering
is like one who presents pig's
blood,
and whoever burns memorial
incense Lev 2:2
is like one who worships an
idol.
They have chosen their own
ways, Isa 57:17
and they delight in their
abominations; Dt 27:15
4 so I also will choose harsh
treatment for them
and will bring on them what
they dread. Pr 10:24
For when I called, no one
answered, Pr 1:24; Jer 7:13
when I spoke, no one
listened.
They did evil in my sight 2Ki 21:2,4,6
and chose what displeases
me." Isa 65:12

5 Hear the word of the LORD,
you who tremble at his word:
"Your own people who hate
you, Ps 38:20
and exclude you because of
my name, have said,
'Let the LORD be glorified,
that we may see your joy!'
Yet they will be put to
shame. Lk 13:17
6 Hear that uproar from the
city,
hear that noise from the
temple!
It is the sound of the LORD Ps 68:33
repaying his enemies all they
deserve. Isa 65:6; Joel 3:7

7 "Before she goes into labor, Isa 54:1
she gives birth;
before the pains come upon
her,
she delivers a son. Rev 12:5
8 Who has ever heard of such
things?
Who has ever seen things
like this? Isa 64:4
Can a country be born in a
day
or a nation be brought forth
in a moment?
Yet no sooner is Zion in labor
than she gives birth to her
children. Isa 49:21
9 Do I bring to the moment of
birth Isa 37:3
and not give delivery?" says
the LORD.
"Do I close up the womb
when I bring to delivery?"
says your God.

10 "Rejoice with Jerusalem and
be glad for her,
Dt 32:43; Ro 15:10
all you who love her; Ps 26:8
rejoice greatly with her,
all you who mourn over her.
Isa 57:19
11 For you will nurse and be
satisfied Isa 60:16
at her comforting breasts;
you will drink deeply
and delight in her
overflowing abundance."

12 For this is what the LORD says:

"I will extend peace to her like
a river, Isa 48:18
and the wealth of nations
like a flooding stream;
Isa 60:5; 61:6
you will nurse and be carried
on her arm Isa 60:4
and dandled on her knees.
13 As a mother comforts her
child,
so will I comfort you;
Isa 40:1; 2Co 1:4
and you will be comforted
over Jerusalem."

14 When you see this, your heart
will rejoice Joel 2:23
and you will flourish like
grass;
the hand of the LORD will be
made known to his
servants, Isa 54:17
but his fury will be shown to
his foes. Isa 10:5
15 See, the LORD is coming with
fire, Isa 1:31
and his chariots are like a
whirlwind; Ps 68:17
he will bring down his anger
with fury,
and his rebuke with flames
of fire. Ps 9:5
16 For with fire and with his
sword Isa 27:1; 30:30
the LORD will execute
judgment on all people,
Eze 36:5
and many will be those slain
by the LORD. Isa 10:4

17 "Those who consecrate and purify themselves to go into the gardens, following one who is among
those who eat the flesh of pigs,
rats and other unclean things —
they will meet their end together
with the one they follow," declares
the LORD. Ps 37:20; Isa 1:28
18 "And I, because of what they
have planned and done, am about
to come[a] and gather the people
of all nations and languages, and
they will come and see my glory.
Isa 59:19
19 "I will set a sign among them,
and I will send some of those who
survive to the nations — to Tarshish, to the Libyans[b] and Lydians
(famous as archers), to Tubal and
Greece, and to the distant islands
that have not heard of my fame or
seen my glory. They will proclaim
my glory among the nations.
20 And they will bring all your peo-

[a] *18* The meaning of the Hebrew for this clause is uncertain. [b] *19* Some Septuagint manuscripts *Put* (Libyans); Hebrew *Pul*

ple, from all the nations, to my
holy mountain in Jerusalem as an
offering to the LORD — on horses,
in chariots and wagons, and on
mules and camels," says the LORD.
"They will bring them, as the Israelites bring their grain offerings,
to the temple of the LORD in ceremonially clean vessels. [21]And I
will select some of them also to
be priests and Levites," says the
LORD. Ex 19:6; Isa 61:6; 1Pe 2:5,9

[22]"As the new heavens and the
new earth that I make will endure
before me," declares the LORD, "so
will your name and descendants
endure. [23]From one New Moon to
another and from one Sabbath to
another, all mankind will come
and bow down before me," says
the LORD. [24]"And they will go out
and look on the dead bodies of
those who rebelled against me;
the worms that eat them will not
die, the fire that burns them will
not be quenched, and they will be
loathsome to all mankind."

Isa 1:31; Mk 9:48*

JEREMIAH

1 The words of Jeremiah son of Hilkiah, one of the priests at Anathoth in the territory of Benjamin. 2The word of the LORD came to him in the thirteenth year of the reign of Josiah son of Amon king of Judah, 3and through the reign of Jehoiakim son of Josiah king of Judah, down to the fifth month of the eleventh year of Zedekiah son of Josiah king of Judah, when the people of Jerusalem went into exile. Jos 21:18; 1Ch 6:60; Jer 52:15

The Call of Jeremiah

4The word of the LORD came to me, saying,

5"Before I formed you in the
womb I knew[a] you, Ps 139:16
before you were born I set
you apart; Isa 49:1
I appointed you as a
prophet to the nations."
ver 10; Jer 25:15-26

6"Alas, Sovereign LORD," I said, "I do not know how to speak; I am too young." Ex 4:10; 1Ki 3:7

7But the LORD said to me, "Do not say, 'I am too young.' You must go to everyone I send you to and say whatever I command you. 8Do not be afraid of them, for I am with you and will rescue you," declares the LORD. Jer 15:20; Eze 2:6

9Then the LORD reached out his hand and touched my mouth and said to me, "I have put my words in your mouth. 10See, today I appoint you over nations and kingdoms to uproot and tear down, to destroy and overthrow, to build and to plant." Jer 18:7-10; Isa 6:7

11The word of the LORD came to me: "What do you see, Jeremiah?" Jer 24:3; Am 7:8

"I see the branch of an almond tree," I replied.

12The LORD said to me, "You have seen correctly, for I am watching[b] to see that my word is fulfilled." Jer 44:27

13The word of the LORD came to me again: "What do you see?" Zec 4:2

"I see a pot that is boiling," I answered. "It is tilting toward us from the north."

14The LORD said to me, "From the north disaster will be poured out on all who live in the land. 15I am about to summon all the peoples of the northern kingdoms," declares the LORD. Isa 14:31

"Their kings will come and set
up their thrones
in the entrance of the gates
of Jerusalem;

[a] 5 Or *chose* [b] 12 The Hebrew for *watching* sounds like the Hebrew for *almond tree.*

they will come against
all her surrounding
walls
and against all the towns of
Judah. Jer 4:16; 9:11
16 I will pronounce my judgments
on my people Jer 4:12
because of their wickedness
in forsaking me,
Dt 28:20; Jer 17:13
in burning incense to other
gods Jer 7:9
and in worshiping what their
hands have made.
Ps 115:4-8

17 "Get yourself ready! Stand up
and say to them whatever I command you. Do not be terrified by
them, or I will terrify you before
them. 18 Today I have made you a
fortified city, an iron pillar and a
bronze wall to stand against the
whole land — against the kings
of Judah, its officials, its priests
and the people of the land. 19 They
will fight against you but will not
overcome you, for I am with you
and will rescue you," declares the
LORD. Isa 50:7; Jer 20:11; Eze 2:6

Israel Forsakes God

2 The word of the LORD came to
me: 2 "Go and proclaim in the
hearing of Jerusalem: Isa 38:4

"This is what the LORD says:
" 'I remember the devotion
of your youth,
Eze 16:8-14,60; Hos 2:15
how as a bride you loved me
and followed me through the
wilderness, Dt 2:7
through a land not sown.
3 Israel was holy to the LORD,
Ex 19:6
the firstfruits of his harvest;
Jas 1:18; Rev 14:4
all who devoured her were held
guilty, Isa 41:11; Jer 50:7
and disaster overtook
them,' "
declares the LORD.

4 Hear the word of the LORD, you
descendants of Jacob,
all you clans of Israel.

5 This is what the LORD says:

"What fault did your ancestors
find in me,
that they strayed so far from
me?
They followed worthless idols
Dt 32:21
and became worthless
themselves. 2Ki 17:15
6 They did not ask, 'Where is the
LORD,
who brought us up out of
Egypt Hos 13:4
and led us through the barren
wilderness,
through a land of deserts
and ravines, Dt 8:15; 32:10
a land of drought and utter
darkness,
a land where no one travels
and no one lives?' Jer 51:43
7 I brought you into a fertile land
to eat its fruit and rich
produce. Nu 13:27; Dt 8:7-9

But you came and defiled my land
and made my inheritance detestable.
Ps 106:34-39; Jer 16:18
8 The priests did not ask,
'Where is the LORD?'
Those who deal with the law did not know me; Jer 4:22
the leaders rebelled against me.
The prophets prophesied by Baal, Jer 23:13
following worthless idols.
Jer 16:19

9 "Therefore I bring charges against you again,"
Eze 20:35-36
declares the LORD.
"And I will bring charges against your children's children.
10 Cross over to the coasts of Cyprus and look, Ge 10:4
send to Kedar[a] and observe closely; Ge 25:13
see if there has ever been anything like this:
11 Has a nation ever changed its gods?
(Yet they are not gods at all.)
Isa 37:19; Jer 16:20
But my people have exchanged their glorious God
Ps 106:20; Ro 1:23
for worthless idols.
12 Be appalled at this, you heavens,
and shudder with great horror,"
declares the LORD.
13 "My people have committed two sins:
They have forsaken me,
the spring of living water,
Ps 36:9; Jn 4:14
and have dug their own cisterns,
broken cisterns that cannot hold water.
14 Is Israel a servant, a slave by birth? Ex 4:22
Why then has he become plunder?
15 Lions have roared; Jer 4:7; 50:17
they have growled at him.
They have laid waste his land;
Isa 1:7
his towns are burned and deserted. 2Ki 25:9
16 Also, the men of Memphis and Tahpanhes
Isa 19:13; Jer 43:7-9
have cracked your skull.
17 Have you not brought this on yourselves Jer 4:18
by forsaking the LORD your God Isa 1:28; Jer 17:13
when he led you in the way?
18 Now why go to Egypt Isa 30:2
to drink water from the Nile[b]? Jos 13:3
And why go to Assyria Hos 5:13
to drink water from the Euphrates? Isa 7:20
19 Your wickedness will punish you;
your backsliding will rebuke you. Jer 3:11,22; Hos 5:5

[a] *10* In the Syro-Arabian desert
[b] *18* Hebrew *Shihor*; that is, a branch of the Nile

Consider then and realize
how evil and bitter it is for
you Job 20:14
when you forsake the LORD
your God Jer 19:4
and have no awe of me,"
Ps 36:1
declares the Lord,
the LORD Almighty.
20 "Long ago you broke off your
yoke Lev 26:13
and tore off your bonds;
you said, 'I will not serve
you!'
Indeed, on every high hill
Isa 57:7; Jer 17:2
and under every spreading
tree Dt 12:2
you lay down as a prostitute.
Isa 1:21
21 I had planted you like a choice
vine Ex 15:17; Ps 80:8
of sound and reliable
stock.
How then did you turn
against me
into a corrupt, wild vine?
Isa 5:4
22 Although you wash yourself
with soap Ps 51:2
and use an abundance of
cleansing powder,
the stain of your guilt is still
before me,"
declares the Sovereign
LORD.
23 "How can you say, 'I am not
defiled; Pr 30:12
I have not run after the
Baals'? Jer 9:14
See how you behaved in the
valley; Jer 7:31
consider what you have
done.
You are a swift she-camel
running here and there,
Jer 31:22
24 a wild donkey accustomed to
the desert, Jer 14:6
sniffing the wind in her
craving —
in her heat who can restrain
her?
Any males that pursue
her need not tire
themselves;
at mating time they will find
her.
25 Do not run until your feet are
bare
and your throat is dry.
But you said, 'It's no use!
I love foreign gods,
Dt 32:16; Jer 3:13; 14:10
and I must go after them.'
26 "As a thief is disgraced when he
is caught, Jer 48:27
so the people of Israel are
disgraced —
they, their kings and their
officials,
their priests and their
prophets. Jer 32:32
27 They say to wood, 'You are my
father,'
and to stone, 'You gave me
birth.' Jer 3:9
They have turned their backs
to me Ps 14:3
and not their faces; Jer 18:17; 32:33

yet when they are in trouble,
they say, Isa 26:16
'Come and save us!' Hos 5:15
28 Where then are the gods you
made for yourselves?
Isa 45:20
Let them come if they can
save you
when you are in trouble!
Dt 32:37
For you, Judah, have as many
gods
as you have towns. Jer 11:13

29 "Why do you bring charges
against me?
You have all rebelled against
me," Jer 5:1; 6:13; Da 9:11
declares the LORD.
30 "In vain I punished your
people;
they did not respond to
correction.
Your sword has devoured
your prophets
Ac 7:52; 1Th 2:15; Ne 9:26
like a ravenous lion.

31 "You of this generation, consider the word of the LORD:

"Have I been a desert to Israel
or a land of great darkness?
Isa 45:19
Why do my people say, 'We are
free to roam;
we will come to you no
more'?
32 Does a young woman forget
her jewelry,
a bride her wedding
ornaments?
Yet my people have
forgotten me, Isa 57:11
days without number.
33 How skilled you are at
pursuing love!
Even the worst of women
can learn from your
ways.
34 On your clothes is found
the lifeblood of the innocent
poor, 2Ki 21:16
though you did not catch
them breaking in. Ex 22:2
Yet in spite of all this
35 you say, 'I am innocent;
Pr 30:12
he is not angry with me.'
But I will pass judgment on
you Jer 25:31
because you say, 'I have not
sinned.' 1Jn 1:8,10
36 Why do you go about so much,
changing your ways? Jer 31:22
You will be disappointed by
Egypt Isa 30:2-3,7
as you were by Assyria.
37 You will also leave that place
with your hands on your
head, 2Sa 13:19
for the LORD has rejected those
you trust;
you will not be helped by
them. Jer 37:7

3 "If a man divorces his wife
Dt 24:1-4
and she leaves him and
marries another man,
should he return to her again?
Would not the land be
completely defiled?

But you have lived as a
prostitute with
many lovers —
Jer 2:20,25; Eze 16:26,29
would you now return to
me?" Hos 2:7
declares the LORD.
2 "Look up to the barren heights
and see.
Is there any place where
you have not been
ravished?
By the roadside you sat waiting
for lovers, Ge 38:14
sat like a nomad in the
desert.
You have defiled the land Jer 2:7
with your prostitution and
wickedness. Isa 1:21
3 Therefore the showers have
been withheld, Lev 26:19
and no spring rains have
fallen. Jer 14:4
Yet you have the brazen look of
a prostitute;
you refuse to blush with
shame. Jer 6:15; 8:12
4 Have you not just called to me:
'My Father, my friend from
my youth, ver 19; Jer 2:2
5 will you always be angry?
Isa 57:16
Will your wrath continue
forever?'
This is how you talk,
but you do all the evil you
can."

Unfaithful Israel

6 During the reign of King Josiah, the LORD said to me, "Have
you seen what faithless Israel has
done? She has gone up on every
high hill and under every spreading tree and has committed adultery there. 7 I thought that after
she had done all this she would
return to me but she did not, and
her unfaithful sister Judah saw
it. 8 I gave faithless Israel her certificate of divorce and sent her
away because of all her adulteries. Yet I saw that her unfaithful
sister Judah had no fear; she also
went out and committed adultery.
9 Because Israel's immorality mat-
tered so little to her, she defiled
the land and committed adultery
with stone and wood. 10 In spite of
all this, her unfaithful sister Judah
did not return to me with all her
heart, but only in pretense," declares the LORD. Jer 12:2; Eze 33:31
11 The LORD said to me, "Faithless
Israel is more righteous than unfaithful Judah. 12 Go, proclaim this
message toward the north:
Eze 16:52; 23:11

" 'Return, faithless Israel,'
declares the LORD,
Jer 31:21-22; Eze 33:11
'I will frown on you no
longer,
for I am faithful,' declares the
LORD, Ps 6:2
'I will not be angry forever.
Ps 86:15
13 Only acknowledge your guilt —
Dt 30:1-3
you have rebelled against the
LORD your God,

you have scattered your
favors to foreign gods
Jer 2:25
under every spreading tree,
Dt 12:2
and have not obeyed me,' "
ver 25
declares the LORD.

14"Return, faithless people," declares the LORD, "for I am your
husband. I will choose you — one
from a town and two from a clan —
and bring you to Zion. 15Then I
will give you shepherds after my
own heart, who will lead you with
knowledge and understanding.
16In those days, when your numbers have increased greatly in the
land," declares the LORD, "people will no longer say, 'The ark of
the covenant of the LORD.' It will
never enter their minds or be remembered; it will not be missed,
nor will another one be made. 17At
that time they will call Jerusalem
The Throne of the LORD, and all
nations will gather in Jerusalem
to honor the name of the LORD.
No longer will they follow the
stubbornness of their evil hearts.
18In those days the people of Judah will join the people of Israel,
and together they will come from
a northern land to the land I gave
your ancestors as an inheritance.
Hos 2:19; Jer 11:8; Am 9:15

19"I myself said,

" 'How gladly would I treat you
like my children
and give you a pleasant land,
the most beautiful
inheritance of any
nation.'
I thought you would call me
'Father' Isa 63:16
and not turn away from
following me.
20But like a woman unfaithful to
her husband,
so you, Israel, have been
unfaithful to me,"
declares the LORD.

21A cry is heard on the barren
heights,
the weeping and pleading of
the people of Israel,
because they have perverted
their ways
and have forgotten the LORD
their God. Isa 57:11

22"Return, faithless people;
Hos 14:4
I will cure you of
backsliding." Hos 6:1

"Yes, we will come to you,
for you are the LORD our God.
23Surely the idolatrous
commotion on the hills
and mountains is a
deception;
surely in the LORD our God
is the salvation of Israel.
Ps 3:8; Jer 17:14
24From our youth shameful gods
have consumed Hos 9:10
the fruits of our ancestors'
labor —
their flocks and herds,
their sons and daughters.

25 Let us lie down in our shame, Ezr 9:6
and let our disgrace cover us.
We have sinned against the
LORD our God, Jdg 10:10
both we and our ancestors; Jer 14:20
from our youth till this day Jer 22:21
we have not obeyed the LORD
our God." Eze 2:3

4 "If you, Israel, will return, Jer 3:1,22; Joel 2:12
then return to me,"
declares the LORD.
"If you put your detestable
idols out of my sight Jer 35:15
and no longer go astray,
2 and if in a truthful, just and
righteous way
you swear, 'As surely as the
LORD lives,' Dt 10:20; Isa 65:16
then the nations will invoke
blessings by him Ge 22:18; Gal 3:8
and in him they will boast."

3 This is what the LORD says to the people of Judah and to Jerusalem:

"Break up your unplowed
ground Hos 10:12
and do not sow among
thorns. Mk 4:18
4 Circumcise yourselves to the
LORD,
circumcise your hearts, Dt 10:16; Jer 9:26; Ro 2:28-29
you people of Judah and
inhabitants of Jerusalem,
or my wrath will flare up and
burn like fire Zep 2:2
because of the evil you have
done— Ex 32:22
burn with no one to quench
it. Am 5:6

Disaster From the North

5 "Announce in Judah and
proclaim in Jerusalem
and say: Jer 5:20
'Sound the trumpet
throughout the land!' Nu 10:2,7
Cry aloud and say:
'Gather together!
Let us flee to the fortified
cities!' Jos 10:20; Jer 8:14
6 Raise the signal to go to Zion! Ps 74:4; Isa 11:10
Flee for safety without
delay!
For I am bringing disaster from
the north, Jer 1:13-15; 50:3
even terrible destruction."
7 A lion has come out of his lair; 2Ki 24:1; Jer 2:15
a destroyer of nations has set
out. Jer 6:26
He has left his place
to lay waste your land. Isa 1:7
Your towns will lie in ruins Jer 25:9
without inhabitant.
8 So put on sackcloth, Isa 22:12; Jer 6:26
lament and wail, Jer 7:29
for the fierce anger of the LORD
has not turned away from us. Jer 30:24

9 "In that day," declares the LORD,
"the king and the officials will lose heart, 1Sa 17:32
the priests will be horrified,
and the prophets will be appalled." Isa 29:9

10 Then I said, "Alas, Sovereign
LORD! How completely you have
deceived this people and Jerusalem by saying, 'You will have
peace,' when the sword is at our
throats!" 2Th 2:11; Jer 14:13
11 At that time this people and Jerusalem will be told, "A scorching
wind from the barren heights in
the desert blows toward my people, but not to winnow or cleanse;
12 a wind too strong for that comes
from me. Now I pronounce my
judgments against them."
Jer 1:16; Eze 17:10; Hos 13:15

13 Look! He advances like the clouds, Isa 19:1
his chariots come like a whirlwind, Isa 5:28
his horses are swifter than eagles. Dt 28:49; Hab 1:8
Woe to us! We are ruined!
Isa 6:11; 24:3
14 Jerusalem, wash the evil from your heart and be saved.
Jas 4:8
How long will you harbor wicked thoughts? Ps 6:3
15 A voice is announcing from Dan, Jer 8:16
proclaiming disaster from the hills of Ephraim.
Jer 31:6
16 "Tell this to the nations,
proclaim concerning Jerusalem:
'A besieging army is coming from a distant land,
raising a war cry against the cities of Judah.
Eze 21:22
17 They surround her like men guarding a field,
2Ki 25:1,4
because she has rebelled against me,'" Jer 5:23
declares the LORD.
18 "Your own conduct and actions
Ps 107:17; Isa 50:1
have brought this on you.
Jer 2:17
This is your punishment.
How bitter it is! Jer 2:19
How it pierces to the heart!"

19 Oh, my anguish, my anguish!
Isa 22:4; Jer 9:10
I writhe in pain.
Oh, the agony of my heart!
My heart pounds within me,
Jer 23:9
I cannot keep silent. Jer 20:9
For I have heard the sound of the trumpet;
Nu 10:2; Job 39:24
I have heard the battle cry.
Nu 10:9; Jer 49:2
20 Disaster follows disaster;
Ps 42:7; Eze 7:26
the whole land lies in ruins.
In an instant my tents are destroyed, Jer 10:20
my shelter in a moment.

21 How long must I see the battle
standard Nu 2:2
and hear the sound of the
trumpet? Jos 6:20; Jer 6:1

22 "My people are fools; Jer 10:8
they do not know me. Jer 2:8
They are senseless children;
they have no
understanding.
They are skilled in doing evil;
Jer 13:23; 1Co 14:20
they know not how to do
good." Ro 16:19

23 I looked at the earth,
and it was formless and
empty; Ge 1:2
and at the heavens,
and their light was gone.
Job 9:7; 30:26
24 I looked at the mountains,
and they were quaking;
Isa 5:25; Eze 38:20
all the hills were swaying.
25 I looked, and there were no
people;
every bird in the sky had
flown away. Jer 9:10; Zep 1:3
26 I looked, and the fruitful land
was a desert; Jer 12:4
all its towns lay in ruins
Isa 6:11
before the LORD, before his
fierce anger. Jer 12:13

27 This is what the LORD says:

"The whole land will be
ruined,
though I will not destroy
it completely.
Jer 5:10,18; 30:11; 46:28
28 Therefore the earth will mourn
Hos 4:3
and the heavens above grow
dark, Isa 5:30; 50:3
because I have spoken and will
not relent, Nu 23:19
I have decided and will not
turn back." Jer 23:20; 30:24

29 At the sound of horsemen and
archers Jer 6:23
every town takes to flight.
2Ki 25:4
Some go into the thickets;
some climb up among the
rocks. 1Sa 26:20
All the towns are deserted;
Isa 6:12
no one lives in them.
30 What are you doing, you
devastated one? Isa 10:3-4
Why dress yourself in
scarlet
and put on jewels of gold?
Eze 23:40
Why highlight your eyes with
makeup? 2Ki 9:30
You adorn yourself in vain.
Your lovers despise you;
La 1:2; Eze 23:9,22
they want to kill you. Ps 35:4
31 I hear a cry as of a woman in
labor, Jer 13:21
a groan as of one bearing her
first child —
the cry of Daughter Zion
gasping for breath,
Isa 42:14
stretching out her hands and
saying, Isa 1:15; La 1:17

"Alas! I am fainting;
my life is given over to
murderers." La 2:21

Not One Is Upright

5 "Go up and down the streets
of Jerusalem, Eze 22:30
look around and consider, Ps 45:10
search through her
squares.
If you can find but one person Ge 18:32
who deals honestly and
seeks the truth, Jer 14:14; Eze 13:6
I will forgive this city. Ge 18:24
2 Although they say, 'As surely as
the LORD lives,' Jer 4:2
still they are swearing
falsely." Lev 19:12
3 LORD, do not your eyes look for
truth? 2Ch 16:9
You struck them, but they
felt no pain; Isa 9:13
you crushed them, but they
refused correction. Jer 2:30; Zep 3:2
They made their faces harder
than stone Jer 7:26; 19:15
and refused to repent. 2Ch 28:22; Isa 1:5
4 I thought, "These are only the
poor;
they are foolish, Jer 4:22
for they do not know the
way of the LORD, Pr 10:21; Jer 8:7
the requirements of their
God.
5 So I will go to the leaders Mic 3:1,9
and speak to them;
surely they know the way of
the LORD,
the requirements of their
God."
But with one accord they too
had broken off the yoke
and torn off the bonds. Ps 2:3; Jer 2:20
6 Therefore a lion from the
forest will attack them, Ps 17:12
a wolf from the desert will
ravage them,
a leopard will lie in wait near
their towns Hos 13:7
to tear to pieces any who
venture out,
for their rebellion is great
and their backslidings many. Jer 30:14

7 "Why should I forgive you?
Your children have
forsaken me
and sworn by gods
that are not gods. Dt 32:21; Jos 23:7; Zep 1:5
I supplied all their needs,
yet they committed adultery Nu 25:1
and thronged to the houses
of prostitutes. Jer 13:27
8 They are well-fed, lusty
stallions,
each neighing for another
man's wife. Eze 22:11
9 Should I not punish them for
this?" Jer 9:9
declares the LORD.

"Should I not avenge myself Isa 57:6
on such a nation as this?

10 "Go through her vineyards and
ravage them,
but do not destroy them
completely. Jer 4:27; Am 9:8
Strip off her branches,
for these people do not
belong to the LORD.
11 The people of Israel and the
people of Judah
have been utterly unfaithful
to me," Jer 3:20
declares the LORD.
12 They have lied about the LORD;
they said, "He will do nothing!
No harm will come to us; Jer 23:17
we will never see sword or
famine. Jer 14:13
13 The prophets are but wind Jer 14:15
and the word is not in them;
so let what they say be done
to them."

14 Therefore this is what the LORD
God Almighty says:

"Because the people have
spoken these words,
I will make my words in
your mouth a fire Jer 1:9; 23:29; Hos 6:5
and these people the wood it
consumes.
15 People of Israel," declares the
LORD,
"I am bringing a distant
nation against you — Dt 28:49; Isa 5:26; Jer 4:16
an ancient and enduring
nation,
a people whose language you
do not know, Isa 28:11
whose speech you do not
understand.
16 Their quivers are like an open
grave;
all of them are mighty
warriors.
17 They will devour your harvests
and food, Lev 26:16; Jer 8:16
devour your sons and
daughters; Dt 28:32
they will devour your flocks
and herds, Dt 28:31
devour your vines and fig
trees. Nu 16:14
With the sword they will
destroy Lev 26:25
the fortified cities in which
you trust. Dt 28:33

18 "Yet even in those days," declares the LORD, "I will not destroy
you completely. 19 And when the
people ask, 'Why has the LORD
our God done all this to us?' you
will tell them, 'As you have forsaken me and served foreign gods
in your own land, so now you will
serve foreigners in a land not your
own.' Dt 28:48; Jer 4:27

20 "Announce this to the
descendants of Jacob
and proclaim it in Judah:
21 Hear this, you foolish and
senseless people, Jer 4:22; Hab 2:18
who have eyes but do not
see, Isa 6:10; Eze 12:2

who have ears but do not
hear: Mt 13:15; Mk 8:18
22 Should you not fear me?"
declares the LORD. Dt 28:58
"Should you not tremble in
my presence? Isa 64:2
I made the sand a boundary for
the sea, Ge 1:9
an everlasting barrier it
cannot cross.
The waves may roll, but they
cannot prevail;
they may roar, but they
cannot cross it. Ps 46:3
23 But these people have stubborn
and rebellious hearts; Dt 21:18
they have turned aside and
gone away. Ps 14:3
24 They do not say to
themselves,
'Let us fear the LORD our
God,
who gives autumn and
spring rains in season, Ps 147:8; Joel 2:23
who assures us of the regular
weeks of harvest.' Ge 8:22; Ac 14:17
25 Your wrongdoings have kept
these away;
your sins have deprived you
of good.

26 "Among my people are the
wicked
who lie in wait like men
who snare birds Ps 10:8; Pr 1:11
and like those who set traps
to catch people. Mic 7:2
27 Like cages full of birds,
their houses are full of
deceit; Jer 9:6
they have become rich and
powerful Jer 12:1
28 and have grown fat and
sleek. Dt 32:15
Their evil deeds have no limit;
they do not seek justice.
They do not promote the
case of the fatherless; Zec 7:10
they do not defend the
just cause of the poor. Isa 1:23; Jer 7:6
29 Should I not punish them for
this?"
declares the LORD.
"Should I not avenge myself
on such a nation as this?
30 "A horrible and shocking thing Hos 6:10
has happened in the land:
31 The prophets prophesy lies, Eze 13:6; Mic 2:11
the priests rule by their own
authority, La 4:13
and my people love it this
way.
But what will you do in the
end?

Jerusalem Under Siege

6 "Flee for safety, people of
Benjamin!
Flee from Jerusalem!
Sound the trumpet in Tekoa! 2Ch 11:6
Raise the signal over Beth
Hakkerem! Ne 3:14

For disaster looms out of the
north, Jer 4:6
even terrible destruction.
2 I will destroy Daughter Zion, Ps 9:14
so beautiful and delicate. La 4:5
3 Shepherds with their flocks
will come against her; Jer 12:10
they will pitch their tents
around her, 2Ki 25:4; Lk 19:43
each tending his own
portion."
4 "Prepare for battle against her!
Arise, let us attack at noon! Jer 15:8
But, alas, the daylight is fading,
and the shadows of evening
grow long.
5 So arise, let us attack at night
and destroy her fortresses!"

6 This is what the LORD Almighty
says:

"Cut down the trees Dt 20:19-20
and build siege ramps
against Jerusalem. Jer 32:24
This city must be punished;
it is filled with oppression. Jer 25:38
7 As a well pours out its water,
so she pours out her
wickedness.
Violence and destruction
resound in her; Ps 55:9; Jer 20:8; Eze 7:11,23
her sickness and wounds are
ever before me.
8 Take warning, Jerusalem,
or I will turn away from you Eze 23:18; Hos 9:12
and make your land desolate
so no one can live in it."

9 This is what the LORD Almighty
says:

"Let them glean the remnant
of Israel
as thoroughly as a vine;
pass your hand over the
branches again,
like one gathering grapes."

10 To whom can I speak and give
warning?
Who will listen to me?
Their ears are closed[a] Ac 7:51
so they cannot hear. Isa 42:20
The word of the LORD is
offensive to them; Jer 20:8
they find no pleasure in it.
11 But I am full of the wrath of
the LORD, Jer 7:20
and I cannot hold it in. Job 32:20

"Pour it out on the children in
the street
and on the young men
gathered together; Jer 9:21
both husband and wife will be
caught in it,
and the old, those weighed
down with years. La 2:21
12 Their houses will be turned
over to others, Dt 28:30
together with their fields and
their wives, Jer 8:10; 38:22

[a] 10 Hebrew *uncircumcised*

when I stretch out my hand Isa 5:25
against those who live in the land,"
declares the LORD.
13 "From the least to the greatest,
all are greedy for gain; Isa 56:11
prophets and priests alike,
all practice deceit. Jer 8:10
14 They dress the wound of my people
as though it were not serious.
'Peace, peace,' they say,
when there is no peace.
Jer 4:10; 8:11; Eze 13:10
15 Are they ashamed of their detestable conduct?
No, they have no shame at all;
they do not even know how to blush. Jer 3:3; 8:10-12
So they will fall among the fallen;
they will be brought down when I punish them,"
2Ch 25:16; Jer 27:15
says the LORD.

16 This is what the LORD says:

"Stand at the crossroads and look;
ask for the ancient paths,
Jer 18:15
ask where the good way is, and walk in it, Ps 119:3
and you will find rest for your souls. Mt 11:29
But you said, 'We will not walk in it.'
17 I appointed watchmen over you and said, Eze 3:17
'Listen to the sound of the trumpet!'
But you said, 'We will not listen.' Jer 11:7-8; 25:4
18 Therefore hear, you nations;
you who are witnesses,
observe what will happen to them.
19 Hear, you earth: Isa 1:2; Jer 22:29
I am bringing disaster on this people, Jos 23:15
the fruit of their schemes, Pr 1:31
because they have not listened to my words
and have rejected my law.
Jer 8:9
20 What do I care about incense from Sheba
or sweet calamus from a distant land? Ex 30:23
Your burnt offerings are not acceptable; Am 5:22
your sacrifices do not please me." Isa 1:11; Mic 6:7-8

21 Therefore this is what the LORD says:

"I will put obstacles before this people.
Parents and children alike
will stumble over them;
Isa 8:14
neighbors and friends will perish."

22 This is what the LORD says:

"Look, an army is coming
from the land of the north;
Jer 1:15; 10:22

a great nation is being
stirred up
from the ends of the earth.
23They are armed with bow and
spear;
they are cruel and show no
mercy. Isa 13:18
They sound like the roaring
sea
as they ride on their horses;
Jer 4:29
they come like men in battle
formation
to attack you, Daughter
Zion."

24We have heard reports about
them,
and our hands hang limp.
Anguish has gripped us, Jer 4:19
pain like that of a woman in
labor. Jer 4:31; 50:41-43
25Do not go out to the fields
or walk on the roads,
for the enemy has a sword,
and there is terror on every
side. Jer 49:29
26Put on sackcloth, my people,
Jer 4:8
and roll in ashes;
Jer 25:34; Mic 1:10
mourn with bitter wailing
as for an only son, Zec 12:10
for suddenly the destroyer
Ex 12:23
will come upon us.

27"I have made you a tester of
metals Jer 9:7
and my people the ore,
that you may observe
and test their ways.
28They are all hardened rebels,
Jer 5:23
going about to slander. Jer 9:4
They are bronze and iron;
Eze 22:18
they all act corruptly.
29The bellows blow fiercely
to burn away the lead with
fire,
but the refining goes on in
vain;
the wicked are not purged
out.
30They are called rejected silver,
because the LORD has
rejected them."
Ps 119:119; Jer 7:29; Hos 9:17

False Religion Worthless

7 This is the word that came
to Jeremiah from the LORD:
2"Stand at the gate of the LORD's
house and there proclaim this
message: Jer 17:19
"'Hear the word of the LORD, all
you people of Judah who come
through these gates to worship
the LORD. 3This is what the LORD
Almighty, the God of Israel, says:
Reform your ways and your actions, and I will let you live in this
place. 4Do not trust in deceptive
words and say, "This is the temple of the LORD, the temple of the
LORD, the temple of the LORD!" 5If
you really change your ways and
your actions and deal with each
other justly, 6if you do not oppress
the foreigner, the fatherless or the
widow and do not shed innocent
blood in this place, and if you do

not follow other gods to your own harm, 7then I will let you live in this place, in the land I gave your ancestors for ever and ever. 8But look, you are trusting in deceptive words that are worthless.

Jer 18:11; 26:13; Mic 3:11

9" 'Will you steal and murder, commit adultery and perjury,[a] burn incense to Baal and follow other gods you have not known, 10and then come and stand before me in this house, which bears my Name, and say, "We are safe" — safe to do all these detestable things? 11Has this house, which bears my Name, become a den of robbers to you? But I have been watching! declares the LORD.

Mk 11:17*; Jer 29:23

12" 'Go now to the place in Shiloh where I first made a dwelling for my Name, and see what I did to it because of the wickedness of my people Israel. 13While you were doing all these things, declares the LORD, I spoke to you again and again, but you did not listen; I called you, but you did not answer. 14Therefore, what I did to Shiloh I will now do to the house that bears my Name, the temple you trust in, the place I gave to you and your ancestors. 15I will thrust you from my presence, just as I did all your fellow Israelites, the people of Ephraim.'

Ps 78:67; Isa 65:12

16"So do not pray for this people nor offer any plea or petition for them; do not plead with me, for I will not listen to you. 17Do you not see what they are doing in the towns of Judah and in the streets of Jerusalem? 18The children gather wood, the fathers light the fire, and the women knead the dough and make cakes to offer to the Queen of Heaven. They pour out drink offerings to other gods to arouse my anger. 19But am I the one they are provoking? declares the LORD. Are they not rather harming themselves, to their own shame?

Ex 32:10; Jer 9:19

20" 'Therefore this is what the Sovereign LORD says: My anger and my wrath will be poured out on this place — on man and beast, on the trees of the field and on the crops of your land — and it will burn and not be quenched.

Jer 42:18; La 2:3-5

21" 'This is what the LORD Almighty, the God of Israel, says: Go ahead, add your burnt offerings to your other sacrifices and eat the meat yourselves! 22For when I brought your ancestors out of Egypt and spoke to them, I did not just give them commands about burnt offerings and sacrifices, 23but I gave them this command: Obey me, and I will be your God and you will be my people. Walk in obedience to all I command you, that it may go well with you. 24But they did not listen or pay attention; instead, they followed the stubborn inclinations of their evil hearts. They went backward and

[a] 9 Or *and swear by false gods*

not forward. 25 From the time your
ancestors left Egypt until now,
day after day, again and again I
sent you my servants the prophets. 26 But they did not listen to
me or pay attention. They were
stiff-necked and did more evil
than their ancestors.’ Ex 19:5; Jer 16:12

27 “When you tell them all this,
they will not listen to you; when
you call to them, they will not answer. 28 Therefore say to them, ‘This
is the nation that has not obeyed
the LORD its God or responded to
correction. Truth has perished; it
has vanished from their lips.

29 “ ‘Cut off your hair and throw
it away; take up a lament on the
barren heights, for the LORD has
rejected and abandoned this generation that is under his wrath.
Jer 6:30; Eze 3:7

The Valley of Slaughter

30 “ ‘The people of Judah have
done evil in my eyes, declares the
LORD. They have set up their detestable idols in the house that
bears my Name and have defiled
it. 31 They have built the high places of Topheth in the Valley of Ben
Hinnom to burn their sons and
daughters in the fire — something
I did not command, nor did it enter my mind. 32 So beware, the days
are coming, declares the LORD,
when people will no longer call it
Topheth or the Valley of Ben Hinnom, but the Valley of Slaughter,
for they will bury the dead in Topheth until there is no more room.
33 Then the carcasses of this people
will become food for the birds and
the wild animals, and there will be
no one to frighten them away. 34 I
will bring an end to the sounds of
joy and gladness and to the voices of bride and bridegroom in the
towns of Judah and the streets of
Jerusalem, for the land will become desolate. Isa 24:8; Rev 18:23

8 “ ‘At that time, declares the
LORD, the bones of the kings
and officials of Judah, the bones
of the priests and prophets, and
the bones of the people of Jerusalem will be removed from their
graves. 2 They will be exposed to
the sun and the moon and all the
stars of the heavens, which they
have loved and served and which
they have followed and consulted and worshiped. They will not
be gathered up or buried, but will
be like dung lying on the ground.
3 Wherever I banish them, all the
survivors of this evil nation will
prefer death to life, declares the
LORD Almighty.’ Job 3:22; Rev 9:6

Sin and Punishment

4 “Say to them, ‘This is what the
LORD says:

“ ‘When people fall down, do
they not get up? Pr 24:16
When someone turns away,
do they not return?
5 Why then have these people
turned away?
Why does Jerusalem always
turn away?

They cling to deceit; Jer 5:27
they refuse to return.
Jer 7:24; 9:6
6 I have listened attentively,
but they do not say what is
right.
None of them repent of their
wickedness, Rev 9:20
saying, "What have I done?"
Each pursues their own course
Ps 14:1-3
like a horse charging into
battle.
7 Even the stork in the sky
knows her appointed
seasons,
and the dove, the swift and the
thrush
observe the time of their
migration.
But my people do not know
Isa 1:3; Jer 5:4-5
the requirements of the
LORD.

8 " 'How can you say, "We are
wise,
for we have the law of the
LORD," Ro 2:17
when actually the lying pen of
the scribes
has handled it falsely?
9 The wise will be put to shame;
Jer 6:15
they will be dismayed and
trapped. Job 5:13
Since they have rejected
the word of the LORD,
Jer 6:19
what kind of wisdom do they
have? Pr 1:7
10 Therefore I will give their
wives to other men
and their fields to new
owners. Jer 6:12
From the least to the greatest,
all are greedy for gain; Isa 56:11
prophets and priests alike,
La 2:14
all practice deceit. Jer 23:11,15
11 They dress the wound of my
people
as though it were not
serious.
"Peace, peace," they say,
when there is no peace. Jer 6:14
12 Are they ashamed of their
detestable conduct?
No, they have no shame at
all; Jer 3:3
they do not even know how
to blush.
So they will fall among the
fallen;
they will be brought down
when they are punished,
Ps 52:5-7; Isa 3:9
says the LORD.
13 " 'I will take away their harvest,
declares the LORD.
There will be no grapes on
the vine. Joel 1:7
There will be no figs on the
tree, Lk 13:6
and their leaves will wither.
Mt 21:19
What I have given them
will be taken from them.[a] ' "
Jer 5:17

[a] 13 The meaning of the Hebrew for this sentence is uncertain.

14 Why are we sitting here?
Gather together!
Let us flee to the fortified cities Jer 4:5; 35:11
and perish there!
For the LORD our God has doomed us to perish
and given us poisoned water to drink, Jer 9:15; 23:15
because we have sinned against him. Jer 14:7,20
15 We hoped for peace ver 11
but no good has come,
for a time of healing
but there is only terror. Jer 14:19
16 The snorting of the enemy's horses
is heard from Dan; Jer 4:15
at the neighing of their stallions
the whole land trembles.
They have come to devour Jer 5:17
the land and everything in it,
the city and all who live there.

17 "See, I will send venomous snakes among you, Nu 21:6; Dt 32:24
vipers that cannot be charmed, Ps 58:5
and they will bite you,"
declares the LORD.

18 You who are my Comforter[a] in sorrow,
my heart is faint within me. La 5:17
19 Listen to the cry of my people
from a land far away: Jer 9:16
"Is the LORD not in Zion?
Is her King no longer there?" Mic 4:9

"Why have they aroused my anger with their images, Jer 44:3
with their worthless foreign idols?" Dt 32:21

20 "The harvest is past,
the summer has ended,
and we are not saved."

21 Since my people are crushed, I am crushed; Ps 94:5
I mourn, and horror grips me. Jer 14:17
22 Is there no balm in Gilead? Ge 37:25
Is there no physician there?
Why then is there no healing Jer 30:12
for the wound of my people?

9

[b] 1 Oh, that my head were a spring of water
and my eyes a fountain of tears! Ps 119:136
I would weep day and night Jer 13:17; La 2:11,18
for the slain of my people. Isa 22:4
2 Oh, that I had in the desert Ps 55:7
a lodging place for travelers,
so that I might leave my people
and go away from them;

[a] *18* The meaning of the Hebrew for this word is uncertain. [b] In Hebrew texts 9:1 is numbered 8:23, and 9:2-26 is numbered 9:1-25.

for they are all adulterers, Jer 5:7-8; 23:10; Hos 4:2
a crowd of unfaithful people. 1Ki 19:10

3 "They make ready their tongue
like a bow, to shoot lies; Ps 64:3
it is not by truth
that they triumph[a] in the
land.
They go from one sin to another;
they do not acknowledge
me," Isa 1:3
declares the LORD.
4 "Beware of your friends; 2Sa 15:12
do not trust anyone in your
clan. Mic 7:5-6
For every one of them is a
deceiver,[b] Ge 27:35
and every friend a slanderer. Ex 20:16
5 Friend deceives friend, Lev 6:2
and no one speaks the truth. Ps 15:2
They have taught their tongues
to lie; Ps 52:3
they weary themselves with
sinning.
6 You[c] live in the midst of
deception; Jer 5:27
in their deceit they refuse to
acknowledge me,"
declares the LORD.

7 Therefore this is what the LORD
Almighty says:

"See, I will refine and test
them, Isa 1:25; Jer 6:27
for what else can I do
because of the sin of my
people?
8 Their tongue is a deadly arrow; ver 3; Ps 35:20
it speaks deceitfully.
With their mouths they all
speak cordially to their
neighbors, Isa 3:5
but in their hearts
they set traps for them. Jer 5:26
9 Should I not punish them for
this?"
declares the LORD.
"Should I not avenge myself Jer 5:9,29
on such a nation as this?"

10 I will weep and wail for the
mountains
and take up a lament
concerning the
wilderness grasslands.
They are desolate and
untraveled,
and the lowing of cattle is
not heard.
The birds have all fled
and the animals are gone. Jer 4:25; 12:4; Hos 4:3

11 "I will make Jerusalem a heap
of ruins,
a haunt of jackals; Isa 34:13
and I will lay waste the towns
of Judah Jer 1:15
so no one can live there." Isa 25:2; Jer 26:9

12 Who is wise enough to understand this? Who has been instructed by the LORD and can explain it?

[a] 3 Or *lies; / they are not valiant for truth*
[b] 4 Or *a deceiving Jacob*
[c] 6 That is, Jeremiah (the Hebrew is singular)

Why has the land been ruined and
laid waste like a desert that no one
can cross? Ps 107:43; Hos 14:9

13 The LORD said, "It is because
they have forsaken my law, which
I set before them; they have not
obeyed me or followed my law.
14 Instead, they have followed the
stubbornness of their hearts; they
have followed the Baals, as their
ancestors taught them." 15 Therefore this is what the LORD Almighty, the God of Israel, says:
"See, I will make this people eat
bitter food and drink poisoned
water. 16 I will scatter them among
nations that neither they nor their
ancestors have known, and I will
pursue them with the sword until
I have made an end of them."
Lev 26:33; Dt 28:64; Jer 44:27

17 This is what the LORD Almighty
says:

"Consider now! Call for the
wailing women to come;
Ecc 12:5; Am 5:16
send for the most skillful of
them.
18 Let them come quickly
and wail over us
till our eyes overflow with tears
and water streams from our
eyelids. Jer 14:17
19 The sound of wailing is heard
from Zion:
'How ruined we are! Jer 4:13
How great is our shame!
We must leave our land
because our houses are in
ruins.'"

20 Now, you women, hear the
word of the LORD;
open your ears to the words
of his mouth.
Teach your daughters how to
wail;
teach one another a lament.
Isa 32:9-13
21 Death has climbed in through
our windows
and has entered our
fortresses;
it has removed the children
from the streets
and the young men from
the public squares.
2Ch 36:17

22 Say, "This is what the LORD declares:

"'Dead bodies will lie
like dung on the open field,
Jer 8:2
like cut grain behind the
reaper,
with no one to gather
them.'"

23 This is what the LORD says:

"Let not the wise boast of their
wisdom Ecc 9:11
or the strong boast of their
strength 1Ki 20:11
or the rich boast of their
riches, Eze 28:4-5
24 but let the one who boasts
boast about this:
1Co 1:31*; Gal 6:14
that they have the
understanding to
know me, Ps 36:10

that I am the LORD, who
exercises kindness,
Ps 51:1; Mic 7:18; 2Co 10:17*
justice and righteousness on
earth, Ps 36:6
for in these I delight,"
declares the LORD.

25"The days are coming," declares the LORD, "when I will punish all who are circumcised only in
the flesh — 26Egypt, Judah, Edom,
Ammon, Moab and all who live in
the wilderness in distant places.[a]
For all these nations are really uncircumcised, and even the whole
house of Israel is uncircumcised
in heart." Lev 26:41; Ro 2:8-9,28

God and Idols

10 Hear what the LORD says to
you, people of Israel. 2This
is what the LORD says:

"Do not learn the ways of the
nations Lev 20:23
or be terrified by signs in the
heavens,
though the nations are
terrified by them.
3For the practices of the peoples
are worthless;
they cut a tree out of the
forest,
and a craftsman shapes
it with his chisel.
Isa 40:19; Jer 44:8
4They adorn it with silver and
gold; Hos 13:2
they fasten it with hammer
and nails
so it will not totter. Isa 41:7
5Like a scarecrow in a cucumber
field,
their idols cannot speak; 1Co 12:2
they must be carried
because they cannot walk.
Ps 115:5,7
Do not fear them;
they can do no harm
nor can they do any good."
Isa 41:24; 46:7

6No one is like you, LORD;
you are great, Ps 48:1
and your name is mighty in
power.
7Who should not fear you,
King of the nations?
Ps 22:28; Rev 15:4
This is your due.
Among all the wise leaders of
the nations
and in all their kingdoms,
there is no one like you.

8They are all senseless and
foolish; Isa 40:19; Jer 4:22
they are taught by worthless
wooden idols. Dt 32:21
9Hammered silver is brought
from Tarshish
and gold from Uphaz.
What the craftsman and
goldsmith have made
Ps 115:4; Isa 40:19
is then dressed in blue and
purple —
all made by skilled workers.
10But the LORD is the true God;
he is the living God, the
eternal King. Ge 21:33; Mt 16:16

[a] *26* Or *wilderness and who clip the hair by their foreheads*

When he is angry, the earth
trembles; Ps 29:8
the nations cannot endure
his wrath. Ps 76:7

11“Tell them this: ‘These gods,
who did not make the heavens
and the earth, will perish from the
earth and from under the heavens.’ ”[a] Ps 96:5; Isa 2:18

12But God made the earth by his
power;
he founded the world by his
wisdom
and stretched out the
heavens by his
understanding.
Ge 1:1,8; Isa 40:22
13When he thunders, the waters
in the heavens roar;
Job 36:29
he makes clouds rise from
the ends of the earth.
He sends lightning with the
rain Ps 135:7
and brings out the wind
from his storehouses.
Dt 28:12
14Everyone is senseless and
without knowledge;
every goldsmith is shamed
by his idols. Isa 1:29
The images he makes are a
fraud; Isa 44:20
they have no breath in them.
15They are worthless, the
objects of mockery;
Isa 41:24; Jer 14:22
when their judgment comes,
they will perish.
16He who is the Portion of
Jacob is not like these,
Dt 32:9; Ps 119:57
for he is the Maker of all
things, ver 12; Jer 32:17
including Israel, the people
of his inheritance —
Ps 74:2
the LORD Almighty is his
name. Jer 51:15-19

Coming Destruction

17Gather up your belongings
to leave the land,
Eze 12:3-12
you who live under siege.
18For this is what the LORD
says:
“At this time I will hurl out
1Sa 25:29
those who live in this land;
I will bring distress on them
Dt 28:52
so that they may be
captured.”

19Woe to me because of my
injury!
My wound is incurable! Jer 14:17
Yet I said to myself,
“This is my sickness, and I
must endure it.” Mic 7:9
20My tent is destroyed; Jer 4:20
all its ropes are snapped.
My children are gone from
me and are no more;
Jer 31:15; La 1:5
no one is left now to pitch
my tent
or to set up my shelter.

[a] 11 The text of this verse is in Aramaic.

21 The shepherds are senseless
Jer 22:22
and do not inquire of the
LORD; Isa 56:10
so they do not prosper
and all their flock is
scattered. Jer 23:2
22 Listen! The report is coming —
a great commotion from the
land of the north!
It will make the towns of Judah
desolate,
a haunt of jackals. Jer 9:11

Jeremiah's Prayer

23 LORD, I know that people's lives
are not their own;
it is not for them to direct
their steps. Pr 20:24
24 Discipline me, LORD, but only
in due measure —
not in your anger, Ps 6:1; 38:1
or you will reduce me to
nothing. Jer 30:11
25 Pour out your wrath on the
nations Zep 3:8
that do not acknowledge you,
on the peoples who do not
call on your name.
Job 18:21; Ps 14:4
For they have devoured Jacob;
Ps 79:7; Jer 8:16
they have devoured him
completely
and destroyed his homeland.
Ps 79:6-7

The Covenant Is Broken

11 This is the word that came
to Jeremiah from the LORD:
2 "Listen to the terms of this covenant and tell them to the people
of Judah and to those who live in
Jerusalem. 3 Tell them that this is
what the LORD, the God of Israel,
says: 'Cursed is the one who does
not obey the terms of this covenant — 4 the terms I commanded your ancestors when I brought
them out of Egypt, out of the iron-
smelting furnace.' I said, 'Obey me
and do everything I command
you, and you will be my people,
and I will be your God. 5 Then I will
fulfill the oath I swore to your ancestors, to give them a land flowing with milk and honey' — the
land you possess today."
Ex 24:8; Jer 7:23
I answered, "Amen, LORD."
Dt 27:26
6 The LORD said to me, "Proclaim
all these words in the towns of Judah and in the streets of Jerusalem: 'Listen to the terms of this
covenant and follow them. 7 From
the time I brought your ancestors up from Egypt until today, I
warned them again and again,
saying, "Obey me." 8 But they did
not listen or pay attention; instead, they followed the stubbornness of their evil hearts. So I
brought on them all the curses of
the covenant I had commanded
them to follow but that they did
not keep.' " Dt 15:5; Ro 2:13; Jas 1:22
9 Then the LORD said to me,
"There is a conspiracy among the
people of Judah and those who live
in Jerusalem. 10 They have returned
to the sins of their ancestors, who

refused to listen to my words. They
have followed other gods to serve
them. Both Israel and Judah have
broken the covenant I made with
their ancestors. 11 Therefore this is
what the LORD says: 'I will bring
on them a disaster they cannot
escape. Although they cry out to
me, I will not listen to them. 12 The
towns of Judah and the people of
Jerusalem will go and cry out to
the gods to whom they burn incense, but they will not help them
at all when disaster strikes. 13 You,
Judah, have as many gods as you
have towns; and the altars you
have set up to burn incense to that
shameful god Baal are as many as
the streets of Jerusalem.'
Eze 22:25; Jdg 2:12-13

14 "Do not pray for this people or
offer any plea or petition for them,
because I will not listen when they
call to me in the time of their distress. Ex 32:10

15 "What is my beloved doing in
my temple
as she, with many others,
works out her evil
schemes?
Can consecrated meat
avert your
punishment?
When you engage in your
wickedness,
then you rejoice.[a]" Jer 7:9-10

16 The LORD called you a thriving
olive tree Ps 1:3
with fruit beautiful in
form.
But with the roar of a mighty
storm
he will set it on fire, Jer 21:14
and its branches will be
broken. Isa 27:11; Ro 11:17-24

17 The LORD Almighty, who planted
you, has decreed disaster for you,
because the people of both Israel and Judah have done evil and
aroused my anger by burning incense to Baal. Isa 5:2; Jer 12:2

Plot Against Jeremiah

18 Because the LORD revealed
their plot to me, I knew it, for at
that time he showed me what they
were doing. 19 I had been like a gentle lamb led to the slaughter; I did
not realize that they had plotted
against me, saying, Jer 18:18; 20:10

"Let us destroy the tree and its
fruit;
let us cut him off from the
land of the living, Isa 53:8
that his name be
remembered no more."
Ps 83:4

20 But you, LORD Almighty, who
judge righteously Ps 7:11
and test the heart and mind,
Ps 7:9
let me see your vengeance on
them, Ps 58:10
for to you I have committed
my cause.

21 Therefore this is what the LORD
says about the people of Anathoth

[a] 15 Or *Could consecrated meat avert your punishment? / Then you would rejoice*

who are threatening to kill you,
saying, "Do not prophesy in the
name of the LORD or you will die
by our hands"— 22therefore this
is what the LORD Almighty says:
"I will punish them. Their young
men will die by the sword, their
sons and daughters by famine.
23Not even a remnant will be left
to them, because I will bring disaster on the people of Anathoth
in the year of their punishment."
Jer 6:9; 23:12

Jeremiah's Complaint

12 You are always righteous,
LORD, Ezr 9:15
when I bring a case before
you.
Yet I would speak with you
about your justice:
Eze 18:25
Why does the way of the
wicked prosper? Jer 5:27-28
Why do all the faithless live
at ease?
2You have planted them, and
they have taken root;
Jer 11:17
they grow and bear fruit.
You are always on their lips
but far from their hearts.
Mt 15:8; Titus 1:16
3Yet you know me, LORD;
you see me and test my
thoughts about you.
Ps 139:1-4; Jer 11:20
Drag them off like sheep to be
butchered!
Set them apart for the day of
slaughter! Jer 17:18
4How long will the land lie
parched Jer 4:28
and the grass in every field
be withered? Joel 1:10-12
Because those who live in it are
wicked,
the animals and birds have
perished. Jer 4:25
Moreover, the people are
saying,
"He will not see what
happens to us."

God's Answer

5"If you have raced with men on
foot
and they have worn you out,
how can you compete with
horses?
If you stumble[a] in safe country,
how will you manage in the
thickets by[b] the Jordan?
Jer 49:19; 50:44
6Your relatives, members of
your own family—
even they have betrayed you;
they have raised a loud
cry against you.
Pr 26:24-25; Jer 9:4
Do not trust them,
though they speak well of
you. Ps 12:2

7"I will forsake my house, 2Ki 21:14
abandon my inheritance;
Jer 7:29
I will give the one I love Isa 5:1
into the hands of her
enemies. Jer 17:4

[a] 5 Or *you feel secure only* [b] 5 Or *the flooding of*

8 My inheritance has become
to me
like a lion in the forest.
She roars at me;
therefore I hate her.
Hos 9:15; Am 6:8
9 Has not my inheritance
become to me
like a speckled bird of prey
that other birds of prey
surround and attack?
Go and gather all the wild
beasts;
bring them to devour.
Isa 56:9; Jer 15:3; Eze 23:25
10 Many shepherds will ruin my
vineyard Jer 23:1
and trample down my field;
they will turn my pleasant field
into a desolate wasteland.
Isa 5:1-7
11 It will be made a wasteland,
parched and desolate before
me; Isa 42:25; Jer 23:10
the whole land will be laid
waste
because there is no one who
cares.
12 Over all the barren heights in
the desert
destroyers will swarm,
for the sword of the LORD will
devour Jer 47:6
from one end of the land to
the other; Jer 3:2
no one will be safe. Jer 7:10
13 They will sow wheat but reap
thorns;
they will wear themselves
out but gain nothing.
Lev 26:20; Dt 28:38; Mic 6:15
They will bear the shame of
their harvest
because of the LORD's fierce
anger." Jer 4:26

14 This is what the LORD says:
"As for all my wicked neighbors
who seize the inheritance I gave
my people Israel, I will uproot
them from their lands and I will
uproot the people of Judah from
among them. 15 But after I uproot
them, I will again have compassion and will bring each of them
back to their own inheritance and
their own country. 16 And if they
learn well the ways of my people
and swear by my name, saying, 'As
surely as the LORD lives' — even
as they once taught my people
to swear by Baal — then they will
be established among my people.
17 But if any nation does not listen,
I will completely uproot and destroy it," declares the LORD.
Isa 60:12; Jer 4:2; Zec 2:7-9

A Linen Belt

13 This is what the LORD said
to me: "Go and buy a linen
belt and put it around your waist,
but do not let it touch water." 2 So I
bought a belt, as the LORD directed, and put it around my waist.
3 Then the word of the LORD
came to me a second time: 4 "Take
the belt you bought and are wearing around your waist, and go now
to Perath[a] and hide it there in a

[a] 4 Or possibly *to the Euphrates*; similarly in verses 5-7

crevice in the rocks." 5 So I went
and hid it at Perath, as the LORD
told me. Ex 40:16

6 Many days later the LORD said
to me, "Go now to Perath and get
the belt I told you to hide there."
7 So I went to Perath and dug up
the belt and took it from the place
where I had hidden it, but now it
was ruined and completely useless.

8 Then the word of the LORD
came to me: 9 "This is what the
LORD says: 'In the same way I will
ruin the pride of Judah and the
great pride of Jerusalem. 10 These
wicked people, who refuse to listen to my words, who follow the
stubbornness of their hearts and
go after other gods to serve and
worship them, will be like this
belt — completely useless! 11 For as
a belt is bound around the waist,
so I bound all the people of Israel
and all the people of Judah to me,'
declares the LORD, 'to be my people for my renown and praise and
honor. But they have not listened.'
Lev 26:19; Jer 7:26; 32:20

Wineskins

12 "Say to them: 'This is what
the LORD, the God of Israel, says:
Every wineskin should be filled
with wine.' And if they say to you,
'Don't we know that every wineskin should be filled with wine?'
13 then tell them, 'This is what the
LORD says: I am going to fill with
drunkenness all who live in this
land, including the kings who sit
on David's throne, the priests, the
prophets and all those living in
Jerusalem. 14 I will smash them
one against the other, parents and
children alike, declares the LORD.
I will allow no pity or mercy or
compassion to keep me from destroying them.' "
Isa 51:17; Jer 16:5; Eze 5:10

Threat of Captivity

15 Hear and pay attention,
  do not be arrogant,
  for the LORD has spoken.
Ps 95:7-8

16 Give glory to the LORD your
    God Jos 7:19
  before he brings the
    darkness,
before your feet stumble Jer 23:12
  on the darkening hills.
You hope for light,
  but he will turn it to utter
    darkness
  and change it to deep gloom.
Isa 59:9

17 If you do not listen, Mal 2:2
  I will weep in secret
  because of your pride;
my eyes will weep bitterly,
  overflowing with tears, Jer 9:1
  because the LORD's flock will
    be taken captive. Jer 14:18

18 Say to the king and to the
    queen mother, Isa 22:17
  "Come down from your
    thrones,
for your glorious crowns
2Sa 12:30; La 5:16
  will fall from your heads."

19 The cities in the Negev will be
shut up,
and there will be no one to
open them.
All Judah will be carried into
exile, Jer 20:4; 52:30
carried completely away.

20 Look up and see
those who are coming from
the north. Jer 6:22; Hab 1:6
Where is the flock that was
entrusted to you, Jer 23:2
the sheep of which you
boasted?
21 What will you say when the
LORD sets over you
those you cultivated
as your special allies?
Jer 38:22
Will not pain grip you
like that of a woman in
labor? Jer 4:31
22 And if you ask yourself,
"Why has this happened to
me?" —
it is because of your many sins
Jer 16:10-12
that your skirts have been
torn off Isa 20:4
and your body mistreated.
Eze 16:37; Na 3:5-6
23 Can an Ethiopian[a] change his
skin
or a leopard its spots?
Neither can you do good
who are accustomed to doing
evil. 2Ch 6:36

24 "I will scatter you like chaff Ps 1:4
driven by the desert wind.
Lev 26:33
25 This is your lot,
the portion I have decreed
for you," Job 20:29; Mt 24:51
declares the LORD,
"because you have forgotten me
Isa 17:10
and trusted in false gods.
Ps 4:2
26 I will pull up your skirts over
your face
that your shame
may be seen —
La 1:8; Eze 16:37; Hos 2:10
27 your adulteries and lustful
neighings,
your shameless prostitution!
Jer 2:20
I have seen your detestable acts
on the hills and in the fields.
Eze 6:13
Woe to you, Jerusalem!
How long will you be
unclean?" Hos 8:5

Drought, Famine, Sword

14 This is the word of the LORD that came to Jeremiah concerning the drought: Isa 5:6

2 "Judah mourns, Isa 3:26; Jer 8:21
her cities languish;
they wail for the land,
and a cry goes up from
Jerusalem.
3 The nobles send their servants
for water;
they go to the cisterns
but find no water.
2Ki 18:31; Job 6:19-20

[a] 23 Hebrew *Cushite* (probably a person from the upper Nile region)

They return with their jars
unfilled;
dismayed and despairing,
they cover their heads. 2Sa 15:30
4 The ground is cracked
because there is no rain in
the land; Jer 3:3
the farmers are dismayed
and cover their heads.
5 Even the doe in the field
deserts her newborn fawn
because there is no grass.
Isa 15:6
6 Wild donkeys stand on
the barren heights
Job 39:5-6; Jer 2:24
and pant like jackals;
their eyes fail
for lack of food."

7 Although our sins testify
against us, Hos 5:5
do something, LORD, for
the sake of your name.
Ps 79:9
For we have often rebelled;
Jer 5:6
we have sinned against you.
Jer 8:14
8 You who are the hope of Israel,
Jer 17:13
its Savior in times of distress,
Ps 46:1
why are you like a stranger in
the land,
like a traveler who stays only
a night?
9 Why are you like a man taken
by surprise,
like a warrior powerless to
save? Isa 50:2
You are among us, LORD, Jer 8:19
and we bear your name;
Isa 63:19; Jer 15:16
do not forsake us! Ps 27:9

10 This is what the LORD says
about this people:

"They greatly love to wander;
they do not restrain their
feet. Ps 119:101; Jer 2:25
So the LORD does not accept
them; Jer 6:20; Am 5:22
he will now remember their
wickedness Hos 9:9
and punish them for their
sins." Hos 8:13

11 Then the LORD said to me, "Do
not pray for the well-being of this
people. 12 Although they fast, I will
not listen to their cry; though they
offer burnt offerings and grain offerings, I will not accept them. Instead, I will destroy them with the
sword, famine and plague."
Ex 32:10; Isa 1:15; Jer 7:21

13 But I said, "Alas, Sovereign
LORD! The prophets keep telling them, 'You will not see the
sword or suffer famine. Indeed, I
will give you lasting peace in this
place.'" Jer 5:12

14 Then the LORD said to me, "The
prophets are prophesying lies in
my name. I have not sent them
or appointed them or spoken to
them. They are prophesying to
you false visions, divinations,
idolatries[a] and the delusions of
their own minds. 15 Therefore this

[a] 14 Or *visions, worthless divinations*

is what the LORD says about the
prophets who are prophesying in
my name: I did not send them,
yet they are saying, 'No sword or
famine will touch this land.' Those
same prophets will perish by
sword and famine. 16 And the people they are prophesying to will
be thrown out into the streets of
Jerusalem because of the famine
and sword. There will be no one to
bury them, their wives, their sons
and their daughters. I will pour
out on them the calamity they deserve. Jer 5:12-13; 27:14

17 "Speak this word to them:

" 'Let my eyes overflow with
tears Jer 9:1
night and day without
ceasing;
for the Virgin Daughter, my
people, 2Ki 19:21
has suffered a grievous
wound,
a crushing blow. Jer 8:21
18 If I go into the country,
I see those slain by the sword;
if I go into the city,
I see the ravages of famine.
Eze 7:15
Both prophet and priest
have gone to a land they
know not.' " 2Ch 36:10

19 Have you rejected Judah
completely? Jer 7:29
Do you despise Zion?
Why have you afflicted us
so that we cannot be healed?
Jer 30:12-13
We hoped for peace
but no good has come,
for a time of healing
but there is only terror. Jer 8:15
20 We acknowledge our
wickedness, LORD, Jer 3:13
and the guilt of our
ancestors; 1Ki 8:47
we have indeed sinned
against you. Da 9:7-8
21 For the sake of your name do
not despise us; Jos 7:9
do not dishonor your
glorious throne. Jer 3:17
Remember your covenant
with us
and do not break it. Ex 2:24
22 Do any of the worthless idols of
the nations bring rain?
Ps 135:7
Do the skies themselves send
down showers?
No, it is you, LORD our God.
Therefore our hope is in
you,
for you are the one who does
all this. Isa 43:10

15 Then the LORD said to me:
"Even if Moses and Samuel
were to stand before me, my heart
would not go out to this people.
Send them away from my presence! Let them go! 2 And if they
ask you, 'Where shall we go?' tell
them, 'This is what the LORD says:
Jer 7:16; Eze 14:14,20

" 'Those destined for death, to
death;
those for the sword, to the
sword; Jer 43:11

those for starvation, to
starvation; Jer 14:12
those for captivity, to captivity.'
Rev 13:10

3"I will send four kinds of destroyers against them," declares
the LORD, "the sword to kill and
the dogs to drag away and the
birds and the wild animals to devour and destroy. 4I will make
them abhorrent to all the kingdoms of the earth because of what
Manasseh son of Hezekiah king of
Judah did in Jerusalem.
Dt 28:25; 2Ki 23:26-27

5"Who will have pity on you,
Jerusalem? Isa 51:19; Jer 13:14
Who will mourn for you?
Who will stop to ask how you
are?
6You have rejected me,"
declares the LORD.
Jer 6:19; 7:24
"You keep on backsliding.
So I will reach out and destroy
you; Zep 1:4
I am tired of holding back.
Jer 7:20; Am 7:8
7I will winnow them with a
winnowing fork
at the city gates of the
land.
I will bring bereavement and
destruction on my
people, Jer 18:21
for they have not changed
their ways. 2Ch 28:22
8I will make their widows more
numerous Isa 47:9
than the sand of the sea.
At midday I will bring a
destroyer Jer 6:4
against the mothers of their
young men;
suddenly I will bring down on
them
anguish and terror. Job 18:11
9The mother of seven will grow
faint 1Sa 2:5
and breathe her last.
Her sun will set while it is still
day;
she will be disgraced and
humiliated. Jer 7:19
I will put the survivors to the
sword Jer 21:7
before their enemies," 2Ki 25:7
declares the LORD.

10Alas, my mother, that you gave
me birth, Job 3:1
a man with whom the
whole land strives and
contends! Jer 1:19
I have neither lent nor
borrowed, Lev 25:36
yet everyone curses me.
Jer 6:10

11The LORD said,

"Surely I will deliver you
for a good purpose;
Jer 40:4
surely I will make your
enemies plead with you
Jer 21:1-2; 37:3; 42:1-3
in times of disaster and
times of distress.

12"Can a man break iron —
iron from the north — or
bronze? Jer 28:14

[13]"Your wealth and your
treasures 2Ki 25:15
I will give as plunder,
without charge, Ps 44:12
because of all your sins
throughout your country.
Jer 17:3
[14]I will enslave you to your
enemies
in[a] a land you do not know,
Jer 16:13
for my anger will kindle a fire
Dt 32:22; Ps 21:9
that will burn against you."

[15]LORD, you understand;
remember me and care
for me.
Avenge me on my
persecutors. Jer 12:3
You are long-suffering — do
not take me away; Ex 34:6
think of how I suffer
reproach for your sake.
Ps 69:7-9
[16]When your words came, I ate
them; Eze 3:3; Rev 10:10
they were my joy and my
heart's delight, Ps 119:72,103
for I bear your name,
Jer 14:9
LORD God Almighty.
[17]I never sat in the company of
revelers, Ps 1:1; 26:4-5; Jer 16:8
never made merry with them;
I sat alone because your hand
was on me 2Ki 3:15
and you had filled me with
indignation.
[18]Why is my pain unending
and my wound grievous and
incurable? Jer 30:15; Mic 1:9
You are to me like a deceptive
brook,
like a spring that fails. Job 6:15

[19]Therefore this is what the
LORD says:

"If you repent, I will restore
you
that you may serve me; Zec 3:7
if you utter worthy, not
worthless, words,
you will be my spokesman.
Ex 4:16
Let this people turn to you,
but you must not turn to
them.
[20]I will make you a wall to this
people,
a fortified wall of bronze;
they will fight against you
but will not overcome you,
for I am with you
to rescue and save you,"
Jer 20:11; Eze 3:8
declares the LORD.
[21]"I will save you from the hands
of the wicked Jer 1:8
and deliver you from the
grasp of the cruel."
Ge 48:16; Jer 50:34

Day of Disaster

16 Then the word of the LORD
came to me: [2]"You must not
marry and have sons or daughters in this place." [3]For this is what
the LORD says about the sons and

[a] *14* Some Hebrew manuscripts, Septuagint and Syriac (see also 17:4); most Hebrew manuscripts *I will cause your enemies to bring you / into*

daughters born in this land and about the women who are their mothers and the men who are their fathers: 4"They will die of deadly diseases. They will not be mourned or buried but will be like dung lying on the ground. They will perish by sword and famine, and their dead bodies will become food for the birds and the wild animals." Ps 83:10; 1Co 7:26-27; Jer 6:21

5For this is what the LORD says: "Do not enter a house where there is a funeral meal; do not go to mourn or show sympathy, because I have withdrawn my blessing, my love and my pity from this people," declares the LORD. 6"Both high and low will die in this land. They will not be buried or mourned, and no one will cut themselves or shave their head for the dead. 7No one will offer food to comfort those who mourn for the dead — not even for a father or a mother — nor will anyone give them a drink to console them.

Jer 15:5; Eze 9:5-6

8"And do not enter a house where there is feasting and sit down to eat and drink. 9For this is what the LORD Almighty, the God of Israel, says: Before your eyes and in your days I will bring an end to the sounds of joy and gladness and to the voices of bride and bridegroom in this place.

Rev 18:23; Hos 2:11

10"When you tell these people all this and they ask you, 'Why has the LORD decreed such a great disaster against us? What wrong have we done? What sin have we committed against the LORD our God?' 11then say to them, 'It is because your ancestors forsook me,' declares the LORD, 'and followed other gods and served and worshiped them. They forsook me and did not keep my law. 12But you have behaved more wickedly than your ancestors. See how all of you are following the stubbornness of your evil hearts instead of obeying me. 13So I will throw you out of this land into a land neither you nor your ancestors have known, and there you will serve other gods day and night, for I will show you no favor.' Dt 29:24; Jer 5:19; 13:10

14"However, the days are coming," declares the LORD, "when it will no longer be said, 'As surely as the LORD lives, who brought the Israelites up out of Egypt,' 15but it will be said, 'As surely as the LORD lives, who brought the Israelites up out of the land of the north and out of all the countries where he had banished them.' For I will restore them to the land I gave their ancestors. Jer 23:7-8; 24:6

16"But now I will send for many fishermen," declares the LORD, "and they will catch them. After that I will send for many hunters, and they will hunt them down on every mountain and hill and from the crevices of the rocks. 17My eyes are on all their ways; they are not hidden from me, nor is their sin concealed from my eyes. 18I will repay them double for their wickedness and their sin, because they have defiled my land with the lifeless forms of their vile images and have filled my inheritance with their detestable idols." Pr 15:3; 1Co 4:5; Heb 4:13

19 LORD, my strength and my fortress,
my refuge in time of distress, Ps 46:1
to you the nations will come Isa 2:2; Jer 3:17
from the ends of the earth and say,
"Our ancestors possessed nothing but false gods, Ps 4:2
worthless idols that did them no good. Isa 40:19
20 Do people make their own gods?
Yes, but they are not gods!" Isa 37:19; Jer 2:11

21 "Therefore I will teach them —
this time I will teach them my power and might.
Then they will know
that my name is the LORD. Ex 3:15

17 "Judah's sin is engraved with an iron tool, Job 19:24
inscribed with a flint point,
on the tablets of their hearts Pr 3:3; 2Co 3:3
and on the horns of their altars. Ex 27:2
2 Even their children remember
their altars and Asherah poles[a] 2Ch 24:18
beside the spreading trees
and on the high hills. Jer 2:20
3 My mountain in the land
and your[b] wealth and all your treasures
I will give away as plunder, 2Ki 24:13
together with your high places, Jer 26:18; Mic 3:12
because of sin throughout your country. Jer 15:13
4 Through your own fault you will lose
the inheritance I gave you. La 5:2
I will enslave you to your enemies Dt 28:48; Jer 12:7
in a land you do not know, Jer 16:13
for you have kindled my anger,
and it will burn forever." Jer 15:14

5 This is what the LORD says:

"Cursed is the one who trusts in man, Isa 2:22; 30:1-3
who draws strength from mere flesh
and whose heart turns away from the LORD. 2Co 1:9
6 That person will be like a bush in the wastelands;
they will not see prosperity when it comes.
They will dwell in the parched places of the desert,
in a salt land where no one lives. Dt 29:23; Job 39:6

[a] 2 That is, wooden symbols of the goddess Asherah [b] 2,3 Or *hills / [3]and the mountains of the land. / Your*

7"But blessed is the one who
trusts in the LORD, Ps 34:8; Pr 16:20
whose confidence is in
him.
8They will be like a tree planted
by the water
that sends out its roots by
the stream.
It does not fear when heat
comes;
its leaves are always green.
It has no worries in a year of
drought Jer 14:1-6
and never fails to bear fruit."
Ps 1:3; 92:12-14

9The heart is deceitful
above all things
Ecc 9:3; Mt 13:15; Mk 7:21-22
and beyond cure.
Who can understand it?

10"I the LORD search the heart
1Sa 16:7; Rev 2:23
and examine the mind,
Jer 20:12; Ro 8:27
to reward each person
according to their
conduct, Jer 32:19
according to what their
deeds deserve." Ro 2:6

11Like a partridge that hatches
eggs it did not lay
are those who gain riches by
unjust means.
When their lives are half gone,
their riches will desert
them,
and in the end they will
prove to be fools. Lk 12:20

12A glorious throne, exalted from
the beginning, Jer 3:17
is the place of our sanctuary.
13LORD, you are the hope of
Israel; Jer 14:8
all who forsake you will be
put to shame. Isa 1:28; Jer 2:17
Those who turn away from you
will be written in the
dust Ps 69:28
because they have forsaken
the LORD,
the spring of living water.
Jn 4:10

14Heal me, LORD, and I will be
healed; Isa 30:26
save me and I will be saved,
Ps 119:94
for you are the one I praise.
Ps 109:1
15They keep saying to me,
"Where is the word of the
LORD?
Let it now be fulfilled!"
Isa 5:19; 2Pe 3:4
16I have not run away from being
your shepherd;
you know I have not desired
the day of despair.
What passes my lips is open
before you.
17Do not be a terror to me;
Ps 88:15-16
you are my refuge in the day
of disaster. Jer 16:19; Na 1:7
18Let my persecutors be put to
shame,
but keep me from shame;
let them be terrified,
but keep me from terror.

Bring on them the day of
disaster;
destroy them with double
destruction. Ps 35:1-8

Keeping the Sabbath Day Holy

19 This is what the LORD said to me: "Go and stand at the Gate of the People,[a] through which the kings of Judah go in and out; stand also at all the other gates of Jerusalem. 20 Say to them, 'Hear the word of the LORD, you kings of Judah and all people of Judah and everyone living in Jerusalem who come through these gates. 21 This is what the LORD says: Be careful not to carry a load on the Sabbath day or bring it through the gates of Jerusalem. 22 Do not bring a load out of your houses or do any work on the Sabbath, but keep the Sabbath day holy, as I commanded your ancestors. 23 Yet they did not listen or pay attention; they were stiff-necked and would not listen or respond to discipline. 24 But if you are careful to obey me, declares the LORD, and bring no load through the gates of this city on the Sabbath, but keep the Sabbath day holy by not doing any work on it, 25 then kings who sit on David's throne will come through the gates of this city with their officials. They and their officials will come riding in chariots and on horses, accompanied by the men of Judah and those living in Jerusalem, and this city will be inhabited forever. 26 People will come from the towns of Judah and the villages around Jerusalem, from the territory of Benjamin and the western foothills, from the hill country and the Negev, bringing burnt offerings and sacrifices, grain offerings and incense, and bringing thank offerings to the house of the LORD. 27 But if you do not obey me to keep the Sabbath day holy by not carrying any load as you come through the gates of Jerusalem on the Sabbath day, then I will kindle an unquenchable fire in the gates of Jerusalem that will consume her fortresses.' "

2Ki 25:9; Jer 22:5; Am 2:5

At the Potter's House

18 This is the word that came to Jeremiah from the LORD: 2 "Go down to the potter's house, and there I will give you my message." 3 So I went down to the potter's house, and I saw him working at the wheel. 4 But the pot he was shaping from the clay was marred in his hands; so the potter formed it into another pot, shaping it as seemed best to him.

5 Then the word of the LORD came to me. 6 He said, "Can I not do with you, Israel, as this potter does?" declares the LORD. "Like clay in the hand of the potter, so are you in my hand, Israel. 7 If at any time I announce that a nation or kingdom is to be uprooted, torn down and destroyed, 8 and if that nation I warned repents of its evil,

[a] 19 Or *Army*

then I will relent and not inflict on
it the disaster I had planned. [9]And
if at another time I announce that
a nation or kingdom is to be built
up and planted, [10]and if it does evil
in my sight and does not obey me,
then I will reconsider the good I
had intended to do for it.
Isa 45:9; Ro 9:20-21; Jer 1:10

[11]"Now therefore say to the people of Judah and those living in
Jerusalem, 'This is what the LORD
says: Look! I am preparing a disaster for you and devising a plan
against you. So turn from your evil
ways, each one of you, and reform
your ways and your actions.' [12]But
they will reply, 'It's no use. We will
continue with our own plans; we
will all follow the stubbornness of
our evil hearts.'"
2Ki 17:13; Isa 57:10; Jer 2:25

[13]Therefore this is what the LORD says:

"Inquire among the nations:
Who has ever heard anything like this? Isa 66:8; Jer 2:10
A most horrible thing has been done Jer 5:30
by Virgin Israel. 2Ki 19:21
[14]Does the snow of Lebanon
ever vanish from its rocky slopes?
Do its cool waters from distant sources
ever stop flowing?[a]
[15]Yet my people have forgotten me; Isa 17:10
they burn incense to worthless idols, Jer 10:15
which made them stumble in their ways,
in the ancient paths. Jer 6:16
They made them walk in byways,
on roads not built up. Isa 57:14; 62:10
[16]Their land will be an object of horror Jer 25:9
and of lasting scorn; Jer 19:8
all who pass by will be appalled
and will shake their heads. Ps 22:7
[17]Like a wind from the east, Jer 13:24
I will scatter them before their enemies;
I will show them my back and not my face Jer 2:27
in the day of their disaster."

[18]They said, "Come, let's make
plans against Jeremiah; for the
teaching of the law by the priest
will not cease, nor will counsel
from the wise, nor the word from
the prophets. So come, let's attack
him with our tongues and pay no
attention to anything he says."
Jer 11:19; Mal 2:7

[19]Listen to me, LORD;
hear what my accusers are saying! Ps 71:13
[20]Should good be repaid with evil? Ge 44:4
Yet they have dug a pit for me. Ps 35:7; 57:6

[a] 14 The meaning of the Hebrew for this sentence is uncertain.

Remember that I stood before
you Jer 15:1
and spoke in their behalf
Ps 106:23
to turn your wrath away
from them.
21 So give their children over to
famine; Jer 11:22
hand them over to the power
of the sword. Ps 63:10
Let their wives be made
childless and widows;
Ps 109:9
let their men be put to
death,
their young men slain by the
sword in battle. Isa 9:17
22 Let a cry be heard from their
houses Jer 6:26
when you suddenly bring
invaders against them,
for they have dug a pit to
capture me
and have hidden snares for
my feet. Ps 140:5
23 But you, LORD, know
all their plots to kill me.
Jer 11:21
Do not forgive their crimes
Ps 109:14
or blot out their sins from
your sight.
Let them be overthrown before
you;
deal with them in the time of
your anger. Jer 10:24

19 This is what the LORD says:
"Go and buy a clay jar from
a potter. Take along some of the
elders of the people and of the
priests 2and go out to the Valley
of Ben Hinnom, near the entrance
of the Potsherd Gate. There proclaim the words I tell you, 3and
say, 'Hear the word of the LORD,
you kings of Judah and people of
Jerusalem. This is what the LORD
Almighty, the God of Israel, says:
Listen! I am going to bring a disaster on this place that will make
the ears of everyone who hears of
it tingle. 4For they have forsaken
me and made this a place of foreign gods; they have burned incense in it to gods that neither
they nor their ancestors nor the
kings of Judah ever knew, and
they have filled this place with
the blood of the innocent. 5They
have built the high places of Baal
to burn their children in the fire
as offerings to Baal — something I
did not command or mention, nor
did it enter my mind. 6So beware,
the days are coming, declares the
LORD, when people will no longer
call this place Topheth or the Valley of Ben Hinnom, but the Valley
of Slaughter. 1Sa 3:11; 2Ki 21:16; Jer 6:19
7" 'In this place I will ruin[a] the
plans of Judah and Jerusalem. I
will make them fall by the sword
before their enemies, at the hands
of those who want to kill them,
and I will give their carcasses as
food to the birds and the wild animals. 8I will devastate this city
and make it an object of horror
and scorn; all who pass by will be

[a] 7 The Hebrew for *ruin* sounds like the Hebrew for *jar* (see verses 1 and 10).

appalled and will scoff because of
all its wounds. 9I will make them
eat the flesh of their sons and
daughters, and they will eat one
another's flesh because their enemies will press the siege so hard
against them to destroy them.'

Dt 28:49-57; Jer 18:16

10"Then break the jar while
those who go with you are watching, 11and say to them, 'This is what
the LORD Almighty says: I will
smash this nation and this city
just as this potter's jar is smashed
and cannot be repaired. They will
bury the dead in Topheth until
there is no more room. 12This is
what I will do to this place and to
those who live here, declares the
LORD. I will make this city like Topheth. 13The houses in Jerusalem
and those of the kings of Judah
will be defiled like this place, Topheth — all the houses where they
burned incense on the roofs to all
the starry hosts and poured out
drink offerings to other gods.' "

Ps 2:9; Jer 7:32

14Jeremiah then returned from
Topheth, where the LORD had sent
him to prophesy, and stood in the
court of the LORD's temple and
said to all the people, 15"This is
what the LORD Almighty, the God
of Israel, says: 'Listen! I am going
to bring on this city and all the
villages around it every disaster
I pronounced against them, because they were stiff-necked and
would not listen to my words.' "

Jer 7:26; 17:23

Jeremiah and Pashhur

20 When the priest Pashhur
son of Immer, the offi-
cial in charge of the temple of the
LORD, heard Jeremiah prophesying these things, 2he had Jeremiah
the prophet beaten and put in the
stocks at the Upper Gate of Benjamin at the LORD's temple. 3The
next day, when Pashhur released
him from the stocks, Jeremiah said
to him, "The LORD's name for you
is not Pashhur, but Terror on Every
Side. 4For this is what the LORD says:
'I will make you a terror to yourself
and to all your friends; with your
own eyes you will see them fall by
the sword of their enemies. I will
give all Judah into the hands of
the king of Babylon, who will carry
them away to Babylon or put them
to the sword. 5I will deliver all the
wealth of this city into the hands of
their enemies — all its products, all
its valuables and all the treasures
of the kings of Judah. They will
take it away as plunder and carry
it off to Babylon. 6And you, Pashhur, and all who live in your house
will go into exile to Babylon. There
you will die and be buried, you and
all your friends to whom you have
prophesied lies.' " 2Ki 20:17; Jer 52:27

Jeremiah's Complaint

7You deceived[a] me, LORD, and I
was deceived[a]; Ex 5:23
you overpowered me and
prevailed. Isa 8:11

[a] 7 Or *persuaded*

I am ridiculed all day long; Job 12:4
everyone mocks me. Job 17:2; Ps 119:21
8 Whenever I speak, I cry out
proclaiming violence and destruction. Jer 6:7
So the word of the LORD has brought me
insult and reproach all day long. 2Ch 36:16; Jer 6:10
9 But if I say, "I will not mention his word
or speak anymore in his name,"
his word is in my heart like a fire, Ps 39:3
a fire shut up in my bones.
I am weary of holding it in; Job 32:18-20; Ac 4:20
indeed, I cannot.
10 I hear many whispering,
"Terror on every side! Jer 6:25
Denounce him! Let's denounce him!" Isa 29:21
All my friends Ps 41:9
are waiting for me to slip, saying, Lk 11:53-54
"Perhaps he will be deceived;
then we will prevail over him 1Ki 19:2
and take our revenge on him." Jer 11:19

11 But the LORD is with me like a mighty warrior;
Jer 1:8; Ro 8:31
so my persecutors will stumble and not prevail.
Jer 15:20; 17:18
They will fail and be thoroughly disgraced;
Jer 23:40
their dishonor will never be forgotten.
12 LORD Almighty, you who examine the righteous
and probe the heart and mind, Jer 17:10
let me see your vengeance on them, Ps 54:7; 59:10
for to you I have committed my cause. Jer 11:20

13 Sing to the LORD! Isa 12:6
Give praise to the LORD!
He rescues the life of the needy Ps 35:10
from the hands of the wicked. Ps 97:10

14 Cursed be the day I was born! Job 3:3; Jer 15:10
May the day my mother bore me not be blessed!
15 Cursed be the man who brought my father the news,
who made him very glad, saying,
"A child is born to you — a son!"
16 May that man be like the towns Ge 19:25
the LORD overthrew without pity.
May he hear wailing in the morning,
a battle cry at noon.
17 For he did not kill me in the womb, Job 10:18-19
with my mother as my grave,
her womb enlarged forever.

18 Why did I ever come out of the
womb Job 3:10-11
to see trouble and sorrow Ge 3:17
and to end my days in
shame? Ps 90:9

God Rejects Zedekiah's Request

21 The word came to Jeremiah
from the LORD when King
Zedekiah sent to him Pashhur son
of Malkijah and the priest Zephaniah son of Maaseiah. They said:
2 "Inquire now of the LORD for us
because Nebuchadnezzar[a] king of
Babylon is attacking us. Perhaps
the LORD will perform wonders for
us as in times past so that he will
withdraw from us." 2Ki 24:18; 25:18
3 But Jeremiah answered them,
"Tell Zedekiah, 4 'This is what the
LORD, the God of Israel, says: I
am about to turn against you
the weapons of war that are in
your hands, which you are using
to fight the king of Babylon and
the Babylonians[b] who are outside the wall besieging you. And
I will gather them inside this city.
5 I myself will fight against you
with an outstretched hand and a
mighty arm in furious anger and
in great wrath. 6 I will strike down
those who live in this city — both
man and beast — and they will
die of a terrible plague. 7 After
that, declares the LORD, I will give
Zedekiah king of Judah, his officials and the people in this city
who survive the plague, sword
and famine, into the hands of
Nebuchadnezzar king of Babylon
and to their enemies who want to
kill them. He will put them to the
sword; he will show them no mercy or pity or compassion.'
2Ch 36:17; Jer 37:17; 39:5
8 "Furthermore, tell the people,
'This is what the LORD says: See, I
am setting before you the way of
life and the way of death. 9 Whoever stays in this city will die by
the sword, famine or plague. But
whoever goes out and surrenders
to the Babylonians who are besieging you will live; they will escape with their lives. 10 I have determined to do this city harm and
not good, declares the LORD. It will
be given into the hands of the king
of Babylon, and he will destroy it
with fire.' Jer 44:11,27; 52:13
11 "Moreover, say to the royal
house of Judah, 'Hear the word of
the LORD. 12 This is what the LORD
says to you, house of David: Jer 13:18

" 'Administer justice every
morning; Jer 22:3
rescue from the hand of the
oppressor Ps 27:11
the one who has been
robbed,
or my wrath will break out and
burn like fire Jer 10:10
because of the evil you have
done — Jer 23:2
burn with no one to
quench it. Isa 1:31

[a] 2 Hebrew *Nebuchadrezzar,* of which *Nebuchadnezzar* is a variant; here and often in Jeremiah and Ezekiel [b] 4 Or *Chaldeans*; also in verse 9

[13]I am against you, Jerusalem, Eze 13:8
you who live above this
valley Ps 125:2
on the rocky plateau,
declares the LORD—
you who say, "Who can come
against us?
Who can enter our refuge?"
Jer 49:4; Ob 1:3-4
[14]I will punish you as your deeds
deserve, Isa 3:10-11
declares the LORD.
I will kindle a fire in your
forests 2Ch 36:19; Eze 20:47
that will consume everything
around you.'"

Judgment Against Wicked Kings

22 This is what the LORD says:
"Go down to the palace of
the king of Judah and proclaim this
message there: [2]'Hear the word of
the LORD to you, king of Judah, you
who sit on David's throne—you,
your officials and your people who
come through these gates. [3]This is
what the LORD says: Do what is just
and right. Rescue from the hand of
the oppressor the one who has been
robbed. Do no wrong or violence
to the foreigner, the fatherless or
the widow, and do not shed innocent blood in this place. [4]For if you
are careful to carry out these commands, then kings who sit on David's throne will come through the
gates of this palace, riding in chariots and on horses, accompanied
by their officials and their people.
[5]But if you do not obey these commands, declares the LORD, I swear
by myself that this palace will become a ruin.'" Jer 17:27; Mic 6:8; Heb 6:13
[6]For this is what the LORD says
about the palace of the king of Judah:

"Though you are like Gilead
to me, Ge 31:21
like the summit of Lebanon,
I will surely make you like a
wasteland, Mic 3:12
like towns not inhabited.
[7]I will send destroyers against
you, Jer 4:7
each man with his weapons,
and they will cut up your fine
cedar beams Isa 10:34
and throw them into the fire.
2Ch 36:19

[8]"People from many nations
will pass by this city and will ask
one another, 'Why has the LORD
done such a thing to this great
city?' [9]And the answer will be: 'Because they have forsaken the covenant of the LORD their God and
have worshiped and served other
gods.'" 2Ki 22:17; 2Ch 34:25

[10]Do not weep for the dead king
or mourn his loss; Ecc 4:2
rather, weep bitterly for him
who is exiled,
because he will never return
Jer 24:9
nor see his native land
again.

[11]For this is what the LORD says
about Shallum[a] son of Josiah, who

[a] 11 Also called *Jehoahaz*

succeeded his father as king of
Judah but has gone from this
place: "He will never return. [12]He
will die in the place where they
have led him captive; he will not
see this land again." 2Ki 23:31,34

[13]"Woe to him who builds
his palace by
unrighteousness, Mic 3:10; Hab 2:9
his upper rooms by injustice,
making his own people work
for nothing,
not paying them for their
labor. Jas 5:4
[14]He says, 'I will build myself a
great palace Isa 5:8-9
with spacious upper
rooms.'
So he makes large windows
in it,
panels it with cedar 2Sa 7:2
and decorates it in red. Eze 23:14

[15]"Does it make you a king
to have more and more
cedar?
Did not your father have food
and drink?
He did what was right and
just, 2Ki 23:25
so all went well with him. Ps 128:2; Isa 3:10
[16]He defended the cause of
the poor and needy, Ps 72:1-4,12-13
and so all went well.
Is that not what it means to
know me?" Ps 36:10
declares the LORD.

[17]"But your eyes and your heart
are set only on dishonest
gain, Isa 56:11
on shedding innocent blood 2Ki 24:4
and on oppression and
extortion." Dt 28:33

[18]Therefore this is what the LORD
says about Jehoiakim son of Josiah king of Judah:

"They will not mourn for him: 2Sa 1:26
'Alas, my brother! Alas, my
sister!'
They will not mourn for him:
'Alas, my master! Alas, his
splendor!'
[19]He will have the burial of a
donkey —
dragged away and thrown Jer 36:30
outside the gates of
Jerusalem."

[20]"Go up to Lebanon and cry
out,
let your voice be heard in
Bashan, Ps 68:15
cry out from Abarim, Nu 27:12
for all your allies are crushed. Jer 30:14
[21]I warned you when you felt
secure,
but you said, 'I will not
listen!'
This has been your way
from your youth; Jer 3:25; 32:30
you have not obeyed me. Jer 7:23-28

22 The wind will drive all your
shepherds away, Dt 28:64
and your allies will go into
exile. ver 20
Then you will be ashamed and
disgraced Jer 7:19
because of all your
wickedness.
23 You who live in 'Lebanon,[a]'
1Ki 7:2
who are nestled in cedar
buildings,
how you will groan when pangs
come upon you,
pain like that of a woman in
labor! Jer 4:31

24 "As surely as I live," declares
the LORD, "even if you, Jehoiachin[b] son of Jehoiakim king of Judah, were a signet ring on my right
hand, I would still pull you off. 25 I
will deliver you into the hands of
those who want to kill you, those
you fear — Nebuchadnezzar king
of Babylon and the Babylonians.[c]
26 I will hurl you and the mother
who gave you birth into another
country, where neither of you was
born, and there you both will die.
27 You will never come back to the
land you long to return to."
2Ki 24:8; 2Ch 36:10

28 Is this man Jehoiachin a
despised, broken pot,
Ps 31:12; Jer 48:38; Hos 8:8
an object no one wants?
Why will he and his children be
hurled out, Jer 15:1
cast into a land they do not
know? Jer 17:4
29 O land, land, land, Jer 6:19; Mic 1:2
hear the word of the LORD!
30 This is what the LORD says:
"Record this man as if
childless, 1Ch 3:18; Mt 1:12
a man who will not prosper
in his lifetime, Jer 10:21
for none of his offspring will
prosper, Job 18:19
none will sit on the throne of
David Ps 94:20
or rule anymore in Judah."

The Righteous Branch

23 "Woe to the shepherds who
are destroying and scattering the sheep of my pasture!" declares the LORD. 2 Therefore this is
what the LORD, the God of Israel,
says to the shepherds who tend
my people: "Because you have
scattered my flock and driven
them away and have not bestowed
care on them, I will bestow punishment on you for the evil you
have done," declares the LORD. 3 "I
myself will gather the remnant
of my flock out of all the countries where I have driven them
and will bring them back to their
pasture, where they will be fruitful and increase in number. 4 I will
place shepherds over them who
will tend them, and they will no
longer be afraid or terrified, nor
will any be missing," declares the
LORD. Jer 3:15; 30:10; Eze 34:23

[a] *23* That is, the palace in Jerusalem (see 1 Kings 7:2) [b] *24* Hebrew *Koniah,* a variant of *Jehoiachin;* also in verse 28 [c] *25* Or *Chaldeans*

5"The days are coming," declares
the LORD,
"when I will raise up for
David[a] a righteous
Branch, Isa 4:2
a King who will reign wisely Isa 9:7
and do what is just and
right in the land.
Isa 11:1; Zec 6:12
6In his days Judah will be
saved
and Israel will live in safety.
This is the name by which
he will be called:
Jer 33:16; Mt 1:21-23
The LORD Our Righteous
Savior. Ro 3:21-22; 1Co 1:30

7"So then, the days are coming,"
declares the LORD, "when people
will no longer say, 'As surely as the
LORD lives, who brought the Israelites up out of Egypt,' 8but they
will say, 'As surely as the LORD
lives, who brought the descendants of Israel up out of the land
of the north and out of all the
countries where he had banished
them.' Then they will live in their
own land." Isa 43:5-6; Am 9:14-15

Lying Prophets

9Concerning the prophets:

My heart is broken within me;
all my bones tremble.
I am like a drunken man,
like a strong man overcome
by wine,
because of the LORD
and his holy words. Jer 20:8-9

10The land is full of adulterers; Jer 9:2
because of the curse[b]
the land lies parched Dt 28:23-24
and the pastures in the
wilderness are withered.
Jer 9:10; Hos 4:2-3
The prophets follow an evil
course
and use their power unjustly.
11"Both prophet and priest are
godless; Jer 6:13; Zep 3:4
even in my temple I find
their wickedness," Jer 7:10
declares the LORD.
12"Therefore their path
will become slippery; Jer 13:16
they will be banished to
darkness
and there they will fall.
I will bring disaster on them
in the year they are
punished," Jer 11:23
declares the LORD.

13"Among the prophets of
Samaria
I saw this repulsive thing:
They prophesied by Baal Jer 2:8
and led my people Israel
astray. Eze 13:10
14And among the prophets of
Jerusalem
I have seen something
horrible: Jer 5:30
They commit adultery and
live a lie. Jer 29:23

[a] *5* Or *up from David's line* [b] *10* Or *because of these things*

They strengthen the hands of
evildoers, Eze 13:22
so that not one of them turns
from their wickedness.
They are all like Sodom to me; Ge 18:20
the people of Jerusalem are
like Gomorrah." Jer 20:16

15 Therefore this is what the LORD Almighty says concerning the prophets:

"I will make them eat bitter food
and drink poisoned water, Jer 8:14; 9:15
because from the prophets of
Jerusalem
ungodliness has spread
throughout the land." Jer 8:10

16 This is what the LORD Almighty says:

"Do not listen to what
the prophets are
prophesying to you; Jer 27:9-10,14; Mt 7:15
they fill you with false hopes.
They speak visions from their
own minds, Jer 14:14
not from the mouth of the
LORD. Jer 9:20
17 They keep saying to those who
despise me,
'The LORD says: You will have
peace.' Jer 8:11
And to all who follow the
stubbornness of their
hearts Jer 13:10
they say, 'No harm will come
to you.' Jer 5:12; Mic 3:11
18 But which of them has stood in
the council of the LORD Ro 11:34
to see or to hear his word?
Who has listened and heard
his word?
19 See, the storm of the LORD Jer 25:32; 30:23
will burst out in wrath,
a whirlwind swirling down Zec 7:14
on the heads of the
wicked.
20 The anger of the LORD will
not turn back 2Ki 23:26; Jer 30:24
until he fully accomplishes
the purposes of his heart.
In days to come
you will understand it
clearly.
21 I did not send these prophets, Jer 14:14; 27:15
yet they have run with their
message;
I did not speak to them,
yet they have prophesied.
22 But if they had stood in my
council, 1Ki 22:19
they would have
proclaimed my
words to my people
and would have turned them
from their evil ways Jer 25:5; Zec 1:4
and from their evil deeds.
23 "Am I only a God nearby," Ps 139:1-10
declares the LORD,
"and not a God far away?

24Who can hide in secret places Job 22:12-14
so that I cannot see them?"
declares the LORD.
"Do not I fill heaven and
earth?" 1Ki 8:27
declares the LORD.

25"I have heard what the prophets say who prophesy lies in my
name. They say, 'I had a dream! I
had a dream!' 26How long will this
continue in the hearts of these lying prophets, who prophesy the
delusions of their own minds?
27They think the dreams they tell
one another will make my people
forget my name, just as their ancestors forgot my name through
Baal worship. 28Let the prophet who has a dream recount the
dream, but let the one who has my
word speak it faithfully. For what
has straw to do with grain?" declares the LORD. 29"Is not my word
like fire," declares the LORD, "and
like a hammer that breaks a rock
in pieces? Jdg 3:7; Jer 14:14

30"Therefore," declares the
LORD, "I am against the prophets who steal from one another
words supposedly from me. 31Yes,"
declares the LORD, "I am against
the prophets who wag their own
tongues and yet declare, 'The
LORD declares.' 32Indeed, I am
against those who prophesy false
dreams," declares the LORD. "They
tell them and lead my people
astray with their reckless lies, yet
I did not send or appoint them.
They do not benefit these people
in the least," declares the LORD.
Dt 18:20; Ps 34:16; Jer 14:15

False Prophecy

33"When these people, or a
prophet or a priest, ask you, 'What
is the message from the LORD?'
say to them, 'What message? I will
forsake you, declares the LORD.'
34If a prophet or a priest or anyone else claims, 'This is a message from the LORD,' I will punish
them and their household. 35This
is what each of you keeps saying
to your friends and other Israelites: 'What is the LORD's answer?'
or 'What has the LORD spoken?'
36But you must not mention 'a
message from the LORD' again,
because each one's word becomes
their own message. So you distort
the words of the living God, the
LORD Almighty, our God. 37This is
what you keep saying to a prophet: 'What is the LORD's answer to
you?' or 'What has the LORD spoken?' 38Although you claim, 'This
is a message from the LORD,' this is
what the LORD says: You used the
words, 'This is a message from the
LORD,' even though I told you that
you must not claim, 'This is a message from the LORD.' 39Therefore, I
will surely forget you and cast you
out of my presence along with the
city I gave to you and your ancestors. 40I will bring on you everlasting disgrace — everlasting shame
that will not be forgotten."
Jer 20:11; Eze 5:14-15

Two Baskets of Figs

24 After Jehoiachin[a] son of Jehoiakim king of Judah and the officials, the skilled workers and the artisans of Judah were carried into exile from Jerusalem to Babylon by Nebuchadnezzar king of Babylon, the LORD showed me two baskets of figs placed in front of the temple of the LORD.
2One basket had very good figs, like those that ripen early; the other basket had very bad figs, so bad they could not be eaten.

Isa 5:4; Am 8:1-2

3Then the LORD asked me, "What do you see, Jeremiah?" Jer 1:11; Am 8:2

"Figs," I answered. "The good ones are very good, but the bad ones are so bad they cannot be eaten."

4Then the word of the LORD
came to me: 5"This is what the
LORD, the God of Israel, says: 'Like these good figs, I regard as good the exiles from Judah, whom I sent away from this place to the
land of the Babylonians.[b] 6My
eyes will watch over them for their good, and I will bring them back to this land. I will build them up and not tear them down; I will plant them and not uproot them.
7I will give them a heart to know me, that I am the LORD. They will be my people, and I will be their God, for they will return to me with all their heart. Jer 31:33; 32:40
8" 'But like the bad figs, which are so bad they cannot be eaten,' says the LORD, 'so will I deal with Zedekiah king of Judah, his officials and the survivors from Jerusalem, whether they remain in
this land or live in Egypt. 9I will
make them abhorrent and an offense to all the kingdoms of the earth, a reproach and a byword, a curse[c] and an object of ridicule, wherever I banish them. 10I
will send the sword, famine and plague against them until they are destroyed from the land I gave to them and their ancestors.' "

Jer 15:4; 32:4-5

Seventy Years of Captivity

25 The word came to Jeremiah concerning all the people of Judah in the fourth year of Jehoiakim son of Josiah king of Judah, which was the first year of Nebuchadnezzar king of Babylon. 2So Jeremiah the prophet
said to all the people of Judah and to all those living in Jerusalem:
3For twenty-three years — from the thirteenth year of Josiah son of Amon king of Judah until this very day — the word of the LORD has come to me and I have spoken to you again and again, but you have not listened. Jer 1:2; 7:26; 36:1
4And though the LORD has sent all his servants the prophets to you again and again, you have not listened or paid any attention.

[a] 1 Hebrew *Jeconiah,* a variant of *Jehoiachin*
[b] 5 Or *Chaldeans*
[c] 9 That is, their names will be used in cursing (see 29:22); or, others will see that they are cursed.

5They said, "Turn now, each of
you, from your evil ways and your
evil practices, and you can stay in
the land the LORD gave to you and
your ancestors for ever and ever.
6Do not follow other gods to serve
and worship them; do not arouse
my anger with what your hands
have made. Then I will not harm
you." Dt 8:19; Jer 7:25

7"But you did not listen to me,"
declares the LORD, "and you have
aroused my anger with what your
hands have made, and you have
brought harm to yourselves."

Dt 32:21; 2Ki 21:15

8Therefore the LORD Almighty
says this: "Because you have not
listened to my words, 9I will summon all the peoples of the north
and my servant Nebuchadnezzar king of Babylon," declares
the LORD, "and I will bring them
against this land and its inhabitants and against all the surrounding nations. I will completely destroy[a] them and make them
an object of horror and scorn, and
an everlasting ruin. 10I will banish
from them the sounds of joy and
gladness, the voices of bride and
bridegroom, the sound of millstones and the light of the lamp.
11This whole country will become
a desolate wasteland, and these
nations will serve the king of Babylon seventy years.

Jer 18:16; 27:6; Rev 18:22-23

12"But when the seventy years
are fulfilled, I will punish the
king of Babylon and his nation,
the land of the Babylonians,[b] for
their guilt," declares the LORD,
"and will make it desolate forever.
13I will bring on that land all the
things I have spoken against it, all
that are written in this book and
prophesied by Jeremiah against
all the nations. 14They themselves
will be enslaved by many nations
and great kings; I will repay them
according to their deeds and the
work of their hands." Jer 50:9; 51:6

The Cup of God's Wrath

15This is what the LORD, the God
of Israel, said to me: "Take from
my hand this cup filled with the
wine of my wrath and make all the
nations to whom I send you drink
it. 16When they drink it, they will
stagger and go mad because of the
sword I will send among them."

Isa 51:17; Na 3:11

17So I took the cup from the
LORD's hand and made all the nations to whom he sent me drink
it: 18Jerusalem and the towns of
Judah, its kings and officials, to
make them a ruin and an object
of horror and scorn, a curse[c] — as
they are today; 19Pharaoh king of
Egypt, his attendants, his officials
and all his people, 20and all the
foreign people there; all the kings
of Uz; all the kings of the Philistines (those of Ashkelon, Gaza,

[a] 9 The Hebrew term refers to the irrevocable giving over of things or persons to the LORD, often by totally destroying them. [b] 12 Or *Chaldeans* [c] 18 That is, their names to be used in cursing (see 29:22); or, to be seen by others as cursed

Ekron, and the people left at Ashdod); 21Edom, Moab and Ammon;
22all the kings of Tyre and Sidon;
the kings of the coastlands across
the sea; 23Dedan, Tema, Buz and all
who are in distant places[a]; 24all the
kings of Arabia and all the kings of
the foreign people who live in the
wilderness; 25all the kings of Zimri, Elam and Media; 26and all the
kings of the north, near and far,
one after the other — all the kingdoms on the face of the earth. And
after all of them, the king of Sheshak[b] will drink it too. Jer 1:10; 44:22

27"Then tell them, 'This is what
the LORD Almighty, the God of Israel, says: Drink, get drunk and
vomit, and fall to rise no more
because of the sword I will send
among you.' 28But if they refuse
to take the cup from your hand
and drink, tell them, 'This is what
the LORD Almighty says: You must
drink it! 29See, I am beginning
to bring disaster on the city that
bears my Name, and will you indeed go unpunished? You will not
go unpunished, for I am calling
down a sword on all who live on
the earth, declares the LORD Almighty.' Eze 21:4; 1Pe 4:17

30"Now prophesy all these words
against them and say to them:

"'The LORD will roar from on
high; Isa 16:10; 42:13
he will thunder from his holy
dwelling Joel 3:16; Am 1:2
and roar mightily against his
land.
He will shout like those who
tread the grapes, Rev 14:19-20
shout against all who live on
the earth.
31The tumult will resound to the
ends of the earth,
for the LORD will bring charges
against the nations; Hos 4:1; Joel 3:2; Mic 6:2
he will bring judgment on all
mankind Jer 2:35
and put the wicked to the
sword,'" Jer 15:9
declares the LORD.

32This is what the LORD Almighty
says:

"Look! Disaster is spreading
from nation to nation; Isa 34:2
a mighty storm is rising Jer 23:19
from the ends of the earth." Dt 28:49

33At that time those slain by the
LORD will be everywhere — from
one end of the earth to the other.
They will not be mourned or gathered up or buried, but will be like
dung lying on the ground. Ps 79:3; Isa 66:16; Jer 16:4

34Weep and wail, you shepherds;
roll in the dust, you leaders
of the flock. Jer 6:26
For your time to be slaughtered
has come; Isa 34:6; Jer 50:27
you will fall like the best of
the rams.[c] Jer 22:28

[a] 23 Or *who clip the hair by their foreheads*
[b] 26 *Sheshak* is a cryptogram for Babylon.
[c] 34 Septuagint; Hebrew *fall and be shattered like fine pottery*

35 The shepherds will have
nowhere to flee,
the leaders of the flock no
place to escape. Job 11:20
36 Hear the cry of the shepherds,
Jer 23:1; Zec 11:3
the wailing of the leaders of
the flock,
for the LORD is destroying
their pasture.
37 The peaceful meadows will be
laid waste
because of the fierce anger of
the LORD.
38 Like a lion he will leave his lair,
Jer 4:7
and their land will become
desolate Jer 44:22
because of the sword[a] of the
oppressor Jer 46:16
and because of the LORD's
fierce anger. Ex 15:7

Jeremiah Threatened With Death

26 Early in the reign of Jehoiakim son of Josiah king of Judah, this word came from the LORD: 2 "This is what the LORD says: Stand in the courtyard of the LORD's house and speak to all the people of the towns of Judah who come to worship in the house of the LORD. Tell them everything I command you; do not omit a word. 3 Perhaps they will listen and each will turn from their evil ways. Then I will relent and not inflict on them the disaster I was planning because of the evil they have done. 4 Say to them, 'This is what the LORD says: If you do not listen to me and follow my law, which I have set before you, 5 and if you do not listen to the words of my servants the prophets, whom I have sent to you again and again (though you have not listened), 6 then I will make this house like Shiloh and this city a curse[b] among all the nations of the earth.' " Lev 26:14; Jer 25:4

7 The priests, the prophets and all the people heard Jeremiah speak these words in the house of the LORD. 8 But as soon as Jeremiah finished telling all the people everything the LORD had commanded him to say, the priests, the prophets and all the people seized him and said, "You must die! 9 Why do you prophesy in the LORD's name that this house will be like Shiloh and this city will be desolate and deserted?" And all the people crowded around Jeremiah in the house of the LORD. Jer 9:11

10 When the officials of Judah heard about these things, they went up from the royal palace to the house of the LORD and took their places at the entrance of the New Gate of the LORD's house. 11 Then the priests and the prophets said to the officials and all the people, "This man should be sentenced to death because he has prophesied against this city. You have heard it with your own ears!"

Jer 38:4; Mt 26:66; Ac 6:11

[a] 38 Some Hebrew manuscripts and Septuagint (see also 46:16 and 50:16); most Hebrew manuscripts *anger* [b] 6 That is, its name will be used in cursing (see 29:22); or, others will see that it is cursed.

12 Then Jeremiah said to all the officials and all the people: "The LORD
sent me to prophesy against this
house and this city all the things
you have heard. 13 Now reform your
ways and your actions and obey the
LORD your God. Then the LORD will
relent and not bring the disaster he
has pronounced against you. 14 As
for me, I am in your hands; do with
me whatever you think is good and
right. 15 Be assured, however, that if
you put me to death, you will bring
the guilt of innocent blood on yourselves and on this city and on those
who live in it, for in truth the LORD
has sent me to you to speak all these
words in your hearing." Jer 7:5; 38:5

16 Then the officials and all the
people said to the priests and the
prophets, "This man should not be
sentenced to death! He has spoken
to us in the name of the LORD our
God." Ac 5:34-39; 23:9,29

17 Some of the elders of the land
stepped forward and said to the entire assembly of people, 18 "Micah of
Moresheth prophesied in the days
of Hezekiah king of Judah. He told
all the people of Judah, 'This is what
the LORD Almighty says: Mic 1:1

"'Zion will be plowed like a
field, Isa 2:3
Jerusalem will become a heap
of rubble, Ne 4:2; Jer 9:11
the temple hill a mound
overgrown with
thickets.'[a] Jer 17:3; Zec 8:3

19 "Did Hezekiah king of Judah or
anyone else in Judah put him to
death? Did not Hezekiah fear the
LORD and seek his favor? And did
not the LORD relent, so that he
did not bring the disaster he pronounced against them? We are
about to bring a terrible disaster
on ourselves!"
2Sa 24:16; 2Ch 32:24-26; Hab 2:10

20 (Now Uriah son of Shemaiah
from Kiriath Jearim was another
man who prophesied in the name
of the LORD; he prophesied the
same things against this city and
this land as Jeremiah did. 21 When
King Jehoiakim and all his officers
and officials heard his words, the
king was determined to put him
to death. But Uriah heard of it and
fled in fear to Egypt. 22 King Jehoiakim, however, sent Elnathan son
of Akbor to Egypt, along with some
other men. 23 They brought Uriah
out of Egypt and took him to King
Jehoiakim, who had him struck
down with a sword and his body
thrown into the burial place of the
common people.) Jer 36:12,25; Mt 10:23

24 Furthermore, Ahikam son of
Shaphan supported Jeremiah, and
so he was not handed over to the
people to be put to death. 2Ki 22:12

Judah to Serve Nebuchadnezzar

27 Early in the reign of Zedekiah[b] son of Josiah king of Judah, this word came to Jeremiah

[a] 18 Micah 3:12 [b] 1 A few Hebrew manuscripts and Syriac (see also 27:3,12 and 28:1); most Hebrew manuscripts *Jehoiakim* (Most Septuagint manuscripts do not have this verse.)

from the LORD: 2This is what the
LORD said to me: "Make a yoke out
of straps and crossbars and put it
on your neck. 3Then send word
to the kings of Edom, Moab, Ammon, Tyre and Sidon through the
envoys who have come to Jerusalem to Zedekiah king of Judah.
4Give them a message for their
masters and say, 'This is what the
LORD Almighty, the God of Israel,
says: "Tell this to your masters:
5With my great power and outstretched arm I made the earth
and its people and the animals
that are on it, and I give it to anyone I please. 6Now I will give all
your countries into the hands of
my servant Nebuchadnezzar king
of Babylon; I will make even the
wild animals subject to him. 7All
nations will serve him and his son
and his grandson until the time
for his land comes; then many nations and great kings will subju-
gate him. Jer 25:12,14; 28:10,13

8" ' "If, however, any nation or
kingdom will not serve Nebuchadnezzar king of Babylon or bow its
neck under his yoke, I will punish
that nation with the sword, famine and plague, declares the LORD,
until I destroy it by his hand. 9So
do not listen to your prophets,
your diviners, your interpreters
of dreams, your mediums or your
sorcerers who tell you, 'You will
not serve the king of Babylon.'
10They prophesy lies to you that
will only serve to remove you far
from your lands; I will banish you
and you will perish. 11But if any
nation will bow its neck under the
yoke of the king of Babylon and
serve him, I will let that nation remain in its own land to till it and
to live there, declares the LORD." ' "
Jer 21:9; 23:25

12I gave the same message to
Zedekiah king of Judah. I said,
"Bow your neck under the yoke
of the king of Babylon; serve him
and his people, and you will live.
13Why will you and your people die
by the sword, famine and plague
with which the LORD has threatened any nation that will not serve
the king of Babylon? 14Do not listen to the words of the prophets
who say to you, 'You will not serve
the king of Babylon,' for they are
prophesying lies to you. 15'I have
not sent them,' declares the LORD.
'They are prophesying lies in my
name. Therefore, I will banish
you and you will perish, both you
and the prophets who prophesy to
you.' " Jer 6:15; 14:14; 23:21

16Then I said to the priests and
all these people, "This is what
the LORD says: Do not listen to
the prophets who say, 'Very soon
now the articles from the LORD's
house will be brought back from
Babylon.' They are prophesying lies to you. 17Do not listen to
them. Serve the king of Babylon,
and you will live. Why should this
city become a ruin? 18If they are
prophets and have the word of
the LORD, let them plead with the
LORD Almighty that the articles

remaining in the house of the
LORD and in the palace of the king
of Judah and in Jerusalem not be
taken to Babylon. 19For this is what
the LORD Almighty says about the
pillars, the bronze Sea, the movable stands and the other articles
that are left in this city, 20which
Nebuchadnezzar king of Babylon
did not take away when he carried Jehoiachin[a] son of Jehoiakim
king of Judah into exile from Jerusalem to Babylon, along with all
the nobles of Judah and Jerusalem — 21yes, this is what the LORD
Almighty, the God of Israel, says
about the things that are left in
the house of the LORD and in the
palace of the king of Judah and
in Jerusalem: 22'They will be taken to Babylon and there they will
remain until the day I come for
them,' declares the LORD. 'Then I
will bring them back and restore
them to this place.'" Ezr 1:7; 7:19

The False Prophet Hananiah

28 In the fifth month of that same year, the fourth year,
early in the reign of Zedekiah king
of Judah, the prophet Hananiah
son of Azzur, who was from Gibeon, said to me in the house of the
LORD in the presence of the priests
and all the people: 2"This is what
the LORD Almighty, the God of Israel, says: 'I will break the yoke of
the king of Babylon. 3Within two
years I will bring back to this place
all the articles of the LORD's house
that Nebuchadnezzar king of Babylon removed from here and took
to Babylon. 4I will also bring back
to this place Jehoiachin[a] son of Jehoiakim king of Judah and all the
other exiles from Judah who went
to Babylon,' declares the LORD, 'for
I will break the yoke of the king of
Babylon.'" 2Ki 24:13; Jer 22:24-27

5Then the prophet Jeremiah replied to the prophet Hananiah before the priests and all the people
who were standing in the house of
the LORD. 6He said, "Amen! May the
LORD do so! May the LORD fulfill
the words you have prophesied by
bringing the articles of the LORD's
house and all the exiles back to
this place from Babylon. 7Nevertheless, listen to what I have to say
in your hearing and in the hearing of all the people: 8From early
times the prophets who preceded
you and me have prophesied war,
disaster and plague against many
countries and great kingdoms.
9But the prophet who prophesies
peace will be recognized as one
truly sent by the LORD only if his
prediction comes true."

Lev 26:14-17; Dt 18:22

10Then the prophet Hananiah
took the yoke off the neck of the
prophet Jeremiah and broke it,
11and he said before all the people, "This is what the LORD says:
'In the same way I will break the
yoke of Nebuchadnezzar king of
Babylon off the neck of all the nations within two years.'" At this,

[a] *20,4* Hebrew *Jeconiah,* a variant of *Jehoiachin*

the prophet Jeremiah went on his
way. Jer 14:14; 27:2,10
12 After the prophet Hananiah had broken the yoke off the
neck of the prophet Jeremiah, the
word of the LORD came to Jeremiah: 13 "Go and tell Hananiah, 'This
is what the LORD says: You have
broken a wooden yoke, but in its
place you will get a yoke of iron.
14 This is what the LORD Almighty,
the God of Israel, says: I will put
an iron yoke on the necks of all
these nations to make them serve
Nebuchadnezzar king of Babylon,
and they will serve him. I will even
give him control over the wild animals.' " Dt 28:48; Jer 27:6
15 Then the prophet Jeremiah
said to Hananiah the prophet,
"Listen, Hananiah! The LORD has
not sent you, yet you have persuaded this nation to trust in lies.
16 Therefore this is what the LORD
says: 'I am about to remove you
from the face of the earth. This
very year you are going to die, because you have preached rebellion
against the LORD.' "
Dt 13:5; Jer 29:32; Eze 13:6
17 In the seventh month of that
same year, Hananiah the prophet
died. 2Ki 1:17

A Letter to the Exiles

29 This is the text of the letter
that the prophet Jeremiah
sent from Jerusalem to the surviving elders among the exiles and
to the priests, the prophets and all
the other people Nebuchadnezzar
had carried into exile from Jerusalem to Babylon. 2 (This was after
King Jehoiachin[a] and the queen
mother, the court officials and the
leaders of Judah and Jerusalem,
the skilled workers and the artisans had gone into exile from Jerusalem.) 3 He entrusted the letter
to Elasah son of Shaphan and to
Gemariah son of Hilkiah, whom
Zedekiah king of Judah sent to
King Nebuchadnezzar in Babylon.
It said: 2Ki 24:12; Jer 22:24-28

4 This is what the LORD Almighty, the God of Israel, says
to all those I carried into exile
from Jerusalem to Babylon:
5 "Build houses and settle
down; plant gardens and eat
what they produce. 6 Marry
and have sons and daughters;
find wives for your sons and
give your daughters in marriage, so that they too may
have sons and daughters. Increase in number there; do
not decrease. 7 Also, seek the
peace and prosperity of the
city to which I have carried
you into exile. Pray to the
LORD for it, because if it prospers, you too will prosper."
8 Yes, this is what the LORD
Almighty, the God of Israel,
says: "Do not let the prophets
and diviners among you deceive you. Do not listen to the
dreams you encourage them

[a] 2 Hebrew *Jeconiah*, a variant of *Jehoiachin*

to have. 9They are prophesying lies to you in my name. I
have not sent them," declares
the LORD. Jer 14:14; 1Ti 2:1-2
10This is what the LORD
says: "When seventy years are
completed for Babylon, I will
come to you and fulfill my
good promise to bring you
back to this place. 11For I know
the plans I have for you," declares the LORD, "plans to
prosper you and not to harm
you, plans to give you hope
and a future. 12Then you will
call on me and come and pray
to me, and I will listen to you.
13You will seek me and find
me when you seek me with all
your heart. 14I will be found by
you," declares the LORD, "and
will bring you back from captivity.[a] I will gather you from
all the nations and places
where I have banished you,"
declares the LORD, "and will
bring you back to the place
from which I carried you into
exile." Jer 24:7; 25:12; Da 9:2
15You may say, "The LORD
has raised up prophets for us
in Babylon," 16but this is what
the LORD says about the king
who sits on David's throne
and all the people who remain in this city, your fellow
citizens who did not go with
you into exile — 17yes, this is
what the LORD Almighty says:
"I will send the sword, famine
and plague against them and
I will make them like figs that
are so bad they cannot be eat-
en. 18I will pursue them with
the sword, famine and plague
and will make them abhor-
rent to all the kingdoms of the
earth, a curse[b] and an object of
horror, of scorn and reproach,
among all the nations where
I drive them. 19For they have
not listened to my words," declares the LORD, "words that I
sent to them again and again
by my servants the proph-
ets. And you exiles have not
listened either," declares the
LORD. Jer 6:19; 25:4
20Therefore, hear the word
of the LORD, all you exiles
whom I have sent away from
Jerusalem to Babylon. 21This
is what the LORD Almighty,
the God of Israel, says about
Ahab son of Kolaiah and Zedekiah son of Maaseiah, who are
prophesying lies to you in my
name: "I will deliver them into
the hands of Nebuchadnezzar
king of Babylon, and he will
put them to death before your
very eyes. 22Because of them,
all the exiles from Judah who
are in Babylon will use this
curse: 'May the LORD treat
you like Zedekiah and Ahab,
whom the king of Babylon
burned in the fire.' 23For they

[a] 14 Or *will restore your fortunes*
[b] 18 That is, their names will be used in cursing (see verse 22); or, others will see that they are cursed.

have done outrageous things
in Israel; they have committed adultery with their neighbors' wives, and in my name
they have uttered lies — which
I did not authorize. I know it
and am a witness to it," declares the LORD. Jer 23:14; Heb 4:13

Message to Shemaiah

24 Tell Shemaiah the Nehelamite,
25 "This is what the LORD Almighty,
the God of Israel, says: You sent
letters in your own name to all
the people in Jerusalem, to the
priest Zephaniah son of Maaseiah,
and to all the other priests. You
said to Zephaniah, 26 'The LORD
has appointed you priest in place
of Jehoiada to be in charge of the
house of the LORD; you should put
any maniac who acts like a prophet into the stocks and neck-irons.
27 So why have you not reprimand-
ed Jeremiah from Anathoth, who
poses as a prophet among you?
28 He has sent this message to us
in Babylon: It will be a long time.
Therefore build houses and settle
down; plant gardens and eat what
they produce.'" 2Ki 25:18; Jer 21:1

29 Zephaniah the priest, however, read the letter to Jeremiah the
prophet. 30 Then the word of the
LORD came to Jeremiah: 31 "Send
this message to all the exiles: 'This
is what the LORD says about Shemaiah the Nehelamite: Because
Shemaiah has prophesied to you,
even though I did not send him,
and has persuaded you to trust in
lies, 32 this is what the LORD says:
I will surely punish Shemaiah
the Nehelamite and his descendants. He will have no one left
among this people, nor will he
see the good things I will do for
my people, declares the LORD, because he has preached rebellion
against me.'" Jer 14:14; 28:15-16

Restoration of Israel

30 This is the word that came
to Jeremiah from the LORD:
2 "This is what the LORD, the God of
Israel, says: 'Write in a book all the
words I have spoken to you. 3 The
days are coming,' declares the
LORD, 'when I will bring my people Israel and Judah back from
captivity[a] and restore them to the
land I gave their ancestors to possess,' says the LORD."
Isa 30:8; Jer 16:15; 29:14

4 These are the words the LORD
spoke concerning Israel and Judah: 5 "This is what the LORD says:

"'Cries of fear are heard — Jer 6:25
terror, not peace.
6 Ask and see:
Can a man bear children?
Then why do I see every strong
man
with his hands on his
stomach like a woman
in labor, Jer 4:31
every face turned deathly
pale? Isa 29:22

[a] 3 *Or will restore the fortunes of my people Israel and Judah*

7 How awful that day will be!
Isa 2:12; Joel 2:11
No other will be like it.
It will be a time of trouble for Jacob, Zep 1:15
but he will be saved out of it.
Jer 23:3

8 " 'In that day,' declares the LORD Almighty,
'I will break the yoke off their necks Isa 9:4
and will tear off their bonds;
Ps 107:14
no longer will foreigners enslave them. Eze 34:27
9 Instead, they will serve the LORD their God
and David their king,
Eze 34:23-24; 37:24; Hos 3:5
whom I will raise up for them.

10 " 'So do not be afraid, Jacob my servant; Isa 43:5; 44:2
do not be dismayed, Israel,'
declares the LORD.
'I will surely save you out of a distant place, Jer 29:14
your descendants from the land of their exile.
Jacob will again have peace and security, Isa 35:9
and no one will make him afraid.
11 I am with you and will save you,'
declares the LORD.
'Though I completely destroy all the nations
among which I scatter you,
I will not completely destroy you. Jer 4:27; 46:28
I will discipline you but only in due measure; Jer 10:24
I will not let you go entirely unpunished.' Am 9:8

12 "This is what the LORD says:
" 'Your wound is incurable,
Jer 10:19
your injury beyond healing.
Jer 15:18
13 There is no one to plead your cause,
no remedy for your sore,
no healing for you.
Jer 8:22; 14:19; 46:11
14 All your allies have forgotten you; La 1:2
they care nothing for you.
I have struck you as an enemy would Job 13:24
and punished you as would the cruel, Job 30:21
because your guilt is so great
and your sins so many. Jer 5:6
15 Why do you cry out over your wound,
your pain that has no cure?
Jer 10:19
Because of your great guilt and many sins
I have done these things to you. Pr 1:31
16 " 'But all who devour you will be devoured; Isa 33:1; Jer 10:25
all your enemies will go into exile. Isa 14:2; Joel 3:4-8
Those who plunder you will be plundered; Jer 50:10
all who make spoil of you I will despoil.

17 But I will restore you to health
and heal your wounds,' Isa 1:5
declares the LORD,
'because you are called an
outcast, Jer 33:24
Zion for whom no one cares.'
Ps 142:4

18 "This is what the LORD says:
" 'I will restore the fortunes of
Jacob's tents Jer 31:23
and have compassion on his
dwellings; Ps 102:13
the city will be rebuilt on her
ruins, Jer 31:4,24,38
and the palace will stand in
its proper place.
19 From them will come songs
of thanksgiving
Isa 35:10; 51:3
and the sound of rejoicing.
Ps 126:1-2; Jer 31:4
I will add to their numbers,
Jer 33:22
and they will not be
decreased;
I will bring them honor, Isa 60:9
and they will not be
disdained.
20 Their children will be as
in days of old,
Isa 54:13; Jer 31:17
and their community will be
established before me;
Isa 54:14
I will punish all who oppress
them. Ex 23:22
21 Their leader will be one of their
own; Jer 23:5-6
their ruler will arise from
among them. Dt 17:15
I will bring him near and he
will come close to me —
Nu 16:5
for who is he who will devote
himself
to be close to me?'
declares the LORD.
22 " 'So you will be my people,
Isa 19:25; Hos 2:23
and I will be your God.' "
Lev 26:12

23 See, the storm of the LORD
Jer 23:19
will burst out in wrath,
a driving wind swirling down
on the heads of the wicked.
24 The fierce anger of the LORD
will not turn back
Jer 4:8,28
until he fully accomplishes
the purposes of his heart.
In days to come
you will understand this.
Jer 23:19-20

31 "At that time," declares the
LORD, "I will be the God of all
the families of Israel, and they will
be my people." Jer 30:22
2 This is what the LORD says:

"The people who survive the
sword
will find favor in the
wilderness; Nu 14:20
I will come to give rest to
Israel." Ex 33:14

3 The LORD appeared to us in the
past,[a] saying:

[a] 3 Or *LORD has appeared to us from afar*

"I have loved you with an
everlasting love; Dt 4:37
I have drawn you with
unfailing kindness.
Hos 11:4
4 I will build you up again,
and you, Virgin Israel, will be
rebuilt. 2Ki 19:21; Jer 1:10
Again you will take up your
timbrels Ge 31:27
and go out to dance with the
joyful. Jer 30:19
5 Again you will plant
vineyards
on the hills of Samaria;
Jer 50:19
the farmers will plant them
and enjoy their fruit.
Isa 65:21; Am 9:14
6 There will be a day when
watchmen cry out
on the hills of Ephraim,
'Come, let us go up to Zion,
to the LORD our God.' "
Isa 2:3; Jer 50:4-5; Mic 4:2
7 This is what the LORD says:

"Sing with joy for Jacob;
shout for the foremost of the
nations. Dt 28:13; Isa 61:9
Make your praises heard, and
say,
'LORD, save your people,
Ps 14:7; 28:9
the remnant of Israel.' Isa 37:31
8 See, I will bring them from
the land of the north
Jer 3:18; 23:8
and gather them from
the ends of the earth.
Dt 30:4; Eze 34:12-14
Among them will be the
blind and the lame,
Isa 42:16; Eze 34:16; Mic 4:6
expectant mothers and
women in labor;
a great throng will return.
9 They will come with weeping;
Ps 126:5
they will pray as I bring
them back.
I will lead them beside streams
of water Isa 63:13
on a level path where they
will not stumble, Isa 49:11
because I am Israel's father,
Ex 4:22; Jer 3:4
and Ephraim is my firstborn
son.

10 "Hear the word of the LORD,
you nations;
proclaim it in distant
coastlands: Isa 66:19; Jer 25:22
'He who scattered Israel will
gather them Jer 50:19
and will watch over his
flock like a shepherd.'
Isa 40:11; Eze 34:12
11 For the LORD will deliver Jacob
and redeem them from
the hand of those
stronger than they.
Ps 142:6; Isa 44:23; 48:20
12 They will come and shout for
joy on the heights of
Zion; Eze 17:23; Mic 4:1
they will rejoice in the
bounty of the LORD —
Joel 3:18
the grain, the new wine and
the olive oil, Hos 2:21-22

the young of the flocks and
herds.
They will be like a well-watered
garden, Isa 58:11
and they will sorrow no more.
Isa 65:19; Jn 16:22; Rev 7:17
13 Then young women will dance
and be glad,
young men and old as well.
I will turn their mourning into
gladness; Isa 61:3
I will give them comfort and
joy instead of sorrow.
Ps 30:11; Isa 51:11
14 I will satisfy the priests with
abundance, Lev 7:35-36
and my people will be
filled with my bounty,"
Isa 30:23
declares the LORD.

15 This is what the LORD says:

"A voice is heard in Ramah,
Jos 18:25
mourning and great
weeping,
Rachel weeping for her
children
and refusing to be
comforted, Ge 37:35
because they are no more."
Mt 2:17-18*

16 This is what the LORD says:

"Restrain your voice from
weeping
and your eyes from tears,
Isa 25:8; 30:19
for your work will be
rewarded," Ru 2:12
declares the LORD.

"They will return from the
land of the enemy. Eze 11:17
17 So there is hope for your
descendants,"
Job 8:7; La 3:29
declares the LORD.
"Your children will return to
their own land. Jer 30:20

18 "I have surely heard Ephraim's
moaning:
'You disciplined me like
an unruly calf,
Job 5:17; Hos 4:16
and I have been disciplined.
Restore me, and I will return,
Ps 80:3
because you are the LORD
my God.
19 After I strayed, Eze 36:31
I repented;
after I came to understand,
I beat my breast. Eze 21:12; Lk 18:13
I was ashamed and humiliated
Ezr 9:6
because I bore the disgrace
of my youth.' Jer 22:21
20 Is not Ephraim my dear son,
the child in whom I
delight?
Though I often speak against
him,
I still remember him.
Hos 4:4; 11:8
Therefore my heart yearns for
him;
I have great compassion for
him," Isa 63:15; Mic 7:18
declares the LORD.

21 "Set up road signs;
put up guideposts.

Take note of the highway, Jer 50:5
the road that you take.
Return, Virgin Israel, Isa 52:11
return to your towns.
22 How long will you wander, Jer 2:23
unfaithful Daughter Israel? Jer 3:6
The LORD will create a new
thing on earth — Isa 43:19
the woman will return to[a]
the man." Dt 32:10

23 This is what the LORD Almighty, the God of Israel, says:
"When I bring them back from
captivity,[b] the people in the land
of Judah and in its towns will once
again use these words: 'The LORD
bless you, you prosperous city, you
sacred mountain.' 24 People will
live together in Judah and all its
towns — farmers and those who
move about with their flocks. 25 I
will refresh the weary and satisfy
the faint." Jn 4:14; Isa 1:26; Zec 8:4-8

26 At this I awoke and looked
around. My sleep had been pleasant to me. Zec 4:1

27 "The days are coming," declares the LORD, "when I will plant
the kingdoms of Israel and Judah
with the offspring of people and
of animals. 28 Just as I watched
over them to uproot and tear
down, and to overthrow, destroy
and bring disaster, so I will watch
over them to build and to plant,"
declares the LORD. 29 "In those days
people will no longer say, Jer 1:10; 18:8; 44:27

'The parents have eaten sour
grapes, La 5:7
and the children's teeth are
set on edge.' Eze 18:2

30 Instead, everyone will die for
their own sin; whoever eats sour
grapes — their own teeth will be
set on edge. Isa 3:11; Gal 6:7

31 "The days are coming," declares
the LORD,
"when I will make a new
covenant Heb 8:8-12*; 10:16-17
with the people of Israel
and with the people of Judah.
32 It will not be like the covenant Ex 24:8
I made with their ancestors Dt 5:3
when I took them by the hand
to lead them out of Egypt, Jer 11:4
because they broke my
covenant,
though I was a husband to[c]
them,[d]" Isa 54:5
declares the LORD.
33 "This is the covenant I will make
with the people of Israel
after that time," declares the
LORD.
"I will put my law in their minds
and write it on their hearts. 2Co 3:3
I will be their God,
and they will be my people. Jer 24:7; Heb 10:16

[a] 22 Or *will protect* [b] 23 Or *I restore their fortunes* [c] 32 Hebrew; Septuagint and Syriac / *and I turned away from* [d] 32 Or *was their master*

34 No longer will they teach their
neighbor, 1Jn 2:27
or say to one another, 'Know
the LORD,'
because they will all know me,
Jn 6:45
from the least of them to the
greatest,"
declares the LORD.
"For I will forgive their
wickedness Isa 54:13; Jer 33:8
and will remember their sins
no more." Mic 7:19; Heb 10:17*

35 This is what the LORD says,

he who appoints the sun Ps 136:7-9
to shine by day,
who decrees the moon and
stars
to shine by night, Ge 1:16
who stirs up the sea Ex 14:21
so that its waves roar — Ps 93:3
the LORD Almighty is his
name: Jer 10:16
36 "Only if these decrees vanish
from my sight," Jer 33:20-26
declares the LORD,
"will Israel ever cease Ps 89:36-37
being a nation before me."

37 This is what the LORD says:

"Only if the heavens above can
be measured Jer 33:22
and the foundations of the
earth below be searched
out
will I reject all the descendants
of Israel Jer 33:24-26; Ro 11:1-5
because of all they have
done,"
declares the LORD.

38 "The days are coming," declares the LORD, "when this city
will be rebuilt for me from the
Tower of Hananel to the Corner
Gate. 39 The measuring line will
stretch from there straight to
the hill of Gareb and then turn to
Goah. 40 The whole valley where
dead bodies and ashes are thrown,
and all the terraces out to the Kidron Valley on the east as far as the
corner of the Horse Gate, will be
holy to the LORD. The city will never again be uprooted or demolished." Joel 3:17; Zec 14:21

Jeremiah Buys a Field

32 This is the word that came
to Jeremiah from the LORD
in the tenth year of Zedekiah king
of Judah, which was the eighteenth year of Nebuchadnezzar.
2 The army of the king of Babylon
was then besieging Jerusalem,
and Jeremiah the prophet was
confined in the courtyard of the
guard in the royal palace of Judah.
2Ki 25:1; Ne 3:25

3 Now Zedekiah king of Judah
had imprisoned him there, saying, "Why do you prophesy as you
do? You say, 'This is what the LORD
says: I am about to give this city
into the hands of the king of Babylon, and he will capture it. 4 Zedekiah king of Judah will not escape
the Babylonians[a] but will certainly be given into the hands of the
king of Babylon, and will speak

[a] 4 Or *Chaldeans*; also in verses 5, 24, 25, 28, 29 and 43

with him face to face and see him
with his own eyes. [5]He will take
Zedekiah to Babylon, where he
will remain until I deal with him,
declares the LORD. If you fight
against the Babylonians, you will
not succeed.'" Jer 34:2-3; 38:18,23; 39:5-7

[6]Jeremiah said, "The word of
the LORD came to me: [7]Hanamel
son of Shallum your uncle is going to come to you and say, 'Buy
my field at Anathoth, because as
nearest relative it is your right and
duty to buy it.'

Lev 25:24-25; Ru 4:3-4; Mt 27:10*

[8]"Then, just as the LORD had
said, my cousin Hanamel came to
me in the courtyard of the guard
and said, 'Buy my field at Anathoth in the territory of Benjamin.
Since it is your right to redeem it
and possess it, buy it for yourself.'

"I knew that this was the word
of the LORD; [9]so I bought the
field at Anathoth from my cousin Hanamel and weighed out for
him seventeen shekels[a] of silver.
[10]I signed and sealed the deed,
had it witnessed, and weighed
out the silver on the scales. [11]I
took the deed of purchase — the
sealed copy containing the terms
and conditions, as well as the unsealed copy — [12]and I gave this
deed to Baruch son of Neriah, the
son of Mahseiah, in the presence
of my cousin Hanamel and of the
witnesses who had signed the
deed and of all the Jews sitting in
the courtyard of the guard.

Jer 36:4; 51:59

[13]"In their presence I gave Baruch these instructions: [14]'This is
what the LORD Almighty, the God
of Israel, says: Take these docu-
ments, both the sealed and unsealed copies of the deed of purchase, and put them in a clay jar
so they will last a long time. [15]For
this is what the LORD Almighty,
the God of Israel, says: Houses,
fields and vineyards will again be
bought in this land.'

Jer 30:18; Am 9:14-15

[16]"After I had given the deed of
purchase to Baruch son of Neriah,
I prayed to the LORD:

[17]"Ah, Sovereign LORD, you
have made the heavens and
the earth by your great power
and outstretched arm. Nothing is too hard for you. [18]You
show love to thousands but
bring the punishment for
the parents' sins into the laps
of their children after them.
Great and mighty God, whose
name is the LORD Almighty,
[19]great are your purposes and
mighty are your deeds. Your
eyes are open to the ways of
all mankind; you reward each
person according to their conduct and as their deeds deserve. [20]You performed signs
and wonders in Egypt and
have continued them to this
day, in Israel and among all
mankind, and have gained

[a] 9 That is, about 7 ounces or about 200 grams

the renown that is still yours.
21You brought your people Israel out of Egypt with signs
and wonders, by a mighty
hand and an outstretched arm
and with great terror. 22You
gave them this land you had
sworn to give their ancestors,
a land flowing with milk and
honey. 23They came in and
took possession of it, but they
did not obey you or follow
your law; they did not do what
you commanded them to do.
So you brought all this disaster on them. Ps 44:2; Jer 11:8; Da 9:14

24"See how the siege ramps
are built up to take the city.
Because of the sword, famine
and plague, the city will be
given into the hands of the
Babylonians who are attacking it. What you said has happened, as you now see. 25And
though the city will be given
into the hands of the Babylonians, you, Sovereign LORD,
say to me, 'Buy the field with
silver and have the transac-
tion witnessed.' "

Dt 4:25-26; Jer 14:12

26Then the word of the LORD
came to Jeremiah: 27"I am the
LORD, the God of all mankind. Is
anything too hard for me? 28There-
fore this is what the LORD says: I
am about to give this city into the
hands of the Babylonians and to
Nebuchadnezzar king of Babylon,
who will capture it. 29The Babylonians who are attacking this city
will come in and set it on fire; they
will burn it down, along with the
houses where the people aroused
my anger by burning incense on
the roofs to Baal and by pouring
out drink offerings to other gods.

Ge 18:14; Jer 21:10

30"The people of Israel and Judah have done nothing but evil
in my sight from their youth; indeed, the people of Israel have
done nothing but arouse my anger with what their hands have
made, declares the LORD. 31From
the day it was built until now, this
city has so aroused my anger and
wrath that I must remove it from
my sight. 32The people of Israel
and Judah have provoked me by
all the evil they have done — they,
their kings and officials, their
priests and prophets, the people
of Judah and those living in Jerusalem. 33They turned their backs
to me and not their faces; though I
taught them again and again, they
would not listen or respond to discipline. 34They set up their vile images in the house that bears my
Name and defiled it. 35They built
high places for Baal in the Valley
of Ben Hinnom to sacrifice their
sons and daughters to Molek,
though I never commanded — nor
did it enter my mind — that they
should do such a detestable thing
and so make Judah sin.

Lev 18:21; Jer 19:5

36"You are saying about this
city, 'By the sword, famine and

plague it will be given into the hands of the king of Babylon'; but this is what the LORD, the God of Israel, says: [37]I will surely gather them from all the lands where I banish them in my furious anger and great wrath; I will bring them back to this place and let them live in safety. [38]They will be my people, and I will be their God. [39]I will give them singleness of heart and action, so that they will always fear me and that all will then go well for them and for their children after them. [40]I will make an everlasting covenant with them: I will never stop doing good to them, and I will inspire them to fear me, so that they will never turn away from me. [41]I will rejoice in doing them good and will assuredly plant them in this land with all my heart and soul.

Dt 30:9; Am 9:15

[42]"This is what the LORD says: As I have brought all this great calamity on this people, so I will give them all the prosperity I have promised them. [43]Once more fields will be bought in this land of which you say, 'It is a desolate waste, without people or animals, for it has been given into the hands of the Babylonians.' [44]Fields will be bought for silver, and deeds will be signed, sealed and witnessed in the territory of Benjamin, in the villages around Jerusalem, in the towns of Judah and in the towns of the hill country, of the western foothills and of the Negev, because I will restore their fortunes,[a] declares the LORD."

Jer 17:26; 33:7,11,26

Promise of Restoration

33 While Jeremiah was still confined in the courtyard of the guard, the word of the LORD came to him a second time: [2]"This is what the LORD says, he who made the earth, the LORD who formed it and established it — the LORD is his name: [3]'Call to me and I will answer you and tell you great and unsearchable things you do not know.' [4]For this is what the LORD, the God of Israel, says about the houses in this city and the royal palaces of Judah that have been torn down to be used against the siege ramps and the sword [5]in the fight with the Babylonians[b]: 'They will be filled with the dead bodies of the people I will slay in my anger and wrath. I will hide my face from this city because of all its wickedness.

Isa 55:6; Jer 29:12

[6]" 'Nevertheless, I will bring health and healing to it; I will heal my people and will let them enjoy abundant peace and security. [7]I will bring Judah and Israel back from captivity[c] and will rebuild them as they were before. [8]I will cleanse them from all the sin they have committed against me and will forgive all their sins of rebellion against me. [9]Then this city

[a] 44 Or *will bring them back from captivity*
[b] 5 Or *Chaldeans*
[c] 7 Or *will restore the fortunes of Judah and Israel*

will bring me renown, joy, praise
and honor before all nations on
earth that hear of all the good
things I do for it; and they will
be in awe and will tremble at the
abundant prosperity and peace I
provide for it.' Heb 9:13-14; Jer 3:17
10"This is what the LORD says:
'You say about this place, "It is a
desolate waste, without people or
animals." Yet in the towns of Judah and the streets of Jerusalem
that are deserted, inhabited by
neither people nor animals, there
will be heard once more 11the
sounds of joy and gladness, the
voices of bride and bridegroom,
and the voices of those who bring
thank offerings to the house of
the LORD, saying, Lev 7:12; Jer 32:43

"Give thanks to the LORD
Almighty,
for the LORD is good; Ps 136:1
his love endures forever."
2Ch 5:13

For I will restore the fortunes of
the land as they were before,' says
the LORD. Ps 14:7; Isa 1:26
12"This is what the LORD Almighty says: 'In this place, desolate and without people or animals — in all its towns there will
again be pastures for shepherds
to rest their flocks. 13In the towns
of the hill country, of the western
foothills and of the Negev, in the
territory of Benjamin, in the villages around Jerusalem and in
the towns of Judah, flocks will
again pass under the hand of the
one who counts them,' says the
LORD. Lev 27:32; Isa 65:10; Jer 17:26
14" 'The days are coming,' declares the LORD, 'when I will fulfill
the good promise I made to the
people of Israel and Judah. Jer 29:10

15" 'In those days and at that
time
I will make a righteous
Branch sprout
from David's line;
Ps 72:2; Isa 4:2; 11:1; Jer 23:5
he will do what is just and
right in the land.
16In those days Judah will be
saved Isa 45:17
and Jerusalem will live in
safety.
This is the name by which
it[a] will be called:
Isa 59:14; Zec 8:3,16
The LORD Our Righteous
Savior.' 1Co 1:30

17For this is what the LORD says:
'David will never fail to have a
man to sit on the throne of Israel,
18nor will the Levitical priests ever
fail to have a man to stand before
me continually to offer burnt offerings, to burn grain offerings
and to present sacrifices.' "
2Sa 7:13; 1Ki 2:4; Lk 1:33
19The word of the LORD came to
Jeremiah: 20"This is what the LORD
says: 'If you can break my covenant
with the day and my covenant
with the night, so that day and
night no longer come at their appointed time, 21then my covenant

[a] *16* Or *he*

with David my servant — and my
covenant with the Levites who are
priests ministering before me —
can be broken and David will no
longer have a descendant to reign
on his throne. 22I will make the
descendants of David my servant
and the Levites who minister before me as countless as the stars in
the sky and as measureless as the
sand on the seashore.' "
Ge 15:5; Ps 89:34

23The word of the LORD came to
Jeremiah: 24"Have you not noticed
that these people are saying, 'The
LORD has rejected the two kingdoms[a] he chose'? So they despise
my people and no longer regard
them as a nation. 25This is what
the LORD says: 'If I have not made
my covenant with day and night
and established the laws of heav-
en and earth, 26then I will reject
the descendants of Jacob and David my servant and will not choose
one of his sons to rule over the descendants of Abraham, Isaac and
Jacob. For I will restore their fortunes[b] and have compassion on
them.' " Ps 74:16-17; Jer 31:35-37

Warning to Zedekiah

34 While Nebuchadnezzar
king of Babylon and all his
army and all the kingdoms and
peoples in the empire he ruled
were fighting against Jerusalem
and all its surrounding towns, this
word came to Jeremiah from the
LORD: 2"This is what the LORD, the
God of Israel, says: Go to Zedekiah
king of Judah and tell him, 'This is
what the LORD says: I am about to
give this city into the hands of the
king of Babylon, and he will burn
it down. 3You will not escape from
his grasp but will surely be captured and given into his hands.
You will see the king of Babylon
with your own eyes, and he will
speak with you face to face. And
you will go to Babylon.
2Ki 25:1; Jer 32:4,29

4" 'Yet hear the LORD's promise
to you, Zedekiah king of Judah.
This is what the LORD says concerning you: You will not die by
the sword; 5you will die peacefully. As people made a funeral fire
in honor of your predecessors, the
kings who ruled before you, so
they will make a fire in your honor
and lament, "Alas, master!" I myself make this promise, declares
the LORD.' " 2Ch 16:14; Jer 22:18

6Then Jeremiah the prophet
told all this to Zedekiah king of
Judah, in Jerusalem, 7while the
army of the king of Babylon was
fighting against Jerusalem and
the other cities of Judah that were
still holding out — Lachish and
Azekah. These were the only fortified cities left in Judah.
Jos 10:3; 2Ch 11:9

Freedom for Slaves

8The word came to Jeremiah
from the LORD after King Zedekiah had made a covenant with all

[a] *24* Or *families* [b] *26* Or *will bring them back from captivity*

the people in Jerusalem to proclaim freedom for the slaves. 9 Everyone was to free their Hebrew slaves, both male and female; no one was to hold a fellow Hebrew in bondage. 10 So all the officials and people who entered into this covenant agreed that they would free their male and female slaves and no longer hold them in bondage. They agreed, and set them free. 11 But afterward they changed their minds and took back the slaves they had freed and enslaved them again. Ex 21:2; Lev 25:39-46

12 Then the word of the LORD came to Jeremiah: 13 "This is what the LORD, the God of Israel, says: I made a covenant with your ancestors when I brought them out of Egypt, out of the land of slavery. I said, 14 'Every seventh year each of you must free any fellow Hebrews who have sold themselves to you. After they have served you six years, you must let them go free.'[a] Your ancestors, however, did not listen to me or pay attention to me. 15 Recently you repented and did what is right in my sight: Each of you proclaimed freedom to your own people. You even made a covenant before me in the house that bears my Name. 16 But now you have turned around and profaned my name; each of you has taken back the male and female slaves you had set free to go where they wished. You have forced them to become your slaves again. Ex 20:7; Lev 19:12; Jer 7:10-11

17 "Therefore this is what the LORD says: You have not obeyed me; you have not proclaimed freedom to your own people. So I now proclaim 'freedom' for you, declares the LORD — 'freedom' to fall by the sword, plague and famine. I will make you abhorrent to all the kingdoms of the earth. 18 Those who have violated my covenant and have not fulfilled the terms of the covenant they made before me, I will treat like the calf they cut in two and then walked between its pieces. 19 The leaders of Judah and Jerusalem, the court officials, the priests and all the people of the land who walked between the pieces of the calf, 20 I will deliver into the hands of their enemies who want to kill them. Their dead bodies will become food for the birds and the wild animals. Dt 28:26; Jer 7:33; 19:7

21 "I will deliver Zedekiah king of Judah and his officials into the hands of their enemies who want to kill them, to the army of the king of Babylon, which has withdrawn from you. 22 I am going to give the order, declares the LORD, and I will bring them back to this city. They will fight against it, take it and burn it down. And I will lay waste the towns of Judah so no one can live there." Jer 37:5; 39:1-2

The Rekabites

35 This is the word that came to Jeremiah from the LORD during the reign of Jehoiakim

[a] 14 Deut. 15:12

son of Josiah king of Judah: 2“Go
to the Rekabite family and invite
them to come to one of the side
rooms of the house of the LORD
and give them wine to drink.”

1Ki 6:5; 2Ki 10:15; 1Ch 2:55

3So I went to get Jaazaniah son
of Jeremiah, the son of Habazzi-
niah, and his brothers and all his
sons — the whole family of the
Rekabites. 4I brought them into
the house of the LORD, into the
room of the sons of Hanan son of
Igdaliah the man of God. It was
next to the room of the officials,
which was over that of Maaseiah
son of Shallum the doorkeeper.
5Then I set bowls full of wine and
some cups before the Rekabites
and said to them, “Drink some
wine.” Dt 33:1; 1Ch 9:19

6But they replied, “We do not
drink wine, because our forefather Jehonadab[a] son of Rekab
gave us this command: ‘Neither
you nor your descendants must
ever drink wine. 7Also you must
never build houses, sow seed or
plant vineyards; you must never
have any of these things, but must
always live in tents. Then you will
live a long time in the land where
you are nomads.’ 8We have obeyed
everything our forefather Jehonadab son of Rekab commanded
us. Neither we nor our wives nor
our sons and daughters have ever
drunk wine 9or built houses to
live in or had vineyards, fields or
crops. 10We have lived in tents and
have fully obeyed everything our
forefather Jehonadab commanded us. 11But when Nebuchadnezzar king of Babylon invaded this
land, we said, ‘Come, we must go
to Jerusalem to escape the Babylonian[b] and Aramean armies.’ So we
have remained in Jerusalem.”

2Ki 10:15; Jer 8:14

12Then the word of the LORD
came to Jeremiah, saying: 13“This
is what the LORD Almighty, the
God of Israel, says: Go and tell the
people of Judah and those living
in Jerusalem, ‘Will you not learn
a lesson and obey my words?’
declares the LORD. 14‘Jehonadab
son of Rekab ordered his descendants not to drink wine and
this command has been kept. To
this day they do not drink wine,
because they obey their forefather’s command. But I have spoken to you again and again, yet
you have not obeyed me. 15Again
and again I sent all my servants
the prophets to you. They said,
“Each of you must turn from your
wicked ways and reform your actions; do not follow other gods to
serve them. Then you will live in
the land I have given to you and
your ancestors.” But you have not
paid attention or listened to me.
16The descendants of Jehonadab
son of Rekab have carried out the
command their forefather gave
them, but these people have not
obeyed me.’ Jer 7:13; 18:11; 32:33

[a] 6 Hebrew *Jonadab*, a variant of *Jehonadab*; here and often in this chapter
[b] 11 Or *Chaldean*

17“Therefore this is what the
LORD God Almighty, the God of
Israel, says: ‘Listen! I am going to
bring on Judah and on everyone
living in Jerusalem every disaster I pronounced against them. I
spoke to them, but they did not
listen; I called to them, but they
did not answer.’ ”

Isa 65:12; Jer 7:13; Pr 1:24

18Then Jeremiah said to the
family of the Rekabites, “This is
what the LORD Almighty, the God
of Israel, says: ‘You have obeyed
the command of your forefather
Jehonadab and have followed all
his instructions and have done everything he ordered.’ 19Therefore
this is what the LORD Almighty,
the God of Israel, says: ‘Jehonadab son of Rekab will never fail to
have a descendant to serve me.’ ”

Jer 15:19; 33:17

Jehoiakim Burns Jeremiah’s Scroll

36 In the fourth year of Jehoiakim son of Josiah king of
Judah, this word came to Jeremiah from the LORD: 2“Take a scroll
and write on it all the words I have
spoken to you concerning Israel,
Judah and all the other nations
from the time I began speaking
to you in the reign of Josiah till
now. 3Perhaps when the people of
Judah hear about every disaster I
plan to inflict on them, they will
each turn from their wicked ways;
then I will forgive their wickedness and their sin.”

Jer 18:8; 26:3; Jnh 3:8

4So Jeremiah called Baruch son
of Neriah, and while Jeremiah
dictated all the words the LORD
had spoken to him, Baruch wrote
them on the scroll. 5Then Jeremiah told Baruch, “I am restricted; I
am not allowed to go to the LORD’s
temple. 6So you go to the house of
the LORD on a day of fasting and
read to the people from the scroll
the words of the LORD that you
wrote as I dictated. Read them to
all the people of Judah who come
in from their towns. 7Perhaps they
will bring their petition before the
LORD and will each turn from their
wicked ways, for the anger and
wrath pronounced against this
people by the LORD are great.”

Jer 32:12; Eze 2:9

8Baruch son of Neriah did everything Jeremiah the prophet
told him to do; at the LORD’s temple he read the words of the LORD
from the scroll. 9In the ninth
month of the fifth year of Jehoiakim son of Josiah king of Judah,
a time of fasting before the LORD
was proclaimed for all the people
in Jerusalem and those who had
come from the towns of Judah.
10From the room of Gemariah son
of Shaphan the secretary, which
was in the upper courtyard at the
entrance of the New Gate of the
temple, Baruch read to all the people at the LORD’s temple the words
of Jeremiah from the scroll.

2Ch 20:3; Jer 26:10

11When Micaiah son of Gemariah, the son of Shaphan, heard all

the words of the LORD from the
scroll, 12he went down to the secretary's room in the royal palace,
where all the officials were sitting:
Elishama the secretary, Delaiah
son of Shemaiah, Elnathan son of
Akbor, Gemariah son of Shaphan,
Zedekiah son of Hananiah, and all
the other officials. 13After Micaiah told them everything he had
heard Baruch read to the people
from the scroll, 14all the officials
sent Jehudi son of Nethaniah, the
son of Shelemiah, the son of Cushi, to say to Baruch, "Bring the
scroll from which you have read
to the people and come." So Baruch son of Neriah went to them
with the scroll in his hand. 15They
said to him, "Sit down, please, and
read it to us." Jer 26:22

So Baruch read it to them.
16When they heard all these words,
they looked at each other in fear
and said to Baruch, "We must report all these words to the king."
17Then they asked Baruch, "Tell
us, how did you come to write all
this? Did Jeremiah dictate it?"

Jer 30:2

18"Yes," Baruch replied, "he dictated all these words to me, and I
wrote them in ink on the scroll."

ver 4

19Then the officials said to Baruch, "You and Jeremiah, go and
hide. Don't let anyone know where
you are." 1Ki 17:3

20After they put the scroll in
the room of Elishama the secretary, they went to the king in the
courtyard and reported everything to him. 21The king sent Jehudi to get the scroll, and Jehudi brought it from the room of
Elishama the secretary and read
it to the king and all the officials
standing beside him. 22It was the
ninth month and the king was
sitting in the winter apartment,
with a fire burning in the firepot
in front of him. 23Whenever Jehudi had read three or four columns
of the scroll, the king cut them
off with a scribe's knife and threw
them into the firepot, until the
entire scroll was burned in the
fire. 24The king and all his attendants who heard all these words
showed no fear, nor did they tear
their clothes. 25Even though Elnathan, Delaiah and Gemariah urged
the king not to burn the scroll, he
would not listen to them. 26In-
stead, the king commanded Jerahmeel, a son of the king, Seraiah son of Azriel and Shelemiah
son of Abdeel to arrest Baruch the
scribe and Jeremiah the prophet.
But the LORD had hidden them.

1Ki 22:8; Jer 15:21

27After the king burned the
scroll containing the words that
Baruch had written at Jeremiah's
dictation, the word of the LORD
came to Jeremiah: 28"Take another
scroll and write on it all the words
that were on the first scroll, which
Jehoiakim king of Judah burned
up. 29Also tell Jehoiakim king of
Judah, 'This is what the LORD says:
You burned that scroll and said,

"Why did you write on it that the
king of Babylon would certainly
come and destroy this land and
wipe from it both man and beast?"
30 Therefore this is what the LORD
says about Jehoiakim king of Judah: He will have no one to sit on
the throne of David; his body will
be thrown out and exposed to the
heat by day and the frost by night.
31 I will punish him and his children and his attendants for their
wickedness; I will bring on them
and those living in Jerusalem and
the people of Judah every disaster
I pronounced against them, because they have not listened.' "

Isa 30:10; Jer 22:19

32 So Jeremiah took another
scroll and gave it to the scribe Baruch son of Neriah, and as Jeremiah dictated, Baruch wrote on it all
the words of the scroll that Jehoiakim king of Judah had burned in
the fire. And many similar words
were added to them. ver 4; Ex 34:1

Jeremiah in Prison

37 Zedekiah son of Josiah was
made king of Judah by Nebuchadnezzar king of Babylon; he
reigned in place of Jehoiachin[a]
son of Jehoiakim. 2 Neither he
nor his attendants nor the people
of the land paid any attention to
the words the LORD had spoken
through Jeremiah the prophet.

2Ch 36:12,14; Jer 22:24

3 King Zedekiah, however, sent
Jehukal son of Shelemiah with the
priest Zephaniah son of Maaseiah
to Jeremiah the prophet with this
message: "Please pray to the LORD
our God for us." Jer 21:1-2; 42:2

4 Now Jeremiah was free to come
and go among the people, for he
had not yet been put in prison.
5 Pharaoh's army had marched out
of Egypt, and when the Babylonians[b] who were besieging Jerusalem heard the report about them,
they withdrew from Jerusalem.

2Ki 24:7; Eze 17:15

6 Then the word of the LORD
came to Jeremiah the prophet:
7 "This is what the LORD, the God
of Israel, says: Tell the king of Judah, who sent you to inquire of
me, 'Pharaoh's army, which has
marched out to support you, will
go back to its own land, to Egypt.
8 Then the Babylonians will return
and attack this city; they will capture it and burn it down.'
9 "This is what the LORD says:
Do not deceive yourselves, thinking, 'The Babylonians will surely
leave us.' They will not! 10 Even if
you were to defeat the entire Babylonian[c] army that is attacking you
and only wounded men were left
in their tents, they would come out
and burn this city down." Jer 34:22
11 After the Babylonian army had
withdrawn from Jerusalem because of Pharaoh's army, 12 Jeremiah started to leave the city to go
to the territory of Benjamin to get
his share of the property among

[a] *1* Hebrew *Koniah*, a variant of *Jehoiachin*
[b] *5* Or *Chaldeans*; also in verses 8, 9, 13 and 14
[c] *10* Or *Chaldean*; also in verse 11

the people there. 13But when he reached the Benjamin Gate, the captain of the guard, whose name was Irijah son of Shelemiah, the son of Hananiah, arrested him and said, “You are deserting to the Babylonians!” Jer 32:9

14“That’s not true!” Jeremiah said. “I am not deserting to the Babylonians.” But Irijah would not listen to him; instead, he arrested Jeremiah and brought him to the officials. 15They were angry with Jeremiah and had him beaten and imprisoned in the house of Jonathan the secretary, which they had made into a prison. Jer 38:26; 40:4

16Jeremiah was put into a vaulted cell in a dungeon, where he remained a long time. 17Then King Zedekiah sent for him and had him brought to the palace, where he asked him privately, “Is there any word from the LORD?” Jer 15:11; 38:16

“Yes,” Jeremiah replied, “you will be delivered into the hands of the king of Babylon.” Jer 21:7

18Then Jeremiah said to King Zedekiah, “What crime have I committed against you or your attendants or this people, that you have put me in prison? 19Where are your prophets who prophesied to you, ‘The king of Babylon will not attack you or this land’? 20But now, my lord the king, please listen. Let me bring my petition before you: Do not send me back to the house of Jonathan the secretary, or I will die there.” 1Sa 26:18; Jn 10:32

21King Zedekiah then gave orders for Jeremiah to be placed in the courtyard of the guard and given a loaf of bread from the street of the bakers each day until all the bread in the city was gone. So Jeremiah remained in the courtyard of the guard. Jer 32:2; 38:6,13,28; 52:6

Jeremiah Thrown Into a Cistern

38 Shephatiah son of Mattan, Gedaliah son of Pashhur, Jehukal[a] son of Shelemiah, and Pashhur son of Malkijah heard what Jeremiah was telling all the people when he said, 2“This is what the LORD says: ‘Whoever stays in this city will die by the sword, famine or plague, but whoever goes over to the Babylonians[b] will live. They will escape with their lives; they will live.’ 3And this is what the LORD says: ‘This city will certainly be given into the hands of the army of the king of Babylon, who will capture it.’ ” Jer 21:4,10; 32:3; 37:3

4Then the officials said to the king, “This man should be put to death. He is discouraging the soldiers who are left in this city, as well as all the people, by the things he is saying to them. This man is not seeking the good of these people but their ruin.” Jer 26:11; 36:12

5“He is in your hands,” King Zedekiah answered. “The king can do nothing to oppose you.” 1Sa 15:24; Jer 26:14

[a] 1 Hebrew *Jukal*, a variant of *Jehukal*
[b] 2 Or *Chaldeans*; also in verses 18, 19 and 23

6 So they took Jeremiah and put
him into the cistern of Malkijah,
the king's son, which was in the
courtyard of the guard. They lowered Jeremiah by ropes into the
cistern; it had no water in it, only
mud, and Jeremiah sank down
into the mud. Jer 37:21; La 3:53
7 But Ebed-Melek, a Cushite,[a] an
official[b] in the royal palace, heard
that they had put Jeremiah into
the cistern. While the king was sitting in the Benjamin Gate, 8 Ebed-
Melek went out of the palace and
said to him, 9 "My lord the king,
these men have acted wickedly in
all they have done to Jeremiah the
prophet. They have thrown him
into a cistern, where he will starve
to death when there is no longer
any bread in the city." Jer 37:21; Ac 8:27
10 Then the king commanded
Ebed-Melek the Cushite, "Take
thirty men from here with you
and lift Jeremiah the prophet out
of the cistern before he dies."
11 So Ebed-Melek took the men
with him and went to a room under the treasury in the palace. He
took some old rags and worn-out
clothes from there and let them
down with ropes to Jeremiah in
the cistern. 12 Ebed-Melek the Cushite said to Jeremiah, "Put these
old rags and worn-out clothes under your arms to pad the ropes."
Jeremiah did so, 13 and they pulled
him up with the ropes and lifted
him out of the cistern. And Jeremiah remained in the courtyard
of the guard. Jer 37:21

Zedekiah Questions Jeremiah Again

14 Then King Zedekiah sent for
Jeremiah the prophet and had
him brought to the third entrance
to the temple of the LORD. "I am
going to ask you something," the
king said to Jeremiah. "Do not
hide anything from me."
1Sa 3:17; Jer 37:3
15 Jeremiah said to Zedekiah,
"If I give you an answer, will you
not kill me? Even if I did give
you counsel, you would not listen
to me."
16 But King Zedekiah swore this
oath secretly to Jeremiah: "As surely as the LORD lives, who has giv-
en us breath, I will neither kill you
nor hand you over to those who
want to kill you." Isa 57:16; Jer 37:17
17 Then Jeremiah said to Zedekiah, "This is what the LORD God
Almighty, the God of Israel, says:
'If you surrender to the officers of
the king of Babylon, your life will
be spared and this city will not be
burned down; you and your family will live. 18 But if you will not
surrender to the officers of the
king of Babylon, this city will be
given into the hands of the Babylonians and they will burn it
down; you yourself will not escape
from them.'" Jer 32:4; 34:3
19 King Zedekiah said to Jeremiah, "I am afraid of the Jews who
have gone over to the Babylonians, for the Babylonians may

[a] 7 Probably from the upper Nile region
[b] 7 Or *a eunuch*

hand me over to them and they
will mistreat me." Isa 51:12; Jn 12:42
20"They will not hand you over,"
Jeremiah replied. "Obey the LORD
by doing what I tell you. Then it
will go well with you, and your life
will be spared. 21But if you refuse
to surrender, this is what the LORD
has revealed to me: 22All the wom-
en left in the palace of the king of
Judah will be brought out to the officials of the king of Babylon. Those
women will say to you: Jer 6:12; 11:4

"'They misled you and
overcame you —
those trusted friends of
yours. Jer 13:21
Your feet are sunk in the mud; Ps 69:14
your friends have deserted
you.'

23"All your wives and children
will be brought out to the Babylonians. You yourself will not escape
from their hands but will be captured by the king of Babylon; and
this city will[a] be burned down."
2Ki 25:6; Jer 41:10
24Then Zedekiah said to Jeremiah, "Do not let anyone know about
this conversation, or you may die.
25If the officials hear that I talked
with you, and they come to you
and say, 'Tell us what you said to
the king and what the king said to
you; do not hide it from us or we
will kill you,' 26then tell them, 'I
was pleading with the king not to
send me back to Jonathan's house
to die there.'" Jer 37:15

27All the officials did come to
Jeremiah and question him, and
he told them everything the king
had ordered him to say. So they
said no more to him, for no one
had heard his conversation with
the king.
28And Jeremiah remained in the
courtyard of the guard until the
day Jerusalem was captured.
Jer 37:21; 39:14

The Fall of Jerusalem

39 This is how Jerusalem was tak-
en: 1In the ninth year of
Zedekiah king of Judah, in
the tenth month, Nebuchadnezzar
king of Babylon marched against
Jerusalem with his whole army
and laid siege to it. 2And on the
ninth day of the fourth month of
Zedekiah's eleventh year, the city
wall was broken through. 3Then all
the officials of the king of Babylon
came and took seats in the Middle Gate: Nergal-Sharezer of Sam-
gar, Nebo-Sarsekim a chief officer,
Nergal-Sharezer a high official and
all the other officials of the king
of Babylon. 4When Zedekiah king
of Judah and all the soldiers saw
them, they fled; they left the city
at night by way of the king's garden, through the gate between the
two walls, and headed toward the
Arabah.[b] Jer 25:29; 2Ch 36:11
5But the Babylonian[c] army pursued them and overtook Zedekiah in the plains of Jericho. They

[a] 23 Or *and you will cause this city to*
[b] 4 Or *the Jordan Valley* [c] 5 Or *Chaldean*

captured him and took him to
Nebuchadnezzar king of Babylon
at Riblah in the land of Hamath,
where he pronounced sentence
on him. 6There at Riblah the king
of Babylon slaughtered the sons
of Zedekiah before his eyes and
also killed all the nobles of Judah. 7Then he put out Zedekiah's
eyes and bound him with bronze
shackles to take him to Babylon.
2Ki 23:33; Jer 32:5; Eze 12:13

8The Babylonians[a] set fire to
the royal palace and the houses
of the people and broke down the
walls of Jerusalem. 9Nebuzaradan
commander of the imperial guard
carried into exile to Babylon the
people who remained in the city,
along with those who had gone
over to him, and the rest of the
people. 10But Nebuzaradan the
commander of the guard left behind in the land of Judah some of
the poor people, who owned nothing; and at that time he gave them
vineyards and fields.
2Ki 25:1-12; Jer 52:4-16

11Now Nebuchadnezzar king of
Babylon had given these orders
about Jeremiah through Nebuzaradan commander of the imperial
guard: 12"Take him and look after
him; don't harm him but do for
him whatever he asks." 13So Nebuzaradan the commander of the
guard, Nebushazban a chief officer, Nergal-Sharezer a high official and all the other officers of
the king of Babylon 14sent and had
Jeremiah taken out of the courtyard of the guard. They turned
him over to Gedaliah son of Ahikam, the son of Shaphan, to take
him back to his home. So he remained among his own people.
Jer 38:28; 1Pe 3:13

15While Jeremiah had been
confined in the courtyard of the
guard, the word of the LORD came
to him: 16"Go and tell Ebed-Melek the Cushite, 'This is what the
LORD Almighty, the God of Israel, says: I am about to fulfill my
words against this city — words
concerning disaster, not prosperity. At that time they will be fulfilled before your eyes. 17But I will
rescue you on that day, declares
the LORD; you will not be given
into the hands of those you fear.
18I will save you; you will not fall
by the sword but will escape with
your life, because you trust in me,
declares the LORD.' " Jer 21:9; 45:5

Jeremiah Freed

40 The word came to Jere-
miah from the LORD after
Nebuzaradan commander of the
imperial guard had released him
at Ramah. He had found Jeremiah bound in chains among all the
captives from Jerusalem and Judah who were being carried into
exile to Babylon. 2When the commander of the guard found Jeremiah, he said to him, "The LORD
your God decreed this disaster for
this place. 3And now the LORD has
brought it about; he has done just

[a] 8 Or *Chaldeans*

as he said he would. All this happened because you people sinned
against the LORD and did not obey
him. 4But today I am freeing you
from the chains on your wrists.
Come with me to Babylon, if you
like, and I will look after you; but
if you do not want to, then don't
come. Look, the whole country
lies before you; go wherever you
please." 5However, before Jeremiah turned to go,[a] Nebuzaradan
added, "Go back to Gedaliah son
of Ahikam, the son of Shaphan,
whom the king of Babylon has
appointed over the towns of Judah, and live with him among the
people, or go anywhere else you
please." Jer 39:11-12; Da 9:11

Then the commander gave him
provisions and a present and let
him go. 6So Jeremiah went to Gedaliah son of Ahikam at Mizpah and
stayed with him among the people who were left behind in the
land. Jdg 20:1; 1Sa 7:5-17

Gedaliah Assassinated

7When all the army officers
and their men who were still in
the open country heard that the
king of Babylon had appointed
Gedaliah son of Ahikam as governor over the land and had put
him in charge of the men, women
and children who were the poorest in the land and who had not
been carried into exile to Babylon, 8they came to Gedaliah at
Mizpah — Ishmael son of Nethaniah, Johanan and Jonathan the
sons of Kareah, Seraiah son of
Tanhumeth, the sons of Ephai the
Netophathite, and Jaazaniah[b] the
son of the Maakathite, and their
men. 9Gedaliah son of Ahikam,
the son of Shaphan, took an oath
to reassure them and their men.
"Do not be afraid to serve the Babylonians,[c]" he said. "Settle down
in the land and serve the king of
Babylon, and it will go well with
you. 10I myself will stay at Mizpah
to represent you before the Babylonians who come to us, but you
are to harvest the wine, summer
fruit and olive oil, and put them
in your storage jars, and live in the
towns you have taken over."
Dt 1:39; Jer 38:20

11When all the Jews in Moab,
Ammon, Edom and all the other countries heard that the king
of Babylon had left a remnant in
Judah and had appointed Gedaliah son of Ahikam, the son of
Shaphan, as governor over them,
12they all came back to the land
of Judah, to Gedaliah at Mizpah,
from all the countries where they
had been scattered. And they harvested an abundance of wine and
summer fruit. Jer 43:5

13Johanan son of Kareah and all
the army officers still in the open
country came to Gedaliah at Mizpah 14and said to him, "Don't you
know that Baalis king of the Ammonites has sent Ishmael son of

[a] 5 Or *Jeremiah answered* [b] 8 Hebrew *Jezaniah,* a variant of *Jaazaniah* [c] 9 Or *Chaldeans*; also in verse 10

Nethaniah to take your life?" But
Gedaliah son of Ahikam did not
believe them. Jer 41:10
15 Then Johanan son of Kareah
said privately to Gedaliah in Mizpah, "Let me go and kill Ishmael
son of Nethaniah, and no one will
know it. Why should he take your
life and cause all the Jews who are
gathered around you to be scattered and the remnant of Judah
to perish?" 2Ki 21:14; Isa 1:9; Ro 11:5
16 But Gedaliah son of Ahikam
said to Johanan son of Kareah,
"Don't do such a thing! What you
are saying about Ishmael is not
true."

41 In the seventh month Ishmael son of Nethaniah,
the son of Elishama, who was of
royal blood and had been one of
the king's officers, came with ten
men to Gedaliah son of Ahikam
at Mizpah. While they were eating
together there, 2 Ishmael son of
Nethaniah and the ten men who
were with him got up and struck
down Gedaliah son of Ahikam, the
son of Shaphan, with the sword,
killing the one whom the king of
Babylon had appointed as governor over the land. 3 Ishmael also
killed all the men of Judah who
were with Gedaliah at Mizpah, as
well as the Babylonian[a] soldiers
who were there. 2Ki 25:22-26; Jer 40:5,8
4 The day after Gedaliah's as-
sassination, before anyone knew
about it, 5 eighty men who had
shaved off their beards, torn their
clothes and cut themselves came
from Shechem, Shiloh and Samaria, bringing grain offerings and
incense with them to the house of
the LORD. 6 Ishmael son of Nethaniah went out from Mizpah to meet
them, weeping as he went. When
he met them, he said, "Come to
Gedaliah son of Ahikam." 7 When
they went into the city, Ishmael son of Nethaniah and the men
who were with him slaughtered
them and threw them into a cistern. 8 But ten of them said to Ishmael, "Don't kill us! We have wheat
and barley, olive oil and honey,
hidden in a field." So he let them
alone and did not kill them with
the others. 9 Now the cistern where
he threw all the bodies of the men
he had killed along with Gedaliah
was the one King Asa had made
as part of his defense against Baasha king of Israel. Ishmael son of
Nethaniah filled it with the dead.
1Ki 15:22; 2Ch 16:1,6
10 Ishmael made captives of all
the rest of the people who were
in Mizpah — the king's daughters
along with all the others who were
left there, over whom Nebuzaradan commander of the imperial
guard had appointed Gedaliah son
of Ahikam. Ishmael son of Nethaniah took them captive and set
out to cross over to the Ammonites. Jer 40:14
11 When Johanan son of Kareah and all the army officers who
were with him heard about all the
crimes Ishmael son of Nethaniah

[a] 3 Or *Chaldean*

had committed, [12]they took all
their men and went to fight Ishmael son of Nethaniah. They
caught up with him near the great
pool in Gibeon. [13]When all the people Ishmael had with him saw Johanan son of Kareah and the army
officers who were with him, they
were glad. [14]All the people Ishmael had taken captive at Mizpah
turned and went over to Johanan
son of Kareah. [15]But Ishmael son
of Nethaniah and eight of his men
escaped from Johanan and fled to
the Ammonites. 2Sa 2:13; Pr 28:17

Flight to Egypt

[16]Then Johanan son of Kareah
and all the army officers who were
with him led away all the people of
Mizpah who had survived, whom
Johanan had recovered from Ishmael son of Nethaniah after Ishmael had assassinated Gedaliah
son of Ahikam — the soldiers,
women, children and court officials he had recovered from Gibeon. [17]And they went on, stopping
at Geruth Kimham near Bethlehem on their way to Egypt [18]to escape the Babylonians.[a] They were
afraid of them because Ishmael
son of Nethaniah had killed Gedaliah son of Ahikam, whom the
king of Babylon had appointed as
governor over the land.

42 Then all the army officers,
including Johanan son of
Kareah and Jezaniah[b] son of Hoshaiah, and all the people from the
least to the greatest approached
[2]Jeremiah the prophet and said to
him, "Please hear our petition and
pray to the LORD your God for this
entire remnant. For as you now
see, though we were once many,
now only a few are left. [3]Pray that
the LORD your God will tell us
where we should go and what we
should do." Ps 86:11; Pr 3:6

[4]"I have heard you," replied Jeremiah the prophet. "I will certainly pray to the LORD your God as
you have requested; I will tell you
everything the LORD says and will
keep nothing back from you."
1Ki 22:14; 1Sa 3:17

[5]Then they said to Jeremiah, "May the LORD be a true and
faithful witness against us if we
do not act in accordance with everything the LORD your God sends
you to tell us. [6]Whether it is favorable or unfavorable, we will obey
the LORD our God, to whom we are
sending you, so that it will go well
with us, for we will obey the LORD
our God." Dt 6:3; Jer 7:23

[7]Ten days later the word of the
LORD came to Jeremiah. [8]So he
called together Johanan son of Kareah and all the army officers who
were with him and all the people
from the least to the greatest. [9]He
said to them, "This is what the
LORD, the God of Israel, to whom
you sent me to present your petition, says: [10]'If you stay in this
land, I will build you up and not
tear you down; I will plant you and

[a] 18 Or *Chaldeans* [b] 1 Hebrew; Septuagint (see also 43:2) *Azariah*

not uproot you, for I have relented concerning the disaster I have
inflicted on you. 11Do not be afraid
of the king of Babylon, whom you
now fear. Do not be afraid of him,
declares the LORD, for I am with
you and will save you and deliver
you from his hands. 12I will show
you compassion so that he will
have compassion on you and restore you to your land.'
Ps 106:44-46; Ro 8:31

13"However, if you say, 'We will
not stay in this land,' and so disobey the LORD your God, 14and if
you say, 'No, we will go and live in
Egypt, where we will not see war
or hear the trumpet or be hungry
for bread,' 15then hear the word of
the LORD, you remnant of Judah.
This is what the LORD Almighty,
the God of Israel, says: 'If you are
determined to go to Egypt and
you do go to settle there, 16then
the sword you fear will overtake
you there, and the famine you
dread will follow you into Egypt,
and there you will die. 17Indeed,
all who are determined to go to
Egypt to settle there will die by
the sword, famine and plague; not
one of them will survive or escape
the disaster I will bring on them.'
18This is what the LORD Almighty,
the God of Israel, says: 'As my anger and wrath have been poured
out on those who lived in Jerusalem, so will my wrath be poured
out on you when you go to Egypt.
You will be a curse[a] and an object
of horror, a curse[a] and an object of
reproach; you will never see this
place again.'
Jer 7:20; 29:18; 44:13

19"Remnant of Judah, the LORD
has told you, 'Do not go to Egypt.'
Be sure of this: I warn you today
20that you made a fatal mistake
when you sent me to the LORD
your God and said, 'Pray to the
LORD our God for us; tell us everything he says and we will do
it.' 21I have told you today, but you
still have not obeyed the LORD
your God in all he sent me to tell
you. 22So now, be sure of this: You
will die by the sword, famine and
plague in the place where you
want to go to settle."
Eze 6:11; Hos 9:6

43 When Jeremiah had finished telling the people all
the words of the LORD their God —
everything the LORD had sent him
to tell them — 2Azariah son of Hoshaiah and Johanan son of Kareah and all the arrogant men said
to Jeremiah, "You are lying! The
LORD our God has not sent you to
say, 'You must not go to Egypt to
settle there.' 3But Baruch son of
Neriah is inciting you against us
to hand us over to the Babylonians,[b] so they may kill us or carry
us into exile to Babylon."
Jer 26:8; 42:1

4So Johanan son of Kareah and
all the army officers and all the
people disobeyed the LORD's command to stay in the land of Judah.
5Instead, Johanan son of Kareah

[a] 18 That is, your name will be used in cursing (see 29:22); or, others will see that you are cursed. [b] 3 Or *Chaldeans*

and all the army officers led away
all the remnant of Judah who had
come back to live in the land of
Judah from all the nations where
they had been scattered. 6They
also led away all those whom
Nebuzaradan commander of the
imperial guard had left with Gedaliah son of Ahikam, the son of
Shaphan — the men, the women,
the children and the king's daughters. And they took Jeremiah the
prophet and Baruch son of Neriah
along with them. 7So they entered
Egypt in disobedience to the LORD
and went as far as Tahpanhes.

Jer 40:12; 44:1

8In Tahpanhes the word of the
LORD came to Jeremiah: 9"While
the Jews are watching, take some
large stones with you and bury
them in clay in the brick pavement at the entrance to Pharaoh's
palace in Tahpanhes. 10Then say
to them, 'This is what the LORD
Almighty, the God of Israel, says:
I will send for my servant Nebuchadnezzar king of Babylon, and
I will set his throne over these
stones I have buried here; he will
spread his royal canopy above
them. 11He will come and attack
Egypt, bringing death to those
destined for death, captivity to
those destined for captivity, and
the sword to those destined for
the sword. 12He will set fire to the
temples of the gods of Egypt; he
will burn their temples and take
their gods captive. As a shepherd
picks his garment clean of lice, so
he will pick Egypt clean and depart. 13There in the temple of the
sun[a] in Egypt he will demolish the
sacred pillars and will burn down
the temples of the gods of Egypt.'"

Jer 15:2; 44:13; 46:13-26

Disaster Because of Idolatry

44 This word came to Jeremiah concerning all the Jews
living in Lower Egypt — in Migdol,
Tahpanhes and Memphis — and
in Upper Egypt: 2"This is what the
LORD Almighty, the God of Israel,
says: You saw the great disaster I
brought on Jerusalem and on all
the towns of Judah. Today they
lie deserted and in ruins 3because
of the evil they have done. They
aroused my anger by burning incense to and worshiping other
gods that neither they nor you nor
your ancestors ever knew. 4Again
and again I sent my servants the
prophets, who said, 'Do not do
this detestable thing that I hate!'
5But they did not listen or pay attention; they did not turn from
their wickedness or stop burning
incense to other gods. 6Therefore,
my fierce anger was poured out;
it raged against the towns of Judah and the streets of Jerusalem
and made them the desolate ruins
they are today. Jer 7:25; 25:4; 26:5

7"Now this is what the LORD God
Almighty, the God of Israel, says:
Why bring such great disaster on
yourselves by cutting off from
Judah the men and women, the

[a] 13 Or *in Heliopolis*

children and infants, and so leave yourselves without a remnant? 8 Why arouse my anger with what your hands have made, burning incense to other gods in Egypt, where you have come to live? You will destroy yourselves and make yourselves a curse[a] and an object of reproach among all the nations on earth. 9 Have you forgotten the wickedness committed by your ancestors and by the kings and queens of Judah and the wickedness committed by you and your wives in the land of Judah and the streets of Jerusalem? 10 To this day they have not humbled themselves or shown reverence, nor have they followed my law and the decrees I set before you and your ancestors. 1Ki 9:6-9

11 "Therefore this is what the LORD Almighty, the God of Israel, says: I am determined to bring disaster on you and to destroy all Judah. 12 I will take away the remnant of Judah who were determined to go to Egypt to settle there. They will all perish in Egypt; they will fall by the sword or die from famine. From the least to the greatest, they will die by sword or famine. They will become a curse and an object of horror, a curse and an object of reproach. 13 I will punish those who live in Egypt with the sword, famine and plague, as I punished Jerusalem. 14 None of the remnant of Judah who have gone to live in Egypt will escape or survive to return to the land of Judah, to which they long to return and live; none will return except a few fugitives."

Jer 21:10; 22:24-27; Am 9:4

15 Then all the men who knew that their wives were burning incense to other gods, along with all the women who were present — a large assembly — and all the people living in Lower and Upper Egypt, said to Jeremiah, 16 "We will not listen to the message you have spoken to us in the name of the LORD! 17 We will certainly do everything we said we would: We will burn incense to the Queen of Heaven and will pour out drink offerings to her just as we and our ancestors, our kings and our officials did in the towns of Judah and in the streets of Jerusalem. At that time we had plenty of food and were well off and suffered no harm. 18 But ever since we stopped burning incense to the Queen of Heaven and pouring out drink offerings to her, we have had nothing and have been perishing by sword and famine." Dt 23:23; Jer 7:18

19 The women added, "When we burned incense to the Queen of Heaven and poured out drink offerings to her, did not our husbands know that we were making cakes impressed with her image and pouring out drink offerings to her?" Jer 7:18

[a] *8* That is, your name will be used in cursing (see 29:22); or, others will see that you are cursed; also in verse 12; similarly in verse 22.

20 Then Jeremiah said to all the
people, both men and women,
who were answering him, 21 "Did
not the LORD remember and call
to mind the incense burned in the
towns of Judah and the streets of
Jerusalem by you and your ancestors, your kings and your officials and the people of the land?
22 When the LORD could no longer
endure your wicked actions and
the detestable things you did, your
land became a curse and a desolate waste without inhabitants,
as it is today. 23 Because you have
burned incense and have sinned
against the LORD and have not
obeyed him or followed his law
or his decrees or his stipulations,
this disaster has come upon you,
as you now see."

1Ki 9:9; Da 9:11-12; Jer 40:2

24 Then Jeremiah said to all the
people, including the women,
"Hear the word of the LORD, all you
people of Judah in Egypt. 25 This is
what the LORD Almighty, the God
of Israel, says: You and your wives
have done what you said you
would do when you promised, 'We
will certainly carry out the vows
we made to burn incense and pour
out drink offerings to the Queen
of Heaven.' Jer 43:7

"Go ahead then, do what you
promised! Keep your vows! 26 But
hear the word of the LORD, all you
Jews living in Egypt: 'I swear by
my great name,' says the LORD,
'that no one from Judah living anywhere in Egypt will ever
again invoke my name or swear,
"As surely as the Sovereign LORD
lives." 27 For I am watching over
them for harm, not for good; the
Jews in Egypt will perish by sword
and famine until they are all destroyed. 28 Those who escape the
sword and return to the land of
Judah from Egypt will be very few.
Then the whole remnant of Judah
who came to live in Egypt will
know whose word will stand —
mine or theirs. Jer 31:28; Eze 20:39

29 " 'This will be the sign to you
that I will punish you in this place,'
declares the LORD, 'so that you will
know that my threats of harm
against you will surely stand.'
30 This is what the LORD says: 'I am
going to deliver Pharaoh Hophra
king of Egypt into the hands of his
enemies who want to kill him, just
as I gave Zedekiah king of Judah
into the hands of Nebuchadnezzar
king of Babylon, the enemy who
wanted to kill him.' " Jer 39:5; 46:26

A Message to Baruch

45 When Baruch son of Neriah
wrote on a scroll the words
Jeremiah the prophet dictated in
the fourth year of Jehoiakim son
of Josiah king of Judah, Jeremiah said this to Baruch: 2 "This is
what the LORD, the God of Israel, says to you, Baruch: 3 You said,
'Woe to me! The LORD has added
sorrow to my pain; I am worn out
with groaning and find no rest.'
4 But the LORD has told me to say
to you, 'This is what the LORD says:

I will overthrow what I have built
and uproot what I have planted,
throughout the earth. 5Should you
then seek great things for yourself? Do not seek them. For I will
bring disaster on all people, declares the LORD, but wherever you
go I will let you escape with your
life.' " Jer 21:9; 36:4,18,32; 38:2; 39:18

A Message About Egypt

46 This is the word of the LORD that came to Jeremiah the prophet concerning the nations: Jer 25:15-38

2Concerning Egypt:

This is the message against the army of Pharaoh Necho king of Egypt, which was defeated at Carchemish on the Euphrates River by Nebuchadnezzar king of Babylon in the fourth year of Jehoiakim son of Josiah king of Judah: 2Ki 23:29; 2Ch 35:20

3"Prepare your shields, both
large and small, Isa 21:5; Jer 51:11-12
and march out for battle!
4Harness the horses,
mount the steeds!
Take your positions
with helmets on!
Polish your spears, Eze 21:9-11
put on your armor! 1Sa 17:5,38; 2Ch 26:14
5What do I see?
They are terrified,
they are retreating,
their warriors are defeated.
They flee in haste Jer 48:44
without looking back,
and there is terror on every
side," Jer 49:29
declares the LORD.
6"The swift cannot flee Isa 30:16
nor the strong escape.
In the north by the River
Euphrates
they stumble and fall. Da 11:19
7"Who is this that rises like the
Nile,
like rivers of surging waters? Jer 47:2
8Egypt rises like the Nile, Eze 29:3,9
like rivers of surging waters.
She says, 'I will rise and cover
the earth;
I will destroy cities and their
people.' Da 11:10
9Charge, you horses!
Drive furiously, you
charioteers! Jer 47:3
March on, you warriors — men
of Cush[a] and Put who
carry shields,
men of Lydia who draw the
bow. Isa 66:19
10But that day belongs to
the Lord, the LORD
Almighty — Joel 1:15
a day of vengeance, for
vengeance on his foes. Dt 32:41
The sword will devour till it is
satisfied, Dt 32:42
till it has quenched its thirst
with blood. Dt 32:42

[a] 9 That is, the upper Nile region

For the Lord, the LORD
Almighty, will offer
sacrifice Zep 1:7
in the land of the north by
the River Euphrates.
Ge 2:14

11 "Go up to Gilead and get balm,
Jer 8:22
Virgin Daughter Egypt. Isa 47:1
But you try many medicines in
vain;
there is no healing for you.
Mic 1:9
12 The nations will hear of your
shame;
your cries will fill the earth.
One warrior will stumble over
another;
both will fall down together."
Isa 19:4; Na 3:8-10

13 This is the message the LORD
spoke to Jeremiah the prophet
about the coming of Nebuchadnezzar king of Babylon to attack
Egypt: Isa 19:1

14 "Announce this in Egypt,
and proclaim it in
Migdol;
proclaim it also in Memphis
and Tahpanhes: Jer 43:8
'Take your positions and get
ready,
for the sword devours those
around you.' Jer 24:8
15 Why will your warriors be laid
low?
They cannot stand, for the
LORD will push them
down. Isa 66:15-16
16 They will stumble repeatedly;
Lev 26:37
they will fall over each other.
They will say, 'Get up, let us go
back
to our own people and our
native lands, Isa 13:14
away from the sword of the
oppressor.' Jer 25:38
17 There they will exclaim,
'Pharaoh king of Egypt is only
a loud noise; 1Ki 20:10-11
he has missed his
opportunity.' Isa 19:11-16

18 "As surely as I live," declares
the King, Jer 48:15
whose name is the LORD
Almighty,
"one will come who is like
Tabor among the
mountains, Jos 19:22
like Carmel by the sea. 1Ki 18:42
19 Pack your belongings for exile,
Isa 20:4
you who live in Egypt,
for Memphis will be laid waste
Eze 29:10,12
and lie in ruins without
inhabitant.

20 "Egypt is a beautiful heifer,
but a gadfly is coming
against her from the north.
Jer 47:2
21 The mercenaries in her ranks
2Ki 7:6
are like fattened calves.
They too will turn and flee
together,
they will not stand their
ground,

for the day of disaster is
coming upon them, Ps 37:13; Jer 18:17
the time for them to be
punished. Job 18:20
22 Egypt will hiss like a fleeing
serpent
as the enemy advances in
force;
they will come against her with
axes,
like men who cut down
trees.
23 They will chop down her
forest,"
declares the LORD,
"dense though it be.
They are more numerous than
locusts, Jdg 7:12
they cannot be counted.
24 Daughter Egypt will be put to
shame,
given into the hands of the
people of the north." Jer 1:15

25 The LORD Almighty, the God of
Israel, says: "I am about to bring
punishment on Amon god of
Thebes, on Pharaoh, on Egypt and
her gods and her kings, and on
those who rely on Pharaoh. 26 I will
give them into the hands of those
who want to kill them — Nebuchadnezzar king of Babylon and
his officers. Later, however, Egypt
will be inhabited as in times past,"
declares the LORD. Eze 29:11-16; 32:11

27 "Do not be afraid, Jacob my
servant; Isa 41:13; 43:5
do not be dismayed, Israel.
I will surely save you out of a
distant place,
your descendants from
the land of their exile. Isa 11:11; Jer 50:19
Jacob will again have peace
and security,
and no one will make him
afraid.
28 Do not be afraid, Jacob my
servant,
for I am with you," declares
the LORD. Isa 8:9-10
"Though I completely
destroy all the nations Jer 4:27
among which I scatter you,
I will not completely destroy
you.
I will discipline you but only in
due measure;
I will not let you go entirely
unpunished."

A Message About the Philistines

47 This is the word of the LORD that came to Jeremiah the prophet concerning the Philistines before Pharaoh attacked Gaza: Am 1:6; Zec 9:5-7

2 This is what the LORD says:

"See how the waters are
rising in the north; Isa 8:7; 14:31
they will become an
overflowing torrent.
They will overflow the land
and everything in it,
the towns and those who live
in them.

The people will cry out;
all who dwell in the land will wail Isa 15:3
3 at the sound of the hooves of galloping steeds,
at the noise of enemy chariots Jer 46:9; Eze 23:24
and the rumble of their wheels.
Parents will not turn to help their children;
their hands will hang limp. Isa 13:7
4 For the day has come
to destroy all the Philistines
and to remove all survivors
who could help Tyre and Sidon. Am 1:9-10; Zec 9:2-4
The LORD is about to destroy the Philistines, Ge 10:14; Joel 3:4
the remnant from the coasts of Caphtor.[a] Dt 2:23
5 Gaza will shave her head in mourning; Jer 41:5; Mic 1:16
Ashkelon will be silenced. Jer 25:20
You remnant on the plain,
how long will you cut yourselves?

6 "'Alas, sword of the LORD, Jer 12:12
how long till you rest?
Return to your sheath;
cease and be still.' Eze 21:30
7 But how can it rest
when the LORD has commanded it,
when he has ordered it
to attack Ashkelon and the coast?" Eze 25:15-17

A Message About Moab

48 Concerning Moab: Ge 19:37

This is what the LORD Almighty, the God of Israel, says:

"Woe to Nebo, for it will be ruined. Nu 32:38
Kiriathaim will be disgraced and captured; Nu 32:37
the stronghold[b] will be disgraced and shattered.
2 Moab will be praised no more; Isa 16:14
in Heshbon[c] people will plot her downfall: Nu 21:25
'Come, let us put an end to that nation.'
You, the people of Madmen,[d] will also be silenced;
the sword will pursue you.
3 Cries of anguish arise from Horonaim, Isa 15:5
cries of great havoc and destruction.
4 Moab will be broken;
her little ones will cry out.[e]
5 They go up the hill to Luhith, Isa 15:5
weeping bitterly as they go;
on the road down to Horonaim
anguished cries over the destruction are heard.

[a] 4 That is, Crete [b] 1 Or *captured; / Misgab* [c] 2 The Hebrew for *Heshbon* sounds like the Hebrew for *plot.* [d] 2 The name of the Moabite town Madmen sounds like the Hebrew for *be silenced.* [e] 4 Hebrew; Septuagint / *proclaim it to Zoar*

6 Flee! Run for your lives;
become like a bush[a] in the desert. Jer 17:6
7 Since you trust in your deeds and riches, Ps 49:6
you too will be taken captive,
and Chemosh will go into exile, Nu 21:29; Isa 46:1-2; Jer 49:3
together with his priests and officials. Am 2:3
8 The destroyer will come against every town, Ex 12:23
and not a town will escape.
The valley will be ruined
and the plateau destroyed, Jos 13:9
because the LORD has spoken.
9 Put salt on Moab, Jdg 9:45
for she will be laid waste[b]; Jer 51:29
her towns will become desolate,
with no one to live in them.

10 "A curse on anyone who is lax in doing the LORD's work!
A curse on anyone who keeps their sword from bloodshed! 1Ki 20:42; 2Ki 13:15-19; Jer 47:6

11 "Moab has been at rest from youth, Zec 1:15
like wine left on its dregs, Zep 1:12
not poured from one jar to another —
she has not gone into exile.
So she tastes as she did,
and her aroma is unchanged.
12 But days are coming,"
declares the LORD,
"when I will send men who pour from pitchers,
and they will pour her out;
they will empty her pitchers
and smash her jars.
13 Then Moab will be ashamed of Chemosh, Hos 10:6
as Israel was ashamed
when they trusted in Bethel. Jos 7:2

14 "How can you say, 'We are warriors, Ps 33:16
men valiant in battle'?
15 Moab will be destroyed and her towns invaded;
her finest young men will go down in the slaughter," Jer 50:27
declares the King, whose name is the LORD Almighty. Jer 46:18; 51:57
16 "The fall of Moab is at hand; Isa 13:22
her calamity will come quickly.
17 Mourn for her, all who live around her,
all who know her fame; 2Ki 3:4-5
say, 'How broken is the mighty scepter, Ps 110:2
how broken the glorious staff!'

18 "Come down from your glory
and sit on the parched ground, Isa 47:1

[a] 6 Or *like Aroer* [b] 9 Or *Give wings to Moab, / for she will fly away*

you inhabitants of Daughter
Dibon, Nu 21:30; Jos 13:9
for the one who destroys Moab
will come up against you
and ruin your fortified cities.
19 Stand by the road and watch,
you who live in Aroer. Dt 2:36
Ask the man fleeing and the
woman escaping,
ask them, 'What has
happened?'
20 Moab is disgraced, for she is
shattered.
Wail and cry out! Isa 16:7
Announce by the Arnon Nu 21:13
that Moab is destroyed.
21 Judgment has come to the
plateau —
to Holon, Jahzah
and Mephaath,
Nu 21:23; Jos 13:18; Isa 15:4
22 to Dibon, Nebo and Beth
Diblathaim, Jos 13:9,17
23 to Kiriathaim, Beth Gamul
and Beth Meon, Jos 13:17
24 to Kerioth and Bozrah —
Am 2:2
to all the towns of Moab, far
and near. Isa 15:1
25 Moab's horn[a] is cut off; Ps 75:10
her arm is broken,"
Ps 10:15; Eze 30:21
declares the LORD.
26 "Make her drunk, Jer 25:16,27
for she has defied the LORD.
1Sa 17:26
Let Moab wallow in her vomit;
Isa 28:8
let her be an object of
ridicule.
27 Was not Israel the object of
your ridicule? Jer 2:26
Was she caught among
thieves, 2Ki 17:3-6
that you shake your head in
scorn Jer 18:16; Mic 7:8-10
whenever you speak of her?
28 Abandon your towns and dwell
among the rocks,
you who live in Moab.
Be like a dove that makes its
nest Ps 55:6-7
at the mouth of a cave. Jdg 6:2
29 "We have heard of Moab's
pride — Isa 16:6
how great is her
arrogance! —
of her insolence, her pride, her
conceit
and the haughtiness of her
heart. Pr 16:18
30 I know her insolence but it is
futile,"
declares the LORD,
"and her boasts accomplish
nothing. Ps 10:3
31 Therefore I wail over Moab,
Isa 15:5-8
for all Moab I cry out,
I moan for the people of Kir
Hareseth. 2Ki 3:25
32 I weep for you, as Jazer weeps,
Jos 13:25
you vines of Sibmah. Isa 16:8-9
Your branches spread as far as
the sea[b];
they reached as far as[c] Jazer.

[a] 25 *Horn* here symbolizes strength.
[b] 32 Probably the Dead Sea [c] 32 Two Hebrew manuscripts and Septuagint; most Hebrew manuscripts *as far as the Sea of*

The destroyer has fallen
on your ripened fruit and grapes.
33 Joy and gladness are gone
from the orchards and fields of Moab.
I have stopped the flow of wine
from the presses; Isa 16:10
no one treads them with shouts of joy. Joel 1:12
Although there are shouts,
they are not shouts of joy.
34 "The sound of their cry rises
from Heshbon to Elealeh and Jahaz, Isa 15:4
from Zoar as far as Horonaim
and Eglath Shelishiyah, Isa 15:5
for even the waters of Nimrim are dried up. Isa 15:6
35 In Moab I will put an end
to those who make offerings on the high places Isa 15:2; 16:12
and burn incense to their gods," Jer 11:13
declares the LORD.
36 "So my heart laments for Moab
like the music of a pipe; Isa 16:11
it laments like a pipe for the people of Kir Hareseth. 2Ki 3:25
The wealth they acquired is gone. Isa 16:6-12
37 Every head is shaved Isa 15:2; Jer 41:5
and every beard cut off; 2Sa 10:4
every hand is slashed
and every waist is covered with sackcloth. Ge 37:34; Isa 3:24
38 On all the roofs in Moab
and in the public squares
there is nothing but mourning,
for I have broken Moab
like a jar that no one wants," Jer 22:28
declares the LORD.
39 "How shattered she is! How they wail!
How Moab turns her back in shame!
Moab has become an object of ridicule,
an object of horror to all those around her."

40 This is what the LORD says:

"Look! An eagle is swooping down, Dt 28:49; Hab 1:8
spreading its wings over Moab. Isa 8:8
41 Kerioth[a] will be captured Isa 15:1
and the strongholds taken.
In that day the hearts of Moab's warriors
will be like the heart of a woman in labor. Isa 21:3
42 Moab will be destroyed as a nation Ps 83:4; Isa 16:14
because she defied the LORD. ver 26
43 Terror and pit and snare await you, Isa 24:17
you people of Moab,"
declares the LORD.

[a] 41 Or *The cities*

44 "Whoever flees from the terror 1Ki 19:17; Isa 24:18
will fall into a pit,
whoever climbs out of the pit
will be caught in a snare;
for I will bring on Moab
the year of her punishment," Jer 11:23
declares the LORD.

45 "In the shadow of Heshbon
the fugitives stand helpless,
for a fire has gone out from
Heshbon,
a blaze from the midst of
Sihon; Nu 21:21,26-28
it burns the foreheads of
Moab,
the skulls of the noisy
boasters. Nu 24:17
46 Woe to you, Moab! Nu 21:29
The people of Chemosh are
destroyed;
your sons are taken into exile
and your daughters into
captivity.

47 "Yet I will restore the fortunes
of Moab Jer 49:6,39
in days to come,"
declares the LORD.

Here ends the judgment on Moab.

A Message About Ammon

49 Concerning the Ammonites: Am 1:13; Zep 2:8-9

This is what the LORD says:

"Has Israel no sons?
Has Israel no heir?
Why then has Molek[a]
taken possession
of Gad? Lev 18:21
Why do his people live in its
towns?
2 But the days are coming,"
declares the LORD,
"when I will sound the battle
cry Jer 4:19
against Rabbah of the
Ammonites; Dt 3:11
it will become a mound of
ruins, Dt 13:16
and its surrounding villages
will be set on fire.
Then Israel will drive out
those who drove her out," Isa 14:2; Eze 21:28-32; 25:2-11
says the LORD.
3 "Wail, Heshbon, for Ai is
destroyed! Jos 8:28
Cry out, you inhabitants of
Rabbah!
Put on sackcloth and mourn;
rush here and there inside
the walls,
for Molek will go into exile, Jer 48:7
together with his priests and
officials.
4 Why do you boast of your
valleys,
boast of your valleys so
fruitful?
Unfaithful Daughter Ammon, Jer 3:6
you trust in your riches and
say, Jer 9:23; 1Ti 6:17
'Who will attack me?' Jer 21:13

[a] 1 Or *their king*; also in verse 3

[5]I will bring terror on you
from all those around you,"
declares the Lord,
the LORD Almighty.
"Every one of you will be
driven away,
and no one will gather the
fugitives.

[6]"Yet afterward, I will restore
the fortunes of the
Ammonites," ver 39; Jer 48:47
declares the LORD.

A Message About Edom

[7]Concerning Edom: Eze 25:12

This is what the LORD Almighty
says:

"Is there no longer wisdom in
Teman? Ge 36:11,15,34
Has counsel perished from
the prudent?
Has their wisdom decayed?
[8]Turn and flee, hide in deep
caves,
you who live in Dedan, Jer 25:23
for I will bring disaster on Esau
at the time when I punish
him.
[9]If grape pickers came to you,
would they not leave a few
grapes?
If thieves came during the night,
would they not steal only as
much as they wanted?
[10]But I will strip Esau bare;
I will uncover his hiding
places,
so that he cannot conceal
himself.
His armed men are destroyed,
also his allies and
neighbors,
so there is no one to say,
Ob 1:5-6; Mal 1:2-5
[11]'Leave your fatherless children;
I will keep them alive.
Hos 14:3
Your widows too can depend
on me.'" Dt 10:18; Jas 1:27

[12]This is what the LORD says: "If
those who do not deserve to drink
the cup must drink it, why should
you go unpunished? You will not
go unpunished, but must drink it.
[13]I swear by myself," declares the
LORD, "that Bozrah will become a
ruin and a curse,[a] an object of horror and reproach; and all its towns
will be in ruins forever."
Isa 34:6; Jer 25:28-29

[14]I have heard a message from
the LORD;
an envoy was sent to the
nations to say,
"Assemble yourselves to
attack it!
Rise up for battle!"

[15]"Now I will make you
small among the
nations,
despised by mankind.
[16]The terror you inspire
and the pride of your heart
have deceived you,
you who live in the clefts of the
rocks,

[a] *13* That is, its name will be used in cursing (see 29:22); or, others will see that it is cursed.

who occupy the heights of
the hill.
Though you build your nest
as high as the eagle's,
Job 39:27; Am 9:2
from there I will bring you
down,"
declares the LORD.
17 "Edom will become an object of
horror;
all who pass by will be
appalled and will scoff
because of all its wounds.
Jer 50:13; Eze 35:7
18 As Sodom and Gomorrah were
overthrown, Ge 19:24; Dt 29:23
along with their neighboring
towns,"
says the LORD,
"so no one will live there;
no people will dwell in it.
Isa 34:10
19 "Like a lion coming up from
Jordan's thickets Jer 12:5
to a rich pastureland,
I will chase Edom from its land
in an instant.
Who is the chosen one I will
appoint for this?
Who is like me and who can
challenge me? Jer 50:44
And what shepherd can
stand against me?"
1Sa 17:35
20 Therefore, hear what the LORD
has planned against
Edom, Isa 34:5
what he has purposed
against those who live in
Teman: Isa 14:27
The young of the flock will be
dragged away; Jer 50:45
their pasture will be appalled
at their fate. Mal 1:3-4
21 At the sound of their fall the
earth will tremble; Eze 26:15
their cry will resound to the
Red Sea.[a] Jer 50:46; Eze 26:18
22 Look! An eagle will soar and
swoop down, Hos 8:1
spreading its wings over
Bozrah. Ge 36:33
In that day the hearts of
Edom's warriors Jer 50:36
will be like the heart of
a woman in labor.
Isa 13:8; Jer 48:40-41

A Message About Damascus

23 Concerning Damascus:
Ge 14:15; 2Ch 16:2; Ac 9:2

"Hamath and Arpad are
dismayed, Isa 10:9
for they have heard bad
news.
They are disheartened,
troubled like[b] the restless
sea. Isa 57:20
24 Damascus has become feeble,
she has turned to flee
and panic has gripped her;
anguish and pain have seized
her,
pain like that of a woman in
labor.
25 Why has the city of renown not
been abandoned,
the town in which I delight?

[a] 21 *Or the Sea of Reeds* [b] 23 Hebrew *on* or *by*

26 Surely, her young men will fall
in the streets;
all her soldiers will be
silenced in that day,"
Jer 50:30
declares the LORD
Almighty.
27 "I will set fire to the walls of
Damascus; Am 1:4
it will consume the fortresses
of Ben-Hadad." 1Ki 15:18

A Message About Kedar and Hazor

28 Concerning Kedar and the
kingdoms of Hazor, which Nebuchadnezzar king of Babylon attacked: Ge 25:13

This is what the LORD says:

"Arise, and attack Kedar
and destroy the people of the
East. Jdg 6:3
29 Their tents and their flocks will
be taken;
their shelters will be carried
off
with all their goods and
camels.
People will shout to them,
'Terror on every side!'
Jer 6:25; 46:5
30 "Flee quickly away!
Stay in deep caves, you who
live in Hazor," Jdg 6:2
declares the LORD.
"Nebuchadnezzar king of
Babylon has plotted
against you; Jer 10:22
he has devised a plan against
you.
31 "Arise and attack a nation at
ease,
which lives in confidence,"
declares the LORD,
"a nation that has neither gates
nor bars; Eze 38:11
its people live far from
danger.
32 Their camels will become
plunder, Jdg 6:5
and their large herds will be
spoils of war.
I will scatter to the winds
those who are in distant
places[a] Jer 9:26
and will bring disaster
on them from every
side,"
declares the LORD.
33 "Hazor will become a haunt of
jackals, Isa 13:22
a desolate place forever.
Jer 10:22
No one will live there;
no people will dwell in it."
ver 18; Jer 51:37

A Message About Elam

34 This is the word of the LORD
that came to Jeremiah the prophet concerning Elam, early in the
reign of Zedekiah king of Judah:
Ge 10:22; 2Ki 24:18

35 This is what the LORD Almighty says:

"See, I will break the bow of
Elam, Isa 22:6
the mainstay of their might.

[a] 32 Or *who clip the hair by their foreheads*

36 I will bring against Elam the
four winds ver 32
from the four quarters of
heaven; Da 11:4
I will scatter them to the four
winds,
and there will not be a nation
where Elam's exiles do
not go.
37 I will shatter Elam before their
foes,
before those who want to kill
them;
I will bring disaster on them,
even my fierce anger," Jer 30:24
declares the LORD.
"I will pursue them with the
sword Jer 9:16
until I have made an end of
them.
38 I will set my throne in Elam
and destroy her king and
officials,"
declares the LORD.
39 "Yet I will restore the fortunes
of Elam Jer 48:47
in days to come,"
declares the LORD.

A Message About Babylon

50 This is the word the LORD spoke through Jeremiah the prophet concerning Babylon and the land of the Babylonians[a]: Ge 10:10; Isa 13:1

2 "Announce and proclaim
among the nations, Jer 4:16
lift up a banner and
proclaim it; Ps 20:5
keep nothing back, but say,
'Babylon will be captured; Jer 51:31
Bel will be put to shame,
Isa 46:1
Marduk filled with terror.
Jer 51:47
Her images will be put to shame
and her idols filled with
terror.' Lev 26:30
3 A nation from the north will
attack her Isa 41:25
and lay waste her land.
No one will live in it; Isa 14:22-23
both people and animals will
flee away. Zep 1:3

4 "In those days, at that time,"
declares the LORD,
"the people of Israel and the
people of Judah together
Hos 1:11
will go in tears to seek
the LORD their God.
Ezr 3:12; Jer 31:9; Hos 3:5
5 They will ask the way to Zion
Jer 31:21
and turn their faces toward it.
They will come and bind
themselves to the LORD
Jer 33:7
in an everlasting covenant
Isa 55:3; Jer 32:40; Heb 8:6-10
that will not be forgotten.

6 "My people have been lost
sheep; Isa 53:6; Mt 9:36; 10:6
their shepherds have
led them astray
Jer 23:32; Eze 13:10
and caused them to roam on
the mountains.

[a] 1 Or *Chaldeans*; also in verses 8, 25, 35 and 45

They wandered over mountain
and hill Jer 3:6; Eze 34:6
and forgot their own resting
place.
7 Whoever found them devoured
them;
their enemies said, 'We are
not guilty, Jer 2:3
for they sinned against the LORD,
their verdant pasture,
the LORD, the hope of their
ancestors.' Jer 14:8

8 "Flee out of Babylon;
Isa 48:20; Jer 51:6; Rev 18:4
leave the land of the
Babylonians,
and be like the goats that
lead the flock.
9 For I will stir up and bring
against Babylon Isa 13:17
an alliance of great nations
from the land of the
north. Isa 41:25; Jer 25:26
They will take up their
positions against her,
and from the north she will
be captured.
Their arrows will be like skilled
warriors Isa 13:18
who do not return empty-
handed.
10 So Babylonia[a] will be
plundered; Jer 30:16
all who plunder her will have
their fill,"
declares the LORD.

11 "Because you rejoice and are
glad,
you who pillage my
inheritance, Isa 47:6
because you frolic like a
heifer threshing grain
Jer 31:18
and neigh like stallions,
12 your mother will be greatly
ashamed;
she who gave you birth will
be disgraced.
She will be the least of the
nations —
a wilderness, a dry land, a
desert. Isa 21:1; Jer 25:12
13 Because of the LORD's anger she
will not be inhabited
but will be completely
desolate. Jer 9:11
All who pass Babylon will be
appalled;
they will scoff because of all
her wounds. Jer 18:16; 49:17

14 "Take up your positions around
Babylon,
all you who draw the bow.
Shoot at her! Spare no arrows,
Isa 13:18
for she has sinned against
the LORD.
15 Shout against her on every
side! Jer 51:14
She surrenders, her towers
fall,
her walls are torn down.
Jer 51:44,58
Since this is the vengeance of
the LORD, Jer 51:6
take vengeance on her;
do to her as she has
done to others.
Ps 137:8; Rev 18:6; Hab 2:7-8

[a] 10 Or *Chaldea*

16 Cut off from Babylon the sower,
and the reaper with his sickle
at harvest.
Because of the sword of the
oppressor Jer 25:38
let everyone return to their
own people, Isa 13:14
let everyone flee to their
own land. Jer 51:9

17 "Israel is a scattered flock Ps 119:176
that lions have chased away. Jer 2:15
The first to devour them
was the king of Assyria; 2Ki 17:6
the last to crush their bones Nu 24:8
was Nebuchadnezzar king of
Babylon." 2Ki 24:10,14; 25:7

18 Therefore this is what the
LORD Almighty, the God of Israel,
says:

"I will punish the king of
Babylon and his land
as I punished the king of
Assyria. Isa 10:12; Eze 31:3
19 But I will bring Israel back
to their own pasture, Jer 31:10; Eze 34:13
and they will graze on
Carmel and Bashan;
their appetite will be satisfied
on the hills of Ephraim and
Gilead. Jer 10:12-16; 33:12
20 In those days, at that time,"
declares the LORD,
"search will be made for Israel's
guilt,
but there will be none,
and for the sins of Judah, Mic 7:18-19
but none will be found,
for I will forgive the remnant
I spare. Isa 1:9; Jer 31:34

21 "Attack the land of Merathaim
and those who live in Pekod. Eze 23:23
Pursue, kill and completely
destroy[a] them,"
declares the LORD.
"Do everything I have
commanded you.
22 The noise of battle is in the
land, Jer 4:19-21; 51:54
the noise of great destruction!
23 How broken and shattered
is the hammer of the whole
earth! Isa 10:5
How desolate is Babylon Isa 14:16
among the nations!
24 I set a trap for you, Babylon, Da 5:30-31
and you were caught before
you knew it;
you were found and captured Jer 51:31
because you opposed the
LORD. Job 9:4
25 The LORD has opened his arsenal
and brought out the
weapons of his wrath, Isa 13:5
for the Sovereign LORD
Almighty has work to do
in the land of the
Babylonians. Jer 51:25,55

[a] *21* The Hebrew term refers to the irrevocable giving over of things or persons to the LORD, often by totally destroying them; also in verse 26.

26 Come against her from afar.
Break open her granaries;
pile her up like heaps of grain.
Completely destroy her Isa 14:22-23
and leave her no remnant.
27 Kill all her young bulls; Ps 68:30
let them go down to the slaughter! Isa 30:25
Woe to them! For their day has come, Job 18:20
the time for them to be punished. Jer 51:6
28 Listen to the fugitives and refugees from Babylon
declaring in Zion Isa 48:20; Jer 51:10
how the LORD our God has taken vengeance, ver 15
vengeance for his temple. 2Ki 24:13; Jer 51:11

29 "Summon archers against Babylon,
all those who draw the bow.
Encamp all around her;
let no one escape. Isa 13:18
Repay her for her deeds; Jer 51:56; Rev 18:6
do to her as she has done.
For she has defied the LORD, Isa 47:10
the Holy One of Israel. Ps 78:41
30 Therefore, her young men will fall in the streets; Isa 13:18; Jer 49:26
all her soldiers will be silenced in that day,"
declares the LORD.
31 "See, I am against you, you arrogant one," Jer 21:13
declares the Lord, the LORD Almighty,
"for your day has come,
the time for you to be punished.
32 The arrogant one will stumble and fall Ps 119:21
and no one will help her up; Am 5:2
I will kindle a fire in her towns Jer 21:14; 49:27
that will consume all who are around her."

33 This is what the LORD Almighty
says:

"The people of Israel are oppressed, Isa 58:6
and the people of Judah as well.
All their captors hold them fast,
refusing to let them go. Isa 14:17
34 Yet their Redeemer is strong; Job 19:25
the LORD Almighty is his name. Jer 51:19
He will vigorously defend their cause Jer 15:21; 51:36
so that he may bring rest to their land, Isa 14:7
but unrest to those who live in Babylon.

35 "A sword against the Babylonians!" Jer 47:6
declares the LORD —
"against those who live in Babylon

and against her officials and
wise men! Da 5:7
36 A sword against her false
prophets!
They will become fools.
A sword against her warriors!
Jer 49:22
They will be filled with
terror.
37 A sword against her horses and
chariots Jer 51:21
and all the foreigners in her
ranks!
They will become weaklings.
Jer 51:30; Na 3:13
A sword against her treasures!
Isa 45:3
They will be plundered.
38 A drought on[a] her waters!
They will dry up. Ps 137:1; Jer 51:13
For it is a land of idols, Jer 51:36
idols that will go mad with
terror.

39 "So desert creatures and
hyenas will live there,
and there the owl will
dwell.
It will never again be
inhabited
or lived in from generation
to generation.
Isa 13:19-22; 34:13-15; Jer 51:37
40 As I overthrew Sodom and
Gomorrah Ge 19:24; Mt 10:15
along with their neighboring
towns,"
declares the LORD,
"so no one will live there;
no people will dwell in it.
Jer 51:62

41 "Look! An army is coming from
the north; Jer 6:22
a great nation and many
kings
are being stirred up from
the ends of the earth.
Isa 13:4; Jer 51:22-28
42 They are armed with bows and
spears;
they are cruel and without
mercy. Isa 13:18
They sound like the roaring sea
Isa 5:30
as they ride on their
horses;
they come like men in battle
formation
to attack you, Daughter
Babylon. Jer 6:23
43 The king of Babylon has
heard reports about
them,
and his hands hang limp.
Jer 47:3
Anguish has gripped him,
pain like that of a woman in
labor. Jer 6:22-24
44 Like a lion coming up from
Jordan's thickets
to a rich pastureland,
I will chase Babylon from its
land in an instant.
Who is the chosen one I will
appoint for this? Nu 16:5
Who is like me and who
can challenge me?
Job 41:10; Jer 49:19
And what shepherd can
stand against me?"

[a] 38 Or *A sword against*

45 Therefore, hear what the LORD
has planned against
Babylon,
what he has purposed
against the land of
the Babylonians:
Isa 14:24; Jer 51:11
The young of the flock will be
dragged away;
their pasture will be appalled
at their fate.
46 At the sound of Babylon's
capture the earth will
tremble; Jer 49:21
its cry will resound
among the nations.
Rev 18:9-10

51

This is what the LORD says:

"See, I will stir up the spirit of a
destroyer Isa 13:17
against Babylon and the
people of Leb Kamai.[a]
Jer 25:12
2 I will send foreigners to
Babylon
to winnow her and to
devastate her land;
Jer 15:7; Mt 3:12
they will oppose her on every
side
in the day of her disaster.
Isa 13:9
3 Let not the archer string his
bow, Jer 50:29
nor let him put on his armor.
Jer 46:4
Do not spare her young men;
completely destroy[b] her
army.
4 They will fall down slain in
Babylon,[c] Isa 13:15
fatally wounded in her
streets. Jer 49:26; 50:30
5 For Israel and Judah have
not been forsaken
Isa 54:6-8
by their God, the LORD
Almighty,
though their land[d] is full of
guilt Hos 4:1
before the Holy One of Israel.

6 "Flee from Babylon! Jer 50:8
Run for your lives!
Do not be destroyed because
of her sins. Rev 18:4
It is time for the LORD's
vengeance; Jer 50:15
he will repay her what she
deserves. Jer 25:14
7 Babylon was a gold cup in
the LORD's hand;
Jer 25:15-16; Rev 14:8-10; 17:4
she made the whole earth
drunk.
The nations drank her wine;
therefore they have now
gone mad.
8 Babylon will suddenly fall
and be broken.
Isa 21:9; Rev 14:8
Wail over her!
Get balm for her pain; Jer 46:11
perhaps she can be healed.

[a] 1 *Leb Kamai* is a cryptogram for Chaldea, that is, Babylonia. [b] 3 The Hebrew term refers to the irrevocable giving over of things or persons to the LORD, often by totally destroying them. [c] 4 Or *Chaldea* [d] 5 Or *Almighty, / and the land of the Babylonians*

9 " 'We would have healed
Babylon,
but she cannot be healed;
let us leave her and each
go to our own land,
Isa 13:14; Jer 50:16
for her judgment reaches to
the skies, Rev 18:4-5
it rises as high as the
heavens.'

10 " 'The LORD has vindicated us;
Mic 7:9
come, let us tell in Zion
what the LORD our God has
done.' Jer 50:28

11 "Sharpen the arrows, Jer 50:9
take up the shields! Jer 46:4
The LORD has stirred up the
kings of the Medes, Isa 41:2
because his purpose is to
destroy Babylon. Jer 50:45
The LORD will take vengeance,
vengeance for his temple.
Jer 50:28
12 Lift up a banner against the
walls of Babylon! Ps 20:5
Reinforce the guard,
station the watchmen, 2Sa 18:24
prepare an ambush! Jer 50:24
The LORD will carry out his
purpose, Ps 33:11
his decree against the people
of Babylon.
13 You who live by many waters
Rev 17:1,15
and are rich in treasures,
Isa 45:3; Hab 2:9
your end has come,
the time for you to be
destroyed. Jer 50:3

14 The LORD Almighty has sworn
by himself: Am 6:8
I will surely fill you with
troops, as with a swarm
of locusts, Na 3:15
and they will shout in
triumph over you. Jer 50:15

15 "He made the earth by his
power;
he founded the world by his
wisdom
and stretched out the
heavens by his
understanding.
Ge 1:1; Ps 104:2; 136:5
16 When he thunders, the waters
in the heavens roar;
Ps 18:11-13
he makes clouds rise from
the ends of the earth.
He sends lightning with the
rain
and brings out the wind
from his storehouses.
Ps 13:7; Jnh 1:4

17 "Everyone is senseless and
without knowledge;
every goldsmith is shamed
by his idols.
The images he makes are a
fraud; Isa 44:20; Hab 2:18-19
they have no breath in them.
18 They are worthless, the objects
of mockery; Jer 18:15
when their judgment comes,
they will perish.
19 He who is the Portion of Jacob
is not like these, Ps 119:57
for he is the Maker of all
things,

including the people of his
inheritance— Ex 34:9
the LORD Almighty is his
name.

20 "You are my war club, Isa 10:5
my weapon for battle—
with you I shatter nations,
Mic 4:13
with you I destroy kingdoms,
21 with you I shatter horse and
rider, Ex 15:1
with you I shatter chariot
and driver, Jer 50:37
22 with you I shatter man and
woman,
with you I shatter old man
and youth,
with you I shatter young
man and young woman,
2Ch 36:17; Isa 13:17-18
23 with you I shatter shepherd
and flock,
with you I shatter farmer
and oxen,
with you I shatter governors
and officials.

24 "Before your eyes I will repay
Babylon and all who live in Babylonia[a] for all the wrong they have
done in Zion," declares the LORD.
Jer 50:15

25 "I am against you, you
destroying mountain,
Jer 21:13
you who destroy the whole
earth,"
declares the LORD.
"I will stretch out my hand
against you,
roll you off the cliffs,
and make you a burned-out
mountain. Zec 4:7
26 No rock will be taken from you
for a cornerstone,
nor any stone for a
foundation,
for you will be desolate
forever,"
declares the LORD.

27 "Lift up a banner in the land!
Isa 13:2; Jer 50:2
Blow the trumpet among the
nations!
Prepare the nations for battle
against her;
summon against her these
kingdoms: Jer 25:14
Ararat, Minni and Ashkenaz.
Ge 8:4; 10:3
Appoint a commander against
her;
send up horses like a swarm
of locusts.
28 Prepare the nations for battle
against her—
the kings of the Medes, ver 11
their governors and all their
officials,
and all the countries they rule.
29 The land trembles and writhes,
Jer 49:21
for the LORD's purposes
against Babylon stand—
Ps 33:11
to lay waste the land of
Babylon Jer 48:9
so that no one will live there.
Isa 13:20

[a] 24 Or *Chaldea*; also in verse 35

30 Babylon's warriors have
stopped fighting; Jer 50:36
they remain in their
strongholds.
Their strength is exhausted;
they have become weaklings.
Isa 19:16
Her dwellings are set on fire;
Isa 47:14
the bars of her gates are
broken. La 2:9; Na 3:13
31 One courier follows another
2Sa 18:19-31
and messenger follows
messenger
to announce to the king of
Babylon
that his entire city is
captured, Jer 50:2
32 the river crossings seized,
the marshes set on fire,
Isa 47:14
and the soldiers terrified."
Jer 50:36

33 This is what the LORD Almighty, the God of Israel, says:

"Daughter Babylon is like a
threshing floor Isa 21:10
at the time it is trampled;
the time to harvest her will
soon come." Isa 17:5; Hos 6:11

34 "Nebuchadnezzar king of
Babylon has
devoured us,
Jer 50:17; Hos 8:8
he has thrown us into
confusion,
he has made us an empty
jar.
Like a serpent he has
swallowed us
and filled his stomach with
our delicacies,
and then has spewed us out.
Lev 18:25
35 May the violence done to our
flesh[a] be on Babylon,"
Hab 2:17
say the inhabitants of Zion.
"May our blood be on those
who live in Babylonia,"
says Jerusalem. Ps 137:8

36 Therefore this is what the
LORD says:

"See, I will defend your cause
Ps 140:12; Jer 50:34
and avenge you; Ro 12:19
I will dry up her sea Jer 50:38
and make her springs dry.
37 Babylon will be a heap of ruins,
a haunt of jackals,
Isa 13:22; Rev 18:2
an object of horror and scorn,
a place where no one lives.
Jer 50:13,39
38 Her people all roar like young
lions,
they growl like lion cubs.
39 But while they are aroused,
I will set out a feast for
them
and make them drunk, Isa 21:5
so that they shout with
laughter —
then sleep forever and not
awake," Ps 13:3
declares the LORD.

[a] 35 Or *done to us and to our children*

40 "I will bring them down
like lambs to the slaughter,
like rams and goats. Eze 39:18

41 "How Sheshak[a] will be
captured, Isa 13:19; Jer 25:26
the boast of the whole earth
seized!
How desolate Babylon will be
among the nations!
42 The sea will rise over
Babylon;
its roaring waves will cover
her. Isa 8:7
43 Her towns will be desolate,
a dry and desert land,
a land where no one lives,
through which no one
travels. Isa 13:20; Jer 2:6
44 I will punish Bel in Babylon
Isa 46:1
and make him spew out
what he has swallowed.
The nations will no longer
stream to him.
And the wall of Babylon will
fall. Jer 50:15

45 "Come out of her, my people!
Rev 18:4
Run for your lives! Jer 50:8
Run from the fierce anger of
the LORD. Ps 76:10
46 Do not lose heart or be afraid
Jer 46:27
when rumors are heard in
the land; 2Ki 19:7
one rumor comes this year,
another the next,
rumors of violence in the
land
and of ruler against ruler.

47 For the time will surely come
when I will punish the
idols of Babylon;
Isa 46:1-2; Jer 50:2
her whole land will be
disgraced Jer 50:12
and her slain will all lie
fallen within her.
48 Then heaven and earth and all
that is in them
will shout for joy over
Babylon, Isa 44:23; Rev 18:20
for out of the north Isa 41:25
destroyers will attack her,"
declares the LORD.

49 "Babylon must fall because of
Israel's slain,
just as the slain in all the
earth
have fallen because of
Babylon. Jer 50:29
50 You who have escaped the
sword,
leave and do not linger! ver 45
Remember the LORD in a
distant land, Ps 137:6
and call to mind Jerusalem."

51 "We are disgraced, Ps 44:13-16; 79:4
for we have been insulted
and shame covers our faces,
because foreigners have
entered
the holy places of the LORD's
house." La 1:10

52 "But days are coming," declares
the LORD,
"when I will punish her
idols,

[a] 41 *Sheshak* is a cryptogram for Babylon.

and throughout her land
the wounded will groan.
53 Even if Babylon ascends to the heavens Isa 14:13-14
and fortifies her lofty stronghold,
I will send destroyers against her," Jer 49:16
declares the LORD.

54 "The sound of a cry comes from Babylon,
the sound of great destruction Jer 50:22
from the land of the Babylonians.[a]
55 The LORD will destroy Babylon;
he will silence her noisy din.
Waves of enemies will rage like great waters; Ps 18:4
the roar of their voices will resound.
56 A destroyer will come against Babylon;
her warriors will be captured,
and their bows will be broken. Ps 46:9
For the LORD is a God of retribution;
he will repay in full. Ps 94:1-2; Hab 2:8
57 I will make her officials and wise men drunk,
her governors, officers and warriors as well;
they will sleep forever and not awake," Ps 76:5; Jer 25:27
declares the King, whose name is the LORD Almighty. Jer 46:18; 48:15

58 This is what the LORD Almighty says:

"Babylon's thick wall will be leveled Isa 15:1
and her high gates set on fire; Isa 13:2
the peoples exhaust themselves for nothing, Isa 47:13
the nations' labor is only fuel for the flames." Hab 2:13

59 This is the message Jeremiah the prophet gave to the staff
officer Seraiah son of Neriah, the
son of Mahseiah, when he went to
Babylon with Zedekiah king of Judah in the fourth year of his reign.
60 Jeremiah had written on a scroll
about all the disasters that would
come upon Babylon — all that had
been recorded concerning Babylon. 61 He said to Seraiah, "When
you get to Babylon, see that you
read all these words aloud. 62 Then
say, 'LORD, you have said you will
destroy this place, so that neither
people nor animals will live in it;
it will be desolate forever.' 63 When
you finish reading this scroll, tie
a stone to it and throw it into the
Euphrates. 64 Then say, 'So will Babylon sink to rise no more because
of the disaster I will bring on her.
And her people will fall.' " Rev 18:21; Jer 50:13,39

The words of Jeremiah end here.

[a] 54 Or *Chaldeans*

The Fall of Jerusalem

52 Zedekiah was twenty-one years old when he became king, and he reigned in Jerusalem eleven years. His mother's name was Hamutal daughter of Jeremiah; she was from Libnah. 2 He did evil in the eyes of the LORD, just as Jehoiakim had done. 3 It was because of the LORD's anger that all this happened to Jerusalem and Judah, and in the end he thrust them from his presence.

2Ki 24:17; Jer 36:30

Now Zedekiah rebelled against the king of Babylon.

2Ki 24:18-20; 2Ch 36:11-16

4 So in the ninth year of Zedekiah's reign, on the tenth day of the tenth month, Nebuchadnezzar king of Babylon marched against Jerusalem with his whole army. They encamped outside the city and built siege works all around it. 5 The city was kept under siege until the eleventh year of King Zedekiah.

2Ki 25:1-7; Jer 39:1

6 By the ninth day of the fourth month the famine in the city had become so severe that there was no food for the people to eat. 7 Then the city wall was broken through, and the whole army fled. They left the city at night through the gate between the two walls near the king's garden, though the Babylonians[a] were surrounding the city. They fled toward the Arabah,[b] 8 but the Babylonian[c] army pursued King Zedekiah and overtook him in the plains of Jericho. All his soldiers were separated from him and scattered, 9 and he was captured.

Jer 32:4

He was taken to the king of Babylon at Riblah in the land of Hamath, where he pronounced sentence on him. 10 There at Riblah the king of Babylon killed the sons of Zedekiah before his eyes; he also killed all the officials of Judah. 11 Then he put out Zedekiah's eyes, bound him with bronze shackles and took him to Babylon, where he put him in prison till the day of his death.

Jer 22:30; Eze 12:13

12 On the tenth day of the fifth month, in the nineteenth year of Nebuchadnezzar king of Babylon, Nebuzaradan commander of the imperial guard, who served the king of Babylon, came to Jerusalem. 13 He set fire to the temple of the LORD, the royal palace and all the houses of Jerusalem. Every important building he burned down. 14 The whole Babylonian army, under the commander of the imperial guard, broke down all the walls around Jerusalem. 15 Nebuzaradan the commander of the guard carried into exile some of the poorest people and those who remained in the city, along with the rest of the craftsmen[d] and those who had deserted to the king of Babylon. 16 But Nebuzaradan left behind the rest of the poorest people of the

[a] 7 Or *Chaldeans*; also in verse 17 [b] 7 Or *the Jordan Valley* [c] 8 Or *Chaldean*; also in verse 14 [d] 15 Or *the populace*

land to work the vineyards and fields. Jer 39:1-10

17 The Babylonians broke up the bronze pillars, the movable stands and the bronze Sea that were at the temple of the LORD and they carried all the bronze to Babylon. 18 They also took away the pots, shovels, wick trimmers, sprinkling bowls, dishes and all the bronze articles used in the temple service. 19 The commander of the imperial guard took away the basins, censers, sprinkling bowls, pots, lampstands, dishes and bowls used for drink offerings — all that were made of pure gold or silver. Jer 27:19-22

20 The bronze from the two pillars, the Sea and the twelve bronze bulls under it, and the movable stands, which King Solomon had made for the temple of the LORD, was more than could be weighed. 21 Each pillar was eighteen cubits high and twelve cubits in circumference[a]; each was four fingers thick, and hollow. 22 The bronze capital on top of one pillar was five cubits[b] high and was decorated with a network and pomegranates of bronze all around. The other pillar, with its pomegranates, was similar. 23 There were ninety-six pomegranates on the sides; the total number of pomegranates above the surrounding network was a hundred. 2Ki 25:1-21; 2Ch 36:17-20

24 The commander of the guard took as prisoners Seraiah the chief priest, Zephaniah the priest next in rank and the three doorkeepers. 25 Of those still in the city, he took the officer in charge of the fighting men, and seven royal advisers. He also took the secretary who was chief officer in charge of conscripting the people of the land, sixty of whom were found in the city. 26 Nebuzaradan the commander took them all and brought them to the king of Babylon at Riblah. 27 There at Riblah, in the land of Hamath, the king had them executed.

2Ki 25:18; Jer 21:1; 37:3

So Judah went into captivity, away from her land. 28 This is the number of the people Nebuchadnezzar carried into exile:

2Ki 24:14-16; 2Ch 36:20

in the seventh year, 3,023
 Jews;
29 in Nebuchadnezzar's eighteenth year,
 832 people from Jerusalem;
30 in his twenty-third year,
 745 Jews taken into exile by
 Nebuzaradan the commander of the imperial
 guard. Jer 43:3
There were 4,600 people in
 all. Jer 13:19

Jehoiachin Released

31 In the thirty-seventh year of the exile of Jehoiachin king of

[a] *21* That is, about 27 feet high and 18 feet in circumference or about 8.1 meters high and 5.4 meters in circumference
[b] *22* That is, about 7 1/2 feet or about 2.3 meters

Judah, in the year Awel-Marduk
became king of Babylon, on the
twenty-fifth day of the twelfth
month, he released Jehoiachin
king of Judah and freed him from
prison. 32 He spoke kindly to him
and gave him a seat of honor higher than those of the other kings
who were with him in Babylon.
33 So Jehoiachin put aside his prison clothes and for the rest of his
life ate regularly at the king's table. 34 Day by day the king of Babylon gave Jehoiachin a regular allowance as long as he lived, till the
day of his death.

2Ki 25:27-30

LAMENTATIONS

1 [a] How deserted lies the city, Lev 26:43
once so full of people! Jer 42:2
How like a widow is she, Isa 47:8
who once was great among the nations! 1Ki 4:21
She who was queen among the provinces
has now become a slave. Isa 3:26; Jer 40:9

2 Bitterly she weeps at night, Ps 6:6
tears are on her cheeks.
Among all her lovers Jer 3:1
there is no one to comfort her.
All her friends have betrayed her; Jer 4:30; Mic 7:5
they have become her enemies. Jer 30:14

3 After affliction and harsh labor,
Judah has gone into exile. Jer 13:19
She dwells among the nations;
she finds no resting place. Dt 28:65
All who pursue her have overtaken her
in the midst of her distress.

4 The roads to Zion mourn, Ps 137:1
for no one comes to her appointed festivals.
All her gateways are desolate, Jer 9:11
her priests groan,
her young women grieve,
and she is in bitter anguish. Joel 1:8-13

5 Her foes have become her masters;
her enemies are at ease.
The LORD has brought her grief Jer 30:15
because of her many sins. Ps 5:10
Her children have gone into exile, Jer 52:28-30
captive before the foe. Ps 137:3

6 All the splendor has departed from Daughter Zion. Jer 13:18
Her princes are like deer
that find no pasture;
in weakness they have fled
before the pursuer.

7 In the days of her affliction and wandering
Jerusalem remembers all the treasures
that were hers in days of old.
When her people fell into enemy hands,
there was no one to help her. Jer 37:7; La 4:17
Her enemies looked at her
and laughed at her destruction.

[a] This chapter is an acrostic poem, the verses of which begin with the successive letters of the Hebrew alphabet.

8 Jerusalem has sinned greatly Isa 59:2-13
and so has become unclean. Jer 2:22
All who honored her despise her,
for they have all seen her naked; Jer 13:22,26
she herself groans Ps 6:6
and turns away.

9 Her filthiness clung to her skirts;
she did not consider her future. Dt 32:28-29; Isa 47:7
Her fall was astounding; Jer 13:18
there was none to comfort her. Ecc 4:1; Jer 16:7
"Look, LORD, on my affliction, Ps 25:18
for the enemy has triumphed."

10 The enemy laid hands
on all her treasures; Isa 64:11
she saw pagan nations
enter her sanctuary— Ps 74:7-8; Jer 51:51
those you had forbidden Dt 23:3
to enter your assembly.

11 All her people groan Ps 38:8
as they search for bread; Jer 52:6
they barter their treasures for food
to keep themselves alive.
"Look, LORD, and consider,
for I am despised."

12 "Is it nothing to you, all you who pass by? Jer 18:16
Look around and see.
Is any suffering like my suffering
that was inflicted on me,
that the LORD brought on me
in the day of his fierce anger? Jer 30:24

13 "From on high he sent fire,
sent it down into my bones. Job 30:30
He spread a net for my feet
and turned me back.
He made me desolate, Jer 44:6
faint all the day long. Hab 3:16

14 "My sins have been bound into a yoke[a]; Dt 28:48; Isa 47:6
by his hands they were woven together.
They have been hung on my neck,
and the Lord has sapped my strength.
He has given me into the hands Jer 32:5
of those I cannot withstand.

15 "The Lord has rejected
all the warriors in my midst; Jer 37:10
he has summoned an army against me Isa 41:2
to[b] crush my young men. Jer 18:21
In his winepress the Lord has trampled Jdg 6:11
Virgin Daughter Judah. Jer 14:17

[a] 14 Most Hebrew manuscripts; many Hebrew manuscripts and Septuagint *He kept watch over my sins* [b] 15 Or *has set a time for me / when he will*

16 "This is why I weep
and my eyes overflow with tears. La 2:11,18; 3:48-49
No one is near to comfort me, Ps 69:20; Ecc 4:1
no one to restore my spirit.
My children are destitute
because the enemy has prevailed." Jer 13:17; 14:17

17 Zion stretches out her hands, Jer 4:31
but there is no one to comfort her.
The LORD has decreed for Jacob
that his neighbors become his foes; Ex 23:21
Jerusalem has become
an unclean thing among them. Lev 18:25-28

18 "The LORD is righteous, Ex 9:27
yet I rebelled against his command. 1Sa 12:14
Listen, all you peoples;
look on my suffering.
My young men and young women
have gone into exile. Dt 28:32,41

19 "I called to my allies
but they betrayed me.
My priests and my elders
perished in the city Jer 14:15; La 2:20
while they searched for food
to keep themselves alive.

20 "See, LORD, how distressed I am! Jer 4:19
I am in torment within, La 2:11
and in my heart I am disturbed,
for I have been most rebellious.
Outside, the sword bereaves;
inside, there is only death. Dt 32:25; Eze 7:15

21 "People have heard my groaning, ver 8; Ps 6:6
but there is no one to comfort me. ver 4
All my enemies have heard of my distress;
they rejoice at what you have done. La 2:15
May you bring the day
you have announced Jer 30:16
so they may become like me.

22 "Let all their wickedness come before you;
deal with them
as you have dealt with me
because of all my sins. Ne 4:5
My groans are many Ps 6:6
and my heart is faint."

2

[a] How the Lord has covered Daughter Zion
with the cloud of his anger[b]! La 3:44
He has hurled down the splendor of Israel
from heaven to earth;
he has not remembered his footstool Ps 99:5; 132:7
in the day of his anger. Jer 12:7

[a] This chapter is an acrostic poem, the verses of which begin with the successive letters of the Hebrew alphabet. [b] 1 Or *How the Lord in his anger / has treated Daughter Zion with contempt*

2 Without pity the Lord
has swallowed up Ps 21:9; La 3:43
all the dwellings of Jacob;
in his wrath he has torn down
the strongholds of Daughter
Judah. Ps 89:39-40; Mic 5:11
He has brought her kingdom
and its princes
down to the ground in
dishonor. Isa 25:12

3 In fierce anger he has cut off
every horn[a,b] of Israel. Ps 75:5,10
He has withdrawn his right
hand Ps 74:11
at the approach of the
enemy.
He has burned in Jacob like a
flaming fire
that consumes
everything around it.
Isa 42:25; Jer 21:4-5,14

4 Like an enemy he has strung
his bow; La 3:12-13
his right hand is ready.
Like a foe he has slain
all who were pleasing to the
eye; Eze 24:16,25
he has poured out his wrath
like fire Jer 7:20
on the tent of Daughter Zion.
Jer 4:20

5 The Lord is like an enemy;
Jer 30:14
he has swallowed up Israel.
He has swallowed up all her
palaces
and destroyed her
strongholds. ver 2
He has multiplied mourning
and lamentation
for Daughter Judah. Jer 9:17-20

6 He has laid waste his dwelling
like a garden;
he has destroyed his place of
meeting. Jer 52:13
The LORD has made Zion
forget
her appointed festivals and
her Sabbaths; Zep 3:18
in his fierce anger he has
spurned
both king and priest. La 4:16

7 The Lord has rejected his altar
and abandoned his
sanctuary. Eze 7:24
He has given the walls of her
palaces
into the hands of the enemy;
Ps 74:7-8; Isa 64:11; Jer 33:4-5
they have raised a shout in the
house of the LORD
as on the day of an
appointed festival.

8 The LORD determined to tear
down
the wall around Daughter
Zion.
He stretched out a measuring
line 2Ki 21:13; Isa 34:11
and did not withhold his
hand from destroying.
He made ramparts and walls
lament; Ps 48:13
together they wasted away.
Isa 3:26

[a] 3 Or *off / all the strength*; or *every king*
[b] 3 *Horn* here symbolizes strength.

9 Her gates have sunk into the
ground; Ne 1:3
their bars he has broken and
destroyed.
Her king and her princes
are exiled among the
nations, Dt 28:36
the law is no more, 2Ch 15:3
and her prophets no longer
find
visions from the LORD. Jer 14:14

10 The elders of Daughter Zion
sit on the ground in silence;
they have sprinkled dust on
their heads Job 2:12
and put on sackcloth. Isa 15:3
The young women of
Jerusalem
have bowed their heads to
the ground. Job 2:13; Isa 3:26

11 My eyes fail from weeping,
La 13:48-51
I am in torment within; La 1:20
my heart is poured out on the
ground ver 19; Ps 22:14
because my people are
destroyed,
because children and infants
faint La 4:4
in the streets of the city.

12 They say to their mothers,
"Where is bread and wine?"
as they faint like the wounded
in the streets of the city,
as their lives ebb away
in their mothers' arms. La 4:4

13 What can I say for you?
With what can I compare you,
Daughter Jerusalem?
To what can I liken you,
that I may comfort you,
Virgin Daughter Zion? Isa 37:22
Your wound is as deep as the
sea. Jer 14:17; La 1:12
Who can heal you?

14 The visions of your prophets
were false and worthless;
Jer 28:15
they did not expose your sin
to ward off your captivity.
Isa 58:1
The prophecies they gave you
were false and misleading.
Jer 2:8; 29:9

15 All who pass your way
clap their hands at you; Eze 25:6
they scoff and shake their
heads Jer 19:8
at Daughter Jerusalem: La 1:21
"Is this the city that was called
the perfection of beauty, Ps 50:2
the joy of the whole earth?"
Ps 48:2

16 All your enemies open their
mouths
wide against you; Ps 56:2; La 3:46
they scoff and gnash their
teeth Job 16:9
and say, "We have swallowed
her up. Ps 35:25
This is the day we have waited
for;
we have lived to see it." Mic 4:11

17 The LORD has done what he
planned;
he has fulfilled his word,
which he decreed long ago.
Dt 28:15-45

He has overthrown you
without pity, ver 2; Eze 5:11
he has let the enemy gloat
over you, Ps 22:17
he has exalted the horn[a] of
your foes. Ps 89:42

18 The hearts of the people
cry out to the Lord. Ps 119:145
You walls of Daughter Zion,
let your tears flow like a river La 1:16
day and night; Jer 9:1
give yourself no relief,
your eyes no rest. La 3:49

19 Arise, cry out in the night,
as the watches of the night
begin;
pour out your heart like water 1Sa 1:15; Ps 62:8
in the presence of the Lord. Isa 26:9
Lift up your hands to him
for the lives of your
children,
who faint from hunger Isa 51:20
at every street corner.

20 "Look, LORD, and consider:
Whom have you ever treated
like this?
Should women eat their
offspring, Jer 19:9
the children they have cared
for? La 4:10
Should priest and prophet be
killed Ps 78:64; Jer 14:15
in the sanctuary of the Lord? La 1:19

21 "Young and old lie together
in the dust of the streets;
my young men and young
women
have fallen by the sword. 2Ch 36:17; Ps 78:62-63; Jer 6:11
You have slain them in the day
of your anger;
you have slaughtered
them without pity. Jer 13:14; La 3:43; Zec 11:6

22 "As you summon to a feast day,
so you summoned against
me terrors on every side. Ps 31:13; Jer 6:25
In the day of the LORD's anger
no one escaped or survived; Jer 11:11
those I cared for and reared Hos 9:13
my enemy has destroyed."

3[b]

I am the man who has seen
affliction
by the rod of the LORD's
wrath. Job 19:21; Ps 88:7
2 He has driven me away and
made me walk
in darkness rather than light; Jer 4:23
3 indeed, he has turned his hand
against me Isa 5:25
again and again, all day long.

4 He has made my skin and my
flesh grow old
and has broken my bones. Ps 51:8; Isa 38:13; Jer 50:17

[a] 17 *Horn* here symbolizes strength.
[b] This chapter is an acrostic poem; the verses of each stanza begin with the successive letters of the Hebrew alphabet, and the verses within each stanza begin with the same letter.

5 He has besieged me and
surrounded me
with bitterness and hardship.
ver 19; Jer 23:15
6 He has made me dwell in
darkness
like those long dead. Ps 88:5-6
7 He has walled me in so I cannot
escape; Job 3:23
he has weighed me down
with chains. Jer 40:4
8 Even when I call out or cry for
help,
he shuts out my prayer.
Job 30:20; Ps 22:2
9 He has barred my way with
blocks of stone;
he has made my paths
crooked. Isa 63:17; Hos 2:6

10 Like a bear lying in wait,
like a lion in hiding,
Hos 13:8; Am 5:18-19
11 he dragged me from the path
and mangled me Hos 6:1
and left me without help.
12 He drew his bow La 2:4
and made me the target
for his arrows.
Job 7:20; Ps 7:12-13; 38:2

13 He pierced my heart
with arrows from his quiver.
Job 6:4
14 I became the laughingstock of
all my people; Jer 20:7
they mock me in song all day
long. Job 30:9
15 He has filled me with bitter herbs
and given me gall to drink.
Jer 9:15

16 He has broken my teeth with
gravel; Pr 20:17
he has trampled me in the
dust. Ps 7:5
17 I have been deprived of peace;
I have forgotten what
prosperity is.
18 So I say, "My splendor is gone
and all that I had hoped
from the LORD." Job 17:15

19 I remember my affliction and
my wandering,
the bitterness and the gall.
20 I well remember them,
and my soul is downcast
within me. Ps 42:5,11
21 Yet this I call to mind
and therefore I have hope:

22 Because of the LORD's great
love we are not
consumed, Ps 103:11; Hos 11:9
for his compassions never
fail. Ps 78:38; Mal 3:6
23 They are new every morning;
great is your faithfulness.
Zep 3:5
24 I say to myself, "The LORD is
my portion; Ps 16:5
therefore I will wait for him."

25 The LORD is good to those
whose hope is in him,
to the one who seeks him;
Isa 25:9; 30:18
26 it is good to wait quietly Isa 30:15
for the salvation of the LORD.
Ps 37:7; 40:1
27 It is good for a man to bear the
yoke
while he is young.

28 Let him sit alone in silence,
Jer 15:17
for the LORD has laid it on him.
29 Let him bury his face in the dust —
there may yet be hope. Jer 31:17
30 Let him offer his cheek to one who would strike him,
Job 16:10; Isa 50:6
and let him be filled with disgrace.

31 For no one is cast off
by the Lord forever.
Ps 94:14; Isa 54:7
32 Though he brings grief, he will show compassion,
so great is his unfailing love.
Ps 78:38; Hos 11:8
33 For he does not willingly bring affliction
or grief to anyone. Eze 33:11

34 To crush underfoot
all prisoners in the land,
35 to deny people their rights
before the Most High,
36 to deprive them of justice —
would not the Lord see such things?
Jer 22:3; Hab 1:13

37 Who can speak and have it happen
if the Lord has not decreed it? Ps 33:9-11
38 Is it not from the mouth of the Most High
that both calamities and good things come?
Job 2:10; Isa 45:7; Jer 32:42
39 Why should the living complain
when punished for their sins? Jer 30:15; Mic 7:9

40 Let us examine our ways and test them, 2Co 13:5
and let us return to the LORD.
Ps 119:59; 139:23-24
41 Let us lift up our hearts and our hands
to God in heaven, and say:
Ps 25:1; 28:2
42 "We have sinned and rebelled
Da 9:5
and you have not forgiven.
Jer 5:7-9

43 "You have covered yourself with anger and pursued us;
you have slain without pity.
La 2:2,17,21
44 You have covered yourself with a cloud Ps 97:2
so that no prayer can get through. Zec 7:13
45 You have made us scum and refuse 1Co 4:13
among the nations.

46 "All our enemies have opened their mouths
wide against us. La 2:16
47 We have suffered terror and pitfalls, Jer 48:43
ruin and destruction."
Isa 24:17-18
48 Streams of tears flow from my eyes La 1:16
because my people are destroyed. La 2:11

49 My eyes will flow unceasingly,
without relief, Jer 14:17
50 until the LORD looks down
from heaven and sees. Isa 63:15
51 What I see brings grief to my
soul
because of all the women of
my city.

52 Those who were my enemies
without cause
hunted me like a bird. Ps 35:7
53 They tried to end my life in a
pit Jer 37:16
and threw stones at me;
54 the waters closed over my
head, Ps 69:2; Jnh 2:3-5
and I thought I was about to
perish. Ps 88:5

55 I called on your name, LORD,
from the depths of the pit.
Ps 130:1; Jnh 2:2
56 You heard my plea: "Do not
close your ears Ps 55:1
to my cry for relief."
57 You came near when I called
you, Ps 46:1
and you said, "Do not fear."
Isa 41:10

58 You, Lord, took up my case;
Jer 51:36
you redeemed my life.
Ps 34:22; Jer 50:34
59 LORD, you have seen the wrong
done to me. Jer 18:19-20
Uphold my cause!
60 You have seen the depth of
their vengeance,
all their plots against me.
Jer 11:20; 18:18

61 LORD, you have heard their
insults, Ps 89:50
all their plots against me —
62 what my enemies whisper and
mutter
against me all day long.
Eze 36:3

63 Look at them! Sitting or
standing,
they mock me in their songs.
64 Pay them back what they
deserve, LORD,
for what their hands have
done. Ps 28:4
65 Put a veil over their hearts,
Isa 6:10
and may your curse be on
them!
66 Pursue them in anger and
destroy them
from under the heavens of
the LORD.

4 [a] How the gold has lost its
luster,
the fine gold become dull!
The sacred gems are scattered
at every street corner. Eze 7:19

2 How the precious children of
Zion, Isa 51:18
once worth their weight in
gold,
are now considered as pots of
clay,
the work of a potter's hands!

3 Even jackals offer their breasts
to nurse their young,

[a] This chapter is an acrostic poem, the verses of which begin with the successive letters of the Hebrew alphabet.

but my people have become
heartless
like ostriches in the desert.
Job 39:16

4 Because of thirst the infant's
tongue
sticks to the roof of its
mouth; Ps 22:15
the children beg for bread,
but no one gives it to them.
La 2:11-12

5 Those who once ate delicacies
are destitute in the streets.
Those brought up in royal
purple Jer 6:2
now lie on ash heaps. Am 6:3-7

6 The punishment of my people
is greater than that of
Sodom, Ge 19:25
which was overthrown in a
moment
without a hand turned to
help her.

7 Their princes were brighter
than snow
and whiter than milk,
their bodies more ruddy than
rubies,
their appearance like lapis
lazuli.

8 But now they are blacker than
soot; Job 30:28
they are not recognized in
the streets.
Their skin has shriveled on
their bones; Ps 102:3-5
it has become as dry as a
stick.

9 Those killed by the sword are
better off
than those who die of
famine;
racked with hunger, they waste
away
for lack of food from the
field. Jer 15:2; 16:4

10 With their own hands
compassionate women
have cooked their own
children, Dt 28:53-57; La 2:20
who became their food
when my people were
destroyed.

11 The LORD has given full vent to
his wrath; Job 20:23
he has poured out his fierce
anger. Zep 2:2; 3:8
He kindled a fire in Zion Jer 17:27
that consumed her
foundations.
Dt 32:22; Jer 7:20

12 The kings of the earth did not
believe,
nor did any of the peoples of
the world,
that enemies and foes could
enter
the gates of Jerusalem.
1Ki 9:9; Jer 21:13

13 But it happened because
of the sins of her
prophets
and the iniquities of her
priests, Jer 6:13; Eze 22:28
who shed within her
the blood of the righteous.
2Ki 21:16

14 Now they grope through the streets
as if they were blind. Isa 59:10
They are so defiled with blood Jer 2:34; 19:4
that no one dares to touch their garments.

15 "Go away! You are unclean!" people cry to them.
"Away! Away! Don't touch us!"
When they flee and wander about,
people among the nations say,
"They can stay here no longer." Lev 13:46

16 The LORD himself has scattered them;
he no longer watches over them. Isa 9:14-16
The priests are shown no honor,
the elders no favor. La 5:12

17 Moreover, our eyes failed,
looking in vain for help; Isa 20:5; La 1:7; Eze 29:16
from our towers we watched
for a nation that could not save us. Jer 37:7

18 People stalked us at every step,
so we could not walk in our streets.
Our end was near, our days were numbered,
for our end had come. Eze 7:2-12; Am 8:2

19 Our pursuers were swifter
than eagles in the sky; Dt 28:49
they chased us over the mountains Isa 5:26-28
and lay in wait for us in the desert. Jer 52:7

20 The LORD's anointed, our very life breath, 2Sa 19:21
was caught in their traps. Jer 39:5; Eze 12:12-13; 19:4,8
We thought that under his shadow
we would live among the nations.

21 Rejoice and be glad, Daughter Edom,
you who live in the land of Uz.
But to you also the cup will be passed; Jer 25:15
you will be drunk and stripped naked. Am 1:11-12; Ob 1:16

22 Your punishment will end, Daughter Zion; Isa 40:2; Jer 33:8
he will not prolong your exile.
But he will punish your sin, Daughter Edom,
and expose your wickedness. Ps 137:7; Mal 1:4

5 Remember, LORD, what has happened to us;
look, and see our disgrace. Ps 44:13-16; 89:50
2 Our inheritance has been turned over to strangers, Ps 79:1
our homes to foreigners. Zep 1:13

3 We have become fatherless,
our mothers are widows. Jer 15:8; 18:21
4 We must buy the water we drink;
our wood can be had only at a price. Isa 3:1
5 Those who pursue us are at our heels;
we are weary and find no rest. Jos 1:13; Ne 9:37
6 We submitted to Egypt and Assyria Hos 9:3
to get enough bread.
7 Our ancestors sinned and are no more,
and we bear their punishment. Jer 14:20; 16:12
8 Slaves rule over us, Ne 5:15
and there is no one to free us from their hands. Zec 11:6
9 We get our bread at the risk of our lives
because of the sword in the desert.
10 Our skin is hot as an oven,
feverish from hunger. La 4:8-9
11 Women have been violated in Zion, Zec 14:2
and virgins in the towns of Judah.
12 Princes have been hung up by their hands;
elders are shown no respect. La 4:16
13 Young men toil at the millstones;
boys stagger under loads of wood.
14 The elders are gone from the city gate;
the young men have stopped their music. Jer 7:34
15 Joy is gone from our hearts;
our dancing has turned to mourning. Jer 25:10
16 The crown has fallen from our head. Ps 89:39
Woe to us, for we have sinned! Isa 3:11
17 Because of this our hearts are faint, Isa 1:5
because of these things our eyes grow dim Ps 6:7
18 for Mount Zion, which lies desolate, Mic 3:12
with jackals prowling over it.

19 You, LORD, reign forever;
your throne endures from generation to generation. Ps 45:6; 102:12,24-27
20 Why do you always forget us? Ps 13:1; 44:24
Why do you forsake us so long?
21 Restore us to yourself, LORD,
that we may return; Ps 80:3
renew our days as of old
22 unless you have utterly rejected us Ps 53:5; 60:1-2
and are angry with us beyond measure. Isa 64:9

EZEKIEL

Ezekiel's Inaugural Vision

1 In my thirtieth year, in the
fourth month on the fifth day,
while I was among the exiles by
the Kebar River, the heavens were
opened and I saw visions of God.
Mt 3:16; Ac 7:56; Ex 24:10
2 On the fifth of the month —
it was the fifth year of the exile
of King Jehoiachin — 3 the word
of the LORD came to Ezekiel the
priest, the son of Buzi, by the Kebar River in the land of the Babylonians.[a] There the hand of the
LORD was on him. 2Ki 3:15; Eze 3:14,22
4 I looked, and I saw a windstorm coming out of the north —
an immense cloud with flashing lightning and surrounded by
brilliant light. The center of the
fire looked like glowing metal,
5 and in the fire was what looked
like four living creatures. In appearance their form was human,
6 but each of them had four faces
and four wings. 7 Their legs were
straight; their feet were like those
of a calf and gleamed like burnished bronze. 8 Under their wings
on their four sides they had human hands. All four of them had
faces and wings, 9 and the wings of
one touched the wings of another. Each one went straight ahead;
they did not turn as they moved.
Rev 4:6; Eze 10:8
10 Their faces looked like this:
Each of the four had the face of
a human being, and on the right
side each had the face of a lion,
and on the left the face of an ox;
each also had the face of an eagle.
11 Such were their faces. They each
had two wings spreading out upward, each wing touching that of
the creature on either side; and
each had two other wings covering its body. 12 Each one went
straight ahead. Wherever the spirit would go, they would go, without turning as they went. 13 The
appearance of the living creatures
was like burning coals of fire or
like torches. Fire moved back and
forth among the creatures; it was
bright, and lightning flashed out
of it. 14 The creatures sped back and
forth like flashes of lightning.
Isa 6:2; Rev 4:5,7
15 As I looked at the living creatures, I saw a wheel on the ground
beside each creature with its four
faces. 16 This was the appearance
and structure of the wheels: They
sparkled like topaz, and all four
looked alike. Each appeared to
be made like a wheel intersecting a wheel. 17 As they moved, they
would go in any one of the four
directions the creatures faced; the
wheels did not change direction

[a] 3 Or *Chaldeans*

as the creatures went. 18 Their rims were high and awesome, and all four rims were full of eyes all around. Eze 10:12; Rev 4:6

19 When the living creatures moved, the wheels beside them moved; and when the living creatures rose from the ground, the wheels also rose. 20 Wherever the spirit would go, they would go, and the wheels would rise along with them, because the spirit of the living creatures was in the wheels. 21 When the creatures moved, they also moved; when the creatures stood still, they also stood still; and when the creatures rose from the ground, the wheels rose along with them, because the spirit of the living creatures was in the wheels. ver 12; Eze 10:17

22 Spread out above the heads of the living creatures was what looked something like a vault, sparkling like crystal, and awesome. 23 Under the vault their wings were stretched out one toward the other, and each had two wings covering its body. 24 When the creatures moved, I heard the sound of their wings, like the roar of rushing waters, like the voice of the Almighty,[a] like the tumult of an army. When they stood still, they lowered their wings. Eze 10:5; Rev 1:15

25 Then there came a voice from above the vault over their heads as they stood with lowered wings. 26 Above the vault over their heads was what looked like a throne of lapis lazuli, and high above on the throne was a figure like that of a man. 27 I saw that from what appeared to be his waist up he looked like glowing metal, as if full of fire, and that from there down he looked like fire; and brilliant light surrounded him. 28 Like the appearance of a rainbow in the clouds on a rainy day, so was the radiance around him. Rev 4:2; 10:1

This was the appearance of the likeness of the glory of the LORD. When I saw it, I fell facedown, and I heard the voice of one speaking. Eze 3:23; 8:4

Ezekiel's Call to Be a Prophet

2 He said to me, "Son of man,[b] stand up on your feet and I will speak to you." 2 As he spoke, the Spirit came into me and raised me to my feet, and I heard him speaking to me. Eze 3:24; Da 8:18

3 He said: "Son of man, I am sending you to the Israelites, to a rebellious nation that has rebelled against me; they and their ancestors have been in revolt against me to this very day. 4 The people to whom I am sending you are obstinate and stubborn. Say to them, 'This is what the Sovereign LORD says.' 5 And whether they listen or fail to listen — for they are a rebellious people — they will know that a prophet has been among them.

[a] 24 Hebrew *Shaddai* [b] 1 The Hebrew phrase *ben adam* means *human being*. The phrase *son of man* is retained as a form of address here and throughout Ezekiel because of its possible association with "Son of Man" in the New Testament.

6And you, son of man, do not be
afraid of them or their words. Do
not be afraid, though briers and
thorns are all around you and you
live among scorpions. Do not be
afraid of what they say or be terrified by them, though they are a rebellious people. 7You must speak
my words to them, whether they
listen or fail to listen, for they are
rebellious. 8But you, son of man,
listen to what I say to you. Do not
rebel like that rebellious people;
open your mouth and eat what I
give you." Jer 3:25; Rev 10:9

9Then I looked, and I saw a hand
stretched out to me. In it was a
scroll, 10which he unrolled before
me. On both sides of it were written words of lament and mourning and woe. Eze 8:3; Rev 8:13

3 And he said to me, "Son of man,
eat what is before you, eat this
scroll; then go and speak to the
people of Israel." 2So I opened my
mouth, and he gave me the scroll
to eat.

3Then he said to me, "Son of
man, eat this scroll I am giving
you and fill your stomach with it."
So I ate it, and it tasted as sweet as
honey in my mouth.
Ps 19:10; Rev 10:9-10

4He then said to me: "Son of
man, go now to the people of Israel and speak my words to them.
5You are not being sent to a people of obscure speech and strange
language, but to the people of Israel — 6not to many peoples of
obscure speech and strange language, whose words you cannot
understand. Surely if I had sent
you to them, they would have listened to you. 7But the people of
Israel are not willing to listen to
you because they are not willing
to listen to me, for all the Israelites are hardened and obstinate.
8But I will make you as unyielding
and hardened as they are. 9I will
make your forehead like the hard-
est stone, harder than flint. Do not
be afraid of them or terrified by
them, though they are a rebellious
people." Isa 50:7; Eze 2:6; Mic 3:8

10And he said to me, "Son of
man, listen carefully and take to
heart all the words I speak to you.
11Go now to your people in exile
and speak to them. Say to them,
'This is what the Sovereign LORD
says,' whether they listen or fail to
listen." Eze 2:4-5,7

12Then the Spirit lifted me up,
and I heard behind me a loud
rumbling sound as the glory of the
LORD rose from the place where it
was standing.[a] 13It was the sound
of the wings of the living creatures brushing against each other
and the sound of the wheels beside them, a loud rumbling sound.
14The Spirit then lifted me up and
took me away, and I went in bitterness and in the anger of my
spirit, with the strong hand of the
LORD on me. 15I came to the exiles

[a] 12 Probable reading of the original Hebrew text; Masoretic Text *sound — may the glory of the LORD be praised from his place*

who lived at Tel Aviv near the Kebar River. And there, where they were living, I sat among them for seven days — deeply distressed.

Eze 8:3; 1Ki 18:12; Ac 8:39

Ezekiel's Task as Watchman

16At the end of seven days the word of the LORD came to me: 17"Son of man, I have made you a watchman for the people of Israel; so hear the word I speak and give them warning from me. 18When I say to a wicked person, 'You will surely die,' and you do not warn them or speak out to dissuade them from their evil ways in order to save their life, that wicked person will die for[a] their sin, and I will hold you accountable for their blood. 19But if you do warn the wicked person and they do not turn from their wickedness or from their evil ways, they will die for their sin; but you will have saved yourself.

Isa 52:8; Jer 6:17; Ac 20:26

20"Again, when a righteous person turns from their righteousness and does evil, and I put a stumbling block before them, they will die. Since you did not warn them, they will die for their sin. The righteous things that person did will not be remembered, and I will hold you accountable for their blood. 21But if you do warn the righteous person not to sin and they do not sin, they will surely live because they took warning, and you will have saved yourself."

Eze 18:24; Ac 20:31

22The hand of the LORD was on me there, and he said to me, "Get up and go out to the plain, and there I will speak to you." 23So I got up and went out to the plain. And the glory of the LORD was standing there, like the glory I had seen by the Kebar River, and I fell facedown.

Eze 1:1; 8:4; Ac 9:6

24Then the Spirit came into me and raised me to my feet. He spoke to me and said: "Go, shut yourself inside your house. 25And you, son of man, they will tie with ropes; you will be bound so that you cannot go out among the people. 26I will make your tongue stick to the roof of your mouth so that you will be silent and unable to rebuke them, for they are a rebellious people. 27But when I speak to you, I will open your mouth and you shall say to them, 'This is what the Sovereign LORD says.' Whoever will listen let them listen, and whoever will refuse let them refuse; for they are a rebellious people.

Eze 24:27; 33:22

Siege of Jerusalem Symbolized

4 "Now, son of man, take a block of clay, put it in front of you and draw the city of Jerusalem on it. 2Then lay siege to it: Erect siege works against it, build a ramp up to it, set up camps against it and put battering rams around it. 3Then take an iron pan, place it as an iron wall between you and the city and turn your face toward it. It will be

[a] 18 Or *in*; also in verses 19 and 20

under siege, and you shall besiege it. This will be a sign to the people of Israel. Eze 12:3-6; 24:24,27; Jer 39:1

4"Then lie on your left side and put the sin of the people of Israel upon yourself.[a] You are to bear their sin for the number of days you lie on your side. 5I have assigned you the same number of days as the years of their sin. So for 390 days you will bear the sin of the people of Israel.

6"After you have finished this, lie down again, this time on your right side, and bear the sin of the people of Judah. I have assigned you 40 days, a day for each year. 7Turn your face toward the siege of Jerusalem and with bared arm prophesy against her. 8I will tie you up with ropes so that you cannot turn from one side to the other until you have finished the days of your siege. Nu 14:34; Eze 3:25

9"Take wheat and barley, beans and lentils, millet and spelt; put them in a storage jar and use them to make bread for yourself. You are to eat it during the 390 days you lie on your side. 10Weigh out twenty shekels[b] of food to eat each day and eat it at set times. 11Also measure out a sixth of a hin[c] of water and drink it at set times. 12Eat the food as you would a loaf of barley bread; bake it in the sight of the people, using human excrement for fuel." 13The LORD said, "In this way the people of Israel will eat defiled food among the nations where I will drive them." Hos 9:3; Am 7:17

14Then I said, "Not so, Sovereign LORD! I have never defiled myself. From my youth until now I have never eaten anything found dead or torn by wild animals. No impure meat has ever entered my mouth." Ex 22:31; Ac 10:14

15"Very well," he said, "I will let you bake your bread over cow dung instead of human excrement."

16He then said to me: "Son of man, I am about to cut off the food supply in Jerusalem. The people will eat rationed food in anxiety and drink rationed water in despair, 17for food and water will be scarce. They will be appalled at the sight of each other and will waste away because of[d] their sin.

Lev 26:39; Eze 24:23; 33:10

God's Razor of Judgment

5 "Now, son of man, take a sharp sword and use it as a barber's razor to shave your head and your beard. Then take a set of scales and divide up the hair. 2When the days of your siege come to an end, burn a third of the hair inside the city. Take a third and strike it with the sword all around the city. And scatter a third to the wind. For I will pursue them with drawn sword. 3But take a few hairs and tuck them away in the folds of your garment. 4Again, take a few of these and throw them into the fire and

[a] 4 Or *upon your side* [b] 10 That is, about 8 ounces or about 230 grams [c] 11 That is, about 2/3 quart or about 0.6 liter [d] 17 Or *away in*

burn them up. A fire will spread
from there to all Israel. Lev 26:33
5"This is what the Sovereign
LORD says: This is Jerusalem, which
I have set in the center of the nations, with countries all around
her. 6Yet in her wickedness she has
rebelled against my laws and decrees more than the nations and
countries around her. She has rejected my laws and has not followed my decrees. Jer 11:10; Zec 7:11
7"Therefore this is what the Sovereign LORD says: You have been
more unruly than the nations
around you and have not followed
my decrees or kept my laws. You
have not even[a] conformed to the
standards of the nations around
you. 2Ch 33:9; Eze 16:47
8"Therefore this is what the
Sovereign LORD says: I myself am
against you, Jerusalem, and I will
inflict punishment on you in the
sight of the nations. 9Because of
all your detestable idols, I will do
to you what I have never done
before and will never do again.
10Therefore in your midst parents
will eat their children, and children will eat their parents. I will
inflict punishment on you and
will scatter all your survivors to
the winds. 11Therefore as surely
as I live, declares the Sovereign
LORD, because you have defiled
my sanctuary with all your vile
images and detestable practices, I myself will shave you; I will
not look on you with pity or spare
you. 12A third of your people will
die of the plague or perish by famine inside you; a third will fall by
the sword outside your walls; and
a third I will scatter to the winds
and pursue with drawn sword.
Da 9:12; Zec 2:6
13"Then my anger will cease and
my wrath against them will subside, and I will be avenged. And
when I have spent my wrath on
them, they will know that I the
LORD have spoken in my zeal.
Isa 1:24; Eze 21:17
14"I will make you a ruin and a reproach among the nations around
you, in the sight of all who pass
by. 15You will be a reproach and a
taunt, a warning and an object of
horror to the nations around you
when I inflict punishment on you
in anger and in wrath and with
stinging rebuke. I the LORD have
spoken. 16When I shoot at you with
my deadly and destructive arrows
of famine, I will shoot to destroy
you. I will bring more and more
famine upon you and cut off your
supply of food. 17I will send famine and wild beasts against you,
and they will leave you childless.
Plague and bloodshed will sweep
through you, and I will bring the
sword against you. I the LORD have
spoken." Ne 2:17; Eze 25:17

Doom for the Mountains of Israel

6 The word of the LORD came
to me: 2"Son of man, set your
face against the mountains of

[a] 7 Most Hebrew manuscripts; some Hebrew manuscripts and Syriac *You have*

Israel; prophesy against them
3and say: 'You mountains of Israel, hear the word of the Sovereign LORD. This is what the Sovereign LORD says to the mountains
and hills, to the ravines and valleys: I am about to bring a sword
against you, and I will destroy
your high places. 4Your altars will
be demolished and your incense
altars will be smashed; and I will
slay your people in front of your
idols. 5I will lay the dead bodies
of the Israelites in front of their
idols, and I will scatter your bones
around your altars. 6Wherever you
live, the towns will be laid waste
and the high places demolished,
so that your altars will be laid
waste and devastated, your idols
smashed and ruined, your incense
altars broken down, and what you
have made wiped out. 7Your people will fall slain among you, and
you will know that I am the LORD.

Lev 26:30; Eze 36:1

8" 'But I will spare some, for
some of you will escape the sword
when you are scattered among
the lands and nations. 9Then in
the nations where they have been
carried captive, those who escape
will remember me — how I have
been grieved by their adulterous
hearts, which have turned away
from me, and by their eyes, which
have lusted after their idols. They
will loathe themselves for the evil
they have done and for all their
detestable practices. 10And they
will know that I am the LORD; I did
not threaten in vain to bring this
calamity on them.

Isa 7:13; Jer 44:28; Eze 14:22

11" 'This is what the Sovereign
LORD says: Strike your hands together and stamp your feet and cry
out "Alas!" because of all the wicked and detestable practices of the
people of Israel, for they will fall
by the sword, famine and plague.
12One who is far away will die of
the plague, and one who is near
will fall by the sword, and anyone
who survives and is spared will
die of famine. So will I pour out
my wrath on them. 13And they will
know that I am the LORD, when
their people lie slain among their
idols around their altars, on every
high hill and on all the mountaintops, under every spreading tree
and every leafy oak — places where
they offered fragrant incense to all
their idols. 14And I will stretch out
my hand against them and make
the land a desolate waste from the
desert to Diblah[a] — wherever they
live. Then they will know that I am
the LORD.' " Eze 21:14,17; Jer 2:20; Hos 4:13

The End Has Come

7 The word of the LORD came to
me: 2"Son of man, this is what
the Sovereign LORD says to the
land of Israel:

" 'The end! The end has come
upon the four corners of the
land!

[a] 14 Most Hebrew manuscripts; a few Hebrew manuscripts *Riblah*

3 The end is now upon you,
and I will unleash my anger
against you.
I will judge you according to
your conduct
and repay you for all your
detestable practices.
4 I will not look on you with pity;
I will not spare you.
I will surely repay you for your
conduct
and for the detestable
practices among you.

" 'Then you will know that I am
the LORD.' Eze 5:11; Am 8:2,10

5 "This is what the Sovereign
LORD says:

" 'Disaster! Unheard-of[a]
disaster!
See, it comes!
6 The end has come!
The end has come!
It has roused itself against you.
See, it comes!
7 Doom has come upon you,
upon you who dwell in the
land.
The time has come! The day is
near!
There is panic, not joy, on the
mountains.
8 I am about to pour out my
wrath on you
and spend my anger against
you.
I will judge you according to
your conduct
and repay you for all your
detestable practices.
9 I will not look on you with pity;
I will not spare you.
I will repay you for your
conduct
and for the detestable
practices among you.

" 'Then you will know that it is I
the LORD who strikes you.
2Ki 21:12; Eze 20:8,21

10 " 'See, the day!
See, it comes!
Doom has burst forth,
the rod has budded,
arrogance has blossomed!
11 Violence has arisen,[b]
a rod to punish the wicked.
None of the people will be
left,
none of that crowd —
none of their wealth,
nothing of value.
12 The time has come!
The day has arrived!
Let not the buyer rejoice
nor the seller grieve,
for my wrath is on the whole
crowd.
13 The seller will not recover
the property that was sold —
as long as both buyer and
seller live.
For the vision concerning the
whole crowd
will not be reversed.
Because of their sins, not one
of them
will preserve their life.

[a] 5 Most Hebrew manuscripts; some Hebrew manuscripts and Syriac *Disaster after* [b] 11 Or *The violent one has become*

14 " 'They have blown the
trumpet,
they have made all things
ready,
but no one will go into battle,
for my wrath is on the
whole crowd.
Lev 25:24-28; Jer 16:6
15 Outside is the sword;
inside are plague and
famine.
Those in the country
will die by the sword;
those in the city
will be devoured by famine
and plague.
16 The fugitives who escape
will flee to the mountains.
Like doves of the valleys,
they will all moan,
each for their own sins.
17 Every hand will go limp;
every leg will be wet with
urine.
18 They will put on sackcloth
and be clothed with terror.
Every face will be covered with
shame,
and every head will be
shaved.
19 " 'They will throw their silver
into the streets,
and their gold will be
treated as a thing
unclean.
Their silver and gold
will not be able to deliver
them
in the day of the LORD's
wrath.
It will not satisfy their
hunger
or fill their stomachs,
for it has caused them to
stumble into sin.
20 They took pride in their
beautiful jewelry
and used it to make their
detestable idols.
They made it into vile
images;
therefore I will make it a
thing unclean for them.
21 I will give their wealth as
plunder to foreigners
and as loot to the wicked of
the earth,
who will defile it.
22 I will turn my face away from
the people,
and robbers will desecrate
the place I treasure.
They will enter it
and will defile it.
Dt 32:25; Eze 39:23-24; Zep 1:7,18

23 " 'Prepare chains!
For the land is full of
bloodshed,
and the city is full of
violence.
24 I will bring the most wicked of
nations
to take possession of their
houses.
I will put an end to the pride of
the mighty,
and their sanctuaries will be
desecrated.
25 When terror comes,
they will seek peace in vain.

26 Calamity upon calamity will come,
and rumor upon rumor.
They will go searching for a vision from the prophet,
priestly instruction in the law will cease,
the counsel of the elders will come to an end.
27 The king will mourn,
the prince will be clothed with despair,
and the hands of the people of the land will tremble.
I will deal with them according to their conduct,
and by their own standards I will judge them.

"'Then they will know that I am
the LORD.'" Eze 24:21; 26:16

Idolatry in the Temple

8 In the sixth year, in the sixth
month on the fifth day, while
I was sitting in my house and the
elders of Judah were sitting before me, the hand of the Sovereign LORD came on me there. 2 I
looked, and I saw a figure like that
of a man.[a] From what appeared to
be his waist down he was like fire,
and from there up his appearance
was as bright as glowing metal.
3 He stretched out what looked
like a hand and took me by the
hair of my head. The Spirit lifted
me up between earth and heaven
and in visions of God he took me
to Jerusalem, to the entrance of
the north gate of the inner court,
where the idol that provokes to
jealousy stood. 4 And there before
me was the glory of the God of Israel, as in the vision I had seen in
the plain. Eze 1:28; 3:22
5 Then he said to me, "Son of
man, look toward the north." So I
looked, and in the entrance north
of the gate of the altar I saw this
idol of jealousy. Jer 32:34
6 And he said to me, "Son of man,
do you see what they are doing —
the utterly detestable things the
Israelites are doing here, things
that will drive me far from my
sanctuary? But you will see things
that are even more detestable."
Eze 5:11; Hos 5:6
7 Then he brought me to the entrance to the court. I looked, and I
saw a hole in the wall. 8 He said to
me, "Son of man, now dig into the
wall." So I dug into the wall and
saw a doorway there.
9 And he said to me, "Go in and
see the wicked and detestable
things they are doing here." 10 So I
went in and looked, and I saw portrayed all over the walls all kinds
of crawling things and unclean
animals and all the idols of Israel. 11 In front of them stood seventy
elders of Israel, and Jaazaniah son
of Shaphan was standing among
them. Each had a censer in his
hand, and a fragrant cloud of incense was rising. Ex 3:16; 20:4

[a] 2 Or *saw a fiery figure*

12 He said to me, "Son of man, have you seen what the elders of Israel are doing in the darkness, each at the shrine of his own idol? They say, 'The LORD does not see us; the LORD has forsaken the land.'" 13 Again, he said, "You will see them doing things that are even more detestable." Ps 10:11; Eze 9:9

14 Then he brought me to the entrance of the north gate of the house of the LORD, and I saw women sitting there, mourning the god Tammuz. 15 He said to me, "Do you see this, son of man? You will see things that are even more detestable than this." Eze 11:12

16 He then brought me into the inner court of the house of the LORD, and there at the entrance to the temple, between the portico and the altar, were about twenty-five men. With their backs toward the temple of the LORD and their faces toward the east, they were bowing down to the sun in the east. Dt 4:19; Jer 2:27

17 He said to me, "Have you seen this, son of man? Is it a trivial matter for the people of Judah to do the detestable things they are doing here? Must they also fill the land with violence and continually arouse my anger? Look at them putting the branch to their nose! 18 Therefore I will deal with them in anger; I will not look on them with pity or spare them. Although they shout in my ears, I will not listen to them." Isa 1:15; Jer 11:11; Mic 3:4

Judgment on the Idolaters

9 Then I heard him call out in a loud voice, "Bring near those who are appointed to execute judgment on the city, each with a weapon in his hand." 2 And I saw six men coming from the direction of the upper gate, which faces north, each with a deadly weapon in his hand. With them was a man clothed in linen who had a writing kit at his side. They came in and stood beside the bronze altar. Lev 16:4; Eze 10:2; Rev 15:6

3 Now the glory of the God of Israel went up from above the cherubim, where it had been, and moved to the threshold of the temple. Then the LORD called to the man clothed in linen who had the writing kit at his side 4 and said to him, "Go throughout the city of Jerusalem and put a mark on the foreheads of those who grieve and lament over all the detestable things that are done in it." Ex 12:7; Rev 7:3; 9:4

5 As I listened, he said to the others, "Follow him through the city and kill, without showing pity or compassion. 6 Slaughter the old men, the young men and women, the mothers and children, but do not touch anyone who has the mark. Begin at my sanctuary." So they began with the old men who were in front of the temple. 2Ch 36:17; 1Pe 4:17

7 Then he said to them, "Defile the temple and fill the courts with the slain. Go!" So they went out

and began killing throughout the city. 8 While they were killing and I was left alone, I fell facedown, crying out, "Alas, Sovereign LORD! Are you going to destroy the entire remnant of Israel in this outpouring of your wrath on Jerusalem?"

Eze 11:13; Am 7:1-6

9 He answered me, "The sin of the people of Israel and Judah is exceedingly great; the land is full of bloodshed and the city is full of injustice. They say, 'The LORD has forsaken the land; the LORD does not see.' 10 So I will not look on them with pity or spare them, but I will bring down on their own heads what they have done."

Eze 8:18; 11:21

11 Then the man in linen with the writing kit at his side brought back word, saying, "I have done as you commanded."

God's Glory Departs From the Temple

10 I looked, and I saw the likeness of a throne of lapis lazuli above the vault that was over the heads of the cherubim. 2 The LORD said to the man clothed in linen, "Go in among the wheels beneath the cherubim. Fill your hands with burning coals from among the cherubim and scatter them over the city." And as I watched, he went in. Eze 1:22; Rev 8:5

3 Now the cherubim were standing on the south side of the temple when the man went in, and a cloud filled the inner court. 4 Then the glory of the LORD rose from above the cherubim and moved to the threshold of the temple. The cloud filled the temple, and the court was full of the radiance of the glory of the LORD. 5 The sound of the wings of the cherubim could be heard as far away as the outer court, like the voice of God Almighty[a] when he speaks.

Eze 1:24,28; 9:3

6 When the LORD commanded the man in linen, "Take fire from among the wheels, from among the cherubim," the man went in and stood beside a wheel. 7 Then one of the cherubim reached out his hand to the fire that was among them. He took up some of it and put it into the hands of the man in linen, who took it and went out. 8 (Under the wings of the cherubim could be seen what looked like human hands.) Eze 1:8

9 I looked, and I saw beside the cherubim four wheels, one beside each of the cherubim; the wheels sparkled like topaz. 10 As for their appearance, the four of them looked alike; each was like a wheel intersecting a wheel. 11 As they moved, they would go in any one of the four directions the cherubim faced; the wheels did not turn about[b] as the cherubim went. The cherubim went in whatever direction the head faced, without turning as they went. 12 Their entire bodies, including their backs, their hands and their wings, were

[a] 5 Hebrew *El-Shaddai* [b] 11 Or *aside*

completely full of eyes, as were
their four wheels. 13I heard the
wheels being called "the whirling
wheels." 14Each of the cherubim
had four faces: One face was that
of a cherub, the second the face of
a human being, the third the face
of a lion, and the fourth the face of
an eagle. Eze 1:10; Rev 4:7

15Then the cherubim rose upward. These were the living creatures I had seen by the Kebar River. 16When the cherubim moved,
the wheels beside them moved;
and when the cherubim spread
their wings to rise from the
ground, the wheels did not leave
their side. 17When the cherubim
stood still, they also stood still;
and when the cherubim rose, they
rose with them, because the spirit of the living creatures was in
them. Eze 1:20-21

18Then the glory of the LORD departed from over the threshold of
the temple and stopped above the
cherubim. 19While I watched, the
cherubim spread their wings and
rose from the ground, and as they
went, the wheels went with them.
They stopped at the entrance of
the east gate of the LORD's house,
and the glory of the God of Israel
was above them. Ps 18:10; Eze 11:1,22

20These were the living creatures I had seen beneath the God
of Israel by the Kebar River, and I
realized that they were cherubim.
21Each had four faces and four
wings, and under their wings was
what looked like human hands.
22Their faces had the same appearance as those I had seen by the Kebar River. Each one went straight
ahead. Eze 1:6

God's Sure Judgment on Jerusalem

11 Then the Spirit lifted me up
and brought me to the gate of
the house of the LORD that faces
east. There at the entrance of the
gate were twenty-five men, and I
saw among them Jaazaniah son
of Azzur and Pelatiah son of Benaiah, leaders of the people. 2The
LORD said to me, "Son of man,
these are the men who are plotting evil and giving wicked advice
in this city. 3They say, 'Haven't our
houses been recently rebuilt? This
city is a pot, and we are the meat
in it.' 4Therefore prophesy against
them; prophesy, son of man."
Eze 3:4,17; 8:16

5Then the Spirit of the LORD
came on me, and he told me to
say: "This is what the LORD says:
That is what you are saying, you
leaders in Israel, but I know what
is going through your mind. 6You
have killed many people in this
city and filled its streets with the
dead. Jer 17:10; Eze 7:23

7"Therefore this is what the Sovereign LORD says: The bodies you
have thrown there are the meat
and this city is the pot, but I will
drive you out of it. 8You fear the
sword, and the sword is what I will
bring against you, declares the
Sovereign LORD. 9I will drive you
out of the city and deliver you into

the hands of foreigners and inflict
punishment on you. 10You will fall
by the sword, and I will execute
judgment on you at the borders
of Israel. Then you will know that
I am the LORD. 11This city will not
be a pot for you, nor will you be the
meat in it; I will execute judgment
on you at the borders of Israel.
12And you will know that I am the
LORD, for you have not followed my
decrees or kept my laws but have
conformed to the standards of the
nations around you." Lev 18:4; Eze 8:10

13Now as I was prophesying, Pelatiah son of Benaiah died. Then I
fell facedown and cried out in a
loud voice, "Alas, Sovereign LORD!
Will you completely destroy the
remnant of Israel?" Eze 9:8; Am 7:2

The Promise of Israel's Return

14The word of the LORD came to
me: 15"Son of man, the people of
Jerusalem have said of your fellow
exiles and all the other Israelites,
'They are far away from the LORD;
this land was given to us as our
possession.' Eze 33:24

16"Therefore say: 'This is what
the Sovereign LORD says: Although
I sent them far away among
the nations and scattered them
among the countries, yet for a little while I have been a sanctuary
for them in the countries where
they have gone.' Ps 90:1; Isa 8:14

17"Therefore say: 'This is what
the Sovereign LORD says: I will
gather you from the nations and
bring you back from the countries
where you have been scattered,
and I will give you back the land
of Israel again.' Jer 24:5-6; Eze 28:25

18"They will return to it and remove all its vile images and detestable idols. 19I will give them
an undivided heart and put a new
spirit in them; I will remove from
them their heart of stone and give
them a heart of flesh. 20Then they
will follow my decrees and be careful to keep my laws. They will be
my people, and I will be their God.
21But as for those whose hearts are
devoted to their vile images and
detestable idols, I will bring down
on their own heads what they
have done, declares the Sovereign
LORD." Jer 32:39; Eze 18:31; 36:26

22Then the cherubim, with the
wheels beside them, spread their
wings, and the glory of the God of
Israel was above them. 23The glory of the LORD went up from within the city and stopped above the
mountain east of it. 24The Spirit
lifted me up and brought me to
the exiles in Babylonia[a] in the vision given by the Spirit of God.
Zec 14:4; 2Co 12:2-4

Then the vision I had seen went
up from me, 25and I told the exiles everything the LORD had
shown me. Eze 3:4,11

The Exile Symbolized

12 The word of the LORD came
to me: 2"Son of man, you are
living among a rebellious people.

[a] 24 Or *Chaldea*

They have eyes to see but do not see and ears to hear but do not hear, for they are a rebellious people.

3"Therefore, son of man, pack your belongings for exile and in the daytime, as they watch, set out and go from where you are to another place. Perhaps they will understand, though they are a rebellious people. 4During the daytime, while they watch, bring out your belongings packed for exile. Then in the evening, while they are watching, go out like those who go into exile. 5While they watch, dig through the wall and take your belongings out through it. 6Put them on your shoulder as they are watching and carry them out at dusk. Cover your face so that you cannot see the land, for I have made you a sign to the Israelites." Isa 8:18; Eze 4:3; 24:24

7So I did as I was commanded. During the day I brought out my things packed for exile. Then in the evening I dug through the wall with my hands. I took my belongings out at dusk, carrying them on my shoulders while they watched. Eze 24:18; 37:10

8In the morning the word of the LORD came to me: 9"Son of man, did not the Israelites, that rebellious people, ask you, 'What are you doing?' Eze 17:12; 24:19

10"Say to them, 'This is what the Sovereign LORD says: This prophecy concerns the prince in Jerusalem and all the Israelites who are there.' 11Say to them, 'I am a sign to you.' Zec 3:8

"As I have done, so it will be done to them. They will go into exile as captives. Jer 15:2; 52:15

12"The prince among them will put his things on his shoulder at dusk and leave, and a hole will be dug in the wall for him to go through. He will cover his face so that he cannot see the land. 13I will spread my net for him, and he will be caught in my snare; I will bring him to Babylonia, the land of the Chaldeans, but he will not see it, and there he will die. 14I will scatter to the winds all those around him — his staff and all his troops — and I will pursue them with drawn sword. 2Ki 25:5; Eze 5:10,12

15"They will know that I am the LORD, when I disperse them among the nations and scatter them through the countries. 16But I will spare a few of them from the sword, famine and plague, so that in the nations where they go they may acknowledge all their detestable practices. Then they will know that I am the LORD."

Jer 22:8-9; Eze 6:8-10; 14:22

17The word of the LORD came to me: 18"Son of man, tremble as you eat your food, and shudder in fear as you drink your water. 19Say to the people of the land: 'This is what the Sovereign LORD says about those living in Jerusalem and in the land of Israel: They will eat their food in anxiety and drink their water in despair, for their

land will be stripped of everything
in it because of the violence of all
who live there. 20The inhabited
towns will be laid waste and the
land will be desolate. Then you
will know that I am the LORD.' "

Isa 7:23-24; Jer 4:7

There Will Be No Delay

21The word of the LORD came
to me: 22"Son of man, what is this
proverb you have in the land of
Israel: 'The days go by and every
vision comes to nothing'? 23Say to
them, 'This is what the Sovereign
LORD says: I am going to put an
end to this proverb, and they will
no longer quote it in Israel.' Say
to them, 'The days are near when
every vision will be fulfilled. 24For
there will be no more false visions
or flattering divinations among
the people of Israel. 25But I the
LORD will speak what I will, and
it shall be fulfilled without delay.
For in your days, you rebellious
people, I will fulfill whatever I say,
declares the Sovereign LORD.' "

Eze 13:23; Zec 13:2-4

26The word of the LORD came to
me: 27"Son of man, the Israelites
are saying, 'The vision he sees is
for many years from now, and he
prophesies about the distant future.' Da 10:14

28"Therefore say to them, 'This
is what the Sovereign LORD says:
None of my words will be delayed
any longer; whatever I say will be
fulfilled, declares the Sovereign
LORD.' "

False Prophets Condemned

13 The word of the LORD came
to me: 2"Son of man, prophesy against the prophets of Israel
who are now prophesying. Say to
those who prophesy out of their
own imagination: 'Hear the word
of the LORD! 3This is what the Sovereign LORD says: Woe to the foolish[a] prophets who follow their
own spirit and have seen nothing!
4Your prophets, Israel, are like
jackals among ruins. 5You have
not gone up to the breaches in the
wall to repair it for the people of
Israel so that it will stand firm in
the battle on the day of the LORD.
6Their visions are false and their
divinations a lie. Even though the
LORD has not sent them, they say,
"The LORD declares," and expect
him to fulfill their words. 7Have
you not seen false visions and uttered lying divinations when you
say, "The LORD declares," though I
have not spoken? Eze 22:28,30; Jer 23:16

8" 'Therefore this is what the
Sovereign LORD says: Because
of your false words and lying visions, I am against you, declares
the Sovereign LORD. 9My hand
will be against the prophets who
see false visions and utter lying
divinations. They will not belong
to the council of my people or be
listed in the records of Israel, nor
will they enter the land of Israel.
Then you will know that I am the
Sovereign LORD. Jer 17:13; Eze 20:38

[a] 3 Or *wicked*

10“ ‘Because they lead my people
astray, saying, “Peace,” when there
is no peace, and because, when a
flimsy wall is built, they cover it
with whitewash, 11therefore tell
those who cover it with whitewash
that it is going to fall. Rain will
come in torrents, and I will send
hailstones hurtling down, and violent winds will burst forth. 12When
the wall collapses, will people not
ask you, “Where is the whitewash
you covered it with?” Eze 22:28; 38:22

13“ ‘Therefore this is what the
Sovereign LORD says: In my wrath
I will unleash a violent wind, and
in my anger hailstones and torrents of rain will fall with destructive fury. 14I will tear down the wall
you have covered with whitewash
and will level it to the ground so
that its foundation will be laid
bare. When it[a] falls, you will be
destroyed in it; and you will know
that I am the LORD. 15So I will pour
out my wrath against the wall and
against those who covered it with
whitewash. I will say to you, “The
wall is gone and so are those who
whitewashed it, 16those prophets
of Israel who prophesied to Jerusalem and saw visions of peace for
her when there was no peace, declares the Sovereign LORD.” ’

Isa 57:21; Jer 6:14

17“Now, son of man, set your face
against the daughters of your people who prophesy out of their own
imagination. Prophesy against
them 18and say, ‘This is what the
Sovereign LORD says: Woe to the
women who sew magic charms
on all their wrists and make veils
of various lengths for their heads
in order to ensnare people. Will
you ensnare the lives of my people but preserve your own? 19You
have profaned me among my people for a few handfuls of barley
and scraps of bread. By lying to
my people, who listen to lies, you
have killed those who should not
have died and have spared those
who should not live. Pr 28:21; Rev 2:20

20“ ‘Therefore this is what the
Sovereign LORD says: I am against
your magic charms with which
you ensnare people like birds and
I will tear them from your arms;
I will set free the people that you
ensnare like birds. 21I will tear off
your veils and save my people
from your hands, and they will
no longer fall prey to your power.
Then you will know that I am the
LORD. 22Because you disheartened
the righteous with your lies, when
I had brought them no grief, and
because you encouraged the wicked not to turn from their evil ways
and so save their lives, 23therefore
you will no longer see false visions
or practice divination. I will save
my people from your hands. And
then you will know that I am the
LORD.’ ” Eze 12:24; Mic 3:6

Idolaters Condemned

14 Some of the elders of Israel
came to me and sat down in
front of me. 2Then the word of the

[a] 14 Or *the city*

LORD came to me: 3"Son of man,
these men have set up idols in
their hearts and put wicked stumbling blocks before their faces.
Should I let them inquire of me
at all? 4Therefore speak to them
and tell them, 'This is what the
Sovereign LORD says: When any of
the Israelites set up idols in their
hearts and put a wicked stumbling
block before their faces and then
go to a prophet, I the LORD will answer them myself in keeping with
their great idolatry. 5I will do this
to recapture the hearts of the people of Israel, who have all deserted
me for their idols.' Eze 7:19; Zec 11:8

6"Therefore say to the people of
Israel, 'This is what the Sovereign
LORD says: Repent! Turn from
your idols and renounce all your
detestable practices! Isa 2:20; 30:22

7" 'When any of the Israelites
or any foreigner residing in Israel separate themselves from me
and set up idols in their hearts
and put a wicked stumbling block
before their faces and then go to
a prophet to inquire of me, I the
LORD will answer them myself. 8I
will set my face against them and
make them an example and a byword. I will remove them from my
people. Then you will know that I
am the LORD. Eze 5:15; 15:7

9" 'And if the prophet is enticed
to utter a prophecy, I the LORD
have enticed that prophet, and I
will stretch out my hand against
him and destroy him from among
my people Israel. 10They will bear
their guilt — the prophet will be
as guilty as the one who consults
him. 11Then the people of Israel will no longer stray from me,
nor will they defile themselves
anymore with all their sins. They
will be my people, and I will be
their God, declares the Sovereign
LORD.' " Eze 11:19-20; 48:11

Jerusalem's Judgment Inescapable

12The word of the LORD came
to me: 13"Son of man, if a country sins against me by being unfaithful and I stretch out my hand
against it to cut off its food supply and send famine upon it and
kill its people and their animals,
14even if these three men — Noah,
Daniel[a] and Job — were in it, they
could save only themselves by
their righteousness, declares the
Sovereign LORD. Jer 15:1; Eze 18:20

15"Or if I send wild beasts
through that country and they
leave it childless and it becomes
desolate so that no one can pass
through it because of the beasts,
16as surely as I live, declares the
Sovereign LORD, even if these
three men were in it, they could
not save their own sons or daughters. They alone would be saved,
but the land would be desolate.
Eze 5:17; 18:20

17"Or if I bring a sword against
that country and say, 'Let the
sword pass throughout the land,'
and I kill its people and their

[a] 14 Or *Danel*, a man of renown in ancient literature; also in verse 20

animals, 18as surely as I live, declares the Sovereign LORD, even
if these three men were in it, they
could not save their own sons or
daughters. They alone would be
saved. Eze 5:12; 21:3-4; 25:13

19"Or if I send a plague into
that land and pour out my wrath
on it through bloodshed, killing
its people and their animals, 20as
surely as I live, declares the Sovereign LORD, even if Noah, Daniel
and Job were in it, they could save
neither son nor daughter. They
would save only themselves by
their righteousness. ver 14; Eze 38:22

21"For this is what the Sovereign
LORD says: How much worse will it
be when I send against Jerusalem
my four dreadful judgments —
sword and famine and wild beasts
and plague — to kill its men and
their animals! 22Yet there will be
some survivors — sons and daughters who will be brought out of it.
They will come to you, and when
you see their conduct and their actions, you will be consoled regarding the disaster I have brought
on Jerusalem — every disaster I
have brought on it. 23You will be
consoled when you see their conduct and their actions, for you will
know that I have done nothing in
it without cause, declares the Sovereign LORD." Jer 22:8-9

Jerusalem as a Useless Vine

15 The word of the LORD came
to me: 2"Son of man, how is
the wood of a vine different from
that of a branch from any of the
trees in the forest? 3Is wood ever
taken from it to make anything
useful? Do they make pegs from
it to hang things on? 4And after it is thrown on the fire as fuel
and the fire burns both ends and
chars the middle, is it then useful
for anything? 5If it was not useful
for anything when it was whole,
how much less can it be made into
something useful when the fire
has burned it and it is charred?
Jn 15:6; Hos 10:1

6"Therefore this is what the Sovereign LORD says: As I have given
the wood of the vine among the
trees of the forest as fuel for the
fire, so will I treat the people living in Jerusalem. 7I will set my
face against them. Although they
have come out of the fire, the fire
will yet consume them. And when
I set my face against them, you
will know that I am the LORD. 8I
will make the land desolate because they have been unfaithful,
declares the Sovereign LORD."
Isa 24:18; Am 9:1-4

Jerusalem as an Adulterous Wife

16 The word of the LORD came
to me: 2"Son of man, con-
front Jerusalem with her detestable practices 3and say, 'This is
what the Sovereign LORD says
to Jerusalem: Your ancestry and
birth were in the land of the Canaanites; your father was an Amorite and your mother a Hittite. 4On
the day you were born your cord

was not cut, nor were you washed
with water to make you clean,
nor were you rubbed with salt or
wrapped in cloths. 5No one looked
on you with pity or had compassion enough to do any of these
things for you. Rather, you were
thrown out into the open field,
for on the day you were born you
were despised. Eze 20:4; 22:2; Hos 2:3

6" 'Then I passed by and saw you
kicking about in your blood, and
as you lay there in your blood I
said to you, "Live!"[a] 7I made you
grow like a plant of the field. You
grew and developed and entered
puberty. Your breasts had formed
and your hair had grown, yet you
were stark naked. Ex 19:4; Dt 1:10

8" 'Later I passed by, and when
I looked at you and saw that
you were old enough for love, I
spread the corner of my garment
over you and covered your naked
body. I gave you my solemn oath
and entered into a covenant with
you, declares the Sovereign LORD,
and you became mine.
Jer 2:2; Hos 2:7,19-20

9" 'I bathed you with water and
washed the blood from you and
put ointments on you. 10I clothed
you with an embroidered dress
and put sandals of fine leather on
you. I dressed you in fine linen
and covered you with costly garments. 11I adorned you with jewelry: I put bracelets on your arms
and a necklace around your neck,
12and I put a ring on your nose,
earrings on your ears and a beautiful crown on your head. 13So you
were adorned with gold and silver; your clothes were of fine linen
and costly fabric and embroidered
cloth. Your food was honey, olive
oil and the finest flour. You became very beautiful and rose to be
a queen. 14And your fame spread
among the nations on account of
your beauty, because the splendor
I had given you made your beauty perfect, declares the Sovereign
LORD. 1Ki 10:24; La 2:15

15" 'But you trusted in your
beauty and used your fame to become a prostitute. You lavished
your favors on anyone who passed
by and your beauty became his.
16You took some of your garments
to make gaudy high places, where
you carried on your prostitution.
You went to him, and he possessed your beauty.[b] 17You also
took the fine jewelry I gave you,
the jewelry made of my gold and
silver, and you made for yourself
male idols and engaged in prostitution with them. 18And you took
your embroidered clothes to put
on them, and you offered my oil
and incense before them. 19Also
the food I provided for you — the
flour, olive oil and honey I gave
you to eat — you offered as fragrant incense before them. That is
what happened, declares the Sovereign LORD. Isa 57:8; Jer 2:20; Eze 23:3

[a] *6* A few Hebrew manuscripts, Septuagint and Syriac; most Hebrew manuscripts repeat *and as you lay there in your blood I said to you, "Live!"* [b] *16* The meaning of the Hebrew for this sentence is uncertain.

20“ ‘And you took your sons and
daughters whom you bore to me
and sacrificed them as food to the
idols. Was your prostitution not
enough? 21You slaughtered my
children and sacrificed them to
the idols. 22In all your detestable
practices and your prostitution
you did not remember the days of
your youth, when you were naked
and bare, kicking about in your
blood. Ps 106:37-38; Jer 2:2; Hos 11:1

23“ ‘Woe! Woe to you, declares the
Sovereign LORD. In addition to all
your other wickedness, 24you built
a mound for yourself and made a
lofty shrine in every public square.
25At every street corner you built
your lofty shrines and degraded your beauty, spreading your
legs with increasing promiscuity
to anyone who passed by. 26You
engaged in prostitution with the
Egyptians, your neighbors with
large genitals, and aroused my anger with your increasing promiscuity. 27So I stretched out my hand
against you and reduced your territory; I gave you over to the greed
of your enemies, the daughters of
the Philistines, who were shocked
by your lewd conduct. 28You engaged in prostitution with the Assyrians too, because you were in-
satiable; and even after that, you
still were not satisfied. 29Then you
increased your promiscuity to include Babylonia,[a] a land of merchants, but even with this you
were not satisfied.
Isa 57:7; Jer 2:20; Eze 20:28

30“ ‘I am filled with fury against
you,[b] declares the Sovereign LORD,
when you do all these things,
acting like a brazen prostitute!
31When you built your mounds
at every street corner and made
your lofty shrines in every public
square, you were unlike a prostitute, because you scorned payment. Jer 3:3

32“ ‘You adulterous wife! You
prefer strangers to your own husband! 33All prostitutes receive
gifts, but you give gifts to all your
lovers, bribing them to come to
you from everywhere for your il-
licit favors. 34So in your prostitution you are the opposite of others; no one runs after you for your
favors. You are the very opposite,
for you give payment and none is
given to you. Hos 8:9-10

35“ ‘Therefore, you prostitute,
hear the word of the LORD! 36This
is what the Sovereign LORD says:
Because you poured out your lust
and exposed your naked body in
your promiscuity with your lovers, and because of all your detestable idols, and because you
gave them your children’s blood,
37therefore I am going to gather
all your lovers, with whom you
found pleasure, those you loved
as well as those you hated. I will
gather them against you from
all around and will strip you in
front of them, and they will see
you stark naked. 38I will sentence

[a] 29 Or *Chaldea* [b] 30 Or *How feverish is your heart,*

you to the punishment of wom-
en who commit adultery and who
shed blood; I will bring on you the
blood vengeance of my wrath and
jealous anger. 39 Then I will deliver you into the hands of your lovers, and they will tear down your
mounds and destroy your lofty
shrines. They will strip you of your
clothes and take your fine jewelry
and leave you stark naked. 40 They
will bring a mob against you, who
will stone you and hack you to
pieces with their swords. 41 They
will burn down your houses and
inflict punishment on you in the
sight of many women. I will put a
stop to your prostitution, and you
will no longer pay your lovers.
42 Then my wrath against you will
subside and my jealous anger will
turn away from you; I will be calm
and no longer angry. Eze 5:13; 39:29

43 " 'Because you did not remember the days of your youth but enraged me with all these things, I
will surely bring down on your
head what you have done, declares the Sovereign LORD. Did you
not add lewdness to all your other
detestable practices?

Ps 78:42; Eze 11:21; 22:31

44 " 'Everyone who quotes proverbs will quote this proverb about
you: "Like mother, like daughter."
45 You are a true daughter of your
mother, who despised her husband and her children; and you are
a true sister of your sisters, who
despised their husbands and their
children. Your mother was a Hittite and your father an Amorite.
46 Your older sister was Samaria,
who lived to the north of you with
her daughters; and your younger
sister, who lived to the south of
you with her daughters, was Sodom. 47 You not only followed their
ways and copied their detestable
practices, but in all your ways you
soon became more depraved than
they. 48 As surely as I live, declares
the Sovereign LORD, your sister
Sodom and her daughters never
did what you and your daughters
have done. Mt 10:15; 11:23-24

49 " 'Now this was the sin of your
sister Sodom: She and her daughters were arrogant, overfed and
unconcerned; they did not help
the poor and needy. 50 They were
haughty and did detestable things
before me. Therefore I did away
with them as you have seen. 51 Samaria did not commit half the
sins you did. You have done more
detestable things than they, and
have made your sisters seem righteous by all these things you have
done. 52 Bear your disgrace, for you
have furnished some justification
for your sisters. Because your sins
were more vile than theirs, they
appear more righteous than you.
So then, be ashamed and bear
your disgrace, for you have made
your sisters appear righteous.

Ge 13:13; Lk 12:16-20

53 " 'However, I will restore
the fortunes of Sodom and her
daughters and of Samaria and
her daughters, and your fortunes

along with them, 54so that you
may bear your disgrace and be
ashamed of all you have done in
giving them comfort. 55And your
sisters, Sodom with her daughters
and Samaria with her daughters,
will return to what they were before; and you and your daughters
will return to what you were before. 56You would not even mention your sister Sodom in the
day of your pride, 57before your
wickedness was uncovered. Even
so, you are now scorned by the
daughters of Edom[a] and all her
neighbors and the daughters of
the Philistines — all those around
you who despise you. 58You will
bear the consequences of your
lewdness and your detestable
practices, declares the LORD.

2Ki 16:6; Eze 23:49

59" 'This is what the Sovereign
LORD says: I will deal with you as
you deserve, because you have
despised my oath by breaking the
covenant. 60Yet I will remember
the covenant I made with you in
the days of your youth, and I will
establish an everlasting covenant
with you. 61Then you will remember your ways and be ashamed
when you receive your sisters,
both those who are older than you
and those who are younger. I will
give them to you as daughters, but
not on the basis of my covenant
with you. 62So I will establish my
covenant with you, and you will
know that I am the LORD. 63Then,
when I make atonement for you
for all you have done, you will remember and be ashamed and never again open your mouth because
of your humiliation, declares the
Sovereign LORD.' " Jer 32:40; Ro 3:19

Two Eagles and a Vine

17 The word of the LORD came
to me: 2"Son of man, set forth
an allegory and tell it to the Israelites as a parable. 3Say to them,
'This is what the Sovereign LORD
says: A great eagle with powerful wings, long feathers and full
plumage of varied colors came to
Lebanon. Taking hold of the top of
a cedar, 4he broke off its topmost
shoot and carried it away to a land
of merchants, where he planted it
in a city of traders. Jer 22:23; Eze 20:49

5" 'He took one of the seedlings
of the land and put it in fertile
soil. He planted it like a willow by
abundant water, 6and it sprouted and became a low, spreading
vine. Its branches turned toward
him, but its roots remained under
it. So it became a vine and produced branches and put out leafy
boughs. Dt 8:7-9; Isa 44:4

7" 'But there was another great
eagle with powerful wings and
full plumage. The vine now sent
out its roots toward him from
the plot where it was planted and
stretched out its branches to him
for water. 8It had been planted in
good soil by abundant water so

[a] 57 Many Hebrew manuscripts and Syriac; most Hebrew manuscripts, Septuagint and Vulgate *Aram*

that it would produce branches,
bear fruit and become a splendid
vine.' Eze 31:4
9“Say to them, ‘This is what
the Sovereign LORD says: Will it
thrive? Will it not be uprooted
and stripped of its fruit so that it
withers? All its new growth will
wither. It will not take a strong
arm or many people to pull it up
by the roots. 10It has been planted,
but will it thrive? Will it not wither completely when the east wind
strikes it — wither away in the plot
where it grew?’ ” Hos 13:15
11Then the word of the LORD
came to me: 12“Say to this rebellious people, ‘Do you not know
what these things mean?’ Say to
them: ‘The king of Babylon went
to Jerusalem and carried off her
king and her nobles, bringing
them back with him to Babylon.
13Then he took a member of the
royal family and made a treaty
with him, putting him under oath.
He also carried away the leading
men of the land, 14so that the kingdom would be brought low, unable
to rise again, surviving only by
keeping his treaty. 15But the king
rebelled against him by sending
his envoys to Egypt to get horses
and a large army. Will he succeed?
Will he who does such things escape? Will he break the treaty and
yet escape? 2Ch 36:13; Eze 12:9; 29:14
16“ ‘As surely as I live, declares
the Sovereign LORD, he shall die
in Babylon, in the land of the king
who put him on the throne, whose
oath he despised and whose treaty he broke. 17Pharaoh with his
mighty army and great horde will
be of no help to him in war, when
ramps are built and siege works
erected to destroy many lives. 18He
despised the oath by breaking the
covenant. Because he had given
his hand in pledge and yet did all
these things, he shall not escape.
1Ch 29:24; Eze 29:6-7
19“ ‘Therefore this is what the
Sovereign LORD says: As surely as
I live, I will repay him for despis-
ing my oath and breaking my covenant. 20I will spread my net for
him, and he will be caught in my
snare. I will bring him to Babylon
and execute judgment on him
there because he was unfaithful
to me. 21All his choice troops will
fall by the sword, and the survivors will be scattered to the winds.
Then you will know that I the
LORD have spoken. Eze 12:13-14; 20:36
22“ ‘This is what the Sovereign
LORD says: I myself will take a
shoot from the very top of a cedar and plant it; I will break off
a tender sprig from its topmost
shoots and plant it on a high and
lofty mountain. 23On the mountain heights of Israel I will plant
it; it will produce branches and
bear fruit and become a splendid cedar. Birds of every kind will
nest in it; they will find shelter in
the shade of its branches. 24All the
trees of the forest will know that I
the LORD bring down the tall tree
and make the low tree grow tall.

I dry up the green tree and make
the dry tree flourish. Ps 96:12; Jer 23:5
"'I the LORD have spoken, and I
will do it.'" Eze 19:12; Am 9:11

The One Who Sins Will Die

18 The word of the LORD came
to me: 2"What do you peo-
ple mean by quoting this proverb
about the land of Israel:

"'The parents eat sour grapes,
and the children's teeth
are set on edge'?
Isa 3:15; Jer 31:29; La 5:7

3"As surely as I live, declares the
Sovereign LORD, you will no longer quote this proverb in Israel.
4For everyone belongs to me, the
parent as well as the child — both
alike belong to me. The one who
sins is the one who will die.
Ro 6:23; Isa 42:5

5"Suppose there is a righteous
man
who does what is just and
right.
6He does not eat at the
mountain shrines Eze 22:9
or look to the idols of Israel.
Dt 4:19; Eze 6:13
He does not defile his
neighbor's wife
or have sexual relations with
a woman during her
period. Lev 12:2
7He does not oppress anyone,
Ex 22:21
but returns what he took in
pledge for a loan. Dt 24:12
He does not commit robbery
Ex 20:15
but gives his food to the
hungry Job 22:7
and provides clothing for the
naked. Dt 15:11; Mt 25:36
8He does not lend to them at
interest
or take a profit from them.
Ex 22:25; Lev 25:35-37; Dt 23:19-20
He withholds his hand from
doing wrong
and judges fairly between
two parties. Zec 8:16
9He follows my decrees Lev 19:37
and faithfully keeps my laws.
That man is righteous; Hab 2:4
he will surely live,
Lev 18:5; Am 5:4
declares the Sovereign
LORD.

10"Suppose he has a violent son,
who sheds blood or does any of
these other things[a] 11(though the
father has done none of them):
Ex 21:12

"He eats at the mountain
shrines.
He defiles his neighbor's wife.
12He oppresses the poor and
needy. Am 4:1
He commits robbery.
He does not return what he
took in pledge.
He looks to the idols.
He does detestable things.
Isa 59:6-7; Eze 8:6,17
13He lends at interest and takes a
profit. Ex 22:25

[a] 10 *Or things to a brother*

Will such a man live? He will not!
Because he has done all these detestable things, he is to be put to
death; his blood will be on his own
head. Eze 33:4-5

[14]"But suppose this son has a
son who sees all the sins his father commits, and though he sees
them, he does not do such things:
2Ch 34:21; Pr 23:24

[15]"He does not eat at the
mountain shrines
or look to the idols of Israel.
He does not defile his
neighbor's wife.
[16]He does not oppress anyone
or require a pledge for a loan.
He does not commit robbery
but gives his food to the
hungry
and provides clothing for the
naked. Ps 41:1; Isa 58:10
[17]He withholds his hand from
mistreating the poor
and takes no interest or
profit from them.
He keeps my laws and follows
my decrees.

He will not die for his father's sin;
he will surely live. [18]But his father
will die for his own sin, because
he practiced extortion, robbed his
brother and did what was wrong
among his people.

[19]"Yet you ask, 'Why does the son
not share the guilt of his father?'
Since the son has done what is just
and right and has been careful to
keep all my decrees, he will surely
live. [20]The one who sins is the one
who will die. The child will not
share the guilt of the parent, nor
will the parent share the guilt of
the child. The righteousness of the
righteous will be credited to them,
and the wickedness of the wicked
will be charged against them.
Dt 24:16; Isa 3:11; Ro 2:9

[21]"But if a wicked person turns
away from all the sins they have
committed and keeps all my decrees and does what is just and
right, that person will surely live;
they will not die. [22]None of the offenses they have committed will
be remembered against them.
Because of the righteous things
they have done, they will live.
[23]Do I take any pleasure in the
death of the wicked? declares the
Sovereign LORD. Rather, am I not
pleased when they turn from their
ways and live? Eze 33:11; 1Ti 2:4

[24]"But if a righteous person
turns from their righteousness
and commits sin and does the
same detestable things the wicked
person does, will they live? None
of the righteous things that person has done will be remembered.
Because of the unfaithfulness they
are guilty of and because of the
sins they have committed, they
will die. Eze 3:20; 20:27; 2Pe 2:20-22

[25]"Yet you say, 'The way of the
Lord is not just.' Hear, you Israelites: Is my way unjust? Is it not
your ways that are unjust? [26]If a
righteous person turns from their
righteousness and commits sin,
they will die for it; because of the

sin they have committed they will
die. 27But if a wicked person turns
away from the wickedness they
have committed and does what is
just and right, they will save their
life. 28Because they consider all the
offenses they have committed and
turn away from them, that person
will surely live; they will not die.
29Yet the Israelites say, 'The way of
the Lord is not just.' Are my ways
unjust, people of Israel? Is it not
your ways that are unjust?

Eze 33:17; Zep 3:5; Mal 2:17

30"Therefore, you Israelites, I
will judge each of you according to
your own ways, declares the Sovereign LORD. Repent! Turn away
from all your offenses; then sin
will not be your downfall. 31Rid
yourselves of all the offenses you
have committed, and get a new
heart and a new spirit. Why will
you die, people of Israel? 32For I
take no pleasure in the death of
anyone, declares the Sovereign
LORD. Repent and live! Eze 7:3; 11:19

A Lament Over Israel's Princes

19 "Take up a lament concerning the princes of Israel
2and say: 2Ki 24:6; Eze 26:17

"'What a lioness was your
mother
among the lions!
She lay down among them
and reared her cubs.
3She brought up one of her
cubs,
and he became a strong lion.
He learned to tear the prey
and he became a man-eater.
4The nations heard about him,
and he was trapped in their
pit.
They led him with hooks
to the land of Egypt.

2Ki 23:33-34; 2Ch 36:4

5"'When she saw her hope
unfulfilled,
her expectation gone,
she took another of her cubs
and made him a strong lion.

2Ki 23:34

6He prowled among the lions,
for he was now a strong
lion.
He learned to tear the prey
and he became a man-eater.

2Ki 24:9; 2Ch 36:9

7He broke down[a] their
strongholds
and devastated their towns.

Eze 30:12

The land and all who were in it
were terrified by his
roaring.
8Then the nations came against
him, 2Ki 24:2
those from regions round
about.
They spread their net for him,
and he was trapped in their
pit. 2Ki 24:11
9With hooks they pulled him
into a cage
and brought him to the king
of Babylon. 2Ch 36:6

[a] 7 Targum (see Septuagint); Hebrew *He knew*

They put him in prison,
so his roar was heard no longer
on the mountains of Israel.
2Ki 24:15

10 " 'Your mother was like a vine
in your vineyard[a]
planted by the water; Ps 80:8-11
it was fruitful and full of branches
because of abundant water.
11 Its branches were strong,
fit for a ruler's scepter.
It towered high
above the thick foliage,
conspicuous for its height
and for its many branches.
Eze 31:3; Da 4:11
12 But it was uprooted in fury
Eze 17:10
and thrown to the ground.
The east wind made it shrivel,
it was stripped of its fruit;
its strong branches withered
and fire consumed them.
Eze 28:17; Hos 13:15
13 Now it is planted in the desert,
Eze 20:35
in a dry and thirsty land.
Hos 2:3
14 Fire spread from one of its main[b] branches
and consumed its fruit.
Eze 20:47
No strong branch is left on it
fit for a ruler's scepter.' Eze 15:4

"This is a lament and is to be used as a lament."

Rebellious Israel Purged

20 In the seventh year, in the
fifth month on the tenth
day, some of the elders of Israel
came to inquire of the LORD, and
they sat down in front of me.
Eze 8:1

2 Then the word of the LORD
came to me: 3 "Son of man, speak
to the elders of Israel and say to
them, 'This is what the Sovereign
LORD says: Have you come to inquire of me? As surely as I live, I
will not let you inquire of me, declares the Sovereign LORD.'
Eze 14:3; Mic 3:7

4 "Will you judge them? Will you
judge them, son of man? Then
confront them with the detestable practices of their ancestors
5 and say to them: 'This is what the
Sovereign LORD says: On the day I
chose Israel, I swore with uplifted
hand to the descendants of Jacob
and revealed myself to them in
Egypt. With uplifted hand I said to
them, "I am the LORD your God."
6 On that day I swore to them that
I would bring them out of Egypt
into a land I had searched out for
them, a land flowing with milk
and honey, the most beautiful
of all lands. 7 And I said to them,
"Each of you, get rid of the vile
images you have set your eyes on,
and do not defile yourselves with
the idols of Egypt. I am the LORD
your God." Ex 6:7; Dt 8:7; Ps 48:2

[a] *10* Two Hebrew manuscripts; most Hebrew manuscripts *your blood*
[b] *14* Or *from under its*

8“ ‘But they rebelled against me
and would not listen to me; they
did not get rid of the vile images
they had set their eyes on, nor did
they forsake the idols of Egypt. So
I said I would pour out my wrath
on them and spend my anger
against them in Egypt. 9But for the
sake of my name, I brought them
out of Egypt. I did it to keep my
name from being profaned in the
eyes of the nations among whom
they lived and in whose sight I
had revealed myself to the Israelites. 10Therefore I led them out of
Egypt and brought them into the
wilderness. 11I gave them my decrees and made known to them
my laws, by which the person who
obeys them will live. 12Also I gave
them my Sabbaths as a sign between us, so they would know that
I the LORD made them holy.

Lev 18:5; Dt 4:7-8; Ro 10:5

13“ ‘Yet the people of Israel rebelled against me in the wilderness. They did not follow my decrees but rejected my laws — by
which the person who obeys
them will live — and they utterly desecrated my Sabbaths. So I
said I would pour out my wrath
on them and destroy them in the
wilderness. 14But for the sake of
my name I did what would keep it
from being profaned in the eyes
of the nations in whose sight I had
brought them out. 15Also with uplifted hand I swore to them in the
wilderness that I would not bring
them into the land I had given
them — a land flowing with milk
and honey, the most beautiful of
all lands — 16because they rejected my laws and did not follow my
decrees and desecrated my Sabbaths. For their hearts were devoted to their idols. 17Yet I looked
on them with pity and did not destroy them or put an end to them
in the wilderness. 18I said to their
children in the wilderness, “Do
not follow the statutes of your
parents or keep their laws or defile yourselves with their idols. 19I
am the LORD your God; follow my
decrees and be careful to keep my
laws. 20Keep my Sabbaths holy,
that they may be a sign between
us. Then you will know that I am
the LORD your God.”

Dt 5:32-33; Am 5:26

21“ ‘But the children rebelled
against me: They did not follow
my decrees, they were not careful
to keep my laws, of which I said,
“The person who obeys them will
live by them,” and they desecrated my Sabbaths. So I said I would
pour out my wrath on them and
spend my anger against them in
the wilderness. 22But I withheld
my hand, and for the sake of my
name I did what would keep it
from being profaned in the eyes
of the nations in whose sight I had
brought them out. 23Also with uplifted hand I swore to them in the
wilderness that I would disperse
them among the nations and scatter them through the countries,
24because they had not obeyed my

laws but had rejected my decrees
and desecrated my Sabbaths, and
their eyes lusted after their parents' idols. 25So I gave them other statutes that were not good and
laws through which they could
not live; 26I defiled them through
their gifts — the sacrifice of every
firstborn — that I might fill them
with horror so they would know
that I am the LORD.'

Lev 26:33; Dt 28:64; Ps 81:12

27"Therefore, son of man, speak
to the people of Israel and say to
them, 'This is what the Sovereign
LORD says: In this also your ancestors blasphemed me by being unfaithful to me: 28When I brought
them into the land I had sworn to
give them and they saw any high
hill or any leafy tree, there they
offered their sacrifices, made offerings that aroused my anger,
presented their fragrant incense
and poured out their drink offerings. 29Then I said to them: What
is this high place you go to?'" (It is
called Bamah[a] to this day.)

Eze 6:13; Ro 2:24

Rebellious Israel Renewed

30"Therefore say to the Israelites: 'This is what the Sovereign
LORD says: Will you defile yourselves the way your ancestors did
and lust after their vile images?
31When you offer your gifts — the
sacrifice of your children in the
fire — you continue to defile yourselves with all your idols to this
day. Am I to let you inquire of me,
you Israelites? As surely as I live,
declares the Sovereign LORD, I will
not let you inquire of me.

Ps 106:37-39; Jer 16:12; Eze 16:20

32" 'You say, "We want to be like
the nations, like the peoples of the
world, who serve wood and stone."
But what you have in mind will
never happen. 33As surely as I live,
declares the Sovereign LORD, I will
reign over you with a mighty hand
and an outstretched arm and with
outpoured wrath. 34I will bring
you from the nations and gather you from the countries where
you have been scattered — with a
mighty hand and an outstretched
arm and with outpoured wrath.
35I will bring you into the wilderness of the nations and there, face
to face, I will execute judgment
upon you. 36As I judged your ancestors in the wilderness of the
land of Egypt, so I will judge you,
declares the Sovereign LORD. 37I
will take note of you as you pass
under my rod, and I will bring you
into the bond of the covenant. 38I
will purge you of those who revolt
and rebel against me. Although
I will bring them out of the land
where they are living, yet they will
not enter the land of Israel. Then
you will know that I am the LORD.

Lev 27:32; Jer 33:13; Eze 16:62

39" 'As for you, people of Israel,
this is what the Sovereign LORD
says: Go and serve your idols, every one of you! But afterward
you will surely listen to me and

[a] 29 *Bamah* means *high place.*

no longer profane my holy name
with your gifts and idols. 40For
on my holy mountain, the high
mountain of Israel, declares the
Sovereign LORD, there in the land
all the people of Israel will serve
me, and there I will accept them.
There I will require your offerings
and your choice gifts,[a] along with
all your holy sacrifices. 41I will accept you as fragrant incense when
I bring you out from the nations
and gather you from the countries where you have been scattered, and I will be proved holy
through you in the sight of the
nations. 42Then you will know that
I am the LORD, when I bring you
into the land of Israel, the land I
had sworn with uplifted hand to
give to your ancestors. 43There you
will remember your conduct and
all the actions by which you have
defiled yourselves, and you will
loathe yourselves for all the evil
you have done. 44You will know
that I am the LORD, when I deal
with you for my name's sake and
not according to your evil ways
and your corrupt practices, you
people of Israel, declares the Sovereign LORD.' " Eze 16:61; Hos 5:15

Prophecy Against the South

45The word of the LORD came to
me: 46"Son of man, set your face
toward the south; preach against
the south and prophesy against
the forest of the southland. 47Say
to the southern forest: 'Hear the
word of the LORD. This is what the
Sovereign LORD says: I am about
to set fire to you, and it will consume all your trees, both green
and dry. The blazing flame will not
be quenched, and every face from
south to north will be scorched by
it. 48Everyone will see that I the
LORD have kindled it; it will not be
quenched.' " Jer 7:20; 21:14

49Then I said, "Sovereign LORD,
they are saying of me, 'Isn't he just
telling parables?' "[b] Mt 13:13; Jn 16:25

Babylon as God's Sword of Judgment

21[c] The word of the LORD
came to me: 2"Son of man,
set your face against Jerusalem
and preach against the sanctuary. Prophesy against the land
of Israel 3and say to her: 'This is
what the LORD says: I am against
you. I will draw my sword from
its sheath and cut off from you
both the righteous and the wicked. 4Because I am going to cut off
the righteous and the wicked, my
sword will be unsheathed against
everyone from south to north.
5Then all people will know that I
the LORD have drawn my sword
from its sheath; it will not return
again.' Eze 20:46-47; Na 1:9

6"Therefore groan, son of man!
Groan before them with broken heart and bitter grief. 7And
when they ask you, 'Why are you

[a] 40 Or *and the gifts of your firstfruits*
[b] 49 In Hebrew texts 20:45-49 is numbered 21:1-5. [c] In Hebrew texts 21:1-32 is numbered 21:6-37.

groaning?' you shall say, 'Because of the news that is coming. Every heart will melt with fear and every hand go limp; every spirit will become faint and every leg will be wet with urine.' It is coming! It will surely take place, declares the Sovereign LORD." Isa 22:4; Eze 7:17

8 The word of the LORD came to
me: 9 "Son of man, prophesy and
say, 'This is what the Lord says:

"'A sword, a sword,
sharpened and polished —
10 sharpened for the slaughter, Ps 110:5-6; Isa 34:5-6
polished to flash like lightning!

"'Shall we rejoice in the scepter of my royal son? The sword despises every such stick.

11 "'The sword is appointed to be polished, Jer 46:4
to be grasped with the hand;
it is sharpened and polished,
made ready for the hand of the slayer.
12 Cry out and wail, son of man,
for it is against my people;
it is against all the princes of Israel.
They are thrown to the sword
along with my people.
Therefore beat your breast. Jer 31:19

13 "'Testing will surely come. And what if even the scepter, which the sword despises, does not continue? declares the Sovereign LORD.'

14 "So then, son of man,
prophesy
and strike your hands together. Nu 24:10
Let the sword strike twice,
even three times.
It is a sword for slaughter —
a sword for great slaughter,
closing in on them from every side. Eze 6:11; 30:24
15 So that hearts may melt with fear 2Sa 17:10
and the fallen be many,
I have stationed the sword for slaughter[a] Ps 22:14
at all their gates.
Look! It is forged to strike like lightning,
it is grasped for slaughter.
16 Slash to the right, you sword,
then to the left,
wherever your blade is turned.
17 I too will strike my hands together, Eze 22:13
and my wrath will subside. Eze 5:13
I the LORD have spoken." Eze 6:11

18 The word of the LORD came to
me: 19 "Son of man, mark out two
roads for the sword of the king
of Babylon to take, both starting
from the same country. Make a
signpost where the road branches off to the city. 20 Mark out one
road for the sword to come against
Rabbah of the Ammonites and another against Judah and fortified

[a] 15 Septuagint; the meaning of the Hebrew for this word is uncertain.

Jerusalem. [21]For the king of Babylon will stop at the fork in the
road, at the junction of the two
roads, to seek an omen: He will
cast lots with arrows, he will consult his idols, he will examine the
liver. [22]Into his right hand will
come the lot for Jerusalem, where
he is to set up battering rams, to
give the command to slaughter, to
sound the battle cry, to set battering rams against the gates, to build
a ramp and to erect siege works.
[23]It will seem like a false omen to
those who have sworn allegiance
to him, but he will remind them of
their guilt and take them captive.
Nu 23:23; Eze 4:2

[24]"Therefore this is what the
Sovereign LORD says: 'Because
you people have brought to mind
your guilt by your open rebellion,
revealing your sins in all that you
do — because you have done this,
you will be taken captive.

[25]" 'You profane and wicked
prince of Israel, whose day has
come, whose time of punishment
has reached its climax, [26]this is
what the Sovereign LORD says:
Take off the turban, remove the
crown. It will not be as it was: The
lowly will be exalted and the exalted will be brought low. [27]A ruin!
A ruin! I will make it a ruin! The
crown will not be restored until
he to whom it rightfully belongs
shall come; to him I will give it.'
Ps 2:6; Eze 37:24; Hag 2:21-22

[28]"And you, son of man, prophesy and say, 'This is what the Sovereign LORD says about the Ammonites and their insults: Zep 2:8

" 'A sword, a sword, Jer 12:12
drawn for the slaughter,
polished to consume
and to flash like lightning!
[29]Despite false visions
concerning you
and lying divinations about
you,
it will be laid on the necks
of the wicked who are to be
slain,
whose day has come,
whose time of punishment
has reached its climax.
Eze 22:28; 35:5

[30]" 'Let the sword return to its
sheath. Jer 47:6
In the place where you were
created,
in the land of your ancestry,
Eze 16:3
I will judge you.
[31]I will pour out my wrath on
you
and breathe out my fiery
anger against you;
Eze 22:20-21
I will deliver you into the
hands of brutal men,
men skilled in destruction.
Jer 51:20-23
[32]You will be fuel for the fire,
Mal 4:1
your blood will be shed in
your land,
you will be remembered no
more; Eze 25:10
for I the LORD have spoken.' "

Judgment on Jerusalem's Sins

22 The word of the LORD came
to me:

2“Son of man, will you judge her?
Will you judge this city of bloodshed? Then confront her with all
her detestable practices 3and say:
‘This is what the Sovereign LORD
says: You city that brings on herself doom by shedding blood in
her midst and defiles herself by
making idols, 4you have become
guilty because of the blood you
have shed and have become defiled by the idols you have made.
You have brought your days to a
close, and the end of your years
has come. Therefore I will make
you an object of scorn to the nations and a laughingstock to all
the countries. 5Those who are near
and those who are far away will
mock you, you infamous city, full
of turmoil. 2Ki 21:16; Eze 5:14; Na 3:1

6“ ‘See how each of the princes
of Israel who are in you uses his
power to shed blood. 7In you they
have treated father and mother
with contempt; in you they have
oppressed the foreigner and mistreated the fatherless and the widow. 8You have despised my holy
things and desecrated my Sabbaths. 9In you are slanderers who
are bent on shedding blood; in you
are those who eat at the mountain
shrines and commit lewd acts. 10In
you are those who dishonor their
father's bed; in you are those who
violate women during their period, when they are ceremonially
unclean. 11In you one man commits a detestable offense with his
neighbor's wife, another shamefully defiles his daughter-in-law,
and another violates his sister, his
own father's daughter. 12In you are
people who accept bribes to shed
blood; you take interest and make
a profit from the poor. You extort
unjust gain from your neighbors.
And you have forgotten me, declares the Sovereign LORD.

Lev 18:15; Dt 27:25; Mic 7:3

13“ ‘I will surely strike my hands
together at the unjust gain you
have made and at the blood you
have shed in your midst. 14Will
your courage endure or your
hands be strong in the day I deal
with you? I the LORD have spoken,
and I will do it. 15I will disperse you
among the nations and scatter you
through the countries; and I will
put an end to your uncleanness.
16When you have been defiled[a] in
the eyes of the nations, you will
know that I am the LORD.’ ”

Dt 4:27; Eze 21:7; 23:27

17Then the word of the LORD
came to me: 18“Son of man, the
people of Israel have become dross
to me; all of them are the copper, tin, iron and lead left inside
a furnace. They are but the dross
of silver. 19Therefore this is what
the Sovereign LORD says: ‘Because
you have all become dross, I will
gather you into Jerusalem. 20As

[a] 16 Or *When I have allotted you your inheritance*

silver, copper, iron, lead and tin
are gathered into a furnace to be
melted with a fiery blast, so will
I gather you in my anger and my
wrath and put you inside the city
and melt you. 21I will gather you
and I will blow on you with my fiery wrath, and you will be melted
inside her. 22As silver is melted in
a furnace, so you will be melted
inside her, and you will know that
I the LORD have poured out my
wrath on you.'"

Jer 6:28-30; Eze 20:8,33; Mal 3:2

23Again the word of the LORD
came to me: 24"Son of man, say to
the land, 'You are a land that has
not been cleansed or rained on in
the day of wrath.' 25There is a conspiracy of her princes[a] within her
like a roaring lion tearing its prey;
they devour people, take treasures
and precious things and make
many widows within her. 26Her
priests do violence to my law and
profane my holy things; they do
not distinguish between the holy
and the common; they teach that
there is no difference between the
unclean and the clean; and they
shut their eyes to the keeping of
my Sabbaths, so that I am profaned among them. 27Her officials
within her are like wolves tearing
their prey; they shed blood and kill
people to make unjust gain. 28Her
prophets whitewash these deeds
for them by false visions and lying divinations. They say, 'This is
what the Sovereign LORD says'—
when the LORD has not spoken.
29The people of the land practice
extortion and commit robbery;
they oppress the poor and needy
and mistreat the foreigner, denying them justice. Ex 23:9; Eze 13:2,6-7

30"I looked for someone among
them who would build up the wall
and stand before me in the gap on
behalf of the land so I would not
have to destroy it, but I found no
one. 31So I will pour out my wrath
on them and consume them with
my fiery anger, bringing down
on their own heads all they have
done, declares the Sovereign
LORD." Jer 5:1; Eze 13:5

Two Adulterous Sisters

23 The word of the LORD came
to me: 2"Son of man, there
were two women, daughters of the
same mother. 3They became prostitutes in Egypt, engaging in prostitution from their youth. In that
land their breasts were fondled
and their virgin bosoms caressed.
4The older was named Oholah,
and her sister was Oholibah. They
were mine and gave birth to sons
and daughters. Oholah is Samaria,
and Oholibah is Jerusalem.

Jer 3:7; Eze 16:45

5"Oholah engaged in prostitution while she was still mine; and
she lusted after her lovers, the
Assyrians—warriors 6clothed in
blue, governors and commanders, all of them handsome young
men, and mounted horsemen.
7She gave herself as a prostitute to

[a] 25 Septuagint; Hebrew *prophets*

all the elite of the Assyrians and
defiled herself with all the idols of
everyone she lusted after. 8She did
not give up the prostitution she
began in Egypt, when during her
youth men slept with her, caressed
her virgin bosom and poured out
their lust on her. 2Ki 16:7; Hos 8:9

9"Therefore I delivered her into
the hands of her lovers, the Assyrians, for whom she lusted. 10They
stripped her naked, took away her
sons and daughters and killed her
with the sword. She became a byword among women, and punishment was inflicted on her.
Eze 16:36; Hos 11:5

11"Her sister Oholibah saw this,
yet in her lust and prostitution
she was more depraved than her
sister. 12She too lusted after the
Assyrians — governors and commanders, warriors in full dress,
mounted horsemen, all handsome
young men. 13I saw that she too
defiled herself; both of them went
the same way. 2Ki 16:7-15; Jer 3:8-11

14"But she carried her prostitution still further. She saw men portrayed on a wall, figures of Chaldeans[a] portrayed in red, 15with belts
around their waists and flowing
turbans on their heads; all of them
looked like Babylonian chariot officers, natives of Chaldea.[b] 16As
soon as she saw them, she lusted
after them and sent messengers to
them in Chaldea. 17Then the Babylonians came to her, to the bed
of love, and in their lust they defiled her. After she had been defiled by them, she turned away
from them in disgust. 18When she
carried on her prostitution openly and exposed her naked body, I
turned away from her in disgust,
just as I had turned away from her
sister. 19Yet she became more and
more promiscuous as she recalled
the days of her youth, when she
was a prostitute in Egypt. 20There
she lusted after her lovers, whose
genitals were like those of donkeys and whose emission was like
that of horses. 21So you longed for
the lewdness of your youth, when
in Egypt your bosom was caressed
and your young breasts fondled.[c]
Jer 40:9; Eze 16:29

22"Therefore, Oholibah, this is
what the Sovereign LORD says: I
will stir up your lovers against
you, those you turned away from
in disgust, and I will bring them
against you from every side —
23the Babylonians and all the Chaldeans, the men of Pekod and Shoa
and Koa, and all the Assyrians with
them, handsome young men, all
of them governors and commanders, chariot officers and men of
high rank, all mounted on horses.
24They will come against you with
weapons,[d] chariots and wagons
and with a throng of people; they
will take up positions against you
on every side with large and small
shields and with helmets. I will

[a] 14 Or *Babylonians* [b] 15 Or *Babylonia*; also in verse 16 [c] 21 Syriac (see also verse 3); Hebrew *caressed because of your young breasts* [d] 24 The meaning of the Hebrew for this word is uncertain.

turn you over to them for punishment, and they will punish you according to their standards. [25]I will direct my jealous anger against you, and they will deal with you in fury. They will cut off your noses and your ears, and those of you who are left will fall by the sword. They will take away your sons and daughters, and those of you who are left will be consumed by fire. [26]They will also strip you of your clothes and take your fine jewelry. [27]So I will put a stop to the lewdness and prostitution you began in Egypt. You will not look on these things with longing or remember Egypt anymore. Eze 16:37,39,41

[28]"For this is what the Sovereign LORD says: I am about to deliver you into the hands of those you hate, to those you turned away from in disgust. [29]They will deal with you in hatred and take away everything you have worked for. They will leave you stark naked, and the shame of your prostitution will be exposed. Your lewdness and promiscuity [30]have brought this on you, because you lusted after the nations and defiled yourself with their idols. [31]You have gone the way of your sister; so I will put her cup into your hand. Jer 34:20; Eze 6:9

[32]"This is what the Sovereign LORD says:

"You will drink your sister's
cup,
a cup large and deep;
it will bring scorn and derision,
for it holds so much.
Ps 60:3; Isa 51:17; Jer 25:15

[33]You will be filled with
drunkenness and sorrow,
the cup of ruin and
desolation,
the cup of your sister
Samaria. Jer 25:15-16
[34]You will drink it and drain it
dry Ps 75:8; Isa 51:17
and chew on its pieces —
and you will tear your
breasts.

I have spoken, declares the Sovereign LORD.

[35]"Therefore this is what the Sovereign LORD says: Since you have forgotten me and turned your back on me, you must bear the consequences of your lewdness and prostitution." 1Ki 14:9; Jer 3:21

[36]The LORD said to me: "Son of man, will you judge Oholah and Oholibah? Then confront them with their detestable practices, [37]for they have committed adultery and blood is on their hands. They committed adultery with their idols; they even sacrificed their children, whom they bore to me, as food for them. [38]They have also done this to me: At that same time they defiled my sanctuary and desecrated my Sabbaths. [39]On the very day they sacrificed their children to their idols, they entered my sanctuary and desecrated it. That is what they did in my house. 2Ki 21:4; Jer 7:10

40 "They even sent messengers
for men who came from far away,
and when they arrived you bathed
yourself for them, applied eye
makeup and put on your jewelry. 41 You sat on an elegant couch,
with a table spread before it on
which you had placed the incense
and olive oil that belonged to me.
Isa 57:9; Am 6:4

42 "The noise of a carefree crowd
was around her; drunkards were
brought from the desert along with
men from the rabble, and they put
bracelets on the wrists of the woman and her sister and beautiful
crowns on their heads. 43 Then I said
about the one worn out by adultery,
'Now let them use her as a prostitute, for that is all she is.' 44 And they
slept with her. As men sleep with a
prostitute, so they slept with those
lewd women, Oholah and Oholibah. 45 But righteous judges will
sentence them to the punishment
of women who commit adultery
and shed blood, because they are
adulterous and blood is on their
hands. Eze 16:38; Hos 6:5

46 "This is what the Sovereign
LORD says: Bring a mob against
them and give them over to terror
and plunder. 47 The mob will stone
them and cut them down with
their swords; they will kill their
sons and daughters and burn down
their houses. 2Ch 36:19; Eze 16:40-41

48 "So I will put an end to lewdness in the land, that all women
may take warning and not imitate
you. 49 You will suffer the penalty for your lewdness and bear the
consequences of your sins of idolatry. Then you will know that I am
the Sovereign LORD." Eze 7:4; 2Pe 2:6

Jerusalem as a Cooking Pot

24 In the ninth year, in the
tenth month on the tenth
day, the word of the LORD came to
me: 2 "Son of man, record this date,
this very date, because the king of
Babylon has laid siege to Jerusalem this very day. 3 Tell this rebellious people a parable and say to
them: 'This is what the Sovereign
LORD says: Jer 39:1; Eze 17:2

" 'Put on the cooking pot;
put it on
and pour water into it.
Jer 1:13; Eze 11:3

4 Put into it the pieces of meat,
all the choice pieces — the
leg and the shoulder.
Fill it with the best of these
bones;
5 take the pick of the flock.
Jer 52:10

Pile wood beneath it for the
bones;
bring it to a boil
and cook the bones in it.
Jer 52:24-27

6 " 'For this is what the Sovereign
LORD says:

" 'Woe to the city of bloodshed,
Eze 22:2

to the pot now encrusted,
whose deposit will not go
away!

Take the meat out piece by piece
in whatever order it comes.
Ob 1:11; Na 3:10

7 " 'For the blood she shed is in her midst:
She poured it on the bare rock;
she did not pour it on the ground,
where the dust would cover it. Lev 17:13
8 To stir up wrath and take revenge
I put her blood on the bare rock,
so that it would not be covered.

9 " 'Therefore this is what the Sovereign LORD says:

" 'Woe to the city of bloodshed!
I, too, will pile the wood high.
10 So heap on the wood
and kindle the fire.
Cook the meat well,
mixing in the spices;
and let the bones be charred.
11 Then set the empty pot on the coals
till it becomes hot and its copper glows,
so that its impurities may be melted
and its deposit burned away.
Jer 21:10; Eze 22:15
12 It has frustrated all efforts;
its heavy deposit has not been removed,
not even by fire.

13 " 'Now your impurity is lewdness. Because I tried to cleanse you but you would not be cleansed from your impurity, you will not be clean again until my wrath against you has subsided.
Jer 6:28-30; Eze 16:42; 22:24

14 " 'I the LORD have spoken. The time has come for me to act. I will not hold back; I will not have pity, nor will I relent. You will be judged according to your conduct and your actions, declares the Sovereign LORD.' " Eze 18:30; 36:19

Ezekiel's Wife Dies

15 The word of the LORD came to
me: 16 "Son of man, with one blow
I am about to take away from you
the delight of your eyes. Yet do not
lament or weep or shed any tears.
17 Groan quietly; do not mourn for
the dead. Keep your turban fastened and your sandals on your feet; do not cover your mustache and beard or eat the customary food of mourners." Jer 13:17; 16:7
18 So I spoke to the people in the morning, and in the evening my wife died. The next morning I did as I had been commanded.
19 Then the people asked me, "Won't you tell us what these things have to do with us? Why are you acting like this?" Eze 12:9
20 So I said to them, "The word of
the LORD came to me: 21 Say to the
people of Israel, 'This is what the Sovereign LORD says: I am about to desecrate my sanctuary — the

stronghold in which you take
pride, the delight of your eyes, the
object of your affection. The sons
and daughters you left behind will
fall by the sword. 22And you will do
as I have done. You will not cover
your mustache and beard or eat
the customary food of mourners.
23You will keep your turbans on
your heads and your sandals on
your feet. You will not mourn or
weep but will waste away because
of[a] your sins and groan among
yourselves. 24Ezekiel will be a sign
to you; you will do just as he has
done. When this happens, you
will know that I am the Sovereign
LORD.' Eze 4:3; 12:11

25"And you, son of man, on the
day I take away their stronghold,
their joy and glory, the delight of
their eyes, their heart's desire, and
their sons and daughters as well —
26on that day a fugitive will come
to tell you the news. 27At that time
your mouth will be opened; you
will speak with him and will no
longer be silent. So you will be a
sign to them, and they will know
that I am the LORD." Jer 11:22; Eze 3:26

A Prophecy Against Ammon

25 The word of the LORD came
to me: 2"Son of man, set
your face against the Ammonites and prophesy against them.
3Say to them, 'Hear the word of
the Sovereign LORD. This is what
the Sovereign LORD says: Because
you said "Aha!" over my sanctuary when it was desecrated and
over the land of Israel when it
was laid waste and over the people of Judah when they went into
exile, 4therefore I am going to
give you to the people of the East
as a possession. They will set up
their camps and pitch their tents
among you; they will eat your
fruit and drink your milk. 5I will
turn Rabbah into a pasture for
camels and Ammon into a resting place for sheep. Then you will
know that I am the LORD. 6For this
is what the Sovereign LORD says:
Because you have clapped your
hands and stamped your feet, rejoicing with all the malice of your
heart against the land of Israel,
7therefore I will stretch out my
hand against you and give you
as plunder to the nations. I will
wipe you out from among the nations and exterminate you from
the countries. I will destroy you,
and you will know that I am the
LORD.'" Zep 2:8-9; Eze 21:31

A Prophecy Against Moab

8"This is what the Sovereign
LORD says: 'Because Moab and
Seir said, "Look, Judah has become like all the other nations,"
9therefore I will expose the flank
of Moab, beginning at its frontier
towns — Beth Jeshimoth, Baal
Meon and Kiriathaim — the glory of that land. 10I will give Moab
along with the Ammonites to the
people of the East as a possession,
so that the Ammonites will not be

[a] 23 Or *away in*

remembered among the nations;
11and I will inflict punishment on
Moab. Then they will know that I
am the LORD.'" Jer 48:1; Am 2:1

A Prophecy Against Edom

12"This is what the Sovereign
LORD says: 'Because Edom took revenge on Judah and became very
guilty by doing so, 13therefore this
is what the Sovereign LORD says: I
will stretch out my hand against
Edom and kill both man and
beast. I will lay it waste, and from
Teman to Dedan they will fall by
the sword. 14I will take vengeance
on Edom by the hand of my people Israel, and they will deal with
Edom in accordance with my anger and my wrath; they will know
my vengeance, declares the Sovereign LORD.'" 2Ch 28:17; Eze 35:11

A Prophecy Against Philistia

15"This is what the Sovereign
LORD says: 'Because the Philistines
acted in vengeance and took revenge with malice in their hearts,
and with ancient hostility sought
to destroy Judah, 16therefore this
is what the Sovereign LORD says: I
am about to stretch out my hand
against the Philistines, and I will
wipe out the Kerethites and destroy those remaining along the
coast. 17I will carry out great vengeance on them and punish them
in my wrath. Then they will know
that I am the LORD, when I take
vengeance on them.'"

2Ch 28:18; Jer 47:1-7

A Prophecy Against Tyre

26 In the eleventh month of
the twelfth[a] year, on the
first day of the month, the word
of the LORD came to me: 2"Son of
man, because Tyre has said of Jerusalem, 'Aha! The gate to the nations is broken, and its doors have
swung open to me; now that she
lies in ruins I will prosper,' 3there-
fore this is what the Sovereign
LORD says: I am against you, Tyre,
and I will bring many nations
against you, like the sea casting
up its waves. 4They will destroy
the walls of Tyre and pull down
her towers; I will scrape away her
rubble and make her a bare rock.
5Out in the sea she will become
a place to spread fishnets, for I
have spoken, declares the Sovereign LORD. She will become plunder for the nations, 6and her settlements on the mainland will be
ravaged by the sword. Then they
will know that I am the LORD.

Isa 23; Eze 27:32

7"For this is what the Sovereign
LORD says: From the north I am
going to bring against Tyre Nebuchadnezzar[b] king of Babylon, king
of kings, with horses and chariots,
with horsemen and a great army.
8He will ravage your settlements
on the mainland with the sword;

[a] *1* Probable reading of the original Hebrew text; Masoretic Text does not have *month of the twelfth.* [b] *7* Hebrew *Nebuchadrezzar,* of which *Nebuchadnezzar* is a variant; here and often in Ezekiel and Jeremiah

he will set up siege works against
you, build a ramp up to your walls
and raise his shields against you.
[9]He will direct the blows of his
battering rams against your walls
and demolish your towers with
his weapons. [10]His horses will be
so many that they will cover you
with dust. Your walls will tremble at the noise of the warhorses, wagons and chariots when
he enters your gates as men enter a city whose walls have been
broken through. [11]The hooves of
his horses will trample all your
streets; he will kill your people
with the sword, and your strong
pillars will fall to the ground.
[12]They will plunder your wealth
and loot your merchandise; they
will break down your walls and
demolish your fine houses and
throw your stones, timber and
rubble into the sea. [13]I will put an
end to your noisy songs, and the
music of your harps will be heard
no more. [14]I will make you a bare
rock, and you will become a place
to spread fishnets. You will never
be rebuilt, for I the LORD have spoken, declares the Sovereign LORD.

Jer 27:6; Mal 1:4

[15]"This is what the Sovereign
LORD says to Tyre: Will not the
coastlands tremble at the sound
of your fall, when the wounded groan and the slaughter takes
place in you? [16]Then all the princes
of the coast will step down from
their thrones and lay aside their
robes and take off their embroidered garments. Clothed with terror, they will sit on the ground,
trembling every moment, appalled at you. [17]Then they will take
up a lament concerning you and
say to you:

Eze 27:32

"'How you are destroyed, city
of renown,
peopled by men of the sea!
You were a power on the seas,
you and your citizens;
you put your terror
on all who lived there.

Isa 14:12

[18]Now the coastlands tremble
on the day of your fall;
the islands in the sea
are terrified at your
collapse.'

Isa 23:5; 41:5; Eze 27:35

[19]"This is what the Sovereign
LORD says: When I make you a
desolate city, like cities no longer inhabited, and when I bring
the ocean depths over you and its
vast waters cover you, [20]then I will
bring you down with those who
go down to the pit, to the people
of long ago. I will make you dwell
in the earth below, as in ancient
ruins, with those who go down to
the pit, and you will not return or
take your place[a] in the land of the
living. [21]I will bring you to a horrible end and you will be no more.
You will be sought, but you will
never again be found, declares the
Sovereign LORD."

Eze 27:36; 28:19; Rev 18:21

[a] 20 Septuagint; Hebrew *return, and I will give glory*

A Lament Over Tyre

27 The word of the LORD came to me: [2]"Son of man, take up a lament concerning Tyre. [3]Say to Tyre, situated at the gateway to the sea, merchant of peoples on many coasts, 'This is what the Sovereign LORD says: Eze 19:1; Hos 9:13

" 'You say, Tyre,
"I am perfect in beauty." Eze 28:2
[4]Your domain was on the high seas;
your builders brought your beauty to perfection.
[5]They made all your timbers
of juniper from Senir[a]; Dt 3:9
they took a cedar from Lebanon Isa 2:13
to make a mast for you.
[6]Of oaks from Bashan Nu 21:33; Jer 22:20; Zec 11:2
they made your oars;
of cypress wood[b] from the coasts of Cyprus Ge 10:4; Isa 23:12
they made your deck,
adorned with ivory.
[7]Fine embroidered linen from Egypt was your sail Ex 26:36
and served as your banner;
your awnings were of blue and purple Ex 25:4; Jer 10:9
from the coasts of Elishah. Ge 10:4
[8]Men of Sidon and Arvad were your oarsmen; Ge 10:18
your skilled men, Tyre, were aboard as your sailors. 1Ki 9:27
[9]Veteran craftsmen of Byblos were on board Jos 13:5; 1Ki 5:18
as shipwrights to caulk your seams.
All the ships of the sea and their sailors
came alongside to trade for your wares.

[10]" 'Men of Persia, Lydia and Put Eze 30:5; 38:5
served as soldiers in your army.
They hung their shields and helmets on your walls,
bringing you splendor.
[11]Men of Arvad and Helek
guarded your walls on every side;
men of Gammad
were in your towers.
They hung their shields around your walls;
they brought your beauty to perfection.

[12]" 'Tarshish did business with
you because of your great wealth
of goods; they exchanged silver,
iron, tin and lead for your merchandise. Ge 10:4
[13]" 'Greece, Tubal and Meshek did
business with you; they traded human beings and articles of bronze
for your wares. Ge 10:2; Rev 18:13
[14]" 'Men of Beth Togarmah exchanged chariot horses, cavalry
horses and mules for your merchandise. Ge 10:3; Eze 38:6

[a] 5 That is, Mount Hermon [b] 6 Targum; the Masoretic Text has a different division of the consonants.

15"'The men of Rhodes[a] traded
with you, and many coastlands
were your customers; they paid
you with ivory tusks and ebony.
Ge 10:7; Rev 18:12
16"'Aram[b] did business with you
because of your many products;
they exchanged turquoise, purple
fabric, embroidered work, fine lin-
en, coral and rubies for your merchandise. Jdg 10:6; Eze 28:13
17"'Judah and Israel traded with
you; they exchanged wheat from
Minnith and confections,[c] honey,
olive oil and balm for your wares.
Jdg 11:33
18"'Damascus did business with
you because of your many products and great wealth of goods.
They offered wine from Helbon,
wool from Zahar 19and casks of
wine from Izal in exchange for
your wares: wrought iron, cassia
and calamus. Ge 10:2; 14:15; Eze 47:16-18
20"'Dedan traded in saddle blankets with you.
21"'Arabia and all the princes of
Kedar were your customers; they
did business with you in lambs,
rams and goats. Ge 25:13; Isa 60:7
22"'The merchants of Sheba and
Raamah traded with you; for your
merchandise they exchanged the
finest of all kinds of spices and
precious stones, and gold.
Ge 10:7,28; 1Ki 10:1-2; Isa 60:6
23"'Harran, Kanneh and Eden
and merchants of Sheba, Ashur
and Kilmad traded with you. 24In
your marketplace they traded with
you beautiful garments, blue fabric, embroidered work and mul-
ticolored rugs with cords twisted
and tightly knotted. 2Ki 19:12; Isa 37:12

25"'The ships of Tarshish serve Isa 2:16 *fn*
as carriers for your wares.
You are filled with heavy cargo
as you sail the sea.
26Your oarsmen take you
out to the high seas.
But the east wind will break
you to pieces Ps 48:7; Jer 18:17
far out at sea.
27Your wealth, merchandise and
wares, Pr 11:4
your mariners, sailors and
shipwrights,
your merchants and all your
soldiers,
and everyone else on board
will sink into the heart of the
sea Eze 28:8
on the day of your shipwreck.
28The shorelands will quake Eze 26:15
when your sailors cry out.
29All who handle the oars
will abandon their ships;
the mariners and all the sailors
will stand on the shore.
30They will raise their voice
and cry bitterly over you;
they will sprinkle dust on their
heads 2Sa 1:2
and roll in ashes.
Jer 6:26; Rev 18:18-19

[a] *15* Septuagint; Hebrew *Dedan*
[b] *16* Most Hebrew manuscripts; some Hebrew manuscripts and Syriac *Edom*
[c] *17* The meaning of the Hebrew for this word is uncertain.

31 They will shave their heads
because of you
and will put on sackcloth.
They will weep over you with
anguish of soul Isa 16:9
and with bitter mourning.
Isa 22:12; Eze 7:18
32 As they wail and mourn over
you,
they will take up a lament
concerning you: Eze 26:17
"Who was ever silenced like
Tyre,
surrounded by the sea?"
Eze 26:5
33 When your merchandise went
out on the seas,
you satisfied many nations;
with your great wealth and
your wares ver 12; Eze 28:4-5
you enriched the kings of the
earth.
34 Now you are shattered by the sea
in the depths of the waters;
your wares and all your
company
have gone down with you.
Zec 9:4
35 All who live in the coastlands
Eze 26:15
are appalled at you; Lev 26:32
their kings shudder with horror
and their faces are distorted
with fear. Eze 26:17-18
36 The merchants among the
nations scoff at you;
Jer 18:16; 19:8
you have come to a horrible
end
and will be no more.'"
Ps 37:10,36; Eze 26:21

A Prophecy Against the King of Tyre

28 The word of the LORD came
to me: 2 "Son of man, say to
the ruler of Tyre, 'This is what the
Sovereign LORD says: Isa 13:11

"'In the pride of your heart
you say, "I am a god;
I sit on the throne of a god
Isa 14:13
in the heart of the seas."
Zep 2:15
But you are a mere mortal and
not a god,
though you think you
are as wise as a god.
Ps 9:20; Isa 31:3; 2Th 2:4
3 Are you wiser than Daniel[a]?
Da 1:20; 5:11-12
Is no secret hidden from you?
4 By your wisdom and
understanding
you have gained wealth for
yourself
and amassed gold and silver
in your treasuries. Zec 9:3
5 By your great skill in trading
Isa 23:8
you have increased your
wealth, Eze 27:33
and because of your wealth
your heart has grown proud.
Ps 52:7; 62:10; Hos 12:8

6 "'Therefore this is what the
Sovereign LORD says:

"'Because you think you are
wise,
as wise as a god,

[a] 3 Or *Danel*, a man of renown in ancient literature

7 I am going to bring foreigners
against you,
the most ruthless of nations; Eze 30:11; 31:12; 32:12
they will draw their swords
against your beauty and
wisdom Jer 9:23
and pierce your shining
splendor.
8 They will bring you down to
the pit, Eze 32:30
and you will die a violent
death
in the heart of the seas. Eze 27:27
9 Will you then say, "I am a god,"
in the presence of those who
kill you?
You will be but a mortal, not a
god, Isa 31:3
in the hands of those who
slay you. Eze 16:49
10 You will die the death of
the uncircumcised Eze 31:18; 32:19,24
at the hands of foreigners.

I have spoken, declares the Sovereign LORD.' "

11 The word of the LORD came to
me: 12 "Son of man, take up a lament concerning the king of Tyre
and say to him: 'This is what the
Sovereign LORD says: Eze 19:1

" 'You were the seal of
perfection,
full of wisdom and perfect in
beauty. Eze 27:2-4
13 You were in Eden,
the garden of God; Eze 31:8-9
every precious stone adorned
you:
carnelian, chrysolite and
emerald,
topaz, onyx and jasper,
lapis lazuli, turquoise and
beryl.[a] Eze 27:16
Your settings and mountings[b]
were made of gold;
on the day you were created
they were prepared. Rev 21:20
14 You were anointed as a
guardian cherub, Ex 25:17-20; 30:26; 40:9
for so I ordained you.
You were on the holy mount of
God;
you walked among the fiery
stones.
15 You were blameless in your
ways
from the day you were
created
till wickedness was found in
you.
16 Through your widespread
trade
you were filled with violence, Hab 2:17
and you sinned.
So I drove you in disgrace from
the mount of God,
and I expelled you, guardian
cherub, Ge 3:24
from among the fiery
stones.

[a] *13* The precise identification of some of these precious stones is uncertain.
[b] *13* The meaning of the Hebrew for this phrase is uncertain.

17 Your heart became proud
Eze 31:10
on account of your beauty,
and you corrupted your wisdom
because of your splendor.
So I threw you to the earth;
I made a spectacle of you
before kings. Eze 19:12
18 By your many sins and
dishonest trade
you have desecrated your
sanctuaries.
So I made a fire come out from
you,
and it consumed you,
and I reduced you to ashes on
the ground Mal 4:3
in the sight of all who were
watching.
19 All the nations who knew you
are appalled at you;
you have come to a horrible end
and will be no more.' "
Eze 26:21; 27:36

A Prophecy Against Sidon

20 The word of the LORD came to
me: 21 "Son of man, set your face
against Sidon; prophesy against
her 22 and say: 'This is what the
Sovereign LORD says: Jer 25:22; Eze 6:2

" 'I am against you, Sidon,
and among you I will display
my glory. Eze 39:13
You will know that I am the
LORD,
when I inflict punishment
on you Eze 30:19
and within you am proved to
be holy. Lev 10:3

23 I will send a plague upon you
and make blood flow in your
streets.
The slain will fall within you,
with the sword against you
on every side.
Then you will know that I am
the LORD. Eze 38:22

24 " 'No longer will the people of
Israel have malicious neighbors
who are painful briers and sharp
thorns. Then they will know that I
am the Sovereign LORD.
Nu 33:55; Jos 23:13; Eze 2:6

25 " 'This is what the Sovereign
LORD says: When I gather the
people of Israel from the nations
where they have been scattered, I
will be proved holy through them
in the sight of the nations. Then
they will live in their own land,
which I gave to my servant Jacob.
26 They will live there in safety and
will build houses and plant vineyards; they will live in safety when
I inflict punishment on all their
neighbors who maligned them.
Then they will know that I am the
LORD their God.' "
Isa 11:12; Jer 23:6; Am 9:14-15

A Prophecy Against Egypt

Judgment on Pharaoh

29 In the tenth year, in the
tenth month on the twelfth
day, the word of the LORD came to
me: 2 "Son of man, set your face
against Pharaoh king of Egypt and
prophesy against him and against
all Egypt. 3 Speak to him and say:

'This is what the Sovereign LORD
says: Isa 19:1-17; Jer 46:2

"'I am against you, Pharaoh
king of Egypt, Jer 44:30
you great monster lying
among your streams.
Ps 74:13; Isa 27:1; Eze 32:2
You say, "The Nile belongs to
me; Jer 46:8
I made it for myself."
4But I will put hooks in your
jaws 2Ki 19:28
and make the fish of your
streams stick to your
scales.
I will pull you out from among
your streams,
with all the fish sticking to
your scales. Eze 38:4
5I will leave you in the desert,
you and all the fish of your
streams.
You will fall on the open field
and not be gathered or
picked up.
I will give you as food
to the beasts of the
earth and the
birds of the sky.
Jer 7:33; 34:20; Eze 32:4-6

6Then all who live in Egypt will
know that I am the LORD.

"'You have been a staff of reed
for the people of Israel. 7When
they grasped you with their hands,
you splintered and you tore open
their shoulders; when they leaned
on you, you broke and their backs
were wrenched.[a] Isa 36:6; Eze 17:15-17

8"'Therefore this is what the
Sovereign LORD says: I will bring
a sword against you and kill both
man and beast. 9Egypt will become a desolate wasteland. Then
they will know that I am the LORD.
Eze 14:17; 32:11-13

"'Because you said, "The Nile
is mine; I made it," 10therefore I
am against you and against your
streams, and I will make the land
of Egypt a ruin and a desolate
waste from Migdol to Aswan, as
far as the border of Cush.[b] 11The
foot of neither man nor beast
will pass through it; no one will
live there for forty years. 12I will
make the land of Egypt desolate
among devastated lands, and her
cities will lie desolate forty years
among ruined cities. And I will
disperse the Egyptians among the
nations and scatter them through
the countries. Eze 30:7,23,26

13"'Yet this is what the Sovereign LORD says: At the end of forty
years I will gather the Egyptians
from the nations where they were
scattered. 14I will bring them back
from captivity and return them to
Upper Egypt, the land of their ancestry. There they will be a lowly
kingdom. 15It will be the lowliest
of kingdoms and will never again
exalt itself above the other nations. I will make it so weak that
it will never again rule over the

[a] 7 Syriac (see also Septuagint and Vulgate); Hebrew *and you caused their backs to stand* [b] 10 That is, the upper Nile region

nations. 16 Egypt will no longer be
a source of confidence for the people of Israel but will be a reminder of their sin in turning to her for
help. Then they will know that I
am the Sovereign LORD.' "
Isa 30:2; Hos 8:13

Nebuchadnezzar's Reward

17 In the twenty-seventh year,
in the first month on the first
day, the word of the LORD came
to me: 18 "Son of man, Nebuchadnezzar king of Babylon drove his
army in a hard campaign against
Tyre; every head was rubbed bare
and every shoulder made raw. Yet
he and his army got no reward
from the campaign he led against
Tyre. 19 Therefore this is what the
Sovereign LORD says: I am going
to give Egypt to Nebuchadnezzar
king of Babylon, and he will carry off its wealth. He will loot and
plunder the land as pay for his
army. 20 I have given him Egypt as
a reward for his efforts because
he and his army did it for me, declares the Sovereign LORD.
Isa 10:6-7; Jer 25:9

21 "On that day I will make a
horn[a] grow for the Israelites, and
I will open your mouth among
them. Then they will know that I
am the LORD." Ps 132:17; Eze 24:27

A Lament Over Egypt

30 The word of the LORD came to me: 2 "Son of man,
prophesy and say: 'This is what
the Sovereign LORD says:

" 'Wail and say, Isa 13:6
"Alas for that day!"
3 For the day is near,
Joel 2:1,11; Ob 1:15
the day of the LORD is near —
Eze 7:12,19
a day of clouds,
a time of doom for the nations.
4 A sword will come against Egypt, Da 11:43
and anguish will come upon Cush.[b] Eze 29:10
When the slain fall in Egypt,
her wealth will be carried away
and her foundations torn down. Eze 29:19

5 Cush and Libya, Lydia and all Arabia, Kub and the people of the covenant land will fall by the sword
along with Egypt. Jer 25:20
6 " 'This is what the LORD says:

" 'The allies of Egypt will fall
and her proud strength will fail.
From Migdol to Aswan Eze 29:10
they will fall by the sword within her,
declares the Sovereign LORD.
7 " 'They will be desolate
among desolate lands,
and their cities will lie
among ruined cities. Eze 29:12

[a] 21 *Horn* here symbolizes strength.
[b] 4 That is, the upper Nile region; also in verses 5 and 9

[8]Then they will know that I am
the LORD,
when I set fire to Egypt
Jer 49:27
and all her helpers are
crushed. Eze 29:9

[9]" 'On that day messengers will
go out from me in ships to fright-
en Cush out of her complacency.
Anguish will take hold of them on
the day of Egypt's doom, for it is
sure to come. Isa 18:1-2; Eze 32:9-10

[10]" 'This is what the Sovereign
LORD says:

" 'I will put an end to the
hordes of Egypt
by the hand of
Nebuchadnezzar king of
Babylon. Eze 29:19
[11]He and his army — the most
ruthless of nations —
Eze 28:7
will be brought in to destroy
the land.
They will draw their swords
against Egypt
and fill the land with the
slain.
[12]I will dry up the waters of the
Nile Isa 19:6; Eze 29:9
and sell the land to an evil
nation;
by the hand of foreigners
I will lay waste the land and
everything in it. Eze 19:7

I the LORD have spoken.

[13]" 'This is what the Sovereign
LORD says:

" 'I will destroy the idols Jer 43:12
and put an end to the images
in Memphis. Isa 19:13
No longer will there be a prince
in Egypt, Zec 10:11
and I will spread fear
throughout the land.
[14]I will lay waste Upper Egypt,
Eze 29:14
set fire to Zoan Ps 78:12,43
and inflict punishment on
Thebes. Jer 46:25
[15]I will pour out my wrath on
Pelusium,
the stronghold of Egypt,
and wipe out the hordes of
Thebes.
[16]I will set fire to Egypt; Jos 7:15
Pelusium will writhe in
agony.
Thebes will be taken by storm;
Memphis will be in constant
distress. Isa 19:13
[17]The young men of Heliopolis
and Bubastis Ge 41:45
will fall by the sword,
and the cities themselves
will go into captivity.
[18]Dark will be the day at
Tahpanhes
when I break the yoke of
Egypt; Lev 26:13; Isa 9:4
there her proud strength will
come to an end.
She will be covered with clouds,
and her villages will go into
captivity.
[19]So I will inflict punishment on
Egypt, Eze 28:22
and they will know that I am
the LORD.' "

Pharaoh's Arms Are Broken

[20]In the eleventh year, in the
first month on the seventh day,
the word of the LORD came to me:
[21]"Son of man, I have broken the
arm of Pharaoh king of Egypt.
It has not been bound up to be
healed or put in a splint so that
it may become strong enough to
hold a sword. [22]Therefore this is
what the Sovereign LORD says:
I am against Pharaoh king of
Egypt. I will break both his arms,
the good arm as well as the broken one, and make the sword fall
from his hand. [23]I will disperse the
Egyptians among the nations and
scatter them through the countries. [24]I will strengthen the arms
of the king of Babylon and put my
sword in his hand, but I will break
the arms of Pharaoh, and he will
groan before him like a mortally
wounded man. [25]I will strengthen
the arms of the king of Babylon,
but the arms of Pharaoh will fall
limp. Then they will know that I
am the LORD, when I put my sword
into the hand of the king of Babylon and he brandishes it against
Egypt. [26]I will disperse the Egyptians among the nations and scatter them through the countries.
Then they will know that I am the
LORD." Zep 2:12; Zec 10:6,12

Pharaoh as a Felled Cedar of Lebanon

31 In the eleventh year, in the
third month on the first day,
the word of the LORD came to me:
[2]"Son of man, say to Pharaoh king
of Egypt and to his hordes:
Jer 52:5; Eze 30:20

" 'Who can be compared with
you in majesty?
[3]Consider Assyria, once a cedar
in Lebanon, Jer 50:18
with beautiful branches
overshadowing the
forest;
it towered on high,
its top above the thick
foliage. Isa 10:34
[4]The waters nourished it, Eze 17:7
deep springs made it grow
tall;
their streams flowed
all around its base
and sent their channels
to all the trees of the field.
Da 4:10
[5]So it towered higher
than all the trees of the
field;
its boughs increased
and its branches grew long,
spreading because of
abundant waters. Eze 17:5
[6]All the birds of the sky
nested in its boughs,
all the animals of the wild
gave birth under its
branches;
all the great nations
lived in its shade.
Eze 17:23; Mt 13:32
[7]It was majestic in beauty,
with its spreading boughs,
for its roots went down
to abundant waters.

8 The cedars in the garden of
God Ps 80:10
could not rival it,
nor could the junipers
equal its boughs,
nor could the plane trees Ge 30:37
compare with its
branches —
no tree in the garden of God
could match its beauty. Ge 2:8-9
9 I made it beautiful
with abundant branches,
the envy of all the trees of
Eden Ge 2:8
in the garden of God. Ge 13:10; Eze 28:13

10 " 'Therefore this is what the
Sovereign LORD says: Because the
great cedar towered over the thick
foliage, and because it was proud
of its height, 11 I gave it into the
hands of the ruler of the nations,
for him to deal with according
to its wickedness. I cast it aside,
12 and the most ruthless of foreign
nations cut it down and left it. Its
boughs fell on the mountains and
in all the valleys; its branches lay
broken in all the ravines of the
land. All the nations of the earth
came out from under its shade
and left it. 13 All the birds settled
on the fallen tree, and all the wild
animals lived among its branches.
14 Therefore no other trees by the
waters are ever to tower proudly
on high, lifting their tops above
the thick foliage. No other trees
so well-watered are ever to reach
such a height; they are all destined for death, for the earth below, among mortals who go down
to the realm of the dead. Eze 28:7; Da 5:20

15 " 'This is what the Sovereign
LORD says: On the day it was
brought down to the realm of the
dead I covered the deep springs
with mourning for it; I held back
its streams, and its abundant waters were restrained. Because of
it I clothed Lebanon with gloom,
and all the trees of the field withered away. 16 I made the nations
tremble at the sound of its fall
when I brought it down to the
realm of the dead to be with those
who go down to the pit. Then all
the trees of Eden, the choicest
and best of Lebanon, the well-watered trees, were consoled in
the earth below. 17 They too, like
the great cedar, had gone down
to the realm of the dead, to those
killed by the sword, along with
the armed men who lived in its
shade among the nations. Ps 9:17; Isa 14:15

18 " 'Which of the trees of Eden
can be compared with you in
splendor and majesty? Yet you,
too, will be brought down with
the trees of Eden to the earth below; you will lie among the uncircumcised, with those killed by the
sword. Eze 32:19,21

" 'This is Pharaoh and all his
hordes, declares the Sovereign
LORD.' "

A Lament Over Pharaoh

32 In the twelfth year, in the
twelfth month on the first
day, the word of the LORD came
to me: 2"Son of man, take up a lament concerning Pharaoh king of
Egypt and say to him: Eze 27:2; 31:1

"'You are like a lion among the
nations; Eze 19:3,6
you are like a monster in the
seas
thrashing about in your streams,
churning the water with your
feet
and muddying the streams.
Eze 29:3; 34:18

3"'This is what the Sovereign
LORD says:

"'With a great throng of people
I will cast my net over you,
and they will haul you up in
my net. Eze 12:13
4I will throw you on the land
and hurl you on the open
field.
I will let all the birds of the sky
settle on you
and all the animals of the
wild gorge themselves
on you. Isa 18:6; Eze 31:12-13
5I will spread your flesh on the
mountains
and fill the valleys with your
remains. Eze 31:12
6I will drench the land with your
flowing blood Isa 34:3
all the way to the mountains,
and the ravines will be filled
with your flesh.
7When I snuff you out, I will
cover the heavens
and darken their stars;
I will cover the sun with a
cloud,
and the moon will not give
its light. Joel 2:2,31; 3:15
8All the shining lights in the
heavens
I will darken over you; Ps 102:26
I will bring darkness over
your land, Joel 2:10
declares the Sovereign
LORD.
9I will trouble the hearts of
many peoples
when I bring about your
destruction among the
nations,
among[a] lands you have not
known.
10I will cause many peoples to be
appalled at you,
and their kings will shudder
with horror because of
you
when I brandish my sword
before them.
On the day of your downfall
Jer 46:10
each of them will tremble
every moment for his life.
Eze 26:16; 27:35

11"'For this is what the Sovereign LORD says:

"'The sword of the king of
Babylon Jer 46:26
will come against you. Eze 29:19

[a] 9 Hebrew; Septuagint *bring you into captivity among the nations, / to*

12 I will cause your hordes to fall
by the swords of mighty
men—
the most ruthless of all
nations. Eze 28:7
They will shatter the pride of
Egypt,
and all her hordes will be
overthrown. Eze 31:11-12
13 I will destroy all her cattle
from beside abundant waters
no longer to be stirred by the
foot of man
or muddied by the hooves of
cattle. Eze 29:8,11
14 Then I will let her waters settle
and make her streams flow
like oil,
declares the Sovereign
LORD.
15 When I make Egypt desolate
and strip the land of
everything in it,
when I strike down all who live
there,
then they will know that I
am the LORD.' Ex 7:5; Eze 6:7

16 "This is the lament they will
chant for her. The daughters of
the nations will chant it; for Egypt
and all her hordes they will chant
it, declares the Sovereign LORD."
2Ch 35:25; Eze 26:17

Egypt's Descent Into the Realm of the Dead

17 In the twelfth year, on the fifteenth day of the month, the word
of the LORD came to me:
18 "Son of
man, wail for the hordes of Egypt
and consign to the earth below
both her and the daughters of
mighty nations, along with those
who go down to the pit.
19 Say
to them, 'Are you more favored
than others? Go down and be laid
among the uncircumcised.'
20 They
will fall among those killed by the
sword. The sword is drawn; let her
be dragged off with all her hordes.
21 From within the realm of the
dead the mighty leaders will say
of Egypt and her allies, 'They have
come down and they lie with the
uncircumcised, with those killed
by the sword.' Isa 14:9; Eze 28:10

22 "Assyria is there with her
whole army; she is surrounded by
the graves of all her slain, all who
have fallen by the sword.
23 Their
graves are in the depths of the
pit and her army lies around her
grave. All who had spread terror
in the land of the living are slain,
fallen by the sword. Isa 14:15

24 "Elam is there, with all her
hordes around her grave. All of
them are slain, fallen by the sword.
All who had spread terror in the
land of the living went down uncircumcised to the earth below.
They bear their shame with those
who go down to the pit.
25 A bed is
made for her among the slain, with
all her hordes around her grave.
All of them are uncircumcised,
killed by the sword. Because their
terror had spread in the land of the
living, they bear their shame with
those who go down to the pit; they
are laid among the slain. Jer 49:37

[26]"Meshek and Tubal are there,
with all their hordes around their
graves. All of them are uncircumcised, killed by the sword because
they spread their terror in the
land of the living. [27]But they do
not lie with the fallen warriors of
old,[a] who went down to the realm
of the dead with their weapons
of war — their swords placed under their heads and their shields[b]
resting on their bones — though
these warriors also had terrorized
the land of the living. Eze 27:13

[28]"You too, Pharaoh, will be broken and will lie among the uncircumcised, with those killed by the
sword.

[29]"Edom is there, her kings and
all her princes; despite their power, they are laid with those killed
by the sword. They lie with the
uncircumcised, with those who go
down to the pit. Isa 34:5-15; Eze 25:12-14

[30]"All the princes of the north
and all the Sidonians are there;
they went down with the slain in
disgrace despite the terror caused
by their power. They lie uncircumcised with those killed by the
sword and bear their shame with
those who go down to the pit.
Eze 38:6; 39:2

[31]"Pharaoh — he and all his
army — will see them and he will
be consoled for all his hordes that
were killed by the sword, declares
the Sovereign LORD. [32]Although I
had him spread terror in the land
of the living, Pharaoh and all his
hordes will be laid among the uncircumcised, with those killed by
the sword, declares the Sovereign
LORD." Eze 31:16

Renewal of Ezekiel's Call as Watchman

33 The word of the LORD came
to me: [2]"Son of man, speak
to your people and say to them:
'When I bring the sword against
a land, and the people of the land
choose one of their men and make
him their watchman, [3]and he sees
the sword coming against the land
and blows the trumpet to warn
the people, [4]then if anyone hears
the trumpet but does not heed
the warning and the sword comes
and takes their life, their blood
will be on their own head. [5]Since
they heard the sound of the trumpet but did not heed the warning, their blood will be on their
own head. If they had heeded the
warning, they would have saved
themselves. [6]But if the watchman
sees the sword coming and does
not blow the trumpet to warn the
people and the sword comes and
takes someone's life, that person's
life will be taken because of their
sin, but I will hold the watchman
accountable for their blood.'
Eze 3:11,18

[7]"Son of man, I have made you a
watchman for the people of Israel;
so hear the word I speak and give

[a] 27 Septuagint; Hebrew *warriors who were uncircumcised* [b] 27 Probable reading of the original Hebrew text; Masoretic Text *punishment*

them warning from me. [8]When I say to the wicked, 'You wicked person, you will surely die,' and you do not speak out to dissuade them from their ways, that wicked person will die for[a] their sin, and I will hold you accountable for their blood. [9]But if you do warn the wicked person to turn from their ways and they do not do so, they will die for their sin, though you yourself will be saved. Eze 3:17-19

[10]"Son of man, say to the Israelites, 'This is what you are saying: "Our offenses and sins weigh us down, and we are wasting away because of[b] them. How then can we live?"' [11]Say to them, 'As surely as I live, declares the Sovereign LORD, I take no pleasure in the death of the wicked, but rather that they turn from their ways and live. Turn! Turn from your evil ways! Why will you die, people of Israel?' Eze 18:32; 2Pe 3:9

[12]"Therefore, son of man, say to your people, 'If someone who is righteous disobeys, that person's former righteousness will count for nothing. And if someone who is wicked repents, that person's former wickedness will not bring condemnation. The righteous person who sins will not be allowed to live even though they were formerly righteous.' [13]If I tell a righteous person that they will surely live, but then they trust in their righteousness and do evil, none of the righteous things that person has done will be remembered; they will die for the evil they have done. [14]And if I say to a wicked person, 'You will surely die,' but they then turn away from their sin and do what is just and right — [15]if they give back what they took in pledge for a loan, return what they have stolen, follow the decrees that give life, and do no evil — that person will surely live; they will not die. [16]None of the sins that person has committed will be remembered against them. They have done what is just and right; they will surely live. Eze 18:22; 20:11

[17]"Yet your people say, 'The way of the Lord is not just.' But it is their way that is not just. [18]If a righteous person turns from their righteousness and does evil, they will die for it. [19]And if a wicked person turns away from their wickedness and does what is just and right, they will live by doing so. [20]Yet you Israelites say, 'The way of the Lord is not just.' But I will judge each of you according to your own ways." Eze 3:20; 18:26

Jerusalem's Fall Explained

[21]In the twelfth year of our exile, in the tenth month on the fifth day, a man who had escaped from Jerusalem came to me and said, "The city has fallen!" [22]Now the evening before the man arrived, the hand of the LORD was on me, and he opened my mouth before the man came to me in the morning.

[a] *8* Or *in*; also in verse 9 [b] *10* Or *away in*

So my mouth was opened and I was no longer silent.
Eze 24:27

23Then the word of the LORD came to me: 24"Son of man, the people living in those ruins in the land of Israel are saying, 'Abraham was only one man, yet he possessed the land. But we are many; surely the land has been given to us as our possession.' 25Therefore say to them, 'This is what the Sovereign LORD says: Since you eat meat with the blood still in it and look to your idols and shed blood, should you then possess the land? 26You rely on your sword, you do detestable things, and each of you defiles his neighbor's wife. Should you then possess the land?'
Eze 22:6,11,27

27"Say this to them: 'This is what the Sovereign LORD says: As surely as I live, those who are left in the ruins will fall by the sword, those out in the country I will give to the wild animals to be devoured, and those in strongholds and caves will die of a plague. 28I will make the land a desolate waste, and her proud strength will come to an end, and the mountains of Israel will become desolate so that no one will cross them. 29Then they will know that I am the LORD, when I have made the land a desolate waste because of all the detestable things they have done.'
1Sa 13:6; Isa 2:19

30"As for you, son of man, your people are talking together about you by the walls and at the doors of the houses, saying to each other, 'Come and hear the message that has come from the LORD.' 31My people come to you, as they usually do, and sit before you to hear your words, but they do not put them into practice. Their mouths speak of love, but their hearts are greedy for unjust gain. 32Indeed, to them you are nothing more than one who sings love songs with a beautiful voice and plays an instrument well, for they hear your words but do not put them into practice.
Mk 6:20; Ps 78:36-37

33"When all this comes true — and it surely will — then they will know that a prophet has been among them."
1Sa 3:20; Eze 2:5

The LORD Will Be Israel's Shepherd

34 The word of the LORD came to me: 2"Son of man, prophesy against the shepherds of Israel; prophesy and say to them: 'This is what the Sovereign LORD says: Woe to you shepherds of Israel who only take care of yourselves! Should not shepherds take care of the flock? 3You eat the curds, clothe yourselves with the wool and slaughter the choice animals, but you do not take care of the flock. 4You have not strengthened the weak or healed the sick or bound up the injured. You have not brought back the strays or searched for the lost. You have ruled them harshly and brutally. 5So they were scattered because there was no shepherd, and

when they were scattered they
became food for all the wild animals. 6My sheep wandered over all
the mountains and on every high
hill. They were scattered over the
whole earth, and no one searched
or looked for them. Jer 23:1; Jn 10:11
7" 'Therefore, you shepherds,
hear the word of the LORD: 8As
surely as I live, declares the Sovereign LORD, because my flock lacks
a shepherd and so has been plundered and has become food for
all the wild animals, and because
my shepherds did not search for
my flock but cared for themselves
rather than for my flock, 9there-
fore, you shepherds, hear the word
of the LORD: 10This is what the Sovereign LORD says: I am against the
shepherds and will hold them accountable for my flock. I will remove them from tending the flock
so that the shepherds can no longer feed themselves. I will rescue
my flock from their mouths, and
it will no longer be food for them.
Jer 21:13; Zec 10:3
11" 'For this is what the Sovereign
LORD says: I myself will search for
my sheep and look after them. 12As
a shepherd looks after his scattered flock when he is with them,
so will I look after my sheep. I will
rescue them from all the places where they were scattered on
a day of clouds and darkness. 13I
will bring them out from the nations and gather them from the
countries, and I will bring them
into their own land. I will pasture
them on the mountains of Israel,
in the ravines and in all the settlements in the land. 14I will tend
them in a good pasture, and the
mountain heights of Israel will be
their grazing land. There they will
lie down in good grazing land, and
there they will feed in a rich pasture on the mountains of Israel.
15I myself will tend my sheep and
have them lie down, declares the
Sovereign LORD. 16I will search for
the lost and bring back the strays.
I will bind up the injured and
strengthen the weak, but the sleek
and the strong I will destroy. I will
shepherd the flock with justice.
Isa 10:16; Lk 5:32
17" 'As for you, my flock, this is
what the Sovereign LORD says: I
will judge between one sheep and
another, and between rams and
goats. 18Is it not enough for you
to feed on the good pasture? Must
you also trample the rest of your
pasture with your feet? Is it not
enough for you to drink clear water? Must you also muddy the rest
with your feet? 19Must my flock
feed on what you have trampled
and drink what you have muddied
with your feet? Mt 25:32-33
20" 'Therefore this is what the
Sovereign LORD says to them:
See, I myself will judge between
the fat sheep and the lean sheep.
21Because you shove with flank
and shoulder, butting all the weak
sheep with your horns until you
have driven them away, 22I will save
my flock, and they will no longer

be plundered. I will judge between
one sheep and another. 23 I will
place over them one shepherd, my
servant David, and he will tend
them; he will tend them and be
their shepherd. 24 I the LORD will be
their God, and my servant David
will be prince among them. I the
LORD have spoken. Isa 40:11; Eze 36:28
25 "'I will make a covenant of
peace with them and rid the land
of savage beasts so that they may
live in the wilderness and sleep in
the forests in safety. 26 I will make
them and the places surrounding my hill a blessing.[a] I will send
down showers in season; there
will be showers of blessing. 27 The
trees will yield their fruit and the
ground will yield its crops; the
people will be secure in their land.
They will know that I am the LORD,
when I break the bars of their yoke
and rescue them from the hands of
those who enslaved them. 28 They
will no longer be plundered by the
nations, nor will wild animals devour them. They will live in safety,
and no one will make them afraid.
29 I will provide for them a land renowned for its crops, and they will
no longer be victims of famine in
the land or bear the scorn of the
nations. 30 Then they will know
that I, the LORD their God, am with
them and that they, the Israelites,
are my people, declares the Sovereign LORD. 31 You are my sheep,
the sheep of my pasture, and I am
your God, declares the Sovereign
LORD.'" Ps 100:3; Jer 23:1

A Prophecy Against Edom

35 The word of the LORD came
to me: 2 "Son of man, set
your face against Mount Seir;
prophesy against it 3 and say: 'This
is what the Sovereign LORD says: I
am against you, Mount Seir, and I
will stretch out my hand against
you and make you a desolate
waste. 4 I will turn your towns into
ruins and you will be desolate.
Then you will know that I am the
LORD. Jer 6:12; Eze 25:12-14
5 "'Because you harbored an ancient hostility and delivered the
Israelites over to the sword at the
time of their calamity, the time
their punishment reached its climax, 6 therefore as surely as I live,
declares the Sovereign LORD, I will
give you over to bloodshed and it
will pursue you. Since you did not
hate bloodshed, bloodshed will
pursue you. 7 I will make Mount
Seir a desolate waste and cut off
from it all who come and go. 8 I
will fill your mountains with the
slain; those killed by the sword
will fall on your hills and in your
valleys and in all your ravines. 9 I
will make you desolate forever;
your towns will not be inhabited.
Then you will know that I am the
LORD. Ps 137:7; Eze 21:29
10 "'Because you have said, "These
two nations and countries will be

[a] 26 Or *I will cause them and the places surrounding my hill to be named in blessings* (see Gen. 48:20); or *I will cause them and the places surrounding my hill to be seen as blessed*

ours and we will take possession
of them," even though I the LORD
was there, 11therefore as surely as I
live, declares the Sovereign LORD,
I will treat you in accordance with
the anger and jealousy you showed
in your hatred of them and I will
make myself known among them
when I judge you. 12Then you will
know that I the LORD have heard
all the contemptible things you
have said against the mountains of
Israel. You said, "They have been
laid waste and have been given
over to us to devour." 13You boasted against me and spoke against
me without restraint, and I heard
it. 14This is what the Sovereign
LORD says: While the whole earth
rejoices, I will make you desolate.
15Because you rejoiced when the
inheritance of Israel became desolate, that is how I will treat you.
You will be desolate, Mount Seir,
you and all of Edom. Then they
will know that I am the LORD.' "

Jer 50:11-13; La 4:21; Ob 1:12

Hope for the Mountains of Israel

36 "Son of man, prophesy
to the mountains of Isra-
el and say, 'Mountains of Israel,
hear the word of the LORD. 2This
is what the Sovereign LORD says:
The enemy said of you, "Aha! The
ancient heights have become our
possession." ' 3Therefore prophesy and say, 'This is what the Sovereign LORD says: Because they
ravaged and crushed you from
every side so that you became
the possession of the rest of the
nations and the object of people's malicious talk and slander,
4therefore, mountains of Israel,
hear the word of the Sovereign
LORD: This is what the Sovereign
LORD says to the mountains and
hills, to the ravines and valleys,
to the desolate ruins and the
deserted towns that have been
plundered and ridiculed by the
rest of the nations around you —
5this is what the Sovereign LORD
says: In my burning zeal I have
spoken against the rest of the
nations, and against all Edom,
for with glee and with malice in
their hearts they made my land
their own possession so that they
might plunder its pastureland.'
6Therefore prophesy concerning
the land of Israel and say to the
mountains and hills, to the ravines and valleys: 'This is what
the Sovereign LORD says: I speak
in my jealous wrath because you
have suffered the scorn of the nations. 7Therefore this is what the
Sovereign LORD says: I swear with
uplifted hand that the nations
around you will also suffer scorn.

Ps 123:3-4; Eze 34:29; 35:10,15

8" 'But you, mountains of Israel, will produce branches and
fruit for my people Israel, for they
will soon come home. 9I am concerned for you and will look on
you with favor; you will be plowed
and sown, 10and I will cause many
people to live on you — yes, all of
Israel. The towns will be inhabited

and the ruins rebuilt. 11I will increase the number of people and
animals living on you, and they
will be fruitful and become numerous. I will settle people on you
as in the past and will make you
prosper more than before. Then
you will know that I am the LORD.
12I will cause people, my people
Israel, to live on you. They will
possess you, and you will be their
inheritance; you will never again
deprive them of their children.

Eze 47:14,22

13" 'This is what the Sovereign
LORD says: Because some say to
you, "You devour people and deprive your nation of its children,"
14therefore you will no longer devour people or make your nation
childless, declares the Sovereign
LORD. 15No longer will I make you
hear the taunts of the nations, and
no longer will you suffer the scorn
of the peoples or cause your nation to fall, declares the Sovereign
LORD.' " Nu 13:32; Eze 34:29

Israel's Restoration Assured

16Again the word of the LORD
came to me: 17"Son of man, when
the people of Israel were living in
their own land, they defiled it by
their conduct and their actions.
Their conduct was like a woman's monthly uncleanness in my
sight. 18So I poured out my wrath
on them because they had shed
blood in the land and because
they had defiled it with their idols.
19I dispersed them among the nations, and they were scattered
through the countries; I judged
them according to their conduct
and their actions. 20And wherever they went among the nations
they profaned my holy name, for
it was said of them, 'These are the
LORD's people, and yet they had to
leave his land.' 21I had concern for
my holy name, which the people
of Israel profaned among the nations where they had gone.

Ps 74:18; Isa 48:9

22"Therefore say to the Israelites, 'This is what the Sovereign LORD says: It is not for your
sake, people of Israel, that I am
going to do these things, but for
the sake of my holy name, which
you have profaned among the
nations where you have gone. 23I
will show the holiness of my great
name, which has been profaned
among the nations, the name
you have profaned among them.
Then the nations will know that I
am the LORD, declares the Sovereign LORD, when I am proved holy
through you before their eyes.

Ps 126:2; Isa 5:16

24" 'For I will take you out of the
nations; I will gather you from all
the countries and bring you back
into your own land. 25I will sprinkle clean water on you, and you
will be clean; I will cleanse you
from all your impurities and from
all your idols. 26I will give you a
new heart and put a new spirit in you; I will remove from you
your heart of stone and give you

a heart of flesh. [27]And I will put
my Spirit in you and move you to
follow my decrees and be careful
to keep my laws. [28]Then you will
live in the land I gave your ancestors; you will be my people, and
I will be your God. [29]I will save
you from all your uncleanness. I
will call for the grain and make it
plentiful and will not bring famine upon you. [30]I will increase the
fruit of the trees and the crops of
the field, so that you will no longer
suffer disgrace among the nations
because of famine. [31]Then you
will remember your evil ways and
wicked deeds, and you will loathe
yourselves for your sins and detestable practices. [32]I want you to
know that I am not doing this for
your sake, declares the Sovereign
LORD. Be ashamed and disgraced
for your conduct, people of Israel!
Jer 24:7; Eze 11:19

[33]" 'This is what the Sovereign
LORD says: On the day I cleanse
you from all your sins, I will resettle your towns, and the ruins will
be rebuilt. [34]The desolate land will
be cultivated instead of lying desolate in the sight of all who pass
through it. [35]They will say, "This
land that was laid waste has become like the garden of Eden; the
cities that were lying in ruins, desolate and destroyed, are now fortified and inhabited." [36]Then the
nations around you that remain
will know that I the LORD have
rebuilt what was destroyed and
have replanted what was desolate.
I the LORD have spoken, and I will
do it.'
Eze 22:14; 37:14; 39:27-28

[37]"This is what the Sovereign
LORD says: Once again I will yield
to Israel's plea and do this for
them: I will make their people as
numerous as sheep, [38]as numerous as the flocks for offerings at
Jerusalem during her appointed
festivals. So will the ruined cities be filled with flocks of people.
Then they will know that I am the
LORD."
1Ki 8:63; 2Ch 35:7-9

The Valley of Dry Bones

37 The hand of the LORD was
on me, and he brought me
out by the Spirit of the LORD and
set me in the middle of a valley; it was full of bones. [2]He led
me back and forth among them,
and I saw a great many bones on
the floor of the valley, bones that
were very dry. [3]He asked me, "Son
of man, can these bones live?"
Eze 1:3; 8:3; 11:24

I said, "Sovereign LORD, you
alone know."
Dt 32:39; 1Sa 2:6

[4]Then he said to me, "Prophesy
to these bones and say to them,
'Dry bones, hear the word of the
LORD! [5]This is what the Sovereign LORD says to these bones: I
will make breath[a] enter you, and
you will come to life. [6]I will attach tendons to you and make
flesh come upon you and cover
you with skin; I will put breath
in you, and you will come to life.

[a] 5 The Hebrew for this word can also mean *wind* or *spirit* (see verses 6-14).

Then you will know that I am the
LORD.'" Ps 104:29-30; Joel 2:27; 3:17
[7]So I prophesied as I was commanded. And as I was prophesying, there was a noise, a rattling
sound, and the bones came together, bone to bone. [8]I looked,
and tendons and flesh appeared
on them and skin covered them,
but there was no breath in them.
[9]Then he said to me, "Prophesy to the breath; prophesy, son of
man, and say to it, 'This is what
the Sovereign LORD says: Come,
breath, from the four winds and
breathe into these slain, that they
may live.'" [10]So I prophesied as he
commanded me, and breath entered them; they came to life and
stood up on their feet — a vast
army. Ps 104:30; Rev 11:11
[11]Then he said to me: "Son of
man, these bones are the people
of Israel. They say, 'Our bones are
dried up and our hope is gone; we
are cut off.' [12]Therefore prophesy
and say to them: 'This is what the
Sovereign LORD says: My people, I
am going to open your graves and
bring you up from them; I will
bring you back to the land of Israel. [13]Then you, my people, will
know that I am the LORD, when I
open your graves and bring you up
from them. [14]I will put my Spirit
in you and you will live, and I will
settle you in your own land. Then
you will know that I the LORD
have spoken, and I have done it,
declares the LORD.'"
Hos 13:14; Joel 2:28-29

One Nation Under One King

[15]The word of the LORD came to
me: [16]"Son of man, take a stick of
wood and write on it, 'Belonging
to Judah and the Israelites associated with him.' Then take another stick of wood, and write on it,
'Belonging to Joseph (that is, to
Ephraim) and all the Israelites associated with him.' [17]Join them together into one stick so that they
will become one in your hand.
Nu 17:2-3; 2Ch 15:9
[18]"When your people ask you,
'Won't you tell us what you mean
by this?' [19]say to them, 'This is
what the Sovereign LORD says: I
am going to take the stick of Joseph — which is in Ephraim's
hand — and of the Israelite tribes
associated with him, and join it
to Judah's stick. I will make them
into a single stick of wood, and
they will become one in my hand.'
[20]Hold before their eyes the sticks
you have written on [21]and say to
them, 'This is what the Sovereign
LORD says: I will take the Israelites out of the nations where they
have gone. I will gather them from
all around and bring them back
into their own land. [22]I will make
them one nation in the land, on
the mountains of Israel. There will
be one king over all of them and
they will never again be two nations or be divided into two kingdoms. [23]They will no longer defile
themselves with their idols and
vile images or with any of their
offenses, for I will save them from

all their sinful backsliding,[a] and I
will cleanse them. They will be my
people, and I will be their God.
Eze 36:25,28

24"'My servant David will be
king over them, and they will all
have one shepherd. They will follow my laws and be careful to keep
my decrees. 25They will live in the
land I gave to my servant Jacob,
the land where your ancestors
lived. They and their children and
their children's children will live
there forever, and David my servant will be their prince forever.
26I will make a covenant of peace
with them; it will be an everlasting covenant. I will establish them
and increase their numbers, and
I will put my sanctuary among
them forever. 27My dwelling place
will be with them; I will be their
God, and they will be my people.
28Then the nations will know that
I the LORD make Israel holy, when
my sanctuary is among them forever.'" Eze 20:12; 2Co 6:16*

The LORD's Great Victory Over the Nations

38 The word of the LORD came
to me: 2"Son of man, set
your face against Gog, of the land
of Magog, the chief prince of[b] Meshek and Tubal; prophesy against
him 3and say: 'This is what the
Sovereign LORD says: I am against
you, Gog, chief prince of[c] Meshek
and Tubal. 4I will turn you around,
put hooks in your jaws and bring
you out with your whole army—
your horses, your horsemen fully armed, and a great horde with
large and small shields, all of them
brandishing their swords. 5Persia,
Cush[d] and Put will be with them,
all with shields and helmets, 6also
Gomer with all its troops, and Beth
Togarmah from the far north with
all its troops—the many nations
with you. Ge 10:2; Eze 39:11

7"'Get ready; be prepared, you
and all the hordes gathered about
you, and take command of them.
8After many days you will be
called to arms. In future years you
will invade a land that has recovered from war, whose people were
gathered from many nations to
the mountains of Israel, which had
long been desolate. They had been
brought out from the nations, and
now all of them live in safety. 9You
and all your troops and the many
nations with you will go up, advancing like a storm; you will be
like a cloud covering the land.
Isa 28:2; Jer 4:13; Joel 2:2

10"'This is what the Sovereign
LORD says: On that day thoughts
will come into your mind and you
will devise an evil scheme. 11You
will say, "I will invade a land of
unwalled villages; I will attack a
peaceful and unsuspecting people—all of them living without
walls and without gates and bars.

[a] *23* Many Hebrew manuscripts (see also Septuagint); most Hebrew manuscripts *all their dwelling places where they sinned*
[b] *2* Or *the prince of Rosh,*
[c] *3* Or *Gog, prince of Rosh,*
[d] *5* That is, the upper Nile region

[12]I will plunder and loot and turn
my hand against the resettled ruins and the people gathered from
the nations, rich in livestock and
goods, living at the center of the
land.[a]" [13]Sheba and Dedan and the
merchants of Tarshish and all her
villages[b] will say to you, "Have
you come to plunder? Have you
gathered your hordes to loot, to
carry off silver and gold, to take
away livestock and goods and to
seize much plunder?" '

Eze 27:22; Jer 15:13

[14]"Therefore, son of man, prophesy and say to Gog: 'This is what
the Sovereign LORD says: In that
day, when my people Israel are
living in safety, will you not take
notice of it? [15]You will come from
your place in the far north, you
and many nations with you, all
of them riding on horses, a great
horde, a mighty army. [16]You will
advance against my people Israel
like a cloud that covers the land.
In days to come, Gog, I will bring
you against my land, so that the
nations may know me when I am
proved holy through you before
their eyes.

Isa 29:23; Eze 39:21

[17]" 'This is what the Sovereign
LORD says: You are the one I spoke
of in former days by my servants
the prophets of Israel. At that
time they prophesied for years
that I would bring you against
them. [18]This is what will happen
in that day: When Gog attacks the
land of Israel, my hot anger will
be aroused, declares the Sovereign LORD. [19]In my zeal and fiery
wrath I declare that at that time
there shall be a great earthquake
in the land of Israel. [20]The fish in
the sea, the birds in the sky, the
beasts of the field, every creature
that moves along the ground,
and all the people on the face of
the earth will tremble at my presence. The mountains will be overturned, the cliffs will crumble and
every wall will fall to the ground.
[21]I will summon a sword against
Gog on all my mountains, declares
the Sovereign LORD. Every man's
sword will be against his brother. [22]I will execute judgment on
him with plague and bloodshed;
I will pour down torrents of rain,
hailstones and burning sulfur on
him and on his troops and on the
many nations with him. [23]And so
I will show my greatness and my
holiness, and I will make myself
known in the sight of many nations. Then they will know that I
am the LORD.'

1Sa 14:20; Hag 2:6,21

39

"Son of man, prophesy
against Gog and say: 'This
is what the Sovereign LORD says: I
am against you, Gog, chief prince
of[c] Meshek and Tubal. [2]I will turn
you around and drag you along. I
will bring you from the far north
and send you against the mountains of Israel. [3]Then I will strike
your bow from your left hand and
make your arrows drop from your

[a] 12 The Hebrew for this phrase means *the navel of the earth.* [b] 13 Or *her strong lions* [c] 1 Or *Gog, prince of Rosh,*

right hand. 4On the mountains
of Israel you will fall, you and all
your troops and the nations with
you. I will give you as food to all
kinds of carrion birds and to the
wild animals. 5You will fall in the
open field, for I have spoken, declares the Sovereign LORD. 6I will
send fire on Magog and on those
who live in safety in the coastlands, and they will know that I
am the LORD. Jer 25:22; Am 1:4

7"'I will make known my holy
name among my people Israel. I
will no longer let my holy name
be profaned, and the nations will
know that I the LORD am the Holy
One in Israel. 8It is coming! It will
surely take place, declares the Sovereign LORD. This is the day I have
spoken of. Ex 20:7; Eze 36:16,23

9"'Then those who live in the
towns of Israel will go out and
use the weapons for fuel and burn
them up — the small and large
shields, the bows and arrows, the
war clubs and spears. For seven
years they will use them for fuel.
10They will not need to gather
wood from the fields or cut it from
the forests, because they will use
the weapons for fuel. And they
will plunder those who plundered
them and loot those who looted them, declares the Sovereign
LORD. Isa 14:2; 33:1; Hab 2:8

11"'On that day I will give Gog a
burial place in Israel, in the valley of those who travel east of the
Sea. It will block the way of travelers, because Gog and all his hordes
will be buried there. So it will be
called the Valley of Hamon Gog.[a]
Eze 38:2

12"'For seven months the Israelites will be burying them in order
to cleanse the land. 13All the people of the land will bury them, and
the day I display my glory will be
a memorable day for them, declares the Sovereign LORD. 14Peo-
ple will be continually employed
in cleansing the land. They will
spread out across the land and,
along with others, they will bury
any bodies that are lying on the
ground. Dt 21:23; Eze 28:22

"'After the seven months they
will carry out a more detailed
search. 15As they go through the
land, anyone who sees a human
bone will leave a marker beside it
until the gravediggers bury it in
the Valley of Hamon Gog, 16near
a town called Hamonah.[b] And so
they will cleanse the land.'

17"Son of man, this is what the
Sovereign LORD says: Call out to
every kind of bird and all the wild
animals: 'Assemble and come together from all around to the sacrifice I am preparing for you, the
great sacrifice on the mountains
of Israel. There you will eat flesh
and drink blood. 18You will eat the
flesh of mighty men and drink the
blood of the princes of the earth as
if they were rams and lambs, goats
and bulls — all of them fattened
animals from Bashan. 19At the

[a] 11 *Hamon Gog* means *hordes of Gog.*
[b] 16 *Hamonah* means *horde.*

sacrifice I am preparing for you,
you will eat fat till you are glutted
and drink blood till you are drunk.
20 At my table you will eat your fill
of horses and riders, mighty men
and soldiers of every kind,' declares the Sovereign LORD.

Ps 22:12; Rev 19:17-18

21 "I will display my glory among
the nations, and all the nations
will see the punishment I inflict and the hand I lay on them.
22 From that day forward the people of Israel will know that I am
the LORD their God. 23 And the nations will know that the people
of Israel went into exile for their
sin, because they were unfaithful
to me. So I hid my face from them
and handed them over to their
enemies, and they all fell by the
sword. 24 I dealt with them according to their uncleanness and their
offenses, and I hid my face from
them. Eze 36:19

25 "Therefore this is what the
Sovereign LORD says: I will now
restore the fortunes of Jacob[a]
and will have compassion on all
the people of Israel, and I will be
zealous for my holy name. 26 They
will forget their shame and all the
unfaithfulness they showed toward me when they lived in safety in their land with no one to
make them afraid. 27 When I have
brought them back from the nations and have gathered them
from the countries of their enemies, I will be proved holy through
them in the sight of many nations. 28 Then they will know that I
am the LORD their God, for though
I sent them into exile among the
nations, I will gather them to their
own land, not leaving any behind.
29 I will no longer hide my face
from them, for I will pour out my
Spirit on the people of Israel, declares the Sovereign LORD."

Joel 2:28; Ac 2:17

The Temple Area Restored

40 In the twenty-fifth year
of our exile, at the beginning of the year, on the tenth of
the month, in the fourteenth year
after the fall of the city — on that
very day the hand of the LORD
was on me and he took me there.
2 In visions of God he took me to
the land of Israel and set me on
a very high mountain, on whose
south side were some buildings
that looked like a city. 3 He took
me there, and I saw a man whose
appearance was like bronze; he
was standing in the gateway with
a linen cord and a measuring rod
in his hand. 4 The man said to me,
"Son of man, look carefully and
listen closely and pay attention
to everything I am going to show
you, for that is why you have been
brought here. Tell the people of Israel everything you see."

Jer 26:2; Eze 44:5

The East Gate to the Outer Court

5 I saw a wall completely surrounding the temple area. The

[a] 25 *Or now bring Jacob back from captivity*

length of the measuring rod in
the man's hand was six long cubits,[a] each of which was a cubit
and a handbreadth. He measured
the wall; it was one measuring rod
thick and one rod high. Eze 42:20
6 Then he went to the east gate.
He climbed its steps and measured
the threshold of the gate; it was
one rod deep. 7 The alcoves for the
guards were one rod long and one
rod wide, and the projecting walls
between the alcoves were five cubits[b] thick. And the threshold of
the gate next to the portico facing
the temple was one rod deep.
ver 36; Eze 8:16
8 Then he measured the portico
of the gateway; 9 it[c] was eight cubits[d] deep and its jambs were two
cubits[e] thick. The portico of the
gateway faced the temple.
10 Inside the east gate were three
alcoves on each side; the three
had the same measurements, and
the faces of the projecting walls
on each side had the same measurements. 11 Then he measured
the width of the entrance of the
gateway; it was ten cubits and its
length was thirteen cubits.[f] 12 In
front of each alcove was a wall
one cubit high, and the alcoves
were six cubits square. 13 Then he
measured the gateway from the
top of the rear wall of one alcove
to the top of the opposite one;
the distance was twenty-five cubits[g] from one parapet opening to
the opposite one. 14 He measured
along the faces of the projecting walls all around the inside of
the gateway — sixty cubits.[h] The
measurement was up to the portico[i] facing the courtyard.[j] 15 The
distance from the entrance of
the gateway to the far end of its
portico was fifty cubits.[k] 16 The alcoves and the projecting walls inside the gateway were surmount-
ed by narrow parapet openings
all around, as was the portico; the
openings all around faced inward.
The faces of the projecting walls
were decorated with palm trees.
Ex 27:9; 2Ch 3:5

The Outer Court

17 Then he brought me into the
outer court. There I saw some
rooms and a pavement that had
been constructed all around the
court; there were thirty rooms
along the pavement. 18 It abutted

[a] *5* That is, about 11 feet or about 3.2 meters; also in verse 12. The long cubit of about 21 inches or about 53 centimeters is the basic unit of measurement of length throughout chapters 40 – 48. [b] *7* That is, about 8 3/4 feet or about 2.7 meters; also in verse 48 [c] *8,9* Many Hebrew manuscripts, Septuagint, Vulgate and Syriac; most Hebrew manuscripts *gateway facing the temple; it was one rod deep. 9Then he measured the portico of the gateway; it*
[d] *9* That is, about 14 feet or about 4.2 meters
[e] *9* That is, about 3 1/2 feet or about 1 meter
[f] *11* That is, about 18 feet wide and 23 feet long or about 5.3 meters wide and 6.9 meters long [g] *13* That is, about 44 feet or about 13 meters; also in verses 21, 25, 29, 30, 33 and 36 [h] *14* That is, about 105 feet or about 32 meters [i] *14* Septuagint; Hebrew *projecting wall* [j] *14* The meaning of the Hebrew for this verse is uncertain.
[k] *15* That is, about 88 feet or about 27 meters; also in verses 21, 25, 29, 33 and 36

the sides of the gateways and was
as wide as they were long; this
was the lower pavement. 19Then
he measured the distance from
the inside of the lower gateway to
the outside of the inner court; it
was a hundred cubits[a] on the east
side as well as on the north.

Eze 41:6; 46:1

The North Gate

20Then he measured the length
and width of the north gate, leading into the outer court. 21Its alcoves — three on each side — its
projecting walls and its portico
had the same measurements as
those of the first gateway. It was
fifty cubits long and twenty-five
cubits wide. 22Its openings, its portico and its palm tree decorations
had the same measurements as
those of the gate facing east. Sev-
en steps led up to it, with its portico opposite them. 23There was a
gate to the inner court facing the
north gate, just as there was on
the east. He measured from one
gate to the opposite one; it was a
hundred cubits.

ver 49

The South Gate

24Then he led me to the south
side and I saw the south gate. He
measured its jambs and its portico, and they had the same measurements as the others. 25The
gateway and its portico had narrow openings all around, like the
openings of the others. It was fifty cubits long and twenty-five cubits wide. 26Seven steps led up to
it, with its portico opposite them;
it had palm tree decorations on
the faces of the projecting walls
on each side. 27The inner court
also had a gate facing south, and
he measured from this gate to the
outer gate on the south side; it
was a hundred cubits.

ver 22,32

The Gates to the Inner Court

28Then he brought me into the
inner court through the south
gate, and he measured the south
gate; it had the same measurements as the others. 29Its alcoves,
its projecting walls and its portico had the same measurements
as the others. The gateway and its
portico had openings all around. It
was fifty cubits long and twenty-
five cubits wide. 30(The porticoes
of the gateways around the inner
court were twenty-five cubits wide
and five cubits deep.) 31Its portico
faced the outer court; palm trees
decorated its jambs, and eight
steps led up to it.

ver 21-22

32Then he brought me to the
inner court on the east side, and
he measured the gateway; it had
the same measurements as the
others. 33Its alcoves, its projecting
walls and its portico had the same
measurements as the others. The
gateway and its portico had openings all around. It was fifty cubits
long and twenty-five cubits wide.
34Its portico faced the outer court;

[a] *19* That is, about 175 feet or about 53 meters; also in verses 23, 27 and 47

palm trees decorated the jambs on
either side, and eight steps led up
to it. ver 22
35Then he brought me to the
north gate and measured it. It had
the same measurements as the
others, 36as did its alcoves, its projecting walls and its portico, and
it had openings all around. It was
fifty cubits long and twenty-five
cubits wide. 37Its portico[a] faced
the outer court; palm trees decorated the jambs on either side,
and eight steps led up to it.
Eze 44:4; 47:2

The Rooms for Preparing Sacrifices

38A room with a doorway was
by the portico in each of the inner
gateways, where the burnt offerings were washed. 39In the portico
of the gateway were two tables on
each side, on which the burnt offerings, sin offerings[b] and guilt offerings were slaughtered. 40By the
outside wall of the portico of the
gateway, near the steps at the entrance of the north gateway were
two tables, and on the other side
of the steps were two tables. 41So
there were four tables on one side
of the gateway and four on the
other — eight tables in all — on
which the sacrifices were slaughtered. 42There were also four tables of dressed stone for the burnt
offerings, each a cubit and a half
long, a cubit and a half wide and a
cubit high.[c] On them were placed
the utensils for slaughtering the
burnt offerings and the other
sacrifices. 43And double-pronged
hooks, each a handbreadth[d] long,
were attached to the wall all
around. The tables were for the
flesh of the offerings. Lev 4:3,28; 7:1

The Rooms for the Priests

44Outside the inner gate, within
the inner court, were two rooms,
one[e] at the side of the north gate
and facing south, and another at
the side of the south[f] gate and
facing north. 45He said to me,
"The room facing south is for the
priests who guard the temple,
46and the room facing north is
for the priests who guard the altar. These are the sons of Zadok,
who are the only Levites who may
draw near to the LORD to minister
before him." 1Ki 2:35; Eze 43:19; 44:15
47Then he measured the court:
It was square — a hundred cubits
long and a hundred cubits wide.
And the altar was in front of the
temple. Eze 41:13-14

The New Temple

48He brought me to the portico
of the temple and measured the
jambs of the portico; they were
five cubits wide on either side.
The width of the entrance was

[a] 37 Septuagint (see also verses 31 and 34); Hebrew *jambs* [b] 39 Or *purification offerings* [c] 42 That is, about 2 2/3 feet long and wide and 21 inches high or about 80 centimeters long and wide and 53 centimeters high [d] 43 That is, about 3 1/2 inches or about 9 centimeters [e] 44 Septuagint; Hebrew *were rooms for singers, which were* [f] 44 Septuagint; Hebrew *east*

fourteen cubits[a] and its projecting walls were[b] three cubits[c] wide
on either side. 49The portico was
twenty cubits[d] wide, and twelve[e]
cubits[f] from front to back. It was
reached by a flight of stairs,[g] and
there were pillars on each side of
the jambs. 1Ki 6:3; 7:15

41 Then the man brought me to
the main hall and measured
the jambs; the width of the jambs
was six cubits[h] on each side.[i] 2The
entrance was ten cubits[j] wide, and
the projecting walls on each side
of it were five cubits[k] wide. He
also measured the main hall; it
was forty cubits long and twenty
cubits wide.[l] ver 23; 2Ch 3:3

3Then he went into the inner sanctuary and measured the
jambs of the entrance; each was
two cubits[m] wide. The entrance
was six cubits wide, and the projecting walls on each side of it
were seven cubits[n] wide. 4And he
measured the length of the inner
sanctuary; it was twenty cubits,
and its width was twenty cubits
across the end of the main hall. He
said to me, "This is the Most Holy
Place." 1Ki 6:20; Heb 9:3-8

5Then he measured the wall of
the temple; it was six cubits thick,
and each side room around the
temple was four cubits[o] wide. 6The
side rooms were on three levels,
one above another, thirty on each
level. There were ledges all around
the wall of the temple to serve as
supports for the side rooms, so
that the supports were not inserted into the wall of the temple. 7The
side rooms all around the temple
were wider at each successive level. The structure surrounding the
temple was built in ascending
stages, so that the rooms widened
as one went upward. A stairway
went up from the lowest floor to
the top floor through the middle
floor. 1Ki 6:5,8; Eze 40:17

8I saw that the temple had a
raised base all around it, forming
the foundation of the side rooms.
It was the length of the rod, six
long cubits. 9The outer wall of the
side rooms was five cubits thick.
The open area between the side
rooms of the temple 10and the
priests' rooms was twenty cubits wide all around the temple.
11There were entrances to the side
rooms from the open area, one
on the north and another on the
south; and the base adjoining the

[a] 48 That is, about 25 feet or about 7.4 meters
[b] 48 Septuagint; Hebrew *entrance was*
[c] 48 That is, about 5 1/4 feet or about 1.6 meters
[d] 49 That is, about 35 feet or about 11 meters
[e] 49 Septuagint; Hebrew *eleven*
[f] 49 That is, about 21 feet or about 6.4 meters
[g] 49 Hebrew; Septuagint *Ten steps led up to it*
[h] 1 That is, about 11 feet or about 3.2 meters; also in verses 3, 5 and 8
[i] 1 One Hebrew manuscript and Septuagint; most Hebrew manuscripts *side, the width of the tent*
[j] 2 That is, about 18 feet or about 5.3 meters
[k] 2 That is, about 8 3/4 feet or about 2.7 meters; also in verses 9, 11 and 12
[l] 2 That is, about 70 feet long and 35 feet wide or about 21 meters long and 11 meters wide
[m] 3 That is, about 3 1/2 feet or about 1.1 meters; also in verse 22
[n] 3 That is, about 12 feet or about 3.7 meters
[o] 5 That is, about 7 feet or about 2.1 meters

open area was five cubits wide all around.

12 The building facing the temple courtyard on the west side was seventy cubits[a] wide. The wall of the building was five cubits thick all around, and its length was ninety cubits.[b]

13 Then he measured the temple; it was a hundred cubits[c] long, and the temple courtyard and the building with its walls were also a hundred cubits long. 14 The width of the temple courtyard on the east, including the front of the temple, was a hundred cubits. Eze 40:47

15 Then he measured the length of the building facing the courtyard at the rear of the temple, including its galleries on each side; it was a hundred cubits. Eze 42:3

The main hall, the inner sanctuary and the portico facing the court, 16 as well as the thresholds and the narrow windows and galleries around the three of them — everything beyond and including the threshold was covered with wood. The floor, the wall up to the windows, and the windows were covered. 17 In the space above the outside of the entrance to the inner sanctuary and on the walls at regular intervals all around the inner and outer sanctuary 18 were carved cherubim and palm trees. Palm trees alternated with cherubim. Each cherub had two faces: 19 the face of a human being toward the palm tree on one side and the face of a lion toward the palm tree on the other. They were carved all around the whole temple. 20 From the floor to the area above the entrance, cherubim and palm trees were carved on the wall of the main hall. 1Ki 6:29; 7:36; Eze 10:14

21 The main hall had a rectangular doorframe, and the one at the front of the Most Holy Place was similar. 22 There was a wooden altar three cubits[d] high and two cubits square[e]; its corners, its base[f] and its sides were of wood. The man said to me, "This is the table that is before the LORD." 23 Both the main hall and the Most Holy Place had double doors. 24 Each door had two leaves — two hinged leaves for each door. 25 And on the doors of the main hall were carved cherubim and palm trees like those carved on the walls, and there was a wooden overhang on the front of the portico. 26 On the sidewalls of the portico were narrow windows with palm trees carved on each side. The side rooms of the temple also had overhangs. Eze 44:16; Mal 1:7,12

The Rooms for the Priests

42 Then the man led me northward into the outer court and brought me to the rooms

[a] *12* That is, about 123 feet or about 37 meters [b] *12* That is, about 158 feet or about 48 meters [c] *13* That is, about 175 feet or about 53 meters; also in verses 14 and 15 [d] *22* That is, about 5 1/4 feet or about 1.5 meters [e] *22* Septuagint; Hebrew *long* [f] *22* Septuagint; Hebrew *length*

opposite the temple courtyard
and opposite the outer wall on the
north side. 2The building whose
door faced north was a hundred
cubits long and fifty cubits wide.[a]
3Both in the section twenty cubits[b]
from the inner court and in the section opposite the pavement of the
outer court, gallery faced gallery
at the three levels. 4In front of the
rooms was an inner passageway
ten cubits wide and a hundred cubits[c] long.[d] Their doors were on the
north. 5Now the upper rooms were
narrower, for the galleries took
more space from them than from
the rooms on the lower and middle
floors of the building. 6The rooms
on the top floor had no pillars, as
the courts had; so they were smaller in floor space than those on the
lower and middle floors. 7There
was an outer wall parallel to the
rooms and the outer court; it extended in front of the rooms for fifty cubits. 8While the row of rooms
on the side next to the outer court
was fifty cubits long, the row on
the side nearest the sanctuary was
a hundred cubits long. 9The lower
rooms had an entrance on the east
side as one enters them from the
outer court. Eze 41:12-14; 44:5

10On the south side[e] along the
length of the wall of the outer
court, adjoining the temple courtyard and opposite the outer wall,
were rooms 11with a passageway
in front of them. These were like
the rooms on the north; they had
the same length and width, with
similar exits and dimensions.
Similar to the doorways on the
north 12were the doorways of the
rooms on the south. There was a
doorway at the beginning of the
passageway that was parallel to
the corresponding wall extending
eastward, by which one enters the
rooms. Eze 41:12-14

13Then he said to me, "The north
and south rooms facing the temple courtyard are the priests'
rooms, where the priests who approach the LORD will eat the most
holy offerings. There they will
put the most holy offerings — the
grain offerings, the sin offerings[f]
and the guilt offerings — for the
place is holy. 14Once the priests
enter the holy precincts, they are
not to go into the outer court until they leave behind the garments
in which they minister, for these
are holy. They are to put on other clothes before they go near the
places that are for the people."
Ex 29:9; Lev 8:7-9

15When he had finished measuring what was inside the temple area, he led me out by the east
gate and measured the area all
around: 16He measured the east
side with the measuring rod; it

[a] 2 That is, about 175 feet long and 88 feet wide or about 53 meters long and 27 meters wide [b] 3 That is, about 35 feet or about 11 meters [c] 4 Septuagint and Syriac; Hebrew *and one cubit* [d] 4 That is, about 18 feet wide and 175 feet long or about 5.3 meters wide and 53 meters long
[e] 10 Septuagint; Hebrew *Eastward*
[f] 13 Or *purification offerings*

was five hundred cubits.[a,b] 17He
measured the north side; it was
five hundred cubits[c] by the measuring rod. 18He measured the
south side; it was five hundred cubits by the measuring rod. 19Then
he turned to the west side and
measured; it was five hundred cubits by the measuring rod. 20So
he measured the area on all four
sides. It had a wall around it, five
hundred cubits long and five hundred cubits wide, to separate the
holy from the common.

Eze 45:2; Rev 21:16

God's Glory Returns to the Temple

43 Then the man brought me
to the gate facing east, 2and
I saw the glory of the God of Israel coming from the east. His voice
was like the roar of rushing waters, and the land was radiant with
his glory. 3The vision I saw was
like the vision I had seen when
he[d] came to destroy the city and
like the visions I had seen by the
Kebar River, and I fell facedown.
4The glory of the LORD entered
the temple through the gate facing east. 5Then the Spirit lifted me
up and brought me into the inner
court, and the glory of the LORD
filled the temple.

Eze 11:24; 8:3

6While the man was stand-
ing beside me, I heard someone
speaking to me from inside the
temple. 7He said: "Son of man, this
is the place of my throne and the
place for the soles of my feet. This
is where I will live among the Israelites forever. The people of Israel will never again defile my holy
name — neither they nor their
kings — by their prostitution and
the funeral offerings[e] for their
kings at their death.[f] 8When they
placed their threshold next to my
threshold and their doorposts beside my doorposts, with only a
wall between me and them, they
defiled my holy name by their detestable practices. So I destroyed
them in my anger. 9Now let them
put away from me their prostitution and the funeral offerings for
their kings, and I will live among
them forever.

Eze 37:26-28

10"Son of man, describe the temple to the people of Israel, that
they may be ashamed of their
sins. Let them consider its perfection, 11and if they are ashamed of
all they have done, make known
to them the design of the temple — its arrangement, its exits
and entrances — its whole design
and all its regulations[g] and laws.
Write these down before them so
that they may be faithful to its design and follow all its regulations.

Eze 16:61; 44:5

[a] *16* See Septuagint of verse 17; Hebrew *rods*; also in verses 18 and 19. [b] *16* Five hundred cubits equal about 875 feet or about 265 meters; also in verses 17, 18 and 19. [c] *17* Septuagint; Hebrew *rods* [d] *3* Some Hebrew manuscripts and Vulgate; most Hebrew manuscripts *I* [e] *7* Or *the memorial monuments*; also in verse 9 [f] *7* Or *their high places* [g] *11* Some Hebrew manuscripts and Septuagint; most Hebrew manuscripts *regulations and its whole design*

12 "This is the law of the temple: All the surrounding area on top of the mountain will be most holy. Such is the law of the temple.

Eze 40:2

The Great Altar Restored

13 "These are the measurements of the altar in long cubits,[a] that cubit being a cubit and a handbreadth: Its gutter is a cubit deep and a cubit wide, with a rim of one span[b] around the edge. And this is the height of the altar: 14 From the gutter on the ground up to the lower ledge that goes around the altar it is two cubits high, and the ledge is a cubit wide.[c] From this lower ledge to the upper ledge that goes around the altar it is four cubits high, and that ledge is also a cubit wide.[d] 15 Above that, the altar hearth is four cubits high, and four horns project upward from the hearth. 16 The altar hearth is square, twelve cubits[e] long and twelve cubits wide. 17 The upper ledge also is square, fourteen cubits[f] long and fourteen cubits wide. All around the altar is a gutter of one cubit with a rim of half a cubit.[b] The steps of the altar face east."

Ex 20:26; 2Ch 4:1

18 Then he said to me, "Son of man, this is what the Sovereign LORD says: These will be the regulations for sacrificing burnt offerings and splashing blood against the altar when it is built: 19 You are to give a young bull as a sin offering[g] to the Levitical priests of the family of Zadok, who come near to minister before me, declares the Sovereign LORD. 20 You are to take some of its blood and put it on the four horns of the altar and on the four corners of the upper ledge and all around the rim, and so purify the altar and make atonement for it. 21 You are to take the bull for the sin offering and burn it in the designated part of the temple area outside the sanctuary.

Ex 29:14; Heb 13:11

22 "On the second day you are to offer a male goat without defect for a sin offering, and the altar is to be purified as it was purified with the bull. 23 When you have finished purifying it, you are to offer a young bull and a ram from the flock, both without defect. 24 You are to offer them before the LORD, and the priests are to sprinkle salt on them and sacrifice them as a burnt offering to the LORD.

Lev 2:13; Mk 9:49-50

25 "For seven days you are to provide a male goat daily for a sin offering; you are also to provide a

[a] *13* That is, about 21 inches or about 53 centimeters; also in verses 14 and 17. The long cubit is the basic unit for linear measurement throughout Ezekiel 40 – 48. [b] *13,17* That is, about 11 inches or about 27 centimeters [c] *14* That is, about 3 1/2 feet high and 1 3/4 feet wide or about 105 centimeters high and 53 centimeters wide [d] *14* That is, about 7 feet high and 1 3/4 feet wide or about 2.1 meters high and 53 centimeters wide [e] *16* That is, about 21 feet or about 6.4 meters [f] *17* That is, about 25 feet or about 7.4 meters [g] *19* Or *purification offering*; also in verses 21, 22 and 25

young bull and a ram from the
flock, both without defect. 26For
seven days they are to make atonement for the altar and cleanse it;
thus they will dedicate it. 27At the
end of these days, from the eighth
day on, the priests are to present
your burnt offerings and fellowship offerings on the altar. Then I
will accept you, declares the Sovereign LORD." Lev 8:33; 17:5

The Priesthood Restored

44 Then the man brought me
back to the outer gate of
the sanctuary, the one facing east,
and it was shut. 2The LORD said to
me, "This gate is to remain shut.
It must not be opened; no one
may enter through it. It is to remain shut because the LORD, the
God of Israel, has entered through
it. 3The prince himself is the only
one who may sit inside the gateway to eat in the presence of the
LORD. He is to enter by way of the
portico of the gateway and go out
the same way." Eze 46:2,8

4Then the man brought me by
way of the north gate to the front
of the temple. I looked and saw
the glory of the LORD filling the
temple of the LORD, and I fell facedown. Eze 1:28; 3:23

5The LORD said to me, "Son of
man, look carefully, listen closely
and give attention to everything I
tell you concerning all the regulations and instructions regarding
the temple of the LORD. Give attention to the entrance to the temple and all the exits of the sanctuary. 6Say to rebellious Israel, 'This
is what the Sovereign LORD says:
Enough of your detestable practices, people of Israel! 7In addition to all your other detestable
practices, you brought foreigners
uncircumcised in heart and flesh
into my sanctuary, desecrating
my temple while you offered me
food, fat and blood, and you broke
my covenant. 8Instead of carrying
out your duty in regard to my holy
things, you put others in charge
of my sanctuary. 9This is what the
Sovereign LORD says: No foreigner
uncircumcised in heart and flesh
is to enter my sanctuary, not even
the foreigners who live among the
Israelites. Lev 26:41; Joel 3:17

10" 'The Levites who went far
from me when Israel went astray
and who wandered from me after
their idols must bear the consequences of their sin. 11They may
serve in my sanctuary, having
charge of the gates of the temple and serving in it; they may
slaughter the burnt offerings and
sacrifices for the people and stand
before the people and serve them.
12But because they served them
in the presence of their idols and
made the people of Israel fall into
sin, therefore I have sworn with
uplifted hand that they must bear
the consequences of their sin, declares the Sovereign LORD. 13They
are not to come near to serve me as
priests or come near any of my holy
things or my most holy offerings;

they must bear the shame of their
detestable practices. 14 And I will
appoint them to guard the temple
for all the work that is to be done
in it. 2Ki 23:8; Nu 18:23

15 "'But the Levitical priests, who
are descendants of Zadok and who
guarded my sanctuary when the
Israelites went astray from me,
are to come near to minister before me; they are to stand before
me to offer sacrifices of fat and
blood, declares the Sovereign
LORD. 16 They alone are to enter my
sanctuary; they alone are to come
near my table to minister before
me and serve me as guards.
Nu 18:5; Eze 40:46

17 "'When they enter the gates of
the inner court, they are to wear
linen clothes; they must not wear
any woolen garment while ministering at the gates of the inner
court or inside the temple. 18 They
are to wear linen turbans on their
heads and linen undergarments
around their waists. They must
not wear anything that makes
them perspire. 19 When they go
out into the outer court where the
people are, they are to take off the
clothes they have been ministering in and are to leave them in the
sacred rooms, and put on other
clothes, so that the people are not
consecrated through contact with
their garments. Eze 42:14; 46:20

20 "'They must not shave their
heads or let their hair grow long,
but they are to keep the hair of
their heads trimmed. 21 No priest is
to drink wine when he enters the
inner court. 22 They must not marry
widows or divorced women; they
may marry only virgins of Israelite descent or widows of priests.
23 They are to teach my people the
difference between the holy and
the common and show them how
to distinguish between the unclean and the clean. Eze 22:26; Mal 2:7

24 "'In any dispute, the priests
are to serve as judges and decide
it according to my ordinances.
They are to keep my laws and my
decrees for all my appointed festivals, and they are to keep my Sabbaths holy. Dt 17:8-9; 2Ch 19:8

25 "'A priest must not defile himself by going near a dead person;
however, if the dead person was
his father or mother, son or daughter, brother or unmarried sister,
then he may defile himself. 26 After
he is cleansed, he must wait sev-
en days. 27 On the day he goes into
the inner court of the sanctuary
to minister in the sanctuary, he is
to offer a sin offering[a] for himself,
declares the Sovereign LORD.
Lev 21:1-4; Nu 19:14

28 "'I am to be the only inheritance the priests have. You are to
give them no possession in Israel;
I will be their possession. 29 They
will eat the grain offerings, the sin
offerings and the guilt offerings;
and everything in Israel devoted[b]

[a] 27 Or *purification offering*; also in verse 29
[b] 29 The Hebrew term refers to the irrevocable giving over of things or persons to the LORD.

to the LORD will belong to them. 30The best of all the firstfruits and of all your special gifts will belong to the priests. You are to give them the first portion of your ground meal so that a blessing may rest on your household. 31The priests must not eat anything, whether bird or animal, found dead or torn by wild animals.

Nu 18:20; Dt 10:9; 18:1-2

Israel Fully Restored

45 " 'When you allot the land as an inheritance, you are to present to the LORD a portion of the land as a sacred district, 25,000 cubits[a] long and 20,000[b] cubits[c] wide; the entire area will be holy. 2Of this, a section 500 cubits[d] square is to be for the sanctuary, with 50 cubits[e] around it for open land. 3In the sacred district, measure off a section 25,000 cubits long and 10,000 cubits[f] wide. In it will be the sanctuary, the Most Holy Place. 4It will be the sacred portion of the land for the priests, who minister in the sanctuary and who draw near to minister before the LORD. It will be a place for their houses as well as a holy place for the sanctuary. 5An area 25,000 cubits long and 10,000 cubits wide will belong to the Levites, who serve in the temple, as their possession for towns to live in.[g]

Eze 47:21-22; 48:13

6" 'You are to give the city as its property an area 5,000 cubits[h] wide and 25,000 cubits long, adjoining the sacred portion; it will belong to all Israel.

Eze 48:15-18

7" 'The prince will have the land bordering each side of the area formed by the sacred district and the property of the city. It will extend westward from the west side and eastward from the east side, running lengthwise from the western to the eastern border parallel to one of the tribal portions. 8This land will be his possession in Israel. And my princes will no longer oppress my people but will allow the people of Israel to possess the land according to their tribes.

Eze 46:18; 48:21

9" 'This is what the Sovereign LORD says: You have gone far enough, princes of Israel! Give up your violence and oppression and do what is just and right. Stop dispossessing my people, declares the Sovereign LORD. 10You are to use accurate scales, an accurate ephah[i] and an accurate bath.[j] 11The ephah and the bath are to be the

[a] *1* That is, about 8 miles or about 13 kilometers; also in verses 3, 5 and 6 [b] *1* Septuagint (see also verses 3 and 5 and 48:9); Hebrew *10,000* [c] *1* That is, about 6 1/2 miles or about 11 kilometers [d] *2* That is, about 875 feet or about 265 meters [e] *2* That is, about 88 feet or about 27 meters [f] *3* That is, about 3 1/3 miles or about 5.3 kilometers; also in verse 5 [g] *5* Septuagint; Hebrew *temple; they will have as their possession 20 rooms* [h] *6* That is, about 1 2/3 miles or about 2.7 kilometers [i] *10* An ephah was a dry measure having the capacity of about 3/5 bushel or about 22 liters. [j] *10* A bath was a liquid measure equaling about 6 gallons or about 22 liters.

same size, the bath containing a
tenth of a homer and the ephah a
tenth of a homer; the homer is to
be the standard measure for both.
12 The shekel[a] is to consist of twenty gerahs. Twenty shekels plus
twenty-five shekels plus fifteen
shekels equal one mina.[b]

Jer 22:3; Zec 7:9-10; 8:16

13 " 'This is the special gift you
are to offer: a sixth of an ephah[c]
from each homer of wheat and a
sixth of an ephah[d] from each homer of barley. 14 The prescribed
portion of olive oil, measured
by the bath, is a tenth of a bath[e]
from each cor (which consists of
ten baths or one homer, for ten
baths are equivalent to a homer).
15 Also one sheep is to be taken
from every flock of two hundred
from the well-watered pastures
of Israel. These will be used for
the grain offerings, burnt offerings and fellowship offerings to
make atonement for the people,
declares the Sovereign LORD. 16 All
the people of the land will be required to give this special offering to the prince in Israel. 17 It will
be the duty of the prince to provide the burnt offerings, grain offerings and drink offerings at the
festivals, the New Moons and the
Sabbaths — at all the appointed
festivals of Israel. He will provide
the sin offerings,[f] grain offerings,
burnt offerings and fellowship
offerings to make atonement for
the Israelites.

1Ki 8:62; 2Ch 31:3

18 " 'This is what the Sovereign
LORD says: In the first month
on the first day you are to take a
young bull without defect and
purify the sanctuary. 19 The priest
is to take some of the blood of
the sin offering and put it on the
doorposts of the temple, on the
four corners of the upper ledge
of the altar and on the gateposts
of the inner court. 20 You are to do
the same on the seventh day of the
month for anyone who sins unintentionally or through ignorance;
so you are to make atonement for
the temple.

Lev 4:27; Eze 43:20

21 " 'In the first month on the
fourteenth day you are to observe
the Passover, a festival lasting sev-
en days, during which you shall eat
bread made without yeast. 22 On
that day the prince is to provide
a bull as a sin offering for himself and for all the people of the
land. 23 Every day during the sev-
en days of the festival he is to provide seven bulls and seven rams
without defect as a burnt offering
to the LORD, and a male goat for a
sin offering. 24 He is to provide as
a grain offering an ephah for each
bull and an ephah for each ram,

[a] *12* A shekel weighed about 2/5 ounce or about 12 grams. [b] *12* That is, 60 shekels; the common mina was 50 shekels. Sixty shekels were about 1 1/2 pounds or about 690 grams. [c] *13* That is, probably about 6 pounds or about 2.7 kilograms [d] *13* That is, probably about 5 pounds or about 2.3 kilograms [e] *14* That is, about 2 1/2 quarts or about 2.2 liters [f] *17* Or *purification offerings*; also in verses 19, 22, 23 and 25

along with a hin[a] of olive oil for
each ephah. Ex 12:11; Lev 23:5-6
25 "'During the seven days of the
festival, which begins in the seventh month on the fifteenth day,
he is to make the same provision
for sin offerings, burnt offerings,
grain offerings and oil.
Lev 23:34-43; Nu 29:12-38

46 "'This is what the Sovereign LORD says: The gate of
the inner court facing east is to be
shut on the six working days, but
on the Sabbath day and on the day
of the New Moon it is to be opened.
2 The prince is to enter from the
outside through the portico of the
gateway and stand by the gate-
post. The priests are to sacrifice
his burnt offering and his fellowship offerings. He is to bow down
in worship at the threshold of the
gateway and then go out, but the
gate will not be shut until evening.
3 On the Sabbaths and New Moons
the people of the land are to worship in the presence of the LORD at
the entrance of that gateway. 4 The
burnt offering the prince brings
to the LORD on the Sabbath day is
to be six male lambs and a ram,
all without defect. 5 The grain offering given with the ram is to be
an ephah,[b] and the grain offering
with the lambs is to be as much
as he pleases, along with a hin[c] of
olive oil for each ephah. 6 On the
day of the New Moon he is to offer a young bull, six lambs and a
ram, all without defect. 7 He is to
provide as a grain offering one
ephah with the bull, one ephah
with the ram, and with the lambs
as much as he wants to give, along
with a hin of oil for each ephah.
8 When the prince enters, he is to
go in through the portico of the
gateway, and he is to come out the
same way. Eze 40:19; 44:3
9 "'When the people of the land
come before the LORD at the appointed festivals, whoever enters
by the north gate to worship is to
go out the south gate; and whoever enters by the south gate is
to go out the north gate. No one
is to return through the gate by
which they entered, but each is
to go out the opposite gate. 10 The
prince is to be among them, going
in when they go in and going out
when they go out. 11 At the feasts
and the appointed festivals, the
grain offering is to be an ephah
with a bull, an ephah with a ram,
and with the lambs as much as he
pleases, along with a hin of oil for
each ephah. Ex 23:14; Ps 42:4
12 "'When the prince provides
a freewill offering to the LORD —
whether a burnt offering or fellowship offerings — the gate facing east is to be opened for him.
He shall offer his burnt offering or
his fellowship offerings as he does
on the Sabbath day. Then he shall
go out, and after he has gone out,
the gate will be shut. Eze 45:17

[a] *24* That is, about 1 gallon or about 3.8 liters [b] *5* That is, probably about 35 pounds or about 16 kilograms; also in verses 7 and 11 [c] *5* That is, about 1 gallon or about 3.8 liters; also in verses 7 and 11

13“ ‘Every day you are to provide
a year-old lamb without defect
for a burnt offering to the LORD;
morning by morning you shall
provide it. 14You are also to provide with it morning by morning
a grain offering, consisting of a
sixth of an ephah[a] with a third of
a hin[b] of oil to moisten the flour.
The presenting of this grain offering to the LORD is a lasting ordinance. 15So the lamb and the grain
offering and the oil shall be provided morning by morning for a
regular burnt offering.
Nu 28:5-6; Ex 29:38,42

16“ ‘This is what the Sovereign
LORD says: If the prince makes a
gift from his inheritance to one
of his sons, it will also belong to
his descendants; it is to be their
property by inheritance. 17If, however, he makes a gift from his inheritance to one of his servants,
the servant may keep it until the
year of freedom; then it will revert
to the prince. His inheritance belongs to his sons only; it is theirs.
18The prince must not take any
of the inheritance of the people,
driving them off their property.
He is to give his sons their inheritance out of his own property, so
that not one of my people will be
separated from their property.’ ”
Eze 45:8; Mic 2:1-2

19Then the man brought me
through the entrance at the side
of the gate to the sacred rooms
facing north, which belonged
to the priests, and showed me a
place at the western end. 20He said
to me, “This is the place where the
priests are to cook the guilt offering and the sin offering[c] and bake
the grain offering, to avoid bringing them into the outer court and
consecrating the people.” Zec 14:20

21He then brought me to the
outer court and led me around to
its four corners, and I saw in each
corner another court. 22In the four
corners of the outer court were
enclosed[d] courts, forty cubits long
and thirty cubits wide;[e] each of
the courts in the four corners was
the same size. 23Around the inside
of each of the four courts was a
ledge of stone, with places for fire
built all around under the ledge.
24He said to me, “These are the
kitchens where those who minister at the temple are to cook the
sacrifices of the people.”

The River From the Temple

47 The man brought me back
to the entrance to the temple, and I saw water coming out
from under the threshold of the
temple toward the east (for the
temple faced east). The water was
coming down from under the
south side of the temple, south of
the altar. 2He then brought me out

[a] 14 That is, probably about 6 pounds or about 2.7 kilograms [b] 14 That is, about 1 1/2 quarts or about 1.3 liters [c] 20 Or *purification offering* [d] 22 The meaning of the Hebrew for this word is uncertain. [e] 22 That is, about 70 feet long and 53 feet wide or about 21 meters long and 16 meters wide

through the north gate and led me around the outside to the outer gate facing east, and the water was trickling from the south side.

Joel 3:18; Rev 22:1

3 As the man went eastward with a measuring line in his hand, he measured off a thousand cubits[a] and then led me through water that was ankle-deep. 4 He measured off another thousand cubits and led me through water that was knee-deep. He measured off another thousand and led me through water that was up to the waist. 5 He measured off another thousand, but now it was a river that I could not cross, because the water had risen and was deep enough to swim in — a river that no one could cross. 6 He asked me, "Son of man, do you see this?"

Isa 11:9; Eze 40:3

Then he led me back to the bank of the river. 7 When I arrived there, I saw a great number of trees on each side of the river. 8 He said to me, "This water flows toward the eastern region and goes down into the Arabah,[b] where it enters the Dead Sea. When it empties into the sea, the salty water there becomes fresh. 9 Swarms of living creatures will live wherever the river flows. There will be large numbers of fish, because this water flows there and makes the salt water fresh; so where the river flows everything will live. 10 Fishermen will stand along the shore; from En Gedi to En Eglaim there will be places for spreading nets. The fish will be of many kinds — like the fish of the Mediterranean Sea. 11 But the swamps and marshes will not become fresh; they will be left for salt. 12 Fruit trees of all kinds will grow on both banks of the river. Their leaves will not wither, nor will their fruit fail. Every month they will bear fruit, because the water from the sanctuary flows to them. Their fruit will serve for food and their leaves for healing."

Ps 1:3; Jer 17:8

The Boundaries of the Land

13 This is what the Sovereign LORD says: "These are the boundaries of the land that you will divide among the twelve tribes of Israel as their inheritance, with two portions for Joseph. 14 You are to divide it equally among them. Because I swore with uplifted hand to give it to your ancestors, this land will become your inheritance.

Dt 1:8; Eze 20:5-6

15 "This is to be the boundary of the land:

"On the north side it will run from the Mediterranean Sea by the Hethlon road past Lebo Hamath to Zedad, 16 Berothah[c] and Sibraim (which lies on the border between Damascus and Hamath), as

[a] *3* That is, about 1,700 feet or about 530 meters [b] *8* Or *the Jordan Valley*
[c] *15,16* See Septuagint and 48:1; Hebrew *road to go into Zedad, 16Hamath, Berothah.*

far as Hazer Hattikon, which
is on the border of Hauran.
17The boundary will extend
from the sea to Hazar Enan,[a]
along the northern border of
Damascus, with the border
of Hamath to the north. This
will be the northern boundary. Eze 48:1
18"On the east side the boundary
will run between Hauran and
Damascus, along the Jordan
between Gilead and the land
of Israel, to the Dead Sea and
as far as Tamar.[b] This will be
the eastern boundary. Eze 27:18
19"On the south side it will run
from Tamar as far as the waters of Meribah Kadesh, then
along the Wadi of Egypt to the
Mediterranean Sea. This will
be the southern boundary.
Eze 48:28
20"On the west side, the Mediterranean Sea will be the boundary to a point opposite Lebo
Hamath. This will be the western boundary. Nu 34:6; Eze 48:1
21"You are to distribute this land
among yourselves according to
the tribes of Israel. 22You are to
allot it as an inheritance for yourselves and for the foreigners residing among you and who have children. You are to consider them as
native-born Israelites; along with
you they are to be allotted an inheritance among the tribes of Israel. 23In whatever tribe a foreigner resides, there you are to give
them their inheritance," declares
the Sovereign LORD. Eph 3:6; Col 3:11

The Division of the Land

48 "These are the tribes, listed by name: At the north-
ern frontier, Dan will have one
portion; it will follow the Hethlon road to Lebo Hamath; Hazar
Enan and the northern border of
Damascus next to Hamath will be
part of its border from the east
side to the west side.
Ge 30:6; Eze 47:20
2"Asher will have one portion;
it will border the territory of Dan
from east to west. Jos 19:24-31
3"Naphtali will have one portion; it will border the territory of
Asher from east to west. Jos 19:32-39
4"Manasseh will have one portion; it will border the territory of
Naphtali from east to west.
Jos 17:1-11
5"Ephraim will have one portion; it will border the territory of
Manasseh from east to west.
Jos 16:5-9
6"Reuben will have one portion; it will border the territory of
Ephraim from east to west.
Jos 13:15-21
7"Judah will have one portion;
it will border the territory of Reuben from east to west. Jos 15:1-63
8"Bordering the territory of Judah from east to west will be the
portion you are to present as a

[a] 17 Hebrew *Enon*, a variant of *Enan*
[b] 18 See Syriac; Hebrew *Israel. You will measure to the Dead Sea.*

special gift. It will be 25,000 cubits[a] wide, and its length from
east to west will equal one of the
tribal portions; the sanctuary will
be in the center of it. ver 21
9“The special portion you are to
offer to the LORD will be 25,000 cubits long and 10,000 cubits[b] wide.
10This will be the sacred portion for
the priests. It will be 25,000 cubits
long on the north side, 10,000 cubits wide on the west side, 10,000
cubits wide on the east side and
25,000 cubits long on the south
side. In the center of it will be the
sanctuary of the LORD. 11This will
be for the consecrated priests, the
Zadokites, who were faithful in
serving me and did not go astray
as the Levites did when the Israelites went astray. 12It will be a special gift to them from the sacred
portion of the land, a most holy
portion, bordering the territory of
the Levites. Eze 44:15
13“Alongside the territory of the
priests, the Levites will have an
allotment 25,000 cubits long and
10,000 cubits wide. Its total length
will be 25,000 cubits and its width
10,000 cubits. 14They must not
sell or exchange any of it. This is
the best of the land and must not
pass into other hands, because it is
holy to the LORD. Lev 25:34; 27:10,28
15“The remaining area, 5,000
cubits[c] wide and 25,000 cubits
long, will be for the common use
of the city, for houses and for pastureland. The city will be in the
center of it 16and will have these
measurements: the north side
4,500 cubits,[d] the south side 4,500
cubits, the east side 4,500 cubits,
and the west side 4,500 cubits.
17The pastureland for the city will
be 250 cubits[e] on the north, 250
cubits on the south, 250 cubits
on the east, and 250 cubits on the
west. 18What remains of the area,
bordering on the sacred portion
and running the length of it, will
be 10,000 cubits on the east side
and 10,000 cubits on the west
side. Its produce will supply food
for the workers of the city. 19The
workers from the city who farm it
will come from all the tribes of Israel. 20The entire portion will be a
square, 25,000 cubits on each side.
As a special gift you will set aside
the sacred portion, along with the
property of the city. Rev 21:16
21“What remains on both sides
of the area formed by the sacred
portion and the property of the
city will belong to the prince. It
will extend eastward from the
25,000 cubits of the sacred portion
to the eastern border, and westward from the 25,000 cubits to the
western border. Both these areas
running the length of the tribal
portions will belong to the prince,

[a] *8* That is, about 8 miles or about 13 kilometers; also in verses 9, 10, 13, 15, 20 and 21 [b] *9* That is, about 3 1/3 miles or about 5.3 kilometers; also in verses 10, 13 and 18 [c] *15* That is, about 1 2/3 miles or about 2.7 kilometers [d] *16* That is, about 1 1/2 miles or about 2.4 kilometers; also in verses 30, 32, 33 and 34 [e] *17* That is, about 440 feet or about 135 meters

and the sacred portion with the
temple sanctuary will be in the
center of them. 22So the property
of the Levites and the property of
the city will lie in the center of the
area that belongs to the prince.
The area belonging to the prince
will lie between the border of Judah and the border of Benjamin.
Eze 45:7
23"As for the rest of the tribes:
Benjamin will have one portion;
it will extend from the east side to
the west side. Jos 18:11-28
24"Simeon will have one portion; it will border the territory of
Benjamin from east to west.
Jos 19:1-9
25"Issachar will have one portion; it will border the territory of
Simeon from east to west. Jos 19:17-23
26"Zebulun will have one portion; it will border the territory of
Issachar from east to west.
Jos 19:10-16
27"Gad will have one portion; it
will border the territory of Zebulun from east to west. Jos 13:24-28
28"The southern boundary of
Gad will run south from Tamar
to the waters of Meribah Kadesh,
then along the Wadi of Egypt to
the Mediterranean Sea. Eze 47:19
29"This is the land you are to allot as an inheritance to the tribes
of Israel, and these will be their
portions," declares the Sovereign
LORD. Eze 45:1

The Gates of the New City

30"These will be the exits of the
city: Beginning on the north side,
which is 4,500 cubits long, 31the
gates of the city will be named after the tribes of Israel. The three
gates on the north side will be the
gate of Reuben, the gate of Judah
and the gate of Levi.
32"On the east side, which
is 4,500 cubits long, will be three
gates: the gate of Joseph, the gate
of Benjamin and the gate of Dan.
33"On the south side, which measures 4,500 cubits, will be three
gates: the gate of Simeon, the gate
of Issachar and the gate of Zebulun.
34"On the west side, which is
4,500 cubits long, will be three
gates: the gate of Gad, the gate of
Asher and the gate of Naphtali.
Rev 21:12-13
35"The distance all around will
be 18,000 cubits.[a]
"And the name of the city from
that time on will be:

THE LORD IS THERE."

[a] 35 That is, about 6 miles or about 9.5 kilometers

DANIEL

Daniel's Training in Babylon

1 In the third year of the reign
of Jehoiakim king of Judah,
Nebuchadnezzar king of Babylon
came to Jerusalem and besieged
it. 2And the Lord delivered Jehoiakim king of Judah into his hand,
along with some of the articles
from the temple of God. These he
carried off to the temple of his god
in Babylonia[a] and put in the treasure house of his god.
2Ch 36:6; Jer 27:19-20; Zec 5:5-11

3Then the king ordered Ashpe-
naz, chief of his court officials, to
bring into the king's service some
of the Israelites from the royal
family and the nobility— 4young
men without any physical defect,
handsome, showing aptitude for
every kind of learning, well informed, quick to understand, and
qualified to serve in the king's
palace. He was to teach them the
language and literature of the
Babylonians.[b] 5The king assigned
them a daily amount of food and
wine from the king's table. They
were to be trained for three years,
and after that they were to enter
the king's service. Isa 39:7

6Among those who were chosen
were some from Judah: Daniel,
Hananiah, Mishael and Azariah.
7The chief official gave them new
names: to Daniel, the name Belteshazzar; to Hananiah, Shadrach;
to Mishael, Meshach; and to Azariah, Abednego. Da 4:8; 5:12

8But Daniel resolved not to defile himself with the royal food
and wine, and he asked the chief
official for permission not to defile himself this way. 9Now God
had caused the official to show
favor and compassion to Daniel,
10but the official told Daniel, "I am
afraid of my lord the king, who
has assigned your[c] food and drink.
Why should he see you looking
worse than the other young men
your age? The king would then
have my head because of you."
Ge 39:21; 1Ki 8:50

11Daniel then said to the guard
whom the chief official had appointed over Daniel, Hananiah,
Mishael and Azariah, 12"Please test
your servants for ten days: Give
us nothing but vegetables to eat
and water to drink. 13Then compare our appearance with that of
the young men who eat the royal food, and treat your servants
in accordance with what you see."
14So he agreed to this and tested
them for ten days. Rev 2:10

15At the end of the ten days
they looked healthier and better

[a] 2 Hebrew *Shinar* [b] 4 Or *Chaldeans*
[c] 10 The Hebrew for *your* and *you* in this verse is plural.

nourished than any of the young men who ate the royal food. 16 So the guard took away their choice food and the wine they were to drink and gave them vegetables instead. Ex 23:25

17 To these four young men God gave knowledge and understanding of all kinds of literature and learning. And Daniel could understand visions and dreams of all kinds. Da 2:19,30; 7:1; 8:1

18 At the end of the time set by the king to bring them into his service, the chief official presented them to Nebuchadnezzar. 19 The king talked with them, and he found none equal to Daniel, Hananiah, Mishael and Azariah; so they entered the king's service. 20 In every matter of wisdom and understanding about which the king questioned them, he found them ten times better than all the magicians and enchanters in his whole kingdom. 1Ki 4:30; Da 2:13,28

21 And Daniel remained there until the first year of King Cyrus. Da 6:28; 10:1

Nebuchadnezzar's Dream

2 In the second year of his reign, Nebuchadnezzar had dreams; his mind was troubled and he could not sleep. 2 So the king summoned the magicians, enchanters, sorcerers and astrologers[a] to tell him what he had dreamed. When they came in and stood before the king, 3 he said to them, "I have had a dream that troubles me and I want to know what it means.[b]" Da 4:5-6

4 Then the astrologers answered the king,[c] "May the king live forever! Tell your servants the dream, and we will interpret it." Ezr 4:7; Da 3:9; 5:10

5 The king replied to the astrologers, "This is what I have firmly decided: If you do not tell me what my dream was and interpret it, I will have you cut into pieces and your houses turned into piles of rubble. 6 But if you tell me the dream and explain it, you will receive from me gifts and rewards and great honor. So tell me the dream and interpret it for me." Da 5:7,16

7 Once more they replied, "Let the king tell his servants the dream, and we will interpret it."

8 Then the king answered, "I am certain that you are trying to gain time, because you realize that this is what I have firmly decided: 9 If you do not tell me the dream, there is only one penalty for you. You have conspired to tell me misleading and wicked things, hoping the situation will change. So then, tell me the dream, and I will know that you can interpret it for me." Est 4:11; Isa 41:22-24

10 The astrologers answered the king, "There is no one on earth

[a] 2 Or *Chaldeans*; also in verses 4, 5 and 10
[b] 3 Or *was*
[c] 4 At this point the Hebrew text has *in Aramaic*, indicating that the text from here through the end of chapter 7 is in Aramaic.

who can do what the king asks! No
king, however great and mighty,
has ever asked such a thing of any
magician or enchanter or astrolo-
ger. 11What the king asks is too difficult. No one can reveal it to the
king except the gods, and they do
not live among humans." Da 5:8,11

12This made the king so angry
and furious that he ordered the
execution of all the wise men of
Babylon. 13So the decree was issued to put the wise men to death,
and men were sent to look for
Daniel and his friends to put them
to death. Da 1:20; 3:13,19

14When Arioch, the commander of the king's guard, had gone
out to put to death the wise men
of Babylon, Daniel spoke to him
with wisdom and tact. 15He asked
the king's officer, "Why did the
king issue such a harsh decree?"
Arioch then explained the matter
to Daniel. 16At this, Daniel went in
to the king and asked for time, so
that he might interpret the dream
for him.

17Then Daniel returned to his
house and explained the matter
to his friends Hananiah, Mishael
and Azariah. 18He urged them to
plead for mercy from the God of
heaven concerning this mystery,
so that he and his friends might
not be executed with the rest of
the wise men of Babylon. 19Dur-
ing the night the mystery was revealed to Daniel in a vision. Then
Daniel praised the God of heaven
20and said: Job 33:15; Da 1:17

"Praise be to the name of God
for ever and ever; Ps 113:2
wisdom and power are his.
Jer 32:19
21He changes times and seasons;
Da 7:25
he deposes kings and raises
up others. Ps 75:6-7
He gives wisdom to the wise
Jas 1:5
and knowledge to the
discerning. 2Sa 14:17
22He reveals deep and hidden
things; Da 5:11
he knows what lies in
darkness, Ps 139:11-12; Heb 4:13
and light dwells with him.
Isa 45:7; Jas 1:17
23I thank and praise you, God of
my ancestors: Ex 3:15
You have given me wisdom
and power, Da 1:17
you have made known to me
what we asked of you,
you have made known to us
the dream of the king."
Eze 28:3

Daniel Interprets the Dream

24Then Daniel went to Arioch,
whom the king had appointed to
execute the wise men of Babylon,
and said to him, "Do not execute
the wise men of Babylon. Take me
to the king, and I will interpret his
dream for him." ver 14

25Arioch took Daniel to the king
at once and said, "I have found a
man among the exiles from Judah who can tell the king what his
dream means." Da 1:6; 5:13; 6:13

26 The king asked Daniel (also
called Belteshazzar), "Are you able
to tell me what I saw in my dream
and interpret it?" Da 1:7

27 Daniel replied, "No wise man,
enchanter, magician or diviner can
explain to the king the mystery
he has asked about, 28 but there is
a God in heaven who reveals mysteries. He has shown King Nebuchadnezzar what will happen in
days to come. Your dream and the
visions that passed through your
mind as you were lying in bed are
these: Da 4:5; Am 4:13

29 "As Your Majesty was lying
there, your mind turned to things
to come, and the revealer of mysteries showed you what is going to
happen. 30 As for me, this mystery
has been revealed to me, not because I have greater wisdom than
anyone else alive, but so that Your
Majesty may know the interpretation and that you may understand
what went through your mind.
Isa 45:3; Da 1:17; Am 4:13

31 "Your Majesty looked, and
there before you stood a large
statue—an enormous, dazzling
statue, awesome in appearance.
32 The head of the statue was made
of pure gold, its chest and arms
of silver, its belly and thighs of
bronze, 33 its legs of iron, its feet
partly of iron and partly of baked
clay. 34 While you were watching,
a rock was cut out, but not by human hands. It struck the statue
on its feet of iron and clay and
smashed them. 35 Then the iron,
the clay, the bronze, the silver and
the gold were all broken to pieces
and became like chaff on a threshing floor in the summer. The wind
swept them away without leaving
a trace. But the rock that struck
the statue became a huge mountain and filled the whole earth.
Hab 1:7; Zec 4:6

36 "This was the dream, and now
we will interpret it to the king.
37 Your Majesty, you are the king of
kings. The God of heaven has giv-
en you dominion and power and
might and glory; 38 in your hands
he has placed all mankind and the
beasts of the field and the birds in
the sky. Wherever they live, he has
made you ruler over them all. You
are that head of gold. Da 4:21-22

39 "After you, another kingdom
will arise, inferior to yours. Next, a
third kingdom, one of bronze, will
rule over the whole earth. 40 Finally, there will be a fourth kingdom,
strong as iron—for iron breaks
and smashes everything—and as
iron breaks things to pieces, so it
will crush and break all the others. 41 Just as you saw that the feet
and toes were partly of baked clay
and partly of iron, so this will be a
divided kingdom; yet it will have
some of the strength of iron in it,
even as you saw iron mixed with
clay. 42 As the toes were partly iron
and partly clay, so this kingdom
will be partly strong and partly
brittle. 43 And just as you saw the
iron mixed with baked clay, so the
people will be a mixture and will

not remain united, any more than iron mixes with clay. Da 7:7,23

44 "In the time of those kings, the God of heaven will set up a kingdom that will never be destroyed, nor will it be left to another people. It will crush all those kingdoms and bring them to an end, but it will itself endure forever. 45 This is the meaning of the vision of the rock cut out of a mountain, but not by human hands — a rock that broke the iron, the bronze, the clay, the silver and the gold to pieces. Isa 9:7; Lk 1:33

"The great God has shown the king what will take place in the future. The dream is true and its interpretation is trustworthy." Ge 41:25

46 Then King Nebuchadnezzar fell prostrate before Daniel and paid him honor and ordered that an offering and incense be presented to him. 47 The king said to Daniel, "Surely your God is the God of gods and the Lord of kings and a revealer of mysteries, for you were able to reveal this mystery." Da 11:36; Ac 10:25

48 Then the king placed Daniel in a high position and lavished many gifts on him. He made him ruler over the entire province of Babylon and placed him in charge of all its wise men. 49 Moreover, at Daniel's request the king appointed Shadrach, Meshach and Abednego administrators over the province of Babylon, while Daniel himself remained at the royal court. Da 4:9; 5:11

The Image of Gold and the Blazing Furnace

3 King Nebuchadnezzar made an image of gold, sixty cubits high and six cubits wide,[a] and set it up on the plain of Dura in the province of Babylon. 2 He then summoned the satraps, prefects, governors, advisers, treasurers, judges, magistrates and all the other provincial officials to come to the dedication of the image he had set up. 3 So the satraps, prefects, governors, advisers, treasurers, judges, magistrates and all the other provincial officials assembled for the dedication of the image that King Nebuchadnezzar had set up, and they stood before it. Isa 46:6; Hab 2:19

4 Then the herald loudly proclaimed, "Nations and peoples of every language, this is what you are commanded to do: 5 As soon as you hear the sound of the horn, flute, zither, lyre, harp, pipe and all kinds of music, you must fall down and worship the image of gold that King Nebuchadnezzar has set up. 6 Whoever does not fall down and worship will immediately be thrown into a blazing furnace." Jer 29:22; Da 6:7

7 Therefore, as soon as they heard the sound of the horn, flute, zither, lyre, harp and all kinds of music, all the nations and peoples of every language fell down and

[a] *1* That is, about 90 feet high and 9 feet wide or about 27 meters high and 2.7 meters wide

worshiped the image of gold that
King Nebuchadnezzar had set up.
8At this time some astrologers[a]
came forward and denounced
the Jews. 9They said to King Nebuchadnezzar, "May the king live
forever! 10Your Majesty has issued
a decree that everyone who hears
the sound of the horn, flute, zither, lyre, harp, pipe and all kinds of
music must fall down and worship
the image of gold, 11and that whoever does not fall down and worship will be thrown into a blazing
furnace. 12But there are some Jews
whom you have set over the affairs
of the province of Babylon — Shadrach, Meshach and Abednego —
who pay no attention to you, Your
Majesty. They neither serve your
gods nor worship the image of
gold you have set up." Da 2:49; 6:13
13Furious with rage, Nebuchadnezzar summoned Shadrach, Meshach and Abednego. So these
men were brought before the
king, 14and Nebuchadnezzar said
to them, "Is it true, Shadrach, Meshach and Abednego, that you
do not serve my gods or worship
the image of gold I have set up?
15Now when you hear the sound of
the horn, flute, zither, lyre, harp,
pipe and all kinds of music, if you
are ready to fall down and worship the image I made, very good.
But if you do not worship it, you
will be thrown immediately into
a blazing furnace. Then what god
will be able to rescue you from my
hand?" Isa 36:18-20
16Shadrach, Meshach and Abednego replied to him, "King Nebuchadnezzar, we do not need to defend ourselves before you in this
matter. 17If we are thrown into the
blazing furnace, the God we serve
is able to deliver us from it, and
he will deliver us[b] from Your Majesty's hand. 18But even if he does
not, we want you to know, Your
Majesty, that we will not serve
your gods or worship the image of
gold you have set up." Ps 27:1-2
19Then Nebuchadnezzar was
furious with Shadrach, Meshach
and Abednego, and his attitude
toward them changed. He ordered the furnace heated sev-
en times hotter than usual 20and
commanded some of the strongest soldiers in his army to tie up
Shadrach, Meshach and Abednego
and throw them into the blazing
furnace. 21So these men, wearing
their robes, trousers, turbans and
other clothes, were bound and
thrown into the blazing furnace.
22The king's command was so urgent and the furnace so hot that
the flames of the fire killed the
soldiers who took up Shadrach,
Meshach and Abednego, 23and
these three men, firmly tied, fell
into the blazing furnace.
Lev 26:18-28; Da 1:7
24Then King Nebuchadnezzar
leaped to his feet in amazement
and asked his advisers, "Weren't

[a] 8 *Or Chaldeans* [b] 17 *Or If the God we serve is able to deliver us, then he will deliver us from the blazing furnace and*

there three men that we tied up
and threw into the fire?"
They replied, "Certainly, Your
Majesty."
25 He said, "Look! I see four men
walking around in the fire, un-
bound and unharmed, and the
fourth looks like a son of the gods."
26 Nebuchadnezzar then approached the opening of the blazing furnace and shouted, "Shadrach, Meshach and Abednego,
servants of the Most High God,
come out! Come here!" Da 4:2,34
So Shadrach, Meshach and
Abednego came out of the fire,
27 and the satraps, prefects, governors and royal advisers crowded
around them. They saw that the
fire had not harmed their bodies, nor was a hair of their heads
singed; their robes were not
scorched, and there was no smell
of fire on them. Heb 11:32-34
28 Then Nebuchadnezzar said,
"Praise be to the God of Shadrach,
Meshach and Abednego, who has
sent his angel and rescued his
servants! They trusted in him
and defied the king's command
and were willing to give up their
lives rather than serve or worship
any god except their own God.
29 Therefore I decree that the people of any nation or language who
say anything against the God of
Shadrach, Meshach and Abednego
be cut into pieces and their houses be turned into piles of rubble,
for no other god can save in this
way." Da 6:27
30 Then the king promoted Shadrach, Meshach and Abednego in
the province of Babylon. Da 2:49

Nebuchadnezzar's Dream of a Tree

4[a] King Nebuchadnezzar,

To the nations and peoples
of every language, who live in
all the earth: Da 3:4

May you prosper greatly!
Da 6:25

2 It is my pleasure to tell
you about the miraculous
signs and wonders that the
Most High God has performed
for me. Ps 74:9; Da 3:26

3 How great are his signs,
how mighty his
wonders! Da 6:27
His kingdom is an eternal
kingdom;
his dominion endures
from generation to
generation. Da 2:44

4 I, Nebuchadnezzar, was at
home in my palace, content-
ed and prosperous. 5 I had a
dream that made me afraid.
As I was lying in bed, the images and visions that passed
through my mind terrified
me. 6 So I commanded that all
the wise men of Babylon be
brought before me to interpret the dream for me. 7 When
the magicians, enchanters,

[a] In Aramaic texts 4:1-3 is numbered 3:31-33, and 4:4-37 is numbered 4:1-34.

astrologers[a] and diviners
came, I told them the dream,
but they could not interpret it
for me. 8Finally, Daniel came
into my presence and I told
him the dream. (He is called
Belteshazzar, after the name
of my god, and the spirit of
the holy gods is in him.)
Da 2:1; 5:11,14
9I said, "Belteshazzar, chief
of the magicians, I know that
the spirit of the holy gods is
in you, and no mystery is too
difficult for you. Here is my
dream; interpret it for me.
10These are the visions I saw
while lying in bed: I looked,
and there before me stood a
tree in the middle of the land.
Its height was enormous.
11The tree grew large and
strong and its top touched
the sky; it was visible to the
ends of the earth. 12Its leaves
were beautiful, its fruit abundant, and on it was food for
all. Under it the wild animals
found shelter, and the birds
lived in its branches; from it
every creature was fed.
Da 2:48; 5:11-12
13"In the visions I saw while
lying in bed, I looked, and
there before me was a holy
one, a messenger,[b] coming
down from heaven. 14He called
in a loud voice: 'Cut down the
tree and trim off its branches;
strip off its leaves and scatter
its fruit. Let the animals flee
from under it and the birds
from its branches. 15But let the
stump and its roots, bound
with iron and bronze, remain
in the ground, in the grass of
the field. Eze 31:12; Mt 3:10
"'Let him be drenched with
the dew of heaven, and let him
live with the animals among
the plants of the earth. 16Let
his mind be changed from
that of a man and let him be
given the mind of an animal,
till seven times[c] pass by for
him. ver 23,32
17"'The decision is an-
nounced by messengers, the
holy ones declare the verdict,
so that the living may know
that the Most High is sovereign over all kingdoms on
earth and gives them to anyone he wishes and sets over
them the lowliest of people.'
Da 5:18-21; Mt 23:12
18"This is the dream that I,
King Nebuchadnezzar, had.
Now, Belteshazzar, tell me
what it means, for none of the
wise men in my kingdom can
interpret it for me. But you
can, because the spirit of the
holy gods is in you."
Ge 41:8; Da 1:20

Daniel Interprets the Dream

19Then Daniel (also called
Belteshazzar) was greatly

[a] 7 Or *Chaldeans* [b] 13 Or *watchman*; also in verses 17 and 23 [c] 16 Or *years*; also in verses 23, 25 and 32

perplexed for a time, and his thoughts terrified him. So the king said, "Belteshazzar, do not let the dream or its meaning alarm you." Da 7:15,28

Belteshazzar answered, "My lord, if only the dream applied to your enemies and its meaning to your adversaries! 20 The tree you saw, which grew large and strong, with its top touching the sky, visible to the whole earth, 21 with beautiful leaves and abundant fruit, providing food for all, giving shelter to the wild animals, and having nesting places in its branches for the birds — 22 Your Majesty, you are that tree! You have become great and strong; your greatness has grown until it reaches the sky, and your dominion extends to distant parts of the earth.

Jer 27:7; Da 5:18-19

23 "Your Majesty saw a holy one, a messenger, coming down from heaven and saying, 'Cut down the tree and destroy it, but leave the stump, bound with iron and bronze, in the grass of the field, while its roots remain in the ground. Let him be drenched with the dew of heaven; let him live with the wild animals, until seven times pass by for him.' Da 5:21

24 "This is the interpretation, Your Majesty, and this is the decree the Most High has issued against my lord the king: 25 You will be driven away from people and will live with the wild animals; you will eat grass like the ox and be drenched with the dew of heaven. Seven times will pass by for you until you acknowledge that the Most High is sovereign over all kingdoms on earth and gives them to anyone he wishes. 26 The command to leave the stump of the tree with its roots means that your kingdom will be restored to you when you acknowledge that Heaven rules. 27 Therefore, Your Majesty, be pleased to accept my advice: Renounce your sins by doing what is right, and your wickedness by being kind to the oppressed. It may be that then your prosperity will continue."

Isa 55:6-7; Eze 18:22

The Dream Is Fulfilled

28 All this happened to King Nebuchadnezzar. 29 Twelve months later, as the king was walking on the roof of the royal palace of Babylon, 30 he said, "Is not this the great Babylon I have built as the royal residence, by my mighty power and for the glory of my majesty?" Da 5:20; Hab 2:4

31 Even as the words were on his lips, a voice came from

heaven, "This is what is decreed for you, King Nebu-
chadnezzar: Your royal authority has been taken from
you. 32You will be driven away
from people and will live with
the wild animals; you will eat
grass like the ox. Seven times
will pass by for you until you
acknowledge that the Most
High is sovereign over all
kingdoms on earth and gives
them to anyone he wishes."
2Sa 22:28; Job 9:12

33Immediately what had
been said about Nebuchad-
nezzar was fulfilled. He was
driven away from people and
ate grass like the ox. His body
was drenched with the dew
of heaven until his hair grew
like the feathers of an eagle
and his nails like the claws of
a bird. Da 5:20-21

34At the end of that time, I,
Nebuchadnezzar, raised my
eyes toward heaven, and my
sanity was restored. Then
I praised the Most High; I
honored and glorified him
who lives forever.
Da 12:7; Rev 4:10

His dominion is an eternal
dominion;
his kingdom endures
from generation to
generation. Lk 1:33
35All the peoples of the earth
are regarded as nothing.
Isa 40:17
He does as he pleases Ps 115:3; 135:6
with the powers of heaven
and the peoples of the earth.
No one can hold back his hand
or say to him: "What have
you done?" Isa 45:9; Ro 9:20

36At the same time that
my sanity was restored, my
honor and splendor were returned to me for the glory of
my kingdom. My advisers and
nobles sought me out, and I
was restored to my throne
and became even greater
than before. 37Now I, Nebuchadnezzar, praise and exalt
and glorify the King of heav-
en, because everything he
does is right and all his ways
are just. And those who walk
in pride he is able to humble.
Da 5:20,23

The Writing on the Wall

5 King Belshazzar gave a great
banquet for a thousand of his
nobles and drank wine with them.
2While Belshazzar was drinking
his wine, he gave orders to bring
in the gold and silver goblets that
Nebuchadnezzar his father[a] had
taken from the temple in Jerusalem, so that the king and his nobles, his wives and his concubines
might drink from them. 3So they
brought in the gold goblets that
had been taken from the temple
of God in Jerusalem, and the king

[a] 2 Or *ancestor*; or *predecessor*; also in verses 11, 13 and 18

and his nobles, his wives and his concubines drank from them. 4As they drank the wine, they praised the gods of gold and silver, of bronze, iron, wood and stone.
Da 1:2; Rev 9:20

5Suddenly the fingers of a human hand appeared and wrote on the plaster of the wall, near the lampstand in the royal palace. The king watched the hand as it wrote. 6His face turned pale and he was so frightened that his legs became weak and his knees were knocking.
Eze 7:17; Da 4:5

7The king summoned the enchanters, astrologers[a] and diviners. Then he said to these wise men of Babylon, "Whoever reads this writing and tells me what it means will be clothed in purple and have a gold chain placed around his neck, and he will be made the third highest ruler in the kingdom."
Da 2:5-6,48

8Then all the king's wise men came in, but they could not read the writing or tell the king what it meant. 9So King Belshazzar became even more terrified and his face grew more pale. His nobles were baffled.
Isa 21:4

10The queen,[b] hearing the voices of the king and his nobles, came into the banquet hall. "May the king live forever!" she said. "Don't be alarmed! Don't look so pale! 11There is a man in your kingdom who has the spirit of the holy gods in him. In the time of your father he was found to have insight and intelligence and wisdom like that of the gods. Your father, King Nebuchadnezzar, appointed him chief of the magicians, enchanters, astrologers and diviners. 12He did this because Daniel, whom the king called Belteshazzar, was found to have a keen mind and knowledge and understanding, and also the ability to interpret dreams, explain riddles and solve difficult problems. Call for Daniel, and he will tell you what the writing means."
Da 1:7; 6:3

13So Daniel was brought before the king, and the king said to him, "Are you Daniel, one of the exiles my father the king brought from Judah? 14I have heard that the spirit of the gods is in you and that you have insight, intelligence and outstanding wisdom. 15The wise men and enchanters were brought before me to read this writing and tell me what it means, but they could not explain it. 16Now I have heard that you are able to give interpretations and to solve difficult problems. If you can read this writing and tell me what it means, you will be clothed in purple and have a gold chain placed around your neck, and you will be made the third highest ruler in the kingdom."
Da 6:13

17Then Daniel answered the king, "You may keep your gifts for yourself and give your rewards to someone else. Nevertheless, I will

[a] 7 Or *Chaldeans*; also in verse 11 [b] *10* Or *queen mother*

read the writing for the king and
tell him what it means. 2Ki 5:16
18"Your Majesty, the Most High
God gave your father Nebuchadnezzar sovereignty and greatness
and glory and splendor. 19Because
of the high position he gave him,
all the nations and peoples of every language dreaded and feared
him. Those the king wanted to put
to death, he put to death; those he
wanted to spare, he spared; those
he wanted to promote, he promoted; and those he wanted to humble, he humbled. 20But when his
heart became arrogant and hardened with pride, he was deposed
from his royal throne and stripped
of his glory. 21He was driven away
from people and given the mind
of an animal; he lived with the
wild donkeys and ate grass like
the ox; and his body was drenched
with the dew of heaven, until he
acknowledged that the Most High
God is sovereign over all kingdoms
on earth and sets over them anyone he wishes. Da 4:16-17,35; Eze 17:24
22"But you, Belshazzar, his son,[a]
have not humbled yourself, though
you knew all this. 23Instead, you
have set yourself up against the
Lord of heaven. You had the goblets from his temple brought to
you, and you and your nobles, your
wives and your concubines drank
wine from them. You praised the
gods of silver and gold, of bronze,
iron, wood and stone, which cannot see or hear or understand. But
you did not honor the God who
holds in his hand your life and all
your ways. 24Therefore he sent the
hand that wrote the inscription.
Ps 115:4-8; Jer 10:23
25"This is the inscription that
was written:

MENE, MENE, TEKEL, PARSIN

26"Here is what these words
mean:

Mene[b]: God has numbered
the days of your reign
and brought it to an
end. Isa 13:6; Jer 27:7
27*Tekel*[c]: You have been
weighed on the scales
and found wanting.
Ps 62:9
28*Peres*[d]: Your kingdom is
divided and given to
the Medes and Per-
sians." Da 6:28

29Then at Belshazzar's command, Daniel was clothed in
purple, a gold chain was placed
around his neck, and he was proclaimed the third highest ruler in
the kingdom. Da 2:6
30That very night Belshazzar,
king of the Babylonians,[e] was
slain, 31and Darius the Mede took
over the kingdom, at the age of
sixty-two.[f] Da 6:1; 9:1

[a] 22 Or *descendant*; or *successor*
[b] 26 *Mene* can mean *numbered* or *mina* (a unit of money).
[c] 27 *Tekel* can mean *weighed* or *shekel.*
[d] 28 *Peres* (the singular of *Parsin*) can mean *divided* or *Persia* or *a half mina* or *a half shekel.*
[e] 30 Or *Chaldeans*
[f] 31 In Aramaic texts this verse (5:31) is numbered 6:1.

Daniel in the Den of Lions

6 [a] It pleased Darius to appoint
120 satraps to rule throughout the kingdom, 2with three administrators over them, one of
whom was Daniel. The satraps
were made accountable to them
so that the king might not suffer
loss. 3Now Daniel so distinguished
himself among the administrators
and the satraps by his exceptional
qualities that the king planned to
set him over the whole kingdom.
4At this, the administrators and
the satraps tried to find grounds
for charges against Daniel in his
conduct of government affairs,
but they were unable to do so.
They could find no corruption in
him, because he was trustworthy
and neither corrupt nor negligent.
5Finally these men said, "We will
never find any basis for charges
against this man Daniel unless it
has something to do with the law
of his God." Est 10:3; Da 5:12-14

6So these administrators and
satraps went as a group to the
king and said: "May King Darius
live forever! 7The royal administrators, prefects, satraps, advisers and governors have all agreed
that the king should issue an edict
and enforce the decree that anyone who prays to any god or human being during the next thirty
days, except to you, Your Majesty,
shall be thrown into the lions' den.
8Now, Your Majesty, issue the decree and put it in writing so that it
cannot be altered — in accordance
with the law of the Medes and Persians, which cannot be repealed."
9So King Darius put the decree in
writing. Ps 59:3; Da 3:6

10Now when Daniel learned that
the decree had been published, he
went home to his upstairs room
where the windows opened toward Jerusalem. Three times a
day he got down on his knees and
prayed, giving thanks to his God,
just as he had done before. 11Then
these men went as a group and
found Daniel praying and asking
God for help. 12So they went to the
king and spoke to him about his
royal decree: "Did you not pub-
lish a decree that during the next
thirty days anyone who prays to
any god or human being except
to you, Your Majesty, would be
thrown into the lions' den?"
Ps 95:6; Ac 5:29

The king answered, "The decree stands — in accordance with
the law of the Medes and Persians,
which cannot be repealed."
Da 3:8-12

13Then they said to the king,
"Daniel, who is one of the exiles
from Judah, pays no attention to
you, Your Majesty, or to the decree you put in writing. He still
prays three times a day." 14When
the king heard this, he was greatly distressed; he was determined
to rescue Daniel and made every
effort until sundown to save him.
Est 3:8; Mk 6:26

[a] In Aramaic texts 6:1-28 is numbered 6:2-29.

15 Then the men went as a
group to King Darius and said to
him, "Remember, Your Majesty,
that according to the law of the
Medes and Persians no decree or
edict that the king issues can be
changed." Est 8:8
16 So the king gave the order, and
they brought Daniel and threw
him into the lions' den. The king
said to Daniel, "May your God,
whom you serve continually, rescue you!" Ps 37:39-40
17 A stone was brought and
placed over the mouth of the den,
and the king sealed it with his own
signet ring and with the rings of
his nobles, so that Daniel's situation might not be changed. 18 Then
the king returned to his palace
and spent the night without eating and without any entertain-
ment being brought to him. And
he could not sleep. Mt 27:66
19 At the first light of dawn, the
king got up and hurried to the lions' den. 20 When he came near
the den, he called to Daniel in an
anguished voice, "Daniel, servant
of the living God, has your God,
whom you serve continually, been
able to rescue you from the lions?"
Da 3:17
21 Daniel answered, "May the
king live forever! 22 My God sent
his angel, and he shut the mouths
of the lions. They have not hurt
me, because I was found innocent
in his sight. Nor have I ever done
any wrong before you, Your Majesty." Heb 11:33; 2Ti 4:17
23 The king was overjoyed and
gave orders to lift Daniel out of
the den. And when Daniel was lifted from the den, no wound was
found on him, because he had
trusted in his God. 1Ch 5:20; Da 3:27
24 At the king's command, the
men who had falsely accused Daniel were brought in and thrown
into the lions' den, along with
their wives and children. And before they reached the floor of the
den, the lions overpowered them
and crushed all their bones.
Dt 24:16; 2Ki 14:6
25 Then King Darius wrote to all
the nations and peoples of every
language in all the earth: Da 3:4

"May you prosper greatly!
Da 4:1

26 "I issue a decree that in every part of my kingdom people must fear and reverence
the God of Daniel. Da 3:29

"For he is the living God Jos 2:11
and he endures forever;
Rev 1:18
his kingdom will not be
destroyed,
his dominion will never end.
Da 2:44
27 He rescues and he saves;
he performs signs and
wonders Da 4:3
in the heavens and on the
earth.
He has rescued Daniel
from the power of the
lions."

28So Daniel prospered during
the reign of Darius and the reign
of Cyrus[a] the Persian. Da 1:21

Daniel's Dream of Four Beasts

7 In the first year of Belshazzar king of Babylon, Daniel
had a dream, and visions passed
through his mind as he was lying
in bed. He wrote down the substance of his dream. Da 1:17; 5:1
2Daniel said: "In my vision at
night I looked, and there before
me were the four winds of heaven
churning up the great sea. 3Four
great beasts, each different from
the others, came up out of the sea.
Rev 13:1
4"The first was like a lion, and it
had the wings of an eagle. I watched
until its wings were torn off and it
was lifted from the ground so that
it stood on two feet like a human
being, and the mind of a human
was given to it. Jer 4:7; Eze 17:3
5"And there before me was a
second beast, which looked like a
bear. It was raised up on one of its
sides, and it had three ribs in its
mouth between its teeth. It was
told, 'Get up and eat your fill of
flesh!' Da 2:39
6"After that, I looked, and there
before me was another beast, one
that looked like a leopard. And
on its back it had four wings like
those of a bird. This beast had four
heads, and it was given authority
to rule. Rev 13:2
7"After that, in my vision at
night I looked, and there before
me was a fourth beast — terrifying and frightening and very powerful. It had large iron teeth; it
crushed and devoured its victims
and trampled underfoot whatever
was left. It was different from all
the former beasts, and it had ten
horns. Da 2:40; Rev 12:3
8"While I was thinking about the
horns, there before me was another horn, a little one, which came
up among them; and three of the
first horns were uprooted before it.
This horn had eyes like the eyes of
a human being and a mouth that
spoke boastfully. Rev 13:5-6
9"As I looked,

"thrones were set in place,
and the Ancient of Days took
his seat. Mt 19:28
His clothing was as white as
snow; Mt 28:3
the hair of his head was
white like wool. Rev 1:14
His throne was flaming with
fire,
and its wheels were all
ablaze. Eze 1:15
10A river of fire was flowing, Ps 50:3
coming out from before him.
Rev 5:11
Thousands upon thousands
attended him;
ten thousand times ten
thousand stood before
him.
The court was seated,
and the books were opened.
Rev 20:11-15

[a] 28 Or *Darius, that is, the reign of Cyrus*

11“Then I continued to watch
because of the boastful words the
horn was speaking. I kept looking until the beast was slain and
its body destroyed and thrown
into the blazing fire. 12(The other
beasts had been stripped of their
authority, but were allowed to live
for a period of time.) Rev 19:20

13“In my vision at night I looked,
and there before me was one like
a son of man,[a] coming with the
clouds of heaven. He approached
the Ancient of Days and was led
into his presence. 14He was giv-
en authority, glory and sovereign
power; all nations and peoples of
every language worshiped him.
His dominion is an everlasting
dominion that will not pass away,
and his kingdom is one that will
never be destroyed. Heb 12:28; Rev 11:15

The Interpretation of the Dream

15“I, Daniel, was troubled in
spirit, and the visions that passed
through my mind disturbed me.
16I approached one of those standing there and asked him the
meaning of all this. Da 4:19

“So he told me and gave me the
interpretation of these things:
17‘The four great beasts are four
kings that will rise from the earth.
18But the holy people of the Most
High will receive the kingdom
and will possess it forever — yes,
for ever and ever.’

Isa 60:12-14; Rev 2:26; 20:4

19“Then I wanted to know the
meaning of the fourth beast, which
was different from all the others
and most terrifying, with its iron
teeth and bronze claws — the beast
that crushed and devoured its
victims and trampled underfoot
whatever was left. 20I also wanted to know about the ten horns
on its head and about the other
horn that came up, before which
three of them fell — the horn that
looked more imposing than the
others and that had eyes and a
mouth that spoke boastfully. 21As I
watched, this horn was waging war
against the holy people and defeating them, 22until the Ancient of
Days came and pronounced judgment in favor of the holy people of
the Most High, and the time came
when they possessed the kingdom.

Rev 13:7

23“He gave me this explanation:
‘The fourth beast is a fourth kingdom that will appear on earth. It
will be different from all the other kingdoms and will devour the
whole earth, trampling it down
and crushing it. 24The ten horns
are ten kings who will come from
this kingdom. After them another
king will arise, different from the
earlier ones; he will subdue three
kings. 25He will speak against the
Most High and oppress his holy
people and try to change the
set times and the laws. The holy
people will be delivered into his

[a] 13 The Aramaic phrase *bar enash* means *human being*. The phrase *son of man* is retained here because of its use in the New Testament as a title of Jesus, probably based largely on this verse.

hands for a time, times and half a
time.[a] Da 2:21; Rev 17:12
26“‘But the court will sit, and
his power will be taken away and
completely destroyed forever.
27Then the sovereignty, power and
greatness of all the kingdoms under heaven will be handed over to
the holy people of the Most High.
His kingdom will be an everlasting kingdom, and all rulers will
worship and obey him.’ Ps 22:27; 72:11
28“This is the end of the matter.
I, Daniel, was deeply troubled by
my thoughts, and my face turned
pale, but I kept the matter to myself.” Da 4:19

Daniel's Vision of a Ram and a Goat

8 In the third year of King Belshazzar's reign, I, Daniel, had
a vision, after the one that had already appeared to me. 2In my vision I saw myself in the citadel of
Susa in the province of Elam; in
the vision I was beside the Ulai
Canal. 3I looked up, and there before me was a ram with two horns,
standing beside the canal, and
the horns were long. One of the
horns was longer than the other
but grew up later. 4I watched the
ram as it charged toward the west
and the north and the south. No
animal could stand against it, and
none could rescue from its power. It did as it pleased and became
great. Da 11:3,16
5As I was thinking about this,
suddenly a goat with a prominent
horn between its eyes came from
the west, crossing the whole earth
without touching the ground. 6It
came toward the two-horned ram
I had seen standing beside the
canal and charged at it in great
rage. 7I saw it attack the ram furiously, striking the ram and shat-
tering its two horns. The ram was
powerless to stand against it; the
goat knocked it to the ground and
trampled on it, and none could
rescue the ram from its power. 8The goat became very great,
but at the height of its power the
large horn was broken off, and in
its place four prominent horns
grew up toward the four winds of
heaven. 2Ch 26:16-21; Rev 7:1
9Out of one of them came another horn, which started small
but grew in power to the south
and to the east and toward the
Beautiful Land. 10It grew until it
reached the host of the heavens,
and it threw some of the starry
host down to the earth and trampled on them. 11It set itself up to
be as great as the commander
of the army of the LORD; it took
away the daily sacrifice from
the LORD, and his sanctuary was
thrown down. 12Because of rebellion, the LORD's people[b] and the
daily sacrifice were given over to
it. It prospered in everything it
did, and truth was thrown to the
ground. Da 11:16,31; 12:11
13Then I heard a holy one speaking, and another holy one said to

[a] 25 Or *for a year, two years and half a year*
[b] 12 Or *rebellion, the armies*

him, "How long will it take for the
vision to be fulfilled — the vision
concerning the daily sacrifice, the
rebellion that causes desolation,
the surrender of the sanctuary
and the trampling underfoot of
the LORD's people?" Da 4:23; 12:6

14 He said to me, "It will take
2,300 evenings and mornings;
then the sanctuary will be recon-
secrated." Da 12:11-12

The Interpretation of the Vision

15 While I, Daniel, was watching
the vision and trying to understand it, there before me stood
one who looked like a man. 16 And
I heard a man's voice from the Ulai
calling, "Gabriel, tell this man the
meaning of the vision."
Da 10:16-18; Lk 1:19

17 As he came near the place
where I was standing, I was terrified and fell prostrate. "Son of
man,"[a] he said to me, "understand
that the vision concerns the time
of the end." Eze 1:28; Rev 1:17

18 While he was speaking to me,
I was in a deep sleep, with my face
to the ground. Then he touched
me and raised me to my feet.
Eze 2:2; Da 10:16-18

19 He said: "I am going to tell you
what will happen later in the time
of wrath, because the vision concerns the appointed time of the
end.[b] 20 The two-horned ram that
you saw represents the kings of
Media and Persia. 21 The shaggy
goat is the king of Greece, and the
large horn between its eyes is the
first king. 22 The four horns that
replaced the one that was broken
off represent four kingdoms that
will emerge from his nation but
will not have the same power.
Hab 2:3

23 "In the latter part of their
reign, when rebels have become completely wicked, a
fierce-looking king, a master of
intrigue, will arise. 24 He will become very strong, but not by
his own power. He will cause astounding devastation and will
succeed in whatever he does.
He will destroy those who are
mighty, the holy people. 25 He
will cause deceit to prosper, and
he will consider himself superi-
or. When they feel secure, he will
destroy many and take his stand
against the Prince of princes. Yet
he will be destroyed, but not by
human power. Da 2:34; 11:21,36

26 "The vision of the evenings
and mornings that has been given
you is true, but seal up the vision,
for it concerns the distant future."
Da 10:1,14

27 I, Daniel, was worn out. I lay
exhausted for several days. Then
I got up and went about the king's
business. I was appalled by the vision; it was beyond understanding. Da 7:28

[a] *17* The Hebrew phrase *ben adam* means *human being*. The phrase *son of man* is retained as a form of address here because of its possible association with "Son of Man" in the New Testament.
[b] *19* Or *because the end will be at the appointed time*

Daniel's Prayer

9 In the first year of Darius son of Xerxes[a] (a Mede by descent), who was made ruler over the Babylonian[b] kingdom — 2 in the first year of his reign, I, Daniel, understood from the Scriptures, according to the word of the LORD given to Jeremiah the prophet, that the desolation of Jerusalem would last seventy years. 3 So I turned to the Lord God and pleaded with him in prayer and petition, in fasting, and in sackcloth and ashes.

2Ch 36:21; Jer 29:12

4 I prayed to the LORD my God and confessed: 1Ki 8:30

"Lord, the great and awesome God, who keeps his covenant of love with those who love him and keep his commandments, 5 we have sinned and done wrong. We have been wicked and have rebelled; we have turned away from your commands and laws. 6 We have not listened to your servants the prophets, who spoke in your name to our kings, our princes and our ancestors, and to all the people of the land.

2Ch 36:16; Ps 106:6

7 "Lord, you are righteous, but this day we are covered with shame — the people of Judah and the inhabitants of Jerusalem and all Israel, both near and far, in all the countries where you have scattered us because of our unfaithfulness to you. 8 We and our kings, our princes and our ancestors are covered with shame, LORD, because we have sinned against you. 9 The Lord our God is merciful and forgiving, even though we have rebelled against him; 10 we have not obeyed the LORD our God or kept the laws he gave us through his servants the prophets. 11 All Israel has transgressed your law and turned away, refusing to obey you. 2Ki 17:13-15; Ne 9:17

"Therefore the curses and sworn judgments written in the Law of Moses, the servant of God, have been poured out on us, because we have sinned against you. 12 You have fulfilled the words spoken against us and against our rulers by bringing on us great disaster. Under the whole heaven nothing has ever been done like what has been done to Jerusalem. 13 Just as it is written in the Law of Moses, all this disaster has come on us, yet we have not sought the favor of the LORD our God by turning from our sins and giving attention to your truth. 14 The LORD did not hesitate to bring the disaster on us, for the LORD our God is righteous in everything he does; yet we have not obeyed him. Isa 1:4-6; Eze 5:9

[a] 1 Hebrew *Ahasuerus* [b] 1 Or *Chaldean*

[15]"Now, Lord our God, who
brought your people out of
Egypt with a mighty hand
and who made for yourself
a name that endures to this
day, we have sinned, we have
done wrong. [16]Lord, in keeping with all your righteous
acts, turn away your anger
and your wrath from Jerusalem, your city, your holy hill.
Our sins and the iniquities of
our ancestors have made Jerusalem and your people an
object of scorn to all those
around us. Ps 31:1; Zec 8:3

[17]"Now, our God, hear the
prayers and petitions of your
servant. For your sake, Lord,
look with favor on your desolate sanctuary. [18]Give ear, our
God, and hear; open your eyes
and see the desolation of the
city that bears your Name. We
do not make requests of you
because we are righteous, but
because of your great mercy.
[19]Lord, listen! Lord, forgive!
Lord, hear and act! For your
sake, my God, do not delay,
because your city and your
people bear your Name."
Isa 37:17; Jer 7:10-12; 25:29

The Seventy "Sevens"

[20]While I was speaking and praying, confessing my sin and the sin
of my people Israel and making
my request to the LORD my God
for his holy hill — [21]while I was
still in prayer, Gabriel, the man
I had seen in the earlier vision,
came to me in swift flight about
the time of the evening sacrifice.
[22]He instructed me and said to me,
"Daniel, I have now come to give
you insight and understanding.
[23]As soon as you began to pray, a
word went out, which I have come
to tell you, for you are highly esteemed. Therefore, consider the
word and understand the vision:
Mt 24:15

[24]"Seventy 'sevens'[a] are decreed
for your people and your holy city
to finish[b] transgression, to put an
end to sin, to atone for wickedness, to bring in everlasting righteousness, to seal up vision and
prophecy and to anoint the Most
Holy Place.[c] Isa 53:10; 56:1

[25]"Know and understand this:
From the time the word goes out
to restore and rebuild Jerusalem until the Anointed One,[d] the
ruler, comes, there will be seven
'sevens,' and sixty-two 'sevens.'
It will be rebuilt with streets and
a trench, but in times of trouble.
[26]After the sixty-two 'sevens,' the
Anointed One will be put to death
and will have nothing.[e] The people of the ruler who will come will
destroy the city and the sanctuary.
The end will come like a flood: War
will continue until the end, and
desolations have been decreed.

[a] 24 Or *'weeks'*; also in verses 25 and 26
[b] 24 Or *restrain* [c] 24 Or *the most holy One* [d] 25 Or *an anointed one*; also in verse 26 [e] 26 Or *death and will have no one*; or *death, but not for himself*

27He will confirm a covenant with
many for one 'seven.'[a] In the middle of the 'seven'[a] he will put an
end to sacrifice and offering. And
at the temple[b] he will set up an
abomination that causes desolation, until the end that is decreed
is poured out on him.[c]"[d]

Isa 10:22; 53:8

Daniel's Vision of a Man

10 In the third year of Cyrus
king of Persia, a revela-
tion was given to Daniel (who was
called Belteshazzar). Its message
was true and it concerned a great
war.[e] The understanding of the
message came to him in a vision.

Da 8:26

2At that time I, Daniel, mourned
for three weeks. 3I ate no choice
food; no meat or wine touched my
lips; and I used no lotions at all
until the three weeks were over.

Ezr 9:4

4On the twenty-fourth day of
the first month, as I was standing
on the bank of the great river, the
Tigris, 5I looked up and there before me was a man dressed in lin-
en, with a belt of fine gold from
Uphaz around his waist. 6His body
was like topaz, his face like lightning, his eyes like flaming torches,
his arms and legs like the gleam
of burnished bronze, and his voice
like the sound of a multitude.

Rev 1:15; 19:12

7I, Daniel, was the only one who
saw the vision; those who were
with me did not see it, but such
terror overwhelmed them that
they fled and hid themselves. 8So I
was left alone, gazing at this great
vision; I had no strength left, my
face turned deathly pale and I was
helpless. 9Then I heard him speaking, and as I listened to him, I fell
into a deep sleep, my face to the
ground.

2Ki 6:17-20; Da 8:18,27

10A hand touched me and set
me trembling on my hands and
knees. 11He said, "Daniel, you who
are highly esteemed, consider
carefully the words I am about to
speak to you, and stand up, for I
have now been sent to you." And
when he said this to me, I stood
up trembling.

Da 9:23; Eze 2:1

12Then he continued, "Do not be
afraid, Daniel. Since the first day
that you set your mind to gain understanding and to humble yourself before your God, your words
were heard, and I have come in
response to them. 13But the prince
of the Persian kingdom resisted
me twenty-one days. Then Michael, one of the chief princes, came
to help me, because I was detained there with the king of Persia. 14Now I have come to explain
to you what will happen to your
people in the future, for the vision
concerns a time yet to come."

Da 2:28; 8:26; Hab 2:3

[a] 27 Or *'week'* [b] 27 Septuagint and Theodotion; Hebrew *wing* [c] 27 Or *it* [d] 27 Or *And one who causes desolation will come upon the wing of the abominable temple, until the end that is decreed is poured out on the desolated city* [e] 1 Or *true and burdensome*

15While he was saying this to
me, I bowed with my face toward the ground and was speechless. 16Then one who looked like
a man[a] touched my lips, and I
opened my mouth and began to
speak. I said to the one standing
before me, "I am overcome with
anguish because of the vision, my
lord, and I feel very weak. 17How
can I, your servant, talk with you,
my lord? My strength is gone and
I can hardly breathe." Jer 1:9; Da 4:19
18Again the one who looked like
a man touched me and gave me
strength. 19"Do not be afraid, you
who are highly esteemed," he said.
"Peace! Be strong now; be strong."
Jdg 6:23; Isa 35:4

When he spoke to me, I was
strengthened and said, "Speak,
my lord, since you have given me
strength." Isa 6:1-8

20So he said, "Do you know why
I have come to you? Soon I will return to fight against the prince of
Persia, and when I go, the prince
of Greece will come; 21but first I
will tell you what is written in the
Book of Truth. (No one supports
me against them except Michael,
11 your prince. 1And in the first
year of Darius the Mede, I
took my stand to support and protect him.) Da 11:2; Jude 1:9

The Kings of the South and the North

2"Now then, I tell you the truth:
Three more kings will arise in Persia, and then a fourth, who will
be far richer than all the others.
When he has gained power by his
wealth, he will stir up everyone
against the kingdom of Greece.
3Then a mighty king will arise,
who will rule with great power
and do as he pleases. 4After he has
arisen, his empire will be broken
up and parceled out toward the
four winds of heaven. It will not
go to his descendants, nor will it
have the power he exercised, because his empire will be uprooted
and given to others. Da 8:4,21-22

5"The king of the South will become strong, but one of his commanders will become even stronger than he and will rule his own
kingdom with great power. 6After
some years, they will become allies. The daughter of the king of
the South will go to the king of
the North to make an alliance, but
she will not retain her power, and
he and his power[b] will not last. In
those days she will be betrayed,
together with her royal escort and
her father[c] and the one who supported her.

7"One from her family line will
arise to take her place. He will attack the forces of the king of the
North and enter his fortress; he
will fight against them and be victorious. 8He will also seize their
gods, their metal images and their

[a] 16 Most manuscripts of the Masoretic Text; one manuscript of the Masoretic Text, Dead Sea Scrolls and Septuagint *Then something that looked like a human hand*
[b] 6 Or *offspring* [c] 6 Or *child* (see Vulgate and Syriac)

valuable articles of silver and gold
and carry them off to Egypt. For
some years he will leave the king
of the North alone. 9Then the king
of the North will invade the realm
of the king of the South but will
retreat to his own country. 10His
sons will prepare for war and assemble a great army, which will
sweep on like an irresistible flood
and carry the battle as far as his
fortress. Isa 8:8; Da 9:26

11"Then the king of the South
will march out in a rage and fight
against the king of the North, who
will raise a large army, but it will
be defeated. 12When the army is
carried off, the king of the South
will be filled with pride and will
slaughter many thousands, yet he
will not remain triumphant. 13For
the king of the North will muster another army, larger than the
first; and after several years, he
will advance with a huge army fully equipped. Da 8:7-8

14"In those times many will rise
against the king of the South.
Those who are violent among
your own people will rebel in fulfillment of the vision, but without success. 15Then the king of
the North will come and build up
siege ramps and will capture a fortified city. The forces of the South
will be powerless to resist; even
their best troops will not have the
strength to stand. 16The invader
will do as he pleases; no one will
be able to stand against him. He
will establish himself in the Beautiful Land and will have the power
to destroy it. 17He will determine
to come with the might of his entire kingdom and will make an alliance with the king of the South.
And he will give him a daughter
in marriage in order to overthrow
the kingdom, but his plans[a] will
not succeed or help him. 18Then
he will turn his attention to the
coastlands and will take many of
them, but a commander will put
an end to his insolence and will
turn his insolence back on him.
19After this, he will turn back toward the fortresses of his own
country but will stumble and fall,
to be seen no more. Ps 27:2; Eze 26:21

20"His successor will send out a
tax collector to maintain the royal
splendor. In a few years, however,
he will be destroyed, yet not in anger or in battle. Isa 60:17

21"He will be succeeded by a
contemptible person who has not
been given the honor of royalty.
He will invade the kingdom when
its people feel secure, and he will
seize it through intrigue. 22Then
an overwhelming army will be
swept away before him; both it
and a prince of the covenant will
be destroyed. 23After coming to
an agreement with him, he will
act deceitfully, and with only a
few people he will rise to power. 24When the richest provinces
feel secure, he will invade them
and will achieve what neither his
fathers nor his forefathers did.

[a] 17 Or *but she*

He will distribute plunder, loot
and wealth among his followers.
He will plot the overthrow of fortresses — but only for a time.

Ne 9:25; Da 8:25

25 “With a large army he will
stir up his strength and courage
against the king of the South.
The king of the South will wage
war with a large and very powerful army, but he will not be able
to stand because of the plots devised against him. 26 Those who
eat from the king’s provisions
will try to destroy him; his army
will be swept away, and many will
fall in battle. 27 The two kings, with
their hearts bent on evil, will sit at
the same table and lie to each other, but to no avail, because an end
will still come at the appointed
time. 28 The king of the North will
return to his own country with
great wealth, but his heart will
be set against the holy covenant.
He will take action against it and
then return to his own country.

Ps 64:6; Hab 2:3

29 “At the appointed time he will
invade the South again, but this
time the outcome will be different
from what it was before. 30 Ships
of the western coastlands will oppose him, and he will lose heart.
Then he will turn back and vent
his fury against the holy covenant.
He will return and show favor to
those who forsake the holy covenant.

Ge 10:4

31 “His armed forces will rise up
to desecrate the temple fortress
and will abolish the daily sacrifice.
Then they will set up the abomination that causes desolation. 32 With
flattery he will corrupt those who
have violated the covenant, but
the people who know their God
will firmly resist him.

Mt 24:15*; Mic 5:7-9

33 “Those who are wise will instruct many, though for a time
they will fall by the sword or be
burned or captured or plundered.
34 When they fall, they will receive
a little help, and many who are
not sincere will join them. 35 Some
of the wise will stumble, so that
they may be refined, purified and
made spotless until the time of
the end, for it will still come at
the appointed time.

Da 12:10; Zec 13:9; Jn 15:2

The King Who Exalts Himself

36 “The king will do as he pleases. He will exalt and magnify himself above every god and will say
unheard-of things against the God
of gods. He will be successful until
the time of wrath is completed, for
what has been determined must
take place. 37 He will show no regard for the gods of his ancestors
or for the one desired by women,
nor will he regard any god, but
will exalt himself above them all.
38 Instead of them, he will honor a
god of fortresses; a god unknown
to his ancestors he will honor with
gold and silver, with precious
stones and costly gifts. 39 He will attack the mightiest fortresses with

the help of a foreign god and will
greatly honor those who acknowledge him. He will make them rulers over many people and will distribute the land at a price.[a]
Da 7:25; Rev 13:5-6

40 "At the time of the end the
king of the South will engage
him in battle, and the king of the
North will storm out against him
with chariots and cavalry and a
great fleet of ships. He will invade many countries and sweep
through them like a flood. 41 He
will also invade the Beautiful
Land. Many countries will fall, but
Edom, Moab and the leaders of
Ammon will be delivered from his
hand. 42 He will extend his power
over many countries; Egypt will
not escape. 43 He will gain control
of the treasures of gold and silver
and all the riches of Egypt, with
the Libyans and Cushites[b] in submission. 44 But reports from the
east and the north will alarm him,
and he will set out in a great rage
to destroy and annihilate many.
45 He will pitch his royal tents between the seas at[c] the beautiful
holy mountain. Yet he will come
to his end, and no one will help
him.
Isa 5:28; 21:1; Eze 38:4

The End Times

12 "At that time Michael, the
great prince who protects
your people, will arise. There will
be a time of distress such as has
not happened from the beginning of nations until then. But at
that time your people — everyone whose name is found written
in the book — will be delivered.
2 Multitudes who sleep in the dust
of the earth will awake: some to
everlasting life, others to shame
and everlasting contempt. 3 Those
who are wise[d] will shine like the
brightness of the heavens, and
those who lead many to righteousness, like the stars for ever
and ever. 4 But you, Daniel, roll up
and seal the words of the scroll
until the time of the end. Many
will go here and there to increase
knowledge."
Isa 8:16; Rev 22:10

5 Then I, Daniel, looked, and
there before me stood two others,
one on this bank of the river and
one on the opposite bank. 6 One of
them said to the man clothed in
linen, who was above the waters
of the river, "How long will it be
before these astonishing things
are fulfilled?"
Da 8:13; 10:4

7 The man clothed in linen, who
was above the waters of the river,
lifted his right hand and his left
hand toward heaven, and I heard
him swear by him who lives forever, saying, "It will be for a time,
times and half a time.[e] When the
power of the holy people has been
finally broken, all these things will
be completed."
Lk 21:24; Rev 10:7

[a] 39 Or *land for a reward* [b] 43 That is, people from the upper Nile region [c] 45 Or *the sea and* [d] 3 Or *who impart wisdom* [e] 7 Or *a year, two years and half a year*

[8]I heard, but I did not understand. So I asked, "My lord, what
will the outcome of all this be?"
[9]He replied, "Go your way, Daniel, because the words are rolled
up and sealed until the time of
the end. [10]Many will be purified,
made spotless and refined, but the
wicked will continue to be wicked.
None of the wicked will understand, but those who are wise will
understand. Isa 32:7; Rev 22:11

[11]"From the time that the daily sacrifice is abolished and the
abomination that causes desolation is set up, there will be 1,290
days. [12]Blessed is the one who
waits for and reaches the end of
the 1,335 days. Isa 30:18; Da 8:14
[13]"As for you, go your way till the
end. You will rest, and then at the
end of the days you will rise to receive your allotted inheritance."
Rev 14:13

HOSEA

1 The word of the LORD that came
to Hosea son of Beeri during
the reigns of Uzziah, Jotham, Ahaz
and Hezekiah, kings of Judah, and
during the reign of Jeroboam son
of Jehoash[a] king of Israel:
Jer 1:2; 2Ki 13:13

Hosea's Wife and Children

2When the LORD began to speak
through Hosea, the LORD said to
him, "Go, marry a promiscuous
woman and have children with
her, for like an adulterous wife
this land is guilty of unfaithfulness to the LORD." 3So he married
Gomer daughter of Diblaim, and
she conceived and bore him a son.
Dt 31:16; Hos 5:3

4Then the LORD said to Hosea,
"Call him Jezreel, because I will
soon punish the house of Jehu for
the massacre at Jezreel, and I will
put an end to the kingdom of Israel. 5In that day I will break Israel's
bow in the Valley of Jezreel."
2Ki 10:1-14; 15:29

6Gomer conceived again and
gave birth to a daughter. Then
the LORD said to Hosea, "Call her
Lo-Ruhamah (which means "not
loved"), for I will no longer show
love to Israel, that I should at all
forgive them. 7Yet I will show love
to Judah; and I will save them —
not by bow, sword or battle, or by
horses and horsemen, but I, the
LORD their God, will save them."
Ps 44:6; Zec 4:6

8After she had weaned Lo-Ruhamah, Gomer had another son.
9Then the LORD said, "Call him Lo-
Ammi (which means "not my people"), for you are not my people,
and I am not your God.[b]
Eze 11:19-20; 1Pe 2:10

10"Yet the Israelites will be like
the sand on the seashore, which
cannot be measured or counted.
In the place where it was said to
them, 'You are not my people,'
they will be called 'children of the
living God.' 11The people of Judah
and the people of Israel will come
together; they will appoint one
leader and will come up out of the
land, for great will be the day of
Jezreel.[c] Ro 9:26*; Jos 3:10

2 [d] "Say of your brothers, 'My
people,' and of your sisters,
'My loved one.' 1Pe 2:10

Israel Punished and Restored

2"Rebuke your mother, rebuke
her, Isa 50:1; Hos 1:2
for she is not my wife,
and I am not her husband.
Let her remove the adulterous
look from her face Eze 23:45

[a] *1* Hebrew *Joash*, a variant of *Jehoash*
[b] *9* Or *your I AM*
[c] *11* In Hebrew texts 1:10,11 is numbered 2:1,2.
[d] In Hebrew texts 2:1-23 is numbered 2:3-25.

and the unfaithfulness
from between her
breasts.
3 Otherwise I will strip her
naked
and make her as bare as on
the day she was born; Eze 16:4,22
I will make her like a desert, Isa 32:13-14
turn her into a parched land,
and slay her with thirst.
4 I will not show my love to her
children, Eze 8:18
because they are the children
of adultery. Hos 5:7
5 Their mother has been
unfaithful
and has conceived them in
disgrace.
She said, 'I will go after my
lovers, Jer 3:6
who give me my food and
my water,
my wool and my linen, my
olive oil and my drink.' Jer 44:17-18
6 Therefore I will block her path
with thornbushes;
I will wall her in so that
she cannot find her way. La 3:9
7 She will chase after her lovers
but not catch them;
she will look for them but
not find them. Hos 5:13
Then she will say,
'I will go back to my husband
as at first, Jer 2:2
for then I was better off than
now.' Eze 16:8
8 She has not acknowledged that
I was the one Isa 1:3
who gave her the grain, the
new wine and oil,
who lavished on her the silver
and gold —
which they used for Baal. Eze 16:15-19; Hos 8:4
9 "Therefore I will take away my
grain when it ripens, Hos 8:7
and my new wine when it is
ready. Hos 9:2
I will take back my wool and
my linen,
intended to cover her naked
body.
10 So now I will expose her
lewdness
before the eyes of her lovers;
no one will take her out of
my hands. Eze 16:37
11 I will stop all her celebrations: Jer 7:34
her yearly festivals, her New
Moons,
her Sabbath days — all her
appointed festivals. Isa 1:14; Am 8:10
12 I will ruin her vines and her fig
trees, Isa 7:23; Jer 8:13
which she said were her pay
from her lovers;
I will make them a thicket, Isa 5:6
and wild animals will devour
them. Hos 13:8
13 I will punish her for the days
she burned incense to the
Baals; Hos 11:2

she decked herself with rings
and jewelry, Eze 16:17
and went after her lovers, Hos 4:13
but me she forgot," Hos 4:6; 8:14
declares the LORD.

14 "Therefore I am now going to
allure her;
I will lead her into the
wilderness
and speak tenderly to her.
15 There I will give her back her
vineyards,
and will make the Valley of
Achor[a] a door of hope. Jos 7:24,26
There she will respond[b] as in
the days of her youth, Jer 2:2
as in the day she came up
out of Egypt. Hos 12:9

16 "In that day," declares the LORD,
"you will call me 'my
husband'; Isa 54:5
you will no longer call me
'my master.[c]'
17 I will remove the names of
the Baals from her lips; Ex 23:13; Ps 16:4
no longer will their names be
invoked. Jos 23:7
18 In that day I will make a
covenant for them
with the beasts of the field,
the birds in the sky
and the creatures that move
along the ground. Job 5:22
Bow and sword and battle
I will abolish from the land, Isa 2:4
so that all may lie down in
safety. Eze 34:25
19 I will betroth you to me
forever; Isa 62:4
I will betroth you in[d]
righteousness and
justice, Isa 1:27
in[d] love and compassion. Isa 54:8
20 I will betroth you in[d]
faithfulness,
and you will acknowledge
the LORD. Jer 31:34; Hos 6:6; 13:4

21 "In that day I will respond,"
declares the LORD—
"I will respond to the skies, Isa 55:10; Zec 8:12
and they will respond to the
earth;
22 and the earth will respond to
the grain,
the new wine and the olive
oil, Jer 31:12; Joel 2:19
and they will respond to
Jezreel.[e] Hos 1:4
23 I will plant her for myself in
the land; Jer 31:27
I will show my love to the
one I called 'Not my
loved one.[f]' Hos 1:6
I will say to those called 'Not
my people,[g]' 'You are my
people'; Hos 1:10
and they will say, 'You are
my God.'" Ro 9:25*; 1Pe 2:10

[a] 15 *Achor* means *trouble.* [b] 15 Or *sing*
[c] 16 Hebrew *baal* [d] 19,20 Or *with*
[e] 22 *Jezreel* means *God plants.*
[f] 23 Hebrew *Lo-Ruhamah* (see 1:6)
[g] 23 Hebrew *Lo-Ammi* (see 1:9)

Hosea's Reconciliation With His Wife

3 The LORD said to me, "Go, show your love to your wife again, though she is loved by another man and is an adulteress. Love her as the LORD loves the Israelites, though they turn to other gods and love the sacred raisin cakes." 2Sa 6:19; Hos 1:2

2 So I bought her for fifteen
shekels[a] of silver and about a homer and a lethek[b] of barley. 3 Then
I told her, "You are to live with me many days; you must not be a prostitute or be intimate with any man, and I will behave the same way toward you."

4 For the Israelites will live many
days without king or prince, without sacrifice or sacred stones, without ephod or household gods.
5 Afterward the Israelites will re-
turn and seek the LORD their God and David their king. They will come trembling to the LORD and to his blessings in the last days. Jer 50:4-5; Eze 34:23-24

The Charge Against Israel

4 Hear the word of the LORD,
you Israelites,
because the LORD has a
charge to bring Jer 2:9
against you who live in the
land: Joel 1:2,14
"There is no faithfulness, no
love, Pr 24:2
no acknowledgment of God
in the land. Jer 7:28
2 There is only cursing,[c] lying
and murder, Hos 6:9; 7:3
stealing and adultery; Hos 7:1
they break all bounds,
and bloodshed follows
bloodshed. 2Ki 21:16; Hos 5:2
3 Because of this the land dries
up, Jer 4:28
and all who live in it waste
away; Isa 33:9
the beasts of the field, the birds
in the sky
and the fish in the sea are
swept away. Jer 4:25; Zep 1:3

4 "But let no one bring a charge,
let no one accuse another,
for your people are like those
who bring charges against a
priest. Dt 17:12; Eze 3:26
5 You stumble day and night,
Eze 14:7
and the prophets stumble
with you.
So I will destroy your mother—
Hos 2:2
6 my people are destroyed
from lack of knowledge.
Hos 2:13; Mal 2:7-8

"Because you have rejected
knowledge,
I also reject you as my
priests;
because you have ignored the
law of your God, Hos 8:1,12
I also will ignore your
children.

[a] 2 That is, about 6 ounces or about 170 grams [b] 2 A homer and a lethek possibly weighed about 430 pounds or about 195 kilograms. [c] 2 That is, to pronounce a curse on

[7]The more priests there
were,
the more they sinned against
me;
they exchanged their
glorious God[a] for
something disgraceful.
Hos 10:1,6; 13:6; Hab 2:16
[8]They feed on the sins of my
people
and relish their wickedness.
Isa 56:11; Mic 3:11
[9]And it will be: Like people, like
priests. Isa 24:2
I will punish both of them
for their ways
and repay them for their
deeds. Jer 5:31; Hos 9:9,15

[10]"They will eat but not have
enough; Lev 26:26; Mic 6:14
they will engage in
prostitution but not
flourish,
because they have deserted the
LORD Hos 7:14; 9:17
to give themselves [11]to
prostitution; Hos 5:4
old wine and new wine
take away their
understanding. Pr 20:1
[12]My people consult a wooden
idol, Jer 2:27
and a diviner's rod speaks to
them. Hab 2:19
A spirit of prostitution leads
them astray; Isa 44:20
they are unfaithful to their
God. Ps 73:27
[13]They sacrifice on the
mountaintops
and burn offerings on the
hills,
under oak, poplar and
terebinth, Isa 1:29
where the shade is pleasant.
Jer 3:6; Hos 11:2
Therefore your daughters
turn to prostitution
Jer 2:20; Am 7:17
and your daughters-in-law to
adultery. Hos 2:13

[14]"I will not punish your
daughters
when they turn to
prostitution,
nor your daughters-in-law
when they commit
adultery,
because the men themselves
consort with harlots ver 11
and sacrifice with shrine
prostitutes — Hos 9:10
a people without
understanding will
come to ruin! Pr 10:21

[15]"Though you, Israel, commit
adultery,
do not let Judah become
guilty.

"Do not go to Gilgal;
Hos 9:15; 12:11; Am 4:4
do not go up to Beth Aven.[b]
Hos 5:8
And do not swear, 'As surely
as the LORD lives!' Jer 4:2

[a] 7 Syriac (see also an ancient Hebrew scribal tradition); Masoretic Text *me; / I will exchange their glory* [b] 15 *Beth Aven* means *house of wickedness* (a derogatory name for Bethel, which means *house of God*).

16 The Israelites are stubborn, Ex 32:9
like a stubborn heifer. Jer 31:18
How then can the LORD pasture them
like lambs in a meadow? Isa 5:17; 7:25
17 Ephraim is joined to idols;
leave him alone!
18 Even when their drinks are gone,
they continue their prostitution;
their rulers dearly love shameful ways.
19 A whirlwind will sweep them away, Hos 12:1; 13:15
and their sacrifices will bring them shame. Isa 1:29

Judgment Against Israel

5 "Hear this, you priests!
Pay attention, you Israelites!
Listen, royal house!
This judgment is against you: Job 10:2
You have been a snare at Mizpah, Hos 6:9; 9:8
a net spread out on Tabor. Jer 5:26
2 The rebels are knee-deep in slaughter. Hos 4:2
I will discipline all of them. Hos 9:15
3 I know all about Ephraim;
Israel is not hidden from me.
Ephraim, you have now turned to prostitution;
Israel is corrupt. Hos 6:10
4 "Their deeds do not permit them
to return to their God.
A spirit of prostitution is in their heart; Hos 4:11
they do not acknowledge the LORD. Hos 4:6
5 Israel's arrogance testifies against them; Hos 7:10
the Israelites, even Ephraim, stumble in their sin; Eze 14:7
Judah also stumbles with them. Hos 14:1
6 When they go with their flocks and herds
to seek the LORD, Mic 6:6-7
they will not find him;
he has withdrawn himself from them. Pr 1:28; Isa 1:15; Eze 8:6
7 They are unfaithful to the LORD; Hos 6:7
they give birth to illegitimate children. Hos 2:4
When they celebrate their New Moon feasts, Isa 1:14
he will devour[a] their fields. Hos 2:11-12
8 "Sound the trumpet in Gibeah, Hos 9:9; 10:9
the horn in Ramah. Isa 10:29
Raise the battle cry in Beth Aven[b]; Hos 4:15
lead on, Benjamin.

[a] 7 Or *Now their New Moon feasts / will devour them and* [b] 8 *Beth Aven* means *house of wickedness* (a derogatory name for Bethel, which means *house of God*).

9 Ephraim will be laid waste
on the day of reckoning. Isa 37:3; Hos 9:11-17
Among the tribes of Israel
I proclaim what is certain. Isa 46:10; Zec 1:6
10 Judah's leaders are like those
who move boundary stones. Dt 19:14
I will pour out my wrath on them
like a flood of water. Eze 7:8
11 Ephraim is oppressed,
trampled in judgment,
intent on pursuing idols.[a] Hos 9:16; Mic 6:16
12 I am like a moth to Ephraim, Isa 51:8
like rot to the people of Judah.

13 "When Ephraim saw his sickness, Isa 7:16
and Judah his sores,
then Ephraim turned to Assyria, Hos 7:11; 8:9
and sent to the great king for help. Hos 10:6
But he is not able to cure you, Hos 14:3
not able to heal your sores. Jer 30:12
14 For I will be like a lion to Ephraim, Am 3:4
like a great lion to Judah.
I will tear them to pieces and go away; Hos 6:1
I will carry them off, with no one to rescue them. Mic 5:8
15 Then I will return to my lair
until they have borne their guilt
and seek my face — Hos 3:5
in their misery
they will earnestly seek me." Isa 64:9; Jer 2:27

Israel Unrepentant

6 "Come, let us return to the LORD. Isa 10:20
He has torn us to pieces Hos 5:14
but he will heal us; Jer 3:22
he has injured us
but he will bind up our wounds. Dt 32:39; Jer 30:17; Hos 14:4
2 After two days he will revive us; Ps 30:5
on the third day he will restore us, Ps 71:20
that we may live in his presence.
3 Let us acknowledge the LORD;
let us press on to acknowledge him.
As surely as the sun rises,
he will appear;
he will come to us like the winter rains, Joel 2:23
like the spring rains that water the earth." Ps 72:6

4 "What can I do with you, Ephraim? Hos 11:8
What can I do with you, Judah?
Your love is like the morning mist,

[a] 11 The meaning of the Hebrew for this word is uncertain.

like the early dew that
disappears. Hos 7:1; 13:3
5 Therefore I cut you in pieces
with my prophets,
I killed you with the words
of my mouth —
Jer 1:9-10; 23:29
then my judgments go forth
like the sun.[a] Heb 4:12
6 For I desire mercy, not sacrifice,
Isa 1:11; Mt 9:13*; 12:7*
and acknowledgment of
God rather than burnt
offerings. Hos 2:20
7 As at Adam,[b] they have broken
the covenant; Hos 8:1
they were unfaithful to me
there. Hos 5:7
8 Gilead is a city of evildoers,
Hos 12:11
stained with footprints of
blood.
9 As marauders lie in ambush for
a victim, Ps 10:8
so do bands of priests;
they murder on the road to
Shechem,
carrying out their
wicked schemes.
Jer 7:9-10; Eze 22:9; Hos 7:1
10 I have seen a horrible thing in
Israel: Jer 5:30
There Ephraim is given to
prostitution,
Israel is defiled. Hos 5:3

11 "Also for you, Judah,
a harvest is appointed. Joel 3:13

"Whenever I would restore the
fortunes of my people,
Ps 126:1; Zep 2:7

7 1 whenever I would heal Israel,
the sins of Ephraim are
exposed
and the crimes of Samaria
revealed. Hos 6:4
They practice deceit,
thieves break into houses,
Hos 4:2
bandits rob in the streets;
Hos 6:9
2 but they do not realize
that I remember all their evil
deeds. Jer 14:10; Hos 8:13
Their sins engulf them; Jer 2:19
they are always before me.

3 "They delight the king with
their wickedness,
the princes with their lies.
Mic 7:3
4 They are all adulterers, Jer 9:2
burning like an oven
whose fire the baker need not
stir
from the kneading of the
dough till it rises.
5 On the day of the festival of our
king
the princes become inflamed
with wine, Isa 28:1,7
and he joins hands with the
mockers. Ps 1:1
6 Their hearts are like an oven;
Ps 21:9
they approach him with
intrigue.
Their passion smolders all
night;

[a] 5 The meaning of the Hebrew for this line is uncertain. [b] 7 Or *Like Adam*; or *Like human beings*

in the morning it blazes like
a flaming fire.
7 All of them are hot as an oven;
they devour their rulers.
All their kings fall, Hos 13:10
and none of them calls on
me. Ps 14:4

8 "Ephraim mixes with the
nations; Ps 106:35; Hos 5:13
Ephraim is a flat loaf not
turned over.
9 Foreigners sap his strength, Isa 1:7; Hos 8:7
but he does not realize it.
His hair is sprinkled with gray,
but he does not notice.
10 Israel's arrogance testifies
against him, Hos 5:5
but despite all this
he does not return to the LORD
his God
or search for him. Isa 9:13

11 "Ephraim is like a dove, Hos 11:11
easily deceived and
senseless —
now calling to Egypt, Hos 9:6
now turning to Assyria. Hos 5:13; 12:1
12 When they go, I will throw
my net over them; Eze 12:13
I will pull them down like
the birds in the sky.
When I hear them flocking
together,
I will catch them.
13 Woe to them, Hos 9:12
because they have
strayed from me! Jer 14:10; Eze 34:4-6; Hos 9:17
Destruction to them,
because they have rebelled
against me!
I long to redeem them
but they speak about me
falsely. Mt 23:37
14 They do not cry out to me from
their hearts Jer 3:10
but wail on their beds.
They slash themselves,[a]
appealing to their gods
for grain and new wine, Am 2:8
but they turn away from me. Hos 13:16
15 I trained them and
strengthened their arms,
but they plot evil against me. Na 1:9,11
16 They do not turn to the Most
High;
they are like a faulty bow. Ps 78:9,57
Their leaders will fall by the
sword
because of their insolent
words.
For this they will be ridiculed Eze 23:32
in the land of Egypt. Hos 9:3

Israel to Reap the Whirlwind

8 "Put the trumpet to your lips!
An eagle is over the house of
the LORD Jer 4:13
because the people have
broken my covenant Jer 11:10

[a] 14 Some Hebrew manuscripts and Septuagint; most Hebrew manuscripts *They gather together*

and rebelled against my law.
Hos 4:6; 6:7
2 Israel cries out to me,
'Our God, we acknowledge you!'
3 But Israel has rejected what is good;
an enemy will pursue him.
Titus 1:16
4 They set up kings without my consent;
they choose princes without my approval.
Hos 13:10
With their silver and gold
they make idols for themselves Hos 2:8
to their own destruction.
5 Samaria, throw out your calf-idol! Hos 10:5
My anger burns against them.
How long will they be incapable of purity?
Jer 13:27
6 They are from Israel!
This calf — a metalworker has made it;
it is not God. Hos 14:3
It will be broken in pieces,
that calf of Samaria. Ex 32:4
7 "They sow the wind
and reap the whirlwind.
Pr 22:8; Isa 66:15; Hos 10:12-13
The stalk has no head;
it will produce no flour.
Hos 9:16
Were it to yield grain,
foreigners would swallow it up. Hos 2:9
8 Israel is swallowed up; Jer 51:34
now she is among the nations
like something no one wants. Jer 22:28
9 For they have gone up to Assyria
like a wild donkey wandering alone.
Ephraim has sold herself to lovers. Eze 23:5; Hos 5:13
10 Although they have sold themselves among the nations,
I will now gather them together. Eze 16:37; 22:20
They will begin to waste away
Jer 42:2
under the oppression of the mighty king.
11 "Though Ephraim built many altars for sin offerings,
these have become altars for sinning. Hos 10:1; 12:11
12 I wrote for them the many things of my law,
but they regarded them as something foreign.
13 Though they offer sacrifices as gifts to me,
and though they eat the meat, Jer 7:21
the LORD is not pleased with them.
Now he will remember their wickedness Hos 7:2
and punish their sins: Hos 4:9
They will return to Egypt.
Hos 9:3,6

14 Israel has forgotten their
Maker Dt 32:18; Hos 2:13
and built palaces;
Judah has fortified many
towns.
But I will send fire on their
cities
that will consume their
fortresses." Jer 17:27

Punishment for Israel

9 Do not rejoice, Israel;
do not be jubilant like the
other nations. Isa 22:12-13
For you have been unfaithful to
your God; Hos 10:5
you love the wages of a
prostitute Ge 30:15
at every threshing floor.
2 Threshing floors and
winepresses will not
feed the people;
the new wine will fail them.
Hos 2:9
3 They will not remain in the
LORD's land; Lev 25:23
Ephraim will return to Egypt
Hos 8:13
and eat unclean food in
Assyria. Eze 4:13; Hos 7:11
4 They will not pour out
wine offerings to the
LORD,
nor will their sacrifices
please him. Hos 8:13
Such sacrifices will be
to them like the
bread of mourners;
Jer 16:7
all who eat them will be
unclean. Hag 2:13-14
This food will be for themselves;
it will not come into the
temple of the LORD.
Eze 4:13-14

5 What will you do on the day of
your appointed festivals,
Isa 10:3; Jer 5:31; Hos 2:11
on the feast days of the
LORD?
6 Even if they escape from
destruction,
Egypt will gather them, Hos 7:11
and Memphis will bury
them. Isa 19:13
Their treasures of silver will be
taken over by briers,
and thorns will overrun their
tents. Isa 5:6; Hos 10:8
7 The days of punishment are
coming, Isa 34:8; Jer 10:15
the days of reckoning are at
hand.
Let Israel know this.
Because your sins are so many
Jer 16:18
and your hostility so great,
the prophet is considered a
fool, Isa 44:25; La 2:14; Eze 14:9-10
the inspired person a
maniac. Hos 14:1
8 The prophet, along with my
God,
is the watchman over
Ephraim,[a]
yet snares await him on all his
paths, Hos 5:1
and hostility in the house of
his God.

[a] 8 Or *The prophet is the watchman over Ephraim, / the people of my God*

9 They have sunk deep into
corruption,
as in the days of Gibeah.
Jdg 19:16-30; Hos 5:8
God will remember their
wickedness Hos 8:13
and punish them for their
sins. Hos 4:9

10 "When I found Israel,
it was like finding grapes in
the desert;
when I saw your ancestors,
it was like seeing the
early fruit on the
fig tree.
But when they came to Baal
Peor, Nu 25:1-5; Ps 106:28-29
they consecrated themselves
to that shameful idol
Jer 11:13; Hos 4:14
and became as vile as the
thing they loved.
11 Ephraim's glory will fly away
like a bird — Hos 4:7; 10:5
no birth, no pregnancy, no
conception.
12 Even if they rear children,
I will bereave them of every
one. Eze 24:21
Woe to them Hos 7:13
when I turn away from
them! Dt 31:17
13 I have seen Ephraim,
like Tyre,
planted in a pleasant place.
Eze 27:3
But Ephraim will bring out
their children to the slayer."

14 Give them, LORD —
what will you give them?
Give them wombs that
miscarry
and breasts that are dry.
Lk 23:29

15 "Because of all their
wickedness in Gilgal,
Hos 4:15
I hated them there.
Because of their sinful deeds,
Hos 7:2
I will drive them out of my
house.
I will no longer love them;
all their leaders are rebellious.
Isa 1:23; Hos 4:9; 5:2
16 Ephraim is blighted, Hos 5:11
their root is withered,
they yield no fruit. Hos 8:7
Even if they bear children,
I will slay their cherished
offspring." ver 12

17 My God will reject them
because they have not
obeyed him; Hos 4:10
they will be wanderers
among the nations.
Dt 28:65; Hos 7:13

10

Israel was a spreading vine;
Eze 15:2
he brought forth fruit for
himself.
As his fruit increased,
he built more altars; 1Ki 14:23
as his land prospered,
he adorned his sacred stones.
Hos 8:11; 12:11
2 Their heart is deceitful, 1Ki 18:21
and now they must bear
their guilt. Hos 13:16

The LORD will demolish their
altars ver 8
and destroy their sacred
stones. Mic 5:13

3 Then they will say, "We have no
king
because we did not revere
the LORD.
But even if we had a king,
what could he do for us?"
4 They make many promises,
take false oaths Hos 4:2
and make agreements; Eze 17:19; Am 5:7
therefore lawsuits spring up
like poisonous weeds in a
plowed field. Am 6:12
5 The people who live in Samaria
fear
for the calf-idol of Beth
Aven.[a] Hos 5:8
Its people will mourn over it,
and so will its idolatrous
priests, 2Ki 23:5
those who had rejoiced over its
splendor,
because it is taken from them
into exile. Hos 8:5; 9:1,3,11
6 It will be carried to Assyria Hos 11:5
as tribute for the great king. Hos 5:13
Ephraim will be disgraced; Hos 4:7
Israel will be ashamed of its
foreign alliances. Jer 48:13
7 Samaria's king will be
destroyed, Hos 13:11
swept away like a twig on the
surface of the waters.
8 The high places of wickedness[b]
will be destroyed — 1Ki 12:28-30; Hos 4:13
it is the sin of Israel.
Thorns and thistles will grow
up
and cover their altars. Isa 32:13; Hos 9:6
Then they will say to the
mountains, "Cover us!"
and to the hills, "Fall on us!" Lk 23:30*; Rev 6:16

9 "Since the days of Gibeah,
you have sinned, Israel, Hos 5:8
and there you have
remained.[c]
Will not war again overtake
the evildoers in Gibeah?
10 When I please, I will punish
them; Eze 5:13; Hos 4:9
nations will be gathered
against them
to put them in bonds for
their double sin.
11 Ephraim is a trained heifer
that loves to thresh;
so I will put a yoke
on her fair neck.
I will drive Ephraim,
Judah must plow,
and Jacob must break up the
ground.
12 Sow righteousness for
yourselves, Pr 11:18

[a] 5 *Beth Aven* means *house of wickedness* (a derogatory name for Bethel, which means *house of God*). [b] 8 Hebrew *aven*, a reference to Beth Aven (a derogatory name for Bethel); see verse 5. [c] 9 Or *there a stand was taken*

reap the fruit of unfailing
love,
and break up your unplowed
ground; Jer 4:3
for it is time to seek the
LORD, Hos 12:6
until he comes
and showers his righteousness
on you. Isa 45:8
13 But you have planted
wickedness,
you have reaped evil,
Job 4:8; Gal 6:7-8
you have eaten the fruit of
deception.
Because you have depended on
your own strength
and on your many warriors,
Ps 33:16
14 the roar of battle will rise
against your people,
so that all your fortresses will
be devastated — Isa 17:3
as Shalman devastated Beth
Arbel on the day of
battle, 2Ki 17:3
when mothers were dashed
to the ground with their
children. Hos 13:16
15 So will it happen to you, Bethel,
because your wickedness is
great.
When that day dawns,
the king of Israel will be
completely destroyed.

God's Love for Israel

11 "When Israel was a child,
I loved him, Jer 2:2
and out of Egypt I called my
son. Hos 12:9,13; Mt 2:15*
2 But the more they were called,
the more they went away
from me.[a]
They sacrificed to the Baals
Hos 2:13
and they burned incense to
images. 2Ki 17:15; Jer 18:15
3 It was I who taught Ephraim to
walk,
taking them by the arms;
Dt 1:31; Hos 7:15
but they did not realize
it was I who healed them.
Jer 30:17
4 I led them with cords of human
kindness,
with ties of love. Jer 31:2-3
To them I was like one who lifts
a little child to the cheek,
and I bent down to feed
them. Ps 78:25
5 "Will they not return to Egypt
Hos 7:16
and will not Assyria rule over
them Hos 10:6
because they refuse to
repent?
6 A sword will flash in their
cities; Hos 13:16
it will devour their false
prophets
and put an end to their
plans.
7 My people are determined to
turn from me. Jer 3:6-7; 8:5
Even though they call me
God Most High,
I will by no means exalt
them.

[a] 2 Septuagint; Hebrew *them*

8 "How can I give you up,
Ephraim? Hos 6:4
How can I hand you over,
Israel?
How can I treat you like
Admah?
How can I make you like
Zeboyim? Ge 14:8
My heart is changed within me;
all my compassion is
aroused. 1Ki 3:26; Ps 25:6
9 I will not carry out my fierce
anger, Dt 13:17; Jer 30:11
nor will I devastate Ephraim
again. Mal 3:6
For I am God, and not a man —
Nu 23:19
the Holy One among you.
Isa 31:1
I will not come against their
cities.
10 They will follow the LORD;
he will roar like a lion.
When he roars,
his children will come
trembling from the
west. Hos 6:1-3
11 They will come from Egypt,
trembling like sparrows,
from Assyria, fluttering like
doves. Isa 11:11
I will settle them in their
homes," Eze 28:26
declares the LORD.

Israel's Sin

12 Ephraim has surrounded me
with lies, Hos 4:2
Israel with deceit.
And Judah is unruly against
God,
even against the faithful
Holy One.[a] Hos 10:13

12

[b] 1 Ephraim feeds on the
wind; Eze 17:10
he pursues the east wind all
day
and multiplies lies and
violence. Hos 4:19
He makes a treaty with Assyria
Hos 5:13
and sends olive oil to Egypt.
2Ki 17:4
2 The LORD has a charge to bring
against Judah; Mic 6:2
he will punish Jacob[c]
according to his ways
and repay him according to
his deeds. Hos 4:9
3 In the womb he grasped his
brother's heel; Ge 25:26
as a man he struggled with
God. Ge 32:24-29
4 He struggled with the angel
and overcame him;
he wept and begged for his
favor.
He found him at Bethel
Ge 28:12-15; 35:15
and talked with him there —
5 the LORD God Almighty,
the LORD is his name! Ex 3:15
6 But you must return to your
God; Isa 19:22
maintain love and justice,
Mic 6:8
and wait for your God always.
Hos 6:1-3; 10:12; Mic 7:7

[a] *12* In Hebrew texts this verse (11:12) is numbered 12:1. [b] In Hebrew texts 12:1-14 is numbered 12:2-15. [c] *2* *Jacob* means *he grasps the heel*, a Hebrew idiom for *he takes advantage of* or *he deceives*.

[7]The merchant uses dishonest
scales Am 8:5
and loves to defraud.
[8]Ephraim boasts,
"I am very rich; I have
become wealthy.
Ps 62:10; Rev 3:17
With all my wealth they will
not find in me
any iniquity or sin."

[9]"I have been the LORD your
God
ever since you came out of
Egypt; Lev 23:43; Hos 11:1
I will make you live in tents
again, Ne 8:17
as in the days of your
appointed festivals.
[10]I spoke to the prophets,
gave them many visions
and told parables through
them." 2Ki 17:13; Eze 20:49

[11]Is Gilead wicked? Hos 6:8
Its people are worthless!
Do they sacrifice bulls in Gilgal?
Hos 4:15
Their altars will be like piles
of stones
on a plowed field. Hos 8:11
[12]Jacob fled to the country of
Aram[a]; Ge 28:5
Israel served to get a
wife,
and to pay for her he tended
sheep. Ge 29:18
[13]The LORD used a prophet to
bring Israel up from
Egypt, Hos 11:1
by a prophet he cared for
him. Isa 63:11-14
[14]But Ephraim has aroused his
bitter anger;
his Lord will leave on
him the guilt of his
bloodshed Eze 18:13
and will repay him for his
contempt. Da 11:18

The LORD's Anger Against Israel

13 When Ephraim spoke,
people trembled; Jdg 12:1
he was exalted in Israel. Jdg 8:1
But he became guilty of Baal
worship and died. Hos 11:2
[2]Now they sin more and more;
they make idols for
themselves from their
silver, Isa 46:6; Jer 10:4
cleverly fashioned images,
all of them the work of
craftsmen.
It is said of these people,
"They offer human sacrifices!
They kiss[b] calf-idols!"
Isa 44:17-20
[3]Therefore they will be like the
morning mist,
like the early dew that
disappears, Hos 6:4
like chaff swirling from
a threshing floor,
Isa 17:13; Da 2:35
like smoke escaping through
a window. Ps 68:2

[4]"But I have been the LORD your
God
ever since you came out of
Egypt. Hos 12:9

[a] 12 That is, Northwest Mesopotamia
[b] 2 Or "*Men who sacrifice / kiss*

You shall acknowledge no God
but me, Ex 20:3
no Savior except me.
Isa 43:11; 45:21-22
5 I cared for you in the
wilderness, Dt 1:19
in the land of burning heat.
6 When I fed them, they were
satisfied;
when they were satisfied,
they became proud;
then they forgot me.
Dt 32:12-15; Hos 2:13
7 So I will be like a lion to
them,
like a leopard I will lurk by
the path.
8 Like a bear robbed of her cubs,
2Sa 17:8
I will attack them and rip
them open;
like a lion I will devour them —
Ps 17:12
a wild animal will tear them
apart. Ps 50:22

9 "You are destroyed, Israel,
because you are against me,
against your helper.
Dt 33:29; Jer 2:17-19
10 Where is your king, that he
may save you? 2Ki 17:4
Where are your rulers in all
your towns,
of whom you said,
'Give me a king and princes'?
Hos 8:4
11 So in my anger I gave you a
king,
and in my wrath I took him
away. 1Ki 14:10; Hos 10:7
12 The guilt of Ephraim is stored
up,
his sins are kept on record.
Dt 32:34
13 Pains as of a woman in
childbirth come to him,
Mic 4:9-10
but he is a child without
wisdom;
when the time arrives, 2Ki 19:3
he doesn't have the sense to
come out of the womb.
Isa 66:9

14 "I will deliver this people from
the power of the grave;
Eze 37:12-13
I will redeem them from
death. Isa 25:8
Where, O death, are your
plagues?
Where, O grave, is your
destruction? 1Co 15:55*

"I will have no compassion,
15 even though he thrives
among his brothers.
Hos 10:1
An east wind from the LORD
will come, Eze 19:12
blowing in from the
desert;
his spring will fail
and his well dry up. Jer 51:36
His storehouse will be
plundered Jer 20:5
of all its treasures.
16 The people of Samaria
must bear their guilt,
Hos 10:2
because they have rebelled
against their God. Hos 7:14

They will fall by the sword; Hos 11:6
their little ones will be dashed to the ground, Hos 10:14
their pregnant women ripped open."[a] 2Ki 15:16

Repentance to Bring Blessing

14 [b] Return, Israel, to the LORD your God. Jer 3:12
Your sins have been your downfall! Hos 5:5
2 Take words with you
and return to the LORD.
Say to him:
"Forgive all our sins
and receive us graciously, Mic 7:18-19
that we may offer the fruit of our lips.[c] Heb 13:15
3 Assyria cannot save us;
we will not mount warhorses. Isa 31:1
We will never again say 'Our gods' Hos 8:6
to what our own hands have made,
for in you the fatherless find compassion." Ps 10:14; 68:5

4 "I will heal their waywardness Hos 6:1
and love them freely, Zep 3:17
for my anger has turned away from them. Job 13:16
5 I will be like the dew to Israel;
he will blossom like a lily. SS 2:1
Like a cedar of Lebanon Isa 35:2
he will send down his roots; Job 29:19
6 his young shoots will grow.
His splendor will be like an olive tree, Ps 52:8; Jer 11:16
his fragrance like a cedar of Lebanon. SS 4:11
7 People will dwell again in his shade; Ps 91:1-4
they will flourish like the grain,
they will blossom like the vine —
Israel's fame will be like the wine of Lebanon. Eze 17:23; Hos 2:22
8 Ephraim, what more have I[d] to do with idols?
I will answer him and care for him.
I am like a flourishing juniper; Isa 37:24
your fruitfulness comes from me."

9 Who is wise? Let them realize these things. Ps 107:43
Who is discerning? Let them understand. Pr 10:29; Isa 1:28
The ways of the LORD are right; Ps 111:7-8; Zep 3:5; Ac 13:10
the righteous walk in them, Isa 26:7
but the rebellious stumble in them.

[a] *16* In Hebrew texts this verse (13:16) is numbered 14:1. [b] In Hebrew texts 14:1-9 is numbered 14:2-10. [c] *2* Or *offer our lips as sacrifices of bulls* [d] *8* Or Hebrew; Septuagint *What more has Ephraim*

JOEL

1 The word of the LORD that came
to Joel son of Pethuel.
Jer 1:2; Ac 2:16

An Invasion of Locusts

2 Hear this, you elders; Hos 5:1
listen, all who live in the
land. Hos 4:1
Has anything like this ever
happened in your days
or in the days of your
ancestors? Joel 2:2
3 Tell it to your children,
Ex 10:2; Ps 78:4
and let your children tell it to
their children,
and their children to the
next generation.
4 What the locust swarm has left
Ex 10:14
the great locusts have eaten;
what the great locusts have left
the young locusts have
eaten;
what the young locusts have
left Ex 10:5
other locusts[a] have eaten.
Dt 28:39; Na 3:15

5 Wake up, you drunkards, and
weep!
Wail, all you drinkers of
wine; Joel 3:3
wail because of the new wine,
for it has been snatched from
your lips.
6 A nation has invaded my land,
a mighty army without
number; Joel 2:2,11,25
it has the teeth of a lion, Rev 9:8
the fangs of a lioness.
7 It has laid waste my vines Isa 5:6
and ruined my fig trees.
Am 4:9
It has stripped off their bark
and thrown it away,
leaving their branches
white.

8 Mourn like a virgin in sackcloth
Isa 22:12; Am 8:10
grieving for the betrothed of
her youth.
9 Grain offerings and drink
offerings Hos 9:4; Joel 2:14,17
are cut off from the house of
the LORD.
The priests are in mourning,
Isa 22:12
those who minister before
the LORD.
10 The fields are ruined,
the ground is dried up; Isa 24:4
the grain is destroyed,
the new wine is dried up,
Hos 9:2
the olive oil fails.

11 Despair, you farmers,
Jer 14:3-4; Am 5:16
wail, you vine growers;

[a] 4 The precise meaning of the four Hebrew words used here for locusts is uncertain.

grieve for the wheat and the barley,
because the harvest of the field is destroyed. Isa 17:11
12 The vine is dried up
and the fig tree is withered;
the pomegranate, the palm and the apple[a] tree —
all the trees of the field — are dried up. Hag 2:19
Surely the people's joy
is withered away.

A Call to Lamentation

13 Put on sackcloth, you priests, and mourn; Jer 4:8
wail, you who minister before the altar. Joel 2:17
Come, spend the night in sackcloth,
you who minister before my God;
for the grain offerings and drink offerings
are withheld from the house of your God.
14 Declare a holy fast; 2Ch 20:3
call a sacred assembly.
Summon the elders
and all who live in the land
to the house of the LORD your God,
and cry out to the LORD. Jnh 3:8

15 Alas for that day! Jer 30:7
For the day of the LORD is near; Joel 2:1,11,31
it will come like destruction from the Almighty.[b] Ge 17:1

16 Has not the food been cut off Isa 3:7
before our very eyes —
joy and gladness
from the house of our God? Dt 12:7
17 The seeds are shriveled beneath the clods.[c] Isa 17:10-11
The storehouses are in ruins,
the granaries have been broken down,
for the grain has dried up.
18 How the cattle moan!
The herds mill about
because they have no pasture;
even the flocks of sheep are suffering. Jer 9:10

19 To you, LORD, I call, Ps 50:15
for fire has devoured
the pastures in the wilderness Jer 9:10; Am 7:4
and flames have burned
up all the trees of the field.
20 Even the wild animals pant for you; Ps 104:21
the streams of water have dried up 1Ki 17:7
and fire has devoured
the pastures in the wilderness.

An Army of Locusts

2 Blow the trumpet in Zion; Jer 4:5
sound the alarm on my holy hill. Ex 15:17

[a] 12 Or possibly *apricot* [b] 15 Hebrew *Shaddai* [c] 17 The meaning of the Hebrew for this word is uncertain.

Let all who live in the land
tremble,
for the day of the LORD is
coming. Zep 1:14-16
It is close at hand — Ob 1:15
2 a day of darkness and gloom,
Da 9:12; Am 5:18
a day of clouds and
blackness. Rev 9:2
Like dawn spreading across the
mountains
a large and mighty army
comes, Joel 1:6
such as never was in ancient
times Joel 1:2
nor ever will be in ages to
come.

3 Before them fire devours,
behind them a flame blazes.
Before them the land is
like the garden of Eden,
Ge 2:8
behind them, a desert
waste — Ps 105:34-35
nothing escapes them.
4 They have the appearance of
horses; Rev 9:7
they gallop along like
cavalry.
5 With a noise like that of
chariots Rev 9:9
they leap over the
mountaintops,
like a crackling fire consuming
stubble, Isa 5:24; 30:30
like a mighty army drawn up
for battle.
6 At the sight of them, nations
are in anguish; Isa 13:8
every face turns pale. Na 2:10
7 They charge like warriors;
they scale walls like soldiers.
They all march in line,
not swerving from their
course. Isa 5:27
8 They do not jostle each other;
each marches straight ahead.
They plunge through defenses
without breaking ranks.
9 They rush upon the city;
they run along the wall.
They climb into the houses;
like thieves they enter
through the windows.
Jer 9:21

10 Before them the earth shakes,
Ps 18:7
the heavens tremble,
the sun and moon are
darkened, Mt 24:29
and the stars no longer
shine. Isa 13:10; Eze 32:8
11 The LORD thunders Joel 1:15
at the head of his army;
his forces are beyond number,
and mighty is the army that
obeys his command.
The day of the LORD is great;
Zep 1:14; Rev 18:8
it is dreadful.
Who can endure it? Eze 22:14

Rend Your Heart

12 "Even now," declares the LORD,
"return to me with all your
heart, Jer 4:1; Hos 12:6
with fasting and weeping
and mourning."
13 Rend your heart Isa 57:15
and not your garments. Job 1:20

Return to the LORD your God, Isa 19:22
for he is gracious and
compassionate, Dt 4:31
slow to anger and abounding
in love, Ex 34:6
and he relents from sending
calamity. Jer 18:8
14 Who knows? He may turn and
relent Jer 26:3
and leave behind a
blessing — Hag 2:19
grain offerings and drink
offerings Joel 1:13
for the LORD your God.

15 Blow the trumpet in Zion,
Nu 10:2
declare a holy fast, Jer 36:9
call a sacred assembly. Joel 1:14
16 Gather the people,
consecrate the assembly;
Ex 19:10,22
bring together the elders, Joel 1:2
gather the children,
those nursing at the breast.
Let the bridegroom leave his
room Ps 19:5
and the bride her chamber.
17 Let the priests, who minister
before the LORD,
weep between the
portico and the altar.
Eze 8:16; Mt 23:35
Let them say, "Spare your
people, LORD.
Do not make your
inheritance an object of
scorn, Ps 44:13
a byword among the nations.
1Ki 9:7
Why should they say among
the peoples,
'Where is their God?'" Ps 42:3

The LORD's Answer

18 Then the LORD was jealous for
his land Zec 1:14
and took pity on his people.
Ps 72:13

19 The LORD replied[a] to them:
"I am sending you grain,
new wine and olive oil,
Jer 31:12
enough to satisfy you fully;
Lev 26:5
never again will I make you
an object of scorn to the
nations. Eze 34:29

20 "I will drive the northern
horde far from you,
Jer 1:14-15
pushing it into a parched
and barren land;
its eastern ranks will drown in
the Dead Sea Zec 14:8
and its western ranks in
the Mediterranean
Sea.
And its stench will go up; Isa 34:3
its smell will rise."

Surely he has done great
things!
21 Do not be afraid, land of
Judah; Isa 54:4; Zep 3:16-17
be glad and rejoice. Ps 9:2
Surely the LORD has done great
things! Ps 126:3

[a] 18,19 *Or LORD will be jealous . . . / and take pity . . . / 19 The LORD will reply*

22 Do not be afraid, you wild
animals,
for the pastures in the
wilderness are becoming
green. Ps 65:12
The trees are bearing their fruit;
the fig tree and the vine
yield their riches.
Joel 1:18-20
23 Be glad, people of Zion,
rejoice in the LORD your God,
Isa 41:16; Hab 3:18; Zec 10:7
for he has given you the
autumn rains
because he is faithful.
He sends you abundant
showers, Eze 34:26
both autumn and spring
rains, as before. Lev 26:4
24 The threshing floors will be
filled with grain;
the vats will overflow with
new wine and oil.
Am 9:13; Mal 3:10
25 "I will repay you for the years
the locusts have eaten —
Dt 28:39
the great locust and the
young locust,
the other locusts and the
locust swarm[a] —
my great army that I sent
among you. Joel 1:6
26 You will have plenty to eat,
until you are full, Lev 26:5
and you will praise the name
of the LORD your God,
Isa 62:9
who has worked wonders for
you; Isa 25:1
never again will my people be
shamed. Isa 29:22
27 Then you will know that I am
in Israel, Ex 6:7
that I am the LORD your God,
Joel 3:17
and that there is no
other;
never again will my people be
shamed. Zep 3:11

The Day of the LORD

28 "And afterward,
I will pour out my Spirit on
all people. Eze 39:29
Your sons and daughters will
prophesy, 1Sa 19:20
your old men will dream
dreams, Jer 23:25
your young men will see
visions.
29 Even on my servants, both
men and women,
1Co 12:13; Gal 3:28
I will pour out my Spirit in
those days. Eze 36:27
30 I will show wonders in the
heavens Lk 21:11
and on the earth, Mk 13:24-25
blood and fire and billows of
smoke.
31 The sun will be turned to
darkness Mt 24:29
and the moon to blood
before the coming of the
great and dreadful
day of the LORD.
Isa 13:9-10; Mal 4:1,5

[a] *25* The precise meaning of the four Hebrew words used here for locusts is uncertain.

[32]And everyone who calls
on the name of the LORD will
be saved; Ro 10:13*
for on Mount Zion and in
Jerusalem Isa 46:13
there will be deliverance,
Ob 1:17
as the LORD has said,
even among the survivors
Mic 4:7; Ro 9:27
whom the LORD calls.[a] Ac 2:39

The Nations Judged

3 [b] "In those days and at that
time,
when I restore the fortunes
of Judah and Jerusalem,
Jer 16:15
[2]I will gather all nations Zep 3:8
and bring them down to the
Valley of Jehoshaphat.[c]
Isa 22:1
There I will put them on trial
Eze 36:5
for what they did to my
inheritance, my people
Israel,
because they scattered my
people among the
nations Lev 26:33
and divided up my land.
[3]They cast lots for my people
Eze 24:6
and traded boys for
prostitutes;
they sold girls for wine to
drink. Am 2:6

[4]"Now what have you against
me, Tyre and Sidon and all you
regions of Philistia? Are you repaying me for something I have
done? If you are paying me back,
I will swiftly and speedily return
on your own heads what you have
done. [5]For you took my silver and
my gold and carried off my finest
treasures to your temples.[d] [6]You
sold the people of Judah and Jerusalem to the Greeks, that you
might send them far from their
homeland. 2Ch 21:16-17; Isa 34:8

[7]"See, I am going to rouse them
out of the places to which you sold
them, and I will return on your
own heads what you have done. [8]I
will sell your sons and daughters
to the people of Judah, and they
will sell them to the Sabeans, a nation far away." The LORD has spoken. Isa 43:5-6; Jer 23:8

[9]Proclaim this among the
nations:
Prepare for war! Isa 8:9
Rouse the warriors! Jer 46:4
Let all the fighting men draw
near and attack.
[10]Beat your plowshares into
swords
and your pruning hooks into
spears. Isa 2:4; Mic 4:3
Let the weakling say, Zec 12:8
"I am strong!" Jos 1:6
[11]Come quickly, all you nations
from every side,
and assemble there.
Eze 38:15-16; Zep 3:8

[a] *32* In Hebrew texts 2:28-32 is numbered 3:1-5. [b] In Hebrew texts 3:1-21 is numbered 4:1-21. [c] *2* *Jehoshaphat* means *the LORD judges*; also in verse 12. [d] *5* Or *palaces*

Bring down your warriors,
LORD! Isa 13:3

12 "Let the nations be roused;
let them advance into the
Valley of Jehoshaphat,
for there I will sit
to judge all the nations on
every side. Isa 2:4
13 Swing the sickle, Mk 4:29
for the harvest is ripe.
Hos 6:11; Mt 13:39; Rev 14:15-19
Come, trample the grapes,
Jer 25:30
for the winepress is full
Rev 14:20
and the vats overflow —
so great is their wickedness!"

14 Multitudes, multitudes
in the valley of decision!
For the day of the LORD is near
Isa 34:2-8; Joel 1:15
in the valley of decision.
Eze 36:5
15 The sun and moon will be
darkened,
and the stars no longer
shine. Eze 32:7
16 The LORD will roar from Zion
and thunder from
Jerusalem; Am 1:2
the earth and the heavens
will tremble. Eze 38:19
But the LORD will be a refuge
for his people, Ps 46:1
a stronghold for the people
of Israel. Jer 16:19

Blessings for God's People

17 "Then you will know that I, the
LORD your God, Joel 2:27
dwell in Zion, my holy hill.
Isa 4:3
Jerusalem will be holy; Jer 31:40
never again will foreigners
invade her. Isa 52:1

18 "In that day the mountains will
drip new wine,
and the hills will flow with
milk; Ex 3:8
all the ravines of Judah
will run with water.
Isa 30:25; 35:6
A fountain will flow out of the
LORD's house Rev 22:1-2
and will water the valley of
acacias.[a] Eze 47:1; Am 9:13
19 But Egypt will be desolate,
Isa 19:1
Edom a desert waste, Isa 11:14
because of violence done to the
people of Judah, Ob 1:10
in whose land they shed
innocent blood.
20 Judah will be inhabited forever
Am 9:15
and Jerusalem through all
generations.
21 Shall I leave their innocent
blood unavenged? Isa 1:15
No, I will not." Eze 36:25

The LORD dwells in Zion!

[a] 18 Or *Valley of Shittim*

AMOS

1 The words of Amos, one of the shepherds of Tekoa — the vision he saw concerning Israel two years before the earthquake, when Uzziah was king of Judah and Jeroboam son of Jehoash[a] was king of Israel. 2Sa 14:2; 2Ki 14:23; Zec 14:5

2 He said:

"The LORD roars from Zion Isa 42:13
 and thunders from
 Jerusalem; Joel 3:16
the pastures of the shepherds
 dry up,
 and the top of Carmel
 withers." Jer 12:4; Am 9:3

Judgment on Israel's Neighbors

3 This is what the LORD says:

"For three sins of Damascus, Isa 8:4; 17:1-3
 even for four, I will not
 relent. Am 2:6
Because she threshed Gilead
 with sledges having iron
 teeth,
4 I will send fire on the house of
 Hazael Jer 49:27
 that will consume the
 fortresses of Ben-Hadad. 2Ki 6:24; Jer 17:27
5 I will break down the gate of
 Damascus; Jer 51:30
 I will destroy the king who is
 in[b] the Valley of Aven[c]
 and the one who holds the
 scepter in Beth Eden.
 The people of Aram will go
 into exile to Kir," 2Ki 16:9
 says the LORD.

6 This is what the LORD says:

"For three sins of Gaza, 1Sa 6:17; Zep 2:4
 even for four, I will not
 relent.
Because she took captive whole
 communities
 and sold them to Edom, Ob 1:11
7 I will send fire on the walls of
 Gaza
 that will consume her
 fortresses.
8 I will destroy the king[d] of
 Ashdod 2Ch 26:6
 and the one who holds the
 scepter in Ashkelon.
I will turn my hand against
 Ekron, Ps 81:14
 till the last of the Philistines
 are dead," Eze 25:16
 says the Sovereign LORD.

9 This is what the LORD says:

"For three sins of Tyre, Isa 23:1-18; Mt 11:21
 even for four, I will not
 relent.

[a] *1* Hebrew *Joash,* a variant of *Jehoash*
[b] *5* Or *the inhabitants of*
[c] *5* *Aven* means *wickedness.*
[d] *8* Or *inhabitants*

Because she sold whole
communities of captives
to Edom,
disregarding a treaty of
brotherhood, 1Ki 5:12
10 I will send fire on the walls of
Tyre
that will consume her
fortresses." Zec 9:1-4

11 This is what the LORD says:

"For three sins of Edom,
Nu 20:14-21; Jer 49:7-22
even for four, I will not
relent.
Because he pursued his brother
with a sword
and slaughtered the women
of the land,
because his anger raged
continually
and his fury flamed
unchecked, Eze 25:12-14
12 I will send fire on Teman Ob 1:9-10
that will consume the
fortresses of Bozrah."
Isa 34:5; 63:1-6

13 This is what the LORD says:

"For three sins of Ammon,
Jer 49:1-6; Eze 21:28; 25:2-7
even for four, I will not
relent.
Because he ripped open the
pregnant women of
Gilead Hos 13:16
in order to extend his borders,
14 I will set fire to the walls of
Rabbah Dt 3:11
that will consume her
fortresses
amid war cries on the day of
battle, Am 2:2
amid violent winds on a
stormy day.
15 Her king[a] will go into exile,
he and his officials together,"
Jer 25:21
says the LORD.

2 This is what the LORD says:

"For three sins of Moab, Isa 16:6
even for four, I will not
relent.
Because he burned to ashes
the bones of Edom's king,
2 I will send fire on Moab
that will consume the
fortresses of Kerioth.[b]
Jer 48:24
Moab will go down in great
tumult
amid war cries and the blast
of the trumpet. Jos 6:20
3 I will destroy her ruler Ps 2:10
and kill all her officials with
him," Isa 40:23
says the LORD.

4 This is what the LORD says:

"For three sins of Judah, 2Ki 17:19
even for four, I will not
relent.
Because they have rejected the
law of the LORD Jer 6:19
and have not kept his
decrees, Eze 20:24
because they have been led
astray by false gods,[c]
Isa 9:16; 28:15

[a] 15 Or / *Molek* [b] 2 Or *of her cities*
[c] 4 Or *by lies*

the gods[a] their ancestors
followed, 2Ki 22:13; Jer 16:12
5 I will send fire on Judah
that will consume the
fortresses of Jerusalem."
Jer 17:27; Hos 8:14

Judgment on Israel

6 This is what the LORD says:

"For three sins of Israel,
even for four, I will not relent.
They sell the innocent for
silver,
and the needy for a pair of
sandals. Joel 3:3; Am 8:6
7 They trample on the heads of
the poor
as on the dust of the ground
and deny justice to the
oppressed.
Father and son use the same
girl
and so profane my holy
name. Am 5:11-12; 8:4
8 They lie down beside every
altar
on garments taken in pledge.
Ex 22:26
In the house of their god
they drink wine taken as
fines. Am 4:1; 6:6
9 "Yet I destroyed the
Amorites before them,
Nu 21:23-26; Jos 10:12
though they were tall as the
cedars
and strong as the oaks. Ps 29:9
I destroyed their fruit above
and their roots below.
Eze 17:9; Mal 4:1

10 I brought you up out of Egypt
Ex 20:2; Am 3:1
and led you forty years in the
wilderness Dt 2:7
to give you the land of the
Amorites. Ex 3:8; Am 9:7
11 "I also raised up prophets from
among your children
Dt 18:18; Jer 7:25
and Nazirites from among
your youths. Nu 6:2-3; Jdg 13:5
Is this not true, people of
Israel?"
declares the LORD.
12 "But you made the Nazirites
drink wine
and commanded
the prophets
not to prophesy.
Isa 30:10; Jer 11:21; Mic 2:6
13 "Now then, I will crush you
as a cart crushes when
loaded with grain.
14 The swift will not escape,
the strong will not muster
their strength, Jer 9:23
and the warrior will not save
his life. Ps 33:16; Isa 30:16-17
15 The archer will not stand his
ground, Eze 39:3
the fleet-footed soldier will
not get away,
and the horseman will not
save his life. Ecc 9:11
16 Even the bravest warriors
Jer 48:41
will flee naked on that day,"
declares the LORD.

[a] 4 Or *lies*

Witnesses Summoned Against Israel

3 Hear this word, people of Israel, the word the LORD has spoken against you — against the whole family I brought up out of Egypt: Am 2:10

2 "You only have I chosen Dt 7:6; Lk 12:47
of all the families of the earth;
therefore I will punish you
for all your sins." Jer 14:10

3 Do two walk together
unless they have agreed to do so?
4 Does a lion roar in the thicket
when it has no prey? Ps 104:21; Hos 5:14
Does it growl in its den
when it has caught nothing?
5 Does a bird swoop down to a trap on the ground
when no bait is there?
Does a trap spring up from the ground
if it has not caught anything?
6 When a trumpet sounds in a city,
do not the people tremble?
When disaster comes to a city,
has not the LORD caused it? Isa 14:24-27; 45:7

7 Surely the Sovereign LORD does nothing
without revealing his plan Ge 18:17; Jn 15:15; Rev 10:7
to his servants the prophets. Jer 23:22

8 The lion has roared —
who will not fear?
The Sovereign LORD has spoken —
who can but prophesy? Jer 20:9; Ac 4:20

9 Proclaim to the fortresses of Ashdod
and to the fortresses of Egypt:
"Assemble yourselves on the mountains of Samaria; Am 4:1; 6:1
see the great unrest within her
and the oppression among her people."

10 "They do not know how to do right," declares the LORD, Jer 4:22; Am 5:7; 6:12
"who store up in their fortresses
what they have plundered and looted." Hab 2:8; Zep 1:9

11 Therefore this is what the Sovereign LORD says:

"An enemy will overrun your land,
pull down your strongholds
and plunder your fortresses." Am 2:5; 6:14

12 This is what the LORD says:

"As a shepherd rescues from the lion's mouth 1Sa 17:34
only two leg bones or a piece of an ear,

so will the Israelites living in
Samaria be rescued,
with only the head of a bed
and a piece of fabric[a] from a
couch.[b]" Am 6:4

13 "Hear this and testify against
the descendants of Jacob," declares the Lord, the LORD God Almighty. Eze 2:7

14 "On the day I punish Israel for
her sins,
I will destroy the altars of
Bethel; Am 5:5-6
the horns of the altar will be
cut off
and fall to the ground.
15 I will tear down the winter
house Jer 36:22
along with the summer
house; Jdg 3:20
the houses adorned with ivory
will be destroyed 1Ki 22:39
and the mansions will be
demolished," Isa 34:5
declares the LORD.

Israel Has Not Returned to God

4 Hear this word, you cows
of Bashan on Mount
Samaria, Ps 22:12; Am 3:9
you women who oppress
the poor and crush the
needy Dt 24:14
and say to your husbands,
"Bring us some drinks!"
Am 2:8; 5:11; 8:6
2 The Sovereign LORD has sworn
by his holiness:
"The time will surely come
Jer 31:31
when you will be taken away
with hooks, Am 6:8
the last of you with
fishhooks.[c]
3 You will each go straight out
through breaches in the wall,
Eze 12:5
and you will be cast out
toward Harmon,[d]"
declares the LORD.
4 "Go to Bethel and sin;
go to Gilgal and sin yet more.
Hos 4:15
Bring your sacrifices every
morning, Nu 28:3
your tithes every three years.[e]
Dt 14:28; Eze 20:39; Am 5:21-22
5 Burn leavened bread as a thank
offering Lev 7:13
and brag about your freewill
offerings — Lev 22:18-21
boast about them, you Israelites,
for this is what you love to do,"
declares the Sovereign
LORD.

6 "I gave you empty stomachs in
every city
and lack of bread in every
town,
yet you have not returned
to me,"
declares the LORD.

[a] 12 The meaning of the Hebrew for this phrase is uncertain. [b] 12 Or *Israelites be rescued, / those who sit in Samaria / on the edge of their beds / and in Damascus on their couches.* [c] 2 Or *away in baskets, / the last of you in fish baskets*
[d] 3 Masoretic Text; with a different word division of the Hebrew (see Septuagint) *out, you mountain of oppression*
[e] 4 Or *days*

7"I also withheld rain from
you
when the harvest was still
three months away.
I sent rain on one town,
but withheld it from another.
Dt 11:17; 2Ch 7:13
One field had rain;
another had none and dried
up.
8 People staggered from town to
town for water Eze 4:16-17
but did not get enough to
drink,
yet you have not returned to
me," Jer 3:7
declares the LORD.

9"Many times I struck your
gardens and vineyards,
destroying them with
blight and mildew.
Dt 28:22
Locusts devoured your fig and
olive trees, Joel 1:7
yet you have not returned to
me," Jer 3:10; Hag 2:17
declares the LORD.

10"I sent plagues among you
Ex 9:3; Dt 28:27
as I did to Egypt. Ex 11:5
I killed your young men with
the sword, Isa 9:17
along with your captured
horses.
I filled your nostrils with the
stench of your camps,
Isa 34:3
yet you have not returned to
me," Dt 28:21
declares the LORD.

11"I overthrew some of you
as I overthrew Sodom
and Gomorrah.
Ge 19:24; Jer 23:14
You were like a burning stick
snatched from the fire,
Isa 7:4
yet you have not returned to
me,"
declares the LORD.

12"Therefore this is what I will do
to you, Israel,
and because I will do this to
you, Israel,
prepare to meet your God."

13 He who forms the mountains,
Ps 65:6
who creates the wind,
and who reveals his
thoughts to mankind,
Da 2:28
who turns dawn to darkness,
and treads on the heights of
the earth — Mic 1:3
the LORD God Almighty is
his name.
Isa 47:4; Am 5:8,27; 9:6

A Lament and Call to Repentance

5 Hear this word, Israel, this lament I take up concerning you:
Eze 19:1

2"Fallen is Virgin Israel, Jer 14:17
never to rise again,
deserted in her own land,
with no one to lift her up."
Jer 50:32; Am 8:14

3 This is what the Sovereign LORD
says to Israel:

"Your city that marches out a thousand strong
will have only a hundred left;
your town that marches out a hundred strong
will have only ten left." Isa 6:13; Am 6:9

4 This is what the LORD says to
Israel:

"Seek me and live; Isa 55:3; Jer 29:13
5 do not seek Bethel,
do not go to Gilgal, Am 4:4
do not journey to Beersheba. Am 8:14
For Gilgal will surely go into exile,
and Bethel will be reduced to nothing.[a]" 1Sa 7:16
6 Seek the LORD and live, Isa 55:6
or he will sweep through the tribes of Joseph like a fire; Dt 4:24
it will devour them,
and Bethel will have no one to quench it. Am 3:14
7 There are those who turn justice into bitterness Am 6:12
and cast righteousness to the ground. Hos 10:4
8 He who made the Pleiades and Orion, Job 9:9
who turns midnight into dawn Isa 42:16
and darkens day into night, Ps 104:20; Am 8:9
who calls for the waters of the sea
and pours them out over the face of the land —
the LORD is his name. Ps 104:6-9; Am 4:13
9 With a blinding flash he destroys the stronghold
and brings the fortified city to ruin. Mic 5:11
10 There are those who hate the one who upholds justice in court Isa 29:21
and detest the one who tells the truth. 1Ki 22:8
11 You levy a straw tax on the poor Am 8:6
and impose a tax on their grain.
Therefore, though you have built stone mansions, Am 3:15
you will not live in them; Mic 1:6
though you have planted lush vineyards,
you will not drink their wine. Mic 6:15
12 For I know how many are your offenses
and how great your sins. Hos 5:3

There are those who oppress the innocent and take bribes
and deprive the poor of justice in the courts. Isa 5:23; Am 2:6-7

[a] 5 Hebrew *aven*, a reference to Beth Aven (a derogatory name for Bethel); see Hosea 4:15.

13 Therefore the prudent keep
quiet in such times,
for the times are evil. Mic 2:3

14 Seek good, not evil,
that you may live. ver 6
Then the LORD God Almighty
will be with you,
just as you say he is.
15 Hate evil, love good; Ro 12:9
maintain justice in the
courts. Isa 1:17
Perhaps the LORD God
Almighty will have
mercy Joel 2:14
on the remnant of Joseph.
Mic 5:7-8

16 Therefore this is what the Lord, the LORD God Almighty, says:

"There will be wailing in all the
streets Jer 9:17
and cries of anguish in every
public square.
The farmers will be summoned
to weep Joel 1:11
and the mourners to wail.
17 There will be wailing in all the
vineyards,
for I will pass through your
midst," Ex 12:12
says the LORD.

The Day of the LORD

18 Woe to you who long
for the day of the LORD!
Joel 1:15
Why do you long for the day of
the LORD?
That day will be darkness,
not light. Isa 5:19,30; Joel 2:2
19 It will be as though a man fled
from a lion
only to meet a bear,
as though he entered his
house
and rested his hand on the
wall
only to have a snake bite
him. Job 20:24; Jer 48:44
20 Will not the day of the LORD be
darkness, not light—
pitch-dark, without a ray
of brightness?
Isa 13:10; Zep 1:15

21 "I hate, I despise your religious
festivals; Lev 26:31
your assemblies are a stench
to me. Isa 1:11-16
22 Even though you bring me
burnt offerings and
grain offerings,
I will not accept them. Ps 40:6
Though you bring choice
fellowship offerings,
I will have no regard for
them. Isa 66:3; Mic 6:6-7
23 Away with the noise of your
songs!
I will not listen to the music
of your harps. Am 6:5
24 But let justice roll on like a
river, Jer 22:3
righteousness like a never-
failing stream! Mic 6:8

25 "Did you bring me sacrifices
and offerings Isa 43:23
forty years in the wilderness,
people of Israel? Dt 32:17
26 You have lifted up the shrine of
your king,

the pedestal of your idols,
the star of your god[a] —
which you made for
yourselves.
27 Therefore I will send you
into exile beyond
Damascus,"
says the LORD, whose
name is God Almighty.
Am 4:13; Ac 7:42-43*

Woe to the Complacent

6 Woe to you who are
complacent in Zion,
Lk 6:24
and to you who feel secure
on Mount Samaria, Am 3:9
you notable men of the
foremost nation,
to whom the people of Israel
come! Isa 32:9-11
2 Go to Kalneh and look at it;
Ge 10:10
go from there to great
Hamath, 2Ki 18:34
and then go down to Gath in
Philistia. 2Ch 26:6
Are they better off than your
two kingdoms? Na 3:8
Is their land larger than
yours?
3 You put off the day of disaster
and bring near a reign of
terror. Isa 56:12; Am 9:10
4 You lie on beds adorned with
ivory
and lounge on your
couches.
You dine on choice lambs
and fattened calves.
Eze 34:2-3; Am 3:12
5 You strum away on your harps
like David Isa 5:12; Am 5:23
and improvise on musical
instruments. 1Ch 15:16
6 You drink wine by the bowlful
Am 2:8
and use the finest lotions,
but you do not grieve
over the ruin of Joseph.
Eze 9:4
7 Therefore you will be among
the first to go into exile;
Am 5:27
your feasting and lounging
will end. Jer 16:9

The LORD Abhors the Pride of Israel

8 The Sovereign LORD has sworn
by himself — the LORD God Almighty declares: Ge 22:16; Heb 6:13

"I abhor the pride of Jacob
Ps 47:4
and detest his fortresses;
I will deliver up the city Am 4:2
and everything in it." Dt 32:19

9 If ten people are left in one
house, they too will die. 10 And
if the relative who comes to carry the bodies out of the house
to burn them[b] asks anyone who
might be hiding there, "Is anyone
else with you?" and he says, "No,"
then he will go on to say, "Hush!
We must not mention the name of
the LORD." Am 5:3; 8:3; 1Sa 31:12

[a] 26 Or *lifted up Sakkuth your king / and Kaiwan your idols, / your star-gods;* Septuagint *lifted up the shrine of Molek / and the star of your god Rephan, / their idols* [b] 10 Or *to make a funeral fire in honor of the dead*

11 For the LORD has given the command,
and he will smash the great house into pieces Am 3:15
and the small house into bits. Isa 55:11

12 Do horses run on the rocky crags?
Does one plow the sea[a] with oxen?
But you have turned justice into poison Hos 10:4
and the fruit of righteousness into bitterness — Am 5:7
13 you who rejoice in the conquest of Lo Debar[b]
and say, "Did we not take Karnaim[c] by our own strength?" Job 8:15; Isa 28:14-15

14 For the LORD God Almighty declares,
"I will stir up a nation against you, Israel, Jer 5:15
that will oppress you all the way from Lebo Hamath to the valley of the Arabah." 1Ki 8:65; Am 3:11

Locusts, Fire and a Plumb Line

7 This is what the Sovereign
LORD showed me: He was preparing swarms of locusts after
the king's share had been harvested and just as the late crops
were coming up. 2 When they had
stripped the land clean, I cried out,
"Sovereign LORD, forgive! How can
Jacob survive? He is so small!"
Isa 37:4; Eze 11:13

3 So the LORD relented.
Dt 32:36; Jnh 3:10
"This will not happen," the LORD
said. Hos 11:8
4 This is what the Sovereign
LORD showed me: The Sovereign
LORD was calling for judgment by
fire; it dried up the great deep and
devoured the land. 5 Then I cried
out, "Sovereign LORD, I beg you,
stop! How can Jacob survive? He
is so small!" Joel 2:17
6 So the LORD relented. Jnh 3:10
"This will not happen either,"
the Sovereign LORD said. Eze 9:8

7 This is what he showed me: The
Lord was standing by a wall that
had been built true to plumb,[d]
with a plumb line[e] in his hand.
8 And the LORD asked me, "What
do you see, Amos?" Am 8:2
"A plumb line," I replied. 2Ki 21:13
Then the Lord said, "Look, I am
setting a plumb line among my
people Israel; I will spare them no
longer. Jer 15:6; Eze 7:2-9

9 "The high places of Isaac will be destroyed
and the sanctuaries of Israel will be ruined; Lev 26:31
with my sword I will rise against the house of Jeroboam." 2Ki 15:9; Hos 10:8

[a] 12 With a different word division of the Hebrew; Masoretic Text *plow there*
[b] 13 *Lo Debar* means *nothing.*
[c] 13 *Karnaim* means *horns; horn* here symbolizes strength.
[d] 7 The meaning of the Hebrew for this phrase is uncertain.
[e] 7 The meaning of the Hebrew for this phrase is uncertain; also in verse 8.

Amos and Amaziah

[10]Then Amaziah the priest of
Bethel sent a message to Jeroboam king of Israel: "Amos is raising
a conspiracy against you in the
very heart of Israel. The land cannot bear all his words. [11]For this is
what Amos is saying:
1Ki 12:32; 2Ki 14:23

"'Jeroboam will die by the
sword,
and Israel will surely go into
exile, Am 5:27
away from their native
land.'" Jer 36:16

[12]Then Amaziah said to Amos,
"Get out, you seer! Go back to the
land of Judah. Earn your bread
there and do your prophesying
there. [13]Don't prophesy anymore
at Bethel, because this is the king's
sanctuary and the temple of the
kingdom." Am 2:12; Ac 4:18
[14]Amos answered Amaziah, "I
was neither a prophet nor the son
of a prophet, but I was a shepherd,
and I also took care of sycamore-
fig trees. [15]But the LORD took me
from tending the flock and said to
me, 'Go, prophesy to my people Israel.' [16]Now then, hear the word of
the LORD. You say, 2Ki 2:5; Eze 2:3-4

"'Do not prophesy against
Israel, Eze 20:46; Mic 2:6
and stop preaching against
the descendants of
Isaac.'

[17]"Therefore this is what the
LORD says:

"'Your wife will become a
prostitute in the city,
Hos 4:13
and your sons and daughters
will fall by the sword.
Your land will be measured
and divided up,
and you yourself will die in a
pagan[a] country.
And Israel will surely go into
exile,
away from their native
land.'" Eze 4:13; Hos 9:3

A Basket of Ripe Fruit

8 This is what the Sovereign
LORD showed me: a basket
of ripe fruit. [2]"What do you see,
Amos?" he asked. Am 7:8
"A basket of ripe fruit," I answered. Ge 40:16
Then the LORD said to me, "The
time is ripe for my people Israel; I
will spare them no longer. Eze 7:2-9
[3]"In that day," declares the Sovereign LORD, "the songs in the
temple will turn to wailing.[b] Many,
many bodies — flung everywhere!
Silence!" Am 5:16; 6:10

[4]Hear this, you who trample the
needy
and do away with the poor of
the land, Ps 14:4; Pr 30:14

[5]saying,

"When will the New Moon be
over
that we may sell grain,

[a] 17 Hebrew *an unclean* [b] 3 Or *"the temple singers will wail*

and the Sabbath be ended
that we may market
wheat?" —
skimping on the measure,
boosting the price
and cheating with
dishonest scales,
Ne 13:15-16; Mic 6:10-11
6 buying the poor with silver
and the needy for a pair of
sandals,
selling even the sweepings
with the wheat. Am 2:6

7 The LORD has sworn by himself, the Pride of Jacob: "I will never forget anything they have done.
Hos 8:13; Am 6:8

8 "Will not the land tremble for
this, Hos 4:3
and all who live in it
mourn?
The whole land will rise like
the Nile;
it will be stirred up and then
sink
like the river of Egypt.
Jer 46:8; Am 9:5

9 "In that day," declares the Sovereign LORD,

"I will make the sun go down
at noon
and darken the earth
in broad daylight.
Jer 15:9; Mic 3:6
10 I will turn your religious
festivals into
mourning
and all your singing into
weeping.
I will make all of you wear
sackcloth Jer 48:37
and shave your heads.
I will make that time like
mourning for an only
son Jer 6:26; Zec 12:10
and the end of it like a bitter
day. Eze 7:18

11 "The days are coming," declares
the Sovereign LORD,
1Sa 3:1; 2Ch 15:3
"when I will send a famine
through the land —
not a famine of food or a thirst
for water,
but a famine of hearing the
words of the LORD.
12 People will stagger from sea to
sea
and wander from north to
east,
searching for the word of the
LORD,
but they will not find it.
Eze 20:3,31

13 "In that day

"the lovely young women and
strong young men
will faint because of thirst.
Isa 41:17; Hos 2:3
14 Those who swear by the sin of
Samaria —
who say, 'As surely as your
god lives, Dan,' 1Ki 12:29
or, 'As surely as the god[a] of
Beersheba lives' — Am 5:5
they will fall, never to rise
again." Am 5:2

[a] 14 Hebrew *the way*

Israel to Be Destroyed

9 I saw the Lord standing by the altar, and he said:

"Strike the tops of the pillars
so that the thresholds shake.
Bring them down on the heads of all the people; Ps 68:21
those who are left I will kill with the sword.
Not one will get away,
none will escape.
2Though they dig down to the depths below, Ps 139:8
from there my hand will take them.
Though they climb up to the heavens above, Jer 51:53
from there I will bring them down. Ob 1:4
3Though they hide themselves on the top of Carmel, Am 1:2
there I will hunt them down and seize them. Ps 139:8-10
Though they hide from my eyes at the bottom of the sea,
there I will command the serpent to bite them. Jer 16:16-17
4Though they are driven into exile by their enemies,
there I will command the sword to slay them. Lev 26:33; Eze 5:12

"I will keep my eye on them
for harm and not for good." Jer 21:10; 39:16

5The Lord, the LORD Almighty —
he touches the earth and it melts, Ps 46:2; Mic 1:4
and all who live in it mourn;
the whole land rises like the Nile,
then sinks like the river of Egypt; Am 8:8
6he builds his lofty palace[a] in the heavens
and sets its foundation[b] on the earth;
he calls for the waters of the sea
and pours them out over the face of the land —
the LORD is his name. Ps 104:1-3,5-6,13; Am 5:8

7"Are not you Israelites
the same to me as the Cushites[c]?" Isa 20:4; 43:3
declares the LORD.
"Did I not bring Israel up from Egypt,
the Philistines from Caphtor[d] Dt 2:23
and the Arameans from Kir? Isa 22:6; Am 1:5; 2:10

8"Surely the eyes of the Sovereign LORD
are on the sinful kingdom.
I will destroy it
from the face of the earth.

[a] 6 The meaning of the Hebrew for this phrase is uncertain. [b] 6 The meaning of the Hebrew for this word is uncertain. [c] 7 That is, people from the upper Nile region [d] 7 That is, Crete

Yet I will not totally destroy
the descendants of Jacob,"
declares the LORD.
9 "For I will give the command,
and I will shake the people of
Israel
among all the nations
as grain is shaken in a sieve,
Isa 30:28; Lk 22:31
and not a pebble will reach
the ground.
10 All the sinners among my
people
will die by the sword,
all those who say,
'Disaster will not overtake or
meet us.' Am 6:3

Israel's Restoration

11 "In that day

"I will restore David's fallen
shelter — Isa 7:2
I will repair its broken walls
and restore its ruins — Ps 53:6
and will rebuild it as it used
to be, Ps 80:12
12 so that they may possess the
remnant of Edom Nu 24:18
and all the nations that bear
my name,[a]"
Isa 43:7
declares the LORD,
who will do these things.

13 "The days are coming," declares
the LORD,

"when the reaper will be
overtaken by the
plowman Lev 26:5
and the planter by the one
treading grapes.
New wine will drip from the
mountains
and flow from all the hills,
Joel 3:18
14 and I will bring my people
Israel back from exile.[b]
Jer 33:7

"They will rebuild the ruined
cities and live in them.
Isa 61:4
They will plant vineyards
and drink their wine;
they will make gardens and
eat their fruit. Jer 30:18; 31:28
15 I will plant Israel in their own
land, Isa 60:21
never again to be uprooted
from the land I have given
them," Isa 65:9

says the LORD your God.

[a] 12 Hebrew; Septuagint *so that the remnant of people / and all the nations that bear my name may seek me* [b] 14 Or *will restore the fortunes of my people Israel*

OBADIAH

Obadiah's Vision

[1]The vision of Obadiah.

This is what the Sovereign LORD says about Edom — Jer 49:7-22; Eze 25:12-14

We have heard a message from
the LORD:
An envoy was sent to the
nations to say, Isa 18:2
"Rise, let us go against her for
battle" — Jer 6:4-5

[2]"See, I will make you small
among the nations;
you will be utterly despised.
[3]The pride of your heart has
deceived you, Isa 16:6
you who live in the clefts of
the rocks[a]
and make your home on the
heights,
you who say to yourself,
'Who can bring me down
to the ground?'
Isa 14:13-15; Rev 18:7
[4]Though you soar like the eagle
and make your nest among
the stars, Hab 2:9
from there I will bring you
down," Jer 49:14-16; Isa 14:13
declares the LORD.
[5]"If thieves came to you,
if robbers in the night —
oh, what a disaster awaits
you! —
would they not steal only as
much as they wanted?
If grape pickers came to you,
would they not leave a few
grapes? Jer 49:9-10
[6]But how Esau will be
ransacked,
his hidden treasures
pillaged!
[7]All your allies will force you to
the border; Jer 30:14
your friends will deceive and
overpower you;
those who eat your bread will
set a trap for you,[b] Ps 41:9
but you will not detect it.

[8]"In that day," declares the
LORD,
"will I not destroy the
wise men of Edom,
Job 5:12; Isa 29:14
those of understanding
in the mountains of
Esau?
[9]Your warriors, Teman, will be
terrified, Ge 36:11,34
and everyone in Esau's
mountains
will be cut down in the
slaughter.
[10]Because of the violence against
your brother Jacob,
Joel 3:19; Am 1:11-12

[a] 3 Or *of Sela* [b] 7 The meaning of the Hebrew for this clause is uncertain.

you will be covered with
shame;
you will be destroyed
forever. Eze 35:9
11 On the day you stood aloof
while strangers carried off
his wealth
and foreigners entered his
gates
and cast lots for Jerusalem, Na 3:10
you were like one of them.
12 You should not gloat over your
brother Pr 24:17
in the day of his misfortune, Job 31:29
nor rejoice over the people of
Judah Eze 35:15
in the day of their
destruction, Pr 17:5
nor boast so much Ps 137:7
in the day of their trouble. Mic 4:11
13 You should not march
through the gates
of my people
in the day of their disaster,
nor gloat over them in their
calamity Eze 35:5
in the day of their disaster,
nor seize their wealth
in the day of their disaster.
14 You should not wait at the
crossroads
to cut down their fugitives,
nor hand over their survivors
in the day of their trouble.

15 "The day of the LORD is near Eze 30:3
for all nations.
As you have done, it will be
done to you;
your deeds will return
upon your own head. Jer 50:29; Hab 2:8
16 Just as you drank on my holy
hill,
so all the nations will
drink continually; Jer 25:15; 49:12
they will drink and drink
and be as if they had never
been.
17 But on Mount Zion will be
deliverance; Am 9:11-15
it will be holy, Isa 4:3
and Jacob will possess his
inheritance. Zec 8:12
18 Jacob will be a fire
and Joseph a flame;
Esau will be stubble,
and they will set him on
fire and destroy him. Zec 12:6
There will be no survivors Jer 49:10
from Esau."
The LORD has spoken.
19 People from the Negev will
occupy
the mountains of Esau,
and people from the foothills
will possess
the land of the Philistines. Isa 11:14
They will occupy the fields of
Ephraim and Samaria, Jer 31:5
and Benjamin will possess
Gilead.

20 This company of Israelite
exiles who are in Canaan
will possess the land as far as
Zarephath; 1Ki 17:9-10
the exiles from Jerusalem who
are in Sepharad
will possess the towns of the
Negev. Jer 33:13

21 Deliverers will go up on[a]
Mount Zion
to govern the mountains of
Esau.
And the kingdom will be the
LORD's. Zec 14:9,16; Rev 11:15

[a] 21 Or *from*

JONAH

Jonah Flees From the LORD

1 The word of the LORD came to Jonah son of Amittai: 2 "Go to the great city of Nineveh and preach against it, because its wickedness has come up before me."

Ge 10:11; Mt 12:39-41

3 But Jonah ran away from the LORD and headed for Tarshish. He went down to Joppa, where he found a ship bound for that port. After paying the fare, he went aboard and sailed for Tarshish to flee from the LORD.

Jos 19:46; Ps 139:7; Ac 9:36,43

4 Then the LORD sent a great wind on the sea, and such a violent storm arose that the ship threatened to break up. 5 All the sailors were afraid and each cried out to his own god. And they threw the cargo into the sea to lighten the ship. Ps 107:23-26; Ac 27:18-19

But Jonah had gone below deck, where he lay down and fell into a deep sleep. 6 The captain went to him and said, "How can you sleep? Get up and call on your god! Maybe he will take notice of us so that we will not perish." Jnh 3:8; Ps 107:28

7 Then the sailors said to each other, "Come, let us cast lots to find out who is responsible for this calamity." They cast lots and the lot fell on Jonah. 8 So they asked him, "Tell us, who is responsible for making all this trouble for us? What kind of work do you do? Where do you come from? What is your country? From what people are you?" Jos 7:10-18; 1Sa 14:42

9 He answered, "I am a Hebrew and I worship the LORD, the God of heaven, who made the sea and the dry land." Ps 146:6; Ac 17:24

10 This terrified them and they asked, "What have you done?" (They knew he was running away from the LORD, because he had already told them so.)

11 The sea was getting rougher and rougher. So they asked him, "What should we do to you to make the sea calm down for us?"

12 "Pick me up and throw me into the sea," he replied, "and it will become calm. I know that it is my fault that this great storm has come upon you." 2Sa 24:17; 1Ch 21:17

13 Instead, the men did their best to row back to land. But they could not, for the sea grew even wilder than before. 14 Then they cried out to the LORD, "Please, LORD, do not let us die for taking this man's life. Do not hold us accountable for killing an innocent man, for you, LORD, have done as you pleased." 15 Then they took Jonah and threw him overboard, and the raging sea grew calm. 16 At this the men greatly feared the LORD, and they

offered a sacrifice to the LORD and
made vows to him. Lk 8:24; Dt 21:8

Jonah's Prayer

17 Now the LORD provided a huge
fish to swallow Jonah, and Jonah
was in the belly of the fish three
2 [a] days and three nights. 1 From
inside the fish Jonah prayed
to the LORD his God. 2 He said:
Mt 12:40; 16:4; Lk 11:30

"In my distress I called to the
LORD, Ps 18:6; 120:1
and he answered me.
From deep in the realm of the
dead I called for help,
and you listened to my cry.
3 You hurled me into the depths, Ps 88:6
into the very heart of the seas,
and the currents swirled
about me;
all your waves and breakers
swept over me. Ps 42:7
4 I said, 'I have been banished
from your sight; Ps 31:22
yet I will look again
toward your holy temple.'
5 The engulfing waters
threatened me,[b]
the deep surrounded me;
seaweed was wrapped
around my head. Ps 69:1-2
6 To the roots of the mountains I
sank down;
the earth beneath barred me
in forever.
But you, LORD my God,
brought my life up from
the pit. Ps 30:3
7 "When my life was ebbing
away,
I remembered you, LORD, Ps 77:11-12
and my prayer rose to you, 2Ch 30:27
to your holy temple. Ps 18:6
8 "Those who cling to
worthless idols 2Ki 17:15; Jer 10:8
turn away from God's love
for them.
9 But I, with shouts of grateful
praise,
will sacrifice to you. Ps 50:14,23
What I have vowed I will make
good. Ecc 5:4-5
I will say, 'Salvation comes
from the LORD.'" Ps 3:8

10 And the LORD commanded the
fish, and it vomited Jonah onto
dry land.

Jonah Goes to Nineveh

3 Then the word of the LORD
came to Jonah a second time:
2 "Go to the great city of Nineveh
and proclaim to it the message I
give you." Jnh 1:1
3 Jonah obeyed the word of the
LORD and went to Nineveh. Now
Nineveh was a very large city; it
took three days to go through it.
4 Jonah began by going a day's
journey into the city, proclaiming, "Forty more days and Nineveh will be overthrown." 5 The

[a] In Hebrew texts 2:1 is numbered 1:17, and 2:1-10 is numbered 2:2-11. [b] 5 Or *waters were at my throat*

Ninevites believed God. A fast was
proclaimed, and all of them, from
the greatest to the least, put on
sackcloth. Da 9:3; Lk 11:32
6When Jonah's warning reached
the king of Nineveh, he rose from
his throne, took off his royal robes,
covered himself with sackcloth
and sat down in the dust. 7This
is the proclamation he issued in
Nineveh: Job 2:8,13; Eze 27:30-31

"By the decree of the king and
his nobles:

Do not let people or ani-
mals, herds or flocks, taste
anything; do not let them eat
or drink. 8But let people and
animals be covered with sackcloth. Let everyone call urgently on God. Let them give
up their evil ways and their
violence. 9Who knows? God
may yet relent and with compassion turn from his fierce
anger so that we will not perish." Joel 2:14; Jnh 1:6

10When God saw what they did
and how they turned from their
evil ways, he relented and did not
bring on them the destruction he
had threatened. Jer 18:8; Am 7:6

Jonah's Anger at the LORD's Compassion

4 But to Jonah this seemed very
wrong, and he became angry.
2He prayed to the LORD, "Isn't this
what I said, LORD, when I was still
at home? That is what I tried to
forestall by fleeing to Tarshish. I
knew that you are a gracious and
compassionate God, slow to anger and abounding in love, a God
who relents from sending calamity. 3Now, LORD, take away my life,
for it is better for me to die than to
live." 1Ki 19:4; Ps 86:5,15
4But the LORD replied, "Is it right
for you to be angry?" Mt 20:11-15
5Jonah had gone out and sat
down at a place east of the city.
There he made himself a shelter,
sat in its shade and waited to see
what would happen to the city.
6Then the LORD God provided
a leafy plant[a] and made it grow
up over Jonah to give shade for
his head to ease his discomfort,
and Jonah was very happy about
the plant. 7But at dawn the next
day God provided a worm, which
chewed the plant so that it withered. 8When the sun rose, God
provided a scorching east wind,
and the sun blazed on Jonah's
head so that he grew faint. He
wanted to die, and said, "It would
be better for me to die than to
live." Joel 1:12
9But God said to Jonah, "Is it
right for you to be angry about the
plant?"

"It is," he said. "And I'm so angry I wish I were dead."

10But the LORD said, "You have
been concerned about this plant,
though you did not tend it or make

[a] 6 The precise identification of this plant is uncertain; also in verses 7, 9 and 10.

it grow. It sprang up overnight and
died overnight. [11]And should I not
have concern for the great city of
Nineveh, in which there are more
than a hundred and twenty thousand people who cannot tell their
right hand from their left — and
also many animals?" Jnh 1:2; 3:10

MICAH

1 The word of the LORD that came
to Micah of Moresheth during
the reigns of Jotham, Ahaz and
Hezekiah, kings of Judah — the
vision he saw concerning Samaria
and Jerusalem. Jer 26:18; Hos 1:1

2 Hear, you peoples, all of you, Ps 50:7
listen, earth and all who live in it, Jer 6:19
that the Sovereign LORD may bear witness against you, Dt 4:26
the Lord from his holy temple. Ps 11:4

Judgment Against Samaria and Jerusalem

3 Look! The LORD is coming from his dwelling place; Isa 18:4
he comes down and treads on the heights of the earth. Am 4:13
4 The mountains melt beneath him Ps 46:2,6
and the valleys split apart, Nu 16:31; Na 1:5
like wax before the fire,
like water rushing down a slope.
5 All this is because of Jacob's transgression,
because of the sins of the people of Israel.
What is Jacob's transgression?
Is it not Samaria? Am 8:14
What is Judah's high place?
Is it not Jerusalem?

6 "Therefore I will make Samaria a heap of rubble,
a place for planting vineyards.
I will pour her stones into the valley Am 5:11
and lay bare her foundations. Eze 13:14
7 All her idols will be broken to pieces; Eze 6:6
all her temple gifts will be burned with fire;
I will destroy all her images. Dt 9:21
Since she gathered her gifts from the wages of prostitutes, Dt 23:17-18
as the wages of prostitutes they will again be used."

Weeping and Mourning

8 Because of this I will weep and wail; Isa 15:3
I will go about barefoot and naked.
I will howl like a jackal
and moan like an owl.
9 For Samaria's plague is incurable; Jer 46:11
it has spread to Judah. 2Ki 18:13
It has reached the very gate of my people, Isa 3:26
even to Jerusalem itself.

10 Tell it not in Gath[a];
weep not at all.
In Beth Ophrah[b]
roll in the dust.
11 Pass by naked and in shame, Eze 23:29
you who live in Shaphir.[c]
Those who live in Zaanan[d]
will not come out.
Beth Ezel is in mourning;
it no longer protects you.
12 Those who live in Maroth[e]
writhe in pain,
waiting for relief, Jer 14:19
because disaster has come
from the LORD, Jer 40:2
even to the gate of
Jerusalem.
13 You who live in Lachish, Jos 10:3
harness fast horses to the
chariot.
You are where the sin of
Daughter Zion began, Ps 9:14
for the transgressions of
Israel were found in
you.
14 Therefore you will give parting
gifts 2Ki 16:8
to Moresheth Gath.
The town of Akzib[f] will prove
deceptive Jos 15:44; Jer 15:18
to the kings of Israel.
15 I will bring a conqueror against
you
who live in Mareshah.[g] Jos 15:44
The nobles of Israel
will flee to Adullam. Jos 12:15
16 Shave your head in mourning Job 1:20
for the children in whom you
delight;
make yourself as bald as the
vulture,
for they will go from you into
exile. Am 5:27

Human Plans and God's Plans

2 Woe to those who plan
iniquity,
to those who plot evil on
their beds! Ps 36:4
At morning's light they carry it
out
because it is in their power to
do it.
2 They covet fields and seize
them, Isa 5:8
and houses, and take them.
They defraud people of their
homes, Jer 22:17
they rob them of their
inheritance. Eze 46:18

3 Therefore, the LORD says:

"I am planning disaster
against this people, Jer 18:11; Am 3:1-2
from which you cannot save
yourselves.
You will no longer walk
proudly, Isa 2:12
for it will be a time of
calamity.

[a] 10 *Gath* sounds like the Hebrew for *tell.*
[b] 10 *Beth Ophrah* means *house of dust.*
[c] 11 *Shaphir* means *pleasant.*
[d] 11 *Zaanan* sounds like the Hebrew for *come out.*
[e] 12 *Maroth* sounds like the Hebrew for *bitter.*
[f] 14 *Akzib* means *deception.*
[g] 15 *Mareshah* sounds like the Hebrew for *conqueror.*

4 In that day people will ridicule you;
they will taunt you with this mournful song:
'We are utterly ruined; Jer 4:13
my people's possession is divided up.
He takes it from me!
He assigns our fields to traitors.'"

5 Therefore you will have no one in the assembly of the LORD
to divide the land by lot. Jos 18:4

False Prophets

6 "Do not prophesy," their prophets say.
"Do not prophesy about these things;
disgrace will not overtake us." Am 2:12; Mic 6:16
7 You descendants of Jacob, should it be said,
"Does the LORD become[a] impatient?
Does he do such things?"

"Do not my words do good Ps 119:65
to the one whose ways are upright? Ps 15:2; 84:11
8 Lately my people have risen up
like an enemy.
You strip off the rich robe
from those who pass by without a care,
like men returning from battle.
9 You drive the women of my people
from their pleasant homes. Jer 10:20
You take away my blessing
from their children forever.
10 Get up, go away!
For this is not your resting place, Dt 12:9
because it is defiled, Lev 18:25-29; Ps 106:38-39
it is ruined, beyond all remedy.
11 If a liar and deceiver comes and says, Jer 5:31
'I will prophesy for you plenty of wine and beer,'
that would be just the prophet for this people! Isa 30:10

Deliverance Promised

12 "I will surely gather all of you, Jacob;
I will surely bring together the remnant of Israel. Mic 4:7; 5:7; 7:18
I will bring them together like sheep in a pen,
like a flock in its pasture;
the place will throng with people.
13 The One who breaks open the way will go up before them; Isa 52:12
they will break through the gate and go out.
Their King will pass through before them,
the LORD at their head."

[a] 7 Or *Is the Spirit of the LORD*

Leaders and Prophets Rebuked

3 Then I said,

"Listen, you leaders of Jacob, Jer 5:5
you rulers of Israel.
Should you not embrace
justice,
2 you who hate good and love
evil;
who tear the skin from my
people
and the flesh from their
bones; Ps 53:4; Eze 22:27
3 who eat my people's flesh, Ps 14:4
strip off their skin
and break their bones in
pieces; Zep 3:3
who chop them up like meat
for the pan, Job 24:14
like flesh for the pot?" Eze 11:7

4 Then they will cry out to the
LORD,
but he will not answer them.
Ps 18:41; Isa 1:15
At that time he will hide his
face from them Dt 31:17
because of the evil they have
done. Eze 8:18

5 This is what the LORD says:

"As for the prophets
who lead my people astray,
Isa 3:12; 9:16
they proclaim 'peace' Jer 4:10
if they have something to
eat,
but prepare to wage war
against anyone
who refuses to feed them.
6 Therefore night will come
over you, without
visions,
and darkness, without
divination. Isa 8:19-22
The sun will set for the
prophets, Isa 29:10
and the day will go dark for
them. Eze 7:26
7 The seers will be ashamed
Mic 7:16
and the diviners disgraced.
Isa 44:25
They will all cover their faces
Lev 13:45
because there is no answer
from God." Eze 20:3
8 But as for me, I am filled with
power,
with the Spirit of the LORD,
and with justice and might,
to declare to Jacob his
transgression,
to Israel his sin. Isa 58:1
9 Hear this, you leaders of Jacob,
you rulers of Israel,
who despise justice
and distort all that is right;
Ps 58:1-2; Isa 1:23
10 who build Zion with bloodshed,
Jer 22:13; Hab 2:12
and Jerusalem with
wickedness. Eze 22:27
11 Her leaders judge for a bribe,
Mal 2:9
her priests teach for a price,
Eze 13:19
and her prophets tell
fortunes for money.
Isa 1:23; Jer 6:13; Hos 4:8,18

Yet they look for the LORD's
support and say,
"Is not the LORD among us?
No disaster will come upon
us." Jer 7:4
12 Therefore because of you,
Zion will be plowed like a
field,
Jerusalem will become a heap
of rubble, Jer 26:18
the temple hill a mound
overgrown with thickets.
Jer 17:3

The Mountain of the LORD

4 In the last days
the mountain of the LORD's
temple will be
established Zec 8:3
as the highest of the
mountains;
it will be exalted above the
hills, Eze 17:22
and peoples will stream to it.
Ps 22:27; Jer 3:17

2 Many nations will come and say,

"Come, let us go up to the
mountain of the LORD,
Jer 31:6
to the temple of the God of
Jacob. Zec 2:11; 14:16
He will teach us his ways,
Ps 25:8-9; Isa 54:13
so that we may walk in his
paths."
The law will go out from Zion,
the word of the LORD from
Jerusalem.
3 He will judge between many
peoples
and will settle disputes for
strong nations far and
wide. Isa 11:4
They will beat their swords into
plowshares
and their spears into pruning
hooks. Joel 3:10
Nation will not take up sword
against nation,
nor will they train for war
anymore. Isa 2:1-4
4 Everyone will sit under their
own vine
and under their own fig tree,
1Ki 4:25
and no one will make them
afraid, Lev 26:6
for the LORD Almighty has
spoken. Isa 1:20; Zec 3:10
5 All the nations may walk
in the name of their gods,
2Ki 17:29
but we will walk in the name of
the LORD
our God for ever and ever.
Zec 10:12

The LORD's Plan

6 "In that day," declares the LORD,

"I will gather the lame;
I will assemble the exiles
Ps 147:2
and those I have brought to
grief. Eze 34:13,16; 37:21; Zep 3:19
7 I will make the lame my
remnant, Mic 2:12
those driven away a strong
nation.

The LORD will rule over them
in Mount Zion
from that day and forever.
Lk 1:33; Rev 11:15

8 As for you, watchtower of the
flock,
stronghold[a] of Daughter
Zion,
the former dominion will be
restored to you; Isa 1:26
kingship will come to
Daughter Jerusalem."

9 Why do you now cry aloud —
have you no king[b]? Jer 8:19
Has your ruler[c] perished,
that pain seizes you like that
of a woman in labor?
Jer 30:6

10 Writhe in agony, Daughter
Zion,
like a woman in labor,
for now you must leave the
city
to camp in the open field.
You will go to Babylon;
2Ki 20:18; Isa 43:14
there you will be rescued.
There the LORD will redeem
you Isa 48:20
out of the hand of your
enemies.

11 But now many nations
are gathered against you.
They say, "Let her be defiled,
let our eyes gloat over Zion!"
La 2:16; Ob 1:12

12 But they do not know
the thoughts of the LORD;
they do not understand his
plan, Isa 55:8; Ro 11:33-34
that he has gathered them
like sheaves to the
threshing floor.

13 "Rise and thresh, Daughter Zion,
for I will give you horns of
iron;
I will give you hooves of bronze,
and you will break to pieces
many nations." Da 2:44
You will devote their ill-gotten
gains to the LORD,
their wealth to the Lord of all
the earth.

A Promised Ruler From Bethlehem

5 [d] Marshal your troops now,
city of troops,
for a siege is laid against us.
They will strike Israel's ruler
on the cheek with a rod. La 3:30

2 "But you, Bethlehem
Ephrathah, Jn 7:42; Ge 48:7
though you are small among
the clans[e] of Judah,
out of you will come for me
one who will be ruler over
Israel, 1Sa 13:14
whose origins are from of old,
Ps 102:25
from ancient times." Mt 2:6*

3 Therefore Israel will be
abandoned
until the time when she who
is in labor bears a son,
and the rest of his brothers
return
to join the Israelites.

[a] 8 Or *hill* [b] 9 Or *King* [c] 9 Or *Ruler*
[d] In Hebrew texts 5:1 is numbered 4:14, and 5:2-15 is numbered 5:1-14. [e] 2 Or *rulers*

4 He will stand and shepherd
his flock
Isa 40:11; Eze 34:11-15,23
in the strength of the LORD,
in the majesty of the name
of the LORD his God.
And they will live securely,
for then his greatness
Isa 52:13; Lk 1:32
will reach to the ends of the
earth.
5 And he will be our peace
Isa 9:6; Lk 2:14; Col 1:19-20
when the Assyrians invade
our land
Isa 8:7
and march through our
fortresses.
We will raise against them
seven shepherds,
even eight commanders,
Isa 10:24-27
6 who will rule[a] the land of
Assyria with the sword,
the land of Nimrod
with drawn sword.[b]
Ge 10:8; Zep 2:13
He will deliver us from the
Assyrians
when they invade our land
and march across our
borders.
Na 2:11-13
7 The remnant of Jacob
will be
in the midst of many peoples
Mic 2:12
like dew from the LORD,
Ps 133:3
like showers on the grass,
Isa 44:4
which do not wait for anyone
or depend on man.
8 The remnant of Jacob will be
among the nations,
in the midst of many peoples,
like a lion among the beasts of
the forest,
Ge 49:9
like a young lion among
flocks of sheep,
which mauls and mangles as it
goes,
Mic 4:13; Zec 10:5
and no one can rescue.
Ps 50:22; Hos 5:14
9 Your hand will be lifted up
in triumph over your
enemies,
Ps 10:12
and all your foes will be
destroyed.

10 "In that day," declares the LORD,

"I will destroy your horses
from among you
and demolish your chariots.
Hos 14:3; Zec 9:10
11 I will destroy the cities of your
land
Isa 6:11
and tear down all your
strongholds.
Hos 10:14; Am 5:9
12 I will destroy your witchcraft
and you will no longer cast
spells.
Dt 18:10-12; Isa 2:6
13 I will destroy your idols
and your sacred stones from
among you;
you will no longer bow down
to the work of your hands.
Eze 6:9; Zec 13:2
14 I will uproot from among you
your Asherah poles[c]
Ex 34:13
when I demolish your cities.

[a] 6 Or *crush* [b] 6 Or *Nimrod in its gates*
[c] 14 That is, wooden symbols of the goddess Asherah

[15]I will take vengeance in anger
and wrath Isa 65:12
on the nations that have not
obeyed me."

The LORD's Case Against Israel

6 Listen to what the LORD says:

"Stand up, plead my case
before the mountains;
Ps 50:1; Eze 6:2
let the hills hear what you
have to say.

[2]"Hear, you mountains, the
LORD's accusation;
Dt 32:1; Hos 12:2
listen, you everlasting
foundations of the
earth.
For the LORD has a case against
his people;
he is lodging a charge
against Israel. Ps 50:7

[3]"My people, what have I done
to you?
How have I burdened you?
Answer me. Jer 2:5
[4]I brought you up out of Egypt
Ex 3:10
and redeemed you
from the land of slavery.
Dt 7:8
I sent Moses to lead you, Ex 4:16
also Aaron and Miriam.
Ex 15:20; Ps 77:20
[5]My people, remember
what Balak king of Moab
plotted Nu 22:5-6
and what Balaam son of Beor
answered.
Remember your journey
from Shittim to Gilgal,
Nu 25:1; Jos 5:9-10
that you may know the
righteous acts of the
LORD." Jdg 5:11; 1Sa 12:7

[6]With what shall I come before
the LORD
and bow down before the
exalted God?
Shall I come before him with
burnt offerings,
with calves a year old?
Ps 40:6-8; 51:16-17
[7]Will the LORD be pleased with
thousands of rams,
Isa 40:16
with ten thousand rivers of
olive oil? Ps 50:8-10
Shall I offer my firstborn
for my transgression,
Lev 18:21
the fruit of my body for the
sin of my soul? 2Ki 16:3
[8]He has shown you, O mortal,
what is good.
And what does the LORD
require of you?
To act justly and to love mercy
Isa 1:17; Jer 22:3
and to walk humbly[a]
with your God.
Dt 10:12-13; Hos 6:6

Israel's Guilt and Punishment

[9]Listen! The LORD is calling to
the city —
and to fear your name is
wisdom —

[a] 8 Or *prudently*

"Heed the rod and the One
who appointed it.[a] Isa 11:4
10 Am I still to forget your ill-
gotten treasures, you
wicked house,
and the short ephah,[b]
which is accursed?
Eze 45:9-10; Am 3:10; 8:4-6
11 Shall I acquit someone with
dishonest scales,
Lev 19:36; Hos 12:7
with a bag of false weights?
12 Your rich people are violent;
Isa 1:23
your inhabitants are liars
Isa 3:8
and their tongues speak
deceitfully. Jer 9:3
13 Therefore, I have begun to
destroy you, Isa 1:7; 6:11
to ruin[c] you because of your
sins.
14 You will eat but not be
satisfied; Isa 9:20
your stomach will still be
empty.[d]
You will store up but save
nothing, Isa 30:6
because what you save[e] I will
give to the sword.
15 You will plant but not harvest;
Dt 28:38; Jer 12:13
you will press olives but not
use the oil,
you will crush grapes but
not drink the wine.
Am 5:11; Zep 1:13
16 You have observed the statutes
of Omri 1Ki 16:25
and all the practices of
Ahab's house; 1Ki 16:29-33
you have followed their
traditions. Jer 7:24
Therefore I will give you over
to ruin Jer 25:9
and your people to derision;
you will bear the scorn of the
nations.[f]" Jer 51:51

Israel's Misery

7 What misery is mine!
I am like one who gathers
summer fruit
at the gleaning of the
vineyard;
there is no cluster of grapes to
eat,
none of the early figs that I
crave.
2 The faithful have been swept
from the land; Ps 12:1
not one upright person
remains. Jer 2:29
Everyone lies in wait to shed
blood; Mic 3:10
they hunt each other with
nets. Jer 5:26
3 Both hands are skilled in doing
evil; Pr 4:16
the ruler demands gifts,
the judge accepts bribes, Eze 22:12
the powerful dictate what
they desire —
they all conspire together.

[a] 9 The meaning of the Hebrew for this line is uncertain. [b] 10 An ephah was a dry measure. [c] 13 Or *Therefore, I will make you ill and destroy you; / I will ruin* [d] 14 The meaning of the Hebrew for this word is uncertain. [e] 14 Or *You will press toward birth but not give birth, / and what you bring to birth* [f] 16 Septuagint; Hebrew *scorn due my people*

4 The best of them is like a brier, Eze 2:6
the most upright worse
than a thorn hedge. 2Sa 23:6
The day God visits you has
come,
the day your watchmen
sound the alarm.
Now is the time of your
confusion. Isa 22:5; Hos 9:7
5 Do not trust a neighbor;
put no confidence in a
friend. Jer 9:4
Even with the woman who lies
in your embrace
guard the words of your
lips.
6 For a son dishonors his father,
a daughter rises up against
her mother, Eze 22:7
a daughter-in-law against her
mother-in-law —
a man's enemies are the
members of his own
household. Mt 10:35-36*

7 But as for me, I watch in
hope for the LORD,
Ps 130:5; Isa 25:9
I wait for God my Savior;
my God will hear me. Ps 4:3

Israel Will Rise

8 Do not gloat over me, my
enemy! Pr 24:17
Though I have fallen, I will
rise. Ps 37:24; Am 9:11
Though I sit in darkness,
the LORD will be my light.
Isa 9:2
9 Because I have sinned against
him,
I will bear the LORD's wrath,
La 3:39-40
until he pleads my case
and upholds my cause.
He will bring me out into the
light;
I will see his righteousness.
Isa 46:13
10 Then my enemy will see it
and will be covered with
shame, Ps 35:26
she who said to me,
"Where is the LORD your
God?"
My eyes will see her downfall;
Isa 51:23
even now she will be
trampled underfoot
Zec 10:5
like mire in the streets.

11 The day for building your walls
will come, Isa 54:11
the day for extending your
boundaries.
12 In that day people will come to
you
from Assyria and the cities of
Egypt,
even from Egypt to the
Euphrates
and from sea to sea
and from mountain to
mountain. Isa 19:23-25
13 The earth will become
desolate because of its
inhabitants,
as the result of their deeds.
Isa 3:10-11

Prayer and Praise

[14]Shepherd your people with
your staff, Ps 23:4; Mic 5:4
the flock of your
inheritance,
which lives by itself in a
forest,
in fertile pasturelands.[a]
Let them feed in Bashan and
Gilead Jer 50:19
as in days long ago.

[15]"As in the days when you came
out of Egypt,
I will show them my
wonders." Ex 3:20; Ps 78:12

[16]Nations will see and be
ashamed, Isa 26:11
deprived of all their power.
They will put their hands over
their mouths
and their ears will become
deaf.
[17]They will lick dust like a
snake,
like creatures that crawl on
the ground.
They will come trembling out
of their dens;
they will turn in fear to
the LORD our God
Isa 49:23; 59:19
and will be afraid of you.
[18]Who is a God like you,
Ex 8:10; 1Sa 2:2
who pardons sin and forgives
the transgression
Isa 43:25; Jer 50:20
of the remnant of his
inheritance? Ex 34:9; Mic 2:12
You do not stay angry forever
Ps 103:9
but delight to show mercy.
Jer 32:41
[19]You will again have
compassion on us;
you will tread our sins
underfoot
and hurl all our iniquities
into the depths of the
sea. Isa 43:25; Jer 31:34
[20]You will be faithful to Jacob,
and show love to Abraham,
Gal 3:16
as you pledged on oath to our
ancestors Dt 7:8; Lk 1:72
in days long ago. Ps 108:4

[a] 14 Or *in the middle of Carmel*

NAHUM

1 A prophecy concerning Nineveh. The book of the vision of
Nahum the Elkoshite. Jnh 1:2; Zep 2:13

The LORD's Anger Against Nineveh

2 The LORD is a jealous and
avenging God; Ex 20:5
the LORD takes vengeance
and is filled with wrath.
Dt 32:41; Ps 94:1
The LORD takes vengeance on
his foes
and vents his wrath against
his enemies.
3 The LORD is slow to anger but
great in power; Ne 9:17
the LORD will not leave the
guilty unpunished. Ex 34:7
His way is in the whirlwind and
the storm,
and clouds are the dust of his
feet. Ps 104:3
4 He rebukes the sea and dries
it up; Ex 14:22
he makes all the rivers run
dry.
Bashan and Carmel wither Isa 33:9
and the blossoms of Lebanon
fade.
5 The mountains quake before
him Ex 19:18
and the hills melt away. Mic 1:4
The earth trembles at his
presence,
the world and all who live
in it. Eze 38:20
6 Who can withstand his
indignation? Ps 130:3
Who can endure his fierce
anger? Mal 3:2
His wrath is poured out like
fire; Jer 10:10
the rocks are shattered
before him. 1Ki 19:11
7 The LORD is good, Jer 33:11
a refuge in times of trouble.
Jer 17:17
He cares for those who trust in
him, Ps 1:6
8 but with an overwhelming
flood
he will make an end of
Nineveh;
he will pursue his foes into
the realm of darkness.
9 Whatever they plot against the
LORD
he will bring[a] to an end;
trouble will not come a
second time.
10 They will be entangled among
thorns 2Sa 23:6
and drunk from their
wine;
they will be consumed like
dry stubble.[b] Isa 5:24; Mal 4:1
11 From you, Nineveh, has one
come forth

[a] 9 Or *What do you foes plot against the LORD? / He will bring it* [b] 10 The meaning of the Hebrew for this verse is uncertain.

who plots evil against the
LORD
and devises wicked plans.

12 This is what the LORD says:

"Although they have allies and
are numerous,
they will be destroyed and
pass away. Isa 10:34
Although I have afflicted you,
Judah,
I will afflict you no more.
Isa 54:6-8; La 3:31-32
13 Now I will break their yoke
from your neck Isa 9:4
and tear your shackles away."
Ps 107:14

14 The LORD has given a
command concerning
you, Nineveh:
"You will have no descendants
to bear your name. Isa 14:22
I will destroy the images and
idols Mic 5:13
that are in the temple of
your gods.
I will prepare your grave,
Eze 32:22-23
for you are vile."

15 Look, there on the mountains,
the feet of one who brings
good news, Ro 10:15
who proclaims peace! Isa 52:7
Celebrate your festivals, Judah,
Lev 23:2-4
and fulfill your vows.
No more will the wicked invade
you; Isa 52:1
they will be completely
destroyed.[a]

Nineveh to Fall

2 [b] An attacker advances against
you, Nineveh. Jer 51:20
Guard the fortress,
watch the road,
brace yourselves,
marshal all your strength!

2 The LORD will restore the
splendor of Jacob
Isa 60:15; Eze 37:23
like the splendor of Israel,
though destroyers have laid
them waste
and have ruined their vines.

3 The shields of the soldiers are
red;
the warriors are clad in
scarlet. Eze 23:14-15
The metal on the chariots
flashes
on the day they are made
ready;
the spears of juniper are
brandished.[c]
4 The chariots storm through the
streets, Jer 4:13
rushing back and forth
through the squares.
They look like flaming torches;
they dart about like
lightning.

5 Nineveh summons her picked
troops,
yet they stumble on their
way. Jer 46:12

[a] *15* In Hebrew texts this verse (1:15) is numbered 2:1. [b] In Hebrew texts 2:1-13 is numbered 2:2-14. [c] *3* Hebrew; Septuagint and Syriac *ready; / the horsemen rush to and fro.*

They dash to the city wall;
the protective shield is put in place.
6 The river gates are thrown open Na 3:13
and the palace collapses.
7 It is decreed[a] that Nineveh
be exiled and carried away.
Her female slaves moan like doves Isa 59:11
and beat on their breasts. Isa 32:12
8 Nineveh is like a pool
whose water is draining away.
"Stop! Stop!" they cry,
but no one turns back.
9 Plunder the silver!
Plunder the gold!
The supply is endless,
the wealth from all its treasures!
10 She is pillaged, plundered, stripped!
Hearts melt, knees give way,
bodies tremble, every face grows pale. Isa 29:22

11 Where now is the lions' den, Isa 5:29
the place where they fed their young,
where the lion and lioness went,
and the cubs, with nothing to fear?
12 The lion killed enough for his cubs Jer 51:34
and strangled the prey for his mate,
filling his lairs with the kill Jer 4:7
and his dens with the prey. Isa 37:18

13 "I am against you," Jer 21:13; Na 3:5
declares the LORD Almighty.
"I will burn up your chariots in smoke, Ps 46:9
and the sword will devour your young lions.
I will leave you no prey on the earth.
The voices of your messengers
will no longer be heard." Mic 5:6

Woe to Nineveh

3 Woe to the city of blood, Eze 22:2; Mic 3:10
full of lies, Ps 12:2
full of plunder,
never without victims!
2 The crack of whips,
the clatter of wheels,
galloping horses
and jolting chariots!
3 Charging cavalry,
flashing swords
and glittering spears!
Many casualties,
piles of dead,
bodies without number,
people stumbling over the corpses — 2Ki 19:35; Isa 34:3
4 all because of the wanton lust of a prostitute,
alluring, the mistress of sorceries, Isa 47:9
who enslaved nations by her prostitution Isa 23:17; Eze 16:25-29
and peoples by her witchcraft.

[a] 7 The meaning of the Hebrew for this word is uncertain.

5 "I am against you," declares the
LORD Almighty. Na 2:13
"I will lift your skirts over
your face. Jer 13:22
I will show the nations your
nakedness Isa 47:3
and the kingdoms your
shame.
6 I will pelt you with filth, Job 9:31
I will treat you with
contempt Jer 51:37
and make you a spectacle.
Isa 14:16
7 All who see you will flee from
you and say, Isa 13:14
'Nineveh is in ruins — who
will mourn for her?'
Jer 15:5
Where can I find anyone to
comfort you?" Isa 51:19

8 Are you better than Thebes,
Jer 46:25; Am 6:2
situated on the Nile, Isa 19:6-9
with water around her?
The river was her defense,
the waters her wall.
9 Cush[a] and Egypt were her
boundless strength;
2Ch 12:3
Put and Libya were among
her allies. Eze 27:10; 30:5
10 Yet she was taken captive Isa 20:4
and went into exile.
Her infants were dashed to
pieces Isa 13:16; Hos 13:16
at every street corner.
Lots were cast for her nobles,
Job 6:27
and all her great men were
put in chains. Jer 40:1

11 You too will become drunk;
the protective shield is put in
Isa 49:26
you will go into hiding Isa 2:10
and seek refuge from the
enemy.

12 All your fortresses are like fig
trees
with their first ripe fruit;
when they are shaken,
the figs fall into the mouth
of the eater. Isa 28:4
13 Look at your troops —
they are all weaklings.
Isa 19:16; Jer 50:37
The gates of your land Na 2:6
are wide open to your
enemies;
fire has consumed the bars
of your gates. Isa 45:2

14 Draw water for the siege, 2Ch 32:4
strengthen your defenses!
Na 2:1

Work the clay,
tread the mortar,
repair the brickwork!
15 There the fire will consume
you;
the sword will cut you
down —
they will devour you like a
swarm of locusts.
Multiply like grasshoppers,
multiply like locusts! Joel 1:4
16 You have increased the
number of your
merchants
till they are more numerous
than the stars in the sky,

[a] 9 That is, the upper Nile region

but like locusts they strip the
land Ex 10:13
and then fly away.
17 Your guards are like locusts, Jer 51:27
your officials like swarms of
locusts
that settle in the walls on a
cold day —
but when the sun appears they
fly away,
and no one knows where.
18 King of Assyria, your
shepherds[a] slumber; Ps 76:5-6
your nobles lie down to rest. Isa 56:10
Your people are scattered on
the mountains 1Ki 22:17
with no one to gather
them.
19 Nothing can heal you; Mic 1:9
your wound is fatal.
All who hear the news about
you
clap their hands at your fall, La 2:15; Zep 2:15
for who has not felt
your endless cruelty? Isa 37:18

[a] *18* That is, rulers

HABAKKUK

1 The prophecy that Habakkuk
the prophet received. Na 1:1

Habakkuk's Complaint

2 How long, LORD, must I call for
help,
but you do not listen?
Ps 13:1-2; 22:1-2
Or cry out to you, "Violence!"
but you do not save? Jer 14:9
3 Why do you make me look at
injustice?
Why do you tolerate
wrongdoing? Job 9:23
Destruction and violence are
before me; Jer 20:8
there is strife, and conflict
abounds. Ps 55:9
4 Therefore the law is paralyzed,
Ps 119:126
and justice never prevails.
The wicked hem in the
righteous,
so that justice is perverted.
Isa 5:20; Eze 9:9

The LORD's Answer

5 "Look at the nations and
watch —
and be utterly amazed. Isa 29:9
For I am going to do something
in your days
that you would not believe,
even if you were told. Ac 13:41*
6 I am raising up the
Babylonians,[a] 2Ki 24:2
that ruthless and impetuous
people,
who sweep across the whole
earth
to seize dwellings not their
own. Jer 13:20
7 They are a feared and dreaded
people; Isa 18:7; Jer 39:5-9
they are a law to themselves
and promote their own honor.
8 Their horses are swifter than
leopards, Jer 4:13
fiercer than wolves at dusk.
Their cavalry gallops headlong;
their horsemen come from
afar.
They fly like an eagle swooping
to devour;
9 they all come intent on
violence.
Their hordes[b] advance like a
desert wind
and gather prisoners like
sand. Hab 2:5
10 They mock kings
and scoff at rulers. 2Ch 36:6
They laugh at all fortified cities;
by building earthen ramps
they capture them.
11 Then they sweep past like the
wind and go on — Jer 4:11-12
guilty people, whose own
strength is their god."
Da 4:30

[a] 6 Or *Chaldeans* [b] 9 The meaning of the Hebrew for this word is uncertain.

Habakkuk's Second Complaint

12 LORD, are you not from
everlasting? Ge 21:33
My God, my Holy One, you[a]
will never die. Isa 31:1
You, LORD, have appointed
them to execute
judgment; Isa 10:6
you, my Rock, have ordained
them to punish. Ex 33:22
13 Your eyes are too pure to look
on evil; Ps 18:26
you cannot tolerate
wrongdoing. La 3:34-36
Why then do you tolerate the
treacherous? Ps 25:3
Why are you silent while the
wicked
swallow up those more
righteous than
themselves? Job 21:7
14 You have made people like the
fish in the sea,
like the sea creatures that
have no ruler.
15 The wicked foe pulls all of
them up with hooks,
Isa 19:8
he catches them in his net,
Jer 16:16
he gathers them up in his
dragnet;
and so he rejoices and is
glad.
16 Therefore he sacrifices to his
net
and burns incense to his
dragnet, Jer 44:8
for by his net he lives in luxury
and enjoys the choicest food.
17 Is he to keep on emptying his
net,
destroying nations without
mercy? Isa 14:6; 19:8

2 I will stand at my watch Isa 21:8
and station myself on the
ramparts; Ps 48:13
I will look to see what he will
say to me, Ps 85:8
and what answer I am to give
to this complaint.[b] Ps 5:3

The LORD's Answer

2 Then the LORD replied:

"Write down the revelation
Rev 1:19
and make it plain on tablets
so that a herald[c] may run
with it.
3 For the revelation awaits an
appointed time; Da 11:27
it speaks of the end Da 8:17; 10:14
and will not prove false.
Though it linger, wait for it;
Ps 27:14
it[d] will certainly come
and will not delay.
Eze 12:25; Heb 10:37-38

4 "See, the enemy is puffed up;
his desires are not upright —
but the righteous person
will live by his
faithfulness[e] —
Ro 1:17*; Gal 3:11*; Heb 10:37-38*

[a] 12 An ancient Hebrew scribal tradition; Masoretic Text *we* [b] 1 Or *and what to answer when I am rebuked* [c] 2 Or *so that whoever reads it* [d] 3 Or *Though he linger, wait for him; / he* [e] 4 Or *faith*

5 indeed, wine betrays him; Pr 20:1
he is arrogant and never at
rest. Isa 2:11
Because he is as greedy as the
grave
and like death is never
satisfied, Pr 27:20; 30:15-16
he gathers to himself all the
nations
and takes captive all the
peoples. Hab 1:9

6 "Will not all of them taunt him
with ridicule and scorn, saying,
Isa 14:4

" 'Woe to him who piles up
stolen goods
and makes himself wealthy
by extortion! Am 2:8
How long must this go on?'
7 Will not your creditors
suddenly arise?
Will they not wake up and
make you tremble?
Then you will become their
prey. Pr 29:1
8 Because you have plundered
many nations,
the peoples who are left
will plunder you.
Isa 33:1; Zec 2:8-9
For you have shed human blood;
you have destroyed lands
and cities and everyone
in them. Eze 39:10

9 "Woe to him who builds his
house by unjust gain,
Jer 22:13
setting his nest on high
to escape the clutches of ruin!
10 You have plotted the ruin of
many peoples, Jer 26:19
shaming your own house
and forfeiting your life.
Na 3:6
11 The stones of the wall will cry
out, Jos 24:27; Lk 19:40
and the beams of the
woodwork will echo it.

12 "Woe to him who builds a city
with bloodshed Mic 3:10
and establishes a town by
injustice!
13 Has not the LORD Almighty
determined
that the people's labor is only
fuel for the fire, Isa 50:11
that the nations exhaust
themselves for nothing?
Isa 47:13
14 For the earth will be filled with
the knowledge of the
glory of the LORD Nu 14:21
as the waters cover the sea.
Isa 11:9

15 "Woe to him who gives drink to
his neighbors,
pouring it from the wineskin
till they are drunk,
so that he can gaze on their
naked bodies!
16 You will be filled with shame
instead of glory.
Eze 23:32-34; Hos 4:7
Now it is your turn! Drink
and let your nakedness
be exposed[a]! La 4:21

[a] *16* Masoretic Text; Dead Sea Scrolls, Aquila, Vulgate and Syriac (see also Septuagint) *and stagger*

The cup from the LORD's right
hand is coming around
to you, Isa 51:22
and disgrace will cover your
glory.
17 The violence you have done to
Lebanon will overwhelm
you, Jer 51:35
and your destruction of
animals will terrify you.
Jer 50:15
For you have shed human
blood;
you have destroyed lands
and cities and everyone
in them.

18 "Of what value is an idol
carved by a craftsman?
Jer 5:21
Or an image that teaches
lies?
For the one who makes it
trusts in his own
creation;
he makes idols that
cannot speak.
Ps 115:4-5; Jer 10:14
19 Woe to him who says to wood,
'Come to life!'
Or to lifeless stone, 'Wake
up!' 1Ki 18:27
Can it give guidance?
It is covered with gold and
silver; Jer 10:4
there is no breath in it."
Hos 4:12

20 The LORD is in his holy temple;
Ps 11:4
let all the earth be silent
before him. Isa 41:1

Habakkuk's Prayer

3 A prayer of Habakkuk the prophet. On *shigionoth*.[a]

2 LORD, I have heard of your
fame; Ps 44:1
I stand in awe of your deeds,
LORD. Ps 119:120
Repeat them in our day, Ps 85:6
in our time make them
known;
in wrath remember mercy.
Isa 54:8

3 God came from Teman,
the Holy One from Mount
Paran.[b]
His glory covered the heavens
Ps 8:1
and his praise filled the
earth. Ps 48:10
4 His splendor was like the
sunrise; Isa 18:4
rays flashed from his hand,
where his power was hidden.
Job 9:6
5 Plague went before him;
pestilence followed his
steps.
6 He stood, and shook the earth;
he looked, and made the
nations tremble.
The ancient mountains
crumbled Ps 46:2
and the age-old hills
collapsed — Ps 114:1-6
but he marches on forever.
Ge 21:33

[a] *1* Probably a literary or musical term
[b] *3* The Hebrew has *Selah* (a word of uncertain meaning) here and at the middle of verse 9 and at the end of verse 13.

7 I saw the tents of Cushan in
distress,
the dwellings of Midian in
anguish. Ex 15:14; Jdg 7:24-25
8 Were you angry with the rivers,
LORD? Ex 7:20
Was your wrath against the
streams?
Did you rage against the sea
when you rode your horses
and your chariots to victory?
Ps 68:17
9 You uncovered your bow,
you called for many arrows.
Ps 7:12-13
You split the earth with
rivers;
10 the mountains saw you and
writhed.
Torrents of water swept by;
the deep roared Ps 98:7
and lifted its waves on high.
Ps 93:3
11 Sun and moon stood still in the
heavens Jos 10:13
at the glint of your flying
arrows, Ps 18:14
at the lightning of your
flashing spear. Zec 9:14
12 In wrath you strode through
the earth
and in anger you threshed
the nations. Isa 41:15
13 You came out to deliver your
people, Ps 20:6; 28:8
to save your anointed one.
2Sa 23:1
You crushed the leader of
the land of wickedness,
Ps 110:6
you stripped him from head
to foot.
14 With his own spear you pierced
his head
when his warriors
stormed out to scatter
us, Jdg 7:22
gloating as though about to
devour
the wretched who were in
hiding. Ps 64:2-5
15 You trampled the sea with your
horses,
churning the great waters.
Ex 15:8; Ps 77:19

16 I heard and my heart
pounded,
my lips quivered at the
sound;
decay crept into my bones,
and my legs trembled.
Yet I will wait patiently
for the day of calamity
Ps 37:7
to come on the nation
invading us.
17 Though the fig tree does not
bud
and there are no grapes on
the vines,
though the olive crop
fails
and the fields produce no
food, Joel 1:10-12,18
though there are no sheep in
the pen
and no cattle in the stalls,
Jer 5:17
18 yet I will rejoice in the LORD,
Isa 61:10; Php 4:4

I will be joyful in God my
Savior. Lk 1:47

[19]The Sovereign LORD is my
strength; Dt 33:29; Ps 46:1-5
he makes my feet like the
feet of a deer,
he enables me to tread
on the heights.
2Sa 22:34; Ps 18:33

For the director of music.
On my stringed
instruments.

ZEPHANIAH

1 The word of the LORD that came
to Zephaniah son of Cushi, the
son of Gedaliah, the son of Amariah, the son of Hezekiah, during
the reign of Josiah son of Amon
king of Judah: 2Ki 22:1; 2Ch 34:1-35:25

Judgment on the Whole Earth in the Day of the LORD

2 "I will sweep away everything
from the face of the earth,"
Ge 6:7
declares the LORD.
3 "I will sweep away both man
and beast; Jer 50:3
I will sweep away the birds in
the sky Jer 4:25
and the fish in the sea —
and the idols that cause the
wicked to stumble."[a]

"When I destroy all mankind
on the face of the earth,"
Hos 4:3
declares the LORD,
4 "I will stretch out my
hand against Judah
Jer 6:12
and against all who live in
Jerusalem.
I will destroy every remnant
of Baal worship in this
place, Mic 5:13
the very names of the
idolatrous priests —
Hos 10:5
5 those who bow down on the
roofs
to worship the starry
host,
those who bow down and
swear by the LORD
and who also swear by
Molek,[b] Jer 5:7
6 those who turn back from
following the LORD
Isa 1:4; Jer 2:13
and neither seek the LORD
nor inquire of him."
Isa 9:13; Hos 7:7

7 Be silent before the Sovereign
LORD, Hab 2:20; Zec 2:13
for the day of the LORD is
near. Isa 13:6
The LORD has prepared a
sacrifice; Jer 46:10
he has consecrated those he
has invited.

8 "On the day of the LORD's
sacrifice
I will punish the officials
Isa 24:21
and the king's sons Jer 39:6
and all those clad
in foreign clothes.
9 On that day I will punish
all who avoid stepping on
the threshold,[c]

[a] 3 The meaning of the Hebrew for this line is uncertain. [b] 5 Hebrew *Malkam* [c] 9 See 1 Samuel 5:5.

who fill the temple of their
gods
with violence and deceit. Am 3:10

10 "On that day,"
declares the LORD, Isa 22:5
"a cry will go up from the Fish
Gate, 2Ch 33:14
wailing from the New
Quarter,
and a loud crash from the
hills.
11 Wail, you who live in the
market district[a]; Jas 5:1
all your merchants will be
wiped out,
all who trade with[b] silver will
be destroyed. Hos 9:6
12 At that time I will search
Jerusalem with lamps
and punish those who are
complacent, Am 6:1
who are like wine left on its
dregs, Jer 48:11
who think, 'The LORD will do
nothing, Eze 8:12
either good or bad.'
13 Their wealth will be plundered,
Jer 15:13
their houses demolished.
Though they build houses,
they will not live in them;
though they plant vineyards,
they will not drink the wine."
Am 5:11; Mic 6:15

14 The great day of the LORD is
near — Eze 7:7; Joel 1:15
near and coming quickly.
The cry on the day of the LORD
is bitter;
the Mighty Warrior shouts
his battle cry.
15 That day will be a day of
wrath —
a day of distress and
anguish,
a day of trouble and ruin,
a day of darkness and
gloom,
a day of clouds and
blackness — Isa 22:5; Joel 2:2
16 a day of trumpet and battle
cry Jer 4:19
against the fortified cities
and against the corner
towers. Isa 2:15

17 "I will bring such distress on all
people Dt 28:52
that they will grope about
like those who are blind,
Isa 59:10
because they have sinned
against the LORD.
Their blood will be poured out
like dust Ps 79:3
and their entrails like dung.
Jer 9:22
18 Neither their silver nor their
gold
will be able to save them
on the day of the LORD's
wrath." Eze 7:19

In the fire of his jealousy Dt 29:20
the whole earth will be
consumed, Zep 3:8
for he will make a sudden end
of all who live on the earth.
Ge 6:7

[a] 11 *Or the Mortar* [b] 11 *Or in*

Judah and Jerusalem Judged Along With the Nations

Judah Summoned to Repent

2 Gather together, gather
yourselves together,
Joel 1:14
you shameful nation, Jer 3:3; 6:15
2 before the decree takes effect
and that day passes like
windblown chaff,
Isa 17:13; Hos 13:3
before the LORD's fierce anger
comes upon you, La 4:11
before the day of the LORD's
wrath
comes upon you. Eze 7:19
3 Seek the LORD, all you humble
of the land, Am 5:6
you who do what he
commands.
Seek righteousness, seek
humility; Ps 45:4; Am 5:14-15
perhaps you will be sheltered
Ps 57:1
on the day of the LORD's
anger.

Philistia

4 Gaza will be abandoned
Am 1:6-8; Zec 9:5-7
and Ashkelon left in ruins.
At midday Ashdod will be
emptied
and Ekron uprooted.
5 Woe to you who live by the sea,
you Kerethite people; Eze 25:16
the word of the LORD is against
you, Am 3:1
Canaan, land of the
Philistines.
He says, "I will destroy you,
and none will be left." Isa 14:30
6 The land by the sea will
become pastures
having wells for shepherds
and pens for flocks. Isa 5:17
7 That land will belong
to the remnant of the people
of Judah; Ge 45:7
there they will find pasture.
In the evening they will lie
down
in the houses of Ashkelon.
The LORD their God will care for
them;
he will restore their
fortunes.[a] Ps 126:4; Jer 32:44

Moab and Ammon

8 "I have heard the insults of
Moab Jer 48:27
and the taunts of the
Ammonites, Eze 21:28
who insulted my people Eze 25:3
and made threats against
their land. La 3:61
9 Therefore, as surely as I live,"
declares the LORD Almighty,
the God of Israel,
"surely Moab will become like
Sodom, Dt 29:23
the Ammonites like
Gomorrah — Jer 49:1-6
a place of weeds and salt pits,
a wasteland forever.
The remnant of my people will
plunder them; Isa 11:14
the survivors of my nation
will inherit their land."
Am 2:1-3

[a] 7 Or *will bring back their captives*

[10]This is what they will get in
return for their pride, Isa 16:6
for insulting and mocking
the people of the LORD
Almighty. Jer 48:27
[11]The LORD will be awesome to
them Joel 2:11
when he destroys all the
gods of the earth. Zep 1:4
Distant nations will bow down
to him, Zep 3:9
all of them in their own
lands.

Cush

[12]"You Cushites,[a] too, Isa 18:1; 20:4
will be slain by my sword."
Jer 46:10

Assyria

[13]He will stretch out his hand
against the north
and destroy Assyria,
leaving Nineveh utterly
desolate
and dry as the desert.
Na 1:1; Mic 5:6
[14]Flocks and herds will lie down
there, Isa 5:17
creatures of every kind.
The desert owl and the screech
owl Ps 102:6; Isa 14:23
will roost on her columns.
Their hooting will echo
through the windows,
rubble will fill the doorways,
the beams of cedar will be
exposed.
[15]This is the city of revelry Isa 32:9
that lived in safety. Isa 47:8
She said to herself,
"I am the one! And there
is none besides me."
Eze 28:2
What a ruin she has become,
a lair for wild beasts!
All who pass by her scoff Na 3:19
and shake their fists.

Jerusalem

3 Woe to the city of oppressors,
rebellious and defiled!
Jer 6:6; Eze 23:30
[2]She obeys no one, Jer 22:21
she accepts no correction.
Jer 7:28
She does not trust in the LORD,
Dt 1:32
she does not draw near to
her God. Ps 73:28; Jer 5:3
[3]Her officials within her
are roaring lions;
her rulers are evening wolves,
Eze 22:27
who leave nothing for the
morning.
[4]Her prophets are unprincipled;
they are treacherous people.
Jer 9:4
Her priests profane the
sanctuary
and do violence to the law.
Eze 22:26
[5]The LORD within her is
righteous; Ezr 9:15
he does no wrong. Dt 32:4
Morning by morning he
dispenses his justice,
Ps 5:3

[a] 12 That is, people from the upper Nile region

and every new day he does
not fail, La 3:23
yet the unrighteous know no
shame. Eze 18:25

Jerusalem Remains Unrepentant

6 "I have destroyed nations;
their strongholds are
demolished.
I have left their streets
deserted,
with no one passing
through.
Their cities are laid waste;
Lev 26:31
they are deserted and empty.
7 Of Jerusalem I thought,
'Surely you will fear me
and accept correction!' Jer 7:28
Then her place of refuge[a]
would not be
destroyed,
nor all my punishments
come upon[b] her.
But they were still eager
to act corruptly in all they
did. Hos 9:9
8 Therefore wait for me,"
declares the LORD, Ps 27:14
"for the day I will stand up to
testify.[c]
I have decided to assemble the
nations, Joel 3:2
to gather the kingdoms
and to pour out my wrath on
them —
all my fierce anger. Jer 10:25
The whole world will be
consumed Zep 1:18
by the fire of my jealous
anger.

Restoration of Israel's Remnant

9 "Then I will purify the lips of
the peoples,
that all of them may call on
the name of the LORD
Zep 2:11
and serve him shoulder to
shoulder. Isa 19:18
10 From beyond the rivers of
Cush[d] Ps 68:31
my worshipers, my scattered
people,
will bring me offerings. Isa 60:7
11 On that day you, Jerusalem,
will not be put to shame
Joel 2:26-27
for all the wrongs you have
done to me, Ge 50:15
because I will remove from you
your arrogant boasters. Ps 59:12
Never again will you be haughty
on my holy hill. Ex 15:17
12 But I will leave within you
the meek and humble. Isa 14:32
The remnant of Israel
will trust in the name of the
LORD. Na 1:7
13 They will do no wrong;
Isa 10:21; Mic 4:7
they will tell no lies. Rev 14:5
A deceitful tongue
will not be found in their
mouths.
They will eat and lie down
Eze 34:15; Zep 2:7
and no one will make them
afraid." Eze 34:25-28

[a] 7 Or *her sanctuary* [b] 7 Or *all those I appointed over* [c] 8 Septuagint and Syriac; Hebrew *will rise up to plunder* [d] 10 That is, the upper Nile region

14 Sing, Daughter Zion; Zec 2:10
shout aloud, Israel! Isa 12:6
Be glad and rejoice with all
your heart, Isa 51:11
Daughter Jerusalem!
15 The LORD has taken away your
punishment,
he has turned back your
enemy.
The LORD, the King of Israel, is
with you; Eze 37:26-28
never again will you fear any
harm. Isa 54:14
16 On that day
they will say to Jerusalem,
"Do not fear, Zion;
do not let your hands hang
limp. Isa 35:3-4; Heb 12:12
17 The LORD your God is with you,
the Mighty Warrior who
saves. Isa 63:1
He will take great delight in
you; Isa 62:4
in his love he will no longer
rebuke you, Hos 14:4
but will rejoice over you with
singing." Isa 40:1

18 "I will remove from you
all who mourn over the
loss of your appointed
festivals,
which is a burden and
reproach for you.
19 At that time I will deal
with all who oppressed you.
I will rescue the lame;
I will gather the exiles.
Eze 34:16; Mic 4:6
I will give them praise and
honor Isa 60:18
in every land where they
have suffered shame.
20 At that time I will gather you;
at that time I will bring you
home. Jer 29:14; Eze 37:12
I will give you honor and praise
Isa 56:5
among all the peoples of the
earth
when I restore your fortunes[a]
Joel 3:1
before your very eyes,"
says the LORD.

[a] 20 Or *I bring back your captives*

HAGGAI

A Call to Build the House of the LORD

1 In the second year of King Darius, on the first day of the sixth
month, the word of the LORD came
through the prophet Haggai to Zerubbabel son of Shealtiel, governor of Judah, and to Joshua son of
Jozadak,[a] the high priest:
Ezr 4:24; 5:3; Mt 1:12-13

2 This is what the LORD Almighty
says: "These people say, 'The time
has not yet come to rebuild the
LORD's house.'" Ezr 1:2
3 Then the word of the LORD
came through the prophet Haggai:
4 "Is it a time for you yourselves to
be living in your paneled houses,
while this house remains a ruin?"
2Sa 7:2; Ezr 5:1; Jer 33:12
5 Now this is what the LORD Almighty says: "Give careful thought
to your ways. 6 You have planted
much, but harvested little. You
eat, but never have enough. You
drink, but never have your fill. You
put on clothes, but are not warm.
You earn wages, only to put them
in a purse with holes in it."
La 3:40; Hag 2:15,18

7 This is what the LORD Almighty
says: "Give careful thought to your
ways. 8 Go up into the mountains
and bring down timber and build
my house, so that I may take pleasure in it and be honored," says the
LORD. 9 "You expected much, but
see, it turned out to be little. What
you brought home, I blew away.
Why?" declares the LORD Almighty.
"Because of my house, which remains a ruin, while each of you
is busy with your own house.
10 Therefore, because of you the
heavens have withheld their dew
and the earth its crops. 11 I called
for a drought on the fields and the
mountains, on the grain, the new
wine, the olive oil and everything
else the ground produces, on people and livestock, and on all the labor of your hands." Ps 132:13-14; Hag 2:17

12 Then Zerubbabel son of Shealtiel, Joshua son of Jozadak, the
high priest, and the whole remnant of the people obeyed the
voice of the LORD their God and
the message of the prophet Haggai, because the LORD their God
had sent him. And the people
feared the LORD. Dt 31:12; Isa 50:10
13 Then Haggai, the LORD's messenger, gave this message of the
LORD to the people: "I am with
you," declares the LORD. 14 So the
LORD stirred up the spirit of Zerubbabel son of Shealtiel, governor of Judah, and the spirit of
Joshua son of Jozadak, the high

[a] 1 Hebrew *Jehozadak*, a variant of *Jozadak*; also in verses 12 and 14

priest, and the spirit of the whole
remnant of the people. They came
and began to work on the house of
the LORD Almighty, their God, 15on
the twenty-fourth day of the sixth
month. Ezr 5:2; Ro 8:31

The Promised Glory of the New House

In the second year of King Da-
2 rius, 1on the twenty-first day
of the seventh month, the
word of the LORD came through
the prophet Haggai: 2"Speak to
Zerubbabel son of Shealtiel, governor of Judah, to Joshua son of
Jozadak,[a] the high priest, and to
the remnant of the people. Ask
them, 3'Who of you is left who
saw this house in its former glory? How does it look to you now?
Does it not seem to you like nothing? 4But now be strong, Zerubbabel,' declares the LORD. 'Be strong,
Joshua son of Jozadak, the high
priest. Be strong, all you people of
the land,' declares the LORD, 'and
work. For I am with you,' declares
the LORD Almighty. 5'This is what
I covenanted with you when you
came out of Egypt. And my Spirit
remains among you. Do not fear.'
1Ch 28:20; Isa 63:11

6"This is what the LORD Almighty says: 'In a little while I will
once more shake the heavens and
the earth, the sea and the dry land.
7I will shake all nations, and what
is desired by all nations will come,
and I will fill this house with glory,'
says the LORD Almighty. 8'The silver is mine and the gold is mine,'
declares the LORD Almighty. 9'The
glory of this present house will
be greater than the glory of the
former house,' says the LORD Almighty. 'And in this place I will
grant peace,' declares the LORD Almighty." Heb 12:26*

Blessings for a Defiled People

10On the twenty-fourth day of
the ninth month, in the second
year of Darius, the word of the
LORD came to the prophet Haggai:
11"This is what the LORD Almighty
says: 'Ask the priests what the law
says: 12If someone carries consecrated meat in the fold of their garment, and that fold touches some
bread or stew, some wine, olive oil
or other food, does it become consecrated?'" Lev 10:10-11; Mt 23:19

The priests answered, "No."

13Then Haggai said, "If a person defiled by contact with a dead
body touches one of these things,
does it become defiled?"

"Yes," the priests replied, "it becomes defiled." Lev 22:4-6

14Then Haggai said, "'So it is
with this people and this nation
in my sight,' declares the LORD.
'Whatever they do and whatever
they offer there is defiled. Isa 1:13

15"'Now give careful thought to
this from this day on[b] — consider
how things were before one stone
was laid on another in the LORD's

[a] 2 Hebrew *Jehozadak*, a variant of *Jozadak*; also in verse 4
[b] 15 Or *to the days past*

temple. 16When anyone came to a
heap of twenty measures, there
were only ten. When anyone went
to a wine vat to draw fifty measures, there were only twenty. 17I
struck all the work of your hands
with blight, mildew and hail, yet
you did not return to me,' declares the LORD. 18'From this day
on, from this twenty-fourth day
of the ninth month, give careful thought to the day when the
foundation of the LORD's temple
was laid. Give careful thought:
19Is there yet any seed left in the
barn? Until now, the vine and the
fig tree, the pomegranate and the
olive tree have not borne fruit.

Hag 1:5-6; Zec 8:9

"'From this day on I will bless
you.'" Joel 2:14

Zerubbabel the LORD's Signet Ring

20The word of the LORD came to
Haggai a second time on the twenty-fourth day of the month: 21"Tell
Zerubbabel governor of Judah
that I am going to shake the heavens and the earth. 22I will over-
turn royal thrones and shatter the
power of the foreign kingdoms. I
will overthrow chariots and their
drivers; horses and their riders
will fall, each by the sword of his
brother. Jdg 7:22; Da 2:44; Mic 5:10

23"'On that day,' declares the
LORD Almighty, 'I will take you, my
servant Zerubbabel son of Shealtiel,' declares the LORD, 'and I will
make you like my signet ring, for
I have chosen you,' declares the
LORD Almighty." Isa 43:10

ZECHARIAH

A Call to Return to the LORD

1 In the eighth month of the second year of Darius, the word
of the LORD came to the prophet
Zechariah son of Berekiah, the son
of Iddo: Ezr 4:24; Ne 12:4

2"The LORD was very angry with
your ancestors. 3Therefore tell the
people: This is what the LORD Almighty says: 'Return to me,' declares the LORD Almighty, 'and I
will return to you,' says the LORD
Almighty. 4Do not be like your
ancestors, to whom the earlier
prophets proclaimed: This is what
the LORD Almighty says: 'Turn
from your evil ways and your evil
practices.' But they would not listen or pay attention to me, declares the LORD. 5Where are your
ancestors now? And the prophets,
do they live forever? 6But did not
my words and my decrees, which
I commanded my servants the
prophets, overtake your ancestors? Mal 3:7; Jas 4:8

"Then they repented and said,
'The LORD Almighty has done to
us what our ways and practices
deserve, just as he determined
to do.'" Jer 12:14-17; La 2:17

The Man Among the Myrtle Trees

7On the twenty-fourth day of
the eleventh month, the month of
Shebat, in the second year of Darius, the word of the LORD came to
the prophet Zechariah son of Berekiah, the son of Iddo.

8During the night I had a vision,
and there before me was a man
mounted on a red horse. He was
standing among the myrtle trees
in a ravine. Behind him were red,
brown and white horses.
Zec 6:2-7; Rev 6:4

9I asked, "What are these, my
lord?"

The angel who was talking with
me answered, "I will show you
what they are." Zec 4:1,4-5

10Then the man standing among
the myrtle trees explained, "They
are the ones the LORD has sent to
go throughout the earth." Zec 6:5-8

11And they reported to the angel of the LORD who was standing
among the myrtle trees, "We have
gone throughout the earth and
found the whole world at rest and
in peace." Isa 14:7

12Then the angel of the LORD
said, "LORD Almighty, how long
will you withhold mercy from Jerusalem and from the towns of
Judah, which you have been angry with these seventy years?" 13So
the LORD spoke kind and comforting words to the angel who talked
with me. Da 9:2; Zec 4:1

14Then the angel who was
speaking to me said, "Proclaim

this word: This is what the LORD
Almighty says: 'I am very jealous
for Jerusalem and Zion, 15and I am
very angry with the nations that
feel secure. I was only a little angry, but they went too far with the
punishment.' Am 1:11; Zec 8:2
16"Therefore this is what the
LORD says: 'I will return to Jerusalem with mercy, and there my
house will be rebuilt. And the
measuring line will be stretched
out over Jerusalem,' declares the
LORD Almighty. Zec 2:1-2
17"Proclaim further: This is what
the LORD Almighty says: 'My towns
will again overflow with prosperity, and the LORD will again comfort Zion and choose Jerusalem.'"
Isa 51:3; Zec 2:12

Four Horns and Four Craftsmen

18Then I looked up, and there
before me were four horns. 19I
asked the angel who was speaking
to me, "What are these?"
He answered me, "These are the
horns that scattered Judah, Israel
and Jerusalem." Am 6:13
20Then the LORD showed me
four craftsmen. 21I asked, "What
are these coming to do?"
He answered, "These are the
horns that scattered Judah so that
no one could raise their head, but
the craftsmen have come to terrify
them and throw down these horns
of the nations who lifted up their
horns against the land of Judah to
scatter its people."[a] Ps 75:4,10

A Man With a Measuring Line

2[b] Then I looked up, and there
before me was a man with
a measuring line in his hand. 2I
asked, "Where are you going?"
He answered me, "To measure
Jerusalem, to find out how wide
and how long it is." Rev 21:15
3While the angel who was
speaking to me was leaving, another angel came to meet him
4and said to him: "Run, tell that
young man, 'Jerusalem will be a
city without walls because of the
great number of people and animals in it. 5And I myself will be a
wall of fire around it,' declares the
LORD, 'and I will be its glory within.' Ps 46:5; Rev 21:23
6"Come! Come! Flee from the
land of the north," declares the
LORD, "for I have scattered you
to the four winds of heaven," declares the LORD. Eze 17:21
7"Come, Zion! Escape, you who
live in Daughter Babylon!" 8For
this is what the LORD Almighty
says: "After the Glorious One has
sent me against the nations that
have plundered you — for whoever touches you touches the apple
of his eye — 9I will surely raise
my hand against them so that
their slaves will plunder them.[c]
Then you will know that the LORD
Almighty has sent me.
Dt 32:10; Zec 4:9

[a] 21 In Hebrew texts 1:18-21 is numbered 2:1-4.
[b] In Hebrew texts 2:1-13 is numbered 2:5-17.
[c] 8,9 Or *says after . . . eye:* 9*"I . . . plunder them."*

10“Shout and be glad, Daughter Zion. For I am coming, and
I will live among you,” declares
the LORD. 11“Many nations will be
joined with the LORD in that day
and will become my people. I will
live among you and you will know
that the LORD Almighty has sent
me to you. 12The LORD will inherit Judah as his portion in the holy
land and will again choose Jerusalem. 13Be still before the LORD, all
mankind, because he has roused
himself from his holy dwelling.”
Hab 2:20; Zec 1:17

Clean Garments for the High Priest

3 Then he showed me Joshua
the high priest standing before the angel of the LORD, and Satan[a] standing at his right side to
accuse him. 2The LORD said to Satan, “The LORD rebuke you, Satan!
The LORD, who has chosen Jerusalem, rebuke you! Is not this man
a burning stick snatched from the
fire?” Ps 109:6; Jude 1:9,23

3Now Joshua was dressed in
filthy clothes as he stood before
the angel. 4The angel said to those
who were standing before him,
“Take off his filthy clothes.”

Then he said to Joshua, “See, I
have taken away your sin, and I
will put fine garments on you.”
Isa 52:1; Mic 7:18

5Then I said, “Put a clean turban
on his head.” So they put a clean
turban on his head and clothed
him, while the angel of the LORD
stood by. Ex 29:6

6The angel of the LORD gave this
charge to Joshua: 7“This is what
the LORD Almighty says: ‘If you
will walk in obedience to me and
keep my requirements, then you
will govern my house and have
charge of my courts, and I will give
you a place among these standing
here. Dt 17:8-11; Eze 44:15-16

8“ ‘Listen, High Priest Joshua,
you and your associates seated before you, who are men symbolic of
things to come: I am going to bring
my servant, the Branch. 9See, the
stone I have set in front of Joshua!
There are seven eyes[b] on that one
stone, and I will engrave an inscription on it,’ says the LORD Almighty,
‘and I will remove the sin of this
land in a single day. Isa 28:16; Eze 12:11

10“ ‘In that day each of you will
invite your neighbor to sit under
your vine and fig tree,’ declares
the LORD Almighty.” 1Ki 4:25; Mic 4:4

The Gold Lampstand and the Two Olive Trees

4 Then the angel who talked
with me returned and woke
me up, like someone awakened
from sleep. 2He asked me, “What
do you see?” Jer 1:13; Da 8:18

I answered, “I see a solid gold
lampstand with a bowl at the top
and seven lamps on it, with seven
channels to the lamps. 3Also there
are two olive trees by it, one on
the right of the bowl and the other on its left.” Rev 4:5; 11:4

[a] *1* Hebrew *satan* means *adversary.*
[b] *9* Or *facets*

4I asked the angel who talked
with me, "What are these, my
lord?"
5He answered, "Do you not
know what these are?"
"No, my lord," I replied. Zec 1:9
6So he said to me, "This is the
word of the LORD to Zerubbabel:
'Not by might nor by power, but
by my Spirit,' says the LORD Almighty. Isa 11:2-4; Hos 1:7
7"What are you, mighty mountain? Before Zerubbabel you will
become level ground. Then he will
bring out the capstone to shouts
of 'God bless it! God bless it!'"
Ps 118:22; Jer 51:25
8Then the word of the LORD
came to me: 9"The hands of Zerubbabel have laid the foundation
of this temple; his hands will also
complete it. Then you will know
that the LORD Almighty has sent
me to you. Zec 2:9; 6:12
10"Who dares despise the day of
small things, since the seven eyes
of the LORD that range throughout
the earth will rejoice when they
see the chosen capstone[a] in the
hand of Zerubbabel?"
Hag 2:3; Zec 3:9; Rev 5:6
11Then I asked the angel, "What
are these two olive trees on the
right and the left of the lampstand?" Rev 11:4
12Again I asked him, "What are
these two olive branches beside
the two gold pipes that pour out
golden oil?"
13He replied, "Do you not know
what these are?"
"No, my lord," I said.
14So he said, "These are the two
who are anointed to[b] serve the
Lord of all the earth."
Ex 29:7; Da 9:24-26; Zec 3:1-7

The Flying Scroll

5 I looked again, and there before me was a flying scroll.
Eze 2:9; Rev 5:1
2He asked me, "What do you
see?"
I answered, "I see a flying scroll,
twenty cubits long and ten cubits
wide.[c]"
3And he said to me, "This is the
curse that is going out over the
whole land; for according to what
it says on one side, every thief
will be banished, and according
to what it says on the other, everyone who swears falsely will be
banished. 4The LORD Almighty declares, 'I will send it out, and it will
enter the house of the thief and
the house of anyone who swears
falsely by my name. It will remain
in that house and destroy it completely, both its timbers and its
stones.'" Lev 14:34-45; Mal 3:5

The Woman in a Basket

5Then the angel who was speaking to me came forward and said
to me, "Look up and see what is
appearing."
6I asked, "What is it?"

[a] 10 Or *the plumb line* [b] 14 Or *two who bring oil and* [c] 2 That is, about 30 feet long and 15 feet wide or about 9 meters long and 4.5 meters wide

He replied, "It is a basket." And
he added, "This is the iniquity[a] of
the people throughout the land."
7Then the cover of lead was
raised, and there in the basket sat
a woman! 8He said, "This is wickedness," and he pushed her back
into the basket and pushed its
lead cover down on it. Mic 6:11
9Then I looked up — and there
before me were two women, with
the wind in their wings! They had
wings like those of a stork, and
they lifted up the basket between
heaven and earth. Lev 11:19
10"Where are they taking the
basket?" I asked the angel who
was speaking to me.
11He replied, "To the country of
Babylonia[b] to build a house for it.
When the house is ready, the basket will be set there in its place."

Ge 10:10; Jer 29:5,28; Da 1:2

Four Chariots

6 I looked up again, and there
before me were four char-
iots coming out from between
two mountains — mountains of
bronze. 2The first chariot had red
horses, the second black, 3the
third white, and the fourth dappled — all of them powerful. 4I
asked the angel who was speaking
to me, "What are these, my lord?"

Rev 6:2,5

5The angel answered me, "These
are the four spirits[c] of heaven,
going out from standing in the
presence of the Lord of the whole
world. 6The one with the black
horses is going toward the north
country, the one with the white
horses toward the west,[d] and the
one with the dappled horses toward the south."

Eze 37:9; Mt 24:31; Rev 7:1

7When the powerful horses
went out, they were straining to
go throughout the earth. And he
said, "Go throughout the earth!"
So they went throughout the
earth. Zec 1:10
8Then he called to me, "Look,
those going toward the north
country have given my Spirit[e] rest
in the land of the north."

Eze 5:13; 24:13

A Crown for Joshua

9The word of the LORD came to
me: 10"Take silver and gold from
the exiles Heldai, Tobijah and Jedaiah, who have arrived from Babylon. Go the same day to the house
of Josiah son of Zephaniah. 11Take
the silver and gold and make a
crown, and set it on the head of
the high priest, Joshua son of Jozadak.[f] 12Tell him this is what the
LORD Almighty says: 'Here is the
man whose name is the Branch,
and he will branch out from his
place and build the temple of the
LORD. 13It is he who will build the
temple of the LORD, and he will be
clothed with majesty and will sit
and rule on his throne. And he[g]

[a] 6 Or *appearance* [b] 11 Hebrew *Shinar* [c] 5 Or *winds* [d] 6 Or *horses after them* [e] 8 Or *spirit* [f] 11 Hebrew *Jehozadak,* a variant of *Jozadak* [g] 13 Or *there*

will be a priest on his throne. And
there will be harmony between
the two.' 14The crown will be given
to Heldai,[a] Tobijah, Jedaiah and
Hen[b] son of Zephaniah as a memorial in the temple of the LORD.
15Those who are far away will come
and help to build the temple of the LORD, and you will know that the LORD Almighty has sent me to you. This will happen if you diligently obey the LORD your God."

Isa 60:10; Zec 2:9-11; 3:7

Justice and Mercy, Not Fasting

7 In the fourth year of King Darius, the word of the LORD came to Zechariah on the fourth day of the ninth month, the month
of Kislev. 2The people of Bethel had sent Sharezer and Regem-Melek, together with their men,
to entreat the LORD 3by asking
the priests of the house of the LORD Almighty and the prophets, "Should I mourn and fast in the fifth month, as I have done for so many years?"

Jer 52:12-14; Zec 8:19

4Then the word of the LORD Almighty came to me: 5"Ask all the
people of the land and the priests, 'When you fasted and mourned in the fifth and seventh months for the past seventy years, was it really for me that you fasted?
6And when you were eating and
drinking, were you not just feasting for yourselves? 7Are these not
the words the LORD proclaimed through the earlier prophets when Jerusalem and its surrounding towns were at rest and prosperous, and the Negev and the western foothills were settled?' "

Jer 22:21; Zec 1:4

8And the word of the LORD came
again to Zechariah: 9"This is what
the LORD Almighty said: 'Administer true justice; show mercy and compassion to one another. 10Do
not oppress the widow or the fatherless, the foreigner or the poor. Do not plot evil against each other.'

Isa 1:17; Zec 8:16

11"But they refused to pay attention; stubbornly they turned their backs and covered their ears.
12They made their hearts as hard
as flint and would not listen to the law or to the words that the LORD Almighty had sent by his Spirit through the earlier prophets. So the LORD Almighty was very angry.

Ne 9:29; Eze 11:19; Da 9:12

13" 'When I called, they did
not listen; so when they called, I would not listen,' says the LORD
Almighty. 14'I scattered them with
a whirlwind among all the nations, where they were strangers. The land they left behind them was so desolate that no one traveled through it. This is how they made the pleasant land desolate.' "

Isa 1:15; Jer 44:6

The LORD Promises to Bless Jerusalem

8 The word of the LORD Almighty came to me.

[a] 14 Syriac; Hebrew *Helem* [b] 14 Or *and the gracious one, the*

[2]This is what the LORD Almighty says: "I am very jealous for Zion; I am burning with jealousy for her." Joel 2:18

[3]This is what the LORD says: "I will return to Zion and dwell in Jerusalem. Then Jerusalem will be called the Faithful City, and the mountain of the LORD Almighty will be called the Holy Mountain." Zec 1:16; 2:10

[4]This is what the LORD Almighty says: "Once again men and women of ripe old age will sit in the streets of Jerusalem, each of them with cane in hand because of their age. [5]The city streets will be filled with boys and girls playing there." Isa 65:20; Jer 30:20

[6]This is what the LORD Almighty says: "It may seem marvelous to the remnant of this people at that time, but will it seem marvelous to me?" declares the LORD Almighty. Ps 118:23; 126:1-3

[7]This is what the LORD Almighty says: "I will save my people from the countries of the east and the west. [8]I will bring them back to live in Jerusalem; they will be my people, and I will be faithful and righteous to them as their God." Zec 2:11; 10:6

[9]This is what the LORD Almighty says: "Now hear these words, 'Let your hands be strong so that the temple may be built.' This is also what the prophets said who were present when the foundation was laid for the house of the LORD Almighty. [10]Before that time there were no wages for people or hire for animals. No one could go about their business safely because of their enemies, since I had turned everyone against their neighbor. [11]But now I will not deal with the remnant of this people as I did in the past," declares the LORD Almighty. Isa 12:1; Hag 2:4

[12]"The seed will grow well, the vine will yield its fruit, the ground will produce its crops, and the heavens will drop their dew. I will give all these things as an inheritance to the remnant of this people. [13]Just as you, Judah and Israel, have been a curse[a] among the nations, so I will save you, and you will be a blessing.[b] Do not be afraid, but let your hands be strong." Ge 12:2; Jer 42:18; Joel 2:22

[14]This is what the LORD Almighty says: "Just as I had determined to bring disaster on you and showed no pity when your ancestors angered me," says the LORD Almighty, [15]"so now I have determined to do good again to Jerusalem and Judah. Do not be afraid. [16]These are the things you are to do: Speak the truth to each other, and render true and sound judgment in your courts; [17]do not plot evil against each other, and do not love to swear falsely. I hate all this," declares the LORD. Pr 3:29; Zec 7:9; Eph 4:25

[a] *13* That is, your name has been used in cursing (see Jer. 29:22); or, you have been regarded as under a curse. [b] *13* Or *and your name will be used in blessings* (see Gen. 48:20); or *and you will be seen as blessed*

18 The word of the LORD Almighty
came to me.
19 This is what the LORD Almighty
says: "The fasts of the fourth, fifth,
seventh and tenth months will become joyful and glad occasions
and happy festivals for Judah.
Therefore love truth and peace."
Ps 30:11
20 This is what the LORD Almighty says: "Many peoples and
the inhabitants of many cities will
yet come, 21 and the inhabitants
of one city will go to another and
say, 'Let us go at once to entreat
the LORD and seek the LORD Almighty. I myself am going.' 22 And
many peoples and powerful nations will come to Jerusalem to
seek the LORD Almighty and to entreat him." Ps 117:1; Zec 2:11
23 This is what the LORD Almighty
says: "In those days ten people
from all languages and nations
will take firm hold of one Jew by
the hem of his robe and say, 'Let
us go with you, because we have
heard that God is with you.'"
Isa 45:14; 1Co 14:25

Judgment on Israel's Enemies

9 A prophecy:

The word of the LORD is
against the land of
Hadrak
and will come to rest on
Damascus — Isa 17:1
for the eyes of all people and
all the tribes of Israel
are on the LORD —[a]
2 and on Hamath too, which
borders on it, Jer 49:23
and on Tyre and Sidon,
though they are very
skillful. Eze 28:1-19
3 Tyre has built herself a
stronghold;
she has heaped up silver like
dust,
and gold like the dirt of the
streets. Job 27:16; Eze 28:4
4 But the Lord will take away her
possessions
and destroy her power on the
sea,
and she will be consumed by
fire. Isa 23:1; Eze 26:3-5
5 Ashkelon will see it and fear;
Jer 47:5
Gaza will writhe in agony,
and Ekron too, for her hope
will wither.
Gaza will lose her king
and Ashkelon will be deserted.
6 A mongrel people will occupy
Ashdod,
and I will put an end to the
pride of the Philistines.
Isa 14:30
7 I will take the blood from their
mouths,
the forbidden food from
between their teeth.
Those who are left will belong
to our God Job 25:2
and become a clan in Judah,
and Ekron will be like the
Jebusites. Jer 47:1

[a] 1 *Or Damascus. / For the eye of the LORD is on all people, / as well as on the tribes of Israel,*

8 But I will encamp at my temple
to guard it against
marauding forces.
Never again will an oppressor
overrun my people,
for now I am keeping watch.
Isa 52:1; 54:14

The Coming of Zion's King

9 Rejoice greatly, Daughter Zion!
Isa 62:11
Shout, Daughter Jerusalem!
See, your king comes to you,
righteous and victorious,
Isa 9:6-7; Zep 3:14-15
lowly and riding on a donkey,
on a colt, the foal of a
donkey. Mt 21:5*; Jn 12:15*
10 I will take away the chariots
from Ephraim
and the warhorses from
Jerusalem,
and the battle bow will be
broken. Hos 1:7; 2:18
He will proclaim peace to the
nations. Isa 2:4
His rule will extend from sea
to sea
and from the River[a] to the
ends of the earth. Ps 72:8
11 As for you, because of the
blood of my covenant
with you, Ex 24:8
I will free your prisoners
from the waterless pit.
Isa 42:7
12 Return to your fortress, you
prisoners of hope; Joel 3:16
even now I announce that
I will restore twice as
much to you. Isa 40:2
13 I will bend Judah as I bend my
bow
and fill it with Ephraim. Isa 49:2
I will rouse your sons, Zion,
against your sons, Greece,
Joel 3:6
and make you like a warrior's
sword. Jer 51:20

The LORD Will Appear

14 Then the LORD will appear over
them; Isa 31:5
his arrow will flash like
lightning. Ps 18:14; Hab 3:11
The Sovereign LORD will sound
the trumpet;
he will march in the storms
of the south, Isa 21:1; 66:15
15 and the LORD Almighty
will shield them.
Isa 37:35; Zec 12:8
They will destroy
and overcome with
slingstones.
They will drink and roar as
with wine;
they will be full like a bowl
used for sprinkling[b]
the corners of the altar.
Ex 27:2
16 The LORD their God will save
his people on that day
as a shepherd saves his
flock.
They will sparkle in his land
like jewels in a crown.
Isa 62:3; Jer 31:11
17 How attractive and beautiful
they will be!

[a] *10* That is, the Euphrates [b] *15* Or *bowl, / like*

Grain will make the young
men thrive,
and new wine the young
women.

The LORD Will Care for Judah

10 Ask the LORD for rain in
the springtime;
it is the LORD who sends the
thunderstorms.
He gives showers of rain to all
people, Lev 26:4
and plants of the field to
everyone. Job 14:9
2 The idols speak deceitfully,
Eze 21:21
diviners see visions that lie;
Isa 44:25
they tell dreams that are false,
they give comfort in vain.
Isa 40:19
Therefore the people wander
like sheep
oppressed for lack of a
shepherd. Eze 34:5; Hos 3:4

3 "My anger burns against the
shepherds,
and I will punish the leaders;
Jer 25:34
for the LORD Almighty will care
for his flock, the people of
Judah,
and make them like a proud
horse in battle. Eze 34:8-10
4 From Judah will come the
cornerstone, Ps 118:22
from him the tent peg,
Isa 22:23
from him the battle bow, Zec 9:10
from him every ruler.
5 Together they[a] will be like
warriors in battle
trampling their enemy into
the mud of the streets.
2Sa 22:43
They will fight because the
LORD is with them,
and they will put the enemy
horsemen to shame.
Am 2:15; Hag 2:22

6 "I will strengthen Judah
and save the tribes of Joseph.
I will restore them
because I have compassion
on them. Zec 8:7-8
They will be as though
I had not rejected them,
for I am the LORD their God
and I will answer them. Zec 13:9
7 The Ephraimites will become
like warriors,
and their hearts will be glad
as with wine. Zec 9:15
Their children will see it and be
joyful;
their hearts will rejoice in
the LORD.
8 I will signal for them Isa 5:26
and gather them in.
Surely I will redeem them;
they will be as numerous as
before. Eze 36:11
9 Though I scatter them among
the peoples,
yet in distant lands they will
remember me. Eze 6:9
They and their children will
survive,
and they will return.

[a] 4,5 Or *ruler, all of them together.* / [5] *They*

10 I will bring them back from
Egypt
and gather them from
Assyria. Isa 11:11
I will bring them to Gilead and
Lebanon, Jer 50:19
and there will not be room
enough for them. Isa 49:19
11 They will pass through the sea
of trouble;
the surging sea will be
subdued
and all the depths of the Nile
will dry up. Isa 19:5-7; 51:10
Assyria's pride will be brought
down Zep 2:13
and Egypt's scepter will pass
away. Eze 30:13
12 I will strengthen them in the
LORD
and in his name they will
live securely," Mic 4:5
declares the LORD.

11 Open your doors, Lebanon,
Eze 31:3
so that fire may devour your
cedars! Zec 12:6
2 Wail, you juniper, for the cedar
has fallen;
the stately trees are ruined!
Wail, oaks of Bashan; Isa 2:13
the dense forest has been cut
down! Isa 32:19
3 Listen to the wail of the
shepherds;
their rich pastures are
destroyed!
Listen to the roar of the lions;
the lush thicket of the Jordan
is ruined! Jer 2:15; 50:44

Two Shepherds

4 This is what the LORD my God
says: "Shepherd the flock marked
for slaughter. 5 Their buyers
slaughter them and go unpunished. Those who sell them say,
'Praise the LORD, I am rich!' Their
own shepherds do not spare them.
6 For I will no longer have pity on
the people of the land," declares
the LORD. "I will give everyone
into the hands of their neighbors
and their king. They will devastate
the land, and I will not rescue anyone from their hands." Mic 5:8; 7:2-6
7 So I shepherded the flock
marked for slaughter, particularly
the oppressed of the flock. Then
I took two staffs and called one
Favor and the other Union, and
I shepherded the flock. 8 In one
month I got rid of the three shepherds. Jer 25:34
The flock detested me, and I
grew weary of them 9 and said, "I
will not be your shepherd. Let the
dying die, and the perishing perish. Let those who are left eat one
another's flesh." Jer 15:2; 43:11
10 Then I took my staff called Favor and broke it, revoking the covenant I had made with all the nations. 11 It was revoked on that day,
and so the oppressed of the flock
who were watching me knew it
was the word of the LORD. Jer 14:21
12 I told them, "If you think it
best, give me my pay; but if not,
keep it." So they paid me thirty
pieces of silver. Ex 21:32; Mt 26:15

13 And the LORD said to me,
"Throw it to the potter" — the
handsome price at which they valued me! So I took the thirty pieces of silver and threw them to the
potter at the house of the LORD.

Mt 27:9-10*; Ac 1:18-19

14 Then I broke my second staff
called Union, breaking the family bond between Judah and Israel.

15 Then the LORD said to me,
"Take again the equipment of a
foolish shepherd. 16 For I am going
to raise up a shepherd over the
land who will not care for the lost,
or seek the young, or heal the injured, or feed the healthy, but will
eat the meat of the choice sheep,
tearing off their hooves.

17 "Woe to the worthless
shepherd, Jer 23:1
who deserts the flock!
May the sword strike his
arm and his right eye!

Eze 30:21-22

May his arm be completely
withered,
his right eye totally blinded!"

Isa 13:1; Jer 23:1

Jerusalem's Enemies to Be Destroyed

12 A prophecy: The word of the
LORD concerning Israel.

The LORD, who stretches out the
heavens, who lays the foundation
of the earth, and who forms the
human spirit within a person, declares: 2 "I am going to make Jerusalem a cup that sends all the surrounding peoples reeling. Judah
will be besieged as well as Jerusalem. 3 On that day, when all the
nations of the earth are gathered
against her, I will make Jerusalem
an immovable rock for all the nations. All who try to move it will
injure themselves. 4 On that day I
will strike every horse with panic and its rider with madness,"
declares the LORD. "I will keep a
watchful eye over Judah, but I will
blind all the horses of the nations.
5 Then the clans of Judah will say
in their hearts, 'The people of Jerusalem are strong, because the
LORD Almighty is their God.'

Ps 75:8; Isa 51:23; Zec 14:14

6 "On that day I will make the
clans of Judah like a firepot in a
woodpile, like a flaming torch
among sheaves. They will consume all the surrounding peoples
right and left, but Jerusalem will
remain intact in her place.

Isa 10:17-18; Ob 1:18

7 "The LORD will save the dwellings of Judah first, so that the
honor of the house of David and of
Jerusalem's inhabitants may not
be greater than that of Judah. 8 On
that day the LORD will shield those
who live in Jerusalem, so that the
feeblest among them will be like
David, and the house of David will
be like God, like the angel of the
LORD going before them. 9 On that
day I will set out to destroy all the
nations that attack Jerusalem.

Zec 9:15; 14:2-3

Mourning for the One They Pierced

10"And I will pour out on the
house of David and the inhabitants of Jerusalem a spirit[a] of
grace and supplication. They will
look on[b] me, the one they have
pierced, and they will mourn for
him as one mourns for an only
child, and grieve bitterly for him
as one grieves for a firstborn son.
11On that day the weeping in Jerusalem will be as great as the
weeping of Hadad Rimmon in
the plain of Megiddo. 12The land
will mourn, each clan by itself,
with their wives by themselves:
the clan of the house of David and
their wives, the clan of the house
of Nathan and their wives, 13the
clan of the house of Levi and their
wives, the clan of Shimei and their
wives, 14and all the rest of the clans
and their wives. Jn 19:34,37*; Rev 1:7

Cleansing From Sin

13 "On that day a fountain will
be opened to the house of
David and the inhabitants of Jerusalem, to cleanse them from sin
and impurity. Ps 51:2; Heb 9:14; Jer 17:13

2"On that day, I will banish the
names of the idols from the land,
and they will be remembered
no more," declares the LORD Almighty. "I will remove both the
prophets and the spirit of impurity from the land. 3And if anyone
still prophesies, their father and
mother, to whom they were born,
will say to them, 'You must die,
because you have told lies in the
LORD's name.' Then their own parents will stab the one who prophesies. Dt 18:20; Jer 23:14-15,34

4"On that day every prophet will
be ashamed of their prophetic vision. They will not put on a prophet's garment of hair in order to
deceive. 5Each will say, 'I am not
a prophet. I am a farmer; the land
has been my livelihood since my
youth.[c]' 6If someone asks, 'What
are these wounds on your body[d]?'
they will answer, 'The wounds
I was given at the house of my
friends.' Mic 3:6-7; Mt 3:4

The Shepherd Struck, the Sheep Scattered

7"Awake, sword, against my
shepherd, Isa 40:11; Jer 47:6
against the man who is close
to me!"
declares the LORD
Almighty.
"Strike the shepherd,
and the sheep will be
scattered, Mt 26:31*
and I will turn my hand
against the little ones.
8In the whole land," declares the
LORD,
"two-thirds will be struck
down and perish;
yet one-third will be left in it.
Eze 5:2-4,12
9This third I will put into the
fire; Mal 3:2

[a] 10 Or *the Spirit* [b] 10 Or *to* [c] 5 Or *farmer; a man sold me in my youth*
[d] 6 Or *wounds between your hands*

I will refine them like silver 1Pe 1:6-7
and test them like gold.
They will call on my name Ps 50:15
and I will answer them; Zec 10:6
I will say, 'They are my people,' Jer 30:22
and they will say, 'The LORD
is our God.'" Jer 29:12

The LORD Comes and Reigns

14 A day of the LORD is coming,
Jerusalem, when your pos-
sessions will be plundered and divided up within your very walls.
Isa 13:9; Mal 4:1

2I will gather all the nations to
Jerusalem to fight against it; the
city will be captured, the houses
ransacked, and the women raped.
Half of the city will go into exile,
but the rest of the people will not
be taken from the city. 3Then the
LORD will go out and fight against
those nations, as he fights on a day
of battle. 4On that day his feet will
stand on the Mount of Olives, east
of Jerusalem, and the Mount of Olives will be split in two from east
to west, forming a great valley,
with half of the mountain moving
north and half moving south. 5You
will flee by my mountain valley,
for it will extend to Azel. You will
flee as you fled from the earthquake[a] in the days of Uzziah king
of Judah. Then the LORD my God
will come, and all the holy ones
with him. Eze 11:23; Am 1:1; Mt 16:27

6On that day there will be neither sunlight nor cold, frosty
darkness. 7It will be a unique
day — a day known only to the
LORD — with no distinction between day and night. When evening comes, there will be light.
Rev 21:23-25; 22:5

8On that day living water will
flow out from Jerusalem, half of it
east to the Dead Sea and half of it
west to the Mediterranean Sea, in
summer and in winter.
Eze 47:1-12; Rev 22:1-2

9The LORD will be king over the
whole earth. On that day there
will be one LORD, and his name
the only name. Eph 4:5-6; Rev 11:15

10The whole land, from Geba to
Rimmon, south of Jerusalem, will
become like the Arabah. But Jerusalem will be raised up high from
the Benjamin Gate to the site of
the First Gate, to the Corner Gate,
and from the Tower of Hananel
to the royal winepresses, and will
remain in its place. 11It will be inhabited; never again will it be destroyed. Jerusalem will be secure.
Am 9:11; Zec 12:6

12This is the plague with which
the LORD will strike all the nations that fought against Jerusalem: Their flesh will rot while they
are still standing on their feet,
their eyes will rot in their sockets, and their tongues will rot in
their mouths. 13On that day people

[a] 5 Or *5My mountain valley will be blocked and will extend to Azel. It will be blocked as it was blocked because of the earthquake*

will be stricken by the LORD with
great panic. They will seize each
other by the hand and attack one
another. 14Judah too will fight at
Jerusalem. The wealth of all the
surrounding nations will be collected — great quantities of gold
and silver and clothing. 15A similar plague will strike the horses
and mules, the camels and donkeys, and all the animals in those
camps. Dt 28:22; Zec 11:6

16Then the survivors from all
the nations that have attacked Jerusalem will go up year after year
to worship the King, the LORD Almighty, and to celebrate the Festival of Tabernacles. 17If any of the
peoples of the earth do not go up
to Jerusalem to worship the King,
the LORD Almighty, they will have
no rain. 18If the Egyptian people
do not go up and take part, they
will have no rain. The LORD[a] will
bring on them the plague he inflicts on the nations that do not
go up to celebrate the Festival
of Tabernacles. 19This will be the
punishment of Egypt and the
punishment of all the nations
that do not go up to celebrate the
Festival of Tabernacles.

Isa 60:6-9; Am 4:7

20On that day HOLY TO THE LORD
will be inscribed on the bells of
the horses, and the cooking pots
in the LORD's house will be like
the sacred bowls in front of the altar. 21Every pot in Jerusalem and
Judah will be holy to the LORD Almighty, and all who come to sacrifice will take some of the pots
and cook in them. And on that day
there will no longer be a Canaanite[b] in the house of the LORD Almighty. 1Co 10:31; Eze 44:9

[a] 18 Or *part, then the LORD*
[b] 21 Or *merchant*

MALACHI

1 A prophecy: The word of the LORD to Israel through Malachi.[a]

Na 1:1; 1Pe 4:11

Israel Doubts God's Love

2 "I have loved you," says the LORD.

Dt 4:37

"But you ask, 'How have you loved us?'

Mal 2:14,17

"Was not Esau Jacob's brother?" declares the LORD. "Yet I have loved Jacob, 3 but Esau I have hated, and I have turned his hill country into a wasteland and left his inheritance to the desert jackals."

Ro 9:13*; Isa 34:10; Eze 35:3-9

4 Edom may say, "Though we have been crushed, we will rebuild the ruins."

Isa 9:10

But this is what the LORD Almighty says: "They may build, but I will demolish. They will be called the Wicked Land, a people always under the wrath of the LORD. 5 You will see it with your own eyes and say, 'Great is the LORD — even beyond the borders of Israel!'

Ps 35:27; Am 1:11-12

Breaking Covenant Through Blemished Sacrifices

6 "A son honors his father, and a slave his master. If I am a father, where is the honor due me? If I am a master, where is the respect due me?" says the LORD Almighty.

Isa 1:2; Mt 15:4

"It is you priests who show contempt for my name.

"But you ask, 'How have we shown contempt for your name?'

7 "By offering defiled food on my altar.

Lev 21:6

"But you ask, 'How have we defiled you?'

"By saying that the LORD's table is contemptible. 8 When you offer blind animals for sacrifice, is that not wrong? When you sacrifice lame or diseased animals, is that not wrong? Try offering them to your governor! Would he be pleased with you? Would he accept you?" says the LORD Almighty.

Lev 22:22; Dt 15:21; Isa 43:23

9 "Now plead with God to be gracious to us. With such offerings from your hands, will he accept you?" — says the LORD Almighty.

Lev 23:33-44

10 "Oh, that one of you would shut the temple doors, so that you would not light useless fires on my altar! I am not pleased with you," says the LORD Almighty, "and I will accept no offering from your hands. 11 My name will be great among the nations, from where the sun rises to where it sets. In every place incense and pure offerings will be brought to me, because my name will be great

[a] *1 Malachi* means *my messenger.*

among the nations," says the LORD
Almighty. Isa 1:11-14; Hos 5:6
[12]"But you profane it by saying,
'The Lord's table is defiled,' and,
'Its food is contemptible.' [13]And
you say, 'What a burden!' and you
sniff at it contemptuously," says
the LORD Almighty. Isa 43:22-24
"When you bring injured, lame
or diseased animals and offer
them as sacrifices, should I accept
them from your hands?" says the
LORD. [14]"Cursed is the cheat who
has an acceptable male in his flock
and vows to give it, but then sacrifices a blemished animal to the
Lord. For I am a great king," says
the LORD Almighty, "and my name
is to be feared among the nations.
Lev 22:18-21; 1Ti 6:15

Additional Warning to the Priests

2 "And now, you priests, this
warning is for you. [2]If you do
not listen, and if you do not re-
solve to honor my name," says the
LORD Almighty, "I will send a curse
on you, and I will curse your blessings. Yes, I have already cursed
them, because you have not resolved to honor me. Dt 28:20
[3]"Because of you I will rebuke
your descendants[a]; I will smear
on your faces the dung from your
festival sacrifices, and you will
be carried off with it. [4]And you
will know that I have sent you
this warning so that my covenant
with Levi may continue," says the
LORD Almighty. [5]"My covenant
was with him, a covenant of life
and peace, and I gave them to
him; this called for reverence and
he revered me and stood in awe of
my name. [6]True instruction was in
his mouth and nothing false was
found on his lips. He walked with
me in peace and uprightness, and
turned many from sin.
Nu 25:12; Jer 23:22
[7]"For the lips of a priest ought
to preserve knowledge, because
he is the messenger of the LORD
Almighty and people seek instruction from his mouth. [8]But you
have turned from the way and by
your teaching have caused many
to stumble; you have violated the
covenant with Levi," says the LORD
Almighty. [9]"So I have caused you
to be despised and humiliated before all the people, because you
have not followed my ways but
have shown partiality in matters
of the law." 1Sa 2:30; Jer 18:15

Breaking Covenant Through Divorce

[10]Do we not all have one Father[b]? Did not one God create us?
Why do we profane the covenant
of our ancestors by being unfaithful to one another? Ex 19:5; 1Co 8:6
[11]Judah has been unfaithful. A
detestable thing has been committed in Israel and in Jerusalem:
Judah has desecrated the sanctuary the LORD loves by marrying
women who worship a foreign
god. [12]As for the man who does

[a] 3 Or *will blight your grain* [b] 10 Or *father*

this, whoever he may be, may the
LORD remove him from the tents
of Jacob[a] — even though he brings
an offering to the LORD Almighty.
Mal 1:10

13Another thing you do: You
flood the LORD's altar with tears.
You weep and wail because he no
longer looks with favor on your
offerings or accepts them with
pleasure from your hands. 14You
ask, "Why?" It is because the LORD
is the witness between you and
the wife of your youth. You have
been unfaithful to her, though she
is your partner, the wife of your
marriage covenant. Pr 5:18; Heb 13:4

15Has not the one God made
you? You belong to him in body
and spirit. And what does the one
God seek? Godly offspring.[b] So be
on your guard, and do not be unfaithful to the wife of your youth.
Mt 19:4-6; 1Co 7:14

16"The man who hates and divorces his wife," says the LORD,
the God of Israel, "does violence
to the one he should protect,"[c]
says the LORD Almighty.
Dt 24:1; Mt 5:31-32; 19:4-9

So be on your guard, and do not
be unfaithful. Ps 51:10

Breaking Covenant Through Injustice

17You have wearied the LORD
with your words. Isa 43:24

"How have we wearied him?"
you ask. Mal 1:2

By saying, "All who do evil are
good in the eyes of the LORD, and
he is pleased with them" or "Where
is the God of justice?" Ps 5:4

3 "I will send my messenger, who
will prepare the way before me.
Then suddenly the Lord you are
seeking will come to his temple;
the messenger of the covenant,
whom you desire, will come," says
the LORD Almighty. Mt 11:10*

2But who can endure the day of
his coming? Who can stand when
he appears? For he will be like a
refiner's fire or a launderer's soap.
3He will sit as a refiner and purifier
of silver; he will purify the Levites
and refine them like gold and silver. Then the LORD will have men
who will bring offerings in righteousness, 4and the offerings of
Judah and Jerusalem will be acceptable to the LORD, as in days
gone by, as in former years.
Rev 6:17; Isa 1:25; Mal 1:11

5"So I will come to put you
on trial. I will be quick to testify against sorcerers, adulterers
and perjurers, against those who
defraud laborers of their wages,
who oppress the widows and the
fatherless, and deprive the foreigners among you of justice, but
do not fear me," says the LORD Almighty. Lev 19:13; Jer 7:9; Jas 5:4

[a] 12 Or 12*May the LORD remove from the tents of Jacob anyone who gives testimony in behalf of the man who does this*

[b] 15 The meaning of the Hebrew for the first part of this verse is uncertain.

[c] 16 Or *"I hate divorce," says the LORD, the God of Israel, "because the man who divorces his wife covers his garment with violence,"*

Breaking Covenant by Withholding Tithes

6 “I the LORD do not change. So you, the descendants of Jacob, are not destroyed. 7 Ever since the time of your ancestors you have turned away from my decrees and have not kept them. Return to me, and I will return to you,” says the LORD Almighty. Ac 7:51; Jas 1:17

“But you ask, ‘How are we to return?’

8 “Will a mere mortal rob God? Yet you rob me.

“But you ask, ‘How are we robbing you?’

“In tithes and offerings. 9 You are under a curse — your whole nation — because you are robbing me. 10 Bring the whole tithe into the storehouse, that there may be food in my house. Test me in this,” says the LORD Almighty, “and see if I will not throw open the floodgates of heaven and pour out so much blessing that there will not be room enough to store it. 11 I will prevent pests from devouring your crops, and the vines in your fields will not drop their fruit before it is ripe,” says the LORD Almighty. 12 “Then all the nations will call you blessed, for yours will be a delightful land,” says the LORD Almighty. Ne 13:10-12; Isa 62:4

Israel Speaks Arrogantly Against God

13 “You have spoken arrogantly against me,” says the LORD. Mal 2:17

“Yet you ask, ‘What have we said against you?’

14 “You have said, ‘It is futile to serve God. What do we gain by carrying out his requirements and going about like mourners before the LORD Almighty? 15 But now we call the arrogant blessed. Certainly evildoers prosper, and even when they put God to the test, they get away with it.’” Isa 58:3; Jer 7:10

The Faithful Remnant

16 Then those who feared the LORD talked with each other, and the LORD listened and heard. A scroll of remembrance was written in his presence concerning those who feared the LORD and honored his name. Ps 34:15; 56:8

17 “On the day when I act,” says the LORD Almighty, “they will be my treasured possession. I will spare them, just as a father has compassion and spares his son who serves him. 18 And you will again see the distinction between the righteous and the wicked, between those who serve God and those who do not. Ps 103:13; Mt 25:32-33,41

Judgment and Covenant Renewal

4 [a] “Surely the day is coming; it will burn like a furnace. All the arrogant and every evildoer will be stubble, and the day that is coming will set them on fire,” says the LORD Almighty. “Not a root or a branch will be left to them.

[a] In Hebrew texts 4:1-6 is numbered 3:19-24.

2But for you who revere my name,
the sun of righteousness will rise
with healing in its rays. And you
will go out and frolic like well-fed
calves. 3Then you will trample on
the wicked; they will be ashes under the soles of your feet on the
day when I act," says the LORD Almighty. Lk 1:78; Eph 5:14

4"Remember the law of my servant Moses, the decrees and laws I
gave him at Horeb for all Israel.
Ex 20:1

5"See, I will send the prophet
Elijah to you before that great and
dreadful day of the LORD comes.
6He will turn the hearts of the
parents to their children, and the
hearts of the children to their parents; or else I will come and strike
the land with total destruction."
Mt 11:14; Lk 1:17

NEW TESTAMENT

MATTHEW

The Genealogy of Jesus the Messiah

1 This is the genealogy[a] of Jesus the Messiah[b] the son of David, the son of Abraham:

Ge 22:18; Isa 11:1; Ro 1:3

2 Abraham was the father of Isaac, Ge 21:3,12
Isaac the father of Jacob, Ge 25:26
Jacob the father of Judah and his brothers, Ge 29:35
3 Judah the father of Perez and Zerah, whose mother was Tamar, Ge 38:27-30
Perez the father of Hezron,
Hezron the father of Ram,
4 Ram the father of Amminadab,
Amminadab the father of Nahshon,
Nahshon the father of Salmon,
5 Salmon the father of Boaz, whose mother was Rahab,
Boaz the father of Obed, whose mother was Ruth,
Obed the father of Jesse,
6 and Jesse the father of King David. Ru 4:18-22; 1Sa 16:1

David was the father of Solomon, whose mother had been Uriah's wife, 2Sa 12:24
7 Solomon the father of Rehoboam,
Rehoboam the father of Abijah,
Abijah the father of Asa,
8 Asa the father of Jehoshaphat,
Jehoshaphat the father of Jehoram,
Jehoram the father of Uzziah,
9 Uzziah the father of Jotham,
Jotham the father of Ahaz,
Ahaz the father of Hezekiah,
10 Hezekiah the father of Manasseh, 2Ki 20:21
Manasseh the father of Amon,
Amon the father of Josiah,
11 and Josiah the father of Jeconiah[c] and his brothers at the time of the exile to Babylon. 1Ch 3:10-17

12 After the exile to Babylon:
Jeconiah was the father of Shealtiel, 1Ch 3:17
Shealtiel the father of Zerubbabel, 1Ch 3:19; Ezr 3:2
13 Zerubbabel the father of Abihud,

[a] *1* Or *is an account of the origin* [b] *1* Or *Jesus Christ. Messiah* (Hebrew) and *Christ* (Greek) both mean *Anointed One*; also in verse 18. [c] *11* That is, Jehoiachin; also in verse 12

Abihud the father of Eliakim,
Eliakim the father of Azor,
14 Azor the father of Zadok,
Zadok the father of Akim,
Akim the father of Elihud,
15 Elihud the father of Eleazar,
Eleazar the father of Matthan,
Matthan the father of Ja-
cob,
16 and Jacob the father of Joseph, the husband of
Mary, and Mary was the
mother of Jesus who is
called the Messiah.

Mt 27:17; Lk 1:27

17 Thus there were fourteen generations in all from Abraham to
David, fourteen from David to the
exile to Babylon, and fourteen
from the exile to the Messiah.

Lk 3:23-38

Joseph Accepts Jesus as His Son

18 This is how the birth of Jesus
the Messiah came about[a]: His
mother Mary was pledged to be
married to Joseph, but before they
came together, she was found to
be pregnant through the Holy
Spirit.
19 Because Joseph her husband was faithful to the law, and
yet[b] did not want to expose her to
public disgrace, he had in mind to
divorce her quietly. Lk 1:35; Dt 24:1

20 But after he had considered
this, an angel of the Lord appeared
to him in a dream and said, "Joseph son of David, do not be afraid
to take Mary home as your wife,
because what is conceived in her
is from the Holy Spirit.
21 She will
give birth to a son, and you are to
give him the name Jesus,[c] because
he will save his people from their
sins." Lk 2:11; Ac 13:23,28

22 All this took place to fulfill
what the Lord had said through
the prophet:
23 "The virgin will
conceive and give birth to a son,
and they will call him Immanuel"[d] (which means "God with us").

Isa 8:8,10

24 When Joseph woke up, he did
what the angel of the Lord had
commanded him and took Mary
home as his wife.
25 But he did not
consummate their marriage until she gave birth to a son. And he
gave him the name Jesus. Lk 1:31

The Magi Visit the Messiah

2 After Jesus was born in Bethlehem in Judea, during the
time of King Herod, Magi[e] from
the east came to Jerusalem
2 and
asked, "Where is the one who has
been born king of the Jews? We
saw his star when it rose and have
come to worship him."

Nu 24:17; Jer 23:5

3 When King Herod heard this he
was disturbed, and all Jerusalem
with him.
4 When he had called to-
gether all the people's chief priests

[a] 18 Or *The origin of Jesus the Messiah was like this* [b] 19 Or *was a righteous man and* [c] 21 *Jesus* is the Greek form of *Joshua*, which means *the LORD saves.* [d] 23 Isaiah 7:14 [e] 1 Traditionally *wise men*

and teachers of the law, he asked
them where the Messiah was to be
born. 5“In Bethlehem in Judea,”
they replied, “for this is what the
prophet has written:

6“ ‘But you, Bethlehem, in the
land of Judah,
are by no means least
among the rulers of
Judah;
for out of you will come a
ruler
who will shepherd my
people Israel.’[a]” Jn 7:42

7Then Herod called the Magi secretly and found out from them
the exact time the star had appeared. 8He sent them to Bethlehem and said, “Go and search
carefully for the child. As soon as
you find him, report to me, so that
I too may go and worship him.”
9After they had heard the king,
they went on their way, and the
star they had seen when it rose
went ahead of them until it
stopped over the place where the
child was. 10When they saw the
star, they were overjoyed. 11On
coming to the house, they saw
the child with his mother Mary,
and they bowed down and worshiped him. Then they opened
their treasures and presented
him with gifts of gold, frankincense and myrrh. 12And having
been warned in a dream not to go
back to Herod, they returned to
their country by another route.
Ps 72:10; Isa 60:3

The Escape to Egypt

13When they had gone, an angel
of the Lord appeared to Joseph in a
dream. “Get up,” he said, “take the
child and his mother and escape
to Egypt. Stay there until I tell you,
for Herod is going to search for the
child to kill him.” Rev 12:4
14So he got up, took the child and
his mother during the night and
left for Egypt, 15where he stayed
until the death of Herod. And so
was fulfilled what the Lord had
said through the prophet: “Out of
Egypt I called my son.”[b] Ex 4:22-23
16When Herod realized that he
had been outwitted by the Magi,
he was furious, and he gave orders to kill all the boys in Bethlehem and its vicinity who were two
years old and under, in accordance
with the time he had learned from
the Magi. 17Then what was said
through the prophet Jeremiah
was fulfilled: Mt 1:22

18“A voice is heard in Ramah,
weeping and great
mourning,
Rachel weeping for her
children
and refusing to be
comforted,
because they are no more.”[c]

The Return to Nazareth

19After Herod died, an angel of
the Lord appeared in a dream to
Joseph in Egypt 20and said, “Get

[a] 6 Micah 5:2,4 [b] 15 Hosea 11:1
[c] 18 Jer. 31:15

up, take the child and his mother and go to the land of Israel, for
those who were trying to take the
child's life are dead." Ex 4:19
[21]So he got up, took the child
and his mother and went to the
land of Israel. [22]But when he heard
that Archelaus was reigning in Judea in place of his father Herod,
he was afraid to go there. Having been warned in a dream, he
withdrew to the district of Galilee,
[23]and he went and lived in a town
called Nazareth. So was fulfilled
what was said through the prophets, that he would be called a Nazarene. Lk 1:26; Jn 1:45-46

John the Baptist Prepares the Way

3 In those days John the Baptist
came, preaching in the wilderness of Judea [2]and saying, "Repent, for the kingdom of heaven
has come near." [3]This is he who
was spoken of through the prophet Isaiah: Mt 4:17

"A voice of one calling in the
wilderness,
'Prepare the way for the Lord,
make straight paths for
him.'"[a] Lk 1:76; Jn 1:23

[4]John's clothes were made of
camel's hair, and he had a leather
belt around his waist. His food was
locusts and wild honey. [5]People
went out to him from Jerusalem
and all Judea and the whole region
of the Jordan. [6]Confessing their
sins, they were baptized by him in
the Jordan River. Lev 11:22; 2Ki 1:8

[7]But when he saw many of the
Pharisees and Sadducees coming
to where he was baptizing, he said
to them: "You brood of vipers!
Who warned you to flee from the
coming wrath? [8]Produce fruit in
keeping with repentance. [9]And
do not think you can say to yourselves, 'We have Abraham as our
father.' I tell you that out of these
stones God can raise up children
for Abraham. [10]The ax is already
at the root of the trees, and every
tree that does not produce good
fruit will be cut down and thrown
into the fire. Mt 7:19; Ac 26:20
[11]"I baptize you with[b] water for
repentance. But after me comes
one who is more powerful than
I, whose sandals I am not worthy
to carry. He will baptize you with[b]
the Holy Spirit and fire. [12]His winnowing fork is in his hand, and
he will clear his threshing floor,
gathering his wheat into the barn
and burning up the chaff with unquenchable fire." Mk 1:3-8; Lk 3:2-17

The Baptism of Jesus

[13]Then Jesus came from Galilee to the Jordan to be baptized
by John. [14]But John tried to deter
him, saying, "I need to be baptized
by you, and do you come to me?"
Mk 1:4
[15]Jesus replied, "Let it be so now;
it is proper for us to do this to fulfill all righteousness." Then John
consented.

[a] *3* Isaiah 40:3 [b] *11* Or *in*

16 As soon as Jesus was baptized,
he went up out of the water. At
that moment heaven was opened,
and he saw the Spirit of God descending like a dove and alighting
on him. 17 And a voice from heaven
said, "This is my Son, whom I love;
with him I am well pleased."

Mk 1:9-11; Lk 3:21-22; Jn 1:31-34

Jesus Is Tested in the Wilderness

4 Then Jesus was led by the Spirit into the wilderness to be
tempted[a] by the devil. 2 After fasting forty days and forty nights, he
was hungry. 3 The tempter came to
him and said, "If you are the Son
of God, tell these stones to become
bread." 1Ki 19:8; 1Th 3:5
4 Jesus answered, "It is written:
'Man shall not live on bread alone,
but on every word that comes
from the mouth of God.'[b]" Jn 4:34
5 Then the devil took him to the
holy city and had him stand on
the highest point of the temple.
6 "If you are the Son of God," he
said, "throw yourself down. For it
is written: Mt 27:53

"'He will command his
angels concerning
you,
and they will lift you up in
their hands,
so that you will not strike
your foot against a
stone.'[c]"

7 Jesus answered him, "It is also
written: 'Do not put the Lord your
God to the test.'[d]"
8 Again, the devil took him to a
very high mountain and showed
him all the kingdoms of the world
and their splendor. 9 "All this I will
give you," he said, "if you will bow
down and worship me."
10 Jesus said to him, "Away from
me, Satan! For it is written: 'Worship the Lord your God, and serve
him only.'[e]"
11 Then the devil left him, and
angels came and attended him.

Mk 1:12-13; Lk 4:1-13

Jesus Begins to Preach

12 When Jesus heard that John
had been put in prison, he withdrew to Galilee. 13 Leaving Nazareth, he went and lived in Capernaum, which was by the lake in
the area of Zebulun and Naphtali— 14 to fulfill what was said
through the prophet Isaiah:

Mt 14:3; Mk 1:21

15 "Land of Zebulun and land of
Naphtali,
the Way of the Sea, beyond
the Jordan,
Galilee of the Gentiles—
16 the people living in
darkness
have seen a great light;
on those living in the land of
the shadow of death
a light has dawned."[f]

Lk 2:32; Jn 1:4-5,9

[a] *1* The Greek for *tempted* can also mean *tested.* [b] *4* Deut. 8:3 [c] *6* Psalm 91:11,12 [d] *7* Deut. 6:16 [e] *10* Deut. 6:13 [f] *16* Isaiah 9:1,2

17 From that time on Jesus began
to preach, "Repent, for the kingdom of heaven has come near."
Mt 3:2

Jesus Calls His First Disciples

18 As Jesus was walking beside
the Sea of Galilee, he saw two
brothers, Simon called Peter and
his brother Andrew. They were
casting a net into the lake, for they
were fishermen. 19 "Come, follow
me," Jesus said, "and I will send
you out to fish for people." 20 At
once they left their nets and followed him. Mk 10:21,28,52
21 Going on from there, he saw
two other brothers, James son of
Zebedee and his brother John.
They were in a boat with their father Zebedee, preparing their nets.
Jesus called them, 22 and immediately they left the boat and their
father and followed him.
Mk 1:16-20; Lk 5:2-11; Jn 1:35-42

Jesus Heals the Sick

23 Jesus went throughout Galilee, teaching in their synagogues,
proclaiming the good news of the
kingdom, and healing every disease and sickness among the people. 24 News about him spread all
over Syria, and people brought
to him all who were ill with various diseases, those suffering severe pain, the demon-possessed,
those having seizures, and the
paralyzed; and he healed them.
25 Large crowds from Galilee, the
Decapolis,[a] Jerusalem, Judea and
the region across the Jordan followed him. Mk 1:14; Ac 10:38

Introduction to the Sermon on the Mount

5 Now when Jesus saw the
crowds, he went up on a mountainside and sat down. His disciples came to him, 2 and he began
to teach them.

The Beatitudes

He said:

3 "Blessed are the poor in
spirit,
for theirs is the kingdom of
heaven. Mt 25:34
4 Blessed are those who
mourn,
for they will be comforted.
Isa 61:2-3; Rev 7:17
5 Blessed are the meek,
for they will inherit the
earth. Ps 37:11; Ro 4:13
6 Blessed are those who
hunger and thirst for
righteousness,
for they will be filled. Isa 55:1-2
7 Blessed are the merciful,
for they will be shown mercy.
Jas 2:13
8 Blessed are the pure in heart,
Ps 24:3-4
for they will see God.
Heb 12:14; Rev 22:4
9 Blessed are the peacemakers,
Ro 14:19; Jas 3:18
for they will be called
children of God. Ro 8:14

[a] 25 That is, the Ten Cities

10 Blessed are those who are
persecuted because
of righteousness, 1Pe 3:14
for theirs is the kingdom of
heaven. Mt 25:34

11 "Blessed are you when people insult you, persecute you and
falsely say all kinds of evil against
you because of me. 12 Rejoice and
be glad, because great is your reward in heaven, for in the same
way they persecuted the prophets
who were before you. Ac 7:52; 1Pe 4:14

Salt and Light

13 "You are the salt of the earth.
But if the salt loses its saltiness,
how can it be made salty again?
It is no longer good for anything,
except to be thrown out and
trampled underfoot.
Mk 9:50; Lk 14:34-35

14 "You are the light of the world.
A town built on a hill cannot be
hidden. 15 Neither do people light
a lamp and put it under a bowl. Instead they put it on its stand, and
it gives light to everyone in the
house. 16 In the same way, let your
light shine before others, that they
may see your good deeds and glorify your Father in heaven.
Jn 8:12; 1Co 10:31

The Fulfillment of the Law

17 "Do not think that I have come
to abolish the Law or the Prophets; I have not come to abolish
them but to fulfill them. 18 For
truly I tell you, until heaven and
earth disappear, not the smallest letter, not the least stroke of a
pen, will by any means disappear
from the Law until everything is
accomplished. 19 Therefore anyone
who sets aside one of the least of
these commands and teaches
others accordingly will be called
least in the kingdom of heaven,
but whoever practices and teaches these commands will be called
great in the kingdom of heaven.
20 For I tell you that unless your
righteousness surpasses that of
the Pharisees and the teachers of
the law, you will certainly not enter the kingdom of heaven.
Lk 16:17; Jas 2:10

Murder

21 "You have heard that it was
said to the people long ago, 'You
shall not murder,[a] and anyone
who murders will be subject to
judgment.' 22 But I tell you that
anyone who is angry with a brother or sister[b,c] will be subject to
judgment. Again, anyone who
says to a brother or sister, 'Raca,'[d]
is answerable to the court. And
anyone who says, 'You fool!' will
be in danger of the fire of hell.
1Jn 3:15

23 "Therefore, if you are offering your gift at the altar and there
remember that your brother or

[a] *21* Exodus 20:13 [b] *22* The Greek word for *brother or sister* (*adelphos*) refers here to a fellow disciple, whether man or woman; also in verse 23. [c] *22* Some manuscripts *brother or sister without cause* [d] *22* An Aramaic term of contempt

sister has something against you, 24 leave your gift there in front of the altar. First go and be reconciled to them; then come and offer your gift.

25 "Settle matters quickly with your adversary who is taking you to court. Do it while you are still together on the way, or your adversary may hand you over to the judge, and the judge may hand you over to the officer, and you may be thrown into prison. 26 Truly I tell you, you will not get out until you have paid the last penny.

Lk 12:58-59

Adultery

27 "You have heard that it was said, 'You shall not commit adultery.'[a] 28 But I tell you that anyone who looks at a woman lustfully has already committed adultery with her in his heart. 29 If your right eye causes you to stumble, gouge it out and throw it away. It is better for you to lose one part of your body than for your whole body to be thrown into hell. 30 And if your right hand causes you to stumble, cut it off and throw it away. It is better for you to lose one part of your body than for your whole body to go into hell.

Mk 9:42-47; Pr 6:25

Divorce

31 "It has been said, 'Anyone who divorces his wife must give her a certificate of divorce.'[b] 32 But I tell you that anyone who divorces his wife, except for sexual immorality, makes her the victim of adultery, and anyone who marries a divorced woman commits adultery.

Lk 16:18

Oaths

33 "Again, you have heard that it was said to the people long ago, 'Do not break your oath, but fulfill to the Lord the vows you have made.' 34 But I tell you, do not swear an oath at all: either by heaven, for it is God's throne; 35 or by the earth, for it is his footstool; or by Jerusalem, for it is the city of the Great King. 36 And do not swear by your head, for you cannot make even one hair white or black. 37 All you need to say is simply 'Yes' or 'No'; anything beyond this comes from the evil one.[c]

Nu 30:2; Jas 5:12

Eye for Eye

38 "You have heard that it was said, 'Eye for eye, and tooth for tooth.'[d] 39 But I tell you, do not resist an evil person. If anyone slaps you on the right cheek, turn to them the other cheek also. 40 And if anyone wants to sue you and take your shirt, hand over your coat as well. 41 If anyone forces you to go one mile, go with them two miles. 42 Give to the one who asks you, and do not turn away from the one who wants to borrow from you.

Lk 6:29-30

[a] 27 Exodus 20:14 [b] 31 Deut. 24:1 [c] 37 Or *from evil* [d] 38 Exodus 21:24; Lev. 24:20; Deut. 19:21

Love for Enemies

[43]"You have heard that it was
said, 'Love your neighbor[a] and
hate your enemy.' [44]But I tell you,
love your enemies and pray for
those who persecute you, [45]that
you may be children of your Father in heaven. He causes his sun
to rise on the evil and the good,
and sends rain on the righteous
and the unrighteous. [46]If you love
those who love you, what reward
will you get? Are not even the tax
collectors doing that? [47]And if you
greet only your own people, what
are you doing more than others?
Do not even pagans do that? [48]Be
perfect, therefore, as your heavenly Father is perfect.

Lev 19:2; Lk 6:27-28

Giving to the Needy

6 "Be careful not to practice
your righteousness in front of
others to be seen by them. If you
do, you will have no reward from
your Father in heaven. Mt 23:5

[2]"So when you give to the needy,
do not announce it with trumpets,
as the hypocrites do in the synagogues and on the streets, to be
honored by others. Truly I tell you,
they have received their reward
in full. [3]But when you give to the
needy, do not let your left hand
know what your right hand is doing, [4]so that your giving may be in
secret. Then your Father, who sees
what is done in secret, will reward
you. Col 3:23-24

Prayer

[5]"And when you pray, do not
be like the hypocrites, for they
love to pray standing in the synagogues and on the street corners
to be seen by others. Truly I tell
you, they have received their reward in full. [6]But when you pray,
go into your room, close the door
and pray to your Father, who is
unseen. Then your Father, who
sees what is done in secret, will reward you. [7]And when you pray, do
not keep on babbling like pagans,
for they think they will be heard
because of their many words. [8]Do
not be like them, for your Father
knows what you need before you
ask him. Lk 18:10-14

[9]"This, then, is how you should
pray:

"'Our Father in heaven, Mal 2:10
hallowed be your name,
[10]your kingdom come, Mt 3:2
your will be done, Mt 26:39
on earth as it is in heaven.
[11]Give us today our daily bread. Pr 30:8
[12]And forgive us our debts,
as we also have forgiven our
debtors. Mt 18:21-35
[13]And lead us not into
temptation,[b] Jas 1:13
but deliver us from the evil
one.[c]'

[a] 43 Lev. 19:18 [b] 13 The Greek for *temptation* can also mean *testing*. [c] 13 Or *from evil*; some late manuscripts *one, / for yours is the kingdom and the power and the glory forever. Amen.*

[14]For if you forgive other people when they sin against you, your heavenly Father will also forgive you. [15]But if you do not forgive others their sins, your Father will not forgive your sins.

Mt 18:21-35; Mk 11:25,26; Luke 11:2-4

Fasting

[16]"When you fast, do not look somber as the hypocrites do, for they disfigure their faces to show others they are fasting. Truly I tell you, they have received their reward in full. [17]But when you fast, put oil on your head and wash your face, [18]so that it will not be obvious to others that you are fasting, but only to your Father, who is unseen; and your Father, who sees what is done in secret, will reward you.

ver 4,6; Isa 58:5

Treasures in Heaven

[19]"Do not store up for yourselves treasures on earth, where moths and vermin destroy, and where thieves break in and steal. [20]But store up for yourselves treasures in heaven, where moths and vermin do not destroy, and where thieves do not break in and steal. [21]For where your treasure is, there your heart will be also.

Lk 12:33-34; Heb 13:5

[22]"The eye is the lamp of the body. If your eyes are healthy,[a] your whole body will be full of light. [23]But if your eyes are unhealthy,[b] your whole body will be full of darkness. If then the light within you is darkness, how great is that darkness!

Lk 11:34-36

[24]"No one can serve two masters. Either you will hate the one and love the other, or you will be devoted to the one and despise the other. You cannot serve both God and money.

Lk 16:13

Do Not Worry

[25]"Therefore I tell you, do not worry about your life, what you will eat or drink; or about your body, what you will wear. Is not life more than food, and the body more than clothes? [26]Look at the birds of the air; they do not sow or reap or store away in barns, and yet your heavenly Father feeds them. Are you not much more valuable than they? [27]Can any one of you by worrying add a single hour to your life[c]?

Mt 10:29-31; 1Pe 5:7

[28]"And why do you worry about clothes? See how the flowers of the field grow. They do not labor or spin. [29]Yet I tell you that not even Solomon in all his splendor was dressed like one of these. [30]If that is how God clothes the grass of the field, which is here today and tomorrow is thrown into the fire, will he not much more clothe you—you of little faith? [31]So do not worry, saying, 'What shall we eat?' or 'What shall we drink?' or 'What shall we wear?' [32]For the pagans run after all these

[a] *22* The Greek for *healthy* here implies *generous.* [b] *23* The Greek for *unhealthy* here implies *stingy.* [c] *27* Or *single cubit to your height*

things, and your heavenly Father
knows that you need them. 33But
seek first his kingdom and his righteousness, and all these things will
be given to you as well. 34Therefore
do not worry about tomorrow, for
tomorrow will worry about itself.
Each day has enough trouble of its
own. Lk 12:22-31

Judging Others

7 “Do not judge, or you too will
be judged. 2For in the same
way you judge others, you will be
judged, and with the measure you
use, it will be measured to you.
Mk 4:24; Lk 6:38

3“Why do you look at the speck
of sawdust in your brother’s eye
and pay no attention to the plank
in your own eye? 4How can you say
to your brother, ‘Let me take the
speck out of your eye,’ when all
the time there is a plank in your
own eye? 5You hypocrite, first take
the plank out of your own eye, and
then you will see clearly to remove
the speck from your brother’s eye.
Lk 6:41-42

6“Do not give dogs what is sacred; do not throw your pearls to
pigs. If you do, they may trample
them under their feet, and turn
and tear you to pieces.

Ask, Seek, Knock

7“Ask and it will be given to you;
seek and you will find; knock and
the door will be opened to you.
8For everyone who asks receives;
the one who seeks finds; and to
the one who knocks, the door will
be opened. Jer 29:12-13; Jn 15:7,16

9“Which of you, if your son asks
for bread, will give him a stone?
10Or if he asks for a fish, will give
him a snake? 11If you, then, though
you are evil, know how to give
good gifts to your children, how
much more will your Father in
heaven give good gifts to those
who ask him! 12So in everything,
do to others what you would have
them do to you, for this sums
up the Law and the Prophets.
Lk 11:9-13

The Narrow and Wide Gates

13“Enter through the narrow
gate. For wide is the gate and
broad is the road that leads to destruction, and many enter through
it. 14But small is the gate and narrow the road that leads to life, and
only a few find it. Lk 13:24; Jn 10:7,9

True and False Prophets

15“Watch out for false prophets.
They come to you in sheep’s clothing, but inwardly they are ferocious
wolves. 16By their fruit you will recognize them. Do people pick grapes
from thornbushes, or figs from
thistles? 17Likewise, every good
tree bears good fruit, but a bad tree
bears bad fruit. 18A good tree cannot bear bad fruit, and a bad tree
cannot bear good fruit. 19Every tree
that does not bear good fruit is cut
down and thrown into the fire.
20Thus, by their fruit you will recognize them. Mk 13:22; Lk 6:44

True and False Disciples

21“Not everyone who says to me,
‘Lord, Lord,’ will enter the kingdom of heaven, but only the one
who does the will of my Father
who is in heaven. 22Many will say
to me on that day, ‘Lord, Lord, did
we not prophesy in your name
and in your name drive out demons and in your name perform
many miracles?’ 23Then I will tell
them plainly, ‘I never knew you.
Away from me, you evildoers!’

Mt 25:12,41; Lk 13:25-27

The Wise and Foolish Builders

24“Therefore everyone who
hears these words of mine and
puts them into practice is like
a wise man who built his house
on the rock. 25The rain came
down, the streams rose, and the
winds blew and beat against that
house; yet it did not fall, because
it had its foundation on the rock.
26But everyone who hears these
words of mine and does not put
them into practice is like a foolish man who built his house on
sand. 27The rain came down, the
streams rose, and the winds blew
and beat against that house, and
it fell with a great crash.”

Lk 6:47-49

28When Jesus had finished saying these things, the crowds were
amazed at his teaching, 29because
he taught as one who had authority, and not as their teachers of
the law.

Lk 4:32; Jn 7:46

Jesus Heals a Man With Leprosy

8 When Jesus came down from
the mountainside, large
crowds followed him. 2A man
with leprosy[a] came and knelt before him and said, “Lord, if you are
willing, you can make me clean.”

Mt 15:25

3Jesus reached out his hand and
touched the man. “I am willing,”
he said. “Be clean!” Immediately he was cleansed of his leprosy. 4Then Jesus said to him, “See
that you don’t tell anyone. But go,
show yourself to the priest and offer the gift Moses commanded, as
a testimony to them.”

Mk 1:40-44; Lk 5:12-14

The Faith of the Centurion

5When Jesus had entered Capernaum, a centurion came to
him, asking for help. 6“Lord,” he
said, “my servant lies at home
paralyzed, suffering terribly.”

Mt 4:24

7Jesus said to him, “Shall I come
and heal him?”

8The centurion replied, “Lord, I
do not deserve to have you come
under my roof. But just say the
word, and my servant will be
healed. 9For I myself am a man
under authority, with soldiers under me. I tell this one, ‘Go,’ and he
goes; and that one, ‘Come,’ and
he comes. I say to my servant, ‘Do
this,’ and he does it.”

Ps 107:20

[a] 2 The Greek word traditionally translated *leprosy* was used for various diseases affecting the skin.

10 When Jesus heard this, he was amazed and said to those following him, "Truly I tell you, I have not found anyone in Israel with such great faith. 11 I say to you that many will come from the east and the west, and will take their places at the feast with Abraham, Isaac and Jacob in the kingdom of heaven. 12 But the subjects of the kingdom will be thrown outside, into the darkness, where there will be weeping and gnashing of teeth." Lk 13:28-29

13 Then Jesus said to the centurion, "Go! Let it be done just as you believed it would." And his servant was healed at that moment. Lk 7:1-10

Jesus Heals Many

14 When Jesus came into Peter's house, he saw Peter's mother-in-law lying in bed with a fever. 15 He touched her hand and the fever left her, and she got up and began to wait on him. Mk 1:29-34; Lk 4:38-41

16 When evening came, many who were demon-possessed were brought to him, and he drove out the spirits with a word and healed all the sick. 17 This was to fulfill what was spoken through the prophet Isaiah: Mt 1:22

"He took up our infirmities
and bore our diseases."[a]

The Cost of Following Jesus

18 When Jesus saw the crowd around him, he gave orders to cross to the other side of the lake. 19 Then a teacher of the law came to him and said, "Teacher, I will follow you wherever you go." Mk 4:35

20 Jesus replied, "Foxes have dens and birds have nests, but the Son of Man has no place to lay his head." Mk 8:31

21 Another disciple said to him, "Lord, first let me go and bury my father."

22 But Jesus told him, "Follow me, and let the dead bury their own dead." Lk 9:57-60

Jesus Calms the Storm

23 Then he got into the boat and his disciples followed him. 24 Suddenly a furious storm came up on the lake, so that the waves swept over the boat. But Jesus was sleeping. 25 The disciples went and woke him, saying, "Lord, save us! We're going to drown!" Mk 4:36-41; Lk 8:22-25

26 He replied, "You of little faith, why are you so afraid?" Then he got up and rebuked the winds and the waves, and it was completely calm. Ps 65:7; 107:29

27 The men were amazed and asked, "What kind of man is this? Even the winds and the waves obey him!" Mt 14:22-33

Jesus Restores Two Demon-Possessed Men

28 When he arrived at the other side in the region of the Gadarenes,[b]

[a] 17 Isaiah 53:4 (see Septuagint)
[b] 28 Some manuscripts *Gergesenes*; other manuscripts *Gerasenes*

two demon-possessed men coming from the tombs met him. They
were so violent that no one could
pass that way. 29“What do you want
with us, Son of God?” they shouted.
“Have you come here to torture us
before the appointed time?”

Mk 1:24; Jn 2:4

30Some distance from them a
large herd of pigs was feeding.
31The demons begged Jesus, “If
you drive us out, send us into the
herd of pigs.”

32He said to them, “Go!” So they
came out and went into the pigs,
and the whole herd rushed down
the steep bank into the lake and
died in the water. 33Those tending
the pigs ran off, went into the town
and reported all this, including
what had happened to the demon-
possessed men. 34Then the whole
town went out to meet Jesus. And
when they saw him, they pleaded
with him to leave their region.

Mk 5:1-17; Lk 8:26-37

Jesus Forgives and Heals a Paralyzed Man

9 Jesus stepped into a boat,
crossed over and came to his
own town. 2Some men brought to
him a paralyzed man, lying on a
mat. When Jesus saw their faith,
he said to the man, “Take heart,
son; your sins are forgiven.”

Lk 7:48; Jn 16:33

3At this, some of the teachers of
the law said to themselves, “This
fellow is blaspheming!”

Mt 26:65; Jn 10:33

4Knowing their thoughts, Jesus
said, “Why do you entertain evil
thoughts in your hearts? 5Which
is easier: to say, ‘Your sins are forgiven,’ or to say, ‘Get up and walk’?
6But I want you to know that the
Son of Man has authority on earth
to forgive sins.” So he said to the
paralyzed man, “Get up, take your
mat and go home.” 7Then the man
got up and went home. 8When the
crowd saw this, they were filled
with awe; and they praised God,
who had given such authority to
man.

Mk 2:3-12; Lk 5:18-26

The Calling of Matthew

9As Jesus went on from there,
he saw a man named Matthew sitting at the tax collector’s booth.
“Follow me,” he told him, and Matthew got up and followed him.

Mt 4:19

10While Jesus was having dinner at Matthew’s house, many tax
collectors and sinners came and
ate with him and his disciples.
11When the Pharisees saw this,
they asked his disciples, “Why
does your teacher eat with tax
collectors and sinners?”

Mt 11:19; Gal 2:15

12On hearing this, Jesus said, “It
is not the healthy who need a doctor, but the sick. 13But go and learn
what this means: ‘I desire mercy,
not sacrifice.’[a] For I have not come
to call the righteous, but sinners.”

Mk 2:14-17; Lk 5:27-32

[a] *13* Hosea 6:6

Jesus Questioned About Fasting

14 Then John's disciples came
and asked him, "How is it that we
and the Pharisees fast often, but
your disciples do not fast?" Lk 18:12
15 Jesus answered, "How can the
guests of the bridegroom mourn
while he is with them? The time
will come when the bridegroom
will be taken from them; then
they will fast. Jn 3:29; Ac 13:2-3
16 "No one sews a patch of un-
shrunk cloth on an old garment,
for the patch will pull away from
the garment, making the tear
worse. 17 Neither do people pour
new wine into old wineskins. If
they do, the skins will burst; the
wine will run out and the wineskins will be ruined. No, they pour
new wine into new wineskins, and
both are preserved."
Mk 2:18-22; Lk 5:33-39

Jesus Raises a Dead Girl and Heals a Sick Woman

18 While he was saying this, a
synagogue leader came and knelt
before him and said, "My daughter has just died. But come and
put your hand on her, and she will
live." 19 Jesus got up and went with
him, and so did his disciples. Mt 8:2
20 Just then a woman who had
been subject to bleeding for
twelve years came up behind him
and touched the edge of his cloak.
21 She said to herself, "If I only
touch his cloak, I will be healed."
Mt 14:36; Mk 3:10
22 Jesus turned and saw her.
"Take heart, daughter," he said,
"your faith has healed you." And
the woman was healed at that moment. Lk 7:50; 17:19; 18:42
23 When Jesus entered the synagogue leader's house and saw the
noisy crowd and people playing
pipes, 24 he said, "Go away. The girl
is not dead but asleep." But they
laughed at him. 25 After the crowd
had been put outside, he went in
and took the girl by the hand, and
she got up. 26 News of this spread
through all that region.
Mk 5:22-43; Lk 8:41-56

Jesus Heals the Blind and the Mute

27 As Jesus went on from there,
two blind men followed him, calling out, "Have mercy on us, Son of
David!" Mt 15:22; Mk 10:47
28 When he had gone indoors,
the blind men came to him, and
he asked them, "Do you believe
that I am able to do this?"
"Yes, Lord," they replied. Ac 14:9
29 Then he touched their eyes and
said, "According to your faith let it
be done to you"; 30 and their sight
was restored. Jesus warned them
sternly, "See that no one knows
about this." 31 But they went out
and spread the news about him all
over that region. Mt 8:4; Mk 7:36
32 While they were going out, a
man who was demon-possessed
and could not talk was brought
to Jesus. 33 And when the demon
was driven out, the man who had
been mute spoke. The crowd was

amazed and said, "Nothing like this has ever been seen in Israel."
Mk 2:12

34 But the Pharisees said, "It is by the prince of demons that he drives out demons." Mt 12:24; Lk 11:15

The Workers Are Few

35 Jesus went through all the towns and villages, teaching in their synagogues, proclaiming the good news of the kingdom and healing every disease and sickness. 36 When he saw the crowds, he had compassion on them, because they were harassed and helpless, like sheep without a shepherd. 37 Then he said to his disciples, "The harvest is plentiful but the workers are few. 38 Ask the Lord of the harvest, therefore, to send out workers into his harvest field." Lk 10:2; Jn 4:35

Jesus Sends Out the Twelve

10 Jesus called his twelve disciples to him and gave them authority to drive out impure spirits and to heal every disease and sickness. Mk 3:13-15

2 These are the names of the twelve apostles: first, Simon (who is called Peter) and his brother Andrew; James son of Zebedee, and his brother John; 3 Philip and Bartholomew; Thomas and Matthew the tax collector; James son of Alphaeus, and Thaddaeus; 4 Simon the Zealot and Judas Iscariot, who betrayed him.
Mk 3:16-19; Lk 6:14-16; Ac 1:13

5 These twelve Jesus sent out with the following instructions: "Do not go among the Gentiles or enter any town of the Samaritans. 6 Go rather to the lost sheep of Israel. 7 As you go, proclaim this message: 'The kingdom of heaven has come near.' 8 Heal the sick, raise the dead, cleanse those who have leprosy,[a] drive out demons. Freely you have received; freely give.

9 "Do not get any gold or silver or copper to take with you in your belts — 10 no bag for the journey or extra shirt or sandals or a staff, for the worker is worth his keep. 11 Whatever town or village you enter, search there for some worthy person and stay at their house until you leave. 12 As you enter the home, give it your greeting. 13 If the home is deserving, let your peace rest on it; if it is not, let your peace return to you. 14 If anyone will not welcome you or listen to your words, leave that home or town and shake the dust off your feet. 15 Truly I tell you, it will be more bearable for Sodom and Gomorrah on the day of judgment than for that town.
Mt 3:2; 15:24; 1Ti 5:18

16 "I am sending you out like sheep among wolves. Therefore be as shrewd as snakes and as innocent as doves. 17 Be on your guard; you will be handed over to the local councils and be flogged

[a] 8 The Greek word traditionally translated *leprosy* was used for various diseases affecting the skin.

in the synagogues. 18On my account you will be brought before
governors and kings as witnesses
to them and to the Gentiles. 19But
when they arrest you, do not worry about what to say or how to say
it. At that time you will be given
what to say, 20for it will not be you
speaking, but the Spirit of your Father speaking through you.

Mk 13:9; Ac 5:40

21"Brother will betray brother to
death, and a father his child; children will rebel against their parents and have them put to death.
22You will be hated by everyone
because of me, but the one who
stands firm to the end will be
saved. 23When you are persecuted
in one place, flee to another. Truly
I tell you, you will not finish going
through the towns of Israel before
the Son of Man comes.

Mk 13:11-13; Lk 21:12-17

24"The student is not above the
teacher, nor a servant above his
master. 25It is enough for students
to be like their teachers, and servants like their masters. If the
head of the house has been called
Beelzebul, how much more the
members of his household!

Mk 3:22; Lk 6:40

26"So do not be afraid of them,
for there is nothing concealed
that will not be disclosed, or hidden that will not be made known.
27What I tell you in the dark, speak
in the daylight; what is whispered
in your ear, proclaim from the
roofs. 28Do not be afraid of those
who kill the body but cannot kill
the soul. Rather, be afraid of the
One who can destroy both soul
and body in hell. 29Are not two
sparrows sold for a penny? Yet not
one of them will fall to the ground
outside your Father's care.[a] 30And
even the very hairs of your head
are all numbered. 31So don't be
afraid; you are worth more than
many sparrows.

Mk 4:22; Heb 10:31

32"Whoever acknowledges me
before others, I will also acknowledge before my Father in heaven.
33But whoever disowns me before
others, I will disown before my Father in heaven.

Lk 12:2-9

34"Do not suppose that I have
come to bring peace to the earth.
I did not come to bring peace, but
a sword. 35For I have come to turn

"'a man against his father,
a daughter against her
mother,
a daughter-in-law against her
mother-in-law —
36 a man's enemies will be the
members of his own
household.'[b]

Mic 7:6

37"Anyone who loves their father
or mother more than me is not
worthy of me; anyone who loves
their son or daughter more than
me is not worthy of me. 38Whoev-
er does not take up their cross and
follow me is not worthy of me.
39Whoever finds their life will lose
it, and whoever loses their life for
my sake will find it.

Lk 14:26; Jn 12:25

[a] 29 Or *will*; or *knowledge* [b] 36 Micah 7:6

40"Anyone who welcomes you
welcomes me, and anyone who
welcomes me welcomes the one
who sent me. 41Whoever welcomes
a prophet as a prophet will receive
a prophet's reward, and whoever
welcomes a righteous person as
a righteous person will receive a
righteous person's reward. 42And
if anyone gives even a cup of cold
water to one of these little ones
who is my disciple, truly I tell you,
that person will certainly not lose
their reward." Lk 9:48; Jn 12:44; Gal 4:14

Jesus and John the Baptist

11 After Jesus had finished instructing his twelve disciples,
he went on from there to teach
and preach in the towns of Galilee.[a] Mt 7:28
2When John, who was in prison,
heard about the deeds of the Messiah, he sent his disciples 3to ask
him, "Are you the one who is to
come, or should we expect someone else?" Mt 14:3; Jn 11:27
4Jesus replied, "Go back and report to John what you hear and
see: 5The blind receive sight, the
lame walk, those who have leprosy[b] are cleansed, the deaf hear, the
dead are raised, and the good news
is proclaimed to the poor. 6Blessed
is anyone who does not stumble on
account of me." Isa 35:4-6; Lk 4:18-19
7As John's disciples were leaving, Jesus began to speak to the
crowd about John: "What did you
go out into the wilderness to see?
A reed swayed by the wind? 8If
not, what did you go out to see? A
man dressed in fine clothes? No,
those who wear fine clothes are
in kings' palaces. 9Then what did
you go out to see? A prophet? Yes,
I tell you, and more than a prophet. 10This is the one about whom it
is written: Lk 1:76

" 'I will send my messenger
ahead of you,
who will prepare your way
before you.'[c]

11Truly I tell you, among those
born of women there has not ris-
en anyone greater than John the
Baptist; yet whoever is least in the
kingdom of heaven is greater than
he. 12From the days of John the
Baptist until now, the kingdom of
heaven has been subjected to violence,[d] and violent people have
been raiding it. 13For all the Prophets and the Law prophesied until
John. 14And if you are willing to
accept it, he is the Elijah who was
to come. 15Whoever has ears, let
them hear. Mal 4:5; Lk 1:17
16"To what can I compare this
generation? They are like children
sitting in the marketplaces and
calling out to others:

17" 'We played the pipe for you,
and you did not dance;
we sang a dirge,
and you did not mourn.'

[a] 1 Greek *in their towns* [b] 5 The Greek word traditionally translated *leprosy* was used for various diseases affecting the skin. [c] 10 Mal. 3:1 [d] 12 Or *been forcefully advancing*

[18]For John came neither eating
nor drinking, and they say, 'He has
a demon.' [19]The Son of Man came
eating and drinking, and they say,
'Here is a glutton and a drunkard,
a friend of tax collectors and sinners.' But wisdom is proved right
by her deeds." Lk 7:18-35

Woe on Unrepentant Towns

[20]Then Jesus began to denounce
the towns in which most of his miracles had been performed, because
they did not repent. [21]"Woe to you,
Chorazin! Woe to you, Bethsaida!
For if the miracles that were performed in you had been performed
in Tyre and Sidon, they would have
repented long ago in sackcloth and
ashes. [22]But I tell you, it will be more
bearable for Tyre and Sidon on
the day of judgment than for you.
[23]And you, Capernaum, will you be
lifted to the heavens? No, you will
go down to Hades.[a] For if the miracles that were performed in you
had been performed in Sodom, it
would have remained to this day.
[24]But I tell you that it will be more
bearable for Sodom on the day of
judgment than for you." Lk 10:13-15

The Father Revealed in the Son

[25]At that time Jesus said, "I
praise you, Father, Lord of heaven
and earth, because you have hidden these things from the wise
and learned, and revealed them
to little children. [26]Yes, Father,
for this is what you were pleased
to do. 1Co 1:26-29

[27]"All things have been committed to me by my Father. No one
knows the Son except the Father,
and no one knows the Father except the Son and those to whom
the Son chooses to reveal him.
Lk 10:21-22

[28]"Come to me, all you who are
weary and burdened, and I will
give you rest. [29]Take my yoke upon
you and learn from me, for I am
gentle and humble in heart, and
you will find rest for your souls.
[30]For my yoke is easy and my burden is light." Jer 6:16; Jn 13:15

Jesus Is Lord of the Sabbath

12 At that time Jesus went
through the grainfields on
the Sabbath. His disciples were
hungry and began to pick some
heads of grain and eat them.
[2]When the Pharisees saw this, they
said to him, "Look! Your disciples
are doing what is unlawful on the
Sabbath." Ex 20:10; Lk 13:14

[3]He answered, "Haven't you
read what David did when he and
his companions were hungry? [4]He
entered the house of God, and he
and his companions ate the consecrated bread — which was not
lawful for them to do, but only for
the priests. [5]Or haven't you read
in the Law that the priests on Sabbath duty in the temple desecrate
the Sabbath and yet are innocent?
[6]I tell you that something greater
than the temple is here. [7]If you had

[a] *23* That is, the realm of the dead

known what these words mean, 'I
desire mercy, not sacrifice,'[a] you
would not have condemned the
innocent. 8For the Son of Man is
Lord of the Sabbath."
Mk 2:23-28; Lk 6:1-5

9Going on from that place, he
went into their synagogue, 10and
a man with a shriveled hand was
there. Looking for a reason to
bring charges against Jesus, they
asked him, "Is it lawful to heal on
the Sabbath?" Lk 13:14; 14:3

11He said to them, "If any of you
has a sheep and it falls into a pit
on the Sabbath, will you not take
hold of it and lift it out? 12How
much more valuable is a person
than a sheep! Therefore it is lawful to do good on the Sabbath."

13Then he said to the man,
"Stretch out your hand." So he
stretched it out and it was completely restored, just as sound as
the other. 14But the Pharisees went
out and plotted how they might
kill Jesus. Mk 3:1-6; Lk 6:6-11

God's Chosen Servant

15Aware of this, Jesus withdrew
from that place. A large crowd followed him, and he healed all who
were ill. 16He warned them not to
tell others about him. 17This was
to fulfill what was spoken through
the prophet Isaiah: Mt 4:23; 8:4

18"Here is my servant whom I
have chosen,
the one I love, in whom I
delight; Mt 3:17
I will put my Spirit on him,
Jn 3:34
and he will proclaim justice
to the nations.
19He will not quarrel or cry out;
no one will hear his voice in
the streets.
20A bruised reed he will not
break,
and a smoldering wick he
will not snuff out,
till he has brought justice
through to victory.
21 In his name the nations will
put their hope."[b] Isa 42:1-4

Jesus and Beelzebul

22Then they brought him a demon-possessed man who was
blind and mute, and Jesus healed
him, so that he could both talk
and see. 23All the people were astonished and said, "Could this be
the Son of David?" Mt 4:24; 9:32-33

24But when the Pharisees heard
this, they said, "It is only by Beelzebul, the prince of demons, that
this fellow drives out demons."
Mt 9:34; Mk 3:22

25Jesus knew their thoughts and
said to them, "Every kingdom divided against itself will be ruined,
and every city or household divided against itself will not stand. 26If
Satan drives out Satan, he is divided against himself. How then
can his kingdom stand? 27And if I
drive out demons by Beelzebul, by
whom do your people drive them

[a] 7 Hosea 6:6 [b] 21 Isaiah 42:1-4

out? So then, they will be your
judges. 28But if it is by the Spirit of
God that I drive out demons, then
the kingdom of God has come
upon you. Mt 9:4; Ac 19:13

29"Or again, how can anyone enter a strong man's house and carry
off his possessions unless he first
ties up the strong man? Then he
can plunder his house.
Mk 3:23-27; Lk 11:17-22

30"Whoever is not with me is
against me, and whoever does not
gather with me scatters. 31And so I
tell you, every kind of sin and slander can be forgiven, but blasphemy
against the Spirit will not be forgiv-
en. 32Anyone who speaks a word
against the Son of Man will be forgiven, but anyone who speaks
against the Holy Spirit will not be
forgiven, either in this age or in the
age to come. Mk 9:40; Lk 12:10

33"Make a tree good and its fruit
will be good, or make a tree bad
and its fruit will be bad, for a tree
is recognized by its fruit. 34You
brood of vipers, how can you who
are evil say anything good? For the
mouth speaks what the heart is
full of. 35A good man brings good
things out of the good stored up in
him, and an evil man brings evil
things out of the evil stored up in
him. 36But I tell you that everyone
will have to give account on the
day of judgment for every empty
word they have spoken. 37For by
your words you will be acquitted,
and by your words you will be condemned." Mt 15:18; Lk 6:45

The Sign of Jonah

38Then some of the Pharisees
and teachers of the law said to him,
"Teacher, we want to see a sign
from you." Mt 16:1; Jn 2:18; 1Co 1:22

39He answered, "A wicked and
adulterous generation asks for a
sign! But none will be given it except the sign of the prophet Jonah.
40For as Jonah was three days and
three nights in the belly of a huge
fish, so the Son of Man will be
three days and three nights in the
heart of the earth. 41The men of
Nineveh will stand up at the judgment with this generation and
condemn it; for they repented at
the preaching of Jonah, and now
something greater than Jonah is
here. 42The Queen of the South
will rise at the judgment with
this generation and condemn it;
for she came from the ends of the
earth to listen to Solomon's wisdom, and now something greater
than Solomon is here. Lk 11:29-32

43"When an impure spirit comes
out of a person, it goes through
arid places seeking rest and does
not find it. 44Then it says, 'I will
return to the house I left.' When
it arrives, it finds the house un-
occupied, swept clean and put in
order. 45Then it goes and takes
with it seven other spirits more
wicked than itself, and they go in
and live there. And the final condition of that person is worse than
the first. That is how it will be with
this wicked generation."
Lk 11:24-26; 2Pe 2:20

Jesus' Mother and Brothers

[46]While Jesus was still talking to the crowd, his mother and
brothers stood outside, wanting
to speak to him. [47]Someone told
him, "Your mother and brothers
are standing outside, wanting to
speak to you." Mt 13:55; Jn 2:12
[48]He replied to him, "Who is my
mother, and who are my broth-
ers?" [49]Pointing to his disciples, he
said, "Here are my mother and my
brothers. [50]For whoever does the
will of my Father in heaven is my
brother and sister and mother."
Mk 3:31-35; Lk 8:19-21

The Parable of the Sower

13 That same day Jesus went
out of the house and sat by
the lake. [2]Such large crowds gathered around him that he got into
a boat and sat in it, while all the
people stood on the shore. [3]Then
he told them many things in parables, saying: "A farmer went out to
sow his seed. [4]As he was scattering
the seed, some fell along the path,
and the birds came and ate it up.
[5]Some fell on rocky places, where
it did not have much soil. It sprang
up quickly, because the soil was
shallow. [6]But when the sun came
up, the plants were scorched, and
they withered because they had no
root. [7]Other seed fell among thorns,
which grew up and choked the
plants. [8]Still other seed fell on good
soil, where it produced a crop — a
hundred, sixty or thirty times what
was sown. [9]Whoever has ears, let
them hear." Ge 26:12; Mt 11:15
[10]The disciples came to him and
asked, "Why do you speak to the
people in parables?"
[11]He replied, "Because the knowledge of the secrets of the kingdom
of heaven has been given to you,
but not to them. [12]Whoever has
will be given more, and they will
have an abundance. Whoever does
not have, even what they have will
be taken from them. [13]This is why
I speak to them in parables:
Lk 19:26; 1Co 2:10,14

"Though seeing, they do not
see;
though hearing, they do not
hear or understand.
Dt 29:4; Jer 5:21; Eze 12:2

[14]In them is fulfilled the prophecy
of Isaiah:

" 'You will be ever hearing but
never understanding;
you will be ever seeing but
never perceiving.
[15]For this people's heart has
become calloused;
they hardly hear with their
ears,
and they have closed their
eyes.
Otherwise they might see with
their eyes,
hear with their ears,
understand with their hearts
and turn, and I would heal
them.'[a]

[a] *15* Isaiah 6:9,10 (see Septuagint)

16 But blessed are your eyes because they see, and your ears because they hear. 17 For truly I tell
you, many prophets and righteous
people longed to see what you see
but did not see it, and to hear what
you hear but did not hear it.

Lk 10:23-24; Heb 11:13

18 "Listen then to what the parable of the sower means: 19 When
anyone hears the message about
the kingdom and does not understand it, the evil one comes and
snatches away what was sown in
their heart. This is the seed sown
along the path. 20 The seed falling
on rocky ground refers to someone who hears the word and at
once receives it with joy. 21 But
since they have no root, they last
only a short time. When trouble or
persecution comes because of the
word, they quickly fall away. 22 The
seed falling among the thorns refers to someone who hears the
word, but the worries of this life
and the deceitfulness of wealth
choke the word, making it unfruitful. 23 But the seed falling on
good soil refers to someone who
hears the word and understands
it. This is the one who produces a
crop, yielding a hundred, sixty or
thirty times what was sown."

Mk 4:13-20; Lk 8:11-15

The Parable of the Weeds

24 Jesus told them another parable: "The kingdom of heaven is
like a man who sowed good seed
in his field. 25 But while everyone
was sleeping, his enemy came and
sowed weeds among the wheat,
and went away. 26 When the wheat
sprouted and formed heads, then
the weeds also appeared.

Mt 18:23; 20:1

27 "The owner's servants came to
him and said, 'Sir, didn't you sow
good seed in your field? Where
then did the weeds come from?'

28 "'An enemy did this,' he replied.

"The servants asked him, 'Do you
want us to go and pull them up?'

29 "'No,' he answered, 'because
while you are pulling the weeds,
you may uproot the wheat with
them. 30 Let both grow together
until the harvest. At that time I
will tell the harvesters: First collect the weeds and tie them in
bundles to be burned; then gather the wheat and bring it into my
barn.'"

Mt 3:12

The Parables of the Mustard Seed and the Yeast

31 He told them another parable:
"The kingdom of heaven is like a
mustard seed, which a man took
and planted in his field. 32 Though
it is the smallest of all seeds, yet
when it grows, it is the largest of
garden plants and becomes a tree,
so that the birds come and perch
in its branches."

Mk 4:30-32

33 He told them still another parable: "The kingdom of heaven is
like yeast that a woman took and
mixed into about sixty pounds[a] of

[a] 33 Or about 27 kilograms

flour until it worked all through the dough." Lk 13:18-21

34 Jesus spoke all these things to the crowd in parables; he did not say anything to them without using a parable. 35 So was fulfilled what was spoken through the prophet: Mk 4:33; Jn 16:25

"I will open my mouth in
    parables,
  I will utter things hidden
    since the creation of the
    world."[a] Ps 78:2; 1Co 2:7

The Parable of the Weeds Explained

36 Then he left the crowd and went into the house. His disciples came to him and said, "Explain to us the parable of the weeds in the field." Mt 15:15

37 He answered, "The one who sowed the good seed is the Son of Man. 38 The field is the world, and the good seed stands for the people of the kingdom. The weeds are the people of the evil one, 39 and the enemy who sows them is the devil. The harvest is the end of the age, and the harvesters are angels. Mt 24:3; Rev 14:15

40 "As the weeds are pulled up and burned in the fire, so it will be at the end of the age. 41 The Son of Man will send out his angels, and they will weed out of his kingdom everything that causes sin and all who do evil. 42 They will throw them into the blazing furnace, where there will be weeping and gnashing of teeth. 43 Then the righteous will shine like the sun in the kingdom of their Father. Whoever has ears, let them hear. Da 12:3; Mt 8:12; 11:15

The Parables of the Hidden Treasure and the Pearl

44 "The kingdom of heaven is like treasure hidden in a field. When a man found it, he hid it again, and then in his joy went and sold all he had and bought that field. Isa 55:1; Php 3:7-8

45 "Again, the kingdom of heaven is like a merchant looking for fine pearls. 46 When he found one of great value, he went away and sold everything he had and bought it. ver 24

The Parable of the Net

47 "Once again, the kingdom of heaven is like a net that was let down into the lake and caught all kinds of fish. 48 When it was full, the fishermen pulled it up on the shore. Then they sat down and collected the good fish in baskets, but threw the bad away. 49 This is how it will be at the end of the age. The angels will come and separate the wicked from the righteous 50 and throw them into the blazing furnace, where there will be weeping and gnashing of teeth. Mt 25:32

51 "Have you understood all these things?" Jesus asked.

"Yes," they replied.

[a] 35 Psalm 78:2

52He said to them, "Therefore
every teacher of the law who has
become a disciple in the kingdom of heaven is like the owner
of a house who brings out of his
storeroom new treasures as well
as old."

A Prophet Without Honor

53When Jesus had finished
these parables, he moved on from
there. 54Coming to his hometown,
he began teaching the people in
their synagogue, and they were
amazed. "Where did this man get
this wisdom and these miraculous powers?" they asked. 55"Isn't
this the carpenter's son? Isn't his
mother's name Mary, and aren't
his brothers James, Joseph, Simon and Judas? 56Aren't all his
sisters with us? Where then did
this man get all these things?"
57And they took offense at him.
Mt 7:28; Jn 6:42

But Jesus said to them, "A
prophet is not without honor except in his own town and in his
own home." Lk 4:24; Jn 4:44

58And he did not do many miracles there because of their lack of
faith. Mk 6:1-6

John the Baptist Beheaded

14 At that time Herod the tetrarch heard the reports
about Jesus, 2and he said to his
attendants, "This is John the Baptist; he has risen from the dead!
That is why miraculous powers
are at work in him." Lk 9:7-9

3Now Herod had arrested John
and bound him and put him in
prison because of Herodias, his
brother Philip's wife, 4for John had
been saying to him: "It is not lawful
for you to have her." 5Herod wanted to kill John, but he was afraid of
the people, because they considered John a prophet. Mt 11:9; Lk 3:19-20

6On Herod's birthday the daughter of Herodias danced for the
guests and pleased Herod so much
7that he promised with an oath
to give her whatever she asked.
8Prompted by her mother, she
said, "Give me here on a platter
the head of John the Baptist." 9The
king was distressed, but because of
his oaths and his dinner guests, he
ordered that her request be granted 10and had John beheaded in
the prison. 11His head was brought
in on a platter and given to the
girl, who carried it to her mother.
12John's disciples came and took
his body and buried it. Then they
went and told Jesus. Mk 6:14-29

Jesus Feeds the Five Thousand

13When Jesus heard what had
happened, he withdrew by boat
privately to a solitary place. Hearing of this, the crowds followed
him on foot from the towns.
14When Jesus landed and saw a
large crowd, he had compassion
on them and healed their sick.
Mt 15:32-38

15As evening approached, the disciples came to him and said, "This
is a remote place, and it's already

getting late. Send the crowds away, so they can go to the villages and buy themselves some food."

16 Jesus replied, "They do not need to go away. You give them something to eat."

17 "We have here only five loaves of bread and two fish," they answered.

18 "Bring them here to me," he said. 19 And he directed the people to sit down on the grass. Taking the five loaves and the two fish and looking up to heaven, he gave thanks and broke the loaves. Then he gave them to the disciples, and the disciples gave them to the people. 20 They all ate and were satisfied, and the disciples picked up twelve basketfuls of broken pieces that were left over. 21 The number of those who ate was about five thousand men, besides women and children. Mk 6:32-44; Lk 9:10-17; Jn 6:1-13

Jesus Walks on the Water

22 Immediately Jesus made the disciples get into the boat and go on ahead of him to the other side, while he dismissed the crowd. 23 After he had dismissed them, he went up on a mountainside by himself to pray. Later that night, he was there alone, 24 and the boat was already a considerable distance from land, buffeted by the waves because the wind was against it. Lk 3:21

25 Shortly before dawn Jesus went out to them, walking on the lake. 26 When the disciples saw him walking on the lake, they were terrified. "It's a ghost," they said, and cried out in fear. Lk 24:37

27 But Jesus immediately said to them: "Take courage! It is I. Don't be afraid." Mt 17:7; Rev 1:17

28 "Lord, if it's you," Peter replied, "tell me to come to you on the water."

29 "Come," he said.

Then Peter got down out of the boat, walked on the water and came toward Jesus. 30 But when he saw the wind, he was afraid and, beginning to sink, cried out, "Lord, save me!"

31 Immediately Jesus reached out his hand and caught him. "You of little faith," he said, "why did you doubt?" Mt 6:30

32 And when they climbed into the boat, the wind died down. 33 Then those who were in the boat worshiped him, saying, "Truly you are the Son of God."

Mk 6:45-51; Jn 6:15-21

34 When they had crossed over, they landed at Gennesaret. 35 And when the men of that place recognized Jesus, they sent word to all the surrounding country. People brought all their sick to him 36 and begged him to let the sick just touch the edge of his cloak, and all who touched it were healed.

Mk 6:53-56

That Which Defiles

15 Then some Pharisees and teachers of the law came to Jesus from Jerusalem and asked,

2 “Why do your disciples break the
tradition of the elders? They don’t
wash their hands before they eat!”
Lk 11:38

3 Jesus replied, “And why do you
break the command of God for
the sake of your tradition? 4 For
God said, ‘Honor your father and
mother’[a] and ‘Anyone who curses their father or mother is to be
put to death.’[b] 5 But you say that if
anyone declares that what might
have been used to help their father or mother is ‘devoted to God,’
6 they are not to ‘honor their father
or mother’ with it. Thus you nullify the word of God for the sake
of your tradition. 7 You hypocrites!
Isaiah was right when he prophesied about you:

8 “ ‘These people honor me with
their lips,
but their hearts are far from
me.
9 They worship me in vain;
their teachings are merely
human rules.’[c]”

Col 2:20-22; Mal 2:2

10 Jesus called the crowd to him
and said, “Listen and understand.
11 What goes into someone’s mouth
does not defile them, but what
comes out of their mouth, that is
what defiles them.” Ac 10:14-15

12 Then the disciples came to
him and asked, “Do you know that
the Pharisees were offended when
they heard this?”

13 He replied, “Every plant that my
heavenly Father has not planted will
be pulled up by the roots. 14 Leave
them; they are blind guides.[d] If the
blind lead the blind, both will fall
into a pit.” Mt 23:16,24; Lk 6:39

15 Peter said, “Explain the parable to us.” Mt 13:36

16 “Are you still so dull?” Jesus
asked them. 17 “Don’t you see that
whatever enters the mouth goes
into the stomach and then out
of the body? 18 But the things that
come out of a person’s mouth
come from the heart, and these
defile them. 19 For out of the heart
come evil thoughts — murder,
adultery, sexual immorality, theft,
false testimony, slander. 20 These
are what defile a person; but eating with unwashed hands does
not defile them.” Mk 7:1-23; Gal 5:19-21

The Faith of a Canaanite Woman

21 Leaving that place, Jesus withdrew to the region of Tyre and Sidon. 22 A Canaanite woman from
that vicinity came to him, crying out, “Lord, Son of David, have
mercy on me! My daughter is demon-possessed and suffering terribly.” Mt 4:24; 9:27

23 Jesus did not answer a word.
So his disciples came to him and
urged him, “Send her away, for she
keeps crying out after us.”

24 He answered, “I was sent only
to the lost sheep of Israel.”

Mt 10:6,23; Ro 15:8

[a] 4 Exodus 20:12; Deut. 5:16
[b] 4 Exodus 21:17; Lev. 20:9
[c] 9 Isaiah 29:13 [d] 14 Some
manuscripts *blind guides of the blind*

[25]The woman came and knelt before him. "Lord, help me!" she said. Mt 8:2

[26]He replied, "It is not right to take the children's bread and toss it to the dogs."

[27]"Yes it is, Lord," she said. "Even the dogs eat the crumbs that fall from their master's table."

[28]Then Jesus said to her, "Woman, you have great faith! Your request is granted." And her daughter was healed at that moment.

Mk 7:24-30

Jesus Feeds the Four Thousand

[29]Jesus left there and went along the Sea of Galilee. Then he went up on a mountainside and sat down. [30]Great crowds came to him, bringing the lame, the blind, the crippled, the mute and many others, and laid them at his feet; and he healed them. [31]The people were amazed when they saw the mute speaking, the crippled made well, the lame walking and the blind seeing. And they praised the God of Israel. Mk 7:31-37

[32]Jesus called his disciples to him and said, "I have compassion for these people; they have already been with me three days and have nothing to eat. I do not want to send them away hungry, or they may collapse on the way."

Mt 9:36

[33]His disciples answered, "Where could we get enough bread in this remote place to feed such a crowd?"

[34]"How many loaves do you have?" Jesus asked.

"Seven," they replied, "and a few small fish."

[35]He told the crowd to sit down on the ground. [36]Then he took the seven loaves and the fish, and when he had given thanks, he broke them and gave them to the disciples, and they in turn to the people. [37]They all ate and were satisfied. Afterward the disciples picked up seven basketfuls of broken pieces that were left over. [38]The number of those who ate was four thousand men, besides women and children. [39]After Jesus had sent the crowd away, he got into the boat and went to the vicinity of Magadan.

Mt 14:13-21; Mk 8:1-10

The Demand for a Sign

16 The Pharisees and Sadducees came to Jesus and tested him by asking him to show them a sign from heaven.

Mt 12:38; Ac 4:1

[2]He replied, "When evening comes, you say, 'It will be fair weather, for the sky is red,' [3]and in the morning, 'Today it will be stormy, for the sky is red and overcast.' You know how to interpret the appearance of the sky, but you cannot interpret the signs of the times.[a] [4]A wicked and adulterous generation looks for a sign, but none will be given it except the

[a] 2,3 Some early manuscripts do not have *When evening comes . . . of the times.*

sign of Jonah." Jesus then left them and went away. Mt 12:39; Lk 12:54-56

The Yeast of the Pharisees and Sadducees

5 When they went across the lake, the disciples forgot to take bread. 6 "Be careful," Jesus said to them. "Be on your guard against the yeast of the Pharisees and Sadducees." Lk 12:1

7 They discussed this among themselves and said, "It is because we didn't bring any bread."

8 Aware of their discussion, Jesus asked, "You of little faith, why are you talking among yourselves about having no bread? 9 Do you still not understand? Don't you remember the five loaves for the five thousand, and how many basketfuls you gathered? 10 Or the seven loaves for the four thousand, and how many basketfuls you gathered? 11 How is it you don't understand that I was not talking to you about bread? But be on your guard against the yeast of the Pharisees and Sadducees." 12 Then they understood that he was not telling them to guard against the yeast used in bread, but against the teaching of the Pharisees and Sadducees. Mk 8:11-21

Peter Declares That Jesus Is the Messiah

13 When Jesus came to the region of Caesarea Philippi, he asked his disciples, "Who do people say the Son of Man is?" Mk 8:27-29; Lk 9:18-20

14 They replied, "Some say John the Baptist; others say Elijah; and still others, Jeremiah or one of the prophets." Mt 14:2; Mk 6:15

15 "But what about you?" he asked. "Who do you say I am?"

16 Simon Peter answered, "You are the Messiah, the Son of the living God." Jn 11:27

17 Jesus replied, "Blessed are you, Simon son of Jonah, for this was not revealed to you by flesh and blood, but by my Father in heaven. 18 And I tell you that you are Peter,[a] and on this rock I will build my church, and the gates of Hades[b] will not overcome it. 19 I will give you the keys of the kingdom of heaven; whatever you bind on earth will be[c] bound in heaven, and whatever you loose on earth will be[c] loosed in heaven." 20 Then he ordered his disciples not to tell anyone that he was the Messiah. Jn 1:42; Eph 2:20

Jesus Predicts His Death

21 From that time on Jesus began to explain to his disciples that he must go to Jerusalem and suffer many things at the hands of the elders, the chief priests and the teachers of the law, and that he must be killed and on the third day be raised to life. Mk 9:31; Lk 17:25

22 Peter took him aside and began to rebuke him. "Never, Lord!"

[a] *18* The Greek word for *Peter* means *rock.* [b] *18* That is, the realm of the dead [c] *19* Or *will have been*

he said. "This shall never happen
to you!"
23 Jesus turned and said to Peter,
"Get behind me, Satan! You are a
stumbling block to me; you do not
have in mind the concerns of God,
but merely human concerns."
Mt 4:10
24 Then Jesus said to his disciples, "Whoever wants to be my disciple must deny themselves and
take up their cross and follow me.
25 For whoever wants to save their
life[a] will lose it, but whoever loses
their life for me will find it. 26 What
good will it be for someone to gain
the whole world, yet forfeit their
soul? Or what can anyone give in
exchange for their soul? 27 For the
Son of Man is going to come in his
Father's glory with his angels, and
then he will reward each person
according to what they have done.
28 "Truly I tell you, some who are
standing here will not taste death
before they see the Son of Man
coming in his kingdom."
Mk 8:31-9:1; Lk 9:22-27

The Transfiguration

17 After six days Jesus took
with him Peter, James and
John the brother of James, and
led them up a high mountain by
themselves. 2 There he was transfigured before them. His face
shone like the sun, and his clothes
became as white as the light. 3 Just
then there appeared before them
Moses and Elijah, talking with
Jesus.
Mt 4:21
4 Peter said to Jesus, "Lord, it is
good for us to be here. If you wish,
I will put up three shelters — one
for you, one for Moses and one for
Elijah."
5 While he was still speaking, a
bright cloud covered them, and a
voice from the cloud said, "This is
my Son, whom I love; with him I
am well pleased. Listen to him!"
Mt 3:17; 2Pe 1:17
6 When the disciples heard this,
they fell facedown to the ground,
terrified. 7 But Jesus came and
touched them. "Get up," he said.
"Don't be afraid." 8 When they
looked up, they saw no one except
Jesus.
Lk 9:28-36
9 As they were coming down the
mountain, Jesus instructed them,
"Don't tell anyone what you have
seen, until the Son of Man has
been raised from the dead."
Mt 16:21; Mk 8:30
10 The disciples asked him, "Why
then do the teachers of the law say
that Elijah must come first?"
11 Jesus replied, "To be sure, Elijah comes and will restore all
things. 12 But I tell you, Elijah has
already come, and they did not
recognize him, but have done to
him everything they wished. In
the same way the Son of Man is
going to suffer at their hands."
13 Then the disciples understood
that he was talking to them about
John the Baptist.
Mk 9:2-13

[a] 25 The Greek word means either *life* or *soul*; also in verse 26.

Jesus Heals a Demon-Possessed Boy

14When they came to the crowd, a man approached Jesus and knelt before him. 15"Lord, have mercy on my son," he said. "He has seizures and is suffering greatly. He often falls into the fire or into the water. 16I brought him to your disciples, but they could not heal him."

Mt 4:24

17"You unbelieving and perverse generation," Jesus replied, "how long shall I stay with you? How long shall I put up with you? Bring the boy here to me." 18Jesus rebuked the demon, and it came out of the boy, and he was healed at that moment.

19Then the disciples came to Jesus in private and asked, "Why couldn't we drive it out?"

Mk 9:14-28; Lk 9:37-42

20He replied, "Because you have so little faith. Truly I tell you, if you have faith as small as a mustard seed, you can say to this mountain, 'Move from here to there,' and it will move. Nothing will be impossible for you." [21][a] Mk 11:23; Lk 17:6

Jesus Predicts His Death a Second Time

22When they came together in Galilee, he said to them, "The Son of Man is going to be delivered into the hands of men. 23They will kill him, and on the third day he will be raised to life." And the disciples were filled with grief.

Mt 16:21; Ac 2:23; 3:13

The Temple Tax

24After Jesus and his disciples arrived in Capernaum, the collectors of the two-drachma temple tax came to Peter and asked, "Doesn't your teacher pay the temple tax?"

Ex 30:13

25"Yes, he does," he replied.

When Peter came into the house, Jesus was the first to speak. "What do you think, Simon?" he asked. "From whom do the kings of the earth collect duty and taxes — from their own children or from others?" Mt 22:17-21; Ro 13:7

26"From others," Peter answered.

"Then the children are exempt," Jesus said to him. 27"But so that we may not cause offense, go to the lake and throw out your line. Take the first fish you catch; open its mouth and you will find a four-drachma coin. Take it and give it to them for my tax and yours."

Jn 6:61

The Greatest in the Kingdom of Heaven

18 At that time the disciples came to Jesus and asked, "Who, then, is the greatest in the kingdom of heaven?"

2He called a little child to him, and placed the child among them. 3And he said: "Truly I tell you, unless you change and become like little children, you will never enter the kingdom of heaven.

[a] *21* Some manuscripts include here words similar to Mark 9:29.

4Therefore, whoever takes the
lowly position of this child is the
greatest in the kingdom of heav-
en. 5And whoever welcomes one
such child in my name welcomes
me. Mt 19:14; 1Pe 2:2

Causing to Stumble

6"If anyone causes one of these
little ones — those who believe in
me — to stumble, it would be better for them to have a large millstone hung around their neck
and to be drowned in the depths
of the sea. 7Woe to the world because of the things that cause
people to stumble! Such things
must come, but woe to the person through whom they come! 8If
your hand or your foot causes you
to stumble, cut it off and throw it
away. It is better for you to enter
life maimed or crippled than to
have two hands or two feet and
be thrown into eternal fire. 9And
if your eye causes you to stumble,
gouge it out and throw it away. It
is better for you to enter life with
one eye than to have two eyes and
be thrown into the fire of hell.

Mt 5:29; Mk 9:43,45; Lk 17:1

The Parable of the Wandering Sheep

10"See that you do not despise
one of these little ones. For I tell
you that their angels in heaven always see the face of my Father in
heaven. [11][a] Ge 48:16; Ps 34:7; Heb 1:14
12"What do you think? If a man
owns a hundred sheep, and one
of them wanders away, will he not
leave the ninety-nine on the hills
and go to look for the one that
wandered off? 13And if he finds it,
truly I tell you, he is happier about
that one sheep than about the
ninety-nine that did not wander
off. 14In the same way your Father
in heaven is not willing that any
of these little ones should perish.

Lk 15:4-7

Dealing With Sin in the Church

15"If your brother or sister[b] sins,[c]
go and point out their fault, just
between the two of you. If they
listen to you, you have won them
over. 16But if they will not listen,
take one or two others along, so
that 'every matter may be established by the testimony of two or
three witnesses.'[d] 17If they still refuse to listen, tell it to the church;
and if they refuse to listen even
to the church, treat them as you
would a pagan or a tax collector.

1Co 6:1-6; Jas 5:19-20

18"Truly I tell you, whatever you
bind on earth will be[e] bound in
heaven, and whatever you loose
on earth will be[e] loosed in heaven.

Mt 16:19; Jn 20:23

19"Again, truly I tell you that if
two of you on earth agree about
anything they ask for, it will be

[a] *11* Some manuscripts include here the words of Luke 19:10. [b] *15* The Greek word for *brother or sister* (*adelphos*) refers here to a fellow disciple, whether man or woman; also in verses 21 and 35.
[c] *15* Some manuscripts *sins against you*
[d] *16* Deut. 19:15 [e] *18* Or *will have been*

done for them by my Father in heaven. 20 For where two or three gather in my name, there am I with them." Mt 7:7

The Parable of the Unmerciful Servant

21 Then Peter came to Jesus and asked, "Lord, how many times shall I forgive my brother or sister who sins against me? Up to seven times?" Lk 17:4

22 Jesus answered, "I tell you, not seven times, but seventy-seven times.[a] Ge 4:24

23 "Therefore, the kingdom of heaven is like a king who wanted to settle accounts with his servants. 24 As he began the settlement, a man who owed him ten thousand bags of gold[b] was brought to him. 25 Since he was not able to pay, the master ordered that he and his wife and his children and all that he had be sold to repay the debt. 2Ki 4:1; Mt 25:19

26 "At this the servant fell on his knees before him. 'Be patient with me,' he begged, 'and I will pay back everything.' 27 The servant's master took pity on him, canceled the debt and let him go. Mt 8:2

28 "But when that servant went out, he found one of his fellow servants who owed him a hundred silver coins.[c] He grabbed him and began to choke him. 'Pay back what you owe me!' he demanded.

29 "His fellow servant fell to his knees and begged him, 'Be patient with me, and I will pay it back.'

30 "But he refused. Instead, he went off and had the man thrown into prison until he could pay the debt. 31 When the other servants saw what had happened, they were outraged and went and told their master everything that had happened.

32 "Then the master called the servant in. 'You wicked servant,' he said, 'I canceled all that debt of yours because you begged me to. 33 Shouldn't you have had mercy on your fellow servant just as I had on you?' 34 In anger his master handed him over to the jailers to be tortured, until he should pay back all he owed.

35 "This is how my heavenly Father will treat each of you unless you forgive your brother or sister from your heart." Mt 6:14; Jas 2:13

Divorce

19 When Jesus had finished saying these things, he left Galilee and went into the region of Judea to the other side of the Jordan. 2 Large crowds followed him, and he healed them there. Mt 4:23; 7:28

3 Some Pharisees came to him to test him. They asked, "Is it lawful for a man to divorce his wife for any and every reason?" Mt 5:31

[a] 22 Or *seventy times seven* [b] 24 Greek *ten thousand talents*; a talent was worth about 20 years of a day laborer's wages. [c] 28 Greek *a hundred denarii*; a denarius was the usual daily wage of a day laborer (see 20:2).

4"Haven't you read," he replied, "that at the beginning the
Creator 'made them male and
female,'[a] 5and said, 'For this reason a man will leave his father
and mother and be united to his
wife, and the two will become
one flesh'[b]? 6So they are no longer two, but one flesh. Therefore
what God has joined together, let
no one separate."

Ge 5:2; 1Co 6:16; Eph 5:31

7"Why then," they asked, "did
Moses command that a man give
his wife a certificate of divorce
and send her away?" Dt 24:1-4; Mt 5:31

8Jesus replied, "Moses permitted you to divorce your wives because your hearts were hard. But it
was not this way from the beginning. 9I tell you that anyone who
divorces his wife, except for sexual immorality, and marries another woman commits adultery."

Mk 10:1-12; Lk 16:18

10The disciples said to him, "If
this is the situation between a
husband and wife, it is better not
to marry."

11Jesus replied, "Not everyone
can accept this word, but only
those to whom it has been given.
12For there are eunuchs who were
born that way, and there are eunuchs who have been made eunuchs by others — and there are
those who choose to live like eunuchs for the sake of the kingdom
of heaven. The one who can accept
this should accept it."

Mt 13:11; 1Co 7:7-9,17

The Little Children and Jesus

13Then people brought little
children to Jesus for him to place
his hands on them and pray for
them. But the disciples rebuked
them. Mk 5:23

14Jesus said, "Let the little children come to me, and do not
hinder them, for the kingdom of
heaven belongs to such as these."
15When he had placed his hands
on them, he went on from there.

Mk 10:13-16; Lk 18:15-17

The Rich and the Kingdom of God

16Just then a man came up to
Jesus and asked, "Teacher, what
good thing must I do to get eternal life?" Mt 25:46; Lk 10:25

17"Why do you ask me about
what is good?" Jesus replied.
"There is only One who is good.
If you want to enter life, keep the
commandments." Lev 18:5

18"Which ones?" he inquired.

Jesus replied, "'You shall not
murder, you shall not commit
adultery, you shall not steal, you
shall not give false testimony,
19honor your father and mother,'[c]
and 'love your neighbor as yourself.'[d]" Lev 19:18; Jas 2:11

20"All these I have kept," the
young man said. "What do I still
lack?"

21Jesus answered, "If you want
to be perfect, go, sell your possessions and give to the poor, and you

[a] 4 Gen. 1:27 [b] 5 Gen. 2:24
[c] 19 Exodus 20:12-16; Deut. 5:16-20
[d] 19 Lev. 19:18

will have treasure in heaven. Then
come, follow me."

Mt 6:20; Lk 12:33; Ac 4:34-35

22 When the young man heard
this, he went away sad, because he
had great wealth.

23 Then Jesus said to his disciples, "Truly I tell you, it is hard for
someone who is rich to enter the
kingdom of heaven. 24 Again I tell
you, it is easier for a camel to go
through the eye of a needle than
for someone who is rich to enter
the kingdom of God."

Mt 13:22; 1Ti 6:9-10

25 When the disciples heard this,
they were greatly astonished and
asked, "Who then can be saved?"

26 Jesus looked at them and said,
"With man this is impossible, but
with God all things are possible."

Ge 18:14; Lk 1:37; Ro 4:21

27 Peter answered him, "We have
left everything to follow you!
What then will there be for us?"

Mt 4:19

28 Jesus said to them, "Truly I tell
you, at the renewal of all things,
when the Son of Man sits on his
glorious throne, you who have followed me will also sit on twelve
thrones, judging the twelve tribes
of Israel. 29 And everyone who has
left houses or brothers or sisters
or father or mother or wife[a] or
children or fields for my sake will
receive a hundred times as much
and will inherit eternal life. 30 But
many who are first will be last, and
many who are last will be first.

Mk 10:17-30; Lk 18:18-30

The Parable of the Workers in the Vineyard

20 "For the kingdom of heav-
en is like a landowner who
went out early in the morning to
hire workers for his vineyard. 2 He
agreed to pay them a denarius[b]
for the day and sent them into his
vineyard.

Mt 21:28,33

3 "About nine in the morning he
went out and saw others standing
in the marketplace doing nothing. 4 He told them, 'You also go
and work in my vineyard, and I
will pay you whatever is right.' 5 So
they went.

"He went out again about noon
and about three in the afternoon
and did the same thing. 6 About
five in the afternoon he went
out and found still others standing around. He asked them, 'Why
have you been standing here all
day long doing nothing?'

7 " 'Because no one has hired us,'
they answered.

"He said to them, 'You also go
and work in my vineyard.'

8 "When evening came, the owner of the vineyard said to his fore-
man, 'Call the workers and pay
them their wages, beginning with
the last ones hired and going on to
the first.'

Lev 19:13; Dt 24:15

9 "The workers who were hired
about five in the afternoon came
and each received a denarius. 10 So
when those came who were hired

[a] *29* Some manuscripts do not have *or wife*.
[b] *2* A denarius was the usual daily wage of a day laborer.

first, they expected to receive more. But each one of them also received a denarius. [11]When they received it, they began to grumble against the landowner. [12]'These who were hired last worked only one hour,' they said, 'and you have made them equal to us who have borne the burden of the work and the heat of the day.' Jnh 4:8; Jas 1:11

[13]"But he answered one of them, 'I am not being unfair to you, friend. Didn't you agree to work for a denarius? [14]Take your pay and go. I want to give the one who was hired last the same as I gave you. [15]Don't I have the right to do what I want with my own money? Or are you envious because I am generous?' Dt 15:9; Mk 7:22

[16]"So the last will be first, and the first will be last." Mt 19:30

Jesus Predicts His Death a Third Time

[17]Now Jesus was going up to Jerusalem. On the way, he took the Twelve aside and said to them, [18]"We are going up to Jerusalem, and the Son of Man will be delivered over to the chief priests and the teachers of the law. They will condemn him to death [19]and will hand him over to the Gentiles to be mocked and flogged and crucified. On the third day he will be raised to life!" Mk 10:32-34; Lk 18:31-33

A Mother's Request

[20]Then the mother of Zebedee's sons came to Jesus with her sons and, kneeling down, asked a favor of him. Mt 4:21; 8:2

[21]"What is it you want?" he asked.

She said, "Grant that one of these two sons of mine may sit at your right and the other at your left in your kingdom." Mt 19:28

[22]"You don't know what you are asking," Jesus said to them. "Can you drink the cup I am going to drink?" Mt 26:39,42; Lk 22:42; Jn 18:11

"We can," they answered.

[23]Jesus said to them, "You will indeed drink from my cup, but to sit at my right or left is not for me to grant. These places belong to those for whom they have been prepared by my Father." Ac 12:2; Rev 1:9

[24]When the ten heard about this, they were indignant with the two brothers. [25]Jesus called them together and said, "You know that the rulers of the Gentiles lord it over them, and their high officials exercise authority over them. [26]Not so with you. Instead, whoever wants to become great among you must be your servant, [27]and whoever wants to be first must be your slave — [28]just as the Son of Man did not come to be served, but to serve, and to give his life as a ransom for many." Mk 10:35-45; Jn 13:13-16

Two Blind Men Receive Sight

[29]As Jesus and his disciples were leaving Jericho, a large crowd followed him. [30]Two blind men were

sitting by the roadside, and when
they heard that Jesus was going
by, they shouted, "Lord, Son of David, have mercy on us!" Mt 9:27
31 The crowd rebuked them and
told them to be quiet, but they
shouted all the louder, "Lord, Son
of David, have mercy on us!"
32 Jesus stopped and called
them. "What do you want me to
do for you?" he asked.
33 "Lord," they answered, "we
want our sight."
34 Jesus had compassion on them
and touched their eyes. Immediately they received their sight and
followed him. Mk 10:46-52; Lk 18:35-43

Jesus Comes to Jerusalem as King

21 As they approached Jerusalem and came to Bethphage
on the Mount of Olives, Jesus sent
two disciples, 2 saying to them, "Go
to the village ahead of you, and at
once you will find a donkey tied
there, with her colt by her. Untie
them and bring them to me. 3 If
anyone says anything to you, say
that the Lord needs them, and he
will send them right away."
Mk 11:1-10
4 This took place to fulfill what
was spoken through the prophet:

5 "Say to Daughter Zion,
'See, your king comes to you,
gentle and riding on a donkey,
and on a colt, the foal of a
donkey.' "[a] Isa 62:11

6 The disciples went and did as
Jesus had instructed them. 7 They
brought the donkey and the colt
and placed their cloaks on them
for Jesus to sit on. 8 A very large
crowd spread their cloaks on the
road, while others cut branches
from the trees and spread them
on the road. 9 The crowds that
went ahead of him and those that
followed shouted, 2Ki 9:13

"Hosanna[b] to the Son of
David!" Mt 9:27
"Blessed is he who comes in
the name of the Lord!"[c]
Lk 19:29-38
"Hosanna[b] in the highest
heaven!" Jn 12:12-15

10 When Jesus entered Jerusalem, the whole city was stirred
and asked, "Who is this?"
11 The crowds answered, "This is
Jesus, the prophet from Nazareth
in Galilee." Jn 6:14; 7:40

Jesus at the Temple

12 Jesus entered the temple
courts and drove out all who were
buying and selling there. He overturned the tables of the money
changers and the benches of those
selling doves. 13 "It is written," he
said to them, " 'My house will be
called a house of prayer,'[d] but you
are making it 'a den of robbers.'[e]"
Ex 30:13; Dt 14:26

[a] 5 Zech. 9:9 [b] 9 A Hebrew expression meaning "Save!" which became an exclamation of praise; also in verse 15
[c] 9 Psalm 118:25,26 [d] 13 Isaiah 56:7
[e] 13 Jer. 7:11

14The blind and the lame came to him at the temple, and he healed them. 15But when the chief priests and the teachers of the law saw the wonderful things he did and the children shouting in the temple courts, "Hosanna to the Son of David," they were indignant.

Mt 9:27; Lk 19:39

16"Do you hear what these children are saying?" they asked him.

"Yes," replied Jesus, "have you never read,

" 'From the lips of children and infants
you, Lord, have called forth your praise'[a]?"

Mk 11:15-18; Lk 19:45-47

17And he left them and went out of the city to Bethany, where he spent the night.

Mt 26:6; Mk 11:1; Lk 24:50

Jesus Curses a Fig Tree

18Early in the morning, as Jesus was on his way back to the city, he was hungry. 19Seeing a fig tree by the road, he went up to it but found nothing on it except leaves. Then he said to it, "May you never bear fruit again!" Immediately the tree withered.

Isa 34:4; Jer 8:13

20When the disciples saw this, they were amazed. "How did the fig tree wither so quickly?" they asked.

21Jesus replied, "Truly I tell you, if you have faith and do not doubt, not only can you do what was done to the fig tree, but also you can say to this mountain, 'Go, throw yourself into the sea,' and it will be done. 22If you believe, you will receive whatever you ask for in prayer."

Mk 11:12-14,20-24; Jas 1:6

The Authority of Jesus Questioned

23Jesus entered the temple courts, and, while he was teaching, the chief priests and the elders of the people came to him. "By what authority are you doing these things?" they asked. "And who gave you this authority?"

Ac 4:7; 7:27

24Jesus replied, "I will also ask you one question. If you answer me, I will tell you by what authority I am doing these things. 25John's baptism — where did it come from? Was it from heaven, or of human origin?"

They discussed it among themselves and said, "If we say, 'From heaven,' he will ask, 'Then why didn't you believe him?' 26But if we say, 'Of human origin' — we are afraid of the people, for they all hold that John was a prophet."

Mk 6:20

27So they answered Jesus, "We don't know."

Then he said, "Neither will I tell you by what authority I am doing these things.

Mk 11:27-33; Lk 20:1-8

The Parable of the Two Sons

28"What do you think? There was a man who had two sons. He went to the first and said, 'Son, go and work today in the vineyard.'

Mt 20:1

[a] *16* Psalm 8:2 (see Septuagint)

29"'I will not,' he answered, but
later he changed his mind and went.
30"Then the father went to the
other son and said the same thing.
He answered, 'I will, sir,' but he did
not go.
31"Which of the two did what his
father wanted?"
"The first," they answered.
Jesus said to them, "Truly I tell
you, the tax collectors and the
prostitutes are entering the kingdom of God ahead of you. 32For
John came to you to show you the
way of righteousness, and you did
not believe him, but the tax collectors and the prostitutes did.
And even after you saw this, you
did not repent and believe him.
Lk 7:29-30,36-50

The Parable of the Tenants

33"Listen to another parable:
There was a landowner who planted a vineyard. He put a wall around
it, dug a winepress in it and built
a watchtower. Then he rented the
vineyard to some farmers and
moved to another place. 34When
the harvest time approached, he
sent his servants to the tenants to
collect his fruit. Ps 80:8; Isa 5:1-7
35"The tenants seized his servants; they beat one, killed another, and stoned a third. 36Then he
sent other servants to them, more
than the first time, and the tenants
treated them the same way. 37Last
of all, he sent his son to them.
'They will respect my son,' he said.
2Ch 24:21; Mt 23:34,37; Heb 11:36-37
38"But when the tenants saw the
son, they said to each other, 'This
is the heir. Come, let's kill him and
take his inheritance.' 39So they
took him and threw him out of the
vineyard and killed him.
Ps 2:8; Mt 12:14; Heb 1:2
40"Therefore, when the owner
of the vineyard comes, what will
he do to those tenants?"
41"He will bring those wretches
to a wretched end," they replied,
"and he will rent the vineyard to
other tenants, who will give him
his share of the crop at harvest
time." Ac 13:46; 18:6; 28:28
42Jesus said to them, "Have you
never read in the Scriptures:

"'The stone the builders
rejected
has become the
cornerstone;
the Lord has done this,
and it is marvelous
in our eyes'[a]?
Ac 4:11; 1Pe 2:7

43"Therefore I tell you that
the kingdom of God will be tak-
en away from you and given to a
people who will produce its fruit.
44Anyone who falls on this stone
will be broken to pieces; anyone
on whom it falls will be crushed."[b]
Mt 8:12; Lk 2:34
45When the chief priests and the
Pharisees heard Jesus' parables,
they knew he was talking about
them. 46They looked for a way to

[a] 42 Psalm 118:22,23 [b] 44 Some manuscripts do not have verse 44.

arrest him, but they were afraid of
the crowd because the people held
that he was a prophet.
Mk 12:1-12; Lk 20:9-19

The Parable of the Wedding Banquet

22 Jesus spoke to them again
in parables, saying: 2“The
kingdom of heaven is like a king
who prepared a wedding banquet
for his son. 3He sent his servants
to those who had been invited to
the banquet to tell them to come,
but they refused to come. Mt 21:34
4“Then he sent some more servants and said, ‘Tell those who
have been invited that I have prepared my dinner: My oxen and fattened cattle have been butchered,
and everything is ready. Come to
the wedding banquet.’ Mt 21:36
5“But they paid no attention
and went off — one to his field,
another to his business. 6The rest
seized his servants, mistreated
them and killed them. 7The king
was enraged. He sent his army
and destroyed those murderers
and burned their city. Lk 19:27
8“Then he said to his servants,
‘The wedding banquet is ready,
but those I invited did not deserve to come. 9So go to the street
corners and invite to the banquet
anyone you find.’ 10So the servants
went out into the streets and gathered all the people they could find,
the bad as well as the good, and
the wedding hall was filled with
guests. Eze 21:21; Mt 13:47-48

11“But when the king came in to
see the guests, he noticed a man
there who was not wearing wedding clothes. 12He asked, ‘How did
you get in here without wedding
clothes, friend?’ The man was
speechless. Mt 20:13; 26:50
13“Then the king told the attendants, ‘Tie him hand and foot, and
throw him outside, into the darkness, where there will be weeping
and gnashing of teeth.’ Mt 8:12
14“For many are invited, but few
are chosen.” Lk 14:6-24

Paying the Imperial Tax to Caesar

15Then the Pharisees went out
and laid plans to trap him in his
words. 16They sent their disciples
to him along with the Herodians.
“Teacher,” they said, “we know
that you are a man of integrity
and that you teach the way of God
in accordance with the truth. You
aren’t swayed by others, because
you pay no attention to who they
are. 17Tell us then, what is your
opinion? Is it right to pay the imperial tax[a] to Caesar or not?”
Mt 17:25; Mk 3:6
18But Jesus, knowing their evil
intent, said, “You hypocrites, why
are you trying to trap me? 19Show
me the coin used for paying the
tax.” They brought him a denarius, 20and he asked them, “Whose
image is this? And whose inscription?”
21“Caesar’s,” they replied.

[a] 17 A special tax levied on subject peoples, not on Roman citizens

Then he said to them, "So give
back to Caesar what is Caesar's,
and to God what is God's." Ro 13:7
22 When they heard this, they
were amazed. So they left him and
went away. Mk 12:13-17; Lk 20:20-26

Marriage at the Resurrection

23 That same day the Sadducees,
who say there is no resurrection,
came to him with a question.
24 "Teacher," they said, "Moses
told us that if a man dies without having children, his brother
must marry the widow and raise
up offspring for him. 25 Now there
were seven brothers among us.
The first one married and died,
and since he had no children, he
left his wife to his brother. 26 The
same thing happened to the second and third brother, right on
down to the seventh. 27 Finally, the
woman died. 28 Now then, at the
resurrection, whose wife will she
be of the seven, since all of them
were married to her?"
Dt 25:5-6; Ac 23:8
29 Jesus replied, "You are in error because you do not know the
Scriptures or the power of God.
30 At the resurrection people will
neither marry nor be given in
marriage; they will be like the angels in heaven. 31 But about the resurrection of the dead — have you
not read what God said to you, 32 'I
am the God of Abraham, the God
of Isaac, and the God of Jacob'[a]?
He is not the God of the dead but
of the living." Ex 3:6; Jn 20:9; Ac 7:32

33 When the crowds heard this,
they were astonished at his teaching. Mk 12:18-27; Lk 20:27-40

The Greatest Commandment

34 Hearing that Jesus had silenced the Sadducees, the Pharisees got together. 35 One of them,
an expert in the law, tested him
with this question: 36 "Teacher,
which is the greatest commandment in the Law?" Lk 7:30; 10:25; 11:45
37 Jesus replied: " 'Love the Lord
your God with all your heart and
with all your soul and with all your
mind.'[b] 38 This is the first and greatest commandment. 39 And the second is like it: 'Love your neighbor
as yourself.'[c] 40 All the Law and the
Prophets hang on these two commandments." Mk 12:28-31

Whose Son Is the Messiah?

41 While the Pharisees were gathered together, Jesus asked them,
42 "What do you think about the
Messiah? Whose son is he?"
"The son of David," they replied.
Mt 9:27
43 He said to them, "How is it
then that David, speaking by the
Spirit, calls him 'Lord'? For he says,

44 " 'The Lord said to my Lord:
"Sit at my right hand
until I put your enemies
under your feet." '[d]

45 If then David calls him 'Lord,'
how can he be his son?" 46 No one

[a] 32 Exodus 3:6 [b] 37 Deut. 6:5
[c] 39 Lev. 19:18 [d] 44 Psalm 110:1

could say a word in reply, and from that day on no one dared to ask him any more questions.

Mk 12:35-37; Lk 20:41-44; Heb 1:13; 10:13

A Warning Against Hypocrisy

23 Then Jesus said to the crowds and to his disciples:
2"The teachers of the law and the
Pharisees sit in Moses' seat. 3So
you must be careful to do everything they tell you. But do not do what they do, for they do not practice what they preach. 4They tie up
heavy, cumbersome loads and put them on other people's shoulders, but they themselves are not willing to lift a finger to move them.

Lk 11:46; Ac 15:10; Gal 6:13

5"Everything they do is done for people to see: They make their phylacteries[a] wide and the tassels on their garments long;
6they love the place of honor at banquets and the most important seats in the synagogues; 7they
love to be greeted with respect in the marketplaces and to be called 'Rabbi' by others.

Mk 12:38-39; Lk 20:45-46

8"But you are not to be called 'Rabbi,' for you have one Teacher, and you are all brothers. 9And do
not call anyone on earth 'father,' for you have one Father, and he is in heaven. 10Nor are you to be
called instructors, for you have one Instructor, the Messiah. 11The
greatest among you will be your servant. 12For those who exalt
themselves will be humbled, and those who humble themselves will be exalted.

Mt 20:26; Lk 14:11

Seven Woes on the Teachers of the Law and the Pharisees

13"Woe to you, teachers of the law and Pharisees, you hypocrites! You shut the door of the kingdom of heaven in people's faces. You yourselves do not enter, nor will you let those enter who are trying to. [14][b]

Lk 11:52

15"Woe to you, teachers of the law and Pharisees, you hypocrites! You travel over land and sea to win a single convert, and when you have succeeded, you make them twice as much a child of hell as you are.

Mt 5:22; Ac 2:11

16"Woe to you, blind guides! You say, 'If anyone swears by the temple, it means nothing; but anyone who swears by the gold of the temple is bound by that oath.' 17You
blind fools! Which is greater: the gold, or the temple that makes the gold sacred? 18You also say, 'If anyone swears by the altar, it means nothing; but anyone who swears by the gift on the altar is bound by that oath.' 19You blind men! Which
is greater: the gift, or the altar that makes the gift sacred? 20Therefore, anyone who swears by the altar swears by it and by everything on it. 21And anyone who swears by
the temple swears by it and by the

[a] 5 That is, boxes containing Scripture verses, worn on forehead and arm
[b] 14 Some manuscripts include here words similar to Mark 12:40 and Luke 20:47.

one who dwells in it. 22And anyone
who swears by heaven swears by
God's throne and by the one who
sits on it. Ex 29:37; Mt 5:34
23"Woe to you, teachers of the
law and Pharisees, you hypocrites! You give a tenth of your
spices—mint, dill and cumin. But
you have neglected the more important matters of the law—justice, mercy and faithfulness. You
should have practiced the latter,
without neglecting the former.
24You blind guides! You strain out
a gnat but swallow a camel.

Lev 27:30; Lk 11:42

25"Woe to you, teachers of the
law and Pharisees, you hypocrites!
You clean the outside of the cup
and dish, but inside they are full of
greed and self-indulgence. 26Blind
Pharisee! First clean the inside of
the cup and dish, and then the
outside also will be clean.

Mk 7:4; Lk 11:39

27"Woe to you, teachers of the
law and Pharisees, you hypocrites!
You are like whitewashed tombs,
which look beautiful on the outside but on the inside are full of
the bones of the dead and everything unclean. 28In the same way,
on the outside you appear to people as righteous but on the inside
you are full of hypocrisy and wickedness. Lk 11:44; Ac 23:3
29"Woe to you, teachers of the
law and Pharisees, you hypocrites!
You build tombs for the prophets
and decorate the graves of the
righteous. 30And you say, 'If we
had lived in the days of our ancestors, we would not have taken
part with them in shedding the
blood of the prophets.' 31So you
testify against yourselves that
you are the descendants of those
who murdered the prophets. 32Go
ahead, then, and complete what
your ancestors started!

Lk 11:47-48; Ac 7:51-52

33"You snakes! You brood of vipers! How will you escape being
condemned to hell? 34Therefore
I am sending you prophets and
sages and teachers. Some of them
you will kill and crucify; others
you will flog in your synagogues
and pursue from town to town.
35And so upon you will come all
the righteous blood that has been
shed on earth, from the blood of
righteous Abel to the blood of
Zechariah son of Berekiah, whom
you murdered between the temple and the altar. 36Truly I tell you,
all this will come on this generation. Lk 11:49-51
37"Jerusalem, Jerusalem, you
who kill the prophets and stone
those sent to you, how often I have
longed to gather your children together, as a hen gathers her chicks
under her wings, and you were not
willing. 38Look, your house is left
to you desolate. 39For I tell you,
you will not see me again until
you say, 'Blessed is he who comes
in the name of the Lord.'[a]"

Lk 13:34-35; 2Ch 24:21

[a] 39 Psalm 118:26

The Destruction of the Temple and Signs of the End Times

24 Jesus left the temple and was walking away when his disciples came up to him to call his attention to its buildings. 2“Do you see all these things?” he asked. “Truly I tell you, not one stone here will be left on another; every one will be thrown down.” Mk 13:1-37; Lk 21:5-36

3As Jesus was sitting on the Mount of Olives, the disciples came to him privately. “Tell us,” they said, “when will this happen, and what will be the sign of your coming and of the end of the age?” Mt 21:1

4Jesus answered: “Watch out that no one deceives you. 5For many will come in my name, claiming, ‘I am the Messiah,’ and will deceive many. 6You will hear of wars and rumors of wars, but see to it that you are not alarmed. Such things must happen, but the end is still to come. 7Nation will rise against nation, and kingdom against kingdom. There will be famines and earthquakes in various places. 8All these are the beginning of birth pains. Isa 19:2; Ac 11:28

9“Then you will be handed over to be persecuted and put to death, and you will be hated by all nations because of me. 10At that time many will turn away from the faith and will betray and hate each other, 11and many false prophets will appear and deceive many people. 12Because of the increase of wickedness, the love of most will grow cold, 13but the one who stands firm to the end will be saved. 14And this gospel of the kingdom will be preached in the whole world as a testimony to all nations, and then the end will come. Ro 10:18; Col 1:6,23

15“So when you see standing in the holy place ‘the abomination that causes desolation,’[a] spoken of through the prophet Daniel — let the reader understand — 16then let those who are in Judea flee to the mountains. 17Let no one on the housetop go down to take anything out of the house. 18Let no one in the field go back to get their cloak. 19How dreadful it will be in those days for pregnant women and nursing mothers! 20Pray that your flight will not take place in winter or on the Sabbath. 21For then there will be great distress, unequaled from the beginning of the world until now — and never to be equaled again.

22“If those days had not been cut short, no one would survive, but for the sake of the elect those days will be shortened. 23At that time if anyone says to you, ‘Look, here is the Messiah!’ or, ‘There he is!’ do not believe it. 24For false messiahs and false prophets will appear and perform great signs and wonders to deceive, if possible, even the elect. 25See, I have told you ahead of time. Lk 17:23; 2Th 2:9-11

[a] *15* Daniel 9:27; 11:31; 12:11

26“So if anyone tells you, ‘There
he is, out in the wilderness,’ do not
go out; or, ‘Here he is, in the inner rooms,’ do not believe it. 27For
as lightning that comes from the
east is visible even in the west, so
will be the coming of the Son of
Man. 28Wherever there is a carcass,
there the vultures will gather.

Lk 17:24,30,37

29“Immediately after the distress of those days

“ ‘the sun will be darkened,
and the moon will not give
its light;
the stars will fall from the sky,
and the heavenly bodies
will be shaken.’[a]

Eze 32:7; Joel 2:10,31

30“Then will appear the sign of
the Son of Man in heaven. And
then all the peoples of the earth[b]
will mourn when they see the Son
of Man coming on the clouds of
heaven, with power and great glory.[c] 31And he will send his angels
with a loud trumpet call, and they
will gather his elect from the four
winds, from one end of the heavens to the other.

Da 7:13; Isa 27:13; 1Co 15:52

32“Now learn this lesson from
the fig tree: As soon as its twigs
get tender and its leaves come out,
you know that summer is near.
33Even so, when you see all these
things, you know that it[d] is near,
right at the door. 34Truly I tell you,
this generation will certainly not
pass away until all these things
have happened. 35Heaven and
earth will pass away, but my words
will never pass away.

Mt 5:18; 16:28

The Day and Hour Unknown

36“But about that day or hour no
one knows, not even the angels in
heaven, nor the Son,[e] but only the
Father. 37As it was in the days of
Noah, so it will be at the coming of
the Son of Man. 38For in the days
before the flood, people were eating and drinking, marrying and
giving in marriage, up to the day
Noah entered the ark; 39and they
knew nothing about what would
happen until the flood came and
took them all away. That is how it
will be at the coming of the Son
of Man. 40Two men will be in the
field; one will be taken and the
other left. 41Two women will be
grinding with a hand mill; one
will be taken and the other left.

Lk 17:26-27,34-35

42“Therefore keep watch, because you do not know on what
day your Lord will come. 43But understand this: If the owner of the
house had known at what time
of night the thief was coming, he
would have kept watch and would
not have let his house be broken
into. 44So you also must be ready,
because the Son of Man will come
at an hour when you do not expect
him.

Mt 25:13; Lk 12:39-40

[a] *29* Isaiah 13:10; 34:4 [b] *30* Or *the tribes of the land* [c] *30* See Daniel 7:13-14. [d] *33* Or *he* [e] *36* Some manuscripts do not have *nor the Son.*

[45]“Who then is the faithful and
wise servant, whom the master
has put in charge of the servants
in his household to give them
their food at the proper time?
[46]It will be good for that servant
whose master finds him doing so
when he returns. [47]Truly I tell you,
he will put him in charge of all his
possessions. [48]But suppose that
servant is wicked and says to himself, ‘My master is staying away a
long time,’ [49]and he then begins to
beat his fellow servants and to eat
and drink with drunkards. [50]The
master of that servant will come
on a day when he does not expect
him and at an hour he is not aware
of. [51]He will cut him to pieces and
assign him a place with the hypocrites, where there will be weeping and gnashing of teeth.
Lk 12:42-46; Rev 16:15

The Parable of the Ten Virgins

25 “At that time the kingdom
of heaven will be like ten
virgins who took their lamps and
went out to meet the bridegroom.
[2]Five of them were foolish and
five were wise. [3]The foolish ones
took their lamps but did not take
any oil with them. [4]The wise ones,
however, took oil in jars along with
their lamps. [5]The bridegroom was
a long time in coming, and they
all became drowsy and fell asleep.
1Th 5:6; Rev 19:7

[6]“At midnight the cry rang out:
‘Here’s the bridegroom! Come out
to meet him!’

[7]“Then all the virgins woke up
and trimmed their lamps. [8]The
foolish ones said to the wise, ‘Give
us some of your oil; our lamps are
going out.’ Lk 12:35

[9]“ ‘No,’ they replied, ‘there may
not be enough for both us and
you. Instead, go to those who sell
oil and buy some for yourselves.’

[10]“But while they were on their
way to buy the oil, the bridegroom
arrived. The virgins who were
ready went in with him to the wedding banquet. And the door was
shut. Rev 19:9

[11]“Later the others also came.
‘Lord, Lord,’ they said, ‘open the
door for us!’

[12]“But he replied, ‘Truly I tell
you, I don’t know you.’ Mt 7:23

[13]“Therefore keep watch, because you do not know the day or
the hour. Mt 24:42,44; Mk 13:35; Lk 12:40

The Parable of the Bags of Gold

[14]“Again, it will be like a man
going on a journey, who called his
servants and entrusted his wealth
to them. [15]To one he gave five bags
of gold, to another two bags, and
to another one bag,[a] each according to his ability. Then he went on
his journey. [16]The man who had
received five bags of gold went at
once and put his money to work
and gained five bags more. [17]So
also, the one with two bags of gold

[a] *15* Greek *five talents . . . two talents . . . one talent*; also throughout this parable; a talent was worth about 20 years of a day laborer’s wage.

gained two more. 18But the man
who had received one bag went
off, dug a hole in the ground and
hid his master's money.
Mt 18:24-25; 21:33; Lk 19:12
19"After a long time the master
of those servants returned and
settled accounts with them. 20The
man who had received five bags of
gold brought the other five. 'Master,' he said, 'you entrusted me
with five bags of gold. See, I have
gained five more.' Mt 18:23
21"His master replied, 'Well
done, good and faithful servant!
You have been faithful with a few
things; I will put you in charge
of many things. Come and share
your master's happiness!'
Mt 24:45,47; Lk 16:10
22"The man with two bags of
gold also came. 'Master,' he said,
'you entrusted me with two bags of
gold; see, I have gained two more.'
23"His master replied, 'Well
done, good and faithful servant!
You have been faithful with a few
things; I will put you in charge
of many things. Come and share
your master's happiness!' ver 21
24"Then the man who had received one bag of gold came. 'Master,' he said, 'I knew that you are
a hard man, harvesting where
you have not sown and gathering
where you have not scattered seed.
25So I was afraid and went out and
hid your gold in the ground. See,
here is what belongs to you.'
26"His master replied, 'You
wicked, lazy servant! So you knew
that I harvest where I have not
sown and gather where I have not
scattered seed? 27Well then, you
should have put my money on
deposit with the bankers, so that
when I returned I would have received it back with interest.
28" 'So take the bag of gold from
him and give it to the one who
has ten bags. 29For whoever has
will be given more, and they will
have an abundance. Whoever does
not have, even what they have will
be taken from them. 30And throw
that worthless servant outside,
into the darkness, where there
will be weeping and gnashing of
teeth.' Lk 19:12-27

The Sheep and the Goats

31"When the Son of Man comes
in his glory, and all the angels
with him, he will sit on his glorious throne. 32All the nations will
be gathered before him, and he
will separate the people one from
another as a shepherd separates
the sheep from the goats. 33He will
put the sheep on his right and the
goats on his left. Eze 34:17,20; Mal 3:18
34"Then the King will say to
those on his right, 'Come, you
who are blessed by my Father;
take your inheritance, the kingdom prepared for you since the
creation of the world. 35For I was
hungry and you gave me something to eat, I was thirsty and you
gave me something to drink, I was
a stranger and you invited me in,
36I needed clothes and you clothed

me, I was sick and you looked after
me, I was in prison and you came
to visit me.' 1Co 15:50; Jas 2:15-16; Rev 13:8
37"Then the righteous will an-
swer him, 'Lord, when did we
see you hungry and feed you, or
thirsty and give you something
to drink? 38When did we see you
a stranger and invite you in, or
needing clothes and clothe you?
39When did we see you sick or in
prison and go to visit you?'
40"The King will reply, 'Truly I
tell you, whatever you did for one
of the least of these brothers and
sisters of mine, you did for me.'
Pr 19:17; Mt 10:40,42
41"Then he will say to those on
his left, 'Depart from me, you who
are cursed, into the eternal fire prepared for the devil and his angels.
42For I was hungry and you gave
me nothing to eat, I was thirsty
and you gave me nothing to drink,
43I was a stranger and you did not
invite me in, I needed clothes and
you did not clothe me, I was sick
and in prison and you did not look
after me.' Mt 7:23; Mk 9:43,48; 2Pe 2:4
44"They also will answer, 'Lord,
when did we see you hungry or
thirsty or a stranger or needing
clothes or sick or in prison, and
did not help you?'
45"He will reply, 'Truly I tell you,
whatever you did not do for one of
the least of these, you did not do
for me.' Pr 14:31; 17:5
46"Then they will go away to
eternal punishment, but the righteous to eternal life." Da 12:2; Jn 5:29

The Plot Against Jesus

26 When Jesus had finished
saying all these things,
he said to his disciples, 2"As you
know, the Passover is two days
away—and the Son of Man will be
handed over to be crucified."
Mt 7:28; Jn 13:1
3Then the chief priests and the
elders of the people assembled
in the palace of the high priest,
whose name was Caiaphas, 4and
they schemed to arrest Jesus secretly and kill him. 5"But not during the festival," they said, "or
there may be a riot among the
people." Mk 14:1-2; Lk 22:1-2

Jesus Anointed at Bethany

6While Jesus was in Bethany in
the home of Simon the Leper, 7a
woman came to him with an alabaster jar of very expensive perfume, which she poured on his
head as he was reclining at the
table. Mt 21:17
8When the disciples saw this,
they were indignant. "Why this
waste?" they asked. 9"This perfume could have been sold at a
high price and the money given
to the poor."
10Aware of this, Jesus said to
them, "Why are you bothering this
woman? She has done a beautiful
thing to me. 11The poor you will always have with you,[a] but you will
not always have me. 12When she
poured this perfume on my body,

[a] *11* See Deut. 15:11.

she did it to prepare me for burial.
13 Truly I tell you, wherever this
gospel is preached throughout the
world, what she has done will also
be told, in memory of her."

Mk 14:3-9; Lk 7:37-38; Jn 12:1-8

Judas Agrees to Betray Jesus

14 Then one of the Twelve — the
one called Judas Iscariot — went
to the chief priests 15 and asked,
"What are you willing to give me
if I deliver him over to you?" So
they counted out for him thirty
pieces of silver. 16 From then on Judas watched for an opportunity to
hand him over. Mk 14:10-11; Lk 22:3-6

The Last Supper

17 On the first day of the Festival
of Unleavened Bread, the disciples
came to Jesus and asked, "Where
do you want us to make preparations for you to eat the Passover?"

Ex 12:18-20

18 He replied, "Go into the city to
a certain man and tell him, 'The
Teacher says: My appointed time
is near. I am going to celebrate the
Passover with my disciples at your
house.' " 19 So the disciples did as
Jesus had directed them and prepared the Passover.

Mk 14:12-16; Lk 22:7-13

20 When evening came, Jesus
was reclining at the table with the
Twelve. 21 And while they were eating, he said, "Truly I tell you, one of
you will betray me." Lk 22:21-23; Jn 13:21

22 They were very sad and began to say to him one after the
other, "Surely you don't mean me,
Lord?"

23 Jesus replied, "The one who
has dipped his hand into the bowl
with me will betray me. 24 The Son
of Man will go just as it is written
about him. But woe to that man
who betrays the Son of Man! It
would be better for him if he had
not been born." Mk 14:17-21; Jn 13:18

25 Then Judas, the one who would
betray him, said, "Surely you don't
mean me, Rabbi?" Mt 23:7

Jesus answered, "You have said
so."

26 While they were eating, Jesus
took bread, and when he had giv-
en thanks, he broke it and gave it
to his disciples, saying, "Take and
eat; this is my body." 1Co 10:16

27 Then he took a cup, and when
he had given thanks, he gave it to
them, saying, "Drink from it, all
of you. 28 This is my blood of the[a]
covenant, which is poured out for
many for the forgiveness of sins.
29 I tell you, I will not drink from
this fruit of the vine from now on
until that day when I drink it new
with you in my Father's kingdom."

Lk 22:17-20; 1Co 11:23-25

30 When they had sung a hymn,
they went out to the Mount of
Olives. Mk 14:22-26

Jesus Predicts Peter's Denial

31 Then Jesus told them, "This
very night you will all fall away on
account of me, for it is written:

Mt 11:6; 13:21

[a] *28* Some manuscripts *the new*

"'I will strike the shepherd,
and the sheep of the flock
will be scattered.'[a]

32 But after I have risen, I will go
ahead of you into Galilee."
Mt 28:7,10,16

33 Peter replied, "Even if all fall
away on account of you, I never
will."
34 "Truly I tell you," Jesus answered, "this very night, before
the rooster crows, you will disown
me three times." Jn 13:37-38
35 But Peter declared, "Even if I
have to die with you, I will never
disown you." And all the other disciples said the same.
Mk 14:27-31; Lk 22:31-34

Gethsemane

36 Then Jesus went with his disciples to a place called Gethsemane,
and he said to them, "Sit here while
I go over there and pray." 37 He took
Peter and the two sons of Zebedee
along with him, and he began to
be sorrowful and troubled. 38 Then
he said to them, "My soul is overwhelmed with sorrow to the point
of death. Stay here and keep watch
with me." Mt 4:21; Jn 12:27
39 Going a little farther, he fell
with his face to the ground and
prayed, "My Father, if it is possible, may this cup be taken from
me. Yet not as I will, but as you
will." Mt 20:22; Jn 6:38
40 Then he returned to his disciples and found them sleeping.
"Couldn't you men keep watch
with me for one hour?" he asked
Peter. 41 "Watch and pray so that
you will not fall into temptation.
The spirit is willing, but the flesh
is weak." Mt 6:13
42 He went away a second time
and prayed, "My Father, if it is not
possible for this cup to be taken
away unless I drink it, may your
will be done."
43 When he came back, he again
found them sleeping, because
their eyes were heavy. 44 So he left
them and went away once more
and prayed the third time, saying
the same thing.
45 Then he returned to the disciples and said to them, "Are you still
sleeping and resting? Look, the
hour has come, and the Son of Man
is delivered into the hands of sinners. 46 Rise! Let us go! Here comes
my betrayer!" Mk 14:32-42; Lk 22:40-46

Jesus Arrested

47 While he was still speaking,
Judas, one of the Twelve, arrived.
With him was a large crowd armed
with swords and clubs, sent from
the chief priests and the elders
of the people. 48 Now the betrayer
had arranged a signal with them:
"The one I kiss is the man; arrest
him." 49 Going at once to Jesus, Judas said, "Greetings, Rabbi!" and
kissed him. Mt 23:7
50 Jesus replied, "Do what you
came for, friend."[b] Mt 20:13; 22:12

[a] 31 Zech. 13:7 [b] 50 Or *"Why have you come, friend?"*

Then the men stepped forward,
seized Jesus and arrested him.
51With that, one of Jesus' companions reached for his sword, drew it
out and struck the servant of the
high priest, cutting off his ear.
Lk 22:36,38; Jn 18:10
52"Put your sword back in its
place," Jesus said to him, "for all
who draw the sword will die by
the sword. 53Do you think I cannot
call on my Father, and he will at
once put at my disposal more than
twelve legions of angels? 54But
how then would the Scriptures be
fulfilled that say it must happen
in this way?" Ge 9:6; Rev 13:10
55In that hour Jesus said to
the crowd, "Am I leading a rebellion, that you have come out
with swords and clubs to capture
me? Every day I sat in the temple
courts teaching, and you did not
arrest me. 56But this has all tak-
en place that the writings of the
prophets might be fulfilled." Then
all the disciples deserted him and
fled. Mk 14:43-50; Lk 22:47-53

Jesus Before the Sanhedrin

57Those who had arrested Jesus
took him to Caiaphas the high
priest, where the teachers of the
law and the elders had assembled.
58But Peter followed him at a distance, right up to the courtyard of
the high priest. He entered and sat
down with the guards to see the
outcome. Jn 18:15
59The chief priests and the
whole Sanhedrin were looking
for false evidence against Jesus so
that they could put him to death.
60But they did not find any, though
many false witnesses came forward. Ps 27:12; 35:11; Ac 6:13
Finally two came forward 61and
declared, "This fellow said, 'I am
able to destroy the temple of God
and rebuild it in three days.'"
Dt 19:15; Jn 2:19
62Then the high priest stood up
and said to Jesus, "Are you not going to answer? What is this testimony that these men are bringing against you?" 63But Jesus
remained silent. Mt 27:12,14
The high priest said to him, "I
charge you under oath by the living God: Tell us if you are the Messiah, the Son of God." Lk 22:67
64"You have said so," Jesus replied. "But I say to all of you:
From now on you will see the Son
of Man sitting at the right hand
of the Mighty One and coming on
the clouds of heaven."[a]
Ps 110:1; Da 7:13; Rev 1:7
65Then the high priest tore his
clothes and said, "He has spoken
blasphemy! Why do we need any
more witnesses? Look, now you
have heard the blasphemy. 66What
do you think?" Mk 14:63
"He is worthy of death," they answered. Lev 24:16; Jn 19:7
67Then they spit in his face and
struck him with their fists. Others
slapped him 68and said, "Prophesy
to us, Messiah. Who hit you?"
Mk 14:53-65; Jn 18:12-13,19-24

[a] 64 See Psalm 110:1; Daniel 7:13.

Peter Disowns Jesus

69 Now Peter was sitting out in
the courtyard, and a servant girl
came to him. "You also were with
Jesus of Galilee," she said.
70 But he denied it before them
all. "I don't know what you're talking about," he said.
71 Then he went out to the gateway, where another servant girl
saw him and said to the people
there, "This fellow was with Jesus
of Nazareth."
72 He denied it again, with an
oath: "I don't know the man!"
73 After a little while, those
standing there went up to Peter
and said, "Surely you are one of
them; your accent gives you away."
74 Then he began to call down
curses, and he swore to them, "I
don't know the man!"
Immediately a rooster crowed.
75 Then Peter remembered the
word Jesus had spoken: "Before
the rooster crows, you will disown
me three times." And he went outside and wept bitterly. ver 34; Jn 13:38

Judas Hangs Himself

27 Early in the morning, all the
chief priests and the elders
of the people made their plans
how to have Jesus executed. 2 So
they bound him, led him away
and handed him over to Pilate the
governor. Mt 20:19; Mk 15:1; Ac 3:13
3 When Judas, who had be-
trayed him, saw that Jesus was
condemned, he was seized with
remorse and returned the thirty
pieces of silver to the chief priests
and the elders. 4 "I have sinned,"
he said, "for I have betrayed innocent blood." Mt 26:14-15
"What is that to us?" they replied. "That's your responsibility."
ver 24
5 So Judas threw the money into
the temple and left. Then he went
away and hanged himself.
Lk 1:9,21; Ac 1:18
6 The chief priests picked up the
coins and said, "It is against the
law to put this into the treasury,
since it is blood money." 7 So they
decided to use the money to buy
the potter's field as a burial place
for foreigners. 8 That is why it has
been called the Field of Blood to
this day. 9 Then what was spoken
by Jeremiah the prophet was fulfilled: "They took the thirty pieces of silver, the price set on him
by the people of Israel, 10 and they
used them to buy the potter's field,
as the Lord commanded me."[a]
Mt 1:22; Ac 1:19

Jesus Before Pilate

11 Meanwhile Jesus stood before
the governor, and the governor
asked him, "Are you the king of
the Jews?" Mt 2:2
"You have said so," Jesus replied.
12 When he was accused by the
chief priests and the elders, he
gave no answer. 13 Then Pilate
asked him, "Don't you hear the testimony they are bringing against

[a] 10 See Zech. 11:12,13; Jer. 19:1-13; 32:6-9.

you?" 14 But Jesus made no reply,
not even to a single charge — to
the great amazement of the governor. Mt 26:62-63; Jn 19:9
15 Now it was the governor's custom at the festival to release a
prisoner chosen by the crowd. 16 At
that time they had a well-known
prisoner whose name was Jesus[a]
Barabbas. 17 So when the crowd
had gathered, Pilate asked them,
"Which one do you want me to release to you: Jesus Barabbas, or
Jesus who is called the Messiah?"
18 For he knew it was out of self-interest that they had handed Jesus
over to him. Jn 18:39
19 While Pilate was sitting on the
judge's seat, his wife sent him this
message: "Don't have anything to
do with that innocent man, for I
have suffered a great deal today in
a dream because of him."
Mt 1:20; Jn 19:13
20 But the chief priests and the
elders persuaded the crowd to ask
for Barabbas and to have Jesus executed. Ac 3:14
21 "Which of the two do you want
me to release to you?" asked the
governor.
"Barabbas," they answered.
22 "What shall I do, then, with
Jesus who is called the Messiah?"
Pilate asked. Mt 1:16
They all answered, "Crucify
him!"
23 "Why? What crime has he committed?" asked Pilate.
But they shouted all the louder,
"Crucify him!"
24 When Pilate saw that he was
getting nowhere, but that instead an uproar was starting, he
took water and washed his hands
in front of the crowd. "I am innocent of this man's blood," he said.
"It is your responsibility!"
Dt 21:6-8; Mt 26:5
25 All the people answered, "His
blood is on us and on our children!" Jos 2:19; Ac 5:28
26 Then he released Barabbas to
them. But he had Jesus flogged,
and handed him over to be cruci-
fied. Mk 15:2-15; Lk 23:2-3,18-25; Jn 18:29-19:16

The Soldiers Mock Jesus

27 Then the governor's soldiers
took Jesus into the Praetorium
and gathered the whole company of soldiers around him. 28 They
stripped him and put a scarlet
robe on him, 29 and then twisted
together a crown of thorns and
set it on his head. They put a staff
in his right hand. Then they knelt
in front of him and mocked him.
"Hail, king of the Jews!" they said.
30 They spit on him, and took the
staff and struck him on the head
again and again. 31 After they had
mocked him, they took off the
robe and put his own clothes on
him. Then they led him away to
crucify him. Mk 15:16-20; Isa 53:3,7

The Crucifixion of Jesus

32 As they were going out, they
met a man from Cyrene, named

[a] 16 Many manuscripts do not have *Jesus*; also in verse 17.

Simon, and they forced him to
carry the cross. 33They came to
a place called Golgotha (which
means "the place of the skull").
34There they offered Jesus wine
to drink, mixed with gall; but after tasting it, he refused to drink
it. 35When they had crucified him,
they divided up his clothes by
casting lots. 36And sitting down,
they kept watch over him there.
37Above his head they placed the
written charge against him: THIS
IS JESUS, THE KING OF THE JEWS.

38Two rebels were crucified with
him, one on his right and one on
his left. 39Those who passed by
hurled insults at him, shaking
their heads 40and saying, "You
who are going to destroy the temple and build it in three days, save
yourself! Come down from the
cross, if you are the Son of God!"
41In the same way the chief priests,
the teachers of the law and the elders mocked him. 42"He saved others," they said, "but he can't save
himself! He's the king of Israel!
Let him come down now from the
cross, and we will believe in him.
43He trusts in God. Let God rescue
him now if he wants him, for he
said, 'I am the Son of God.'" 44In
the same way the rebels who were
crucified with him also heaped insults on him.

Mk 15:22-32; Lk 23:33-43; Jn 19:17-24

The Death of Jesus

45From noon until three in the
afternoon darkness came over all
the land. 46About three in the afternoon Jesus cried out in a loud
voice, *"Eli, Eli,*[a] *lema sabachthani?"*
(which means "My God, my God,
why have you forsaken me?").[b]

Am 8:9

47When some of those standing
there heard this, they said, "He's
calling Elijah."

48Immediately one of them ran
and got a sponge. He filled it with
wine vinegar, put it on a staff, and
offered it to Jesus to drink. 49The
rest said, "Now leave him alone.
Let's see if Elijah comes to save
him." Ps 69:21

50And when Jesus had cried out
again in a loud voice, he gave up
his spirit. Jn 19:30

51At that moment the curtain of
the temple was torn in two from
top to bottom. The earth shook,
the rocks split 52and the tombs
broke open. The bodies of many
holy people who had died were
raised to life. 53They came out of
the tombs after Jesus' resurrection and[c] went into the holy city
and appeared to many people.

Ex 26:31-33; Mt 4:5

54When the centurion and those
with him who were guarding
Jesus saw the earthquake and all
that had happened, they were terrified, and exclaimed, "Surely he
was the Son of God!" Mt 4:3; 17:5

55Many women were there,
watching from a distance. They

[a] 46 Some manuscripts *Eloi, Eloi*
[b] 46 Psalm 22:1 [c] 53 Or *tombs, and after Jesus' resurrection they*

had followed Jesus from Galilee to care for his needs. 56 Among them were Mary Magdalene, Mary the mother of James and Joseph,[a] and the mother of Zebedee's sons.

Mk 15:33-41; Lk 23:44-49

The Burial of Jesus

57 As evening approached, there came a rich man from Arimathea, named Joseph, who had himself become a disciple of Jesus. 58 Going to Pilate, he asked for Jesus' body, and Pilate ordered that it be given to him. 59 Joseph took the body, wrapped it in a clean linen cloth, 60 and placed it in his own new tomb that he had cut out of the rock. He rolled a big stone in front of the entrance to the tomb and went away. 61 Mary Magdalene and the other Mary were sitting there opposite the tomb.

Mk 15:42-47; Lk 23:50-56; Jn 19:38-42

The Guard at the Tomb

62 The next day, the one after Preparation Day, the chief priests and the Pharisees went to Pilate. 63 "Sir," they said, "we remember that while he was still alive that deceiver said, 'After three days I will rise again.' 64 So give the order for the tomb to be made secure until the third day. Otherwise, his disciples may come and steal the body and tell the people that he has been raised from the dead. This last deception will be worse than the first."

Mt 16:21; 28:13

65 "Take a guard," Pilate answered. "Go, make the tomb as secure as you know how." 66 So they went and made the tomb secure by putting a seal on the stone and posting the guard.

Da 6:17; Mt 28:11

Jesus Has Risen

28 After the Sabbath, at dawn on the first day of the week, Mary Magdalene and the other Mary went to look at the tomb.

Mt 27:56

2 There was a violent earthquake, for an angel of the Lord came down from heaven and, going to the tomb, rolled back the stone and sat on it. 3 His appearance was like lightning, and his clothes were white as snow. 4 The guards were so afraid of him that they shook and became like dead men.

Da 10:6; Mk 9:3

5 The angel said to the women, "Do not be afraid, for I know that you are looking for Jesus, who was crucified. 6 He is not here; he has risen, just as he said. Come and see the place where he lay. 7 Then go quickly and tell his disciples: 'He has risen from the dead and is going ahead of you into Galilee. There you will see him.' Now I have told you."

Mk 16:1-8; Lk 24:1-10

8 So the women hurried away from the tomb, afraid yet filled with joy, and ran to tell his disciples. 9 Suddenly Jesus met them. "Greetings," he said. They came to

[a] *56* Greek *Joses,* a variant of *Joseph*

him, clasped his feet and worshiped
him. [10]Then Jesus said to them, "Do
not be afraid. Go and tell my brothers to go to Galilee; there they will
see me." Ro 8:29; Heb 2:11-13,17

The Guards' Report

[11]While the women were on
their way, some of the guards
went into the city and reported to
the chief priests everything that
had happened. [12]When the chief
priests had met with the elders
and devised a plan, they gave the
soldiers a large sum of money,
[13]telling them, "You are to say, 'His
disciples came during the night
and stole him away while we were
asleep.' [14]If this report gets to the
governor, we will satisfy him and
keep you out of trouble." [15]So the
soldiers took the money and did
as they were instructed. And this
story has been widely circulated
among the Jews to this very day.
Mt 27:2,65-66

The Great Commission

[16]Then the eleven disciples went
to Galilee, to the mountain where
Jesus had told them to go. [17]When
they saw him, they worshiped
him; but some doubted. [18]Then
Jesus came to them and said, "All
authority in heaven and on earth
has been given to me. [19]Therefore
go and make disciples of all nations, baptizing them in the name
of the Father and of the Son and
of the Holy Spirit, [20]and teaching
them to obey everything I have
commanded you. And surely I am
with you always, to the very end
of the age." Mk 16:15-16; Php 2:9-10

MARK

John the Baptist Prepares the Way

1 The beginning of the good
news about Jesus the Messiah,[a]
the Son of God,[b] 2as it is written in
Isaiah the prophet: Mt 4:3

"I will send my messenger
ahead of you,
who will prepare
your way"[c] —
Mal 3:1; Mt 11:10; Lk 7:27

3"a voice of one calling in the
wilderness,
'Prepare the way for the
Lord,
make straight paths for
him.' "[d]

4And so John the Baptist appeared
in the wilderness, preaching a
baptism of repentance for the forgiveness of sins. 5The whole Judean countryside and all the people of Jerusalem went out to him.
Confessing their sins, they were
baptized by him in the Jordan
River. 6John wore clothing made
of camel's hair, with a leather belt
around his waist, and he ate locusts and wild honey. 7And this
was his message: "After me comes
the one more powerful than I, the
straps of whose sandals I am not
worthy to stoop down and untie.
8I baptize you with[e] water, but he
will baptize you with[e] the Holy
Spirit." Mt 3:1-11; Lk 3:2-16

The Baptism and Testing of Jesus

9At that time Jesus came from
Nazareth in Galilee and was baptized by John in the Jordan. 10Just
as Jesus was coming up out of the
water, he saw heaven being torn
open and the Spirit descending
on him like a dove. 11And a voice
came from heaven: "You are my
Son, whom I love; with you I am
well pleased." Mt 3:13-17; Lk 3:21-22

12At once the Spirit sent him
out into the wilderness, 13and he
was in the wilderness forty days,
being tempted[f] by Satan. He was
with the wild animals, and angels
attended him. Mt 4:1-11; Lk 4:1-13

Jesus Announces the Good News

14After John was put in prison, Jesus went into Galilee, proclaiming the good news of God.
15"The time has come," he said.
"The kingdom of God has come
near. Repent and believe the good
news!" Ac 20:21; Gal 4:4; Eph 1:10

Jesus Calls His First Disciples

16As Jesus walked beside the Sea
of Galilee, he saw Simon and his
brother Andrew casting a net into

[a] *1* Or *Jesus Christ. Messiah* (Hebrew) and *Christ* (Greek) both mean *Anointed One.*
[b] *1* Some manuscripts do not have *the Son of God.*
[c] *2* Mal. 3:1
[d] *3* Isaiah 40:3
[e] *8* Or *in*
[f] *13* The Greek for *tempted* can also mean *tested.*

the lake, for they were fishermen.
17“Come, follow me,” Jesus said,
“and I will send you out to fish for
people.” 18At once they left their
nets and followed him. Mt 4:19
19When he had gone a little farther, he saw James son of Zebedee
and his brother John in a boat,
preparing their nets. 20Without
delay he called them, and they left
their father Zebedee in the boat
with the hired men and followed
him. Mt 4:18-22; Lk 5:2-11; Jn 1:35-42

Jesus Drives Out an Impure Spirit

21They went to Capernaum, and
when the Sabbath came, Jesus
went into the synagogue and began to teach. 22The people were
amazed at his teaching, because
he taught them as one who had
authority, not as the teachers of
the law. 23Just then a man in their
synagogue who was possessed by
an impure spirit cried out, 24“What
do you want with us, Jesus of Nazareth? Have you come to destroy
us? I know who you are — the
Holy One of God!”
Mt 7:28-29; 8:29; Lk 1:35
25“Be quiet!” said Jesus sternly.
“Come out of him!” 26The impure
spirit shook the man violently and
came out of him with a shriek.
Mk 9:20
27The people were all so amazed
that they asked each other, “What
is this? A new teaching — and with
authority! He even gives orders
to impure spirits and they obey
him.” 28News about him spread
quickly over the whole region of
Galilee. Lk 4:31-37

Jesus Heals Many

29As soon as they left the synagogue, they went with James and
John to the home of Simon and
Andrew. 30Simon’s mother-in-law
was in bed with a fever, and they
immediately told Jesus about
her. 31So he went to her, took her
hand and helped her up. The fever
left her and she began to wait on
them. Mt 8:14-15; Lk 4:38-39
32That evening after sunset the
people brought to Jesus all the
sick and demon-possessed. 33The
whole town gathered at the door,
34and Jesus healed many who had
various diseases. He also drove
out many demons, but he would
not let the demons speak because
they knew who he was.
Mt 8:16-17; Lk 4:40-41

Jesus Prays in a Solitary Place

35Very early in the morning,
while it was still dark, Jesus got
up, left the house and went off to
a solitary place, where he prayed.
36Simon and his companions went
to look for him, 37and when they
found him, they exclaimed: “Everyone is looking for you!” Lk 3:21
38Jesus replied, “Let us go somewhere else — to the nearby villages — so I can preach there also.
That is why I have come.” 39So
he traveled throughout Galilee,
preaching in their synagogues
and driving out demons. Lk 4:42-43

Jesus Heals a Man With Leprosy

40A man with leprosy[a] came to
him and begged him on his knees,
"If you are willing, you can make
me clean." Mk 10:17

41Jesus was indignant.[b] He
reached out his hand and touched
the man. "I am willing," he said.
"Be clean!" 42Immediately the leprosy left him and he was cleansed.
43Jesus sent him away at once
with a strong warning: 44"See that
you don't tell this to anyone. But
go, show yourself to the priest
and offer the sacrifices that Moses
commanded for your cleansing, as
a testimony to them." 45Instead he
went out and began to talk freely, spreading the news. As a result,
Jesus could no longer enter a town
openly but stayed outside in lonely places. Yet the people still came
to him from everywhere.
Mt 8:2-4; Lk 5:12-14

Jesus Forgives and Heals a Paralyzed Man

2 A few days later, when Jesus
again entered Capernaum, the
people heard that he had come
home. 2They gathered in such
large numbers that there was no
room left, not even outside the
door, and he preached the word to
them. 3Some men came, bringing
to him a paralyzed man, carried
by four of them. 4Since they could
not get him to Jesus because of
the crowd, they made an opening
in the roof above Jesus by digging
through it and then lowered the
mat the man was lying on. 5When
Jesus saw their faith, he said to the
paralyzed man, "Son, your sins are
forgiven." Mt 4:24; Lk 7:48

6Now some teachers of the law
were sitting there, thinking to
themselves, 7"Why does this fellow talk like that? He's blaspheming! Who can forgive sins but God
alone?" Isa 43:25

8Immediately Jesus knew in his
spirit that this was what they were
thinking in their hearts, and he
said to them, "Why are you thinking these things? 9Which is easier:
to say to this paralyzed man, 'Your
sins are forgiven,' or to say, 'Get
up, take your mat and walk'? 10But
I want you to know that the Son of
Man has authority on earth to forgive sins." So he said to the man,
11"I tell you, get up, take your mat
and go home." 12He got up, took
his mat and walked out in full
view of them all. This amazed everyone and they praised God, saying, "We have never seen anything
like this!" Mt 9:2-8; Lk 5:18-26

Jesus Calls Levi and Eats With Sinners

13Once again Jesus went out beside the lake. A large crowd came
to him, and he began to teach
them. 14As he walked along, he

[a] *40* The Greek word traditionally translated *leprosy* was used for various diseases affecting the skin. [b] *41* Many manuscripts *Jesus was filled with compassion*

saw Levi son of Alphaeus sitting
at the tax collector's booth. "Follow me," Jesus told him, and Levi
got up and followed him.
Mt 4:19; Mk 1:45

15 While Jesus was having dinner at Levi's house, many tax collectors and sinners were eating
with him and his disciples, for
there were many who followed
him. 16 When the teachers of the
law who were Pharisees saw him
eating with the sinners and tax
collectors, they asked his disciples: "Why does he eat with tax
collectors and sinners?"
Mt 9:11; Ac 23:9

17 On hearing this, Jesus said to
them, "It is not the healthy who
need a doctor, but the sick. I have
not come to call the righteous, but
sinners." Mt 9:9-13; Lk 5:27-32

Jesus Questioned About Fasting

18 Now John's disciples and the
Pharisees were fasting. Some people came and asked Jesus, "How is
it that John's disciples and the disciples of the Pharisees are fasting,
but yours are not?" Mt 6:16-18; Ac 13:2

19 Jesus answered, "How can
the guests of the bridegroom fast
while he is with them? They cannot, so long as they have him with
them. 20 But the time will come
when the bridegroom will be tak-
en from them, and on that day
they will fast. Lk 17:22

21 "No one sews a patch of un-
shrunk cloth on an old garment.
Otherwise, the new piece will pull
away from the old, making the
tear worse. 22 And no one pours
new wine into old wineskins.
Otherwise, the wine will burst the
skins, and both the wine and the
wineskins will be ruined. No, they
pour new wine into new wineskins." Mt 9:14-17; Lk 5:33-38

Jesus Is Lord of the Sabbath

23 One Sabbath Jesus was going
through the grainfields, and as his
disciples walked along, they began
to pick some heads of grain. 24 The
Pharisees said to him, "Look, why
are they doing what is unlawful
on the Sabbath?" Dt 23:25; Mt 12:2

25 He answered, "Have you never
read what David did when he and
his companions were hungry and
in need? 26 In the days of Abiathar
the high priest, he entered the
house of God and ate the consecrated bread, which is lawful only
for priests to eat. And he also gave
some to his companions."
Lev 24:5-9; 1Sa 21:1-6; 2Sa 8:17

27 Then he said to them, "The
Sabbath was made for man, not
man for the Sabbath. 28 So the Son
of Man is Lord even of the Sabbath." Mt 12:1-8; Lk 6:1-5

Jesus Heals on the Sabbath

3 Another time Jesus went into
the synagogue, and a man with
a shriveled hand was there. 2 Some
of them were looking for a reason
to accuse Jesus, so they watched
him closely to see if he would heal
him on the Sabbath. 3 Jesus said to

the man with the shriveled hand, "Stand up in front of everyone."

Mk 1:21; Lk 14:1

4Then Jesus asked them, "Which is lawful on the Sabbath: to do good or to do evil, to save life or to kill?" But they remained silent.

5He looked around at them in anger and, deeply distressed at their stubborn hearts, said to the man, "Stretch out your hand." He stretched it out, and his hand was completely restored. 6Then the Pharisees went out and began to plot with the Herodians how they might kill Jesus. Mt 12:9-14; Lk 6:6-11

Crowds Follow Jesus

7Jesus withdrew with his disciples to the lake, and a large crowd from Galilee followed. 8When they heard about all he was doing, many people came to him from Judea, Jerusalem, Idumea, and the regions across the Jordan and around Tyre and Sidon. 9Because of the crowd he told his disciples to have a small boat ready for him, to keep the people from crowding him. 10For he had healed many, so that those with diseases were pushing forward to touch him. 11Whenever the impure spirits saw him, they fell down before him and cried out, "You are the Son of God." 12But he gave them strict orders not to tell others about him. Mt 12:15-16; Lk 6:17-19

Jesus Appoints the Twelve

13Jesus went up on a mountainside and called to him those he wanted, and they came to him. 14He appointed twelve[a] that they might be with him and that he might send them out to preach 15and to have authority to drive out demons. 16These are the twelve he appointed: Simon (to whom he gave the name Peter), 17James son of Zebedee and his brother John (to them he gave the name Boanerges, which means "sons of thunder"), 18Andrew, Philip, Bartholomew, Matthew, Thomas, James son of Alphaeus, Thaddaeus, Simon the Zealot 19and Judas Iscariot, who betrayed him.

Mt 10:2-4; Lk 6:14-16; Ac 1:13

Jesus Accused by His Family and by Teachers of the Law

20Then Jesus entered a house, and again a crowd gathered, so that he and his disciples were not even able to eat. 21When his family[b] heard about this, they went to take charge of him, for they said, "He is out of his mind."

Jn 10:20; Ac 26:24

22And the teachers of the law who came down from Jerusalem said, "He is possessed by Beelzebul! By the prince of demons he is driving out demons."

Mt 9:34; 10:25; Jn 7:20

23So Jesus called them over to him and began to speak to them in parables: "How can Satan drive out Satan? 24If a kingdom is

[a] 14 Some manuscripts *twelve—designating them apostles—* [b] 21 Or *his associates*

divided against itself, that kingdom cannot stand. 25If a house is
divided against itself, that house
cannot stand. 26And if Satan opposes himself and is divided, he
cannot stand; his end has come.
27In fact, no one can enter a strong
man's house without first tying
him up. Then he can plunder the
strong man's house. 28Truly I tell
you, people can be forgiven all
their sins and every slander they
utter, 29but whoever blasphemes
against the Holy Spirit will never
be forgiven; they are guilty of an
eternal sin." Mt 12:25-29; Lk 11:17-22

30He said this because they were
saying, "He has an impure spirit."

31Then Jesus' mother and brothers arrived. Standing outside, they
sent someone in to call him. 32A
crowd was sitting around him,
and they told him, "Your mother
and brothers are outside looking
for you." ver 21

33"Who are my mother and my
brothers?" he asked.

34Then he looked at those seated in a circle around him and
said, "Here are my mother and my
brothers! 35Whoever does God's
will is my brother and sister and
mother." Mt 12:46-50; Lk 8:19-21

The Parable of the Sower

4 Again Jesus began to teach by
the lake. The crowd that gathered around him was so large that
he got into a boat and sat in it out
on the lake, while all the people
were along the shore at the water's edge. 2He taught them many
things by parables, and in his
teaching said: 3"Listen! A farmer went out to sow his seed. 4As
he was scattering the seed, some
fell along the path, and the birds
came and ate it up. 5Some fell on
rocky places, where it did not have
much soil. It sprang up quickly,
because the soil was shallow. 6But
when the sun came up, the plants
were scorched, and they withered
because they had no root. 7Oth-
er seed fell among thorns, which
grew up and choked the plants,
so that they did not bear grain.
8Still other seed fell on good soil.
It came up, grew and produced
a crop, some multiplying thirty, some sixty, some a hundred
times." Mk 3:23; Jn 15:5; Col 1:6

9Then Jesus said, "Whoever has
ears to hear, let them hear."
Mt 11:15

10When he was alone, the Twelve
and the others around him asked
him about the parables. 11He told
them, "The secret of the kingdom
of God has been given to you. But
to those on the outside everything
is said in parables 12so that,
1Co 5:12-13; Col 4:5; 1Th 4:12

" 'they may be ever seeing but
never perceiving,
and ever hearing but never
understanding;
otherwise they might turn
and be forgiven!'[a]"
Mt 13:1-15; Lk 8:4-10

[a] 12 Isaiah 6:9,10

[13]Then Jesus said to them,
"Don't you understand this parable? How then will you understand any parable? [14]The farmer
sows the word. [15]Some people are
like seed along the path, where
the word is sown. As soon as they
hear it, Satan comes and takes
away the word that was sown in
them. [16]Others, like seed sown on
rocky places, hear the word and at
once receive it with joy. [17]But since
they have no root, they last only a
short time. When trouble or persecution comes because of the word,
they quickly fall away. [18]Still others, like seed sown among thorns,
hear the word; [19]but the worries
of this life, the deceitfulness of
wealth and the desires for other things come in and choke the
word, making it unfruitful. [20]Oth-
ers, like seed sown on good soil,
hear the word, accept it, and produce a crop — some thirty, some
sixty, some a hundred times what
was sown." Mt 13:18-23; Lk 8:11-15

A Lamp on a Stand

[21]He said to them, "Do you bring
in a lamp to put it under a bowl
or a bed? Instead, don't you put it
on its stand? [22]For whatever is hidden is meant to be disclosed, and
whatever is concealed is meant to
be brought out into the open. [23]If
anyone has ears to hear, let them
hear." Mt 5:15; 10:26; 11:15
[24]"Consider carefully what you
hear," he continued. "With the
measure you use, it will be measured to you — and even more.
[25]Whoever has will be given more;
whoever does not have, even
what they have will be taken from
them." Mt 25:29; Lk 6:38

The Parable of the Growing Seed

[26]He also said, "This is what
the kingdom of God is like. A
man scatters seed on the ground.
[27]Night and day, whether he sleeps
or gets up, the seed sprouts and
grows, though he does not know
how. [28]All by itself the soil produces grain — first the stalk, then
the head, then the full kernel in
the head. [29]As soon as the grain
is ripe, he puts the sickle to it, because the harvest has come."
Mt 13:24; Rev 14:15

The Parable of the Mustard Seed

[30]Again he said, "What shall we
say the kingdom of God is like,
or what parable shall we use to
describe it? [31]It is like a mustard
seed, which is the smallest of all
seeds on earth. [32]Yet when planted, it grows and becomes the largest of all garden plants, with such
big branches that the birds can
perch in its shade."
Mt 13:31-32; Lk 13:18-19
[33]With many similar parables
Jesus spoke the word to them, as
much as they could understand.
[34]He did not say anything to them
without using a parable. But when
he was alone with his own disciples, he explained everything.
Jn 16:12,25

Jesus Calms the Storm

35 That day when evening came,
he said to his disciples, "Let us go
over to the other side." 36 Leaving
the crowd behind, they took him
along, just as he was, in the boat.
There were also other boats with
him. 37 A furious squall came up,
and the waves broke over the boat,
so that it was nearly swamped.
38 Jesus was in the stern, sleeping
on a cushion. The disciples woke
him and said to him, "Teacher,
don't you care if we drown?"

Mk 3:9; 5:2,21; 6:32,45

39 He got up, rebuked the wind
and said to the waves, "Quiet! Be
still!" Then the wind died down
and it was completely calm.

40 He said to his disciples, "Why
are you so afraid? Do you still have
no faith?" Mt 14:31; Mk 16:14

41 They were terrified and asked
each other, "Who is this? Even the
wind and the waves obey him!"

Mt 8:18,23-27; Lk 8:22-25

Jesus Restores a Demon-Possessed Man

5 They went across the lake to
the region of the Gerasenes.[a]
2 When Jesus got out of the boat,
a man with an impure spirit came
from the tombs to meet him. 3 This
man lived in the tombs, and no
one could bind him anymore, not
even with a chain. 4 For he had often been chained hand and foot,
but he tore the chains apart and
broke the irons on his feet. No one
was strong enough to subdue him.
5 Night and day among the tombs
and in the hills he would cry out
and cut himself with stones.

Mk 1:23; 4:1

6 When he saw Jesus from a distance, he ran and fell on his knees
in front of him. 7 He shouted at
the top of his voice, "What do you
want with me, Jesus, Son of the
Most High God? In God's name
don't torture me!" 8 For Jesus had
said to him, "Come out of this
man, you impure spirit!"

Mt 8:29; Ac 16:17; Heb 7:1

9 Then Jesus asked him, "What is
your name?"

"My name is Legion," he replied, "for we are many." 10 And he
begged Jesus again and again not
to send them out of the area.

11 A large herd of pigs was feeding on the nearby hillside. 12 The
demons begged Jesus, "Send us
among the pigs; allow us to go into
them." 13 He gave them permission,
and the impure spirits came out
and went into the pigs. The herd,
about two thousand in number,
rushed down the steep bank into
the lake and were drowned.

14 Those tending the pigs ran off
and reported this in the town and
countryside, and the people went
out to see what had happened.
15 When they came to Jesus, they
saw the man who had been possessed by the legion of demons,
sitting there, dressed and in his
right mind; and they were afraid.

[a] *1* Some manuscripts *Gadarenes*; other manuscripts *Gergesenes*

16Those who had seen it told the
people what had happened to the
demon-possessed man — and told
about the pigs as well. 17Then the
people began to plead with Jesus
to leave their region.
Mt 8:28-34; Lk 8:26-37

18As Jesus was getting into the
boat, the man who had been demon-possessed begged to go with
him. 19Jesus did not let him, but
said, "Go home to your own people and tell them how much the
Lord has done for you, and how he
has had mercy on you." 20So the
man went away and began to tell
in the Decapolis[a] how much Jesus
had done for him. And all the people were amazed. Lk 8:38-39

Jesus Raises a Dead Girl and Heals a Sick Woman

21When Jesus had again crossed
over by boat to the other side of
the lake, a large crowd gathered
around him while he was by the
lake. 22Then one of the synagogue
leaders, named Jairus, came, and
when he saw Jesus, he fell at his
feet. 23He pleaded earnestly with
him, "My little daughter is dying.
Please come and put your hands
on her so that she will be healed
and live." 24So Jesus went with
him. Mk 6:5; Lk 13:14

A large crowd followed and
pressed around him. 25And a woman was there who had been subject to bleeding for twelve years.
26She had suffered a great deal under the care of many doctors and
had spent all she had, yet instead
of getting better she grew worse.
27When she heard about Jesus, she
came up behind him in the crowd
and touched his cloak, 28because
she thought, "If I just touch his
clothes, I will be healed." 29Imme-
diately her bleeding stopped and
she felt in her body that she was
freed from her suffering.
Lev 15:25-30; Mt 9:20

30At once Jesus realized that
power had gone out from him. He
turned around in the crowd and
asked, "Who touched my clothes?"
Lk 5:17; 6:19

31"You see the people crowding against you," his disciples answered, "and yet you can ask, 'Who
touched me?' "

32But Jesus kept looking around
to see who had done it. 33Then the
woman, knowing what had happened to her, came and fell at his
feet and, trembling with fear, told
him the whole truth. 34He said
to her, "Daughter, your faith has
healed you. Go in peace and be
freed from your suffering."
Mt 9:22; Ac 15:33

35While Jesus was still speaking, some people came from the
house of Jairus, the synagogue
leader. "Your daughter is dead,"
they said. "Why bother the teacher anymore?"

36Overhearing[b] what they said,
Jesus told him, "Don't be afraid;
just believe."

[a] 20 That is, the Ten Cities [b] 36 Or *Ignoring*

[37]He did not let anyone follow him except Peter, James and John the brother of James. [38]When they came to the home of the synagogue leader, Jesus saw a commotion, with people crying and wailing loudly. [39]He went in and said to them, "Why all this commotion and wailing? The child is not dead but asleep." [40]But they laughed at him. Mt 4:21; 9:24

After he put them all out, he took the child's father and mother and the disciples who were with him, and went in where the child was. [41]He took her by the hand and said to her, "*Talitha koum!*" (which means "Little girl, I say to you, get up!"). [42]Immediately the girl stood up and began to walk around (she was twelve years old). At this they were completely astonished. [43]He gave strict orders not to let anyone know about this, and told them to give her something to eat. Mt 9:18-26; Lk 8:41-56

A Prophet Without Honor

6 Jesus left there and went to his hometown, accompanied by his disciples. [2]When the Sabbath came, he began to teach in the synagogue, and many who heard him were amazed. Mt 4:23; 7:28

"Where did this man get these things?" they asked. "What's this wisdom that has been given him? What are these remarkable miracles he is performing? [3]Isn't this the carpenter? Isn't this Mary's son and the brother of James, Joseph,[a] Judas and Simon? Aren't his sisters here with us?" And they took offense at him. Mt 11:6; 12:46

[4]Jesus said to them, "A prophet is not without honor except in his own town, among his relatives and in his own home." [5]He could not do any miracles there, except lay his hands on a few sick people and heal them. [6]He was amazed at their lack of faith. Mt 13:54-58

Jesus Sends Out the Twelve

Then Jesus went around teaching from village to village. [7]Calling the Twelve to him, he began to send them out two by two and gave them authority over impure spirits. Mt 10:1; Mk 3:13; Lk 13:22

[8]These were his instructions: "Take nothing for the journey except a staff — no bread, no bag, no money in your belts. [9]Wear sandals but not an extra shirt. [10]Whenever you enter a house, stay there until you leave that town. [11]And if any place will not welcome you or listen to you, leave that place and shake the dust off your feet as a testimony against them." Mt 10:1,9-14; Lk 9:1,3-5

[12]They went out and preached that people should repent. [13]They drove out many demons and anointed many sick people with oil and healed them. Lk 9:6; Jas 5:14

John the Baptist Beheaded

[14]King Herod heard about this, for Jesus' name had become well

[a] 3 Greek *Joses,* a variant of *Joseph*

known. Some were saying,[a] "John
the Baptist has been raised from
the dead, and that is why miraculous powers are at work in him."
Mt 3:1
15 Others said, "He is Elijah."
Mal 4:5
And still others claimed, "He is
a prophet, like one of the prophets
of long ago." Mt 16:14; Mk 8:28
16 But when Herod heard this, he
said, "John, whom I beheaded, has
been raised from the dead!" Lk 9:7-9
17 For Herod himself had given
orders to have John arrested, and
he had him bound and put in prison. He did this because of Herodias, his brother Philip's wife, whom
he had married. 18 For John had
been saying to Herod, "It is not
lawful for you to have your brother's wife." 19 So Herodias nursed a
grudge against John and wanted
to kill him. But she was not able
to, 20 because Herod feared John
and protected him, knowing him
to be a righteous and holy man.
When Herod heard John, he was
greatly puzzled[b]; yet he liked to
listen to him. Lev 18:16; Mt 21:26
21 Finally the opportune time
came. On his birthday Herod gave
a banquet for his high officials
and military commanders and the
leading men of Galilee. 22 When
the daughter of[c] Herodias came
in and danced, she pleased Herod
and his dinner guests. Est 1:3; Lk 3:1
The king said to the girl, "Ask
me for anything you want, and I'll
give it to you." 23 And he promised
her with an oath, "Whatever you
ask I will give you, up to half my
kingdom." Est 5:3,6; 7:2
24 She went out and said to her
mother, "What shall I ask for?"
"The head of John the Baptist,"
she answered.
25 At once the girl hurried in to
the king with the request: "I want
you to give me right now the head
of John the Baptist on a platter."
26 The king was greatly distressed, but because of his oaths
and his dinner guests, he did not
want to refuse her. 27 So he immediately sent an executioner with
orders to bring John's head. The
man went, beheaded John in the
prison, 28 and brought back his
head on a platter. He presented
it to the girl, and she gave it to
her mother. 29 On hearing of this,
John's disciples came and took his
body and laid it in a tomb. Mt 14:1-12

Jesus Feeds the Five Thousand

30 The apostles gathered around
Jesus and reported to him all they
had done and taught. 31 Then, because so many people were coming and going that they did not
even have a chance to eat, he said
to them, "Come with me by yourselves to a quiet place and get
some rest." Lk 9:10; Ac 1:2,26
32 So they went away by themselves in a boat to a solitary place.

[a] 14 Some early manuscripts *He was saying*
[b] 20 Some early manuscripts *he did many things*
[c] 22 Some early manuscripts *When his daughter*

33But many who saw them leaving
recognized them and ran on foot
from all the towns and got there
ahead of them. 34When Jesus landed and saw a large crowd, he had
compassion on them, because they
were like sheep without a shepherd. So he began teaching them
many things. Mt 14:13-21; Mk 4:36

35By this time it was late in the
day, so his disciples came to him.
"This is a remote place," they said,
"and it's already very late. 36Send
the people away so that they can
go to the surrounding countryside
and villages and buy themselves
something to eat." Mk 8:2-9

37But he answered, "You give
them something to eat."

They said to him, "That would
take more than half a year's wages[a]! Are we to go and spend that
much on bread and give it to them
to eat?" 2Ki 4:42-44

38"How many loaves do you
have?" he asked. "Go and see."

When they found out, they said,
"Five — and two fish." Lk 9:10-17

39Then Jesus directed them to
have all the people sit down in
groups on the green grass. 40So
they sat down in groups of hundreds and fifties. 41Taking the five
loaves and the two fish and looking up to heaven, he gave thanks
and broke the loaves. Then he
gave them to his disciples to distribute to the people. He also divided the two fish among them
all. 42They all ate and were satisfied, 43and the disciples picked up
twelve basketfuls of broken pieces
of bread and fish. 44The number of
the men who had eaten was five
thousand. Jn 6:5-13

Jesus Walks on the Water

45Immediately Jesus made his
disciples get into the boat and
go on ahead of him to Bethsaida, while he dismissed the crowd.
46After leaving them, he went up
on a mountainside to pray.
Mt 11:21; Lk 3:21

47Later that night, the boat was
in the middle of the lake, and he
was alone on land. 48He saw the
disciples straining at the oars, because the wind was against them.
Shortly before dawn he went out
to them, walking on the lake. He
was about to pass by them, 49but
when they saw him walking on the
lake, they thought he was a ghost.
They cried out, 50because they
all saw him and were terrified.
Lk 24:37

Immediately he spoke to them
and said, "Take courage! It is I.
Don't be afraid." 51Then he climbed
into the boat with them, and the
wind died down. They were completely amazed, 52for they had not
understood about the loaves; their
hearts were hardened.
Mt 14:22-32; Jn 6:15-21

53When they had crossed over,
they landed at Gennesaret and an-
chored there. 54As soon as they got
out of the boat, people recognized
Jesus. 55They ran throughout that

[a] 37 Greek *take two hundred denarii*

whole region and carried the sick
on mats to wherever they heard
he was. 56And wherever he went —
into villages, towns or countryside — they placed the sick in the
marketplaces. They begged him
to let them touch even the edge of
his cloak, and all who touched it
were healed. Mt 14:34-36

That Which Defiles

7 The Pharisees and some of
the teachers of the law who
had come from Jerusalem gathered around Jesus 2and saw some
of his disciples eating food with
hands that were defiled, that is,
unwashed. 3(The Pharisees and
all the Jews do not eat unless they
give their hands a ceremonial
washing, holding to the tradition
of the elders. 4When they come
from the marketplace they do not
eat unless they wash. And they observe many other traditions, such
as the washing of cups, pitchers
and kettles.[a]) Mt 23:25; Ac 10:14,28
5So the Pharisees and teachers
of the law asked Jesus, "Why don't
your disciples live according to
the tradition of the elders instead
of eating their food with defiled
hands?" Gal 1:14; Col 2:8
6He replied, "Isaiah was right
when he prophesied about you
hypocrites; as it is written:

"'These people honor me with
their lips,
but their hearts are far
from me.
7They worship me in vain;
their teachings are merely
human rules.'[b]

8You have let go of the commands
of God and are holding on to human traditions."
9And he continued, "You have a
fine way of setting aside the commands of God in order to observe[c]
your own traditions! 10For Moses said, 'Honor your father and
mother,'[d] and, 'Anyone who curses
their father or mother is to be put
to death.'[e] 11But you say that if anyone declares that what might have
been used to help their father or
mother is Corban (that is, devoted
to God) — 12then you no longer let
them do anything for their father
or mother. 13Thus you nullify the
word of God by your tradition that
you have handed down. And you
do many things like that."
Mt 23:16,18; Heb 4:12
14Again Jesus called the crowd
to him and said, "Listen to me,
everyone, and understand this.
15Nothing outside a person can
defile them by going into them.
Rather, it is what comes out of a
person that defiles them." [16][f]
17After he had left the crowd
and entered the house, his disciples asked him about this parable. 18"Are you so dull?" he asked.

[a] 4 Some early manuscripts *pitchers, kettles and dining couches* [b] 6,7 Isaiah 29:13 [c] 9 Some manuscripts *set up* [d] 10 Exodus 20:12; Deut. 5:16 [e] 10 Exodus 21:17; Lev. 20:9 [f] 16 Some manuscripts include here the words of 4:23.

"Don't you see that nothing that
enters a person from the outside
can defile them? 19 For it doesn't
go into their heart but into their
stomach, and then out of the
body." (In saying this, Jesus declared all foods clean.)
Ac 10:15; 1Ti 4:3-5

20 He went on: "What comes out
of a person is what defiles them.
21 For it is from within, out of a
person's heart, that evil thoughts
come — sexual immorality, theft,
murder, 22 adultery, greed, malice,
deceit, lewdness, envy, slander, arrogance and folly. 23 All these evils
come from inside and defile a person." Mt 15:1-20

Jesus Honors a Syrophoenician Woman's Faith

24 Jesus left that place and went
to the vicinity of Tyre.[a] He entered
a house and did not want anyone to know it; yet he could not
keep his presence secret. 25 In fact,
as soon as she heard about him,
a woman whose little daughter
was possessed by an impure spirit came and fell at his feet. 26 The
woman was a Greek, born in Syrian Phoenicia. She begged Jesus to
drive the demon out of her daughter. Mt 4:24; 11:21

27 "First let the children eat all
they want," he told her, "for it is
not right to take the children's
bread and toss it to the dogs."

28 "Lord," she replied, "even the
dogs under the table eat the children's crumbs."

29 Then he told her, "For such a
reply, you may go; the demon has
left your daughter."

30 She went home and found her
child lying on the bed, and the demon gone. Mt 15:21-28

Jesus Heals a Deaf and Mute Man

31 Then Jesus left the vicinity
of Tyre and went through Sidon,
down to the Sea of Galilee and into
the region of the Decapolis.[b] 32 There
some people brought to him a man
who was deaf and could hardly talk,
and they begged Jesus to place his
hand on him. Mk 5:23; Lk 11:14

33 After he took him aside, away
from the crowd, Jesus put his fingers into the man's ears. Then he
spit and touched the man's tongue.
34 He looked up to heaven and with a
deep sigh said to him, *"Ephphatha!"*
(which means "Be opened!"). 35 At
this, the man's ears were opened,
his tongue was loosened and he began to speak plainly. Isa 35:5-6

36 Jesus commanded them not
to tell anyone. But the more he
did so, the more they kept talking about it. 37 People were overwhelmed with amazement. "He
has done everything well," they
said. "He even makes the deaf hear
and the mute speak." Mt 15:29-31

Jesus Feeds the Four Thousand

8 During those days another
large crowd gathered. Since
they had nothing to eat, Jesus

[a] 24 Many early manuscripts *Tyre and Sidon*
[b] 31 That is, the Ten Cities

called his disciples to him and said,
2“I have compassion for these people; they have already been with
me three days and have nothing
to eat. 3If I send them home hungry, they will collapse on the way,
because some of them have come
a long distance.” Mt 9:36
4His disciples answered, “But
where in this remote place can
anyone get enough bread to feed
them?”
5“How many loaves do you
have?” Jesus asked.
“Seven,” they replied.
6He told the crowd to sit down
on the ground. When he had tak-
en the seven loaves and given
thanks, he broke them and gave
them to his disciples to distribute to the people, and they did
so. 7They had a few small fish as
well; he gave thanks for them also
and told the disciples to distribute them. 8The people ate and
were satisfied. Afterward the disciples picked up seven basketfuls
of broken pieces that were left
over. 9About four thousand were
present. After he had sent them
away, 10he got into the boat with
his disciples and went to the region of Dalmanutha.
Mt 15:32-39; Mk 6:32-44
11The Pharisees came and began to question Jesus. To test him,
they asked him for a sign from
heaven. 12He sighed deeply and
said, “Why does this generation
ask for a sign? Truly I tell you, no
sign will be given to it.” 13Then he
left them, got back into the boat
and crossed to the other side.
Mt 12:38; Mk 7:34

The Yeast of the Pharisees and Herod

14The disciples had forgotten to
bring bread, except for one loaf
they had with them in the boat.
15“Be careful,” Jesus warned them.
“Watch out for the yeast of the
Pharisees and that of Herod.”
Mt 14:1; Lk 12:1; 1Co 5:6-8
16They discussed this with one
another and said, “It is because we
have no bread.”
17Aware of their discussion,
Jesus asked them: “Why are you
talking about having no bread?
Do you still not see or understand?
Are your hearts hardened? 18Do
you have eyes but fail to see, and
ears but fail to hear? And don’t you
remember? 19When I broke the
five loaves for the five thousand,
how many basketfuls of pieces did
you pick up?” Isa 6:9-10; Mk 6:52
“Twelve,” they replied.
Mt 14:20; Mk 6:41-44
20“And when I broke the seven
loaves for the four thousand, how
many basketfuls of pieces did you
pick up?”
They answered, “Seven.” Mt 15:37
21He said to them, “Do you still
not understand?”
Mk 6:52

Jesus Heals a Blind Man at Bethsaida

22They came to Bethsaida, and
some people brought a blind

man and begged Jesus to touch
him. 23 He took the blind man by
the hand and led him outside the
village. When he had spit on the
man's eyes and put his hands on
him, Jesus asked, "Do you see anything?" Mk 5:23; 7:33

24 He looked up and said, "I see
people; they look like trees walking around."

25 Once more Jesus put his hands
on the man's eyes. Then his eyes
were opened, his sight was restored, and he saw everything
clearly. 26 Jesus sent him home,
saying, "Don't even go into[a] the
village."

Peter Declares That Jesus Is the Messiah

27 Jesus and his disciples went
on to the villages around Caesarea Philippi. On the way he asked
them, "Who do people say I am?"

28 They replied, "Some say John
the Baptist; others say Elijah; and
still others, one of the prophets."
Mt 3:1; Mal 4:5

29 "But what about you?" he
asked. "Who do you say I am?"

Peter answered, "You are the
Messiah." Mt 16:13-16; Lk 9:18-20

30 Jesus warned them not to tell
anyone about him. Mt 8:4; 16:20; 17:9

Jesus Predicts His Death

31 He then began to teach them
that the Son of Man must suffer
many things and be rejected by
the elders, the chief priests and
the teachers of the law, and that
he must be killed and after three
days rise again. 32 He spoke plainly about this, and Peter took him
aside and began to rebuke him.
Mt 16:21; Jn 18:20

33 But when Jesus turned and
looked at his disciples, he rebuked
Peter. "Get behind me, Satan!" he
said. "You do not have in mind the
concerns of God, but merely human concerns." Mt 4:10

The Way of the Cross

34 Then he called the crowd to
him along with his disciples and
said: "Whoever wants to be my
disciple must deny themselves
and take up their cross and follow
me. 35 For whoever wants to save
their life[b] will lose it, but whoever loses their life for me and
for the gospel will save it. 36 What
good is it for someone to gain the
whole world, yet forfeit their soul?
37 Or what can anyone give in exchange for their soul? 38 If anyone
is ashamed of me and my words
in this adulterous and sinful generation, the Son of Man will be
ashamed of them when he comes
in his Father's glory with the holy
angels." Mt 10:33; Jn 12:25

9 And he said to them, "Truly I
tell you, some who are standing here will not taste death before they see that the kingdom of
God has come with power."
Mt 16:21-28; Lk 9:22-27

[a] 26 Some manuscripts *go and tell anyone in*
[b] 35 The Greek word means either *life* or
soul; also in verses 36 and 37.

The Transfiguration

2After six days Jesus took Peter,
James and John with him and led
them up a high mountain, where
they were all alone. There he was
transfigured before them. 3His
clothes became dazzling white,
whiter than anyone in the world
could bleach them. 4And there appeared before them Elijah and Moses, who were talking with Jesus.
Mt 28:3

5Peter said to Jesus, "Rabbi, it is
good for us to be here. Let us put
up three shelters — one for you,
one for Moses and one for Elijah."
6(He did not know what to say,
they were so frightened.) Mt 23:7

7Then a cloud appeared and covered them, and a voice came from
the cloud: "This is my Son, whom I
love. Listen to him!" Ex 24:16; Mt 3:17

8Suddenly, when they looked
around, they no longer saw anyone with them except Jesus.
Lk 9:28-36

9As they were coming down the
mountain, Jesus gave them orders not to tell anyone what they
had seen until the Son of Man had
risen from the dead. 10They kept
the matter to themselves, discussing what "rising from the dead"
meant. Mt 8:20; Mk 8:30

11And they asked him, "Why do
the teachers of the law say that
Elijah must come first?"

12Jesus replied, "To be sure, Elijah does come first, and restores
all things. Why then is it written
that the Son of Man must suffer
much and be rejected? 13But I tell
you, Elijah has come, and they
have done to him everything they
wished, just as it is written about
him." Mt 17:1-13

Jesus Heals a Boy Possessed by an Impure Spirit

14When they came to the other
disciples, they saw a large crowd
around them and the teachers of
the law arguing with them. 15As
soon as all the people saw Jesus,
they were overwhelmed with
wonder and ran to greet him.

16"What are you arguing with
them about?" he asked.

17A man in the crowd answered,
"Teacher, I brought you my son,
who is possessed by a spirit that
has robbed him of speech. 18When-
ever it seizes him, it throws him
to the ground. He foams at the
mouth, gnashes his teeth and becomes rigid. I asked your disciples
to drive out the spirit, but they
could not."

19"You unbelieving generation,"
Jesus replied, "how long shall I
stay with you? How long shall I put
up with you? Bring the boy to me."

20So they brought him. When
the spirit saw Jesus, it immediately threw the boy into a convulsion.
He fell to the ground and rolled
around, foaming at the mouth.
Mk 1:26

21Jesus asked the boy's father,
"How long has he been like this?"

"From childhood," he answered.
22"It has often thrown him into

fire or water to kill him. But if you
can do anything, take pity on us
and help us.”
23“‘If you can’?” said Jesus. “Everything is possible for one who
believes.” Mk 11:23; Jn 11:40
24Immediately the boy’s father
exclaimed, “I do believe; help me
overcome my unbelief!”
25When Jesus saw that a crowd
was running to the scene, he rebuked the impure spirit. “You
deaf and mute spirit,” he said, “I
command you, come out of him
and never enter him again.”
26The spirit shrieked, convulsed
him violently and came out. The
boy looked so much like a corpse
that many said, “He’s dead.” 27But
Jesus took him by the hand and
lifted him to his feet, and he
stood up.
28After Jesus had gone indoors,
his disciples asked him privately,
“Why couldn’t we drive it out?”
Mt 17:14-19; Mk 7:17
29He replied, “This kind can
come out only by prayer.[a]”

Jesus Predicts His Death a Second Time

30They left that place and
passed through Galilee. Jesus did
not want anyone to know where
they were, 31because he was
teaching his disciples. He said to
them, “The Son of Man is going
to be delivered into the hands of
men. They will kill him, and after three days he will rise.” 32But
they did not understand what he
meant and were afraid to ask him
about it. Lk 9:37-45
33They came to Capernaum.
When he was in the house, he
asked them, “What were you arguing about on the road?” 34But
they kept quiet because on the
way they had argued about who
was the greatest. Mt 4:13; Lk 22:24
35Sitting down, Jesus called the
Twelve and said, “Anyone who
wants to be first must be the very
last, and the servant of all.”
Mt 20:26; Mk 10:43
36He took a little child whom he
placed among them. Taking the
child in his arms, he said to them,
37“Whoever welcomes one of these
little children in my name welcomes me; and whoever welcomes
me does not welcome me but the
one who sent me.” Mt 18:1-5; Lk 9:46-48

Whoever Is Not Against Us Is for Us

38“Teacher,” said John, “we saw
someone driving out demons
in your name and we told him
to stop, because he was not one
of us.” Nu 11:27-29
39“Do not stop him,” Jesus said.
“For no one who does a miracle
in my name can in the next moment say anything bad about me,
40for whoever is not against us is
for us. 41Truly I tell you, anyone
who gives you a cup of water in
my name because you belong to
the Messiah will certainly not lose
their reward. Mt 10:42; Mt 12:30; Lk 11:23

[a] 29 Some manuscripts *prayer and fasting*

Causing to Stumble

42"If anyone causes one of these
little ones — those who believe in
me — to stumble, it would be better for them if a large millstone
were hung around their neck and
they were thrown into the sea. 43If
your hand causes you to stumble, cut it off. It is better for you
to enter life maimed than with
two hands to go into hell, where
the fire never goes out. [44][a] 45And
if your foot causes you to stumble, cut it off. It is better for you
to enter life crippled than to have
two feet and be thrown into hell.
[46][a] 47And if your eye causes you
to stumble, pluck it out. It is better for you to enter the kingdom
of God with one eye than to have
two eyes and be thrown into hell,
48where

> " 'the worms that eat them do
> not die,
> and the fire is not
> quenched.'[b]

49Everyone will be salted with fire.
Mt 5:29; 18:9

50"Salt is good, but if it loses
its saltiness, how can you make
it salty again? Have salt among
yourselves, and be at peace with
each other." Mt 5:13; Ro 12:18

Divorce

10 Jesus then left that place
and went into the region
of Judea and across the Jordan.
Again crowds of people came to
him, and as was his custom, he
taught them. Jn 10:40; 11:7

2Some Pharisees came and tested him by asking, "Is it lawful for
a man to divorce his wife?" Mk 2:16

3"What did Moses command
you?" he replied.

4They said, "Moses permitted
a man to write a certificate of divorce and send her away."
Dt 24:1-4; Mt 5:31

5"It was because your hearts
were hard that Moses wrote you
this law," Jesus replied. 6"But at
the beginning of creation God
'made them male and female.'[c]
7'For this reason a man will leave
his father and mother and be united to his wife,[d] 8and the two will
become one flesh.'[e] So they are no
longer two, but one flesh. 9There-
fore what God has joined together,
let no one separate." Ge 5:2; 1Co 6:16

10When they were in the house
again, the disciples asked Jesus
about this. 11He answered, "Anyone who divorces his wife and
marries another woman commits
adultery against her. 12And if she
divorces her husband and marries
another man, she commits adultery." Mt 19:1-9; Lk 16:18; Ro 7:3

The Little Children and Jesus

13People were bringing little children to Jesus for him to

[a] 44,46 Some manuscripts include here the words of verse 48. [b] 48 Isaiah 66:24
[c] 6 Gen. 1:27 [d] 7 Some early manuscripts do not have *and be united to his wife.*
[e] 8 Gen. 2:24

place his hands on them, but the
disciples rebuked them. 14 When
Jesus saw this, he was indignant.
He said to them, "Let the little
children come to me, and do not
hinder them, for the kingdom
of God belongs to such as these.
15 Truly I tell you, anyone who will
not receive the kingdom of God
like a little child will never enter it." 16 And he took the children
in his arms, placed his hands on
them and blessed them.

Mt 19:13-15; Lk 18:15-17

The Rich and the Kingdom of God

17 As Jesus started on his way, a
man ran up to him and fell on his
knees before him. "Good teacher,"
he asked, "what must I do to inherit eternal life?" Lk 10:25; Ac 20:32

18 "Why do you call me good?"
Jesus answered. "No one is good—
except God alone. 19 You know the
commandments: 'You shall not
murder, you shall not commit
adultery, you shall not steal, you
shall not give false testimony, you
shall not defraud, honor your father and mother.'[a]"

Ex 20:12-16; Dt 5:16-20

20 "Teacher," he declared, "all
these I have kept since I was a
boy."

21 Jesus looked at him and loved
him. "One thing you lack," he said.
"Go, sell everything you have and
give to the poor, and you will have
treasure in heaven. Then come,
follow me." Mt 6:20; Lk 12:33

22 At this the man's face fell. He
went away sad, because he had
great wealth.

23 Jesus looked around and said
to his disciples, "How hard it is for
the rich to enter the kingdom of
God!" Ps 52:7; 1Ti 6:9-10,17

24 The disciples were amazed at
his words. But Jesus said again,
"Children, how hard it is[b] to enter
the kingdom of God! 25 It is easier
for a camel to go through the eye
of a needle than for someone who
is rich to enter the kingdom of
God." Mt 7:13-14; Lk 12:16-20

26 The disciples were even more
amazed, and said to each other,
"Who then can be saved?"

27 Jesus looked at them and said,
"With man this is impossible, but
not with God; all things are possible with God." Mt 19:26

28 Then Peter spoke up, "We have
left everything to follow you!"

Mt 4:19

29 "Truly I tell you," Jesus replied, "no one who has left home
or brothers or sisters or mother
or father or children or fields for
me and the gospel 30 will fail to receive a hundred times as much in
this present age: homes, brothers, sisters, mothers, children
and fields—along with persecutions—and in the age to come
eternal life. 31 But many who are
first will be last, and the last first."

Mt 19:16-30; Lk 18:18-30

[a] *19* Exodus 20:12-16; Deut. 5:16-20
[b] *24* Some manuscripts *is for those who trust in riches*

Jesus Predicts His Death a Third Time

[32]They were on their way up to
Jerusalem, with Jesus leading the
way, and the disciples were astonished, while those who followed
were afraid. Again he took the
Twelve aside and told them what
was going to happen to him. [33]"We
are going up to Jerusalem," he
said, "and the Son of Man will be
delivered over to the chief priests
and the teachers of the law. They
will condemn him to death and
will hand him over to the Gentiles,
[34]who will mock him and spit on
him, flog him and kill him. Three
days later he will rise."

Mt 20:17-19; Lk 18:31-33

The Request of James and John

[35]Then James and John, the sons
of Zebedee, came to him. "Teacher," they said, "we want you to do
for us whatever we ask."

[36]"What do you want me to do
for you?" he asked.

[37]They replied, "Let one of us sit
at your right and the other at your
left in your glory." Mt 19:28

[38]"You don't know what you are
asking," Jesus said. "Can you drink
the cup I drink or be baptized with
the baptism I am baptized with?"

Mt 20:22; Lk 12:50

[39]"We can," they answered.

Jesus said to them, "You will
drink the cup I drink and be baptized with the baptism I am baptized with, [40]but to sit at my right
or left is not for me to grant. These
places belong to those for whom
they have been prepared."

Ac 12:2; Rev 1:9

[41]When the ten heard about this,
they became indignant with James
and John. [42]Jesus called them together and said, "You know that
those who are regarded as rulers
of the Gentiles lord it over them,
and their high officials exercise
authority over them. [43]Not so with
you. Instead, whoever wants to
become great among you must be
your servant, [44]and whoever wants
to be first must be slave of all. [45]For
even the Son of Man did not come
to be served, but to serve, and to
give his life as a ransom for many."

Mt 20:20-28; Mk 9:35

Blind Bartimaeus Receives His Sight

[46]Then they came to Jericho. As
Jesus and his disciples, together
with a large crowd, were leaving
the city, a blind man, Bartimae-
us (which means "son of Timae-
us"), was sitting by the roadside
begging. [47]When he heard that it
was Jesus of Nazareth, he began to
shout, "Jesus, Son of David, have
mercy on me!" Mt 9:27; Mk 1:24

[48]Many rebuked him and told
him to be quiet, but he shouted
all the more, "Son of David, have
mercy on me!"

[49]Jesus stopped and said, "Call
him."

So they called to the blind man,
"Cheer up! On your feet! He's calling
you." [50]Throwing his cloak aside,

he jumped to his feet and came to
Jesus.
51“What do you want me to do
for you?” Jesus asked him.
The blind man said, “Rabbi, I
want to see.” Mt 23:7
52“Go,” said Jesus, “your faith
has healed you.” Immediately he
received his sight and followed
Jesus along the road.
Mt 20:29-34; Lk 18:35-43

Jesus Comes to Jerusalem as King

11 As they approached Jerusalem and came to Bethphage
and Bethany at the Mount of Olives, Jesus sent two of his disciples, 2saying to them, “Go to the
village ahead of you, and just as
you enter it, you will find a colt
tied there, which no one has ever
ridden. Untie it and bring it here.
3If anyone asks you, ‘Why are you
doing this?’ say, ‘The Lord needs it
and will send it back here shortly.’ ” Nu 19:2; Dt 21:3; Mt 21:1
4They went and found a colt outside in the street, tied at a doorway. As they untied it, 5some people standing there asked, “What
are you doing, untying that colt?”
6They answered as Jesus had told
them to, and the people let them
go. 7When they brought the colt
to Jesus and threw their cloaks
over it, he sat on it. 8Many people
spread their cloaks on the road,
while others spread branches they
had cut in the fields. 9Those who
went ahead and those who followed shouted, Mt 23:39; Mk 14:16

“Hosanna![a]”

“Blessed is he who comes in
the name of the Lord!”[b]
10“Blessed is the coming kingdom
of our father David!”

“Hosanna in the
highest heaven!”
Mt 21:1-9; Lk 19:29-38; Jn 12:12-15

11Jesus entered Jerusalem and
went into the temple courts. He
looked around at everything, but
since it was already late, he went
out to Bethany with the Twelve.
Mt 21:12,17

Jesus Curses a Fig Tree and Clears the Temple Courts

12The next day as they were leaving Bethany, Jesus was hungry.
13Seeing in the distance a fig tree
in leaf, he went to find out if it had
any fruit. When he reached it, he
found nothing but leaves, because
it was not the season for figs.
14Then he said to the tree, “May no
one ever eat fruit from you again.”
And his disciples heard him say it.
Mt 21:18-22
15On reaching Jerusalem, Jesus
entered the temple courts and
began driving out those who
were buying and selling there.
He overturned the tables of the
money changers and the benches of those selling doves, 16and
would not allow anyone to carry

[a] 9 A Hebrew expression meaning “Save!” which became an exclamation of praise; also in verse 10 [b] 9 Psalm 118:25,26

merchandise through the temple
courts. 17And as he taught them,
he said, "Is it not written: 'My
house will be called a house of
prayer for all nations'[a]? But you
have made it 'a den of robbers.'[b]"
Mt 21:12-16; Lk 19:45-47

18The chief priests and the
teachers of the law heard this and
began looking for a way to kill
him, for they feared him, because
the whole crowd was amazed at
his teaching. Jn 2:13-16

19When evening came, Jesus
and his disciples[c] went out of the
city. Lk 21:37

20In the morning, as they went
along, they saw the fig tree withered from the roots. 21Peter remembered and said to Jesus, "Rabbi, look! The fig tree you cursed
has withered!" Mt 23:7

22"Have faith in God," Jesus answered. 23"Truly[d] I tell you, if anyone says to this mountain, 'Go,
throw yourself into the sea,' and
does not doubt in their heart but
believes that what they say will
happen, it will be done for them.
24Therefore I tell you, whatever
you ask for in prayer, believe that
you have received it, and it will be
yours. 25And when you stand praying, if you hold anything against
anyone, forgive them, so that your
Father in heaven may forgive you
your sins." [26][e] Mt 21:19-22

The Authority of Jesus Questioned

27They arrived again in Jerusalem, and while Jesus was walking in the temple courts, the chief
priests, the teachers of the law and
the elders came to him. 28"By what
authority are you doing these
things?" they asked. "And who
gave you authority to do this?"

29Jesus replied, "I will ask you
one question. Answer me, and I
will tell you by what authority I
am doing these things. 30John's
baptism — was it from heaven, or
of human origin? Tell me!"

31They discussed it among
themselves and said, "If we say,
'From heaven,' he will ask, 'Then
why didn't you believe him?' 32But
if we say, 'Of human origin' . . ."
(They feared the people, for everyone held that John really was a
prophet.) Mt 11:9

33So they answered Jesus, "We
don't know."

Jesus said, "Neither will I tell
you by what authority I am doing
these things." Mt 21:23-27; Lk 20:1-8

The Parable of the Tenants

12 Jesus then began to speak
to them in parables: "A man
planted a vineyard. He put a wall
around it, dug a pit for the winepress and built a watchtower. Then
he rented the vineyard to some
farmers and moved to another
place. 2At harvest time he sent a
servant to the tenants to collect

[a] 17 Isaiah 56:7 [b] 17 Jer. 7:11 [c] 19 Some early manuscripts *came, Jesus*
[d] *22,23* Some early manuscripts *"If you have faith in God," Jesus answered, 23"truly*
[e] *26* Some manuscripts include here words similar to Matt. 6:15.

from them some of the fruit of the
vineyard. 3 But they seized him,
beat him and sent him away empty-handed. 4 Then he sent another
servant to them; they struck this
man on the head and treated him
shamefully. 5 He sent still another,
and that one they killed. He sent
many others; some of them they
beat, others they killed. Isa 5:1-7

6 "He had one left to send, a son,
whom he loved. He sent him last
of all, saying, 'They will respect
my son.' Heb 1:1-3

7 "But the tenants said to one another, 'This is the heir. Come, let's
kill him, and the inheritance will
be ours.' 8 So they took him and
killed him, and threw him out of
the vineyard.

9 "What then will the owner of
the vineyard do? He will come
and kill those tenants and give the
vineyard to others. 10 Haven't you
read this passage of Scripture:

> " 'The stone the builders
> rejected
> has become the
> cornerstone;
> 11 the Lord has done this,
> and it is marvelous in our
> eyes'[a]?" Ac 4:11

12 Then the chief priests, the
teachers of the law and the elders
looked for a way to arrest him because they knew he had spoken
the parable against them. But they
were afraid of the crowd; so they
left him and went away.
Mt 21:33-46; Lk 20:9-19

Paying the Imperial Tax to Caesar

13 Later they sent some of the
Pharisees and Herodians to Jesus
to catch him in his words. 14 They
came to him and said, "Teacher,
we know that you are a man of integrity. You aren't swayed by others, because you pay no attention
to who they are; but you teach the
way of God in accordance with the
truth. Is it right to pay the imperial tax[b] to Caesar or not? 15 Should
we pay or shouldn't we?"
Mt 12:10; 22:16

But Jesus knew their hypocrisy. "Why are you trying to trap
me?" he asked. "Bring me a denarius and let me look at it." 16 They
brought the coin, and he asked
them, "Whose image is this? And
whose inscription?"

"Caesar's," they replied.

17 Then Jesus said to them, "Give
back to Caesar what is Caesar's and
to God what is God's." Ro 13:7

And they were amazed at him.
Mt 22:15-22; Lk 20:20-26

Marriage at the Resurrection

18 Then the Sadducees, who say
there is no resurrection, came to
him with a question. 19 "Teacher,"
they said, "Moses wrote for us that
if a man's brother dies and leaves
a wife but no children, the man
must marry the widow and raise
up offspring for his brother. 20 Now
there were seven brothers. The

[a] *11* Psalm 118:22,23 [b] *14* A special tax levied on subject peoples, not on Roman citizens

first one married and died without leaving any children. 21The second one married the widow, but he also died, leaving no child. It was the same with the third. 22In fact, none of the seven left any children. Last of all, the woman died too. 23At the resurrection[a] whose wife will she be, since the seven were married to her?" Dt 25:5; Ac 23:8

24Jesus replied, "Are you not in error because you do not know the Scriptures or the power of God? 25When the dead rise, they will neither marry nor be given in marriage; they will be like the angels in heaven. 26Now about the dead rising — have you not read in the Book of Moses, in the account of the burning bush, how God said to him, 'I am the God of Abraham, the God of Isaac, and the God of Jacob'[b]? 27He is not the God of the dead, but of the living. You are badly mistaken!" Mt 22:23-33; Lk 20:27-38

The Greatest Commandment

28One of the teachers of the law came and heard them debating. Noticing that Jesus had given them a good answer, he asked him, "Of all the commandments, which is the most important?" Lk 10:25-28; 20:39

29"The most important one," answered Jesus, "is this: 'Hear, O Israel: The Lord our God, the Lord is one.[c] 30Love the Lord your God with all your heart and with all your soul and with all your mind and with all your strength.'[d] 31The second is this: 'Love your neighbor as yourself.'[e] There is no commandment greater than these." Mt 5:43

32"Well said, teacher," the man replied. "You are right in saying that God is one and there is no other but him. 33To love him with all your heart, with all your understanding and with all your strength, and to love your neighbor as yourself is more important than all burnt offerings and sacrifices." 1Sa 15:22; Mic 6:6-8

34When Jesus saw that he had answered wisely, he said to him, "You are not far from the kingdom of God." And from then on no one dared ask him any more questions. Mt 22:34-40; Lk 20:40

Whose Son Is the Messiah?

35While Jesus was teaching in the temple courts, he asked, "Why do the teachers of the law say that the Messiah is the son of David? 36David himself, speaking by the Holy Spirit, declared:

"'The Lord said to my Lord:
"Sit at my right hand
until I put your enemies
under your feet."'[f]

37David himself calls him 'Lord.' How then can he be his son?" Mt 22:41-46; Lk 20:41-44

The large crowd listened to him with delight. Mt 9:27; 22:44

[a] 23 Some manuscripts *resurrection, when people rise from the dead,* [b] 26 Exodus 3:6
[c] 29 Or *The Lord our God is one Lord*
[d] 30 Deut. 6:4,5 [e] 31 Lev. 19:18
[f] 36 Psalm 110:1

Warning Against the Teachers of the Law

38As he taught, Jesus said,
"Watch out for the teachers of the
law. They like to walk around in
flowing robes and be greeted with
respect in the marketplaces, 39and
have the most important seats in
the synagogues and the places of
honor at banquets. 40They devour
widows' houses and for a show
make lengthy prayers. These men
will be punished most severely."
Mt 23:1-7; Lk 20:45-47

The Widow's Offering

41Jesus sat down opposite the
place where the offerings were
put and watched the crowd putting their money into the temple
treasury. Many rich people threw
in large amounts. 42But a poor
widow came and put in two very
small copper coins, worth only a
few cents. 2Ki 12:9; Jn 8:20
43Calling his disciples to him,
Jesus said, "Truly I tell you, this
poor widow has put more into the
treasury than all the others. 44They
all gave out of their wealth; but
she, out of her poverty, put in everything — all she had to live on."
2Co 8:12

The Destruction of the Temple and Signs of the End Times

13 As Jesus was leaving the
temple, one of his disciples
said to him, "Look, Teacher! What
massive stones! What magnificent
buildings!"
2"Do you see all these great
buildings?" replied Jesus. "Not one
stone here will be left on another;
every one will be thrown down."
Lk 19:44
3As Jesus was sitting on the
Mount of Olives opposite the temple, Peter, James, John and Andrew asked him privately, 4"Tell
us, when will these things happen? And what will be the sign
that they are all about to be fulfilled?" Mt 4:21; 21:1
5Jesus said to them: "Watch out
that no one deceives you. 6Many
will come in my name, claiming,
'I am he,' and will deceive many.
7When you hear of wars and rumors of wars, do not be alarmed.
Such things must happen, but the
end is still to come. 8Nation will
rise against nation, and kingdom
against kingdom. There will be
earthquakes in various places,
and famines. These are the beginning of birth pains.
Eph 5:6; 2Th 2:3,10-12
9"You must be on your guard.
You will be handed over to the
local councils and flogged in the
synagogues. On account of me you
will stand before governors and
kings as witnesses to them. 10And
the gospel must first be preached
to all nations. 11Whenever you are
arrested and brought to trial, do
not worry beforehand about what
to say. Just say whatever is given
you at the time, for it is not you
speaking, but the Holy Spirit.
Mt 10:19-20; Lk 12:11-12

12“Brother will betray brother to
death, and a father his child. Children will rebel against their parents and have them put to death.
13Everyone will hate you because
of me, but the one who stands
firm to the end will be saved.

Mic 7:6; Mt 10:21-22

14“When you see ‘the abomination that causes desolation’[a]
standing where it[b] does not belong — let the reader understand — then let those who are
in Judea flee to the mountains.
15Let no one on the housetop go
down or enter the house to take
anything out. 16Let no one in the
field go back to get their cloak.
17How dreadful it will be in those
days for pregnant women and
nursing mothers! 18Pray that this
will not take place in winter, 19be-
cause those will be days of distress
unequaled from the beginning,
when God created the world, until now — and never to be equaled
again.

20“If the Lord had not cut short
those days, no one would survive.
But for the sake of the elect, whom
he has chosen, he has shortened
them. 21At that time if anyone says
to you, ‘Look, here is the Messiah!’
or, ‘Look, there he is!’ do not believe it. 22For false messiahs and
false prophets will appear and
perform signs and wonders to deceive, if possible, even the elect.
23So be on your guard; I have told
you everything ahead of time.

Jn 4:48; 2Pe 3:17

24“But in those days, following
that distress,

“ ‘the sun will be darkened,
and the moon will not give
its light;
25the stars will fall from the
sky,
and the heavenly bodies will
be shaken.’[c]

Mt 24:29

26“At that time people will see
the Son of Man coming in clouds
with great power and glory. 27And
he will send his angels and gather his elect from the four winds,
from the ends of the earth to the
ends of the heavens.

Da 7:13; Zec 2:6; Rev 1:7

28“Now learn this lesson from
the fig tree: As soon as its twigs
get tender and its leaves come out,
you know that summer is near.
29Even so, when you see these
things happening, you know that
it[b] is near, right at the door. 30Truly
I tell you, this generation will certainly not pass away until all these
things have happened. 31Heaven
and earth will pass away, but my
words will never pass away.

Mt 5:18; Mk 9:1

The Day and Hour Unknown

32“But about that day or hour no
one knows, not even the angels in
heaven, nor the Son, but only the
Father. 33Be on guard! Be alert[d]!
You do not know when that time

[a] *14* Daniel 9:27; 11:31; 12:11 [b] *14,29* Or *he*
[c] *25* Isaiah 13:10; 34:4 [d] *33* Some
manuscripts *alert and pray*

will come. 34 It's like a man going
away: He leaves his house and
puts his servants in charge, each
with their assigned task, and tells
the one at the door to keep watch.
Mt 25:14; Ac 1:7; 1Th 5:6

35 "Therefore keep watch because you do not know when the
owner of the house will come
back — whether in the evening, or
at midnight, or when the rooster
crows, or at dawn. 36 If he comes
suddenly, do not let him find you
sleeping. 37 What I say to you, I say
to everyone: 'Watch!'" Lk 12:35-40

Jesus Anointed at Bethany

14 Now the Passover and the
Festival of Unleavened
Bread were only two days away,
and the chief priests and the
teachers of the law were scheming to arrest Jesus secretly and kill
him. 2 "But not during the festival," they said, "or the people may
riot." Mt 12:14; Jn 11:55; 13:1

3 While he was in Bethany, reclining at the table in the home of
Simon the Leper, a woman came
with an alabaster jar of very expensive perfume, made of pure
nard. She broke the jar and poured
the perfume on his head.
Mt 21:17; Lk 7:37-39

4 Some of those present were
saying indignantly to one another, "Why this waste of perfume?
5 It could have been sold for more
than a year's wages[a] and the money given to the poor." And they rebuked her harshly.

6 "Leave her alone," said Jesus.
"Why are you bothering her?
She has done a beautiful thing
to me. 7 The poor you will always
have with you,[b] and you can help
them any time you want. But you
will not always have me. 8 She did
what she could. She poured perfume on my body beforehand to
prepare for my burial. 9 Truly I
tell you, wherever the gospel is
preached throughout the world,
what she has done will also be
told, in memory of her."
Jn 12:1-8; Dt 15:11

10 Then Judas Iscariot, one of the
Twelve, went to the chief priests
to betray Jesus to them. 11 They
were delighted to hear this and
promised to give him money. So
he watched for an opportunity to
hand him over. Mt 26:2-16; Lk 22:1-6

The Last Supper

12 On the first day of the Festival
of Unleavened Bread, when it was
customary to sacrifice the Passover lamb, Jesus' disciples asked
him, "Where do you want us to go
and make preparations for you to
eat the Passover?"
Ex 12:1-11; Dt 16:1-4; 1Co 5:7

13 So he sent two of his disciples,
telling them, "Go into the city, and
a man carrying a jar of water will
meet you. Follow him. 14 Say to
the owner of the house he enters,
'The Teacher asks: Where is my
guest room, where I may eat the

[a] 5 Greek *than three hundred denarii*
[b] 7 See Deut. 15:11.

Passover with my disciples?' [15]He
will show you a large room upstairs, furnished and ready. Make
preparations for us there." Ac 1:13
[16]The disciples left, went into
the city and found things just as
Jesus had told them. So they prepared the Passover.
[17]When evening came, Jesus
arrived with the Twelve. [18]While
they were reclining at the table
eating, he said, "Truly I tell you,
one of you will betray me — one
who is eating with me."
[19]They were saddened, and one
by one they said to him, "Surely
you don't mean me?"
[20]"It is one of the Twelve," he replied, "one who dips bread into the
bowl with me. [21]The Son of Man
will go just as it is written about
him. But woe to that man who betrays the Son of Man! It would be
better for him if he had not been
born." Mt 8:20; Jn 13:18-27
[22]While they were eating, Jesus
took bread, and when he had giv-
en thanks, he broke it and gave it
to his disciples, saying, "Take it;
this is my body." Mt 14:19
[23]Then he took a cup, and when
he had given thanks, he gave it to
them, and they all drank from it. 1Co 10:16
[24]"This is my blood of the[a] covenant, which is poured out for
many," he said to them. [25]"Truly
I tell you, I will not drink again
from the fruit of the vine until
that day when I drink it new in the
kingdom of God." 1Co 11:23-25
[26]When they had sung a hymn,
they went out to the Mount of Olives. Mt 26:17-30; Lk 22:7-23

Jesus Predicts Peter's Denial

[27]"You will all fall away," Jesus
told them, "for it is written:

"'I will strike the shepherd,
and the sheep will be
scattered.'[b]

[28]But after I have risen, I will go
ahead of you into Galilee." Mk 16:7
[29]Peter declared, "Even if all fall
away, I will not."
[30]"Truly I tell you," Jesus answered, "today — yes, tonight —
before the rooster crows twice[c]
you yourself will disown me three
times." Lk 22:34; Jn 13:38
[31]But Peter insisted emphatical-
ly, "Even if I have to die with you,
I will never disown you." And all
the others said the same. Mt 26:31-35

Gethsemane

[32]They went to a place called
Gethsemane, and Jesus said to his
disciples, "Sit here while I pray."
[33]He took Peter, James and John
along with him, and he began to
be deeply distressed and troubled.
[34]"My soul is overwhelmed with
sorrow to the point of death," he
said to them. "Stay here and keep
watch." Jn 12:27
[35]Going a little farther, he fell

[a] 24 Some manuscripts *the new*
[b] 27 Zech. 13:7 [c] 30 Some early manuscripts do not have *twice*.

to the ground and prayed that if
possible the hour might pass from
him. 36 "*Abba*,[a] Father," he said,
"everything is possible for you.
Take this cup from me. Yet not
what I will, but what you will."
Mt 26:39; Ro 8:15

37 Then he returned to his disciples and found them sleeping.
"Simon," he said to Peter, "are you
asleep? Couldn't you keep watch
for one hour? 38 Watch and pray so
that you will not fall into temptation. The spirit is willing, but the
flesh is weak." Mt 6:13; Ro 7:22-23

39 Once more he went away and
prayed the same thing. 40 When he
came back, he again found them
sleeping, because their eyes were
heavy. They did not know what to
say to him.

41 Returning the third time, he
said to them, "Are you still sleeping and resting? Enough! The
hour has come. Look, the Son of
Man is delivered into the hands
of sinners. 42 Rise! Let us go! Here
comes my betrayer!"
Mt 26:36-46; Lk 22:40-46

Jesus Arrested

43 Just as he was speaking, Judas, one of the Twelve, appeared.
With him was a crowd armed with
swords and clubs, sent from the
chief priests, the teachers of the
law, and the elders. Mt 10:4

44 Now the betrayer had arranged
a signal with them: "The one I kiss
is the man; arrest him and lead
him away under guard." 45 Going at
once to Jesus, Judas said, "Rabbi!"
and kissed him. 46 The men seized
Jesus and arrested him. 47 Then
one of those standing near drew
his sword and struck the servant
of the high priest, cutting off his
ear. Mt 23:7

48 "Am I leading a rebellion,"
said Jesus, "that you have come
out with swords and clubs to
capture me? 49 Every day I was
with you, teaching in the temple
courts, and you did not arrest me.
But the Scriptures must be fulfilled." 50 Then everyone deserted
him and fled.
Mt 26:47-56; Lk 22:47-50; Jn 18:3-11

51 A young man, wearing nothing but a linen garment, was following Jesus. When they seized
him, 52 he fled naked, leaving his
garment behind.

Jesus Before the Sanhedrin

53 They took Jesus to the high
priest, and all the chief priests,
the elders and the teachers of the
law came together. 54 Peter followed him at a distance, right into
the courtyard of the high priest.
There he sat with the guards and
warmed himself at the fire.
Mt 26:3; Jn 18:18

55 The chief priests and the
whole Sanhedrin were looking
for evidence against Jesus so that
they could put him to death, but
they did not find any. 56 Many testified falsely against him, but their
statements did not agree. Mt 5:22

[a] *36* Aramaic for *father*

[57]Then some stood up and gave this false testimony against him: [58]"We heard him say, 'I will destroy this temple made with human hands and in three days will build another, not made with hands.'" [59]Yet even then their testimony did not agree.

Mk 15:29; Jn 2:19

[60]Then the high priest stood up before them and asked Jesus, "Are you not going to answer? What is this testimony that these men are bringing against you?" [61]But Jesus remained silent and gave no answer. Isa 53:7; Mt 27:12,14

Again the high priest asked him, "Are you the Messiah, the Son of the Blessed One?" Mt 16:16; Jn 4:25-26

[62]"I am," said Jesus. "And you will see the Son of Man sitting at the right hand of the Mighty One and coming on the clouds of heaven."

Rev 1:7

[63]The high priest tore his clothes. "Why do we need any more witnesses?" he asked. [64]"You have heard the blasphemy. What do you think?" Lk 22:67-71

They all condemned him as worthy of death. [65]Then some began to spit at him; they blindfolded him, struck him with their fists, and said, "Prophesy!" And the guards took him and beat him.

Mt 26:57-68; Jn 18:12-13,19-24

Peter Disowns Jesus

[66]While Peter was below in the courtyard, one of the servant girls of the high priest came by. [67]When she saw Peter warming himself, she looked closely at him. ver 54

"You also were with that Nazarene, Jesus," she said. Mk 1:24

[68]But he denied it. "I don't know or understand what you're talking about," he said, and went out into the entryway.[a]

[69]When the servant girl saw him there, she said again to those standing around, "This fellow is one of them." [70]Again he denied it.

After a little while, those standing near said to Peter, "Surely you are one of them, for you are a Galilean." Ac 2:7

[71]He began to call down curses, and he swore to them, "I don't know this man you're talking about."

[72]Immediately the rooster crowed the second time.[b] Then Peter remembered the word Jesus had spoken to him: "Before the rooster crows twice[c] you will disown me three times." And he broke down and wept.

Mt 26:69-75; Lk 22:56-62; Jn 18:16-18,25-27

Jesus Before Pilate

15 Very early in the morning, the chief priests, with the elders, the teachers of the law and the whole Sanhedrin, made their plans. So they bound Jesus, led him away and handed him over to Pilate. Mt 27:1-2

[a] 68 Some early manuscripts *entryway and the rooster crowed* [b] 72 Some early manuscripts do not have *the second time.* [c] 72 Some early manuscripts do not have *twice.*

2"Are you the king of the Jews?" asked Pilate. Mt 2:2

"You have said so," Jesus replied.

3The chief priests accused him of many things. 4So again Pilate asked him, "Aren't you going to answer? See how many things they are accusing you of."

5But Jesus still made no reply, and Pilate was amazed. Mk 14:61

6Now it was the custom at the festival to release a prisoner whom the people requested. 7A man called Barabbas was in prison with the insurrectionists who had committed murder in the uprising. 8The crowd came up and asked Pilate to do for them what he usually did.

9"Do you want me to release to you the king of the Jews?" asked Pilate, 10knowing it was out of self-interest that the chief priests had handed Jesus over to him. 11But the chief priests stirred up the crowd to have Pilate release Barabbas instead. Ac 3:14

12"What shall I do, then, with the one you call the king of the Jews?" Pilate asked them.

13"Crucify him!" they shouted.

14"Why? What crime has he committed?" asked Pilate.

But they shouted all the louder, "Crucify him!"

15Wanting to satisfy the crowd, Pilate released Barabbas to them. He had Jesus flogged, and handed him over to be crucified.

Mt 27:11-26; Lk 23:2-3,18-25; Jn 18:29-19:16

The Soldiers Mock Jesus

16The soldiers led Jesus away into the palace (that is, the Praetorium) and called together the whole company of soldiers. 17They put a purple robe on him, then twisted together a crown of thorns and set it on him. 18And they began to call out to him, "Hail, king of the Jews!" 19Again and again they struck him on the head with a staff and spit on him. Falling on their knees, they paid homage to him. 20And when they had mocked him, they took off the purple robe and put his own clothes on him. Then they led him out to crucify him. Mt 27:27-31; Heb 13:12

The Crucifixion of Jesus

21A certain man from Cyrene, Simon, the father of Alexander and Rufus, was passing by on his way in from the country, and they forced him to carry the cross. 22They brought Jesus to the place called Golgotha (which means "the place of the skull"). 23Then they offered him wine mixed with myrrh, but he did not take it. 24And they crucified him. Dividing up his clothes, they cast lots to see what each would get.

Ps 22:18; Lk 23:26

25It was nine in the morning when they crucified him. 26The written notice of the charge against him read: THE KING OF THE JEWS.

27They crucified two rebels with him, one on his right and one on

his left. [28][a] 29Those who passed
by hurled insults at him, shaking their heads and saying, "So!
You who are going to destroy the
temple and build it in three days,
30come down from the cross and
save yourself!" 31In the same way
the chief priests and the teachers
of the law mocked him among
themselves. "He saved others,"
they said, "but he can't save himself! 32Let this Messiah, this king
of Israel, come down now from
the cross, that we may see and believe." Those crucified with him
also heaped insults on him.

Mt 27:33-44; Lk 23:33-43; Jn 19:17-24

The Death of Jesus

33At noon, darkness came over
the whole land until three in the
afternoon. 34And at three in the afternoon Jesus cried out in a loud
voice, *"Eloi, Eloi, lema sabachthani?"* (which means "My God,
my God, why have you forsaken
me?").[b] Am 8:9

35When some of those standing
near heard this, they said, "Listen,
he's calling Elijah."

36Someone ran, filled a sponge
with wine vinegar, put it on a staff,
and offered it to Jesus to drink.
"Now leave him alone. Let's see if
Elijah comes to take him down,"
he said. Ps 69:21

37With a loud cry, Jesus breathed
his last. Jn 19:30

38The curtain of the temple was
torn in two from top to bottom.
39And when the centurion, who
stood there in front of Jesus, saw
how he died,[c] he said, "Surely this
man was the Son of God!"

Mt 4:3; Heb 10:19-20

40Some women were watching
from a distance. Among them
were Mary Magdalene, Mary
the mother of James the younger and of Joseph,[d] and Salome.
41In Galilee these women had
followed him and cared for his
needs. Many other women who
had come up with him to Jerusalem were also there.

Mt 27:45-46; Lk 23:44-49

The Burial of Jesus

42It was Preparation Day (that
is, the day before the Sabbath).
So as evening approached, 43Jo-
seph of Arimathea, a prominent
member of the Council, who was
himself waiting for the kingdom
of God, went boldly to Pilate and
asked for Jesus' body. 44Pilate was
surprised to hear that he was already dead. Summoning the centurion, he asked him if Jesus had
already died. 45When he learned
from the centurion that it was so,
he gave the body to Joseph. 46So
Joseph bought some linen cloth,
took down the body, wrapped it in
the linen, and placed it in a tomb
cut out of rock. Then he rolled a
stone against the entrance of the

[a] *28* Some manuscripts include here words similar to Luke 22:37. [b] *34* Psalm 22:1 [c] *39* Some manuscripts *saw that he died with such a cry* [d] *40* Greek *Joses*, a variant of *Joseph*; also in verse 47

tomb. 47 Mary Magdalene and Mary
the mother of Joseph saw where
he was laid.

Mt 27:57-61; Lk 23:50-56; Jn 19:38-42

Jesus Has Risen

16 When the Sabbath was over,
Mary Magdalene, Mary the
mother of James, and Salome
bought spices so that they might
go to anoint Jesus' body. 2 Very
early on the first day of the week,
just after sunrise, they were on
their way to the tomb 3 and they
asked each other, "Who will roll
the stone away from the entrance
of the tomb?"

Mk 15:46; Lk 23:56; Jn 19:39-40

4 But when they looked up,
they saw that the stone, which
was very large, had been rolled
away. 5 As they entered the tomb,
they saw a young man dressed in
a white robe sitting on the right
side, and they were alarmed.

Jn 20:12

6 "Don't be alarmed," he said.
"You are looking for Jesus the
Nazarene, who was crucified. He
has risen! He is not here. See the
place where they laid him. 7 But go,
tell his disciples and Peter, 'He is
going ahead of you into Galilee.
There you will see him, just as he
told you.'"

Mk 1:24; 14:28

8 Trembling and bewildered, the
women went out and fled from the
tomb. They said nothing to anyone, because they were afraid.[a]

Mt 28:1-8; Lk 24:1-10

[The earliest manuscripts and
some other ancient witnesses
do not have verses 9 – 20.]

*9 When Jesus rose early on the first
day of the week, he appeared first to
Mary Magdalene, out of whom he had
driven seven demons. 10 She went and
told those who had been with him
and who were mourning and weeping. 11 When they heard that Jesus
was alive and that she had seen him,
they did not believe it.*

Lk 24:11; Jn 20:11-18

*12 Afterward Jesus appeared in a dif-
ferent form to two of them while they
were walking in the country. 13 These
returned and reported it to the rest;
but they did not believe them either.*

Lk 24:13-32

*14 Later Jesus appeared to the Elev-
en as they were eating; he rebuked
them for their lack of faith and their
stubborn refusal to believe those who
had seen him after he had risen.*

Lk 24:36-43

*15 He said to them, "Go into all the
world and preach the gospel to all creation. 16 Whoever believes and is baptized will be saved, but whoever does
not believe will be condemned. 17 And
these signs will accompany those who
believe: In my name they will drive
out demons; they will speak in new*

[a] 8 Some manuscripts have the following ending between verses 8 and 9, and one manuscript has it after verse 8 (omitting verses 9-20): *Then they quickly reported all these instructions to those around Peter. After this, Jesus himself also sent out through them from east to west the sacred and imperishable proclamation of eternal salvation. Amen.*

tongues; [18]*they will pick up snakes with their hands; and when they drink deadly poison, it will not hurt them at all; they will place their hands on sick people, and they will get well."*

Mt 28:18-20; Lk 24:47-48

[19]*After the Lord Jesus had spoken to them, he was taken up into heaven and he sat at the right hand of God.* [20]*Then the disciples went out and preached everywhere, and the Lord worked with them and confirmed his word by the signs that accompanied it.*

Lk 24:50-51; Ps 110:1

LUKE

Introduction

1 Many have undertaken to draw
up an account of the things that
have been fulfilled[a] among us,
2just as they were handed down
to us by those who from the first
were eyewitnesses and servants
of the word. 3With this in mind,
since I myself have carefully investigated everything from the
beginning, I too decided to write
an orderly account for you, most
excellent Theophilus, 4so that you
may know the certainty of the
things you have been taught.
Ac 1:1; 11:4; Heb 2:3

The Birth of John the Baptist Foretold

5In the time of Herod king of
Judea there was a priest named
Zechariah, who belonged to the
priestly division of Abijah; his
wife Elizabeth was also a descendant of Aaron. 6Both of them were
righteous in the sight of God, observing all the Lord's commands
and decrees blamelessly. 7But they
were childless because Elizabeth
was not able to conceive, and they
were both very old. Ge 7:1; 1Ch 24:10
8Once when Zechariah's division
was on duty and he was serving as
priest before God, 9he was chosen
by lot, according to the custom of
the priesthood, to go into the temple of the Lord and burn incense.
10And when the time for the burning of incense came, all the assembled worshipers were praying outside. Ex 30:7-8; Lev 16:17; 1Ch 24:19
11Then an angel of the Lord appeared to him, standing at the
right side of the altar of incense.
12When Zechariah saw him, he was
startled and was gripped with fear.
13But the angel said to him: "Do not
be afraid, Zechariah; your prayer
has been heard. Your wife Elizabeth will bear you a son, and you
are to call him John. 14He will be a
joy and delight to you, and many
will rejoice because of his birth,
15for he will be great in the sight of
the Lord. He is never to take wine
or other fermented drink, and he
will be filled with the Holy Spirit
even before he is born. 16He will
bring back many of the people of
Israel to the Lord their God. 17And
he will go on before the Lord, in
the spirit and power of Elijah, to
turn the hearts of the parents to
their children and the disobedient
to the wisdom of the righteous —
to make ready a people prepared
for the Lord." Jer 1:5; Mt 11:14
18Zechariah asked the angel,
"How can I be sure of this? I am an
old man and my wife is well along
in years." Ge 17:17

[a] *1* Or *been surely believed*

19The angel said to him, "I am
Gabriel. I stand in the presence
of God, and I have been sent to
speak to you and to tell you this
good news. 20And now you will be
silent and not able to speak until
the day this happens, because you
did not believe my words, which
will come true at their appointed
time." Eze 3:26; Da 8:16; 9:21

21Meanwhile, the people were
waiting for Zechariah and wondering why he stayed so long in
the temple. 22When he came out,
he could not speak to them. They
realized he had seen a vision in
the temple, for he kept making
signs to them but remained unable to speak.

23When his time of service was
completed, he returned home.
24After this his wife Elizabeth
became pregnant and for five
months remained in seclusion.
25"The Lord has done this for me,"
she said. "In these days he has
shown his favor and taken away
my disgrace among the people."
Ge 30:23; Isa 4:1

The Birth of Jesus Foretold

26In the sixth month of Elizabeth's pregnancy, God sent the angel Gabriel to Nazareth, a town in
Galilee, 27to a virgin pledged to be
married to a man named Joseph, a
descendant of David. The virgin's
name was Mary. 28The angel went
to her and said, "Greetings, you
who are highly favored! The Lord
is with you." Mt 1:16,18,20; 2:23

29Mary was greatly troubled at
his words and wondered what
kind of greeting this might be.
30But the angel said to her, "Do not
be afraid, Mary; you have found
favor with God. 31You will conceive
and give birth to a son, and you are
to call him Jesus. 32He will be great
and will be called the Son of the
Most High. The Lord God will give
him the throne of his father David,
33and he will reign over Jacob's descendants forever; his kingdom
will never end." Da 2:44; 7:14,27; Mic 4:7

34"How will this be," Mary asked
the angel, "since I am a virgin?"

35The angel answered, "The
Holy Spirit will come on you, and
the power of the Most High will
overshadow you. So the holy one
to be born will be called[a] the Son
of God. 36Even Elizabeth your relative is going to have a child in
her old age, and she who was said
to be unable to conceive is in her
sixth month. 37For no word from
God will ever fail." Mt 19:26

38"I am the Lord's servant,"
Mary answered. "May your word
to me be fulfilled." Then the angel
left her.

Mary Visits Elizabeth

39At that time Mary got ready and
hurried to a town in the hill coun-
try of Judea, 40where she entered
Zechariah's home and greeted
Elizabeth. 41When Elizabeth heard
Mary's greeting, the baby leaped in

a 35 Or So the child to be born will be called holy,

her womb, and Elizabeth was filled
with the Holy Spirit. 42In a loud
voice she exclaimed: "Blessed are
you among women, and blessed is
the child you will bear! 43But why
am I so favored, that the mother of
my Lord should come to me? 44As
soon as the sound of your greeting
reached my ears, the baby in my
womb leaped for joy. 45Blessed is
she who has believed that the Lord
would fulfill his promises to her!"
Jdg 5:24; Jn 13:13

Mary's Song

46And Mary said:

"My soul glorifies the Lord Ps 34:2-3
47 and my spirit rejoices in God
my Savior, 1Ti 1:1; 2:3
48for he has been mindful
of the humble state of his
servant. Ps 138:6
From now on all generations
will call me blessed, Lk 11:27
49 for the Mighty One has done
great things for me — Ps 71:19
holy is his name. Ps 111:9
50His mercy extends to those
who fear him,
from generation to
generation. Ex 20:6; Ps 103:17
51He has performed mighty
deeds with his arm; Ps 98:1; Isa 40:10
he has scattered those who
are proud in their inmost
thoughts. Ge 11:8; Jer 13:9
52He has brought down rulers
from their thrones
but has lifted up the humble. Mt 23:12
53He has filled the hungry with
good things Ps 107:9
but has sent the rich away
empty. 1Sa 2:1-10
54He has helped his servant
Israel,
remembering to be merciful Ps 98:3
55to Abraham and his
descendants forever, Ge 17:19; Ps 132:11; Gal 3:16
just as he promised our
ancestors."

56Mary stayed with Elizabeth for
about three months and then returned home.

The Birth of John the Baptist

57When it was time for Elizabeth to have her baby, she gave
birth to a son. 58Her neighbors and
relatives heard that the Lord had
shown her great mercy, and they
shared her joy.

59On the eighth day they came
to circumcise the child, and they
were going to name him after his
father Zechariah, 60but his mother
spoke up and said, "No! He is to be
called John." Ge 17:12; Lk 2:21

61They said to her, "There is no
one among your relatives who has
that name."

62Then they made signs to his
father, to find out what he would
like to name the child. 63He asked

for a writing tablet, and to everyone's astonishment he wrote, "His
name is John." 64 Immediately his
mouth was opened and his tongue
set free, and he began to speak,
praising God. 65 All the neighbors
were filled with awe, and throughout the hill country of Judea people were talking about all these
things. 66 Everyone who heard this
wondered about it, asking, "What
then is this child going to be?" For
the Lord's hand was with him.
Ge 39:2; Ac 11:21

Zechariah's Song

67 His father Zechariah was filled
with the Holy Spirit and prophesied: Joel 2:28

68 "Praise be to the Lord, the God
of Israel, Ps 72:18
because he has come to his
people and redeemed
them. Ps 111:9; Lk 7:16
69 He has raised up a horn[a] of
salvation for us Ps 18:2; 132:17
in the house of his servant
David Mt 1:1
70 (as he said through his holy
prophets of long ago),
Jer 23:5
71 salvation from our enemies
and from the hand of all who
hate us —
72 to show mercy to our ancestors
Mic 7:20
and to remember his holy
covenant, Ps 105:8-9; 106:45
73 the oath he swore to our
father Abraham: Ge 22:16-18
74 to rescue us from the hand of
our enemies,
and to enable us to serve him
without fear Heb 9:14; 1Jn 4:18
75 in holiness and
righteousness before
him all our days. Eph 4:24

76 And you, my child, will be
called a prophet of the
Most High; Mt 11:9
for you will go on before the
Lord to prepare the way
for him, Mal 3:1
77 to give his people the
knowledge of salvation
through the forgiveness of
their sins, Jer 31:34; Mk 1:4
78 because of the tender mercy of
our God,
by which the rising sun will
come to us from heaven
Mal 4:2
79 to shine on those living in
darkness
and in the shadow of death,
Isa 9:2; Mt 4:16
to guide our feet into the path
of peace." Lk 2:14

80 And the child grew and became strong in spirit[b]; and he
lived in the wilderness until he appeared publicly to Israel. Lk 2:40,52

The Birth of Jesus

2 In those days Caesar Augustus issued a decree that a census should be taken of the entire

[a] 69 *Horn* here symbolizes a strong king.
[b] 80 Or *in the Spirit*

Roman world. 2(This was the first census that took place while[a] Quirinius was governor of Syria.) 3And everyone went to their own town to register. Mt 24:14; Lk 3:1

4So Joseph also went up from the town of Nazareth in Galilee to Judea, to Bethlehem the town of David, because he belonged to the house and line of David. 5He went there to register with Mary, who was pledged to be married to him and was expecting a child. 6While they were there, the time came for the baby to be born, 7and she gave birth to her firstborn, a son. She wrapped him in cloths and placed him in a manger, because there was no guest room available for them. Jn 7:42

8And there were shepherds living out in the fields nearby, keeping watch over their flocks at night. 9An angel of the Lord appeared to them, and the glory of the Lord shone around them, and they were terrified. 10But the angel said to them, "Do not be afraid. I bring you good news that will cause great joy for all the people. 11Today in the town of David a Savior has been born to you; he is the Messiah, the Lord. 12This will be a sign to you: You will find a baby wrapped in cloths and lying in a manger."

Isa 7:14; Mt 1:21

13Suddenly a great company of the heavenly host appeared with the angel, praising God and saying,

14"Glory to God in the highest
heaven,
and on earth peace to those
on whom his favor
rests." Ro 5:1; Eph 2:14,17

15When the angels had left them and gone into heaven, the shepherds said to one another, "Let's go to Bethlehem and see this thing that has happened, which the Lord has told us about."

16So they hurried off and found Mary and Joseph, and the baby, who was lying in the manger. 17When they had seen him, they spread the word concerning what had been told them about this child, 18and all who heard it were amazed at what the shepherds said to them. 19But Mary treasured up all these things and pondered them in her heart. 20The shepherds returned, glorifying and praising God for all the things they had heard and seen, which were just as they had been told.

Mt 9:8

21On the eighth day, when it was time to circumcise the child, he was named Jesus, the name the angel had given him before he was conceived. Lk 1:31,59

Jesus Presented in the Temple

22When the time came for the purification rites required by the Law of Moses, Joseph and Mary took him to Jerusalem to present him to the Lord 23(as it is written

[a] 2 Or *This census took place before*

in the Law of the Lord, "Every
firstborn male is to be consecrated to the Lord"[a]), 24and to offer a
sacrifice in keeping with what is
said in the Law of the Lord: "a pair
of doves or two young pigeons."[b]
Ex 13:2,12,15; Lev 12:8

25Now there was a man in Jerusalem called Simeon, who was
righteous and devout. He was
waiting for the consolation of Israel, and the Holy Spirit was on him.
26It had been revealed to him by
the Holy Spirit that he would not
die before he had seen the Lord's
Messiah. 27Moved by the Spirit, he
went into the temple courts. When
the parents brought in the child
Jesus to do for him what the custom of the Law required, 28Simeon
took him in his arms and praised
God, saying: Lk 1:6; 23:51

29"Sovereign Lord, as you have
promised, ver 26
you may now dismiss[c] your
servant in peace. Ac 2:24
30For my eyes have seen your
salvation, Isa 52:10
31 which you have prepared in
the sight of all nations:
32a light for revelation to the
Gentiles,
and the glory of your people
Israel." Isa 42:6; 49:6; Ac 13:47

33The child's father and mother
marveled at what was said about
him. 34Then Simeon blessed them
and said to Mary, his mother: "This
child is destined to cause the falling and rising of many in Israel,
and to be a sign that will be spoken against, 35so that the thoughts
of many hearts will be revealed.
And a sword will pierce your own
soul too." Mt 21:44; 1Co 1:23; 1Pe 2:7-8

36There was also a prophet,
Anna, the daughter of Penuel, of
the tribe of Asher. She was very
old; she had lived with her husband seven years after her marriage, 37and then was a widow until she was eighty-four.[d] She never
left the temple but worshiped
night and day, fasting and praying. 38Coming up to them at that
very moment, she gave thanks to
God and spoke about the child to
all who were looking forward to
the redemption of Jerusalem.
Lk 1:68; 1Ti 5:5

39When Joseph and Mary had
done everything required by the
Law of the Lord, they returned to
Galilee to their own town of Nazareth. 40And the child grew and
became strong; he was filled with
wisdom, and the grace of God was
on him. Mt 2:23; Lk 1:80

The Boy Jesus at the Temple

41Every year Jesus' parents went
to Jerusalem for the Festival of the
Passover. 42When he was twelve
years old, they went up to the festival, according to the custom.
43After the festival was over, while
his parents were returning home,

[a] 23 Exodus 13:2,12 [b] 24 Lev. 12:8
[c] 29 *Or promised, / now dismiss*
[d] 37 *Or then had been a widow for eighty-four years.*

the boy Jesus stayed behind in Jerusalem, but they were unaware of
it. 44Thinking he was in their company, they traveled on for a day.
Then they began looking for him
among their relatives and friends.
45When they did not find him, they
went back to Jerusalem to look for
him. 46After three days they found
him in the temple courts, sitting
among the teachers, listening to
them and asking them questions.
47Everyone who heard him was
amazed at his understanding and
his answers. 48When his parents
saw him, they were astonished.
His mother said to him, "Son, why
have you treated us like this? Your
father and I have been anxiously
searching for you."

Ex 23:15; Dt 16:1-8; Mt 12:46

49"Why were you searching for
me?" he asked. "Didn't you know I
had to be in my Father's house?"[a]
50But they did not understand
what he was saying to them.

Mk 9:32; Jn 2:16

51Then he went down to Nazareth with them and was obedient
to them. But his mother treasured
all these things in her heart. 52And
Jesus grew in wisdom and stature,
and in favor with God and man.

Mt 2:23; Lk 1:80

John the Baptist Prepares the Way

3 In the fifteenth year of the
reign of Tiberius Caesar—
when Pontius Pilate was governor
of Judea, Herod tetrarch of Galilee, his brother Philip tetrarch of
Iturea and Traconitis, and Lysa-
nias tetrarch of Abilene— 2dur-
ing the high-priesthood of Annas
and Caiaphas, the word of God
came to John son of Zechariah in
the wilderness. 3He went into all
the country around the Jordan,
preaching a baptism of repentance for the forgiveness of sins.
4As it is written in the book of the
words of Isaiah the prophet:

Mk 1:4; Jn 18:13; Ac 4:6

"A voice of one calling in the
wilderness,
'Prepare the way for the Lord,
make straight paths for
him.
5Every valley shall be filled in,
every mountain and hill
made low.
The crooked roads shall
become straight,
the rough ways smooth.
6And all people will see
God's salvation.' "[b]

Ps 98:2; Isa 52:10; Lk 2:30

7John said to the crowds coming
out to be baptized by him, "You
brood of vipers! Who warned you
to flee from the coming wrath?
8Produce fruit in keeping with
repentance. And do not begin to
say to yourselves, 'We have Abraham as our father.' For I tell you
that out of these stones God can
raise up children for Abraham.
9The ax is already at the root of
the trees, and every tree that does

[a] 49 Or *be about my Father's business*
[b] 6 Isaiah 40:3-5

not produce good fruit will be cut
down and thrown into the fire."
Jn 8:33,39; Gal 3:7
10"What should we do then?" the
crowd asked. Mt 3:1-10; Mk 1:3-5
11John answered, "Anyone who
has two shirts should share with
the one who has none, and anyone who has food should do the
same." Isa 58:7
12Even tax collectors came to be
baptized. "Teacher," they asked,
"what should we do?" Lk 7:29
13"Don't collect any more than
you are required to," he told them.
Lk 19:8
14Then some soldiers asked him,
"And what should we do?"

He replied, "Don't extort money
and don't accuse people falsely—
be content with your pay."
Ex 23:1; Lev 19:11

15The people were waiting expectantly and were all wondering in their hearts if John might
possibly be the Messiah. 16John
answered them all, "I baptize
you with[a] water. But one who is
more powerful than I will come,
the straps of whose sandals I am
not worthy to untie. He will baptize you with[a] the Holy Spirit and
fire. 17His winnowing fork is in his
hand to clear his threshing floor
and to gather the wheat into his
barn, but he will burn up the chaff
with unquenchable fire." 18And
with many other words John ex-
horted the people and proclaimed
the good news to them.
Mt 3:11-12; Mk 1:7-8

19But when John rebuked Herod
the tetrarch because of his marriage to Herodias, his brother's
wife, and all the other evil things
he had done, 20Herod added this
to them all: He locked John up in
prison. Mt 14:3-4; Mk 6:17-18

The Baptism and Genealogy of Jesus

21When all the people were being baptized, Jesus was baptized
too. And as he was praying, heav-
en was opened 22and the Holy
Spirit descended on him in bodily form like a dove. And a voice
came from heaven: "You are my
Son, whom I love; with you I am
well pleased." Mt 3:13-17; Mk 1:9-11
23Now Jesus himself was about
thirty years old when he began
his ministry. He was the son, so it
was thought, of Joseph,
Mt 4:17; Lk 1:27; Ac 1:1

the son of Heli, 24the son of Matthat,
the son of Levi, the son of Melki,
the son of Jannai, the son of Joseph,
25the son of Mattathias, the son of Amos,
the son of Nahum, the son of Esli,
the son of Naggai, 26the son of Maath,
the son of Mattathias, the son of Semein,
the son of Josek, the son of Joda,

[a] 16 Or *in*

27 the son of Joanan, the son of Rhesa,
the son of Zerubbabel, the son of Shealtiel, Mt 1:12
the son of Neri, 28 the son of Melki,
the son of Addi, the son of Cosam,
the son of Elmadam, the son of Er,
29 the son of Joshua, the son of Eliezer,
the son of Jorim, the son of Matthat,
the son of Levi, 30 the son of Simeon,
the son of Judah, the son of Joseph,
the son of Jonam, the son of Eliakim,
31 the son of Melea, the son of Menna,
the son of Mattatha, the son of Nathan, 2Sa 5:14; 1Ch 3:5
the son of David, 32 the son of Jesse,
the son of Obed, the son of Boaz,
the son of Salmon,[a] the son of Nahshon,
33 the son of Amminadab, the son of Ram,[b]
the son of Hezron, the son of Perez, Ru 4:18-22; 1Ch 2:10-12
the son of Judah, 34 the son of Jacob,
the son of Isaac, the son of Abraham,
the son of Terah, the son of Nahor, Ge 11:24,26
35 the son of Serug, the son of Reu,
the son of Peleg, the son of Eber,
the son of Shelah, 36 the son of Cainan,
the son of Arphaxad, the son of Shem, Ge 11:12
the son of Noah, the son of Lamech, Ge 5:28-32
37 the son of Methuselah, the son of Enoch,
the son of Jared, the son of Mahalalel,
the son of Kenan, 38 the son of Enosh, Ge 5:12-25
the son of Seth, the son of Adam,
the son of God. Mt 1:1-17

Jesus Is Tested in the Wilderness

4 Jesus, full of the Holy Spirit, left the Jordan and was
led by the Spirit into the wilderness, 2 where for forty days he
was tempted[c] by the devil. He ate
nothing during those days, and at
the end of them he was hungry.
Ex 34:28; Lk 2:27

3 The devil said to him, "If you
are the Son of God, tell this stone
to become bread." Mt 4:3

4 Jesus answered, "It is written: 'Man shall not live on bread
alone.'[d]" Dt 8:3

[a] 32 Some early manuscripts *Sala*
[b] 33 Some manuscripts *Amminadab, the son of Admin, the son of Arni*; other manuscripts vary widely.
[c] 2 The Greek for *tempted* can also mean *tested*.
[d] 4 Deut. 8:3

5The devil led him up to a high
place and showed him in an instant all the kingdoms of the
world. 6And he said to him, "I will
give you all their authority and
splendor; it has been given to me,
and I can give it to anyone I want
to. 7If you worship me, it will all be
yours." Jn 12:31; 14:30; 1Jn 5:19
8Jesus answered, "It is written:
'Worship the Lord your God and
serve him only.'[a]" Dt 6:13
9The devil led him to Jerusalem
and had him stand on the highest
point of the temple. "If you are
the Son of God," he said, "throw
yourself down from here. 10For it
is written:

"'He will command his angels
concerning you
to guard you carefully;
11they will lift you up in their
hands,
so that you will not strike
your foot against a
stone.'[b]" Ps 91:11-12

12Jesus answered, "It is said: 'Do
not put the Lord your God to the
test.'[c]" Dt 6:16
13When the devil had finished
all this tempting, he left him until
an opportune time. Mt 4:1-11; Mk 1;12-13

Jesus Rejected at Nazareth

14Jesus returned to Galilee
in the power of the Spirit, and
news about him spread through
the whole countryside. 15He was
teaching in their synagogues, and
everyone praised him. Mt 4:12; 9:26
16He went to Nazareth, where
he had been brought up, and on
the Sabbath day he went into the
synagogue, as was his custom. He
stood up to read, 17and the scroll
of the prophet Isaiah was handed
to him. Unrolling it, he found the
place where it is written: Mt 13:54

18"The Spirit of the Lord is on
me, Jn 3:34
because he has anointed me
to proclaim good news to the
poor. Mk 16:15
He has sent me to proclaim
freedom for the
prisoners
and recovery of sight for the
blind,
to set the oppressed free,
19 to proclaim the year of the
Lord's favor."[d] Lev 25:10

20Then he rolled up the scroll,
gave it back to the attendant and
sat down. The eyes of everyone
in the synagogue were fastened
on him. 21He began by saying to
them, "Today this scripture is fulfilled in your hearing." Mt 26:55
22All spoke well of him and were
amazed at the gracious words that
came from his lips. "Isn't this Joseph's son?" they asked.
Mt 13:54-55; Jn 6:42; 7:15
23Jesus said to them, "Surely
you will quote this proverb to me:
'Physician, heal yourself!' And
you will tell me, 'Do here in your

[a] *8* Deut. 6:13 [b] *11* Psalm 91:11,12
[c] *12* Deut. 6:16 [d] *19* Isaiah 61:1,2
(see Septuagint); Isaiah 58:6

hometown what we have heard that you did in Capernaum.'"

Mk 1:21-28; 2:1-12

24"Truly I tell you," he continued, "no prophet is accepted in his hometown. 25I assure you that there were many widows in Israel in Elijah's time, when the sky was shut for three and a half years and there was a severe famine throughout the land. 26Yet Elijah was not sent to any of them, but to a widow in Zarephath in the region of Sidon. 27And there were many in Israel with leprosy[a] in the time of Elisha the prophet, yet not one of them was cleansed — only Naaman the Syrian."

Mt 13:57; Jn 4:44

28All the people in the synagogue were furious when they heard this. 29They got up, drove him out of the town, and took him to the brow of the hill on which the town was built, in order to throw him off the cliff. 30But he walked right through the crowd and went on his way. Jn 8:59; 10:39

Jesus Drives Out an Impure Spirit

31Then he went down to Capernaum, a town in Galilee, and on the Sabbath he taught the people. 32They were amazed at his teaching, because his words had authority. Mt 7:28-29

33In the synagogue there was a man possessed by a demon, an impure spirit. He cried out at the top of his voice, 34"Go away! What do you want with us, Jesus of Nazareth? Have you come to destroy us? I know who you are — the Holy One of God!" Mk 1:24; Jas 2:19

35"Be quiet!" Jesus said sternly. "Come out of him!" Then the demon threw the man down before them all and came out without injuring him.

36All the people were amazed and said to each other, "What words these are! With authority and power he gives orders to impure spirits and they come out!" 37And the news about him spread throughout the surrounding area.

Mk 1:21-28

Jesus Heals Many

38Jesus left the synagogue and went to the home of Simon. Now Simon's mother-in-law was suffering from a high fever, and they asked Jesus to help her. 39So he bent over her and rebuked the fever, and it left her. She got up at once and began to wait on them.

40At sunset, the people brought to Jesus all who had various kinds of sickness, and laying his hands on each one, he healed them. 41Moreover, demons came out of many people, shouting, "You are the Son of God!" But he rebuked them and would not allow them to speak, because they knew he was the Messiah. Mt 8:14-17; Mk 5:23

42At daybreak, Jesus went out to a solitary place. The people were

[a] 27 The Greek word traditionally translated *leprosy* was used for various diseases affecting the skin.

looking for him and when they
came to where he was, they tried
to keep him from leaving them.
43But he said, "I must proclaim the
good news of the kingdom of God
to the other towns also, because
that is why I was sent." 44And he
kept on preaching in the synagogues of Judea. Mt 3:2; 4:23

Jesus Calls His First Disciples

5 One day as Jesus was standing
by the Lake of Gennesaret,[a] the
people were crowding around him
and listening to the word of God.
2He saw at the water's edge two
boats, left there by the fishermen,
who were washing their nets. 3He
got into one of the boats, the one
belonging to Simon, and asked him
to put out a little from shore. Then
he sat down and taught the people
from the boat. Mt 13:2; Heb 4:12

4When he had finished speaking, he said to Simon, "Put out
into deep water, and let down the
nets for a catch." Jn 21:6

5Simon answered, "Master,
we've worked hard all night and
haven't caught anything. But because you say so, I will let down
the ncts." Lk 8:24,45; 9:33,49; 17:13

6When they had done so, they
caught such a large number of
fish that their nets began to break.
7So they signaled their partners in
the other boat to come and help
them, and they came and filled
both boats so full that they began
to sink. Jn 21:11

8When Simon Peter saw this, he
fell at Jesus' knees and said, "Go
away from me, Lord; I am a sinful
man!" 9For he and all his companions were astonished at the catch
of fish they had taken, 10and so
were James and John, the sons of
Zebedee, Simon's partners.
Ge 18:27; Job 42:6; Isa 6:5

Then Jesus said to Simon, "Don't
be afraid; from now on you will
fish for people." 11So they pulled
their boats up on shore, left everything and followed him.
Mt 4:18-22; Mk 1:16-20; Jn 1:40-42

Jesus Heals a Man With Leprosy

12While Jesus was in one of the
towns, a man came along who
was covered with leprosy.[b] When
he saw Jesus, he fell with his face
to the ground and begged him,
"Lord, if you are willing, you can
make me clean." Mt 8:2

13Jesus reached out his hand
and touched the man. "I am willing," he said. "Be clean!" And immediately the leprosy left him.

14Then Jesus ordered him,
"Don't tell anyone, but go, show
yourself to the priest and offer the
sacrifices that Moses commanded
for your cleansing, as a testimony
to them." Mt 8:2-4; Mk 1:40-44

15Yet the news about him spread
all the more, so that crowds of
people came to hear him and
to be healed of their sicknesses.

[a] 1 That is, the Sea of Galilee [b] 12 The Greek word traditionally translated *leprosy* was used for various diseases affecting the skin.

16 But Jesus often withdrew to
lonely places and prayed.
Mt 14:23; Lk 3:21

Jesus Forgives and Heals a Paralyzed Man

17 One day Jesus was teaching,
and Pharisees and teachers of the
law were sitting there. They had
come from every village of Galilee and from Judea and Jerusalem. And the power of the Lord
was with Jesus to heal the sick.
18 Some men came carrying a paralyzed man on a mat and tried to
take him into the house to lay him
before Jesus. 19 When they could
not find a way to do this because
of the crowd, they went up on the
roof and lowered him on his mat
through the tiles into the middle of the crowd, right in front of
Jesus. Mk 5:30; Lk 6:19
20 When Jesus saw their faith, he
said, "Friend, your sins are forgiv-
en." Lk 7:48-49
21 The Pharisees and the teachers of the law began thinking to
themselves, "Who is this fellow
who speaks blasphemy? Who can
forgive sins but God alone?"
Isa 43:25
22 Jesus knew what they were
thinking and asked, "Why are
you thinking these things in your
hearts? 23 Which is easier: to say,
'Your sins are forgiven,' or to say,
'Get up and walk'? 24 But I want
you to know that the Son of Man
has authority on earth to forgive
sins." So he said to the paralyzed
man, "I tell you, get up, take your
mat and go home." 25 Immediately he stood up in front of them,
took what he had been lying on
and went home praising God.
26 Everyone was amazed and gave
praise to God. They were filled
with awe and said, "We have seen
remarkable things today."
Mt 9:2-8; Mk 2:3-12

Jesus Calls Levi and Eats With Sinners

27 After this, Jesus went out and
saw a tax collector by the name of
Levi sitting at his tax booth. "Follow me," Jesus said to him, 28 and
Levi got up, left everything and
followed him. Mt 4:19
29 Then Levi held a great banquet for Jesus at his house, and a
large crowd of tax collectors and
others were eating with them.
30 But the Pharisees and the teachers of the law who belonged to
their sect complained to his disciples, "Why do you eat and drink
with tax collectors and sinners?"
Lk 15:1; Ac 23:9
31 Jesus answered them, "It is
not the healthy who need a doctor, but the sick. 32 I have not come
to call the righteous, but sinners
to repentance." Mt 9:9-13; Mk 2:14-17

Jesus Questioned About Fasting

33 They said to him, "John's disciples often fast and pray, and so do
the disciples of the Pharisees, but
yours go on eating and drinking."
Lk 7:18; Jn 1:35; 3:25-26

34 Jesus answered, "Can you
make the friends of the bridegroom fast while he is with them?
35 But the time will come when the
bridegroom will be taken from
them; in those days they will fast."

Lk 17:22; Jn 16:5-7

36 He told them this parable: "No
one tears a piece out of a new garment to patch an old one. Otherwise, they will have torn the new
garment, and the patch from the
new will not match the old. 37 And
no one pours new wine into old
wineskins. Otherwise, the new
wine will burst the skins; the wine
will run out and the wineskins
will be ruined. 38 No, new wine
must be poured into new wineskins. 39 And no one after drinking
old wine wants the new, for they
say, 'The old is better.'"

Mt 9:14-17; Mk 2:18-22

Jesus Is Lord of the Sabbath

6 One Sabbath Jesus was going
through the grainfields, and
his disciples began to pick some
heads of grain, rub them in their
hands and eat the kernels. 2 Some
of the Pharisees asked, "Why are
you doing what is unlawful on the
Sabbath?"

Dt 23:25

3 Jesus answered them, "Have
you never read what David did
when he and his companions were
hungry? 4 He entered the house of
God, and taking the consecrated
bread, he ate what is lawful only
for priests to eat. And he also gave
some to his companions." 5 Then
Jesus said to them, "The Son of
Man is Lord of the Sabbath."

Lev 24:5,9; 1Sa 21:6

6 On another Sabbath he went
into the synagogue and was teaching, and a man was there whose
right hand was shriveled. 7 The
Pharisees and the teachers of the
law were looking for a reason to
accuse Jesus, so they watched him
closely to see if he would heal on
the Sabbath. 8 But Jesus knew what
they were thinking and said to the
man with the shriveled hand, "Get
up and stand in front of everyone." So he got up and stood there.

Mt 12:2,10

9 Then Jesus said to them, "I ask
you, which is lawful on the Sabbath: to do good or to do evil, to
save life or to destroy it?"

10 He looked around at them all,
and then said to the man, "Stretch
out your hand." He did so, and his
hand was completely restored.
11 But the Pharisees and the teachers of the law were furious and
began to discuss with one another
what they might do to Jesus.

Mt 12:1-14; Mk 2:23-3:6

The Twelve Apostles

12 One of those days Jesus went
out to a mountainside to pray, and
spent the night praying to God.
13 When morning came, he called his
disciples to him and chose twelve
of them, whom he also designated apostles: 14 Simon (whom he
named Peter), his brother Andrew,
James, John, Philip, Bartholomew,

15Matthew, Thomas, James son of
Alphaeus, Simon who was called
the Zealot, 16Judas son of James,
and Judas Iscariot, who became a
traitor. Mt 10:2-4; Mk 3:16-19; Ac 1:13

Blessings and Woes

17He went down with them and
stood on a level place. A large
crowd of his disciples was there
and a great number of people
from all over Judea, from Jerusalem,
and from the coastal region
around Tyre and Sidon, 18who had
come to hear him and to be healed
of their diseases. Those troubled
by impure spirits were cured,
19and the people all tried to touch
him, because power was coming
from him and healing them all.
Mt 14:36; Lk 5:17

20Looking at his disciples, he
said:

"Blessed are you who are poor,
for yours is the kingdom of
God. Mt 25:34
21Blessed are you who hunger
now,
for you will be satisfied.
Isa 55:1-2; Mt 5:6

Blessed are you who weep now,
for you will laugh.
Isa 61:2-3; Mt 5:4; Rev 7:17
22Blessed are you when people
hate you,
when they exclude you and
insult you Jn 9:22; 16:2
and reject your name as evil,
because of the Son of Man.
Jn 15:21

23"Rejoice in that day and leap for
joy, because great is your reward
in heaven. For that is how their
ancestors treated the prophets.
Mt 5:12

24"But woe to you who are rich,
Jas 5:1
for you have already received
your comfort. Lk 16:25
25Woe to you who are well fed
now,
for you will go hungry. Isa 65:13
Woe to you who laugh now,
for you will mourn and weep.
Pr 14:13
26Woe to you when everyone
speaks well of you,
for that is how their
ancestors treated the
false prophets. Mt 7:15

Love for Enemies

27"But to you who are listening I
say: Love your enemies, do good to
those who hate you, 28bless those
who curse you, pray for those who
mistreat you. 29If someone slaps
you on one cheek, turn to them
the other also. If someone takes
your coat, do not withhold your
shirt from them. 30Give to everyone
who asks you, and if anyone
takes what belongs to you, do not
demand it back. 31Do to others as
you would have them do to you.
Mt 5:39-42

32"If you love those who love you,
what credit is that to you? Even
sinners love those who love them.
33And if you do good to those who

are good to you, what credit is that
to you? Even sinners do that. 34And
if you lend to those from whom
you expect repayment, what credit is that to you? Even sinners lend
to sinners, expecting to be repaid
in full. 35But love your enemies, do
good to them, and lend to them
without expecting to get anything
back. Then your reward will be
great, and you will be children of
the Most High, because he is kind
to the ungrateful and wicked. 36Be
merciful, just as your Father is
merciful. Jas 2:13; Mt 5:48

Judging Others

37"Do not judge, and you will
not be judged. Do not condemn,
and you will not be condemned.
Forgive, and you will be forgiven.
38Give, and it will be given to you.
A good measure, pressed down,
shaken together and running
over, will be poured into your lap.
For with the measure you use, it
will be measured to you."

Mt 7:1; Mk 4:24

39He also told them this parable:
"Can the blind lead the blind? Will
they not both fall into a pit? 40The
student is not above the teacher,
but everyone who is fully trained
will be like their teacher.

Mt 10:24; Jn 13:16

41"Why do you look at the speck
of sawdust in your brother's eye
and pay no attention to the plank
in your own eye? 42How can you
say to your brother, 'Brother, let
me take the speck out of your eye,'
when you yourself fail to see the
plank in your own eye? You hypocrite, first take the plank out of
your eye, and then you will see
clearly to remove the speck from
your brother's eye. Mt 7:1-5

A Tree and Its Fruit

43"No good tree bears bad fruit,
nor does a bad tree bear good
fruit. 44Each tree is recognized by
its own fruit. People do not pick
figs from thornbushes, or grapes
from briers. 45A good man brings
good things out of the good stored
up in his heart, and an evil man
brings evil things out of the evil
stored up in his heart. For the
mouth speaks what the heart is
full of. Mt 12:33-35

The Wise and Foolish Builders

46"Why do you call me, 'Lord,
Lord,' and do not do what I say?
47As for everyone who comes to
me and hears my words and puts
them into practice, I will show you
what they are like. 48They are like
a man building a house, who dug
down deep and laid the foundation on rock. When a flood came,
the torrent struck that house but
could not shake it, because it was
well built. 49But the one who hears
my words and does not put them
into practice is like a man who
built a house on the ground without a foundation. The moment
the torrent struck that house, it
collapsed and its destruction was
complete." Mt 7:24-27

The Faith of the Centurion

7 When Jesus had finished saying all this to the people who
were listening, he entered Capernaum. 2There a centurion's servant, whom his master valued
highly, was sick and about to die.
3The centurion heard of Jesus and
sent some elders of the Jews to
him, asking him to come and heal
his servant. 4When they came to
Jesus, they pleaded earnestly with
him, "This man deserves to have
you do this, 5because he loves our
nation and has built our synagogue." 6So Jesus went with them.

Mt 7:28

He was not far from the house
when the centurion sent friends
to say to him: "Lord, don't trouble yourself, for I do not deserve
to have you come under my roof.
7That is why I did not even consider myself worthy to come to you.
But say the word, and my servant
will be healed. 8For I myself am
a man under authority, with soldiers under me. I tell this one,
'Go,' and he goes; and that one,
'Come,' and he comes. I say to my
servant, 'Do this,' and he does it."

Ps 107:20

9When Jesus heard this, he was
amazed at him, and turning to
the crowd following him, he said,
"I tell you, I have not found such
great faith even in Israel." 10Then
the men who had been sent returned to the house and found the
servant well.

Mt 8:5-13

Jesus Raises a Widow's Son

11Soon afterward, Jesus went to
a town called Nain, and his disciples and a large crowd went along
with him. 12As he approached the
town gate, a dead person was being carried out — the only son of
his mother, and she was a widow.
And a large crowd from the town
was with her. 13When the Lord saw
her, his heart went out to her and
he said, "Don't cry."

Jn 11:1-44

14Then he went up and touched
the bier they were carrying him
on, and the bearers stood still. He
said, "Young man, I say to you, get
up!" 15The dead man sat up and
began to talk, and Jesus gave him
back to his mother.

1Ki 17:17-24; 2Ki 4:32-37

16They were all filled with awe
and praised God. "A great prophet has appeared among us," they
said. "God has come to help his
people." 17This news about Jesus
spread throughout Judea and the
surrounding country.

Mk 5:21-24,35-43

Jesus and John the Baptist

18John's disciples told him about
all these things. Calling two of
them, 19he sent them to the Lord
to ask, "Are you the one who is to
come, or should we expect someone else?"

Mt 3:1; Lk 5:33

20When the men came to Jesus,
they said, "John the Baptist sent
us to you to ask, 'Are you the one
who is to come, or should we expect someone else?' "

21 At that very time Jesus cured
many who had diseases, sicknesses and evil spirits, and gave sight
to many who were blind. 22 So he
replied to the messengers, "Go
back and report to John what you
have seen and heard: The blind receive sight, the lame walk, those
who have leprosy[a] are cleansed,
the deaf hear, the dead are raised,
and the good news is proclaimed
to the poor. 23 Blessed is anyone
who does not stumble on account
of me." Isa 29:18-19; Lk 4:18

24 After John's messengers left,
Jesus began to speak to the crowd
about John: "What did you go
out into the wilderness to see? A
reed swayed by the wind? 25 If not,
what did you go out to see? A man
dressed in fine clothes? No, those
who wear expensive clothes and
indulge in luxury are in palaces.
26 But what did you go out to see? A
prophet? Yes, I tell you, and more
than a prophet. 27 This is the one
about whom it is written: Mt 11:9

"'I will send my messenger
ahead of you,
who will prepare your way
before you.'[b]

28 I tell you, among those born of
women there is no one greater
than John; yet the one who is least
in the kingdom of God is greater
than he." Mt 3:2; 11:10; Mk 1:2

29 (All the people, even the tax
collectors, when they heard Jesus'
words, acknowledged that God's
way was right, because they had
been baptized by John. 30 But the
Pharisees and the experts in the
law rejected God's purpose for
themselves, because they had not
been baptized by John.)
Mt 22:35; Lk 3:12

31 Jesus went on to say, "To what,
then, can I compare the people
of this generation? What are they
like? 32 They are like children sitting in the marketplace and calling out to each other:

"'We played the pipe for you,
and you did not dance;
we sang a dirge,
and you did not cry.'

33 For John the Baptist came neither eating bread nor drinking
wine, and you say, 'He has a demon.' 34 The Son of Man came eating and drinking, and you say,
'Here is a glutton and a drunkard, a friend of tax collectors and
sinners.' 35 But wisdom is proved
right by all her children."
Mt 11:2-19; Lk 1:15

Jesus Anointed by a Sinful Woman

36 When one of the Pharisees invited Jesus to have dinner with
him, he went to the Pharisee's
house and reclined at the table.
37 A woman in that town who lived
a sinful life learned that Jesus was
eating at the Pharisee's house, so
she came there with an alabaster jar of perfume. 38 As she stood

[a] *22* The Greek word traditionally translated *leprosy* was used for various diseases affecting the skin. [b] *27* Mal. 3:1

behind him at his feet weeping, she began to wet his feet with her tears. Then she wiped them with her hair, kissed them and poured perfume on them.

39 When the Pharisee who had invited him saw this, he said to himself, "If this man were a prophet, he would know who is touching him and what kind of woman she is — that she is a sinner." Mt 21:11

40 Jesus answered him, "Simon, I have something to tell you."

"Tell me, teacher," he said.

41 "Two people owed money to a certain moneylender. One owed him five hundred denarii,[a] and the other fifty. 42 Neither of them had the money to pay him back, so he forgave the debts of both. Now which of them will love him more?"

43 Simon replied, "I suppose the one who had the bigger debt forgiven."

"You have judged correctly," Jesus said.

44 Then he turned toward the woman and said to Simon, "Do you see this woman? I came into your house. You did not give me any water for my feet, but she wet my feet with her tears and wiped them with her hair. 45 You did not give me a kiss, but this woman, from the time I entered, has not stopped kissing my feet. 46 You did not put oil on my head, but she has poured perfume on my feet. 47 Therefore, I tell you, her many sins have been forgiven — as her great love has shown. But whoever has been forgiven little loves little." Ge 18:4; Ps 23:5; 1Ti 5:10

48 Then Jesus said to her, "Your sins are forgiven." Mt 9:2

49 The other guests began to say among themselves, "Who is this who even forgives sins?"

50 Jesus said to the woman, "Your faith has saved you; go in peace." Mk 5:34; Lk 8:48; Ac 15:33

The Parable of the Sower

8 After this, Jesus traveled about from one town and village to another, proclaiming the good news of the kingdom of God. The Twelve were with him, 2 and also some women who had been cured of evil spirits and diseases: Mary (called Magdalene) from whom seven demons had come out; 3 Joanna the wife of Chuza, the manager of Herod's household; Susanna; and many others. These women were helping to support them out of their own means.

Mt 4:23; 14:1; 27:55-56

4 While a large crowd was gathering and people were coming to Jesus from town after town, he told this parable: 5 "A farmer went out to sow his seed. As he was scattering the seed, some fell along the path; it was trampled on, and the birds ate it up. 6 Some fell on rocky ground, and when it came up, the plants withered because they had no moisture. 7 Other seed

[a] 41 A denarius was the usual daily wage of a day laborer (see Matt. 20:2).

fell among thorns, which grew
up with it and choked the plants.
8Still other seed fell on good soil.
It came up and yielded a crop, a
hundred times more than was
sown."

When he said this, he called
out, "Whoever has ears to hear, let
them hear." Mt 11:15

9His disciples asked him what
this parable meant. 10He said, "The
knowledge of the secrets of the
kingdom of God has been given to
you, but to others I speak in parables, so that, Mt 13:11

> " 'though seeing, they may not
> see;
> though hearing, they may
> not understand.'[a]

Isa 6:9; Mt 13:13-14

11"This is the meaning of the
parable: The seed is the word
of God. 12Those along the path
are the ones who hear, and then
the devil comes and takes away
the word from their hearts, so
that they may not believe and
be saved. 13Those on the rocky
ground are the ones who receive
the word with joy when they hear
it, but they have no root. They believe for a while, but in the time of
testing they fall away. 14The seed
that fell among thorns stands for
those who hear, but as they go on
their way they are choked by life's
worries, riches and pleasures, and
they do not mature. 15But the seed
on good soil stands for those with
a noble and good heart, who hear
the word, retain it, and by perse-
vering produce a crop.

Mt 13:2-23; Mk 4:1-20

A Lamp on a Stand

16"No one lights a lamp and
hides it in a clay jar or puts it under a bed. Instead, they put it on
a stand, so that those who come
in can see the light. 17For there is
nothing hidden that will not be
disclosed, and nothing concealed
that will not be known or brought
out into the open. 18Therefore
consider carefully how you listen.
Whoever has will be given more;
whoever does not have, even what
they think they have will be taken
from them." Mt 5:15; Mk 4:22; Lk 19:26

Jesus' Mother and Brothers

19Now Jesus' mother and brothers came to see him, but they were
not able to get near him because
of the crowd. 20Someone told him,
"Your mother and brothers are
standing outside, wanting to see
you." Jn 7:5

21He replied, "My mother and
brothers are those who hear God's
word and put it into practice."

Mt 12:46-50; Mk 3:31-35

Jesus Calms the Storm

22One day Jesus said to his disciples, "Let us go over to the other
side of the lake." So they got into a
boat and set out. 23As they sailed,
he fell asleep. A squall came down

[a] 10 Isaiah 6:9

on the lake, so that the boat was
being swamped, and they were in
great danger.
24The disciples went and woke
him, saying, "Master, Master, we're
going to drown!" Mk 6:47-52; Jn 6:16-21
He got up and rebuked the
wind and the raging waters; the
storm subsided, and all was calm.
25"Where is your faith?" he asked
his disciples. Mt 8:23-27
In fear and amazement they
asked one another, "Who is this?
He commands even the winds and
the water, and they obey him."
Mk 4:36-41

Jesus Restores a Demon-Possessed Man

26They sailed to the region of
the Gerasenes,[a] which is across the
lake from Galilee. 27When Jesus
stepped ashore, he was met by a
demon-possessed man from the
town. For a long time this man
had not worn clothes or lived in a
house, but had lived in the tombs.
28When he saw Jesus, he cried out
and fell at his feet, shouting at
the top of his voice, "What do you
want with me, Jesus, Son of the
Most High God? I beg you, don't
torture me!" 29For Jesus had commanded the impure spirit to come
out of the man. Many times it had
seized him, and though he was
chained hand and foot and kept
under guard, he had broken his
chains and had been driven by the
demon into solitary places.
Mt 8:29; Mk 5:7
30Jesus asked him, "What is your
name?"
"Legion," he replied, because
many demons had gone into him.
31And they begged Jesus repeatedly not to order them to go into the
Abyss. Rev 9:1-2,11; 11:7
32A large herd of pigs was feeding there on the hillside. The demons begged Jesus to let them
go into the pigs, and he gave
them permission. 33When the demons came out of the man, they
went into the pigs, and the herd
rushed down the steep bank into
the lake and was drowned.
ver 22-23
34When those tending the pigs
saw what had happened, they ran
off and reported this in the town
and countryside, 35and the people went out to see what had happened. When they came to Jesus,
they found the man from whom
the demons had gone out, sitting
at Jesus' feet, dressed and in his
right mind; and they were afraid.
36Those who had seen it told the
people how the demon-possessed
man had been cured. 37Then all
the people of the region of the
Gerasenes asked Jesus to leave
them, because they were overcome with fear. So he got into the
boat and left. Mt 8:28-34
38The man from whom the demons had gone out begged to
go with him, but Jesus sent him
away, saying, 39"Return home and

[a] 26 Some manuscripts *Gadarenes*; other manuscripts *Gergesenes*; also in verse 37

tell how much God has done for
you." So the man went away and
told all over town how much Jesus
had done for him. Mk 5:1-20

Jesus Raises a Dead Girl and Heals a Sick Woman

40 Now when Jesus returned, a
crowd welcomed him, for they
were all expecting him. 41 Then a
man named Jairus, a synagogue
leader, came and fell at Jesus' feet,
pleading with him to come to his
house 42 because his only daughter,
a girl of about twelve, was dying.
Mk 5:22

As Jesus was on his way, the
crowds almost crushed him. 43 And
a woman was there who had been
subject to bleeding for twelve
years,[a] but no one could heal her.
44 She came up behind him and
touched the edge of his cloak,
and immediately her bleeding
stopped. Lev 15:25-30; Mt 9:20

45 "Who touched me?" Jesus
asked.

When they all denied it, Peter said, "Master, the people are
crowding and pressing against
you." Lk 5:5

46 But Jesus said, "Someone
touched me; I know that power
has gone out from me." Lk 5:17; 6:19

47 Then the woman, seeing that
she could not go unnoticed, came
trembling and fell at his feet. In
the presence of all the people, she
told why she had touched him
and how she had been instantly healed.
48 Then he said to her,
"Daughter, your faith has healed
you. Go in peace." Mt 9:22; Ac 15:33

49 While Jesus was still speaking,
someone came from the house
of Jairus, the synagogue leader.
"Your daughter is dead," he said.
"Don't bother the teacher anymore."
ver 41

50 Hearing this, Jesus said to Jairus, "Don't be afraid; just believe,
and she will be healed."

51 When he arrived at the house
of Jairus, he did not let anyone
go in with him except Peter, John
and James, and the child's father
and mother. 52 Meanwhile, all the
people were wailing and mourning for her. "Stop wailing," Jesus
said. "She is not dead but asleep."
Jn 11:11,13

53 They laughed at him, knowing that she was dead. 54 But he
took her by the hand and said,
"My child, get up!" 55 Her spirit returned, and at once she stood up.
Then Jesus told them to give her
something to eat. 56 Her parents
were astonished, but he ordered
them not to tell anyone what had
happened. Mt 9:18-26; Mk 5:22-43

Jesus Sends Out the Twelve

9 When Jesus had called the
Twelve together, he gave
them power and authority to
drive out all demons and to cure
diseases, 2 and he sent them out to
proclaim the kingdom of God and
to heal the sick. 3 He told them:

[a] 43 Many manuscripts *years, and she had spent all she had on doctors*

"Take nothing for the journey —
no staff, no bag, no bread, no
money, no extra shirt. [4]Whatever
house you enter, stay there until
you leave that town. [5]If people do
not welcome you, leave their town
and shake the dust off your feet
as a testimony against them." [6]So
they set out and went from village
to village, proclaiming the good
news and healing people everywhere. Mt 10:9-15; Mk 6:8-11

[7]Now Herod the tetrarch heard
about all that was going on. And he
was perplexed because some were
saying that John had been raised
from the dead, [8]others that Elijah
had appeared, and still others that
one of the prophets of long ago
had come back to life. [9]But Herod
said, "I beheaded John. Who, then,
is this I hear such things about?"
And he tried to see him.
Mt 14:1-2; Mk 6:14-16

Jesus Feeds the Five Thousand

[10]When the apostles returned,
they reported to Jesus what they
had done. Then he took them with
him and they withdrew by themselves to a town called Bethsaida,
[11]but the crowds learned about it
and followed him. He welcomed
them and spoke to them about
the kingdom of God, and healed
those who needed healing.
Mt 11:21; Mk 6:30

[12]Late in the afternoon the
Twelve came to him and said,
"Send the crowd away so they
can go to the surrounding villages and countryside and find food
and lodging, because we are in a
remote place here."

[13]He replied, "You give them
something to eat."
Mt 14:13-21; Mk 6:32-44

They answered, "We have only
five loaves of bread and two fish —
unless we go and buy food for all
this crowd." [14](About five thousand men were there.) Jn 6:5-13

But he said to his disciples,
"Have them sit down in groups of
about fifty each." [15]The disciples
did so, and everyone sat down.
[16]Taking the five loaves and the
two fish and looking up to heaven,
he gave thanks and broke them.
Then he gave them to the disciples
to distribute to the people. [17]They
all ate and were satisfied, and the
disciples picked up twelve basketfuls of broken pieces that were left
over. 2Ki 4:42-44

Peter Declares That Jesus Is the Messiah

[18]Once when Jesus was praying
in private and his disciples were
with him, he asked them, "Who do
the crowds say I am?" Lk 3:21

[19]They replied, "Some say John
the Baptist; others say Elijah; and
still others, that one of the prophets of long ago has come back to
life." Mt 3:1

[20]"But what about you?" he
asked. "Who do you say I am?"
Mt 16:13-16

Peter answered, "God's Messiah."
Mk 8:27-29; Jn 6:66-69

Jesus Predicts His Death

21 Jesus strictly warned them
not to tell this to anyone. 22 And
he said, "The Son of Man must
suffer many things and be rejected by the elders, the chief priests
and the teachers of the law, and
he must be killed and on the third
day be raised to life."

Mt 16:20-21; Mk 8:30

23 Then he said to them all:
"Whoever wants to be my disciple
must deny themselves and take
up their cross daily and follow me.
24 For whoever wants to save their
life will lose it, but whoever loses
their life for me will save it. 25 What
good is it for someone to gain the
whole world, and yet lose or forfeit their very self? 26 Whoever is
ashamed of me and my words,
the Son of Man will be ashamed of
them when he comes in his glory
and in the glory of the Father and
of the holy angels.

27 "Truly I tell you, some who are
standing here will not taste death
before they see the kingdom of
God." Mt 16:21-28; Mk 8:31-9:1

The Transfiguration

28 About eight days after Jesus
said this, he took Peter, John and
James with him and went up onto
a mountain to pray. 29 As he was
praying, the appearance of his face
changed, and his clothes became
as bright as a flash of lightning.
30 Two men, Moses and Elijah, appeared in glorious splendor, talking with Jesus. 31 They spoke about
his departure,[a] which he was about
to bring to fulfillment at Jerusalem. 32 Peter and his companions
were very sleepy, but when they
became fully awake, they saw his
glory and the two men standing
with him. 33 As the men were leaving Jesus, Peter said to him, "Master, it is good for us to be here. Let
us put up three shelters — one for
you, one for Moses and one for
Elijah." (He did not know what he
was saying.) Lk 3:21; 2Pe 1:15

34 While he was speaking, a cloud
appeared and covered them, and
they were afraid as they entered
the cloud. 35 A voice came from
the cloud, saying, "This is my Son,
whom I have chosen; listen to
him." 36 When the voice had spoken, they found that Jesus was
alone. The disciples kept this to
themselves and did not tell anyone at that time what they had
seen. Mt 17:1-8; Mk 9:2-8

Jesus Heals a Demon-Possessed Boy

37 The next day, when they came
down from the mountain, a large
crowd met him. 38 A man in the
crowd called out, "Teacher, I beg
you to look at my son, for he is
my only child. 39 A spirit seizes
him and he suddenly screams;
it throws him into convulsions
so that he foams at the mouth.
It scarcely ever leaves him and is

[a] *31* Greek *exodos*

destroying him. 40 I begged your disciples to drive it out, but they could not." Mt 17:14-18,22-23

41 "You unbelieving and perverse generation," Jesus replied, "how long shall I stay with you and put up with you? Bring your son here." Dt 32:5

42 Even while the boy was coming, the demon threw him to the ground in a convulsion. But Jesus rebuked the impure spirit, healed the boy and gave him back to his father. 43 And they were all amazed at the greatness of God.

Jesus Predicts His Death a Second Time

While everyone was marveling at all that Jesus did, he said to his disciples, 44 "Listen carefully to what I am about to tell you: The Son of Man is going to be delivered into the hands of men." 45 But they did not understand what this meant. It was hidden from them, so that they did not grasp it, and they were afraid to ask him about it. Mk 9:14-27,30-32

46 An argument started among the disciples as to which of them would be the greatest. 47 Jesus, knowing their thoughts, took a little child and had him stand beside him. 48 Then he said to them, "Whoever welcomes this little child in my name welcomes me; and whoever welcomes me welcomes the one who sent me. For it is the one who is least among you all who is the greatest." Mt 18:1-5

49 "Master," said John, "we saw someone driving out demons in your name and we tried to stop him, because he is not one of us." Lk 5:5

50 "Do not stop him," Jesus said, "for whoever is not against you is for you." Mt 12:30; Lk 11:23

Samaritan Opposition

51 As the time approached for him to be taken up to heaven, Jesus resolutely set out for Jerusalem. 52 And he sent messengers on ahead, who went into a Samaritan village to get things ready for him; 53 but the people there did not welcome him, because he was heading for Jerusalem. 54 When the disciples James and John saw this, they asked, "Lord, do you want us to call fire down from heaven to destroy them[a]?" 55 But Jesus turned and rebuked them. 56 Then he and his disciples went to another village. 2Ki 1:10,12; Mk 16:19; Lk 13:22

The Cost of Following Jesus

57 As they were walking along the road, a man said to him, "I will follow you wherever you go."

58 Jesus replied, "Foxes have dens and birds have nests, but the Son of Man has no place to lay his head."

59 He said to another man, "Follow me."

But he replied, "Lord, first let me go and bury my father."

[a] 54 Some manuscripts *them, just as Elijah did*

60Jesus said to him, "Let the
dead bury their own dead, but you
go and proclaim the kingdom of
God." Mt 8:19-22

61Still another said, "I will follow
you, Lord; but first let me go back
and say goodbye to my family."

1Ki 19:20

62Jesus replied, "No one who
puts a hand to the plow and looks
back is fit for service in the kingdom of God."

Jesus Sends Out the Seventy-Two

10 After this the Lord appointed seventy-two[a] others
and sent them two by two ahead
of him to every town and place
where he was about to go. 2He told
them, "The harvest is plentiful,
but the workers are few. Ask the
Lord of the harvest, therefore, to
send out workers into his harvest
field. 3Go! I am sending you out
like lambs among wolves. 4Do not
take a purse or bag or sandals; and
do not greet anyone on the road.

Mt 9:37-38; 10:16; Jn 4:35

5"When you enter a house, first
say, 'Peace to this house.' 6If someone who promotes peace is there,
your peace will rest on them; if
not, it will return to you. 7Stay
there, eating and drinking whatever they give you, for the worker
deserves his wages. Do not move
around from house to house.

Mt 10:10; 1Co 9:14; 1Ti 5:18

8"When you enter a town and
are welcomed, eat what is offered
to you. 9Heal the sick who are
there and tell them, 'The kingdom
of God has come near to you.' 10But
when you enter a town and are not
welcomed, go into its streets and
say, 11'Even the dust of your town
we wipe from our feet as a warning to you. Yet be sure of this: The
kingdom of God has come near.' 12I
tell you, it will be more bearable
on that day for Sodom than for
that town. Lk 9:3-5; 1Co 10:27

13"Woe to you, Chorazin! Woe
to you, Bethsaida! For if the miracles that were performed in you
had been performed in Tyre and
Sidon, they would have repented
long ago, sitting in sackcloth and
ashes. 14But it will be more bearable for Tyre and Sidon at the
judgment than for you. 15And you,
Capernaum, will you be lifted to
the heavens? No, you will go down
to Hades.[b] Mt 4:13; Rev 11:3

16"Whoever listens to you listens
to me; whoever rejects you rejects
me; but whoever rejects me rejects him who sent me."

Mt 10:40; Jn 13:20

17The seventy-two returned with
joy and said, "Lord, even the demons submit to us in your name."

Mk 16:17

18He replied, "I saw Satan fall
like lightning from heaven. 19I
have given you authority to trample on snakes and scorpions and
to overcome all the power of the
enemy; nothing will harm you.

[a] *1* Some manuscripts *seventy*; also in verse 17 [b] *15* That is, the realm of the dead

20However, do not rejoice that the
spirits submit to you, but rejoice
that your names are written in
heaven." Ex 32:32; Heb 12:23; Rev 13:8
21At that time Jesus, full of joy
through the Holy Spirit, said, "I
praise you, Father, Lord of heaven
and earth, because you have hidden these things from the wise
and learned, and revealed them to
little children. Yes, Father, for this
is what you were pleased to do. 1Co 1:26-29
22"All things have been committed to me by my Father. No one
knows who the Son is except the
Father, and no one knows who the
Father is except the Son and those
to whom the Son chooses to reveal
him." Mt 11:21-23,25-27
23Then he turned to his disciples and said privately, "Blessed
are the eyes that see what you see.
24For I tell you that many prophets
and kings wanted to see what you
see but did not see it, and to hear
what you hear but did not hear it." Mt 13:16-17

The Parable of the Good Samaritan

25On one occasion an expert
in the law stood up to test Jesus.
"Teacher," he asked, "what must I
do to inherit eternal life?" Mt 19:16; Lk 18:18
26"What is written in the Law?"
he replied. "How do you read it?"
27He answered, "'Love the Lord
your God with all your heart and
with all your soul and with all your
strength and with all your mind'[a];
and, 'Love your neighbor as yourself.'[b]" Lev 19:18; Dt 6:5
28"You have answered correctly," Jesus replied. "Do this and you
will live." Mt 22:34-40; Mk 12:28-31
29But he wanted to justify himself, so he asked Jesus, "And who
is my neighbor?" Lk 16:15
30In reply Jesus said: "A man
was going down from Jerusalem
to Jericho, when he was attacked
by robbers. They stripped him of
his clothes, beat him and went
away, leaving him half dead. 31A
priest happened to be going down
the same road, and when he saw
the man, he passed by on the other side. 32So too, a Levite, when he
came to the place and saw him,
passed by on the other side. 33But
a Samaritan, as he traveled, came
where the man was; and when he
saw him, he took pity on him. 34He
went to him and bandaged his
wounds, pouring on oil and wine.
Then he put the man on his own
donkey, brought him to an inn
and took care of him. 35The next
day he took out two denarii[c] and
gave them to the innkeeper. 'Look
after him,' he said, 'and when I return, I will reimburse you for any
extra expense you may have.' Mt 10:5; Lev 21:1-3
36"Which of these three do you
think was a neighbor to the man
who fell into the hands of robbers?"

[a] 27 Deut. 6:5 [b] 27 Lev. 19:18
[c] 35 A denarius was the usual daily wage of a day laborer (see Matt. 20:2).

37 The expert in the law replied,
"The one who had mercy on him."
Jesus told him, "Go and do like-
wise."

At the Home of Martha and Mary

38 As Jesus and his disciples
were on their way, he came to a
village where a woman named
Martha opened her home to him.
39 She had a sister called Mary, who
sat at the Lord's feet listening to
what he said. 40 But Martha was
distracted by all the preparations
that had to be made. She came to
him and asked, "Lord, don't you
care that my sister has left me to
do the work by myself? Tell her to
help me!" Lk 8:35; Jn 11:1
41 "Martha, Martha," the Lord answered, "you are worried and upset about many things, 42 but few
things are needed — or indeed
only one.[a] Mary has chosen what
is better, and it will not be taken
away from her."

Ps 27:4; Mt 6:25-34; Lk 12:11,22

Jesus' Teaching on Prayer

11 One day Jesus was praying in
a certain place. When he finished, one of his disciples said to
him, "Lord, teach us to pray, just
as John taught his disciples."

Lk 3:21; Jn 13:13

2 He said to them, "When you
pray, say:

"'Father,[b]
hallowed be your name,
your kingdom come.[c] Mt 3:2
3 Give us each day our daily
bread.
4 Forgive us our sins,
for we also forgive
everyone who
sins against us.[d]

Mt 18:35; Mk 11:25

And lead us not into
temptation.[e]'" Mt 6:9-13

5 Then Jesus said to them, "Suppose you have a friend, and you
go to him at midnight and say,
'Friend, lend me three loaves of
bread; 6 a friend of mine on a journey has come to me, and I have no
food to offer him.' 7 And suppose
the one inside answers, 'Don't
bother me. The door is already
locked, and my children and I are
in bed. I can't get up and give you
anything.' 8 I tell you, even though
he will not get up and give you
the bread because of friendship,
yet because of your shameless au-
dacity[f] he will surely get up and
give you as much as you need.

Lk 18:1-6

9 "So I say to you: Ask and it will
be given to you; seek and you will
find; knock and the door will be
opened to you. 10 For everyone who
asks receives; the one who seeks
finds; and to the one who knocks,
the door will be opened. Mt 7:7

[a] 42 Some manuscripts *but only one thing is needed* [b] 2 Some manuscripts *Our Father in heaven* [c] 2 Some manuscripts *come. May your will be done on earth as it is in heaven.* [d] 4 Greek *everyone who is indebted to us* [e] 4 Some manuscripts *temptation, but deliver us from the evil one* [f] 8 Or *yet to preserve his good name*

[11]"Which of you fathers, if your
son asks for[a] a fish, will give him
a snake instead? [12]Or if he asks
for an egg, will give him a scorpion? [13]If you then, though you are
evil, know how to give good gifts
to your children, how much more
will your Father in heaven give the
Holy Spirit to those who ask him!"

Jesus and Beelzebul

[14]Jesus was driving out a demon
that was mute. When the demon
left, the man who had been mute
spoke, and the crowd was amazed.
[15]But some of them said, "By Beelzebul, the prince of demons, he
is driving out demons." [16]Others
tested him by asking for a sign
from heaven. Mt 12:22,24

[17]Jesus knew their thoughts
and said to them: "Any kingdom
divided against itself will be ruined, and a house divided against
itself will fall. [18]If Satan is divided
against himself, how can his kingdom stand? I say this because you
claim that I drive out demons by
Beelzebul. [19]Now if I drive out demons by Beelzebul, by whom do
your followers drive them out?
So then, they will be your judges.
[20]But if I drive out demons by the
finger of God, then the kingdom
of God has come upon you.

Mt 12:25-28

[21]"When a strong man, fully
armed, guards his own house, his
possessions are safe. [22]But when
someone stronger attacks and
overpowers him, he takes away
the armor in which the man trusted and divides up his plunder.

Mk 3:23-27

[23]"Whoever is not with me is
against me, and whoever does not
gather with me scatters.

Mt 12:30; Lk 9:50

[24]"When an impure spirit comes
out of a person, it goes through
arid places seeking rest and does
not find it. Then it says, 'I will return to the house I left.' [25]When it
arrives, it finds the house swept
clean and put in order. [26]Then it
goes and takes seven other spirits
more wicked than itself, and they
go in and live there. And the final
condition of that person is worse
than the first." Mt 12:43-45

[27]As Jesus was saying these
things, a woman in the crowd
called out, "Blessed is the mother who gave you birth and nursed
you." Lk 23:29

[28]He replied, "Blessed rather are
those who hear the word of God
and obey it." Lk 8:21; Jn 14:21

The Sign of Jonah

[29]As the crowds increased, Jesus
said, "This is a wicked generation.
It asks for a sign, but none will be
given it except the sign of Jonah.
[30]For as Jonah was a sign to the
Ninevites, so also will the Son of
Man be to this generation. [31]The
Queen of the South will rise at the
judgment with the people of this
generation and condemn them,

[a] *11* Some manuscripts *for bread, will give him a stone? Or if he asks for*

for she came from the ends of the earth to listen to Solomon's wisdom; and now something greater than Solomon is here. 32 The men of Nineveh will stand up at the judgment with this generation and condemn it, for they repented at the preaching of Jonah; and now something greater than Jonah is here. Mt 12:39-42

The Lamp of the Body

33 "No one lights a lamp and puts it in a place where it will be hidden, or under a bowl. Instead they put it on its stand, so that those who come in may see the light. 34 Your eye is the lamp of your body. When your eyes are healthy,[a] your whole body also is full of light. But when they are unhealthy,[b] your body also is full of darkness. 35 See to it, then, that the light within you is not darkness. 36 Therefore, if your whole body is full of light, and no part of it dark, it will be just as full of light as when a lamp shines its light on you." Mt 6:22-23; Mk 4:21; Lk 8:16

Woes on the Pharisees and the Experts in the Law

37 When Jesus had finished speaking, a Pharisee invited him to eat with him; so he went in and reclined at the table. 38 But the Pharisee was surprised when he noticed that Jesus did not first wash before the meal. Mk 7:3-4

39 Then the Lord said to him, "Now then, you Pharisees clean the outside of the cup and dish, but inside you are full of greed and wickedness. 40 You foolish people! Did not the one who made the outside make the inside also? 41 But now as for what is inside you — be generous to the poor, and everything will be clean for you.

Mt 23:25-26; Lk 12:33

42 "Woe to you Pharisees, because you give God a tenth of your mint, rue and all other kinds of garden herbs, but you neglect justice and the love of God. You should have practiced the latter without leaving the former undone.

Mic 6:8; Mt 23:23

43 "Woe to you Pharisees, because you love the most important seats in the synagogues and respectful greetings in the marketplaces.

Mt 23:6-7; Mk 12:38-39

44 "Woe to you, because you are like unmarked graves, which people walk over without knowing it."

Mt 23:27

45 One of the experts in the law answered him, "Teacher, when you say these things, you insult us also." Mt 22:35

46 Jesus replied, "And you experts in the law, woe to you, because you load people down with burdens they can hardly carry, and you yourselves will not lift one finger to help them. Mt 23:4

47 "Woe to you, because you build tombs for the prophets, and it was your ancestors who killed them.

[a] 34 The Greek for *healthy* here implies *generous*. [b] 34 The Greek for *unhealthy* here implies *stingy*.

48So you testify that you approve
of what your ancestors did; they
killed the prophets, and you build
their tombs. 49Because of this, God
in his wisdom said, 'I will send
them prophets and apostles, some
of whom they will kill and others
they will persecute.' 50Therefore
this generation will be held responsible for the blood of all the
prophets that has been shed since
the beginning of the world, 51from
the blood of Abel to the blood of
Zechariah, who was killed between the altar and the sanctuary.
Yes, I tell you, this generation will
be held responsible for it all.

Mt 23:29-32,34-36

52"Woe to you experts in the law,
because you have taken away the
key to knowledge. You yourselves
have not entered, and you have
hindered those who were entering." Mt 23:13

53When Jesus went outside, the
Pharisees and the teachers of the
law began to oppose him fiercely and to besiege him with questions, 54waiting to catch him in
something he might say. Mk 12:13

Warnings and Encouragements

12 Meanwhile, when a crowd of
many thousands had gath-
ered, so that they were trampling
on one another, Jesus began to
speak first to his disciples, saying:
"Be[a] on your guard against the
yeast of the Pharisees, which is
hypocrisy. 2There is nothing concealed that will not be disclosed,
or hidden that will not be made
known. 3What you have said in the
dark will be heard in the daylight,
and what you have whispered in
the ear in the inner rooms will be
proclaimed from the roofs.

Mk 4:22; Lk 8:17

4"I tell you, my friends, do not
be afraid of those who kill the
body and after that can do no
more. 5But I will show you whom
you should fear: Fear him who, after your body has been killed, has
authority to throw you into hell.
Yes, I tell you, fear him. 6Are not
five sparrows sold for two pen-
nies? Yet not one of them is forgotten by God. 7Indeed, the very
hairs of your head are all numbered. Don't be afraid; you are
worth more than many sparrows.

Mt 10:30; Jn 15:14,15; Heb 10:31

8"I tell you, whoever publicly
acknowledges me before others,
the Son of Man will also acknowledge before the angels of God.
9But whoever disowns me before
others will be disowned before the
angels of God. 10And everyone who
speaks a word against the Son of
Man will be forgiven, but anyone
who blasphemes against the Holy
Spirit will not be forgiven.

Mt 10:26-33; 1Jn 5:16

11"When you are brought before
synagogues, rulers and authorities, do not worry about how you
will defend yourselves or what
you will say, 12for the Holy Spirit

[a] 1 *Or speak to his disciples, saying: "First of all, be*

will teach you at that time what you should say." Mt 10:20; Mk 13:11

The Parable of the Rich Fool

13Someone in the crowd said to him, "Teacher, tell my brother to divide the inheritance with me."

14Jesus replied, "Man, who appointed me a judge or an arbiter between you?" 15Then he said to them, "Watch out! Be on your guard against all kinds of greed; life does not consist in an abundance of possessions."

Job 20:20; Ps 62:10

16And he told them this parable: "The ground of a certain rich man yielded an abundant harvest. 17He thought to himself, 'What shall I do? I have no place to store my crops.'

18"Then he said, 'This is what I'll do. I will tear down my barns and build bigger ones, and there I will store my surplus grain. 19And I'll say to myself, "You have plenty of grain laid up for many years. Take life easy; eat, drink and be merry."'

20"But God said to him, 'You fool! This very night your life will be demanded from you. Then who will get what you have prepared for yourself?' Ps 39:6; Jer 17:11

21"This is how it will be with whoever stores up things for themselves but is not rich toward God." ver 33

Do Not Worry

22Then Jesus said to his disciples: "Therefore I tell you, do not worry about your life, what you will eat; or about your body, what you will wear. 23For life is more than food, and the body more than clothes. 24Consider the ravens: They do not sow or reap, they have no storeroom or barn; yet God feeds them. And how much more valuable you are than birds! 25Who of you by worrying can add a single hour to your life[a]? 26Since you cannot do this very little thing, why do you worry about the rest?

Job 38:41; Ps 147:9

27"Consider how the wild flowers grow. They do not labor or spin. Yet I tell you, not even Solomon in all his splendor was dressed like one of these. 28If that is how God clothes the grass of the field, which is here today, and tomorrow is thrown into the fire, how much more will he clothe you — you of little faith! 29And do not set your heart on what you will eat or drink; do not worry about it. 30For the pagan world runs after all such things, and your Father knows that you need them. 31But seek his kingdom, and these things will be given to you as well.

Mt 6:25-33

32"Do not be afraid, little flock, for your Father has been pleased to give you the kingdom. 33Sell your possessions and give to the poor. Provide purses for yourselves that will not wear out, a treasure in heaven that will never fail, where no thief comes near

[a] 25 Or *single cubit to your height*

and no moth destroys. 34For where
your treasure is, there your heart
will be also. Mt 6:20-21; 14:27

Watchfulness

35"Be dressed ready for service
and keep your lamps burning,
36like servants waiting for their
master to return from a wedding
banquet, so that when he comes
and knocks they can immediately open the door for him. 37It will
be good for those servants whose
master finds them watching when
he comes. Truly I tell you, he will
dress himself to serve, will have
them recline at the table and will
come and wait on them. 38It will
be good for those servants whose
master finds them ready, even
if he comes in the middle of the
night or toward daybreak. 39But
understand this: If the owner of
the house had known at what hour
the thief was coming, he would
not have let his house be broken
into. 40You also must be ready, because the Son of Man will come at
an hour when you do not expect
him." Mt 25:1-13; Mk 13:33-37

41Peter asked, "Lord, are you
telling this parable to us, or to everyone?"

42The Lord answered, "Who then
is the faithful and wise manager,
whom the master puts in charge
of his servants to give them their
food allowance at the proper
time? 43It will be good for that servant whom the master finds doing so when he returns. 44Truly I
tell you, he will put him in charge
of all his possessions. 45But suppose the servant says to himself,
'My master is taking a long time
in coming,' and he then begins
to beat the other servants, both
men and women, and to eat and
drink and get drunk. 46The master
of that servant will come on a day
when he does not expect him and
at an hour he is not aware of. He
will cut him to pieces and assign
him a place with the unbelievers.
Mt 24:43-51

47"The servant who knows the
master's will and does not get
ready or does not do what the
master wants will be beaten with
many blows. 48But the one who
does not know and does things deserving punishment will be beat-
en with few blows. From everyone
who has been given much, much
will be demanded; and from the
one who has been entrusted with
much, much more will be asked.
Lev 5:17; Dt 25:2

Not Peace but Division

49"I have come to bring fire on
the earth, and how I wish it were
already kindled! 50But I have a
baptism to undergo, and what
constraint I am under until it is
completed! 51Do you think I came
to bring peace on earth? No, I tell
you, but division. 52From now on
there will be five in one family
divided against each other, three
against two and two against three.
53They will be divided, father

against son and son against father,
mother against daughter and
daughter against mother, mother-in-law against daughter-in-
law and daughter-in-law against
mother-in-law." Mt 10:34-36

Interpreting the Times

54He said to the crowd: "When
you see a cloud rising in the west,
immediately you say, 'It's going to
rain,' and it does. 55And when the
south wind blows, you say, 'It's
going to be hot,' and it is. 56Hypo-
crites! You know how to interpret
the appearance of the earth and
the sky. How is it that you don't
know how to interpret this present time? Mt 16:2-3
57"Why don't you judge for yourselves what is right? 58As you are
going with your adversary to the
magistrate, try hard to be reconciled on the way, or your adversary
may drag you off to the judge, and
the judge turn you over to the officer, and the officer throw you into
prison. 59I tell you, you will not get
out until you have paid the last
penny." Mt 5:25-26; Mk 12:42

Repent or Perish

13 Now there were some present at that time who told
Jesus about the Galileans whose
blood Pilate had mixed with
their sacrifices. 2Jesus answered,
"Do you think that these Galileans were worse sinners than all
the other Galileans because they
suffered this way? 3I tell you, no!
But unless you repent, you too
will all perish. 4Or those eighteen
who died when the tower in Siloam fell on them — do you think
they were more guilty than all the
others living in Jerusalem? 5I tell
you, no! But unless you repent,
you too will all perish."
Mt 27:2; Jn 9:2-3,7,11
6Then he told this parable: "A
man had a fig tree growing in his
vineyard, and he went to look for
fruit on it but did not find any. 7So
he said to the man who took care
of the vineyard, 'For three years
now I've been coming to look for
fruit on this fig tree and haven't
found any. Cut it down! Why
should it use up the soil?'
Mt 3:10; 21:19
8"'Sir,' the man replied, 'leave it
alone for one more year, and I'll
dig around it and fertilize it. 9If it
bears fruit next year, fine! If not,
then cut it down.'"

Jesus Heals a Crippled Woman on the Sabbath

10On a Sabbath Jesus was teaching in one of the synagogues,
11and a woman was there who
had been crippled by a spirit for
eighteen years. She was bent
over and could not straighten up
at all. 12When Jesus saw her, he
called her forward and said to her,
"Woman, you are set free from
your infirmity." 13Then he put his
hands on her, and immediately
she straightened up and praised
God. Mt 4:23; Mk 5:23

14 Indignant because Jesus had
healed on the Sabbath, the synagogue leader said to the people,
"There are six days for work. So
come and be healed on those days,
not on the Sabbath."
Ex 20:9; Mk 5:22; Lk 14:3

15 The Lord answered him, "You
hypocrites! Doesn't each of you on
the Sabbath untie your ox or donkey from the stall and lead it out
to give it water? 16 Then should not
this woman, a daughter of Abraham, whom Satan has kept bound
for eighteen long years, be set free
on the Sabbath day from what
bound her?" Lk 14:5; 19:9

17 When he said this, all his opponents were humiliated, but the
people were delighted with all the
wonderful things he was doing.
Isa 66:5

The Parables of the Mustard Seed and the Yeast

18 Then Jesus asked, "What is the
kingdom of God like? What shall I
compare it to? 19 It is like a mustard
seed, which a man took and planted in his garden. It grew and became a tree, and the birds perched
in its branches." Mk 4:30-32

20 Again he asked, "What shall
I compare the kingdom of God
to? 21 It is like yeast that a woman
took and mixed into about sixty
pounds[a] of flour until it worked
all through the dough." Mt 13:31-33

The Narrow Door

22 Then Jesus went through the
towns and villages, teaching as
he made his way to Jerusalem.
23 Someone asked him, "Lord,
are only a few people going to be
saved?" Lk 9:51

He said to them, 24 "Make every effort to enter through the
narrow door, because many, I tell
you, will try to enter and will not
be able to. 25 Once the owner of the
house gets up and closes the door,
you will stand outside knocking
and pleading, 'Sir, open the door
for us.' Mt 7:13

"But he will answer, 'I don't
know you or where you come
from.' Mt 7:23; 25:10-12

26 "Then you will say, 'We ate and
drank with you, and you taught in
our streets.'

27 "But he will reply, 'I don't
know you or where you come
from. Away from me, all you evildoers!' Mt 7:23; 25:41

28 "There will be weeping there,
and gnashing of teeth, when you
see Abraham, Isaac and Jacob and
all the prophets in the kingdom of
God, but you yourselves thrown
out. 29 People will come from east
and west and north and south,
and will take their places at the
feast in the kingdom of God. 30 Indeed there are those who are last
who will be first, and first who will
be last." Mt 19:30

Jesus' Sorrow for Jerusalem

31 At that time some Pharisees
came to Jesus and said to him,

[a] 21 Or about 27 kilograms

"Leave this place and go somewhere else. Herod wants to kill
you." Mt 14:1
32 He replied, "Go tell that fox, 'I
will keep on driving out demons
and healing people today and tomorrow, and on the third day I
will reach my goal.' 33 In any case,
I must press on today and tomorrow and the next day — for surely
no prophet can die outside Jerusalem! Mt 21:11; Heb 2:10
34 "Jerusalem, Jerusalem, you
who kill the prophets and stone
those sent to you, how often I have
longed to gather your children together, as a hen gathers her chicks
under her wings, and you were
not willing. 35 Look, your house is
left to you desolate. I tell you, you
will not see me again until you
say, 'Blessed is he who comes in
the name of the Lord.'[a]"
Mt 23:37-39; Lk 19:41

Jesus at a Pharisee's House

14 One Sabbath, when Jesus
went to eat in the house of a
prominent Pharisee, he was being
carefully watched. 2 There in front
of him was a man suffering from
abnormal swelling of his body.
3 Jesus asked the Pharisees and
experts in the law, "Is it lawful to
heal on the Sabbath or not?" 4 But
they remained silent. So taking
hold of the man, he healed him
and sent him on his way.
Mt 12:2; 22:35
5 Then he asked them, "If one of
you has a child[b] or an ox that falls
into a well on the Sabbath day, will
you not immediately pull it out?"
6 And they had nothing to say.
Lk 13:15
7 When he noticed how the
guests picked the places of honor
at the table, he told them this parable: 8 "When someone invites you
to a wedding feast, do not take the
place of honor, for a person more
distinguished than you may have
been invited. 9 If so, the host who
invited both of you will come and
say to you, 'Give this person your
seat.' Then, humiliated, you will
have to take the least important
place. 10 But when you are invited, take the lowest place, so that
when your host comes, he will say
to you, 'Friend, move up to a better place.' Then you will be honored in the presence of all the other guests. 11 For all those who exalt
themselves will be humbled, and
those who humble themselves
will be exalted." Pr 25:6-7
12 Then Jesus said to his host,
"When you give a luncheon or
dinner, do not invite your friends,
your brothers or sisters, your relatives, or your rich neighbors; if you
do, they may invite you back and
so you will be repaid. 13 But when
you give a banquet, invite the
poor, the crippled, the lame, the
blind, 14 and you will be blessed.
Although they cannot repay you,
you will be repaid at the resurrection of the righteous." Ac 24:15

[a] 35 Psalm 118:26 [b] 5 Some manuscripts *donkey*

The Parable of the Great Banquet

15When one of those at the table with him heard this, he said to
Jesus, "Blessed is the one who will
eat at the feast in the kingdom of
God." Rev 19:9

16Jesus replied: "A certain man
was preparing a great banquet and
invited many guests. 17At the time
of the banquet he sent his servant
to tell those who had been invited, 'Come, for everything is now
ready.'

18"But they all alike began to
make excuses. The first said, 'I
have just bought a field, and I must
go and see it. Please excuse me.'

19"Another said, 'I have just
bought five yoke of oxen, and I'm
on my way to try them out. Please
excuse me.'

20"Still another said, 'I just got
married, so I can't come.'

21"The servant came back and
reported this to his master. Then
the owner of the house became
angry and ordered his servant, 'Go
out quickly into the streets and al-
leys of the town and bring in the
poor, the crippled, the blind and
the lame.' ver 13

22" 'Sir,' the servant said, 'what
you ordered has been done, but
there is still room.'

23"Then the master told his
servant, 'Go out to the roads and
country lanes and compel them to
come in, so that my house will be
full. 24I tell you, not one of those
who were invited will get a taste
of my banquet.' " Mt 22:2-14; Ac 13:46

The Cost of Being a Disciple

25Large crowds were traveling
with Jesus, and turning to them
he said: 26"If anyone comes to
me and does not hate father and
mother, wife and children, brothers and sisters — yes, even their
own life — such a person cannot
be my disciple. 27And whoever
does not carry their cross and follow me cannot be my disciple.
Mt 10:37-38; Lk 9:23

28"Suppose one of you wants to
build a tower. Won't you first sit
down and estimate the cost to see
if you have enough money to complete it? 29For if you lay the foundation and are not able to finish it,
everyone who sees it will ridicule
you, 30saying, 'This person began
to build and wasn't able to finish.'

31"Or suppose a king is about to
go to war against another king.
Won't he first sit down and consider whether he is able with ten
thousand men to oppose the one
coming against him with twenty
thousand? 32If he is not able, he
will send a delegation while the
other is still a long way off and
will ask for terms of peace. 33In the
same way, those of you who do not
give up everything you have cannot be my disciples. Php 3:7-8

34"Salt is good, but if it loses its
saltiness, how can it be made salty
again? 35It is fit neither for the
soil nor for the manure pile; it is
thrown out. Mt 5:13; Mk 9:50

"Whoever has ears to hear, let
them hear." Mt 11:15

The Parable of the Lost Sheep

15 Now the tax collectors and sinners were all gathering around to hear Jesus. 2But the Pharisees and the teachers of the law muttered, "This man welcomes sinners and eats with them."

Mt 9:11; Lk 5:29

3Then Jesus told them this parable: 4"Suppose one of you has a hundred sheep and loses one of them. Doesn't he leave the ninety-nine in the open country and go after the lost sheep until he finds it? 5And when he finds it, he joyfully puts it on his shoulders 6and goes home. Then he calls his friends and neighbors together and says, 'Rejoice with me; I have found my lost sheep.' 7I tell you that in the same way there will be more rejoicing in heaven over one sinner who repents than over ninety-nine righteous persons who do not need to repent.

Mt 18:12-14

The Parable of the Lost Coin

8"Or suppose a woman has ten silver coins[a] and loses one. Doesn't she light a lamp, sweep the house and search carefully until she finds it? 9And when she finds it, she calls her friends and neighbors together and says, 'Rejoice with me; I have found my lost coin.' 10In the same way, I tell you, there is rejoicing in the presence of the angels of God over one sinner who repents."

ver 6-7

The Parable of the Lost Son

11Jesus continued: "There was a man who had two sons. 12The younger one said to his father, 'Father, give me my share of the estate.' So he divided his property between them.

Dt 21:17; Mt 21:28

13"Not long after that, the younger son got together all he had, set off for a distant country and there squandered his wealth in wild living. 14After he had spent everything, there was a severe famine in that whole country, and he began to be in need. 15So he went and hired himself out to a citizen of that country, who sent him to his fields to feed pigs. 16He longed to fill his stomach with the pods that the pigs were eating, but no one gave him anything.

Lev 11:7; Lk 16:1

17"When he came to his senses, he said, 'How many of my father's hired servants have food to spare, and here I am starving to death! 18I will set out and go back to my father and say to him: Father, I have sinned against heaven and against you. 19I am no longer worthy to be called your son; make me like one of your hired servants.' 20So he got up and went to his father.

Lev 26:40; Mt 3:2

"But while he was still a long way off, his father saw him and was filled with compassion for him; he ran to his son, threw his arms around him and kissed him.

Ge 45:14-15; Ac 20:37

[a] 8 Greek *ten drachmas*, each worth about a day's wages

21“The son said to him, ‘Father,
I have sinned against heaven and
against you. I am no longer worthy to be called your son.’ Ps 51:4

22“But the father said to his servants, ‘Quick! Bring the best robe
and put it on him. Put a ring on
his finger and sandals on his feet.
23Bring the fattened calf and kill
it. Let’s have a feast and celebrate.
24For this son of mine was dead
and is alive again; he was lost and
is found.’ So they began to celebrate. Eph 2:1,5; 5:14; 1Ti 5:6

25“Meanwhile, the older son
was in the field. When he came
near the house, he heard music
and dancing. 26So he called one of
the servants and asked him what
was going on. 27‘Your brother has
come,’ he replied, ‘and your father has killed the fattened calf
because he has him back safe and
sound.’

28“The older brother became
angry and refused to go in. So his
father went out and pleaded with
him. 29But he answered his father,
‘Look! All these years I’ve been
slaving for you and never disobeyed your orders. Yet you never gave me even a young goat so
I could celebrate with my friends.
30But when this son of yours who
has squandered your property
with prostitutes comes home, you
kill the fattened calf for him!’
Pr 29:3; Jnh 4:1

31“ ‘My son,’ the father said, ‘you
are always with me, and everything I have is yours. 32But we had
to celebrate and be glad, because
this brother of yours was dead and
is alive again; he was lost and is
found.’ ” Mal 3:17

The Parable of the Shrewd Manager

16 Jesus told his disciples:
“There was a rich man whose
manager was accused of wasting
his possessions. 2So he called him
in and asked him, ‘What is this I
hear about you? Give an account
of your management, because you
cannot be manager any longer.’
Lk 15:13,30

3“The manager said to himself,
‘What shall I do now? My master is taking away my job. I’m not
strong enough to dig, and I’m
ashamed to beg— 4I know what
I’ll do so that, when I lose my job
here, people will welcome me into
their houses.’

5“So he called in each one of his
master’s debtors. He asked the
first, ‘How much do you owe my
master?’

6“ ‘Nine hundred gallons[a] of olive oil,’ he replied.

“The manager told him, ‘Take
your bill, sit down quickly, and
make it four hundred and fifty.’

7“Then he asked the second,
‘And how much do you owe?’

“ ‘A thousand bushels[b] of wheat,’
he replied.

“He told him, ‘Take your bill and
make it eight hundred.’

[a] 6 Or about 3,000 liters [b] 7 Or about 30 tons

8“The master commended the
dishonest manager because he
had acted shrewdly. For the people of this world are more shrewd
in dealing with their own kind
than are the people of the light.
9I tell you, use worldly wealth to
gain friends for yourselves, so that
when it is gone, you will be welcomed into eternal dwellings.
Mt 19:21; Jn 12:36

10“Whoever can be trusted with
very little can also be trusted with
much, and whoever is dishonest
with very little will also be dishonest with much. 11So if you have
not been trustworthy in handling
worldly wealth, who will trust you
with true riches? 12And if you have
not been trustworthy with someone else’s property, who will give
you property of your own?
Mt 25:21,23; Lk 19:17

13“No one can serve two masters. Either you will hate the one
and love the other, or you will be
devoted to the one and despise
the other. You cannot serve both
God and money.” Mt 6:24

14The Pharisees, who loved
money, heard all this and were
sneering at Jesus. 15He said to
them, “You are the ones who justify yourselves in the eyes of others,
but God knows your hearts. What
people value highly is detestable
in God’s sight. 1Sa 16:7; Lk 23:35; 1Ti 3:3

Additional Teachings

16“The Law and the Prophets
were proclaimed until John. Since
that time, the good news of the
kingdom of God is being preached,
and everyone is forcing their way
into it. 17It is easier for heaven and
earth to disappear than for the
least stroke of a pen to drop out of
the Law. Mt 5:18; 11:12-13

18“Anyone who divorces his wife
and marries another woman commits adultery, and the man who
marries a divorced woman commits adultery. Mt 5:31-32; 1Co 7:10-11

The Rich Man and Lazarus

19“There was a rich man who was
dressed in purple and fine linen
and lived in luxury every day. 20At
his gate was laid a beggar named
Lazarus, covered with sores 21and
longing to eat what fell from the
rich man’s table. Even the dogs
came and licked his sores.
Eze 16:49; Ac 3:2

22“The time came when the beggar died and the angels carried
him to Abraham’s side. The rich
man also died and was buried. 23In
Hades, where he was in torment,
he looked up and saw Abraham
far away, with Lazarus by his side.
24So he called to him, ‘Father Abraham, have pity on me and send
Lazarus to dip the tip of his finger
in water and cool my tongue, because I am in agony in this fire.’
Mt 5:22; Lk 3:8

25“But Abraham replied, ‘Son,
remember that in your lifetime
you received your good things,
while Lazarus received bad things,
but now he is comforted here and

you are in agony. 26 And besides all
this, between us and you a great
chasm has been set in place, so
that those who want to go from
here to you cannot, nor can anyone cross over from there to us.'
Ps 17:14; Lk 6:21,24-25

27 "He answered, 'Then I beg you,
father, send Lazarus to my family, 28 for I have five brothers. Let
him warn them, so that they will
not also come to this place of torment.' Ac 2:40; 1Th 4:6

29 "Abraham replied, 'They have
Moses and the Prophets; let them
listen to them.' Lk 4:17; Jn 5:45-47

30 " 'No, father Abraham,' he said,
'but if someone from the dead
goes to them, they will repent.'
Lk 3:8

31 "He said to him, 'If they do not
listen to Moses and the Prophets,
they will not be convinced even if
someone rises from the dead.' "

Sin, Faith, Duty

17 Jesus said to his disciples:
"Things that cause people
to stumble are bound to come,
but woe to anyone through whom
they come. 2 It would be better for
them to be thrown into the sea
with a millstone tied around their
neck than to cause one of these
little ones to stumble. 3 So watch
yourselves. Mt 18:7; Mk 10:24; Lk 10:21

"If your brother or sister[a] sins
against you, rebuke them; and if
they repent, forgive them. 4 Even if
they sin against you seven times
in a day and seven times come
back to you saying 'I repent,' you
must forgive them." Mt 18:15,21-22

5 The apostles said to the Lord,
"Increase our faith!" Mk 6:30; Lk 7:13

6 He replied, "If you have faith as
small as a mustard seed, you can
say to this mulberry tree, 'Be uprooted and planted in the sea,' and
it will obey you. Mt 17:20; 21:21

7 "Suppose one of you has a servant plowing or looking after the
sheep. Will he say to the servant
when he comes in from the field,
'Come along now and sit down to
eat'? 8 Won't he rather say, 'Prepare
my supper, get yourself ready and
wait on me while I eat and drink;
after that you may eat and drink'?
9 Will he thank the servant because he did what he was told to
do? 10 So you also, when you have
done everything you were told to
do, should say, 'We are unworthy
servants; we have only done our
duty.' " Lk 12:37; 1Co 9:16

Jesus Heals Ten Men With Leprosy

11 Now on his way to Jerusalem,
Jesus traveled along the border
between Samaria and Galilee. 12 As
he was going into a village, ten
men who had leprosy[b] met him.
They stood at a distance 13 and
called out in a loud voice, "Jesus,
Master, have pity on us!"
Lk 5:5; 9:51; Jn 4:3-4

[a] 3 The Greek word for *brother or sister* (*adelphos*) refers here to a fellow disciple, whether man or woman. [b] 12 The Greek word traditionally translated *leprosy* was used for various diseases affecting the skin.

14When he saw them, he said,
"Go, show yourselves to the
priests." And as they went, they
were cleansed. Lev 14:2; Mt 8:4
15One of them, when he saw he
was healed, came back, praising
God in a loud voice. 16He threw
himself at Jesus' feet and thanked
him — and he was a Samaritan.
Mt 9:8; 10:5
17Jesus asked, "Were not all
ten cleansed? Where are the other nine? 18Has no one returned to
give praise to God except this foreigner?" 19Then he said to him,
"Rise and go; your faith has made
you well." Mt 9:22

The Coming of the Kingdom of God

20Once, on being asked by the
Pharisees when the kingdom of
God would come, Jesus replied,
"The coming of the kingdom of
God is not something that can be
observed, 21nor will people say,
'Here it is,' or 'There it is,' because
the kingdom of God is in your
midst."[a] ver 23; Mt 3:2
22Then he said to his disciples,
"The time is coming when you
will long to see one of the days
of the Son of Man, but you will
not see it. 23People will tell you,
'There he is!' or 'Here he is!' Do
not go running off after them.
24For the Son of Man in his day[b]
will be like the lightning, which
flashes and lights up the sky
from one end to the other. 25But
first he must suffer many things
and be rejected by this generation. Mt 9:15; Lk 9:22; 21:8
26"Just as it was in the days of
Noah, so also will it be in the days
of the Son of Man. 27People were
eating, drinking, marrying and
being given in marriage up to the
day Noah entered the ark. Then
the flood came and destroyed
them all. Ge 7:6-24; Mt 24:37-39
28"It was the same in the days of
Lot. People were eating and drinking, buying and selling, planting
and building. 29But the day Lot
left Sodom, fire and sulfur rained
down from heaven and destroyed
them all. Ge 19:1-28
30"It will be just like this on the
day the Son of Man is revealed.
31On that day no one who is on the
housetop, with possessions inside,
should go down to get them. Likewise, no one in the field should go
back for anything. 32Remember
Lot's wife! 33Whoever tries to keep
their life will lose it, and whoever
loses their life will preserve it. 34I
tell you, on that night two people
will be in one bed; one will be tak-
en and the other left. 35Two wom-
en will be grinding grain together; one will be taken and the other
left." [36][c] Mt 24:41; Mk 13:15-16
37"Where, Lord?" they asked.
He replied, "Where there is a
dead body, there the vultures will
gather." Mt 24:28

[a] 21 Or *is within you* [b] 24 Some manuscripts do not have *in his day.* [c] 36 Some manuscripts include here words similar to Matt. 24:40.

The Parable of the Persistent Widow

18 Then Jesus told his disciples a parable to show them
that they should always pray and
not give up. 2He said: "In a certain
town there was a judge who neither feared God nor cared what
people thought. 3And there was a
widow in that town who kept coming to him with the plea, 'Grant
me justice against my adversary.'
Isa 40:31; Lk 11:5-8

4"For some time he refused. But
finally he said to himself, 'Even
though I don't fear God or care
what people think, 5yet because
this widow keeps bothering me,
I will see that she gets justice, so
that she won't eventually come
and attack me!'" Lk 11:8

6And the Lord said, "Listen to
what the unjust judge says. 7And
will not God bring about justice
for his chosen ones, who cry out
to him day and night? Will he keep
putting them off? 8I tell you, he
will see that they get justice, and
quickly. However, when the Son of
Man comes, will he find faith on
the earth?" Mt 8:20; Rev 6:10

The Parable of the Pharisee and the Tax Collector

9To some who were confident
of their own righteousness and
looked down on everyone else,
Jesus told this parable: 10"Two
men went up to the temple to
pray, one a Pharisee and the other a tax collector. 11The Pharisee
stood by himself and prayed: 'God,
I thank you that I am not like other people — robbers, evildoers,
adulterers — or even like this tax
collector. 12I fast twice a week and
give a tenth of all I get.'
Isa 65:5; Lk 16:15

13"But the tax collector stood at
a distance. He would not even look
up to heaven, but beat his breast
and said, 'God, have mercy on me,
a sinner.' Lk 5:32; 23:48

14"I tell you that this man, rather
than the other, went home justified before God. For all those who
exalt themselves will be humbled,
and those who humble themselves will be exalted."
Mt 23:12; Lk 14:11

The Little Children and Jesus

15People were also bringing babies to Jesus for him to place his
hands on them. When the disciples saw this, they rebuked them.
16But Jesus called the children to
him and said, "Let the little children come to me, and do not hinder them, for the kingdom of God
belongs to such as these. 17Truly I
tell you, anyone who will not receive the kingdom of God like a
little child will never enter it."
Mt 18:3

The Rich and the Kingdom of God

18A certain ruler asked him,
"Good teacher, what must I do to
inherit eternal life?" Lk 10:25
19"Why do you call me good?"
Jesus answered. "No one is good —

except God alone. 20You know the
commandments: 'You shall not
commit adultery, you shall not
murder, you shall not steal, you
shall not give false testimony,
honor your father and mother.'[a]"

Ex 20:12-16; Dt 5:16-20; Ro 13:9

21"All these I have kept since I
was a boy," he said.

22When Jesus heard this, he said
to him, "You still lack one thing.
Sell everything you have and give
to the poor, and you will have
treasure in heaven. Then come,
follow me." Mt 6:20; Ac 2:45

23When he heard this, he became very sad, because he was
very wealthy. 24Jesus looked at
him and said, "How hard it is for
the rich to enter the kingdom of
God! 25Indeed, it is easier for a
camel to go through the eye of a
needle than for someone who is
rich to enter the kingdom of God."

Pr 11:28

26Those who heard this asked,
"Who then can be saved?"

27Jesus replied, "What is impossible with man is possible with
God." Mt 19:26

28Peter said to him, "We have
left all we had to follow you!"

Mt 4:19

29"Truly I tell you," Jesus said to
them, "no one who has left home
or wife or brothers or sisters or
parents or children for the sake
of the kingdom of God 30will fail
to receive many times as much in
this age, and in the age to come
eternal life." Mt 19:16-29; Mk 10:17-30

Jesus Predicts His Death a Third Time

31Jesus took the Twelve aside and
told them, "We are going up to Jerusalem, and everything that is written by the prophets about the Son
of Man will be fulfilled. 32He will be
delivered over to the Gentiles. They
will mock him, insult him and spit
on him; 33they will flog him and kill
him. On the third day he will rise
again." Mt 20:17-19; Mk 10:32-34

34The disciples did not understand any of this. Its meaning was
hidden from them, and they did
not know what he was talking
about. Mk 9:32; Lk 9:45

A Blind Beggar Receives His Sight

35As Jesus approached Jericho, a
blind man was sitting by the roadside begging. 36When he heard
the crowd going by, he asked what
was happening. 37They told him,
"Jesus of Nazareth is passing by."

Lk 19:1,4

38He called out, "Jesus, Son of
David, have mercy on me!"

Mt 9:27; 17:15; Lk 18:13

39Those who led the way rebuked him and told him to be quiet, but he shouted all the more,
"Son of David, have mercy on me!"

40Jesus stopped and ordered the
man to be brought to him. When
he came near, Jesus asked him,
41"What do you want me to do for
you?"

"Lord, I want to see," he replied.

[a] 20 Exodus 20:12-16; Deut. 5:16-20

42 Jesus said to him, "Receive your sight; your faith has healed you." 43 Immediately he received his sight and followed Jesus, praising God. When all the people saw it, they also praised God.

Mt 20:29-34; Mk 10:46-52

Zacchaeus the Tax Collector

19 Jesus entered Jericho and was passing through. 2 A man was there by the name of Zacchaeus; he was a chief tax collector and was wealthy. 3 He wanted to see who Jesus was, but because he was short he could not see over the crowd. 4 So he ran ahead and climbed a sycamore-fig tree to see him, since Jesus was coming that way.

1Ki 10:27; 1Ch 27:28

5 When Jesus reached the spot, he looked up and said to him, "Zacchaeus, come down immediately. I must stay at your house today." 6 So he came down at once and welcomed him gladly.

7 All the people saw this and began to mutter, "He has gone to be the guest of a sinner."

Mt 9:11

8 But Zacchaeus stood up and said to the Lord, "Look, Lord! Here and now I give half of my possessions to the poor, and if I have cheated anybody out of anything, I will pay back four times the amount."

Ex 22:1; Lk 7:13

9 Jesus said to him, "Today salvation has come to this house, because this man, too, is a son of Abraham. 10 For the Son of Man came to seek and to save the lost."

Lk 3:8; Jn 3:17

The Parable of the Ten Minas

11 While they were listening to this, he went on to tell them a parable, because he was near Jerusalem and the people thought that the kingdom of God was going to appear at once. 12 He said: "A man of noble birth went to a distant country to have himself appointed king and then to return. 13 So he called ten of his servants and gave them ten minas.[a] 'Put this money to work,' he said, 'until I come back.'

Mk 13:34; Lk 17:20

14 "But his subjects hated him and sent a delegation after him to say, 'We don't want this man to be our king.'

15 "He was made king, however, and returned home. Then he sent for the servants to whom he had given the money, in order to find out what they had gained with it.

16 "The first one came and said, 'Sir, your mina has earned ten more.'

17 " 'Well done, my good servant!' his master replied. 'Because you have been trustworthy in a very small matter, take charge of ten cities.'

Pr 27:18; Lk 16:10

18 "The second came and said, 'Sir, your mina has earned five more.'

19 "His master answered, 'You take charge of five cities.'

20 "Then another servant came and said, 'Sir, here is your mina; I

[a] 13 A mina was about three months' wages.

have kept it laid away in a piece of
cloth. [21]I was afraid of you, because
you are a hard man. You take out
what you did not put in and reap
what you did not sow.' Mt 25:24
[22]"His master replied, 'I will
judge you by your own words, you
wicked servant! You knew, did
you, that I am a hard man, taking out what I did not put in, and
reaping what I did not sow? [23]Why
then didn't you put my money on
deposit, so that when I came back,
I could have collected it with interest?' 2Sa 1:16; Mt 25:26
[24]"Then he said to those standing by, 'Take his mina away from
him and give it to the one who has
ten minas.'
[25]"'Sir,' they said, 'he already
has ten!'
[26]"He replied, 'I tell you that
to everyone who has, more will
be given, but as for the one who
has nothing, even what they have
will be taken away. [27]But those enemies of mine who did not want
me to be king over them — bring
them here and kill them in front
of me.'" Mt 25:14-30

Jesus Comes to Jerusalem as King

[28]After Jesus had said this, he
went on ahead, going up to Jerusalem. [29]As he approached Bethphage and Bethany at the hill called
the Mount of Olives, he sent two
of his disciples, saying to them,
[30]"Go to the village ahead of you,
and as you enter it, you will find a
colt tied there, which no one has
ever ridden. Untie it and bring it
here. [31]If anyone asks you, 'Why
are you untying it?' say, 'The Lord
needs it.'" Mt 21:1-9; Mk 10:32
[32]Those who were sent ahead
went and found it just as he had
told them. [33]As they were untying
the colt, its owners asked them,
"Why are you untying the colt?" Lk 22:13
[34]They replied, "The Lord
needs it."
[35]They brought it to Jesus, threw
their cloaks on the colt and put
Jesus on it. [36]As he went along,
people spread their cloaks on the
road. Mk 11:1-10; 2Ki 9:13
[37]When he came near the place
where the road goes down the
Mount of Olives, the whole crowd
of disciples began joyfully to
praise God in loud voices for all
the miracles they had seen: Mt 21:1

[38]"Blessed is the king who comes
in the name of the
Lord!"[a] Ps 118:26; Lk 13:35

"Peace in heaven and glory in
the highest!" Jn 12:12-15

[39]Some of the Pharisees in the
crowd said to Jesus, "Teacher, rebuke your disciples!" Mt 21:15-16
[40]"I tell you," he replied, "if they
keep quiet, the stones will cry
out." Hab 2:11
[41]As he approached Jerusalem
and saw the city, he wept over it
[42]and said, "If you, even you, had
only known on this day what

[a] *38* Psalm 118:26

would bring you peace — but now it is hidden from your eyes. [43]The days will come upon you when your enemies will build an embankment against you and encircle you and hem you in on every side. [44]They will dash you to the ground, you and the children within your walls. They will not leave one stone on another, because you did not recognize the time of God's coming to you." Lk 21:6; 1Pe 2:12

Jesus at the Temple

[45]When Jesus entered the temple courts, he began to drive out those who were selling. [46]"It is written," he said to them, "'My house will be a house of prayer'[a]; but you have made it 'a den of robbers.'[b]" Mt 21:12-16; Isa 56:7; Jer 7:11

[47]Every day he was teaching at the temple. But the chief priests, the teachers of the law and the leaders among the people were trying to kill him. [48]Yet they could not find any way to do it, because all the people hung on his words. Mt 26:55; Mk 11:18

The Authority of Jesus Questioned

20 One day as Jesus was teaching the people in the temple courts and proclaiming the good news, the chief priests and the teachers of the law, together with the elders, came up to him. [2]"Tell us by what authority you are doing these things," they said. "Who gave you this authority?" Lk 8:1; Ac 4:7

[3]He replied, "I will also ask you a question. Tell me: [4]John's baptism — was it from heaven, or of human origin?" Mk 1:4

[5]They discussed it among themselves and said, "If we say, 'From heaven,' he will ask, 'Why didn't you believe him?' [6]But if we say, 'Of human origin,' all the people will stone us, because they are persuaded that John was a prophet." Mt 11:9; Lk 7:29

[7]So they answered, "We don't know where it was from."

[8]Jesus said, "Neither will I tell you by what authority I am doing these things." Mt 21:23-27; Mk 11:27-33

The Parable of the Tenants

[9]He went on to tell the people this parable: "A man planted a vineyard, rented it to some farmers and went away for a long time. [10]At harvest time he sent a servant to the tenants so they would give him some of the fruit of the vineyard. But the tenants beat him and sent him away empty-handed. [11]He sent another servant, but that one also they beat and treated shamefully and sent away empty-handed. [12]He sent still a third, and they wounded him and threw him out. Isa 5:1-7; Mt 25:14

[13]"Then the owner of the vineyard said, 'What shall I do? I will send my son, whom I love; perhaps they will respect him.' Mt 3:17

[14]"But when the tenants saw him, they talked the matter over.

[a] 46 Isaiah 56:7 [b] 46 Jer. 7:11

'This is the heir,' they said. 'Let's
kill him, and the inheritance will
be ours.' 15So they threw him out
of the vineyard and killed him.
"What then will the owner of
the vineyard do to them? 16He will
come and kill those tenants and
give the vineyard to others." Lk 19:27
When the people heard this,
they said, "God forbid!"
17Jesus looked directly at them
and asked, "Then what is the
meaning of that which is written:

"'The stone the builders
rejected
has become the
cornerstone'[a]?

18Everyone who falls on that stone
will be broken to pieces; anyone
on whom it falls will be crushed."
Isa 8:14-15; Ac 4:11
19The teachers of the law and the
chief priests looked for a way to
arrest him immediately, because
they knew he had spoken this parable against them. But they were
afraid of the people.
Mt 21:33-46; Mk 12:1-12

Paying Taxes to Caesar

20Keeping a close watch on him,
they sent spies, who pretended to
be sincere. They hoped to catch
Jesus in something he said, so that
they might hand him over to the
power and authority of the governor. 21So the spies questioned
him: "Teacher, we know that you
speak and teach what is right, and
that you do not show partiality
but teach the way of God in accordance with the truth. 22Is it right
for us to pay taxes to Caesar or
not?" Mt 12:10; Jn 3:2
23He saw through their duplicity and said to them, 24"Show me
a denarius. Whose image and inscription are on it?"
"Caesar's," they replied.
25He said to them, "Then give
back to Caesar what is Caesar's,
and to God what is God's."
Lk 23:2; Ro 13:7
26They were unable to trap him
in what he had said there in public. And astonished by his answer,
they became silent.
Mt 22:15-22; Mk 12:13-17

The Resurrection and Marriage

27Some of the Sadducees, who
say there is no resurrection, came
to Jesus with a question. 28"Teacher," they said, "Moses wrote for us
that if a man's brother dies and
leaves a wife but no children, the
man must marry the widow and
raise up offspring for his brother.
29Now there were seven brothers.
The first one married a woman
and died childless. 30The second
31and then the third married her,
and in the same way the seven
died, leaving no children. 32Fi-
nally, the woman died too. 33Now
then, at the resurrection whose
wife will she be, since the seven
were married to her?" Dt 25:5; Ac 23:8
34Jesus replied, "The people of
this age marry and are given in

[a] 17 Psalm 118:22

marriage. 35But those who are considered worthy of taking part in
the age to come and in the resurrection from the dead will neither
marry nor be given in marriage,
36and they can no longer die; for
they are like the angels. They are
God's children, since they are children of the resurrection. 37But in
the account of the burning bush,
even Moses showed that the dead
rise, for he calls the Lord 'the God
of Abraham, and the God of Isaac,
and the God of Jacob.'[a] 38He is not
the God of the dead, but of the living, for to him all are alive."

Ex 3:6; 1Jn 3:1-2

39Some of the teachers of the
law responded, "Well said, teacher!" 40And no one dared to ask him
any more questions.

Mt 22:23-33; Mk 12:18-27

Whose Son Is the Messiah?

41Then Jesus said to them, "Why
is it said that the Messiah is the
son of David? 42David himself declares in the Book of Psalms: Mt 1:1

"'The Lord said to my Lord:
"Sit at my right hand
43until I make your enemies
a footstool for your feet."'[b]

Ps 110:1; Mt 22:44

44David calls him 'Lord.' How then
can he be his son?"

Warning Against the Teachers of the Law

45While all the people were listening, Jesus said to his disciples,
46"Beware of the teachers of the
law. They like to walk around in
flowing robes and love to be greeted with respect in the marketplaces and have the most important seats in the synagogues and
the places of honor at banquets.
47They devour widows' houses and
for a show make lengthy prayers.
These men will be punished most
severely." Mt 22:41-23:7; Mk 12:35-40

The Widow's Offering

21 As Jesus looked up, he saw
the rich putting their gifts
into the temple treasury. 2He also
saw a poor widow put in two very
small copper coins. 3"Truly I tell
you," he said, "this poor widow
has put in more than all the others. 4All these people gave their
gifts out of their wealth; but she
out of her poverty put in all she
had to live on." Mk 12:41-44

The Destruction of the Temple and Signs of the End Times

5Some of his disciples were re-
marking about how the temple
was adorned with beautiful stones
and with gifts dedicated to God.
But Jesus said, 6"As for what you
see here, the time will come when
not one stone will be left on another; every one of them will be
thrown down." Lk 19:44

7"Teacher," they asked, "when
will these things happen? And
what will be the sign that they are
about to take place?"

[a] 37 Exodus 3:6 [b] 43 Psalm 110:1

8He replied: "Watch out that
you are not deceived. For many
will come in my name, claiming,
'I am he,' and, 'The time is near.'
Do not follow them. 9When you
hear of wars and uprisings, do not
be frightened. These things must
happen first, but the end will not
come right away." Lk 17:23

10Then he said to them: "Nation
will rise against nation, and kingdom against kingdom. 11There will
be great earthquakes, famines
and pestilences in various places,
and fearful events and great signs
from heaven. 2Ch 15:6; Isa 29:6

12"But before all this, they will
seize you and persecute you. They
will hand you over to synagogues
and put you in prison, and you will
be brought before kings and governors, and all on account of my
name. 13And so you will bear testimony to me. 14But make up your
mind not to worry beforehand how
you will defend yourselves. 15For I
will give you words and wisdom
that none of your adversaries will
be able to resist or contradict. 16You
will be betrayed even by parents,
brothers and sisters, relatives and
friends, and thcy will put some of
you to death. 17Everyone will hate
you because of me. 18But not a hair
of your head will perish. 19Stand
firm, and you will win life. Mt 10:17-22

20"When you see Jerusalem being surrounded by armies, you will
know that its desolation is near.
21Then let those who are in Judea
flee to the mountains, let those in
the city get out, and let those in
the country not enter the city. 22For
this is the time of punishment in
fulfillment of all that has been
written. 23How dreadful it will be
in those days for pregnant women
and nursing mothers! There will be
great distress in the land and wrath
against this people. 24They will fall
by the sword and will be taken as
prisoners to all the nations. Jerusalem will be trampled on by the
Gentiles until the times of the Gentiles are fulfilled. Isa 63:18; Da 8:13

25"There will be signs in the sun,
moon and stars. On the earth, nations will be in anguish and per-
plexity at the roaring and tossing
of the sea. 26People will faint from
terror, apprehensive of what is
coming on the world, for the heavenly bodies will be shaken. 27At
that time they will see the Son of
Man coming in a cloud with power and great glory. 28When these
things begin to take place, stand
up and lift up your heads, because
your redemption is drawing near."
Lk 18:7; Rev 1:7

29He told them this parable:
"Look at the fig tree and all the
trees. 30When they sprout leaves,
you can see for yourselves and
know that summer is near. 31Even
so, when you see these things happening, you know that the kingdom of God is near. Mt 3:2

32"Truly I tell you, this generation will certainly not pass away
until all these things have happened. 33Heaven and earth will

pass away, but my words will never pass away. Mt 5:18; Lk 11:50
34“Be careful, or your hearts will
be weighed down with carousing,
drunkenness and the anxieties of
life, and that day will close on you
suddenly like a trap. 35For it will
come on all those who live on the
face of the whole earth. 36Be always on the watch, and pray that
you may be able to escape all that
is about to happen, and that you
may be able to stand before the
Son of Man.” Mk 4:19; 1Th 5:2-7
37Each day Jesus was teaching
at the temple, and each evening
he went out to spend the night on
the hill called the Mount of Olives,
38and all the people came early in
the morning to hear him at the
temple. Mk 11:19; Jn 8:2

Judas Agrees to Betray Jesus

22 Now the Festival of Unleavened Bread, called the Passover, was approaching, 2and the
chief priests and the teachers of
the law were looking for some way
to get rid of Jesus, for they were
afraid of the people. 3Then Satan
entered Judas, called Iscariot, one
of the Twelve. 4And Judas went
to the chief priests and the officers of the temple guard and discussed with them how he might
betray Jesus. 5They were delighted and agreed to give him money.
6He consented, and watched for an
opportunity to hand Jesus over to
them when no crowd was present.
Mt 26:2-5; Mk 14:1-2,10-11

The Last Supper

7Then came the day of Unleavened Bread on which the Passover
lamb had to be sacrificed. 8Jesus
sent Peter and John, saying, “Go
and make preparations for us to
eat the Passover.” Dt 16:5-8; Ac 3:1,11
9“Where do you want us to prepare for it?” they asked.
10He replied, “As you enter the
city, a man carrying a jar of water will meet you. Follow him to
the house that he enters, 11and say
to the owner of the house, ‘The
Teacher asks: Where is the guest
room, where I may eat the Passover with my disciples?’ 12He will
show you a large room upstairs,
all furnished. Make preparations
there.”
13They left and found things just
as Jesus had told them. So they
prepared the Passover.
Mt 26:17-19; Mk 14:12-16
14When the hour came, Jesus
and his apostles reclined at the table. 15And he said to them, “I have
eagerly desired to eat this Passover with you before I suffer. 16For
I tell you, I will not eat it again until it finds fulfillment in the kingdom of God.” Lk 14:15; Rev 19:9
17After taking the cup, he gave
thanks and said, “Take this and
divide it among you. 18For I tell
you I will not drink again from the
fruit of the vine until the kingdom
of God comes.”
19And he took bread, gave
thanks and broke it, and gave it
to them, saying, “This is my body

given for you; do this in remembrance of me."

Mt 26:26-29; Mk 14:22-25; 1Co 11:23-25

20 In the same way, after the
supper he took the cup, saying,
"This cup is the new covenant in
my blood, which is poured out for
you.[a] 21 But the hand of him who
is going to betray me is with mine
on the table. 22 The Son of Man
will go as it has been decreed.
But woe to that man who betrays
him!" 23 They began to question
among themselves which of them
it might be who would do this.

Mt 26:21-24; Mk 14:18-21; Jn 13:21-30

24 A dispute also arose among
them as to which of them was
considered to be greatest. 25 Jesus
said to them, "The kings of the
Gentiles lord it over them; and
those who exercise authority over
them call themselves Benefactors.
26 But you are not to be like that.
Instead, the greatest among you
should be like the youngest, and
the one who rules like the one
who serves. 27 For who is greater, the one who is at the table or
the one who serves? Is it not the
one who is at the table? But I am
among you as one who serves.
28 You are those who have stood
by me in my trials. 29 And I con-
fer on you a kingdom, just as my
Father conferred one on me, 30 so
that you may eat and drink at my
table in my kingdom and sit on
thrones, judging the twelve tribes
of Israel. Mt 20:25-28; Mk 10:42-45

31 "Simon, Simon, Satan has
asked to sift all of you as wheat.
32 But I have prayed for you, Simon, that your faith may not fail.
And when you have turned back,
strengthen your brothers."

Jn 21:15-17

33 But he replied, "Lord, I am
ready to go with you to prison and
to death." Jn 11:16

34 Jesus answered, "I tell you, Peter, before the rooster crows today,
you will deny three times that you
know me."

Mt 26:33-35; Mk 14:29-31; Jn 13:37-38

35 Then Jesus asked them, "When
I sent you without purse, bag or
sandals, did you lack anything?"

Mt 10:9-10; Lk 9:3; 10:4

"Nothing," they answered.

36 He said to them, "But now
if you have a purse, take it, and
also a bag; and if you don't have
a sword, sell your cloak and buy
one. 37 It is written: 'And he was
numbered with the transgressors'[b]; and I tell you that this
must be fulfilled in me. Yes, what
is written about me is reaching its
fulfillment." Isa 53:12

38 The disciples said, "See, Lord,
here are two swords."

"That's enough!" he replied.

Jesus Prays on the Mount of Olives

39 Jesus went out as usual to the
Mount of Olives, and his disciples
followed him. 40 On reaching the
place, he said to them, "Pray that

[a] 19,20 Some manuscripts do not have *given for you . . . poured out for you.*
[b] 37 Isaiah 53:12

you will not fall into temptation."
41He withdrew about a stone's
throw beyond them, knelt down
and prayed, 42"Father, if you are
willing, take this cup from me; yet
not my will, but yours be done."
43An angel from heaven appeared
to him and strengthened him.
44And being in anguish, he prayed
more earnestly, and his sweat was
like drops of blood falling to the
ground.[a] Mt 4:11; 6:13; Lk 21:37

45When he rose from prayer
and went back to the disciples,
he found them asleep, exhausted from sorrow. 46"Why are you
sleeping?" he asked them. "Get up
and pray so that you will not fall
into temptation."

Mt 26:36-46; Mk 14:32-42

Jesus Arrested

47While he was still speaking
a crowd came up, and the man
who was called Judas, one of the
Twelve, was leading them. He approached Jesus to kiss him, 48but
Jesus asked him, "Judas, are you
betraying the Son of Man with a
kiss?"

49When Jesus' followers saw
what was going to happen, they
said, "Lord, should we strike with
our swords?" 50And one of them
struck the servant of the high
priest, cutting off his right ear.

51But Jesus answered, "No more
of this!" And he touched the man's
ear and healed him.

52Then Jesus said to the chief
priests, the officers of the temple
guard, and the elders, who had
come for him, "Am I leading a rebellion, that you have come with
swords and clubs? 53Every day I
was with you in the temple courts,
and you did not lay a hand on me.
But this is your hour — when darkness reigns."

Mt 26:47-56; Mk 14:43-50; Jn 18:3-11

Peter Disowns Jesus

54Then seizing him, they led
him away and took him into the
house of the high priest. Peter followed at a distance. 55And when
some there had kindled a fire in
the middle of the courtyard and
had sat down together, Peter sat
down with them. 56A servant girl
saw him seated there in the fire-
light. She looked closely at him
and said, "This man was with
him." Mt 26:57-58; Mk 14:53-54

57But he denied it. "Woman, I
don't know him," he said.

58A little later someone else saw
him and said, "You also are one of
them."

"Man, I am not!" Peter replied.

59About an hour later another asserted, "Certainly this fellow
was with him, for he is a Galilean."

Lk 23:6

60Peter replied, "Man, I don't
know what you're talking about!"
Just as he was speaking, the rooster crowed. 61The Lord turned and
looked straight at Peter. Then
Peter remembered the word the

[a] 43,44 Many early manuscripts do not have verses 43 and 44.

Lord had spoken to him: "Before
the rooster crows today, you will
disown me three times." 62And he
went outside and wept bitterly.
Mt 26:69-75; Mk 14:66-72; Jn 18:16-18,25-27

The Guards Mock Jesus

63The men who were guarding
Jesus began mocking and beating
him. 64They blindfolded him and
demanded, "Prophesy! Who hit
you?" 65And they said many other
insulting things to him.
Mt 26:67-68; Mk 14:65; Jn 18:22-23

Jesus Before Pilate and Herod

66At daybreak the council of
the elders of the people, both the
chief priests and the teachers of
the law, met together, and Jesus
was led before them. 67"If you are
the Messiah," they said, "tell us."
Mt 27:1; Mk 15:1

Jesus answered, "If I tell you,
you will not believe me, 68and if I
asked you, you would not answer.
69But from now on, the Son of Man
will be seated at the right hand of
the mighty God." Mk 16:19; Lk 20:3-8

70They all asked, "Are you then
the Son of God?" Mt 4:3

He replied, "You say that I am."
Mt 27:11; Lk 23:3

71Then they said, "Why do we
need any more testimony? We
have heard it from his own lips."
Mt 26:63-66; Mk 14:61-63; Jn 18:19-21

23 Then the whole assembly
rose and led him off to Pilate. 2And they began to accuse
him, saying, "We have found this
man subverting our nation. He opposes payment of taxes to Caesar
and claims to be Messiah, a king."
Lk 20:22; Jn 19:12

3So Pilate asked Jesus, "Are you
the king of the Jews?"

"You have said so," Jesus re-
plied. Mt 27:11-14; Mk 15:2-5; Jn 18:29-37

4Then Pilate announced to the
chief priests and the crowd, "I find
no basis for a charge against this
man." Mt 27:23; 2Co 5:21

5But they insisted, "He stirs up
the people all over Judea by his
teaching. He started in Galilee
and has come all the way here."
Mk 1:14

6On hearing this, Pilate asked if
the man was a Galilean. 7When he
learned that Jesus was under Herod's jurisdiction, he sent him to
Herod, who was also in Jerusalem
at that time. Mt 14:1; Lk 3:1

8When Herod saw Jesus, he was
greatly pleased, because for a long
time he had been wanting to see
him. From what he had heard
about him, he hoped to see him
perform a sign of some sort. 9He
plied him with many questions,
but Jesus gave him no answer.
10The chief priests and the teachers of the law were standing there,
vehemently accusing him. 11Then
Herod and his soldiers ridiculed
and mocked him. Dressing him
in an elegant robe, they sent him
back to Pilate. 12That day Herod
and Pilate became friends — before this they had been enemies.
Mk 15:17-19; Lk 9:9; Ac 4:27

13 Pilate called together the chief
priests, the rulers and the people,
14 and said to them, "You brought
me this man as one who was inciting the people to rebellion. I
have examined him in your presence and have found no basis for
your charges against him. 15 Neither has Herod, for he sent him
back to us; as you can see, he has
done nothing to deserve death.
16 Therefore, I will punish him and
then release him." [17][a]

Mt 27:26; Jn 19:1

18 But the whole crowd shouted,
"Away with this man! Release Barabbas to us!" 19 (Barabbas had been
thrown into prison for an insurrection in the city, and for murder.) Ac 3:13-14

20 Wanting to release Jesus, Pilate appealed to them again. 21 But
they kept shouting, "Crucify him!
Crucify him!"

22 For the third time he spoke to
them: "Why? What crime has this
man committed? I have found
in him no grounds for the death
penalty. Therefore I will have him
punished and then release him."

ver 16

23 But with loud shouts they in-
sistently demanded that he be
crucified, and their shouts prevailed. 24 So Pilate decided to grant
their demand. 25 He released the
man who had been thrown into
prison for insurrection and murder, the one they asked for, and
surrendered Jesus to their will.

Mt 27:15-26; Mk 15:6-15; Jn 18:39-19:16

The Crucifixion of Jesus

26 As the soldiers led him away,
they seized Simon from Cyrene,
who was on his way in from the
country, and put the cross on him
and made him carry it behind
Jesus. 27 A large number of people
followed him, including women
who mourned and wailed for him.
28 Jesus turned and said to them,
"Daughters of Jerusalem, do not
weep for me; weep for yourselves
and for your children. 29 For the
time will come when you will say,
'Blessed are the childless women,
the wombs that never bore and
the breasts that never nursed!'
30 Then

Mt 24:19; Lk 19:41-44

"'they will say to the
mountains, "Fall on us!"
and to the hills, "Cover us!"'[b]

31 For if people do these things
when the tree is green, what will
happen when it is dry?"

Eze 20:47; Hos 10:8; Rev 6:16

32 Two other men, both criminals, were also led out with him
to be executed. 33 When they came
to the place called the Skull, they
crucified him there, along with
the criminals — one on his right,
the other on his left. 34 Jesus said,
"Father, forgive them, for they do
not know what they are doing."[c]
And they divided up his clothes by
casting lots.

Ps 22:18; Mt 27:38

[a] *17* Some manuscripts include here words similar to Matt. 27:15 and Mark 15:6.
[b] *30* Hosea 10:8
[c] *34* Some early manuscripts do not have this sentence.

35 The people stood watching,
and the rulers even sneered at
him. They said, "He saved others;
let him save himself if he is God's
Messiah, the Chosen One."
Ps 22:17; Isa 42:1
36 The soldiers also came up
and mocked him. They offered
him wine vinegar 37 and said, "If
you are the king of the Jews, save
yourself." Mt 27:48; Lk 4:3,9
38 There was a written notice
above him, which read: THIS IS THE
KING OF THE JEWS. Mt 2:2
39 One of the criminals who
hung there hurled insults at him:
"Aren't you the Messiah? Save
yourself and us!" ver 35,37
40 But the other criminal rebuked him. "Don't you fear God,"
he said, "since you are under the
same sentence? 41 We are punished
justly, for we are getting what our
deeds deserve. But this man has
done nothing wrong."
42 Then he said, "Jesus, remember me when you come into your
kingdom.[a]" Mt 16:27
43 Jesus answered him, "Truly I
tell you, today you will be with me
in paradise."
Mt 27:33-44; Mk 15:22-32; Jn 19:17-24

The Death of Jesus

44 It was now about noon, and
darkness came over the whole
land until three in the afternoon,
45 for the sun stopped shining. And
the curtain of the temple was torn
in two. 46 Jesus called out with
a loud voice, "Father, into your
hands I commit my spirit."[b] When
he had said this, he breathed his
last. Ps 31:5; Jn 19:30
47 The centurion, seeing what
had happened, praised God and
said, "Surely this was a righteous
man." 48 When all the people who
had gathered to witness this sight
saw what took place, they beat
their breasts and went away. 49 But
all those who knew him, including
the women who had followed him
from Galilee, stood at a distance,
watching these things.
Mt 27:45-56; Mk 15:33-41

The Burial of Jesus

50 Now there was a man named
Joseph, a member of the Council,
a good and upright man, 51 who
had not consented to their decision and action. He came from
the Judean town of Arimathea,
and he himself was waiting for
the kingdom of God. 52 Going to
Pilate, he asked for Jesus' body.
53 Then he took it down, wrapped
it in linen cloth and placed it in a
tomb cut in the rock, one in which
no one had yet been laid. 54 It was
Preparation Day, and the Sabbath
was about to begin.
Mt 27:62; Lk 2:25,38
55 The women who had come
with Jesus from Galilee followed
Joseph and saw the tomb and how
his body was laid in it. 56 Then they
went home and prepared spices
and perfumes. But they rested on

[a] 42 Some manuscripts *come with your kingly power* [b] 46 Psalm 31:5

the Sabbath in obedience to the commandment.

Mt 27:57-61; Mk 15:42-47; Jn 19:38-42

Jesus Has Risen

24 On the first day of the week, very early in the morning, the women took the spices they had prepared and went to the tomb. 2They found the stone rolled away from the tomb, 3but when they entered, they did not find the body of the Lord Jesus. 4While they were wondering about this, suddenly two men in clothes that gleamed like lightning stood beside them. 5In their fright the women bowed down with their faces to the ground, but the men said to them, "Why do you look for the living among the dead? 6He is not here; he has risen! Remember how he told you, while he was still with you in Galilee: 7'The Son of Man must be delivered over to the hands of sinners, be crucified and on the third day be raised again.' " 8Then they remembered his words.

Mt 28:1-8

9When they came back from the tomb, they told all these things to the Eleven and to all the others. 10It was Mary Magdalene, Joanna, Mary the mother of James, and the others with them who told this to the apostles. 11But they did not believe the women, because their words seemed to them like nonsense. 12Peter, however, got up and ran to the tomb. Bending over, he saw the strips of linen lying by themselves, and he went away, wondering to himself what had happened.

Mk 16:1-8; Jn 20:1-8

On the Road to Emmaus

13Now that same day two of them were going to a village called Emmaus, about seven miles[a] from Jerusalem. 14They were talking with each other about everything that had happened. 15As they talked and discussed these things with each other, Jesus himself came up and walked along with them; 16but they were kept from recognizing him.

Jn 20:14; 21:4

17He asked them, "What are you discussing together as you walk along?"

They stood still, their faces downcast. 18One of them, named Cleopas, asked him, "Are you the only one visiting Jerusalem who does not know the things that have happened there in these days?"

Jn 19:25

19"What things?" he asked.

"About Jesus of Nazareth," they replied. "He was a prophet, powerful in word and deed before God and all the people. 20The chief priests and our rulers handed him over to be sentenced to death, and they crucified him; 21but we had hoped that he was the one who was going to redeem Israel. And what is more, it is the third day since all this took place. 22In addition, some of our women amazed us. They went to the

[a] 13 Or about 11 kilometers

tomb early this morning [23]but
didn't find his body. They came
and told us that they had seen a
vision of angels, who said he was
alive. [24]Then some of our companions went to the tomb and
found it just as the women had
said, but they did not see Jesus."
Mt 21:11; Mk 1:24

[25]He said to them, "How foolish
you are, and how slow to believe
all that the prophets have spoken!
[26]Did not the Messiah have to suffer these things and then enter
his glory?" [27]And beginning with
Moses and all the Prophets, he explained to them what was said in
all the Scriptures concerning himself. Jn 1:45

[28]As they approached the village
to which they were going, Jesus
continued on as if he were going farther. [29]But they urged him
strongly, "Stay with us, for it is
nearly evening; the day is almost
over." So he went in to stay with
them.

[30]When he was at the table
with them, he took bread, gave
thanks, broke it and began to
give it to them. [31]Then their eyes
were opened and they recognized
him, and he disappeared from
their sight. [32]They asked each other, "Were not our hearts burning
within us while he talked with us
on the road and opened the Scriptures to us?" Ps 39:3; Mt 14:19

[33]They got up and returned at
once to Jerusalem. There they
found the Eleven and those with
them, assembled together [34]and
saying, "It is true! The Lord has
risen and has appeared to Simon."
[35]Then the two told what had happened on the way, and how Jesus
was recognized by them when he
broke the bread. 1Co 15:5

Jesus Appears to the Disciples

[36]While they were still talking
about this, Jesus himself stood
among them and said to them,
"Peace be with you." Jn 20:19,21,26

[37]They were startled and frightened, thinking they saw a ghost.
[38]He said to them, "Why are you
troubled, and why do doubts rise
in your minds? [39]Look at my hands
and my feet. It is I myself! Touch
me and see; a ghost does not have
flesh and bones, as you see I have."
Mk 6:49; Jn 20:27

[40]When he had said this, he
showed them his hands and feet.
[41]And while they still did not believe it because of joy and amazement, he asked them, "Do you
have anything here to eat?" [42]They
gave him a piece of broiled fish,
[43]and he took it and ate it in their
presence. Ac 10:41

[44]He said to them, "This is what
I told you while I was still with
you: Everything must be fulfilled
that is written about me in the
Law of Moses, the Prophets and
the Psalms." Mt 18:31-33

[45]Then he opened their minds
so they could understand the
Scriptures. [46]He told them, "This
is what is written: The Messiah

will suffer and rise from the dead
on the third day, 47 and repentance for the forgiveness of sins
will be preached in his name to
all nations, beginning at Jerusalem. 48 You are witnesses of these
things. 49 I am going to send you
what my Father has promised;
but stay in the city until you have
been clothed with power from on
high." Ac 1:4,8

The Ascension of Jesus

50 When he had led them out to
the vicinity of Bethany, he lifted
up his hands and blessed them.
51 While he was blessing them, he
left them and was taken up into
heaven. 52 Then they worshiped
him and returned to Jerusalem
with great joy. 53 And they stayed
continually at the temple, praising God. 2Ki 2:11; Ac 2:46

JOHN

The Word Became Flesh

1 In the beginning was the Word,
and the Word was with God, and
the Word was God. 2He was with
God in the beginning. 3Through
him all things were made; without him nothing was made that
has been made. 4In him was life,
and that life was the light of all
mankind. 5The light shines in the
darkness, and the darkness has
not overcome[a] it.

Jn 3:19; 5:26; Php 2:6; Col 1:16; 1Jn 1:2

6There was a man sent from God
whose name was John. 7He came
as a witness to testify concerning
that light, so that through him all
might believe. 8He himself was
not the light; he came only as a
witness to the light.

9The true light that gives light
to everyone was coming into
the world. 10He was in the world,
and though the world was made
through him, the world did not recognize him. 11He came to that which
was his own, but his own did not
receive him. 12Yet to all who did receive him, to those who believed in
his name, he gave the right to become children of God— 13children
born not of natural descent, nor
of human decision or a husband's
will, but born of God. Jn 3:6; 1Pe 1:23

14The Word became flesh and
made his dwelling among us. We
have seen his glory, the glory of
the one and only Son, who came
from the Father, full of grace and
truth. Gal 4:4; 1Ti 3:16

15(John testified concerning
him. He cried out, saying, "This is
the one I spoke about when I said,
'He who comes after me has surpassed me because he was before
me.'") 16Out of his fullness we have
all received grace in place of grace
already given. 17For the law was
given through Moses; grace and
truth came through Jesus Christ.
18No one has ever seen God, but
the one and only Son, who is himself God and[b] is in closest relationship with the Father, has made
him known. Ex 33:20; 1Jn 4:9

John the Baptist Denies Being the Messiah

19Now this was John's testimony
when the Jewish leaders[c] in Jerusalem sent priests and Levites to ask
him who he was. 20He did not fail to
confess, but confessed freely, "I am
not the Messiah." Lk 3:15-16; Jn 2:18

21They asked him, "Then who
are you? Are you Elijah?" Mt 11:14

[a] 5 Or *understood* [b] 18 Some manuscripts *but the only Son, who* [c] 19 The Greek term traditionally translated *the Jews* (*hoi Ioudaioi*) refers here and elsewhere in John's Gospel to those Jewish leaders who opposed Jesus; also in 5:10, 15, 16; 7:1, 11, 13; 9:22; 18:14, 28, 36; 19:7, 12, 31, 38; 20:19.

He said, "I am not."
"Are you the Prophet?" Dt 18:15
He answered, "No."
22Finally they said, "Who are
you? Give us an answer to take
back to those who sent us. What
do you say about yourself?"
23John replied in the words of
Isaiah the prophet, "I am the voice
of one calling in the wilderness,
'Make straight the way for the
Lord.'"[a] Isa 40:3; Mt 3:1
24Now the Pharisees who had
been sent 25questioned him, "Why
then do you baptize if you are not
the Messiah, nor Elijah, nor the
Prophet?"
26"I baptize with[b] water," John
replied, "but among you stands
one you do not know. 27He is the
one who comes after me, the
straps of whose sandals I am not
worthy to untie." Mk 1:4,7
28This all happened at Bethany
on the other side of the Jordan,
where John was baptizing.
Jn 3:26; 10:40

John Testifies About Jesus

29The next day John saw Jesus
coming toward him and said,
"Look, the Lamb of God, who
takes away the sin of the world!
30This is the one I meant when
I said, 'A man who comes after
me has surpassed me because he
was before me.' 31I myself did not
know him, but the reason I came
baptizing with water was that he
might be revealed to Israel."
Isa 53:7; 1Pe 1:19

32Then John gave this testimony: "I saw the Spirit come down
from heaven as a dove and remain on him. 33And I myself did
not know him, but the one who
sent me to baptize with water told
me, 'The man on whom you see
the Spirit come down and remain
is the one who will baptize with
the Holy Spirit.' 34I have seen and
I testify that this is God's Chosen
One."[c] Mt 3:11,16; Mk 1:10

John's Disciples Follow Jesus

35The next day John was there
again with two of his disciples.
36When he saw Jesus passing by,
he said, "Look, the Lamb of God!"
ver 29
37When the two disciples heard
him say this, they followed Jesus.
38Turning around, Jesus saw them
following and asked, "What do
you want?"
They said, "Rabbi" (which means
"Teacher"), "where are you staying?" Mt 23:7
39"Come," he replied, "and you
will see."
So they went and saw where he
was staying, and they spent that
day with him. It was about four in
the afternoon.
40Andrew, Simon Peter's brother, was one of the two who heard
what John had said and who
had followed Jesus. 41The first
thing Andrew did was to find his

[a] 23 Isaiah 40:3 [b] 26 Or *in*; also in verses 31 and 33 (twice) [c] 34 See Isaiah 42:1; many manuscripts *is the Son of God.*

brother Simon and tell him, "We
have found the Messiah" (that is,
the Christ). 42 And he brought him
to Jesus. Jn 4:25

Jesus looked at him and said,
"You are Simon son of John. You
will be called Cephas" (which,
when translated, is Peter[a]).
Mt 4:18-22; Mk 1:16-20; Lk 5:2-11

Jesus Calls Philip and Nathanael

43 The next day Jesus decided to
leave for Galilee. Finding Philip,
he said to him, "Follow me."
Mt 10:3; Jn 14:8-9

44 Philip, like Andrew and Peter,
was from the town of Bethsaida.
45 Philip found Nathanael and told
him, "We have found the one Moses wrote about in the Law, and
about whom the prophets also
wrote — Jesus of Nazareth, the
son of Joseph." Mt 2:23; Lk 3:23

46 "Nazareth! Can anything good
come from there?" Nathanael
asked. Jn 7:41-42,52

"Come and see," said Philip.

47 When Jesus saw Nathanael approaching, he said of him,
"Here truly is an Israelite in
whom there is no deceit."
Ps 32:2; Ro 9:4,6

48 "How do you know me?" Nathanael asked.

Jesus answered, "I saw you
while you were still under the fig
tree before Philip called you."

49 Then Nathanael declared,
"Rabbi, you are the Son of God;
you are the king of Israel."
Mt 4:3; Jn 12:13

50 Jesus said, "You believe[b] because I told you I saw you under the
fig tree. You will see greater things
than that." 51 He then added, "Very
truly I tell you,[c] you[c] will see 'heav-
en open, and the angels of God ascending and descending on'[d] the
Son of Man." Ge 28:12; Mt 3:16; 8:20

Jesus Changes Water Into Wine

2 On the third day a wedding
took place at Cana in Galilee.
Jesus' mother was there, 2 and
Jesus and his disciples had also
been invited to the wedding.
3 When the wine was gone, Jesus'
mother said to him, "They have no
more wine." Mt 12:46; Jn 4:46

4 "Woman,[e] why do you involve
me?" Jesus replied. "My hour has
not yet come."
Jn 7:6; 19:26

5 His mother said to the servants,
"Do whatever he tells you." Ge 41:55

6 Nearby stood six stone water
jars, the kind used by the Jews for
ceremonial washing, each holding
from twenty to thirty gallons.[f]
Mk 7:3-4; Jn 3:25

7 Jesus said to the servants, "Fill
the jars with water"; so they filled
them to the brim.

8 Then he told them, "Now draw
some out and take it to the master
of the banquet."

They did so, 9 and the master
of the banquet tasted the water

[a] 42 *Cephas* (Aramaic) and *Peter* (Greek) both mean *rock*. [b] 50 Or *Do you believe . . . ?* [c] 51 The Greek is plural. [d] 51 Gen. 28:12 [e] 4 The Greek for *Woman* does not denote any disrespect. [f] 6 Or from about 75 to about 115 liters

that had been turned into wine.
He did not realize where it had
come from, though the servants
who had drawn the water knew.
Then he called the bridegroom
aside 10and said, "Everyone brings
out the choice wine first and then
the cheaper wine after the guests
have had too much to drink; but
you have saved the best till now."
Jn 4:46

11What Jesus did here in Cana of
Galilee was the first of the signs
through which he revealed his
glory; and his disciples believed
in him. Ex 14:31; Jn 1:14

12After this he went down to
Capernaum with his mother and
brothers and his disciples. There
they stayed for a few days. Mt 12:46

Jesus Clears the Temple Courts

13When it was almost time for the
Jewish Passover, Jesus went up to
Jerusalem. 14In the temple courts
he found people selling cattle,
sheep and doves, and others sitting
at tables exchanging money. 15So
he made a whip out of cords, and
drove all from the temple courts,
both sheep and cattle; he scattered
the coins of the money changers
and overturned their tables. 16To
those who sold doves he said, "Get
these out of here! Stop turning
my Father's house into a market!"
17His disciples remembered that it
is written: "Zeal for your house will
consume me."[a] Ps 69:9

18The Jews then responded to
him, "What sign can you show us
to prove your authority to do all
this?" Mt 12:38

19Jesus answered them, "Destroy this temple, and I will raise
it again in three days."
Mt 26:61; 27:40; Mk 14:58

20They replied, "It has taken
forty-six years to build this temple, and you are going to raise it
in three days?" 21But the temple he
had spoken of was his body. 22After he was raised from the dead,
his disciples recalled what he had
said. Then they believed the scripture and the words that Jesus had
spoken. Lk 24:5-8; 1Co 6:19

23Now while he was in Jerusalem at the Passover Festival,
many people saw the signs he was
performing and believed in his
name.[b] 24But Jesus would not entrust himself to them, for he knew
all people. 25He did not need any
testimony about mankind, for he
knew what was in each person.
Jn 6:61,64; 13:11

Jesus Teaches Nicodemus

3 Now there was a Pharisee, a
man named Nicodemus who
was a member of the Jewish ruling council. 2He came to Jesus at
night and said, "Rabbi, we know
that you are a teacher who has
come from God. For no one could
perform the signs you are doing if
God were not with him."
Jn 9:16,33; Ac 2:22

3Jesus replied, "Very truly I tell
you, no one can see the kingdom

[a] 17 Psalm 69:9 [b] 23 Or *in him*

of God unless they are born
again.[a]" Jn 1:13; 1Pe 1:23
4"How can someone be born
when they are old?" Nicodemus
asked. "Surely they cannot enter
a second time into their mother's
womb to be born!"
5Jesus answered, "Very truly I
tell you, no one can enter the kingdom of God unless they are born of
water and the Spirit. 6Flesh gives
birth to flesh, but the Spirit[b] gives
birth to spirit. 7You should not be
surprised at my saying, 'You[c] must
be born again.' 8The wind blows
wherever it pleases. You hear its
sound, but you cannot tell where
it comes from or where it is going.
So it is with everyone born of the
Spirit."[d] Jn 1:13; Titus 3:5
9"How can this be?" Nicodemus
asked. Jn 6:52,60
10"You are Israel's teacher," said
Jesus, "and do you not understand these things? 11Very truly
I tell you, we speak of what we
know, and we testify to what we
have seen, but still you people do
not accept our testimony. 12I have
spoken to you of earthly things
and you do not believe; how then
will you believe if I speak of heavenly things? 13No one has ever
gone into heaven except the one
who came from heaven — the Son
of Man.[e] 14Just as Moses lifted up
the snake in the wilderness, so
the Son of Man must be lifted up,[f]
15that everyone who believes may
have eternal life in him."[g]
Nu 21:8-9; Jn 8:28

16For God so loved the world that
he gave his one and only Son, that
whoever believes in him shall not
perish but have eternal life. 17For
God did not send his Son into the
world to condemn the world, but
to save the world through him.
18Whoever believes in him is not
condemned, but whoever does
not believe stands condemned already because they have not believed in the name of God's one
and only Son. 19This is the verdict:
Light has come into the world, but
people loved darkness instead of
light because their deeds were
evil. 20Everyone who does evil
hates the light, and will not come
into the light for fear that their
deeds will be exposed. 21But whoever lives by the truth comes into
the light, so that it may be seen
plainly that what they have done
has been done in the sight of God.
Ro 5:8; 1Jn 4:9-10

John Testifies Again About Jesus

22After this, Jesus and his disciples went out into the Judean
countryside, where he spent some
time with them, and baptized.
23Now John also was baptizing at
Aenon near Salim, because there
was plenty of water, and people

[a] 3 The Greek for *again* also means *from above*; also in verse 7. [b] 6 Or *but spirit* [c] 7 The Greek is plural. [d] 8 The Greek for *Spirit* is the same as that for *wind*. [e] 13 Some manuscripts *Man, who is in heaven* [f] 14 The Greek for *lifted up* also means *exalted*. [g] 15 Some interpreters end the quotation with verse 21.

were coming and being baptized.
24(This was before John was put in
prison.) 25An argument developed
between some of John's disciples
and a certain Jew over the matter of
ceremonial washing. 26They came
to John and said to him, "Rabbi,
that man who was with you on the
other side of the Jordan — the one
you testified about — look, he is
baptizing, and everyone is going
to him." Jn 1:7; 4:2

27To this John replied, "A person can receive only what is giv-
en them from heaven. 28You yourselves can testify that I said, 'I am
not the Messiah but am sent ahead
of him.' 29The bride belongs to the
bridegroom. The friend who at-
tends the bridegroom waits and
listens for him, and is full of joy
when he hears the bridegroom's
voice. That joy is mine, and it is
now complete. 30He must become
greater; I must become less."[a]
Jn 1:20,23; 16:24

31The one who comes from
above is above all; the one who
is from the earth belongs to the
earth, and speaks as one from the
earth. The one who comes from
heaven is above all. 32He testifies
to what he has seen and heard,
but no one accepts his testimony. 33Whoever has accepted it has
certified that God is truthful. 34For
the one whom God has sent speaks
the words of God, for God[b] gives
the Spirit without limit. 35The Father loves the Son and has placed
everything in his hands. 36Who-
ever believes in the Son has eternal life, but whoever rejects the
Son will not see life, for God's
wrath remains on them.
Mt 28:18; Jn 5:20,22; 17:2

Jesus Talks With a Samaritan Woman

4 Now Jesus learned that the
Pharisees had heard that he
was gaining and baptizing more
disciples than John — 2although
in fact it was not Jesus who baptized, but his disciples. 3So he left
Judea and went back once more to
Galilee. Jn 3:22,26

4Now he had to go through Samaria. 5So he came to a town in
Samaria called Sychar, near the
plot of ground Jacob had given to
his son Joseph. 6Jacob's well was
there, and Jesus, tired as he was
from the journey, sat down by the
well. It was about noon.
Ge 33:19; 48:22; Jos 24:32

7When a Samaritan woman
came to draw water, Jesus said to
her, "Will you give me a drink?"
8(His disciples had gone into the
town to buy food.) Ge 24:17; 1Ki 17:10

9The Samaritan woman said to
him, "You are a Jew and I am a Samaritan woman. How can you ask
me for a drink?" (For Jews do not
associate with Samaritans.[c])
Lk 9:52-53

10Jesus answered her, "If you
knew the gift of God and who it

[a] *30* Some interpreters end the quotation with verse 36. [b] *34* Greek *he* [c] *9* Or *do not use dishes Samaritans have used*

is that asks you for a drink, you
would have asked him and he
would have given you living water.” Isa 44:3; Rev 21:6; 22:1,17
11“Sir,” the woman said, “you
have nothing to draw with and
the well is deep. Where can you
get this living water? 12Are you
greater than our father Jacob, who
gave us the well and drank from it
himself, as did also his sons and
his livestock?” ver 6
13Jesus answered, “Every-
one who drinks this water will
be thirsty again, 14but whoever
drinks the water I give them will
never thirst. Indeed, the water I
give them will become in them a
spring of water welling up to eternal life.” Jn 6:35; 7:38
15The woman said to him, “Sir,
give me this water so that I won’t
get thirsty and have to keep coming here to draw water.” Jn 6:34
16He told her, “Go, call your husband and come back.”
17“I have no husband,” she replied.
Jesus said to her, “You are right
when you say you have no husband. 18The fact is, you have had
five husbands, and the man you
now have is not your husband.
What you have just said is quite
true.”
19“Sir,” the woman said, “I can
see that you are a prophet. 20Our
ancestors worshiped on this
mountain, but you Jews claim that
the place where we must worship
is in Jerusalem.” Dt 11:29; Lk 9:53
21“Woman,” Jesus replied, “believe me, a time is coming when
you will worship the Father neither on this mountain nor in Jerusalem. 22You Samaritans worship
what you do not know; we worship
what we do know, for salvation is
from the Jews. 23Yet a time is coming and has now come when the
true worshipers will worship the
Father in the Spirit and in truth,
for they are the kind of worshipers
the Father seeks. 24God is spirit, and
his worshipers must worship in the
Spirit and in truth.” Mal 1:11; Php 3:3
25The woman said, “I know that
Messiah” (called Christ) “is coming.
When he comes, he will explain everything to us.” Mt 1:16; Jn 1:41
26Then Jesus declared, “I, the
one speaking to you—I am he.”
Jn 8:24; 9:35-37

The Disciples Rejoin Jesus

27Just then his disciples returned and were surprised to find
him talking with a woman. But no
one asked, “What do you want?”
or “Why are you talking with her?”
ver 8
28Then, leaving her water jar,
the woman went back to the town
and said to the people, 29“Come,
see a man who told me everything
I ever did. Could this be the Messiah?” 30They came out of the town
and made their way toward him.
Jn 7:26,31
31Meanwhile his disciples urged
him, “Rabbi, eat something.”
Mt 23:7

32 But he said to them, "I have
food to eat that you know nothing
about." Job 23:12; Mt 4:4; Jn 6:27
33 Then his disciples said to
each other, "Could someone have
brought him food?"
34 "My food," said Jesus, "is to do
the will of him who sent me and to
finish his work. 35 Don't you have a
saying, 'It's still four months until
harvest'? I tell you, open your eyes
and look at the fields! They are
ripe for harvest. 36 Even now the
one who reaps draws a wage and
harvests a crop for eternal life, so
that the sower and the reaper may
be glad together. 37 Thus the saying
'One sows and another reaps' is
true. 38 I sent you to reap what you
have not worked for. Others have
done the hard work, and you have
reaped the benefits of their labor."
Mt 9:37; Jn 6:38; Ro 1:13

Many Samaritans Believe

39 Many of the Samaritans from
that town believed in him because of the woman's testimony, "He told me everything I ever
did." 40 So when the Samaritans
came to him, they urged him to
stay with them, and he stayed two
days. 41 And because of his words
many more became believers.
ver 5,29
42 They said to the woman, "We
no longer believe just because of
what you said; now we have heard
for ourselves, and we know that
this man really is the Savior of the
world." Lk 2:11; 1Jn 4:14

Jesus Heals an Official's Son

43 After the two days he left for
Galilee. 44 (Now Jesus himself had
pointed out that a prophet has no
honor in his own country.) 45 When
he arrived in Galilee, the Galileans
welcomed him. They had seen all
that he had done in Jerusalem at
the Passover Festival, for they also
had been there. Mt 13:57; Jn 2:23
46 Once more he visited Cana in
Galilee, where he had turned the
water into wine. And there was a
certain royal official whose son lay
sick at Capernaum. 47 When this
man heard that Jesus had arrived
in Galilee from Judea, he went
to him and begged him to come
and heal his son, who was close to
death. Jn 2:1-11
48 "Unless you people see signs
and wonders," Jesus told him,
"you will never believe."
Da 4:2-3; Jn 2:11; Heb 2:4
49 The royal official said, "Sir,
come down before my child dies."
50 "Go," Jesus replied, "your son
will live."
The man took Jesus at his word
and departed. 51 While he was still
on the way, his servants met him
with the news that his boy was living. 52 When he inquired as to the
time when his son got better, they
said to him, "Yesterday, at one in
the afternoon, the fever left him."
53 Then the father realized that
this was the exact time at which
Jesus had said to him, "Your son
will live." So he and his whole
household believed. Ac 11:14

54This was the second sign Jesus
performed after coming from Judea to Galilee. Jn 2:11

The Healing at the Pool

5 Some time later, Jesus went
up to Jerusalem for one of the
Jewish festivals. 2Now there is in
Jerusalem near the Sheep Gate a
pool, which in Aramaic is called
Bethesda[a] and which is surrounded by five covered colonnades.
3Here a great number of disabled
people used to lie — the blind, the
lame, the paralyzed. [4][b] 5One who
was there had been an invalid for
thirty-eight years. 6When Jesus
saw him lying there and learned
that he had been in this condition
for a long time, he asked him, "Do
you want to get well?"

Ne 3:1; 12:39; Jn 19:13,17,20

7"Sir," the invalid replied, "I
have no one to help me into the
pool when the water is stirred.
While I am trying to get in, someone else goes down ahead of me."
8Then Jesus said to him, "Get
up! Pick up your mat and walk."
9At once the man was cured; he
picked up his mat and walked.

Mt 9:5-6; Mk 2:11; Lk 5:24

The day on which this took place
was a Sabbath, 10and so the Jewish
leaders said to the man who had
been healed, "It is the Sabbath;
the law forbids you to carry your
mat." Ne 13:15-22; Mt 12:2; Jn 9:14
11But he replied, "The man who
made me well said to me, 'Pick up
your mat and walk.'"
12So they asked him, "Who is
this fellow who told you to pick it
up and walk?"
13The man who was healed had
no idea who it was, for Jesus had
slipped away into the crowd that
was there.
14Later Jesus found him at the
temple and said to him, "See, you
are well again. Stop sinning or
something worse may happen to
you." 15The man went away and
told the Jewish leaders that it was
Jesus who had made him well.

Jn 1:19; 8:11

The Authority of the Son

16So, because Jesus was doing
these things on the Sabbath, the
Jewish leaders began to persecute
him. 17In his defense Jesus said to
them, "My Father is always at his
work to this very day, and I too am
working." 18For this reason they
tried all the more to kill him; not
only was he breaking the Sabbath,
but he was even calling God his
own Father, making himself equal
with God. Jn 7:1; 10:30,33
19Jesus gave them this answer:
"Very truly I tell you, the Son can
do nothing by himself; he can do
only what he sees his Father doing,

[a] 2 Some manuscripts *Bethzatha*; other manuscripts *Bethsaida* [b] 3,4 Some manuscripts include here, wholly or in part, *paralyzed — and they waited for the moving of the waters. 4From time to time an angel of the Lord would come down and stir up the waters. The first one into the pool after each such disturbance would be cured of whatever disease they had.*

because whatever the Father does
the Son also does. 20For the Father
loves the Son and shows him all
he does. Yes, and he will show him
even greater works than these, so
that you will be amazed. 21For just
as the Father raises the dead and
gives them life, even so the Son
gives life to whom he is pleased
to give it. 22Moreover, the Father
judges no one, but has entrusted
all judgment to the Son, 23that all
may honor the Son just as they
honor the Father. Whoever does
not honor the Son does not honor
the Father, who sent him.

Ac 10:42; 1Jn 2:23

24"Very truly I tell you, whoever
hears my word and believes him
who sent me has eternal life and
will not be judged but has crossed
over from death to life. 25Very truly I tell you, a time is coming and
has now come when the dead will
hear the voice of the Son of God
and those who hear will live. 26For
as the Father has life in himself,
so he has granted the Son also to
have life in himself. 27And he has
given him authority to judge because he is the Son of Man.

Jn 3:18; 1Jn 3:14

28"Do not be amazed at this, for
a time is coming when all who are
in their graves will hear his voice
29and come out — those who have
done what is good will rise to live,
and those who have done what is
evil will rise to be condemned. 30By
myself I can do nothing; I judge
only as I hear, and my judgment
is just, for I seek not to please myself but him who sent me.

Da 12:2; Mt 25:46; 26:39

Testimonies About Jesus

31"If I testify about myself, my
testimony is not true. 32There is
another who testifies in my favor,
and I know that his testimony
about me is true. Jn 8:14

33"You have sent to John and
he has testified to the truth. 34Not
that I accept human testimony;
but I mention it that you may
be saved. 35John was a lamp that
burned and gave light, and you
chose for a time to enjoy his light.

Jn 1:7; 2Pe 1:19

36"I have testimony weightier
than that of John. For the works
that the Father has given me to
finish — the very works that I am
doing — testify that the Father
has sent me. 37And the Father who
sent me has himself testified concerning me. You have never heard
his voice nor seen his form, 38nor
does his word dwell in you, for you
do not believe the one he sent.
39You study[a] the Scriptures diligently because you think that in
them you have eternal life. These
are the very Scriptures that testify about me, 40yet you refuse to
come to me to have life.

Jn 8:18; 10:25; Ro 2:17-18

41"I do not accept glory from
human beings, 42but I know you.
I know that you do not have the
love of God in your hearts. 43I have

[a] 39 Or 39*Study*

come in my Father's name, and you do not accept me; but if someone else comes in his own name, you will accept him. 44 How can you believe since you accept glory from one another but do not seek the glory that comes from the only God[a]? Ro 2:29

45 "But do not think I will accuse you before the Father. Your accuser is Moses, on whom your hopes are set. 46 If you believed Moses, you would believe me, for he wrote about me. 47 But since you do not believe what he wrote, how are you going to believe what I say?" Lk 16:29,31; Jn 9:28; Ro 2:17

Jesus Feeds the Five Thousand

6 Some time after this, Jesus crossed to the far shore of the Sea of Galilee (that is, the Sea of Tiberias), 2 and a great crowd of people followed him because they saw the signs he had performed by healing the sick. 3 Then Jesus went up on a mountainside and sat down with his disciples. 4 The Jewish Passover Festival was near. Jn 2:11; 11:55

5 When Jesus looked up and saw a great crowd coming toward him, he said to Philip, "Where shall we buy bread for these people to eat?" 6 He asked this only to test him, for he already had in mind what he was going to do. Jn 1:43

7 Philip answered him, "It would take more than half a year's wages[b] to buy enough bread for each one to have a bite!"

8 Another of his disciples, Andrew, Simon Peter's brother, spoke up, 9 "Here is a boy with five small barley loaves and two small fish, but how far will they go among so many?" 2Ki 4:43; Jn 1:40

10 Jesus said, "Have the people sit down." There was plenty of grass in that place, and they sat down (about five thousand men were there). 11 Jesus then took the loaves, gave thanks, and distributed to those who were seated as much as they wanted. He did the same with the fish. Mt 14:19

12 When they had all had enough to eat, he said to his disciples, "Gather the pieces that are left over. Let nothing be wasted." 13 So they gathered them and filled twelve baskets with the pieces of the five barley loaves left over by those who had eaten.

Mt 14:13-21; Mk 6:32-44; Lk 9:10-17

14 After the people saw the sign Jesus performed, they began to say, "Surely this is the Prophet who is to come into the world." 15 Jesus, knowing that they intended to come and make him king by force, withdrew again to a mountain by himself.

Mt 14:23; Jn 18:36; Dt 18:15,18

Jesus Walks on the Water

16 When evening came, his disciples went down to the lake, 17 where they got into a boat and set off across the lake for Capernaum.

[a] 44 Some early manuscripts *the Only One*
[b] 7 Greek *take two hundred denarii*

By now it was dark, and Jesus had
not yet joined them. 18A strong
wind was blowing and the waters grew rough. 19When they had
rowed about three or four miles,[a]
they saw Jesus approaching the
boat, walking on the water; and
they were frightened. 20But he said
to them, "It is I; don't be afraid."
21Then they were willing to take
him into the boat, and immediately the boat reached the shore
where they were heading.

Mt 14:22-33; Mk 6:47-51

22The next day the crowd that
had stayed on the opposite shore
of the lake realized that only one
boat had been there, and that
Jesus had not entered it with his
disciples, but that they had gone
away alone. 23Then some boats
from Tiberias landed near the
place where the people had eaten
the bread after the Lord had given
thanks. 24Once the crowd realized
that neither Jesus nor his disciples
were there, they got into the boats
and went to Capernaum in search
of Jesus.

Jesus the Bread of Life

25When they found him on the
other side of the lake, they asked
him, "Rabbi, when did you get
here?" Mt 23:7

26Jesus answered, "Very truly I
tell you, you are looking for me,
not because you saw the signs I
performed but because you ate
the loaves and had your fill. 27Do
not work for food that spoils, but
for food that endures to eternal
life, which the Son of Man will
give you. For on him God the Father has placed his seal of approval." Isa 55:2; Jn 4:14; Ro 4:11

28Then they asked him, "What
must we do to do the works God
requires?"

29Jesus answered, "The work of
God is this: to believe in the one
he has sent." Jn 3:17; 1Jn 3:23

30So they asked him, "What
sign then will you give that we
may see it and believe you? What
will you do? 31Our ancestors ate
the manna in the wilderness; as
it is written: 'He gave them bread
from heaven to eat.'[b]"

Ex 16:4,15; Nu 11:7-9; Mt 12:38

32Jesus said to them, "Very truly
I tell you, it is not Moses who has
given you the bread from heaven,
but it is my Father who gives you
the true bread from heaven. 33For
the bread of God is the bread that
comes down from heaven and
gives life to the world." Jn 3:13,31

34"Sir," they said, "always give us
this bread." Jn 4:15

35Then Jesus declared, "I am
the bread of life. Whoever comes
to me will never go hungry, and
whoever believes in me will never be thirsty. 36But as I told you,
you have seen me and still you
do not believe. 37All those the Father gives me will come to me,
and whoever comes to me I will
never drive away. 38For I have

[a] *19* Or about 5 or 6 kilometers
[b] *31* Exodus 16:4; Neh. 9:15; Psalm 78:24,25

come down from heaven not to
do my will but to do the will of
him who sent me. 39And this is
the will of him who sent me, that
I shall lose none of all those he
has given me, but raise them up
at the last day. 40For my Father's
will is that everyone who looks to
the Son and believes in him shall
have eternal life, and I will raise
them up at the last day."

Jn 3:15-16; 10:28

41At this the Jews there began
to grumble about him because he
said, "I am the bread that came
down from heaven." 42They said,
"Is this not Jesus, the son of Joseph, whose father and mother
we know? How can he now say, 'I
came down from heaven'?"

Lk 4:22; Jn 7:27-28

43"Stop grumbling among
yourselves," Jesus answered.
44"No one can come to me unless
the Father who sent me draws
them, and I will raise them up at
the last day. 45It is written in the
Prophets: 'They will all be taught
by God.'[a] Everyone who has heard
the Father and learned from him
comes to me. 46No one has seen
the Father except the one who is
from God; only he has seen the
Father. 47Very truly I tell you, the
one who believes has eternal life.
48I am the bread of life. 49Your
ancestors ate the manna in the
wilderness, yet they died. 50But
here is the bread that comes
down from heaven, which anyone may eat and not die. 51I am
the living bread that came down
from heaven. Whoever eats this
bread will live forever. This bread
is my flesh, which I will give for
the life of the world."

Isa 54:13; Jn 1:18; Heb 10:10

52Then the Jews began to argue
sharply among themselves, "How
can this man give us his flesh to
eat?"

Jn 9:16; 10:19

53Jesus said to them, "Very truly I tell you, unless you eat the
flesh of the Son of Man and drink
his blood, you have no life in
you. 54Whoever eats my flesh and
drinks my blood has eternal life,
and I will raise them up at the last
day. 55For my flesh is real food and
my blood is real drink. 56Whoever
eats my flesh and drinks my blood
remains in me, and I in them.
57Just as the living Father sent me
and I live because of the Father,
so the one who feeds on me will
live because of me. 58This is the
bread that came down from heav-
en. Your ancestors ate manna and
died, but whoever feeds on this
bread will live forever." 59He said
this while teaching in the synagogue in Capernaum.

1Jn 3:24; 4:15; Jn 3:36

Many Disciples Desert Jesus

60On hearing it, many of his disciples said, "This is a hard teaching. Who can accept it?"

61Aware that his disciples were
grumbling about this, Jesus said
to them, "Does this offend you?

[a] 45 Isaiah 54:13

62 Then what if you see the Son of Man ascend to where he was before! 63 The Spirit gives life; the flesh counts for nothing. The words I have spoken to you — they are full of the Spirit[a] and life. 64 Yet there are some of you who do not believe." For Jesus had known from the beginning which of them did not believe and who would betray him. 65 He went on to say, "This is why I told you that no one can come to me unless the Father has enabled them."

Jn 2:25; 3:13; 2Co 3:6

66 From this time many of his disciples turned back and no longer followed him. ver 60

67 "You do not want to leave too, do you?" Jesus asked the Twelve.

Mt 10:2

68 Simon Peter answered him, "Lord, to whom shall we go? You have the words of eternal life. 69 We have come to believe and to know that you are the Holy One of God." Mk 8:29; Lk 9:20

70 Then Jesus replied, "Have I not chosen you, the Twelve? Yet one of you is a devil!" 71 (He meant Judas, the son of Simon Iscariot, who, though one of the Twelve, was later to betray him.)

Jn 13:27; 15:16,19

Jesus Goes to the Festival of Tabernacles

7 After this, Jesus went around in Galilee. He did not want[b] to go about in Judea because the Jewish leaders there were looking for a way to kill him. 2 But when the Jewish Festival of Tabernacles was near, 3 Jesus' brothers said to him, "Leave Galilee and go to Judea, so that your disciples there may see the works you do. 4 No one who wants to become a public figure acts in secret. Since you are doing these things, show yourself to the world." 5 For even his own brothers did not believe in him.

Mt 12:46; Jn 5:18; Lev 23:34

6 Therefore Jesus told them, "My time is not yet here; for you any time will do. 7 The world cannot hate you, but it hates me because I testify that its works are evil. 8 You go to the festival. I am not[c] going up to this festival, because my time has not yet fully come." 9 After he had said this, he stayed in Galilee.

Mt 26:18; Jn 3:19-20

10 However, after his brothers had left for the festival, he went also, not publicly, but in secret. 11 Now at the festival the Jewish leaders were watching for Jesus and asking, "Where is he?" Jn 11:56

12 Among the crowds there was widespread whispering about him. Some said, "He is a good man."

Others replied, "No, he deceives the people." 13 But no one would say anything publicly about him for fear of the leaders.

Jn 9:22; 12:42; 19:38

[a] 63 Or *are Spirit*; or *are spirit* [b] 1 Some manuscripts *not have authority* [c] 8 Some manuscripts *not yet*

Jesus Teaches at the Festival

14 Not until halfway through the festival did Jesus go up to the temple courts and begin to teach. 15 The Jews there were amazed and asked, "How did this man get such learning without having been taught?" Mt 13:54; Jn 1:19; Ac 26:24

16 Jesus answered, "My teaching is not my own. It comes from the one who sent me. 17 Anyone who chooses to do the will of God will find out whether my teaching comes from God or whether I speak on my own. 18 Whoever speaks on their own does so to gain personal glory, but he who seeks the glory of the one who sent him is a man of truth; there is nothing false about him. 19 Has not Moses given you the law? Yet not one of you keeps the law. Why are you trying to kill me?"

Jn 5:41; 8:50,54; 14:24

20 "You are demon-possessed," the crowd answered. "Who is trying to kill you?"

21 Jesus said to them, "I did one miracle, and you are all amazed. 22 Yet, because Moses gave you circumcision (though actually it did not come from Moses, but from the patriarchs), you circumcise a boy on the Sabbath. 23 Now if a boy can be circumcised on the Sabbath so that the law of Moses may not be broken, why are you angry with me for healing a man's whole body on the Sabbath? 24 Stop judging by mere appearances, but instead judge correctly." Jn 8:15,48; 10:20

Division Over Who Jesus Is

25 At that point some of the people of Jerusalem began to ask, "Isn't this the man they are trying to kill? 26 Here he is, speaking publicly, and they are not saying a word to him. Have the authorities really concluded that he is the Messiah? 27 But we know where this man is from; when the Messiah comes, no one will know where he is from." Mt 13:55; Lk 4:22

28 Then Jesus, still teaching in the temple courts, cried out, "Yes, you know me, and you know where I am from. I am not here on my own authority, but he who sent me is true. You do not know him, 29 but I know him because I am from him and he sent me."

Mt 11:27; Jn 8:14,26,42

30 At this they tried to seize him, but no one laid a hand on him, because his hour had not yet come. 31 Still, many in the crowd believed in him. They said, "When the Messiah comes, will he perform more signs than this man?" Jn 2:11; 8:30

32 The Pharisees heard the crowd whispering such things about him. Then the chief priests and the Pharisees sent temple guards to arrest him.

33 Jesus said, "I am with you for only a short time, and then I am going to the one who sent me. 34 You will look for me, but you will not find me; and where I am, you cannot come." Jn 8:21; 13:33

35 The Jews said to one another, "Where does this man intend to go

that we cannot find him? Will he
go where our people live scattered
among the Greeks, and teach the
Greeks? [36]What did he mean when
he said, 'You will look for me, but
you will not find me,' and 'Where I
am, you cannot come'?" Jas 1:1; 1Pe 1:1

[37]On the last and greatest day of
the festival, Jesus stood and said
in a loud voice, "Let anyone who
is thirsty come to me and drink.
[38]Whoever believes in me, as Scripture has said, rivers of living water
will flow from within them."[a] [39]By
this he meant the Spirit, whom
those who believed in him were
later to receive. Up to that time
the Spirit had not been given,
since Jesus had not yet been glorified. Isa 55:1; Joel 2:28; Jn 12:23

[40]On hearing his words, some of
the people said, "Surely this man
is the Prophet." Mt 21:11; Jn 1:21

[41]Others said, "He is the Messiah."

Still others asked, "How can the
Messiah come from Galilee? [42]Does
not Scripture say that the Messiah
will come from David's descendants and from Bethlehem, the
town where David lived?" [43]Thus
the people were divided because
of Jesus. [44]Some wanted to seize
him, but no one laid a hand on
him. Mic 5:2; Jn 9:16; 10:19

Unbelief of the Jewish Leaders

[45]Finally the temple guards
went back to the chief priests and
the Pharisees, who asked them,
"Why didn't you bring him in?"

[46]"No one ever spoke the way
this man does," the guards replied. Mt 7:28

[47]"You mean he has deceived
you also?" the Pharisees retorted.
[48]"Have any of the rulers or of the
Pharisees believed in him? [49]No!
But this mob that knows nothing
of the law — there is a curse on
them." Jn 12:42

[50]Nicodemus, who had gone to
Jesus earlier and who was one of
their own number, asked, [51]"Does
our law condemn a man without
first hearing him to find out what
he has been doing?" Jn 3:1; 19:39

[52]They replied, "Are you from
Galilee, too? Look into it, and you
will find that a prophet does not
come out of Galilee."

[The earliest manuscripts and many other ancient witnesses do not have John 7:53 — 8:11. A few manuscripts include these verses, wholly or in part, after John 7:36, John 21:25, Luke 21:38 or Luke 24:53.]

8 *[53]Then they all went home, [1]but
Jesus went to the Mount of Olives.
[2]At dawn he appeared again in
the temple courts, where all the people gathered around him, and he sat
down to teach them. [3]The teachers of
the law and the Pharisees brought in a
woman caught in adultery. They made
her stand before the group [4]and said*

[a] 37,38 Or *me. And let anyone drink [38]who believes in me." As Scripture has said, "Out of him (or them) will flow rivers of living water."*

to Jesus, "Teacher, this woman was
caught in the act of adultery. 5In the
Law Moses commanded us to stone
such women. Now what do you say?"
6They were using this question as a
trap, in order to have a basis for accus-
ing him. Lev 20:10; Dt 22:22; Mt 12:10
But Jesus bent down and started to
write on the ground with his finger.
7When they kept on questioning him,
he straightened up and said to them,
"Let any one of you who is without sin
be the first to throw a stone at her."
8Again he stooped down and wrote on
the ground. Dt 17:7; Ro 2:1,22
9At this, those who heard began to
go away one at a time, the older ones
first, until only Jesus was left, with the
woman still standing there. 10Jesus
straightened up and asked her, "Wom-
an, where are they? Has no one con-
demned you?"
11"No one, sir," she said.
"Then neither do I condemn you,"
Jesus declared. "Go now and leave your
life of sin." Jn 3:17; 5:14

Dispute Over Jesus' Testimony

12When Jesus spoke again to the
people, he said, "I am the light of
the world. Whoever follows me
will never walk in darkness, but
will have the light of life."
Jn 1:4; 6:35; Pr 4:18; Mt 5:14
13The Pharisees challenged him,
"Here you are, appearing as your
own witness; your testimony is
not valid." Jn 5:31
14Jesus answered, "Even if I testify on my own behalf, my testimony is valid, for I know where I
came from and where I am going.
But you have no idea where I come
from or where I am going. 15You
judge by human standards; I pass
judgment on no one. 16But if I do
judge, my decisions are true, because I am not alone. I stand with
the Father, who sent me. 17In your
own Law it is written that the testimony of two witnesses is true. 18I
am one who testifies for myself;
my other witness is the Father,
who sent me." Mt 18:16; Jn 5:37; 7:28
19Then they asked him, "Where
is your father?"
"You do not know me or my Father," Jesus replied. "If you knew
me, you would know my Father
also." 20He spoke these words while
teaching in the temple courts near
the place where the offerings were
put. Yet no one seized him, because his hour had not yet come.
Mk 12:41; Jn 16:3; 1Jn 2:23

Dispute Over Who Jesus Is

21Once more Jesus said to them,
"I am going away, and you will
look for me, and you will die in
your sin. Where I go, you cannot
come." Jn 7:34; 13:33
22This made the Jews ask, "Will
he kill himself? Is that why he says,
'Where I go, you cannot come'?"
23But he continued, "You are
from below; I am from above. You
are of this world; I am not of this
world. 24I told you that you would
die in your sins; if you do not believe that I am he, you will indeed
die in your sins." Jn 3:31; 4:26

[25]"Who are you?" they asked.
"Just what I have been telling
you from the beginning," Jesus
replied. [26]"I have much to say in
judgment of you. But he who sent
me is trustworthy, and what I have
heard from him I tell the world."

Jn 3:32; 7:28; 15:15

[27]They did not understand that
he was telling them about his Father. [28]So Jesus said, "When you
have lifted up[a] the Son of Man,
then you will know that I am he
and that I do nothing on my own
but speak just what the Father has
taught me. [29]The one who sent
me is with me; he has not left me
alone, for I always do what pleases him." [30]Even as he spoke, many
believed in him. Jn 4:34; 7:31; 12:32

Dispute Over Whose Children Jesus' Opponents Are

[31]To the Jews who had believed
him, Jesus said, "If you hold to my
teaching, you are really my disciples. [32]Then you will know the
truth, and the truth will set you
free." Jn 15:7; Ro 8:2; Jas 2:12

[33]They answered him, "We are
Abraham's descendants and have
never been slaves of anyone. How
can you say that we shall be set
free?" Mt 3:9

[34]Jesus replied, "Very truly I tell
you, everyone who sins is a slave
to sin. [35]Now a slave has no permanent place in the family, but
a son belongs to it forever. [36]So if
the Son sets you free, you will be
free indeed. [37]I know that you are
Abraham's descendants. Yet you
are looking for a way to kill me,
because you have no room for my
word. [38]I am telling you what I
have seen in the Father's presence,
and you are doing what you have
heard from your father.[b]"

Jn 5:19,30; Ro 6:16; Gal 4:30

[39]"Abraham is our father," they
answered.

"If you were Abraham's children," said Jesus, "then you
would[c] do what Abraham did. [40]As
it is, you are looking for a way to
kill me, a man who has told you
the truth that I heard from God.
Abraham did not do such things.
[41]You are doing the works of your
own father." Ro 9:7; Gal 3:7

"We are not illegitimate children," they protested. "The only
Father we have is God himself."

Isa 63:16; 64:8

[42]Jesus said to them, "If God
were your Father, you would love
me, for I have come here from God.
I have not come on my own; God
sent me. [43]Why is my language not
clear to you? Because you are unable to hear what I say. [44]You belong to your father, the devil, and
you want to carry out your father's
desires. He was a murderer from
the beginning, not holding to the
truth, for there is no truth in him.
When he lies, he speaks his native

[a] 28 The Greek for *lifted up* also means *exalted*. [b] 38 Or *presence. Therefore do what you have heard from the Father.* [c] 39 Some early manuscripts *"If you are Abraham's children," said Jesus, "then*

language, for he is a liar and the
father of lies. 45Yet because I tell
the truth, you do not believe me!
46Can any of you prove me guilty
of sin? If I am telling the truth,
why don't you believe me? 47Who-
ever belongs to God hears what
God says. The reason you do not
hear is that you do not belong to
God." Jn 18:37; 1Jn 4:6

Jesus' Claims About Himself

48The Jews answered him,
"Aren't we right in saying that you
are a Samaritan and demon-possessed?" Mt 10:5; Jn 7:20
49"I am not possessed by a demon," said Jesus, "but I honor my
Father and you dishonor me. 50I
am not seeking glory for myself;
but there is one who seeks it, and
he is the judge. 51Very truly I tell
you, whoever obeys my word will
never see death." Jn 5:41; 11:26
52At this they exclaimed, "Now
we know that you are demon-possessed! Abraham died and so did
the prophets, yet you say that whoever obeys your word will never
taste death. 53Are you greater than
our father Abraham? He died, and
so did the prophets. Who do you
think you are?" Mk 3:22; Jn 4:12
54Jesus replied, "If I glorify myself, my glory means nothing. My
Father, whom you claim as your
God, is the one who glorifies me.
55Though you do not know him,
I know him. If I said I did not, I
would be a liar like you, but I do
know him and obey his word.
56Your father Abraham rejoiced at
the thought of seeing my day; he
saw it and was glad." Jn 7:28-29; Heb 11:13
57"You are not yet fifty years
old," they said to him, "and you
have seen Abraham!"
58"Very truly I tell you," Jesus
answered, "before Abraham was
born, I am!" 59At this, they picked
up stones to stone him, but Jesus
hid himself, slipping away from
the temple grounds. Ex 3:14; Jn 10:31; 11:8

Jesus Heals a Man Born Blind

9 As he went along, he saw a
man blind from birth. 2His
disciples asked him, "Rabbi, who
sinned, this man or his parents,
that he was born blind?" Ex 20:5; Mt 23:7
3"Neither this man nor his parents sinned," said Jesus, "but this
happened so that the works of God
might be displayed in him. 4As
long as it is day, we must do the
works of him who sent me. Night
is coming, when no one can work.
5While I am in the world, I am the
light of the world." Jn 8:12; 12:46
6After saying this, he spit on
the ground, made some mud with
the saliva, and put it on the man's
eyes. 7"Go," he told him, "wash
in the Pool of Siloam" (this word
means "Sent"). So the man went
and washed, and came home seeing. Mk 7:33; 8:23; Jn 11:37
8His neighbors and those who
had formerly seen him begging

asked, "Isn't this the same man
who used to sit and beg?" 9 Some
claimed that he was. Ac 3:2,10

Others said, "No, he only looks
like him."

But he himself insisted, "I am
the man."

10 "How then were your eyes
opened?" they asked.

11 He replied, "The man they call
Jesus made some mud and put it
on my eyes. He told me to go to
Siloam and wash. So I went and
washed, and then I could see."
ver 7

12 "Where is this man?" they
asked him.

"I don't know," he said.

The Pharisees Investigate the Healing

13 They brought to the Pharisees the man who had been blind.
14 Now the day on which Jesus had
made the mud and opened the
man's eyes was a Sabbath. 15 Therefore the Pharisees also asked him
how he had received his sight. "He
put mud on my eyes," the man replied, "and I washed, and now I
see." Jn 5:9

16 Some of the Pharisees said,
"This man is not from God, for he
does not keep the Sabbath." Mt 12:2

But others asked, "How can a
sinner perform such signs?" So
they were divided. Jn 7:43; 10:19

17 Then they turned again to the
blind man, "What have you to say
about him? It was your eyes he
opened."

The man replied, "He is a prophet." Mt 21:11

18 They still did not believe that
he had been blind and had received his sight until they sent for
the man's parents. 19 "Is this your
son?" they asked. "Is this the one
you say was born blind? How is it
that now he can see?" Jn 1:19

20 "We know he is our son," the
parents answered, "and we know
he was born blind. 21 But how he
can see now, or who opened his
eyes, we don't know. Ask him. He
is of age; he will speak for himself." 22 His parents said this because they were afraid of the
Jewish leaders, who already had
decided that anyone who acknowledged that Jesus was the
Messiah would be put out of the
synagogue. 23 That was why his
parents said, "He is of age; ask
him." Jn 7:13; 12:42

24 A second time they summoned the man who had been
blind. "Give glory to God by telling
the truth," they said. "We know
this man is a sinner." ver 16; Jos 7:19

25 He replied, "Whether he is a
sinner or not, I don't know. One
thing I do know. I was blind but
now I see!"

26 Then they asked him, "What
did he do to you? How did he open
your eyes?"

27 He answered, "I have told you
already and you did not listen.
Why do you want to hear it again?
Do you want to become his disciples too?"

28Then they hurled insults at
him and said, "You are this fellow's disciple! We are disciples of
Moses! 29We know that God spoke
to Moses, but as for this fellow, we
don't even know where he comes
from." Jn 5:45; 8:14
30The man answered, "Now that
is remarkable! You don't know
where he comes from, yet he
opened my eyes. 31We know that
God does not listen to sinners.
He listens to the godly person
who does his will. 32Nobody has
ever heard of opening the eyes
of a man born blind. 33If this man
were not from God, he could do
nothing." Ps 34:15-16; Pr 15:29; Isa 1:15
34To this they replied, "You were
steeped in sin at birth; how dare
you lecture us!" And they threw
him out. Isa 66:5

Spiritual Blindness

35Jesus heard that they had
thrown him out, and when he
found him, he said, "Do you believe
in the Son of Man?" Mt 8:20; Jn 3:15
36"Who is he, sir?" the man
asked. "Tell me so that I may believe in him." Ro 10:14
37Jesus said, "You have now seen
him; in fact, he is the one speaking with you." Jn 4:26
38Then the man said, "Lord, I
believe," and he worshiped him.
Mt 28:9
39Jesus said,[a] "For judgment I
have come into this world, so that
the blind will see and those who
see will become blind." Mt 13:13; Jn 5:22
40Some Pharisees who were
with him heard him say this and
asked, "What? Are we blind too?"
Ro 2:19
41Jesus said, "If you were blind,
you would not be guilty of sin; but
now that you claim you can see,
your guilt remains. Jn 15:22,24

The Good Shepherd and His Sheep

10 "Very truly I tell you Pharisees, anyone who does not
enter the sheep pen by the gate,
but climbs in by some other way,
is a thief and a robber. 2The one
who enters by the gate is the shepherd of the sheep. 3The gatekeeper opens the gate for him, and the
sheep listen to his voice. He calls
his own sheep by name and leads
them out. 4When he has brought
out all his own, he goes on ahead
of them, and his sheep follow him
because they know his voice. 5But
they will never follow a stranger;
in fact, they will run away from
him because they do not recognize a stranger's voice." 6Jesus
used this figure of speech, but
the Pharisees did not understand
what he was telling them.
Mk 9:32; Jn 16:25
7Therefore Jesus said again,
"Very truly I tell you, I am the gate
for the sheep. 8All who have come
before me are thieves and robbers,
but the sheep have not listened
to them. 9I am the gate; whoever

[a] 38,39 Some early manuscripts do not have *Then the man said . . . 39Jesus said.*

enters through me will be saved.[a]
They will come in and go out, and
find pasture. 10 The thief comes
only to steal and kill and destroy;
I have come that they may have
life, and have it to the full.

Jn 1:4; Ro 5:17

11 "I am the good shepherd. The
good shepherd lays down his life
for the sheep. 12 The hired hand
is not the shepherd and does not
own the sheep. So when he sees
the wolf coming, he abandons the
sheep and runs away. Then the
wolf attacks the flock and scatters
it. 13 The man runs away because
he is a hired hand and cares nothing for the sheep.

Isa 40:11; Eze 34:11-16,23; Heb 13:20

14 "I am the good shepherd; I
know my sheep and my sheep
know me — 15 just as the Father
knows me and I know the Father — and I lay down my life for
the sheep. 16 I have other sheep
that are not of this sheep pen. I
must bring them also. They too
will listen to my voice, and there
shall be one flock and one shepherd. 17 The reason my Father loves
me is that I lay down my life —
only to take it up again. 18 No one
takes it from me, but I lay it down
of my own accord. I have authority to lay it down and authority to
take it up again. This command I
received from my Father."

Mt 11:27; Jn 15:10; Eph 2:11-19

19 The Jews who heard these
words were again divided. 20 Many
of them said, "He is demon-possessed and raving mad. Why listen
to him?"

Jn 7:20,43

21 But others said, "These are not
the sayings of a man possessed by
a demon. Can a demon open the
eyes of the blind?"

Ex 4:11; Jn 9:32-33

Further Conflict Over Jesus' Claims

22 Then came the Festival of Dedication[b] at Jerusalem. It was winter, 23 and Jesus was in the temple courts walking in Solomon's
Colonnade. 24 The Jews who were
there gathered around him, saying, "How long will you keep us in
suspense? If you are the Messiah,
tell us plainly."

Jn 16:25,29; Ac 3:11

25 Jesus answered, "I did tell
you, but you do not believe. The
works I do in my Father's name
testify about me, 26 but you do not
believe because you are not my
sheep. 27 My sheep listen to my
voice; I know them, and they follow me. 28 I give them eternal life,
and they shall never perish; no
one will snatch them out of my
hand. 29 My Father, who has given
them to me, is greater than all[c]; no
one can snatch them out of my Father's hand. 30 I and the Father are
one."

Jn 17:21-23

31 Again his Jewish opponents
picked up stones to stone him,
32 but Jesus said to them, "I have
shown you many good works from
the Father. For which of these do
you stone me?"

Jn 8:59

[a] 9 Or *kept safe* [b] 22 That is, Hanukkah
[c] 29 Many early manuscripts *What my Father has given me is greater than all*

33“We are not stoning you for any good work,” they replied, “but for blasphemy, because you, a mere man, claim to be God.” Lev 24:16; Jn 5:18

34Jesus answered them, “Is it not written in your Law, ‘I have said you are “gods” ’[a]? 35If he called them ‘gods,’ to whom the word of God came — and Scripture cannot be set aside — 36what about the one whom the Father set apart as his very own and sent into the world? Why then do you accuse me of blasphemy because I said, ‘I am God’s Son’? 37Do not believe me unless I do the works of my Father. 38But if I do them, even though you do not believe me, believe the works, that you may know and understand that the Father is in me, and I in the Father.” 39Again they tried to seize him, but he escaped their grasp. Jn 14:10-11,20; 15:24

40Then Jesus went back across the Jordan to the place where John had been baptizing in the early days. There he stayed, 41and many people came to him. They said, “Though John never performed a sign, all that John said about this man was true.” 42And in that place many believed in Jesus. Jn 1:28; 7:31

The Death of Lazarus

11 Now a man named Lazarus was sick. He was from Bethany, the village of Mary and her sister Martha. 2(This Mary, whose brother Lazarus now lay sick, was the same one who poured perfume on the Lord and wiped his feet with her hair.) 3So the sisters sent word to Jesus, “Lord, the one you love is sick.” Lk 10:38; Jn 12:3

4When he heard this, Jesus said, “This sickness will not end in death. No, it is for God’s glory so that God’s Son may be glorified through it.” 5Now Jesus loved Martha and her sister and Lazarus. 6So when he heard that Lazarus was sick, he stayed where he was two more days, 7and then he said to his disciples, “Let us go back to Judea.” Jn 9:3; 10:40

8“But Rabbi,” they said, “a short while ago the Jews there tried to stone you, and yet you are going back?” Mt 23:7; Jn 10:31

9Jesus answered, “Are there not twelve hours of daylight? Anyone who walks in the daytime will not stumble, for they see by this world’s light. 10It is when a person walks at night that they stumble, for they have no light.” Jn 9:4; 12:35

11After he had said this, he went on to tell them, “Our friend Lazarus has fallen asleep; but I am going there to wake him up.” Ac 7:60

12His disciples replied, “Lord, if he sleeps, he will get better.” 13Jesus had been speaking of his death, but his disciples thought he meant natural sleep. Mt 9:24

14So then he told them plainly, “Lazarus is dead, 15and for your

[a] 34 Psalm 82:6

sake I am glad I was not there, so
that you may believe. But let us go
to him."

16Then Thomas (also known as
Didymus[a]) said to the rest of the
disciples, "Let us also go, that we
may die with him."

Mt 10:3; Jn 14:5; 20:24-28

Jesus Comforts the Sisters of Lazarus

17On his arrival, Jesus found
that Lazarus had already been
in the tomb for four days. 18Now
Bethany was less than two miles[b]
from Jerusalem, 19and many Jews
had come to Martha and Mary to
comfort them in the loss of their
brother. 20When Martha heard
that Jesus was coming, she went
out to meet him, but Mary stayed
at home. Job 2:11; Lk 10:38-42

21"Lord," Martha said to Jesus,
"if you had been here, my brother
would not have died. 22But I know
that even now God will give you
whatever you ask." Jn 9:31

23Jesus said to her, "Your brother will rise again."

24Martha answered, "I know he
will rise again in the resurrection
at the last day." Jn 5:28-29; Ac 24:15

25Jesus said to her, "I am the
resurrection and the life. The one
who believes in me will live, even
though they die; 26and whoever
lives by believing in me will never die. Do you believe this?"

Jn 1:4; 3:15

27"Yes, Lord," she replied, "I believe that you are the Messiah, the
Son of God, who is to come into
the world." Mt 16:16; Jn 6:14

28After she had said this, she
went back and called her sister Mary aside. "The Teacher is
here," she said, "and is asking for
you." 29When Mary heard this, she
got up quickly and went to him.
30Now Jesus had not yet entered
the village, but was still at the
place where Martha had met him.
31When the Jews who had been
with Mary in the house, comforting her, noticed how quickly she
got up and went out, they followed her, supposing she was going to the tomb to mourn there.

Mt 26:18; Jn 13:13

32When Mary reached the place
where Jesus was and saw him, she
fell at his feet and said, "Lord, if
you had been here, my brother
would not have died."

33When Jesus saw her weeping, and the Jews who had come
along with her also weeping, he
was deeply moved in spirit and
troubled. 34"Where have you laid
him?" he asked. Jn 12:27

"Come and see, Lord," they replied.

35Jesus wept. Lk 19:41

36Then the Jews said, "See how
he loved him!"

37But some of them said, "Could
not he who opened the eyes of
the blind man have kept this man
from dying?" Jn 9:6-7

[a] 16 *Thomas* (Aramaic) and *Didymus* (Greek) both mean *twin*. [b] 18 Or about 3 kilometers

Jesus Raises Lazarus From the Dead

38 Jesus, once more deeply
moved, came to the tomb. It was
a cave with a stone laid across the
entrance. 39 "Take away the stone,"
he said. Mt 27:60; Lk 24:2; Jn 20:1

"But, Lord," said Martha, the sister of the dead man, "by this time there is a bad odor, for he has been there four days."

40 Then Jesus said, "Did I not tell
you that if you believe, you will
see the glory of God?" ver 23-25

41 So they took away the stone.
Then Jesus looked up and said,
"Father, I thank you that you have
heard me. 42 I knew that you always hear me, but I said this for
the benefit of the people standing
here, that they may believe that
you sent me." Jn 3:17; 12:30

43 When he had said this, Jesus
called in a loud voice, "Lazarus,
come out!" 44 The dead man came
out, his hands and feet wrapped
with strips of linen, and a cloth
around his face. Jn 19:40; 20:7

Jesus said to them, "Take off the grave clothes and let him go."

The Plot to Kill Jesus

45 Therefore many of the Jews
who had come to visit Mary, and
had seen what Jesus did, believed
in him. 46 But some of them went
to the Pharisees and told them
what Jesus had done. 47 Then the
chief priests and the Pharisees
called a meeting of the Sanhedrin.
Mt 26:3; Jn 2:23; 7:31

"What are we accomplishing?"
they asked. "Here is this man performing many signs. 48 If we let
him go on like this, everyone will
believe in him, and then the Romans will come and take away
both our temple and our nation."
Jn 2:11

49 Then one of them, named Caiaphas, who was high priest that
year, spoke up, "You know nothing at all! 50 You do not realize that
it is better for you that one man
die for the people than that the
whole nation perish."
Mt 26:3; Jn 18:13-14

51 He did not say this on his
own, but as high priest that year
he prophesied that Jesus would
die for the Jewish nation, 52 and
not only for that nation but also
for the scattered children of God,
to bring them together and make
them one. 53 So from that day on
they plotted to take his life.
Isa 49:6; Mt 12:14; Jn 10:16

54 Therefore Jesus no longer
moved about publicly among the
people of Judea. Instead he withdrew to a region near the wilderness, to a village called Ephraim,
where he stayed with his disciples.
Jn 7:1

55 When it was almost time for
the Jewish Passover, many went
up from the country to Jerusalem for their ceremonial cleansing before the Passover. 56 They
kept looking for Jesus, and as they
stood in the temple courts they
asked one another, "What do you

think? Isn't he coming to the festival at all?" 57 But the chief priests
and the Pharisees had given orders that anyone who found out
where Jesus was should report it
so that they might arrest him.
2Ch 30:17-18; Mk 14:1; Jn 7:11

Jesus Anointed at Bethany

12 Six days before the Passover, Jesus came to Bethany,
where Lazarus lived, whom Jesus
had raised from the dead. 2 Here a
dinner was given in Jesus' honor.
Martha served, while Lazarus was
among those reclining at the table
with him. 3 Then Mary took about
a pint[a] of pure nard, an expensive
perfume; she poured it on Jesus'
feet and wiped his feet with her
hair. And the house was filled with
the fragrance of the perfume.
Jn 11:2,55

4 But one of his disciples, Judas Iscariot, who was later to betray him, objected, 5 "Why wasn't
this perfume sold and the money given to the poor? It was worth
a year's wages.[b]" 6 He did not say
this because he cared about the
poor but because he was a thief; as
keeper of the money bag, he used
to help himself to what was put
into it. Mt 10:4; Jn 13:29

7 "Leave her alone," Jesus replied. "It was intended that she
should save this perfume for the
day of my burial. 8 You will always
have the poor among you,[c] but
you will not always have me."
Mt 26:6-13; Mk 14:3-9; Lk 7:37-39

9 Meanwhile a large crowd of
Jews found out that Jesus was
there and came, not only because
of him but also to see Lazarus,
whom he had raised from the
dead. 10 So the chief priests made
plans to kill Lazarus as well, 11 for
on account of him many of the
Jews were going over to Jesus and
believing in him. Jn 7:31; 11:43-44

Jesus Comes to Jerusalem as King

12 The next day the great crowd
that had come for the festival
heard that Jesus was on his way
to Jerusalem. 13 They took palm
branches and went out to meet
him, shouting, Lev 23:40

"Hosanna![d]"
"Blessed is he who comes in
the name of the Lord!"[e]
Ps 118:25-26

"Blessed is the king of Israel!"

14 Jesus found a young donkey and
sat on it, as it is written:

15 "Do not be afraid, Daughter
Zion;
see, your king is coming,
seated on a donkey's colt."[f]
Mt 21:4-9; Mk 11:7-10; Lk 19:35-38

16 At first his disciples did not
understand all this. Only after
Jesus was glorified did they realize that these things had been

[a] *3* Or about 0.5 liter [b] *5* Greek *three hundred denarii* [c] *8* See Deut. 15:11.
[d] *13* A Hebrew expression meaning "Save!" which became an exclamation of praise
[e] *13* Psalm 118:25,26 [f] *15* Zech. 9:9

written about him and that these
things had been done to him.
Jn 7:39; 14:26

17 Now the crowd that was with
him when he called Lazarus from
the tomb and raised him from
the dead continued to spread the
word. 18 Many people, because
they had heard that he had performed this sign, went out to
meet him. 19 So the Pharisees said
to one another, "See, this is getting us nowhere. Look how the
whole world has gone after him!"
Jn 11:42,47-48

Jesus Predicts His Death

20 Now there were some Greeks
among those who went up to worship at the festival. 21 They came to
Philip, who was from Bethsaida in
Galilee, with a request. "Sir," they
said, "we would like to see Jesus."
22 Philip went to tell Andrew; Andrew and Philip in turn told Jesus.
Mt 11:21; Jn 1:44; 7:35

23 Jesus replied, "The hour has
come for the Son of Man to be glorified. 24 Very truly I tell you, unless a kernel of wheat falls to the
ground and dies, it remains only
a single seed. But if it dies, it produces many seeds. 25 Anyone who
loves their life will lose it, while
anyone who hates their life in this
world will keep it for eternal life.
26 Whoever serves me must follow
me; and where I am, my servant
also will be. My Father will honor
the one who serves me.
Mt 10:39; Jn 13:32; 14:3

27 "Now my soul is troubled, and
what shall I say? 'Father, save me
from this hour'? No, it was for this
very reason I came to this hour.
28 Father, glorify your name!"
Mt 26:38-39; Jn 11:33,38

Then a voice came from heav-
en, "I have glorified it, and will
glorify it again." 29 The crowd that
was there and heard it said it had
thundered; others said an angel
had spoken to him.
Mt 3:17

30 Jesus said, "This voice was for
your benefit, not mine. 31 Now is the
time for judgment on this world;
now the prince of this world will
be driven out. 32 And I, when I am
lifted up[a] from the earth, will draw
all people to myself." 33 He said this
to show the kind of death he was
going to die.
Jn 11:42; 14:30; 18:32

34 The crowd spoke up, "We have
heard from the Law that the Messiah will remain forever, so how
can you say, 'The Son of Man must
be lifted up'? Who is this 'Son of
Man'?"
Ps 110:4; Eze 37:25

35 Then Jesus told them, "You are
going to have the light just a little
while longer. Walk while you have
the light, before darkness overtakes you. Whoever walks in the
dark does not know where they are
going. 36 Believe in the light while
you have the light, so that you may
become children of light." When
he had finished speaking, Jesus
left and hid himself from them.
Jn 8:59; Eph 5:8; 1Jn 2:11

[a] *32* The Greek for *lifted up* also means *exalted*.

Belief and Unbelief Among the Jews

37 Even after Jesus had performed so many signs in their
presence, they still would not believe in him. 38 This was to fulfill
the word of Isaiah the prophet:
Jn 2:11

> "Lord, who has believed our
> message
> and to whom has the
> arm of the Lord been
> revealed?"[a] Ro 10:16

39 For this reason they could not
believe, because, as Isaiah says
elsewhere:

> 40 "He has blinded their eyes
> and hardened their hearts,
> so they can neither see with
> their eyes,
> nor understand with their
> hearts,
> nor turn—and I would heal
> them."[b]

41 Isaiah said this because he saw
Jesus' glory and spoke about him.
Isa 6:1-4; Mt 13:13,15

42 Yet at the same time many
even among the leaders believed
in him. But because of the Pharisees they would not openly acknowledge their faith for fear
they would be put out of the synagogue; 43 for they loved human
praise more than praise from God.
Jn 5:44; 7:13; 9:22

44 Then Jesus cried out, "Whoever believes in me does not believe in me only, but in the one
who sent me. 45 The one who looks
at me is seeing the one who sent
me. 46 I have come into the world
as a light, so that no one who believes in me should stay in darkness. Mt 10:40; Jn 3:19; 14:9

47 "If anyone hears my words but
does not keep them, I do not judge
that person. For I did not come to
judge the world, but to save the
world. 48 There is a judge for the
one who rejects me and does not
accept my words; the very words
I have spoken will condemn them
at the last day. 49 For I did not speak
on my own, but the Father who
sent me commanded me to say all
that I have spoken. 50 I know that
his command leads to eternal life.
So whatever I say is just what the
Father has told me to say."
Jn 3:17; 14:31

Jesus Washes His Disciples' Feet

13 It was just before the Passover Festival. Jesus knew
that the hour had come for him
to leave this world and go to the
Father. Having loved his own who
were in the world, he loved them
to the end. Jn 11:55; 16:28

2 The evening meal was in progress, and the devil had already
prompted Judas, the son of Simon
Iscariot, to betray Jesus. 3 Jesus
knew that the Father had put all
things under his power, and that
he had come from God and was returning to God; 4 so he got up from
the meal, took off his outer clothing, and wrapped a towel around

[a] *38* Isaiah 53:1 [b] *40* Isaiah 6:10

his waist. 5 After that, he poured water into a basin and began to wash his disciples' feet, drying them with the towel that was wrapped around him.

Mt 28:18; Jn 8:42

6 He came to Simon Peter, who said to him, "Lord, are you going to wash my feet?"

7 Jesus replied, "You do not realize now what I am doing, but later you will understand."

8 "No," said Peter, "you shall never wash my feet."

Jesus answered, "Unless I wash you, you have no part with me."

9 "Then, Lord," Simon Peter replied, "not just my feet but my hands and my head as well!"

10 Jesus answered, "Those who have had a bath need only to wash their feet; their whole body is clean. And you are clean, though not every one of you." 11 For he knew who was going to betray him, and that was why he said not every one was clean. Jn 15:3

12 When he had finished washing their feet, he put on his clothes and returned to his place. "Do you understand what I have done for you?" he asked them. 13 "You call me 'Teacher' and 'Lord,' and rightly so, for that is what I am. 14 Now that I, your Lord and Teacher, have washed your feet, you also should wash one another's feet. 15 I have set you an example that you should do as I have done for you. 16 Very truly I tell you, no servant is greater than his master, nor is a messenger greater than the one who sent him. 17 Now that you know these things, you will be blessed if you do them.

Mt 10:24; Php 2:11; Jas 1:25

Jesus Predicts His Betrayal

18 "I am not referring to all of you; I know those I have chosen. But this is to fulfill this passage of Scripture: 'He who shared my bread has turned[a] against me.'[b]

Ps 41:9; Jn 6:70; 15:16,19

19 "I am telling you now before it happens, so that when it does happen you will believe that I am who I am. 20 Very truly I tell you, whoever accepts anyone I send accepts me; and whoever accepts me accepts the one who sent me."

Lk 10:16; Jn 14:29; 16:4

21 After he had said this, Jesus was troubled in spirit and testified, "Very truly I tell you, one of you is going to betray me."

Mt 26:21; Jn 12:27

22 His disciples stared at one another, at a loss to know which of them he meant. 23 One of them, the disciple whom Jesus loved, was reclining next to him. 24 Simon Peter motioned to this disciple and said, "Ask him which one he means."

Jn 19:26; 20:2; 21:7,20

25 Leaning back against Jesus, he asked him, "Lord, who is it?"

Jn 21:20

26 Jesus answered, "It is the one to whom I will give this piece of

[a] *18* Greek *has lifted up his heel*
[b] *18* Psalm 41:9

bread when I have dipped it in the
dish." Then, dipping the piece of
bread, he gave it to Judas, the son
of Simon Iscariot. 27As soon as Judas took the bread, Satan entered
into him. Lk 22:3

So Jesus told him, "What you
are about to do, do quickly."
28But no one at the meal understood why Jesus said this to
him. 29Since Judas had charge of
the money, some thought Jesus
was telling him to buy what was
needed for the festival, or to give
something to the poor. 30As soon
as Judas had taken the bread, he
went out. And it was night.
Lk 22:53; Jn 12:6

Jesus Predicts Peter's Denial

31When he was gone, Jesus said,
"Now the Son of Man is glorified
and God is glorified in him. 32If
God is glorified in him,[a] God will
glorify the Son in himself, and will
glorify him at once. Jn 14:13; 1Pe 4:11

33"My children, I will be with
you only a little longer. You will
look for me, and just as I told the
Jews, so I tell you now: Where I
am going, you cannot come.
Jn 7:33-34

34"A new command I give you:
Love one another. As I have loved
you, so you must love one another. 35By this everyone will know
that you are my disciples, if you
love one another."
Lev 19:18; 1Jn 2:7-11; 4:20

36Simon Peter asked him, "Lord,
where are you going?"

Jesus replied, "Where I am going, you cannot follow now, but
you will follow later."
Jn 21:18-19; 2Pe 1:14

37Peter asked, "Lord, why can't
I follow you now? I will lay down
my life for you."

38Then Jesus answered, "Will
you really lay down your life for
me? Very truly I tell you, before
the rooster crows, you will disown
me three times!
Mt 26:33-35; Mk 14:29-31; Lk 22:33-34

Jesus Comforts His Disciples

14 "Do not let your hearts be
troubled. You believe in
God[b]; believe also in me. 2My Father's house has many rooms;
if that were not so, would I have
told you that I am going there to
prepare a place for you? 3And if
I go and prepare a place for you,
I will come back and take you to
be with me that you also may be
where I am. 4You know the way to
the place where I am going."
Jn 12:26; 13:33,36

Jesus the Way to the Father

5Thomas said to him, "Lord, we
don't know where you are going,
so how can we know the way?"
Jn 11:16

6Jesus answered, "I am the way
and the truth and the life. No
one comes to the Father except
through me. 7If you really know

[a] 32 Many early manuscripts do not have *If God is glorified in him.* [b] 1 Or *Believe in God*

me, you will know[a] my Father as
well. From now on, you do know
him and have seen him."
Jn 1:14; 10:9; 11:25
8 Philip said, "Lord, show us the
Father and that will be enough
for us." Jn 1:43
9 Jesus answered: "Don't you
know me, Philip, even after I have
been among you such a long time?
Anyone who has seen me has seen
the Father. How can you say, 'Show
us the Father'? 10 Don't you believe
that I am in the Father, and that
the Father is in me? The words I
say to you I do not speak on my
own authority. Rather, it is the Father, living in me, who is doing his
work. 11 Believe me when I say that
I am in the Father and the Father
is in me; or at least believe on the
evidence of the works themselves.
12 Very truly I tell you, whoever believes in me will do the works I
have been doing, and they will do
even greater things than these,
because I am going to the Father.
13 And I will do whatever you ask in
my name, so that the Father may
be glorified in the Son. 14 You may
ask me for anything in my name,
and I will do it. Jn 10:38; 12:45

Jesus Promises the Holy Spirit

15 "If you love me, keep my commands. 16 And I will ask the Father,
and he will give you another advocate to help you and be with you
forever— 17 the Spirit of truth. The
world cannot accept him, because
it neither sees him nor knows
him. But you know him, for he
lives with you and will be[b] in you.
18 I will not leave you as orphans; I
will come to you. 19 Before long, the
world will not see me anymore,
but you will see me. Because I live,
you also will live. 20 On that day
you will realize that I am in my
Father, and you are in me, and I
am in you. 21 Whoever has my commands and keeps them is the one
who loves me. The one who loves
me will be loved by my Father, and
I too will love them and show myself to them." Jn 15:10; 1Jn 5:3
22 Then Judas (not Judas Iscariot) said, "But, Lord, why do you
intend to show yourself to us and
not to the world?" Lk 6:16; Ac 10:41
23 Jesus replied, "Anyone who
loves me will obey my teaching.
My Father will love them, and we
will come to them and make our
home with them. 24 Anyone who
does not love me will not obey my
teaching. These words you hear
are not my own; they belong to
the Father who sent me.
Jn 7:16; 1Jn 2:24
25 "All this I have spoken while
still with you. 26 But the Advocate,
the Holy Spirit, whom the Father
will send in my name, will teach
you all things and will remind you
of everything I have said to you.
27 Peace I leave with you; my peace
I give you. I do not give to you as
the world gives. Do not let your

[a] 7 Some manuscripts *If you really knew me, you would know*
[b] 17 Some early manuscripts *and is*

hearts be troubled and do not be
afraid. Jn 15:26; Php 4:7; 1Jn 2:20,27
28“You heard me say, ‘I am going away and I am coming back to
you.’ If you loved me, you would
be glad that I am going to the
Father, for the Father is greater
than I. 29I have told you now before it happens, so that when it
does happen you will believe. 30I
will not say much more to you, for
the prince of this world is coming. He has no hold over me, 31but
he comes so that the world may
learn that I love the Father and do
exactly what my Father has commanded me. Jn 10:18; 12:31; 13:19
“Come now; let us leave.

The Vine and the Branches

15 “I am the true vine, and my
Father is the gardener. 2He
cuts off every branch in me that
bears no fruit, while every branch
that does bear fruit he prunes[a] so
that it will be even more fruitful.
3You are already clean because of
the word I have spoken to you.
4Remain in me, as I also remain in
you. No branch can bear fruit by
itself; it must remain in the vine.
Neither can you bear fruit unless
you remain in me. Isa 5:1-7; 1Jn 2:6
5“I am the vine; you are the
branches. If you remain in me and
I in you, you will bear much fruit;
apart from me you can do nothing.
6If you do not remain in me, you
are like a branch that is thrown
away and withers; such branches are picked up, thrown into the
fire and burned. 7If you remain in
me and my words remain in you,
ask whatever you wish, and it will
be done for you. 8This is to my Father’s glory, that you bear much
fruit, showing yourselves to be my
disciples. Mt 7:7; Jn 8:31
9“As the Father has loved me,
so have I loved you. Now remain
in my love. 10If you keep my commands, you will remain in my
love, just as I have kept my Father’s commands and remain in
his love. 11I have told you this so
that my joy may be in you and that
your joy may be complete. 12My
command is this: Love each other
as I have loved you. 13Greater love
has no one than this: to lay down
one’s life for one’s friends. 14You
are my friends if you do what I
command. 15I no longer call you
servants, because a servant does
not know his master’s business.
Instead, I have called you friends,
for everything that I learned from
my Father I have made known to
you. 16You did not choose me, but
I chose you and appointed you
so that you might go and bear
fruit — fruit that will last — and so
that whatever you ask in my name
the Father will give you. 17This is
my command: Love each other.
Jn 13:18,34; 14:15

The World Hates the Disciples

18“If the world hates you, keep
in mind that it hated me first.

[a] 2 The Greek for *he prunes* also means *he cleans.*

[19]If you belonged to the world, it
would love you as its own. As it is,
you do not belong to the world,
but I have chosen you out of the
world. That is why the world hates
you. [20]Remember what I told you:
'A servant is not greater than his
master.'[a] If they persecuted me,
they will persecute you also. If
they obeyed my teaching, they
will obey yours also. [21]They will
treat you this way because of my
name, for they do not know the
one who sent me. [22]If I had not
come and spoken to them, they
would not be guilty of sin; but
now they have no excuse for their
sin. [23]Whoever hates me hates my
Father as well. [24]If I had not done
among them the works no one
else did, they would not be guilty
of sin. As it is, they have seen, and
yet they have hated both me and
my Father. [25]But this is to fulfill
what is written in their Law: 'They
hated me without reason.'[b]

Jn 9:41; 1Jn 3:13

The Work of the Holy Spirit

[26]"When the Advocate comes,
whom I will send to you from the
Father — the Spirit of truth who
goes out from the Father — he will
testify about me. [27]And you also
must testify, for you have been
with me from the beginning.

Jn 14:17; 1Jn 5:7

16 "All this I have told you so
that you will not fall away.
[2]They will put you out of the synagogue; in fact, the time is coming
when anyone who kills you will
think they are offering a service
to God. [3]They will do such things
because they have not known the
Father or me. [4]I have told you this,
so that when their time comes you
will remember that I warned you
about them. I did not tell you this
from the beginning because I was
with you, [5]but now I am going to
him who sent me. None of you
asks me, 'Where are you going?'
[6]Rather, you are filled with grief
because I have said these things.
[7]But very truly I tell you, it is for
your good that I am going away.
Unless I go away, the Advocate will
not come to you; but if I go, I will
send him to you. [8]When he comes,
he will prove the world to be in
the wrong about sin and righteousness and judgment: [9]about
sin, because people do not believe
in me; [10]about righteousness, because I am going to the Father,
where you can see me no longer;
[11]and about judgment, because the
prince of this world now stands
condemned.

Jn 7:33,39; 14:16,26

[12]"I have much more to say to
you, more than you can now bear.
[13]But when he, the Spirit of truth,
comes, he will guide you into all
the truth. He will not speak on his
own; he will speak only what he
hears, and he will tell you what is
yet to come. [14]He will glorify me
because it is from me that he will
receive what he will make known
to you. [15]All that belongs to the

[a] *20* John 13:16 [b] *25* Psalms 35:19; 69:4

Father is mine. That is why I said
the Spirit will receive from me
what he will make known to you."
Jn 14:17,26; 17:10

The Disciples' Grief Will Turn to Joy

16 Jesus went on to say, "In a little while you will see me no more,
and then after a little while you
will see me." Jn 14:18-24
17 At this, some of his disciples
said to one another, "What does he
mean by saying, 'In a little while
you will see me no more, and then
after a little while you will see me,'
and 'Because I am going to the Father'?" 18 They kept asking, "What
does he mean by 'a little while'?
We don't understand what he is
saying."
19 Jesus saw that they wanted to
ask him about this, so he said to
them, "Are you asking one another what I meant when I said, 'In
a little while you will see me no
more, and then after a little while
you will see me'? 20 Very truly I
tell you, you will weep and mourn
while the world rejoices. You will
grieve, but your grief will turn to
joy. 21 A woman giving birth to a
child has pain because her time
has come; but when her baby is
born she forgets the anguish because of her joy that a child is
born into the world. 22 So with
you: Now is your time of grief, but
I will see you again and you will
rejoice, and no one will take away
your joy. 23 In that day you will
no longer ask me anything. Very
truly I tell you, my Father will
give you whatever you ask in my
name. 24 Until now you have not
asked for anything in my name.
Ask and you will receive, and your
joy will be complete.
Mt 7:7; Jn 15:11,16
25 "Though I have been speaking figuratively, a time is coming
when I will no longer use this kind
of language but will tell you plainly about my Father. 26 In that day
you will ask in my name. I am not
saying that I will ask the Father on
your behalf. 27 No, the Father himself loves you because you have
loved me and have believed that I
came from God. 28 I came from the
Father and entered the world; now
I am leaving the world and going
back to the Father." Jn 10:6; 14:21,23
29 Then Jesus' disciples said,
"Now you are speaking clearly and without figures of speech.
30 Now we can see that you know
all things and that you do not
even need to have anyone ask you
questions. This makes us believe
that you came from God." Jn 13:3
31 "Do you now believe?" Jesus
replied. 32 "A time is coming and
in fact has come when you will be
scattered, each to your own home.
You will leave me all alone. Yet
I am not alone, for my Father is
with me. Mt 26:31; Jn 8:16,29
33 "I have told you these things,
so that in me you may have peace.
In this world you will have trouble. But take heart! I have overcome the world." Jn 14:27; Ro 8:37

Jesus Prays to Be Glorified

17 After Jesus said this, he looked toward heaven and prayed: Jn 11:41

"Father, the hour has come. Glorify your Son, that your Son may glorify you. [2]For you granted him authority over all people that he might give eternal life to all those you have given him. [3]Now this is eternal life: that they know you, the only true God, and Jesus Christ, whom you have sent. [4]I have brought you glory on earth by finishing the work you gave me to do. [5]And now, Father, glorify me in your presence with the glory I had with you before the world began. Jn 1:2; Php 2:6

Jesus Prays for His Disciples

[6]"I have revealed you[a] to those whom you gave me out of the world. They were yours; you gave them to me and they have obeyed your word. [7]Now they know that everything you have given me comes from you. [8]For I gave them the words you gave me and they accepted them. They knew with certainty that I came from you, and they believed that you sent me. [9]I pray for them. I am not praying for the world, but for those you have given me, for they are yours. [10]All I have is yours, and all you have is mine. And glory has come to me through them. [11]I will remain in the world no longer, but they are still in the world, and I am coming to you. Holy Father, protect them by the power of[b] your name, the name you gave me, so that they may be one as we are one. [12]While I was with them, I protected them and kept them safe by[c] that name you gave me. None has been lost except the one doomed to destruction so that Scripture would be fulfilled. Jn 6:39,70; 7:33

[13]"I am coming to you now, but I say these things while I am still in the world, so that they may have the full measure of my joy within them. [14]I have given them your word and the world has hated them, for they are not of the world any more than I am of the world. [15]My prayer is not that you take them out of the world but that you protect them from the evil one. [16]They are not of the world, even as I am not of it. [17]Sanctify them by[d] the truth; your word is truth. [18]As you sent me into the world, I have sent them into the world.

[a] 6 *Greek* your name [b] 11 *Or* Father, keep them faithful to [c] 12 *Or* kept them faithful to [d] 17 *Or* them to live in accordance with

[19]For them I sanctify myself,
that they too may be truly
sanctified. Jn 8:23; 20:21

Jesus Prays for All Believers

[20]"My prayer is not for
them alone. I pray also for
those who will believe in me
through their message, [21]that
all of them may be one, Father, just as you are in me and
I am in you. May they also be
in us so that the world may
believe that you have sent me.
[22]I have given them the glory
that you gave me, that they
may be one as we are one —
[23]I in them and you in me —
so that they may be brought
to complete unity. Then the
world will know that you sent
me and have loved them even
as you have loved me.
Jn 10:38; 14:20

[24]"Father, I want those you
have given me to be with me
where I am, and to see my glory, the glory you have given
me because you loved me before the creation of the world.
Jn 12:26

[25]"Righteous Father, though
the world does not know you,
I know you, and they know
that you have sent me. [26]I
have made you[a] known to
them, and will continue to
make you known in order that
the love you have for me may
be in them and that I myself
may be in them." Jn 15:9,21; 16:27

Jesus Arrested

18 When he had finished praying, Jesus left with his disciples and crossed the Kidron Valley.
On the other side there was a garden, and he and his disciples went
into it. 2Sa 15:23; Mt 21:1
[2]Now Judas, who betrayed him,
knew the place, because Jesus had
often met there with his disciples.
[3]So Judas came to the garden,
guiding a detachment of soldiers
and some officials from the chief
priests and the Pharisees. They
were carrying torches, lanterns
and weapons. Lk 21:37; 22:39; Ac 1:16
[4]Jesus, knowing all that was going to happen to him, went out
and asked them, "Who is it you
want?"
Jn 6:64; 13:1,11
[5]"Jesus of Nazareth," they replied. Mk 1:24
"I am he," Jesus said. (And Judas the traitor was standing there
with them.) [6]When Jesus said, "I
am he," they drew back and fell to
the ground.
[7]Again he asked them, "Who is
it you want?"
"Jesus of Nazareth," they said.
[8]Jesus answered, "I told you
that I am he. If you are looking
for me, then let these men go."
[9]This happened so that the words
he had spoken would be fulfilled:
"I have not lost one of those you
gave me."[b]
Jn 17:12
[10]Then Simon Peter, who had a
sword, drew it and struck the high

[a] 26 Greek *your name* [b] 9 John 6:39

priest's servant, cutting off his right ear. (The servant's name was Malchus.)
[11]Jesus commanded Peter, "Put your sword away! Shall I not drink the cup the Father has given me?"

Mt 26:47-56; Mk 14:43-50; Lk 22:47-53

[12]Then the detachment of soldiers with its commander and the Jewish officials arrested Jesus. They bound him [13]and brought him first to Annas, who was the father-in-law of Caiaphas, the high priest that year. [14]Caiaphas was the one who had advised the Jewish leaders that it would be good if one man died for the people.

Mt 26:57; Jn 11:49-51

Peter's First Denial

[15]Simon Peter and another disciple were following Jesus. Because this disciple was known to the high priest, he went with Jesus into the high priest's courtyard, [16]but Peter had to wait outside at the door. The other disciple, who was known to the high priest, came back, spoke to the servant girl on duty there and brought Peter in.

Mt 26:58; Mk 14:54; Lk 22:54

[17]"You aren't one of this man's disciples too, are you?" she asked Peter.

He replied, "I am not."

[18]It was cold, and the servants and officials stood around a fire they had made to keep warm. Peter also was standing with them, warming himself.

Mt 26:69-70; Mk 14:66-68; Lk 22:55-57

The High Priest Questions Jesus

[19]Meanwhile, the high priest questioned Jesus about his disciples and his teaching.

[20]"I have spoken openly to the world," Jesus replied. "I always taught in synagogues or at the temple, where all the Jews come together. I said nothing in secret. [21]Why question me? Ask those who heard me. Surely they know what I said."

Mt 26:55; Jn 7:26

[22]When Jesus said this, one of the officials nearby slapped him in the face. "Is this the way you answer the high priest?" he demanded.

Jn 19:3

[23]"If I said something wrong," Jesus replied, "testify as to what is wrong. But if I spoke the truth, why did you strike me?" [24]Then Annas sent him bound to Caiaphas the high priest.

Mt 26:59-68; Mk 14:55-65; Lk 22:63-71

Peter's Second and Third Denials

[25]Meanwhile, Simon Peter was still standing there warming himself. So they asked him, "You aren't one of his disciples too, are you?"

He denied it, saying, "I am not."

[26]One of the high priest's servants, a relative of the man whose ear Peter had cut off, challenged him, "Didn't I see you with him in the garden?" [27]Again Peter denied it, and at that moment a rooster began to crow.

Mt 26:71-75; Mk 14:69-72; Lk 22:58-62

Jesus Before Pilate

28Then the Jewish leaders took
Jesus from Caiaphas to the palace
of the Roman governor. By now it
was early morning, and to avoid
ceremonial uncleanness they did
not enter the palace, because they
wanted to be able to eat the Passover. 29So Pilate came out to them
and asked, "What charges are you
bringing against this man?"
Mt 27:2; Mk 15:1; Jn 11:55

30"If he were not a criminal,"
they replied, "we would not have
handed him over to you."

31Pilate said, "Take him yourselves and judge him by your own
law."

"But we have no right to execute anyone," they objected. 32This
took place to fulfill what Jesus had
said about the kind of death he
was going to die. Mt 20:19; Jn 12:32-33

33Pilate then went back inside
the palace, summoned Jesus and
asked him, "Are you the king of
the Jews?" Lk 23:3; Jn 19:9

34"Is that your own idea," Jesus
asked, "or did others talk to you
about me?"

35"Am I a Jew?" Pilate replied.
"Your own people and chief priests
handed you over to me. What is it
you have done?"

36Jesus said, "My kingdom is not
of this world. If it were, my servants would fight to prevent my
arrest by the Jewish leaders. But
now my kingdom is from another
place." Mt 26:53; Jn 6:15

37"You are a king, then!" said Pilate.

Jesus answered, "You say that
I am a king. In fact, the reason I
was born and came into the world
is to testify to the truth. Everyone
on the side of truth listens to me."
Jn 8:47; 1Jn 4:6

38"What is truth?" retorted Pilate. With this he went out again to
the Jews gathered there and said,
"I find no basis for a charge against
him. 39But it is your custom for me
to release to you one prisoner at
the time of the Passover. Do you
want me to release 'the king of the
Jews'?" Lk 23:4; Jn 19:4,6

40They shouted back, "No, not
him! Give us Barabbas!" Now Barabbas had taken part in an uprising. Ac 3:14

Jesus Sentenced to Be Crucified

19 Then Pilate took Jesus and
had him flogged. 2The soldiers twisted together a crown of
thorns and put it on his head. They
clothed him in a purple robe 3and
went up to him again and again,
saying, "Hail, king of the Jews!"
And they slapped him in the face.
Mt 27:26,29; Jn 18:22

4Once more Pilate came out and
said to the Jews gathered there,
"Look, I am bringing him out to
you to let you know that I find no
basis for a charge against him."
5When Jesus came out wearing
the crown of thorns and the purple robe, Pilate said to them, "Here
is the man!" Lk 23:4; Jn 18:38

6As soon as the chief priests and
their officials saw him, they shouted, "Crucify! Crucify!"
But Pilate answered, "You take
him and crucify him. As for me, I
find no basis for a charge against
him." Lk 23:4; Ac 3:13
7The Jewish leaders insisted,
"We have a law, and according to
that law he must die, because he
claimed to be the Son of God."
Lev 24:16; Mt 26:63-66
8When Pilate heard this, he was
even more afraid, 9and he went
back inside the palace. "Where do
you come from?" he asked Jesus,
but Jesus gave him no answer.
10"Do you refuse to speak to me?"
Pilate said. "Don't you realize I
have power either to free you or
to crucify you?" Mk 14:61; Jn 18:33
11Jesus answered, "You would
have no power over me if it were
not given to you from above.
Therefore the one who handed me
over to you is guilty of a greater
sin." Jn 18:28-30; Ac 3:13; Ro 13:1
12From then on, Pilate tried to
set Jesus free, but the Jewish leaders kept shouting, "If you let this
man go, you are no friend of Caesar. Anyone who claims to be a
king opposes Caesar." Lk 23:2
13When Pilate heard this, he
brought Jesus out and sat down on
the judge's seat at a place known
as the Stone Pavement (which in
Aramaic is Gabbatha). 14It was the
day of Preparation of the Passover; it was about noon.
Mt 27:62; Mk 15:25; Jn 5:2
"Here is your king," Pilate said
to the Jews.
15But they shouted, "Take him
away! Take him away! Crucify
him!"
"Shall I crucify your king?" Pilate asked.
"We have no king but Caesar,"
the chief priests answered.
16Finally Pilate handed him over
to them to be crucified.
Mt 27:27-31; Mk 15:16-20

The Crucifixion of Jesus

So the soldiers took charge of
Jesus. 17Carrying his own cross, he
went out to the place of the Skull
(which in Aramaic is called Golgotha). 18There they crucified him,
and with him two others — one on
each side and Jesus in the middle.
Lk 23:26,32-33; Jn 5:2
19Pilate had a notice prepared
and fastened to the cross. It read:
JESUS OF NAZARETH, THE KING OF
THE JEWS. 20Many of the Jews read
this sign, for the place where Jesus
was crucified was near the city, and
the sign was written in Aramaic,
Latin and Greek. 21The chief priests
of the Jews protested to Pilate, "Do
not write 'The King of the Jews,'
but that this man claimed to be
king of the Jews." Mk 1:24; Heb 13:12
22Pilate answered, "What I have
written, I have written."
23When the soldiers crucified
Jesus, they took his clothes, dividing them into four shares,
one for each of them, with the
undergarment remaining. This

garment was seamless, woven in
one piece from top to bottom.
24“Let’s not tear it,” they said to
one another. “Let’s decide by lot
who will get it.”

This happened that the scripture might be fulfilled that said,

Mt 1:22

“They divided my clothes
among them
and cast lots for my
garment.”[a]

Ps 22:18

So this is what the soldiers did.

Mt 27:33-44; Mk 15:22-32; Lk 23:33-43

25Near the cross of Jesus stood
his mother, his mother’s sister,
Mary the wife of Clopas, and Mary
Magdalene. 26When Jesus saw his
mother there, and the disciple
whom he loved standing nearby,
he said to her, “Woman,[b] here is
your son,” 27and to the disciple,
“Here is your mother.” From that
time on, this disciple took her into
his home.

Mk 15:40-41; Lk 24:18; Jn 13:23

The Death of Jesus

28Later, knowing that everything had now been finished, and
so that Scripture would be fulfilled, Jesus said, “I am thirsty.”
29A jar of wine vinegar was there,
so they soaked a sponge in it, put
the sponge on a stalk of the hyssop plant, and lifted it to Jesus’
lips. 30When he had received the
drink, Jesus said, “It is finished.”
With that, he bowed his head and
gave up his spirit.

Mt 27:48,50; Mk 15:36-37; Lk 23:36

31Now it was the day of Preparation, and the next day was to be a
special Sabbath. Because the Jewish leaders did not want the bodies left on the crosses during the
Sabbath, they asked Pilate to have
the legs broken and the bodies
taken down. 32The soldiers therefore came and broke the legs of
the first man who had been crucified with Jesus, and then those
of the other. 33But when they came
to Jesus and found that he was already dead, they did not break his
legs. 34Instead, one of the soldiers
pierced Jesus’ side with a spear,
bringing a sudden flow of blood
and water. 35The man who saw it
has given testimony, and his testimony is true. He knows that he
tells the truth, and he testifies so
that you also may believe. 36These
things happened so that the scripture would be fulfilled: “Not one
of his bones will be broken,”[c]
37and, as another scripture says,
“They will look on the one they
have pierced.”[d]

1Jn 5:6,8; Rev 1:7

The Burial of Jesus

38Later, Joseph of Arimathea
asked Pilate for the body of Jesus.
Now Joseph was a disciple of Jesus,
but secretly because he feared the
Jewish leaders. With Pilate’s permission, he came and took the
body away. 39He was accompanied

[a] 24 Psalm 22:18 [b] 26 The Greek for *Woman* does not denote any disrespect.
[c] 36 Exodus 12:46; Num. 9:12; Psalm 34:20
[d] 37 Zech. 12:10

by Nicodemus, the man who earlier had visited Jesus at night. Nicodemus brought a mixture of myrrh
and aloes, about seventy-five
pounds.[a] [40]Taking Jesus' body, the
two of them wrapped it, with the
spices, in strips of linen. This was
in accordance with Jewish burial
customs. [41]At the place where Jesus
was crucified, there was a garden,
and in the garden a new tomb, in
which no one had ever been laid.
[42]Because it was the Jewish day of
Preparation and since the tomb
was nearby, they laid Jesus there.

Mt 27:57-61; Mk 15:42-47; Lk 23:50-56

The Empty Tomb

20 Early on the first day of
the week, while it was still
dark, Mary Magdalene went to the
tomb and saw that the stone had
been removed from the entrance.
[2]So she came running to Simon
Peter and the other disciple, the
one Jesus loved, and said, "They
have taken the Lord out of the
tomb, and we don't know where
they have put him!"

[3]So Peter and the other disciple
started for the tomb. [4]Both were
running, but the other disciple
outran Peter and reached the tomb
first. [5]He bent over and looked in at
the strips of linen lying there but
did not go in. [6]Then Simon Peter
came along behind him and went
straight into the tomb. He saw the
strips of linen lying there, [7]as well
as the cloth that had been wrapped
around Jesus' head. The cloth was
still lying in its place, separate
from the linen. [8]Finally the other disciple, who had reached the
tomb first, also went inside. He saw
and believed. [9](They still did not
understand from Scripture that
Jesus had to rise from the dead.)
[10]Then the disciples went back to
where they were staying.

Mt 28:1-8; Mk 16:1-8; Lk 24:1-10

Jesus Appears to Mary Magdalene

[11]Now Mary stood outside the
tomb crying. As she wept, she bent
over to look into the tomb [12]and
saw two angels in white, seated
where Jesus' body had been, one
at the head and the other at the
foot. Mk 16:5; Lk 24:4; Ac 5:19

[13]They asked her, "Woman, why
are you crying?"

"They have taken my Lord
away," she said, "and I don't know
where they have put him." [14]At
this, she turned around and saw
Jesus standing there, but she did
not realize that it was Jesus.

Mk 16:9; Jn 21:4

[15]He asked her, "Woman, why
are you crying? Who is it you are
looking for?"

Thinking he was the gardener,
she said, "Sir, if you have carried
him away, tell me where you have
put him, and I will get him."

[16]Jesus said to her, "Mary."

She turned toward him and
cried out in Aramaic, "Rabboni!"
(which means "Teacher").

Mt 23:7; Jn 5:2

[a] 39 Or about 34 kilograms

[17]Jesus said, "Do not hold on to
me, for I have not yet ascended to
the Father. Go instead to my brothers and tell them, 'I am ascending
to my Father and your Father, to
my God and your God.'"
Mt 28:10; Jn 7:33
[18]Mary Magdalene went to the
disciples with the news: "I have
seen the Lord!" And she told them
that he had said these things to
her. Lk 24:10,22-23

Jesus Appears to His Disciples

[19]On the evening of that first
day of the week, when the disciples were together, with the doors
locked for fear of the Jewish leaders, Jesus came and stood among
them and said, "Peace be with you!"
[20]After he said this, he showed
them his hands and side. The disciples were overjoyed when they saw
the Lord. Lk 24:36-39; Jn 16:20,22
[21]Again Jesus said, "Peace be
with you! As the Father has sent
me, I am sending you." [22]And with
that he breathed on them and
said, "Receive the Holy Spirit. [23]If
you forgive anyone's sins, their
sins are forgiven; if you do not forgive them, they are not forgiven."
Mt 16:19; 18:18; 28:19

Jesus Appears to Thomas

[24]Now Thomas (also known as
Didymus[a]), one of the Twelve, was
not with the disciples when Jesus
came. [25]So the other disciples told
him, "We have seen the Lord!"
Jn 11:16
But he said to them, "Unless I
see the nail marks in his hands
and put my finger where the nails
were, and put my hand into his
side, I will not believe." Mk 16:11
[26]A week later his disciples were
in the house again, and Thomas
was with them. Though the doors
were locked, Jesus came and stood
among them and said, "Peace be
with you!" [27]Then he said to Thomas, "Put your finger here; see my
hands. Reach out your hand and
put it into my side. Stop doubting
and believe." Lk 24:40; Jn 14:27
[28]Thomas said to him, "My Lord
and my God!"
[29]Then Jesus told him, "Because
you have seen me, you have believed; blessed are those who have
not seen and yet have believed."
Jn 3:15; 1Pe 1:8

The Purpose of John's Gospel

[30]Jesus performed many other
signs in the presence of his disciples, which are not recorded in
this book. [31]But these are written
that you may believe[b] that Jesus
is the Messiah, the Son of God, and
that by believing you may have
life in his name. Jn 3:15; 21:25

Jesus and the Miraculous Catch of Fish

21 Afterward Jesus appeared
again to his disciples, by the
Sea of Galilee.[c] It happened this

[a] 24 *Thomas* (Aramaic) and *Didymus* (Greek) both mean *twin.* [b] 31 Or *may continue to believe* [c] 1 Greek *Tiberias*

way: 2Simon Peter, Thomas (also
known as Didymus[a]), Nathanael
from Cana in Galilee, the sons of
Zebedee, and two other disciples
were together. 3"I'm going out to
fish," Simon Peter told them, and
they said, "We'll go with you." So
they went out and got into the
boat, but that night they caught
nothing. Mt 4:21; Lk 5:5
4Early in the morning, Jesus
stood on the shore, but the disciples did not realize that it was
Jesus. Lk 24:16; Jn 20:14
5He called out to them, "Friends,
haven't you any fish?"

"No," they answered.

6He said, "Throw your net on
the right side of the boat and you
will find some." When they did,
they were unable to haul the net
in because of the large number of
fish. Lk 5:4-7
7Then the disciple whom Jesus
loved said to Peter, "It is the Lord!"
As soon as Simon Peter heard him
say, "It is the Lord," he wrapped his
outer garment around him (for he
had taken it off) and jumped into
the water. 8The other disciples
followed in the boat, towing the
net full of fish, for they were not
far from shore, about a hundred
yards.[b] 9When they landed, they
saw a fire of burning coals there
with fish on it, and some bread.
Jn 13:23; 18:18
10Jesus said to them, "Bring
some of the fish you have just
caught." 11So Simon Peter climbed
back into the boat and dragged the
net ashore. It was full of large fish,
153, but even with so many the net
was not torn. 12Jesus said to them,
"Come and have breakfast." None
of the disciples dared ask him,
"Who are you?" They knew it was
the Lord. 13Jesus came, took the
bread and gave it to them, and did
the same with the fish. 14This was
now the third time Jesus appeared
to his disciples after he was raised
from the dead. Jn 20:19,26

Jesus Reinstates Peter

15When they had finished eating, Jesus said to Simon Peter, "Simon son of John, do you love me
more than these?"

"Yes, Lord," he said, "you know
that I love you." Mt 26:33,35; Jn 13:37

Jesus said, "Feed my lambs."
Lk 12:32
16Again Jesus said, "Simon son
of John, do you love me?"

He answered, "Yes, Lord, you
know that I love you."

Jesus said, "Take care of my
sheep." Ac 20:28; 1Pe 5:2-3
17The third time he said to
him, "Simon son of John, do you
love me?"

Peter was hurt because Jesus
asked him the third time, "Do
you love me?" He said, "Lord, you
know all things; you know that I
love you." Jn 16:30

Jesus said, "Feed my sheep.
18Very truly I tell you, when you
were younger you dressed yourself

[a] 2 *Thomas* (Aramaic) and *Didymus* (Greek) both mean *twin.* [b] 8 Or about 90 meters

and went where you wanted; but
when you are old you will stretch
out your hands, and someone else
will dress you and lead you where
you do not want to go." 19 Jesus said
this to indicate the kind of death
by which Peter would glorify God.
Then he said to him, "Follow me!"
2Pe 1:14

20 Peter turned and saw that the
disciple whom Jesus loved was
following them. (This was the one
who had leaned back against Jesus
at the supper and had said, "Lord,
who is going to betray you?")
21 When Peter saw him, he asked,
"Lord, what about him?" Jn 13:23,25

22 Jesus answered, "If I want
him to remain alive until I return,
what is that to you? You must follow me." 23 Because of this, the
rumor spread among the believers that this disciple would not
die. But Jesus did not say that he
would not die; he only said, "If I
want him to remain alive until I
return, what is that to you?"
Mt 16:27; Ac 1:16

24 This is the disciple who testifies to these things and who wrote
them down. We know that his testimony is true. Jn 19:35

25 Jesus did many other things
as well. If every one of them were
written down, I suppose that even
the whole world would not have
room for the books that would be
written. Jn 20:30

ACTS

Jesus Taken Up Into Heaven

1 In my former book, Theophilus, I wrote about all that Jesus
began to do and to teach 2until the
day he was taken up to heaven,
after giving instructions through
the Holy Spirit to the apostles he
had chosen. 3After his suffering,
he presented himself to them
and gave many convincing proofs
that he was alive. He appeared to
them over a period of forty days
and spoke about the kingdom of
God. 4On one occasion, while he
was eating with them, he gave
them this command: "Do not
leave Jerusalem, but wait for the
gift my Father promised, which
you have heard me speak about.
5For John baptized with[a] water,
but in a few days you will be baptized with[a] the Holy Spirit."

Lk 1:1-4; Jn 14:16

6Then they gathered around
him and asked him, "Lord, are you
at this time going to restore the
kingdom to Israel?" Mt 17:11

7He said to them: "It is not for
you to know the times or dates
the Father has set by his own authority. 8But you will receive power when the Holy Spirit comes on
you; and you will be my witnesses
in Jerusalem, and in all Judea and
Samaria, and to the ends of the
earth." Mt 24:36; Lk 24:48

9After he said this, he was tak-
en up before their very eyes, and a
cloud hid him from their sight.

Mk 16:19

10They were looking intently
up into the sky as he was going,
when suddenly two men dressed
in white stood beside them. 11"Men
of Galilee," they said, "why do you
stand here looking into the sky?
This same Jesus, who has been tak-
en from you into heaven, will come
back in the same way you have seen
him go into heaven." Mt 16:27; Jn 20:12

Matthias Chosen to Replace Judas

12Then the apostles returned to
Jerusalem from the hill called the
Mount of Olives, a Sabbath day's
walk[b] from the city. 13When they
arrived, they went upstairs to the
room where they were staying.
Those present were Peter, John,
James and Andrew; Philip and
Thomas, Bartholomew and Matthew; James son of Alphaeus and
Simon the Zealot, and Judas son
of James. 14They all joined together constantly in prayer, along with
the women and Mary the mother
of Jesus, and with his brothers.

Ac 2:42; 9:37; Lk 23:49,55

15In those days Peter stood up
among the believers (a group

[a] 5 Or *in* [b] 12 That is, about 5/8 mile or about 1 kilometer

numbering about a hundred and
twenty) 16 and said, "Brothers and
sisters,[a] the Scripture had to be
fulfilled in which the Holy Spirit spoke long ago through David
concerning Judas, who served
as guide for those who arrested
Jesus. 17 He was one of our number
and shared in our ministry."

Jn 6:70-71; 13:18

18 (With the payment he received
for his wickedness, Judas bought
a field; there he fell headlong, his
body burst open and all his intestines spilled out. 19 Everyone in Jerusalem heard about this, so they
called that field in their language
Akeldama, that is, Field of Blood.)

Mt 26:14-15; 27:3-10

20 "For," said Peter, "it is written
in the Book of Psalms:

> " 'May his place be deserted;
> let there be no one to
> dwell in it,'[b] Ps 69:25

and,

> " 'May another take his place of
> leadership.'[c]

21 Therefore it is necessary to
choose one of the men who have
been with us the whole time the
Lord Jesus was living among us,
22 beginning from John's baptism
to the time when Jesus was taken
up from us. For one of these must
become a witness with us of his
resurrection." Mk 1:4; Lk 24:48

23 So they nominated two men:
Joseph called Barsabbas (also
known as Justus) and Matthias.
24 Then they prayed, "Lord, you
know everyone's heart. Show
us which of these two you have
chosen 25 to take over this apos-
tolic ministry, which Judas left
to go where he belongs." 26 Then
they cast lots, and the lot fell to
Matthias; so he was added to the
eleven apostles.

1Sa 16:7; Jer 17:10; Rev 2:23

The Holy Spirit Comes at Pentecost

2 When the day of Pentecost
came, they were all together
in one place. 2 Suddenly a sound
like the blowing of a violent wind
came from heaven and filled the
whole house where they were sitting. 3 They saw what seemed to be
tongues of fire that separated and
came to rest on each of them. 4 All
of them were filled with the Holy
Spirit and began to speak in other tongues[d] as the Spirit enabled
them. Mk 16:17; 1Co 12:10

5 Now there were staying in Jerusalem God-fearing Jews from every nation under heaven. 6 When
they heard this sound, a crowd
came together in bewilderment,
because each one heard their
own language being spoken. 7 Utterly amazed, they asked: "Aren't
all these who are speaking Galileans? 8 Then how is it that each

[a] *16* The Greek word for *brothers and sisters* (*adelphoi*) refers here to believers, both men and women, as part of God's family; also in 6:3; 11:29; 12:17; 16:40; 18:18, 27; 21:7, 17; 28:14, 15. [b] *20* Psalm 69:25 [c] *20* Psalm 109:8 [d] *4* Or *languages*; also in verse 11

of us hears them in our native
language? 9 Parthians, Medes and
Elamites; residents of Mesopotamia, Judea and Cappadocia, Pontus and Asia,[a] 10 Phrygia and Pamphylia, Egypt and the parts of
Libya near Cyrene; visitors from
Rome 11 (both Jews and converts
to Judaism); Cretans and Arabs — we hear them declaring the wonders of God in our own tongues!"
12 Amazed and perplexed, they
asked one another, "What does
this mean?" Ac 1:11; 16:6
13 Some, however, made fun of
them and said, "They have had too
much wine." 1Co 14:23

Peter Addresses the Crowd

14 Then Peter stood up with the
Eleven, raised his voice and addressed the crowd: "Fellow Jews
and all of you who live in Jerusalem, let me explain this to you; listen carefully to what I say. 15 These
people are not drunk, as you suppose. It's only nine in the morning! 16 No, this is what was spoken
by the prophet Joel: 1Th 5:7

17 " 'In the last days, God says,
I will pour out my Spirit on
all people. Jn 7:37-39; Ac 10:45
Your sons and daughters will
prophesy, Ac 21:9
your young men will see
visions,
your old men will dream
dreams.
18 Even on my servants, both
men and women,
I will pour out my Spirit in
those days,
and they will prophesy.
Ac 21:9-12
19 I will show wonders in the
heavens above
and signs on the earth below,
blood and fire and billows of
smoke.
20 The sun will be turned to
darkness
and the moon to blood Mt 24:29
before the coming of the
great and glorious day of
the Lord.
21 And everyone who calls
on the name of the Lord will
be saved.'[b] Ro 10:13; 2Ti 2:22

22 "Fellow Israelites, listen to
this: Jesus of Nazareth was a man
accredited by God to you by miracles, wonders and signs, which
God did among you through him,
as you yourselves know. 23 This
man was handed over to you by
God's deliberate plan and foreknowledge; and you, with the
help of wicked men,[c] put him to
death by nailing him to the cross.
24 But God raised him from the
dead, freeing him from the agony
of death, because it was impossible for death to keep its hold on
him. 25 David said about him:
Jn 4:48; 2Co 4:14; Eph 1:20

" 'I saw the Lord always
before me.

[a] *9* That is, the Roman province by that name [b] *21* Joel 2:28-32 [c] *23* Or *of those not having the law* (that is, Gentiles)

Because he is at my right
hand,
I will not be shaken.
26 Therefore my heart is glad and
my tongue rejoices;
my body also will rest in hope,
27 because you will not abandon
me to the realm of the
dead,
you will not let your holy one
see decay. Ac 13:35
28 You have made known to me
the paths of life;
you will fill me with joy in
your presence.'[a] Ps 16:8-11

29 "Fellow Israelites, I can tell you
confidently that the patriarch David died and was buried, and his
tomb is here to this day. 30 But he
was a prophet and knew that God
had promised him on oath that
he would place one of his descendants on his throne. 31 Seeing what
was to come, he spoke of the resurrection of the Messiah, that he
was not abandoned to the realm of
the dead, nor did his body see decay. 32 God has raised this Jesus to
life, and we are all witnesses of it.
33 Exalted to the right hand of God,
he has received from the Father
the promised Holy Spirit and has
poured out what you now see and
hear. 34 For David did not ascend to
heaven, and yet he said, Ac 10:45; 13:36

" 'The Lord said to my Lord:
"Sit at my right hand
35 until I make your enemies
a footstool for your feet." '[b]
Mt 22:44

36 "Therefore let all Israel be assured of this: God has made this
Jesus, whom you crucified, both
Lord and Messiah." Lk 2:11
37 When the people heard this,
they were cut to the heart and said
to Peter and the other apostles,
"Brothers, what shall we do?"
Lk 3:10,12,14
38 Peter replied, "Repent and be
baptized, every one of you, in the
name of Jesus Christ for the forgiveness of your sins. And you will
receive the gift of the Holy Spirit.
39 The promise is for you and your
children and for all who are far
off — for all whom the Lord our
God will call." Lk 24:47; Ac 3:19; Eph 2:13
40 With many other words he
warned them; and he pleaded
with them, "Save yourselves from
this corrupt generation." 41 Those
who accepted his message were
baptized, and about three thousand were added to their number
that day. Dt 32:5; Php 2:15

The Fellowship of the Believers

42 They devoted themselves to
the apostles' teaching and to fellowship, to the breaking of bread
and to prayer. 43 Everyone was
filled with awe at the many wonders and signs performed by the
apostles. 44 All the believers were
together and had everything in
common. 45 They sold property
and possessions to give to anyone
who had need. 46 Every day they

[a] *28* Psalm 16:8-11 (see Septuagint)
[b] *35* Psalm 110:1

continued to meet together in the
temple courts. They broke bread in
their homes and ate together with
glad and sincere hearts, 47 praising
God and enjoying the favor of all
the people. And the Lord added
to their number daily those who
were being saved. Ac 5:14; Ro 14:18

Peter Heals a Lame Beggar

3 One day Peter and John were
going up to the temple at the
time of prayer — at three in the
afternoon. 2 Now a man who was
lame from birth was being carried
to the temple gate called Beautiful, where he was put every day
to beg from those going into the
temple courts. 3 When he saw Peter
and John about to enter, he asked
them for money. 4 Peter looked
straight at him, as did John. Then
Peter said, "Look at us!" 5 So the
man gave them his attention, expecting to get something from
them. Ps 55:17; Ac 14:8

6 Then Peter said, "Silver or gold
I do not have, but what I do have
I give you. In the name of Jesus
Christ of Nazareth, walk." 7 Taking
him by the right hand, he helped
him up, and instantly the man's
feet and ankles became strong.
8 He jumped to his feet and began
to walk. Then he went with them
into the temple courts, walking
and jumping, and praising God.
9 When all the people saw him
walking and praising God, 10 they
recognized him as the same man
who used to sit begging at the
temple gate called Beautiful, and
they were filled with wonder and
amazement at what had happened
to him. Ac 4:10,16,21

Peter Speaks to the Onlookers

11 While the man held on to Peter and John, all the people were
astonished and came running
to them in the place called Solomon's Colonnade. 12 When Peter
saw this, he said to them: "Fellow Israelites, why does this surprise you? Why do you stare at us
as if by our own power or godliness we had made this man walk?
13 The God of Abraham, Isaac and
Jacob, the God of our fathers, has
glorified his servant Jesus. You
handed him over to be killed, and
you disowned him before Pilate,
though he had decided to let him
go. 14 You disowned the Holy and
Righteous One and asked that
a murderer be released to you.
15 You killed the author of life, but
God raised him from the dead. We
are witnesses of this. 16 By faith
in the name of Jesus, this man
whom you see and know was
made strong. It is Jesus' name
and the faith that comes through
him that has completely healed
him, as you can all see.
Mk 1:24; Jn 10:23; Ac 2:24

17 "Now, fellow Israelites, I know
that you acted in ignorance, as
did your leaders. 18 But this is how
God fulfilled what he had foretold through all the prophets, saying that his Messiah would suffer.

[19]Repent, then, and turn to God, so
that your sins may be wiped out,
that times of refreshing may come
from the Lord, [20]and that he may
send the Messiah, who has been
appointed for you — even Jesus.
[21]Heaven must receive him until
the time comes for God to restore
everything, as he promised long
ago through his holy prophets.
[22]For Moses said, 'The Lord your
God will raise up for you a prophet like me from among your own
people; you must listen to everything he tells you. [23]Anyone who
does not listen to him will be completely cut off from their people.'[a]

Dt 18:15,18; Ac 7:37

[24]"Indeed, beginning with Samuel, all the prophets who have
spoken have foretold these days.
[25]And you are heirs of the prophets and of the covenant God made
with your fathers. He said to Abraham, 'Through your offspring all
peoples on earth will be blessed.'[b]
[26]When God raised up his servant,
he sent him first to you to bless
you by turning each of you from
your wicked ways." Ac 13:46; Ro 1:16

Peter and John Before the Sanhedrin

4 The priests and the captain
of the temple guard and the
Sadducees came up to Peter and
John while they were speaking to
the people. [2]They were greatly disturbed because the apostles were
teaching the people, proclaiming
in Jesus the resurrection of the
dead. [3]They seized Peter and John
and, because it was evening, they
put them in jail until the next day.
[4]But many who heard the message
believed; so the number of men
who believed grew to about five
thousand. Lk 22:4; Ac 5:18

[5]The next day the rulers, the elders and the teachers of the law
met in Jerusalem. [6]Annas the high
priest was there, and so were Caiaphas, John, Alexander and others
of the high priest's family. [7]They
had Peter and John brought before them and began to question
them: "By what power or what
name did you do this?"

Mt 26:3; Lk 3:2; 23:13

[8]Then Peter, filled with the
Holy Spirit, said to them: "Rulers
and elders of the people! [9]If we
are being called to account today
for an act of kindness shown to a
man who was lame and are being
asked how he was healed, [10]then
know this, you and all the people
of Israel: It is by the name of Jesus
Christ of Nazareth, whom you crucified but whom God raised from
the dead, that this man stands before you healed. [11]Jesus is

Lk 23:13; Ac 2:24

"'the stone you builders
rejected,
which has become the
cornerstone.'[c]

[12]Salvation is found in no one else,
for there is no other name under

[a] 23 Deut. 18:15,18,19 [b] 25 Gen. 22:18; 26:4 [c] 11 Psalm 118:22

heaven given to mankind by which
we must be saved."
Mt 1:21; Ac 10:43; 1Ti 2:5

13 When they saw the courage of
Peter and John and realized that
they were unschooled, ordinary
men, they were astonished and
they took note that these men had
been with Jesus. 14 But since they
could see the man who had been
healed standing there with them,
there was nothing they could say.
15 So they ordered them to withdraw from the Sanhedrin and
then conferred together. 16 "What
are we going to do with these
men?" they asked. "Everyone living in Jerusalem knows they have
performed a notable sign, and we
cannot deny it. 17 But to stop this
thing from spreading any further
among the people, we must warn
them to speak no longer to anyone in this name."
Mt 11:25; Jn 11:47; Ac 3:6-10

18 Then they called them in again
and commanded them not to
speak or teach at all in the name
of Jesus. 19 But Peter and John replied, "Which is right in God's
eyes: to listen to you, or to him?
You be the judges! 20 As for us, we
cannot help speaking about what
we have seen and heard." Ac 5:29,40

21 After further threats they let
them go. They could not decide
how to punish them, because all
the people were praising God for
what had happened. 22 For the man
who was miraculously healed was
over forty years old. Ac 5:26

The Believers Pray

23 On their release, Peter and
John went back to their own people and reported all that the chief
priests and the elders had said
to them. 24 When they heard this,
they raised their voices together
in prayer to God. "Sovereign Lord,"
they said, "you made the heavens
and the earth and the sea, and everything in them. 25 You spoke by
the Holy Spirit through the mouth
of your servant, our father David:
Ac 1:16

"'Why do the nations rage
and the peoples plot in vain?
26 The kings of the earth rise up
and the rulers band together
against the Lord
and against his anointed
one.'[a,b]

27 Indeed Herod and Pontius Pilate
met together with the Gentiles
and the people of Israel in this
city to conspire against your holy
servant Jesus, whom you anointed. 28 They did what your power
and will had decided beforehand
should happen. 29 Now, Lord, consider their threats and enable your
servants to speak your word with
great boldness. 30 Stretch out your
hand to heal and perform signs
and wonders through the name of
your holy servant Jesus."
Lk 4:18; Ac 2:23; 10:38; Php 1:14

31 After they prayed, the place
where they were meeting was

[a] 26 That is, Messiah or Christ
[b] 26 Psalm 2:1,2

shaken. And they were all filled
with the Holy Spirit and spoke the
word of God boldly. Ac 2:2; Heb 4:12

The Believers Share Their Possessions

32All the believers were one in
heart and mind. No one claimed
that any of their possessions was
their own, but they shared everything they had. 33With great
power the apostles continued to
testify to the resurrection of the
Lord Jesus. And God's grace was
so powerfully at work in them all
34that there were no needy persons among them. For from time
to time those who owned land or
houses sold them, brought the
money from the sales 35and put
it at the apostles' feet, and it was
distributed to anyone who had
need. Ac 2:44-45; 6:1

36Joseph, a Levite from Cyprus,
whom the apostles called Barnabas (which means "son of encouragement"), 37sold a field he owned
and brought the money and put it
at the apostles' feet. Ac 5:2; 9:27

Ananias and Sapphira

5 Now a man named Ananias, together with his wife Sapphira,
also sold a piece of property. 2With
his wife's full knowledge he kept
back part of the money for himself, but brought the rest and put
it at the apostles' feet. Ac 4:35,37

3Then Peter said, "Ananias, how
is it that Satan has so filled your
heart that you have lied to the Holy
Spirit and have kept for yourself
some of the money you received
for the land? 4Didn't it belong to
you before it was sold? And after it
was sold, wasn't the money at your
disposal? What made you think of
doing such a thing? You have not
lied just to human beings but to
God." Lev 6:2; Dt 23:21

5When Ananias heard this, he
fell down and died. And great fear
seized all who heard what had
happened. 6Then some young
men came forward, wrapped up
his body, and carried him out and
buried him. Jn 19:40

7About three hours later his
wife came in, not knowing what
had happened. 8Peter asked her,
"Tell me, is this the price you and
Ananias got for the land?"

"Yes," she said, "that is the
price."

9Peter said to her, "How could
you conspire to test the Spirit of
the Lord? Listen! The feet of the
men who buried your husband
are at the door, and they will carry
you out also."

10At that moment she fell down
at his feet and died. Then the
young men came in and, finding
her dead, carried her out and buried her beside her husband. 11Great
fear seized the whole church and
all who heard about these events.
Ac 19:17

The Apostles Heal Many

12The apostles performed many
signs and wonders among the

people. And all the believers
used to meet together in Solomon's Colonnade. 13No one else
dared join them, even though
they were highly regarded by the
people. 14Nevertheless, more and
more men and women believed
in the Lord and were added to
their number. 15As a result, people
brought the sick into the streets
and laid them on beds and mats
so that at least Peter's shadow
might fall on some of them as he
passed by. 16Crowds gathered also
from the towns around Jerusalem, bringing their sick and those
tormented by impure spirits, and
all of them were healed.

Ac 2:47; 3:11; 19:12

The Apostles Persecuted

17Then the high priest and all his
associates, who were members of
the party of the Sadducees, were
filled with jealousy. 18They arrested the apostles and put them in
the public jail. 19But during the
night an angel of the Lord opened
the doors of the jail and brought
them out. 20"Go, stand in the temple courts," he said, "and tell the
people all about this new life."

Jn 6:63,68; Ac 4:1

21At daybreak they entered the
temple courts, as they had been
told, and began to teach the people.

When the high priest and his
associates arrived, they called together the Sanhedrin — the full
assembly of the elders of Israel —
and sent to the jail for the apostles.
22But on arriving at the jail, the
officers did not find them there.
So they went back and reported, 23"We found the jail securely
locked, with the guards standing
at the doors; but when we opened
them, we found no one inside."
24On hearing this report, the captain of the temple guard and the
chief priests were at a loss, wondering what this might lead to.

Ac 4:1,5-6

25Then someone came and said,
"Look! The men you put in jail
are standing in the temple courts
teaching the people." 26At that, the
captain went with his officers and
brought the apostles. They did not
use force, because they feared that
the people would stone them.

Ac 4:21

27The apostles were brought in
and made to appear before the
Sanhedrin to be questioned by
the high priest. 28"We gave you
strict orders not to teach in this
name," he said. "Yet you have
filled Jerusalem with your teaching and are determined to make
us guilty of this man's blood."

Mt 23:35; Ac 2:23,36

29Peter and the other apostles
replied: "We must obey God rather than human beings! 30The God
of our ancestors raised Jesus from
the dead — whom you killed by
hanging him on a cross. 31God exalted him to his own right hand as
Prince and Savior that he might
bring Israel to repentance and

forgive their sins. 32 We are witnesses of these things, and so is the Holy Spirit, whom God has given to those who obey him."

Jn 15:26; Ac 3:13; 4:19

33 When they heard this, they were furious and wanted to put them to death. 34 But a Pharisee named Gamaliel, a teacher of the law, who was honored by all the people, stood up in the Sanhedrin and ordered that the men be put outside for a little while. 35 Then he addressed the Sanhedrin: "Men of Israel, consider carefully what you intend to do to these men. 36 Some time ago Theudas appeared, claiming to be somebody, and about four hundred men rallied to him. He was killed, all his followers were dispersed, and it all came to nothing. 37 After him, Judas the Galilean appeared in the days of the census and led a band of people in revolt. He too was killed, and all his followers were scattered. 38 Therefore, in the present case I advise you: Leave these men alone! Let them go! For if their purpose or activity is of human origin, it will fail. 39 But if it is from God, you will not be able to stop these men; you will only find yourselves fighting against God."

Ac 7:51; 11:17

40 His speech persuaded them. They called the apostles in and had them flogged. Then they ordered them not to speak in the name of Jesus, and let them go.

Mt 10:17

41 The apostles left the Sanhedrin, rejoicing because they had been counted worthy of suffering disgrace for the Name. 42 Day after day, in the temple courts and from house to house, they never stopped teaching and proclaiming the good news that Jesus is the Messiah.

Jn 15:21; Ac 2:46

The Choosing of the Seven

6 In those days when the number of disciples was increasing, the Hellenistic Jews[a] among them complained against the Hebraic Jews because their widows were being overlooked in the daily distribution of food. 2 So the Twelve gathered all the disciples together and said, "It would not be right for us to neglect the ministry of the word of God in order to wait on tables. 3 Brothers and sisters, choose seven men from among you who are known to be full of the Spirit and wisdom. We will turn this responsibility over to them 4 and will give our attention to prayer and the ministry of the word."

Ac 4:35; 9:29

5 This proposal pleased the whole group. They chose Stephen, a man full of faith and of the Holy Spirit; also Philip, Procorus, Nicanor, Timon, Parmenas, and Nicolas from Antioch, a convert to Judaism. 6 They presented these men to the apostles, who prayed and laid their hands on them.

Ac 1:24; 9:17; 1Ti 4:14

[a] *1* That is, Jews who had adopted the Greek language and culture

7 So the word of God spread. The
number of disciples in Jerusalem increased rapidly, and a large
number of priests became obedient to the faith. Ac 12:24; 19:20

Stephen Seized

8 Now Stephen, a man full of
God's grace and power, performed
great wonders and signs among
the people. 9 Opposition arose,
however, from members of the
Synagogue of the Freedmen (as it
was called) — Jews of Cyrene and
Alexandria as well as the provinces of Cilicia and Asia — who began
to argue with Stephen. 10 But they
could not stand up against the
wisdom the Spirit gave him as he
spoke. Lk 21:15; Jn 4:48

11 Then they secretly persuaded
some men to say, "We have heard
Stephen speak blasphemous
words against Moses and against
God." Mt 26:59-61; 1Ki 21:10

12 So they stirred up the people
and the elders and the teachers of
the law. They seized Stephen and
brought him before the Sanhedrin.
13 They produced false witnesses,
who testified, "This fellow never
stops speaking against this holy
place and against the law. 14 For we
have heard him say that this Jesus
of Nazareth will destroy this place
and change the customs Moses
handed down to us." Mt 5:22; Ac 15:1

15 All who were sitting in the Sanhedrin looked intently at Stephen,
and they saw that his face was like
the face of an angel. Mt 5:22

Stephen's Speech to the Sanhedrin

7 Then the high priest asked Stephen, "Are these charges true?"

2 To this he replied: "Brothers and fathers, listen to me! The
God of glory appeared to our father Abraham while he was still in
Mesopotamia, before he lived in
Harran. 3 'Leave your country and
your people,' God said, 'and go to
the land I will show you.'[a]
Ac 22:1; Ge 11:31; 15:7

4 "So he left the land of the Chaldeans and settled in Harran. After
the death of his father, God sent
him to this land where you are
now living. 5 He gave him no inheritance here, not even enough
ground to set his foot on. But God
promised him that he and his descendants after him would possess
the land, even though at that time
Abraham had no child. 6 God spoke
to him in this way: 'For four hundred years your descendants will
be strangers in a country not their
own, and they will be enslaved
and mistreated. 7 But I will punish
the nation they serve as slaves,'
God said, 'and afterward they will
come out of that country and worship me in this place.'[b] 8 Then he
gave Abraham the covenant of circumcision. And Abraham became
the father of Isaac and circumcised
him eight days after his birth. Later Isaac became the father of Jacob, and Jacob became the father
of the twelve patriarchs.
Ge 29:31-35; Ex 3:12

[a] 3 Gen. 12:1 [b] 7 Gen. 15:13,14

9“Because the patriarchs were
jealous of Joseph, they sold him
as a slave into Egypt. But God was
with him 10and rescued him from
all his troubles. He gave Joseph
wisdom and enabled him to gain
the goodwill of Pharaoh king of
Egypt. So Pharaoh made him ruler over Egypt and all his palace.

Ge 41:37-43; Ps 105:20-22

11“Then a famine struck all Egypt
and Canaan, bringing great suffering, and our ancestors could not
find food. 12When Jacob heard that
there was grain in Egypt, he sent
our forefathers on their first visit. 13On their second visit, Joseph
told his brothers who he was, and
Pharaoh learned about Joseph’s
family. 14After this, Joseph sent
for his father Jacob and his whole
family, seventy-five in all. 15Then
Jacob went down to Egypt, where
he and our ancestors died. 16Their
bodies were brought back to Shechem and placed in the tomb that
Abraham had bought from the
sons of Hamor at Shechem for a
certain sum of money.

Ge 45:1-4; Dt 10:22; Jos 24:32

17“As the time drew near for God
to fulfill his promise to Abraham,
the number of our people in Egypt
had greatly increased. 18Then ‘a
new king, to whom Joseph meant
nothing, came to power in Egypt.’[a]
19He dealt treacherously with our
people and oppressed our ancestors by forcing them to throw out
their newborn babies so that they
would die.

Ex 1:10-22

20“At that time Moses was born,
and he was no ordinary child.[b] For
three months he was cared for by
his family. 21When he was placed
outside, Pharaoh’s daughter took
him and brought him up as her
own son. 22Moses was educated in
all the wisdom of the Egyptians
and was powerful in speech and
action.

1Ki 4:30; Isa 19:11

23“When Moses was forty years
old, he decided to visit his own
people, the Israelites. 24He saw
one of them being mistreated by
an Egyptian, so he went to his defense and avenged him by killing
the Egyptian. 25Moses thought
that his own people would realize
that God was using him to rescue
them, but they did not. 26The next
day Moses came upon two Israelites who were fighting. He tried to
reconcile them by saying, ‘Men,
you are brothers; why do you want
to hurt each other?’

27“But the man who was mistreating the other pushed Moses
aside and said, ‘Who made you
ruler and judge over us? 28Are you
thinking of killing me as you killed
the Egyptian yesterday?’[c] 29When
Moses heard this, he fled to Midian, where he settled as a foreigner
and had two sons.

Ex 2:11-15

30“After forty years had passed,
an angel appeared to Moses in the
flames of a burning bush in the
desert near Mount Sinai. 31When
he saw this, he was amazed at the

[a] *18* Exodus 1:8 [b] *20* Or *was fair in the sight of God* [c] *28* Exodus 2:14

sight. As he went over to get a
closer look, he heard the Lord say:
32 'I am the God of your fathers, the
God of Abraham, Isaac and Jacob.'[a]
Moses trembled with fear and did
not dare to look. Ex 3:1-4,6

33 "Then the Lord said to him,
'Take off your sandals, for the
place where you are standing is
holy ground. 34 I have indeed seen
the oppression of my people in
Egypt. I have heard their groaning
and have come down to set them
free. Now come, I will send you
back to Egypt.'[b] Ex 3:5,7-10

35 "This is the same Moses they
had rejected with the words, 'Who
made you ruler and judge?' He was
sent to be their ruler and deliverer
by God himself, through the angel
who appeared to him in the bush.
36 He led them out of Egypt and
performed wonders and signs in
Egypt, at the Red Sea and for forty
years in the wilderness.

Ex 12:41; 14:21

37 "This is the Moses who told
the Israelites, 'God will raise up for
you a prophet like me from your
own people.'[c] 38 He was in the assembly in the wilderness, with the
angel who spoke to him on Mount
Sinai, and with our ancestors; and
he received living words to pass
on to us. Dt 18:15,18; Ro 3:2

39 "But our ancestors refused to
obey him. Instead, they rejected
him and in their hearts turned
back to Egypt. 40 They told Aaron, 'Make us gods who will go before us. As for this fellow Moses
who led us out of Egypt—we
don't know what has happened
to him!'[d] 41 That was the time
they made an idol in the form of
a calf. They brought sacrifices to
it and reveled in what their own
hands had made. 42 But God turned
away from them and gave them
over to the worship of the sun,
moon and stars. This agrees with
what is written in the book of the
prophets:

"'Did you bring me sacrifices
and offerings
forty years in the wilderness,
people of Israel?
Ex 32:4-6; Ps 106:19-20

43 You have taken up the
tabernacle of Molek
and the star of your god
Rephan,
the idols you made to
worship.
Therefore I will send you into
exile'[e] beyond Babylon.
Am 5:25-27

44 "Our ancestors had the tabernacle of the covenant law with
them in the wilderness. It had
been made as God directed Moses,
according to the pattern he had
seen. 45 After receiving the tabernacle, our ancestors under Joshua
brought it with them when they
took the land from the nations
God drove out before them. It remained in the land until the time

[a] 32 Exodus 3:6 [b] 34 Exodus 3:5,7,8,10
[c] 37 Deut. 18:15 [d] 40 Exodus 32:1
[e] 43 Amos 5:25-27 (see Septuagint)

of David, 46who enjoyed God's
favor and asked that he might
provide a dwelling place for the
God of Jacob.[a] 47But it was Solomon who built a house for him.

Jos 3:14-17; 2Sa 7:8-16

48"However, the Most High does
not live in houses made by human
hands. As the prophet says:

1Ki 8:27; 2Ch 2:6

49" 'Heaven is my throne,
and the earth is my footstool.

Mt 5:34-35

What kind of house will you
build for me?
says the Lord.
Or where will my resting
place be?
50Has not my hand made
all these things?'[b]

Isa 66:1-2

51"You stiff-necked people!
Your hearts and ears are still uncircumcised. You are just like
your ancestors: You always resist the Holy Spirit! 52Was there
ever a prophet your ancestors did
not persecute? They even killed
those who predicted the coming
of the Righteous One. And now
you have betrayed and murdered
him — 53you who have received
the law that was given through
angels but have not obeyed it."

Ac 3:14; Gal 3:19

The Stoning of Stephen

54When the members of the
Sanhedrin heard this, they were
furious and gnashed their teeth
at him. 55But Stephen, full of the
Holy Spirit, looked up to heav-
en and saw the glory of God, and
Jesus standing at the right hand
of God. 56"Look," he said, "I see
heaven open and the Son of Man
standing at the right hand of God."

Mt 3:16; Ac 5:33

57At this they covered their ears
and, yelling at the top of their
voices, they all rushed at him,
58dragged him out of the city and
began to stone him. Meanwhile,
the witnesses laid their coats at
the feet of a young man named
Saul.

Lev 24:14,16; Dt 13:9

59While they were stoning him,
Stephen prayed, "Lord Jesus, receive my spirit." 60Then he fell on
his knees and cried out, "Lord, do
not hold this sin against them."
When he had said this, he fell
asleep.

Ps 31:5; Ac 9:40

8 And Saul approved of their
killing him.

Ac 7:58

The Church Persecuted and Scattered

On that day a great persecution
broke out against the church in Jerusalem, and all except the apostles were scattered throughout
Judea and Samaria. 2Godly men
buried Stephen and mourned
deeply for him. 3But Saul began
to destroy the church. Going from
house to house, he dragged off
both men and women and put
them in prison.

Ac 11:19; 1Co 15:9

[a] 46 Some early manuscripts *the house of Jacob* [b] 50 Isaiah 66:1,2

Philip in Samaria

4Those who had been scattered
preached the word wherever they
went. 5Philip went down to a city
in Samaria and proclaimed the
Messiah there. 6When the crowds
heard Philip and saw the signs he
performed, they all paid close attention to what he said. 7For with
shrieks, impure spirits came out
of many, and many who were paralyzed or lame were healed. 8So
there was great joy in that city.

Ac 6:5; 15:35

Simon the Sorcerer

9Now for some time a man
named Simon had practiced sorcery in the city and amazed all
the people of Samaria. He boasted that he was someone great,
10and all the people, both high
and low, gave him their attention
and exclaimed, "This man is rightly called the Great Power of God."
11They followed him because he
had amazed them for a long time
with his sorcery. 12But when they
believed Philip as he proclaimed
the good news of the kingdom of
God and the name of Jesus Christ,
they were baptized, both men and
women. 13Simon himself believed
and was baptized. And he followed
Philip everywhere, astonished by
the great signs and miracles he
saw. Ac 13:6; 19:11

14When the apostles in Jerusalem heard that Samaria had accepted the word of God, they sent
Peter and John to Samaria. 15When
they arrived, they prayed for the
new believers there that they
might receive the Holy Spirit, 16be-
cause the Holy Spirit had not yet
come on any of them; they had
simply been baptized in the name
of the Lord Jesus. 17Then Peter and
John placed their hands on them,
and they received the Holy Spirit.

Ac 6:6; 19:2

18When Simon saw that the Spirit was given at the laying on of the
apostles' hands, he offered them
money 19and said, "Give me also
this ability so that everyone on
whom I lay my hands may receive
the Holy Spirit."

20Peter answered: "May your
money perish with you, because
you thought you could buy the
gift of God with money! 21You have
no part or share in this ministry,
because your heart is not right before God. 22Repent of this wickedness and pray to the Lord in the
hope that he may forgive you for
having such a thought in your
heart. 23For I see that you are full
of bitterness and captive to sin."

2Ki 5:16; Mt 10:8; Ac 2:38

24Then Simon answered, "Pray
to the Lord for me so that nothing
you have said may happen to me."

Ex 8:8; Nu 21:7; 1Ki 13:6

25After they had further proclaimed the word of the Lord
and testified about Jesus, Peter
and John returned to Jerusalem,
preaching the gospel in many Samaritan villages. Ac 13:48

Philip and the Ethiopian

26Now an angel of the Lord said
to Philip, "Go south to the road —
the desert road — that goes down
from Jerusalem to Gaza." 27So he
started out, and on his way he met
an Ethiopian[a] eunuch, an important official in charge of all the
treasury of the Kandake (which
means "queen of the Ethiopians").
This man had gone to Jerusalem
to worship, 28and on his way home
was sitting in his chariot reading
the Book of Isaiah the prophet.
29The Spirit told Philip, "Go to that
chariot and stay near it."
Jn 12:20; Ac 5:19

30Then Philip ran up to the chariot and heard the man reading
Isaiah the prophet. "Do you understand what you are reading?"
Philip asked.

31"How can I," he said, "unless
someone explains it to me?" So he
invited Philip to come up and sit
with him.

32This is the passage of Scripture
the eunuch was reading:

"He was led like a sheep to the slaughter,
and as a lamb before its shearer is silent,
so he did not open his mouth.
33In his humiliation he was deprived of justice.
Who can speak of his descendants?
For his life was taken from the earth."[b] Isa 53:7-8

34The eunuch asked Philip, "Tell
me, please, who is the prophet
talking about, himself or someone else?" 35Then Philip began
with that very passage of Scripture and told him the good news
about Jesus. Lk 24:27; Ac 18:28

36As they traveled along the
road, they came to some water
and the eunuch said, "Look, here
is water. What can stand in the
way of my being baptized?" [37][c]
38And he gave orders to stop the
chariot. Then both Philip and the
eunuch went down into the water
and Philip baptized him. 39When
they came up out of the water, the
Spirit of the Lord suddenly took
Philip away, and the eunuch did
not see him again, but went on his
way rejoicing. 40Philip, however,
appeared at Azotus and traveled
about, preaching the gospel in all
the towns until he reached Caesarea. 1Ki 18:12; 2Ki 2:16; Ac 10:47

Saul's Conversion

9 Meanwhile, Saul was still
breathing out murderous
threats against the Lord's disciples. He went to the high priest
2and asked him for letters to the
synagogues in Damascus, so that
if he found any there who belonged to the Way, whether men
or women, he might take them

[a] 27 That is, from the southern Nile region
[b] 33 Isaiah 53:7,8 (see Septuagint)
[c] 37 Some manuscripts include here *Philip said, "If you believe with all your heart, you may." The eunuch answered, "I believe that Jesus Christ is the Son of God."*

as prisoners to Jerusalem. 3As
he neared Damascus on his journey, suddenly a light from heaven
flashed around him. 4He fell to the
ground and heard a voice say to
him, "Saul, Saul, why do you persecute me?" Ac 8:3; 19:9,23; 1Co 15:8

5"Who are you, Lord?" Saul
asked.

"I am Jesus, whom you are persecuting," he replied. 6"Now get
up and go into the city, and you
will be told what you must do."
Eze 3:22

7The men traveling with Saul
stood there speechless; they heard
the sound but did not see anyone.
8Saul got up from the ground, but
when he opened his eyes he could
see nothing. So they led him by the
hand into Damascus. 9For three
days he was blind, and did not eat
or drink anything. Da 10:7; Ac 22:9

10In Damascus there was a disciple named Ananias. The Lord
called to him in a vision, "Ananias!" Ac 10:3,17,19

"Yes, Lord," he answered.

11The Lord told him, "Go to the
house of Judas on Straight Street
and ask for a man from Tarsus
named Saul, for he is praying. 12In
a vision he has seen a man named
Ananias come and place his hands
on him to restore his sight."
Ac 21:39; 22:3

13"Lord," Ananias answered, "I
have heard many reports about
this man and all the harm he has
done to your holy people in Jerusalem. 14And he has come here
with authority from the chief
priests to arrest all who call on
your name." Ro 1:7; 16:2,15

15But the Lord said to Ananias,
"Go! This man is my chosen instrument to proclaim my name to
the Gentiles and their kings and to
the people of Israel. 16I will show
him how much he must suffer for
my name." Ac 13:2; 20:23; Ro 11:13

17Then Ananias went to the
house and entered it. Placing his
hands on Saul, he said, "Brother
Saul, the Lord—Jesus, who appeared to you on the road as you
were coming here—has sent me
so that you may see again and be
filled with the Holy Spirit." 18Im-
mediately, something like scales
fell from Saul's eyes, and he could
see again. He got up and was baptized, 19and after taking some
food, he regained his strength.
Ac 22:4-16; 26:9-18

Saul in Damascus and Jerusalem

Saul spent several days with the
disciples in Damascus. 20At once
he began to preach in the synagogues that Jesus is the Son of
God. 21All those who heard him
were astonished and asked, "Isn't
he the man who raised havoc in
Jerusalem among those who call
on this name? And hasn't he come
here to take them as prisoners to
the chief priests?" 22Yet Saul grew
more and more powerful and baffled the Jews living in Damascus by proving that Jesus is the
Messiah. Ac 8:3; 18:5,28

23After many days had gone by,
there was a conspiracy among the
Jews to kill him, 24but Saul learned
of their plan. Day and night they
kept close watch on the city gates
in order to kill him. 25But his followers took him by night and lowered him in a basket through an
opening in the wall. 1Sa 19:12; Ac 20:3,19

26When he came to Jerusalem,
he tried to join the disciples, but
they were all afraid of him, not believing that he really was a disciple. 27But Barnabas took him and
brought him to the apostles. He
told them how Saul on his journey had seen the Lord and that
the Lord had spoken to him, and
how in Damascus he had preached
fearlessly in the name of Jesus.
28So Saul stayed with them and
moved about freely in Jerusalem,
speaking boldly in the name of
the Lord. 29He talked and debat-
ed with the Hellenistic Jews,[a] but
they tried to kill him. 30When the
believers learned of this, they took
him down to Caesarea and sent
him off to Tarsus. Ac 6:1; 22:17

31Then the church throughout
Judea, Galilee and Samaria enjoyed a time of peace and was
strengthened. Living in the fear
of the Lord and encouraged by the
Holy Spirit, it increased in numbers. Ac 8:1

Aeneas and Dorcas

32As Peter traveled about the
country, he went to visit the Lord's
people who lived in Lydda. 33There
he found a man named Aeneas,
who was paralyzed and had been
bedridden for eight years. 34"Aeneas," Peter said to him, "Jesus Christ
heals you. Get up and roll up your
mat." Immediately Aeneas got up.
35All those who lived in Lydda and
Sharon saw him and turned to the
Lord. Ac 3:6,16; 11:21

36In Joppa there was a disciple named Tabitha (in Greek her
name is Dorcas); she was always
doing good and helping the poor.
37About that time she became
sick and died, and her body was
washed and placed in an upstairs
room. 38Lydda was near Joppa;
so when the disciples heard that
Peter was in Lydda, they sent
two men to him and urged him,
"Please come at once!"
1Ti 2:10; Titus 3:8

39Peter went with them, and
when he arrived he was taken upstairs to the room. All the widows stood around him, crying and
showing him the robes and other clothing that Dorcas had made
while she was still with them. Ac 6:1

40Peter sent them all out of the
room; then he got down on his
knees and prayed. Turning toward
the dead woman, he said, "Tabitha,
get up." She opened her eyes, and
seeing Peter she sat up. 41He took
her by the hand and helped her to
her feet. Then he called for the believers, especially the widows, and
presented her to them alive. 42This

[a] *29* That is, Jews who had adopted the Greek language and culture

became known all over Joppa, and
many people believed in the Lord.
43 Peter stayed in Joppa for some
time with a tanner named Simon.
Lk 7:14; Ac 7:60; 10:6

Cornelius Calls for Peter

10 At Caesarea there was a
man named Cornelius, a
centurion in what was known as
the Italian Regiment. 2 He and all
his family were devout and God-
fearing; he gave generously to
those in need and prayed to God
regularly. 3 One day at about three
in the afternoon he had a vision.
He distinctly saw an angel of God,
who came to him and said, "Cornelius!"
Ac 3:1; 5:19

4 Cornelius stared at him in fear.
"What is it, Lord?" he asked.

The angel answered, "Your
prayers and gifts to the poor have
come up as a memorial offering
before God. 5 Now send men to
Joppa to bring back a man named
Simon who is called Peter. 6 He is
staying with Simon the tanner,
whose house is by the sea."
Ac 9:43; Rev 8:4

7 When the angel who spoke to
him had gone, Cornelius called
two of his servants and a devout
soldier who was one of his attendants. 8 He told them everything
that had happened and sent them
to Joppa.
Ac 9:36

Peter's Vision

9 About noon the following day
as they were on their journey and
approaching the city, Peter went
up on the roof to pray. 10 He became hungry and wanted something to eat, and while the meal
was being prepared, he fell into
a trance. 11 He saw heaven opened
and something like a large sheet
being let down to earth by its four
corners. 12 It contained all kinds
of four-footed animals, as well as
reptiles and birds. 13 Then a voice
told him, "Get up, Peter. Kill and
eat."
Mt 24:17; Ac 22:17

14 "Surely not, Lord!" Peter replied. "I have never eaten anything impure or unclean."
Dt 14:3-20; Eze 4:14

15 The voice spoke to him a second time, "Do not call anything
impure that God has made clean."
Ro 14:14,17,20; 1Co 10:25; 1Ti 4:3-4

16 This happened three times,
and immediately the sheet was
taken back to heaven.

17 While Peter was wondering
about the meaning of the vision,
the men sent by Cornelius found
out where Simon's house was
and stopped at the gate. 18 They
called out, asking if Simon who
was known as Peter was staying
there.

19 While Peter was still thinking
about the vision, the Spirit said
to him, "Simon, three[a] men are
looking for you. 20 So get up and go
downstairs. Do not hesitate to go
with them, for I have sent them."
Ac 8:29; 15:7-9

[a] 19 One early manuscript *two*; other manuscripts do not have the number.

21 Peter went down and said to
the men, "I'm the one you're looking for. Why have you come?"
22 The men replied, "We have
come from Cornelius the centurion. He is a righteous and God-
fearing man, who is respected by
all the Jewish people. A holy angel
told him to ask you to come to his
house so that he could hear what
you have to say." 23 Then Peter invited the men into the house to be
his guests. Ac 11:14

Peter at Cornelius's House

The next day Peter started out
with them, and some of the believers from Joppa went along.
24 The following day he arrived in
Caesarea. Cornelius was expecting them and had called together
his relatives and close friends. 25 As
Peter entered the house, Cornelius
met him and fell at his feet in reverence. 26 But Peter made him get
up. "Stand up," he said, "I am only
a man myself." Rev 19:10
27 While talking with him, Peter went inside and found a large
gathering of people. 28 He said to
them: "You are well aware that it
is against our law for a Jew to associate with or visit a Gentile. But
God has shown me that I should
not call anyone impure or unclean. 29 So when I was sent for,
I came without raising any ob-
jection. May I ask why you sent
for me?" Jn 4:9; Ac 15:8-9
30 Cornelius answered: "Three
days ago I was in my house praying at this hour, at three in the afternoon. Suddenly a man in shining clothes stood before me 31 and
said, 'Cornelius, God has heard
your prayer and remembered your
gifts to the poor. 32 Send to Joppa
for Simon who is called Peter. He is
a guest in the home of Simon the
tanner, who lives by the sea.' 33 So
I sent for you immediately, and it
was good of you to come. Now we
are all here in the presence of God
to listen to everything the Lord
has commanded you to tell us."
Ac 11:5-14
34 Then Peter began to speak: "I
now realize how true it is that God
does not show favoritism 35 but accepts from every nation the one
who fears him and does what is
right. 36 You know the message
God sent to the people of Israel, announcing the good news of
peace through Jesus Christ, who is
Lord of all. 37 You know what has
happened throughout the province of Judea, beginning in Galilee after the baptism that John
preached — 38 how God anointed
Jesus of Nazareth with the Holy
Spirit and power, and how he went
around doing good and healing all
who were under the power of the
devil, because God was with him.
Mt 28:18; Jn 3:2
39 "We are witnesses of everything he did in the country of
the Jews and in Jerusalem. They
killed him by hanging him on a
cross, 40 but God raised him from
the dead on the third day and

caused him to be seen. 41He was
not seen by all the people, but
by witnesses whom God had already chosen — by us who ate and
drank with him after he rose from
the dead. 42He commanded us to
preach to the people and to testify
that he is the one whom God appointed as judge of the living and
the dead. 43All the prophets testify
about him that everyone who believes in him receives forgiveness
of sins through his name."

Isa 53:11; Ac 2:24; 5:30

44While Peter was still speaking these words, the Holy Spirit
came on all who heard the message. 45The circumcised believers
who had come with Peter were astonished that the gift of the Holy
Spirit had been poured out even
on Gentiles. 46For they heard them
speaking in tongues[a] and praising
God. Mk 16:17; Ac 11:18

Then Peter said, 47"Surely no
one can stand in the way of their
being baptized with water. They
have received the Holy Spirit just
as we have." 48So he ordered that
they be baptized in the name of
Jesus Christ. Then they asked Peter to stay with them for a few
days. Ac 2:38; 8:36; 11:17

Peter Explains His Actions

11 The apostles and the believers throughout Judea heard
that the Gentiles also had received
the word of God. 2So when Peter
went up to Jerusalem, the circumcised believers criticized him 3and
said, "You went into the house of
uncircumcised men and ate with
them." Ac 10:25,28; Gal 2:12

4Starting from the beginning,
Peter told them the whole story:
5"I was in the city of Joppa praying, and in a trance I saw a vision.
I saw something like a large sheet
being let down from heaven by its
four corners, and it came down to
where I was. 6I looked into it and
saw four-footed animals of the
earth, wild beasts, reptiles and
birds. 7Then I heard a voice telling
me, 'Get up, Peter. Kill and eat.'

Ac 10:9-32

8"I replied, 'Surely not, Lord!
Nothing impure or unclean has
ever entered my mouth.'

9"The voice spoke from heaven a
second time, 'Do not call anything
impure that God has made clean.'
10This happened three times, and
then it was all pulled up to heaven
again. Ac 10:15

11"Right then three men who
had been sent to me from Caesarea stopped at the house where I
was staying. 12The Spirit told me
to have no hesitation about going with them. These six brothers also went with me, and we entered the man's house. 13He told
us how he had seen an angel appear in his house and say, 'Send
to Joppa for Simon who is called
Peter. 14He will bring you a message through which you and all
your household will be saved.'

Ac 8:29; 15:9

[a] 46 Or *other languages*

15 "As I began to speak, the Holy
Spirit came on them as he had
come on us at the beginning.
16 Then I remembered what the
Lord had said: 'John baptized
with[a] water, but you will be baptized with[a] the Holy Spirit.' 17 So if
God gave them the same gift he
gave us who believed in the Lord
Jesus Christ, who was I to think
that I could stand in God's way?"

Ac 2:4; 10:45,47

18 When they heard this, they
had no further objections and
praised God, saying, "So then,
even to Gentiles God has granted
repentance that leads to life."

Ro 10:12-13; 2Co 7:10

The Church in Antioch

19 Now those who had been scattered by the persecution that
broke out when Stephen was
killed traveled as far as Phoenicia,
Cyprus and Antioch, spreading the
word only among Jews. 20 Some of
them, however, men from Cyprus
and Cyrene, went to Antioch and
began to speak to Greeks also, telling them the good news about the
Lord Jesus. 21 The Lord's hand was
with them, and a great number of
people believed and turned to the
Lord. Lk 1:66; Ac 2:47

22 News of this reached the
church in Jerusalem, and they sent
Barnabas to Antioch. 23 When he
arrived and saw what the grace of
God had done, he was glad and encouraged them all to remain true
to the Lord with all their hearts.
24 He was a good man, full of the
Holy Spirit and faith, and a great
number of people were brought to
the Lord. Ac 5:14; 13:43

25 Then Barnabas went to Tarsus
to look for Saul, 26 and when he
found him, he brought him to Antioch. So for a whole year Barnabas
and Saul met with the church and
taught great numbers of people.
The disciples were called Christians first at Antioch.

Ac 9:11; 26:28; 1Pe 4:16

27 During this time some prophets came down from Jerusalem to
Antioch. 28 One of them, named
Agabus, stood up and through
the Spirit predicted that a severe
famine would spread over the
entire Roman world. (This happened during the reign of Claudius.) 29 The disciples, as each one
was able, decided to provide help
for the brothers and sisters living
in Judea. 30 This they did, sending
their gift to the elders by Barnabas
and Saul. Ac 12:25; Ro 15:26; 1Co 12:28-29

Peter's Miraculous Escape From Prison

12 It was about this time that
King Herod arrested some
who belonged to the church, intending to persecute them. 2 He
had James, the brother of John,
put to death with the sword.
3 When he saw that this met with
approval among the Jews, he proceeded to seize Peter also. This
happened during the Festival of

[a] 16 Or *in*

Unleavened Bread. 4After arresting him, he put him in prison,
handing him over to be guarded
by four squads of four soldiers
each. Herod intended to bring
him out for public trial after the
Passover. Ex 12:15; 23:15; Mt 4:21

5So Peter was kept in prison, but
the church was earnestly praying
to God for him. Eph 6:18

6The night before Herod was
to bring him to trial, Peter was
sleeping between two soldiers,
bound with two chains, and sen-
tries stood guard at the entrance.
7Suddenly an angel of the Lord
appeared and a light shone in the
cell. He struck Peter on the side
and woke him up. "Quick, get up!"
he said, and the chains fell off Peter's wrists. Ac 5:19; 16:26

8Then the angel said to him,
"Put on your clothes and sandals."
And Peter did so. "Wrap your cloak
around you and follow me," the
angel told him. 9Peter followed
him out of the prison, but he had
no idea that what the angel was
doing was really happening; he
thought he was seeing a vision.
10They passed the first and second guards and came to the iron
gate leading to the city. It opened
for them by itself, and they went
through it. When they had walked
the length of one street, suddenly
the angel left him. Ac 16:26

11Then Peter came to himself
and said, "Now I know without a
doubt that the Lord has sent his
angel and rescued me from Herod's clutches and from everything
the Jewish people were hoping
would happen." Da 3:28; 6:22

12When this had dawned on
him, he went to the house of Mary
the mother of John, also called
Mark, where many people had
gathered and were praying. 13Pe-
ter knocked at the outer entrance,
and a servant named Rhoda came
to answer the door. 14When she
recognized Peter's voice, she was
so overjoyed she ran back without
opening it and exclaimed, "Peter
is at the door!" Lk 24:41; Jn 18:16-17

15"You're out of your mind," they
told her. When she kept insisting
that it was so, they said, "It must
be his angel." Mt 18:10

16But Peter kept on knocking,
and when they opened the door
and saw him, they were astonished. 17Peter motioned with his
hand for them to be quiet and described how the Lord had brought
him out of prison. "Tell James
and the other brothers and sisters
about this," he said, and then he
left for another place. Ac 13:16; 19:33

18In the morning, there was no
small commotion among the soldiers as to what had become of Peter. 19After Herod had a thorough
search made for him and did not
find him, he cross-examined the
guards and ordered that they be
executed. Ac 16:27

Herod's Death

Then Herod went from Judea
to Caesarea and stayed there. 20He

had been quarreling with the
people of Tyre and Sidon; they
now joined together and sought
an audience with him. After secur-
ing the support of Blastus, a trusted personal servant of the king,
they asked for peace, because they
depended on the king's country
for their food supply.

1Ki 5:9,11; Eze 27:17; Ac 8:40

21 On the appointed day Herod,
wearing his royal robes, sat on his
throne and delivered a public address to the people. 22 They shouted, "This is the voice of a god, not
of a man." 23 Immediately, because
Herod did not give praise to God,
an angel of the Lord struck him
down, and he was eaten by worms
and died. 1Sa 25:38; 2Sa 24:16-17

24 But the word of God continued to spread and flourish.

Ac 6:7; Heb 4:12

Barnabas and Saul Sent Off

25 When Barnabas and Saul had
finished their mission, they returned from[a] Jerusalem, taking
with them John, also called Mark.

13 1 Now in the church at Antioch there were prophets
and teachers: Barnabas, Simeon
called Niger, Lucius of Cyrene,
Manaen (who had been brought
up with Herod the tetrarch) and
Saul. 2 While they were worshiping the Lord and fasting, the Holy
Spirit said, "Set apart for me Barnabas and Saul for the work to
which I have called them." 3 So
after they had fasted and prayed,
they placed their hands on them
and sent them off.

Ac 11:30; 14:26; 22:21

On Cyprus

4 The two of them, sent on their
way by the Holy Spirit, went down
to Seleucia and sailed from there
to Cyprus. 5 When they arrived
at Salamis, they proclaimed the
word of God in the Jewish synagogues. John was with them as
their helper. Ac 12:12; Heb 4:12

6 They traveled through the
whole island until they came to
Paphos. There they met a Jewish
sorcerer and false prophet named
Bar-Jesus, 7 who was an attendant
of the proconsul, Sergius Pau-
lus. The proconsul, an intelligent
man, sent for Barnabas and Saul
because he wanted to hear the
word of God. 8 But Elymas the sorcerer (for that is what his name
means) opposed them and tried to
turn the proconsul from the faith.
9 Then Saul, who was also called
Paul, filled with the Holy Spirit, looked straight at Elymas and
said, 10 "You are a child of the devil
and an enemy of everything that
is right! You are full of all kinds of
deceit and trickery. Will you never stop perverting the right ways
of the Lord? 11 Now the hand of the
Lord is against you. You are going
to be blind for a time, not even
able to see the light of the sun."

1Sa 5:6-7; Ac 4:8; 6:7

[a] 25 Some manuscripts *to*

Immediately mist and darkness came over him, and he groped about, seeking someone to lead him by the hand. 12When the proconsul saw what had happened, he believed, for he was amazed at the teaching about the Lord.

In Pisidian Antioch

13From Paphos, Paul and his companions sailed to Perga in Pamphylia, where John left them to return to Jerusalem. 14From Perga they went on to Pisidian Antioch. On the Sabbath they entered the synagogue and sat down. 15After the reading from the Law and the Prophets, the leaders of the synagogue sent word to them, saying, "Brothers, if you have a word of exhortation for the people, please speak." Ac 14:19,21; 16:13

16Standing up, Paul motioned with his hand and said: "Fellow Israelites and you Gentiles who worship God, listen to me! 17The God of the people of Israel chose our ancestors; he made the people prosper during their stay in Egypt; with mighty power he led them out of that country; 18for about forty years he endured their conduct[a] in the wilderness; 19and he overthrew seven nations in Canaan, giving their land to his people as their inheritance. 20All this took about 450 years.

Dt 1:31; 7:6-8; Jos 19:51

"After this, God gave them judges until the time of Samuel the prophet. 21Then the people asked for a king, and he gave them Saul son of Kish, of the tribe of Benjamin, who ruled forty years. 22After removing Saul, he made David their king. God testified concerning him: 'I have found David son of Jesse, a man after my own heart; he will do everything I want him to do.' 1Sa 13:14; 15:23,26

23"From this man's descendants God has brought to Israel the Savior Jesus, as he promised. 24Before the coming of Jesus, John preached repentance and baptism to all the people of Israel. 25As John was completing his work, he said: 'Who do you suppose I am? I am not the one you are looking for. But there is one coming after me whose sandals I am not worthy to untie.'

Mt 1:21; 3:11; Jn 1:27

26"Fellow children of Abraham and you God-fearing Gentiles, it is to us that this message of salvation has been sent. 27The people of Jerusalem and their rulers did not recognize Jesus, yet in condemning him they fulfilled the words of the prophets that are read every Sabbath. 28Though they found no proper ground for a death sentence, they asked Pilate to have him executed. 29When they had carried out all that was written about him, they took him down from the cross and laid him in a tomb. 30But God raised him from the dead, 31and for many days he was seen by those who had

[a] *18* Some manuscripts *he cared for them*

traveled with him from Galilee
to Jerusalem. They are now his
witnesses to our people.
Mt 28:16; Lk 24:48; Ac 3:17

32“We tell you the good news:
What God promised our ancestors
33he has fulfilled for us, their children, by raising up Jesus. As it is
written in the second Psalm:
Ac 5:42; Ro 4:13

“ ‘You are my son;
today I have become your
father.’[a]

34God raised him from the dead so
that he will never be subject to decay. As God has said,

“ ‘I will give you the holy and
sure blessings promised
to David.’[b]

35So it is also stated elsewhere:

“ ‘You will not let your holy
one see decay.’[c]
Ps 16:10; Ac 2:27

36“Now when David had served
God’s purpose in his own generation, he fell asleep; he was buried
with his ancestors and his body
decayed. 37But the one whom God
raised from the dead did not see
decay. Ac 2:24,29; 1Ki 2:10

38“Therefore, my friends, I want
you to know that through Jesus
the forgiveness of sins is proclaimed to you. 39Through him
everyone who believes is set free
from every sin, a justification you
were not able to obtain under
the law of Moses. 40Take care that
what the prophets have said does
not happen to you:
Lk 24:47; Jn 3:15; Ro 3:28

41“ ‘Look, you scoffers,
wonder and perish,
for I am going to do something
in your days
that you would never
believe,
even if someone told you.’[d]”
Hab 1:5

42As Paul and Barnabas were
leaving the synagogue, the people invited them to speak further
about these things on the next
Sabbath. 43When the congregation
was dismissed, many of the Jews
and devout converts to Judaism
followed Paul and Barnabas, who
talked with them and urged them
to continue in the grace of God.
Ac 11:23; 14:22

44On the next Sabbath almost
the whole city gathered to hear
the word of the Lord. 45When the
Jews saw the crowds, they were
filled with jealousy. They began to
contradict what Paul was saying
and heaped abuse on him.
Ac 18:6; 1Th 2:16

46Then Paul and Barnabas answered them boldly: “We had to
speak the word of God to you first.
Since you reject it and do not consider yourselves worthy of eternal
life, we now turn to the Gentiles.

[a] *33* Psalm 2:7 [b] *34* Isaiah 55:3
[c] *35* Psalm 16:10 (see Septuagint)
[d] *41* Hab. 1:5

47 For this is what the Lord has
commanded us: Ac 3:26; 18:6; 28:28

> "'I have made you[a] a light for
> the Gentiles,
> that you[a] may bring
> salvation to the ends of
> the earth.'[b]" Lk 2:32; Isa 49:6

48 When the Gentiles heard this,
they were glad and honored the
word of the Lord; and all who were
appointed for eternal life believed.
Ac 8:25

49 The word of the Lord spread
through the whole region. 50 But
the Jewish leaders incited the
God-fearing women of high standing and the leading men of the
city. They stirred up persecution
against Paul and Barnabas, and
expelled them from their region.
51 So they shook the dust off their
feet as a warning to them and
went to Iconium. 52 And the disciples were filled with joy and with
the Holy Spirit. Mt 10:14; Lk 1:15

In Iconium

14 At Iconium Paul and Barnabas went as usual into
the Jewish synagogue. There they
spoke so effectively that a great
number of Jews and Greeks believed. 2 But the Jews who refused
to believe stirred up the other
Gentiles and poisoned their minds
against the brothers. 3 So Paul and
Barnabas spent considerable time
there, speaking boldly for the
Lord, who confirmed the message
of his grace by enabling them to
perform signs and wonders. 4 The
people of the city were divided;
some sided with the Jews, others with the apostles. 5 There was
a plot afoot among both Gentiles
and Jews, together with their leaders, to mistreat them and stone
them. 6 But they found out about
it and fled to the Lycaonian cities of Lystra and Derbe and to the
surrounding country, 7 where they
continued to preach the gospel.
Jn 4:48; Heb 2:4

In Lystra and Derbe

8 In Lystra there sat a man who
was lame. He had been that way
from birth and had never walked.
9 He listened to Paul as he was
speaking. Paul looked directly at
him, saw that he had faith to be
healed 10 and called out, "Stand
up on your feet!" At that, the man
jumped up and began to walk.
Mt 9:28-29; Ac 3:8

11 When the crowd saw what Paul
had done, they shouted in the Lycaonian language, "The gods have
come down to us in human form!"
12 Barnabas they called Zeus, and
Paul they called Hermes because he
was the chief speaker. 13 The priest
of Zeus, whose temple was just
outside the city, brought bulls and
wreaths to the city gates because
he and the crowd wanted to offer
sacrifices to them. Ac 8:10; 28:6

14 But when the apostles Barnabas and Paul heard of this, they

[a] 47 The Greek is singular.
[b] 47 Isaiah 49:6

tore their clothes and rushed
out into the crowd, shouting:
15“Friends, why are you doing this?
We too are only human, like you.
We are bringing you good news,
telling you to turn from these
worthless things to the living God,
who made the heavens and the
earth and the sea and everything
in them. 16In the past, he let all
nations go their own way. 17Yet he
has not left himself without testimony: He has shown kindness by
giving you rain from heaven and
crops in their seasons; he provides
you with plenty of food and fills
your hearts with joy.” 18Even with
these words, they had difficulty
keeping the crowd from sacrificing to them. Ac 10:26; Jas 5:17; Ro 1:20

19Then some Jews came from
Antioch and Iconium and won
the crowd over. They stoned Paul
and dragged him outside the city,
thinking he was dead. 20But after
the disciples had gathered around
him, he got up and went back into
the city. The next day he and Barnabas left for Derbe.

Ac 13:45; 2Co 11:25; 2Ti 3:11

The Return to Antioch in Syria

21They preached the gospel in
that city and won a large number
of disciples. Then they returned
to Lystra, Iconium and Antioch,
22strengthening the disciples and
encouraging them to remain true
to the faith. “We must go through
many hardships to enter the kingdom of God,” they said. 23Paul and
Barnabas appointed elders[a] for
them in each church and, with
prayer and fasting, committed
them to the Lord, in whom they
had put their trust. 24After going
through Pisidia, they came into
Pamphylia, 25and when they had
preached the word in Perga, they
went down to Attalia.

2Ti 3:12; Titus 1:5

26From Attalia they sailed back
to Antioch, where they had been
committed to the grace of God for
the work they had now completed.
27On arriving there, they gathered
the church together and reported all that God had done through
them and how he had opened a
door of faith to the Gentiles. 28And
they stayed there a long time with
the disciples. Ac 13:1,3; 1Co 16:9; 2Co 2:12

The Council at Jerusalem

15 Certain people came down
from Judea to Antioch and
were teaching the believers: “Unless you are circumcised, according to the custom taught by Moses, you cannot be saved.” 2This
brought Paul and Barnabas into
sharp dispute and debate with
them. So Paul and Barnabas were
appointed, along with some other believers, to go up to Jerusalem to see the apostles and elders
about this question. 3The church
sent them on their way, and as
they traveled through Phoenicia
and Samaria, they told how the

[a] 23 Or *Barnabas ordained elders*; or *Barnabas had elders elected*

Gentiles had been converted. This
news made all the believers very
glad. 4When they came to Jerusalem, they were welcomed by the
church and the apostles and elders, to whom they reported everything God had done through
them. Ac 14:27; Gal 5:2-3

5Then some of the believers
who belonged to the party of the
Pharisees stood up and said, "The
Gentiles must be circumcised and
required to keep the law of Moses." Ac 5:17

6The apostles and elders met
to consider this question. 7After
much discussion, Peter got up
and addressed them: "Brothers,
you know that some time ago
God made a choice among you
that the Gentiles might hear from
my lips the message of the gospel and believe. 8God, who knows
the heart, showed that he accepted them by giving the Holy Spirit
to them, just as he did to us. 9He
did not discriminate between us
and them, for he purified their
hearts by faith. 10Now then, why
do you try to test God by putting
on the necks of Gentiles a yoke
that neither we nor our ancestors
have been able to bear? 11No! We
believe it is through the grace of
our Lord Jesus that we are saved,
just as they are."

Mt 23:4; Ac 10:44,47; Ro 3:24

12The whole assembly became
silent as they listened to Barnabas
and Paul telling about the signs
and wonders God had done among
the Gentiles through them. 13When
they finished, James spoke up.
"Brothers," he said, "listen to me.
14Simon[a] has described to us how
God first intervened to choose a
people for his name from the Gentiles. 15The words of the prophets
are in agreement with this, as it is
written: Ac 12:17; 14:27

16" 'After this I will return
and rebuild David's fallen
tent.
Its ruins I will rebuild,
and I will restore it,
17that the rest of mankind may
seek the Lord,
even all the Gentiles who
bear my name,
says the Lord, who does these
things'[b] — Am 9:11-12
18 things known from long
ago.[c] Isa 45:21

19"It is my judgment, therefore,
that we should not make it difficult for the Gentiles who are turning to God. 20Instead we should
write to them, telling them to abstain from food polluted by idols,
from sexual immorality, from the
meat of strangled animals and
from blood. 21For the law of Moses has been preached in every
city from the earliest times and is
read in the synagogues on every
Sabbath." Ac 13:15; 1Co 10:14-28

[a] *14* Greek *Simeon*, a variant of *Simon*; that is, Peter [b] *17* Amos 9:11,12 (see Septuagint) [c] *17,18* Some manuscripts *things' — / 18the Lord's work is known to him from long ago*

The Council's Letter to Gentile Believers

22 Then the apostles and elders,
with the whole church, decided
to choose some of their own men
and send them to Antioch with
Paul and Barnabas. They chose
Judas (called Barsabbas) and Silas,
men who were leaders among the
believers. 23 With them they sent
the following letter: Ac 16:19,25,29

> The apostles and elders, your
> brothers,
>
> To the Gentile believers in
> Antioch, Syria and Cilicia:
> Ac 6:9; 11:19
>
> Greetings. Jas 1:1
>
> 24 We have heard that some
> went out from us without
> our authorization and dis-
> turbed you, troubling your
> minds by what they said. 25 So
> we all agreed to choose some
> men and send them to you
> with our dear friends Barna-
> bas and Paul — 26 men who
> have risked their lives for the
> name of our Lord Jesus Christ.
> 27 Therefore we are sending
> Judas and Silas to confirm by
> word of mouth what we are
> writing. 28 It seemed good to
> the Holy Spirit and to us not
> to burden you with anything
> beyond the following require-
> ments: 29 You are to abstain
> from food sacrificed to idols,
> from blood, from the meat of
> strangled animals and from
> sexual immorality. You will
> do well to avoid these things.
> Ac 14:19; 21:25
>
> Farewell.

30 So the men were sent off and
went down to Antioch, where they
gathered the church together and
delivered the letter. 31 The people
read it and were glad for its encouraging message. 32 Judas and
Silas, who themselves were prophets, said much to encourage and
strengthen the believers. 33 After
spending some time there, they
were sent off by the believers with
the blessing of peace to return
to those who had sent them. [34][a]
35 But Paul and Barnabas remained
in Antioch, where they and many
others taught and preached the
word of the Lord. Ac 8:4; 1Co 16:11

Disagreement Between Paul and Barnabas

36 Some time later Paul said to
Barnabas, "Let us go back and visit the believers in all the towns
where we preached the word of
the Lord and see how they are
doing." 37 Barnabas wanted to
take John, also called Mark, with
them, 38 but Paul did not think it
wise to take him, because he had
deserted them in Pamphylia and
had not continued with them in
the work. 39 They had such a sharp

[a] 34 Some manuscripts include here *But Silas decided to remain there.*

disagreement that they parted
company. Barnabas took Mark and
sailed for Cyprus, 40but Paul chose
Silas and left, commended by the
believers to the grace of the Lord.
41He went through Syria and Cilicia, strengthening the churches.
Ac 12:12; 13:13; 16:5

Timothy Joins Paul and Silas

16 Paul came to Derbe and
then to Lystra, where a disciple named Timothy lived, whose
mother was Jewish and a believer but whose father was a Greek.
2The believers at Lystra and Iconium spoke well of him. 3Paul
wanted to take him along on the
journey, so he circumcised him
because of the Jews who lived in
that area, for they all knew that
his father was a Greek. 4As they
traveled from town to town, they
delivered the decisions reached by
the apostles and elders in Jerusalem for the people to obey. 5So the
churches were strengthened in
the faith and grew daily in numbers. Ac 9:31; 11:30; 15:28-29

Paul's Vision of the Man of Macedonia

6Paul and his companions traveled throughout the region of
Phrygia and Galatia, having been
kept by the Holy Spirit from
preaching the word in the province
of Asia. 7When they came to the
border of Mysia, they tried to enter Bithynia, but the Spirit of Jesus
would not allow them to. 8So they
passed by Mysia and went down to
Troas. 9During the night Paul had
a vision of a man of Macedonia
standing and begging him, "Come
over to Macedonia and help us."
10After Paul had seen the vision,
we got ready at once to leave for
Macedonia, concluding that God
had called us to preach the gospel
to them. Ac 9:10; Ro 8:9; 2Co 2:12

Lydia's Conversion in Philippi

11From Troas we put out to sea
and sailed straight for Samo-
thrace, and the next day we went
on to Neapolis. 12From there we
traveled to Philippi, a Roman colo-
ny and the leading city of that district[a] of Macedonia. And we stayed
there several days. Php 1:1; 1Th 2:2
13On the Sabbath we went outside the city gate to the river,
where we expected to find a place
of prayer. We sat down and began
to speak to the women who had
gathered there. 14One of those listening was a woman from the city
of Thyatira named Lydia, a dealer
in purple cloth. She was a worshiper of God. The Lord opened her
heart to respond to Paul's message. 15When she and the members of her household were baptized, she invited us to her home.
"If you consider me a believer in
the Lord," she said, "come and stay
at my house." And she persuaded us. Lk 24:45; Ac 13:14

[a] *12* The text and meaning of the Greek for *the leading city of that district* are uncertain.

Paul and Silas in Prison

[16]Once when we were going to
the place of prayer, we were met
by a female slave who had a spirit
by which she predicted the future.
She earned a great deal of money for her owners by fortune-tell-
ing. [17]She followed Paul and the
rest of us, shouting, "These men
are servants of the Most High God,
who are telling you the way to be
saved." [18]She kept this up for many
days. Finally Paul became so an-
noyed that he turned around and
said to the spirit, "In the name of
Jesus Christ I command you to
come out of her!" At that moment
the spirit left her. Mk 16:17; 1Sa 28:3,7

[19]When her owners realized that
their hope of making money was
gone, they seized Paul and Silas
and dragged them into the marketplace to face the authorities.
[20]They brought them before the
magistrates and said, "These men
are Jews, and are throwing our city
into an uproar [21]by advocating customs unlawful for us Romans to
accept or practice." Ac 17:6; 19:25-26

[22]The crowd joined in the attack against Paul and Silas, and
the magistrates ordered them to
be stripped and beaten with rods.
[23]After they had been severely
flogged, they were thrown into
prison, and the jailer was commanded to guard them carefully.
[24]When he received these orders,
he put them in the inner cell and
fastened their feet in the stocks.

Jer 20:2-3; 2Co 11:25; 1Th 2:2

[25]About midnight Paul and Silas
were praying and singing hymns
to God, and the other prisoners
were listening to them. [26]Sudden-
ly there was such a violent earthquake that the foundations of the
prison were shaken. At once all
the prison doors flew open, and
everyone's chains came loose.
[27]The jailer woke up, and when
he saw the prison doors open, he
drew his sword and was about to
kill himself because he thought
the prisoners had escaped. [28]But
Paul shouted, "Don't harm yourself! We are all here!"

Ac 4:31; 12:19; Eph 5:19

[29]The jailer called for lights,
rushed in and fell trembling before
Paul and Silas. [30]He then brought
them out and asked, "Sirs, what
must I do to be saved?" Ac 2:37

[31]They replied, "Believe in
the Lord Jesus, and you will be
saved — you and your household."
[32]Then they spoke the word of the
Lord to him and to all the others
in his house. [33]At that hour of the
night the jailer took them and
washed their wounds; then immediately he and all his household
were baptized. [34]The jailer brought
them into his house and set a meal
before them; he was filled with joy
because he had come to believe in
God — he and his whole household. Jn 3:15; Ro 11:14

[35]When it was daylight, the
magistrates sent their officers to
the jailer with the order: "Release
those men." [36]The jailer told Paul,

“The magistrates have ordered
that you and Silas be released.
Now you can leave. Go in peace.”
Ac 15:33
37 But Paul said to the officers:
“They beat us publicly without a
trial, even though we are Roman
citizens, and threw us into prison.
And now do they want to get rid
of us quietly? No! Let them come
themselves and escort us out.”
Ac 22:25-29
38 The officers reported this to
the magistrates, and when they
heard that Paul and Silas were Roman citizens, they were alarmed.
39 They came to appease them and
escorted them from the prison,
requesting them to leave the city.
40 After Paul and Silas came out of
the prison, they went to Lydia’s
house, where they met with the
brothers and sisters and encouraged them. Then they left.
Mt 8:34; Ac 1:16

In Thessalonica

17 When Paul and his companions had passed through
Amphipolis and Apollonia, they
came to Thessalonica, where
there was a Jewish synagogue. 2 As
was his custom, Paul went into
the synagogue, and on three Sabbath days he reasoned with them
from the Scriptures, 3 explaining and proving that the Messiah had to suffer and rise from the
dead. “This Jesus I am proclaiming to you is the Messiah,” he said.
4 Some of the Jews were persuaded and joined Paul and Silas, as
did a large number of God-fearing
Greeks and quite a few prominent
women.
Ac 15:22; 18:28
5 But other Jews were jealous;
so they rounded up some bad
characters from the marketplace,
formed a mob and started a riot
in the city. They rushed to Jason’s
house in search of Paul and Silas
in order to bring them out to the
crowd.[a] 6 But when they did not
find them, they dragged Jason
and some other believers before
the city officials, shouting: “These
men who have caused trouble all
over the world have now come
here, 7 and Jason has welcomed
them into his house. They are all
defying Caesar’s decrees, saying
that there is another king, one
called Jesus.” 8 When they heard
this, the crowd and the city officials were thrown into turmoil.
9 Then they made Jason and the
others post bond and let them go.
Lk 23:2; Ro 16:21

In Berea

10 As soon as it was night, the believers sent Paul and Silas away
to Berea. On arriving there, they
went to the Jewish synagogue.
11 Now the Berean Jews were of
more noble character than those
in Thessalonica, for they received
the message with great eagerness
and examined the Scriptures every day to see if what Paul said was
true. 12 As a result, many of them

[a] 5 Or *the assembly of the people*

believed, as did also a number
of prominent Greek women and
many Greek men.

Lk 16:29; Jn 5:39; Ac 20:4

13But when the Jews in Thessalonica learned that Paul was
preaching the word of God at Berea, some of them went there too,
agitating the crowds and stirring
them up. 14The believers immediately sent Paul to the coast, but
Silas and Timothy stayed at Berea.
15Those who escorted Paul brought
him to Athens and then left with
instructions for Silas and Timothy
to join him as soon as possible.

Ac 16:1; 18:5

In Athens

16While Paul was waiting for
them in Athens, he was greatly distressed to see that the city
was full of idols. 17So he reasoned
in the synagogue with both Jews
and God-fearing Greeks, as well
as in the marketplace day by day
with those who happened to be
there. 18A group of Epicurean and
Stoic philosophers began to debate with him. Some of them
asked, “What is this babbler trying to say?” Others remarked,
“He seems to be advocating foreign gods.” They said this because
Paul was preaching the good news
about Jesus and the resurrection.
19Then they took him and brought
him to a meeting of the Areopagus, where they said to him, “May
we know what this new teaching
is that you are presenting? 20You
are bringing some strange ideas
to our ears, and we would like to
know what they mean.” 21(All the
Athenians and the foreigners who
lived there spent their time doing
nothing but talking about and listening to the latest ideas.)

Ac 4:2; 9:20

22Paul then stood up in the
meeting of the Areopagus and
said: “People of Athens! I see that
in every way you are very religious. 23For as I walked around
and looked carefully at your objects of worship, I even found an
altar with this inscription: TO AN
UNKNOWN GOD. So you are ignorant of the very thing you worship — and this is what I am going
to proclaim to you. Jn 4:22
24“The God who made the world
and everything in it is the Lord of
heaven and earth and does not live
in temples built by human hands.
25And he is not served by human
hands, as if he needed anything.
Rather, he himself gives everyone
life and breath and everything
else. 26From one man he made
all the nations, that they should
inhabit the whole earth; and he
marked out their appointed times
in history and the boundaries of
their lands. 27God did this so that
they would seek him and perhaps reach out for him and find
him, though he is not far from
any one of us. 28‘For in him we live
and move and have our being.’[a]

[a] 28 From the Cretan philosopher Epimenides

As some of your own poets have
said, ‘We are his offspring.’[a]
Dt 32:8; Ac 14:17

29 “Therefore since we are God’s
offspring, we should not think
that the divine being is like gold
or silver or stone — an image
made by human design and skill.
30 In the past God overlooked such
ignorance, but now he commands
all people everywhere to repent.
31 For he has set a day when he will
judge the world with justice by
the man he has appointed. He has
given proof of this to everyone by
raising him from the dead.”
Lk 24:47; Titus 2:11-12

32 When they heard about the
resurrection of the dead, some
of them sneered, but others said,
“We want to hear you again on
this subject.” 33 At that, Paul left
the Council. 34 Some of the people
became followers of Paul and believed. Among them was Diony-
sius, a member of the Areopagus,
also a woman named Damaris,
and a number of others. ver 19,22

In Corinth

18 After this, Paul left Athens
and went to Corinth. 2 There
he met a Jew named Aquila, a native of Pontus, who had recently come from Italy with his wife
Priscilla, because Claudius had ordered all Jews to leave Rome. Paul
went to see them, 3 and because
he was a tentmaker as they were,
he stayed and worked with them.
4 Every Sabbath he reasoned in the
synagogue, trying to persuade
Jews and Greeks.
Ro 16:3; 1Co 16:19; 2Ti 4:19

5 When Silas and Timothy came
from Macedonia, Paul devoted
himself exclusively to preaching,
testifying to the Jews that Jesus
was the Messiah. 6 But when they
opposed Paul and became abusive, he shook out his clothes in
protest and said to them, “Your
blood be on your own heads! I am
innocent of it. From now on I will
go to the Gentiles.” Ac 13:46; 20:26

7 Then Paul left the synagogue
and went next door to the house of
Titius Justus, a worshiper of God.
8 Crispus, the synagogue leader,
and his entire household believed
in the Lord; and many of the Corinthians who heard Paul believed
and were baptized. Mk 5:22; 1Co 1:14

9 One night the Lord spoke to
Paul in a vision: “Do not be afraid;
keep on speaking, do not be silent.
10 For I am with you, and no one
is going to attack and harm you,
because I have many people in
this city.” 11 So Paul stayed in Corinth for a year and a half, teaching
them the word of God. Mt 28:20

12 While Gallio was proconsul
of Achaia, the Jews of Corinth
made a united attack on Paul and
brought him to the place of judgment. 13 “This man,” they charged,
“is persuading the people to worship God in ways contrary to the
law.” Ro 15:26; 1Co 16:15

[a] *28* From the Cilician Stoic philosopher Aratus

14 Just as Paul was about to speak,
Gallio said to them, "If you Jews
were making a complaint about
some misdemeanor or serious
crime, it would be reasonable for
me to listen to you. 15 But since it in-
volves questions about words and
names and your own law — settle
the matter yourselves. I will not
be a judge of such things." 16 So he
drove them off. 17 Then the crowd
there turned on Sosthenes the
synagogue leader and beat him in
front of the proconsul; and Gallio
showed no concern whatever.

Ac 23:29; 1Co 1:1

Priscilla, Aquila and Apollos

18 Paul stayed on in Corinth for
some time. Then he left the brothers and sisters and sailed for Syria,
accompanied by Priscilla and Aquila. Before he sailed, he had his
hair cut off at Cenchreae because
of a vow he had taken. 19 They arrived at Ephesus, where Paul left
Priscilla and Aquila. He himself
went into the synagogue and reasoned with the Jews. 20 When they
asked him to spend more time
with them, he declined. 21 But as
he left, he promised, "I will come
back if it is God's will." Then he
set sail from Ephesus. 22 When he
landed at Caesarea, he went up to
Jerusalem and greeted the church
and then went down to Antioch.

Ac 11:19; 1Co 4:19

23 After spending some time in
Antioch, Paul set out from there
and traveled from place to place
throughout the region of Galatia
and Phrygia, strengthening all the
disciples.

Ac 14:22; 16:6

24 Meanwhile a Jew named Apollos, a native of Alexandria, came
to Ephesus. He was a learned man,
with a thorough knowledge of
the Scriptures. 25 He had been instructed in the way of the Lord,
and he spoke with great fervor[a]
and taught about Jesus accurately,
though he knew only the baptism
of John. 26 He began to speak boldly in the synagogue. When Priscilla and Aquila heard him, they
invited him to their home and
explained to him the way of God
more adequately.

Ac 19:3; 1Co 1:12; Titus 3:13

27 When Apollos wanted to go to
Achaia, the brothers and sisters
encouraged him and wrote to the
disciples there to welcome him.
When he arrived, he was a great
help to those who by grace had believed. 28 For he vigorously refuted
his Jewish opponents in public debate, proving from the Scriptures
that Jesus was the Messiah.

Ac 9:22; 17:2

Paul in Ephesus

19 While Apollos was at Corinth, Paul took the road
through the interior and arrived
at Ephesus. There he found some
disciples 2 and asked them, "Did
you receive the Holy Spirit when[b]
you believed?"

Ac 18:1,19

[a] 25 Or *with fervor in the Spirit* [b] 2 Or *after*

They answered, "No, we have
not even heard that there is a Holy
Spirit."
3So Paul asked, "Then what baptism did you receive?"
"John's baptism," they replied.
4Paul said, "John's baptism
was a baptism of repentance. He
told the people to believe in the
one coming after him, that is,
in Jesus." 5On hearing this, they
were baptized in the name of the
Lord Jesus. 6When Paul placed his
hands on them, the Holy Spirit
came on them, and they spoke in
tongues[a] and prophesied. 7There
were about twelve men in all.

Ac 2:4; 6:6; 10:46

8Paul entered the synagogue
and spoke boldly there for three
months, arguing persuasively
about the kingdom of God. 9But
some of them became obstinate;
they refused to believe and publicly maligned the Way. So Paul left
them. He took the disciples with
him and had discussions daily in
the lecture hall of Tyrannus. 10This
went on for two years, so that all
the Jews and Greeks who lived
in the province of Asia heard the
word of the Lord. Ac 1:3; 9:2; 20:31

11God did extraordinary miracles through Paul, 12so that even
handkerchiefs and aprons that
had touched him were taken to
the sick, and their illnesses were
cured and the evil spirits left
them. Ac 5:15; 8:13

13Some Jews who went around
driving out evil spirits tried to invoke the name of the Lord Jesus
over those who were demon-possessed. They would say, "In the
name of the Jesus whom Paul
preaches, I command you to come
out." 14Seven sons of Sceva, a Jewish chief priest, were doing this.
15One day the evil spirit answered
them, "Jesus I know, and Paul I
know about, but who are you?"
16Then the man who had the evil
spirit jumped on them and overpowered them all. He gave them
such a beating that they ran out of
the house naked and bleeding.

Mt 12:27; Mk 9:38

17When this became known
to the Jews and Greeks living
in Ephesus, they were all seized
with fear, and the name of the
Lord Jesus was held in high hon-
or. 18Many of those who believed
now came and openly confessed
what they had done. 19A number who had practiced sorcery
brought their scrolls together
and burned them publicly. When
they calculated the value of the
scrolls, the total came to fifty
thousand drachmas.[b] 20In this
way the word of the Lord spread
widely and grew in power.

Ac 5:5,11; 6:7; 12:24

21After all this had happened,
Paul decided[c] to go to Jerusalem,
passing through Macedonia and
Achaia. "After I have been there,"
he said, "I must visit Rome also."

[a] 6 Or *other languages* [b] 19 A drachma was a silver coin worth about a day's wages.
[c] 21 Or *decided in the Spirit*

22 He sent two of his helpers, Timothy and Erastus, to Macedonia,
while he stayed in the province of
Asia a little longer. Ro 15:25; 16:23

The Riot in Ephesus

23 About that time there arose a
great disturbance about the Way.
24 A silversmith named Demetrius, who made silver shrines of
Artemis, brought in a lot of business for the craftsmen there. 25 He
called them together, along with
the workers in related trades, and
said: "You know, my friends, that
we receive a good income from
this business. 26 And you see and
hear how this fellow Paul has convinced and led astray large numbers of people here in Ephesus and
in practically the whole province
of Asia. He says that gods made by
human hands are no gods at all.
27 There is danger not only that our
trade will lose its good name, but
also that the temple of the great
goddess Artemis will be discredit-
ed; and the goddess herself, who
is worshiped throughout the province of Asia and the world, will be
robbed of her divine majesty."

Ps 115:4; Isa 44:10-20; Jer 10:3-5

28 When they heard this, they
were furious and began shouting:
"Great is Artemis of the Ephesians!" 29 Soon the whole city was in
an uproar. The people seized Gaius and Aristarchus, Paul's traveling companions from Macedonia,
and all of them rushed into the
theater together. 30 Paul wanted to
appear before the crowd, but the
disciples would not let him. 31 Even
some of the officials of the province, friends of Paul, sent him a
message begging him not to venture into the theater.

Ac 20:4; 27:2; Col 4:10

32 The assembly was in confusion: Some were shouting one
thing, some another. Most of the
people did not even know why
they were there. 33 The Jews in the
crowd pushed Alexander to the
front, and they shouted instructions to him. He motioned for silence in order to make a defense
before the people. 34 But when
they realized he was a Jew, they
all shouted in unison for about
two hours: "Great is Artemis of the
Ephesians!" Ac 12:17; 21:34

35 The city clerk quieted the
crowd and said: "Fellow Ephesians, doesn't all the world know
that the city of Ephesus is the
guardian of the temple of the
great Artemis and of her image,
which fell from heaven? 36 Therefore, since these facts are undeni-
able, you ought to calm down and
not do anything rash. 37 You have
brought these men here, though
they have neither robbed temples nor blasphemed our goddess.
38 If, then, Demetrius and his fellow craftsmen have a grievance
against anybody, the courts are
open and there are proconsuls.
They can press charges. 39 If there
is anything further you want to
bring up, it must be settled in a

legal assembly. 40As it is, we are in
danger of being charged with ri-
oting because of what happened
today. In that case we would not
be able to account for this commotion, since there is no reason
for it." 41After he had said this, he
dismissed the assembly.

Ac 18:19; Ro 2:22

Through Macedonia and Greece

20 When the uproar had ended, Paul sent for the disciples and, after encouraging them,
said goodbye and set out for Macedonia. 2He traveled through that
area, speaking many words of encouragement to the people, and
finally arrived in Greece, 3where
he stayed three months. Because
some Jews had plotted against him
just as he was about to sail for Syria, he decided to go back through
Macedonia. 4He was accompanied
by Sopater son of Pyrrhus from
Berea, Aristarchus and Secundus
from Thessalonica, Gaius from
Derbe, Timothy also, and Tychicus
and Trophimus from the province
of Asia. 5These men went on ahead
and waited for us at Troas. 6But we
sailed from Philippi after the Festival of Unleavened Bread, and five
days later joined the others at Troas, where we stayed seven days.

Ac 9:23-24; 16:9

Eutychus Raised From the Dead at Troas

7On the first day of the week we
came together to break bread. Paul
spoke to the people and, because
he intended to leave the next day,
kept on talking until midnight.
8There were many lamps in the
upstairs room where we were
meeting. 9Seated in a window was
a young man named Eutychus,
who was sinking into a deep sleep
as Paul talked on and on. When
he was sound asleep, he fell to the
ground from the third story and
was picked up dead. 10Paul went
down, threw himself on the young
man and put his arms around
him. "Don't be alarmed," he said.
"He's alive!" 11Then he went upstairs again and broke bread and
ate. After talking until daylight, he
left. 12The people took the young
man home alive and were greatly
comforted.

Mt 9:23-24; Ac 1:13; 1Co 16:2

Paul's Farewell to the Ephesian Elders

13We went on ahead to the ship
and sailed for Assos, where we
were going to take Paul aboard. He
had made this arrangement because he was going there on foot.
14When he met us at Assos, we took
him aboard and went on to Mityle-
ne. 15The next day we set sail from
there and arrived off Chios. The
day after that we crossed over to
Samos, and on the following day
arrived at Miletus. 16Paul had decided to sail past Ephesus to avoid
spending time in the province of
Asia, for he was in a hurry to reach
Jerusalem, if possible, by the day
of Pentecost.

Ac 2:1; 19:21

17 From Miletus, Paul sent to
Ephesus for the elders of the
church. 18 When they arrived, he
said to them: "You know how I
lived the whole time I was with
you, from the first day I came into
the province of Asia. 19 I served the
Lord with great humility and with
tears and in the midst of severe
testing by the plots of my Jewish
opponents. 20 You know that I have
not hesitated to preach anything
that would be helpful to you but
have taught you publicly and from
house to house. 21 I have declared
to both Jews and Greeks that they
must turn to God in repentance
and have faith in our Lord Jesus.
Ac 2:38; 18:5

22 "And now, compelled by the
Spirit, I am going to Jerusalem,
not knowing what will happen to
me there. 23 I only know that in every city the Holy Spirit warns me
that prison and hardships are facing me. 24 However, I consider my
life worth nothing to me; my only
aim is to finish the race and complete the task the Lord Jesus has
given me — the task of testifying
to the good news of God's grace.
Ac 21:13; Gal 1:1

25 "Now I know that none of you
among whom I have gone about
preaching the kingdom will ever
see me again. 26 Therefore, I declare
to you today that I am innocent
of the blood of any of you. 27 For I
have not hesitated to proclaim to
you the whole will of God. 28 Keep
watch over yourselves and all the
flock of which the Holy Spirit has
made you overseers. Be shepherds
of the church of God,[a] which he
bought with his own blood.[b] 29 I
know that after I leave, savage
wolves will come in among you
and will not spare the flock. 30 Even
from your own number men will
arise and distort the truth in order
to draw away disciples after them.
31 So be on your guard! Remember
that for three years I never stopped
warning each of you night and day
with tears.
Ac 19:10; 1Pe 5:2

32 "Now I commit you to God and
to the word of his grace, which can
build you up and give you an inheritance among all those who
are sanctified. 33 I have not coveted
anyone's silver or gold or clothing.
34 You yourselves know that these
hands of mine have supplied my
own needs and the needs of my
companions. 35 In everything I did,
I showed you that by this kind of
hard work we must help the weak,
remembering the words the Lord
Jesus himself said: 'It is more
blessed to give than to receive.' "
Ac 18:3; 1Co 9:12; Col 1:12

36 When Paul had finished speaking, he knelt down with all of
them and prayed. 37 They all wept
as they embraced him and kissed
him. 38 What grieved them most
was his statement that they would
never see his face again. Then they
accompanied him to the ship.
Lk 15:20; Ac 21:5

[a] 28 Many manuscripts *of the Lord*
[b] 28 Or *with the blood of his own Son*

On to Jerusalem

21 After we had torn ourselves
away from them, we put out
to sea and sailed straight to Kos.
The next day we went to Rhodes
and from there to Patara. 2We
found a ship crossing over to Phoenicia, went on board and set sail.
3After sighting Cyprus and passing to the south of it, we sailed on
to Syria. We landed at Tyre, where
our ship was to unload its cargo.
4We sought out the disciples there
and stayed with them seven days.
Through the Spirit they urged
Paul not to go on to Jerusalem.
5When it was time to leave, we left
and continued on our way. All of
them, including wives and children, accompanied us out of the
city, and there on the beach we
knelt to pray. 6After saying goodbye to each other, we went aboard
the ship, and they returned home.
Ac 20:23,36

7We continued our voyage from
Tyre and landed at Ptolemais,
where we greeted the brothers
and sisters and stayed with them
for a day. 8Leaving the next day,
we reached Caesarea and stayed
at the house of Philip the evangelist, one of the Seven. 9He had four
unmarried daughters who prophesied. Ac 6:5; Eph 4:11; 2Ti 4:5

10After we had been there a
number of days, a prophet named
Agabus came down from Judea.
11Coming over to us, he took Paul's
belt, tied his own hands and feet
with it and said, "The Holy Spirit
says, 'In this way the Jewish leaders in Jerusalem will bind the
owner of this belt and will hand
him over to the Gentiles.'"
1Ki 22:11; Ac 11:28

12When we heard this, we and
the people there pleaded with
Paul not to go up to Jerusalem.
13Then Paul answered, "Why are
you weeping and breaking my
heart? I am ready not only to be
bound, but also to die in Jerusalem for the name of the Lord
Jesus." 14When he would not be
dissuaded, we gave up and said,
"The Lord's will be done."
Ac 9:16; 20:24

15After this, we started on our
way up to Jerusalem. 16Some of
the disciples from Caesarea accompanied us and brought us to
the home of Mnason, where we
were to stay. He was a man from
Cyprus and one of the early disciples. Ac 8:40; 19:21

Paul's Arrival at Jerusalem

17When we arrived at Jerusalem, the brothers and sisters received us warmly. 18The next day
Paul and the rest of us went to
see James, and all the elders were
present. 19Paul greeted them and
reported in detail what God had
done among the Gentiles through
his ministry. Ac 1:17; 15:4

20When they heard this, they
praised God. Then they said to
Paul: "You see, brother, how many
thousands of Jews have believed,
and all of them are zealous for the

law. 21They have been informed
that you teach all the Jews who
live among the Gentiles to turn
away from Moses, telling them
not to circumcise their children
or live according to our customs.
22What shall we do? They will certainly hear that you have come,
23so do what we tell you. There are
four men with us who have made
a vow. 24Take these men, join in
their purification rites and pay
their expenses, so that they can
have their heads shaved. Then
everyone will know there is no
truth in these reports about you,
but that you yourself are living in
obedience to the law. 25As for the
Gentile believers, we have written to them our decision that they
should abstain from food sacrificed to idols, from blood, from
the meat of strangled animals and
from sexual immorality."

Ac 18:18; 22:3; 1Co 7:18-19

26The next day Paul took the
men and purified himself along
with them. Then he went to the
temple to give notice of the date
when the days of purification
would end and the offering would
be made for each of them.

Nu 6:13-20; Ac 24:18

Paul Arrested

27When the seven days were
nearly over, some Jews from the
province of Asia saw Paul at the
temple. They stirred up the whole
crowd and seized him, 28shouting,
"Fellow Israelites, help us! This is
the man who teaches everyone
everywhere against our people
and our law and this place. And
besides, he has brought Greeks
into the temple and defiled this
holy place." 29(They had previously seen Trophimus the Ephesian
in the city with Paul and assumed
that Paul had brought him into
the temple.)

Ac 20:4; 24:18

30The whole city was aroused,
and the people came running
from all directions. Seizing Paul,
they dragged him from the temple, and immediately the gates
were shut. 31While they were trying to kill him, news reached the
commander of the Roman troops
that the whole city of Jerusalem
was in an uproar. 32He at once took
some officers and soldiers and ran
down to the crowd. When the ri-
oters saw the commander and
his soldiers, they stopped beating
Paul.

Ac 23:27; 26:21

33The commander came up and
arrested him and ordered him to
be bound with two chains. Then
he asked who he was and what
he had done. 34Some in the crowd
shouted one thing and some another, and since the commander
could not get at the truth because
of the uproar, he ordered that Paul
be taken into the barracks. 35When
Paul reached the steps, the violence of the mob was so great he
had to be carried by the soldiers.
36The crowd that followed kept
shouting, "Get rid of him!"

Lk 23:18; Ac 22:22

Paul Speaks to the Crowd

37 As the soldiers were about to
take Paul into the barracks, he
asked the commander, "May I say
something to you?"

"Do you speak Greek?" he replied. 38 "Aren't you the Egyptian
who started a revolt and led four
thousand terrorists out into the
wilderness some time ago?"
Mt 24:26; Ac 5:36

39 Paul answered, "I am a Jew,
from Tarsus in Cilicia, a citizen
of no ordinary city. Please let me
speak to the people." Ac 9:11; 22:3

40 After receiving the commander's permission, Paul stood on the
steps and motioned to the crowd.
When they were all silent, he
22 said to them in Aramaic[a]:
1 "Brothers and fathers, listen now to my defense." Ac 7:2; 12:17

2 When they heard him speak
to them in Aramaic, they became
very quiet. Jn 5:2; Ac 21:40

Then Paul said: 3 "I am a Jew,
born in Tarsus of Cilicia, but
brought up in this city. I studied
under Gamaliel and was thoroughly trained in the law of our
ancestors. I was just as zealous for
God as any of you are today. 4 I persecuted the followers of this Way
to their death, arresting both men
and women and throwing them
into prison, 5 as the high priest and
all the Council can themselves testify. I even obtained letters from
them to their associates in Damascus, and went there to bring these
people as prisoners to Jerusalem
to be punished. Ac 21:20; 26:5

6 "About noon as I came near
Damascus, suddenly a bright light
from heaven flashed around me.
7 I fell to the ground and heard a
voice say to me, 'Saul! Saul! Why
do you persecute me?' Ac 9:3

8 " 'Who are you, Lord?' I asked.

" 'I am Jesus of Nazareth, whom
you are persecuting,' he replied.
9 My companions saw the light, but
they did not understand the voice
of him who was speaking to me.
Ac 9:7; 26:13

10 " 'What shall I do, Lord?' I
asked.

" 'Get up,' the Lord said, 'and
go into Damascus. There you will
be told all that you have been assigned to do.' 11 My companions led
me by the hand into Damascus,
because the brilliance of the light
had blinded me. Ac 9:8; 16:30

12 "A man named Ananias came
to see me. He was a devout observ-
er of the law and highly respected
by all the Jews living there. 13 He
stood beside me and said, 'Brother Saul, receive your sight!' And
at that very moment I was able to
see him. Ac 9:17; 10:22

14 "Then he said: 'The God of
our ancestors has chosen you to
know his will and to see the Righteous One and to hear words from
his mouth. 15 You will be his witness to all people of what you
have seen and heard. 16 And now

[a] 40 Or possibly *Hebrew*; also in 22:2

what are you waiting for? Get up,
be baptized and wash your sins
away, calling on his name.'
Ac 9:1-22; 26:9-18

17 "When I returned to Jerusalem and was praying at the temple, I fell into a trance 18 and saw
the Lord speaking to me. 'Quick!'
he said. 'Leave Jerusalem immediately, because the people here
will not accept your testimony
about me.' Ac 9:26; 10:10

19 " 'Lord,' I replied, 'these people know that I went from one
synagogue to another to impris-
on and beat those who believe
in you. 20 And when the blood of
your martyr[a] Stephen was shed,
I stood there giving my approval
and guarding the clothes of those
who were killing him.' Ac 8:1,3

21 "Then the Lord said to me,
'Go; I will send you far away to the
Gentiles.' " Ac 9:15; 13:46

Paul the Roman Citizen

22 The crowd listened to Paul until he said this. Then they raised
their voices and shouted, "Rid the
earth of him! He's not fit to live!"
Ac 21:36; 25:24

23 As they were shouting and
throwing off their cloaks and
flinging dust into the air, 24 the
commander ordered that Paul be
taken into the barracks. He directed that he be flogged and interro-
gated in order to find out why the
people were shouting at him like
this. 25 As they stretched him out
to flog him, Paul said to the centurion standing there, "Is it legal for
you to flog a Roman citizen who
hasn't even been found guilty?"
2Sa 16:13; Ac 16:37

26 When the centurion heard
this, he went to the commander
and reported it. "What are you going to do?" he asked. "This man is
a Roman citizen."

27 The commander went to Paul
and asked, "Tell me, are you a Roman citizen?"

"Yes, I am," he answered.

28 Then the commander said, "I
had to pay a lot of money for my
citizenship."

"But I was born a citizen," Paul
replied.

29 Those who were about to in-
terrogate him withdrew immediately. The commander himself was
alarmed when he realized that he
had put Paul, a Roman citizen, in
chains. Ac 16:38

Paul Before the Sanhedrin

30 The commander wanted to
find out exactly why Paul was being accused by the Jews. So the
next day he released him and ordered the chief priests and all the
members of the Sanhedrin to assemble. Then he brought Paul and
had him stand before them.
Mt 5:22; Ac 23:28

23 Paul looked straight at the
Sanhedrin and said, "My
brothers, I have fulfilled my duty
to God in all good conscience to
this day." 2 At this the high priest

[a] *20* Or *witness*

Ananias ordered those standing near Paul to strike him on the mouth. 3 Then Paul said to him, "God will strike you, you whitewashed wall! You sit there to judge me according to the law, yet you yourself violate the law by commanding that I be struck!" Dt 25:1-2; Jn 7:51

4 Those who were standing near Paul said, "How dare you insult God's high priest!"

5 Paul replied, "Brothers, I did not realize that he was the high priest; for it is written: 'Do not speak evil about the ruler of your people.'[a]" Ex 22:28

6 Then Paul, knowing that some of them were Sadducees and the others Pharisees, called out in the Sanhedrin, "My brothers, I am a Pharisee, descended from Pharisees. I stand on trial because of the hope of the resurrection of the dead." 7 When he said this, a dispute broke out between the Pharisees and the Sadducees, and the assembly was divided. 8 (The Sadducees say that there is no resurrection, and that there are neither angels nor spirits, but the Pharisees believe all these things.) Mt 22:23; Ac 22:5; 26:5

9 There was a great uproar, and some of the teachers of the law who were Pharisees stood up and argued vigorously. "We find nothing wrong with this man," they said. "What if a spirit or an angel has spoken to him?" 10 The dispute became so violent that the commander was afraid Paul would be torn to pieces by them. He ordered the troops to go down and take him away from them by force and bring him into the barracks. Ac 21:34; 22:7,17-18

11 The following night the Lord stood near Paul and said, "Take courage! As you have testified about me in Jerusalem, so you must also testify in Rome." Ac 18:9; 19:21

The Plot to Kill Paul

12 The next morning some Jews formed a conspiracy and bound themselves with an oath not to eat or drink until they had killed Paul. 13 More than forty men were involved in this plot. 14 They went to the chief priests and the elders and said, "We have taken a solemn oath not to eat anything until we have killed Paul. 15 Now then, you and the Sanhedrin petition the commander to bring him before you on the pretext of wanting more accurate information about his case. We are ready to kill him before he gets here." Ac 22:30

16 But when the son of Paul's sister heard of this plot, he went into the barracks and told Paul. Ac 21:34

17 Then Paul called one of the centurions and said, "Take this young man to the commander; he has something to tell him." 18 So he took him to the commander.

The centurion said, "Paul, the prisoner, sent for me and asked

[a] 5 Exodus 22:28

me to bring this young man to
you because he has something to
tell you." Eph 3:1
19 The commander took the
young man by the hand, drew him
aside and asked, "What is it you
want to tell me?"
20 He said: "Some Jews have
agreed to ask you to bring Paul
before the Sanhedrin tomorrow
on the pretext of wanting more
accurate information about him.
21 Don't give in to them, because
more than forty of them are waiting in ambush for him. They have
taken an oath not to eat or drink
until they have killed him. They
are ready now, waiting for your
consent to their request." ver 14-15
22 The commander dismissed
the young man with this warning:
"Don't tell anyone that you have
reported this to me."

Paul Transferred to Caesarea

23 Then he called two of his centurions and ordered them, "Get
ready a detachment of two hundred soldiers, seventy horsemen
and two hundred spearmen[a] to go
to Caesarea at nine tonight. 24 Provide horses for Paul so that he may
be taken safely to Governor Felix."
Ac 24:1-3,10
25 He wrote a letter as follows:

26 Claudius Lysias,

To His Excellency, Governor
Felix: Ac 24:3

Greetings. Ac 15:23

27 This man was seized by
the Jews and they were about
to kill him, but I came with
my troops and rescued him,
for I had learned that he is a
Roman citizen. 28 I wanted to
know why they were accusing
him, so I brought him to their
Sanhedrin. 29 I found that the
accusation had to do with
questions about their law, but
there was no charge against
him that deserved death or
imprisonment. 30 When I was
informed of a plot to be carried out against the man, I
sent him to you at once. I also
ordered his accusers to present to you their case against
him. Ac 24:19; 26:31

31 So the soldiers, carrying out
their orders, took Paul with them
during the night and brought him
as far as Antipatris. 32 The next day
they let the cavalry go on with
him, while they returned to the
barracks. 33 When the cavalry arrived in Caesarea, they delivered
the letter to the governor and
handed Paul over to him. 34 The
governor read the letter and asked
what province he was from. Learning that he was from Cilicia, 35 he
said, "I will hear your case when
your accusers get here." Then he
ordered that Paul be kept under
guard in Herod's palace.
Ac 21:39; 24:27; 25:16

[a] *23* The meaning of the Greek for this word is uncertain.

Paul's Trial Before Felix

24 Five days later the high priest Ananias went down to Caesarea with some of the elders and a lawyer named Tertullus, and they brought their charges against Paul before the governor. 2When Paul was called in, Tertullus presented his case before Felix: "We have enjoyed a long period of peace under you, and your foresight has brought about reforms in this nation. 3Everywhere and in every way, most excellent Felix, we acknowledge this with profound gratitude. 4But in order not to weary you further, I would request that you be kind enough to hear us briefly. Ac 23:2,24

5"We have found this man to be a troublemaker, stirring up riots among the Jews all over the world. He is a ringleader of the Nazarene sect 6and even tried to desecrate the temple; so we seized him. [7][a] 8By examining him yourself you will be able to learn the truth about all these charges we are bringing against him." Ac 16:20; 21:28

9The other Jews joined in the accusation, asserting that these things were true. 1Th 2:16

10When the governor motioned for him to speak, Paul replied: "I know that for a number of years you have been a judge over this nation; so I gladly make my defense. 11You can easily verify that no more than twelve days ago I went up to Jerusalem to worship. 12My accusers did not find me arguing with anyone at the temple, or stirring up a crowd in the synagogues or anywhere else in the city. 13And they cannot prove to you the charges they are now making against me. 14However, I admit that I worship the God of our ancestors as a follower of the Way, which they call a sect. I believe everything that is in accordance with the Law and that is written in the Prophets, 15and I have the same hope in God as these men themselves have, that there will be a resurrection of both the righteous and the wicked. 16So I strive always to keep my conscience clear before God and man. Ac 9:2; 23:1; 25:8

17"After an absence of several years, I came to Jerusalem to bring my people gifts for the poor and to present offerings. 18I was ceremonially clean when they found me in the temple courts doing this. There was no crowd with me, nor was I involved in any disturbance. 19But there are some Jews from the province of Asia, who ought to be here before you and bring charges if they have anything against me. 20Or these who are here should state what crime they found in me when I stood before the Sanhedrin — 21unless it was this one

[a] 6-8 Some manuscripts include here *him, and we would have judged him in accordance with our law. 7But the commander Lysias came and took him from us with much violence, 8ordering his accusers to come before you.*

thing I shouted as I stood in their
presence: 'It is concerning the resurrection of the dead that I am on
trial before you today.'"

Ac 11:29-30; 23:6; 2Co 8:1-4

22 Then Felix, who was well acquainted with the Way, adjourned
the proceedings. "When Lysias
the commander comes," he said,
"I will decide your case." 23 He ordered the centurion to keep Paul
under guard but to give him some
freedom and permit his friends
to take care of his needs.

Ac 27:3; 28:16

24 Several days later Felix came
with his wife Drusilla, who was
Jewish. He sent for Paul and listened to him as he spoke about
faith in Christ Jesus. 25 As Paul
talked about righteousness, self-
control and the judgment to come,
Felix was afraid and said, "That's
enough for now! You may leave.
When I find it convenient, I will
send for you." 26 At the same time
he was hoping that Paul would offer him a bribe, so he sent for him
frequently and talked with him.

Ac 20:21; 2Pe 1:6

27 When two years had passed,
Felix was succeeded by Porcius
Festus, but because Felix wanted
to grant a favor to the Jews, he left
Paul in prison. Ac 12:3; 25:1,4,9,14

Paul's Trial Before Festus

25 Three days after arriving in
the province, Festus went
up from Caesarea to Jerusalem,
2 where the chief priests and the
Jewish leaders appeared before
him and presented the charges against Paul. 3 They requested
Festus, as a favor to them, to have
Paul transferred to Jerusalem, for
they were preparing an ambush
to kill him along the way. 4 Festus answered, "Paul is being held
at Caesarea, and I myself am going there soon. 5 Let some of your
leaders come with me, and if the
man has done anything wrong,
they can press charges against
him there." Ac 24:1,23

6 After spending eight or ten
days with them, Festus went down
to Caesarea. The next day he convened the court and ordered
that Paul be brought before him.
7 When Paul came in, the Jews who
had come down from Jerusalem
stood around him. They brought
many serious charges against him,
but they could not prove them.

Mk 15:3; Ac 24:5-6

8 Then Paul made his defense: "I
have done nothing wrong against
the Jewish law or against the temple or against Caesar."

Ac 6:13; 24:12; 28:17

9 Festus, wishing to do the Jews
a favor, said to Paul, "Are you willing to go up to Jerusalem and
stand trial before me there on
these charges?" Ac 12:3; 24:27

10 Paul answered: "I am now
standing before Caesar's court,
where I ought to be tried. I have
not done any wrong to the Jews,
as you yourself know very well.
11 If, however, I am guilty of doing

anything deserving death, I do
not refuse to die. But if the charges brought against me by these
Jews are not true, no one has the
right to hand me over to them. I
appeal to Caesar!" Ac 26:32; 28:19
12After Festus had conferred
with his council, he declared: "You
have appealed to Caesar. To Caesar
you will go!"

Festus Consults King Agrippa

13A few days later King Agrippa and Bernice arrived at Caesarea to pay their respects to Festus.
14Since they were spending many
days there, Festus discussed Paul's
case with the king. He said: "There
is a man here whom Felix left as a
prisoner. 15When I went to Jerusalem, the chief priests and the elders of the Jews brought charges
against him and asked that he be
condemned. Ac 24:1,27
16"I told them that it is not the
Roman custom to hand over anyone before they have faced their
accusers and have had an opportunity to defend themselves
against the charges. 17When they
came here with me, I did not delay the case, but convened the
court the next day and ordered
the man to be brought in. 18When
his accusers got up to speak, they
did not charge him with any of the
crimes I had expected. 19Instead,
they had some points of dispute
with him about their own religion
and about a dead man named
Jesus who Paul claimed was alive.
20I was at a loss how to investigate such matters; so I asked if he
would be willing to go to Jerusalem and stand trial there on these
charges. 21But when Paul made
his appeal to be held over for the
Emperor's decision, I ordered him
held until I could send him to Caesar." Ac 18:15; 23:29
22Then Agrippa said to Festus, "I
would like to hear this man myself."

He replied, "Tomorrow you will
hear him." Ac 9:15

Paul Before Agrippa

23The next day Agrippa and Bernice came with great pomp and
entered the audience room with
the high-ranking military officers and the prominent men of
the city. At the command of Festus, Paul was brought in. 24Festus
said: "King Agrippa, and all who
are present with us, you see this
man! The whole Jewish community has petitioned me about him
in Jerusalem and here in Caesarea, shouting that he ought not to
live any longer. 25I found he had
done nothing deserving of death,
but because he made his appeal
to the Emperor I decided to send
him to Rome. 26But I have nothing definite to write to His Majesty about him. Therefore I have
brought him before all of you,
and especially before you, King
Agrippa, so that as a result of this
investigation I may have something to write. 27For I think it is

unreasonable to send a prisoner
on to Rome without specifying
the charges against him."

Ac 22:22; 23:9

26 Then Agrippa said to Paul,
"You have permission to
speak for yourself." Ac 9:15; 25:22

So Paul motioned with his hand
and began his defense: [2]"King
Agrippa, I consider myself fortu-
nate to stand before you today as
I make my defense against all the
accusations of the Jews, [3]and especially so because you are well
acquainted with all the Jewish
customs and controversies. Therefore, I beg you to listen to me patiently. Ac 6:14; 25:19

[4]"The Jewish people all know
the way I have lived ever since I
was a child, from the beginning
of my life in my own country,
and also in Jerusalem. [5]They have
known me for a long time and can
testify, if they are willing, that I
conformed to the strictest sect of
our religion, living as a Pharisee.
[6]And now it is because of my hope
in what God has promised our ancestors that I am on trial today.
[7]This is the promise our twelve
tribes are hoping to see fulfilled
as they earnestly serve God day
and night. King Agrippa, it is because of this hope that these Jews
are accusing me. [8]Why should any
of you consider it incredible that
God raises the dead?

1Th 3:10; 1Ti 5:5; Jas 1:1

[9]"I too was convinced that I
ought to do all that was possible
to oppose the name of Jesus of
Nazareth. [10]And that is just what I
did in Jerusalem. On the authority of the chief priests I put many
of the Lord's people in prison, and
when they were put to death, I
cast my vote against them. [11]Many
a time I went from one synagogue
to another to have them punished, and I tried to force them
to blaspheme. I was so obsessed
with persecuting them that I even
hunted them down in foreign
cities. Ac 8:3; 1Ti 1:13

[12]"On one of these journeys I
was going to Damascus with the
authority and commission of the
chief priests. [13]About noon, King
Agrippa, as I was on the road, I
saw a light from heaven, brighter
than the sun, blazing around me
and my companions. [14]We all fell
to the ground, and I heard a voice
saying to me in Aramaic,[a] 'Saul,
Saul, why do you persecute me? It
is hard for you to kick against the
goads.' Ac 9:7

[15]"Then I asked, 'Who are you,
Lord?'

"'I am Jesus, whom you are
persecuting,' the Lord replied.
[16]'Now get up and stand on your
feet. I have appeared to you to
appoint you as a servant and as
a witness of what you have seen
and will see of me. [17]I will rescue
you from your own people and
from the Gentiles. I am sending
you to them [18]to open their eyes
and turn them from darkness to

[a] 14 Or *Hebrew*

light, and from the power of Satan to God, so that they may receive forgiveness of sins and a place among those who are sanctified by faith in me.'

Isa 35:5; 42:7,16; 1Pe 2:9

19 "So then, King Agrippa, I was not disobedient to the vision from heaven. 20 First to those in Damascus, then to those in Jerusalem and in all Judea, and then to the Gentiles, I preached that they should repent and turn to God and demonstrate their repentance by their deeds. 21 That is why some Jews seized me in the temple courts and tried to kill me. 22 But God has helped me to this very day; so I stand here and testify to small and great alike. I am saying nothing beyond what the prophets and Moses said would happen— 23 that the Messiah would suffer and, as the first to rise from the dead, would bring the message of light to his own people and to the Gentiles."

Lk 2:32; Ac 21:27,30; 1Co 15:20,23

24 At this point Festus interrupted Paul's defense. "You are out of your mind, Paul!" he shouted. "Your great learning is driving you insane." Jn 10:20; 1Co 4:10

25 "I am not insane, most excellent Festus," Paul replied. "What I am saying is true and reasonable. 26 The king is familiar with these things, and I can speak freely to him. I am convinced that none of this has escaped his notice, because it was not done in a corner. 27 King Agrippa, do you believe the prophets? I know you do." Ac 23:26

28 Then Agrippa said to Paul, "Do you think that in such a short time you can persuade me to be a Christian?" Ac 11:26

29 Paul replied, "Short time or long—I pray to God that not only you but all who are listening to me today may become what I am, except for these chains." Ac 21:33

30 The king rose, and with him the governor and Bernice and those sitting with them. 31 After they left the room, they began saying to one another, "This man is not doing anything that deserves death or imprisonment." Ac 23:9; 25:23

32 Agrippa said to Festus, "This man could have been set free if he had not appealed to Caesar."

Ac 25:11; 28:18

Paul Sails for Rome

27 When it was decided that we would sail for Italy, Paul and some other prisoners were handed over to a centurion named Julius, who belonged to the Imperial Regiment. 2 We boarded a ship from Adramyttium about to sail for ports along the coast of the province of Asia, and we put out to sea. Aristarchus, a Macedonian from Thessalonica, was with us.

Ac 19:29; 25:12,25

3 The next day we landed at Sidon; and Julius, in kindness to Paul, allowed him to go to his friends so they might provide for his needs. 4 From there we put out

to sea again and passed to the lee
of Cyprus because the winds were
against us. 5When we had sailed
across the open sea off the coast
of Cilicia and Pamphylia, we landed at Myra in Lycia. 6There the
centurion found an Alexandrian
ship sailing for Italy and put us
on board. 7We made slow head-
way for many days and had difficulty arriving off Cnidus. When
the wind did not allow us to hold
our course, we sailed to the lee
of Crete, opposite Salmone. 8We
moved along the coast with difficulty and came to a place called
Fair Havens, near the town of La-
sea. Ac 24:23; 28:11

9Much time had been lost, and
sailing had already become dan-
gerous because by now it was after the Day of Atonement.[a] So
Paul warned them, 10"Men, I can
see that our voyage is going to be
disastrous and bring great loss to
ship and cargo, and to our own
lives also." 11But the centurion,
instead of listening to what Paul
said, followed the advice of the pilot and of the owner of the ship.
12Since the harbor was unsuitable
to winter in, the majority decided
that we should sail on, hoping to
reach Phoenix and winter there.
This was a harbor in Crete, facing
both southwest and northwest.

Lev 23:27-29; Nu 29:7

The Storm

13When a gentle south wind began to blow, they saw their opportunity; so they weighed anchor and sailed along the shore of
Crete. 14Before very long, a wind
of hurricane force, called the
Northeaster, swept down from
the island. 15The ship was caught
by the storm and could not head
into the wind; so we gave way to
it and were driven along. 16As we
passed to the lee of a small island
called Cauda, we were hardly able
to make the lifeboat secure, 17so
the men hoisted it aboard. Then
they passed ropes under the ship
itself to hold it together. Because
they were afraid they would run
aground on the sandbars of Syr-
tis, they lowered the sea anchor[b]
and let the ship be driven along.
18We took such a violent battering from the storm that the next
day they began to throw the cargo
overboard. 19On the third day, they
threw the ship's tackle overboard
with their own hands. 20When
neither sun nor stars appeared
for many days and the storm continued raging, we finally gave up
all hope of being saved.

Jnh 1:5; Mk 4:37

21After they had gone a long
time without food, Paul stood up
before them and said: "Men, you
should have taken my advice not
to sail from Crete; then you would
have spared yourselves this damage and loss. 22But now I urge
you to keep up your courage, because not one of you will be lost;
only the ship will be destroyed.

[a] 9 That is, Yom Kippur [b] 17 Or *the sails*

23 Last night an angel of the God
to whom I belong and whom I
serve stood beside me 24 and said,
'Do not be afraid, Paul. You must
stand trial before Caesar; and God
has graciously given you the lives
of all who sail with you.' 25 So keep
up your courage, men, for I have
faith in God that it will happen
just as he told me. 26 Nevertheless,
we must run aground on some island." Ac 23:11; 28:1

The Shipwreck

27 On the fourteenth night we
were still being driven across the
Adriatic[a] Sea, when about midnight the sailors sensed they were
approaching land. 28 They took
soundings and found that the
water was a hundred and twenty
feet[b] deep. A short time later they
took soundings again and found
it was ninety feet[c] deep. 29 Fearing
that we would be dashed against
the rocks, they dropped four anchors from the stern and prayed
for daylight. 30 In an attempt to
escape from the ship, the sailors let the lifeboat down into the
sea, pretending they were going
to lower some anchors from the
bow. 31 Then Paul said to the centurion and the soldiers, "Unless
these men stay with the ship, you
cannot be saved." 32 So the soldiers cut the ropes that held the
lifeboat and let it drift away.
ver 16,24

33 Just before dawn Paul urged
them all to eat. "For the last fourteen days," he said, "you have been
in constant suspense and have
gone without food — you haven't
eaten anything. 34 Now I urge you
to take some food. You need it to
survive. Not one of you will lose a
single hair from his head." 35 After
he said this, he took some bread
and gave thanks to God in front of
them all. Then he broke it and began to eat. 36 They were all encouraged and ate some food themselves. 37 Altogether there were 276
of us on board. 38 When they had
eaten as much as they wanted,
they lightened the ship by throwing the grain into the sea.
Mt 10:30; 14:19

39 When daylight came, they did
not recognize the land, but they
saw a bay with a sandy beach,
where they decided to run the
ship aground if they could. 40 Cutting loose the anchors, they left
them in the sea and at the same
time untied the ropes that held
the rudders. Then they hoisted the foresail to the wind and
made for the beach. 41 But the ship
struck a sandbar and ran aground.
The bow stuck fast and would not
move, and the stern was broken
to pieces by the pounding of the
surf. Ac 28:1; 2Co 11:25

42 The soldiers planned to kill
the prisoners to prevent any of
them from swimming away and

[a] 27 In ancient times the name referred to an area extending well south of Italy.
[b] 28 Or about 37 meters [c] 28 Or about 27 meters

escaping. 43But the centurion
wanted to spare Paul's life and
kept them from carrying out their
plan. He ordered those who could
swim to jump overboard first and
get to land. 44The rest were to get
there on planks or on other pieces
of the ship. In this way everyone
reached land safely. ver 22,31

Paul Ashore on Malta

28 Once safely on shore, we
found out that the island
was called Malta. 2The islanders showed us unusual kindness.
They built a fire and welcomed
us all because it was raining and
cold. 3Paul gathered a pile of
brushwood and, as he put it on
the fire, a viper, driven out by the
heat, fastened itself on his hand.
4When the islanders saw the snake
hanging from his hand, they said
to each other, "This man must be a
murderer; for though he escaped
from the sea, the goddess Justice
has not allowed him to live." 5But
Paul shook the snake off into the
fire and suffered no ill effects.
6The people expected him to swell
up or suddenly fall dead; but after waiting a long time and seeing
nothing unusual happen to him,
they changed their minds and
said he was a god. Lk 10:19; Ac 14:11

7There was an estate nearby that
belonged to Publius, the chief official of the island. He welcomed us
to his home and showed us generous hospitality for three days.
8His father was sick in bed, suffering from fever and dysentery.
Paul went in to see him and, after
prayer, placed his hands on him
and healed him. 9When this had
happened, the rest of the sick on
the island came and were cured.
10They honored us in many ways;
and when we were ready to sail,
they furnished us with the supplies we needed. Ac 9:40; Jas 5:14-15

Paul's Arrival at Rome

11After three months we put out
to sea in a ship that had wintered
in the island — it was an Alexandrian ship with the figurehead of
the twin gods Castor and Pollux.
12We put in at Syracuse and stayed
there three days. 13From there
we set sail and arrived at Rhegi-
um. The next day the south wind
came up, and on the following
day we reached Puteoli. 14There
we found some brothers and sisters who invited us to spend a
week with them. And so we came
to Rome. 15The brothers and sisters there had heard that we were
coming, and they traveled as far
as the Forum of Appius and the
Three Taverns to meet us. At the
sight of these people Paul thanked
God and was encouraged. 16When
we got to Rome, Paul was allowed
to live by himself, with a soldier to
guard him. Ac 1:16; 24:23; 27:6

Paul Preaches at Rome Under Guard

17Three days later he called together the local Jewish leaders.

When they had assembled, Paul
said to them: "My brothers, although I have done nothing
against our people or against the
customs of our ancestors, I was
arrested in Jerusalem and handed over to the Romans. [18]They examined me and wanted to release
me, because I was not guilty of
any crime deserving death. [19]The
Jews objected, so I was compelled
to make an appeal to Caesar. I certainly did not intend to bring any
charge against my own people.
[20]For this reason I have asked to
see you and talk with you. It is because of the hope of Israel that I
am bound with this chain."

Ac 25:11; 26:6-7

[21]They replied, "We have not
received any letters from Judea
concerning you, and none of our
people who have come from there
has reported or said anything bad
about you. [22]But we want to hear
what your views are, for we know
that people everywhere are talking against this sect." Ac 22:5; 24:5,14

[23]They arranged to meet Paul
on a certain day, and came in even
larger numbers to the place where
he was staying. He witnessed to
them from morning till evening,
explaining about the kingdom of
God, and from the Law of Moses
and from the Prophets he tried
to persuade them about Jesus.
[24]Some were convinced by what
he said, but others would not believe. [25]They disagreed among
themselves and began to leave after Paul had made this final statement: "The Holy Spirit spoke the
truth to your ancestors when he
said through Isaiah the prophet:

Ac 14:4; 19:8

[26]" 'Go to this people and say,
"You will be ever hearing but
never understanding;
you will be ever seeing but
never perceiving."
[27]For this people's heart has
become calloused; Ps 119:70
they hardly hear with their
ears,
and they have closed their
eyes.
Otherwise they might see with
their eyes,
hear with their ears,
understand with their hearts
and turn, and I would heal
them.'[a] Mt 13:15

[28]"Therefore I want you to know
that God's salvation has been sent
to the Gentiles, and they will listen!" [29][b]

Ac 13:46

[30]For two whole years Paul
stayed there in his own rented
house and welcomed all who came
to see him. [31]He proclaimed the
kingdom of God and taught about
the Lord Jesus Christ — with all
boldness and without hindrance!

Ac 4:29

[a] 27 Isaiah 6:9,10 (see Septuagint)
[b] 29 Some manuscripts include here *After he said this, the Jews left, arguing vigorously among themselves.*

ROMANS

1 Paul, a servant of Christ Jesus, called to be an apostle and set apart for the gospel of God — 2the gospel he promised beforehand through his prophets in the Holy Scriptures 3regarding his Son, who as to his earthly life[a] was a descendant of David, 4and who through the Spirit of holiness was appointed the Son of God in power[b] by his resurrection from the dead: Jesus Christ our Lord. 5Through him we received grace and apostleship to call all the Gentiles to the obedience that comes from[c] faith for his name's sake. 6And you also are among those Gentiles who are called to belong to Jesus Christ.

Ac 6:7; 9:15; Rev 17:14

7To all in Rome who are loved by God and called to be his holy people: Ro 8:39

Grace and peace to you from God our Father and from the Lord Jesus Christ. 1Co 1:3; 1Pe 1:2

Paul's Longing to Visit Rome

8First, I thank my God through Jesus Christ for all of you, because your faith is being reported all over the world. 9God, whom I serve in my spirit in preaching the gospel of his Son, is my witness how constantly I remember you 10in my prayers at all times; and I pray that now at last by God's will the way may be opened for me to come to you.

Ro 15:32; 2Ti 1:3

11I long to see you so that I may impart to you some spiritual gift to make you strong — 12that is, that you and I may be mutually encouraged by each other's faith. 13I do not want you to be unaware, brothers and sisters,[d] that I planned many times to come to you (but have been prevented from doing so until now) in order that I might have a harvest among you, just as I have had among the other Gentiles. Ro 15:22-23

14I am obligated both to Greeks and non-Greeks, both to the wise and the foolish. 15That is why I am so eager to preach the gospel also to you who are in Rome.

Ro 15:20; 1Co 9:16

16For I am not ashamed of the gospel, because it is the power of God that brings salvation to everyone who believes: first to the Jew, then to the Gentile. 17For in the gospel the righteousness of God is revealed — a righteousness that is

[a] 3 Or *who according to the flesh* [b] 4 Or *was declared with power to be the Son of God* [c] 5 Or *that is* [d] 13 The Greek word for *brothers and sisters* (*adelphoi*) refers here to believers, both men and women, as part of God's family; also in 7:1, 4; 8:12, 29; 10:1; 11:25; 12:1; 15:14, 30; 16:14, 17.

by faith from first to last,[a] just as
it is written: "The righteous will
live by faith."[b] Ro 3:21; 1Co 1:18; Gal 3:11

God's Wrath Against Sinful Humanity

18The wrath of God is being revealed from heaven against all
the godlessness and wickedness
of people, who suppress the truth
by their wickedness, 19since what
may be known about God is plain
to them, because God has made it
plain to them. 20For since the creation of the world God's invisible
qualities — his eternal power and
divine nature — have been clearly
seen, being understood from what
has been made, so that people are
without excuse. Ps 19:1-6; Ac 14:17

21For although they knew God,
they neither glorified him as God
nor gave thanks to him, but their
thinking became futile and their
foolish hearts were darkened.
22Although they claimed to be
wise, they became fools 23and exchanged the glory of the immortal
God for images made to look like
a mortal human being and birds
and animals and reptiles.
Ps 106:20; Jer 2:5

24Therefore God gave them over
in the sinful desires of their hearts
to sexual impurity for the degrad-
ing of their bodies with one another. 25They exchanged the truth
about God for a lie, and worshiped
and served created things rather
than the Creator — who is forever
praised. Amen. Jer 10:14; Eph 4:19

26Because of this, God gave them
over to shameful lusts. Even their
women exchanged natural sexual relations for unnatural ones.
27In the same way the men also
abandoned natural relations with
women and were inflamed with
lust for one another. Men committed shameful acts with other
men, and received in themselves
the due penalty for their error.
Lev 18:22; 1Th 4:5

28Furthermore, just as they did
not think it worthwhile to retain
the knowledge of God, so God gave
them over to a depraved mind, so
that they do what ought not to be
done. 29They have become filled
with every kind of wickedness,
evil, greed and depravity. They
are full of envy, murder, strife, deceit and malice. They are gossips,
30slanderers, God-haters, insolent,
arrogant and boastful; they invent
ways of doing evil; they disobey
their parents; 31they have no understanding, no fidelity, no love,
no mercy. 32Although they know
God's righteous decree that those
who do such things deserve death,
they not only continue to do these
very things but also approve of
those who practice them.
Ro 6:23; 2Ti 3:2

God's Righteous Judgment

2 You, therefore, have no excuse, you who pass judgment
on someone else, for at whatever

[a] 17 Or *is from faith to faith* [b] 17 Hab. 2:4

point you judge another, you are
condemning yourself, because
you who pass judgment do the
same things. 2Now we know that
God's judgment against those who
do such things is based on truth.
3So when you, a mere human being, pass judgment on them and
yet do the same things, do you
think you will escape God's judgment? 4Or do you show contempt
for the riches of his kindness, forbearance and patience, not realizing that God's kindness is intended to lead you to repentance?

Ex 34:6; Ro 3:25; 2Pe 3:9

5But because of your stubbornness and your unrepentant heart,
you are storing up wrath against
yourself for the day of God's
wrath, when his righteous judgment will be revealed. 6God "will
repay each person according to
what they have done."[a] 7To those
who by persistence in doing good
seek glory, honor and immortality, he will give eternal life. 8But
for those who are self-seeking
and who reject the truth and follow evil, there will be wrath and
anger. 9There will be trouble and
distress for every human being
who does evil: first for the Jew,
then for the Gentile; 10but glory,
honor and peace for everyone who
does good: first for the Jew, then
for the Gentile. 11For God does not
show favoritism. Ac 10:34; 2Th 2:12

12All who sin apart from the law
will also perish apart from the law,
and all who sin under the law will
be judged by the law. 13For it is not
those who hear the law who are
righteous in God's sight, but it is
those who obey the law who will
be declared righteous. 14(Indeed,
when Gentiles, who do not have
the law, do by nature things required by the law, they are a law for
themselves, even though they do
not have the law. 15They show that
the requirements of the law are
written on their hearts, their consciences also bearing witness, and
their thoughts sometimes accusing them and at other times even
defending them.) 16This will take
place on the day when God judges people's secrets through Jesus
Christ, as my gospel declares.

Ac 10:42; Jas 1:22-23,25

The Jews and the Law

17Now you, if you call yourself
a Jew; if you rely on the law and
boast in God; 18if you know his will
and approve of what is superior
because you are instructed by the
law; 19if you are convinced that you
are a guide for the blind, a light for
those who are in the dark, 20an instructor of the foolish, a teacher of
little children, because you have in
the law the embodiment of knowledge and truth— 21you, then, who
teach others, do you not teach
yourself? You who preach against
stealing, do you steal? 22You who
say that people should not commit adultery, do you commit adultery? You who abhor idols, do you

[a] 6 Psalm 62:12; Prov. 24:12

rob temples? 23You who boast in
the law, do you dishonor God by
breaking the law? 24As it is written: "God's name is blasphemed
among the Gentiles because of
you."[a] Isa 52:5; Mic 3:11

25Circumcision has value if
you observe the law, but if you
break the law, you have become
as though you had not been circumcised. 26So then, if those who
are not circumcised keep the law's
requirements, will they not be regarded as though they were circumcised? 27The one who is not
circumcised physically and yet
obeys the law will condemn you
who, even though you have the[b]
written code and circumcision,
are a lawbreaker. Mt 12:41-42; Gal 5:3

28A person is not a Jew who is
one only outwardly, nor is circumcision merely outward and physical. 29No, a person is a Jew who is
one inwardly; and circumcision is
circumcision of the heart, by the
Spirit, not by the written code.
Such a person's praise is not from
other people, but from God.
2Co 10:18; Gal 6:15

God's Faithfulness

3 What advantage, then, is there
in being a Jew, or what value
is there in circumcision? 2Much
in every way! First of all, the Jews
have been entrusted with the very
words of God. Dt 4:8; Ps 147:19

3What if some were unfaithful?
Will their unfaithfulness nullify
God's faithfulness? 4Not at all! Let
God be true, and every human be-
ing a liar. As it is written:
Ps 116:11; Heb 4:2

"So that you may be proved
right when you speak
and prevail when you
judge."[c] Ps 51:4

5But if our unrighteousness
brings out God's righteousness
more clearly, what shall we say?
That God is unjust in bringing his
wrath on us? (I am using a human
argument.) 6Certainly not! If that
were so, how could God judge the
world? 7Someone might argue,
"If my falsehood enhances God's
truthfulness and so increases his
glory, why am I still condemned as
a sinner?" 8Why not say — as some
slanderously claim that we say —
"Let us do evil that good may result"? Their condemnation is just!
Ge 18:25; Gal 3:15

No One Is Righteous

9What shall we conclude then?
Do we have any advantage? Not
at all! For we have already made
the charge that Jews and Gentiles
alike are all under the power of
sin. 10As it is written: Gal 3:22

"There is no one righteous, not
even one;
11 there is no one who
understands;
there is no one who seeks
God.

[a] 24 Isaiah 52:5 (see Septuagint); Ezek. 36:20,22 [b] 27 Or *who, by means of a* [c] 4 Psalm 51:4

12 All have turned away,
they have together become worthless;
there is no one who does good,
not even one."[a] Ps 14:1-3
13 "Their throats are open graves;
their tongues practice deceit."[b] Ps 5:9
"The poison of vipers is on their lips."[c] Ps 140:3
14 "Their mouths are full of cursing and bitterness."[d] Ps 10:7
15 "Their feet are swift to shed blood;
16 ruin and misery mark their ways,
17 and the way of peace they do not know."[e] Isa 59:7-8
18 "There is no fear of God before their eyes."[f] Ps 36:1

19 Now we know that whatever
the law says, it says to those who
are under the law, so that every
mouth may be silenced and the
whole world held accountable to
God. 20 Therefore no one will be
declared righteous in God's sight
by the works of the law; rather,
through the law we become conscious of our sin. Ac 13:39; Ro 7:7

Righteousness Through Faith

21 But now apart from the law
the righteousness of God has been
made known, to which the Law
and the Prophets testify. 22 This
righteousness is given through
faith in[g] Jesus Christ to all who
believe. There is no difference between Jew and Gentile, 23 for all
have sinned and fall short of the
glory of God, 24 and all are justified
freely by his grace through the
redemption that came by Christ
Jesus. 25 God presented Christ as a
sacrifice of atonement,[h] through
the shedding of his blood—to be
received by faith. He did this to
demonstrate his righteousness,
because in his forbearance he had
left the sins committed beforehand unpunished— 26 he did it to
demonstrate his righteousness at
the present time, so as to be just
and the one who justifies those
who have faith in Jesus.

Ro 1:17; 4:16; 10:12

27 Where, then, is boasting? It is
excluded. Because of what law?
The law that requires works? No,
because of the law that requires
faith. 28 For we maintain that a person is justified by faith apart from
the works of the law. 29 Or is God
the God of Jews only? Is he not the
God of Gentiles too? Yes, of Gentiles too, 30 since there is only one
God, who will justify the circumcised by faith and the uncircumcised through that same faith. 31 Do
we, then, nullify the law by this
faith? Not at all! Rather, we uphold the law. 1Co 1:29-31; Gal 3:8

[a] *12* Psalms 14:1-3; 53:1-3; Eccles. 7:20
[b] *13* Psalm 5:9 [c] *13* Psalm 140:3
[d] *14* Psalm 10:7 (see Septuagint)
[e] *17* Isaiah 59:7,8 [f] *18* Psalm 36:1
[g] *22* Or *through the faithfulness of*
[h] *25* The Greek for *sacrifice of atonement* refers to the atonement cover on the ark of the covenant (see Lev. 16:15,16).

Abraham Justified by Faith

4 What then shall we say that
Abraham, our forefather according to the flesh, discovered in
this matter? 2If, in fact, Abraham
was justified by works, he had
something to boast about — but
not before God. 3What does Scripture say? "Abraham believed God,
and it was credited to him as righteousness."[a] Ge 15:6; 1Co 1:31; Gal 3:6

4Now to the one who works,
wages are not credited as a gift but
as an obligation. 5However, to the
one who does not work but trusts
God who justifies the ungodly,
their faith is credited as righteousness. 6David says the same thing
when he speaks of the blessedness
of the one to whom God credits
righteousness apart from works:
Ro 11:6

7"Blessed are those
whose transgressions are
forgiven,
whose sins are covered.
8Blessed is the one
whose sin the Lord will
never count against
them."[b] Ps 32:1-2; 2Co 5:19

9Is this blessedness only for the
circumcised, or also for the uncircumcised? We have been saying
that Abraham's faith was credited to him as righteousness. 10Un-
der what circumstances was it
credited? Was it after he was circumcised, or before? It was not after, but before! 11And he received
circumcision as a sign, a seal of
the righteousness that he had by
faith while he was still uncircumcised. So then, he is the father of
all who believe but have not been
circumcised, in order that righteousness might be credited to
them. 12And he is then also the father of the circumcised who not
only are circumcised but who also
follow in the footsteps of the faith
that our father Abraham had before he was circumcised.
Ge 17:10-11; Lk 19:9

13It was not through the law that
Abraham and his offspring received the promise that he would
be heir of the world, but through
the righteousness that comes by
faith. 14For if those who depend
on the law are heirs, faith means
nothing and the promise is worthless, 15because the law brings
wrath. And where there is no law
there is no transgression.
Ro 3:20; 7:7-25; Gal 3:18

16Therefore, the promise comes
by faith, so that it may be by grace
and may be guaranteed to all
Abraham's offspring — not only
to those who are of the law but
also to those who have the faith of
Abraham. He is the father of us all.
17As it is written: "I have made you
a father of many nations."[c] He is
our father in the sight of God, in
whom he believed — the God who
gives life to the dead and calls into
being things that were not.
Ro 3:24; 1Co 1:28

[a] *3* Gen. 15:6; also in verse 22
[b] *8* Psalm 32:1,2 [c] *17* Gen. 17:5

18 Against all hope, Abraham in hope believed and so became the father of many nations, just as it had been said to him, "So shall your offspring be."[a] 19 Without weakening in his faith, he faced the fact that his body was as good as dead — since he was about a hundred years old — and that Sarah's womb was also dead. 20 Yet he did not waver through unbelief regarding the promise of God, but was strengthened in his faith and gave glory to God, 21 being fully persuaded that God had power to do what he had promised. 22 This is why "it was credited to him as righteousness." 23 The words "it was credited to him" were written not for him alone, 24 but also for us, to whom God will credit righteousness — for us who believe in him who raised Jesus our Lord from the dead. 25 He was delivered over to death for our sins and was raised to life for our justification.

Ac 2:24; Ro 15:4; Heb 11:19

Peace and Hope

5 Therefore, since we have been justified through faith, we[b] have peace with God through our Lord Jesus Christ, 2 through whom we have gained access by faith into this grace in which we now stand. And we[c] boast in the hope of the glory of God. 3 Not only so, but we[c] also glory in our sufferings, because we know that suffering produces perseverance; 4 perseverance, character; and character, hope. 5 And hope does not put us to shame, because God's love has been poured out into our hearts through the Holy Spirit, who has been given to us.

Eph 2:18; Jas 1:2-3

6 You see, at just the right time, when we were still powerless, Christ died for the ungodly. 7 Very rarely will anyone die for a righteous person, though for a good person someone might possibly dare to die. 8 But God demonstrates his own love for us in this: While we were still sinners, Christ died for us.

Jn 15:13; 1Pe 3:18

9 Since we have now been justified by his blood, how much more shall we be saved from God's wrath through him! 10 For if, while we were God's enemies, we were reconciled to him through the death of his Son, how much more, having been reconciled, shall we be saved through his life! 11 Not only is this so, but we also boast in God through our Lord Jesus Christ, through whom we have now received reconciliation.

Ro 11:28; 2Co 5:18-19

Death Through Adam, Life Through Christ

12 Therefore, just as sin entered the world through one man, and death through sin, and in this way death came to all people, because all sinned —

13 To be sure, sin was in the world before the law was given, but sin is

[a] *18* Gen. 15:5 [b] *1* Many manuscripts *let us* [c] *2,3* Or *let us*

not charged against anyone's account where there is no law. 14Nevertheless, death reigned from the time of Adam to the time of Moses, even over those who did not sin by breaking a command, as did Adam, who is a pattern of the one to come. Ge 2:17; 1Co 15:22,45

15But the gift is not like the trespass. For if the many died by the trespass of the one man, how much more did God's grace and the gift that came by the grace of the one man, Jesus Christ, overflow to the many! 16Nor can the gift of God be compared with the result of one man's sin: The judgment followed one sin and brought condemnation, but the gift followed many trespasses and brought justification. 17For if, by the trespass of the one man, death reigned through that one man, how much more will those who receive God's abundant provision of grace and of the gift of righteousness reign in life through the one man, Jesus Christ! Ac 15:11

18Consequently, just as one trespass resulted in condemnation for all people, so also one righteous act resulted in justification and life for all people. 19For just as through the disobedience of the one man the many were made sinners, so also through the obedience of the one man the many will be made righteous.

Ro 4:25; Php 2:8

20The law was brought in so that the trespass might increase. But where sin increased, grace increased all the more, 21so that, just as sin reigned in death, so also grace might reign through righteousness to bring eternal life through Jesus Christ our Lord.

Gal 3:19; 1Ti 1:13-14

Dead to Sin, Alive in Christ

6 What shall we say, then? Shall we go on sinning so that grace may increase? 2By no means! We are those who have died to sin; how can we live in it any longer? 3Or don't you know that all of us who were baptized into Christ Jesus were baptized into his death? 4We were therefore buried with him through baptism into death in order that, just as Christ was raised from the dead through the glory of the Father, we too may live a new life. Col 2:12; 3:10

5For if we have been united with him in a death like his, we will certainly also be united with him in a resurrection like his. 6For we know that our old self was crucified with him so that the body ruled by sin might be done away with,[a] that we should no longer be slaves to sin — 7because anyone who has died has been set free from sin.

Ro 7:24; Gal 2:20

8Now if we died with Christ, we believe that we will also live with him. 9For we know that since Christ was raised from the dead, he cannot die again; death no longer has mastery over him.

[a] 6 Or *be rendered powerless*

10 The death he died, he died to sin
once for all; but the life he lives,
he lives to God. Ac 2:24; Rev 1:18

11 In the same way, count yourselves dead to sin but alive to God
in Christ Jesus. 12 Therefore do not
let sin reign in your mortal body
so that you obey its evil desires.
13 Do not offer any part of yourself
to sin as an instrument of wickedness, but rather offer yourselves
to God as those who have been
brought from death to life; and offer every part of yourself to him as
an instrument of righteousness.
14 For sin shall no longer be your
master, because you are not under
the law, but under grace.

Ro 3:24; Gal 5:18

Slaves to Righteousness

15 What then? Shall we sin because we are not under the law but
under grace? By no means! 16 Don't
you know that when you offer
yourselves to someone as obedient slaves, you are slaves of the
one you obey — whether you are
slaves to sin, which leads to death,
or to obedience, which leads to
righteousness? 17 But thanks be to
God that, though you used to be
slaves to sin, you have come to
obey from your heart the pattern
of teaching that has now claimed
your allegiance. 18 You have been
set free from sin and have become
slaves to righteousness.

Jn 8:34; Ro 8:2; 2Ti 1:13

19 I am using an example from
everyday life because of your human limitations. Just as you used
to offer yourselves as slaves to
impurity and to ever-increasing
wickedness, so now offer yourselves as slaves to righteousness
leading to holiness. 20 When you
were slaves to sin, you were free
from the control of righteousness.
21 What benefit did you reap at that
time from the things you are now
ashamed of? Those things result
in death! 22 But now that you have
been set free from sin and have
become slaves of God, the benefit
you reap leads to holiness, and the
result is eternal life. 23 For the wages of sin is death, but the gift of
God is eternal life in[a] Christ Jesus
our Lord. Ro 5:12; Gal 6:7-8

Released From the Law, Bound to Christ

7 Do you not know, brothers and
sisters — for I am speaking to
those who know the law — that
the law has authority over someone only as long as that person
lives? 2 For example, by law a married woman is bound to her husband as long as he is alive, but if
her husband dies, she is released
from the law that binds her to
him. 3 So then, if she has sexual
relations with another man while
her husband is still alive, she is
called an adulteress. But if her
husband dies, she is released from
that law and is not an adulteress if
she marries another man.

Ro 1:13; 1Co 7:39

[a] 23 Or *through*

4So, my brothers and sisters, you
also died to the law through the
body of Christ, that you might belong to another, to him who was
raised from the dead, in order that
we might bear fruit for God. 5For
when we were in the realm of the
flesh,[a] the sinful passions aroused
by the law were at work in us, so
that we bore fruit for death. 6But
now, by dying to what once bound
us, we have been released from the
law so that we serve in the new way
of the Spirit, and not in the old way
of the written code. Ro 2:29; 6:13

The Law and Sin

7What shall we say, then? Is the
law sinful? Certainly not! Nevertheless, I would not have known what
sin was had it not been for the law.
For I would not have known what
coveting really was if the law had
not said, "You shall not covet."[b]
8But sin, seizing the opportunity
afforded by the commandment,
produced in me every kind of coveting. For apart from the law, sin
was dead. 9Once I was alive apart
from the law; but when the commandment came, sin sprang to life
and I died. 10I found that the very
commandment that was intended
to bring life actually brought death.
11For sin, seizing the opportunity
afforded by the commandment,
deceived me, and through the
commandment put me to death.
12So then, the law is holy, and the
commandment is holy, righteous
and good. Lev 18:5; 1Ti 1:8

13Did that which is good, then,
become death to me? By no
means! Nevertheless, in order that
sin might be recognized as sin, it
used what is good to bring about
my death, so that through the
commandment sin might become
utterly sinful. Ro 6:23

14We know that the law is spiritual; but I am unspiritual, sold
as a slave to sin. 15I do not understand what I do. For what I want
to do I do not do, but what I hate I
do. 16And if I do what I do not want
to do, I agree that the law is good.
17As it is, it is no longer I myself
who do it, but it is sin living in me.
18For I know that good itself does
not dwell in me, that is, in my sinful nature.[c] For I have the desire to
do what is good, but I cannot carry
it out. 19For I do not do the good I
want to do, but the evil I do not
want to do — this I keep on doing.
20Now if I do what I do not want to
do, it is no longer I who do it, but
it is sin living in me that does it.
2Ki 17:17; Gal 5:17

21So I find this law at work: Although I want to do good, evil is
right there with me. 22For in my
inner being I delight in God's
law; 23but I see another law at
work in me, waging war against
the law of my mind and making
me a prisoner of the law of sin at

[a] *5* In contexts like this, the Greek word for *flesh* (*sarx*) refers to the sinful state of human beings, often presented as a power in opposition to the Spirit.
[b] *7* Exodus 20:17; Deut. 5:21 [c] *18* Or *my flesh*

work within me. 24What a wretched man I am! Who will rescue me
from this body that is subject to
death? 25Thanks be to God, who
delivers me through Jesus Christ
our Lord! Ro 6:6; Gal 5:17
So then, I myself in my mind
am a slave to God's law, but in my
sinful nature[a] a slave to the law of
sin. Ro 6:16,22

Life Through the Spirit

8 Therefore, there is now no
condemnation for those
who are in Christ Jesus, 2because
through Christ Jesus the law of
the Spirit who gives life has set
you[b] free from the law of sin and
death. 3For what the law was powerless to do because it was weakened by the flesh,[c] God did by
sending his own Son in the likeness of sinful flesh to be a sin offering.[d] And so he condemned
sin in the flesh, 4in order that the
righteous requirement of the law
might be fully met in us, who do
not live according to the flesh but
according to the Spirit.
1Co 15:45; Gal 5:16; Heb 7:18
5Those who live according to the
flesh have their minds set on what
the flesh desires; but those who
live in accordance with the Spirit have their minds set on what
the Spirit desires. 6The mind governed by the flesh is death, but the
mind governed by the Spirit is life
and peace. 7The mind governed by
the flesh is hostile to God; it does
not submit to God's law, nor can it
do so. 8Those who are in the realm
of the flesh cannot please God.
Gal 6:8; Jas 4:4
9You, however, are not in the
realm of the flesh but are in the
realm of the Spirit, if indeed the
Spirit of God lives in you. And if
anyone does not have the Spirit of Christ, they do not belong
to Christ. 10But if Christ is in you,
then even though your body is
subject to death because of sin,
the Spirit gives life[e] because of
righteousness. 11And if the Spirit of him who raised Jesus from
the dead is living in you, he who
raised Christ from the dead will
also give life to your mortal bodies because of[f] his Spirit who lives
in you. Ac 2:24; Gal 4:6
12Therefore, brothers and sisters, we have an obligation — but
it is not to the flesh, to live according to it. 13For if you live according to the flesh, you will die; but if
by the Spirit you put to death the
misdeeds of the body, you will live.
14For those who are led by the
Spirit of God are the children of
God. 15The Spirit you received does
not make you slaves, so that you
live in fear again; rather, the Spirit
you received brought about your

[a] 25 Or *in the flesh* [b] 2 The Greek is singular; some manuscripts *me* [c] 3 In contexts like this, the Greek word for *flesh* (*sarx*) refers to the sinful state of human beings, often presented as a power in opposition to the Spirit; also in verses 4-13. [d] 3 Or *flesh, for sin* [e] 10 Or *you, your body is dead because of sin, yet your spirit is alive* [f] 11 Some manuscripts *bodies through*

adoption to sonship.[a] And by him
we cry, *"Abba,*[b] Father." 16The Spirit himself testifies with our spirit
that we are God's children. 17Now
if we are children, then we are
heirs — heirs of God and co-heirs
with Christ, if indeed we share
in his sufferings in order that we
may also share in his glory.

Gal 4:7; 1Pe 4:13

Present Suffering and Future Glory

18I consider that our present sufferings are not worth comparing
with the glory that will be revealed
in us. 19For the creation waits in eager expectation for the children of
God to be revealed. 20For the creation was subjected to frustration,
not by its own choice, but by the
will of the one who subjected it, in
hope 21that[c] the creation itself will
be liberated from its bondage to
decay and brought into the freedom and glory of the children of
God.

Ac 3:21; 2Pe 3:13; Jn 1:12

22We know that the whole creation has been groaning as in the
pains of childbirth right up to the
present time. 23Not only so, but we
ourselves, who have the firstfruits
of the Spirit, groan inwardly as
we wait eagerly for our adoption
to sonship, the redemption of our
bodies. 24For in this hope we were
saved. But hope that is seen is no
hope at all. Who hopes for what
they already have? 25But if we
hope for what we do not yet have,
we wait for it patiently.

2Co 5:2,4; Gal 5:5

26In the same way, the Spirit
helps us in our weakness. We do
not know what we ought to pray
for, but the Spirit himself inter-
cedes for us through wordless
groans. 27And he who searches
our hearts knows the mind of the
Spirit, because the Spirit inter-
cedes for God's people in accordance with the will of God.

Eph 6:18; Rev 2:23

28And we know that in all things
God works for the good of those
who love him, who[d] have been
called according to his purpose.
29For those God foreknew he also
predestined to be conformed
to the image of his Son, that he
might be the firstborn among
many brothers and sisters. 30And
those he predestined, he also
called; those he called, he also justified; those he justified, he also
glorified.

1Co 6:11; Eph 1:5,11; Php 3:21

More Than Conquerors

31What, then, shall we say in
response to these things? If God
is for us, who can be against us?
32He who did not spare his own
Son, but gave him up for us all —
how will he not also, along with
him, graciously give us all things?

[a] *15* The Greek word for *adoption to sonship* is a term referring to the full legal standing of an adopted male heir in Roman culture; also in verse 23. [b] *15* Aramaic for *father*
[c] *20,21* Or *subjected it in hope.* [21]*For*
[d] *28* Or *that all things work together for good to those who love God, who*; or *that in all things God works together with those who love him to bring about what is good — with those who*

33 Who will bring any charge against those whom God has chosen? It is God who justifies. 34 Who then is the one who condemns? No one. Christ Jesus who died — more than that, who was raised to life — is at the right hand of God and is also interceding for us. 35 Who shall separate us from the love of Christ? Shall trouble or hardship or persecution or famine or nakedness or danger or sword? 36 As it is written:

Ps 118:6; Jn 3:16; Heb 7:25

"For your sake we face death all
  day long;
 we are considered as sheep
  to be slaughtered."[a]

37 No, in all these things we are more than conquerors through him who loved us. 38 For I am convinced that neither death nor life, neither angels nor demons,[b] neither the present nor the future, nor any powers, 39 neither height nor depth, nor anything else in all creation, will be able to separate us from the love of God that is in Christ Jesus our Lord.

Ps 44:22; 1Co 15:57; 2Co 4:11

Paul's Anguish Over Israel

9 I speak the truth in Christ — I am not lying, my conscience confirms it through the Holy Spirit — 2 I have great sorrow and unceasing anguish in my heart. 3 For I could wish that I myself were cursed and cut off from Christ for the sake of my people, those of my own race, 4 the people of Israel. Theirs is the adoption to sonship; theirs the divine glory, the covenants, the receiving of the law, the temple worship and the promises. 5 Theirs are the patriarchs, and from them is traced the human ancestry of the Messiah, who is God over all, forever praised![c] Amen.

Jn 1:1; Heb 9:1

God's Sovereign Choice

6 It is not as though God's word had failed. For not all who are descended from Israel are Israel. 7 Nor because they are his descendants are they all Abraham's children. On the contrary, "It is through Isaac that your offspring will be reckoned."[d] 8 In other words, it is not the children by physical descent who are God's children, but it is the children of the promise who are regarded as Abraham's offspring. 9 For this was how the promise was stated: "At the appointed time I will return, and Sarah will have a son."[e]

Ge 18:10,14; Gal 6:16

10 Not only that, but Rebekah's children were conceived at the same time by our father Isaac. 11 Yet, before the twins were born or had done anything good or bad — in order that God's purpose in election might stand: 12 not by works but by him who calls — she

[a] *36* Psalm 44:22 [b] *38* Or *nor heavenly rulers* [c] *5* Or *Messiah, who is over all. God be forever praised!* Or *Messiah. God who is over all be forever praised!* [d] *7* Gen. 21:12 [e] *9* Gen. 18:10,14

was told, "The older will serve the
younger."[a] 13 Just as it is written:
"Jacob I loved, but Esau I hated."[b]

Ge 25:21,23; Ro 8:28

14 What then shall we say? Is God
unjust? Not at all! 15 For he says to
Moses,

2Ch 19:7

"I will have mercy on whom
I have mercy,
and I will have compassion
on whom I have
compassion."[c]

16 It does not, therefore, depend
on human desire or effort, but on
God's mercy. 17 For Scripture says
to Pharaoh: "I raised you up for
this very purpose, that I might
display my power in you and that
my name might be proclaimed in
all the earth."[d] 18 Therefore God
has mercy on whom he wants
to have mercy, and he hardens
whom he wants to harden.

Ex 4:21; 9:16; 33:19

19 One of you will say to me:
"Then why does God still blame
us? For who is able to resist his
will?" 20 But who are you, a human
being, to talk back to God? "Shall
what is formed say to the one who
formed it, 'Why did you make me
like this?'"[e] 21 Does not the potter
have the right to make out of the
same lump of clay some pottery
for special purposes and some for
common use?

2Ti 2:20

22 What if God, although choosing to show his wrath and make
his power known, bore with great
patience the objects of his wrath—
prepared for destruction? 23 What
if he did this to make the riches
of his glory known to the objects
of his mercy, whom he prepared
in advance for glory— 24 even
us, whom he also called, not only
from the Jews but also from the
Gentiles? 25 As he says in Hosea:

Ro 3:29; 8:30

"I will call them 'my people'
who are not my people;
and I will call her 'my loved
one' who is not my
loved one,"[f]

26 and,

"In the very place where it was
said to them,
'You are not my people,'
there they will be called
'children of the
living God.'"[g]

Mt 16:16; Ro 8:14; 1Pe 2:10

27 Isaiah cries out concerning Israel:

"Though the number of
the Israelites be like
the sand by the sea,

Ge 22:17; Hos 1:10

only the remnant will be
saved.

Ro 11:5

28 For the Lord will carry out
his sentence on earth with
speed and finality."[h]

Isa 10:22-23

[a] 12 Gen. 25:23 [b] 13 Mal. 1:2,3
[c] 15 Exodus 33:19 [d] 17 Exodus 9:16
[e] 20 Isaiah 29:16; 45:9 [f] 25 Hosea 2:23
[g] 26 Hosea 1:10 [h] 28 Isaiah 10:22,23
(see Septuagint)

29 It is just as Isaiah said previously:

"Unless the Lord Almighty
Jas 5:4
had left us descendants,
we would have become like
Sodom,
we would have been
like Gomorrah."[a]
Isa 13:19; Jer 50:40

Israel's Unbelief

30 What then shall we say? That
the Gentiles, who did not pursue
righteousness, have obtained it,
a righteousness that is by faith;
31 but the people of Israel, who pursued the law as the way of righteousness, have not attained their
goal. 32 Why not? Because they pursued it not by faith but as if it were
by works. They stumbled over the
stumbling stone. 33 As it is written:
Ro 1:17; 10:2-3; Gal 5:4

"See, I lay in Zion a stone
that causes people to
stumble
and a rock that makes them
fall,
and the one who believes in
him will never be put to
shame."[b] Isa 28:16; Ro 10:11

10 Brothers and sisters, my
heart's desire and prayer to
God for the Israelites is that they
may be saved. 2 For I can testify
about them that they are zealous
for God, but their zeal is not based
on knowledge. 3 Since they did not
know the righteousness of God
and sought to establish their own,
they did not submit to God's righteousness. 4 Christ is the culmination of the law so that there may
be righteousness for everyone
who believes. Ac 21:20; Ro 1:17; Gal 3:24

5 Moses writes this about the
righteousness that is by the law:
"The person who does these
things will live by them."[c] 6 But the
righteousness that is by faith says:
"Do not say in your heart, 'Who
will ascend into heaven?'"[d] (that
is, to bring Christ down) 7 "or 'Who
will descend into the deep?'"[e]
(that is, to bring Christ up from
the dead). 8 But what does it say?
"The word is near you; it is in your
mouth and in your heart,"[f] that
is, the message concerning faith
that we proclaim: 9 If you declare
with your mouth, "Jesus is Lord,"
and believe in your heart that God
raised him from the dead, you will
be saved. 10 For it is with your heart
that you believe and are justified,
and it is with your mouth that you
profess your faith and are saved.
11 As Scripture says, "Anyone who
believes in him will never be put
to shame."[g] 12 For there is no difference between Jew and Gentile —
the same Lord is Lord of all and
richly blesses all who call on him,
13 for, "Everyone who calls on the
name of the Lord will be saved."[h]
Ac 2:21

[a] *29* Isaiah 1:9 [b] *33* Isaiah 8:14; 28:16
[c] *5* Lev. 18:5 [d] *6* Deut. 30:12
[e] *7* Deut. 30:13 [f] *8* Deut. 30:14
[g] *11* Isaiah 28:16 (see Septuagint)
[h] *13* Joel 2:32

14 How, then, can they call on the
one they have not believed in?
And how can they believe in the
one of whom they have not heard?
And how can they hear without
someone preaching to them?
15 And how can anyone preach unless they are sent? As it is written: "How beautiful are the feet
of those who bring good news!"[a]

Isa 52:7; Na 1:15

16 But not all the Israelites accepted the good news. For Isaiah
says, "Lord, who has believed our
message?"[b] 17 Consequently, faith
comes from hearing the message,
and the message is heard through
the word about Christ. 18 But I ask:
Did they not hear? Of course they
did:

Col 3:16; Gal 3:2,5

"Their voice has gone out into
all the earth,
their words to the ends of
the world."[c]

19 Again I ask: Did Israel not understand? First, Moses says,

"I will make you envious by
those who are not a
nation;
I will make you angry by
a nation that has no
understanding."[d]

Ro 11:11,14

20 And Isaiah boldly says,

"I was found by those who did
not seek me;
I revealed myself to
those who did not
ask for me."[e]

21 But concerning Israel he says,

"All day long I have held out
my hands
to a disobedient and
obstinate people."[f]

Isa 65:1-2; Jer 35:17; Ro 9:30

The Remnant of Israel

11 I ask then: Did God reject his
people? By no means! I am
an Israelite myself, a descendant
of Abraham, from the tribe of
Benjamin. 2 God did not reject his
people, whom he foreknew. Don't
you know what Scripture says in
the passage about Elijah — how
he appealed to God against Israel: 3 "Lord, they have killed your
prophets and torn down your altars; I am the only one left, and
they are trying to kill me"[g]? 4 And
what was God's answer to him?
"I have reserved for myself sev-
en thousand who have not bowed
the knee to Baal."[h] 5 So too, at the
present time there is a remnant
chosen by grace. 6 And if by grace,
then it cannot be based on works;
if it were, grace would no longer
be grace.

Ro 4:4; 9:27

7 What then? What the people
of Israel sought so earnestly they
did not obtain. The elect among
them did, but the others were
hardened, 8 as it is written:

Ro 9:18,31

[a] 15 Isaiah 52:7
[b] 16 Isaiah 53:1
[c] 18 Psalm 19:4
[d] 19 Deut. 32:21
[e] 20 Isaiah 65:1
[f] 21 Isaiah 65:2
[g] 3 1 Kings 19:10,14
[h] 4 1 Kings 19:18

"God gave them a spirit of
stupor,
eyes that could not see
and ears that could not hear,
Mt 13:13-15
to this very day."[a]
9 And David says:

"May their table become a
snare and a trap,
a stumbling block
and a retribution
for them.
10 May their eyes be darkened so
they cannot see,
and their backs be bent
forever."[b] Ps 69:22-23

Ingrafted Branches

11 Again I ask: Did they stumble so as to fall beyond recovery?
Not at all! Rather, because of their
transgression, salvation has come
to the Gentiles to make Israel envious. 12 But if their transgression
means riches for the world, and
their loss means riches for the
Gentiles, how much greater riches
will their full inclusion bring!
Ac 13:46; Ro 10:19

13 I am talking to you Gentiles.
Inasmuch as I am the apostle to
the Gentiles, I take pride in my
ministry 14 in the hope that I may
somehow arouse my own people
to envy and save some of them.
15 For if their rejection brought
reconciliation to the world, what
will their acceptance be but life
from the dead? 16 If the part of
the dough offered as firstfruits
is holy, then the whole batch is
holy; if the root is holy, so are the
branches. Lk 15:24,32; Ac 9:15

17 If some of the branches have
been broken off, and you, though
a wild olive shoot, have been grafted in among the others and now
share in the nourishing sap from
the olive root, 18 do not consider
yourself to be superior to those
other branches. If you do, consider
this: You do not support the root,
but the root supports you. 19 You
will say then, "Branches were broken off so that I could be grafted
in." 20 Granted. But they were broken off because of unbelief, and
you stand by faith. Do not be arrogant, but tremble. 21 For if God did
not spare the natural branches, he
will not spare you either.
1Co 10:12; 1Ti 6:17; 1Pe 1:17

22 Consider therefore the kindness and sternness of God: sternness to those who fell, but kindness to you, provided that you
continue in his kindness. Otherwise, you also will be cut off. 23 And
if they do not persist in unbelief,
they will be grafted in, for God is
able to graft them in again. 24 After all, if you were cut out of an
olive tree that is wild by nature,
and contrary to nature were grafted into a cultivated olive tree, how
much more readily will these, the
natural branches, be grafted into
their own olive tree!
Jn 15:2; 1Co 15:2; 2Co 3:16

[a] *8* Deut. 29:4; Isaiah 29:10
[b] *10* Psalm 69:22,23

All Israel Will Be Saved

25I do not want you to be ignorant of this mystery, brothers and
sisters, so that you may not be
conceited: Israel has experienced
a hardening in part until the full
number of the Gentiles has come
in, 26and in this way[a] all Israel will
be saved. As it is written:
Lk 21:24; Isa 45:17

"The deliverer will come from
Zion;
he will turn godlessness
away from Jacob.
27And this is[b] my covenant with
them
when I take away their sins."[c]
Heb 8:10,12

28As far as the gospel is concerned, they are enemies for your
sake; but as far as election is concerned, they are loved on account
of the patriarchs, 29for God's gifts
and his call are irrevocable. 30Just
as you who were at one time disobedient to God have now received mercy as a result of their
disobedience, 31so they too have
now become disobedient in order
that they too may now[d] receive
mercy as a result of God's mercy
to you. 32For God has bound everyone over to disobedience so that
he may have mercy on them all.
Dt 7:8; Ro 3:9; Heb 7:21

Doxology

33Oh, the depth of the riches
of the wisdom and[e]
knowledge of God! Ps 92:5
How unsearchable his
judgments,
and his paths beyond tracing
out! Job 11:7
34"Who has known the mind of
the Lord?
Or who has been his
counselor?"[f]
Isa 40:13-14; Job 36:22
35"Who has ever given to God,
that God should repay
them?"[g] Job 35:7
36For from him and through
him and for him are all
things. 1Co 8:6; Col 1:16
To him be the glory forever!
Amen. Ro 16:27

A Living Sacrifice

12 Therefore, I urge you, brothers and sisters, in view of
God's mercy, to offer your bodies as a living sacrifice, holy and
pleasing to God — this is your true
and proper worship. 2Do not conform to the pattern of this world,
but be transformed by the renew-
ing of your mind. Then you will
be able to test and approve what
God's will is — his good, pleasing
and perfect will. Eph 4:23; 5:17; 1Pe 1:14

Humble Service in the Body of Christ

3For by the grace given me I say
to every one of you: Do not think

[a] 26 Or *and so* [b] 27 Or *will be*
[c] 27 Isaiah 59:20,21; 27:9 (see Septuagint); Jer. 31:33,34 [d] 31 Some manuscripts do not have *now.* [e] 33 Or *riches and the wisdom and the* [f] 34 Isaiah 40:13
[g] 35 Job 41:11

of yourself more highly than you
ought, but rather think of yourself with sober judgment, in accordance with the faith God has
distributed to each of you. 4For
just as each of us has one body
with many members, and these
members do not all have the same
function, 5so in Christ we, though
many, form one body, and each
member belongs to all the others. 6We have different gifts, according to the grace given to each
of us. If your gift is prophesying,
then prophesy in accordance with
your[a] faith; 7if it is serving, then
serve; if it is teaching, then teach;
8if it is to encourage, then give encouragement; if it is giving, then
give generously; if it is to lead,[b] do
it diligently; if it is to show mercy,
do it cheerfully.

Ac 15:32; 2Co 9:5-13; Eph 4:11

Love in Action

9Love must be sincere. Hate
what is evil; cling to what is good.
10Be devoted to one another in
love. Honor one another above
yourselves. 11Never be lacking in
zeal, but keep your spiritual fervor, serving the Lord. 12Be joyful in
hope, patient in affliction, faithful
in prayer. 13Share with the Lord's
people who are in need. Practice
hospitality. 1Ti 3:2; Heb 10:32,36

14Bless those who persecute you;
bless and do not curse. 15Rejoice
with those who rejoice; mourn
with those who mourn. 16Live in
harmony with one another. Do not
be proud, but be willing to associate with people of low position.[c]
Do not be conceited. Mt 5:44; Ro 15:5

17Do not repay anyone evil for
evil. Be careful to do what is right
in the eyes of everyone. 18If it is
possible, as far as it depends on
you, live at peace with everyone.
19Do not take revenge, my dear
friends, but leave room for God's
wrath, for it is written: "It is mine
to avenge; I will repay,"[d] says the
Lord. 20On the contrary:

Lev 19:18; Ro 14:19; 2Co 8:21

"If your enemy is hungry, feed
him;
if he is thirsty, give him
something to drink.
In doing this, you will heap
burning coals on his
head."[e] Mt 5:44; Lk 6:27

21Do not be overcome by evil, but
overcome evil with good.

Submission to Governing Authorities

13 Let everyone be subject to
the governing authorities,
for there is no authority except
that which God has established.
The authorities that exist have
been established by God. 2Conse-
quently, whoever rebels against
the authority is rebelling against
what God has instituted, and those
who do so will bring judgment on
themselves. 3For rulers hold no

[a] 6 *Or the* [b] 8 *Or to provide for others*
[c] 16 *Or willing to do menial work*
[d] 19 Deut. 32:35 [e] 20 Prov. 25:21,22

terror for those who do right, but
for those who do wrong. Do you
want to be free from fear of the
one in authority? Then do what is
right and you will be commended.
4For the one in authority is God's
servant for your good. But if you
do wrong, be afraid, for rulers do
not bear the sword for no reason.
They are God's servants, agents of
wrath to bring punishment on the
wrongdoer. 5Therefore, it is necessary to submit to the authorities,
not only because of possible punishment but also as a matter of
conscience. 1Th 4:6; 1Pe 2:14

6This is also why you pay taxes,
for the authorities are God's servants, who give their full time to
governing. 7Give to everyone what
you owe them: If you owe taxes,
pay taxes; if revenue, then revenue; if respect, then respect; if
honor, then honor. Mt 22:17,21; Lk 23:2

Love Fulfills the Law

8Let no debt remain outstanding, except the continuing debt
to love one another, for whoever
loves others has fulfilled the law.
9The commandments, "You shall
not commit adultery," "You shall
not murder," "You shall not steal,"
"You shall not covet,"[a] and whatever other command there may
be, are summed up in this one
command: "Love your neighbor
as yourself."[b] 10Love does no harm
to a neighbor. Therefore love is
the fulfillment of the law.
Mt 19:19; 22:39-40

The Day Is Near

11And do this, understanding
the present time: The hour has
already come for you to wake
up from your slumber, because
our salvation is nearer now than
when we first believed. 12The
night is nearly over; the day is almost here. So let us put aside the
deeds of darkness and put on the
armor of light. 13Let us behave
decently, as in the daytime, not
in carousing and drunkenness,
not in sexual immorality and debauchery, not in dissension and
jealousy. 14Rather, clothe yourselves with the Lord Jesus Christ,
and do not think about how to
gratify the desires of the flesh.[c]
Gal 3:27; 5:19-21

The Weak and the Strong

14 Accept the one whose faith
is weak, without quarreling
over disputable matters. 2One person's faith allows them to eat anything, but another, whose faith is
weak, eats only vegetables. 3The
one who eats everything must
not treat with contempt the one
who does not, and the one who
does not eat everything must not
judge the one who does, for God
has accepted them. 4Who are you
to judge someone else's servant?
To their own master, servants

[a] 9 Exodus 20:13-15,17; Deut. 5:17-19,21
[b] 9 Lev. 19:18 [c] 14 In contexts like this, the Greek word for *flesh* (*sarx*) refers to the sinful state of human beings, often presented as a power in opposition to the Spirit.

stand or fall. And they will stand,
for the Lord is able to make them
stand. Lk 18:9; Jas 4:12
5One person considers one day
more sacred than another; another considers every day alike. Each
of them should be fully convinced
in their own mind. 6Whoever regards one day as special does so to
the Lord. Whoever eats meat does
so to the Lord, for they give thanks
to God; and whoever abstains does
so to the Lord and gives thanks to
God. 7For none of us lives for ourselves alone, and none of us dies
for ourselves alone. 8If we live, we
live for the Lord; and if we die, we
die for the Lord. So, whether we
live or die, we belong to the Lord.
9For this very reason, Christ died
and returned to life so that he
might be the Lord of both the dead
and the living. Gal 2:20; Php 1:20
10You, then, why do you judge
your brother or sister[a]? Or why do
you treat them with contempt?
For we will all stand before God's
judgment seat. 11It is written:
Mt 7:1; 2Co 5:10

"'As surely as I live,' says the
Lord, Isa 49:18
'every knee will bow before
me;
every tongue will
acknowledge God.'"[b]

12So then, each of us will give an
account of ourselves to God.
Isa 45:23; Mt 12:36; Php 2:10-11; 1Pe 4:5
13Therefore let us stop passing
judgment on one another. Instead,
make up your mind not to put any
stumbling block or obstacle in the
way of a brother or sister. 14I am
convinced, being fully persuaded
in the Lord Jesus, that nothing is
unclean in itself. But if anyone regards something as unclean, then
for that person it is unclean. 15If
your brother or sister is distressed
because of what you eat, you are
no longer acting in love. Do not
by your eating destroy someone
for whom Christ died. 16There-
fore do not let what you know is
good be spoken of as evil. 17For the
kingdom of God is not a matter of
eating and drinking, but of righteousness, peace and joy in the
Holy Spirit, 18because anyone who
serves Christ in this way is pleasing to God and receives human
approval.
Ro 15:13; 1Co 8:8; 2Co 8:21
19Let us therefore make every effort to do what leads to peace and
to mutual edification. 20Do not destroy the work of God for the sake
of food. All food is clean, but it is
wrong for a person to eat anything
that causes someone else to stumble. 21It is better not to eat meat or
drink wine or to do anything else
that will cause your brother or sister to fall. 1Co 8:9-13
22So whatever you believe about
these things keep between yourself and God. Blessed is the one

[a] *10* The Greek word for *brother or sister* (*adelphos*) refers here to a believer, whether man or woman, as part of God's family; also in verses 13, 15 and 21. [b] *11* Isaiah 45:23

who does not condemn himself
by what he approves. [23]But whoever has doubts is condemned if
they eat, because their eating is
not from faith; and everything
that does not come from faith is
sin.[a]

15 We who are strong ought
to bear with the failings of
the weak and not to please ourselves. [2]Each of us should please
our neighbors for their good, to
build them up. [3]For even Christ
did not please himself but, as it is
written: "The insults of those who
insult you have fallen on me."[b]
[4]For everything that was written
in the past was written to teach
us, so that through the endurance
taught in the Scriptures and the
encouragement they provide we
might have hope. Ro 14:1,19; 1Co 10:33

[5]May the God who gives endurance and encouragement give you
the same attitude of mind toward
each other that Christ Jesus had,
[6]so that with one mind and one
voice you may glorify the God and
Father of our Lord Jesus Christ.
Ps 34:3; Ro 12:16; Rev 1:6

[7]Accept one another, then, just
as Christ accepted you, in order to
bring praise to God. [8]For I tell you
that Christ has become a servant
of the Jews[c] on behalf of God's
truth, so that the promises made
to the patriarchs might be confirmed [9]and, moreover, that the
Gentiles might glorify God for his
mercy. As it is written:
Mt 15:24; Ro 14:1; 2Co 1:20

"Therefore I will praise you
among the Gentiles;
I will sing the praises of your
name."[d]

[10]Again, it says,

"Rejoice, you Gentiles, with his
people."[e]

[11]And again,

"Praise the Lord, all you
Gentiles;
let all the peoples extol
him."[f]

[12]And again, Isaiah says,

"The Root of Jesse will
spring up, Rev 5:5
one who will arise to rule
over the nations;
in him the Gentiles will
hope."[g] Dt 32:43; 2Sa 22:50; Ps 18:49; Isa 11:10

[13]May the God of hope fill you
with all joy and peace as you trust
in him, so that you may overflow
with hope by the power of the
Holy Spirit. Ro 14:17; 1Th 1:5

Paul the Minister to the Gentiles

[14]I myself am convinced, my
brothers and sisters, that you
yourselves are full of goodness,
filled with knowledge and competent to instruct one another.

[a] *23* Some manuscripts place 16:25-27 here; others after 15:33. [b] *3* Psalm 69:9 [c] *8* Greek *circumcision* [d] *9* 2 Samuel 22:50; Psalm 18:49 [e] *10* Deut. 32:43 [f] *11* Psalm 117:1 [g] *12* Isaiah 11:10 (see Septuagint)

[15]Yet I have written you quite
boldly on some points to remind
you of them again, because of the
grace God gave me [16]to be a minister of Christ Jesus to the Gentiles.
He gave me the priestly duty of
proclaiming the gospel of God, so
that the Gentiles might become
an offering acceptable to God,
sanctified by the Holy Spirit.

Ro 1:1; 12:3

[17]Therefore I glory in Christ
Jesus in my service to God. [18]I
will not venture to speak of anything except what Christ has accomplished through me in leading the Gentiles to obey God by
what I have said and done — [19]by
the power of signs and wonders,
through the power of the Spirit of
God. So from Jerusalem all the way
around to Illyricum, I have fully
proclaimed the gospel of Christ.
[20]It has always been my ambition
to preach the gospel where Christ
was not known, so that I would
not be building on someone else's
foundation. [21]Rather, as it is written:

Ac 21:19; 2Co 10:15-16

"Those who were not told
about him will see,
and those who have not
heard will understand."[a]

[22]This is why I have often been
hindered from coming to you.

Isa 52:15; Ro 1:13

Paul's Plan to Visit Rome

[23]But now that there is no more
place for me to work in these regions, and since I have been longing for many years to visit you, [24]I
plan to do so when I go to Spain.
I hope to see you while passing
through and to have you assist me
on my journey there, after I have
enjoyed your company for a while.
[25]Now, however, I am on my way
to Jerusalem in the service of the
Lord's people there. [26]For Macedonia and Achaia were pleased to
make a contribution for the poor
among the Lord's people in Jerusalem. [27]They were pleased to do it,
and indeed they owe it to them. For
if the Gentiles have shared in the
Jews' spiritual blessings, they owe
it to the Jews to share with them
their material blessings. [28]So after I have completed this task and
have made sure that they have received this contribution, I will go
to Spain and visit you on the way.
[29]I know that when I come to you, I
will come in the full measure of the
blessing of Christ.

Ro 1:10-11; 1Co 9:11

[30]I urge you, brothers and sisters, by our Lord Jesus Christ and
by the love of the Spirit, to join
me in my struggle by praying to
God for me. [31]Pray that I may be
kept safe from the unbelievers in
Judea and that the contribution I
take to Jerusalem may be favorably received by the Lord's people
there, [32]so that I may come to you
with joy, by God's will, and in your
company be refreshed. [33]The God
of peace be with you all. Amen.

Ro 16:20; 2Co 13:11; Php 4:9

[a] *21* Isaiah 52:15 (see Septuagint)

Personal Greetings

16 I commend to you our sister Phoebe, a deacon[a,b] of the church in Cenchreae. 2I ask you to receive her in the Lord in a way worthy of his people and to give her any help she may need from you, for she has been the benefactor of many people, including me.
Ac 18:18; Php 2:29

3Greet Priscilla[c] and Aquila, my co-workers in Christ Jesus.
4They risked their lives for me. Not only I but all the churches of the Gentiles are grateful to them. Ac 18:2; Ro 8:1,39
5Greet also the church that meets at their house. 1Co 16:19; Col 4:15
Greet my dear friend Epenetus, who was the first convert to Christ in the province of Asia.
1Co 16:15
6Greet Mary, who worked very hard for you.
7Greet Andronicus and Junia, my fellow Jews who have been in prison with me. They are outstanding among[d] the apostles, and they were in Christ before I was. ver 11,21
8Greet Ampliatus, my dear friend in the Lord.
9Greet Urbanus, our co-worker in Christ, and my dear friend Stachys. ver 3
10Greet Apelles, whose fidelity to Christ has stood the test. ver 3
Greet those who belong to the household of Aristobulus.
Ac 11:14
11Greet Herodion, my fellow Jew.
ver 7,21
Greet those in the household of Narcissus who are in the Lord.
Ac 11:14
12Greet Tryphena and Tryphosa, those women who work hard in the Lord.
Greet my dear friend Persis, another woman who has worked very hard in the Lord.
13Greet Rufus, chosen in the Lord, and his mother, who has been a mother to me, too. Mk 15:21
14Greet Asyncritus, Phlegon, Hermes, Patrobas, Hermas and the other brothers and sisters with them.
15Greet Philologus, Julia, Nereus and his sister, and Olympas and all the Lord's people who are with them. Ac 9:13
16Greet one another with a holy kiss.
All the churches of Christ send greetings.
1Co 16:20; 2Co 13:12; 1Th 5:26

17I urge you, brothers and sisters, to watch out for those who cause divisions and put obstacles in your way that are contrary to the teaching you have learned. Keep away from them.
18For such people are not serving our Lord Christ, but their own appetites.

[a] *1* Or *servant* [b] *1* The word *deacon* refers here to a Christian designated to serve with the overseers/elders of the church in a variety of ways; similarly in Phil. 1:1 and 1 Tim. 3:8,12. [c] *3* Greek *Prisca*, a variant of *Priscilla* [d] *7* Or *are esteemed by*

By smooth talk and flattery they
deceive the minds of naive people. [19]Everyone has heard about
your obedience, so I rejoice because of you; but I want you to be
wise about what is good, and innocent about what is evil.

Mt 10:16; 1Co 14:20

[20]The God of peace will soon
crush Satan under your feet.

Ge 3:15; Ro 15:33

The grace of our Lord Jesus be
with you. 1Th 5:28

[21]Timothy, my co-worker, sends
his greetings to you, as do Lucius, Jason and Sosipater, my fellow
Jews. Ac 13:1; 16:1; 17:5

[22]I, Tertius, who wrote down
this letter, greet you in the Lord.

[23]Gaius, whose hospitality I
and the whole church here enjoy,
sends you his greetings. Ac 19:29

Erastus, who is the city's director of public works, and our brother Quartus send you their greetings. [24][a] Ac 19:22; 2Ti 4:20

[25]Now to him who is able to establish you in accordance with my
gospel, the message I proclaim
about Jesus Christ, in keeping
with the revelation of the mystery
hidden for long ages past, [26]but
now revealed and made known
through the prophetic writings
by the command of the eternal
God, so that all the Gentiles might
come to the obedience that comes
from[b] faith — [27]to the only wise
God be glory forever through
Jesus Christ! Amen.

Ro 11:36; Eph 1:9; Col 1:26-27

[a] 24 Some manuscripts include here *May the grace of our Lord Jesus Christ be with all of you. Amen.* [b] 26 Or *that is*

1 CORINTHIANS

1 Paul, called to be an apostle of
Christ Jesus by the will of God,
and our brother Sosthenes,
Ro 1:1; Eph 1:1

[2]To the church of God in Corinth, to those sanctified in Christ
Jesus and called to be his holy
people, together with all those everywhere who call on the name of
our Lord Jesus Christ — their Lord
and ours: Ac 18:1; Ro 1:7

[3]Grace and peace to you from
God our Father and the Lord Jesus
Christ. Ro 1:7

Thanksgiving

[4]I always thank my God for you
because of his grace given you in
Christ Jesus. [5]For in him you have
been enriched in every way — with
all kinds of speech and with all
knowledge — [6]God thus confirming
our testimony about Christ among
you. [7]Therefore you do not lack any
spiritual gift as you eagerly wait for
our Lord Jesus Christ to be revealed.
[8]He will also keep you firm to the
end, so that you will be blameless
on the day of our Lord Jesus Christ.
[9]God is faithful, who has called you
into fellowship with his Son, Jesus
Christ our Lord. Isa 49:7; 2Pe 3:12

A Church Divided Over Leaders

[10]I appeal to you, brothers and
sisters,[a] in the name of our Lord
Jesus Christ, that all of you agree
with one another in what you say
and that there be no divisions
among you, but that you be perfectly united in mind and thought.
[11]My brothers and sisters, some
from Chloe's household have informed me that there are quarrels
among you. [12]What I mean is this:
One of you says, "I follow Paul";
another, "I follow Apollos"; another, "I follow Cephas[b]"; still another, "I follow Christ."
Jn 1:42; 1Co 3:4,22

[13]Is Christ divided? Was Paul
crucified for you? Were you baptized in the name of Paul? [14]I
thank God that I did not baptize
any of you except Crispus and Gaius, [15]so no one can say that you
were baptized in my name. [16](Yes,
I also baptized the household of
Stephanas; beyond that, I don't
remember if I baptized anyone
else.) [17]For Christ did not send me
to baptize, but to preach the gospel — not with wisdom and eloquence, lest the cross of Christ be
emptied of its power.
Jn 4:2; 1Co 2:1,4,13

[a] *10* The Greek word for *brothers and sisters* (*adelphoi*) refers here to believers, both men and women, as part of God's family; also in verses 11 and 26; and in 2:1; 3:1; 4:6; 6:8; 7:24, 29; 10:1; 11:33; 12:1; 14:6, 20, 26, 39; 15:1, 6, 50, 58; 16:15, 20. [b] *12* That is, Peter

Christ Crucified Is God's Power and Wisdom

18For the message of the cross is
foolishness to those who are perishing, but to us who are being
saved it is the power of God. 19For
it is written: Ro 1:16; 2Co 2:15

"I will destroy the wisdom of
the wise;
the intelligence of the
intelligent I will
frustrate."[a] Isa 29:14

20Where is the wise person?
Where is the teacher of the law?
Where is the philosopher of this
age? Has not God made foolish the
wisdom of the world? 21For since
in the wisdom of God the world
through its wisdom did not know
him, God was pleased through the
foolishness of what was preached
to save those who believe. 22Jews
demand signs and Greeks look for
wisdom, 23but we preach Christ
crucified: a stumbling block to
Jews and foolishness to Gentiles, 24but to those whom God
has called, both Jews and Greeks,
Christ the power of God and the
wisdom of God. 25For the foolishness of God is wiser than human
wisdom, and the weakness of God
is stronger than human strength.
2Co 13:4; Col 2:3

26Brothers and sisters, think of
what you were when you were
called. Not many of you were wise
by human standards; not many
were influential; not many were
of noble birth. 27But God chose
the foolish things of the world to
shame the wise; God chose the
weak things of the world to shame
the strong. 28God chose the lowly
things of this world and the despised things — and the things
that are not — to nullify the things
that are, 29so that no one may boast
before him. 30It is because of him
that you are in Christ Jesus, who
has become for us wisdom from
God — that is, our righteousness,
holiness and redemption. 31There-
fore, as it is written: "Let the one
who boasts boast in the Lord."[b]
2Co 10:17; Eph 1:7,14; 2:9

2 And so it was with me, brothers and sisters. When I came to
you, I did not come with eloquence
or human wisdom as I proclaimed
to you the testimony about God.[c]
2For I resolved to know nothing
while I was with you except Jesus
Christ and him crucified. 3I came
to you in weakness with great fear
and trembling. 4My message and
my preaching were not with wise
and persuasive words, but with a
demonstration of the Spirit's power, 5so that your faith might not
rest on human wisdom, but on
God's power. Ro 15:19; 2Co 4:7; 6:7

God's Wisdom Revealed by the Spirit

6We do, however, speak a message of wisdom among the mature, but not the wisdom of this

[a] *19* Isaiah 29:14 [b] *31* Jer. 9:24
[c] *1* Some manuscripts *proclaimed to you God's mystery*

age or of the rulers of this age,
who are coming to nothing. 7No,
we declare God's wisdom, a mystery that has been hidden and that
God destined for our glory before
time began. 8None of the rulers of
this age understood it, for if they
had, they would not have crucified
the Lord of glory. 9However, as it is
written: Ac 7:2; 1Co 1:20; Eph 4:13

"What no eye has seen,
what no ear has heard,
and what no human mind has
conceived"[a] —
the things God has prepared
for those who love
him —

10these are the things God has revealed to us by his Spirit.

Isa 65:17; Jn 14:26

The Spirit searches all things,
even the deep things of God. 11For
who knows a person's thoughts
except their own spirit within
them? In the same way no one
knows the thoughts of God except the Spirit of God. 12What we
have received is not the spirit of
the world, but the Spirit who is
from God, so that we may understand what God has freely given
us. 13This is what we speak, not in
words taught us by human wisdom but in words taught by the
Spirit, explaining spiritual realities with Spirit-taught words.[b]
14The person without the Spirit
does not accept the things that
come from the Spirit of God but
considers them foolishness, and
cannot understand them because
they are discerned only through
the Spirit. 15The person with the
Spirit makes judgments about all
things, but such a person is not
subject to merely human judgments, 16for, 1Co 1:17-18

"Who has known the mind of
the Lord
so as to instruct him?"[c]

Isa 40:13

But we have the mind of Christ.

Jn 15:15

The Church and Its Leaders

3 Brothers and sisters, I could
not address you as people
who live by the Spirit but as people who are still worldly — mere
infants in Christ. 2I gave you
milk, not solid food, for you were
not yet ready for it. Indeed, you
are still not ready. 3You are still
worldly. For since there is jealousy and quarreling among you, are
you not worldly? Are you not acting like mere humans? 4For when
one says, "I follow Paul," and another, "I follow Apollos," are you
not mere human beings?

Gal 5:20; Heb 5:13

5What, after all, is Apollos?
And what is Paul? Only servants,
through whom you came to believe — as the Lord has assigned to
each his task. 6I planted the seed,
Apollos watered it, but God has

[a] 9 Isaiah 64:4 [b] 13 Or *Spirit, interpreting spiritual truths to those who are spiritual*
[c] 16 Isaiah 40:13

been making it grow. 7So neither the one who plants nor the one who waters is anything, but only God, who makes things grow. 8The one who plants and the one who waters have one purpose, and they will each be rewarded according to their own labor. 9For we are co-workers in God's service; you are God's field, God's building.

2Co 6:1; Eph 2:20-22

10By the grace God has given me, I laid a foundation as a wise builder, and someone else is building on it. But each one should build with care. 11For no one can lay any foundation other than the one already laid, which is Jesus Christ. 12If anyone builds on this foundation using gold, silver, costly stones, wood, hay or straw, 13their work will be shown for what it is, because the Day will bring it to light. It will be revealed with fire, and the fire will test the quality of each person's work. 14If what has been built survives, the builder will receive a reward. 15If it is burned up, the builder will suffer loss but yet will be saved — even though only as one escaping through the flames.

2Th 1:7-10; Jude 23

16Don't you know that you yourselves are God's temple and that God's Spirit dwells in your midst? 17If anyone destroys God's temple, God will destroy that person; for God's temple is sacred, and you together are that temple.

2Co 6:16

18Do not deceive yourselves. If any of you think you are wise by the standards of this age, you should become "fools" so that you may become wise. 19For the wisdom of this world is foolishness in God's sight. As it is written: "He catches the wise in their craftiness"[a]; 20and again, "The Lord knows that the thoughts of the wise are futile."[b] 21So then, no more boasting about human leaders! All things are yours, 22whether Paul or Apollos or Cephas[c] or the world or life or death or the present or the future — all are yours, 23and you are of Christ, and Christ is of God.

2Co 10:7; Gal 3:29

The Nature of True Apostleship

4 This, then, is how you ought to regard us: as servants of Christ and as those entrusted with the mysteries God has revealed. 2Now it is required that those who have been given a trust must prove faithful. 3I care very little if I am judged by you or by any human court; indeed, I do not even judge myself. 4My conscience is clear, but that does not make me innocent. It is the Lord who judges me. 5Therefore judge nothing before the appointed time; wait until the Lord comes. He will bring to light what is hidden in darkness and will expose the motives of the heart. At that time each will receive their praise from God.

Ro 2:1,29

[a] 19 Job 5:13 [b] 20 Psalm 94:11
[c] 22 That is, Peter

6 Now, brothers and sisters, I
have applied these things to myself and Apollos for your benefit,
so that you may learn from us the
meaning of the saying, "Do not go
beyond what is written." Then you
will not be puffed up in being a
follower of one of us over against
the other. 7 For who makes you different from anyone else? What do
you have that you did not receive?
And if you did receive it, why do
you boast as though you did not?
Jn 3:27; 1Co 1:12

8 Already you have all you want!
Already you have become rich!
You have begun to reign — and
that without us! How I wish that
you really had begun to reign so
that we also might reign with you!
9 For it seems to me that God has
put us apostles on display at the
end of the procession, like those
condemned to die in the arena. We
have been made a spectacle to the
whole universe, to angels as well
as to human beings. 10 We are fools
for Christ, but you are so wise in
Christ! We are weak, but you are
strong! You are honored, we are
dishonored! 11 To this very hour we
go hungry and thirsty, we are in
rags, we are brutally treated, we are
homeless. 12 We work hard with our
own hands. When we are cursed,
we bless; when we are persecuted,
we endure it; 13 when we are slandered, we answer kindly. We have
become the scum of the earth, the
garbage of the world — right up to
this moment. Ac 17:18; Ro 8:35

Paul's Appeal and Warning

14 I am writing this not to shame
you but to warn you as my dear
children. 15 Even if you had ten
thousand guardians in Christ, you
do not have many fathers, for in
Christ Jesus I became your father
through the gospel. 16 Therefore I
urge you to imitate me. 17 For this
reason I have sent to you Timothy,
my son whom I love, who is faithful in the Lord. He will remind you
of my way of life in Christ Jesus,
which agrees with what I teach everywhere in every church.
1Co 7:17; 1Th 1:6; 2:11

18 Some of you have become arrogant, as if I were not coming to
you. 19 But I will come to you very
soon, if the Lord is willing, and
then I will find out not only how
these arrogant people are talking,
but what power they have. 20 For
the kingdom of God is not a matter of talk but of power. 21 What do
you prefer? Shall I come to you
with a rod of discipline, or shall
I come in love and with a gentle
spirit? Ro 15:13; 2Co 1:15-16

Dealing With a Case of Incest

5 It is actually reported that
there is sexual immorality
among you, and of a kind that even
pagans do not tolerate: A man is
sleeping with his father's wife.
2 And you are proud! Shouldn't you
rather have gone into mourning
and have put out of your fellowship the man who has been doing
this? 3 For my part, even though I

am not physically present, I am
with you in spirit. As one who is
present with you in this way, I
have already passed judgment in
the name of our Lord Jesus on the
one who has been doing this. 4So
when you are assembled and I am
with you in spirit, and the power
of our Lord Jesus is present, 5hand
this man over to Satan for the destruction of the flesh,[a,b] so that his
spirit may be saved on the day of
the Lord. 1Ti 1:20; 2Th 3:6

6Your boasting is not good.
Don't you know that a little
yeast leavens the whole batch of
dough? 7Get rid of the old yeast,
so that you may be a new unleavened batch — as you really are.
For Christ, our Passover lamb, has
been sacrificed. 8Therefore let us
keep the Festival, not with the old
bread leavened with malice and
wickedness, but with the unleavened bread of sincerity and truth.
Gal 5:9; 1Pe 1:19

9I wrote to you in my letter not
to associate with sexually immoral people — 10not at all meaning
the people of this world who are
immoral, or the greedy and swindlers, or idolaters. In that case you
would have to leave this world.
11But now I am writing to you that
you must not associate with anyone who claims to be a brother or
sister[c] but is sexually immoral or
greedy, an idolater or slanderer,
a drunkard or swindler. Do not
even eat with such people.
1Co 10:27; Eph 5:11

12What business is it of mine to
judge those outside the church?
Are you not to judge those inside?
13God will judge those outside.
"Expel the wicked person from
among you."[d] Mk 4:11; 1Co 6:1-4

Lawsuits Among Believers

6 If any of you has a dispute with
another, do you dare to take it
before the ungodly for judgment
instead of before the Lord's people? 2Or do you not know that
the Lord's people will judge the
world? And if you are to judge the
world, are you not competent to
judge trivial cases? 3Do you not
know that we will judge angels?
How much more the things of
this life! 4Therefore, if you have
disputes about such matters, do
you ask for a ruling from those
whose way of life is scorned in the
church? 5I say this to shame you.
Is it possible that there is nobody
among you wise enough to judge
a dispute between believers? 6But
instead, one brother takes another
to court — and this in front of unbelievers! Mt 19:28; 2Co 6:14-15

7The very fact that you have lawsuits among you means you have
been completely defeated already.

[a] *5* In contexts like this, the Greek word for *flesh* (*sarx*) refers to the sinful state of human beings, often presented as a power in opposition to the Spirit. [b] *5* Or *of his body* [c] *11* The Greek word for *brother or sister* (*adelphos*) refers here to a believer, whether man or woman, as part of God's family; also in 8:11, 13. [d] *13* Deut. 13:5; 17:7; 19:19; 21:21; 22:21,24; 24:7

Why not rather be wronged? Why
not rather be cheated? 8Instead,
you yourselves cheat and do
wrong, and you do this to your
brothers and sisters. 9Or do you
not know that wrongdoers will not
inherit the kingdom of God? Do
not be deceived: Neither the sexually immoral nor idolaters nor
adulterers nor men who have sex
with men[a] 10nor thieves nor the
greedy nor drunkards nor slanderers nor swindlers will inherit
the kingdom of God. 11And that is
what some of you were. But you
were washed, you were sanctified,
you were justified in the name of
the Lord Jesus Christ and by the
Spirit of our God. 1Co 1:2; Gal 5:21

Sexual Immorality

12"I have the right to do anything," you say — but not everything is beneficial. "I have the
right to do anything" — but I will
not be mastered by anything.
13You say, "Food for the stomach
and the stomach for food, and
God will destroy them both." The
body, however, is not meant for
sexual immorality but for the
Lord, and the Lord for the body.
14By his power God raised the
Lord from the dead, and he will
raise us also. 15Do you not know
that your bodies are members of
Christ himself? Shall I then take
the members of Christ and unite
them with a prostitute? Never!
16Do you not know that he who
unites himself with a prostitute
is one with her in body? For it is
said, "The two will become one
flesh."[b] 17But whoever is united
with the Lord is one with him in
spirit.[c] Jn 17:21-23; Gal 2:20

18Flee from sexual immorality.
All other sins a person commits
are outside the body, but whoever
sins sexually, sins against their
own body. 19Do you not know that
your bodies are temples of the
Holy Spirit, who is in you, whom
you have received from God? You
are not your own; 20you were
bought at a price. Therefore hon-
or God with your bodies.
Ro 6:12; Heb 13:4; Rev 5:9

Concerning Married Life

7 Now for the matters you wrote
about: "It is good for a man
not to have sexual relations with
a woman." 2But since sexual immorality is occurring, each man
should have sexual relations with
his own wife, and each woman with her own husband. 3The
husband should fulfill his marital duty to his wife, and likewise
the wife to her husband. 4The
wife does not have authority over
her own body but yields it to her
husband. In the same way, the
husband does not have authority over his own body but yields it
to his wife. 5Do not deprive each
other except perhaps by mutual

[a] 9 The words *men who have sex with men* translate two Greek words that refer to the passive and active participants in homosexual acts. [b] 16 Gen. 2:24 [c] 17 Or *in the Spirit*

consent and for a time, so that you
may devote yourselves to prayer.
Then come together again so
that Satan will not tempt you because of your lack of self-control.
6I say this as a concession, not as
a command. 7I wish that all of you
were as I am. But each of you has
your own gift from God; one has
this gift, another has that.

1Co 9:5; 12:4,11

8Now to the unmarried[a] and the
widows I say: It is good for them
to stay unmarried, as I do. 9But if
they cannot control themselves,
they should marry, for it is better
to marry than to burn with passion.

1Ti 5:14

10To the married I give this command (not I, but the Lord): A wife
must not separate from her husband. 11But if she does, she must
remain unmarried or else be reconciled to her husband. And a husband must not divorce his wife.

Mal 2:14-16; Mt 5:32; Lk 16:18

12To the rest I say this (I, not the
Lord): If any brother has a wife
who is not a believer and she is
willing to live with him, he must
not divorce her. 13And if a woman
has a husband who is not a believer and he is willing to live with
her, she must not divorce him.
14For the unbelieving husband has
been sanctified through his wife,
and the unbelieving wife has been
sanctified through her believing
husband. Otherwise your children
would be unclean, but as it is, they
are holy.

Mal 2:15

15But if the unbeliever leaves, let
it be so. The brother or the sister is
not bound in such circumstances;
God has called us to live in peace.
16How do you know, wife, whether you will save your husband?
Or, how do you know, husband,
whether you will save your wife?

Ro 14:19; 1Pe 3:1

Concerning Change of Status

17Nevertheless, each person
should live as a believer in whatever
situation the Lord has assigned to
them, just as God has called them.
This is the rule I lay down in all the
churches. 18Was a man already circumcised when he was called? He
should not become uncircumcised.
Was a man uncircumcised when he
was called? He should not be circumcised. 19Circumcision is nothing and uncircumcision is nothing.
Keeping God's commands is what
counts. 20Each person should remain in the situation they were in
when God called them.

21Were you a slave when you
were called? Don't let it trouble
you — although if you can gain
your freedom, do so. 22For the one
who was a slave when called to
faith in the Lord is the Lord's freed
person; similarly, the one who was
free when called is Christ's slave.
23You were bought at a price; do
not become slaves of human beings. 24Brothers and sisters, each
person, as responsible to God,

[a] 8 Or *widowers*

should remain in the situation they were in when God called them. 1Co 6:20; Eph 6:6

Concerning the Unmarried

25Now about virgins: I have no
command from the Lord, but I
give a judgment as one who by
the Lord's mercy is trustworthy.
26Because of the present crisis, I
think that it is good for a man to
remain as he is. 27Are you pledged
to a woman? Do not seek to be released. Are you free from such a
commitment? Do not look for a
wife. 28But if you do marry, you
have not sinned; and if a virgin
marries, she has not sinned. But
those who marry will face many
troubles in this life, and I want to
spare you this. 1Ti 1:13,16

29What I mean, brothers and sisters, is that the time is short. From
now on those who have wives
should live as if they do not; 30those
who mourn, as if they did not;
those who are happy, as if they were
not; those who buy something, as
if it were not theirs to keep; 31those
who use the things of the world,
as if not engrossed in them. For
this world in its present form is
passing away. Ro 13:11-12; 1Jn 2:17

32I would like you to be free
from concern. An unmarried man
is concerned about the Lord's affairs — how he can please the
Lord. 33But a married man is concerned about the affairs of this
world — how he can please his
wife — 34and his interests are divided. An unmarried woman or
virgin is concerned about the
Lord's affairs: Her aim is to be devoted to the Lord in both body
and spirit. But a married woman
is concerned about the affairs of
this world — how she can please
her husband. 35I am saying this for
your own good, not to restrict you,
but that you may live in a right
way in undivided devotion to the
Lord. Ps 86:11; 1Ti 5:5

36If anyone is worried that he
might not be acting honorably toward the virgin he is engaged to,
and if his passions are too strong[a]
and he feels he ought to marry, he
should do as he wants. He is not
sinning. They should get married.
37But the man who has settled
the matter in his own mind, who
is under no compulsion but has
control over his own will, and who
has made up his mind not to marry the virgin — this man also does
the right thing. 38So then, he who
marries the virgin does right, but
he who does not marry her does
better.[b] Heb 13:4

[a] 36 Or *if she is getting beyond the usual age for marriage* [b] 36-38 Or *36If anyone thinks he is not treating his daughter properly, and if she is getting along in years (or if her passions are too strong), and he feels she ought to marry, he should do as he wants. He is not sinning. He should let her get married. 37But the man who has settled the matter in his own mind, who is under no compulsion but has control over his own will, and who has made up his mind to keep the virgin unmarried — this man also does the right thing. 38So then, he who gives his virgin in marriage does right, but he who does not give her in marriage does better.*

[39]A woman is bound to her husband as long as he lives. But if her husband dies, she is free to marry anyone she wishes, but he must belong to the Lord. [40]In my judgment, she is happier if she stays as she is — and I think that I too have the Spirit of God. Ro 7:2-3; 2Co 6:14

Concerning Food Sacrificed to Idols

8 Now about food sacrificed to idols: We know that "We all possess knowledge." But knowledge puffs up while love builds up. [2]Those who think they know something do not yet know as they ought to know. [3]But whoever loves God is known by God.[a]

Ac 15:20; 1Co 13:8-9,12; Gal 4:9

[4]So then, about eating food sacrificed to idols: We know that "An idol is nothing at all in the world" and that "There is no God but one." [5]For even if there are so-called gods, whether in heaven or on earth (as indeed there are many "gods" and many "lords"), [6]yet for us there is but one God, the Father, from whom all things came and for whom we live; and there is but one Lord, Jesus Christ, through whom all things came and through whom we live.

Ro 11:36; Mal 2:10

[7]But not everyone possesses this knowledge. Some people are still so accustomed to idols that when they eat sacrificial food they think of it as having been sacrificed to a god, and since their conscience is weak, it is defiled. [8]But food does not bring us near to God; we are no worse if we do not eat, and no better if we do. Ro 14:14,17

[9]Be careful, however, that the exercise of your rights does not become a stumbling block to the weak. [10]For if someone with a weak conscience sees you, with all your knowledge, eating in an idol's temple, won't that person be emboldened to eat what is sacrificed to idols? [11]So this weak brother or sister, for whom Christ died, is destroyed by your knowledge. [12]When you sin against them in this way and wound their weak conscience, you sin against Christ. [13]Therefore, if what I eat causes my brother or sister to fall into sin, I will never eat meat again, so that I will not cause them to fall.

Mt 18:6; Ro 14:21; Gal 5:13

Paul's Rights as an Apostle

9 Am I not free? Am I not an apostle? Have I not seen Jesus our Lord? Are you not the result of my work in the Lord? [2]Even though I may not be an apostle to others, surely I am to you! For you are the seal of my apostleship in the Lord. 1Co 3:6; 2Co 3:2-3

[3]This is my defense to those who sit in judgment on me. [4]Don't we have the right to food and drink? [5]Don't we have the right to take a

[a] *2,3* An early manuscript and another ancient witness *think they have knowledge do not yet know as they ought to know. [3]But whoever loves truly knows.*

believing wife along with us, as do
the other apostles and the Lord's
brothers and Cephas[a]? 6Or is it
only I and Barnabas who lack the
right to not work for a living?
Ac 4:36; 1Th 2:6

7Who serves as a soldier at his
own expense? Who plants a vineyard and does not eat its grapes?
Who tends a flock and does not
drink the milk? 8Do I say this merely on human authority? Doesn't
the Law say the same thing? 9For
it is written in the Law of Moses: "Do not muzzle an ox while
it is treading out the grain."[b] Is it
about oxen that God is concerned?
10Surely he says this for us, doesn't
he? Yes, this was written for us, because whoever plows and threshes
should be able to do so in the hope
of sharing in the harvest. 11If we
have sown spiritual seed among
you, is it too much if we reap a
material harvest from you? 12If
others have this right of support
from you, shouldn't we have it all
the more? Ro 15:27; 2Ti 2:6

But we did not use this right. On
the contrary, we put up with anything rather than hinder the gospel of Christ.

13Don't you know that those who
serve in the temple get their food
from the temple, and that those
who serve at the altar share in
what is offered on the altar? 14In
the same way, the Lord has commanded that those who preach the
gospel should receive their living
from the gospel. Mt 10:10; 1Ti 5:18

15But I have not used any of
these rights. And I am not writing this in the hope that you will
do such things for me, for I would
rather die than allow anyone to
deprive me of this boast. 16For
when I preach the gospel, I cannot boast, since I am compelled
to preach. Woe to me if I do not
preach the gospel! 17If I preach
voluntarily, I have a reward; if not
voluntarily, I am simply discharg-
ing the trust committed to me.
18What then is my reward? Just
this: that in preaching the gospel
I may offer it free of charge, and so
not make full use of my rights as a
preacher of the gospel.
1Co 3:8,14; Gal 2:7

Paul's Use of His Freedom

19Though I am free and belong
to no one, I have made myself a
slave to everyone, to win as many
as possible. 20To the Jews I became like a Jew, to win the Jews.
To those under the law I became
like one under the law (though
I myself am not under the law),
so as to win those under the law.
21To those not having the law I became like one not having the law
(though I am not free from God's
law but am under Christ's law),
so as to win those not having the
law. 22To the weak I became weak,
to win the weak. I have become
all things to all people so that by
all possible means I might save
some. 23I do all this for the sake of

[a] 5 That is, Peter [b] 9 Deut. 25:4

the gospel, that I may share in its
blessings. Ro 2:12,14; 1Co 10:33

The Need for Self-Discipline

24 Do you not know that in a race
all the runners run, but only one
gets the prize? Run in such a way
as to get the prize. 25 Everyone who
competes in the games goes into
strict training. They do it to get
a crown that will not last, but we
do it to get a crown that will last
forever. 26 Therefore I do not run
like someone running aimlessly;
I do not fight like a boxer beating
the air. 27 No, I strike a blow to my
body and make it my slave so that
after I have preached to others, I
myself will not be disqualified for
the prize. Ro 8:13; 2Ti 4:7

Warnings From Israel's History

10 For I do not want you to be
ignorant of the fact, brothers and sisters, that our ancestors
were all under the cloud and that
they all passed through the sea.
2 They were all baptized into Moses
in the cloud and in the sea. 3 They
all ate the same spiritual food 4 and
drank the same spiritual drink; for
they drank from the spiritual rock
that accompanied them, and that
rock was Christ. 5 Nevertheless,
God was not pleased with most of
them; their bodies were scattered
in the wilderness. Nu 14:29; Heb 3:17

6 Now these things occurred as
examples to keep us from setting
our hearts on evil things as they
did. 7 Do not be idolaters, as some
of them were; as it is written: "The
people sat down to eat and drink
and got up to indulge in revelry."[a]
8 We should not commit sexual immorality, as some of them did —
and in one day twenty-three thousand of them died. 9 We should
not test Christ,[b] as some of them
did — and were killed by snakes.
10 And do not grumble, as some of
them did — and were killed by the
destroying angel. Ex 12:23; Nu 21:5-6

11 These things happened to
them as examples and were written down as warnings for us, on
whom the culmination of the
ages has come. 12 So, if you think
you are standing firm, be careful
that you don't fall! 13 No temptation[c] has overtaken you except
what is common to mankind. And
God is faithful; he will not let you
be tempted[c] beyond what you can
bear. But when you are tempted,[c]
he will also provide a way out so
that you can endure it.
Ro 11:20; 2Pe 2:9

Idol Feasts and the Lord's Supper

14 Therefore, my dear friends,
flee from idolatry. 15 I speak to
sensible people; judge for yourselves what I say. 16 Is not the cup
of thanksgiving for which we give
thanks a participation in the blood
of Christ? And is not the bread
that we break a participation in

[a] 7 Exodus 32:6 [b] 9 Some manuscripts *test the Lord* [c] 13 The Greek for *temptation* and *tempted* can also mean *testing* and *tested*.

the body of Christ? 17Because there
is one loaf, we, who are many, are
one body, for we all share the one
loaf. Mt 26:26-28; 1Co 12:27

18Consider the people of Israel:
Do not those who eat the sacrifices participate in the altar? 19Do I
mean then that food sacrificed to
an idol is anything, or that an idol
is anything? 20No, but the sacrifices of pagans are offered to demons, not to God, and I do not
want you to be participants with
demons. 21You cannot drink the
cup of the Lord and the cup of demons too; you cannot have a part
in both the Lord's table and the table of demons. 22Are we trying to
arouse the Lord's jealousy? Are we
stronger than he? Dt 32:16,21; Isa 45:9

The Believer's Freedom

23"I have the right to do anything," you say — but not everything is beneficial. "I have the
right to do anything" — but not
everything is constructive. 24No
one should seek their own good,
but the good of others.
Ro 15:1-2; 1Co 6:12

25Eat anything sold in the meat
market without raising questions
of conscience, 26for, "The earth is
the Lord's, and everything in it."[a]
Ps 24:1; Ac 10:15

27If an unbeliever invites you
to a meal and you want to go,
eat whatever is put before you
without raising questions of conscience. 28But if someone says to
you, "This has been offered in
sacrifice," then do not eat it, both
for the sake of the one who told
you and for the sake of conscience.
29I am referring to the other person's conscience, not yours. For
why is my freedom being judged
by another's conscience? 30If I
take part in the meal with thankfulness, why am I denounced because of something I thank God
for? Lk 10:7; Ro 14:6

31So whether you eat or drink or
whatever you do, do it all for the
glory of God. 32Do not cause anyone to stumble, whether Jews,
Greeks or the church of God —
33even as I try to please everyone
in every way. For I am not seeking my own good but the good of
many, so that they may be saved.

11 1Follow my example, as I follow the example of Christ.
Ro 11:14; 15:2

On Covering the Head in Worship

2I praise you for remembering
me in everything and for holding
to the traditions just as I passed
them on to you. 3But I want you
to realize that the head of every
man is Christ, and the head of the
woman is man,[b] and the head of
Christ is God. 4Every man who
prays or prophesies with his head
covered dishonors his head. 5But
every woman who prays or prophesies with her head uncovered
dishonors her head — it is the
same as having her head shaved.

[a] 26 Psalm 24:1 [b] 3 Or *of the wife is her husband*

[6]For if a woman does not cover her head, she might as well have her hair cut off; but if it is a disgrace for a woman to have her hair cut off or her head shaved, then she should cover her head. 1Co 4:17; 15:2-3

[7]A man ought not to cover his head,[a] since he is the image and glory of God; but woman is the glory of man. [8]For man did not come from woman, but woman from man; [9]neither was man created for woman, but woman for man. [10]It is for this reason that a woman ought to have authority over her own[b] head, because of the angels. [11]Nevertheless, in the Lord woman is not independent of man, nor is man independent of woman. [12]For as woman came from man, so also man is born of woman. But everything comes from God. Ge 2:21-23; Jas 3:9

[13]Judge for yourselves: Is it proper for a woman to pray to God with her head uncovered? [14]Does not the very nature of things teach you that if a man has long hair, it is a disgrace to him, [15]but that if a woman has long hair, it is her glory? For long hair is given to her as a covering. [16]If anyone wants to be contentious about this, we have no other practice — nor do the churches of God. Ro 11:36; 1Co 7:17

Correcting an Abuse of the Lord's Supper

[17]In the following directives I have no praise for you, for your meetings do more harm than good. [18]In the first place, I hear that when you come together as a church, there are divisions among you, and to some extent I believe it. [19]No doubt there have to be differences among you to show which of you have God's approval. [20]So then, when you come together, it is not the Lord's Supper you eat, [21]for when you are eating, some of you go ahead with your own private suppers. As a result, one person remains hungry and another gets drunk. [22]Don't you have homes to eat and drink in? Or do you despise the church of God by humiliating those who have nothing? What shall I say to you? Shall I praise you? Certainly not in this matter! 1Co 1:10-12; 1Jn 2:19

[23]For I received from the Lord what I also passed on to you: The Lord Jesus, on the night he was betrayed, took bread, [24]and when he had given thanks, he broke it and said, "This is my body, which is for you; do this in remembrance of me." [25]In the same way, after supper he took the cup, saying, "This cup is the new covenant in my blood; do this, whenever you drink it, in remembrance of me."

[a] 4-7 Or [4]*Every man who prays or prophesies with long hair dishonors his head.* [5]*But every woman who prays or prophesies with no covering of hair dishonors her head — she is just like one of the "shorn women."* [6]*If a woman has no covering, let her be for now with short hair; but since it is a disgrace for a woman to have her hair shorn or shaved, she should grow it again.* [7]*A man ought not to have long hair*

[b] 10 Or *have a sign of authority on her*

26 For whenever you eat this bread
and drink this cup, you proclaim
the Lord's death until he comes.

Mt 26:26-28; Mk 14:22-24; Lk 22:17-20

27 So then, whoever eats the
bread or drinks the cup of the
Lord in an unworthy manner
will be guilty of sinning against
the body and blood of the Lord.
28 Everyone ought to examine
themselves before they eat of the
bread and drink from the cup.
29 For those who eat and drink
without discerning the body of
Christ eat and drink judgment on
themselves. 30 That is why many
among you are weak and sick,
and a number of you have fallen
asleep. 31 But if we were more discerning with regard to ourselves,
we would not come under such
judgment. 32 Nevertheless, when
we are judged in this way by the
Lord, we are being disciplined so
that we will not be finally condemned with the world.

Ps 94:12; Heb 12:7-10; Rev 3:19

33 So then, my brothers and sisters, when you gather to eat, you
should all eat together. 34 Anyone
who is hungry should eat something at home, so that when you
meet together it may not result in
judgment. ver 21-22

And when I come I will give further directions. 1Co 4:19

Concerning Spiritual Gifts

12 Now about the gifts of the
Spirit, brothers and sisters, I
do not want you to be uninformed.
2 You know that when you were
pagans, somehow or other you
were influenced and led astray
to mute idols. 3 Therefore I want
you to know that no one who is
speaking by the Spirit of God says,
"Jesus be cursed," and no one can
say, "Jesus is Lord," except by the
Holy Spirit. Ro 1:11; 1Th 1:9; 1Jn 4:2-3

4 There are different kinds of
gifts, but the same Spirit distributes them. 5 There are different
kinds of service, but the same
Lord. 6 There are different kinds
of working, but in all of them and
in everyone it is the same God at
work. Ro 12:4-8; Eph 4:11; Heb 2:4

7 Now to each one the manifes-
tation of the Spirit is given for
the common good. 8 To one there
is given through the Spirit a message of wisdom, to another a message of knowledge by means of
the same Spirit, 9 to another faith
by the same Spirit, to another gifts
of healing by that one Spirit, 10 to
another miraculous powers, to
another prophecy, to another distinguishing between spirits, to another speaking in different kinds
of tongues,[a] and to still another
the interpretation of tongues.[a]
11 All these are the work of one and
the same Spirit, and he distributes
them to each one, just as he determines. Eph 4:12; 1Co 2:6

Unity and Diversity in the Body

12 Just as a body, though one, has
many parts, but all its many parts

[a] *10* Or *languages*; also in verse 28

form one body, so it is with Christ.
13 For we were all baptized by[a] one
Spirit so as to form one body—
whether Jews or Gentiles, slave or
free—and we were all given the
one Spirit to drink. 14 Even so the
body is not made up of one part
but of many. Gal 3:28; Col 3:11

15 Now if the foot should say, "Because I am not a hand, I do not belong to the body," it would not for
that reason stop being part of the
body. 16 And if the ear should say,
"Because I am not an eye, I do not
belong to the body," it would not
for that reason stop being part of
the body. 17 If the whole body were
an eye, where would the sense of
hearing be? If the whole body were
an ear, where would the sense of
smell be? 18 But in fact God has
placed the parts in the body, every one of them, just as he wanted
them to be. 19 If they were all one
part, where would the body be?
20 As it is, there are many parts, but
one body. Ro 12:5

21 The eye cannot say to the hand,
"I don't need you!" And the head
cannot say to the feet, "I don't need
you!" 22 On the contrary, those parts
of the body that seem to be weaker
are indispensable, 23 and the parts
that we think are less honorable
we treat with special honor. And
the parts that are unpresentable
are treated with special modesty,
24 while our presentable parts need
no special treatment. But God
has put the body together, giving
greater honor to the parts that
lacked it, 25 so that there should be
no division in the body, but that
its parts should have equal concern for each other. 26 If one part
suffers, every part suffers with it;
if one part is honored, every part
rejoices with it.

27 Now you are the body of
Christ, and each one of you is a
part of it. 28 And God has placed in
the church first of all apostles, second prophets, third teachers, then
miracles, then gifts of healing, of
helping, of guidance, and of different kinds of tongues. 29 Are all
apostles? Are all prophets? Are all
teachers? Do all work miracles?
30 Do all have gifts of healing? Do
all speak in tongues[b]? Do all interpret? 31 Now eagerly desire the
greater gifts. 1Co 14:1,39; Eph 4:11

Love Is Indispensable

And yet I will show you the most
excellent way.

13 If I speak in the tongues[c] of
men or of angels, but do not
have love, I am only a resounding gong or a clanging cymbal.
2 If I have the gift of prophecy and
can fathom all mysteries and all
knowledge, and if I have a faith
that can move mountains, but do
not have love, I am nothing. 3 If I
give all I possess to the poor and
give over my body to hardship
that I may boast,[d] but do not have
love, I gain nothing. Mt 6:2; 1Co 14:2

[a] 13 Or *with;* or *in* [b] 30 Or *other languages* [c] 1 Or *languages* [d] 3 Some manuscripts *body to the flames*

4 Love is patient, love is kind. It does not envy, it does not boast, it is not proud. 5 It does not dishonor others, it is not self-seeking, it is not easily angered, it keeps no record of wrongs. 6 Love does not delight in evil but rejoices with the truth. 7 It always protects, always trusts, always hopes, always perseveres. 1Co 10:24; 2Jn 4

8 Love never fails. But where there are prophecies, they will cease; where there are tongues, they will be stilled; where there is knowledge, it will pass away. 9 For we know in part and we prophesy in part, 10 but when completeness comes, what is in part disappears. 11 When I was a child, I talked like a child, I thought like a child, I reasoned like a child. When I became a man, I put the ways of childhood behind me. 12 For now we see only a reflection as in a mirror; then we shall see face to face. Now I know in part; then I shall know fully, even as I am fully known.

1Co 8:3; 2Co 5:7; 1Jn 3:2

13 And now these three remain: faith, hope and love. But the greatest of these is love. 1Co 16:14; Gal 5:5-6

Intelligibility in Worship

14 Follow the way of love and eagerly desire gifts of the Spirit, especially prophecy. 2 For anyone who speaks in a tongue[a] does not speak to people but to God. Indeed, no one understands them; they utter mysteries by the Spirit. 3 But the one who prophesies speaks to people for their strengthening, encouraging and comfort. 4 Anyone who speaks in a tongue edifies themselves, but the one who prophesies edifies the church. 5 I would like every one of you to speak in tongues,[b] but I would rather have you prophesy. The one who prophesies is greater than the one who speaks in tongues,[b] unless someone interprets, so that the church may be edified. Nu 11:29; 1Co 12:31

6 Now, brothers and sisters, if I come to you and speak in tongues, what good will I be to you, unless I bring you some revelation or knowledge or prophecy or word of instruction? 7 Even in the case of lifeless things that make sounds, such as the pipe or harp, how will anyone know what tune is being played unless there is a distinction in the notes? 8 Again, if the trumpet does not sound a clear call, who will get ready for battle? 9 So it is with you. Unless you speak intelligible words with your tongue, how will anyone know what you are saying? You will just be speaking into the air. 10 Undoubtedly there are all sorts of languages in the world, yet none of them is without meaning. 11 If then I do not grasp the meaning of what someone is saying, I am a foreigner to the speaker, and the speaker is a foreigner to me. 12 So it is with you.

[a] 2 Or *in another language*; also in verses 4, 13, 14, 19, 26 and 27 [b] 5 Or *in other languages*; also in verses 6, 18, 22, 23 and 39

Since you are eager for gifts of the
Spirit, try to excel in those that
build up the church. Nu 10:9; Jer 4:19
13 For this reason the one who
speaks in a tongue should pray
that they may interpret what they
say. 14 For if I pray in a tongue, my
spirit prays, but my mind is unfruitful. 15 So what shall I do? I will
pray with my spirit, but I will also
pray with my understanding; I
will sing with my spirit, but I will
also sing with my understanding.
16 Otherwise when you are praising
God in the Spirit, how can someone else, who is now put in the position of an inquirer,[a] say "Amen"
to your thanksgiving, since they
do not know what you are saying? 17 You are giving thanks well
enough, but no one else is edified.
1Ch 16:36; 1Co 11:24
18 I thank God that I speak in
tongues more than all of you. 19 But
in the church I would rather speak
five intelligible words to instruct
others than ten thousand words in
a tongue. ver 6
20 Brothers and sisters, stop
thinking like children. In regard
to evil be infants, but in your
thinking be adults. 21 In the Law it
is written: Jn 10:34; Eph 4:14

"With other tongues
and through the lips of
foreigners
I will speak to this people,
but even then they will not
listen to me, Isa 28:11-12
says the Lord."[b]

22 Tongues, then, are a sign, not
for believers but for unbelievers;
prophecy, however, is not for unbelievers but for believers. 23 So if
the whole church comes together
and everyone speaks in tongues,
and inquirers or unbelievers come
in, will they not say that you are
out of your mind? 24 But if an unbeliever or an inquirer comes in
while everyone is prophesying,
they are convicted of sin and are
brought under judgment by all,
25 as the secrets of their hearts are
laid bare. So they will fall down
and worship God, exclaiming,
"God is really among you!"
Isa 45:14; Zec 8:23; Ac 2:13

Good Order in Worship

26 What then shall we say, brothers and sisters? When you come together, each of you has a hymn, or
a word of instruction, a revelation,
a tongue or an interpretation. Everything must be done so that the
church may be built up. 27 If anyone speaks in a tongue, two — or
at the most three — should speak,
one at a time, and someone must
interpret. 28 If there is no interpreter, the speaker should keep quiet
in the church and speak to himself
and to God. Ro 14:19; 1Co 12:7-10
29 Two or three prophets should
speak, and the others should
weigh carefully what is said. 30 And

[a] *16* The Greek word for *inquirer* is a technical term for someone not fully initiated into a religion; also in verses 23 and 24. [b] *21* Isaiah 28:11,12

if a revelation comes to someone who is sitting down, the first
speaker should stop. 31For you can
all prophesy in turn so that everyone may be instructed and encouraged. 32The spirits of prophets are
subject to the control of prophets.
33For God is not a God of disorder
but of peace — as in all the congregations of the Lord's people.

1Co 12:10; 1Jn 4:1

34Women[a] should remain silent
in the churches. They are not allowed to speak, but must be in
submission, as the law says. 35If
they want to inquire about something, they should ask their own
husbands at home; for it is disgraceful for a woman to speak in
the church.[b] 1Ti 2:11-12

36Or did the word of God origi-
nate with you? Or are you the only
people it has reached? 37If anyone
thinks they are a prophet or otherwise gifted by the Spirit, let them
acknowledge that what I am writing to you is the Lord's command.
38But if anyone ignores this, they
will themselves be ignored.[c]

2Co 10:7; 1Jn 4:6

39Therefore, my brothers and
sisters, be eager to prophesy, and
do not forbid speaking in tongues.
40But everything should be done
in a fitting and orderly way.

1Co 12:31

The Resurrection of Christ

15 Now, brothers and sisters, I
want to remind you of the
gospel I preached to you, which
you received and on which you
have taken your stand. 2By this
gospel you are saved, if you hold
firmly to the word I preached to
you. Otherwise, you have believed
in vain. Ro 1:16; 11:22

3For what I received I passed on
to you as of first importance[d]: that
Christ died for our sins according to the Scriptures, 4that he was
buried, that he was raised on the
third day according to the Scriptures, 5and that he appeared to
Cephas,[e] and then to the Twelve.
6After that, he appeared to more
than five hundred of the brothers
and sisters at the same time, most
of whom are still living, though
some have fallen asleep. 7Then
he appeared to James, then to all
the apostles, 8and last of all he appeared to me also, as to one ab-
normally born. Ac 1:3-4; 9:3-6,17

9For I am the least of the apostles and do not even deserve to be
called an apostle, because I persecuted the church of God. 10But by
the grace of God I am what I am,
and his grace to me was not without effect. No, I worked harder
than all of them — yet not I, but
the grace of God that was with me.
11Whether, then, it is I or they, this
is what we preach, and this is what
you believed. 2Co 11:23; Php 2:13

[a] 33,34 Or *peace. As in all the congregations of the Lord's people, 34women* [b] 34,35 In a few manuscripts these verses come after verse 40.
[c] 38 Some manuscripts *But anyone who is ignorant of this will be ignorant* [d] 3 Or *you at the first* [e] 5 That is, Peter

The Resurrection of the Dead

12 But if it is preached that Christ
has been raised from the dead,
how can some of you say that
there is no resurrection of the
dead? 13 If there is no resurrection
of the dead, then not even Christ
has been raised. 14 And if Christ has
not been raised, our preaching is
useless and so is your faith. 15 More
than that, we are then found to be
false witnesses about God, for we
have testified about God that he
raised Christ from the dead. But
he did not raise him if in fact the
dead are not raised. 16 For if the
dead are not raised, then Christ
has not been raised either. 17 And
if Christ has not been raised, your
faith is futile; you are still in your
sins. 18 Then those also who have
fallen asleep in Christ are lost. 19 If
only for this life we have hope in
Christ, we are of all people most to
be pitied. Ac 2:24; Ro 4:25

20 But Christ has indeed been
raised from the dead, the firstfruits
of those who have fallen asleep.
21 For since death came through a
man, the resurrection of the dead
comes also through a man. 22 For
as in Adam all die, so in Christ all
will be made alive. 23 But each in
turn: Christ, the firstfruits; then,
when he comes, those who belong
to him. 24 Then the end will come,
when he hands over the kingdom
to God the Father after he has destroyed all dominion, authority
and power. 25 For he must reign until he has put all his enemies under
his feet. 26 The last enemy to be destroyed is death. 27 For he "has put
everything under his feet."[a] Now
when it says that "everything" has
been put under him, it is clear that
this does not include God himself,
who put everything under Christ.
28 When he has done this, then the
Son himself will be made subject
to him who put everything under
him, so that God may be all in all.

1Co 3:23; Php 3:21

29 Now if there is no resurrection, what will those do who are
baptized for the dead? If the dead
are not raised at all, why are people baptized for them? 30 And as for
us, why do we endanger ourselves
every hour? 31 I face death every
day—yes, just as surely as I boast
about you in Christ Jesus our Lord.
32 If I fought wild beasts in Ephesus
with no more than human hopes,
what have I gained? If the dead
are not raised, 2Co 1:8; 11:26

"Let us eat and drink,
 for tomorrow we die."[b]

33 Do not be misled: "Bad company
corrupts good character."[c] 34 Come
back to your senses as you ought,
and stop sinning; for there are
some who are ignorant of God—I
say this to your shame.

Isa 22:13; Lk 12:19

The Resurrection Body

35 But someone will ask, "How are
the dead raised? With what kind of

[a] 27 Psalm 8:6 [b] 32 Isaiah 22:13
[c] 33 From the Greek poet Menander

body will they come?" 36How foolish! What you sow does not come
to life unless it dies. 37When you
sow, you do not plant the body that
will be, but just a seed, perhaps of
wheat or of something else. 38But
God gives it a body as he has determined, and to each kind of seed he
gives its own body. 39Not all flesh
is the same: People have one kind
of flesh, animals have another,
birds another and fish another.
40There are also heavenly bodies
and there are earthly bodies; but
the splendor of the heavenly bodies is one kind, and the splendor of
the earthly bodies is another. 41The
sun has one kind of splendor, the
moon another and the stars another; and star differs from star in
splendor. Eze 37:3; Jn 12:24

42So will it be with the resurrection of the dead. The body that is
sown is perishable, it is raised imperishable; 43it is sown in dishon-
or, it is raised in glory; it is sown in
weakness, it is raised in power; 44it
is sown a natural body, it is raised
a spiritual body. Mt 13:43; Php 3:21

If there is a natural body, there is
also a spiritual body. 45So it is written: "The first man Adam became
a living being"[a]; the last Adam, a
life-giving spirit. 46The spiritual
did not come first, but the natural, and after that the spiritual.
47The first man was of the dust of
the earth; the second man is of
heaven. 48As was the earthly man,
so are those who are of the earth;
and as is the heavenly man, so
also are those who are of heaven.
49And just as we have borne the
image of the earthly man, so shall
we[b] bear the image of the heavenly man. Ge 5:3; Ro 8:29

50I declare to you, brothers and
sisters, that flesh and blood cannot inherit the kingdom of God,
nor does the perishable inherit the
imperishable. 51Listen, I tell you a
mystery: We will not all sleep, but
we will all be changed— 52in a
flash, in the twinkling of an eye,
at the last trumpet. For the trumpet will sound, the dead will be
raised imperishable, and we will
be changed. 53For the perishable
must clothe itself with the imperishable, and the mortal with immortality. 54When the perishable
has been clothed with the imperishable, and the mortal with immortality, then the saying that is
written will come true: "Death has
been swallowed up in victory."[c]
Mt 24:31; 2Co 5:2,4

55"Where, O death, is your
victory?
Where, O death, is your
sting?"[d]

56The sting of death is sin, and
the power of sin is the law. 57But
thanks be to God! He gives us the
victory through our Lord Jesus
Christ. Hos 13:14; Ro 4:15; 8:37

58Therefore, my dear brothers
and sisters, stand firm. Let nothing

[a] 45 Gen. 2:7 [b] 49 Some early manuscripts *so let us* [c] 54 Isaiah 25:8 [d] 55 Hosea 13:14

move you. Always give yourselves
fully to the work of the Lord, because you know that your labor in
the Lord is not in vain. 1Co 16:10

The Collection for the Lord's People

16 Now about the collection for
the Lord's people: Do what I
told the Galatian churches to do.
2On the first day of every week,
each one of you should set aside
a sum of money in keeping with
your income, saving it up, so that
when I come no collections will
have to be made. 3Then, when I
arrive, I will give letters of intro-
duction to the men you approve
and send them with your gift to
Jerusalem. 4If it seems advisable
for me to go also, they will accompany me. Ac 20:7; 24:17

Personal Requests

5After I go through Macedonia, I
will come to you — for I will be going through Macedonia. 6Perhaps
I will stay with you for a while, or
even spend the winter, so that you
can help me on my journey, wherever I go. 7For I do not want to see
you now and make only a passing
visit; I hope to spend some time
with you, if the Lord permits. 8But
I will stay on at Ephesus until
Pentecost, 9because a great door
for effective work has opened to
me, and there are many who oppose me. Ac 18:21; 1Co 4:19
10When Timothy comes, see to it
that he has nothing to fear while
he is with you, for he is carrying on
the work of the Lord, just as I am.
11No one, then, should treat him
with contempt. Send him on his
way in peace so that he may return
to me. I am expecting him along
with the brothers. 1Co 15:58; 1Ti 4:12
12Now about our brother Apollos: I strongly urged him to go
to you with the brothers. He was
quite unwilling to go now, but he
will go when he has the opportunity. Ac 18:24; 1Co 1:12
13Be on your guard; stand firm
in the faith; be courageous; be
strong. 14Do everything in love.
1Co 14:1; Php 1:27
15You know that the household
of Stephanas were the first converts in Achaia, and they have devoted themselves to the service
of the Lord's people. I urge you,
brothers and sisters, 16to submit
to such people and to everyone
who joins in the work and labors
at it. 17I was glad when Stephanas,
Fortunatus and Achaicus arrived,
because they have supplied what
was lacking from you. 18For they
refreshed my spirit and yours also.
Such men deserve recognition.
2Co 11:9; Php 2:29

Final Greetings

19The churches in the province
of Asia send you greetings. Aquila
and Priscilla[a] greet you warmly in
the Lord, and so does the church
that meets at their house. 20All the
brothers and sisters here send you

[a] *19* Greek *Prisca,* a variant of *Priscilla*

greetings. Greet one another with
a holy kiss. Ro 16:5,16
21I, Paul, write this greeting in
my own hand. Gal 6:11; Col 4:18
22If anyone does not love the
Lord, let that person be cursed!
Come, Lord[a]! Ro 9:3; Eph 6:24
23The grace of the Lord Jesus be
with you. Ro 16:20
24My love to all of you in Christ
Jesus. Amen.[b]

[a] 22 The Greek for *Come, Lord* reproduces an Aramaic expression (*Marana tha*) used by early Christians. [b] 24 Some manuscripts do not have *Amen*.

2 CORINTHIANS

1 Paul, an apostle of Christ Jesus
by the will of God, and Timothy
our brother, Col 1:1; 2Ti 1:1

To the church of God in Corinth,
together with all his holy people
throughout Achaia: Ac 18:12; 1Co 10:32

2 Grace and peace to you from
God our Father and the Lord Jesus
Christ. Ro 1:7

Praise to the God of All Comfort

3 Praise be to the God and Father
of our Lord Jesus Christ, the Father
of compassion and the God of all
comfort, 4 who comforts us in all
our troubles, so that we can comfort those in any trouble with the
comfort we ourselves receive from
God. 5 For just as we share abundantly in the sufferings of Christ,
so also our comfort abounds
through Christ. 6 If we are distressed, it is for your comfort and
salvation; if we are comforted, it
is for your comfort, which produces in you patient endurance of the
same sufferings we suffer. 7 And
our hope for you is firm, because
we know that just as you share in
our sufferings, so also you share in
our comfort. 2Co 4:10,15; Eph 1:3

8 We do not want you to be uninformed, brothers and sisters,[a]
about the troubles we experienced
in the province of Asia. We were
under great pressure, far beyond
our ability to endure, so that we
despaired of life itself. 9 Indeed,
we felt we had received the sentence of death. But this happened
that we might not rely on ourselves but on God, who raises the
dead. 10 He has delivered us from
such a deadly peril, and he will
deliver us again. On him we have
set our hope that he will continue to deliver us, 11 as you help us by
your prayers. Then many will give
thanks on our behalf for the gracious favor granted us in answer
to the prayers of many.
Ro 15:30; 2Co 4:15

Paul's Change of Plans

12 Now this is our boast: Our conscience testifies that we have con-
ducted ourselves in the world, and
especially in our relations with
you, with integrity[b] and godly
sincerity. We have done so, rely-
ing not on worldly wisdom but on
God's grace. 13 For we do not write
you anything you cannot read or
understand. And I hope that, 14 as
you have understood us in part,
you will come to understand fully
that you can boast of us just as we

[a] 8 The Greek word for *brothers and sisters* (*adelphoi*) refers here to believers, both men and women, as part of God's family; also in 8:1; 13:11. [b] 12 Many manuscripts *holiness*

will boast of you in the day of the
Lord Jesus. 1Co 1:8; 2:1,4,13
15Because I was confident of this,
I wanted to visit you first so that
you might benefit twice. 16I wanted to visit you on my way to Macedonia and to come back to you
from Macedonia, and then to have
you send me on my way to Judea.
17Was I fickle when I intended to
do this? Or do I make my plans in
a worldly manner so that in the
same breath I say both "Yes, yes"
and "No, no"? 1Co 16:5-7; 2Co 10:2-3
18But as surely as God is faithful,
our message to you is not "Yes"
and "No." 19For the Son of God,
Jesus Christ, who was preached
among you by us — by me and Silas[a] and Timothy — was not "Yes"
and "No," but in him it has always
been "Yes." 20For no matter how
many promises God has made,
they are "Yes" in Christ. And so
through him the "Amen" is spoken
by us to the glory of God. 21Now it
is God who makes both us and you
stand firm in Christ. He anointed
us, 22set his seal of ownership on
us, and put his Spirit in our hearts
as a deposit, guaranteeing what is
to come. 2Co 5:5; 1Jn 2:20,27
23I call God as my witness — and
I stake my life on it — that it was
in order to spare you that I did not
return to Corinth. 24Not that we
lord it over your faith, but we work
with you for your joy, because it is
2 by faith you stand firm. 1So I
made up my mind that I would
not make another painful visit to
you. 2For if I grieve you, who is left
to make me glad but you whom I
have grieved? 3I wrote as I did, so
that when I came I would not be
distressed by those who should
have made me rejoice. I had confidence in all of you, that you would
all share my joy. 4For I wrote you
out of great distress and anguish
of heart and with many tears, not
to grieve you but to let you know
the depth of my love for you.
2Co 7:8,12; 12:21

Forgiveness for the Offender

5If anyone has caused grief, he
has not so much grieved me as he
has grieved all of you to some extent — not to put it too severely.
6The punishment inflicted on him
by the majority is sufficient. 7Now
instead, you ought to forgive and
comfort him, so that he will not be
overwhelmed by excessive sorrow.
8I urge you, therefore, to reaffirm
your love for him. 9Another reason I wrote you was to see if you
would stand the test and be obedient in everything. 10Anyone you
forgive, I also forgive. And what I
have forgiven — if there was anything to forgive — I have forgiven
in the sight of Christ for your sake,
11in order that Satan might not
outwit us. For we are not unaware
of his schemes. 2Co 10:6; Gal 6:1

Ministers of the New Covenant

12Now when I went to Troas to
preach the gospel of Christ and

a 19 Greek *Silvanus*, a variant of *Silas*

found that the Lord had opened a door for me, 13I still had no peace of mind, because I did not find my brother Titus there. So I said goodbye to them and went on to Macedonia. Ac 16:8; 2Co 7:5-6,13

14But thanks be to God, who always leads us as captives in Christ's triumphal procession and uses us to spread the aroma of the knowledge of him everywhere. 15For we are to God the pleasing aroma of Christ among those who are being saved and those who are perishing. 16To the one we are an aroma that brings death; to the other, an aroma that brings life. And who is equal to such a task? 17Unlike so many, we do not peddle the word of God for profit. On the contrary, in Christ we speak before God with sincerity, as those sent from God. Lk 2:34; 2Co 1:12

3 Are we beginning to commend ourselves again? Or do we need, like some people, letters of recommendation to you or from you? 2You yourselves are our letter, written on our hearts, known and read by everyone. 3You show that you are a letter from Christ, the result of our ministry, written not with ink but with the Spirit of the living God, not on tablets of stone but on tablets of human hearts. Jer 31:33; Eze 11:19

4Such confidence we have through Christ before God. 5Not that we are competent in ourselves to claim anything for ourselves, but our competence comes from God. 6He has made us competent as ministers of a new covenant — not of the letter but of the Spirit; for the letter kills, but the Spirit gives life. Jn 6:63; 1Co 15:10

The Greater Glory of the New Covenant

7Now if the ministry that brought death, which was engraved in letters on stone, came with glory, so that the Israelites could not look steadily at the face of Moses because of its glory, transitory though it was, 8will not the ministry of the Spirit be even more glorious? 9If the ministry that brought condemnation was glorious, how much more glorious is the ministry that brings righteousness! 10For what was glorious has no glory now in comparison with the surpassing glory. 11And if what was transitory came with glory, how much greater is the glory of that which lasts! Ex 34:29-35; Ro 1:17

12Therefore, since we have such a hope, we are very bold. 13We are not like Moses, who would put a veil over his face to prevent the Israelites from seeing the end of what was passing away. 14But their minds were made dull, for to this day the same veil remains when the old covenant is read. It has not been removed, because only in Christ is it taken away. 15Even to this day when Moses is read, a veil covers their hearts. 16But whenever anyone turns to the Lord, the

veil is taken away. 17Now the Lord
is the Spirit, and where the Spirit of the Lord is, there is freedom.
18And we all, who with unveiled
faces contemplate[a] the Lord's glory, are being transformed into his
image with ever-increasing glory,
which comes from the Lord, who
is the Spirit. Ro 8:29; 1Co 13:12

Present Weakness and Resurrection Life

4 Therefore, since through
God's mercy we have this ministry, we do not lose heart. 2Rath-
er, we have renounced secret and
shameful ways; we do not use
deception, nor do we distort the
word of God. On the contrary, by
setting forth the truth plainly we
commend ourselves to everyone's
conscience in the sight of God.
3And even if our gospel is veiled,
it is veiled to those who are perishing. 4The god of this age has
blinded the minds of unbelievers, so that they cannot see the
light of the gospel that displays
the glory of Christ, who is the image of God. 5For what we preach
is not ourselves, but Jesus Christ
as Lord, and ourselves as your
servants for Jesus' sake. 6For God,
who said, "Let light shine out of
darkness,"[b] made his light shine
in our hearts to give us the light
of the knowledge of God's glory
displayed in the face of Christ.
Ge 1:3; 2Pe 1:19

7But we have this treasure in
jars of clay to show that this all-
surpassing power is from God and
not from us. 8We are hard pressed
on every side, but not crushed;
perplexed, but not in despair;
9persecuted, but not abandoned;
struck down, but not destroyed.
10We always carry around in our
body the death of Jesus, so that
the life of Jesus may also be revealed in our body. 11For we who
are alive are always being given
over to death for Jesus' sake, so
that his life may also be revealed
in our mortal body. 12So then,
death is at work in us, but life is
at work in you.
1Co 2:5; 2Co 7:5; Heb 13:5

13It is written: "I believed; therefore I have spoken."[c] Since we
have that same spirit of[d] faith, we
also believe and therefore speak,
14because we know that the one
who raised the Lord Jesus from
the dead will also raise us with
Jesus and present us with you
to himself. 15All this is for your
benefit, so that the grace that is
reaching more and more people
may cause thanksgiving to overflow to the glory of God.
2Co 1:11; Eph 5:27

16Therefore we do not lose heart.
Though outwardly we are wasting away, yet inwardly we are being renewed day by day. 17For our
light and momentary troubles are
achieving for us an eternal glory that far outweighs them all.

[a] 18 Or *reflect* [b] 6 Gen. 1:3
[c] 13 Psalm 116:10 (see Septuagint) [d] 13 Or
Spirit-given

18So we fix our eyes not on what is
seen, but on what is unseen, since
what is seen is temporary, but
what is unseen is eternal.

Ro 8:24; Heb 11:1

Awaiting the New Body

5 For we know that if the earthly tent we live in is destroyed,
we have a building from God,
an eternal house in heaven, not
built by human hands. 2Mean-
while we groan, longing to be
clothed instead with our heavenly dwelling, 3because when we
are clothed, we will not be found
naked. 4For while we are in this
tent, we groan and are burdened,
because we do not wish to be un-
clothed but to be clothed instead
with our heavenly dwelling, so
that what is mortal may be swallowed up by life. 5Now the one
who has fashioned us for this
very purpose is God, who has giv-
en us the Spirit as a deposit, guaranteeing what is to come.

Ro 8:23; 1Co 15:53-54

6Therefore we are always confident and know that as long as
we are at home in the body we
are away from the Lord. 7For we
live by faith, not by sight. 8We are
confident, I say, and would prefer
to be away from the body and at
home with the Lord. 9So we make
it our goal to please him, whether we are at home in the body or
away from it. 10For we must all appear before the judgment seat of
Christ, so that each of us may receive what is due us for the things
done while in the body, whether
good or bad.

Ro 14:10; Eph 6:8

The Ministry of Reconciliation

11Since, then, we know what it
is to fear the Lord, we try to persuade others. What we are is plain
to God, and I hope it is also plain
to your conscience. 12We are not
trying to commend ourselves to
you again, but are giving you an
opportunity to take pride in us,
so that you can answer those who
take pride in what is seen rather
than in what is in the heart. 13If we
are "out of our mind," as some say,
it is for God; if we are in our right
mind, it is for you. 14For Christ's
love compels us, because we are
convinced that one died for all,
and therefore all died. 15And he
died for all, that those who live
should no longer live for themselves but for him who died for
them and was raised again.

Ro 14:7-9; Gal 2:20

16So from now on we regard no
one from a worldly point of view.
Though we once regarded Christ
in this way, we do so no longer.
17Therefore, if anyone is in Christ,
the new creation has come:[a] The
old has gone, the new is here! 18All
this is from God, who reconciled
us to himself through Christ and
gave us the ministry of reconciliation: 19that God was reconciling
the world to himself in Christ, not
counting people's sins against

[a] 17 Or *Christ, that person is a new creation.*

them. And he has committed to
us the message of reconciliation.
[20]We are therefore Christ's ambassadors, as though God were making his appeal through us. We im-
plore you on Christ's behalf: Be
reconciled to God. [21]God made him
who had no sin to be sin[a] for us, so
that in him we might become the
righteousness of God.

1Pe 2:22,24; 1Jn 3:5

6 As God's co-workers we urge
you not to receive God's grace
in vain. [2]For he says, 1Co 3:9; 2Co 5:20

> "In the time of my favor I
> heard you,
> and in the day of salvation I
> helped you."[b]

I tell you, now is the time of God's
favor, now is the day of salvation.

Ps 69:13; Isa 55:6

Paul's Hardships

[3]We put no stumbling block
in anyone's path, so that our
ministry will not be discredit-
ed. [4]Rather, as servants of God
we commend ourselves in every way: in great endurance; in
troubles, hardships and distress-
es; [5]in beatings, imprisonments
and riots; in hard work, sleepless
nights and hunger; [6]in purity, understanding, patience and kindness; in the Holy Spirit and in sincere love; [7]in truthful speech and
in the power of God; with weapons of righteousness in the right
hand and in the left; [8]through
glory and dishonor, bad report
and good report; genuine, yet
regarded as impostors; [9]known,
yet regarded as unknown; dying,
and yet we live on; beaten, and
yet not killed; [10]sorrowful, yet always rejoicing; poor, yet making
many rich; having nothing, and
yet possessing everything.

Ro 8:32; 2Co 1:8-10

[11]We have spoken freely to you,
Corinthians, and opened wide our
hearts to you. [12]We are not withholding our affection from you,
but you are withholding yours
from us. [13]As a fair exchange — I
speak as to my children — open
wide your hearts also.

1Co 4:14; 2Co 7:3

Warning Against Idolatry

[14]Do not be yoked together with
unbelievers. For what do righteousness and wickedness have in
common? Or what fellowship can
light have with darkness? [15]What
harmony is there between Christ
and Belial[c]? Or what does a believer have in common with an unbeliever? [16]What agreement is there
between the temple of God and
idols? For we are the temple of the
living God. As God has said:

> "I will live with them
> and walk among them,
> and I will be their God,
> and they will be my people."[d]

1Co 3:16; 5:9-10

[a] 21 Or *be a sin offering* [b] 2 Isaiah 49:8
[c] 15 Greek *Beliar*, a variant of *Belial*
[d] 16 Lev. 26:12; Jer. 32:38; Ezek. 37:27

17 Therefore,

"Come out from them Rev 18:4
and be separate,
says the Lord.
Touch no unclean thing,
and I will receive you."[a]

18 And,

"I will be a Father to you,
and you will be my sons and
daughters,
says the Lord
Almighty."[b]

7 Therefore, since we have these
promises, dear friends, let us
purify ourselves from everything
that contaminates body and spirit, perfecting holiness out of reverence for God. 2Co 6:17-18

Paul's Joy Over the Church's Repentance

2 Make room for us in your
hearts. We have wronged no one,
we have corrupted no one, we
have exploited no one. 3 I do not
say this to condemn you; I have
said before that you have such a
place in our hearts that we would
live or die with you. 4 I have spoken to you with great frankness; I
take great pride in you. I am greatly encouraged; in all our troubles
my joy knows no bounds.
2Co 6:10-13

5 For when we came into Macedonia, we had no rest, but we were
harassed at every turn — conflicts
on the outside, fears within. 6 But
God, who comforts the downcast,
comforted us by the coming of Titus, 7 and not only by his coming
but also by the comfort you had
given him. He told us about your
longing for me, your deep sorrow,
your ardent concern for me, so
that my joy was greater than ever.
2Co 2:13; 4:8

8 Even if I caused you sorrow
by my letter, I do not regret it.
Though I did regret it — I see that
my letter hurt you, but only for a
little while — 9 yet now I am happy, not because you were made
sorry, but because your sorrow
led you to repentance. For you
became sorrowful as God intended and so were not harmed in any
way by us. 10 Godly sorrow brings
repentance that leads to salvation
and leaves no regret, but worldly
sorrow brings death. 11 See what
this godly sorrow has produced
in you: what earnestness, what
eagerness to clear yourselves,
what indignation, what alarm,
what longing, what concern, what
readiness to see justice done.
At every point you have proved
yourselves to be innocent in this
matter. 12 So even though I wrote
to you, it was neither on account
of the one who did the wrong nor
on account of the injured party,
but rather that before God you
could see for yourselves how devoted to us you are. 13 By all this
we are encouraged.
1Co 5:1-2; 2Co 2:2,4

[a] 17 Isaiah 52:11; Ezek. 20:34,41
[b] 18 2 Samuel 7:14; 7:8

In addition to our own encouragement, we were especially delighted to see how happy Titus was, because his spirit has been refreshed by all of you. 14 I had boasted to him about you, and you have not embarrassed me. But just as everything we said to you was true, so our boasting about you to Titus has proved to be true as well. 15 And his affection for you is all the greater when he remembers that you were all obedient, receiving him with fear and trembling. 16 I am glad I can have complete confidence in you.

2Co 2:9; Php 2:12

The Collection for the Lord's People

8 And now, brothers and sisters, we want you to know about the grace that God has given the Macedonian churches. 2 In the midst of a very severe trial, their overflowing joy and their extreme poverty welled up in rich generosity. 3 For I testify that they gave as much as they were able, and even beyond their ability. Entirely on their own, 4 they urgently pleaded with us for the privilege of sharing in this service to the Lord's people. 5 And they exceeded our expectations: They gave themselves first of all to the Lord, and then by the will of God also to us. 6 So we urged Titus, just as he had earlier made a beginning, to bring also to completion this act of grace on your part. 7 But since you excel in everything — in faith, in speech, in knowledge, in complete earnestness and in the love we have kindled in you[a] — see that you also excel in this grace of giving.

1Co 1:5; 2Co 9:8

8 I am not commanding you, but I want to test the sincerity of your love by comparing it with the earnestness of others. 9 For you know the grace of our Lord Jesus Christ, that though he was rich, yet for your sake he became poor, so that you through his poverty might become rich.

1Co 7:6; Php 2:6-8

10 And here is my judgment about what is best for you in this matter. Last year you were the first not only to give but also to have the desire to do so. 11 Now finish the work, so that your eager willingness to do it may be matched by your completion of it, according to your means. 12 For if the willingness is there, the gift is acceptable according to what one has, not according to what one does not have.

Mk 12:43-44; Lk 21:3; 1Co 7:25,40

13 Our desire is not that others might be relieved while you are hard pressed, but that there might be equality. 14 At the present time your plenty will supply what they need, so that in turn their plenty will supply what you need. The goal is equality, 15 as it is written: "The one who gathered much did

[a] 7 Some manuscripts *and in your love for us*

not have too much, and the one who gathered little did not have too little."[a] Ex 16:18; 2Co 9:12

Titus Sent to Receive the Collection

16 Thanks be to God, who put into the heart of Titus the same concern I have for you. 17 For Titus not only welcomed our appeal, but he is coming to you with much enthusiasm and on his own initiative. 18 And we are sending along with him the brother who is praised by all the churches for his service to the gospel. 19 What is more, he was chosen by the churches to accompany us as we carry the offering, which we administer in order to honor the Lord himself and to show our eagerness to help. 20 We want to avoid any criticism of the way we administer this liberal gift. 21 For we are taking pains to do what is right, not only in the eyes of the Lord but also in the eyes of man. Ro 12:17; 14:18; 1Co 16:3-4

22 In addition, we are sending with them our brother who has often proved to us in many ways that he is zealous, and now even more so because of his great confidence in you. 23 As for Titus, he is my partner and co-worker among you; as for our brothers, they are representatives of the churches and an honor to Christ. 24 Therefore show these men the proof of your love and the reason for our pride in you, so that the churches can see it. 2Co 9:2; Php 2:25

9 There is no need for me to write to you about this service to the Lord's people. 2 For I know your eagerness to help, and I have been boasting about it to the Macedonians, telling them that since last year you in Achaia were ready to give; and your enthusiasm has stirred most of them to action. 3 But I am sending the brothers in order that our boasting about you in this matter should not prove hollow, but that you may be ready, as I said you would be. 4 For if any Macedonians come with me and find you unprepared, we — not to say anything about you — would be ashamed of having been so confident. 5 So I thought it necessary to urge the brothers to visit you in advance and finish the arrangements for the generous gift you had promised. Then it will be ready as a generous gift, not as one grudgingly given. Php 4:17; 2Co 12:17-18

Generosity Encouraged

6 Remember this: Whoever sows sparingly will also reap sparingly, and whoever sows generously will also reap generously. 7 Each of you should give what you have decided in your heart to give, not reluctantly or under compulsion, for God loves a cheerful giver. 8 And God is able to bless you abundantly, so that in all things at all times, having all that you

[a] 15 Exodus 16:18

need, you will abound in every
good work. [9]As it is written:

Eph 3:20; Php 4:19

"They have freely scattered
their gifts to the poor;
Mal 3:10
their righteousness endures
forever."[a]

[10]Now he who supplies seed to the
sower and bread for food will also
supply and increase your store of
seed and will enlarge the harvest
of your righteousness. [11]You will
be enriched in every way so that
you can be generous on every occasion,
and through us your generosity
will result in thanksgiving
to God. Ps 112:9; Isa 55:10; Hos 10:12

[12]This service that you perform
is not only supplying the needs of
the Lord's people but is also overflowing
in many expressions of
thanks to God. [13]Because of the
service by which you have proved
yourselves, others will praise God
for the obedience that accompanies
your confession of the gospel
of Christ, and for your generosity
in sharing with them and with everyone
else. [14]And in their prayers
for you their hearts will go out to
you, because of the surpassing
grace God has given you. [15]Thanks
be to God for his indescribable
gift! Mt 9:8; Ro 5:15-16; 2Co 2:12

Paul's Defense of His Ministry

10 By the humility and gentleness
of Christ, I appeal
to you — I, Paul, who am "timid"
when face to face with you, but
"bold" toward you when away! [2]I
beg you that when I come I may
not have to be as bold as I expect
to be toward some people who
think that we live by the standards
of this world. [3]For though we live
in the world, we do not wage war
as the world does. [4]The weapons
we fight with are not the weapons
of the world. On the contrary, they
have divine power to demolish
strongholds. [5]We demolish arguments
and every pretension that
sets itself up against the knowledge
of God, and we take captive
every thought to make it obedient
to Christ. [6]And we will be ready to
punish every act of disobedience,
once your obedience is complete.

Jer 1:10; 2Co 2:9

[7]You are judging by appearances.[b]
If anyone is confident that
they belong to Christ, they should
consider again that we belong to
Christ just as much as they do. [8]So
even if I boast somewhat freely
about the authority the Lord gave
us for building you up rather than
tearing you down, I will not be
ashamed of it. [9]I do not want to
seem to be trying to frighten you
with my letters. [10]For some say,
"His letters are weighty and forceful,
but in person he is unimpressive
and his speaking amounts
to nothing." [11]Such people should
realize that what we are in our
letters when we are absent, we

[a] 9 Psalm 112:9 [b] 7 Or *Look at the obvious facts*

will be in our actions when we are
present. 1Co 1:17; 2:3

12We do not dare to classify or
compare ourselves with some who
commend themselves. When they
measure themselves by themselves and compare themselves
with themselves, they are not
wise. 13We, however, will not boast
beyond proper limits, but will confine our boasting to the sphere of
service God himself has assigned
to us, a sphere that also includes
you. 14We are not going too far
in our boasting, as would be the
case if we had not come to you,
for we did get as far as you with
the gospel of Christ. 15Neither do
we go beyond our limits by boasting of work done by others. Our
hope is that, as your faith continues to grow, our sphere of activity among you will greatly expand,
16so that we can preach the gospel
in the regions beyond you. For we
do not want to boast about work
already done in someone else's
territory. 17But, "Let the one who
boasts boast in the Lord."[a] 18For
it is not the one who commends
himself who is approved, but the
one whom the Lord commends.

Ro 2:29; 1Co 4:5

Paul and the False Apostles

11 I hope you will put up with
me in a little foolishness. Yes,
please put up with me! 2I am jealous for you with a godly jealousy.
I promised you to one husband,
to Christ, so that I might present
you as a pure virgin to him. 3But I
am afraid that just as Eve was deceived by the serpent's cunning,
your minds may somehow be led
astray from your sincere and pure
devotion to Christ. 4For if someone
comes to you and preaches a Jesus
other than the Jesus we preached,
or if you receive a different spirit
from the Spirit you received, or a
different gospel from the one you
accepted, you put up with it easily
enough.

5I do not think I am in the least
inferior to those "super-apostles."[b]
6I may indeed be untrained as a
speaker, but I do have knowledge.
We have made this perfectly clear
to you in every way. 7Was it a sin
for me to lower myself in order to
elevate you by preaching the gospel of God to you free of charge? 8I
robbed other churches by receiving support from them so as to
serve you. 9And when I was with
you and needed something, I was
not a burden to anyone, for the
brothers who came from Macedonia supplied what I needed. I have
kept myself from being a burden
to you in any way, and will continue to do so. 10As surely as the
truth of Christ is in me, nobody in
the regions of Achaia will stop this
boasting of mine. 11Why? Because I
do not love you? God knows I do!

1Co 1:17; Eph 3:4

12And I will keep on doing what
I am doing in order to cut the

[a] 17 Jer. 9:24 [b] 5 Or *to the most eminent apostles*

ground from under those who want an opportunity to be considered equal with us in the things they boast about. 13For such people are false apostles, deceitful workers, masquerading as apostles of Christ. 14And no wonder, for Satan himself masquerades as an angel of light. 15It is not surprising, then, if his servants also masquerade as servants of righteousness. Their end will be what their actions deserve. Php 3:19; Rev 2:2

Paul Boasts About His Sufferings

16I repeat: Let no one take me for a fool. But if you do, then tolerate me just as you would a fool, so that I may do a little boasting. 17In this self-confident boasting I am not talking as the Lord would, but as a fool. 18Since many are boasting in the way the world does, I too will boast. 19You gladly put up with fools since you are so wise! 20In fact, you even put up with anyone who enslaves you or exploits you or takes advantage of you or puts on airs or slaps you in the face. 21To my shame I admit that we were too weak for that!

1Co 4:10; Php 3:3-4

Whatever anyone else dares to boast about — I am speaking as a fool — I also dare to boast about. 22Are they Hebrews? So am I. Are they Israelites? So am I. Are they Abraham's descendants? So am I. 23Are they servants of Christ? (I am out of my mind to talk like this.) I am more. I have worked much harder, been in prison more frequently, been flogged more severely, and been exposed to death again and again. 24Five times I received from the Jews the forty lashes minus one. 25Three times I was beaten with rods, once I was pelted with stones, three times I was shipwrecked, I spent a night and a day in the open sea, 26I have been constantly on the move. I have been in danger from rivers, in danger from bandits, in danger from my fellow Jews, in danger from Gentiles; in danger in the city, in danger in the country, in danger at sea; and in danger from false believers. 27I have labored and toiled and have often gone without sleep; I have known hunger and thirst and have often gone without food; I have been cold and naked. 28Besides everything else, I face daily the pressure of my concern for all the churches. 29Who is weak, and I do not feel weak? Who is led into sin, and I do not inwardly burn?

Ro 9:4; 1Co 15:10

30If I must boast, I will boast of the things that show my weakness. 31The God and Father of the Lord Jesus, who is to be praised forever, knows that I am not lying. 32In Damascus the governor under King Aretas had the city of the Damascenes guarded in order to arrest me. 33But I was lowered in a basket from a window in the wall and slipped through his hands.

Ac 9:24-25; 1Co 2:3

Paul's Vision and His Thorn

12 I must go on boasting. Although there is nothing to
be gained, I will go on to visions
and revelations from the Lord. 2I
know a man in Christ who fourteen years ago was caught up to
the third heaven. Whether it was
in the body or out of the body I
do not know — God knows. 3And I
know that this man — whether in
the body or apart from the body
I do not know, but God knows —
4was caught up to paradise and
heard inexpressible things, things
that no one is permitted to tell. 5I
will boast about a man like that,
but I will not boast about myself, except about my weaknesses.
6Even if I should choose to boast,
I would not be a fool, because
I would be speaking the truth.
But I refrain, so no one will think
more of me than is warranted by
what I do or say, 7or because of
these surpassingly great revelations. Therefore, in order to keep
me from becoming conceited, I
was given a thorn in my flesh, a
messenger of Satan, to torment
me. 8Three times I pleaded with
the Lord to take it away from me.
9But he said to me, "My grace is
sufficient for you, for my power is
made perfect in weakness." Therefore I will boast all the more gladly about my weaknesses, so that
Christ's power may rest on me.
10That is why, for Christ's sake, I
delight in weaknesses, in insults,
in hardships, in persecutions, in
difficulties. For when I am weak,
then I am strong. 2Co 13:4; 2Th 1:4

Paul's Concern for the Corinthians

11I have made a fool of myself,
but you drove me to it. I ought to
have been commended by you, for
I am not in the least inferior to the
"super-apostles,"[a] even though I
am nothing. 12I persevered in dem-
onstrating among you the marks
of a true apostle, including signs,
wonders and miracles. 13How were
you inferior to the other churches,
except that I was never a burden
to you? Forgive me this wrong!
1Co 9:12,18; 2Co 11:7

14Now I am ready to visit you
for the third time, and I will not
be a burden to you, because what
I want is not your possessions but
you. After all, children should not
have to save up for their parents,
but parents for their children. 15So
I will very gladly spend for you everything I have and expend myself as well. If I love you more, will
you love me less? 16Be that as it
may, I have not been a burden to
you. Yet, crafty fellow that I am, I
caught you by trickery! 17Did I exploit you through any of the men
I sent to you? 18I urged Titus to go
to you and I sent our brother with
him. Titus did not exploit you, did
he? Did we not walk in the same
footsteps by the same Spirit?
2Co 8:18; 11:9; Php 2:17

19Have you been thinking all
along that we have been defending

[a] 11 *Or the most eminent apostles*

ourselves to you? We have been
speaking in the sight of God as
those in Christ; and everything
we do, dear friends, is for your
strengthening. 20For I am afraid
that when I come I may not find
you as I want you to be, and you
may not find me as you want me
to be. I fear that there may be discord, jealousy, fits of rage, selfish
ambition, slander, gossip, arrogance and disorder. 21I am afraid
that when I come again my God
will humble me before you, and
I will be grieved over many who
have sinned earlier and have not
repented of the impurity, sexual sin and debauchery in which
they have indulged.

1Co 14:33; 2Co 13:2

Final Warnings

13 This will be my third visit
to you. "Every matter must
be established by the testimony
of two or three witnesses."[a] 2I already gave you a warning when
I was with you the second time. I
now repeat it while absent: On my
return I will not spare those who
sinned earlier or any of the others,
3since you are demanding proof
that Christ is speaking through
me. He is not weak in dealing with
you, but is powerful among you.
4For to be sure, he was crucified
in weakness, yet he lives by God's
power. Likewise, we are weak in
him, yet by God's power we will
live with him in our dealing with
you.

Ro 1:4; Php 2:7-8; 1Pe 3:18

5Examine yourselves to see
whether you are in the faith; test
yourselves. Do you not realize that
Christ Jesus is in you — unless, of
course, you fail the test? 6And I
trust that you will discover that
we have not failed the test. 7Now
we pray to God that you will not
do anything wrong — not so that
people will see that we have stood
the test but so that you will do
what is right even though we may
seem to have failed. 8For we cannot do anything against the truth,
but only for the truth. 9We are glad
whenever we are weak but you are
strong; and our prayer is that you
may be fully restored. 10This is why
I write these things when I am absent, that when I come I may not
have to be harsh in my use of authority — the authority the Lord
gave me for building you up, not
for tearing you down.

1Co 11:28; 2Co 10:8

Final Greetings

11Finally, brothers and sisters,
rejoice! Strive for full restoration,
encourage one another, be of one
mind, live in peace. And the God
of love and peace will be with you.

Ro 15:33; Eph 6:23

12Greet one another with a holy
kiss. 13All God's people here send
their greetings. Ro 16:16; Php 4:22

14May the grace of the Lord Jesus
Christ, and the love of God, and
the fellowship of the Holy Spirit
be with you all. Ro 16:20; Php 2:1

[a] 1 Deut. 19:15

GALATIANS

1 Paul, an apostle — sent not
from men nor by a man, but by
Jesus Christ and God the Father,
who raised him from the dead —
2 and all the brothers and sisters[a]
with me, Ac 2:24; Php 4:21

To the churches in Galatia: 1Co 16:1

3 Grace and peace to you from
God our Father and the Lord Jesus
Christ, 4 who gave himself for our
sins to rescue us from the present
evil age, according to the will of
our God and Father, 5 to whom be
glory for ever and ever. Amen.
Mt 20:28; Ro 4:25; Php 4:20

No Other Gospel

6 I am astonished that you are
so quickly deserting the one who
called you to live in the grace of
Christ and are turning to a different gospel — 7 which is really no
gospel at all. Evidently some people are throwing you into confusion and are trying to pervert the
gospel of Christ. 8 But even if we
or an angel from heaven should
preach a gospel other than the
one we preached to you, let them
be under God's curse! 9 As we have
already said, so now I say again: If
anybody is preaching to you a gospel other than what you accepted,
let them be under God's curse!
Ro 9:3; 16:17

10 Am I now trying to win the
approval of human beings, or of
God? Or am I trying to please people? If I were still trying to please
people, I would not be a servant of
Christ. Ro 2:29; 1Th 2:4

Paul Called by God

11 I want you to know, brothers and sisters, that the gospel
I preached is not of human origin. 12 I did not receive it from any
man, nor was I taught it; rather,
I received it by revelation from
Jesus Christ. 1Co 11:23; 15:1
13 For you have heard of my previous way of life in Judaism, how
intensely I persecuted the church
of God and tried to destroy it. 14 I
was advancing in Judaism beyond
many of my own age among my
people and was extremely zealous for the traditions of my fathers. 15 But when God, who set me
apart from my mother's womb and
called me by his grace, was pleased
16 to reveal his Son in me so that I
might preach him among the Gentiles, my immediate response was
not to consult any human being. 17 I
did not go up to Jerusalem to see
those who were apostles before I

[a] 2 The Greek word for *brothers and sisters* (*adelphoi*) refers here to believers, both men and women, as part of God's family; also in verse 11; and in 3:15; 4:12, 28, 31; 5:11, 13; 6:1, 18.

was, but I went into Arabia. Later I
returned to Damascus. Mt 15:2; 16:17
18Then after three years, I went
up to Jerusalem to get acquainted with Cephas[a] and stayed with
him fifteen days. 19I saw none of
the other apostles — only James,
the Lord's brother. 20I assure you
before God that what I am writing
you is no lie.
21Then I went to Syria and Cilicia. 22I was personally unknown
to the churches of Judea that are
in Christ. 23They only heard the
report: "The man who formerly
persecuted us is now preaching
the faith he once tried to destroy."
24And they praised God because
of me. Ro 9:1; 1Th 2:14

Paul Accepted by the Apostles

2 Then after fourteen years, I
went up again to Jerusalem,
this time with Barnabas. I took Titus along also. 2I went in response
to a revelation and, meeting privately with those esteemed as
leaders, I presented to them the
gospel that I preach among the
Gentiles. I wanted to be sure I was
not running and had not been
running my race in vain. 3Yet not
even Titus, who was with me, was
compelled to be circumcised, even
though he was a Greek. 4This matter arose because some false believers had infiltrated our ranks
to spy on the freedom we have
in Christ Jesus and to make us
slaves. 5We did not give in to them
for a moment, so that the truth of
the gospel might be preserved for
you. Ac 15:1; 2Co 11:26
6As for those who were held in
high esteem — whatever they were
makes no difference to me; God
does not show favoritism — they
added nothing to my message.
7On the contrary, they recognized
that I had been entrusted with the
task of preaching the gospel to
the uncircumcised,[b] just as Peter
had been to the circumcised.[c] 8For
God, who was at work in Peter as
an apostle to the circumcised, was
also at work in me as an apostle to
the Gentiles. 9James, Cephas[d] and
John, those esteemed as pillars,
gave me and Barnabas the right
hand of fellowship when they recognized the grace given to me.
They agreed that we should go to
the Gentiles, and they to the circumcised. 10All they asked was that
we should continue to remember
the poor, the very thing I had been
eager to do all along. Ac 24:17; Ro 12:3

Paul Opposes Cephas

11When Cephas came to Antioch,
I opposed him to his face, because
he stood condemned. 12For before
certain men came from James,
he used to eat with the Gentiles.
But when they arrived, he began
to draw back and separate himself from the Gentiles because he
was afraid of those who belonged
to the circumcision group. 13The

[a] 18 That is, Peter [b] 7 That is, Gentiles
[c] 7 That is, Jews; also in verses 8 and 9
[d] 9 That is, Peter; also in verses 11 and 14

other Jews joined him in his hypocrisy, so that by their hypocrisy
even Barnabas was led astray.
Ac 4:36; 11:3

14 When I saw that they were not
acting in line with the truth of the
gospel, I said to Cephas in front of
them all, "You are a Jew, yet you
live like a Gentile and not like a
Jew. How is it, then, that you force
Gentiles to follow Jewish customs?
Ac 10:28

15 "We who are Jews by birth and
not sinful Gentiles 16 know that
a person is not justified by the
works of the law, but by faith in
Jesus Christ. So we, too, have put
our faith in Christ Jesus that we
may be justified by faith in[a] Christ
and not by the works of the law,
because by the works of the law no
one will be justified. Ac 13:39; Ro 9:30

17 "But if, in seeking to be justified in Christ, we Jews find ourselves also among the sinners,
doesn't that mean that Christ promotes sin? Absolutely not! 18 If I
rebuild what I destroyed, then I
really would be a lawbreaker.

19 "For through the law I died to
the law so that I might live for God.
20 I have been crucified with Christ
and I no longer live, but Christ
lives in me. The life I now live in
the body, I live by faith in the Son
of God, who loved me and gave
himself for me. 21 I do not set aside
the grace of God, for if righteousness could be gained through the
law, Christ died for nothing!"[b]
2Co 5:15; 1Pe 4:2

Faith or Works of the Law

3 You foolish Galatians! Who has
bewitched you? Before your
very eyes Jesus Christ was clearly portrayed as crucified. 2 I would
like to learn just one thing from
you: Did you receive the Spirit by
the works of the law, or by believing what you heard? 3 Are you so
foolish? After beginning by means
of the Spirit, are you now trying
to finish by means of the flesh?[c]
4 Have you experienced[d] so much
in vain — if it really was in vain?
5 So again I ask, does God give
you his Spirit and work miracles
among you by the works of the
law, or by your believing what you
heard? 6 So also Abraham "believed
God, and it was credited to him as
righteousness."[e] Ro 10:17; 1Co 12:10

7 Understand, then, that those
who have faith are children of
Abraham. 8 Scripture foresaw that
God would justify the Gentiles by
faith, and announced the gospel in
advance to Abraham: "All nations
will be blessed through you."[f]
9 So those who rely on faith are
blessed along with Abraham, the
man of faith. Ac 3:25; Ro 4:3

10 For all who rely on the works
of the law are under a curse, as it

[a] 16 Or *but through the faithfulness of . . . justified on the basis of the faithfulness of*
[b] 21 Some interpreters end the quotation after verse 14.
[c] 3 In contexts like this, the Greek word for *flesh* (*sarx*) refers to the sinful state of human beings, often presented as a power in opposition to the Spirit.
[d] 4 Or *suffered*
[e] 6 Gen. 15:6
[f] 8 Gen. 12:3; 18:18; 22:18

is written: "Cursed is everyone who
does not continue to do everything
written in the Book of the Law."[a]
11Clearly no one who relies on the
law is justified before God, because
"the righteous will live by faith."[b]
12The law is not based on faith; on
the contrary, it says, "The person
who does these things will live by
them."[c] 13Christ redeemed us from
the curse of the law by becoming a curse for us, for it is written:
"Cursed is everyone who is hung
on a pole."[d] 14He redeemed us in order that the blessing given to Abraham might come to the Gentiles
through Christ Jesus, so that by
faith we might receive the promise
of the Spirit. Ac 2:33; Ro 4:9,16

The Law and the Promise

15Brothers and sisters, let me
take an example from everyday
life. Just as no one can set aside or
add to a human covenant that has
been duly established, so it is in this
case. 16The promises were spoken
to Abraham and to his seed. Scripture does not say "and to seeds,"
meaning many people, but "and to
your seed,"[e] meaning one person,
who is Christ. 17What I mean is this:
The law, introduced 430 years later, does not set aside the covenant
previously established by God and
thus do away with the promise.
18For if the inheritance depends on
the law, then it no longer depends
on the promise; but God in his
grace gave it to Abraham through
a promise. Ex 12:40; Ro 4:14

19Why, then, was the law given at
all? It was added because of transgressions until the Seed to whom
the promise referred had come.
The law was given through angels
and entrusted to a mediator. 20A
mediator, however, implies more
than one party; but God is one.
Ac 7:53; Heb 8:6

21Is the law, therefore, opposed
to the promises of God? Absolutely not! For if a law had been given
that could impart life, then righteousness would certainly have
come by the law. 22But Scripture
has locked up everything under
the control of sin, so that what was
promised, being given through
faith in Jesus Christ, might be giv-
en to those who believe.
Ro 11:32; Gal 2:17

Children of God

23Before the coming of this
faith,[f] we were held in custody
under the law, locked up until
the faith that was to come would
be revealed. 24So the law was our
guardian until Christ came that
we might be justified by faith.
25Now that this faith has come, we
are no longer under a guardian.
Ro 10:4; 11:32

26So in Christ Jesus you are all
children of God through faith, 27for
all of you who were baptized into
Christ have clothed yourselves

[a] *10* Deut. 27:26 [b] *11* Hab. 2:4
[c] *12* Lev. 18:5 [d] *13* Deut. 21:23
[e] *16* Gen. 12:7; 13:15; 24:7 [f] *22,23* Or *through the faithfulness of Jesus . . . 23Before faith came*

with Christ. 28There is neither Jew
nor Gentile, neither slave nor free,
nor is there male and female, for
you are all one in Christ Jesus.
29If you belong to Christ, then you
are Abraham's seed, and heirs according to the promise.
Ro 8:14; Eph 2:14-15

4 What I am saying is that as
long as an heir is underage,
he is no different from a slave, although he owns the whole estate.
2The heir is subject to guardians
and trustees until the time set by
his father. 3So also, when we were
underage, we were in slavery under the elemental spiritual forces[a] of the world. 4But when the set
time had fully come, God sent his
Son, born of a woman, born under the law, 5to redeem those under the law, that we might receive
adoption to sonship.[b] 6Because
you are his sons, God sent the
Spirit of his Son into our hearts,
the Spirit who calls out, "*Abba*,[c]
Father." 7So you are no longer a
slave, but God's child; and since
you are his child, God has made
you also an heir. Ro 5:5; 8:15-17

Paul's Concern for the Galatians

8Formerly, when you did not
know God, you were slaves to those
who by nature are not gods. 9But
now that you know God — or rather are known by God — how is it
that you are turning back to those
weak and miserable forces[d]? Do
you wish to be enslaved by them
all over again? 10You are observing
special days and months and seasons and years! 11I fear for you, that
somehow I have wasted my efforts
on you. Eph 2:12; 1Th 3:5; 4:5

12I plead with you, brothers
and sisters, become like me, for
I became like you. You did me
no wrong. 13As you know, it was
because of an illness that I first
preached the gospel to you, 14and
even though my illness was a trial
to you, you did not treat me with
contempt or scorn. Instead, you
welcomed me as if I were an angel of God, as if I were Christ Jesus
himself. 15Where, then, is your
blessing of me now? I can testify that, if you could have done
so, you would have torn out your
eyes and given them to me. 16Have
I now become your enemy by telling you the truth? 1Co 2:3; Gal 6:18

17Those people are zealous to
win you over, but for no good.
What they want is to alienate you
from us, so that you may have zeal
for them. 18It is fine to be zealous,
provided the purpose is good, and
to be so always, not just when I am
with you. 19My dear children, for
whom I am again in the pains of
childbirth until Christ is formed in
you, 20how I wish I could be with
you now and change my tone, because I am perplexed about you!
1Co 4:15; Eph 4:13

[a] 3 Or *under the basic principles* [b] 5 The Greek word for *adoption to sonship* is a legal term referring to the full legal standing of an adopted male heir in Roman culture. [c] 6 Aramaic for *Father*
[d] 9 Or *principles*

Hagar and Sarah

21 Tell me, you who want to be
under the law, are you not aware
of what the law says? 22 For it is
written that Abraham had two
sons, one by the slave woman and
the other by the free woman. 23 His
son by the slave woman was born
according to the flesh, but his son
by the free woman was born as the
result of a divine promise.

Ro 9:7-8; Heb 11:11

24 These things are being taken
figuratively: The women represent two covenants. One covenant
is from Mount Sinai and bears
children who are to be slaves: This
is Hagar. 25 Now Hagar stands for
Mount Sinai in Arabia and corre-
sponds to the present city of Jerusalem, because she is in slavery
with her children. 26 But the Jerusalem that is above is free, and she
is our mother. 27 For it is written:

Heb 12:22; Rev 3:12

"Be glad, barren woman,
you who never bore a child;
shout for joy and cry aloud,
you who were never in labor;
because more are the children
of the desolate woman
than of her who has a
husband."[a]

Isa 54:1

28 Now you, brothers and sisters,
like Isaac, are children of promise.
29 At that time the son born according to the flesh persecuted the son
born by the power of the Spirit. It
is the same now. 30 But what does
Scripture say? "Get rid of the slave
woman and her son, for the slave
woman's son will never share
in the inheritance with the free
woman's son."[b] 31 Therefore, brothers and sisters, we are not children
of the slave woman, but of the free
woman.

Ge 21:9-10

Freedom in Christ

5 It is for freedom that Christ has
set us free. Stand firm, then,
and do not let yourselves be burdened again by a yoke of slavery.

1Co 16:13; Gal 2:4

2 Mark my words! I, Paul, tell you
that if you let yourselves be circumcised, Christ will be of no value to you at all. 3 Again I declare
to every man who lets himself be
circumcised that he is obligated to
obey the whole law. 4 You who are
trying to be justified by the law
have been alienated from Christ;
you have fallen away from grace.
5 For through the Spirit we eagerly await by faith the righteousness
for which we hope. 6 For in Christ
Jesus neither circumcision nor
uncircumcision has any value. The
only thing that counts is faith expressing itself through love.

Ro 8:23-24; Heb 12:15; Jas 2:22

7 You were running a good race.
Who cut in on you to keep you
from obeying the truth? 8 That
kind of persuasion does not
come from the one who calls you.
9 "A little yeast works through the

[a] 27 Isaiah 54:1 [b] 30 Gen. 21:10

whole batch of dough." 10I am confident in the Lord that you will
take no other view. The one who
is throwing you into confusion,
whoever that may be, will have
to pay the penalty. 11Brothers and
sisters, if I am still preaching circumcision, why am I still being
persecuted? In that case the offense of the cross has been abolished. 12As for those agitators,
I wish they would go the whole
way and emasculate themselves!

Gal 1:7; 6:12

Life by the Spirit

13You, my brothers and sisters,
were called to be free. But do not
use your freedom to indulge the
flesh[a]; rather, serve one another
humbly in love. 14For the entire
law is fulfilled in keeping this one
command: "Love your neighbor as
yourself."[b] 15If you bite and devour
each other, watch out or you will
be destroyed by each other.

Mt 22:39; 1Co 9:19

16So I say, walk by the Spirit,
and you will not gratify the desires of the flesh. 17For the flesh
desires what is contrary to the
Spirit, and the Spirit what is contrary to the flesh. They are in conflict with each other, so that you
are not to do whatever[c] you want.
18But if you are led by the Spirit,
you are not under the law.

Ro 7:15-23; 1Ti 1:9

19The acts of the flesh are obvious: sexual immorality, impurity
and debauchery; 20idolatry and
witchcraft; hatred, discord, jealousy, fits of rage, selfish ambition,
dissensions, factions 21and envy;
drunkenness, orgies, and the like.
I warn you, as I did before, that
those who live like this will not inherit the kingdom of God.

Ro 13:13; 1Co 6:18

22But the fruit of the Spirit
is love, joy, peace, forbearance,
kindness, goodness, faithfulness,
23gentleness and self-control.
Against such things there is no
law. 24Those who belong to Christ
Jesus have crucified the flesh with
its passions and desires. 25Since
we live by the Spirit, let us keep
in step with the Spirit. 26Let us not
become conceited, provoking and
envying each other.

Eph 5:9; Php 2:3; Col 3:12-15

Doing Good to All

6 Brothers and sisters, if someone is caught in a sin, you who
live by the Spirit should restore
that person gently. But watch
yourselves, or you also may be
tempted. 2Carry each other's burdens, and in this way you will fulfill the law of Christ. 3If anyone
thinks they are something when
they are not, they deceive themselves. 4Each one should test their
own actions. Then they can take
pride in themselves alone, without

[a] 13 In contexts like this, the Greek word for *flesh* (*sarx*) refers to the sinful state of human beings, often presented as a power in opposition to the Spirit; also in verses 16, 17, 19 and 24; and in 6:8. [b] 14 Lev. 19:18
[c] 17 Or *you do not do what*

comparing themselves to someone else, [5]for each one should carry their own load. [6]Nevertheless,
the one who receives instruction
in the word should share all good
things with their instructor.

1Co 9:11,14

[7]Do not be deceived: God cannot be mocked. A man reaps what
he sows. [8]Whoever sows to please
their flesh, from the flesh will
reap destruction; whoever sows
to please the Spirit, from the Spirit will reap eternal life. [9]Let us not
become weary in doing good, for
at the proper time we will reap
a harvest if we do not give up.
[10]Therefore, as we have opportunity, let us do good to all people,
especially to those who belong to
the family of believers.

1Co 15:58; Eph 2:19

Not Circumcision but the New Creation

[11]See what large letters I use as
I write to you with my own hand!

1Co 16:21

[12]Those who want to impress
people by means of the flesh are
trying to compel you to be circumcised. The only reason they
do this is to avoid being persecuted for the cross of Christ. [13]Not
even those who are circumcised
keep the law, yet they want you
to be circumcised that they may
boast about your circumcision in
the flesh. [14]May I never boast except in the cross of our Lord Jesus
Christ, through which[a] the world
has been crucified to me, and I
to the world. [15]Neither circumcision nor uncircumcision means
anything; what counts is the new
creation. [16]Peace and mercy to all
who follow this rule — to[b] the Israel of God. Ro 6:2,6; Gal 5:11

[17]From now on, let no one cause
me trouble, for I bear on my body
the marks of Jesus. Isa 44:5; 2Co 1:5

[18]The grace of our Lord Jesus
Christ be with your spirit, brothers and sisters. Amen.

Ro 16:20; 2Ti 4:22

[a] 14 Or *whom* [b] 16 Or *rule and to*

EPHESIANS

1 Paul, an apostle of Christ Jesus
by the will of God, 1Co 1:1; 2Co 1:1

To God's holy people in Ephesus,[a] the faithful in Christ Jesus:
Col 1:2

2Grace and peace to you from
God our Father and the Lord Jesus
Christ. Ro 1:7

Praise for Spiritual Blessings in Christ

3Praise be to the God and Father
of our Lord Jesus Christ, who has
blessed us in the heavenly realms
with every spiritual blessing in
Christ. 4For he chose us in him
before the creation of the world
to be holy and blameless in his
sight. In love 5he[b] predestined us
for adoption to sonship[c] through
Jesus Christ, in accordance with
his pleasure and will— 6to the
praise of his glorious grace, which
he has freely given us in the One
he loves. 7In him we have redemption through his blood, the
forgiveness of sins, in accordance
with the riches of God's grace
8that he lavished on us. With all
wisdom and understanding, 9he[d]
made known to us the mystery of
his will according to his good pleasure, which he purposed in Christ,
10to be put into effect when the
times reach their fulfillment—to
bring unity to all things in heaven
and on earth under Christ.
Ro 8:29-30; 2Co 1:3

11In him we were also chosen,[e]
having been predestined according to the plan of him who works
out everything in conformity with
the purpose of his will, 12in order
that we, who were the first to put
our hope in Christ, might be for
the praise of his glory. 13And you
also were included in Christ when
you heard the message of truth,
the gospel of your salvation. When
you believed, you were marked in
him with a seal, the promised Holy
Spirit, 14who is a deposit guaranteeing our inheritance until
the redemption of those who are
God's possession—to the praise of
his glory. Eph 3:11; 4:30

Thanksgiving and Prayer

15For this reason, ever since I
heard about your faith in the Lord
Jesus and your love for all God's
people, 16I have not stopped giving thanks for you, remembering
you in my prayers. 17I keep asking

[a] *1* Some early manuscripts do not have *in Ephesus.* [b] *4,5* Or *sight in love. 5He* [c] *5* The Greek word for *adoption to sonship* is a legal term referring to the full legal standing of an adopted male heir in Roman culture. [d] *8,9* Or *us with all wisdom and understanding. 9And he* [e] *11* Or *were made heirs*

that the God of our Lord Jesus
Christ, the glorious Father, may
give you the Spirit[a] of wisdom
and revelation, so that you may
know him better. 18 I pray that the
eyes of your heart may be enlightened in order that you may know
the hope to which he has called
you, the riches of his glorious inheritance in his holy people, 19 and
his incomparably great power for
us who believe. That power is the
same as the mighty strength 20 he
exerted when he raised Christ
from the dead and seated him
at his right hand in the heavenly
realms, 21 far above all rule and authority, power and dominion, and
every name that is invoked, not
only in the present age but also in
the one to come. 22 And God placed
all things under his feet and appointed him to be head over everything for the church, 23 which is
his body, the fullness of him who
fills everything in every way.

Php 2:9-10; Col 1:4,9

Made Alive in Christ

2 As for you, you were dead
in your transgressions and
sins, 2 in which you used to live
when you followed the ways of
this world and of the ruler of the
kingdom of the air, the spirit who
is now at work in those who are
disobedient. 3 All of us also lived
among them at one time, gratify-
ing the cravings of our flesh[b] and
following its desires and thoughts.
Like the rest, we were by nature
deserving of wrath. 4 But because
of his great love for us, God, who
is rich in mercy, 5 made us alive
with Christ even when we were
dead in transgressions — it is by
grace you have been saved. 6 And
God raised us up with Christ and
seated us with him in the heavenly realms in Christ Jesus, 7 in order
that in the coming ages he might
show the incomparable riches of
his grace, expressed in his kindness to us in Christ Jesus. 8 For it
is by grace you have been saved,
through faith — and this is not
from yourselves, it is the gift of
God — 9 not by works, so that no
one can boast. 10 For we are God's
handiwork, created in Christ Jesus
to do good works, which God prepared in advance for us to do.

Isa 29:23; Eph 4:24; Titus 2:14

Jew and Gentile Reconciled Through Christ

11 Therefore, remember that formerly you who are Gentiles by
birth and called "uncircumcised"
by those who call themselves "the
circumcision" (which is done in
the body by human hands) — 12 remember that at that time you
were separate from Christ, excluded from citizenship in Israel
and foreigners to the covenants
of the promise, without hope
and without God in the world.

[a] 17 Or *a spirit* [b] 3 In contexts like this, the Greek word for *flesh* (*sarx*) refers to the sinful state of human beings, often presented as a power in opposition to the Spirit.

[13]But now in Christ Jesus you who
once were far away have been
brought near by the blood of Christ.
Ac 2:39; Col 1:20

[14]For he himself is our peace,
who has made the two groups one
and has destroyed the barrier,
the dividing wall of hostility, [15]by
setting aside in his flesh the law
with its commands and regulations. His purpose was to create in
himself one new humanity out of
the two, thus making peace, [16]and
in one body to reconcile both of
them to God through the cross,
by which he put to death their
hostility. [17]He came and preached
peace to you who were far away
and peace to those who were near.
[18]For through him we both have
access to the Father by one Spirit.

[19]Consequently, you are no longer foreigners and strangers, but
fellow citizens with God's people
and also members of his household, [20]built on the foundation of
the apostles and prophets, with
Christ Jesus himself as the chief
cornerstone. [21]In him the whole
building is joined together and
rises to become a holy temple in
the Lord. [22]And in him you too are
being built together to become a
dwelling in which God lives by his
Spirit. Mt 16:18; 1Co 3:16-17

God's Marvelous Plan for the Gentiles

3 For this reason I, Paul, the prisoner of Christ Jesus for the
sake of you Gentiles — Ac 23:18; Eph 4:1

[2]Surely you have heard about
the administration of God's grace
that was given to me for you,
[3]that is, the mystery made known
to me by revelation, as I have already written briefly. [4]In reading this, then, you will be able to
understand my insight into the
mystery of Christ, [5]which was not
made known to people in other
generations as it has now been revealed by the Spirit to God's holy
apostles and prophets. [6]This mystery is that through the gospel the
Gentiles are heirs together with
Israel, members together of one
body, and sharers together in the
promise in Christ Jesus.
Gal 3:29; Eph 2:15-16

[7]I became a servant of this gospel by the gift of God's grace giv-
en me through the working of his
power. [8]Although I am less than
the least of all the Lord's people,
this grace was given me: to preach
to the Gentiles the boundless riches of Christ, [9]and to make plain to
everyone the administration of
this mystery, which for ages past
was kept hidden in God, who created all things. [10]His intent was
that now, through the church, the
manifold wisdom of God should
be made known to the rulers
and authorities in the heavenly realms, [11]according to his eternal purpose that he accomplished
in Christ Jesus our Lord. [12]In him
and through faith in him we may
approach God with freedom and
confidence. [13]I ask you, therefore,

not to be discouraged because of
my sufferings for you, which are
your glory. Eph 2:18; Heb 4:16

A Prayer for the Ephesians

14For this reason I kneel before the Father, 15from whom every family[a] in heaven and on
earth derives its name. 16I pray
that out of his glorious riches he
may strengthen you with power
through his Spirit in your inner
being, 17so that Christ may dwell
in your hearts through faith. And
I pray that you, being rooted and
established in love, 18may have
power, together with all the Lord's
holy people, to grasp how wide
and long and high and deep is the
love of Christ, 19and to know this
love that surpasses knowledge —
that you may be filled to the measure of all the fullness of God.

Eph 1:23; Col 2:10

20Now to him who is able to do
immeasurably more than all we
ask or imagine, according to his
power that is at work within us,
21to him be glory in the church and
in Christ Jesus throughout all generations, for ever and ever! Amen.

Ro 11:36; 16:25

Unity and Maturity in the Body of Christ

4 As a prisoner for the Lord,
then, I urge you to live a life
worthy of the calling you have received. 2Be completely humble
and gentle; be patient, bearing
with one another in love. 3Make
every effort to keep the unity of
the Spirit through the bond of
peace. 4There is one body and one
Spirit, just as you were called to
one hope when you were called;
5one Lord, one faith, one baptism;
6one God and Father of all, who is
over all and through all and in all.

Ro 11:36; Col 1:10

7But to each one of us grace has
been given as Christ apportioned
it. 8This is why it[b] says:

Ro 12:3; 1Co 12:7,11

"When he ascended on high,
he took many captives Col 2:15
and gave gifts to his people."[c]

9(What does "he ascended" mean
except that he also descended to
the lower, earthly regions[d]? 10He
who descended is the very one
who ascended higher than all the
heavens, in order to fill the whole
universe.) 11So Christ himself
gave the apostles, the prophets,
the evangelists, the pastors and
teachers, 12to equip his people for
works of service, so that the body
of Christ may be built up 13until we
all reach unity in the faith and in
the knowledge of the Son of God
and become mature, attaining to
the whole measure of the fullness
of Christ. 1Co 12:27-28; Col 1:28

14Then we will no longer be infants, tossed back and forth by
the waves, and blown here and

[a] 15 The Greek for *family* (*patria*) is derived from the Greek for *father* (*pater*). [b] 8 Or *God* [c] 8 Psalm 68:18 [d] 9 Or *the depths of the earth*

there by every wind of teaching
and by the cunning and craftiness of people in their deceitful
scheming. 15Instead, speaking the
truth in love, we will grow to become in every respect the mature
body of him who is the head, that
is, Christ. 16From him the whole
body, joined and held together by
every supporting ligament, grows
and builds itself up in love, as each
part does its work. 1Co 14:20; Eph 1:22

Instructions for Christian Living

17So I tell you this, and insist
on it in the Lord, that you must
no longer live as the Gentiles do,
in the futility of their thinking.
18They are darkened in their understanding and separated from
the life of God because of the ignorance that is in them due to the
hardening of their hearts. 19Hav-
ing lost all sensitivity, they have
given themselves over to sensual-
ity so as to indulge in every kind
of impurity, and they are full of
greed. Ro 1:21; 1Ti 4:2

20That, however, is not the way of
life you learned 21when you heard
about Christ and were taught in
him in accordance with the truth
that is in Jesus. 22You were taught,
with regard to your former way of
life, to put off your old self, which
is being corrupted by its deceitful
desires; 23to be made new in the
attitude of your minds; 24and to
put on the new self, created to be
like God in true righteousness and
holiness. Ro 6:4; Col 3:10

25Therefore each of you must
put off falsehood and speak truth-
fully to your neighbor, for we are
all members of one body. 26"In
your anger do not sin"[a]: Do not let
the sun go down while you are still
angry, 27and do not give the devil a
foothold. 28Anyone who has been
stealing must steal no longer, but
must work, doing something useful with their own hands, that they
may have something to share with
those in need. Zec 8:16; Lk 3:11

29Do not let any unwholesome
talk come out of your mouths, but
only what is helpful for building
others up according to their needs,
that it may benefit those who listen. 30And do not grieve the Holy
Spirit of God, with whom you were
sealed for the day of redemption.
31Get rid of all bitterness, rage and
anger, brawling and slander, along
with every form of malice. 32Be
kind and compassionate to one
another, forgiving each other, just
as in Christ God forgave you.
5 1Follow God's example, therefore, as dearly loved children 2and
walk in the way of love, just as
Christ loved us and gave himself
up for us as a fragrant offering
and sacrifice to God.

Col 3:8; 1Th 5:19; Lk 6:36; 2Co 2:15

3But among you there must not
be even a hint of sexual immorality, or of any kind of impurity, or of
greed, because these are improper
for God's holy people. 4Nor should
there be obscenity, foolish talk or

[a] 26 Psalm 4:4 (see Septuagint)

coarse joking, which are out of
place, but rather thanksgiving.
5For of this you can be sure: No immoral, impure or greedy person —
such a person is an idolater — has
any inheritance in the kingdom
of Christ and of God.[a] 6Let no one
deceive you with empty words, for
because of such things God's wrath
comes on those who are disobedient. 7Therefore do not be partners
with them. Ro 1:18; 1Co 6:9
8For you were once darkness,
but now you are light in the Lord.
Live as children of light 9(for the
fruit of the light consists in all
goodness, righteousness and
truth) 10and find out what pleases the Lord. 11Have nothing to do
with the fruitless deeds of darkness, but rather expose them. 12It
is shameful even to mention what
the disobedient do in secret. 13But
everything exposed by the light
becomes visible — and everything that is illuminated becomes
a light. 14This is why it is said:

Lk 16:8; Gal 5:22

"Wake up, sleeper, Ro 13:11
rise from the dead, Jn 5:25
and Christ will shine on you."
Isa 60:1

15Be very careful, then, how you
live — not as unwise but as wise,
16making the most of every opportunity, because the days are evil.
17Therefore do not be foolish, but
understand what the Lord's will is.
18Do not get drunk on wine, which
leads to debauchery. Instead, be
filled with the Spirit, 19speak-
ing to one another with psalms,
hymns, and songs from the Spirit.
Sing and make music from your
heart to the Lord, 20always giving
thanks to God the Father for everything, in the name of our Lord
Jesus Christ. Ps 34:1; Col 3:16

Instructions for Christian Households

21Submit to one another out of
reverence for Christ. Gal 5:13
22Wives, submit yourselves to
your own husbands as you do to
the Lord. 23For the husband is the
head of the wife as Christ is the
head of the church, his body, of
which he is the Savior. 24Now as
the church submits to Christ, so
also wives should submit to their
husbands in everything.
1Co 11:3; Eph 6:5
25Husbands, love your wives,
just as Christ loved the church
and gave himself up for her 26to
make her holy, cleansing[b] her by
the washing with water through
the word, 27and to present her to
himself as a radiant church, without stain or wrinkle or any other blemish, but holy and blameless. 28In this same way, husbands
ought to love their wives as their
own bodies. He who loves his wife
loves himself. 29After all, no one
ever hated their own body, but
they feed and care for their body,
just as Christ does the church —

[a] 5 Or *kingdom of the Messiah and God*
[b] 26 Or *having cleansed*

30 for we are members of his body.
31 "For this reason a man will leave
his father and mother and be united to his wife, and the two will become one flesh."[a] 32 This is a profound mystery — but I am talking
about Christ and the church.
33 However, each one of you also
must love his wife as he loves himself, and the wife must respect her
husband. Mt 19:5; Col 1:22

6 Children, obey your parents
in the Lord, for this is right.
2 "Honor your father and mother" — which is the first commandment with a promise — 3 "so that it
may go well with you and that you
may enjoy long life on the earth."[b]
Ex 20:12; Col 3:20

4 Fathers,[c] do not exasperate
your children; instead, bring them
up in the training and instruction
of the Lord. Ge 18:19; Col 3:21

5 Slaves, obey your earthly masters with respect and fear, and
with sincerity of heart, just as you
would obey Christ. 6 Obey them
not only to win their favor when
their eye is on you, but as slaves of
Christ, doing the will of God from
your heart. 7 Serve wholeheartedly, as if you were serving the Lord,
not people, 8 because you know
that the Lord will reward each
one for whatever good they do,
whether they are slave or free.
Col 3:22,24

9 And masters, treat your slaves
in the same way. Do not threaten
them, since you know that he who
is both their Master and yours is
in heaven, and there is no favoritism with him. Col 3:18-4:1

The Armor of God

10 Finally, be strong in the Lord
and in his mighty power. 11 Put on
the full armor of God, so that you
can take your stand against the
devil's schemes. 12 For our struggle is not against flesh and blood,
but against the rulers, against the
authorities, against the powers of
this dark world and against the
spiritual forces of evil in the heavenly realms. 13 Therefore put on
the full armor of God, so that when
the day of evil comes, you may be
able to stand your ground, and after you have done everything, to
stand. 14 Stand firm then, with the
belt of truth buckled around your
waist, with the breastplate of righteousness in place, 15 and with your
feet fitted with the readiness that
comes from the gospel of peace.
16 In addition to all this, take up the
shield of faith, with which you can
extinguish all the flaming arrows
of the evil one. 17 Take the helmet
of salvation and the sword of the
Spirit, which is the word of God.

18 And pray in the Spirit on all
occasions with all kinds of prayers
and requests. With this in mind,
be alert and always keep on praying for all the Lord's people. 19 Pray
also for me, that whenever I speak,
words may be given me so that I
will fearlessly make known the

[a] 31 Gen. 2:24 [b] 3 Deut. 5:16 [c] 4 Or *Parents*

mystery of the gospel, [20]for which
I am an ambassador in chains.
Pray that I may declare it fearless-
ly, as I should. 2Co 3:12; 5:20

Final Greetings

[21]Tychicus, the dear brother and
faithful servant in the Lord, will
tell you everything, so that you
also may know how I am and what
I am doing. [22]I am sending him to
you for this very purpose, that you
may know how we are, and that he
may encourage you. Ac 20:4; Col 4:7-9
[23]Peace to the brothers and sisters,[a] and love with faith from
God the Father and the Lord Jesus
Christ. [24]Grace to all who love our
Lord Jesus Christ with an undying
love.[b] Gal 6:16; 1Pe 5:14

[a] 23 The Greek word for *brothers and sisters* (*adelphoi*) refers here to believers, both men and women, as part of God's family.
[b] 24 Or *Grace and immortality to all who love our Lord Jesus Christ.*

PHILIPPIANS

1 Paul and Timothy, servants of
Christ Jesus, Ac 16:1; 2Co 1:1

To all God's holy people in Christ
Jesus at Philippi, together with
the overseers and deacons[a]: 1Ti 3:1,8

2 Grace and peace to you from
God our Father and the Lord Jesus
Christ. Ro 1:7

Thanksgiving and Prayer

3 I thank my God every time I remember you. 4 In all my prayers for
all of you, I always pray with joy
5 because of your partnership in
the gospel from the first day until
now, 6 being confident of this, that
he who began a good work in you
will carry it on to completion until
the day of Christ Jesus.
Ac 16:12-40; 1Co 1:8

7 It is right for me to feel this way
about all of you, since I have you
in my heart and, whether I am in
chains or defending and confirming the gospel, all of you share in
God's grace with me. 8 God can testify how I long for all of you with
the affection of Christ Jesus.
Ro 1:9; 2Pe 1:13

9 And this is my prayer: that
your love may abound more and
more in knowledge and depth of
insight, 10 so that you may be able
to discern what is best and may
be pure and blameless for the day
of Christ, 11 filled with the fruit of
righteousness that comes through
Jesus Christ — to the glory and
praise of God. 1Co 1:8; 1Th 3:12

Paul's Chains Advance the Gospel

12 Now I want you to know, brothers and sisters,[b] that what has happened to me has actually served to
advance the gospel. 13 As a result,
it has become clear throughout
the whole palace guard[c] and to
everyone else that I am in chains
for Christ. 14 And because of my
chains, most of the brothers and
sisters have become confident in
the Lord and dare all the more to
proclaim the gospel without fear.
Ac 4:29; 21:33

15 It is true that some preach
Christ out of envy and rivalry, but
others out of goodwill. 16 The latter do so out of love, knowing that
I am put here for the defense of
the gospel. 17 The former preach
Christ out of selfish ambition, not
sincerely, supposing that they can
stir up trouble for me while I am in
chains. 18 But what does it matter?

[a] *1* The word *deacons* refers here to Christians designated to serve with the overseers/elders of the church in a variety of ways; similarly in Romans 16:1 and 1 Tim. 3:8,12. [b] *12* The Greek word for *brothers and sisters* (*adelphoi*) refers here to believers, both men and women, as part of God's family; also in verse 14; and in 3:1, 13, 17; 4:1, 8, 21. [c] *13* Or *whole palace*

The important thing is that in every way, whether from false motives or true, Christ is preached.
And because of this I rejoice. Php 2:3

Yes, and I will continue to rejoice, 19for I know that through
your prayers and God's provision
of the Spirit of Jesus Christ what
has happened to me will turn out
for my deliverance.[a] 20I eagerly expect and hope that I will in no way
be ashamed, but will have sufficient courage so that now as always
Christ will be exalted in my body,
whether by life or by death. 21For
to me, to live is Christ and to die is
gain. 22If I am to go on living in the
body, this will mean fruitful labor
for me. Yet what shall I choose? I
do not know! 23I am torn between
the two: I desire to depart and be
with Christ, which is better by far;
24but it is more necessary for you
that I remain in the body. 25Con-
vinced of this, I know that I will remain, and I will continue with all
of you for your progress and joy in
the faith, 26so that through my being with you again your boasting
in Christ Jesus will abound on account of me. 2Co 5:8; 2Ti 4:6

Life Worthy of the Gospel

27Whatever happens, conduct
yourselves in a manner worthy of
the gospel of Christ. Then, whether I come and see you or only
hear about you in my absence, I
will know that you stand firm in
the one Spirit,[b] striving together as one for the faith of the gospel 28without being frightened in
any way by those who oppose you.
This is a sign to them that they will
be destroyed, but that you will be
saved — and that by God. 29For it
has been granted to you on behalf of Christ not only to believe
in him, but also to suffer for him,
30since you are going through the
same struggle you saw I had, and
now hear that I still have.

Ac 16:19-40; 1Th 2:2

Imitating Christ's Humility

2 Therefore if you have any encouragement from being united with Christ, if any comfort from
his love, if any common sharing
in the Spirit, if any tenderness
and compassion, 2then make my
joy complete by being like-mind-
ed, having the same love, being
one in spirit and of one mind. 3Do
nothing out of selfish ambition
or vain conceit. Rather, in humility value others above yourselves,
4not looking to your own interests
but each of you to the interests of
the others. Ro 12:10; Gal 5:26

5In your relationships with one
another, have the same mindset
as Christ Jesus: Mt 11:29

6Who, being in very nature[c]
God, Jn 1:1; 14:9
did not consider equality
with God something
to be used to his own
advantage; Jn 5:18

[a] 19 Or *vindication*; or *salvation* [b] 27 Or *in one spirit* [c] 6 Or *in the form of*

7 rather, he made himself
nothing 2Co 8:9
by taking the very nature[a] of
a servant, Mt 20:28
being made in human
likeness. Jn 1:14; Heb 2:17
8 And being found in appearance
as a man,
he humbled himself
by becoming obedient to
death — Mt 26:39; Heb 5:8
even death on a cross!
1Co 1:23

9 Therefore God exalted him
to the highest place
Ac 2:33; Heb 2:9
and gave him the name that
is above every name,
Eph 1:20-21
10 that at the name of Jesus every
knee should bow, Ro 14:11
in heaven and on earth and
under the earth, Mt 28:18
11 and every tongue acknowledge
that Jesus Christ is Lord,
Jn 13:13
to the glory of God the Father.

Do Everything Without Grumbling

12 Therefore, my dear friends,
as you have always obeyed — not
only in my presence, but now
much more in my absence — continue to work out your salvation
with fear and trembling, 13 for it is
God who works in you to will and
to act in order to fulfill his good
purpose. 2Co 7:15; Ezr 1:5
14 Do everything without grumbling or arguing, 15 so that you
may become blameless and pure,
"children of God without fault in a
warped and crooked generation."[b]
Then you will shine among them
like stars in the sky 16 as you hold
firmly to the word of life. And
then I will be able to boast on the
day of Christ that I did not run or
labor in vain. 17 But even if I am
being poured out like a drink offering on the sacrifice and service
coming from your faith, I am glad
and rejoice with all of you. 18 So
you too should be glad and rejoice
with me. Ro 15:16; 2Ti 4:6

Timothy and Epaphroditus

19 I hope in the Lord Jesus to
send Timothy to you soon, that
I also may be cheered when I receive news about you. 20 I have no
one else like him, who will show
genuine concern for your welfare.
21 For everyone looks out for their
own interests, not those of Jesus
Christ. 22 But you know that Timothy has proved himself, because as
a son with his father he has served
with me in the work of the gospel.
23 I hope, therefore, to send him as
soon as I see how things go with
me. 24 And I am confident in the
Lord that I myself will come soon.
1Co 10:24; Php 1:25
25 But I think it is necessary to
send back to you Epaphroditus,
my brother, co-worker and fellow
soldier, who is also your messenger, whom you sent to take care of

[a] 7 Or *the form* [b] 15 Deut. 32:5

my needs. 26For he longs for all of
you and is distressed because you
heard he was ill. 27Indeed he was
ill, and almost died. But God had
mercy on him, and not on him
only but also on me, to spare me
sorrow upon sorrow. 28Therefore
I am all the more eager to send
him, so that when you see him
again you may be glad and I may
have less anxiety. 29So then, welcome him in the Lord with great
joy, and honor people like him,
30because he almost died for the
work of Christ. He risked his life
to make up for the help you yourselves could not give me.
1Co 16:17-18; 1Ti 5:17

No Confidence in the Flesh

3 Further, my brothers and sisters, rejoice in the Lord! It is no
trouble for me to write the same
things to you again, and it is a
safeguard for you. 2Watch out for
those dogs, those evildoers, those
mutilators of the flesh. 3For it is
we who are the circumcision, we
who serve God by his Spirit, who
boast in Christ Jesus, and who
put no confidence in the flesh—
4though I myself have reasons for
such confidence. Ps 22:16,20; Gal 6:15

If someone else thinks they
have reasons to put confidence in
the flesh, I have more: 5circum-
cised on the eighth day, of the
people of Israel, of the tribe of
Benjamin, a Hebrew of Hebrews;
in regard to the law, a Pharisee; 6as
for zeal, persecuting the church;
as for righteousness based on the
law, faultless. Ro 11:1; 2Co 11:22

7But whatever were gains to me
I now consider loss for the sake
of Christ. 8What is more, I consider everything a loss because of
the surpassing worth of knowing
Christ Jesus my Lord, for whose
sake I have lost all things. I consider them garbage, that I may
gain Christ 9and be found in him,
not having a righteousness of my
own that comes from the law, but
that which is through faith in[a]
Christ—the righteousness that
comes from God on the basis of
faith. 10I want to know Christ—
yes, to know the power of his resurrection and participation in his
sufferings, becoming like him in
his death, 11and so, somehow, attaining to the resurrection from
the dead. Ro 6:3-5; 8:17

12Not that I have already obtained all this, or have already arrived at my goal, but I press on to
take hold of that for which Christ
Jesus took hold of me. 13Broth-
ers and sisters, I do not consider
myself yet to have taken hold of
it. But one thing I do: Forgetting
what is behind and straining toward what is ahead, 14I press on toward the goal to win the prize for
which God has called me heaven-
ward in Christ Jesus. Lk 9:62; Heb 6:1

Following Paul's Example

15All of us, then, who are mature
should take such a view of things.

[a] 9 Or *through the faithfulness of*

And if on some point you think
differently, that too God will make
clear to you. 16Only let us live up to
what we have already attained.
1Co 2:6; Gal 5:10

17Join together in following my
example, brothers and sisters,
and just as you have us as a model, keep your eyes on those who
live as we do. 18For, as I have often told you before and now tell
you again even with tears, many
live as enemies of the cross of
Christ. 19Their destiny is destruction, their god is their stomach,
and their glory is in their shame.
Their mind is set on earthly
things. 20But our citizenship is in
heaven. And we eagerly await a
Savior from there, the Lord Jesus
Christ, 21who, by the power that
enables him to bring everything
under his control, will transform
our lowly bodies so that they will
be like his glorious body.
1Co 15:43-53; Eph 1:19

Closing Appeal for Steadfastness and Unity

4 Therefore, my brothers and
sisters, you whom I love and
long for, my joy and crown, stand
firm in the Lord in this way, dear
friends! Php 1:8,27

2I plead with Euodia and I plead
with Syntyche to be of the same
mind in the Lord. 3Yes, and I ask
you, my true companion, help
these women since they have contended at my side in the cause of
the gospel, along with Clement
and the rest of my co-workers,
whose names are in the book of
life. Php 2:2,25

Final Exhortations

4Rejoice in the Lord always. I
will say it again: Rejoice! 5Let your
gentleness be evident to all. The
Lord is near. 6Do not be anxious
about anything, but in every situation, by prayer and petition,
with thanksgiving, present your
requests to God. 7And the peace of
God, which transcends all understanding, will guard your hearts
and your minds in Christ Jesus.
Jn 14:27; Col 3:15

8Finally, brothers and sisters,
whatever is true, whatever is noble, whatever is right, whatever
is pure, whatever is lovely, whatever is admirable — if anything is
excellent or praiseworthy — think
about such things. 9Whatever you
have learned or received or heard
from me, or seen in me — put it
into practice. And the God of peace
will be with you. Ro 15:33; Php 3:17

Thanks for Their Gifts

10I rejoiced greatly in the Lord
that at last you renewed your concern for me. Indeed, you were concerned, but you had no opportunity to show it. 11I am not saying this
because I am in need, for I have
learned to be content whatever
the circumstances. 12I know what
it is to be in need, and I know what
it is to have plenty. I have learned
the secret of being content in any

and every situation, whether well
fed or hungry, whether living in
plenty or in want. 13I can do all
this through him who gives me
strength. 2Co 12:9; 1Ti 6:6,8

14Yet it was good of you to share
in my troubles. 15Moreover, as you
Philippians know, in the early days
of your acquaintance with the gospel, when I set out from Macedonia, not one church shared with
me in the matter of giving and
receiving, except you only; 16for
even when I was in Thessalonica,
you sent me aid more than once
when I was in need. 17Not that I desire your gifts; what I desire is that
more be credited to your account.
18I have received full payment
and have more than enough. I am
amply supplied, now that I have
received from Epaphroditus the
gifts you sent. They are a fragrant
offering, an acceptable sacrifice,
pleasing to God. 19And my God will
meet all your needs according to
the riches of his glory in Christ
Jesus. Ps 23:1; Ro 2:4

20To our God and Father be glory for ever and ever. Amen.

Ro 11:36; Gal 1:4

Final Greetings

21Greet all God's people in Christ
Jesus. The brothers and sisters
who are with me send greetings.
22All God's people here send you
greetings, especially those who
belong to Caesar's household.

Ac 9:13; Gal 1:2

23The grace of the Lord Jesus
Christ be with your spirit. Amen.[a]

Ro 16:20

[a] 23 Some manuscripts do not have *Amen.*

COLOSSIANS

1 Paul, an apostle of Christ Jesus
by the will of God, and Timothy
our brother, 1Co 1:1; 2Co 1:1

2 To God's holy people in Colos-
sae, the faithful brothers and sisters[a] in Christ:

Grace and peace to you from
God our Father.[b] Ro 1:7; Col 4:18

Thanksgiving and Prayer

3 We always thank God, the Father of our Lord Jesus Christ,
when we pray for you, 4 because we
have heard of your faith in Christ
Jesus and of the love you have for
all God's people — 5 the faith and
love that spring from the hope
stored up for you in heaven and
about which you have already
heard in the true message of the
gospel 6 that has come to you. In
the same way, the gospel is bearing fruit and growing throughout
the whole world — just as it has
been doing among you since the
day you heard it and truly understood God's grace. 7 You learned it
from Epaphras, our dear fellow
servant,[c] who is a faithful minister of Christ on our[d] behalf, 8 and
who also told us of your love in
the Spirit. Ro 15:30; 1Th 5:8

9 For this reason, since the day
we heard about you, we have not
stopped praying for you. We continually ask God to fill you with
the knowledge of his will through
all the wisdom and understanding that the Spirit gives,[e] 10 so that
you may live a life worthy of the
Lord and please him in every way:
bearing fruit in every good work,
growing in the knowledge of God,
11 being strengthened with all power according to his glorious might
so that you may have great endurance and patience, 12 and giving
joyful thanks to the Father, who
has qualified you[f] to share in the
inheritance of his holy people in
the kingdom of light. 13 For he has
rescued us from the dominion of
darkness and brought us into the
kingdom of the Son he loves, 14 in
whom we have redemption, the
forgiveness of sins. Eph 1:7; 6:12

The Supremacy of the Son of God

15 The Son is the image of the invisible God, the firstborn over all
creation. 16 For in him all things
were created: things in heaven
and on earth, visible and invisible, whether thrones or powers

[a] 2 The Greek word for *brothers and sisters* (*adelphoi*) refers here to believers, both men and women, as part of God's family; also in 4:15. [b] 2 Some manuscripts *Father and the Lord Jesus Christ* [c] 7 Or *slave* [d] 7 Some manuscripts *your* [e] 9 Or *all spiritual wisdom and understanding* [f] 12 Some manuscripts *us*

or rulers or authorities; all things
have been created through him
and for him. [17]He is before all
things, and in him all things hold
together. [18]And he is the head of
the body, the church; he is the beginning and the firstborn from
among the dead, so that in everything he might have the su-
premacy. [19]For God was pleased
to have all his fullness dwell in
him, [20]and through him to reconcile to himself all things, whether
things on earth or things in heav-
en, by making peace through his
blood, shed on the cross.

2Co 5:18; Eph 2:13

[21]Once you were alienated from
God and were enemies in your
minds because of[a] your evil behavior. [22]But now he has reconciled you by Christ's physical body
through death to present you holy
in his sight, without blemish and
free from accusation— [23]if you
continue in your faith, established
and firm, and do not move from
the hope held out in the gospel.
This is the gospel that you heard
and that has been proclaimed to
every creature under heaven, and
of which I, Paul, have become a
servant. Ro 10:18; 1Co 3:5; Eph 3:17

Paul's Labor for the Church

[24]Now I rejoice in what I am suffering for you, and I fill up in my
flesh what is still lacking in regard
to Christ's afflictions, for the sake
of his body, which is the church.
[25]I have become its servant by the
commission God gave me to present to you the word of God in its
fullness— [26]the mystery that has
been kept hidden for ages and
generations, but is now disclosed
to the Lord's people. [27]To them
God has chosen to make known
among the Gentiles the glorious
riches of this mystery, which is
Christ in you, the hope of glory.

Ro 8:10; Eph 3:2

[28]He is the one we proclaim, ad-
monishing and teaching everyone
with all wisdom, so that we may
present everyone fully mature in
Christ. [29]To this end I strenuously
contend with all the energy Christ
so powerfully works in me.

1Co 15:10; Eph 1:19; Col 2:1

2 I want you to know how hard I
am contending for you and for
those at Laodicea, and for all who
have not met me personally. [2]My
goal is that they may be encouraged in heart and united in love,
so that they may have the full
riches of complete understanding,
in order that they may know the
mystery of God, namely, Christ,
[3]in whom are hidden all the treasures of wisdom and knowledge.
[4]I tell you this so that no one may
deceive you by fine-sounding arguments. [5]For though I am absent
from you in body, I am present
with you in spirit and delight to
see how disciplined you are and
how firm your faith in Christ is.

1Co 14:40; 1Th 2:17; 1Pe 5:9

[a] 21 Or *minds, as shown by*

Spiritual Fullness in Christ

6 So then, just as you received
Christ Jesus as Lord, continue to
live your lives in him, 7 rooted and
built up in him, strengthened in
the faith as you were taught, and
overflowing with thankfulness.

Eph 3:17; Col 1:10

8 See to it that no one takes you
captive through hollow and deceptive philosophy, which depends on human tradition and the
elemental spiritual forces[a] of this
world rather than on Christ.

Gal 4:3; 1Ti 6:20

9 For in Christ all the fullness
of the Deity lives in bodily form,
10 and in Christ you have been
brought to fullness. He is the head
over every power and authority.
11 In him you were also circumcised
with a circumcision not performed
by human hands. Your whole self
ruled by the flesh[b] was put off
when you were circumcised by[c]
Christ, 12 having been buried with
him in baptism, in which you were
also raised with him through your
faith in the working of God, who
raised him from the dead.

Ac 2:24; Ro 2:29; 6:5

13 When you were dead in your
sins and in the uncircumcision of
your flesh, God made you[d] alive
with Christ. He forgave us all our
sins, 14 having canceled the charge
of our legal indebtedness, which
stood against us and condemned
us; he has taken it away, nailing
it to the cross. 15 And having dis-
armed the powers and authorities, he made a public spectacle of
them, triumphing over them by
the cross.[e]

Eph 2:15; 6:12

Freedom From Human Rules

16 Therefore do not let anyone judge you by what you eat
or drink, or with regard to a religious festival, a New Moon celebration or a Sabbath day. 17 These
are a shadow of the things that
were to come; the reality, however, is found in Christ. 18 Do not let
anyone who delights in false humility and the worship of angels
disqualify you. Such a person also
goes into great detail about what
they have seen; they are puffed
up with idle notions by their unspiritual mind. 19 They have lost
connection with the head, from
whom the whole body, supported
and held together by its ligaments
and sinews, grows as God causes it
to grow.

Eph 1:22; 4:16

20 Since you died with Christ to
the elemental spiritual forces of
this world, why, as though you
still belonged to the world, do you
submit to its rules: 21 "Do not handle! Do not taste! Do not touch!"?
22 These rules, which have to do
with things that are all destined

[a] 8 Or *the basic principles*; also in verse 20
[b] 11 In contexts like this, the Greek word for *flesh* (*sarx*) refers to the sinful state of human beings, often presented as a power in opposition to the Spirit; also in verse 13.
[c] 11 Or *put off in the circumcision of*
[d] 13 Some manuscripts *us*
[e] 15 Or *them in him*

to perish with use, are based on
merely human commands and
teachings. 23 Such regulations indeed have an appearance of wisdom, with their self-imposed worship, their false humility and their
harsh treatment of the body, but
they lack any value in restraining
sensual indulgence.

Mt 15:9; 1Co 6:13; Titus 1:14

Living as Those Made Alive in Christ

3 Since, then, you have been
raised with Christ, set your
hearts on things above, where
Christ is, seated at the right hand
of God. 2 Set your minds on things
above, not on earthly things. 3 For
you died, and your life is now hidden with Christ in God. 4 When
Christ, who is your[a] life, appears,
then you also will appear with him
in glory. Ro 6:2; 1Jn 3:2

5 Put to death, therefore, whatever belongs to your earthly nature: sexual immorality, impurity,
lust, evil desires and greed, which
is idolatry. 6 Because of these, the
wrath of God is coming.[b] 7 You
used to walk in these ways, in the
life you once lived. 8 But now you
must also rid yourselves of all
such things as these: anger, rage,
malice, slander, and filthy language from your lips. 9 Do not lie
to each other, since you have tak-
en off your old self with its practices 10 and have put on the new self,
which is being renewed in knowledge in the image of its Creator.
11 Here there is no Gentile or Jew,
circumcised or uncircumcised,
barbarian, Scythian, slave or free,
but Christ is all, and is in all.

Ro 12:2; Gal 3:28; Eph 1:23

12 Therefore, as God's chosen
people, holy and dearly loved,
clothe yourselves with compassion, kindness, humility, gentleness and patience. 13 Bear with
each other and forgive one another if any of you has a grievance
against someone. Forgive as the
Lord forgave you. 14 And over all
these virtues put on love, which
binds them all together in perfect
unity. Eph 4:3; Php 2:3

15 Let the peace of Christ rule
in your hearts, since as members
of one body you were called to
peace. And be thankful. 16 Let the
message of Christ dwell among
you richly as you teach and admonish one another with all wisdom through psalms, hymns, and
songs from the Spirit, singing to
God with gratitude in your hearts.
17 And whatever you do, whether in
word or deed, do it all in the name
of the Lord Jesus, giving thanks to
God the Father through him.

1Co 10:31; Eph 5:19

Instructions for Christian Households

18 Wives, submit yourselves to
your husbands, as is fitting in the
Lord. Eph 5:22

[a] 4 Some manuscripts *our* [b] 6 Some early manuscripts *coming on those who are disobedient*

19 Husbands, love your wives and
do not be harsh with them.
20 Children, obey your parents
in everything, for this pleases the
Lord.
21 Fathers,[a] do not embitter your
children, or they will become discouraged.
22 Slaves, obey your earthly masters in everything; and do it, not
only when their eye is on you and
to curry their favor, but with sincerity of heart and reverence for
the Lord. 23 Whatever you do, work
at it with all your heart, as working for the Lord, not for human
masters, 24 since you know that
you will receive an inheritance
from the Lord as a reward. It is
the Lord Christ you are serving.
25 Anyone who does wrong will be
repaid for their wrongs, and there
is no favoritism. Ac 10:34; 20:32

4 Masters, provide your slaves
with what is right and fair, because you know that you also have
a Master in heaven. Eph 5:22-6:9

Further Instructions

2 Devote yourselves to prayer,
being watchful and thankful.
3 And pray for us, too, that God
may open a door for our message,
so that we may proclaim the mystery of Christ, for which I am in
chains. 4 Pray that I may proclaim
it clearly, as I should. 5 Be wise in
the way you act toward outsiders;
make the most of every opportunity. 6 Let your conversation be always full of grace, seasoned with
salt, so that you may know how to
answer everyone.
Mk 9:50; Eph 5:16; 1Pe 3:15

Final Greetings

7 Tychicus will tell you all the
news about me. He is a dear brother, a faithful minister and fellow
servant[b] in the Lord. 8 I am sending him to you for the express
purpose that you may know about
our[c] circumstances and that he
may encourage your hearts. 9 He is
coming with Onesimus, our faithful and dear brother, who is one
of you. They will tell you everything that is happening here.
Eph 6:21-22

10 My fellow prisoner Aristarchus sends you his greetings, as
does Mark, the cousin of Barnabas. (You have received instructions about him; if he comes to
you, welcome him.) 11 Jesus, who is
called Justus, also sends greetings.
These are the only Jews[d] among
my co-workers for the kingdom
of God, and they have proved a
comfort to me. 12 Epaphras, who is
one of you and a servant of Christ
Jesus, sends greetings. He is always wrestling in prayer for you,
that you may stand firm in all the
will of God, mature and fully assured. 13 I vouch for him that he
is working hard for you and for
those at Laodicea and Hierapolis.

[a] *21* Or *Parents* [b] *7* Or *slave*; also in verse 12 [c] *8* Some manuscripts *that he may know about your* [d] *11* Greek *only ones of the circumcision group*

14 Our dear friend Luke, the doctor,
and Demas send greetings. 15 Give
my greetings to the brothers and
sisters at Laodicea, and to Nym-
pha and the church in her house.
Ac 4:36; Ro 15:30
16 After this letter has been read
to you, see that it is also read in
the church of the Laodiceans and
that you in turn read the letter
from Laodicea. 2Th 3:14
17 Tell Archippus: "See to it that
you complete the ministry you
have received in the Lord."
2Ti 4:5; Phm 2
18 I, Paul, write this greeting in my
own hand. Remember my chains.
Grace be with you. Heb 13:3,25

1 THESSALONIANS

1 Paul, Silas[a] and Timothy,
Ac 16:1; 2Th 1:1

To the church of the Thessaloni-
ans in God the Father and the Lord
Jesus Christ: Ac 17:1

Grace and peace to you. Ro 1:7

Thanksgiving for the Thessalonians' Faith

2We always thank God for all of
you and continually mention you
in our prayers. 3We remember
before our God and Father your
work produced by faith, your labor prompted by love, and your
endurance inspired by hope in our
Lord Jesus Christ. Ro 1:8; 8:25
4For we know, brothers and sisters[b] loved by God, that he has chosen you, 5because our gospel came
to you not simply with words but
also with power, with the Holy
Spirit and deep conviction. You
know how we lived among you for
your sake. 6You became imitators
of us and of the Lord, for you welcomed the message in the midst of
severe suffering with the joy giv-
en by the Holy Spirit. 7And so you
became a model to all the believers in Macedonia and Achaia. 8The
Lord's message rang out from you
not only in Macedonia and Achaia — your faith in God has become
known everywhere. Therefore we
do not need to say anything about
it, 9for they themselves report
what kind of reception you gave
us. They tell how you turned to
God from idols to serve the living
and true God, 10and to wait for his
Son from heaven, whom he raised
from the dead — Jesus, who rescues us from the coming wrath.
Ac 2:24; Ro 5:9

Paul's Ministry in Thessalonica

2 You know, brothers and sisters, that our visit to you was
not without results. 2We had previously suffered and been treated outrageously in Philippi, as
you know, but with the help of
our God we dared to tell you his
gospel in the face of strong opposition. 3For the appeal we make
does not spring from error or impure motives, nor are we trying
to trick you. 4On the contrary, we
speak as those approved by God
to be entrusted with the gospel.
We are not trying to please people but God, who tests our hearts.
5You know we never used flattery,
nor did we put on a mask to cover up greed — God is our witness.

[a] *1* Greek *Silvanus*, a variant of *Silas*
[b] 4 The Greek word for *brothers and sisters* (*adelphoi*) refers here to believers, both men and women, as part of God's family; also in 2:1, 9, 14, 17; 3:7; 4:1, 10, 13; 5:1, 4, 12, 14, 25, 27.

6We were not looking for praise
from people, not from you or anyone else, even though as apostles
of Christ we could have asserted
our authority. 7Instead, we were
like young children[a] among you.

Gal 1:10; 1Th 1:5,9

Just as a nursing mother cares
for her children, 8so we cared
for you. Because we loved you
so much, we were delighted to
share with you not only the gospel of God but our lives as well.
9Surely you remember, brothers
and sisters, our toil and hardship; we worked night and day
in order not to be a burden to
anyone while we preached the
gospel of God to you. 10You are
witnesses, and so is God, of how
holy, righteous and blameless we
were among you who believed.
11For you know that we dealt with
each of you as a father deals with
his own children, 12encouraging,
comforting and urging you to live
lives worthy of God, who calls you
into his kingdom and glory.

Eph 4:1; 1Th 1:5

13And we also thank God continually because, when you received
the word of God, which you heard
from us, you accepted it not as a
human word, but as it actually is,
the word of God, which is indeed
at work in you who believe. 14For
you, brothers and sisters, became
imitators of God's churches in Judea, which are in Christ Jesus: You
suffered from your own people the
same things those churches suffered from the Jews 15who killed
the Lord Jesus and the prophets
and also drove us out. They displease God and are hostile to everyone 16in their effort to keep us
from speaking to the Gentiles so
that they may be saved. In this
way they always heap up their sins
to the limit. The wrath of God has
come upon them at last.[b]

Mt 23:32; Ac 13:45,50

Paul's Longing to See the Thessalonians

17But, brothers and sisters, when
we were orphaned by being separated from you for a short time (in
person, not in thought), out of our
intense longing we made every
effort to see you. 18For we wanted to come to you — certainly I,
Paul, did, again and again — but
Satan blocked our way. 19For what
is our hope, our joy, or the crown
in which we will glory in the presence of our Lord Jesus when he
comes? Is it not you? 20Indeed,
you are our glory and joy.

2Co 1:14; 1Th 3:10

3 So when we could stand it no
longer, we thought it best to
be left by ourselves in Athens. 2We
sent Timothy, who is our brother
and co-worker in God's service in
spreading the gospel of Christ, to
strengthen and encourage you in
your faith, 3so that no one would
be unsettled by these trials. For
you know quite well that we are

[a] 7 Some manuscripts *were gentle*
[b] 16 Or *them fully*

destined for them. 4In fact, when
we were with you, we kept telling
you that we would be persecuted.
And it turned out that way, as you
well know. 5For this reason, when
I could stand it no longer, I sent
to find out about your faith. I was
afraid that in some way the tempter had tempted you and that our
labors might have been in vain.

Ac 9:16; Gal 2:2

Timothy's Encouraging Report

6But Timothy has just now come
to us from you and has brought
good news about your faith and
love. He has told us that you always have pleasant memories of
us and that you long to see us, just
as we also long to see you. 7There-
fore, brothers and sisters, in all our
distress and persecution we were
encouraged about you because
of your faith. 8For now we really
live, since you are standing firm
in the Lord. 9How can we thank
God enough for you in return for
all the joy we have in the presence of our God because of you?
10Night and day we pray most earnestly that we may see you again
and supply what is lacking in your
faith.

1Th 1:2; 2Ti 1:3

11Now may our God and Father
himself and our Lord Jesus clear
the way for us to come to you.
12May the Lord make your love
increase and overflow for each
other and for everyone else, just
as ours does for you. 13May he
strengthen your hearts so that
you will be blameless and holy in
the presence of our God and Father when our Lord Jesus comes
with all his holy ones.

1Co 1:8; 1Th 4:9-10

Living to Please God

4 As for other matters, brothers
and sisters, we instructed you
how to live in order to please God,
as in fact you are living. Now we
ask you and urge you in the Lord
Jesus to do this more and more.
2For you know what instructions
we gave you by the authority of
the Lord Jesus.

2Co 5:9; 13:11

3It is God's will that you should
be sanctified: that you should
avoid sexual immorality; 4that
each of you should learn to control your own body[a] in a way that
is holy and honorable, 5not in passionate lust like the pagans, who
do not know God; 6and that in this
matter no one should wrong or
take advantage of a brother or sister.[b] The Lord will punish all those
who commit such sins, as we told
you and warned you before. 7For
God did not call us to be impure,
but to live a holy life. 8Therefore,
anyone who rejects this instruction does not reject a human being but God, the very God who
gives you his Holy Spirit.

Ro 5:5; Gal 4:6

[a] 4 Or *learn to live with your own wife*; or *learn to acquire a wife* [b] 6 The Greek word for *brother or sister* (*adelphos*) refers here to a believer, whether man or woman, as part of God's family.

9 Now about your love for one
another we do not need to write to
you, for you yourselves have been
taught by God to love each other. 10 And in fact, you do love all of
God's family throughout Macedonia. Yet we urge you, brothers and
sisters, to do so more and more,
11 and to make it your ambition to
lead a quiet life: You should mind
your own business and work with
your hands, just as we told you,
12 so that your daily life may win
the respect of outsiders and so
that you will not be dependent on
anybody. Eph 4:28; 2Th 3:10-12

Believers Who Have Died

13 Brothers and sisters, we do not
want you to be uninformed about
those who sleep in death, so that
you do not grieve like the rest of
mankind, who have no hope. 14 For
we believe that Jesus died and
rose again, and so we believe that
God will bring with Jesus those
who have fallen asleep in him.
15 According to the Lord's word,
we tell you that we who are still
alive, who are left until the coming of the Lord, will certainly not
precede those who have fallen
asleep. 16 For the Lord himself will
come down from heaven, with a
loud command, with the voice of
the archangel and with the trumpet call of God, and the dead in
Christ will rise first. 17 After that,
we who are still alive and are left
will be caught up together with
them in the clouds to meet the
Lord in the air. And so we will be
with the Lord forever. 18 Therefore
encourage one another with these
words. 1Co 15:52; Ac 1:9; Rev 11:12

The Day of the Lord

5 Now, brothers and sisters,
about times and dates we do
not need to write to you, 2 for you
know very well that the day of the
Lord will come like a thief in the
night. 3 While people are saying,
"Peace and safety," destruction
will come on them suddenly, as
labor pains on a pregnant woman,
and they will not escape.
1Th 4:9; 2Pe 3:10

4 But you, brothers and sisters,
are not in darkness so that this day
should surprise you like a thief.
5 You are all children of the light
and children of the day. We do
not belong to the night or to the
darkness. 6 So then, let us not be
like others, who are asleep, but let
us be awake and sober. 7 For those
who sleep, sleep at night, and
those who get drunk, get drunk
at night. 8 But since we belong to
the day, let us be sober, putting on
faith and love as a breastplate, and
the hope of salvation as a helmet.
9 For God did not appoint us to suffer wrath but to receive salvation
through our Lord Jesus Christ.
10 He died for us so that, whether
we are awake or asleep, we may
live together with him. 11 Therefore
encourage one another and build
each other up, just as in fact you
are doing. 1Th 4:18; Eph 4:29

Final Instructions

12 Now we ask you, brothers and
sisters, to acknowledge those who
work hard among you, who care
for you in the Lord and who admonish you. 13 Hold them in the
highest regard in love because
of their work. Live in peace with
each other. 14 And we urge you,
brothers and sisters, warn those
who are idle and disruptive, encourage the disheartened, help
the weak, be patient with everyone. 15 Make sure that nobody pays
back wrong for wrong, but always
strive to do what is good for each
other and for everyone else.

Eph 4:32; 2Th 3:6-7,11

16 Rejoice always, 17 pray continually, 18 give thanks in all circumstances; for this is God's will for
you in Christ Jesus. Php 4:4

19 Do not quench the Spirit. 20 Do
not treat prophecies with contempt 21 but test them all; hold on
to what is good, 22 reject every kind
of evil. 1Co 14:29; Eph 4:30

23 May God himself, the God of
peace, sanctify you through and
through. May your whole spirit,
soul and body be kept blameless
at the coming of our Lord Jesus
Christ. 24 The one who calls you is
faithful, and he will do it.

1Co 1:9; Php 1:6

25 Brothers and sisters, pray for
us. 26 Greet all God's people with a
holy kiss. 27 I charge you before the
Lord to have this letter read to all
the brothers and sisters.

Ro 16:16; Col 4:16

28 The grace of our Lord Jesus
Christ be with you. Ro 16:20

2 THESSALONIANS

1 Paul, Silas[a] and Timothy,
1Th 1:1; Ac 15:22

To the church of the Thessaloni-
ans in God our Father and the Lord
Jesus Christ: Ac 17:1

2 Grace and peace to you from
God the Father and the Lord Jesus
Christ. Ro 1:7

Thanksgiving and Prayer

3 We ought always to thank God
for you, brothers and sisters,[b] and
rightly so, because your faith is
growing more and more, and the
love all of you have for one another is increasing. 4 Therefore,
among God's churches we boast
about your perseverance and faith
in all the persecutions and trials
you are enduring. 1Th 3:12; 2:14
5 All this is evidence that God's
judgment is right, and as a result
you will be counted worthy of the
kingdom of God, for which you are
suffering. 6 God is just: He will pay
back trouble to those who trouble
you 7 and give relief to you who are
troubled, and to us as well. This
will happen when the Lord Jesus
is revealed from heaven in blazing
fire with his powerful angels. 8 He
will punish those who do not know
God and do not obey the gospel of
our Lord Jesus. 9 They will be punished with everlasting destruction
and shut out from the presence of
the Lord and from the glory of his
might 10 on the day he comes to be
glorified in his holy people and to
be marveled at among all those
who have believed. This includes
you, because you believed our testimony to you. 1Th 4:16; Jude 14
11 With this in mind, we constantly pray for you, that our God
may make you worthy of his calling, and that by his power he may
bring to fruition your every desire
for goodness and your every deed
prompted by faith. 12 We pray this
so that the name of our Lord Jesus
may be glorified in you, and you in
him, according to the grace of our
God and the Lord Jesus Christ.[c]
Php 2:9-11; 1Th 1:3

The Man of Lawlessness

2 Concerning the coming of our
Lord Jesus Christ and our being gathered to him, we ask you,
brothers and sisters, 2 not to become easily unsettled or alarmed
by the teaching allegedly from
us — whether by a prophecy or by
word of mouth or by letter — asserting that the day of the Lord

[a] *1* Greek *Silvanus*, a variant of *Silas*
[b] *3* The Greek word for *brothers and sisters* (*adelphoi*) refers here to believers, both men and women, as part of God's family; also in 2:1, 13, 15; 3:1, 6, 13.
[c] *12* Or *God and Lord, Jesus Christ*

has already come. 3Don't let anyone deceive you in any way, for
that day will not come until the
rebellion occurs and the man of
lawlessness[a] is revealed, the man
doomed to destruction. 4He will
oppose and will exalt himself over
everything that is called God or is
worshiped, so that he sets himself
up in God's temple, proclaiming
himself to be God. Isa 14:13-14; 1Co 8:5

5Don't you remember that when
I was with you I used to tell you
these things? 6And now you know
what is holding him back, so that
he may be revealed at the proper
time. 7For the secret power of lawlessness is already at work; but the
one who now holds it back will
continue to do so till he is taken
out of the way. 8And then the lawless one will be revealed, whom
the Lord Jesus will overthrow with
the breath of his mouth and destroy by the splendor of his coming. 9The coming of the lawless
one will be in accordance with
how Satan works. He will use all
sorts of displays of power through
signs and wonders that serve the
lie, 10and all the ways that wickedness deceives those who are perishing. They perish because they
refused to love the truth and so be
saved. 11For this reason God sends
them a powerful delusion so that
they will believe the lie 12and so
that all will be condemned who
have not believed the truth but
have delighted in wickedness.
Jn 4:48; Ro 1:32

Stand Firm

13But we ought always to thank
God for you, brothers and sisters loved by the Lord, because
God chose you as firstfruits[b] to
be saved through the sanctifying
work of the Spirit and through belief in the truth. 14He called you to
this through our gospel, that you
might share in the glory of our
Lord Jesus Christ.

15So then, brothers and sisters,
stand firm and hold fast to the
teachings[c] we passed on to you,
whether by word of mouth or by
letter. 1Co 11:2; 16:13

16May our Lord Jesus Christ
himself and God our Father, who
loved us and by his grace gave us
eternal encouragement and good
hope, 17encourage your hearts
and strengthen you in every good
deed and word. Jn 3:16; 1Th 3:2

Request for Prayer

3 As for other matters, brothers
and sisters, pray for us that the
message of the Lord may spread
rapidly and be honored, just as it
was with you. 2And pray that we
may be delivered from wicked and
evil people, for not everyone has
faith. 3But the Lord is faithful, and
he will strengthen you and protect
you from the evil one. 4We have
confidence in the Lord that you
are doing and will continue to do
the things we command. 5May the

[a] 3 Some manuscripts *sin* [b] 13 Some manuscripts *because from the beginning God chose you* [c] 15 Or *traditions*

Lord direct your hearts into God's
love and Christ's perseverance.
1Ch 29:18; 1Co 1:9

Warning Against Idleness

6In the name of the Lord Jesus
Christ, we command you, brothers and sisters, to keep away from
every believer who is idle and disruptive and does not live according to the teaching[a] you received
from us. 7For you yourselves know
how you ought to follow our example. We were not idle when we
were with you, 8nor did we eat
anyone's food without paying for
it. On the contrary, we worked
night and day, laboring and toiling so that we would not be a burden to any of you. 9We did this, not
because we do not have the right
to such help, but in order to offer
ourselves as a model for you to
imitate. 10For even when we were
with you, we gave you this rule:
"The one who is unwilling to work
shall not eat." 1Co 9:4-14; 1Th 4:11
11We hear that some among
you are idle and disruptive. They
are not busy; they are busybodies. 12Such people we command
and urge in the Lord Jesus Christ
to settle down and earn the food
they eat. 13And as for you, brothers and sisters, never tire of doing
what is good. Gal 6:9; 1Ti 5:13
14Take special note of anyone
who does not obey our instruction in this letter. Do not associate
with them, in order that they may
feel ashamed. 15Yet do not regard
them as an enemy, but warn them
as you would a fellow believer.
Gal 6:1; 1Th 5:14

Final Greetings

16Now may the Lord of peace
himself give you peace at all times
and in every way. The Lord be with
all of you. Ro 15:33
17I, Paul, write this greeting in
my own hand, which is the distinguishing mark in all my letters.
This is how I write. 1Co 16:21
18The grace of our Lord Jesus
Christ be with you all. Ro 16:20

[a] 6 Or *tradition*

1 TIMOTHY

1 Paul, an apostle of Christ Jesus
by the command of God our
Savior and of Christ Jesus our
hope, Col 1:27; Titus 1:3

2To Timothy my true son in the
faith: Ac 16:1; 2Ti 1:2

Grace, mercy and peace from
God the Father and Christ Jesus
our Lord. Ro 1:7

Timothy Charged to Oppose False Teachers

3As I urged you when I went
into Macedonia, stay there in Ephesus so that you may command
certain people not to teach false
doctrines any longer 4or to devote
themselves to myths and endless
genealogies. Such things promote
controversial speculations rather than advancing God's work —
which is by faith. 5The goal of this
command is love, which comes
from a pure heart and a good conscience and a sincere faith. 6Some
have departed from these and
have turned to meaningless talk.
7They want to be teachers of the
law, but they do not know what
they are talking about or what
they so confidently affirm.

2Ti 2:22; Titus 1:14

8We know that the law is good if
one uses it properly. 9We also know
that the law is made not for the
righteous but for lawbreakers and
rebels, the ungodly and sinful, the
unholy and irreligious, for those
who kill their fathers or mothers,
for murderers, 10for the sexually immoral, for those practicing
homosexuality, for slave traders
and liars and perjurers — and for
whatever else is contrary to the
sound doctrine 11that conforms to
the gospel concerning the glory of
the blessed God, which he entrusted to me. Gal 2:7; 2Ti 4:3

The Lord's Grace to Paul

12I thank Christ Jesus our Lord,
who has given me strength, that
he considered me trustworthy, ap-
pointing me to his service. 13Even
though I was once a blasphemer and a persecutor and a violent
man, I was shown mercy because
I acted in ignorance and unbelief.
14The grace of our Lord was poured
out on me abundantly, along with
the faith and love that are in Christ
Jesus. Ac 8:3; 2Ti 1:13

15Here is a trustworthy saying that deserves full acceptance:
Christ Jesus came into the world to
save sinners — of whom I am the
worst. 16But for that very reason I
was shown mercy so that in me,
the worst of sinners, Christ Jesus
might display his immense patience as an example for those who

would believe in him and receive
eternal life. 17 Now to the King eternal, immortal, invisible, the only
God, be honor and glory for ever
and ever. Amen. Ro 11:36; Col 1:15; Rev 15:3

The Charge to Timothy Renewed

18 Timothy, my son, I am giving
you this command in keeping with
the prophecies once made about
you, so that by recalling them you
may fight the battle well, 19 holding
on to faith and a good conscience,
which some have rejected and so
have suffered shipwreck with regard to the faith. 20 Among them
are Hymenaeus and Alexander,
whom I have handed over to Satan to be taught not to blaspheme.
1Ti 4:14; 2Ti 2:3

Instructions on Worship

2 I urge, then, first of all, that
petitions, prayers, intercession and thanksgiving be made
for all people — 2 for kings and all
those in authority, that we may
live peaceful and quiet lives in all
godliness and holiness. 3 This is
good, and pleases God our Savior,
4 who wants all people to be saved
and to come to a knowledge of the
truth. 5 For there is one God and
one mediator between God and
mankind, the man Christ Jesus,
6 who gave himself as a ransom for
all people. This has now been witnessed to at the proper time. 7 And
for this purpose I was appointed
a herald and an apostle — I am
telling the truth, I am not lying —
and a true and faithful teacher of
the Gentiles. 1Co 1:6; Gal 3:20
8 Therefore I want the men everywhere to pray, lifting up holy
hands without anger or disputing.
9 I also want the women to dress
modestly, with decency and propriety, adorning themselves, not
with elaborate hairstyles or gold
or pearls or expensive clothes,
10 but with good deeds, appropriate for women who profess to worship God. Pr 31:13; 1Pe 3:3
11 A woman[a] should learn in quietness and full submission. 12 I do
not permit a woman to teach or
to assume authority over a man;[b]
she must be quiet. 13 For Adam was
formed first, then Eve. 14 And Adam
was not the one deceived; it was
the woman who was deceived and
became a sinner. 15 But women[c]
will be saved through childbearing — if they continue in faith,
love and holiness with propriety.
Ge 3:1-6,13; 1Co 11:8

Qualifications for Overseers and Deacons

3 Here is a trustworthy saying:
Whoever aspires to be an overseer desires a noble task. 2 Now the
overseer is to be above reproach,
faithful to his wife, temperate,
self-controlled, respectable, hospitable, able to teach, 3 not given to
drunkenness, not violent but gentle, not quarrelsome, not a lover of
money. 4 He must manage his own

[a] 11 Or *wife;* also in verse 12 [b] 12 Or *over her husband* [c] 15 Greek *she*

family well and see that his children obey him, and he must do so
in a manner worthy of full[a] respect.
5(If anyone does not know how to
manage his own family, how can
he take care of God's church?) 6He
must not be a recent convert, or
he may become conceited and fall
under the same judgment as the
devil. 7He must also have a good
reputation with outsiders, so that
he will not fall into disgrace and
into the devil's trap. 1Ti 6:4; 2Ti 2:26

8In the same way, deacons[b]
are to be worthy of respect, sincere, not indulging in much wine,
and not pursuing dishonest gain.
9They must keep hold of the deep
truths of the faith with a clear conscience. 10They must first be tested; and then if there is nothing
against them, let them serve as
deacons. 1Ti 1:19; Titus 2:3

11In the same way, the women[c]
are to be worthy of respect, not
malicious talkers but temperate
and trustworthy in everything.
Titus 2:3

12A deacon must be faithful to
his wife and must manage his
children and his household well.
13Those who have served well gain
an excellent standing and great
assurance in their faith in Christ
Jesus.

Reasons for Paul's Instructions

14Although I hope to come to
you soon, I am writing you these
instructions so that, 15if I am delayed, you will know how people ought to conduct themselves
in God's household, which is the
church of the living God, the pillar and foundation of the truth.
16Beyond all question, the mystery
from which true godliness springs
is great: Ro 16:25; Eph 2:21

He appeared in the flesh, Jn 1:14
was vindicated by the Spirit,[d]
was seen by angels,
was preached among the nations, Col 1:23
was believed on in the world,
was taken up in glory. Mk 16:19

4 The Spirit clearly says that in
later times some will aban-
don the faith and follow deceiving spirits and things taught by
demons. 2Such teachings come
through hypocritical liars, whose
consciences have been seared as
with a hot iron. 3They forbid people to marry and order them to
abstain from certain foods, which
God created to be received with
thanksgiving by those who believe and who know the truth.
4For everything God created is
good, and nothing is to be rejected
if it is received with thanksgiving, 5because it is consecrated by
the word of God and prayer.
Ro 14:14-18

[a] 4 Or *him with proper* [b] 8 The word *deacons* refers here to Christians designated to serve with the overseers/elders of the church in a variety of ways; similarly in verse 12; and in Romans 16:1 and Phil. 1:1. [c] 11 Possibly deacons' wives or women who are deacons [d] 16 Or *vindicated in spirit*

[6]If you point these things out
to the brothers and sisters,[a] you
will be a good minister of Christ
Jesus, nourished on the truths of
the faith and of the good teaching that you have followed. [7]Have
nothing to do with godless myths
and old wives' tales; rather, train
yourself to be godly. [8]For physical training is of some value, but
godliness has value for all things,
holding promise for both the present life and the life to come. [9]This
is a trustworthy saying that deserves full acceptance. [10]That is
why we labor and strive, because
we have put our hope in the living
God, who is the Savior of all people, and especially of those who
believe. 1Ti 1:15

[11]Command and teach these
things. [12]Don't let anyone look
down on you because you are
young, but set an example for the
believers in speech, in conduct, in
love, in faith and in purity. [13]Until I
come, devote yourself to the public reading of Scripture, to preaching and to teaching. [14]Do not neglect your gift, which was given
you through prophecy when the
body of elders laid their hands on
you. 1Ti 1:14,18; Titus 2:7

[15]Be diligent in these matters;
give yourself wholly to them, so
that everyone may see your progress. [16]Watch your life and doctrine closely. Persevere in them,
because if you do, you will save
both yourself and your hearers.
Ro 11:14

Widows, Elders and Slaves

5 Do not rebuke an older man
harshly, but exhort him as if
he were your father. Treat younger
men as brothers, [2]older women as
mothers, and younger women as
sisters, with absolute purity.
Lev 19:32; Titus 2:6

[3]Give proper recognition to
those widows who are really in
need. [4]But if a widow has children
or grandchildren, these should
learn first of all to put their religion into practice by caring for
their own family and so repaying
their parents and grandparents,
for this is pleasing to God. [5]The
widow who is really in need and
left all alone puts her hope in God
and continues night and day to
pray and to ask God for help. [6]But
the widow who lives for pleasure
is dead even while she lives. [7]Give
the people these instructions, so
that no one may be open to blame.
[8]Anyone who does not provide for
their relatives, and especially for
their own household, has denied
the faith and is worse than an unbeliever. 1Ti 4:11; Titus 1:16

[9]No widow may be put on the
list of widows unless she is over
sixty, has been faithful to her
husband, [10]and is well known for
her good deeds, such as bringing
up children, showing hospitality, washing the feet of the Lord's
people, helping those in trouble

[a] 6 The Greek word for *brothers and sisters* (*adelphoi*) refers here to believers, both men and women, as part of God's family.

and devoting herself to all kinds
of good deeds. Lk 7:44; 1Pe 2:12
11 As for younger widows, do not
put them on such a list. For when
their sensual desires overcome
their dedication to Christ, they
want to marry. 12 Thus they bring
judgment on themselves, because
they have broken their first pledge.
13 Besides, they get into the habit of
being idle and going about from
house to house. And not only do
they become idlers, but also busybodies who talk nonsense, saying
things they ought not to. 14 So I
counsel younger widows to marry,
to have children, to manage their
homes and to give the enemy no
opportunity for slander. 15 Some
have in fact already turned away
to follow Satan. 1Co 7:9; 2Th 3:11

16 If any woman who is a believer
has widows in her care, she should
continue to help them and not
let the church be burdened with
them, so that the church can help
those widows who are really in
need. ver 3-5

17 The elders who direct the affairs of the church well are worthy
of double honor, especially those
whose work is preaching and
teaching. 18 For Scripture says, "Do
not muzzle an ox while it is treading out the grain,"[a] and "The worker deserves his wages."[b] 19 Do not
entertain an accusation against an
elder unless it is brought by two
or three witnesses. 20 But those elders who are sinning you are to
reprove before everyone, so that
the others may take warning. 21 I
charge you, in the sight of God and
Christ Jesus and the elect angels,
to keep these instructions without
partiality, and to do nothing out of
favoritism. 1Ti 6:13; 2Ti 4:1

22 Do not be hasty in the laying
on of hands, and do not share in
the sins of others. Keep yourself
pure. Ac 6:6; Eph 5:11

23 Stop drinking only water, and
use a little wine because of your
stomach and your frequent illnesses. 1Ti 3:8

24 The sins of some are obvious,
reaching the place of judgment
ahead of them; the sins of others
trail behind them. 25 In the same
way, good deeds are obvious, and
even those that are not obvious
cannot remain hidden forever.

6 All who are under the yoke of
slavery should consider their
masters worthy of full respect, so
that God's name and our teaching
may not be slandered. 2 Those who
have believing masters should not
show them disrespect just because
they are fellow believers. Instead,
they should serve them even better because their masters are dear
to them as fellow believers and are
devoted to the welfare[c] of their
slaves.

False Teachers and the Love of Money

These are the things you are
to teach and insist on. 3 If anyone

[a] 18 Deut. 25:4 [b] 18 Luke 10:7 [c] 2 Or *and benefit from the service*

teaches otherwise and does not
agree to the sound instruction of
our Lord Jesus Christ and to godly
teaching, 4they are conceited and
understand nothing. They have an
unhealthy interest in controversies and quarrels about words that
result in envy, strife, malicious
talk, evil suspicions 5and constant
friction between people of corrupt
mind, who have been robbed of
the truth and who think that godliness is a means to financial gain.

1Ti 1:10; Titus 1:15

6But godliness with con-
tentment is great gain. 7For we
brought nothing into the world,
and we can take nothing out of
it. 8But if we have food and clothing, we will be content with that.
9Those who want to get rich fall
into temptation and a trap and
into many foolish and harmful desires that plunge people into ruin
and destruction. 10For the love of
money is a root of all kinds of evil.
Some people, eager for money,
have wandered from the faith and
pierced themselves with many
griefs. 1Ti 3:3; Heb 13:5

Final Charge to Timothy

11But you, man of God, flee from
all this, and pursue righteousness, godliness, faith, love, endurance and gentleness. 12Fight the
good fight of the faith. Take hold
of the eternal life to which you
were called when you made your
good confession in the presence of
many witnesses. 13In the sight of
God, who gives life to everything,
and of Christ Jesus, who while testifying before Pontius Pilate made
the good confession, I charge you
14to keep this command without
spot or blame until the appearing
of our Lord Jesus Christ, 15which
God will bring about in his own
time — God, the blessed and only
Ruler, the King of kings and Lord
of lords, 16who alone is immortal and who lives in unapproach-
able light, whom no one has seen
or can see. To him be honor and
might forever. Amen.

Jn 18:33-37; 1Ti 5:21

17Command those who are rich
in this present world not to be
arrogant nor to put their hope
in wealth, which is so uncertain,
but to put their hope in God, who
richly provides us with everything for our enjoyment. 18Com-
mand them to do good, to be rich
in good deeds, and to be generous
and willing to share. 19In this way
they will lay up treasure for themselves as a firm foundation for the
coming age, so that they may take
hold of the life that is truly life.

Lk 12:20-21; Ac 14:17

20Timothy, guard what has been
entrusted to your care. Turn away
from godless chatter and the opposing ideas of what is falsely
called knowledge, 21which some
have professed and in so doing
have departed from the faith.

2Ti 1:12,14; 2:18

Grace be with you all. Col 4:18

2 TIMOTHY

1 Paul, an apostle of Christ Jesus
by the will of God, in keeping
with the promise of life that is in
Christ Jesus, 2Co 1:1

2To Timothy, my dear son:
Ac 16:1; 1Ti 1:2

Grace, mercy and peace from
God the Father and Christ Jesus
our Lord. Ro 1:7

Thanksgiving

3I thank God, whom I serve,
as my ancestors did, with a clear
conscience, as night and day I
constantly remember you in my
prayers. 4Recalling your tears, I
long to see you, so that I may be
filled with joy. 5I am reminded of
your sincere faith, which first lived
in your grandmother Lois and in
your mother Eunice and, I am persuaded, now lives in you also.

Appeal for Loyalty to Paul and the Gospel

6For this reason I remind you
to fan into flame the gift of God,
which is in you through the laying
on of my hands. 7For the Spirit God
gave us does not make us timid,
but gives us power, love and self-
discipline. 8So do not be ashamed
of the testimony about our Lord
or of me his prisoner. Rather, join
with me in suffering for the gospel, by the power of God. 9He has
saved us and called us to a holy
life — not because of anything we
have done but because of his own
purpose and grace. This grace was
given us in Christ Jesus before the
beginning of time, 10but it has now
been revealed through the appearing of our Savior, Christ Jesus,
who has destroyed death and has
brought life and immortality to
light through the gospel. 11And of
this gospel I was appointed a herald and an apostle and a teacher.
12That is why I am suffering as I
am. Yet this is no cause for shame,
because I know whom I have believed, and am convinced that he
is able to guard what I have entrusted to him until that day.
1Ti 2:7; 6:20

13What you heard from me, keep
as the pattern of sound teaching,
with faith and love in Christ Jesus.
14Guard the good deposit that was
entrusted to you — guard it with
the help of the Holy Spirit who
lives in us. 1Ti 1:14; Titus 1:9

Examples of Disloyalty and Loyalty

15You know that everyone in the
province of Asia has deserted me,
including Phygelus and Hermoge-
nes. 2Ti 4:10-11,16

16May the Lord show mercy to
the household of Onesiphorus,

because he often refreshed me
and was not ashamed of my
chains. 17On the contrary, when he
was in Rome, he searched hard for
me until he found me. 18May the
Lord grant that he will find mercy from the Lord on that day! You
know very well in how many ways
he helped me in Ephesus.

2Ti 4:19; Heb 6:10

The Appeal Renewed

2 You then, my son, be strong
in the grace that is in Christ
Jesus. 2And the things you have
heard me say in the presence of
many witnesses entrust to reliable
people who will also be qualified
to teach others. 3Join with me in
suffering, like a good soldier of
Christ Jesus. 4No one serving as a
soldier gets entangled in civilian
affairs, but rather tries to please
his commanding officer. 5Simi-
larly, anyone who competes as an
athlete does not receive the victor's crown except by competing
according to the rules. 6The hard-
working farmer should be the first
to receive a share of the crops. 7Re-
flect on what I am saying, for the
Lord will give you insight into all
this. 1Co 9:25; 1Ti 1:18

8Remember Jesus Christ,
raised from the dead, descended from David. This is my gospel,
9for which I am suffering even to
the point of being chained like a
criminal. But God's word is not
chained. 10Therefore I endure everything for the sake of the elect,
that they too may obtain the salvation that is in Christ Jesus, with
eternal glory. Ro 2:16; 2Co 4:17

11Here is a trustworthy saying:

1Ti 1:15

If we died with him,
  we will also live with him;

Ro 6:2-11

12if we endure,
  we will also reign with him.

Ro 8:17; 1Pe 4:13

If we disown him,
  he will also disown us; Mt 10:33
13if we are faithless,
  he remains faithful,

Nu 23:19; Ro 3:3

for he cannot disown
  himself.

Dealing With False Teachers

14Keep reminding God's people
of these things. Warn them before God against quarreling about
words; it is of no value, and only
ruins those who listen. 15Do your
best to present yourself to God
as one approved, a worker who
does not need to be ashamed and
who correctly handles the word of
truth. 16Avoid godless chatter, because those who indulge in it will
become more and more ungodly.
17Their teaching will spread like
gangrene. Among them are Hymenaeus and Philetus, 18who have
departed from the truth. They say
that the resurrection has already
taken place, and they destroy
the faith of some. 19Nevertheless,
God's solid foundation stands

firm, sealed with this inscription:
"The Lord knows those who are
his," and, "Everyone who confesses the name of the Lord must turn
away from wickedness."

Jn 10:14; 1Co 1:2

[20]In a large house there are articles not only of gold and silver, but
also of wood and clay; some are
for special purposes and some for
common use. [21]Those who cleanse
themselves from the latter will be
instruments for special purposes, made holy, useful to the Master and prepared to do any good
work. Ro 9:21; 2Ti 3:17

[22]Flee the evil desires of youth
and pursue righteousness, faith,
love and peace, along with those
who call on the Lord out of a pure
heart. [23]Don't have anything to
do with foolish and stupid arguments, because you know they
produce quarrels. [24]And the Lord's
servant must not be quarrelsome
but must be kind to everyone,
able to teach, not resentful. [25]Op-
ponents must be gently instructed, in the hope that God will grant
them repentance leading them to
a knowledge of the truth, [26]and
that they will come to their senses and escape from the trap of the
devil, who has taken them captive
to do his will. 1Ti 1:5; 3:7

3 But mark this: There will be
terrible times in the last days.
[2]People will be lovers of themselves, lovers of money, boastful, proud, abusive, disobedient
to their parents, ungrateful, unholy, [3]without love, unforgiving,
slanderous, without self-control,
brutal, not lovers of the good,
[4]treacherous, rash, conceited, lovers of pleasure rather than lovers
of God — [5]having a form of godliness but denying its power. Have
nothing to do with such people.

Ro 1:30; 1Ti 4:1

[6]They are the kind who worm
their way into homes and gain
control over gullible women, who
are loaded down with sins and are
swayed by all kinds of evil desires,
[7]always learning but never able to
come to a knowledge of the truth.
[8]Just as Jannes and Jambres opposed Moses, so also these teachers oppose the truth. They are
men of depraved minds, who, as
far as the faith is concerned, are
rejected. [9]But they will not get
very far because, as in the case of
those men, their folly will be clear
to everyone. Ex 7:12; 1Ti 6:5

A Final Charge to Timothy

[10]You, however, know all about
my teaching, my way of life, my
purpose, faith, patience, love, endurance, [11]persecutions, sufferings — what kinds of things happened to me in Antioch, Iconium
and Lystra, the persecutions I endured. Yet the Lord rescued me
from all of them. [12]In fact, everyone who wants to live a godly life
in Christ Jesus will be persecuted,
[13]while evildoers and impostors
will go from bad to worse, deceiving and being deceived. [14]But as

for you, continue in what you have
learned and have become convinced of, because you know those
from whom you learned it, [15]and
how from infancy you have known
the Holy Scriptures, which are able
to make you wise for salvation
through faith in Christ Jesus. [16]All
Scripture is God-breathed and is
useful for teaching, rebuking, cor-
recting and training in righteousness, [17]so that the servant of God[a]
may be thoroughly equipped for
every good work. 2Pe 1:20-21

4 In the presence of God and of
Christ Jesus, who will judge
the living and the dead, and in
view of his appearing and his
kingdom, I give you this charge:
[2]Preach the word; be prepared in
season and out of season; correct,
rebuke and encourage — with
great patience and careful instruction. [3]For the time will come
when people will not put up with
sound doctrine. Instead, to suit
their own desires, they will gather around them a great number of
teachers to say what their itching
ears want to hear. [4]They will turn
their ears away from the truth
and turn aside to myths. [5]But you,
keep your head in all situations,
endure hardship, do the work of
an evangelist, discharge all the
duties of your ministry.

Ac 21:8; 1Ti 1:10

[6]For I am already being poured
out like a drink offering, and the
time for my departure is near. [7]I
have fought the good fight, I have
finished the race, I have kept the
faith. [8]Now there is in store for me
the crown of righteousness, which
the Lord, the righteous Judge, will
award to me on that day — and
not only to me, but also to all who
have longed for his appearing.

1Ti 1:18; 2Ti 1:12

Personal Remarks

[9]Do your best to come to me
quickly, [10]for Demas, because he
loved this world, has deserted
me and has gone to Thessalonica.
Crescens has gone to Galatia, and
Titus to Dalmatia. [11]Only Luke is
with me. Get Mark and bring him
with you, because he is helpful to
me in my ministry. [12]I sent Tychicus to Ephesus. [13]When you come,
bring the cloak that I left with Car-
pus at Troas, and my scrolls, especially the parchments. Col 4:14; 2Ti 1:15

[14]Alexander the metalworker
did me a great deal of harm. The
Lord will repay him for what he
has done. [15]You too should be on
your guard against him, because
he strongly opposed our message.

Ac 19:33; Ro 12:19

[16]At my first defense, no one
came to my support, but everyone
deserted me. May it not be held
against them. [17]But the Lord stood
at my side and gave me strength,
so that through me the message
might be fully proclaimed and all
the Gentiles might hear it. And
I was delivered from the lion's
mouth. [18]The Lord will rescue me

[a] 17 Or *that you, a man of God,*

from every evil attack and will
bring me safely to his heavenly
kingdom. To him be glory for ever
and ever. Amen. Ps 121:7; Ro 11:36

Final Greetings

19Greet Priscilla[a] and Aquila and
the household of Onesiphorus.
20Erastus stayed in Corinth, and
I left Trophimus sick in Miletus.
21Do your best to get here before
winter. Eubulus greets you, and so
do Pudens, Linus, Claudia and all
the brothers and sisters.[b]
Ac 19:22; 20:4

22The Lord be with your spirit.
Grace be with you all. Gal 6:18; Col 4:18

[a] 19 Greek *Prisca*, a variant of *Priscilla*

[b] 21 The Greek word for *brothers and sisters* (*adelphoi*) refers here to believers, both men and women, as part of God's family.

TITUS

1 Paul, a servant of God and an
apostle of Jesus Christ to further the faith of God's elect and
their knowledge of the truth that
leads to godliness — 2in the hope
of eternal life, which God, who
does not lie, promised before the
beginning of time, 3and which
now at his appointed season he
has brought to light through the
preaching entrusted to me by the
command of God our Savior,

2Ti 1:1,10

4To Titus, my true son in our
common faith: 2Co 2:13

Grace and peace from God the
Father and Christ Jesus our Savior.

Ro 1:7

Appointing Elders Who Love What Is Good

5The reason I left you in Crete
was that you might put in order
what was left unfinished and appoint[a] elders in every town, as I
directed you. 6An elder must be
blameless, faithful to his wife, a
man whose children believe[b] and
are not open to the charge of being wild and disobedient. 7Since
an overseer manages God's household, he must be blameless — not
overbearing, not quick-tempered,
not given to drunkenness, not violent, not pursuing dishonest gain.
8Rather, he must be hospitable,
one who loves what is good, who is
self-controlled, upright, holy and
disciplined. 9He must hold firmly
to the trustworthy message as it
has been taught, so that he can encourage others by sound doctrine
and refute those who oppose it.

1Ti 3:2-4

Rebuking Those Who Fail to Do Good

10For there are many rebellious
people, full of meaningless talk
and deception, especially those
of the circumcision group. 11They
must be silenced, because they
are disrupting whole households
by teaching things they ought not
to teach — and that for the sake
of dishonest gain. 12One of Crete's
own prophets has said it: "Cretans
are always liars, evil brutes, lazy
gluttons."[c] 13This saying is true.
Therefore rebuke them sharply,
so that they will be sound in the
faith 14and will pay no attention
to Jewish myths or to the merely
human commands of those who
reject the truth. 15To the pure, all
things are pure, but to those who
are corrupted and do not believe,
nothing is pure. In fact, both their

[a] 5 Or *ordain* [b] 6 Or *children are trustworthy* [c] 12 From the Cretan philosopher Epimenides

minds and consciences are corrupted. 16They claim to know God,
but by their actions they deny
him. They are detestable, disobedient and unfit for doing anything
good. 1Ti 1:4; 1Jn 2:4

Doing Good for the Sake of the Gospel

2 You, however, must teach
what is appropriate to sound
doctrine. 2Teach the older men to
be temperate, worthy of respect,
self-controlled, and sound in faith,
in love and in endurance.
1Ti 1:10; Titus 1:13

3Likewise, teach the older wom-
en to be reverent in the way they
live, not to be slanderers or ad-
dicted to much wine, but to teach
what is good. 4Then they can urge
the younger women to love their
husbands and children, 5to be self-
controlled and pure, to be busy at
home, to be kind, and to be subject to their husbands, so that no
one will malign the word of God.
Eph 5:22; 1Ti 6:1

6Similarly, encourage the young
men to be self-controlled. 7In everything set them an example by
doing what is good. In your teaching show integrity, seriousness
8and soundness of speech that cannot be condemned, so that those
who oppose you may be ashamed
because they have nothing bad to
say about us. 1Ti 4:12; 1Pe 2:12

9Teach slaves to be subject to
their masters in everything, to try
to please them, not to talk back
to them, 10and not to steal from
them, but to show that they can be
fully trusted, so that in every way
they will make the teaching about
God our Savior attractive.
Mt 5:16; Eph 6:5

11For the grace of God has appeared that offers salvation to all
people. 12It teaches us to say "No"
to ungodliness and worldly passions, and to live self-controlled,
upright and godly lives in this
present age, 13while we wait for
the blessed hope — the appearing
of the glory of our great God and
Savior, Jesus Christ, 14who gave
himself for us to redeem us from
all wickedness and to purify for
himself a people that are his very
own, eager to do what is good.
2Ti 3:12; 2Pe 1:1

15These, then, are the things you
should teach. Encourage and rebuke with all authority. Do not let
anyone despise you.

Saved in Order to Do Good

3 Remind the people to be subject to rulers and authorities,
to be obedient, to be ready to do
whatever is good, 2to slander no
one, to be peaceable and considerate, and always to be gentle toward everyone. Eph 4:31; 2Ti 2:24

3At one time we too were foolish, disobedient, deceived and
enslaved by all kinds of passions
and pleasures. We lived in malice
and envy, being hated and hating
one another. 4But when the kindness and love of God our Savior

appeared, 5he saved us, not because of righteous things we had
done, but because of his mercy. He
saved us through the washing of
rebirth and renewal by the Holy
Spirit, 6whom he poured out on us
generously through Jesus Christ
our Savior, 7so that, having been
justified by his grace, we might
become heirs having the hope of
eternal life. 8This is a trustworthy
saying. And I want you to stress
these things, so that those who
have trusted in God may be careful to devote themselves to doing
what is good. These things are excellent and profitable for everyone. 1Ti 1:15; Titus 2:14

9But avoid foolish controversies
and genealogies and arguments
and quarrels about the law, because these are unprofitable and
useless. 10Warn a divisive person
once, and then warn them a second time. After that, have nothing
to do with them. 11You may be sure
that such people are warped and
sinful; they are self-condemned.

1Ti 1:4; 2Ti 2:14

Final Remarks

12As soon as I send Artemas or
Tychicus to you, do your best to
come to me at Nicopolis, because
I have decided to winter there.
13Do everything you can to help
Zenas the lawyer and Apollos on
their way and see that they have
everything they need. 14Our people must learn to devote themselves to doing what is good, in
order to provide for urgent needs
and not live unproductive lives.

Ac 18:24; 20:4

15Everyone with me sends you
greetings. Greet those who love us
in the faith. 1Ti 1:2

Grace be with you all. Col 4:18

PHILEMON

1Paul, a prisoner of Christ Jesus,
and Timothy our brother, Eph 3:1

To Philemon our dear friend
and fellow worker — 2also to Ap-
phia our sister and Archippus our
fellow soldier — and to the church
that meets in your home:
Ro 16:5; Php 2:25; Col 4:17

3Grace and peace to you[a] from
God our Father and the Lord Jesus
Christ. Ro 1:7

Thanksgiving and Prayer

4I always thank my God as I remember you in my prayers, 5be-
cause I hear about your love for
all his holy people and your faith
in the Lord Jesus. 6I pray that
your partnership with us in the
faith may be effective in deepen-
ing your understanding of every
good thing we share for the sake
of Christ. 7Your love has given me
great joy and encouragement, because you, brother, have refreshed
the hearts of the Lord's people.
2Co 7:4,13; Col 1:4

Paul's Plea for Onesimus

8Therefore, although in Christ I
could be bold and order you to do
what you ought to do, 9yet I prefer to appeal to you on the basis
of love. It is as none other than
Paul — an old man and now also
a prisoner of Christ Jesus — 10that
I appeal to you for my son Onesimus,[b] who became my son while
I was in chains. 11Formerly he was
useless to you, but now he has
become useful both to you and
to me. 1Co 4:15; Col 4:9

12I am sending him — who is
my very heart — back to you. 13I
would have liked to keep him
with me so that he could take
your place in helping me while I
am in chains for the gospel. 14But I
did not want to do anything without your consent, so that any favor you do would not seem forced
but would be voluntary. 15Perhaps
the reason he was separated from
you for a little while was that you
might have him back forever —
16no longer as a slave, but better
than a slave, as a dear brother. He
is very dear to me but even dearer
to you, both as a fellow man and
as a brother in the Lord.
2Co 9:7; 1Ti 6:2

17So if you consider me a partner, welcome him as you would
welcome me. 18If he has done you
any wrong or owes you anything,
charge it to me. 19I, Paul, am writing this with my own hand. I will
pay it back — not to mention that

[a] *3* The Greek is plural; also in verses 22 and 25; elsewhere in this letter "you" is singular. [b] *10* *Onesimus* means *useful.*

you owe me your very self. [20]I do
wish, brother, that I may have
some benefit from you in the
Lord; refresh my heart in Christ.
[21]Confident of your obedience, I
write to you, knowing that you
will do even more than I ask.
2Co 2:3; 8:23

[22]And one thing more: Prepare a
guest room for me, because I hope
to be restored to you in answer to
your prayers. 2Co 1:11; Php 1:25

[23]Epaphras, my fellow prisoner
in Christ Jesus, sends you greetings. [24]And so do Mark, Aristarchus, Demas and Luke, my fellow
workers. Ac 12:12; Col 1:7

[25]The grace of the Lord Jesus
Christ be with your spirit. 2Ti 4:22

HEBREWS

God's Final Word: His Son

1 In the past God spoke to our ancestors through the prophets at
many times and in various ways,
2 but in these last days he has spoken to us by his Son, whom he
appointed heir of all things, and
through whom also he made the
universe. 3 The Son is the radiance
of God's glory and the exact representation of his being, sustaining
all things by his powerful word.
After he had provided purification
for sins, he sat down at the right
hand of the Majesty in heaven.
4 So he became as much superior
to the angels as the name he has
inherited is superior to theirs.
Php 2:9-10; Heb 7:27

The Son Superior to Angels

5 For to which of the angels did
God ever say,

> "You are my Son;
> today I have become your
> Father"[a]? Ps 2:7

Or again,

> "I will be his Father,
> and he will be my Son"[b]? 2Sa 7:14

6 And again, when God brings his
firstborn into the world, he says,
Heb 10:5

> "Let all God's angels worship
> him."[c] Ps 97:7

7 In speaking of the angels he says,

> "He makes his angels spirits,
> and his servants flames of
> fire."[d] Ps 104:4

8 But about the Son he says,

> "Your throne, O God, will last
> for ever and ever; Lk 1:33
> a scepter of justice will be the
> scepter of your kingdom.
> 9 You have loved righteousness
> and hated wickedness;
> therefore God, your God,
> has set you above your
> companions Php 2:9
> by anointing you with the oil
> of joy."[e] Isa 61:1,3

10 He also says,

> "In the beginning, Lord, you
> laid the foundations of
> the earth,
> and the heavens are the work
> of your hands. Ps 8:6; Zec 12:1
> 11 They will perish, but you
> remain;
> they will all wear out like a
> garment. Isa 34:4; Heb 12:27
> 12 You will roll them up like a
> robe;
> like a garment they will be
> changed.

[a] 5 Psalm 2:7 [b] 5 2 Samuel 7:14; 1 Chron. 17:13 [c] 6 Deut. 32:43 (see Dead Sea Scrolls and Septuagint) [d] 7 Psalm 104:4 [e] 9 Psalm 45:6,7

But you remain the same,
Heb 13:8
and your years will never
end."[a] Ps 102:25-27

[13]To which of the angels did God ever say,

"Sit at my right hand Mk 16:19
until I make your enemies
a footstool for your feet"[b]?

[14]Are not all angels ministering spirits sent to serve those who will inherit salvation?
Jos 10:24; Ps 103:20; Mt 22:44

Warning to Pay Attention

2 We must pay the most careful
attention, therefore, to what
we have heard, so that we do not
drift away. [2]For since the message
spoken through angels was binding, and every violation and disobedience received its just punishment, [3]how shall we escape if
we ignore so great a salvation?
This salvation, which was first
announced by the Lord, was confirmed to us by those who heard
him. [4]God also testified to it by
signs, wonders and various miracles, and by gifts of the Holy Spirit
distributed according to his will.
Lk 1:2; Heb 10:29

Jesus Made Fully Human

[5]It is not to angels that he has
subjected the world to come,
about which we are speaking. [6]But
there is a place where someone
has testified: Heb 4:4

"What is mankind that you are
mindful of them,
a son of man that you care
for him? Job 7:17; Ps 144:3
[7]You made them a little[c] lower
than the angels;
you crowned them with
glory and honor
[8] and put everything under
their feet."[d,e] 1Co 15:25

In putting everything under
them,[f] God left nothing that is not
subject to them.[f] Yet at present we
do not see everything subject to
them.[f] [9]But we do see Jesus, who
was made lower than the angels
for a little while, now crowned
with glory and honor because
he suffered death, so that by the
grace of God he might taste death
for everyone. Jn 3:16; Ac 2:33; Php 2:7-9

[10]In bringing many sons and
daughters to glory, it was fitting
that God, for whom and through
whom everything exists, should
make the pioneer of their salvation
perfect through what he suffered.
[11]Both the one who makes people
holy and those who are made holy
are of the same family. So Jesus is
not ashamed to call them brothers
and sisters.[g] [12]He says, Jn 20:17; Ro 11:36

[a] *12* Psalm 102:25-27 [b] *13* Psalm 110:1
[c] *7* Or *them for a little while*
[d] *6-8* Psalm 8:4-6 [e] *7,8* Or *[7]You made him a little lower than the angels;/ you crowned him with glory and honor/ [8]and put everything under his feet."* [f] *8* Or *him*
[g] *11* The Greek word for *brothers and sisters* (*adelphoi*) refers here to believers, both men and women, as part of God's family; also in verse 12; and in 3:1, 12; 10:19; 13:22.

"I will declare your name to my
brothers and sisters;
in the assembly I will sing
your praises."[a]

13 And again,

"I will put my trust in him."[b]

Isa 8:17

And again he says,

"Here am I, and the children
God has given me."[c]

Isa 8:18; Jn 10:29

14 Since the children have flesh
and blood, he too shared in their
humanity so that by his death he
might break the power of him who
holds the power of death — that is,
the devil — 15 and free those who
all their lives were held in slavery
by their fear of death. 16 For surely
it is not angels he helps, but Abraham's descendants. 17 For this reason he had to be made like them,[d]
fully human in every way, in order
that he might become a merciful
and faithful high priest in service
to God, and that he might make
atonement for the sins of the
people. 18 Because he himself suffered when he was tempted, he is
able to help those who are being
tempted. Heb 4:15; 1Jn 3:8

Jesus Greater Than Moses

3 Therefore, holy brothers and
sisters, who share in the heavenly calling, fix your thoughts on
Jesus, whom we acknowledge as
our apostle and high priest. 2 He
was faithful to the one who appointed him, just as Moses was
faithful in all God's house. 3 Jesus
has been found worthy of greater honor than Moses, just as the
builder of a house has greater hon-
or than the house itself. 4 For every
house is built by someone, but God
is the builder of everything. 5 "Moses was faithful as a servant in all
God's house,"[e] bearing witness to
what would be spoken by God in
the future. 6 But Christ is faithful
as the Son over God's house. And
we are his house, if indeed we hold
firmly to our confidence and the
hope in which we glory. Heb 2:11,17

Warning Against Unbelief

7 So, as the Holy Spirit says:

Heb 9:8

"Today, if you hear his voice,
8 do not harden your hearts

Heb 4:7

as you did in the rebellion,
during the time of testing in
the wilderness,
9 where your ancestors tested
and tried me,
though for forty years they
saw what I did. Ac 7:36
10 That is why I was angry with
that generation;
I said, 'Their hearts are
always going astray,
and they have not known my
ways.'

[a] 12 Psalm 22:22 [b] 13 Isaiah 8:17
[c] 13 Isaiah 8:18 [d] 17 Or *like his brothers*
[e] 5 Num. 12:7

11 So I declared on oath in my
anger, Dt 1:34-35
'They shall never enter my
rest.'"[a] Ps 95:7-11; Heb 4:3,5

12 See to it, brothers and sisters,
that none of you has a sinful, unbelieving heart that turns away
from the living God. 13 But encourage one another daily, as long as
it is called "Today," so that none
of you may be hardened by sin's
deceitfulness. 14 We have come to
share in Christ, if indeed we hold
our original conviction firmly to
the very end. 15 As has just been
said: Eph 4:22; Heb 10:24-25

"Today, if you hear his voice,
do not harden your hearts
as you did in the rebellion."[b]
Ps 95:7-8

16 Who were they who heard and
rebelled? Were they not all those
Moses led out of Egypt? 17 And
with whom was he angry for forty
years? Was it not with those who
sinned, whose bodies perished in
the wilderness? 18 And to whom did
God swear that they would never
enter his rest if not to those who
disobeyed? 19 So we see that they
were not able to enter, because of
their unbelief.
Jn 3:36; Nu 14:20-23; Ps 106:26

A Sabbath-Rest for the People of God

4 Therefore, since the promise of entering his rest still
stands, let us be careful that none
of you be found to have fallen
short of it. 2 For we also have had
the good news proclaimed to us,
just as they did; but the message
they heard was of no value to
them, because they did not share
the faith of those who obeyed.[c]
3 Now we who have believed enter
that rest, just as God has said,
1Th 2:13; Heb 12:15

"So I declared on oath in my
anger,
'They shall never enter my
rest.'"[d] Ps 95:11; Heb 3:11

And yet his works have been finished since the creation of the
world. 4 For somewhere he has
spoken about the seventh day in
these words: "On the seventh day
God rested from all his works."[e]
5 And again in the passage above
he says, "They shall never enter
my rest." Ex 20:11; Ps 95:11
6 Therefore since it still remains
for some to enter that rest, and
since those who formerly had the
good news proclaimed to them
did not go in because of their disobedience, 7 God again set a certain
day, calling it "Today." This he did
when a long time later he spoke
through David, as in the passage
already quoted: Heb 3:18

"Today, if you hear his voice,
do not harden your hearts."[b]

[a] *11* Psalm 95:7-11 [b] *15,7* Psalm 95:7,8
[c] *2* Some manuscripts *because those who heard did not combine it with faith*
[d] *3* Psalm 95:11; also in verse 5
[e] *4* Gen. 2:2

8 For if Joshua had given them
rest, God would not have spoken
later about another day. 9 There
remains, then, a Sabbath-rest for
the people of God; 10 for anyone
who enters God's rest also rests
from their works,[a] just as God did
from his. 11 Let us, therefore, make
every effort to enter that rest, so
that no one will perish by following their example of disobedience.
Heb 1:1; 3:18

12 For the word of God is alive and
active. Sharper than any double-
edged sword, it penetrates even to
dividing soul and spirit, joints and
marrow; it judges the thoughts
and attitudes of the heart. 13 Nothing in all creation is hidden from
God's sight. Everything is uncovered and laid bare before the eyes
of him to whom we must give account. Ps 33:13-15; 1Co 14:24-25

Jesus the Great High Priest

14 Therefore, since we have a
great high priest who has ascended into heaven,[b] Jesus the Son of
God, let us hold firmly to the faith
we profess. 15 For we do not have a
high priest who is unable to em-
pathize with our weaknesses, but
we have one who has been tempted in every way, just as we are —
yet he did not sin. 16 Let us then approach God's throne of grace with
confidence, so that we may receive
mercy and find grace to help us in
our time of need. 2Co 5:21; Heb 3:1

5 Every high priest is selected
from among the people and is
appointed to represent the people
in matters related to God, to offer
gifts and sacrifices for sins. 2 He
is able to deal gently with those
who are ignorant and are going
astray, since he himself is subject
to weakness. 3 This is why he has to
offer sacrifices for his own sins, as
well as for the sins of the people.
4 And no one takes this honor on
himself, but he receives it when
called by God, just as Aaron was.
Heb 7:27-28

5 In the same way, Christ did not
take on himself the glory of becoming a high priest. But God said
to him, Jn 8:54; Heb 1:1

"You are my Son;
today I have become your
Father."[c]

6 And he says in another place,

"You are a priest forever,
in the order of
Melchizedek."[d]

Ps 110:4; Heb 7:17,21

7 During the days of Jesus' life
on earth, he offered up prayers
and petitions with fervent cries
and tears to the one who could
save him from death, and he was
heard because of his reverent submission. 8 Son though he was, he
learned obedience from what he
suffered 9 and, once made perfect,
he became the source of eternal
salvation for all who obey him

[a] 10 Or *labor* [b] 14 Greek *has gone through the heavens* [c] 5 Psalm 2:7
[d] 6 Psalm 110:4

[10]and was designated by God to
be high priest in the order of Melchizedek. Mk 14:36; Heb 2:10

Warning Against Falling Away

[11]We have much to say about
this, but it is hard to make it
clear to you because you no longer try to understand. [12]In fact,
though by this time you ought to
be teachers, you need someone to
teach you the elementary truths
of God's word all over again. You
need milk, not solid food! [13]Any-
one who lives on milk, being still
an infant, is not acquainted with
the teaching about righteousness.
[14]But solid food is for the mature,
who by constant use have trained
themselves to distinguish good
from evil. 1Co 2:6; 3:2

6 Therefore let us move beyond
the elementary teachings
about Christ and be taken forward
to maturity, not laying again the
foundation of repentance from
acts that lead to death,[a] and of
faith in God, [2]instruction about
cleansing rites,[b] the laying on
of hands, the resurrection of the
dead, and eternal judgment. [3]And
God permitting, we will do so.
Php 3:12-14; Heb 5:12

[4]It is impossible for those who
have once been enlightened, who
have tasted the heavenly gift,
who have shared in the Holy Spirit, [5]who have tasted the goodness
of the word of God and the powers of the coming age [6]and who
have fallen[c] away, to be brought
back to repentance. To their loss
they are crucifying the Son of
God all over again and subjecting him to public disgrace. [7]Land
that drinks in the rain often falling on it and that produces a
crop useful to those for whom it
is farmed receives the blessing
of God. [8]But land that produces
thorns and thistles is worthless
and is in danger of being cursed.
In the end it will be burned.
Ge 3:17-18; Isa 5:6

[9]Even though we speak like
this, dear friends, we are convinced of better things in your
case — the things that have to do
with salvation. [10]God is not unjust; he will not forget your work
and the love you have shown him
as you have helped his people and
continue to help them. [11]We want
each of you to show this same
diligence to the very end, so that
what you hope for may be fully
realized. [12]We do not want you to
become lazy, but to imitate those
who through faith and patience
inherit what has been promised.
1Th 1:3; Heb 3:6

The Certainty of God's Promise

[13]When God made his promise to Abraham, since there was
no one greater for him to swear
by, he swore by himself, [14]saying,
"I will surely bless you and give
you many descendants."[d] [15]And so

[a] *1* Or *from useless rituals* [b] *2* Or *about baptisms* [c] *6* Or *age,* [6]*if they fall*
[d] *14* Gen. 22:17

after waiting patiently, Abraham
received what was promised.

Ge 22:16; Lk 1:73

16 People swear by someone
greater than themselves, and the
oath confirms what is said and
puts an end to all argument. 17 Because God wanted to make the
unchanging nature of his purpose
very clear to the heirs of what was
promised, he confirmed it with
an oath. 18 God did this so that,
by two unchangeable things in
which it is impossible for God to
lie, we who have fled to take hold
of the hope set before us may be
greatly encouraged. 19 We have
this hope as an anchor for the
soul, firm and secure. It enters
the inner sanctuary behind the
curtain, 20 where our forerunner,
Jesus, has entered on our behalf.
He has become a high priest forever, in the order of Melchizedek.

Heb 2:17; 4:14; 5:6

Melchizedek the Priest

7 This Melchizedek was king of
Salem and priest of God Most
High. He met Abraham returning
from the defeat of the kings and
blessed him, 2 and Abraham gave
him a tenth of everything. First,
the name Melchizedek means
"king of righteousness"; then also,
"king of Salem" means "king of
peace." 3 Without father or mother, without genealogy, without
beginning of days or end of life,
resembling the Son of God, he remains a priest forever.

Ge 14:18-20

4 Just think how great he was:
Even the patriarch Abraham gave
him a tenth of the plunder! 5 Now
the law requires the descendants
of Levi who become priests to collect a tenth from the people —
that is, from their fellow Israelites — even though they also are
descended from Abraham. 6 This
man, however, did not trace his
descent from Levi, yet he collected a tenth from Abraham and
blessed him who had the promises. 7 And without doubt the lesser
is blessed by the greater. 8 In the
one case, the tenth is collected by
people who die; but in the other case, by him who is declared
to be living. 9 One might even say
that Levi, who collects the tenth,
paid the tenth through Abraham,
10 because when Melchizedek met
Abraham, Levi was still in the
body of his ancestor.

Ro 4:13; Heb 5:6; 6:20

Jesus Like Melchizedek

11 If perfection could have been
attained through the Levitical
priesthood — and indeed the law
given to the people established
that priesthood — why was there
still need for another priest to
come, one in the order of Melchizedek, not in the order of Aaron? 12 For when the priesthood is
changed, the law must be changed
also. 13 He of whom these things
are said belonged to a different
tribe, and no one from that tribe
has ever served at the altar. 14 For

it is clear that our Lord descended
from Judah, and in regard to that
tribe Moses said nothing about
priests. 15 And what we have said is
even more clear if another priest
like Melchizedek appears, 16 one
who has become a priest not on
the basis of a regulation as to his
ancestry but on the basis of the
power of an indestructible life.
17 For it is declared: Isa 11:1; Lk 3:33

> "You are a priest forever,
> in the order of
> Melchizedek."[a]

Ps 110:4; Heb 5:6

18 The former regulation is set
aside because it was weak and useless 19 (for the law made nothing
perfect), and a better hope is introduced, by which we draw near
to God. Ro 3:20; Heb 4:16
20 And it was not without an
oath! Others became priests without any oath, 21 but he became a
priest with an oath when God said
to him:

> "The Lord has sworn
> and will not change his
> mind: 1Sa 15:29; Ro 11:29
> 'You are a priest forever.' "[a]

22 Because of this oath, Jesus has
become the guarantor of a better
covenant. Heb 5:6; 8:6
23 Now there have been many of
those priests, since death prevented them from continuing in office;
24 but because Jesus lives forever,
he has a permanent priesthood.
25 Therefore he is able to save completely[b] those who come to God
through him, because he always
lives to intercede for them.

Ro 8:34; 11:14

26 Such a high priest truly meets
our need — one who is holy, blameless, pure, set apart from sinners,
exalted above the heavens. 27 Unlike the other high priests, he does
not need to offer sacrifices day after day, first for his own sins, and
then for the sins of the people. He
sacrificed for their sins once for all
when he offered himself. 28 For the
law appoints as high priests men
in all their weakness; but the oath,
which came after the law, appointed the Son, who has been made
perfect forever. Heb 2:10; 5:2

The High Priest of a New Covenant

8 Now the main point of what
we are saying is this: We do
have such a high priest, who sat
down at the right hand of the
throne of the Majesty in heaven,
2 and who serves in the sanctuary,
the true tabernacle set up by the
Lord, not by a mere human being.

Heb 9:11,24

3 Every high priest is appointed
to offer both gifts and sacrifices,
and so it was necessary for this
one also to have something to offer. 4 If he were on earth, he would
not be a priest, for there are already priests who offer the gifts
prescribed by the law. 5 They serve
at a sanctuary that is a copy and

[a] 17,21 Psalm 110:4 [b] 25 Or *forever*

shadow of what is in heaven. This
is why Moses was warned when
he was about to build the tabernacle: "See to it that you make everything according to the pattern
shown you on the mountain."[a]
6 But in fact the ministry Jesus has
received is as superior to theirs as
the covenant of which he is mediator is superior to the old one,
since the new covenant is established on better promises.

Ex 25:40; Lk 22:20

7 For if there had been nothing
wrong with that first covenant, no
place would have been sought for
another. 8 But God found fault with
the people and said[b]: Heb 7:11,18

"The days are coming, declares
the Lord,
when I will make a new
covenant Jer 31:31
with the people of Israel
and with the people of
Judah.
9 It will not be like the covenant
I made with their ancestors
Ex 19:5-6
when I took them by the hand
to lead them out of Egypt,
because they did not remain
faithful to my covenant,
and I turned away from
them,
declares the Lord.
10 This is the covenant I will
establish with the
people of Israel Ro 11:27
after that time, declares the
Lord.
I will put my laws in their
minds
and write them on their
hearts. Heb 10:16
I will be their God,
and they will be my people.
Zec 8:8
11 No longer will they teach their
neighbor,
or say to one another,
'Know the Lord,'
because they will all
know me,
from the least of them
to the greatest.
Isa 54:13; Jn 6:45
12 For I will forgive their
wickedness
and will remember their
sins no more."[c]
Ro 11:27; Heb 10:17

13 By calling this covenant "new,"
he has made the first one obsolete; and what is obsolete and out-
dated will soon disappear. 2Co 5:17

Worship in the Earthly Tabernacle

9 Now the first covenant had
regulations for worship and
also an earthly sanctuary. 2 A tabernacle was set up. In its first room
were the lampstand and the table
with its consecrated bread; this
was called the Holy Place. 3 Behind
the second curtain was a room
called the Most Holy Place, 4 which
had the golden altar of incense
and the gold-covered ark of the

[a] 5 Exodus 25:40 [b] 8 Some manuscripts may be translated *fault and said to the people.* [c] 12 Jer. 31:31-34

covenant. This ark contained the
gold jar of manna, Aaron's staff
that had budded, and the stone
tablets of the covenant. 5Above
the ark were the cherubim of the
Glory, overshadowing the atonement cover. But we cannot discuss
these things in detail now.

Ex 25:8,23-29

6When everything had been
arranged like this, the priests
entered regularly into the outer room to carry on their ministry. 7But only the high priest entered the inner room, and that
only once a year, and never without blood, which he offered for
himself and for the sins the people had committed in ignorance.
8The Holy Spirit was showing by
this that the way into the Most
Holy Place had not yet been disclosed as long as the first tabernacle was still functioning. 9This
is an illustration for the present
time, indicating that the gifts and
sacrifices being offered were not
able to clear the conscience of the
worshiper. 10They are only a matter of food and drink and various
ceremonial washings — external
regulations applying until the
time of the new order.

Col 2:16; Heb 7:16

The Blood of Christ

11But when Christ came as high
priest of the good things that
are now already here,[a] he went
through the greater and more perfect tabernacle that is not made
with human hands, that is to say, is
not a part of this creation. 12He did
not enter by means of the blood
of goats and calves; but he entered
the Most Holy Place once for all by
his own blood, thus obtaining[b]
eternal redemption. 13The blood
of goats and bulls and the ashes
of a heifer sprinkled on those who
are ceremonially unclean sanctify
them so that they are outwardly
clean. 14How much more, then, will
the blood of Christ, who through
the eternal Spirit offered himself
unblemished to God, cleanse our
consciences from acts that lead to
death,[c] so that we may serve the
living God!

Heb 6:1; 1Pe 3:18

15For this reason Christ is the
mediator of a new covenant, that
those who are called may receive
the promised eternal inheritance — now that he has died as a
ransom to set them free from the
sins committed under the first
covenant.

1Ti 2:5; Heb 7:22

16In the case of a will,[d] it is necessary to prove the death of the
one who made it, 17because a
will is in force only when somebody has died; it never takes effect while the one who made it is
living. 18This is why even the first
covenant was not put into effect
without blood. 19When Moses had
proclaimed every command of
the law to all the people, he took

[a] 11 Some early manuscripts *are to come*
[b] 12 Or *blood, having obtained* [c] 14 Or *from useless rituals* [d] 16 Same Greek word as *covenant*; also in verse 17

the blood of calves, together with
water, scarlet wool and branches of hyssop, and sprinkled the
scroll and all the people. 20 He
said, "This is the blood of the covenant, which God has commanded you to keep."[a] 21 In the same
way, he sprinkled with the blood
both the tabernacle and everything used in its ceremonies. 22 In
fact, the law requires that nearly everything be cleansed with
blood, and without the shedding
of blood there is no forgiveness.
Ex 24:8; Mt 26:28

23 It was necessary, then, for the
copies of the heavenly things to be
purified with these sacrifices, but
the heavenly things themselves
with better sacrifices than these.
24 For Christ did not enter a sanctuary made with human hands that
was only a copy of the true one;
he entered heaven itself, now to
appear for us in God's presence.
25 Nor did he enter heaven to offer
himself again and again, the way
the high priest enters the Most
Holy Place every year with blood
that is not his own. 26 Otherwise
Christ would have had to suffer
many times since the creation of
the world. But he has appeared
once for all at the culmination of
the ages to do away with sin by
the sacrifice of himself. 27 Just as
people are destined to die once,
and after that to face judgment,
28 so Christ was sacrificed once to
take away the sins of many; and
he will appear a second time, not
to bear sin, but to bring salvation
to those who are waiting for him.
2Co 5:10; 1Pe 2:24

Christ's Sacrifice Once for All

10 The law is only a shadow
of the good things that are
coming — not the realities themselves. For this reason it can never, by the same sacrifices repeated endlessly year after year, make
perfect those who draw near to
worship. 2 Otherwise, would they
not have stopped being offered?
For the worshipers would have
been cleansed once for all, and
would no longer have felt guilty
for their sins. 3 But those sacrifices
are an annual reminder of sins. 4 It
is impossible for the blood of bulls
and goats to take away sins.
Heb 9:7,11,23

5 Therefore, when Christ came
into the world, he said: Heb 1:6

"Sacrifice and offering you did
not desire,
but a body you prepared for
me; 1Pe 2:24
6 with burnt offerings and sin
offerings
you were not pleased.
7 Then I said, 'Here I am — it is
written about me in the
scroll — Jer 36:2
I have come to do your will,
my God.' "[b]

8 First he said, "Sacrifices and offerings, burnt offerings and sin

[a] 20 Exodus 24:8 [b] 7 Psalm 40:6-8
(see Septuagint)

offerings you did not desire, nor
were you pleased with them" —
though they were offered in accordance with the law. [9]Then he
said, "Here I am, I have come to do
your will." He sets aside the first
to establish the second. [10]And by
that will, we have been made holy
through the sacrifice of the body
of Jesus Christ once for all.

Jn 17:19; Heb 7:27; 1Pe 2:24

[11]Day after day every priest
stands and performs his religious
duties; again and again he offers
the same sacrifices, which can never take away sins. [12]But when this
priest had offered for all time one
sacrifice for sins, he sat down at
the right hand of God, [13]and since
that time he waits for his enemies
to be made his footstool. [14]For by
one sacrifice he has made perfect
forever those who are being made
holy.

Eph 5:26; Heb 1:13

[15]The Holy Spirit also testifies to
us about this. First he says:

Heb 3:7

[16]"This is the covenant I will
make with them
after that time, says the Lord.
I will put my laws in their
hearts,
and I will write them on
their minds."[a]

[17]Then he adds:

"Their sins and lawless acts
I will remember no more."[b]

[18]And where these have been forgiven, sacrifice for sin is no longer
necessary.

Jer 31:33; Heb 8:10,12

A Call to Persevere in Faith

[19]Therefore, brothers and sisters, since we have confidence to
enter the Most Holy Place by the
blood of Jesus, [20]by a new and living way opened for us through
the curtain, that is, his body, [21]and
since we have a great priest over
the house of God, [22]let us draw
near to God with a sincere heart
and with the full assurance that
faith brings, having our hearts
sprinkled to cleanse us from a
guilty conscience and having
our bodies washed with pure water. [23]Let us hold unswervingly to
the hope we profess, for he who
promised is faithful. [24]And let us
consider how we may spur one
another on toward love and good
deeds, [25]not giving up meeting
together, as some are in the habit of doing, but encouraging one
another — and all the more as you
see the Day approaching.

Ac 2:42; 1Co 1:9

[26]If we deliberately keep on sinning after we have received the
knowledge of the truth, no sacrifice for sins is left, [27]but only a
fearful expectation of judgment
and of raging fire that will consume the enemies of God. [28]Any-
one who rejected the law of Moses
died without mercy on the testimony of two or three witnesses.
[29]How much more severely do
you think someone deserves to
be punished who has trampled

[a] 16 Jer. 31:33 [b] 17 Jer. 31:34

the Son of God underfoot, who has treated as an unholy thing the blood of the covenant that sanctified them, and who has insulted the Spirit of grace? 30For we know him who said, "It is mine to avenge; I will repay,"[a] and again, "The Lord will judge his people."[b] 31It is a dreadful thing to fall into the hands of the living God.

Eph 4:30; Heb 6:6

32Remember those earlier days after you had received the light, when you endured in a great conflict full of suffering. 33Sometimes you were publicly exposed to insult and persecution; at other times you stood side by side with those who were so treated. 34You suffered along with those in prison and joyfully accepted the confiscation of your property, because you knew that you yourselves had better and lasting possessions. 35So do not throw away your confidence; it will be richly rewarded.

1Co 4:9; Php 1:29-30

36You need to persevere so that when you have done the will of God, you will receive what he has promised. 37For,

"In just a little while,

Lk 21:19; Heb 12:1

he who is coming will come
and will not delay."[c]

Mt 11:3; Rev 22:20

38And,

"But my righteous[d] one will
live by faith. Ro 1:17; Gal 3:11
And I take no pleasure
in the one who shrinks
back."[e]

39But we do not belong to those who shrink back and are destroyed, but to those who have faith and are saved.

Hab 2:3-4

Faith in Action

11 Now faith is confidence in what we hope for and assurance about what we do not see. 2This is what the ancients were commended for.

Ro 8:24; 2Co 4:18

3By faith we understand that the universe was formed at God's command, so that what is seen was not made out of what was visible.

Ge 1; 2Pe 3:5

4By faith Abel brought God a better offering than Cain did. By faith he was commended as righteous, when God spoke well of his offerings. And by faith Abel still speaks, even though he is dead.

Ge 4:4; Heb 12:24

5By faith Enoch was taken from this life, so that he did not experience death: "He could not be found, because God had taken him away."[f] For before he was taken, he was commended as one who pleased God. 6And without faith it is impossible to please God, because anyone who comes to him must believe that he exists

[a] *30* Deut. 32:35 [b] *30* Deut. 32:36; Psalm 135:14 [c] *37* Isaiah 26:20; Hab. 2:3 [d] *38* Some early manuscripts *But the righteous* [e] *38* Hab. 2:4 (see Septuagint) [f] *5* Gen. 5:24

and that he rewards those who
earnestly seek him.
Ge 5:21-24; Heb 7:19
7By faith Noah, when warned
about things not yet seen, in holy
fear built an ark to save his family. By his faith he condemned
the world and became heir of the
righteousness that is in keeping
with faith. Ge 6:13-22; 1Pe 3:20
8By faith Abraham, when called
to go to a place he would later receive as his inheritance, obeyed
and went, even though he did
not know where he was going.
9By faith he made his home in
the promised land like a stranger
in a foreign country; he lived in
tents, as did Isaac and Jacob, who
were heirs with him of the same
promise. 10For he was looking
forward to the city with foundations, whose architect and builder
is God. 11And by faith even Sarah,
who was past childbearing age,
was enabled to bear children because she[a] considered him faithful who had made the promise.
12And so from this one man, and
he as good as dead, came descendants as numerous as the stars
in the sky and as countless as the
sand on the seashore.
Ge 22:17; Ro 4:19
13All these people were still living by faith when they died. They
did not receive the things promised; they only saw them and welcomed them from a distance, ad-
mitting that they were foreigners
and strangers on earth. 14People
who say such things show that
they are looking for a country
of their own. 15If they had been
thinking of the country they had
left, they would have had opportunity to return. 16Instead, they
were longing for a better country — a heavenly one. Therefore
God is not ashamed to be called
their God, for he has prepared a
city for them. Ex 3:6,15; Heb 13:14
17By faith Abraham, when God
tested him, offered Isaac as a
sacrifice. He who had embraced
the promises was about to sacrifice his one and only son, 18even
though God had said to him, "It is
through Isaac that your offspring
will be reckoned."[b] 19Abraham
reasoned that God could even
raise the dead, and so in a manner of speaking he did receive
Isaac back from death.
Ge 22:1-10; Ro 4:21
20By faith Isaac blessed Jacob
and Esau in regard to their future.
Ge 27:27-29,39-40
21By faith Jacob, when he was
dying, blessed each of Joseph's
sons, and worshiped as he leaned
on the top of his staff. Ge 48:1,8-22
22By faith Joseph, when his end
was near, spoke about the exodus
of the Israelites from Egypt and
gave instructions concerning the
burial of his bones.
Ge 50:24-25; Ex 13:19

[a] *11* Or *By faith Abraham, even though he was too old to have children — and Sarah herself was not able to conceive — was enabled to become a father because he*
[b] *18* Gen. 21:12

23 By faith Moses' parents hid him for three months after he was born, because they saw he was no ordinary child, and they were not afraid of the king's edict.

Ex 1:16,22; 2:2

24 By faith Moses, when he had grown up, refused to be known as the son of Pharaoh's daughter. 25 He chose to be mistreated along with the people of God rather than to enjoy the fleeting pleasures of sin. 26 He regarded disgrace for the sake of Christ as of greater value than the treasures of Egypt, because he was looking ahead to his reward. 27 By faith he left Egypt, not fearing the king's anger; he persevered because he saw him who is invisible. 28 By faith he kept the Passover and the application of blood, so that the destroyer of the firstborn would not touch the firstborn of Israel. Ex 12:21-23; Heb 13:13

29 By faith the people passed through the Red Sea as on dry land; but when the Egyptians tried to do so, they were drowned.

Ex 14:21-31

30 By faith the walls of Jericho fell, after the army had marched around them for seven days.

Jos 6:12-20

31 By faith the prostitute Rahab, because she welcomed the spies, was not killed with those who were disobedient.[a] Jos 6:22-25; Jas 2:25

32 And what more shall I say? I do not have time to tell about Gideon, Barak, Samson and Jephthah, about David and Samuel and the prophets, 33 who through faith conquered kingdoms, administered justice, and gained what was promised; who shut the mouths of lions, 34 quenched the fury of the flames, and escaped the edge of the sword; whose weakness was turned to strength; and who became powerful in battle and routed foreign armies. 35 Women received back their dead, raised to life again. There were others who were tortured, refusing to be released so that they might gain an even better resurrection. 36 Some faced jeers and flogging, and even chains and imprisonment. 37 They were put to death by stoning;[b] they were sawed in two; they were killed by the sword. They went about in sheepskins and goatskins, destitute, persecuted and mistreated— 38 the world was not worthy of them. They wandered in deserts and mountains, living in caves and in holes in the ground.

1Ki 18:4; 2Ki 1:8

39 These were all commended for their faith, yet none of them received what had been promised, 40 since God had planned something better for us so that only together with us would they be made perfect. Heb 2:10

12 Therefore, since we are surrounded by such a great cloud of witnesses, let us throw off everything that hinders and

[a] 31 Or *unbelieving* [b] 37 Some early manuscripts *stoning; they were put to the test;*

the sin that so easily entangles.
And let us run with perseverance
the race marked out for us, 2fixing
our eyes on Jesus, the pioneer and
perfecter of faith. For the joy set
before him he endured the cross,
scorning its shame, and sat down
at the right hand of the throne of
God. 3Consider him who endured
such opposition from sinners, so
that you will not grow weary and
lose heart. Gal 6:9; Php 2:8-9

God Disciplines His Children

4In your struggle against sin,
you have not yet resisted to the
point of shedding your blood.
5And have you completely forgotten this word of encouragement
that addresses you as a father addresses his son? It says, Heb 10:32-34

"My son, do not make
light of the Lord's
discipline,
and do not lose heart when
he rebukes you,
6because the Lord disciplines
the one he loves, Ps 94:12
and he chastens everyone
he accepts as his son."[a]
Pr 3:11-12

7Endure hardship as discipline;
God is treating you as his children. For what children are not
disciplined by their father? 8If
you are not disciplined — and everyone undergoes discipline —
then you are not legitimate, not
true sons and daughters at all.
9Moreover, we have all had human
fathers who disciplined us and we
respected them for it. How much
more should we submit to the
Father of spirits and live! 10They
disciplined us for a little while as
they thought best; but God disciplines us for our good, in order
that we may share in his holiness.
11No discipline seems pleasant at
the time, but painful. Later on,
however, it produces a harvest of
righteousness and peace for those
who have been trained by it.
Isa 38:16; Jas 3:17-18

12Therefore, strengthen your
feeble arms and weak knees.
13"Make level paths for your feet,"[b]
so that the lame may not be disabled, but rather healed.
Pr 4:26; Gal 6:1

Warning and Encouragement

14Make every effort to live in
peace with everyone and to be
holy; without holiness no one will
see the Lord. 15See to it that no
one falls short of the grace of God
and that no bitter root grows up
to cause trouble and defile many.
16See that no one is sexually immoral, or is godless like Esau, who
for a single meal sold his inheritance rights as the oldest son.
17Afterward, as you know, when
he wanted to inherit this blessing, he was rejected. Even though
he sought the blessing with tears,
he could not change what he had
done. Ge 25:29-34; 27:30-40

[a] *5,6* Prov. 3:11,12 (see Septuagint)
[b] *13* Prov. 4:26

The Mountain of Fear and the Mountain of Joy

18 You have not come to a mountain that can be touched and that
is burning with fire; to darkness,
gloom and storm; 19 to a trumpet
blast or to such a voice speaking words that those who heard
it begged that no further word
be spoken to them, 20 because
they could not bear what was
commanded: "If even an animal
touches the mountain, it must be
stoned to death."[a] 21 The sight was
so terrifying that Moses said, "I
am trembling with fear."[b]

Ex 20:19; Dt 5:5,25

22 But you have come to Mount
Zion, to the city of the living God,
the heavenly Jerusalem. You
have come to thousands upon
thousands of angels in joyful assembly, 23 to the church of the
firstborn, whose names are written in heaven. You have come to
God, the Judge of all, to the spirits of the righteous made perfect,
24 to Jesus the mediator of a new
covenant, and to the sprinkled
blood that speaks a better word
than the blood of Abel.

Php 3:12; Heb 11:4

25 See to it that you do not refuse
him who speaks. If they did not escape when they refused him who
warned them on earth, how much
less will we, if we turn away from
him who warns us from heaven?
26 At that time his voice shook the
earth, but now he has promised,
"Once more I will shake not only
the earth but also the heavens."[c]
27 The words "once more" indicate
the removing of what can be shak-
en — that is, created things — so
that what cannot be shaken may
remain.

1Co 7:31; 2Pe 3:10

28 Therefore, since we are receiving a kingdom that cannot be
shaken, let us be thankful, and so
worship God acceptably with reverence and awe, 29 for our "God is a
consuming fire."[d]

Dt 4:24; Heb 13:15

Concluding Exhortations

13 Keep on loving one another
as brothers and sisters. 2 Do
not forget to show hospitality to
strangers, for by so doing some
people have shown hospitality to
angels without knowing it. 3 Continue to remember those in prison
as if you were together with them
in prison, and those who are mistreated as if you yourselves were
suffering.

Ge 18:1-33; Col 4:18

4 Marriage should be honored
by all, and the marriage bed kept
pure, for God will judge the adulterer and all the sexually immoral. 5 Keep your lives free from the
love of money and be content
with what you have, because God
has said,

1Co 6:9; Php 4:11

"Never will I leave you;
never will I forsake you."[e]

6 So we say with confidence,

[a] 20 Exodus 19:12,13 [b] 21 See Deut. 9:19.
[c] 26 Haggai 2:6 [d] 29 Deut. 4:24
[e] 5 Deut. 31:6

"The Lord is my helper; I will
not be afraid.
What can mere mortals do
to me?"[a]

Dt 31:6,8; Jos 1:5; Ps 118:6-7

7Remember your leaders, who
spoke the word of God to you. Consider the outcome of their way of
life and imitate their faith. 8Jesus
Christ is the same yesterday and
today and forever. Heb 1:12; 6:12

9Do not be carried away by all
kinds of strange teachings. It is
good for our hearts to be strengthened by grace, not by eating ceremonial foods, which is of no benefit to those who do so. 10We have
an altar from which those who
minister at the tabernacle have no
right to eat. 1Co 9:13; Eph 4:14

11The high priest carries the
blood of animals into the Most
Holy Place as a sin offering, but
the bodies are burned outside the
camp. 12And so Jesus also suffered
outside the city gate to make
the people holy through his own
blood. 13Let us, then, go to him
outside the camp, bearing the disgrace he bore. 14For here we do
not have an enduring city, but we
are looking for the city that is to
come. Php 3:20; Heb 12:22

15Through Jesus, therefore, let
us continually offer to God a sacrifice of praise — the fruit of lips
that openly profess his name.
16And do not forget to do good and
to share with others, for with such
sacrifices God is pleased.

Php 4:18; Hos 14:2

17Have confidence in your leaders and submit to their authority, because they keep watch over
you as those who must give an account. Do this so that their work
will be a joy, not a burden, for that
would be of no benefit to you.

Isa 62:6; Ac 20:28

18Pray for us. We are sure that
we have a clear conscience and
desire to live honorably in every
way. 19I particularly urge you to
pray so that I may be restored to
you soon. 1Th 5:25; Phm 22

Benediction and Final Greetings

20Now may the God of peace,
who through the blood of the eternal covenant brought back from
the dead our Lord Jesus, that great
Shepherd of the sheep, 21equip
you with everything good for doing his will, and may he work in us
what is pleasing to him, through
Jesus Christ, to whom be glory for
ever and ever. Amen. Php 2:13; Jn 3:22

22Brothers and sisters, I urge
you to bear with my word of exhortation, for in fact I have written to you quite briefly. 1Pe 5:12

23I want you to know that our
brother Timothy has been released. If he arrives soon, I will
come with him to see you. Ac 16:1

24Greet all your leaders and all
the Lord's people. Those from Italy send you their greetings. Ac 18:2

25Grace be with you all. Col 4:18

[a] 6 Psalm 118:6,7

JAMES

1 James, a servant of God and of
the Lord Jesus Christ,
Ac 15:13; Titus 1:1

To the twelve tribes scattered
among the nations: Jn 7:35; 1Pe 1:1

Greetings. Ac 15:23

Trials and Temptations

2Consider it pure joy, my brothers and sisters,[a] whenever you
face trials of many kinds, 3be-
cause you know that the testing of
your faith produces perseverance.
4Let perseverance finish its work
so that you may be mature and
complete, not lacking anything.
5If any of you lacks wisdom, you
should ask God, who gives generously to all without finding fault,
and it will be given to you. 6But
when you ask, you must believe
and not doubt, because the one
who doubts is like a wave of the
sea, blown and tossed by the wind.
7That person should not expect to
receive anything from the Lord.
8Such a person is double-minded
and unstable in all they do.
1Ki 3:9-10; Mk 11:24

9Believers in humble circumstances ought to take pride in
their high position. 10But the rich
should take pride in their humiliation — since they will pass away
like a wild flower. 11For the sun rises with scorching heat and withers
the plant; its blossom falls and its
beauty is destroyed. In the same
way, the rich will fade away even
while they go about their business. Ps 102:4,11; Isa 40:6-8

12Blessed is the one who perseveres under trial because, having
stood the test, that person will
receive the crown of life that the
Lord has promised to those who
love him. 1Co 9:25; Jas 2:5

13When tempted, no one should
say, "God is tempting me." For God
cannot be tempted by evil, nor
does he tempt anyone; 14but each
person is tempted when they are
dragged away by their own evil desire and enticed. 15Then, after desire has conceived, it gives birth to
sin; and sin, when it is full-grown,
gives birth to death. Job 15:35; Ps 7:14

16Don't be deceived, my dear
brothers and sisters. 17Every good
and perfect gift is from above,
coming down from the Father of
the heavenly lights, who does not
change like shifting shadows. 18He
chose to give us birth through the
word of truth, that we might be a
kind of firstfruits of all he created.
Jn 1:13; Rev 14:4

[a] 2 The Greek word for *brothers and sisters* (*adelphoi*) refers here to believers, both men and women, as part of God's family; also in verses 16 and 19; and in 2:1, 5, 14; 3:10, 12; 4:11; 5:7, 9, 10, 12, 19.

Listening and Doing

[19]My dear brothers and sisters,
take note of this: Everyone should
be quick to listen, slow to speak and
slow to become angry, [20]because
human anger does not produce
the righteousness that God desires.
[21]Therefore, get rid of all moral filth
and the evil that is so prevalent and
humbly accept the word planted in
you, which can save you. Eph 1:13; 4:22

[22]Do not merely listen to the
word, and so deceive yourselves. Do
what it says. [23]Anyone who listens
to the word but does not do what
it says is like someone who looks
at his face in a mirror [24]and, after
looking at himself, goes away and
immediately forgets what he looks
like. [25]But whoever looks intently
into the perfect law that gives freedom, and continues in it—not forgetting what they have heard, but
doing it—they will be blessed in
what they do. Jn 13:17; Jas 2:12

[26]Those who consider themselves religious and yet do not
keep a tight rein on their tongues
deceive themselves, and their religion is worthless. [27]Religion that
God our Father accepts as pure
and faultless is this: to look after
orphans and widows in their distress and to keep oneself from being polluted by the world.

Isa 1:17,23; 1Pe 3:10

Favoritism Forbidden

2 My brothers and sisters, believers in our glorious Lord
Jesus Christ must not show favoritism. [2]Suppose a man comes into
your meeting wearing a gold ring
and fine clothes, and a poor man
in filthy old clothes also comes in.
[3]If you show special attention to
the man wearing fine clothes and
say, "Here's a good seat for you,"
but say to the poor man, "You
stand there" or "Sit on the floor by
my feet," [4]have you not discriminated among yourselves and become judges with evil thoughts?

Jn 7:24; 1Co 2:8

[5]Listen, my dear brothers and
sisters: Has not God chosen those
who are poor in the eyes of the
world to be rich in faith and to
inherit the kingdom he promised those who love him? [6]But
you have dishonored the poor. Is
it not the rich who are exploiting
you? Are they not the ones who
are dragging you into court? [7]Are
they not the ones who are blaspheming the noble name of him
to whom you belong?

Lk 12:21; 1Co 11:22

[8]If you really keep the royal law
found in Scripture, "Love your
neighbor as yourself,"[a] you are doing right. [9]But if you show favoritism, you sin and are convicted by
the law as lawbreakers. [10]For whoever keeps the whole law and yet
stumbles at just one point is guilty
of breaking all of it. [11]For he who
said, "You shall not commit adultery,"[b] also said, "You shall not
murder."[c] If you do not commit

[a] *8* Lev. 19:18 [b] *11* Exodus 20:14; Deut. 5:18 [c] *11* Exodus 20:13; Deut. 5:17

adultery but do commit murder,
you have become a lawbreaker.
Mt 5:19; Gal 3:10

12Speak and act as those who
are going to be judged by the
law that gives freedom, 13because
judgment without mercy will be
shown to anyone who has not
been merciful. Mercy triumphs
over judgment. Mt 5:7; Jas 1:25

Faith and Deeds

14What good is it, my brothers
and sisters, if someone claims to
have faith but has no deeds? Can
such faith save them? 15Suppose
a brother or a sister is without
clothes and daily food. 16If one of
you says to them, "Go in peace;
keep warm and well fed," but
does nothing about their physical needs, what good is it? 17In the
same way, faith by itself, if it is not
accompanied by action, is dead.
Mt 7:26; 1Jn 3:17-18

18But someone will say, "You
have faith; I have deeds."

Show me your faith without
deeds, and I will show you my
faith by my deeds. 19You believe
that there is one God. Good! Even
the demons believe that — and
shudder. Mt 8:29; Jas 3:13

20You foolish person, do you
want evidence that faith without
deeds is useless[a]? 21Was not our
father Abraham considered righteous for what he did when he offered his son Isaac on the altar?
22You see that his faith and his actions were working together, and
his faith was made complete by
what he did. 23And the scripture
was fulfilled that says, "Abraham
believed God, and it was credited
to him as righteousness,"[b] and he
was called God's friend. 24You see
that a person is considered righteous by what they do and not by
faith alone. 2Ch 20:7; Ro 4:3

25In the same way, was not even
Rahab the prostitute considered
righteous for what she did when
she gave lodging to the spies and
sent them off in a different direction? 26As the body without the
spirit is dead, so faith without
deeds is dead. Heb 11:31

Taming the Tongue

3 Not many of you should become teachers, my fellow believers, because you know that
we who teach will be judged more
strictly. 2We all stumble in many
ways. Anyone who is never at fault
in what they say is perfect, able to
keep their whole body in check.
Mt 12:37; Jas 1:26

3When we put bits into the
mouths of horses to make them
obey us, we can turn the whole
animal. 4Or take ships as an example. Although they are so large
and are driven by strong winds,
they are steered by a very small
rudder wherever the pilot wants
to go. 5Likewise, the tongue is
a small part of the body, but it
makes great boasts. Consider

[a] 20 Some early manuscripts *dead*
[b] 23 Gen. 15:6

what a great forest is set on fire by
a small spark. 6The tongue also is
a fire, a world of evil among the
parts of the body. It corrupts the
whole body, sets the whole course
of one's life on fire, and is itself set
on fire by hell. Pr 16:27; Mt 15:11,18-19

7All kinds of animals, birds, reptiles and sea creatures are being
tamed and have been tamed by
mankind, 8but no human being
can tame the tongue. It is a restless evil, full of deadly poison.
Ps 140:3; Ro 3:13

9With the tongue we praise our
Lord and Father, and with it we
curse human beings, who have
been made in God's likeness. 10Out
of the same mouth come praise
and cursing. My brothers and sisters, this should not be. 11Can both
fresh water and salt water flow
from the same spring? 12My brothers and sisters, can a fig tree bear
olives, or a grapevine bear figs?
Neither can a salt spring produce
fresh water. Ge 1:26-27; Mt 7:16

Two Kinds of Wisdom

13Who is wise and understanding among you? Let them show it
by their good life, by deeds done
in the humility that comes from
wisdom. 14But if you harbor bitter envy and selfish ambition in
your hearts, do not boast about
it or deny the truth. 15Such "wisdom" does not come down from
heaven but is earthly, unspiritual, demonic. 16For where you have
envy and selfish ambition, there
you find disorder and every evil
practice. 1Ti 4:1; Jas 2:18

17But the wisdom that comes
from heaven is first of all pure;
then peace-loving, considerate,
submissive, full of mercy and
good fruit, impartial and sincere.
18Peacemakers who sow in peace
reap a harvest of righteousness.
Pr 11:18; Ro 12:9

Submit Yourselves to God

4 What causes fights and quarrels among you? Don't they
come from your desires that battle within you? 2You desire but do
not have, so you kill. You covet but
you cannot get what you want, so
you quarrel and fight. You do not
have because you do not ask God.
3When you ask, you do not receive, because you ask with wrong
motives, that you may spend what
you get on your pleasures.
Ro 7:23; 1Jn 3:22

4You adulterous people,[a] don't
you know that friendship with the
world means enmity against God?
Therefore, anyone who chooses to
be a friend of the world becomes
an enemy of God. 5Or do you think
Scripture says without reason that
he jealously longs for the spirit he
has caused to dwell in us[b]? 6But he
gives us more grace. That is why
Scripture says: Jn 15:19; 1Jn 2:15

[a] 4 An allusion to covenant unfaithfulness; see Hosea 3:1. [b] 5 Or *that the spirit he caused to dwell in us envies intensely;* or *that the Spirit he caused to dwell in us longs jealously*

"God opposes the proud
but shows favor to the
humble."[a] Pr 3:34; Mt 23:12

7Submit yourselves, then, to
God. Resist the devil, and he will
flee from you. 8Come near to God
and he will come near to you.
Wash your hands, you sinners,
and purify your hearts, you double-minded. 9Grieve, mourn and
wail. Change your laughter to
mourning and your joy to gloom.
10Humble yourselves before the
Lord, and he will lift you up.

Isa 1:16; 1Pe 5:6-9

11Brothers and sisters, do not
slander one another. Anyone who
speaks against a brother or sister[b]
or judges them speaks against
the law and judges it. When you
judge the law, you are not keeping
it, but sitting in judgment on it.
12There is only one Lawgiver and
Judge, the one who is able to save
and destroy. But you — who are
you to judge your neighbor?

Mt 10:28; Ro 14:4

Boasting About Tomorrow

13Now listen, you who say, "Today or tomorrow we will go to this
or that city, spend a year there,
carry on business and make money." 14Why, you do not even know
what will happen tomorrow. What
is your life? You are a mist that
appears for a little while and then
vanishes. 15Instead, you ought
to say, "If it is the Lord's will, we
will live and do this or that." 16As
it is, you boast in your arrogant
schemes. All such boasting is evil.
17If anyone, then, knows the good
they ought to do and doesn't do it,
it is sin for them. Lk 12:47; 1Co 5:6

Warning to Rich Oppressors

5 Now listen, you rich people, weep and wail because
of the misery that is coming on
you. 2Your wealth has rotted, and
moths have eaten your clothes.
3Your gold and silver are corrod-
ed. Their corrosion will testify
against you and eat your flesh
like fire. You have hoarded wealth
in the last days. 4Look! The wages you failed to pay the workers
who mowed your fields are crying
out against you. The cries of the
harvesters have reached the ears
of the Lord Almighty. 5You have
lived on earth in luxury and self-
indulgence. You have fattened
yourselves in the day of slaughter.[c] 6You have condemned and
murdered the innocent one, who
was not opposing you.

Heb 10:38; Jas 4:2

Patience in Suffering

7Be patient, then, brothers and
sisters, until the Lord's coming.
See how the farmer waits for the
land to yield its valuable crop, patiently waiting for the autumn and

[a] *6* Prov. 3:34 [b] *11* The Greek word for *brother or sister* (*adelphos*) refers here to a believer, whether man or woman, as part of God's family. [c] *5* Or *yourselves as in a day of feasting*

spring rains. 8You too, be patient
and stand firm, because the Lord's
coming is near. 9Don't grumble
against one another, brothers and
sisters, or you will be judged. The
Judge is standing at the door!

Mt 24:33; Jas 4:11

10Brothers and sisters, as an example of patience in the face of
suffering, take the prophets who
spoke in the name of the Lord.
11As you know, we count as blessed
those who have persevered. You
have heard of Job's perseverance
and have seen what the Lord finally brought about. The Lord is full
of compassion and mercy.

Job 42:10,12-17; Mt 5:12

12Above all, my brothers and sisters, do not swear — not by heav-
en or by earth or by anything else.
All you need to say is a simple
"Yes" or "No." Otherwise you will
be condemned. Mt 5:34-37

The Prayer of Faith

13Is anyone among you in trouble? Let them pray. Is anyone happy? Let them sing songs of praise.
14Is anyone among you sick? Let
them call the elders of the church
to pray over them and anoint
them with oil in the name of the
Lord. 15And the prayer offered
in faith will make the sick person well; the Lord will raise them
up. If they have sinned, they will
be forgiven. 16Therefore confess
your sins to each other and pray
for each other so that you may be
healed. The prayer of a righteous
person is powerful and effective.

Jn 9:31; 1Pe 2:24

17Elijah was a human being,
even as we are. He prayed earnestly that it would not rain, and it did
not rain on the land for three and
a half years. 18Again he prayed,
and the heavens gave rain, and
the earth produced its crops.

1Ki 18:41-45; Ac 14:15

19My brothers and sisters, if one
of you should wander from the
truth and someone should bring
that person back, 20remember
this: Whoever turns a sinner from
the error of their way will save
them from death and cover over a
multitude of sins.

Mt 18:15; Ro 11:14; 1Pe 4:8

1 PETER

1 Peter, an apostle of Jesus Christ,
2Pe 1:1

To God's elect, exiles scattered
throughout the provinces of Pontus, Galatia, Cappadocia, Asia and
Bithynia, [2]who have been chosen
according to the foreknowledge
of God the Father, through the
sanctifying work of the Spirit, to
be obedient to Jesus Christ and
sprinkled with his blood:
2Th 2:13; Heb 10:22

Grace and peace be yours in
abundance. Ro 1:7

Praise to God for a Living Hope

[3]Praise be to the God and Father
of our Lord Jesus Christ! In his
great mercy he has given us new
birth into a living hope through
the resurrection of Jesus Christ
from the dead, [4]and into an inheritance that can never perish, spoil
or fade. This inheritance is kept
in heaven for you, [5]who through
faith are shielded by God's power
until the coming of the salvation
that is ready to be revealed in the
last time. [6]In all this you greatly rejoice, though now for a little
while you may have had to suffer
grief in all kinds of trials. [7]These
have come so that the proven
genuineness of your faith — of
greater worth than gold, which
perishes even though refined by
fire — may result in praise, glory
and honor when Jesus Christ is
revealed. [8]Though you have not
seen him, you love him; and even
though you do not see him now,
you believe in him and are filled
with an inexpressible and glorious joy, [9]for you are receiving the
end result of your faith, the salvation of your souls. Jn 20:29; Ro 6:22

[10]Concerning this salvation, the
prophets, who spoke of the grace
that was to come to you, searched
intently and with the greatest
care, [11]trying to find out the time
and circumstances to which the
Spirit of Christ in them was pointing when he predicted the sufferings of the Messiah and the glories
that would follow. [12]It was revealed to them that they were not
serving themselves but you, when
they spoke of the things that have
now been told you by those who
have preached the gospel to you
by the Holy Spirit sent from heav-
en. Even angels long to look into
these things. Lk 24:49; 2Pe 1:21

Be Holy

[13]Therefore, with minds that are
alert and fully sober, set your hope
on the grace to be brought to you
when Jesus Christ is revealed at
his coming. [14]As obedient children,

do not conform to the evil desires
you had when you lived in ignorance. 15But just as he who called
you is holy, so be holy in all you
do; 16for it is written: "Be holy, because I am holy."[a] Ro 12:2; Eph 4:18

17Since you call on a Father who
judges each person's work impartially, live out your time as foreigners here in reverent fear. 18For you
know that it was not with perishable things such as silver or gold
that you were redeemed from the
empty way of life handed down
to you from your ancestors, 19but
with the precious blood of Christ,
a lamb without blemish or defect.
20He was chosen before the creation of the world, but was revealed
in these last times for your sake.
21Through him you believe in God,
who raised him from the dead and
glorified him, and so your faith and
hope are in God. 1Co 6:20; Heb 12:28

22Now that you have purified
yourselves by obeying the truth
so that you have sincere love for
each other, love one another deeply, from the heart.[b] 23For you have
been born again, not of perishable
seed, but of imperishable, through
the living and enduring word of
God. 24For, Jn 1:13; Heb 13:1

"All people are like grass,
  and all their glory is like the
    flowers of the field;
the grass withers and the
    flowers fall,
25 but the word of the Lord
    endures forever."[c] Jas 1:10-11

And this is the word that was
preached to you.

2 Therefore, rid yourselves of
all malice and all deceit, hypocrisy, envy, and slander of every kind. 2Like newborn babies,
crave pure spiritual milk, so that
by it you may grow up in your salvation, 3now that you have tasted
that the Lord is good. 1Co 3:2; Heb 6:5

The Living Stone and a Chosen People

4As you come to him, the living Stone — rejected by humans
but chosen by God and precious
to him — 5you also, like living
stones, are being built into a spiritual house[d] to be a holy priesthood, offering spiritual sacrifices
acceptable to God through Jesus
Christ. 6For in Scripture it says:
Php 4:18; Heb 13:15

"See, I lay a stone in Zion,
  a chosen and precious
    cornerstone, Eph 2:20
and the one who trusts in him
  will never be put to shame."[e]

7Now to you who believe, this
stone is precious. But to those who
do not believe, 2Co 2:16

"The stone the builders
    rejected
  has become the
    cornerstone,"[f]

[a] 16 Lev. 11:44,45; 19:2 [b] 22 Some early manuscripts *from a pure heart*
[c] 25 Isaiah 40:6-8 (see Septuagint)
[d] 5 Or *into a temple of the Spirit*
[e] 6 Isaiah 28:16 [f] 7 Psalm 118:22

8 and,

> "A stone that causes people to
> stumble
> and a rock that makes them
> fall."[a]

They stumble because they disobey the message — which is also
what they were destined for.

Ps 118:22; Isa 28:16; 1Co 1:23

9 But you are a chosen people,
a royal priesthood, a holy nation,
God's special possession, that you
may declare the praises of him
who called you out of darkness
into his wonderful light. 10 Once
you were not a people, but now
you are the people of God; once
you had not received mercy, but
now you have received mercy.

Hos 1:9-10; Ac 26:18

Living Godly Lives in a Pagan Society

11 Dear friends, I urge you, as
foreigners and exiles, to abstain
from sinful desires, which wage
war against your soul. 12 Live such
good lives among the pagans that,
though they accuse you of doing
wrong, they may see your good
deeds and glorify God on the day
he visits us.

Mt 5:16; Php 2:15; Jas 4:1; 1Pe 3:16

13 Submit yourselves for the
Lord's sake to every human authority: whether to the emperor,
as the supreme authority, 14 or to
governors, who are sent by him to
punish those who do wrong and
to commend those who do right.
15 For it is God's will that by doing
good you should silence the ignorant talk of foolish people. 16 Live
as free people, but do not use your
freedom as a cover-up for evil; live
as God's slaves. 17 Show proper respect to everyone, love the family
of believers, fear God, honor the
emperor.

Ro 12:10; 13:7; 1Pe 3:17

18 Slaves, in reverent fear of God
submit yourselves to your masters, not only to those who are
good and considerate, but also
to those who are harsh. 19 For it is
commendable if someone bears
up under the pain of unjust suffering because they are conscious of
God. 20 But how is it to your credit
if you receive a beating for doing
wrong and endure it? But if you
suffer for doing good and you endure it, this is commendable before God. 21 To this you were called,
because Christ suffered for you,
leaving you an example, that you
should follow in his steps.

Mt 16:24; Eph 6:5; 1Pe 3:14,17

> 22 "He committed no sin,
> and no deceit was found in
> his mouth."[b]

Isa 53:9

23 When they hurled their insults
at him, he did not retaliate; when
he suffered, he made no threats.
Instead, he entrusted himself to
him who judges justly. 24 "He himself bore our sins" in his body on
the cross, so that we might die
to sins and live for righteousness; "by his wounds you have

[a] 8 Isaiah 8:14 [b] 22 Isaiah 53:9

been healed." 25For "you were like
sheep going astray,"[a] but now you
have returned to the Shepherd
and Overseer of your souls.
Isa 53:6; Jn 10:11

3 Wives, in the same way submit yourselves to your own
husbands so that, if any of them
do not believe the word, they may
be won over without words by the
behavior of their wives, 2when
they see the purity and reverence
of your lives. 3Your beauty should
not come from outward adorn-
ment, such as elaborate hairstyles
and the wearing of gold jewelry
or fine clothes. 4Rather, it should
be that of your inner self, the un-
fading beauty of a gentle and quiet spirit, which is of great worth
in God's sight. 5For this is the way
the holy women of the past who
put their hope in God used to
adorn themselves. They submitted themselves to their own husbands, 6like Sarah, who obeyed
Abraham and called him her lord.
You are her daughters if you do
what is right and do not give way
to fear. Ge 18:12; 1Ti 5:5

7Husbands, in the same way be
considerate as you live with your
wives, and treat them with respect as the weaker partner and as
heirs with you of the gracious gift
of life, so that nothing will hinder
your prayers. Eph 5:25-33

Suffering for Doing Good

8Finally, all of you, be like-
minded, be sympathetic, love one
another, be compassionate and
humble. 9Do not repay evil with
evil or insult with insult. On the
contrary, repay evil with blessing,
because to this you were called so
that you may inherit a blessing.
10For, Heb 6:14; 1Pe 2:21

"Whoever would love life
and see good days
must keep their tongue from
evil
and their lips from deceitful
speech.
11They must turn from evil and
do good;
they must seek peace and
pursue it.
12For the eyes of the Lord are on
the righteous
and his ears are attentive to
their prayer,
but the face of the Lord is
against those who do
evil."[b] Ps 34:12-16

13Who is going to harm you if
you are eager to do good? 14But
even if you should suffer for what
is right, you are blessed. "Do not
fear their threats[c]; do not be
frightened."[d] 15But in your hearts
revere Christ as Lord. Always be
prepared to give an answer to
everyone who asks you to give
the reason for the hope that you
have. But do this with gentleness
and respect, 16keeping a clear conscience, so that those who speak

[a] *24,25* Isaiah 53:4,5,6 (see Septuagint)
[b] *12* Psalm 34:12-16 [c] *14* Or *fear what they fear* [d] *14* Isaiah 8:12

maliciously against your good behavior in Christ may be ashamed of their slander. [17]For it is better, if it is God's will, to suffer for doing good than for doing evil. [18]For Christ also suffered once for sins, the righteous for the unrighteous, to bring you to God. He was put to death in the body but made alive in the Spirit. [19]After being made alive,[a] he went and made proclamation to the imprisoned spirits— [20]to those who were disobedient long ago when God waited patiently in the days of Noah while the ark was being built. In it only a few people, eight in all, were saved through water, [21]and this water symbolizes baptism that now saves you also—not the removal of dirt from the body but the pledge of a clear conscience toward God.[b] It saves you by the resurrection of Jesus Christ, [22]who has gone into heaven and is at God's right hand—with angels, authorities and powers in submission to him.

Ro 8:38; 1Pe 1:3

Living for God

4 Therefore, since Christ suffered in his body, arm yourselves also with the same attitude, because whoever suffers in the body is done with sin. [2]As a result, they do not live the rest of their earthly lives for evil human desires, but rather for the will of God. [3]For you have spent enough time in the past doing what pagans choose to do—living in debauchery, lust, drunkenness, orgies, carousing and detestable idolatry. [4]They are surprised that you do not join them in their reckless, wild living, and they heap abuse on you. [5]But they will have to give account to him who is ready to judge the living and the dead. [6]For this is the reason the gospel was preached even to those who are now dead, so that they might be judged according to human standards in regard to the body, but live according to God in regard to the spirit.

Ac 10:42; 1Pe 3:19

[7]The end of all things is near. Therefore be alert and of sober mind so that you may pray. [8]Above all, love each other deeply, because love covers over a multitude of sins. [9]Offer hospitality to one another without grumbling. [10]Each of you should use whatever gift you have received to serve others, as faithful stewards of God's grace in its various forms. [11]If anyone speaks, they should do so as one who speaks the very words of God. If anyone serves, they should do so with the strength God provides, so that in all things God may be praised through Jesus Christ. To him be the glory and the power for ever and ever. Amen.

Pr 10:12; Ro 12:6-7

[a] 18,19 Or *but made alive in the spirit,* [19]*in which also* [b] 21 Or *but an appeal to God for a clear conscience*

Suffering for Being a Christian

12 Dear friends, do not be surprised at the fiery ordeal that
has come on you to test you, as
though something strange were
happening to you. 13 But rejoice inasmuch as you participate in the
sufferings of Christ, so that you
may be overjoyed when his glory is revealed. 14 If you are insulted because of the name of Christ,
you are blessed, for the Spirit of
glory and of God rests on you.
15 If you suffer, it should not be as
a murderer or thief or any other kind of criminal, or even as a
meddler. 16 However, if you suffer
as a Christian, do not be ashamed,
but praise God that you bear that
name. 17 For it is time for judgment
to begin with God's household;
and if it begins with us, what will
the outcome be for those who do
not obey the gospel of God? 18 And,
Ac 5:41; Ro 8:17

> "If it is hard for the righteous
> to be saved,
> what will become of the
> ungodly and the
> sinner?"[a] Pr 11:31; Lk 23:31

19 So then, those who suffer according to God's will should commit themselves to their faithful
Creator and continue to do good.
1Pe 2:15; 3:17

To the Elders and the Flock

5 To the elders among you, I
appeal as a fellow elder and a
witness of Christ's sufferings who
also will share in the glory to be
revealed: 2 Be shepherds of God's
flock that is under your care,
watching over them — not because you must, but because you
are willing, as God wants you to
be; not pursuing dishonest gain,
but eager to serve; 3 not lording it
over those entrusted to you, but
being examples to the flock. 4 And
when the Chief Shepherd appears,
you will receive the crown of glory
that will never fade away.
1Co 9:25; 1Ti 3:3; Rev 1:9

5 In the same way, you who are
younger, submit yourselves to
your elders. All of you, clothe
yourselves with humility toward
one another, because, Eph 5:21

> "God opposes the proud
> but shows favor to the
> humble."[b]

6 Humble yourselves, therefore,
under God's mighty hand, that he
may lift you up in due time. 7 Cast
all your anxiety on him because
he cares for you. Heb 13:5; Jas 4:6,10

8 Be alert and of sober mind.
Your enemy the devil prowls
around like a roaring lion looking
for someone to devour. 9 Resist
him, standing firm in the faith,
because you know that the family
of believers throughout the world
is undergoing the same kind of
sufferings. Ac 14:22; Col 2:5

10 And the God of all grace, who
called you to his eternal glory in

[a] *18* Prov. 11:31 (see Septuagint)
[b] *5* Prov. 3:34

Christ, after you have suffered a
little while, will himself restore
you and make you strong, firm
and steadfast. 11 To him be the
power for ever and ever. Amen.

Ro 11:36; 2Co 4:17

Final Greetings

12 With the help of Silas,[a] whom I
regard as a faithful brother, I have
written to you briefly, encouraging you and testifying that this is
the true grace of God. Stand fast
in it. 2Co 1:19; Heb 13:22

13 She who is in Babylon, chosen together with you, sends you
her greetings, and so does my son
Mark. 14 Greet one another with a
kiss of love. Ac 12:12; Ro 16:16

Peace to all of you who are in
Christ. Eph 6:23

[a] 12 Greek *Silvanus*, a variant of *Silas*

2 PETER

1 Simon Peter, a servant and apostle of Jesus Christ, Ro 1:1; 1Pe 1:1

To those who through the righteousness of our God and Savior
Jesus Christ have received a faith
as precious as ours:
Ro 3:21-26; Titus 2:13

2 Grace and peace be yours in
abundance through the knowledge of God and of Jesus our Lord.
Php 3:8

Confirming One's Calling and Election

3 His divine power has given
us everything we need for a godly life through our knowledge of
him who called us by his own glory and goodness. 4 Through these
he has given us his very great and
precious promises, so that through
them you may participate in the
divine nature, having escaped the
corruption in the world caused by
evil desires. 2Co 7:1; 1Pe 1:5

5 For this very reason, make every effort to add to your faith goodness; and to goodness, knowledge;
6 and to knowledge, self-control;
and to self-control, perseverance;
and to perseverance, godliness;
7 and to godliness, mutual affection; and to mutual affection, love.
8 For if you possess these qualities
in increasing measure, they will
keep you from being ineffective
and unproductive in your knowledge of our Lord Jesus Christ. 9 But
whoever does not have them is
nearsighted and blind, forgetting
that they have been cleansed from
their past sins. 1Jn 2:11; Eph 5:26

10 Therefore, my brothers and
sisters,[a] make every effort to confirm your calling and election. For
if you do these things, you will
never stumble, 11 and you will receive a rich welcome into the eternal kingdom of our Lord and Savior Jesus Christ. 2Pe 3:17

Prophecy of Scripture

12 So I will always remind you
of these things, even though you
know them and are firmly established in the truth you now have.
13 I think it is right to refresh your
memory as long as I live in the
tent of this body, 14 because I know
that I will soon put it aside, as our
Lord Jesus Christ has made clear
to me. 15 And I will make every effort to see that after my departure
you will always be able to remember these things. 2Co 5:1,4; 1Jn 2:21

16 For we did not follow cleverly
devised stories when we told you
about the coming of our Lord Jesus

[a] *10* The Greek word for *brothers and sisters* (*adelphoi*) refers here to believers, both men and women, as part of God's family.

Christ in power, but we were eyewitnesses of his majesty. 17 He received honor and glory from God
the Father when the voice came to
him from the Majestic Glory, saying, "This is my Son, whom I love;
with him I am well pleased."[a] 18 We
ourselves heard this voice that
came from heaven when we were
with him on the sacred mountain.

Mt 3:17; 17:1-8

19 We also have the prophetic
message as something completely reliable, and you will do well
to pay attention to it, as to a light
shining in a dark place, until the
day dawns and the morning star
rises in your hearts. 20 Above all,
you must understand that no
prophecy of Scripture came about
by the prophet's own interpretation of things. 21 For prophecy
never had its origin in the human
will, but prophets, though human,
spoke from God as they were carried along by the Holy Spirit.

Ac 1:16; 2Ti 3:16

False Teachers and Their Destruction

2 But there were also false
prophets among the people,
just as there will be false teachers among you. They will secretly introduce destructive heresies,
even denying the sovereign Lord
who bought them — bringing
swift destruction on themselves.
2 Many will follow their depraved
conduct and will bring the way
of truth into disrepute. 3 In their
greed these teachers will exploit
you with fabricated stories. Their
condemnation has long been
hanging over them, and their destruction has not been sleeping.

2Co 2:17; Jude 4

4 For if God did not spare angels
when they sinned, but sent them
to hell,[b] putting them in chains of
darkness[c] to be held for judgment;
5 if he did not spare the ancient
world when he brought the flood
on its ungodly people, but protected Noah, a preacher of righteousness, and seven others; 6 if he condemned the cities of Sodom and
Gomorrah by burning them to
ashes, and made them an example of what is going to happen to
the ungodly; 7 and if he rescued
Lot, a righteous man, who was
distressed by the depraved conduct of the lawless 8 (for that righteous man, living among them
day after day, was tormented in
his righteous soul by the lawless
deeds he saw and heard) — 9 if this
is so, then the Lord knows how to
rescue the godly from trials and
to hold the unrighteous for punishment on the day of judgment.
10 This is especially true of those
who follow the corrupt desire of
the flesh[d] and despise authority.

1Co 10:13; 2Pe 3:3

[a] 17 Matt. 17:5; Mark 9:7; Luke 9:35
[b] 4 Greek *Tartarus* [c] 4 Some manuscripts *in gloomy dungeons* [d] 10 In contexts like this, the Greek word for *flesh* (*sarx*) refers to the sinful state of human beings, often presented as a power in opposition to the Spirit; also in verse 18.

Bold and arrogant, they are not
afraid to heap abuse on celestial
beings; 11yet even angels, although
they are stronger and more powerful, do not heap abuse on such beings when bringing judgment on
them from[a] the Lord. 12But these
people blaspheme in matters they
do not understand. They are like
unreasoning animals, creatures
of instinct, born only to be caught
and destroyed, and like animals
they too will perish. Jude 8-10

13They will be paid back with
harm for the harm they have
done. Their idea of pleasure is to
carouse in broad daylight. They
are blots and blemishes, reveling in their pleasures while they
feast with you.[b] 14With eyes full
of adultery, they never stop sinning; they seduce the unstable;
they are experts in greed — an accursed brood! 15They have left the
straight way and wandered off to
follow the way of Balaam son of
Bezer,[c] who loved the wages of
wickedness. 16But he was rebuked
for his wrongdoing by a donkey —
an animal without speech — who
spoke with a human voice and restrained the prophet's madness.
Nu 22:21-30

17These people are springs without water and mists driven by a
storm. Blackest darkness is reserved for them. 18For they mouth
empty, boastful words and, by appealing to the lustful desires of
the flesh, they entice people who
are just escaping from those who
live in error. 19They promise them
freedom, while they themselves
are slaves of depravity — for "people are slaves to whatever has
mastered them." 20If they have escaped the corruption of the world
by knowing our Lord and Savior
Jesus Christ and are again entangled in it and are overcome, they
are worse off at the end than they
were at the beginning. 21It would
have been better for them not to
have known the way of righteousness, than to have known it and
then to turn their backs on the sacred command that was passed on
to them. 22Of them the proverbs
are true: "A dog returns to its vomit,"[d] and, "A sow that is washed
returns to her wallowing in the
mud." Mt 12:45; Heb 6:4-6

The Day of the Lord

3 Dear friends, this is now my
second letter to you. I have
written both of them as remind-
ers to stimulate you to wholesome
thinking. 2I want you to recall the
words spoken in the past by the
holy prophets and the command
given by our Lord and Savior
through your apostles. 2Pe 1:13

3Above all, you must understand that in the last days scoffers
will come, scoffing and following
their own evil desires. 4They will
say, "Where is this 'coming' he

[a] *11* Many manuscripts *beings in the presence of* [b] *13* Some manuscripts *in their love feasts* [c] *15* Greek *Bosor*
[d] *22* Prov. 26:11

promised? Ever since our ancestors died, everything goes on as
it has since the beginning of creation." 5But they deliberately forget
that long ago by God's word the
heavens came into being and the
earth was formed out of water and
by water. 6By these waters also the
world of that time was deluged
and destroyed. 7By the same word
the present heavens and earth are
reserved for fire, being kept for
the day of judgment and destruction of the ungodly. Eze 12:22; 2Pe 2:10

8But do not forget this one
thing, dear friends: With the Lord
a day is like a thousand years, and
a thousand years are like a day.
9The Lord is not slow in keeping
his promise, as some understand
slowness. Instead he is patient
with you, not wanting anyone to
perish, but everyone to come to
repentance. Ps 90:4; Heb 10:37

10But the day of the Lord will
come like a thief. The heavens
will disappear with a roar; the elements will be destroyed by fire,
and the earth and everything
done in it will be laid bare.[a]
Mt 24:35; Rev 21:1

11Since everything will be destroyed in this way, what kind of
people ought you to be? You ought
to live holy and godly lives 12as you
look forward to the day of God and
speed its coming.[b] That day will
bring about the destruction of the
heavens by fire, and the elements
will melt in the heat. 13But in keeping with his promise we are looking forward to a new heaven and
a new earth, where righteousness
dwells. Isa 65:17; 1Co 1:7

14So then, dear friends, since you
are looking forward to this, make
every effort to be found spotless,
blameless and at peace with him.
15Bear in mind that our Lord's patience means salvation, just as our
dear brother Paul also wrote you
with the wisdom that God gave
him. 16He writes the same way in
all his letters, speaking in them of
these matters. His letters contain
some things that are hard to understand, which ignorant and unstable people distort, as they do
the other Scriptures, to their own
destruction. Eph 3:3; 2Pe 2:14

17Therefore, dear friends, since
you have been forewarned, be on
your guard so that you may not
be carried away by the error of the
lawless and fall from your secure
position. 18But grow in the grace
and knowledge of our Lord and
Savior Jesus Christ. To him be glory both now and forever! Amen.
2Pe 1:11; Rev 2:5

[a] 10 Some manuscripts *be burned up*
[b] 12 Or *as you wait eagerly for the day of God to come*

1 JOHN

The Incarnation of the Word of Life

1 That which was from the beginning, which we have heard,
which we have seen with our eyes,
which we have looked at and our
hands have touched — this we proclaim concerning the Word of life.
2The life appeared; we have seen it
and testify to it, and we proclaim
to you the eternal life, which was
with the Father and has appeared
to us. 3We proclaim to you what
we have seen and heard, so that
you also may have fellowship with
us. And our fellowship is with the
Father and with his Son, Jesus
Christ. 4We write this to make our[a]
joy complete. Jn 3:29; 1Jn 2:1

Light and Darkness, Sin and Forgiveness

5This is the message we have
heard from him and declare to
you: God is light; in him there is
no darkness at all. 6If we claim to
have fellowship with him and yet
walk in the darkness, we lie and
do not live out the truth. 7But if
we walk in the light, as he is in the
light, we have fellowship with one
another, and the blood of Jesus,
his Son, purifies us from all[b] sin.
Heb 9:14; Rev 1:5

8If we claim to be without sin,
we deceive ourselves and the truth
is not in us. 9If we confess our sins,
he is faithful and just and will forgive us our sins and purify us from
all unrighteousness. 10If we claim
we have not sinned, we make him
out to be a liar and his word is not
in us. 1Jn 2:14; 5:10

2 My dear children, I write this
to you so that you will not sin.
But if anybody does sin, we have
an advocate with the Father —
Jesus Christ, the Righteous One.
2He is the atoning sacrifice for our
sins, and not only for ours but also
for the sins of the whole world.
Ro 3:25; Heb 7:25

Love and Hatred for Fellow Believers

3We know that we have come
to know him if we keep his commands. 4Whoever says, "I know
him," but does not do what he
commands is a liar, and the truth
is not in that person. 5But if anyone obeys his word, love for God[c]
is truly made complete in them.
This is how we know we are in
him: 6Whoever claims to live in
him must live as Jesus did.
1Pe 2:21; 1Jn 4:12

7Dear friends, I am not writing
you a new command but an old
one, which you have had since the
beginning. This old command is

[a] 4 Some manuscripts *your* [b] 7 Or *every*
[c] 5 Or *word, God's love*

the message you have heard. 8 Yet
I am writing you a new command;
its truth is seen in him and in you,
because the darkness is passing
and the true light is already shining. Jn 1:9; 13:34
9 Anyone who claims to be in the
light but hates a brother or sister[a]
is still in the darkness. 10 Anyone
who loves their brother and sister[b] lives in the light, and there
is nothing in them to make them
stumble. 11 But anyone who hates a
brother or sister is in the darkness
and walks around in the darkness.
They do not know where they are
going, because the darkness has
blinded them. Jn 12:35; 1Jn 3:14

Reasons for Writing

12 I am writing to you, dear
children,
because your sins have been
forgiven on account of
his name. 1Jn 3:23
13 I am writing to you, fathers,
because you know him who
is from the beginning.
Jn 1:1
I am writing to you, young
men,
because you have overcome
the evil one. Mt 5:37; Jn 16:33
14 I write to you, dear children,
because you know the
Father.
I write to you, fathers,
because you know him who
is from the beginning.
Jn 1:1
I write to you, young men,
because you are strong,
Eph 6:10
and the word of God lives in
you, Jn 5:38; 1Jn 1:10
and you have overcome the
evil one. ver 13

On Not Loving the World

15 Do not love the world or anything in the world. If anyone loves
the world, love for the Father[c] is
not in them. 16 For everything in
the world — the lust of the flesh,
the lust of the eyes, and the pride
of life — comes not from the Father but from the world. 17 The
world and its desires pass away,
but whoever does the will of God
lives forever. Pr 27:20; Ro 12:2; 1Co 7:31

Warnings Against Denying the Son

18 Dear children, this is the last
hour; and as you have heard that
the antichrist is coming, even now
many antichrists have come. This
is how we know it is the last hour.
19 They went out from us, but they
did not really belong to us. For
if they had belonged to us, they
would have remained with us; but
their going showed that none of
them belonged to us. 1Co 11:19; 1Jn 4:1

[a] 9 The Greek word for *brother or sister* (*adelphos*) refers here to a believer, whether man or woman, as part of God's family; also in verse 11; and in 3:15, 17; 4:20; 5:16.
[b] 10 The Greek word for *brother and sister* (*adelphos*) refers here to a believer, whether man or woman, as part of God's family; also in 3:10; 4:20, 21.
[c] 15 Or *world, the Father's love*

20 But you have an anointing
from the Holy One, and all of you
know the truth.[a] 21 I do not write to
you because you do not know the
truth, but because you do know it
and because no lie comes from the
truth. 22 Who is the liar? It is whoever denies that Jesus is the Christ.
Such a person is the antichrist —
denying the Father and the Son.
23 No one who denies the Son has
the Father; whoever acknowledges the Son has the Father also.
2Pe 1:12; 1Jn 4:15

24 As for you, see that what you
have heard from the beginning remains in you. If it does, you also
will remain in the Son and in the
Father. 25 And this is what he promised us — eternal life. Jn 14:23; 1Jn 1:3

26 I am writing these things to
you about those who are trying to
lead you astray. 27 As for you, the
anointing you received from him
remains in you, and you do not
need anyone to teach you. But as
his anointing teaches you about
all things and as that anointing is
real, not counterfeit — just as it has
taught you, remain in him. 2Jn 7

God's Children and Sin

28 And now, dear children, continue in him, so that when he appears we may be confident and
unashamed before him at his
coming. 1Jn 3:2; 4:17

29 If you know that he is righteous, you know that everyone
who does what is right has been
born of him.

3 See what great love the Father
has lavished on us, that we
should be called children of God!
And that is what we are! The reason the world does not know us
is that it did not know him. 2 Dear
friends, now we are children of
God, and what we will be has not
yet been made known. But we
know that when Christ appears,[b]
we shall be like him, for we shall
see him as he is. 3 All who have this
hope in him purify themselves,
just as he is pure. Jn 1:12; 16:3

4 Everyone who sins breaks the
law; in fact, sin is lawlessness. 5 But
you know that he appeared so that
he might take away our sins. And
in him is no sin. 6 No one who lives
in him keeps on sinning. No one
who continues to sin has either
seen him or known him.
2Co 5:21; 1Jn 5:17

7 Dear children, do not let anyone lead you astray. The one who
does what is right is righteous,
just as he is righteous. 8 The one
who does what is sinful is of the
devil, because the devil has been
sinning from the beginning. The
reason the Son of God appeared
was to destroy the devil's work.
9 No one who is born of God will
continue to sin, because God's
seed remains in them; they cannot go on sinning, because they
have been born of God. 10 This is
how we know who the children
of God are and who the children

[a] 20 Some manuscripts *and you know all things* [b] 2 Or *when it is made known*

of the devil are: Anyone who does
not do what is right is not God's
child, nor is anyone who does not
love their brother and sister.

1Jn 4:8; 5:18

More on Love and Hatred

11 For this is the message you
heard from the beginning: We
should love one another. 12 Do not
be like Cain, who belonged to the
evil one and murdered his brother. And why did he murder him?
Because his own actions were evil
and his brother's were righteous.
13 Do not be surprised, my brothers
and sisters,[a] if the world hates you.
14 We know that we have passed
from death to life, because we love
each other. Anyone who does not
love remains in death. 15 Anyone
who hates a brother or sister is a
murderer, and you know that no
murderer has eternal life residing
in him.

Mt 5:21-22; Gal 5:20-21

16 This is how we know what love
is: Jesus Christ laid down his life
for us. And we ought to lay down
our lives for our brothers and sisters. 17 If anyone has material possessions and sees a brother or
sister in need but has no pity on
them, how can the love of God be
in that person? 18 Dear children, let
us not love with words or speech
but with actions and in truth.

19 This is how we know that we
belong to the truth and how we set
our hearts at rest in his presence:
20 If our hearts condemn us, we
know that God is greater than our
hearts, and he knows everything.
21 Dear friends, if our hearts do not
condemn us, we have confidence
before God 22 and receive from him
anything we ask, because we keep
his commands and do what pleases him. 23 And this is his command:
to believe in the name of his Son,
Jesus Christ, and to love one another as he commanded us. 24 The
one who keeps God's commands
lives in him, and he in them. And
this is how we know that he lives
in us: We know it by the Spirit he
gave us.

1Jn 2:6; 4:13

On Denying the Incarnation

4 Dear friends, do not believe
every spirit, but test the spirits
to see whether they are from God,
because many false prophets have
gone out into the world. 2 This is
how you can recognize the Spirit
of God: Every spirit that acknowledges that Jesus Christ has come
in the flesh is from God, 3 but every
spirit that does not acknowledge
Jesus is not from God. This is the
spirit of the antichrist, which you
have heard is coming and even
now is already in the world.

1Co 12:3; 2Jn 7

4 You, dear children, are from
God and have overcome them,
because the one who is in you is
greater than the one who is in the
world. 5 They are from the world

[a] *13* The Greek word for *brothers and sisters* (*adelphoi*) refers here to believers, both men and women, as part of God's family; also in verse 16.

and therefore speak from the
viewpoint of the world, and the
world listens to them. 6 We are
from God, and whoever knows
God listens to us; but whoever is
not from God does not listen to us.
This is how we recognize the Spirit[a] of truth and the spirit of falsehood. Jn 8:47; 14:17

God's Love and Ours

7 Dear friends, let us love one
another, for love comes from God.
Everyone who loves has been born
of God and knows God. 8 Whoever
does not love does not know God,
because God is love. 9 This is how
God showed his love among us: He
sent his one and only Son into the
world that we might live through
him. 10 This is love: not that we
loved God, but that he loved us
and sent his Son as an atoning sacrifice for our sins. 11 Dear friends,
since God so loved us, we also
ought to love one another. 12 No
one has ever seen God; but if we
love one another, God lives in us
and his love is made complete
in us. 1Jn 2:2,5

13 This is how we know that we
live in him and he in us: He has
given us of his Spirit. 14 And we
have seen and testify that the Father has sent his Son to be the
Savior of the world. 15 If anyone
acknowledges that Jesus is the
Son of God, God lives in them and
they in God. 16 And so we know and
rely on the love God has for us.
God is love. Whoever lives in
love lives in God, and God in
them. 17 This is how love is made
complete among us so that we
will have confidence on the day
of judgment: In this world we are
like Jesus. 18 There is no fear in
love. But perfect love drives out
fear, because fear has to do with
punishment. The one who fears is
not made perfect in love.
Ro 8:15; 1Jn 2:5

19 We love because he first loved
us. 20 Whoever claims to love God
yet hates a brother or sister is a
liar. For whoever does not love
their brother and sister, whom
they have seen, cannot love God,
whom they have not seen. 21 And
he has given us this command:
Anyone who loves God must also
love their brother and sister.
Mt 5:43; 1Jn 2:4

Faith in the Incarnate Son of God

5 Everyone who believes that
Jesus is the Christ is born of
God, and everyone who loves the
father loves his child as well. 2 This
is how we know that we love the
children of God: by loving God
and carrying out his commands.
3 In fact, this is love for God: to
keep his commands. And his commands are not burdensome, 4 for
everyone born of God overcomes
the world. This is the victory that
has overcome the world, even our
faith. 5 Who is it that overcomes

Ro 10:9

[a] 6 Or *spirit*

the world? Only the one who believes that Jesus is the Son of God.
Jn 14:15; 16:33

6 This is the one who came by
water and blood—Jesus Christ. He
did not come by water only, but by
water and blood. And it is the Spirit who testifies, because the Spirit is the truth. 7 For there are three
that testify: 8 the[a] Spirit, the water
and the blood; and the three are
in agreement. 9 We accept human
testimony, but God's testimony is
greater because it is the testimony
of God, which he has given about
his Son. 10 Whoever believes in the
Son of God accepts this testimony. Whoever does not believe God
has made him out to be a liar, because they have not believed the
testimony God has given about
his Son. 11 And this is the testimony: God has given us eternal life,
and this life is in his Son. 12 Whoever has the Son has life; whoever
does not have the Son of God does
not have life. Jn 3:15-16,36; 1Jn 2:25

Concluding Affirmations

13 I write these things to you who
believe in the name of the Son of
God so that you may know that
you have eternal life. 14 This is the
confidence we have in approaching God: that if we ask anything
according to his will, he hears us.
15 And if we know that he hears
us—whatever we ask—we know
that we have what we asked of
him. Jn 20:31; 1Jn 3:21

16 If you see any brother or sister
commit a sin that does not lead to
death, you should pray and God
will give them life. I refer to those
whose sin does not lead to death.
There is a sin that leads to death.
I am not saying that you should
pray about that. 17 All wrongdoing
is sin, and there is sin that does
not lead to death. Jas 5:15; 1Jn 3:4

18 We know that anyone born of
God does not continue to sin; the
One who was born of God keeps
them safe, and the evil one cannot harm them. 19 We know that
we are children of God, and that
the whole world is under the control of the evil one. 20 We know
also that the Son of God has come
and has given us understanding,
so that we may know him who
is true. And we are in him who
is true by being in his Son Jesus
Christ. He is the true God and eternal life. Lk 24:45; Jn 17:3

21 Dear children, keep yourselves
from idols. 1Co 10:14; 1Th 1:9

[a] 7,8 Late manuscripts of the Vulgate *testify in heaven: the Father, the Word and the Holy Spirit, and these three are one. 8 And there are three that testify on earth: the* (not found in any Greek manuscript before the fourteenth century)

2 JOHN

1 The elder, 3Jn 1

To the lady chosen by God and
to her children, whom I love in the
truth — and not I only, but also all
who know the truth — 2 because
of the truth, which lives in us and
will be with us forever: Jn 8:32; 1Jn 1:8

3 Grace, mercy and peace from
God the Father and from Jesus
Christ, the Father's Son, will be
with us in truth and love. Ro 1:7

4 It has given me great joy to
find some of your children walking in the truth, just as the Father
commanded us. 5 And now, dear
lady, I am not writing you a new
command but one we have had
from the beginning. I ask that
we love one another. 6 And this is
love: that we walk in obedience to
his commands. As you have heard
from the beginning, his command is that you walk in love.
1Jn 2:5; 3:11

7 I say this because many deceivers, who do not acknowledge Jesus
Christ as coming in the flesh, have
gone out into the world. Any such
person is the deceiver and the antichrist. 8 Watch out that you do
not lose what we[a] have worked for,
but that you may be rewarded fully. 9 Anyone who runs ahead and
does not continue in the teaching
of Christ does not have God; whoever continues in the teaching has
both the Father and the Son. 10 If
anyone comes to you and does not
bring this teaching, do not take
them into your house or welcome
them. 11 Anyone who welcomes
them shares in their wicked work.
Ro 16:17; 1Jn 2:23

12 I have much to write to you,
but I do not want to use paper and
ink. Instead, I hope to visit you
and talk with you face to face, so
that our joy may be complete.
3Jn 13-14

13 The children of your sister,
who is chosen by God, send their
greetings. ver 1

[a] 8 Some manuscripts *you*

3 JOHN

1The elder, 2Jn 1

To my dear friend Gaius, whom
I love in the truth.

2Dear friend, I pray that you
may enjoy good health and that
all may go well with you, even as
your soul is getting along well. 3It
gave me great joy when some believers came and testified about
your faithfulness to the truth, telling how you continue to walk in it.
4I have no greater joy than to hear
that my children are walking in
the truth. 1Co 4:15; 2Jn 4
5Dear friend, you are faithful in
what you are doing for the brothers and sisters,[a] even though they
are strangers to you. 6They have
told the church about your love.
Please send them on their way in
a manner that honors God. 7It was
for the sake of the Name that they
went out, receiving no help from
the pagans. 8We ought therefore
to show hospitality to such people
so that we may work together for
the truth. Ac 20:33,35; Ro 12:13
9I wrote to the church, but Diot-
rephes, who loves to be first, will
not welcome us. 10So when I come,
I will call attention to what he is
doing, spreading malicious nonsense about us. Not satisfied with
that, he even refuses to welcome
other believers. He also stops
those who want to do so and puts
them out of the church.
Jn 9:22,34; 2Jn 12
11Dear friend, do not imitate
what is evil but what is good. Anyone who does what is good is from
God. Anyone who does what is evil
has not seen God. 12Demetrius is
well spoken of by everyone — and
even by the truth itself. We also
speak well of him, and you know
that our testimony is true.
Jn 21:24; 1Ti 3:7
13I have much to write you, but I
do not want to do so with pen and
ink. 14I hope to see you soon, and
we will talk face to face. 2Jn 12

15Peace to you. The friends here
send their greetings. Greet the
friends there by name. Jn 10:3

[a] 5 The Greek word for *brothers and sisters* (*adelphoi*) refers here to believers, both men and women, as part of God's family.

JUDE

1Jude, a servant of Jesus Christ
and a brother of James, Ac 1:13

To those who have been called,
who are loved in God the Father
and kept for[a] Jesus Christ:

Jn 17:12; Ro 1:6-7

2Mercy, peace and love be yours
in abundance. 2Pe 1:2

The Sin and Doom of Ungodly People

3Dear friends, although I was
very eager to write to you about
the salvation we share, I felt compelled to write and urge you to
contend for the faith that was once
for all entrusted to God's holy people. 4For certain individuals whose
condemnation was written about[b]
long ago have secretly slipped in
among you. They are ungodly
people, who pervert the grace of
our God into a license for immorality and deny Jesus Christ our
only Sovereign and Lord.

Gal 2:4; 2Pe 2:1

5Though you already know all
this, I want to remind you that
the Lord[c] at one time delivered
his people out of Egypt, but later
destroyed those who did not believe. 6And the angels who did not
keep their positions of authority but abandoned their proper
dwelling — these he has kept in
darkness, bound with everlasting
chains for judgment on the great
Day. 7In a similar way, Sodom
and Gomorrah and the surrounding towns gave themselves up to
sexual immorality and perversion. They serve as an example of
those who suffer the punishment
of eternal fire.

Dt 29:23; 2Pe 2:6

8In the very same way, on the
strength of their dreams these
ungodly people pollute their own
bodies, reject authority and heap
abuse on celestial beings. 9But
even the archangel Michael, when
he was disputing with the devil
about the body of Moses, did not
himself dare to condemn him for
slander but said, "The Lord rebuke
you!"[d] 10Yet these people slander
whatever they do not understand,
and the very things they do understand by instinct — as irrational
animals do — will destroy them.

2Pe 2:10,12

11Woe to them! They have taken
the way of Cain; they have rushed
for profit into Balaam's error; they
have been destroyed in Korah's rebellion. Nu 16:1-3,31-35; 1Jn 3:12

[a] *1* Or *by*; or *in* [b] *4* Or *individuals who were marked out for condemnation*
[c] *5* Some early manuscripts *Jesus*
[d] *9* Jude is alluding to the Jewish *Testament of Moses* (approximately the first century A.D.).

[12]These people are blemishes at
your love feasts, eating with you
without the slightest qualm —
shepherds who feed only themselves. They are clouds without
rain, blown along by the wind;
autumn trees, without fruit and
uprooted — twice dead. [13]They are
wild waves of the sea, foaming up
their shame; wandering stars, for
whom blackest darkness has been
reserved forever. Isa 57:20; Php 3:19
[14]Enoch, the seventh from Adam,
prophesied about them: "See, the
Lord is coming with thousands
upon thousands of his holy ones
[15]to judge everyone, and to convict all of them of all the ungodly
acts they have committed in their
ungodliness, and of all the defiant
words ungodly sinners have spoken against him."[a] [16]These people
are grumblers and faultfinders;
they follow their own evil desires;
they boast about themselves and
flatter others for their own advantage. Dt 33:2; 2Pe 2:18

A Call to Persevere

[17]But, dear friends, remember what the apostles of our Lord
Jesus Christ foretold. [18]They said
to you, "In the last times there will
be scoffers who will follow their
own ungodly desires." [19]These are
the people who divide you, who
follow mere natural instincts and
do not have the Spirit. 1Ti 4:1; 2Pe 2:1
[20]But you, dear friends, by building yourselves up in your most
holy faith and praying in the Holy
Spirit, [21]keep yourselves in God's
love as you wait for the mercy of
our Lord Jesus Christ to bring you
to eternal life. Titus 2:13; 2Pe 3:12
[22]Be merciful to those who
doubt; [23]save others by snatching
them from the fire; to others show
mercy, mixed with fear — hating
even the clothing stained by corrupted flesh.[b] Am 4:11; Zec 3:2-5

Doxology

[24]To him who is able to keep
you from stumbling and to present you before his glorious presence without fault and with great
joy — [25]to the only God our Savior
be glory, majesty, power and authority, through Jesus Christ our
Lord, before all ages, now and forevermore! Amen. Ro 11:36; Col 1:22

[a] *14,15* From the Jewish *First Book of Enoch* (approximately the first century B.C.)
[b] *22,23* The Greek manuscripts of these verses vary at several points.

REVELATION

Prologue

1 The revelation from Jesus Christ, which God gave him to show his servants what must soon take place. He made it known by sending his angel to his servant John, 2who testifies to everything he saw — that is, the word of God and the testimony of Jesus Christ. 3Blessed is the one who reads aloud the words of this prophecy, and blessed are those who hear it and take to heart what is written in it, because the time is near.
Lk 11:28; 1Co 1:6

Greetings and Doxology

4John,

To the seven churches in the province of Asia:
ver 11,20

Grace and peace to you from him who is, and who was, and who is to come, and from the seven spirits[a] before his throne, 5and from Jesus Christ, who is the faithful witness, the firstborn from the dead, and the ruler of the kings of the earth.
Col 1:18; Rev 17:14

To him who loves us and has freed us from our sins by his blood, 6and has made us to be a kingdom and priests to serve his God and Father — to him be glory and power for ever and ever! Amen.
Ro 11:36; 1Pe 2:5

7"Look, he is coming with the
clouds,"[b]
Da 7:13
and "every eye will see him,
even those who pierced him";
Jn 19:34,37
and all peoples on earth "will
mourn because of him."[c]
So shall it be! Amen.

8"I am the Alpha and the Omega," says the Lord God, "who is, and who was, and who is to come, the Almighty."
Rev 4:8; 21:6

John's Vision of Christ

9I, John, your brother and companion in the suffering and kingdom and patient endurance that are ours in Jesus, was on the island of Patmos because of the word of God and the testimony of Jesus. 10On the Lord's Day I was in the Spirit, and I heard behind me a loud voice like a trumpet, 11which said: "Write on a scroll what you see and send it to the seven churches: to Ephesus, Smyrna, Pergamum, Thyatira, Sardis, Philadelphia and Laodicea."
2Ti 2:12; Rev 4:1

12I turned around to see the voice that was speaking to me. And when I turned I saw seven golden lampstands, 13and among the lampstands was someone like

[a] 4 That is, the sevenfold Spirit
[b] 7 Daniel 7:13 [c] 7 Zech. 12:10

a son of man,[a] dressed in a robe
reaching down to his feet and
with a golden sash around his
chest. 14 The hair on his head was
white like wool, as white as snow,
and his eyes were like blazing fire.
15 His feet were like bronze glowing in a furnace, and his voice was
like the sound of rushing waters.
16 In his right hand he held sev-
en stars, and coming out of his
mouth was a sharp, double-edged
sword. His face was like the sun
shining in all its brilliance.

Heb 4:12; Rev 2:12,16

17 When I saw him, I fell at his
feet as though dead. Then he
placed his right hand on me and
said: “Do not be afraid. I am the
First and the Last. 18 I am the Living One; I was dead, and now look,
I am alive for ever and ever! And I
hold the keys of death and Hades.

Ro 6:9; Rev 20:1

19 “Write, therefore, what you
have seen, what is now and what
will take place later. 20 The mystery of the seven stars that you
saw in my right hand and of the
seven golden lampstands is this:
The seven stars are the angels[b]
of the seven churches, and the
seven lampstands are the seven
churches.

Mt 5:14-15

To the Church in Ephesus

2 “To the angel[c] of the church in
Ephesus write:

Ac 18:19

These are the words of him
who holds the seven stars in his
right hand and walks among
the seven golden lampstands.
2 I know your deeds, your hard
work and your perseverance. I
know that you cannot tolerate
wicked people, that you have
tested those who claim to be
apostles but are not, and have
found them false. 3 You have
persevered and have endured
hardships for my name, and
have not grown weary.

1Jn 4:1; Rev 1:16

4 Yet I hold this against you:
You have forsaken the love
you had at first. 5 Consider
how far you have fallen! Repent and do the things you
did at first. If you do not repent, I will come to you and
remove your lampstand from
its place. 6 But you have this in
your favor: You hate the practices of the Nicolaitans, which
I also hate.

Mt 24:12; Rev 1:20

7 Whoever has ears, let them
hear what the Spirit says to
the churches. To the one who
is victorious, I will give the
right to eat from the tree of
life, which is in the paradise
of God.

Ge 2:9; Rev 3:6,13,22

To the Church in Smyrna

8 “To the angel of the church in
Smyrna write:

Rev 1:11

These are the words of him
who is the First and the Last,

[a] *13* See Daniel 7:13. [b] *20* Or *messengers*
[c] *1* Or *messenger*; also in verses 8, 12 and 18

who died and came to life again. 9I know your afflictions and your poverty — yet you are rich! I know about the slander of those who say they are Jews and are not, but are a synagogue of Satan. 10Do not be afraid of what you are about to suffer. I tell you, the devil will put some of you in prison to test you, and you will suffer persecution for ten days. Be faithful, even to the point of death, and I will give you life as your victor's crown. Da 1:12,14; Jas 2:5

11Whoever has ears, let them hear what the Spirit says to the churches. The one who is victorious will not be hurt at all by the second death. Rev 21:8

To the Church in Pergamum

12"To the angel of the church in Pergamum write: Rev 1:11

These are the words of him who has the sharp, double-edged sword. 13I know where you live — where Satan has his throne. Yet you remain true to my name. You did not renounce your faith in me, not even in the days of Antipas, my faithful witness, who was put to death in your city — where Satan lives. Rev 1:16; 14:12

14Nevertheless, I have a few things against you: There are some among you who hold to the teaching of Balaam, who taught Balak to entice the Israelites to sin so that they ate food sacrificed to idols and committed sexual immorality. 15Likewise, you also have those who hold to the teaching of the Nicolaitans. 16Repent therefore! Otherwise, I will soon come to you and will fight against them with the sword of my mouth. 2Th 2:8; Rev 1:16

17Whoever has ears, let them hear what the Spirit says to the churches. To the one who is victorious, I will give some of the hidden manna. I will also give that person a white stone with a new name written on it, known only to the one who receives it. Rev 19:12

To the Church in Thyatira

18"To the angel of the church in Thyatira write: Rev 1:11

These are the words of the Son of God, whose eyes are like blazing fire and whose feet are like burnished bronze. 19I know your deeds, your love and faith, your service and perseverance, and that you are now doing more than you did at first. Rev 1:14-15

20Nevertheless, I have this against you: You tolerate that woman Jezebel, who calls herself a prophet. By her teaching she misleads my servants into sexual immorality

and the eating of food sacrificed to idols. 21 I have given
her time to repent of her immorality, but she is unwilling.
22 So I will cast her on a bed
of suffering, and I will make
those who commit adultery
with her suffer intensely, unless they repent of her ways.
23 I will strike her children
dead. Then all the churches
will know that I am he who
searches hearts and minds,
and I will repay each of you
according to your deeds.

24 Now I say to the rest of
you in Thyatira, to you who
do not hold to her teaching
and have not learned Satan's
so-called deep secrets, 'I will
not impose any other burden
on you, 25 except to hold on to
what you have until I come.'

Ac 15:28; Rev 9:20

26 To the one who is victorious and does my will to the
end, I will give authority over
the nations — 27 that one 'will
rule them with an iron scepter
and will dash them to pieces
like pottery'[a] — just as I have
received authority from my
Father. 28 I will also give that
one the morning star. 29 Whoever has ears, let them hear
what the Spirit says to the
churches. Rev 22:16

To the Church in Sardis

3 "To the angel[b] of the church in
Sardis write: Rev 1:11

These are the words of him
who holds the seven spirits[c]
of God and the seven stars. I
know your deeds; you have
a reputation of being alive,
but you are dead. 2 Wake up!
Strengthen what remains
and is about to die, for I have
found your deeds unfinished
in the sight of my God. 3 Remember, therefore, what
you have received and heard;
hold it fast, and repent. But
if you do not wake up, I will
come like a thief, and you will
not know at what time I will
come to you. 2Pe 3:10; Rev 1:4,16

4 Yet you have a few people
in Sardis who have not soiled
their clothes. They will walk
with me, dressed in white,
for they are worthy. 5 The one
who is victorious will, like
them, be dressed in white. I
will never blot out the name
of that person from the book
of life, but will acknowledge
that name before my Father
and his angels. 6 Whoever has
ears, let them hear what the
Spirit says to the churches.

Mt 10:32; Rev 2:7

To the Church in Philadelphia

7 "To the angel of the church in
Philadelphia write: Rev 1:11

These are the words of him
who is holy and true, who

[a] *27* Psalm 2:9 [b] *1* Or *messenger*; also in verses 7 and 14 [c] *1* That is, the sevenfold Spirit

holds the key of David. What
he opens no one can shut,
and what he shuts no one can
open. [8]I know your deeds.
See, I have placed before you
an open door that no one can
shut. I know that you have
little strength, yet you have
kept my word and have not
denied my name. [9]I will make
those who are of the synagogue of Satan, who claim to
be Jews though they are not,
but are liars — I will make
them come and fall down at
your feet and acknowledge
that I have loved you. [10]Since
you have kept my command
to endure patiently, I will
also keep you from the hour
of trial that is going to come
on the whole world to test the
inhabitants of the earth.

Rev 6:10; 17:8

[11]I am coming soon. Hold
on to what you have, so that
no one will take your crown.
[12]The one who is victorious I
will make a pillar in the temple of my God. Never again
will they leave it. I will write
on them the name of my God
and the name of the city of
my God, the new Jerusalem,
which is coming down out
of heaven from my God; and
I will also write on them my
new name. [13]Whoever has
ears, let them hear what the
Spirit says to the churches.

Gal 2:9; Rev 22:4

To the Church in Laodicea

[14]"To the angel of the church in Laodicea write:

Rev 1:11

These are the words of the
Amen, the faithful and true
witness, the ruler of God's
creation. [15]I know your deeds,
that you are neither cold nor
hot. I wish you were either
one or the other! [16]So, because
you are lukewarm — neither
hot nor cold — I am about to
spit you out of my mouth.
[17]You say, 'I am rich; I have
acquired wealth and do not
need a thing.' But you do not
realize that you are wretched,
pitiful, poor, blind and naked.
[18]I counsel you to buy from
me gold refined in the fire,
so you can become rich; and
white clothes to wear, so you
can cover your shameful nakedness; and salve to put on
your eyes, so you can see.

Hos 12:8; 1Co 4:8; Col 1:16,18

[19]Those whom I love I rebuke and discipline. So be
earnest and repent. [20]Here I
am! I stand at the door and
knock. If anyone hears my
voice and opens the door, I
will come in and eat with that
person, and they with me.

Lk 12:36; Heb 12:5-6

[21]To the one who is victorious, I will give the right to sit
with me on my throne, just as
I was victorious and sat down
with my Father on his throne.

22Whoever has ears, let them
hear what the Spirit says to
the churches." Mt 19:28; Rev 2:7

The Throne in Heaven

4 After this I looked, and there
before me was a door standing open in heaven. And the voice
I had first heard speaking to me
like a trumpet said, "Come up
here, and I will show you what
must take place after this." 2At
once I was in the Spirit, and there
before me was a throne in heaven
with someone sitting on it. 3And
the one who sat there had the
appearance of jasper and ruby. A
rainbow that shone like an emerald encircled the throne. 4Sur-
rounding the throne were twenty-four other thrones, and seated
on them were twenty-four elders.
They were dressed in white and
had crowns of gold on their heads.
5From the throne came flashes of
lightning, rumblings and peals of
thunder. In front of the throne,
seven lamps were blazing. These
are the seven spirits[a] of God. 6Also
in front of the throne there was
what looked like a sea of glass,
clear as crystal. Rev 11:16; 15:2

In the center, around the throne,
were four living creatures, and they
were covered with eyes, in front
and in back. 7The first living creature was like a lion, the second was
like an ox, the third had a face like
a man, the fourth was like a flying
eagle. 8Each of the four living creatures had six wings and was covered with eyes all around, even under its wings. Day and night they
never stop saying: Isa 6:2; Eze 1:10

"'Holy, holy, holy
is the Lord God Almighty,'[b]
who was, and is, and is to come."

9Whenever the living creatures
give glory, honor and thanks to
him who sits on the throne and
who lives for ever and ever, 10the
twenty-four elders fall down before him who sits on the throne
and worship him who lives for ever
and ever. They lay their crowns before the throne and say: Rev 5:8,14

11"You are worthy, our Lord and
God,
to receive glory and honor
and power, Rev 5:12
for you created all things,
and by your will they were
created
and have their being." Rev 10:6

The Scroll and the Lamb

5 Then I saw in the right hand
of him who sat on the throne
a scroll with writing on both sides
and sealed with seven seals. 2And
I saw a mighty angel proclaiming
in a loud voice, "Who is worthy
to break the seals and open the
scroll?" 3But no one in heaven or
on earth or under the earth could
open the scroll or even look inside it. 4I wept and wept because

[a] 5 That is, the sevenfold Spirit
[b] 8 Isaiah 6:3

no one was found who was worthy
to open the scroll or look inside.
5 Then one of the elders said to me,
"Do not weep! See, the Lion of the
tribe of Judah, the Root of David,
has triumphed. He is able to open
the scroll and its seven seals."
Ge 49:9; Isa 11:1,10

6 Then I saw a Lamb, looking as
if it had been slain, standing at the
center of the throne, encircled by
the four living creatures and the
elders. The Lamb had seven horns
and seven eyes, which are the sev-
en spirits[a] of God sent out into
all the earth. 7 He went and took
the scroll from the right hand of
him who sat on the throne. 8 And
when he had taken it, the four living creatures and the twenty-four
elders fell down before the Lamb.
Each one had a harp and they
were holding golden bowls full
of incense, which are the prayers
of God's people. 9 And they sang a
new song, saying: Ps 40:3; Rev 14:2

"You are worthy to take the
scroll Rev 4:11
and to open its seals,
because you were slain,
and with your blood you
purchased for God 1Co 6:20
persons from every tribe and
language and people
and nation. Rev 13:7
10 You have made them to be a
kingdom and priests to
serve our God, 1Pe 2:5
and they will reign[b] on the
earth."

11 Then I looked and heard the
voice of many angels, numbering
thousands upon thousands, and
ten thousand times ten thousand.
They encircled the throne and the
living creatures and the elders.
12 In a loud voice they were saying:
Da 7:10; Heb 12:22

"Worthy is the Lamb, who was
slain, ver 9,13
to receive power and wealth
and wisdom and
strength
and honor and glory and
praise!" Rev 4:11

13 Then I heard every creature in
heaven and on earth and under
the earth and on the sea, and all
that is in them, saying: Php 2:10

"To him who sits on the
throne and to the Lamb
ver 1,7; Rev 6:16
be praise and honor and
glory and power,
for ever and ever!"

14 The four living creatures said,
"Amen," and the elders fell down
and worshiped. 1Ch 29:11; Rev 4:10

The Seals

6 I watched as the Lamb opened
the first of the seven seals.
Then I heard one of the four living
creatures say in a voice like thunder, "Come!" 2 I looked, and there
before me was a white horse! Its
rider held a bow, and he was given

[a] 6 That is, the sevenfold Spirit
[b] 10 Some manuscripts *they reign*

a crown, and he rode out as a conqueror bent on conquest.
Zec 6:11; Rev 19:11

3When the Lamb opened the second seal, I heard the second living
creature say, "Come!" 4Then another horse came out, a fiery red one.
Its rider was given power to take
peace from the earth and to make
people kill each other. To him was
given a large sword. Rev 4:7

5When the Lamb opened the
third seal, I heard the third living
creature say, "Come!" I looked,
and there before me was a black
horse! Its rider was holding a pair
of scales in his hand. 6Then I heard
what sounded like a voice among
the four living creatures, saying,
"Two pounds[a] of wheat for a day's
wages,[b] and six pounds[c] of barley for a day's wages,[b] and do not
damage the oil and the wine!"
Rev 4:7; 9:4

7When the Lamb opened the
fourth seal, I heard the voice of
the fourth living creature say,
"Come!" 8I looked, and there before me was a pale horse! Its rider
was named Death, and Hades was
following close behind him. They
were given power over a fourth of
the earth to kill by sword, famine
and plague, and by the wild beasts
of the earth. Zec 6:3; Rev 4:7

9When he opened the fifth seal,
I saw under the altar the souls
of those who had been slain because of the word of God and the
testimony they had maintained.
10They called out in a loud voice,
"How long, Sovereign Lord, holy
and true, until you judge the inhabitants of the earth and avenge
our blood?" 11Then each of them
was given a white robe, and they
were told to wait a little longer,
until the full number of their fellow servants, their brothers and
sisters,[d] were killed just as they
had been. Heb 11:40; Rev 20:4

12I watched as he opened the
sixth seal. There was a great earthquake. The sun turned black like
sackcloth made of goat hair, the
whole moon turned blood red,
13and the stars in the sky fell to
earth, as figs drop from a fig tree
when shaken by a strong wind.
14The heavens receded like a scroll
being rolled up, and every mountain and island was removed from
its place. Jer 4:24; Rev 8:10

15Then the kings of the earth,
the princes, the generals, the
rich, the mighty, and everyone
else, both slave and free, hid in
caves and among the rocks of the
mountains. 16They called to the
mountains and the rocks, "Fall on
us and hide us[e] from the face of
him who sits on the throne and
from the wrath of the Lamb! 17For
the great day of their[f] wrath has
come, and who can withstand it?"
Ps 76:7; Zep 1:14-15

[a] 6 Or about 1 kilogram [b] 6 Greek *a denarius* [c] 6 Or about 3 kilograms
[d] 11 The Greek word for *brothers and sisters* (*adelphoi*) refers here to believers, both men and women, as part of God's family; also in 12:10; 19:10. [e] 16 See Hosea 10:8.
[f] 17 Some manuscripts *his*

144,000 Sealed

7 After this I saw four angels
standing at the four corners of
the earth, holding back the four
winds of the earth to prevent any
wind from blowing on the land or
on the sea or on any tree. 2Then
I saw another angel coming up
from the east, having the seal of
the living God. He called out in a
loud voice to the four angels who
had been given power to harm the
land and the sea: 3"Do not harm
the land or the sea or the trees until we put a seal on the foreheads
of the servants of our God." 4Then
I heard the number of those who
were sealed: 144,000 from all the
tribes of Israel. Rev 9:16; 14:1,3

5From the tribe of Judah
12,000 were sealed,
from the tribe of Reuben
12,000,
from the tribe of Gad 12,000,
6from the tribe of Asher 12,000,
from the tribe of Naphtali
12,000,
from the tribe of Manasseh
12,000,
7from the tribe of Simeon
12,000,
from the tribe of Levi 12,000,
from the tribe of Issachar
12,000,
8from the tribe of Zebulun
12,000,
from the tribe of Joseph
12,000,
from the tribe of Benjamin
12,000.

The Great Multitude in White Robes

9After this I looked, and there
before me was a great multitude
that no one could count, from every nation, tribe, people and language, standing before the throne
and before the Lamb. They were
wearing white robes and were
holding palm branches in their
hands. 10And they cried out in a
loud voice: Rev 5:9

"Salvation belongs to our God,
Ps 3:8; Rev 12:10; 19:1
who sits on the throne, Rev 5:1
and to the Lamb."

11All the angels were standing
around the throne and around
the elders and the four living
creatures. They fell down on their
faces before the throne and worshiped God, 12saying: Rev 4:4,6,10

"Amen!
Praise and glory
and wisdom and thanks and
honor
and power and strength
be to our God for ever and ever.
Amen!" Rev 5:12-14

13Then one of the elders asked
me, "These in white robes — who
are they, and where did they come
from?" Rev 3:4

14I answered, "Sir, you know."
And he said, "These are they
who have come out of the great
tribulation; they have washed
their robes and made them white

in the blood of the Lamb. [15]Therefore, Heb 9:14; 1Jn 1:7

"they are before the throne of
God ver 9
and serve him day and night
in his temple; Rev 11:19
and he who sits on the throne
will shelter them with his
presence. Rev 21:3
[16]'Never again will they hunger;
never again will they thirst.
Jn 6:35
The sun will not beat down on
them,'[a]
nor any scorching heat.
Isa 49:10
[17]For the Lamb at the center of
the throne
will be their shepherd;
Ps 23:1; Jn 10:11
'he will lead them to springs of
living water.'[a] Jn 4:10
'And God will wipe away
every tear from their
eyes.'[b]" Isa 25:8; Rev 21:4

The Seventh Seal and the Golden Censer

8 When he opened the seventh
seal, there was silence in heav-
en for about half an hour. Rev 6:1
[2]And I saw the seven angels who
stand before God, and seven trumpets were given to them.
Mt 24:31; Rev 9:1,13
[3]Another angel, who had a
golden censer, came and stood at
the altar. He was given much incense to offer, with the prayers
of all God's people, on the gold-
en altar in front of the throne.
[4]The smoke of the incense, together with the prayers of God's
people, went up before God from
the angel's hand. [5]Then the angel
took the censer, filled it with fire
from the altar, and hurled it on
the earth; and there came peals
of thunder, rumblings, flashes of
lightning and an earthquake.
Ex 30:1-6; Rev 5:8

The Trumpets

[6]Then the seven angels who had
the seven trumpets prepared to
sound them. ver 2
[7]The first angel sounded his
trumpet, and there came hail and
fire mixed with blood, and it was
hurled down on the earth. A third
of the earth was burned up, a third
of the trees were burned up, and
all the green grass was burned up.
Eze 38:22; Rev 9:4
[8]The second angel sounded his
trumpet, and something like a
huge mountain, all ablaze, was
thrown into the sea. A third of
the sea turned into blood, [9]a third
of the living creatures in the sea
died, and a third of the ships were
destroyed. Jer 51:25; Rev 16:3
[10]The third angel sounded his
trumpet, and a great star, blazing like a torch, fell from the sky
on a third of the rivers and on the
springs of water— [11]the name of
the star is Wormwood.[c] A third
of the waters turned bitter, and

[a] *16,17* Isaiah 49:10 [b] *17* Isaiah 25:8
[c] *11* Wormwood is a bitter substance.

many people died from the waters
that had become bitter.
Isa 14:12; Rev 16:4

12 The fourth angel sounded his
trumpet, and a third of the sun
was struck, a third of the moon,
and a third of the stars, so that a
third of them turned dark. A third
of the day was without light, and
also a third of the night.
Ex 10:21-23; Rev 6:12-13

13 As I watched, I heard an eagle
that was flying in midair call out
in a loud voice: "Woe! Woe! Woe to
the inhabitants of the earth, because of the trumpet blasts about
to be sounded by the other three
angels!" Rev 9:12; 14:6

9 The fifth angel sounded his
trumpet, and I saw a star that
had fallen from the sky to the
earth. The star was given the key
to the shaft of the Abyss. 2 When
he opened the Abyss, smoke rose
from it like the smoke from a gi-
gantic furnace. The sun and sky
were darkened by the smoke from
the Abyss. 3 And out of the smoke
locusts came down on the earth
and were given power like that of
scorpions of the earth. 4 They were
told not to harm the grass of the
earth or any plant or tree, but only
those people who did not have
the seal of God on their foreheads.
5 They were not allowed to kill
them but only to torture them for
five months. And the agony they
suffered was like that of the sting
of a scorpion when it strikes. 6 During those days people will seek
death but will not find it; they will
long to die, but death will elude
them. Jer 8:3; Rev 8:7

7 The locusts looked like horses
prepared for battle. On their heads
they wore something like crowns
of gold, and their faces resembled human faces. 8 Their hair was
like women's hair, and their teeth
were like lions' teeth. 9 They had
breastplates like breastplates of
iron, and the sound of their wings
was like the thundering of many
horses and chariots rushing into
battle. 10 They had tails with sting-
ers, like scorpions, and in their
tails they had power to torment
people for five months. 11 They had
as king over them the angel of the
Abyss, whose name in Hebrew is
Abaddon and in Greek is Apollyon
(that is, Destroyer). Joel 1:6; 2:5

12 The first woe is past; two other
woes are yet to come. Rev 8:13

13 The sixth angel sounded his
trumpet, and I heard a voice coming from the four horns of the
golden altar that is before God. 14 It
said to the sixth angel who had the
trumpet, "Release the four angels
who are bound at the great river
Euphrates." 15 And the four angels
who had been kept ready for this
very hour and day and month and
year were released to kill a third
of mankind. 16 The number of the
mounted troops was twice ten
thousand times ten thousand. I
heard their number. Rev 7:4; 16:12

17 The horses and riders I saw in
my vision looked like this: Their

breastplates were fiery red, dark
blue, and yellow as sulfur. The
heads of the horses resembled the
heads of lions, and out of their
mouths came fire, smoke and
sulfur. 18A third of mankind was
killed by the three plagues of fire,
smoke and sulfur that came out of
their mouths. 19The power of the
horses was in their mouths and in
their tails; for their tails were like
snakes, having heads with which
they inflict injury. Rev 11:5

20The rest of mankind who
were not killed by these plagues
still did not repent of the work
of their hands; they did not stop
worshiping demons, and idols
of gold, silver, bronze, stone and
wood — idols that cannot see or
hear or walk. 21Nor did they repent
of their murders, their magic arts,
their sexual immorality or their
thefts. Ps 115:4-7; 1Co 10:20

The Angel and the Little Scroll

10 Then I saw another mighty
angel coming down from
heaven. He was robed in a cloud,
with a rainbow above his head;
his face was like the sun, and his
legs were like fiery pillars. 2He was
holding a little scroll, which lay
open in his hand. He planted his
right foot on the sea and his left
foot on the land, 3and he gave a
loud shout like the roar of a lion.
When he shouted, the voices of
the seven thunders spoke. 4And
when the seven thunders spoke,
I was about to write; but I heard
a voice from heaven say, "Seal up
what the seven thunders have said
and do not write it down."
Da 8:26; Mt 17:2

5Then the angel I had seen
standing on the sea and on the
land raised his right hand to heav-
en. 6And he swore by him who
lives for ever and ever, who created the heavens and all that is in
them, the earth and all that is in it,
and the sea and all that is in it, and
said, "There will be no more delay!
7But in the days when the seventh
angel is about to sound his trumpet, the mystery of God will be accomplished, just as he announced
to his servants the prophets."
Rev 4:11; 16:17

8Then the voice that I had heard
from heaven spoke to me once
more: "Go, take the scroll that lies
open in the hand of the angel who
is standing on the sea and on the
land." ver 2,4

9So I went to the angel and asked
him to give me the little scroll. He
said to me, "Take it and eat it. It
will turn your stomach sour, but
'in your mouth it will be as sweet
as honey.'[a]" 10I took the little scroll
from the angel's hand and ate it.
It tasted as sweet as honey in my
mouth, but when I had eaten it,
my stomach turned sour. 11Then
I was told, "You must prophesy
again about many peoples, nations, languages and kings."
Jer 15:16; Eze 2:8-3:3

[a] 9 Ezek. 3:3

The Two Witnesses

11 I was given a reed like a measuring rod and was told, "Go
and measure the temple of God
and the altar, with its worshipers. [2]But exclude the outer court;
do not measure it, because it has
been given to the Gentiles. They
will trample on the holy city for
42 months. [3]And I will appoint
my two witnesses, and they will
prophesy for 1,260 days, clothed
in sackcloth." [4]They are "the two
olive trees" and the two lampstands, and "they stand before
the Lord of the earth."[a] [5]If anyone
tries to harm them, fire comes
from their mouths and devours
their enemies. This is how anyone
who wants to harm them must
die. [6]They have power to shut up
the heavens so that it will not rain
during the time they are prophesying; and they have power to
turn the waters into blood and to
strike the earth with every kind of
plague as often as they want.
Rev 13:5; Zec 4:14

[7]Now when they have finished
their testimony, the beast that
comes up from the Abyss will attack them, and overpower and kill
them. [8]Their bodies will lie in the
public square of the great city—
which is figuratively called Sodom
and Egypt—where also their Lord
was crucified. [9]For three and a half
days some from every people,
tribe, language and nation will
gaze on their bodies and refuse
them burial. [10]The inhabitants of
the earth will gloat over them and
will celebrate by sending each other gifts, because these two prophets had tormented those who live
on the earth. Est 9:19,22; Da 7:21

[11]But after the three and a half
days the breath[b] of life from God
entered them, and they stood on
their feet, and terror struck those
who saw them. [12]Then they heard
a loud voice from heaven saying
to them, "Come up here." And
they went up to heaven in a cloud,
while their enemies looked on.
Eze 37:5,9-10,14; Ac 1:9

[13]At that very hour there was a
severe earthquake and a tenth of
the city collapsed. Seven thousand
people were killed in the earthquake, and the survivors were terrified and gave glory to the God of
heaven. Rev 6:12; 16:11

[14]The second woe has passed;
the third woe is coming soon.
Rev 8:13

The Seventh Trumpet

[15]The seventh angel sounded
his trumpet, and there were loud
voices in heaven, which said:
Rev 10:7; 16:17

"The kingdom of the world has
become
the kingdom of our Lord and
of his Messiah, Rev 12:10
and he will reign for ever and
ever."

[a] 4 See Zech. 4:3,11,14. [b] 11 Or *Spirit* (see Ezek. 37:5,14)

16And the twenty-four elders, who
were seated on their thrones before God, fell on their faces and
worshiped God, 17saying: Rev 4:4

"We give thanks to you, Lord
God Almighty, Rev 1:8
the One who is and who was,
Rev 1:4
because you have taken your
great power
and have begun to reign.
Rev 19:6
18The nations were angry, Ps 2:1
and your wrath has come.
The time has come for judging
the dead,
and for rewarding your
servants the prophets
Rev 10:7
and your people who revere
your name,
both great and small— Rev 19:5
and for destroying those who
destroy the earth."

19Then God's temple in heaven
was opened, and within his temple was seen the ark of his covenant. And there came flashes
of lightning, rumblings, peals of
thunder, an earthquake and a severe hailstorm. Rev 15:5,8; 16:21

The Woman and the Dragon

12 A great sign appeared in
heaven: a woman clothed
with the sun, with the moon under her feet and a crown of twelve
stars on her head. 2She was pregnant and cried out in pain as she
was about to give birth. 3Then another sign appeared in heaven: an
enormous red dragon with seven
heads and ten horns and seven
crowns on its heads. 4Its tail swept
a third of the stars out of the sky
and flung them to the earth. The
dragon stood in front of the woman who was about to give birth, so
that it might devour her child the
moment he was born. 5She gave
birth to a son, a male child, who
"will rule all the nations with an
iron scepter."[a] And her child was
snatched up to God and to his
throne. 6The woman fled into the
wilderness to a place prepared for
her by God, where she might be
taken care of for 1,260 days.
Da 8:10; Rev 11:2

7Then war broke out in heav-
en. Michael and his angels fought
against the dragon, and the dragon and his angels fought back.
8But he was not strong enough,
and they lost their place in heav-
en. 9The great dragon was hurled
down — that ancient serpent
called the devil, or Satan, who
leads the whole world astray. He
was hurled to the earth, and his
angels with him. Jn 12:31; Rev 20:3,8,10
10Then I heard a loud voice in
heaven say: Rev 11:15

"Now have come the salvation
and the power
and the kingdom of our God,
Rev 7:10
and the authority of his
Messiah.

[a] 5 Psalm 2:9

For the accuser of our brothers
and sisters, Job 1:9-11; Zec 3:1
who accuses them before our
God day and night,
has been hurled down.
[11]They triumphed over him Jn 16:33
by the blood of the Lamb
Rev 7:14
and by the word of their
testimony; Rev 6:9
they did not love their lives so
much
as to shrink from death.
Lk 14:26
[12]Therefore rejoice, you heavens
Ps 96:11; Rev 18:20
and you who dwell in them!
But woe to the earth and the
sea, Rev 10:6
because the devil has gone
down to you!
He is filled with fury,
because he knows that his
time is short."

[13]When the dragon saw that he
had been hurled to the earth, he
pursued the woman who had giv-
en birth to the male child. [14]The
woman was given the two wings
of a great eagle, so that she might
fly to the place prepared for her
in the wilderness, where she
would be taken care of for a time,
times and half a time, out of the
serpent's reach. [15]Then from his
mouth the serpent spewed water
like a river, to overtake the woman and sweep her away with the
torrent. [16]But the earth helped
the woman by opening its mouth
and swallowing the river that the
dragon had spewed out of his
mouth. [17]Then the dragon was enraged at the woman and went off
to wage war against the rest of her
offspring — those who keep God's
commands and hold fast their testimony about Jesus.

The Beast out of the Sea

13 The dragon[a] stood on the
shore of the sea. And I saw
a beast coming out of the sea. It
had ten horns and seven heads,
with ten crowns on its horns,
and on each head a blasphemous
name. [2]The beast I saw resembled
a leopard, but had feet like those
of a bear and a mouth like that of
a lion. The dragon gave the beast
his power and his throne and great
authority. [3]One of the heads of the
beast seemed to have had a fatal
wound, but the fatal wound had
been healed. The whole world was
filled with wonder and followed
the beast. [4]People worshiped the
dragon because he had given authority to the beast, and they also
worshiped the beast and asked,
"Who is like the beast? Who can
wage war against it?" Da 7:1-6; Rev 17:8
[5]The beast was given a mouth
to utter proud words and blasphemies and to exercise its authority
for forty-two months. [6]It opened
its mouth to blaspheme God,
and to slander his name and his
dwelling place and those who live
in heaven. [7]It was given power to

[a] *1* Some manuscripts *And I*

wage war against God's holy people and to conquer them. And it
was given authority over every
tribe, people, language and nation. 8 All inhabitants of the earth
will worship the beast — all whose
names have not been written in
the Lamb's book of life, the Lamb
who was slain from the creation
of the world.[a] Mt 25:34; Rev 20:12

9 Whoever has ears, let them
hear. Rev 2:7

10 "If anyone is to go into
captivity,
into captivity they will go.
If anyone is to be killed[b] with
the sword,
with the sword they will be
killed."[c] Jer 15:2; 43:11

This calls for patient endurance
and faithfulness on the part of
God's people. Heb 6:12; Rev 14:12

The Beast out of the Earth

11 Then I saw a second beast,
coming out of the earth. It had
two horns like a lamb, but it spoke
like a dragon. 12 It exercised all the
authority of the first beast on its
behalf, and made the earth and
its inhabitants worship the first
beast, whose fatal wound had been
healed. 13 And it performed great
signs, even causing fire to come
down from heaven to the earth in
full view of the people. 14 Because
of the signs it was given power
to perform on behalf of the first
beast, it deceived the inhabitants
of the earth. It ordered them to set
up an image in honor of the beast
who was wounded by the sword
and yet lived. 15 The second beast
was given power to give breath to
the image of the first beast, so that
the image could speak and cause
all who refused to worship the image to be killed. 16 It also forced all
people, great and small, rich and
poor, free and slave, to receive
a mark on their right hands or
on their foreheads, 17 so that they
could not buy or sell unless they
had the mark, which is the name
of the beast or the number of its
name. Rev 12:9; 14:11

18 This calls for wisdom. Let the
person who has insight calculate
the number of the beast, for it is
the number of a man.[d] That number is 666. Rev 15:2; 17:9

The Lamb and the 144,000

14 Then I looked, and there
before me was the Lamb,
standing on Mount Zion, and with
him 144,000 who had his name
and his Father's name written on
their foreheads. 2 And I heard a
sound from heaven like the roar
of rushing waters and like a loud
peal of thunder. The sound I heard
was like that of harpists playing
their harps. 3 And they sang a new
song before the throne and before the four living creatures and
the elders. No one could learn the

[a] 8 Or *written from the creation of the world in the book of life belonging to the Lamb who was slain* [b] 10 Some manuscripts *anyone kills* [c] 10 Jer. 15:2 [d] 18 Or is *humanity's number*

song except the 144,000 who had been redeemed from the earth. 4These are those who did not defile themselves with women, for they remained virgins. They follow the Lamb wherever he goes. They were purchased from among mankind and offered as firstfruits to God and the Lamb. 5No lie was found in their mouths; they are blameless. Ps 32:2; Eph 5:27

The Three Angels

6Then I saw another angel flying in midair, and he had the eternal gospel to proclaim to those who live on the earth — to every nation, tribe, language and people. 7He said in a loud voice, "Fear God and give him glory, because the hour of his judgment has come. Worship him who made the heavens, the earth, the sea and the springs of water." Rev 8:10; 15:4

8A second angel followed and said, "'Fallen! Fallen is Babylon the Great,'[a] which made all the nations drink the maddening wine of her adulteries." Isa 21:9; Jer 51:8

9A third angel followed them and said in a loud voice: "If anyone worships the beast and its image and receives its mark on their forehead or on their hand, 10they, too, will drink the wine of God's fury, which has been poured full strength into the cup of his wrath. They will be tormented with burning sulfur in the presence of the holy angels and of the Lamb. 11And the smoke of their torment will rise for ever and ever. There will be no rest day or night for those who worship the beast and its image, or for anyone who receives the mark of its name." 12This calls for patient endurance on the part of the people of God who keep his commands and remain faithful to Jesus. Isa 34:10; Rev 13:10

13Then I heard a voice from heaven say, "Write this: Blessed are the dead who die in the Lord from now on." 1Co 15:18; 1Th 4:16

"Yes," says the Spirit, "they will rest from their labor, for their deeds will follow them." Rev 2:7; 22:17

Harvesting the Earth and Trampling the Winepress

14I looked, and there before me was a white cloud, and seated on the cloud was one like a son of man[b] with a crown of gold on his head and a sharp sickle in his hand. 15Then another angel came out of the temple and called in a loud voice to him who was sitting on the cloud, "Take your sickle and reap, because the time to reap has come, for the harvest of the earth is ripe." 16So he who was seated on the cloud swung his sickle over the earth, and the earth was harvested. Jer 51:33; Joel 3:13

17Another angel came out of the temple in heaven, and he too had a sharp sickle. 18Still another angel, who had charge of the fire, came from the altar and called in a loud voice to him who had the sharp

[a] 8 Isaiah 21:9 [b] 14 See Daniel 7:13.

sickle, "Take your sharp sickle and
gather the clusters of grapes from
the earth's vine, because its grapes
are ripe." 19The angel swung his
sickle on the earth, gathered its
grapes and threw them into the
great winepress of God's wrath.
20They were trampled in the winepress outside the city, and blood
flowed out of the press, rising as
high as the horses' bridles for a
distance of 1,600 stadia.[a]

Heb 13:12; Rev 19:15

Seven Angels With Seven Plagues

15 I saw in heaven another great and marvelous sign:
seven angels with the seven last
plagues — last, because with them
God's wrath is completed. 2And I
saw what looked like a sea of glass
glowing with fire and, standing
beside the sea, those who had
been victorious over the beast and
its image and over the number of
its name. They held harps given
them by God 3and sang the song
of God's servant Moses and of the
Lamb: Rev 4:6; 13:14

"Great and marvelous are your
deeds, Ps 111:2
Lord God Almighty. Rev 1:8
Just and true are your ways, Ps 145:17
King of the nations.[b]
4Who will not fear you, Lord, Jer 10:7
and bring glory to your
name? Ps 86:9
For you alone are holy.
All nations will come
and worship before you, Isa 66:23
for your righteous acts have
been revealed."[c] Rev 19:8

5After this I looked, and I saw in
heaven the temple — that is, the
tabernacle of the covenant law —
and it was opened. 6Out of the temple came the seven angels with the
seven plagues. They were dressed
in clean, shining linen and wore
golden sashes around their chests.
7Then one of the four living creatures gave to the seven angels seven
golden bowls filled with the wrath
of God, who lives for ever and ever.
8And the temple was filled with
smoke from the glory of God and
from his power, and no one could
enter the temple until the seven
plagues of the seven angels were
completed. Ex 40:34-35; Rev 4:6

The Seven Bowls of God's Wrath

16 Then I heard a loud voice from the temple saying to
the seven angels, "Go, pour out the
seven bowls of God's wrath on the
earth." Rev 15:1
2The first angel went and
poured out his bowl on the land,
and ugly, festering sores broke out
on the people who had the mark
of the beast and worshiped its image. Rev 8:7; 13:15-17

[a] *20* That is, about 180 miles or about 300 kilometers [b] *3* Some manuscripts *ages* [c] *3,4* Phrases in this song are drawn from Psalm 111:2,3; Deut. 32:4; Jer. 10:7; Psalms 86:9; 98:2.

3The second angel poured out
his bowl on the sea, and it turned
into blood like that of a dead person, and every living thing in the
sea died. Ex 7:17-21; Rev 8:8-9
4The third angel poured out his
bowl on the rivers and springs of
water, and they became blood.
5Then I heard the angel in charge
of the waters say: Ex 7:17-21; Rev 8:10

"You are just in these
judgments, O Holy One,
Rev 1:4; 15:3; 15:4
you who are and who were;
Rev 6:10
6for they have shed the blood
of your holy people and
your prophets, Lk 11:49-51
and you have given them
blood to drink as they
deserve."

7And I heard the altar respond:
Rev 6:9

"Yes, Lord God Almighty, Rev 1:8
true and just are
your judgments."
Isa 49:26; Rev 15:3

8The fourth angel poured out
his bowl on the sun, and the sun
was allowed to scorch people with
fire. 9They were seared by the intense heat and they cursed the
name of God, who had control
over these plagues, but they refused to repent and glorify him.
Rev 11:13
10The fifth angel poured out his
bowl on the throne of the beast,
and its kingdom was plunged into
darkness. People gnawed their
tongues in agony 11and cursed the
God of heaven because of their
pains and their sores, but they refused to repent of what they had
done. Rev 9:2; 13:2
12The sixth angel poured out his
bowl on the great river Euphrates,
and its water was dried up to prepare the way for the kings from
the East. 13Then I saw three impure spirits that looked like frogs;
they came out of the mouth of the
dragon, out of the mouth of the
beast and out of the mouth of the
false prophet. 14They are demonic spirits that perform signs, and
they go out to the kings of the
whole world, to gather them for
the battle on the great day of God
Almighty. 1Ti 4:1; Rev 17:14

15"Look, I come like a thief!
Blessed is the one who stays
awake and remains clothed,
so as not to go naked and be
shamefully exposed."

16Then they gathered the kings together to the place that in Hebrew
is called Armageddon.
2Ki 23:29-30; Rev 9:11
17The seventh angel poured
out his bowl into the air, and out
of the temple came a loud voice
from the throne, saying, "It is
done!" 18Then there came flashes
of lightning, rumblings, peals of
thunder and a severe earthquake.
No earthquake like it has ever occurred since mankind has been
on earth, so tremendous was the

quake. 19The great city split into
three parts, and the cities of the
nations collapsed. God remembered Babylon the Great and gave
her the cup filled with the wine of
the fury of his wrath. 20Every island fled away and the mountains
could not be found. 21From the sky
huge hailstones, each weighing
about a hundred pounds,[a] fell on
people. And they cursed God on
account of the plague of hail, because the plague was so terrible.
Ex 9:23-25; Rev 14:10

Babylon, the Prostitute on the Beast

17 One of the seven angels who
had the seven bowls came
and said to me, "Come, I will show
you the punishment of the great
prostitute, who sits by many waters. 2With her the kings of the
earth committed adultery, and
the inhabitants of the earth were
intoxicated with the wine of her
adulteries." Jer 51:13; Rev 16:19

3Then the angel carried me
away in the Spirit into a wilderness. There I saw a woman sitting
on a scarlet beast that was covered
with blasphemous names and had
seven heads and ten horns. 4The
woman was dressed in purple and
scarlet, and was glittering with
gold, precious stones and pearls.
She held a golden cup in her hand,
filled with abominable things and
the filth of her adulteries. 5The
name written on her forehead was
a mystery: Jer 51:7; 12:6,14

BABYLON THE GREAT
THE MOTHER OF PROSTITUTES
AND OF THE ABOMINATIONS
OF THE EARTH.

6I saw that the woman was drunk
with the blood of God's holy people, the blood of those who bore
testimony to Jesus. Rev 18:24

When I saw her, I was greatly
astonished. 7Then the angel said
to me: "Why are you astonished?
I will explain to you the mystery
of the woman and of the beast she
rides, which has the seven heads
and ten horns. 8The beast, which
you saw, once was, now is not, and
yet will come up out of the Abyss
and go to its destruction. The inhabitants of the earth whose
names have not been written in
the book of life from the creation
of the world will be astonished
when they see the beast, because
it once was, now is not, and yet
will come. Rev 13:3,10

9"This calls for a mind with
wisdom. The seven heads are sev-
en hills on which the woman sits.
10They are also seven kings. Five
have fallen, one is, the other has
not yet come; but when he does
come, he must remain for only a
little while. 11The beast who once
was, and now is not, is an eighth
king. He belongs to the seven and
is going to his destruction.
Rev 13:18

12"The ten horns you saw are ten
kings who have not yet received a

[a] 21 Or about 45 kilograms

kingdom, but who for one hour
will receive authority as kings
along with the beast. 13They have
one purpose and will give their
power and authority to the beast.
14They will wage war against the
Lamb, but the Lamb will triumph
over them because he is Lord of
lords and King of kings — and
with him will be his called, chosen
and faithful followers."
1Ti 6:15; Rev 16:14

15Then the angel said to me,
"The waters you saw, where the
prostitute sits, are peoples, multitudes, nations and languages.
16The beast and the ten horns you
saw will hate the prostitute. They
will bring her to ruin and leave
her naked; they will eat her flesh
and burn her with fire. 17For God
has put it into their hearts to accomplish his purpose by agree-
ing to hand over to the beast their
royal authority, until God's words
are fulfilled. 18The woman you saw
is the great city that rules over the
kings of the earth." Rev 10:7; 16:19

Lament Over Fallen Babylon

18 After this I saw another
angel coming down from
heaven. He had great authority,
and the earth was illuminated by
his splendor. 2With a mighty voice
he shouted: Eze 43:2; Rev 17:1

"'Fallen! Fallen is Babylon the
Great!'[a] Rev 14:8
She has become a dwelling
for demons
and a haunt for every impure
spirit, Rev 16:13
a haunt for every unclean
bird,
a haunt for every unclean
and detestable animal.
Isa 13:21-22; Jer 50:39
3For all the nations have
drunk
the maddening wine of her
adulteries. Rev 14:8
The kings of the earth
committed adultery
with her, Rev 17:2
and the merchants of the
earth grew rich from
her excessive luxuries."
Eze 27:9-25

Warning to Escape Babylon's Judgment

4Then I heard another voice
from heaven say:

"'Come out of her, my people,'[b]
Jer 50:8; 2Co 6:17
so that you will not share in
her sins,
so that you will not
receive any of her
plagues; Ge 19:15
5for her sins are piled up to
heaven, Jer 51:9
and God has remembered
her crimes. Rev 16:19
6Give back to her as she has
given;
pay her back double for
what she has done.
Ps 137:8; Jer 50:15,29

[a] 2 Isaiah 21:9 [b] 4 Jer. 51:45

Pour her a double portion
from her own cup. Rev 14:10; 16:19
7 Give her as much torment and grief
as the glory and luxury she gave herself. Eze 28:2-8
In her heart she boasts,
'I sit enthroned as queen.
I am not a widow;[a]
I will never mourn.' Zep 2:15
8 Therefore in one day her plagues will overtake her: Isa 47:9
death, mourning and famine.
She will be consumed by fire, Rev 17:16
for mighty is the Lord God
who judges her.

Threefold Woe Over Babylon's Fall

9 "When the kings of the earth
who committed adultery with
her and shared her luxury see the
smoke of her burning, they will
weep and mourn over her. 10 Terrified at her torment, they will
stand far off and cry:
Eze 26:17-18; Rev 19:3

" 'Woe! Woe to you, great city,
you mighty city of Babylon!
In one hour your doom has
come!' Rev 17:12

11 "The merchants of the earth
will weep and mourn over her because no one buys their cargoes
anymore — 12 cargoes of gold, silver, precious stones and pearls;
fine linen, purple, silk and scarlet
cloth; every sort of citron wood,
and articles of every kind made
of ivory, costly wood, bronze, iron
and marble; 13 cargoes of cinnamon and spice, of incense, myrrh
and frankincense, of wine and olive oil, of fine flour and wheat;
cattle and sheep; horses and car-
riages; and human beings sold as
slaves. Eze 27:13; Rev 17:4
14 "They will say, 'The fruit you
longed for is gone from you. All
your luxury and splendor have
vanished, never to be recovered.'
15 The merchants who sold these
things and gained their wealth
from her will stand far off, terrified at her torment. They will
weep and mourn 16 and cry out:
Eze 27:31

" 'Woe! Woe to you, great city,
dressed in fine linen, purple and scarlet,
and glittering with gold,
precious stones and pearls! Rev 17:4
17 In one hour such great wealth
has been brought to ruin!' Rev 17:12,16

"Every sea captain, and all who
travel by ship, the sailors, and all
who earn their living from the
sea, will stand far off. 18 When they
see the smoke of her burning,
they will exclaim, 'Was there ever
a city like this great city?' 19 They
will throw dust on their heads,
and with weeping and mourning
cry out: Eze 27:28-30; Rev 13:4

[a] 7 See Isaiah 47:7,8.

"'Woe! Woe to you, great city, Rev 17:18
where all who had ships on
the sea
became rich through her
wealth!
In one hour she has been
brought to ruin!' Rev 17:16

20 "Rejoice over her, you heavens!
Jer 51:48
Rejoice, you people of God!
Rejoice, apostles and
prophets!
For God has judged her
with the judgment she
imposed on you." Rev 19:2

The Finality of Babylon's Doom

21 Then a mighty angel picked up
a boulder the size of a large millstone and threw it into the sea,
and said: Jer 51:63; Rev 5:2

"With such violence
the great city of Babylon
will be thrown down,
Rev 17:18
never to be found again.
22 The music of harpists and
musicians, pipers and
trumpeters,
will never be heard in you
again. Eze 26:13
No worker of any trade
will ever be found in you
again.
The sound of a millstone
will never be heard in you
again. Jer 25:10
23 The light of a lamp
will never shine in you again.
The voice of bridegroom and
bride
will never be heard in you
again. Jer 7:34
Your merchants were the
world's important
people. Isa 23:8
By your magic spell all the
nations were led astray.
Na 3:4
24 In her was found the blood
of prophets and
of God's holy people,
Rev 17:6
of all who have been
slaughtered on the
earth." Jer 51:49

Threefold Hallelujah Over Babylon's Fall

19 After this I heard what
sounded like the roar of a
great multitude in heaven shouting: Rev 11:15

"Hallelujah!
Salvation and glory and power
belong to our God,
Rev 4:11; 7:10
2 for true and just are his
judgments. Rev 16:7
He has condemned the great
prostitute Rev 17:1
who corrupted the earth by
her adulteries.
He has avenged on her the
blood of his servants."
Dt 32:43; Rev 6:10

3 And again they shouted:
"Hallelujah!

The smoke from her goes
up for ever and ever."
Isa 34:10; Rev 14:11

4The twenty-four elders and the four living creatures fell down and worshiped God, who was seated on the throne. And they cried:
Rev 4:4,6; 5:14

"Amen, Hallelujah!"

5Then a voice came from the throne, saying:

"Praise our God,
all you his servants, Ps 134:1
you who fear him,
both great and small!" Rev 11:18

6Then I heard what sounded like a great multitude, like the roar of rushing waters and like loud peals of thunder, shouting: Rev 11:15

"Hallelujah!
For our Lord God Almighty
reigns. Rev 1:8
7Let us rejoice and be glad
and give him glory! Rev 11:13
For the wedding of the Lamb
has come, Mt 22:2; Eph 5:32
and his bride has made
herself ready. Rev 21:2,9
8Fine linen, bright and clean,
Rev 15:6
was given her to wear."

(Fine linen stands for the righteous acts of God's holy people.)
Rev 15:4

9Then the angel said to me, "Write this: Blessed are those who are invited to the wedding supper of the Lamb!" And he added, "These are the true words of God."
Lk 14:15; Rev 1:19

10At this I fell at his feet to worship him. But he said to me, "Don't do that! I am a fellow servant with you and with your brothers and sisters who hold to the testimony of Jesus. Worship God! For it is the Spirit of prophecy who bears testimony to Jesus." Rev 22:8-9

The Heavenly Warrior Defeats the Beast

11I saw heaven standing open
and there before me was a white
horse, whose rider is called Faithful and True. With justice he judges and wages war. 12His eyes are
like blazing fire, and on his head
are many crowns. He has a name
written on him that no one knows
but he himself. 13He is dressed in
a robe dipped in blood, and his
name is the Word of God. 14The
armies of heaven were following
him, riding on white horses and
dressed in fine linen, white and
clean. 15Coming out of his mouth
is a sharp sword with which to
strike down the nations. "He
will rule them with an iron scepter."[a] He treads the winepress of
the fury of the wrath of God Almighty. 16On his robe and on his
thigh he has this name written:
Isa 11:4; Rev 6:2

KING OF KINGS AND
LORD OF LORDS.

[a] *15* Psalm 2:9

17 And I saw an angel standing in
the sun, who cried in a loud voice
to all the birds flying in midair,
"Come, gather together for the
great supper of God, 18 so that you
may eat the flesh of kings, generals, and the mighty, of horses and
their riders, and the flesh of all
people, free and slave, great and
small." Eze 39:17-20
19 Then I saw the beast and the
kings of the earth and their armies gathered together to wage
war against the rider on the horse
and his army. 20 But the beast was
captured, and with it the false
prophet who had performed the
signs on its behalf. With these
signs he had deluded those who
had received the mark of the beast
and worshiped its image. The two
of them were thrown alive into
the fiery lake of burning sulfur.
21 The rest were killed with the
sword coming out of the mouth of
the rider on the horse, and all the
birds gorged themselves on their
flesh. Da 7:11; Rev 13:12

The Thousand Years

20 And I saw an angel coming down out of heaven,
having the key to the Abyss and
holding in his hand a great chain.
2 He seized the dragon, that ancient serpent, who is the devil, or
Satan, and bound him for a thousand years. 3 He threw him into
the Abyss, and locked and sealed
it over him, to keep him from deceiving the nations anymore until
the thousand years were ended.
After that, he must be set free for
a short time. Da 6:17; Rev 12:9
4 I saw thrones on which were
seated those who had been given
authority to judge. And I saw the
souls of those who had been beheaded because of their testimony about Jesus and because of the
word of God. They[a] had not worshiped the beast or its image and
had not received its mark on their
foreheads or their hands. They
came to life and reigned with
Christ a thousand years. 5 (The
rest of the dead did not come to
life until the thousand years were
ended.) This is the first resurrection. 6 Blessed and holy are those
who share in the first resurrection.
The second death has no power
over them, but they will be priests
of God and of Christ and will reign
with him for a thousand years.
Rev 1:6; 2:11

The Judgment of Satan

7 When the thousand years are
over, Satan will be released from his
prison 8 and will go out to deceive
the nations in the four corners of
the earth — Gog and Magog — and
to gather them for battle. In number they are like the sand on the
seashore. 9 They marched across
the breadth of the earth and surrounded the camp of God's people, the city he loves. But fire
came down from heaven and devoured them. 10 And the devil, who

[a] 4 Or *God; I also saw those who*

deceived them, was thrown into the lake of burning sulfur, where the beast and the false prophet had been thrown. They will be tormented day and night for ever and ever. Eze 38:9,16; Rev 14:10-11

The Judgment of the Dead

11Then I saw a great white throne and him who was seated on it. The earth and the heavens fled from his presence, and there was no place for them. 12And I saw the dead, great and small, standing before the throne, and books were opened. Another book was opened, which is the book of life. The dead were judged according to what they had done as recorded in the books. 13The sea gave up the dead that were in it, and death and Hades gave up the dead that were in them, and each person was judged according to what they had done. 14Then death and Hades were thrown into the lake of fire. The lake of fire is the second death. 15Anyone whose name was not found written in the book of life was thrown into the lake of fire. Mt 16:27; 1Co 15:26

A New Heaven and a New Earth

21 Then I saw "a new heaven and a new earth,"[a] for the first heaven and the first earth had passed away, and there was no longer any sea. 2I saw the Holy City, the new Jerusalem, coming down out of heaven from God, prepared as a bride beautifully dressed for her husband. 3And I heard a loud voice from the throne saying, "Look! God's dwelling place is now among the people, and he will dwell with them. They will be his people, and God himself will be with them and be their God. 4'He will wipe every tear from their eyes. There will be no more death'[b] or mourning or crying or pain, for the old order of things has passed away."

Isa 35:10; 1Co 15:26

5He who was seated on the throne said, "I am making everything new!" Then he said, "Write this down, for these words are trustworthy and true."

Rev 4:9; 19:9; 20:11

6He said to me: "It is done. I am the Alpha and the Omega, the Beginning and the End. To the thirsty I will give water without cost from the spring of the water of life. 7Those who are victorious will inherit all this, and I will be their God and they will be my children. 8But the cowardly, the unbelieving, the vile, the murderers, the sexually immoral, those who practice magic arts, the idolaters and all liars — they will be consigned to the fiery lake of burning sulfur. This is the second death."

Rev 1:8; 16:17

The New Jerusalem, the Bride of the Lamb

9One of the seven angels who had the seven bowls full of the

[a] 1 Isaiah 65:17 [b] 4 Isaiah 25:8

seven last plagues came and said
to me, "Come, I will show you the
bride, the wife of the Lamb." 10 And
he carried me away in the Spirit to
a mountain great and high, and
showed me the Holy City, Jerusalem, coming down out of heaven
from God. 11 It shone with the glory of God, and its brilliance was
like that of a very precious jewel,
like a jasper, clear as crystal. 12 It
had a great, high wall with twelve
gates, and with twelve angels at
the gates. On the gates were written the names of the twelve tribes
of Israel. 13 There were three gates
on the east, three on the north,
three on the south and three on
the west. 14 The wall of the city had
twelve foundations, and on them
were the names of the twelve
apostles of the Lamb.

Eze 48:30-34; Rev 15:1,6-7

15 The angel who talked with me
had a measuring rod of gold to
measure the city, its gates and its
walls. 16 The city was laid out like
a square, as long as it was wide.
He measured the city with the rod
and found it to be 12,000 stadia[a] in
length, and as wide and high as it
is long. 17 The angel measured the
wall using human measurement,
and it was 144 cubits[b] thick.[c] 18 The
wall was made of jasper, and the
city of pure gold, as pure as glass.
19 The foundations of the city walls
were decorated with every kind
of precious stone. The first foundation was jasper, the second sap-
phire, the third agate, the fourth
emerald, 20 the fifth onyx, the sixth
ruby, the seventh chrysolite, the
eighth beryl, the ninth topaz, the
tenth turquoise, the eleventh jacinth, and the twelfth amethyst.[d]
21 The twelve gates were twelve
pearls, each gate made of a single
pearl. The great street of the city
was of gold, as pure as transparent
glass. Isa 54:11-12; Rev 11:1

22 I did not see a temple in the
city, because the Lord God Almighty and the Lamb are its temple. 23 The city does not need the
sun or the moon to shine on it,
for the glory of God gives it light,
and the Lamb is its lamp. 24 The nations will walk by its light, and the
kings of the earth will bring their
splendor into it. 25 On no day will
its gates ever be shut, for there
will be no night there. 26 The glory
and honor of the nations will be
brought into it. 27 Nothing impure
will ever enter it, nor will anyone who does what is shameful
or deceitful, but only those whose
names are written in the Lamb's
book of life. Isa 24:23; 52:1; Rev 22:14-15

Eden Restored

22 Then the angel showed
me the river of the water
of life, as clear as crystal, flowing
from the throne of God and of the
Lamb 2 down the middle of the
great street of the city. On each

[a] *16* That is, about 1,400 miles or about 2,200 kilometers [b] *17* That is, about 200 feet or about 65 meters [c] *17* Or *high* [d] *20* The precise identification of some of these precious stones is uncertain.

side of the river stood the tree of
life, bearing twelve crops of fruit,
yielding its fruit every month.
And the leaves of the tree are for
the healing of the nations. 3No
longer will there be any curse. The
throne of God and of the Lamb
will be in the city, and his servants
will serve him. 4They will see his
face, and his name will be on their
foreheads. 5There will be no more
night. They will not need the light
of a lamp or the light of the sun,
for the Lord God will give them
light. And they will reign for ever
and ever. Eze 47:1; Zec 14:11; Rev 21:23

John and the Angel

6The angel said to me, "These
words are trustworthy and true.
The Lord, the God who inspires
the prophets, sent his angel to
show his servants the things that
must soon take place."
Rev 1:1; 19:9; 21:5

7"Look, I am coming soon!
Blessed is the one who keeps the
words of the prophecy written in
this scroll." Rev 1:3; 3:11

8I, John, am the one who heard
and saw these things. And when
I had heard and seen them, I fell
down to worship at the feet of
the angel who had been showing
them to me. 9But he said to me,
"Don't do that! I am a fellow servant with you and with your fellow prophets and with all who
keep the words of this scroll. Worship God!" Rev 19:10

10Then he told me, "Do not seal
up the words of the prophecy of
this scroll, because the time is
near. 11Let the one who does wrong
continue to do wrong; let the vile
person continue to be vile; let the
one who does right continue to do
right; and let the holy person continue to be holy." Eze 3:27; Da 8:26

Epilogue: Invitation and Warning

12"Look, I am coming soon! My
reward is with me, and I will give
to each person according to what
they have done. 13I am the Alpha
and the Omega, the First and the
Last, the Beginning and the End.
Isa 40:10; Rev 1:8; 21:6

14"Blessed are those who wash
their robes, that they may have
the right to the tree of life and
may go through the gates into the
city. 15Outside are the dogs, those
who practice magic arts, the sexually immoral, the murderers, the
idolaters and everyone who loves
and practices falsehood.
Gal 5:19-21; Php 3:2

16"I, Jesus, have sent my angel
to give you[a] this testimony for the
churches. I am the Root and the
Offspring of David, and the bright
Morning Star." 2Pe 1:19; Rev 1:1

17The Spirit and the bride say,
"Come!" And let the one who hears
say, "Come!" Let the one who is
thirsty come; and let the one who
wishes take the free gift of the water of life. Rev 2:7

[a] *16* The Greek is plural.

18 I warn everyone who hears
the words of the prophecy of this
scroll: If anyone adds anything
to them, God will add to that person the plagues described in this
scroll. 19 And if anyone takes words
away from this scroll of prophecy,
God will take away from that person any share in the tree of life
and in the Holy City, which are described in this scroll. Dt 4:2; Pr 30:6
20 He who testifies to these things
says, "Yes, I am coming soon." Rev 1:2

Amen. Come, Lord Jesus. 1Co 16:22

21 The grace of the Lord Jesus be
with God's people. Amen. Ro 16:20

TABLE OF WEIGHTS AND MEASURES

	Biblical Unit	Approximate American Equivalent	Approximate Metric Equivalent
Weights	talent (60 minas)	75 pounds	34 kilograms
	mina (50 shekels)	1 1/4 pounds	560 grams
	shekel (2 bekas)	2/5 ounce	11.5 grams
	pim (2/3 shekel)	1/4 ounce	7.8 grams
	beka (10 gerahs)	1/5 ounce	5.7 grams
	gerah	1/50 ounce	0.6 gram
	daric	1/3 ounce	8.4 grams
Length	cubit	18 inches	45 centimeters
	span	9 inches	23 centimeters
	handbreadth	3 inches	7.5 centimeters
	stadion (pl. stadia)	600 feet	183 meters
Capacity			
Dry Measure	cor [homer] (10 ephahs)	6 bushels	220 liters
	lethek (5 ephahs)	3 bushels	110 liters
	ephah (10 omers)	3/5 bushel	22 liters
	seah (1/3 ephah)	7 quarts	7.5 liters
	omer (1/10 ephah)	2 quarts	2 liters
	cab (1/18 ephah)	1 quart	1 liter
Liquid Measure	bath (1 ephah)	6 gallons	22 liters
	hin (1/6 bath)	1 gallon	3.8 liters
	log (1/72 bath)	1/3 quart	0.3 liter

The figures of the table are calculated on the basis of a shekel equaling 11.5 grams, a cubit equaling 18 inches and an ephah equaling 22 liters. The quart referred to is either a dry quart (slightly larger than a liter) or a liquid quart (slightly smaller than a liter), whichever is applicable. The ton referred to in the footnotes is the American ton of 2,000 pounds. These weights are calculated relative to the particular commodity involved. Accordingly, the same measure of capacity in the text may be converted into different weights in the footnotes.

This table is based upon the best available information, but it is not intended to be mathematically precise; like the measurement equivalents in the footnotes, it merely gives approximate amounts and distances. Weights and measures differed somewhat at various times and places in the ancient world. There is uncertainty particularly about the ephah and the bath; further discoveries may shed more light on these units of capacity.

DICTIONARY–CONCORDANCE

A

Aaron — the brother of Moses; he served as Moses' spokesman before Pharaoh (Ex 4:14–16, 27–31; 7:1–2); he was Israel's first high priest (Ex 28:1; Nu 17; Heb 5:1–4).

abandon — to leave completely; to desert.

Abba — the word for *father* in Aramaic, one of the three languages Jesus spoke.

Ro 8:15	And by him we cry, "*A*, Father."
Gal 4:6	the Spirit who calls out, "*A*, Father."

Abel — the second son of Adam (Ge 4:2); he offered a pleasing sacrifice to God (Ge 4:4; Heb 11:4) but was murdered by his brother Cain (Ge 4:8; Mt 23:35; 1Jn 3:12).

abhor — to hate or to turn away from.

Ps 26:5	I *a* the assembly of evildoers
Am 6:8	"I *a* the pride of Jacob

Abigail — the wife of Nabal; she helped save David's life (1Sa 25:14–35) and later became his wife (1Sa 25:36–42).

abolish — to destroy completely; to put an end to.

abomination — a thing to be hated.

abound — to be more than enough; to overflow.

Ex 34:6	slow to anger, *a* in love
Php 1:9	that your love may *a* more

Abraham — the father of the Jewish nation and of all believers. God promised that he would make a mighty nation of Abraham's children and would give them the land of Canaan (Ge 15; 17; 22; Ro 4; Heb 6:13–15). As a test, God told him to offer his son Isaac as a sacrifice (Ge 22; Heb 11:17–19) but withdrew this command when Abraham showed that he would trust God and obey him.

Absalom — a son of David (2Sa 3:3); he plotted to take David's throne. He died when his long hair became tangled in an oak tree and Joab, David's commander, plunged javelins into his heart (2Sa 14—18).

abstain — to keep from doing something.

abundance, abundant — having plenty; more than enough.

Jude 2	Mercy, peace and love be yours in *a*.

Abyss — the place of the dead; the place where evil spirits live.

Achan — an Israelite who kept spoil from the conquest of Jericho for himself; as a result of Achan's stealing what belonged to God, the Israelites were defeated at Ai and he and his family were stoned to death (Jos 7; 22:20).

acknowledge — to know and to say that something is true; to recognize.

Mt 10:32	I will also *a* before my Father in heaven.
1Jn 4:3	spirit that does not *a* Jesus is not from God.

acts — deeds.

Ps 150:2	Praise him for his *a* of power
Isa 64:6	all our righteous *a* are like filthy rags

Adam — the first person God created (Ge 1:26–2:25); he sinned by disobeying God (Ge 3) and in that way brought all people under the curse of sin (Ro 5:12–21).

admonish — to give warning or advice in a caring way.

adorn — to make more beautiful.

adultery — having sexual relations with someone other than one's husband or wife. Spiritual adultery means being unfaithful to God (Jer 3).

Ex 20:14	"You shall not commit *a*.
Mt 5:28	lustfully has already committed *a*

adversary — enemy; opponent.

advice — an opinion given about a decision to be made.

1Ki 12:14	he followed the *a* of the young men
Pr 20:18	Plans are established by seeking *a*;

advocate — 1. *(v.)* to speak in favor of; 2. *(n.)* someone who speaks in another person's defense; 3. *(n.)* another name for the Holy Spirit.

Jn 14:16	he will give you another *a* to help you
Jn 14:26	But the *A*, the Holy Spirit,
Jn 15:26	"When the *A* comes, whom I will

affliction — trouble or pain that lasts a long time.

Ro 12:12	patient in *a*, faithful in prayer.

agony — extreme pain of mind or body.

Ahab — a wicked king of Israel; the husband of Jezebel (1Ki 16:31). He caused Israel to worship Baal rather than God (1Ki 16:31–33) and was opposed by God's prophet Elijah (1Ki 17:1; 18; 21).

alabaster — a hard marble-like material that can be made into jars, vases or sculptures.

alienate — to make unfriendly; to turn a person's interest or affection away from another person or thing.

allot — to divide and give away in parts. In Old Testament times the land of Canaan was allotted to the twelve tribes of Israel.

Almighty — a name used to show how strong and powerful God is.

Ge 17:1 — "I am God *A*; walk before me
Isa 6:3 — "Holy, holy, holy is the LORD *A*;

altar — a raised platform made of stones, metal, dirt or wood, on which sacrifices were made.

ambush — the act of hiding in order to attack by surprise.

Amen — Hebrew word that means "so be it" or "let it become true."

Amos — a prophet of Israel who lived about the same time as Hosea and Jonah; he spoke about God's justice and righteousness.

Ananias — 1. the husband of Sapphira; he was struck dead for lying to God (Ac 5:1–11); 2. the disciple who baptized Saul (Ac 9:10–19); 3. the high priest before whom Paul was tried in Jerusalem (Ac 22:30–24:1).

ancestor — a person from whom someone is descended.

Ps 78:5 — commanded our *a* to teach their children,

ancient — very old.

Andrew — one of the twelve apostles; the brother of Peter (Mt 4:18; 10:2; Ac 1:13).

angel — a heavenly being.

Ps 34:7 — The *a* of the LORD encamps
Heb 1:14 — Are not all *a* ministering spirits
Heb 2:7 — made them a little lower than the *a*;
1Pe 1:12 — Even *a* long to look

anger — a strong feeling of displeasure; rage; fury.

Ps 103:8 — slow to *a*, abounding in love.
Jas 1:20 — human *a* does not produce the righteousness

anguish — extreme pain or distress of mind or body.

Jer 49:24 — *a* and pain have seized her;

annihilate — to destroy completely.

anoint — to pour oil on a person's head, either for a physical benefit (Jas 5:14) or to set someone apart for service to God (Ex 28:41).

antichrist — a person who is against Christ.

1Jn 2:18 — you have heard that the *a* is coming,
1Jn 2:22 — Such a person is the *a*

anxiety — worry.

1Pe 5:7 — Cast all your *a* on him

Apollos — a Christian from Alexandria who knew the Scriptures well (Ac 18:24–28) and helped Paul to minister in Corinth (Ac 19:1; 1Co 1:12).

apostle — 1. any of the twelve men Jesus chose to work with him during his earthly ministry; after being equipped by the Holy Spirit, they were sent out to preach about Jesus; 2. later, someone who had been with Jesus, had seen his miracles and then taught others about him.

Mt 10:2 — These are the names of the twelve *a*:
1Co 12:28 — God has placed in the church first of all *a*,
1Co 15:9 — For I am the least of the *a*

appalled — overcome with shock or horror.

appeal — to make an earnest request.

1Pe 5:1 — I *a* as a fellow elder

appoint — to assign someone officially to a job or position.

Aquila — the husband of Priscilla; Aquila and Priscilla were co-workers with Paul in Corinth (Ac 18; Ro 16:3).

Aramaic — the language that was commonly spoken in the countries east of the Mediterranean Sea during Jesus' earthly ministry.

ark of the covenant law — also called the ark of the covenant; a large gold-covered box, which contained the Ten Commandments (tablets of the covenant law), a jar of manna and Aaron's staff, and was kept inside the Most Holy Place in the tabernacle (tent of meeting). It was a reminder to the Israelites of God's presence with them.

armor — protective clothing worn in battle, usually made of metal.

Eph 6:11 — Put on the full *a* of God

aroma — an odor or smell, usually pleasant.

arouse — to excite; to stir to action.

arrest — to officially or lawfully make a prisoner of someone.

arrogant — proud; conceited.

arrow — See bow.

ascend — to go up. Jesus ascended to heaven to return to God the Father.

ascribe — to think of as caused by, coming from or belonging to.

1Ch 16:28 *a* to the LORD glory and strength,

Asherah poles — wooden poles honoring Asherah, the Canaanite goddess of love and war.

Dt 12:3 burn their *A* in the fire;

assemble — to bring a group of people together; to meet together.

Assyria — one of the powerful nations of biblical times; it often attacked the Israelites; its capital was Nineveh.

astray — mistaken; not on the right path; lost.

Isa 53:6 We all, like sheep, have gone *a*,

atone — to make right, by paying the penalty, the relationship between God and humans that was broken through sin. In the Old Testament, people atoned symbolically for their sins by offering sacrifices to God. In the New Testament, Jesus corrected the relationship between God and people once and for all by dying to take away sins.

atonement — the payment that corrects the relationship between God and humans that was broken through sin.

Lev 17:11 it is the blood that makes *a*
Lev 23:27 this seventh month is the Day of *A*.
Ro 3:25 God presented Christ as a sacrifice of *a*,
Heb 2:17 that he might make *a* for the sins

attack — to set upon with force, as in a battle.

authority — the right and power to give orders.

Mt 9:6 the Son of Man has *a* on earth
Mt 28:18 "All *a* in heaven and on earth has
Ro 13:1 for there is no *a* except that which
Heb 13:17 your leaders and submit to their *a*,

avenge — to get back at or punish someone who has done wrong.

Dt 32:35 It is mine to *a*; I will repay.

avoid — to keep away from.

Pr 20:19 *a* anyone who talks too much.

awe — respect and wonder; a holy fear of God because of his great power.

Ps 65:8 earth is filled with *a* at your wonders;

B

Baal — the name of many false gods in Canaan.

1Ki 18:25 Elijah said to the prophets of *B*,

Babel — a tower built soon after the flood; the builders were attempting to reach up to God, but God confused their language so that the building was stopped.

Babylon — the beautiful capital of Babylonia; it was a powerful and influential city in the Near East from the eighteenth to the sixth centuries BC. In the New Testament, Babylon represents the godless city.

Ps 137:1 By the rivers of *B* we sat and wept
Rev 14:8 Fallen is *B* the Great,

Balaam — a seer who tried to curse Israel during their journey to the promised land, but God would not allow it (Nu 22—24).

balm — a skin cream used to heal sores and relieve pain.

Jer 8:22 Is there no *b* in Gilead?

banish — to force a person away from a place.

banquet — a formal meal, usually for a large group of people.

baptize — a religious ceremony in which water is used as a symbol of cleansing from sin. Churches today baptize by sprinkling or pouring or immersing in water. Baptism is a sign that sin is washed away.

Mk 1:9 and was *b* by John in the Jordan.
Ac 1:5 but in a few days you will be *b*
Ac 2:38 "Repent and be *b*, every one of you,

Barabbas — the Jews chose this criminal, rather than Jesus, to be released by Pilate (Mt 27:26).

Barnabas — an apostle; he was a co-worker with Paul on his first missionary journey (Ac 9:27; Ac 13—15).

barren — 1. unable to have children; 2. unable to produce crops.

Bartholomew — one of the twelve apostles (Mt 10:3; Ac 1:13). He was also probably known as Nathanael (Jn 1:45–49; 21:2).

Bathsheba — the wife of Uriah; she committed adultery with David and later became his wife (2Sa 11); she was the mother of Solomon (2Sa 12:24).

Beelzebul — the prince of demons; Satan.

Lk 11:19 if I drive out demons by *B*,

Beersheba — an important town that marked the southern boundary of Judah.

believe — to accept as true; to trust; to have faith.

Mk 1:15 Repent and *b* the good news!"
Mk 9:24 "I do *b*; help me overcome my
Jn 1:7 that through him all might *b*.
Jn 3:18 does not *b* stands condemned
Jn 20:27 Stop doubting and *b*."
Ac 16:31 They replied, "*B* in the Lord Jesus,
Ro 3:22 faith in Jesus Christ to all who *b*.
1Th 4:14 we *b* that Jesus died and rose again

Benjamin — the twelfth son of Jacob. Rachel was his mother, and he was the younger brother of Joseph (Ge 35:16–24; Ge 42—45).

besiege — to surround a city or town completely with an army, so that nothing can go in or out.

bestow — to give.

Bethlehem — the city in Judea where Jesus was born (Mt 2:1).

betray — to turn a friend over to his or her enemies; to be unfaithful to.

Mt 27:3 When Judas, who had *b* him,
1Co 11:23 on the night he was *b*, took bread,

betroth — to promise to marry.

bewildered — confused; puzzled.

bind — 1. to tie with a rope or string; 2. to make tight or firm.

Dt 6:8 and *b* them on your foreheads.
Mt 16:19 whatever you *b* on earth will be

birthright — the special rights of the firstborn son. In the Old Testament, after the father died, the oldest son received the father's power and right to make decisions for the entire family. He also got twice as much money and property as each of his brothers.

bitter — having harsh or hateful feelings.

Eph 4:31 Get rid of all *b*, rage
Heb 12:15 and that no *b* root grows up

blameless — without fault.

Ge 17:1 walk before me faithfully and be *b*.
1Co 1:8 so that you will be *b* on the day

blaspheme — to speak carelessly, falsely or insultingly about God or holy things.

Mk 3:29 whoever *b* against the Holy Spirit

blemish — a spot or mark that makes something imperfect.

1Pe 1:19 a lamb without *b* or defect.

bless — 1. to make holy; 2. to show favor to; 3. to ask God to show favor to.

Ge 2:3 Then God *b* the seventh day
Ge 12:3 I will *b* those who *b* you,
Mt 5:3 "*B* are the poor in spirit
Ro 12:14 *b* those who persecute you; *b*

blight — a disease in plants that makes them shrivel up and die.

blind — unable to see. Spiritual blindness is an inability to understand the things of God.

Mt 11:5 The *b* receive sight, the lame walk,
Jn 9:25 I was *b* but now I see!"

blood — as the life-giving fluid in the body, it represents life itself. In the Old Testament, the blood of sacrifices symbolized the giving of life for life. Through the blood of Jesus on the cross, believers are saved from death for their sins.

Ex 12:13 and when I see the *b*, I will pass
Lev 17:11 For the life of a creature is in the *b*,
Mt 26:28 This is my *b* of the covenant,
Eph 1:7 we have redemption through his *b*,
Heb 9:12 once for all by his own *b*,

blot — to erase or get rid of.

Ex 32:32 then *b* me out of the book you have
Ps 51:1 *b* out my transgressions.

boast — to brag; to call attention to.

Ps 44:8 In God we make our *b*
Gal 6:14 May I never *b* except in the cross

Boaz — a wealthy man who lived in Bethlehem in the days of the judges; he married Ruth (Ru 2; 4).

body — 1. physical part of a person; 2. a group working as a unit.

Pr 3:8 This will bring health to your *b*
Ro 12:1 to offer your *b* as a living sacrifice,
1Co 6:19 not know that your *b* are temples
Eph 5:30 for we are members of his *b*.

bondage — slavery.

Ezr 9:9 God has not forsaken us in our *b*.

born again — refers to the experience of salvation; entering God's family through faith in Christ.

Jn 3:3 no one can see the kingdom of God unless they are *b*.
1Pe 1:23 For you have been *b*,

bow — a weapon made of a strip of flexible material with a cord connecting the two ends and holding the strip bent; used to shoot arrows.

branch — an extension of another body or system.

Jer 33:15 I will make a righteous *B* sprout
Jn 15:5 "I am the vine; you are the *b*.

bread — in Bible times the most important food in the diet.

Dt 8:3 that man does not live on *b* alone
Mt 6:11 Give us today our daily *b*.
Jn 6:35 Jesus declared, "I am the *b* of life.

breastpiece — a decorated square of linen cloth worn by the high priest when he entered the Holy Place.

breastplate — a chest-covering made of metal or leather, worn by soldiers for protection.

bribe — money or favor given to influence judgment or conduct.

Ex 23:8 "Do not accept a *b*,

bride — a woman who is about to get married. The church is called Jesus' bride.

bridegroom — a man who is about to get married. Christ is called the church's bridegroom.

bronze — a metal, the combination of copper and tin, used to make tools, weapons and ornamental articles.

brother — a male who has the same parents as another person.

Ge 4:9 "Am I my *b* keeper?"
Mt 18:15 "If your *b* or sister sins,
2Co 13:11 Finally, *b* and sisters, rejoice!

burden — a heavy load.

Mt 11:30 my yoke is easy and my *b* is light.
Gal 6:2 Carry each other's *b*,

burnt offering — in the Old Testament a sacrifice to the Lord that expressed devotion and complete surrender (Ge 8:20; Ex 29:18).

C

Caesar — the title of many Roman emperors.

Lk 2:1 In those days *C* Augustus
Mt 22:21 "Give back to *C* what is Caesar's,

Cain — Adam and Eve's firstborn son; he murdered his brother Abel (Ge 4:1–16).

calamity — a disaster, usually causing great loss and suffering.

Caleb — one of the twelve men who was sent to spy on Canaan. He came back with a positive report and encouraged the Israelites to take possession of Canaan (Nu 13:6–14:38; Dt 1:36).

call — 1. (*v.*) to ask to come; 2. to give a name to; 3. (*n.*) a summons for a particular purpose or job.

2Ch 7:14 if my people, who are *c*
Ps 145:18 near to all who *c* on him,
Mt 9:13 not come to *c* the righteous,
Ro 8:30 And those he predestined, he also *c*;
Ro 11:29 gifts and his *c* are irrevocable.
1Pe 2:9 of him who *c* you out of darkness

camel — a large animal, able to travel long distances and used for transportation of people and goods.

Canaan — 1. the land God promised to the nation of Israel; 2. the promised land.

capstone — the stone that holds two walls together; the stone that finishes a wall.

1Pe 2:7 has become the *c*,"

care — to show concern for.

Ps 8:4 human beings that you *c* for them?
1Pe 5:7 on him because he *c* for you.

cavalry — a group of soldiers riding horses.

censer — a bowl or dish used for carrying hot coals or for burning incense.

census — a count of the population of a group of people.

centurion — a Roman army officer in charge of one hundred soldiers.

chaff — the seed covering of a grain such as wheat. In Bible times, the grain and chaff were separated by tossing the grain into the air so the wind could blow the chaff away.

Ps 1:4 They are like *c*
Mt 3:12 up the *c* with unquenchable fire."

chariot — a two-wheeled vehicle pulled by horses.

2Ki 6:17 and *c* of fire all around Elisha.

cheerful — full of joy; pleasant.

Pr 15:13 A happy heart makes the face *c*,
2Co 9:7 for God loves a *c* giver.

cherub (pl. cherubim) — an angel, with an appearance something like a human being.

children — sons and daughters.

Mt 19:14 "Let the little *c* come to me,
Eph 6:1 *C*, obey your parents in the Lord,
1Jn 3:1 that we should be called *c* of God!

choose (chosen) — to select.

Jos 24:15 then *c* for yourselves this day
Mt 22:14 "For many are invited, but few are *c*."
Jn 15:16 You did not *c* me,
Eph 1:4 he *c* us in him before the creation
1Pe 2:9 But you are a *c* people, a royal

Christ — the official title of Jesus, meaning "the Anointed One." It is a Greek word, and it means the same as the Hebrew word *Messiah*.

Jn 1:17 grace and truth came through Jesus *C*.
Ac 3:6 name of Jesus *C* of Nazareth, walk."
Ro 5:8 While we were still sinners, *C* died
Eph 5:23 as *C* is the head of the church,
Php 1:21 to live is *C* and to die is gain.

Christian — a believer in or follower of Christ.

Ac 11:26 The disciples were called *C* first
1Pe 4:16 as a *C*, do not be ashamed,

chronicles — a history of events in the order in which they took place.

church — the entire group of people who believe in Christ.

Mt 16:18 and on this rock I will build my *c*,
Eph 5:23 as Christ is the head of the *c*,
Col 1:24 the sake of his body, which is the *c*.

circumcision — the cutting off of the loose fold of skin at the end of the penis; it symbolized the agreement God made with the Israelites, and they came to be known as "the circumcision" (Eph 2:11).

Ge 17:10	Every male among you shall be *c*.

cistern — a pit dug into the ground for storing rainwater.

citadel — a tower or building, especially in a city, equipped for war.

city of refuge — one of six cities set aside by Moses and Joshua for those who had accidentally killed someone. Such people would be safe there until a fair trial could be held (Nu 35:9–15).

clan — a group of people belonging to the same extended family.

Ge 24:38	to my father's family and to my own *c*,
Zec 12:12	The land will mourn, each *c* by itself,

clean animals — animals God allowed the Israelites to sacrifice and eat.

cleanse — to make clean; to wash.

cloak — a loose-fitting coat without sleeves.

comfort — to relieve from distress; to console.

Ps 23:4	rod and your staff, they *c* me.
2Co 1:4	so that we can *c* those

commandment — an order given by God. God gave the Ten Commandments to the Israelites while they were encamped in the area of Mount Sinai.

Ex 20:6	who love me and keep my *c*.
Ecc 12:13	Fear God and keep his *c*,
Mt 22:38	This is the first and greatest *c*.

commend — 1. to praise; 2. to hand over to someone for safekeeping.

Ps 145:4	One generation *c* your works

companion — one who is a friend or associate or helper.

compassion (compassionate) — sympathy; pity.

Ne 9:17	gracious and *c*, slow to anger
Ps 103:4	and crowns you with love and *c*,
Mt 9:36	When he saw the crowds, he had *c*
Ro 9:15	and I will have *c* on whom I have *c*."
Col 3:12	clothe yourselves with *c*, kindness,

conceive — 1. to become pregnant; 2. to think up or imagine.

Mt 1:20	what is *c* in her is from the Holy
1Co 2:9	no human mind has *c*

concubine — in Bible times, a woman who belonged to a man but did not have the rights of a wife. She was often one of the spoils of war, and her primary purpose was to bear children for the man.

condemn (condemnation) — to punish; to pronounce guilty.

Jn 3:17	Son into the world to *c* the world,
Ro 8:1	there is now no *c* for those who are

confess — 1. to say what you believe; 2. to tell your sins to someone.

2Ti 2:19	"Everyone who *c* the name of the Lord
1Jn 1:9	If we *c* our sins, he is faithful

conform — to agree with and try to be like someone; to do what others say to do.

Ro 8:29	predestined to be *c* to the image
1Pe 1:14	do not *c* to the evil desires you had

conscience — the sense of knowing if something is good or bad; a sense of right and wrong.

Ro 2:15	their *c* also bearing witness,
Titus 1:15	their minds and *c* are corrupted.
Heb 9:14	cleanse our *c* from acts that lead

consecrate — to set aside or dedicate for God's use.

Ex 13:2	"*C* to me every firstborn male.
Lev 20:7	"*C* yourselves and be holy,

consider — to think about carefully.

Ps 8:3	When I *c* your heavens,

console — to comfort.

conspire — to plan together to do wrong.

consult — to ask the advice or opinion of someone.

consume — 1. to use up or eat up; 2. to destroy completely.

Jn 2:17	"Zeal for your house will *c* me."
Heb 12:29	for our "God is a *c* fire."

contempt — lack of respect; looking down on someone or something as being worthless.

Pr 14:31	Whoever oppresses the poor shows *c*
1Th 5:20	Do not treat prophecies with *c*

contend — to struggle, as in a contest or against difficulties.

content — satisfied.

Php 4:11	to be *c* whatever the circumstances.
Heb 13:5	and be *c* with what you have,

contrite — to feel sorry for one's sins; to feel repentant.

Ps 51:17	a broken and *c* heart,
Isa 66:2	those who are humble and *c* in spirit,

convert — a person who has changed from one belief to another.

1Ti 3:6 He must not be a recent *c*,

convict — 1. to prove one guilty; 2. to make a person feel sorrow.

Jas 2:9 and are *c* by the law as lawbreakers.

copper — a common metal, easy to work with; often used to make coins.

Cornelius — a Roman to whom Peter preached the gospel; he became the first Gentile Christian (Ac 10).

cornerstone — the first or most important stone laid when constructing a building.

Eph 2:20 with Christ Jesus himself as the chief *c*.

corrupt — 1. (*v.*) to change something from good to bad; 2. (*adj.*) wicked.

Ge 6:11 Now the earth was *c* in God's sight
1Co 15:33 "Bad company *c* good character."

counsel — to give advice to.

Pr 15:22 Plans fail for lack of *c*,

covenant — 1. an agreement between two people or two groups of people, in which both usually make specific promises; 2. the promises of God for salvation.

Ge 9:9 "I now establish my *c* with you
Ex 19:5 if you obey me fully and keep my *c*,
Jer 31:31 "when I will make a new *c*
1Co 11:25 "This cup is the new *c* in my blood;
Heb 9:15 Christ is the mediator of a new *c*,

covet — to want for oneself something that belongs to another person.

Ex 20:17 "You shall not *c* your neighbor's

crafty — sly, clever.

Ge 3:1 Now the serpent was more *c*

crave — to desire strongly; to feel a deep need for.

1Pe 2:2 newborn babies, *c* pure spiritual

create — to make; to bring into being.

Ge 1:1 In the beginning God *c* the heavens
Ps 51:10 *C* in me a pure heart, O God,
Col 1:16 For in him all things were *c*:
Rev 10:6 who *c* the heavens and all that is

crime — an unlawful act.

criminal — someone who commits an unlawful act.

Lk 23:32 Two other men, both *c*,

cripple — a disabled person or animal.

cross — a tall beam with a crossbar on which a criminal was hung or tied to die.

Mt 10:38 Whoever does not take up their *c*
Gal 6:14 in the *c* of our Lord Jesus Christ,
Php 2:8 even death on a *c*!
Col 2:14 taken it away, nailing it to the *c*.
Heb 12:2 set before him he endured the *c*,

crown — a headpiece worn to symbolize glory, honor and victory.

1Co 9:25 it to get a *c* that will last forever.
2Ti 4:8 store for me the *c* of righteousness,
Rev 2:10 life as your victor's crown.

crucify — to put to death by nailing or tying a person's body to a cross.

Mt 27:22 They all answered, "*C* him!"
1Co 1:23 but we preach Christ *c*: a stumbling
Gal 2:20 I have been *c* with Christ

cruel — causing envy, grief or pain.

cubit — a measure of length in Bible times; about 18 inches.

cupbearer — an officer of considerable responsibility who tasted the king's food and wine before serving them to him (Ne 1:11).

curse — 1. (*v.*) to ask God to bring evil or injury to; 2. (*n.*) a prayer or desire that evil or injury come upon someone.

Lev 20:9 "Anyone who *c* their father or mother
Lk 6:28 bless those who *c* you, pray
Gal 3:13 "*C* is everyone who is hung on a pole."

custom — a practice common to a particular place or group of people.

Mk 15:6 Now it was the *c* at the festival
Ac 17:2 As was his *c*, Paul went into the synagogue

cymbals — a musical instrument; round metal disks either struck with a stick or struck together to produce a clanging sound.

cypress — an evergreen tree of the pine family.

D

Daniel — a young Jewish exile; he lived in Babylon during the reign of several kings, including Nebuchadnezzar. He prayed to God rather than obey an order to pray only to the king and was thrown into a lion's den (Da 1—6).

daughter — a female descendant.

Job 1:2 He had seven sons and three *d*,

David — the son of Jesse; anointed by Samuel to become king of Israel (1Sa 16:1–13); killed the giant Goliath (1Sa 17); during his reign Israel's place in the land of Canaan was made secure.

day — 1. the period of time between dawn and darkness; 2. a specified time.

Ge 1:5	God called the light "*d*,"
Ecc 12:1	Creator in the *d* of your youth,
Joel 2:31	and dreadful *d* of the LORD.
Mic 4:1	In the last *d*
Lk 11:3	Give us each *d* our daily bread.
Lk 18:33	On the third *d* he will rise
Heb 1:2	in these last *d* he has spoken to us
2Pe 3:8	With the Lord a *d* is like

deacon — a church officer whose qualifications are given in 1Ti 3:8–13.

death — the end of physical life; also the penalty for sin (Ro 6:23).

Ecc 7:2	for *d* is the destiny of everyone;
Isa 25:8	he will swallow up *d* forever.
1Co 15:21	For since *d* came through a man,
1Co 15:55	Where, O *d*, is your sting?"
Rev 21:4	There will be no more *d*

debauchery — living an immoral life or a life without religion; living to please only oneself.

Deborah — a prophetess who led Israel to victory over the Canaanites (Jdg 4—5).

debt — something that one person owes another.

Mt 6:12	And forgive us our *d*,

deceive — to fool or trick; to lie.

Ge 3:13	"The serpent *d* me, and I ate."
Gal 6:7	Do not be *d*: God cannot be
1Jn 1:8	we *d* ourselves and the truth is not

declare — to make known formally; to state forcefully.

Ps 19:1	The heavens *d* the glory of God;
Eph 6:20	Pray that I may *d* it fearlessly,

decree — 1. (*v.*) to order or command; 2. (*n.*) an order or law given by someone with power and authority.

dedicate — to set apart for a special purpose, often for God's use.

defect — imperfection; fault.

defile — to make something that is good and pure into something impure or unclean.

defraud — to cheat someone by trickery.

Deity — God.

Col 2:9	of the *D* lives in bodily form,

delight — finding great pleasure in something.

Ps 119:47	for I *d* in your commands
Mt 12:18	the one I love, in whom I *d*;

deliver — to rescue; to set free.

demon — evil spirit. A demon-possessed person is one who is controlled by evil spirits.

Mk 5:15	possessed by the legion of *d*,
Jas 2:19	Good! Even the *d* believe that

denarius — a small Roman coin made of silver. During Jesus' earthly ministry, one denarius was the payment for about one day's work.

denounce — to say a person or thing is evil.

deposit — something pledged or given as part of the payment.

Eph 1:14	who is a *d* guaranteeing our

depraved (depravity) — evil or sinful.

2Ti 3:8	They are men of *d* minds,
2Pe 2:19	they themselves are slaves of *d*

deprive — to take something away from.

Am 5:12	and *d* the poor of justice

depths — the deepest part of a thing.

Ps 130:1	Out of the *d* I cry
La 3:55	from the *d* of the pit.

descendant — a member of a particular family line.

desecrate — to treat without respect or reverence.

desolate — not lived in; lonely; deserted.

despise — to look down on with contempt.

Pr 1:7	but fools *d* wisdom
Titus 2:15	Do not let anyone *d* you.

destiny — a predetermined course of events.

Php 3:19	Their *d* is destruction,

destitute — not having necessary things such as money and food.

destroy — to ruin completely.

detest — to hate.

devastate — to bring to ruin by violent action.

Jer 19:8	I will *d* this city

devil — the great enemy of God and tempter of people.

Lk 4:2	forty days he was tempted by the *d*.
Eph 6:11	stand against the *d* schemes.
2Ti 2:26	and escape from the trap of the *d*,
Jas 4:7	Resist the *d*, and he will flee
1Pe 5:8	Your enemy the *d* prowls

devote — to set apart for a special person or for a special reason; to set apart for God's use.

devour — 1. to eat up greedily; 2. to destroy.

1Pe 5:8	looking for someone to *d*.

devout — religious; giving much time to prayer and worship.

die — 1. to lose life; 2. to become insensitive to, as to die to the law (Gal 2:19).

Ge 2:17	when you eat from it you will certainly *d.*"
Ecc 3:2	a time to be born and a time to *d,*
Eze 18:4	one who sins is the one who will *d.*
Jn 11:26	by believing in me will never *d.*
1Co 15:22	in Adam all *d,* so in Christ all will
Php 1:21	to live is Christ and to *d* is gain.

diligence (diligent) — characterized by hard work or earnest effort.

disaster — a sudden event bringing great damage, loss or destruction.

Dt 31:29	*d* will fall on you

discern — to understand; to come to know the difference between two or more things.

Php 1:10	you may be able to *d* what is best

disciple — a follower or student, especially one who believes what the leader teaches. Anyone who believes in Jesus is his disciple.

Lk 14:27	and follow me cannot be my *d.*
Jn 13:35	everyone will know that you are my *d,*

discipline — 1. (*v.*) to correct; to teach what is right; 2. (*n.*) training that corrects, molds or perfects moral character.

Pr 29:17	*D* your children, and they will give you
Heb 12:6	the Lord *d* the one he loves,
Rev 3:19	Those whom I love I rebuke and *d.*

disgrace — to bring shame to.

disobey (disobedient) — to fail to obey.

1Pe 2:8	because they *d* the message

disown — to reject someone or something so completely that it no longer belongs to you.

Mt 26:34	you will *d* me three times."
2Ti 2:12	If we *d* him,

disperse — to scatter; to spread around.

dispute — to argue irritably.

dissension — disagreement; quarreling.

distress — suffering, misery, agony.

Ps 57:6	I was bowed down in *d.*
Ro 2:9	There will be trouble and *d*

divination — seeing into the future by magic.

Lev 19:26	"Do not practice *d* or seek omens.

divine — given by God; belonging to God.

Ro 1:20	his eternal power and *d* nature

divorce — to legally dissolve a marriage.

Mal 2:16	who hates and *d* his wife,"
Mt 19:3	for a man to *d* his wife for any
1Co 7:11	And a husband must not *d* his wife.

doctrine — teachings or beliefs about God.

1Ti 4:16	Watch your life and *d* closely.
Titus 2:1	what is appropriate to sound *d.*

dominion — power; rule.

Ps 22:28	for *d* belongs to the LORD
Eph 1:21	far above all rule and authority, power and *d,*

doom — 1. (*v.*) to make certain something will fail or be destroyed; 2. (*n.*) fate; condemnation; ruin.

Rev 18:10	In one hour your *d* has come!'

door — a barrier that can be opened and closed; Christians open the doors of their hearts to Jesus.

Mt 7:7	and the *d* will be opened to you.
Rev 3:20	I stand at the *d* and knock.

doubt — uncertainty.

Mt 21:21	if you have faith and do not *d,*
Mk 11:23	and does not *d* in their heart
Jas 1:6	you must believe and not *d,*

dread — great fear.

dream — thoughts, images or emotion occurring during sleep; God sometimes spoke to his people through dreams.

Da 2:4	Tell your servants the *d,*

dross — the impure scum that floats on the surface of molten metals; sometimes used as a picture of the wicked.

Ps 119:119	you discard like *d;*

drought — a long period of time without rain.

drunkard — a person who is often or usually drunk.

Pr 23:21	for *d* and gluttons become poor,

dwelling — place in which people live; house; in Scripture usually refers to the place where God lives.

1Ki 8:30	Hear from heaven, your *d* place,
Ps 84:1	How lovely is your *d* place,

E

earth — the place that God created for human beings to live.

Ge 1:1	God created the heavens and the *e.*
Ps 24:1	*e* is the LORD's, and everything
Mt 6:10	done, on *e* as it is in heaven.
Mt 24:35	Heaven and *e* will pass away,
Lk 2:14	on *e* peace to those
Php 2:10	in heaven and on *e* and under the *e,*
2Pe 3:13	to a new heaven and a new *e,*

Eden — the location of the beautiful garden God created for Adam and Eve.

edict — an order or law made by a person who has the power to enforce it.

Est 2:8 the king's order and *e*

edify — to teach someone to live a godly life, or to help someone to live in such a way.

1Co 14:4 but the one who prophesies *e* the church.

Egypt — one of the most powerful nations of ancient times, located in the northeast corner of Africa; the Israelites were captives in Egypt at the beginning of the book of Exodus.

elders — 1. the older men of a town or nation; they were the leaders of their community and made all the important decisions; 2. the leaders of the church.

1Ti 5:17 The *e* who direct the affairs
Titus 1:5 and appoint *e* in every town,

election — the choosing of Christians by God, as people who belong to him. Christians are called "the elect" (2Ti 2:10).

Ro 9:11 God's purpose in *e* might stand:
2Pe 1:10 to confirm your calling and *e*.

Eli — the high priest with whom Samuel spent the early years of his life (1Sa 2:11–26).

Elijah — a prophet of the Lord who predicted a famine in Israel (1Ki 17:1) and defeated the prophets of Baal in the test of whose God would set fire to the altar (1Ki 18:16–46).

Elisha — the prophet who succeeded Elijah. He was present when God took Elijah to heaven, and he took his place as prophet to Israel (2Ki 2:1–18).

Elizabeth — the mother of John the Baptist. Mary went to visit her when she found out she, too, was pregnant (Lk 1:5–58).

enchanter — a magician or snake charmer.

encourage — to inspire with courage or hope.

2Sa 19:7 Now go out and *e* your men.
1Th 4:18 Therefore *e* one another with these words.

endure — to continue; to keep on going; to bear something that is difficult or painful.

Ps 136:1 His love *e* forever.
Mal 3:2 who can *e* the day of his coming?
1Co 10:13 so that you can *e* it.

enemy — a person who opposes another person or a cause.

Mt 5:44 Love your *e* and pray
Php 3:18 many live as *e* of the cross of Christ.

enjoy — to take pleasure in.

Jdg 19:9 Stay and *e* yourself.
Jer 33:6 and will let them *e* abundant peace
3Jn 2 I pray that you may *e* good health

enmity — a feeling of antagonism, hostility or hatred.

Ge 3:15 put *e* between you and the woman,

Enoch — a man who "walked with God." Later in life, God "took him away" (Ge 5:18–24).

entice — to tempt or lure.

envoy — a person who represents one government in its dealings with another.

envy — to want for oneself something that belongs to another person.

1Co 13:4 It does not *e*, it does not boast,

ephod — a linen apron worn by a priest over his robe. It was decorated with gold, blue, purple and scarlet yarns.

Ephraim — 1. one of Joseph's sons; 2. the tribe of Israel whose members were descendants of Ephraim; 3. a name for the northern kingdom of Israel after the ten tribes of Israel and the two tribes of Judah separated from each other.

Esau — the firstborn son of Isaac and twin of Jacob (Ge 25:21–26). He sold his birthright to Jacob for a pot of stew (Ge 25:29–34) and was tricked out of his blessing by this same brother (Ge 27).

esteem — 1. (*v.*) to value; to consider important; 2. (*n.*) high regard or respect.

Pr 22:1 to be *e* is better than silver or gold.
Isa 53:3 and we held him in low *e*.

Esther — a Jewish woman who lived in Persia (Est 2:7) and became queen (Est 2:8–18). Upon being told of a plot to kill the Jews, she went to the king and pleaded for the Jewish people and thus saved them (Est 3—4; 7—9).

eternal — without beginning or end; forever; timeless.

Dt 33:27 The *e* God is your refuge,
Jn 3:16 him shall not perish but have *e* life.
Ro 6:23 but the gift of God is *e* life
1Jn 5:13 you may know that you have *e* life.

eunuch — a man whose sex organs have been removed so that he cannot produce children. Often in Bible times these men were important officials in royal palaces.

Eve — the first woman God created (Ge 2:20–24). Her name means "mother of all the living" (Ge 3:20).

everlasting — forever; without end.

Ps 90:2 from *e* to *e* you are God.
Isa 9:6 *E* Father, Prince of Peace.
Isa 55:3 I will make an *e* covenant with you,
2Th 1:9 punished with *e* destruction

evil — wicked; doing things against God's will.

Ge 2:9 of the knowledge of good and *e*.
Ps 23:4 I will fear no *e*,
Mt 6:13 but deliver us from the *e* one.'
Ro 12:9 Hate what is *e*; cling
Ro 12:17 Do not repay anyone *e* for *e*.
Eph 6:16 all the flaming arrows of the *e* one.

exalt — to praise; to raise to an important position.

Ps 118:28 you are my God, and I will *e* you.
Ps 148:13 for his name alone is *e*;
Pr 14:34 Righteousness *e* a nation,
Mt 23:12 For those who *e* themselves

examine — to look over carefully; to test.

1Co 11:28 Everyone ought to *e* themselves

exclaim — to cry out or speak in sudden or strong emotion.

Lk 1:42 In a loud voice she *e*: "Blessed

exclude — to leave out.

execute — to put to death, especially as punishment for an illegal act.

Lk 23:32 were also led out with him to be *e*.

exile — 1. (*v.*) to force someone to leave his or her country or home; 2. (*n.*) forced removal from one's country or home.

Ezr 6:19 the *e* celebrated the Passover.
1Pe 1:1 To God's elect, *e* scattered

exodus — the departure of a large group of people from one place to go to another. The book of Exodus is the story of the Israelites' journey from Egypt to Canaan.

exploit — to take unfair advantage of.

Pr 22:22 Do not *e* the poor

extol — to praise.

Ps 34:1 I will *e* the LORD at all times;
Ps 95:2 and *e* him with music and song.

extortion — something gotten from a person by force or by using other illegal means.

Ezekiel — a priest who was called to be a prophet to the Jewish people when they were in exile in Babylon (Eze 1—3). He had many visions from the Lord (Eze 37; 40).

Ezra — a priest and teacher of the Law; he led a group of Jewish exiles back to Israel and helped them reestablish the temple of God and restore proper worship (Ezr 7—8).

F

fail — to be unsuccessful.

Ecc 6:6 but *f* to enjoy his prosperity.
1Co 13:8 Love never *f*.

faint — 1. (*adj.*) lacking courage; 2. (*v.*) to lose courage.

Ps 142:3 When my spirit grows *f* within me,
Lk 21:26 People will *f* from terror,

faith — belief and trust in God; knowing that God is real, even though one can't see him.

Mt 17:20 if you have *f* as small as a mustard
Lk 7:9 I have not found such great *f*
Ro 1:17 "The righteous will live by *f*."
Ro 3:22 given through *f* in Jesus Christ
1Co 13:2 and if I have a *f* that can move
2Co 5:7 we live by *f*, not by sight.
Eph 6:16 to all this, take up the shield of *f*,
1Ti 6:12 Fight the good fight of the *f*.
Heb 11:1 *f* is confidence in what we hope for
Heb 11:8 By *f* Abraham, when called to go
Heb 12:2 the pioneer and perfecter of *f*
Jas 2:26 so *f* without deeds is dead.

faithful (faithfulness) — trustworthy; loyal.

Ps 145:13 and *f* in all he does.
La 3:23 great is your *f*.
Mt 25:21 'Well done, good and *f* servant!
Ro 12:12 patient in affliction, *f* in prayer.
1Co 10:13 And God is *f*; he will not let you
1Jn 1:9 he is *f* and just and will forgive us
Rev 1:5 who is the *f* witness, the firstborn

false (falsehood) — a lie.

Ex 20:16 "You shall not give *f* testimony

family — a group of people who are related to each other.

Ps 68:6 God sets the lonely in *f*,
Lk 9:61 go back and say goodbye to my *f*."
1Ti 3:4 He must manage his own *f* well

famine — 1. a time when there is not enough food; 2. any severe shortage.

Am 8:11 but a *f* of hearing the words
Mt 24:7 There will be *f* and earthquakes

fast — 1. (*adj.*) firmly fixed; not movable; 2. (*v.*) to go without food for a period of time.

Ps 139:10 your right hand will hold me *f*.
Mt 6:16 "When you *f*, do not look somber

father — a male parent; God is also known as one's father.

Ge 2:24 why a man leaves his *f*
Ge 17:4 You will be the *f* of many nations.
Ex 20:12 "Honor your *f* and your mother,
Mt 6:9 "'Our *F* in heaven,

Lk 11:11 "Which of you *f*, if your son asks
Jn 10:30 I and the *F* are one."
Jn 14:6 No one comes to the *F*

favor — goodwill; a positive attitude toward another person.

1Sa 20:3 I have found *f* in your eyes,

fear — (*v.*) 1. to respect highly; to feel reverence and awe for; 2. to be afraid of; (*n.*) 1. profound reverence toward God; 2. anticipation or awareness of danger.

Dt 6:13 *F* the LORD your God, serve him
Ps 91:5 You will not *f* the terror of night,
Ps 111:10 *f* of the LORD is the beginning
Isa 41:10 So do not *f*, for I am with you;
Php 2:12 to work out your salvation with *f*

fellowship — companionship or friendship.

1Jn 1:6 claim to have *f* with him yet walk
1Jn 1:7 we have *f* with one another,

fertile — producing fruit in great quantities; productive.

Nu 13:20 How is the soil? Is it *f* or poor?

festival — a religious celebration.

Nu 29:12 Celebrate a *f* to the LORD
Ezr 6:22 with joy the *F* of Unleavened Bread,
Jn 4:45 in Jerusalem at the Passover *F*,

fig — 1. a brownish pear-shaped fruit that grows in countries near the Mediterranean Sea; 2. the tree that grows this fruit.

Joel 2:22 the *f* tree and the vine yield their riches.

firstborn — a family's first child. The firstborn son in an Israelite family became the head of the family when his father died, and he received twice as much money and property as each of his brothers.

Ex 11:5 Every *f* son in Egypt will die,

firstfruits — the first vegetables, fruits and grains harvested from the field.

Ex 23:19 "Bring the best of the *f* of your soil

flesh — 1. the soft parts of the bodies of humans and animals; 2. the believer's sinful nature.

Job 6:12 Is my *f* bronze?
Php 3:3 put no confidence in the *f*
Ro 8:13 live according to the *f*, you will die;
Ro 13:14 gratify the desires of the *f*.

flock — a collection of sheep under the care of a shepherd.

Ps 65:13 The meadows are covered with *f*
Isa 40:11 He tends his *f* like a shepherd:

flog — to beat with a stick or a whip.

flood — a large amount of water that covers the ground, as in the time of Noah (Ge 6—8).

foe — an enemy.

Ps 61:3 a strong tower against the *f*.

folly — foolishness; the lack of wisdom.

Pr 26:5 Answer a fool according to his *f*,
2Ti 3:9 their *f* will be clear to everyone.

fool — a person who is not wise.

Ps 14:1 The *f* says in his heart,
Lk 12:20 "But God said to him, 'You *f*!

forbearance — patient endurance; self-control; not enforcing a right.

Gal 5:22 love, joy, peace, *f*, kindness,

forefather — a male ancestor.

forever — for a limitless time.

Dt 32:40 As surely as I live *f*,
Ps 136:1 His love endures *f*.

forgive — to pardon or excuse; to no longer blame or be angry with someone who has done you wrong.

Mt 6:14 For if you *f* other people
Lk 23:34 Jesus said, "Father, *f* them,
Col 3:13 *F* as the Lord forgave you.
1Jn 1:9 and just and will *f* us our sins

forsake — to leave another completely alone; to abandon

Jos 1:5 I will never leave you nor *f* you.
Isa 55:7 Let the wicked *f* their ways
Mt 27:46 my God, why have you *f* me?"

fortified — to make strong, such as a town with a wall.

fortress — a city that is fortified.

fragrance (fragrant) — a sweet or pleasant odor.

SS 4:10 the *f* of your perfume
Php 4:18 They are a *f* offering,

free (freedom) — not bound; liberated.

Jn 8:32 and the truth will set you *f*."
Ro 6:18 You have been set *f* from sin
2Co 3:17 the Spirit of the Lord is, there is *f*.

friend — a person who loves and respects another person.

Pr 18:24 there is a *f* who sticks closer
Jn 15:13 to lay down one's life for one's *f*.
Jas 4:4 Anyone who chooses to be a *f*

fruitful — productive; yielding much fruit.

Ge 1:22 "Be *f* and increase in number
Jn 15:2 prunes so that it will be even more *f*.

fulfill (fulfillment) — to complete a promise or project.

Ps 116:14	I will *f* my vows to the LORD
Mk 14:49	But the Scriptures must be *f*."
Ro 13:10	Therefore love is the *f* of the law.

fury — intense anger.

Pr 6:34	jealousy arouses a husband's *f*,

G

Gabriel — the angel who announced the births of John the Baptist and Jesus (Lk 1:11–20, 26–38).

Galilee — the northern part of Palestine. Jesus grew up, preached and did most of his miracles there. Today this area is in northern Israel.

gall — 1. a plant with an extremely bitter-tasting fruit; 2. the liquid made by the liver.

Mt 27:34	mixed with *g*; but after tasting it,

genealogy — a list of a person's ancestors or descendants; a family tree.

generation — the entire number of people born and living at about the same time. Grandparents, parents and children are three different generations.

Ps 102:12	your renown endures through all *g*.
Lk 1:48	now on all *g* will call me blessed,

Gentile — anyone who is not a Jew.

Ro 3:9	and *G* alike are all under
Ro 11:13	as I am the apostle to the *G*,

Gideon — a judge who freed Israel from the rule and terror of the Midianites (Jdg 6—8). He asked for a sign from God, and God showed him his will by means of dew and a fleece (Jdg 6:36–40).

gift — 1. a present; 2. a talent or ability.

Ro 6:23	but the *g* of God is eternal life
1Co 12:4	There are different kinds of *g*,
2Co 9:15	be to God for his indescribable *g*!

glean — to pick up the grain or fruit left behind after harvesting; usually a way for the poor to get food.

Ruth 2:8	Don't go and *g* in another field

gloat — to look at or think about something or someone with malicious satisfaction.

Mic 7:8	Do not *g* over me, my enemy!

glorify — to praise and honor in worship.

Ps 34:3	*G* the LORD with me;
Jn 17:1	*G* your Son, that your Son may

glory — 1. honor; praise; 2. a source of pride or worthiness.

Ps 8:5	and crowned them with *g* and honor.
Ps 19:1	The heavens declare the *g* of God;
Lk 2:14	"*G* to God in the highest heaven,
Jn 1:14	We have seen his *g*, the *g* of the one
1Co 10:31	whatever you do, do it all for the *g*
Rev 4:11	to receive *g* and honor and power,

glutton — a person who eats too much.

Dt 21:20	He is a *g* and a drunkard."

gnash — to grind (one's teeth) together.

Mt 8:12	there will be weeping and *g* of teeth."

goat — an animal raised for its meat and milk; sometimes used in religious sacrifices.

God — the supreme Creator and the powerful force of the universe; the One who is to be worshiped.

Ge 1:1	In the beginning *G* created
Ex 20:5	the LORD your *G*, am a jealous *G*,
Nu 23:19	*G* is not human, that he should lie,
Dt 6:4	LORD our *G*, the LORD is one.
Dt 6:5	Love the LORD your *G*
Ps 46:1	*G* is our refuge and strength,
Jn 1:18	ever seen *G*, but the one
Jn 3:16	For *G* so loved the world that he
Jn 4:24	*G* is spirit, and his worshipers must
1Jn 4:16	*G* is love.
Rev 4:8	holy is the Lord *G* Almighty,

godly — to be devoted and loving toward God, wanting to do his will.

1Ti 4:7	train yourself to be *g*.
2Pe 3:11	live holy and *g* lives

Golgotha — the hill outside Jerusalem where Jesus was hung on a cross.

Goliath — the Philistine giant who was killed by David (1Sa 17; 21:9).

gospel — 1. the good news that Jesus died for sins and rose again; 2. any of the first four books of the New Testament.

Ro 1:16	I am not ashamed of the *g*,
1Co 9:16	Woe to me if I do not preach the *g*!
1Co 15:2	By this *g* you are saved,

gossip — to talk too much about others, especially in a way that is hurtful.

2Co 12:20	slander, *g*, arrogance and disorder.

grace — an undeserved favor or gift; the undeserved forgiveness, kindness and mercy that God gives us.

Ro 3:24	all are justified freely by his *g*
Ro 5:20	where sin increased, *g* increased all
2Co 12:9	"My *g* is sufficient for you,
Eph 2:5	it is by *g* you have been saved.
Titus 3:7	having been justified by his *g*,

greed — selfish desire for more money or possessions than one needs.

Lk 12:15 on your guard against all kinds of *g*;
Col 3:5 evil desires and *g*, which is idolatry.

grieve — to cause someone pain or sorrow.

Jn 16:20 You will *g*, but your grief will turn
Eph 4:30 do not *g* the Holy Spirit of God,

guarantee — a pledge that something will take place.

Eph 1:14 who is a deposit *g* our inheritance

guardian-redeemer — in Old Testament times a close male relative who had the responsibility to marry a widow and buy her husband's property (Dt 25:5–6).

Ruth 3:9 since you are a *g* of our family.

guide — to direct or point out the way.

Ps 23:3 He *g* me along the right paths

guilty — deserving punishment for having broken a law or commandment.

Ex 34:7 does not leave the *g* unpunished;
Heb 10:22 to cleanse us from a *g* conscience
Jas 2:10 at just one point is *g* of breaking all

H

Hades — hell; the place where the spirits of the dead live.

Mt 16:18 the gates of *H* will not overcome it.

Hagar — a slave of Sarah and one of Abraham's wives; the mother of Ishmael (Ge 16:1–6; 25:12).

Haggai — a prophet who encouraged the Israelites returning from exile in Babylon to rebuild the temple (Ezr 5:1; Hag 1—2).

hallelujah — praise the Lord; a song of praise.

Rev 19:1 "*H!* Salvation and glory and power

hallowed — holy; sacred.

Mt 6:9 *h* be your name,

Ham — the youngest of Noah's three sons (Ge 5:32).

Hannah — she prayed for a son, and God gave her Samuel. She dedicated him to God; he lived in the temple as a boy and became a prophet and judge (1Sa 1—2).

harp — a musical instrument with twelve strings for strumming; frequently used in religious ceremonies.

Ps 71:22 I will praise you with the *h*

harvest — the season for gathering in crops.

Ge 8:22 "As long as the earth endures, seedtime and *h*,

hate — to detest, to have extreme dislike for.

Ps 5:5 You *h* all who do wrong;
Mk 13:13 Everyone will *h* you because of me,

haughty — proud.

Pr 16:18 a *h* spirit before a fall.

heal — to make well again.

Lk 8:43 but no one could *h* her.
Ac 28:27 and I would *h* them.'

heart — the center of a person's life, including the mind, the will and the emotions.

Dt 6:5 LORD your God with all your *h*
1Sa 16:7 but the LORD looks at the *h*."
Ps 51:10 Create in me a pure *h*, O God,
Ps 119:11 I have hidden your word in my *h*
Ps 139:23 Search me, O God, and know my *h*;
Eze 36:26 I will give you a new *h*
Mt 5:8 Blessed are the pure in *h*,

heaven — 1. the place where God lives; 2. the sky.

Ge 14:19 Creator of *h* and earth.
Mt 19:23 to enter the kingdom of *h*.
Lk 24:51 and was taken up into *h*.
Php 3:20 But our citizenship is in *h*.
Rev 21:1 Then I saw "a new *h* and a new earth,"

Hebrew — 1. another name for an Israelite; a descendant of Abraham; 2. the language spoken by the Jews. The Old Testament was written in Hebrew.

heir — someone who receives the property or blessings of a person who has died.

Ro 8:17 then we are *h* — *h* of God
Eph 3:6 gospel the Gentiles are *h* together

herd — a large number of animals of one kind kept together in a group.

Herod — the family name of five kings who ruled Palestine under the Roman emperor: Herod the Great (Mt 2:16); Herod Antipas (Mk 6:14–29); Herod Philip (Mt 14:3; Mk 6:17); Herod Agrippa I (Ac 12:1–4, 19–23); Herod Agrippa II (Ac 23:35; 25:13–26:32).

Herodias — the wife of Herod Antipas; she persuaded her daughter to ask Antipas for the head of John the Baptist (Mk 6:17).

Hezekiah — a king of Judah; he restored the temple, reinstituted proper worship and sought the Lord's help against the Assyrians.

high priest — the chief religious official in the Jewish religion. In the Old Testament he offered the most important sacrifices to God in behalf of the people.

Heb 4:14 a great high *p* who has ascended
Heb 7:26 a high *p* truly meets our need

hinder — to hold back; to prevent; to delay.

Mt 19:14 come to me, and do not *h* them,

holy — set apart for God; belonging to God; pure; godly.

Ex 20:8 the Sabbath day by keeping it *h.*
Lev 11:44 and be *h*, because I am *h.*
Isa 6:3 "*H, h, h* is the LORD Almighty;
Ro 12:1 as a living sacrifice, *h* and pleasing
Rev 4:8 "*H, h, h* is the Lord God Almighty,

Holy Spirit — the third person of the Trinity; he lives and works in the hearts and minds of believers; he came at Pentecost in a powerful way (Ac 2). Other names are: the Spirit, Counselor and Comforter.

Ps 51:11 or take your *H* from me.
Jn 14:26 But the Advocate, the *H*,
Jn 20:22 and said, "Receive the *H.*
Ac 2:4 of them were filled with the *H*
Gal 5:22 But the fruit of the *S* is love, joy,

honor — to show respect to; to give credit to.

Ex 20:12 "*H* your father and your mother,
Ps 8:5 and crowned them with glory and *h.*

hope — the anticipation of something good.

Ps 42:5 Put your *h* in God,
Isa 40:31 but those who *h* in the LORD
Ro 8:24 But *h* that is seen is no *h* at all.
1Co 15:19 for this life we have *h* in Christ,
Heb 11:1 faith is confidence in what we *h* for

hordes — a loosely organized or disorderly crowd of people; usually committing harmful acts.

Hab 1:9 Their *h* advance like a desert wind

horror — strong and painful fear or dread.

Jer 8:21 I mourn, and *h* grips me.

hosanna — a Hebrew word of praise meaning "save."

Mt 21:9 "*H* in the highest heaven!"

hospitality — welcoming people into one's home; sharing one's home and food with others.

Ro 12:13 Practice *h.*
1Pe 4:9 Offer *h* to one another

hostile — like an enemy; unfriendly.

human — like people rather than animals, in actions or thoughts or appearance.

humble — 1. (*v.*) to make lower; 2. (*adj.*) not proud; not pretending to be important.

Ps 147:6 The LORD sustains the *h*
Mt 23:12 who exalt themselves will be *h*,
Jas 4:10 *H* yourselves before the Lord,

humiliate — to make humble; to reduce to a lower position; to make ashamed.

1Co 11:22 by *h* those who have nothing?

humility — the absence of pride.

Php 2:3 but in *h* value others above
1Pe 5:5 clothe yourselves with *h*

hymn — a song of praise to God.

Eph 5:19 with psalms, *h*, and songs

hypocrite — a person who pretends to be better than he or she is.

Mt 6:5 when you pray, do not be like the *h*,
Mt 7:5 You *h*, first take the plank out

hyssop — a plant used to sprinkle water or blood for religious cleansing.

Ps 51:7 with *h*, and I will be clean;

I

idle — 1. lacking worth or basis; 2. lazy.

Dt 32:47 They are not just *i* words
1Th 5:14 warn those who are *i*

idol — a statue made by people and worshiped as if it had the power of a god; anything that takes the place of God in a person's life. Worshiping idols is called idolatry.

1Co 8:4 We know that "An *i* is nothing at all
Col 3:5 evil desires and greed, which is *i.*

image — likeness.

Ge 1:27 God created mankind in his own *i*,
Da 3:12 nor worship the *i* of gold you have set up."

Immanuel — a name for Jesus meaning "God with us."

Mt 1:23 and they will call him *I*"

immoral (immorality) — wicked; not living by right standards.

1Co 6:18 Flee from sexual *i.*
Eph 5:5 No *i*, impure or greedy person

immortal (immortality) — free from death; not able to die.

1Co 15:53 and the mortal with *i.*
1Ti 1:17 Now to the King eternal, *i*,

imperishable — not able to die or to be destroyed.

1Pe 1:23 not of perishable seed, but of *i*,

impure — not pure; not clean.

Ac 10:15 not call anything *i* that God has
1Th 4:7 For God did not call us to be *i*,

incense — 1. spices burned to make a sweet-smelling smoke, as a way of worshiping God; 2. the sweet smell or the smoke of burning spices.

Ps 141:2 my prayer be set before you like *i*;
Rev 8:3 He was given much *i* to offer,

indignation — anger.

Na 1:6 Who can withstand his *i?*

infirmity — physical weakness; disease.

Lk 13:12 set free from your *i.*"

inflict — to cause to be endured.

Eze 5:8 I will *i* punishment on you
2Co 2:6 The punishment *i* on him by

inhabitant — one who lives in a particular place.

Nu 33:55 drive out all the *i* of the land
Rev 6:10 the *i* of the earth and avenge

inherit — to receive money, property or keepsakes from a person after his or her death.

Mt 5:5 for they will *i* the earth.
Mk 10:17 "what must I do to *i* eternal life?"

inheritance — money, property or keepsakes received from a person after his or her death.

Dt 4:20 to be the people of his *i*,
1Pe 1:4 and into an *i* that can never perish,

iniquity — sin; wickedness.

Ps 51:2 Wash away all my *i*
Ps 103:10 or repay us according to our *i.*
Isa 53:6 the *i* of us all.

injustice — unfairness.

Pr 22:8 Whoever sows *i* reaps calamity,

inscription — 1. the writing on a coin; 2. a written title or message.

instruct — to give knowledge or information; to teach.

Pr 9:9 *I* the wise and they will be wiser
1Th 4:1 we *i* you how to live

instruction — the action of a teacher; a lesson.

Ac 1:2 after giving *i* through the Holy Spirit
2Ti 4:2 with great patience and careful *i*

insult — 1. (*v.*) to treat with contempt by word or action; to offend; 2. (*n.*) an act or speech of contempt.

Ps 69:9 the *i* of those who *i* you fall on me
Mt 5:11 "Blessed are you when people *i* you,

insurrection — revolt or rebellion against a government.

integrity — complete honesty.

Ps 25:21 May *i* and uprightness protect me,

intercede — to beg or plead for another person.

Ro 8:26 but the Spirit himself *i* for us

intercession — the plea made on behalf of another person.

Isa 53:12 and made *i* for the transgressors.

intermarry — to marry someone from a different race or religion.

Dt 7:3 Do not *i* with them.

interpret — to explain the meaning of.

Mt 16:3 you cannot *i* the signs of the times.
1Co 12:30 Do all speak in tongues? Do all *i?*

invoke — to call for help or support.

Ac 19:13 to *i* the name of the Lord Jesus

Isaac — the promised son of Abraham and Sarah (Ge 17:19; 21:1–7); offered as a sacrifice by Abraham (Ge 22); married Rebekah (Ge 24) and was the father of Esau and Jacob (Ge 25).

Isaiah — a prophet called by God (Isa 6) to prophesy to Judah (Isa 1:1). Some of his prophesies were about the coming Messiah (Isa 53).

Ishmael — the son of Abraham and Hagar (Ge 16); he was not to be the son of the covenant (Ge 17:18–21).

Israel — 1. the new name God gave to Jacob (Ge 32:28); 2. the nation made up of descendants of the twelve sons of Jacob; 3. the northern ten tribes after they separated from Judah and Benjamin.

Ge 37:3 Now *I* loved Joseph more than
Dt 6:4 Hear, O *I*: The LORD our God,
Lk 22:30 judging the twelve tribes of *I.*
Eph 3:6 Gentiles are heirs together with *I*,

Israelites — the people of Israel.

Ex 14:22 and the *I* went through the sea
Ro 9:27 the number of the *I* be like the sand

J

Jacob — the son of Isaac and Rebekah; he was the twin brother of Esau (Ge 25:21–26); he bought Esau's birthright for a pot of stew (Ge 25:29–34); he wrestled with God, and his name was changed to Israel (Ge 32:22–32); the descendants of his twelve sons became the nation of Israel.

James — 1. one of the twelve apostles; the brother of John (Mt 4:21–22); 2. one of the twelve apostles; the son of Alphaeus (Mt 10:3); 3. the brother of Jesus (Mk 6:3); the author of the letter of James (Jas 1:1).

Japheth — one of the sons of Noah (Ge 5:32); he was blessed because he covered his father's nakedness (Ge 9:18–28).

jealous (jealousy) — 1. afraid of losing someone's love or affection; 2. angry or unhappy because of what someone else has; 3. careful to guard or keep what one has.

Joel 2:18 Then the LORD was *j* for his land
2Co 11:2 I am *j* for you with a godly *j.*
Gal 5:20 hatred, discord, *j*, fits of rage,

Jeremiah — a prophet called by God to prophesy to Judah (Jer 1:1–3). He is often referred to as the prophet of gloom, because he prophesied about the destruction of Judah.

Jericho — the ancient city destroyed by Joshua when the Hebrews entered Canaan (Jos 6).

Jeroboam — an official in Solomon's court; he rebelled and became the first king of the northern ten tribes of Israel (1Ki 11:26–40; 12:1–20).

Jerusalem — the political and religious center of the Jews; it was the site of many important events in the Bible; also called "Zion" and "the City of David."

2Ki 23:27	and I will reject *J*, the city I chose,
Ne 2:17	Come, let us rebuild the wall of *J*,
Ps 137:5	If I forget you, O *J*,
Jn 4:20	where we must worship is in *J*."
Rev 21:2	I saw the Holy City, the new *J*,

Jesse — the father of David, king of Israel (1Sa 16:10–13).

Jesus — The Son of God; the Savior of the world; the Messiah, through whom people can be saved.

Mt 1:21	you are to give him the name *J*,
Mk 11:22	"Have faith in God," *J* answered.
Php 2:10	name of *J* every knee should bow,

Jew — an Israelite; one of the chosen people of God; a descendant of Abraham through Jacob.

Mt 2:2	who has been born king of the *J*?
Ro 3:29	Or is God the God of *J* only?
Gal 3:28	There is neither *J* nor Gentile,

Jezebel — the wife of King Ahab (1Ki 16:31). She promoted Baal worship in Israel (1Ki 16:32–33), had many prophets of God killed (1Ki 18:4,13) and opposed the prophet Elijah (1Ki 19:1–2).

Joab — the commander of the armies of King David.

Joash — the boy-king of Judah; he repaired the temple (2Ki 12).

Job — a wealthy man from the land of Uz who feared God (Job 1:1–5). His righteousness was tested by disaster (Job 1:6–22) and personal affliction (Job 2), but in the end God restored wealth and honor to him (Job 42).

John — 1. the Baptist (Mk 1:2–8); the son of Zechariah and Elizabeth (Lk 1). He preached in the desert, preparing the people for Jesus (Mt 3:11–12); baptized Jesus in the Jordan River (Mt 3:13–17); executed by Herod (Mk 6:14–29); 2. one of the twelve apostles; brother of the apostle James (Lk 5:1–10); wrote the Gospel of John, the letters of John (2Jn 1; 3Jn 1) and the book of Revelation (Rev 1:1; 22:8).

John Mark (see Mark, John).

Jonah — a prophet who was called to preach to Nineveh but instead fled to Tarshish (Jnh 1:1–3). While at sea a great storm arose because of his disobedience; he was thrown into the sea and was swallowed by a large fish (Jnh 1:4–17). He then repented and went to Nineveh and preached, telling the people to repent (Jnh 3).

Jonathan — a son of King Saul (1Sa 13:16) who had a close friendship with David (1Sa 18:1–4; 19—20; 23:16–18). When he was killed (1Sa 31) David mourned greatly for him (2Sa 1).

Joppa — an ancient walled town on the coast of Palestine.

Jordan — a river in Palestine that flows between the Sea of Galilee and the Dead Sea.

Jos 4:22	'Israel crossed the *J* on dry ground.'
Mt 3:6	baptized by him in the *J* River.

Joseph — 1. the son of Jacob and Rachel (Ge 30:24), who was favored by his father but hated by his brothers (Ge 37:3–4). He was sold into slavery (Ge 37:12–36), taken to Egypt and eventually given a high position under Pharaoh (Ge 41:41–57); 2. the husband of Mary and childhood father of Jesus (Mt 1:16–24; 2:13–19); 3. a disciple of Jesus from Arimathea; he gave his tomb for Jesus' burial (Mt 27:57–61); 4. the original name of Barnabas (Ac 4:36).

Joshua — 1. the son of Nun (Nu 13:8); Moses' aide and later his successor (Dt 31:1–18); he led the Israelites across the Jordan River into Canaan (Jos 3—4); was the commander in the conquest of Jericho (Jos 6), Ai (Jos 7—8), and a large part of Canaan (Jos 10—12); oversaw the dividing up of the promised land among the twelve tribes of Israel (Jos 13—22); 2. the high priest in Israel during the rebuilding of both the temple (Hag 1—2) and the altar (Ezr 3:2,8); also called Jeshua.

Josiah — godly king of Judah for thirty-one years shortly before the destruction of Jerusalem.

Judah — 1. Jacob's fourth son; 2. the tribe of Israel whose members were descendants of Judah; 3. a name for the southern kingdom after Judah and Benjamin separated from the northern ten tribes.

Ge 29:35	So she named him *J*.
Zec 10:4	From *J* will come the cornerstone,
Mt 2:6	Bethlehem, in the land of *J*,
Rev 5:5	See, the Lion of the tribe of *J*,

Judaism — the teachings of the Jewish religion.

Judas — 1. one of the twelve apostles (Lk 6:16; Ac 1:13); was probably also called Thaddaeus (Mt 10:3); 2. one of the brothers of Jesus (Mt 13:55); author of the last letter in the New Testament

(Jude 1); 3. one of the twelve apostles, also called Iscariot; he betrayed Jesus (Mk 3:19; 14:10–50) and then hung himself (Mt 27:3–5).

Judea — the area of Palestine where the tribe of Judah lived after the exile.

Mk 10:1 into the region of *J* and across the Jordan.
Gal 1:22 to the churches of *J* that are in Christ.

judge — to decide if something is good or bad; to condemn.

Ps 9:8 and *j* the peoples with equity.
Mt 7:1 "Do not *j*, or you too will be judged.
2Ti 4:1 who will *j* the living and the dead,

judgment — 1. a decision or opinion; 2. a decision of guilt or innocence made by a judge in a court of law; punishment decided on by a court; 3. a decision from God, especially the final judgment when God will reward those who believe in him and condemn all others to hell.

Dt 1:17 of anyone, for *j* belongs to God.
Ps 119:66 Teach me knowledge and good *j*,
Isa 66:16 the LORD will execute *j*
Mt 5:21 who murders will be subject to *j*.'
Mt 12:36 have to give account on the day of *j*
Jn 5:22 but has entrusted all *j* to the Son,
Ro 14:10 stand before God's *j* seat.
2Co 5:10 appear before the *j* seat of Christ,

just — righteous, legally correct.

Ps 111:7 The works of his hands are faithful and *j*;
Rev 16:7 true and *j* are your judgments."

justice — fairness.

Isa 30:18 For the LORD is a God of *j*.
Isa 61:8 "For I, the LORD, love *j*;
Zec 7:9 'Administer true *j*; show mercy
Lk 11:42 you neglect *j* and the love of God.

justify (justification) — to erase someone's sins; to declare righteous.

Ac 13:39 a *j* you were not able to obtain
Ro 3:24 and all are *j* freely by his grace
Ro 4:25 and was raised to life for our *j*.
Ro 5:1 since we have been *j* through faith,
Gal 3:24 Christ came that we might be *j* by faith.

K

kind — considerate, loving.

Eph 4:32 Be *k* and compassionate

king — ruler over a country or kingdom; Christ is often referred to as the King of kings.

1Ki 22:3 The *k* of Israel had said
1Ti 6:15 the *K* of *k* and Lord of lords,

kingdom — an area or group of people headed by a king; God's kingdom, or the kingdom of heaven, is made up of all believers.

Ex 19:6 you will be for me a *k* of priests
Mt 3:2 "Repent, for the *k* of heaven has come
Mt 5:3 for theirs is the *k* of heaven.
Mt 6:33 But seek first his *k* and his
Mt 16:19 the keys of the *k* of heaven;
Jn 18:36 "My *k* is not of this world.
1Co 15:24 hands over the *k* to God the Father
Rev 11:15 "The *k* of the world has become the *k*

Kish — the father of King Saul, the first king of Israel.

knowledge — possessing the facts, understanding.

Pr 1:7 of the LORD is the beginning of *k*,
Hos 4:6 are destroyed from lack of *k*.
1Co 8:1 *k* puffs up while love builds up.

L

Laban — the brother of Rebekah (Ge 24:29–51) and father of Rachel and Leah (Ge 29—31).

labor — 1. (*v.*) to work; 2. (*n.*) a task; 3. (*n.*) the time just before giving birth.

Ge 5:29 the *l* and painful toil of our hands
Ex 20:9 Six days you shall *l* and do all your work,
Jer 13:21 like that of a woman in *l*?

lack — 1. (*v.*) to stand in need of; 2. (*n.*) the state of being in need of something.

Ps 34:9 those who fear him *l* nothing.

lamb — a principal sacrificial animal in the Old Testament; since Jesus is the supreme sacrifice of God, he is called the "Lamb of God."

Isa 53:7 he was led like a *l* to the slaughter,
Jn 1:29 *L* of God, who takes away the sin
1Co 5:7 our Passover *l*, has been sacrificed.
Rev 5:6 Then I saw a *L*, looking

lament, lamentation — a cry of grief.

Ps 5:1 LORD, consider my *l*.

law — 1. God's rules, which help his people know what is right and wrong (the Ten Commandments are part of God's law); 2. (cap.) the first five books of the Bible, written by Moses.

Ps 1:2 and who meditates on his *l*
Ps 19:7 The *l* of the LORD is perfect,
Ps 119:97 Oh, how I love your *l*!

Mt 22:40	All the *L* and the Prophets hang
Ro 8:3	For what the *l* was powerless to do
Ro 13:10	love is the fulfillment of the *l*.
Gal 3:24	So the *l* was our guardian

Lazarus — 1. the poor man in one of Jesus' parables (Lk 16:19–31); 2. the brother of Mary and Martha; Jesus raised him from the dead (Jn 11:1–12:19).

Leah — the wife of Jacob; she had six sons and one daughter (Ge 29:16–30:21).

leprosy — a word used in the Bible for many different skin diseases and infections.

Mk 1:42	Immediately the *l* left him

Levite — a member of the tribe of Levi. The Levites took care of the temple. Only Levites could become priests, but not all Levites were priests.

lewd — indecent; wicked.

life — the total substance of a person's existence; can refer to both physical and spiritual existence.

Ge 2:7	into his nostrils the breath of *l*,
Jn 3:16	shall not perish but have eternal *l*.
Jn 11:25	"I am the resurrection and the *l*.
Jn 14:6	am the way and the truth and the *l*.
Ro 6:23	but the gift of God is eternal *l*

light — the form of energy that allows a person to see; in the Old Testament it symbolized life and blessing.

Ge 1:3	"Let there be *l*," and there was *l*.
Ps 27:1	The LORD is my *l* and my salvation
Ps 119:105	a *l* on my path.
Isa 9:2	have seen a great *l*;
Mt 5:16	let your *l* shine before others,
Jn 8:12	he said, "I am the *l* of the world.
1Jn 1:5	God is *l*; in him there is no

linen — cloth made from the fiber of flax plants.

live — to be alive; may refer to both physical and spiritual existence.

Ex 20:12	so that you may *l* long
Ro 1:17	"The righteous will *l* by faith."
2Co 5:7	For we *l* by faith, not by sight.
Php 1:21	to *l* is Christ and to die is gain.

loathe — to feel disgust or hatred.

Job 10:1	"I *l* my very life;

locusts — a type of grasshopper. When they settle in a grain field, orchard or other cultivated area, they eat and can destroy the crop.

Lord — refers to God as the master. (See also LORD.)

Mt 3:3	'Prepare the way for the *L*,
Lk 2:9	glory of the *L* shone around them,
Ac 16:31	replied, "Believe in the *L* Jesus,
Ro 10:13	on the name of the *L* will be saved."
Php 2:11	acknowledge that Jesus Christ is *L*,
2Pe 1:16	the coming of our *L* Jesus Christ,
Rev 17:14	he is *L* of lords and King of kings
Rev 22:20	Come, *L* Jesus.

LORD (Yahweh) — the intimate and personal name of God; it emphasizes his role as Israel's Redeemer and covenant Lord. (See also Lord.)

Ge 2:4	when the *L* God made the earth
Ex 20:2	"I am the *L* your God, who
Ps 23:1	The *L* is my shepherd, I lack
Ps 103:1	Praise the *L*, my soul;
Pr 1:7	The fear of the *L* is the beginning
Isa 6:3	"Holy, holy, holy is the *L* Almighty;
Isa 55:6	Seek the *L* while he may be found;

Lot — the nephew of Abraham (Ge 12:5). He chose to live in Sodom (Ge 13); Abraham pleaded with God for Lot's life when God was about to destroy Sodom (Ge 19:1–29).

lot — one of the ways used in Bible times to find out God's will about something. It is somewhat like drawing straws.

Mt 27:35	divided up his clothes by casting *l*.
Ac 1:26	Then they cast *l*, and the *l* fell

love — wanting good to come to another person; being concerned and willing to work for another person's benefit.

Ex 20:6	showing *l* to a thousand generations
Ps 23:6	Surely your goodness and *l* will follow
Ps 136:1–26	His *l* endures forever.
Mt 3:17	"This is my Son, whom I *l*;
Mt 5:44	*l* your enemies and pray
Mt 19:19	and '*l* your neighbor as yourself.'"
Jn 13:34	I give you: *L* one another.
Jn 15:13	Greater *l* has no one than this:
Ro 13:10	Therefore *l* is the fulfillment
Gal 5:22	But the fruit of the Spirit is *l*, joy,
Eph 1:4–5	In *l* he predestined us
1Jn 3:10	anyone who does not *l* their brother.
1Jn 3:16	This is how we know what *l* is:
1Jn 4:7	for *l* comes from God.
1Jn 4:10	This is *l*: not that we loved God,
1Jn 4:16	God is *l*.

Luke — a co-worker with Paul; he wrote the books of Luke and Acts (Col 4:14).

lust — a strong desire for something wrong.

Pr 6:25	Do not *l* in your heart
Ro 1:26	God gave them over to shameful *l*.

lyre — a small lap harp with three to twelve strings.

1Sa 18:10	David was playing the *l*,

M

Macedonia — a Roman province; the first part of Europe to receive Christianity.

Magi — men of Arabia and Persia who studied the stars. People thought they had the power to tell the meaning of dreams.

Mt 2:1 — *M* from the east came to Jerusalem

maimed — crippled; having lost a part of one's body, such as an arm or leg.

majestic (majesty) — great and powerful.

Ex 15:6 — was *m* in power.
Ps 8:1 — how *m* is your name in all the earth!
Ps 111:3 — Glorious and *m* are his deeds,

malice — hatred; wishing harm on someone else.

1Pe 2:1 — rid yourselves of all *m*

Manasseh — 1. the older son of Joseph and the tribe descended from him (Ge 41:51; Nu 1:34); 2. one of the kings of Judah (2Ki 21:1).

manger — a feed box for cows or other animals.

Lk 2:7 — placed him in a *m*, because there

maniac — an insane person; an overly enthusiastic person.

2Ki 9:20 — he drives like a *m*."

manna — the special food God gave daily to the Israelites until they reached the promised land.

Ex 16:31 — people of Israel called the bread *m*.
Jn 6:49 — Your ancestors ate the *m*

Mark, John — the cousin of Barnabas (Col 4:10); a helper to Paul and Barnabas (Ac 13:5); later a co-worker with Barnabas (Ac 15:39) and then Paul (Phm 24); author of the second Gospel, according to early church tradition.

marriage — the joining together before God and other people of a man and a woman to form a new family.

Ge 29:26 — younger daughter in *m* before the older
Mt 22:30 — neither marry nor be given in *m*;
Heb 13:4 — by all, and the *m* bed kept pure,

Martha — the sister of Mary and Lazarus, the man whom Jesus raised from the dead (Jn 11; 12:2).

marvelous — something that surprises, that fills one with wonder.

Ps 118:23 — and it is *m* in our eyes.
Rev 15:3 — "Great and *m* are your deeds,

Mary — 1. the mother of Jesus (Mt 1:16–25); 2. Mary Magdalene — a woman whom Jesus freed from demons (Lk 8:2), who was present at the cross (Mk 15:40) and who came on Easter morning to the tomb (Mt 27:61); 3. the sister of Martha and Lazarus; she washed Jesus' feet with expensive perfume (Jn 12:1–8).

master — one who rules over others.

Mt 6:24 — "No one can serve two *m*.
Jn 13:16 — no servant is greater than his *m*,

Matthew — a tax collector who became one of the twelve apostles (Mt 9:9–13); also called Levi (Mk 2:14–17).

mediator — one who makes peace between two people or two groups who are displeased and/or angry with each other. Jesus is the mediator between us and God.

1Ti 2:5 — and one *m* between God and mankind,
Heb 9:15 — For this reason Christ is the *m*

meditate — to think seriously and carefully.

Ps 1:2 — who *m* on his law day and night.
Ps 119:15 — I *m* on your precepts

medium — a person who can supposedly talk with the spirits of people who have died.

1Sa 28:7 — "Find me a woman who is a *m*,

meek — patient; mild; gentle.

Ps 37:11 — But the *m* will inherit the land
Mt 5:5 — Blessed are the *m*,

Melchizedek — a priest and king of early Salem (Jerusalem); Jesus was said to be a priest like Melchizedek (Heb 5:6).

Mephibosheth — son of Jonathan and grandson of Saul; he lived out his life under King David's protection (2Sa 9:11).

mercy — kindness and forgiveness, especially when given to a person who doesn't deserve it.

Mic 6:8 — To act justly and to love *m*
Ro 9:15 — "I will have *m* on whom I have *m*,
1Pe 1:3 — In his great *m* he has given us new

Messiah — the "Anointed One"; Christ; the one the Jews expected to come and be their king.

Lk 9:20 — Peter answered, "God's *M*."
Jn 1:41 — "We have found the *M*"

Methuselah — a man in early Bible times who lived 969 years (Ge 5:27).

Michal — daughter of Saul, wife of David, both of whom were kings of Israel.

midwives — women who helped with the birth of a baby.

Ex 1:17 — The *m*, however, feared God

millstone — one of a pair of stones used to crush grain for flour.

Lk 17:2 — sea with a *m* tied around their neck

minister — 1. (*v.*) to serve; to give care or attention to; 2. (*n.*) one who serves others as God directs.

2Co 3:6 as *m* of a new covenant
1Ti 4:6 you will be a good *m*

miracle — an unusual event, one that goes against the normal laws of nature. Miracles are done by the power of God.

Ps 77:14 You are the God who performs *m*;
Mk 6:2 What are these remarkable *m* he is
Ac 2:22 accredited by God to you by *m*,
Heb 2:4 it by signs, wonders and various *m*,

Miriam — the sister of Moses and Aaron (Nu 26:59); led the Israelites in praising God in dance and song after he had parted the waters of the Red Sea (Ex 15:20–21); later temporarily struck with leprosy because she criticized Moses (Nu 12).

Moab — 1. a son of Lot whose descendants became bitter enemies of the Israelites; 2. the land occupied by the Moabites, to the east of the Dead Sea.

money — a medium of exchange.

Ecc 5:10 Whoever loves *m* never has
Mt 6:24 You cannot serve both God and *m*.
1Co 16:2 set aside a sum of *m* in keeping
1Ti 6:10 For the love of *m* is a root

Mordecai — cousin of Esther, queen of Persia; he and Esther saved the Jews from a plot to put them all to death.

mortal — human; able to die.

Ps 9:20 the nations know they are only *m*.
Ps 103:15 The life of *m* is like grass,
1Co 15:53 and the *m* with immortality,

Moses — the leader of Israel in the exodus out of Egypt, ending in their passing through the Red Sea (Ex 12—14). He received the law of God at Sinai (Ex 19—23) and gave it to the people of Israel. Moses was allowed to view the land of Canaan from the top of Mount Nebo, but he died without entering it (Nu 20:1–13; Dt 34:5–12).

mother — the female parent.

Ge 2:24 and *m* and is united to his wife,
Dt 5:16 "Honor your father and your *m*,

mourn — to feel deep sorrow; to grieve.

Mt 5:4 Blessed are those who *m*,

murder — to kill someone illegally.

Ex 20:13 "You shall not *m*.

muster — to gather together, especially to gather soldiers for war.

mute — unable to speak.

Mt 9:33 the man who had been *m* spoke.

myrrh — the sweet-smelling sap of the myrrh bush. It was used to make the sacred anointing oil.

Mt 2:11 gifts of gold, frankincense and *m*.

N

Nabal — a rich sheepherder in Judah who insulted David; when David planned to take revenge, Nabal's wife Abigail brought gifts to calm David; Nabal died shortly afterwards, and Abigail married David (1Sa 25:1–42).

Naboth — owner of a vineyard that King Ahab wanted and gained by having Naboth accused of blasphemy and stoned (1Ki 21:1–29).

Naomi — the mother-in-law of Ruth (Ru 1); she advised Ruth to seek marriage with Boaz (Ru 2—4).

Naphtali — a son of Jacob and father of the tribe of Naphtali (Nu 1:42–43).

nard — an expensive, pleasant-smelling oil from the spikenard, a plant that grew in India.

Mk 14:3 perfume, made of pure *n*.

Nathan — the prophet of God who exposed David's sin with Bathsheba, causing David to repent (2Sa 12:1–25).

Nathanael — one of the twelve apostles (Jn 1:45–49); was probably also called Bartholomew (Mt 10:3).

Nazarene — a person who lived in or came from the town of Nazareth in Galilee.

Mk 16:6 looking for Jesus the *N*,

Nazirite — a person who separated himself or herself by taking a vow to do special work for God. This included a promise not to cut one's hair and not to drink wine.

Jdg 16:17 I have been a *N* dedicated to God

Nebuchadnezzar — king of Babylon who took Judah into captivity.

Negev — the desert region south of Judea.

Ge 24:62 for he was living in the *N*.

Nehemiah — the Jewish cupbearer of King Artaxerxes of Persia (Ne 2:1); while in Jerusalem rebuilt the walls of the city (Ne 2—6) and with Ezra reestablished the worship of God there after the exile in Babylon (Ne 8).

neighbor — 1. someone who lives nearby; 2. any fellow human being.

Lev 19:18 but love your *n* as yourself.
Lk 10:36 of these three do you think was a *n*

Nicodemus — a Pharisee who visited Jesus at night (Jn 3) and learned about being born again.

Nile — the primary river in Egypt.

Nineveh — the city to which Jonah was sent to preach (Jnh 1:2); the ancient capital of Assyria.

Noah — "a righteous man" in early Bible times; he built an ark, as God commanded him (Ge 6—8). God made a covenant with him never again to cover the entire earth with a flood (Ge 9).

nullify — to make of no value; to make unimportant.

Mk 7:13 Thus you *n* the word of God

O

oath — a promise in which one asks God to witness that something is true.

Dt 10:20 take your *o* in his name.

obey (obedience) — to do as asked; to follow someone's commands or wishes.

Dt 6:3 careful to *o* so that it may go well
1Sa 15:22 To *o* is better than sacrifice,
Jn 14:23 who loves me will *o* my teaching.
Ac 5:29 "We must *o* God rather than human
Eph 6:1 *o* your parents in the Lord,

offense — an act that makes someone angry by what was done.

offering — 1. something given to God as an act of worship; 2. the sacrifice of an animal to make the relationship between God and human beings right again. In the Old Testament, animals and grains were regularly used as offerings in an attempt to bring the people closer to God.

Ge 22:8 provide the lamb for the burnt *o*,
Isa 53:10 the LORD makes his life an *o*
Mk 12:33 is more important than all burnt *o*
Eph 5:2 as a fragrant *o* and sacrifice to God.

offspring — children.

Ge 3:15 and between your *o* and hers;
Ge 12:7 "To your *o* I will give this land."

oil — almost always refers to olive oil; used to anoint someone for a physical benefit or to set someone apart for service.

2Ki 9:6 prophet poured the *o* on Jehu's head
Lk 7:46 You did not put *o* on my head,

olive — a tree whose fruit gives olive oil, which was used for varied purposes.

oppress — to control people unfairly and cruelly by the use of one's power.

Isa 53:7 He was *o* and afflicted,
Zec 7:10 Do not *o* the widow

oracle — 1. a saying or answer; 2. the word of the Lord.

ordain — 1. to set apart for a specific office or duty; 2. to order or command.

Ps 111:9 he *o* his covenant forever

ordinance — 1. an official law; 2. a law made or commanded by God.

1Sa 30:25 a statute and *o* for Israel

ornate — elaborately decorated or adorned.

Ge 37:3 he made an *o* robe for him.

overseer — one of the terms used for leaders in the early church.

Ac 20:28 the Holy Spirit has made you *o*.
1Ti 3:2 Now the *o* is to be above reproach,

oxen — strong animals that were used in various ways in farming communities.

P

pagan — a person who does not worship God, especially someone who worships idols.

1Pe 2:12 such good lives among the *p* that,

papyrus — 1. a large water plant, similar to the reed, which grows in marshes and lakes. Moses' mother put him in a basket made from papyrus (Ex 2:3); 2. a paper made from this plant.

parable — a story that tells a special lesson or truth. Jesus told many parables.

paralyzed — unable to move certain parts of one's body.

Mk 2:3 bringing to him a *p* man,

parents — fathers and mothers.

Pr 17:6 and *p* are the pride of their children.
Eph 6:1 Children, obey your *p* in the Lord,
Col 3:20 obey your *p* in everything,

Passover — an annual holiday that still today reminds the Jewish people of how God freed them from slavery in Egypt. The Lord "passed over" the homes marked with the blood of a lamb on their doorframes, but he killed all the other firstborn in Egypt.

Ex 12:11 Eat it in haste; it is the LORD's *P*.

Passover lamb — the lamb killed on the Passover as a sacrifice. Jesus is our Passover lamb, because he was sacrificed for our deliverance from sin, in the same way a lamb was sacrificed when the Israelites were delivered from Egypt.

1Co 5:7 our *P* lamb, has been sacrificed.

pasture — a plot or section of grassy land used for grazing cattle.

patient (patience) — able to put up with problems or pain without complaining or becoming angry.

Ro 12:12	Be joyful in hope, *p* in affliction,
1Co 13:4	Love is *p*, love is kind.
Col 3:12	kindness, humility, gentleness and *p*.

patriarch — the father and ruler of a family; the head of a tribe.

Paul — a Pharisee from Tarsus (Ac 9:11); named Saul at birth (Ac 13:9). Jesus appeared to him on the road to Damascus (Ac 9:4–9), and he became a powerful apostle (Gal 1). His writings make up a large part of the New Testament, ranging from intricate theology to passionate letters to struggling churches.

peace — freedom from disturbance; calm.

Isa 9:6	Everlasting Father, Prince of *P*.
Lk 2:14	on earth *p* to those on whom his
Jn 14:27	*P* I leave with you; my *p*
Ro 5:1	we have *p* with God
Gal 5:22	joy, *p*, forbearance, kindness,

Pentecost — a Jewish feast celebrated fifty days after the Passover. Today the Christian church celebrates Pentecost because it was the day the Holy Spirit came to dwell with Christ's followers (Ac 2:1–4).

people — a collective group.

2Ch 7:14	if my *p*, who are called by my name,
1Pe 2:9	you are a chosen *p*,

perfect — flawless; without defect.

Mt 5:48	Be *p*, therefore, as your heavenly

perish — to spoil; to be destroyed.

Ps 102:26	They will *p*, but you remain;

persecute (persecution) — to continually treat someone cruelly and unfairly. The early Christians were persecuted for believing in Jesus as the Son of God.

Jn 15:20	they *p* me, they will *p* you
Ac 26:14	'Saul, Saul, why do you *p* me?
Ro 12:14	Bless those who *p* you; bless

persevere (perseverance) — to refuse to give up; to keep on trying; to continue in one's actions or beliefs in spite of problems.

Ro 5:3	we know that suffering produces *p*;
Heb 10:36	You need to *p* so that
Heb 12:1	let us run with *p* the race

Persia — ancient geographical area and kingdom located north of the Persian Gulf.

pervert — to use wrongly; to turn from what is right.

pestilence — a plague; a disease that spreads quickly and kills many people.

Ps 91:3	snare and from the deadly *p*.

Peter — one of the twelve apostles; the brother of Andrew; also called Simon (Lk 6:14) and Cephas (Jn 1:42); he denied Jesus three times (Mk 14:66–72) but became a bold evangelist. He wrote the books of 1 and 2 Peter.

petition — to make a formal request.

pharaoh — the title given to the ruler of Egypt.

Pharisees — a group of Jews who obeyed very strictly both God's laws and all their own rules about God's laws.

Mt 5:20	surpasses that of the *P*

Philip — 1. one of the twelve apostles (Mt 10:3); 2. a deacon (Ac 6:1–7) and evangelist in Samaria; he witnessed to an Ethiopian (Ac 8:4–40).

Philistines — enemies of the Israelites throughout much of Old Testament history; they were especially powerful during the reigns of Saul and David.

Pilate — the governor of Judea who questioned Jesus (Lk 22:66–23:25) and then sent him to Herod (Lk 23:6–12). Pilate finally consented to Jesus' crucifixion when the crowds chose Barabbas rather than Jesus to be released (Lk 23:13–25).

pity — a sympathy or sorrow for the suffering of another.

Mk 9:22	take *p* on us and help us."

plague — 1. a disease that kills many people, such as the plague of boils (Ex 9:8–11); 2. an event that causes much suffering or loss, such as the plague of locusts (Ex 10:1–14).

plead — to appeal earnestly; to beg.

Job 16:21	he *p* with God as one *p* for a friend.

pledge — a binding promise or agreement.

1Ti 5:12	they have broken their first *p*.

plot — to plan, usually secretly; to scheme.

Ps 83:5	With one mind they *p* together;

plowshare — the pointed part of the plow; it cuts into the soil to make rows.

Mic 4:3	will beat their swords into *p*

plunder — 1. (*v.*) to loot or rob during a war; 2. (*n.*) property taken by plundering.

pomegranate — a reddish fruit about the size of an orange. It has many seeds and a juicy pulp.

poor — those who have little money.

Dt 15:4	there need be no *p* people
Isa 61:1	me to proclaim good news to the *p*.
Mt 26:11	The *p* you will always have

1Co 13:3	If I give all I possess to the *p*
2Co 8:9	yet for your sake he became *p*,

portico — a porch, usually at the front of a building.

2Ch 3:4	The *p* at the front of the temple

praise — 1. (*v.*) to glorify; to say good things about someone or something; 2. (*n.*) approval; worship.

Ex 15:2	He is my God, and I will *p* him,
Ps 119:175	Let me live that I may *p* you,
Eph 1:12	might be for the *p* of his glory.

pray — to talk with God.

2Ch 7:14	will humble themselves and *p*
Mt 6:5	"And when you *p*, do not be like
Ro 8:26	do not know what we ought to *p*
1Th 5:16–17	Rejoice always, *p* continually,

preach — to tell the message of the gospel in public; to deliver a sermon.

Mt 11:1	and *p* in the towns of Galilee.
Ro 10:15	how can they *p* unless they are sent?

precept — command; law; rule.

Ps 19:8	The *p* of the LORD are right,
Ps 119:69	I keep your *p* with all my heart.

precious — valuable; of great worth.

Ps 139:17	How *p* to me are your thoughts,

predestine — to decide or decree ahead of time.

Ro 8:30	And those he *p*, he also called;
Eph 1:5	he *p* us for adoption

pregnant — carrying an unborn child within a woman's body.

Lk 1:24	his wife Elizabeth became *p*

prevail — to triumph or succeed.

pride — 1. (negative) the attitude that one is better than others; 2. (positive) a healthy self-respect or sense of satisfaction.

Pr 16:18	*P* goes before destruction,
Gal 6:4	they can take *p* in themselves

priest (priesthood) — a Levite who offered sacrifices and prayers to God for the people.

1Pe 2:9	you are a chosen people, a royal *p*,

prince — a male member of a royal family.

prison — a building where people are held, usually for committing a crime.

proclaim — to announce or declare.

1Ch 16:23	*p* his salvation day after day.
Ps 19:1	the skies *p* the work of his hands.
Isa 61:1	to *p* good news to the poor.
1Co 11:26	you *p* the Lord's death

profane — to make a holy thing impure by treating it with disrespect or irreverence.

Lev 22:32	Do not *p* my holy name,

prophecy — a message from God that a prophet brings to the people.

1Co 13:8	where there are *p*, they will cease;
2Pe 1:20	you must understand that no *p*

prophesy — to give the message of God to the people.

Joel 2:28	Your sons and daughters will *p*,
1Co 14:39	brothers and sisters, be eager to *p*,

prophet — a person who receives messages from God to tell to his people. A prophet is called by God to speak for him.

Dt 18:18	up for them a *p* like you
Lk 24:25	believe all that the *p* have spoken!
Ac 10:43	All the *p* testify about him that
Heb 1:1	through the *p* at many times

prosper — to succeed; achieve economic success.

Pr 11:25	A generous person will *p*;

prostitute — a person who offers his or her body for sexual relations in exchange for money.

Jos 2:1	house of a *p* named Rahab

prostrate — lying facedown on the ground.

proud — to have pride.

Ro 12:16	Do not be *p*, but be willing
Jas 4:6	"God opposes the *p*

proverbs — 1. wise sayings; 2. (Proverbs) a book of the Bible that contains many wise sayings.

1Ki 4:32	He spoke three thousand *p*

provoke — to make angry; to cause trouble.

prudent — wise.

Pr 19:14	a *p* wife is from the LORD.

psalms — 1. poetry written to praise God; 2. (Psalms) a book of the Bible that contains many psalms.

Eph 5:19	speaking to one another with *p*,

punish (punishment) — to cause someone to suffer for doing wrong.

Ge 4:13	"My *p* is more than I can bear.
Ex 20:5	jealous God, *p* the children for the sin

pure — perfectly free from fault or blemish.

Ps 51:10	Create in me a *p* heart, O God,

purify — to make pure or clean.

1Jn 1:7	of Jesus, his Son, *p* us from all sin.
1Jn 1:9	and *p* us from all unrighteousness.

Purim — an annual Jewish holiday celebrating Queen Esther's rescue of the Jews when Haman plotted to destroy them.

pursue — 1. to follow in order to overtake; to chase; 2. to seek a goal.

Lev 26:7	You will *p* your enemies,
1Ti 6:11	and *p* righteousness, godliness,

Q

quail — a small spotted bird similar to the partridge; God provided quail and manna to the Israelites when they wandered in the wilderness.

Nu 11:32	people went out and gathered *q*.

quake — 1. (*v.*) to shake or tremble; 2. (*n.*) an earthquake.

Ps 75:3	the earth and all its people *q*,
Rev 16:18	so tremendous was the *q*.

queen — 1. the female ruler of a country; 2. the wife of a king.

R

Rabbi — a teacher of Jewish law.

Rachel — the daughter of Laban (Ge 29:16); she became Jacob's wife (Ge 29:28) and bore him two sons, Joseph and Benjamin (Ge 30:22–24; 35:16–24).

rage — a fit of anger.

Eph 4:31	Get rid of all bitterness, *r*

ram — a male sheep.

ransom — the price paid to get back a person who is held as a slave. Because people are slaves of sin, a ransom had to be paid, which was the death of the sinless one, Jesus.

Mt 20:28	and to give his life as a *r* for many."
Heb 9:15	as a *r* to set them free

reap — 1. to cut down grain at harvest time; to gather a crop together; 2. to get as a result or reward.

Gal 6:7	A man *r* what he sows.

Rebekah — Isaac's wife (Ge 24); the mother of Esau and Jacob (Ge 25:19–26). With her encouragement, Jacob tricked his father into giving him the blessing that belonged to Esau (Ge 27:1–17).

rebel — 1. (*v.*) to disobey and turn against those in authority; 2. (*n.*) a person who disobeys and flaunts authority.

Ro 13:2	whoever *r* against the authority

rebuke — to scold sharply.

2Ti 4:2	correct, *r* and encourage
Rev 3:19	Those whom I love I *r*

reconcile (reconciliation) — to return to friendship after a quarrel; human beings are "reconciled" to God through Christ.

Mt 5:24	First go and be *r* to them;
Ro 5:10	we were *r* to him through the death
2Co 5:18	and gave us the ministry of *r*:

redeem (redemption) — 1. to free from evil by paying a price (Gal 3:13); 2. to buy back.

Ex 21:30	the owner may *r* his life
Gal 3:13	Christ *r* us from the curse
Eph 1:7	In him we have *r* through his blood,
Col 1:14	in whom we have *r*, the forgiveness

Red Sea — the body of water the Israelites crossed in a miraculous way when they were escaping from slavery in Egypt.

refuge — a place of shelter and safety.

Ps 46:1	God is our *r* and strength,

regard — to pay attention to.

Ps 41:1	Blessed are those who have *r* for the weak;

regulations — rules dealing with procedure or ceremony.

Rehoboam — the son of Solomon; he became king after his father's death (1Ki 11:43). Because of his harsh treatment of the people, Israel was divided into two kingdoms (1Ki 12:1–24; 14:21–31).

reign — the time during which a king or other official rules.

rejoice — to express joy or gladness.

Ps 118:24	let us *r* today be glad.
Lk 1:47	and my spirit *r* in God my Savior,
Php 4:4	*R* in the Lord always.

remnant — a small part remaining; a small surviving group.

Isa 10:21	A *r* will return,

repent (repentance) — to turn away from sin; to be sorry for what one has done and to promise not to do it again.

Mt 4:17	"*R*, for the kingdom of heaven
Lk 3:8	Produce fruit in keeping with *r*.
Ac 2:38	Peter replied, "*R* and be baptized,

reproach — 1. (*v.*) to blame or accuse; 2. (*n.*) something for which one can be blamed or criticized.

Job 27:6	my conscience will not *r* me

require (requirement) — to demand as necessary.

1Ki 8:31	is *r* to take an oath
Zec 3:7	obedience to me and keep my *r*,

rescue — to save or deliver.

Ps 140:1 — *R* me, LORD from evildoers;

respect — to look up to or hold in high esteem.

1Pe 2:17 — Show proper *r* to everyone,

restitution — to restore or pay back for damage, loss or injury.

Nu 5:7 — must make full *r* for the wrong

restore — to bring back; to return something to its former condition.

Ps 51:12 — *R* to me the joy of your salvation
Ac 3:21 — time comes for God to *r* everything,

resurrection — the act of coming back to life after being dead.

Jn 11:25 — Jesus said to her, "I am the *r*
Ro 1:4 — in power by his *r* from the dead:
1Co 15:12 — some of you say that there is no *r*

retribution — punishment for doing wrong.

Jer 51:56 — For the LORD is a God of *r*;

Reuben — oldest son of Jacob and founder of the tribe of the same name.

revelation — the act of making known or telling about.

Gal 1:12 — I received it by *r* from Jesus Christ.
Rev 1:1 — *r* from Jesus Christ, which God gave

revenge — to hurt or punish a person who has wronged you; to get back at someone who has hurt you.

Lev 19:18 — " 'Do not seek *r* or bear a grudge
Ro 12:19 — Do not take *r*, my dear friends,

reverence (revere) — a deep respect, honor and awe.

Ps 5:7 — in *r* I bow down
Col 3:22 — of heart and *r* for the Lord.

reward — 1. (*v.*) to repay with good for something someone has done; 2. (*n.*) the gift one receives for good behavior or character.

Ps 127:3 — offspring a *r* from him.
Jer 17:10 — to *r* each person according to
Mt 5:12 — because great is your *r* in heaven,
Mt 6:5 — they have received their *r* in full.

righteous (righteousness) — being in a right relationship to God; not guilty before God.

Isa 64:6 — and all our *r* acts are like filthy rags;
Ro 3:10 — "There is no one *r*, not even one;

Rome — 1. the empire that controlled much of the known world at the time of Christ; 2. the capital city of the Roman Empire, located in Italy.

royal — of or belonging to the ruler of a country and his family.

Ruth — a Moabite widow who went with her mother-in-law Naomi to Bethlehem (Ru 1). There she gathered the gleanings from the field of Boaz (Ru 2), whom she later married (Ru 3—4:12). She was an ancestor of David (Ru 4:13–22) and of Jesus (Mt 1:5).

ruthless — merciless; cruel.

Ps 54:3 — *r* people are trying to kill me
Hab 1:6 — that *r* and impetuous people,

S

Sabbath — the seventh day of the week; the Jewish day of rest and worship. It extended from Friday sunset until Saturday sunset.

Ex 20:8 — "Remember the *S* day

sackcloth — a rough cloth, usually woven from goats' hair. Clothing made of sackcloth was worn as a sign of mourning for the dead or as a sign that a person was sorry for his or her sins.

sacred — holy; set apart for God in a special way.

1Co 3:17 — God's temple is *s*,

sacrifice — 1. (*v.*) to offer something as a gift to God; 2. (*n.*) an offering given to God. In the Old Testament God commanded the people to pay for their sins by sacrificing the blood of cattle, lambs, goats, doves or pigeons. These sacrifices were pictures of Jesus' coming as a once-for-all sacrifice for sinners.

Ex 12:27 — 'It is the Passover *s* to the LORD,
1Sa 15:22 — To obey is better than *s*,
Ro 12:1 — to offer your bodies as a living *s*,
Heb 9:28 — so Christ was *s* once
1Jn 2:2 — He is the atoning *s* for our sins,

Sadducees — a group of Jewish leaders, many of them priests. Unlike the Pharisees, the Sadducees did not believe in a resurrection of the dead, but they agreed with the Pharisees in their hatred of Jesus.

Mk 12:18 — *S*, who say there is no resurrection,

salvation — deliverance from the guilt and power of sin. By his death and resurrection, Jesus brings salvation to people who believe in him.

Ps 27:1 — The LORD is my light and my *s*
Lk 2:30 — For my eyes have seen your *s*,
Ac 4:12 — *S* is found in no one else,
2Co 7:10 — brings repentance that leads to *s*
Php 2:12 — to work out your *s* with fear
Heb 2:3 — escape if we ignore so great a *s*?

Samaritan — a person who lived in or came from Samaria. Because the Samaritans were only partly Jewish and worshiped God differently from the Jews, Jews from Judea and Galilee hated the Samaritans. They would go out of their way to travel around Samaria (Lk 10:30–37).

Samson — an Israelite judge who was known for his great strength. He was betrayed by Delilah but in the end was used by God to punish the Philistines (Jdg 16).

Samuel — often called the last of Israel's judges and the first of Israel's prophets (see also Heb 11:32). His birth was earnestly prayed for by his mother Hannah (1Sa 1:10–18), and when he was old enough, she brought him to the temple and he was dedicated to the Lord (1Sa 1:21–28). There he was raised by Eli (1Sa 2:11; 18—26) and was called to be a prophet (1Sa 3).

sanctify (sanctification) — to make holy; sanctification is the ongoing work of the Holy Spirit in the hearts of believers.

Ro 15:16 to God, *s* by the Holy Spirit.
1Th 5:23 *s* you through and through.
2Th 2:13 through the *s* work of the Spirit

sanctuary — a place where God is worshiped; a holy place.

Ps 150:1 Praise God in his *s*;

Sanhedrin — the ruling council of the Jews in Jesus' time. It was made up of seventy men, and the leader was the high priest. The Sanhedrin could decide whether someone was innocent or guilty of breaking a Jewish law, but it could not put anyone to death without the permission of the Roman governor.

Mk 14:55 the whole *S* were looking for evidence

Sarah — the wife of Abraham and mother of Isaac; first called Sarai (Ge 11:29–31). God promised her that, though she had been barren throughout her life, she would give birth to a son in her old age (Ge 17:15–21; 18:10–15).

Satan — the devil; the leader of the fallen spirits; the most powerful enemy of God and humans.

Mk 4:15 *S* comes and takes away the word
2Co 11:14 for *S* himself masquerades
Rev 12:9 serpent called the devil, or *S*,

satisfy — 1. to please, to make happy; 2. to fulfill a condition.

Ps 103:5 who *s* your desires with good things

satrap — the governor of a province in ancient Persia.

Saul — 1. the first king of Israel (1Sa 9—10). He was anointed by Samuel but was later rejected by God because of disobedience; David was chosen to be his successor; 2. see Paul.

saved — 1. (*v.*) rescued from danger; 2. (*n.*) people who acknowledge that by Jesus' death they have been rescued from the punishment of death that their sins deserve.

Ro 10:13 on the name of the Lord will be *s*."
Eph 2:8 For it is by grace you have been *s*,

Savior — a name for Jesus that means he saves his people from sin.

Lk 1:47 and my spirit rejoices in God my *S*,
1Ti 4:10 who is the *S* of all people,
1Jn 4:14 Son to be the *S* of the world.

scarlet — the color bright red.

scepter — a rod or stick held by a king or queen as a sign of royal power and authority.

Ge 49:10 The *s* will not depart from Judah,

scoff — to mock or sneer at.

Ps 2:4 the Lord *s* at them.

scorn — to despise, to reject with anger or contempt.

Ps 69:20 *S* has broken my heart

scorpion — a spider-like animal with a poisonous stinger at the end of its tail.

scoundrel — a mean, worthless person; a villain.

Pr 16:27 A *s* plots evil,

scourge — to whip.

2Ch 10:11 My father *s* you with whips;

scribe — a person with the important task of copying letters, books and legal papers.

Scripture — all or part of the Bible. When the Bible uses this word it means the Old Testament, since the New Testament had not yet been written. Today we call the Old and New Testaments the Bible or Scripture.

Jn 10:35 and *S* cannot be set aside
2Ti 3:16 All *S* is God-breathed
2Pe 1:20 that no prophecy of *S* came about

scroll — a book made of a long piece of leather or paper that was rolled around a stick at both ends.

Jos 18:9 They wrote its description on a *s*,

seal — 1. a tool with a design raised on it or cut into it; 2. the mark made by pressing this tool onto wax, paper or other soft material. A seal was used to close a letter or legal paper or to prove the authority of the paper.

2Co 1:22 set his *s* of ownership on us,
Rev 5:2 "Who is worthy to break the *s*

sect — a group of people who hold one or more beliefs in common; especially, a small religious group that has separated from a larger group.

seer — a prophet; a person who, with God's help, can see what will happen in the future.

1Sa 9:19 "I am the *s*," Samuel replied.

self-control — the ability to control one's own actions and feelings.

Gal 5:23 gentleness and *s*.
2Pe 1:6 and to knowledge, *s*; and to *s*,

selfish — centered on oneself; not interested in others.

Php 2:3 Do nothing out of *s* ambition

Sennacherib — an Assyrian king who raided Judah during the time of Hezekiah.

sexual immorality — using sex in ways God says are wrong.

1Co 6:13 body, however, is not meant for *s*,
1Th 4:3 that you should avoid *s*;

shame — a painful emotion caused by an awareness of guilt or shortcoming.

Pr 19:26 a child who brings *s* and disgrace.
1Co 15:34 I say this to your *s*.

sheep — the animal most often mentioned in Scripture, probably because it was the animal most often raised in Bible times; used for meat, for cloth, and for religious sacrifice.

Isa 53:6 We all, like *s*, have gone astray,

shekel — a specific weight of silver, used as money.

Shem — one of the three sons of Noah (Ge 5:32). He, along with his brother Japheth, covered his father when he was naked (Ge 9:21–31). Abraham was one of his descendants (Ge 11:10–32).

shepherd — someone who takes care of a flock of sheep. It is often used in the Bible as a figure of speech for anyone who cares for a group of people.

Ps 23:1 The LORD is my *s*, I lack nothing.
Jer 31:10 will watch over his flock like a *s*.'
Jn 10:11 The good *s* lays down his life
Ac 20:28 Be *s* of the church of God,

shield — a piece of defensive armor, usually carried on the arm; often a figure of speech in the Bible used to describe God's protection of his people.

Ps 7:10 My *s* is God Most High,

shrine — a dwelling for a god.

sickle — a tool with a long, curved blade and a short handle, used for cutting grain.

siege — see besiege.

signet — a ring with a design on it. The design was stamped in wax to seal a letter or legal paper. Signet rings were usually worn by people in authority.

Silas — a member of the church in Jerusalem; he traveled with Paul.

Simon — 1. see Peter; 2. one of the twelve apostles; also called the Zealot (Mt 10:4; Ac 1:13); 3. a sorcerer in Samaria who had great influence on the Samaritan people during the early days of the church; he was severely rebuked by Peter (Ac 8:9–24) for attempting to buy the power of the Holy Spirit.

sin — 1. (*v.*) to break the law of God; 2. (*n.*) the act of not doing what God wants.

Nu 32:23 be sure that your *s* will find you
Ps 51:2 and cleanse me from my *s*.
Ps 119:11 that I might not *s* against you.
Isa 1:18 "Though your *s* are like scarlet,
Mt 1:21 he will save his people from their *s*."
Lk 11:4 Forgive us our *s*,
Jn 1:29 who takes away the *s* of the world!
Ro 3:23 for all have *s* and fall short
Ro 6:23 For the wages of *s* is death,
2Co 5:21 God made him who had no *s* to be *s*
1Jn 1:9 If we confess our *s*, he is faithful

Sinai, Mount — the mountain where Moses received the Ten Commandments (Ex 19—20).

sinner — a person who breaks the law of God.

Ps 1:1 or stand in the way that *s* take
Mt 9:13 come to call the righteous, but *s*."
Lk 15:7 in heaven over one *s* who repents
Lk 18:13 'God, have mercy on me, a *s*.'
Ro 5:8 While we were still *s*, Christ died

slander — 1. (*v.*) saying untrue things about another person in order to hurt him or her; 2. (*n.*) false charges or misrepresentations about another person.

Lev 19:16 " 'Do not go about spreading *s*
Titus 3:2 to *s* no one, to be peaceable

slaughter — 1. the butchering of livestock for food; 2. the killing of great numbers of human beings, as in a battle.

slave — 1. a person who is owned by another; 2. a person who is dominated or controlled by an outside force.

Ro 7:14 I am unspiritual, sold as a *s* to sin.
Gal 3:28 *s* nor free, male nor female,

slay, slain — to kill violently or in great numbers.

sluggard — a lazy person.

Pr 19:24 A *s* buries his hand in the dish;

slumber — to sleep.

snare — a trap; something risky that tempts or endangers a person.

snatch — to grab suddenly, often without permission or right.

Sodom and Gomorrah — the two cities destroyed by God because the people were so wicked.

Ge 19:24	rained down burning sulfur on *S*

Solomon — the son of David and Bathsheba (2Sa 12:24). He became king of Israel after David died (1Ki 1). He asked God for wisdom and was given it (1Ki 3), and he built the temple (1Ki 5—7). His many foreign wives turned his heart away from God (1Ki 11:1–13).

son — a male descendant.

Pr 10:1	A wise *s* brings joy to his father,
Joel 2:28	Your *s* and daughters will prophesy,
2Co 6:18	you will be my *s* and daughters,
Heb 2:10	many *s* and daughters to glory,
1Jn 4:9	only *S* into the world that we might

Son of Man — a title Jesus used for himself to show his humanity as distinct from his divinity. It was also a reference to the Messiah prophesied about in Daniel 7:13.

Mt 20:18	and the *S* will be delivered
Mk 14:62	you will see the *S* sitting
Lk 19:10	For the *S* came to seek
Jn 3:14	so the *S* must be lifted up,

sorcery — the use of magic and supernatural powers that are evil; witchcraft.

Dt 18:10	practices divination or *s*,

soul — the spiritual part of a person; the part of a person that does not die.

Dt 6:5	with all your *s* and with all your
Ps 23:3	he refreshes my *s*.
Mt 10:28	kill the body but cannot kill the *s*.
Mt 11:29	and you will find rest for your *s*.
Mt 16:26	yet forfeit their *s*? Or what can
Mt 22:37	with all your *s* and with all your

sovereign — having authority over everything; often used in Scripture as a descriptive title for God, "Sovereign LORD."

sow — to plant seeds. In Jesus' time seeds were sown by scattering them by hand over the ground.

Job 4:8	and those who *s* trouble reap it.
Mk 4:3	A farmer went out to *s* his seed.
Gal 6:7	A man reaps what he *s*.

spear — a weapon with a long handle and a sharp point, usually thrown.

spirit — 1. the part of a person that is not the body; the soul; 2. a being who does not have a body; 3. (cap.) see Holy Spirit.

Ps 31:5	Into your hands I commit my *s*;
Eze 36:26	you a new heart and put a new *s*
Mt 5:3	"Blessed are the poor in *s*,
Mt 26:41	*s* is willing, but the flesh is weak."
1Jn 4:1	Dear friends, do not believe every *s*,

splendor — something magnificent or splendid.

spoils — booty or plunder taken from an enemy in war.

springs — a source of water coming up from the ground.

Dt 8:7	streams, and deep *s* gushing out
Rev 7:17	lead them to *s* of living water.

staff — a stick used to lean on; a rod used by a shepherd.

Ps 23:4	your rod and your *s*,

starry hosts — the stars and other heavenly bodies.

2Ki 21:3	He bowed down to all the *s*

statutes — established rules or laws.

Ps 19:7	*s* of the LORD are trustworthy,

steadfast — settled; not changing or wavering.

Ps 51:10	and renew a *s* spirit within me.

steal — to rob; to take what belongs to someone else.

Ex 20:15	"You shall not *s*.
Eph 4:28	must *s* no longer,

stench — a terrible smell.

Stephen — one of the first seven men to serve the Jerusalem church (Ac 6:5); he became the first Christian martyr (Ac 7:60).

stiff-necked — stubborn.

Ac 7:51	"You *s* people!

stone — to kill or to try to kill someone by throwing rocks or stones.

strength — power; forcefulness.

Ex 15:2	"The LORD is my *s* and my defense;
Dt 6:5	all your soul and with all your *s*.
Ps 46:1	God is our refuge and *s*,
Isa 40:31	will renew their *s*.
Php 4:13	through him who gives me *s*.

strife — bitter and sometimes violent conflict.

Pr 30:33	stirring up anger produces *s*."

stronghold — a fortified place; a place of security.

1Sa 24:22	David and his men went up to the *s*.
Ps 27:1	The LORD is the *s* of my life

subdue — to bring under control; to conquer.

Ps 81:14	how quickly I would *s* their enemies

submission — humbleness; obedience.

1Co 14:34 but must be in *s*, as the law says.
1Ti 2:11 learn in quietness and full *s*.

submit — to willingly yield to another.

Pr 3:6 in all your ways *s* to him,
Eph 5:21 *S* to one another out of reverence
Col 3:18 Wives, *s* yourselves to your husbands,
Jas 4:7 *S* yourselves, then, to God.

succeed — 1. to turn out well; 2. to follow another as heir or successor of a title or rank.

suffer — to bear or endure something painful.

Mk 8:31 the Son of Man must *s* many things
Lk 24:26 the Messiah have to *s* these things
1Co 12:26 If one part *s*, every part *s* with it;

suffering — the experience of enduring pain.

Isa 53:3 of *s*, and familiar with pain.
Ac 5:41 worthy of *s* disgrace for the Name.
Ro 8:17 share in his *s* in order that we may
2Ti 1:8 Rather, join with me in *s* for the gospel,

summon — to issue a call to come together; to send for.

Isa 43:1 I have *s* you by name; you are mine.

sustain — to give support; to help; to comfort.

Ps 18:35 and your right hand *s* me;
Ps 146:9 and *s* the fatherless and the widow,

swear — to promise forcefully or earnestly.

1Sa 30:15 "*S* to me before God that you will

swindler — someone who cheats another person out of money or other possessions.

1Co 6:10 nor *s* will inherit the kingdom

sword — a weapon with a long blade for cutting or thrusting.

symbol — an object or action that stands for or suggests something else. The cross is a symbol of Jesus' death.

synagogue — the Jewish place of worship and religious teaching.

Lk 4:16 the Sabbath day he went into the *s*,
Ac 17:2 his custom, Paul went into the *s*,

T

tabernacle — the tent used by the Israelites for meeting with God; the place where God chose to show his presence. The tabernacle was made by God's command and according to his plans. It is described in detail in Exodus 26. Also called the tent of meeting.

Ex 40:34 the glory of the LORD filled the *t*.

talent — a large amount (75 lbs or 34 kg) of silver or gold, worth very much money.

Ex 25:39 A *t* of pure gold is to be used

tax — money a government requires its citizens to pay.

Mt 22:19 the coin used for paying the *t*."

teach — to instruct; to help someone learn.

Ex 33:13 *t* me your ways so I may know you
Ps 90:12 *T* us to number our days,
Lk 11:1 said to him, "Lord, *t* us to pray,
Jn 14:26 will *t* you all things and will remind

tempest — a violent storm.

temple — 1. the place where the Jewish people worshiped and sacrificed in Jerusalem; the first temple was built by King Solomon as a house for God; 2. any place of worship. In this sense, the human body is referred to as a temple (1Co 6:19).

1Ki 8:27 How much less this *t* I have built!
Ac 17:24 not live in *t* built by human hands.
2Co 6:16 For we are the *t* of the living God.

tempt (temptation) — trying to get someone to do wrong.

Mt 4:1 the wilderness to be *t* by the devil.
1Co 10:13 No *t* has overtaken you except

tenant — one who rents land or a house from a landlord.

testimony — a statement made by a witness to prove that something is true.

Lk 18:20 not give false *t*, honor your father

tetrarch — a ruler over one-fourth of a kingdom.

Thaddaeus — one of the twelve apostles (Mk 3:18); son of James and probably also known as Judas (Lk 6:16; Ac 1:13).

thanks — the expression of gratitude.

1Ch 16:34 Give *t* to the LORD, for
Ps 100:4 give *t* to him and praise his name.
1Co 15:57 *t* be to God! He gives us the victory
2Co 9:15 *T* be to God for his indescribable
1Th 5:18 give *t* in all circumstances;

thanksgiving — recognizing and thanking the one who has provided a gift.

Ps 100:4 Enter his gates with *t*
Php 4:6 by prayer and petition, with *t*,

Thomas — one of the twelve apostles (Lk 6:15; Ac 1:13); at first he doubted Jesus' resurrection, but when he saw Jesus, he believed (Jn 20:24–28).

thrive — to grow vigorously.

Thummim — see Urim.

threshing floor — the place where grain was trampled by oxen or beaten with a stick to separate it from the stalk.

Ru 3:6 So she went down to the *t*

Timothy — fellow-traveler and official representative of the apostle Paul. He joined Paul on his second missionary journey (Ac 16—20), and at one point in this journey Paul sent him to minister to the church at Corinth (1Co 4:17; 16:10). He was the leader of the church at Ephesus (1Ti 1:3) and a co-writer with Paul (1Th 1:1; 2Th 1:1; Phm 1).

tithe — the giving to God of one-tenth of what one earns.

Lev 27:30 " 'A *t* of everything from the land,
Mal 3:10 the whole *t* into the storehouse,

Titus — a Gentile co-worker with Paul (Gal 2:1–3; 2Ti 4:10). Paul sent him to Corinth to help solve some of the problems there (2Co 2:13; 7—8; 12:18).

toil — 1. (*n.*) strenuous and tiring work; 2. (*v.*) to work long and hard.

Ecc 3:9 What do workers gain from their *t?*

tomb — a burial place. In Bible times, a tomb was often either a cave or a cavity dug into a stone cliff, with a large stone rolled in front to close it.

Mt 27:65 make the *t* as secure as you know
Lk 24:2 the stone rolled away from the *t*,
Jn 11:17 been in the *t* for four days.

tongue — 1. the organ of speech in the mouth; 2. a language.

Ps 39:1 and keep my *t* from sin;
Ac 2:4 and began to speak in other *t*
Php 2:11 every *t* acknowledge that Jesus
Jas 1:26 do not keep a tight rein on their *t*

torment — extreme pain or anguish; agony.

2Co 12:7 a messenger of Satan, to *t* me.

tradition — the handing down of information and beliefs from one generation to another.

Mt 15:2 break the *t* of the elders?

trample — to walk heavily causing injury or damage.

Ps 60:12 he will *t* down our enemies.

transfigure — to change the appearance of; to make bright and glorious.

Mt 17:2 There he was *t* before them.

transgression — sin; disobeying the law of God.

Ps 32:1 whose *t* are forgiven,
Isa 53:5 But he was pierced for our *t*,
Eph 2:1 you were dead in your *t* and sins,

treacherous — untrustworthy, unreliable, faithless.

tread — to step or walk on or over.

Job 24:11 they *t* the winepresses,

treasure — 1. (*n.*) wealth that is stored up or hidden away; 2. (*v.*) to hold or keep something precious, something of value; to cherish.

Mt 6:21 your *t* is, there your heart will be also.

treaty — an agreement between two people or groups or nations.

Ex 34:12 Be careful not to make a *t*

trespass — sin; wrongdoing.

Ro 5:17 For if, by the *t* of the one man,

tribe — a social group made up of a particular branch of a family.

tribute — payment by one ruler or nation to another as an act of submission or in order to guarantee protection.

Isa 16:1 Send lambs as *t* to the ruler

triumph — a victory; a notable success.

Pr 28:12 the righteous *t*, there is great elation;

true — certain; exactly right.

Ps 119:160 All your words are *t*;
Jn 17:3 the only *t* God, and Jesus Christ,
Ro 3:4 Let God be *t*, and every human
Php 4:8 whatever is *t*, whatever is noble,

trust — firm belief or faith in another.

Ps 37:3 *T* in the LORD and do good;
Pr 3:5 *T* in the LORD with all your heart
Isa 26:3 because they *t* in you.
Isa 30:15 in quietness and *t* is your strength,
1Co 4:2 been given a *t* must prove faithful.

trustworthy — deserving of trust; reliable.

Ps 19:7 The statutes of the LORD are *t*,
1Ti 1:15 Here is a *t* saying that deserves full

truth — that which conforms to the facts.

Ps 145:18 to all who call on him in *t*.
Zec 8:16 are to do: Speak the *t* to each other,
Jn 8:32 know the *t*, and the *t*
Jn 14:6 I am the way and the *t* and the life.
Ro 1:25 They exchanged the *t* about God
1Co 13:6 in evil but rejoices with the *t*.
Eph 4:15 Instead, speaking the *t* in love,
Heb 10:26 received the knowledge of the *t*,
1Jn 1:6 we lie and do not live out the *t*.
1Jn 1:8 deceive ourselves and the *t* is not

tunic — a long shirt worn by men in Bible times.

Ezr 9:3 When I heard this, I tore my *t*

turban — a head-covering made by winding a cloth around the head.

U

unbelief — doubt.

Mk 9:24 help me overcome my *u!"*

unbeliever — one who does not believe in Jesus.

2Co 6:14 Do not be yoked together with *u.*

unclean — morally or spiritually impure; unclean animals were those that the Israelites were not allowed to sacrifice or to eat.

unity — being one.

Ps 133:1 God's people live together in *u!*
Col 3:14 them all together in perfect *u.*

unleavened bread — bread made without yeast. It is usually flat, like a pancake or cracker.

Ex 12:17 "Celebrate the Festival of *U,*

uphold — to give support to.

Ps 37:17 the LORD *u* the righteous.

upright — honest; doing what is right and good.

Urim and Thummim — objects that were placed on the vest of the high priest; used to determine God's will for the nation of Israel.

utter — to pronounce, to speak.

Ps 78:2 I will *u* hidden things,
Jer 15:19 if you *u* worthy, not worthless, words,

utterly — completely, totally.

V

vain — worthless; unsuccessful; foolish. "In vain" means without success or result.

valiant — courageous.

vast — very great in size or amount; huge.

vault — the atmosphere or sky as seen from the earth.

Ge 1:8 God called the *v* "sky."

vengeance — hurt or punishment done to another person who has done something wrong against another.

Isa 34:8 For the LORD has a day of *v,*

vigor — strength and health in the body and its growth.

Job 20:11 The youthful *v* that fills his bones

vile — disgusting, evil.

Rev 22:11 let the *v* person continue to be *v;*

vindicate — to defend; to provide justice for; to set free.

Ps 135:4 For the LORD will *v* his people

violate — 1. to rape; 2. to make something unholy; 3. to fail to obey.

viper — 1. a venomous snake; 2. a treacherous or vicious person.

virgin — a woman or girl who has never had sexual intercourse.

Isa 7:14 The *v* will conceive
Mt 1:23 "The *v* will conceive

vision — a dream from God.

Nu 12:6 reveal myself to them in *v,*
Joel 2:28 your young men will see *v.*
Ac 26:19 disobedient to the *v* from heaven.

vow — a solemn promise made before God or to God.

Jdg 11:30 Jephthah made a *v* to the LORD:
Ps 116:14 I will fulfill my *v* to the LORD

W

wages — payment received for work completed.

Ro 6:23 For the *w* of sin is death,

wail — to cry loudly.

walk — to follow a certain course.

Ps 1:1 who does not *w* in step
Isa 2:5 let us *w* in the light of the LORD.
Mic 6:8 and to *w* humbly with your God.
2Jn 6 his command is that you *w* in love.

wander — to move about without a fixed course.

Nu 32:13 he made them *w* in the wilderness
Jas 5:19 if one of you should *w* from the truth

warn — to give notice beforehand of danger or evil.

warrior — a soldier.

Isa 9:3 as *w* rejoice when dividing

wash — to clean.

Ps 51:7 *w* me, and I will be whiter
Ac 22:16 be baptized and *w* your sins away,

watch — to be on the lookout for someone or something.

Jer 31:10 will *w* over his flock like a shepherd.'
Mt 26:41 "*W* and pray so that you will not fall

way — the means of getting somewhere; the path.

2Sa 22:31 "As for God, his *w* is perfect:
Ps 1:1 or stand in the *w* that sinners
Ps 37:5 Commit your *w* to the LORD;
Isa 53:6 each of us has turned to our own *w;*
Jn 14:6 "I am the *w* and the truth
1Co 12:31 will show you the most excellent *w.*

wean — to help a child or animal begin to eat solid food rather than his or her mother's milk.

weapon — an object used for fighting.

weary — 1. tired; 2. having one's patience or tolerance exhausted.

Dt 25:18 When you were *w* and worn out,
Zec 11:8 and I grew *w* of them

weep, wept — to cry.

Jn 11:35 Jesus *w*.

welcome — 1. to greet a person pleasantly; 2. to make a person feel at home.

Jdg 19:20 "You are *w* at my house,"

wholehearted — sincere; devoted without holding anything back.

wicked — sinful.

Ps 1:1 walk in step with the *w*
Isa 55:7 Let the *w* forsake their ways

widow — a woman whose husband has died.

will — desire; seeking God's will means looking for what God wants to be done.

Ps 143:10 Teach me to do your *w*,
Isa 53:10 Yet it was the LORD's *w*
Mt 6:10 your *w* be done,
Mt 26:39 Yet not as I *w*, but as you *w*."
Ro 12:2 and approve what God's *w* is
Eph 5:17 understand what the Lord's *w* is.
1Jn 5:14 we ask anything according to his *w*,
Rev 4:11 and by your *w* they were created

winepress — a vat or tub in which the juice of grapes is pressed out. Used in the Bible as a symbol for the anger of God against wickedness.

Rev 14:19 into the great *w* of God's wrath.

wisdom — the understanding that comes from God.

Lk 2:52 And Jesus grew in *w* and stature,
Jas 1:5 of you lacks *w*, you should ask God,

witchcraft — practices using evil spirits, magic, or sorcery.

Mic 5:12 I will destroy your *w*

wither — to dry or shrivel up, usually from a lack of moisture.

witness — one who personally sees an event take place.

Ac 22:15 You will be his *w* to all people

woe — great misery; distress.

Isa 6:5 "*W* to me!" I cried.
Lk 11:42 "*W* to you Pharisees, because you

womb — the organ within a woman's body where a child grows before birth.

Lk 1:44 the baby in my *w* leaped for joy.

word — 1. the means of expressing oneself through language; 2. the Bible, as God's written message to people; 3. (cap.) Jesus is the Word sent from God because his life on earth told the message of God.

Jn 1:14 The *W* became flesh and made his
Heb 4:12 For the *w* of God is alive

work — 1. (*n.*) employment; duty; 2. (*v.*) to bring about; to try to achieve a goal.

Ex 23:12 "Six days do your *w*,
Jn 9:4 we must do the *w* of him who sent
Php 2:12 continue to *w* out your salvation
2Ti 3:17 equipped for every good *w*.

world — 1. the earth and those who live in it; 2. the secular, as opposed to the spiritual or religious.

Mt 5:14 "You are the light of the *w*.
Jn 1:29 who takes away the sin of the *w*!
Jn 3:16 so loved the *w* that he gave is one
Jn 8:12 he said, "I am the light of the *w*.
Ro 12:2 Do not conform to the pattern of this *w*,
1Jn 2:15 not love the *w* or anything in the *w*.

worldly — loving the things of the world more than the things of God.

Titus 2:12 to ungodliness and *w* passions,

worry — to feel anxious and uneasy.

Mt 6:25 I tell you, do not *w* about your life,

worship — 1. (*v.*) to give praise, honor and respect to God; 2. (*n.*) reverence given to God.

Ps 95:6 Come, let us bow down in *w*,
Jn 4:24 his worshipers must *w* in the Spirit

worthy — having value; honorable; deserving.

1Ch 16:25 For great is the LORD and most *w*
Eph 4:1 to live a life *w* of the calling you
Rev 5:2 "Who is *w* to break the seals

wrath — great anger; the strong anger of God.

Pr 15:1 A gentle answer turns away *w*,
Ro 5:9 saved from God's *w* through him!

X

Xerxes — king of Persia; he made Esther, a young Jewess, his queen (Est 2:15–18).

Y

yearn — to long for; to want very much.

yeast — the ingredient that makes dough rise; sometimes a figure of speech for the influence someone has over others.

Mt 16:6	guard against the *y* of the Pharisees
Gal 5:9	little *y* works through the whole

yield — 1. to submit; 2. to grow or produce fruit.

Ps 67:6	The land *y* its harvest;
Isa 48:11	I will not *y* my glory to another.

yoke — 1. (*v.*) to join together; 2. (*n.*) a wooden bar that goes over the necks of two animals, usually oxen. The yoke holds the animals together as they pull an object, such as a plow or a cart.

Mt 11:29	Take my *y* upon you and learn
2Co 6:14	Do not be *y* together

youth — the time when a person is young.

Ecc 12:1	Creator in the days of your *y*,

Z

Zacchaeus — a tax collector who climbed a tree in order to see Jesus (Lk 19:1–5).

zeal — eagerness; strong desire.

Ro 12:11	Never be lacking in *z*,

Zealot — a member of the Jewish group that wanted to fight against and overthrow the Roman government.

Zechariah — a prophet and priest who returned to Jerusalem from the Babylonian captivity; he encouraged the Jews to rebuild the temple (Ezr 5:1; 6:14; Zec 1:1).

Zerubbabel — a descendant of David (1Ch 3:19); he led the return of the Jews from the Babylonian captivity (Ezr 1—3; Ne 7:7; Hag 1—2; Zec 4).

Zion — 1. the hill on which the city of Jerusalem first stood; David's royal palace and the temple were both built on Mount Zion; 2. the entire city of Jerusalem.

Jer 50:5	They will ask the way to *Z*
Ro 11:26	"The deliverer will come from *Z*;